CQ's
Politics in America
2010
THE 111TH CONGRESS

By Congressional Quarterly Staff
Chuck McCutcheon and
Christina L. Lyons, Editors

★

In-depth Profiles of Members of Congress
Biographical Data and Key Votes
Election Results and District Snapshots

★

Robert W. Merry, President and Editor-in-Chief
Michael Riley, Editor and Senior Vice President
Keith White, Publisher and Senior Vice President
John A. Jenkins, President and Publisher, CQ Press, a division of SAGE

Published by Congressional Quarterly Inc.
Paul C. Tash, Chairman
Andrew P. Corty, Vice Chairman
Nelson Poynter (1903–1978), Founder

Congressional Quarterly Inc.
1255 22nd Street N.W.
Washington, DC 20037
202-419-8500; toll-free, 1-800-432-2250
www.cq.com

The paper used in this publication exceeds the requirements of the American National Standard for Information Sciences — Permanence of Paper for Printed Library Materials, ANSI Z39.48-1992.

Printed and bound in the United States of America

11 10 09 08 07   5 4 3 2 1

ISBN 978-1-60426-602-3 (cloth)   ISBN 978-1-60426-603-0 (paper)

ISSN 1064-6809

The Library of Congress catalogued an earlier edition of this title as follows:

Congressional Quarterly's Politics in America: 1994, the 103rd Congress / by CQ's political staff: Phil Duncan, Editor

p.   cm.

Includes index.

1. United States. Congress — Biography.   2. United States. Congress — Committees.   3. United States. Congress — Election districts — Handbooks, manuals, etc.   I. Duncan, Phil. II. Congressional Quarterly Inc. III. Title: Politics in America.
JK1010.C67 1993   328.73'073'45'0202

Politics in America 2010
THE 111TH CONGRESS

EDITORS
Chuck McCutcheon, Christina L. Lyons

DEPUTY EDITOR
Martha Angle

MANAGING EDITOR
Kimberly Hallock

SENIOR EDITORS
Amanda H. Allen, Stephanie M. Kanowitz, Brian Nutting, Chris White

CONTRIBUTING EDITORS
Christine C. Lawrence, Kathleen Murphy, Kathleen Silvassy

SENIOR WRITERS
John M. Donnelly, Marc Rehmann, Richard Rubin,
Seth Stern, Alex Wayne, Shawn Zeller

POLITICAL ANALYSIS
John Cranford (vote studies), Greg Giroux (district vote for president)

CONTRIBUTING WRITERS
David Baumann, Adriel Bettelheim, Emily Cadei, David Clarke,
Edward Epstein, Karen Foerstel, Lydia Gensheimer, Libby George,
Benton Ives, Bart Jansen, Adrianne Kroepsch, Gebe Martinez,
Phil Mattingly, David Nather, Alan K. Ota, Avery Palmer, Keith Perine,
Josh Rogin, William Scally, Joseph J. Schatz, Stacey Skotzko,
Miriam Straus, Greg Vadala, Kerry Young

REPORTERS AND RESEARCHERS
Adjoa Adofo, Rebecca Adams, Alan Ahlrich, Joanna Anderson, Nell Benton,
Rachel Bloom, Miranda Blue, Alecia Burke, Leah Carliner, Samuel Collins Jr.,
Jessica Benton Cooney, Susannah Clark, Coral Davenport, Kate Davidson,
Karoun Demirjian, Emma Dumain, Emily Ethridge, Sasha Ghosh-Siminoff,
Liriel Higa, Molly Hooper, Colby Itkowitz, Annie Johnson,
Matthew M. Johnson, Ryan Kelly, Noella Kertes, Anne L. Kim, Peter H. King,
Alex Knott, Jody Kyle, Matthew Lockeed, Rob Margetta, Will Matthews,
Meghan McCarthy, Courtney McCarty, John Mellyn, Sarah Molenkamp,
Amrit Naresh, Leah Nylen, Christina C. Parisi, Lauren Phillips, Fiona Reeves,
Catharine Richert, John J. Ryan, Jennifer Scholtes, Gabriella Schwarz,
Marghuerita Scott, Annie Shuppy, Megan Sowder-Staley, Jesse Stanchak,
Tim Starks, Frances Symes, Michael Teitelbaum, Neda Toloui-Semnani,
Robert Tomkin, Derek Wallbank, Joe Warminsky, Caitlin Webber,
Matthew Weinstein, Ben Weyl, Chris Wright, Alexander Yamet

COPY EDITORS
Pat Joy, Chris Kapler, Melinda W. Nahmias, Jennifer Rubio,
Melanie Starkey, Chris Wright

PHOTOGRAPHY AND GRAPHICS
Scott J. Ferrell, Jamey Fry, Marilyn Gates-Davis, John Irons

DISTRICT MAPS
SpatiaLogic Mapping (Charlottesville, Va.), Kimberly Hallock

PUBLISHING SOFTWARE
Mark Logic (San Carlos, Calif.), Erin Miller, Frank Rubino

IT SUPPORT
Ron Brodmann, John Hanna, Melissa Howard, Pat Joy

PIA ONLINE EDITION
CQ Press, a division of SAGE (Thousand Oaks, Calif.),
Andrew Boney, Jerry Orvedahl

PRODUCTION MANAGER
CQ Press, a division of SAGE, Paul Pressau

BUSINESS MANAGER
Julie S. Kimbro

Politics in America

THE 15TH EDITION

At times, historic is a convenient adjective, easy to toss out and much overused. But there's no doubt that historic is a perfect word to use when describing this nation's 2008 election. As voters put Democratic Illinois Sen. Barack Obama in the White House as the country's first African-American president, they also significantly expanded Democratic majorities in both chambers of Congress. This newly unified government, operating against the backdrop of a devastating global economic crisis, raises a possibility that the tectonic plates of American government could shift, perhaps abruptly, and reshape the political and policy landscape for years to come.

While no one possesses a crystal ball, it is certain that the members of the 111th Congress, faced with a staggering array of monumental issues and decisions, will play a vital role in shaping the course of this country. That reality is what makes this 15th edition of *Politics in America* a crucial resource for understanding Congress, its decisions and its ultimate impact on public policy. This book will help you fathom the motivations of key players, assess the impact of issues that matter to them, and give you an authoritative roadmap to follow the political drama as it plays out on Capitol Hill.

Last fall's election returned Democrats to one-party rule for the first time in 15 years and enhanced their ability to move an ambitious legislative agenda. In the House, they built on their dominance, but with an expanded majority, Speaker Nancy Pelosi will be challenged to corral together an increasingly diverse party to drive the agenda. In the Senate, the story will revolve around the Democrat's quest for the political Holy Grail: 60 certain votes to beat back GOP filibuster threats.

Beyond institutional dynamics, there looms a set of intertwined issues certain to affect the course of policy making. Beyond the sputtering economy stands a panoply of other vital matters: health care overhaul, energy independence, wars in Iraq and Afghanistan, an unstable Pakistan and an unpredictable Iran. To understand how it all fits together, CQ journalists blanketed the Capitol to interview members of Congress and learn about their goals, experiences and perspectives. We delved into their politics, and we assessed exactly what kind of influence they have on the Hill.

Since 1945, Congressional Quarterly, which operates at the nexus of politics, legislation and public policy, has been an authoritative chronicler of Washington's governmental business. In a city known for its extremes, we play it down the middle. We are nonpartisan and independent. We don't say where members should stand on issues; we simply assess, as nearly as possible, how effective they are at achieving their stated goals.

In 1981, CQ published the first version of *Politics in America,* an insider's guide to the people who participate in one of the world's largest democracies. Leaf through these pages and you'll find that each lawmaker's section contains an in-depth political profile, key statistics on votes and positions, and a demographic description of the member's district.

Every day, CQ's editorial operation of more than 160 staffers brings an unparalleled expertise to the information published in our online news service, CQ.com, and in our print publications. Online, we have a robust twin to *Politics in America,* namely the Members section of CQ.com. The profiles you find here also live on the Internet, and, during the next two years, they will be updated regularly online to reflect the latest significant events.

Under the excellent editorial direction of Chuck McCutcheon and Christy Lyons, we think we have produced the most objective, authoritative, comprehensive and insightful volume of political analysis on the 111th Congress. We trust you'll agree.

Michael Riley
Editor and Senior Vice President
Congressional Quarterly Inc.

www.cqpress.com

From Problem to Solution?

C ongress is a much-maligned institution. Unwieldy, unpredictable and unable to pass bills — or stop them — as quickly as some voters would like, it is often entrenched in the lower reaches of opinion polls. In the weeks leading up to the 2008 presidential election, when Democratic candidate Barack Obama's message of hope was resonating with a broad cross-section of the public, more than three-quarters of those surveyed said they disapproved of the job the House and Senate were doing.

Political scholars don't have much positive to say about Congress, either. They dissect its alleged dysfunction at length and point to the persistence of partisanship, the decline in deliberation and the parochial self-interest among its members. The oft-quoted experts Thomas Mann and Norman Ornstein titled their 2006 indictment of Congress' failure to live up to its constitutional responsibilities "The Broken Branch."

But as has happened in the past, major events have made Capitol Hill a place of considerable consequence. Two wars, a severe economic crisis, looming concerns over health care, energy prices, the environment and other pressing issues have focused attention on the House and Senate as perhaps being part of the solution, rather than just the problem.

One way for Congress to try to solve problems is through its power of the purse. Lawmakers showed their willingness to provide money — shelving other concerns and turning back strenuous objections from both sides of the aisle — in approving a $700 billion rescue of the financial services industry in October 2008. That significant spending exercise was followed in short order during Obama's early months in office by a $410 billion spending bill for the 2009 fiscal year, a $787 billion economic stimulus law and a $3.56 trillion budget blueprint for the next fiscal year, all pushed to enactment by the Democratic leadership. Republicans adamantly opposed such moves, citing a lack of input as well as concerns over the magnitude of the actions. Observers noted with widely contrasting degrees of admiration and scorn that such moves thrust the federal government more deeply into American life than at any other time in recent decades.

And Congress' involvement by no means ends there. Aware of lawmakers' tendency toward anger when excluded from doing business, Obama turned to them to shape his biggest policy proposals. He outlined his general goals on health care reform, global warming legislation and other issues, but permitted Capitol Hill to fill in the details.

That provided an opening for some of Washington's most distinctive personalities to put an imprint on the president's priorities. They include, to name just a few, new House Energy and Commerce Chairman Henry A. Waxman of California, a liberal known as a shrewd dealmaker; Ways and Means Chairman Charles B. Rangel of New York, another crafty veteran bogged down in an ethics investigation; and the Senate tandem of Iowa Republican Charles E. Grassley and Montana Democrat Max Baucus atop the Finance Committee, exceptionally close-knit even by that chamber's clubby standards.

The relatively agreeable working arrangement between the White House and Congress was made possible by the 2008 election — the first since 1992 in which voters elected a Democratic president, House and Senate. At the outset of Obama's administration, the party controlled almost exactly as many seats as it did when Bill Clinton became president in 1993. But the two eras aren't exactly parallel. Clinton was a former governor who never served in Congress; his vice president, Al Gore, was the

Congress has helped thrust the federal government more deeply into American life than at any other time in recent decades.

About the Editors

Chuck McCutcheon has been covering Congress since 1995, initially as Washington correspondent for the Albuquerque Journal. He later became a reporter for Congressional Quarterly covering the Senate, national security and energy issues, then was a national correspondent and news editor for Newhouse News Service before returning to CQ in 2008 to serve as member profiles editor. He is the author of two books: *Nuclear Reactions: The Politics of Opening a Radioactive Waste Disposal Site* and the forthcoming *Global Warming and Climate Change*. He has a journalism degree from Northwestern University and lives in Washington, D.C., with his wife Liisa.

Christina L. Lyons has held a variety of positions at Congressional Quarterly since 1994, when she helped produce a documentary on Congress and the media in concert with the Freedom Forum. She subsequently became a news editor and senior editor for CQ's New Media department. After a stint as a freelance writer and editor, she returned to CQ as a news editor in 2002 and became managing editor of member profiles in 2008. She also covered Capitol Hill as a reporter for several newsletters, specializing in environmental and health policy, and covered local and state politics for the Frederick (Md.) News-Post. She holds a bachelor's degree from the University of the Pacific and a master's degree in political science from American University. She lives in Germantown, Md., with her husband Louis and their two children, Jack and Josie.

one with the substantial record of service in the House and Senate. Many of Clinton's early stumblings — most notably on health care — were widely attributed to an inability to bring Congress aboard as a partner.

Obama, meanwhile, spent four years in the Senate and forged alliances with members of both parties there. His vice president, Joseph R. Biden Jr., was a 36-year veteran of the chamber, with a formidable record on foreign policy and legal issues. The new president put a heavy emphasis on Hill experience in choosing his other lieutenants. His chief of staff, Rahm Emanuel, was a former chairman of the House Democratic Caucus. Four Cabinet officials came directly from Congress: Hillary Rodham Clinton at State, Ray LaHood at Transportation, Hilda L. Solis at Labor and Ken Salazar at Interior. And the head of Obama's Office of Management and Budget, Peter R. Orszag, was a former director of the Congressional Budget Office.

With so much intermingling between the executive and legislative branches, the characteristics of the latter merit especially close scrutiny. On average, senators and House members in the 111th Congress are older than their predecessors in previous Congresses dating back more than a century. As life expectancies have increased, members of Congress are serving with greater frequency at ages when most of their peers have long since retired. The average age for a senator in 2009 is slightly over 63; the average for a House member is 57.

Three of the four longest-serving senators in history took their seats when the Congress convened: Democrat Robert C. Byrd of West Virginia, Massachusetts Democrat Edward M. Kennedy and Hawaii Democrat Daniel K. Inouye. Across the Capitol, Michigan Democrat John D. Dingell reached a milestone in February 2009 by becoming the longest-serving House member ever. With each nearing the end of their careers, each was determined to craft legislation to help cement their legacies.

The 111th Congress includes a record 90 women (73 in the House, 17 in the Senate). Many, led by Speaker Nancy Pelosi of California, were in position to have a substantial imprint on shaping legislation. The Senate Small Business and Entrepreneurship Committee had women serving as both its chair (Louisiana's Mary L. Landrieu) and ranking Republican (Maine's Olympia J. Snowe) — the first occurrence of that in either chamber.

But the most significant demographic feature of the 111th Congress is the extreme regionalization of the two parties. The Democratic Party saw its caucus shrink sharply in the South. At the outset of Clinton's presidency, one-third of the Democratic caucus came from that region; now the region represents less than one-fourth of the caucus. The majority party drew a larger share from the more liberal-leaning Pacific Coast and Northeast, with not a single Republican member of the House hailing from New England. And many of those Democrats hold a large share of the leadership positions.

All of this has led Republicans to examine how to regroup as the party of opposition. As Senate Minority Leader Mitch McConnell of Kentucky lamented in January 2009: "The Republican Party seems to be slipping into a position of being more of a regional party than a national one."

Because of such a variety of issues, ideologies and personalities at play, Congress bears watching to see how it responds to the challenges it faces. Obviously, far more than just its approval ratings are at stake.

Chuck McCutcheon
May 2009

A Bigger Role in the Economy

Long before the 111th Congress was sworn in, it was clear that the weakened state of the U.S. economy would make the task of governing more challenging than Washington had seen in many generations.

Public opinion surveys had shown large majorities of the American public were apprehensive about their ability to find adequate jobs or to afford to live the way they wanted. One poll in mid-2008 financed by the Rockefeller Foundation showed that eight in 10 people agreed with this statement: "The social contract of the 20th century has been broken and needs to be rewritten to reflect the current realities of life today."

Most in that survey blamed Washington policy-makers for their troubles and said the rules of the game were rigged against them.

No doubt as a consequence of the banking and mortgage crisis, and possibly because of a growing distaste at the income gap between rich and poor, public opinion had turned after years of encouraging a hands-off approach by government. In particular, the tone was now one that favored greater regulation of business.

The electoral consequences that fall were immense. That was true both for the losers, many of whom were not in tune with the increasing desire for change expressed by the voters, and for the winners, who found themselves confronting a political-economic landscape unlike anything seen in decades. There was little doubt the American people had handed the new Congress and the new president the responsibility to address a wide range of economic and fiscal policy concerns that were perceived to have been largely ignored by those previously in charge.

The challenge ahead had been evident from the outset of the 2008 campaign. As the year progressed, the economy increasingly showed itself to be in far worse shape than almost anyone had imagined. Home foreclosures mounted, as did big bank failures. Consumer spending slowed to a trickle, and residential construction came to a halt.

Throughout the year, incumbent lawmakers and challengers of both parties were forced to address the building crisis, though it fell to the presidential campaigns to set the themes. Barack Obama, the Democratic nominee for president, offered a plan for middle-class tax relief and wide-ranging economic assistance. For his part, John McCain, the Republican standard-bearer, seemed to barely acknowledge rising middle-class angst and in particular the housing crisis, and tied his economic program principally to preserving the Bush-era tax cuts that were scheduled to expire in two years.

By Election Day, the economy was in a full-scale retreat unlike anything seen in at least a generation. The unemployment rate had climbed above 6 percent for the first time in five years and was headed much higher as companies eliminated hundreds of thousands of jobs every month. The National Bureau of Economic Research, a nonpartisan think tank based in Cambridge, Mass., pronounced the recession official in early December, saying the economy had been undergoing a broad decline for a year.

The news, however, was anti-climactic for the country and for its angry and disillusioned electorate. By that time, congressional Democrats had increased their majorities in the House and Senate, and Obama had been elected president, promising bold steps to put the economy back on a path to growth.

Democrats were not shy in advocating a bigger role for the federal government in remaking the economy. In a sweeping policy address two weeks before taking office, Obama asked the nation to adopt "a sense of common purpose above the same narrow partisanship and insist that the

Before taking office, Obama asked the nation to adopt "a sense of common purpose above the same narrow partisanship and insist that the first question each of us asks isn't 'What's good for me?' but 'What's good for the country my children will inherit?'"

Gross Domestic Product

Although the recession was judged to have begun in December 2007, U.S. gross domestic product didn't begin shrinking in earnest until the third quarter of 2008. By May of 2009, it was clear that GDP was contracting consistently and rapidly. GDP fell at a 6.3 percent annual rate in the final three months of 2008, and early estimates showed it fell at a 6.1 percent rate in the first quarter of 2009. It was the first time since 1974 that the United States had experienced three straight quarters of declining GDP, and the economy's decline so far was greater than in any recession since 1957-58.

Quarterly change, seasonally adjusted annual rate

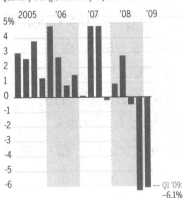

first question each of us asks isn't 'What's good for me?' but 'What's good for the country my children will inherit?' "

This call for change was seen by many observers as the beginnings of a renegotiation of the social contract between the government and the American people. As much as anything, it was a swing away from the individualist, anti-government ideal articulated by President Ronald Reagan, and embraced to a greater or lesser degree by the presidents who followed him — particularly George W. Bush and his "ownership society."

This evolution in ideals had been underway for some time and was not merely the dream of liberal activists. It was evident before the election in the attitudes of voters who said they feared they were being abandoned by their government. It was manifest in Washington's earliest responses to the nation's economic woes, and clear even in the decisions of the Bush administration during its final months in office and in calls by conservative economists for government intervention.

Lawmakers had begun 2008 by talking of handing out tens of billions of dollars in tax relief to give a lift to what was then seen as merely sluggish economic growth. By fall, that early economic stimulus measure looked like a pittance alongside increasingly aggressive government actions.

Early that October, Congress voted to give the Bush Treasury Department hundreds of billions of dollars with very few strings attached to prevent a wholesale collapse of the financial system. Leading up to that step, two of the largest investment banks in the country and the largest savings and loan institution had failed, the Treasury had taken control of Fannie Mae and Freddie Mac, the two largest mortgage financing companies, and the Federal Reserve had used emergency powers to rescue the world's largest insurance company. Moreover, many large commercial banks were feared to be in jeopardy.

Not only were the sums being borrowed for these endeavors almost beyond comprehension — the total amount of federal debt grew by $1.5 trillion, or 16 percent, in 2008 alone — but also the government's hand reached deep inside financial enterprises to help steer the economy in ways never before seen.

The first order of business for the 111th Congress was a request from the not-yet-inaugurated president for roughly $800 billion in spending increases and tax cuts that, it was hoped, would provide additional economic stimulus and prevent the deepest recession since World War II from worsening. Lawmakers pared Obama's request back a bit, added some sweeteners of their own, and in mid-February, a $787 billion package became law.

Beyond the stimulus measure, the early months of 2009 saw few signs that the Obama administration would temper its intention to expand the government's role in the economy in significant ways. Even as there were fleeting suggestions that the recession might bottom out by mid-year, the president kept up the heat on Congress, and Democrats on Capitol Hill appeared willing to stay the course.

Obama's Treasury joined with the Fed and other banking regulators to keep a close eye on the largest banks, forcing some to devise plans to increase their capital cushions through private means or risk an increased government role in their business. At the same time, lawmakers began early discussions with the administration about strengthening supervision of the financial industry to prevent a recurrence of the disaster that befell global credit markets in 2008.

With the seeming acquiescence of lawmakers, the White House played a crucial role in shrinking the U.S. auto industry in a bid to preserve it. Obama essentially ousted the chief executive of General Motors Corp. as part of a move to reorganize the largest domestic car company. And the administration engineered an orderly bankruptcy of No. 3 Chrysler, including its sale to a group that included the Italian car manufacturer Fiat. Bankruptcy for GM, too, seemed inevitable at the end of May.

In a budget for fiscal 2010 delivered to Capitol Hill just weeks after he took office, Obama proposed a whopping deficit of $1.2 trillion. Were it not for the fact that the fiscal 2009 shortfall already had been projected to come in at $1.7 trillion, Obama's proposal would have been stunning, amounting to two and a half times the previous record of $454 billion set in 2008. Even so, the volume of red ink requested for 2010 was still twice as large in inflation-adjusted terms as the biggest shortfall incurred during World War II.

The Democratic Congress went along, although the budget won not a single Republican vote. Congress gave the president almost everything he requested, including money to overhaul the nation's health insurance system and require most employers to cover their workers. The congressionally approved budget even incorporated a process to end-run objections to the health care overhaul plan from Senate Republicans and avoid a potentially killing filibuster.

Obama also chose to pick fights with lawmakers on sensitive economic issues that he said were critical for the nation's long-term success. For instance, he called on Congress to revise the way multinational corporations are taxed, a proposal that was met with immediate questioning on Capitol Hill. And he said he would press ahead with a demand for an overhaul of immigration laws that had stalled in prior years.

He also signaled that at some point, when the economy was back on track, he would turn his attention to the cost of government and work to move the budget closer to balance. As a small part of that effort, Obama proposed about $17 billion in program terminations and cutbacks for fiscal 2010, most of which were apt to face close scrutiny in Congress.

The legislative outcome for each of those contentious issues remained far from clear. Similarly, a push to make it easier for union organizers to operate — which had been at the top of labor's legislative agenda and was a chief concern of the U.S. Chamber of Commerce and other business groups — ran into early objections on Capitol Hill and was seemingly side-tracked. The administration did not show evidence of wanting to engage in a bitter battle over that issue in the early part of 2009, preferring to preserve its political capital for the coming debates on health care, global warming and other economic issues.

In rhetoric, Obama and many lawmakers on Capitol Hill plainly began 2009 by underscoring the notion that the social contract between the government and the people needed a renewal. How that renewal would play out was dependent both on the strength of the push-back by conservatives trying to reinvigorate President Reagan's legacy, and on the willingness of those on the left to agree to inevitable calls for compromise.

The course of the economy, too, was destined to be critical in any expansion of government's reach. Were the recession to persist and perhaps deepen, the opening for Washington to step in would widen. If, as seemed possible in early 2009, the economy touched bottom and began to recover by year's end, calls for a bigger federal role in the economy might abate.

Still, for some time to come, it was likely to be conventionally understood that it was a failure of government that allowed financial markets to crash and to bring on a global recession. That presented Obama and his allies in Congress both the opportunity and the challenge to act to prevent such failures from occurring in the future.

John Cranford
CQ Weekly Columnist, Political Economy
Managing Editor for Enterprise
May 2009

Total Payrolls

U.S. employers began eliminating jobs in January 2008, and by April 2009 the economy had lost 5.7 million positions. By then, the total number of non-farm jobs had fallen to 132.4 million, below the number that existed in January 2005 and below the peak of 132.5 million positions that existed before the recession of 2001. The jobless rate was at an almost 26-year high of 8.9 percent in April 2009, and many economists expected unemployment would reach 10 percent before it stopped rising in 2010.

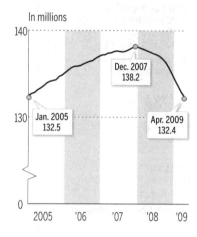

In millions

140

Dec. 2007
138.2

130 Jan. 2005
132.5

Apr. 2009
132.4

0

2005   '06   '07   '08   '09

Table of Contents

Preface v
Explanation of Statistics xvi

ALABAMA

Gov. Bob Riley (R) 1
Statistics 1
Map 2

U.S. SENATE
Richard C. Shelby (R) 3
Jeff Sessions (R) 5

U.S. HOUSE OF REPRESENTATIVES
1. Jo Bonner (R) 7
2. Bobby Bright (D) 9
3. Mike D. Rogers (R) 10
4. Robert B. Aderholt (R) 12
5. Parker Griffith (D) 14
6. Spencer Bachus (R) 15
7. Artur Davis (D) 17

ALASKA

Gov. Sarah Palin (R) 19
Statistics 19
Map 20

U.S. SENATE
Lisa Murkowski (R) 21
Mark Begich (D) 23

U.S. HOUSE OF REPRESENTATIVES
AL Don Young (R) 25

AMERICAN SAMOA

U.S. HOUSE OF REPRESENTATIVES
Eni F.H. Faleomavaega (D) 1127

ARIZONA

Gov. Jan Brewer (R) 27
Statistics 27
Map 28
Phoenix area map 29

U.S. SENATE
John McCain (R) 30
Jon Kyl (R) 32

U.S. HOUSE OF REPRESENTATIVES
1. Ann Kirkpatrick (D) 34
2. Trent Franks (R) 35
3. John Shadegg (R) 37
4. Ed Pastor (D) 39
5. Harry E. Mitchell (D) 41
6. Jeff Flake (R) 43
7. Raúl M. Grijalva (D) 45
8. Gabrielle Giffords (D) 47

ARKANSAS

Gov. Mike Beebe (D) 49
Statistics 49
Map 50

U.S. SENATE
Blanche Lincoln (D) 51
Mark Pryor (D) 53

U.S. HOUSE OF REPRESENTATIVES
1. Marion Berry (D) 55
2. Vic Snyder (D) 57
3. John Boozman (R) 59
4. Mike Ross (D) 61

CALIFORNIA

Gov. Arnold Schwarzenegger (R) . . . 63
Statistics 63
San Francisco area map 64
Los Angeles area map 65
San Diego area map 66
Map 67

U.S. SENATE
Dianne Feinstein (D) 68
Barbara Boxer (D) 70

U.S. HOUSE OF REPRESENTATIVES
1. Mike Thompson (D) 72
2. Wally Herger (R) 74
3. Dan Lungren (R) 76
4. Tom McClintock (R) 78
5. Doris Matsui (D) 79
6. Lynn Woolsey (D) 81
7. George Miller (D) 83
8. Nancy Pelosi (D) 85
9. Barbara Lee (D) 88
10. Expected vacancy (Tauscher) . . . 90
11. Jerry McNerney (D) 91
12. Jackie Speier (D) 93
13. Pete Stark (D) 95
14. Anna G. Eshoo (D) 97
15. Michael M. Honda (D) 99
16. Zoe Lofgren (D) 101
17. Sam Farr (D) 103
18. Dennis Cardoza (D) 105
19. George Radanovich (R) 107
20. Jim Costa (D) 109
21. Devin Nunes (R) 111
22. Kevin McCarthy (R) 113
23. Lois Capps (D) 115
24. Elton Gallegly (R) 117
25. Howard P. "Buck" McKeon (R) . . 119
26. David Dreier (R) 121
27. Brad Sherman (D) 123
28. Howard L. Berman (D) 125
29. Adam B. Schiff (D) 127
30. Henry A. Waxman (D) 129
31. Xavier Becerra (D) 131
32. Vacant (Solis) 133
33. Diane Watson (D) 134
34. Lucille Roybal-Allard (D) 136
35. Maxine Waters (D) 138
36. Jane Harman (D) 140
37. Laura Richardson (D) 142
38. Grace F. Napolitano (D) 144
39. Linda T. Sánchez (D) 146
40. Ed Royce (R) 148
41. Jerry Lewis (R) 150
42. Gary G. Miller (R) 152
43. Joe Baca (D) 154
44. Ken Calvert (R) 156
45. Mary Bono Mack (R) 158
46. Dana Rohrabacher (R) 160
47. Loretta Sanchez (D) 162
48. John Campbell (R) 164
49. Darrell Issa (R) 166
50. Brian P. Bilbray (R) 168
51. Bob Filner (D) 170
52. Duncan Hunter (R) 172
53. Susan A. Davis (D) 173

COLORADO

Gov. Bill Ritter Jr. (D) 175
Statistics 175
Map 176
Denver area map 176

U.S. SENATE
Mark Udall (D) 177
Michael Bennet (D) 179

U.S. HOUSE OF REPRESENTATIVES
1. Diana DeGette (D) 181
2. Jared Polis (D) 183
3. John Salazar (D) 184
4. Betsy Markey (D) 186
5. Doug Lamborn (R) 187
6. Mike Coffman (R) 189
7. Ed Perlmutter (D) 190

CONNECTICUT

Gov. M. Jodi Rell (R) 192
Statistics 192
Map 193

U.S. SENATE
Christopher J. Dodd (D) 194
Joseph I. Lieberman (I) 196

U.S. HOUSE OF REPRESENTATIVES
1. John B. Larson (D) 198
2. Joe Courtney (D) 200
3. Rosa DeLauro (D) 202
4. Jim Himes (D) 204
5. Christopher S. Murphy (D) 205

DELAWARE

Gov. Jack Markell (D) 207
Statistics 207
Map 208

U.S. SENATE
Thomas R. Carper (D) 209
Ted Kaufman (D) 211

www.cqpress.com

U.S. HOUSE OF REPRESENTATIVES
AL Michael N. Castle (R) 213

DISTRICT OF COLUMBIA

U.S. HOUSE OF REPRESENTATIVES
Eleanor Holmes Norton (D) 1128

FLORIDA

Gov. Charlie Crist (R) 215
Statistics 215
Map 216
Miami area map 217
Orlando area map 217

U.S. SENATE
Bill Nelson (D) 218
Mel Martinez (R) 220

U.S. HOUSE OF REPRESENTATIVES
1. Jeff Miller (R) 222
2. Allen Boyd (D) 224
3. Corrine Brown (D) 226
4. Ander Crenshaw (R) 228
5. Ginny Brown-Waite (R) 230
6. Cliff Stearns (R) 232
7. John L. Mica (R) 234
8. Alan Grayson (D) 236
9. Gus Bilirakis (R) 237
10. C.W. Bill Young (R) 239
11. Kathy Castor (D) 241
12. Adam H. Putnam (R) 243
13. Vern Buchanan (R) 245
14. Connie Mack (R) 247
15. Bill Posey (R) 249
16. Tom Rooney (R) 250
17. Kendrick B. Meek (D) 251
18. Ileana Ros-Lehtinen (R) 253
19. Robert Wexler (D) 255
20. Debbie Wasserman Schultz (D) . 257
21. Lincoln Diaz-Balart (R) 259
22. Ron Klein (D) 261
23. Alcee L. Hastings (D) 263
24. Suzanne M. Kosmas (D) 265
25. Mario Diaz-Balart (R) 266

GEORGIA

Gov. Sonny Perdue (R) 268
Statistics 268
Map 269
Atlanta area map 270

U.S. SENATE
Saxby Chambliss (R) 271
Johnny Isakson (R) 273

U.S. HOUSE OF REPRESENTATIVES
1. Jack Kingston (R) 275
2. Sanford D. Bishop Jr. (D) 277
3. Lynn Westmoreland (R) 279
4. Hank Johnson (D) 281
5. John Lewis (D) 283

6. Tom Price (R) 285
7. John Linder (R) 287
8. Jim Marshall (D) 289
9. Nathan Deal (R) 291
10. Paul Broun (R) 293
11. Phil Gingrey (R) 295
12. John Barrow (D) 297
13. David Scott (D) 299

GUAM

U.S. HOUSE OF REPRESENTATIVES
Madeleine Z. Bordallo (D) 1129

HAWAII

Gov. Linda Lingle (R) 301
Statistics 301
Map 302

U.S. SENATE
Daniel K. Inouye (D) 303
Daniel K. Akaka (D) 305

U.S. HOUSE OF REPRESENTATIVES
1. Neil Abercrombie (D) 307
2. Mazie K. Hirono (D) 309

IDAHO

Gov. C. L. "Butch" Otter (R) 311
Statistics 311
Map 312

U.S. SENATE
Michael D. Crapo (R) 313
Jim Risch (R) 315

U.S. HOUSE OF REPRESENTATIVES
1. Walt Minnick (D) 317
2. Mike Simpson (R) 318

ILLINOIS

Gov. Pat Quinn (D) 320
Statistics 320
Map 321
Chicago area map 322

U.S. SENATE
Richard J. Durbin (D) 323
Roland W. Burris (D) 325

U.S. HOUSE OF REPRESENTATIVES
1. Bobby L. Rush (D) 327
2. Jesse L. Jackson Jr. (D) 329
3. Daniel Lipinski (D) 331
4. Luis V. Gutierrez (D) 333
5. Mike Quigley (D) 335
6. Peter Roskam (R) 336
7. Danny K. Davis (D) 338
8. Melissa Bean (D) 340
9. Jan Schakowsky (D) 342
10. Mark Steven Kirk (R) 344
11. Debbie Halvorson (D) 346

12. Jerry F. Costello (D) 347
13. Judy Biggert (R) 349
14. Bill Foster (D) 351
15. Timothy V. Johnson (R) 353
16. Donald Manzullo (R) 355
17. Phil Hare (D) 357
18. Aaron Schock (R) 359
19. John Shimkus (R) 360

INDIANA

Gov. Mitch Daniels (R) 362
Statistics 362
Map 363

U.S. SENATE
Richard G. Lugar (R) 364
Evan Bayh (D) 366

U.S. HOUSE OF REPRESENTATIVES
1. Peter J. Visclosky (D) 368
2. Joe Donnelly (D) 370
3. Mark Souder (R) 372
4. Steve Buyer (R) 374
5. Dan Burton (R) 376
6. Mike Pence (R) 378
7. André Carson (D) 380
8. Brad Ellsworth (D) 382
9. Baron P. Hill (D) 384

IOWA

Gov. Chet Culver (D) 386
Statistics 386
Map 387

U.S. SENATE
Charles E. Grassley (R) 388
Tom Harkin (D) 390

U.S. HOUSE OF REPRESENTATIVES
1. Bruce Braley (D) 392
2. Dave Loebsack (D) 394
3. Leonard L. Boswell (D) 396
4. Tom Latham (R) 398
5. Steve King (R) 400

KANSAS

Gov. Mark Parkinson (D) 402
Statistics 402
Map 403

U.S. SENATE
Sam Brownback (R) 404
Pat Roberts (R) 406

U.S. HOUSE OF REPRESENTATIVES
1. Jerry Moran (R) 408
2. Lynn Jenkins (R) 410
3. Dennis Moore (D) 411
4. Todd Tiahrt (R) 413

KENTUCKY

Gov. Steven L. Beshear (D) 415
Statistics 415
Map 416

U.S. SENATE
Mitch McConnell (R) 417
Jim Bunning (R) 420

U.S. HOUSE OF REPRESENTATIVES
1. Ed Whitfield (R) 422
2. Brett Guthrie (R) 424
3. John Yarmuth (D) 425
4. Geoff Davis (R) 427
5. Harold Rogers (R) 429
6. Ben Chandler (D) 431

LOUISIANA

Gov. Bobby Jindal (R) 433
Statistics 433
Map 434

U.S. SENATE
Mary L. Landrieu (D) 435
David Vitter (R) 437

U.S. HOUSE OF REPRESENTATIVES
1. Steve Scalise (R) 439
2. Anh "Joseph" Cao (R) 441
3. Charlie Melancon (D) 442
4. John Fleming (R) 444
5. Rodney Alexander (R) 445
6. Bill Cassidy (R) 447
7. Charles Boustany Jr. (R) 448

MAINE

Gov. John Baldacci (D) 450
Statistics 450
Map 451

U.S. SENATE
Olympia J. Snowe (R) 452
Susan Collins (R) 454

U.S. HOUSE OF REPRESENTATIVES
1. Chellie Pingree (D) 456
2. Michael H. Michaud (D) 457

MARYLAND

Gov. Martin O'Malley (D) 459
Statistics 459
Map 460
Baltimore area map 460

U.S. SENATE
Barbara A. Mikulski (D) 461
Benjamin L. Cardin (D) 463

U.S. HOUSE OF REPRESENTATIVES
1. Frank Kratovil Jr. (D) 465
2. C.A. Dutch Ruppersberger (D) . 466
3. John Sarbanes (D) 468
4. Donna Edwards (D) 470

5. Steny H. Hoyer (D) 472
6. Roscoe G. Bartlett (R) 474
7. Elijah E. Cummings (D) 476
8. Chris Van Hollen (D) 478

MASSACHUSETTS

Gov. Deval Patrick (D) 480
Statistics 480
Map 481
Boston area map 481

U.S. SENATE
Edward M. Kennedy (D) 482
John Kerry (D) 484

U.S. HOUSE OF REPRESENTATIVES
1. John W. Olver (D) 486
2. Richard E. Neal (D) 488
3. Jim McGovern (D) 490
4. Barney Frank (D) 492
5. Niki Tsongas (D) 494
6. John F. Tierney (D) 496
7. Edward J. Markey (D) 498
8. Michael E. Capuano (D) 500
9. Stephen F. Lynch (D) 502
10 Bill Delahunt (D) 504

MICHIGAN

Gov. Jennifer M. Granholm (D) 506
Statistics 506
Detroit area map 507
Map 507

U.S. SENATE
Carl Levin (D) 508
Debbie Stabenow (D) 510

U.S. HOUSE OF REPRESENTATIVES
1. Bart Stupak (D) 512
2. Peter Hoekstra (R) 514
3. Vernon J. Ehlers (R) 516
4. Dave Camp (R) 518
5. Dale E. Kildee (D) 520
6. Fred Upton (R) 522
7. Mark Schauer (D) 524
8. Mike Rogers (R) 525
9. Gary Peters (D) 527
10. Candice S. Miller (R) 528
11. Thaddeus McCotter (R) 530
12. Sander M. Levin (D) 532
13. Carolyn Cheeks Kilpatrick (D) . 534
14. John Conyers Jr. (D) 536
15. John D. Dingell (D) 538

MINNESOTA

Gov. Tim Pawlenty (R) 540
Statistics 540
Map 541
Twin Cities area map 541

U.S. SENATE
Amy Klobuchar (D) 542
Al Franken (D) 544
Norm Coleman (R) 545

U.S. HOUSE OF REPRESENTATIVES
1. Tim Walz (D) 546
2. John Kline (R) 548
3. Erik Paulsen (R) 550
4. Betty McCollum (D) 551
5. Keith Ellison (D) 553
6. Michele Bachmann (R) 555
7. Collin C. Peterson (D) 557
8. James L. Oberstar (D) 559

MISSISSIPPI

Gov. Haley Barbour (R) 561
Statistics 561
Map 562

U.S. SENATE
Thad Cochran (R) 563
Roger Wicker (R) 565

U.S. HOUSE OF REPRESENTATIVES
1. Travis W. Childers (D) 567
2. Bennie Thompson (D) 569
3. Gregg Harper (R) 571
4. Gene Taylor (D) 572

MISSOURI

Gov. Jay Nixon (D) 574
Statistics 574
Map 575

U.S. SENATE
Christopher S. Bond (R) 576
Claire McCaskill (D) 578

U.S. HOUSE OF REPRESENTATIVES
1. William Lacy Clay (D) 580
2. Todd Akin (R) 582
3. Russ Carnahan (D) 584
4. Ike Skelton (D) 586
5. Emanuel Cleaver II (D) 588
6. Sam Graves (R) 590
7. Roy Blunt (R) 592
8. Jo Ann Emerson (R) 594
9. Blaine Luetkemeyer (R) 596

MONTANA

Gov. Brian Schweitzer (D) 597
Statistics 597
Map 598

U.S. SENATE
Max Baucus (D) 599
Jon Tester (D) 601

U.S. HOUSE OF REPRESENTATIVES
AL Denny Rehberg (R) 603

NEBRASKA

Gov. Dave Heineman (R) 605
Statistics 605
Map 606

U.S. SENATE
Ben Nelson (D) 607
Mike Johanns (R) 609

U.S. HOUSE OF REPRESENTATIVES
1. Jeff Fortenberry (R) 611
2. Lee Terry (R) 613
3. Adrian Smith (R) 615

NEVADA

Gov. Jim Gibbons (R) 617
Statistics 617
Map 618

U.S. SENATE
Harry Reid (D) 619
John Ensign (R) 622

U.S. HOUSE OF REPRESENTATIVES
1. Shelley Berkley (D) 624
2. Dean Heller (R) 626
3. Dina Titus (D) 628

NEW HAMPSHIRE

Gov. John Lynch (D) 629
Statistics 629
Map 630

U.S. SENATE
Judd Gregg (R) 631
Jeanne Shaheen (D) 633

U.S. HOUSE OF REPRESENTATIVES
1. Carol Shea-Porter (D) 635
2. Paul W. Hodes (D) 637

NEW JERSEY

Gov. Jon Corzine (D) 639
Statistics 639
Map 640
Northern New Jersey map 640

U.S. SENATE
Frank R. Lautenberg (D) 641
Robert Menendez (D) 643

U.S. HOUSE OF REPRESENTATIVES
1. Robert E. Andrews (D) 645
2. Frank A. LoBiondo (R) 647
3. John Adler (D) 649
4. Christopher H. Smith (R) 650
5. Scott Garrett (R) 652
6. Frank Pallone Jr. (D) 654
7. Leonard Lance (R) 656
8. Bill Pascrell Jr. (D) 657
9. Steven R. Rothman (D) 659
10. Donald M. Payne (D) 661
11. Rodney Frelinghuysen (R) 663
12. Rush D. Holt (D) 665
13. Albio Sires (D) 667

NEW MEXICO

Gov. Bill Richardson (D) 669
Statistics 669
Map 670

U.S. SENATE
Jeff Bingaman (D) 671
Tom Udall (D) 673

U.S. HOUSE OF REPRESENTATIVES
1. Martin Heinrich (D) 675
2. Harry Teague (D) 676
3. Ben Ray Luján (D) 677

NEW YORK

Gov. David A. Paterson (D) 678
Statistics 678
Map 679
New York City area map 680

U.S. SENATE
Charles E. Schumer (D) 681
Kirsten Gillibrand (D) 683

U.S. HOUSE OF REPRESENTATIVES
1. Timothy H. Bishop (D) 685
2. Steve Israel (D) 687
3. Peter T. King (R) 689
4. Carolyn McCarthy (D) 691
5. Gary L. Ackerman (D) 693
6. Gregory W. Meeks (D) 695
7. Joseph Crowley (D) 697
8. Jerrold Nadler (D) 699
9. Anthony Weiner (D) 701
10. Edolphus Towns (D) 703
11. Yvette D. Clarke (D) 705
12. Nydia M. Velázquez (D) 707
13. Michael E. McMahon (D) 709
14. Carolyn B. Maloney (D) 710
15. Charles B. Rangel (D) 712
16. José E. Serrano (D) 714
17. Eliot L. Engel (D) 716
18. Nita M. Lowey (D) 718
19. John Hall (D) 720
20. Scott Murphy (D) 722
21. Paul Tonko (D) 723
22. Maurice D. Hinchey (D) 724
23. John M. McHugh (R) 726
24. Michael Arcuri (D) 728
25. Dan Maffei (D) 730
26. Christopher Lee (R) 731
27. Brian Higgins (D) 732
28. Louise M. Slaughter (D) 734
29. Eric Massa (D) 736

NORTH CAROLINA

Gov. Bev Perdue (D) 737
Statistics 737
Map 738

U.S. SENATE
Richard M. Burr (R) 739
Kay Hagan (D) 741

U.S. HOUSE OF REPRESENTATIVES
1. G.K. Butterfield (D) 743
2. Bob Etheridge (D) 745
3. Walter B. Jones (R) 747
4. David E. Price (D) 749
5. Virginia Foxx (R) 751
6. Howard Coble (R) 753
7. Mike McIntyre (D) 755
8. Larry Kissell (D) 757
9. Sue Myrick (R) 758
10. Patrick T. McHenry (R) 760
11. Heath Shuler (D) 762
12. Melvin Watt (D) 764
13. Brad Miller (D) 766

NORTH DAKOTA

Gov. John Hoeven (R) 768
Statistics 768
Map 769

U.S. SENATE
Kent Conrad (D) 770
Byron L. Dorgan (D) 772

U.S. HOUSE OF REPRESENTATIVES
AL Earl Pomeroy (D) 774

NORTHERN MARIANAS

U.S. HOUSE OF REPRESENTATIVES
Gregorio Kilili Camacho Sablan (D) . . 1130

OHIO

Gov. Ted Strickland (D) 776
Statistics 776
Map 777

U.S. SENATE
George V. Voinovich (R) 778
Sherrod Brown (D) 780

U.S. HOUSE OF REPRESENTATIVES
1. Steve Driehaus (D) 782
2. Jean Schmidt (R) 783
3. Michael R. Turner (R) 785
4. Jim Jordan (R) 787

5. Bob Latta (R). 789
6. Charlie Wilson (D) 791
7. Steve Austria (R) 793
8. John A. Boehner (R). 794
9. Marcy Kaptur (D) 797
10. Dennis J. Kucinich (D) 799
11. Marcia L. Fudge (D) 801
12. Pat Tiberi (R) 803
13. Betty Sutton (D) 805
14. Steven C. LaTourette (R) 807
15. Mary Jo Kilroy (D) 809
16. John Boccieri (D) 810
17. Tim Ryan (D). 811
18. Zack Space (D) 813

OKLAHOMA

Gov. Brad Henry (D). 815
Statistics 815
Map. 816

U.S. SENATE
James M. Inhofe (R) 817
Tom Coburn (R) 819

U.S. HOUSE OF REPRESENTATIVES
1. John Sullivan (R) 821
2. Dan Boren (D). 823
3. Frank D. Lucas (R). 825
4. Tom Cole (R) 827
5. Mary Fallin (R) 829

OREGON

Gov. Theodore R. Kulongoski (D) . . 831
Statistics 831
Map. 832

U.S. SENATE
Ron Wyden (D) 833
Jeff Merkley (D) 835

U.S. HOUSE OF REPRESENTATIVES
1. David Wu (D) 837
2. Greg Walden (R) 839
3. Earl Blumenauer (D). 841
4. Peter A. DeFazio (D) 843
5. Kurt Schrader (D) 845

PENNSYLVANIA

Gov. Edward G. Rendell (D). 846
Statistics 846
Philadelphia area map 847
Map. 848

U.S. SENATE
Arlen Specter (D). 849
Bob Casey (D) 851

U.S. HOUSE OF REPRESENTATIVES
1. Robert A. Brady (D) 853
2. Chaka Fattah (D). 855
3. Kathy Dahlkemper (D) 857
4. Jason Altmire (D). 858
5. Glenn Thompson (R) 860

6. Jim Gerlach (R) 861
7. Joe Sestak (D) 863
8. Patrick J. Murphy (D). 865
9. Bill Shuster (R) 867
10. Christopher Carney (D). 869
11. Paul E. Kanjorski (D). 871
12. John P. Murtha (D) 873
13. Allyson Y. Schwartz (D) 875
14. Mike Doyle (D) 877
15. Charlie Dent (R) 879
16. Joe Pitts (R) 881
17. Tim Holden (D) 883
18. Tim Murphy (R) 885
19. Todd R. Platts (R) 887

PUERTO RICO

U.S. HOUSE OF REPRESENTATIVES
Pedro R. Pierluisi (D). 1131

RHODE ISLAND

Gov. Donald L. Carcieri (R) 889
Statistics 889
Map. 890

U.S. SENATE
Jack Reed (D) 891
Sheldon Whitehouse (D). 893
U.S. HOUSE OF REPRESENTATIVES
1. Patrick J. Kennedy (D) 895
2. Jim Langevin (D) 897

SOUTH CAROLINA

Gov. Mark Sanford (R). 899
Statistics 899
Map. 900

U.S. SENATE
Lindsey Graham (R) 901
Jim DeMint (R) 903

U.S. HOUSE OF REPRESENTATIVES
1. Henry E. Brown Jr. (R) 905
2. Joe Wilson (R) 907
3. J. Gresham Barrett (R) 909
4. Bob Inglis (R) 911
5. John M. Spratt Jr. (D) 913
6. James E. Clyburn (D) 915

SOUTH DAKOTA

Gov. Michael Rounds (R). 917
Statistics 917
Map. 918

U.S. SENATE
Tim Johnson (D) 919
John Thune (R) 921

U.S. HOUSE OF REPRESENTATIVES
AL Stephanie Herseth Sandlin (D). 923

TENNESSEE

Gov. Phil Bredesen (D) 925
Statistics 925
Map. 926

U.S. SENATE
Lamar Alexander (R) 927
Bob Corker (R) 929

U.S. HOUSE OF REPRESENTATIVES
1. Phil Roe (R). 931
2. John J. "Jimmy" Duncan Jr. (R). 932
3. Zach Wamp (R). 934
4. Lincoln Davis (D) 936
5. Jim Cooper (D) 938
6. Bart Gordon (D) 940
7. Marsha Blackburn (R) 942
8. John Tanner (D) 944
9. Steve Cohen (D) 946

TEXAS

Gov. Rick Perry (R). 948
Statistics 948
Map. 949
Dallas area map 950
Houston area map. 950

U.S. SENATE
Kay Bailey Hutchison (R). 951
John Cornyn (R). 953

U.S. HOUSE OF REPRESENTATIVES
1. Louie Gohmert (R) 955
2. Ted Poe (R). 957
3. Sam Johnson (R) 959
4. Ralph M. Hall (R) 961
5. Jeb Hensarling (R) 963
6. Joe L. Barton (R). 965
7. John Culberson (R). 967
8. Kevin Brady (R) 969
9. Al Green (D) 971
10. Michael McCaul (R) 973
11. K. Michael Conaway (R). 975
12. Kay Granger (R) 977
13. William M. "Mac" Thornberry (R) 979
14. Ron Paul (R) 981
15. Rubén Hinojosa (D) 983
16. Silvestre Reyes (D) 985
17. Chet Edwards (D) 987
18. Sheila Jackson Lee (D). 989
19. Randy Neugebauer (R). 991
20. Charlie Gonzalez (D). 993
21. Lamar Smith (R) 995
22. Pete Olson (R). 997
23. Ciro D. Rodriguez (D) 998
24. Kenny Marchant (R). 1000
25. Lloyd Doggett (D) 1002
26. Michael C. Burgess (R). 1004
27. Solomon P. Ortiz (D) 1006
28. Henry Cuellar (D) 1008
29. Gene Green (D) 1010
30. Eddie Bernice Johnson (D). . . 1012

31. John Carter (R) 1014
32. Pete Sessions (R) 1016

UTAH

Gov. Jon Huntsman Jr. (R) 1018
Statistics 1018
Map 1019

U.S. SENATE
Orrin G. Hatch (R) 1020
Robert F. Bennett (R) 1022

U.S. HOUSE OF REPRESENTATIVES
1. Rob Bishop (R) 1024
2. Jim Matheson (D) 1026
3. Jason Chaffetz (R) 1028

VERMONT

Gov. Jim Douglas (R) 1029
Statistics 1029
Map 1030

U.S. SENATE
Patrick J. Leahy (D) 1031
Bernard Sanders (I) 1033

U.S. HOUSE OF REPRESENTATIVES
AL Peter Welch (D) 1035

VIRGIN ISLANDS

U.S. HOUSE OF REPRESENTATIVES
Donna M.C. Christensen (D) 1132

VIRGINIA

Gov. Tim Kaine (D) 1037
Statistics 1037
Northern Virginia area map 1038
Map 1038

U.S. SENATE
Jim Webb (D) 1039
Mark Warner (D) 1041

U.S. HOUSE OF REPRESENTATIVES
1. Rob Wittman (R) 1043
2. Glenn Nye (D) 1045
3. Robert C. Scott (D) 1046
4. J. Randy Forbes (R) 1048
5. Tom Perriello (D) 1050
6. Robert W. Goodlatte (R) 1051
7. Eric Cantor (R) 1053
8. James P. Moran (D) 1055
9. Rick Boucher (D) 1057
10. Frank R. Wolf (R) 1059
11. Gerald E. Connolly (D) 1061

WASHINGTON

Gov. Christine Gregoire (D) 1062
Statistics 1062
Seattle area map 1063
Map 1063

U.S. SENATE
Patty Murray (D) 1064
Maria Cantwell (D) 1066

U.S. HOUSE OF REPRESENTATIVES
1. Jay Inslee (D) 1068
2. Rick Larsen (D) 1070
3. Brian Baird (D) 1072
4. Doc Hastings (R) 1074
5. Cathy McMorris Rodgers (R) . 1076
6. Norm Dicks (D) 1078
7. Jim McDermott (D) 1080
8. Dave Reichert (R) 1082
9. Adam Smith (D) 1084

WEST VIRGINIA

Gov. Joe Manchin III (D) 1086
Statistics 1086
Map 1087

U.S. SENATE
Robert C. Byrd (D) 1088
John D. Rockefeller IV (D) 1090

U.S. HOUSE OF REPRESENTATIVES
1. Alan B. Mollohan (D) 1092
2. Shelley Moore Capito (R) 1094
3. Nick J. Rahall II (D) 1096

WISCONSIN

Gov. James E. Doyle (D) 1098
Statistics 1098
Map 1099

U.S. SENATE
Herb Kohl (D) 1100
Russ Feingold (D) 1102

U.S. HOUSE OF REPRESENTATIVES
1. Paul D. Ryan (R) 1104
2. Tammy Baldwin (D) 1106
3. Ron Kind (D) 1108
4. Gwen Moore (D) 1110
5. F. James Sensenbrenner Jr. (R) . 1112
6. Tom Petri (R) 1114
7. David R. Obey (D) 1116
8. Steve Kagen (D) 1118

WYOMING

Gov. Dave Freudenthal (D) 1120
Statistics 1120
Map 1121

U.S. SENATE
Michael B. Enzi (R) 1122
John Barrasso (R) 1124

U.S. HOUSE OF REPRESENTATIVES
AL Cynthia M. Lummis (R) 1126

MEMBER STATISTICS

BY THE NUMBERS 1133
HOUSE SENIORITY 1134
SENATE SENIORITY 1138
WOMEN IN CONGRESS 1140
OLDEST/YOUNGEST 1140
MINORITIES IN CONGRESS . . . 1141
FORMER HILL AIDES 1142
MILITARY SERVICE 1144
MOST & LEAST LEGISLATION . 1146
FAMILIES IN CONGRESS 1147
PRONUNCIATION GUIDE 1148
NEW TO CONGRESS 1149
SENATORS UP IN 2008 1149
OCCUPATIONS 1152
RELIGIONS 1153
SENATE VOTE STUDIES 1154
HOUSE VOTE STUDIES 1156
INFORMAL CAUCUSES 1158
DISTRICT DEMOGRAPHICS . . . 1162
DID YOU KNOW? 1206

ELECTIONS

CLOSEST ELECTIONS 1164
SPLIT TICKETS 1165

CAMPAIGN FINANCE

TOP SPENDERS 1166
CAMPAIGN FINANCE 1168

COMMITTEES

HOUSE COMMITTEES 1184
SENATE COMMITTEES 1197
JOINT COMMITTEES 1205
COMMITTEE FACTS 1161

MEMBER NAME INDEX

INDEX 1209

Explanation of Statistics

State Profiles

State profile pages contain information on governors, compositions of state legislatures and information about major cities. Details about the makeup of the state legislatures, salaries, the legislative schedule, registered voters and state term limits were obtained from state officials and reflect their status as of May 2009.

POPULATION AND URBAN STATISTICS

Demographic information was obtained from the U.S. Census Bureau and the Bureau of Economic Analysis, both within the Commerce Department. Violent crime rates are from 2000, the poverty rate is from 1999 and federal workers and military personnel statistics are from 2001.

STATISTICS BY DISTRICT

Demographic information relates to current congressional district lines. The figures for racial composition, Hispanic origin, median household income, types of employment, age, education, urban versus rural residence and size of each congressional district are from the Census Bureau.

The racial composition figures reflect census respondents who described themselves as of one race. The white population figure is for non-Hispanic whites. The median household income figure is for 1999.

The occupational breakdown combines figures from the Census Bureau's management, professional and related occupations category and its sales and office occupations category to make up the white-collar category. The blue-collar category includes three bureau categories: farming, fishing and forestry; construction, extraction and maintenance; and production, transportation and material moving occupations.

The college education table shows the percentage of people age 25 and older who have earned at least a bachelor's degree. The district's area is presented in square miles of land area.

LOUISIANA STATE PROFILES

Data for Louisiana is also based on the 2000 census, but because of the demographic shifts caused by hurricane-related devastation in 2005 it should be used with care until it is recalculated as part of the 2010 census. An asterisk denotes those districts that would merit additional attention.

Other states were either directly impacted by the storm or altered by the influx of Gulf Coast evacuees, but they have roughly returned to pre-hurricane standards, and so data for Mississippi, Texas, Alabama, Florida and other affected states have not been flagged.

District Descriptions

In most states, congressional district lines were redrawn in 2001 or 2002 to reflect reapportionment and changes in population patterns revealed in the 2000 census. Maine's constitution calls for redistricting in the third year of each decade, and so new lines were drawn in 2003 for the 2004 election. Other mid-decade changes were in response to legal challenges.

A second set of Pennsylvania district lines drawn in 2002 was not effective until the 2004 election. Georgia districts were reconfigured in 2005 for the 2006 election. Texas had five districts — the 15th, 21st, 23rd, 25th and 28th — redrawn by a federal court for the 2006 election. No congressional district lines changed for the 2008 election.

The district description briefly sets forth the economic, sociological, demographic and political forces that are the keys to elections and that influence the legislative agenda of the district's member of Congress. City population figures are from the U.S. Census Bureau.

Presidential Vote by District

CQ determined the 2008 presidential vote in each House district by acquiring and calculating vote returns from state and county election offices in the 43 states that have more than one House district. In seven of those states — Connecticut, Kentucky, Maine, Minnesota, Nebraska, North Carolina and Virginia — CQ used the presidential district vote calculations produced by state election officials. Seven states — Alaska, Delaware, Montana, North Dakota, South Dakota, Vermont and Wyoming — have only one House district.

Key to Party Abbreviations

AC	American Constitution
ADBP	All-Day Breakfast Party
AKI	Alaskan Independence
AMI	American Independent
BLU	Blue Enigma
BTB	Back to Basics
C	Conservative
CFL	Connecticut for Lieberman
CNSTP	Constitution
CS	Common Sense
CRE	Cheap Renewable Energy
D	Democratic
EINDC	Energy Independence
ELIM	Eliminate the Primary
FTP	For the People
GREEN	Green
HFC	Hsing for Congress
I	Independent
IA	Independent American
IGREEN	Independent Green
INDC	Independence
IGWT	In God We Trust
LFC	Lindsay for Congress
LIBERT	Libertarian
LU	Liberty Union
MOUNT	Mountain
NEB	Nebraska
NL	Natural Law

continued on next page

Military base figures are compiled by CQ from information provided by each base and from annual Defense Department reports. Military base listings do not include Coast Guard, National Guard or reserve bases, and do not include all depots and arsenals due to space limitations.

Member Profiles

Committees

Committee assignments are as of May 2009, and a complete roster for each panel begins on page 1184.

Career and Political Highlights

The member's principal occupations before becoming a full-time public official are given, with the most recent occupation listed first. Often, lawmakers' prior political offices were part-time jobs, and the member continued working at his or her "career" job. Political highlights listed include elected positions in government, high party posts, posts requiring legislative confirmation and unsuccessful candidacies for public office. Dates given cover years of service, not election dates.

Elections

Results for 2006 and 2008 are listed for House members, with primary results for 2008. For senators and governors, the most recent election results are listed. Because candidates who received less than 1 percent of the vote are not listed and percentages have been rounded, election results do not always add up to 100 percent.

Earlier election victories are noted for members of the House and Senate, with the member's percentage of the vote given. If no percentage is given for a year, the member either did not run or lost the election.

For special elections and primaries where a candidate would have won outright if he or she had received a majority of the votes, two election tallies are given, one for the initial election and one for the subsequent runoff.

PRIMARY ELECTIONS

Prior to 2009 Louisiana held its primary on Election Day. It was an open primary, with candidates from all parties on the ballot. Any candidate who received more than half the votes, or who was unopposed, was elected. If no candidate received an outright majority, the top two vote-getters, regardless of party, advanced to a runoff election to decide the winner.

In March 2008, the Washington state Supreme Court upheld the "top two" primary system in which voters are able to vote for one candidate from among all candidates running for each office without having to declare a party affiliation or select a party ballot. The two candidates in each race who receive the most votes qualify for the general election, provided the candidate received at least 1 percent of the total votes cast for that office. Candidates for partisan office have the opportunity to state a political party preference on the primary ballot, but that preference is not an indication of approval, support, nomination, endorsement or association by the party that is listed.

Key Votes

Profiles of members who served in the 110th Congress (2007-08) are accompanied by key votes chosen by CQ editors from that Congress. Following is a description of those votes, including President George W. Bush's position on that particular vote, if he unambiguously took one beforehand.

continued from previous page

PACGRN	Pacific Green
PC	Personal Choice
PFP	Peace and Freedom
POP	Populist
POPDEM	Popular Democratic
PPC	Poor People's Campaign
PRI	Puerto Rican Independence
PRO	Progressive
PROS	Prosperity Not War
PTY	Term Limits for U.S. Congress
QRT	Quit Raising Taxes
R	Republican
REF	Reform
RTB	Rock the Boat
S	Socialist
SW	Socialist Workers
TI	Think Independently
UNT	Unity
USTAX	U.S. Taxpayers
VGE	Vermont Green
VPC	Vote People Change
WFM	Working Families
WG	Wisconsin Greens
WTN	Withdraw Troops Now
WTP	We The People
X	Not applicable

Key Votes

CQ editors selected key votes from roll-call votes taken during the 110th Congress. The following symbols are used:

Y   voted for (yes)

N   voted against (no)

\#   paired for

\+   announced for

X   paired against

−   announced against

P   voted "present"

C   voted "present" to avoid possible conflict of interest

?   did not vote or otherwise make a position known

I   ineligible

S   Speaker exercised her discretion to not vote

Senate Key Votes

2008

Prohibit discrimination based on genetic information (Senate Vote 113): Passage of a bill (HR 493) that would prohibit insurance companies, employers, employment agencies and labor unions from discriminating on the basis of genetic information. It would bar health plans from requiring genetic testing. Insurers could not adjust premiums or base enrollment decisions on genetic information. It also would provide legal protection to employers who contract with insurers to provide health insurance from being sued for a violation committed by the insurer. Before passage, the Senate adopted the Snowe, R-Maine, substitute amendment by voice vote. Passed 95-0: R 46-0; D 47-0; I 2-0. April 24, 2008.

Reauthorize farm and nutrition programs for five years (Senate Vote 130): Adoption of the conference report on the bill (HR 2419) that would reauthorize federal farm and nutrition programs for five years, including crop subsidies and food stamps, as well as conservation, rural development and agricultural trade programs. It would authorize a $10 billion increase for nutrition programs, offset by extending customs user fees. It also would cut direct payment subsidies overall by $313 million, in part by reducing the percentage of acres for which a farmer can collect those payments from 85 percent to 83.3 percent. Farmers making more than $750,000 a year in farm-related income and those with more than $500,000 a year in non-farm-related income would not be eligible for federal subsidies. It would provide a $65,000 limit for countercyclical payments, authorize $1.3 billion to enroll new acreage in the Wetlands Reserve Program and reduce the Conservation Reserve Program to 32 million acres. Country-of-origin labels for all meat would be required by September 2008. It also would extend the Milk Income Loss Contract Program through fiscal 2012 and provide a subsidy for the purchase of excess sugar in the U.S. market to make sugar-based ethanol. A no was a vote in support of the president's position. Adopted (thus cleared for the president) 81-15: R 35-13; D 44-2; I 2-0. May 15, 2008.

Limit debate on "cap and trade" system for greenhouse gas emissions (Senate Vote 145): Motion to invoke cloture (thus limiting debate) on the Boxer, D-Calif., substitute amendment to S 3036. The amendment would cap greenhouse gas emissions nationwide and set up a trading system for companies to buy and sell emissions allowances. Three-fifths of the total Senate (60) is required to invoke cloture. A no was a vote in support of the president's position. Motion rejected 48-36: R 7-32; D 39-4; I 2-0. June 6, 2008.

Allow lawsuits against companies that participated in warrantless wiretapping (Senate Vote 164): Dodd, D-Conn., amendment to HR 6304 that would strike the provisions providing retroactive immunity from civil liability to telecommunications companies that have participated in the National Security Agency's warrantless surveillance program. A no was a vote in support of the president's position. Rejected 32-66: R 0-48; D 31-17; I 1-1. July 9, 2008.

Limit debate on a bill to block a scheduled cut in Medicare payments to doctors (Senate Vote 169): Motion to invoke cloture (thus limiting debate) on the motion to proceed to the bill (HR 6331) that would prevent a 10.6 percent cut in Medicare physician payments scheduled to take effect on July 1, 2008, by holding payments at current rates for 18 months. It would give doctors a 1.1 percent increase in payments in 2009 and provide $16.6 billion over 10 years for changes to Medicare beneficiary programs. The costs would be partially offset by provisions to reduce the cost of Medicare Advantage plans. Support of three-fifths of the total

Senate (60) is required to invoke cloture. (By unanimous consent, the motion to proceed was agreed to and the bill was passed by voice vote.) A no was a vote in support of the president's position. Motion agreed to 69-30: R 18-30; D 49-0; I 2-0. July 9, 2008.

Grant mortgage relief to homeowners and funding for Fannie Mae and Freddie Mac (Senate Vote 186): Reid, D-Nev., motion to concur in the House amendment to the Senate amendment to the House amendments to the Senate amendment. The House amendment to the bill (HR 3221) would grant authority to the Treasury Department to extend new credit and buy stock in Fannie Mae and Freddie Mac. It would create an independent regulator for the two mortgage giants and the Federal Home Loan Bank System. It would overhaul the Federal Housing Administration and allow it to insure up to $300 billion worth of new, refinanced loans for struggling mortgage borrowers. It also includes a $7,500 tax credit for some first-time homebuyers, higher loan limits for FHA-backed loans, a standard tax deduction for property taxes and revenue-raisers to offset part of the costs. It also would authorize $3.9 billion in grants to states and localities to purchase and rehabilitate foreclosed properties and increase the federal debt limit to $10.6 trillion. A yes was a vote in support of the president's position. Motion agreed to (thus clearing the bill for the president), 72-13: R 27-13; D 43-0; I 2-0. July 26, 2008.

Approve a nuclear cooperation agreement with India (Senate Vote 211): Passage of the bill (HR 7081) that would grant congressional approval to the U.S.-India nuclear cooperation agreement. It would require that the president determine and certify to Congress that certain actions have occurred before the Nuclear Regulatory Commission could issue licenses for transfers of nuclear-related goods and services, including that India has provided the International Atomic Energy Agency with a credible plan to separate civilian and military nuclear facilities, materials and programs. By unanimous consent, the Senate agreed to raise the majority requirement for passage of the bill to 60 votes. A yes was a vote in support of the president's position. Passed 86-13: R 49-0; D 36-12; I 1-1. Oct. 1, 2008.

Approve final $700 billion program to stabilize financial markets (Senate Vote 213): Passage of the bill (HR 1424) that would allow the Treasury to use up to $700 billion, in installments, to buy certain mortgage assets. The bill would require the Treasury to create a program to insure mortgage assets, would provide for congressional oversight and would limit compensation for executives whose troubled assets are purchased. It would call on Treasury to implement a plan to reduce foreclosures and encourage servicers of mortgages to modify mortgage terms. The bill would allow the department to immediately use $250 billion in authority to buy assets, with an additional $100 billion if the president certifies such an expansion. The president would have to provide a written request for the remaining $350 billion, which would be subject to congressional disapproval and subsequent veto override. It would temporarily expand federal deposit insurance to $250,000 per bank account. It also would extend dozens of expired or expiring tax provisions, including several energy tax provisions. It would provide a one-year adjustment to exempt roughly 22 million taxpayers from paying the alternative minimum tax on 2008 income and require private insurance plans to put mental health benefits on par with other medical benefits. By unanimous consent, the Senate agreed to raise the majority requirement for passage of the bill to 60 votes. A yes was a vote in support of the president's position. Passed 74-25: R 34-15; D 39-9; I 1-1. Oct. 1, 2008.

Allow consideration of a $14 billion auto industry loan package (Senate Vote 215): Motion to invoke cloture (thus limiting debate) on the motion to proceed to the bill (HR 7005) on the alternative minimum

Key Votes

CQ editors selected key votes from roll-call votes taken during the 110th Congress. The following symbols are used:

Y voted for (yes)

N voted against (no)

paired for

+ announced for

X paired against

− announced against

P voted "present"

C voted "present" to avoid possible conflict of interest

? did not vote or otherwise make a position known

I ineligible

S Speaker exercised her discretion to not vote

tax, which would serve as the vehicle for an emergency loan package for domestic automakers. Three-fifths of the total Senate (60) is required to invoke cloture. Motion rejected 52-35: R 10-31; D 40-4; I 2-0. Dec. 11, 2008.

2007

Increase minimum wage by $2.10 an hour (Senate Vote 42): Passage of the bill (HR 2) that would raise the minimum wage to $7.25 per hour over two years and provide $8.3 billion in small-business tax incentives, including extending the work opportunity tax credit for five years, and the small-business expensing deduction through 2010. It also would set minimum wage requirements for the Northern Mariana Islands and extend the 15-year depreciation of improvements on leased property for three months. The tax provisions would be offset with revenue increases, including a $1 million cap on the amount of executive compensation that can be tax-deferred in any year and an extension of backward restrictions on certain sale-in-lease-out deals. A yes was a vote in support of the president's position. Passed 94-3: R 45-3; D 47-0; I 2-0. Feb. 1, 2007.

Limit debate on a comprehensive immigration bill (Senate Vote 235): Motion to invoke cloture (thus limiting debate) on the bill (S 1639) that would overhaul U.S. immigration policies, provide for a temporary guest worker program and institute new border security measures, including an electronic verification system. Three-fifths of the total Senate (60) is required to invoke cloture. A yes was a vote in support of the president's position. Motion rejected 46-53: R 12-37; D 33-15; I 1-1. June 28, 2007.

Overhaul congressional lobbying and ethics rules for members and their staffs (Senate Vote 294): Reid, D-Nev., motion to concur in the House amendment to the bill (S 1) that would overhaul congressional lobbying and ethics rules for members and their staffs and require the disclosure of "bundled" campaign contributions that exceed $15,000 in a six-month period. Former senators would have to wait two years before becoming lobbyists. It would require quarterly disclosure reports on lobbying activities and deny congressional pensions to members convicted of certain felonies committed after the date of enactment. It would require senators, candidates for Senate and presidential candidates to pay charter rates for trips on private planes while barring House candidates from accepting trips on private planes. Among changes to House and Senate rules, it would prohibit a member's staff from having lobbying contact with the member's spouse and impose new earmark disclosure requirements in the Senate. Civil penalties for failure to comply with lobbying disclosure requirements would be raised to $200,000. Motion agreed to (thus clearing the bill for the president), 83-14: R 34-14; D 47-0 (ND 42-0, SD 5-0); I 2-0. Aug. 2, 2007.

Limit debate on considering a bill to add House seats for the District of Columbia and Utah (Senate Vote 339): Motion to invoke cloture (thus limiting debate) on the Reid, D-Nev., motion to proceed to the bill (S 1257) that would increase the membership of the House of Representatives to 437, by granting a seat to the District of Columbia and an additional seat to Utah. Three-fifths of the total Senate (60) is required to invoke cloture. A no was a vote in support of the president's position. Motion rejected 57-42: R 8-41; D 47-1; I 2-0. Sept. 11, 2007.

Limit debate on restoring habeas corpus rights to detainees (Senate Vote 340): Motion to invoke cloture (thus limiting debate) on the Specter, R-Pa., amendment to the Levin, D-Mich., substitute amendment to HR 1585. The Specter amendment would restore habeas corpus rights to enemy combatants under U.S. detention, as well as to those awaiting military reviews that will determine their legal status. The substitute would authorize $648.3 billion for defense programs in fiscal 2008, including $127.5 billion for the wars in Iraq and Afghanistan. It also would authorize

$143.5 billion for operations and maintenance; $109.9 billion for procurement; $122.9 billion for military personnel and $74.7 billion for research development, testing and evaluation. Three-fifths of the total Senate (60) is required to invoke cloture. A no was a vote in support of the president's position. Motion rejected 56-43: R 6-42; D 49-0; I 1-1. Sept. 19, 2007.

Mandate minimum breaks for troops between deployments to Iraq or Afghanistan (Senate Vote 341): Webb, D-Va., amendment to the Levin, D-Mich., substitute amendment to HR 1585. The Webb amendment would mandate minimum intervals between deployments for troops serving in Iraq and Afghanistan. It would require active duty forces to be guaranteed as much time at home as they served while deployed. National Guard and reservists would be guaranteed three years at home between deployments. The substitute would authorize $648.3 billion for defense programs in fiscal 2008, including $127.5 billion for the wars in Iraq and Afghanistan. It also would authorize $143.5 billion for operations and maintenance; $109.9 billion for procurement; $122.9 billion for military personnel and $74.7 billion for research development, testing and evaluation. By unanimous consent, the Senate agreed to raise the majority requirement for adoption of the amendment to 60 votes. A no was a vote in support of the president's position. Rejected 56-44: R 6-43; D 49-0; I 1-1. (Subsequently, the Webb amendment was withdrawn.) Sept. 19, 2007.

Override Bush veto of $23.2 billion water projects authorization bill (Senate Vote 406): Passage, over President Bush's Nov. 2, 2007, veto, of the bill (HR 1495) that would authorize $23.2 billion for more than 900 water resource development projects and studies by the Army Corps of Engineers for flood control, navigation, beach erosion control and environmental restoration. The bill would require independent peer review for certain projects that exceed $45 million. It would authorize $3.9 billion for a system of new locks and dams and environmental restoration for the Upper Mississippi River and Illinois waterway system. It also would authorize hurricane recovery activities along the Gulf Coast. A two-thirds majority of those present and voting (62 in this case) of both chambers is required to override a veto. A no was a vote in support of the president's position. Passed (thus enacted into law) 79-14: R 34-12; D 43-2; I 2-0. Nov. 8, 2007.

Confirm Michael B. Mukasey as attorney general (Senate Vote 407): Confirmation of President Bush's nomination of Michael B. Mukasey of New York to be attorney general. A yes was a vote in support of the president's position. Confirmed 53-40: R 46-0; D 6-39; I 1-1. Nov. 8, 2007.

Limit debate on an energy policy overhaul containing $21.8 billion in tax incentives and reduced oil and gas subsidies (Senate Vote 425): Motion to invoke cloture (thus limiting debate) on the Reid, D-Nev., motion to concur in the House amendment to the Senate amendment with an additional amendment to HR 6 that would require new Corporate Average Fuel Economy standards of 35 miles per gallon for cars and light trucks, and require the production and use of 36 billion gallons of biofuels by 2022. It would direct the Energy Department to set new energy efficiency standards. The additional amendment would strike a provision that would require utilities to produce 15 percent of their electricity from alternative sources by 2020. It also would increase to $21.8 billion a package of tax incentives that would be offset in part by eliminating or reducing $13 billion in subsidies for major oil and gas companies. Three-fifths of the total Senate (60) is required to invoke cloture. A no was a vote in support of the president's position. Motion rejected 59-40: R 9-39; D 48-1; I 2-0. Dec. 13, 2007.

Key Votes

CQ editors selected key votes from roll-call votes taken during the 110th Congress. The following symbols are used:

Y   voted for (yes)

N   voted against (no)

\#   paired for

\+   announced for

X   paired against

−   announced against

P   voted "present"

C   voted "present" to avoid possible conflict of interest

?   did not vote or otherwise make a position known

I   ineligible

S   Speaker exercised her discretion to not vote

House Key Votes

2008

Delay consideration of Colombia free-trade agreement (House Vote 181): Adoption of the resolution that would suspend "fast-track" requirements for considering a bill (HR 5724) that would implement a U.S.-Colombia free-trade agreement. A no was a vote in support of the president's position. Adopted 224-195: R 6-185; D 218-10. April 10, 2008.

Override Bush veto of federal farm and nutrition programs reauthorization bill (House Vote 346): Passage, over President Bush's May 21, 2008, veto, of the bill (HR 2419) that would reauthorize federal farm and nutrition programs for five years, including crop subsidies and food stamps, as well as conservation and rural development. It would authorize a $10.4 billion increase for nutrition programs, offset by extending customs user fees. It also would cut direct payment subsidies overall by $313 million, in part by reducing the percentage of acres for which a farmer can collect those payments from 85 percent to 83.3 percent. Farmers making more than $750,000 a year in farm-related income and those with more than $500,000 a year in non-farm-related income would not be eligible for federal subsidies. It would provide a $65,000 limit for countercyclical payments, authorize $1.3 billion to enroll new acreage in the Wetlands Reserve Program and reduce the Conservation Reserve Program to 32 million acres. Country-of-origin labels for all meat would be required by September 2008. It also would extend the Milk Income Loss Contract Program through fiscal 2012. A two-thirds majority of those present and voting (283 in this case for the House) of both chambers is required to override a veto. A no was a vote in support of the president's position. Passed 316-108: R 100-94; D 216-14. May 21, 2008.

Overhaul surveillance laws and permit dismissal of suits against companies that conducted warrantless wiretapping (House Vote 437): Passage of the bill (HR 6304) that would overhaul the Foreign Intelligence Surveillance Act (FISA), which governs electronic surveillance of foreign terrorism suspects. The bill would allow investigations of up to one year that involved surveillance targeting those who are not U.S. persons and who are reasonably believed to be outside the United States. The FISA court would have to approve procedures for conducting the surveillance. Warrantless surveillance would be allowed as long as it does not intentionally target U.S. persons or those located within the United States, excluding foreign agents. It would allow for retroactive liability immunity for telecommunications companies that have participated in the National Security Agency's warrantless surveillance program. The bill's provisions would expire on Dec. 31, 2012, but warrants would remain in effect until they expire. A yes was a vote in support of the president's position. Passed 293-129: R 188-1; D 105-128. June 20, 2008.

Grant mortgage relief to homeowners and funding for Fannie Mae and Freddie Mac (House Vote 519): Frank, D-Mass., motion to concur in the Senate amendment with the House amendment to HR 3221 that would grant authority to the Treasury Department to extend new credit and buy stock in Fannie Mae and Freddie Mac. It also would create an independent regulator for the two mortgage giants and the Federal Home Loan Bank System. It would overhaul the Federal Housing Administration and allow it to insure up to $300 billion worth of new, refinanced loans for struggling mortgage borrowers. It also includes a $7,500 tax credit to some first-time homebuyers, higher loan limits for FHA-backed loans, a standard tax deduction for property taxes and revenue-raisers to offset part of the costs. It also would authorize $3.92 billion in grants to states and localities to purchase and rehabilitate foreclosed properties and increase the federal debt limit to $10.6 trillion. A yes was a vote in support of the president's position. Adopted 272-152: R 45-149; D 227-3. July 23, 2008.

Approve initial $700 billion program to stabilize financial markets (House Vote 674): Frank, D-Mass., motion to concur in the Senate amendment to the House amendment to the Senate amendment to HR 3997, with an additional House amendment. The House amendment would allow the Treasury to use up to $700 billion, in installments, to buy certain mortgage assets. It would require the department to insure the assets and set up systems for congressional oversight. It would direct the Treasury to set limits on compensation for executives of companies whose troubled assets it purchases, and call on the department to develop programs to reduce foreclosures and encourage lenders to modify mortgage terms. It would prohibit the purchase of certain assets at a higher price than the seller paid for the asset. The measure would allow the department to immediately use $250 billion in authority to buy assets, with an additional $100 billion if the president certifies such an expansion. The president would have to provide a written request for the remaining $350 billion, which could be subject to congressional disapproval. A yes was a vote in support of the president's position. Motion rejected 205-228: R 65-133; D 140-95. Sept. 29, 2008.

Approve final $700 billion program to stabilize financial markets (House Vote 681): Frank, D-Mass., motion to concur in the Senate amendments to HR 1424 that would allow the Treasury to use up to $700 billion, in installments, to buy certain mortgage assets. The bill would require the Treasury to create a program to insure mortgage assets, would provide for congressional oversight and would limit compensation for executives whose troubled assets are purchased. It would call on Treasury to implement a plan to reduce foreclosures and encourage servicers of mortgages to modify mortgage terms. The bill would allow the department to immediately use $250 billion in authority to buy assets, with an additional $100 billion if the president certifies such an expansion. The president would have to provide a written request for the remaining $350 billion, which would be subject to congressional disapproval and subsequent veto override. It would temporarily increase federal deposit insurance to $250,000 per bank account. It also would extend dozens of expired or expiring tax provisions, including several energy tax provisions. It would provide a one-year adjustment to exempt roughly 22 million taxpayers from paying the alternative minimum tax on 2008 income and require private insurance plans to put mental health benefits on par with other medical benefits. A yes was a vote in support of the president's position. Motion agreed to (thus clearing the bill for the president), 263-171: R 91-108; D 172-63. Oct. 3, 2008.

Provide $14 billion in loans to automakers (House Vote 690): Passage of the bill (HR 7321) that would allow up to $14 billion in loans to eligible domestic automakers. One or more presidentially appointed administrators would be empowered to bring together auto companies, unions, creditors and others to negotiate long-term restructuring plans, which auto companies would have to submit by March 31, 2009. Administrators could recall the loans if they do not approve the plans. Companies getting loans would have to submit any planned investment or transaction of $100 million or more for review. Loan interest rates would be set at 5 percent for the first five years and 9 percent each subsequent year. The bill would give the government warrants in each participating company worth at least 20 percent of the loan's value, and the option of obtaining up to 20 percent in non-voting stock in the company. It also would prohibit loan recipients from giving bonuses to its 25 most highly-compensated employees while the loan was outstanding. A yes was a vote in support of the president's position. Passed 237-170: R 32-150; D 205-20. Dec. 10, 2008.

Key Votes

CQ editors selected key votes from roll-call votes taken during the 110th Congress. The following symbols are used:

Y   voted for (yes)
N   voted against (no)
paired for
+   announced for
X   paired against
−   announced against
P   voted "present"
C   voted "present" to avoid possible conflict of interest
?   did not vote or otherwise make a position known
I   ineligible
S   Speaker exercised her discretion to not vote

2007

Increase minimum wage by $2.10 an hour (House Vote 18): Passage of the bill (HR 2) that would increase the federal minimum wage by $2.10 over two years — from the current level of $5.15 an hour to $7.25 an hour. The minimum wage would increase 60 days after enactment, from $5.15 to $5.85 an hour. It would rise to $6.55 an hour a year later, and to $7.25 an hour the next year. The bill also would extend federal minimum wage requirements to the Commonwealth of the Northern Mariana Islands and set it at $3.55 an hour, 60 days after enactment. The wage would rise in 50 cent increments every six months until it reached the $7.25 per hour level. A no was a vote in support of the president's position. Passed 315-116: R 82-116; D 233-0. Jan. 10, 2007.

Approve $124.2 billion in emergency war spending and set goal for redeployment of troops from Iraq (House Vote 265): Adoption of the conference report on the bill (HR 1591) that would provide $124.2 billion in fiscal 2007 emergency funding, as well as set a goal of redeploying most U.S. combat troops in Iraq by the end of March 2008, if the president can certify the Iraq government is meeting benchmarks, and by the end of 2007 if he cannot. The measure would provide $95.5 billion for military operations in Iraq and Afghanistan, $6.8 billion for hurricane recovery and relief, $3.5 billion in crop and livestock disaster assistance and $2.25 billion for homeland security anti-terrorism programs. It also would raise the minimum wage to $7.25 per hour over two years and provide $4.8 billion in small-business tax incentives. A no was a vote in support of the president's position. Adopted (thus sent to the Senate) 218-208: R 2-195; D 216-13. April 25, 2007.

Reject federal contraceptive assistance to international family planning groups (House Vote 534): Smith, R-N.J., amendment to HR 2764 that would strike language in the bill to clarify that no contract or grant to provide donated contraceptives in developing countries would be denied to any nongovernmental organization solely on the basis of the Mexico City policy, which bars U.S. aid to international family planning organizations that perform or promote abortions, even if they use their own funds to do so. A yes was a vote in support of the president's position. Rejected in Committee of the Whole 205-218: R 180-12; D 25-206. June 21, 2007.

Override Bush veto of $23.2 billion water projects authorization bill (House Vote 1040): Passage, over President Bush's Nov. 2, 2007, veto of the bill (HR 1495) that would authorize $23.2 billion for more than 900 water resource development projects and studies by the Army Corps of Engineers for flood control, navigation, beach erosion control and environmental restoration. The bill would require independent peer review for certain projects that exceed $45 million. It would authorize $3.9 billion for a system of new locks and dams and environmental restoration for the Upper Mississippi River and Illinois waterway system. It also would authorize hurricane recovery activities along the Gulf Coast. A two-thirds majority of those present and voting (277 in this case) of both chambers is required to override a veto. A no was a vote in support of the president's position. Passed 361-54: R 138-54; D 223-0. Nov. 6, 2007.

Implement Peru free-trade agreement (House Vote 1060): Passage of the bill (HR 3688) that would implement a free-trade agreement between the United States and Peru. The agreement would reduce most tariffs and duties on goods traded between the two countries, increase protections for intellectual property and require Peru to take steps to strengthen its labor and environmental enforcement standards. A yes was a vote in support of the president's position. Passed 285-132: R 176-16; D 109-116. Nov. 8, 2007.

Approve energy policy overhaul with new fuel economy standard (House Vote 1177): Dingell, D-Mich., motion to concur in the Senate amendment to the House amendment to the Senate amendment to HR 6 that would require new Corporate Average Fuel Economy (CAFE) standards of 35 miles per gallon for cars and light trucks, and require 36 billion gallons of biofuels to be used by 2022. It also would direct the Energy Department to set new energy efficiency standards. It would include a $2.1 billion tax package to cover the cost of the new CAFE standards. A yes was a vote in support of the president's position. Motion agreed to (thus clearing the bill for the president), 314-100: R 95-96; D 219-4. Dec. 18, 2007.

Clear $473.5 billion omnibus spending bill, including $70 billion for military operations (House Vote 1186): Obey, D-Wis., motion to concur in the Senate amendment to the House amendments to the Senate amendment to HR 2764 that would provide $473.5 billion in discretionary spending in fiscal 2008 for all federal departments and agencies whose regular fiscal 2008 spending bills have not been enacted. The measure incorporates 11 previously separate appropriations bills: Agriculture; Commerce-Justice-Science; Energy-Water; Financial Services; Homeland Security; Interior-Environment; Labor-HHS-Education; Legislative Branch; Military Construction-VA; State-Foreign Operations; and Transportation-HUD. The total includes $3.7 billion in emergency funding for veterans' programs. It would provide $70 billion for military operations in Afghanistan and Iraq. A yes was a vote in support of the president's position. Motion agreed to (thus clearing the bill for the president), 272-142: R 194-1; D 78-141. Dec. 19, 2007.

Vote Studies

Each year, CQ studies the frequency with which each member of Congress supports or opposes a given position. Scores are based only on votes cast; failure to vote does not alter a member's score, and all votes have equal statistical weight in the analysis. Scores are rounded to the nearest whole percentage point, although rounding is not used to increase any score to 100 percent or to reduce any score to zero.

PARTY UNITY

Party unity votes are defined as votes in the Senate and House that split the parties — a majority of voting Democrats opposing a majority of voting Republicans. Votes on which the parties agree, or on which either party divides evenly, are excluded. Party unity scores represent the percentage of party unity votes on which a member voted yes or no in agreement with a majority of the member's party. Opposition-to-party scores represent the percentage of party unity votes on which a member voted yes or no in disagreement with a majority of the member's party.

PRESIDENTIAL SUPPORT

CQ tries to determine what the president personally, as distinct from other administration officials, does and does not want in the way of legislative action. This is done by analyzing his messages to Congress, news conference remarks and other public statements and documents.

Occasionally, important bills are so extensively amended that it is impossible to characterize final passage as a victory or a defeat for the president. These votes have been excluded from the study. Votes on motions to recommit, to reconsider or to table (kill) often are key tests that govern the outcome. Such votes are included in the presidential support tabulations.

BUSH ERA SCORES

CQ completed a study of all roll call votes during President George W. Bush's two terms up to Congress' Oct. 3, 2008, recess. CQ calculated both

Congress by its Numbers

A new Congress is elected in each even-numbered year and convenes at the beginning of each odd-numbered year. As a shorthand, this book frequently refers to the actions of a particular Congress by its number. The sequence began with the 1st Congress, which was elected in 1788.

	Elected:	Met in:
111th Congress	2008	2009 and 2010
110th Congress	2006	2007 and 2008
109th Congress	2004	2005 and 2006
108th Congress	2002	2003 and 2004
107th Congress	2000	2001 and 2002
106th Congress	1998	1999 and 2000
105th Congress	1996	1997 and 1998
104th Congress	1994	1995 and 1996
103rd Congress	1992	1993 and 1994
102nd Congress	1990	1991 and 1992
101st Congress	1988	1989 and 1990
100th Congress	1986	1987 and 1988

party unity and presidential support scores over the entire Bush presidency for individual lawmakers who were then serving in the 110th Congress.

The party unity scores include all roll call votes where an absolute majority of one party voted against an absolute majority of the other party. There were 2,731 such votes in the House during the period (52 percent of the total) and 1,509 such votes in the Senate (58 percent). On average, House Democrats voted with their caucus on such party unity votes 93 percent of the time over the period, while Republicans were unified 92 percent of the time. In the Senate, Democrats stayed united on 91 percent of party unity votes, while Republicans voted together 90 percent of the time.

To determine the presidential support scores the analysis uses all votes where CQ editors determined that President Bush had taken a clear position prior to the vote. There were 454 such votes in the House during the period (9 percent of the total) and 569 such votes in the Senate (22 percent). On average, House Republicans supported Bush on 80 percent of such votes, and Democrats supported the president on just 20 percent. In the Senate, where votes on confirmations tend to elevate presidential support scores, Republicans voted with Bush 88 percent of the time, and Democrats gave him their support on 51 percent of the relevant votes.

Interest Group Ratings

Ratings for members by four advocacy groups are chosen to reflect labor, liberal, business and conservative viewpoints.

AFL-CIO

The AFL-CIO was formed when the American Federation of Labor and the Congress of Industrial Organizations merged in 1955. For senators, the ratings are based on nine votes in 1999, eight in 2000, 16 in 2001, 13 in 2002 and 2003, 12 in 2004, 14 in 2005, 15 in 2006, 19 in 2007 and 11 in 2008. For House members, ratings are based on 15 in 2004 and 2005, 14 in 2006, 24 in 2007 and 18 in 2008. (www.aflcio.org)

ADA

Americans for Democratic Action was founded in 1947 by a group of liberal Democrats that included Minnesota Sen. Hubert H. Humphrey and Eleanor Roosevelt. The ADA ratings are based on 20 votes each year in each chamber of Congress. (www.adaction.org)

CCUS

The Chamber of Commerce of the United States represents local, regional and state chambers as well as trade and professional groups. It was founded in 1912 to be "a voice for organized business." For senators, the ratings are based on 17 votes in 1999, 15 in 2000, 14 in 2001, 20 in 2002, 23 in 2003, 17 in 2004, 18 in 2005, 12 in 2006, 11 in 2007 and 8 in 2008. For members of the House, the ratings are based on 21 votes in 2004, 27 in 2005, 15 in 2006, 20 in 2007 and 18 in 2008. (www.uschamber.com)

ACU

The American Conservative Union was founded in 1964 "to mobilize resources of responsible conservative thought across the country and further the general cause of conservatism." The organization intends to provide education in political activity, "prejudice in the press," foreign and military policy, domestic economic policy, the arts, professions and sciences. For senators, the ratings are based on 24 votes in 1999, 2000 and 2001, 20 in 2002, 19 in 2003, and 25 in each of the last five years. For members of the House, the ratings are based on 25 votes each of the last five years. (www.conservative.org)

Gov. Bob Riley (R)

First elected: 2002
Length of term: 4 years
Term expires: 1/11
Salary: $112,895
Phone: (334) 242-7100

Residence: Montgomery
Born: Oct. 3, 1944; Ashland, Ala.
Religion: Baptist
Family: Wife, Patsy Riley; four children (one deceased)
Education: U. of Alabama, B.A. 1965 (business administration)
Career: Auto dealer; trucking company executive; farmer
Political highlights: Ashland City Council, 1972-76; candidate for mayor of Ashland, 1976; U.S. House, 1997-2003

Election results:
2006 GENERAL

Bob Riley (R)	718,327	57.4%
Lucy Baxley (D)	519,827	41.6%
write-ins	12,247	1.0%

Lt. Gov. Jim Folsom Jr. (D)

First elected: 2006
Length of term: 4 years
Term expires: 1/11
Salary: $61,714
Phone: (334) 242-7900

LEGISLATURE

Legislature: Annually, limit of 30 legislative days within 105 calendar days

Senate: 35 members, 4-year terms
2009 ratios: 19 D, 13 R, 3 vacancies; 28 men, 4 women
Salary: $10/day; $50 for each 3-day week; $4,108/month expenses
Phone: (334) 242-7800

House: 105 members, 4-year terms
2009 ratios: 62 D, 43 R; 91 men, 14 women
Salary: $10/day; $50 for each 3-day week; $4,108/month expenses
Phone: (334) 242-7600

TERM LIMITS

Governor: 2 consecutive terms
Senate: No
House: No

URBAN STATISTICS

CITY	POPULATION
Birmingham	242,820
Montgomery	201,568
Mobile	198,915
Huntsville	158,216
Tuscaloosa	77,906

REGISTERED VOTERS

Voters do not register by party.

POPULATION

2008 population (est.)	4,661,900
2000 population	4,447,100
1990 population	4,040,587
Percent change (1990-2000)	+10.1%
Rank among states (2008)	23

Median age	35.8
Born in state	73.4%
Foreign born	2%
Violent crime rate	486/100,000
Poverty level	16.1%
Federal workers	50,081
Military	38,706

ELECTIONS

STATE ELECTION OFFICIAL
(334) 242-7210
DEMOCRATIC PARTY
(334) 262-2221
REPUBLICAN PARTY
(205) 212-5900

MISCELLANEOUS

Web: www.alabama.gov
Capital: Montgomery

U.S. CONGRESS

Senate: 2 Republicans
House: 4 Republicans, 3 Democrats

2000 Census Statistics by District

DIST.	2008 VOTE FOR PRESIDENT OBAMA	MCCAIN	WHITE	BLACK	ASIAN	HISP	MEDIAN INCOME	WHITE COLLAR	BLUE COLLAR	SERVICE INDUSTRY	OVER 64	UNDER 18	COLLEGE EDUCATION	RURAL	SQ. MILES
1	38%	61%	68%	28%	1%	1%	$34,739	55%	31%	15%	13%	27%	19%	36%	6,317
2	37	63	67	29	1	2	$32,460	55	31	14	13	26	18	50	10,502
3	43	56	65	32	1	1	$30,806	52	34	14	13	25	17	47	7,834
4	22	76	90	5	0	3	$31,344	46	42	12	15	24	11	73	8,372
5	38	61	78	17	1	2	$38,054	57	30	13	12	25	24	41	4,486
6	25	74	89	8	1	2	$46,946	68	22	10	12	24	30	38	4,564
7	71	29	36	62	1	1	$26,672	53	29	17	13	26	15	28	8,669
STATE	39	60	70	26	1	2	$34,135	55	31	13	13	25	19	45	50,744
U.S.	53	46	69	12	4	13	$41,994	60	25	15	12	26	24	21	3,537,438

Sen. Richard C. Shelby (R)

Elected 1986; 4th term

CAPITOL OFFICE
224-5744
shelby.senate.gov
304 Russell Bldg. 20510-0103; fax 224-3416

COMMITTEES
Appropriations
Banking, Housing & Urban Affairs - ranking
member
Special Aging

RESIDENCE
Tuscaloosa

BORN
May 6, 1934; Birmingham, Ala.

RELIGION
Presbyterian

FAMILY
Wife, Annette Nevin Shelby; two children

EDUCATION
U. of Alabama, A.B. 1957, LL.B. 1963

CAREER
Lawyer; city prosecutor

POLITICAL HIGHLIGHTS
Ala. Senate, 1971-79 (served as a Democrat);
U.S. House, 1979-87 (served as a Democrat)

ELECTION RESULTS

2004 GENERAL

Richard C. Shelby (R)	1,242,200	67.6%
Wayne Sowell (D)	595,018	32.4%

2004 PRIMARY

Richard C. Shelby (R)	unopposed

PREVIOUS WINNING PERCENTAGES*
1998 (63%); 1992 (65%); 1986 (50%); 1984 House
Election (97%); 1982 House Election (97%); 1980
House Election (73%); 1978 House Election (94%)
* Elected as a Democrat 1978-92

Shelby is a cagey legislator who has long been willing to go his own way. He was one of Congress' first party-switchers in the 1990s, stood largely alone in demanding the CIA director's firing after the Sept. 11 attacks and — in 2008 — refused to be involved with George W. Bush administration plans to help ailing financial services firms as the top-ranking Republican on the committee overseeing the industry.

"I think people at times like some independence," he once said. "They like independent thought, not someone to be a rubber stamp for either party."

Shelby regularly asserts his independence as the Banking, Housing and Urban Affairs Committee's ranking member. He is a frequent skeptic of government regulation, and during the 110th Congress (2007-08) his support was often critical to getting bills through the committee. He could prove a formidable opponent of legislation that severely curtails market activity, though the enlarged Democratic majority in the Senate in the 111th Congress (2009-10) may weaken his hand.

Shelby was a leading critic of the Bush administration's $700 billion proposal to shore up the financial services sector from the moment it was announced in fall 2008. He said the plan was "aimed at rescuing the same financial institutions that created this crisis" and that it was "neither workable nor comprehensive despite its enormous price tag." His opposition forced Minority Leader Mitch McConnell to tap New Hampshire Republican Judd Gregg to represent the Senate GOP at the negotiating table.

Shelby also contended that Congress was being asked to act on the rescue plan too hastily — a concern he has often voiced on Banking. He prefers to conduct exhaustive hearings and offstage reviews before drafting legislation.

His deliberate approach avoids roiling the financial markets with quick fixes to problems, but it can also slow the legislative response to serious abuses. It took Congress more than two years to crack down on unscrupulous financial services and insurance companies that prey on members of the military, in large part because Shelby insisted on waiting for a series of reports on the abuses from government agencies. "He may be slow, he may be cautious, he may be frustrating," Banking Chairman Christopher J. Dodd of Connecticut told The New York Times in May 2008. "But once he makes the deal, it happens."

Shelby has worked with Dodd on several major pieces of legislation, including a 2008 bill to throw a lifeline to home mortgage giants Fannie Mae and Freddie Mac as well as provide relief to homeowners facing foreclosure. Shelby — who had warned for years that the government-chartered firms were taking on too much risk — insisted on keeping the measure as inexpensive as possible, getting Dodd and other Democrats to use Fannie Mae and Freddie Mac to cover some of the costs of the relief effort out of contributions already planned for an affordable-housing trust fund.

While he prefers free-market solutions to government regulation, Shelby occasionally behaves like the Democrat he once was. He departs from the GOP mainstream most often on questions of privacy, predatory lending and stock market regulation. "People have to have confidence in the banking system and financial markets," he said. "That's why transparency is so important." Legislation is not always the answer, he said; sometimes vigorous oversight alone can spur change in targeted industries.

Shelby is among his party's most prodigious fundraisers, using his Banking Committee position to collect generous contributions from the financial and insurance industries. Some critics say he has received so much money that it has distorted his perspective. In June 2007, he said in an interview that Congress should not increase taxes on private equity firms like Blackstone Group; within a week, Blackstone executives contributed nearly $25,000. But he insisted his vote is not for sale. "That is not relevant to any decision I made, whether I raise money or don't raise money," he told The New York Times.

Before taking the helm of the Banking panel when the GOP controlled the Senate in 2003, Shelby had served as the chairman and then the vice chairman of the Intelligence Committee. He called the Sept. 11 terrorist attacks "an intelligence failure of unprecedented magnitude" and singled out the CIA for relying too much on technological tools and not enough on agents in the field. He regularly called for the resignation of then-CIA Director George J. Tenet despite support for Tenet from President Bush and many other senior Republicans.

Fallout from that period in his career continued into the 109th Congress (2005-06) with a Select Ethics Committee investigation into allegations that Shelby leaked secret government information to the media. The information, which infuriated top Bush administration officials when it was made public, was the National Security Agency's interception of two messages on the eve of the attacks that were not translated until Sept. 12, 2001. The Arabic-language messages said, "The match is about to begin" and "Tomorrow is zero hour." The Ethics panel cleared Shelby of any wrongdoing in 2005.

Shelby steers vast sums of federal money to Alabama. He is a longtime Appropriations Committee member, and an analysis of fiscal 2008 spending bills by Taxpayers for Common Sense ranked Shelby fifth among senators in earmarks, or funding set-asides for special projects, with more than $427 million obtained either alone or with other members.

When it comes to earmarking, Shelby has "made a kind of art form out of it," former Alabama GOP Rep. Jack Edwards told the Mobile Press-Register. He has helped foster the space and defense economy in Huntsville, home to NASA's Marshall Space Flight Center and the Army's Redstone Arsenal. The Army was so grateful for Shelby's help in securing a new 200,000-square-foot, $33 million scientific and technical center that it named the facility the Richard C. Shelby Center for Missile Intelligence. A building at the biomedical research complex at the University of Alabama-Birmingham is named for Shelby and his wife, Annette, in gratitude for the millions of dollars the senator steered to the complex.

Shelby got his Appropriations seat after he switched parties following the Republican takeover of Congress in 1994. Although the switch struck many as opportunistic — just a few months earlier, he said he had "no intention of switching parties" — Shelby said he made the move because of what he described as the demise of the pro-defense, conservative wing of the Democratic Party. His move also followed an attempt by the Clinton administration to move some space programs out of Alabama after Shelby had audaciously criticized President Clinton's budget while standing next to Vice President Al Gore in front of television cameras.

Shelby spent most of the 1960s as a municipal prosecutor in Tuscaloosa. He served eight years in the state Senate, where he was often at odds with Gov. George C. Wallace Jr. Though he was initially interested in running for lieutenant governor in 1978, more than a dozen other Democrats had the same idea. When one of his former law partners, Democrat Walter Flowers, gave up his House seat that year to run for the Senate, Shelby was easily persuaded to change course and run for Congress.

Shelby operated largely behind the scenes in the House for eight years, working on projects for his district and often siding with Republicans. His election to the Senate as a Democrat in 1986 was a slim victory over one-term incumbent Jeremiah Denton, the first Republican elected statewide in Alabama since Reconstruction. His re-elections have been by comfortable margins.

KEY VOTES

2008
Yes   Prohibit discrimination based on genetic information
Yes   Reauthorize farm and nutrition programs for five years
No   Limit debate on "cap and trade" system for greenhouse gas emissions
No   Allow lawsuits against companies that participated in warrantless wiretapping
No   Limit debate on a bill to block a scheduled cut in Medicare payments to doctors
Yes   Grant mortgage relief to homeowners and funding for Fannie Mae and Freddie Mac
Yes   Approve a nuclear cooperation agreement with India
No   Approve final $700 billion program to stabilize financial markets
No   Allow consideration of a $14 billion auto industry loan package

2007
Yes   Increase minimum wage by $2.10 an hour
No   Limit debate on a comprehensive immigration bill
Yes   Overhaul congressional lobbying and ethics rules for members and their staffs
No   Limit debate on considering a bill to add House seats for the District of Columbia and Utah
No   Limit debate on restoring habeas corpus rights to detainees
No   Mandate minimum breaks for troops between deployments to Iraq or Afghanistan
Yes   Override Bush veto of $23.2 billion water projects authorization bill
Yes   Confirm Michael B. Mukasey as attorney general
No   Limit debate on an energy policy overhaul containing $21.8 billion in tax incentives and reduced oil and gas subsidies

CQ VOTE STUDIES

	PARTY UNITY		PRESIDENTIAL SUPPORT	
	SUPPORT	OPPOSE	SUPPORT	OPPOSE
2008	95%	5%	74%	26%
2007	88%	12%	80%	20%
2006	88%	12%	86%	14%
2005	94%	6%	89%	11%
2004	94%	6%	86%	14%
2003	96%	4%	95%	5%
2002	80%	20%	87%	13%
2001	88%	12%	97%	3%
2000	97%	3%	45%	55%
1999	89%	11%	38%	62%

INTEREST GROUPS

	AFL-CIO	ADA	CCUS	ACU
2008	20%	15%	75%	84%
2007	21%	20%	73%	88%
2006	7%	10%	83%	74%
2005	23%	10%	89%	88%
2004	25%	20%	88%	84%
2003	15%	10%	82%	90%
2002	38%	10%	85%	80%
2001	19%	5%	93%	100%
2000	0%	0%	93%	100%
1999	22%	10%	71%	84%

Sen. Jeff Sessions (R)

Elected 1996; 3nd term

CAPITOL OFFICE
224-4124
sessions.senate.gov
335 Russell Bldg. 20510-0104; fax 224-3149

COMMITTEES
Armed Services
Budget
Energy & Natural Resources
Judiciary - ranking member

RESIDENCE
Mobile

BORN
Dec. 24, 1946; Hybart, Ala.

RELIGION
Methodist

FAMILY
Wife, Mary Sessions; three children

EDUCATION
Huntingdon College, B.A. 1969 (history);
U. of Alabama, J.D. 1973

MILITARY SERVICE
Army Reserve, 1973-86

CAREER
Lawyer; teacher

POLITICAL HIGHLIGHTS
Assistant U.S. attorney, 1975-77; U.S. attorney,
1981-93; Ala. attorney general, 1995-97

ELECTION RESULTS

2008 GENERAL

Jeff Sessions (R)	1,305,383	63.4%
Vivian Davis Figures (D)	752,391	36.5%

2008 PRIMARY

Jeff Sessions (R)	199,690	92.3%
Earl Mack Gavin (R)	16,718	7.7%

PREVIOUS WINNING PERCENTAGES
2002 (59%); 1996 (52%)

The mild-mannered but tenacious Sessions has become widely admired among conservatives for his unyielding stance against illegal immigration, fervent support of the Iraq War and crusades against what he considers excessive spending.

At a glance, Sessions doesn't cut an imposing figure; he is slight in stature, courtly and unpretentious. "He's down to earth — what you see is what you get," President George W. Bush said of Sessions while campaigning for him in 2007. But he does not back down from a fight. "Sen. Sessions is a scrapper," said John Cornyn of Texas, a like-minded GOP colleague on the Judiciary Committee.

Sessions is well positioned to propound his views, especially after taking over as Judiciary's top-ranking Republican in May 2009 after Arlen Specter of Pennsylvania switched parties. The move puts Sessions in the unusual position of being at the forefront of a committee that rejected him for a federal judgeship in 1986; the panel's chairman, Patrick J. Leahy of Vermont, was among those voting against him. Right-wing activists count on him to carry their banner against Leahy and the Obama administration on hot-button issues ranging from Supreme Court nominations to investigations of alleged misdeeds by Bush's administration.

Sessions' ongoing battles on immigration have brought him the most attention. When a bipartisan Senate majority passed a bill in 2006 offering guest worker permits and a path to citizenship for those in the country illegally, he called it "the worst piece of legislation to come before the Senate since I've been here." After the bill died in a standoff with the House, he was among those who pushed through legislation, signed into law, authorizing construction of a 700-mile fence along the Mexican border instead.

The following year, Sessions strenuously objected to a Democratic proposal to put some children of illegal immigrants on a path to citizenship. And in March 2008, he led a dozen GOP senators in introducing a package of enforcement-oriented immigration bills, even as presidential candidate and Arizona Sen. John McCain supported a more comprehensive overhaul of the system with a less harsh approach toward illegal immigrants.

Sessions' emergence as a leader on immigration is unusual because it wasn't something he had shown much interest in earlier in his career. "But as I watched and studied and looked around and saw nobody else willing to pick up the issue and run with it, I felt like I was doing the right thing," he told The Birmingham News.

A former Alabama attorney general and U.S. attorney, Sessions has been on familiar turf dealing with the Judiciary Committee's other issues. He has been an ardent advocate of sweeping executive authority in the war on terrorism; in 2005, he was one of nine Senate Republicans to vote against a ban on "cruel, inhuman or degrading treatment" of suspected terrorists. He has been active in the committee's fights over confirming judges and promoted the confirmation of William H. Pryor — a former Alabama attorney general and protégé of his — to a permanent seat on the 11th Circuit Court of Appeals.

Sessions has come down on both sides of the filibuster issue when it comes to confirming judges. While he was one of a number of Republicans demanding that President Clinton's judicial nominees clear the Senate's 60-vote threshold, he was also one of the top critics of Democrats when they sought to filibuster Bush's nominees.

He was only the second candidate for the federal bench in 48 years to have the Judiciary Committee kill his nomination in 1986. President Reagan nominated Sessions, then the chief prosecutor for the Southern District of Alabama, but critics accused Sessions of "gross insensitivity" on racial issues. According to sworn statements by Justice Department lawyers, he called the NAACP and the American Civil Liberties Union "communist-inspired" and said they tried to "force civil rights down the throats of people." Sessions said his words were misrepresented.

Sessions expressed reservations about several of Obama's nominees at the Justice Department and said he was concerned about the president packing the agency with "far-left" nominees. "I believe the president deserves deference, but he's about used all the deference he's going to get out of me," he said in April 2009.

When the Senate took up a $48 billion bill in 2008 to expand the U.S. role in the global fight against AIDS and other diseases, Sessions wanted to remove language that repealed a ban on HIV-positive visitors to the United States. He finally dropped his demand in exchange for an amendment to encourage blood safety programs, clearing the way for the measure to become law.

He did show a desire to work with Democrats to equalize federal sentences for offenses involving crack and powdered cocaine. The lower sentencing threshold for crack has disproportionately affected African-Americans.

From his seat on the Budget Committee, Sessions has long promoted spending controls, smaller government and tax cuts. In 2005, he helped lead a push to pare entitlement program spending in order to boost funding for the military and other discretionary programs. He also called for legislation to enforce a cap on spending on the Medicare prescription drug benefit enacted in 2003. In fall 2008, he was one of 15 Senate Republicans to oppose the $700 billion bill to shore up the ailing financial services sector, saying it would "require the work of an entire generation of Americans to pay back."

On Armed Services, Sessions keeps an eye out for military installations in his state, including Maxwell Air Force Base near Montgomery. He is an advocate for a missile defense system and seeks more development of space-based devices, which could help his state's aerospace industry.

He was a leading defender of Bush's conduct of the Iraq War. In 2007, he pushed through the Senate a bill to ensure that members of the armed forces discharged because of injuries sustained in combat still receive the bonuses they would have gotten had they continued to serve. The House later passed similar legislation, but Congress failed to clear a final measure into law before the end of the 110th Congress (2007-08).

From his seat on the Energy and Natural Resources panel, he wants to clear away regulatory hurdles for new construction of nuclear power plants while providing government incentives and investing in methods to recycle waste.

He grew up in the tiny towns of Hybart and Camden, southwest of Montgomery. His father owned a general store and then a farm equipment dealership. Sessions worked in both. He joined the Young Republicans and served as student body president at Huntingdon College in Alabama. After earning a law degree, he joined a law firm in Russellville, Ala., becoming assistant U.S. attorney in 1975 and U.S. attorney for the Southern District of Alabama in 1981.

In 1994, he ran for state attorney general. With a corruption scandal raging in Montgomery, he rode to victory on a vow to clean up the mess. Two years later, Sessions entered the Senate race to succeed retiring Democrat Howell Heflin. He won a seven-way primary, then faced Roger Bedford, chairman of the state Senate Judiciary Committee. Sessions appealed to Alabama's conservative Christian activists and prevailed with 52 percent of the vote, giving Alabama two Republican senators for the first time since Reconstruction. Benefitting from his state's deep conservatism, he won his next two elections easily.

KEY VOTES

2008

Yes	Prohibit discrimination based on genetic information
Yes	Reauthorize farm and nutrition programs for five years
No	Limit debate on "cap and trade" system for greenhouse gas emissions
No	Allow lawsuits against companies that participated in warrantless wiretapping
No	Limit debate on a bill to block a scheduled cut in Medicare payments to doctors
Yes	Grant mortgage relief to homeowners and funding for Fannie Mae and Freddie Mac
Yes	Approve a nuclear cooperation agreement with India
No	Approve final $700 billion program to stabilize financial markets
No	Allow consideration of a $14 billion auto industry loan package

2007

Yes	Increase minimum wage by $2.10 an hour
No	Limit debate on a comprehensive immigration bill
Yes	Overhaul congressional lobbying and ethics rules for members and their staffs
No	Limit debate on considering a bill to add House seats for the District of Columbia and Utah
No	Limit debate on restoring habeas corpus rights to detainees
No	Mandate minimum breaks for troops between deployments to Iraq or Afghanistan
No	Override Bush veto of $23.2 billion water projects authorization bill
Yes	Confirm Michael B. Mukasey as attorney general
No	Limit debate on an energy policy overhaul containing $21.8 billion in tax incentives and reduced oil and gas subsidies

CQ VOTE STUDIES

	PARTY UNITY		PRESIDENTIAL SUPPORT	
	SUPPORT	OPPOSE	SUPPORT	OPPOSE
2008	98%	2%	74%	26%
2007	92%	8%	85%	15%
2006	96%	4%	91%	9%
2005	97%	3%	90%	10%
2004	97%	3%	96%	4%
2003	98%	2%	99%	1%
2002	87%	13%	88%	12%
2001	95%	5%	97%	3%
2000	97%	3%	42%	58%
1999	94%	6%	24%	76%

INTEREST GROUPS

	AFL-CIO	ADA	CCUS	ACU
2008	10%	20%	50%	84%
2007	16%	10%	40%	83%
2006	20%	0%	92%	92%
2005	14%	0%	78%	100%
2004	8%	10%	88%	96%
2003	0%	0%	100%	75%
2002	25%	10%	84%	90%
2001	20%	5%	86%	96%
2000	0%	0%	86%	100%
1999	11%	0%	88%	100%

Rep. Jo Bonner (R)

Elected 2002; 4th term

Bonner spent years working as a congressional aide and still follows staffers' key tenets of survival: He lets others seek the spotlight and keeps his Republican superiors happy by faithfully toeing the party line.

Like many Southern politicians, he began his career as a Democrat but switched to the Republican Party in the 1990s. His voting record reflects his loyalty to his adopted party: From 2003, when he joined Congress, through October 2008, Bonner sided with his party 97 percent of the time on votes that pitted Republicans against Democrats.

One of his infrequent departures from the GOP majority came in fall 2008, when Bonner supported the Bush administration's $700 billion plan to shore up the financial services industry. That vote drew him criticism from some constituents — and the threat of a 2010 primary challenge from Orange Beach real estate developer Peter Gounares, who said in 2009, "Voting to support the bank bailout last year goes against everything a conservative believes in."

A scion of an old Southern family, Bonner came to Congress bent on perpetuating a tradition in his district of sending federal dollars back home. He earned that chance in February 2008, when he won a seat on the Appropriations Committee. He replaced Mississippi Republican Roger Wicker, who was appointed to the Senate. Bonner beat out a half dozen other Republicans for the seat. He was a former aide to the committee while working for Republican Sonny Callahan, an Appropriations chairman on energy and water projects who groomed Bonner as his successor.

Bonner had been Callahan's aide for almost 18 years, and before that he interned for longtime appropriator Jack Edwards. "They both made a name for themselves taking care of the people back home, so I've had two very good teachers," he said.

Still, in his campaign for the coveted slot, Bonner spoke of the need for fiscal discipline. He vowed to be a "vigilant guardian of the taxpayers' money, helping to expose and eliminate wasteful or questionable spending." Bonner further helped his cause by giving $65,000 to the National Republican Congressional Committee in the 2007-08 cycle prior to his appointment. He subsequently gave it another $135,000, along with $70,000 to assorted GOP colleagues and challengers.

He also paid his dues by agreeing to take an unpopular assignment on the House ethics committee, assuming the top Republican seat on that panel in the 111th Congress and serving on a special subcommittee investigating allegations of financial improprieties lodged against Ways and Means Chairman Charles B. Rangel of New York.

Much of Bonner's time in the 110th Congress (2007-08) was devoted to dealing with a thorny defense contracting dispute. In 2007, he traveled to France to meet with officials of Northrop Grumman Corp. and the North American division of European Aeronautic Defence and Space Co. (EADS). The Air Force awarded EADS a $35 billion contract to build new aerial refueling tankers. But the Government Accountability Office determined the service made an error in choosing EADS over Boeing Co., leading the Pentagon to scrap the award with plans to order a new competition in 2009.

Bonner's family is among the most prominent in southern Alabama. His grandfather was a banker in Wilcox County and his great-uncles were a doctor, a lawyer and a local newspaper publisher. Bonner, whose given name is Josiah Robins Bonner Jr., is named for his father, a Georgetown-trained

CAPITOL OFFICE
225-4931
bonner.house.gov
2236 Rayburn Bldg. 20515-0101; fax 225-0562

COMMITTEES
Appropriations
Standards of Official Conduct - ranking member

RESIDENCE
Mobile

BORN
Nov. 19, 1959; Selma, Ala.

RELIGION
Episcopalian

FAMILY
Wife, Janee Bonner; two children

EDUCATION
U. of Alabama, B.A. 1982 (journalism),
attended 1998 (law)

CAREER
Congressional and campaign aide

POLITICAL HIGHLIGHTS
No previous office

ELECTION RESULTS

2008 GENERAL

Jo Bonner (R)	210,652	98.3%
write-ins	3,707	1.7%

2008 PRIMARY

Jo Bonner (R)	unopposed

2006 GENERAL

Jo Bonner (R)	112,944	68.1%
Vivian Sheffield Beckerle (D)	52,770	31.8%

PREVIOUS WINNING PERCENTAGES
2004 (63%); 2002 (61%)

attorney who was a county judge, a powerful local post.

Bonner's district is anchored by Mobile, an old Confederate port city that exudes charm. To the north are Mayberry-style towns, which have produced a remarkable number of great Southern writers. Monroeville was home to both Truman Capote and Harper Lee, who used the town as inspiration for the fictional Maycomb in her classic novel "To Kill a Mockingbird."

At one time, Bonner thought he'd be a journalist. As a kid in Camden, Bonner launched a community newspaper with the loan of a press from the local newspaper editor, whose son was a playmate. In high school, Bonner was a broadcast announcer at basketball games and student council president.

He earned a college degree in journalism, then followed his interest in politics to the 1982 gubernatorial campaign of Democrat George McMillan, who was challenging Democratic incumbent George C. Wallace Jr. To young professionals such as Bonner, McMillan represented a "new chapter" for Alabama after the race-tinged politics of Wallace and the state's history of violence during the civil rights movement.

McMillan lost to Wallace, but Bonner had met Callahan, who was a candidate for lieutenant governor. Callahan also lost, but two years later he won a race for a House seat and hired Bonner to be his press secretary. Bonner eventually rose to become chief of staff.

Callahan quietly encouraged his trusted aide to eventually run for the seat himself. In 1997, Bonner moved from Washington to the state district, a rarity for a chief of staff, most of whom work on Capitol Hill. He paid close attention to constituent service, joining the local Rotary Club and board of the local Junior League. When Callahan announced his retirement in 2002, Bonner was primed to run.

His toughest competition came from Tom Young, a Mobile native and a fellow Republican who, like Bonner, was a career congressional aide. Young was chief of staff for the state's Republican Sen. Richard C. Shelby. It was one of the most expensive and hotly contested races of the season. Bonner led in a seven-way June primary but fell short of a majority, forcing a runoff. He went on to win 62 percent of the vote to Young's 38 percent. In November, Bonner easily defeated Democratic businesswoman Judy McCain Belk.

Setting up shop was a breeze for Bonner. He kept all but two of Callahan's staff members. In 2004, after Belk challenged him in a rematch, Bonner won with 63 percent of the vote. Two years later, he boosted his total to 68 percent. He did not face an opponent in the 2008 general election.

KEY VOTES

2008

No   Delay consideration of Colombia free-trade agreement

Yes   Override Bush veto of federal farm and nutrition programs reauthorization bill

Yes   Overhaul surveillance laws and permit dismissal of suits against companies that conducted warrantless wiretapping

No   Grant mortgage relief to homeowners and funding for Fannie Mae and Freddie Mac

Yes   Approve initial $700 billion program to stabilize financial markets

Yes   Approve final $700 billion program to stabilize financial markets

No   Provide $14 billion in loans to automakers

2007

Yes   Increase minimum wage by $2.10 an hour

No   Approve $124.2 billion in emergency war spending and set goal for redeployment of troops from Iraq

?   Reject federal contraceptive assistance to international family planning groups

Yes   Override Bush veto of $23.2 billion water projects authorization bill

Yes   Implement Peru free-trade agreement

Yes   Approve energy policy overhaul with new fuel economy standards

Yes   Clear $473.5 billion omnibus spending bill, including $70 billion for military operations

CQ VOTE STUDIES

	PARTY UNITY		PRESIDENTIAL SUPPORT	
	SUPPORT	OPPOSE	SUPPORT	OPPOSE
2008	97%	3%	76%	24%
2007	93%	7%	83%	17%
2006	96%	4%	93%	7%
2005	96%	4%	83%	17%
2004	97%	3%	92%	8%

INTEREST GROUPS

	AFL-CIO	ADA	CCUS	ACU
2008	13%	15%	94%	83%
2007	13%	15%	85%	83%
2006	7%	0%	100%	88%
2005	7%	0%	89%	100%
2004	15%	0%	100%	95%

ALABAMA 1
Southwest — Mobile

Mobile anchors the solidly GOP 1st, Alabama's only Gulf Coast district. The beaches of southern Mobile County and resorts in Baldwin County give way to pine forests and cotton and soybean fields to the north.

The shipping and manufacturing industries in Mobile remain strong. International Shipholding relocated from New Orleans in 2005 following Hurricane Katrina, which left Mobile relatively unharmed. ST Mobile Aerospace Engineering — still the county's largest industrial employer — converts planes for FedEx at its Mobile facility. A new industrial shipping container terminal at the city's port opened in late 2008.

Other expansion in the district includes production at a new Berg Steel facility and a planned ThyssenKrupp manufacturing plant. Construction of the Alabama Motorsports Park near the Mobile suburb of Prichard is expected to provide thousands of jobs. The multi-use park will attract visitors to racing venues and commercial and outdoor recreation sites.

Growing Baldwin County thrives on tourism and agriculture. Condomini-

um and resort development continues, and sod, peanut and wheat dominate the county's agricultural economy. Development in the district's eastern reaches includes a new gaming and entertainment establishment in Escambia County — Wind Creek Casino and Hotel opened in early 2009 and plans to expand.

Rural Monroe County relies on timber production and manufacturing, while Washington County, west of the Tombigbee River, is home to several major chemical plants.

The South's shift to the GOP took root early in Alabama's 1st. Republicans have held the U.S. House seat since 1965, and the district has overwhelmingly favored Republican presidential candidates for decades. In 2008, John McCain won every county that falls wholly within the 1st.

MAJOR INDUSTRY
Commercial shipping, aerospace, timber, distribution, agriculture

CITIES
Mobile, 198,915; Prichard, 28,633; Daphne, 16,581; Tillmans Corner, 15,685

NOTABLE
Author Harper Lee based the fictional setting of "To Kill a Mockingbird" on her hometown of Monroeville.

Rep. Bobby Bright (D)

Elected 2008; 1st term

Bright is the first Democrat to capture this southeast Alabama seat in nearly half a century, but he promises not to stray too far from the policies of his fiscally conservative Republican predecessors.

The 13th of 14 children born to a Dale County sharecropper in the wire-grass region of southern Alabama, Bright hopes to bring a calming voice to what is expected to be a heated debate on the economy. A member of the fiscally conservative Blue Dog Coalition, he said he hopes to rein in spending and work to balance the national budget. "As mayor of Montgomery, I balanced the budget in each of my nine years in office," he said. "I also believe economic development is extremely important as we try to energize our economy."

Bright had an early chance to show his Blue Dog credentials in 2009, when he was one of just seven House Democrats to vote against the $787 billion economic stimulus law. Congress should have simply focused on "investments in infrastructure and targeted tax relief for individuals and small businesses, but this legislation includes billions in additional spending that will have little effect on the economy," he told the Montgomery Advertiser.

Bright also sits on the Armed Services Committee, where he can watch out for Fort Rucker and Maxwell-Gunter Air Force Base in his district. As mayor, Bright was a leader in a successful community effort in 2005 to rebuff a proposal before the Base Realignment and Closure Commission that could have cost Maxwell-Gunter thousands of jobs. He serves on the Armed Services subcommittee that oversees the base closure process.

Bright also serves on the Small Business and Agriculture committees. The 2nd District is the nation's No. 2 producer of peanuts. His first bill in the House was to provide tax breaks for certain small businesses.

Bright has spent his entire life in Alabama, and one measure of the adjustments he must make as a freshman came when he discovered there were few restaurants in the Washington area that could prepare grits to his liking. "I did find one place up there that has decent grits, but at most places, when you ask for them, they'll look at you and say, 'Oh, no, not another one,'" he told the Montgomery Advertiser.

CAPITOL OFFICE
225-2901
bright.house.gov
1205 Longworth Bldg. 20515-0102; fax 225-8913

COMMITTEES
Agriculture
Armed Services
Small Business

RESIDENCE
Montgomery

BORN
July 21, 1952; Midland City, Ala.

RELIGION
Baptist

FAMILY
Wife, Lynn Clardy Bright; three children

EDUCATION
Enterprise State Junior College, attended 1970-72;
Auburn U., B.A. 1975 (political science);
Troy State U., M.S. 1977 (criminal justice);
Faulkner U., J.D. 1982

CAREER
Lawyer; prison guard

POLITICAL HIGHLIGHTS
Mayor of Montgomery, 1999-2009

ELECTION RESULTS

2008 GENERAL

Bobby Bright (D)	144,368	50.2%
Jay Love (R)	142,578	49.6%

2008 PRIMARY

Bobby Bright (D)	19,456	66.6%
Cendie Crawley (D)	5,110	17.5%
Cheryl Sabel (D)	4,631	15.9%

ALABAMA 2

Southeast — part of Montgomery, Dothan

The 2nd takes in a chunk of Montgomery, the growing city of Dothan, and small towns that dot the southern Alabama coastal plain. Agriculture, still vital to the economy in rural areas here, includes peanut, cotton and soybean farming — the 2nd is the nation's second-ranked peanut-producing district.

Defense and state government still provide many jobs in the Montgomery area, and Maxwell Air Force Base and its Gunter Annex host many of the Air Force's computer systems and training centers. Dothan, in the southeast, relies on manufacturing and is a regional distribution hub. Fort Rucker, 20 miles to the northwest, is an Army aviation training center and supports activities at the Dothan Regional Airport.

Tourism is a steadily increasing business,

and antebellum homes in Eufaula and fishing on Lake Eufaula, on the border with Georgia, lure visitors to the area.

A large military retiree population underscores the 2nd's conservative bent. In 2008, the district sent conservative Democrat Bobby Bright to the U.S. House. Of the 15 counties wholly in the 2nd, only black-majority Bullock and Lowndes voted for Democrat Barack Obama in the 2008 presidential election.

MAJOR INDUSTRY
Agriculture, defense, manufacturing, government

MILITARY BASES
Fort Rucker (Army), 4,265 military, 2,136 civilian (2007); Maxwell-Gunter Air Force Base, 3,133 military, 2,233 civilian (2007)

CITIES
Montgomery (pt.), 127,986; Dothan, 57,737; Prattville, 24,303

NOTABLE
The Boll Weevil Monument in Enterprise honors the insect, whose taste for cotton induced local farmers to grow peanuts.

Rep. Mike D. Rogers (R)

Elected 2002; 4th term

CAPITOL OFFICE
225-3261
www.house.gov/mike-rogers
324 Cannon Bldg. 20515-0103; fax 226-8485

COMMITTEES
Agriculture
Armed Services
Homeland Security

RESIDENCE
Anniston

BORN
July 16, 1958; Hammond, Ind.

RELIGION
Baptist

FAMILY
Wife, Donna Elizabeth "Beth" Rogers;
three children

EDUCATION
Jacksonville State U., B.A. 1981 (political science
& psychology), M.P.A. 1985; Birmingham School
of Law, J.D. 1991

CAREER
Lawyer; laid-off worker assistance program
director; psychiatric counselor

POLITICAL HIGHLIGHTS
Calhoun County Commission, 1987-91; candidate
for Ala. House, 1990; Ala. House, 1995-2002
(minority leader, 1998-2000)

ELECTION RESULTS

2008 GENERAL

Mike D. Rogers (R)	150,819	53.4%
Joshua Segall (D)	131,299	46.5%

2008 PRIMARY

Mike D. Rogers (R)	unopposed

2006 GENERAL

Mike D. Rogers (R)	98,257	59.4%
Greg A. Pierce (D)	63,559	38.4%
Mark Edwin Layfield (I)	3,414	2.1%

PREVIOUS WINNING PERCENTAGES
2004 (61%); 2002 (50%)

Rogers is a fervent conservative on both fiscal and social policy who lets his constituents know he isn't a complacent Beltway insider; his 2008 campaign slogan was "Mike Rogers is our way of fighting back." At the same time, he harbors ambitions for a role in the GOP leadership.

"The fact is, if you want to be in leadership in Congress...you've got to demonstrate you're a leader, not just on policy or subject-matter expertise, but in doing the things that get you in the majority," Rogers told The Birmingham News shortly after starting his American Security Political Action Committee in 2007.

Among the things he believes are required is raising money. While his new PAC had raised only about $23,270 for the 2007-08 election cycle and donated just $15,500 of that, Rogers' own campaign committee was far more active and more generous, giving $125,300 to other GOP units or candidates. His contributions to the House Republicans' campaign committee totalled $91,500 for that cycle, an impressive showing for a rank-and-file member — especially when Rogers was in a competitive re-election fight of his own.

From his seat on the Agriculture Committee, Rogers split with the Bush administration in 2008 over farm policy, backing the successful override of President George W. Bush's veto of a five-year bill to authorize agriculture and nutrition programs. He also subsequently opposed an unsuccessful $14 billion bailout of U.S. automakers. He bucked the majority of his party in 2009 to support a reauthorization of the State Children's Health Insurance Program.

His district in eastern Alabama has a fair number of Democrats and is home to many military families, many of which have a member serving in Iraq. He said support for the U.S. effort in Iraq is "rock solid" in his area. "Folks know that I'm representing their view of the world," said Rogers, a member of the Armed Services Committee.

Rogers also uses his seat on that committee to look out for the interests of Anniston Army Depot, which is located in his hometown and refers to itself as the "Pit Crew of the American Warfighter," and of nearby Maxwell-Gunter Air Force Base northwest of Montgomery and Fort Benning, across the border in Georgia. While Republicans were in power, he helped secure $24 million for building Army ground combat vehicles at the Anniston Depot. He also worked to get $55 million in federal funds for domestic security training at the old Fort McClellan base, shuttered in 1999.

He is the top-ranking Republican on the Homeland Security Committee's panel on emergency preparedness and response. He previously served as chairman and then ranking Republican on the Management, Investigations and Oversight Subcommittee. In 2007, he successfully promoted a $62.5 million earmark for the Homeland Security Department's Center for Domestic Preparedness, located in Anniston. In 2008, Rogers won House passage of his measure to promote domestic breeding and training of bomb-sniffing dogs. Auburn University's well-regarded dog-training facility sparked his interest.

Border security is an issue that riles his constituents, Rogers said: "People are upset about the fact that we have so many millions of illegals here and nobody knows who they are." He voted in 2005 to make it a crime to be in the United States without legal documentation, and in 2006 supported successful legislation authorizing construction of a 700-mile fence along the border with Mexico.

Rogers is the son of a textile worker and defends that diminished industry in his state. He opposes free trade with China and is wary of any trade pacts that might hurt the domestic textile industry. But he voted for the 2005 Central America Free Trade Agreement after he and fellow Alabama Republican Spencer Bachus secured protections for their state's textile industry.

Rogers faced some controversy in his first term when he supported the burning of chemical agents and munitions at a new federal incinerator at the Anniston Depot, even though local school officials said their buildings were not prepared for an accidental release of air toxins. GOP Sen. Richard C. Shelby of Alabama favored a delay. Ultimately, all sides agreed to a timetable to begin destroying more than 2,000 tons of chemicals stored in aging, leaky igloos.

Rogers traces his ancestry back five generations in eastern Alabama. His father was a firefighter at the Anniston Depot, while his mother worked in a textile factory. Neither graduated from high school, but Rogers earned a degree from the Birmingham School of Law. While working for the United Way as a career counselor, he met his wife, who worked for a local power company. They attended law school at night, and after graduating, she stayed at the power company while he started his own law practice in Anniston.

Rogers says his parents were conservatives who supported Gov. George C. Wallace Jr. and President Nixon. He recalls watching the Republican and Democratic national conventions in 1968 and 1972, from the moment he got home from school. He later volunteered for Ronald Reagan and recalls "working in his presidential campaign and thinking when my contemporaries became adults, this would be a Republican South because he had so captivated people in the South."

At 28, Rogers became the first Republican elected to the Calhoun County Commission. He was elected to the Alabama House in 1994, where he focused on health care and wrote a bill forcing every insurance plan to cover payments to doctors not in their networks. He eventually became minority leader.

When Republican Rep. Bob Riley ran successfully for governor in 2002, Rogers jumped into the race for his House seat. He faced Joe Turnham, a businessman aided by national Democratic Party organizations that saw an opportunity to take away a GOP seat. Rogers won by a slim 2 percentage points.

In 2004, he faced Bill Fuller, a veteran state legislator. The district is one-third African-American, and two of the state's leading black political groups endorsed Fuller. But Rogers raised more than $2 million and won with 61 percent of the vote. In 2006, he cruised to re-election, but in 2008 faced his closest re-election, facing Joshua Segall, a Montgomery attorney who ran a well-funded race. He won with 53 percent of the vote.

KEY VOTES

2008

Yes Delay consideration of Colombia free-trade agreement
Yes Override Bush veto of federal farm and nutrition programs reauthorization bill
Yes Overhaul surveillance laws and permit dismissal of suits against companies that conducted warrantless wiretapping
Yes Grant mortgage relief to homeowners and funding for Fannie Mae and Freddie Mac
Yes Approve initial $700 billion program to stabilize financial markets
Yes Approve final $700 billion program to stabilize financial markets
No Provide $14 billion in loans to automakers

2007

Yes Increase minimum wage by $2.10 an hour
No Approve $124.2 billion in emergency war spending and set goal for redeployment of troops from Iraq
Yes Reject federal contraceptive assistance to international family planning groups
Yes Override Bush veto of $23.2 billion water projects authorization bill
Yes Implement Peru free-trade agreement
Yes Approve energy policy overhaul with new fuel economy standards
Yes Clear $473.5 billion omnibus spending bill, including $70 billion for military operations

CQ VOTE STUDIES

	PARTY UNITY		PRESIDENTIAL SUPPORT	
	SUPPORT	OPPOSE	SUPPORT	OPPOSE
2008	88%	12%	53%	47%
2007	90%	10%	74%	26%
2006	96%	4%	83%	17%
2005	94%	6%	83%	17%
2004	95%	5%	76%	24%

INTEREST GROUPS

	AFL-CIO	ADA	CCUS	ACU
2008	40%	50%	89%	50%
2007	21%	20%	90%	80%
2006	36%	10%	87%	84%
2005	31%	10%	85%	88%
2004	13%	10%	100%	88%

ALABAMA 3

East — part of Montgomery, Anniston, Auburn

From the capital city to rural Appalachia, the 3rd enjoys a diversified economy that includes technology, manufacturing, government and universities. Among the district's many significant historical sites and tourist attractions, its section of Montgomery hosts the State Capitol Complex, the first White House of the Confederacy and the Dexter Avenue Baptist Church, where the 1955 bus boycott was launched.

To the north, Anniston, the Calhoun County seat, relies heavily on federal government jobs. FEMA operates a training site for first-responders to chemical, biological and nuclear terrorist attacks at the former Fort McClellan Army base, and the Anniston Army Depot hosts a chemical weapons incinerator and combat vehicle maintenance facilities.

Auburn University, one of the state's largest employers and a national leader in agricultural research, has partnered with the city of Auburn and the state of Alabama to develop a research park that has begun to attract major firms. The city also has undertaken efforts to lure new companies and diversify economically beyond reliance on the university.

The district's industrial sector includes a Honda plant in Lincoln and Hyundai's first U.S. plant, south of Montgomery. The collapse of the once-thriving textile and construction industries has hit Chambers County particularly hard.

The Republican-leaning 3rd is home to many conservative voters who generally favor GOP presidential candidates, as well as a substantial black population and small pockets of university liberals. Although Macon County gave Democrat Barack Obama his highest percentage of any county in the state (87 percent), Republican John McCain took 56 percent of the district's 2008 presidential vote overall.

MAJOR INDUSTRY
Higher education, technology, manufacturing, defense

MILITARY BASES
Anniston Army Depot, 11 military, 5,045 civilian (2007)

CITIES
Montgomery (pt.), 73,582; Auburn, 42,987; Phenix City, 28,265; Anniston, 24,276; Opelika, 23,498

NOTABLE
Tuskegee University, founded in 1881, was the first historically black college to be recognized as a National Historic Landmark.

Rep. Robert B. Aderholt (R)

Elected 1996; 7th term

CAPITOL OFFICE
225-4876
aderholt.house.gov
1433 Longworth Bldg. 20515-0104; fax 225-5587

COMMITTEES
Appropriations
Budget

RESIDENCE
Haleyville

BORN
July 22, 1965; Haleyville, Ala.

RELIGION
Congregationalist Baptist

FAMILY
Wife, Caroline Aderholt; two children

EDUCATION
Birmingham Southern U., B.A. 1987 (history &
political science); Samford U., J.D. 1990

CAREER
Lawyer; gubernatorial aide

POLITICAL HIGHLIGHTS
Republican nominee for Ala. House, 1990;
Haleyville municipal judge, 1992-96

ELECTION RESULTS

2008 GENERAL

Robert B. Aderholt (R)	196,741	74.8%
Nicholas B. Sparks (D)	66,077	25.1%

2008 PRIMARY

Robert B. Aderholt (R)	unopposed

2006 GENERAL

Robert B. Aderholt (R)	128,484	70.2%
Barbara Bobo (D)	54,382	29.7%

PREVIOUS WINNING PERCENTAGES
2004 (75%); 2002 (87%); 2000 (61%); 1998 (56%);
1996 (50%)

Aderholt is an economic and social conservative who would prefer to see the government tax and spend less. But unlike some of his GOP colleagues, he defends Congress' power of the purse and — with his judicious and straight-laced manner — resists others' efforts to eliminate earmarks, funding set-asides for projects in members' districts.

In the 110th Congress (2007-08), many of his fellow members of the Republican Study Committee, a group of the House's most conservative members, pressed for an end to earmarking. But Aderholt (ADD-er-holt) joined a small band of GOP appropriators led by Frank R. Wolf of Virginia in proposing an alternative: a temporary moratorium on the member-driven funding set-asides and the creation of a bipartisan, bicameral select committee to study the earmark issue. Neither plan went anywhere, and earmarks continued to slip into spending bills.

In fiscal 2008, Aderholt helped snare nearly $44 million in earmarks, according to Taxpayers for Common Sense. His rural, sparsely populated district is relatively poor compared to the rest of Alabama, and Aderholt considers the practice an important way to improve the quality of life there. "We aren't asking the federal government to fund the entire project," he said. "We're just asking for some help, because on our own it would be almost impossible."

In 2006, Aderholt was one of just 15 House Republicans to vote against giving the president enhanced power to eliminate line items in spending bills, subject to a final vote of Congress. "Congress needs to continue to take responsibility for spending and not pass the buck to the president," he said.

Aderholt is the top Republican on the Legislative Branch Appropriations Subcommittee and serves on the Commerce-Justice-Science Appropriations panel. He zealously promotes funding for NASA's Marshall Space Flight Center in Huntsville, located in the nearby 5th District. Many of his constituents work at the facility. He also continues to press for completion of "Corridor X," an interstate route following U.S. 78 across his district from Mississippi. He said the nearly $1.1 billion project, first championed by his predecessor, Democratic Rep. Tom Bevill, "is going to be lifeblood for us."

The son of a judge who also was a Baptist pastor, Aderholt was raised in a deeply conservative community. He is best known for his efforts to bring religious values into the public sphere and has fought to permit public displays of the Ten Commandments. It is a mission he embraced soon after he arrived in 1997 when a federal judge, citing the First Amendment, ordered a judge in Aderholt's district to remove a copy of the commandments from his courtroom wall.

In 2003, when another federal judge ordered the removal of a stone display of the Ten Commandments from Montgomery's state judicial complex, Aderholt said it was a "scene one would expect to see in the former Soviet Union, not the United States of America." In 2005, he introduced legislation that would bar court action against government officials as a result of their "acknowledgement of God as the sovereign source of law, liberty or government."

Aderholt is staunchly opposed to abortion. He favors constitutional amendments to outlaw all abortions except to save the life of the woman and opposes human cloning and embryonic stem cell research. He also has opposed measures to expand gay rights, voting in 2007 against House legislation to bar employment discrimination based on sexual orientation.

As a member of the Helsinki Commission monitoring human rights in Europe and the countries of the former Soviet Union, Aderholt has extended his campaign for freedom of religious expression overseas, particularly in Georgia and Turkmenistan. In 2008 he supported Georgia in its struggles to repel a Russian invasion and backed U.S. aid to help the country rebuild.

He irked the Bush administration when he joined two other House Republicans on a 2007 trip to Syria to meet with leaders there. "We were not coming as the head of state. We weren't going to make any offers to the Syrians," he said. "We saw our role as reaching out to the Syrians and those from the Middle East to say, 'Hey, it's in everyone's interest to have peace in this part of the world.'"

Aderholt regards most trade deals with a wary eye. Foreign competition has clobbered steel and textile industries in his area. After a Gulf States Steel plant in Gadsden closed in 2000, eliminating 1,700 jobs, he backed legislation providing loan guarantees for steel companies hurt by foreign imports, part of an effort to attract a buyer to reopen the plant.

The next year, when VF Corp., manufacturer of Lee and Wrangler jeans, closed four factories in and around the 4th District, Aderholt voted against granting the president fast-track authority to negotiate trade deals. Seven months later, he voted for the final version of the bill, reversing course after House leaders promised to fight against lifting tariffs on socks made in the Caribbean — an issue of parochial importance because of the major role textile mills play in the local economy.

He voted for the 2005 Central America Free Trade Agreement, but only after receiving written assurances from top administration officials — and a personal phone call from President Bush — that they would help protect domestic sockmakers from import surges. The trade pact passed the House by two votes. Aderholt was upset it took until 2008 for the government to confirm what he already knew — that the accord had led to a surge in imports and a drop in domestic production.

Aderholt grew up with politics. When he was 5, he wrote a campaign letter touting his father in a local election, and he recalls meeting Republican Sen. Bob Dole of Kansas when he was about 11. A month after his law school graduation, he was nominated for a state House seat but lost the general election. He was appointed to a municipal court judgeship in 1992 and went to work for Republican Gov. Fob James Jr. in 1995.

When Bevill retired in 1996 after 15 terms, Aderholt made a run for the seat. He took 49 percent of the primary vote against four rivals; he won the nomination when the second-place finisher declined to demand a runoff. Democrats backed former state Sen. Robert T. "Bob" Wilson Jr., who was nearly as conservative as Aderholt on social issues. Aderholt prevailed by 2 percentage points. He has won handily since.

KEY VOTES

2008

Yes Delay consideration of Colombia free-trade agreement

Yes Override Bush veto of federal farm and nutrition programs reauthorization bill

Yes Overhaul surveillance laws and permit dismissal of suits against companies that conducted warrantless wiretapping

No Grant mortgage relief to homeowners and funding for Fannie Mae and Freddie Mac

No Approve initial $700 billion program to stabilize financial markets

No Approve final $700 billion program to stabilize financial markets

No Provide $14 billion in loans to automakers

2007

Yes Increase minimum wage by $2.10 an hour

No Approve $124.2 billion in emergency war spending and set goal for redeployment of troops from Iraq

Yes Reject federal contraceptive assistance to international family planning groups

Yes Override Bush veto of $23.2 billion water projects authorization bill

No Implement Peru free-trade agreement

Yes Approve energy policy overhaul with new fuel economy standards

Yes Clear $473.5 billion omnibus spending bill, including $70 billion for military operations

CQ VOTE STUDIES

	PARTY UNITY		PRESIDENTIAL SUPPORT	
	SUPPORT	OPPOSE	SUPPORT	OPPOSE
2008	96%	4%	67%	33%
2007	89%	11%	75%	25%
2006	95%	5%	87%	13%
2005	97%	3%	93%	7%
2004	93%	7%	85%	15%

INTEREST GROUPS

	AFL-CIO	ADA	CCUS	ACU
2008	21%	25%	82%	92%
2007	17%	20%	79%	84%
2006	21%	10%	87%	84%
2005	13%	0%	85%	92%
2004	7%	0%	100%	92%

ALABAMA 4

North central — Gadsden, part of Decatur

Taking in mountains, foothills, flatlands and large waterways, the rural 4th runs the width of the state, bordering both Mississippi and Georgia. A small black population and the absence of a major city distinguish the relatively poor district from the rest of Alabama.

The 4th relies on assistance from the Appalachian Regional Commission, a decades-old federal-state partnership to aid development and reduce poverty in the area. Completion of "Corridor X," an interstate route following U.S. 78 across the 4th from Mississippi, is a priority of the commission and of local officials, who hope the route will attract new midsize businesses. Many local residents work in nearby metropolitan areas, such as Huntsville (in the 5th) and Birmingham (in the 6th and 7th).

Textiles, mining and rubber and other manufacturing are still major job sources here despite volatility in the coal market and the loss of some manufacturing and textile jobs abroad. The industrial sector has diversified beyond steel and textiles to include food processing and wood products. The Tennessee Valley Authority's Guntersville Reservoir, shared

with the 5th, supports a shipping-based economy in Guntersville. Gadsden, the district's only sizable city, has had some success with economic diversification efforts following manufacturing plant closures.

Agribusinesses, especially cattle and poultry enterprises, form a significant sector of the local economy, and tourism is growing. The mountainous landscape provides opportunities for outdoor recreation, and Smith Lake in Cullman, Walker and Winston counties lures visitors to the 4th.

Once a Democratic stronghold, the 4th's conservative population tends to support GOP candidates nationally, but still elects Democrats to state and local offices. In 1996, voters sent a Republican to Congress for just the second time since Reconstruction, and have re-elected GOP Rep. Robert B. Aderholt with strong margins since.

MAJOR INDUSTRY
Manufacturing, textiles, mining, agriculture, tourism

CITIES
Gadsden, 38,978; Albertville, 17,247; Jasper, 14,052; Cullman, 13,995

NOTABLE
Dry Cullman County hosts an Oktoberfest celebration where only non-alcoholic beverages, including one called "Oktoberzest," are served.

Rep. Parker Griffith (D)

Elected 2008; 1st term

Griffith, a member of the Blue Dog Coalition of fiscally conservative Democrats, promises to fill the shoes left by his predecessor, Democrat Robert E. "Bud" Cramer. Early in his first term, he gave ample evidence he won't hesitate to buck his party.

He was one of a handful of Democrats to vote against two key labor bills addressing pay disparities between men and women. He also cast votes against releasing the second $350 billion of funds authorized under a financial services industry rescue law Congress cleared in fall 2008. And he was one of seven House Democrats to oppose the $787 billion economic stimulus law in February 2009. "We need to jump-start our economy and create new jobs," he said. But he said the bill would not do enough to "cut taxes, support small businesses or invest in our research and development programs."

Griffith prefers a middle ground between regulation and free markets. "The role of the government in America is a role that is [similar to] a partner with business — a facilitator with business in a global economy," he said.

After spending much of his life treating cancer patients, Griffith hopes to focus his congressional labors on access to and affordability of health care, a hot topic for President Obama and the 111th Congress (2009-10). He hopes to devise a program to help pay medical school tuition for doctors who pledge to work in underserved areas or opt for specialties where there is a shortage of providers.

The 5th District supports a large military and defense industry and is home to NASA's Marshall Space Flight Center and a Boeing satellite rocket booster plant. Griffith was unable to gain a spot on the Armed Services Committee, but he will be able to look out for the flight center from his post on the Science panel. On the Transportation and Infrastructure panel, he plans to work to alleviate clogged roads and traffic problems in his district.

Griffith is the oldest member of the House freshman class. He retired as a radiation oncologist in the 1990s and, with his brother, built a business that included a number of funeral homes and health care facilities. He lost a close race for mayor of Huntsville in 2004. In 2006 he won election to the state Senate, where he worked on tax cuts, alternative fuel sources and health care.

CAPITOL OFFICE
225-4801
griffith.house.gov
417 Cannon Bldg. 20515-0105; fax 225-4392

COMMITTEES
Science & Technology
Small Business
Transportation & Infrastructure

RESIDENCE
Huntsville

BORN
Aug. 6, 1942; Shreveport, La.

RELIGION
Episcopalian

FAMILY
Wife, Virginia Griffith; five children

EDUCATION
Loyola U. (La.), attended 1962-64 (dentistry); Louisiana State U., B.S. 1966 (zoology & chemistry), M.D. 1970

MILITARY SERVICE
Army Reserve, 1970-73

CAREER
Physician; funeral and nursing homes owner; real estate developer

POLITICAL HIGHLIGHTS
Candidate for mayor of Huntsville, 2004; Ala. Senate, 2006-08

ELECTION RESULTS

2008 GENERAL

Parker Griffith (D)	156,642	51.3%
Wayne Parker (R)	147,314	48.2%

2008 PRIMARY

Parker Griffith (D)	3,874	89.9%
David Maker (D)	3,874	10.1%

ALABAMA 5

North — Huntsville

The Tennessee River winds through the 5th, which stretches across the state's northern tier and borders Mississippi, Tennessee and Georgia. The Tennessee Valley Authority maintains a strong presence along the river, and the government and industrial facilities lining its famous shores are vital to the 5th.

Huntsville relies on federal government, defense and contracting jobs. NASA's Marshall Space Flight Center develops rocket propulsion technology and space flight vehicles, and the Army's Redstone Arsenal is home to rocket and missile programs.

Strong manufacturing, research and technology sectors bolster the 5th's economy. Huntsville's Cummings Research Park has 25,000 employees, and a Toyota engine plant employs almost 900. Nearly one in five workers in Huntsville is employed in high-technology manufacturing or services.

Decatur's industrial economy boasts a United Launch Alliance satellite rocket booster plant, a 3M chemical plant and a Nucor steel mill. Agriculture represents a healthy portion of the 5th's rural economy, and crops include corn, cotton and soybeans.

The generally conservative voters in the 5th elect many Democrats to state and local offices, have never sent a Republican to Congress and favor GOP presidential candidates.

MAJOR INDUSTRY
Defense, government, manufacturing, technology, agriculture

MILITARY BASES
Redstone Arsenal (Army), 1,800 military, 15,049 civilian (2009)

CITIES
Huntsville, 158,216; Decatur (pt.), 44,655; Florence, 36,264; Madison, 29,329

NOTABLE
Muscle Shoals' Fame Recording Studios merged rhythm and blues, country and gospel to create the "Muscle Shoals Sound."

Rep. Spencer Bachus (R)

Elected 1992; 9th term

CAPITOL OFFICE
225-4921
bachus.house.gov
2246 Rayburn Bldg. 20515-0106; fax 225-2082

COMMITTEES
Financial Services - ranking member

RESIDENCE
Vestavia Hills

BORN
Dec. 28, 1947; Birmingham, Ala.

RELIGION
Baptist

FAMILY
Wife, Linda Bachus; five children

EDUCATION
Auburn U., B.A. 1969; U. of Alabama, J.D. 1972

MILITARY SERVICE
Ala. National Guard, 1969-71

CAREER
Lawyer; sawmill owner

POLITICAL HIGHLIGHTS
Ala. Senate, 1983; Ala. House, 1983-87;
Ala. Board of Education, 1987-91; candidate for
Ala. attorney general, 1990; Ala. Republican Party
chairman, 1991-92

ELECTION RESULTS

2008 GENERAL

Spencer Bachus (R)	280,902	97.8%
write-ins	6,335	2.2%

2008 PRIMARY

Spencer Bachus (R)	unopposed

2006 GENERAL

Spencer Bachus (R)	163,514	98.3%
write-ins	2,786	1.7%

PREVIOUS WINNING PERCENTAGES
2004 (99%); 2002 (90%); 2000 (88%); 1998 (72%);
1996 (71%); 1994 (79%); 1992 (52%)

Bachus is typically in step with conservatives on everything from abortion rights to tax cuts. But recently he has seen his political fortunes rise and dip along with — and in large part because of — the economy.

Bachus (BACK-us) is the top-ranking Republican on the Financial Services Committee, a position he secured at the start of the 110th Congress (2007-08) through stepped-up fundraising for Republicans in tight races and his conservative bona fides as a member of the Republican Study Committee. But as the economy and housing markets tumbled and the GOP divided on solutions, Bachus found himself alone among GOP leaders in negotiating a Bush White House financial services industry rescue plan.

In fall 2008, his decision to work with Democratic leaders on the $700 billion plan to stabilize the economy led conservatives to accuse him of "drinking the Kool-Aid," and eventually forced Minority Leader John A. Boehner to strip him of his power to speak for the GOP at the deliberations.

"Politically, I would have been much better off just saying, 'I don't like this,' and staying out of it," Bachus told the Birmingham News. But on the House floor, he insisted that "failure to act on this imperfect legislation would have severe consequences for our economy and would harm the people I represent." He went as far as to suggest, along with Treasury Secretary Henry M. Paulson Jr., that the plan could be a revenue-raiser.

While the position was maddening to many conservatives, Bachus said the leadership had assured him that his place as top-ranking member is safe. He was more in sync with the GOP as President Obama took office; in February 2009, he dismissed a proposal by Treasury Secretary Timothy F. Geithner to bolster the rescue law, saying it was "just a broad outline" needing more work.

Bachus frequently stands against government intervention and regulation, but the growth of subprime mortgage lending had him investigating action long before the troubles came. He ordered studies on the lending, drafted bills to tighten regulation and ultimately supported a plan by Financial Services Chairman Barney Frank of Massachusetts to keep more bad mortgages from being issued. Late in 2008, he said even more stringent rules might be needed.

But Bachus, who in 2006 contributed more than $550,000 of his own campaign funds to the National Republican Congressional Committee, the House GOP's political arm, is still a reliable conservative. He opposes abortion, opposed a 2007 bill to ban job discrimination based on sexual preference, and was an early supporter of President George W. Bush's 2001 and 2003 tax cuts. He likes to remind people the American Civil Liberties Union rates him one of the worst Alabama congressmen.

He also has proved he is not "Barney's lapdog," as implied by the more senior Richard H. Baker of Louisiana during their battle for Financial Services' top GOP post. Bachus stood against Frank in 2008 on a bill to keep mortgage giants Fannie Mae and Freddie Mac afloat. Bachus went so far as to send Bush a letter requesting a veto of the plan, which he said could threaten the long-term solvency of the two government-sponsored enterprises.

While Bachus lost that battle, as well as another struggle over his opposition to an affordable-housing trust fund, he has won a few others. In 2008, he fought Frank's plan to dismantle an online gambling bill. Bachus also got his way, with the help of the Senate, on a more measured yet temporary renewal of the federal terrorism insurance program.

Bachus is attuned to the rapidly changing environment for handling confidential financial information, driven by advances in computer and Internet technology. He wants Financial Services to address problems with e-mail scams and with security of personal information. He also wants to crack down on lenders who prey on consumers with high-interest, low-value loans.

A devout Baptist, Bachus' religious beliefs have led to his support of Third World debt relief and education investments, and therefore to unusual alliances with the likes of U2 frontman Bono and liberal California Democrat Maxine Waters. Bachus, whose son served in the Marines, said canceling the debt of poorer countries can help stabilize their governments, combat poverty and prevent terrorism. "Young people who are reading books aren't building bombs," he said in 2007.

He has supported economic sanctions on Sudan in the hope of halting the killings of Christians in the southern region. He sponsored legislation in 2004 to prevent foreign oil companies from raising capital through U.S. financial markets if the companies continue to do business in Sudan. The Bush administration said it preferred to negotiate with the oil companies, and the bill went nowhere.

Bachus keeps an eye on local concerns as well. He helped secure a new national veterans' center in Birmingham, and won a provision setting aside 30,000 acres for a wildlife refuge along a stretch of the Cahaba River. A $25 million appropriation in 2004 for an upgrade of U.S. 78 between Birmingham and Memphis also bears his mark. And he and the Alabama delegation successfully lobbied the Base Realignment and Closure Commission to retain the Birmingham International Airport Air Guard Station, home to the 117th Air Refueling Wing. In 2008, Bachus also pressed the federal government to take action on a financial crisis in Jefferson County, Ala., which teetered on bankruptcy due to bad debts.

Bachus played a role in the 2008 GOP convention by serving on the committee that drafted the rules and laid out the party platform.

Early in his career, Bachus owned a sawmill, but for the most part, he earned a living as a trial lawyer. He began his career in elective office in 1983, serving first in the state legislature, then on the state board of education and then as chairman of the Alabama GOP.

In his first House bid, Bachus benefited from the post-1990 census remapping of Alabama's congressional districts that transformed the district held for five terms by Democratic Rep. Ben Erdreich into a Republican bastion. Bachus took 52 percent of the vote in 1992 and since then has been re-elected with at least 70 percent. In redistricting after the 2000 census, the district became even more securely Republican. He had no major party opposition in 2002 and ran unopposed in 2004, 2006 and 2008.

KEY VOTES

2008

No   Delay consideration of Colombia free-trade agreement
Yes Override Bush veto of federal farm and nutrition programs reauthorization bill
Yes Overhaul surveillance laws and permit dismissal of suits against companies that conducted warrantless wiretapping
No   Grant mortgage relief to homeowners and funding for Fannie Mae and Freddie Mac
Yes Approve initial $700 billion program to stabilize financial markets
Yes Approve final $700 billion program to stabilize financial markets
No   Provide $14 billion in loans to automakers

2007

Yes Increase minimum wage by $2.10 an hour
No   Approve $124.2 billion in emergency war spending and set goal for redeployment of troops from Iraq
Yes Reject federal contraceptive assistance to international family planning groups
No   Override Bush veto of $23.2 billion water projects authorization bill
Yes Implement Peru free-trade agreement
No   Approve energy policy overhaul with new fuel economy standards
Yes Clear $473.5 billion omnibus spending bill, including $70 billion for military operations

CQ VOTE STUDIES

	PARTY UNITY		PRESIDENTIAL SUPPORT	
	SUPPORT	OPPOSE	SUPPORT	OPPOSE
2008	94%	6%	68%	32%
2007	93%	7%	83%	17%
2006	97%	3%	97%	3%
2005	98%	2%	88%	12%
2004	95%	5%	88%	12%

INTEREST GROUPS

	AFL-CIO	ADA	CCUS	ACU
2008	20%	20%	94%	84%
2007	14%	10%	79%	92%
2006	21%	0%	93%	88%
2005	20%	5%	93%	92%
2004	13%	5%	100%	96%

ALABAMA 6

Central — suburban Birmingham and Tuscaloosa

Some of the sweetest homes in Alabama are found in the 6th District, a mix of white and wealthy suburbs of Birmingham and Tuscaloosa, parts of the cities themselves and nearby rural areas in central Alabama. The U-shaped 6th surrounds a thin peninsula of land in the adjacent 7th that stretches southwest from downtown Birmingham to Tuscaloosa.

Decades of population decline in Birmingham contrast with the overall growth of the metropolitan area. The 6th takes in much of the area's suburbs, while the city is mostly in the 7th. Commuters reside in historically wealthy areas in southern Jefferson County, particularly Mountain Brook and Homewood. Shelby County, mainly south of Birmingham, has seen significant suburban growth over the past three decades and has been known for having the highest median income of any county in the state.

The 6th includes a section of Tuscaloosa north of the Black Warrior River, which bisects the city and separates it from the county's biggest employer, the University of Alabama in the 7th. On autumn Saturdays, more than 92,000 fans from across the state wind up just south of the river from the 6th at the University of Alabama's Bryant-Denny Stadium to watch "Crimson Tide" football.

Birmingham's suburbs are encroaching on the district's rural areas, but agriculture, manufacturing and mining remain key to economic health in some areas. Agricultural production has slowed, but peaches remain a point of pride in Chilton County. Mercedes-Benz vehicles are produced in Vance, within the strip of the 7th bordered on both sides by the 6th.

The growing conservative, white-collar Birmingham suburbs that account for much of the district's population have kept the 6th reliably Republican. Democrats have not fielded a candidate to face Rep. Spencer Bachus since 1998.

MAJOR INDUSTRY
Manufacturing, higher education, mining, agriculture

CITIES
Hoover, 62,742; Birmingham (pt.), 26,723; Vestavia Hills, 24,476; Alabaster, 22,619; Mountain Brook, 20,604

NOTABLE
The Cahaba River National Wildlife Refuge is a natural habitat for longleaf pine and hosts the largest known stand of endangered shoals lily.

Rep. Artur Davis (D)

Elected 2002; 4th term

CAPITOL OFFICE
225-2665
www.house.gov/arturdavis
208 Cannon Bldg. 20515-0107; fax 226-9567

COMMITTEES
House Administration
Ways & Means

RESIDENCE
Birmingham

BORN
Oct. 9, 1967; Montgomery, Ala.

RELIGION
Lutheran

FAMILY
Wife, Tara Davis

EDUCATION
Harvard U., A.B. 1990 (government), J.D. 1993

CAREER
Lawyer

POLITICAL HIGHLIGHTS
Assistant U.S. attorney, 1994-98; sought
Democratic nomination for U.S. House, 2000

ELECTION RESULTS

2008 GENERAL

Artur Davis (D)	228,518	98.6%
write-ins	3,183	1.4%

2008 PRIMARY

Artur Davis (D)	unopposed

2006 GENERAL

Artur Davis (D)	133,870	99.0%
write-ins	1,294	1.0%

PREVIOUS WINNING PERCENTAGES
2004 (75%); 2002 (92%)

Davis is a politically savvy, middle-of-the-road Democrat who advocates both an activist federal government and culturally conservative policies. He says his views and voting record represent the mainstream in his district and in the country, and he is eager to test his appeal statewide.

"I came to the House to serve a period of time and in part to seek for higher office," he said. Davis (his first name is pronounced ar-TOUR) had contemplated a run for the Senate in 2008, but opted instead to focus on Illinois Sen. Barack Obama's presidential campaign. Obama is a former law school classmate of Davis, who was often mentioned as a possible candidate for attorney general in Obama's administration.

Davis turned his eye in 2009 to the governor's seat in 2010; Republican Gov. Bob Riley is term-limited. Even in Alabama, a state with a history of troubled race relations, Davis sees fresh opportunity for black politicians. "Race tells us less than it ever has in American political life," he said. "Those hurdles are coming down, and the change that is producing in American society is as profound as the collapse of the Berlin Wall was in Europe." If elected, Davis would be the first black governor of a state in the Deep South.

Davis insists he could win over voters based on shared views and values. "When I drive down I-95 to visit my mother in Montgomery, I see a giant Confederate flag. That's part of our history that we live with every day. We were...the first Confederate capital and the first capital of the civil rights movement," he said. "It's not my task to repudiate history; it's my task to find common ground based on our shared history."

Davis' votes typically vacillate; he is a member of both the liberal Congressional Black Caucus and the politically moderate New Democrat Coalition. He was one of four vice chairmen of the New Democrats in the 110th Congress (2007-08). Davis also serves on the Democratic Steering Committee, which makes committee assignments.

He supports a constitutional amendment to ban same-sex marriage, and in 2007 he voted against a bill to prohibit workplace discrimination against gays. He was one of 63 Democrats in 2003 to vote for a conservative-backed ban on what opponents call "partial birth" abortion.

In 2005, he supported a renewal of the 2001 anti-terrorism law known as the Patriot Act; he also supported an overhaul of the law allowing the government to eavesdrop on foreign terrorists in 2008. He was among 27 House Democrats voting in 2006 to allow oil and gas drilling in Alaska's Arctic National Wildlife Refuge — a proposal that did not become law.

From his seat on the Judiciary Committee, Davis in 2007 helped pass a bill sponsored by Chairman John Conyers Jr. of Michigan to toughen sentencing for hate crimes. Under the bill, those convicted of hate crimes could face life in prison if the incident resulted in death or involved a kidnapping, sexual assault or attempted murder. Republicans argued the legislation undermined the principle of equality, and they unsuccessfully tried to amend it to include the elderly, children, members of the armed forces and police officers. "It was probably the most distorted, misunderstood bill I have encountered since being in Congress," Davis said. "If you don't like people because of who they are, this bill says we are offended by that as a community."

Davis thinks the government should help lift people out of poverty — his district is the fifth-poorest in the nation. From his seat on the powerful Ways and Means Committee, he backed passage in early 2009 of a law expanding the State Children's Health Insurance Program, which covers chldren from low-income families that don't qualify for Medicaid. In 2004, Davis was a chief sponsor of a measure to help people buy their first homes. Congress included the provision in a spending law, reducing the required amount of upfront money from buyers taking part in the government's single-family guaranteed loan program. With the change, borrowers could finance loan fees along with the rest of the loan rather than paying for them at closing time.

That same year, he worked with Democrat Charles B. Rangel of New York, now Ways and Means chairman, on expanding the child tax credit for poor families. While their efforts failed to expand Bush's $1,000-per-child tax credit to all families who pay little or no taxes, they won a modified version of the proposal that made 6.5 million low-income families eligible for a refundable credit.

Davis earned nationwide recognition when, as a junior member of the Budget Committee in the 108th Congress (2003-04), he engineered a change in the funding formula for black colleges. He noted Bush's 2004 budget would have cut funding for 1890 land-grant schools, which are predominately black, while maintaining funding for 1862 land-grant colleges, which are predominately white. Two of the country's 17 black schools are in Alabama. Casting it as an issue of racial fairness, he won adoption of a House amendment that reversed the proposed cuts.

Davis grew up in the hard-pressed west end of Montgomery near downtown. His parents divorced when he was young, and Davis, an only child, was raised by his grandmother and his mother, an elementary school teacher. As a boy, he was a voracious reader and loved history. He graduated magna cum laude from Harvard in 1990 and went on to earn his law degree there. Davis worked his way through college and took out student loans.

After graduation, Davis returned to Montgomery and worked as an assistant U.S. attorney from 1994 to 1998. He launched his first bid for the House in 2000 and lost. But two years later, voters in the 7th District had grown weary of Democrat Earl F. Hilliard, and the mayors of Selma and Birmingham backed Davis, who raised more than $1.5 million.

Davis finished second to Hilliard in a three-candidate primary and won the runoff with 56 percent of the vote. No Republican ran in his heavily Democratic district. By the time of his first re-election campaign, Davis had opened five offices across the district and hired eight times as many staff as his predecessor. He also launched a public-private initiative aimed at bringing new businesses to the district. He handily turned back primary challengers and sailed to re-election in 2004. He was unopposed in 2006 and 2008.

KEY VOTES

2008

Yes Delay consideration of Colombia free-trade agreement

Yes Override Bush veto of federal farm and nutrition programs reauthorization bill

Yes Overhaul surveillance laws and permit dismissal of suits against companies that conducted warrantless wiretapping

Yes Grant mortgage relief to homeowners and funding for Fannie Mae and Freddie Mac

Yes Approve initial $700 billion program to stabilize financial markets

Yes Approve final $700 billion program to stabilize financial markets

No Provide $14 billion in loans to automakers

2007

Yes Increase minimum wage by $2.10 an hour

Yes Approve $124.2 billion in emergency war spending and set goal for redeployment of troops from Iraq

No Reject federal contraceptive assistance to international family planning groups

Yes Override Bush veto of $23.2 billion water projects authorization bill

Yes Implement Peru free-trade agreement

Yes Approve energy policy overhaul with new fuel economy standards

Yes Clear $473.5 billion omnibus spending bill, including $70 billion for military operations

CQ VOTE STUDIES

	PARTY UNITY		PRESIDENTIAL SUPPORT	
	SUPPORT	OPPOSE	SUPPORT	OPPOSE
2008	96%	4%	24%	76%
2007	94%	6%	12%	88%
2006	80%	20%	53%	47%
2005	83%	17%	46%	54%
2004	87%	13%	44%	56%

INTEREST GROUPS

	AFL-CIO	ADA	CCUS	ACU
2008	93%	85%	67%	12%
2007	96%	90%	70%	4%
2006	100%	75%	73%	44%
2005	87%	80%	70%	28%
2004	73%	75%	71%	24%

ALABAMA 7

West central — parts of Birmingham and Tuscaloosa

Marked by stark regional contrasts, the 7th includes chunks of Birmingham and Tuscaloosa, as well as struggling rural areas in west central Alabama. Health care and banking sectors have taken root in parts of the district, but the 7th remains Alabama's poorest district overall.

Economic growth in the 7th's part of Birmingham, the densely populated downtown area, has trailed the rest of the city and its suburbs since the collapse of the steel industry in the 1970s. Decades of redevelopment efforts have yielded some success, and the sprawling University of Alabama at Birmingham continues to expand. Downtown also includes a Civil Rights District featuring historic sites and museums.

To the west, manufacturing, medical services and the University of Alabama's flagship campus anchor Tuscaloosa's thriving, diversified economy. Nearby Vance is home to a Mercedes-Benz plant.

Almost all of the rest of the 7th District falls into Alabama's portion of the Black Belt, a region of rich soil that stretches from Texas to Virginia. This poverty-filled area has not known prosperity since before the Civil War, when cotton plantation owners made fortunes from slave labor. Although agricultural diversification efforts have been modestly successful, jobs remain scarce, and the population has been declining for decades.

In contrast to its white, well-to-do neighbor — the Republican 6th — the bulk of the 7th's residents are poor to middle class blacks who vote overwhelmingly Democratic. The district, as redrawn after the 1990 census, has been held by two African-American representatives, including the state's first black U.S. House member since Reconstruction.

MAJOR INDUSTRY
Agriculture, manufacturing, higher education, health care

CITIES
Birmingham (pt.), 216,097; Tuscaloosa (pt.), 68,928; Bessemer (pt.), 27,599

NOTABLE
Edmund Pettus Bridge in Selma was the site of "Bloody Sunday," when Alabama state troopers beat and gassed peaceful civil rights marchers — who were co-led by current Georgia Democratic Rep. John Lewis — on their way from Selma to Montgomery in 1965.

Gov. Sarah Palin (R)

Pronounced: PAY-lin
First elected: 2006
Length of term: 4 years
Term expires: 12/10
Salary: $125,000
Phone: (907) 465-3500

Residence: Wasilla
Born: Feb. 11, 1964;
Sandpoint, Idaho
Religion: Christian non-denominational
Family: Husband, Todd Palin; five children
Education: U. of Idaho, B.S. 1987
(journalism)
Career: Commercial fishing company owner;
outdoor recreational equipment company
owner; sports reporter
Political highlights: Wasilla City Council,
1992-96; mayor of Wasilla, 1996-2002;
sought Republican nomination for lieutenant
governor, 2002; Alaska Oil and Gas
Conservation Commission, 2003-04;
Republican nominee for vice president, 2008

Election results:
2006 GENERAL

Sarah Palin (R)	114,697	48.3%
Tony Knowles (D)	97,238	41.0%
Andrew Halcro (I)	22,443	9.5%

Lt. Gov. Sean Parnell (R)

First elected: 2006
Length of term: 4 years
Term expires: 12/10
Salary: $100,000
Phone: (907) 465-3520

LEGISLATURE

Legislature: January-May, limit of
90 calendar days

Senate: 20 members, 4-year terms
2009 ratios: 10 R, 10 D; 17 men,
3 women
Salary: $50,400
Phone: (907) 465-3701

House: 40 members, 2-year terms
2009 ratios: 22 R, 18 D; 31 men,
9 women
Salary: $50,400
Phone: (907) 465-3725

TERM LIMITS

Governor: 2 consecutive terms
Senate: No
House: No

URBAN STATISTICS

CITY	POPULATION
Anchorage	260,283
Juneau	30,711
Fairbanks	30,224
Sitka	8,835
Ketchikan	7,922

REGISTERED VOTERS

Unaffiliated	53%
Republican	27%
Democrat	16%
Others	4%

POPULATION

2008 population (est.)	686,293
2000 population	626,932
1990 population	550,043
Percent change (1990-2000)	+14%
Rank among states (2008)	47

Median age	32.4
Born in state	38.1%
Foreign born	5.9%
Violent crime rate	567/100,000
Poverty level	9.4%
Federal workers	16,363
Military	22,786

ELECTIONS

STATE ELECTION OFFICIAL
(907) 465-4611
DEMOCRATIC PARTY
(907) 258-3050
REPUBLICAN PARTY
(907) 276-4467

MISCELLANEOUS

Web: www.state.ak.us
Capital: Juneau

U.S. CONGRESS

Senate: 1 Republican, 1 Democrat
House: 1 Republican

2000 Census Statistics by District

DIST.	2008 VOTE FOR PRESIDENT OBAMA	MCCAIN	WHITE	BLACK	ASIAN	HISP	MEDIAN INCOME	WHITE COLLAR	BLUE COLLAR	SERVICE INDUSTRY	OVER 64	UNDER 18	COLLEGE EDUCATION	RURAL	SQ. MILES
AL	38%	59%	68%	3%	4%	4%	$51,571	61%	24%	16%	6%	30%	25%	34%	571,951
STATE	38	59	68	3	4	4	$51,571	61	24	16	6	30	25	34	571,951
U.S.	53	46	69	12	4	13	$41,994	60	25	15	12	26	24	21	3,537,438

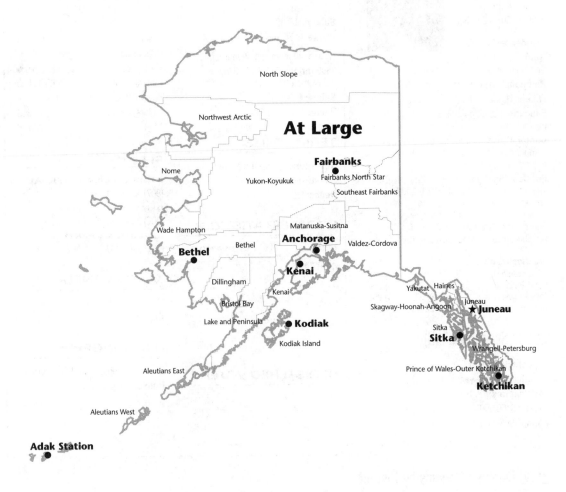

North Slope

Northwest Arctic

At Large

Nome

Fairbanks

Yukon-Koyukuk

Fairbanks North Star

Southeast Fairbanks

Wade Hampton

Matanuska-Susitna

Anchorage

Bethel

Valdez-Cordova

Bethel

Kenai

Dillingham

Yakutat   Haines

Kenai

Skagway-Hoonah-Angoon

Juneau

★**Juneau**

Bristol Bay

Lake and Peninsula

Kodiak

Sitka

Sitka

Kodiak Island

Wrangell-Petersburg

Aleutians East

Prince of Wales-Outer Ketchikan

Ketchikan

Aleutians West

Adak Station

Sen. Lisa Murkowski (R)

Elected 2004; 1st full term
Appointed December 2002

CAPITOL OFFICE
224-6665
murkowski.senate.gov
709 Hart Bldg. 20510-0202; fax 224-5301

COMMITTEES
Appropriations
Energy & Natural Resources - ranking member
Health, Education, Labor & Pensions
Indian Affairs

RESIDENCE
Girdwood

BORN
May 22, 1957; Ketchikan, Alaska

RELIGION
Roman Catholic

FAMILY
Husband, Verne Martell; two children

EDUCATION
Willamette U., attended 1975-77;
Georgetown U., B.A. 1980 (economics);
Willamette U., J.D. 1985

CAREER
Lawyer; state legislative aide

POLITICAL HIGHLIGHTS
Anchorage district attorney, 1987-89; Alaska
House, 1999-2002

ELECTION RESULTS

2004 GENERAL

Lisa Murkowski (R)	149,773	48.6%
Tony Knowles (D)	140,424	45.6%
Marc J. Millican (NON)	8,885	2.9%
Jerry Sanders (AKI)	3,785	1.2%

2004 PRIMARY

Lisa Murkowski (R)	45,710	58.1%
Mike Miller (R)	29,313	37.3%
Wev Shea (R)	2,857	3.6%

With the equivalent of just one term under her belt, Murkowski is the most powerful member of Alaska's once-mighty delegation. A lawyer who supports abortion rights and works with colleagues across the aisle on issues ranging from energy to health care, she is a contrast to the state's other prominent female — Gov. Sarah Palin, who courted social conservatives as GOP presidential candidate John McCain's running mate in 2008.

Murkowski came to office in controversy — she was initially appointed by her father to take his seat after he was elected governor in 2002 — but has subsequently avoided the negative publicity that has afflicted her fellow Alaskans. Her GOP colleague Ted Stevens, a longtime force on the Appropriations Committee, lost his 2008 bid for a seventh Senate term after being convicted of corruption charges (the charges were later dropped). And the state's only House member, 18-term Republican Don Young, yielded his top-ranking slot on the Natural Resources Committee in December 2008 amid ethics questions, though he vowed to seek to reclaim the spot when his name is cleared.

Murkowski is filling the shoes of retired veteran New Mexico Sen. Pete V. Domenici as the Energy and Natural Resources Committee's top Republican. "There's a lot of weight" to taking over for Domenici and Stevens, she acknowledged. "But I look at it this way: What if I only had had two years of working with Ted, or two years of working with Pete? Then maybe I wouldn't feel I'm as prepared as I am now."

Republican leaders are doing what they can to help her. She received a coveted seat on the Appropriations Committee at the outset of the 111th. She also was named a counsel to Minority Leader Mitch McConnell to provide behind-the-scenes advice.

Murkowski will be at the center of efforts to enact comprehensive energy legislation in the 111th. On that issue, she has a broader focus than Palin, who touts oil and gas drilling — mainstays of Alaska's economy — as the main solution. "How have we gotten to this point where Republicans are just for drilling and Democrats are just for conserving or locking everything up? That's not the way things should be," she said. "Energy security should mean a diversification of our energy resources, whether it's renewables or more nuclear or more domestic production."

Murkowski has a good relationship with Energy Chairman Jeff Bingaman of New Mexico, another pragmatist. But she is keen on furthering Domenici's legacy as a champion of nuclear energy and is likely to push more aggressively for its use than many Democrats would like. She shares Bingaman's concerns over global warming and signed on as a cosponsor to his legislation in the 110th Congress (2007-08) to set up a "cap and trade" system of limiting greenhouse gas emissions that was more industry-friendly than the version the Senate considered but did not pass in 2008.

Murkowski's priorities extend well beyond energy. She has introduced or cosponsored several health-related bills, including one to combat fetal alcohol syndrome, a major problem in her state. A member of the Health, Education, Labor and Pensions Committee, she has frequently teamed with Democrats to push proposals to improve prevention and treatment of cardiovascular disease in women and to get junk food out of schools.

She also has been involved in efforts to reshape the 2001 No Child Left Behind education law to ensure its benchmarks for student progress are met in Alaska and other rural states that lack qualified teachers. On the Indian Affairs panel, where she was the top Republican in the 110th Congress, she has teamed with Chairman Byron L. Dorgan of North Dakota on efforts to improve American Indian housing and health care. She also worked with Barack Obama when he was in the Senate on a bill to ban exports of mercury — which can make fish unsafe to eat — that was signed into law in 2008.

After serving two years as an appointed senator, she began her first full term in 2005 in a strengthened position politically after winning the seat in her own right. The election lifted the nepotism cloud from her appointment by her father, Frank H. Murkowski, who quit the Senate when he was elected governor. As an appointed senator, she had chalked up several legislative victories with the help of Stevens, for whom she once interned. Stevens has called Murkowski "a hell of a lot better senator than her dad ever was."

Although more moderate than the senior Murkowski, she usually votes with the GOP leadership. However, she supports abortion rights and in 2003 joined eight other Senate Republicans voting to affirm support of the Supreme Court decision in *Roe v. Wade*, which legalized abortion. She backs some abortion restrictions, however; she voted in 2003 to ban a procedure opponents call "partial birth" abortion.

Murkowski also is more labor-friendly than most Republican senators. During the 109th Congress (2005-06), she backed Democratic proposals to extend unemployment benefits by 26 weeks and cosponsored a Republican bill to give workers looking for jobs an extra 13 weeks of pay.

Murkowski can claim several Senate firsts. She is the first native-born Alaskan to serve in the chamber and the first daughter of a senator to serve. She is also the only senator to be appointed by a parent.

The second of six children, Murkowski grew up in Ketchikan in the Alaskan Panhandle and attended high school in Fairbanks. She interned for Stevens in her senior year, then went to Georgetown University, graduating in 1980. Her father was just launching his first Senate campaign, and she and her siblings joined the effort. Later, with a law degree from Willamette University in Oregon, she spent two years as Anchorage's district attorney before opening a solo law practice.

She ran successfully for the state House in 1998, was re-elected twice and was chosen by her peers late in 2002 as majority leader, a post she never filled because of her subsequent appointment to the U.S. Senate.

In the state legislature, when Alaska suffered a funding shortfall, she joined a bipartisan coalition that advocated raising taxes and was instrumental in the passage of a boost in the state's alcohol tax to a dime a drink, at the time the highest rate in the nation. She also supported public funding for abortions.

During her 2004 campaign, she faced Democrat Tony Knowles, a former two-term governor, a former mayor of Anchorage, a Vietnam veteran and a one-time oil rig worker. Murkowski tried to distance herself politically from her father, who was proving to be an unpopular governor due to his support for a tax increase and his attempt to use federal homeland security funds for a jet to carry him around the state.

Under the banner "Team Alaska," Murkowski played up her working relationships with Stevens and Young, who chaired the Transportation and Infrastructure Committee. As Republican George W. Bush swept 61 percent of Alaska's vote for president, Murkowski squeaked past Knowles by 3 percentage points.

Murkowski is up for re-election in 2010, and there has been speculation her challengers could include Palin, who defeated Murkowski's father in the governor's race in 2006. But she said she's confident her seniority and accomplishments have won over her constituents. "I really do think Alaskans of all different stripes have come to look at me without that lens of nepotism," she said. "I will get an e-mail almost every day where it says, 'I didn't like how you got there, but I'm sure liking the job you're doing.'"

KEY VOTES

2008
Yes   Prohibit discrimination based on genetic information
No   Reauthorize farm and nutrition programs for five years
?   Limit debate on "cap and trade" system for greenhouse gas emissions
No   Allow lawsuits against companies that participated in warrantless wiretapping
Yes   Limit debate on a bill to block a scheduled cut in Medicare payments to doctors
Yes   Grant mortgage relief to homeowners and funding for Fannie Mae and Freddie Mac
Yes   Approve a nuclear cooperation agreement with India
Yes   Approve final $700 billion program to stabilize financial markets
No   Allow consideration of a $14 billion auto industry loan package

2007
Yes   Increase minimum wage by $2.10 an hour
No   Limit debate on a comprehensive immigration bill
Yes   Overhaul congressional lobbying and ethics rules for members and their staffs
No   Limit debate on considering a bill to add House seats for the District of Columbia and Utah
No   Limit debate on restoring habeas corpus rights to detainees
No   Mandate minimum breaks for troops between deployments to Iraq or Afghanistan
Yes   Override Bush veto of $23.2 billion water projects authorization bill
Yes   Confirm Michael B. Mukasey as attorney general
Yes   Limit debate on an energy policy overhaul containing $21.8 billion in tax incentives and reduced oil and gas subsidies

CQ VOTE STUDIES

	PARTY UNITY		PRESIDENTIAL SUPPORT	
	SUPPORT	OPPOSE	SUPPORT	OPPOSE
2008	72%	28%	72%	28%
2007	71%	29%	77%	23%
2006	82%	18%	89%	11%
2005	93%	7%	87%	13%
2004	92%	8%	87%	13%
2003	94%	6%	93%	7%

INTEREST GROUPS

	AFL-CIO	ADA	CCUS	ACU
2008	40%	25%	86%	58%
2007	32%	30%	91%	67%
2006	13%	5%	100%	71%
2005	14%	20%	100%	83%
2004	50%	35%	94%	74%
2003	15%	20%	86%	70%

Sen. Mark Begich (D)

Elected 2008; 1st term

CAPITOL OFFICE
224-3004
begich.senate.gov
144 Russell Bldg. 20510; fax 224-2354

COMMITTEES
Armed Services
Commerce, Science & Transportation
Veterans' Affairs

RESIDENCE
Anchorage

BORN
March 30, 1962; Anchorage, Alaska

RELIGION
Roman Catholic

FAMILY
Wife, Deborah Bonito; one child

EDUCATION
U. of Alaska, Anchorage, attended 1981-88

CAREER
Property development company owner;
city government employee

POLITICAL HIGHLIGHTS
Anchorage Assembly, 1988-98 (chairman, 1993, 1996-98); candidate for mayor of Anchorage, 1994, 2000; mayor of Anchorage, 2003-09

ELECTION RESULTS

2008 GENERAL

Mark Begich (D)	151,767	47.8%
Ted Stevens (R)	147,814	46.5%
Bob Bird (AKI)	13,197	4.2%

2008 PRIMARY

Mark Begich (D)	63,747	90.8%
Ray Metcalfe (D)	5,480	7.8%
Frank Vondersaar (D)	965	1.4%

The first Democrat to represent Alaska in the Senate in nearly three decades, Begich portrays himself as a moderate and touts his "consensus-building" skills developed in local and state politics.

He believes his compromising manner will be more effective in the Senate than the often abrasive personality of his predecessor, Republican Ted Stevens. But he does hope to emulate Stevens' skill in bringing federal dollars to his state.

"Senator Stevens' style was if you disagreed with him on that one issue, you would be demonized. That's not healthy," Begich said. "What I would rather do is recognize where some people are, and show them where we have great potential. Yes, we have serious issues, but we have to deal with them with some realistic viewpoints in life and who we are as people."

The 47-year-old Begich was known affectionately as the "boy mayor" of Anchorage, Alaska's largest city. He barely outran the 85-year-old Stevens in an acrimonious race that was still too close to call for weeks after Election Day. The tight race came despite the fact that, just days before the election, Stevens had been found guilty on seven corruption charges of making false statements on financial disclosure forms. The Justice Department decided in April 2009 to drop the case after the judge criticized prosecutors for failing to turn over documents to defense lawyers, a decision Begich called "reasonable."

As a Hill newcomer, Begich will have to work with the other two members of the Alaska delegation, both of whom are Republicans: Sen. Lisa Murkowski and Rep. Don Young. Yet he also will have to distance himself from the state's political past. Both Young and Stevens, experts at steering federal funds to Alaskan projects, were known for obtaining vast sums for the state, including the infamous Gravina Island Bridge, often derided as the "Bridge to Nowhere" and held up as a symbol of Congress' misuse of taxpayer money.

Begich sits on the Commerce, Science and Transportation Committee, where Stevens served and where he hopes to work on climate change legislation. He said he became aware of the gravity of global warming at the annual Sundance Summit for mayors in 2005. Afterward, he implemented policies in Anchorage that were intended to reduce greenhouse gas emissions and save energy. He supports the creation of a nationwide "cap-and-trade" system to reduce emissions.

Begich favors both an expansion of energy development and increased federal spending on energy-efficient practices. Like Stevens, Begich favors opening more of Alaska to energy development and drilling for oil in the Arctic National Wildlife Refuge, partially as a way to create new jobs. But like many Democrats, he also believes energy exploration should be complemented by an expansion of renewable energy.

As mayor, Begich led a citywide push to phase in energy-efficient streetlights. By using up to 50 percent less energy, the new lights are expected to save money for a city that turns dark in the early afternoon during the winter.

The Commerce panel also is expected to take up a renewal of the 2005 surface transportation bill, a measure that traditionally is a vehicle for funding local projects. Begich favors building a light rail to ease the commute for workers traveling between Anchorage and the Palmer-Wasilla region.

On the Armed Services Committee, Begich is expected to look out for his state's numerous military bases and robust defense industry. He said he supports bringing an end to the Iraq War and a responsible withdrawal of U.S. troops from Iraq while boosting the number of troops in Afghanistan.

He also sits on the Veterans' Affairs Committee. Early in 2009 he backed a bill by Democrat Daniel K. Akaka of Hawaii to require that veterans' health care be funded one year in advance of the regular appropriations process, and launched a series of "veterans listening sessions" in Anchorage and Fairbanks.

Begich often talks about his former career as a small-businessman, which began at age 16 when he and his brother started several businesses, including a nightclub for teens and a venture in vending machine businesses. He later managed apartment buildings that catered to low-income renters and became a real estate agent in the 1990s.

Begich said small businesses should get more federal assistance in offering employees health care. He supports a buy-in program for the uninsured similar to the Federal Employee Health Benefit Plan, which serves members of Congress as well as federal employees and retirees. Begich says the competitive nature of the plan helps keep costs down.

On social issues, Begich is expected to align with Democrats to support abortion rights, and he favors allowing same-sex couples to receive benefits through their partners. But as a lifetime member of the National Rifle Association, he is expected to buck party leaders on gun-owners' rights.

Begich is the third of six children born to schoolteachers who moved from Minnesota to Alaska in the late 1950s. His father, Nick Begich, was elected as Alaska's at-large House member in 1970. The senior Begich disappeared in 1972 with House Majority Leader Hale Boggs aboard a plane that was never found. (Young, who had lost to Begich in the 1972 election, won the seat in a special election in early 1973.) Begich was only 10 years old.

Begich never graduated from college, instead getting a business license at the age of 16. His political career started in the 1980s, when he worked for then-Anchorage Mayor Tony Knowles, who later served two terms as Alaska's governor. At the age of 26, Begich was elected to the Anchorage Assembly and served 10 years, including three years as chairman and two as vice chairman.

Begich lost 1994 and 2000 mayoral races before being elected in 2003, becoming the first Alaskan-born citizen to serve as Anchorage's top elected official. During his more than five years in that role, the city's bond ratings improved to among the top 5 percent in the country, and voters approved a new $100 million civic and convention center.

Knowing Stevens' popularity back home, where he is called "Uncle Ted," Begich rarely discussed his predecessor's criminal case during his 2008 race. Stevens touted his seniority and close relationships with other "old bulls." Begich countered by saying he would differ from Stevens' sometimes irascible style by offering a more compromising approach.

In campaign speeches, Begich often highlighted how much he respected Stevens, but said that the state would benefit from a changing of the guard. "I just saw Alaska moving and shifting and changing, and he was not in touch [with] what was going on," he said.

Just weeks before election day, the Anchorage Daily News wrote an article that said both Begich and Stevens enjoyed financial ties to Alaska's biggest commercial real estate developers. The article didn't have much effect, however, as more pressing news came the day after, when Stevens was convicted in a Washington courtroom.

Stevens led by more than 3,000 votes at the end of Election Day, but the race wasn't called until late November. Thousands of absentee ballots allowed Begich to defeat the 40-year incumbent by fewer than 4,000 votes in a state that favored Republican presidential nominee John McCain over Barack Obama with just under 60 percent of the vote.

Begich is the first person of Croatian stock in the Senate; his father was the first in the House. Since being elected to the Senate, the younger Begich says he has done interviews with more than half a dozen Croatian news outlets.

Rep. Don Young (R)

Elected March 1973; 18th full term

The acerbic Young, who calls himself the "alpha wolf," pours his energy into delivering funds to his federally dependent state and keeping a vigilant eye on public-lands issues. Well into his fourth decade in Congress, he ranks second to C.W. Bill Young of Florida in GOP seniority and is the seventh-most-senior House member overall.

Like most Western Republicans, Young is an eager ally of energy, mining and timber interests and a vigorous advocate of private property holders' rights. But his influence over lands policy has waned now that Democrats are in control and he no longer serves as the Natural Resources Committee's top Republican.

Heading into the 111th Congress (2009-10), Young dropped his bid for a second term as the panel's top Republican amid questions about possible ethics problems but vowed to eventually reclaim the position from Washington's Doc Hastings. "For the good of the Republican Party, the right thing for me to do is temporarily step down from my post as ranking member on the House Committee on Natural Resources while my name is cleared," Young said in December 2008. "At that time, I look forward to regaining my post."

During the 2008 campaign, news reports indicated that Young was under scrutiny by the Justice Department for his ties to VECO Corp., an oil services company at the center of the public-corruption probe of his home-state ally, Sen. Ted Stevens. While Stevens was defeated for re-election soon after being convicted of failing to report gifts from VECO and other business interests (though the Justice Department subsequently decided to drop the charges), Young insisted he had not accepted personal gifts and had not done favors for the company. His campaign spent more than $1 million on his legal expenses and tried to reimburse a VECO executive for $37,626 in expenses for annual pig roasts the executive had sponsored for Young over 10 years.

Young played a role in promoting a $10 million design study for the "Coconut Road" highway interchange off Interstate 75 in Florida in a 2005 highway law. In 2008 the Senate included a provision in a technical corrections law that directed the Justice Department to examine the earmark's origin. Young denied that the funding set-aside,which was revised after the bill had cleared both chambers, was intended to aid a developer and other interests that donated to his campaign.

Young has long made clear he does not intend to end his pursuit of funding for his state. In a 2007 floor fight with Republican Scott Garrett of New Jersey, Young defended funding for Alaska Native education by likening himself to an Alaskan mink: "Those that bite me will be bitten back."

Young sometimes joins with Democrats in promoting routine measures such as public land swaps and funding to fight forest fires, but he typically takes the opposing side on broad land management and environmental issues. He has pushed in vain to open Alaska's Arctic National Wildlife Refuge to oil drilling and to provide tax incentives for private property owners who implement plans to aid the recovery of animals listed under the Endangered Species Act. He warned that the May 2008 listing of the polar bear as a threatened species would lead to lawsuits that could "stop development and traditional activities the Alaska Natives have conducted for thousands of years."

He remains a staunch defender of a short-lived provision authorizing two "bridges to nowhere" in Alaska — one of which was to be named for him — in the 2005 highway law. In 2008, Young backed a one-time supporter of the project who later opposed it: Alaska Gov. Sarah Palin.

CAPITOL OFFICE
225-5765
donyoung.house.gov
2111 Rayburn Bldg. 20515-0201; fax 225-0425

COMMITTEES
Natural Resources
Transportation & Infrastructure

RESIDENCE
Fort Yukon

BORN
June 9, 1933; Meridian, Calif.

RELIGION
Episcopalian

FAMILY
Wife, Lula Young; two children

EDUCATION
Yuba Junior College, A.A. 1952;
California State U., Chico, B.A. 1958

MILITARY SERVICE
Army, 1955-57

CAREER
Elementary school teacher; riverboat captain

POLITICAL HIGHLIGHTS
Fort Yukon City Council, 1960-64; mayor of Fort Yukon, 1964-68; Alaska House, 1967-70; Alaska Senate, 1971-73; Republican nominee for U.S. House, 1972

ELECTION RESULTS

2008 GENERAL

Don Young (R)	158,939	50.1%
Ethan Berkowitz (D)	142,560	45.0%
Don Wright (AKI)	14,274	4.5%

2008 PRIMARY

Don Young (R)	48,195	45.5%
Sean Parnell (R)	47,891	45.2%
Gabrielle LeDoux (R)	9,901	9.3%

2006 GENERAL

Don Young (R)	132,743	56.6%
Diane E. Benson (D)	93,879	40.0%
Alexander Crawford (LIBERT)	4,029	1.7%

PREVIOUS WINNING PERCENTAGES
2004 (71%); 2002 (75%); 2000 (70%); 1998 (63%); 1996 (59%); 1994 (57%); 1992 (47%); 1990 (52%); 1988 (63%); 1986 (56%); 1984 (55%); 1982 (71%); 1980 (74%); 1978 (55%); 1976 (71%); 1974 (54%); 1973 Special Election (51%)

As chairman of the Transportation and Infrastructure Committee in the 109th Congress (2005-06), he steered a six-year, $286.5 billion renewal of highway and mass transit programs to enactment after several years of effort, though he had to settle for a far smaller package than he wanted. In the 108th Congress (2003-04), he proposed a $375 billion bill that would have increased the 18.4-cents-per-gallon federal tax on gasoline to help pay for transportation projects. But President George W. Bush refused to support a gas tax increase, and Young had to cut the proposed spending significantly.

He takes a conservative stance on tax cuts and opposed the $700 billion financial sector rescue package in 2008. He swings to the center on a few union-related and civil-liberties issues. He backed a 2007 minimum wage increase and voted for a "card check" proposal to permit unions to organize workplaces with petition drives instead of full-blown elections. And he voted in 2006 against legislation to authorize the National Security Agency's warrantless electronic surveillance program. "I still believe that we can go after the terrorists without the invasion of privacy this bill advocates," he declared.

Raised on a farm in California, Young got an introduction to Alaska through his favorite book, Jack London's "Call of the Wild." After completing college and military service, he headed for Alaska in 1959 and settled in as a fifth-grade teacher for Alaska Native students at a school in Fort Yukon, seven miles above the Arctic Circle. He taught school in the winter and captained his own tug and barge operation along the Yukon in the summer, ferrying supplies to villages along the river. He is the only licensed mariner in Congress.

He served as mayor of Fort Yukon and as a state House member before moving up to a state Senate seat in 1970. The only election he has ever lost was his first U.S. House race, in 1972. His opponent, freshman Democrat Nick Begich, disappeared without a trace, along with House Majority Leader Hale Boggs, during an October airplane flight from Anchorage to Juneau. Begich still beat Young by almost 12,000 votes in November. When Begich's seat was declared vacant a few weeks later, Young edged out Emil Notti, the former state Democratic chairman, in a 1973 special election. (The late Begich's son, Mark, defeated Stevens for re-election in 2008.)

On the campaign trail in 2008, Young made the case that Alaskans needed him to take care of the state's interests with Democrats gaining clout in Washington. "You need me now more than ever to fight Obama and Hillary Clinton and George Miller and Nancy Pelosi," he told a gathering of the Alaska Republican Party. He survived a Palin-backed 2008 primary challenge by Lt. Gov. Sean Parnell by just 304 votes and edged Democrat Ethan Berkowitz, a former state legislator, in the general election with 50 percent of the vote.

KEY VOTES

2008

No Delay consideration of Colombia free-trade agreement

Yes Override Bush veto of federal farm and nutrition programs reauthorization bill

Yes Overhaul surveillance laws and permit dismissal of suits against companies that conducted warrantless wiretapping

No Grant mortgage relief to homeowners and funding for Fannie Mae and Freddie Mac

No Approve initial $700 billion program to stabilize financial markets

No Approve final $700 billion program to stabilize financial markets

Yes Provide $14 billion in loans to automakers

2007

Yes Increase minimum wage by $2.10 an hour

No Approve $124.2 billion in emergency war spending and set goal for redeployment of troops from Iraq

Yes Reject federal contraceptive assistance to international family planning groups

Yes Override Bush veto of $23.2 billion water projects authorization bill

Yes Implement Peru free-trade agreement

No Approve energy policy overhaul with new fuel economy standards

Yes Clear $473.5 billion omnibus spending bill, including $70 billion for military operations

CQ VOTE STUDIES

	PARTY UNITY		PRESIDENTIAL SUPPORT	
	SUPPORT	OPPOSE	SUPPORT	OPPOSE
2008	88%	12%	54%	46%
2007	83%	17%	65%	35%
2006	92%	8%	90%	10%
2005	91%	9%	78%	22%
2004	92%	8%	87%	13%

INTEREST GROUPS

	AFL-CIO	ADA	CCUS	ACU
2008	77%	55%	73%	71%
2007	64%	30%	88%	65%
2006	36%	25%	100%	72%
2005	21%	5%	96%	83%
2004	17%	0%	100%	95%

ALASKA

At Large

Alaska's remoteness belies its dependence on Washington, D.C. While state and local government is Alaska's largest employer, a never-ending battle for control over the local economy has made voters hostile to Washington despite billions of dollars in annual federal spending directed to the state.

The state's proximity to Russia and the Far East makes it a military stronghold, and its vulnerable economic boosters — oil and gas, minerals and timber — lie mostly on federally owned land. Most Alaskans and local lawmakers view opening land to oil and gas exploration as the best way to independence and heavily favor drilling in the Arctic National Wildlife Refuge. But economic turmoil nationwide might delay construction of a natural gas pipeline from Prudhoe Bay through Canada to the lower 48 states.

The state continues to build a privatized economy in the health care, retail and tourism sectors. Alaska has not had state sales and income taxes since black gold was discovered near Prudhoe Bay in the 1970s.

Alaska tends to support Republicans at the federal level, but voters in some cities, the panhandle and the isolated tundra are more Democratic. Moderates dominate the state legislature. Most residents in this cold, conservative frontier state pay more attention to personality than to party affiliation and register as either third-party or unaffiliated voters.

A sense of loyalty to elected officials led many voters here to support embattled longtime incumbent Republican Sen. Ted Stevens, who was ousted by Democrat Mark Begich in 2008, and overwhelmingly support the GOP presidential ticket, which included popular Gov. Sarah Palin.

MAJOR INDUSTRY
Oil and gas, defense, government, tourism, fishing, timber, mining

MILITARY BASES
Fort Richardson (Army), 6,100 military, 1,179 civilian (2008); Elmendorf Air Force Base, 5,848 military, 1,122 civilian (2009); Fort Wainwright (Army), 7,214 military, 1,330 civilian; Eielson Air Force Base, 2,016 military, 632 civilian; Fort Greely (Army), 200 military, 825 civilian (2008)

CITIES
Anchorage, 260,283; Juneau, 30,711; Fairbanks, 30,224

NOTABLE
Mt. McKinley is the highest point in North America, at 20,320 feet.

Gov. Jan Brewer (R)

Assumed Office: Jan. 21, 2009, due to the resignation of Janet Napolitano, D, to become Homeland Security secretary.

Length of term: 4 years
Term expires: 1/11
Salary: $95,000
Phone: (602) 542-4331
Residence: Glendale
Born: September 26, 1944; Los Angeles, Calif.
Religion: Lutheran – Missouri Synod
Family: Husband, John Brewer; three children (one deceased)
Education: Verdugo Hills H.S., graduated 1962
Career: Homemaker; office manager
Political highlights: Ariz. House, 1983-87; Ariz. Senate, 1987-96 (majority whip, 1993-96); Maricopa County Board of Supervisors, 1997-2002; secretary of State, 2003-09

Recent election results:

2006 GENERAL

Janet Napolitano (D)	959,830	62.6%
Len Munsil (R)	543,528	35.4%
Barry Hess (LIBERT)	30,268	2.0%

Secretary of State Ken Bennett (R)*

(no lieutenant governor)
Assumed office: 2009
Length of term: 4 years
Term expires: 1/11
Salary: $70,000
Phone: (602) 542-4285

* Bennett is not eligible to replace Brewer as governor. The state attorney general is the next-highest ranking elected constitutional officer in Arizona.

LEGISLATURE

Legislature: 100 days January-April
Senate: 30 members, 2-year terms
2009 ratios: 18 R, 12 D; 18 men, 12 women
Salary: $24,000
Phone: (602) 926-3559

House: 60 members, 2-year terms
2009 ratios: 35 R, 25 D; 45 men, 15 women
Salary: $24,000
Phone: (602) 926-4221

TERM LIMITS

Governor: 2 consecutive terms
Senate: 4 consecutive terms
House: 4 consecutive terms

URBAN STATISTICS

CITY	POPULATION
Phoenix	1,321,045
Tucson	486,699
Mesa	396,375
Glendale	218,812
Scottsdale	202,705

REGISTERED VOTERS

Republican	37%
Democrat	34%
Others	28%
Third parties	1%

POPULATION

2008 population (est.)	6,500,180
2000 population	5,130,632
1990 population	3,665,228
Percent change (1990-2000)	+40%
Rank among states (2008)	14

Median age	34.2
Born in state	34.7%
Foreign born	12.8%
Violent crime rate	532/100,000
Poverty level	13.9%
Federal workers	46,967
Military	33,485

ELECTIONS

STATE ELECTION OFFICIAL
(602) 542-8683
DEMOCRATIC PARTY
(602) 298-4200
REPUBLICAN PARTY
(602) 957-7770

MISCELLANEOUS

Web: www.az.gov
Capital: Phoenix

U.S. CONGRESS

Senate: 2 Republicans
House: 5 Democrats, 3 Republicans

2000 Census Statistics by District

DIST.	2008 VOTE FOR PRESIDENT OBAMA	MCCAIN	WHITE	BLACK	ASIAN	HISP	MEDIAN INCOME	WHITE COLLAR	BLUE COLLAR	SERVICE INDUSTRY	OVER 64	UNDER 18	COLLEGE EDUCATION	RURAL	SQ. MILES
1	44%	54%	58%	1%	1%	16%	$32,979	53%	27%	20%	14%	28%	18%	45%	58,608
2	38	61	78	2	2	14	$42,432	60	23	17	20	24	19	11	20,220
3	42	56	79	2	2	14	$48,108	68	18	14	10	25	30	4	598
4	66	33	29	7	1	58	$30,624	44	36	20	7	33	10	0	199
5	47	52	77	3	3	13	$51,780	73	14	13	10	23	40	3	1,406
6	38	61	77	2	2	17	$47,976	63	23	14	14	28	24	3	724
7	57	42	39	3	1	51	$30,828	51	29	20	11	30	13	16	22,873
8	46	52	74	3	2	18	$40,656	67	17	16	17	23	31	13	9,007
STATE	45	54	64	3	2	25	$40,558	61	23	16	13	27	24	12	113,635
U.S.	53	46	69	12	4	13	$41,994	60	25	15	12	26	24	21	3,537,438

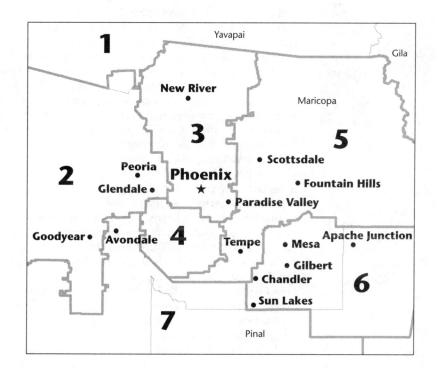

Sen. John McCain (R)

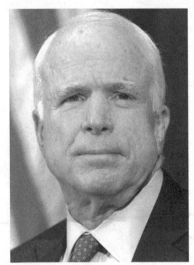

CAPITOL OFFICE
224-2235
mccain.senate.gov
241 Russell Bldg. 20510-0303; fax 228-2862

COMMITTEES
Armed Services - ranking member
Energy & Natural Resources
Health, Education, Labor & Pensions
Homeland Security & Governmental Affairs
Indian Affairs

RESIDENCE
Phoenix

BORN
Aug. 29, 1936; Panama Canal Zone, Panama

RELIGION
Episcopalian

FAMILY
Wife, Cindy McCain; seven children

EDUCATION
U.S. Naval Academy, B.S. 1958; National War
College, attended 1974

CAREER
Navy officer; Navy Senate liaison; beer distributor

MILITARY SERVICE
Navy, 1958-81

POLITICAL HIGHLIGHTS
U.S. House, 1983-87; sought Republican nomination
for president, 2000; Republican nominee for
president, 2008

ELECTION RESULTS

2004 GENERAL

John McCain (R)	404,507	76.7%
Stuart Starky (D)	404,507	20.6%
Ernest Hancock (LIBERT)	51,798	2.6%

2004 PRIMARY

John McCain (R)	unopposed

PREVIOUS WINNING PERCENTAGES
1998 (69%); 1992 (56%); 1986 (61%); 1984 House
Election (78%); 1982 House Election (66%)

Elected 1986; 4th term

McCain can be hard to categorize, despite a quarter of a century in national politics. He is conservative on fundamental issues, including national security and government spending. He has been an ardent supporter of the Iraq War and consistently voted against timetables to withdraw troops. He is also known for using Senate floor time to read lengthy lists of "pork barrel" spending in appropriations bills. But McCain racks up enough exceptions to the party line to often be viewed as a moderate.

He was one of the authors of the 2002 campaign finance overhaul that many conservative groups deplore. He developed immigration legislation that included ways for illegal immigrants to earn citizenship, an idea many Republicans called "amnesty." And he has worked with one of his closest friends, Independent Joseph I. Lieberman of Connecticut, on climate change legislation that many Republicans consider too expensive for businesses.

McCain did little to end the apparent confusion upon returning from the 2008 presidential campaign trail. He made peace with Democrat Barack Obama, the man who defeated him and whose stances and experience he had often belittled. In January 2009 McCain gave a floor speech urging rapid confirmation of Hillary Rodham Clinton for secretary of State, undermining efforts by Republican Sen. John Cornyn of Texas to delay the confirmation to seek greater scrutiny of possible conflicts of interest.

But McCain also spoke out against Obama. He and a group of Republicans proposed an alternative to the president's stimulus plan, which they said would spend a lot of money without fixing the economy. He also voted against releasing the second half of the $700 billion in financial rescue funds approved in 2008. And when Obama signed an order requiring the detention camp at Guantánamo Bay, Cuba, to be closed, McCain applauded the move, but said it was a mistake to put the process in motion before deciding what to do with the prisoners.

He told Fox News he sees his role as "the loyal opposition — help and work together where I can, and stand up for the principles and the party and the philosophy that I campaigned on and have stood for for many years."

McCain can be blunt, funny and testy — often in the same sitting. Several of his colleagues have been subjected to his aggressive, obscenity-laced tirades. He is also famously self-deprecating; a favorite campaign line of his was, "I am older than dirt and have more scars than Frankenstein."

He has signaled he will run for a fifth Senate term in 2010, and he continues to work on the issues that have been central to much of his career, such as fighting government waste. In January 2009, he reunited with Democrat Russ Feingold of Wisconsin — his partner on the 2002 rewrite of campaign finance laws — to crack down on earmarks by improving disclosure and making it easier to challenge them on the Senate floor.

In the 111th Congress (2009-10), McCain has three new committee assignments: Energy and Natural Resources, Homeland Security and Governmental Affairs, and Health, Education, Labor, and Pensions. He retained his position as the ranking Republican on Armed Services and continues to serve on Indian Affairs. He dropped off the Commerce, Science and Transportation Committee, a panel he had once chaired.

McCain voted against President George W. Bush's 2001 and 2003 tax cuts that expire at the end of 2010, but since then he has said he wants to see them made permanent. In 2004 and 2006, he voted against a constitutional ban on gay marriage. He also voted in 2006 to expand embryonic stem cell research. In 1999, he voted against a bill to mandate criminal background checks for customers at gun shows, but two years later joined with Lieberman to push for a less restrictive version of the legislation.

McCain often finds himself in the company of moderates because of disagreements with his party. In May 2005, for example, he helped broker a deal among a bipartisan group of senators, known as the Gang of 14, to prevent a showdown over Democrats' ability to filibuster conservative judicial nominees. The seven Republicans and seven Democrats, mostly moderates, pledged to vote against the GOP leadership's "nuclear option," a procedural force play that could have barred all future filibusters of judicial nominations.

Later that year, McCain — who endured five and a half years of brutal physical abuse as a prisoner of war in Vietnam — pushed Congress to ban torture of overseas detainees, a move Bush initially opposed. Bush eventually backed down and signed the legislation.

On Armed Services, McCain was a frequent critic of the Bush administration's handling of the Iraq War, but from the right rather than the left. He wanted the administration to send far more troops than it felt comfortable with. When reports indicated Bush's 2007 decision to send more than 21,000 additional troops into Iraq had helped decrease the violence, McCain felt vindicated.

McCain's voting record doesn't perturb colleagues as much as his attitude does. In a chamber where members are expected to treat one another with deference, McCain comes off as self-righteous and quick to discard courtesies. He describes himself as a "pro-life, small-government, anti-spending, foreign-policy-hawk conservative." But he's also a fan of Theodore Roosevelt and doesn't worry about conservative attacks when he emulates TR's progressivism. "When I know what the right thing to do is, and I do it, it always turns out fine," McCain said in April 2006. "If I do something for political reasons, it always turns out badly. It's just the way my political life has unfolded."

The son of an admiral and grandson of another, McCain went to the Naval Academy in Annapolis with great family expectations but didn't prove to be admiral material. He finished fifth from the bottom in the class of 1958. During the Vietnam War his Navy fighter plane was shot down and he was captured by the North Vietnamese. Both arms and a leg broken, McCain was dragged from the crash and thrown, without benefit of medical treatment, into a cell. He spent the next five and a half years enduring torture and solitary confinement, an experience recounted in his best-selling memoir, "Faith of My Fathers," and the subject of a 2005 movie on the A&E cable network.

After a stint as the Navy's Senate liaison, McCain ran for Congress in 1982, winning the seat of retiring House Minority Leader John J. Rhodes. After two terms, McCain entered the race to succeed retiring GOP Sen. Barry Goldwater in 1986 and drew 61 percent of the vote. During his first Senate term, McCain was one of five senators accused of interceding with federal regulators on behalf of wealthy savings and loan operator Charles H. Keating Jr. After a protracted Ethics Committee investigation, McCain received a mild rebuke in 1991, the low point of his Senate career.

The black mark hurt; in 1992, he won re-election with only 56 percent. He rebounded in 1998 with 69 percent. Two years later, 5 million people chose McCain over Bush in the GOP primary. But Bush ultimately overtook McCain in South Carolina. In 2004, McCain won a fourth Senate term with 77 percent of the vote.

In the 2008 presidential race, McCain was the last man standing in a GOP field that included several figures initially seen as having a better chance. His surprise selection of Alaska Gov. Sarah Palin as his running mate energized conservatives but was met negatively by the independents and Democrats he had hoped to capture. McCain was unable to overcome Obama's superior fundraising operation and message as a candidate of change, and he ended up losing to the Illinois Democrat by 7 percentage points. He failed to hold key swing states, such as Florida and Ohio, that went for Bush in 2000 and 2004.

KEY VOTES

2008
? Prohibit discrimination based on genetic information
? Reauthorize farm and nutrition programs for five years
+ Limit debate on "cap and trade" system for greenhouse gas emissions
? Allow lawsuits against companies that participated in warrantless wiretapping
? Limit debate on a bill to block a scheduled cut in Medicare payments to doctors
? Grant mortgage relief to homeowners and funding for Fannie Mae and Freddie Mac
Yes Approve a nuclear cooperation agreement with India
Yes Approve final $700 billion program to stabilize financial markets
No Allow consideration of a $14 billion auto industry loan package

2007
Yes Increase minimum wage by $2.10 an hour
Yes Limit debate on a comprehensive immigration bill
No Overhaul congressional lobbying and ethics rules for members and their staffs
No Limit debate on considering a bill to add House seats for the District of Columbia and Utah
No Limit debate on restoring habeas corpus rights to detainees
No Mandate minimum breaks for troops between deployments to Iraq or Afghanistan
? Override Bush veto of $23.2 billion water projects authorization bill
? Confirm Michael B. Mukasey as attorney general
? Limit debate on an energy policy overhaul containing $21.8 billion in tax incentives and reduced oil and gas subsidies

CQ VOTE STUDIES

	PARTY UNITY		PRESIDENTIAL SUPPORT	
	SUPPORT	OPPOSE	SUPPORT	OPPOSE
2008	93%	7%	89%	11%
2007	90%	10%	95%	5%
2006	76%	24%	89%	11%
2005	84%	16%	77%	23%
2004	79%	21%	92%	8%
2003	86%	14%	91%	9%
2002	80%	20%	90%	10%
2001	67%	33%	91%	9%
2000	83%	17%	38%	62%
1999	90%	10%	38%	62%

INTEREST GROUPS

	AFL-CIO	ADA	CCUS	ACU
2008	0%	5%	100%	63%
2007	0%	10%	100%	80%
2006	7%	15%	100%	65%
2005	7%	10%	72%	80%
2004	33%	35%	67%	72%
2003	15%	35%	61%	75%
2002	33%	20%	79%	78%
2001	27%	40%	50%	68%
2000	14%	5%	75%	81%
1999	0%	5%	75%	77%

Sen. Jon Kyl (R)

Elected 1994; 3rd term

Kyl has become an influential part of the Senate Republican leadership's upper ranks after two decades of quietly crafting legislation. His rise is a tribute to his policy smarts, his hard work and a stridency-free dedication to conservative principles that has earned the respect of senators on both sides of the aisle.

He has served as the Senate GOP whip since 2007; before that he was spokesman for his caucus as chairman of the Republican Conference. He is a familiar face on cable news and Sunday talk shows. Kyl (KILE) even appeared as a surrogate in Denver during the 2008 Democratic National Convention on behalf of his fellow Arizona Republican and presidential candidate John McCain.

Yet Kyl has preferred to operate behind the scenes during much of his career, unlike McCain or the man he replaced as whip, Mississippi's Trent Lott. Kyl can claim credit — but rarely does — for derailing many legislative initiatives, such as the 1999 Comprehensive Nuclear Test Ban Treaty and Harriet Miers' nomination to the Supreme Court in 2005.

Dubbed "The Operator" by Time magazine, which named him one of the 10 best senators in 2006, Kyl explains his success this way: "You can accomplish a lot if you're not necessarily out in front on everything." Nor does he seek the role of political lightning rod. "I have made an effort not to be partisan in an in-your-face sense," he once said. "Ordinarily, I don't talk about Republicans and Democrats. I talk about ideas."

Kyl did fall victim to partisan sentiment during the 110th Congress (2007-08) when he took the lead in an unsuccessful attempt to broker comprehensive immigration legislation with Democrats and George W. Bush's administration. Conservatives were outraged that Kyl, who previously took a hard line against illegal immigration, would support a measure that included a path toward citizenship. Republican officials in his home state accused him of betrayal, and angry callers overloaded his office phone lines. But Kyl offered no apologies. "Obviously, I wasn't thinking of my political career when I took the leadership role I did in the immigration debate," he told The Arizona Republic. "Sometimes you do what you have to do."

Kyl will have to adjust to a far different relationship with a Democratic administration after eight years of enjoying close ties to Vice President Dick Cheney, his political mentor from their days together in the House. "My father said you should find somebody you can trust," Kyl recalled. "So I went to Dick Cheney." The two stayed in touch over the years, becoming close friends.

On the Judiciary Committee, Kyl frequently blocked legislation the Bush administration opposed, including a reporter's shield law. That prompted the Arizona Republic to dub him "Senator Secrecy." He proved a thorn in the side of Chairman Patrick J. Leahy of Vermont, opposing a patent law overhaul and an effort to strengthen the Freedom of Information Act.

But Kyl also had repeatedly thwarted the panel's previous chairman, Arlen Specter of Pennsylvania, when the GOP controlled the Senate. Operating in the shadows, Kyl helped block the Supreme Court nomination of Miers, Bush's White House counsel, whom conservatives viewed as unreliable. He also torpedoed Specter's efforts to oversee the president's domestic surveillance programs.

Kyl's voting record has been uniformly conservative. He has gone against the majority of his party on only a few occasions; in July 2008, he was one of just 13 GOP senators to oppose housing legislation aimed at assisting mortgage giants Fannie Mae and Freddie Mac, saying it would place "an immense financial burden on every American taxpayer." He has been the lead Senate sponsor of bills to repeal the estate tax and to ban Internet gambling.

Kyl has long been one of the GOP's pre-eminent advocates of a robust national security posture. Since his time in the House, where he served on the Armed Services Committee, he has advocated a national missile defense system. He strongly supported Bush's decision in 2002 to withdraw from the 1972 Anti-Ballistic Missile Treaty, which banned nationwide anti-missile defense. Kyl successfully pushed to include $7.4 billion for missile defense in the 2002 defense spending law.

Kyl favors unilateral steps rather than negotiated agreements to neutralize emerging military threats, contending that the United States should rely on its military to guarantee its national security. He called the U.S. invasion of Iraq "one of the most ambitious and important missions in world history." His support for the war effort has remained unwavering.

He demonstrated an interest in combating terrorism at home long before the attacks of Sept. 11. As chairman of the Judiciary Subcommittee on Terrorism, Technology and Homeland Security, Kyl led the effort to rewrite wiretapping laws to make it easier for law enforcement officials to track and capture terrorists. Ideas he had long advocated, such as allowing investigators to use roving wiretaps to follow suspects using multiple cell phones, were included in the controversial 2001 anti-terrorism law known as the Patriot Act.

Kyl has worked with California Democrat Dianne Feinstein to win passage of a constitutional amendment to guarantee crime victims the right to speak at proceedings that determine prison sentences and consider the potential release of a convict. In 2004, they decided to abandon the amendment in favor of a stand-alone victims' rights bill. Kyl favors expanded use of DNA evidence, and in 2008 lauded new Justice Department rules to expand DNA tests to immigration detainees and others arrested for federal crimes, not just those convicted. But he opposed a move to give inmates access to DNA testing, arguing it would become too easy for them to secure post-conviction DNA tests and win new trials.

Kyl was born in northeastern Nebraska near the small college town of Wayne, where his father, John H. Kyl, was a school principal and led the local Chamber of Commerce. In the 1950s, the family moved to Iowa, where the elder Kyl joined his brother in a clothing business, and later was elected to the U.S. House, serving 11 years. He helped prepare his son for a life in politics by coaching him in public speaking, and he brought young Kyl to spend the summer of 1963 with him in Washington.

Kyl went to college at the University of Arizona, inspired by the state's GOP icon, Sen. Barry Goldwater. He read and reread Goldwater's "Conscience of a Conservative" and William F. Buckley's "Up from Liberalism."

After law school, he joined a Phoenix law firm. In 1985 he became president of the Phoenix Chamber of Commerce, building strong business community ties that helped him win a 1986 GOP primary over John Conlon, a former House member trying for a comeback. Kyl handily won the general election.

Kyl won three easy re-elections to the House and launched a Senate bid in 1994 even before incumbent Democrat Dennis DeConcini announced his retirement. He breezed to the GOP nomination as first-term Rep. Sam Coppersmith struggled to secure the Democratic nomination. Voters in Arizona liked the themes Kyl stressed — smaller government, lower taxes and reduced regulation. He prevailed over Coppersmith by 14 percentage points. Six years later, the Democrats did not even field a candidate.

But in 2006, Kyl faced millionaire shopping-mall developer Jim Pederson, a former state Democratic Party chairman. Bush, Cheney and other GOP bigwigs went all-out to help Kyl, and he bucked the year's strong Democratic tide to win a third term by almost 10 percentage points.

KEY VOTES

2008
Yes Prohibit discrimination based on genetic information
No Reauthorize farm and nutrition programs for five years
No Limit debate on "cap and trade" system for greenhouse gas emissions
No Allow lawsuits against companies that participated in warrantless wiretapping
No Limit debate on a bill to block a scheduled cut in Medicare payments to doctors
No Grant mortgage relief to homeowners and funding for Fannie Mae and Freddie Mac
Yes Approve a nuclear cooperation agreement with India
Yes Approve final $700 billion program to stabilize financial markets
No Allow consideration of a $14 billion auto industry loan package

2007
No Increase minimum wage by $2.10 an hour
Yes Limit debate on a comprehensive immigration bill
No Overhaul congressional lobbying and ethics rules for members and their staffs
No Limit debate on considering a bill to add House seats for the District of Columbia and Utah
No Limit debate on restoring habeas corpus rights to detainees
No Mandate minimum breaks for troops between deployments to Iraq or Afghanistan
No Override Bush veto of $23.2 billion water projects authorization bill
Yes Confirm Michael B. Mukasey as attorney general
No Limit debate on an energy policy overhaul containing $21.8 billion in tax incentives and reduced oil and gas subsidies

CQ VOTE STUDIES

	PARTY UNITY		PRESIDENTIAL SUPPORT	
	SUPPORT	OPPOSE	SUPPORT	OPPOSE
2008	100%	0%	83%	17%
2007	93%	7%	89%	11%
2006	95%	5%	90%	10%
2005	98%	2%	89%	11%
2004	98%	2%	100%	0%
2003	99%	1%	99%	1%
2002	96%	4%	96%	4%
2001	98%	2%	99%	1%
2000	99%	1%	41%	59%
1999	97%	3%	34%	66%

INTEREST GROUPS

	AFL-CIO	ADA	CCUS	ACU
2008	0%	0%	63%	96%
2007	0%	5%	60%	100%
2006	13%	0%	92%	92%
2005	0%	5%	83%	100%
2004	0%	5%	88%	100%
2003	0%	10%	96%	90%
2002	15%	0%	90%	100%
2001	6%	5%	100%	100%
2000	0%	0%	85%	100%
1999	0%	0%	82%	100%

Rep. Ann Kirkpatrick (D)

Elected 2008; 1st term

Kirkpatrick seeks to be a pragmatic voice for a rural and sprawling district she believes sorely needs assistance from Washington. She said many of her constituents, which include the largest American Indian population of any district in the nation, lack such basic infrastructure as electricity and running water. Better schools, health care and economic development are high on her agenda.

Raised in the midst of Indian country — her parents ran a general store in Whiteriver, in the middle of the Fort Apache Indian Reservation — Kirkpatrick said the first words she uttered as a child were in Apache.

After graduating from the University of Arizona, she became a substitute teacher to supplement the income of her family, struggling to cope with the unexpected death of her father during her junior year. She later obtained a law degree and worked as a county prosecutor before opening a small law firm.

A member of the Small Business Committee, Kirkpatrick touts her experience opening her own firm. "That was a leap of faith," she recalled. "The first 24 hours we didn't know if the phone would ring. I know what it's like to try to keep the doors open and not be sure if anyone will come."

Kirkpatrick favors allowing small businesses to form large groups to gain greater purchasing power for health care plans.

She is the only Arizona lawmaker on the House Homeland Security panel. She supports an overhaul of immigration policy to increase resources for border patrol agents and sensor technology, and favors penalties for employers who hire illegal immigrants. But she also backs a path to citizenship and a temporary-worker program for farms in the South.

Kirkpatrick is the daughter of a World War II veteran and sits on the Veterans' Affairs Committee, where she will advocate expanding health care coverage to soldiers returning from combat. When sworn into the House, she used the same bible her father carried with him during the war.

She won a challenge against a GOP incumbent in a 2004 state House race. She focused on such issues as children's health care and methamphetamine abuse until mid-2007, when she launched her successful U.S. House campaign.

CAPITOL OFFICE
225-2315
kirkpatrick.house.gov
1123 Longworth Bldg. 20515-0301; fax 226-9739

COMMITTEES
Homeland Security
Small Business
Veterans' Affairs

RESIDENCE
Flagstaff

BORN
March 24, 1950; McNary, Ariz.

RELIGION
Roman Catholic

FAMILY
Engaged to Roger Curley; two children

EDUCATION
U. of Arizona, B.A. 1972 (secondary education), J.D. 1979

CAREER
Lawyer; county prosecutor; teacher

POLITICAL HIGHLIGHTS
Ariz. House, 2005-07

ELECTION RESULTS

2008 GENERAL

Ann Kirkpatrick (D)	155,791	55.9%
Sydney Hay (R)	109,924	39.4%
Brent Maupin (I)	9,394	3.4%
Thane Eichenauer (LIBERT)	3,678	1.3%

2008 PRIMARY

Ann Kirkpatrick (D)	26,734	47.2%
Mary Kim Titla (D)	18,428	32.6%
Howard Shanker (D)	8,056	14.2%
Jeffrey Brown (D)	3,376	6.0%

ARIZONA 1

North and east – Flagstaff, Prescott, Navajo reservation

A population that includes rural conservatives, artistic liberals and a large American Indian population makes Arizona's immense 1st District appear ripe for unpredictable elections. Sprawling across much of northern and eastern Arizona, the 58,608-square-mile swath is larger than 30 states.

Democrats have a slight voter registration advantage, and many locals call themselves environmentalists in a district that includes both sides of the Grand Canyon. Despite the Democrats' seeming advantage, Arizona Sen. John McCain captured 54 percent of the district's 2008 presidential vote. But, Rep. Ann Kirkpatrick defeated Republican Sydney Hay with 56 percent of the vote following Republican Rick Renzi's retirement in 2008.

Sedona, a tourist destination renowned for its natural beauty, is home to art galleries and luxury resorts. The 1st also features mining and timber operations, but drought and fires, which hit the area hard in the last decade, worry residents and officials.

The district has the nation's largest American Indian population (23 percent), and high rates of poverty and unemployment continue to be problems in the American Indian communities. Because of longstanding land disputes, the 1st is missing a chunk of land in its northern section to avoid placing the Hopi Nation in the same district as the Navajo Nation.

MAJOR INDUSTRY
Tourism, agriculture, timber, mining

CITIES
Flagstaff, 52,894; Prescott, 33,938; Casa Grande, 25,224; Prescott Valley, 23,535

NOTABLE
Sedona claims the only place in the world where you can find a McDonald's without the golden arches — the city's artistically inclined residents painted them turquoise.

Rep. Trent Franks (R)

Elected 2002; 4th term

CAPITOL OFFICE
225-4576
www.house.gov/franks
2435 Rayburn Bldg. 20515-0302; fax 225-6328

COMMITTEES
Armed Services
Judiciary

RESIDENCE
Peoria

BORN
June 19, 1957; Uravan, Colo.

RELIGION
Baptist

FAMILY
Wife, Josephine Franks; two children

EDUCATION
Ottawa U. (Ariz.), attended 1989-90

CAREER
Oil company executive; conservative think tank
president; state children's programs director

POLITICAL HIGHLIGHTS
Ariz. House, 1985-87; defeated for re-election to
Ariz. House, 1986; sought Republican nomination
for U.S. House, 1994

ELECTION RESULTS

2008 GENERAL

Trent Franks (R)	200,914	59.4%
John Thrasher (D)	125,611	37.2%
Powell Gammill (LIBERT)	7,882	2.3%
William Crum (GREEN)	3,616	1.1%

2008 PRIMARY

Trent Franks (R)	unopposed

2006 GENERAL

Trent Franks (R)	135,150	58.6%
John Thrasher (D)	89,671	38.9%
Powell Gammill (LIBERT)	5,734	2.5%

PREVIOUS WINNING PERCENTAGES
2004 (59%); 2002 (60%)

An ardent social conservative, small-government advocate and defense hawk, Franks' views are rarely in sync with the House majority these days. He is particularly unhappy that the government is spending billions of dollars to prop up ailing banks, auto makers and Wall Street financiers.

Franks voted against all the legislative efforts providing federal funds to staunch the economic downturn. After voting no in December 2008 on a $14 billion measure aimed at keeping the auto makers in business, Franks said, "People are beginning to awaken to the fact that over the past several months, this Democratic-led Congress has begun to plummet down a slippery slope of ineffective, government-managed, taxpayer-funded bailouts; and there is no telling where the stampede will end."

He also had little good to say about President Obama and the Democrats' push in early 2009 to revive the economy. After voting against the initial House version of the $700 billion economic stimulus plan, Franks said: "Obviously there is no limit to Democrats' capacity to contort the English language in their attempt to depict today's bill, a massive government spending spree, as a 'stimulus' for an ailing economy." Franks would prefer taxpayer money be spent on the U.S. military. He sponsored a joint resolution in 2007 to mandate that the Pentagon's budget never go below 4 percent of the gross national product, which would currently provide an additional $40 billion to the Defense Department.

On the Armed Services Committee, he presses for the creation of a ballistic missile shield. He said the deployment of an anti-missile system in Eastern Europe could help deter Iran from building and deploying ballistic missiles. During 2008 consideration of the defense authorization measure, GOP funding requests for an antimissile shield in Europe and for the Army's next generation of weapons, the Future Combat Systems, were continually reduced. Franks said the reduced spending could embolden Iran in its pursuit of nuclear weapons and long-range ballistic missiles. It would give Teheran a "head start that will be difficult for us to address," he said.

As ranking member of the Judiciary panel's Constitution subcommittee he defended the coercive interrogation techniques authorized by George W. Bush's administration for use with terrorist suspects. He said giving suspects the right to challenge their detention would be "a disaster waiting to happen."

Franks claimed few victories during the 110th Congress (2007-08) to add to his already modest set of legislative achievements. He has attracted little support to replicate a program he promoted as a state legislator: tax credits for charitable contributions to groups that provide tuition vouchers for children enrolled in private or parochial schools. Franks drafted an Arizona law in 1997 creating such scholarships, and has repeatedly sponsored legislation to create a similar national program. The measure has never reached the House floor.

On his signature social issue, Franks supports rolling back the Supreme Court's *Roe v. Wade* decision legalizing abortion, which he calls "the greatest genocide in the history of mankind." In Arizona, he was known around the statehouse for wearing a tie tack in the shape of a fetus's feet. Franks would outlaw abortion except to save the life of the woman. He remains skeptical of government's ability to solve thorny social problems. He initially opposed Bush's 2003 Medicare prescription drug benefit program for the elderly until the very last minute, when, in a dramatic vote tally that lasted through the night, he changed his mind.

True to his belief that smaller government is better government, Franks continues to attack the practice of earmarking funds for projects back home, and he pushes for deep spending cuts to reduce the deficit. With fellow Arizona Republican Jeff Flake, he sponsored a bill to take money spent on "pork barrel" projects and put it into defense and homeland security. Unlike many members who decry excessive spending while quietly lobbying for every federal dollar they can get, Franks doesn't try to earmark funds for projects for his district. But he also doesn't entirely shy away from helping his district. Working from his seat on Armed Services, he secured $14 million in 2003 for land acquisition around Luke Air Force Base to keep local development from encroaching on the facility.

Before entering politics, Franks made a living in the oil and gas exploration business. Right out of high school and starting with just a truck-mounted rig, he and his brother went looking for oil in Texas. The two were so young they had to hire an 18-year-old friend to get a drilling permit. They drilled a lot of dry holes and lived out of a trailer. But when Franks was 17, they struck oil, a modest well that produced a few barrels and earnings of $100 a day. Today, Liberty Petroleum Corp. — managed by Franks' two brothers — is going strong with exploration projects around the world.

Franks grew up in the small vanadium and uranium mining town of Uravan, Colo. (now a ghost town), the son of a geologist and a nurse. The eldest of five children, he was born with a severe cleft lip and palate that took nine surgeries to correct. He is an active booster of Operation Smile, which provides free surgeries to babies with birth defects in 25 countries.

Franks never finished college. He finally settled in the Phoenix suburbs after he married. Josephine Franks, who is from the Philippines, liked the weather and vegetation.

He made a successful 1984 bid for a statehouse seat, but lost after one term. He then founded a think tank called the Arizona Family Research Institute, a group affiliated with Christian syndicated radio host James Dobson and his Focus on the Family organization.

He tried in 1994 for a U.S. House seat, but lost the GOP primary to John Shadegg, with whom he now serves in the Arizona delegation. Franks tried again in 2002 and edged past Lisa Atkins, former chief of staff for retiring GOP Rep. Bob Stump, by just 797 votes and handily won the November election.

In early 2004, Franks appeared to be the most endangered of the first-term GOP incumbents. He took 64 percent of the vote in the GOP primary against radio station owner Rick L. Murphy and went on to win in November with 59 percent — a vote share he matched in his 2006 and 2008 re-elections.

KEY VOTES

2008

No Delay consideration of Colombia free-trade agreement
No Override Bush veto of federal farm and nutrition programs reauthorization bill
Yes Overhaul surveillance laws and permit dismissal of suits against companies that conducted warrantless wiretapping
No Grant mortgage relief to homeowners and funding for Fannie Mae and Freddie Mac
No Approve initial $700 billion program to stabilize financial markets
No Approve final $700 billion program to stabilize financial markets
No Provide $14 billion in loans to automakers

2007

No Increase minimum wage by $2.10 an hour
No Approve $124.2 billion in emergency war spending and set goal for redeployment of troops from Iraq
Yes Reject federal contraceptive assistance to international family planning groups
No Override Bush veto of $23.2 billion water projects authorization bill
Yes Implement Peru free-trade agreement
No Approve energy policy overhaul with new fuel economy standards
Yes Clear $473.5 billion omnibus spending bill, including $70 billion for military operations

CQ VOTE STUDIES

	PARTY UNITY		PRESIDENTIAL SUPPORT	
	SUPPORT	OPPOSE	SUPPORT	OPPOSE
2008	99%	1%	87%	13%
2007	99%	1%	95%	5%
2006	96%	4%	90%	10%
2005	98%	2%	91%	9%
2004	98%	2%	91%	9%

INTEREST GROUPS

	AFL-CIO	ADA	CCUS	ACU
2008	0%	0%	76%	100%
2007	4%	0%	70%	100%
2006	7%	10%	93%	100%
2005	14%	5%	81%	100%
2004	0%	0%	95%	100%

ARIZONA 2

Northwest and central — most of Glendale, Peoria, Lake Havasu City; Hopi reservation

The 2nd spans the northwest corner of Arizona, but Republicans living in the western Phoenix suburbs to the southeast dominate its politics. Home to the vast majority of the 2nd's residents, this area takes in a corner of the city and suburbs such as rapidly growing Peoria and Surprise, most of Glendale and the retirement community of Sun City.

The district's diverse economy includes manufacturing jobs in the aerospace, electronics, communications and chemical industries. A Glendale-based Honeywell Aerospace division provides many of these jobs. Luke Air Force Base, a training center for F-16 pilots nearly 20 miles west of downtown Phoenix, is the 2nd's largest employer and contributes roughly $2 billion to the local economy annually, and efforts aim to keep the expanding metropolitan area from encroaching on the base. National economic downturns have not caused significant hardships here yet.

Most of the district's land is in Mohave County, where Lake Havasu City,

Bullhead City and Kingman are located. Democrats maintain isolated areas of influence among American Indians in the northwest, where younger, lower-income and larger minority populations live. Overall, the district is almost 80 percent white and gave Arizona Republican John McCain 61 percent of its 2008 presidential vote.

The 2nd also includes the Hopi reservation, an appendage separated from the surrounding Navajo reservation (located in the 1st). Redistricting following the 2000 census kept the tribes in different districts due to historical tensions between them. To reach the Hopi land in northeastern Arizona, the 2nd follows the Colorado River through the Grand Canyon, both sides of which are in the 1st.

MAJOR INDUSTRY
Retail, manufacturing, tourism

MILITARY BASES
Luke Air Force Base, 4,948 military, 1,040 civilian (2007)

CITIES
Glendale (pt.), 146,483; Peoria, 108,364; Phoenix (pt.), 47,199; Lake Havasu City, 41,938; Sun City (unincorporated), 38,309; Bullhead City, 33,769

NOTABLE
The Hopi have used "dry farming" to grow crops in the rough terrain.

Rep. John Shadegg (R)

Elected 1994; 8th term

Shadegg is a fiscal conservative who believes in a limited government. A skilled lawyer who relishes the details of the legislative process, he has a penchant for going against the grain; he and his wife built a house on a golf course, even though they don't like golf.

Shadegg (SHAD-egg) said he has become disillusioned with the Republican Party. He said he signed the GOP's "Contract With America" manifesto in 1994 because it promised to restore "the bonds of trust between the American people and the U.S. Congress." Instead, he said, "I have watched as the institution has protected and defended corrupt members and corrupt practices." He fought against earmarks — funding set-asides for special projects. But such spending ballooned during GOP rule. And he saw the federal budget go into the red.

Disappointed with what he sees as the Republicans' failure to meet its commitments and stymied in his efforts to advance in the House leadership, Shadegg was ready to call it quits at the end of the 110th Congress (2007-08). But he changed his mind after 146 of his colleagues signed a letter begging him to reconsider. "The Republican Conference needs you here, the conservative movement needs you here, and the country needs you here," the letter said.

Shadegg said he was "stunned and deeply humbled" by the reaction to his announcement, including a letter from 33 conservative organizations and thousands of calls to his office urging him to reconsider. He said he had never intended to be a "professional politician," and that his decision to retire had been a personal one made between him and his family, who nevertheless backed his decision to seek re-election for an eighth term.

In the 111th Congress (2009-10), his seat on the Energy and Commerce Committee will place him in the center of continued debates on health care, oil drilling and global warming.

He continues to battle against loosening the federal purse strings. He dismissed President Obama's $787 billion stimulus bill in February 2009 as "nothing more than a sordid wish list of paybacks, kickbacks and pork spending for special interests."

He also joined with most Republicans in July 2008 to vote against a sweeping housing finance package — signed into law by President George W. Bush — aimed at stabilizing the financial markets and battered housing sector by providing a backstop for Fannie Mae and Freddie Mac and establishing a new regulator for the two mortgage finance giants. He was one of only 25 Republicans to vote in 2003 against expanding the Medicare program to cover prescription drugs.

The Arizona Republic, Shadegg's hometown newspaper, summed him up this way in 2006: "By Washington standards, John Shadegg is a throwback, an artifact from an era when Republicans truly were committed to easily identifiable GOP principles like preservation of free markets, lower taxes and, above all else, spending restraint."

His high principles have failed to garner him a higher leadership post. In 2006, he dropped his post as chairman of the Republican Policy Committee to enter the race to succeed GOP leader Tom DeLay after DeLay was indicted on state finance charges. But he came in a distant third. Three months later, Shadegg lost his deputy whip position when Minority Whip Roy Blunt of Missouri tossed him out for voting with other Republican Steering Committee members against the rule governing debate of a funding bill for the Iraq War

CAPITOL OFFICE
225-3361
johnshadegg.house.gov
436 Cannon Bldg. 20515-0303; fax 225-3462

COMMITTEES
Energy & Commerce
Select Energy Independence & Global Warming

RESIDENCE
Phoenix

BORN
Oct. 22, 1949; Phoenix, Ariz.

RELIGION
Episcopalian

FAMILY
Wife, Shirley Shadegg; two children

EDUCATION
U. of Arizona, B.A. 1972, J.D. 1975

MILITARY SERVICE
Ariz. Air National Guard, 1969-75

CAREER
State prosecutor; lawyer

POLITICAL HIGHLIGHTS
No previous office

ELECTION RESULTS

2008 GENERAL

John Shadegg (R)	148,800	54.1%
Bob Lord (D)	115,759	42.1%
Michael Shoen (LIBERT)	10,602	3.8%

2008 PRIMARY

John Shadegg (R)	unopposed

2006 GENERAL

John Shadegg (R)	112,519	59.3%
Herb Paine (D)	72,586	38.2%
Mark Yannone (LIBERT)	4,744	2.5%

PREVIOUS WINNING PERCENTAGES
2004 (80%); 2002 (67%); 2000 (64%); 1998 (65%); 1996 (67%); 1994 (60%)

and Gulf Coast recovery efforts. The group was protesting the rule because it barred them from offering amendments. Following the November 2006 elections, he made an unsuccessful bid for Blunt's whip job.

Yet since 1999, Shadegg has held a coveted seat on Energy and Commerce, which has jurisdiction over a wide range of issues, including health care and the ongoing debate on universal coverage. He advocates providing a health tax credit to enable people to make their own health decisions. Minority Leader John A. Boehner of Ohio tapped him in February 2009 to serve on a 16-member group to devise a GOP health care overhaul.

Shadegg is a member of Energy and Commerce's panels on Health and Energy and the Environment. He also sits on the Select Committee on Energy Independence and Global Warming. He said he has not been convinced man-made greenhouse gases are responsible for global warming. He favors action to improve energy efficiency and reduce greenhouse gas emissions, but said launching a cap-and-trade system to reduce emissions should wait until "the case has been made."

In August 2008 he joined a small group of Republicans on the floor protesting the Democrats' refusal to vote on a GOP energy plan that would end a moratorium on drilling along the outer continental shelf. He is a staunch supporter of hydroelectric power; according to the Washington Times, he has used elementary-school textbooks to teach its principles to colleagues.

Shadegg's family name is well known in Arizona GOP circles. His late father, Stephen, was a longtime political adviser to Barry Goldwater, the five-term Arizona senator and 1964 Republican presidential nominee. The younger Shadegg developed his own political connections, working in the state attorney general's office and then serving as counsel to the House Republican Caucus in the Arizona Legislature. The election law expertise he gained in Phoenix came in handy when he wrote a position paper for House Republican leaders on the application of law in the disputed 2000 presidential contest. He went to Florida, the locus of the dispute, and was a prominent spokesman for Bush's position.

Shadegg's only election struggle was in his initial primary in 1994. For most of the race, he was thought to be trailing former Maricopa County Supervisor Jim Bruner and former state Rep. Trent Franks, now his colleague in Congress. But Shadegg won with 43 percent of the vote to 30 percent for Franks and 21 percent for Bruner. He took the general election with 60 percent, capturing the House seat vacated when Republican Jon Kyl won election to the Senate. Shadegg has won re-election handily since, though in 2006 and 2008 his winning percentages dipped as Democrats ran spirited races against him.

KEY VOTES

2008
No Delay consideration of Colombia free-trade agreement
No Override Bush veto of federal farm and nutrition programs reauthorization bill
Yes Overhaul surveillance laws and permit dismissal of suits against companies that conducted warrantless wiretapping
No Grant mortgage relief to homeowners and funding for Fannie Mae and Freddie Mac
No Approve initial $700 billion program to stabilize financial markets
Yes Approve final $700 billion program to stabilize financial markets
No Provide $14 billion in loans to automakers

2007
No Increase minimum wage by $2.10 an hour
No Approve $124.2 billion in emergency war spending and set goal for redeployment of troops from Iraq
Yes Reject federal contraceptive assistance to international family planning groups
No Override Bush veto of $23.2 billion water projects authorization bill
Yes Implement Peru free-trade agreement
No Approve energy policy overhaul with new fuel economy standards
Yes Clear $473.5 billion omnibus spending bill, including $70 billion for military operations

CQ VOTE STUDIES

	PARTY UNITY		PRESIDENTIAL SUPPORT	
	SUPPORT	OPPOSE	SUPPORT	OPPOSE
2008	99%	1%	83%	17%
2007	98%	2%	94%	6%
2006	95%	5%	90%	10%
2005	98%	2%	96%	4%
2004	99%	1%	97%	3%

INTEREST GROUPS

	AFL-CIO	ADA	CCUS	ACU
2008	0%	0%	83%	96%
2007	4%	0%	70%	100%
2006	7%	10%	100%	100%
2005	8%	0%	81%	100%
2004	7%	0%	95%	100%

ARIZONA 3

Northern Phoenix; Paradise Valley

The 3rd, which takes in a large chunk of northern Phoenix and the hills and suburbs north of the city, remains Arizona's least minority-influenced district. Although 79 percent of district residents were white in 2000, a booming Hispanic population in the 3rd — as in much of the state — has cut significantly into that majority.

Northern Phoenix is home to many large planned communities, including North Gateway Village — 45 square miles of what was mostly open land approximately 25 miles north of downtown Phoenix. Significant population growth has caused the political dynamics of the northern part of the district to fluctuate. Young liberal professionals moving into planned communities such as New River are mixed with conservative residents in such areas as the large community of Anthem.

Many of the state's most affluent and politically active residents live east of Phoenix in Paradise Valley, where the median household income is more than $150,000. The town is exclusively zoned for single-family residential use and collects no property taxes. Democrats are concentrated in the

southern part of the 3rd, where the district extends to downtown Phoenix. Resorts and tourist attractions provide some district jobs, but the economy relies on manufacturing companies, including producers of electronics and aerospace equipment. Aerospace manufacturer Honeywell, which has locations throughout the area, is one of the district's largest employers. The 3rd also is home to the Mayo Clinic Hospital, and health care accounts for a significant portion of the district's economy.

While most district voters tend to support economically and socially conservative candidates at the local and federal levels, residents have shown increasing support for Democrats. Arizonan John McCain got only 57 percent of the 2008 presidential vote here — roughly a percentage point less than George W. Bush captured in 2004 — and Rep. John Shadegg has won re-election by tighter margins in recent years.

MAJOR INDUSTRY
Technology, manufacturing, electronics, health care, construction

CITIES
Phoenix (pt.), 603,604; Paradise Valley, 13,664; New River, 10,740

NOTABLE
Locally brewed Cave Creek Chili Beer has a pepper in every bottle.

Rep. Ed Pastor (D)

Elected September 1991; 9th full term

The senior member of Arizona's House delegation and the state's only appropriator, Pastor has to look out for the interests of more than just his Phoenix-based district. And his job isn't made any easier by the anti-earmark attitude of some of his GOP colleagues.

Arizona's Republican Sen. John McCain has spent years attacking the funding set-asides for home-state projects that most lawmakers pursue. And Grand Canyon State Reps. Jeff Flake and John Shadegg are leaders of the anti-earmark movement among House Republicans. All of them refuse to seek earmarks for their districts or for Arizona.

That leaves Pastor (pas-TORE) to bring home the bacon. He has steered hundreds of millions of dollars to his district and state over the years, especially for transportation projects. Phoenix's rapid population growth is creating serious strains, he says. "When I was a county supervisor, the biggest scare was that Phoenix was going to one day wake up and be like L.A.," Pastor says. "We looked like L.A. in size, but we didn't in freeways."

From the Appropriations subcommittees dealing with transportation, energy and water funding, he has kept a steady stream of grants and contracts flowing to his district. He helped get a federal commitment of $587 million for a light-rail project for the city that began operating in late 2008. And Pastor has helped direct funds to several local habitat restoration programs, including $8.4 million to restore animal habitat and control flooding along the Salt River. When endorsing him in October 2006 for an eighth full term, The Arizona Republic called him the " 'go to' guy" for Phoenix.

Pastor is also a trusted insider in the Democratic leadership. He has been one of his party's chief deputy whips since 1999.

With Democrats in control of the White House as well as Congress, Pastor hopes the 111th Congress (2009-10) will return to the issue of immigration policy, something Democrats essentially put on hold during the 110th Congress (2007-08). Nowhere are tensions higher over the issue than in Pastor's home state. Its congressional delegation is split between those who want a crackdown on illegal immigration and those who, like Pastor, tend to view immigrants as an important economic engine. The first Hispanic elected to Congress from Arizona, Pastor has long held naturalization workshops in his district and staffed them with volunteers including local lawyers to help legal immigrants apply for citizenship.

Pastor roundly criticized the House Republican majority's immigration proposal in the 109th Congress (2005-06), which would have made it a felony to be in the United States illegally or to hire undocumented workers. He backed a bill by two Arizona GOP colleagues, Jim Kolbe and Flake, that was similar to an approach taken by McCain and Senate Democrats combining border security and work site enforcement with a guest worker program and a path to citizenship for most illegal immigrants. The Senate passed the measure, but House Republicans deemed it too lenient and refused to negotiate a final bill.

Pastor chaired the Congressional Hispanic Caucus from 1995 to 1996. He has opposed GOP efforts to roll back bilingual education and make English the official language of the federal government. His wife, Verma, was the longtime director of bilingual programs for the Arizona Department of Education.

The oldest son of a copper miner, Pastor grew up in a working-class household about 85 miles east of Phoenix. Many of his peers were destined for jobs in the mines, but Pastor's parents wanted him to go to college, so they saved their money and bought encyclopedias for him to read. His father pushed him

CAPITOL OFFICE
225-4065
www.house.gov/pastor
2465 Rayburn Bldg. 20515-0304; fax 225-1655

COMMITTEES
Appropriations

RESIDENCE
Phoenix

BORN
June 28, 1943; Claypool, Ariz.

RELIGION
Roman Catholic

FAMILY
Wife, Verma Mendez Pastor; two children

EDUCATION
Arizona State U., B.A. 1966 (chemistry), J.D. 1974

CAREER
Teacher; gubernatorial aide; public policy consultant

POLITICAL HIGHLIGHTS
Maricopa County Board of Supervisors, 1977-91

ELECTION RESULTS

2008 GENERAL

Ed Pastor (D)	89,721	72.1%
Don Karg (R)	26,435	21.2%
Rebecca DeWitt (GREEN)	4,464	3.6%
Joe Cobb (LIBERT)	3,807	3.1%

2008 PRIMARY

Ed Pastor (D)	unopposed

2006 GENERAL

Ed Pastor (D)	56,464	72.5%
Don Karg (R)	18,627	23.9%
Ronald Harders (LIBERT)	2,770	3.6%

PREVIOUS WINNING PERCENTAGES
2004 (70%); 2002 (67%); 2000 (69%); 1998 (68%); 1996 (65%); 1994 (62%); 1992 (66%); 1991 Special Election (56%)

to deliver newspapers for The Arizona Republic so he could qualify for a college scholarship the newspaper was sponsoring. From sixth grade through high school, Pastor delivered papers. He also lettered in football and baseball and was elected senior class president. He went to Arizona State University on a scholarship and was the first member of his family to attend college. He worked in the mines during the summers to help pay his expenses.

After graduating with an undergraduate degree in chemistry and a teaching certificate, Pastor taught high school for a time and worked nights helping adults learn to read and write. He got involved with a nonprofit group, The Guadalupe Organization Inc., and eventually became its deputy director.

During that time, Pastor got interested in the Chicano movement and its charismatic leader, César Chávez. Believing Mexican-Americans needed more decisive political leadership, he started volunteering for Mexican-American candidates in south Phoenix. He also went to law school.

After working for the successful gubernatorial campaign of Democrat Raúl Castro in 1974, he became one of the governor's aides.

Pastor was elected to the Maricopa County Board of Supervisors in 1976. Often the only Democrat on the board, he generally got along with the GOP majority and was able to achieve much of his legislative agenda. He said being in the minority party taught him patience and sharpened his negotiating skills.

Pastor had been eyeing a run for the 2nd District ever since it was drawn in 1982 as the state's most Hispanic district. Democratic Rep. Morris K. Udall, who suffered from Parkinson's disease, resigned in May 1991. Two days later, Pastor quit his post on the board to campaign for the seat. He was the establishment's choice, having built up a healthy war chest and solid name recognition as a supervisor. In the five-person special primary, he prevailed by 5 percentage points over Tucson Mayor Tom Volgy. His 11-percentage-point victory in the special election over Republican Pat Conner, a Yuma County supervisor, remains his closest House election.

Reapportionment after the 2000 census gave Arizona two additional House seats, and Pastor chose to run in the newly drawn 4th District nestled in the suburbs of Phoenix. Its population was slightly less Hispanic than his old one, but that caused him no difficulty.

He drew some unflattering attention in 2007 when The Arizona Republic reported he had funneled some $1 million in earmarks to a local community-college scholarship program just months before his daughter was hired to direct it. The controversy may have hurt her when she ran for the Phoenix City Council later in the year. She lost that race, but it did no harm to her father's political standing. Pastor won his ninth full term in 2008 with 72 percent.

KEY VOTES

2008

Yes Delay consideration of Colombia free-trade agreement

Yes Override Bush veto of federal farm and nutrition programs reauthorization bill

No Overhaul surveillance laws and permit dismissal of suits against companies that conducted warrantless wiretapping

Yes Grant mortgage relief to homeowners and funding for Fannie Mae and Freddie Mac

No Approve initial $700 billion program to stabilize financial markets

Yes Approve final $700 billion program to stabilize financial markets

Yes Provide $14 billion in loans to automakers

2007

Yes Increase minimum wage by $2.10 an hour

Yes Approve $124.2 billion in emergency war spending and set goal for redeployment of troops from Iraq

No Reject federal contraceptive assistance to international family planning groups

? Override Bush veto of $23.2 billion water projects authorization bill

No Implement Peru free-trade agreement

? Approve energy policy overhaul with new fuel economy standards

? Clear $473.5 billion omnibus spending bill, including $70 billion for military operations

CQ VOTE STUDIES

	PARTY UNITY		PRESIDENTIAL SUPPORT	
	SUPPORT	OPPOSE	SUPPORT	OPPOSE
2008	99%	1%	13%	87%
2007	98%	2%	2%	98%
2006	90%	10%	20%	80%
2005	93%	7%	15%	85%
2004	93%	7%	18%	82%

INTEREST GROUPS

	AFL-CIO	ADA	CCUS	ACU
2008	100%	100%	50%	4%
2007	96%	95%	47%	0%
2006	93%	100%	33%	8%
2005	93%	100%	37%	8%
2004	100%	100%	29%	4%

ARIZONA 4

Downtown and south Phoenix; part of Glendale

The 4th District, located solely within Maricopa County in Arizona's "Valley of the Sun," includes southern and central Phoenix, as well as Guadalupe and part of Glendale. Overall, the 4th, a Democratic stronghold, has the state's highest percentage of Hispanic residents and its highest percentage of black residents. Much of the recent growth in the Hispanic-majority district has been among the Latino population.

Despite high home foreclosure rates in Maricopa County, downtown revitalization continues in Phoenix. Office complexes, hotels, restaurants and shops are still opening up near residential buildings. City officials are trying to improve pedestrian access to all parts of the sprawling downtown area and are encouraging energy-conscious development — several venues sport solar panels. The initial 20-mile segment of the Valley Metro light-rail line that will connect Tempe and Mesa to downtown Phoenix opened in late 2008.

Other projects in the city include completion of an expanded downtown campus for Arizona State University and the Copper Square urban development district. But amid nationwide economic slowdowns, local retail industries may contract, and Phoenix Sky Harbor International Airport will be postponing some previously scheduled terminal and infrastructure expansion, including a rail link to the Valley Metro line.

Glendale (shared with the 2nd) is a growing white-collar, conservative community. Few agricultural areas remain in the 4th as a decade of development in Phoenix has encroached on the district's southwestern edge.

Arizona's Hispanic voters tend to support Democratic candidates on immigration but break from the Democratic Party on some social issues, opposing abortion rights and favoring some traditionally Republican "family values" type legislation. Barack Obama earned his highest percentage statewide here, taking 66 percent of the district's 2008 presidential vote.

MAJOR INDUSTRY
Retail, manufacturing, education

CITIES
Phoenix (pt.) 558,408; Glendale (pt.), 72,329; Guadalupe, 5,228

NOTABLE
The 4th's portion of Phoenix includes City Hall, the state Capitol, Chase Field, US Airways Center and Mystery Castle.

Rep. Harry E. Mitchell (D)

Elected 2006; 2nd term

CAPITOL OFFICE
225-2190
mitchell.house.gov
1410 Longworth Bldg. 20515-0305; fax 225-3263

COMMITTEES
Science & Technology
Transportation & Infrastructure
Veterans' Affairs
 (Oversight & Investigations - chairman)

RESIDENCE
Tempe

BORN
July 18, 1940; Phoenix, Ariz.

RELIGION
Roman Catholic

FAMILY
Wife, Marianne Mitchell; two children

EDUCATION
Arizona State U., B.A. 1962 (political science),
M.P.A. 1980

CAREER
High school teacher; college instructor

POLITICAL HIGHLIGHTS
Tempe City Council, 1970-78; mayor of Tempe,
1978-94; sought Democratic nomination for
superintendent of public instruction, 1994; Ariz.
Senate, 1999-2006 (assistant minority leader,
2005-06); Ariz. Democratic Party chairman, 2005-06

ELECTION RESULTS

2008 GENERAL

Harry E. Mitchell (D)	149,033	53.2%
David Schweikert (R)	122,165	43.6%
Warren Severin (LIBERT)	9,158	3.3%

2008 PRIMARY

Harry E. Mitchell (D)	unopposed

2006 GENERAL

Harry E. Mitchell (D)	101,838	50.4%
J.D. Hayworth (R)	93,815	46.4%
Warren Severin (LIBERT)	6,357	3.2%

A self-proclaimed "social moderate, fiscal conservative," Mitchell takes care to keep in mind the interests of his district, long a GOP stronghold where the economy caters to wealthy business class travelers and resort vacationers.

Mitchell is a member of the New Democrat Coalition, a group of pro-business moderates, as well as the Blue Dogs, whose members have a generally conservative fiscal outlook. He bucks party leaders on certain issues, he says, to better reflect the voters in his heavily suburban district.

In late 2008, he was one of 20 House Democrats who voted against a federal bailout of the automobile industry. He also bucked the majority of his party to vote against an initial $700 billion financial industry rescue bill, but then voted for a modified version that he said provided more taxpayer protections. Then in early 2009, he was one of 17 Democrats who voted against President Obama's $3.56 trillion budget blueprint for fiscal 2010.

House Democratic leaders tolerate his tendency to stray, given the makeup of his district and his need to retain hold of a House seat he took from J.D. Hayworth, a boisterous conservative and veteran of the GOP class of 1994.

Early in 2009, he and Republican Ron Paul of Texas offered legislation to prevent House members from receiving an automatic cost-of-living pay raise. He noted that "as millions of Americans watch their incomes shrink, a pay raise for members of Congress would have seemed glaringly out of touch." A few weeks later Democratic leaders announced that, indeed, members would have to forgo a cost-of-living increase that year.

Mitchell also supports estate tax cuts and in both 2007 and 2009 has sponsored legislation to make permanent the 2003 reduction in capital gains tax rates from 20 percent to 15 percent. "I think half of Americans today own stock. It's not just the wealthy," Mitchell says. "I think for the middle class it was important."

Mitchell's votes on many social issues are more in line with those of his party. In 2007 he supported a bill to ban job discrimination based on an individual's sexual orientation. He supports an Arizona law that bars same-sex marriage, but opposes a marriage amendment to the Constitution, arguing that it is not the federal government's role to regulate in that sphere.

At 66, he was the oldest new member to be sworn into Congress in 2007. He had already spent 32 years in public office, and Democratic leaders gave him the gavel of the Veterans' Affairs panel on Oversight and Investigations.

Mitchell led the panel in more hearings during the 110th Congress (2007-08) than were held in the two previous Congresses combined. He was among the first members to criticize former Veterans Affairs Secretary Jim Nicholson, who resigned in 2007 after a tumultuous tenure that included budget shortfalls and poor management of patients at Walter Reed Army Medical Center in Washington. "Unless you hold people's feet to the fire, these things will continue to go on," he said.

Mitchell was successful in overturning a long-standing VA policy that barred the department from using TV advertisements. In July 2008, the VA announced the launch of a three-month pilot program to boost public awareness about a veterans' suicide hotline. He also teamed with Virginia Democratic Sen. Jim Webb, a military veteran, on a measure that expanded the GI bill to benefit troops who served in the wars in Afghanistan and Iraq. It was signed into law in June 2008 as part of a supplemental spending bill.

As the first Arizonan to sit on the House Transportation and Infrastructure Committee in nearly 20 years, Mitchell doesn't hide his pleasure in bringing federal dollars home. During his first year, Mitchell obtained more than $34 million in earmarks — funding set-asides for members' projects. The funds were used to improve Phoenix-Mesa Gateway Airport and bus facilities in Tempe. In the 111th Congress (2009-10), the committee is expected to take up a renewal of the 2005 surface transportation bill — traditionally a vehicle for funding local projects. Mitchell is on the panel's highways subcommittee.

Mitchell's future goals include improving Arizona's returns from the Highway Trust Fund, from which the state now receives 92 cents for every dollar it contributes in user-paid taxes.

Mitchell is a lifelong Tempe resident. His father worked for Southern Pacific as a railroad engineer; his mother was a homemaker. His paternal grandfather served in the state legislature when Mitchell was growing up.

After graduating from Tempe High School, where he later spent 28 years teaching government and economics, Mitchell attended Arizona State University, earning a degree in political science. He was a college instructor at ASU in the late 1990s. "When I decided to run, it wasn't because I was mad with anyone or had any axes to grind," Mitchell says. "I've just always been a student, teacher and practitioner of government."

He won a seat on the Tempe City Council in 1970, in his first bid for public office. Eight years later he became the city's mayor. As the city's chief executive for 16 years, Mitchell helped revitalize downtown Tempe and increased public transportation as it grew from a suburban community to an urban center. In gratitude, city officials established the Harry E. Mitchell Municipal Complex and erected a 35-foot abstract steel statue in honor of him near City Hall.

He made a failed bid for state superintendent of public instruction in 1994 but returned to public life four years later when he won a seat in the Arizona Senate. He served as both the chamber's assistant minority leader and Democratic state party chairman from 2005 to 2006.

Term-limited in the state Senate, and seeing Hayworth's favorable ratings falling, Mitchell jumped into the House race in 2006. Hayworth, a hard-liner on immigration, claimed Mitchell's views on the issue were too liberal. Mitchell supported a guest worker program coupled with heightened border security and surveillance. Throughout the campaign, Mitchell accused Hayworth of being too cozy with lobbyists, especially Jack Abramoff, who later was sentenced to four years in prison for bribery and defrauding some of his clients.

Mitchell prevailed by 4 percentage points, and boosted that margin to nearly 10 percentage points in 2008.

KEY VOTES

2008

Yes Delay consideration of Colombia free-trade agreement

No   Override Bush veto of federal farm and nutrition programs reauthorization bill

Yes Overhaul surveillance laws and permit dismissal of suits against companies that conducted warrantless wiretapping

Yes Grant mortgage relief to homeowners and funding for Fannie Mae and Freddie Mac

No   Approve initial $700 billion program to stabilize financial markets

Yes Approve final $700 billion program to stabilize financial markets

No   Provide $14 billion in loans to automakers

2007

Yes Increase minimum wage by $2.10 an hour

Yes Approve $124.2 billion in emergency war spending and set goal for redeployment of troops from Iraq

No   Reject federal contraceptive assistance to international family planning groups

Yes Override Bush veto of $23.2 billion water projects authorization bill

Yes Implement Peru free-trade agreement

Yes Approve energy policy overhaul with new fuel economy standards

Yes Clear $473.5 billion omnibus spending bill, including $70 billion for military operations

CQ VOTE STUDIES

	PARTY UNITY		PRESIDENTIAL SUPPORT	
	SUPPORT	OPPOSE	SUPPORT	OPPOSE
2008	80%	20%	25%	75%
2007	83%	17%	13%	87%

INTEREST GROUPS

	AFL-CIO	ADA	CCUS	ACU
2008	87%	75%	67%	32%
2007	83%	80%	60%	8%

ARIZONA 5

Scottsdale; Tempe; parts of Phoenix and Mesa

Wealth, beautiful sunsets and conservative politics abound in the 5th, which takes in a sliver of Phoenix and spreads east to Tempe, Scottsdale and the western parts of Chandler and Mesa. The 5th also encompasses towns such as Sunflower and Fountain Hills that highlight the area's trademarks — nature and leisure.

With luxury resorts, golf courses, museums, art galleries and spring training baseball, the district relies on the success of its hospitality and tourism industries, and caters to both business travelers and vacationers. Scottsdale's many stylish lodgings have been successful at hosting visitors to events like the PGA Tour's FBR Open. The 5th's part of Phoenix includes the zoo and the Desert Botanical Garden.

American Indians comprise only 2.1 percent of the majority-white district, but casinos and resorts at Salt River and Fort McDowell Indian reservations lure guests to the district. Scottsdale Pavilions shopping mall, inside Salt River, is an example of local development between private business and American Indian communities.

Health care represents a growing sector of the economy, and Mayo Clinic research facilities and Caremark, a pharmaceutical benefits management firm, are among the businesses that employ many 5th District residents.

Scottsdale and Fountain Hills draw retirees and their bank accounts — both places have higher incomes and median ages than the state and nation — to the wealthiest district in the state. Farther south, Tempe, home of Arizona State University, has a median age under 30.

Tempe's more liberal voters can offset the 5th's overall GOP bent, but there are nearly as many independents registered to vote in the district as Democrats. John McCain won the district by almost 5 percentage points in the 2008 presidential election, but Democrat Harry E. Mitchell has represented the 5th since ousting a Republican incumbent in 2006.

MAJOR INDUSTRY
Tourism, education, health care

CITIES
Scottsdale, 202,705; Tempe, 158,625; Mesa (pt.), 96,622; Phoenix (pt.), 85,765; Chandler (pt.), 66,823; Fountain Hills, 20,235

NOTABLE
Taliesin West in Scottsdale was Frank Lloyd Wright's winter home.

Rep. Jeff Flake (R)

Elected 2000; 5th term

Flake is a strict Barry Goldwater conservative who has long waged a lonely war against what he sees as wasteful spending, offering scores of amendments to strip legislation of earmarks — funding set-asides for projects in lawmakers' districts. His own party has been little help to him, though, and it wasn't until Democrats took over Congress that he managed to win a battle.

In 2007, during debate on a Financial Services spending bill, the House adopted a Flake amendment to kill a $129,000 earmark for a foundation called the Perfect Christmas Tree Project. But for Flake, it was a Pyrrhic victory; the earmark was the work of Republican Patrick T. McHenry of North Carolina, a fellow conservative. "I didn't expect to get my first win by friendly fire," Flake said at the time.

The GOP had paused in its crusade against the dangers of deficits and too much federal power, but Flake still hewed to a personal political philosophy of small government and reduced spending. Earmarks make an easy target, as they are often important only to a single member of Congress. But his opposition to the funding mechanism has won him few friends. "I'm sick and tired of phony amendments that act like they are going to save money," Republican John Culberson of Texas complained in 2007 after Flake tried to eliminate a $300,000 Culberson earmark for the Houston Zoo.

In early 2009, he joined his party in opposing President Obama's economic stimulus plan, which became law. Before final passage, he highlighted what he called "egregious earmarks," including $222,000 for greenhouse lettuce germplasm in Salinas, California. "Lettuce allow this earmark to wilt," he quipped. In late 2008, he opposed two $700 billion measures — the second of which became law — intended to shore up the ailing financial services industry, and voted against a $14 billion loan which later stalled in the Senate to bail out the auto industry.

Flake said his fellow Republicans often have trampled on the principle of federalism, overriding states on everything from social policy to regulatory matters. "You can't be a fair-weather federalist," he said. He has voted against such broadly popular initiatives as the 2001 education overhaul known as No Child Left Behind, the 2003 Medicare prescription drug benefit, and both the 2002 and 2008 farm bills, which authorized agriculture and nutrition programs.

In 2007, he was one of only 35 Republicans to vote for a bill to prohibit workplace discrimination against gays. "If we accept the premise of the Civil Rights Act — and I do — and the Voting Rights Act that followed, we can't extend protections to some groups and deny them for others," he said. Flake antagonized his party's leadership with his public support for an immigration overhaul that would allow many of the estimated 13 million illegal immigrants in the country to gain legal status. In 2006, he was stripped of his assignment to the Judiciary Committee. Flake told the San Antonio Express-News the move was punishment for his support of what proponents call "comprehensive" immigration reform and opponents call "amnesty."

Undeterred, he partnered in 2007 with Illinois Democrat Luis V. Gutierrez on legislation to strengthen border security and interior immigration enforcement, create a temporary guest worker program, and provide illegal immigrants a path to citizenship.

Flake asked Minority Leader John A. Boehner to appoint him to the Appropriations Committee when a seat came open in 2008. An array of budget watchdog groups lined up behind Flake. Freedom Works, a conservative interest group of former House Majority Leader Dick Armey of Texas, start-

CAPITOL OFFICE
225-2635
www.house.gov/flake
240 Cannon Bldg. 20515-0306; fax 226-4386

COMMITTEES
Foreign Affairs
Natural Resources
Oversight & Government Reform

RESIDENCE
Mesa

BORN
Dec. 31, 1962; Snowflake, Ariz.

RELIGION
Mormon

FAMILY
Wife, Cheryl Flake; five children

EDUCATION
Brigham Young U., B.A. 1986 (international relations), M.A. 1987 (political science)

CAREER
Public policy think tank director;
African business trade representative; lobbyist

POLITICAL HIGHLIGHTS
No previous office

ELECTION RESULTS

2008 GENERAL

Jeff Flake (R)	208,582	62.4%
Rebecca Schneider (D)	115,457	34.6%
Rick Biondi (LIBERT)	10,137	3%

2008 PRIMARY

Jeff Flake (R)	unopposed

2006 GENERAL

Jeff Flake (R)	51,285	74.8%
Jason M. Blair (LIBERT)	51,285	25.2%

PREVIOUS WINNING PERCENTAGES
2004 (79%); 2002 (66%); 2000 (54%)

ed a "Make it Flake" campaign. But in January 2009 he was again passed over. Instead, leaders put him on the Oversight and Government Reform Committee, where Flake hopes to have a greater impact on earmark reform. He also sits on the Natural Resources Committee, where he fights against what he calls "a new vehicle for earmarks" — National Heritage Areas, which he says siphon money away from the national park system.

Flake evinces misgivings about his party's direction on issues beyond spending and immigration. The day after the November 2008 election, when Republicans lost more seats in the House, he called for the replacement of House GOP leaders. "Let's face it, we've really not run on a message for years," he told the Arizona Republic.

On the Foreign Affairs panel, he has expressed doubts about military progress in Iraq, though he has largely supported his party in votes related to the war. He is a defender of civil liberties, and said George W. Bush's administration "overstepped" with its policy of warrantless wiretapping of terrorism suspects.

Flake has led Republicans seeking to end restrictions on travel to Cuba by U.S. citizens, calling instead for a policy of robust economic engagement.

Although a hard-liner politically, Flake is easygoing and personable. When he's not with his wife and five children, he spends his free time in the House gym playing basketball and is a star of the GOP's team in the annual congressional charity baseball game.

Flake and 10 siblings grew up on the family ranch near Snowflake, about 100 miles northeast of Phoenix. Established in 1878, the town is named after its Mormon settler founders, Erastus Snow and William Flake, the lawmaker's great-great-grandfather. A Mormon himself, Flake went on a two-year church mission to Zimbabwe and South Africa in 1982. He majored in international relations at Brigham Young University, and in 1989 moved to Namibia as director of the Foundation for Democracy, a group trying to help the country develop a constitution after its break from South Africa. He returned to Arizona in 1992 to take the helm of the Goldwater Institute, a think tank that led the way to create state charter schools and a tax credit plan to fund private-school scholarships. It is named for the state's famed conservative trailblazer, former Sen. Barry Goldwater — Flake's own political model. Flake also attributes his success to Arizona Sen. John McCain, another anti-earmark crusader.

Flake first ran for the U.S. House in 2000, when GOP Rep. Matt Salmon retired. With Salmon's endorsement, Flake won a five-way primary. In the general election, Flake bested Democratic labor lobbyist David Mendoza. He won the 2002 election by 34 percentage points and didn't face another Democratic challenger until 2008, when he won with more than 62 percent of the vote.

KEY VOTES

2008

No   Delay consideration of Colombia free-trade agreement

No   Override Bush veto of federal farm and nutrition programs reauthorization bill

Yes   Overhaul surveillance laws and permit dismissal of suits against companies that conducted warrantless wiretapping

No   Grant mortgage relief to homeowners and funding for Fannie Mae and Freddie Mac

No   Approve initial $700 billion program to stabilize financial markets

No   Approve final $700 billion program to stabilize financial markets

No   Provide $14 billion in loans to automakers

2007

No   Increase minimum wage by $2.10 an hour

No   Approve $124.2 billion in emergency war spending and set goal for redeployment of troops from Iraq

Yes   Reject federal contraceptive assistance to international family planning groups

No   Override Bush veto of $23.2 billion water projects authorization bill

Yes   Implement Peru free-trade agreement

No   Approve energy policy overhaul with new fuel economy standards

Yes   Clear $473.5 billion omnibus spending bill, including $70 billion for military operations

CQ VOTE STUDIES

	PARTY UNITY		PRESIDENTIAL SUPPORT	
	SUPPORT	OPPOSE	SUPPORT	OPPOSE
2008	99%	1%	85%	15%
2007	95%	5%	89%	11%
2006	86%	14%	72%	28%
2005	91%	9%	74%	26%
2004	93%	7%	74%	26%

INTEREST GROUPS

	AFL-CIO	ADA	CCUS	ACU
2008	0%	0%	61%	100%
2007	4%	5%	68%	100%
2006	0%	20%	79%	100%
2005	7%	0%	70%	96%
2004	13%	15%	81%	96%

ARIZONA 6

Southeast Phoenix suburbs — most of Mesa and Chandler, Gilbert, Apache Junction

Rooted in the conservative leanings of an affluent, historically Mormon population, the suburban 6th favors Republican candidates. The district still has a significant population of Mormons, as well as a mix of young couples who commute to Phoenix. The area's warm sunny days have helped draw an established population of retirees from other states.

East of Phoenix, the district takes in all but the westernmost segments of Mesa and Chandler. Adjacent to the two cities is Gilbert, and the district spreads east to take in part of still largely rural Pinal County, including Apache Junction near the county's northern border.

The southeastern Phoenix suburbs experienced decades of population growth that is characteristic of the area, and local officials hope that the Santan Freeway corridor, traversing Chandler, Gilbert and Mesa, will support further growth. Construction in the area continues despite housing market slowdowns. Retail also is an important sector of the district's

economy, and Wal-Mart is a major employer in the 6th. Manufacturing aids the economy in fast-growing Mesa, and the city hosts a large Boeing facility. Technology manufacturing plays a role here as well: Intel has two locations in Chandler and employs 10,000 people. Agriculture, especially alfalfa and dairy operations, figures in the district's economy but is being replaced due to sprawling development.

Republicans hold a 20-percentage-point edge in party registration here, and the 6th gave John McCain 61 percent of its 2008 presidential vote, his highest percentage in the state. In 2006, GOP Sen. Jon Kyl received his highest statewide percentage (62 percent) in the district, while Democratic Gov. Janet Napolitano received her lowest statewide percentage (54 percent) here.

MAJOR INDUSTRY
Manufacturing, technology, retail, construction

CITIES
Mesa (pt.), 299,753; Chandler (pt.), 109,758; Gilbert, 109,697; Apache Junction, 31,814

NOTABLE
Chandler's Ostrich Festival, held each March, features ostrich races and a parade.

Rep. Raúl M. Grijalva (D)

Elected 2002; 4th term

CAPITOL OFFICE
225-2435
www.house.gov/grijalva
1440 Longworth Bldg. 20515-0307; fax 225-1541

COMMITTEES
Education & Labor
Natural Resources
(National Parks, Forests & Public Lands -
chairman)

RESIDENCE
Tucson

BORN
Feb. 19, 1948; Tucson, Ariz.

RELIGION
Roman Catholic

FAMILY
Wife, Mona Grijalva; three children

EDUCATION
U. of Arizona, B.A. 1987 (sociology)

CAREER
University dean; community center director

POLITICAL HIGHLIGHTS
Candidate for Tucson Unified School District
Governing Board, 1972; Tucson Unified School
District Governing Board, 1974-86; Pima County
Board of Supervisors, 1989-2002 (chairman,
1997, 2001-02)

ELECTION RESULTS

2008 GENERAL

Raúl M. Grijalva (D)	124,304	63.3%
Joseph Sweeney (R)	64,425	32.8%
Raymond Patrick Petrulsky (LIBERT)	80,354	3.9%

2008 PRIMARY

Raúl M. Grijalva (D)	unopposed

2006 GENERAL

Raúl M. Grijalva (D)	80,354	61.1%
Ron Drake (R)	46,498	35.4%
Joe Cobb (LIBERT)	4,673	3.6%

PREVIOUS WINNING PERCENTAGES
2004 (62%); 2002 (59%)

Grijalva's background as a social worker and community-center director makes him a fierce advocate for Democratic priorities such as education, health care and worker rights. He has seen firsthand the struggles ordinary people face, and remains rooted in the Tucson neighborhood where he grew up.

He also is a favorite of environmentalists for the strong conservationist views he espouses from his seat as chairman of the Natural Resources subcommittee that oversees public lands. They and the Congressional Hispanic Caucus strongly urged President Obama to select Grijalva (gree-HAHL-va) to be his Interior secretary, but Obama opted for Colorado Sen. Ken Salazar instead.

Despite his disappointment, Grijalva said he remains committed to pursuing his desire to preserve public lands. He even turned down a spot on the exclusive Ways and Means Committee for the 111th Congress (2009-10), a seat he once sought and that would have given him a larger role on tax and health policy. But he was unwilling to give up his chairmanship on the Natural Resources subcommittee, where one of his top priorities going forward is a rewrite of the 1872 Mining Law that governs hard-rock mining on public lands. The House passed an overhaul bill in 2007 that would impose a royalty for the first time on minerals such as gold, copper and uranium, but the measure died in the Senate.

He also plans to push back against public-lands policies pursued by George W. Bush's administration, which favored oil and gas drilling, mining and other resource-use activities over conservation. "We're talking about creating a balance between the extraction that's available on public lands and the protection that's necessary of those resources," he said.

In 2005, Bush signed into law Grijalva's bill returning 16,000 acres of land to four Colorado River Indian tribes who lost the property to the government in 1915 after they refused to lease it for mining. Grijalva also steered to passage a bill to spur economic growth on Gila River Indian lands. Grijalva's district has seven tribes; on his office wall he displays a carved mask from the Yaquis.

Grijalva has served on the Education and Labor Committee since he arrived in Congress, and has pushed to fully fund the federal No Child Left Behind Act to improve test scores in public schools. When Congress resumes its effort to overhaul that Bush-era law, Grijalva plans to seek greater local flexibility in executing its mandates.

In 2003, he fought GOP-inspired changes to Head Start aimed at giving states more control over the preschool program. When Congress reauthorized the program in 2007, he worked to ensure funding priorities to help children with limited English proficiency and those of American Indian and migrant worker families.

Grijalva maintains a keen interest in immigration and border issues. His southwestern Arizona district shares 300 miles with Mexico, second only to Texas' 23rd. In recent years, hundreds of people trying to evade border police have died in the vast Sonoran Desert. He opposes punitive immigration policies and guest worker proposals that would not lead to permanent legal residency. He said the guest worker idea is reminiscent of the bracero program, under which migrant Mexican workers flocked to low-wage U.S. farm jobs created by World War II labor shortages. Grijalva's father, a Mexican cowboy, was a bracero and later married a U.S. citizen.

During the immigration debate in the 109th Congress (2005-06), Grijalva backed legislation by Republican Sen. John McCain, a fellow Arizonan, and Democratic Sen. Edward M. Kennedy of Massachusetts to create a guest worker program that included a path to U.S. citizenship. GOP opposition eventually killed the measure, and Congress instead voted to authorize a 700-mile fence along the border with Mexico, a plan Grijalva opposed. "That infrastructure has taken away from other infrastructure needs along the border—including port-of-entry improvement, technology improvement, transportation issues," he said in October 2008.

Grijalva is no fan of recent trade deals. He opposed the 2005 bill to implement the Central America Free Trade Agreement, as well as a 2007 free-trade pact with Peru. He assailed "this destructive process of corporate globalization that has done so much harm to this nation and our neighbors."

He also vigorously opposes the war in Iraq and refuses to vote for war funding bills. "I will not vote for any bill that funds anything other than beginning the safe, orderly and rapid withdrawal of our troops from Iraq," he said.

On health care issues, he supports efforts to expand the Clinton-era State Children's Health Insurance Program, which provides insurance for children from low-income families that do not qualify for Medicaid, to include their parents. He also would extend Medicare to people between the ages of 55 and 64, who are often unable to obtain affordable health insurance if they lose their jobs.

Grijalva dislikes the nonstop fundraising of modern campaigns, and his staff has to badger him to keep at it. Advised to hold a golf tournament to raise money, he instead threw a bowl-a-thon.

He still lives in the working-class, heavily Latino section of south Tucson where he was born and raised. He attended the University of Arizona, but quit to get married. Grijalva and his school librarian wife, Mona, had three daughters, and he became a social worker and community activist.

He ran for the Tucson school board in 1972 and was "embarrassingly" defeated. In his second attempt in 1974, he followed through with voter ID work and door-to-door mailings. He served 12 years on the board, then won election to the Pima County Board of Supervisors. While in local government, he frequently advised young people to stay in school. To set an example, he finished nine credit hours left on his sociology degree, graduating from the University of Arizona at 39.

When redistricting created a new Hispanic-majority district in southern Arizona, Grijalva jumped into the crowded 2002 primary race. He prevailed against one incumbent and two former state senators. In the general election, the Hispanic makeup of the district ensured Grijalva's victory. He defeated Republican Ross Hieb, a farmer and forester, with 59 percent of the vote and has won re-election easily ever since.

KEY VOTES

2008
Yes Delay consideration of Colombia free-trade agreement
Yes Override Bush veto of federal farm and nutrition programs reauthorization bill
No Overhaul surveillance laws and permit dismissal of suits against companies that conducted warrantless wiretapping
Yes Grant mortgage relief to homeowners and funding for Fannie Mae and Freddie Mac
No Approve initial $700 billion program to stabilize financial markets
No Approve final $700 billion program to stabilize financial markets
Yes Provide $14 billion in loans to automakers

2007
Yes Increase minimum wage by $2.10 an hour
Yes Approve $124.2 billion in emergency war spending and set goal for redeployment of troops from Iraq
No Reject federal contraceptive assistance to international family planning groups
Yes Override Bush veto of $23.2 billion water projects authorization bill
No Implement Peru free-trade agreement
Yes Approve energy policy overhaul with new fuel economy standards
No Clear $473.5 billion omnibus spending bill, including $70 billion for military operations

CQ VOTE STUDIES

	PARTY UNITY		PRESIDENTIAL SUPPORT	
	SUPPORT	OPPOSE	SUPPORT	OPPOSE
2008	99%	1%	10%	90%
2007	99%	1%	4%	96%
2006	99%	1%	10%	90%
2005	98%	2%	13%	87%
2004	99%	1%	12%	88%

INTEREST GROUPS

	AFL-CIO	ADA	CCUS	ACU
2008	100%	100%	44%	8%
2007	96%	100%	50%	0%
2006	93%	100%	27%	4%
2005	93%	100%	30%	0%
2004	100%	100%	10%	0%

ARIZONA 7
Southwest — part of Tucson, Yuma, Avondale

Stretching mainly south and west from Phoenix, the Hispanic-majority, strongly Democratic 7th crosses large reservations and rural areas to take in Yuma, downtown Tucson and most of Arizona's border with Mexico. It also includes the Mexican border town of Nogales and runs up the California border. The district's chunk of Tucson is home to the University of Arizona — one of southern Arizona's top employers.

A large population of seasonal immigrant workers — particularly in vegetable farming — buttresses the agriculture and service industries but boosts the district's poverty statistics. The 7th has more blue-collar workers and fewer college graduates than most Arizona districts.

Illegal immigration is a major problem here. Crossing the border in this vast desert region is especially dangerous, due to the extreme heat and lack of water, and it also hampers military training activities on the Barry M. Goldwater Range, which covers more than 100 miles of the border.

The Tohono O'odham and Gila River reservations are the 7th's largest,

and American Indians make up 6 percent of the population here. Gila River, south of Phoenix, and Tohono O'odham, at the district's southern edge, host resorts and casinos, but also have invested in commercial and industrial parks to diversify economically.

Republicans are competitive in most of the 7th's counties, but Democrats dominate in Pima County, the district's most populous, which includes the 7th's portion of Tucson and many American Indian residents. Overall, Barack Obama took 57 percent of the district's vote for president in 2008.

MAJOR INDUSTRY
Agriculture, tourism, education

MILITARY BASES
Marine Corps Air Station Yuma, 4,761 military, 542 civilian (2007); Yuma Proving Ground (Army), 97 military, 663 civilian (2007)

CITIES
Tucson (pt.), 230,164; Yuma, 77,515; Avondale, 35,883; Phoenix (pt.), 26,069

NOTABLE
Yuma Territorial Prison — a late-19th-century penitentiary — was turned into a high school, then a shelter for railroad vagrants, and now is a state historic park.

Rep. Gabrielle Giffords (D)

Elected 2006; 2nd term

CAPITOL OFFICE
225-2542
giffords.house.gov
1728 Longworth Bldg. 20515-0308; fax 225-0378

COMMITTEES
Armed Services
Foreign Affairs
Science & Technology
   (Space & Aeronautics - chairwoman)

RESIDENCE
Tucson

BORN
June 8, 1970; Tucson, Ariz.

RELIGION
Jewish

FAMILY
Husband, Mark Kelly

EDUCATION
Scripps College, B.A. 1993 (sociology & Latin American history); Cornell U., M.R.P. 1997 (regional planning)

CAREER
Property management company owner; retail tire company president; regional economic and employment analyst

POLITICAL HIGHLIGHTS
Ariz. House, 2001-03; Ariz. Senate, 2003-05

ELECTION RESULTS

2008 GENERAL

Gabrielle Giffords (D)	179,629	54.7%
Timothy S. Bee (R)	140,553	42.8%
Paul Davis (LIBERT)	8,081	2.5%

2008 PRIMARY

Gabrielle Giffords (D)	unopposed

2006 GENERAL

Gabrielle Giffords (D)	137,655	54.2%
Randy Graf (R)	106,790	42.1%
David F. Nolan (LIBERT)	4,849	1.9%
Jay Quick (I)	4,408	1.7%

Giffords is seen as a pragmatic go-getter, focusing largely on immigration reform and border control, alternative-energy policy and relations with Latin America. She hews to the center of her party, particularly on social issues, while calling for fiscal discipline. She is a member of the Blue Dog Coalition, a group of fiscally conservative Democrats.

Giffords' views on immigration are influenced by the 100-mile border that her district shares with Mexico. She wants to control the entrance of illegal immigrants, while recognizing that the hospitality and agriculture employers in her district rely on non-U.S. workers. She advocates stronger penalties against employers who hire illegal immigrants and a guest worker program allowing foreign citizens to work seasonally in the United States. "We don't have the American workers who want to pick chili peppers," she says.

The 8th District's border with Mexico was for years the only one with a roaming checkpoint, she says. The other 34 border checkpoints were permanent. "We had a wide-open gap, like 'Enter Here!' " Giffords says, and Tucson was a magnet for smugglers. When the Border Patrol announced a change to a permanent, enlarged checkpoint near a densely populated area in Santa Cruz County, local residents objected. Giffords formed a group consisting of business owners, residents and environmentalists that worked with the Border Patrol on a compromise to move the checkpoint six miles to the south of its proposed location. The Arizona Republic in a September 2007 editorial praised Giffords for "an effective effort by a first-term lawmaker."

She also has been pushing a measure to help employers check whether their employees are legal. The federal government currently uses a software program called E-Verify that checks for an employee's eligibility criteria. Giffords has criticized the system, saying it has been used mainly on a voluntary basis over the 12 years it's been operational. She is the main Democratic sponsor of a bill by Texas Republican Sam Johnson that would turn over employer enforcement to privately run companies administered by state governments.

Giffords, who speaks Spanish and owns a home in Mexico, sits on the Foreign Affairs Committee's Western Hemisphere Subcommittee.

She also has a seat on Science and Technology, where she serves as chairwoman of the Space and Aeronautics Subcommittee. She is particularly interested in developing solar and renewable energy sources. Arizona has 300 days of sunshine each year, she said. "We have the land, the technology, the concentrated sunshine," Giffords says. "I want to see south Arizona be the 'Solarcon Valley' of the United States." She introduced legislation, which became part of the sweeping energy package in the 110th Congress (2007-08), to authorize $43 million through fiscal 2012 for research to help solar plants generate more energy in low-light situations.

Giffords also sits on Armed Services, which allows her to look out for the interests of her district's two military installations. She was the first Democratic freshman to visit Iraq in February 2007, where during a stopover in Israel, she learned F-14 parts from U.S. planes were being sold to Iran. Once home, Giffords introduced a bill to ban the sale of F-14 parts, which passed the House. Iran's air force is the only one that still flies the F-14.

Giffords votes with her party on most social issues. In 2007, she voted to override President George W. Bush's veto on a bill to expand the State Children's Health Insurance Program, which covers children from low-income families that do not qualify for Medicaid, and voted against allowing faith-based Head Start pre-school program providers to take religion into account when hiring. And she supports abortion rights. But in 2008, she backed a measure to roll back District of Columbia gun control laws.

In the fall of 2008, she was one of four Blue Dogs to change their vote on a $700 billion proposal aimed at shoring up the nation's financial services sector. Having opposed an initial measure, she supported a revised version that ultimately became law. But later that year she opposed a $14 billion bailout bill for U.S. automakers, saying she remained unconvinced of the need for a bailout.

On the first anniversary of her House election, Giffords married Mark Kelly, 43, a NASA astronaut and former Navy pilot. Their wedding was a "low-carbon-footprint" event held at an organic produce farm south of Tucson. The ceremony was Jewish, and the food Mexican.

Giffords is a third-generation Arizonan, who grew up in Tucson. Her father owned a tire business and served on the school board. Her mother is an art conservator, specializing in Latin American art. Giffords grew up riding horses and racing motorcycles competitively, and loves working on old cars.

At 18, Giffords registered as a Republican as she was inspired by Arizona Supreme Court Justice Sandra Day O'Connor. She attended Scripps College in California, and after graduation was awarded a Fulbright grant to study in Chihuahua, Mexico. Giffords also spent a year in San Diego studying a border control program initiated along the California-Mexico border.

After earning a master's degree in regional planning and completing a consulting stint in New York, Giffords returned to Tucson when her father became ill to take over the family tire and automotive business.

She says she became politically motivated when she realized how poorly Arizona ranked nationally on many social indicators — teenage pregnancy, dropout rates and teen suicide. In 1999, she changed her party affiliation after realizing she was more moderate on social issues than most Arizona Republicans. She was elected to the Arizona House in 2000. In 2002, she became the youngest woman elected to the state Senate.

When GOP Rep. Jim Kolbe decided to retire, Giffords seized the opportunity. She beat out five primary challengers and in the general election faced former state GOP Rep. Randy Graf, who touted a tough enforcement-first approach to immigration. But Graf had fallen out of favor with local Republicans. Giffords prevailed with 54 percent of the vote.

In 2008, she beat GOP state Senate President Timothy S. Bee by 12 percentage points.

KEY VOTES

2008

Yes Delay consideration of Colombia free-trade agreement

Yes Override Bush veto of federal farm and nutrition programs reauthorization bill

Yes Overhaul surveillance laws and permit dismissal of suits against companies that conducted warrantless wiretapping

Yes Grant mortgage relief to homeowners and funding for Fannie Mae and Freddie Mac

No Approve initial $700 billion program to stabilize financial markets

Yes Approve final $700 billion program to stabilize financial markets

No Provide $14 billion in loans to automakers

2007

Yes Increase minimum wage by $2.10 an hour

Yes Approve $124.2 billion in emergency war spending and set goal for redeployment of troops from Iraq

No Reject federal contraceptive assistance to international family planning groups

Yes Override Bush veto of $23.2 billion water projects authorization bill

+ Implement Peru free-trade agreement

Yes Approve energy policy overhaul with new fuel economy standards

Yes Clear $473.5 billion omnibus spending bill, including $70 billion for military operations

CQ VOTE STUDIES

	PARTY UNITY		PRESIDENTIAL SUPPORT	
	SUPPORT	OPPOSE	SUPPORT	OPPOSE
2008	86%	14%	19%	81%
2007	87%	13%	6%	94%

INTEREST GROUPS

	AFL-CIO	ADA	CCUS	ACU
2008	87%	80%	67%	20%
2007	96%	80%	61%	4%

ARIZONA 8
Southeast — part of Tucson and northern suburbs

Nestled in the state's southeast corner, the 8th District is home to many swing voters and independents. The more conservative Cochise County takes up most of the 8th's land, but most residents live in Pima County in the Tucson area. The district runs along more than 100 miles of Arizona's border with Mexico, and immigration and border security are major issues here.

Tucson is surrounded by mountain ranges and "sky islands" towering over the desert, but the majestic Santa Catalinas north of the city are the local landmark. Although population growth north of the city is slowing, water resources and water services remain major concerns in this arid region. South of the city, Green Valley is known for retirement communities, and nearly three-fourths of the population is older than 65.

Military jets flying past Tucson on their way to or from Davis-Monthan Air Force Base, southeast of the city, reveal one the area's economic engines: the military. Defense and aerospace contractor Raytheon Missile Systems is a major district employer. In Sierra Vista to the south, Fort Huachuca — home to the The U.S. Military Intelligence Center — employs thousands of contractors in high-technology fields.

Although its flagship campus is in the neighboring 7th, the University of Arizona has a campus in Sierra Vista and is one of the largest employers in the district. Service industries and tourism account for a significant portion of the district's economy.

In one of the state's closest presidential contests in 2008, Republican John McCain took 52 percent of the district's vote.

MAJOR INDUSTRY
Service, manufacturing, military, aerospace

MILITARY BASES
Davis-Monthan Air Force Base, 5,998 military, 1,486 civilian (2007); Fort Huachuca (Army), 5,472 military, 2,638 civilian (2007)

CITIES
Tucson (pt.), 256,535; Casas Adobes (unincorporated), 54,011; Catalina Foothills (unincorporated), 53,794; Sierra Vista, 37,775

NOTABLE
Tombstone, "the town too tough to die," was notorious for its boomtown lawlessness in the late 1800s.

ARKANSAS

Gov. Mike Beebe (D)

Pronounced: BEE-bee
First elected: 2006
Length of term: 4 years
Term expires: 1/11
Salary: $87,352
Phone: (501) 682-2345

Residence: Searcy
Born: Dec. 28, 1946; Amagon, Ark.
Religion: Episcopalian
Family: Wife, Ginger Beebe; three children
Education: Arkansas State U., B.A. 1968 (political science); U. of Arkansas, J.D. 1972
Military service: Army Reserve, 1968-74
Career: Lawyer
Political highlights: Ark. Senate, 1983-2003 (president pro tempore, 2001-03); Ark. attorney general, 2003-07

Election results:
2006 GENERAL

Mike Beebe (D)	430,765	55.6%
Asa Hutchinson (R)	315,040	40.7%
Rod Bryan (I)	15,767	2.0%
Jim Lendall (GREEN)	12,774	1.6%

Lt. Gov. Bill Halter (D)

First elected: 2006
Length of term: 4 years
Term expires: 1/11
Salary: $42,219
Phone: (501) 682-2144

LEGISLATURE

General Assembly: At least 60 calendar days January-March in odd-numbered years

Senate: 35 members, mixed 4-year and two-year terms
2009 ratios: 27 D, 8 R; 28 men, 7 women
Salary: $15,953
Phone: (501) 682-6107

House: 100 members, 2-year terms
2009 ratios: 72 D, 28 R; 75 men, 25 women
Salary: $14,765
Phone: (501) 682-7771

TERM LIMITS

Governor: 2 terms
Senate: 2 terms
House: 3 terms

URBAN STATISTICS

CITY	POPULATION
Little Rock	183,133
Fort Smith	80,268
North Little Rock	60,433
Fayetteville	58,047
Jonesboro	55,515

REGISTERED VOTERS

Voters do not register by party.

POPULATION

2008 population (est.)	2,855,390
2000 population	2,673,400
1990 population	2,350,725
Percent change (1990-2000)	+13.7%
Rank among states (2008)	32

Median age	36
Born in state	63.9%
Foreign born	2.8%
Violent crime rate	445/100,000
Poverty level	15.8%
Federal workers	20,543
Military	18,894

ELECTIONS

STATE ELECTION OFFICIAL
(501) 682-5070
DEMOCRATIC PARTY
(501) 374-2361
REPUBLICAN PARTY
(501) 372-7301

MISCELLANEOUS

Web: www.arkansas.gov
Capital: Little Rock

U.S. CONGRESS

Senate: 2 Democrats
House: 3 Democrats, 1 Republican

2000 Census Statistics by District

DIST.	2008 VOTE FOR PRESIDENT OBAMA	MCCAIN	WHITE	BLACK	ASIAN	HISP	MEDIAN INCOME	WHITE COLLAR	BLUE COLLAR	SERVICE INDUSTRY	OVER 64	UNDER 18	COLLEGE EDUCATION	RURAL	SQ. MILES
1	38%	59%	80%	17%	0%	2%	$28,940	49%	37%	14%	15%	26%	12%	56%	17,151
2	44	54	76	19	1	2	$37,221	60	26	14	12	25	23	34	5,922
3	33	64	87	2	1	6	$33,915	53	33	14	13	26	18	46	8,490
4	39	58	71	24	0	3	$29,675	48	37	15	16	25	13	55	20,505
STATE	39	59	79	16	1	3	$32,182	53	33	14	14	25	17	47	52,068
U.S.	53	46	69	12	4	13	$41,994	60	25	15	12	26	24	21	3,537,438

Sen. Blanche Lincoln (D)

Elected 1998; 2nd term

CAPITOL OFFICE
224-4843
lincoln.senate.gov
355 Dirksen Bldg. 20510-0404; fax 228-1371

COMMITTEES
Agriculture, Nutrition & Forestry
Energy & Natural Resources
Finance
  (Social Security, Pensions & Family Policy -
  chairwoman)
Special Aging

RESIDENCE
Little Rock

BORN
Sept. 30, 1960; Helena, Ark.

RELIGION
Episcopalian

FAMILY
Husband, Steve Lincoln; two children

EDUCATION
Randolph-Macon Woman's College, B.A. 1982
(biology)

CAREER
Lobbyist; congressional aide

POLITICAL HIGHLIGHTS
U.S. House, 1993-97

ELECTION RESULTS

2004 GENERAL
Blanche Lincoln (D)	580,973	55.8%
Jim Holt (R)	458,036	44.2%

2004 PRIMARY
Blanche Lincoln (D)	231,037	83.1%
Lisa Burks (D)	47,010	16.9%

PREVIOUS WINNING PERCENTAGES
1998 (55%); 1994 House Election (53%);
1992 House Election (70%)

Lincoln is a leading advocate for rural America and a key centrist who searches for bipartisan "common sense" solutions on contentious issues. Her outgoing personality and ability to relate to constituents make her a popular politician in a state that has voted Republican in the last three presidential elections.

The wife of a physician and the mother of twin boys entering their teenage years, Lincoln must juggle the demands of career and family. She carves out time from work to be with her children, taking on such tasks as chaperoning an overnight trip to the Washington Navy Yard with their Cub Scout troop.

She insists her balancing act is nothing special — that millions of Americans do the same thing, often with fewer resources. "I'm like any other working parent, and I try really hard not to forget that," she said, explaining why she has pushed for refundable child tax credits, Internet safety measures, health insurance for small businesses and other policies that benefit families.

Lincoln was among the early advocates for Democrats focusing on faith, family and pocketbook issues that appeal to rural voters — a strategy that helped the party recapture control of both chambers in 2006. She launched a legislative advocacy group, dubbed the Third Way, with Sens. Thomas R. Carper of Delaware and Evan Bayh of Indiana. Formed as a nonprofit lobbying group in January 2005, it pushes initiatives backed by moderate Democrats.

Lincoln often works closely with the state's junior senator, Democrat Mark Pryor, another moderate. The two participated in the "gang of 20" seeking a bipartisan consensus on energy legislation in 2008. She also sought a middle ground on Iraq in 2007, joining 13 other senators who sought a redeployment of U.S. troops without the timetables favored by many Democrats.

She has shown a willingness to join Republicans on major legislation. She sided with President George W. Bush on the 2001 education overhaul that tied federal funds to student performance on tests, and on the 2003 Medicare bill that created a prescription drug benefit for the elderly. She was one of just 11 Senate Democrats supporting the final Medicare measure, which she said "wasn't perfect" but represented a step in the right direction. She brings that same perspective to issues ranging from a Social Security overhaul to updating the Endangered Species Act, saying it is important to get things done even if compromises are required. "My philosophy is really that we don't produce a work of art here, we produce a work in progress," she said.

On the Finance Committee, she has complained about her colleagues' failure to pay for at least a portion of proposed tax breaks. "Pay for three-quarters of it. Pay for whatever," she said in 2008. "You gotta pay for something. You can't just not pay for any of this stuff."

Lincoln knows how to talk to her state's rural residents. Duck hunting is among her leisure pursuits, and she made clear she thought the Supreme Court did the right thing in 2008 when it declared that the Second Amendment guaranteed an individual's right to bear arms. She has fared equally well on Capitol Hill; in its annual survey of 1,700 congressional aides in September 2008, Washingtonian magazine ranked her as the "nicest" senator.

Raised in eastern Arkansas, where her family has farmed for seven generations, Lincoln describes herself as a "daughter of the east Arkansas Delta" and speaks passionately about the need to improve tax breaks, health care and other services in rural areas.

As a subcommittee chairwoman on the Agriculture Committee, she served on the conference committee that produced a major farm policy overhaul enacted in 2008. Her pro-agriculture positions won her a "Golden Plow" award in February 2008 from the American Farm Bureau Federation. But her views also have drawn fire from environmentalists and watchdog groups, who have criticized her staunch defense of farm subsidies.

In 2001, she helped win authorization of the eight-state Delta Regional Authority, modeled after the Appalachian Regional Commission, with initial funding of $20 million to spur economic development in the South. During a trip on Air Force One in 2001, when Bush lobbied her to support his first major tax cut, Lincoln requested disaster relief for Arkansas farmers and increased anti-poverty efforts in the Mississippi Delta region. "Agriculture is really my base, not only for my state's economy but also my heritage," she said.

Lincoln also is a strong supporter of nuclear power, saying it has been a reliable energy source for her constituents. She favors action to combat global warming, but has preached caution. When the Senate took up climate change legislation in 2008, she joined nine other Democrats from Midwestern and Southern states circulating a letter saying the measure should treat states equitably, contain costs, clarify the role of state and federal governments and ensure accountability for the money spent.

Shortly after graduating from college, Lincoln (then Blanche Lambert) interned briefly for Sotheby's auction house before getting her start on Capitol Hill in 1982 as a staff assistant for Democratic Arkansas Rep. Bill Alexander. (While Lincoln went east, her oldest sister headed west to Hollywood where she became a director of music videos and films.)

Lincoln left Capitol Hill after two years for a series of research jobs with lobbying firms. In 1991, she decided to challenge Alexander in a race that drew little notice until news broke that Alexander was among the top 10 abusers in the House overdraft scandal. In that scandal, members wrote checks from House bank accounts even if they didn't have money on deposit to cover them; because the accounts had overdraft protection, members essentially received interest-free loans. Lincoln took 61 percent of the vote in the 1992 primary and coasted to victory in November. She married Steve Lincoln, an obstetrician and gynecologist, in 1993, and won re-election to the House the next year.

Seen as a rising star in Arkansas, she decided not to seek a third House term in 1996 after becoming pregnant with twins. But her career pause did not last long. When Democratic Sen. Dale Bumpers announced his retirement in 1998, Lincoln jumped at the chance to run for a Senate seat. In the general election, she benefited from a stumble by her Republican opponent, state Sen. Fay Boozman, who said a woman was unlikely to become pregnant when she is raped because of hormonal responses in her body that he referred to as "God's little protective shield." Lincoln accused Boozman of insensitivity to rape victims, and he later apologized for the remarks. Lincoln won by 13 percentage points, becoming at age 38 the youngest woman ever elected to the Senate.

She told her constituents she was moving the family to Washington. "I want to watch my family grow up. I want to see their school plays. We'll be back here every holiday and every chance I get, but I'm not going to sacrifice my family for this job," she said. Her constituents approved; in 2004, Lincoln raised $6 million for her re-election campaign and won 56 percent of the vote to defeat Republican state Sen. Jim Holt.

Lincoln said she takes inspiration from Hattie Caraway of Arkansas, who in 1932 became the first woman popularly elected to the U.S. Senate and is the only other woman senator ever elected from Arkansas. Lincoln carried a quote from Caraway with her when she ran in 1998. It said, "If I can hold on to my sense of humor and a modicum of dignity, I shall have a wonderful time running for office whether I get there or not."

KEY VOTES

2008

Yes Prohibit discrimination based on genetic information

Yes Reauthorize farm and nutrition programs for five years

Yes Limit debate on "cap and trade" system for greenhouse gas emissions

No Allow lawsuits against companies that participated in warrantless wiretapping

Yes Limit debate on a bill to block a scheduled cut in Medicare payments to doctors

Yes Grant mortgage relief to homeowners and funding for Fannie Mae and Freddie Mac

Yes Approve a nuclear cooperation agreement with India

Yes Approve final $700 billion program to stabilize financial markets

No Allow consideration of a $14 billion auto industry loan package

2007

Yes Increase minimum wage by $2.10 an hour

Yes Limit debate on a comprehensive immigration bill

Yes Overhaul congressional lobbying and ethics rules for members and their staffs

Yes Limit debate on considering a bill to add House seats for the District of Columbia and Utah

Yes Limit debate on restoring habeas corpus rights to detainees

Yes Mandate minimum breaks for troops between deployments to Iraq or Afghanistan

Yes Override Bush veto of $23.2 billion water projects authorization bill

No Confirm Michael B. Mukasey as attorney general

Yes Limit debate on an energy policy overhaul containing $21.8 billion in tax incentives and reduced oil and gas subsidies

CQ VOTE STUDIES

	PARTY UNITY		PRESIDENTIAL SUPPORT	
	SUPPORT	OPPOSE	SUPPORT	OPPOSE
2008	81%	19%	41%	59%
2007	87%	13%	46%	54%
2006	81%	19%	59%	41%
2005	81%	19%	50%	50%
2004	79%	21%	72%	28%
2003	81%	19%	61%	39%
2002	61%	39%	89%	11%
2001	79%	21%	71%	29%
2000	80%	20%	84%	16%
1999	83%	17%	80%	20%

INTEREST GROUPS

	AFL-CIO	ADA	CCUS	ACU
2008	90%	80%	75%	8%
2007	89%	90%	55%	10%
2006	73%	90%	67%	8%
2005	79%	95%	89%	16%
2004	100%	95%	71%	20%
2003	77%	75%	78%	20%
2002	77%	70%	75%	40%
2001	88%	85%	79%	28%
2000	50%	70%	86%	20%
1999	89%	95%	65%	12%

Sen. Mark Pryor (D)

Elected 2002; 2nd term

CAPITOL OFFICE
224-2353
pryor.senate.gov
255 Dirksen Bldg. 20510; fax 228-0908

COMMITTEES
Appropriations
Commerce, Science & Transportation
(Consumer Affairs, Product Safety & Insurance - chairman)
Homeland Security & Governmental Affairs
(State, Local & Private Sector Preparedness - chairman)
Rules & Administration
Small Business & Entrepreneurship
Select Ethics

RESIDENCE
Little Rock

BORN
Jan. 10, 1963; Fayetteville, Ark.

RELIGION
Christian

FAMILY
Wife, Jill Pryor; two children

EDUCATION
U. of Arkansas, B.A. 1985 (history), J.D. 1988

CAREER
Lawyer

POLITICAL HIGHLIGHTS
Ark. House, 1991-95; sought Democratic nomination for Ark. attorney general, 1994; Ark. attorney general, 1999-2003

ELECTION RESULTS

2008 GENERAL

Mark Pryor (D)	804,678	79.5%
Rebekah Kennedy (GREEN)	207,076	20.5%

2008 PRIMARY

Mark Pryor (D)	unopposed

PREVIOUS WINNING PERCENTAGES
2002 (54%)

Pryor has emerged as a leader of his party's centrist faction, often serving as a magnetic hub for ad hoc coalitions that form to pressure the leaders of both parties to give an inch or two and resolve partisan stalemates.

By temperament, training and political necessity, he is a bridge builder, not a bomb thrower. His focus on finding middle ground often takes him well outside his party's liberal mainstream. "I'm not as partisan as maybe some would like me to be on our side. That's just not my motivation. I think we need people who can put that aside and try to get things done," Pryor said.

His approach has paid off politically. After former Arkansas Gov. Mike Huckabee ran unsuccessfully for the 2008 GOP presidential nomination and elected not to run for Senate, Pryor found himself as the only incumbent senator without major party opposition in 2008. With trademark modesty, he attributed his good fortune not to his record but to quirky Arkansas politics and offered to share his ample war chest with his colleagues.

Although he remains one of the youngest senators, Pryor is a fierce defender of Senate tradition. The son of David H. Pryor, a former Arkansas governor and three-term senator, he grew up at a time when the Senate was still a big family, with friendships that went beyond politics. He follows that model. Like his father, Mark Pryor moved his family to Washington when he first got elected, something few members of Congress do these days. His children are about the same age as those of his home-state Democratic colleague, Blanche Lincoln, and their families are close.

Pryor works to recruit new members to the cause of coalition building. Since 2004, he has sponsored a post-election orientation session in the Capitol for new senators with Democrat Thomas R. Carper of Delaware and Republicans Lamar Alexander of Tennessee and George V. Voinovich of Ohio. "I hope it will serve to acclimate them to work in a bipartisan way," he said.

Pryor gained a seat on the Appropriations Committee for the 111th Congress (2009-10), but he had to leave the Armed Services panel, where he had immersed himself in defense issues. His nuts-and-bolts approach to consensus building helped him clinch a measure extending military leaves from 15 to 20 days after 15-month tours of duty. He also helped to ensure that soldiers receiving combat pay can still qualify for the earned-income tax credit.

He is chairman of the Commerce, Science and Transportation Committee's Consumer Affairs panel, where during the 110th Congress (2007-08) he steered through a law to ban lead in children's products, protect whistleblowers and outlaw the use of certain plastic softeners, called phthalates, in toys. It grew out of a series of 2007 product recalls including Chinese-made toys that contained dangerous levels of lead. He also won permanent extension of the National Do Not Call Registry to limit telemarketing calls to consumers and enactment of a law imposing new safety standards for drain covers for pools.

Pryor made his first big mark in 2005 as one of seven Democrats and seven Republicans who formed a "Gang of 14" to end most Democratic filibusters of President George W. Bush's judicial nominees while blocking GOP leaders from using a parliamentary "nuclear option" to abolish such filibusters for good. That prompted many senators to seek him out for other bipartisan coalitions.

He joined one such group in mid-2008 to promote compromise legislation to address soaring energy costs and high gasoline prices, but election year politics made dealmaking difficult. A former state attorney general, Pryor maintains an interest in law enforcement and related issues, but he declined an invitation to join the Judiciary Committee, calling it a "partisan quagmire." Although he voted to confirm Attorney General Alberto R. Gonzales in 2005, he joined other Democrats in pressing for Gonzales' resignation in 2007 after evidence emerged that nine U.S. attorneys, including Bud Cummins, a U.S. attorney for eastern Arkansas, had been fired for political reasons.

Pryor's voting record sometimes puts him at odds with his party. During the 110th, he supported Bush's position more often than all but two other Democrats. But at the start of the 111th Congress (2009-10), he seemed inclined to stick with his party. He supported several bills put forward by the Democrats, including President Obama's push for an economic stimulus package. The Senate measure, which passed in February 2009, grew out of negotiations led by the chamber's moderates, and Pryor said after it passed: "While not perfect, the overall bill offers a balanced mix of tax cuts and investments. I'm optimistic it will provide the jolt to our economy that we need now and for the future."

He also voted for an expansion of a children's health insurance program, which Republicans said was too costly, and a bill making it easier for workers to sue for wage discrimination, one of the first measures signed into law by Obama.

But he will part with his party majority on social issues such as gun control and abortion rights. During his first campaign for the Senate, Pryor declined to declare himself either "pro-choice" or "pro-life," because he said neither label fits.

In 2006, he was one of just six Democrats to support a bill making it a crime to take a minor across state lines to obtain an abortion in order to circumvent state parental consent laws. And in another vote, Pryor declined to affirm the principles of *Roe v. Wade*, the Supreme Court case that legalized abortion. "I can't in good conscience say that *Roe v. Wade* should never be overturned," he told the Arkansas Democrat-Gazette.

Pryor is more sympathetic to business concerns than many Democrats. In 2005, he voted for the Central America Free Trade Agreement and an overhaul of bankruptcy law that clamped down on debtors. He calls himself a deficit hawk and in 2003 voted against an omnibus spending bill that contained nearly $300 million in projects for his state. In 2006, he was one of just two Democrats who sided with Republicans to block drought-relief funding that would have added $4.8 billion to the deficit.

Pryor was 15 when his family moved to the Washington area after his father's 1978 election to the Senate. He got an early start in politics, serving as a class president at Walt Whitman High School in Bethesda. He also was a congressional page, as his father had been. After high school, Pryor, hoping for a career in politics, returned to his hometown of Fayetteville and earned undergraduate and law degrees from the University of Arkansas.

Elected to the state House in 1990 at age 27, Pryor lost the Democratic primary for attorney general in 1994. Shortly thereafter, he was diagnosed with sarcoma, a rare form of cancer, and was unable to walk unassisted for more than a year after surgery. After the disease went into remission, Pryor relaunched his career. He was elected attorney general in 1998. In that position, he sued tobacco companies for smoking-related health care costs and made it possible for Arkansans to block telemarketing calls.

Pryor defeated conservative Republican Sen. Tim Hutchinson by 8 percentage points in 2002. Hutchinson, a Baptist minister who had campaigned as a "traditional values" Republican, had divorced his wife of 29 years and married a former Senate aide. Pryor never spoke directly about the divorce but touted his own commitment to his religion and his family.

KEY VOTES

2008
Yes Prohibit discrimination based on genetic information

Yes Reauthorize farm and nutrition programs for five years

Yes Limit debate on "cap and trade" system for greenhouse gas emissions

No Allow lawsuits against companies that participated in warrantless wiretapping

Yes Limit debate on a bill to block a scheduled cut in Medicare payments to doctors

Yes Grant mortgage relief to homeowners and funding for Fannie Mae and Freddie Mac

Yes Approve a nuclear cooperation agreement with India

Yes Approve final $700 billion program to stabilize financial markets

Yes Allow consideration of a $14 billion auto industry loan package

2007
Yes Increase minimum wage by $2.10 an hour

No Limit debate on a comprehensive immigration bill

Yes Overhaul congressional lobbying and ethics rules for members and their staffs

Yes Limit debate on considering a bill to add House seats for the District of Columbia and Utah

Yes Limit debate on restoring habeas corpus rights to detainees

Yes Mandate minimum breaks for troops between deployments to Iraq or Afghanistan

Yes Override Bush veto of $23.2 billion water projects authorization bill

No Confirm Michael B. Mukasey as attorney general

Yes Limit debate on an energy policy overhaul containing $21.8 billion in tax incentives and reduced oil and gas subsidies

CQ VOTE STUDIES

	PARTY UNITY		PRESIDENTIAL SUPPORT	
	SUPPORT	OPPOSE	SUPPORT	OPPOSE
2008	79%	21%	46%	54%
2007	81%	19%	46%	54%
2006	76%	24%	64%	36%
2005	80%	20%	58%	42%
2004	81%	19%	68%	32%
2003	84%	16%	60%	40%

INTEREST GROUPS

	AFL-CIO	ADA	CCUS	ACU
2008	100%	85%	75%	4%
2007	84%	70%	45%	12%
2006	73%	75%	75%	20%
2005	79%	90%	78%	24%
2004	92%	85%	71%	20%
2003	85%	70%	61%	30%

Rep. Marion Berry (D)

Elected 1996; 7th term

CAPITOL OFFICE
225-4076
www.house.gov/berry
2305 Rayburn Bldg. 20515-0401; fax 225-5602

COMMITTEES
Appropriations
Budget

RESIDENCE
Gillette

BORN
Aug. 27, 1942; Stuttgart, Ark.

RELIGION
Methodist

FAMILY
Wife, Carolyn Berry; two children

EDUCATION
U. of Arkansas, attended 1962 (pre-pharmacy);
U. of Arkansas, Little Rock, B.S. 1965 (pharmacy)

CAREER
Farmer; White House aide; pharmacist

POLITICAL HIGHLIGHTS
Gillett City Council, 1976-80; Ark. Soil and
Water Conservation Commission, 1986-94
(chairman, 1992)

ELECTION RESULTS

2008 GENERAL
Marion Berry (D)   unopposed

2008 PRIMARY
Marion Berry (D)   unopposed

2006 GENERAL

Marion Berry (D)	127,577	69.3%
Mickey Stumbaugh (R)	56,611	30.7%

PREVIOUS WINNING PERCENTAGES
2004 (67%); 2002 (67%); 2000 (60%); 1998 (100%);
1996 (53%)

Berry is known for his blunt speaking style and fierce advocacy of funding to benefit his home district, one of the country's poorest regions. He once described himself to a local audience as a "farmer who got more involved in politics than maybe I should have."

Yet he is also one of the House's most conservative Democrats, particularly on budget issues. He has been a longtime member of the Blue Dog Coalition, a group of fiscally conservative Democrats that intends to keep a check on just how far left the agenda of the newly expanded Democratic majority will go in concert with the Obama administration. Berry has a strong interest in a balanced budget and backs a mandate for a two-thirds majority vote to raise taxes.

He is vocal on the Blue Dogs' positions. In 2005, he drew attention during an acrimonious budget debate when he took issue with one Republican's characterization of the Blue Dogs as "lap dogs." Berry looked at Florida GOP Rep. Adam H. Putnam, then 31, and declared, "I wonder what you're going to be when you grow up." He then turned to Republican Jeb Hensarling of Texas and called him a "Howdy Doody-looking nimrod." The Arkansas Democrat-Gazette withheld its endorsement of Berry in the 2006 election, citing the name-calling incident.

Despite his fiscal conservatism, Berry takes advantage of his seat on the Appropriations Committee to aid his district. For fiscal 2008, he secured more than $123 million in earmarks, or funding set-asides for special projects, either alone or with other members, ranking him seventh in the House, according to Taxpayers for Common Sense. "Being an appropriator, I like earmarks, make no apologies for them," Berry told a local audience in a March 2008 speech.

Berry serves on the Appropriations subcommittee for transportation and housing projects. An original backer of the Delta Regional Authority, established in 2000 to spur economic development in the eight-state Mississippi Delta region, Berry continues to push for his state's share. One of Berry's goals is to bring commercial air service to the Ozark Regional Airport in Mountain Home.

He tends to be more conservative than his party on certain social issues. He backs gun owners' rights and a constitutional amendment permitting prayer in schools. But he aligns more closely with his party on the issue of health care. As Congress' only pharmacist, he can provide a unique perspective on on any health care legislation. He supports Democratic proposals to curb prescription drug and health care insurance costs.

In early 2009, Berry again supported a bill to expand the State Children's Health Insurance Program, which covers children from low-income families that do not qualify for Medicaid; President George W. Bush had twice vetoed bills similar to the one President Obama signed into law.

During the 110th Congress (2007-08), Berry also voted to reverse a planned cut in Medicare reimbursement rates for doctors. When Republicans objected to a 2007 bill forcing the federal government to negotiate with drugmakers for lower Medicare prescription drug costs, he said his GOP opponents "don't know turnip greens from butter beans about what they are talking about."

He sharply opposed the 2003 law establishing a drug benefit under Medicare, calling it "the single sorriest piece of legislation written in my lifetime." The then-majority Republicans refused to let Democrats attend negotiations on the final bill, and Berry and New York's Charles B. Rangel, who were Democratic conferees, dramatically barged into a room where the GOP-only talks were being held.

Berry had served on the Agriculture Committee until 2003 and can still help shape long-range farm policy from his positions as one of two vice chairmen of the Democratic Steering and Policy Committee and as a senior whip. He worked much of his life on a rice farm and co-owns with his brothers a soybean and rice farm in Gillett.

From 1995 through 2005, Berry's farm partnership received nearly $2.4 million in government farm subsidies, according to a USA Today report — the most for congressional members during that time period.

He joins lawmakers from other agribusiness states in supporting an end to the more than 45-year-old economic embargo against Cuba, a change that could create a new market for poultry, rice and soybeans.

As a youth, Berry recalls going with his father to the One Horse Store general store in the town of Bayou Meto, where men gathered to talk about politics. Though his father and grandfather never held elective office, Berry said their involvement in civic affairs set an example. While attending pharmacy school at the University of Arkansas, Berry frequented a family friend's drugstore in Little Rock, where many of the state's movers and shakers gathered.

He worked as a pharmacist for only two years after college, but that background appealed to party leaders years later when they tapped him to represent the rural and conservative factions among House Democrats on health care and prescription drug issues. Berry began his political career in 1976, when he was elected to the Gillett City Council.

In 1982, he became Bill Clinton's gubernatorial campaign coordinator in Arkansas County, a post he also held in 1986 and 1990. As governor, Clinton in 1986 named Berry to the state Soil and Water Conservation Commission, where he served eight years. He moved to Washington when Clinton was elected president and appointed him as a special assistant for agricultural trade and food assistance issues.

When Democratic Rep. Blanche Lincoln decided not to seek a third term in 1996 after becoming pregnant with twins, Berry won a close contest to fill her seat against Republican Warren Dupwe, a former Jonesboro city attorney who had held Lincoln to 53 percent of the vote in 1994. In a district that has not elected a Republican since Reconstruction, Berry has easily sailed through five re-election campaigns, usually winning by a 2-to-1 ratio or better. He was unopposed in 2008.

KEY VOTES

2008
Yes Delay consideration of Colombia free-trade agreement

Yes Override Bush veto of federal farm and nutrition programs reauthorization bill

Yes Overhaul surveillance laws and permit dismissal of suits against companies that conducted warrantless wiretapping

Yes Grant mortgage relief to homeowners and funding for Fannie Mae and Freddie Mac

Yes Approve initial $700 billion program to stabilize financial markets

Yes Approve final $700 billion program to stabilize financial markets

Yes Provide $14 billion in loans to automakers

2007
Yes Increase minimum wage by $2.10 an hour

Yes Approve $124.2 billion in emergency war spending and set goal for redeployment of troops from Iraq

No Reject federal contraceptive assistance to international family planning groups

Yes Override Bush veto of $23.2 billion water projects authorization bill

Yes Implement Peru free-trade agreement

Yes Approve energy policy overhaul with new fuel economy standards

Yes Clear $473.5 billion omnibus spending bill, including $70 billion for military operations

CQ VOTE STUDIES

	PARTY UNITY		PRESIDENTIAL SUPPORT	
	SUPPORT	OPPOSE	SUPPORT	OPPOSE
2008	96%	4%	21%	79%
2007	94%	6%	11%	89%
2006	76%	24%	50%	50%
2005	75%	25%	37%	63%
2004	81%	19%	36%	64%

INTEREST GROUPS

	AFL-CIO	ADA	CCUS	ACU
2008	86%	75%	56%	13%
2007	96%	90%	55%	8%
2006	93%	50%	73%	56%
2005	87%	65%	63%	52%
2004	100%	60%	45%	36%

ARKANSAS 1
Northeast – Jonesboro, West Memphis

Settled in the Natural State's northeastern corner, the 1st stretches from the Mississippi Delta through fertile plains and into the hilly north where the Ozark Mountains begin. The district, the poorest in the state, borders Missouri to the north and Tennessee and Mississippi to the east.

Rising fuel and transportation costs may harm farming operations in the alluvial cotton delta and fertile rice lands of the farming-dependent district. Jonesboro, the district's most populous city, is the hub for northeast Arkansas' agricultural production. Riceland Foods, one of the world's leading rice millers, is based in Stuttgart, and cattle and poultry farms prosper in the north. A volatile market may endanger steel production plants near Blytheville and manufacturing plants in Stuttgart, Jonesboro and Batesville.

Poverty is most notably present in the largely white, older populations in the northwest and within the former sharecropping communities in the Democratic Delta. The Delta Regional Authority, which aims to increase economic development in the areas around the Mississippi River, gives government support to some of the 1st's nonprofit organizations and local communities. These communities continually rank below national averages, with many residents undereducated and unemployed.

The White River National Wildlife Refuge, located in the southeastern portion of the 1st and shared with the 4th, is one of the few areas in the district that routinely attracts tourists. Each year, thousands of fishermen, hunters and watchers travel to the migratory bird preserve.

Despite electing few Republicans at either the state or federal level, the socially conservative and heavily Christian 1st gave John McCain 59 percent of its 2008 presidential vote. Western Lonoke County, home to Little Rock suburbanites and some military personnel, leans Republican, although no Republican has represented the district since 1875.

MAJOR INDUSTRY
Agriculture, manufacturing, steel production

CITIES
Jonesboro, 55,515; West Memphis, 27,666; Paragould, 22,017; Blytheville, 18,272; Cabot, 15,261; Forrest City, 14,774

NOTABLE
Hattie Caraway, who in 1932 became the first woman elected to the U.S. Senate, lived in Jonesboro.

Rep. Vic Snyder (D)

Elected 1996; 7th term

Snyder pursues his focus on U.S. troops and veterans with quiet determination, avoiding the limelight and partisan sniping that often consumes Congress. He often uses his floor speeches to praise others. "Every little tiff doesn't have to turn into a bar fight," he said during one Armed Services meeting in July 2007 when members fell to squabbling.

Snyder is a former Marine who served 13 months in Vietnam at the height of the war in the late 1960s. He holds degrees in both medicine and law, and as a family-practice doctor has volunteered extensively in refugee camps abroad.

His seats on both the Armed Services and Veterans' Affairs committees position him well to press his twin goals of ensuring U.S. troops are fully prepared for combat and that they are properly recognized for their service once they return home. He is a leading champion of the GI Bill and a staunch advocate for improved benefits for members of the National Guard and reserves.

He also is a legislator who sees the big picture and asks questions that go beyond the nitty-gritty of the bill before him. As chairman of the Armed Services Subcommittee on Oversight and Investigations, Snyder held a series of hearings during the 110th Congress (2007-08) on developments in Iraq after President George W. Bush in 2007 sent an additional 21,000 troops there. But he ranged well beyond specific war-related topics, launching a new set of hearings in mid-2008 titled "A New U.S. Grand Strategy." It was, he admitted, an amorphous topic. "The term 'grand strategy' is one that I think several of us on the committee are still trying to get our hands around," he said. "Particularly, do we currently have one? Do we need one? And if so, what should it be?"

In the 111th Congress (2009-10), Armed Services will have to grapple with cuts to the defense budget in response to the nation's economic crisis. Even before the meltdown on Wall Street, many lawmakers predicted a slowdown in defense spending after 11 years of increases. The committee is likely to decrease spending on future weapons systems, Snyder said, adding that keeping weapons within budget "is something we've really struggled with as a country."

In 2008, he hailed the enactment of a war spending bill that greatly expanded benefits under the GI Bill and granted equal veterans' education benefits to Guard and reserve members who have served at least three years on active duty.

During his own medical training, Snyder worked at two Veterans Administration hospitals, and he is a champion of the VA health care system. A member of the Veterans' Affairs Health Subcommittee, Snyder has pushed for better care for Iraq War veterans. But he also has pressured the Defense and Veterans Affairs departments to do more to address Gulf War syndrome, a mysterious range of ailments reported by veterans of the 1991 military campaign in the Persian Gulf.

In the 108th Congress (2003-04), Snyder fought a Pentagon plan to issue a single medal for service in Afghanistan and Iraq, successfully pressing a bill for separate medals. "As a Vietnam veteran and former Marine, one of the first things I look for on a soldier's uniform is the campaign ribbon that notes where the soldier served," he said.

Snyder counts as a major achievement his role in the 106th Congress (1999-2000) in overturning a Medicare regulation that halted coverage for immunosuppressive drugs after less than four years. When organ transplant

CAPITOL OFFICE
225-2506
www.house.gov/snyder
2210 Rayburn Bldg. 20515-0402; fax 225-5903

COMMITTEES
Armed Services
  (Oversight & Investigations - chairman)
Veterans' Affairs
Joint Economic

RESIDENCE
Little Rock

BORN
Sept. 27, 1947; Medford, Ore.

RELIGION
Methodist

FAMILY
Wife, Betsy Singleton; four children

EDUCATION
Willamette U., B.A. 1975 (chemistry);
U. of Oregon Health Sciences Center, M.D. 1979;
U. of Arkansas, Little Rock, J.D. 1988

MILITARY SERVICE
Marine Corps, 1967-69

CAREER
Physician

POLITICAL HIGHLIGHTS
Ark. Senate, 1991-96

ELECTION RESULTS

2008 GENERAL
Vic Snyder (D)	212,303	76.5%
Deb McFarland (GREEN)	64,398	23.2%

2008 PRIMARY
Vic Snyder (D)	unopposed

2006 GENERAL
Vic Snyder (D)	124,871	60.5%
Andy Mayberry (R)	81,432	39.5%

PREVIOUS WINNING PERCENTAGES
2004 (58%); 2002 (93%); 2000 (58%); 1998 (58%);
1996 (52%)

recipients stopped buying the expensive drugs, it sometimes led to organ rejection and another costly transplant — which Medicare covered.

Over the years, Snyder has been among the lawmakers from agribusiness states agitating for an end to the more than 45-year-old economic embargo against Cuba, a change that could create a new market for poultry, rice and soybeans. He contends that U.S. credibility is undermined by the inconsistency of trading with communist-led China and Vietnam.

Snyder's parents divorced when he was 2, and his mother raised him in Medford, Ore. After high school, Snyder attended Willamette University in Salem, Ore., for two years, then dropped out to join the Marines. He served a year in Vietnam, and after he returned home, he spent four years working odd jobs. He was an aide at a Colorado school for children with mental health problems and also worked at a gas station. Returning to Oregon, he became an emergency medical technician, which triggered his interest in medicine. He worked in a nursing home and as a part-time nurse's aide at a hospital.

He went back to Willamette University in 1973, earned a degree in chemistry, and then went to medical school at the University of Oregon Health Sciences Center in Portland. Under the GI Bill, most of his education was paid for by the government. Snyder did his residency in Little Rock, then settled in Arkansas as a family practitioner. He served as a volunteer doctor in refugee camps abroad, often for months at a time, in Thailand, Honduras, Sudan and Sierra Leone.

Snyder earned his law degree in 1988, and although he's never practiced, he put the knowledge to use as a member of the Arkansas Senate from 1991 to 1996. He sponsored two strict drunken-driving bills that became law.

When Democratic Rep. Ray Thornton announced his retirement from Congress in 1996, Snyder entered the 2nd District race as an underdog, facing two tough opponents in the primary. He finished second to prosecuting attorney Mark Stodola but surged to a narrow victory in the runoff. In the fall, he embraced national Democratic themes, pledging to oppose GOP initiatives on Medicare, education and the environment. He squeaked past Republican Bud Cummins, a businessman and lawyer, with 52 percent of the vote as President Bill Clinton carried the 2nd District by 18 percentage points. He has since won re-election by double-digit margins.

In 2003, Snyder ended his long bachelorhood by marrying the Rev. Betsy Singleton, pastor of the United Methodist Church in Little Rock. That same year, he underwent heart surgery for a faulty mitral valve. The Snyders had a son in 2006, named Charles Pennington Snyder, Penn for short. His wife delivered triplets, all boys, in December 2008.

KEY VOTES

2008

Yes Delay consideration of Colombia free-trade agreement

Yes Override Bush veto of federal farm and nutrition programs reauthorization bill

Yes Overhaul surveillance laws and permit dismissal of suits against companies that conducted warrantless wiretapping

Yes Grant mortgage relief to homeowners and funding for Fannie Mae and Freddie Mac

Yes Approve initial $700 billion program to stabilize financial markets

Yes Approve final $700 billion program to stabilize financial markets

? Provide $14 billion in loans to automakers

2007

Yes Increase minimum wage by $2.10 an hour

Yes Approve $124.2 billion in emergency war spending and set goal for redeployment of troops from Iraq

No Reject federal contraceptive assistance to international family planning groups

Yes Override Bush veto of $23.2 billion water projects authorization bill

Yes Implement Peru free-trade agreement

Yes Approve energy policy overhaul with new fuel economy standards

Yes Clear $473.5 billion omnibus spending bill, including $70 billion for military operations

CQ VOTE STUDIES

	PARTY UNITY		PRESIDENTIAL SUPPORT	
	SUPPORT	OPPOSE	SUPPORT	OPPOSE
2008	97%	3%	20%	80%
2007	95%	5%	12%	88%
2006	86%	14%	45%	55%
2005	86%	14%	33%	67%
2004	85%	15%	41%	59%

INTEREST GROUPS

	AFL-CIO	ADA	CCUS	ACU
2008	100%	90%	67%	5%
2007	96%	85%	60%	4%
2006	93%	75%	43%	17%
2005	80%	80%	59%	8%
2004	80%	95%	57%	20%

ARKANSAS 2
Central — Little Rock

An urban hub in a relatively rural state, the state capital of Little Rock is the focal point of the 2nd District. More than half of the district's population is concentrated in the Little Rock area, the governmental and economic center of the state. The district has the state's largest white-collar population and its highest median household income.

Despite national economic instability, Little Rock's unemployment rates remain low and some retail and manufacturing businesses are expanding. A University of Arkansas campus and the system's medical school lead a regional health care, education and research hub, employing thousands of district residents.

Little Rock's River Market District is a magnet for partygoers looking for club and bar venues, and the Quapaw Quarter's Victorian buildings draw historians to downtown. The nearby Clinton Presidential Center is also along the Arkansas River, and the entertainment district now spills across the Big Dam Bridge to North Little Rock where the 18,000-seat multipurpose Alltel Arena is located.

Saline County is south and west of Little Rock's Pulaski County, along the foothills of the Ouachita Mountains. Perry and Faulkner County to the north have gained residents, with Republicans increasing in popularity as the suburbs in all three counties expand. White County is home to Church of Christ-affiliated Harding University.

Democratic support is concentrated in Pulaski County, among poor and working-class neighborhoods, and in strong union and university populations. Although the district twice supported favorite-son Bill Clinton in presidential elections, Republican George W. Bush narrowly carried it in both 2000 and 2004, and John McCain won with a nearly 10-percentage-point margin over Democrat Barack Obama in 2008.

MAJOR INDUSTRY
Government, higher education, retail, health care, military

MILITARY BASES
Little Rock Air Force Base, 5,021 military, 773 civilian (2007)

CITIES
Little Rock, 183,133; North Little Rock, 60,433; Conway, 43,167

NOTABLE
Little Rock Air Force Base has the largest C-130 training and airlift facility in the world.

Rep. John Boozman (R)

Elected 2001; 4th full term

CAPITOL OFFICE
225-4301
www.boozman.house.gov
1519 Longworth Bldg. 20515; fax 225-5713

COMMITTEES
Foreign Affairs
Transportation & Infrastructure
Veterans' Affairs

RESIDENCE
Rogers

BORN
Dec. 10, 1950; Shreveport, La.

RELIGION
Baptist

FAMILY
Wife, Cathy Boozman; three children

EDUCATION
U. of Arkansas, attended 1972; Southern
College of Optometry, O.D. 1977

CAREER
Optometrist; cattle farm owner

POLITICAL HIGHLIGHTS
Rogers Public Schools Board of Education,
1994-2001

ELECTION RESULTS

2008 GENERAL

John Boozman (R)	215,196	78.5%
Abel Noah Tomlinson (GREEN)	58,850	21.5%

2008 PRIMARY

John Boozman (R)	unopposed

2006 GENERAL

John Boozman (R)	125,039	62.2%
Woodrow Anderson (D)	75,885	37.8%

PREVIOUS WINNING PERCENTAGES
2004 (59%); 2002 (99%); 2001 Special Election (56%)

Boozman, the lone optometrist in Congress, enjoys another distinction he often jokes about: "I am in a unique situation. I am the senior Republican and the junior Republican from Arkansas." Every other House member and both senators from the state are Democrats.

Boozman (BOZE-man) represents a rural and small-town district covering the northwest corner of Arkansas. It has been in GOP hands for more than 40 years; its footnote in history is its snub of Bill Clinton in 1974, when the future Democratic president was defeated in a bid for the House seat, his first loss of a political race.

Boozman is still a bit amazed to find himself where he is. He had never been to Washington, D.C., before he won his 2001 special-election race to succeed GOP Rep. Asa Hutchinson, who took a job in the George W. Bush administration. "I didn't think I would ever see a president firsthand, much less be sitting in the limo making small talk while he sticks his face to the window and is waving to everybody," Boozman said.

He has patterned his career after that of former Republican Rep. John Paul Hammerschmidt, who held the seat from 1967 until 1993. He focuses intently on parochial issues, including those affecting two big companies headquartered in the 3rd District, Wal-Mart Stores Inc. in Bentonville and Tyson Foods Inc. in Springdale, as well as the University of Arkansas.

In Boozman's first term, GOP leaders gave him a seat on the Transportation and Infrastructure Committee, and in 2007 he became the top Republican on its Water Resources and Environment Subcommittee. He backed the big reauthorization of the Water Resources and Development Act that Congress enacted later in the year over President Bush's veto, joining in the override effort.

Boozman earlier used his committee post to secure politically popular funding for the Interstate 49 project. Planned to be a north-south artery between Kansas City, Mo., and port cities in Louisiana, it would cut through western Arkansas. With the panel gearing up to write a multi-year surface transportation bill in the 111th Congress (2009-10), Boozman vows to "ensure that Arkansas receives as much money as possible specifically designated for projects in the 3rd District...as well as for the state's highway needs."

Boozman also wants to secure federal funds for the Northwest Arkansas Regional Airport and promote the port system capabilities of Fort Smith and Russellville, two growing communities on the Arkansas River.

A social and fiscal conservative in tune with his district and the national GOP, he nonetheless works comfortably with Democrats on issues of concern to his district. "Partisanship doesn't build roads, create jobs or feed families. Common-sense ideas do," he said. But occasionally, his efforts to look out for 3rd District interests put him at sharp odds with Democrats.

Boozman came under fire in March 2005 for an amendment to the year's surface transportation bill that would have extended the maximum workday for truckers to 16 hours, including an unpaid two-hour break. The issue was of great interest to trucking-dependent retailers such as Wal-Mart. Critics dubbed Boozman's proposal the "sweatshop-on-wheels amendment," and Boozman was eventually forced to withdraw it.

Boozman said that though he grew up among Southern Democrats, he was drawn to the Republican Party by President Reagan in the 1980s. Boozman calls himself "pro-life, pro-gun, conservative on social issues and pretty conservative fiscally."

A member of the Foreign Affairs Committee, he focuses on trade issues and ways to combat drug smuggling. He has pushed for more federal aid to stamp out the rapid growth of domestic methamphetamine drug labs. He also advocates ending the U.S. trade embargo against Cuba, a priority for the state's rice and poultry farmers who seea potentially lucrative market.

On the Veterans' Affairs panel, Boozman is the senior Republican on the Economic Opportunity Subcommittee. In the 109th Congress (2005-06), Boozman and Chairwoman Stephanie Herseth Sandlin of South Dakota pushed through the House a bill to require the Veterans Affairs Department to set annual contracting goals for small businesses owned by former military servicemembers. In the 110th (2007-08), he backed an expansion of GI Bill education benefits for veterans and championed a provision to allow spouses of severely disabled vets to use their GI Bill benefits.

Boozman is the second of three children of an Air Force master sergeant. The family moved around with his father's Air Force assignments, and Boozman spent his early childhood in London, attending an all-boys British school. Eventually, the family returned to Fort Smith, Ark., where it had roots dating to the late 19th century. The 6-foot-3-inch Boozman was a standout football player at Northside High School in Fort Smith and went on to be an offensive tackle for the University of Arkansas' vaunted Razorbacks.

Boozman was going to be a dentist until his brother, Fay, who was studying ophthalmology, convinced him to go to optometry school so they could practice together. They co-founded Boozman-Hof Regional Eye Clinic in 1977 in their hometown of Rogers.

Fay Boozman, who died in a March 2005 accident while working on his farm in Rogers, was always the higher-profile politician. He had served in the state Senate and eventually ran against Democrat Blanche Lincoln in the 1998 open-seat U.S. Senate race, but lost. John Boozman started his political career on the Rogers school board, where he served roughly six years.

When Bush appointed Hutchinson to head the Drug Enforcement Administration, Fay Boozman passed on a chance to seek the seat. John jumped in. He finished first in the four-candidate GOP primary but was forced into a runoff by state Sen. Gunner DeLay, a distant cousin of then-Majority Leader Tom DeLay, a Texas Republican.

Endorsed by GOP Gov. Mike Huckabee, Boozman won both the primary runoff and the 2001 special election. He has cemented his grip on the seat since then. He ran without major-party opposition in 2008.

KEY VOTES

2008

No   Delay consideration of Colombia free-trade agreement

Yes Override Bush veto of federal farm and nutrition programs reauthorization bill

Yes Overhaul surveillance laws and permit dismissal of suits against companies that conducted warrantless wiretapping

No   Grant mortgage relief to homeowners and funding for Fannie Mae and Freddie Mac

Yes Approve initial $700 billion program to stabilize financial markets

Yes Approve final $700 billion program to stabilize financial markets

No   Provide $14 billion in loans to automakers

2007

Yes Increase minimum wage by $2.10 an hour

No   Approve $124.2 billion in emergency war spending and set goal for redeployment of troops from Iraq

Yes Reject federal contraceptive assistance to international family planning groups

Yes Override Bush veto of $23.2 billion water projects authorization bill

Yes Implement Peru free-trade agreement

Yes Approve energy policy overhaul with new fuel economy standards

Yes Clear $473.5 billion omnibus spending bill, including $70 billion for military operations

CQ VOTE STUDIES

	PARTY UNITY		PRESIDENTIAL SUPPORT	
	SUPPORT	OPPOSE	SUPPORT	OPPOSE
2008	95%	5%	71%	29%
2007	91%	9%	74%	26%
2006	97%	3%	92%	8%
2005	96%	4%	77%	23%
2004	96%	4%	82%	18%

INTEREST GROUPS

	AFL-CIO	ADA	CCUS	ACU
2008	13%	25%	94%	84%
2007	13%	15%	90%	92%
2006	21%	5%	100%	92%
2005	15%	0%	93%	96%
2004	13%	10%	100%	96%

ARKANSAS 3

Northwest – Fort Smith, Fayetteville

Arkansas' hilly northwest subscribes to a blend of rugged and religious conservatism rooted in both mountain ranges and suburbia. Rough terrain gives way to retail outlets, interstates and the Arkansas River valley at the southern edge of the district.

Bentonville, Rogers, Springdale and Fayetteville, all in the state's northwest corner, sit at the commercial hub of the district. Hometown giants Wal-Mart in Bentonville and Tyson Foods stores in Springdale provide jobs, as does the University of Arkansas' flagship campus in Fayetteville, but this fast-growing metropolitan corridor is not immune to economic instability. Further south, Fort Smith — the state's manufacturing hub, focusing on appliances and home improvement products — has experienced significant job losses and a housing market downturn.

The 3rd has prospered from tourism. Anchored by the lush Ozark National Forest, located in the district's south, and Beaver Lake, located in the north, the area attracts thousands of visitors each year. Outdoor enthusiasts take in the gorgeous scenery and history buffs visit Civil War sites

such as Pea Ridge National Military Park, as well as the museums and landmarks in Fort Smith, which cover everything from the founding of the namesake fort to the Belle Grove Historic District.

Religion-oriented tourism in Carroll County conveys the conservative, Bible Belt character of the district. The small Ozarks town of Eureka Springs boasts the Thorncrown Chapel, nearby creation-themed Museum of Earth History and an outdoor drama, The Great Passion Play, which is centered around the 67-foot-tall Christ of the Ozarks statue.

The 3rd is the most Republican district in the state, giving more than 64 percent support to John McCain in 2008. It was the state's only district to withhold hearty support from native son Bill Clinton in 1996.

MAJOR INDUSTRY

Retail, tourism, agriculture, manufacturing

CITIES

Fort Smith, 80,268; Fayetteville, 58,047; Springdale, 45,798; Rogers, 38,829; Russellville, 23,682; Bentonville, 19,730

NOTABLE

Miss Laura's Social Club, now the Fort Smith visitor's center, was the first former bordello to be listed on the National Register of Historic Places.

Rep. Mike Ross (D)

Elected 2000; 5th term

CAPITOL OFFICE
225-3772
www.ross.house.gov
2436 Rayburn Bldg. 20515-0404; fax 225-1314

COMMITTEES
Energy & Commerce
Foreign Affairs

RESIDENCE
Prescott

BORN
Aug. 2, 1961; Texarkana, Ark.

RELIGION
Methodist

FAMILY
Wife, Holly Ross; two children

EDUCATION
Texarkana Community College, attended 1981;
U. of Arkansas, Little Rock, B.A. 1987 (political science)

CAREER
Pharmacy owner; wholesale drug and medical supply company field representative; aide to lieutenant governor

POLITICAL HIGHLIGHTS
Nevada County Quorum Court, 1983-85;
Ark. Senate, 1991-2001

ELECTION RESULTS

2008 GENERAL

Mike Ross (D)	203,178	86.2%
Joshua Drake (GREEN)	32,603	13.8%

2008 PRIMARY

Mike Ross (D)	unopposed

2006 GENERAL

Mike Ross (D)	128,236	74.7%
Joe Ross (R)	43,360	25.3%

PREVIOUS WINNING PERCENTAGES
2004 (100%); 2002 (61%); 2000 (51%)

Ross brings a moderate tone to the Democratic contingent in the House, advocating a conservative stance on fiscal and social issues but voting in step with colleagues on issues that impact his rural, economically disadvantaged district. "I am committed to providing a helping hand, but not a handout," he said. "It's about helping those who want to help themselves."

Ross is a member of the Blue Dog Coalition, a group of roughly 50 fiscally conservative Democrats, and served as the group's communications co-chairman in the 110th Congress (2007-08). He repeatedly warns fellow Democrats not to abandon fiscally conservative policies, and in early 2007 he touted the reinstatement of pay-as-you-go budget rules that require offsets to any new direct spending or tax cuts. And with expectations set for the Obama administration's initiatives on a variety of issues, Ross is expected to take a role in pushing the brakes if he thinks spending gets too high.

Yet Ross voted for the $787 billion economic stimulus bill in February 2009. The Daily Siftings Herald in Arkadelphia quoted him saying that recession was "the most significant event to occur since 9/11...and quite frankly the most challenging. I don't think we can sit by and idly do nothing."

In late 2008, he supported two $700 billion bills to help the ailing financial services industry. After the second became law, he said the bipartisan solution was necessary to prevent a domino effect that could force the country into a 1930s-era economic depression. "No one of us wanted to vote for it, and it wasn't politically popular, but it was one of those things you have to put politics on the side for and do what is in the best interest of the country," Ross said.

During the 110th, Ross advocated improved fiscal responsibility to bring down the national deficit and address the economic crisis. In December 2007, he was one of 64 Democrats who opposed a bill to provide a one-year "patch" exempting an additional 21 million people from the alternative minimum tax, which was originally intended to target only wealthy taxpayers but was not indexed for inflation. Ross criticized the exemption, which was signed into law, for violating pay-as-you-go rules. But he voted for a similar bill in 2008.

He has consistently opposed the annual cost-of-living pay raise for lawmakers until the minimum wage is increased. He directs the pay raise to a scholarship fund for two 4th District college students. In the 110th, he supported a bill to increase the $5.15 hourly minimum wage to $7.25 over two years.

As a member of the Energy and Commerce Committee, Ross hopes to attract new industries to revive the economy in his district, where about 25 percent of the residents live below the poverty line. A member of the Energy and Environment Subcommittee, he plans to push for more energy research initiatives leading to the development of alternative, renewable fuels. He backed the 2008 farm bill, a $289 billion measure to reauthorize agriculture and nutrition programs for five years. Ross touted the measure's $1 billion in loan guarantees for the development of refineries that process renewable fuels and $7.9 billion to enable farmers to convert highly erodible cropland and other environmentally sensitive land to vegetative cover.

A former pharmacy owner, Ross also sits on the Health Subcommittee, where he pushes for improvements to rural health care. In 2008, he voted to reverse a planned cut in Medicare reimbursement rates for doctors. In 2009, he supported the expansion of the State Children's Health Insurance Program, which covers children from low-income families that do not qualify for Medicaid.

In 2009, Ross picked up a seat on the Foreign Affairs Committee, where he hopes to keep an eye on the global economy. "While our armed forces do a terrific job of protecting our country, national security involves much more than military might," he said. "The economy and security of this nation are dependent on working with our allies around the world."

Ross attracted national attention in 2006 when he criticized the Federal Emergency Management Agency for parking more than 10,000 new manufactured homes in a hay meadow near the airport in Hope, Ark., after the homes were not delivered to Hurricane Katrina victims in Louisiana. Ross and Arkansas Democratic Sen. Mark Pryor later sought approval for the homes to be sold or donated to local governments and nonprofit organizations.

On certain social issues, Ross aligns with the GOP. He opposes same-sex marriage and abortion rights, though he voted to lift restrictions on federally funded embryonic stem cell research. In 2007, he was one of 25 Democrats to oppose a bill to prohibit job discrimination based on sexual orientation. An avid hunter, Ross also is a fierce opponent of gun control legislation. But he backs laws to keep weapons out of schools. Ross has led efforts to overturn gun control laws in the District of Columbia.

Ross was born in Texarkana, the son of two schoolteachers who encouraged him to get involved in public service. At the age of 21, Ross drove Bill Clinton around the state for more than a year as the future president campaigned for governor and Ross ran for a term on Nevada County's legislative body, the Quorum Court. Both of them won. "It was me and him in a Chevy Citation," Ross recalls. "I learned a lot...He never forgot where he was from, and he never forgot about trying to help the little people."

Ross worked his way through college as a radio announcer and graduated at 25, while working as a top aide to Arkansas' lieutenant governor, Winston Bryant. In 1988, he was a regional coordinator for Democrat Michael S. Dukakis' presidential campaign. He worked as a field representative for a wholesale drug and medical supply company, and later, he and his pharmacist wife, Holly Ross, opened their own pharmacy in the small town of Prescott. They sold it in 2007.

He stayed active in politics, winning a 1990 election to the state Senate. In 2000, he challenged four-term GOP Rep. Jay Dickey. Ross was widely regarded as the front-runner for the Democratic nomination but faced three opponents in a bitter primary. Two of his primary foes later endorsed Dickey. Ross' win, by 2 percentage points, was the Democrats' only victory over an incumbent outside California that year.

Some Republicans explained away Dickey's defeat as the revenge of Clinton, whose impeachment Dickey had supported in 1998. Ross handily defeated Dickey in 2002 with 61 percent of the vote, and he has easily won re-election since.

KEY VOTES

2008
Yes Delay consideration of Colombia free-trade agreement
Yes Override Bush veto of federal farm and nutrition programs reauthorization bill
Yes Overhaul surveillance laws and permit dismissal of suits against companies that conducted warrantless wiretapping
Yes Grant mortgage relief to homeowners and funding for Fannie Mae and Freddie Mac
Yes Approve initial $700 billion program to stabilize financial markets
Yes Approve final $700 billion program to stabilize financial markets
Yes Provide $14 billion in loans to automakers

2007
Yes Increase minimum wage by $2.10 an hour
Yes Approve $124.2 billion in emergency war spending and set goal for redeployment of troops from Iraq
No   Reject federal contraceptive assistance to international family planning groups
Yes Override Bush veto of $23.2 billion water projects authorization bill
Yes Implement Peru free-trade agreement
Yes Approve energy policy overhaul with new fuel economy standards
Yes Clear $473.5 billion omnibus spending bill, including $70 billion for military operations

CQ VOTE STUDIES

	PARTY UNITY		PRESIDENTIAL SUPPORT	
	SUPPORT	OPPOSE	SUPPORT	OPPOSE
2008	95%	5%	24%	76%
2007	89%	11%	11%	89%
2006	74%	26%	53%	47%
2005	78%	22%	49%	51%
2004	82%	18%	53%	47%

INTEREST GROUPS

	AFL-CIO	ADA	CCUS	ACU
2008	93%	85%	67%	12%
2007	96%	85%	70%	28%
2006	86%	50%	67%	60%
2005	85%	75%	65%	52%
2004	87%	65%	62%	44%

ARKANSAS 4
South — Pine Bluff, Hot Springs

Planted across most of Arkansas' southern half, the 4th is the state's largest district in area and features an abundant timber industry, small farming communities and one of the state's most lucrative tourist areas.

Local tourism revolves around Hot Springs and the nearby Ouachita Mountains. Hot Springs, heralded as America's first resort, attracts tourists to its national park, and visitors hope the warm waters that were once used to treat illness will still promote relaxation.

The timber industry, located mostly in the district's western portion in and around the Ouachita Mountains, employs thousands of district residents. East of Hot Springs, the Pine Bluff Arsenal, which once produced the nation's supply of biological weapons, is home to an emergency preparedness center and a center for toxicological research, as well as a chemical weapons disposal facility.

Rice, soybeans, cotton and rural poverty characterize the eastern edge of the 4th, where many Mississippi River communities have majority

black populations. Most of Arkansas' catfish production — a prime aquaculture product of the state — is in Chicot County.

Democrats receive their most faithful support from the Delta region. Republicans fare better in the district's oil- and chemical-producing south, as well as in military and white-collar areas near Pine Bluff and Hot Springs. The socially conservative 4th elected its first GOP representative of the 20th century in 1992, but overwhelmingly supported Hope-born and Hot Springs-raised Bill Clinton in both of his presidential bids. The district gave John McCain 58 percent of its 2008 presidential vote, but most of the area's state legislators are Democrats.

MAJOR INDUSTRY
Timber, agriculture, livestock, tourism

MILITARY BASES
Pine Bluff Arsenal (Army), 200 military, 1,366 civilian (2007)

CITIES
Pine Bluff, 55,085; Hot Springs, 35,750; Texarkana, 26,448

NOTABLE
Hot Springs, once a getaway for mobsters such as Charles "Lucky" Luciano and Al Capone in the 1930s, now hosts the Gangster Museum of America.

Gov. Arnold Schwarzenegger (R)

First elected: 2003
Length of term: 4 years
Term expires: 1/11
Salary: $212,179
Phone: (916) 445-2841

Residence: Los Angeles
Born: July 30, 1947;
Thal, Austria
Religion: Unspecified
Family: Wife, Maria Shriver; four children
Education: U. of Wisconsin, Superior, B.A.
1979 (business & international economics)
Career: Actor; real estate investor;
bodybuilder; weight training supplies
salesman
Political highlights: No previous office

Election results:
2006 GENERAL

Arnold Schwarzenegger (R)	4,850,157	55.9%
Phil Angelides (D)	3,376,732	38.9%
Peter Miguel Camejo (GREEN)	205,995	2.4%
Art Olivier (LIBERT)	114,329	1.3%

Lt. Gov. John Garamendi (D)

First elected: 2006
Length of term: 4 years
Term expires: 1/11
Salary: $159,134
Phone: (916) 445-8994

LEGISLATURE

Legislature: Year-round with recess

Senate: 40 members, 4-year terms
2009 ratios: 24 D, 15 R, 1 vacancy;
26 men, 13 women
Salary: $116,208
Phone: (916) 445-4251

Assembly: 80 members, 2-year terms
2009 ratios: 51 D, 29 R; 60 men,
20 women
Salary: $116,208
Phone: (916) 445-3614

TERM LIMITS

Governor: 2 terms
Senate: 2 terms
Assembly: 3 terms

URBAN STATISTICS

CITY	POPULATION
Los Angeles	3,694,820
San Diego	1,223,400
San Jose	894,943
San Francisco	776,733
Long Beach	461,522

REGISTERED VOTERS

Democrat	45%
Republican	31%
Unaffiliated	20%
Others	4%

POPULATION

2008 population (est.)	36,756,666
2000 population	33,871,648
1990 population	29,760,021
Percent change (1990-2000)	+13.8%
Rank among states (2008)	1

Median age	33.3
Born in state	50.2%
Foreign born	26.2%
Violent crime rate	622/100,000
Poverty level	14.2%
Federal workers	246,152
Military	228,903

ELECTIONS

STATE ELECTION OFFICIAL
(916) 657-2166
DEMOCRATIC PARTY
(916) 442-5707
REPUBLICAN PARTY
(818) 841-5210

MISCELLANEOUS

Web: www.ca.gov
Capital: Sacramento

U.S. CONGRESS

Senate: 2 Democrats
House: 33 Democrats, 19
Republicans
The 32nd District seat is vacant.

2000 Census Statistics by District

DIST.	2008 VOTE FOR PRESIDENT OBAMA	MCCAIN	WHITE	BLACK	ASIAN	HISP	MEDIAN INCOME	WHITE COLLAR	BLUE COLLAR	SERVICE INDUSTRY	OVER 64	UNDER 18	COLLEGE EDUCATION	RURAL	SQ. MILES
1	66%	32%	71%	1%	4%	18%	$38,918	58%	24%	18%	13%	25%	25%	24%	11,006
2	43	55	76	1	4	14	$33,559	55	27	18	15	26	17	32	21,758
3	49	49	74	4	6	11	$51,313	68	19	13	12	26	27	14	3,374
4	44	54	84	1	2	9	$49,387	63	20	16	14	26	25	33	16,453
5	70	28	43	14	15	21	$36,719	63	20	17	11	28	21	0	147
6	76	22	76	2	4	15	$59,115	68	18	14	13	23	38	10	1,625
7	72	26	43	17	13	21	$52,778	60	23	17	10	27	22	1	349
8	85	12	43	9	29	16	$52,322	73	12	15	13	14	44	0	35
9	88	10	35	26	15	19	$44,314	69	17	14	11	23	37	0	132
10	65	33	65	6	9	15	$65,243	69	18	13	12	27	36	3	1,013
11	54	44	64	3	9	20	$61,996	68	21	11	10	29	29	10	2,277
12	74	24	48	3	29	16	$70,307	73	15	12	14	21	41	0	117
13	74	24	38	6	28	21	$62,415	67	22	11	10	25	32	1	221
14	73	25	60	3	16	18	$77,985	77	13	10	12	22	52	6	826
15	68	30	47	2	29	17	$74,947	74	17	9	10	24	42	1	286

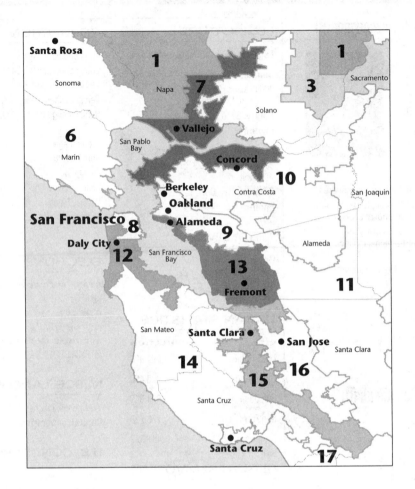

2000 Census Statistics by District

DIST.	2008 VOTE FOR PRESIDENT OBAMA	MCCAIN	WHITE	BLACK	ASIAN	HISP	MEDIAN INCOME	WHITE COLLAR	BLUE COLLAR	SERVICE INDUSTRY	OVER 64	UNDER 18	COLLEGE EDUCATION	RURAL	SQ. MILES
16	70%	29%	32%	3%	23%	38%	$67,689	61%	25%	14%	8%	27%	27%	1%	230
17	72	26	46	3	5	43	$49,234	55	28	16	10	27	25	10	4,820
18	59	39	39	6	9	42	$34,211	46	37	17	10	34	10	9	3,052
19	46	52	60	3	4	28	$41,225	59	25	15	12	28	20	19	6,692
20	60	39	21	7	6	63	$26,800	38	43	19	7	35	6	9	4,982
21	42	56	46	2	5	43	$36,047	53	31	16	10	32	15	20	8,026
22	38	60	67	6	3	21	$41,801	58	25	17	11	29	18	18	10,417
23	66	32	49	2	5	42	$44,874	57	26	17	12	25	26	2	1,042
24	51	48	69	2	4	22	$61,453	68	19	14	11	28	30	6	3,883
25	49	48	57	8	4	27	$49,002	60	24	16	8	32	19	12	21,484
26	51	47	53	4	15	24	$58,968	71	17	12	11	27	32	1	752
27	66	32	45	4	11	36	$46,781	66	20	14	11	26	26	0	151
28	76	22	31	4	6	56	$40,439	58	26	16	9	29	24	0	77
29	68	30	39	6	24	26	$43,895	70	16	14	13	23	33	1	101
30	70	28	76	3	9	8	$60,713	84	7	9	15	17	54	2	286

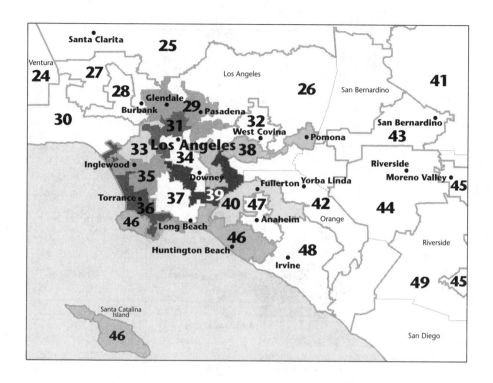

2000 Census Statistics by District

DIST.	2008 VOTE FOR PRESIDENT OBAMA	MCCAIN	WHITE	BLACK	ASIAN	HISP	MEDIAN INCOME	WHITE COLLAR	BLUE COLLAR	SERVICE INDUSTRY	OVER 64	UNDER 18	COLLEGE EDUCATION	RURAL	SQ. MILES
31	80%	18%	10%	4%	14%	70%	$26,093	44%	34%	22%	7%	30%	14%	0%	39
32	68	30	15	3	18	62	$41,394	51	33	16	9	31	14	0	92
33	87	12	20	30	12	35	$31,655	64	18	18	10	24	27	0	48
34	75	23	11	4	5	77	$29,863	44	40	16	8	32	9	0	58
35	84	14	10	34	6	47	$32,156	53	28	19	8	33	13	0	55
36	64	34	48	4	13	30	$51,633	71	16	13	10	23	37	0	75
37	80	19	17	25	11	43	$34,006	54	29	17	8	33	15	0	75
38	71	27	14	4	10	71	$42,488	51	34	15	9	32	13	0	104
39	65	32	21	6	10	61	$45,307	55	31	14	8	33	15	0	65
40	47	51	49	2	16	30	$54,356	65	22	13	11	27	26	0	100
41	44	54	64	5	4	23	$38,721	57	25	17	14	28	18	11	13,314
42	45	53	54	3	16	24	$70,463	74	15	11	8	28	35	1	314
43	68	30	23	12	3	58	$37,390	46	37	17	6	37	9	1	191
44	50	49	51	5	5	35	$51,578	59	27	14	8	31%	21	2	522
45	52	47	50	6	3	38	$40,468	53	26	21	16	29	17	10	5,980

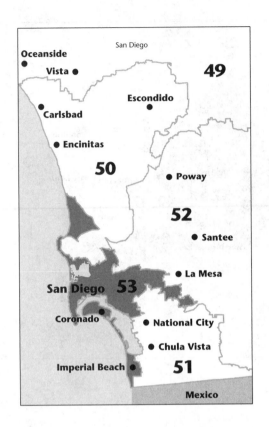

2000 Census Statistics by District

DIST.	2008 VOTE FOR PRESIDENT OBAMA	MCCAIN	WHITE	BLACK	ASIAN	HISP	MEDIAN INCOME	WHITE COLLAR	BLUE COLLAR	SERVICE INDUSTRY	OVER 64	UNDER 18	COLLEGE EDUCATION	RURAL	SQ. MILES
46	48%	50%	63%	1%	15%	17%	$61,567	73%	16%	12%	13%	22%	36%	0%	264
47	60	38	17	1	14	65	$41,618	41	39	20	6	33	10	0	55
48	49	49	68	1	13	15	$69,663	80	10	10	12	23	47	0	212
49	45	53	58	5	3	30	$46,445	58	26	16	13	29	21	10	1,690
50	51	47	66	2	10	19	$59,813	71	16	13	12	25	40	2	300
51	63	35	21	9	12	53	$39,243	55	26	20	10	31	15	4	4,582
52	45	53	73	4	5	14	$52,940	68	18	14	11	27	29	6	2,113
53	68	30	51	7	8	29	$36,637	65	17	19	10	21	32	0	95
STATE	61	37	47	6	11	32	$47,493	63	22	15	11	27	27	6	155,959
U.S.	53	46	69	12	4	13	$41,994	60	25	15	12	26	24	21	3,537,438

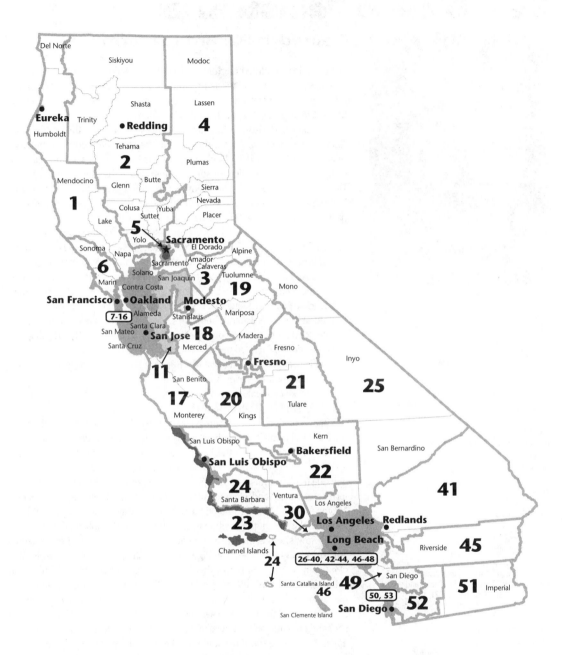

Sen. Dianne Feinstein (D)

Elected 1992; 3rd full term

CAPITOL OFFICE
224-3841
feinstein.senate.gov
331 Hart Bldg. 20510-0504; fax 228-3954

COMMITTEES
Appropriations
  (Interior-Environment - chairwoman)
Judiciary
Rules & Administration
Select Intelligence - chairwoman

RESIDENCE
San Francisco

BORN
June 22, 1933; San Francisco, Calif.

RELIGION
Jewish

FAMILY
Husband, Richard Blum; one child,
three stepchildren

EDUCATION
Stanford U., A.B. 1955 (history)

CAREER
Civic board official

POLITICAL HIGHLIGHTS
San Francisco Board of Supervisors, 1970-78
(president, 1970-71, 1974-75, 1978); candidate
for mayor of San Francisco, 1971, 1975; mayor
of San Francisco, 1978-89; Democratic nominee
for governor, 1990

ELECTION RESULTS

2006 GENERAL

Dianne Feinstein (D)	5,076,289	59.4%
Richard "Dick" Mountjoy (R)	2,990,822	35.0%
Todd Chretien (GREEN)	147,074	1.7%
Michael S. Metti (LIBERT)	133,851	1.6%
Marsha Feinland (PFP)	117,764	1.4%

2006 PRIMARY

Dianne Feinstein (D)	2,176,888	87.0%
Colleen Fernald (D)	199,180	8.0%
Martin Luther Church (D)	127,301	5.1%

PREVIOUS WINNING PERCENTAGES
2000 (56%); 1994 (47%); 1992 Special Election (54%)

Feinstein is a calm, thoughtful legislator interested in reaching across the Senate's partisan divide to make compromises. Sometimes that has meant teaming with conservatives with whom she usually disagrees, and sometimes it means questioning her party's leaders.

Feinstein (FINE-stine) has never fit the stereotype of the soft-hearted "San Francisco liberal," even though she rose to prominence as the city's mayor from 1978 to 1989. Back home, she is thought of as a moderate and even a conservative voice on some issues. While she often votes with her Democratic colleagues, she is known for often protracted deliberations before making up her mind — something that makes her seem less overtly partisan than many of her colleagues.

Feinstein broke with teachers unions to support a school voucher program in Washington, D.C., in 2004. Two years later, she was the sole Democrat on the Judiciary Committee to support a constitutional amendment to protect the flag. And in 2007, she supported the nomination of Michael B. Mukasey as President George W. Bush's attorney general despite liberals' opposition.

She irked Majority Leader Harry Reid in January 2009, by declaring Illinois Democrat Roland W. Burris should be seated to replace Barack Obama in the Senate. Reid and other senior Democrats argued that Gov. Rod R. Blagojevich's selection was tainted because federal prosecutors said the governor tried to sell the seat. "If you don't seat Mr. Burris, it has ramifications for gubernatorial appointments all over America," she said.

"She'll take political heat to find common ground," South Carolina Republican Sen. Lindsey Graham told The Wall Street Journal.

That reputation for pragmatism and centrism has helped her regularly top the list of California's most-admired officeholders. A 2008 survey showed that if Feinstein were to seek the Democratic gubernatorial nomination in 2010 — Republican Gov. Arnold Schwarzenegger will be ineligible to seek re-election due to term limits — she would swamp a primary field that could include former governor and current Attorney General Jerry Brown, Los Angeles Mayor Antonio Villaraigosa and San Francisco Mayor Gavin Newsom. Feinstein initially sought the position in 1990, but lost to Republican Pete Wilson.

For now, she has plenty to keep her busy. In the 111th Congress (2009-10), she chairs the Select Intelligence Committee and wields considerable clout as a senior member of the Appropriations, Judiciary and Rules and Administration committees. Early in 2009, she ruffled some feathers by questioning President Obama's selection of former California Rep. Leon E. Panetta to head the CIA. She said Panetta — a former White House chief of staff and one-time political rival of hers in the 1990 governor's race — lacked any intelligence experience and that she had not been consulted about his appointment. She eventually relented and said she would back Panetta.

Subsequently, Feinstein declared intentions for the intelligence panel to review the administration's detention and interrogation tactics at the military detention facility at Guantánamo Bay, Cuba. She also could revisit the 2008 update to the Foreign Intelligence Surveillance Act, which expands administration authority to spy on suspected terrorists and permits retroactive legal immunity for telecommunications companies that assisted the Bush administration's warrantless surveillance program.

Feinstein was a supporter of Obama's $787 billion economic stimulus plan, and supported a $700 billion measure, which Bush signed into law in 2008, aimed at shoring up the nation's financial services sector. In early

2009, she joined with Maine Republican Olympia J. Snowe on legislation to prohibit companies from using their relief funds to lobby. Feinstein also introduced a bill to impose government supervision over the business-travel costs of companies receiving such funds.

As chairwoman of the Interior and Environment Appropriations Subcommittee, she has helped preserve the CalFed program that protects water quality in the San Francisco Bay and Sacramento-San Joaquin River Delta — where most of the state's freshwater comes from — while preserving the water supply for the state's enormous agricultural interests. She also has worked with Schwarzenegger to get more money for the state's efforts to fight wildfires.

With Democrat Daniel K. Inouye of Hawaii, Snowe and Republican Ted Stevens, then the senior Alaska senator, she cosponsored a provision in the Democrats' 2007 energy bill that mandated the first increase in fuel economy standards for cars and trucks in two decades. With Snowe and Democrat Carl Levin of Michigan, she wrote legislation — included in the reauthorization of agriculture programs enacted in May 2008 — closing the "Enron loophole" that had allowed manipulation of energy markets, including in Feinstein's home state early in the decade.

She also played a lead role in the Senate's 2007 investigation into allegations that the Justice Department under Attorney General Alberto R. Gonzales had politicized the offices of many U.S. attorneys across the country. The investigation led to Gonzales' resignation that year, and Feinstein helped push to enactment laws bolstering the Senate's role in confirming U.S. attorneys and requiring prosecutors to live in the districts where they are appointed to serve.

In 2008, her measure to ban phthalates — chemicals used to make plastics softer — in children's toys was included in a Consumer Product Safety Commission bill enacted in August 2008. Phthalates have been tied to possible reproductive problems, especially in males.

Feinstein, a longtime champion of gun restrictions, was upset in June 2008 when the U.S. Supreme Court struck down the District of Columbia's handgun ban. "With this decision, 70 years of precedent has gone out the window. And I believe the people of this great country will be less safe because of it," said Feinstein, the author of a federal assault weapons ban that lapsed. In February 2009, the Senate included in a District voting rights bill an amendment to repeal the District's ban on semiautomatic weapons. Feinstein lambasted her colleagues for the vote and vowed to push legislation to reinstate the federal assault weapons ban.

Feinstein came to support gun control through painful personal experience. In 1978, while serving as president of San Francisco's Board of Supervisors, Feinstein discovered the body of Mayor George Moscone in his City Hall office after he and Harvey Milk, the city's first openly gay city supervisor, were gunned down by former Supervisor Dan White. (The incident was depicted — with an archival news clip of Feinstein — in the 2008 film "Milk.")

As board president, Feinstein succeeded Moscone as mayor, a job she had sought unsuccessfully at the ballot box. As mayor, she defeated a recall effort that groups against gun control put on the ballot. She left City Hall in 1989 and prepared for her 1990 gubernatorial race against Wilson.

In 1992, she defeated Sen. John Seymour, whom Wilson had appointed to succeed himself in the U.S. Senate. In 1994, Feinstein got a scare from then-Rep. Michael Huffington, an oil family scion, who spent millions of his own dollars. But she prevailed, as she did six years later against Rep. Tom Campbell, a moderate Republican who had difficulty getting traction in the race. In 2006, she coasted to victory over former Sen. Richard "Dick" Mountjoy, a conservative who could raise only enough money to mount a nominal campaign.

KEY VOTES

2008

Yes Prohibit discrimination based on genetic information

Yes Reauthorize farm and nutrition programs for five years

Yes Limit debate on "cap-and-trade" system for greenhouse gas emissions

No Allow lawsuits against companies that participated in warrantless wiretapping

Yes Limit debate on a bill to block a scheduled cut in Medicare payments to doctors

Yes Grant mortgage relief to homeowners and funding for Fannie Mae and Freddie Mac

Yes Approve a nuclear cooperation agreement with India

Yes Approve final $700 billion program to stabilize financial markets

Yes Allow consideration of a $14 billion auto industry loan package

2007

Yes Increase minimum wage by $2.10 an hour

Yes Limit debate on a comprehensive immigration bill

Yes Overhaul congressional lobbying and ethics rules for members and their staffs

Yes Limit debate on considering a bill to add House seats for the District of Columbia and Utah

Yes Limit debate on restoring habeas corpus rights to detainees

Yes Mandate minimum breaks for troops between deployments to Iraq or Afghanistan

Yes Override Bush veto of $23.2 billion water projects authorization bill

Yes Confirm Michael B. Mukasey as attorney general

Yes Limit debate on an energy policy overhaul containing $21.8 billion in tax incentives and reduced oil and gas subsidies

CQ VOTE STUDIES

	PARTY UNITY		PRESIDENTIAL SUPPORT	
	SUPPORT	OPPOSE	SUPPORT	OPPOSE
2008	91%	9%	38%	62%
2007	93%	7%	39%	61%
2006	90%	10%	54%	46%
2005	92%	8%	40%	60%
2004	95%	5%	62%	38%
2003	91%	9%	49%	51%
2002	83%	17%	76%	24%
2001	85%	15%	71%	29%
2000	88%	12%	84%	16%
1999	91%	9%	87%	13%

INTEREST GROUPS

	AFL-CIO	ADA	CCUS	ACU
2008	100%	100%	63%	4%
2007	89%	90%	45%	0%
2006	100%	90%	50%	0%
2005	62%	95%	50%	12%
2004	100%	100%	65%	4%
2003	92%	90%	39%	5%
2002	92%	80%	55%	20%
2001	94%	85%	71%	12%
2000	50%	70%	54%	28%
1999	78%	100%	53%	4%

Sen. Barbara Boxer (D)

Elected 1992; 3rd term

CAPITOL OFFICE
224-3553
boxer.senate.gov
112 Hart Bldg. 20510-0505; fax 228-3972

COMMITTEES
Commerce, Science & Transportation
Environment & Public Works - chairwoman
Foreign Relations
  (International Operations & Organizations -
  chairwoman)
Select Ethics - chairwoman

RESIDENCE
Rancho Mirage

BORN
Nov. 11, 1940; Brooklyn, N.Y.

RELIGION
Jewish

FAMILY
Husband, Stewart Boxer; two children

EDUCATION
Brooklyn College, B.A. 1962 (economics)

CAREER
Congressional aide; journalist; stockbroker

POLITICAL HIGHLIGHTS
Candidate for Marin County Board of Supervisors, 1972; Marin County Board of Supervisors, 1977-83 (president, 1980); U.S. House, 1983-93

ELECTION RESULTS

2004 GENERAL

Barbara Boxer (D)	6,955,728	57.7%
Bill Jones (R)	4,555,922	37.8%
Marsha Feinland (PFP)	243,846	2.0%
James P. "Jim" Gray (LIBERT)	216,522	1.8%

2004 PRIMARY

Barbara Boxer (D)	unopposed

PREVIOUS WINNING PERCENTAGES
1998 (53%); 1992 (48%); 1990 House Election (68%); 1988 House Election (73%); 1986 House Election (74%); 1984 House Election (68%); 1982 House Election (52%)

As chairwoman of the Environment and Public Works Committee, Boxer has sparked more than a few YouTube moments in which she has brassily put down her opponents. That is hardly surprising, given her repeated outspokenness during her quarter-century on Capitol Hill.

Boxer's brash liberalism, environmentalism, feminist sympathies and anti-war sentiment have made her an icon of the political left. She often displays little patience for those who don't share her views. "When I believe in something, I believe in it strongly," she once said.

In March 2007, not long after assuming the Environment post, Boxer hosted a hearing for former Vice President Al Gore to allow him to discuss his well-known views on how global warming must be confronted. When the committee's ranking Republican, global warming skeptic James M. Inhofe of Oklahoma, asked Gore to respond to his questions in writing, Boxer ordered Inhofe to allow the Nobel Prize winner to speak. "You're not making the rules anymore. You used to when you had this," she told the former GOP committee chairman, holding up the gavel. "Elections have consequences."

Boxer is likely to be a strong ally of President Obama's administration after having tangled with George W. Bush's appointees. She called for EPA administrator Stephen L. Johnson's resignation for his agency's decision under Bush to black out information in documents her panel had sought as it investigated the Bush administration's opposition to California's bid for a waiver from federal rules limiting its ability to regulate car and truck emissions. Relations between the two grew so bad that for much of 2008 he refused to appear before her committee. When he and some of his top aides didn't show up for a September hearing on the administration's environmental record, Boxer let loose. "They're cowardly and they have been a danger to this country," she said.

The incidents showed Boxer's often-blunt style with opponents while demonstrating her commitment to combating global warming, a topic she calls her top legislative priority. She has had trouble, though, finding any consensus on the divisive issue.

The closest she came was in June 2008, when the Senate almost took up a sweeping bill that would have created a mandatory "cap and trade" program to deal with global warming. Instead, the bipartisan legislation was never debated, as parliamentary wrangling left it shelved.

In February 2009, Boxer predicted her committee would move a global warming bill in time to bring to international climate talks in Copenhagen that December. She said she needed time to ensure the bill has wide support. "We want to get a bill out there that is straightforward," she said, and "doesn't have so much weight that it sinks."

Getting major legislation passed has not been the trademark of Boxer's career. Heading into the 110th Congress (2007-08), only one Boxer-sponsored Senate bill had ever been enacted into law. That 1994 measure allowed states to conduct seismic retrofitting of bridges without regard to whether the bridges could be fixed or replaced under an existing federal program.

Nevertheless, she keeps a busy agenda. She has pushed legislation to protect people from exposure to perchlorate, a toxic component in rocket fuel that has contaminated drinking water in 35 states. She has tangled with the Bush administration over its refusal to list polar bears as endangered species and its decision to end the ban on offshore drilling, a significant environmental concern in California.

A key legislative victory for Boxer came in November 2007, when the Senate voted to override Bush's veto of the $23.2 billion Water Resources Development Act, a popular piece of legislation authorizing water projects but that Bush criticized as too expensive. His veto prompted a rare legislative moment in which Boxer and Inhofe worked together to reverse the president.

She has taken up the cause of the nation's vanishing honeybees, which have been suffering from "colony collapse disorder." In seeking funding to study the decline in the insect that is a vital pollinator for many crops, Boxer has warned that the bees' decline could cause a $15 billion direct loss in crop production, including in such important California crops as almonds.

Boxer also has proposed putting anti-missile technology on U.S. commercial aircraft. And as an almost weekly cross-country commuter, she has pushed for enactment of an air passengers' bill of rights.

Boxer has another portfolio, as chairwoman of the Select Ethics Committee. In that role, she oversaw the committee process that in February 2008 resulted in a decision to admonish Republican Sen. Larry E. Craig of Idaho. The committee said he brought discredit upon the Senate by his efforts to escape charges in June 2007 when he was arrested in a Minnesota airport rest room for allegedly soliciting an undercover police officer for a sexual encounter.

Boxer also serves on the Foreign Relations Committee, where she chairs the subcommittee on international operations and organizations, human rights, democracy and global women's issues. She wants Obama's administration to seek to end violence and discrimination against women globally. She has been a consistent critic of the Iraq War; in October 2002, she was one of 23 senators to vote against the resolution authorizing Bush to use force to oust Saddam Hussein, and she hasn't let up in her criticism.

Boxer's other committee assignment is Commerce, Science and Transportation. During a 2008 debate on consumer product safety legislation, she responded to GOP resistance about a ban on certain phthalates — compounds commonly used to make plastics more flexible — by putting 90 scientific studies on the dangers of phthalates into the record. House and Senate conferees eventually reached a deal in which several of the compounds were banned.

Boxer's fiery stands have been popular in California, where she was reelected to her third term in 2004 by a 20 percentage point margin over former Secretary of State Bill Jones. Six years earlier, she had a similarly easy time beating state Treasurer Matt Fong by 10 points. To ward off challengers in 2010, she raised nearly $4.7 million during the 2008 election cycle.

Her initial Senate run proved more difficult. In 1992, the "Year of the Woman" in national politics, she defeated conservative TV commentator Bruce Herschensohn by 5 percentage points.

Boxer, a Brooklyn-born stockbroker, got her political start in Marin County, just across the Golden Gate Bridge from San Francisco, after she moved there at age 27 with her husband Stewart, an Oakland labor attorney. She won a county board of supervisors seat in 1976, on her second try, and won a House seat in 1982, taking over from longtime friend and mentor Rep. John L. Burton after he decided to retire.

Boxer is a friend of House Speaker Nancy Pelosi, a fellow Bay Area Democrat, dating back to the time in the 1980s when they represented adjoining districts in the House. Boxer is also friends with former President Bill Clinton and his wife, Secretary of State Hillary Rodham Clinton. Boxer's daughter, Nicole, married Tony Rodham, the former first lady's brother. The couple had a son, Zachary, in 1996, but divorced in 2000. Zachary Rodham is the only person ever to have a grandmother and an aunt serving in the Senate.

Boxer hasn't limited her energies to politics. She published a well-reviewed novel, "A Time to Run," with author Mary-Rose Hayes in 2005. It tells the story of a female senator whose former lover attempts to sabotage her career.

KEY VOTES

2008
Yes Prohibit discrimination based on genetic information
Yes Reauthorize farm and nutrition programs for five years
Yes Limit debate on "cap and trade" system for greenhouse gas emissions
Yes Allow lawsuits against companies that participated in warrantless wiretapping
Yes Limit debate on a bill to block a scheduled cut in Medicare payments to doctors
Yes Grant mortgage relief to homeowners and funding for Fannie Mae and Freddie Mac
No   Approve a nuclear cooperation agreement with India
Yes Approve final $700 billion program to stabilize financial markets
Yes Allow consideration of a $14 billion auto industry loan package

2007
Yes Increase minimum wage by $2.10 an hour
Yes Limit debate on a comprehensive immigration bill
Yes Overhaul congressional lobbying and ethics rules for members and their staffs
Yes Limit debate on considering a bill to add House seats for the District of Columbia and Utah
Yes Limit debate on restoring habeas corpus rights to detainees
Yes Mandate minimum breaks for troops between deployments to Iraq or Afghanistan
Yes Override Bush veto of $23.2 billion water projects authorization bill
No   Confirm Michael B. Mukasey as attorney general
Yes Limit debate on an energy policy overhaul containing $21.8 billion in tax incentives and reduced oil and gas subsidies

CQ VOTE STUDIES

	PARTY UNITY		PRESIDENTIAL SUPPORT	
	SUPPORT	OPPOSE	SUPPORT	OPPOSE
2008	99%	1%	30%	70%
2007	97%	3%	34%	66%
2006	97%	3%	47%	53%
2005	99%	1%	30%	70%
2004	96%	4%	65%	35%
2003	99%	1%	44%	56%
2002	95%	5%	65%	35%
2001	98%	2%	64%	36%
2000	100%	0%	92%	8%
1999	97%	3%	84%	16%

INTEREST GROUPS

	AFL-CIO	ADA	CCUS	ACU
2008	100%	95%	57%	4%
2007	100%	80%	33%	4%
2006	100%	95%	25%	8%
2005	92%	100%	24%	12%
2004	100%	95%	56%	4%
2003	100%	95%	22%	10%
2002	100%	90%	40%	5%
2001	100%	95%	42%	0%
2000	67%	85%	41%	4%
1999	100%	100%	47%	4%

Rep. Mike Thompson (D)

Elected 1998; 6th term

CAPITOL OFFICE
225-3311
mikethompson.house.gov
231 Cannon Bldg. 20515-0501; fax 225-4335

COMMITTEES
Ways & Means
Select Intelligence
(Terrorism, Human Intelligence, Analysis &
(Counterintelligence - chairman)

RESIDENCE
St. Helena

BORN
Jan. 24, 1951; St. Helena, Calif.

RELIGION
Roman Catholic

FAMILY
Wife, Janet Thompson; two children

EDUCATION
California State U., Chico, B.A. 1982
(political science), M.A. 1996 (public administration)

MILITARY SERVICE
Army 1969-73

CAREER
Grape farmer; winery maintenance supervisor;
state legislative aide; college instructor

POLITICAL HIGHLIGHTS
Calif. Senate, 1990-98

ELECTION RESULTS

2008 GENERAL

Mike Thompson (D)	197,812	68.1%
Zane Starkewolf (R)	67,853	23.4%
Carol Wolman (GREEN)	24,793	8.5%

2008 PRIMARY

Mike Thompson (D)	57,778	88.0%
Mitchell Clogg (D)	7,897	12.0%

2006 GENERAL

Mike Thompson (D)	144,409	66.2%
John W. Jones (R)	63,194	29.0%
Pamela Elizondo (GREEN)	6,899	3.2%
Timothy J. Stock (PFP)	3,503	1.6%

PREVIOUS WINNING PERCENTAGES
2004 (67%); 2002 (64%); 2000 (65%); 1998 (62%)

Thompson's close friendship with Speaker Nancy Pelosi, his work with the fiscally conservative Blue Dog Coalition and his skill at building partnerships have enabled him to emerge as a leading Democratic voice on tax, intelligence, agriculture and environment issues.

Thompson comes from a family of grape growers, and he owns a 30-acre vineyard where he grows organic sauvignon blanc grapes. His long, coastal district stretches from the Napa Valley north to the Oregon border. In his D.C. office, he keeps a wine closet full of bottles of the Bonterra sauvignon blanc made from his grapes. Pelosi owns a vineyard in his hometown of St. Helena.

Although Thompson is a loyal ally on most of his party's priorities, he can veer away on fiscal issues as he aligns with the Blue Dogs. He supports pay-as-you-go rules requiring offsets for tax cuts and spending increases, for example, but he is reluctant to divide the Democratic caucus on such issues as immigration. "I'm a Blue Dog from back in the days where there was one issue that made us Blue Dogs, and that was fiscal responsibility," he said.

He was reluctant at first in fall 2008 to support a $700 billion measure, ultimately signed into law, to shore up the ailing financial services industry. He voted no on its first iteration, but when it came back to the House a second time, he changed his mind and voted yes. With credit markets tightening, he said, "it's a different time" than when the first vote was taken.

He was more certain about the need for President Obama's $787 billion economic stimulus measure that cleared Congress in February 2009. "We're hemorrhaging jobs all across the country, and in my district it's bad," Thompson told the San Francisco Chronicle. Thompson said some of the bill's items "are pretty doggone good," especially those promoting renewable energy.

Thompson is an advocate for environmental protection and land preservation. In early 2009, he was considered a possibility for Interior secretary. The job ultimately went to Sen. Ken Salazar of Colorado.

Thompson and California Democratic Sen. Barbara Boxer gained enactment of a bill in 2006 setting aside 273,000 acres of northern California as wilderness land, spanning parts of five counties in his district. Thompson won over a key ally in California Republican Richard W. Pombo, then-chairman of the Resources Committee, by including provisions to allow access in certain areas for off-road vehicles and to retain some roads.

He is particularly concerned about the reduction in salmon runs in the Klamath River — a problem caused, he says, by the George W. Bush administration's diversion of water to other areas. He helped enact a measure in 2006 that aimed to restore salmon runs. And in 2008, he and Pelosi helped get $170 million in disaster assistance for the salmon industry into the farm bill.

As a former Vietnam combat veteran, Thompson has a deep interest in the war in Iraq. He opposed both the war's authorization in 2002 and Bush's proposal in early 2007 to send more than 20,000 additional U.S. combat troops into Iraq. In 2006 and 2007, he offered unsuccessful bills calling for troop withdrawals. In the 110th Congress (2007-08), he gained a coveted spot on the Select Intelligence Committee, where he serves as chairman of the Terrorism, Human Intelligence, Analysis and Counterintelligence Subcommittee. He opposed legislation that gave telecommunications companies retroactive immunity for assisting a warrantless surveillance program.

A member of the Ways and Means Committee since 2005, Thompson has argued for measures to improve rural health care, including legislation to fund programs that offer health care advice and doctor consultations via computer and telephone. In the 110th, he successfully incorporated into the 2007 farm bill his proposals for tax incentives to help encourage land conservation and protect endangered species.

Thompson is usually willing to expend effort and money for the benefit of the vineyards in his district. He has worked to expand trade markets for California's wine and produce, and pressed for federal dollars to fight insect-borne crop diseases. He co-founded the Congressional Wine Caucus in 1999 and calls his fundraising arm the VINE PAC.

A prolific fundraiser, Thompson led the Democratic Congressional Campaign Committee's effort to protect endangered incumbents in the 2006 elections. He also helped launch the committee's business council, an outreach program designed to bring the party closer to the business community. But he was passed over for the committee chairmanship in the 2008 cycle.

He traces his business-friendly values back to his grandfathers, a butcher and a vineyard owner. Thompson grew up in his district before the wine boom, picking walnuts and prunes to make extra money. During his lifetime, winemaking turned from a sleepy profession into a major industry.

As a young man, he worked as a maintenance supervisor at the Beringer Vineyard in Napa Valley. "I was the guy the Hispanic field laborers would come to with their problems," he said. When he once sought to intervene on behalf of a Hispanic worker who had been cheated by a mechanic, Thompson recalled, "The guy in the repair shop said: 'What do you care? The guy's just a Mexican.'"

Outraged by the incident, Thompson says he realized that to be able to help people effectively, he would have to complete his education. He had dropped out of high school and joined the Army, serving as a staff sergeant and platoon leader with the 173rd Airborne Brigade in Vietnam, where he was wounded and received a Purple Heart. In his late 20s and early 30s, he earned his high school diploma and then a college degree.

One of his political science professors suggested he apply for a fellowship with the state legislature. He later served as chief of staff for Assemblyman Lou Papan. When Papan left, Thompson packed up his office and prepared to leave the legislature, agreeing only to help Papan's successor, Jackie Speier, find a replacement. She ultimately convinced him to stay. Thompson supported Speier's successful bid for Congress in a special election in 2008.

Thompson ran for elective office in 1990, winning a seat in the state Senate. California's legislative term limits forced him to set his sights on Congress in 1998. He easily defeated his underfunded Republican opponent, Napa County Supervisor Mark Luce. He has gone on to win re-election handily.

KEY VOTES

2008

Yes Delay consideration of Colombia free-trade agreement

Yes Override Bush veto of federal farm and nutrition programs reauthorization bill

No Overhaul surveillance laws and permit dismissal of suits against companies that conducted warrantless wiretapping

Yes Grant mortgage relief to homeowners and funding for Fannie Mae and Freddie Mac

No Approve initial $700 billion program to stabilize financial markets

Yes Approve final $700 billion program to stabilize financial markets

Yes Provide $14 billion in loans to automakers

2007

Yes Increase minimum wage by $2.10 an hour

Yes Approve $124.2 billion in emergency war spending and set goal for redeployment of troops from Iraq

No Reject federal contraceptive assistance to international family planning groups

Yes Override Bush veto of $23.2 billion water projects authorization bill

Yes Implement Peru free-trade agreement

+ Approve energy policy overhaul with new fuel economy standards

− Clear $473.5 billion omnibus spending bill, including $70 billion for military operations

CQ VOTE STUDIES

	PARTY UNITY		PRESIDENTIAL SUPPORT	
	SUPPORT	OPPOSE	SUPPORT	OPPOSE
2008	95%	5%	15%	85%
2007	96%	4%	4%	96%
2006	93%	7%	23%	77%
2005	92%	8%	18%	82%
2004	91%	9%	24%	76%

INTEREST GROUPS

	AFL-CIO	ADA	CCUS	ACU
2008	100%	90%	56%	8%
2007	96%	90%	55%	0%
2006	86%	90%	47%	20%
2005	87%	90%	48%	16%
2004	87%	90%	48%	13%

CALIFORNIA 1

Northern Coast — Eureka; Napa, Davis

The 1st District is notable for its breadth and diversity. Even the weather patterns vary across the district, with a rainy north and arid farmland in the south. It takes about nine hours to travel the length of the district, a journey that starts in Yolo County, across the river from Sacramento, moves through Napa Valley's famous wineries and the northern coast's towering redwood forests, and ends at the Oregon border in Del Norte County, one of the district's three coastal counties.

In the north, Mendocino, Humboldt and Del Norte counties historically have been a battleground for environmentalists and the timber industry, although the isolated protests are less intense than they were two decades ago. East of Mendocino, Lake County has a mix of ranching, farming and tourism. Once attractive to retirees for its relatively low cost of living compared with Bay Area cities, the county is suffering from rising unemployment and home foreclosures.

South of Mendocino, the 1st takes in part of wine-producing Sonoma County and all of Napa County. More than 300 wineries are in the 1st, a

large segment of the state's total. In addition to wine sales, winery tours also bring revenue. Napa is the second-most popular tourist destination in California after Disneyland.

Apart from wine, timber and tourism, the 1st's economy extends to commercial fishing in Crescent City, Eureka and Fort Bragg. The University of California, Davis, in Yolo County is a major employer, although just one-quarter of district residents have a college degree.

Politically, the district can show an independent streak, but it remains mostly liberal. Democrats have a substantial lead in voter registration in every county except Del Norte. Barack Obama won the 1st with 66 percent of the vote in the 2008 presidential election, and Del Norte was also the only county wholly in the 1st to vote for Republican John McCain.

MAJOR INDUSTRY
Agriculture, timber, tourism

CITIES
Napa, 72,585; Davis, 60,308; Woodland (pt.), 39,455

NOTABLE
At more than 5,000 acres, the campus in Davis is the largest in the University of California system.

Rep. Wally Herger (R)

Elected 1986; 12th term

Herger has a modest national profile and mediocre fundraising record, but his solid conservative credentials over the past two decades have made him a "go to" guy on the Ways and Means Committee for Republican leaders. He favors a simpler tax code, free trade, and a free-market approach to improving health care and lowering costs.

After a long and steady climb on Ways and Means, he became the senior Republican on the panel's Health Subcommittee in January 2009. The assignment came after he was unable to overcome a challenge from Michigan Republican Dave Camp to succeed the retiring Jim McCrery as the full committee's top Republican in the 111th Congress (2009-10).

In February 2009, Herger was named to a group created to develop the GOP's health care overhaul plan. Minority Leader John A. Boehner charged the group with devising arguments against an expansion of government programs such as Medicaid and Medicare, a key element of many Democratic health care plans. "I strongly oppose plans that will take health care out of the hands of doctors and patients and put them in the hands of faceless bureaucrats," Herger said later that month. He was also critical of a bill, signed into law in 2009, to expand the State Children's Health Insurance Program, which covers children from low-income families that don't quality for Medicaid.

He is a member of the Republican Study Committee, a group of the most conservative House Republicans, and GOP leaders can usually count on his support. However, in 2008, he initially voted against a Democratic bill that prevented cuts to Medicare physician payments. When the bill moved forward in a way he didn't expect, he let local physicians know he regretted his vote.

During the 110th Congress (2007-08), Herger was the Republicans' standard-bearer on free trade as the top GOP member of the Ways and Means Trade Subcommittee. In Herger's Northern California district, agriculture dominates the economy. "As Americans, we can't consume all that we grow. We need to be able to export," he said, noting his district is a major supplier of rice, almonds and walnuts — along with 60 percent of the world's prunes.

He fought for free-trade deals with Colombia, Peru, South Korea and Panama while trying to preserve fast-track authority, which allows the president to send Congress trade deals for simple up-or-down votes. He also tried to contain the costs of a revision to the Trade Adjustment Assistance program, which helps companies and workers hurt by international trade agreements. But with Democrats in charge, only the Peru deal became law, and a bipartisan agreement announced in 2007 on including labor and environmental standards in trade deals didn't seem to yield a long-term consensus. Meanwhile, Congress allowed fast-track authority to expire.

On another big Ways and Means issue, Herger favors a simpler tax code. He is top-ranking Republican on the Joint Taxation Committee. On behalf of local and state governments and contractors, he has worked with Democrats, including Kendrick B. Meek of Florida, to postpone a law requiring 3 percent of many government contract payments to be withheld to prevent tax evasion.

In fall 2008, he voted for two versions of a $700 billion plan to shore up the financial services sector — the second of which became law — against constituent calls, arguing the bill was necessary to protect the local economy. And he opposed President Obama's $787 billion economic stimulus plan in February 2009, saying people "are not looking for a handout, and they know that we can not spend and borrow our way back to prosperity." He backed a GOP plan that relied more on tax relief for workers and small businesses.

CAPITOL OFFICE
225-3076
www.house.gov/herger
242 Cannon Bldg. 20515-0502; fax 226-8852

COMMITTEES
Ways & Means
Joint Taxation - ranking member

RESIDENCE
Chico

BORN
May 20, 1945; Sutter County, Calif.

RELIGION
Mormon

FAMILY
Wife, Pamela Herger; nine children (one deceased)

EDUCATION
American River College, A.A. 1967;
California State U., Sacramento, attended 1969

CAREER
Rancher; gas company executive

POLITICAL HIGHLIGHTS
Calif. Assembly, 1980-86

ELECTION RESULTS

2008 GENERAL
Wally Herger (R)	163,459	57.9%
Jeff Morris (D)	118,878	42.1%

2008 PRIMARY
Wally Herger (R)	unopposed

2006 GENERAL
Wally Herger (R)	134,911	64.2%
A.J. Sekhon (D)	68,234	32.5%
E. Kent Hinesley (LIBERT)	7,057	3.3%

PREVIOUS WINNING PERCENTAGES
2004 (67%); 2002 (66%); 2000 (66%); 1998 (63%);
1996 (61%); 1994 (64%); 1992 (65%); 1990 (64%);
1988 (59%); 1986 (58%)

Herger was chairman of the Ways and Means subcommittee on welfare in the 109th Congress (2005-06). He tried to impose tougher work requirements on recipients, continuing a trend started in the mid-1990s when congressional conservatives struck an agreement with President Clinton that ended 60 years of guaranteed federal assistance and created work requirements. But Herger was blocked by GOP moderates who thought his work rules went too far.

A converted Mormon with a large family, Herger said he wants to remain active in the welfare debate and believes preserving traditional family structure is the surest way to reduce the welfare rolls. He takes particular interest in federal programs aimed at children, especially the more than 500,000 children in foster care. In 2001, he sponsored legislation, which became law, to increase funding for adoption, foster care and post-adoption services. In 2006, Herger's subcommittee produced a bill renewing several programs to combat child abuse and neglect. It gave the states $345 million annually, including $40 million that Herger insisted be set aside to pay for once-a-month visits by social workers.

One of Herger's main missions is to prevent environmentalists from encroaching on the interests of loggers, ranchers and private property owners. He's taken a particular interest in what he calls the "government-caused disaster" in the Klamath River basin in which water needed by farmers for irrigation was withheld to protect two species of fish.

Herger grew up on his family's 200-acre cattle ranch and plum farm in the Northern California town of Rio Oso. His grandparents purchased the land after their arrival from Switzerland in 1907. Financially well-to-do, Herger made his money in ranching and running Herger Gas, a propane company in Rio Oso, with his father. Herger married young and had two children, but the marriage broke up. He remarried months after meeting his present wife, Pamela. She was a nurse who, like him, was divorced, had a child and had converted to the Mormon faith. They both wanted a big family, and eventually they had six children, one of whom died of a stroke at age 2.

In the late 1970s, high inflation and interest rates spurred him to volunteer for local GOP candidates. "The next thing I knew, I was running for the State Assembly," he said. "And then once I got in, I thought, 'What am I doing?'"

In 1980, he won his Assembly seat in the Reagan Revolution, and was in his third term when GOP Rep. Gene Chappie announced his retirement. Linking himself to President Reagan, Herger won the 1986 general election with 58 percent of the vote. He has had little electoral difficulty since. Redistricting in 2001 shifted his district to the west, but left him with his two major population centers, Redding and Chico, and presented him with no re-election worries.

KEY VOTES

2008

No Delay consideration of Colombia free-trade agreement

Yes Override Bush veto of federal farm and nutrition programs reauthorization bill

Yes Overhaul surveillance laws and permit dismissal of suits against companies that conducted warrantless wiretapping

No Grant mortgage relief to homeowners and funding for Fannie Mae and Freddie Mac

Yes Approve initial $700 billion program to stabilize financial markets

Yes Approve final $700 billion program to stabilize financial markets

No Provide $14 billion in loans to automakers

2007

No Increase minimum wage by $2.10 an hour

No Approve $124.2 billion in emergency war spending and set goal for redeployment of troops from Iraq

Yes Reject federal contraceptive assistance to international family planning groups

Yes Override Bush veto of $23.2 billion water projects authorization bill

Yes Implement Peru free-trade agreement

No Approve energy policy overhaul with new fuel economy standards

Yes Clear $473.5 billion omnibus spending bill, including $70 billion for military operations

CQ VOTE STUDIES

	PARTY UNITY		PRESIDENTIAL SUPPORT	
	SUPPORT	OPPOSE	SUPPORT	OPPOSE
2008	97%	3%	78%	22%
2007	95%	5%	85%	15%
2006	100%	0%	95%	5%
2005	97%	3%	85%	15%
2004	99%	1%	88%	12%

INTEREST GROUPS

	AFL-CIO	ADA	CCUS	ACU
2008	0%	10%	89%	88%
2007	4%	5%	80%	96%
2006	14%	0%	93%	92%
2005	13%	0%	93%	96%
2004	7%	5%	100%	100%

CALIFORNIA 2
North central — Redding, Chico

The mountainous 2nd forms a north-south strip down the center of northern California, from the Oregon border through the Sacramento Valley. It includes the Sutter Buttes mountain range west of Yuba City.

Agriculture dominates the sprawling 2nd, the largest district in California at almost 22,000 square miles. Almost one-third of the district is rural, with rice farms and orchards that produce walnuts, almonds and peaches. Sunsweet Growers, headquartered in Yuba City, operates the world's largest dried fruit packing plant.

The 2nd endures harsh weather, and conditions cause major fires every year, especially in the northern counties of Shasta, Trinity and Siskiyou, and in the valley county of Butte. Much of the district is extremely dry and temperatures soar during the summer. Water also is a perennial issue: Two-thirds of the state's supply comes from the upper third of the state, which has caused tension between northern and southern California.

Much of the district's economic activity is centered in Shasta County,

which has seen rising unemployment rates. Redding is about 160 miles north of Sacramento in Shasta County and attracts tourists who visit nearby Shasta Lake, the state's largest man-made reservoir. In Butte County, health care and higher education are major employers in Chico. More than 17,000 students attend California State University, Chico.

The 2nd is largely white, Republican and relatively poor. The district has seen a steady influx of Sikhs in the Yuba City area, as well as an infusion of Democratic-leaning Hispanic farm workers. Chico has a large Democratic presence, but Republican John McCain won the district comfortably in the 2008 presidential election.

MAJOR INDUSTRY
Agriculture, timber, tourism, health care

MILITARY BASES
Beale Air Force Base, 4,000 military, 1,200 civilian (2009)

CITIES
Redding, 80,865; Chico, 59,954; Yuba City, 36,758

NOTABLE
Redding's Sundial Bridge at Turtle Bay, a pedestrian bridge that spans the Sacramento River, functions as a working sundial but only gives the accurate time one day a year — on the summer solstice in June.

Rep. Dan Lungren (R)

Elected 2004; 8th term
Also served 1979-89

Lungren is a conservative yet cooperative Republican who skillfully bridges partisan divides to leave his imprint on national security issues that he says propelled his return to the House in 2004.

His legislative views are much in keeping with his previous tenure from 1979 to 1989 — when he pushed for stronger border security and tax cuts, helped pass the 1981 extensions of the Voting Rights Act and led efforts to include a catchall crime package in a 1984 spending bill. A self-described "Reagan conservative," Lungren has adorned his office walls with photos of the 40th president and framed letters from Reagan.

Lungren advocates a limited role for government, reduced taxes and a strong national defense. He supports extending George W. Bush's sweeping tax cuts of 2001 and 2003 that are set to expire in 2011, and he opposes pay-as-you-go budget rules that require offsets to be found for new mandatory expenditures. He said the rules "make it more difficult to stop taxes from going up."

His commitment to limited government and concern about costs prompted his "no" vote on the Democrats' $289 billion renewal of agriculture and nutrition programs in 2008, despite the fact that his district is heavily reliant on agriculture. "At some point," he said, "you just have to say, 'Wait a minute ... we have blown any sense of fiscal responsibility.'" He also opposed an unsuccessful $14 billion measure to bail out U.S. automakers.

He did, however, back two $700 billion proposals — the second of which became law — in fall 2008 to aid the ailing financial services industry, contending something had to be done to stem the crisis on Wall Street.

After the GOP's dismal showing at the polls in 2008, Lungren launched a surprise challenge to John A. Boehner for Minority Leader. His entry was seen largely as a means for the Republican Study Committee — the House GOP's conservative wing — to pressure Boehner to embrace more of the group's priorities and give its members more choice committee assignments.

Though Boehner won easily, the Study Committee did see several of its goals realized. For Lungren, the result meant becoming the ranking Republican on the House Administration Committee in January 2009. The panel's mission includes settling election questions, oversight of the Capitol Police and Capitol Visitor Center and personnel matters.

Lungren said he holds the institution of Congress and its traditions in high esteem and is disappointed in what he sees as members' growing disregard for legislative decorum. He doesn't hesitate to upbraid his colleagues for violating certain standards of dress — whether it is showing up to vote without a tie or bringing teenagers in torn jeans into the well during votes. He was considered among the most strident of Republicans during his early years in the House, but now he laments the "harder edge to the partisanship" that exists today compared with the 1980s, when, he said, members were more cordial.

He can be as critical of his party or its leaders. In 2006, he joined forces with New York Republican John E. Sweeney in calling for every GOP leader except Speaker J. Dennis Hastert to stand for re-election in order to be held accountable after a series of ethics scandals. The caucus rejected the proposal, 85-107.

In 2007, Lungren supported the lobbying and ethics reform law that put new restrictions on the ways members and lobbyists interact. Yet he opposed, unsuccessfully, the bill's ban on privately financed travel for lawmakers.

In May 2008, ABC News aired an unflattering report about a transportation industry conference he attended in Hawaii the previous winter. Lungren said he abided by the law and funded the trip through his campaign committee, not

CAPITOL OFFICE
225-5716
lungren.house.gov
2262 Rayburn Bldg. 20515-0503; fax 226-1298

COMMITTEES
Homeland Security
House Administration - ranking member
Judiciary

RESIDENCE
Gold River

BORN
Sept. 22, 1946; Long Beach, Calif.

RELIGION
Roman Catholic

FAMILY
Wife, Bobbi Lungren; three children

EDUCATION
U. of Notre Dame, B.A. 1968 (English);
Georgetown U., J.D. 1971

CAREER
Lawyer

POLITICAL HIGHLIGHTS
Republican nominee for U.S. House, 1976;
U.S. House, 1979-89; Calif. attorney general,
1991-99; Republican nominee for governor, 1998

ELECTION RESULTS

2008 GENERAL

Dan Lungren (R)	155,424	49.5%
Bill Durston (D)	137,971	43.9%
Dina J. Padilla (PFP)	13,378	4.3%
Douglas Arthur Tuma (LIBERT)	7,273	2.3%

2008 PRIMARY

Dan Lungren (R)	unopposed

2006 GENERAL

Dan Lungren (R)	135,709	59.5%
Bill Durston (D)	86,318	37.8%
Douglas Arthur Tuma (LIBERT)	3,772	1.6%
Michael Roskey (PFP)	2,370	1.0%

PREVIOUS WINNING PERCENTAGES
2004 (62%); 1986 (73%); 1984 (73%); 1982 (69%);
1980 (72%); 1978 (54%)

with taxpayer or private funds. Asked if he would have gone if the conference had been in Pittsburgh, Lungren responded, "I probably wouldn't have been in Pittsburgh in January. Do I look like I would go to Pittsburgh in January?"

From his posts on the Homeland Security and Judiciary committees he has worked with Democrats on national security issues. He is the ranking Republican on Homeland Security's Subcommittee on Emerging Threats, Cybersecurity, and Science and Technology.

He worked to forge a compromise with Democrats on the rewrite of the Foreign Intelligence Surveillance Act, which became law in July 2008. And he has joined with liberal Democrat Jim McGovern of Massachusetts to promote efforts to reduce nuclear weapons in the United States and Russia. During the 109th Congress (2005-06), he worked with California Democrat Jane Harman to pass a massive port security bill, which became law in 2006.

Also during the 109th, he sponsored a bill to tighten chemical plant security. The bill didn't pass, but his efforts helped pressure appropriators to add chemical facility security provisions in a 2007 spending bill.

Lungren helped steer to passage the 1986 Immigration Reform Act that tightened border enforcement but provided one-time amnesty for illegal immigrants in the country prior to 1982. In 2005, he cosponsored a border security bill to add thousands of enforcement agents at the borders. The provision was later incorporated into the House immigration bill.

The second of seven children, Lungren remembers walking precincts for Republican candidates at age 6, when his father was President Nixon's personal physician. Lungren originally wanted to follow his dad into medicine, but discovered early in college he wasn't academically suited for medical school.

He made an unsuccessful bid for the House in 1976, but two years later won a rematch and served in Congress for 10 years before leaving to serve as California's state treasurer. But Lungren was accused of being overly partisan and didn't win state Senate confirmation. He bounced back, winning election to become California attorney general, a position he held from 1991 to 1999.

In 1998, he made a failed bid for the governorship, suffering a 20-percentage-point defeat. After that race, he stayed in the Sacramento area and jumped into the 2004 House race when three-term Republican incumbent Doug Ose announced his retirement.

In the primary, Lungren defeated two well-financed candidates, including Mary Ose, the incumbent's sister. He cruised to a general election victory in the GOP-dominated district. In the 2006 race against Democrat Bill Durston, a physician and Vietnam veteran, he garnered 60 percent of the vote. He again held off Durston in a 2008 rematch.

KEY VOTES

2008

No Delay consideration of Colombia free-trade agreement

No Override Bush veto of federal farm and nutrition programs reauthorization bill

Yes Overhaul surveillance laws and permit dismissal of suits against companies that conducted warrantless wiretapping

Yes Grant mortgage relief to homeowners and funding for Fannie Mae and Freddie Mac

Yes Approve initial $700 billion program to stabilize financial markets

Yes Approve final $700 billion program to stabilize financial markets

No Provide $14 billion in loans to automakers

2007

No Increase minimum wage by $2.10 an hour

No Approve $124.2 billion in emergency war spending and set goal for redeployment of troops from Iraq

Yes Reject federal contraceptive assistance to international family planning groups

Yes Override Bush veto of $23.2 billion water projects authorization bill

? Implement Peru free-trade agreement

No Approve energy policy overhaul with new fuel economy standards

Yes Clear $473.5 billion omnibus spending bill, including $70 billion for military operations

CQ VOTE STUDIES

	PARTY UNITY		PRESIDENTIAL SUPPORT	
	SUPPORT	OPPOSE	SUPPORT	OPPOSE
2008	95%	5%	86%	14%
2007	96%	4%	87%	13%
2006	94%	6%	93%	7%
2005	97%	3%	91%	9%

INTEREST GROUPS

	AFL-CIO	ADA	CCUS	ACU
2008	7%	5%	94%	88%
2007	4%	0%	83%	96%
2006	21%	10%	80%	84%
2005	13%	0%	93%	92%

CALIFORNIA 3
Central – Sacramento suburbs

The 3rd stretches west from Alpine County on the Nevada border, bends around Sacramento and reaches Solano County, near Napa. It experiences periodic flooding from the Sacramento and American rivers, making water and flood control important local issues. The politically competitive district is predominantly white and white-collar.

More than 85 percent of the 3rd's population comes from a chunk of Sacramento County that includes the Sacramento suburbs of Citrus Heights and Rio Linda. Many residents here moved to the 3rd to work in state government or to escape the state's more crowded urban areas while still working in the technology industries. Folsom, to Sacramento's northeast, is home to an Intel campus that hosts the company's information technology division, but the Sacramento suburbs will be looking to rebound from falling home values and rising unemployment.

Wineries and agriculture dominate the 3rd's economy. Amador County, southeast of Sacramento, is home to several large wineries. Elsewhere, growers rely on grape, almond and prune production, except in forestry-

heavy Alpine County, where mountains and skiing are prevalent. McClellan Air Force Base closed in 2001 and was converted into a business park (shared with the 5th) that attracted high-tech businesses.

While Sacramento County in the district's western arm is the politically competitive heart of the 3rd, its surrounding areas tend to be largely rural and Republican. Republicans George W. Bush, in 2004, and Gov. Arnold Schwarzenegger, in 2006, each won re-election here easily. But, the 3rd was one of only 34 districts in the nation to vote both for Democrat Barack Obama and for a Republican U.S. House member in 2008. Obama carried the district by less than 1 percentage point in the presidential election, and Rep. Dan Lungren won re-election without reaching 50 percent of the vote.

MAJOR INDUSTRY
Agriculture, timber, technology

CITIES
Citrus Heights, 85,071; Arden-Arcade (unincorporated) (pt.), 53,597; Folsom, 51,884; Carmichael, 49,742

NOTABLE
Folsom Powerhouse, finished in 1895 and now a state park, was the nation's first long-distance hydroelectric power plant.

Rep. Tom McClintock (R)

Elected 2008; 1st term

McClintock is a strict conservative who supports tax cuts, a balanced budget and smaller government — all priorities he pursued during nearly 30 years in California politics. "I think freedom is a vastly superior policy to the authoritarianism that the Democrats have offered in every field of governance," he said. "I intend to continue to press that case as long as I am drawing breath."

In February 2009, he joined all House Republicans in opposing President Obama's $787 billion economic stimulus bill, and then balked at a subsequent $410 billion catchall spending bill. "The supporters of this policy have not been able to cite a single example in all of recorded history where massive government spending has stimulated an economy. And there are plenty of examples where it has ruined economies and brought down great nations," he said.

He also opposed expansion of the State Children's Health Insurance Program, which covers children whose families don't qualify for Medicaid. "This is no longer a program for the children of poor people," he said. "It is being used to insinuate government into the medical care of every American." He said families earning six-figure incomes are pushed into the program.

From his seat on the Natural Resources Committee, he hopes to loosen federal restrictions on timber clearing, which he believes will prevent forest fires and help the timber industry. On Education and Labor, he plans to advocate a repeal of the No Child Left Behind education law. The panel is expected during the 111th Congress (2009-10) to take up renewal of the program.

McClintock represented suburban Los Angeles for more than 20 years in the California Legislature. He had a tough time in his 2008 bid to replace GOP Rep. John Doolittle, who was under federal scrutiny for his ties to now-convicted lobbyist Jack Abramoff. Both his primary opponent, former Rep. Doug Ose, and general election opponent, Democrat Charlie Brown, accused McClintock of being a "carpetbagger." McClintock had moved his family to the Sacramento area in the mid-1990s to be with them during the legislative season. California law required him to retain his legal residence in Thousand Oaks. But he touted his legislative record and eked out a victory over Brown in a race that wasn't called until weeks after Election Day.

CAPITOL OFFICE
225-2511
mcclintock.house.gov
508 Cannon Bldg. 20515-0504; fax 225-5444

COMMITTEES
Education & Labor
Natural Resources

RESIDENCE
Thousand Oaks

BORN
July 10, 1956; Bronxville, N.Y.

RELIGION
Baptist

FAMILY
Wife, Lori McClintock; two children

EDUCATION
U. of California, Los Angeles, B.A. 1978 (political science)

CAREER
Conservative public policy group director; state legislative aide; newspaper columnist

POLITICAL HIGHLIGHTS
Ventura County Republican Central Committee chairman, 1979-81; Calif. Assembly, 1982-92; Republican nominee for U.S. House, 1992; Republican nominee for Calif. controller, 1994; Calif. Assembly, 1996-2000; Calif. Senate, 2000-08; Republican nominee for Calif. controller, 2002; candidate for governor (recall election), 2003; Republican nominee for lieutenant governor, 2006

ELECTION RESULTS

2008 GENERAL

Tom McClintock (R)	185,790	50.3%
Charlie Brown (D)	183,990	49.7%

2008 PRIMARY

Tom McClintock (R)	51,655	53.5%
Doug Ose (R)	37,802	39.1%
Suzanne Jones (R)	4,920	5.1%
Theodore Terbolizard (R)	2,249	2.3%

CALIFORNIA 4

Northeast — Roseville, Rocklin

The largely rural 4th, featuring lakes, rivers and mountains, starts at the Oregon border and drops down the Nevada border to Lake Tahoe. The district also takes in areas near Sacramento in the southwestern corner.

The mining counties of El Dorado and Placer give the 4th a Gold Rush feel, but the modern industry here is based in technology. Placer, El Dorado and Nevada counties host more than three-fourths of the district's population and the facilities for big technology firms like Hewlett-Packard and Oracle. These areas draw residents who want to leave crowded cities but still work in technology fields.

Timber and agriculture also play important roles in the economy, and the 4th is a popular vacation destination. Ski resorts dot the Sierra Nevada mountain range, and Lake Tahoe in eastern El Dorado and Placer counties offers skiing, hiking, shopping and golf.

Here, visitors may opt for resorts, condominiums or cabins. Placer's abundant natural beauty is a draw for retirees. Economic uncertainty leaves the local technology, tourism and retail markets vulnerable.

The 4th has Califoria's highest percentage of white residents (84 percent) and was safe Republican territory for decades. Republican John McCain won here by a 10-percentage-point margin in the 2008 presidential election, and his two highest percentages statewide were in Modoc and Lassen counties. But Republican Rep. Tom McClintock defeated Democrat Charlie Brown, who also had run in 2006, by fewer than 2,000 votes in one of the nation's closest elections.

MAJOR INDUSTRY
Technology, agriculture, mining, tourism

CITIES
Roseville, 79,921; Rocklin, 36,330

NOTABLE
Lake Tahoe is the second-deepest lake in the nation and 10th-deepest in the world.

Rep. Doris Matsui (D)

Elected March 2005; 2nd full term

CAPITOL OFFICE
225-7163
matsui.house.gov
222 Cannon Bldg. 20515-0505; fax 225-0566

COMMITTEES
Energy & Commerce
Rules

RESIDENCE
Sacramento

BORN
Sept. 25, 1944; Poston, Ariz.

RELIGION
Methodist

FAMILY
Widowed; one child

EDUCATION
U. of California, Berkeley, B.A. 1966 (psychology)

CAREER
Lobbyist; White House aide; homemaker;
state computer systems analyst

POLITICAL HIGHLIGHTS
No previous office

ELECTION RESULTS

2008 GENERAL

Doris Matsui (D)	164,242	74.3%
Paul A. Smith (R)	46,002	20.8%
L. R. Roberts (PFP)	10,731	4.8%

2008 PRIMARY

Doris Matsui (D)	unopposed

2006 GENERAL

Doris Matsui (D)	105,676	70.8%
Claire Yan (R)	35,106	23.5%
Jeff Kravitz (GREEN)	6,466	4.3%
John C. Reiger (PFP)	2,018	1.4%

PREVIOUS WINNING PERCENTAGES
2005 Special Election (68%)

While many members of Congress aim to distance themselves from Washington, Matsui makes no bones about being an insider. Her government connections have sometimes stirred criticism, but she balances that by showing a willingness to go her own way.

Matsui won the seat held by her late husband Robert T. Matsui, who died days before he was to be sworn in for his 14th term. She knew her way around Washington not only as a congressional spouse, but as a member of President Clinton's staff and as a K Street lobbyist. She says her connections have helped her. "I think every one of us [uses] what we have," she said.

The Matsuis came to know Nancy Pelosi, now Speaker, in the 1970s when she was active in the state party and Robert was campaigning for a seat in Congress. When he passed away suddenly in 2005, Pelosi, then serving as minority leader, led the way in coalescing Democratic Party support behind his wife's run for his seat.

When Doris Matsui won the special election, Pelosi gave her a seat on the Rules Committee that shapes debate on major bills. Matsui also sits on the Democratic Steering Committee, which makes committee assignments. In June 2008, she was given a coveted seat on the Energy and Commerce Committee, although it required a waiver from the Democratic leadership for her to sit on two exclusive committees.

Matsui is a loyal Democrat, and has supported President Obama's early initiatives to right the economy and limit the damages from the falling housing market. When Obama's $787 billion economic stimulus bill passed the House in February 2009, she said, "Millions of people across our country are suffering too much for this House to shy away from its responsibility to lead."

Her insider reputation has occasionally generated criticism from more ideologically driven Democrats in her district, but she has displayed a willingness to break from the Sacramento establishment at times. In 2008, despite opposition from local developers and the mayor, she refused to challenge the Federal Emergency Management Agency's designation of parts of northern Sacramento as a floodplain. Critics said the decision would limit development and the resulting tax revenue. "We've gotten beyond the point where you can develop anywhere," Matsui said. "We really need to be aware of where we're living."

Before leaving her seat on the Transportation and Infrastructure Committee in May 2008 to take the Energy and Commerce slot, Matsui had focused on water and land use, as well as flood control. She gained support for an amendment, included in the Democratic farm bill in May 2008, which made the Sacramento River Watershed eligible for funding under a new $280 million program aimed at improving water quality. She originally had pushed a broader amendment that also focused on farmland conservation and flood control, but scaled it back in response to stiff opposition from farmers in her district.

Pelosi also appointed Matsui to the Smithsonian Institution's Board of Regents. Soon after her appointment, the head of the museum complex stepped down amid criticism of his lavish expense-account spending. Matsui oversaw an internal review in the wake of the scandal that resulted in recommendations to overhaul the structure of the Smithsonian's board and senior management and to encourage greater transparency.

As part of her husband's legacy, Matsui promotes legislation to preserve the World War II Japanese-American internment camps as historic sites. But she differs on one of his signature issues: free trade. Matsui, who helped push through the North American Free Trade Agreement when she was part of the Clinton White House, voted against the Central America Free Trade Agreement in 2005. She said it lacked adequate labor and environmental protection and suggested her husband had similar reservations. She voted for the Peru Free Trade Agreement in November 2007.

Matsui and her husband came from similar backgrounds, both having spent part of their childhoods in internment camps that housed detained Japanese-Americans during World War II. She was born in the Poston internment camp in Arizona, but was too young to remember the experience; her family moved out when she was 3 months old. Her parents tried to shield her from their painful memories. "They never lost hope in the idea that this country is the best country in the world," she said.

Matsui drew on that background in 2006 when speaking against legislation allowing the George W. Bush administration to aggressively interrogate and prosecute terrorism suspects. "I know something about what can happen to the rights of Americans when the executive branch overreaches in a time of war," she said.

Matsui met her husband at a college dance, while she attended the University of California at Berkeley and he studied law at the University of California at Hastings. They married in 1966. While her husband pursued a political career, Matsui raised their son and worked with Sacramento-area nonprofit organizations before they moved to Washington.

In 1992, Clinton rewarded her for her early support of his campaign with a spot on his eight-member presidential transition committee. She became a deputy assistant to the president and the highest-ranking Asian-American official in the White House. After leaving the White House in 1998, she went to work as a lobbyist and as government relations director at the Washington law firm Collier Shannon Scott, representing communications and high-tech companies, a job she held until running for Congress.

Taking her husband's seat was an unexpected turn for Matsui. Though he had been diagnosed with a rare bone disease, he had been re-elected in November 2004. A few weeks later, the Matsuis brought their 18-month-old granddaughter, Anna, to the House floor to prepare the toddler for attending the congressman's swearing-in. The next day, he was admitted to the hospital with pneumonia. He died just eight days later, on New Year's Day 2005.

As he lay in the hospital with an increasingly grim prognosis, Matsui encouraged his wife to run for his seat. Some eight weeks later, she emerged victorious in a special election from a crowded field of a dozen candidates, winning 68 percent of the vote. She has since won easily, taking more than 70 percent of the vote in her last two elections.

KEY VOTES

2008

Yes Delay consideration of Colombia free-trade agreement

Yes Override Bush veto of federal farm and nutrition programs reauthorization bill

No   Overhaul surveillance laws and permit dismissal of suits against companies that conducted warrantless wiretapping

Yes Grant mortgage relief to homeowners and funding for Fannie Mae and Freddie Mac

Yes Approve initial $700 billion program to stabilize financial markets

Yes Approve final $700 billion program to stabilize financial markets

Yes Provide $14 billion in loans to automakers

2007

Yes Increase minimum wage by $2.10 an hour

Yes Approve $124.2 billion in emergency war spending and set goal for redeployment of troops from Iraq

No   Reject federal contraceptive assistance to international family planning groups

Yes Override Bush veto of $23.2 billion water projects authorization bill

Yes Implement Peru free-trade agreement

Yes Approve energy policy overhaul with new fuel economy standards

No   Clear $473.5 billion omnibus spending bill, including $70 billion for military operations

CQ VOTE STUDIES

	PARTY UNITY		PRESIDENTIAL SUPPORT	
	SUPPORT	OPPOSE	SUPPORT	OPPOSE
2008	99%	1%	13%	87%
2007	99%	1%	5%	95%
2006	97%	3%	25%	75%
2005	98%	2%	14%	86%

INTEREST GROUPS

	AFL-CIO	ADA	CCUS	ACU
2008	100%	100%	56%	0%
2007	96%	95%	55%	0%
2006	93%	95%	33%	4%
2005	93%	100%	46%	0%

CALIFORNIA 5

Sacramento

California state politics and triple-digit temperatures dominate the 5th, located in the hot Central Valley. It's home to the state capital, Sacramento, and reaches east and south to include a few upper-middle-class suburbs such as Arden-Arcade and Elk Grove (both are shared with the 3rd).

Sacramento first attracted fortune hunters after gold was found on the banks of the nearby Sacramento River in 1849. For decades, the presence of cheaper land kept local housing prices below those of San Francisco and elsewhere in the area, and the cost of living was only slightly above the national average. A national housing market crisis, however, forced foreclosure on many district residents.

State government has provided the lion's share of the 5th's employment, but local budget shortfalls have caused layoffs. Sacramento is home to a California State University campus, and, outside of government, the city's largest employer is the University of California, Davis, medical center.

Other key employers include large technology firms such as Intel and

Hewlett-Packard, but high-tech unemployment rates in the area have climbed. The nearby Port of Sacramento (located in the 1st), which handles more than 1 million tons of cargo each year and is linked to the San Francisco Bay and Pacific Ocean, is another economic driver.

The city works to lure tourists to the Old Sacramento neighborhood on the waterfront, home to museums, restaurants, shopping and an annual jazz festival. The California State Fair also attracts visitors.

The 5th is racially diverse, with Hispanics making up 21 percent of residents and Asians and blacks each accounting for at least 14 percent of the total population. Barack Obama won 70 percent of the 5th's vote in the 2008 presidential election.

MAJOR INDUSTRY
State government, technology, health care

CITIES
Sacramento, 407,018; Arden-Arcade (unincorporated) (pt.), 42,428; Parkway-South Sacramento (unincorporated), 36,468

NOTABLE
Founded in 1885, the Crocker Art Museum in Sacramento is the oldest public art museum west of the Mississippi River.

Rep. Lynn Woolsey (D)

Elected 1992; 9th term

CAPITOL OFFICE
225-5161
woolsey.house.gov
2263 Rayburn Bldg. 20515-0506; fax 225-5163

COMMITTEES
Education & Labor
 (Workforce Protections - chairwoman)
Foreign Affairs
Science & Technology

RESIDENCE
Petaluma

BORN
Nov. 3, 1937; Seattle, Wash.

RELIGION
Presbyterian

FAMILY
Divorced; four children

EDUCATION
U. of Washington, attended 1955-57 (business);
U. of San Francisco, B.S. 1980 (human resources
& organizational behavior)

CAREER
Employment placement company owner;
human resources manager

POLITICAL HIGHLIGHTS
Petaluma City Council, 1985-93

ELECTION RESULTS

2008 GENERAL

Lynn Woolsey (D)	229,672	71.7%
Mike Halliwell (R)	77,073	24.1%
Joel R. Smolen (LIBERT)	13,617	4.2%

2008 PRIMARY

Lynn Woolsey (D)	88,969	100.0%

2006 GENERAL

Lynn Woolsey (D)	173,190	70.2%
Todd Hooper (R)	64,405	26.1%
Richard W. Friesen (LIBERT)	9,028	3.7%

PREVIOUS WINNING PERCENTAGES
2004 (73%); 2002 (67%); 2000 (64%); 1998 (68%);
1996 (62%); 1994 (58%); 1992 (65%)

Woolsey is an unambiguous liberal and persistent voice on issues affecting racial minorities and women, workforce protections, a single-payer national health care system and the Iraq War. She stirs up publicity with curt comments and untraditional tactics. Yet when it comes to shaping national policy, some critics within her party say she is ineffectual, and even too liberal for her left-leaning San Francisco Bay district.

One of her most famous moments in Congress was in 1999, when she was booted out of a Senate hearing room by conservative Sen. Jesse Helms of North Carolina for attempting to protest Helms' failure to support a global treaty condemning discrimination against women. During the House debate in 2003 on President George W. Bush's bill to create a Medicare prescription drug benefit for the elderly — a bill Woolsey (WOOL-zee) considered inadequate — she led 84 Democratic lawmakers in publicly renouncing their membership in the AARP to protest the organization's support of the bill. The bill still became law.

During Bush's presidency she was one of the most outspoken critics of the Iraq War, frustrated that Democrats and the White House wouldn't go further to end U.S. involvement immediately. But during the 110th Congress (2007-08), she proved more successful at generating anti-war publicity than actually curtailing military involvement. In 2007, she joined two other liberal congresswomen from California, Barbara Lee and Maxine Waters. They nicknamed themselves "The Triad" as they spoke out against the war at a series of rallies in states holding early presidential primaries. But she angered centrist colleagues that year when she told anti-war activists that they should "go after Democrats" for not being tough enough about ending the war, even if it cost them their congressional majority.

Her guest at the 2006 State of the Union address, activist Cindy Sheehan, wore a T-shirt bearing an anti-war message and was arrested by Capitol police. Woolsey was unbowed. "Stifling the truth will not blind Americans to the immorality of sending young Americans to die in an unnecessary war," she said.

She viewed President Obama's 2008 campaign pledge to bring troops home as promising. But she quickly criticized the president's plan, announced in February 2009, to draw down the number of troops over 18 months and leave between 35,000 and 50,000 troops in Iraq after August 2010. Woolsey, a leader of the 70-odd member Out of Iraq Caucus, called the announcement "totally unacceptable." She said leaving any large presence in the country would signal the United States intends to remain "as an enduring occupational force."

Woolsey has achieved some success as chairwoman of the Education and Labor Subcommittee on Workforce Protections. During the 110th Congress, she introduced a measure to provide job-protected leave for family members who need to take time off of work to care for injured soldiers. Her legislation was folded into the fiscal 2008 defense authorization bill that Bush signed into law in January 2008.

Woolsey, the mother of a gay man, also helped move legislation in 2007 aimed at protecting gays and lesbians from workplace discrimination. The measure passed the House, but without the amendment Woolsey sought to protect transgender people. The House in 2007 also passed Woolsey's bill that would increase fines for companies and individuals who violate child labor laws.

A member of the Science and Technology Committee, Woolsey has unsuccessfully pushed "Go Girl" legislation to encourage girls to study science and math. She also advocates federal investment in energy efficiency and conservation.

Woolsey is co-chairwoman of the Congressional Progressive Caucus. Early in the 111th Congress (2009-10), she led the group's call for an economic stimulus package costing an estimated $1 trillion. She said that "anything much less than $1 trillion would be like trying to put out a forest fire with a squirt gun." She supported the $787 billion plan that became law but said she remained "concerned that this legislation is not large enough to confront the crisis we face."

Woolsey grew up in Seattle in a Republican family. Her mother and her stepfather, a veterinarian, ran a small-animal clinic. (Her biological father was not involved in her life after her parents divorced.) She said that, as a young adult, she was influenced by the election of President Kennedy and drawn to the Democratic Party.

She dropped out of the University of Washington to get married and moved with her stockbroker husband to the suburbs of San Francisco. But the marriage fractured, and at age 29 she was divorced with three preschool children. She became a secretary, supplementing her income for three years with Aid to Families with Dependent Children, the national welfare program. "I know firsthand what a difference it makes," says Woolsey, who opposed the 1996 welfare overhaul that set new limits on benefits.

She returned to school and at 42 graduated from the University of San Francisco. When a group of engineers left the company she worked for to start a telecommunications company, they took Woolsey with them. She eventually became the human resources manager of Harris Digital Telephone Systems and later started her own human resources consulting company.

In 1981, she joined a local effort to control fast-paced development in Petaluma. After failing to get an appointment to the planning commission, she ran for city council. In 1992, she ran for the open district seat vacated by Democrat Barbara Boxer, who was running for the Senate. Woolsey won the nomination out of a field of nine candidates. She faced a tough race against Republican Bill Filante, a liberal assemblyman, until Filante fell ill with cancer and ended his campaign. She was among a record number of women elected to Congress that year.

Though she typically has had easy re-elections, her campaign in 2004 suffered from news reports she had tried to persuade a Marin County judge to reduce the sentence for an aide's son, convicted of rape. She later apologized, and ended up taking 73 percent of the vote that year.

KEY VOTES

2008

Yes Delay consideration of Colombia free-trade agreement

Yes Override Bush veto of federal farm and nutrition programs reauthorization bill

No Overhaul surveillance laws and permit dismissal of suits against companies that conducted warrantless wiretapping

Yes Grant mortgage relief to homeowners and funding for Fannie Mae and Freddie Mac

No Approve initial $700 billion program to stabilize financial markets

Yes Approve final $700 billion program to stabilize financial markets

Yes Provide $14 billion in loans to automakers

2007

Yes Increase minimum wage by $2.10 an hour

No Approve $124.2 billion in emergency war spending and set goal for redeployment of troops from Iraq

No Reject federal contraceptive assistance to international family planning groups

Yes Override Bush veto of $23.2 billion water projects authorization bill

No Implement Peru free-trade agreement

+ Approve energy policy overhaul with new fuel economy standards

? Clear $473.5 billion omnibus spending bill, including $70 billion for military operations

CQ VOTE STUDIES

	PARTY UNITY		PRESIDENTIAL SUPPORT	
	SUPPORT	OPPOSE	SUPPORT	OPPOSE
2008	98%	2%	16%	84%
2007	99%	1%	6%	94%
2006	98%	2%	7%	93%
2005	99%	1%	13%	87%
2004	98%	2%	15%	85%

INTEREST GROUPS

	AFL-CIO	ADA	CCUS	ACU
2008	100%	80%	56%	4%
2007	96%	80%	40%	0%
2006	93%	100%	20%	4%
2005	93%	100%	33%	8%
2004	93%	95%	0%	8%

CALIFORNIA 6

Northern Bay Area – Sonoma and Marin counties

Travel north across the Golden Gate Bridge and the scenery changes from the cityscape of San Francisco to the Pacific coastline and inland hills that make up the 6th District.

The 6th has all of Marin County, a very affluent area filled with highly educated residents who are self-employed or San Francisco commuters with high-tech or other white-collar jobs. Marin's suburban population is primarily divided between towns in the foothills of Mt. Tamalpais and waterfront destinations like tony Sausalito, Tiburon and Stinson Beach. Median home prices rose to near $1 million before the U.S. housing market crash, but unemployment rates here remain lower than many regions of the state. Marin also is home to San Quentin State Prison — the oldest correctional facility in California — as well as San Rafael and popular getaway spots such as Point Reyes National Seashore and Muir Woods.

Wine and dairy ranching are key to the district's economy, and Sonoma County is one of the nation's leading producers of wine. Sonoma (shared with the 1st) has hundreds of wineries and is home to a California State University campus and Santa Rosa, the district's largest city. Vineyard tours, tastings and sales form the bedrock of the local tourism industry.

Some technology companies had made inroads in the district, but Marin County officials have acknowledged difficulty retaining firms, due in part to the high cost of housing and lack of developable land for expansion. Although Lucasfilm's Skywalker Ranch is tucked among the hills in a remote area of Marin, the production company has followed many video game and software developers to San Francisco.

Solidly Democratic, the district's affluent residents, despite their wealth, tend to have progressive views. Democrats outnumber Republicans more than 2-to-1 in voter registration, and Democrat Barack Obama received 76 percent of the 6th's vote in the 2008 presidential election.

MAJOR INDUSTRY
Agriculture, telecommunications, tourism

CITIES
Santa Rosa, 147,595; San Rafael, 56,063; Petaluma, 54,548

NOTABLE
The Charles M. Schulz Museum in Santa Rosa celebrates the work of the "Peanuts" creator.

Rep. George Miller (D)

Elected 1974; 18th term

CAPITOL OFFICE
225-2095
www.house.gov/georgemiller
2205 Rayburn Bldg. 20515-0507; fax 225-5609

COMMITTEES
Education & Labor - chairman
Natural Resources

RESIDENCE
Martinez

BORN
May 17, 1945; Richmond, Calif.

RELIGION
Roman Catholic

FAMILY
Wife, Cynthia Miller; two children

EDUCATION
San Francisco State U., B.A. 1968;
U. of California, Davis, J.D. 1972

CAREER
Lawyer; state legislative aide

POLITICAL HIGHLIGHTS
Democratic nominee for Calif. Senate, 1969

ELECTION RESULTS

2008 GENERAL

George Miller (D)	170,962	72.8%
Roger Allen Petersen (R)	51,166	21.8%
Bill Callison (PFP)	6,695	2.8%
Camden McConnell (LIBERT)	5,950	2.5%

2008 PRIMARY

George Miller (D)	unopposed

2006 GENERAL

George Miller (D)	118,000	84.0%
Camden McConnell (LIBERT)	22,486	16.0%

PREVIOUS WINNING PERCENTAGES
2004 (76%); 2002 (71%); 2000 (76%); 1998 (77%);
1996 (72%); 1994 (70%); 1992 (70%); 1990 (61%);
1988 (68%); 1986 (67%); 1984 (66%); 1982 (67%);
1980 (63%); 1978 (63%); 1976 (75%); 1974 (56%)

Miller has long been a stalwart champion of progressive causes, seeking more funding for public education, stronger workers' rights and tougher consumer safety and environmental regulation. One of three remaining "Watergate babies" of 1974 and founder of the Congressional Progressive Caucus, he has done what's necessary to push his priorities whether he's in the majority or under the hand of Republicans with a vastly different agenda.

He was once seen as a fiery partisan willing to butt heads with anyone in his path, but since taking the helm of the Education and Labor Committee in 2007, he has adopted a more inclusive style, seeking the input of other leading Democrats as well as Republicans. And with staunch allies in the Obama administration, he is seeing some progress on his agenda.

In early 2009, Miller was a central player in obtaining more than $100 billion for education in the $787 billion economic stimulus bill. In final negotiations, he helped restore funds for some education programs that had been removed from the bill in the Senate. In the end, the bill included billions of dollars to shore up local school budgets and more money for Pell grants, as well as money for school modernization and construction. The No Child Left Behind program also received its full authorized funding for the first time — a matter that had been high on Miller's agenda since the law was enacted in 2002.

Miller saw some successes early in the 111th Congress (2009-10) on the labor front as well, shepherding to enactment legislation dealing with wage discrimination against women. The bill had passed the House in 2007, but stalled in the Senate. In March 2009, he and Democratic Sen. Tom Harkin of Iowa pushed legislation to make it easier to unionize workplaces.

Miller has more on his plate for the 111th — including rewriting the No Child Left Behind law, which sets elementary and secondary school policy — but recognizes he will have to carefully pick his battles if he hopes to get over the speed bumps presented by the Senate and the nation's flagging economy. "I've been around long enough to know, if nothing else, this place will always surprise you," he said in early 2009.

Miller is a close ally of Speaker Nancy Pelosi, whose district is just across the San Francisco Bay. He was one of her earliest backers, encouraging her to run for a party leadership post in 2001 and setting up her eventual run for Speaker. In exchange, Pelosi named him co-chairman of the Democratic Steering and Policy Committee, giving him a coveted seat in the room when leaders hone policy and message. He has headed the policy side of the operation since 2003 and he has the Speaker's ear on key education and labor policy matters.

When Democrats regained power in the House in 2007, he brought to fruition two items on the Democrats' "Six for '06" agenda: student loan interest rate cuts and a minimum wage increase. On labor issues, he made good on promises for greater protections, mine safety legislation and working to gain passage of a bill to ban job discrimination against gay and lesbian individuals.

Some of Miller's successes have stemmed from his willingness to bring in other leaders and GOP members when drafting legislation. Working on an overhaul of the Higher Education Act in 2007, he allowed subcommittee chairmen and influential GOP committee members to take the lead on substantial portions of the rewrite. The result was a successful bill, and House-Senate negotiations on the final version were a self-described "lovefest." The bill again increased Pell grant funding, tightened the ethical and legal restrictions on private lenders and made colleges and universities more accountable for tuition increases.

Even in the most rancorous debates, Miller tries to involve the GOP. When he gained the power to depose witnesses in an investigation into a Utah mining collapse at Crandall Canyon — an effort the minority called premature, dangerous and irresponsible — he helped craft the rules so the majority had to consult with the minority no later than three days before issuing any notice of a subpoena or deposition. His style was not as effective in his effort in the 110th Congress (2007-08) to rewrite the No Child Left Behind Act. He helped write the original law, but Miller and Democrats long complained it was severely underfunded by the George W. Bush administration. Miller posted his behemoth draft on the panel's Web site, presenting it for commentary from anyone interested. That prompted a horde of responses and exposed the draft to public lambasting before Miller could coalesce congressional support. Freshman Democrats defected, and Republicans flocked to an alternative bill that would have essentially made the law voluntary.

If the defeat stung, Miller didn't show it. He has frequently warned opponents that if they want to go head-to-head with him, "they better bring lunch."

Miller is known for his rants against Republicans with whom he disagrees. A longtime aide remembers when Miller lost his cool during the GOP's talk of its "Contract With America" in the early 1990s. Miller railed against the policies from the podium on the floor, refusing to relinquish his time. The aide said the chairman "was banging the gavel so hard that the head of the gavel came off." The aide remembers watching on C-SPAN as the head of the gavel bounced off the dais and onto the floor.

He's also on the Natural Resources panel, where he previously battled GOP attempts to revise major environmental laws. He opposes drilling for oil off the California coast and in Alaska's Arctic National Wildlife Refuge.

Miller developed an interest in politics when he was growing up and watching his father, George Jr., broker legislative deals on water issues and education as a state senator for 20 years. A seeming physical testament to the father and son's complementary work — although decades apart — is a bridge named for the younger Miller that opened in 2007 alongside an older bridge named for his father. His grandfather, George Miller Sr., was also in public service, as the assistant civil engineer in Richmond.

Miller was a law student in 1969 when his father died. He went to work as a legislative aide to state Sen. George Moscone, the Democratic floor leader and later San Francisco mayor. He was 29 in 1974 when he was elected to succeed Democratic Rep. Jerome Waldie, who chose to run for governor. Miller won his seat in part by exploiting the Watergate scandal. He took 56 percent of the vote and has won re-election easily ever since.

KEY VOTES

2008

Yes Delay consideration of Colombia free-trade agreement

Yes Override Bush veto of federal farm and nutrition programs reauthorization bill

No Overhaul surveillance laws and permit dismissal of suits against companies that conducted warrantless wiretapping

Yes Grant mortgage relief to homeowners and funding for Fannie Mae and Freddie Mac

Yes Approve initial $700 billion program to stabilize financial markets

Yes Approve final $700 billion program to stabilize financial markets

Yes Provide $14 billion in loans to automakers

2007

Yes Increase minimum wage by $2.10 an hour

Yes Approve $124.2 billion in emergency war spending and set goal for redeployment of troops from Iraq

No Reject federal contraceptive assistance to international family planning groups

Yes Override Bush veto of $23.2 billion water projects authorization bill

No Implement Peru free-trade agreement

Yes Approve energy policy overhaul with new fuel economy standards

No Clear $473.5 billion omnibus spending bill, including $70 billion for military operations

CQ VOTE STUDIES

	PARTY UNITY		PRESIDENTIAL SUPPORT	
	SUPPORT	OPPOSE	SUPPORT	OPPOSE
2008	99%	1%	13%	87%
2007	99%	1%	5%	95%
2006	98%	2%	13%	87%
2005	99%	1%	16%	84%
2004	98%	2%	21%	79%

INTEREST GROUPS

	AFL-CIO	ADA	CCUS	ACU
2008	100%	95%	50%	0%
2007	96%	100%	42%	0%
2006	92%	90%	29%	4%
2005	93%	100%	35%	0%
2004	93%	100%	21%	4%

CALIFORNIA 7

Northeastern Bay Area — Vallejo, Richmond

Situated along the San Pablo Bay and the marshes and deltas where the Sacramento and San Joaquin rivers merge, the 7th combines industrial and suburban areas of northern Contra Costa County with the western end of more rural Solano County.

In Contra Costa County, the district takes in residential Concord (shared with the 10th) and the industrial cities of Richmond and Martinez along San Pablo Bay, home to oil, steel and biotech interests. Chevron facilities in Richmond are major employers, and Martinez, the Contra Costa County seat, is reliant on petroleum processing. Cities in Contra Costa have seen rising unemployment and foreclosure rates.

The 7th's military footprint, firmly stamped down during World War II, is almost gone. Some of Richmond's former Kaiser Shipyards — one of the largest World War II shipbuilding operations — has been redeveloped. The inland half of Concord Naval Weapons Station closed in 1999, and its port, transferred in 2008 to the Army as Military Ocean Terminal, Concord, is the only remaining active military installation in the district.

Health care also is important to the district's economy. The medical system implemented during World War II at the Kaiser Shipyards was the foundation for the modern Kaiser Permanente health organization. Still a key employer, the company has had to cut some jobs and delay construction of regional hospitals. Pittsburg was once known for a thriving steel industry, but recent layoffs have stalled local diversification and redevelopment efforts.

The 7th is safe Democratic territory, as just 20 percent of its voters are registered Republicans. The district gave 72 percent of its presidential vote to Democrat Barack Obama in 2008.

MAJOR INDUSTRY
Petrochemicals, steel, biotech, agriculture, health care

MILITARY BASES
Military Ocean Terminal, Concord, 7 military, 96 civilian (2009)

CITIES
Vallejo, 116,760; Richmond, 99,216; Vacaville, 88,625; Pittsburg, 56,769

NOTABLE
The Rosie the Riveter World War II Home Front National Historical Park in Richmond commemorates the contributions of women who held industrial jobs in support of the war effort.

Rep. Nancy Pelosi (D)

Elected June 1987; 11th full term

CAPITOL OFFICE
225-4965
www.house.gov/pelosi
235 Cannon Bldg. 20515-0508; fax 225-4188

COMMITTEES
Speaker of the House - no committee assignments

RESIDENCE
San Francisco

BORN
March 26, 1940; Baltimore, Md.

RELIGION
Roman Catholic

FAMILY
Husband, Paul Pelosi; five children

EDUCATION
Trinity College (D.C.), A.B. 1962

CAREER
Public relations consultant; senatorial campaign committee finance chairwoman; homemaker

POLITICAL HIGHLIGHTS
Calif. Democratic Party chairwoman, 1981-83

ELECTION RESULTS

2008 GENERAL

Nancy Pelosi (D)	204,996	71.9%
Cindy Sheehan (I)	46,118	16.2%
Dana Walsh (R)	27,614	9.7%
Philip Z. Berg (LIBERT)	6,504	2.3%

2008 PRIMARY

Nancy Pelosi (D)	83,510	89.2%
Shirley Golub (D)	10,105	10.8%

2006 GENERAL

Nancy Pelosi (D)	148,435	80.4%
Mike DeNunzio (R)	19,800	10.7%
Krissy Keefer (GREEN)	13,653	7.4%
Philip Z. Berg (LIBERT)	2,751	1.5%

PREVIOUS WINNING PERCENTAGES
2004 (83%); 2002 (80%); 2000 (84%); 1998 (86%); 1996 (84%); 1994 (82%); 1992 (82%); 1990 (77%); 1988 (76%); 1987 Special Runoff Election (63%)

The first female Speaker of the House, Pelosi is always impeccably dressed and polished in front of TV cameras and combines the style of Jackie Kennedy with the iron will of Margaret Thatcher. She has a ready smile and studied graciousness, but can be as hard-nosed as any high-level figure in Washington. She inspires admiration among Democrats — and loathing among conservatives.

Pelosi (pa-LO-see) spent her first two years in charge of the House berating an unpopular president from the opposing party while trying to keep her modest majority unified in staving off his lame-duck round of legislative priorities. She assumed a much different role in 2009, holding together a larger collection of Democrats behind President Obama's ambitious agenda while acting as his cheerleader-in-chief at the Capitol.

Pointing to her past work on such high-profile issues as gay rights and China's human rights, critics often caricature her as an extremist "San Francisco liberal" out of touch with the rest of the nation. But she has brought a degree of unity to a group that had been known for infighting. By the end of March 2009, House Democrats voted with their party's majority an average of 93 percent of the time — a notch above their record-setting 92 percent party-unity average of the previous two years, when the focus was opposition to President George W. Bush.

She stresses reaching down through the ranks at the expense of letting committee chairs call all the shots, as was often the case under Democratic rule in the years before the GOP took over the House in 1994. "We work hard to build consensus in our caucus and then go forward," she once said. "People tell me it's a woman's way, talking and talking until you reach consensus. But I figure you can spend your time trying to get votes or getting consensus first."

Beyond her talk of inclusion is a fierce determination to advance her agenda. She readily thrusts her leadership team and cadre of committee chairs into the role of legislative field marshals. In April 2009 she directed her members to communicate with constituents to sell the White House and congressional plans to overhaul the nation's health care system through town hall meetings.

She also cajoles her lieutenants into sticking with her. When Maryland Rep. Chris Van Hollen, the top House Democratic election strategist, hinted in November 2008 that he might step down after a single term as chairman of the Democratic Congressional Campaign Committee, he got a phone call from Pelosi. By the next day, Van Hollen had reversed course. Her allies also helped elect her former handpicked assistant, Xavier Becerra of California, as vice chairman of the Democratic Caucus — and then she persuaded him not to accept an offer to become Obama's U.S. trade representative in 2009.

Pelosi has had a long and at times awkward relationship with her most senior leadership colleague, Maryland's Steny H. Hoyer. The two first met in the early 1960s when they both worked for then-Maryland Democratic Sen. Daniel B. Brewster. After the 2006 elections, Pelosi strongly backed John P. Murtha of Pennsylvania over Hoyer for the majority leader's post, but Hoyer easily defeated Murtha.

Pelosi now goes to great lengths to appear in sync with Hoyer, just as she does with the White House. She and Obama coordinate closely on message and agenda. Every weekday morning, two of her top communications aides talk with their White House counterpart. Her senior staffers also are in close touch with Obama's chief of staff, Rahm Emanuel, who was one of Pelosi's top advisers when he was in the House. The result of the consultation is tightly scripted message delivery. When Obama signed a $410 billion catch-all spending bill for fiscal 2009, he simultaneously announced his plans for new procedural changes to make the earmarking process for setting aside funds for special projects more transparent; House Democratic leaders announced their support for such changes just before Obama's remarks.

More than most of her predecessors, Pelosi often participates in floor debate and isn't afraid to throw partisan zingers at Republicans. She complained in April 2009 about a "radical right-wing element" that exerts power within the GOP. She rebuffed criticism about a lack of minority input into a $787 billion economic stimulus law — a measure that drew no House Republican votes — by citing the more than 25 hours of markups in committees and a rule that allowed the GOP to offer a substitute, a motion to recommit and a few floor amendments. "When you can't win on policy, you always turn to process, and then you turn to personalities," she said.

Republicans have determinedly sought to make her Public Enemy No. 1 among voters. With Obama riding high in the polls in early 2009, the GOP directed their fire at her; the National Republican Congressional Committee sent out a fundraising letter that March referring to the nation's economic crisis as the "Pelosi Recession." Alabama Republican Rep. Mike D. Rogers told constituents in April 2009 that Pelosi was "crazy" and "mean as a snake."

Republicans pounced on Pelosi in spring 2009 over the extent of her knowledge on the use of waterboarding on arrested terrorist suspects. They accused her of hypocrisy, saying she was briefed in September 2002 on the controversial technique, which simulates drowning, and did not object. But Pelosi accused the CIA and Bush administration of lying to her about its use and denied she had become complicit in their use of techniques she condemned as torture by not speaking out after she learned they were being used. She said confidentiality requirements made it impossible for her to go public with her objections. GOP lawmakers reacted angrily, accusing her of smearing spy agencies and insisting she still wasn't telling the truth.

She defied the expectations of many GOP critics in the 110th Congress. She shelved causes dear to her liberal allies, like pursuing the impeachment of Bush or strengthening gun control. Instead, she focused on issues that could protect her "majority makers," the largely moderate and conservative freshmen whose victories helped Democrats end 12 years of GOP control in 2006.

Pelosi's ascent to the speakership came as a result of her tireless fundraising and her well-honed political skills. She entered leadership in 2001, when she was elected minority whip. After the 2002 election, when Minority Leader Richard A. Gephardt quit, she was easily elected her party's House leader. Pelosi said she was well aware of the historic nature of her rise to the speakership, which she calls breaking the Capitol's "marble ceiling."

Not long after she became Speaker in 2007, the House quickly passed a poll-tested "Six for '06" package that included the first federal minimum wage increase in a decade and congressional ethics reform. She moved quickly to reinstate the House's pay-as-you-go rules — a matter of the highest importance to the fiscally conservative "Blue Dogs," who insist increased spending has to be offset with increased revenue or spending cuts. While that rule was often subsequently ignored, she and Hoyer reiterated their support for the concept in 2009.

She also got through a $700 billion rescue of the financial services sector in fall 2008, but only after an initial failed vote that some Republicans said partly stemmed from a sharply partisan speech she gave shortly before the vote.

Pelosi freely admits her biggest disappointment in the 110th was Congress' failure to end the Iraq War. The House repeatedly voted for a timetable for troop withdrawal, but the bills usually ran into a GOP Senate roadblock or Bush's veto, much to the disappointment of hard-core Democrats, who blamed

On being the first female Speaker:

"This is an historic moment — for the Congress, and for the women of this country. It is a moment for which we have waited more than 200 years."

– January 2007

On her style:

"We don't go in and say, 'Here's the proposal — now who's on board?' We have a great deal of discussion on issues."

– March 2009

On Obama:

"The difference between being the Speaker without a president of your party and the Speaker with Barack Obama as president is night and day."

– March 2009

On Republicans:

"By and large I say to Republicans across the country: Take back your party, the party of protecting the environment, the party of protecting individual rights. Our country needs a strong, diverse Republican Party."

– April 2009

Pelosi. But she boasted of a long list of other accomplishments, including the first increase in vehicle fuel efficiency standards in 32 years, a big increase in veterans' spending, the largest expansion of college aid in six decades and protecting 25 million families from being hit by the alternative minimum tax, which was originally intended to target only wealthy taxpayers but was not indexed for inflation. Many more House initiatives stalled in the Senate.

For Pelosi, a mother of five and grandmother of nine who waited to run for office until her youngest child was almost ready to graduate from high school, the choice of a political career seemed pre-ordained. She is the sole daughter of Thomas D'Alesandro Jr., a Democratic congressman from Baltimore who served three terms as mayor. Politics and constituent service were a way of life for Nancy and her brothers. She remembers taking turns with her brothers manning a desk in the D'Alesandro home where needy constituents would stop by for help in getting food, a job or a doctor. She learned such favors could make friends and supporters for life.

She attended Trinity College in Washington and remembers as a student being inspired by President Kennedy's inauguration, which she attended. She often recites stretches of his inaugural address from memory to explain her own commitment to public service. While in Washington, she met Paul Pelosi, a Georgetown student who hailed from San Francisco. The two married in 1963 and Pelosi gave birth to her five children over the next six years.

The family moved back to Paul Pelosi's home in San Francisco, and she became increasingly active in Democratic Party affairs in a city that was becoming more and more Democratic. She eventually rose to become state party chairwoman, a job that drew on her fundraising prowess. Along the way, she became close to Rep. Phillip Burton, the San Francisco liberal firebrand who narrowly lost a race for House majority leader.

When Burton died in 1983, he was succeeded by his widow, Sala Burton, also a close Pelosi friend. Sala Burton became terminally ill with cancer in 1987 and personally asked Pelosi to run for the seat. Pelosi dove in, winning a wild special election on her first run for public office.

Pelosi has been re-elected ever since by overwhelming margins in a district that now covers about three-quarters of the 47-square-mile city and is amazingly diverse, including large and well-organized Asian and gay populations. She also has played a lead role in preserving the scenic Presidio of San Francisco as a national park, getting money for the protracted toxics cleanup at the Navy's shuttered Hunters Point shipyard and hundreds of millions of dollars over the years for San Francisco's Municipal Railway and a rail extension to San Francisco International Airport.

KEY VOTES

2008
Yes Delay consideration of Colombia free-trade agreement
Yes Override Bush veto of federal farm and nutrition programs reauthorization bill
Yes Overhaul surveillance laws and permit dismissal of suits against companies that conducted warrantless wiretapping
Yes Grant mortgage relief to homeowners and funding for Fannie Mae and Freddie Mac
Yes Approve initial $700 billion program to stabilize financial markets
Yes Approve final $700 billion program to stabilize financial markets
Yes Provide $14 billion in loans to automakers

2007
Yes Increase minimum wage by $2.10 an hour
Yes Approve $124.2 billion in emergency war spending and set goal for redeployment of troops from Iraq
S Reject federal contraceptive assistance to international family planning groups
S Override Bush veto of $23.2 billion water projects authorization bill
Yes Implement Peru free-trade agreement
Yes Approve energy policy overhaul with new fuel economy standards
S Clear $473.5 billion omnibus spending bill, including $70 billion for military operations

CQ VOTE STUDIES

	PARTY UNITY		PRESIDENTIAL SUPPORT	
	SUPPORT	OPPOSE	SUPPORT	OPPOSE
2008	98%	2%	25%	75%
2007	99%	1%	5%	95%
2006	98%	2%	25%	75%
2005	99%	1%	16%	84%
2004	97%	3%	21%	79%

INTEREST GROUPS

	AFL-CIO	ADA	CCUS	ACU
2008	100%	50%	38%	0%
2007	100%	–	22%	0%
2006	93%	95%	40%	8%
2005	93%	95%	36%	0%
2004	93%	100%	35%	8%

CALIFORNIA 8
Most of San Francisco

San Francisco is famous for its landmarks, food and diverse collection of neighborhoods, from the Italian and Hispanic centers of North Beach and the Mission District to spots such as Chinatown, hippie haven Haight-Ashbury and the gay mecca of Castro.

More than 80 percent of the city's residents live in the 8th, which takes in the city's north and east and is the state's smallest district. The 8th's Asian population is the third-largest in the nation. The Chinatown neighborhood is one of the largest Chinese communities in North America.

The city boasts many tourist destinations. Alcatraz prison — used as a federal maximum-security facility from 1934 to 1963 and where Al Capone, George "Machine Gun" Kelly and Robert "Birdman" Stroud were once jailed — receives more than 1 million visitors annually. Other popular attractions include: Fisherman's Wharf, on the city's northern waterfront; the Golden Gate Bridge, which connects San Francisco to Marin County; and the Bay Bridge, which traverses the neck of the bay over Treasure Island to Oakland. The city's part of the Golden Gate

National Recreation Area hosts a Lucasfilm facility that opened in 2005 on the site of the former Letterman Army Medical Center at the Presidio.

The 8th also is home to San Francisco's financial district along Montgomery Street, known as the "Wall Street of the West." The Federal Reserve Bank of San Francisco is there, as is the Transamerica Pyramid and the headquarters of brokerage firm Charles Schwab. The city also has a biomedical industry led by the University of California at San Francisco, the city's second-largest employer after local government.

The 8th is safely Democratic. Phil Angelides took 64 percent of the 2006 gubernatorial vote here, despite winning only 39 percent statewide. In the 2008 presidential election, Democrat Barack Obama sailed to victory here with 85 percent of the district's vote.

MAJOR INDUSTRY
Tourism, financial services, health care

CITIES
San Francisco (pt.), 639,088

NOTABLE
The city's famous cable cars were developed by Andrew Smith Hallidie after he witnessed an accident involving a horse-drawn streetcar.

Rep. Barbara Lee (D)

Elected April 1998; 6th full term

Lee occupies the far-left wing of her party, championing gay rights and promoting a social-justice agenda. She represents Oakland and Berkeley, two of the most liberal and diverse communities in California and the nation. Her voting record reflects her district, and she is enormously popular there, consistently winning re-election with more than 80 percent of the vote.

She is chairwoman of the Congressional Black Caucus (CBC) in the 111th Congress (2009-10). Even with the election of the nation's first African-American president, Lee said the CBC will still need to lobby for remedies to problems faced by the African-American community, such as high home foreclosure and unemployment rates. "We have some huge moral gaps that need to be addressed," she said.

She proved early in 2009 that she would not be giving President Obama a free ride when she expressed concern about his selection of New Hampshire GOP Sen. Judd Gregg to head the Commerce Department. She questioned Gregg's suitability for the job because he had opposed President Clinton's request for additional funding for the 2000 census and because he had voted in favor of abolishing the Commerce Department. Gregg later withdrew his nomination, prompting Lee to say his decision was the right one.

Lee was also not that pleased with the final outcome of Obama's $787 billion economic stimulus plan that cleared Congress in February 2009. When the measure returned to the House after passing the Senate, Lee was unhappy with the spending cuts for school construction and education made to appease the three Senate Republicans whose votes were needed for passage. Yet she voted for the final version, saying it was necessary because of "the disastrous economic policies of the previous administration."

Lee was the only member of Congress to vote against authorizing President George W. Bush to use "all necessary and appropriate" force against those he deemed implicated in the Sept. 11 terrorist attacks. But that did nothing to diminish her standing at home. She was pilloried elsewhere, and for a time had to have police protection because of death threats against her. But she remained steadfast. "If I had to do it again, I would do it again," she said in a 2006 interview. "For the life of me, I can't understand blind faith in a president, Democrat or Republican."

A member of the Appropriations Committee, Lee during the 110th Congress (2007-08) helped attach to funding bills provisions to force a U.S. troop withdrawal from Iraq. Although she was thwarted in efforts to set a timeline for withdrawal, she had more luck with proposals to put constraints on the U.S. role in Iraq. In July 2007, the House passed her bill to ban permanent U.S. bases there, a prohibition that became law in a war funding bill enacted a year later. She also won House adoption, during 2008 consideration of the annual defense authorization bill, of her amendment requiring that any U.S. agreement to defend Iraq be expressly authorized by Congress or come in the form of a treaty requiring the consent of the Senate. But her provision was later removed in conference after facing a White House veto threat.

A leader in the battle against AIDS at home and abroad, Lee was an original cosponsor of a five-year, $19 billion international AIDS measure Bush signed into law in 2003. She also cosponsored a huge expansion of the program in 2008, regaining a seat on the Foreign Affairs Committee — where she had served earlier in her career — the day before the panel tackled that overhaul. She won elimination of a statutory ban on travel to the United States by foreigners infected with HIV/AIDS, among other changes, and proudly attended the

CAPITOL OFFICE
225-2661
www.house.gov/lee
2444 Rayburn Bldg. 20515-0509; fax 225-9817

COMMITTEES
Appropriations
Foreign Affairs

RESIDENCE
Oakland

BORN
July 16, 1946; El Paso, Texas

RELIGION
Baptist

FAMILY
Divorced; two children

EDUCATION
Mills College, B.A. 1973 (psychology);
U. of California, Berkeley, M.S.W. 1975

CAREER
Congressional aide

POLITICAL HIGHLIGHTS
Calif. Assembly, 1990-96; Calif. Senate, 1996-98

ELECTION RESULTS

2008 GENERAL
Barbara Lee (D)	238,915	86.1%
Charles Hargrave (R)	26,917	9.7%
James M. Eyer (LIBERT)	11,704	4.2%

2008 PRIMARY
Barbara Lee (D)	80,466	99.9%

2006 GENERAL
Barbara Lee (D)	167,245	86.3%
John "J.D." denDulk (R)	20,786	10.7%
James M. Eyer (LIBERT)	5,655	2.9%

PREVIOUS WINNING PERCENTAGES
2004 (85%); 2002 (81%); 2000 (85%); 1998 (83%);
1998 Special Election (67%)

White House signing ceremony. "Despite his failings on so many critical issues, the president deserves recognition for working with Congress to enact this important legislation," she said. She vowed to use her Appropriations seat to fund the new law's $48 billion, five-year commitment.

Lee has been a strong voice against the Sudanese government for its support of violence carried out in the Darfur region by the Janjaweed militias. In May 2006, she was one of seven members of the Black Caucus arrested at the Sudanese Embassy for disorderly conduct in protest of the government's policies. In February 2007, Bush signed into law her bill barring foreign companies from receiving U.S. government contracts if they invested in Sudan.

Lee is a strong supporter of gay rights and is a founding member of the House Lesbian, Gay, Bisexual and Transgender Equality Caucus. Her politics grew out of her early memories of discrimination. Her grandmother told her that her mother initially was refused treatment at an El Paso, Texas, hospital when in labor with her, and then was left unattended for so long that Lee had to be delivered using forceps. She said for many years she had a mark on her forehead from the forceps.

She spent her early years in El Paso, where the school system was segregated. She and her sister attended a Catholic school where Lee said they were often the only black students. In 1960, the family moved to Southern California. Her public high school had never chosen a black cheerleader, so Lee set about becoming the first. She enlisted the help of the NAACP to put pressure on the selection committee before her tryout. Once she was selected, a riot broke out at the school.

Lee had never even registered to vote when, while studying at Oakland's Mills College, she was faced with a course requirement to work for a political campaign during the presidential election year of 1972. She signed on with Democratic Rep. Shirley Chisholm of New York, the nation's first notable black candidate for president. Lee rose quickly through the ranks, eventually running Chisholm's Northern California campaign. She said she received an "A" in the course.

While earning a master's degree in social work, Lee helped start a community health center in Berkeley before going to work for Democrat Ronald V. Dellums, her predecessor in the House, in 1975. She worked for him in both California and Washington before running for the state legislature, where she served six years in the Assembly. She then spent 17 months in the Senate. When Dellums decided resign in early 1998, he endorsed Lee to succeed him, and she easily won the special election. She has coasted to re-election ever since.

KEY VOTES

2008

Yes	Delay consideration of Colombia free-trade agreement
Yes	Override Bush veto of federal farm and nutrition programs reauthorization bill
No	Overhaul surveillance laws and permit dismissal of suits against companies that conducted warrantless wiretapping
Yes	Grant mortgage relief to homeowners and funding for Fannie Mae and Freddie Mac
No	Approve initial $700 billion program to stabilize financial markets
Yes	Approve final $700 billion program to stabilize financial markets
Yes	Provide $14 billion in loans to automakers

2007

Yes	Increase minimum wage by $2.10 an hour
No	Approve $124.2 billion in emergency war spending and set goal for redeployment of troops from Iraq
No	Reject federal contraceptive assistance to international family planning groups
Yes	Override Bush veto of $23.2 billion water projects authorization bill
No	Implement Peru free-trade agreement
Yes	Approve energy policy overhaul with new fuel economy standards
No	Clear $473.5 billion omnibus spending bill, including $70 billion for military operations

CQ VOTE STUDIES

	PARTY UNITY		PRESIDENTIAL SUPPORT	
	SUPPORT	OPPOSE	SUPPORT	OPPOSE
2008	99%	1%	14%	86%
2007	98%	2%	9%	91%
2006	99%	1%	7%	93%
2005	98%	2%	13%	87%
2004	99%	1%	15%	85%

INTEREST GROUPS

	AFL-CIO	ADA	CCUS	ACU
2008	100%	100%	41%	4%
2007	96%	90%	45%	0%
2006	93%	100%	20%	4%
2005	93%	100%	31%	4%
2004	100%	95%	5%	0%

CALIFORNIA 9
Northwest Alameda County — Oakland, Berkeley

Across the bay from San Francisco, the 9th District is anchored by Oakland and Berkeley, two racially diverse, liberal communities.

More than 60 percent of district residents live in Oakland, which is roughly one-third black. Neighborhoods in the city's eastern hills tend to be wealthy and less diverse. Oakland's unemployment rate is slightly above the national average, and crime is a major concern here. But urban revitalization efforts and the development of downtown have encouraged new residents and businesses to move into the area and have bolstered the local economy. Critics claim that these same development projects threaten to displace low-income residents.

The 9th also includes the fast-growing bayside city of Emeryville, which is home to commercial development and biotech firms. Other high-tech companies include animation studio Pixar, educational technology developer LeapFrog, and software and wireless technology firms.

Just north of Oakland, Berkeley is home to the flagship campus of the University of California system and looks out over the bay from the Berkeley Hills. The rest of the district includes smaller communities such as Albany, a liberal suburb at the north end of the district; Piedmont, a residential "suburb in the city" in Oakland's hills; and unincorporated sections of Alameda County southeast of Oakland — Ashland, Castro Valley, Cherryland and Fairview.

With a core constituency in left-leaning Oakland and Berkeley, the 9th is a Democratic stronghold where Republicans account for less than 10 percent of registered voters. Barack Obama had his best showing in the state here in the 2008 presidential election, capturing 88 percent of the district's vote.

MAJOR INDUSTRY
Biotech, shipping

CITIES
Oakland, 399,484; Berkeley, 102,743; Castro Valley (unincorporated) (pt.), 57,224; Ashland (unincorporated), 20,793

NOTABLE
Wham-O Toys, based in Emeryville, marketed many famous toys, including the Frisbee, Hula Hoop, Hacky Sack and Slip 'n Slide; The synthetic element Berkelium was created at UC-Berkeley.

Expected Vacancy

Rep. Ellen O. Tauscher (D)
Pending Confirmation

Tauscher is a pro-business, pro-defense Democrat who has mastered not only national security policy but also House parliamentary procedure. Her tough-minded, steady approach to both has increased her standing among her colleagues and led President Obama to nominate her as undersecretary of State for arms control and international security in early 2009.

"Keeping nuclear weapons out of the hands of terrorists, making sure other countries do not obtain them and one day, I hope, ridding the world of these terrible weapons has become my passion and, I hope, my life's work," Tauscher (TAU — rhymes with "now" — sher) said in a message explaining her decision to leave Congress to accept the nomination to the State Department, if confirmed.

Advocates of nuclear arms reductions will look to Tauscher to negotiate not only with foreign countries, but also with Senate Republicans to drum up support for efforts to diminish the threat such arms pose.

A former Wall Street investment banker who moved to Northern California two decades ago, Tauscher was first elected in 1996. A charter member and chairwoman of the New Democrat Coalition, a group of business-friendly centrists, the San Francisco Chronicle once described her as "about the closest thing the Bay Area has to a Republican." Democrats were heavily favored to retain the seat.

Democratic Lieutenant Gov. John Garamendi early on was the best-known candidate in the race to succeed Tauscher, but he faced competition from Democratic state Sen. Mark DeSaulnier, whom Tauscher had endorsed before Garamendi declared his candidacy, as well as that of state Assemblywoman Joan Buchanan and others. Republicans hoped Contra Costa County Sheriff Warren Rupf would jump into the special-election field.

As a member of the Armed Services Committee and chairwoman of its Strategic Forces Subcommittee, Tauscher kept a wary eye on Russia. "On Iran, non-proliferation, missile defense, NATO enlargement, pretty much all roads lead through Moscow on some level," she said at the 45th Munich Security Conference in February 2009. She has been a major supporter of the C-17 transport plane, based at Travis Air Force Base in her district, among other places.

Tauscher also will leave open a seat on the Transportation and Infrastructure Committee, where she has aggressively pursued funds to ease traffic congestion in her district.

The eldest daughter of an Irish Catholic grocery store manager in New Jersey, she was the first person in her family to attend college, majoring in early-childhood education. By age 25, she was one of the first women to hold a seat on the New York Stock Exchange. During a 14-year career, she was a vice president of the investment banking firm Bear Stearns and a vice president of the American Stock Exchange.

Tauscher moved to Northern California in 1989 after marrying ComputerLand executive Bill Tauscher. They had a daughter in 1991 and subsequently divorced. Unhappy with the child care options available to her, Tauscher founded a business that screened prospective child care workers. She also published a child care guidebook.

In 1996, Tauscher took on Republican incumbent Bill Baker and won by less than 2 percentage points, but soon cemented her grip on the seat. She took 65 percent of the vote in 2008.

CALIFORNIA 10
East Bay suburbs — Fairfield, Antioch, Livermore

Travel through the Caldecott Tunnel across the Alameda-Contra Costa county line or on Interstate 680 during rush hour and 10th District residents commuting to and from San Francisco or San Jose probably will surround your car. Separated from the rest of the Bay Area by the hills east of Oakland, the 10th's residents are mainly well-educated, wealthy professionals who work outside the district.

Residents here are a mix of an older generation that moved in from Oakland and newer, younger commuters who identify more with San Francisco or Berkeley. Almost two-thirds of residents live in the 10th District's portion of Contra Costa County, including Antioch and most of Concord (shared with the 7th). Housing market concerns and job losses have affected the East Bay. The district's Solano County portion, which includes Fairfield, is a growing but still largely agricultural area where commuters may head south to the Bay Area or northeast to Sacramento.

Although many residents leave the district for work, the 10th is home to two Energy Department defense program laboratories: Lawrence Livermore National Laboratory — one of the country's leading centers of experimental physics research and defense analysis — and the California branch of the Sandia National Laboratory, which provides engineering support and systems integration for nuclear weapons.

The 10th has a relatively moderate political character — residents tend to be more fiscally conservative but share their Bay Area neighbors' views on the environment and other quality-of-life issues. The combination of the working-class agricultural sector and more moderate, but still largely liberal, suburbanites helps tilt the 10th Democratic. Barack Obama received 65 percent of the district's presidential vote in 2008.

MAJOR INDUSTRY
Research, health care, agriculture, service

MILITARY BASES
Travis Air Force Base, 6,762 military, 1,828 civilian (2007)

CITIES
Fairfield, 96,178; Antioch, 90,532; Livermore, 73,345; Concord (pt.), 72,540

NOTABLE
The world's oldest known working light bulb, first installed in 1901, is housed by the Livermore-Pleasanton Fire Department.

PRIOR ELECTION RESULTS

2008 GENERAL		
Ellen O. Tauscher (D)	192,226	65.1%
Nicholas Gerber (R)	91,877	31.1%
Eugene E. Ruyle (PFP)	11,062	3.7%
2006 GENERAL		
Ellen O. Tauscher (D)	130,859	66.4%
Darcy Linn (R)	66,069	33.5%
2004 GENERAL		
Ellen O. Tauscher (D)	182,750	65.7%
Jeff Ketelson (R)	95,349	34.3%

Rep. Jerry McNerney (D)

Elected 2006; 2nd term

CAPITOL OFFICE
225-1947
mcnerney.house.gov
312 Cannon Bldg. 20515-0511; fax 225-4060

COMMITTEES
Energy & Commerce
Veterans' Affairs

RESIDENCE
Pleasanton

BORN
June 18, 1951; Albuquerque, N.M.

RELIGION
Roman Catholic

FAMILY
Wife, Mary McNerney; three children

EDUCATION
U.S. Military Academy, attended 1969-71;
U. of New Mexico, B.S. 1973 (mathematics),
M.S. 1975 (mathematics), Ph.D. 1981 (mathematics)

CAREER
Wind engineering company owner; wind engineer;
renewable energy consultant and researcher

POLITICAL HIGHLIGHTS
Democratic nominee for U.S. House, 2004

ELECTION RESULTS

2008 GENERAL

Jerry McNerney (D)	164,500	55.3%
Dean Andal (R)	133,104	44.7%

2008 PRIMARY

Jerry McNerney (D)	unopposed

2006 GENERAL

Jerry McNerney (D)	109,868	53.3%
Richard W. Pombo (R)	96,396	46.7%

A loyal Democrat who is a relative novice to the political scene, McNerney spends his time working on parochial issues to ensure a hold on his seat in a formerly Republican-leaning district. His professional experience in the renewable-energy field should give him additional exposure during debate on energy issues.

McNerney, a former wind turbine company executive whose interest in energy issues was sparked during the oil embargo of the 1970s, advocates greater use of ethanol, biodiesel and other renewable-energy sources. He is skeptical of expanding the country's drilling of oil and natural gas.

His stances on energy, complemented by his relationships with Speaker Nancy Pelosi and Energy and Commerce Chairman Henry A. Waxman, both from California, and a seat on the Democratic Steering Committee earned him a spot on Waxman's powerful committee.

He supported the Democrats' 2007 energy bill, signed into law, that included new fuel economy standards and emphasized conservation. McNerney, who drives a Toyota Camry hybrid, said the measure will strengthen national security by reducing U.S. dependence on foreign oil and develop new technologies to reduce energy costs and help create new jobs.

McNerney's interest in energy issues extended to his work on the Science and Technology Committee during the 110th Congress (2007-08), where he pushed through a bill in 2007 to authorize $80 million annually through fiscal 2012 to support the development and use of geothermal energy technologies.

Despite bipartisan committee support, Democratic leaders didn't move it to the floor. In March 2007, he obtained bipartisan support in the House for a bill to authorize $125 million to extend a pilot program aimed at developing alternative water source projects. But the measure stalled in the Senate.

Despite the failure of those measures, McNerney isn't discouraged. "It was always fun to speak up on these issues," he said. "And I could show up a little bit, even though I was this little freshman back here in the very last chair of the committee."

He left the Science Committee in 2009 but still sits on Veterans Affairs, where he supported a 2008 bill that called for a new 10-year veterans' education plan at a cost of almost $62 billion. He also pushed through the committee a bill to create a special panel within the Department of Veterans Affairs to assess the ability of the federal government to treat veterans with traumatic brain injury.

Among the issues that spurred McNerney's decision to run for Congress was his frustration with the Iraq War. Throughout his 2006 campaign, which was fueled by donations from anti-war activists, McNerney touted his opposition to the war and advocated a withdrawal.

Yet he angered those supporters in late 2007, when after returning from his sole visit to Iraq, he said he was willing to negotiate the details of a phased withdrawal.

McNerney is typically a reliable vote for party leaders. During his first term, he backed his party on 92 percent of the votes that pitted a majority of Democrats against a majority of Republicans. Among the Democratic measures he backed was a bill to increase the minimum wage and another prohibiting job discrimination based on sexual orientation.

In fall 2008, he supported two proposals intended to shore up the ailing financial services industry. He considered both measures — the second of which became law in October of that year — to be recovery packages that helped ordinary citizens and small businesses. McNerney subsequently supported another bailout bill for the ailing auto industry, although that bill stalled in the Senate.

When McNerney does stray from Democratic leadership, it's usually on an issue that is strongly supported by his conservative-leaning constituency, which includes Silicon Valley executives and multigenerational farm owners. In 2007, he supported a Republican-sponsored bill to repeal the estate tax.

McNerney was born in Albuquerque, N.M., the youngest of five children. His father was a civil engineer; his mother was a secretary at a local high school. His political roots stem from his dad, who was a San Francisco union organizer before serving in the Philippines during World War II and eventually earning his degree.

McNerney and his twin brother, John, attended St. Joseph's Military Academy in Hays, Kan. He was appointed to the U.S. Military Academy in 1969 but left West Point two years later because he opposed the Vietnam War. He registered for the draft but was not called. Subsequently, he enrolled at the University of New Mexico, eventually earning a Ph.D. in mathematics — making him the only member of Congress to earn a doctorate in that field.

He worked several years for Sandia National Laboratories in New Mexico before moving to Massachusetts, then to California for a senior engineering position with U.S. Windpower (later called Kenetech Corp.). Prior to his election to Congress, he served as an energy consultant and CEO of a start-up company that manufactures wind turbines.

A quiet frustration with national politics probably would have remained masked had McNerney's son not urged him to challenge Republican Richard W. Pombo in the 2004 election. An Air Force reservist, McNerney's son had received an absentee ballot and was furious to see Pombo — a blunt-talking conservative who frequently clashed with environmentalists — running unopposed. McNerney lost to Pombo in the general election by 23 percentage points. But in 2006, with strong backing from environmental groups, he defeated Pombo, the House Resources Committee chairman, by 7 percentage points. McNerney was the first candidate in more than a decade to oust a sitting chairman.

Soon after being elected, McNerney countered Republican attacks by traveling the five-hour plane ride home from Washington to Pleasanton each week and offering voters one-on-one time in his "Congress at Your Corner" sessions. In 2008, he won by 10 percentage points.

KEY VOTES

2008

Yes Delay consideration of Colombia free-trade agreement

Yes Override Bush veto of federal farm and nutrition programs reauthorization bill

Yes Overhaul surveillance laws and permit dismissal of suits against companies that conducted warrantless wiretapping

Yes Grant mortgage relief to homeowners and funding for Fannie Mae and Freddie Mac

Yes Approve initial $700 billion program to stabilize financial markets

Yes Approve final $700 billion program to stabilize financial markets

Yes Provide $14 billion in loans to automakers

2007

Yes Increase minimum wage by $2.10 an hour

Yes Approve $124.2 billion in emergency war spending and set goal for redeployment of troops from Iraq

No Reject federal contraceptive assistance to international family planning groups

Yes Override Bush veto of $23.2 billion water projects authorization bill

No Implement Peru free-trade agreement

Yes Approve energy policy overhaul with new fuel economy standards

No Clear $473.5 billion omnibus spending bill, including $70 billion for military operations

CQ VOTE STUDIES

	PARTY UNITY		PRESIDENTIAL SUPPORT	
	SUPPORT	OPPOSE	SUPPORT	OPPOSE
2008	93%	7%	17%	83%
2007	91%	9%	4%	96%

INTEREST GROUPS

	AFL-CIO	ADA	CCUS	ACU
2008	100%	85%	61%	13%
2007	96%	95%	50%	4%

CALIFORNIA 11

San Joaquin Valley; inland East Bay; part of Stockton

A mix of commuter bedroom communities east of the San Francisco Bay and inland agricultural country, the wrench-shaped 11th runs along Interstate 680 and south past San Jose, while the north end surrounds Stockton on three sides (central Stockton is in the 18th District).

The 11th includes more than 40 percent of Stockton's residents and almost all of surrounding San Joaquin County, where high-end development is overtaking farmland. Gridlock plagued Stockton during the technology boom, as Bay Area commuters were pushed to the city. Traffic remains a concern here, and hourlong drives to San Jose or San Francisco can take twice as long during rush hour. The high-tech bust in the early part of the decade left the Stockton area vulnerable to an extended housing market crisis and rising unemployment rates.

Dairy products and wine grapes are the primary agricultural goods here. Lodi and Woodbridge produce nearly 40 percent of the state's premium wine grapes, many of which are shipped to the Napa Valley for bottling. The agriculture sector in San Joaquin County has come under scrutiny because of local air pollution resulting from the raising of livestock and transportation of farm products. Agricultural exports travel through the trucking centers of Lodi and Tracy on their way out of the 11th. The port of Stockton on the San Joaquin River specializes in bulk cargo, and cement is the main import.

Historically friendly to GOP candidates at the state and federal levels, the moderate 11th has moved to the left in recent years. In 2004, George W. Bush took 54 percent of the 11th's presidential vote, but in 2008, Democrat Barack Obama won the district with the same percentage.

MAJOR INDUSTRY
Agriculture, technology, service

MILITARY BASES
Defense Distribution Depot San Joaquin, 27 military, 2,677 civilian (2007)

CITIES
Stockton (pt.), 104,409; Pleasanton (pt.), 58,432; Lodi, 56,999; Tracy, 56,929

NOTABLE
The museum operated by the San Joaquin County Historical Society, in Lodi, boasts a working blacksmith's shop.

Rep. Jackie Speier (D)

Elected April 2008; 1st full term

Speier can be the same bold, brash liberal she was during nearly two decades in a bitterly partisan state legislature. But she also has shown she can reach out to her ideological opposites on issues that move her.

Speier (SPEAR) was elected in April 2008 in a special election to succeed the late Tom Lantos, who had served since 1981. For the rest of that year, she took her party's side on 99 percent of the floor votes in which Democrats diverged from Republicans.

But she has become a strong advocate of reining in congressional earmarks — funding set-asides for special projects. She even joined forces with conservative Republican Jeff Flake of Arizona, a longstanding critic of the practice. Her concerns led her in February 2009 to join 19 other House Democrats in opposing a $410 billion catchall spending bill for fiscal 2009. "For all the talk of reform, Congress continues to pass spending bills loaded with earmarks without enough time to fully examine where the money is going," she said.

Speier holds a seat on the Financial Services Committee, where she pursues the consumer privacy issues that became one of her trademarks as a state legislator. She also was given Lantos' seat on the Oversight and Government Reform Committee.

She joined her Bay Area Democratic colleague Anna G. Eshoo in introducing a bill in January 2009 requesting help for cities and counties that lost money in the collapse of Lehman Brothers Holdings Inc. The investment banking firm's bankruptcy in September 2008 left Golden State cities, counties and state pensions funds in jeopardy of losing $978 million, according to the League of California Cities.

Speier ran on a platform that highlighted ending the war in Iraq and repairing the economy she said was damaged by actions taken by the George W. Bush administration and costs tied to the war. She also advocated an expansion of health care coverage and financial privacy rights — two issues on which she focused at the state level when she took on such powerful giants as the banking, credit card and pharmaceutical industries. And she championed an environmental platform emphasizing support for California's efforts to crack down on carbon emissions and opposition to oil drilling off the California coast.

In recognition of her work on the latter, House Democratic leaders named Speier in January 2009 to the Select Committee on Energy Independence and Global Warming. She has long championed mass transit; the Caltrain commuter rail line even named a locomotive after her.

Speier's dogged advocacy of issues stems from a philosophy she developed after many hard-learned life lessons. "Never give up. Don't be afraid and remember there is a greater purpose," she said.

Speier has led a life of hard-to-believe twists and turns. In November 1978, while working for Democratic Rep. Leo Ryan of California she was shot five times and left for dead on an airstrip in Guyana by gunmen associated with Peoples Temple cult leader Jim Jones. Years later, her first husband, physician Steve Sierra, was killed by a drunk driver near the couple's home, leaving Speier a widow pregnant with her second child after suffering two miscarriages.

Before he was killed, Sierra and Speier had also adopted a baby whom Speier introduced to her colleagues on the state Assembly floor in Sacramento. But a short while later, the baby's birth mother changed her mind.

CAPITOL OFFICE
225-3531
speier.house.gov
211 Cannon Bldg. 20515-0512; fax 226-4183

COMMITTEES
Financial Services
Oversight & Government Reform
Select Energy Independence & Global Warming

RESIDENCE
Hillsborough

BORN
May 14, 1950; San Francisco, Calif.

RELIGION
Roman Catholic

FAMILY
Husband, Barry Dennis; two children

EDUCATION
U. of California, Davis, B.A. 1972 (political science);
U. of California, Hastings, J.D. 1976

CAREER
Lawyer; game software company executive; disability services nonprofit officer; congressional aide

POLITICAL HIGHLIGHTS
Candidate for U.S. House (special election), 1979;
San Mateo County Board of Supervisors, 1981-86;
Calif. Assembly, 1986-96; Calif. Senate, 1998-2006;
sought Democratic nomination for lieutenant governor, 2006

ELECTION RESULTS

2008 GENERAL

Jackie Speier (D)	200,442	75.1%
Greg Conlon (R)	49,258	18.5%
Nathalie Hrizi (PFP)	5,793	2.2%
Barry Hermanson (GREEN)	5,776	2.2%
Kevin Dempsey Peterson (LIBERT)	5,584	2.1%

2008 PRIMARY

Jackie Speier (D)	60,393	89.5%
Michelle T. McMurry (D)	3,827	5.7%
Frank Henry Wade (D)	1,652	2.4%
Robert M. Barrows (D)	1,594	2.4%

2008 SPECIAL

Jackie Speier (D)	66,279	77.7%
Greg Conlon (R)	7,990	9.4%
Michelle T. McMurry (D)	4,546	5.3%
Michael Moloney (R)	4,517	5.3%
Barry Hermanson (GREEN)	1,947	2.3%

With two co-authors, she drew on her life experiences in writing a book in 2007, "This Is Not the Life I Ordered: 50 Ways to Keep Your Head Above Water When Life Keeps Dragging You Down."

Speier is a San Francisco native whose working-class parents moved south to San Mateo County when she was a child. She took the name Jackie for her Catholic confirmation in honor of former First Lady Jacqueline Kennedy. She met Ryan when she was 16, working as a volunteer in his 1966 re-election campaign for the state Assembly.

Speier went on to study at the University of California at Davis. During her freshman year, Ryan offered her an academic internship. That led to a full-time job working for him in Sacramento, and she followed him to Washington after he won the district seat in 1972. Speier first was a legislative aide, then legal counsel after earning her law degree.

When Speier was serving as his legal counsel, Ryan launched an investigation of Jones, founder of a San Francisco church that was initially praised but that became increasingly cult-like. Jones had moved to the small South American country of Guyana with hundreds of his followers, and Ryan began to investigate reports from constituents who said Jones was holding their relatives against their will.

Speier was among a group of aides and reporters who accompanied Ryan to Guyana. When the group was preparing to leave after four days, gunfire broke out. Speier and nine others were wounded, and Ryan was among five who were killed. Speier was flown to Washington for treatment. Later that day, Jones and more than 900 people died in a mass suicide.

After recovering from several serious wounds and a bacterial infection, she entered the crowded 1979 special election race to succeed Ryan. But she lost to Republican Bill Royer, who was defeated by Lantos the following year.

Speier in 1981 ran a successful campaign for the San Mateo County Board of Supervisors, where she served five years. In 1986, she sought a state Assembly seat, winning the Democratic nomination by just 500 votes. She served 18 years in the state Assembly and Senate, earning a reputation as an advocate of consumers, children and women.

In 2006, Speier lost a hotly contested Democratic primary for lieutenant governor. She then briefly worked for a San Francisco law firm.

When Lantos died in February 2008, just a few months after he was diagnosed with cancer of the esophagus, she took another run for the seat in a special election. She romped to victory in April with 78 percent of the vote in which she needed a minimum of 50 percent to avoid a runoff. In November, she nearly duplicated her showing by taking 75 percent.

KEY VOTES

2008

Yes   Delay consideration of Colombia free-trade agreement

Yes   Override Bush veto of federal farm and nutrition programs reauthorization bill

No   Overhaul surveillance laws and permit dismissal of suits against companies that conducted warrantless wiretapping

Yes   Grant mortgage relief to homeowners and funding for Fannie Mae and Freddie Mac

Yes   Approve initial $700 billion program to stabilize financial markets

Yes   Approve final $700 billion program to stabilize financial markets

Yes   Provide $14 billion in loans to automakers

CQ VOTE STUDIES

	PARTY UNITY		PRESIDENTIAL SUPPORT	
	SUPPORT	OPPOSE	SUPPORT	OPPOSE
2008	99%	1%	10%	90%

INTEREST GROUPS

	AFL-CIO	ADA	CCUS	ACU
2008	100%	60%	43%	0%

CALIFORNIA 12

Part of San Mateo County; most of western San Francisco

A mix of scenic coastal mountains and bayside commuter traffic jams, California's 12th District lies between its two well-known neighbors, downtown San Francisco and the Silicon Valley. To the west of the district is the Pacific Ocean and to the east, the San Francisco Bay.

The wishbone-shaped district includes southwestern San Francisco, and the heavily-populated San Mateo County suburbs, either in Daly City or between two main commuter routes — the Junipero Serra and U.S. Route 101. The 12th's western spur runs south along the Pacific coastline from the Great Highway in San Francisco through Pacifica to Moss Beach, while the eastern spur stretches along the bay to San Carlos and part of Redwood City, about halfway to San Jose.

After an early-2000s downturn in the district's technology economy and in Silicon Valley to the south, the region has begun to rebound. Redwood Shores is home to software giants Oracle and Electronic Arts, and the

popular Internet video site YouTube was founded in San Mateo. South San Francisco, home to several biotech firms, anchors the northern part of the district. San Francisco Airport remains a key employer, although cargo traffic decreased in 2008.

The 12th has the fourth-largest Asian population in the nation at more than 28 percent, and Daly City has the largest concentration of Filipinos in the United States. The Farallon Islands — a national wildlife refuge 28 miles west of San Francisco and a popular destination for whale watchers and shark divers — also belong to the district.

Democrats hold an overwhelming edge here, as less than 20 percent of voters have registered Republican. The district gave 74 percent of its vote to Democrat Barack Obama in the 2008 presidential election.

MAJOR INDUSTRY
Biotech, airport, software

CITIES
San Francisco (pt.), 137,645; Daly City, 103,621; San Mateo, 92,482

NOTABLE
The most lucrative big-wave surfing competition in the world is held at a wave break called Maverick's, off Half Moon Bay.

Rep. Pete Stark (D)

Elected 1972; 19th term

CAPITOL OFFICE
225-5065
www.house.gov/stark
239 Cannon Bldg. 20515-0513; fax 226-3805

COMMITTEES
Ways & Means
  (Health - chairman)
Joint Taxation

RESIDENCE
Fremont

BORN
Nov. 11, 1931; Milwaukee, Wis.

RELIGION
Unitarian

FAMILY
Wife, Deborah Roderick Stark; seven children

EDUCATION
Massachusetts Institute of Technology,
B.S. 1953 (engineering); U. of California,
Berkeley, M.B.A. 1960

MILITARY SERVICE
Air Force, 1955-57

CAREER
Banker

POLITICAL HIGHLIGHTS
Sought Democratic nomination for Calif. Senate,
1969

ELECTION RESULTS

2008 GENERAL

Pete Stark (D)	166,829	76.4%
Raymond Chui (R)	51,447	23.6%

2008 PRIMARY

Pete Stark (D)	unopposed

2006 GENERAL

Pete Stark (D)	110,756	74.9%
George I. Bruno (R)	37,141	25.1%

PREVIOUS WINNING PERCENTAGES
2004 (72%); 2002 (71%); 2000 (70%); 1998 (71%);
1996 (65%); 1994 (65%); 1992 (60%); 1990 (58%);
1988 (73%); 1986 (70%); 1984 (70%); 1982 (61%);
1980 (55%); 1978 (65%); 1976 (71%); 1974 (71%);
1972 (53%)

Stark has little patience for those who don't agree with his liberal views. His verbal lashings of opponents in either party often put him in the media spotlight — much to the chagrin of Democratic leaders. But he can compromise when he wants, and as one of Congress' leading experts on health care policy he has checked off several successes on his agenda for broader and more affordable health care.

Stark has served on the powerful Ways and Means Committee for 35 years, and is chairman of its Health panel — a position he held for 10 years when Democrats previously controlled the House. He has a faith in the ability of government to help the underprivileged and has led his party's fight for universal health care coverage, a Medicare prescription drug benefit and improved regulation of providers.

He is a key player as the 111th Congress (2009-10) begins to look at a plan for universal health care coverage that would meet the call of President Obama. But he took a step in his own direction on that issue in December 2008 when he said any such plan must include a new government-run health insurance option, modeled on Medicare, that would compete with private insurers. "We're not going to have the insurance companies on board, but they're the easiest ones to roll because nobody likes insurance companies," he said in a conference call with reporters.

That idea differs from early proposals by Obama and Senate Finance Chairman Max Baucus of Montana, and it irked insurance companies across the nation.

Stark is known on Capitol Hill and beyond for his verbal zingers and temperamental outbursts, which often overshadow his policy achievements.

In October 2007, Stark's diatribe against President George W. Bush nearly led to his censure on the House floor. Amid the debate over Democrats' failed effort to override Bush's veto of legislation to expand a health care program for children, Stark lashed out: "You don't have money to fund the war or children. But you're going to spend it to blow up innocent people if we can get enough kids to grow old enough for you to send to Iraq to get their heads blown off for the president's amusement."

Republicans demanded an apology. Stark initially refused, despite pressure from Speaker Nancy Pelosi of California. But after the effort to censure him failed, Stark backed down.

Such broadsides are common for Stark. When Democrats fared poorly in the 2002 congressional elections, he urged Minority Leader Richard A. Gephardt to resign, saying he had done "a lousy job." He once called Republican Bill Thomas of California a "fascist," Republican Scott McInnis of Colorado a "little wimp" and "fruitcake," and Republican Nancy L. Johnson of Connecticut a "whore for the insurance industry."

"I shouldn't let my emotions get the best of me, but they do," Stark told the San Jose Mercury News in 2005.

Just as often, Stark has made news simply by breaking the mold. Early in his career, black Democrats rebuffed his request to join the Congressional Black Caucus. Stark, a Caucasian, said his constituency and personal views should make him eligible. The caucus' African-American members respectfully declined. And in 2007 he drew media attention when he acknowledged — after the Secular Coalition of America sponsored a contest to find the highest-ranking atheist in elected office — that he doesn't believe in a supreme being.

Stark has taken an interest in fighting global warming, introducing a bill in January 2009 placing a $10-per-ton tax on carbon that would increase until greenhouse gas emissions have dropped 80 percent from 1990 levels. He called such a tax "the best and most sensible solution."

Despite his reputation, Stark has achieved several legislative successes. A leading critic of private Medicare plans, he claimed victory in July 2007 when the House passed legislation to cut funding for them. He also helped shepherd legislation, enacted into law in 2008, that protects patients against discrimination by health insurance providers and employers based on their genes or genetic predisposition to disease or chronic conditions.

He may be best known for two laws enacted in 1989 and 1993 known as Stark I and Stark II. They strictly regulate physician referrals of Medicare patients to medical facilities in which the doctors have a financial interest, such as laboratories and physical therapy clinics.

During the 12 years the GOP held majority control, he showed a willingness to work across party lines when necessary, helping to win new preventive care benefits for Medicare beneficiaries and push Congress to reduce out-of-pocket costs for hospital outpatient services. He also won passage of a bill requiring medical facilities to use safer blood-drawing devices.

Stark has been less successful at pushing his design for an expansive new prescription drug benefit for Medicare beneficiaries. Congress passed a more limited bill in late 2003 that gave private insurers, rather than the government, the responsibility to negotiate drug prices for seniors.

As Health Subcommittee chairman in 2007, he championed his party's efforts to force the administration to negotiate Medicare drug prices and quickly rejected a health care tax plan that Bush rolled out. "If I could just deep-six it, they'd build a statue of me in Health Care Square," he said.

Stark grew up in Wisconsin and graduated from the Massachusetts Institute of Technology. After serving in the Air Force in the 1950s, he moved west and got a master's degree in business from the University of California at Berkeley. At age 31, he had already founded two banks.

In 1969, he made his first bid for public office, losing a primary for a state legislative seat to George Miller, then a young law school student and now a House colleague. Three years later, Stark took on another George Miller, who had represented Oakland in Congress as a Democrat for 28 years.

Stark spent his money generously and made Miller's support of the Vietnam War a major issue on the way to a primary victory, followed by an election win with 53 percent of the vote. He has won his past six elections with at least 70 percent of the vote.

KEY VOTES

2008

Yes	Delay consideration of Colombia free-trade agreement
No	Override Bush veto of federal farm and nutrition programs reauthorization bill
?	Overhaul surveillance laws and permit dismissal of suits against companies that conducted warrantless wiretapping
Yes	Grant mortgage relief to homeowners and funding for Fannie Mae and Freddie Mac
No	Approve initial $700 billion program to stabilize financial markets
No	Approve final $700 billion program to stabilize financial markets
No	Provide $14 billion in loans to automakers

2007

Yes	Increase minimum wage by $2.10 an hour
P	Approve $124.2 billion in emergency war spending and set goal for redeployment of troops from Iraq
No	Reject federal contraceptive assistance to international family planning groups
Yes	Override Bush veto of $23.2 billion water projects authorization bill
No	Implement Peru free-trade agreement
Yes	Approve energy policy overhaul with new fuel economy standards
No	Clear $473.5 billion omnibus spending bill, including $70 billion for military operations

CQ VOTE STUDIES

	PARTY UNITY		PRESIDENTIAL SUPPORT	
	SUPPORT	OPPOSE	SUPPORT	OPPOSE
2008	94%	6%	13%	87%
2007	97%	3%	12%	88%
2006	99%	1%	5%	95%
2005	98%	2%	11%	89%
2004	99%	1%	15%	85%

INTEREST GROUPS

	AFL-CIO	ADA	CCUS	ACU
2008	93%	90%	47%	13%
2007	95%	80%	47%	4%
2006	92%	95%	8%	4%
2005	93%	90%	32%	0%
2004	100%	90%	5%	0%

CALIFORNIA 13

East Bay — Fremont, Hayward, Alameda

Tucked between the San Francisco Bay to the west, Silicon Valley to the south and Oakland to the north, the 13th is an industrially and culturally diverse suburban area. The district is dotted with working-class communities, and although it is described as the less glamorous side of the bay, its large Hispanic and Asian populations — including immigrants from India, China, Afghanistan and the Philippines — have flourished culturally. Asians, concentrated in Fremont, make up 28 percent of the population, which gives the 13th the nation's fifth-largest percentage of Asian residents.

Fremont's joint General Motors-Toyota auto plant is the city's key employer, although downturns in the national auto industry and job losses at the plant have affected the local economy. Both Fremont and Hayward have become more oriented toward high-tech industries as Silicon Valley has extended its influence to the East Bay. Corsair and Lexar, manufacturers of computer memory devices, are based in Fremont. Hayward also is home to a California State University campus.

San Leandro, just south of Oakland, is home to Ghirardelli Chocolate, Otis Spunkmeyer's cookie empire, and The North Face, which produces outdoor equipment. Cargill Salt has a refinery and production facility in Newark.

The 13th includes Oakland International Airport, although Oakland itself is located in the neighboring 9th District. The airport has expanded its terminals and operations, but overall cargo and passenger traffic is down, adding to the economic uncertainty in the district.

Two-thirds of the district's workers are considered white collar, but the area's blue-collar industry historically has given Democrats a solid base of support. Hayward gave Barack Obama 78 percent of its vote in the 2008 presidential race, and Obama won the district as a whole with 74 percent.

MAJOR INDUSTRY
Electronics, manufacturing, food product processing

CITIES
Fremont, 203,413; Hayward, 140,030; San Leandro, 79,452

NOTABLE
Ghirardelli Chocolate is the nation's longest continually operating chocolate manufacturer.

Rep. Anna G. Eshoo (D)

Elected 1992; 9th term

CAPITOL OFFICE
225-8104
eshoo.house.gov
205 Cannon Bldg. 20515-0514; fax 225-8890

COMMITTEES
Energy & Commerce
Select Intelligence
  (Intelligence Community Management
  - chairwoman)

RESIDENCE
Menlo Park

BORN
Dec. 13, 1942; New Britain, Conn.

RELIGION
Roman Catholic

FAMILY
Divorced; two children

EDUCATION
Canada College, A.A. 1975 (English literature)

CAREER
State legislative aide; homemaker

POLITICAL HIGHLIGHTS
Candidate for San Mateo County Community
College Board of Trustees, 1977; Democratic
National Committee, 1980-92; San Mateo County
Board of Supervisors, 1982-92 (president, 1986);
Democratic nominee for U.S. House, 1988

ELECTION RESULTS

2008 GENERAL

Anna G. Eshoo (D)	190,301	69.8%
Ronny Santana (R)	60,610	22.2%
Brian Holtz (LIBERT)	11,929	4.4%
Carol Brouillet (GREEN)	9,926	3.6%

2008 PRIMARY

Anna G. Eshoo (D)	unopposed

2006 GENERAL

Anna G. Eshoo (D)	141,153	71.1%
Rob Smith (R)	48,097	24.2%
Brian Holtz (LIBERT)	4,692	2.4%
Carol Brouillet (GREEN)	4,633	2.3%

PREVIOUS WINNING PERCENTAGES
2004 (70%); 2002 (68%); 2000 (70%); 1998 (69%);
1996 (65%); 1994 (61%); 1992 (57%)

In her 2008 autobiography, Speaker Nancy Pelosi describes Eshoo, whom she has known for more than 30 years, as "one of my dearest friends in the world." It's a relationship that puts Eshoo in the inner circle of her fellow Bay Area liberal, helping her further the interests of the high-tech businesses that have made her Silicon Valley district south of San Francisco an international economic powerhouse.

It's hard to overstate how close Eshoo is with Pelosi, Pelosi's husband, Paul, and their five adult children. When Pelosi's daughter Christine married Peter Kaufman, son of movie director Phil Kaufman, in a swank San Francisco ceremony in February 2008, the rite was performed by Eshoo. In Eshoo's office, photos of Pelosi's family are interspersed with those of her own.

Eshoo and Pelosi met at a Democratic Party fundraiser at the home of Madeleine Haas Russell, a philanthropist who was the great-grandniece of Levi Strauss. Since then, they have risen together through the political ranks. The Speaker often hands her the gavel to preside over the House when a tough floor fight is expected.

Now in her ninth term, Eshoo holds a coveted seat on the Energy and Commerce Committee, where she serves on the subcommittee for technology and the Internet. She has championed causes favorable to her district's industries, such as Internet neutrality — the idea that broadband providers, including telephone companies and cable television providers, should be barred from blocking certain traffic or establishing tiered pathways for Internet content. In 2007, Eshoo helped push through Congress a bill to extend indefinitely a ban on Internet access taxes, and she has worked to license a free nationwide wireless Internet service. Eshoo also repeatedly has tried to push through legislation requiring doctors, hospitals and other health care providers to adopt electronic medical records — a cause boosted in the $787 billion economic stimulus bill enacted in early 2009.

Eshoo has also taken up more-populist causes in the area of telecommunications. In 2008, she made national headlines when she proposed rules to bar television broadcasters from increasing the volume of advertising spots. "The advertisements that follow programming just about blow everyone out of the room they're in because of the volume. It hits a nerve," Eshoo said.

Eshoo was a driving force behind House Democrats' adoption of an "innovation agenda" that Pelosi touted when the party successfully campaigned to retake control of the chamber in 2006. That agenda also helped Democrats raise campaign cash in Silicon Valley. In 2005, Eshoo arranged a private meeting at Stanford University for Pelosi and other lawmakers to discuss ideas for legislation with such high-tech powerhouses as Cisco Systems CEO John Chambers. The meeting resulted in proposals to make the research and development tax credit permanent, create incentives for broadband development and get the federal government to foster new nanotechnology industries. President Obama has embraced much of that agenda.

Eshoo also serves on the Select Intelligence Committee and has fiercely criticized President George W. Bush's policies regarding the treatment of terrorist detainees and his efforts to expand executive powers under the Foreign Intelligence Surveillance Act, the law governing electronic spying. She led an unsuccessful effort in 2008 to override Bush's veto of intelligence authorization legislation that would have limited permissible interrogation techniques to those mentioned in the Army Field Manual. She said Bush has deeply damaged America's reputation. "I think when historians write about this period of American life, this chapter is going to be entitled one of the darkest in American history," she said.

Eshoo is the only Assyrian member of Congress. Her parents were immigrants from Armenia and Iran. "In our prayers at dinner we thanked God for the food and also thanked God for this country," she said. In 2007, she was a driving force behind the unsuccessful effort, opposed furiously by the Turkish government, urging Bush to recognize the deaths of 1.5 million Armenians in 1915 as a genocide committed by the Ottoman Turks.

Eshoo is a reliable supporter of the Democratic leadership. She has voted to cut off funding for the Iraq War and supported the $700 billion financial industry rescue package in fall 2008. She supports abortion rights and gun control. She and other Catholic Democrats tried earlier this decade to reach out to church leaders who oppose abortion. She helped organize an informal caucus of Catholic House Democrats; they issued a statement of principles in 2006 affirming their strong Catholic faith but saying they disagreed with bishops on how to promote church teachings against abortion.

But her pro-business stance occasionally leads her to team with conservative Republicans. She was active in unsuccessful efforts to block a proposed accounting rule that requires companies to treat employee stock options as an expense they have to deduct from earnings. In 1995, she helped override President Clinton's veto of a bill to limit lawsuits by angry investors.

Eshoo was drawn to politics in her native New Britain, Conn. Her father was a big supporter of Presidents Franklin D. Roosevelt and Harry S. Truman. He hung portraits of the two Democrats in the family's home and named his daughter after Roosevelt's wife, whose full name was Anna Eleanor Roosevelt. One day as she walked home from school, a man in a big car with a police escort stopped and offered young Eshoo a ride. She accepted the lift — from Truman.

The family moved west to California. Eshoo married (she has been divorced since the 1980s) and devoted herself to motherhood while earning a two-year associate's degree in English literature from a local college. Yet she continued her political activity, taking an internship with California Assembly Speaker Leo T. McCarthy, who was also a close Pelosi friend, and later serving as his chief of staff. In 1982, McCarthy urged her to make a run for the San Mateo County Board of Supervisors, where she served for a decade.

In 1988, she lost a House race to Republican Tom Campbell. She was successful four years later, when Campbell was running for the U.S. Senate. She has won easily ever since, aided by the Bay Area's seemingly inexorable Democratic trend.

KEY VOTES

2008
Yes Delay consideration of Colombia free-trade agreement
Yes Override Bush veto of federal farm and nutrition programs reauthorization bill
No Overhaul surveillance laws and permit dismissal of suits against companies that conducted warrantless wiretapping
Yes Grant mortgage relief to homeowners and funding for Fannie Mae and Freddie Mac
Yes Approve initial $700 billion program to stabilize financial markets
Yes Approve final $700 billion program to stabilize financial markets
Yes Provide $14 billion in loans to automakers

2007
Yes Increase minimum wage by $2.10 an hour
Yes Approve $124.2 billion in emergency war spending and set goal for redeployment of troops from Iraq
No Reject federal contraceptive assistance to international family planning groups
Yes Override Bush veto of $23.2 billion water projects authorization bill
Yes Implement Peru free-trade agreement
Yes Approve energy policy overhaul with new fuel economy standards
No Clear $473.5 billion omnibus spending bill, including $70 billion for military operations

CQ VOTE STUDIES

	PARTY UNITY		PRESIDENTIAL SUPPORT	
	SUPPORT	OPPOSE	SUPPORT	OPPOSE
2008	99%	1%	14%	86%
2007	98%	2%	5%	95%
2006	96%	4%	23%	77%
2005	97%	3%	19%	81%
2004	94%	6%	35%	65%

INTEREST GROUPS

	AFL-CIO	ADA	CCUS	ACU
2008	100%	90%	61%	0%
2007	96%	95%	55%	0%
2006	93%	95%	40%	4%
2005	93%	100%	38%	4%
2004	93%	100%	38%	12%

CALIFORNIA 14

Southern San Mateo and northwestern Santa Clara counties; most of Santa Cruz County

The 14th District stretches south from northern San Mateo County on the Pacific coast, taking in the majority of Santa Cruz County and a C-shaped arc of northwestern Santa Clara County just south of the San Francisco Bay. The district is home to Stanford University, technology firms and fruit orchards.

Workers in the 14th are largely wealthy, educated and professional. More than half of residents here have earned a college degree, and more than three-quarters of the local workforce hold white-collar jobs. Very high incomes and relatively stable job and housing markets have helped insulate the district from national economic downturns.

Technology is a dominant industry in the district. Several major firms have their headquarters in the 14th, including Google in Mountain View, Hewlett-Packard and Facebook in Palo Alto, and Yahoo, Palm and AMD in Sunnyvale. NASA's Ames Research Center just outside of Mountain

View collaborates with local technology firms and colleges on high-tech research and development projects.

Voters in the 14th are liberal on many social and environmental issues, particularly in Santa Cruz County. Many residents are more conservative economically, however, and conservative voting blocs exist in wealthy areas such as Saratoga and Monte Sereno in Santa Clara County. Democrats hold an overall 23-percentage-point edge in voter registration, and the district gave Barack Obama 73 percent of its vote in the 2008 presidential election.

MAJOR INDUSTRY
Computers, biotechnology, defense, agriculture

MILITARY BASES
Onizuka Air Force Station, 9 military, 150 civilian (2007)

CITIES
Sunnyvale, 131,760; Mountain View, 70,708; Palo Alto, 58,598; Redwood City (pt.), 52,873; Menlo Park, 30,785

NOTABLE
Stanford University's Cantor Arts Center has the nation's largest concentration of bronze sculptures by Auguste Rodin; Stanford's Linear Accelerator Center claims to be the "world's straightest object."

Rep. Michael M. Honda (D)

Elected 2000; 5th term

CAPITOL OFFICE
225-2631
www.honda.house.gov
1713 Longworth Bldg. 20515-0515; fax 225-2699

COMMITTEES
Appropriations

RESIDENCE
San Jose

BORN
June 27, 1941; Stockton, Calif.

RELIGION
Protestant

FAMILY
Widowed; two children

EDUCATION
San Jose State U., B.S. 1969 (biological sciences),
B.A. 1970 (Spanish), M.A. 1973 (education)

CAREER
Teacher; principal; Peace Corps volunteer

POLITICAL HIGHLIGHTS
San Jose School Board, 1981-90; Santa Clara
County Board of Supervisors, 1990-96;
Calif. Assembly, 1996-2000

ELECTION RESULTS

2008 GENERAL

Michael M. Honda (D)	170,977	71.7%
Joyce Stoer Cordi (R)	55,489	23.3%
Peter Myers (GREEN)	12,123	5.1%

2008 PRIMARY

Michael M. Honda (D)	unopposed

2006 GENERAL

Michael M. Honda (D)	115,532	72.3%
Raymond L. Chukwu (R)	44,186	27.7%

PREVIOUS WINNING PERCENTAGES
2004 (72%); 2002 (66%); 2000 (54%)

Family history and his own experiences as a young man have shaped Honda's career in politics. Born to Japanese-American farm workers just before the start of World War II, he fights against all forms of discrimination and works to address economic disparities.

Honda was just a few months old when the Japanese bombed Pearl Harbor. He and his family, who were living in what is now a part of Silicon Valley, were shipped off to an internment camp in Colorado, where they spent about two and a half years before they were able to move to Chicago when his father joined Navy intelligence.

The family returned to California in 1953, and his parents became strawberry sharecroppers. Honda took janitorial and delivery jobs to pay his way through San Jose State University. He was one credit shy of graduation when he joined the Peace Corps in 1965. After two years in El Salvador, where he built schools and medical clinics, he returned to California to finish college. He took a job as a science teacher, later serving as a principal.

His family's internment and his own Peace Corps experience profoundly influenced Honda. "I think since I came back from the Peace Corps in '67, I saw the niche that I needed to fill ... I had to teach myself to learn from others, then try to figure out through the political process or educational process to seek change, reconciliation," he said.

Honda remembers little of his internment. But he was a key participant in the Japanese-American lobbying campaign that culminated in a 1988 law providing a formal apology and compensation to interned Japanese-Americans. That effort inspired Honda, once he reached Congress, to work for reparations for Americans who were prisoners of the Japanese during World War II. He was also a leading sponsor of legislation signed into law by President George W. Bush in late 2006 to provide $38 million in grant money to preserve the remnants of the internment camps.

In 2007, Honda introduced and won House adoption of a resolution calling on the Japanese government to acknowledge and apologize for the use of sex slaves, known as "comfort women," during World War II. Citing the 1988 official U.S. apology to Japanese-Americans, Honda said, "I know firsthand that we must not be ignorant of the past, and that reconciliation through government actions is long-lasting." The Japanese government lobbied against his resolution, but that did little to slow its adoption.

When terrorists carried out the Sept. 11 attacks, Honda worked to ensure that Arab-Americans were not treated the way his family was during World War II. He wrote to Bush expressing concern about "government-sanctioned racial profiling." And he denounced reports of harassment and attacks on Arab-Americans, Muslims and members of other ethnic groups.

In 2006, Honda came to the defense of Minnesota Democrat Keith Ellison, Congress' first Muslim member, who was criticized by some lawmakers for using a Koran when being ceremonially sworn in. Honda wrote to Virginia Republican Virgil H. Goode Jr., one of Ellison's critics, saying, "As one of the many Japanese-Americans who were interned during World War II because of war hysteria and racial prejudice, I find it particularly offensive that you are equating Rep.-elect Ellison's beliefs with those of radical extremists and condemning him based on their actions."

Honda gained a coveted seat on the Appropriations Committee in 2007. From his seat on the Legislative Branch Subcommittee, he has pushed for creation of a safer, quicker plan for evacuating the U.S. Capitol and its office buildings in case of another terrorist attack. He recalls the chaotic evacuation on Sept. 11, with people running out of the Capitol without a clear sense of where to go for safety. Honda also serves on the subcommittee that provides funding for science and space programs. He makes sure the NASA-Ames Research Center near his district receives its share of government funds.

Representing a district with a healthy slice of Silicon Valley, Honda looks out for the high-tech industry. He favors the repeal of export controls on high-performance computers and permanent renewal of the research and development tax credit. In 2008, he introduced legislation to coordinate various initiatives to improve science, mathematics, engineering, and technology education. President Obama, when he was a senator from Illinois, sponsored a similar bill in the Senate, but neither saw action.

In late 2008, Honda held two competitions for constituents interested in the 20 tickets to the presidential inauguration allotted to his office. One competition was for ideas for innovative education reform, the other was for entries on the Facebook Web site detailing why the constituent wanted to attend. As a result of the competitions, he tried unsuccessfully to include in the $787 billion economic stimulus bill, passed in February 2009, a provision to create an "Educational Innovation Board" that would award $10 million in grants for innovative ideas to help improve the nation's schools.

Also during the 110th Congress (2007-08), Honda successfully pushed for congressional hearings into the 2004 death in Afghanistan of Army Cpl. Pat Tillman and the Bush administration's handling of the announcement of his death. Tillman, hailed for giving up a lucrative National Football League career to enlist just months after the Sept. 11 attacks, was initially reported killed in battle. It was weeks before the Pentagon notified his family, who live in Honda's district, that he was the victim of friendly fire.

Honda got his start in public service more than three decades ago, when he went to Norman Y. Mineta, a fellow Japanese-American who was then a San Jose city councilman, to volunteer his services. When Mineta was elected mayor, he named Honda to the city planning commission in 1971. In 1981, Honda won election to the local school board, and later to the county board of supervisors and the California Assembly.

When moderate GOP Rep. Tom Campbell left the 15th District open in 2000 to pursue another run for the Senate, Honda entered the race. A phone call from President Clinton convinced him the national party would back his bid. Honda won the race by 12 points. Bolstered by redistricting and his ties to the Asian and Hispanic communities in a district where almost half the residents are from those constituencies, Honda has cruised to re-election ever since.

KEY VOTES

2008

Yes   Delay consideration of Colombia free-trade agreement

Yes   Override Bush veto of federal farm and nutrition programs reauthorization bill

No   Overhaul surveillance laws and permit dismissal of suits against companies that conducted warrantless wiretapping

Yes   Grant mortgage relief to homeowners and funding for Fannie Mae and Freddie Mac

Yes   Approve initial $700 billion program to stabilize financial markets

Yes   Approve final $700 billion program to stabilize financial markets

Yes   Provide $14 billion in loans to automakers

2007

Yes   Increase minimum wage by $2.10 an hour

Yes   Approve $124.2 billion in emergency war spending and set goal for redeployment of troops from Iraq

No   Reject federal contraceptive assistance to international family planning groups

Yes   Override Bush veto of $23.2 billion water projects authorization bill

Yes   Implement Peru free-trade agreement

Yes   Approve energy policy overhaul with new fuel economy standards

No   Clear $473.5 billion omnibus spending bill, including $70 billion for military operations

CQ VOTE STUDIES

	PARTY UNITY		PRESIDENTIAL SUPPORT	
	SUPPORT	OPPOSE	SUPPORT	OPPOSE
2008	100%	0%	15%	85%
2007	99%	1%	5%	95%
2006	97%	3%	23%	77%
2005	99%	1%	18%	82%
2004	97%	3%	23%	77%

INTEREST GROUPS

	AFL-CIO	ADA	CCUS	ACU
2008	100%	95%	50%	0%
2007	100%	95%	58%	0%
2006	93%	95%	33%	4%
2005	93%	100%	37%	4%
2004	93%	95%	39%	10%

CALIFORNIA 15

Santa Clara County – part of San Jose

Home to one-third of San Jose's residents, the 15th touches the southern tip of the San Francisco Bay in the north, then descends inland through Silicon Valley to still-rural but fast-growing farm towns and the San Benito County border. Fruit orchards that once covered much of the district were converted into housing and businesses after World War II.

Lying in the heart of Silicon Valley, the 15th is home to several prominent technology firms — Apple in Cupertino and Intel and Sun Microsystems in Santa Clara — and Internet ventures like online auction house eBay in San Jose and Netflix in Los Gatos. The downturn in the area's technology industry, particularly within smaller companies, increased unemployment rates in the affluent suburbs west of San Jose. Demand from research universities and the federal government has helped stabilize the software and semiconductor sectors, although employment levels have not matched the increase in production.

Agriculture also is important here. Gilroy, located in the southern part of the district and known as the "Garlic Capital of the World," is home to a

ConAgra food processing plant.

The diverse 15th includes the nation's second-highest percentage of Asian residents (31 percent). The population here is predominately affluent, although wealth here is vulnerable to economic uncertainty. It also has a high percentage of white-collar workers and has one of the state's lowest percentages of service industry workers.

Some residents are concerned about illegal immigration, but voters in the 15th tend to be liberal on social and environmental issues. Barack Obama won easily here, with 68 percent of the 15th's 2008 presidential vote.

MAJOR INDUSTRY
Computers, biotechnology, health care, agriculture

CITIES
San Jose (pt.), 295,018; Santa Clara, 102,361; Milpitas, 62,698

NOTABLE
Two tons of garlic are consumed during Gilroy's annual Garlic Festival, which features garlic french fries, garlic ice cream — and free gum; The Winchester Mystery House in San Jose, designed by the Winchester rifle heiress, took 38 years to build and has 160 rooms and contains structural oddities.

Rep. Zoe Lofgren (D)

Elected 1994; 8th term

CAPITOL OFFICE
225-3072
www.house.gov/lofgren
102 Cannon Bldg. 20515-0516; fax 225-3336

COMMITTEES
Homeland Security
House Administration
(Elections - chairwoman)
Judiciary
(Immigration, Citizenship, Refugees, Border
Security & International Law - chairwoman)
Standards of Official Conduct - chairwoman
Joint Library

RESIDENCE
San Jose

BORN
Dec. 21, 1947; San Mateo, Calif.

RELIGION
Lutheran

FAMILY
Husband, John Marshall Collins; two children

EDUCATION
Stanford U., A.B. 1970 (political science);
U. of Santa Clara, J.D. 1975

CAREER
Lawyer; professor; congressional aide; nonprofit
housing development director

POLITICAL HIGHLIGHTS
San Jose-Evergreen Community College District
Board of Trustees, 1979-81; Santa Clara County
Board of Supervisors, 1981-95

ELECTION RESULTS

2008 GENERAL

Zoe Lofgren (D)	146,481	71.3%
Charel Winston (R)	49,399	24.1%
Steven Wells (LIBERT)	9,447	4.6%

2008 PRIMARY

Zoe Lofgren (D)	unopposed

2006 GENERAL

Zoe Lofgren (D)	98,929	72.7%
Charel Winston (R)	37,130	27.3%

PREVIOUS WINNING PERCENTAGES
2004 (71%); 2002 (67%); 2000 (72%); 1998 (73%);
1996 (66%); 1994 (65%)

Lofgren is an active legislator who seeks to address immigration, telecommunications, technology and election law issues. One of the few Democrats elected in the GOP sweep of 1994, she relishes the chance to advance her legislative priorities after years of frustration in the minority.

Those issues are expected to dominate much of her time during the 111th Congress (2009-10). But she also has taken on the rather uncomfortable role of chairing the ethics committee. The committee in early 2009 was forced to investigate allegations of financial impropriety involving Ways and Means Chairman Charles B. Rangel of New York.

Lofgren earlier served eight years on the committee, and took part in the investigation that led to a 420-1 House vote in July 2002 to expel Democrat James A. Traficant Jr. of Ohio following his conviction on bribery, racketeering and tax fraud charges. "It is not a fun assignment," she said of her chairmanship.

Lofgren will have to balance her new role as ethics chairwoman with her legislative interests, particularly her top priority — helping enact a "middle of the road" immigration policy overhaul.

A one-time immigration lawyer and former congressional staffer, Lofgren supports a "comprehensive" approach to immigration that combines border security, workplace enforcement and a path to legal status for illegal immigrants working in the United States. Chairwoman of the key Immigration Subcommittee on the Judiciary panel, she calls the current immigration system a "mess." "Americans don't realize how bulky and inefficient and counterintuitive it is until someone they know gets involved, and then people are stunned at how ridiculous the rules are," she said.

At the start of the 110th Congress (2007-08), expectations were high for passage of an immigration bill. The House decided to let the Senate go first, but in June 2007, the Senate measure bogged down. Lofgren and House Democrats then shifted to a piecemeal strategy, introducing a series of more-limited measures designed to fix specific problems with the immigration system. They included Lofgren's ideas to help foreign medical students stay after graduation, extend a visa program for religious workers, and extend a program providing permanent-resident cards to foreigners starting businesses. Except for the medical-student bill, none of them became law.

Lofgren's district has one of the largest concentrations of Vietnamese-Americans, and she advocates using economic pressure on Vietnam on human rights issues. She played a part in the 2008 release of Nguyen Quoc Quan, a California democracy activist who was detained in Vietnam for six months.

As chairwoman of the Elections Subcommittee on the House Administration Committee during the 110th, she sponsored legislation to reimburse states and local governments for the cost of providing backup paper ballots, and to limit political robocalls.

When Lofgren was in the minority, she had more success with amendments to other people's bills than with her own measures. Her provision to accelerate the development of fusion as a long-term energy source was included in the GOP-authored energy bill of 2005. And her amendment to the 2005 revision of the 2001 anti-terrorism law requires the Justice Department to review the detention of material witnesses who are held without charges.

She sometimes aligns with Republicans on issues that affect her technology-driven district in and around San Jose, the capital of Silicon Valley. Though not an expert in computer technology (she was a political science major in college) she has boned up and made herself knowledgeable.

On the social issues that get her attention, Lofgren will not shy from a fight. In 2004, she tried unsuccessfully to stop House approval of a GOP-backed measure giving distinct legal status to fetuses and establishing a separate offense for a crime against a pregnant woman that harms the fetus. She said the Republicans' ultimate aim was to reclassify a fetus as a human. Lofgren sponsored a Democratic alternative creating additional penalties for crimes against pregnant women, but without separate legal status for fetuses.

Lofgren grew up in a blue-collar neighborhood in south Palo Alto. Her father was a truck driver and her mother was a secretary and a school cafeteria cook. "I didn't meet a Republican until I went to junior high school," she said. While other mothers went door-to-door collecting for the March of Dimes, Lofgren's mother went after "dollars for Democrats." Lofgren would spend hours talking politics with her Swedish immigrant grandfather. Instead of going to dances, she and her friends went to political rallies.

After completing her undergraduate studies at Stanford University on a scholarship, she headed to Washington, D.C., landing an internship with Democratic Rep. Don Edwards. She stayed on as a staffer through the 1970s, and was inspired to go to law school when a draft bill of hers was "ripped to shreds" by the House legislative counsel. (Lofgren's husband is a lawyer in San Jose whom she met one election night while working for Edwards.) She practiced immigration law as a partner in the firm of Webber & Lofgren, and taught the subject at the University of Santa Clara.

She was the first executive director of San Jose's Community Housing Developers, a nonprofit group that created low-income housing. In 1979, a colleague urged her to run for the local community college board of trustees, and she won. The campaign came soon after her wedding, and her lists of supporters and guests mixed. "For years," she recalled, "we'd have little index cards that would be like: 'Gave $100, walked three precincts, silver tray.' "

In 1980, she was elected to the Santa Clara County Board of Supervisors, where she stayed for 14 years and was often in conflict with San Jose Mayor Tom McEnery, a Democrat, who pushed downtown redevelopment while Lofgren argued for more money for education and human services.

When Edwards retired from the House after 32 years, the 1994 Democratic primary saw a face-off between Lofgren and McEnery. She benefited from an uproar that ensued when state election officials barred her from describing herself as "county supervisor/mother" on the ballot. The flap drew national attention to her candidacy, and she went on to win the primary. She won handily that November and has coasted to re-election since.

KEY VOTES

2008
Yes Delay consideration of Colombia free-trade agreement
Yes Override Bush veto of federal farm and nutrition programs reauthorization bill
No Overhaul surveillance laws and permit dismissal of suits against companies that conducted warrantless wiretapping
Yes Grant mortgage relief to homeowners and funding for Fannie Mae and Freddie Mac
Yes Approve initial $700 billion program to stabilize financial markets
Yes Approve final $700 billion program to stabilize financial markets
Yes Provide $14 billion in loans to automakers

2007
Yes Increase minimum wage by $2.10 an hour
Yes Approve $124.2 billion in emergency war spending and set goal for redeployment of troops from Iraq
No Reject federal contraceptive assistance to international family planning groups
Yes Override Bush veto of $23.2 billion water projects authorization bill
Yes Implement Peru free-trade agreement
Yes Approve energy policy overhaul with new fuel economy standards
No Clear $473.5 billion omnibus spending bill, including $70 billion for military operations

CQ VOTE STUDIES

	PARTY UNITY		PRESIDENTIAL SUPPORT	
	SUPPORT	OPPOSE	SUPPORT	OPPOSE
2008	99%	1%	14%	86%
2007	99%	1%	6%	94%
2006	97%	3%	23%	77%
2005	97%	3%	13%	87%
2004	94%	6%	30%	70%

INTEREST GROUPS

	AFL-CIO	ADA	CCUS	ACU
2008	100%	100%	56%	0%
2007	96%	95%	55%	0%
2006	93%	100%	33%	4%
2005	93%	100%	37%	4%
2004	93%	95%	33%	12%

CALIFORNIA 16

Most of San Jose

The 16th includes two-thirds of San Jose, California's third-largest city, where 92 percent of district residents live. The remainder live in unincorporated areas of Santa Clara County.

The tremendous growth during the tech boom of the 1990s — which earned San Jose the reputation as "the capital of Silicon Valley" — created a largely white-collar workforce and established the area as a leading exporter of high-tech goods. Unemployment levels had rebounded after an industry downturn a decade ago, but recent economic uncertainty has struck the district again. Santa Clara County has the area's highest median income, but homeowners have struggled with high foreclosure rates.

Major tech firms in the 16th include Cisco Systems, Adobe, IBM's Almaden Research Center and a Hitachi unit focused on supply-chain management. San Jose also has several large medical centers, including Good Samaritan Hospital, and is home to financial management software company Intacct. Local government and San Jose State University are major public sector employers.

One of the most ethnically diverse districts in the Bay Area, the 16th's Asian population includes the nation's second-largest Vietnamese community. Hispanics constitute a plurality of district residents (38 percent), and whites make up 32 percent of the population. The district's recent growth has resulted in one of the state's lowest percentages of population over the age of 64.

The 16th is solidly Democratic, and an influx of Hispanics has helped to keep it that way. Republican Gov. Arnold Schwarzenegger was held under 50 percent of the vote here during his 2006 re-election while capturing 56 percent of the vote statewide. Barack Obama commanded 70 percent of the district's vote in the 2008 presidential election.

MAJOR INDUSTRY
Technology, health care, finance

CITIES
San Jose (pt.), 590,306; Alum Rock (unincorporated), 13,479

NOTABLE
The Tech Museum of Innovation, a mango-colored building in downtown San Jose, welcomes hundreds of thousands of visitors to its exhibits, galleries and educational center.

Rep. Sam Farr (D)

CAPITOL OFFICE
225-2861
farr.house.gov
1126 Longworth Bldg. 20515-0517; fax 225-6791

COMMITTEES
Appropriations

RESIDENCE
Carmel

BORN
July 4, 1941; San Francisco, Calif.

RELIGION
Episcopalian

FAMILY
Wife, Shary Baldwin Farr; one child

EDUCATION
Willamette U., B.S. 1963 (biology)

CAREER
State legislative aide; Peace Corps volunteer

POLITICAL HIGHLIGHTS
Monterey County Board of Supervisors, 1975-80;
Calif. Assembly, 1980-93

ELECTION RESULTS

2008 GENERAL

Sam Farr (D)	168,907	73.9%
Jeff Taylor (R)	59,037	25.8%

2008 PRIMARY

Sam Farr (D)	unopposed

2006 GENERAL

Sam Farr (D)	120,750	75.8%
Anthony R. De Maio (R)	35,932	22.6%
Jeff Edward Taylor (I)	2,611	1.6%

PREVIOUS WINNING PERCENTAGES
2004 (67%); 2002 (68%); 2000 (69%); 1998 (65%);
1996 (59%); 1994 (52%); 1993 Special Runoff
Election (54%)

Elected June 1993; 8th full term

Farr is the quintessential coastal California liberal. He's a fierce environmentalist, a foe of the Iraq War and an advocate for gay rights.

But he is also an outspoken advocate for the agribusiness in his Salinas Valley district, home to America's $3 billion-a-year "salad bowl" — some 85 crops grown year-round that include strawberries, lettuce, spinach and peppers. He also works to protect the 10 military facilities in his district that have a total annual budget of about $750 million. They include the Defense Language Institute Foreign Language Center and the Naval Postgraduate School in Monterey, a center for computer research in intelligence gathering.

Farr also has worked for the successful conversion to civilian use of the Army's once-vast Fort Ord north of Monterey. Among other uses, the base now houses a California State University campus and below-market housing for the area's workers.

A fifth-generation Californian, Farr has long advocated for his area's natural resources, which include the stunning vistas of the Big Sur coastline and the second-largest national marine sanctuary outside of Hawaii. As co-chairman of the House Oceans Caucus, he has sought funding for the dozen research institutions located near the Monterey Bay coastline.

That coastline also is key to the district's $2 billion-a-year tourist industry, centered around Monterey's Cannery Row. The home of the now-vanished sardine-packing industry was made famous in the novel of the same name written by local son and Nobel Prize winner John Steinbeck. Not far south is the little storybook town of Carmel, whose former mayor is movie star Clint Eastwood, and the ultra-rich coastal enclave of Pebble Beach, home to a yearly golf tournament popularized by the late crooner Bing Crosby.

Early in the 110th Congress (2007-08), Farr introduced bipartisan legislation to implement the top recommendations of the 16-member U.S. Commission on Ocean Policy, which he helped create in the late 1990s. The panel recommended creating a stronger ocean agency that would use an ecosystem-based approach to improving protection for oceans and coasts. The legislation stalled because of Republican efforts to use it as a vehicle to authorize oil drilling along the Alaskan coast.

Since 2004, Farr has tried unsuccessfully to push through legislation to protect the southern sea otter, a star attraction along Monterey's coast. He said in a 2006 interview with the nonprofit Otter Project that Congress was more concerned with funneling money into other areas, such as the Iraq War.

A member of the Appropriations Committee, Farr made national news in April 2007 when he inserted a $25 million earmark for his district's spinach growers — hard hit by an E. coli outbreak — into an emergency spending bill for the wars in Iraq and Afghanistan. The group Citizens Against Government Waste named him "Porker of the Month," and the money was dropped by House and Senate negotiators.

Farr, whose district's growers are dependent on migrant laborers, also stirred controversy at a Homeland Security Appropriations hearing in February 2008 when he compared the Immigration and Customs Enforcement agency to the brutal Gestapo secret police of Nazi Germany. "What happens is the public image of you becomes one of not this compassionate law enforcement agency but essentially a Gestapo-type agency that is knocking on doors," he said.

Farr also has used his Appropriations seat to try, so far without success, to eliminate a Food and Drug Administration rule that bars any man who has engaged in homosexual sex since 1977 from donating blood. During an April 2008 hearing, Farr called the rule "discriminatory" and outdated. "The science doesn't support that policy decision," he said.

Farr has cosponsored legislation to reclassify medical marijuana under federal law so it can be legally prescribed. And he has cosponsored legislation to allow people accused of violating federal marijuana laws to introduce evidence in federal court that they followed state law — such as that in California — that allows them to use marijuana for medical reasons.

He successfully persuaded the Agriculture Department in 2008 to drop its plan to aerially spray areas in California where the light-brown apple moth was threatening the state's apple industry. Instead, Farr and other California officials convinced the federal department to release sterile moths.

Farr is a staunch party loyalist and a firm supporter of the leadership of his fellow Californian, Speaker Nancy Pelosi. But he wasn't much impressed by President Obama's professed commitment to bipartisanship at the start of his tenure. "Every new president begins by reaching out to the opposition party. It isn't too long before they realize the role of the opposition party is to kick you in the teeth," he said in January 2009.

Farr was born in San Francisco on July Fourth. His father was a longtime California state senator and the first national director of highway beautification under President Johnson. He grew up surrounded by people who influenced his path in life, including California's powerhouse liberal Gov. Edmund G. "Pat" Brown and landscape photographer Ansel Adams, a family friend. Due to Adams' influence, Farr is an avid photographer known for snapping pictures of his colleagues at work and play.

Farr graduated from Willamette University in Salem, Ore., in 1963, then joined the Peace Corps and spent two years in Colombia. His mother died from cancer while he was serving. After that, his family came to visit him in Colombia and, while on an outing, his younger sister was thrown from a horse and hit her head. She died on the operating table.

After leaving the Peace Corps, Farr got a staff job in the California State Assembly in Sacramento. He later won election to the Monterey County Board of Supervisors, where he served five years. He was then elected to the Assembly, where he served more than a dozen years.

In 1993, he won a special election to replace veteran Democratic Rep. Leon E. Panetta, who had become President Clinton's budget director and now serves as Obama's CIA director. Farr took 54 percent of the vote in a runoff against the GOP nominee, Pebble Beach lawyer Bill McCampbell. He hung on in their 1994 rematch, and has been re-elected easily since.

KEY VOTES

2008

Yes Delay consideration of Colombia free-trade agreement

Yes Override Bush veto of federal farm and nutrition programs reauthorization bill

No Overhaul surveillance laws and permit dismissal of suits against companies that conducted warrantless wiretapping

Yes Grant mortgage relief to homeowners and funding for Fannie Mae and Freddie Mac

Yes Approve initial $700 billion program to stabilize financial markets

Yes Approve final $700 billion program to stabilize financial markets

Yes Provide $14 billion in loans to automakers

2007

Yes Increase minimum wage by $2.10 an hour

Yes Approve $124.2 billion in emergency war spending and set goal for redeployment of troops from Iraq

No Reject federal contraceptive assistance to international family planning groups

Yes Override Bush veto of $23.2 billion water projects authorization bill

Yes Implement Peru free-trade agreement

Yes Approve energy policy overhaul with new fuel economy standards

No Clear $473.5 billion omnibus spending bill, including $70 billion for military operations

CQ VOTE STUDIES

	PARTY UNITY		PRESIDENTIAL SUPPORT	
	SUPPORT	OPPOSE	SUPPORT	OPPOSE
2008	99%	1%	13%	87%
2007	98%	2%	4%	96%
2006	97%	3%	13%	87%
2005	98%	2%	18%	82%
2004	96%	4%	24%	76%

INTEREST GROUPS

	AFL-CIO	ADA	CCUS	ACU
2008	100%	100%	61%	0%
2007	100%	95%	55%	0%
2006	93%	95%	27%	4%
2005	93%	100%	42%	8%
2004	93%	100%	43%	4%

CALIFORNIA 17

Monterey, San Benito and Santa Cruz counties — Salinas, Santa Cruz

The 17th takes in the most populated part of Santa Cruz County, with its namesake city and several sizable seaside communities, and stretches south to include San Benito and Monterey counties, where Monterey attracts tourists and exclusive Pebble Beach is home to celebrities and Silicon Valley executives.

South of Santa Cruz County, agriculture drives the economy. The Salinas Valley supplies nearly 80 percent of America's artichokes, as well as lettuce, spinach, cauliflower, cut flowers and other crops. Major wineries and vineyards also dot the landscape. The valley is home to most of the district's 43 percent Hispanic population.

More than 60 percent of district residents live in Monterey County. The region has developed as a center for marine sciences, with more than a dozen major research institutions located near the Monterey Bay coastline. The county also attracts tourists to its coastline, wineries and

Cannery Row, a former site of fishing and canning businesses and now a shopping center. Several colleges and universities are in the 17th, including the University of California, Santa Cruz, and California State University Monterey Bay.

Santa Cruz County is a Democratic stronghold, and the party has a strong voter registration edge in Monterey and San Benito counties. Barack Obama took 72 percent of the district's 2008 presidential vote.

MAJOR INDUSTRY
Agriculture, tourism, higher education

MILITARY BASES
Fort Hunter Liggett (Army), 3,793 military, 2,160 civilian (2009); Defense Language Institute Foreign Language Center/Presidio of Monterey (Army), 5,419 military, 2,481 civilian (2007); Naval Postgraduate School, 1,144 military, 129 civilian (2009); Fleet Numerical Meteorology and Oceanography Center, 61 military, 173 civilian (2007)

CITIES
Salinas, 151,060; Santa Cruz, 54,593; Watsonville, 44,265; Hollister, 34,413

NOTABLE
Monterey Canyon is the deepest submarine canyon off the North American coast of the Pacific Ocean.

Rep. Dennis Cardoza (D)

Elected 2002; 4th term

CAPITOL OFFICE
225-6131
www.house.gov/cardoza
1224 Longworth Bldg. 20515-0518; fax 225-0819

COMMITTEES
Agriculture
  (Horticulture & Organic Agriculture - chairman)
Rules

RESIDENCE
Atwater

BORN
March 31, 1959; Merced, Calif.

RELIGION
Roman Catholic

FAMILY
Wife, Kathleen McLoughlin; three children

EDUCATION
U. of Maryland, B.A. 1982 (government & politics)

CAREER
Bowling alley executive; Realtor; state legislative
aide; congressional aide

POLITICAL HIGHLIGHTS
Atwater City Council, 1984-87; Merced City Council,
1994-95; Calif. Assembly, 1996-2002

ELECTION RESULTS

2008 GENERAL

Dennis Cardoza (D)	unopposed	

2008 PRIMARY

Dennis Cardoza (D)	unopposed	

2006 GENERAL

Dennis Cardoza (D)	71,182	65.5%
John A. Kanno (R)	37,531	34.5%

PREVIOUS WINNING PERCENTAGES
2004 (67%); 2002 (51%)

Cardoza is a mild-mannered man who serves as a crucial link between the fiscally conservative Blue Dog Coalition of House Democrats and his party's more liberal House leadership.

At the request of Speaker Nancy Pelosi, the former co-chairman of the Blue Dogs regularly attends leadership meetings where he presents their concerns and seeks to resolve disagreements before votes are scheduled on legislation that might split the party. Cardoza said his role is to "try to act as salve on eruptions and bring sides together."

In 2007, Pelosi put him on the Rules Committee, which sets ground rules for floor debates on major legislation and translates the leadership's wishes into a procedural framework designed to ensure the majority party gets its way. That sometimes puts him on the spot, when his own views clash with those of Pelosi and her team. But he has generally been a loyal soldier.

He has not always been a reliable vote for his party, however, and in 2006, the final year of Republican control, Cardoza supported his own party only 79 percent of the time on votes pitting the parties against each other. By 2008 his party unity score hit 97 percent, his personal high.

But he split with the majority of his party in December 2008 and voted against the proposed $14 billion bailout for the nation's auto industry. The bailout bill ultimately died in the Senate. Yet he agreed with President Obama that the U.S. economy needed a jolt of federal money, and he supported the $787 billion stimulus package that cleared Congress in February 2009.

At the start of the 110th Congress (2007-08), Cardoza and the Blue Dogs successfully pushed for adoption of pay-as-you-go budget rules requiring Congress to find offsets for new tax cuts or increased spending. Cardoza would like to see that requirement written into law, not just House rules subject to reconsideration every two years.

Although House Democrats largely stuck to their budget rule in the 110th, the narrowly divided Senate did not. Tempers flared at the end of 2007 when the Senate refused to offset a one-year "patch" to limit the alternative minimum tax, which was originally intended to target only wealthy taxpayers but was not indexed for inflation. Cardoza voted against the final bill negotiated with the Senate, but the measure was enacted anyway. He also was disappointed in 2008 when Congress cleared a supplemental war spending bill creating a costly new veterans' education benefit and extending unemployment benefits for 13 weeks, both without offsets. But he didn't blame his party. "The problem is the Republicans in the Senate aren't willing to pay the freight," he said.

Cardoza has been looking forward to a new dynamic in the 111th Congress (2009-10) because he expects the increased Democratic majority on Capitol Hill to make it easier to enforce fiscal discipline. "The budget process is a disaster and needs a major overhaul to re-establish soundness," he says.

Though more a party loyalist than he used to be, Cardoza still sides with Republicans on some energy and environmental issues. He supports oil and gas drilling in Alaska's Arctic National Wildlife Refuge, and he would allow other states to decide whether to permit drilling on public lands within their borders and off their coasts. Twice Cardoza has tried but failed to garner support for a bill to make it harder for the federal government to designate vast tracts of land as "critical habitat" for endangered species.

He had to give up other committee assignments to serve on the Rules panel, but was allowed to stay on Agriculture and became chairman of its Subcommittee on Horticulture and Organic Agriculture. He zealously promoted the interests of his state as a five-year reauthorization of agriculture and nutrition programs was drafted. When it was enacted in 2008, he hailed its "historic investments" in specialty crops, conservation and nutrition programs. "California agriculture is finally getting the respect and treatment it deserves," he said.

Fixing the foster care system is Cardoza's passion as a lawmaker. In 2000, he and his wife, Kathleen McLoughlin, a physician with a family practice in Merced, adopted a sibling pair, Joey and Elaina, when the children were 6 and 3. (They have one biological child, Brittany, and "she wanted brothers and sisters," he says.) "We didn't know much about foster care back then, but now we are intimately familiar with the plight of foster children in America," he says. In 2008, the Child Welfare League of America awarded Cardoza its annual Congressional Voice for Youth Award in recognition of his efforts to improve the foster care system.

Cardoza grew up in the small town of Atwater, the grandson of immigrants who came from Portugal's Azores Islands in the 1920s. They revered President Franklin D. Roosevelt, whose programs they believed got them through the Depression. When the government began minting Roosevelt dimes, his grandmother refused to spend any of them. "When she died, there were bags of them in her closet," he says.

Cardoza's parents were dairy and sweet potato farmers who later opened bowling alleys in Atwater and Merced. Interested in politics as a youth, he earned a degree in government and politics from the University of Maryland, then interned for Democratic Rep. Martin Frost of Texas.

After college, Cardoza went home to manage the family's bowling business. In 1984, he was elected to the Atwater City Council. He volunteered in the campaign of then-California Assemblyman Gary A. Condit, who became a political mentor. He made it to the Assembly himself in 1996, serving six years. Foreshadowing his role in the U.S. House, he was a leader of a moderate Democratic faction and chaired the Rules Committee.

Condit moved up to the U.S. House but saw his career cut short after he admitted to an extramarital affair with intern Chandra Levy. The young woman from Modesto disappeared in 2002 and was later found slain in a Washington, D.C., park, the victim of an assault while she was jogging. Condit refused to bow out of the 2002 Democratic primary, so Cardoza challenged him. Both of Condit's grown children circulated letters in the district calling Cardoza a "traitor." But he had the Democratic establishment on his side. He won the primary, then prevailed over GOP state Sen. Dick Monteith by 8 percentage points that November. He has had no primary opposition since then, and in 2008 he also faced no opposition in the general election.

KEY VOTES

2008
Yes Delay consideration of Colombia free-trade agreement
Yes Override Bush veto of federal farm and nutrition programs reauthorization bill
Yes Overhaul surveillance laws and permit dismissal of suits against companies that conducted warrantless wiretapping
Yes Grant mortgage relief to homeowners and funding for Fannie Mae and Freddie Mac
Yes Approve initial $700 billion program to stabilize financial markets
Yes Approve final $700 billion program to stabilize financial markets
No Provide $14 billion in loans to automakers

2007
Yes Increase minimum wage by $2.10 an hour
Yes Approve $124.2 billion in emergency war spending and set goal for redeployment of troops from Iraq
No Reject federal contraceptive assistance to international family planning groups
Yes Override Bush veto of $23.2 billion water projects authorization bill
Yes Implement Peru free-trade agreement
Yes Approve energy policy overhaul with new fuel economy standards
No Clear $473.5 billion omnibus spending bill, including $70 billion for military operations

CQ VOTE STUDIES

	PARTY UNITY		PRESIDENTIAL SUPPORT	
	SUPPORT	OPPOSE	SUPPORT	OPPOSE
2008	97%	3%	16%	84%
2007	94%	6%	7%	93%
2006	79%	21%	50%	50%
2005	79%	21%	39%	61%
2004	81%	19%	45%	55%

INTEREST GROUPS

	AFL-CIO	ADA	CCUS	ACU
2008	93%	85%	65%	8%
2007	96%	90%	63%	4%
2006	85%	60%	79%	46%
2005	100%	85%	67%	44%
2004	93%	85%	65%	25%

CALIFORNIA 18

Central Valley – Merced, part of Stockton and Modesto

The Democratic 18th takes in most of Stockton in San Joaquin County, then dives south to pick up half of Stanislaus County and Merced County, which make up the district's agricultural base. A narrow strip stretches through Madera and Fresno counties to almost reach Fresno. Modesto, the Stanislaus County seat, experienced years of growth as businesses fled California's congested coastal cities. The Central Valley's successful agriculture industry also supported a stable economy that has been beset by rising unemployment and foreclosure rates.

Many of the district's blue-collar workers — the 18th has one of the highest percentages in the state (37 percent) — work in the canning and food-processing industry. The district's portion of Modesto includes the headquarters of Foster Farms Dairy, the largest privately owned dairy in California, as well as a full-service plant. National companies such as Del Monte and Frito-Lay also have facilities in the district. Hometown Gallo Winery is the nation's second-largest winery.

Although dominated by agriculture, the district also includes the central portion of the diverse and Democratic port city of Stockton (shared with the 11th), which is a transportation hub on the San Joaquin River. Almost 60 percent of Stockton's residents live in the 18th. In 2005, a University of California campus opened in Merced, the system's 10th and the first U.S. public research university to be built in the 21st century.

The area has a long history of sending Democrats to Congress, having done so for decades, and Barack Obama carried the 18th with 59 percent of the vote in the 2008 presidential election. Hispanics enjoy a plurality of the district's population, while whites make up 39 percent of residents. Stockton has one of the largest Sikh populations in the United States.

MAJOR INDUSTRY
Agriculture, wine, food processing

CITIES
Stockton (pt.), 139,362; Modesto (pt.), 133,975; Merced, 63,893; Ceres, 34,609; Los Banos, 25,869

NOTABLE
Stockton hosts an annual asparagus festival, during which more than 40,000 pounds of asparagus are consumed.

Rep. George Radanovich (R)

Elected 1994; 8th term

CAPITOL OFFICE
225-4540
www.house.gov/radanovich
2410 Rayburn Bldg. 20515-0519; fax 225-3402

COMMITTEES
Energy & Commerce

RESIDENCE
Mariposa

BORN
June 20, 1955; Mariposa, Calif.

RELIGION
Roman Catholic

FAMILY
Wife, Ethie Radanovich; one child

EDUCATION
California Polytechnic State U., San Luis Obispo,
B.S. 1978 (agriculture business management)

CAREER
Bank manager; vintner; carpenter

POLITICAL HIGHLIGHTS
Mariposa County Board of Supervisors, 1989-92
(chairman, 1991); sought Republican nomination
for U.S. House, 1992

ELECTION RESULTS

2008 GENERAL

George Radanovich (R)	179,245	98.4%
Peter Leinau (D)	2,490	1.4%

2008 PRIMARY

George Radanovich (R)	unopposed

2006 GENERAL

George Radanovich (R)	110,246	60.6%
TJ Cox (D)	71,748	39.4%

PREVIOUS WINNING PERCENTAGES
2004 (66%); 2002 (67%); 2000 (65%); 1998 (79%);
1996 (67%); 1994 (57%)

Radanovich is a party loyalist, but he devotes most of his energy to fighting for the interests of his drought-parched district in the San Joaquin Valley, where fish and farmers compete for precious water and the agricultural economy depends on the labor of immigrant workers. In this respect, he espouses a common GOP theme calling for a limited role for the federal government.

He is a member of the Republican Study Committee, a group of the most conservative House Republicans, which has been growing in intraparty influence over the years. Since entering the House with the large GOP Class of 1994, Radanovich (ruh-DON-o-vitch) has been a reliable vote for party leaders. His annual "party unity" scores — the percentage of votes on which he backed a majority of Republicans in opposition to a majority of Democrats — has never dropped below 95 percent.

But there were two votes in late 2008 on which Radanovich broke with his party that he quickly came to regret. He supported two versions of a $700 billion plan to aid the financial services sector, the second of which became law. He reasoned that, although it was far from perfect, "it was the best available option, considering the makeup of this Congress, to shore up our toxic credit markets and bringing confidence back into the market."

He quickly came under fire back home, particularly from conservatives, just before the 2008 election. Radanovich wryly noted it was good he was unopposed on the ballot. After the election, he told a local group, "That's it for me," and vowed to vote against a bailout of the auto industry — which he did.

In early 2009, he stuck with his party to oppose President Obama's $787 billion economic stimulus plan, which became law. "The idea behind an economic stimulus should be to help the American people create and retain jobs — not spend more taxpayer money on big-government programs," he stated.

That comment was more in line with Radanovich's typical philosophy of a limited government. He has long criticized what he regards as the federal government's unreasonable, East Coast-dominated policies on water and land use. He wants to permit suspension of the 1973 Endangered Species Act during times of drought so that more water can be taken by two pumping plants from the Sacramento-San Joaquin River Delta to irrigate fields and keep faucets flowing.

A court ruling on a suit brought under the Endangered Species Act (ESA) mandates reduced pumping to protect the threatened delta smelt, a small fish that lives only in the delta formed by the two rivers. It shares water sources that irrigate some of the nation's most productive cropland and serve 22 million Californians. "We cannot afford to let our state dry up and blow away simply for the sake of protecting a few small fish," Radanovich said.

Radanovich is likely to find it difficult to get traction for his California Drought Alleviation Act in the 111th Congress (2009-10). "It's not getting a lot of attention from the Democrat leadership, of course, because of the ESA reform," he said. But it's "something that maybe should be pushed" because of the prospect of tough drought conditions in the state.

There are better prospects for another Radanovich priority: legislation to implement a historic 2006 settlement of an 18-year dispute between environmentalists, state water authorities and federal agencies to restore 150 miles of the San Joaquin River. Under the accord, salmon could return to the river below the federally owned Friant Dam — a large part of which is now dry for much of the year — while water supplies for 15,000 farms would be protected. Implementing legislation came close to enactment in the 110th Congress.

He had more influence on water issues as chairman of a Natural Resources subcommittee on water in the 109th Congress (2005-06). And earlier, as chairman of its national parks panel, he held hearings to bludgeon the EPA and National Park Service for permitting toxic discharges into the Potomac River. But when the Democrats took over in 2007, he gave up his Natural Resources seat to stay on Energy and Commerce, on which he has served since 2001.

That committee will have jurisdiction over several major pieces of legislation to address domestic energy production and global warming in the 111th Congress. But the ascension of Democrat Henry A. Waxman of California to the chairman's seat "is a signal that that committee is going to move hard left, and we're going to try to bring some balance to this, what I think will be some extreme legislation," Radanovich said.

He is the ranking Republican on the committee's panel on trade and supports free-trade agreements that he says will further boost the state's agricultural exports. In 2005, he backed implementation of the Central America Free Trade Agreement and voted for a free-trade agreement with Peru in 2007.

Radanovich has broken with the GOP leadership on the issue of immigration. He supports securing the nation's borders from illegal immigrants but wants a guest worker program that would ensure migrant labor, which his district's farmers and other agricultural interests depend upon.

Radanovich's district includes Yosemite National Park, and he has clashed more than once with the National Park Service over its plans to reduce overcrowding that he said could hurt tourist-dependent towns and businesses nearby. He says he cherishes the time he spends in the scenic, mountainous park and aims to trek in the high country at least once a year.

The fifth of eight children of a Croatian immigrant who owned a clothing store in Mariposa, he spent his teens on the family's small ranch outside town. He got his degree in agriculture business management and after working as a banker, carpenter and substitute teacher, he pursued his first love: farming.

Inspired by memories of his grandfather making wine in the cellar, he established a winery in the Mariposa County foothills of the Sierra Nevada. At one time the Radanovich Winery shipped about 6,000 cases of wine annually, but he closed it in 2003 after big financial losses.

Radanovich won a seat on the Mariposa County Board of Supervisors in 1989, and in 1992 he made a bid for Congress. Mariposa is far from the district's population center in Fresno County, where he was largely unknown. He lost a close primary, but two years later, aided by a GOP tilt in the district from the post-1990 census remapping, Radanovich beat incumbent Democratic Rep. Richard H. Lehman. He has won easily since.

KEY VOTES

2008
No   Delay consideration of Colombia free-trade agreement
Yes Override Bush veto of federal farm and nutrition programs reauthorization bill
Yes Overhaul surveillance laws and permit dismissal of suits against companies that conducted warrantless wiretapping
No   Grant mortgage relief to homeowners and funding for Fannie Mae and Freddie Mac
Yes Approve initial $700 billion program to stabilize financial markets
Yes Approve final $700 billion program to stabilize financial markets
No   Provide $14 billion in loans to automakers

2007
No   Increase minimum wage by $2.10 an hour
No   Approve $124.2 billion in emergency war spending and set goal for redeployment of troops from Iraq
Yes Reject federal contraceptive assistance to international family planning groups
No   Override Bush veto of $23.2 billion water projects authorization bill
Yes Implement Peru free-trade agreement
No   Approve energy policy overhaul with new fuel economy standards
Yes Clear $473.5 billion omnibus spending bill, including $70 billion for military operations

CQ VOTE STUDIES

| | PARTY UNITY | | PRESIDENTIAL SUPPORT | |
	SUPPORT	OPPOSE	SUPPORT	OPPOSE
2008	97%	3%	77%	23%
2007	96%	4%	88%	12%
2006	97%	3%	95%	5%
2005	96%	4%	86%	14%
2004	95%	5%	91%	9%

INTEREST GROUPS

	AFL-CIO	ADA	CCUS	ACU
2008	7%	20%	94%	87%
2007	9%	0%	68%	100%
2006	7%	5%	100%	88%
2005	21%	0%	96%	92%
2004	7%	0%	100%	100%

CALIFORNIA 19

Central Valley — part of Fresno and Modesto, Turlock, Madera

A fertile farm district, the 19th includes the heart of Central California's San Joaquin Valley. It takes in about half of Stanislaus County, grabbing a portion of Modesto. East of Stanislaus, it moves south from Tuolumne to Mariposa County into almost all of Madera County and part of the city of Fresno, home to large Hispanic, Hmong and Armenian populations.

The district's portion of Stanislaus County includes less than one-third of Modesto's population and the growing city of Turlock. Tuolumne and Mariposa counties, which along with Madera County to the south are home to Yosemite National Park, are sparsely populated areas that make up only roughly one-tenth of the 19th's population. The counties feature ski slopes and forests of the Sierra Nevada range in the east and former Gold Rush towns such as Jamestown, Sonora and Mariposa in the west.

This agricultural district — boasting the nation's third-highest orchard acreage and approximately 10 percent of California's milk cows — has a

Foster Farms Dairy milk and juice processing plant in the 19th's portion of Fresno and a ConAgra plant in Oakdale. Madera County, whose vines account for 10 percent of the state's wine grapes, has several notable wineries, and Yosemite National Park brings tourists here. Turlock's status as a growing bedroom community for San Jose and San Francisco has spurred local debate over issues of smart growth and business development to the north and west.

The 19th is rural, reliably Republican and mostly white, although Hispanics make up 28 percent of residents. Republicans hold a double-digit lead in party registration here. The district gave Arnold Schwarzenegger 69 percent of its 2006 gubernatorial vote, but John McCain took only 52 percent here in the 2008 presidential election.

MAJOR INDUSTRY
Agriculture, dairy, tourism

CITIES
Fresno (pt.), 189,836; Turlock, 55,810; Modesto (pt.), 54,881; Madera, 43,207

NOTABLE
Yosemite National Park was created in 1890, and its El Capitan rock formation is the world's largest granite monolith; Fresno's Forestiere Underground Gardens features plants growing 22 feet below ground.

Rep. Jim Costa (D)

Elected 2004; 3rd term

CAPITOL OFFICE
225-3341
www.house.gov/costa
1314 Longworth Bldg. 20515-0520; fax 225-9308

COMMITTEES
Agriculture
Foreign Affairs
Natural Resources
(Energy & Mineral Resources - chairman)

RESIDENCE
Fresno

BORN
April 13, 1952; Fresno, Calif.

RELIGION
Roman Catholic

FAMILY
Single

EDUCATION
California State U., Fresno, B.A. 1974
(political science)

CAREER
Lobbyist; state legislative aide; congressional
district aide; almond orchard owner

POLITICAL HIGHLIGHTS
Calif. Assembly, 1978-94; Democratic nominee
for Calif. Senate, 1993; Calif. Senate, 1994-2002

ELECTION RESULTS

2008 GENERAL

Jim Costa (D)	93,023	74.3%
Jim Lopez (R)	32,118	25.7%

2008 PRIMARY

Jim Costa (D)	unopposed

2006 GENERAL

Jim Costa (D)	unopposed

PREVIOUS WINNING PERCENTAGES
2004 (53%)

Costa has a deep knowledge of agricultural and natural resources issues, having served 24 years in the California Legislature. He seeks to balance environmental and farm interests. Though he resists labels, he has become an increasingly reliable Democratic vote.

Costa sits on the Natural Resources Committee, where he chairs the Energy and Minerals Resources. He expects to be involved in efforts to draft broad energy legislation in the 111th Congress (2009-10) that meets his goals of being both clean and sustainable. In 2008, he got a measure passed into law enabling the EPA to continue funding clean-diesel projects as part of its enforcement settlements with polluters.

He managed to anger both the mining and oil and gas industries soon after taking over the chairmanship in the 110th Congress (2007-08). Costa pushed to require mining companies to pay royalties on mines near national parks where they currently pay no fees. He told McClatchy Newspapers that Congress "needs to bring a 135-year-old law into the 21st century." The House passed the measure in November 2007, but it stalled in the Senate with the threat of a White House veto. Democrats plan to revive it in the 111th.

He also proposed to fund the $170 million restoration of California's San Joaquin River with a $3.75-per-acre fee on outer continental shelf leases in the Gulf of Mexico that are not producing oil or gas. The river restoration would return salmon to the river, but has area farmers concerned about their future water supplies. The full committee approved the bill, but the House did not take it up in the 110th. However, the Senate passed an omnibus public lands bill January 2009 that includes $88 million for the work necessary to restore water flows and the salmon population for the river.

Costa worked hard on the 2008 reauthorization of agriculture programs, keeping an eye on how it deals with the specialty crops that are abundant in California's Central Valley. He ultimately supported the five-year, $289 billion measure that reauthorized crop subsidies, tightened income eligibility limits for payments and expanded conservation programs.

His agricultural roots run deep. His immigrant grandfather started milking cows on the very day he arrived in the Central Valley a century ago from the Portuguese Azores island of Terceira. Costa's father and uncle later ran the roughly 500-acre farm, located nine miles west of Fresno. Costa started helping out at age 7. The family sold its dairy herd in the 1970s, and after his father and uncle died they divided up the farm. Costa still owns 240 acres of the property, now an almond orchard. He gives out 1-pound bags of the almonds to visitors to his congressional office.

Costa also sits on the Foreign Affairs panel, where he took up the cause of Armenian-Americans who want to condemn the Ottoman Empire's alleged genocide of Armenians in the early 20th century. In 2007 he was a vocal supporter of a non-binding resolution that called upon President George W. Bush to use the word "genocide" when issuing statements about events in Armenia.

Costa has become more vocal about the war in Iraq. In 2007, he joined with a group of 28 moderate Democrats and Republicans who offered their own plan for withdrawing U.S. troops from Iraq without a set date for ending U.S. involvement there.

He is a member of the Blue Dog Coalition of fiscally conservative Democrats. He has voted in favor of Republican bills to permanently repeal the estate tax, weaken the Endangered Species Act and stop minors from crossing state borders to get an abortion without parental consent. But he sided with most Democrats in opposing the 2005 Central America Free Trade Agreement and voted in 2006 against authorization of the Bush administration's warrantless electronic surveillance program.

Though Costa once said, "I don't like being labeled," his support for his party on floor votes which pitted Democrats against Republicans has increased steadily since Democrats assumed control of the House in 2007. He supported the party 76 percent of the time in 2006; that figure jumped to 92 percent in 2007 and 94 percent in 2008.

Politics and government are nothing new for the Costa family. His father served as treasurer for a friend running for the local county board of supervisors. His mother, who died at 90 in 2006, served on a county social services board and as a school trustee. She belonged to Democratic clubs and thought Harry S Truman was "a heck of a guy," Costa told the Fresno Bee when his mother passed away.

Despite his parents' civic nature, working on the farm and skiing occupied most of Costa's attention in high school and college. It wasn't until he interned in the office of Democratic Rep. B.F. Sisk in the summer of 1973 and attended the Senate Watergate hearings that Costa caught the political bug.

He worked on the winning 1974 House campaign of California Democrat John Krebs, and then was an aide in his Washington office before returning to California to help on a state legislative race. After 18 months as the state legislator's administrative assistant, Costa decided to run for the Assembly himself in 1978, when the incumbent in his old home district made a run for governor. He was only 26 when he was elected.

When term limits forced him out of the state Senate in 2002, Costa opened his own lobbying firm. Having flirted with a House run three previous times, Costa quickly declared his candidacy after six-term Democratic Rep. Cal Dooley announced he would not run again. Getting to know the electorate was not a problem; the state Senate district Costa represented for eight years included the entire congressional district. "I'm like an old shoe who's been working with those folks for a long time," Costa said.

Costa trounced former Dooley chief of staff Lisa Quigley in the 2004 primary, which turned ugly when she ran a television ad citing Costa's 1986 arrest in a prostitution sting, for which he had earlier apologized, and a 1994 incident in which police found marijuana in his apartment. (The drug was never linked to him and no charges were filed.) He faced a tough challenge in November from well-funded Republican state Sen. Roy Ashburn. But Costa won by 7 percentage points and was re-elected without opposition in 2006. He easily won re-election in 2008.

KEY VOTES

2008

Yes Delay consideration of Colombia free-trade agreement

Yes Override Bush veto of federal farm and nutrition programs reauthorization bill

Yes Overhaul surveillance laws and permit dismissal of suits against companies that conducted warrantless wiretapping

Yes Grant mortgage relief to homeowners and funding for Fannie Mae and Freddie Mac

Yes Approve initial $700 billion program to stabilize financial markets

Yes Approve final $700 billion program to stabilize financial markets

? Provide $14 billion in loans to automakers

2007

Yes Increase minimum wage by $2.10 an hour

+ Approve $124.2 billion in emergency war spending and set goal for redeployment of troops from Iraq

No Reject federal contraceptive assistance to international family planning groups

Yes Override Bush veto of $23.2 billion water projects authorization bill

Yes Implement Peru free-trade agreement

Yes Approve energy policy overhaul with new fuel economy standards

Yes Clear $473.5 billion omnibus spending bill, including $70 billion for military operations

CQ VOTE STUDIES

	PARTY UNITY		PRESIDENTIAL SUPPORT	
	SUPPORT	OPPOSE	SUPPORT	OPPOSE
2008	94%	6%	26%	74%
2007	92%	8%	8%	92%
2006	76%	24%	47%	53%
2005	79%	21%	42%	58%

INTEREST GROUPS

	AFL-CIO	ADA	CCUS	ACU
2008	100%	80%	67%	9%
2007	96%	90%	65%	4%
2006	86%	70%	93%	56%
2005	93%	80%	70%	32%

CALIFORNIA 20

Central Valley — Kings County, parts of Fresno and Bakersfield

The Hispanic-majority 20th reaches from Fresno to Bakersfield, through rural portions of Fresno, Kings and Kern counties. Roughly 40 percent of Fresno's residents live in the 20th, which takes in much of downtown and Hispanic areas in the southern section of the city.

Federal water projects in the Westlands have spawned vast farms with battalions of workers and a wide variety of crops, including alfalfa, cotton, fruits, sugar beets, wheat and nuts. Fresno's agricultural contribution is more industrial, with fruit and other food processing plants, a Foster Farms poultry farm and several dairy farms. The district also has attracted public and privately run prisons that assist the area's economy.

The 20th bears much of the burden of the San Joaquin Valley's urban and rural poor and is beset by unemployment and crime. Its residents have the nation's sixth-lowest median income, and the district has the state's lowest rate of college education (6 percent), as well as the country's third-highest number of residents without a high school diploma (just under 50 percent). With the only blue-collar plurality in the state, many district workers are Hispanic and Hmong immigrants who work in the local farming communities that have been hurt by agricultural losses after sustained drought conditions. Overall, the district has the nation's fourth-largest orchard acreage.

Democrats enjoy a distinct voter registration advantage in the 20th, and Barack Obama easily won the district's presidential vote in 2008 with 60 percent. The 20th is the nation's third-youngest district, with its median age just a shade under 27.

MAJOR INDUSTRY
Agriculture, dairy, prisons

MILITARY BASES
Naval Air Station Lemoore, 6,000 military, 985 civilian (2008)

CITIES
Fresno (pt.), 154,998; Bakersfield (pt.), 43,284; Hanford, 41,686; Delano, 38,824

NOTABLE
The Fresno Sanitary Landfill is the country's oldest sanitary landfill.

Rep. Devin Nunes (R)

Elected 2002; 4th term

CAPITOL OFFICE
225-2523
nunes.house.gov
1013 Longworth Bldg. 20515-0521; fax 225-3404

COMMITTEES
Budget
Ways & Means

RESIDENCE
Tulare

BORN
Oct. 1, 1973; Tulare, Calif.

RELIGION
Roman Catholic

FAMILY
Wife, Elizabeth Nunes; one child

EDUCATION
College of the Sequoias, A.A. 1993 (agriculture);
California Polytechnic State U., San Luis Obispo,
B.S. 1995 (agricultural business), M.S. 1996
(agriculture)

CAREER
Farmer; U.S. Agriculture Department program
administrator

POLITICAL HIGHLIGHTS
College of the Sequoias Board of Trustees, 1996-
2002; sought Republican nomination for U.S.
House, 1998

ELECTION RESULTS

2008 GENERAL

Devin Nunes (R)	143,498	68.4%
Larry Johnson (D)	66,317	31.6%

2008 PRIMARY

Devin Nunes (R)	unopposed

2006 GENERAL

Devin Nunes (R)	95,214	66.7%
Steven Haze (D)	42,718	29.9%
John Roger Miller (GREEN)	4,729	3.3%

PREVIOUS WINNING PERCENTAGES
2004 (73%); 2002 (70%)

Nunes is a hard-line conservative and a tough advocate when it comes to issues affecting his district. A descendant of dairy farmers from the middle of California, he battles environmentalists, Democrats and even Republicans to protect the water and agricultural interests of his constituents.

He is attentive to party fundraising and has built strategic alliances within his leadership. He was part of a group that successfully backed underdog John A. Boehner in his initial 2006 contest for Republican leader. So far that hasn't helped him move up the leadership ladder; when he ran for GOP conference chairman at the start of the 111th Congress (2009-10), he lost to Mike Pence of Indiana. But he's got time — in his mid-30s, he already ranks eighth out of 15 Republicans on the Ways and Means Committee, where he snagged a seat in 2005. He also sits on the Budget Committee.

Republican leaders can almost always rely on Nunes as there is not much he likes about the Democrats' agenda. He voted against an expansion of a children's health insurance program that was one of first measures in 2009 to clear Congress and be signed by President Obama. He also opposed Obama's $787 billion economic stimulus package, signed into law in February 2009, stating: "It is little more than a magician's grab-bag, loaded with tricks and treats but totally lacking in substance."

In 2007, he voted against a Democratic bill to reauthorize agriculture and nutrition programs for five years, and also a minimum wage increase. The fiscal conservative announced in 2008 that he would stop requesting earmarks, provisions placed into bills that specifically benefit a member's district, declaring the process "totally corrupt."

When Nunes gained a seat on Ways and Means, he had to give up his senior GOP slot on the Natural Resources Committee's panel on national parks, where he typically sided with landowners in their frequent disputes with environmentalists. Yet he has continued to remain firmly involved in local concerns, shrugging off any criticism for his firm stances. He says he doesn't mind being called "brash." But what he doesn't like is what he calls the "populist rhetoric nonsense" that he finds in Congress. "I'm not a populist. I'm a realist," he says.

Nunes spent much of the 110th Congress (2007-08) embroiled in a dispute with other members of the California delegation on water allocations from the San Joaquin River. The issue stems from a court settlement reached by environmentalists and some local officials aimed at restoring water to a 60-mile dry stretch of the river, in the hope of returning Chinook salmon to the area. Nunes in 2006 had joined with many of his California colleagues in announcing legislation to implement the settlement.

But he soon turned against the deal. He complained that under the court settlement "my district will provide the bulk of water used to restore the river. Perhaps this is the reason so many other valley legislators were willing to move forward without finding ways to offset water losses."

The dispute put Nunes at odds with fellow Republican George Radanovich, of the neighboring 19th District, who is a key supporter of the court settlement. When the Senate in January 2009 passed a measure agreeing with the court settlement, Nunes wasn't happy. He said the Senate action "will deprive our region of precious surface water at a time of critical shortage."

In 2006, Nunes won passage of a measure forcing dairy producers to operate in a federally regulated system. The bill was aimed at an Arizona-based dairy, Sarah Farms, which was operating outside the system and selling milk for a lower price in California. Nunes' district is a top milk producer, and he has received substantial campaign contributions from the dairy industry.

Although he is an outspoken advocate for the Sequoia and Kings Canyon national parks in his district, he is frequently at odds with environmental groups that oppose commercial logging.

Nunes' family hails from the Azores, the nine-island chain off the coast of Portugal, where several hundred years ago everyone "had three cows, fished and made wine," he said. His immigrant grandfather established the 640-acre family farm, where his grandmother still runs a dairy operation with the help of two of Nunes' uncles. Nunes and his brother, Anthony, once ran an alfalfa hay harvesting business. Nunes' only involvement in agriculture today is in wine; he is part-owner of the Alpha Omega winery.

The district is home to a concentration of Portuguese-Americans, many of them related by blood or marriage and most Roman Catholic. They share food traditions, festivals and other cultural elements. In 2003, Nunes married Elizabeth Tamariz, a Portuguese-American who teaches elementary school and whom he's known since childhood. The district also has concentrations of Armenians, Mexicans, Sikhs, Hmong and Dutch immigrants. His office wall features a soccer jersey from Portuguese star Luis Figo.

After graduating from California Polytechnic State University with a master's degree in 1996, Nunes volunteered to help a candidate for the board of the two-year College of the Sequoias, which he had attended. The candidate unexpectedly quit, and Nunes, then 22, decided to run himself. He wound up ousting a seasoned incumbent. The next day Nunes, wearing work clothes and fixing his grandmother's water heater, was surprised when a local television crew drove out to interview him. He was hooked on politics.

While on the school board, he met Bill Thomas, the local congressman. In 1998, he agreed to an all-but-hopeless challenge to Democratic incumbent Cal Dooley in the 20th District and lost. In 2000, Nunes campaigned for George W. Bush and was rewarded when Thomas helped him get appointed state director for the U.S. Agriculture Department's rural development program when Bush became president in 2001.

Reapportionment gave California an additional seat, and the 21st District was created. In 2002, Nunes beat two better-known Republicans in the primary, Fresno Mayor Jim Patterson and state Rep. Mike Briggs. His two competitors split the GOP vote in the Fresno area, to Nunes' advantage. He also benefited from a Hispanic-sounding name and the solid support of Portuguese-American voters in Tulare County. He cruised to victory in the general election and has easily won re-election since.

KEY VOTES

2008

No   Delay consideration of Colombia free-trade agreement

No   Override Bush veto of federal farm and nutrition programs reauthorization bill

Yes   Overhaul surveillance laws and permit dismissal of suits against companies that conducted warrantless wiretapping

No   Grant mortgage relief to homeowners and funding for Fannie Mae and Freddie Mac

No   Approve initial $700 billion program to stabilize financial markets

No   Approve final $700 billion program to stabilize financial markets

No   Provide $14 billion in loans to automakers

2007

No   Increase minimum wage by $2.10 an hour

No   Approve $124.2 billion in emergency war spending and set goal for redeployment of troops from Iraq

Yes   Reject federal contraceptive assistance to international family planning groups

No   Override Bush veto of $23.2 billion water projects authorization bill

Yes   Implement Peru free-trade agreement

No   Approve energy policy overhaul with new fuel economy standards

Yes   Clear $473.5 billion omnibus spending bill, including $70 billion for military operations

CQ VOTE STUDIES

	PARTY UNITY		PRESIDENTIAL SUPPORT	
	SUPPORT	OPPOSE	SUPPORT	OPPOSE
2008	97%	3%	83%	17%
2007	97%	3%	81%	19%
2006	98%	2%	95%	5%
2005	96%	4%	87%	13%
2004	95%	5%	91%	9%

INTEREST GROUPS

	AFL-CIO	ADA	CCUS	ACU
2008	7%	0%	94%	100%
2007	5%	5%	79%	100%
2006	8%	0%	100%	84%
2005	29%	5%	96%	84%
2004	13%	0%	100%	96%

CALIFORNIA 21

Central Valley – Tulare County, part of Fresno

The agriculture-dominated 21st is home to all of Tulare and part of Fresno counties, which vie each year for the title of top farm-goods-producing county in the nation. The 21st ranks first in the country in both orchard acreage and total number of milk cows. In addition to about 20 percent of the city of Fresno, the district takes in some of the mountains and forests of the Sierra Nevada chain on its eastern edge.

Tulare County is the world's largest dairy-producing area and the nation's second-largest agricultural county. Land O'Lakes has a large cheese processing plant here, and the county produces more than 250 other agricultural goods, including oranges, grapes, nuts and cotton. Continued drought conditions have hurt production. Tulare also is developing an ethanol industry.

The city of Tulare hosts the annual World Ag Expo, the world's largest agricultural expo, which draws more than 100,000 people from more than 60 countries annually. Visalia is the site of a Provisions Food Company cheese manufacturing plant at a former Kraft Foods dairy facility.

The 21st includes the eastern portion of Fresno, including Fresno Yosemite International Airport. Fresno also is home to a solar-powered Gap clothing distribution center and the Foster Farms turkey hatchery. Tourists are attracted to the district's location in the Sequoia Valley: The Giant Sequoia National Monument and the Sequoia National Forest are located east of Porterville and offer camping, hiking, kayaking or mountain biking either in the forest or in the nearby Sierra Nevada range.

The district's share of Fresno is the more conservative area of the city, and the rest of the 21st is reliably Republican. Republicans hold a solid edge in voter registration in the district's portion of Fresno and in Tulare, and the 21st's residents gave John McCain 56 percent of the vote in the 2008 presidential election, his second-best showing in the state.

MAJOR INDUSTRY
Agriculture, dairy, transportation, tourism

CITIES
Visalia, 91,565; Fresno (pt.), 82,818; Clovis, 68,468; Tulare, 43,994; Porterville, 39,615

NOTABLE
The Porterville High School marching band is said to be the oldest high school band in California.

Rep. Kevin McCarthy (R)

Elected 2006; 2nd term

CAPITOL OFFICE
225-2915
kevinmccarthy.house.gov
1523 Longworth Bldg. 20515-0522; fax 225-8798

COMMITTEES
Financial Services
House Administration

RESIDENCE
Bakersfield

BORN
Jan. 26, 1965; Bakersfield, Calif.

RELIGION
Baptist

FAMILY
Wife, Judy McCarthy; two children

EDUCATION
Bakersfield College, attended 1984-85;
California State U., Bakersfield, B.S. 1989
(business administration), M.B.A. 1994;

CAREER
Congressional district director; sandwich shop
owner

POLITICAL HIGHLIGHTS
Kern County Republican Central Committee,
1992-2002; Kern County Community College
District Board of Trustees, 2000-2002; Calif.
Assembly, 2002-06 (minority leader, 2004-06)

ELECTION RESULTS

2008 GENERAL

Kevin McCarthy (R)		unopposed

2008 PRIMARY

Kevin McCarthy (R)		unopposed

2006 GENERAL

Kevin McCarthy (R)	133,278	70.7%
Sharon M. Beery (D)	55,226	29.3%

Politically savvy and ambitious, McCarthy knows how to raise funds, make friends and do his homework — all qualities Republicans hope will help them take back some House seats and reshape the party's agenda even while coping with the priorities of the Democratic majority and the Obama administration.

McCarthy is the GOP's chief deputy whip for the 111th Congress (2009-10) and will be responsible not only for helping Minority Whip Eric Cantor of Virginia count votes, but also helping lead the party's disparate factions to consensus. He also serves on the executive committee of the National Republican Congressional Committee, and — as a virtual shoo-in for the 2010 midterm election — McCarthy is in charge of recruiting House candidates.

In early 2009, he immediately led a push to recruit moderates to oppose Democrats in divided districts, believing they would be more likely to stick with the party on key issues. And he began to think of the need for the party to appeal to traditionally Democratic groups, such as Hispanics and blacks. "This is not the top of where the Republican Party has been in the past, but it's not the bottom, either," he told The Tribune of San Luis Obispo.

He's expected to raise funds for them, too; during the 2008 election cycle, he gave more than $265,000 to other GOP candidates. He also served as chairman of the Republican Platform Committee for the 2008 presidential election.

In his early 40s, McCarthy has spent nearly his entire adult life in politics, serving as an aide to his predecessor, Republican Bill Thomas, before easily winning the seat upon Thomas' retirement in 2006. Like Thomas, McCarthy is a fiscal conservative who tends to be less engaged on the issues that preoccupy social conservatives. And like Thomas, he immerses himself in the policy details of legislation as well as the politics of his House colleagues. Republican Devin Nunes, a longtime friend who represents the adjoining 21st District, told the Los Angeles Times in January 2009, "Kevin lives and breathes politics."

Instead of sleeping during his weekly five-hour plane ride from Washington to Bakersfield, McCarthy studies the economic and political characteristics of his colleagues' districts, looking for ways to market his policy ideas. "Hopefully I can get to where I understand their districts better than them," McCarthy said. "They may be able to be part of some legislation and not know it."

But McCarthy is much less abrasive than Thomas, who as chairman and ranking member of the Ways and Means Committee was often condescending to his colleagues. McCarthy is congenial and approachable; whether it is a staff member or a stranger, he greets a visitor with a pat on the back and is more likely than not to conduct a meeting with his feet propped on the desk.

At the start of 2009, he picked up a seat on the Financial Services Committee. In the fall of 2008, he voted against two $700 billion measures — the second of which became law — aimed at shoring up the nation's financial services sector. "I cannot support a bailout using tax dollars to throw our hard-earned money at bad decisions with just the hope that the problem gets fixed," he said. He also opposed a subsequent $14 billion bailout measure for the auto industry, which did not become law. And he opposed the Democrats' economic stimulus bill at the start of the 111th, helping craft alternative legislation as a member of a GOP working group.

McCarthy sits on the House Administration Committee, where he is the ranking Republican on the Elections Subcommittee. During his four years in the California Assembly, McCarthy sponsored a bill to take the politics out of congressional redistricting by transferring the power to draw new boundaries from the Assembly to an independent commission. His legislation failed to move through the Democrat-controlled legislature, but Republican Gov. Arnold Schwarzenegger made it part of his agenda.

During his first year in the House, McCarthy was his freshman class representative to the Republican Steering Committee, the panel that makes committee assignments. He had the chance to sample six different committees during various seat reorganizations — including Agriculture, Natural Resources, Homeland Security and Joint Printing. From his seat on Agriculture, he had a hand in redrafting farm policy. At that time, he was the panel's only Republican from California, the nation's largest agricultural producer.

McCarthy's mother was a dental assistant, who then stayed home to raise her three children. His father was a full-time firefighter who supplemented the family income by working as a furniture mover. The younger McCarthy also was a certified firefighter for three summers after he turned 18.

In high school, McCarthy was class president. He supported President Reagan's re-election in 1984, despite strong pro-union sentiment in his family. His father belonged to the firefighters union, and his grandfather was a railroad worker.

To help pay for college, McCarthy bought cars at an auction in Los Angeles and resold them in Bakersfield at a profit. On the second day of the California state lottery, McCarthy, then 19, won $5,000 from a scratch-off ticket. He invested part of his winnings in the stock market and opened Kevin O's Deli. He eventually sold the deli to pay for college, after which he worked as an unpaid intern in Thomas' California office. The internship turned into a full-time position. He eventually held almost every post in that office, from clipping newspapers to handling casework to serving as district director.

In 2000, McCarthy won election to the Kern County Community College board. Two years later, he was elected to the state Assembly, where he was the first freshman to be elected Republican leader in California. As leader, he was included in California's "Big 5," an informal decision-making group that also included Schwarzenegger, the Senate president pro tempore, the GOP Senate leader and the Speaker of the Assembly.

During his four years there, McCarthy helped craft legislation that reduced California's budget deficit. The spending plan avoided new taxes but depended heavily on borrowing money through bonds, fund transfers and loans and cutting funding for foster care and other child welfare programs.

In the race to succeed Thomas in 2006, McCarthy defeated two lesser-known candidates in the GOP primary and breezed past Democrat Sharon M. Beery in the general election with 71 percent of the vote. McCarthy raised $1.2 million to Beery's $27,000. He was unopposed in the 2008 general election.

KEY VOTES

2008

No   Delay consideration of Colombia free-trade agreement

No   Override Bush veto of federal farm and nutrition programs reauthorization bill

Yes Overhaul surveillance laws and permit dismissal of suits against companies that conducted warrantless wiretapping

No   Grant mortgage relief to homeowners and funding for Fannie Mae and Freddie Mac

No   Approve initial $700 billion program to stabilize financial markets

No   Approve final $700 billion program to stabilize financial markets

No   Provide $14 billion in loans to automakers

2007

No   Increase minimum wage by $2.10 an hour

No   Approve $124.2 billion in emergency war spending and set goal for redeployment of troops from Iraq

Yes Reject federal contraceptive assistance to international family planning groups

Yes Override Bush veto of $23.2 billion water projects authorization bill

Yes Implement Peru free-trade agreement

No   Approve energy policy overhaul with new fuel economy standards

Yes Clear $473.5 billion omnibus spending bill, including $70 billion for military operations

CQ VOTE STUDIES

	PARTY UNITY		PRESIDENTIAL SUPPORT	
	SUPPORT	OPPOSE	SUPPORT	OPPOSE
2008	97%	3%	73%	27%
2007	97%	3%	85%	15%

INTEREST GROUPS

	AFL-CIO	ADA	CCUS	ACU
2008	13%	10%	94%	100%
2007	8%	5%	85%	100%

CALIFORNIA 22
Kern and San Luis Obispo counties — Bakersfield

The 22nd District stretches inland from San Luis Obispo County near the coast to Ridgecrest in Kern County before dipping south into northwest Los Angeles County. It then turns north again to take in most of Bakersfield and most of the remaining parts of Kern. More than two-thirds of its residents live in Kern County.

Kern is known for oil production and a strong agricultural base. Along with vineyards and cattle in the San Luis Obispo area (the city itself is in the coastal 23rd), the two counties annually produce billions of dollars' worth of crops such as grapes, citrus, cotton and nuts. Kern County is expanding its renewable-energy base, with solar, wind, natural gas, geothermal and biomass facilities. Kern is also home to the Hyundai-Kia California Proving Ground testing facility in the Mojave Desert area north of Edwards Air Force Base.

Bakersfield (shared with the 20th) is Kern County's largest city and sits in the southern end of the San Joaquin Valley. The city, along with Lancaster (shared with the 25th) in Los Angeles County, continues to

grow. Oil and agriculture dominate, but Bakersfield is trying to diversify with a technology sector.

The 22nd is thoroughly GOP territory, and northern San Luis Obispo County is home to many conservative Democrats. In 2006, Republican Gov. Arnold Schwarzenegger won his highest vote percentages in the state here. Republican candidate John McCain took 60 percent of the district's 2008 vote for president, his highest percentage statewide.

MAJOR INDUSTRY
Agriculture, oil, military

MILITARY BASES
Edwards Air Force Base, 3,500 military, 3,100 civilian (2009) (shared with the 25th); Naval Air Warfare Center Weapons Division, China Lake, 707 military, 3,247 civilian (2007) (shared with the 25th)

CITIES
Bakersfield (pt.), 203,773; Lancaster (pt.), 65,976; Oildale (unincorporated), 27,885; Ridgecrest, 24,927

NOTABLE
Edwards Air Force Base was the site of Chuck Yeager's 1947 flight that broke the sound barrier.

Rep. Lois Capps (D)

Elected March 1998; 6th full term

CAPITOL OFFICE
225-3601
www.house.gov/capps
1110 Longworth Bldg. 20515-0523; fax 225-5632

COMMITTEES
Energy & Commerce
Natural Resources

RESIDENCE
Santa Barbara

BORN
Jan. 10, 1938; Ladysmith, Wis.

RELIGION
Lutheran

FAMILY
Widowed; three children (one deceased)

EDUCATION
Pacific Lutheran U., B.S. 1959 (nursing);
Yale U., M.A. 1964 (religion); U. of California,
Santa Barbara, M.A. 1990 (education)

CAREER
Elementary school nurse; college instructor

POLITICAL HIGHLIGHTS
No previous office

ELECTION RESULTS

2008 GENERAL
Lois Capps (D)	171,403	68.1%
Matt T. Kokkonen (R)	80,385	31.9%

2008 PRIMARY
Lois Capps (D)	50,385	99.7%

2006 GENERAL
Lois Capps (D)	114,661	65.2%
Victor D. Tognazzini (R)	61,272	34.8%

PREVIOUS WINNING PERCENTAGES
2004 (63%); 2002 (59%); 2000 (53%); 1998 (55%);
1998 Special Runoff Election (53%)

A former elementary school nurse, Capps is warm and cheerful. But her soothing ways can mask a steely resolve. Over the past decade in the House, she has earned a reputation of standing firm when advocating for her signature issues: health care and environmental protection.

Capps keeps her registered nurse's license current, studying and taking a new exam every two years, even though it is no longer her primary occupation. She knows that being a registered nurse enhances her credibility on health care issues. "My long life as a nurse and being able to, as I frame it, continue to be a nurse through advocacy for health in Congress" is what is important, she said. The loss of her 35-year-old daughter, Lisa, to lung cancer in 2000 drove her to forge a role in Congress as a tenacious fighter for better awareness of health issues and improvements in treatment. She serves as the vice chairwoman of the Energy and Commerce Health Subcommittee.

In the 110th Congress (2007-08), Capps pushed legislation to provide more information on stroke prevention and treatment, to ease the transition from cancer patient to cancer survivor, and to educate health care professionals about female cardiovascular disease and how treatment for women might differ from that for men. Early in 2009, Capps and California Republican Mary Bono Mack introduced a bill to provide low-income and uninsured women, including those who recently lost their jobs and health benefits, with greater access to health screening and counseling.

She is also not afraid to take on the federal health bureaucracy. As officials from the Centers for Medicare and Medicaid Services hailed a program they said has collected hundreds of millions of dollars in improper payments to hospitals and other Medicare providers, Capps sponsored legislation in 2008 to put a moratorium on the program. She said the program has hurt the solvency of health care providers in her state and across the country.

Capps is a firm supporter of President Obama's agenda. She praised his early action to enact a children's health insurance bill, and backed his $787 billion economic stimulus that cleared Congress in February 2009. "As we craft policies to bring our economy back to life, it's important to remember that this recession didn't 'just happen,'" Capps wrote in a Feb. 15 opinion piece for the Ventura County Star. "It is the result of economic policies willfully pursued for some time — and with special vigor over the last eight years — that wishfully proclaimed tax cuts mostly benefiting the wealthy and relentless deregulation were the solution to every economic problem."

Capps also focuses on environmental issues as a result of the spectacular geography of her district — a strip of the Southern California coast that includes Santa Barbara. A 1969 oil well rupture that fouled pristine beaches along the coast made her a determined foe of offshore oil drilling. In 2006, she voted against a GOP bill to allow drilling off most of the nation's coasts, and she continues to press for a permanent ban on new drilling. She was none too pleased when President George W. Bush announced in June 2008 that he would seek to allow more offshore oil drilling to help increase the nation's energy production and ease high gasoline prices. Capps said Bush's "half-baked" plan would only continue America's addiction to oil.

In 2005, she nearly outmaneuvered Republican Majority Leader Tom DeLay of Texas over potential liability for cleanup costs of water contaminated by a fuel additive made mostly in Texas. When the GOP's energy policy bill was on the House floor, Capps ambushed DeLay by challenging a provision exempting U.S. producers of the fuel additive methyl tertiary butyl ether (MTBE) from lawsuits over water contamination. Capps had an example of MTBE contamination in her own district, where drinking water in the city of Cambria had been affected. Democrats, led by Capps, said a liability shield would shift potentially billions of dollars in cleanup costs to local governments, and so it violated the 1995 unfunded mandates law. That law bars imposition of new costs on states and localities without federal money to help meet the mandates. Though her challenge failed, 213-219, the debate called new attention to MTBE contamination.

Capps won a different showdown with the elder California Republican Duncan Hunter over public access to Santa Rosa Island, part of Channel Islands National Park. Hunter won enactment of a bill in 2006 to limit access so military veterans could hunt there. But Capps successfully repealed Hunter's provision via language in the fiscal 2008 Interior-Environment spending bill.

She has increasingly turned her attention to foreign affairs. In the spring of 2008, she visited six African countries, where she said she discovered many people living on less than $2 a day. "It's overwhelming to see up close and in very personal ways the fact that adults regularly die from preventable disease and children so horribly malnourished," she told the House on her return. She has worked to support women's global health initiatives, including introducing a resolution to support worldwide efforts at preventing maternal mortality that the House passed unanimously in May 2008.

The daughter and granddaughter of Lutheran ministers, Capps grew up in small towns in Wisconsin and Montana. She earned a master's degree in religion from Yale. She worked as a nurse for many years in Santa Barbara schools and ran the county's teen pregnancy counseling project.

When her husband, Walter Capps, ran for the House in 1996, she stood in for him at campaign events while he recovered from injuries suffered in a car accident caused by a drunken driver. When he had a fatal heart attack less than a year into his first term, Lois Capps ran for his seat in what was then the 22nd District. She benefited from his political organization and disunity among Republicans. A primary contest on the GOP side between conservative state Rep. Tom Bordonaro Jr. and moderate state Rep. Brooks Firestone was a bitter struggle that Bordonaro finally won.

Capps stayed focused on local issues and stressed Democratic themes of protecting the environment and improving education and health care. She eventually won by 9 percentage points over Bordonaro in a runoff. She won a full term in November 1998, again besting Bordonaro, this time by 12 percentage points. Republicans targeted her district in 2000, but she held on. Redistricting gave her a boost, and she has won easily since 2002.

KEY VOTES

2008
Yes   Delay consideration of Colombia free-trade agreement
Yes   Override Bush veto of federal farm and nutrition programs reauthorization bill
No   Overhaul surveillance laws and permit dismissal of suits against companies that conducted warrantless wiretapping
Yes   Grant mortgage relief to homeowners and funding for Fannie Mae and Freddie Mac
Yes   Approve initial $700 billion program to stabilize financial markets
Yes   Approve final $700 billion program to stabilize financial markets
Yes   Provide $14 billion in loans to automakers

2007
Yes   Increase minimum wage by $2.10 an hour
Yes   Approve $124.2 billion in emergency war spending and set goal for redeployment of troops from Iraq
No   Reject federal contraceptive assistance to international family planning groups
Yes   Override Bush veto of $23.2 billion water projects authorization bill
Yes   Implement Peru free-trade agreement
Yes   Approve energy policy overhaul with new fuel economy standards
No   Clear $473.5 billion omnibus spending bill, including $70 billion for military operations

CQ VOTE STUDIES

	PARTY UNITY		PRESIDENTIAL SUPPORT	
	SUPPORT	OPPOSE	SUPPORT	OPPOSE
2008	99%	1%	14%	86%
2007	99%	1%	3%	97%
2006	98%	2%	15%	85%
2005	98%	2%	11%	89%
2004	98%	2%	21%	79%

INTEREST GROUPS

	AFL-CIO	ADA	CCUS	ACU
2008	100%	100%	61%	0%
2007	100%	95%	55%	0%
2006	93%	95%	27%	4%
2005	93%	95%	32%	0%
2004	100%	100%	24%	0%

CALIFORNIA 23

Central Coast — Oxnard, Santa Barbara, Santa Maria, San Luis Obispo

The Democratic 23rd is a sliver of coastline stretching south from the Monterey County line through San Luis Obispo, Santa Barbara and Oxnard into Ventura County, which lies northwest of Los Angeles.

Agriculture is a mainstay in the San Luis Obispo area. Fast-growing Santa Maria in Santa Barbara County is known for its manufacturing sector as well as its impressive agricultural output of strawberries, broccoli and wine grapes. The Goleta Valley, just north of Santa Barbara, was previously a farming region but is now attracting high-tech research.

Oxnard is home to large biotechnology companies as well as the Port of Hueneme, the only international port on the central coast. It is responsible for importing the majority of California's bananas and cars, and handles more than $700 billion worth of cargo annually. The largest single employer in the county is the Naval Base Ventura County near the port. Tourism also bolsters this beachfront district's economy.

Strongly Democratic Oxnard is home to a significant portion of the 23rd's Hispanic population — 42 percent of district residents are Hispanic. The 23rd's college students, such as those at University of California, Santa Barbara, and California Polytechnic State University in San Luis Obispo, mix with the Hollywood elite to form a left-leaning district. Democrat Barack Obama easily won the district by a 2-to-1 margin in the 2008 presidential election.

MAJOR INDUSTRY
Agriculture, military, tourism

MILITARY BASES
Naval Base Ventura County, 7,646 military, 10,634 civilian (2008) (shared with the 24th); Vandenberg Air Force Base, 5,221 military, 4,240 civilian (2005) (shared with the 24th)

CITIES
Oxnard, 170,358; Santa Barbara, 92,325; Santa Maria, 77,423; Goleta (unincorporated), 55,204; San Luis Obispo, 44,174

NOTABLE
Hearst Castle, a historic house museum at San Simeon, was home to William Randolph Hearst; Channel Islands National Park is home to 145 unique species of flora and fauna and 2,000 other species.

Rep. Elton Gallegly (R)

Elected 1986; 12th term

CAPITOL OFFICE
225-5811
www.house.gov/gallegly
2309 Rayburn Bldg. 20515-0524; fax 225-1100

COMMITTEES
Foreign Affairs
Judiciary
Natural Resources
Select Intelligence

RESIDENCE
Simi Valley

BORN
March 7, 1944; Huntington Park, Calif.

RELIGION
Protestant

FAMILY
Wife, Janice Gallegly; four children

EDUCATION
California State U., Los Angeles, attended 1962-63

CAREER
Real estate broker

POLITICAL HIGHLIGHTS
Simi Valley City Council, 1979-86;
mayor of Simi Valley, 1980-86

ELECTION RESULTS

2008 GENERAL

Elton Gallegly (R)	174,492	58.2%
Marta Ann Jorgensen (D)	125,560	41.8%

2008 PRIMARY

Elton Gallegly (R)	45,124	77.0%
Michael Tenenbaum (R)	13,446	23.0%

2006 GENERAL

Elton Gallegly (R)	129,812	62.0%
Jill M. Martinez (D)	79,461	38.0%

PREVIOUS WINNING PERCENTAGES
2004 (63%); 2002 (65%); 2000 (54%); 1998 (60%);
1996 (60%); 1994 (66%); 1992 (54%); 1990 (58%);
1988 (69%); 1986 (68%)

Gallegly has settled into comfortable obscurity as a member of a shrunken GOP House minority. A traditional Western conservative, he looks after his district's local interests on issues including water and immigration. But even with posts on four committees — an unusually large workload, and he ranks within the top four in GOP seniority on all of them — he usually flies below the public radar in Washington.

Shortly before winning re-election in 2008, he pledged to work with Democrats in the 111th Congress (2009-10). "The problems confronting our country are greater than anything I've seen in my political life," Gallegly (GAL-uh-glee) told the Ventura County Star two days before the election."I'm committed … to being a part of the attempt to bridge the partisan divide."

Gallegly's inclination to do so might be greater than that of his Republican colleagues, given his treatment in recent years by his own leadership. He has twice been passed over for the top GOP slot on what is now called the Natural Resources Committee. In late 2002, he waged an aggressive campaign to become chairman of the panel, but GOP leaders skipped over a number of more senior Republicans, including Gallegly, to elevate Richard W. Pombo of California, a protégé of Majority Leader Tom DeLay, to the chairmanship. "That process was one that left a bitter taste in a lot of mouths," Gallegly said in 2006.

In 2008, as the GOP organized for the 111th, Gallegly pre-emptively announced he wouldn't be a candidate for top-ranking Republican on the Natural Resources panel, saying he didn't want to give up his seat on the Select Intelligence Committee in order to take the post.

Gallegly is one of the few non-lawyers to sit on the Judiciary Committee, where he takes a hard line on illegal immigrants, a signature issue. He led an unsuccessful 1996 effort to allow local school districts to decide whether to provide a public school education to the children of illegal immigrants. He argued that states such as California could not afford public education for those children and that the promise of free schooling was a magnet drawing illegal immigrants into the country.

After leading a 1995 task force on immigration laws, Gallegly proposed an electronic employment eligibility verification program called E-Verify for immigrants that was enacted into law and has been in use since then. The program remains controversial, however, and Gallegly and other supporters were bracing to fight for its reauthorization in 2009.

In 2005, he helped win enactment of a national security measure, known as the Real ID Act, which set minimum security requirements that states must meet for their driver's licenses to be accepted as identification to board commercial flights or enter federal facilities.

Gallegly occasionally casts his lot with Democrats. As the former mayor of Simi Valley, a community close enough to Los Angeles that many of its residents are concerned about the spread of urban crime, Gallegly has voted for gun restrictions opposed by many Republicans.

From his seat on Natural Resources, Gallegly has sought to limit federal restrictions on land use. He has looked after his state's water interests and helped landowners butting up against federal environmental laws that protect certain species of animals. He also sits on the Foreign Affairs Committee.

Gallegly takes great pride in representing the district that contains the Ronald Reagan Presidential Library. Among his prized possessions is a photo with the former president taken aboard Air Force One. The two are looking out the window at the future site of the library in Simi Valley. In 2008, the House passed a Gallegly bill to create an 11-member commission to plan the commemoration of Reagan's 100th birthday in 2011. Although the Senate did not act that year, Gallegly reintroduced the bill in 2009.

When he was growing up in Southeast Los Angeles, Gallegly followed the political persuasions of his father, a lifelong Democrat. He described his father in an interview with the Los Angeles Times as "an FDR Democrat, and they're much different from the Democrats of today. He believed in government helping people who couldn't help themselves, but not those who could." His parents were poor Dust Bowl migrants from southeastern Oklahoma, he said, who never "worked for a penny above minimum wage."

After dropping out of college because he couldn't afford it, Gallegly went into the real estate business and built a successful brokerage. He also operated a couple of antique shops, specializing in old coin-operated machines and brass cash registers. Frustrated in his dealings with local government, he decided to run for office himself in 1979.

Gallegly won a seat on the Simi Valley City Council and served concurrently as mayor for six years before running for Congress in 1986. Touting his record of boosting Simi Valley's economic development, Gallegly defeated Tony Hope, comedian Bob Hope's son, in the GOP primary and won the general election by 40 percentage points. The area Gallegly represented in the 1990s was more competitive politically; in 2000, Democrat Al Gore carried the district in the presidential race and Gallegly was held to 54 percent of the vote.

Congressional district lines were redrawn in 2001 with incumbent protection in mind. Gallegly's district became more reliably Republican, and he easily won re-election in 2002 and 2004. Gallegly announced in early 2006 he would not run for an 11th term in the House, citing an unspecified medical issue. But he changed his mind after entreaties by California Republican leaders and President George W. Bush. He returned to the campaign trail and won easily. In 2008, Gallegly submitted his re-election papers on the first day of the filing period. He said he had passed his most recent physical exam with flying colors. He won re-election that year with 58 percent of the vote.

Since his first trip to Washington while serving as a local city council member three decades ago, Gallegly has been enamored of Washington and public service. He drove around the Capitol in a rented car several times during that trip. In 2006, Gallegly said, "I'm still as awestruck as I was 29 years ago." And he indicated in 2008 that he still had "fire in the belly" to serve, even while jokingly promising he did "not intend to be there as long as Strom Thurmond," who served in Congress until he was 100 in 2002.

KEY VOTES

2008

No Delay consideration of Colombia free-trade agreement

Yes Override Bush veto of federal farm and nutrition programs reauthorization bill

Yes Overhaul surveillance laws and permit dismissal of suits against companies that conducted warrantless wiretapping

Yes Grant mortgage relief to homeowners and funding for Fannie Mae and Freddie Mac

No Approve initial $700 billion program to stabilize financial markets

No Approve final $700 billion program to stabilize financial markets

No Provide $14 billion in loans to automakers

2007

No Increase minimum wage by $2.10 an hour

No Approve $124.2 billion in emergency war spending and set goal for redeployment of troops from Iraq

Yes Reject federal contraceptive assistance to international family planning groups

Yes Override Bush veto of $23.2 billion water projects authorization bill

Yes Implement Peru free-trade agreement

? Approve energy policy overhaul with new fuel economy standards

Yes Clear $473.5 billion omnibus spending bill, including $70 billion for military operations

CQ VOTE STUDIES

	PARTY UNITY		PRESIDENTIAL SUPPORT	
	SUPPORT	OPPOSE	SUPPORT	OPPOSE
2008	96%	4%	63%	37%
2007	94%	6%	86%	14%
2006	96%	4%	94%	6%
2005	97%	3%	85%	15%
2004	94%	6%	82%	18%

INTEREST GROUPS

	AFL-CIO	ADA	CCUS	ACU
2008	13%	15%	89%	92%
2007	13%	5%	89%	92%
2006	14%	0%	100%	84%
2005	13%	0%	92%	80%
2004	13%	0%	100%	96%

CALIFORNIA 24

Ventura and Santa Barbara counties — Thousand Oaks, Simi Valley

North and west of the close-in Los Angeles suburbs, the 24th includes ski-friendly mountains, fertile valleys and a slice of coastline with excellent surfing. The district takes in nearly all of Ventura County and inland Santa Barbara County.

Ventura County, where more than four-fifths of district residents live, is a mix of lower-income farming communities — many workers in the local agricultural industry are immigrants — and more-upscale residential neighborhoods, such as Moorpark. Ventura's insurance, finance and electronics sectors, as well as the health care and construction industries, supported what had been a steady economy before the housing market began struggling and unemployment rates began rising.

Citrus fruit thrives in the sunshine and fertile soil of Ventura County, while the central and western portions of the 24th in Santa Barbara County produce grapes, broccoli and strawberries. Western Ventura includes

most of the Los Padres National Forest. San Nicolas Island, the Anacapa Islands and part of the Santa Monica Mountains National Recreation Area also fall within the 24th's boundaries.

Despite a GOP lean in the district, Democrat Barack Obama edged out Republican John McCain here, taking 51 percent of the district's 2008 vote for president. The 24th's conservatism primarily comes from interior Santa Barbara. Military retirees and Vandenberg Air Force Base, as well as southern Ventura cities such as Simi Valley and Thousand Oaks, also contribute to the GOP base.

MAJOR INDUSTRY
Biotech, aerospace, service, agriculture

MILITARY BASES
Naval Base Ventura County, 7,646 military, 10,634 civilian (2008) (shared with the 23rd); Vandenberg Air Force Base, 5,221 military, 4,240 civilian (2005) (shared with the 23rd)

CITIES
Thousand Oaks, 117,005; Simi Valley, 111,351; Ventura (pt.), 79,416; Camarillo, 57,077; Lompoc, 41,103; Moorpark, 31,415

NOTABLE
The Ronald Reagan Presidential Library is in Simi Valley.

Rep. Howard P. "Buck" McKeon (R)

Elected 1992; 9th term

CAPITOL OFFICE
225-1956
mckeon.house.gov
2184 Rayburn Bldg. 20515-0525; fax 226-0683

COMMITTEES
Armed Services
Education & Labor - ranking member

RESIDENCE
Santa Clarita

BORN
Sept. 9, 1939; Los Angeles, Calif.

RELIGION
Mormon

FAMILY
Wife, Patricia McKeon; six children

EDUCATION
Brigham Young U., B.S. 1985

CAREER
Clothing store owner

POLITICAL HIGHLIGHTS
William S. Hart School Board, 1978-87;
Santa Clarita City Council, 1987-92 (mayor, 1987-88)

ELECTION RESULTS

2008 GENERAL

Howard P. "Buck" McKeon (R)	144,660	57.7%
Jackie Conaway (D)	105,929	42.3%

2008 PRIMARY

Howard P. "Buck" McKeon (R)	unopposed

2006 GENERAL

Howard P. "Buck" McKeon (R)	93,987	60.0%
Robert Rodriguez (D)	55,913	35.7%
David W. Erickson (LIBERT)	6,873	4.4%

PREVIOUS WINNING PERCENTAGES
2004 (64%); 2002 (65%); 2000 (62%); 1998 (75%);
1996 (62%); 1994 (65%); 1992 (52%)

McKeon is a reliable conservative who pushes for education reform, reduced college costs and tax cuts and looks out for the large defense industry in his district. Generally unpretentious and non-confrontational, he has had mixed success with his priorities as he has dealt with a string of unforeseen twists and turns in the legislative and political arenas.

Having spent years in the majority, and having briefly held the gavel of the committee in charge of education and labor policies, adjusting to life in the minority has been a challenge for the former businessman. As chairman, he had set the pace of the panel and guided legislative policy. Now, as top-ranking Republican on the Education and Labor Committee, he said he's "pretty much just playing defense." With a Democratic White House in place, his frustrations are rising, even though he voiced some optimism following President Obama's February 2009 address to Congress. He applauded Obama's desire to "take on the education establishment" through his willingness to consider such strategies as teacher performance pay and his support for charter schools.

But his dissatisfaction with some early Democratic initiatives led to some unusual partisan outbursts on his part. He was displeased that the Democrats' catchall spending bill for 2009 placed several conditions on a school voucher program for District of Columbia public school students, including limiting the length of its funding. He complained the program was being phased out. "Democrats have crafted another massive federal spending package in secret, this time advancing their partisan agenda at the expense of some of the poorest children in some of the most troubled schools in the country," he said.

He and other Republicans on the committee also raised questions about the inclusion of $100 billion in education spending in the $787 billion economic stimulus law in early 2009. The GOP supports most of the programs that would benefit from the funding, such as Pell grants and school modernization and construction. But McKeon questioned the immediate economic benefit, and joined his colleagues in pressing the Education Department to ensure the dollars are spent wisely. "With so much at stake, Republicans are lining up to protect the interests of students and taxpayers," he said.

During the 110th Congress, he had little choice but to watch as his California colleague George Miller, chairman of the committee and a close ally of Speaker Nancy Pelosi, guided bills to boost mine safety and raise the minimum wage, despite his objections. He also could do little as Democrats made some sweeping changes to federal student loan programs, cutting more than $20 billion from subsidies given to private lenders who offer federally backed student loans. While McKeon, a supporter of that program, warned of dire consequences, scandals in the loan industry helped propel the cuts into law.

But there have been bright points for McKeon, whose brief tenure as chairman began in February 2006 after his predecessor, John A. Boehner of Ohio, was elected majority leader. Long concerned with rapidly increasing college tuition, he won inclusion in the 2006 higher education bill of a requirement that the Education Department assign an "affordability index" to every college that uses federal financial aid programs and compile reports on the tuition increases. That bill never made it in the Senate. But in the 110th, as college costs continued to climb, the new Democratic majority took a cue from the former chairman and included college cost provisions in their new bill to renew the Higher Education Act, which cleared Congress in July 2008.

Another quasi-victory for McKeon was the passage of a law during the

110th Congress to renew the Head Start early-childhood development program for the first time in 10 years. While he supports that program, and its renewal, he was disappointed it did not include language allowing providers to hire employees based on religious preference.

On the committee's major agenda item — a renewal of the Bush administration's landmark elementary and secondary education law known as No Child Left Behind — McKeon has had no clear victory. But the panel is expected to tackle a rewrite of the law during the 111th Congress (2009-10).

A member of the Armed Services Committee, he supported the George W. Bush administration's policy on the war in Iraq and during the 110th rejected Democratic efforts to set a timeline for withdrawal of U.S. troops. He also uses his seat to look out for the defense industry in his district, helping to secure $9.4 million for defense companies in his district for fiscal 2008, according to Taxpayers for Common Sense.

On the issue of immigration, he supports a guest worker program but does not support a pathway to citizenship for illegal immigrants.

Before he became immersed in politics, McKeon worked in his family's business, a chain of Western wear stores based in Santa Clarita that was founded by his parents in 1962 and that at its peak had 500 employees and 52 stores. But Howard & Phil's Western Wear fell on hard times in the 1990s, a casualty, the family said, of declining Japanese tourism and the drop in popularity of country line-dancing. The business closed in 1999, though McKeon still has a soft spot for ostrich-skin cowboy boots.

Fears that his oldest daughter would be bused from their Santa Clarita home into a neighboring school district prompted his first foray into elected office in 1978. But after winning the 14-person race for the school board, he learned the board didn't even have the power to bus his daughter elsewhere.

Years later, after serving as a city council member, the first mayor of Santa Clarita and start-up bank chairman, naïveté drove his bid for a newly created congressional district in suburban Los Angeles. A mayor of a neighboring town called and asked for his support for the seat, but instead McKeon decided in 1991 to launch his own campaign. "I thought, 'If he could do it, I could do it,' " McKeon said. "I didn't know what a congressman did. I'd only met two."

After a fierce campaign, McKeon narrowly defeated a 14-year state Assembly veteran, Phillip D. Wyman, in the primary. In November, McKeon had a sizable spending edge and defeated Democratic lawyer and rancher James H. "Gil" Gilmartin by 19 percentage points. His re-elections have usually been easy, but in 2008, a difficult year for many Republicans, he earned less than 60 percent of the vote for the first time since 1992.

KEY VOTES

2008

No   Delay consideration of Colombia free-trade agreement

No   Override Bush veto of federal farm and nutrition programs reauthorization bill

Yes Overhaul surveillance laws and permit dismissal of suits against companies that conducted warrantless wiretapping

Yes Grant mortgage relief to homeowners and funding for Fannie Mae and Freddie Mac

Yes Approve initial $700 billion program to stabilize financial markets

Yes Approve final $700 billion program to stabilize financial markets

No   Provide $14 billion in loans to automakers

2007

No   Increase minimum wage by $2.10 an hour

No   Approve $124.2 billion in emergency war spending and set goal for redeployment of troops from Iraq

Yes Reject federal contraceptive assistance to international family planning groups

No   Override Bush veto of $23.2 billion water projects authorization bill

Yes Implement Peru free-trade agreement

No   Approve energy policy overhaul with new fuel economy standards

Yes Clear $473.5 billion omnibus spending bill, including $70 billion for military operations

CQ VOTE STUDIES

	PARTY UNITY		PRESIDENTIAL SUPPORT	
	SUPPORT	OPPOSE	SUPPORT	OPPOSE
2008	97%	3%	78%	22%
2007	95%	5%	87%	13%
2006	96%	4%	95%	5%
2005	97%	3%	89%	11%
2004	96%	4%	85%	15%

INTEREST GROUPS

	AFL-CIO	ADA	CCUS	ACU
2008	7%	5%	100%	88%
2007	9%	10%	80%	96%
2006	14%	5%	100%	80%
2005	13%	0%	93%	84%
2004	20%	0%	100%	88%

CALIFORNIA 25

Northern Los Angeles and San Bernardino counties; Inyo and Mono counties

The vast 25th stretches from east-central California on the Nevada border south along the mountains and through Death Valley before crossing the Mojave Desert and San Bernardino County into northern suburban Los Angeles County, where nearly three-fourths of residents live.

The Antelope Valley desert due north of Los Angeles experienced rapid growth for decades, but home foreclosures and an economic downturn have stalled growth. The valley includes Lancaster (shared with the 22nd) and Palmdale, which is California's largest "desert city" and is the commercial and transportation center for the high desert. Palmdale also has a research, development and flight testing site for the aerospace industry, and is home to major Lockheed Martin and Boeing facilities, although unemployment is rising across the Antelope Valley.

Most of the land in Inyo and Mono counties is government-owned, and a few towns rely on mining, agriculture and tourism. Suburban Santa

Clarita Valley on the district's southwestern edge has manufacturing, aerospace and defense industries, but can struggle when there are fewer visitors to Six Flags Magic Mountain, a key employer in the region.

Historically Republican, the 25th's mix of upper middle class residents and more-conservative working class whites supported Democrat Barack Obama by slightly more than one percentage point in the 2008 presidential election.

MAJOR INDUSTRY
Tourism, manufacturing, construction, aerospace, military

MILITARY BASES
Edwards Air Force Base, 3,500 military, 3,100 civilian (2009) (shared with the 22nd); Fort Irwin (Army), 4,709 military, 5,646 civilian (2008); Naval Air Warfare Center Weapons Division, China Lake, 707 military, 3,247 civilian (2007) (shared with the 22nd); Marine Corps Logistics Base Barstow, 148 military, 1,595 civilian (2007)

CITIES
Santa Clarita, 151,088; Palmdale, 116,670; Victorville, 64,029; Lancaster (pt.), 52,742; Los Angeles (pt.), 22,882

NOTABLE
Badwater Basin in Death Valley is the lowest point in North America.

Rep. David Dreier (R)

Elected 1980; 15th term

CAPITOL OFFICE
225-2305
dreier.house.gov
233 Cannon Bldg. 20515-0526; fax 225-7018

COMMITTEES
Rules - ranking member

RESIDENCE
San Dimas

BORN
July 5, 1952; Kansas City, Mo.

RELIGION
Christian Scientist

FAMILY
Single

EDUCATION
Claremont Men's College, B.A. 1975
(political science); Claremont Graduate U., M.A.
1976 (American government)

CAREER
Real estate developer; university fundraiser

POLITICAL HIGHLIGHTS
Republican nominee for U.S. House, 1978

ELECTION RESULTS

2008 GENERAL

David Dreier (R)	140,615	52.6%
Russ Warner (D)	108,039	40.4%
Ted Brown (LIBERT)	18,476	6.9%

2008 PRIMARY

David Dreier (R)	29,627	74.5%
S. Sonny Sardo (R)	10,158	25.5%

2006 GENERAL

David Dreier (R)	102,028	57.0%
Cynthia Rodriguez Matthews (D)	67,878	37.9%
Ted Brown (LIBERT)	5,887	3.3%
Elliott Graham (AMI)	3,351	1.9%

PREVIOUS WINNING PERCENTAGES
2004 (54%); 2002 (64%); 2000 (57%); 1998 (58%);
1996 (61%); 1994 (67%); 1992 (58%); 1990 (64%);
1988 (69%); 1986 (72%); 1984 (71%); 1982 (65%);
1980 (52%)

Dreier has a deep knowledge of the legislative process and a relentless commitment to his work and his small-government ideals. He is a constant thorn in the Democrats' side; as the Republicans' top procedural strategist, he wields his parliamentary skills to help his party win as many tactical victories as possible.

He also is one of the chamber's most cordial members. His trademark of introducing members on the floor by announcing the names of their home-towns (if he doesn't know them by memory, he has staff look them up) often evokes smiles — and sometimes quizzical looks — during even contentious debates with Democrats.

Dreier, who spent eight years chairing the Rules Committee and now serves as its ranking member, was optimistic after the election of President Obama that a new bipartisan atmosphere might prevail. Obama and Dreier had worked together in Congress on projects in Africa. Shortly after the election, Obama called Dreier to renew their connection and invite him to talk to leaders of the incoming administration. Dreier was also impressed when Obama in early January 2009 visited Republicans on Capitol Hill to discuss issues.

But at the start of the 111th Congress (2009-10), his optimism faded. Democrats passed new House rules lifting term limits for committee chair-men and restricting the minority's ability to offer alternative legislation. He accused them of undermining Obama's pledge for a new era of bipartisan-ship. He said the rules package "shreds the Obama vision."

Dreier spent much of the 110th Congress (2007-08) maneuvering — through the repeated use of "motions to recommit" — to defeat legislation and bring floor action to a standstill. He was constantly frustrated by what he viewed as Democratic strategies to ram bills through without bipartisan assent.

After Democrats regained control of the House in 2007, Dreier led week-ly training sessions for his colleagues dubbed "Parliamentary Bootcamp." Among the lessons he offered were "Decorum and Civility in the House," "The Germaneness Rule," and "Roadblocks at the Final Legislative Stages." He also created a committee Web site specifically for Republican members.

Dreier's expertise in procedural maneuvering also won him the position of parliamentarian during the 2008 Republican National Convention — the third time he has been given that honor.

He is close to Republican California Gov. Arnold Schwarzenegger; he was among the actor's strongest supporters in his bid for governor and chaired his transition team after his election in 2003. Whenever Schwarzenegger visits Washington, the two get together to smoke cigars.

Dreier can split with conservatives on some issues. In 2008, he success-fully argued during a GOP leadership meeting to strike the term "Com-munist China" from a policy paper. He was one of just 35 Republicans in 2007 who voted to prohibit job discrimination on the basis of sexual orienta-tion, and he has twice broken with his party to vote against proposed con-stitutional amendments to outlaw same-sex marriage. In 2006, he voted to override President George W. Bush's veto of legislation expanding federal funding for embryonic stem cell research.

On tax-and-spend issues, Dreier is a traditional Republican and a true believer in small government. In 2008, he introduced the Fair and Simple Tax Act to cut the current tax bracket in half, eliminate the inheritance tax, lower capital gains taxes and shrink the top corporate tax rate from 35 percent to 25 percent. The House did not act on the bill, but Dreier promised to continue pushing for major tax cuts, saying they are desperately needed to jump-start the U.S. economy.

Despite his small-government beliefs, Dreier backed both versions of the Bush administration's $700 billion legislation in fall 2008 to shore up the ailing financial services industry, saying it was necessary for the economy. Yet he opposed Obama's $787 billion economic stimulus bill, and later Democrats' $410 billion catchall spending bill for 2009.

Dreier believes expanded trade is needed to help overcome the country's economic downturn. He fought to fast-track a free-trade accord with Colombia during the 110th. When Democrats changed House rules in 2008 to prevent a vote on the trade measure, criticizing the Colombian government for not doing enough to stop violence against union members, he joined other Republicans to unveil a "Colombia Tariff Ticker" that counts off the days and estimated tariffs imposed on U.S. exports due to the lack of a pact.

Dreier also focuses on fighting illegal immigration, an important issue to his distict. He backed legislation introduced by fellow Californian Republican Duncan Hunter — father of the current congressman of the same name — in 2008 to build a 700-mile double-layered fence along the U.S.-Mexico border.

He has worked with colleagues to spread the democratic process. He and Democratic Rep. David E. Price of North Carolina founded the House Democracy Assistance Commission, which teaches government officials from developing countries about constituent services, the legislative process and government operations. Working with parliaments in 12 countries, including East Timor, Georgia, Kenya and Mongolia, Dreier has hosted visiting parliamentarians to help them learn from his congressional activities.

Dreier first fell in love with the congressional process in college, when he was an intern for former GOP Rep. Barry Goldwater Jr. of California in the mid-1970s. He launched his first House bid in 1978 from a dorm at his alma mater while working in the school's planning and development office.

Dreier's father, a Marine Corps drill instructor, figured his son would come home to Kansas City, Mo., to work in the family's real estate business. But Dreier, whose stake in the company makes him one of the richest members of Congress, had been bitten by the political bug. Two years after he lost to Democratic incumbent James F. Lloyd, he swamped the incumbent in fundraising and rode the Reagan wave to victory. He generally has had little trouble since, defeating Democrat Russ Warner in 2008 by 12 percentage points.

During the 110th, he led an effort to encourage colleagues to transfer personal campaign funds to the National Republican Congressional Committee. He ended up giving more than $1.3 million to the committee in 2007 and 2008.

KEY VOTES

2008
No Delay consideration of Colombia free-trade agreement
No Override Bush veto of federal farm and nutrition programs reauthorization bill
Yes Overhaul surveillance laws and permit dismissal of suits against companies that conducted warrantless wiretapping
Yes Grant mortgage relief to homeowners and funding for Fannie Mae and Freddie Mac
Yes Approve initial $700 billion program to stabilize financial markets
Yes Approve final $700 billion program to stabilize financial markets
No Provide $14 billion in loans to automakers

2007
No Increase minimum wage by $2.10 an hour
No Approve $124.2 billion in emergency war spending and set goal for redeployment of troops from Iraq
Yes Reject federal contraceptive assistance to international family planning groups
Yes Override Bush veto of $23.2 billion water projects authorization bill
Yes Implement Peru free-trade agreement
Yes Approve energy policy overhaul with new fuel economy standards
Yes Clear $473.5 billion omnibus spending bill, including $70 billion for military operations

CQ VOTE STUDIES

	PARTY UNITY		PRESIDENTIAL SUPPORT	
	SUPPORT	OPPOSE	SUPPORT	OPPOSE
2008	96%	4%	78%	22%
2007	95%	5%	87%	13%
2006	94%	6%	93%	7%
2005	96%	4%	89%	11%
2004	92%	8%	94%	6%

INTEREST GROUPS

	AFL-CIO	ADA	CCUS	ACU
2008	13%	10%	100%	86%
2007	4%	20%	85%	88%
2006	14%	10%	100%	72%
2005	13%	0%	93%	84%
2004	13%	5%	100%	88%

CALIFORNIA 26
Northeastern Los Angeles suburbs

Set in the foothills of the San Gabriel Mountains, the 26th District is a mix of Los Angeles bedroom communities and the mountainous Angeles National Forest, which makes up its northern half. The commuter-heavy district takes in middle- to upper-class suburbs, many of which have retained their own identities and quaint downtowns.

In the far western part of the 26th, a high-tech flavor is set by La Cañada Flintridge and Pasadena (in the neighboring 29th), which is home to NASA's Jet Propulsion Laboratory and the California Institute of Technology. Monrovia boasts engineering firms and start-up technology companies that employ a highly educated workforce. In Arcadia, revenue from the Santa Anita racetrack has supported capital improvements for the city. Areas such as Glendora that were hit by rapid foreclosures have seen an increase in lower-priced home sales.

Rancho Cucamonga, in the 26th's chunk of San Bernardino County, is a destination for young, middle-class families. Corporate call centers and technology firms fill the San Bernardino Inland Valley suburbs. Small

defense subcontractors also provide jobs. Traffic congestion caused by district residents who commute to Los Angeles or technology jobs in the areas surrounding the 26th continues to be a hot issue locally.

While not as diverse as most of its neighbors, the 26th is one-fourth Hispanic, and parts of the district have seen an increase in Asian residents, notably in Arcadia. Rapid development in communities surrounding Pasadena and in other Los Angeles County cities — particularly Arcadia, Glendora, Monrovia and San Dimas — initially brought young, wealthy, fiscally minded, socially moderate Republicans to the district. Republicans carry a slight edge in party registration here, but the 26th swung narrowly Democratic in the 2008 presidential election, giving Barack Obama 51 percent of its vote.

MAJOR INDUSTRY
Service, manufacturing, health care, biotech

CITIES
Rancho Cucamonga, 127,743; Upland, 68,393; Arcadia, 53,054; Glendora, 49,415; Monrovia, 36,929; San Dimas, 34,980; Claremont, 33,998

NOTABLE
The collection at the Huntington Library in San Marino includes Thomas Gainsborough's painting, "The Blue Boy," and a Gutenberg Bible.

Rep. Brad Sherman (D)

Elected 1996; 7th term

CAPITOL OFFICE
225-5911
www.house.gov/sherman
2242 Rayburn Bldg. 20515-0527; fax 225-5879

COMMITTEES
Financial Services
Foreign Affairs
  (Terrorism, Nonproliferation & Trade - chairman)
Judiciary

RESIDENCE
Sherman Oaks

BORN
Oct. 24, 1954; Los Angeles, Calif.

RELIGION
Jewish

FAMILY
Wife, Lisa N. K. Sherman; one child

EDUCATION
U. of California, Los Angeles, B.A. 1974
(political communication); Harvard U., J.D. 1979

CAREER
Accountant; lawyer

POLITICAL HIGHLIGHTS
Calif. State Board of Equalization, 1991-97
(chairman, 1991-95)

ELECTION RESULTS

2008 GENERAL

Brad Sherman (D)	145,812	68.5%
Navraj Singh (R)	52,852	24.8%
Tim Denton (LIBERT)	14,171	6.7%

2008 PRIMARY

Brad Sherman (D)	unopposed

2006 GENERAL

Brad Sherman (D)	92,650	68.8%
Peter Hankwitz (R)	42,074	31.2%

PREVIOUS WINNING PERCENTAGES
2004 (62%); 2002 (62%); 2000 (66%); 1998 (57%);
1996 (50%)

No one can accuse Sherman of taking himself too seriously. The balding, self-deprecating lawmaker has been known to give away plastic combs emblazoned with his name and phone number. "You'll have more use for a comb than I do," he once quipped to a group of constituents leaving his Capitol Hill office.

He's also been known to start speeches by joking that he's drawn to jobs held in declining public esteem, which explains why he went from a certified public accountant to lawyer, then to simultaneous stints as politician and tax collector.

But he turns serious when discussing his chief preoccupation in Congress: nuclear non-proliferation. As chairman of the Foreign Affairs panel's Subcommittee on Terrorism, Nonproliferation and Trade, Sherman sees Iran as the No. 1 security threat in the world, with North Korea as a close second. "The spread of nuclear weapons is perhaps the only thing that poses a national security threat to ordinary Americans and a threat to their safety and to our way of life," he said in February 2009. "We should be prioritizing non-proliferation at a higher level."

For years, Sherman badgered President George W. Bush about the threat posed by Iran, talking to him about the issue whenever he saw the president — including at holiday parties. After President Obama took office, Sherman called for his administration to work closely with Russia on the matter. "We need Russia's help to stop Iran's nuclear program," he said at a Foreign Affairs hearing in early 2009. "The fault for the present circumstances and chilliness between the two countries lies in Washington as well as Moscow."

At the same time, he said Obama must enlist China in pressuring North Korea. "The key way to do that," he said at another February committee hearing, "is to at least begin to make Beijing believe that access to the U.S. market is contingent upon a greater level of cooperation on the North Korea issue and, if necessary, a Chinese government willing to inform the North Koreans that continued subsidies from Beijing could be cut off if they won't move toward a fair, verifiable and permanent renunciation and abandonment and destruction of existing stockpiles of nuclear weapons."

Sherman favors an aggressive U.S. foreign policy, particularly when it comes to Israel. In 2006, he advocated cutting off funding for the Palestinian government after the militant group Hamas won a majority vote in the Palestinian elections. Three years later, he spoke out strongly when the House passed a resolution condemning Hamas for its role in the conflict in Gaza and southern Israel. "While Israel seeks to lie aside a Palestinian state, Hamas seeks to kill or expel every Jew in the Middle East," he said.

Sherman also sits on the Financial Services Committee, where he has found his background as a CPA invaluable, especially during the panel's investigations and response to corporate accounting scandals such as the one at Enron Corp. earlier this decade. In the 108th Congress (2003-04), he pushed for new federal rules forcing companies to account for stock options on their annual reports of revenues and expenses.

A hard-liner on a balanced budget and a former member of the Budget Committee, Sherman opposed both versions — the second of which became law — of $700 billion legislation in fall 2008 to aid the ailing financial services sector. "Our economy will not do well in the months to come, and dropping $700 billion on Wall Street is not going to make things much better," he said. But he said the bill's faults could be lessened if lawmakers and the news media undertake "an unprecedented level of ferocious oversight."

Sherman expressed exasperation over Bush's 2001 and 2003 tax cuts at a time of deepening deficits. Set to expire in 2011, the cuts substantially reduced income and capital gains tax rates. When Federal Reserve Chairman Alan Greenspan told Congress in 2003 that he "would prefer to find the situation in which spending was constrained, the economy was growing and tax cuts were capable of being initiated without creating fiscal problems," Sherman shot back: "I would prefer a world in which Julia Roberts was calling me, but that is not likely to occur."

What did occur — "miraculously," as Sherman put it — was his December 2006 marriage to Lisa Nicola Kaplan, a State Department expert on human rights. He announced on the House floor in January 2009 that he had to miss a vote to expand the State Children's Health Insurance Program — a measure he co-sponsored to provide insurance for children from low-income families who do not qualify for Medicaid — because he was at the hospital while his wife gave birth to their first child, a girl.

Sherman's other committee assignment is Judiciary, where he has sought to address intellectual property issues such as protecting movies from unauthorized copying. His Los Angeles-area district is the capital of the adult film industry. In his 2006 appearance on "The Colbert Report," Sherman riffed on his nerdiness and feigned shock when host Stephen Colbert quizzed him on the district's pornography industry.

One of Sherman's pet projects is altering the order of presidential succession. In 2007, he reintroduced his bill to ensure the presidency remains in the hands of the same political party by allowing the president to designate either the Speaker of the House or the House minority leader as second in line after the vice president, followed by either the majority or minority leader of the Senate, rather than the Senate president pro tempore.

He got his start in politics as a child, stuffing envelopes for Democratic Rep. George E. Brown Jr., a family friend. A tax law specialist, Sherman was elected to the California State Board of Equalization in 1990 and 1994. That's when he started giving away the combs, which he now orders by the crate.

The board administers tax programs that account for more than a third of the state's revenues, and Sherman led a successful drive during his tenure to repeal the unpopular tax on snacks. In 1996, he ran for the seat of retiring Democratic Rep. Anthony C. Beilenson, who endorsed him. He won the nomination with 54 percent of the vote, besting six other candidates, and carried the general election by 8 percentage points. Since then, he has won re-election comfortably.

KEY VOTES

2008

Yes Delay consideration of Colombia free-trade agreement

Yes Override Bush veto of federal farm and nutrition programs reauthorization bill

Yes Overhaul surveillance laws and permit dismissal of suits against companies that conducted warrantless wiretapping

Yes Grant mortgage relief to homeowners and funding for Fannie Mae and Freddie Mac

No Approve initial $700 billion program to stabilize financial markets

No Approve final $700 billion program to stabilize financial markets

Yes Provide $14 billion in loans to automakers

2007

Yes Increase minimum wage by $2.10 an hour

Yes Approve $124.2 billion in emergency war spending and set goal for redeployment of troops from Iraq

No Reject federal contraceptive assistance to international family planning groups

Yes Override Bush veto of $23.2 billion water projects authorization bill

No Implement Peru free-trade agreement

Yes Approve energy policy overhaul with new fuel economy standards

No Clear $473.5 billion omnibus spending bill, including $70 billion for military operations

CQ VOTE STUDIES

	PARTY UNITY		PRESIDENTIAL SUPPORT	
	SUPPORT	OPPOSE	SUPPORT	OPPOSE
2008	98%	2%	14%	86%
2007	98%	2%	5%	95%
2006	94%	6%	28%	72%
2005	95%	5%	15%	85%
2004	96%	4%	27%	73%

INTEREST GROUPS

	AFL-CIO	ADA	CCUS	ACU
2008	100%	85%	61%	9%
2007	96%	100%	50%	0%
2006	100%	95%	33%	4%
2005	93%	100%	41%	0%
2004	100%	95%	33%	4%

CALIFORNIA 27

Part of the San Fernando Valley; part of Burbank

While most of the 27th is within Los Angeles, people who live here do not generally think of themselves as residents of the city. Instead, they view themselves as part of the Los Angeles communities of Van Nuys, Encino or Sherman Oaks in the San Fernando Valley north of central Los Angeles. The valley's portion of the city lies primarily in the 27th and 28th districts.

Biomedical firms and entertainment ventures located just outside Hollywood drive the economy here. Health testing company Quest Diagnostics has a clinical trials site in Northridge, and other firms are in Sylmar, Van Nuys and North Hollywood. Toymaker MGA Entertainment has its corporate office in Van Nuys, while the San Fernando Valley is home to much of the nation's adult entertainment industry.

The valley has a stable hospitality industry — particularly its hotels and small conference sites — because of its proximity to Hollywood and the local airports. The flat, grid-like streets of much of the 27th take in both the Bob Hope (Burbank) and Van Nuys airports. There are several colleges here as well, including California State University, Northridge.

Reservoirs and aqueducts in the northwest provide water to millions of Los Angeles County residents, and regional efforts continue to conserve water resources. In 2008, heavy wildfires damaged many homes in Sylmar and other parts of the valley.

Asian immigrants, particularly from India and Pakistan, have made the mostly white and Hispanic district home. This rise of immigration increased demand for housing, which in turn led to higher housing rates — the median home price here has previously been as much as three times the national average. But, some new developments and established areas have felt the sting of high foreclosure rates.

A majority of the district's workers are employed in white-collar jobs, and the district is solidly Democratic. Residents here gave Barack Obama 66 percent of the vote in the 2008 presidential election.

MAJOR INDUSTRY
Biotech, service

CITIES
Los Angeles (pt.), 591,573; Burbank (pt.), 45,436

NOTABLE
Van Nuys Airport is the world's busiest general aviation airport.

Rep. Howard L. Berman (D)

Elected 1982; 14th term

The cerebral and serious-minded Berman has become one of the chamber's most effective dealmakers. He puts his skills to use as chairman of the Foreign Affairs Committee, which he runs in a non-confrontational style despite his avowed liberalism, and as a senior member of the Judiciary Committee, where he also avoids partisan squabbles.

Berman is a close ally of fellow Californian and Speaker Nancy Pelosi and is known as an institutionalist, someone who puts his concern for the integrity of Congress above politics. He enjoys tackling a range of complicated issues, from technology to the functioning of the State Department's foreign assistance programs.

Berman assumed the helm of Foreign Affairs in March 2008 after another fellow Californian, Tom Lantos, died of cancer. Before long, he orchestrated a delicate compromise on President George W. Bush's global anti-AIDS program, increasing funding above what Republicans wanted but leaving in the legislation some restrictions on family planning that they favored.

In September, he worked out another deal with Bush, helping steer to enactment a bill approving a civilian nuclear cooperation agreement with India after Secretary of State Condoleezza Rice assured him that she would seek a global ban on transferring enrichment and reprocessing technology to countries that do not already have it.

In the 111th Congress (2009-10), Berman seeks to revamp U.S. foreign aid to Pakistan to emphasize economic development. He also wants to advance a new approach to Iran. He has promoted a deal in which the United States would grant diplomatic recognition to Iran in exchange for its pledge to eliminate its nuclear program, stop aiding terrorist groups and stop interfering with U.S. efforts in Afghanistan and Iraq. In the meantime, though, he remains committed to undermining Iran's nuclear regime.

He is an unswerving supporter of Israel and leapt to its defense when fighting erupted in Gaza in early 2009. "I have no trouble justifying the war Israel has undertaken. I am deeply troubled, however, by the suffering, destruction and loss of innocent life that war inevitably entails," he told the House.

Berman praised President Obama's 2009 proposal to boost the State Department's budget, saying it would help "address fundamental shortages in resources and personnel that are impairing our country's ability to carry out the diplomacy and development pillars of our national security strategy."

From his seat on the Judiciary Committee, Berman looks out for the entertainment industry — an important constituency in his district — and is a leading expert on copyrights and patents and a defender of online freedom of speech. He served as chairman of what was then the Subcommittee on Courts, the Internet and Intellectual Property in the 110th Congress (2007-08) but gave up that gavel in 2009 because of his Foreign Affairs post.

On Judiciary, Berman looks out for Southern California's writers, composers and other content creators and has tried to curb Internet piracy. He is the nemesis of high-tech companies that have accused the entertainment industry of using copyright protection to scuttle the development of new technologies. But he sees the issue as a simple one: "When people can't get rewarded for their works, they won't produce them."

In the 111th, Berman is expected to resume efforts to pass legislation to require radio stations to compensate performers for songs played over the airwaves. Radio stations have long paid songwriters whose music is used, but not the musicians. In 2007, he was the lead House Democrat on bipar-

CAPITOL OFFICE
225-4695
www.house.gov/berman
2221 Rayburn Bldg. 20515-0528; fax 225-3196

COMMITTEES
Foreign Affairs - chairman
Judiciary

RESIDENCE
Valley Village

BORN
April 15, 1941; Los Angeles, Calif.

RELIGION
Jewish

FAMILY
Wife, Janis Berman; two children

EDUCATION
U. of California, Los Angeles, B.A. 1962 (international relations), LL.B. 1965

CAREER
Lawyer

POLITICAL HIGHLIGHTS
Calif. Assembly, 1972-82 (majority leader, 1973-79)

ELECTION RESULTS

2008 GENERAL

Howard L. Berman (D)		unopposed

2008 PRIMARY

Howard L. Berman (D)		unopposed

2006 GENERAL

Howard L. Berman (D)	79,866	73.9%
Stanley Kimmel Kesselman (R)	20,629	19.1%
Byron De Lear (GREEN)	3,868	3.6%
Kelley L. Ross (LIBERT)	3,679	3.4%

PREVIOUS WINNING PERCENTAGES
2004 (71%); 2002 (71%); 2000 (84%); 1998 (82%); 1996 (66%); 1994 (63%); 1992 (61%); 1990 (61%); 1988 (70%); 1986 (65%); 1984 (63%); 1982 (60%)

tisan legislation to overhaul the U.S. patent system, which critics said fostered excessive infringement lawsuits and stifled innovation.

Berman is passionate about immigration issues. In 2005, he and Republican moderate Jim Kolbe of Arizona tried to bridge the polarized debate on immigration with a proposal to create a guest worker program similar to a plan offered by Bush. It would have allowed more immigrants to come in legally to work in low-skilled, low-paying jobs U.S. workers tend to shun. Their effort failed when the House adopted a more conservative bill.

Berman was Pelosi's choice when she needed someone in 2006 to step into the party's senior slot on the ethics committee, which had broken down amid partisan warfare. Berman had served in the role from 1997 to 2003, when the committee investigated several high-profile cases.

Berman drew criticism from Republicans and bloggers in early 2009 when the House passed a $410 billion catchall spending bill that included $200,000 he sought for tattoo removal to help gang members erase signs of their past.

The son of a Polish immigrant who sold textiles in Los Angeles, Berman credits a high school teacher with igniting his career in politics. "My parents weren't political, so she was the person who moved me to challenge assumptions and to debate issues," he said. At UCLA, he had an internship with the California Assembly's Agriculture Committee, where he worked on labor issues with Cesar Chavez's United Farm Workers. And he met Henry A. Waxman, then president of the school's Federation of Young Democrats and now chairman of the Energy and Commerce Committee. The two became fast friends and card-playing buddies. Berman helped Waxman win a seat in the state Assembly, marking the start of the Berman-Waxman political network of like-minded politicians and activists who helped their hand-picked candidates with money and organization. The alliance was a power in Los Angeles County for years.

In 1972, he won an Assembly seat by defeating an GOP incumbent. He rose to majority leader, but lost a bid for Speaker to Democrat Willie L. Brown Jr. Brown then approved a congressional map with an ideal district for Berman. Since his first win in 1982, he has won re-election easily. He contemplated running for mayor of Los Angeles in 1993 and 1997 but decided against it.

In California's redistricting after 2000, House Democrats hired Berman's brother, Michael Berman, as a consultant to draft new post-census lines. The map that was eventually approved carved several Hispanic communities out of Berman's district, making it less likely he would face a primary challenge by a Hispanic in future elections. The move angered Hispanics in the state who wanted a map that would favor electing a Hispanic.

KEY VOTES

2008

Yes Delay consideration of Colombia free-trade agreement

Yes Override Bush veto of federal farm and nutrition programs reauthorization bill

Yes Overhaul surveillance laws and permit dismissal of suits against companies that conducted warrantless wiretapping

Yes Grant mortgage relief to homeowners and funding for Fannie Mae and Freddie Mac

Yes Approve initial $700 billion program to stabilize financial markets

Yes Approve final $700 billion program to stabilize financial markets

Yes Provide $14 billion in loans to automakers

2007

Yes Increase minimum wage by $2.10 an hour

Yes Approve $124.2 billion in emergency war spending and set goal for redeployment of troops from Iraq

No Reject federal contraceptive assistance to international family planning groups

Yes Override Bush veto of $23.2 billion water projects authorization bill

Yes Implement Peru free-trade agreement

Yes Approve energy policy overhaul with new fuel economy standards

Yes Clear $473.5 billion omnibus spending bill, including $70 billion for military operations

CQ VOTE STUDIES

	PARTY UNITY		PRESIDENTIAL SUPPORT	
	SUPPORT	OPPOSE	SUPPORT	OPPOSE
2008	98%	2%	20%	80%
2007	98%	2%	7%	93%
2006	96%	4%	29%	71%
2005	96%	4%	18%	82%
2004	97%	3%	31%	69%

INTEREST GROUPS

	AFL-CIO	ADA	CCUS	ACU
2008	100%	85%	69%	4%
2007	100%	85%	53%	4%
2006	92%	90%	43%	8%
2005	93%	95%	41%	4%
2004	100%	90%	29%	0%

CALIFORNIA 28

Part of the San Fernando Valley

The 28th is centered in the San Fernando Valley north of Los Angeles, where it takes in the small city of San Fernando and includes parts of the Los Angeles communities of Pacoima, Arleta, Panorama City, Van Nuys and North Hollywood. The southern border follows in part iconic Mulholland Drive, taking in Encino, Sherman Oaks and Studio City in the Hollywood Hills north of Beverly Hills.

Economic downturns have struck the 28th's commercial district. Centered on financial services along famed Ventura Boulevard, just south of Route 101, bank branches in office towers compete with miles of strip malls, fast-food outlets, restaurants and residential developments. Traffic congestion is a major concern in the area, and Interstate 405, one of the most congested highways in the country, runs through the southwestern arm of the district.

The technology and entertainment industries fueled the district's economy for the last decade. The CBS Studio Center in Studio City is off Ventura Boulevard just south of the Los Angeles River. Local officials and environmentalists have targeted the river for conservation and urban revitalization. The manufacturing sector here declined in the 1990s after a General Motors plant closed, but the Pepsi Bottling Group still has a facility in San Fernando. Although some biomedical and medical equipment firms are leaving the district, Kaiser Permanente opened a large hospital in Panorama City in 2008.

New immigrants are driving service industry growth here. Once mainly middle-class and white, suburban city communities have attracted many Hispanics, who make up 56 percent of the 28th's population. This influx keeps the 28th in the Democratic column, and the district gave Barack Obama 76 percent of its presidential vote in 2008. Overall, 44 percent of residents were born outside of the United States, the eighth-highest percentage in the nation.

MAJOR INDUSTRY
Service, entertainment, health care, manufacturing

CITIES
Los Angeles (pt.), 615,523; San Fernando, 23,564

NOTABLE
The Academy of Television Arts and Sciences, which presents the annual Emmy Awards, is based in North Hollywood.

Rep. Adam B. Schiff (D)

Elected 2000; 5th term

CAPITOL OFFICE
225-4176
schiff.house.gov/HoR/ca29
2447 Rayburn Bldg. 20515; fax 225-5828

COMMITTEES
Appropriations
Judiciary
Select Intelligence

RESIDENCE
Burbank

BORN
June 22, 1960; Framingham, Mass.

RELIGION
Jewish

FAMILY
Wife, Eve Schiff; two children

EDUCATION
Stanford U., A.B. 1982 (political science
& pre-med); Harvard U., J.D. 1985

CAREER
Federal prosecutor; lawyer

POLITICAL HIGHLIGHTS
Assistant U.S. attorney, 1987-93; Democratic
nominee for Calif. Assembly (special election),
1994; Democratic nominee for Calif. Assembly,
1994; Calif. Senate, 1996-2000

ELECTION RESULTS

2008 GENERAL

Adam B. Schiff (D)	146,198	68.9%
Charles Hahn (R)	56,727	26.7%
Alan Pyeatt (LIBERT)	9,219	4.3%

2008 PRIMARY

Adam B. Schiff (D)	unopposed

2006 GENERAL

Adam B. Schiff (D)	91,014	63.5%
William J. Bodell (R)	39,321	27.4%
William M. Paparian (GREEN)	8,197	5.7%
Lynda L. Llamas (PFP)	2,599	1.8%
Jim Keller (LIBERT)	2,258	1.6%

PREVIOUS WINNING PERCENTAGES
2004 (65%); 2002 (63%); 2000 (53%)

Schiff is helping to shape a new Democratic approach to national security, using his posts on key committees to promote a greater emphasis on combating nuclear proliferation and encouraging economic development in countries where poverty and corruption foment instability.

A former federal prosecutor and Harvard Law School graduate, Schiff is thoughtful and nuanced in his views. He founded a group called the Democratic Study Group on National Security "to get Democrats to speak more knowledgeably, more forcefully" on those issues.

He sees nuclear proliferation as the gravest threat facing the United States. "If there is a nuclear 9/11, it will be of a wholly different order of magnitude from anything we have ever seen," he said. In 2008, he won House and Senate passage of his bill to develop techniques for "fingerprinting" nuclear materials in order to trace them to their point of origin. "We are not going to deter terrorists from using the bomb," Schiff said. "If al Qaeda ever got it, they would use it. But we can deter countries from supplying them if they know it will be traced back to them and they will be held accountable." The measure did not clear in the 110th Congress (2007-08), however.

Schiff wants to do more than play defense. He is working to promote press freedom and economic development around the world. "We have seen in Afghanistan and elsewhere that the economic development, rule of law issues are intertwined with national security issues," he said. He is pushing for a large increase in the number of foreign service officers along with a major boost in U.S. development aid.

In the 110th, Schiff won a seat on the Appropriations Committee. Although an assignment to Appropriations often requires members to give up seats on other panels, Speaker Nancy Pelosi gave Schiff a waiver to remain on the Judiciary Committee. She also appointed him to the Select Intelligence Committee. "I think I have the three best assignments in the place," he said in 2008. But he admits he was startled by the "staggering" time commitment of Intelligence panel work. "I never had so many hearings to go to and had so much I couldn't talk about," he said.

In addition to his committee work, Schiff was named in September 2008 to chair a Judiciary impeachment task force to investigate allegations that G. Thomas Porteous, a U.S. district judge for the Eastern District of Louisiana, committed perjury by signing false financial disclosure forms under oath.

While he supports tough anti-terror laws, Schiff also wants to protect civil liberties. In 2006 and again in the 110th, he teamed with conservative Republican Jeff Flake of Arizona on efforts to rein in a controversial warrantless surveillance program. They contended that domestic surveillance to catch terrorists should be conducted under the careful watch of a special court, and a provision making such review mandatory was part of the 2008 overhaul of the Foreign Intelligence Surveillance Act that President George W. Bush signed into law.

In 2003, Schiff sponsored legislation to authorize military tribunals for prosecuting terrorists, setting specific rules aimed at averting abuses of suspects, including granting public access and providing for Supreme Court review.

Schiff is more moderate than some in his party as he aligns himself with the fiscally conservative Blue Dog Coalition. He was one of four Blue Dogs who changed their vote from no to yes on the $700 billion law that Congress cleared in fall 2008 to assist the ailing financial services industry. He was more favorably disposed to President Obama's economic stimulus measure, which

Congress cleared in February 2009, providing $787 billion in federal funds to revive the economy. "This package is a crucial step in reigniting the economic engine that has made America the most productive and innovative economy in the world," Schiff said after the House vote. "It will not solve all of our problems, but it is a start."

His votes on tax legislation typify his financial views. Schiff was one of 28 Democrats who voted to enact Bush's tax cuts in 2001, but he opposed the next round in 2003, saying it was "fiscally irresponsible" to cut taxes further when the nation was at war and racking up huge annual deficits. He also opposed the 2004 corporate tax package and the 2005 tax cut extensions.

In the 108th Congress (2003-04), Schiff's bill increasing criminal penalties for identity theft was signed into law, and he cosponsored successful legislation to foster the use of DNA analysis in criminal investigations and to expand the national DNA database. In 2008, he steered through the House a bill reauthorizing a grant program aimed at reducing a backlog of DNA evidence awaiting analysis. The bill cleared Congress at the end of 2008.

Schiff was born in Massachusetts; when he was 11, his family moved to northern California, where his father bought a lumber yard. He and his brother had to help out in the business. "There's nothing like working in a lumber yard to make you want to go to grad school," he said.

When he entered Stanford University, Schiff could not decide between medicine and law, so he majored in both pre-med and political science and was accepted to both medical school and law school. Although his parents urged him to become a doctor, Schiff chose law.

After getting his law degree, he returned to California and clerked for a federal judge, then worked in the U.S. attorney's office for six years. A colleague there, Tom Umberg, who was elected to the California Assembly, was the inspiration for his shift into politics. "I wanted to deal with the root causes of the problems I was dealing with as a U.S. attorney," Schiff said.

He was unsuccessful in his first attempt to enter politics, losing to Republican James E. Rogan in 1994 in a contest for an Assembly seat. He rebounded in 1996, winning a state Senate seat. In 2000 he again faced Rogan, by then a U.S. House member who had played a high-profile role in the GOP attempt to impeach President Clinton. Schiff and Rogan raised more than $11 million between them, a House race record. And their race was viewed nationally as a referendum on the impeachment proceedings against Clinton. But Schiff said the race actually turned on local concerns, as the district was so evenly divided on the impeachment issue. He defeated Rogan by 9 percentage points and has been re-elected easily since then.

KEY VOTES

2008

Yes Delay consideration of Colombia free-trade agreement

Yes Override Bush veto of federal farm and nutrition programs reauthorization bill

Yes Overhaul surveillance laws and permit dismissal of suits against companies that conducted warrantless wiretapping

Yes Grant mortgage relief to homeowners and funding for Fannie Mae and Freddie Mac

No Approve initial $700 billion program to stabilize financial markets

Yes Approve final $700 billion program to stabilize financial markets

Yes Provide $14 billion in loans to automakers

2007

Yes Increase minimum wage by $2.10 an hour

Yes Approve $124.2 billion in emergency war spending and set goal for redeployment of troops from Iraq

No Reject federal contraceptive assistance to international family planning groups

Yes Override Bush veto of $23.2 billion water projects authorization bill

Yes Implement Peru free-trade agreement

Yes Approve energy policy overhaul with new fuel economy standards

No Clear $473.5 billion omnibus spending bill, including $70 billion for military operations

CQ VOTE STUDIES

	PARTY UNITY		PRESIDENTIAL SUPPORT	
	SUPPORT	OPPOSE	SUPPORT	OPPOSE
2008	98%	2%	14%	86%
2007	98%	2%	6%	94%
2006	94%	6%	35%	65%
2005	94%	6%	24%	76%
2004	93%	7%	38%	62%

INTEREST GROUPS

	AFL-CIO	ADA	CCUS	ACU
2008	100%	90%	61%	4%
2007	96%	95%	60%	0%
2006	86%	85%	47%	12%
2005	93%	85%	42%	0%
2004	93%	95%	43%	12%

CALIFORNIA 29

Glendale; Pasadena; Alhambra; part of Burbank

Set in the foothills of the San Gabriel Mountains, the 29th includes the largely residential Los Angeles suburbs of Glendale, Pasadena, Alhambra and part of Burbank. The district suffers from heavy traffic congestion, and although Glendale and Pasadena are part of the Los Angeles area, they have their own downtowns.

Television and movie production studios drive much of the economy in both Burbank, home to Walt Disney Studios, and Glendale, containing DreamWorks Animation SKG. NBC announced in late 2007 that it is planning on moving from its 34-acre complex in Burbank to a site near Universal Studios, which is in the adjacent 28th District. Glendale also is home to the corporate headquarters of Nestlé USA and the International House of Pancakes. A technology community has sprung up near a number of colleges and universities in the area, including the California Institute of Technology and NASA's Jet Propulsion Laboratory.

The region includes a wide mix of ethnicities, with none holding a majority of district residents. The 29th has one of the highest percentages of

Asian residents in California and in the nation, and is slightly more than one-fourth Hispanic. Monterey Park (shared with the 32nd) is known as "Little Taipei" for its Taiwanese and other Asian immigrants. Glendale is home to about 85,000 Armenians, one of the largest such communities outside of Armenia, and Alhambra is heavily Asian and Hispanic.

Over the years, immigration and the nearby Hollywood economy have transformed once-WASPish neighborhoods, giving the district a strong Democratic lean. The 29th gave Barack Obama 68 percent of its 2008 presidential vote.

MAJOR INDUSTRY
Entertainment, technology, engineering

CITIES
Glendale, 194,973; Pasadena, 133,936; Alhambra, 85,804; Burbank (pt.), 54,880; San Gabriel, 39,804; Altadena (unincorporated) (pt.), 38,306

NOTABLE
More people have looked through the Zeiss Telescope at the Griffith Observatory than any other telescope in the world; Pasadena's annual Tournament of Roses Parade is never held on a Sunday; The first Church of Scientology was founded in Glendale in 1954; The first satellite launched by the United States was built at the Jet Propulsion Laboratory.

Rep. Henry A. Waxman (D)

Elected 1974; 18th term

CAPITOL OFFICE
225-3976
www.house.gov/waxman
2204 Rayburn Bldg. 20515-0530; fax 225-4099

COMMITTEES
Energy & Commerce - chairman

RESIDENCE
Beverly Hills

BORN
Sept. 12, 1939; Los Angeles, Calif.

RELIGION
Jewish

FAMILY
Wife, Janet Waxman; two children

EDUCATION
U. of California, Los Angeles, B.A. 1961
(political science), J.D. 1964

CAREER
Lawyer

POLITICAL HIGHLIGHTS
Calif. Assembly, 1968-74

ELECTION RESULTS

2008 GENERAL

Henry A. Waxman (D)		unopposed

2008 PRIMARY

Henry A. Waxman (D)		unopposed

2006 GENERAL

Henry A. Waxman (D)	151,284	71.4%
David Nelson Jones (R)	55,904	26.4%
Adele M. Cannon (PFP)	4,546	2.1%

PREVIOUS WINNING PERCENTAGES
2004 (71%); 2002 (70%); 2000 (76%); 1998 (74%);
1996 (68%); 1994 (68%); 1992 (61%); 1990 (69%);
1988 (72%); 1986 (88%); 1984 (63%); 1982 (65%);
1980 (64%); 1978 (63%); 1976 (68%); 1974 (64%)

Waxman is one of Washington's shrewdest operators. Friends and enemies describe him — with varying degrees of admiration — as dogged and tenacious, and he has extensive knowledge of a broad policy portfolio and the ability to be both partisan and patient. He has called himself a "proud, self-confessed, unapologetic liberal."

He uses his skills as chairman of the Energy and Commerce Committee, where he is a major player on several of President Obama's chief priorities: health care, energy and global warming. Waxman also has purview over telecommunications policy and favors institutional change at the Federal Communications Commission.

He enjoys several advantages in getting what he wants, including a like-minded colleague in Speaker Nancy Pelosi, a fellow Californian. His longtime aide, Philip Schiliro, is Obama's congressional relations director.

The 5-foot-5-inch Waxman — with his mustache, wire-rimmed spectacles, thick black eyebrows and bald pate — is not a physically intimidating figure; Time magazine described him as having "all the panache of your parents' dentist." But Republicans have learned to respect him. Former Wyoming GOP Sen. Alan Simpson once griped that he was "tougher than a boiled owl."

Waxman is single-mindedly focused on his job; he has few hobbies and avoids socializing with colleagues. He also doesn't evince much of an ego. "I don't care whether the world knows about me," he told The Washington Post in 2002. "I just want the world to care about some of these issues and care about some of these things that I care about."

Waxman ousted Michigan's John D. Dingell — the House's longest- serving member and Energy and Commerce's top Democrat since 1981 — from the chairmanship in 2008 by taking a page from Obama's playbook and casting himself as an agent of change. In a campaign that flew in the face of the chamber's tradition of seniority, Waxman appealed to younger Democrats who wanted to push an aggressive agenda on environmental and energy issues. They had criticized Dingell, an ardent defender of his state's auto industry, for moving too slowly on restricting greenhouse gas emissions.

In addition to making a philosophical appeal, Waxman quietly gave financial help to the campaigns of younger Democrats, using his political action committee (PAC) to donate two to five times as much as Dingell to individual candidates.

Waxman's rivalry with Dingell dates to the 1980s, when the two clashed on environmental issues. An uneasy truce collapsed in 2008 when Dingell revived a proposal to bar Waxman's home state and others from setting tougher vehicle emissions standards than the federal government. Waxman took it as a personal affront and vowed he and Dingell would "have a fight" over it.

But after taking over the chairmanship, Waxman didn't completely ban Dingell to the sidelines. Instead, he let him take the lead on national health care legislation for the committee during the 111th Congress (2009-10). It was in part a recognition of the clout Dingell still holds; he has had a hand in virtually every major health care debate over the past half-century.

Waxman has had extensive experience in the health policy arena as well. Prior to challenging Dingell, he had made the committee's Health and Environment Subcommittee his main base of operations. He chaired the panel for 16 years before the GOP takeover of 1995.

He has excoriated a provision of the 2003 Medicare prescription drug law that barred the government from negotiating with pharmaceutical companies to obtain discounts for seniors. The GOP-sponsored law instead allowed private insurance companies to negotiate prices with the drugmakers.

Waxman has been a leading congressional crusader against tobacco. At a 1994 hearing, Waxman — a former smoker who had a tough time quitting — grilled the chief executives of the nation's seven largest tobacco companies. All testified under oath that they did not believe nicotine was addictive. The hearing helped lay the groundwork for multibillion-dollar lawsuits against the industry. In March 2009 he renewed efforts to give the Food and Drug Administration broad powers to regulate tobacco advertising and marketing.

Waxman also has had a strong interest in environmental issues. He once blocked an effort to weaken the Clean Air Act by filing 600 amendments that were wheeled in on shopping carts. As Energy chairman in 2009, he sought to win support from skeptical Democrats on climate change legislation by relaxing the early target for reducing greenhouse gas emissions.

Waxman had drawn the most attention in the 110th Congress (2007-08) as chairman of the Oversight and Government Reform Committee, where he was a constant thorn in President George W. Bush's side. He conducted hearings on a number of issues, including the huge compensation packages doled out to executives of firms involved in the subprime mortgage crisis.

Despite his reputation in front of the camera, Waxman can cut deals with Republicans. In the 110th, he and the Oversight Committee's top Republican, Virginia's Thomas M. Davis III, sent pointed inquiries to federal agencies on such subjects as flu vaccine shortages. They also released a report on former lobbyist Jack Abramoff's dealings with the executive branch.

Waxman grew up in an apartment above a Los Angeles grocery store run by his father, who was the son of Russian immigrants and a New Deal Democrat who influenced his son's early thinking about politics and government. Waxman's political career began at UCLA in the 1960s, when he and fellow student — and now House colleague — Howard L. Berman became active in California's Federation of Young Democrats. In 1968, after a term as chairman of the state federation, Waxman, with Berman's support, challenged Democratic state Assemblyman Lester McMillan in a primary and beat him with 64 percent of the vote.

Waxman's district takes in most of the entertainment industry's geography. His constituents in Beverly Hills and part of West Hollywood are politically involved, and many donated generously to Waxman's PAC. His own campaigns are formalities; he has consistently won re-election with more than 60 percent of the vote and ran unopposed in 2008.

KEY VOTES

2008

Yes Delay consideration of Colombia free-trade agreement

No Override Bush veto of federal farm and nutrition programs reauthorization bill

No Overhaul surveillance laws and permit dismissal of suits against companies that conducted warrantless wiretapping

Yes Grant mortgage relief to homeowners and funding for Fannie Mae and Freddie Mac

Yes Approve initial $700 billion program to stabilize financial markets

Yes Approve final $700 billion program to stabilize financial markets

Yes Provide $14 billion in loans to automakers

2007

Yes Increase minimum wage by $2.10 an hour

Yes Approve $124.2 billion in emergency war spending and set goal for redeployment of troops from Iraq

No Reject federal contraceptive assistance to international family planning groups

Yes Override Bush veto of $23.2 billion water projects authorization bill

Yes Implement Peru free-trade agreement

Yes Approve energy policy overhaul with new fuel economy standards

No Clear $473.5 billion omnibus spending bill, including $70 billion for military operations

CQ VOTE STUDIES

	PARTY UNITY		PRESIDENTIAL SUPPORT	
	SUPPORT	OPPOSE	SUPPORT	OPPOSE
2008	99%	1%	16%	84%
2007	99%	1%	7%	93%
2006	98%	2%	8%	92%
2005	98%	2%	16%	84%
2004	97%	3%	13%	87%

INTEREST GROUPS

	AFL-CIO	ADA	CCUS	ACU
2008	100%	95%	61%	4%
2007	100%	90%	53%	0%
2006	100%	95%	33%	4%
2005	93%	100%	38%	0%
2004	100%	100%	20%	0%

CALIFORNIA 30

West Los Angeles County – Santa Monica, West Hollywood, part of Los Angeles

With such glamorous locales as Beverly Hills, Malibu, Bel Air and Pacific Palisades, few places in the 30th have not been immortalized by a movie or television show. The Democratic district stretches west from Santa Monica along the Pacific Coast Highway, past Malibu to the Ventura County line. It also extends north across the Santa Monica Mountains to Calabasas and Hidden Hills on the north side of the range.

The entertainment industry drives the economy here. Many movie and television studios have facilities in the 30th, including MGM, HBO Films, Fox Broadcasting and CBS Studios. Tourism also brings revenue to the district. The 30th is home to attractions such as Grauman's Chinese Theater and several blocks of the Hollywood Walk of Fame. The famed Hollywood Bowl also is in the district.

Even during economic downturns, exclusive Rodeo Drive offers ample high-end shopping, and international tourism helps prop up the luxury retail sector on the posh street. Health care is another economic driver here. The 30th has several medical campuses, including the Cedars-Sinai Medical Center and a Department of Veterans Affairs-run site.

The district, about three-fourths white, has an active gay community in West Hollywood and a large Jewish population. Its economy is overwhelmingly white-collar, and it has the state's highest percentage of college-educated residents, which also is the fourth-highest percentage in the nation. The 30th's colleges and universities, including Pepperdine University and UCLA, provide tens of thousands of jobs.

The district votes overwhelmingly Democratic in elections at all levels and gave Barack Obama 70 percent of its presidential vote in 2008.

MAJOR INDUSTRY
Entertainment, higher education, health care, tourism

CITIES
Los Angeles (pt.), 399,622; Santa Monica, 84,084; West Hollywood, 35,716

NOTABLE
The Rancho La Brea Tar Pits Museum boasts 3 million Ice Age fossils; Santa Monica Airport, formerly Clover Field, was the takeoff and landing point in 1924 for the first circumnavigation of the Earth by air.

Rep. Xavier Becerra (D)

Elected 1992; 9th term

CAPITOL OFFICE
225-6235
becerra.house.gov/HoR/CA31
1119 Longworth Bldg. 20515-0531; fax 225-2202

COMMITTEES
Budget
Ways & Means

RESIDENCE
Los Angeles

BORN
Jan. 26, 1958; Sacramento, Calif.

RELIGION
Roman Catholic

FAMILY
Wife, Carolina Reyes; three children

EDUCATION
Stanford U., A.B. 1980 (economics), J.D. 1984

CAREER
State prosecutor; state legislative aide; lawyer

POLITICAL HIGHLIGHTS
Calif. Assembly, 1990-92; candidate for mayor
of Los Angeles, 2001

ELECTION RESULTS

2008 GENERAL

Xavier Becerra (D)	unopposed

2008 PRIMARY

Xavier Becerra (D)	unopposed

2006 GENERAL

Xavier Becerra (D)	unopposed

PREVIOUS WINNING PERCENTAGES
2004 (80%); 2002 (81%); 2000 (83%); 1998 (81%);
1996 (72%); 1994 (66%); 1992 (58%)

Becerra is part of the House inner circle and one of Speaker Nancy Pelosi's young, loyal lieutenants as vice chairman of the Democratic Caucus, the group of all House Democrats. He represents the views of the party's most liberal wing, its Progressive Caucus, especially in providing health and tax benefits to low-income families.

His loyalty to Pelosi is such that he decided in December 2008 against becoming President Obama's U.S. trade representative. "I have a lot of things I want to achieve in the House," Becerra said of his decision. He also expressed doubts about Obama's willingness to make trade policy a top priority.

Becerra (full name: HAH-vee-air beh-SEH-ra) had vigorously campaigned for the caucus vice chairmanship in 2006, but dropped his bid when John B. Larson of Connecticut, another Pelosi ally, decided to keep the post. Pelosi responded by creating a new position for Becerra, "assistant to the Speaker," giving him a seat in leadership meetings. When Larson moved up to become caucus chairman in late 2008, Becerra won the job over the more centrist Marcy Kaptur of Ohio by a 175-67 vote.

One of Becerra's most important duties is to raise money to help his party. In early 2009 he joined several of his California colleagues in transferring $100,000 from his personal campaign coffers to the Democratic Congressional Campaign Committee.

An opponent of the Iraq War, he supports withdrawing U.S. troops immediately and votes — as he did in June 2008 — against supplemental funding for the wars in Iraq and Afghanistan. A former chairman of the Congressional Hispanic Caucus, Becerra also favors immigration legislation that would emphasize keeping families together and providing a legal route to permanent U.S. residency for current undocumented workers and future immigrants.

He is a reliable Democratic vote, following the party line on 99 percent of votes during President George W. Bush's administration that pitted a majority of Republicans against a majority of Democrats. In his nine terms, Becerra's liberalism has been a sure-fire match for his district, which has California's lowest median income according to 2000 census data, a growing number of immigrants, and is home to some of Los Angeles' entertainment industry, including Paramount Studios.

He joined other liberals in fall 2008 in opposing two $700 billion measures — the second of which became law — to assist the ailing financial services sector. A member of the Budget Committee, he said the legislation didn't do enough for taxpayers or businesses. But he praised Obama's subsequent $787 billion economic stimulus law, signed in February 2009, for its emphasis on "jobs, jobs, jobs."

Becerra's rise through the House ranks means increasingly he can get things done. He has long championed the idea of a Smithsonian museum honoring American Latinos. His persistence paid off in May 2008 when Bush signed legislation creating a 23-member commission to conduct a two-year feasibility study for such a museum in Washington, D.C.

The first Hispanic to serve on the powerful Ways and Means Committee, Becerra sits on its panels on health, oversight and Social Security. He has shown he isn't afraid to tangle with government officials he feels aren't performing. At an April 2008 hearing, he scolded Social Security Commissioner Michael J. Astrue over his agency's backlog of disability applications, which had swollen to some 1.3 million cases because of manpower shortages.

Becerra's district includes some of Los Angeles' most gang-plagued areas and he says he frequently sees the cost of gun violence. He recalls consoling the parents of a 14-year-old girl who was shot and killed in his district when her family's SUV was caught in the cross-fire of a gang gunfight. "Anything I can do to help provide a more stable, secure neighborhood is critical," he told the Los Angeles Times in March 2008. The previous month, he had introduced "gun microstamping" legislation that would require any weapon sold after January 2010 to be internally etched with its make, model and serial number, which would then be stamped on the bullet casing when the weapon is fired. That would help law enforcement match a spent cartridge to the weapon that fired it. He sponsored similar measures in 2000, 2001 and 2003.

With one of the nation's largest seaports in the Los Angeles area, Becerra generally has backed trade deals, including the 1993 North American Free Trade Agreement. But in 2005, he opposed the Central America Free Trade Agreement, citing a lack of worker protections. Months later, he voted against the Oman Free Trade Agreement, again citing labor rights and port security concerns. But he backed the 2007 Peru trade deal after a compromise between the Bush administration and Democrats created additional protections for workers and the environment.

Becerra was born in Sacramento. But his mother was born in Mexico, and his American-born father spent much of his early life moving back and forth across the border to earn money. Becerra still wears his father's wedding ring so he will never forget his humble origins.

The first member of his family to obtain a degree from a four-year college, he earned a bachelor's in economics and a law degree from Stanford. He helped pay his way by working summers on road construction crews in Sacramento and tutoring students in the community during the school year.

A state Senate fellowship cemented his interest in advocacy and policy work. He then worked with a legal services firm in Worcester, Mass., that specialized in helping mentally ill clients. After returning to California, Becerra was an aide for a state senator and worked for the state attorney general.

In 1990, Becerra ran a successful race for a state Assembly seat. Two years later his interest in the "bigger picture issues" of national and foreign policy led him to run for Congress. He easily outdistanced nine other candidates in the 1992 primary, then bested a Republican and three minor-party candidates in November with 58 percent of the vote. He has been re-elected handily ever since, although a 2001 run for Los Angeles mayor ended badly when he raised and spent $1.7 million, only to finish fifth in a field of 14 candidates.

KEY VOTES

2008

Yes	Delay consideration of Colombia free-trade agreement
Yes	Override Bush veto of federal farm and nutrition programs reauthorization bill
No	Overhaul surveillance laws and permit dismissal of suits against companies that conducted warrantless wiretapping
Yes	Grant mortgage relief to homeowners and funding for Fannie Mae and Freddie Mac
No	Approve initial $700 billion program to stabilize financial markets
No	Approve final $700 billion program to stabilize financial markets
Yes	Provide $14 billion in loans to automakers

2007

Yes	Increase minimum wage by $2.10 an hour
Yes	Approve $124.2 billion in emergency war spending and set goal for redeployment of troops from Iraq
No	Reject federal contraceptive assistance to international family planning groups
Yes	Override Bush veto of $23.2 billion water projects authorization bill
Yes	Implement Peru free-trade agreement
Yes	Approve energy policy overhaul with new fuel economy standards
No	Clear $473.5 billion omnibus spending bill, including $70 billion for military operations

CQ VOTE STUDIES

	PARTY UNITY		PRESIDENTIAL SUPPORT	
	SUPPORT	OPPOSE	SUPPORT	OPPOSE
2008	99%	1%	10%	90%
2007	99%	1%	4%	96%
2006	99%	1%	21%	79%
2005	99%	1%	16%	84%
2004	99%	1%	18%	82%

INTEREST GROUPS

	AFL-CIO	ADA	CCUS	ACU
2008	100%	100%	50%	8%
2007	96%	95%	58%	0%
2006	100%	95%	21%	4%
2005	92%	100%	37%	0%
2004	93%	95%	29%	0%

CALIFORNIA 31
Northeast and South Los Angeles

The only district set entirely within the city of Los Angeles, the 31st is densely populated, heavily Hispanic and staunchly Democratic. The district wraps around west of downtown to extend south into South Los Angeles (south central) and northeast toward Pasadena. Hispanics (70 percent) and Asians (14 percent) outnumber whites (10 percent) here.

Rapid immigration has changed many of the district's already diverse communities, and some newcomers are finding a mixed reception. Many Hispanics are among the new residents, and Pico Union and Westlake are dominated by Central American and Mexican immigrants. Other heavily Hispanic communities include Glassell Park and Highland Park, which boasts numerous historic homes along its streets. The eastern side of the district includes Lincoln Heights and El Sereno — heavily Hispanic, blue-collar areas with a significant Mexican immigrant presence. Filipinotown, between Echo Park and Westlake, also has a predominately Mexican and Central American presence — the traditional Filipino presence in the neighborhood has dwindled.

Directly west of Elysian Park, where Dodger Stadium is located, is the artsy Echo Park. In the northeast sits Eagle Rock, a hilly, middle-class pocket of relative affluence that votes Democratic but leans more toward the political center than other parts of the 31st. The still trendy neighborhood, home to Occidental College, recently has seen commercial slowdowns and some residential units stand empty.

Despite economic contributions from Paramount Studios, a slew of area hospitals and white-collar businesses along the Wilshire Boulevard central business corridor, the 31st has the lowest median income in the state, and fourth-lowest in the country, at slightly more than $26,000 per year. Only 14 percent of residents here have a college education, and more than 52 percent do not have a high school diploma.

The 31st supports Democrats, although voter turnout is traditionally low. Barack Obama received 80 percent of the district's 2008 presidential vote.

MAJOR INDUSTRY
Service, entertainment, tourism, health care

CITIES
Los Angeles (pt.), 639,088

NOTABLE
Dedicated in 1886, 575-acre Elysian Park is the city's oldest public park.

Vacant Seat

Rep. Hilda L. Solis (D)
Resigned effective Feb. 24, 2009

The seat representing the overwhelmingly Democratic 32nd District, which includes east Los Angeles and some near-in suburbs, was left open in February 2009 when Hilda L. Solis became President Obama's Labor secretary.

A dozen candidates of all parties appeared together on the May 2009 special primary election ballot to replace Solis. However, none came close to achieving the majority vote needed to win the seat outright under California law governing special-election primaries, thus sending the top vote-getter from each party on to a July 2009 special general election.

The strong favorite to represent the largely working-class district coming out of the primary was Democrat Judy Chu, a member of California's tax equalization board. The Republican nominee was Betty Tom Chu, a Monterey Park city councilwoman. Local news reports said the two are related by marriage.

The district is heavily comprised of Hispanics; the 2000 census indicated 62 percent of the residents were Hispanic, while 18 percent were Asian. It also has a large immigrant population, for whom health care and the environment are important. District voters favored Barack Obama over Republican John McCain with 68 percent of the vote in the 2008 presidential election.

The Democratic Chu, an Asian-American, earned high-profile endorsements from members of the Latino community such as Los Angeles Mayor Antonio Villaraigosa. She defeated Democratic state Sen. Gil Cedillo, who was backed by La Opinion, the largest Spanish-language newspaper in the country, along with members of the Congressional Hispanic Caucus.

Democratic Rep. Loretta Sanchez broke with fellow Hispanic House members to endorse Judy Chu. An aide to Sanchez said she and Chu are longtime friends and that she had endorsed her in all of her races.

Chu stressed her experience representing parts of the district and her background in fiscal matters. Her Republican counterpart, meanwhile, told the San Gabriel Valley Tribune she decided to run because she couldn't support any of the other candidates and wanted to offer voters an alternative.

Solis had previously held the seat for just more than four terms. She was active in the effort to increase the minimum wage in 2007 and was a strong backer of "card check" legislation to allow unions to win recognition when a majority of employees in a workplace sign cards supporting that move. She also sought to ensure that low-income and minority groups aren't disproportionately harmed by pollution. One of her signature accomplishments was a 2003 law that gives citizenship rights to non-citizens who have served one year in the military. The law allows swearing-in ceremonies to be held in overseas bases, consulates and embassies.

Solis worked as a newsletter editor for the Carter administration's White House Office of Hispanic Affairs. At the start of the Reagan administration, she moved to the Office of Management and Budget's civil rights division, but the undoing of Carter's policies drove her back home. She got a job with a state program helping disadvantaged students prepare for college.

Her first election was in 1985, to the Rio Hondo Community College board. She moved on to the California Assembly in 1992 and to the state Senate in 1994, becoming its youngest member and first Hispanic woman. She won her first House election in 2000 when she took on incumbent Democrat Matthew G. Martinez, who was considerably more conservative.

CALIFORNIA 32
East Los Angeles; El Monte; West Covina

The 32nd takes in a small chunk of the city of Los Angeles and extends east into largely Hispanic and Asian working-class suburbs. It includes the southern and central San Gabriel Valley, and goes east to Azusa and Covina, capturing a few good-size cities.

The district lacks a dominant industry, although manufacturing is key in several areas. Many residents commute out of the 32nd for work, but cities in the San Gabriel Valley have suffered from higher unemployment rates than the rest of the nation despite consistent population growth. Once a small farming town, El Monte became home to some small aerospace factories, and is now a light manufacturing area with a retail auto complex. Irwindale, dominated by rock quarries and landfills, is among the district's industrial centers. Rosemead has a large ethnic Chinese population, and it is the headquarters for the Panda Express food chain. The 32nd's small piece of the city of Los Angeles hosts a California State University campus.

As city dwellers continue to leave Los Angeles, local officials in the 32nd have focused on residential and commercial development over the past decade. Two-fifths of the population here is foreign-born, and many residents speak a language other than English at home. The area has several daily Spanish- and Chinese-language papers. Monterey Park (shared with the 29th) is known as "Little Taipei" for its Taiwanese and other Asian immigrants. Another large Asian population lives in wealthy, Democratic-leaning West Covina.

El Monte, in the heart of the San Gabriel Valley, and Baldwin Park, to the east, are blue-collar cities that form the 32nd's Democratic base. Although there had been pockets of Republicans and older white voters in Azusa, these groups are shrinking and the city supported Democrat Barack Obama in the 2008 presidential election. Obama took 68 percent of the district's presidential vote.

MAJOR INDUSTRY
Service, light manufacturing, higher education

CITIES
El Monte, 115,965; West Covina, 105,080; Baldwin Park, 75,837; Rosemead, 53,505; Covina, 46,837; Azusa, 44,712

NOTABLE
The first In-N-Out Burger restaurant opened in 1948 in Baldwin Park.

PRIOR ELECTION RESULTS

2008 GENERAL		
Hilda L. Solis (D)	130,142	100.0%
2006 GENERAL		
Hilda L. Solis (D)	76,059	83.0%
Leland Faegre (LIBERT)	15,627	17.0%
2004 GENERAL		
Hilda L. Solis (D)	119,144	85.0%
Leland Faegre (LIBERT)	21,002	15.0%

Rep. Diane Watson (D)

Elected June 2001; 4th full term

CAPITOL OFFICE
225-7084
www.house.gov/watson
2430 Rayburn Bldg. 20515-0533; fax 225-2422

COMMITTEES
Foreign Affairs
Oversight & Government Reform
(Government Management, Organization &
Procurement - chairwoman)

RESIDENCE
Los Angeles

BORN
Nov. 12, 1933; Los Angeles, Calif.

RELIGION
Roman Catholic

FAMILY
Single

EDUCATION
U. of California, Los Angeles, B.A. 1954
(education); California State U., Los Angeles,
M.S. 1968 (school psychology); Harvard U.,
attended 1981-82; Claremont Graduate School,
Ph.D. 1987 (educational administration)

CAREER
School administrator; state education department
official; teacher; school psychologist

POLITICAL HIGHLIGHTS
Los Angeles County Board of Education,
1975-78; Calif. Senate, 1978-98; candidate for
Los Angeles County Board of Supervisors, 1992;
U.S. ambassador to the Federal States of
Micronesia, 1999-2001

ELECTION RESULTS

2008 GENERAL

Diane Watson (D)	186,924	87.6%
David C. Crowley II (R)	26,536	12.4%

2008 PRIMARY

Diane Watson (D)	44,934	88.1%
Felicia Ford (D)	3,738	7.3%
Mervin Leon Evans (D)	2,315	4.5%

2006 GENERAL

Diane Watson (D)	unopposed

PREVIOUS WINNING PERCENTAGES
2004 (89%); 2002 (83%); 2001 Special Runoff
Election (75%)

Watson is a seasoned legislator who is eager to put her political muscle behind efforts to help the poor and disadvantaged. But she has found the path to power in Congress frustratingly steep.

She serves on the Foreign Affairs Committee, where she advocates for human rights and opposes the Iraq War, and on the Oversight and Government Reform Committee, where she has been involved in investigations into the financial credit crisis. But she wants to serve on a panel where she can tackle issues like health care, one of her top interests.

She says the seniority system and the leadership's emphasis on campaign fundraising have kept her waiting for that kind of assignment. "You're ranked here by how much money you raise for the DCCC," she observed in 2008, referring to the House Democratic fundraising arm, the Democratic Congressional Campaign Committee. Her own fundraising efforts are modest, and her contributions to the party unit and other Democratic campaigns totaled just over $41,000 in the 2007-08 election cycle.

She introduced several health care bills in the 110th Congress (2007-08), but none advanced. "Unless you are in the chief committee that handles them, you have to wait your turn in line," she said glumly.

She was named chairwoman of Oversight and Government Reform's Government Management, Organization and Procurement panel in February 2009. The assignment enables her to scrutinize waste, fraud and abuse in federal spending.

She spent 20 years in the California Senate, most of them as a committee chairwoman. In her self-described role as an agitator for people with little voice in government, she learned how to shelve rhetoric and work quietly to achieve her goals. She can point to a number of legislative successes in other areas, even during the years when Republicans controlled the House, although most came on targeted, non-controversial measures. In the 108th Congress (2003-04), she won enactment of a bill to award a Congressional Gold Medal to civil rights activist Dorothy Height. In the next Congress, her bill to authorize $5 million to protect intellectual property from piracy was wrapped into a foreign aid bill enacted in 2005. Also in that period, the House adopted her amendment to anti-gang legislation that added 200 federal agents.

From her seat on Foreign Affairs in the 110th, Watson won enactment of her bill to reauthorize the U.S. Advisory Commission on Public Diplomacy, and the House passed her bill — which the Senate failed to take up — to ensure libraries and resource centers at U.S. embassies around the world remain fully operational and provide access to films showcasing American values, culture and history. "I represent Hollywood," she said, so she wanted to be sure that "the State Department uses films as diplomacy."

Watson was given a seat on Foreign Affairs when she first arrived in the House after a two-year stint as ambassador to Micronesia, a federation of more than 600 islands in the Pacific. President Clinton appointed her to that post after term limits ended her state Senate career in 1998.

She has been an unswerving opponent of the Iraq War and an ardent champion of human rights around the globe, vigorously supporting a resolution approved by the committee and adopted by the House that called on the Japanese government to apologize for the country's sexual enslavement of thousands of "comfort women" during World War II.

A former Los Angeles public school teacher and the first African-American woman elected to the Los Angeles County school board, Watson is a strong advocate for inner-city children in Head Start, the early-childhood development program for low-income preschoolers, and for youths threatened by gang violence. In an attempt to reduce youth and gang violence, she sponsored a bill in 2007 to increase community service by students at risk of education failure.

In 2008, Watson was one of 13 members of the Congressional Black Caucus to oppose the $700 billion plan to shore up the financial services sector the first time it reached the House floor, but she supported a second, slightly modified version. She called her switch "one of the most difficult votes of my congressional career." Afterward, she joined other members of the Oversight Committee in grilling executives about how and why the credit collapse had occurred.

Watson grew up in the area she now represents in Congress. Her parents were lured to Hollywood by the usual hopes for fame and fortune. Her mother wanted to be an actress, while her father aspired to become "the next Joe Lewis," she said. But Watson's father became a police officer and her mother was a postal worker. She put in time at the local post office herself, sorting Christmas mail for seven seasons. But she had set her sights on a career in education. She earned bachelor's and master's degrees and a Ph.D. in education-related disciplines, and went on to become a teacher and psychologist in Los Angeles' school system.

Watson entered politics in 1975 when she won the school board seat. Three years later, she became the first black woman elected to the California Senate, where she shook up the mostly white-male institution. The California Political Almanac said Watson "seemed to specialize in crashing the party and opening the windows." She chaired the Health and Human Services Committee for 17 years and was the first non-lawyer to serve on its Judiciary Committee. She was credited with helping rebuild her community after the 1992 riots sparked by the acquittal of police charged with beating motorist Rodney King.

When 12-term Democratic Rep. Julian C. Dixon died in December 2000, Dixon's supporters urged Watson to run for the seat. In her special-election bid, she took 33 percent of the vote, defeating 10 other Democrats in the primary. She took 75 percent of the vote in the June general election, besting Republican Noel Irwin Hentschel. Redistricting shifted the boundaries of Watson's district slightly east and north and renumbered it the 33rd, but it remained Democratic. She bested her Republican opponent with 83 percent of the vote in 2002 and did not face another GOP challenger until 2008, when she tallied an even more one-sided victory.

KEY VOTES

2008

Yes Delay consideration of Colombia free-trade agreement

Yes Override Bush veto of federal farm and nutrition programs reauthorization bill

No Overhaul surveillance laws and permit dismissal of suits against companies that conducted warrantless wiretapping

Yes Grant mortgage relief to homeowners and funding for Fannie Mae and Freddie Mac

No Approve initial $700 billion program to stabilize financial markets

Yes Approve final $700 billion program to stabilize financial markets

? Provide $14 billion in loans to automakers

2007

Yes Increase minimum wage by $2.10 an hour

Yes Approve $124.2 billion in emergency war spending and set goal for redeployment of troops from Iraq

No Reject federal contraceptive assistance to international family planning groups

Yes Override Bush veto of $23.2 billion water projects authorization bill

No Implement Peru free-trade agreement

Yes Approve energy policy overhaul with new fuel economy standards

No Clear $473.5 billion omnibus spending bill, including $70 billion for military operations

CQ VOTE STUDIES

	PARTY UNITY		PRESIDENTIAL SUPPORT	
	SUPPORT	OPPOSE	SUPPORT	OPPOSE
2008	99%	1%	10%	90%
2007	99%	1%	5%	95%
2006	98%	2%	9%	91%
2005	98%	2%	9%	91%
2004	98%	2%	23%	77%

INTEREST GROUPS

	AFL-CIO	ADA	CCUS	ACU
2008	100%	100%	53%	4%
2007	96%	95%	47%	0%
2006	100%	80%	33%	0%
2005	93%	95%	37%	4%
2004	92%	85%	16%	0%

CALIFORNIA 33

West Los Angeles; Culver City

The 33rd is an ethnically diverse, Democratic district that begins about one mile inland from Venice Beach, runs east through Culver City and ends up in South Los Angeles (south central). The northern part of the district includes a section of Wilshire Boulevard from the "Miracle Mile" district to Koreatown and hooks north and east through Hollywood.

Blacks, Hispanics and Asians account for more than three-fourths of the population, but the 33rd has no single racial majority. Over the past decade there has been an influx of Hispanics, who now account for the largest part of the population, at 35 percent. The 33rd has a solid middle class, as well as some sharply contrasting areas such as wealthy Hancock Park — where the Los Angeles mayor's official residence is located — and the city's poor South Los Angeles neighborhood.

The largest business sector is the service industry, with health care also providing jobs for many residents. The University of Southern California is in the 33rd's portion of Los Angeles, along with university-affiliated hospitals such as Children's Hospital Los Angeles. Although the 33rd is no longer the film production hub it used to be, it is home to the real Tinseltown — Hollywood — and entertainment continues to be a factor in its overall economy. Sony Pictures Studios (formerly MGM Studios) makes its home in Culver City, which now has a blossoming art scene. The Kodak Theater is the site of the annual Academy Awards.

For recreation, residents and tourists flock to Exposition Park in downtown Los Angeles. In addition to the Los Angeles County Natural History Museum and the California Science Center, the park boasts the Los Angeles Memorial Coliseum, which hosted two Olympiads.

Democrats have an overwhelming advantage in the 33nd, both in the portions of the district in Los Angeles and in Culver City. Barack Obama took 87 percent of the district's vote in the 2008 presidential election, his second-highest percentage in the state.

MAJOR INDUSTRY
Service, entertainment, health care

CITIES
Los Angeles (pt.), 582,746; Culver City, 38,816

NOTABLE
Howard Hughes built the H-4 Hercules "Spruce Goose" in Culver City.

Rep. Lucille Roybal-Allard (D)

Elected 1992; 9th term

CAPITOL OFFICE
225-1766
www.house.gov/roybal-allard
2330 Rayburn Bldg. 20515-0534; fax 226-0350

COMMITTEES
Appropriations

RESIDENCE
East Los Angeles

BORN
June 12, 1941; Boyle Heights, Calif.

RELIGION
Roman Catholic

FAMILY
Husband, Edward Allard; four children

EDUCATION
California State U., Los Angeles, B.A. 1965
(speech)

CAREER
Nonprofit worker

POLITICAL HIGHLIGHTS
Calif. Assembly, 1986-92

ELECTION RESULTS

2008 GENERAL

Lucille Roybal-Allard (D)	98,503	77.1%
Christopher Balding (R)	29,266	22.9%

2008 PRIMARY

Lucille Roybal-Allard (D)	12,622	100.0%

2006 GENERAL

Lucille Roybal-Allard (D)	57,459	76.8%
Wayne Miller (R)	17,359	23.2%

PREVIOUS WINNING PERCENTAGES
2004 (74%); 2002 (74%); 2000 (85%); 1998 (87%);
1996 (82%); 1994 (81%); 1992 (63%)

Roybal-Allard is a loyal liberal foot soldier in Speaker Nancy Pelosi's House. She seeks to balance the related but not always overlapping needs of her two chief constituencies: a minority underclass mired in chronic poverty and a substantial Hispanic working class of laborers and shop owners.

Roybal-Allard almost always votes with her party; her only significant breaks have come when she feared a bill would give too much power to a Republican administration. That led her in fall 2008 to oppose two measures — the second of which became law — granting the White House $700 billion to shore up ailing financial institutions. When Barack Obama came out in favor of extending emergency loans to Detroit's automakers before his inauguration as president, Roybal-Allard voted for that relief measure, although it failed to move in the Senate.

She and Pelosi share a legacy: They are the only two Democratic women ever to follow their fathers to the House. Her father was Edward R. Roybal, one of only three Hispanic members of the House when he arrived in 1963. Pelosi's father, Thomas D'Alesandro Jr., represented Maryland in the 1940s.

Roybal-Allard is the first Mexican-American woman elected to Congress and the first woman to head the Congressional Hispanic Caucus, which her father founded. She said that when she first came to Washington, her constituents "expected me to be just like my dad — pick up the phone and get something done." But she has worked to forge her own identity.

As her father did, Roybal-Allard serves on the Appropriations Committee, where she looks out for her district and the surrounding area. In 2008, she secured more than $90 million in earmarks — funding set-asides for special projects. After joining the Homeland Security Appropriations Subcommittee in 2003, she urged her colleagues to boost funding for state and local governments that bear much of the cost when terror threats require heightened security. In 2006, Los Angeles Mayor Antonio Villaraigosa singled her out for special thanks after the award of more than $80 million to boost local efforts to prepare for and respond to a terrorist attack.

She takes a particular interest in the health care needs of the poor. In 2007, she sponsored a bill to establish grant programs to expand health assessments of newborns, which President George W. Bush signed into law in April 2008.

She is particularly sensitive to the problems of immigrants due to the discrimination and discouragement she said she faced growing up. She recalls being punished for speaking Spanish in school, and her parents being stopped and questioned when they tried to enter hotels. Even when her father began serving on the Los Angeles City Council in the 1950s, he met with resistance. "The racial slurs and not-so-quiet whispers directed at him and our family when we attended events and dinners remain vivid in our minds even today," she said in September 2008.

During the 109th Congress (2005-06), Roybal-Allard voted against GOP bills authorizing a 700-mile fence along the border with Mexico, tightening asylum requirements and making it a felony to be in the United States without valid legal papers. She called the bills "Band-Aids with harmful provisions that will not make us safer or fix our broken immigration system," she said on the House floor.

Before entering politics, Roybal-Allard worked for the United Way and then served as an assistant director on the Alcoholism Council of East Los Angeles. In Congress, she has focused much of her legislative energy on fighting underage drinking. "While we have an extensive campaign to combat illegal drug use, the fact remains that alcohol kills more teens than all other drugs combined," she said. Her efforts have drawn praise from Mothers Against Drunk Driving and other organizations.

A member of the Appropriations Labor, Health and Human Services, and Education Subcommittee, Roybal-Allard won a $1 million provision in 2001 for the Health and Human Services Department to develop new programs to curb underage drinking. She built on that over the years, and in 2006 she won enactment of legislation to coordinate all federal programs and research efforts on underage drinking and provide grants to colleges, states and nonprofit organizations to combat the problem.

Roybal-Allard drew plaudits in the late 1990s for her role in awakening the power of the California congressional delegation, which had been divided and ineffective. As the first elected chairwoman of the California Democratic delegation, she worked with her GOP counterpart, Jerry Lewis, to find issues on which the majority of the delegation could agree.

In 2003, she agreed to take a seat on the House ethics committee at Pelosi's request. Because its membership is evenly divided between Republicans and Democrats, the committee has long struggled to police the ethics violations of members. In 2008, Roybal-Allard briefly oversaw an investigation, later short-circuited, of former GOP Rep. Rick Renzi, who is facing criminal charges related to a land-swap scheme. She was term-limited off the panel in 2009.

The wife of a Marine who did two tours in Vietnam and the stepmother of a son who served in Iraq with the Army, Roybal-Allard voted against the 2002 resolution authorizing the use of force in Iraq and remains fiercely opposed to the U.S. involvement there.

She is an ally of labor unions and takes a protectionist tack on trade issues. She voted against free-trade deals with Peru, the Dominican Republic and Central American countries in recent years.

Her own family tried to dampen her ambitions when she was young. Her father's relatives ridiculed him for sending his daughters to college, saying all that was expected of them was marriage and children. Later, her siblings discouraged her from entering politics, citing the difficulties their father faced.

Roybal-Allard served six years in the California Assembly before winning election to the House in 1992. As a result of redistricting, her father had hoped she could serve beside him in Congress. But her mother's poor health and the strain of constant travel prompted him to retire. Democrat Xavier Becerra won her father's old seat that year, while she captured a neighboring Hispanic district by a 2-to-1 margin. She has won with no less than 74 percent of the vote in each re-election in the heavily Democratic district.

KEY VOTES

2008

Yes Delay consideration of Colombia free-trade agreement

Yes Override Bush veto of federal farm and nutrition programs reauthorization bill

No Overhaul surveillance laws and permit dismissal of suits against companies that conducted warrantless wiretapping

Yes Grant mortgage relief to homeowners and funding for Fannie Mae and Freddie Mac

No Approve initial $700 billion program to stabilize financial markets

No Approve final $700 billion program to stabilize financial markets

Yes Provide $14 billion in loans to automakers

2007

Yes Increase minimum wage by $2.10 an hour

Yes Approve $124.2 billion in emergency war spending and set goal for redeployment of troops from Iraq

No Reject federal contraceptive assistance to international family planning groups

Yes Override Bush veto of $23.2 billion water projects authorization bill

No Implement Peru free-trade agreement

Yes Approve energy policy overhaul with new fuel economy standards

No Clear $473.5 billion omnibus spending bill, including $70 billion for military operations

CQ VOTE STUDIES

	PARTY UNITY		PRESIDENTIAL SUPPORT	
	SUPPORT	OPPOSE	SUPPORT	OPPOSE
2008	99%	1%	11%	89%
2007	99%	1%	3%	97%
2006	93%	7%	27%	73%
2005	97%	3%	15%	85%
2004	98%	2%	24%	76%

INTEREST GROUPS

	AFL-CIO	ADA	CCUS	ACU
2008	100%	95%	44%	8%
2007	96%	100%	55%	0%
2006	100%	100%	33%	4%
2005	93%	95%	43%	0%
2004	100%	100%	35%	0%

CALIFORNIA 34

East central Los Angeles; Downey; Bellflower

The Democratic 34th takes in the heart and southeastern part of Los Angeles and has an overwhelming Hispanic majority. At 77 percent, the district has the largest concentration of Hispanics in California and the fourth-largest percentage in the country. Nearly 54 percent of residents here do not have a high school diploma, the highest rate in the nation.

The economy here relies on businesses in revitalized downtown areas and in nearby light manufacturing centers such as Vernon and Commerce. Downtown hosts toy, jewelry and garment manufacturers and retailers. Some space downtown is being converted into mixed-use units, creating residential loft space. Many of Los Angeles' civic buildings, including city hall, the county prison and courthouses, are in the 34th. The district also is attracting new "green" industries. Despite redevelopment and many small businesses, crime continues to be an issue.

Although crime and unemployment rates have increased in parts of the district, brighter spots include Walt Disney Concert Hall, home of the Los Angeles Philharmonic; the Dorothy Chandler Pavilion, home of the Los

Angeles Opera; the Los Angeles Convention Center; and Staples Center, home to basketball's Lakers, Clippers and Sparks, and hockey's Kings. Transportation hub Union Station and the terminus of the 20-mile Alameda Corridor rail link connecting the city to the ports of Los Angeles and Long Beach also are in the district.

Vernon's population explodes during the workday as workers head to its food-processing and furniture and garment manufacturing plants. Southeast of the city, Downey's economy is driven in part by the Rancho Los Amigos National Rehabilitation Center.

The 34th averages some of California's youngest, poorest and least-educated residents and generally has low voter turnout. Even slightly more suburban and conservative Bellflower and Downey in the south supported Democrat Barack Obama in the 2008 election, and Obama took 75 percent of the district's presidential vote overall.

MAJOR INDUSTRY
Government, manufacturing, service, retail

CITIES
Los Angeles (pt.), 188,018; Downey, 107,323; Bellflower, 72,878

NOTABLE
The first Taco Bell opened in 1962 in Downey.

Rep. Maxine Waters (D)

Elected 1990; 10th term

CAPITOL OFFICE
225-2201
www.house.gov/waters
2344 Rayburn Bldg. 20515-0535; fax 225-7854

COMMITTEES
Financial Services
(Housing & Community Opportunity -
chairwoman)
Judiciary

RESIDENCE
Los Angeles

BORN
Aug. 15, 1938; St. Louis, Mo.

RELIGION
Christian

FAMILY
Husband, Sidney Williams; two children

EDUCATION
California State U., Los Angeles, B.A. 1970

CAREER
City council aide; public relations firm owner;
Head Start program coordinator; telephone
company service representative

POLITICAL HIGHLIGHTS
Calif. Assembly, 1976-90

ELECTION RESULTS

2008 GENERAL

Maxine Waters (D)	150,778	82.6%
Ted Hayes (R)	24,169	13.2%
Herb Peters (LIBERT)	7,632	4.2%

2008 PRIMARY

Maxine Waters (D)	unopposed

2006 GENERAL

Maxine Waters (D)	82,498	83.7%
Gordon Michael Mego (AMI)	8,343	8.5%
Paul T. Ireland (LIBERT)	7,665	7.8%

PREVIOUS WINNING PERCENTAGES
2004 (81%); 2002 (78%); 2000 (87%); 1998 (89%);
1996 (86%); 1994 (78%); 1992 (83%); 1990 (79%)

Waters is an avowed liberal who has no qualms taking on the party establishment when its actions are contrary to her ideals. None of her colleagues doubt her commitment to her causes, which range from helping those on the lowest rung of America's economy to fighting for human rights in China, but they are sometimes put off by her abrasive nature.

She has been known to verbally blast opponents and even allies, telling them to "shut up." She says she has no time to use nuance to make Washingtonians more comfortable when her poor and mostly minority constituents are counting on her. Her tactics can be successful — though not always.

Waters chairs the Financial Services Subcommittee on Housing and Community Opportunity, and in 2008 she was in a pivotal position as lawmakers tried to deal with an ongoing crisis in the residential housing sector and wider financial markets. Waters and committee Chairman Barney Frank of Massachusetts ushered through bills to renew a variety of low-income housing programs. And they pushed through a massive bill — enacted in August 2008 — that included a Federal Housing Administration overhaul, housing tax breaks, and authorization for the government to purchase stock in mortgage giants Fannie Mae and Freddie Mac.

The most important pieces for Waters were the creation of a federal housing trust fund and the inclusion of $3.9 billion in grants to states and localities to buy and rehabilitate foreclosed homes. President George W. Bush initially threatened to veto any measure that included either provision, but Waters and Frank stared down the threat as financial markets and the foreclosure crisis worsened. "The president is attempting to get a lot in this bill," Waters said. "You don't give him all this and not get something else."

She felt the same way about giving Treasury Secretary Henry M. Paulson Jr. $700 billion to aid the failing financial industry in the fall of 2008. Although she voted to release the funding, she later said she was having second thoughts. It wasn't clear to her, she said, where all the money was going or whether it was being effectively deployed.

"If there is one thing I regret," she said at a December 2008 hearing, "I regret attempting to be cooperative in providing to Treasury the flexibility to deal with our economic crisis." She put things more bluntly at another December Financial Services hearing when she told Neel Kashkari, the assistant Treasury secretary responsible for the rescue program, "Please don't come here and ask for another penny, because if you do, I'm going to work 24 hours a day with the same people that I worked with" to make sure that they don't give the program additional money.

The New York Times reported in March 2009 that top Treasury officials were startled when Waters helped set up a meeting in which the chief executive of a bank with financial ties to her family asked for up to $50 million in assistance. The bank, OneUnited, got $12 million the previous December through the rescue program. Waters' staff released letters to The Times showing the meeting was called to discuss broader industry concerns and not just OneUnited.

She received the most attention in 2008 for her incendiary remarks during a Judiciary hearing on record oil company profits when she called for nationalizing the oil industry, and for her calls on the White House to boycott the Olympics in Beijing because of that country's reported human rights abuses.

An ally of House Speaker Nancy Pelosi, a fellow Californian, Waters is one of nine chief deputy whips and serves on the leadership's Steering and

Policy Committee, which makes committee assignments. Waters has been frustrated with Democrats in conservative-leaning districts who have voted in favor of GOP procedural maneuvers to amend bills — frequently housing-related — on the floor. She penned a "Dear Colleague" letter eviscerating party leaders for allowing the votes, which she said "are designed to divide our Caucus and undermine our work."

Waters does not apologize for her outbursts. "The political argument about what one needs to do to be elected is always difficult for me to absorb," she said. "Fundamentally, I believe that if you have to do a lot of things to stay in office that you don't agree with, why are you there?"

When the GOP ruled the House prior to 2007, she seldom found sympathy for her pleas for federal dollars for inner cities. In the majority, she has stepped up her fight for job training, community development funding and the fight against AIDS. She also has worked to stop banks from engaging in predatory lending practices, in which customers in low-income communities pay higher rates and fees than customers in wealthier areas.

Waters has been a constant critic of the war in Iraq. In the 109th Congress (2005-06), she cosponsored a bill to ban funding for the war and in June 2005 founded the Out of Iraq Caucus with a group of fellow liberals to press for a redeployment of U.S. troops. In 2008, she forced Pelosi to move war funding separately from domestic funding so that Democrats could vote against the former while supporting the latter.

Born in St. Louis as one of 13 children in a family on welfare, Waters bused tables in a segregated restaurant as a teenager. She married just after high school and moved in 1961 with her first husband and children to Los Angeles, where she worked in a clothing factory and for the telephone company.

Her public career began in 1965 when she took a job as a program coordinator in the new Head Start early-childhood development program while attending college. She got involved in community organizing, which led her to politics. After working as a volunteer and a consultant to several candidates, she won an upset victory in 1976 for a seat in the California Assembly. "I kind of figured out that some of the things that needed to be done were not being done. And I figured I could do some of those things," Waters said.

In 1990, Waters ran for the seat of Democratic Rep. Augustus F. Hawkins, who was retiring after 14 terms. She had been preparing for the move for years. During redistricting debates in the Assembly in 1982, Waters maneuvered to remove from Hawkins' district a blue-collar, mainly white suburb she saw as unfriendly territory. She won the 1990 race with 79 percent of the vote, and has won every election since with at least 75 percent.

KEY VOTES

2008
Yes Delay consideration of Colombia free-trade agreement
Yes Override Bush veto of federal farm and nutrition programs reauthorization bill
No Overhaul surveillance laws and permit dismissal of suits against companies that conducted warrantless wiretapping
Yes Grant mortgage relief to homeowners and funding for Fannie Mae and Freddie Mac
Yes Approve initial $700 billion program to stabilize financial markets
Yes Approve final $700 billion program to stabilize financial markets
Yes Provide $14 billion in loans to automakers

2007
Yes Increase minimum wage by $2.10 an hour
No Approve $124.2 billion in emergency war spending and set goal for redeployment of troops from Iraq
No Reject federal contraceptive assistance to international family planning groups
Yes Override Bush veto of $23.2 billion water projects authorization bill
No Implement Peru free-trade agreement
Yes Approve energy policy overhaul with new fuel economy standards
No Clear $473.5 billion omnibus spending bill, including $70 billion for military operations

CQ VOTE STUDIES

	PARTY UNITY		PRESIDENTIAL SUPPORT	
	SUPPORT	OPPOSE	SUPPORT	OPPOSE
2008	98%	2%	18%	82%
2007	97%	3%	10%	90%
2006	96%	4%	13%	87%
2005	96%	4%	14%	86%
2004	97%	3%	13%	87%

INTEREST GROUPS

	AFL-CIO	ADA	CCUS	ACU
2008	100%	95%	47%	0%
2007	95%	85%	42%	0%
2006	100%	90%	31%	4%
2005	93%	95%	32%	8%
2004	100%	95%	12%	4%

CALIFORNIA 35
South and Southeast Los Angeles; Inglewood

The overwhelmingly Democratic 35th District is centered in South and Southeast Los Angeles (south central) and is bordered by downtown Los Angeles to the north, Los Angeles International Airport to the west, Torrance to the south and the industrial Alameda Corridor to the east.

Although the 35th is mostly poor, Inglewood and the South Bay cities of Hawthorne, Gardena and Lawndale have growing middle class areas. Gardena allows poker parlors and enjoys a revenue stream from gambling. Local officials in Inglewood hope to lure commercial and residential developers to the Hollywood Park area. West of Inglewood, Los Angeles International Airport is one of the region's largest employers.

A precipitous decline in the district's manufacturing base has allowed poverty, crime and street gangs to dominate the area. Police-community relations, public safety and economic development continue to be central public policy concerns. Riots put the 35th in the headlines in 1992, following the acquittal of white police officers accused of beating black motorist Rodney King. Subsequently, the area became part of a

successful federal empowerment zone and local revitalization zone to help areas affected by the riots. The tax credits and incentives available to local employers have helped increase the number of jobs, but the area still struggles with infrastructure problems, such as street maintenance and development of recreational space.

The 35th leads the state in Democratic party registration — 67 percent of voters have aligned themselves with the party — and Barack Obama captured 84 percent of the vote in the 2008 presidential election, his fourth-highest percentage statewide. Once predominantly black, the district is seeing a huge influx of Hispanics, but it still has the state's largest black population at 34 percent. Gardena also has a large and politically influential Japanese community.

MAJOR INDUSTRY
Aerospace, service, manufacturing

CITIES
Los Angeles (pt.), 280,597; Inglewood, 112,580; Hawthorne, 84,112

NOTABLE
Central Avenue, on the district's eastern edge, was the West Coast hub of African-American entertainment during the jazz age; Hawthorne is the birthplace of The Beach Boys.

Rep. Jane Harman (D)

CAPITOL OFFICE
225-8220
www.house.gov/harman
2400 Rayburn Bldg. 20515-0536; fax 226-7290

COMMITTEES
Energy & Commerce
Homeland Security
(Intelligence, Information Sharing & Terrorism
Risk Assessment - chairwoman)

RESIDENCE
Venice

BORN
June 28, 1945; Queens, N.Y.

RELIGION
Jewish

FAMILY
Husband, Sidney Harman; four children

EDUCATION
Smith College, B.A. 1966 (government);
Harvard U., J.D. 1969

CAREER
Lawyer; White House aide; congressional aide

POLITICAL HIGHLIGHTS
U.S. House, 1993-99; sought Democratic
nomination for governor, 1998

ELECTION RESULTS

2008 GENERAL

Jane Harman (D)	171,948	68.6%
Brian Gibson (R)	78,543	31.4%

2008 PRIMARY

Jane Harman (D)	unopposed

2006 GENERAL

Jane Harman (D)	105,323	63.4%
Brian Gibson (R)	53,068	31.9%
James R. Smith (PFP)	4,592	2.8%
Mike Binkley (LIBERT)	3,170	1.9%

PREVIOUS WINNING PERCENTAGES
2004 (62%); 2002 (61%); 2000 (48%); 1996 (52%);
1994 (48%); 1992 (48%)

Elected 1992; 8th term
Did not serve 1999-2001

Harman is relentlessly energetic and ambitious, overcoming disappointments to establish an influential position for herself in the House. She would prefer to lead the Select Intelligence Committee, a post Democratic leaders once denied her, but has carved out a niche to flex her expertise on spying and other issues on the Homeland Security Committee.

She is serving her second stint in the House; she opted against re-election to run for governor in 1998, losing the primary to Gray Davis, who went on to win. She returned to Congress two years later, and when Democrats recaptured the majority in 2006, she openly expressed her eagerness to head the Intelligence panel. But Speaker-to-be Nancy Pelosi took her off the panel. Pelosi said she removed Harman because of term limits, but she privately viewed her as too close to the Bush administration and too hawkish on defense.

Harman did get the chairmanship of the Homeland Security Committee's intelligence panel. She has a strong interest in improving communications systems for police, firefighters and other emergency responders. And in early 2009 she took a step toward meeting President Obama's interests and introduced the Democrats' version of a bill calling for closure of the U.S. detention center at Guantánamo Bay, Cuba, within one year. Harman said the legislation would "begin a long-needed course correction in U.S. interrogation policies."

In 2009, the House passed her bill aimed at cracking down on what she considers the "overclassification" of information by federal agencies. It was identical to a bill the House passed in July 2008 but which the Senate didn't take up. The Senate in 2008 also didn't act on a similar bill by Harman, passed by the House, aimed at encouraging the flow of unclassified information to state and local law enforcement authorities, first-responders and the public.

In 2007, she pushed through a bill designed to help local authorities deter "homegrown" terrorism by investigating the roots of radicalism. She also was a leading voice during debate on the extension of the Foreign Intelligence Surveillance Act governing electronic spying. In August 2007, she opposed a six-month expansion of the White House's warrantless wiretapping program. After its enactment, Harman said the administration had spurred lawmakers to rush the bill with a "bogus claim" there had been increased "chatter" about a possible imminent terrorist attack on Washington. She ultimately joined 104 of her fellow Democrats in supporting the final version, enacted in July 2008.

She was an early advocate of the Homeland Security Department's creation, stemming from her service on the 10-member, congressionally mandated National Commission on Terrorism, which she joined after losing the primary for governor. She helped write the commission's report warning the threat to the U.S. was increasing and "today's terrorists seek to inflict mass casualties." It was released a little over a year before the Sept. 11 terrorist attacks.

Harman also sits on the Energy and Commerce panel, where she focuses on entertainment and broadcast issues important to her suburban Los Angeles district, as well as energy independence and global warming. As part of a massive energy package in 2007, the House included language by Harman to ban 100-watt incandescent light bulbs nationwide by 2012.

Before her party's takeover of the House, Harman was the top Democrat on Intelligence. She had pursued the Intelligence chairmanship so doggedly she drew the attention of federal investigators. Time magazine reported the FBI looked into whether the American Israel Public Affairs Committee lobbied House leaders to keep her as top-ranking Democrat in exchange for the promise of favors from Harman. She dismissed the allegations as "irresponsible, laughable and scurrilous," and officials found no evidence of wrongdoing.

From her seat on Intelligence, she helped guide the 2004 enactment of a major reorganization of spy agencies in line with recommendations of the commission that investigated the Sept. 11 attacks. She was also one of the few members of Congress who knew about secret CIA interrogation videotapes of top al Qaeda suspects in 2003. In early 2008, she revealed her declassified 2003 letter urging the CIA to reconsider destroying the tapes. The agency didn't heed her warning.

During a visit to a Veterans Administration health care center in West Los Angeles in early 2008, she was stunned by the high percentage of female veterans who said they were victims of sexual assault and rape during their military service. She sponsored a resolution calling on the Defense secretary to develop a strategy to end assault and rape in the military, but it didn't move.

Harman appeals to the swing voters in her district with moderate fiscal stands and liberal social views, including unflagging support for abortion rights. She is among the wealthiest members of Congress, with a net worth of at least $236 million in 2007, according to the Center for Responsive Politics. In 2008, her second husband, Sidney Harman, retired as chairman of Harman International Industries, a multibillion-dollar manufacturer of high-end sound equipment he founded in 1953. The couple is a fixture on Washington's social and philanthropic circuits.

Harman is a disciplined runner and athlete. Her passion for politics was sparked in 1960, when she was a volunteer usher at the Democratic National Convention and met Eleanor Roosevelt. She had considered following her father's path as a doctor, but instead studied government at Smith College. She obtained a law degree from Harvard, and worked for Democratic Sen. John V. Tunney of California and the Senate Judiciary Committee. In 1977, she worked in the Carter White House, then served as a special counsel at the Pentagon.

In 1991, she and her husband returned to California and settled in the 36th District, where incumbent Rep. Democrat Mel Levine had decided to run for the Senate. The opposition pegged Harman as a carpetbagger and opportunist, but she made an issue of GOP candidate Joan Milke Flores' anti-abortion stance. She spent heavily and won by 6 percentage points.

Harman's re-elections in 1994 and 1996 were hard-fought affairs. After losing the gubernatorial race in 1998, Democrats pleaded with her to run for her old seat, then held by Republican Steven T. Kuykendall. She won a five-way race with 48 percent of the vote. Remapping before the 2002 election gave the district a heavier Democratic tilt, and Harman has won handily since. She took 69 percent of the vote in 2008.

KEY VOTES

2008
Yes	Delay consideration of Colombia free-trade agreement
No	Override Bush veto of federal farm and nutrition programs reauthorization bill
Yes	Overhaul surveillance laws and permit dismissal of suits against companies that conducted warrantless wiretapping
Yes	Grant mortgage relief to homeowners and funding for Fannie Mae and Freddie Mac
Yes	Approve initial $700 billion program to stabilize financial markets
Yes	Approve final $700 billion program to stabilize financial markets
Yes	Provide $14 billion in loans to automakers

2007
Yes	Increase minimum wage by $2.10 an hour
Yes	Approve $124.2 billion in emergency war spending and set goal for redeployment of troops from Iraq
No	Reject federal contraceptive assistance to international family planning groups
Yes	Override Bush veto of $23.2 billion water projects authorization bill
Yes	Implement Peru free-trade agreement
Yes	Approve energy policy overhaul with new fuel economy standards
No	Clear $473.5 billion omnibus spending bill, including $70 billion for military operations

CQ VOTE STUDIES

	PARTY UNITY		PRESIDENTIAL SUPPORT	
	SUPPORT	OPPOSE	SUPPORT	OPPOSE
2008	98%	2%	18%	82%
2007	95%	5%	4%	96%
2006	91%	9%	25%	75%
2005	90%	10%	26%	74%
2004	91%	9%	34%	66%

INTEREST GROUPS

	AFL-CIO	ADA	CCUS	ACU
2008	100%	95%	65%	0%
2007	95%	95%	56%	0%
2006	93%	90%	40%	12%
2005	82%	75%	58%	5%
2004	87%	95%	55%	13%

CALIFORNIA 36

Southwest Los Angeles County – Torrance, Redondo Beach, part of Los Angeles

The 36th is home to some of Los Angeles' most famous beaches and biggest aerospace firms. The district begins in the Venice area of the city, then runs along the Pacific coast south through El Segundo to Manhattan, Hermosa and Redondo beaches before hitting Torrance. It then skirts inland, picking up parts of the Wilmington and San Pedro neighborhoods.

Torrance, the district's largest whole city, is dotted with oil wells and derricks. The ExxonMobil refinery in the north end of the city, along with Chevron in El Segundo, help fuel southern California. Torrance is also home to the sales headquarters of several major automakers, and its Del Amo Fashion Center is one of the largest malls in the country.

Despite an economic downturn affecting retail, the auto industry, construction and manufacturing, the aerospace firms in Torrance and El Segundo continue to drive the local economy. The district has some of the state's most-educated residents, and many firms converted some jobs to non-defense projects in order to diversify the economy. The posh, white-collar areas of the district are not immune to rising unemployment and home foreclosure rates.

Torrance is split politically: It is wealthier toward the coast, but inland sections include middle and working class areas that have conservative and labor-heavy pockets. Venice's eclectic beaches are considered the state's most liberal havens outside of Berkeley, while Manhattan Beach and Marina del Rey are ritzier. Overall, the 36th is trending more Democratic and gave Barack Obama 64 percent of its 2008 presidential vote.

MAJOR INDUSTRY
Aerospace, technology, manufacturing

MILITARY BASES
Los Angeles Air Force Base, 1,575 military, 1,152 civilian (2009)

CITIES
Los Angeles (pt.), 295,807; Torrance, 137,946; Redondo Beach, 63,261; Manhattan Beach, 33,852

NOTABLE
The Hyperion sewage treatment plant in Playa del Rey, the former focus of a lengthy lawsuit, is now one of the cleanest plants in the region.

Rep. Laura Richardson (D)

Elected August 2007; 1st full term

CAPITOL OFFICE
225-7924
richardson.house.gov
1725 Longworth Bldg. 20515-0537; fax 225-7926

COMMITTEES
Homeland Security
Transportation & Infrastructure

RESIDENCE
Long Beach

BORN
April 14, 1962; Los Angeles, Calif.

RELIGION
Christian non-denominational

FAMILY
Divorced

EDUCATION
U. of California, Santa Barbara, attended
1980-81; U. of California, Los Angeles, B.A.
1984 (political science); U. of Southern
California, M.B.A. 1996

CAREER
Lieutenant gubernatorial aide; congressional
district aide; document management company
marketing director; customized clothing company
owner; teacher

POLITICAL HIGHLIGHTS
Sought Democratic nomination for Calif.
Assembly, 1996; Long Beach City Council,
2000-2006; Calif. Assembly, 2006-07

ELECTION RESULTS

2008 GENERAL

Laura Richardson (D)	131,342	74.9%
Nicholas "Nick" Dibs (I)	42,774	24.4%

2008 PRIMARY

Laura Richardson (D)	25,713	74.4%
Peter Mathews (D)	5,860	17.0%
Lee Davis (D)	2,983	8.6%

2007 SPECIAL RUNOFF

Laura Richardson (D)	15,559	67.0%
John M. Kanaley (R)	5,837	25.1%
Daniel Abraham Brezenoff (GREEN)	1,274	5.5%
Herb Peters (LIBERT)	538	2.3%

Richardson is a former business owner with a background in local and state government who seeks to shore up her working-class district's ports and roads — as well as her political image. She endured a rocky first term in which revelations about her financial problems overshadowed her legislative work, though they did not hinder her re-election.

Richardson's difficulties began with news stories in May 2008 about her losing her Sacramento home to foreclosure. The property was sold at auction, but the action was reversed after Richardson said she hadn't received proper notice. Subsequent articles said Richardson defaulted on loans on two other California homes and owed $9,000 in property taxes. And the Long Beach Press-Telegram reported she failed to pay a mechanic for hundreds of dollars in car repairs and then abandoned the car at another shop — while leasing the most expensive car among House members, at taxpayer expense.

Richardson found herself fending off criticism from watchdog groups as well as Republicans. But House Democratic leaders rallied to her side; Majority Leader Steny H. Hoyer held a June fundraiser for her. In November, she told the Press-Telegram that she paid up the delinquent loans, lowered her car lease and took responsibility for "personal mistakes" she had made. "What I didn't do is take care of myself and take care of my issues," she told the newspaper.

Though she is a member of the centrist New Democrat Coalition, Richardson's voting record is in the liberal mold of her predecessor and mentor, Democrat Juanita Millender-McDonald, who died of cancer in April 2007. Millender-McDonald was a powerful presence in the House and a strong advocate on a wide range of issues. She was Richardson's former boss and helped her launch a political career of her own in local office and the California Assembly. Richardson shares her support of social programs, having been raised by a single mother dependent on government assistance.

One of Richardson's first legislative successes was a bill in July 2008 — subsequently signed into law — to designate a portion of California State Route 91 in Los Angeles in Millender-McDonald's honor. "She left us way too soon, and I'll work as hard as I can to keep her name in a positive light," Richardson said.

Like her predecessor, Richardson was granted a seat on the Transportation and Infrastructure Committee. Road issues are a primary concern in the 37th, which borders two large seaports and includes major highways that carry cargo inland. Richardson will seek her share of money in a five-year reauthorization of surface transportation programs to come up in the 111th Congress (2009-10). She worked on the issue as a Long Beach City Council member, initiating the planning process for a transportation program for senior citizens.

She introduced a bill in October 2008 to have cargo interests pay a national container fee, with money used to improve freight transportation, protect shipped goods more carefully and lessen the environmental harm caused by freight transportation. It did not make it out of committee.

Richardson also is involved in cargo issues as a member of the Homeland Security Committee, which she joined in 2009 after unsuccessfully vying for a slot on the Ways and Means Committee. At a February 2009 hearing, she urged new Homeland Security Secretary Janet Napolitano to focus special attention on protecting her area's ports because they are so busy. "We really need the commitment that the view is going to be, not everything around the Christmas tree [has] national significance," she said.

Richardson said her path toward politics was set at a young age. A child of an African-American father and Caucasian mother, she recalls asking her divorced mother as a child why strangers threw eggs at their car and cursed at them while they shopped at stores. "My mother tried to explain all those things to me, but eventually she just said to me, 'You should be a person who makes better laws,' " she said. "And that's what got me since the age of about 6 ... wanting to be a public servant."

Richardson was able to attend the University of California, Santa Barbara — where she earned a spot on the basketball team — thanks to California's Educational Opportunity Program, which is designed to improve access for and retention of historically low-income and educationally disadvantaged students. She eventually transferred to UCLA, earning a political science degree.

Over the next 15 years, she dabbled in a range of professions — as a marketing manager for Xerox, owner of a T-shirt design company and a teacher. She then worked as a field deputy for Millender-McDonald. While working for Democratic Lt. Gov. Cruz Bustamante, she entered her first successful political race in 2000 — a seat on the Long Beach City Council — and defeated Dee Andrews, a well-known local sports hero, by a six-vote margin.

Six years later Richardson was elected to the state Assembly, but within a year decided to run for Congress to succeed Millender-McDonald. She was one of three front-runners, along with her predecessor's daughter, Valerie McDonald, in a contest that received national attention for its political competitiveness and racial divisiveness. Running in an all-party ballot in June 2007, Richardson prevailed with 37 percent of the vote, but it was not enough to avoid a runoff.

But her first place finish was tantamount to victory in the strongly Democratic district and she told a crowd of supporters she hoped to be a facilitator in building racial harmony in her diverse district. "There is no longer one color, one perspective, one issue," she said. "There are many." She had little trouble in the runoff, easily winning with just over two-thirds of the vote.

The publicity about Richardson's foreclosure came on the eve of the 2008 Democratic primary, but Richardson trounced college professor Peter Mathews and community newspaper publisher Lee Davis with 74 percent of the vote. As more news emerged about her finances, Mathews and Davis both decided to run as write-in candidates in the general. She also faced an Independent Party candidate, teacher Nicholas Dibs. But Richardson again cruised to victory with 75 percent of the vote.

KEY VOTES

2008
Yes Delay consideration of Colombia free-trade agreement
Yes Override Bush veto of federal farm and nutrition programs reauthorization bill
Yes Overhaul surveillance laws and permit dismissal of suits against companies that conducted warrantless wiretapping
Yes Grant mortgage relief to homeowners and funding for Fannie Mae and Freddie Mac
Yes Approve initial $700 billion program to stabilize financial markets
Yes Approve final $700 billion program to stabilize financial markets
Yes Provide $14 billion in loans to automakers

2007
Yes Override Bush veto of $23.2 billion water projects authorization bill
No   Implement Peru free-trade agreement
Yes Approve energy policy overhaul with new fuel economy standards
No   Clear $473.5 billion omnibus spending bill, including $70 billion for military operations

CQ VOTE STUDIES

	PARTY UNITY		PRESIDENTIAL SUPPORT	
	SUPPORT	OPPOSE	SUPPORT	OPPOSE
2008	99%	1%	16%	84%
2007	99%	1%	7%	93%

INTEREST GROUPS

	AFL-CIO	ADA	CCUS	ACU
2008	100%	100%	59%	0%
2007	100%	—	67%	0%

CALIFORNIA 37
Southern Los Angeles County — most of Long Beach, Compton, Carson

The 37th combines some of the state's poorest and most Democratic areas with a large chunk of middle class Long Beach. Minorities make up almost 85 percent of the population, with Hispanics as the dominant group, totaling 43 percent of residents. The district is one-fourth black and more than one-tenth Asian.

The district contains a sliver of Los Angeles, as well as the lower and middle class suburbs of Compton and Carson to the south. These communities boost Democratic presidential candidates to high margins of victory in the 37th: in 2008, Compton gave Barack Obama 95 percent — his highest margin in Los Angeles County — and Carson gave 76 percent.

Compton has a multiracial and ethnic population, and its poverty, crime rate and ongoing gang activity often lead it to be labeled as an "inner-city" community. But, commercial and residential development in areas previously thought undevelopable, along with police action, has propped up the economy and brought down notoriously high murder rates. Factories, refineries and other industrial sites occupy a large portion of Carson.

The non-coastal portion of Long Beach (the port is in the 46th) contains a more suburban, politically mixed community, and dozens of languages are spoken in local schools. The area has grown with the development of high-tech and aerospace industries, although Boeing's C-17 jet facility remains slated for closure in 2010 and the city struggles with investment and budget shortfalls. The multibillion-dollar Alameda Corridor project, which runs through the district linking the ports of Long Beach and Los Angeles to the south with distribution areas in Los Angeles to the north, created construction jobs. But, port activity has slowed and the economic boost expected from transportation and warehousing jobs is uncertain.

MAJOR INDUSTRY
Service, manufacturing, oil

CITIES
Long Beach (pt.), 368,591; Compton, 93,493; Carson, 89,730; Los Angeles (pt.), 33,808

NOTABLE
The Home Depot Center's multi-use sports complex in Carson is home to soccer's Chivas USA and LA Galaxy.

Rep. Grace F. Napolitano (D)

Elected 1998; 6th term

CAPITOL OFFICE
225-5256
www.napolitano.house.gov
1610 Longworth Bldg. 20515-0538; fax 225-0027

COMMITTEES
Natural Resources
  (Water & Power - chairwoman)
Transportation & Infrastructure

RESIDENCE
Norwalk

BORN
Dec. 4, 1936; Brownsville, Texas

RELIGION
Roman Catholic

FAMILY
Husband, Frank Napolitano; five children

EDUCATION
Brownsville H.S., graduated 1954

CAREER
Regional transportation claims agent

POLITICAL HIGHLIGHTS
Norwalk City Council, 1986-92 (mayor, 1989-90);
Calif. Assembly, 1992-98

ELECTION RESULTS

2008 GENERAL

Grace F. Napolitano (D)	130,211	81.7%
Christopher M. Agrella (LIBERT)	29,113	18.3%

2008 PRIMARY

Grace F. Napolitano (D)	unopposed

2006 GENERAL

Grace F. Napolitano (D)	75,181	75.3%
Sidney W. Street (R)	24,620	24.7%

PREVIOUS WINNING PERCENTAGES
2004 (100%); 2002 (71%); 2000 (71%); 1998 (68%)

Napolitano's solicitous image, enhanced by her silvery hair and fondness for talking about her family — five grown children, 14 grandchildren and one great-grandson — can be deceptive. She can be a fierce political fighter who is protective of the interests of her mostly Hispanic constituents.

Though a solidly Democratic vote, Napolitano doesn't hesitate to make her displeasure known when she sees fit. She blasted a $700 billion financial rescue law in fall 2008, ignoring pleas from her party leadership and insisting Wall Street be held accountable. "We already bailed out several other entities," she said. "Who's next? At the taxpayers' expense? I don't think so."

An avid supporter of New York Sen. Hillary Rodham Clinton's 2008 presidential bid, Napolitano stood by her during the Democratic convention. She was given a speaking role at the Denver convention, during which she proclaimed in Spanish, "¡Votemos por Obama para presidente!" But she admitted later that during the convention's roll call, she cast her ballot for Clinton. She did subsequently campaign for Barack Obama, helping him court Latino voters who overwhelmingly supported Clinton during the primary elections.

The daughter of a Mexican immigrant who raised her two children on a shoestring budget, Napolitano has cultivated a strong connection to her mother's homeland. A former chair of the Congressional Hispanic Caucus, Napolitano expressed her disappointment to party leaders in 2006 that Democrats did not include immigration in their "Six for '06" campaign platform.

As a result, Speaker Nancy Pelosi asked Napolitano to help craft a comprehensive immigration overhaul package in 2007. And later that year, Napolitano and others met with President George W. Bush to promote their bill to create a guest worker program to help immigrants find legal employment in the United States and to provide a pathway for undocumented immigrants to gain legal status. She remains hopeful Congress can someday comprehensively overhaul the immigration system, paying special attention to poverty, the lack of opportunity south of the border and long processing times for legal immigrants.

Napolitano is chairwoman of the Natural Resources Subcommittee on Water and Power. She touts the bipartisanship of her panel, saying it passed 46 bills through the House during the 110th Congress (2007-08) — 28 sponsored by Republicans, 18 by Democrats. She worked closely with California Republican David Dreier to pass legislation in 2007 authorizing an additional $11.2 million for groundwater cleanup in the San Gabriel Basin — an important piece of Southern California's strategy to generate its own clean water supply and ease dependence upon the Colorado River or the San Francisco Bay and Delta.

From her seat on the Transportation and Infrastructure Committee, Napolitano helped push through the House a railroad safety bill she wrote in response to five derailments that had occurred in or near her district. The language was signed into law in October 2008. Napolitano says constituent service is her main driver in Congress. She often calls constituents back personally to answer their requests. "You will never — hardly ever — see me write a letter. I'll pick up the phone," she said. "This is ... the way I represent my district, the way I know my district responds."

Napolitano has a passion for mental health issues that stems from her work on the Norwalk City Council in the 1980s, when hospitals in her area started closing and sending mentally ill patients out on the streets. She co-chairs the

Congressional Mental Health Caucus and has focused particularly on the special needs of children. In 2008, Napolitano secured a $390,000 funding set-aside for a school-based counseling program for her district that assists more than 100 students. Napolitano said several of her House colleagues have requested her help in launching similar programs in their districts.

During a national radio address in 2008, Napolitano — in Spanish — praised passage of legislation that ensures mental health receives the same insurance coverage as other medical illnesses, such as diabetes, asthma or high blood pressure.

Napolitano also has worked to help Iraq War veterans suffering from post-traumatic stress disorder (PTSD). She has gathered several articles on the psychological problems suffered by veterans and given them to John P. Murtha, D-Pa., chairman of the Defense Appropriations Subcommittee. "Every time I'd get an article, I'd go down to John Murtha and I'd give John a copy of that. Then he says, 'Well, Grace, I don't know, maybe I'll start looking.' Two years later, he says, 'I'm putting $400 million in PTSD.'"

Napolitano married at age 18 and had five children by age 23. She caught the political bug as a volunteer in Norwalk's efforts to cultivate a sister-city relationship with Hermosillo, Mexico. She says she joined the effort to show her children and "other youngsters on this side how lucky they were" compared with Mexican children.

She launched her first political campaign, for city council, with $35,000 she borrowed against her home and won by just 28 votes. She served six years, two of them as mayor, before moving up to the state legislature for six years.

In 1998, she ran for the House seat of retiring Democrat Rep. Esteban E. Torres, challenging his hand-picked successor — who was also his son-in-law — for the Democratic nomination. She won the primary by just 618 votes, but sailed to victory in the general election and has easily won re-election ever since.

She drew some unfavorable scrutiny in 2009 when Bloomberg News revealed she had pocketed more than $200,000 in interest over the years on a $150,000 loan she had made to her initial 1998 campaign from money she had withdrawn from a retirement fund — and she still hadn't paid off the loan. The debt, according to Bloomberg, was the biggest asset listed on Napolitano's personal financial disclosure forms.

In Washington, she has tried to win political supporters much the same way she and her second husband, Frank, won customers to their Italian restaurant — through their stomachs. She makes tacos, guacamole and other dishes for her staff and caters her own fundraisers.

KEY VOTES

2008

Yes Delay consideration of Colombia free-trade agreement

Yes Override Bush veto of federal farm and nutrition programs reauthorization bill

No Overhaul surveillance laws and permit dismissal of suits against companies that conducted warrantless wiretapping

Yes Grant mortgage relief to homeowners and funding for Fannie Mae and Freddie Mac

No Approve initial $700 billion program to stabilize financial markets

No Approve final $700 billion program to stabilize financial markets

Yes Provide $14 billion in loans to automakers

2007

Yes Increase minimum wage by $2.10 an hour

Yes Approve $124.2 billion in emergency war spending and set goal for redeployment of troops from Iraq

No Reject federal contraceptive assistance to international family planning groups

Yes Override Bush veto of $23.2 billion water projects authorization bill

No Implement Peru free-trade agreement

Yes Approve energy policy overhaul with new fuel economy standards

No Clear $473.5 billion omnibus spending bill, including $70 billion for military operations

CQ VOTE STUDIES

	PARTY UNITY		PRESIDENTIAL SUPPORT	
	SUPPORT	OPPOSE	SUPPORT	OPPOSE
2008	99%	1%	10%	90%
2007	99%	1%	3%	97%
2006	98%	2%	21%	79%
2005	98%	2%	14%	86%
2004	98%	2%	21%	79%

INTEREST GROUPS

	AFL-CIO	ADA	CCUS	ACU
2008	100%	95%	44%	8%
2007	96%	100%	45%	0%
2006	100%	100%	33%	8%
2005	100%	100%	35%	0%
2004	100%	95%	33%	0%

CALIFORNIA 38
East Los Angeles County — Pomona, Norwalk

The Democratic 38th is a growing middle- and working-class Hispanic-majority district. A sideways "L" shape, the district takes in the city of Norwalk in southeastern Los Angeles County, then stretches north along Interstate 5 to include nearly half of East Los Angeles. It then runs east through Montebello, Pico Rivera and La Puente, before extending a thin arm parallel to the California 60 freeway into the Inland Valley to take in Pomona, the district's largest city, at the county's eastern edge.

The 38th relies on the many small businesses in the district, which includes the East Los Angeles business district. Economic downturns have hurt local retail operations, many of which are owned and operated by Hispanics. Unemployment-rate spikes in the city of Industry, an almost entirely industrial area with no business tax, have hit the few thousand businesses that the city claims once provided more than 80,000 jobs. Like the many commuter towns around Industry, Norwalk is a bedroom community. The city received a publicity boost in 2006 when the multi-agency Joint Regional Intelligence Center opened.

Although it has a large blue-collar workforce, the district contains some affluent and conservative areas such as Hacienda Heights, Rowland Heights (shared with the 42nd) and a narrow sliver of Whittier. Montebello is a middle-class Hispanic area with an Armenian community. Southeast Pomona is densely populated and has experienced some crime problems in recent years. Efforts to revitalize the city's dilapidated downtown are ongoing.

The 38th's working-class residents ensure that the district votes reliably Democratic. Barack Obama received 71 percent of the vote here in 2008 presidential election. California State Polytechnic University, Pomona, and Cerritos College (shared with the 39th) add students to the Democratic mix.

MAJOR INDUSTRY
Manufacturing, oil

CITIES
Pomona, 149,473; Norwalk, 103,298; Pico Rivera, 63,428; Montebello, 62,150; East Los Angeles (unincorporated) (pt.), 53,349

NOTABLE
The Pomona Swap Meet and Car Show is billed as the largest collection of antique cars, parts and accessories on the West Coast.

Rep. Linda T. Sánchez (D)

Elected 2002; 4th term

CAPITOL OFFICE
225-6676
www.lindasanchez.house.gov
1222 Longworth Bldg. 20515-0539; fax 226-1012

COMMITTEES
Judiciary
Ways & Means

RESIDENCE
Lakewood

BORN
Jan. 28, 1969; Orange, Calif.

RELIGION
Roman Catholic

FAMILY
Husband, Jim Sullivan; one child

EDUCATION
U. of California, Berkeley, B.A. 1991 (Spanish literature); U. of California, Los Angeles, J.D. 1995

CAREER
Union official; campaign aide; lawyer

POLITICAL HIGHLIGHTS
No previous office

ELECTION RESULTS

2008 GENERAL

Linda T. Sánchez (D)	125,289	69.7%
Diane A. Lenning (R)	54,533	30.3%

2008 PRIMARY

Linda T. Sánchez (D)	unopposed

2006 GENERAL

Linda T. Sánchez (D)	72,149	65.9%
James L. Andion (R)	37,384	34.1%

PREVIOUS WINNING PERCENTAGES
2004 (61%); 2002 (55%)

Sánchez is a funny yet fiercely committed liberal who has begun to emerge from the shadow of her older sister Loretta, who blazed her way into the House six years ahead of her. A former labor union official, the younger Sánchez puts workers and their families at the center of her chief legislative interests.

She has a prominent forum from which to articulate her views as a member of the powerful Ways and Means Committee, which has jurisdiction over tax, trade and health care policy. She is the first Hispanic woman to serve on the panel.

Sánchez opposed free-trade agreements during President George W. Bush's administration, arguing they failed to protect workers' rights. And she wants to expand health care coverage for the uninsured. "No family should have to forego needed health care because of money," she said in September 2008. "Health care should not be a privilege to be reserved for the wealthy few."

Sánchez also continues to serve on the Judiciary Committee, where she also was the first Hispanic female, though she had to relinquish the gavel of the Subcommittee on Commercial and Administrative Law that she chaired in the 110th Congress (2007-08). From that panel, she conducted a high-profile investigation into the Justice Department's 2006 politically motivated firings of nine U.S. attorneys. "I simply cannot overstate how dangerous a threat this is," she said at a May 2007 hearing on the firings. "Partisanship in our justice system is a cancer; it threatens our very democracy and system of laws."

In addition to her work on Judiciary, which she joined in part to tackle immigration issues, Sánchez devoted considerable effort in the 110th Congress to education. She won inclusion of provisions on bullying and gang prevention in a draft rewrite of the No Child Left Behind Act governing elementary and secondary education. Although the legislation did not make it through Congress, she will again press her concerns in 2009.

Before coming to the House, Sánchez practiced civil rights and labor law; her sister, Loretta, was a businesswoman with an MBA. The sisters spell their last name differently: Linda uses an accent, and Loretta does not. (They pronounce it the same way: SAN-chez.)

Although their voting records are similar, Sánchez was an enthusiastic supporter of Barack Obama in the 2008 Democratic presidential primaries; her sister was a Hillary Rodham Clinton loyalist. Their personal styles are different, too. Linda is a night owl, while Loretta is an early riser. Linda is messy, Loretta neat.

In addition, Linda is funnier than her big sister. "I grew up in a family of seven, and my brothers teased me unmercifully, so I learned to be quick with a comeback," she said. A hit at charity fundraisers, she has a stand-up comedy routine that in 2006 won her the title of "Funniest Celebrity in Washington, D.C." But Connecticut Democratic Rep. John B. Larson, a friend, described her to The New York Times as "a sensitive soul who carries her heart on her sleeve."

For all their differences, the sisters are fiercely loyal to each other. When Loretta Sanchez quit the Congressional Hispanic Caucus in 2007, charging that its chairman, Democrat Joe Baca of California, had been demeaning to women, Linda swiftly did likewise. Linda returned to the caucus in early 2009 when Nydia M. Velázquez of New York became the chairwoman. The sisters also co-authored two books, including "Dream in Color: How the Sánchez Sisters Are Making History in Congress," a 2008 account of their childhoods that explains how their values and traditions helped them succeed.

Sánchez also made some personal news in November 2008 by announcing she was pregnant. She was not married to the father, Jim Sullivan, a government and public relations consultant, when she made the announcement.

Sánchez's House colleagues got a sense of her views on gender equality when she joined the all-male roster of players in the annual House baseball game between Democrats and Republicans. The back of her shirt bore the Roman numerals IX, for Title IX, shorthand for the landmark 1972 law that mandated equal treatment for women in education programs and led to the dramatic growth of women's sports.

Sánchez had no experience in local or state government before her election in 2002, having worked in the labor movement instead. Her father, Ignacio, was a mechanic at a tire shop, where he met her mother, Maria Macias, who was working in its accounting office. Her mother began organizing for a union and met her father as she sought workers to sign up.

Sánchez often questioned why their traditional Latino family gave males special status. "There was a very clear distinction between what boys could do and what girls could do," she said. "Boys were served first and girls served them. They had a lot more freedom and a lot fewer responsibilities."

Her mother told Sánchez to either accept the way things were or try to change them. She once took Sánchez to hear farm labor organizer Cesar Chavez speak. Sánchez, who had worked her way through college as a nanny, security guard, bilingual teacher's aide and ESL instructor, was inspired by Chavez's words to go back to school for a law degree and get involved in organizing labor. She later became executive secretary-treasurer of the AFL-CIO in Orange County, the county's top union post.

Her political activism started in high school in Anaheim. Upset by her gaffe-prone local congressman, conservative Republican Robert K. Dornan, Sánchez knocked on doors for Democratic challenger Dave Carter. Carter lost, but in 1996, Sánchez was the field organizer for sister Loretta's successful campaign against Dornan.

After the 2000 census, the California Legislature drew a new district south of downtown Los Angeles that favored a Hispanic Democratic candidate. In 2002, incumbent Republican Rep. Steve Horn declined to run for the seat. Sánchez jumped in, winning a six-way primary contest with help from Loretta's fundraising network and vigorous campaigning by her family. She has had no trouble maintaining her grip on the seat.

KEY VOTES

2008

Yes Delay consideration of Colombia free-trade agreement

Yes Override Bush veto of federal farm and nutrition programs reauthorization bill

No Overhaul surveillance laws and permit dismissal of suits against companies that conducted warrantless wiretapping

Yes Grant mortgage relief to homeowners and funding for Fannie Mae and Freddie Mac

No Approve initial $700 billion program to stabilize financial markets

No Approve final $700 billion program to stabilize financial markets

Yes Provide $14 billion in loans to automakers

2007

Yes Increase minimum wage by $2.10 an hour

Yes Approve $124.2 billion in emergency war spending and set goal for redeployment of troops from Iraq

No Reject federal contraceptive assistance to international family planning groups

Yes Override Bush veto of $23.2 billion water projects authorization bill

No Implement Peru free-trade agreement

Yes Approve energy policy overhaul with new fuel economy standards

No Clear $473.5 billion omnibus spending bill, including $70 billion for military operations

CQ VOTE STUDIES

	PARTY UNITY		PRESIDENTIAL SUPPORT	
	SUPPORT	OPPOSE	SUPPORT	OPPOSE
2008	99%	1%	10%	90%
2007	99%	1%	3%	97%
2006	98%	2%	15%	85%
2005	99%	1%	13%	87%
2004	99%	1%	15%	85%

INTEREST GROUPS

	AFL-CIO	ADA	CCUS	ACU
2008	100%	100%	50%	8%
2007	100%	100%	55%	0%
2006	93%	100%	33%	4%
2005	93%	100%	30%	0%
2004	100%	100%	20%	0%

CALIFORNIA 39

Southeast Los Angeles County – South Gate, Lakewood, most of Whittier

The U-shaped 39th starts in South Gate and Lynwood, just south of Los Angeles, before stretching south and east to take in Lakewood and Cerritos, then northeast through La Mirada to South Whittier and Whittier. Despite external similarities — ethnic populations and working class economic bases — most of these communities have little interaction with one another. The district is 61 percent Hispanic.

Whittier (shared mainly with the 42nd) and South Whittier are home to many second- and third-generation Hispanic families, and pockets of wealth exist there. Growing La Mirada and the Asian American-heavy Cerritos are more conservative communities that resemble cities in neighboring, wealthier Orange County — former farm areas now dependent on an array of aerospace and technology jobs. Lakewood is more blue-collar. South Gate, Lynwood and Paramount are heavily working class and include many new immigrants, and those cities voted overwhelmingly for Democrat Barack Obama in the 2008 presidential election.

The district has a strong organized-labor movement. Towns like Whittier and Lakewood have a number of industrial and retail centers, and more residents work in the district or nearby rather than commuting to downtown Los Angeles, Orange County or Long Beach. Whittier, an area once dominated by car dealerships, is feeling the impact of a national decline in auto sales.

Democrats control the 39th, which gave Barack Obama 65 percent of its presidential vote in 2008, but the district is not as strongly Democratic as in most of Los Angeles County. La Mirada supported Republican John McCain, and Obama's 33-percentage-point margin here was his second-closest among the 13 districts contained entirely in the county.

MAJOR INDUSTRY
Manufacturing, aerospace

CITIES
South Gate, 96,375; Lakewood, 79,345; Lynwood, 69,845; Whittier (pt.), 56,918; Paramount, 55,266; South Whittier (unincorporated), 55,193

NOTABLE
Paramount is home to Zamboni, maker of the ice resurfacing machines used at skating and hockey rinks; Cerritos built the nation's first solar-heated city hall in 1978.

Rep. Ed Royce (R)

Elected 1992; 9th term

Royce is an uncompromising conservative dedicated to a concept of limited government and a commitment to international cooperation and free trade. For more than 15 years, he has crusaded against what he views as wasteful spending, including foreign aid to countries he says could better benefit from a free-market system.

Since Democrats took control of Congress, Royce has remained true to his principles; from his seat on the Financial Services Committee he was among the leading GOP critics of Democratic efforts to revive the economy. "If higher government spending led automatically to robust economic growth, we'd be experiencing great economic activity today instead of entering into a recession," he said on a Fox News talk show in October 2008.

Royce opposed President Obama's $787 billion economic stimulus package in early 2009, saying, "Most of the spending in this legislation is social spending, which is of questionable benefit to our economy." Yet he also opposed George W. Bush's 2008 plan to shore up ailing banks with a $700 billion package. Royce, who holds seats on the subcommittees overseeing financial institutions and capital markets, called it "state socialism."

He said he was displeased with the Bush administration's handling of the financial downfall of government-sponsored mortgage companies Fannie Mae and Freddie Mac. In 2003, he introduced a bill that would have assigned a government agency to oversee their lending practices. If that had passed, Royce said, Fannie and Freddie's problems likely would have been averted. In 2008 he voted against a massive housing bill that included a financial lifeline potentially worth hundreds of billions of dollars to the troubled mortgage giants.

That same year, he opposed a $289 billion farm bill and legislation that stopped scheduled cuts in Medicare reimbursements for doctors. He was one of only 28 Republicans to vote, early in 2008, against providing tax rebates to help spur the economy, and one of only 54 in 2007 to vote against overriding Bush's veto of a bill authorizing billions in water resources projects.

Throughout the 1990s, Royce was co-chairman of the Congressional Porkbusters Coalition, which opposes appropriations earmarks — funding set-asides to specific projects in members' districts — and in 2005 was one of just eight House members, all Republicans, to vote against the surface transportation law stuffed with funding for such projects.

Royce said he urged John McCain's advisers to consider conservative Alaska Gov. Sarah Palin as his 2008 running mate before he chose her, telling the Orange County Register he regards Palin as a "proven reformer."

Royce has reached across the aisle, however, joining forces with Democrats seeking improved insurance regulation. Currently, the industry is regulated by the states, creating a patchwork quilt of rules that critics say causes uncertainty for consumers. Big insurers advocate a federal option but have been opposed by smaller companies that do business only in certain states. "We may have caught AIG with a national regulator," said Royce, referring to the huge insurer shored up with billions in taxpayer dollars in 2008.

In January 2009, Royce joined Democrat Melissa Bean of Illinois and five other members in urging Timothy F. Geithner, then under consideration for Treasury secretary, to boost oversight of insurance companies by creating an office within Treasury or assigning the task to a high-level appointee.

Royce is the top Republican on the Foreign Affairs panel on Terrorism, Nonproliferation and Trade, where he focuses on the risk posed by Islamic extremism in Pakistan, a nuclear power and major recipient of U.S. foreign

CAPITOL OFFICE
225-4111
royce.house.gov
2185 Rayburn Bldg. 20515-0540; fax 226-0335

COMMITTEES
Financial Services
Foreign Affairs

RESIDENCE
Fullerton

BORN
Oct. 12, 1951; Los Angeles, Calif.

RELIGION
Roman Catholic

FAMILY
Wife, Marie Royce

EDUCATION
California State U., Fullerton, B.A. 1977
(accounting & finance)

CAREER
Tax manager

POLITICAL HIGHLIGHTS
Calif. Senate, 1982-92

ELECTION RESULTS

2008 GENERAL

Ed Royce (R)	144,923	62.5%
Christina Avalos (D)	86,772	37.4%

2008 PRIMARY

Ed Royce (R)	unopposed

2006 GENERAL

Ed Royce (R)	100,995	66.8%
Florice Orea Hoffman (D)	46,418	30.7%
Philip H. Inman (LIBERT)	3,876	2.6%

PREVIOUS WINNING PERCENTAGES
2004 (68%); 2002 (68%); 2000 (63%); 1998 (63%); 1996 (63%); 1994 (66%); 1992 (57%)

aid. Royce would make that aid conditional on steps taken by the Pakistani government to crack down on terrorism.

Royce also is co-chairman of the Caucus on India with Democrat Jim McDermott of Washington. He takes pride in Congress' approval in 2008 of a trade deal permitting the sale of civilian nuclear materials to India; he had led the successful 2006 effort to pass legislation permitting the president to complete negotiations on the treaty.

Royce supports stepped-up border enforcement on immigration, and backed construction of a 700-mile fence along the border of Mexico. He advocates legislation to impose sanctions on employers who hire illegal immigrants.

Royce also has been a leading voice on Africa policy, having chaired the panel on Africa from 1997 to 2005 and fought for economic liberalization and free trade. His victories included a 2004 law authorizing $18.6 million to promote eco-tourism along the Congo River basin and a 2000 law reducing tariffs and quotas on imports from sub-Saharan Africa.

Royce grew up in a blue-collar Democratic household but developed a conservative economic viewpoint early. In high school, he became intrigued by the free-market message in Henry Hazlitt's book "Economics in One Lesson." The author challenged prevailing economic thinking that gave the government a central role. That spurred Royce to read similar books. At California State University in Fullerton, Royce joined the College Republicans.

Royce spent 10 years in the California Senate, where he was the guiding force behind a 1990 ballot proposition, approved by voters, setting forth rights for crime victims. He also wrote the nation's first law making it a felony to stalk or threaten someone with injury. In Washington, he won enactment of a similar bill, signed into law in 1996, that made it a crime to cross state lines with the intent to stalk or harass. In 1999, he helped win enactment of a bill expanding the definition of stalking. In subsequent years, he introduced a victim's rights amendment to the Constitution.

He jumped at the chance to run for the House in 1992 when iconoclastic Republican William E. Dannemeyer decided to run for the Senate. He drew no primary opposition and his Democratic opponent, Molly McClanahan, proved too liberal for Orange County. He won by almost 20 percentage points.

In redistricting after the 2000 census, the Los Angeles County portion of Royce's old 39th District was removed and the district was renumbered the 40th. Regardless of the remapping, Royce continues to win with ease. In February 2009, he was among 10 House incumbents with the most cash on hand — recording nearly $2.2 million in campaign funds, according to a CQ MoneyLine study of campaign reports.

KEY VOTES

2008

No	Delay consideration of Colombia free-trade agreement
No	Override Bush veto of federal farm and nutrition programs reauthorization bill
Yes	Overhaul surveillance laws and permit dismissal of suits against companies that conducted warrantless wiretapping
No	Grant mortgage relief to homeowners and funding for Fannie Mae and Freddie Mac
No	Approve initial $700 billion program to stabilize financial markets
No	Approve final $700 billion program to stabilize financial markets
No	Provide $14 billion in loans to automakers

2007

No	Increase minimum wage by $2.10 an hour
No	Approve $124.2 billion in emergency war spending and set goal for redeployment of troops from Iraq
Yes	Reject federal contraceptive assistance to international family planning groups
No	Override Bush veto of $23.2 billion water projects authorization bill
Yes	Implement Peru free-trade agreement
No	Approve energy policy overhaul with new fuel economy standards
Yes	Clear $473.5 billion omnibus spending bill, including $70 billion for military operations

CQ VOTE STUDIES

	PARTY UNITY		PRESIDENTIAL SUPPORT	
	SUPPORT	OPPOSE	SUPPORT	OPPOSE
2008	99%	1%	82%	18%
2007	97%	3%	90%	10%
2006	94%	6%	93%	7%
2005	97%	3%	89%	11%
2004	94%	6%	82%	18%

INTEREST GROUPS

	AFL-CIO	ADA	CCUS	ACU
2008	0%	0%	83%	100%
2007	8%	0%	70%	100%
2006	7%	5%	100%	96%
2005	0%	0%	77%	96%
2004	20%	15%	90%	96%

CALIFORNIA 40

North central Orange County -- Orange, Fullerton

Like most of Orange County, the 40th is historically wealthy and Republican, although these inland areas are less affluent than the coast, and have trended away from the GOP recently. The district forms a half circle that contains Orange County's northern and western midsize cities. It extends north from Los Alamitos on the Los Angeles County border to take in most of Fullerton before turning southeast to reach Orange and Villa Park. It wraps around Anaheim and Garden Grove, taking in small chunks of each.

Before massive growth a generation ago, Orange County was largely agricultural and blanketed with orange and lemon groves, and many cities were dairy farm communities — there are no longer any orange juice processing plants in the county. Relying heavily on aerospace and defense, the 40th's economy achieved more diversity. Technology firms settled in the district, and, despite economic slowdowns, Knott's Berry Farm amusement park and other venues in Buena Park still lure tourists.

Fullerton is home to a Raytheon facility and a Kimberly-Clark paper mill,

as well as a California State University campus that is one of the city's major employers. Adams Rite Aerospace in Fullerton makes airplane cockpit security doors, which Congress mandated after the Sept. 11 terrorist attacks. Orange is a health care center, and the district is home to four major hospitals. Cypress is the headquarters of Pacificare Health Systems.

Orange, the solidly suburban district's largest city, and Fullerton are both upper middle class; Stanton is a more blue-collar community. While whites make up about half of the district's population, an influx of wealthier Hispanics and Asians are shifting the 40th's demographics. Republicans tend to dominate local, state and national elections here, but John McCain earned only 51 percent of the district's 2008 presidential vote.

MAJOR INDUSTRY
Aerospace, defense, manufacturing, health care

CITIES
Orange, 128,821; Fullerton (pt.), 108,151; Anaheim (pt.), 87,082; Buena Park, 78,282; Cypress, 46,229; Stanton, 37,403; Placentia (pt.), 37,356

NOTABLE
Fullerton is the center of the influential Orange County punk rock scene.

Rep. Jerry Lewis (R)

Elected 1978; 16th term

A former insurance salesman, Lewis can turn on the charm with his distinguished toothpaste-commercial smile and buoyant personality. But it can disappear in an instant, as Pentagon officials learned when he repeatedly challenged their budgets during the six years he presided over the Defense Appropriations Subcommittee.

Lewis is now the full Appropriations Committee's top-ranking GOP member, a job with limited influence with Democrats in control. During the 110th Congress (2007-08), Democrats bypassed the committee on funding for the war in Iraq and other key legislation, causing Lewis to complain the majority party was denying Republicans a voice and destroying the comity that has defined the spending panel. And as Democrats quickly pushed through large spending packages in early 2009, he voiced concern about them heading down a path with no direction.

The situation was much different for Lewis a few years ago, when his career was at its zenith. He achieved his dream job of Appropriations chairman in 2005 after beating out a more senior Republican, Ralph Regula of Ohio, to succeed C.W. Bill Young of Florida, who relinquished the gavel under party-mandated term limits. House GOP leaders chose Lewis for his track record of raising money for the party and his willingness to let them exert more control over appropriations.

His short tenure was marked by a career accomplishment: He coordinated with the Senate to get every spending bill through Congress in 2005, something appropriators rarely achieve. But that milestone was accompanied by ongoing issues about his personal ethics. News broke in 2006 that the Justice Department was looking into Lewis' relationship with Bill Lowery, a lobbyist and friend who hired several Lewis aides and their relatives while seeking favors in spending bills. Lewis has maintained he has done nothing wrong, and little emerged about the investigation in the years that followed.

His tenure as chairman also ended on a sour note when Republicans decided not to complete work on most spending bills following the 2006 election.

Within his own party, Lewis and his fellow appropriators are viewed warily by conservatives, who contend the growth of earmarks, or funding set-asides for projects in member districts, during the GOP-controlled Congress contributed to the party's loss of power. The Republican Study Committee, a group of the most conservative House members, has pushed to have the party forgo earmarks as part of a return to its small-government roots. Though Lewis has signed onto the idea that the process should be overhauled, he doesn't want it abandoned. He makes no apologies for securing funding that benefits his district, such as a cancer treatment center at Loma Linda University and money to combat the ever-present danger of wildfires. "My intention is to do everything I can to see that Southern California and our district get their share," he told Riverside's Press-Enterprise in January 2009.

In more than two decades on the Appropriations panel, Lewis generally has pushed to limit the growth of government spending. From 1995 to 1999, when he was in charge of the subcommittee that funds housing and veterans' programs, he cut spending more deeply than other "cardinals," as the subcommittee chairmen are known.

He called for caution early in the 111th Congress (2009-10) when the House passed a $410 billion catchall spending measure for fiscal 2009. "Even as the president talks about the need to put our economic house in order, this House continues to spend and spend and spend and spend. Clearly, this Congress

CAPITOL OFFICE
225-5861
www.house.gov/jerrylewis
2112 Rayburn Bldg. 20515-0541; fax 225-6498

COMMITTEES
Appropriations - ranking member

RESIDENCE
Redlands

BORN
Oct. 21, 1934; Seattle, Wash.

RELIGION
Presbyterian

FAMILY
Wife, Arlene Willis; seven children

EDUCATION
U. of California, Los Angeles, B.A. 1956 (government)

CAREER
Insurance executive

POLITICAL HIGHLIGHTS
San Bernardino School Board, 1965-68; Calif. Assembly, 1968-78; Republican nominee for Calif. Senate, 1973

ELECTION RESULTS

2008 GENERAL

Jerry Lewis (R)	159,486	61.6%
Tim Prince (D)	99,214	38.4%

2008 PRIMARY

Jerry Lewis (R)	36,663	82.5%
Eric R. Stone (R)	4,330	9.7%
Pamela Zander (R)	3,455	7.8%

2006 GENERAL

Jerry Lewis (R)	109,761	66.9%
Louie A. Contreras (D)	54,235	33.1%

PREVIOUS WINNING PERCENTAGES
2004 (83%); 2002 (67%); 2000 (80%); 1998 (65%); 1996 (65%); 1994 (71%); 1992 (63%); 1990 (61%); 1988 (70%); 1986 (77%); 1984 (85%); 1982 (68%); 1980 (72%); 1978 (61%)

has lost its way," he said. And when the House considered a multibillion-dollar economic stimulus law, he warned against "creating an untenable situation down the line" through a dramatic increase in government spending. He suggested requiring federal agencies to submit individual spending plans before receiving funds to "ensure that every dollar is spent as intended."

Lewis' relationship with Chairman David R. Obey of Wisconsin is often tense. While Lewis refers to Obey as his friend, they often have trouble communicating, with Lewis sometimes writing letters to get Obey's attention. A Democratic decision during the 110th to bring war funding bills directly to the House floor, bypassing the committee, was a particular sore spot. Lewis said Obey doesn't confer with him enough, and at one point in 2008 resorted to showing up in the lobby of Obey's office hoping for a meeting. "Somebody else walked out, and he couldn't help but see me, so he invited me in," Lewis said.

Later in the year, the entire process broke down over whether to end a moratorium on gas and oil drilling in some areas. At a meeting in June, Lewis used a legislative maneuver to force the panel to bring up the bill funding the Interior Department, which carried the moratorium language. An enraged Obey canceled the markup and all subsequent committee meetings, arguing Lewis' maneuver was dirty pool and that he wasn't going to join Lewis in his "play pen." Lewis countered Obey was putting off work on the Interior bill to deny Republicans a vote on the moratorium and that he was well within his rights to offer an amendment.

In the past, Lewis has called on the Defense Department to modernize more quickly to meet post-Cold War threats to security, even if it means scrapping ongoing projects. In 1999, he waged a losing battle to deny $1.9 billion for the chronically overbudget F-22 jet fighter, designed to fight the Soviet Union. Ultimately, lobbying by the Air Force and the plane's contractors led Congress to approve the money.

Over the years, Lewis tried to move up the leadership ladder but was edged out by conservatives who were more confrontational in dealing with the Democrats. After Republicans took control of the House in 1995, Lewis strained his relations with Democratic appropriators by dutifully enforcing the new GOP leadership's cuts in domestic programs.

Lewis dates his interest in government to a trip he made to Washington in 1955. He left the insurance business to enter GOP politics in the early 1960s, winning a seat on the San Bernardino School Board. After three years there, he won a state Assembly seat that he held for a decade.

Lewis' seat has usually been safe. His San Bernardino County-based district has given him at least 61 percent of the vote in 16 elections, including 2008.

KEY VOTES

2008

No Delay consideration of Colombia free-trade agreement

No Override Bush veto of federal farm and nutrition programs reauthorization bill

Yes Overhaul surveillance laws and permit dismissal of suits against companies that conducted warrantless wiretapping

Yes Grant mortgage relief to homeowners and funding for Fannie Mae and Freddie Mac

Yes Approve initial $700 billion program to stabilize financial markets

Yes Approve final $700 billion program to stabilize financial markets

No Provide $14 billion in loans to automakers

2007

No Increase minimum wage by $2.10 an hour

No Approve $124.2 billion in emergency war spending and set goal for redeployment of troops from Iraq

Yes Reject federal contraceptive assistance to international family planning groups

No Override Bush veto of $23.2 billion water projects authorization bill

Yes Implement Peru free-trade agreement

No Approve energy policy overhaul with new fuel economy standards

Yes Clear $473.5 billion omnibus spending bill, including $70 billion for military operations

CQ VOTE STUDIES

	PARTY UNITY		PRESIDENTIAL SUPPORT	
	SUPPORT	OPPOSE	SUPPORT	OPPOSE
2008	94%	6%	82%	18%
2007	84%	16%	80%	20%
2006	94%	6%	90%	10%
2005	95%	5%	89%	11%
2004	93%	7%	91%	9%

INTEREST GROUPS

	AFL-CIO	ADA	CCUS	ACU
2008	20%	20%	100%	84%
2007	13%	10%	80%	88%
2006	21%	15%	93%	67%
2005	13%	0%	93%	76%
2004	13%	0%	100%	88%

CALIFORNIA 41
Most of San Bernardino County – Redlands

The 41st includes vast desert and mountain stretches and most of the nation's largest county, San Bernardino, although it is home to less than one-third of the massive county's residents. The western quarter of the 41st, where the district's Inland Empire, Victor Valley and Riverside County areas are located, contains the vast majority of its population. As the 41st moves east, development is difficult, as high desert, dry lakes and mountains dominate the landscape to the Arizona and Nevada state lines. Local hospitals, government and the military are major employers.

The district begins in a sliver of northwestern Riverside County, including the San Jacinto Valley, Banning, San Jacinto, Beaumont and Calimesa, before crossing into San Bernardino County to pick up communities south of the San Bernardino Mountains. Redlands, Highland, Yucaipa and part of San Bernardino (shared with the 43rd) are here, and Highland's San Manuel Indian Reservation resort casino is now a key employer.

The 41st has a large population of day laborers, many of whom are Hispanic immigrants. There has been a recent local police force emphasis

on reducing gang-related crime, and an expanded border patrol presence has led to increased deportation efforts in the Inland Empire region.

On the north side of the mountains are the growing Victor Valley cities of Hesperia and Apple Valley, communities that are attractive to Los Angeles and Orange county commuters. The local housing market remains volatile following a nationwide collapse and a rise in the number of foreclosures here.

Republicans enjoy a nearly 11-point edge in voter registration, and the district gave John McCain 54 percent of its 2008 presidential vote.

MAJOR INDUSTRY
Service, manufacturing, military

MILITARY BASES
Marine Corps Air Ground Combat Center, Twentynine Palms, 11,174 military, 1,009 civilian (2007)

CITIES
Redlands, 63,591; Hesperia, 62,582; San Bernardino (pt.), 54,789; Apple Valley, 54,239; Highland, 44,605; Yucaipa, 41,207

NOTABLE
The Mojave National Preserve features the Devils Playground dunes.

Rep. Gary G. Miller (R)

Elected 1998; 6th term

CAPITOL OFFICE
225-3201
www.house.gov/garymiller
2349 Rayburn Bldg. 20515-0542; fax 226-6962

COMMITTEES
Financial Services
Transportation & Infrastructure

RESIDENCE
Diamond Bar

BORN
Oct. 16, 1948; Huntsville, Ark.

RELIGION
Protestant

FAMILY
Wife, Cathy Miller; four children

EDUCATION
Mt. San Antonio Community College,
attended 1968-70

MILITARY SERVICE
Army 1967-68

CAREER
Real estate developer

POLITICAL HIGHLIGHTS
Diamond Bar Municipal Advisory Council,
1988-89; Diamond Bar City Council, 1989-90;
sought Republican nomination for Calif. Senate,
1990; Diamond Bar City Council, 1991-95 (mayor,
1993-94); sought Republican nomination for Calif.
Senate (special election), 1994; Calif. Assembly,
1995-98

ELECTION RESULTS

2008 GENERAL

Gary G. Miller (R)	158,404	60.2%
Edwin "Ed" Chau (D)	104,909	39.8%

2008 PRIMARY

Gary G. Miller (R)	unopposed

2006 GENERAL

Gary G. Miller (R)	unopposed

PREVIOUS WINNING PERCENTAGES
2004 (68%); 2002 (68%); 2000 (59%); 1998 (53%)

A self-made millionaire with extensive real estate investments, Miller expresses frustration with myriad federal environmental and business regulations. He is a fiscal and social conservative who aims to pry away some of the regulations he believes can hinder business. But his easygoing nature enables him to make friends and form alliances with Democrats.

Miller sits on the Financial Services Committee, where he is the top-ranking Republican on the International Monetary Policy and Trade Sub-committee. He teamed with its liberal chairman, Democrat Barney Frank of Massachusetts, on a bill the House passed in 2007 to help communities clean up property contaminated by pollutants, although it stalled in the Senate.

But Miller can claim some successes, such as a 2008 housing mortgage rescue bill he backed that became law. Miller successfully inserted in the bill a provision to increase the size of the home loans — from $417,000 to $730,000 — that government-sponsored mortgage giants Fannie Mae and Freddie Mac can purchase, while increasing to the same level the size of loans that the Federal Housing Administration can insure. A compromise with the Senate before the bill's final passage set the figure at $625,000, but Miller said he was satisfied. The change, he said, ensured that people in areas with high housing costs, such as Southern California, "are able to continue having access to safe, affordable mortgages."

His fiscal conservatism was tested early in the 111th Congress when Congress cleared President's Obama $787 billion economic stimulus plan without any House Republican votes. Calling the bill "outrageous," Miller said in a statement the Democratic leadership "rushed to pass a bill that wastes billions of taxpayer dollars on pet projects and payouts to special interest groups."

Miller also has been outspoken on illegal immigration and the increase in undocumented workers, a big issue for voters in his district. In the 110th Congress (2007-08), he backed bills to deny citizenship to the children of illegal immigrants born in the United States, require workers to resolve discrepancies if their names and Social Security numbers do not match and bar illegal immigrants from receiving Social Security benefits. Early in 2009, he cosponsored a measure requiring that all official U.S. business be printed in English and another mandating that ballots for federal elections be printed only in English.

From his seat on Transportation and Infrastructure, Miller works to preserve water quality in parched Southern California. Although usually a loyal Republican, in November 2007 he supported an override of President George W. Bush's veto of a $23.2 billion bill authorizing water-related projects, including $35 million for his district.

Miller's district is home to the Richard Nixon Library in Yorba Linda, and he secured $4 million in 2004 to house Nixon's presidential papers and tapes. The funds secured by Miller paid for the transfer of the papers from the National Archives facility in Maryland to California, and for a new building.

Miller is a Civil War history buff and keeps a large collection of history books in his office, which he reads during his six-hour flights back to California. In 2002, he won enactment of a law to provide federal grants to states and localities to preserve battle sites. He pushed for the law's reauthorization in 2008. The House in March 2009 passed his measure to direct the Interior secretary to establish a program to provide grants for the preservation of Civil War battle sites.

Miller was distracted from his legislative agenda early in the 110th when the federal government turned its eye on him. Shortly after the 2006 election,

Miller came under FBI scrutiny for a provision he added to a 2005 surface transportation bill that improved land a mile from property he owned. The bureau also looked into his deferral of capital gains taxes on land sales he made to the city of Monrovia in 2002 and to Fontana in 2005 and 2006. Miller contended he sold the land under threat of eminent domain; city officials disputed that account. Miller said he paid all necessary taxes, and added that he had provided House Republican leaders with documents showing he did nothing wrong. He said in July 2008 that he had never been contacted by the FBI.

Dealing with these questions took up much of Miller's time early in the 110th Congress, but he was able to claim some successes.

Miller was raised by his mother and grandparents. At an early age, his family moved from Arkansas, where he was born, to Whittier, east of Los Angeles, where many other poor families from Oklahoma and Arkansas had settled. His mother worked as a checker at a grocery store; his grandfather was a custodian for the local school district. Miller said he aspired to be a musician as a child as he was an accomplished trumpet player.

He attended community college for a while but did not earn a degree. He then formed a partnership with a building contractor, and they bid on home improvement contracts with the U.S. Housing and Urban Development Department. He says he learned construction skills on the job, and moved on to build single-family homes and eventually planned communities.

Miller began his political career on the Diamond Bar Municipal Advisory Council. He was a member of Diamond Bar's first city council after the city was incorporated in 1989, and became mayor in 1993.

He lost primary bids for the California Senate in 1990 and 1994. Early in 1995, when voters forced a recall election of state Assemblyman Paul Horcher, who left the Republican Party and backed liberal Democrat Willie L. Brown Jr. for Assembly Speaker, Miller ran for the seat and won.

In 1998, three-term Rep. Jay C. Kim was convicted of violating campaign finance laws, and Miller challenged him in the GOP primary. He won by almost 4,000 votes, and won the general election by nearly 13 percentage points. Miller helped bankroll his campaign with his own money. In remapping after the 2000 census, the district shifted to the south and west and was renumbered the 42nd. Miller won by 39 percentage points in 2002, and almost as much in 2004. In 2006, he was unopposed.

But in 2008, Miller's perceived vulnerability after the FBI inquiry sparked a rare Democratic primary race in the heavily GOP district, eventually won by Montebello School Board Member Edwin "Ed" Chau. But Miller won again easily by 20 percentage points.

KEY VOTES

2008

No   Delay consideration of Colombia free-trade agreement

No   Override Bush veto of federal farm and nutrition programs reauthorization bill

Yes   Overhaul surveillance laws and permit dismissal of suits against companies that conducted warrantless wiretapping

Yes   Grant mortgage relief to homeowners and funding for Fannie Mae and Freddie Mac

Yes   Approve initial $700 billion program to stabilize financial markets

Yes   Approve final $700 billion program to stabilize financial markets

?   Provide $14 billion in loans to automakers

2007

?   Increase minimum wage by $2.10 an hour

No   Approve $124.2 billion in emergency war spending and set goal for redeployment of troops from Iraq

Yes   Reject federal contraceptive assistance to international family planning groups

Yes   Override Bush veto of $23.2 billion water projects authorization bill

Yes   Implement Peru free-trade agreement

?   Approve energy policy overhaul with new fuel economy standards

?   Clear $473.5 billion omnibus spending bill, including $70 billion for military operations

CQ VOTE STUDIES

	PARTY UNITY		PRESIDENTIAL SUPPORT	
	SUPPORT	OPPOSE	SUPPORT	OPPOSE
2008	97%	3%	79%	21%
2007	96%	4%	86%	14%
2006	98%	2%	95%	5%
2005	98%	2%	89%	11%
2004	98%	2%	85%	15%

INTEREST GROUPS

	AFL-CIO	ADA	CCUS	ACU
2008	27%	5%	100%	81%
2007	10%	0%	89%	100%
2006	7%	0%	100%	88%
2005	14%	0%	92%	96%
2004	13%	0%	100%	100%

CALIFORNIA 42

Parts of Orange, Los Angeles and San Bernardino counties — Mission Viejo, Chino

Although most of its population lives in Orange County, the Republican 42nd is centered around the suburbs where Orange, Los Angeles and San Bernardino counties come together east of Los Angeles proper. From there, the 42nd has a long arm that stretches southeast and then southwest farther into Orange County to Mission Viejo and Rancho Santa Margarita. A chunk of eastern Anaheim also falls within the district's borders.

Chino and Chino Hills in San Bernardino County have an agricultural heritage, but the economic influence of dairy production is waning due to residential development and the increasing presence of manufacturing and service sectors. There have been significant downturns in retail and residential growth in the San Bernardino portions of the district.

Diamond Bar and Rowland Heights (shared with the 38th) in Los Angeles

County have large Asian populations. Hispanics and Asians also live in the northern Orange County cities of Brea — which has experienced downturns in the commercial and financial sectors — La Habra and Placentia (shared with the 40th), although this segment of Orange County is predominately white-collar and white. Overall, the district is mostly middle and upper class and dominated by residential communities. Many residents work in technology firms and commute to Los Angeles or Irvine (which is located in the 48th).

Conservatism persists even among non-whites, and Republicans maintain a significant lead in voter registration. The district gave John McCain 53 percent of its 2008 presidential vote.

MAJOR INDUSTRY

Service, light manufacturing, dairy

CITIES

Mission Viejo, 93,102; Chino, 67,168; Chino Hills, 66,787; La Habra, 58,974; Yorba Linda, 58,918; Diamond Bar, 56,287; Anaheim (pt.), 55,395

NOTABLE

Yorba Linda, the birthplace and burial site of President Nixon, is the home of the Nixon Library; La Habra has hosted an annual Corn Festival since 1949; Chino is home to the Planes of Fame museum.

Rep. Joe Baca (D)

Elected 1999; 5th full term

The first Hispanic elected to Congress from the part of Southern California known as the Inland Empire, Baca inserts himself into debates ranging from immigration to the financial crisis. He is outspoken, aggressive and often ruffles feathers, typically with no apology.

Having catapulted himself from shoeshine boy to congressman, he calls himself "working Joe Baca," which could apply both to his work ethic and his strong backing of Hispanics, migrant workers and organized labor. "I'm a fighter because I know what it's like to struggle," he once said.

Baca has long been a strong advocate for immigrants, both legal and illegal, sometimes angering law enforcement in the process. He has kept the issue of immigration reform before his colleagues via a series of speeches and inserts in the Congressional Record honoring the contributions of immigrants. His district is nearly 60 percent Hispanic, and he has often referred to "hardworking" immigrant mothers who "sometimes work three jobs" and fathers who "wake up at 4 a.m. to go to work, earn below minimum wages, and manage to provide for their families."

And early in the 111th Congress (2009-10), he appeared on the House floor every few days to push for a comprehensive overhaul of the nation's immigration laws. He argues against "enforcement-only approaches that create a mistrust of law enforcement amongst the public."

Baca also led the efforts for immigration reform as chairman of the Hispanic Caucus during the 110th Congress (2007-08). But the caucus spent more time fending off crackdowns on illegal immigrants and measures targeting non-English-speakers than it did advancing legislation to help them. The caucus also held up passage of a fiscal 2008 spending bill because it included language that would forbid the Equal Employment Opportunity Commission from suing companies that impose English-only requirements on their workplaces. The language was eventually removed.

Baca also had to deal with disruptions in the caucus after he alienated its female members soon after taking the helm. Fellow California Democrat Loretta Sanchez complained he had referred to her as a "whore" in a conversation with a California state legislator. Sanchez and her sister, Linda T. Sánchez, both quit the caucus in 2007 after the dispute. He denied Sanchez's accusation, although he acknowledged calling Hilda L. Solis, another California Hispanic Democrat, a "kiss-up" to Speaker Nancy Pelosi. He apologized to Solis, but the grumbling continued within the caucus.

Baca made some efforts to reassure his female constituents. He sponsored a financial literacy summit for women in his district and touted his 100 percent voting rating from the American Association of University Women. But it wasn't enough; New York's Nydia M. Velázquez became chairwoman in 2009.

Baca has sought to help immigrant families and farmers from the Agriculture Committee, where he chairs the subcommittee on oversight and nutrition. He successfully included in the 2008 reauthorization of agriculture and nutrition programs provisions to boost food stamp aid, particularly for families with high day care costs, and to expand a fruit and vegetable pilot program to all 50 states. He also helped include increased federal aid for food banks and soup kitchens. But he was unable to expand nutrition benefits for adult legal immigrants; currently, they must be in the country at least five years to be eligible for food stamps.

Baca is a member of both the Financial Services Committee and the fiscally conservative Blue Dog Coalition. As with many Blue Dogs, he has

CAPITOL OFFICE
225-6161
www.house.gov/baca
2245 Rayburn Bldg. 20515-0543; fax 225-8671

COMMITTEES
Agriculture
(Operations, Oversight, Nutrition & Forestry - chairman)
Financial Services
Natural Resources

RESIDENCE
Rialto

BORN
Jan. 23, 1947; Belen, N.M.

RELIGION
Roman Catholic

FAMILY
Wife, Barbara Baca; four children

EDUCATION
California State U., Los Angeles, B.A. 1971 (sociology)

MILITARY SERVICE
Army 1966-68

CAREER
Travel agency owner; corporate community relations executive

POLITICAL HIGHLIGHTS
San Bernardino Community College District Board of Trustees, 1979-93; sought Democratic nomination for Calif. Assembly, 1988, 1990; Calif. Assembly, 1992-98 (Speaker pro tempore, 1995); Calif. Senate, 1998-99

ELECTION RESULTS

2008 GENERAL

Joe Baca (D)	108,259	69.1%
John Roberts (R)	48,312	30.9%

2008 PRIMARY

Joe Baca (D)	13,177	66.3%
Joanne T. Gilbert (D)	6,701	33.7%

2006 GENERAL

Joe Baca (D)	52,791	64.5%
Scott Folkens (R)	29,069	35.5%

PREVIOUS WINNING PERCENTAGES
2004 (66%); 2002 (66%); 2000 (60%); 1999 Special Runoff Election (51%)

been a skeptic of the government's interventions with financial services industry. He first voted against a $700 billion measure to shore up the nation's financial sector in September 2008, saying it didn't do enough to help homeowners facing foreclosure. But he changed his mind three days later, along with four other Blue Dogs, and voted for a similar measure that included increased limits for federally insured bank deposits. He also backed President Obama's $787 billion economic stimulus.

Baca is a strong supporter of organized labor, which in turn has backed him. The AFL-CIO gives him a lifetime voting score of 97 percent. But he sides with Republicans on some issues, including supporting gun owners' rights. He also breaks with his party on environmental issues. He supports oil drilling in Alaska's Arctic National Wildlife Refuge, aligning himself with the Teamsters, who value the jobs the drilling would create. In 2009, he was named to a Blue Dog task force to craft energy policy.

Baca, a member of the Natural Resources Committee, does want the federal government to help protect the water quality in his district. He has pressured the EPA to issue strict standards for perchlorate levels.

Baca was born in tiny Belen, N.M., south of Albuquerque. The son of a railroad laborer and the youngest of 15 children in a house where little English was spoken, Baca as a boy moved with his family to Barstow, Calif. He shined shoes, delivered newspapers and worked as a janitor. He was a laborer for the Santa Fe Railroad between his high school graduation and getting drafted into the Army in 1966. He served as a paratrooper with the 101st and 82nd Airborne divisions but was not sent to Vietnam.

After completing his service, he earned a sociology degree, then worked as a community affairs representative for a phone company. His political career began in 1979 with election to the San Bernardino community college board, where he served 14 years. After two failed attempts to oust a fellow Democrat in the state Assembly, he won the seat in 1992 when the incumbent retired. He was re-elected twice and then won a state Senate seat in 1998.

The following year, when U.S. Rep. George Brown died midway through his 18th term, Baca ran against his widow, Marta Macias Brown, in the special election primary. He defeated her, then posted a 6-percentage-point win over GOP businessman Elia Pirozzi in the runoff. He has won handily ever since.

As a child Baca aspired to a career in baseball. Well into his 30s, he was a catcher for a semi-pro fast-pitch softball team. The 5-foot-6-inch Baca is a spark plug for the Democrats in the annual congressional baseball game. In 2008, he pitched and was named co-most valuable player. Baseball is not his only sport: Golf Digest in 2005 rated him one of the top golfers in Washington.

KEY VOTES

2008
Yes Delay consideration of Colombia free-trade agreement
Yes Override Bush veto of federal farm and nutrition programs reauthorization bill
Yes Overhaul surveillance laws and permit dismissal of suits against companies that conducted warrantless wiretapping
Yes Grant mortgage relief to homeowners and funding for Fannie Mae and Freddie Mac
No Approve initial $700 billion program to stabilize financial markets
Yes Approve final $700 billion program to stabilize financial markets
Yes Provide $14 billion in loans to automakers

2007
Yes Increase minimum wage by $2.10 an hour
Yes Approve $124.2 billion in emergency war spending and set goal for redeployment of troops from Iraq
No Reject federal contraceptive assistance to international family planning groups
Yes Override Bush veto of $23.2 billion water projects authorization bill
No Implement Peru free-trade agreement
Yes Approve energy policy overhaul with new fuel economy standards
No Clear $473.5 billion omnibus spending bill, including $70 billion for military operations

CQ VOTE STUDIES

	PARTY UNITY		PRESIDENTIAL SUPPORT	
	SUPPORT	OPPOSE	SUPPORT	OPPOSE
2008	98%	2%	19%	81%
2007	97%	3%	6%	94%
2006	91%	9%	35%	65%
2005	88%	12%	34%	66%
2004	92%	8%	32%	68%

INTEREST GROUPS

	AFL-CIO	ADA	CCUS	ACU
2008	100%	90%	67%	8%
2007	96%	100%	55%	0%
2006	100%	95%	47%	20%
2005	100%	90%	58%	32%
2004	93%	90%	43%	12%

CALIFORNIA 43

Southwest San Bernardino County – Ontario, Fontana, most of San Bernardino

The San Bernardino County communities of Ontario, Fontana and San Bernardino form the base of the 43rd, which lies in the heart of the Inland Empire east of Los Angeles. The district has retained a diverse and working class feel despite decades of explosive growth that resulted in several years of economic prosperity similar to that of its neighbors in Orange and Los Angeles counties.

The area relied on a strong home construction sector to drive further growth and bolster the region's economy. But, state and local government budget shortfalls and rising foreclosure and unemployment rates affect the local workforce. Some residents commute into Los Angeles along the Pomona and San Bernardino freeways, and technology, manufacturing and aerospace industries will play a large role in economic recovery here. Homeowners in Fontana have been hit particularly hard, although the widespread foreclosure crisis may result in a glut of lower-priced homes in these established suburbs.

The renovated Ontario airport is part of a transportation and container warehousing sector and serves as a hub for FedEx and UPS, but decreases in air travel demand have cut into airport traffic. The large Ontario Mills mall still hosts several major retail anchors, but reduced consumer activity in the region has driven out some stores. The manufacturing sector supports companies such as Mag Instrument, the maker of the Maglite flashlight. Rialto, which is nearly two-thirds Hispanic, is home to regional distribution centers for Staples and Toys "R" Us.

The district is nearly 60 percent Hispanic, and registered Democrats outnumber Republicans by 21 percentage points. The 43rd favors Democrats on all levels, and gave Barack Obama 68 percent of its 2008 presidential vote. Traffic congestion and illegal immigration are big issues among residents here.

MAJOR INDUSTRY
Manufacturing, electronics, agriculture

CITIES
Ontario, 158,007; San Bernardino (pt.), 130,612; Fontana, 128,929; Rialto, 91,873; Colton (pt.), 43,349

NOTABLE
Fontana is the birthplace of the Hells Angels motorcycle club.

Rep. Ken Calvert (R)

Elected 1992; 9th term

CAPITOL OFFICE
225-1986
calvert.house.gov
2201 Rayburn Bldg. 20515-0544; fax 225-2004

COMMITTEES
Appropriations

RESIDENCE
Corona

BORN
June 8, 1953; Corona, Calif.

RELIGION
Protestant

FAMILY
Divorced

EDUCATION
Chaffey College, A.A. 1973 (business);
San Diego State U., B.A. 1975 (economics)

CAREER
Real estate executive; restaurant executive

POLITICAL HIGHLIGHTS
Sought Republican nomination for U.S. House,
1982; Riverside County Republican Party
chairman, 1984-88

ELECTION RESULTS

2008 GENERAL

Ken Calvert (R)	129,937	51.2%
Bill Hedrick (D)	123,890	48.8%

2008 PRIMARY

Ken Calvert (R)	unopposed

2006 GENERAL

Ken Calvert (R)	89,555	60.0%
Louis Vandenberg (D)	55,275	37.0%
Kevin Akin (PFP)	4,486	3.0%

PREVIOUS WINNING PERCENTAGES
2004 (62%); 2002 (64%); 2000 (74%); 1998 (56%);
1996 (55%); 1994 (55%); 1992 (47%)

Calvert is among a dwindling number of Republicans elected in 1992 before the groundswell that achieved the GOP takeover of the House two years later. He remains as committed to the conservative principles that led to that GOP success, including limited federal regulation of private property, stricter controls on immigration and less government spending.

But he does seek federal support for concerns vital to his Southern California district, particularly for water resources, the aviation and aerospace industry, highway improvements, and agriculture. His seat on the Appropriations Committee gives him a role on funding for a range of such issues.

Early in the 111th Congress, Calvert suggested Republicans might find common ground with President Obama and the House Democratic majority. Following Obama's February 2009 address to Congress on his economic and fiscal priorities, Calvert said there could be some agreement on three issues: energy, health care and education. But he told the Orange County Register that "the devil is in the details. We've got to understand the cost of this."

Calvert had voted against the Democrats' early initiatives of the 111th, including Obama's $787 billion economic stimulus plan. "The strategy under this bill is to throw billions of dollars in every bureaucratic direction, cross our fingers and hope for the best," he said.

He also complained that negotiators pulled from the final bill his provision to reauthorize an online program called E-Verify that allows employers to confirm the employment eligibility of new hires. Calvert, an early champion of the program created under a broad 1996 immigration bill, said: "If the stimulus package creates millions of jobs...I want to be absolutely sure that those jobs are going to American workers or legal residents, not illegal aliens."

He had similar concerns when voting against a bill, signed into law in early 2009, to expand the State Children's Health Insurance Program. "I find it unconscionable that Speaker [Nancy] Pelosi has hijacked a successful program...in an effort to provide benefits to illegal immigrants and bring the U.S. one step closer to a nationalized system of health care," he said after the vote. SCHIP covers children from low-income families that do not qualify for Medicaid.

Yet Calvert in the 110th Congress (2007-08) split with most of his GOP colleagues and voted for a housing finance package that called for a new regulator for mortgage giants Fannie Mae and Freddie Mac and provided financial aid for homeowners. "My area has suffered more than most in the country in terms of foreclosures and difficulties in the real estate industry," he said. He also voted in 2008 for a $700 billion package to shore up the financial sector.

But it was his votes on SCHIP and the economic stimulus bill that made him the target of radio ads sponsored by the DCCC in early 2009. Democratic strategists began plotting the 2010 midterm election in his district after the 2008 race, the 10th-closest contest in the nation by percentage margin; Calvert won re-election by a narrow 2 percentage points.

Before the 2008 campaign, Calvert had been under increasing criticism from bloggers who objected to his selection for Appropriations in mid-2007. They pointed to a 2006 Los Angeles Times story that reported he and a partner held numerous properties near transportation projects that Calvert had supported with federal earmarks, funding set-asides for special projects. Some of the properties sold for substantial profits. Calvert denied wrongdoing, and an FBI review of public documents never led to any action. He said he took the seat to protect California's interests on Appropriations.

In the 111th, Calvert sits on the panels overseeing spending for Energy and

Water, Interior and Environment, and Homeland Security. He has long focused on water issues. As chairman of Natural Resources' Water and Power panel in 2004, he worked with California Democrtic Sen. Dianne Feinstein to win enactment of a bill to reauthorize and restructure the California Federal Bay-Delta Program, which aims to enhance the state's water supply, reliability and quality.

A former real estate agent, he typically sides with property owners against environmentalists. Early in his career, he criticized protections for endangered species for unduly restricting property owners' rights. He supported the end of the congressional moratorium on offshore oil and gas drilling in 2008.

A social conservative, Calvert opposes gay marriage and opposed a 2007 bill to ban job discrimination based on sexual orientation. He also voted for a bill to allow faith-based service providers for Head Start, an early-childhood development program for low-income preschoolers, to take religion into account when hiring.

Calvert was born in Corona, just west of Riverside. His family owned the Jolly Fox restaurant for nearly half a century, diversifying into other ventures such as a motel and a bowling alley. His father, who changed parties to become a Republican in the 1960s, won election to the city council and then served as Corona's mayor. The younger Calvert remembers working on Richard Nixon's 1968 presidential campaign, and as a college student, Calvert interned in the Capitol Hill office of GOP Rep. Victor Veysey.

At 28, Calvert in 1982 jumped into an open-seat House race in a district that contained most of Riverside County. He lost the GOP primary by just 868 votes. But he stayed active in party affairs, helping run the gubernatorial campaigns of Republicans George Deukmejian and Pete Wilson.

When reapportionment created a new 43rd District for western Riverside County in 1992, Calvert ran again and won narrowly by relying on write-in ballots to reverse an apparent defeat. But personal tragedy marred his triumph. At the peak of the campaign, Calvert's father committed suicide.

Calvert had a rough start in his first term when a tryst with a prostitute drew widespread notice. He had said his "inappropriate" behavior stemmed from depression over his recent divorce and his father's suicide. Following the publicity, Calvert won the 1994 primary by just 2 percentage points, and the national surge that delivered the House to the GOP carried him to victory with 55 percent. In 2000, he won with 74 percent. In 2002, in redistricted territory, numbered the 44th, Calvert took 70 percent in a three-way primary and cruised to a sixth term. He won easily in 2004 and 2006. But the Democratic tidal wave of 2008 held him to a narrow victory over Democrat Bill Hedrick, a local school board president.

KEY VOTES

2008

No Delay consideration of Colombia free-trade agreement

No Override Bush veto of federal farm and nutrition programs reauthorization bill

Yes Overhaul surveillance laws and permit dismissal of suits against companies that conducted warrantless wiretapping

Yes Grant mortgage relief to homeowners and funding for Fannie Mae and Freddie Mac

Yes Approve initial $700 billion program to stabilize financial markets

Yes Approve final $700 billion program to stabilize financial markets

No Provide $14 billion in loans to automakers

2007

No Increase minimum wage by $2.10 an hour

No Approve $124.2 billion in emergency war spending and set goal for redeployment of troops from Iraq

Yes Reject federal contraceptive assistance to international family planning groups

Yes Override Bush veto of $23.2 billion water projects authorization bill

Yes Implement Peru free-trade agreement

Yes Approve energy policy overhaul with new fuel economy standards

Yes Clear $473.5 billion omnibus spending bill, including $70 billion for military operations

CQ VOTE STUDIES

	PARTY UNITY		PRESIDENTIAL SUPPORT	
	SUPPORT	OPPOSE	SUPPORT	OPPOSE
2008	96%	4%	76%	24%
2007	91%	9%	83%	17%
2006	95%	5%	95%	5%
2005	98%	2%	89%	11%
2004	93%	7%	82%	18%

INTEREST GROUPS

	AFL-CIO	ADA	CCUS	ACU
2008	13%	15%	100%	83%
2007	5%	15%	89%	88%
2006	14%	5%	100%	80%
2005	13%	0%	93%	84%
2004	21%	0%	100%	88%

CALIFORNIA 44
Northwestern Riverside County -- Riverside, Corona

A residential district that lies east of Los Angeles and north of San Diego, the 44th contains about one-third of Riverside County's residents and takes in the southeastern portion of Orange County that borders San Diego County. The Orange County areas include coastal San Clemente, a premier surfing spot, and Santa Ana Mountain forests.

The district experienced decades of growth as young, white-collar families moved into its cities. Commuters who work in Orange or Los Angeles counties arrived in these bedroom communities and increased traffic along Route 91. Traffic congestion remains an issue, and the area's high levels of air pollution make it part of the greater-Los Angeles "smog belt." Recently rising levels of unemployment and home foreclosure rates trouble residents and local officials.

Despite population growth, manufacturing and agriculture — dairy, citrus, grapes, dates and avocados — still contribute to the economy.

Farmland is being driven farther east and out of the district, however, as the Los Angeles area continues to expand.

The district's portion of Orange County is staunchly Republican, but the more blue-collar Riverside communities and the areas around the University of California, Riverside, lean Democratic. Registered Republicans outnumber Democrats in the district overall, but incumbent GOP Rep. Ken Calvert barely withstood a challenge by Democrat Bill Hedrick in the 2008 election, taking only 51 percent of the vote. Democrat Barack Obama edged Republican John McCain here by less than 1 percentage point in the 2008 presidential election.

MAJOR INDUSTRY
Manufacturing, agriculture, health care

MILITARY BASES
Naval Surface Warfare Center, Corona Division, 7 military, 843 civilian (2007)

CITIES
Riverside, 255,166; Corona, 124,966; San Clemente, 49,936

NOTABLE
Riverside's Mission Inn was where Richard and Pat Nixon were married, and Ronald and Nancy Reagan stopped there on their honeymoon.

Rep. Mary Bono Mack (R)

Elected April 1998; 6th full term

CAPITOL OFFICE
225-5330
bono.house.gov
104 Cannon Bldg. 20515-0545; fax 225-2961

COMMITTEES
Energy & Commerce

RESIDENCE
Palm Springs

BORN
Oct. 24, 1961; Cleveland, Ohio

RELIGION
Protestant

FAMILY
Husband, Rep. Connie Mack, R-Fla.; two children, three stepchildren

EDUCATION
U. of Southern California, B.F.A. 1984 (art history)

CAREER
Homemaker; restaurateur

POLITICAL HIGHLIGHTS
No previous office

ELECTION RESULTS

2008 GENERAL

Mary Bono Mack (R)	155,166	58.3%
Julie Bornstein (D)	111,026	41.7%

2008 PRIMARY

Mary Bono Mack (R)	38,726	89.3%
George Pearne (R)	4,618	10.6%

2006 GENERAL

Mary Bono Mack (R)	99,638	60.7%
David Roth (D)	64,613	39.3%

PREVIOUS WINNING PERCENTAGES
2004 (67%); 2002 (65%); 2000 (59%); 1998 (60%);
1998 Special Election (64%)

Bono Mack has a fairly conservative voting record — but she's a moderate by the standards of California's right-leaning GOP delegation. Elected in 1998 after the death of her husband, entertainer-turned-politician Sonny Bono, she works across the aisle and is unafraid to abandon her party on major legislation, especially as the economy has worsened.

During President George W. Bush's two terms, Bono Mack took her party's side on 88 percent of the votes in which Democrats diverged from Republicans — less than any other Golden State Republican in office at the end of the Bush administration. "I'm not a partisan bomb-thrower," she told The Desert Sun of Palm Springs.

Reflecting her district's socially liberal tendencies, she is likely to go her own way on health and social issues. She was one of 82 Republicans to vote for a 2007 Democratic measure raising the minimum wage and one of 40 Republicans in February 2009 to favor an expansion of the State Children's Health Insurance Program, which covers children from low-income families that do not qualify for Medicaid.

Even on fiscal matters, she has shown an increased willingness to cross party lines. She supported two $700 billion measures — the second of which became law — in fall 2008 to aid the ailing financial services sector. Though she joined House Republicans in opposing President Obama's $787 billion economic stimulus bill, she was the only California Republican to back a $410 billion catchall spending bill for 2009 a few weeks later. "There are simply too many vitally important priorities contained in this bill not to support it during these difficult economic times," she said.

She also was one of only 35 Republicans to vote for a 2007 measure prohibiting job discrimination on the basis of an individual's actual or perceived sexual orientation. This vote reflects the demographics of her district. Palm Springs has a growing homosexual population and the city elected its first gay mayor in 2003. She also opposed the GOP's effort in 2004 to amend the Constitution to ban same-sex marriage.

Bono Mack has not been visible on many high-level Capitol Hill debates, but has been willing to wield her celebrity on behalf of causes in which she believes, such as fighting drug abuse. In February 2009, she and her son Chesare gave a candid interview to People magazine about Chesare's addiction to heroin and the painkiller OxyContin and his subsequent recovery. Bush signed a bill into law sponsored by Bono Mack in 2008 that bans online pharmacies from selling controlled substances without valid prescriptions.

She has had some other modest successes in recent years. After wildfires blamed on arson swept through her district, she introduced legislation in 2007 to require arsonists to register with local law enforcement offices just like sex offenders. It passed the House but never made it through the Senate. She also joined with California Democratic Sen. Barbara Boxer to include in a Senate-passed package of public lands bills in early 2009 a measure to designate some 190,000 acres in Riverside County as federally protected wilderness. And in the 109th Congress (2005-06), she sponsored a bill signed into law shifting some AIDS funding from urban centers to less-populated rural areas, which helped districts like hers.

She supports federal funding for medical research using embryonic stem cells, which are harvested from surplus embryos at in vitro fertilization clinics. Opponents liken their use to abortion. She says her physician father and chemist mother influenced her thinking on the issue.

A member of the powerful Energy and Commerce Committee, she supports expanding alternative energy sources as well as nuclear power. She said she wants to be a "reasoned voice" on efforts to curb global warming, warning of the need to protect businesses affected by legislation.

In her early years in the House, Bono Mack pursued legacy issues of her late husband, who died in a 1998 skiing accident. An early effort was helping to pass a copyright extension bill, first championed by and eventually named for Sonny. Ever since the 108th Congress (2003-04), she has focused on intellectual property issues of interest to the entertainment industry.

Bono Mack has cultivated an image of a plain-speaking, unpretentious legislator who is ready to roll up her sleeves. She focuses on the day-to-day issues of her Inland Empire and Coachella Valley constituents, such as high energy bills, the availability of low-income housing, access to water, and resolution of longstanding American Indian land claims.

A top priority has been obtaining funding to restore the Salton Sea, a southern California man-made lake threatened by pollution from agricultural and industrial runoff. In 2007, she voted to override Bush's veto of a $23.2 billion water projects bill, which included $30 million for the restoration project.

Bono Mack grew up in South Pasadena, Calif., the daughter of a surgeon and a chemist, who put her husband through medical school. She worked her way through college as a cocktail waitress, majoring in art history.

As she was celebrating her college graduation at Sonny Bono's West Hollywood restaurant, she met the owner and the two began a relationship. They married two years later, in 1986, when she was 24 — about half Sonny's age. Mary helped manage the restaurant, which he relocated to their new home in Palm Springs, and other companies associated with his entertainment royalties. The first time she voted was for Sonny, who was elected mayor of Palm Springs in 1988.

She came to Washington after he was elected to the House in 1994, and was a stay-at-home mother of their two children. When he died in a skiing accident four years later, GOP leaders urged her to run for his seat. Her Democratic opponent, Ralph Waite, was an actor who appeared on the popular television show "The Waltons"; Bono Mack won a special election in April with almost two-thirds of the vote. She has not been seriously threatened in her re-election bids.

Bono divorced her second husband, Glenn Baxley, the founder of a Western wear company, in September 2005 after a little less than four years of marriage. Just over two years later, she married Rep. Connie Mack, a Florida Republican.

KEY VOTES

2008
No   Delay consideration of Colombia free-trade agreement
Yes   Override Bush veto of federal farm and nutrition programs reauthorization bill
Yes   Overhaul surveillance laws and permit dismissal of suits against companies that conducted warrantless wiretapping
Yes   Grant mortgage relief to homeowners and funding for Fannie Mae and Freddie Mac
Yes   Approve initial $700 billion program to stabilize financial markets
Yes   Approve final $700 billion program to stabilize financial markets
No   Provide $14 billion in loans to automakers

2007
Yes   Increase minimum wage by $2.10 an hour
No   Approve $124.2 billion in emergency war spending and set goal for redeployment of troops from Iraq
No   Reject federal contraceptive assistance to international family planning groups
Yes   Override Bush veto of $23.2 billion water projects authorization bill
Yes   Implement Peru free-trade agreement
Yes   Approve energy policy overhaul with new fuel economy standards
Yes   Clear $473.5 billion omnibus spending bill, including $70 billion for military operations

CQ VOTE STUDIES

	PARTY UNITY		PRESIDENTIAL SUPPORT	
	SUPPORT	OPPOSE	SUPPORT	OPPOSE
2008	90%	10%	64%	36%
2007	85%	15%	58%	42%
2006	85%	15%	81%	19%
2005	93%	7%	80%	20%
2004	86%	14%	58%	42%

INTEREST GROUPS

	AFL-CIO	ADA	CCUS	ACU
2008	29%	40%	88%	74%
2007	25%	30%	89%	65%
2006	17%	25%	86%	68%
2005	20%	15%	93%	71%
2004	27%	35%	100%	56%

CALIFORNIA 45

Riverside County — Moreno Valley, Palm Springs

Desert resorts, a service industry workforce and agriculture fuel the economy of the 45th District, whose residents generally are split between Riverside County's Inland Empire areas, such as Moreno Valley, Hemet and Murrieta, and the resort-filled Coachella Valley cities farther east. Home foreclosures and unemployment have hit the district's large, exurban communities particularly hard, and commercial and business centers struggle with low occupancy rates. Air pollution in the Los Angeles exurbs are a concern for residents and officials.

The Palm Springs area, including Cathedral City, Indian Wells, La Quinta and Indio, draws visitors to its golf courses. Once known as a playground for the rich and retired — the district still has a high percentage of residents over the age of 64 — a younger, middle-class population has begun to populate the area. Beyond tourism and service sectors across the district, the resort region also has health care, shopping and gambling industries. Wind turbine generators are becoming more common in the area as renewable-energy sources.

Fiscally conservative and socially liberal, Palm Springs has a growing gay population — the city elected its first gay mayor in 2003 — and has sizable Jewish and Hispanic communities. Migrant farm laborers, the majority of whom are Hispanic, work in the agricultural communities of the Temecula wine country and the Coachella and San Jacinto valleys, which produce citrus, dates, alfalfa and grapes. The gambling industry supports the economies of the district's American Indian reservations. Health care service providers and small educational institutions have also begun to settle in the 45th.

Although the district tends to lean Republican, pockets in Rancho Mirage and Palm Springs vote Democratic. Overall, the district gave Barack Obama 52 percent of its 2008 presidential vote.

MAJOR INDUSTRY
Service, tourism, agriculture

CITIES
Moreno Valley, 142,381; Hemet, 58,812; Indio, 49,116; Murrieta, 44,282; Palm Springs, 42,807; Cathedral City, 42,647

NOTABLE
The world's largest rotating tramcars are at the Palm Springs Aerial Tramway.

Rep. Dana Rohrabacher (R)

Elected 1988; 11th term

CAPITOL OFFICE
225-2415
rohrabacher.house.gov
2300 Rayburn Bldg. 20515-0546; fax 225-0145

COMMITTEES
Foreign Affairs
Science & Technology

RESIDENCE
Huntington Beach

BORN
June 21, 1947; Coronado, Calif.

RELIGION
Christian

FAMILY
Wife, Rhonda Rohrabacher; three children

EDUCATION
Los Angeles Harbor College, attended 1965-67;
California State U., Long Beach, B.A. 1969
(history); U. of Southern California, M.A. 1971
(American studies)

CAREER
White House speechwriter; newspaper reporter

POLITICAL HIGHLIGHTS
No previous office

ELECTION RESULTS

2008 GENERAL

Dana Rohrabacher (R)	149,818	52.5%
Debbie Cook (D)	122,891	43.1%
Tom Lash (GREEN)	8,257	2.9%
Ernst P. Gasteiger (LIBERT)	4,311	1.5%

2008 PRIMARY

Dana Rohrabacher (R)	43,693	86.6%
Ronald R. St. John (R)	6,751	13.4%

2006 GENERAL

Dana Rohrabacher (R)	116,176	59.6%
Jim Brandt (D)	71,573	36.7%
Dennis Chang (LIBERT)	7,303	3.7%

PREVIOUS WINNING PERCENTAGES
2004 (62%); 2002 (62%); 2000 (62%); 1998 (59%);
1996 (61%); 1994 (69%); 1992 (55%); 1990 (59%);
1988 (64%)

A free-spirited and colorful conservative with a libertarian streak, Rohrabacher hasn't been much affected by his party's minority status. His specialty has always been speaking his mind, regardless of who is in charge.

Few lawmakers can unleash a sound bite with as much ferocity. Rohrabacher (ROAR-ah-BAH-ker) once described illegal immigration as an "invasion of the United States," and said a Senate provision that repealed the ban on HIV-positive visitors to the United States "adds insanity to irresponsibility."

Just days after President Obama took office, Rohrabacher said at a Republican retreat: "The president is a naive man. He is naive about what to expect from enemies of the United States overseas and about what to expect from the left wing of his party." He joined Minority Whip Eric Cantor of Virginia and John Culberson of Texas in vowing that a united GOP minority could force Obama — and possibly House Democratic leaders — to take a closer look at Republican proposals.

But Rohrabacher isn't exactly a team player. He raised eyebrows in September 2008 when he publicly sided with Russia when it invaded Georgia, putting himself at odds with President George W. Bush's administration and politicians of both parties. Earlier in the year, he joined Democrats in criticizing the administration for being unwilling to seek congressional approval for an agreement on Iraq. "I am a Republican, and at times I am embarrassed by the lack of cooperation that this president and his appointees have had with the legislative branch," he said.

Rohrabacher is a senior member of the Foreign Affairs Committee, where he has long been a critic of China's Communist regime. He was a vigorous opponent of the law, enacted in 2000, permanently permitting Chinese goods to enter the United States under the same low tariffs afforded most countries. He teamed with liberal California Democrat Maxine Waters in cosponsoring a 2007 resolution calling for a boycott of the 2008 Olympic Games in Beijing.

In February 2009, a Beijing-based company lost a contract to provide scanning units to the Port of Los Angeles to screen incoming containers for dangerous cargo. Officials said the scanners didn't meet performance standards. Rohrabacher said he didn't want that company or any other Chinese company to get another shot at the contract. "The most important factor in purchasing security equipment should be that it is not coming from a potential enemy," he said, according to the Daily Pilot of Costa Mesa.

Rohrabacher took up the cause of a pair of Border Patrol agents sentenced to prison in October 2006 for the non-fatal 2005 shooting in Texas of a man who turned out to be a drug smuggler attempting to flee across the Mexican border. The trial showed the agents hid evidence of the shooting, and the suspect was given immunity from prosecution for his testimony against them.

The case swiftly became a conservative cause. Rohrabacher angrily denounced Bush for refusing to intervene, calling him arrogant and aloof, and rounded up lawmakers to press for a pardon of the two agents. An appeals court judge upheld their sentences in July 2008, but Bush commuted them.

Rohrabacher, who has called for aggressive steps to combat illegal immigration at every point from the border to the workplace, called Bush "the lamest of lame ducks" for supporting a compromise Senate immigration measure that conservatives worked to derail in 2007. In the 108th Congress (2003-04), he unsuccessfully sought to pass a bill to require hospitals to report to authorities the names of illegal aliens they treated. House leaders promised him a floor vote on the bill in return for his vote for a 2003 bill creating a new prescription drug benefit under Medicare. But the GOP leadership showed little enthusiasm for Rohrabacher's bill, and more Republicans voted against it than for it.

Rohrabacher has split with his party on some other high-profile issues. In 2005, he was one of 15 Republicans voting to protect states that chose to permit medical use of marijuana. And, as the father of triplets conceived through in vitro fertilization, he voted in 2006 to override Bush's veto of a bill expanding embryonic stem cell research, which uses discarded embryos created for in vitro fertilization.

He sided with his party more than 90 percent of the time on votes that split the two parties during Bush's tenure. He is among the GOP's loudest critics of legislation to reduce greenhouse gas emissions, accusing proponents of presenting misleading information about whether it is caused by humans. "When it comes to bait and switch, used car salesmen are paragons of virtue compared to this global warming crowd," he said in May 2008.

Science fascinates Rohrabacher, particularly space, and Boeing Co.'s space division is a prominent employer in his district.

As entrepreneurs began building private aircraft he decided to help these businessmen-explorers. Rohrabacher was chairman of the Science and Technology Committee's Space and Aeronautics Subcommittee from 1997 to 2005 and introduced bills intended to foster private space flight. One bill would have offered a prize of up to $100 million for the first private spacecraft to make three orbits of the Earth. That one went nowhere, but he did push through a law supporting the development of commercial space projects and allowing the Federal Aviation Administration to regulate private spacecraft.

Rohrabacher represents Huntington Beach, a surfing community, and is an avid surfer. Among his friends are writers, artists and musicians from his era, including heavy metal vocalist Sammy Hagar and folk singer Joan Baez. A plaque in his office reads: "Fighting for Freedom…and Having Fun."

During his younger days, Rohrabacher was a hard-drinking, banjo-playing wanderer who worked as a house painter. He later found steady work as a reporter for City News Service and editorial writer for the Orange County Register. He served as assistant press secretary for Ronald Reagan's presidential campaigns, then became a White House speechwriter for Reagan.

In his first bid for elective office, in 1988, Rohrabacher ran for the House seat being vacated by GOP Rep. Dan Lungren. He won despite primary competitors who had both name recognition and Lungren's support. He won re-election with no less than 55 percent of the vote until 2008, when he faced a tough challenge from Democratic Huntington Beach Mayor Debbie Cook and was kept to 53 percent of the vote.

KEY VOTES

2008
No Delay consideration of Colombia free-trade agreement
No Override Bush veto of federal farm and nutrition programs reauthorization bill
Yes Overhaul surveillance laws and permit dismissal of suits against companies that conducted warrantless wiretapping
No Grant mortgage relief to homeowners and funding for Fannie Mae and Freddie Mac
No Approve initial $700 billion program to stabilize financial markets
No Approve final $700 billion program to stabilize financial markets
? Provide $14 billion in loans to automakers

2007
No Increase minimum wage by $2.10 an hour
No Approve $124.2 billion in emergency war spending and set goal for redeployment of troops from Iraq
Yes Reject federal contraceptive assistance to international family planning groups
Yes Override Bush veto of $23.2 billion water projects authorization bill
Yes Implement Peru free-trade agreement
No Approve energy policy overhaul with new fuel economy standards
Yes Clear $473.5 billion omnibus spending bill, including $70 billion for military operations

CQ VOTE STUDIES

	PARTY UNITY		PRESIDENTIAL SUPPORT	
	SUPPORT	OPPOSE	SUPPORT	OPPOSE
2008	95%	5%	74%	26%
2007	95%	5%	83%	17%
2006	90%	10%	90%	10%
2005	94%	6%	80%	20%
2004	91%	9%	84%	16%

INTEREST GROUPS

	AFL-CIO	ADA	CCUS	ACU
2008	14%	10%	82%	96%
2007	13%	5%	75%	96%
2006	7%	15%	93%	88%
2005	7%	5%	81%	96%
2004	29%	15%	85%	91%

CALIFORNIA 46

Coastal Los Angeles and Orange counties — Huntington Beach, Costa Mesa

The 46th runs along the coast south of Los Angeles with an eclectic mix of residents — including senior citizens, surfers and aerospace workers — that live in several different areas. The mountainous peninsula in the district's northwest is home to ultra-wealthy areas such as Rancho Palos Verdes. In the center is a more blue-collar community around Long Beach Harbor, home to one of the nation's largest port complexes. To the southeast, the district takes in Orange County communities such as Huntington Beach and Costa Mesa.

The 46th's economy relies on aerospace and technology. Wealthy Huntington Beach is a hub for both water sports enthusiasts and aerospace workers. Boeing's Huntington Beach campus has employed thousands in defense, space and research programs, although job cuts by the high-tech giant and a slated facility closure may affect the local economy. The housing construction sector had benefited from a residential real estate boom in Orange County but has seen a recent downswing. Costa Mesa

hosts pharmaceutical firms, and manufacturing remains important to many residents in 46th — high-skilled aircraft assemblage and technology development positions have replaced textile factory jobs here.

The 46th is more than three-fifths white, and senior citizens are a significant constituency. Some areas in the district's interior, which includes most of Westminster — home to a large Vietnamese population and shared with the 40th District — tend to be less affluent than coastal cities. The once comfortably conservative district gave GOP Gov. Arnold Schwarzenegger 69 percent of the vote in 2006 but supported John McCain with less than 50 percent of its 2008 presidential vote.

MAJOR INDUSTRY
Aerospace, technology, manufacturing

MILITARY BASES
Naval Weapons Station Seal Beach, 81 military, 326 civilian (2007)

CITIES
Huntington Beach, 189,594; Costa Mesa, 108,724; Long Beach (pt.), 83,666; Westminster (pt.), 60,399; Fountain Valley, 54,978

NOTABLE
Huntington Beach is home to the International Surfing Museum; the 46th includes two channel islands: Santa Catalina and San Clemente.

Rep. Loretta Sanchez (D)

Elected 1996; 7th term

CAPITOL OFFICE
225-2965
lorettasanchez.house.gov
1114 Longworth Bldg. 20515-0547; fax 225-5859

COMMITTEES
Armed Services
Homeland Security
(Border, Maritime & Global Counterterrorism -
chairwoman)
Joint Economic

RESIDENCE
Garden Grove

BORN
Jan. 7, 1960; Lynwood, Calif.

RELIGION
Roman Catholic

FAMILY
Divorced

EDUCATION
Chapman College, B.S. 1982 (economics);
American U., M.B.A. 1984 (finance)

CAREER
Financial adviser; strategic management
associate

POLITICAL HIGHLIGHTS
Candidate for Anaheim City Council, 1994

ELECTION RESULTS

2008 GENERAL

Loretta Sanchez (D)	85,878	69.5%
Rosemarie "Rosie" Avila (R)	31,432	25.4%
Robert Lauten (AMI)	6,274	5.1%

2008 PRIMARY

Loretta Sanchez (D)	unopposed

2006 GENERAL

Loretta Sanchez (D)	47,134	62.3%
Tan Nguyen (R)	28,485	37.7%

PREVIOUS WINNING PERCENTAGES
2004 (60%); 2002 (61%); 2000 (60%); 1998 (56%);
1996 (47%)

Sanchez is an increasingly influential figure on such high-profile issues as border security and immigration and a strong partisan voice on areas affecting women, Hispanics and organized labor. Her ascent over the past dozen years has been buoyed by her close relationship with Speaker Nancy Pelosi and fundraising abilities — she gave out more than $300,000 to other Democrats from her personal campaign account in the 2007-08 cycle.

But it is her personality — gregarious, candid and opinionated — and her presence on the political talk show circuit that have boosted her profile to the point that she is considering a run for governor of California in 2010.

Sanchez's background is in investment banking, but she has carved out a national security niche in Congress. Pelosi, one of the few national politicians to back her long-shot bid for Congress in 1996, granted Sanchez the Democrats' No. 2 position on the Homeland Security Committee when it was created in 2003. When the Democrats took control of the House in 2007, Sanchez became chairwoman of the committee's panel on Border, Maritime and Global Counterterrorism. She has helped chart the party's position on immigration, a three-pronged approach addressing border security, the demand for temporary workers and illegal immigrants already in the country.

From her seat on the Armed Services Committee, she has opposed the war in Iraq. While she has supported war spending bills, she has repeatedly called for benchmarks to evaluate U.S. military progress in Iraq. She also has focused attention on the topic of sexual assault in the military and service academies. In 2005, her proposal to make it easier to press sexual assault charges in the military was enacted into law.

The daughter of Mexican immigrants, Sanchez considers herself a spokesperson for women and America's growing population of Latinos. She and her sister, Rep. Linda T. Sánchez, are the first set of sisters elected to Congress and published a book in 2008 called "Dream in Color: How the Sánchez Sisters Are Making History in Congress." They said the book was intended "to inspire others to pursue a career in public service, and to ultimately speed up the sluggish transition to a more representative government."

The sisters had a public split from Washington's Hispanic establishment in early 2007, owing to a feud with Congressional Hispanic Caucus Chairman Joe Baca. Sanchez and her sister resigned their memberships in the caucus, charging that Baca, a fellow California Democrat, had demeaned women, abused the group's political action committee and held improper elections. Baca denied the allegations, but the episode bitterly divided Hispanic Democrats just as they were about to assert greater power in the 110th Congress (2007-08). In early 2009, Linda T. Sánchez rejoined the caucus after Nydia M. Velázquez of New York became chairwoman, succeeding Baca. Loretta Sanchez did not follow suit, however.

The sisters have appeared on talk shows to discuss their efforts on behalf of women and Hispanics. Loretta was an early backer of New York Sen. Hillary Rodham Clinton for the Democratic presidential nomination, while her sister backed Illinois Sen. Barack Obama. "Our mother brought us up to be independent people," Loretta Sanchez said during a February 2008 appearance on NBC's "Today." "And I'm right and she's wrong, as usual."

Sanchez is known for standing her ground, even when her behavior is viewed as unconventional. In 2000, she embarrassed some Democrats on the eve of their national convention in Los Angeles by at first refusing to cancel a fundraiser at the Playboy mansion, relenting only at the last minute. Her annual Christmas cards usually generate a buzz; the 2006 version featured her lounging in her bed with her pet cat.

Sanchez is a reliable vote for the House Democratic leadership on most issues. She is a member of the Blue Dog Coalition, a group of fiscally conservative Democrats, and backs the pay-as-you-go budget rule that requires offsets for new tax cuts or increased mandatory spending. She voted against a 2007 "patch" to limit the alternative minimum tax (AMT) that lacked offsets. She also voted against the October 2008 $700 billion financial sector rescue plan that carried another AMT patch, again without offsets.

Her Orange County-based district is home to one of the largest Vietnamese communities in the nation, and Sanchez has been a vocal advocate of human rights in Vietnam. She backed House passage of a bill in 2007 to block increases in non-humanitarian U.S. aid to Vietnam unless that government improves its human rights record, but the bill did not move in the Senate.

Sanchez said she grew up a "shy, quiet girl" who did not speak English. Her parents both worked at a manufacturing plant, where her father was a machinist and her mother was a secretary. The second of seven children, she remains close to her family. In October 2008, the Sánchez sisters suffered a devastating loss when their older brother Henry was killed in a boating accident off the coast of Southern California.

Sanchez credits government with her success. "I am a Head Start child, a public school kid, a Pell grant recipient," she said. She opposed the GOP's unsuccessful effort to restructure Head Start, an early-childhood development program for low-income preschoolers, in the 108th Congress (2003-04), invoking her experience growing up poor and challenged by a speech impediment. "I know about these kids, because I am one of those kids," she said during debate on the bill.

She worked her way through college and earned a master's degree in business administration. Feeling isolated as a Hispanic woman in the investment world, she made her first foray into politics in 1994, losing a race for an Anaheim City Council seat. In 1996, she took on conservative GOP Rep. Robert K. Dornan. After winning a four-way primary with 35 percent of the vote, she drew attention from liberal groups. A more Hispanic district and a backlash against a ballot initiative to end state affirmative action programs helped Sanchez score a 984-vote upset.

Dornan claimed he lost to illegal voting by non-citizens, but a House task force said it didn't find enough such instances to prove they altered the outcome. In a 1998 rematch, Sanchez defeated Dornan by 17 percentage points. Her re-elections since have been by larger margins.

KEY VOTES

2008

Yes   Delay consideration of Colombia free-trade agreement
Yes   Override Bush veto of federal farm and nutrition programs reauthorization bill
No   Overhaul surveillance laws and permit dismissal of suits against companies that conducted warrantless wiretapping
Yes   Grant mortgage relief to homeowners and funding for Fannie Mae and Freddie Mac
No   Approve initial $700 billion program to stabilize financial markets
No   Approve final $700 billion program to stabilize financial markets
Yes   Provide $14 billion in loans to automakers

2007

Yes   Increase minimum wage by $2.10 an hour
Yes   Approve $124.2 billion in emergency war spending and set goal for redeployment of troops from Iraq
?   Reject federal contraceptive assistance to international family planning groups
Yes   Override Bush veto of $23.2 billion water projects authorization bill
No   Implement Peru free-trade agreement
Yes   Approve energy policy overhaul with new fuel economy standards
No   Clear $473.5 billion omnibus spending bill, including $70 billion for military operations

CQ VOTE STUDIES

	PARTY UNITY		PRESIDENTIAL SUPPORT	
	SUPPORT	OPPOSE	SUPPORT	OPPOSE
2008	96%	4%	9%	91%
2007	99%	1%	5%	95%
2006	95%	5%	26%	74%
2005	93%	7%	24%	76%
2004	94%	6%	33%	67%

INTEREST GROUPS

	AFL-CIO	ADA	CCUS	ACU
2008	93%	80%	41%	8%
2007	100%	100%	60%	0%
2006	93%	100%	47%	12%
2005	87%	90%	52%	16%
2004	93%	100%	40%	12%

CALIFORNIA 47

Orange County — most of Santa Ana, Anaheim and Garden Grove

An inland chunk of Orange County full of older suburban homes and younger families, the Hispanic-majority 47th is unlike its mostly affluent, Republican neighbors in the county. Located roughly 30 miles southeast of Los Angeles, it takes in parts of four cities: Santa Ana, Anaheim, Garden Grove and Fullerton. A growing number of Hispanics, Vietnamese and other ethnic minorities are changing the demographics here and creating a strong Democratic base.

Almost half of the district's population is in Santa Ana (the Orange County seat), which has higher unemployment and more blue-collar jobs than surrounding areas. Aerospace subcontractors and small businesses are scattered throughout the district, but apart from Disneyland, no single employer drives the area's economy. Despite recent economic downturns, district residents are hoping that Disney will help them ride out the crisis. Recent growth in biomedical and information technology companies broadens the economic base in the 47th.

Three-fourths of Garden Grove's culturally diverse residents live in the 47th, which has an equal mix of Caucasians, Asians and Hispanics. Many years of refugees arriving from Southeast Asia caused concerns that increased demand for social services would lead to higher taxes.

Santa Ana is one of only two Orange County cities that trends Democratic, and the 47th also has some of Anaheim's most Democratic areas. The small part of Fullerton in the district's northern end is heavily Hispanic, although the city overall leans Republican. The Asian community, some of which is heavily Christian, also has a conservative side. Democrat Barack Obama won here easily, taking 60 percent of the district's 2008 presidential vote.

MAJOR INDUSTRY
Small business, service, defense, tourism

CITIES
Santa Ana (pt.), 299,552; Anaheim (pt.), 185,537; Garden Grove (pt.), 125,336; Fullerton (pt.), 17,852

NOTABLE
The 47th's part of Anaheim is home to Disneyland, baseball's Angels and hockey's Ducks; The 10,000-member Crystal Cathedral Ministries megachurch is located in Garden Grove.

Rep. John Campbell (R)

Elected December 2005; 2nd full term

CAPITOL OFFICE
225-5611
www.house.gov/campbell
1507 Longworth Bldg. 20515; fax 225-9177

COMMITTEES
Budget
Financial Services
Joint Economic

RESIDENCE
Irvine

BORN
July 19, 1955; Los Angeles, Calif.

RELIGION
Presbyterian

FAMILY
Wife, Catherine Campbell; two children

EDUCATION
U. of California, Los Angeles, B.A. 1976
(economics); U. of Southern California,
M.S. 1977 (business taxation)

CAREER
Car dealership president; accountant

POLITICAL HIGHLIGHTS
Calif. Assembly, 2000-2004; Calif. Senate, 2004-05

ELECTION RESULTS

2008 GENERAL

John Campbell (R)	171,658	55.6%
Steve Young (D)	125,537	40.7%
Don Patterson (LIBERT)	11,507	3.7%

2008 PRIMARY

John Campbell (R)	unopposed

2006 GENERAL

John Campbell (R)	120,130	59.9%
Steve Young (D)	74,647	37.2%
Bruce Cohen (LIBERT)	5,750	2.9%

PREVIOUS WINNING PERCENTAGES
2005 Special Election (44%)

Campbell is a button-down conservative and self-described "numbers guy" who thinks the numbers in the federal budget are altogether too big. He has spent his time going after spending that has helped to balloon those figures, especially funds set aside, or earmarked, by his fellow lawmakers for specific home-state projects.

When he arrived in Congress after a 2005 special election, he recalled, more than 90 percent of the people who came to see him during his first months in office were looking for some type of handout from the government. But as his vehement anti-earmarking views became known, he said, that traffic trailed off.

Campbell is a member of the Republican Study Committee (RSC), a sizeable group of the most conservative House Republicans. In the 110th Congress (2007-08) he headed the group's budget and spending task force, making him a high-profile critic of the Democratic majority's spending policies, and he was regarded as a front-runner for the committee's chairmanship in fall 2008.

But then he backed the George W. Bush administration's $700 billion proposal to shore up the ailing financial services industry. Fellow RSC members vigorously opposed the measure as unwelcome and unworkable, and after voting in favor of the two bills — the second of which became law — he abandoned his candidacy. But Campbell, whose district had been hit hard by subprime mortgage problems, had no regrets. "During the course of the last 10 days, our financial trading markets have basically become dysfunctional," he told the Orange County Register in September 2008. "That dysfunction, if allowed to continue, could affect everyone in America with a bank account, a pension plan or a mutual fund. We can't just let it run its course and see what happens, because the consequences are unconscionable."

Campbell is still involved in fiscal policy as a member of the Budget Committee, where he continues his anti-earmark crusade. In 2007, he even took the floor to assail a $2 million earmark sought by Democrat John P. Murtha of Pennsylvania, the powerful chairman of the Defense Appropriations Subcommittee and the leading House earmarker. When the House took up a spending bill for military construction and veterans' affairs in 2008, Arizona Republican Jeff Flake and Campbell offered an amendment to delete 103 congressional earmarks from the legislation. Their bid failed, drawing only 63 votes. Even among Republicans, twice as many members voted against them as with them. "Clearly members of Congress do not yet understand what the vast majority of Americans know — earmarks must be ended or reformed," Campbell said on his blog, Green Eyeshade.

Campbell also serves on the Joint Economic and Financial Services committees, a good fit for his background as a businessman and certified public accountant. "I try and fiddle around with other things, but I always wind up back with numbers," he said.

Budgeting terms such as "dynamic scoring" and "pay as you go" rules are part of his lexicon. In 2008, he proposed a constitutional amendment to limit total federal spending to growth in the gross domestic product, unless a two-thirds majority in Congress votes to spend more. He wants to make permanent the tax cuts enacted in 2001 and 2003, during President Bush's first term. He said raising taxes is counterproductive, encouraging individuals and businesses to look for ways to avoid the hit. "When you raise taxes a dollar, the government doesn't see a dollar" in new revenue, he said.

Campbell spent almost 25 years in the automobile business, as a corporate officer and owner of franchises that sold Nissan, Mazda, Ford, Saturn, Porsche and Saab models. His Capitol Hill office is accented with photographs of cars and a model of a 1957 Corvette convertible (he has three Corvettes in California), representing a boyhood passion that turned into a career owning automobile dealerships.

Campbell is a member of the Sons of Union Veterans and has occasionally participated in Civil War re-enactments. He grew up in the Hancock Park area of Los Angeles, in a house built in 1922 by his maternal grandfather. An Irvine resident for more than 30 years, Campbell lives in a house he designed and built with his wife. He said will "never, ever move to Washington. I'm a Californian through and through."

Campbell's great-grandfather on his father's side, Alexander, was elected to the California Assembly in 1860 on the same GOP ticket as Abraham Lincoln. The congressman's father, also named Alexander, ran unsuccessfully for the state Senate when John Campbell was 11. Although he lost, Campbell did his best to help his dad's campaign. Campbell's father was a classic-car collector and dealership investor, spurring Campbell's own interest in cars.

In 1978, after receiving an economics degree from UCLA and a graduate degree in business taxation from the University of Southern California, Campbell moved to Orange County to be a corporate comptroller for car dealerships. He became a GOP volunteer and campaign donor and a second tenor for the Irvine Presbyterian Church.

In 2000, Campbell was recruited to run for the Assembly and won. He was named "freshman of the year" by the National Republican Legislators Association. When term limits forced out the sitting GOP state senator from his area in 2004, Campbell moved up.

But he didn't stay in Sacramento for long. Although he harbored aspirations for higher state office, the 48th District House seat opened up in 2005 when Republican Christopher Cox left to become chairman of the Securities and Exchange Commission. Campbell said he was peppered with calls from people urging him to seek the seat.

In the 10-candidate open special primary to fill Cox's House seat, Campbell got 45 percent of the vote. He prevailed in the special election with 44 percent — a relatively modest share in a district where Republicans regularly get 60 percent or more. In 2006, Campbell won with 60 percent, and had little trouble winning re-election two years later despite the Democratic tide. In early 2009 he underwent surgery for diverticulitis, causing him to miss several weeks of House votes.

KEY VOTES

2008

No	Delay consideration of Colombia free-trade agreement
No	Override Bush veto of federal farm and nutrition programs reauthorization bill
Yes	Overhaul surveillance laws and permit dismissal of suits against companies that conducted warrantless wiretapping
Yes	Grant mortgage relief to homeowners and funding for Fannie Mae and Freddie Mac
Yes	Approve initial $700 billion program to stabilize financial markets
Yes	Approve final $700 billion program to stabilize financial markets
P	Provide $14 billion in loans to automakers

2007

No	Increase minimum wage by $2.10 an hour
No	Approve $124.2 billion in emergency war spending and set goal for redeployment of troops from Iraq
Yes	Reject federal contraceptive assistance to international family planning groups
No	Override Bush veto of $23.2 billion water projects authorization bill
Yes	Implement Peru free-trade agreement
Yes	Approve energy policy overhaul with new fuel economy standards
Yes	Clear $473.5 billion omnibus spending bill, including $70 billion for military operations

CQ VOTE STUDIES

	PARTY UNITY		PRESIDENTIAL SUPPORT	
	SUPPORT	OPPOSE	SUPPORT	OPPOSE
2008	97%	3%	89%	11%
2007	97%	3%	92%	8%
2006	95%	5%	90%	10%
2005	100%	0%	100%	0%

INTEREST GROUPS

	AFL-CIO	ADA	CCUS	ACU
2008	0%	5%	76%	86%
2007	4%	10%	70%	92%
2006	7%	0%	87%	88%
2005	0%	0%	50%	100%

CALIFORNIA 48

Southern Orange County — Irvine, Newport Beach

The 48th covers the Orange County coast from Newport Beach south through Laguna Beach to Dana Point, and it takes in a chunk of the county inland from the coast through Irvine to the foothills of the Santa Ana mountains. The district is distinguished by its large white-collar labor force and its historically high median income.

Newport Beach is known for its beautiful sandy beaches, luxurious housing and solid Republicanism. Picturesque Laguna Beach attracts tourists and scuba divers. Inland is Laguna Woods, home to a significant number of senior citizens, Laguna Niguel and Laguna Hills. Nearly 70 percent of district residents are white.

The engineering and biomedical research programs at the University of California, Irvine, have attracted a large number of high-tech and biotech firms to the area, and the university is the district's largest employer. The national housing market crisis affected the region's foreclosure rates, home prices and unemployment — a major mortgage lender based in Irvine collapsed, taking thousands of local jobs with it.

Smog, crime and other problems endemic to Los Angeles generally do not affect these areas. Irvine consistently rates as the nation's safest city with more than 100,000 people, based on the FBI's crime reporting statistics. But the sheer number of people who commute into the district from the north and east makes transportation among the toughest problems here, as traffic backs up and increases the threat of pollution. Toll roads in the area have helped, and more funding for road improvements aims to ease congestion. Rising gas prices have led to increased use of the expanding regional mass transit rail and bus system.

While registered Republicans outnumber Democrats by 16 percentage points, pockets of Democratic strength can be found in the district's inland sections and in the more liberal-leaning community surrounding the university. Democrat Barack Obama won the 48th by just less than 1 percentage point in the 2008 presidential election.

MAJOR INDUSTRY
Technology, research, tourism

CITIES
Irvine, 143,072; Newport Beach, 70,032; Tustin, 67,504

NOTABLE
The Ayn Rand Institute is located in Irvine.

Rep. Darrell Issa (R)

Elected 2000; 5th term

CAPITOL OFFICE
225-3906
issa.house.gov
2347 Rayburn Bldg. 20515-0549; fax 225-3303

COMMITTEES
Judiciary
Oversight & Government Reform - ranking member

RESIDENCE
Vista

BORN
Nov. 1, 1953; Cleveland, Ohio

RELIGION
Antioch Orthodox Christian Church

FAMILY
Wife, Kathy Issa; one child

EDUCATION
Kent State U., A.A. 1976 (general studies); Siena
Heights College, B.A. 1976 (business administration
and management)

MILITARY SERVICE
Army 1970-72; Army 1976-80; Army Reserve 1980-88

CAREER
Car alarm company owner; electronics
manufacturing company executive

POLITICAL HIGHLIGHTS
Sought Republican nomination for
U.S. Senate, 1998

ELECTION RESULTS

2008 GENERAL

Darrell Issa (R)	140,300	58.3%
Robert Hamilton (D)	90,138	37.4%
Lars R. Grossmith (LIBERT)	10,232	4.2%

2008 PRIMARY

Darrell Issa (R)	unopposed

2006 GENERAL

Darrell Issa (R)	98,831	63.3%
Jeeni Criscenzo (D)	52,227	33.4%
Lars R. Grossmith (LIBERT)	4,952	3.2%

PREVIOUS WINNING PERCENTAGES
2004 (63%); 2002 (77%); 2000 (61%)

Issa's life story isn't a classic Horatio Alger tale, but it's close. As a young man, he turned a small investment into a multimillion-dollar car alarm company. Since then, he's used his considerable fortune — one of the largest in Congress — to become a major player in California Republican politics.

Ambitious to the point that some critics call him arrogant, Issa (EYE-sah) also has risen quickly in the House, where he is the top Republican on the Oversight and Government Reform Committee for the 111th Congress (2009-10). The role in the past has been mostly a highly politicized one, but Issa hopes to work with the committee's new Democratic chairman, Edolphus Towns of New York, to make it more businesslike and bipartisan in rooting out executive branch waste, fraud and abuse.

If history is any guide, though, Issa may have to abandon that approach. He had a confrontational relationship with Towns' predecessor, Henry A. Waxman of California, who was intent on rooting out wrongdoing in the George W. Bush administration.

Issa may have more luck finding bipartisan comity on foreign policy, where he shares President Obama's interest in reviving the Israeli-Palestinian peace process. In a body sometimes accused of being too one-sided in its support of Israel, Issa is a moderating voice, and his Lebanese Christian heritage gives him a unique perspective on the Middle East conflicts.

But Issa's focus, at least initially, will be on the Oversight panel. He worked hard to win the slot, leapfrogging more senior members by throwing himself into his work and mastering unglamorous subjects, such as government procurement reform, to win the favor of the former top Republican, Thomas M. Davis III of Virginia, who retired at the end of 2008. Issa also schmoozed top GOP leaders, hosting a big fundraiser for the party in March 2008. His bid got a boost when another aspirant, Connecticut's Christopher Shays, lost his re-election bid.

With the job in hand, Issa set out to make the committee staff his own, replacing many of the committee's Republican staffers with seasoned investigators. Issa said he stood "ready to proactively probe any critical failures of government neglected by the committee majority."

Issa has shown he is up to that task. At a May 2008 hearing, tempers flared when he demanded Waxman give panel Republicans equal time to question EPA Administrator Stephen L. Johnson about new ozone standards. Waxman threatened to throw Issa from the committee room. Issa said Waxman was "arrogant and unprofessional."

During the final year of the Bush administration, as Waxman pressed for investigations of administration interference into the regulatory process, Issa charged Waxman with unfairness. When Waxman investigated whether Transportation Department officials lobbied EPA civil servants to decide against allowing California to enforce clean air rules more stringent than the federal government's, Issa pressed him to also determine whether EPA staffers lobbied agency decision-makers to side with California. And when Waxman launched an inquiry into executive compensation in the wake of the subprime mortgage crisis in 2008, Issa said he was trying to "scapegoat a few wealthy individuals in a complex crisis where there's plenty of blame to go around."

But Issa didn't shy away from criticizing the Bush administration when he felt it was warranted. He voted twice against giving the administration $700 billion to shore up the financial services sector; after Congress passed the bill, and again at the start of the 111th, he introduced legislation to create an independent panel to study how to address the financial crisis.

Issa also sits on the Judiciary Committee, where during the 110th he was a key player in an ill-fated bid to revamp the country's patent approval process to protect high-tech companies from infringement litigation. The House passed the bill, but the Senate didn't take it up.

Issa has spent much time condemning Middle East terrorists, but he also wants the United States to reach out to friendly Arab nations. His sympathetic approach to Arab nations draws condemnations from pro-Israel advocates. At the same time, Arab commentators complain about his pro-Israel votes.

A major player in California politics, Issa bankrolled the recall effort in 2003 that ousted Democratic Gov. Gray Davis and put Republican Arnold Schwarzenegger in his place. Although Issa wanted to replace Davis himself, several GOP House colleagues persuaded him to step aside for Schwarzenegger, whom they believed to be more likely to win.

In 2007, Issa helped fund an ill-fated effort to convince Californians to award their electoral votes in presidential elections by congressional district, a potential boon to GOP presidential aspirants, since no Republican has won the state since George Bush in 1988. The initiative died when organizers failed to gather enough signatures.

Issa was born in Cleveland, where his Lebanese-American father was a salesman and an X-ray technician. He quit high school at 17 and joined the Army. After Issa had served two years, the Army paid for his college education with the understanding that he would return to active duty upon graduation.

In 1972, he and his older brother, William, were arrested for allegedly stealing a Maserati from a car dealership. The charges were dropped. In 1980, the two were charged with faking the theft of Issa's Mercedes-Benz; again, the charges were dropped. In both cases, Issa blamed his brother.

After fulfilling his Army obligation, Issa returned to Cleveland and used his $7,000 in savings to purchase assets from a struggling electronics business. He and his wife turned those into a highly profitable operation that gained renown as the maker of the popular Viper anti-theft device. In 1985, they moved the business to Vista. In 1999 and 2000, Issa was chairman of the board of the Consumer Electronics Association. He sold the business in 2000.

In 1998, Issa spent $11 million on a failed bid for the GOP Senate nod. He hit the campaign trail again in 2000, when GOP Rep. Ron Packard announced his retirement from the 48th District, a reliably GOP district that was home to President Nixon. Issa weathered a nine-candidate primary, sinking $2 million into the race, then won the general election with 61 percent of the vote. His re-elections have been easy in what is now the 49th District.

KEY VOTES

2008

No   Delay consideration of Colombia free-trade agreement

No   Override Bush veto of federal farm and nutrition programs reauthorization bill

Yes   Overhaul surveillance laws and permit dismissal of suits against companies that conducted warrantless wiretapping

No   Grant mortgage relief to homeowners and funding for Fannie Mae and Freddie Mac

No   Approve initial $700 billion program to stabilize financial markets

No   Approve final $700 billion program to stabilize financial markets

No   Provide $14 billion in loans to automakers

2007

No   Increase minimum wage by $2.10 an hour

No   Approve $124.2 billion in emergency war spending and set goal for redeployment of troops from Iraq

Yes   Reject federal contraceptive assistance to international family planning groups

No   Override Bush veto of $23.2 billion water projects authorization bill

Yes   Implement Peru free-trade agreement

Yes   Approve energy policy overhaul with new fuel economy standards

Yes   Clear $473.5 billion omnibus spending bill, including $70 billion for military operations

CQ VOTE STUDIES

	PARTY UNITY		PRESIDENTIAL SUPPORT	
	SUPPORT	OPPOSE	SUPPORT	OPPOSE
2008	99%	1%	79%	21%
2007	96%	4%	86%	14%
2006	94%	6%	95%	5%
2005	95%	5%	89%	11%
2004	95%	5%	85%	15%

INTEREST GROUPS

	AFL-CIO	ADA	CCUS	ACU
2008	7%	10%	94%	100%
2007	8%	20%	74%	88%
2006	21%	5%	100%	80%
2005	13%	0%	93%	84%
2004	20%	0%	100%	92%

CALIFORNIA 49

North San Diego County; West Riverside County

Based in northwestern San Diego County and western Riverside County, the heavily residential 49th is home to many bedroom communities, including Vista and Oceanside.

While some residents work in the district, others commute to jobs in San Diego (a sliver of which falls in the 49th) or, to a lesser extent, Orange County. The massive Camp Pendleton Marine Corps Base sits near Oceanside, on the largest undeveloped portion of coast in Southern California, but the local economy relies less on military contracts than its San Diego or Orange County neighbors. In northeast San Diego County, Rancho Bernardo has manufacturing and defense sectors, including Hewlett-Packard and Northrop Grumman, many of which are located at a large industrial park in the nearby 50th. Visitors to Oceanside and the beaches along the coast also boost the local economy.

Most residents live in San Diego County, but more than a decade of prodigious growth in Temecula in Riverside County established tourism and retail bases — economic downturns, however, have hurt those

sectors. Old Town Temecula still welcomes tourists who visit the area's wineries, and the desert terrain of the Temecula Valley also has become known for balloon rides, skydiving and golf. The Pechanga Resort and Casino near Temecula employs thousands and lures visitors to the area, but a recent dropoff in the number of visitors has led to job losses.

Some areas here have significant Hispanic populations, but nearly 60 percent of the district is white. The 49th supports Republicans, and John McCain took 53 percent of its 2008 presidential vote. Perris, with a large retirement community, is one of the few places Democrats hold an edge.

MAJOR INDUSTRY
Medical devices, services, manufacturing, defense

MILITARY BASES
Camp Pendleton Marine Corps Base, Air Station and Naval Hospital, 38,000 military, 65,000 civilian (2007); Naval Weapons Station Seal Beach, Detachment Fallbrook, 64 military, 224 civilian (2006)

CITIES
Oceanside, 161,029; Vista, 89,857; Temecula, 57,716; Perris, 36,189

NOTABLE
Oceanside's Mission San Luis Rey de Francia, dedicated in 1798, has been restored to its original design.

Rep. Brian P. Bilbray (R)

Elected June 2006; 5th full term
Also served 1995-2001

Bilbray is a former lifeguard who still surfs the coastal waters of Southern California. Born and raised in the San Diego area he has represented for half his life, he knows his district well and has focused much of his attention on two topics important to his constituents: combating illegal immigration and promoting veterans' benefits.

He said his passion for dealing with immigration stems from growing up with a backyard "full of illegal immigrants hiding from Border Patrol agents." Later, he recalled, he would see cars hit migrants from Mexico while they tried to cross highways. "It felt like a sin to be quiet about what was happening," he said.

Chairman of the Immigration Reform Caucus, an informal group of lawmakers who support tougher immigration laws, Bilbray worked hard in 2007 to stop a bill backed by the Senate and the George W. Bush administration that would have offered the nation's 12 million illegal immigrants a path to citizenship. "The way you stop illegal immigration is not to start by announcing that you're going to reward illegal immigration," he said.

In 2007, he introduced legislation with Democrat Heath Shuler of North Carolina calling for the hire of thousands more Border Patrol agents, increasing technology to secure the country's borders and establishing a program to recruit former military personnel to serve in U.S. Customs and Border Protection.

Bilbray tries to use his position as the top-ranking Republican on the Oversight and Government Reform Subcommittee on Government Management, Organization and Procurement to ensure local governments are reimbursed for the costs of illegal immigration.

His immigration stance and his voting record could lead one to mistake Bilbray for a staunch conservative. During the Bush administration, he sided with his party 94 percent of the time on votes that pitted a majority of each party against each other. He opposed both versions of the $700 billion package to shore up the ailing financial services sector, saying they did nothing to help taxpayers or fix the root causes of the country's economic problems. He called on House leaders to bring the Financial Services Committee back into session in late 2008 to develop plans to rebuild the markets.

But his politics are moderate on some social issues; he has supported some gun control measures and has generally voted for abortion rights. But in 2008, he joined his party in voting for a House bill to repeal District of Columbia laws prohibiting firearm possession, including the possession of semiautomatic firearms. He also was among the few Republicans to vote against repealing the ban on semiautomatic assault-style weapons in 1996. And while he opposed what critics call "partial birth" abortion and federal funding for most abortions, he did not support overturning *Roe v. Wade*, which legalized abortion.

Bilbray's San Diego-area district is home to several military installations, two veterans' hospitals and more than 64,000 veterans. A multitude of defense contractors underpin the local economy.

A member of the Veterans' Affairs Committee, Bilbray backed a suicide prevention bill, signed into law in 2007, that requires the Veterans Affairs Department to train its medical staff to evaluate veterans for signs of depression or post-traumatic stress disorder. He also backed bills to provide tuition credits for reservists and to create a veterans' home loan program.

CAPITOL OFFICE
225-0508
www.house.gov/bilbray
2348 Rayburn Bldg. 20515-0550; fax 225-2558

COMMITTEES
Oversight & Government Reform
Science & Technology
Veterans' Affairs

RESIDENCE
Carlsbad

BORN
Jan. 28, 1951; Coronado, Calif.

RELIGION
Roman Catholic

FAMILY
Wife, Karen Bilbray; six children (one deceased)

EDUCATION
Southwestern College (Calif.), attended 1970-74 (history)

CAREER
Lobbyist; tax firm owner; lifeguard

POLITICAL HIGHLIGHTS
Imperial Beach City Council, 1976-78; mayor of Imperial Beach, 1978-85; San Diego County Board of Supervisors, 1985-95; U.S. House, 1995-2001; defeated for re-election to U.S. House, 2000

ELECTION RESULTS

2008 GENERAL

Brian P. Bilbray (R)	157,502	50.2%
Nick Leibham (D)	141,635	45.2%
Wayne Dunlap (LIBERT)	14,365	4.6%

2008 PRIMARY

Brian P. Bilbray (R)	unopposed

2006 GENERAL

Brian P. Bilbray (R)	118,018	53.1%
Francine Busby (D)	96,612	43.5%
Paul King (LIBERT)	4,119	1.8%
Miriam E. Clark (PFP)	3,353	1.5%

PREVIOUS WINNING PERCENTAGES
2006 Special Election (50%); 1998 (49%); 1996 (53%); 1994 (49%)

On environmental issues, Bilbray tends to vote green. A staple of his political biography is the story of how, as the young mayor of Imperial Beach, he became so frustrated with the federal response to complaints that the Tijuana River was carrying pollution from Mexico onto U.S. beaches that he climbed aboard a bulldozer and dammed the offending stream.

In 2007, he sponsored a measure to require government agencies to update their criteria for water quality and establish national standards for beach monitoring. The bill also called for a three-year EPA study on the benefits of implementing new technology to produce more-efficient testing of water quality. Bilbray also secured an amendment to a House-passed water pollution control to allow the use of special molecular testing to assess coastal recreation waters.

Bilbray scored another clean-water success in 2008, when the House passed his bill calling for $35 million for a water treatment, recycling and reclamation project in San Diego County. The Senate did not take up the measure, however.

And while Bilbray sides with his party to allow offshore drilling in Alabama and Mississippi, he opposes offshore drilling in California, fearing it would harm the region's tourism industry.

Bilbray also is a member of the Science and Technology Committee. He has championed nuclear energy as a way to both meet future electricity demand and reduce greenhouse gas emissions.

Bilbray first won election to the House — in the old 49th District — as part of the GOP wave in 1994 by ousting a Democratic freshman despite being outspent 2-to-1. He never won re-election with more than 53 percent of the vote and finally lost the seat in 2000 to the Democrats. He said he spent the next six years doing a lot of "sailing and surfing," and served as co-chairman of the National Board of Advisors for the Federation for American Immigration Reform, a group that advocates limiting immigration and beefing-up border security.

In 2006, he returned in a special election to fill the 50th District seat of GOP Rep. Randy "Duke" Cunningham, who was sent to prison after admitting to taking more than $2 million in bribes from defense contractors. His former district had encompassed a similar slice of Southern California, and many voters remembered him. Furthermore, the new district was more Republican than his old one. Democrats hoped the taint from the Cunningham scandal would overcome that tilt, but Bilbray won by 5 percentage points, then defeated the same opponent by 10 points in the November general election. He won again in 2008 with 50 percent of the vote.

KEY VOTES

2008

No Delay consideration of Colombia free-trade agreement

No Override Bush veto of federal farm and nutrition programs reauthorization bill

Yes Overhaul surveillance laws and permit dismissal of suits against companies that conducted warrantless wiretapping

No Grant mortgage relief to homeowners and funding for Fannie Mae and Freddie Mac

No Approve initial $700 billion program to stabilize financial markets

No Approve final $700 billion program to stabilize financial markets

No Provide $14 billion in loans to automakers

2007

No Increase minimum wage by $2.10 an hour

No Approve $124.2 billion in emergency war spending and set goal for redeployment of troops from Iraq

Yes Reject federal contraceptive assistance to international family planning groups

No Override Bush veto of $23.2 billion water projects authorization bill

Yes Implement Peru free-trade agreement

No Approve energy policy overhaul with new fuel economy standards

Yes Clear $473.5 billion omnibus spending bill, including $70 billion for military operations

CQ VOTE STUDIES

	PARTY UNITY		PRESIDENTIAL SUPPORT	
	SUPPORT	OPPOSE	SUPPORT	OPPOSE
2008	94%	6%	67%	33%
2007	95%	5%	85%	15%
2006	93%	7%	93%	7%
2000	76%	24%	38%	62%
1999	72%	28%	39%	61%

INTEREST GROUPS

	AFL-CIO	ADA	CCUS	ACU
2008	20%	15%	88%	92%
2007	8%	10%	80%	92%
2006	11%	5%	100%	94%
2000	10%	25%	80%	68%
1999	38%	50%	68%	68%

CALIFORNIA 50
North San Diego; Escondido; Carlsbad

With its beach communities and upper-class neighborhoods, the San Diego-area 50th District combines affluent suburbs like Carlsbad, coastal areas such as Encinitas, the northern part of San Diego itself, and inland Escondido and San Marcos, which are tucked within the district's northeast curve.

The area's wealth is a testament to one of the state's top technology sectors. With national economic downturns, the technology industry in San Diego has suffered losses, and San Diego County has seen rising unemployment. But, the area has weathered the recession better than other regions because of its diversified economy. The growth of cellular technology companies and computer firms, combined with established military and defense contracting, has helped stabilize the area.

Northern San Diego hosts some of the city's renewable-energy firms. Home construction has long been profitable in the north San Diego region but has slowed recently. The mild climate of the coastal area is friendly to commercial production of flowers and fruits.

Unlike San Diego's south side, the 50th is mostly white, although there is a growing Hispanic population and illegal immigration is an issue here. The 50th's conservative corridor runs north and south along Interstate 15, including the Marine Corps base in Miramar (shared with the 52nd). Coastal cities such as Del Mar, Carlsbad and Encinitas, where beach pollution and the environment are issues, add liberals to the district.

In the traditionally Republican stronghold, Democrat Barack Obama narrowly edged out John McCain in the presidential election — and Democratic candidate Nick Leibham nearly unseated incumbent GOP Rep. Brian P. Bilbray — in 2008.

MAJOR INDUSTRY
Technology, defense, manufacturing, tourism, agriculture

MILITARY BASES
Marine Corps Air Station Miramar, 10,000 military, 400 civilian (2008) (shared with the 52nd)

CITIES
San Diego (pt.), 262,523; Escondido, 133,559; Carlsbad, 78,247; Encinitas, 58,014; San Marcos, 54,977

NOTABLE
Carlsbad is home to the Legoland theme park.

Rep. Bob Filner (D)

CAPITOL OFFICE
225-8045
www.house.gov/filner
2428 Rayburn Bldg. 20515-0551; fax 225-9073

COMMITTEES
Transportation & Infrastructure
Veterans' Affairs - chairman

RESIDENCE
Chula Vista

BORN
Sept. 4, 1942; Pittsburgh, Pa.

RELIGION
Jewish

FAMILY
Wife, Jane Filner; two children

EDUCATION
Cornell U., B.A. 1963 (chemistry);
U. of Delaware, M.A. 1969 (history);
Cornell U., Ph.D. 1973 (history of science)

CAREER
Congressional aide; professor

POLITICAL HIGHLIGHTS
San Diego Unified School District Board of
Education, 1979-83 (president, 1982); candidate
for San Diego City Council, 1983; San Diego City
Council, 1987-92 (deputy mayor, 1990-91)

ELECTION RESULTS

2008 GENERAL

Bob Filner (D)	148,281	72.7%
David Lee Joy (R)	49,345	24.2%
Dan "Frodo" Litwin (LIBERT)	6,199	3.0%

2008 PRIMARY

Bob Filner (D)	31,690	75.7%
Daniel C. "Danny" Ramirez (D)	10,182	24.3%

2006 GENERAL

Bob Filner (D)	78,114	67.4%
Blake L. Miles (R)	34,931	30.2%
Dan "Frodo" Litwin (LIBERT)	2,790	2.4%

PREVIOUS WINNING PERCENTAGES
2004 (62%); 2002 (58%); 2000 (68%); 1998 (99%);
1996 (62%); 1994 (57%); 1992 (57%)

Elected 1992; 9th term

Filner is a liberal disciple of former Minnesota senator and vice president Hubert H. Humphrey, but he doesn't share Humphrey's mild-mannered persona. His temper has drawn as much attention as his strenuous advocacy for returning servicemembers from Iraq and Afghanistan along with aging veterans of the Vietnam War and earlier conflicts.

As chairman of the Veterans' Affairs Committee, Filner has regularly ignited partisan fireworks at committee hearings in clashing with the panel's top-ranking Republican, Steve Buyer of Indiana. He can at times be volatile outside of Congress as well: Filner launched into a profanity-laced tirade outside the Department of Veterans Affairs (VA) headquarters in June 2007 over the department's failure to protect veterans' personal data from computer theft and other potential threats.

Filner again made headlines two months later when he got into an altercation with an airline employee who claimed the congressman screamed and pushed past her to find his luggage at Dulles International Airport outside of Washington. Loudoun County, Va., authorities eventually reduced assault and battery charges to trespassing and levied a $100 fine. The House ethics committee established a special investigative subcommittee to review the charge before concluding Filner was not guilty of wrongdoing.

He is expected to have an easy working relationship with President Obama's administration. Obama has promised to make the VA more efficient and better able to serve its constituents. In 2009, he introduced legislation to alter the VA's fiscal planning so that it drafts budgets for the next two years, ensuring funding does not run out and thereby limit veterans' access to health care. He also wants to boost medical and psychological evaluations for returning veterans.

During the 110th Congress (2007-08), Filner saw his agenda on veterans' care furthered thanks to a series of 2007 news reports of unsatisfactory conditions, outpatient neglect and mismanagement at Washington's Walter Reed Army Medical Center. He helped secure record VA budgets in 2008 and 2009 spending bills in the wake of the scandals, then called for Congress to scrupulously monitor the sprawling department's activities.

Filner has fought for years to secure full benefits for Filipino veterans who served with U.S. forces in World War II. His efforts, inspired by the large Filipino community in his San Diego-area district, won him the gratitude of the Philippine government, especially when he was arrested with Filipino-American protesters who chained themselves to the White House fence in 1997. In 2003, President George W. Bush signed his measure to give the veterans full access to VA medical facilities, restore burial benefits to Filipino scouts and boost the compensation for Filipino veterans and their widows. In the 110th, he won House approval of a bill to grant compensation payments to the veterans, only to see it neglected in the Senate. But Obama's $787 billion economic stimulus plan, signed into law in early 2009, included $198 million of already-appropriated money to make such payments to about 18,000 surviving Filipino veterans. Yet, even though he voted for the stimulus, he said the bill didn't provide enough for all veterans.

A 1960s civil rights activist who by his own account avoided the draft with repeated student deferments, Filner landed on Veterans' Affairs almost by accident. Soon after he was elected in 1992, he ran into Democratic Sen. Alan Cranston of California, who was heading into retirement. Cranston, who had chaired the Senate's panel, urged Filner to seek the House assignment, telling him it was good politics for a liberal to champion the cause of veterans.

The newly minted panel member showed up at a reception hosted by Chairman G.V. Sonny Montgomery of Mississippi, a legend in the veterans' community. Filner had never heard of him. "Mr. Chairman," he said, "I was once a tourist through your state. I took a Greyhound bus to your capital, Jackson. I got off and the police chief showed me around his jail. The sheriff in Hines County showed me around his jail, and then I spent a couple of months in your state penitentiary. I was one of the first Freedom Riders." Montgomery did not bat an eyelash. "I was the head of the National Guard that arrested you," he replied. The two men became close.

As the representative of a district on the U.S.-Mexico border, Filner often is in the middle of congressional debates over immigration controls and border security, often looking out for the plight of immigrants. As a member of the Transportation and Infrastructure Committee he supported distributing biometric "smart cards" that could be scanned at entry points to reduce lengthy waiting times at border crossings. He has put more money into surface transportation bills for first-responders and hospitals that treat illegal immigrants needing emergency services. He favors a program in the style of the Marshall Plan to create jobs and improve roads, schools and hospitals in Mexico, believing better conditions would stanch illegal emigration to the United States.

At the start of the 111th Congress (2009-10), he introduced several immigration bills, including a measure to avoid detention of legal immigrants for minor crimes. And he and fellow California Democrat Susan A. Davis joined with local officials and groups to write a letter to Obama in February 2009 asking him to reconsider the construction of a 700-mile fence along the border that would block off a San Diego access point where families reunite.

A native Pennsylvanian, Filner is the son of a former union organizer and businessman who was an early fundraiser for the Rev. Martin Luther King Jr. Filner met King as a teenager and participated in his first civil rights march in 1957. He left college to join the Freedom Riders in 1961. He was arrested during a sit-in at a Mississippi lunch counter with John Lewis, now a House colleague from Georgia. After his release from prison, he finished college and later earned a doctorate in the history of science.

Filner taught history at San Diego State University starting in the 1970s. After working for Minnesota Democrats Humphrey and Rep. Donald M. Fraser, he spent four years on the local school board and five on the city council. He then ran for a newly created 50th District House seat in 1992. His single-minded devotion to fundraising and tireless campaigning helped him overcome five Democratic primary foes. The Democratic makeup of his district — now the 51st — has allowed him a string of easy general election victories.

KEY VOTES

2008
Yes Delay consideration of Colombia free-trade agreement
Yes Override Bush veto of federal farm and nutrition programs reauthorization bill
No   Overhaul surveillance laws and permit dismissal of suits against companies that conducted warrantless wiretapping
Yes Grant mortgage relief to homeowners and funding for Fannie Mae and Freddie Mac
No   Approve initial $700 billion program to stabilize financial markets
No   Approve final $700 billion program to stabilize financial markets
No   Provide $14 billion in loans to automakers

2007
Yes Increase minimum wage by $2.10 an hour
Yes Approve $124.2 billion in emergency war spending and set goal for redeployment of troops from Iraq
No   Reject federal contraceptive assistance to international family planning groups
Yes Override Bush veto of $23.2 billion water projects authorization bill
No   Implement Peru free-trade agreement
Yes Approve energy policy overhaul with new fuel economy standards
No   Clear $473.5 billion omnibus spending bill, including $70 billion for military operations

CQ VOTE STUDIES

	PARTY UNITY		PRESIDENTIAL SUPPORT	
	SUPPORT	OPPOSE	SUPPORT	OPPOSE
2008	95%	5%	13%	87%
2007	99%	1%	4%	96%
2006	97%	3%	18%	82%
2005	98%	2%	15%	85%
2004	98%	2%	23%	77%

INTEREST GROUPS

	AFL-CIO	ADA	CCUS	ACU
2008	93%	100%	47%	12%
2007	100%	90%	45%	0%
2006	92%	95%	33%	12%
2005	93%	100%	37%	4%
2004	93%	95%	22%	9%

CALIFORNIA 51

Central and southern San Diego; Imperial County

The part-urban, part-rural 51st runs east along almost the entire length of California's border with Mexico, except for the western tip at the Pacific Ocean. In the east, it takes in all of Imperial County, and near the Pacific, it climbs north from the border to include part of central San Diego and some close-in suburbs.

The 51st's part of San Diego, which starts south and east of downtown, is working-class, crime ridden and heavily Hispanic. Mexican shoppers who had been drawn to the local shopping centers have been crossing the border less frequently. Chula Vista attracted upscale housing developers in the last decade but recently has experienced high foreclosure rates. South of Chula Vista and across the border from Tijuana, Otay Mesa is known for manufacturing plants that have twin sites in Mexico.

Imperial County is heavily agricultural, with an annual crop yield worth more than $1 billion, and tends to have very high unemployment. The county is more than two-thirds Hispanic. Voters here are more conservative than their city cousins, but still lean heavily Democratic.

Water is another concern in the 51st. Both San Diego and Imperial counties are under pressure to reduce their dependency on the Colorado River, and a proposed solution — to lower the Salton Sea's high salinity and pesticide levels — has environmentalists concerned about the local ecosystem and migratory birds.

The Hispanic-majority district gave 63 percent of its vote to Democrat Barack Obama in the 2008 presidential election. Border issues, particularly illegal immigration — which fills agricultural labor jobs — is a key issue in the 50th District. Ranchers and growers see illegal immigration as a necessary source of labor, while others say it threatens the district's quality of life.

MAJOR INDUSTRY
Service, manufacturing, agriculture, retail

MILITARY BASES
Naval Station San Diego (shared with the 53rd), 28,754 military, 6,222 civilian (2008); El Centro Naval Air Facility, 330 military, 500 civilian (2007)

CITIES
San Diego (pt.), 239,457; Chula Vista, 173,556; National City, 54,260

NOTABLE
El Centro is the winter training home of the Navy's Blue Angels.

Rep. Duncan Hunter (R)

Elected 2008; 1st term

Like his father and predecessor, whose name he shares, Hunter defines the core of his political mission in terms of national defense. And like his father, the younger Hunter — a Marine combat veteran — can be outspoken in expressing strong conservative beliefs.

Hunter joins other conservatives in contending that defense spending should be no less than 4 percent of the gross domestic product. Wars in Iraq and Afghanistan have pushed it slightly above that level, though many lawmakers say money should be redirected to bolster the struggling economy. But Hunter said, "How much is it worth not to have another 9/11?"

Republican leaders gave Hunter a seat on the Armed Services Committee, where his father served his entire 28-year career. He intends to seek to restore combat-worn Army inventories — from unmanned planes to armored vehicles — while trying to boost U.S. warship manufacturing. He criticized the Obama administration's decision in early 2009 to move terrorist inmates from the military detention facility on the U.S. naval base at Guantánamo Bay, Cuba.

Hunter serves on the Education and Labor Committee, where he wants to promote "Buy American" laws. He opposes abortion, backs gun rights and supports a freeze on government spending, except for entitlements, infrastructure and defense. He also strongly favors a security fence along the southwestern U.S. border. His expected loyalty earned him a position on the GOP leadership ladder as an assistant minority whip.

Hunter was 4 years old when his father came to Washington, but he attended schools in the district and later earned a business administration degree from San Diego State University. He was a business analyst when he decided to join the Marines; he served in Iraq twice and Afghanistan once.

His father made it known in early 2007 that he planned to leave the House, paving the way for his son's bid. The younger Hunter cruised through a four-person primary. In the general election, he faced Mike Lumpkin, a retired Navy SEAL commander, but took 56 percent of the vote after raising $1.3 million to Lumpkin's $482,000.

CAPITOL OFFICE
225-5672
hunter.house.gov
1429 Longworth Bldg. 20515-0552; fax 225-0235

COMMITTEES
Armed Services
Education & Labor

RESIDENCE
Lakeside

BORN
Dec. 7, 1976; San Diego, Calif.

RELIGION
Protestant

FAMILY
Wife, Margaret Hunter; three children

EDUCATION
San Diego State U., B.S. 2001
(business administration)

MILITARY SERVICE
Marine Corps 2002-05; Marine Corps Reserve 2005-08

CAREER
Residential real estate developer; business strategies analyst

POLITICAL HIGHLIGHTS
No previous office

ELECTION RESULTS

2008 GENERAL

Duncan Hunter (R)	160,724	56.4%
Mike Lumpkin (D)	111,051	38.9%
Michael Benoit (LIBERT)	13,316	4.7%

2008 PRIMARY

Duncan Hunter (R)	47,930	72.2%
Brian Jones (R)	10,862	16.4%
Bob Watkins (R)	5,539	8.3%
Rick L. Powell (R)	2,074	3.1%

CALIFORNIA 52

Eastern San Diego; inland San Diego County

The 52nd wraps around the east side of San Diego from Poway in the north to east of Otay Mesa in the south, and stretches about 100 miles east and north through mountains and desert parks to reach San Diego County's borders with Riverside and Imperial counties. Most residents live in the predominately wealthy, conservative suburbs or the roughly 15 percent of San Diego that is in the district.

An economic downturn has affected suburban developments, where property values had been increasing for a decade. Poway, whose economic roots lie in agriculture, has a wealthier, more rural feel to it than the surrounding sprawl. Just outside of Poway is an expanse of evenly developed areas that includes part of Rancho Bernardo (shared with the 49th and 50th) and Scripps Ranch. Recent wildfires have damaged homes here.

San Diego's large military and defense-related workforce contributes to both the district's conservatism and its economy. Although most of the area's military bases are in the 53rd, many residents commute to nearby defense contracting jobs.

The district is nearly three-fourths white, and blue- and white-collar workers alike tend to vote Republican and support GOP House members. John McCain took 53 percent of the 2008 presidential vote here.

MAJOR INDUSTRY
Technology, manufacturing, defense

MILITARY BASES
Marine Corps Air Station Miramar, 10,000 military, 500 civilian (2008) (shared with the 50th)

CITIES
San Diego (pt.), 164,554; El Cajon, 94,869; La Mesa, 54,749; Santee, 52,975; Poway, 48,044

NOTABLE
The Unarius Academy of Science believes UFOs will bring technologies that will rid human civilization of pollution and poverty.

Rep. Susan A. Davis (D)

Elected 2000; 5th term

CAPITOL OFFICE
225-2040
www.house.gov/susandavis
1526 Longworth Bldg. 20515-0553; fax 225-2948

COMMITTEES
Armed Services
 (Military Personnel - chairwoman)
Education & Labor
House Administration

RESIDENCE
San Diego

BORN
April 13, 1944; Cambridge, Mass.

RELIGION
Jewish

FAMILY
Husband, Steve Davis; two children

EDUCATION
U. of California, Berkeley, B.A. 1965 (sociology);
U. of North Carolina, M.A. 1968 (social work)

CAREER
High school leadership program director;
public television producer; social worker

POLITICAL HIGHLIGHTS
San Diego Unified School District Board
of Education, 1983-92 (president, 1989-92);
Calif. Assembly, 1994-00

ELECTION RESULTS

2008 GENERAL

Susan A. Davis (D)	161,315	68.5%
Michael Crimmins (R)	64,658	27.4%
Edward M. Teyssier (LIBERT)	9,569	4.1%

2008 PRIMARY

Susan A. Davis (D)	43,171	87.6%
Mike Copass (D)	6,113	12.4%

2006 GENERAL

Susan A. Davis (D)	97,541	67.6%
John "Woody" Woodrum (R)	43,312	30.0%
Ernie Lippe (LIBERT)	3,534	2.4%

PREVIOUS WINNING PERCENTAGES
2004 (66%); 2002 (62%); 2000 (50%)

Davis takes what she describes as a "consistent and quiet approach" to public service. Though she is active on education and defense issues and chairs an Armed Services subcommittee, she is happy to remain in the background. "I'm not a big publicity seeker," she said.

As chairwoman of the Armed Services Subcommittee on Military Personnel, Davis has convened hearings on subjects that are often overlooked or avoided, such as the military's "don't ask, don't tell" stance toward gay servicemembers. During the 110th Congress (2007-08), she cosponsored legislation that would replace the policy with one of non-discrimination with regard to sexual orientation. "I think we're missing out on the services of many people in our country who really do want to serve our country," she said.

Davis, who has a master's degree in social work, also focuses on improving troops' quality of life in housing, pay and health care. She has pushed legislation to maintain military families' eligibility for such government programs as free or reduced-cost school lunches and Supplemental Security Income, which provides payments to the poor, elderly and disabled. She has sought to expand veterans' home loans and disability benefits. Her subcommittee's portion of the 2009 defense authorization bill established a tuition assistance program for military spouses. And early in 2009, she held a hearing on sexual assaults in the armed forces. "The incidents of sexual assault and the stories of the lack of support for the victims are unacceptable," Davis said at the hearing.

With three universities in her district, Davis is a strong proponent of federal education funding. Like many Democrats, she believes President George W. Bush's No Child Left Behind signature 2001 education law should be backed with more money to help states meet the law's mandates. Similarly, she says the federal government should pick up more of the cost of educating students with disabilities. She also sits on the Education and Labor Committee.

Davis combines her interests in education and the military at times. She sponsored a bill — included in a broader veterans' benefits package the House passed in July 2008 — to require colleges to refund any tuition or fees students paid for education interrupted by military service. Her language also would allow such students a temporary deferment from repaying student loans when they return and caps interest rates on their loans. The bill did not move in the Senate, however.

Davis expanded her portfolio in the 110th Congress to include election reform. She was appointed to the House Administration Committee, which oversees federal elections as well as the internal operations of the House. Davis won the committee's approval of a bill to prohibit states from requiring voters to declare an excuse in order to vote absentee. She wrote the bill after her chief of staff, volunteering in Ohio during the 2006 elections, observed voters lined up outside polls late at night because they couldn't take off from work to vote.

One of Davis' longstanding concerns is the regulation of diet supplements. As a member of the California Assembly, she wrote state legislation to restrict sales of supplements containing ephedrine and to more closely regulate supplements in general. An ephedrine-labeling bill written by Davis passed, only to be vetoed by former Democratic Gov. Gray Davis, who called it a federal matter. Once in Congress, she took the governor's hint: She wrote bills requiring dietary supplement manufacturers to provide the Food and Drug Administration with a list of their products and reports of serious adverse reactions. Late in 2003, the FDA announced it was banning the sale of ephedrine.

Davis is an ally of fellow Californian Speaker Nancy Pelosi, who first urged Davis to run for the House and helped her raise money. Davis returned the favor by voting with Democrats on 95 percent of the votes that pitted the majority of each party against each other during the Bush administration. She supported President Obama's 2009 economic stimulus plan.

Davis sometimes breaks with her party on trade issues, which has not made organized labor happy. In 2001, she was among only 21 Democrats (and one of only two from California) who voted in favor of giving the president authority to negotiate trade agreements that cannot be amended by Congress. Several of her pro-trade colleagues in the moderate New Democrat Coalition voted against it, saying the timing was wrong. She said that on balance, the bill would benefit her district. She also broke with her party in 2003 to back trade agreements with Chile and Singapore, but in 2005 she opposed the Central America Free Trade Agreement.

Davis was raised in Richmond, Calif., the daughter of a pediatrician father. She said a desire to help people led her to the mental health field. She was studying social work in graduate school in North Carolina when she met Steve Davis, who was studying to be a psychiatrist. They married and spent two years in Japan while he served in the Air Force.

When the family returned stateside and settled in San Diego, Davis became active in community affairs. She joined the League of Women Voters, serving as the president of the San Diego chapter. She also worked at the local public TV station.

In 1983, when California Democrat Bob Filner, who now represents the neighboring 51st District, left the San Diego school board to run for the city council, Davis won the election to replace him. While still on the school board, she helped start a local fellowship program for preteens and teenagers to learn about how business and government work. She did not seek re-election to the board in 1992 and became the fellowship program's first executive director.

Two years later, Davis won the first of three terms in the California Assembly. A California law on term limits barred her from running again for the Assembly in 2000, so Pelosi urged her to run for Congress.

The political vulnerability of the 49th District's GOP incumbent, Brian P. Bilbray, who had twice won with less than 50 percent of the vote, handed Davis an opportunity. She took advantage, capturing the seat by a 3-percentage-point margin. In her first re-election bid, her vote in favor of Bush's trade legislation cost her the support of the AFL-CIO, which had pumped almost $250 million dollars into her 2000 campaign. But she benefited from the newly drawn 53rd District and won with 62 percent. She has been re-elected easily since.

KEY VOTES

2008
Yes Delay consideration of Colombia free-trade agreement
Yes Override Bush veto of federal farm and nutrition programs reauthorization bill
No Overhaul surveillance laws and permit dismissal of suits against companies that conducted warrantless wiretapping
Yes Grant mortgage relief to homeowners and funding for Fannie Mae and Freddie Mac
Yes Approve initial $700 billion program to stabilize financial markets
Yes Approve final $700 billion program to stabilize financial markets
Yes Provide $14 billion in loans to automakers

2007
Yes Increase minimum wage by $2.10 an hour
Yes Approve $124.2 billion in emergency war spending and set goal for redeployment of troops from Iraq
No Reject federal contraceptive assistance to international family planning groups
Yes Override Bush veto of $23.2 billion water projects authorization bill
Yes Implement Peru free-trade agreement
Yes Approve energy policy overhaul with new fuel economy standards
Yes Clear $473.5 billion omnibus spending bill, including $70 billion for military operations

CQ VOTE STUDIES

	PARTY UNITY		PRESIDENTIAL SUPPORT	
	SUPPORT	OPPOSE	SUPPORT	OPPOSE
2008	99%	1%	15%	85%
2007	97%	3%	7%	93%
2006	94%	6%	26%	74%
2005	96%	4%	20%	80%
2004	95%	5%	33%	67%

INTEREST GROUPS

	AFL-CIO	ADA	CCUS	ACU
2008	100%	95%	56%	0%
2007	100%	90%	55%	0%
2006	86%	90%	33%	8%
2005	93%	90%	41%	0%
2004	93%	100%	43%	4%

CALIFORNIA 53
Downtown San Diego; Imperial Beach

The coastal 53rd is the economic engine that drives surrounding districts. It includes San Diego's downtown, large employers and most of its military bases. The district also runs south along the Pacific Coast through Coronado and Imperial Beach to the Mexican border.

The defense industry, based around the military installations, is a major economic contributor. The mild climate, wide beaches and attractions — such as SeaWorld, Balboa Park (including the San Diego Zoo) and PETCO Park, where baseball's Padres play — draw tourists, but environmentalists are split over long-term solutions to pollution and sewage that still cause occasional beach closures. Foreclosure rates and weakened employment rates have affected the city's downtown area.

Colleges in the district include the University of California, San Diego, in the north, San Diego State University and the University of San Diego. Some private companies have formed research agreements with the schools, and residents in the district hope local biotech and telecommunications firms will stabilize the economy.

The 53rd includes Hispanic Democratic sections east of the city in places such as Lemon Grove. It also contains blue-collar, central city areas like North Park, City Heights, Barrio Logan and Hillcrest, which is one of the area's most liberal and Democratic neighborhoods and the center of the city's gay community. Overall, the 53rd District is less than one-third Hispanic, and Democrat Barack Obama took 68 percent of the district's 2008 presidential vote.

MAJOR INDUSTRY
Defense, tourism, biotech, telecommunications, higher education

MILITARY BASES
Naval Station San Diego (shared with the 51st), 28,460 military, 8,423 civilian (2005); Naval Air Station North Island/Naval Amphibious Base Coronado, 27,000 military, 8,000 civilian (2006); Naval Base Point Loma, 5,942 military, 13,631 civilian (2005); Naval Medical Center San Diego, 3,270 military, 2,260 civilian (2007); Marine Corps Recruit Depot San Diego, 1,450 military, 1,230 civilian (2007)

CITIES
San Diego (pt.), 542,356; Imperial Beach, 26,992; Lemon Grove, 24,918

NOTABLE
Imperial Beach is home to the U.S. Open Sandcastle Competition.

Gov. Bill Ritter Jr. (D)

First elected: 2006
Length of term: 4 years
Term expires: 1/11
Salary: $90,000
Phone: (303) 866-2471

Residence: Denver
Born: Sept. 6, 1956; Aurora, Colo.
Religion: Roman Catholic
Family: Wife, Jeannie Ritter; four children
Education: Colorado State U., B.A. 1978 (political science); U. of Colorado, J.D. 1981
Career: Lawyer; state prosecutor
Political highlights: Assistant U.S. attorney, 1990-92; Denver district attorney, 1993-2005

Election results:
2006 GENERAL

Bill Ritter Jr. (D)	888,096	57.0%
Bob Beauprez (R)	625,886	40.2%
D. Winkler-Kinateder (LIBERT)	23,323	1.5%

Lt. Gov. Barbara O'Brien (D)

First elected: 2006
Length of term: 4 years
Term expires: 1/11
Salary: $68,500
Phone: (303) 866-2087

LEGISLATURE

General Assembly: 120 days January-May

Senate: 35 members, 4-year terms
2009 ratios: 21 D, 14 R; 22 men, 13 women
Salary: $30,000
Phone: (303) 866-2316

House: 65 members, 2-year terms
2009 ratios: 38 D, 27 R; 40 men, 25 women
Salary: $30,000
Phone: (303) 866-2904

TERM LIMITS

Governor: 2 terms
Senate: 2 consecutive terms
House: 4 consecutive terms

URBAN STATISTICS

CITY	POPULATION
Denver	554,636
Colorado Springs	360,890
Aurora	276,393
Lakewood	144,126
Fort Collins	118,652

REGISTERED VOTERS

Others/unaffiliated	34%
Republican	33%
Democrat	33%

POPULATION

2008 population (est.)	4,939,456
2000 population	4,301,261
1990 population	3,294,394
Percent change (1990-2000)	+30.6%
Rank among states (2008)	22
Median age	34.3
Born in state	41.1%
Foreign born	8.6%
Violent crime rate	334/100,000
Poverty level	9.3%
Federal workers	51,455
Military	42,802

ELECTIONS

STATE ELECTION OFFICIAL
(303) 894-2200
DEMOCRATIC PARTY
(303) 623-4762
REPUBLICAN PARTY
(303) 758-3333

MISCELLANEOUS

Web: www.colorado.gov
Capital: Denver

U.S. CONGRESS

Senate: 2 Democrats
House: 5 Democrats, 2 Republicans

2000 Census Statistics by District

DIST.	2008 VOTE FOR PRESIDENT OBAMA	MCCAIN	WHITE	BLACK	ASIAN	HISP	MEDIAN INCOME	WHITE COLLAR	BLUE COLLAR	SERVICE INDUSTRY	OVER 64	UNDER 18	COLLEGE EDUCATION	RURAL	SQ. MILES
1	74%	24%	54%	10%	3%	30%	$39,658	64%	21%	15%	11%	22%	34%	0%	171
2	64	34	79	1	3	15	$55,204	66	21	13	7	25	39	13	5,615
3	48	50	75	1	0	21	$35,970	56	26	17	13	25	24	39	53,963
4	49	50	79	1	1	17	$43,389	60	26	14	10	26	29	25	30,898
5	40	59	77	6	2	11	$45,454	63	21	15	9	27	30	14	7,708
6	46	52	88	2	3	6	$73,393	77	13	9	7	29	47	15	4,104
7	59	39	69	6	3	20	$46,149	63	24	13	10	25	26	2	1,258
STATE	54	45	74	4	2	17	$47,203	65	22	14	10	26	33	16	103,718
U.S.	53	46	69	12	4	13	$41,994	60	25	15	12	26	24	21	3,537,438

Sen. Mark Udall (D)

CAPITOL OFFICE
224-5941
markudall.senate.gov
317 Hart Bldg. 20510; fax 224-6471

COMMITTEES
Armed Services
Energy & Natural Resources
(National Parks - chairman)
Special Aging

RESIDENCE
Eldorado Springs

BORN
July 18, 1950; Tucson, Ariz.

RELIGION
Christian

FAMILY
Wife, Maggie Fox; two children

EDUCATION
Williams College, B.A. 1972 (American civilization)

CAREER
Colo. Outward Bound School executive director

POLITICAL HIGHLIGHTS
Colo. House, 1997-99; U.S. House, 1999-2009

ELECTION RESULTS

2008 GENERAL

Mark Udall (D)	1,230,994	52.8%
Bob Schaffer (R)	990,755	42.5%
Douglas "Dayhorse" Campbell (AC)	59,733	2.6%
Bob Kinsey (GREEN)	50,004	2.1%

2008 PRIMARY

Mark Udall (D)	unopposed

PREVIOUS WINNING PERCENTAGES
2006 House Election (68%); 2004 House Election
(67%); 2002 House Election (60%); 2000 House
Election (55%); 1998 House Election (50%)

Elected 2008; 1st term

An outdoorsman and avid mountain climber, Udall personifies both the West's rugged individualism and its increased willingness to support Democrats. He has described his political philosophy by invoking his experiences in scaling mountain peaks. "You have to be independent-minded to stay alive in those situations, and that reflects who I am," Udall said.

Tall and telegenic, Udall has benefited by being part of what can be considered the West's first family of politics. His father, Morris K. Udall, was an Arizona congressman and 1976 presidential contender; his uncle Stewart L. Udall was Interior secretary under Presidents Kennedy and Johnson and served in the House. And Mark Udall was elected to the House — and later the Senate — at the same times as his cousin Tom, a Democrat from neighboring New Mexico. (Oregon Republican Sen. Gordon H. Smith, who lost his bid for a third term in November 2008, is a second cousin.)

Although they were elected to the House and Senate on the same dates, Mark Udall edged Tom to become the senior freshman senator in the 111th Congress (2009-10), by virtue of his state's population. Within weeks, he abruptly found himself Colorado's senior senator, when President Obama named Udall's Democratic colleague Ken Salazar as Interior secretary.

Of the two Udalls, Mark has a slightly more moderate voting record; he sided with his party 94 percent of the time during the George W. Bush administration on votes in which the two parties diverged, compared with Tom's 97 percent. He is not hesitant to cross party lines to form alliances on legislation he wants to pass. "I'd like to believe that it's hard to pin me down, that I'm not beholden to any particular political philosophy," he said.

Both Udalls voted with fellow Democrats to clear the $787 billion 2009 economic stimulus package. Both split with a majority of their party to oppose the 2008 financial sector rescue plan and to support a gun-rights amendment to a 2009 bill to give the District of Columbia voting rights in the House.

Environmental and energy issues will command Udall's attention in the Senate, much as they did in the House; he serves on the Energy and Natural Resources Committee. He has called for boosting federal investment in renewable energy and raising fuel efficiency standards. During his Senate race, he showed a willingness to accept GOP positions on increased off-shore drilling and more widespread use of nuclear power as part of a larger effort to end U.S. dependence on foreign oil.

In 2004, Udall helped lead a successful ballot initiative boosting the portion of electricity produced by in-state utilities that is derived from renewable energy sources. A member of the House Natural Resources Committee in the 110th Congress (2007-08), he promoted bills to create a program encouraging volunteers to help federal agencies preserve parks, forests and other sensitive tracts. "Some of the traditional uses of our public lands are being pushed off; hunting, fishing, climbing, skiing — those are all important to us as Westerners," he told Bloomberg News.

He angered Colorado environmentalists in 2006 by sponsoring a bill to ease environmental reviews of tree-cutting in forests damaged by an over-abundance of bark beetles. Local officials wanted to get rid of dying trees that could lead to forest fires, but environmentalists feared it would hasten timber harvests without adequate review of the impact on the environment. Udall cites that as an example of where he has "looked to be a problem solver and not blindly embrace a philosophy."

In 2005, Udall voted for a get-tough immigration bill that was mainly written by conservatives and that encouraged local police to arrest immigration violators. Also in 2005, he joined with some of the House's most conservative members in backing legislation to give the president power to remove specific items from appropriations bills, followed by an up-or-down vote by Congress. Udall said Democrats deserved as much credit as Republicans for the idea, noting he had introduced a similar bill earlier that year. Early in the 110th, he offered the bill again.

As a House member in 2007, Udall became chairman of the Science and Technology Committee's Space and Aeronautics Subcommittee. Colorado's space program, which Udall championed, got a big boost in 2006 when Lockheed Martin Corp. won a contract to build the next generation of "Orion" space capsules intended to take an astronaut to the moon. Colorado has surpassed Florida as the third-leading aerospace state, behind Texas and California.

Udall's other House committee assignment was Armed Services; he sits on the same panel in the Senate. In both chambers, he has worked with others in the Colorado delegation to limit a proposed Army expansion of the Pinon Canyon Maneuver Site in southeast Colorado.

Udall was 10 years old when his father, a legendary wit and energetic liberal, first won election to the House from Arizona in 1961. He remembers being rousted from sleep to join his five pajama-clad siblings to celebrate. One of his proudest moments was witnessing "Mo" Udall, as he was known, become the first prominent House Democrat to come out against President Johnson's troop buildup in Vietnam, during a speech at the University of Arizona in 1967.

The junior Udall purposely waited until later in life to get into politics. He said he wanted to step in when he felt ready, not simply to follow his father. After graduating from Williams College in 1972 with a degree in American civilization, Udall didn't go home to Arizona, but rather moved to Colorado's Western Slope and launched a career with the Colorado Outward Bound School. He was a course director for 10 years, then served as executive director from 1985 to 1995.

He was an avid mountain climber, scaling Kanchenjunga, the world's third-highest peak, and attempting to reach the summit of Mount Everest in 1994 via a route that has been climbed only once. He says he gave up mountain climbing out of concern for his two young children.

In his first House race for the seat that Democrat David E. Skaggs gave up after a dozen years, Udall hammered hard when his GOP opponent, former Boulder Mayor Bob Greenlee, questioned the scientific validity of global warming. Udall also campaigned door-to-door to prove he was a "legitimate Coloradan" and not trying to capitalize on a famous name. In one of the more costly House races of 1998, he prevailed by just 5,500 votes. A month after the election, Mo Udall died of Parkinson's disease.

In subsequent elections, Udall's victory margins steadily increased to comfortably safe levels. He briefly entered the 2004 Colorado Senate race when Republican Sen. Ben Nighthorse Campbell retired, but withdrew once Salazar, who was then state attorney general, decided to run. Udall announced in early 2005 that in 2008, he would try for the Senate seat then occupied by Republican Wayne Allard, who announced in 2007 that he would retire from the Senate.

Udall's GOP opponent was Bob Schaffer, a conservative former House member serving on the state board of education. Schaffer sought to paint Udall as a "Boulder liberal," an allusion to the left-leaning reputation of his political base, the home of the University of Colorado's main campus. But Schaffer was at a disadvantage because of the difficult national political environment for Republicans and Udall's superior fundraising ability. Udall won with about 53 percent of the vote in a field that included several minor-party candidates.

KEY VOTES

House Service:

2008
Yes Delay consideration of Colombia free-trade agreement
Yes Override Bush veto of federal farm and nutrition programs reauthorization bill
Yes Overhaul surveillance laws and permit dismissal of suits against companies that conducted warrantless wiretapping
Yes Grant mortgage relief to homeowners and funding for Fannie Mae and Freddie Mac
No Approve initial $700 billion program to stabilize financial markets
No Approve final $700 billion program to stabilize financial markets
Yes Provide $14 billion in loans to automakers

2007
Yes Increase minimum wage by $2.10 an hour
Yes Approve $124.2 billion in emergency war spending and set goal for redeployment of troops from Iraq
No Reject federal contraceptive assistance to international family planning groups
Yes Override Bush veto of $23.2 billion water projects authorization bill
Yes Implement Peru free-trade agreement
Yes Approve energy policy overhaul with new fuel economy standards
Yes Clear $473.5 billion omnibus spending bill, including $70 billion for military operations

CQ VOTE STUDIES

House Service:

	PARTY UNITY		PRESIDENTIAL SUPPORT	
	SUPPORT	OPPOSE	SUPPORT	OPPOSE
2008	94%	6%	21%	79%
2007	94%	6%	8%	92%
2006	92%	8%	30%	70%
2005	91%	9%	20%	80%
2004	94%	6%	32%	68%
2003	95%	5%	24%	76%
2002	93%	7%	33%	67%
2001	96%	4%	30%	70%
2000	93%	7%	77%	23%
1999	93%	7%	80%	20%

INTEREST GROUPS

House Service:

	AFL-CIO	ADA	CCUS	ACU
2008	93%	80%	61%	13%
2007	96%	90%	60%	4%
2006	93%	85%	53%	16%
2005	87%	90%	37%	8%
2004	93%	100%	53%	8%
2003	83%	80%	32%	18%
2002	89%	95%	40%	4%
2001	100%	100%	35%	0%
2000	90%	85%	47%	12%
1999	100%	100%	28%	4%

Sen. Michael Bennet (D)

Appointed January 2009; 1st term

CAPITOL OFFICE
224-5852
bennet.senate.gov
702 Hart Bldg. 20510-0605; fax 228-5036

COMMITTEES
Agriculture, Nutrition & Forestry
Banking, Housing & Urban Affairs
Homeland Security & Governmental Affairs
Special Aging

RESIDENCE
Denver

BORN
Nov. 28, 1964; New Delhi, India

RELIGION
Unspecified

FAMILY
Wife, Susan Daggett; three children

EDUCATION
Wesleyan U., B.A. 1987 (history); Yale U., J.D. 1993

CAREER
School superintendent; investment company executive; laywer; mayoral and gubernatorial aide

POLITICAL HIGHLIGHTS
No previous office

Bennet portrays himself as a confident centrist whose intellectual style has earned him comparisons to President Obama. The former Denver schools superintendent is a political neophyte whose surprise appointment to succeed Sen. Ken Salazar, who was named Obama's Interior secretary, means he must persuade constituents who never elected him he is worthy of keeping the job.

Bennet, who was sworn into office in January 2009, has made clear he will run in 2010 for a full six-year term. Republicans, critical of his selection by Colorado Gov. Bill Ritter Jr., have vowed a determined effort to unseat Bennet and likely will seek to define him as a big-city liberal to win over rural voters. But Bennet downplays his party affiliation and promises to replicate Salazar's reputation for political independence.

Bennet, the second-youngest senator in the 111th Congress (2009-10), displayed such independence early on. He joined a group of 22 Democrats — most from Western or conservative-leaning states — in backing Nevada Republican John Ensign's proposal to codify a 2008 Supreme Court ruling that struck down a District of Columbia gun ownership ban and declared for the first time that the Second Amendment includes an individual's right to bear arms. In February 2009, the measure was adopted as an amendment to legislation granting District residents a representative full voting rights in the House. The vote came one day after Attorney General Eric H. Holder Jr. said the Obama administration would work to reinstate the nationwide assault weapons ban that expired in 2004.

But Bennet stuck with his Democratic colleagues in backing Obama's $787 billion economic stimulus law, which Obama signed in Denver. Bennet, hoping to increase his voter recognition, was invited to the signing ceremony before he toured his state to explain his vote. He admitted to a crowd in Sterling that 80 percent of the constituents who called his office urged him to oppose it, according to the Journal-Advocate in Sterling. But he said he did what he thought was right. "Nobody would have written the bill as it passed," he said. "It is a compromise." He applauded in particular the bill's funding for education to prevent teacher layoffs.

"One time or another we are going to have to address the fact that we are not educating our kids, that we don't have healthcare and are losing it…we have a war on terrorism that is serious business. We have an economic crisis that is choking off the financial health of this country," he told a gathering at the Delta Montrose Technical College, according to the Montrose Daily Press. "I'm just not going to be a senator that is going to fool around with stuff that doesn't have to deal with those things because we do not have the time. For my three daughters, I don't want them living in a world where we failed to solve the problems."

He also acknowledged the package doesn't solve the bank, foreclosure and housing crises — an issue he will be able to address from his seat on the Banking, Housing and Urban Affairs Committee. Bennet told The Denver Post he probably would have voted against the George W. Bush administration's $700 billion package in fall 2008 to shore up the financial services industry. He cited a lack of transparency and oversight.

And he sits on the Agriculture, Nutrition and Forestry panel — the one assignment he requested in order to help shape U.S. agricultural policy and ensure proper implementation of the 2008 farm bill. Bennet's other assignments are Homeland Security and Governmental Affairs and Special Aging.

Given his background, he is also likely to be in the center of debates on education. He was highly regarded enough as Denver schools superinten-dent that Obama nearly tapped him to be his secretary of Education.

In Denver, Bennet promoted a "merit pay" system that increased teachers' starting salaries and linked teacher bonuses to student achievement. He closed low and underperforming schools and won praise from African-American ministers and activists who initially had labeled him a "dictator" by working to reopen one high school serving a mostly minority student body.

Though Denver's student assessment scores remain well below the aver-age for the rest of the state, Colorado's school accountability reports for 2008 showed 140 of the city's 164 school programs either kept pace or exceeded the state in academic growth. Enrollment also grew to its highest levels in three decades. "He's a visionary, able to look far and wide and very deep into the issues at hand," Lucia Guzman, a former Denver school board member, told The Denver Post. The newspaper reported, however, that current school board evaluations have criticized him for a lack of communication.

Congress is expected to consider a renewal of Bush's 2001 No Child Left Behind education law that sought to increase public schools' accountabil-ity. Bennet called the law, which links annual primary and secondary school achievement tests to school funding, "an incredibly crude instru-ment in how to measure achievement."

Bennet promised to work closely with Democrat Mark Udall, who began serving in the Senate in January 2009 after serving five terms in the House. Udall and Bennet are the first pair to represent a state in the Senate as freshmen since 1995, when Republicans Bill Frist and Fred Thompson represented Tennessee.

Despite his lack of political experience, Bennet is no stranger to Washing-ton. He attended St. Albans college preparatory school and was a Capitol Hill page. His father, Doug, was an aide to the U.S. ambassador in India, where Michael Bennet was born, and later served as president of National Public Radio and Wesleyan University. The younger Bennet's brother, James, is a former New York Times political reporter and editor of the Atlantic Monthly.

After law school at Yale, Bennet worked briefly in private practice, then as a counsel in the Clinton administration's Justice Department, where — as part of his job — he wrote speeches for Attorney General Janet Reno.

He went on to serve as a managing director of an investment company headed by Colorado billionaire financier Philip Anschutz, then served as chief of staff to Denver Mayor John Hickenlooper, whom Bennet describes as some-thing of a "big brother." Hickenlooper promoted Bennet for the school super-intendent job, for which he was selected unanimously by the school board.

"I've taken a series of jobs in my life not knowing what they would lead to, and I've made the best decisions based on my gut," Bennet told the Rocky Mountain News in 2005, just before he became schools chief. "The ones where I didn't base the decision on my gut, I've regretted it."

When Gov. Ritter announced his appointment of Bennet to fill Salazar's Senate seat, some residents reacted skeptically. In blue-collar Pueblo, near the state's southern border, they pointedly asked Ritter why he didn't choose someone better-known. But in other cities, such as Loveland, he won positive marks after describing what attracted him to the job: "A very deep concern that our generation is at risk of leaving less opportunity to the children that are coming after us than we ourselves enjoy."

After a series of such appointments to fill congressional seats, Sen. Russ Feingold of Wisconsin proposed a constitutional amendment barring gov-ernors from making appointments. He then set about trying to gain sup-port from the newly appointed senators, but Bennet wouldn't go along with the plan, which would mandate special elections to fill vacancies. "I think it's better left to the states," said Bennet.

Rep. Diana DeGette (D)

Elected 1996; 7th term

CAPITOL OFFICE
225-4431
www.house.gov/degette
2335 Rayburn Bldg. 20515-0601; fax 225-5657

COMMITTEES
Energy & Commerce
Natural Resources

RESIDENCE
Denver

BORN
July 29, 1957; Tachikawa, Japan

RELIGION
Presbyterian

FAMILY
Husband, Lino Lipinsky; two children

EDUCATION
Colorado College, B.A. 1979 (political science);
New York U., J.D. 1982

CAREER
Lawyer; state public defender

POLITICAL HIGHLIGHTS
Colo. House, 1993-96 (assistant minority leader,
1995-96)

ELECTION RESULTS

2008 GENERAL

Diana DeGette (D)	203,755	71.9%
George C. Lilly (R)	67,345	23.8%
Martin L. Buchanan (LIBERT)	12,135	4.3%

2008 PRIMARY

Diana DeGette (D)	unopposed

2006 GENERAL

Diana DeGette (D)	129,446	79.8%
Thomas D. Kelly (GREEN)	32,825	20.2%

PREVIOUS WINNING PERCENTAGES
2004 (74%); 2002 (66%); 2000 (69%); 1998 (67%);
1996 (57%)

When DeGette sets her mind to something — such as promoting stem cell research, children's health insurance or product safety — she goes at it with the perseverance of a practiced attorney, which she is. And now that Democrats are running the show in Washington, she's seeing tangible results.

As a member of the powerful Energy and Commerce Committee, DeGette (De-GET) is in the thick of debate over health care reform in the 111th Congress (2009-10). DeGette is a protege of Michigan Democrat John D. Dingell, the House's longest-serving member, who she said was "instrumental" in getting her a seat on the committee in 1997, her freshman year. For decades the top Democrat on Energy and Commerce, he made her the panel's vice chairwoman in 2007.

California's Henry A. Waxman successfully challenged Dingell for the gavel in the 111th; DeGette vigorously backed Dingell in the power struggle but was able to retain her title. She has no regrets about siding with Dingell. "As my dad used to say, you've got to dance with the one who brung you," she said.

DeGette is not only loyal; she is also persistent. For years, she battled President George W. Bush's restrictions on federally funded embryonic stem cell research, which uses discarded embryos created for in vitro fertilization. DeGette refused to be silenced by Bush's two vetoes, and the election of Barack Obama made her goal a reality.

DeGette's activism on the subject was shaped in part by personal experience: One of her daughters has diabetes and could one day benefit from stem cell-based therapies. After her first defeat in 2006, DeGette helped campaign for a number of pro-stem cell candidates and picked up 14 votes when she pushed her bill through the House a second time in 2007. The final count was still short of the two-thirds majority required to override a veto, however. She published a book on the saga, titled "Sex, Science and Stem Cells: Inside the Right Wing's Assault on Reason." It was released just before the Democratic National Convention kicked off in her Denver district in August 2008.

One of the House's nine chief deputy whips, DeGette is the only Coloradoan in a leadership position. She loves to lasso votes, she says, and counts her bipartisan whip effort on a renewable-energy standard in 2007 as one of her biggest successes, although it fell one vote short in the Senate. She also helped steer an expansion of the State Children's Health Insurance Program, which covers children from low-income families that do not qualify for Medicaid, through the House in the 110th Congress (2007-08), only to see it fall victim to Bush's veto. The legislation sailed through Congress in 2009 and was swiftly signed into law by Obama. DeGette also played a leading role in the 2008 overhaul of the Consumer Product Safety Commission that set stronger safety standards for toys and other consumer products.

DeGette has no scientific training, but she is a staunch advocate of sound science in governance. "When I started getting involved in health care issues and environmental issues, I started seeing how some of our public policy comes out — and it's not based on science. First, that's a waste of taxpayer money. Second, it can really be a risk to people's health," she said.

The Denver area is home to telecommunications, wireless and satellite companies, and DeGette is one of many members eager to rewrite the 1996 Telecommunications Act. "Technology has developed so much since then. and the competitive environment has grown and changed," she noted.

On one key telecommunications issue, DeGette in 2008 opposed electronic surveillance legislation that granted legal protection to telecommunications carriers such as AT&T that cooperated with wiretapping activities by the Bush administration after the Sept. 11 terrorist attacks. DeGette said she still thinks the phone companies should be held accountable for their actions.

It wasn't the first time she advocated corporate responsibility. DeGette took on one of her district's biggest employers, Qwest Communications International Inc., when a multimillion-dollar accounting scandal that implicated the company broke during the slew of corporate shakeouts that began with Enron Corp.'s demise in 2002.

Born in Japan, where her father was stationed with the Air Force, DeGette spent most of her childhood in the Denver area. She was deeply affected, at age 10, by news coverage of the assassination of the Rev. Dr. Martin Luther King Jr. "It hit me, the whole idea of social justice and fighting for equality. I decided I was going to become a lawyer."

After earning a law degree at New York University, DeGette became a public defender in Denver and then went into private practice, specializing in cases about discrimination based on disability, sex and age.

She volunteered in the mayoral campaign of Federico Peña, who later served in President Clinton's Cabinet. That spurred her interest in public service. "I can do these cases one at a time," she recalls thinking, "or I can get elected to office and I can affect many people by changing the laws."

She won a Colorado House seat in 1992. As a freshman member of the minority party, DeGette won enactment of a law — upheld by the Supreme Court in 2000 — requiring protesters to stay eight feet from anyone within 100 feet of entrances to clinics where abortions are performed. That so-called bubble bill made her a target of abortion opponents who have continued to protest at her home over the years. The demonstrations taught her to stand up to fierce criticism, she says.

While in the state House, DeGette moved up to the party leadership. But she resigned from the legislature in early 1996 to concentrate on her bid to succeed liberal Democratic Rep. Patricia Schroeder in Congress.

DeGette won a highly publicized battle with Republican nominee Joe Rogers, a lawyer and former aide to Colorado GOP Sen. Hank Brown. Outspending her opponent 2-to-1, she prevailed by 17 percentage points. Her six reelections have been with two-thirds or more of the vote.

When Obama named Colorado Sen. Ken Salazar as Interior secretary, DeGette figured in speculation about a successor. But she took herself out of the running, saying she could be more effective as Colorado's senior House member.

KEY VOTES

2008

Yes   Delay consideration of Colombia free-trade agreement

Yes   Override Bush veto of federal farm and nutrition programs reauthorization bill

No   Overhaul surveillance laws and permit dismissal of suits against companies that conducted warrantless wiretapping

Yes   Grant mortgage relief to homeowners and funding for Fannie Mae and Freddie Mac

Yes   Approve initial $700 billion program to stabilize financial markets

Yes   Approve final $700 billion program to stabilize financial markets

Yes   Provide $14 billion in loans to automakers

2007

Yes   Increase minimum wage by $2.10 an hour

Yes   Approve $124.2 billion in emergency war spending and set goal for redeployment of troops from Iraq

No   Reject federal contraceptive assistance to international family planning groups

Yes   Override Bush veto of $23.2 billion water projects authorization bill

Yes   Implement Peru free-trade agreement

Yes   Approve energy policy overhaul with new fuel economy standards

No   Clear $473.5 billion omnibus spending bill, including $70 billion for military operations

CQ VOTE STUDIES

	PARTY UNITY		PRESIDENTIAL SUPPORT	
	SUPPORT	OPPOSE	SUPPORT	OPPOSE
2008	99%	1%	13%	87%
2007	99%	1%	5%	95%
2006	98%	2%	25%	75%
2005	96%	4%	16%	84%
2004	97%	3%	29%	71%

INTEREST GROUPS

	AFL-CIO	ADA	CCUS	ACU
2008	100%	80%	59%	0%
2007	100%	90%	55%	0%
2006	100%	95%	33%	4%
2005	87%	90%	37%	0%
2004	100%	90%	37%	0%

COLORADO 1

Denver

The capital city of Denver takes up most of the 1st District, which stretches north and east following the city limits to reach the airport. The 1st, a bastion of liberalism in the once-conservative state, is Colorado's smallest district in size, but Denver's presence allows the district to set the tone for the Centennial State's economic future.

Denver was once dependent on the region's oil and gas industries, but the city boomed during the 1990s as its economy broadened to include technology and telecommunications. These industries now rival state government as the major employers here, although fossil fuel energy remains important. State and local officials are encouraging futher diversification, working to attract renewable-energy firms to the area.

Health care is also important to Denver's economic well-being. There are several hospitals and service providers downtown or in surrounding areas, but the region's health industry is anchored by the University of Colorado Denver Health Sciences Center campus and bioscience research park at the former Fitzsimons Army Medical Center, located just

outside the district's borders in Aurora (in the 7th). Concerns over foreclosures and job losses in several sectors trouble some residents.

Revitalization efforts to the city's lower downtown district, known by locals as "LoDo," have helped attract tourists. Large entertainment venues and a robust nightlife make Denver one of the premier cities to visit between the West Coast and Midwest. Denver International Airport, which opened in 1995, has become one of the nation's busiest.

Denver has the state's most diverse population — the district's growing Hispanic community makes up nearly one-third of residents while blacks make up more than one-tenth of the city's population. Ninety percent of the 1st's residents live in Denver. Barack Obama won 74 percent of the 1st's 2008 presidential vote, easily his highest percentage in the state.

MAJOR INDUSTRY

Telecommunications, computers, government, health care, tourism

CITIES

Denver, 554,636; Englewood, 31,727

NOTABLE

The Great American Beer Festival is the nation's largest and oldest annual brewing competition.

Rep. Jared Polis (D)

Elected 2008; 1st term

Polis has spent his life marching to the beat of his own drum, and as one of the youngest, wealthiest and most Web-savvy members of Congress, Polis (POE-liss) has indicated his time in Congress will be no different.

The openly gay Internet entrepreneur-turned-education-philanthropist — who prefers "Jared" to "congressman" — blogs about his life as a congressman from his laptop computer, which sports an "Obama Pride" sticker. He wears a turtleneck to work most days, changing into a suit only when he has to go to the House floor to vote.

From the Education and Labor panel, he intends to use his background in education to focus on the rewrite of President George W. Bush's signature No Child Left Behind education law, with an emphasis on accountability and resources for the poorest schools. Viewed as a dependable leadership ally, he also serves on the Rules Committee as one of two freshman Democrats.

Polis was 25 when he began a six-year stint on the Colorado State Board of Education. In 2004, he launched a charter school for high-school-aged immigrants, where he served as superintendent for several years, and in 2005, he founded another charter school for homeless children. He said he'll also focus on environmental issues important to voters in the Mountain West, such as management of land, water and forests. He serves as the vice chair whip of the Renewable Energy and Environmental Caucus.

Polis is one of the youngest and wealthiest members of the House. After launching an Internet access company as a sophomore at Princeton, Polis helped spin his family's greeting card company into BlueMountain.com and founded one of the largest online floral companies.

Polis was introduced to political activism at a young age. His journalist-turned-poet mother and physicist-turned-artist father, who had been anti-war activists during the 1960s, took their young son with them to demonstrations against nuclear proliferation. Polis spent summers in Colorado and the school year in San Diego, where he founded a Democratic Club. At 16, he entered Princeton, where he was active in Jewish community activities, student government, the College Democrats and the ROTC.

CAPITOL OFFICE
225-2161
polis.house.gov
501 Cannon Bldg. 20515-0602; fax 226-7840

COMMITTEES
Education & Labor
Rules

RESIDENCE
Boulder

BORN
May 12, 1975; Boulder, Colo.

RELIGION
Jewish

FAMILY
Partner, Marlon Reis

EDUCATION
Princeton U., A.B. 1996 (politics)

CAREER
Internet entrepreneur and venture capitalist; at-risk charter schools founder

POLITICAL HIGHLIGHTS
Colo. Board of Education, 2001-07 (chairman, 2004-05)

ELECTION RESULTS

2008 GENERAL

Jared Polis (D)	215,571	62.6%
Scott Starin (R)	116,591	33.9%
J.A. Calhoun (GREEN)	10,026	2.9%

2008 PRIMARY

Jared Polis (D)	20,493	41.7%
Joan Fitz-Gerald (D)	18,599	37.8%
Will Shafroth (D)	10,075	20.5%

COLORADO 2

Northwest Denver suburbs; Boulder

The 2nd takes in suburbs north and west of Denver, along with Boulder, before heading into the mountains, crossing the Continental Divide and scooping up national forests, wilderness areas, reservoirs and part of ski country. Boulder's liberal culture pulls the generally moderate district to the left, and environmental issues play heavily here.

Boulder, at the foothills of the majestic Rocky Mountains, is home to the University of Colorado's flagship campus and a committed corps of environmentalists. Outdoor sports remain the city's most popular pastime, and bicycling is highly regarded in the city. The city center also boasts a vibrant shopping and nightlife district.

Several federal research laboratories and biotechnology companies have facilities in the district in order to take advantage of the well-educated workforce.

The district also includes the northern part of Jefferson and western Adams counties, where a plurality of residents live, including nearly all of Westminster, the 2nd's most populated city, as well as growing suburbs between Boulder and Denver. Urban sprawl has gained attention here.

Skiing is king in the mountain counties of Eagle — home to the resort city of Vail — Grand and Summit, located in the western part of the district. These skiing communities and other towns along Interstate 70 make it a tourist magnet year-round.

MAJOR INDUSTRY
Technology, research, higher education, tourism

CITIES
Westminster (pt.), 100,850; Boulder, 94,673; Thornton (pt.), 82,378

NOTABLE
Eisenhower Memorial Tunnel, which takes Interstate 70 across the Continental Divide, is the world's highest vehicular tunnel.

Rep. John Salazar (D)

Elected 2004; 3rd term

CAPITOL OFFICE
225-4761
www.house.gov/salazar
326 Cannon Bldg. 20515-0603; fax 226-9669

COMMITTEES
Appropriations
Select Energy Independence & Global Warming

RESIDENCE
Manassa

BORN
July 21, 1953; Alamosa, Colo.

RELIGION
Roman Catholic

FAMILY
Wife, Mary Lou Salazar; three children

EDUCATION
Colorado State U., attended 1971-72;
Adams State College, B.S. 1981 (business)

MILITARY SERVICE
Army, 1973-76

CAREER
Farmer; rancher; seed potato business owner

POLITICAL HIGHLIGHTS
Colo. Agricultural Commission, 1999-2002;
Colo. House, 2003-04

ELECTION RESULTS

2008 GENERAL

John Salazar (D)	203,455	61.6%
Wayne Wolf (R)	126,762	38.4%

2008 PRIMARY

John Salazar (D)	unopposed

2006 GENERAL

John Salazar (D)	146,488	61.6%
Scott Tipton (R)	86,930	36.5%
Bert L. Sargent (LIBERT)	4,417	1.9%

PREVIOUS WINNING PERCENTAGES
2004 (51%)

John Salazar is not as well known as his younger brother, Ken, former Colorado senator and current secretary of Interior. But he doesn't seem to mind. He says his brother is the politician in the family; he'd rather be known as a farmer and rancher who fell unexpectedly into public service.

The Salazar brothers and their three sisters grew up in a tiny house on the family's 52-acre homestead ranch; the five boys slept in a single room and electricity didn't arrive until the 1980s. Their father grew alfalfa and potatoes using a horse-drawn cultivator. "We were raised very poor," said Salazar, who, along with his siblings, rode the family plow as ballast.

Though Salazar's father hoped at least one of his sons would enter the priesthood, that dream went unfulfilled. But the two sons' simultaneous election to Congress in 2004 was a remarkable triumph for a family of Mexican-American farmers who first arrived in Colorado's San Luis Valley in the 1850s.

His childhood, coupled with his later experience as a potato seed farmer, continues to inform Salazar's priorities in Congress, where he looks out for Colorado's agricultural interests and conservation efforts. He has the chance to do so in the 111th Congress (2009-10) from a coveted seat on the Appropriations Committee, where he sits on the panels responsible for funding energy and water programs as well as veterans' affairs and military construction. He has proposed a federally funded water easement program for Colorado's agricultural land and presses for development of renewable energy from biofuels.

Salazar also was named to the Select Energy Independence and Global Warming Committee. The panel gives him a forum for concerns about water quality and quantity; scientists say climate change will reduce both in states like Colorado that get their drinking water from mountain snow runoff. He also seeks to protect the interests of coal-fired electricity providers wanting to improve technology to curtail greenhouse gas emissions, though environmentalists are deeply skeptical of such efforts.

In the 110th Congress (2007-08), Salazar fought the expansion of an Army training area in his district that he said would drive ranchers and farmers off their land. The Army scaled back its request in 2008 from 414,000 to 100,000 additional acres, but announced plans to go forward with the planned purchase despite a ban on expansion that Salazar and his brother helped enact. Salazar successfully pushed to extend the ban in the fiscal 2009 military construction bill passed by the House in August 2008.

Salazar also battled the George W. Bush administration's plans to auction off leases for land in the pristine but natural-gas-rich Roan Plateau for energy development. While he initially pressed for a moratorium or ban, Salazar later pressed the Interior Department to lease less environmentally sensitive areas first. Nonetheless, the department pressed ahead with the scheduled August 2008 auction as planned.

He is among the biggest beneficiaries of campaign contributions from agricultural businesses, ranking 17th among House members with $230,250 in donations over a three-year period, according to a May 2008 analysis by The Denver Post. Salazar defended his advocacy of agricultural interests. "There are only four, maybe six of us [farmers] here in Congress," Salazar told the Post. "If we can't stand up for farmers, we shouldn't be here."

Salazar previously served on the Veterans' Affairs Committee, where he feels a deep personal commitment. A military veteran himself, he also has a son who served in the Colorado National Guard, and his father, a World War II veteran, came to him at age 84 after contracting Alzheimer's disease and asked Salazar to promise that he'd be buried in his uniform.

Salazar has sought to punish those who falsely claim to be recipients of military awards. He sponsored legislation that Bush signed into law in 2006 that made such a false claim a crime. He sponsored a 2007 bill to create a national database containing the names of all military servicemembers and veterans awarded military decorations authorized by Congress, from the Medal of Honor to the Purple Heart.

Salazar has a centrist voting record in line with his Republican-leaning district. A lifelong hunter, he voted for legislation shielding the gun industry from lawsuits. He praised the Supreme Court's 2008 decision that said the Second Amendment encompasses an individual right to bear arms.

He supported elimination of the estate tax, an overhaul of bankruptcy laws and legislation to bar the transport of minors across state lines to evade parental-notification abortion laws. He also opposed two $700 billion measures — the second of which became law — in fall 2008 to aid the ailing financial services sector. "I've never been a pawn for any party," Salazar told the Rocky Mountain News.

In 2007, he joined fellow Blue Dog Democrats in pressing Democratic leaders to find new revenue to offset the cost of an income tax cut for middle-income families rather than increase the national debt.

Salazar, like all of his brothers, spent time at a Catholic seminary in Cincinnati, where Franciscan priests woke him daily at 5:30 a.m. with cowbells and packed almost every minute with study or prayer. After that three-year stint, Salazar said, military basic training "was a piece of cake."

After nearly four years in the Army's Criminal Investigations Division, Salazar earned a business degree. He settled in as a potato seed farmer on part of the family land where he grew up. He participated in a Colorado leadership program for people in agriculture that took him to Washington, D.C., and overseas. He returned home and served on the Rio Grande Water Conservation District. He was appointed to the state Agriculture Commission in 1999 and won a seat in the state legislature in 2002.

Salazar was unopposed for the Democratic U.S. House nomination in 2004, while Republican Greg Walcher, a former director of the state Department of Natural Resources, survived a fractious primary. Salazar won by 4 percentage points, using the campaign slogan "Send a farmer to Congress." He was re-elected easily in 2006 and 2008.

KEY VOTES

2008

Yes Delay consideration of Colombia free-trade agreement

Yes Override Bush veto of federal farm and nutrition programs reauthorization bill

Yes Overhaul surveillance laws and permit dismissal of suits against companies that conducted warrantless wiretapping

Yes Grant mortgage relief to homeowners and funding for Fannie Mae and Freddie Mac

No Approve initial $700 billion program to stabilize financial markets

No Approve final $700 billion program to stabilize financial markets

Yes Provide $14 billion in loans to automakers

2007

Yes Increase minimum wage by $2.10 an hour

Yes Approve $124.2 billion in emergency war spending and set goal for redeployment of troops from Iraq

No Reject federal contraceptive assistance to international family planning groups

Yes Override Bush veto of $23.2 billion water projects authorization bill

Yes Implement Peru free-trade agreement

Yes Approve energy policy overhaul with new fuel economy standards

Yes Clear $473.5 billion omnibus spending bill, including $70 billion for military operations

CQ VOTE STUDIES

	PARTY UNITY		PRESIDENTIAL SUPPORT	
	SUPPORT	OPPOSE	SUPPORT	OPPOSE
2008	96%	4%	19%	81%
2007	93%	7%	9%	91%
2006	76%	24%	57%	43%
2005	81%	19%	46%	54%

INTEREST GROUPS

	AFL-CIO	ADA	CCUS	ACU
2008	93%	85%	61%	12%
2007	96%	90%	60%	8%
2006	77%	60%	64%	44%
2005	80%	75%	67%	44%

COLORADO 3

Western Slope; Pueblo

Spanning 29 counties, the 3rd includes more than half of Colorado's land area, moving from the Wyoming border in the north to the Ute Mountain Indian Reservation and Four Corners area in the southwest, before heading east to include all but one county on the state's southern edge. It displays some of the variety found outside the state's urban centers: rural poor, resort rich, old steel-mill towns and isolated Hispanic counties.

Most of the state's rivers flow down the Western Slope to Nevada and California, and residents here would like to see more of the water stored for local use. Manufacturing in the 3rd has declined, but a new wind energy turbine plant may counter job losses in other skilled manufacturing sectors. Former robust mining areas have dwindled, and western cattle ranchers have seen their profits shrink. The San Luis Valley and rural areas west of Interstate 25 have been hardest hit. Pueblo's Colorado State University campus is thriving, though, and officials in the district hope to diversify the 3rd's economy by creating a more educated workforce.

Pueblo, the district's most populous county, was once dependent on its

steel industry but is beginning to attract people back to its namesake city's downtown area. Both the Historic Arkansas Riverwalk and Union Avenue Historic District lure in locals and tourists. In the north and west parts of the district, national parks, such as Black Canyon of the Gunnison, and ski resorts combine to support the area's hottest economic mainstay: tourism. Visitors hike, bike or raft through the San Juan and Sawatch Mountains, the latter of which include Aspen's ski resort.

Residential Colorado has spilled over the Continental Divide onto the Western Slope. Independent-minded baby boomers in rustic retirement homes along this mountainous terrain tend to give the 3rd a Republican lean. But Pueblo County, heavily unionized and more than one-third Hispanic, keeps the district competitive. Overall, Republican John McCain took the 3rd with barely more than 50 percent of the presidential vote here in 2008, while Rep. John Salazar won comfortably.

MAJOR INDUSTRY
Tourism, skiing, agriculture

CITIES
Pueblo, 102,121; Grand Junction, 41,986; Clifton (unincorporated), 17,345

NOTABLE
The Federal Citizen Information Center is in Pueblo.

Rep. Betsy Markey (D)

Elected 2008; 1st term

Markey seeks to draw on her experience as a business owner and government worker as she focuses on economic issues while charting a centrist course.

She said her business background has influenced her beliefs on fiscal restraint. She co-founded an Internet consulting and Web site development firm, Syscom Services Inc., that evolved into a business with more than 40 employees and annual sales of more than $7 million. She also owned a coffee and ice cream shop in Fort Collins.

"I always had to make sure that you didn't spend more money than you made," she said. She supports pay-as-you-go budget rules and vows to fight "pork barrel spending" and to reduce earmarks, the member-driven funding set-asides to benefit their districts.

Markey in early 2009 promoted a $787 billion economic stimulus bill, signed into law by President Obama, as providing needed assistance to strained transportation and education systems in her state. "Bridges and highways are falling in disrepair. Schools are unable to modernize, and many of them are laying off teachers," said Markey, who received a slot on the Transportation and Infrastructure Committee.

Markey represents Colorado's vast eastern plains, and she plans to use her Agriculture Committee seat to tend to the concerns of farmers and ranchers. On immigration, she has called for securing the borders and opposes "amnesty," though she also has called for "civility in the immigration discussion."

Markey worked on Capitol Hill three decades ago when, just out of college, she got a job with the House Post Office and Civil Service Committee. She stayed in Washington after that, taking jobs at the Treasury and State departments after earning a master's in public administration.

Years later, in Colorado, she ventured into public life as the founder of the Northern Colorado Democratic Business Coalition. In 2002, she was elected chairwoman of the Larimer County Democratic Party, then went to work for Democratic Sen. Ken Salazar after his election in 2004. She worked in Salazar's Colorado office for more than two years before launching her successful bid to unseat GOP Rep. Marilyn Musgrave in 2008.

CAPITOL OFFICE
225-4676
betsymarkey.house.gov
1229 Longworth Bldg. 20515-0604; fax 225-5870

COMMITTEES
Agriculture
Transportation & Infrastructure

RESIDENCE
Fort Collins

BORN
April 27, 1956; Cresskill, N.J.

RELIGION
Roman Catholic

FAMILY
Husband, Jim Kelly; three children

EDUCATION
U. of Florida, B.A. 1978 (political science);
American U., M.P.A. 1983

CAREER
Congressional district director; ice cream and coffee shop owner; Web services company owner; U.S. State Department computer security director; college fundraising assistant

POLITICAL HIGHLIGHTS
Larimer County Democratic Party chairwoman, 2002-05

ELECTION RESULTS

2008 GENERAL

Betsy Markey (D)	187,347	56.2%
Marilyn Musgrave (R)	146,028	43.8%

2008 PRIMARY

Betsy Markey (D)	unopposed

COLORADO 4

North and east — Fort Collins; Greeley

The 4th, which covers Colorado's eastern plains and touches five other states, looks more like the Kansas prairies than the rugged Rockies of much of the rest of the state.

Thanks to intensive irrigation, the 4th's southern and eastern portions include productive wheat and corn fields, but some ranchers and farmers have faced hard times in the face of falling prices. The southern part of the district is spread across mainly small rural communities, and with roughly 9,000 residents, Lamar is the only town or city in the 4th's southern half with more than 3,000 people.

The northwestern part of the district, including Larimer and almost all of Weld counties, along with the 4th's small part of Boulder County, holds 80 percent of the district's population while occupying less than a third of its land. Despite rising unemployment rates in Larimer, Fort Collins, the district's most populous city, is home to Colorado State University, and its research facilities and the local workforce lure technology firms.

Despite taking in mostly rural Republican territory and a history of sending GOP members to the House, federal elections have become more competitive in the once strongly GOP district. The U.S. House seat flipped to Democratic control in 2008, and Republican John McCain won here — eight of his top 10 counties in the state were in rural parts of the 4th — by less than 1 percentage point.

MAJOR INDUSTRY
Agriculture, meatpacking, higher education

CITIES
Fort Collins, 118,652; Greeley, 76,930; Longmont, 71,093; Loveland, 50,608

NOTABLE
Greeley hosts the Greeley Stampede rodeo and music festival each year leading up to July Fourth.

Rep. Doug Lamborn (R)

Elected 2006; 2nd term

CAPITOL OFFICE
225-4422
lamborn.house.gov
437 Cannon Bldg. 20515-0605; fax 225-1942

COMMITTEES
Armed Services
Natural Resources
Veterans' Affairs

RESIDENCE
Colorado Springs

BORN
May 24, 1954; Leavenworth, Kan.

RELIGION
Christian

FAMILY
Wife, Jeanie Lamborn; five children

EDUCATION
U. of Kansas, B.S. 1978 (journalism), J.D. 1985

CAREER
Lawyer

POLITICAL HIGHLIGHTS
Republican nominee for Kan. House, 1982;
Colo. House, 1995-98; Colo. Senate, 1998-2007
(president pro tempore, 1999-2000)

ELECTION RESULTS

2008 GENERAL

Doug Lamborn (R)	183,178	60.0%
Hal Bidlack (D)	113,025	37.0%
Brian X. Scott (AC)	8,894	2.9%

2008 PRIMARY

Doug Lamborn (R)	24,995	44.0%
Jeff Crank (R)	16,794	29.6%
Bentley Rayburn (R)	14,986	26.4%

2006 GENERAL

Doug Lamborn (R)	123,264	59.6%
Jay Fawcett (D)	83,431	40.3%

Lamborn is a devout conservative who opposes abortion and gun control and battles federal intrusions into local land use. A fierce party loyalist representing a district that is home to several nationally prominent right-wing groups, he sees no reason to compromise.

Lamborn is a member of the Republican Study Committee, the House GOP's most conservative faction. During his first term, he sided with Republicans on 99 percent of the votes that pitted the majority of each party against one another. A fiscal conservative, he stuck with his entire party in February 2009 to vote against Obama's $787 billion economic stimulus law, calling it a "Porkulus Package." According to the Canon City Daily Record, he told an audience at a local Lincoln Day Dinner: "I'll always vote no on excess spending."

In fall 2008, he sided with most Study Committee colleagues by opposing two $700 billion measures intended to aid the ailing financial services industry. He said both measures — the second of which became law — relied too heavily on taxpayer dollars to bail out reckless investors. That December, he also voted against a $14 billion loan for the auto industry.

His aim for belt tightening extended to the National Endowment for the Arts. He pushed, unsuccessfully, in 2007 to eliminate its funding, saying such spending shouldn't be permitted in dire economic times. On the Veterans' Affairs Committee, he opposed an overhaul of the Veterans Affairs Department's disability claims system in April 2008, saying it would go too far and create new costs that would conflict with House rules requiring offsets for new spending.

Most of his views are in line with those of his district, where constituents include cattle ranchers, resort workers and social conservatives. But he has faced a series of criticisms since taking office. He was a subject of news reports in early 2009 that focused on a potential connection between campaign contributions from the now defunct lobbying firm The PMA Group and earmarks — funding set-asides for special projects — it secured for clients. The Seattle Times reported Lamborn (LAMB-born) received $2,000 from Lockheed Martin Corp., and he helped obtain $1 million for Lockheed's Senior Scout Integrated Mission Trainer, an Air Force project. But Lamborn told the Colorado Independent that "campaign contributions have absolutely nothing to do with appropriations requests or any other legislative matter."

In September 2007, he attracted attention for leaving a message on one Colorado Springs couple's phone, saying there would be "consequences" if the couple didn't withdraw a letter criticizing him for accepting money from the Nevada-based International Gaming Technology. Lamborn, who had returned the $1,000 check, later apologized to the couple, saying he only meant he would report the matter to the county GOP chairman. He also was criticized for spending more than $135,000 during his first year on franking, a privilege allowing lawmakers to send out mail using public funds.

Local residents took after him when the House passed a bill barring Fort Carson from expanding its Piñon Canyon military training site for one year. Many felt Lamborn should have persuaded farmers and other landowners to drop their opposition to the project. Others noted he wasn't granted a seat on the Armed Services Committee, where his predecessor, Republican Joel Hefley, served. Lamborn got that boost in October 2007, when he was appointed to the committee after the death of Republican Jo Ann Davis of Virginia.

He backed President George W. Bush on Iraq and in 2007 challenged calls for an immediate withdrawal of U.S. troops from the country. In early 2009, after Obama decided to close the Guantánamo Bay, Cuba, detention facility, he introduced a bill to bar the transfer of the prisoners to a prison in Colorado.

From his seat on Veterans' Affairs, Lamborn during the 110th Congress (2007-08) opposed Democratic proposals requiring the Veterans Affairs Department to do physiological testing on each soldier who returned to civilian life after receiving a combat-related injury. He argued the new requirement could further impact the government's already backlogged benefits claims.

He also serves on the Natural Resources panel, where he defends private property rights and denounces increased governmental powers of eminent domain. He favors a comprehensive energy plan that includes an expansion of the nation's wind, solar, nuclear, and domestic oil and natural gas drilling. In early 2009, he criticized Interior Secretary Ken Salazar's decision to void leases, granted by the Bush administration, for oil-shale development on 1.9 million acres of federal land in Colorado, Utah and Wyoming. Lamborn told The Associated Press the decision would cost Colorado billions of dollars in royalties and taxes and the opportunity to become a "world leader" in oil-shale development.

Lamborn is an avid climber. During the 110th, he led an effort to turn Colorado's famous Pikes Peak into a national monument. After he formed an exploratory committee, local agencies criticized him for not telling them first. Some officials said it would have little impact on the mountain or protection of the land; he later abandoned the effort.

Lamborn grew up on a small family farm near Leavenworth, Kan. His mother was a homemaker; his father was a farmer, who supplemented the family income by working at a federal penitentiary. He and his three brothers attended a three-room school near Fairmount before graduating from Lansing High School. Lamborn was his class valedictorian and went to the University of Kansas as a National Merit Scholar. He graduated with a journalism degree and later earned a law degree, then worked for a law firm in Omaha. As a young lawyer, he once snuck out in the middle of the night to repossess a client's car from an ex-girlfriend, according to the Colorado Springs Gazette Telegraph.

Lamborn said he was inspired to enter political office when Ronald Reagan was elected president. In 1982, Lamborn ran unsuccessfully for a seat in the Kansas legislature. Five years later, he moved to Colorado Springs with his wife, and he won a seat in the Colorado House in 1994.

Hefley's retirement in 2006 sparked a free-for-all in the GOP primary. Backed by the conservative Club for Growth, Lamborn edged ex-Hefley aide Jeff Crank. In November, Lamborn defeated retired Air Force Lt. Col. Jay Fawcett by nearly 20 percentage points. Crank challenged Lamborn again two years later, but Lamborn won by a decisive 14-percentage-point margin and took 60 percent in the general election.

KEY VOTES

2008

No Delay consideration of Colombia free-trade agreement

No Override Bush veto of federal farm and nutrition programs reauthorization bill

Yes Overhaul surveillance laws and permit dismissal of suits against companies that conducted warrantless wiretapping

No Grant mortgage relief to homeowners and funding for Fannie Mae and Freddie Mac

No Approve initial $700 billion program to stabilize financial markets

No Approve final $700 billion program to stabilize financial markets

No Provide $14 billion in loans to automakers

2007

No Increase minimum wage by $2.10 an hour

No Approve $124.2 billion in emergency war spending and set goal for redeployment of troops from Iraq

Yes Reject federal contraceptive assistance to international family planning groups

No Override Bush veto of $23.2 billion water projects authorization bill

Yes Implement Peru free-trade agreement

No Approve energy policy overhaul with new fuel economy standards

Yes Clear $473.5 billion omnibus spending bill, including $70 billion for military operations

CQ VOTE STUDIES

	PARTY UNITY		PRESIDENTIAL SUPPORT	
	SUPPORT	OPPOSE	SUPPORT	OPPOSE
2008	99%	1%	83%	17%
2007	99%	1%	95%	5%

INTEREST GROUPS

	AFL-CIO	ADA	CCUS	ACU
2008	0%	0%	83%	100%
2007	4%	0%	70%	100%

COLORADO 5
South central – Colorado Springs

God and country dominate the 5th, an overwhelmingly conservative district in the shadows of the Rocky Mountains in central Colorado. Military bases employ tens of thousands in the Colorado Springs area, and James Dobson's Focus on the Family and other evangelical groups are based in the 5th.

The district has made itself an indispensable arm of the modern military, and Colorado Springs in El Paso County houses the U.S. Space Command, the North American Aerospace Defense Command and some of the country's satellite defense research. The city has broadened its economic base beyond the military, although much of the 5th's new industry, including superconductor and computer development, depends on the defense industry.

The Colorado Springs area is a prime destination for tourists who stop at spots such as the U.S. Air Force Academy, Pikes Peak — the most visited mountain in North America — Glen Eyrie, the 19th-century castle formerly owned by Colorado Springs founder Gen. William Jackson Palmer,

and the nearby Garden of the Gods. More than 80 percent of district residents live in El Paso County, and Kiplinger's Magazine in 2008 named Colorado Springs as one of the nation's best big cities to live in.

El Paso, the largest county in the 5th, gave Republican John McCain 59 percent of its vote — the same percentage with which he took the overall district — in a state that Barack Obama carried in the 2008 presidential election. Democratic Sen. Mark Udall was held to less than 40 percent in El Paso, Teller and Fremont counties and, of districts wholly within the 5th, won only in Lake County.

MAJOR INDUSTRY
Military, defense, tourism, technology

MILITARY BASES
Fort Carson (Army), 24,600 military, 2,300 civilian (2009); U.S. Air Force Academy, 6,192 military, 1,481 civilian (2007); Peterson Air Force Base, 5,266 military, 2,305 civilian (2008); Schriever Air Force Base, 1,928 military, 627 civilian (2009)

CITIES
Colorado Springs, 360,890; Security-Widefield (unincorporated), 29,845

NOTABLE
The U.S. Olympic Committee headquarters are in Colorado Springs.

Rep. Mike Coffman (R)

CAPITOL OFFICE
225-7882
coffman.house.gov
1508 Longworth Bldg. 20515-0606; fax 226-4623

COMMITTEES
Armed Services
Natural Resources
Small Business

RESIDENCE
Aurora

BORN
March 19, 1955; Fort Leonard Wood, Mo.

RELIGION
United Methodist

FAMILY
Wife, Cynthia Coffman

EDUCATION
U. of Colorado, B.A. 1979 (political science)

MILITARY SERVICE
Army, 1972-74; Army Reserve, 1975-79;
Marine Corps, 1979-83; Marine Corps Reserve,
1983-94, 2005-06

CAREER
Property management company owner

POLITICAL HIGHLIGHTS
Candidate for Aurora City Council, 1985;
Colo. House, 1989-94; Colo. Senate, 1994-98;
Colo. treasurer, 1999-2007; Colo. secretary of state,
2007-08

ELECTION RESULTS

2008 GENERAL

Mike Coffman (R)	250,877	60.7%
Hank Eng (D)	162,639	39.3%

2008 PRIMARY

Mike Coffman (R)	28,509	40.1%
Wil Armstrong (R)	23,213	32.7%
Ted Harvey (R)	10,886	15.3%
Steve Ward (R)	8,452	11.9%

Elected 2008; 1st term

Coffman has shown an independent streak throughout his more than two decades in public office. Though a fiscal and social conservative on most issues, he is willing to part ways with other Republicans. "Principle trumps party," he said.

As state treasurer and lawmaker in both chambers of the Colorado General Assembly, he often chided fellow Republicans, including former Gov. Bill Owens, for being fiscally out of line. He also said GOP lawmakers were lax in conducting oversight during George W. Bush's administration. "I really challenge some of those assumptions that everyone [in other countries] is just like us and wants everything we want," he said of Bush's foreign policy.

Coffman most recently served as Colorado's secretary of state, where he angered GOP activists for leaving in the middle of his term to run for the seat of departing Republican Rep. Tom Tancredo. Coffman's election enabled Democratic Gov. Bill Ritter Jr. to appoint a Democrat to replace him.

Coffman brings a decorated military record to Capitol Hill. He dropped out of high school at 17 to enlist in the Army and later served in the Marines. He eventually led combat troops in the first Gulf War and helped organize local elections in Iraq in 2005 and 2006. His experience influenced party leaders to give him a seat on the Armed Services Committee, where he says he'll push for a "more realistic and less idealistic" approach overseas.

Coffman also sits on the Natural Resources Committee, where he seeks a comprehensive energy plan with "the appropriate balance" between environmental and economic concerns.

A former chairman of the state Senate's Finance Committee, Coffman wants more action to cope with the banking crisis. He sided with all Republicans in February 2009 by opposing a $787 billion economic stimulus bill that, he said, didn't live up to the bipartisan rhetoric President Obama had heralded.

After winning a tight four-person primary, Coffman was accused of "purging" voters in statewide races in a controversy that became the subject of a court challenge; he said he was only carrying out his job. In the end, though, he coasted with 61 percent of the vote in a heavily Republican district.

COLORADO 6

Denver suburbs — part of Aurora; Douglas County

White-collar suburbs south of Denver make up the heart of the 6th, where nearly half of residents have earned at least a bachelor's degree. Like much of Colorado, the district experienced two decades of dramatic population growth. Commuters complain about traffic going to and from the Mile High City, but an expansion of metropolitan light rail, as well as highway improvements, has eased some of the gridlock.

Technology-sector manufacturing makes up the economic base of the district. Employers include Raytheon and Lockheed Martin. In addition, Greenwood Village is home to the corporate headquarters of First Data, a financial transaction technology firm.

A plurality of district residents lives in Arapahoe County, which is mostly urbanized in the west and more rural in the east. A small portion of Aurora, Colorado's third-most-populous city, is in the 6th.

Minorities total 12 percent of residents in the district, making the 6th the state's only district where minorities are less than 20 percent of the population. Douglas County accounts for only 30 percent of the district's residents, but it is a GOP stronghold that supported both Republican Rep. Mike Coffman and U.S. Senate candidate Bob Schaffer. John McCain took 53 percent of the 6th's 2008 presidential vote.

MAJOR INDUSTRY
Manufacturing, technology

CITIES
Aurora (pt.), 78,878; Highlands Ranch (unincorporated), 70,931; Southglenn (unincorporated), 43,520; Littleton, 40,340

NOTABLE
The Comanche Crossing Railroad Site near Strasburg marks the place where the last spike was driven in 1870 to create the first continuous transcontinental railroad.

Rep. Ed Perlmutter (D)

Elected 2006; 2nd term

CAPITOL OFFICE
225-2645
perlmutter.house.gov
415 Cannon Bldg. 20515-0607; fax 225-5278

COMMITTEES
Financial Services
Rules

RESIDENCE
Golden

BORN
May 1, 1953; Denver, Colo.

RELIGION
Protestant

FAMILY
Divorced; three children

EDUCATION
U. of Colorado, B.A. 1975 (political science),
J.D. 1978

CAREER
Lawyer

POLITICAL HIGHLIGHTS
Colo. Senate, 1995-2003 (president pro tempore, 2001-03)

ELECTION RESULTS

2008 GENERAL

Ed Perlmutter (D)	173,931	63.5%
John W. Lerew (R)	100,055	36.5%

2008 PRIMARY

Ed Perlmutter (D)	unopposed

2006 GENERAL

Ed Perlmutter (D)	103,918	54.9%
Rick O'Donnell (R)	79,571	42.1%
Dave Chandler (GREEN)	3,073	1.6%
Roger McCarville (AC)	2,605	1.4%

Perlmutter is a party loyalist and a formidable fundraiser who is a reliable Democratic vote, but he is hardly a partisan. He came to Congress with a reputation for crossing party lines in the Colorado General Assembly and says he's struck by the "great senses of humor" among his House colleagues.

Such regard for others will help him get along with Republicans in his new assignment for the 111th Congress (2009-10) on the Rules Committee, where he is charged with carrying out the leadership's wishes on setting terms for floor debate, often over the GOP's objections. His amiability extends to his staff: He takes the rare step of posting his aides' biographies on his Web site along with his own.

Upon entering Congress, though, Perlmutter was faced with a decidedly humorless problem. After years of stagnant budgets, the National Renewable Energy Laboratory, which employs about 1,200 people in Perlmutter's district, faced layoffs. But he and fellow Colorado Democrat Mark Udall were able to persuade Democratic leaders to include another $300 million for the Energy Department's Office of Energy Efficiency and Renewable Energy — the lab's major sponsor — in a 2007 spending bill. From the funding, the department directed $100 million to the lab, saving the jobs. "I felt like I could retire after that one," he said.

Perlmutter likens the goal of energy independence to John F. Kennedy's challenge to land a man on the moon. He advocates the creation of a federal research program akin to the Apollo Project. One likely beneficiary of such a program would be his district's lab.

He praised President Obama's $787 billion economic stimulus law in February 2009 for its investments in mass transit and energy-efficient upgrades to public housing. He said it would help his state's burgeoning renewable energy sector: "This bill gives Colorado's green businesses the shot in the arm they need to grow and expand."

In his first term, Perlmutter was assigned to the Financial Services and Homeland Security committees, common stations for freshman representatives. Neither committee, however, has much to do with energy policy. That didn't stop Perlmutter from legislating on the issue.

On Financial Services, Perlmutter won adoption of an amendment to a bill tightening regulation of Fannie Mae and Freddie Mac that would encourage the two mortgage companies to support energy efficiency standards for low- and moderate-income housing. The committee's chairman, Barney Frank of Massachusetts, asked Perlmutter to chair an energy efficiency task force. The task force's work resulted in a new directive to public-housing authorities: institute energy-efficient building standards in all new public housing built under the HOPE VI program, which is aimed at revitalizing the nation's public-housing stock. Both the Fannie and Freddie bill and the HOPE VI bill passed the House but stalled in the Senate.

In the homeland security arena, Perlmutter won House passage of a bill to require the Homeland Security Department to analyze critical infrastructure for its vulnerability to terrorist attacks and share the results with governments and private owners. The idea is to figure out what information is readily available to potential saboteurs.

But unlike his party's most liberal constituency, he does not favor an immediate and complete withdrawal of U.S. forces from Iraq. He has instead adopted a more nuanced position, supporting withdrawal "in a way that will not create more ruin to our credibility in the world or further endanger our national security," he told The Denver Post. He wants security responsibilities transferred to the Iraqi military and police while a "multi-national reconstruction effort" is established, with U.S. forces stationed in nearby countries "in case a quick strike is necessary."

Aside from renewable energy, Perlmutter said his main interest is sticking up for his constituents. And he is a strong supporter of expanded embryonic stem cell research, as his oldest daughter has epilepsy.

Perlmutter drew headlines in early 2009, when he and other Colorado lawmakers were a subject of news reports focused on a potential connection between campaign contributions from the now-defunct lobbying firm The PMA Group and earmarks — funding set-asides for special projects — it secured for clients. He denied any wrongdoing in obtaining an earmark for IHS Inc., a defense consulting firm and PMA client. His spokeswoman said he did not receive money from IHS, but from PMA's political action committee. He gave the money to charity.

Perlmutter's grandfather and father ran a cement business in the Denver area, where Perlmutter was born and raised, for decades. His father was active in the Democratic Party, and Perlmutter's first taste of politics came by walking precincts with his family and handing out fliers.

He worked his way through law school as a laborer on the family business' construction projects, then spent nearly 30 years at the same law firm, mostly focusing on bankruptcy cases.

Perlmutter was elected to the Colorado state Senate in 1994 in a district traditionally held by Republicans. He served two terms and eventually became president pro tempore. He considered a run for Congress in 2002 but decided to spend more time with his family; in 2004, he co-chaired John Kerry's presidential campaign operation in Colorado.

He saw an opportunity to run for the House in 2006 when GOP Rep. Bob Beauprez launched an ill-fated bid for governor. Perlmutter's GOP opponent was Rick O'Donnell, a former state education commissioner. But O'Donnell's suggestion that high school boys spend part of their senior year in public service, performing such duties as securing the border, hurt him, as did the anti-Republican tide. What was originally a toss-up race turned into a resounding victory for Perlmutter.

He notched another resounding victory over Republican John W. Lerew, founder of a financial planning center, in his 2008 re-election race. He raised nearly $1.8 million, compared with Lerew's $37,100, and gave nearly $300,000 to other Democratic campaigns.

KEY VOTES

2008
Yes Delay consideration of Colombia free-trade agreement
Yes Override Bush veto of federal farm and nutrition programs reauthorization bill
Yes Overhaul surveillance laws and permit dismissal of suits against companies that conducted warrantless wiretapping
Yes Grant mortgage relief to homeowners and funding for Fannie Mae and Freddie Mac
Yes Approve initial $700 billion program to stabilize financial markets
Yes Approve final $700 billion program to stabilize financial markets
Yes Provide $14 billion in loans to automakers

2007
Yes Increase minimum wage by $2.10 an hour
Yes Approve $124.2 billion in emergency war spending and set goal for redeployment of troops from Iraq
No   Reject federal contraceptive assistance to international family planning groups
Yes Override Bush veto of $23.2 billion water projects authorization bill
Yes Implement Peru free-trade agreement
Yes Approve energy policy overhaul with new fuel economy standards
No   Clear $473.5 billion omnibus spending bill, including $70 billion for military operations

CQ VOTE STUDIES

	PARTY UNITY		PRESIDENTIAL SUPPORT	
	SUPPORT	OPPOSE	SUPPORT	OPPOSE
2008	97%	3%	16%	84%
2007	94%	6%	8%	92%

INTEREST GROUPS

	AFL-CIO	ADA	CCUS	ACU
2008	93%	95%	59%	0%
2007	96%	95%	60%	4%

COLORADO 7

Denver suburbs — Lakewood, parts of Aurora and Arvada

Surrounding Denver (and the 1st District) on three sides, the suburban 7th had been politically competitive for most of the decade since it was created following the 2000 census. But a comfortable win by Democrat Barack Obama in the 2008 presidential election and an easy re-election for Rep. Ed Perlmutter indicate a shift to the left here. Minorities total nearly one-third of residents, giving the 7th the second-highest percentage in the state.

The 7th includes parts of Adams, Arapahoe and Jefferson counties, with more than half its residents in Jefferson. The 7th's portion of Jefferson includes Golden, most of Arvada and Lakewood, a middle class area just west of Denver that is home to a large concentration of federal agencies. The Denver Federal Center in Lakewood hosts 26 different federal agencies and more than 6,000 federal employees.

Commerce City, a Hispanic-majority, lower-middle class area just north

of Denver in Adams County, and most of Aurora (shared with the 6th), in Arapahoe County, also are in the 7th. Commerce City is home to the Colorado Rapids soccer stadium.

Decommissioned military facilities have received new life here, as the former Fitzsimons Army Medical Center has been revived by the University of Colorado Denver to serve as the region's health industry anchor with several hospital and research facilities. Also, the former weapons-producing Rocky Mountain Arsenal is now a national wildlife refuge and the largest contiguous open space in the Denver area. Buckley Air Force Base remains a link in the Air Force Space Command satellite tracking system.

MAJOR INDUSTRY
Health care, aerospace, manufacturing, telecommunications

MILITARY BASES
Buckley Air Force Base, 2,971 military, 3,240 civilian (2007)

CITIES
Aurora (pt.), 197,515; Lakewood, 144,126; Arvada (pt.), 98,941; Wheat Ridge, 32,913; Commerce City, 20,991

NOTABLE
The MillerCoors brewery in Golden features free tours and tastings.

CONNECTICUT

Gov. M. Jodi Rell (R)

First elected: 2006; assumed office July 1, 2004, due to resignation of John G. Rowland, R
Length of term: 4 years
Term expires: 1/11
Salary: $150,000
Phone: (860) 566-4840

Residence: Brookfield
Born: June 16, 1946; Norfolk, Va.
Religion: Protestant
Family: Husband, Lou Rell; two children
Education: Old Dominion College, attended 1965-66; Western Connecticut State U., attended 1982-84
Career: Homemaker; investment firm office clerk
Political highlights: Conn. House, 1985-95 (deputy minority leader 1991-1995); lieutenant governor, 1995-2004

Election results:
2006 GENERAL
M. Jodi Rell (R)	710,048	63.2%
John DeStefano (D)	398,220	35.4%

Lt. Gov. Michael Fedele (R)

First elected: 2006
Length of term: 4 years
Term expires: 1/11
Salary: $110,000
Phone: (860) 524-7384

LEGISLATURE

General Assembly: January-June in odd-numbered years; February-May in even-numbered years

Senate: 36 members, 2-year terms
2009 ratios: 24 D, 12 R; 28 men, 8 women
Salary: $28,000
Phone: (860) 240-0500

House: 151 members, 2-year terms
2009 ratios: 114 D, 37 R; 100 men, 51 women
Salary: $28,000
Phone: (860) 240-0400

TERM LIMITS

Governor: No
Senate: No
House: No

URBAN STATISTICS

CITY	POPULATION
Bridgeport	139,529
New Haven	123,626
Hartford	121,578
Stamford	117,083

REGISTERED VOTERS

Others/unaffiliated	43%
Democrat	37%
Republican	20%

POPULATION

2008 population (est.)	3,501,252
2000 population	3,405,565
1990 population	3,287,116
Percent change (1990-2000)	+3.6%
Rank among states (2008)	29
Median age	37.4
Born in state	57%
Foreign born	10.9%
Violent crime rate	325/100,000
Poverty level	7.9%
Federal workers	21,296
Military	16,675

ELECTIONS

STATE ELECTION OFFICIAL
(860) 509-6100
DEMOCRATIC PARTY
(860) 560-1775
REPUBLICAN PARTY
(860) 547-0589

MISCELLANEOUS

Web: www.ct.gov
Capital: Hartford

U.S. CONGRESS

Senate: 1 Democrat, 1 independent
House: 5 Democrats

2000 Census Statistics by District

DIST.	2008 VOTE FOR PRESIDENT OBAMA	MCCAIN	WHITE	BLACK	ASIAN	HISP	MEDIAN INCOME	WHITE COLLAR	BLUE COLLAR	SERVICE INDUSTRY	OVER 64	UNDER 18	COLLEGE EDUCATION	RURAL	SQ. MILES
1	66%	33%	72%	13%	2%	11%	$50,227	66%	20%	14%	15%	24%	28%	7%	653
2	58	40	89	3	2	4	$54,498	63	21	16	12	24	29	33	2,028
3	62	36	76	11	3	8	$49,752	65	21	14	15	24	28	3	459
4	60	40	71	11	3	13	$66,598	72	16	13	13	26	42	4	457
5	56	42	80	5	2	11	$53,118	63	23	14	14	25	30	14	1,248
STATE	61	38	77	9	2	9	$53,935	66	20	14	14	25	31	12	4,845
U.S.	53	46	69	12	4	13	$41,994	60	25	15	12	26	24	21	3,537,438

Sen. Christopher J. Dodd (D)

Elected 1980; 5th term

CAPITOL OFFICE
224-2823
dodd.senate.gov
448 Russell Bldg. 20510-0702; fax 224-1083

COMMITTEES
Banking, Housing & Urban Affairs - chairman
Foreign Relations
   (Western Hemisphere, Peace Corps & Global
   Narcotics Affairs - chairman)
Health, Education, Labor & Pensions
Rules & Administration

RESIDENCE
East Haddam

BORN
May 27, 1944; Willimantic, Conn.

RELIGION
Roman Catholic

FAMILY
Wife, Jackie Clegg Dodd; two children

EDUCATION
Providence College, B.A. 1966;
U. of Louisville, J.D. 1972

MILITARY SERVICE
Army Reserve 1969-75

CAREER
Lawyer; Peace Corps volunteer

POLITICAL HIGHLIGHTS
U.S. House, 1975-81; sought Democratic
nomination for president, 2008

ELECTION RESULTS

2004 GENERAL

Christopher J. Dodd (D)	945,347	66.4%
Jack Orchulli (R)	457,749	32.1%

2004 PRIMARY

Christopher J. Dodd (D)	unopposed

PREVIOUS WINNING PERCENTAGES
1998 (65%); 1992 (59%); 1986 (65%); 1980 (56%);
1978 House Election (70%); 1976 House Election
(65%); 1974 House Election (59%)

Dodd's long experience and practiced skill at cultivating friendships and cutting deals make him a key player on Capitol Hill on issues addressing the struggling housing and financial sectors, as well as health care. He constantly seeks to balance the interests of consumers with those of the industries he oversees as chairman of the Banking, Housing and Urban Affairs Committee.

His finesse at fundraising also has kept him secure in his seat for nearly 30 years, although even that didn't help him much as a 2008 presidential hopeful. He raised more than $18 million in that bid but was little-noticed on the campaign trail and pulled out early in the campaign season. He's been in the center of debates over the ailing economy since then.

Dodd's state has been home to major insurance companies and other financial services firms, and early in 2009, Dodd began to look into a sweeping overhaul of the regulatory system that failed to prevent their collapse. "I pledge that over the coming months, we will rebuild the nation's financial architecture from the bottom up," Dodd said, vowing to put the interests of consumers and shareholders first.

Though the election of Delaware Sen. Joseph R. Biden Jr. as vice president opened up the Foreign Relations Committee chairmanship for Dodd, he decided to keep his Banking post. "Putting our country back on a sound economic footing is our defining challenge of the moment," Dodd said.

Dodd is also the No. 2 Democrat on the Health, Education, Labor and Pensions Committee headed by his close friend, Massachusetts' Edward M. Kennedy, who is battling brain cancer. Kennedy named him his chief deputy for the 2009 push to overhaul the nation's health care system.

Dodd plans to maintain vigorous oversight of the $700 billion financial sector rescue law he helped steer to passage in October 2008. He didn't draw as much attention as his House counterpart, Financial Services Chairman Barney Frank of Massachusetts, but he won praise from colleagues for his work on the package. His proposal to limit executive compensation at companies that participate in the program became part of the final bill.

Earlier in 2008, Dodd helped win enactment of legislation that included a modernization of the Federal Housing Administration and a $300 billion expansion of the FHA's loan insurance programs aimed at helping borrowers avoid foreclosure. The measure also included provisions to overhaul mortgage giants Fannie Mae and Freddie Mac.

His diminished popularity in his home state will complicate his work as he seeks a sixth term in 2010. A Hartford Courant/University of Connecticut poll in October 2008 found 48 percent of residents disapproved and 42 percent approved of his performance, a dip Dodd said did not surprise him. "People are angry," he told the newspaper. "This is the most difficult time economically in my political life."

His stature was not helped by his frequent absences from the state during his presidential bid, which ended in January 2008 after he finished sixth in the Iowa caucuses. Though he temporarily moved his wife and children to a rented home in West Des Moines to strengthen his presence there, his name recognition proved almost non-existent in early polls and his fundraising efforts stagnated, despite efforts to swing Wall Street to his side.

Another negative for Dodd was the controversy over whether he received a sweetheart deal on two mortgages in 2003 from Countrywide Financial Corp., a lender. The Senate ethics committee said in June 2008 that it had begun an initial investigation into whether Dodd and North Dakota Democratic Sen. Kent Conrad got preferential treatment, a probe that continued in 2009. Dodd said that even though he had been told he was put in a "VIP program," he did not assume he would get any special favors.

During the 110th Congress (2007-08), Dodd led Senate liberals in a fight to block retroactive immunity for telecommunications companies that cooperated with the George W. Bush administration's warrantless surveillance of suspected terrorists following the Sept. 11 attacks. The fight dragged on for months, but Dodd's amendment to delete the immunity provision from a bill rewriting electronic surveillance rules was defeated in July 2008. The version enacted into law granted the immunity.

Dodd was more successful during the 110th in pushing through a reauthorization of the Terrorism Risk Insurance Act, which provides a federal backstop for private property insurers writing policies against the threat of terrorism. Dodd also helped write the original 2002 law.

Dodd has said he wants to explore creation of a federal charter option for the nation's larger insurance companies, a priority for large firms because it would spare them from having to comply with 50 different state insurance laws. At the same time, he has sought to defend consumers, taking aim at abusive credit card and predatory lending practices.

In 2008, Dodd steered an overhaul of the nation's flood insurance program through the Senate, but negotiations with the House stalled as committee leaders focused on the financial rescue effort instead.

Although Dodd originally supported the resolution in 2002 authorizing the invasion of Iraq, he became a critic of the Bush administration's handling of the war and has called for the withdrawal of U.S. troops.

Dodd has spent more than half his life in politics. His congressional career includes such milestones as sponsorship of the Family and Medical Leave Act, which guarantees employees time off to care for children and elderly family members. He also led the fight to strengthen voting procedures after the bitterly contested 2000 presidential election. The resulting law set the first federal standards for the conduct of elections.

Despite his Democratic National Committee chairmanship from 1995-97, Dodd has been disappointed in attempts to move up in the leadership. He explored a run against Harry Reid for minority leader in the 109th Congress (2005-06), but bowed out when it was clear Reid had the votes locked up. Ten years earlier, Tom Daschle of South Dakota bested Dodd for the job by just one vote.

With his booming voice, white mane and thick eyebrows, Dodd is easily picked out on the Senate floor. He loves a good joke and can be seen laughing with everyone from fellow senators to reporters to Capitol Hill elevator operators. His easy, comfortable way with people is in part derived from his background as a child of the Senate. His father, Thomas J. Dodd, was a Democratic senator from Connecticut for two terms, though his career declined after his censure in 1967 for misusing political contributions. (The senator believes his father was mistreated by his colleagues, so casts votes to signal his belief that fellow senators should get the benefit of the doubt.)

Dodd served two years in the Peace Corps in the Dominican Republic after college. He won his first House election in 1974 at age 30 on a family name that still resonated with older state voters. It was the post-Watergate election, and he captured an open seat that had been held by a Republican.

When Democrat Abraham Ribicoff retired six years later, Dodd became the youngest person ever elected to the Senate from Connecticut. He took 56 percent of the vote against former New York Sen. James L. Buckley. Dodd has since won re-election more easily, taking almost two-thirds of the vote in his 1998 contest and again in 2004, when he defeated his GOP foe, former clothing company executive Jack Orchulli, with 66 percent of the vote.

KEY VOTES

2008

Yes Prohibit discrimination based on genetic information

Yes Reauthorize farm and nutrition programs for five years

Yes Limit debate on "cap and trade" system for greenhouse gas emissions

Yes Allow lawsuits against companies that participated in warrantless wiretapping

Yes Limit debate on a bill to block a scheduled cut in Medicare payments to doctors

Yes Grant mortgage relief to homeowners and funding for Fannie Mae and Freddie Mac

Yes Approve a nuclear cooperation agreement with India

Yes Approve final $700 billion program to stabilize financial markets

Yes Allow consideration of a $14 billion auto industry loan package

2007

Yes Increase minimum wage by $2.10 an hour

Yes Limit debate on a comprehensive immigration bill

Yes Overhaul congressional lobbying and ethics rules for members and their staffs

Yes Limit debate on considering a bill to add House seats for the District of Columbia and Utah

Yes Limit debate on restoring habeas corpus rights to detainees

Yes Mandate minimum breaks for troops between deployments to Iraq or Afghanistan

? Override Bush veto of $23.2 billion water projects authorization bill

? Confirm Michael B. Mukasey as attorney general

Yes Limit debate on an energy policy overhaul containing $21.8 billion in tax incentives and reduced oil and gas subsidies

CQ VOTE STUDIES

	PARTY UNITY		PRESIDENTIAL SUPPORT	
	SUPPORT	OPPOSE	SUPPORT	OPPOSE
2008	96%	4%	31%	69%
2007	97%	3%	40%	60%
2006	95%	5%	49%	51%
2005	94%	6%	33%	67%
2004	95%	5%	60%	40%
2003	95%	5%	47%	53%
2002	94%	6%	68%	32%
2001	98%	2%	66%	34%
2000	95%	5%	98%	2%
1999	90%	10%	86%	14%

INTEREST GROUPS

	AFL-CIO	ADA	CCUS	ACU
2008	100%	100%	50%	4%
2007	100%	70%	17%	0%
2006	100%	95%	42%	8%
2005	79%	95%	39%	8%
2004	100%	100%	41%	4%
2003	100%	95%	32%	15%
2002	100%	80%	40%	5%
2001	94%	95%	36%	16%
2000	75%	95%	53%	13%
1999	88%	95%	53%	0%

Sen. Joseph I. Lieberman (I)

Elected 1988; 4th term

CAPITOL OFFICE
224-4041
lieberman.senate.gov
706 Hart Bldg. 20510-0703; fax 224-9750

COMMITTEES
Armed Services
 (Airland - chairman)
Homeland Security & Governmental Affairs
 - chairman
Small Business & Entrepreneurship

RESIDENCE
Stamford

BORN
Feb. 24, 1942; Stamford, Conn.

RELIGION
Jewish

FAMILY
Wife, Hadassah Lieberman; four children

EDUCATION
Yale U., B.A. 1964 (politics & economics), LL.B. 1967

CAREER
Lawyer

POLITICAL HIGHLIGHTS
Conn. Senate, 1971-80 (served as a Democrat; majority leader, 1975-80); Democratic nominee for U.S. House, 1980; Conn. attorney general, 1983-89 (served as a Democrat); Democratic nominee for vice president, 2000; sought Democratic nomination for president, 2004

ELECTION RESULTS

2006 GENERAL

Joseph I. Lieberman (CFL)	564,095	49.7%
Ned Lamont (D)	450,844	39.7%
Alan Schlesinger (R)	109,198	9.6%

2006 GENERAL

Ned Lamont (D)	146,404	51.8%
Joseph I. Lieberman (D)	136,490	48.2%

PREVIOUS WINNING PERCENTAGES *
2000 (63%); 1994 (67%); 1988 (50%)
* Elected as a Democrat 1998-2000

There are two Liebermans: One is a pro-labor, pro-abortion rights senator with a strong environmental record who contributed thousands of dollars to his Democratic colleagues heading into the 2008 elections. The other is an unwavering supporter of the Iraq War who accepted a speaking slot at the Republican National Convention to sing the praises of his close friend, Sen. John McCain of Arizona.

The latter Lieberman confounds and infuriates many Democrats. But party leaders have been reluctant to chastise him too strongly. And despite his status as an independent he remains chairman of the Homeland Security and Governmental Affairs Committee — a job giving him as much power as anyone in Washington to ask the tough questions and otherwise conduct oversight of the Obama administration.

As chairman, Lieberman has drawn criticism from Democrats for taking a noticeably quieter approach to oversight than Rep. Henry A. Waxman of California, who went after the George W. Bush administration on multiple fronts when he chaired the House Oversight and Government Reform Committee in the 110th Congress (2007-08). Waxman relinquished the gavel in 2009 to chair the House Energy and Commerce Committee, but his successor, Edolphus Towns of New York, intends to follow Waxman's model.

Lieberman said he's more interested in using his committee to "produce legislation that matters" rather than as a bully pulpit. "I'm always going to try to do something that is very constructive," he said in January 2009. "I never just want to do a hearing to play gotcha, that doesn't lead to something."

Lieberman said some legacies of the Bush administration bear examining, including the state of the Homeland Security Department. But he promised to take on his work just as any true independent would — neutrally and across party lines.

He already works closely with top-ranking Republican Susan Collins of Maine, one of the GOP's few remaining moderates. In 2004, when Collins held the gavel, the pair pushed to enactment an overhaul of the nation's intelligence agencies that conservatives had stalled for months.

Lieberman was an early proponent of creating a Homeland Security Department, pushing such a proposal long before Bush embraced the idea in 2002. He also pressed Bush to accept the creation of the independent commission to investigate government failures that may have opened the nation to the Sept. 11 terrorist attacks.

Lieberman joined Bernard Sanders of Vermont as an independent in the 110th Congress (2007-08), siding with the Democrats for organizational purposes and giving the party its bare 51-49 operational edge. The switch came after Lieberman's lifetime service as a Democrat, including a stint in 2000 as his party's vice presidential nominee. But his hawkishness on Iraq led Connecticut voters to reject him in the 2006 Democratic primary. He promptly ran as an independent and won a fourth term anyway.

Many of his colleagues backed Democrat Ned Lamont, who beat Lieberman in the primary. After winning the November general election, Lieberman wanted to be known as an Independent Democrat, but Senate record-keepers forced him to choose between Democrat and independent. He opted for the latter. And he said it was possible he could someday switch to the GOP.

His chairmanship may have helped stave off any thoughts Lieberman had about defecting to the Republicans, but it wasn't enough to pull him back into the Democrats' camp. "The Democratic Party today is not the party it was in 2000," he told ABC's "This Week" in March 2008. "It's not the Bill Clinton-Al Gore party, which was strong internationalists, strong on defense, pro-trade, pro-reform in our domestic government. It's been effectively taken over by a small group on the left of the party that is protectionist, isolationist…and very, very hyperpartisan."

Another reason Lieberman has remained aloof from the Democratic fold is his friendship with McCain. The two, longtime colleagues on the Armed Services Committee, share a belief that a strong U.S. troop presence in Iraq is essential to success there. Lieberman endorsed McCain's presidential bid in December 2007 and campaigned with him in many states, particularly those with large numbers of Jewish voters. Post-election news reports indicated he was McCain's choice as a running mate before the Arizonan selected Alaska Gov. Sarah Palin to shore up his support among conservatives.

But on most domestic issues, from taxes to civil rights, the New Englander is a reliable Democratic vote. During Bush's two terms, Lieberman scored higher on party unity than 14 Senate Democrats who stayed in office through 2008, including Robert C. Byrd of West Virginia, a former majority leader. Lieberman hasn't forgotten his Democratic friends when it comes to fundraising, either. Just three days after endorsing McCain, he transferred $100,000 to the Democratic Senatorial Campaign Committee.

As a member of the Environment and Public Works Committee during the 110th, Lieberman and Republican John W. Warner of Virginia were chief sponsors of the leading proposal to reduce greenhouse gas emissions that contribute to global warming. The measure stalled in the Senate in June 2008.

When describing his advocacy of environmental stewardship, he often cites *tikkun olam*, the Jewish belief that it is every person's duty to protect all of God's creations.

Lieberman works to build company in the center of the Senate's political spectrum. In the 109th Congress (2005-06), he was one of seven Democrats and seven Republicans who formed a pivotal "Gang of 14" to deter Democratic filibusters against Bush's conservative judicial nominees while blocking Republican leadership threats to use a parliamentary "nuclear option" ending such filibusters forever. Lieberman and other members of the gang continue to touch base often.

Lieberman soared to national prominence in the 2000 presidential campaign, when Al Gore tapped him as his running mate, the first Jew to be on a national ticket. Lieberman charmed voters with his broad smile and gee-whiz attitude. But four years later, when he attempted to win the presidential nomination himself after Gore decided against a second try, his campaign never caught fire. He dropped out in early February 2004.

His religious faith is a driving force for Lieberman. He has been a fervent supporter of Israel and was more open than most Democrats to Bush's proposal to give faith-based organizations funds to provide social services.

Before the 2000 campaign, Lieberman was perhaps best known nationally for a September 1998 speech criticizing President Clinton's behavior in the Monica Lewinsky sex scandal as "immoral." But he never called for the president's resignation, and like all other Senate Democrats, he voted against convicting Clinton in the 1999 impeachment trial.

Lieberman always has been politically ambitious. He won a state Senate seat in 1970 — helped by Clinton, then a 24-year-old campaign aide and Yale Law School student — and soon rose to majority leader. He lost a race for the U.S. House in the Reagan landslide of 1980 but rebounded in 1982 to become Connecticut attorney general.

Six years later, Lieberman mounted a Senate campaign and won a narrow upset victory over Lowell P. Weicker Jr., a three-term liberal Republican. He has prevailed comfortably ever since, with the exception of the 2006 election.

KEY VOTES

2008

Yes Prohibit discrimination based on genetic information

Yes Reauthorize farm and nutrition programs for five years

Yes Limit debate on "cap and trade" system for greenhouse gas emissions

No Allow lawsuits against companies that participated in warrantless wiretapping

Yes Limit debate on a bill to block a scheduled cut in Medicare payments to doctors

Yes Grant mortgage relief to homeowners and funding for Fannie Mae and Freddie Mac

Yes Approve a nuclear cooperation agreement with India

Yes Approve final $700 billion program to stabilize financial markets

Yes Allow consideration of a $14 billion auto industry loan package

2007

Yes Increase minimum wage by $2.10 an hour

Yes Limit debate on a comprehensive immigration bill

Yes Overhaul congressional lobbying and ethics rules for members and their staffs

Yes Limit debate on considering a bill to add House seats for the District of Columbia and Utah

No Limit debate on restoring habeas corpus rights to detainees

No Mandate minimum breaks for troops between deployments to Iraq or Afghanistan

Yes Override Bush veto of $23.2 billion water projects authorization bill

Yes Confirm Michael B. Mukasey as attorney general

Yes Limit debate on an energy policy overhaul containing $21.8 billion in tax incentives and reduced oil and gas subsidies

CQ VOTE STUDIES

	PARTY UNITY		PRESIDENTIAL SUPPORT	
	SUPPORT	OPPOSE	SUPPORT	OPPOSE
2008	81%	19%	52%	48%
2007	81%	19%	62%	38%
2006	85%	15%	62%	38%
2005	90%	10%	46%	54%
2004	89%	11%	63%	37%
2003	95%	5%	32%	68%
2002	85%	15%	77%	23%
2001	93%	7%	69%	31%
2000	88%	12%	94%	6%
1999	87%	13%	89%	11%

INTEREST GROUPS

	AFL-CIO	ADA	CCUS	ACU
2008	100%	85%	75%	8%
2007	84%	70%	73%	8%
2006	77%	75%	44%	17%
2005	92%	80%	61%	8%
2004	83%	75%	79%	0%
2003	100%	70%	25%	0%
2002	92%	85%	60%	20%
2001	93%	95%	43%	28%
2000	80%	75%	33%	20%
1999	78%	95%	47%	0%

Rep. John B. Larson (D)

Elected 1998; 6th term

CAPITOL OFFICE
225-2265
www.house.gov/larson
106 Cannon Bldg. 20515-0701; fax 225-1031

COMMITTEES
Select Energy Independence & Global Warming
Ways & Means

RESIDENCE
East Hartford

BORN
July 22, 1948; Hartford, Conn.

RELIGION
Roman Catholic

FAMILY
Wife, Leslie Larson; three children

EDUCATION
Central Connecticut State U., B.S. 1971 (history)

CAREER
Insurance company owner; high school teacher

POLITICAL HIGHLIGHTS
East Hartford Board of Education, 1978-79;
East Hartford Town Council, 1979-83; Conn. Senate,
1983-95 (president pro tempore, 1987-95); sought
Democratic nomination for governor, 1994

ELECTION RESULTS

2008 GENERAL

John B. Larson (D)	211,493	71.6%
Joe Visconti (R)	76,860	26.0%
Stephen E.D. Fournier (GREEN)	7,201	2.4%

2008 PRIMARY

John B. Larson (D)	unopposed

2006 GENERAL

John B. Larson (D)	154,539	74.4%
Scott MacLean (R)	53,010	25.5%

PREVIOUS WINNING PERCENTAGES
2004 (73%); 2002 (67%); 2000 (72%); 1998 (58%)

In the House Democrats' leadership hierarchy, Larson serves as a release valve for rank-and-file members who want their gripes aired before top party leaders. As chairman of the Democratic Caucus, a group that includes all House Democrats, his affable nature and ability to communicate with every faction of the party makes him an invaluable, honest broker.

Even as vice chairman during the 110th Congress (2007-08), he was seen as the one who takes the heat. "People have no problem unloading on me, where they might have a problem unloading on the Speaker," Larson said. He offered a demonstration, using fake voices to act out a typical scene on the House floor. In Larson's retelling, a gruff-sounding member blasts Larson for the leadership's incompetence at scheduling House business. Then, spying Nancy Pelosi nearby, the same lawmaker kowtows to the Speaker, gushing about her recent TV appearances. The member then turns back to Larson: "And another thing, Larson, let me tell you this: You guys absolutely stink."

Larson, himself a Pelosi fan, accepts the abuse cheerfully. "What most members, want, I think, is to be heard," he said, noting that he travels frequently to districts across the country to understand where his colleagues come from. "They don't necessarily think that you're going to accept their idea. Some do. Some think that every time they espouse something, this is going to be law. But most members, I think, want to be heard."

With the departure of Caucus Chairman Rahm Emanuel of Illinois, who agreed after the 2008 elections to become President Obama's chief of staff, Larson moved up from the vice chairmanship unopposed. He had won the lesser post in early 2006, outmaneuvering two better-known candidates, Jan Schakowsky of Illinois and Joseph Crowley of New York. During the race, Larson quietly picked off votes one by one, aided by his longtime ally John P. Murtha of Pennsylvania. Larson was also able to cash chits he had earned by doing favors for colleagues as the top-ranking Democrat on the perks-disbursing House Administration Committee from 2003 to 2005.

In early 2009 Larson came under scrutiny for funding set-asides, or earmarks, he had won in appropriations bills for clients of The PMA Group. The now-defunct lobbying firm, closely associated with Murtha, was raided by the FBI as part of a probe into its campaign contributions. Larson collected nearly $38,000 in contributions from PMA since 2001, according to CQ MoneyLine.

Larson, a business-friendly Democrat, was inspired to enter public service by President Kennedy, another Catholic from a large New England family. But the current economic crisis has caused him to look further back in history for a role model. He says Democrats now have a rare Rooseveltian moment to craft a new New Deal redefining the pact between citizens and government. He wants his party to attack the challenges of global economics, global warming and global terrorism by focusing on education, health care and jobs.

That approach shapes his work on the Ways and Means Committee, where he has served since 2005. Even as he presses for middle-class tax cuts, health care reform and other Democratic priorities, he supports pay-as-you-go budgeting rules, pushing for revenue-raising offsets to tax cuts. He voted in 2007 against a one-year "patch" to limit the reach of the of the alternative minimum tax because it did not contain offsets.

Larson also worked on energy issues during the 110th, pushing a bill to limit speculation in the oil futures market. He serves on a select global warming panel, and is a member of the Democratic Steering and Policy Committee, which makes committee assignments.

During his first three terms, Larson served on the Armed Services Committee and tried to protect a major employer in his hometown, Pratt & Whitney Aircraft, which makes engines for military aircraft. He fought proposed funding cuts for the F-22 jet fighter, whose engine is made by Pratt & Whitney. In 2008, he argued against an Air Force decision to award a tanker contract to a team that did not include the company.

Larson also used to sit on the Science Committee, where he championed legislation to increase funding for aerospace research and development. In 2004, Larson and Connecticut's two senators obtained funding to create a National Center for Aerospace Leadership in his Hartford-based district.

Closely aligned with Murtha, the first prominent House Democrat to call for a prompt withdrawal from Iraq, Larson used his leadership slot to help drive Democratic opposition to the George W. Bush administration's war policy.

Larson grew up in an East Hartford public-housing project originally built for workers for United Aircraft, precursor to United Technologies Corp., the parent company of Pratt & Whitney. His father was a Pratt & Whitney fireman who moonlighted as an auto mechanic and butcher to support the family. His mother, a state employee, served on the town council. Larson and his seven siblings shared a single bathroom in what they laughingly refer to as the "brick mansion at 10 Chandler."

After graduating from Central Connecticut State University, Larson taught high school history and coached for about five years. He left to join an insurance company that he eventually bought. After stints on the East Hartford school board and town council, he was elected in 1982 to the state Senate, where he served a dozen years. His proudest achievement as a state legislator was Connecticut's Family and Medical Leave Act, the first such law enacted in the country.

Larson made an unsuccessful bid for governor in 1994, gaining endorsements of party leaders but losing the primary to state Comptroller Bill Curry. In 1996, he led a statewide volunteer drive to wire schools and libraries to the Internet. Later, in Congress, he founded the Digital Divide Caucus, which aims to make technology available to all Americans, regardless of income or location.

When veteran 1st District Democratic Rep. Barbara B. Kennelly announced she was running for governor in 1998, Larson was the first Democrat to file for her seat. He edged past Connecticut Secretary of State Miles S. Rapoport in the primary, then built on the lessons from his own 1994 defeat to win the general election. He rolled to a 17-percentage-point victory and has not been seriously threatened since.

KEY VOTES

2008
+	Delay consideration of Colombia free-trade agreement
Yes	Override Bush veto of federal farm and nutrition programs reauthorization bill
No	Overhaul surveillance laws and permit dismissal of suits against companies that conducted warrantless wiretapping
Yes	Grant mortgage relief to homeowners and funding for Fannie Mae and Freddie Mac
Yes	Approve initial $700 billion program to stabilize financial markets
Yes	Approve final $700 billion program to stabilize financial markets
Yes	Provide $14 billion in loans to automakers

2007
Yes	Increase minimum wage by $2.10 an hour
Yes	Approve $124.2 billion in emergency war spending and set goal for redeployment of troops from Iraq
No	Reject federal contraceptive assistance to international family planning groups
Yes	Override Bush veto of $23.2 billion water projects authorization bill
Yes	Implement Peru free-trade agreement
Yes	Approve energy policy overhaul with new fuel economy standards
No	Clear $473.5 billion omnibus spending bill, including $70 billion for military operations

CQ VOTE STUDIES

	PARTY UNITY		PRESIDENTIAL SUPPORT	
	SUPPORT	OPPOSE	SUPPORT	OPPOSE
2008	99%	1%	13%	87%
2007	99%	1%	4%	96%
2006	97%	3%	24%	76%
2005	98%	2%	15%	85%
2004	95%	5%	24%	76%

INTEREST GROUPS

	AFL-CIO	ADA	CCUS	ACU
2008	100%	95%	65%	0%
2007	96%	95%	55%	0%
2006	100%	95%	43%	8%
2005	93%	100%	44%	0%
2004	93%	100%	38%	16%

CONNECTICUT 1

Central – Hartford, Bristol

Resembling a backward "C," the 1st District carves a path from the state's sparsely populated northwestern towns along the Massachusetts border to the capital of Hartford before winding west to take in the central city of Bristol. Situated midway between Boston and New York — roughly 100 miles from each — the staunchly Democratic district is a commercial center for the Northeast Corridor.

Insurance, financial services and state government traditionally formed the backbone of the 1st's economy. Once recognized as the international insurance capital, Hartford still hosts the headquarters or offices of some firms, but recent layoffs in the financial sector have contributed to rising unemployment and emptying office buildings. Hometown company Colt firearms continues area operations, but the 1st's manufacturing base has contracted. Many city residents also struggle, and test scores in the city's school system lag behind the rest of the region.

Aerospace and defense firms also provide a significant source of employment for the district — United Technologies' Pratt & Whitney,

which builds aircraft engines, is headquartered in East Hartford. Bristol is the home of ESPN, and the network is also a job source.

Reflecting a state trend, the 1st's predominately white and wealthy suburbs thrive, while cities such as Hartford depopulate and decay. Local officials hope that efforts to renew the city's historic downtown and riverfront — and to continue construction of certified "green" residential and commercial buildings — draw residents and retail investment.

Hartford-area voters have not sent a Republican to the U.S. House since 1956, and the city's large minority population, mostly Hispanics of Puerto Rican descent, is firmly Democratic. In the 2008 presidential election, the 1st gave Democrat Barack Obama nearly 66 percent overall, his highest statewide vote percentage.

MAJOR INDUSTRY
Insurance, banking, defense, government

CITIES
Hartford, 121,578; West Hartford (unincorporated), 63,589; Bristol, 60,062; East Hartford (unincorporated), 49,575

NOTABLE
Hartford's Wadsworth Atheneum is the nation's oldest public art museum.

Rep. Joe Courtney (D)

Elected 2006; 2nd term

CAPITOL OFFICE
225-2076
courtney.house.gov
215 Cannon Bldg. 20515-0702; fax 225-4977

COMMITTEES
Armed Services
Education & Labor

RESIDENCE
Vernon

BORN
April 6, 1953; Hartford, Conn.

RELIGION
Roman Catholic

FAMILY
Wife, Audrey Budarz Courtney; two children

EDUCATION
Tufts U., B.A. 1975 (history); U. of Connecticut,
J.D. 1978

CAREER
Lawyer; public defender

POLITICAL HIGHLIGHTS
Conn. House, 1987-95; Democratic nominee
for lieutenant governor, 1998; Democratic
nominee for U.S. House, 2002

ELECTION RESULTS

2008 GENERAL

Joe Courtney (D)	212,148	65.7%
Sean Sullivan (R)	104,574	32.4%
G. Scott Deshefy (GREEN)	6,300	2.0%

2008 PRIMARY

Joe Courtney (D)	unopposed

2006 GENERAL

Joe Courtney (D)	121,248	50.0%
Rob Simmons (R)	121,165	50.0%

A former Connecticut state legislator who enjoys the nuts and bolts of the legislative process, Courtney has delved into helping his district's schools, drug manufacturers and defense contractors and has seen success that is typically rare for a newcomer to Capitol Hill.

His efforts helped him solidify his position and get easily re-elected, two years after winning the closest House race of the 2006 elections. He was dubbed "Landslide Joe" that year for unseating three-term Republican Rob Simmons by 83 votes out of more than 242,000 votes cast.

Courtney is on the Armed Services Committee, where he serves a major employer in his district. Senior committee members and Democratic appropriators helped him as a freshman to secure $588 million in fiscal 2008 defense spending for advanced work on nuclear submarines for General Dynamics' Electric Boat facility in Groton. Electric Boat had cut 1,400 jobs, and another 2,000 of the 10,200 jobs were considered at-risk before the spending boost.

Courtney, with the help of fellow Connecticut Democrat John B. Larson, was credited with convincing Defense Appropriations Chairman John P. Murtha of Pennsylvania to visit the Electric Boat plant and then to include funding for the project in his bill.

Subsequent talk among some Democrats of cutting spending on military procurement left Courtney determined to protect submarines. In December 2008, he led more than a dozen House members in urging President-elect Obama to double production of two new *Virginia*-class subs starting in 2011, one year ahead of the Navy's previous schedule.

Courtney also successfully fought in 2008 to have the Eightmile River, running through the towns of East Haddam, Lyme and Salem, recognized as a federal Wild and Scenic River, providing it with greater environmental protection.

Courtney's other seat is on the Education and Labor Committee, where he uses his experience on health care policy. Connecticut faced a budget crisis in the 1990s, and Courtney, a state legislator at the time and the husband of a nurse practitioner, helped tackle the complex long-term care reimbursement process, a multi-year legislative effort. "About six of us understood it," he said, adding, "It's not something that people are going to get their blood racing to hear about."

In the House, he has championed legislation that would shorten the waiting time for people with serious medical conditions to receive health insurance. His bill would reduce from 12 months to three months the waiting period for people with diagnosed illnesses to obtain new health care insurance. He joined home state Democratic Sen. Christopher J. Dodd in December 2008 in urging drug manufacturer Pfizer Inc. to reconsider hiring foreign workers to replace some local contractors in his district.

On education, Courtney also advocates changes to the No Child Left Behind Act, President George W. Bush's signature 2001 education law that ties federal aid to student performance. He says the law sets unfair standards for measuring schools' success, and instead Courtney favors the idea of a "growth model" that would establish a continuum for grading teachers and schools. He has also called for adequate federal funding to meet the law's requirements.

During debate on Obama's $787 billion economic stimulus bill in early 2009, he highlighted the help it would provide school districts. "If Congress fails to stabilize their budgets, we will damage not only this country in the short term, but we will damage it in terms of our ability to compete and thrive and grow as a nation," he said.

Courtney has been a reliable Democrat, voting with his caucus 98 percent of the time in the 110th Congress (2007-08) on votes that pitted a majority of Democrats against a majority of Republicans. But he broke with party leaders to vote against an effort to include funds for the Iraq War in an emergency supplemental spending bill in May 2008.

He also opposed the Peru free-trade pact in November 2007 because he believed the Bush administration failed to follow through on a promise to support legislation to help workers whose jobs are affected by trade deals. And although the deal followed a pact between Democratic leaders and the administration to ensure labor standards are included in all trade agreements, Courtney did not believe the administration would enforce such provisions.

In fall 2008, he opposed a $700 billion proposal, which became law, to aid the ailing financial services sector. He said the measure did not address the underlying causes of the fiscal crisis.

Courtney grew up as a "political junkie" in West Hartford, influenced by his four brothers and the tumultuous 1960s. "I was an Irish Catholic kid who remembered John F. Kennedy — the nuns actually prayed for him during the election in second grade," he said. He became a Democrat, even though his father was a moderate Republican. But he did follow in his father's footsteps by pursuing a law degree at the University of Connecticut and practicing law. His mother was a homemaker.

While in law school, Courtney worked as an aide to Democrat Sam Gejdenson when he was in the General Assembly. Courtney later ran for the state House, where he served from 1987 to 1995; he left to spend time with his family after the birth of his second child.

He made an unsuccessful bid for lieutenant governor in 1998 and for the U.S. House seat in 2002, when Simmons bested him by 8 percentage points. But Courtney was able to knock off Simmons in 2006. In that campaign, Courtney and many Democrats argued that if their opponents could not be held responsible for such issues as the war in Iraq, their re-election would be seen as empowering Republicans to pursue their agenda.

Despite Courtney's narrow victory, Simmons decided not to challenge him in 2008. In that election Courtney raised almost six times as much as his GOP opponent, Norwich attorney Sean Sullivan, and won with more than 65 percent of the vote.

KEY VOTES

2008

Yes	Delay consideration of Colombia free-trade agreement
Yes	Override Bush veto of federal farm and nutrition programs reauthorization bill
No	Overhaul surveillance laws and permit dismissal of suits against companies that conducted warrantless wiretapping
Yes	Grant mortgage relief to homeowners and funding for Fannie Mae and Freddie Mac
No	Approve initial $700 billion program to stabilize financial markets
No	Approve final $700 billion program to stabilize financial markets
Yes	Provide $14 billion in loans to automakers

2007

Yes	Increase minimum wage by $2.10 an hour
Yes	Approve $124.2 billion in emergency war spending and set goal for redeployment of troops from Iraq
No	Reject federal contraceptive assistance to international family planning groups
Yes	Override Bush veto of $23.2 billion water projects authorization bill
No	Implement Peru free-trade agreement
Yes	Approve energy policy overhaul with new fuel economy standards
No	Clear $473.5 billion omnibus spending bill, including $70 billion for military operations

CQ VOTE STUDIES

	PARTY UNITY		PRESIDENTIAL SUPPORT	
	SUPPORT	OPPOSE	SUPPORT	OPPOSE
2008	99%	1%	10%	90%
2007	97%	3%	3%	97%

INTEREST GROUPS

	AFL-CIO	ADA	CCUS	ACU
2008	100%	95%	50%	8%
2007	96%	100%	50%	0%

CONNECTICUT 2
East — Norwich, New London, Storrs

The 2nd, the state's largest district, runs from coastal Middlesex and New London counties north to the Massachusetts border through small former mill towns and the main campus of the University of Connecticut in Storrs.

Defense and tourism steer the 2nd's ship. General Dynamics' Electric Boat Corporation in Groton and the New London Naval Submarine Base are major employers. The Navy's declining demand for submarine production has forced some shipyard layoffs, but the New London base has been fighting for years to avoid closing and keep the base viable.

Once the engine in the 2nd's economy, the massive American Indian-owned casino resorts are vulnerable to economic instability. Both Foxwoods and Mohegan Sun — the resort casino in Uncasville that hosts the state's only major league sports team, the WNBA's Connecticut Sun — have seen recent employment cuts.

Casinos and surrounding towns also have quarreled over taxes and the application of regulations to reservation land. A significant portion of

Connecticut's state revenue comes from tax on casinos, and declines in gaming will hurt state funding.

Home foreclosures, job losses and pay freezes have hurt the district's economy, especially mainstays of local tourism, such as the attractions in historic Mystic Seaport. Officials hope to use federal funding to address chronic transportation issues in the region, some of which have been caused by years of heavy traffic to and from the casinos.

The predominately middle-class 2nd is largely white, with growing black and Hispanic communities. Barack Obama took 58 percent of the 2008 presidential vote here, winning by wide margins in areas such as New London and Mansfield.

MAJOR INDUSTRY
Casinos, defense, tourism, health care

MILITARY BASES
New London Naval Submarine Base, 7,541 military, 1,000 civilian (2009)

CITIES
Norwich, 36,117; New London, 25,671

NOTABLE
New London is home to the U.S. Coast Guard Academy.

Rep. Rosa DeLauro (D)

Elected 1990; 10th term

CAPITOL OFFICE
225-3661
www.house.gov/delauro
2413 Rayburn Bldg. 20515-0703; fax 225-4890

COMMITTEES
Appropriations
  (Agriculture - chairwoman)
Budget

RESIDENCE
New Haven

BORN
March 2, 1943; New Haven, Conn.

RELIGION
Roman Catholic

FAMILY
Husband, Stanley Greenberg; three children

EDUCATION
London School of Economics, attended
1962-63; Marymount College (N.Y.), B.A. 1964;
Columbia U., M.A. 1966 (international politics)

CAREER
Political activist; congressional and mayoral aide

POLITICAL HIGHLIGHTS
No previous office

ELECTION RESULTS

2008 GENERAL

Rosa DeLauro (D)	230,172	77.4%
Bo Itshaky (R)	58,583	19.7%
Ralph A. Ferrucci (GREEN)	8,613	2.9%

2008 PRIMARY

Rosa DeLauro (D)	unopposed

2006 GENERAL

Rosa DeLauro (D)	150,436	76.0%
Joseph Vollano (R)	44,386	22.4%
Daniel A. Sumrall (GREEN)	3,089	1.6%

PREVIOUS WINNING PERCENTAGES
2004 (72%); 2002 (66%); 2000 (72%); 1998 (71%);
1996 (71%); 1994 (63%); 1992 (66%); 1990 (52%)

DeLauro is an ardent and aggressive liberal advocate for women and working families. She has been a voice for the party on national issues such as abortion rights, equal pay for women and women's health parity. And she works to ensure her party doesn't take for granted the female voters who are one of its strongest constituencies.

Typically bespectacled in colorful eyeglasses and clad in bright suits, scarves or baubles, DeLauro (da-LAUR-o) is difficult to miss on Capitol Hill. And her demeanor is as lively as her dress. From her post atop of the Agriculture Appropriations Subcommittee, she runs a tight meeting and a rigorous oversight hearing. And she knows how to deliver a feisty sound bite. When news reports in 2008 detailed the George W. Bush administration's recruitment of retired generals to push its Iraq policy on television talk shows, DeLauro blasted the move as "a propaganda program, a secret program — the American people should never have been taken down this road."

Her views are much more in line with those of President Obama, whom she helped in the crucial last hours of the 2008 presidential primary campaign. She tapped her political network on his behalf just before he squeaked through Connecticut's primary with a narrow win. She emerged as a contender for two Cabinet posts in his White House — secretary of Labor and secretary of Health and Human Services — but was selected for neither.

A member of the Budget Committee, she supported Obama's $787 billion economic stimulus bill in early 2009. And she backed his $3.55 trillion fiscal 2010 budget blueprint. "The president inherited a mess — an economy in the midst of the worst recession since the Great Depression and a growing deficit — a result of mistaken policies and eight years of irresponsibility that avoided the hard decisions," she said. "But with this budget, President Obama responds to these challenges."

DeLauro has made a name for herself as a tireless crusader for food safety. In 2007 and 2008, after a spate of tainted drug imports from China, several E. coli and salmonella scares in the food supply and the biggest beef recall in U.S. history, she became a leading voice on how to correct the problem. "We're seeing the effects of an outmoded, outdated system," she said. In early 2009, in the wake of a massive recall of peanuts, she said, "There is no one person, no individual today who is responsible for food safety."

DeLauro wants to strip the Food and Drug Administration and the Agriculture Department of food safety responsibilities and move those duties to a new agency, and she, along with Connecticut Democratic Sen. Christopher J. Dodd, has been trying to pass legislation to that effect since 1999. Agriculture Secretary Tom Vilsack said in February 2009 he supports a single, combined food safety agency.

She also serves on two other Appropriations subcommittees: Labor, Health and Human Services and Education; and Financial Services.

In early 2009, Obama signed into law her bill that aims to equalize pay for women. It would require employers seeking to justify unequal pay for male and female workers to prove such disparities are job-related and required by a business necessity. She also hopes to push forward a bill to make it mandatory for insurance companies to allow women to stay in the hospital up to 48 hours after surgery for breast cancer. Both measures gained House support in 2008, but didn't make it through the Senate. DeLauro's interest in women's health issues stems in part from her own battle with ovarian cancer more than 20 years ago.

She is hawkish on funding for the UH-60 Black Hawk helicopter, a product of the Stratford-based Sikorsky Aircraft Corp., and for aircraft that use engines built by East Hartford-based Pratt & Whitney. Ups and downs at those companies are felt acutely in DeLauro's district.

A Catholic, DeLauro tries to refocus the "values debate" onto an array of issues where Democrats are strong, such as poverty and the environment. She is staunchly pro-abortion rights and wants Congress to take a "common-ground approach" to abortion that would favor contraception programs, expanded health coverage for women and children, more child care, adoption help and income support for the working poor.

DeLauro is deeply involved in party politics. In the 107th Congress (2001-02), she ran the party's communications arm as the hand-picked assistant of Minority Leader Richard A. Gephardt. When Democrats met late to organize for the 108th Congress (2003-04), DeLauro lost the caucus chief race by one vote. But new Minority Leader Nancy Pelosi appointed her co-chairwoman of the Democratic Steering Committee, which makes committee assignments.

DeLauro's rise from working-class Italian roots to the Democratic leadership's inner circle has been both smart and deliberate. She grew up in Wooster Square, a tight-knit Italian neighborhood in New Haven. Her father, Ted, was an immigrant, and her mother, Luisa, was a factory worker. Both her parents served on the New Haven council, and their home was the hub of neighborhood meetings about issues related to the schools, jobs and immigration officials. When her father first ran for the city council, he kept a file box filled with voters' names and their concerns, then walked door-to-door to seek their votes.

In the 1960s, DeLauro became a community organizer in President Johnson's War on Poverty, then worked for the mayor of New Haven. She ran Dodd's first Senate campaign, then became his chief of staff for seven years. She also took the helm of EMILY's List, the fundraising group that supports pro-abortion rights female candidates for higher office.

In 1990, DeLauro ran for the seat of Democratic Rep. Bruce Morrison, who chose to run for governor of Connecticut. Her political contacts enabled her to raise money quickly and shoo away intraparty competition. She went on to defeat GOP state Sen. Thomas Scott, an energetic conservative opposed to gun control and abortion rights. In a 1992 rematch, she defeated him with 66 percent of the vote. She has been re-elected easily ever since.

Along the way, she married Stanley Greenberg, a prominent Democratic pollster and adviser to President Clinton. In early 2009, tax experts and conservative bloggers questioned the living arrangement — rent-free in the basement of their Capitol Hill home — that the couple had created for White House Chief of Staff Rahm Emanuel, who served in the House with DeLauro.

KEY VOTES

2008

Yes Delay consideration of Colombia free-trade agreement

Yes Override Bush veto of federal farm and nutrition programs reauthorization bill

No Overhaul surveillance laws and permit dismissal of suits against companies that conducted warrantless wiretapping

Yes Grant mortgage relief to homeowners and funding for Fannie Mae and Freddie Mac

Yes Approve initial $700 billion program to stabilize financial markets

Yes Approve final $700 billion program to stabilize financial markets

Yes Provide $14 billion in loans to automakers

2007

Yes Increase minimum wage by $2.10 an hour

Yes Approve $124.2 billion in emergency war spending and set goal for redeployment of troops from Iraq

No Reject federal contraceptive assistance to international family planning groups

Yes Override Bush veto of $23.2 billion water projects authorization bill

No Implement Peru free-trade agreement

Yes Approve energy policy overhaul with new fuel economy standards

No Clear $473.5 billion omnibus spending bill, including $70 billion for military operations

CQ VOTE STUDIES

	PARTY UNITY		PRESIDENTIAL SUPPORT	
	SUPPORT	OPPOSE	SUPPORT	OPPOSE
2008	99%	1%	13%	87%
2007	99%	1%	4%	96%
2006	98%	2%	13%	87%
2005	98%	2%	9%	91%
2004	98%	2%	21%	79%

INTEREST GROUPS

	AFL-CIO	ADA	CCUS	ACU
2008	100%	100%	56%	0%
2007	96%	100%	45%	0%
2006	100%	100%	27%	8%
2005	93%	95%	37%	0%
2004	100%	100%	29%	4%

CONNECTICUT 3
South — New Haven, Milford

The 3rd includes coastal New Haven County towns such as Guilford on Long Island Sound and the port city of New Haven, and takes in Stratford in Fairfield County and most of inland Middletown in Middlesex County.

Like other cities in the state, New Haven is far poorer than its affluent suburbs. Yale University is the city's largest employer, but labor issues have long caused tension between the school and the city's blue-collar workers. Tax issues further strain the relationship between the city and the school — in order to ease tension, Yale has invested millions of dollars into development and infrastructure improvements.

Construction of a research park attracted some biotechnology firms to the area in order to collaborate with Yale's scientific research departments, and expansion of the park includes plans for residential, commercial and parking structures. Although some firms grew and contracted with pharmaceutical giants, critics charge that the companies do not provide jobs for the city's working-class residents. And economic downturns have hindered the university's continued expansion.

Beyond Yale's influence, the economy relies on the defense industry, manufacturing and technology. Stratford-based Sikorsky Aircraft, which manufactures helicopters such as the Army's Black Hawk model, depends on military contracts. Professionals commute from the district's suburbs throughout the state and as far away as New York City. Also, the city of New Haven has begun a revitalization of downtown, attempting to lure visitors to the waterfront and convention centers.

The 3rd's working-class constituents and liberal ivory-tower elite, along with New Haven's Hispanic and black residents, combine to make the district strongly Democratic. Many Italian-Americans still reside in the district's suburbs. Overall, Democrat Barack Obama took nearly 63 percent of the district's 2008 presidential vote.

MAJOR INDUSTRY
Higher education, defense, biotechnology, manufacturing

CITIES
New Haven, 123,626; West Haven, 52,360; Milford, 52,305; Stratford (unincorporated), 49,976; Middletown (pt.), 34,329; Naugatuck, 30,989

NOTABLE
New Haven, home to strong Italian communities, claims to be the birthplace of pizza in America.

Rep. Jim Himes (D)

CAPITOL OFFICE
225-5541
himes.house.gov
214 Cannon Bldg. 20515-0704; fax 225-9629

COMMITTEES
Financial Services
Homeland Security

RESIDENCE
Greenwich

BORN
July 5, 1966; Lima, Peru

RELIGION
Presbyterian

FAMILY
Wife, Mary Himes; two children

EDUCATION
Harvard U., A.B. 1988 (social studies);
Oxford U., M.Phil. 1990 (Rhodes scholar)

CAREER
Affordable housing nonprofit executive;
investment banker

POLITICAL HIGHLIGHTS
Housing Authority of the Town of Greenwich,
2003-06 (chairman, 2003-06); Greenwich
Democratic Town Committee chairman,
2004-08; Greenwich Board of Estimate
and Taxation, 2006-07

ELECTION RESULTS

2008 GENERAL

Jim Himes (D)	158,475	51.3%
Christopher Shays (R)	146,854	47.6%

2008 PRIMARY

Jim Himes (D)	12,260	87.0%
L. Lee Whitnum (D)	1,840	13.0%

Elected 2008; 1st term

Himes is a Harvard graduate, Rhodes scholar and former investment banker who calls himself "a product of the American dream." He said he wants to give others the same opportunities that were available to him.

"Out of a single-working-mom household and a public school, I had all kinds of doors open, and [recent policies] have increasingly closed doors economically for American families," he said. "We need to reverse that now."

Himes came to Congress by unseating moderate Christopher Shays, who had served just over 10 terms and was the last House Republican to represent New England. He sits on the Financial Services Committee and is a member of the centrist New Democrat Coalition, where he was assigned to co-chair a task force on financial services with Illinois Democrat Melissa Bean. His priorities include developing a comprehensive program to prevent home foreclosures.

Himes also sits on the Homeland Security Committee. He wants to tighten port security and conduct close scrutiny of the Homeland Security Department. His other goals include improving energy and health care, which he called the "critical issues of the decade."

Himes grew up in South America, where his father worked for the Ford Foundation. When his parents divorced, he moved to New Jersey with his mother and two sisters. He eventually earned a social studies degree from Harvard before becoming a Rhodes scholar; he is one of five members of the 111th Congress (2009-10) who hold that distinction.

Upon returning to the United States, Himes wanted to work at the State Department, but took a job at investment banking giant Goldman Sachs, which was opening up a Latin America group. He stayed there until he switched careers and worked for a nonprofit low-income housing foundation.

He was a commissioner of the Greenwich Housing Authority and later became an elected member of his town's finance board. He also served as the city's Democratic Town Committee chairman.

Himes defeated Shays — who had survived several previous tough challenges — with 51 percent of the vote. His win was fueled by a strong fundraising effort; he brought in more than $3.9 million.

CONNECTICUT 4

Southwest — Bridgeport, Stamford

The 4th runs from the outskirts of New York City along the wealthy "Gold Coast" towns on Long Island Sound. It takes in the industrial city of Norwalk, white-collar Stamford, and, in stark contrast to the coastal affluence, Bridgeport, the state's largest city.

Financial workers riding commuter trains and Interstate 95 long brought wealth from Wall Street to the 4th's tony suburbs. But now Greenwich, home of the hedge fund industry, is feeling the effects of high-end housing and financial market collapses.

Bridgeport has suffered the fate of many post-industrial cities and registers an unemployment rate above the national average. The South End has seen marked progress, as apartments and businesses take over abandoned factories, but crime and drugs have plagued the city, and development

efforts have achieved only mixed success. Layoffs by municipal and health care employers, and a stalling construction sector, contribute to economic uncertainty in the 4th.

The 4th District's extremes create difficult terrain for politicians to navigate. Several affluent suburbs still elect GOP mayors, while Stamford and Bridgeport have Democrats at the helm. The 4th preferred the last four Democratic presidential candidates overall, and most of the urban poor vote Democratic. Barack Obama — who took 84 percent of the vote in Bridgeport — won the district with 60 percent of its 2008 presidential vote.

MAJOR INDUSTRY
Banking, manufacturing, health care

CITIES
Bridgeport, 139,529; Stamford, 117,083; Norwalk, 82,951; Trumbull (unincorporated), 34,243; Shelton (pt.), 28,192

NOTABLE
The Barnum Museum in Bridgeport houses many of the showman's exhibits.

Rep. Christopher S. Murphy (D)

Elected 2006; 2nd term

CAPITOL OFFICE
225-4476
chrismurphy.house.gov
412 Cannon Bldg. 20515-0705; fax 225-5933

COMMITTEES
Energy & Commerce
Oversight & Government Reform

RESIDENCE
Cheshire

BORN
Aug. 3, 1973; White Plains, N.Y.

RELIGION
Protestant

FAMILY
Wife, Cathy Holahan; one child

EDUCATION
Williams College, B.A. 1996 (history & political science); U. of Connecticut, J.D. 2002

CAREER
Lawyer; state legislative and campaign aide

POLITICAL HIGHLIGHTS
Southington Planning & Zoning Commission, 1997-99; Conn. House, 1999-2003; Conn. Senate, 2003-07

ELECTION RESULTS

2008 GENERAL
Christopher S. Murphy (D, WFM)	179,327	59.2%
David J. Cappiello (R)	117,914	39.0%
Thomas Winn (I)	3,082	1.0%

2008 PRIMARY
Christopher S. Murphy (D)	unopposed

2006 GENERAL
Christopher S. Murphy (D, WFM)	122,980	56.5%
Nancy L. Johnson (R)	94,824	43.5%

One of the House's youngest members, Murphy also is among its most driven. He came to Capitol Hill in his early 30s, having held several local and state government offices — though he never stayed in any longer than four years. Before that, Murphy managed the congressional campaign of a virtual unknown who almost beat the incumbent Republican he ousted a decade later.

Murphy has shown a knack for making friends among fellow Democrats in his state's increasingly influential delegation, including John B. Larson, Democratic Caucus chairman, and Rosa DeLauro, co-chairwoman of the panel that makes Democratic committee assignments. With their help, he landed a seat on the powerful Energy and Commerce Committee in the 111th Congress (2009-10).

Murphy serves on the committee's panel on health. In the state Senate, he chaired the Public Health Committee, where he authored legislation funding stem cell research in Connecticut.

He shares new Energy and Commerce Chairman Henry A. Waxman's belief in universal health coverage, contending that it would cost less than the current "bloated and inefficient" system. In 2007, he pushed, unsuccessfully, legislation to establish a government-run Medicare drug plan that would allow the federal government to use savings from negotiations with pharmaceutical companies to reduce gaps among those not covered. In early 2009, he backed a bill to expand the State Children's Health Insurance Program, which covers children from low-income families who do not qualify for Medicaid.

Murphy also largely echoes the Democratic vision for energy policy. He supports a nationwide mandate for states to provide at least 15 percent of their electricity from wind, solar and other renewable resources. That mandate was the basis of a measure that passed the House in 2007 but stalled in the Senate. Unlike some liberal Democrats, though, he supports increased domestic offshore drilling if it can affect prices and be done in an environmentally responsible fashion.

To fight global warming, he backs a "cap and trade" system among polluters that creates incentives for commercializing renewable energy products. He followed the example of fellow Democrat Peter Welch of Vermont by spending out of his own pocket to ensure his offices in Washington and Connecticut do not emit excess carbon. Congressional rules prohibit members from using office funds for such purposes.

Murphy is a member of the 30-Something Working Group, a collection of young Democratic lawmakers who take to the House floor regularly to sound off about the issues of the day. In May 2007, he led an effort of 21 freshmen members to support an independent panel to investigate members of Congress accused of wrongdoing. His bill passed the House the following March.

He also sits on the Oversight and Government Reform Committee. Like Waxman, the panel's former chairman, he pushes for transparency and accountability in government. Murphy shepherded a bill through the House to require large government contractors that receive more than 80 percent of their annual gross revenue from federal contracts to disclose the names and salaries of their most highly compensated officers.

He said the large profits of companies like the controversial State Department security contractor Blackwater Worldwide led him to sponsor the bill.

"This legislation was meant to give Congress more teeth," he said. The Senate never took up the bill.

Murphy sat on the Financial Services Committee in the 110th Congress (2007-08). He supported two $700 billion measures in fall 2008 that were intended to shore up the ailing financial industry, viewing both measures — the second of which became law in October of that year — as vital to prevent the economy from collapsing. "You know you are voting on a product you don't completely believe in, but in this case the alternative to Congress not passing that legislation was disastrous," he said.

In February 2009, Murphy supported President Obama's $787 billion economic stimulus law, calling it "a bold plan for tough times."

Murphy attributes his political stances to his relatives. His mother grew up in public housing, while his father came from a more affluent background. His grandfather and great-grandfather worked at a New Britain ball bearing factory, which he said is why he supports organized labor.

"My family is tied to the industrial past," Murphy said. "While some people are willing to give up on manufacturing, I am not. Maybe my family prejudices me." Murphy credits his mother with instilling a sense of obligation to give back to society in all three of her children. His brother works for Save the Children, and his sister is a social worker.

Murphy attended Williams College, where he earned a dual degree in history and political science. Shortly after graduating, he managed the congressional campaign of activist Charlotte Koskoff, who came within 1,600 votes of upsetting veteran Republican Nancy L. Johnson. Ten years later, Murphy finished the job, ousting Johnson by a solid margin as part of the Democrats' dominating year nationwide.

In the decade in between, Murphy captured a seat in the state House, unseating a 14-year incumbent, and won election to the state Senate four years later. He did it all while working and attending law school. "I think it's a miracle that I passed the bar," he said, because on the first day of the exam, "I left immediately to cast a vote, and the second day I left immediately to announce I was running for state Senate."

Murphy's 2006 victory over Johnson came during a watershed election season that heavily favored his party. In 2008, he beat GOP state senator David J. Cappiello by a nearly 20-percentage-point margin after raising more than twice as much money.

Murphy's wife, Cathy Holahan, went into labor with their first child when President-elect Barack Obama was giving his acceptance speech at the 2008 Democratic convention. Their son, Owen Edward, was born the next day.

KEY VOTES

2008
Yes Delay consideration of Colombia free-trade agreement
Yes Override Bush veto of federal farm and nutrition programs reauthorization bill
No   Overhaul surveillance laws and permit dismissal of suits against companies that conducted warrantless wiretapping
Yes Grant mortgage relief to homeowners and funding for Fannie Mae and Freddie Mac
Yes Approve initial $700 billion program to stabilize financial markets
Yes Approve final $700 billion program to stabilize financial markets
Yes Provide $14 billion in loans to automakers

2007
Yes Increase minimum wage by $2.10 an hour
Yes Approve $124.2 billion in emergency war spending and set goal for redeployment of troops from Iraq
No   Reject federal contraceptive assistance to international family planning groups
Yes Override Bush veto of $23.2 billion water projects authorization bill
No   Implement Peru free-trade agreement
Yes Approve energy policy overhaul with new fuel economy standards
No   Clear $473.5 billion omnibus spending bill, including $70 billion for military operations

CQ VOTE STUDIES

	PARTY UNITY		PRESIDENTIAL SUPPORT	
	SUPPORT	OPPOSE	SUPPORT	OPPOSE
2008	98%	2%	17%	83%
2007	96%	4%	5%	95%

INTEREST GROUPS

	AFL-CIO	ADA	CCUS	ACU
2008	100%	95%	61%	0%
2007	96%	100%	50%	0%

CONNECTICUT 5
West — Danbury, New Britain, most of Waterbury

Based in the bucolic western part of the state, the 5th is a mix of rolling farmland along the Housatonic River in the Litchfield Hills and midsize industrial cities. Its old manufacturing cities are struggling through the transition into successful centers of technology and skilled manufacturing.

Waterbury is the district's most populous city, with about 80 percent of its residents living in the 5th (the rest live in the 3rd). It is middle-class and diverse, with blacks and Hispanics together totaling 40 percent of the population. East of Waterbury, on the 5th's southeastern edge, are Cheshire, an upper-income, liberal-leaning but competitive area, and Meriden, a Democratic-voting area.

Southwest of Waterbury, Middlebury faces factory closings, white-collar job losses and municipal shortfalls. Growing Danbury, located in the 5th's southwestern corner, has experienced a recent influx of immigrants, resulting in both changes in municipal regulations and community development investment. Employers in Danbury include Praxair, which makes industrial gases, and Scholastic Library Publishing.

North and east of Waterbury, the district branches off to take in New Britain. Although the Hand Tools Division of Stanley Works still operates out of New Britain, continuing manufacturing job losses have hurt the area. New Britain votes Democratic and is home to both a very large Polish community and an ample Hispanic community.

The 5th has grown increasingly liberal. Although Democrat John Kerry barely won the 2004 presidential vote here, Barack Obama took a comfortable 56 percent in 2008. Kerry's 2004 Republican opponent, George W. Bush, carried several towns north and east of Danbury, including burgeoning New Milford and Newtown, but both towns supported Obama in 2008. The House seat changed hands in 2006, and Rep. Christopher S. Murphy won re-election by a wider margin in 2008.

MAJOR INDUSTRY
Manufacturing, health care

CITIES
Waterbury (pt.), 88,624; Danbury, 74,848; New Britain, 71,538; Meriden, 58,244; Torrington (pt.), 20,202

NOTABLE
Cheshire was designated the "Bedding Plant Capital of Connecticut" by the state legislature.

DELAWARE

Gov. Jack Markell (D)

First elected: 2008
Length of term: 4 years
Term expires: 1/13
Salary: $171,000
Phone: (302) 739-4101

Residence: Wilmington
Born: November 26, 1960; Wilmington, Del.
Religion: Jewish
Family: Wife, Carla Markell; two children
Education: Brown U., B.A. 1982 (development studies & economics); U. of Chicago, M.B.A. 1985
Career: Telecommunications company executive; banker
Political highlights: Del. treasurer, 1999-2009

Election results:

2008 GENERAL
Jack Markell (D)	266,861	67.5%
William Swain Lee (R)	126,662	32.0%

Lt. Gov. Matthew Denn (D)

First elected: 2008
Length of term: 4 years
Term expires: 1/13
Salary: $75,500
Phone: (302) 744-4333

LEGISLATURE

General Assembly: January-June

Senate: 21 members, 4-year terms
2009 ratios: 16 D, 5 R; 13 men, 8 women
Salary: $42,000
Phone: (302) 744-4129

House: 41 members, two-year terms
2009 ratios: 24 D, 17 R; 34 men, 7 women
Salary: $42,000
Phone: (302) 744-4087

TERM LIMITS

Governor: 2 terms
Senate: No
House: No

URBAN STATISTICS

CITY	POPULATION
Wilmington	72,664
Dover	32,135
Newark	28,547
Milford	6,732
Seaford	6,699

REGISTERED VOTERS

Democrat	47%
Republican	30%
Others/unaffiliated	23%

POPULATION

2008 population (est.)	873,092
2000 population	783,600
1990 population	666,168
Percent change (1990-2000)	+17.6%
Rank among states (2008)	45

Median age	36
Born in state	48.3%
Foreign born	5.7%
Violent crime rate	684/100,000
Poverty level	9.2%
Federal workers	5,438
Military	8,799

ELECTIONS

STATE ELECTION OFFICIAL
(302) 739-4277
DEMOCRATIC PARTY
(302) 328-9036
REPUBLICAN PARTY
(302) 651-0260

MISCELLANEOUS

Web: www.delaware.gov
Capital: Dover

U.S. CONGRESS

Senate: 2 Democrats
House: 1 Republican

2000 Census Statistics by District

DIST.	2008 VOTE FOR PRESIDENT OBAMA	MCCAIN	WHITE	BLACK	ASIAN	HISP	MEDIAN INCOME	WHITE COLLAR	BLUE COLLAR	SERVICE INDUSTRY	OVER 64	UNDER 18	COLLEGE EDUCATION	RURAL	SQ. MILES
AL	62%	37%	72%	19%	2%	5%	$47,381	63%	23%	15%	13%	25%	25%	20%	1,954
STATE	62	37	72	19	2	5	$47,381	63	23	15	13	25	25	20	1,954
U.S.	53	46	69	12	4	13	$41,994	60	25	15	12	26	24	21	3,537,438

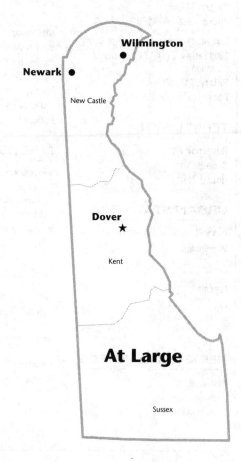

Wilmington

Newark

New Castle

Dover

Kent

At Large

Sussex

Sen. Thomas R. Carper (D)

Elected 2000; 2nd term

CAPITOL OFFICE
224-2441
carper.senate.gov
513 Hart Bldg. 20510-0803; fax 228-2190

COMMITTEES
Environment & Public Works
(Clean Air & Nuclear Safety - chairman)
Finance
Homeland Security & Governmental Affairs
(Federal Financial Management - chairman)

RESIDENCE
Wilmington

BORN
Jan. 23, 1947; Beckley, W.Va.

RELIGION
Presbyterian

FAMILY
Wife, Martha Carper; two children

EDUCATION
Ohio State U., B.A. 1968 (economics);
U. of Delaware, M.B.A. 1975

MILITARY SERVICE
Navy, 1968-73; Naval Reserve, 1973-91

CAREER
State economic development official

POLITICAL HIGHLIGHTS
Del. treasurer, 1977-83; U.S. House, 1983-93;
governor, 1993-2001

ELECTION RESULTS

2006 GENERAL

Thomas R. Carper (D)	170,567	67.1%
Jan Ting (R)	69,734	27.4%
Christine O'Donnell (X)	11,127	4.4%
William E. Morris (LIBERT)	2,671	1.0%

2006 PRIMARY

Thomas R. Carper (D)	unopposed

PREVIOUS WINNING PERCENTAGES
2000 (56%); 1990 House Election (66%); 1988 House
Election (68%); 1986 House Election (66%); 1984
House Election (58%); 1982 House Election (52%)

Delaware voters like Carper, a centrist who is committed to finding what he calls "common-sense solutions." A former state treasurer, governor and House member, he has won more statewide elections than anyone in the state's history. He also is popular among his colleagues, who like his quick wit.

When the Environment and Public Works Committee considered Lisa P. Jackson's nomination to head the EPA in January 2009, Carper jokingly warned her husband Kenneth that she would be busy. "When you bring her home from the inaugural ball ... take a real good look at her," he said. "That's the last time you'll see her until Christmas. Make sure your kids have plenty of pictures of her." At a news conference a month later, when aides removed the box that diminutive California Sen. Barbara Boxer uses behind the lectern for such events, Carper quipped, "Actually, I'd like the box. I want people to say, 'He's a giant among the supporters of doing something about global warming.'"

But Carper is serious about trying to ensure politics isn't all about the extremes at either end. In 2004, he co-founded a group called the Third Way with the idea of giving moderates a higher profile and serving as a think tank to generate middle-of-the-road legislation. In mid-2005, he was named vice chairman of the moderate Democratic Leadership Council once headed by Bill Clinton. Democratic party leaders tapped him as a deputy whip, and he continues to push for moderate solutions.

The early years of Clinton's presidency when Democrats controlled Congress "were not good years for our party," Carper said in July 2008. "We need to remember a lesson that we didn't remember then: For our party to be successful, we need to govern from the middle."

Carper is chairman of Environment and Public Works' Clean Air and Nuclear Safety Subcommittee, where he has been central to the panel's struggle to rewrite the landmark Clean Air Act. He is an original sponsor of a bipartisan climate change measure that would cap emissions of carbon dioxide and other gases that scientists say contribute to global warming at 19 percent below current levels by 2020 and 71 percent by 2050. Under the bill, utilities and other polluters could reduce their own emissions or buy allowances on a so-called carbon market.

He has suggested that revenues from such a "cap and trade" system could be used to research solutions to another thorny environmental problem — the waste piling up at commercial nuclear power plants. He was named in February 2009 to a new Environment Committee panel charged with finding ways to create more energy-efficient "green jobs."

Carper is also committed to a bipartisan solution to overhaul the nation's health care system. He supports Oregon Democratic Sen. Ron Wyden's plan to replace the current employer-based health insurance system with a system in which people would buy coverage directly from insurers through new state-run "purchasing pools." Premiums would be paid through the tax system, with a fixed deduction for the costs of insurance.

Carper has a chance to have more say on health matters as a member of the powerful Finance Committee, which also is responsible for tax and trade legislation. Coming from business-friendly Delaware, he generally favors free-trade agreements.

Carper also serves on the Homeland Security and Governmental Affairs Committee, where as chairman of the panel on federal financial management he will be immersed in efforts to improve the 2010 census. He also has been critical of the U.S. Postal Service's proposals to cut back on the number of days it delivers mail, saying in January 2009 that such a move should be the option of last resort and not the first.

In 2008, Carper departed from his party on one out of every five votes where Democrats and Republicans were pitted against each other. Only four other Senate Democrats broke ranks more often. But he generally toes the line on key votes.

Carper said his consensus-building skills were sharpened by his work with the National Governors Association, and he continues to organize brainstorming sessions with other senators who are also former governors. In 2004, he joined with them to fight a proposed four-year ban on taxes on Internet access that he argued would drain state treasuries of telecommunications taxes. They pushed a two-year ban instead, winning some concessions. Carper's backing was crucial in 2005 to a successful GOP bill tightening the rules for class action lawsuits and shifting them from state to federal courts, which many Democrats opposed as a bad deal for plaintiffs.

Carper attends a bipartisan and non-denominational Thursday Bible study group, where he has forged friendships. He also keeps a list of several hundred birthdays of current and former colleagues, staffers and others, dialing them on that day to wish them well. "It gives me a chance to talk to them outside the course of their normal business…and just to talk to them on a personal level," he told the Wilmington News Journal.

Carper was raised in Roanoke, Va., and moved with his family to Columbus, Ohio, in high school. His father worked for an insurance company while his mother held a variety of jobs. As a boy, Carper was active in the Civil Air Patrol and Boy Scouts and earned an ROTC scholarship to attend Ohio State University.

In college, he underwent a political transformation. Carper said he first held the Republican views of his parents. In 1964, he had campaigned for GOP presidential candidate Barry Goldwater. But by 1968, his senior year, his skepticism about the Vietnam War led him to volunteer in the anti-war presidential campaign of Democrat Eugene McCarthy.

Despite his anti-war sentiments, he wore his Navy uniform to his college graduation and went on to serve in the Navy for five years, flying P-3 submarine-hunting planes in Southeast Asia. He served another 18 years in the Naval Reserve, retiring as a captain in 1991.

After the Navy Carper enrolled in the University of Delaware's business school, where he earned a master's degree in business administration. When Jim Soles, a favorite professor, ran for Congress in 1974, Carper worked as his campaign treasurer and fundraiser. Soles lost to incumbent Pete DuPont, but the taste of politics remained with Carper.

One day in 1976, he was lying on the sandy shores of Dewey Beach, listening to his transistor radio, when a news report said Democrats could not find a candidate for state treasurer. He entered the race and, at age 29, beat a strongly favored Republican.

In 1982, Carper ran for the House after Democrats again had trouble finding someone to take on Republican Rep. Thomas B. Evans. Delaware's economic woes at the time and revelations that Evans was romantically involved with lobbyist Paula Parkinson boosted Carper's campaign, and Delaware's House seat went Democratic for the first time since 1966.

He ran successfully for governor in 1992, swapping jobs with moderate Republican Michael N. Castle, who is still in the House. After two terms as governor, Carper in 2000 returned to Washington in a battle-of-the-titans challenge to five-term Republican Sen. William V. Roth Jr., the Finance Committee chairman who was the architect of the Individual Retirement Account plan named for him. In 2006, he faced nominal opposition.

KEY VOTES

2008

Yes	Prohibit discrimination based on genetic information
Yes	Reauthorize farm and nutrition programs for five years
Yes	Limit debate on "cap and trade" system for greenhouse gas emissions
No	Allow lawsuits against companies that participated in warrantless wiretapping
Yes	Limit debate on a bill to block a scheduled cut in Medicare payments to doctors
+	Grant mortgage relief to homeowners and funding for Fannie Mae and Freddie Mac
Yes	Approve a nuclear cooperation agreement with India
Yes	Approve final $700 billion program to stabilize financial markets
Yes	Allow consideration of a $14 billion auto industry loan package

2007

Yes	Increase minimum wage by $2.10 an hour
Yes	Limit debate on a comprehensive immigration bill
Yes	Overhaul congressional lobbying and ethics rules for members and their staffs
Yes	Limit debate on considering a bill to add House seats for the District of Columbia and Utah
Yes	Limit debate on restoring habeas corpus rights to detainees
Yes	Mandate minimum breaks for troops between deployments to Iraq or Afghanistan
Yes	Override Bush veto of $23.2 billion water projects authorization bill
Yes	Confirm Michael B. Mukasey as attorney general
Yes	Limit debate on an energy policy overhaul containing $21.8 billion in tax incentives and reduced oil and gas subsidies

CQ VOTE STUDIES

	PARTY UNITY		PRESIDENTIAL SUPPORT	
	SUPPORT	OPPOSE	SUPPORT	OPPOSE
2008	80%	20%	45%	55%
2007	88%	12%	46%	54%
2006	79%	21%	64%	36%
2005	77%	23%	38%	62%
2004	86%	14%	66%	34%
2003	81%	19%	53%	47%
2002	74%	26%	79%	21%
2001	80%	20%	72%	28%
House Service:				
1992	76%	24%	32%	68%

INTEREST GROUPS

	AFL-CIO	ADA	CCUS	ACU
2008	100%	85%	63%	0%
2007	89%	85%	55%	8%
2006	87%	90%	58%	20%
2005	64%	90%	72%	8%
2004	100%	95%	71%	12%
2003	77%	75%	70%	10%
2002	85%	80%	50%	25%
2001	93%	90%	58%	24%
House Service:				
1992	67%	75%	63%	40%

Sen. Ted Kaufman (D)

Appointed 2009; 1st term

CAPITOL OFFICE
224-5042
kaufman.senate.gov
383 Russell Bldg. 20510; fax 224-0139

COMMITTEES
Foreign Relations
Judiciary

RESIDENCE
Greenville

BORN
March 15, 1939; Philadelphia, Pa.

RELIGION
Roman Catholic

FAMILY
Wife, Lynne Kaufman; three children

EDUCATION
Duke U., B.S.E. 1960 (mechanical engineering);
U. of Pennsylvania, M.B.A. 1966

CAREER
Congressional and campaign aide;
college instructor; political consultant;
marketing representative

POLITICAL HIGHLIGHTS
Broadcasting Board of Governors, 1995-2008

Kaufman has never held elected office, but his political-insider bona fides and more than three decades' worth of connections enabled him to easily slip into the seat of his former boss and predecessor, Vice President Joseph R. Biden Jr.

Kaufman was appointed to fill Biden's seat until 2010, when a special election will be held to fill the remaining four years of the six-year term Biden won in November 2008 at the same time he was elected vice president. (Delaware is one of several states that permit a candidate on the national ticket to run for another office at the same time.) The appointment was seen by many as a move to pave the way for a Senate bid by Biden's son, Delaware Attorney General Beau Biden.

Kaufman immediately announced he wouldn't post a challenge for the seat. "I do not think Delaware's appointed senator should spend the next two years running for office," he said after his appointment was announced. "I will do this job to the fullest of my ability."

He has made few waves in the Democratic Party. A former chief of staff to Biden, Kaufman said his views are similar on many issues and that since he is serving out his term, it is appropriate for him to consider what Biden would do in making decisions.

Once he was sworn into office in January 2009, he wasted no time embracing the Obama administration's agenda, focusing his first floor speech on the president's economic stimulus plan. After passage of the $787 billion law, he wrote in a February 2009 article in the Wilmington News Journal: "We must tackle this economic crisis now. This bill is large enough to jolt the economy back to life, to convince businesses to invest and hire and encourage consumers to spend and be confident, in anticipation of better times. Action now is the best way to reverse the slide of our economy into a deeper recession."

He also backed an expansion of the State Children's Health Insurance Program, which covers children from low-income families that do not qualify for Medicaid. And he backed legislation, also signed into law, that makes it easier for workers to challenge wage discrimination.

Kaufman sits on two committees where his predecessor had gained prominence: Judiciary and Foreign Relations. On Judiciary, he sits on all but one of the six subcommittees.

He quickly backed a bill sponsored by Judiciary Chairman Patrick J. Leahy of Vermont aimed at uncovering and prosecuting financial fraud in the banking and mortgage industries. Among other things, it would authorize increased resources for the FBI to investigate potential crimes that contributed to the economic crisis. "If people rob a bank, they go to jail. If bankers rob people, they should go to jail, too," he wrote in a March 2009 commentary in the Philadelphia Inquirer.

In a speech on the Senate floor, Kaufman — one of the two senators who hold a degree in engineering (the other is Democrat Jack Reed of Rhode Island) — also urged a shift away from Wall Street careers by building new industries, businesses and products. "To do that, we must put science, engineering and innovation back in their rightful place in our economy," he said.

Kaufman also has said he wants to improve campaign finance reform.

Following announcement of his appointment, Kaufman expressed his own surprise and awe to the News Journal: "To be able to go down and to vote just totally on what you think is right is a gift that I'm not going to mess up."

Kaufman has a wide-ranging background that includes stints in the business world as well as in government and academia.

He received a bachelor's degree in mechanical engineering from Duke and went on to earn a masters in business administration from the Wharton School of the University of Pennsylvania.

From 1966 to 1973, he worked for DuPont Co., the huge chemical manufacturer, in a variety of finance, technical and marketing positions. He made his first foray into politics in 1972 by signing up for Biden's first Senate campaign.

From 1973 to 1995, he served as a Biden aide. Most of that time was as chief of staff, a position that enabled him to develop relationships with numerous lawmakers and lobbyists.

"I used to pinch myself then," he told the Duke University Chronicle. "I thought working in the Senate was such a great honor."

Three years before leaving Biden's office, Kaufman became a senior lecturing fellow at Duke's School of Law. He has taught classes for the School of Law and the Fuqua School of Business. He also served as co-chair of the law school's Center for the Study of Congress. Among the subjects of his lectures was John F. Kennedy's "Profiles in Courage," which outlines how politicians make important decisions.

Kaufman also was teaching a weekly class in Washington, D.C., on Wednesday nights for Duke law students working in the capital during the spring 2009 semester.

In 1995, he was appointed to be a charter member of the Broadcasting Board of Governors, a bipartisan, nine-member board that supervises all U.S. international, non-military broadcasting. During Kaufman's tenure, the broadcasting board came under scrutiny for funding an Arab-language television and radio network, intended to promote a positive image of the United States, that aired anti-American and anti-Israeli viewpoints.

In 2007, members of Congress threatened to withhold funding for the TV network, Alhurra, or "The Free One," after it aired a report on a Holocaust deniers conference in Iran. A joint investigation by the nonprofit journalism organization ProPublica and CBS's "60 Minutes" found the networks employed an untrained, largely foreign staff that lacked in-depth knowledge of the country they were hired to promote. There appeared to be little oversight of the daily operations. Members of the broadcasting board testified at a hearing that year that editorial safety nets had been put in place.

From 1995 until 2008, Kaufman operated Public Strategies, a political and management consulting firm based in Wilmington. He recently served as co-chair of Biden's transition team.

Kaufman's willingness to serve a foreshortened tenure could help Beau Biden to seek the Senate seat after he completes a round of duty in Iraq with the Delaware Army National Guard. The younger Biden was elected in 2006 to a four-year term as state attorney general.

Democratic Gov. Ruth Ann Minner defended her appointment of Kaufman, saying he shared the elder Biden's political views and could focus solely on doing the people's work. "He doesn't need any on-the-job training," she said. "He'll be an effective senator for Delaware from day one."

But the selection disappointed allies of Lt. Gov. John Carney, a favorite of many state party insiders, who narrowly lost the Democratic primary for governor to state Treasurer Jack Markell, the eventual winner of the 2008 general election. Carney had figured prominently in the speculation about an interim replacement for Biden.

Kaufman was sworn in after most of the other Senate freshmen in the 111th Congress (2009-10), because the elder Biden wanted to take the oath for a seventh term on Jan. 6, 2009, before resigning.

Rep. Michael N. Castle (R)

Elected 1992; 9th term

CAPITOL OFFICE
225-4165
www.castle.house.gov
1233 Longworth Bldg. 20515-0801; fax 225-2291

COMMITTEES
Education & Labor
Financial Services

RESIDENCE
Wilmington

BORN
July 2, 1939; Wilmington, Del.

RELIGION
Roman Catholic

FAMILY
Wife, Jane Castle

EDUCATION
Hamilton College, B.A. 1961 (economics);
Georgetown U., LL.B. 1964

CAREER
Lawyer; state prosecutor

POLITICAL HIGHLIGHTS
Del. House, 1967-69; Del. Senate, 1969-77
(minority leader, 1976-77); lieutenant governor,
1981-85; governor, 1985-93

ELECTION RESULTS

2008 GENERAL

Michael N. Castle (R)	235,437	61.1%
Karen M. Hartley-Nagle (D)	146,434	38.0%

2008 PRIMARY

Michael N. Castle (R)	unopposed

2006 GENERAL

Michael N. Castle (R)	143,897	57.2%
Denni Spivack (D)	97,565	38.8%
Karen M. Hartley-Nagle (I)	5,769	2.3%
Michael Berg (GREEN)	4,463	1.8%

PREVIOUS WINNING PERCENTAGES
2004 (69%); 2002 (72%); 2000 (68%); 1998 (66%);
1996 (70%); 1994 (71%); 1992 (55%)

Castle is a low-key former governor who is vastly popular with both his state's Democratic-leaning voters and the handful of fellow moderate Republicans left in the House. "My politics fit Delaware's politics," he said. "They appreciate the fact that I'm independent."

He believes being a social moderate with fiscally conservative views is the only way to get things done in Congress. That means he often votes in opposition to his party. During President George W. Bush's two terms, he departed from the GOP on one-quarter of the floor votes in which the two parties were pitted against each other.

Castle was one of only three House Republicans to vote for all six of the new Democratic majority's signature bills at the start of the 110th Congress (2007-08). He also subsequently broke with the Bush administration in supporting such measures as a troop withdrawal from Iraq within 30 days, reauthorizing the Amtrak national passenger railroad and preventing a scheduled cut in payments to physicians treating Medicare patients.

Castle is the lead Republican in favor of embryonic stem cell research, which uses discarded embryos created for in vitro fertilization. He cosponsored legislation that would have overturned the Bush administration's ban on federal funding of certain kinds of such research. He lauded President Obama's decision in March 2009 to lift the ban but said he would continue to move his legislation to make it difficult for a future president to overturn.

He also is eager to pass legislation to limit greenhouse gas emissions to combat the effects of global warming. He said the shared commitment of Obama and new Energy and Commerce Chairman Henry A. Waxman of California, plus growing cooperation from businesses, left him encouraged.

A series of high-profile achievements could be helpful for Castle in a potential Senate race in 2010. He has avoided running against Democrats Thomas R. Carper or Joseph R. Biden Jr., but Biden's ascension to the vice presidency provides a possible opening for Castle — even though it could mean facing Biden's son Beau, Delaware's attorney general. In addition, such a run would force him to give up his power in the House, where he uses his senior committee posts and good relations with Democrats to influence legislation.

As a senior Republican on the Education and Labor Committee, Castle was one of the architects of federal education policy in recent years. He was a lead sponsor of the No Child Left Behind law, the 2001 legislation initiated by Bush that tied federal education aid to improvements in student test scores. He said he still believes in the concepts of the 2001 law, but thinks any renewal should also include a revamping. Castle also shepherded through Congress a bill calling for disabled students to be treated the same as non-disabled students when being punished for violations of school policy. Advocates for the disabled decried the move as a potential violation of civil rights, but Castle said it would give localities more flexibility.

One of his crusades is the troubling trend of childhood obesity in the United States, which Castle believes can be fought in part by providing healthier foods in schools. He sponsored a bill in the 108th Congress (2003-04) directing the Agriculture Department to develop nutrition guidelines for foods sold in schools and to make $30 million available for nutrition awareness and physical fitness programs.

Castle is the second-ranking Republican on the Financial Services Committee, where he has promoted affordable housing. He backed both versions of the $700 billion effort in fall 2008 to aid the financial services industry — the second of which became law — and a subsequent failed effort to bail out domestic automakers. But with typical understatement, he acknowledged in December 2008 that the financial rescue was an area where "perhaps we did not distinguish ourselves," and that lawmakers should keep close tabs on the industry.

A fan of coin collecting, Castle has promoted creation of new collectible U.S. coins. He was the lead House sponsor of a 2005 law that authorized the minting of a series of $1 coins, starting in 2007, bearing the likenesses of all the U.S. presidents. Four coins a year are issued, with presidents featured in chronological order. In 2008, Bush signed into law his bill authorizing quarters with designs of national parks or other national sites to be issued starting in 2010.

He also looks out for the credit card companies that make their home in Delaware. Castle strongly opposes banning several credit card billing practices, instead arguing that the Federal Reserve should handle the issue through regulation.

Though relatively quiet, Castle nonetheless can be bold in confronting his leadership. In 2006, Castle fought to toughen a lobbying and ethics bill put together by GOP leaders. In 2001, he was one of six Republicans who signed a petition to force Speaker J. Dennis Hastert to bring campaign finance legislation to the floor. In 1998, he was among the dozen GOP lawmakers who voted against three of the four articles of impeachment against President Clinton, who was embroiled in a sex scandal involving a White House intern. In 2005, Republicans eager to open up Alaska's Arctic National Wildlife Refuge to oil drilling included such a provision in a filibuster-proof budget savings bill, pushing it through the Senate. But Castle and other moderates threatened to sink the entire budget measure unless the drilling provision was dropped. They forced its removal from the final budget bill.

The 6-foot-4-inch Castle was a basketball star in high school. He went to Georgetown University Law School after college, "sort of because I didn't know what I was doing," he said. In private practice, he worked for a former Delaware attorney general who encouraged him to take the part-time position of deputy attorney general, a post he assumed at age 26. In 1966, he ran for the state House in a Democratic-leaning district. He won and later ousted an incumbent state senator. After 10 years in the General Assembly, he won election as lieutenant governor for one term and governor for two terms.

With his stint as governor ending, Castle ran for the state's at-large congressional seat in 1992. He won a tough, four-way GOP primary and in November prevailed with 55 percent of the vote. Castle has coasted to re-election since. He was slowed only briefly in his 2006 campaign by two small strokes he suffered in September.

KEY VOTES

2008
No   Delay consideration of Colombia free-trade agreement

No   Override Bush veto of federal farm and nutrition programs reauthorization bill

Yes Overhaul surveillance laws and permit dismissal of suits against companies that conducted warrantless wiretapping

Yes Grant mortgage relief to homeowners and funding for Fannie Mae and Freddie Mac

Yes Approve initial $700 billion program to stabilize financial markets

Yes Approve final $700 billion program to stabilize financial markets

Yes Provide $14 billion in loans to automakers

2007
Yes Increase minimum wage by $2.10 an hour

No   Approve $124.2 billion in emergency war spending and set goal for redeployment of troops from Iraq

No   Reject federal contraceptive assistance to international family planning groups

Yes Override Bush veto of $23.2 billion water projects authorization bill

Yes Implement Peru free-trade agreement

Yes Approve energy policy overhaul with new fuel economy standards

Yes Clear $473.5 billion omnibus spending bill, including $70 billion for military operations

CQ VOTE STUDIES

	PARTY UNITY		PRESIDENTIAL SUPPORT	
	SUPPORT	OPPOSE	SUPPORT	OPPOSE
2008	70%	30%	41%	59%
2007	71%	29%	41%	59%
2006	77%	23%	78%	22%
2005	76%	24%	65%	35%
2004	79%	21%	74%	26%

INTEREST GROUPS

	AFL-CIO	ADA	CCUS	ACU
2008	73%	65%	78%	28%
2007	58%	50%	75%	20%
2006	36%	40%	83%	52%
2005	20%	40%	78%	28%
2004	35%	50%	85%	52%

DELAWARE

At Large

Delaware's coastal terrain and inland agricultural sector contrast with the state's urban center near Wilmington and its suburbs. A string of beach resorts in the state's southeast corner — from Cape Henlopen State Park and Rehoboth Beach south to Fenwick Island on the Maryland border — draws hordes of tourists to the state.

Used to unemployment rates below the national average, Delaware's retail and corporate sectors are struggling in the face of national economic downturns. Favorable tax rates attracted financial services companies, especially credit card firms, and Delaware has been the on-paper home to hundreds of Fortune 500 companies capitalizing on the state's liberal incorporation rules. Delaware's specialized business court, historically busy with new and expanding companies, has seen a flood of bankruptcy cases and corporate realignments.

Strongly Democratic New Castle County is the population center of the state. The county's largest city, Wilmington, is the state's economic hub, and there has been redevelopment there along the Delaware River. But even the DuPont Company, the hometown chemical giant, has seen job cuts recently. Once known for manufacturing, the state capital of Dover has lower unemployment rates than Wilmington, but the gambling and racing facility Dover Downs, a mainstay of the local tourism industry, faces revenue loss.

Immigration, legal and illegal, is changing communities across the state as new residents have made the traditionally dominant Anglo-Saxon population a minority in some towns. The increasingly Democratic-leaning state supported Barack Obama and Delaware's favorite son, Joseph R. Biden Jr., in the 2008 presidential election, and Democratic Gov. Jack Markell won an overwhelming victory in 2008. Democrats also now control both chambers of the state legislature.

MAJOR INDUSTRY
Financial services, manufacturing, tourism, chemicals

MILITARY BASES
Dover Air Force Base, 3,357 military, 1,040 civilian (2009)

CITIES
Wilmington, 72,664; Dover, 32,135; Newark, 28,547

NOTABLE
In 1787, Delaware was the first state to ratify the U.S. Constitution.

FLORIDA

Gov. Charlie Crist (R)

First elected: 2006
Length of term: 4 years
Term expires: 1/11
Salary: $130,273
Phone: (850) 488-4441

Residence: St. Petersburg
Born: July 24, 1956; Altoona, Pa.
Religion: Methodist
Family: Wife, Carole Crist
Education: Wake Forest U., attended 1974-76; Florida State U., B.S. 1978 (government); Samford U., J.D. 1981
Career: State government official; lawyer; congressional state aide
Political highlights: Sought Republican nomination for Fla. Senate, 1986; Fla. Senate, 1992-98; Republican nominee for U.S. Senate, 1998; Fla. Education commissioner, 2001-03; Fla. attorney general, 2003-07

Election results:

2006 GENERAL
Charlie Crist (R)	2,519,845	52.2%
Jim Davis (D)	2,178,289	45.1%
Max Linn (REF)	92,595	1.9%

Lt. Gov. Jeff Kottkamp (R)

First Elected: 2006
Length of term: 4 years
Term expires: 1/11
Salary: $124,851
Phone: (850) 488-4711

LEGISLATURE

Legislature: 60 days March-May; session is often extended

Senate: 40 members; 4-year terms
2009 ratios: 26 R, 14 D; 31 men, 9 women
Salary: $30,336
Phone: (850) 487-5270

House: 120 members; 2-year terms
2009 ratios: 76 R, 44 D; 91 men, 29 women
Salary: $30,336
Phone: (850) 488-1157

TERM LIMITS

Governor: 2 terms
Senate: 2 consecutive terms
House: 4 consecutive terms

URBAN STATISTICS

CITY	POPULATION
Jacksonville	735,617
Miami	362,470
Tampa	303,447
St. Petersburg	248,232
Hialeah	226,419

REGISTERED VOTERS

Democrat	42%
Republican	36%
Unaffiliated	19%
Others	3%

POPULATION

2008 population (est.)	18,328,340
2000 population	15,982,378
1990 population	12,937,926
Percent change (1990-2000)	+23.5%
Rank among states (2008)	4

Median age	38.7
Born in state	32.7%
Foreign born	16.7%
Violent crime rate	812/100,000
Poverty level	12.5%
Federal workers	118,600
Military	106,092

ELECTIONS

STATE ELECTION OFFICIAL
(850) 245-6200
DEMOCRATIC PARTY
(850) 222-3411
REPUBLICAN PARTY
(850) 222-7920

MISCELLANEOUS

Web: www.myflorida.com
Capital: Tallahassee

U.S. CONGRESS

Senate: 1 Democrat, 1 Republican
House: 15 Republicans, 10 Democrats

2000 Census Statistics by District

DIST.	2008 VOTE FOR PRESIDENT OBAMA	MCCAIN	WHITE	BLACK	ASIAN	HISP	MEDIAN INCOME	WHITE COLLAR	BLUE COLLAR	SERVICE INDUSTRY	OVER 64	UNDER 18	COLLEGE EDUCATION	RURAL	SQ. MILES
1	32%	67%	78%	14%	2%	3%	$36,738	57%	25%	18%	13%	24%	20%	23%	4,642
2	45	54	72	22	1	3	$34,718	62	21	18	12	23	24	38	9,425
3	71	28	38	49	2	8	$29,785	52	27	21	11	28	13	10	1,796
4	37	62	78	14	2	4	$43,947	65	21	14	11	24	24	22	4,118
5	43	56	88	5	1	6	$34,815	55	27	17	26	20	14	36	4,044
6	43	56	79	12	2	5	$36,846	61	23	16	15	23	21	31	2,912
7	46	53	81	9	1	7	$40,525	63	21	16	18	22	25	13	1,797
8	52	47	70	7	3	18	$41,568	64	20	17	14	23	26	8	987
9	47	52	85	4	2	8	$40,742	68	18	14	20	22	25	6	634
10	52	47	88	4	2	4	$37,168	65	20	15	23	18	23	0	175
11	66	33	48	27	2	20	$33,559	61	22	17	12	25	21	0	244
12	49	50	72	13	1	12	$37,769	56	28	16	17	25	17	16	1,956
13	47	52	86	4	1	8	$40,187	59	24	18	29	18	24	11	2,599
14	42	57	84	5	1	9	$42,541	60	22	19	27	18	24	9	1,057
15	48	51	78	7	2	11	$39,397	58	22	19	20	22	22	10	2,545

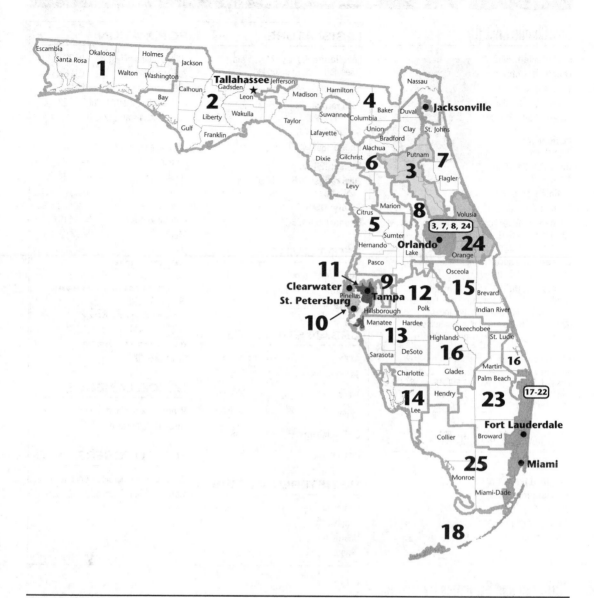

2000 Census Statistics by District

DIST.	2008 VOTE FOR PRESIDENT OBAMA	MCCAIN	WHITE	BLACK	ASIAN	HISP	MEDIAN INCOME	WHITE COLLAR	BLUE COLLAR	SERVICE INDUSTRY	OVER 64	UNDER 18	COLLEGE EDUCATION	RURAL	SQ. MILES
16	47%	52%	82%	6%	1%	10%	$39,408	58%	25%	17%	25%	21%	20%	15%	4,538
17	87	12	18	55	2	21	$30,426	52	24	23	11	29	14	0	97
18	51	49	30	6	1	63	$32,298	60	21	18	18	19	26	1	355
19	65	34	77	6	2	13	$42,237	67	17	15	30	19	26	0	231
20	63	36	67	8	2	21	$44,034	69	16	14	17	21	30	0	160
21	49	51	21	7	2	70	$41,426	64	23	14	13	24	23	0	135
22	52	48	82	4	2	11	$51,200	69	16	14	21	19	34	1	268
23	83	17	29	51	1	14	$31,309	48	28	24	12	28	13	2	3,362
24	49	51	80	6	2	10	$43,954	65	20	15	15	23	26	9	1,583
25	49	50	24	10	2	62	$44,489	62	23	15	9	29	20	6	4,268
STATE	51	48	65	14	2	17	$38,819	61	22	17	18	23	22	11	53,927
U.S.	53	46	69	12	4	13	$41,994	60	25	15	12	26	24	21	3,537,438

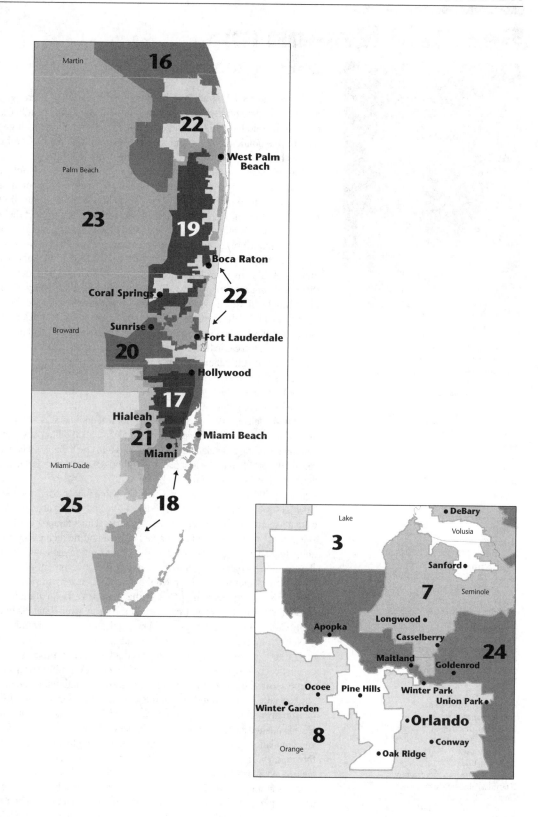

Sen. Bill Nelson (D)

Elected 2000; 2nd term

CAPITOL OFFICE
224-5274
billnelson.senate.gov
716 Hart Bldg. 20510-0905; fax 228-2183

COMMITTEES
Armed Services
(Strategic Forces - chairman)
Budget
Commerce, Science & Transportation
(Science & Space - chairman)
Finance
Select Intelligence
Special Aging

RESIDENCE
Orlando

BORN
Sept. 29, 1942; Miami, Fla.

RELIGION
Protestant

FAMILY
Wife, Grace C. Nelson; two children

EDUCATION
Yale U., B.A. 1965 (political science);
U. of Virginia, J.D. 1968

MILITARY SERVICE
Army Reserve 1965-71; Army 1968-70

CAREER
Lawyer

POLITICAL HIGHLIGHTS
Fla. House, 1972-78; U.S. House, 1979-91;
sought Democratic nomination for governor,
1990; Fla. treasurer and insurance commissioner,
1995-2001

ELECTION RESULTS

2006 GENERAL

Bill Nelson (D)	2,890,548	60.3%
Katherine Harris (R)	1,826,127	38.1%

2006 PRIMARY

Bill Nelson (D)	unopposed

PREVIOUS WINNING PERCENTAGES
2000 (51%); 1988 House Election (61%); 1986 House
Election (73%); 1984 House Election (61%); 1982
House Election (71%); 1980 House Election (70%);
1978 House Election (61%)

Nelson takes a deliberate, middle-of-the-road approach to addressing the needs of his state that typically has kept him out of national headlines. But nearing the middle of his second term, he shows a readiness to engage in high-profile political battles, and his new seat on the Finance Committee thrusts him into the center of debate on the nation's fiscal woes.

Nelson's seats on Finance and five other committees give him many angles from which to watch out for Florida. His role as chairman of the Commerce subcommittee on space enables him to look out for the Kennedy Space Center. His seat on Armed Services lets him protect the interests of the state's military bases and installations, and as a member of the Special Aging Committee, he keeps up on issues of concern to the senior citizen population. He also sits on the Budget and Select Intelligence committees. And he uses his influence in the Senate to try to protect areas off the Florida coast from energy drilling. His new role as a deputy whip also helps him drum up support for his party's measures heading to the floor.

Early in the 111th Congress (2009-10), he fought to secure millions of dollars in stimulus funding for energy, education and law enforcement projects to help struggling areas in his state facing the same economic downturn as communities across the nation. He conducted numerous media interviews to promote President Obama's stimulus package. He told MSNBC in early February 2009 that the bill, which was signed into law, wasn't perfect, adding, "We're learning as we're going. We're making it up as we go. But we've got to try."

Yet in the fall of 2008 — prior to taking his seat on Finance — Nelson was one of nine Senate Democrats to vote against a $700 billion law aimed at helping the ailing financial industry. "We shouldn't be bailing out banks that caused the problem in the first place — without guaranteeing that taxpayers don't get the short end of the stick," he said.

In early 2009, Nelson — along with Florida Republican Mel Martinez and New Jersey Democrat Robert Menendez — voiced strong objections that a catchall spending bill, signed into law by Obama, included a provision loosening some restrictions on the export of food and medicine to Cuba. He ultimately supported passage after the administration indicated the provision wouldn't weaken the embargo against the government of Fidel and Raúl Castro. Another provision would allow U.S. citizens to visit family in Cuba once a year, changing policy of the George W. Bush administration that limited visits to every three years. But Nelson, whose state is home to many Cuban-American families, said he supported increased family travel.

Nelson entered the stage on another national issue that hit home during the 110th Congress (2007-08): the presidential election process. In 2007, he unsuccessfully sued the Democratic National Committee over its decision to strip the state of its delegates to the 2008 national convention as punishment for the state's scheduling of an early presidential primary. Nelson argued the sanction disenfranchised Democratic primary voters. He has pushed a constitutional amendment to abolish the Electoral College and legislation to establish a rotating primary schedule for six regions of the country. He said the process should not permit a candidate who has lost the popular vote to win the Electoral College and become president.

In his first term, Nelson used Senate rules to block a bill to open coastal areas off the Gulf of Mexico to energy drilling. He threatened a filibuster and held up one of Bush's Interior Department appointments. But when gas prices hit $3 a gallon and Congress came under pressure to allow more exploration, Nelson and Martinez negotiated a deal. The bill that came out of the Senate in 2006 opened the eastern Gulf to drilling but banned wells along the Florida coast. The law also guarantees Gulf states a share of the new revenue for coastal preservation. Nelson has pushed legislation to ban unregulated trading of energy futures in a bid to combat rising gasoline prices.

Nelson also is a protector of Florida's "Space Coast." In 1986, he spent six days orbiting Earth aboard the space shuttle *Columbia*, two weeks before the *Challenger* explosion. (He subsequently wrote a book about the experience, which some critics dismissed as a junket.) He advocates for funding increases for NASA, and was one of the first in Congress to warn of the dangers of delaying upgrades to the space shuttles, a point tragically driven home in 2003 when *Columbia* exploded while attempting to re-enter Earth's atmosphere.

In 2007, as chairman of the Science and Space Subcommittee on the Commerce, Science and Transportation panel, Nelson was among the lawmakers who called for the resignation of NASA's inspector general amid allegations he had abused his authority. Nelson also called on NASA's general counsel to resign after he told congressional aides he had destroyed meeting records.

In speaking up for the space agency in 2009, Nelson wrote Appropriations Chairman Daniel K. Inouye of Hawaii a letter in which he argued there would be a gap of at least five years "during which we will lack a U.S. vehicle capable of taking our astronauts to and from the International Space Station. As a result, we will have no choice but to pay Russia for seats on their spacecraft — even as we lay off thousands of U.S. aerospace workers across the country."

Appealing to Florida's senior citizen population, Nelson has cultivated an expertise in consumer protection and privacy issues from his seat on the Commerce panel as well as on Aging. Formerly the state's insurance commissioner, he has sought to prevent insurance companies and financial institutions from sharing customers' medical and financial data without their consent.

A member of the Armed Services Committee, Nelson became disillusioned with Bush's policy in Iraq, even though he voted for the use of force against Iraq in 2002. He drew the Bush administration's ire by going to Syria in 2006 to discuss diplomatic issues with its rulers, including security along the Iraq-Syria border. Speaking before the Council on Foreign Relations in 2007, Nelson said most senators "have been, and will continue to be, fierce defenders of our military...But in retrospect, over and over again, we haven't been told the truth" about the Iraq War.

Nelson is a fifth-generation Floridian. His great-great-grandfather immigrated to America from Denmark in 1829, settling near Chipley in the Florida Panhandle, where much of Nelson's family still lives. Nelson's father was a lawyer; his mother was a schoolteacher.

Nelson majored in political science at Yale and wrote his senior thesis about the Kennedy Space Center. After law school and a brief stint in the Army, he won a seat in the state legislature that he held for six years.

In 1978, he won a bid for an open U.S. House seat. He was an early member of the moderate Democratic Leadership Council that helped boost Bill Clinton to the national stage. Yet, despite a string of re-elections and the publicity attending his adventure as an astronaut, Nelson lost the 1990 Democratic primary for governor, his only electoral defeat.

Four years later, he was elected state insurance commissioner, and he dealt with the aftermath of Hurricane Andrew, which ravaged southern Florida and the state's insurance market in 1992. From the time he announced his run for the Senate, Nelson was the front-runner for the seat Republican Connie Mack had held for two terms. Nelson portrayed his opponent, 10-term congressman Bill McCollum, as too far to the right for Florida, and won with 51 percent of the vote. In 2006, he glided to a 22-percentage-point victory over Florida Republican Rep. Katherine Harris of 2000 Florida presidential recount fame.

KEY VOTES

2008

Yes Prohibit discrimination based on genetic information
Yes Reauthorize farm and nutrition programs for five years
Yes Limit debate on "cap and trade" system for greenhouse gas emissions
No   Allow lawsuits against companies that participated in warrantless wiretapping
Yes Limit debate on a bill to block a scheduled cut in Medicare payments to doctors
Yes Grant mortgage relief to homeowners and funding for Fannie Mae and Freddie Mac
Yes Approve a nuclear cooperation agreement with India
No   Approve final $700 billion program to stabilize financial markets
Yes Allow consideration of a $14 billion auto industry loan package

2007

Yes Increase minimum wage by $2.10 an hour
Yes Limit debate on a comprehensive immigration bill
Yes Overhaul congressional lobbying and ethics rules for members and their staffs
Yes Limit debate on considering a bill to add House seats for the District of Columbia and Utah
Yes Limit debate on restoring habeas corpus rights to detainees
Yes Mandate minimum breaks for troops between deployments to Iraq or Afghanistan
Yes Override Bush veto of $23.2 billion water projects authorization bill
No   Confirm Michael B. Mukasey as attorney general
Yes Limit debate on an energy policy overhaul containing $21.8 billion in tax incentives and reduced oil and gas subsidies

CQ VOTE STUDIES

	PARTY UNITY		PRESIDENTIAL SUPPORT	
	SUPPORT	OPPOSE	SUPPORT	OPPOSE
2008	89%	11%	42%	58%
2007	90%	10%	42%	58%
2006	76%	24%	60%	40%
2005	84%	16%	47%	53%
2004	92%	8%	62%	38%
2003	90%	10%	56%	44%
2002	77%	23%	78%	22%
2001	92%	8%	70%	30%

INTEREST GROUPS

	AFL-CIO	ADA	CCUS	ACU
2008	100%	95%	50%	8%
2007	95%	90%	45%	4%
2006	60%	60%	83%	40%
2005	71%	80%	50%	20%
2004	100%	80%	65%	4%
2003	77%	80%	48%	20%
2002	85%	70%	70%	30%
2001	100%	95%	43%	16%

Sen. Mel Martinez (R)

Elected 2004; 1st term

CAPITOL OFFICE
224-3041
martinez.senate.gov
356 Russell Bldg. 20510-0903; fax 228-5171

COMMITTEES
Armed Services
Banking, Housing & Urban Affairs
Commerce, Science & Transportation
Special Aging - ranking member

RESIDENCE
Orlando

BORN
Oct. 23, 1946; Sagua La Grande, Cuba

RELIGION
Roman Catholic

FAMILY
Wife, Kitty Martinez; three children

EDUCATION
Orlando Junior College, A.A. 1967; Florida State U.,
B.A. 1969 (international affairs), J.D. 1973

CAREER
Lawyer

POLITICAL HIGHLIGHTS
Sought Republican nomination for lieutenant
governor, 1994; Orange County chairman,
1998-2001; Housing and Urban Development
secretary, 2001-03

ELECTION RESULTS

2004 GENERAL

Mel Martinez (R)	3,672,864	49.4%
Betty Castor (D)	3,590,201	48.3%
Dennis F. Bradley (VET)	166,642	2.2%

2004 PRIMARY

Mel Martinez (R)	522,994	44.9%
Bill McCollum (R)	360,474	30.9%
Doug Gallagher (R)	158,360	13.6%
Johnnie Byrd (R)	68,982	5.9%
Karen Saull (R)	20,365	1.8%
Sonya March (R)	17,804	1.5%
Larry Klayman (R)	13,257	1.1%

A former Cuban refugee who escaped Fidel Castro's regime at the age of 15, Martinez is a self-starter with an assertive style that melds idealism with pragmatism. His background and social conservative ideology appeal to the party establishment as it seeks to woo Hispanic voters. But his willingness to compromise — particularly on immigration — has cost him the support of the GOP's conservative wing in the Senate.

That support may now matter less to him, as he intends to retire from the Senate in 2010. Martinez faced a difficult campaign to hold his seat, which had been heavily targeted since his narrow win in 2004 with just 49 percent of the vote. Martinez also was a close ally of President George W. Bush, but isn't always a sure vote for his party — which made him an obvious target of President Obama as he sought support within the GOP early in the 111th Congress (2009-10).

In February 2009, Martinez did join nine Republicans to help Senate Democrats usher into law an expansion of the State Children's Health Insurance Program, which covers children whose families do not quality for Medicaid.

But Obama couldn't persuade him to support a $787 billion economic stimulus package, which ultimately became law. "The majority of the spending in this package is not stimulus spending," Martinez said. "That which is, isn't enough to meet the current economic challenge." He instead tried to find bipartisan support for an alternative that included spending but also focused more heavily on tax cuts.

Martinez, along with Democratic Sens. Bill Nelson of Florida and Robert Menendez of New Jersey, also was displeased that a catchall spending law for 2009 included provisions to loosen rules on travel and imports of food and medicine to Cuba. In a lengthy floor speech, Martinez said it was misguided to set foreign policy in a spending bill. And he asked, "As we consider changing U.S. policy toward Cuba, why are we doing this without asking anything?" He suggested demanding the release of political prisoners, for example.

Treasury Secretary Timothy F. Geithner indicated the provisions would be narrowly interpreted and wouldn't weaken the embargo against the government of Fidel and Raúl Castro — assurances that satisfied Martinez and his colleagues. Still, Martinez opposed the final law, criticizing its inclusion of billions of dollars in earmarks. Martinez will have an opportunity to further address trade and other issues vital to his state during the 111th from his seat on the Commerce, Science and Transportation Committee.

He and Obama may be closer on the issue of offshore drilling for oil. In 2006, after the House passed a sweeping measure that permitted drilling off virtually any U.S. coast, Martinez had helped draft a more restrictive plan that opened 8.3 million more acres in the Gulf of Mexico to drilling while protecting Florida's beaches, and his compromise became law. When high gasoline prices in 2008 raised public support for expanded offshore drilling, Martinez — then a member of the Energy and Natural Resources Committee — argued drilling should occur in Alaska and in the West, but not in Florida, and not without first developing alternative energy supplies.

The first Cuban-American elected to the Senate, Martinez still hopes to address immigration reform in his final years — an issue Obama has pledged to address. But the debate has been a bit uncomfortable for Martinez, who sought bipartisanship when he was a key negotiator on a broad immigration proposal in 2006 and 2007. The legislation — backed by Bush and drafted by Democrat Edward M. Kennedy of Massachusetts and

Republican John McCain of Arizona — would have combined tighter border security and immigration laws with a temporary worker program and created a path to citizenship for most illegal immigrants. Martinez stared down conservatives who wanted to further limit family reunification, but House GOP opposition ultimately doomed the bill.

Republican critics of the measure then set up a MartinezWatch.com Web site in an unsuccessful effort to block his election in 2007 as general chairman of the Republican National Committee. Martinez ultimately served only 10 months in the position; the rift between the senator and social conservatives on immigration — repeated in 2007 — appeared to outweigh their agreement on other issues. The chairmanship was a "misguided adventure," Martinez joked on "The Daily Show With Jon Stewart" on Aug. 12, 2008, when he was promoting his autobiography, "A Sense of Belonging."

His ascendancy to the post had been swift, coming just three years after his election to the Senate and thanks to Bush. Martinez had served as one of the Bush campaign's multiple chairmen in Florida in 2000, and afterward the president tapped him to be his first secretary of Housing and Urban Development. Later Bush encouraged him to run for the Senate, then pushed for Martinez for the RNC job to appeal to Hispanics who abandoned Republicans in the 2006 elections, partly because of the party's harsh immigration stance.

A devout Catholic, Martinez opposes abortion and same-sex marriage. As HUD secretary, he launched a Center for Faith-Based and Community Services to help religious-oriented groups compete for federal grants.

When Congress was negotiating a sweeping mortgage relief bill in 2008, Martinez, who sits on the Banking, Housing and Urban Affairs Committee, and Democratic Sen. Dianne Feinstein of California worked on a provision requiring residential mortgage loan originators to meet minimum national licensing standards. He authored another section of the law with Democratic Sen. Bob Casey of Pennsylvania that imposes stricter appraisal standards for Federal Housing Administration-backed loans.

Florida's large elderly population and Martinez's assignment to the Special Aging panel, where he is the ranking member, have placed him at the forefront of a Republican effort to combat Medicare fraud before government payments are made to those scamming the system, not afterward. He plans to insert the provision into any future debates on overhauling the health care system.

Martinez, a Democrat until the Reagan administration, was once a trial attorney who specialized in helping poor clients and fellow immigrants win handsome settlements from companies. He now wants jury awards limited to "pain and suffering," with a $500,000 ceiling.

As a child in Cuba in 1958, Martinez and his younger brother huddled together in fear on the floor of their bedroom as machine-gun fire rang out in the streets. Four years later, Martinez escaped Cuba and arrived at a refugee camp in the United States not knowing the language or culture. He detailed his escape from Cuba through "Operation Pedro Pan"—jointly sponsored by the U.S. government and the Catholic Church — in his 2008 autobiography.

When Martinez arrived in Florida, his name was Melquiades. But a foster mother shortened it to Mel — a tidbit that proved a compelling backdrop for his 2004 Senate campaign. As he moved from one foster home to another, he worked to save money for college, and later for his family, with whom he was eventually reunited.

Martinez is known for his charisma and approachability, but he can occasionally lose his cool. During the 2004 general election, Martinez accused his Democratic opponent, Betty Castor, the state's former education commissioner, of being soft on terrorism because she did not suspend a professor with suspected ties to Islamic Jihad while she was president of the University of Southern Florida.

KEY VOTES

2008

Yes Prohibit discrimination based on genetic information

Yes Reauthorize farm and nutrition programs for five years

Yes Limit debate on "cap and trade" system for greenhouse gas emissions

No   Allow lawsuits against companies that participated in warrantless wiretapping

Yes Limit debate on a bill to block a scheduled cut in Medicare payments to doctors

Yes Grant mortgage relief to homeowners and funding for Fannie Mae and Freddie Mac

Yes Approve a nuclear cooperation agreement with India

Yes Approve final $700 billion program to stabilize financial markets

No   Allow consideration of a $14 billion auto industry loan package

2007

Yes Increase minimum wage by $2.10 an hour

Yes Limit debate on a comprehensive immigration bill

Yes Overhaul congressional lobbying and ethics rules for members and their staffs

No   Limit debate on considering a bill to add House seats for the District of Columbia and Utah

No   Limit debate on restoring habeas corpus rights to detainees

No   Mandate minimum breaks for troops between deployments to Iraq or Afghanistan

Yes Override Bush veto of $23.2 billion water projects authorization bill

Yes Confirm Michael B. Mukasey as attorney general

No   Limit debate on an energy policy overhaul containing $21.8 billion in tax incentives and reduced oil and gas subsidies

CQ VOTE STUDIES

	PARTY UNITY		PRESIDENTIAL SUPPORT	
	SUPPORT	OPPOSE	SUPPORT	OPPOSE
2008	78%	22%	67%	33%
2007	87%	13%	85%	15%
2006	86%	14%	92%	8%
2005	94%	6%	91%	9%

INTEREST GROUPS

	AFL-CIO	ADA	CCUS	ACU
2008	30%	30%	88%	60%
2007	16%	20%	100%	80%
2006	7%	0%	100%	84%
2005	14%	5%	83%	100%

Rep. Jeff Miller (R)

Elected October 2001; 4th full term

A former deputy sheriff, Miller appears as comfortable in cowboy boots as a business suit. Although his conservative philosophy on most domestic policies puts him at odds with the Democratic majority, he is able to make headway on issues important to his district's many veterans.

The Florida Panhandle houses the Naval Air Station in Pensacola and Eglin Air Force Base. From his seats on the Armed Services and Veterans' Affairs committees, he watches out for active-duty and former servicemembers.

In January 2009, Miller was named the top Republican on Armed Services' Terrorism, Unconventional Threats and Capabilities Subcommittee. The post gives him a say over an array of programs dealing with fighting terrorism — including chemical, biological and nuclear weapons and computer warfare — that have become a priority since the Sept. 11 terrorist attacks. He also gained a seat on the Select Intelligence Committee.

He gave up the top GOP spot on the Veterans Affairs' Health Subcommittee, where during the 110th Congress (2007-08) he advocated for quicker, more responsive treatment of veterans. A long backlog of service-connected disability claims led him to call for an overhaul of the VA. But he opposed Democratic attempts to authorize an array of new programs for homeless veterans, complaining their plans would scrap help for groups already providing care and create a potentially unnecessary therapeutic readjustment program.

After The Washington Post disclosed in early 2007 widespread problems at Walter Reed Army Medical Center, Miller criticized the Pentagon's failure to address the shortcomings sooner. In a letter to Defense Secretary Robert M. Gates, he "strongly recommended" the firing of the Army's surgeon general, Lt. Gen. Kevin Kiley, the former commander at Walter Reed. Miller, an ardent supporter of the Iraq War, was one of many calling for Kiley's head; he soon retired under pressure.

Miller has worked to improve benefits for military personnel and their families since he arrived in Congress. He successfully added an amendment to the annual defense authorization bill in 2004 that eliminated the so-called widows' tax on surviving spouses of military retirees.

Under the military's Survivor Benefit Plan, enacted in the 1970s, spouses of deceased career military retirees initially received 55 percent of the soldier's annual retirement pay, but that payment was cut to 35 percent when the spouse reached age 62. That is when individuals first become eligible for Social Security, but anyone starting Social Security at age 62 faces reduced benefits for life. Miller's provision allowed military spouses older than 62 to retain 55 percent of their deceased spouse's military retirement pay.

In 2003, he cosponsored a measure allowing disabled veterans to simultaneously receive both military pension checks and veterans' disability benefits. A version of the plan was rolled into that year's defense authorization bill. The House passed his bill in 2007 to waive a co-payment requirement for veterans receiving hospice care at a non-VA facility, but it didn't advance in the Senate.

Miller is a member of the conservative Republican Study Committee and the National Republican Congressional Committee, the campaign arm of the House GOP that raises money and recruits candidates. But he keeps a low profile, issuing few news releases. He did draw attention in September 2008 when Sears unveiled a new sportswear line, the All American Army Brand's First Infantry Division collection. The clothing line featuring the 1st Division's official patches had the military's approval, but Miller remained critical. "These are honored insignias that mean something to the people

CAPITOL OFFICE
225-4136
jeffmiller.house.gov
2439 Rayburn Bldg. 20515; fax 225-3414

COMMITTEES
Armed Services
Veterans' Affairs
Select Intelligence

RESIDENCE
Chumuckla

BORN
June 27, 1959; St. Petersburg, Fla.

RELIGION
Methodist

FAMILY
Wife, Vicki Miller; two children

EDUCATION
U. of Florida, B.A. 1984 (journalism)

CAREER
Real estate broker; state agriculture department official; deputy county sheriff

POLITICAL HIGHLIGHTS
Fla. House, 1998-2001

ELECTION RESULTS

2008 GENERAL

Jeff Miller (R)	232,559	70.2%
James "Jim" Bryan (D)	98,797	29.8%

2008 PRIMARY

Jeff Miller (R)	unopposed

2006 GENERAL

Jeff Miller (R)	135,786	68.5%
Jeff Roberts (D)	62,340	31.5%

PREVIOUS WINNING PERCENTAGES
2004 (77%); 2002 (75%); 2001 Special Election (66%)

that wore them, and they should not be commercialized," he told the Northwest Florida Daily News. "What's next, the Congressional Medal of Honor?"

A sixth-generation Floridian whose parents sold real estate and operated a cattle ranch near Clearwater, Miller understands the needs of the culturally Southern 1st District, which is dotted with rural farm towns.

Conservative on both social and fiscal policy, he opposes abortion, embryonic stem cell research and gun control while supporting school vouchers and strict immigration controls. In fall 2008, he opposed a $700 billion measure to shore up the nation's fiscal sector. He said he was unhappy the George W. Bush administration passed the problem along to Congress with little guidance and didn't protect taxpayers enough.

A former small-business owner, Miller is close to the business leaders in his community, many of whom rely on a robust tourism economy. He had fought the Bush administration's plan to open gas and oil drilling within 20 miles of the coast, complaining it would interfere with military training and weapons testing. He said he supports current policy that requires the Defense and Interior departments to coordinate on any oil and gas leases that might affect the military's training in the Gulf of Mexico.

In January 2003, Miller was one of just four House lawmakers to vote against an extension of unemployment benefits that had expired Dec. 28, 2002. "At what point do we quit providing a check to someone without a job?" he asked. "I'm afraid that extending these benefits will diminish the desire to go out and find a job," he said, according to The Associated Press.

A former real estate broker and political aide, Miller has an eclectic résumé. While in high school, he was a disc jockey for the local radio station. Later, he had a stint as a deputy county sheriff and held part-time jobs as a stock car racer and auctioneer.

He studied journalism at the University of Florida. He served as president of the university's education fraternity, Alpha Gamma Rho, and then president of the school's fraternity system. Later he was elected president of college fraternities for southeast Florida. He remains an enthusiastic supporter of the Florida Gators football team, a passion he shares with his two grown sons.

After college, Miller joined the staff of Florida Agriculture Commissioner Doyle Connor. He later served as a state representative for the heavily Republican north Florida district he now represents in Congress.

Miller came to Congress in October 2001, after winning a special election to replace GOP Rep. Joe Scarborough, who had resigned from the House to spend more time with his family. (Scarborough later began a television career.) Miller had garnered 66 percent of the vote. He has coasted to re-election since.

KEY VOTES

2008

No	Delay consideration of Colombia free-trade agreement
No	Override Bush veto of federal farm and nutrition programs reauthorization bill
Yes	Overhaul surveillance laws and permit dismissal of suits against companies that conducted warrantless wiretapping
No	Grant mortgage relief to homeowners and funding for Fannie Mae and Freddie Mac
No	Approve initial $700 billion program to stabilize financial markets
No	Approve final $700 billion program to stabilize financial markets
No	Provide $14 billion in loans to automakers

2007

No	Increase minimum wage by $2.10 an hour
No	Approve $124.2 billion in emergency war spending and set goal for redeployment of troops from Iraq
Yes	Reject federal contraceptive assistance to international family planning groups
No	Override Bush veto of $23.2 billion water projects authorization bill
?	Implement Peru free-trade agreement
Yes	Approve energy policy overhaul with new fuel economy standards
Yes	Clear $473.5 billion omnibus spending bill, including $70 billion for military operations

CQ VOTE STUDIES

	PARTY UNITY		PRESIDENTIAL SUPPORT	
	SUPPORT	OPPOSE	SUPPORT	OPPOSE
2008	99%	1%	85%	15%
2007	97%	3%	88%	12%
2006	97%	3%	92%	8%
2005	96%	4%	85%	15%
2004	99%	1%	92%	8%

INTEREST GROUPS

	AFL-CIO	ADA	CCUS	ACU
2008	7%	5%	89%	100%
2007	13%	10%	58%	92%
2006	14%	5%	93%	92%
2005	15%	0%	80%	92%
2004	8%	5%	100%	100%

FLORIDA 1

Panhandle — Pensacola, Fort Walton Beach

Occupying the western portion of the Panhandle — wedged between Alabama and the Gulf of Mexico — the 1st District stretches from Washington County north of Panama City to Pensacola and the Perdido River. Often dubbed "Lower Alabama," the 1st's Bible Belt culture is much closer to the Old South than to Florida's big cities.

A strong defense presence stabilizes the economy in the 1st, which is home to several large military bases. Eglin Air Force Base is the military's center for air-delivered weaponry and, as the future home of the F-35 Joint Strike Fighter training school, the base is slated to bring thousands of military, civilian and contractor jobs to the area. Naval Air Station Pensacola contributes more than $1 billion to the local economy every year.

Tourism and the area's building boom created economic and population growth here as condominiums and retirement communities popped up in previously rural areas. Big-ticket construction and military development have partially buoyed workers from collapses in the manufacturing and homebuilding sectors. Bucolic open spaces and the white-sand beaches

of Emerald Coast towns such as Destin (a small part of which is in the 2nd) draw vacationers, but hurricanes and widespread economic slow-downs can stall the district's tourism industry.

The 1st, even more conservative than its GOP registration edge would indicate, gave John McCain 67 percent of its 2008 presidential vote, his highest percentage statewide. The 1st's Democrats are more "Dixiecrat" than liberal, and the political ideology of the predominately white district is heavily influenced by the military.

MAJOR INDUSTRY
Defense, tourism, health care

MILITARY BASES
Naval Air Station Pensacola, 16,000 military, 7,400 civilian (2008); Eglin Air Force Base, 7,928 military, 5,435 civilian (2009); Hurlburt Field (Air Force), 7,588 military, 900 civilian; Naval Technical Training Center Corry Station, 783 military, 80 civilian (2008); Naval Air Station Whiting Field, 1,738 military, 1,382 civilian (2006)

CITIES
Pensacola, 56,255; Ferry Pass (unincorporated), 27,176

NOTABLE
The Blue Angels flight group is housed at Naval Air Station Pensacola.

Rep. Allen Boyd (D)

Elected 1996; 7th term

CAPITOL OFFICE
225-5235
www.house.gov/boyd
1227 Longworth Bldg. 20515-0902; fax 225-5615

COMMITTEES
Appropriations
Budget

RESIDENCE
Monticello

BORN
June 6, 1945; Valdosta, Ga.

RELIGION
Methodist

FAMILY
Wife, Cissy Boyd; three children

EDUCATION
North Florida Junior College, A.A. 1966;
Florida State U., B.S. 1969 (accounting)

MILITARY SERVICE
Army 1969-71

CAREER
Farmer

POLITICAL HIGHLIGHTS
Sought Democratic nomination for Jefferson
County Board of County Commissioners, 1972;
Fla. House, 1989-96

ELECTION RESULTS

2008 GENERAL
Allen Boyd (D)	216,804	61.9%
Mark Mulligan (R)	133,404	38.1%

2008 PRIMARY
Allen Boyd (D)	unopposed

2006 GENERAL
Allen Boyd (D)	unopposed

PREVIOUS WINNING PERCENTAGES
2004 (62%); 2002 (67%); 2000 (72%); 1998 (95%);
1996 (59%)

A "Blue Dog" through and through, Boyd's work for the fiscally conservative Democratic coalition consumed most of his energy in recent years.

He calls the group the "fiscal police." First and foremost among the group's principles is the pay-as-you-go budget rule, which requires new spending on entitlement programs or new tax breaks to be offset by spending cuts or tax increases elsewhere. Boyd wants the rule to be written into law, as it was before Republicans allowed it to lapse in 2002 when they controlled Congress.

As one of three co-chairmen of the coalition during the 110th Congress (2007-08), Boyd pressured top Democratic leaders to move an agenda palatable to conservative Democrats and swing voters in districts like his Tallahassee-based 2nd District. Looking toward the challenges facing the incoming Obama administration — the economy, health care, the environment and the wars in Iraq and Afghanistan, Boyd said in November 2008, "I think Obama will do a great job…But we have to guard against lurching too far to the left."

Boyd, who sits on both the Budget and Appropriations committees, and other Blue Dogs were heavily courted by President Obama as he began to move spending bills through Congress in early 2009. Boyd initially was one of 11 Democrats who voted against Obama's economic stimulus bill, and Obama worked hard to sway those votes back. Boyd ultimately supported the final version, saying he was satisfied the original cost, which topped $800 billion, had been reduced to $787 billion. "Back then we were in the third inning of a nine-inning game," he said after final passage of the law. "You were playing with real bullets. This is the ninth inning of the game. This is the bill going to the president."

He also supported a $410 billion catchall spending bill for 2009, which included several earmarks for his own areas, including millions in funding he said he obtained for local transportation and water-related projects. And he applauded Obama's proposed $3.6 trillion budget blueprint for 2010 for including projected costs for overseas military operations, national disaster response and the cost of the alternative minimum tax.

Boyd sits on Appropriations' Financial Services Subcommittee. In fall 2008, before he took a seat on that panel, he supported a $700 billion measure, signed into law, aimed at shoring up the nation's financial services sector.

A rifle platoon leader during the Vietnam War, Boyd also sits on the Defense Appropriations Subcommittee, which writes the annual Pentagon spending bills and legislation to provide supplemental funding for the Iraq War. That seat helps him protect the interests of Tyndall Air Force Base and other nearby military installations. He has worked to speed runway upgrades and other improvements at Tyndall in preparation for the arrival of a second squadron of the Air Force's F/A-22 combat planes.

Although critical of the way the George W. Bush administration waged the war in Iraq, Boyd has supported war funding bills. He voted for the 2008 war supplemental that also extended unemployment benefits for 13 weeks and greatly expanded GI Bill education benefits for veterans. But he grumbled when Democratic leaders bowed to the Senate and allowed those entitlements to be created without offsetting cuts elsewhere. And he is among the Democrats demanding that Iraq pick up more of the cost of its own security and reconstruction.

Boyd, a fifth-generation farmer, uses his seat on the Agriculture Appropriations Subcommittee to advocate for Florida's farmers. When a severe drought hit the Southeast in 2008, he was upset by the water-sharing plan put forward by the Army Corps of Engineers because he felt low flows into the affected rivers could hurt his district. He pushed legislation to study water management issues in the Apalachicola-Chattahoochee-Flint river system.

Boyd isn't afraid to break from his party on hot-button issues — particularly on immigration. He has taken a tough stance on immigration, voting in the 109th Congress (2005-06) to impose stricter identification and asylum requirements on immigrants and to build 700 miles of fencing along the U.S. border with Mexico. In the 110th, he was one of 49 House Democrats cosponsoring a get-tough immigration bill put forward by conservative Democrat Heath Shuler of North Carolina. But he did not join Shuler in signing a discharge petition Republicans circulated in an unsuccessful attempt to force a floor vote on the bill.

Boyd supported a temporary extension in 2007 of the Bush administration's warrantless wiretapping authority, and he backed a 2008 overhaul of the Foreign Intelligence Surveillance Act that set guidelines for electronic surveillance. He was one of 25 House Democrats who signed a letter urging that the bill include retroactive immunity for telecommunications companies that had cooperated with the Bush administration's earlier warrantless spying program. The immunity provision was opposed by most Democrats but was in the final bill at Bush's insistence.

Boyd is a product of rural Jefferson County, just east of Tallahassee. He went to Florida State University, spent two years in the Army and returned home to help his family raise cattle, cotton, sod and peanuts. He became involved in agricultural organizations and civic groups.

He lost a 1972 bid for an open county commission seat but was successful when he won a 1989 special election to the state House and served seven years, cultivating good relations with the business community.

He won his U.S. House seat in 1996, after the retirement of three-term Democrat Pete Peterson. Boyd demonstrated he could hold together the district's traditional Democratic coalition: Tallahassee-area voters with jobs in state and local government and higher education, African-Americans, and the portion of the white electorate still clinging to an inherited aversion to the GOP dating back to the Civil War. He defeated Republican Bill Sutton, a former bank president and one-time state commerce secretary, by 19 percentage points.

Boyd won re-election easily until 2004, when he drew a well-funded challenger in state Rep. Bev Kilmer, who tried to cast him as a liberal. Boyd was the only incumbent Democrat in Florida with a GOP foe, and it was the state's only truly competitive House race. But his popularity took him to a comfortable 62 percent victory. He was unopposed in 2006 and won easily in 2008.

KEY VOTES

2008

No	Delay consideration of Colombia free-trade agreement
Yes	Override Bush veto of federal farm and nutrition programs reauthorization bill
Yes	Overhaul surveillance laws and permit dismissal of suits against companies that conducted warrantless wiretapping
Yes	Grant mortgage relief to homeowners and funding for Fannie Mae and Freddie Mac
Yes	Approve initial $700 billion program to stabilize financial markets
Yes	Approve final $700 billion program to stabilize financial markets
No	Provide $14 billion in loans to automakers

2007

Yes	Increase minimum wage by $2.10 an hour
Yes	Approve $124.2 billion in emergency war spending and set goal for redeployment of troops from Iraq
No	Reject federal contraceptive assistance to international family planning groups
Yes	Override Bush veto of $23.2 billion water projects authorization bill
Yes	Implement Peru free-trade agreement
Yes	Approve energy policy overhaul with new fuel economy standards
Yes	Clear $473.5 billion omnibus spending bill, including $70 billion for military operations

CQ VOTE STUDIES

	PARTY UNITY		PRESIDENTIAL SUPPORT	
	SUPPORT	OPPOSE	SUPPORT	OPPOSE
2008	92%	8%	23%	77%
2007	91%	9%	14%	86%
2006	67%	33%	62%	38%
2005	75%	25%	42%	58%
2004	67%	33%	61%	39%

INTEREST GROUPS

	AFL-CIO	ADA	CCUS	ACU
2008	71%	75%	67%	12%
2007	88%	80%	74%	12%
2006	86%	50%	93%	63%
2005	77%	80%	70%	42%
2004	60%	70%	75%	46%

FLORIDA 2

Panhandle – part of Tallahassee, Panama City

The 2nd stretches around Florida's Big Bend, connecting the Panhandle and the state capital of Tallahassee (a sliver of which is in the 4th District) to the north-central part of the state. Taking in all or part of 16 counties, the 2nd features tobacco and peanut farms, forests and small towns.

The district's natural resources — from the Gulf Coast beaches where oysters are harvested to abundant farmland — drive its economy. Although agriculture has struggled occasionally due to drought and high energy prices, a steady base of government employees working in the state capital buffers any long-term economic effects.

Florida's forestry industry also maintains a strong presence in the district. Panama City, in Bay County, relies on tourism and the economic benefits of the military community around Tyndall Air Force Base. The 2nd has the third-largest percentage (28 percent) of government workers in any district in the nation. Not surprisingly, given its reliance on farming and the military, agriculture and veterans' affairs dominate the district's politics.

While Democratic, the 2nd is not as liberal as districts in southeast Florida. Many of the district's Democrats, including farmers and retirees, often hold conservative views on fiscal and social issues. The exception is the Tallahassee area (Leon County), home to Florida State University and Florida A&M University. Bay County has a stronger conservative element, as do the smaller communities that ring the Gulf Coast. Black residents — the majority of whom live in the Tallahassee area or in neighboring Gadsden County — make up more than one-fifth of the district's population. Barack Obama took 69 percent of Gadsden's 2008 presidential vote, but John McCain won 54 percent of the district's vote overall.

MAJOR INDUSTRY
Agriculture, government, manufacturing

MILITARY BASES
Tyndall Air Force Base, 3,901 military, 729 civilian (2007)

CITIES
Tallahassee (pt.), 147,167; Panama City, 36,417; Callaway, 14,233

NOTABLE
The Suwannee River was made famous by Stephen Foster's song, "Old Folks at Home"; Tallahassee's National High Magnetic Field Laboratory is the highest-powered magnet laboratory in the world.

Rep. Corrine Brown (D)

Elected 1992; 9th term

CAPITOL OFFICE
225-0123
www.house.gov/corrinebrown
2336 Rayburn Bldg. 20515-0903; fax 225-2256

COMMITTEES
Transportation & Infrastructure
(Railroads, Pipelines & Hazardous Materials -
chairwoman)
Veterans' Affairs

RESIDENCE
Jacksonville

BORN
Nov. 11, 1946; Jacksonville, Fla.

RELIGION
Baptist

FAMILY
Single; one child

EDUCATION
Florida A&M U., B.S. 1969 (sociology),
M.A. 1971 (education); U. of Florida, Ed.S. 1974

CAREER
College guidance counselor; travel agency owner

POLITICAL HIGHLIGHTS
Candidate for Fla. House, 1980; Fla. House, 1982-92

ELECTION RESULTS

2008 GENERAL
Corrine Brown (D)   unopposed
2008 PRIMARY
Corrine Brown (D)   unopposed
2006 GENERAL
Corrine Brown (D)   unopposed

PREVIOUS WINNING PERCENTAGES
2004 (99%); 2002 (59%); 2000 (58%); 1998 (55%);
1996 (61%); 1994 (58%); 1992 (59%)

In her district, Brown's slogan is "Corrine Delivers," a reference to her success in procuring federal money for local projects. As a fiercely loyal and sharp-tongued Democrat, what she delivers in Washington can be vociferous and partisan.

When Brown gets worked up — particularly about Republicans' behavior — she is apt to hold nothing back. She briefly lost her speaking privileges on the House floor in 2004 after accusing GOP lawmakers of participating in a "coup d'etat" and of stealing the contested 2000 presidential election in Florida. Unapologetic after the incident, she said, "If they're going to take my words down for telling the truth, that's OK. . . . We had a coup d'etat. Straight out, they stole the election."

Brown may be acerbic, but she is attentive to her district. A Taxpayers for Common Sense study ranked her third in the Florida House delegation for earmarks for 2008, putting her ahead of more senior lawmakers and some who sit on the Appropriations Committee. The watchdog organization found that Brown, working alone and with colleagues, secured $40.7 million. Winning earmarks, funding set-asides for projects in member states, "is a priority for me," she has said.

She initially claimed dissatisfaction with President Obama's economic stimulus bill in early 2009 for not including more for infrastructure projects, but Brown ultimately supported it.

And the city of Jacksonville is counting on Brown too, as chairwoman of the Transportation and Infrastructure Committee's Railroads, Pipelines and Hazardous Materials Subcommittee, to ensure more federal funds head its way. Jacksonville's deepwater cargo port is growing and the city needs funds to complete road projects planned a decade ago. Jacksonville Mayor John Peyton told the Florida Times-Union: "We're relying on her to come through for us."

Brown has long focused on transportation issues. She pushed to enactment in October 2008 a major rail safety and Amtrak reauthorization bill.

She has been a strong supporter of transportation giant CSX Corp., which is located in her district and is one of her largest contributors. Her subcommittee held a hearing on investment in railroads in March 2008, just as CSX faced hedge fund efforts to oust members of its board. Around the same time, CSX donated $25,000, and CSX chief executive Michael Ward donated $1 million to Edward Waters College in Brown's district, a school where she has taught and where she chaired the inaugural committee for a new president in 2008.

Brown sided with CSX in her harsh criticism of the hedge funds, comparing their efforts to a hostile takeover. "A short-term money grab like this recalls memories of the actions leading up to the mortgage crisis that we have today," she said.

Brown has stirred controversy in other ways. During Tropical Storm Fay in 2008, her staff called local officials to ask for sandbags for her Jacksonville home near the Trout River. That set off a furor about special treatment, and she repaid the city for the $886.04 in labor and sandbags. Brown's staff said she asked for the help, thinking that it was offered to all citizens.

Brown also raised eyebrows in 2007 when Citizens for Responsibility and Ethics in Washington pointed out she had paid her son-in-law, Tyree Fields, $5,500 for political consulting during the 2006 election cycle. Fields is married to Brown's daughter, Shantrel Brown Fields, who has been connected to controversy in the past because she is a lobbyist and because she accepted a car from an African businessman who sought help from Brown. Fields has worked for Alcade & Fay, a suburban Washington law firm with numerous Florida clients, and has lobbied on transportation issues. But Brown's staff has said she does not lobby her mother.

A member of the Veterans' Affairs Committee, Brown supports more spending for veterans' health programs. She joined other Florida lawmakers in successfully pushing for funding for a new Veterans' Administration hospital in Orlando.

Brown also has pushed for temporary protected status for Haitians and complained those refugees are treated differently than Cuban refugees. And she describes herself as a "bitter opponent" of the Iraq War and has spoken out against supplemental funding for it.

Brown has sponsored legislation to set up a commission to look at the needs of children after disasters. "Children are not little adults. Their needs are unique and cannot be easily inferred from emergency plans," she said.

She has been vigilant on voter access issues ever since the 2000 presidential recount in Florida. In 2008, she pressed Florida Republican Gov. Charlie Crist to delay a new "no match, no vote" law in Florida to invalidate new voter registrations for voters who can't produce identification that matches state records.

Brown earned two degrees from Florida A&M University — an undergraduate degree and a master's in education — and worked as a college teacher and guidance counselor. She was steered into politics by one of her sorority sisters at the university, Gwendolyn Sawyer Cherry, who went on to become Florida's first black state representative. Although Brown lost her first state House race in 1980, Cherry kept after her to try again, and Brown won a seat in 1982. She served in the state House for a decade.

When a black-majority 3rd District was created by redistricting for the 1990s, Brown was one of four candidates in the bitter 1992 Democratic primary for the seat. She survived a runoff with 64 percent of the vote. Latent acrimony over ethics charges raised in the primary helped hold her share of the vote to 59 percent in November against Republican Don Weidner.

Until recently, Brown had to work for most of her election victories. She won more than three-fifths of the vote — a traditional threshold for having a safe seat — in only one of her first six general elections, when she got a lift on President Clinton's coattails in 1996. Republicans ran a black candidate against Brown in three of her re-election contests, seeking to eliminate race as a factor. Her fortunes have since improved. In 2004, Brown faced only a write-in opponent, and in 2006 and 2008 she was unopposed.

KEY VOTES

2008

Yes   Delay consideration of Colombia free-trade agreement

?   Override Bush veto of federal farm and nutrition programs reauthorization bill

Yes   Overhaul surveillance laws and permit dismissal of suits against companies that conducted warrantless wiretapping

Yes   Grant mortgage relief to homeowners and funding for Fannie Mae and Freddie Mac

Yes   Approve initial $700 billion program to stabilize financial markets

Yes   Approve final $700 billion program to stabilize financial markets

Yes   Provide $14 billion in loans to automakers

2007

Yes   Increase minimum wage by $2.10 an hour

Yes   Approve $124.2 billion in emergency war spending and set goal for redeployment of troops from Iraq

No   Reject federal contraceptive assistance to international family planning groups

Yes   Override Bush veto of $23.2 billion water projects authorization bill

Yes   Implement Peru free-trade agreement

Yes   Approve energy policy overhaul with new fuel economy standards

Yes   Clear $473.5 billion omnibus spending bill, including $70 billion for military operations

CQ VOTE STUDIES

	PARTY UNITY		PRESIDENTIAL SUPPORT	
	SUPPORT	OPPOSE	SUPPORT	OPPOSE
2008	98%	2%	17%	83%
2007	97%	3%	6%	94%
2006	95%	5%	33%	67%
2005	96%	4%	16%	84%
2004	94%	6%	32%	68%

INTEREST GROUPS

	AFL-CIO	ADA	CCUS	ACU
2008	100%	95%	69%	0%
2007	100%	90%	60%	0%
2006	100%	100%	40%	20%
2005	92%	95%	42%	0%
2004	92%	90%	37%	8%

FLORIDA 3

North — parts of Jacksonville, Orlando and Gainesville

The Democratic, blue-collar 3rd bounces among three of Florida's northern cities and includes both heavily urban areas and long stretches of swamps and lakes along the St. Johns River. It slithers south along the river into a large portion of working-class Putnam County, where bass fishing is prevalent, before taking in part of Gainesville, home to the University of Florida (in the 6th), and continuing southeast to Orlando (shared with the 8th and 24th). Most of the area in between the northern cities is dominated by agricultural land and lacks major private employers, contributing to the 3rd's overall underdeveloped economic profile.

The district relies on Jacksonville's port, Naval Air Station Jacksonville (in the 4th District) and other area government facilities for jobs. Transportation company CSX Corp. also is based in the 3rd's portion of Jacksonville. The local financial services sector has held relatively steady amid recent economic slowdowns and rising unemployment rates and has buoyed the city's economy.

At the district's southern end, many Orlando residents work in the volatile tourism industry at locations such as Walt Disney World (in the 8th). Renovations at the Florida Citrus Bowl have stalled as city tax revenues dropped during the recent economic downturn, but construction of a new arena for basketball's Magic has brought jobs to the area.

Blacks make up a plurality (49 percent) of district residents, and the 3rd has the lowest median income (just under $30,000) of any Florida district. Democrats dominate the 3rd, heavily outnumbering Republicans in party registration. Some rural areas in Clay County and in the Palatka area (shared with the 7th) on the St. Johns River are home to Republicans and old-line conservative Democrats, but not enough to counter the 3rd's strong proclivity toward Democrats in federal elections. Barack Obama won 71 percent of the district's 2008 presidential vote.

MAJOR INDUSTRY
Defense, government, transportation, higher education

CITIES
Jacksonville (pt.), 251,892; Orlando (pt.), 61,906; Pine Hills (unincorporated), 41,764; Gainesville (pt.), 35,540

NOTABLE
The St. Johns River and its tributaries flow north to Jacksonville.

Rep. Ander Crenshaw (R)

Elected 2000; 5th term

CAPITOL OFFICE
225-2501
crenshaw.house.gov
440 Cannon Bldg. 20515-0904; fax 225-2504

COMMITTEES
Appropriations

RESIDENCE
Jacksonville

BORN
Sept. 1, 1944; Jacksonville, Fla.

RELIGION
Episcopalian

FAMILY
Wife, Kitty Crenshaw; two children

EDUCATION
U. of Georgia, A.B. 1966 (political science);
U. of Florida, J.D. 1969

CAREER
Investment bank executive; lawyer

POLITICAL HIGHLIGHTS
Fla. House, 1972-78; candidate for Fla. secretary
of state, 1978; sought Republican nomination for
U.S. Senate, 1980; Fla. Senate, 1986-94 (president,
1992-93); sought Republican nomination for
governor, 1994

ELECTION RESULTS

2008 GENERAL

Ander Crenshaw (R)	224,112	65.2%
Jay McGovern (D)	119,330	34.7%

2008 PRIMARY

Ander Crenshaw (R)	unopposed

2006 GENERAL

Ander Crenshaw (R)	141,759	69.7%
Robert J. Harms (D)	61,704	30.3%

PREVIOUS WINNING PERCENTAGES
2004 (100%); 2002 (100%); 2000 (67%)

Crenshaw is a loyal Republican who pursues the parochial interests of his military-driven district and rarely compromises his conservative principles on fiscal and social issues.

He works quietly from his seat on the Appropriations Committee to funnel millions of dollars back home, primarily for defense projects. In the 2008 spending bills, according to Taxpayers for Common Sense, he obtained either by himself or with colleagues nearly $38 million in earmarks — funding requests for special projects. It was the second-highest amount among Florida's House delegation. Those funds include $6 million to replace a communications facility for the Florida Air National Guard and $2.7 million for the construction of a naval slipway barrier.

In January 2009 he saw a longtime plan come to fruition when Jacksonville VA National Cemetery conducted its first burial. He helped champion the effort to build the cemetery.

But Crenshaw largely focuses on Jacksonville's robust Navy sector. In November 2008, he applauded indications by the U.S. Navy that the Mayport naval station might be the home of a nuclear aircraft carrier, a multi-hundred million dollar project for updating the 3,400-acre facility. "We always knew that one day our aircraft carrier fleet was going to be all nuclear, knew there would be a day when the *Kennedy* would leave," Crenshaw told the Florida Times Union. In the 109th Congress (2005-06), the Florida delegation failed in its effort to keep the Navy from retiring the *USS John F. Kennedy*, an aircraft carrier docked at the Naval Station Mayport. The Pentagon had proposed in 2005 to retire one of its 12 carriers to save $1 billion and chose the *Kennedy*, the oldest and likeliest target for retirement.

From his seat on the State-Foreign Operations Subcommittee, Crenshaw inserted a provision to the 2008 catchall spending bill that states the president should devote $60 million in foreign aid to promoting democracy within Iran.

Crenshaw also serves on the Financial Services Appropriations Subcommittee, which will be part of the debate on continued aid to financial institutions. In the fall of 2008, he supported two $700 billion measures — the second of which became law — to shore up the ailing financial services industry.

Both in committee and on the floor, Crenshaw is careful to keep his footing with the party after a couple slips that set back his career, which had rapidly taken off in his early years in the House. An investment banker by trade, he had secured a seat on the Budget Committee in his first term and the powerful Appropriations panel in his second term. He was in line for the ranking Republican spot on Budget at the start of the 110th Congress (2007-08), but leaders passed him over for Paul D. Ryan of Wisconsin, who had less seniority. He then resigned from the panel.

Crenshaw had lost some favorability among the leadership after reports he had accompanied then-Majority Leader Tom DeLay, his wife and others on an expense-paid trip to South Korea in 2001, sponsored by a nonprofit Korean group later identified as a front for a foreign lobbying campaign. News reports indicated the group was operated by a Washington lobbying firm run by DeLay's former chief of staff. House rules prohibit lawmakers form taking trips financed by lobbyists or foreign agents. In a further error of judgment, Crenshaw later backed Roy Blunt of Missouri over John A. Boehner of Ohio to succeed DeLay, who resigned under an ethics cloud in 2006. Boehner won.

But Crenshaw has maintained his support for the party. During his first four terms he sided with Republicans 95 percent of the time on votes that pitted the parties against each other. He voted against expanding funding for global AIDS programs, opposed a bill to ban job discrimination based on sexual preference, and voted to allow Head Start providers to take religion into account when hiring. He voted for George W. Bush's 2001 and 2003 tax cuts, and opposed a 2008 budget that added $23 billion more in discretionary spending to Bush's plan. He also opposed President Obama's $787 billion economic stimulus law in early 2009, calling it a "long list of big government spending that will not work."

Crenshaw is a member of the Congressional Down Syndrome Caucus, and has pushed legislation to provide savings accounts for the care of family members with disabilities. The accounts, in which after-tax contributions could grow tax-free, would be similar to 529 college savings or retirement plans. His bill did not gain any traction during the 110th Congress, and he reintroduced it at the start of the 111th Congress (2009-10).

His family has been in the Jacksonville area since 1901. The son of a lawyer, he was senior class president at Robert E. Lee High School. A lanky 6-foot-4 inches, he went to the University of Georgia on a basketball scholarship and was the third member of his family, following his father and brother, to letter in a sport for the Bulldogs. The first name he uses, Ander, is a shortened version of his given name Alexander and was coined by his older brother.

Of draft age during the Vietnam War, Crenshaw served in the ROTC but avoided combat through a student deferment and high draft lottery number.

While working on a law degree at the University of Florida, he formed a Campus Crusade for Christ chapter. He eventually found he wasn't interested in practicing law and turned to investment banking. He said he began thinking about running for political office after he started dating Kitty Kirk, the daughter of former Florida Gov. Claude R. Kirk Jr. The two later married.

In 1972, Crenshaw won election to the state House and moved up to the state Senate in 1986. In 1993, he became the first Republican to preside over the Florida Senate in 118 years. He led a chamber split evenly between the two parties, preventing total acrimony by his reputation for seeking consensus.

Over time, Crenshaw lost three statewide elections — a bid for secretary of state in 1978, the Republican primary for Senate in 1980 and the GOP primary for governor in 1994. In the latter race, he drew attention for condemning homosexuals but said he would hire gay people if elected.

After leaving the state Senate in 1994, he stayed out of politics until a chance to run for Congress came in 2000, when GOP Rep. Tillie Fowler stuck to her term-limit pledge and retired. Crenshaw won the primary easily, ensuring him victory in the solidly Republican district. He has won re-election easily since.

KEY VOTES

2008

No	Delay consideration of Colombia free-trade agreement
?	Override Bush veto of federal farm and nutrition programs reauthorization bill
Yes	Overhaul surveillance laws and permit dismissal of suits against companies that conducted warrantless wiretapping
No	Grant mortgage relief to homeowners and funding for Fannie Mae and Freddie Mac
Yes	Approve initial $700 billion program to stabilize financial markets
Yes	Approve final $700 billion program to stabilize financial markets
No	Provide $14 billion in loans to automakers

2007

Yes	Increase minimum wage by $2.10 an hour
No	Approve $124.2 billion in emergency war spending and set goal for redeployment of troops from Iraq
Yes	Reject federal contraceptive assistance to international family planning groups
Yes	Override Bush veto of $23.2 billion water projects authorization bill
Yes	Implement Peru free-trade agreement
Yes	Approve energy policy overhaul with new fuel economy standards
Yes	Clear $473.5 billion omnibus spending bill, including $70 billion for military operations

CQ VOTE STUDIES

	PARTY UNITY		PRESIDENTIAL SUPPORT	
	SUPPORT	OPPOSE	SUPPORT	OPPOSE
2008	97%	3%	74%	26%
2007	90%	10%	79%	21%
2006	96%	4%	97%	3%
2005	97%	3%	89%	11%
2004	95%	5%	88%	12%

INTEREST GROUPS

	AFL-CIO	ADA	CCUS	ACU
2008	7%	10%	100%	90%
2007	18%	15%	87%	83%
2006	7%	0%	100%	84%
2005	13%	5%	89%	92%
2004	13%	0%	100%	92%

FLORIDA 4

North — part of Jacksonville, sliver of Tallahassee

The solidly Republican 4th is anchored in Jacksonville and the surrounding beach communities of Duval County. It wraps around the northeast corner of the state and then runs across the northern border counties as far west as Leon County, where it narrows to a finger to take in a small part of eastern Tallahassee, the state capital. Much of the 4th shadows Interstate 10, a highway that traverses the 150 miles of rural territory between Jacksonville and Tallahassee.

Defense, agriculture, inland water and coastal issues dominate the 4th's politics. Republicans hold a slight but growing edge in voter registration after decades of Democratic dominance. Many nominal Democrats in the more rural areas of the district are old-line conservatives who now side with GOP candidates. One such example is Baker County, where Democrats account for 56 percent of registered voters but gave John McCain 78 percent in the 2008 presidential election, his third-highest percentage in a county statewide. Overall, McCain took 62 percent of the 4th's vote.

Jacksonville is a major city, with health care and financial services sectors, and the local economy is still partly supported by manufacturing. The Port of Jacksonville (located in the 3rd District) is the southern hub for international importers and exporters. The Navy's strong presence along the St. Johns River, which slashes through the center of Jacksonville, bolsters the city's economy and provides many jobs. This area depends on the tourism and hospitality industries — visitors have come to the district's plentiful beaches and golf courses for decades, and many residents work for hotels, resorts and other vacation spots.

MAJOR INDUSTRY
Defense, financial services, tourism, health care

MILITARY BASES
Naval Air Station Jacksonville, 8,792 military, 6,867 civilian (2009); Naval Station Mayport, 7,866 military, 892 civilian (2008)

CITIES
Jacksonville (pt.), 396,879; Jacksonville Beach, 20,990

NOTABLE
Fernandina Beach is the only part of the current United States to have existed under eight flags: France, Spain (twice), England, "Patriot," "Green Cross of Florida," Mexico, Confederate States and United States.

Rep. Ginny Brown-Waite (R)

Elected 2002; 4th term

CAPITOL OFFICE
225-1002
brown-waite.house.gov
414 Cannon Bldg. 20515-0905; fax 226-6559

COMMITTEES
Ways & Means

RESIDENCE
Brooksville

BORN
Oct. 5, 1943; Albany, N.Y.

RELIGION
Roman Catholic

FAMILY
Widowed; three children

EDUCATION
State U. of New York, Albany, B.S. 1976;
Russell Sage College, M.A. 1984
(public administration)

CAREER
Health care consultant; state legislative aide

POLITICAL HIGHLIGHTS
Hernando County Board of Commissioners,
1991-93; Fla. Senate, 1992-2002 (president pro
tempore, 2001-02)

ELECTION RESULTS

2008 GENERAL

Ginny Brown-Waite (R)	265,186	61.2%
John Russell (D)	168,446	38.8%

2008 PRIMARY

Ginny Brown-Waite (R)	49,134	80.1%
Jim King (R)	12,232	19.9%

2006 GENERAL

Ginny Brown-Waite (R)	162,421	59.8%
John Russell (D)	108,959	40.1%

PREVIOUS WINNING PERCENTAGES
2004 (66%); 2002 (48%)

Brown-Waite is independent, feisty and not easily intimidated — traits that don't always endear her to her party leadership. Yet she sticks with her party often enough and looks out for her district, which keeps her safe in her seat.

She won a plum assignment to the Ways and Means Committee at the start of the 111th Congress (2009-10). House Minority Leader John A. Boehner of Ohio also named her to a Republican task force on a health care overhaul.

But she has not always agreed with her party on health-related issues. She split with most House Republicans and with President George W. Bush in consistently voting for legislation to expand federally supported embryonic stem cell research. She was one of 51 Republicans voting to override Bush's 2006 veto of a stem cell bill.

She also defied Republican leaders by voting for five of six signature bills the Democrats rushed to the floor in the early days of their new majority in 2007. The only measure she didn't support was a proposal to force drug companies to negotiate their prices with the Medicare program.

And when House Republicans tried in 2005 to block the removal of a feeding tube from Terri Schiavo, a severely brain-damaged Florida woman, Brown-Waite marched into the House chamber and sat next to Florida Democrat Debbie Wasserman Schultz, a leading opponent of the GOP-sponsored bill. As Republicans glared, she spoke out against the measure, then cast one of just five Republican no votes. "The woman has a backbone of steel," Wasserman Schultz told the Miami Herald.

Brown-Waite sparked another controversy in late 2007 when she resigned her post on the House board overseeing the high school page program after only 10 months on the job. She complained that the board was not notified in a timely manner about certain pages' sexual misbehavior and shoplifting allegations. She accused Speaker Nancy Pelosi of failing to provide adequate oversight of the page program, particularly in the wake of revelations that former Florida Rep. Mark Foley had inappropriate communications with pages.

Coupled with her independence is a sharp tongue. In January 2008 she drew fire when she explained she was only reluctantly supporting an economic stimulus package because it entitled "foreign citizens" in Puerto Rico and Guam to receive tax rebate checks. While residents of the territories do not pay federal income tax, those living in Puerto Rico and Guam are U.S. citizens. Instead of apologizing, Brown-Waite accused Democrats of engaging in "race-baiting politics."

Brown-Waite earned a reputation for outspokenness soon after entering politics in her adopted state of Florida. While she was serving in the state Senate the Florida nursing home industry tried to slip into one of her bills a provision relaxing standards for family notification when a patient is released. Brown-Waite denounced nursing home lobbyists as "slimy bastards," according to the Miami Herald.

With a track record of getting bills passed in a big, populous state, Brown-Waite adapted quickly to legislating at the national level. But she also has kept her focus on issues important to her constituents. Her district has one of the largest contingents of veterans in the nation, and in prior Congresses, she used her seat on the Veterans' Affairs Committee to look after their needs.

The signature effort of her first term was a proposal to require that VA hospitals provide treatment to veterans within 30 days of their seeking care or allow them to be treated by a private facility. In the 109th Congress (2005-06), she helped push through a $100,000 increase in the death benefit paid to survivors of those killed in action. She also lobbied successfully for two new VA clinics in her district and major improvements at three others.

To join Ways and Means, she had to give up her seats not only on the Veterans Affairs' panel, but also on Financial Services and Homeland Security.

On most issues, Brown-Waite sticks to the party line. She supports some restrictions on abortion and a constitutional ban on same-sex marriage. She voted for Bush's 2003 tax cut, and in 2005 and 2006 backed renewal of the 2001 anti-terrorism law known as the Patriot Act. She stood with the president in 2007 on a measure reauthorizing a children's health insurance program even though she faced intense pressure to vote to override his veto. She supports gun owners' rights and carries a .38-caliber handgun.

Brown-Waite worked for the 2005 reauthorization of the Violence Against Women Act. Her interest is both deep and personal. She grew up in Albany, N.Y., the daughter of a file clerk who threw her abusive husband out of the house. "It has made me . . . a very strong, outspoken person who believes we need to provide the kind of funds so that abuse victims have a place to get away from the abuser," she said.

She married young, divorced and later married Harvey F. Waite, then a New York state trooper. For 17 years, she served as an aide in the New York state Senate. Even after her husband retired and the couple moved to Florida in 1985, she continued to commute to the job in New York, quitting only when her mother became ill and moved in with them in Florida.

Brown-Waite won election in 1990 to the Hernando County Board of Commissioners. She went on to serve a decade in the state Senate, rising to a leadership position and chairing major committees. She pushed bills to give patients more access to information through physician profiles and to tighten controls on health maintenance organizations. Her record on health care was marred, however, by a 2000 Tampa Tribune story about a too-cozy relationship with a Tampa HMO that paid her an annual salary of nearly $24,000 to "interpret" legislation that she'd had a hand in passing.

When term limits barred her from continuing in the state Senate, her GOP allies redrew the lines of Democratic U.S. Rep. Karen L. Thurman's district to favor a 2002 challenge by Brown-Waite. After an easy primary win, Brown-Waite won that November by a scant 2 percentage points. She has won re-election easily ever since. In 2008, she won by a 22 percentage-point margin, just months after her husband died. He had been battling prostate cancer.

At home, Brown-Waite's favorite getaway is cruising Florida's scenic coast in her red 1959 MG. But she said it is hard to find replacement parts for a vehicle that is almost 50 years old.

KEY VOTES

2008

No	Delay consideration of Colombia free-trade agreement
Yes	Override Bush veto of federal farm and nutrition programs reauthorization bill
?	Overhaul surveillance laws and permit dismissal of suits against companies that conducted warrantless wiretapping
?	Grant mortgage relief to homeowners and funding for Fannie Mae and Freddie Mac
No	Approve initial $700 billion program to stabilize financial markets
No	Approve final $700 billion program to stabilize financial markets
No	Provide $14 billion in loans to automakers

2007

Yes	Increase minimum wage by $2.10 an hour
No	Approve $124.2 billion in emergency war spending and set goal for redeployment of troops from Iraq
Yes	Reject federal contraceptive assistance to international family planning groups
Yes	Override Bush veto of $23.2 billion water projects authorization bill
Yes	Implement Peru free-trade agreement
Yes	Approve energy policy overhaul with new fuel economy standards
Yes	Clear $473.5 billion omnibus spending bill, including $70 billion for military operations

CQ VOTE STUDIES

	PARTY UNITY		PRESIDENTIAL SUPPORT	
	SUPPORT	OPPOSE	SUPPORT	OPPOSE
2008	87%	13%	60%	40%
2007	88%	12%	69%	31%
2006	89%	11%	90%	10%
2005	91%	9%	83%	17%
2004	95%	5%	87%	13%

INTEREST GROUPS

	AFL-CIO	ADA	CCUS	ACU
2008	31%	35%	79%	77%
2007	25%	20%	90%	72%
2006	29%	15%	87%	88%
2005	14%	10%	88%	87%
2004	14%	5%	100%	96%

FLORIDA 5
Northern west coast — Pasco, Hernando counties

Located north of Tampa on Florida's west coast, the 5th includes Hernando, Citrus and Sumter counties, as well as portions of Pasco and four other counties. The district takes in the southern half of Florida's Nature Coast along the Gulf of Mexico, and the district's eastern edge, in Lake County, extends to the greater Orlando area. Parts of Pasco and Lake counties serve as bedroom communities for Tampa and Orlando.

Tourism, integral to the 5th's economy, is centered on the Nature Coast. Gated communities and golf courses clustered on the coast served as havens for retirees, while the area's beaches, snorkeling spots and historic towns attract visitors. The Nature Coast also is home to numerous preserves and parks, which boast panthers, bears and manatees. A decline in tourism statewide has hurt the district's once robust economy.

Agriculture is a mainstay in the district's less developed areas. Levy County in the north depends on cattle, dairy and nuts, while the southeast part of the 5th relies on citrus. Industrial parks in Pasco and Hernando have hosted small manufacturing companies for years, but rising

unemployment here recently has affected the construction, retail and manufacturing sectors. Controlled growth was important to district residents for decades as the region expanded with a steady influx of retirees and young professionals, but a real estate market downturn and widespread job loss has halted much of that growth.

Social Security, prescription drugs and veterans' affairs dominate politics in the 5th, where more than one-fourth of residents are 65 or older. The 5th's electorate is largely conservative, especially on fiscal issues. Republicans outnumber Democrats in voter registration — although many Democrats are conservative Southern Democrats — and 26 percent of voters are registered independents. John McCain took 56 percent of the 5th's 2008 presidential vote.

MAJOR INDUSTRY
Tourism, service, agriculture, health care, manufacturing

CITIES
Spring Hill (unincorporated), 69,078; Land O' Lakes (unincorporated), 20,971

NOTABLE
Weeki Wachee Springs water park, established in 1947, is known for its live, underwater performances by "mermaids."

Rep. Cliff Stearns (R)

Elected 1988; 11th term

CAPITOL OFFICE
225-5744
www.house.gov/stearns
2370 Rayburn Bldg. 20515-0906; fax 225-3973

COMMITTEES
Energy & Commerce
Veterans' Affairs

RESIDENCE
Ocala

BORN
April 16, 1941; Washington, D.C.

RELIGION
Presbyterian

FAMILY
Wife, Joan Stearns; three children

EDUCATION
George Washington U., B.S. 1963
(electrical engineering)

MILITARY SERVICE
Air Force 1963-67

CAREER
Hotel and restaurant executive; advertising
account executive

POLITICAL HIGHLIGHTS
No previous office

ELECTION RESULTS

2008 GENERAL

Cliff Stearns (R)	228,302	60.9%
Tim Cunha (D)	146,655	39.1%

2008 PRIMARY

Cliff Stearns (R)	unopposed

2006 GENERAL

Cliff Stearns (R)	136,601	59.9%
David E. Bruderly (D)	91,528	40.1%

PREVIOUS WINNING PERCENTAGES
2004 (64%); 2002 (65%); 2000 (100%); 1998 (100%);
1996 (67%); 1994 (99%); 1992 (65%); 1990 (59%);
1988 (53%)

Stearns may take inspiration from Moses and Ronald Reagan and display a penchant for quixotic crusades, but he is also a pragmatist who does not allow his conservative ideology to stand in the way of negotiation to achieve a legislative goal.

He receives top ratings from conservative groups for his positions on their issues — tight fiscal policies, gun rights, abortion and pornography. He credits Reagan's dominance of national politics in the 1980s with his decision to join the GOP. As a businessman in Florida, he said he took from Reagan "the belief in the importance of freedom and the opportunity to choose, free markets and owning your own property." But he has an inclusive style and does his homework.

Stearns is a member of the Energy and Commerce Committee, where he has made clear his distaste for regulation. At a November 2007 drafting of Consumer Product Safety Commission legislation, he said requiring new regulations for an industry with voluntary product standards would reduce the industry's willingness to develop its own benchmarks. "I owned a business and I know the burden of unnecessary regulations," said Stearns, who owned a hotel and restaurant management business for nearly 30 years.

But Stearns had no doubts about extending indefinitely the do-not-call registry under which phone customers are shielded from unwanted solicitation calls. "This is one of the most popular laws we've ever enacted," he said in October 2007. Stearns won approval of his proposal — which was included in a bill President George W. Bush signed in 2008 — to extend funding for the program indefinitely instead of through 2012 as originally proposed.

Stearns in 2009 became ranking Republican on the Energy and Commerce panel on Communications, Technology and the Internet. He joined the full committee's ranking GOP member, Joe L. Barton of Texas, in unsuccessfully arguing against a delay for the February 2009 date for switching to digital television. They said changing the date would confuse consumers and burden TV stations that were prepared to turn off their analog feeds.

Stearns has been at the center of efforts to bolster data security on the Internet. But he has found himself at odds with the panel's liberal Democrats on other issues, including so-called network neutrality, under which Internet service providers would be barred from imposing restrictions or conditions on subscribers' use. Stearns criticized a 2008 bill by Massachusetts Democrat Edward J. Markey that many said failed to reach a middle ground. The bill essentially aimed to declare that the Internet should remain open and free of interference by network operators, and to urge the Federal Communications Commission to assess broadband services and consumer rights. Stearns said the measure was more than merely a study and would not allow for "legitimate network management."

To help car buyers, he re-introduced legislation in 2009 to require vehicle identification numbers of totaled vehicles to be sent immediately to car history databases to give consumers better data on salvaged or flooded cars.

He also advocates setting national standards for the protection and care of racehorses. Stearns developed concerns about the welfare of racehorses following the death of Eight Belles at the 2008 Kentucky Derby and the death of Barbaro, the Derby winner in 2006. Both horses had sustained career-ending injuries and had to be put down immediately after the races.

As a member of the Veterans' Affairs Committee, Stearns in 2008 backed bills to expand GI benefits, boosting educational benefits and providing a monthly housing stipend — provisions of which were included in the war spending bill sent to the president in July. When he was chairman of the committee's Health panel from 1997 through 2000, he won passage of a bill to improve access to long-term care for disabled veterans and expanded the Veterans Affairs Department's obligation to provide alternatives to nursing home care.

A fiscal conservative, Stearns earns plaudits from budget watchdog groups. When he does stray from the party line, it is because he objects to the price tag. He opposed in fall 2008 two $700 billion bills — the second of which became law — aimed at shoring up the financial services sector, saying the proposal "puts taxpayers at risk with little or no benefit."

But he will sometimes side with Democrats. He backed a 2007 increase in the minimum wage as well as bills in 2008 to prevent a cut in payments to physicians treating Medicare patients and a requirement for health insurers to cover mental illness the same as other medical conditions.

Stearns' conservative credentials go far back. He was the chief sponsor of a bill enacted in 2005 that shields firearms manufacturers and dealers from liability lawsuits when their products are used in crimes. In the 108th Congress (2003-04), he championed a provision to make it easier for the FCC to fine individual performers for indecent actions.

The son of a Justice Department lawyer, Stearns was born and raised in Washington, D.C., where he was a basketball and track star at Woodrow Wilson High School. He attended George Washington University on an Air Force ROTC scholarship. After graduation, he was stationed at Vandenberg Air Force base in California, serving four years as a specialist in aerospace engineering and satellite reconnaissance.

When he got out of the service, Stearns worked in advertising before he took over a dilapidated motel in Massachusetts and renovated it. In the 1970s, spotting what he viewed as an undervalued Howard Johnson motel for sale in northern Florida, Stearns moved to the Sunshine State. He built a small motel and restaurant management business in Ocala that ultimately employed 120 people. He served on the board of the Monroe, Fla., regional hospital and was director of the local Chamber of Commerce.

In 1988, Stearns ran for an open U.S. House seat and, through his local alliances and political savvy, was able to win the Republican nomination.

Though he was an underdog in the general election against Democratic state House Speaker Jon Mills, Stearns' limited political background gave him a salient, populist theme, as he called himself "a citizen congressman." In his last nine elections, he has captured at least 60 percent of the vote.

KEY VOTES

2008
No Delay consideration of Colombia free-trade agreement

No Override Bush veto of federal farm and nutrition programs reauthorization bill

Yes Overhaul surveillance laws and permit dismissal of suits against companies that conducted warrantless wiretapping

No Grant mortgage relief to homeowners and funding for Fannie Mae and Freddie Mac

No Approve initial $700 billion program to stabilize financial markets

No Approve final $700 billion program to stabilize financial markets

No Provide $14 billion in loans to automakers

2007
Yes Increase minimum wage by $2.10 an hour

No Approve $124.2 billion in emergency war spending and set goal for redeployment of troops from Iraq

Yes Reject federal contraceptive assistance to international family planning groups

No Override Bush veto of $23.2 billion water projects authorization bill

Yes Implement Peru free-trade agreement

No Approve energy policy overhaul with new fuel economy standards

Yes Clear $473.5 billion omnibus spending bill, including $70 billion for military operations

CQ VOTE STUDIES

	PARTY UNITY		PRESIDENTIAL SUPPORT	
	SUPPORT	OPPOSE	SUPPORT	OPPOSE
2008	97%	3%	76%	24%
2007	94%	6%	81%	19%
2006	93%	7%	85%	15%
2005	94%	6%	87%	13%
2004	96%	4%	85%	15%

INTEREST GROUPS

	AFL-CIO	ADA	CCUS	ACU
2008	13%	15%	89%	100%
2007	13%	5%	80%	92%
2006	21%	10%	93%	96%
2005	33%	10%	89%	88%
2004	20%	0%	100%	96%

FLORIDA 6

North central — parts of Jacksonville, Gainesville and Ocala

The landlocked and boomerang-shaped 6th District takes in large swaths of rural territory along with suburbs of northern cities. Stretching from western Duval County (Jacksonville), the district takes in portions of Gainesville before swinging southeast into Marion County. The 6th's southern tip is along the western shore of Lake Harris in Leesburg, which is within Orlando's sphere in central Florida.

The 6th contains three regions with distinct interests. The northern end, centered in Jacksonville (shared with the 3rd and 4th districts), is heavily influenced by the military and the city's busy port. Gainesville, in the middle of the district and shared with the 3rd, is home to the University of Florida and the Malcolm Randall VA Medical Center, a major veterans' hospital. The area south of Ocala, famed for its thoroughbred horse farms, is a haven for retirees and roughly an hour from either Florida coast. Gainesville has mostly escaped the widespread unemployment and real estate market collapse that Ocala has experienced.

The district includes all of two small counties — Gilchrist and Bradford — and parts of six others, including Alachua (Gainesville) and Marion (Ocala), each of which contains about one-fourth of the 6th's population. Alachua is the biggest Democratic outpost in the district, while Republicans have their strongest registration edge in the Clay County Jacksonville suburbs and exurbs west of the St. Johns River. The district's political agenda is dominated by defense interests.

The 6th is firmly conservative, and although the GOP maintains a clear edge in most federal races, registered Republicans maintain only a slight advantage over Democrats. Regardless of party affiliation, voters are willing to support some moderate Democratic candidates. John McCain took 56 percent of the district's vote in the 2008 presidential election — 5 percentage points less than George W. Bush won in 2004.

MAJOR INDUSTRY
Higher education, defense, health care, agriculture

CITIES
Jacksonville (pt.), 86,846; Gainesville (pt.), 59,907; Lakeside (unincorporated), 30,927; Ocala (pt.), 29,559

NOTABLE
The University of Florida hosts the Florida Museum of Natural History.

Rep. John L. Mica (R)

Elected 1992; 9th term

CAPITOL OFFICE
225-4035
www.house.gov/mica
2313 Rayburn Bldg. 20515-0907; fax 226-0821

COMMITTEES
Oversight & Government Reform
Transportation & Infrastructure - ranking member

RESIDENCE
Winter Park

BORN
Jan. 27, 1943; Binghamton, N.Y.

RELIGION
Episcopalian

FAMILY
Wife, Pat Mica; two children

EDUCATION
Miami-Dade Community College, A.A. 1965;
U. of Florida, B.A. 1967 (political science &
education)

CAREER
Cellular telephone company executive; lobbyist;
trade consultant; real estate investor;
congressional aide;

POLITICAL HIGHLIGHTS
Fla. House, 1976-80; Republican nominee
for Fla. Senate, 1980

ELECTION RESULTS

2008 GENERAL
John L. Mica (R)	238,721	62.0%
Faye Armitage (D)	146,292	38.0%

2008 PRIMARY
John L. Mica (R)	unopposed

2006 GENERAL
John L. Mica (R)	149,656	63.1%
John F. Chagnon (D)	87,584	36.9%

PREVIOUS WINNING PERCENTAGES
2004 (100%); 2002 (60%); 2000 (63%); 1998 (100%);
1996 (62%); 1994 (73%); 1992 (56%)

To Mica, who has few interests outside his job in Congress, it's all about politics. And even while he holds a minority seat during a time of intense partisanship, he finds ways to bridge divides on his top issue: transportation.

He's generally a loyal party supporter on other issues. But when it comes to getting funding for transportation projects — especially those that will benefit his district — he will do what it takes to get the money to flow.

As the top Republican on the powerful Transportation and Infrastructure Committee, Mica (MY-cah) has a close working relationship with Chairman James L. Oberstar of Minnesota. He frequently served as the committee's liaison to the George W. Bush administration, more often seeking to persuade Bush to see the committee's point of view rather than the other way around. He said he often found the administration unduly rigid.

With a Democrat in the White House, he may actually see more progress on some of his goals. Early on he saw promise in President Obama's interest in infrastructure funding to help jump-start the economy, and was encouraged that Obama might help guide his goal for high-speed rail around the country. But he doesn't always agree with Obama's methods.

At the start of 2009, Mica was unsatisfied with a $787 billion economic stimulus plan Obama signed into law, saying it didn't provide enough improvements to infrastructure, and he voted against it. But he was happy the bill included $8 billion for high-speed rail projects, and issued press releases saying it would help finance a commuter train project in his Central Florida district.

That February, Transportation Secretary Ray LaHood said he had submitted a report to Obama on a plan for high-speed passenger rail service across the country. He said Obama recognized funding would have to go well beyond that provided in the stimulus package. Mica was thrilled. "If we could put a man on the moon, we should be able to move people from city to city quickly instead of wasting time on a congested highway," he said. "I applaud President Obama's recognition that high-speed rail should be part of America's future."

In 2008, Mica worked with Oberstar to advance through the House a long-stalled five-year reauthorization of Amtrak, the nation's passenger rail system, which called for major new investments in the railroad. It also included a provision Mica initially drafted to allow private companies to bid on a high-speed rail project to connect Washington, D.C., and New York City.

Bush, with the support of Republicans when they held the House majority, had long targeted Amtrak for budget cuts. Amtrak usually ended up with just enough funding to limp along. Mica worked for weeks on negotiations on the final $13 billion bill, pushing for the high-speed rail language to be retained and successfully persuading Bush not to veto the measure.

It wasn't the first time he swayed the panel in a direction opposed to Bush's. In 2007, all but one of the panel's 34 Republicans — including a jubilant Mica — joined unified Democrats in voting to override Bush's veto of a bill drafted by the committee that authorized about $23.2 billion in navigation, flood control and environmental restoration projects around the country. "I loved it," Mica said of the override battle. (The water resources bill became the first law enacted over Bush's veto.)

Mica's committee will get a chance to take a closer look at transportation projects when it tackles an overhaul of the 2005 law that governs spending on highways, bridges and mass transit. But funding could still be a problem. Mica previously had said he wouldn't consider one solution advocated by a bipartisan commission in the 110th Congress (2007-08): a big increase in the 18.4-cents-per-gallon federal gasoline tax, unchanged since 1993. That idea, he said, does not stand a "snowball's chance in hell" of passing Congress. But as the economic crisis worsened in early 2009, he said he might support a second commission recommendation: indexing an increase on the tax to inflation. Ultimately, Mica — who envisions a $1.5 trillion multiyear spending package — wants to combine federal tax revenues, public-private partnerships and bond financing.

The committee also must reauthorize the Federal Aviation Administration and modernize the nation's air traffic control system. An FAA overhaul stalled in the 110th Congress due to an impasse over financing for the upgrades. Mica, who chaired the Aviation Subcommittee before the Democrats took over, voted against the FAA bill in the 110th Congress because he vehemently opposed two labor-related provisions.

After the Sept. 11 terrorist attacks, Mica's subcommittee became a hub of new security measures that have changed the way Americans travel. He championed the effort to arm airline pilots and helped write the law establishing the Transportation Security Administration under the Homeland Security Department. But he has criticized the agency repeatedly for being unresponsive to local concerns and slow to utilize high technology.

Mica is also a senior member of the Oversight and Government Reform panel, but his work on Transportation absorbs most of his time and energy.

He says he has no particular recreational interests. "I'm a pretty dull guy," he said. "I don't have a lot of hobby activities. But I love politics."

Mica calls Florida home now, but he grew up in upstate New York. After years of trips back and forth, the family settled in Florida when Mica was high school age. His father's health was poor, and Mica and his brothers interrupted their schooling to work and help support the family.

Mica's other family members are largely Democrats, including his brother Daniel A. Mica, who served in the House from 1979 to 1989. His other brother worked for Lawton Chiles, a former Democratic U.S. senator and Florida governor. But the first campaign Mica worked in was Republican Richard Nixon's 1960 presidential race against John F. Kennedy.

Mica served in the state legislature from 1976 to 1980, then came to Washington as chief of staff for GOP Sen. Paula Hawkins. After Hawkins lost her re-election bid in 1986, Mica turned to business ventures, including international trade consulting and the cellular telephone business, and became a millionaire. In 1992, GOP Rep. Craig T. James decided not to seek a third term, and Mica went after the seat. He won by 13 percentage points and has been re-elected easily ever since.

KEY VOTES

2008
No   Delay consideration of Colombia free-trade agreement
No   Override Bush veto of federal farm and nutrition programs reauthorization bill
Yes Overhaul surveillance laws and permit dismissal of suits against companies that conducted warrantless wiretapping
No   Grant mortgage relief to homeowners and funding for Fannie Mae and Freddie Mac
No   Approve initial $700 billion program to stabilize financial markets
No   Approve final $700 billion program to stabilize financial markets
No   Provide $14 billion in loans to automakers

2007
No   Increase minimum wage by $2.10 an hour
No   Approve $124.2 billion in emergency war spending and set goal for redeployment of troops from Iraq
Yes Reject federal contraceptive assistance to international family planning groups
Yes Override Bush veto of $23.2 billion water projects authorization bill
Yes Implement Peru free-trade agreement
No   Approve energy policy overhaul with new fuel economy standards
Yes Clear $473.5 billion omnibus spending bill, including $70 billion for military operations

CQ VOTE STUDIES

	PARTY UNITY		PRESIDENTIAL SUPPORT	
	SUPPORT	OPPOSE	SUPPORT	OPPOSE
2008	93%	7%	77%	23%
2007	97%	3%	83%	17%
2006	99%	1%	95%	5%
2005	97%	3%	91%	9%
2004	95%	5%	85%	15%

INTEREST GROUPS

	AFL-CIO	ADA	CCUS	ACU
2008	0%	10%	94%	100%
2007	4%	5%	89%	100%
2006	14%	0%	100%	92%
2005	7%	0%	92%	100%
2004	13%	0%	100%	84%

FLORIDA 7
East — St. John's County, Daytona Beach

The 7th parallels Interstate 95 from southeast of Jacksonville to northern Daytona Beach, where it turns to follow Interstate 4 southwest into the Orlando area. It includes all of Flagler and St. Johns counties, as well as much of Volusia County, parts of Putnam and Seminole counties, and a tiny sliver of Orange County. Two-fifths of the district's population lives in Volusia, mostly between Ormond Beach and Daytona Beach.

A steady influx of people into the 7th spurred the district's economy in recent years and pushed growth-management issues to the top of the local agenda. Retirees flocked to once-small towns near the ocean, drawing retail shops but not as many larger employers. A growing aerospace industry near Daytona Beach, helped by Embry-Riddle Aeronautical University, has broadened the tourism-based economy. But, layoffs, fewer visitors to area hotels and resorts, and a housing market collapse have hurt the district's economy.

Once a major agricultural area, Seminole County now serves as the suburban home to middle- and upper-class Orlando commuters and their

families. But some inland portions maintain an agrarian heritage, especially in bucolic Flagler County. The Daytona Beach area still attracts millions of visitors annually, and although its popularity as a spring break destination for college students has decreased, it draws bikers and race car fans to its beaches and sporting events, including the Daytona 500 stock car race, which is held in the nearby 24th District.

Although Republicans hold a slight registration edge and have won the 7th's presidential vote since 1992, some moderate Democratic candidates also have success with voters here, and the district is home to many independent voters. Republican John McCain took 53 percent of the presidential vote here in 2008.

MAJOR INDUSTRY
Tourism, aerospace, service

CITIES
Daytona Beach (pt.), 53,629; Deltona, 47,033; Ormond Beach, 36,301; Palm Coast, 32,732; Wekiwa Springs (unincorporated), 23,169

NOTABLE
Jackie Robinson Ballpark is a minor league stadium in Daytona Beach where Robinson was the first black baseball player to play in a spring training game.

Rep. Alan Grayson (D)

Elected 2008; 1st term

CAPITOL OFFICE
225-2176
grayson.house.gov
1605 Longworth Bldg. 20515-0908; fax 225-0999

COMMITTEES
Financial Services
Science & Technology

RESIDENCE
Orlando

BORN
March 13, 1958; Bronx, N.Y.

RELIGION
Jewish

FAMILY
Wife, Lolita Grayson; five children

EDUCATION
Harvard U., A.B. 1978 (urban studies), M.P.P. 1983, J.D. 1983

CAREER
Lawyer; telecommunications company owner

POLITICAL HIGHLIGHTS
Sought Democratic nomination for U.S. House, 2006

ELECTION RESULTS

2008 GENERAL

Alan Grayson (D)	172,854	52.0%
Ric Keller (R)	159,490	48.0%

2008 PRIMARY

Alan Grayson (D)	16,104	48.5%
Charlie Stuart (D)	9,146	27.5%
Mike Smith (D)	5,727	17.2%
Quoc Ba Van (D)	1,219	3.7%
Alexander Fry (D)	1,030	3.1%

With his cowboy boots and ready grin, Grayson comes across as an easy-going character. But he quickly turns serious, ready to get to work — and he knows he has little time to prove himself in Congress.

After he ousted Republican Ric Keller, Grayson said he put his new-member badge on his bureau every night for a month, so he could wake up looking at it in the morning. Republicans targeted the vulnerable central Florida seat within weeks of his victory, but to thwart them, Grayson has worked to bring home more federal dollars. He backed the $787 billion economic stimulus bill in early 2009 and proudly touted the millions it provided to his Orlando-based district for highways, transit and schools.

He serves on the Financial Services Committee, where he has sharply criticized the Treasury Department's management of the $700 billion financial rescue plan enacted in October 2008. An attorney who specialized in government contracting law and representing whistleblowers, he won notice from The Wall Street Journal for "waging a one-man war against contractor fraud in Iraq."

Grayson sits on the Space and Aeronautics Subcommittee of the Science and Technology Committee. Aerospace is one of his district's major industries, with Lockheed Martin and the University of Central Florida's Institute for Simulation and Training serving as economic boosters for the area.

On the House floor, Grayson looks to make legislative issues personal. In his first speech, he urged passage of legislation reauthorizing and expanding the State Children's Health Insurance Program, which covers children whose families do not qualify for Medicaid. The measure became law. "I was a very sick child," he told the House. "I had to go to the hospital four times a week for treatment. If it weren't for my parents' union health benefits, I would not be here today for this vote."

Grayson's campaign against Keller left him with a campaign debt of more than $2.7 million. But personally, Grayson is one of the wealthier members of Congress, reporting a net worth of about $29 million — much of it from a telecommunications company and Internet company he founded.

FLORIDA 8

Central — most of Orlando

One of Florida's few landlocked districts, the 8th is powered by the presence of Walt Disney World, Sea World and Universal Studios' resort in the Orlando area. The district surrounds western Orlando and includes upscale parts of the region, much of the city's downtown area, and the Walt Disney World complex. It then pushes north to take in parts of Lake and Marion counties.

Local tourism relies on out-of-state visitors and is vulnerable to economic slowdowns, but the industry is the 8th's undisputed economic leader. The local economy has broadened to include a technology sector headed by Oracle and defense and aerospace contractor Lockheed Martin. New health care and medical research facilities in the southern part of the district may help insulate the 8th District.

Economic growth and redevelopment of downtown Orlando brought office parks and upscale condominiums to the city. A housing market collapse hurt the more well-to-do areas of the district, but a declining cost of living and plummeting home values have made once out-of-reach areas available for some of the tourism-based workforce.

Residents of suburban Orange County tend to back Republicans on social and economic issues. The 8th's population here is younger, wealthier and more educated than in most Florida districts, and the county's Hispanic population, which is mostly of Democratic-leaning Puerto Rican heritage, has put the county within political reach of Democratic candidates. Barack Obama won 52 percent of the district's presidential vote in 2008.

MAJOR INDUSTRY
Tourism, technology, aerospace

CITIES
Orlando (pt.), 123,842; Ocoee (pt.), 23,591

NOTABLE
There are more than 100 lakes in the Orlando metropolitan area.

Rep. Gus Bilirakis (R)

Elected 2006; 2nd term

CAPITOL OFFICE
225-5755
bilirakis.house.gov
1124 Longworth Bldg. 20515-0909; fax 225-4085

COMMITTEES
Foreign Affairs
Homeland Security
Veterans' Affairs

RESIDENCE
Palm Harbor

BORN
Feb. 8, 1963; Gainesville, Fla.

RELIGION
Greek Orthodox

FAMILY
Wife, Eva Bilirakis; four children

EDUCATION
St. Petersburg Junior College, attended 1981-83;
U. of Florida, B.A. 1986 (political science);
Stetson U., J.D. 1989

CAREER
Lawyer; college instructor

POLITICAL HIGHLIGHTS
Fla. House, 1998-2006

ELECTION RESULTS

2008 GENERAL

Gus Bilirakis (R)	216,591	62.2%
Bill Mitchell (D)	126,346	36.3%
John "Johnny K" Kalimnios (X)	3,394	1.0%

2008 PRIMARY

Gus Bilirakis (R)	unopposed

2006 GENERAL

Gus Bilirakis (R)	123,016	55.9%
Phyllis Busansky (D)	96,978	44.1%

Bilirakis has the same unassuming demeanor as his father, former GOP Rep. Michael Bilirakis, a popular pragmatist who represented the Tampa-area district for 24 years before all but bequeathing it to his son in 2006. A lawyer who specialized in estate planning, the younger Bilirakis has continued his father's work on health care issues.

But Gus Bilirakis (bil-uh-RACK-iss) also has focused on security concerns as a member of the Foreign Affairs and Homeland Security committees. He is the only Floridian on Homeland Security; in 2009 he became ranking member on its Management, Investigations and Oversight Subcomittee. The job enables him to investigate operations of an agency that lawmakers in both parties agree has had trouble finding its way since its establishment in 2003. He told the Tampa Tribune the assignment is "not flashy" but important to the nation's defense against terrorism.

In 2008, he sponsored a bill, passed by the House, to authorize a Coast Guard pilot program to test mobile biometric screening systems to verify that people on boats are not attempting to enter the United States unlawfully. The Senate never took up the measure, and he reintroduced similar legislation in 2009.

Bilirakis also championed legislation to create a nationwide "Silver Alert" system to help find missing senior citizens, much like the Amber Alert for missing children. His proposal was incorporated into other legislation that passed the House but not the Senate. The House passed similar legislation in February 2009.

On Foreign Affairs, Bilirakis supported the George W. Bush administration's approach to the Iraq War. He sponsored a measure that became the basis for a House-passed resolution in September 2008 condemning Middle East-based media for broadcasting terrorism recruitment videos and other incitements to violence. The Senate never took up the measure.

Like his father, he is a champion of Greek causes and periodically takes to the House floor to criticize the Turks who control northern Cyprus.

Most of the time, though, Bilirakis prefers to work behind the scenes, moving his priorities forward by way of amendments on legislation and by building friendships with other lawmakers. He has described himself as "a consensus builder." He did once call attention to himself, though it was for a noble cause: He and his staff shaved their heads and went bald for a few days in 2007 as part of a fundraiser for cancer research. "I would love to see everyone shave their heads in D.C.," he told the St. Petersburg Times.

On Veterans' Affairs, Bilirakis has pressed for bills to boost veterans' benefits and to provide tax incentives for businesses that hire reservists or National Guard members.

Bilirakis is generally a loyal Republican vote. He joined many of his GOP colleagues in opposing two bills to aid the ailing financial services industry in fall 2008 — the second of which became law. And he stuck with his party in voting against President Obama's $787 billion economic stimulus legislation in February 2009. He said the measure, which became law, "is simply a long wish list of big government spending" that "will hand a huge 'IOU' to our children and grandchildren."

He has strayed from the GOP leadership on some issues. He supported the 2007 increase in the minimum wage and the following year's legislation to prevent a scheduled cut in Medicare payments to physicians and to have insurers treat mental illness the same as any other illness. He opposes oil drilling in Alaska's Arctic National Wildlife Refuge and supports a buffer on drilling around Florida's coast.

Bilirakis grew up in Tarpon Springs, a resort town where his ancestors settled after leaving Greece a century ago. Bilirakis says he always wanted to follow his father's example of a career in politics. He attended public schools, then studied at a community college in St. Petersburg before finishing his undergraduate degree at the University of Florida with a major in political science. After getting a law degree from the Stetson College of Law, he worked in his father's Palm Harbor practice.

Bilirakis' first foray into electoral politics on his own was a successful run in 1998 for the seat representing Tampa in the state House. He didn't have much in the way of competition. His Democratic opponent was a self-described legal assistant who would not divulge her place of business and, during the campaign, made the bizarre claim that the real Gus Bilirakis had died and was being represented by an imposter she called Danny DeVito. She was denounced by the local Democratic party and Bilirakis went on to easily win the seat. "My wife wishes it was Tom Cruise, not Danny DeVito," Bilirakis jokingly recalled.

During his eight years in legislature, he chaired committees on crime prevention and public safety.

His opportunity to move up to the U.S. House came in 2006 with his father's retirement. Bilirakis breezed past his primary opponent, but the general-election campaign was tougher. Democrats targeted the district as a potential takeover and put up Phyllis Busansky, a former Hillsborough County commissioner with a solid reputation for innovative local programs.

She was also a strong fundraiser, attracting more than $1.4 million for her race although Bilirakis outraised her significantly with $2.6 million. Republicans also sent in a bevy of blockbuster political names to boost Bilirakis' efforts, including Bush, Vice President Dick Cheney and House Speaker J. Dennis Hastert. Bilirakis also was helped immeasurably by his name recognition and a political legacy from his father, who rarely faced a serious Democratic challenge and ran unopposed four times. Bilirakis won by a convincing 12 percentage points.

His 2008 opponent was Bill Mitchell, a Navy veteran and lawyer who led an investigation into offshore drilling practices as a Federal Trade Commission attorney in the 1970s. He criticized Bilirakis' vote against the financial rescue and said the congressman did not exercise leadership on economic issues. But he couldn't compete financially with Bilirakis, who raised five times as much money and won with 62 percent of the vote.

KEY VOTES

2008

No   Delay consideration of Colombia free-trade agreement

Yes   Override Bush veto of federal farm and nutrition programs reauthorization bill

Yes   Overhaul surveillance laws and permit dismissal of suits against companies that conducted warrantless wiretapping

No   Grant mortgage relief to homeowners and funding for Fannie Mae and Freddie Mac

No   Approve initial $700 billion program to stabilize financial markets

No   Approve final $700 billion program to stabilize financial markets

No   Provide $14 billion in loans to automakers

2007

Yes   Increase minimum wage by $2.10 an hour

No   Approve $124.2 billion in emergency war spending and set goal for redeployment of troops from Iraq

Yes   Reject federal contraceptive assistance to international family planning groups

Yes   Override Bush veto of $23.2 billion water projects authorization bill

Yes   Implement Peru free-trade agreement

Yes   Approve energy policy overhaul with new fuel economy standards

Yes   Clear $473.5 billion omnibus spending bill, including $70 billion for military operations

CQ VOTE STUDIES

	PARTY UNITY		PRESIDENTIAL SUPPORT	
	SUPPORT	OPPOSE	SUPPORT	OPPOSE
2008	89%	11%	63%	37%
2007	90%	10%	71%	29%

INTEREST GROUPS

	AFL-CIO	ADA	CCUS	ACU
2008	13%	30%	83%	88%
2007	29%	20%	90%	80%

FLORIDA 9

West — suburbs north of Tampa

Suburban and rural areas northwest of Tampa Bay and St. Petersburg form the bulk of Florida's mostly residential 9th District, which encompasses coastal areas of Pinellas and Pasco counties as well as a large chunk of mostly suburban Hillsborough County.

With a large number of retirees from the North, one-fifth of the population is 65 or older. Clearwater (shared with the 10th) is known as a beach resort and is the "spiritual headquarters" of the Church of Scientology, which has a large community here. Palm Harbor and Tarpon Springs have long-established Greek Orthodox populations.

For decades, the 9th's economy was driven by tourism, fueled by "snowbirds" who spend winters here and visitors to its beaches. Plant City is the exception, as families move in from out of state and settle in the mid-size city. Many year-round residents commute to nearby Tampa or St. Petersburg. Explosive growth in Hillsborough, Pasco, and Pinellas counties encouraged a local real estate boom that has since collapsed. Service-oriented industries had supplemented the construction and hospi-

tality industries, but layoffs in retail sectors have hurt the 9th's once-growing economy. Hillsborough was hit particularly hard by the recent housing market crisis: the county had the fifth-highest foreclosure rate in the state, and one of the highest in the nation, in 2008.

The 9th District has long been a home for mostly GOP retirees, and Republicans retain an edge here due to their dominance in Hillsborough. Many of the county's most heavily Republican precincts are in the 9th despite a strong lean in favor of Democratic candidates in Hillsborough overall. The district's part of Pinellas also is decidedly Republican, while the two parties are nearly even in registration in its share of Pasco County. In 2008, Republican John McCain won the district with 52 percent of its presidential vote.

MAJOR INDUSTRY
Tourism, service, health care, technology

CITIES
Clearwater (pt.), 79,189; Palm Harbor (unincorporated) (pt.), 30,806

NOTABLE
Tarpon Springs, still known as the "Sponge Capital of the World," was settled in the late 19th century by Greek immigrants who came to dive for the natural sponges.

Rep. C.W. Bill Young (R)

Elected 1970; 20th term

CAPITOL OFFICE
225-5961
www.house.gov/young
2407 Rayburn Bldg. 20515-0910; fax 225-9764

COMMITTEES
Appropriations

RESIDENCE
Indian Shores

BORN
Dec. 16, 1930; Harmarville, Pa.

RELIGION
Methodist

FAMILY
Wife, Beverly Young; six children

EDUCATION
St. Petersburg H.S., graduated 1948

MILITARY SERVICE
Fla. National Guard 1948-57

CAREER
Insurance executive; public official

POLITICAL HIGHLIGHTS
Fla. Senate, 1960-70 (minority leader, 1966-70)

ELECTION RESULTS

2008 GENERAL

C.W. Bill Young (R)	182,781	60.7%
Bob Hackworth (D)	118,430	39.3%

2008 PRIMARY

C.W. Bill Young (R)	unopposed

2006 GENERAL

C.W. Bill Young (R)	131,488	65.9%
Samm Simpson (D)	67,950	34.1%

PREVIOUS WINNING PERCENTAGES
2004 (69%); 2002 (100%); 2000 (76%); 1998 (100%);
1996 (67%); 1994 (100%); 1992 (57%); 1990 (100%);
1988 (73%); 1986 (100%); 1984 (80%); 1982 (100%);
1980 (100%); 1978 (79%); 1976 (65%); 1974 (76%);
1972 (76%); 1970 (67%)

Young is the House's longest-serving Republican, having succeeded in his political and legislative quests primarily by using friendliness as a secret weapon. Now in his late 70s, he has worked closely with his Democratic colleagues over the years, especially on the tight-knit Appropriations Committee, where he has specialized in funneling billions of dollars to the Defense Department and millions to his constituents.

Young's typically non-confrontational style personifies the go-along, get-along culture of Appropriations, where there is an unwritten agreement to accede to others' parochial spending projects in exchange for their approval of yours. But his manner is also the product of 24 years in the House minority before the GOP takeover in 1995. He learned then that working with Democrats was a prerequisite for getting legislation passed.

When Republicans took the majority, Speaker Newt Gingrich skipped over Young and two other senior members for the Appropriations chairmanship because they were considered too willing to hike spending. Young settled for chairing the Defense Subcommittee. When he finally got the full panel's gavel in 1999, he allowed conservatives to dominate the early stages of budget negotiations until legislative reality — the need to gain Democratic President Clinton's signature — set in. Clinton refused to sign bills he said cut spending too far, so Young and the GOP met his demands.

Term limits forced him back to the panel's chair in 2005, a slot he held until the Democratic takeover in 2007. He's now the full panel's top-ranking Republican. But it doesn't matter whether he or Pennsylvania Democrat John P. Murtha is chairman of the Defense panel; they're a bipartisan team. With panel members from both parties, they gave a green light to the defense buildup that followed the Sept. 11 attacks, directing hundreds of billions of dollars to the Pentagon for its regular operations and wars in Iraq and Afghanistan.

The pair also has teamed up with their Appropriations colleagues to obtain earmarks — spending targeted for special projects in a particular district or state. Murtha and Young far outpace their House colleagues in this regard. Taxpayers for Common Sense reported that in the fiscal 2008 spending bills, Young ranked third to Mississippi Republican Roger Wicker and Murtha in obtaining earmarks, netting $169 million for 87 projects.

In September 2008, Congress cleared a stopgap 2009 spending bill that included thousands of earmarks worth billions of dollars, according to the watchdog group. Young called the abbreviated appropriations process of the year "terrible" but said he's happy to get his earmarks. "A lot of these projects are related to the national defense needs," he said. "These things are going to be done somewhere, so my attitude is, why not in my district?" Following a devastating quartet of hurricanes in 2004, Young delivered more than $13 billion in federal aid, mostly for his state. With the presidential election approaching that year, Young persuaded the George W. Bush administration to increase its relief request by almost $2 billion.

The practice of earmarking has brought Young scrutiny back home. In 2008, he confirmed a St. Petersburg Times report that he had directed $44.6 million since fiscal 2004 to a Florida defense contractor that employs his son Patrick, and $28.6 million over nine years to another firm that employs his son Billy. Young told the paper the earmarks were worthy of federal funding regardless of the fact his sons worked for those companies.

But Young took a more cautious approach when the House in late 2008 took up two bills — the second of which became law — to provide $700 billion to shore up the nation's financial sector. He told the Times' editorial board the legislation was rushed to a vote without proper scrutiny.

Young breaks with the party's dominant conservatives on several key issues. He has supported a minimum wage increase, a ban on semiautomatic assault-style weapons, and protection of Florida's beaches from erosion and offshore oil and gas drilling. And when he chaired Appropriations, he resisted demands that chairmen raise large amounts of political cash for the party.

Young also sits in the Military Construction- Veterans Affairs Appropriations Subcommittee, where he works to deliver aid to wounded veterans. He and his wife, Beverly, regularly visit wounded service personnel at National Naval Medical Center in Bethesda, Md., or Walter Reed Army Medical Center in Washington, D.C. Nonetheless, Young found himself on the defensive in 2007 when concerns arose about mismanagement and soldiers' poor living conditions at Walter Reed. Young said he knew of the problems as early as 2003, but that he preferred to privately confront the hospital commander rather than go public or wield his appropriator's clout.

Young also works to fund bone marrow transplant research and build a federally sponsored bone marrow donor registry. He became interested in the issue in the 1980s after he met a 10-year-old constituent at risk of dying. After adopting the cause, he learned in 1990 that his daughter had a leukemia treatable only by a bone marrow transplant that ultimately saved her life. In late 2008, his son Patrick had a benign tumor removed from behind his lung.

Young was born into hardscrabble poverty in Pennsylvania's coal country during the Depression. His father, an alcoholic, abandoned the family when Young was a boy. After his mother became ill, the family stayed with relatives in St. Petersburg. Young never went to college, but worked his way to success in the insurance business. He entered politics in 1960, when he was elected as the sole Republican in the Florida Senate, rising to minority leader.

In 1970, he inherited the most dependable Republican House seat from William C. Cramer, who ran for the Senate. The 10th District has tilted Democratic but Young has been re-elected with ease more often than not. Since 1982, Democrats have fielded a candidate only about half the time.

Now in his 20th term, Young no longer finds the House a comfortable home. He is weary of the unrelenting partisanship, ethics scandals and the political money chase. "I will admit to having given some serious thought to retiring," he said in an interview. "I had a serious debate with myself." Young said in 2008 he decided to run at least one more time to help wounded veterans and a U.S. military that is under stress and in transition. In November, he beat Dunedin Mayor Bob Hackworth with 61 percent of the vote.

KEY VOTES

2008

No   Delay consideration of Colombia free-trade agreement

No   Override Bush veto of federal farm and nutrition programs reauthorization bill

Yes Overhaul surveillance laws and permit dismissal of suits against companies that conducted warrantless wiretapping

No   Grant mortgage relief to homeowners and funding for Fannie Mae and Freddie Mac

No   Approve initial $700 billion program to stabilize financial markets

No   Approve final $700 billion program to stabilize financial markets

No   Provide $14 billion in loans to automakers

2007

Yes Increase minimum wage by $2.10 an hour

No   Approve $124.2 billion in emergency war spending and set goal for redeployment of troops from Iraq

Yes Reject federal contraceptive assistance to international family planning groups

No   Override Bush veto of $23.2 billion water projects authorization bill

Yes Implement Peru free-trade agreement

Yes Approve energy policy overhaul with new fuel economy standards

Yes Clear $473.5 billion omnibus spending bill, including $70 billion for military operations

CQ VOTE STUDIES

| | PARTY UNITY | | PRESIDENTIAL SUPPORT | |
	SUPPORT	OPPOSE	SUPPORT	OPPOSE
2008	92%	8%	64%	36%
2007	83%	17%	64%	36%
2006	90%	10%	87%	13%
2005	92%	8%	82%	18%
2004	91%	9%	87%	13%

INTEREST GROUPS

	AFL-CIO	ADA	CCUS	ACU
2008	33%	25%	83%	88%
2007	33%	30%	90%	72%
2006	43%	10%	87%	84%
2005	15%	5%	92%	87%
2004	20%	10%	95%	87%

FLORIDA 10
West — most of Pinellas County, St. Petersburg

The 10th has sandy beaches, a modern urban center, moderate politics, and an economy reeling from financial crisis. The district takes in about 70 percent of Pinellas County's residents, including most of St. Petersburg and its upscale beachfront communities. It skirts most of Clearwater (shared with the 9th) in the central part of the county and captures Dunedin and half of Palm Harbor at its northern tip. Nearly one-fourth of the district's residents are 65 or older, and many retirees live in Largo and the Gulf Coast towns. Pinellas Park and St. Petersburg attract younger residents who want to live closer to major employers and Tampa.

A large part of the district's economy relies on tourism, a job sector that has been vulnerable to nationwide economic downturns. Attractions such as The Pier and Sunken Gardens still lure visitors, and the area received some economic benefit in early 2009 when nearby Tampa Bay hosted the Super Bowl. Financial services and an emerging technology sector centered on the computer and defense industries diversified the 10th's economy and brought more white-collar jobs to the area in the last

decade but did not insulate Pinellas from rising unemployment rates.

Downtown St. Petersburg experienced a cultural revival with renovations to the Mahaffey Theater and the Ponce de Leon hotel, and locals flock to the area's museums, orchestra performances, theaters and nightclubs. Residents also take pride in the preservation of the area's white-sand beaches and wildlife areas.

Republicans hold a slight voter registration advantage and the majority of locally elected officials are Republican: the Pinellas County Board of Commissioners has been controlled by the GOP since 1951. Twenty-five percent of district voters are registered as independent, however, and the 10th's loyalties can flip between parties in presidential races. In 2008, Democrat Barack Obama carried the 10th with 52 percent of its vote.

MAJOR INDUSTRY
Tourism, health care, retail, technology

CITIES
St. Petersburg (pt.), 179,087; Largo, 69,371; Pinellas Park, 45,658

NOTABLE
The Salvador Dalí Museum in St. Petersburg houses the largest collection of art by the Spanish surrealist outside of Europe.

Rep. Kathy Castor (D)

Elected 2006; 2nd term

CAPITOL OFFICE
225-3376
castor.house.gov
317 Cannon Bldg. 20515-0911; fax 225-5652

COMMITTEES
Energy & Commerce
Standards of Official Conduct

RESIDENCE
Tampa

BORN
Aug. 20, 1966; Miami, Fla.

RELIGION
Presbyterian

FAMILY
Husband, Bill Lewis; two children

EDUCATION
Emory U., B.A. 1988 (political science);
Florida State U., J.D. 1991

CAREER
Lawyer

POLITICAL HIGHLIGHTS
Democratic nominee for Fla. Senate, 2000;
Hillsborough County Board of Commissioners,
2002-06

ELECTION RESULTS

2008 GENERAL

Kathy Castor (D)	184,106	71.7%
Eddie Adams Jr. (R)	72,825	28.3%

2008 PRIMARY

Kathy Castor (D)	unopposed

2006 GENERAL

Kathy Castor (D)	97,470	69.6%
Eddie Adams Jr. (R)	42,454	30.3%

Castor is a member of a prominent South Florida political family who has caught the eye of Democratic leaders as a loyal voice and vote for the party. She has a plum assignment on the Energy and Commerce Committee, where she works on improving health care and furthering alternative energy.

Castor was seen as a rising star as soon as she entered the House. She was appointed by Speaker Nancy Pelosi to serve as the freshman class representative on the Democratic Steering Committee, which makes committee assignments. She also furthered Pelosi's agenda as a member of the Rules Committee, which sets the party's terms for floor debate on legislation, in the 110th Congress (2007-08).

As a member of Energy and Commerce's Health Subcommittee, Castor will be involved in shaping Democrats' health legislation in the 111th Congress (2009-10). "The time is now to improve access to quality, affordable health care," she said in December 2008.

She led the 2008 floor debate on a bill to expand the State Children's Health Insurance Program, which provides insurance to children from low-income families who do not qualify for Medicaid, by $35 billion over five years, but voted no on the original version because it stripped provisions she said would have made it easier for parents to sign up their children. The bill also included an increase in cigar taxes, which would have hurt Tampa's cigar-making industry. But Castor eventually supported a failed override to George W. Bush's veto of the bill. The expansion eventually cleared in early 2009 and was one of the first measures signed into law by President Obama.

On energy debates, she brings a background as an attorney who practiced environmental law for a decade and as chairwoman of the Environmental Protection Commission when she was a Hillsborough County commissioner. She opposes efforts to drill for oil and natural gas off the Florida coast, as her district includes part of Manatee County's Gulf Coast.

When gasoline prices were on the rise in the fall of 2008, House Republicans pushed through a bill to lift a 26-year-old moratorium on drilling off the Atlantic and Pacific coasts. Castor and other coastal district members opposed the measure, saying they were worried about the impact of drilling on tourism, fishing and even military exercises. A year earlier, she urged, "It's time for this House to get to work on new alternative energy and not to continue to fuel our addiction to oil and gas." She also introduced legislation that called for a permanent drilling ban within 125 miles of the coast.

Castor also looks out for her constituents by trying to improve travel options between Florida and Cuba, and she wants to allow flights between the Tampa airport and Havana. She said the move would improve travel prospects for thousands of Cuban-Americans. She applauded when Congress approved language in the 2009 catchall spending bill that would allow Cuban-Americans to visit relatives on the island once a year rather than once every three years, the policy under the Bush administration.

Castor also serves on the House ethics panel, where she is in the sometimes uncomfortable position of policing her colleagues' behavior. She strongly backed the House-passed ethics reforms in 2007 and lists the local projects for which she is seeking funding on her official Web site.

During her first term, Castor had a seat on the Armed Services Committee, and her district is home to MacDill Air Force Base, headquarters for U.S. Central Command and U.S. Special Operations Command. With House leaders well aware of her district's needs, Castor was asked to lead her party in debate on a May 2007 rule to the 2008 defense authorization bill. She hammered home her party's theme for the measure: readiness. The bill, which ultimately passed the House almost entirely along party lines, focused on improved training, pay benefits and equipment for military personnel fighting in Iraq and Afghanistan. To increase those accounts, it cut authorized funds from some of the president's requests for future weapons systems. "The readiness of our armed forces has suffered because of the strains imposed by four years of the war," Castor said. "We've got to provide the troops on the ground with the equipment they need to stay safe and survive."

Castor's parents, who divorced when she was 11, were active in Florida politics. Her father was a county judge and helped found Bay Area Legal Services, a nonprofit group that serves low-income families. Castor's mother, Betty, was the first woman to serve on the Hillsborough County Board of Commissioners, and later became one of the first women to sit in the Florida Senate and the first to serve in the state cabinet, where she was education commissioner. From 1993 to 1999, Castor's mother served as the president of the University of South Florida, and in 2004 ran an unsuccessful campaign for the U.S. Senate, losing to Mel Martinez by 1 percentage point.

After graduating from Emory University in Atlanta and earning a law degree from Florida State, Kathy Castor worked in the Department of Community Affairs in Tallahassee. She returned to Tampa in the mid-1990s to work in a law firm representing the city on zoning and code enforcement issues.

She then tried her hand at politics, losing a 2000 bid to the state Senate but winning a 2002 election to the Hillsborough County board, where she was a progressive voice on the conservative-majority board. She won support for greater disclosure on commissioners' meetings with lobbyists and on board members' travel expenses. In 2005, she was the lone dissenting vote when the commission passed a measure forbidding the county government from recognizing gay pride displays or events.

Her path to the House opened when Democratic Rep. Jim Davis made a failed bid for governor in 2006. She became the early favorite by capitalizing on her name recognition and financial support from EMILY's List, a political committee that backs Democratic women who support abortion rights.

She won the five-way primary, which included Leslie Miller, an African-American and state Senate minority leader. While Miller had the backing of the black community, Castor's coffers were too much to overcome. She took 54 percent of the primary vote. Two months later she trounced GOP architect Eddie Adams Jr. in the general election with 70 percent of the vote. In 2008 she again ran against Adams and won with 72 percent of the vote.

KEY VOTES

2008

Yes Delay consideration of Colombia free-trade agreement

\+ Override Bush veto of federal farm and nutrition programs reauthorization bill

Yes Overhaul surveillance laws and permit dismissal of suits against companies that conducted warrantless wiretapping

Yes Grant mortgage relief to homeowners and funding for Fannie Mae and Freddie Mac

No Approve initial $700 billion program to stabilize financial markets

No Approve final $700 billion program to stabilize financial markets

Yes Provide $14 billion in loans to automakers

2007

Yes Increase minimum wage by $2.10 an hour

Yes Approve $124.2 billion in emergency war spending and set goal for redeployment of troops from Iraq

No Reject federal contraceptive assistance to international family planning groups

Yes Override Bush veto of $23.2 billion water projects authorization bill

Yes Implement Peru free-trade agreement

Yes Approve energy policy overhaul with new fuel economy standards

No Clear $473.5 billion omnibus spending bill, including $70 billion for military operations

CQ VOTE STUDIES

	PARTY UNITY		PRESIDENTIAL SUPPORT	
	SUPPORT	OPPOSE	SUPPORT	OPPOSE
2008	99%	1%	14%	86%
2007	98%	2%	7%	93%

INTEREST GROUPS

	AFL-CIO	ADA	CCUS	ACU
2008	100%	95%	63%	9%
2007	96%	95%	55%	0%

FLORIDA 11

West – Tampa, south St. Petersburg

The 11th, one of the state's younger and more racially diverse districts, ranges from Tampa's urban center and part of Bradenton across the bay to south St. Petersburg. The Tampa area's service and technology sectors helped make it the commercial, industrial and financial hub of Florida's west coast, and its skyline grew significantly during the last decade.

The area experienced rapid growth for much of the 2000s, but the recent economic downturn hit the area hard, and Tampa has endured rising unemployment rates across construction, retail and white-collar sectors. Although the city's airport and seaport make it a major shipping and transit hub, the hospitality industry centered around the major cruise lines hosted at the port depends on a high volume of visitors. The University of South Florida is one of the state's largest schools and still an economic engine for the city.

Tampa Bay has a rich history as "Cigar City," one of the nation's biggest producers of cigars, and the Tampa History Center in the Channel District recently opened a permanent exhibit on the city's cigar industry — at its

height, Tampa produced more than 400 million cigars annually. The influence of Cuban and Spanish culture is pronounced in Ybor City, a downtown Tampa neighborhood, and its success at reinventing itself as a nighttime hot spot has given the area new life.

Blacks and Hispanics make up about half of the 11th's population, with heavy concentrations of blacks in south St. Petersburg, east Tampa and parts of Bradenton, and Hispanics in west Tampa and the Egypt Lake-Leto and Town 'n' Country areas just northwest of the city. Democrats outnumber Republicans more than 2-to-1 in the strongly Democratic 11th, and Barack Obama took 66 percent of the district's 2008 presidential vote.

MAJOR INDUSTRY
Service, health care, finance, tourism

MILITARY BASES
MacDill Air Force Base, 5,641 military, 1,621 civilian (2007)

CITIES
Tampa (pt.), 284,199; Town 'n' Country (unincorporated), 72,523; St. Petersburg (pt.), 69,145; University (unincorporated), 30,736

NOTABLE
The Sunshine Skyway Bridge is the world's longest cable-stayed concrete bridge.

Rep. Adam H. Putnam (R)

Elected 2000; 5th term

CAPITOL OFFICE
225-1252
www.house.gov/putnam
442 Cannon Bldg. 20515-0912; fax 226-0585

COMMITTEES
Financial Services

RESIDENCE
Bartow

BORN
July 31, 1974; Bartow, Fla.

RELIGION
Episcopalian

FAMILY
Wife, Melissa Putnam; four children

EDUCATION
U. of Florida, B.S. 1995 (economics)

CAREER
State legislator; citrus farmer and cattle rancher

POLITICAL HIGHLIGHTS
Fla. House, 1996-2000

ELECTION RESULTS

2008 GENERAL

Adam H. Putnam (R)	185,698	57.5%
Doug Tudor (D)	137,465	42.5%

2008 PRIMARY

Adam H. Putnam (R)	unopposed

2006 GENERAL

Adam H. Putnam (R)	124,452	69.1%
Joe Viscusi (X)	34,976	19.4%
Ed Bowlin (X)	20,636	11.5%

PREVIOUS WINNING PERCENTAGES
2004 (65%); 2002 (100%); 2000 (57%)

The boyish-looking yet tough-talking Putnam rose rapidly up the House Republican leadership ladder. But his party's dismal showing in the 2008 elections led him to announce he would not seek another term as chief framer of the party's message, and he has refocused on becoming Florida agricultural commissioner as a possible stepping stone to a future gubernatorial bid.

Putnam, scion of a family known for its cattle and orange groves, said the frustration with being relegated to the minority after years of calling the shots factored in his decision. "If you're going to knock on doors and stand on street corners and stuff a bunch of envelopes for a campaign, you want to have an impact," he told the Miami Herald after launching his run in February 2009.

His departure after the 110th Congress (2007-08) as GOP Conference chairman, the No. 3 job in the Republican leadership, deprived the party of one of its leading political strategists — as well as one of its top fundraisers. During the 2007-08 election cycle, his campaign committee's more than $700,000 in donations to the National Republican Congressional Committee made him the fifth-most-generous contributor among House GOP members.

Putnam was sometimes called the party's attack dog, and proved to be a fierce combatant in a few high-profile cases. He took on Democratic House Speaker Nancy Pelosi early in 2007 for commuting in a military jet back to her San Francisco district, even though the House sergeant at arms had requested the plane for security reasons. During the August 2008 congressional recess, Putnam led a series of floor protests against the Democratic leadership for failing to approve offshore drilling for oil and natural gas.

But in announcing he would not continue in the GOP leadership, Putnam said he wanted to put partisan warfare aside. "With the issues before us today come bipartisan opportunities and partisan differences," he said. "My current role obligates me to the latter and too often excludes me from the former."

In early 2009, he aligned with Democrats in introducing a variety of bills. A member of the Financial Services Committee, he joined liberal Edward J. Markey of Massachusetts on legislation to make the government-sponsored mortgage giants Fannie Mae and Freddie Mac subject to additional federal disclosure regulations. He also joined Connecticut Democrat Joe Courtney on a proposal to establish tax incentives for long-term care expenses and California Democrat Jim Costa on a measure to toughen food safety laws.

Shortly before President Obama took office, Putnam expressed hope he could support the new president's economic stimulus plan. But he ended up joining the rest of his House GOP colleagues in opposing the final $787 billion package, arguing that because much of the money wouldn't be spent immediately, the law "won't even do what its supporters claim its purpose is." He also voted against a $410 billion catchall spending bill and an extension of the State Children's Health Insurance Program, which covers children whose families do not qualify for Medicaid.

When he took the Republican Conference job, Putnam said his goal was to "rebrand" or "redefine the core values and vision" of the House GOP. He reached out to reporters from smaller newspapers, and in 2008 organized a series of debates between Republicans and their Democratic counterparts.

But some of Putnam's tasks proved more challenging than others. He was the party's spokesman in the midst of the scandal surrounding Florida GOP Rep. Mark Foley, who resigned in 2006 after it was discovered that he had sent lewd e-mail messages to teenage students who serve in the House as pages. He defended Bush after the president commuted the sentence of

I. Lewis "Scooter" Libby, a former aide to Vice President Dick Cheney, in 2007 after Libby's conviction on perjury charges.

Putnam was just 26 when he was elected to the House in 2000, at the time the youngest representative in the chamber. Youthful and red-haired, he endured nicknames ranging from "Opie" to "Howdy Doody." But Putnam had a powerful ally: then-House Speaker J. Dennis Hastert of Illinois, whom Putnam had impressed. Hastert asked Putnam to organize younger members in what came to be known as the "Putnam Group" and gave him coveted assignments on the Rules and Budget committees.

Putnam quickly mastered the multilayered parliamentary intricacies of managing bills on the floor and, in early 2006, won the chairmanship of the Republican Policy Committee, placing him fourth in the House GOP hierarchy. Nine months later, he beat out Jack Kingston of Georgia for the conference chairman slot.

In the 110th Congress (2007-08), Putnam took a seat on Financial Services. He supported legislation in October 2008 to rescue ailing Wall Street banks caught up in the subprime mortgage crisis, though he opposed a subsequent bailout of major U.S. automakers.

His voting record is conservative, and he's almost unfailingly loyal to his caucus. Since 2001 he has sided with the GOP on roughly 97 percent of votes that pitted the majority of each party against each other. Early on he strayed on some trade votes he said would hurt Florida's farmers, but supported the 2005 Central America Free Trade Agreement and a 2007 deal with Peru.

Putnam is a fifth-generation Floridian from the small town of Bartow, southwest of Orlando, and remains deeply rooted there. His brother lives across the street and his parents just down the road. When Putnam was 11 years old, he told his grandfather he would run for governor some day, an ambition he still harbors.

He began planning for his first political race during his last year at the University of Florida, where he got an economics degree. A year later, in 1996, he was elected to the state legislature — despite his opponent's argument that Floridians didn't want a representative who'd just left the "frat house." He stayed in the job for four years, chairing the House Agriculture Committee.

In 2000, Republican Rep. Charles T. Canady, for whom Putnam had interned as a college student, stepped down. The Democratic candidate, auto dealer Michael Stedem, tried again to make Putnam's youth an issue, but Putnam won with 57 percent of the vote. He was unopposed for re-election in 2002 and has won easily since then, taking 69 percent of the vote in 2006 and just over 57 percent in 2008.

KEY VOTES

2008

No Delay consideration of Colombia free-trade agreement
Yes Override Bush veto of federal farm and nutrition programs reauthorization bill
Yes Overhaul surveillance laws and permit dismissal of suits against companies that conducted warrantless wiretapping
Yes Grant mortgage relief to homeowners and funding for Fannie Mae and Freddie Mac
Yes Approve initial $700 billion program to stabilize financial markets
Yes Approve final $700 billion program to stabilize financial markets
No Provide $14 billion in loans to automakers

2007

No Increase minimum wage by $2.10 an hour
No Approve $124.2 billion in emergency war spending and set goal for redeployment of troops from Iraq
Yes Reject federal contraceptive assistance to international family planning groups
No Override Bush veto of $23.2 billion water projects authorization bill
Yes Implement Peru free-trade agreement
Yes Approve energy policy overhaul with new fuel economy standards
Yes Clear $473.5 billion omnibus spending bill, including $70 billion for military operations

CQ VOTE STUDIES

| | PARTY UNITY | | PRESIDENTIAL SUPPORT | |
	SUPPORT	OPPOSE	SUPPORT	OPPOSE
2008	95%	5%	75%	25%
2007	97%	3%	88%	12%
2006	97%	3%	97%	3%
2005	97%	3%	89%	11%
2004	97%	3%	91%	9%

INTEREST GROUPS

	AFL-CIO	ADA	CCUS	ACU
2008	7%	15%	94%	83%
2007	4%	10%	80%	92%
2006	7%	0%	100%	84%
2005	13%	5%	85%	92%
2004	13%	0%	100%	100%

FLORIDA 12
West central — Polk and Hillsborough counties

Florida's 12th District has plenty of land, but much of it is covered by citrus groves and natural lakes rather than beaches. Unlike most of western Florida, the 12th does not have an abundance of residential developments. Centered east of Tampa and southwest of Orlando, the district includes almost all of Polk County, suburban and exurban portions of southern and eastern Hillsborough County, and a very small slice of western Osceola County.

Agriculture in Polk County drives the 12th's economy. Polk is the state's top producer of citrus, while the Hillsborough County portion of the district cultivates tomatoes and strawberries. Publix Supermarkets is headquartered in Lakeland, and financial and insurance companies also have large offices in the area. The district's central location makes it a distribution hub, as well as home to a sizable health care sector. As another slice of the economic pie, the district continues to attract retirees to its retirement communities, including Sun City Center.

Despite a thriving agriculture sector and steady growth for a decade in

the area's secondary industries — both blue- and white-collar jobs — the Polk County economy was hit hard recently by rising unemployment rates and a contraction of commercial and industrial interests.

Although the GOP used to have the edge among a third of the district's population in Hillsborough County, Democrats now outnumber Republicans in the portions of all three counties in the 12th. The growing Democratic registration advantage belies the social and economic conservatism of most residents here, and traditional Southern Democratic voters make state and local elections here competitive. The district has backed GOP presidential candidates since 1992, but Republican John McCain won the district with only 50 percent of its 2008 presidential vote, edging Barack Obama by fewer than 4,000 votes.

MAJOR INDUSTRY
Agriculture, financial services, mining

CITIES
Brandon (unincorporated) (pt.), 72,878; Lakeland (pt.), 71,079; Winter Haven, 26,487

NOTABLE
Cypress Gardens Adventure Park in Winter Haven was Florida's first theme park.

Rep. Vern Buchanan (R)

Elected 2006; 2nd term

CAPITOL OFFICE
225-5015
buchanan.house.gov
218 Cannon Bldg. 20515-0913; fax 226-0828

COMMITTEES
Small Business
Transportation & Infrastructure
Veterans' Affairs

RESIDENCE
Longboat Key

BORN
May 8, 1951; Detroit, Mich.

RELIGION
Baptist

FAMILY
Wife, Sandy Buchanan; two children

EDUCATION
Cleary College, B.B.A. 1975 (business administration); U. of Detroit, M.B.A. 1986

MILITARY SERVICE
Mich. Air National Guard 1970-76

CAREER
Car dealership owner; copy and printing company owner; marketing representative

POLITICAL HIGHLIGHTS
No previous office

ELECTION RESULTS

2008 GENERAL

Vern Buchanan (R)	204,382	55.5%
Christine Jennings (D)	137,967	37.5%
Jan Schneider (X)	20,289	5.5%
Don Baldauf (X)	5,358	1.5%

2008 PRIMARY

Vern Buchanan (R)	unopposed

2006 GENERAL

Vern Buchanan (R)	119,309	50.1%
Christine Jennings (D)	118,940	49.9%

Buchanan made a vast fortune in the auto dealership business and is a strongly pro-business fiscal conservative. But like any good car salesman, he knows how to tailor his pitch to his audience. He often departs from GOP orthodoxy on health care, the environment and other issues he considers important to constituents.

Buchanan said his political philosophy is aligned with Reagan-era conservatism in that he believes in small government and that "everyone who can work should work." He said national defense should be the federal government's highest priority. At the same time, though, he dislikes hewing to ideology. "I think it is a problem in our country when people are hard-core partisan," he said.

During the 110th Congress (2007-08), Buchanan broke ranks with the GOP on 14 percent of the votes that pitted the parties against each other. His independent streak, along with his wealth and Florida political connections, has fueled speculation he might be a candidate in 2010 for the open Senate seat now held by retiring Republican Mel Martinez.

Early in the 110th, Buchanan was one of 19 Republicans to support five of the first six Democratic bills introduced, including a measure allowing the federal government to negotiate prescription drug prices on behalf of Medicare recipients. He subsequently voted with Democrats to override President George W. Bush's veto of a bill to expand the State Children's Health Insurance Program, which covers children whose families do not qualify for Medicaid. And he supported bills to prevent a steep cut in payments to physicians treating Medicare patients and to require health insurers that cover mental illness to do so on par with physical illness.

Buchanan's fiscal conservatism led him initially to oppose the Bush administration's $700 billion proposal to shore up the ailing financial services sector. But he supported a reworked version a few days later that became law, saying constituents told him they were worried about their retirement savings.

He once owned Ford and Dodge dealerships, but refused to support a failed effort in late 2008 to aid U.S. automakers. He said he favored an alternative by Senate Republicans to allow the car companies access to $25 billion in federally subsidized loans to help them retool plants to build fuel-efficient vehicles.

Buchanan doesn't mind spending federal dollars to benefit Florida. He wants to increase Florida's return in tax dollars and should get an opportunity in the 111th Congress (2009-10), when the Transportation and Infrastructure Committee takes up a renewal of the massive highway bill that is traditionally a vehicle for funding local projects. During his first year, he used his seat on its highway and transit subcommittee to obtain funding for Sarasota County's Area Transit and enhancements to Interstate 75 and U.S. Highway 41.

Buchanan's concern for the national debt also led him in February 2008 to oppose sending to the House floor a bill authorizing $48 billion toward global AIDS programs, a figure well above the Bush administration's original proposal. "I'm sensitive; I'd like to help Africa," he said. "But we just went from $15 billion to $50 billion. That's crazy." He voted against final passage of the bill as well, though it ultimately became law.

Buchanan supports Republican proposals to increase nuclear production and open Alaska's Arctic National Wildlife Refuge to oil drilling, but he opposes expanded drilling off the Gulf of Mexico, contending it would put Florida's thriving tourism economy at risk. In 2008, he backed legislation by fellow Floridian Kathy Castor, a Democrat, calling for a permanent ban of drilling within 125 miles of the state's coast. That bill did not see action.

From his seat on the Veterans' Affairs Committee, Buchanan looks after a core constituency: retired veterans. In his first term, he finished a long-fought battle started by his predecessors to obtain federal funds for a new national veterans cemetery in Sarasota.

His other committee assignment is Small Business. He has owned printing companies, offshore reinsurance companies, a charter boat business, an aircraft leasing company and numerous real estate holdings in addition to auto dealerships. He is the ranking member of Small Business' Finance and Tax Subcommittee and strongly favors lowering taxes to help small companies.

Buchanan was born into a blue-collar family with five siblings that lived in Inkster, a small city near Detroit. His father was a factory foreman for a computer company; his mother was a stay-at-home mom. He earned an MBA from the University of Detroit after working his way through college. He served six years in the Air National Guard.

In his early 20s, Buchanan started American Speedy Printing Centers, which grew to about 750 outlets nationwide. In 1992 he resigned his last duties at the company, which entered bankruptcy. He has since paid millions of dollars to settle allegations of fraud and taking excessive compensation.

In 1990, he moved from Michigan to Florida, where he built an empire of auto dealerships. When he was elected to Congress, his Buchanan Automotive Group was one of the nation's largest privately owned car dealerships. His minimum net worth of $69 million in 2007 made him one of the 10 wealthiest members of Congress, according to the Center for Responsive Politics.

Buchanan had some background in politics prior to running for office: He gave nearly $100,000 to the Republican National Committee and served as fundraising chairman for Martinez's 2004 campaign and as chairman of the Florida Chamber of Commerce.

In the 2006 general election, he faced Democrat Christine Jennings, his former banker. Democrats accused him of avoiding taxes in purchasing, then selling, a luxury condominium. He attacked Jennings for being weak on taxes and immigration. Buchanan won by 369 votes in the third-closest race of the 2006 election cycle. Jennings contested the results, claiming widespread voting irregularities, including malfunctions of electronic voting machines. But in early 2008, the Government Accountability Office concluded the touchscreen voting machines appeared to have worked properly.

Jennings challenged Buchanan again two years later. Despite the Democratic tide across the nation and in Florida, Buchanan cruised to an 18-percentage-point victory, outraising Jennings by more than 50 percent.

KEY VOTES

2008

No   Delay consideration of Colombia free-trade agreement

Yes   Override Bush veto of federal farm and nutrition programs reauthorization bill

Yes   Overhaul surveillance laws and permit dismissal of suits against companies that conducted warrantless wiretapping

Yes   Grant mortgage relief to homeowners and funding for Fannie Mae and Freddie Mac

No   Approve initial $700 billion program to stabilize financial markets

Yes   Approve final $700 billion program to stabilize financial markets

No   Provide $14 billion in loans to automakers

2007

Yes   Increase minimum wage by $2.10 an hour

No   Approve $124.2 billion in emergency war spending and set goal for redeployment of troops from Iraq

Yes   Reject federal contraceptive assistance to international family planning groups

Yes   Override Bush veto of $23.2 billion water projects authorization bill

Yes   Implement Peru free-trade agreement

Yes   Approve energy policy overhaul with new fuel economy standards

Yes   Clear $473.5 billion omnibus spending bill, including $70 billion for military operations

CQ VOTE STUDIES

	PARTY UNITY		PRESIDENTIAL SUPPORT	
	SUPPORT	OPPOSE	SUPPORT	OPPOSE
2008	80%	20%	44%	56%
2007	90%	10%	66%	34%

INTEREST GROUPS

	AFL-CIO	ADA	CCUS	ACU
2008	40%	50%	83%	60%
2007	33%	35%	85%	84%

FLORIDA 13
Southwest — Sarasota, most of Bradenton

Retirees from the North flock to the 13th District's Gulf Coast cities of Sarasota and Bradenton. Sarasota and Manatee counties have nearly 90 percent of the district's population; the more affluent tend to live near Sarasota, with middle-class residents more prevalent around Bradenton. Overall, the 13th has the nation's highest median age and is a popular home for older part-time residents.

Most residents live near the coast, while farmland and citrus groves are inland. Coastal Sarasota County cultivates a refined image with its art museums, theater and symphony performances. The John and Mable Ringling Museum of Art, located on the Sarasota Bay, features gardens, museums and the mansion once owned by John Ringling. It generally draws a more highly educated and wealthier class of retirees than most other west coast communities in Florida.

Bradenton (shared with the 11th) is the retail center of Manatee County. The city is partly a Tampa-St. Petersburg-area suburb, and has a more noticeable mix of incomes and ethnic groups than Sarasota. It also is home to the IMG Academies — residential sports-training and academic facilities for top athletes in several sports.

Service industries, including investment companies, and trade make up much of the labor force, although several sectors have cut jobs recently. The 13th's agricultural base is strong, with large tomato and citrus crops, but disease and hurricanes are always threats. The area's Gulf beaches, barrier islands and state park make environmental policy a bipartisan concern here.

Republicans hold a decided advantage in party registration, and voters here routinely favor GOP candidates in statewide races. Despite the strong GOP base in the 13th, Democrat Barack Obama fell only 211 votes short of capturing Sarasota County in the 2008 presidential election, and John McCain took the district with only 52 percent overall.

MAJOR INDUSTRY
Agriculture, tourism, health care, service

CITIES
Sarasota, 52,715; Bradenton (pt.), 39,385

NOTABLE
Since 1927, the Ringling Bros. circus sets up shop in Sarasota in winter.

Rep. Connie Mack (R)

Elected 2004; 3rd term

CAPITOL OFFICE
225-2536
mack.house.gov
115 Cannon Bldg. 20515-0914; fax 226-0439

COMMITTEES
Budget
Foreign Affairs
Transportation & Infrastructure

RESIDENCE
Fort Myers

BORN
Aug. 12, 1967; Fort Myers, Fla.

RELIGION
Roman Catholic

FAMILY
Wife, Rep. Mary Bono Mack, R-Calif.;
two children, two stepchildren

EDUCATION
U. of Florida, B.S. 1993 (advertising)

CAREER
Marketing consultant; health products sales
representative

POLITICAL HIGHLIGHTS
Fla. House, 2000-2003

ELECTION RESULTS

2008 GENERAL

Connie Mack (R)	224,602	59.4%
Robert M. Neeld (D)	93,590	24.8%
Burt Saunders (X)	54,750	14.5%
Jeff George (X)	4,949	1.3%

2008 PRIMARY

Connie Mack (R)	unopposed

2006 GENERAL

Connie Mack (R)	151,615	64.4%
Robert M. Neeld (D)	83,920	35.6%

PREVIOUS WINNING PERCENTAGES
2004 (68%)

Mack is an adamant fiscal conservative much like his father and namesake, who served 18 years in Congress. With Democrats controlling the House and White House, the younger Mack is often relegated to the role of critic, though he also helps his district obtain funding for transportation and other needs.

He rarely supports new government spending and opposed all the major economic recovery bills of late 2008 and early 2009, voting against legislation aimed at rescuing ailing banks and automobile companies as well as President Obama's economic stimulus. He called the final $787 billion stimulus measure "little more than a massive spending plan filled with earmarks and liberal social-planning programs." In an open letter to the president published in two newspapers prior to Obama's February visit to Mack's district, Mack wrote, "History has proven that we can't spend our way to prosperity."

Mack is sure to be a thorn in the side of the Democratic leadership on the Budget Committee, which will try to shape Obama's spending priorities. "We need to enact fiscally responsible measures that will help families and businesses grow and prosper, but in a way that does not expand the size, scope and role of government," Mack said in February 2009.

His 14th District consists almost entirely of a portion of Florida's Gulf Coast that was represented from 1983 to 1989 by his father, a conservative who was in the Senate leadership in the mid-1990s. On the Transportation and Infrastructure Committee, Mack shares his father's view that Floridians are shortchanged on federal highway taxes, paying more to the federal government than they receive in return. "We need to allow states, and not bureaucrats in Washington, to keep more of their money and decide where it should go," he said. He also has successfully sought money to expand Interstate 75, which runs through the district.

Mack also battles Democrats on environmental, foreign policy and social issues. During his first term, he cosponsored a bill to permanently ban offshore oil and gas drilling along Florida's coast. But when the issue moved atop the GOP agenda in 2008, he said he had second thoughts. "Circumstances have changed, I have changed, and I believe the people of Florida have changed," he said.

Mack opposed key provisions of the George W. Bush-era anti-terrorism law known as the Patriot Act because he said it "tramples on the civil liberties that are part of the foundation of this country." But he later supported Bush's controversial warrantless wiretapping program of foreign terrorism suspects.

Mack differs from most conservatives on the issue of embryonic stem cell research, which abortion opponents like him generally oppose on the grounds it requires the destruction of human embryos. Like his father, he has felt keenly the toll cancer has wreaked on his family and believes the research could help find a cure. Both of his grandparents on his father's side, as well as an uncle, died of the disease. His mother and sister nearly did as well.

Mack uses his seat on the Foreign Affairs Committee, where he is ranking member on the Western Hemisphere panel, to focus on Latin American issues. He has focused on Venezuelan strongman Hugo Chávez, whom he views as a threat to U.S. interests in the region. In 2008, Mack introduced a resolution declaring Venezuela a state sponsor of terrorism.

Like his father, Mack is a defender of Israel. He rang alarm bells in early 2009 when Chávez expelled the Israeli ambassador from Venezuela.

Mack comes from a family of politicians. His great-great-grandfather, John L. Sheppard, was a Democratic House member from Texas; his great-grandfather, Morris Sheppard, also served in the House, then moved on to a 28-year tenure in the Senate. His father, Connie Mack III, spent three terms in the House and two in the Senate before retiring from Congress in 2000.

But it was another relative who provided Mack with enviable name recognition when he got into politics: His great-grandfather was the original Connie Mack, the legendary owner and manager of the Philadelphia Athletics baseball team. And like him, Mack uses the familiar rather than the given version of his name: Cornelius McGillicuddy IV.

An emphasis on "family values" defined Mack's initial race for Congress in 2004. But his first term in Washington turned out to be difficult for his own family. Mack split from Ann, his wife of nine years, in August 2005, and weeks later, he was linked romantically to another member of Congress, Republican Mary Bono of California — the widow of Sonny Bono, a pop star-turned-congressman — who was divorcing her second husband. Mack married Bono, who's since taken his name (she goes by "Bono Mack"), in 2007.

Mack grew up in southwestern Florida and was a student at Cape Coral High School when his father was elected to Congress. The Macks moved to the nation's capital, settling in the affluent suburb of McLean, Va. Mack graduated from Massanutten Military Academy in Woodstock, Va.

Mack had "stuffed envelopes and walked precincts" for his father, but he hated the sometimes-critical appraisals of the elder Mack in the press. "I think that some of the shots taken at my father really had a negative impact on me," he said. "But as you get older, you realize that's just part of politics these days."

After the military academy, he attended the University of Florida and earned a degree in advertising. He was a health products salesman and marketing consultant, but he soon thought of following in his father's footsteps. At age 33, he was elected to the Florida House in 2000 from Fort Lauderdale. During three years as a state legislator, he organized a group of members opposed to all new taxes and government fees.

When Republican Porter J. Goss resigned just before the end of his eighth term to become CIA director, Mack moved from Fort Lauderdale to Fort Myers to run in the 2004 race in the overwhelmingly Republican 14th District. He eked out a primary victory in a four-way race marked by opponents' jabs about his ties to the area. Voters didn't seem to care.

After winning the primary, he cruised to a lopsided general-election victory. He won re-election in 2008 with nearly 60 percent of the vote. Rumors have floated that Mack might try to follow in his father's footsteps to the Senate by aiming to replace retiring Republican Mel Martinez in 2010, but Mack has been noncommittal.

KEY VOTES

2008

No Delay consideration of Colombia free-trade agreement

No Override Bush veto of federal farm and nutrition programs reauthorization bill

Yes Overhaul surveillance laws and permit dismissal of suits against companies that conducted warrantless wiretapping

No Grant mortgage relief to homeowners and funding for Fannie Mae and Freddie Mac

No Approve initial $700 billion program to stabilize financial markets

No Approve final $700 billion program to stabilize financial markets

No Provide $14 billion in loans to automakers

2007

No Increase minimum wage by $2.10 an hour

No Approve $124.2 billion in emergency war spending and set goal for redeployment of troops from Iraq

Yes Reject federal contraceptive assistance to international family planning groups

Yes Override Bush veto of $23.2 billion water projects authorization bill

Yes Implement Peru free-trade agreement

No Approve energy policy overhaul with new fuel economy standards

Yes Clear $473.5 billion omnibus spending bill, including $70 billion for military operations

CQ VOTE STUDIES

	PARTY UNITY		PRESIDENTIAL SUPPORT	
	SUPPORT	OPPOSE	SUPPORT	OPPOSE
2008	98%	2%	77%	23%
2007	95%	5%	85%	15%
2006	93%	7%	87%	13%
2005	96%	4%	80%	20%

INTEREST GROUPS

	AFL-CIO	ADA	CCUS	ACU
2008	7%	10%	88%	100%
2007	5%	5%	79%	88%
2006	8%	25%	93%	84%
2005	13%	5%	81%	92%

FLORIDA 14
Southwest — Cape Coral, Fort Myers, Naples

Traditionally a haven for retirees and tourists, the solidly Republican 14th features Gulf Coast beaches and golf courses. The district's population is centered in Lee County, where migration of families and young professionals from the North and from Florida's east coast have added to the mix. The 14th also takes in the coastal edge of Collier County and a small slice of Charlotte County. Most residents live near the coast, between the shore and Interstate 75, which runs through the district before turning east into the Everglades.

The population in Collier and Lee counties grew significantly in the 1990s — Cape Coral in Lee County saw its population grow by at least one-third in the last decade — but growth has slowed. Originally a retirement community built on undeveloped rural land, Cape Coral began attracting young professionals with white-collar job opportunities, and many business relocated to the area. The city long relied on its service and home construction industries. Fort Myers' Florida Gulf Coast University, with its environmental and science programs, and the nearby Everglades help promote marine biology and an eco-tourism industry. Wealthier retirees live around Naples in Collier, where golf courses and high-rise condos are plentiful, and a decade of construction raised the tax base for the area.

A collapse of the housing market in Lee and Collier counties caused property values to plummet. The supply of residential units was based on growth patterns that have now stalled, and many homes will be left vacant even as rising foreclosure rates lead to more home sales.

Small Democratic pockets exist within Lee County, but the 14th has the largest Republican voter-registration advantage in the state, and residents here regularly give GOP candidates large vote percentages. John McCain won the district's 2008 presidential vote with 57 percent.

MAJOR INDUSTRY
Tourism, health care, service

CITIES
Cape Coral, 102,286; Fort Myers, 48,208; North Fort Myers (unincorporated), 40,214; Lehigh Acres (unincorporated), 33,430

NOTABLE
The J.N. "Ding" Darling National Wildlife Refuge on Sanibel Island, an area barrier island, hosts migratory birds in its mangrove forests.

Rep. Bill Posey (R)

CAPITOL OFFICE
225-3671
posey.house.gov
132 Cannon Bldg. 20515-0915; fax 225-3516

COMMITTEES
Financial Services

RESIDENCE
Rockledge

BORN
Dec. 18, 1947; Washington, D.C.

RELIGION
Methodist

FAMILY
Wife, Katie Posey; two children

EDUCATION
Brevard Junior College, A.A. 1969

CAREER
Realtor; insurance claims adjuster; space program engineering inspector

POLITICAL HIGHLIGHTS
Rockledge City Council, 1976-86; Fla. House, 1992-2000; Fla. Senate, 2000-08

ELECTION RESULTS

2008 GENERAL

Bill Posey (R)	192,151	53.1%
Stephen Blythe (D)	151,951	42.0%
Frank Zilaitis (X)	14,274	3.9%

2008 PRIMARY

Bill Posey (R)	40,892	76.8%
Alan Bergman (R)	7,809	14.7%
Kevin Lehoullier (R)	4,519	8.5%

Elected 2008; 1st term

The conservative Posey's nickname is "Mr. Accountability." He made accountability his mantra during his 16 years as a Florida state lawmaker, and is especially proud of a law he wrote that requires each state agency to create a summary of its budget, what it does and what it spends.

He wasted no time in bringing his passion to Congress. The Financial Services Committee, on which Posey serves, unanimously approved his "accountability amendment" to its rules package in early 2009. To promote transparency, it requires the panel to post all votes on its Web site within two days.

Despite his concern about accountability, Posey was wary of new regulations to combat the kind of lapses that led to the collapse of the financial system in 2008. "I think that it's not a matter of too few regulations. I think it's a matter of regulations we have not being enforced," he said at a 2009 Financial Services hearing.

Posey is a staunch fiscal conservative who opposed President Obama's $787 billion economic stimulus package, which he criticized as the "biggest generational theft ever." He is a member of the Republican Study Committee, a coalition of House GOP conservatives. Being a conservative, he said, "means you don't spend $2 when $1 will do."

With the Cape Canaveral Air Force Station in his district and Kennedy Space Center right next door, Posey will work to promote NASA, where he once worked as a contractor. He also is an accomplished stock-car racer and won an award for short-track driver achievement.

Posey's move from Tallahassee to Capitol Hill came about after seven-term GOP Rep. Dave Weldon retired. Weldon had asked Posey to run for his seat several times, but Posey resisted. His family initially vetoed a run for Congress, but one of his daughters changed her mind. "She said, 'You trying to do something is better than no one doing anything,'" he recalled.

He received the strong backing of business interests and had little trouble in the GOP primary or the general election against Democratic physician Stephen Blythe.

FLORIDA 15

East central – Indian River County; parts of Brevard, Osceola and Polk counties

Most residents of the 15th live along the Atlantic Coast in Brevard and Indian River counties between Merritt Island and Vero Beach. In addition to all of Indian River and three-fourths of Brevard, the 15th contains regional agricultural hubs in inland Osceola County and in its slice of Polk County. Melbourne and Palm Bay are on the Treasure Coast along the district's central shore.

The Cape Canaveral Air Force Station, Patrick Air Force Base, and the Kennedy Space Center (located in the neighboring 24th) are the Space Coast's economic engines. NASA's presence has provided high-paying jobs, lucrative contracts and tourist attractions, but faces an uncertain future here.

Tourism also is important, and the 15th's beaches include prime Atlantic surfing spot Sebastian Inlet. Disney's Vero Beach Resort draws visitors. Kissimmee, which has a large Hispanic population, depends on Orlando's now-stalling tourism industry.

Although registered Democrats outnumber Republicans in the 15th's portions of Osceola and Polk, the GOP has a slight registration edge overall in the district. Voters have favored GOP presidential candidates since 1992, but John McCain won only 51 percent of the district's 2008 presidential vote.

MAJOR INDUSTRY
Technology, defense, tourism, agriculture

MILITARY BASES
Patrick Air Force Base, 1,319 military, 1,309 civilian (2008)

CITIES
Palm Bay, 79,413; Melbourne, 71,382; Kissimmee, 47,814

NOTABLE
An early name of Yeehaw Junction, at a crossroads of what is now the Florida turnpike, was "Jackass Crossing."

Rep. Tom Rooney (R)

Elected 2008; 1st term

Rooney, an advocate of limited government and fiscal conservatism, hopes to better serve the interests of his traditionally Republican district than his predecessor, Democrat Tim Mahoney. Rooney said he disagreed with Mahoney's position on social issues and the degree of government involvement in the private sector. "I don't believe the government is the answer to everything under the sun. I'm not for bailouts or anything like that," he said.

He also said "it was time to put someone back in the seat that my children believe holds onto values near and dear." Before losing his re-election bid, Mahoney admitted to two extramarital affairs. His predecessor, Republican Mark Foley, departed in 2006 when sexually explicit online messages to teenage House pages were splashed across the news. Rooney was one of only five Republicans to unseat incumbent House Democrats in 2008.

In early 2009, Rooney opposed a series of measures pushed by Democrats and the Obama administration. He voted against a bill — signed into law — to expand the State Children's Health Insurance Program, which covers children whose families do not qualify for Medicaid. He also opposed a $787 billion economic stimulus law and a $410 billion catchall spending bill.

A military veteran and former instructor at the U.S. Military Academy at West Point, Rooney sits on the Armed Services Committee. He hopes to address the needs of military personnel, particularly health care and treatment of post-traumatic stress disorder.

He also is an attorney and sits on the Judiciary Committee, where he is on the Constitution, Civil Rights and Civil Liberties panel. He advocates gun owners' rights and opposes both abortion rights and creating a path to citizenship for illegal immigrants.

Rooney is perhaps best known as the grandson of Pittsburgh Steelers founder Art Rooney. As a youth, he spent summers working as a ball boy. He played football at Washington and Jefferson College and Syracuse University.

During the 2008 race, Rooney was the target of attacks over his father Pat Rooney Sr.'s alleged involvement with the gambling industry. Regardless, Rooney took 60 percent of the vote.

CAPITOL OFFICE
225-5792
rooney.house.gov
1529 Longworth Bldg. 20515-0916; fax 225-3132

COMMITTEES
Armed Services
Judiciary

RESIDENCE
Tequesta

BORN
Nov. 21, 1970; Philadelphia, Pa.

RELIGION
Roman Catholic

FAMILY
Wife, Tara Rooney; three children

EDUCATION
Syracuse U., attended 1989-89; Washington & Jefferson College, B.A. 1993 (English literature); U. of Florida, M.A. 1996 (political science); U. of Miami, J.D. 1999

MILITARY SERVICE
Army 2000-2004

CAREER
Lawyer; children's services organization director; military and state prosecutor; college instructor; congressional aide

POLITICAL HIGHLIGHTS
No previous office

ELECTION RESULTS

2008 GENERAL

Tom Rooney (R)	209,874	60.1%
Tim Mahoney (D)	139,373	39.9%

2008 PRIMARY

Tom Rooney (R)	20,637	36.7%
Gayle Harrell (R)	19,626	34.9%
Hal Valeche (R)	15,916	28.3%

FLORIDA 16

South central — Port St. Lucie, parts of Port Charlotte and Wellington

The 16th sprawls over south-central Florida, connecting wealthy east coast communities with Charlotte Harbor on the west coast. In between, rural Floridians raise cattle and grow sugar cane, particularly around Lake Okeechobee. The 16th envelops the west side of the lake and also takes in most of St. Lucie County's white population near the Atlantic Ocean. With the lake and beaches, the environment is a significant issue here.

The 16th District's coast-to-coast geography has proved to be more of a curse than a blessing in recent years as hurricanes come ashore, causing billions of dollars in damage. Although armed with federal aid, local agriculture is still very vulnerable to both storms and fires.

Port St. Lucie is within commuting distance to major area cities, and it attracted many new residents fleeing skyrocketing housing prices in southern Florida. The district has experienced exceptionally high foreclosure rates recently, however.

St. Lucie County, the 16th's most populous jurisdiction, accounts for about one-fourth of residents. The 16th's share of St. Lucie — including all of Port St. Lucie and some of Fort Pierce and Lakewood Park — has many independent voters. The district's portion of Martin County is older and more Republican. Rep. Tom Rooney put the usually Republican 16th back in GOP hands after brief representation by a Democrat in the U.S. House.

MAJOR INDUSTRY
Agriculture, government, health care

CITIES
Port St. Lucie, 88,769; Port Charlotte (pt.) (unincorp.), 39,610; Wellington (pt.), 35,797

NOTABLE
LaBelle hosts the Swamp Cabbage Festival at the end of each February.

Rep. Kendrick B. Meek (D)

Elected 2002; 4th term

CAPITOL OFFICE
225-4506
kendrickmeek.house.gov
1039 Longworth Bldg. 20515-0917; fax 226-0777

COMMITTEES
Ways & Means

RESIDENCE
Miami

BORN
Sept. 6, 1966; Miami, Fla.

RELIGION
Baptist

FAMILY
Wife, Leslie A. Meek; two children

EDUCATION
Florida A&M U., B.S. 1988 (criminal justice)

CAREER
Security firm business development aide;
state trooper

POLITICAL HIGHLIGHTS
Fla. House, 1994-98; Fla. Senate, 1998-2002

ELECTION RESULTS

2008 GENERAL
Kendrick B. Meek (D)   unopposed
2008 PRIMARY
Kendrick B. Meek (D)   unopposed
2006 GENERAL
Kendrick B. Meek (D)   90,663   100.0%
PREVIOUS WINNING PERCENTAGES
2004 (100%); 2002 (100%)

Only in his fourth term, Meek has superseded the lawmaker he replaced — his mother Carrie P. Meek — in terms of influence and prominence. Having become one of the House's swiftest-rising young Democrats, he hopes his accomplishments and appeal can translate statewide as a candidate for the Senate in 2010.

Meek wasted little time jumping into the race in January 2009 after Florida Republican Sen. Mel Martinez announced his retirement. He touted his service as a Florida Highway Patrol trooper and state legislator in addition to his House service and sought to play off President Obama's 2008 success in articulating a message of change. "I believe that message will continue into the 2010 elections," Meek told The Associated Press. "If you look at my past, it's always been on the side of the everyday person here in Florida, no matter what their background."

He also hired as his chief strategist Steve Hildebrand, a Democratic veteran who focused on Florida while serving as Obama's deputy campaign manager. And he picked up endorsements from two unions while employing his connections to former New York Sen. Hillary Rodham Clinton to have her husband, former President Clinton, raise money for him.

In Washington, Meek has a prominent forum from which to further his standing — the Ways and Means Committee, which handles health care, tax and trade policy. In February 2009, he responded to the public furor over Bernard L. Madoff — who pleaded guilty to a vast Ponzi scheme that bilked investors of billions of dollars — by introducing a bill to provide tax relief to individuals harmed by the investment scam based on paying early investors with money from later ones.

Meek was given the Ways and Means seat as a reward for his prodigious fundraising. In the 2006 and 2008 election cycles, he gave more than $325,000 to the Democratic Congressional Campaign Committee. He also chairs the Congressional Black Caucus Foundation, the organization's policy and educational arm.

Meek previously served on the Armed Services panel, where he repeatedly pushed for a deadline to withdraw U.S. troops from Iraq. He also pressed senior Pentagon officials to diversify the military's top ranks.

Meek's district is more than 50 percent black and has the largest Haitian population in the United States, including residents of Miami's Little Haiti neighborhood. (He issues news releases on Haiti-related topics in both English and Haitian Creole.) Many constituents have friends or relatives on the island nation 600 miles southeast of Florida. Meek visits the country frequently and has fought to liberalize treatment for Haitian refugees.

Meek won approval of a measure giving Haitian-made apparel duty-free access to U.S. markets even if it was made with fabric from third countries such as China. A catchall tax and trade bill cleared by Congress in December 2006 granted such access, within certain limits.

An avid cigar smoker who presents boxes of his favorite as gifts, Meek looks out for cigar makers in his district. He helped arrange meetings between House Democratic leaders and cigar makers upset about a plan in 2008 legislation to pay for an expansion of children's health insurance by increasing cigar taxes. The Miami Herald reported that one Florida cigar maker, Jorge Padron, hosted a $1,000 per person fundraiser for Meek in December 2007.

The Herald also revealed Meek sought $4 million in federal funds in 2007 for a developer of a Florida biotech park who had paid Carrie P. Meek

$40,000 for consulting work. After allegations that money was misspent on the project, Meek later that year publicly called for Miami-Dade County not to rely on federal funds.

Meek represents the mostly poor and working-class neighborhoods of northeast Miami-Dade and southeastern Broward counties. He is well-known for his very public fights with Florida's former governor, the ex-president's brother, Jeb Bush, over education and affirmative action during his days in the state legislature. Meek advocates smaller class sizes in public schools as a way to raise test scores and deter dropouts.

Meek was born into politics the way some children inherit the family business. His mother was the first African American elected to the U.S. House from Florida since Reconstruction. Meek remembers curling up to sleep under her desk — when she served in the state House — as she read bills late into the night. Carrie, a divorced mother of three, was a strong role model, coaching him through early learning difficulties stemming from dyslexia. When he was 12, she made him a page at the state Capitol.

Meek graduated from his mother's alma mater, Florida A&M University, where he studied criminal justice. He went to work as a state trooper, and with his mother's help, rose quickly to captain and was placed on Democratic Lt. Gov. Buddy MacKay's security detail.

After just five years on the force, in 1994, he challenged Rep. Elaine Gordon, a veteran Democratic state House member. Gordon retired, avoiding a primary battle, and Meek was elected. In 1998, Meek, at 32, elbowed out another Democratic incumbent to capture his mother's old state Senate seat. When Gov. Bush refused to meet with him on minority preferences in state contracts and university admissions, Meek staged an overnight "sit in" at Bush's office.

Meek traveled the state promoting an "Arrive with Five" campaign urging women and minorities to register to vote in 2000 and to bring five new voters with them. It helped turn out the largest number of black voters in state history, according to the Orlando Sentinel. He then reconstituted his forces into a successful campaign to amend the state constitution in 2002 to make smaller class sizes mandatory, overcoming fierce opposition from Gov. Bush. That year, his mother announced her retirement less than two weeks before the candidate filing deadline, giving her son a jump-start. Would-be challengers stayed away and Meek was easily elected.

In 2006, Meek faced a primary challenge from Dufirstson Neree, a Haitian-born international development expert who grew up in Miami. Meek trounced the challenger with almost 90 percent of the vote and was unopposed in November; he also was unopposed in 2008.

KEY VOTES

2008

Yes Delay consideration of Colombia free-trade agreement

Yes Override Bush veto of federal farm and nutrition programs reauthorization bill

No Overhaul surveillance laws and permit dismissal of suits against companies that conducted warrantless wiretapping

Yes Grant mortgage relief to homeowners and funding for Fannie Mae and Freddie Mac

Yes Approve initial $700 billion program to stabilize financial markets

Yes Approve final $700 billion program to stabilize financial markets

Yes Provide $14 billion in loans to automakers

2007

Yes Increase minimum wage by $2.10 an hour

Yes Approve $124.2 billion in emergency war spending and set goal for redeployment of troops from Iraq

No Reject federal contraceptive assistance to international family planning groups

Yes Override Bush veto of $23.2 billion water projects authorization bill

Yes Implement Peru free-trade agreement

Yes Approve energy policy overhaul with new fuel economy standards

No Clear $473.5 billion omnibus spending bill, including $70 billion for military operations

CQ VOTE STUDIES

	PARTY UNITY		PRESIDENTIAL SUPPORT	
	SUPPORT	OPPOSE	SUPPORT	OPPOSE
2008	99%	1%	18%	82%
2007	97%	3%	7%	93%
2006	89%	11%	37%	63%
2005	93%	7%	26%	74%
2004	94%	6%	39%	61%

INTEREST GROUPS

	AFL-CIO	ADA	CCUS	ACU
2008	100%	95%	61%	4%
2007	96%	95%	55%	0%
2006	100%	95%	57%	8%
2005	93%	95%	52%	9%
2004	93%	85%	45%	9%

FLORIDA 17

Southeast — parts of Miami and Hollywood

The black-majority and solidly Democratic 17th is a compact district that takes in part of northeast Miami-Dade County and a slice of southeast Broward County. It stretches south from Hollywood and Pembroke Pines into Miami, taking in part of Miramar and North Miami, and it includes an array of neighborhoods that are ethnically and economically diverse.

The district has the state's highest percentage of black residents (55 percent), including many from the West Indies. Whites and Hispanics each make up about one-fifth of the residents. Little Haiti, the cultural heart of southern Florida's thriving Haitian community, is located in the 17th. There is a sizable population of Cuban-Americans, although the community is not as large here as elsewhere in southern Florida. More than 40 percent of district residents speak a language other than English at home, and more than one-third were born outside of the United States.

Overtown, once the region's hub of African-American wealth, spent decades in decline. Miami has pledged millions of dollars to develop affordable housing and new business space in Overtown and to revital-

ize the historic neighborhood, but improvement efforts have stalled.

Infrastructure is important to the district: Miami International Airport is located just outside the 17th, and the Opa-Locka Airport serves as a base for civilian pilots. Interstate 95 — a major hurricane evacuation route — runs through the district. Health concerns are a major topic for residents, many of whom are uninsured. In addition, the HIV/AIDS epidemic has hit the 17th hard, particularly in the black community.

Democrats win at all levels in the 17th — there are nearly twice as many independent voters here as Republicans and statewide GOP candidates often receive less than 25 percent of the vote. Democrat Barack Obama won 87 percent of the 17th's 2008 presidential vote, his highest percentage in Florida, and John McCain did not win any precincts in the district.

MAJOR INDUSTRY
Transportation, service, entertainment

CITIES
Miami (pt.), 81,688; Hollywood (pt.), 57,267; North Miami (pt.), 50,514; Miramar (pt.), 41,272; Carol City (unincorporated) (pt.), 35,858

NOTABLE
Opa-Locka's architecture is based on an Arabian theme.

Rep. Ileana Ros-Lehtinen (R)

Elected August 1989; 10th full term

CAPITOL OFFICE
225-3931
www.house.gov/ros-lehtinen
2470 Rayburn Bldg. 20515; fax 225-5620

COMMITTEES
Foreign Affairs - ranking member

RESIDENCE
Miami

BORN
July 15, 1952; Havana, Cuba

RELIGION
Episcopalian

FAMILY
Husband, Dexter Lehtinen; two children,
two stepchildren

EDUCATION
Miami-Dade Community College, A.A. 1972
(English); Florida International U., B.A. 1975
(English & education), M.S. 1986 (education);
U. of Miami, Ph.D. 2004 (education)

CAREER
Teacher; private school administrator

POLITICAL HIGHLIGHTS
Fla. House, 1982-86; Fla. Senate, 1986-89

ELECTION RESULTS

2008 GENERAL

Ileana Ros-Lehtinen (R)	140,617	57.9%
Annette Taddeo (D)	102,372	42.1%

2008 PRIMARY

Ileana Ros-Lehtinen (R)	unopposed

2006 GENERAL

Ileana Ros-Lehtinen (R)	79,631	62.1%
David "Big Dave" Patlak (D)	48,499	37.8%

PREVIOUS WINNING PERCENTAGES
2004 (65%); 2002 (69%); 2000 (100%); 1998 (100%);
1996 (100%); 1994 (100%); 1992 (67%); 1990 (60%);
1989 Special Election (53%)

Ros-Lehtinen is one of the strongest anti-Fidel Castro voices on Capitol Hill. But she also seeks to shape U.S. foreign policy in regions beyond Cuba; as top-ranking Republican on the Foreign Affairs Committee, she advocates pro-Israel policies and seeks to penalize nations that coddle terrorism, violate human rights and pose a nuclear threat.

A conservative on most fiscal and social issues as well, Ros-Lehtinen (full name: il-ee-AH-na ross-LAY-tin-nen) tends to keep in the mainstream of her party — except when it comes to attempts to set restrictive immigration polices. The first Cuban-American and first Hispanic woman elected to Congress, she looks out for the thousands of immigrants seeking to flee the Cuban communist regime, just as her family did when she was a young girl.

In recent years she moved away from the GOP party line as she feared a backlash at the polls; her party unity score in 2008 was 18 percentage points lower than it was for the entire eight years of the George W. Bush presidency. In 2007, Ros-Lehtinen bucked her party by backing an increase the minimum wage, a Democratic energy bill that included new fuel efficiency standards for automobiles and legislation to prohibit job discrimination based on sexual preference. She has always been an ardent supporter of equal rights for gays and lesbians, a reflection of her South Florida district that includes the Florida Keys, home to a large gay population. She was one of 27 Republicans to vote against a 2006 proposal to ban same-sex marriage.

Her fears of losing her seat proved unfounded — she took 58 percent of the vote in November 2008. She puts a priority on serving constituents and knows how to work a room; one pollster described her to the Miami Herald as "a very touchy-feely congresswoman."

As a leading conservative voice on foreign policy, she was among a group of Republicans that President Obama tried to reach out to before he took office in order to set a spirit of bipartisanship. But when he first called her in December 2008, Ros-Lehtinen hung up on him — and subsequently did the same to Obama's chief of staff, Rahm Emanuel. "I thought it was one of the radio stations in South Florida playing an incredible, elaborate, terrific prank on me," she told the Miami Herald. Foreign Affairs Chairman Howard L. Berman of California eventually convinced her the call was real. "I thought: 'Why would Obama want to call a little slug on the planet like me?'" she said.

Yet early in the 111th Congress (2009-10), she appeared unlikely to embrace much of Obama's initial agenda. She is a leading opponent of Obama's policy to lift travel restrictions to Cuba and remove limits on remittances sent by exiles to their families and friends there. And she opposes Obama's desire to increase foreign aid; in December 2008 she drafted a letter, signed by Minority Leader John A. Boehner and 10 other House Republicans, calling on Obama to freeze the foreign assistance budget at 2008 levels for 2009 and 2010.

Ros-Lehtinen was a strong defender of Bush's conduct of the war in Iraq, where her stepson, a Marine, and his wife served in 2006. "The war in Iraq is part of a far larger struggle, a global struggle, the struggle against Islamist extremist militants," she said during a 2007 House debate on Iraq.

But she criticized the Bush administration's October 2008 decision to remove North Korea from a list of state sponsors of terrorism to keep alive a deal with North Korea to denuclearize. Months earlier, Ros-Lehtinen had included in the Security Assistance and Arms Export Control Reform law a requirement that North Korea take verifiable action to end its proliferation activities, such as its nuclear assistance to Syria and Iran, before it could be considered for removal from the list. And just days earlier, Bush had signed into law her measure advancing human rights in North Korea and speeding up resettlement of North Korean refugees in China who are often exploited.

She opposes House GOP leaders' hard line on immigration and was one of only six Republicans to vote against construction of a 700-mile fence on the U.S.-Mexico border. She backs proposals to combine border enforcement with an expansion of visas and earned legalization for illegal immigrants.

Human rights are a cornerstone of her foreign policy initiatives. Ros-Lehtinen pushed a 2008 law expanding the United States' commitment to fight the global HIV/AIDS pandemic. In 2007, the House passed her bill condemning the use of human shields, a form of violence practiced by Islamic groups.

On international trade, which is vital to Florida's economy, Ros-Lehtinen switched her stance once Bush took office. In 1995, she opposed granting President Clinton the power to negotiate trade agreements that Congress could approve or reject but not amend; in 2002, she backed such authority for Bush. In 2000, she voted against granting China normal trade status. After Bush was in office, she backed most of his trade proposals, including the 2005 Central America Free Trade Agreement.

Ros-Lehtinen's concern for Cuba and its treatment of political dissidents shaped her rise in politics, and she remains isolationist toward the island. In 1999 and 2000, she led the argument that 5-year-old Elián González, who was rescued at sea along with a disabled boat full of refugees, should be allowed to stay with his U.S. relatives. Elián's mother drowned in the tragedy. Other social conservatives favored having the boy returned to his father in Cuba, which was the eventual outcome. The island's state-run newspaper, Granma, called Ros-Lehtinen a "ferocious wolf disguised as a woman," and she had "loba feroz" (shortened to "loba frz") stamped on a vanity license plate.

She was 8 years old when her family fled Cuba. After growing up in Miami and graduating from college, she became a teacher and ran a bilingual private school in southern Florida. In 2004 she completed a doctorate in education. Her dissertation studied House members' perspectives on educational testing.

In 1982, at age 30, she was the first Hispanic woman elected to the state legislature. In a 1989 special election to replace the late Democratic U.S. Rep. Claude Pepper, Ros-Lehtinen defeated three candidates to win the Republican nomination. With the national party's generous support, she beat Democrat Gerald Richman, a Miami Beach lawyer.

Ros-Lehtinen's husband is Dexter Lehtinen, a former state legislator and U.S. attorney for Miami who is now in private practice. He often surfaces in the news as general counsel for South Florida's Miccosukee Tribe.

KEY VOTES

2008

No Delay consideration of Colombia free-trade agreement
Yes Override Bush veto of federal farm and nutrition programs reauthorization bill
Yes Overhaul surveillance laws and permit dismissal of suits against companies that conducted warrantless wiretapping
Yes Grant mortgage relief to homeowners and funding for Fannie Mae and Freddie Mac
No Approve initial $700 billion program to stabilize financial markets
Yes Approve final $700 billion program to stabilize financial markets
No Provide $14 billion in loans to automakers

2007

Yes Increase minimum wage by $2.10 an hour
No Approve $124.2 billion in emergency war spending and set goal for redeployment of troops from Iraq
Yes Reject federal contraceptive assistance to international family planning groups
Yes Override Bush veto of $23.2 billion water projects authorization bill
Yes Implement Peru free-trade agreement
Yes Approve energy policy overhaul with new fuel economy standards
Yes Clear $473.5 billion omnibus spending bill, including $70 billion for military operations

CQ VOTE STUDIES

	PARTY UNITY		PRESIDENTIAL SUPPORT	
	SUPPORT	OPPOSE	SUPPORT	OPPOSE
2008	67%	33%	33%	67%
2007	79%	21%	63%	37%
2006	89%	11%	85%	15%
2005	91%	9%	79%	21%
2004	89%	11%	84%	16%

INTEREST GROUPS

	AFL-CIO	ADA	CCUS	ACU
2008	67%	65%	78%	32%
2007	46%	25%	90%	60%
2006	15%	15%	87%	63%
2005	20%	10%	93%	88%
2004	14%	15%	95%	80%

FLORIDA 18

Southeast — most of Miami; Florida Keys

The 18th features the glitz of downtown Miami and the southern part of Miami Beach, but its political base comes from the Hispanic-dominated areas west of downtown. The district winds its way south along the coast from Miami, follows U.S. 1 through the Florida Keys, taking in downtrodden sections of Little Havana, as well as wealthy Coral Gables (home to the University of Miami), Key Biscayne and Fisher Island.

The Keys — a 120-mile-long island chain between the Gulf of Mexico and the Atlantic Ocean — and in particular Key West, have a significant gay and lesbian population, in addition to older natives who adhere to the independence and environmentalism of the "Conch Republic." The Keys are vulnerable to hurricanes, and the economy depends on out-of-state visitors. The Port of Miami and Miami International Airport, which is nearby in the 21st, are major transportation centers that feed the local trade and tourism industries.

Despite this bedrock industry, falling real estate values and rising foreclosure rates are having a deep impact on Miami-Dade County and

Miami in particular. Local officials hope that a proposed stadium for baseball's Marlins and redevelopment projects in midtown Miami, focused on retail and the arts, will give an economic boost to the area.

A majority of district residents were born outside of the United States, and more than three-fifths of the population is Hispanic. While the older Cuban-American base in this district is reliably Republican and stridently anti-Fidel Castro, issues such as the economy are increasingly more important to younger voters. Overall, residents tend to be conservative on foreign policy issues but more in line with Democrats on welfare and other social issues. Democrat Barack Obama won 51 percent of the district's 2008 presidential vote, although there are still pockets of GOP support in areas such as Little Havana and Coral Gables.

MAJOR INDUSTRY
Trade, transportation, tourism

CITIES
Miami (pt.), 270,214; Miami Beach (pt.), 75,172; Coral Gables, 42,249; Westchester (unincorporated), 30,271; Key West, 25,478

NOTABLE
"Independence Day" celebrations in the Conch Republic honor the one-minute rebellion of Key West residents against a 1982 federal blockade.

Rep. Robert Wexler (D)

Elected 1996; 7th term

CAPITOL OFFICE
225-3001
www.house.gov/wexler
2241 Rayburn Bldg. 20515-0919; fax 225-5974

COMMITTEES
Foreign Affairs
(Europe - chairman)
Judiciary

RESIDENCE
Boca Raton

BORN
Jan. 2, 1961; Queens, N.Y.

RELIGION
Jewish

FAMILY
Wife, Laurie Wexler; three children

EDUCATION
Emory U., attended 1978-79; U. of Florida, B.A.
1982 (political science); George Washington U.,
J.D. 1985

CAREER
Lawyer

POLITICAL HIGHLIGHTS
Fla. Senate, 1990-96

ELECTION RESULTS

2008 GENERAL

Robert Wexler (D)	202,465	66.2%
Edward J. Lynch (R)	83,357	27.2%
Ben Graber (X)	20,214	6.6%

2008 PRIMARY

Robert Wexler (D)	unopposed

2006 GENERAL

Robert Wexler (D)	unopposed

PREVIOUS WINNING PERCENTAGES
2004 (100%); 2002 (72%); 2000 (72%); 1998 (100%);
1996 (66%)

Bombastic and partisan, Wexler is at least self-aware. He titled his 2008 book "Fire-Breathing Liberal," a chronicle of his often intense disagreements with conservatives. The cover shows him with fists raised, as if about to deliver a punch.

In the book, he said, "Right-wing Republicans have done everything possible to destroy the progressive movement in America ...by creating and utilizing an effective propaganda machine intended to turn the word *liberal*, or even simply *Democrat*, into a synonym for traitor." He evokes strong reactions from both sides of the partisan media — the liberal Nation magazine named him "Most Valuable Congressman," while conservative talk radio host Rush Limbaugh derided him as "disgusting."

Wexler was an early supporter of President Obama and campaigned heavily for him, but he is unlikely to help Obama with his pledge to reach out to both sides of the aisle. And Obama almost certainly will want nothing to do with Wexler's plan to reopen debate on the alleged sins of President George W. Bush's administration, ranging from mistreatment of detainees at a military detention facility on the U.S. naval base at Guantánamo Bay, Cuba, to the justification of the Iraq War. But Wexler, who is unlikely to win much support even among House colleagues for the plan, said it remains necessary. "We owe it to the American people and history to pursue the wrongdoings" of the Bush administration "whether or not it helps us politically," he said.

On the other hand, Wexler may find he's to the right of Obama on the Middle East peace process. A member of the Foreign Affairs Committee, Wexler is an uncompromising advocate for Israel, while Obama has pledged a more even-handed course. Wexler sits on the panel's Middle East subcommittee and vigorously defended Israel's 2008 invasion of the Gaza Strip, speaking at Israel solidarity rallies while much of the international community condemned the assault as disproportionate to the Hamas rocket attacks that prompted it. His district has a large Jewish population that applauds his uncompromising views.

As chairman of the Subcommittee on Europe, Wexler wants to strengthen NATO, improve relations with the European Union and Russia and address energy security and climate change.

He's also on the Judiciary Committee, where he backed an unsuccessful effort to impeach Bush for, among other things, allegedly misleading the country into the war in Iraq. He supported the resolution authorizing the president to go to war, but later became a vocal opponent of the U.S. involvement.

He is perhaps best known for his rage, directed at committee Republicans, during the impeachment hearings on President Clinton in 1998. Nearly as notable, two years later, were his blistering attacks on Bush during the Florida voting fiasco that ended with Bush defeating Al Gore to become president.

Wexler subsequently launched an ill-fated legal campaign to force Florida to stop using touch-screen voting machines because they don't provide a paper record of ballots cast. After the courts declined to intervene, he convinced Florida lawmakers in 2007 to approve a bill guaranteeing a paper trail in state elections. He pledged to pursue similar legislation in Congress.

In 2008 he gained Judiciary's support for his bill that aimed to mitigate the nation's nursing shortage by providing 20,000 visas per year for three years specifically for nurses. But the measure never made it to the House floor.

Wexler sat on the Financial Services Committee during the 110th Congress (2007-08). In the fall of 2008, he backed passage of a $700 billion law aimed at shoring up the nation's financial sector, and later that year supported a bill — which ultimately failed — to help the domestic auto industry.

Wexler also usually votes with his party on social and environmental issues. He supported a 2009 law to expand the State Children's Health Insurance Program, which provides insurance for children from low-income families that do not qualify for Medicaid, and he supports federal funding of embryonic stem cell research. He also opposes expanding offshore drilling.

Wexler loves the camera so much he allowed a film crew from the Sundance Channel to shadow him and his staff for a year and a half for a cable TV reality series called "The Hill" that aired in 2006. He did so, he said, to give the public a chance to "try to unlock, to a degree, the mystery of Congress."

But Wexler's penchant for publicity sometimes trips him up. In July 2006, during an appearance on Comedy Central's "Colbert Report," he was asked to say a few things that would "really lose the election for you if you were contested." It resulted in him saying, "I enjoy cocaine because it's a fun thing to do." Numerous people scolded him afterward, but the worst blow came from his teenage children. "They thought I was foolish," he said.

In 2008, Fox News Channel ambushed him outside his Maryland home to show he no longer maintained a residence in his district. A chastened Wexler — who'd been giving his in-laws' retirement address in Florida as his own — leased a Florida residence, but chalked up the controversy to "politics."

Born in Queens, Wexler was best friends as a young boy with the son of Republican Rep. Norman Lent. He recalls that at age 8 or 9 the two used to play a board game in which they pretended to run a presidential campaign. "I knew every state's Electoral College vote count when I was 9 years old," he said. A year later, when he was 10, his family moved to southern Florida.

After earning his law degree at George Washington University, Wexler returned to Florida and practiced law in Boca Raton. In 1990, he unseated a 16-year veteran of the state Senate. During the ensuing six years, he won generally favorable reviews, but he also drew fire for some controversial proposals. As chairman of the state Senate's Criminal Justice Committee, he proposed castration (via a chemical process) for two-time rapists and electrocution for a third rape conviction.

When four-term Democratic Rep. Harry A. Johnston decided not to seek re-election in 1996, Wexler jumped into a four-way primary. He won a plurality of the vote, then handily defeated state Senate Majority Leader Peter Weinstein in the runoff. He took two-thirds of the general-election vote against Republican Beverly Kennedy, a Pompano Beach financial consultant. He has won re-election easily since.

KEY VOTES

2008
Yes Delay consideration of Colombia free-trade agreement
? Override Bush veto of federal farm and nutrition programs reauthorization bill
No Overhaul surveillance laws and permit dismissal of suits against companies that conducted warrantless wiretapping
Yes Grant mortgage relief to homeowners and funding for Fannie Mae and Freddie Mac
Yes Approve initial $700 billion program to stabilize financial markets
Yes Approve final $700 billion program to stabilize financial markets
Yes Provide $14 billion in loans to automakers

2007
Yes Increase minimum wage by $2.10 an hour
Yes Approve $124.2 billion in emergency war spending and set goal for redeployment of troops from Iraq
No Reject federal contraceptive assistance to international family planning groups
Yes Override Bush veto of $23.2 billion water projects authorization bill
No Implement Peru free-trade agreement
? Approve energy policy overhaul with new fuel economy standards
? Clear $473.5 billion omnibus spending bill, including $70 billion for military operations

CQ VOTE STUDIES

	PARTY UNITY		PRESIDENTIAL SUPPORT	
	SUPPORT	OPPOSE	SUPPORT	OPPOSE
2008	99%	1%	15%	85%
2007	98%	2%	3%	97%
2006	93%	7%	30%	70%
2005	97%	3%	22%	78%
2004	97%	3%	32%	68%

INTEREST GROUPS

	AFL-CIO	ADA	CCUS	ACU
2008	100%	90%	54%	5%
2007	100%	95%	55%	0%
2006	100%	90%	33%	8%
2005	93%	100%	26%	0%
2004	85%	95%	37%	0%

FLORIDA 19
Southeast — parts of Coral Springs, Margate and Boca Raton

Two-thirds of the heavily Democratic 19th's residents live in Palm Beach County and one-third live in Broward County, mostly west of Interstate 95, where subdivisions and gated communities dot the landscape. The 19th has no coastline in either county, and it stretches from a small part of West Palm Beach as far south as a sliver of Fort Lauderdale, taking in parts of Boca Raton, Margate and Deerfield Beach.

Older, white, upper-middle-class residents make the 19th one of the most-educated and white-collar districts in the state. Despite a high percentage of residents age 65 or older and a history as a home to retirees — elderly voters still make up a significant majority of the electorate in the 19th's portion of Palm Beach County — the district has seen a shift toward a more middle-aged population in the last decade. The 19th's aging residents make health care an important industry in the district, and, with 44 percent of residents receiving Social Security, federal assistance for the elderly dominates the political agenda. A large Jewish

community, primarily in condominium communities that replaced previously rural land in the district, adds foreign policy concerns and U.S. relations with Israel to the political discussion.

Despite rising unemployment rates across the state, the health care facilities in Palm Beach and Broward counties support the economy in the district. The 19th's portion of Boca Raton long has been home to corporate headquarters and has an established business atmosphere. But, revenue losses and layoffs have hurt some Boca Raton-based companies.

Retirees and the politically active Jewish community provide a consistent base of Democratic support throughout much of the district. In 2008, Barack Obama won 65 percent of the district's presidential vote.

MAJOR INDUSTRY
Health care, financial services

CITIES
Coral Springs (pt.), 74,195; Margate (pt.), 42,284; Greenacres, 27,569; Tamarac (pt.), 25,756; Coconut Creek (pt.), 24,901

NOTABLE
Coconut Creek is home to the world's largest butterfly aviary, called Butterfly World.

Rep. Debbie Wasserman Schultz (D)

Elected 2004; 3rd term

CAPITOL OFFICE
225-7931
www.house.gov/wassermanschultz
118 Cannon Bldg. 20515-0920; fax 226-2052

COMMITTEES
Appropriations
(Legislative Branch - chairwoman)
Judiciary

RESIDENCE
Weston

BORN
Sept. 27, 1966; Queens, N.Y.

RELIGION
Jewish

FAMILY
Husband, Steve Schultz; three children

EDUCATION
U. of Florida, B.A. 1988 (political science), M.A.
1990 (political science)

CAREER
University program administrator;
college instructor; state legislative aide

POLITICAL HIGHLIGHTS
Fla. House, 1992-2000 (Democratic leader pro
tempore, 2000); Fla. Senate, 2000-04

ELECTION RESULTS

2008 GENERAL

Debbie Wasserman Schultz (D)	202,832	77.5%
Margaret Hostetter (X)	58,958	22.5%

2008 PRIMARY

Debbie Wasserman Schultz (D)	unopposed

2006 GENERAL

Debbie Wasserman Schultz (D)	unopposed

PREVIOUS WINNING PERCENTAGES
2004 (70%)

Forceful and articulate, Wasserman Schultz plays the Washington game with ease. Her stern leadership of the Appropriations panel overseeing Congress' budget, her fierce partisanship on the Judiciary Committee and her fundraising skills have earned her admiration among her Democratic colleagues and increasing responsibility for the party's future in the House.

In just her third term, she is one of the nine chief deputy whips tasked with gathering support for party initiatives. And in December 2008 she became one of the three vice chairs for the Democratic Congressional Campaign Committee. Her assignment is to focus on retaining incumbent members in 2010, a task certain to keep her busy; history has shown the party in power generally loses seats in midterm elections.

Before becoming a DCCC vice chairwoman, Wasserman Schultz led the campaign committee's "Frontline" program, which focuses logistical and financial resources on key 2008 House races. Election day results proved the effort successful, but she faced criticism from Florida Democratic activists and liberal bloggers for refusing to campaign against a trio of Cuban-American Republican House members from Miami Dade County. One contributor to the Daily Kos blog accused her of "kneecapping strong challengers and damaging the Democratic Party's prospects" of defeating Ileana Ros-Lehtinen, as well as Lincoln and Mario Diaz-Balart — all of whom ultimately won re-election.

Wasserman Schultz is a vocal defender of Israel; her district includes the third-largest concentration of Jewish Americans in the country. The Jewish Daily Forward, a New York-based Yiddish and English newspaper, once described her as "articulate with a trademark halo of curly blond locks." She helped maintain Jewish voters' support for Barack Obama's bid for the presidency after Hillary Rodham Clinton dropped out of the race in mid-2008.

Appropriations Chairman David R. Obey of Wisconsin calls Wasserman Schultz "the pistol." She frequently complained about the over-budget Capitol Visitors Center, which opened in 2008 after years of delays, and once described it as "one of the most mismanaged entities I've ever encountered." And when Republicans on both sides of the Hill complained President Obama failed to follow through on his pledge of bipartisanship as he pushed major spending bills through Congress, Wasserman Schultz called the complaints "malarkey." She told the Miami Herald, "Bipartisanship means you get to participate and provide input and some of your input will be accepted and some of it won't."

In January 2009, she picked up a seat on Appropriations' Financial Services Subcommittee, tasked with helping resolve an ongoing financial crisis. In fall 2008, she backed both versions — the second of which became law — of a $700 billion package to shore up the troubled financial services sector.

On the Judiciary Committee, Wasserman Schultz holds her own with conservatives on many of her priorities, such as separation of church and state. During committee debate in 2006 on a bill aimed at preserving the phrase "under God" in the Pledge of Allegiance, which had been ruled unconstitutional by a federal court, she scolded Republicans for ignoring "the things that people actually have to deal with in their daily lives, like gas prices, health care costs, fiscal responsibility, a real debate on Iraq."

She also stood up to conservatives in 2005 when they wanted to intervene in the case of Terri Schiavo, a severely brain-damaged Florida woman who was the subject of a major court case over end-of-life medical decisions. Well-versed in the long legal battle from her days in the state legislature, she became a forceful opponent of intervention in the nationally watched case.

By that time, she had already become a familiar figure on TV programs such as "Face the Nation" and the "Today Show." "I had a lot of specific knowledge that kind of thrust me into a more public spotlight," she said.

Policy affecting children is important to Wasserman Schultz, who has three young children, including a set of twins. She often flies to Washington on Tuesday mornings and back home on Thursday nights to maximize her time with her family. Her husband, Steve Schultz, a banker, stays with their children in Florida during the week.

In December 2007, President George W. Bush signed into law her bill giving federal grants to states that require fences around pools and devices that prevent children from becoming trapped in drains. The House in November 2007 passed her bill expanding investigations of computer-generated pornography, authorizing more than $1 billion over eight years to hire federal and state investigators and establish a special counsel's office in the Justice Department. The measure was later wrapped into a broader Senate bill and signed into law.

She grew up in Lido Beach on Long Island. Her father was the chief financial officer for a girls' clothing company, Roanna Togs; her mother was a horticulturist. She attended the University of Florida, her father's alma mater. There, she abandoned her childhood dream of becoming a veterinarian — chemistry was her undoing — and shifted her studies to public policy.

After graduation, she took a job as chief of staff with state Rep. Peter Deutsch, who became her mentor. When he left to campaign for the U.S. House in 1992, he persuaded her to run to replace him in the state legislature.

Local party bosses dismissed her, and she raised only $21,000. Deutsch told her to ignore all that and apply the shoe leather. She estimates she knocked on 25,000 doors, taking notes about the conversations after she left, then mailing personal follow-up letters. She prevailed in a six-way Democratic primary, avoiding a runoff, and went on to become, at 26, the youngest woman ever to serve in the Florida House. Eight years later, she moved up to the state Senate.

When Deutsch decided to run for the U.S. Senate in 2004, Wasserman Schultz again ran for his seat. Name recognition and early fundraising deterred potential primary foes. She donated $100,000 from her campaign funds to help other candidates, and still had cash to spare. Her general election win over Republican Margaret Hostetter, a social-conservative activist, was never in doubt. The GOP didn't field a challenger in 2006 or 2008. And she has continued to raise funds for other candidates. She donated more than $170,000 to Democrats with tough re-election battles in 2006. In the 2008 election cycle, she raised more than $1.7 million and contributed nearly $800,000 to other candidates and the DCCC.

KEY VOTES

2008

Yes Delay consideration of Colombia free-trade agreement

Yes Override Bush veto of federal farm and nutrition programs reauthorization bill

No Overhaul surveillance laws and permit dismissal of suits against companies that conducted warrantless wiretapping

Yes Grant mortgage relief to homeowners and funding for Fannie Mae and Freddie Mac

Yes Approve initial $700 billion program to stabilize financial markets

Yes Approve final $700 billion program to stabilize financial markets

Yes Provide $14 billion in loans to automakers

2007

Yes Increase minimum wage by $2.10 an hour

Yes Approve $124.2 billion in emergency war spending and set goal for redeployment of troops from Iraq

No Reject federal contraceptive assistance to international family planning groups

Yes Override Bush veto of $23.2 billion water projects authorization bill

Yes Implement Peru free-trade agreement

Yes Approve energy policy overhaul with new fuel economy standards

No Clear $473.5 billion omnibus spending bill, including $70 billion for military operations

CQ VOTE STUDIES

	PARTY UNITY		PRESIDENTIAL SUPPORT	
	SUPPORT	OPPOSE	SUPPORT	OPPOSE
2008	99%	1%	13%	87%
2007	98%	2%	6%	94%
2006	94%	6%	33%	67%
2005	94%	6%	24%	76%

INTEREST GROUPS

	AFL-CIO	ADA	CCUS	ACU
2008	100%	100%	59%	0%
2007	100%	90%	55%	0%
2006	100%	95%	40%	4%
2005	93%	100%	44%	0%

FLORIDA 20

Southeast — parts of Hollywood, Sunrise, Davie and Fort Lauderdale

Middle-class suburbs mix with beach communities as the 20th snakes through Broward and Miami-Dade counties from as far north as Tamarac to as far south as Miami Beach. The district takes in part of Fort Lauderdale and accounts for about one-third of Broward's population, much of it in suburbs such as Sunrise, Plantation and Davie.

In addition to western Broward suburbs, the 20th wraps around to reach some coastal northeastern Miami suburbs, with their golf courses and condominium developments. It twists through portions of Hollywood and Hallandale and moves south into Aventura and North Miami before jumping the Intracoastal Waterway to take in highly developed Bal Harbor and a chunk of northern Miami Beach.

Economic downturns have hit Broward hard, and the county experienced recent population loss related to the rising cost of living in the area. The collapse of the housing market in southern Florida has resulted in high foreclosure rates, stagnating home sales and vacant residential units in the district. Residents and officials are concerned about widespread layoffs in the once-thriving financial services sector.

Two-thirds of residents are white and about one-fifth are Hispanic, most of Cuban descent and strongly anti-Fidel Castro. The 20th's large Jewish population makes U.S.-Israel relations politically important. Wilton Manors has a significant gay and lesbian community, and Dania Beach is becoming a more prominent gay resort area. Davie, with its cattle ranches in the central part of the 20th, has retained some of its rural feel. Plantation has more-expensive homes and light industry. Democrats tend to win elections in the 20th at all levels, and Barack Obama received 63 percent of the vote here in the 2008 presidential election.

MAJOR INDUSTRY
Tourism, business services, retail

CITIES
Hollywood (pt.), 81,921; Sunrise (pt.), 71,670; Davie (pt.), 70,142; Plantation (pt.), 66,264; Weston, 49,286; Pembroke Pines (pt.), 37,466

NOTABLE
Dania Beach has an active community for the Basque game jai-alai, and its fronton, or playing arena, opened in 1953.

Rep. Lincoln Diaz-Balart (R)

Elected 1992; 9th term

CAPITOL OFFICE
225-4211
diaz-balart.house.gov
2244 Rayburn Bldg. 20515; fax 225-8576

COMMITTEES
Rules

RESIDENCE
Miami

BORN
Aug. 13, 1954; Havana, Cuba

RELIGION
Roman Catholic

FAMILY
Wife, Cristina Diaz-Balart; two children

EDUCATION
U. of South Florida, B.A. 1976 (international relations); Case Western Reserve U., J.D. 1979

CAREER
Lawyer; state prosecutor

POLITICAL HIGHLIGHTS
Democratic nominee for Fla. House, 1982; Fla. House, 1986-89; Fla. Senate, 1989-92

ELECTION RESULTS

2008 GENERAL

Lincoln Diaz-Balart (R)	137,226	57.9%
Raúl L. Martinez (D)	99,776	42.1%

2008 PRIMARY

Lincoln Diaz-Balart (R)	unopposed

2006 GENERAL

Lincoln Diaz-Balart (R)	66,784	59.5%
Frank J. Gonzalez (D)	45,522	40.5%

PREVIOUS WINNING PERCENTAGES
2004 (73%); 2002 (100%); 2000 (100%); 1998 (75%); 1996 (100%); 1994 (100%); 1992 (100%)

A former prosecutor, Diaz-Balart is a skilled inside player who moves easily in the arcane world of House rules and can be persuasive in face-to-face meetings. His career-long quest has been to rid Cuba of its Communist government, but he hopes to be known for more.

Facing the toughest re-election campaign of his career in 2008, Diaz-Balart (DEE-az ba-LART) emphasized his longtime work on behalf of immigrants. He talked about the need to bring jobs and federal money to his South Florida district, such as the military's Southern Command headquarters, rather than just outlining his stance on Cuba.

Diaz-Balart's influence has waned since Democrats took control, relegating him to a minority seat on the Rules Committee where all power resides with the party in charge. During the George W. Bush administration, he often opposed Democratic initiatives and defended Bush. But early in the 111th Congress (2009-10), he showed some support for President Obama's early agenda items. While he opposed Obama's $787 billion economic stimulus plan, he did change his earlier position and supported a bill to expand the State Children's Health Insurance Program, which covers children whose families don't qualify for Medicaid. He said he backed the legislation, signed into law in February 2009, because it contains provisions to allow legal immigrants who have been in the country less than five years to enroll in the program. His Miami-area district has a large population of immigrants, many from Latin America, and services for non-citizens is a major local issue.

He also was one of seven House Republicans who backed a measure in March 2009 that incorporates several initiatives Obama detailed in his $75 billion housing plan the previous month. The bill includes a provision to allow bankruptcy judges to modify the terms of troubled mortgages.

But Diaz-Balart and Obama may not see perfectly eye-to-eye on Cuba. Diaz-Balart believes there should be no easing of sanctions until Cuba frees its political prisoners, legalizes opposition parties and promises free elections. Before Obama took office, Diaz-Balart warned that "if the new president seeks to unilaterally reduce the main sanctions, we're going to fight in Congress strongly and we have a significant bipartisan coalition."

The economic crisis has started to drive some lobbyists and Democrats to push the idea of revising the issue of sanctions that deny the Castro regime access to tourism dollars and U.S. food supplies. Obama has not indicated a strong willingness to lift a four-decade-old trade embargo against Cuba, but said he is willing to consider easing restrictions on U.S. citizens' travel there. Provisions in a catchall spending bill cleared in 2009 would loosen rules on travel and imports of food and medicine to Cuba, but after an outcry among several members, the administration said the provisions would be interpreted narrowly.

Diaz-Balart views his recent re-election as a vindication of his hard-line approach. "It shows the community is very, very strong in its support for freedom for our oppressed brothers and sisters" in Cuba, he said.

When the GOP ruled the House, Diaz-Balart frequently led floor debates for the Republicans as a member of Rules, a plus for a party eager to showcase its few Hispanic members. He in turn leveraged the party's interest in wooing Hispanic voters to press for liberalized immigration policies out of the Republican mainstream. He bucked his party on the 1996 welfare overhaul that imposed new restrictions on benefits to legal and illegal immigrants. And he still proudly touts his work on a 1997 law that helped prevent the deportation of an estimated 150,000 Nicaraguans.

He was among a minority of Republicans in 2006 who voted against legislation to build a 700-mile fence along the U.S.-Mexico border and to classify illegal immigrants as criminals. He also broke with conservatives in 2006 to support renewing a provision of the landmark 1965 Voting Rights Act that requires local governments to offer assistance to non-English speakers.

He was one of the few GOP House candidates in 1994 who declined to sign the "Contract with America," its political manifesto that year, because of a provision that would have cut off benefits to legal immigrants.

Diaz-Balart hails from a prominent family of pre-revolutionary politicians who fled Cuba when Castro took power, and now represents the fervently anti-Castro Cuban-American community in South Florida. (His brother, Mario, also represents a South Florida district.) Neither Castro's terminal illness, made public in 2006, nor his resignation in 2008 softened those sentiments. Diaz-Balart insists little has changed in Cuba since Castro's brother, Raúl, assumed power, at least in name. "Fidel Castro is still the source of power in that regime," Diaz-Balart said.

Diaz-Balart's grandfather, father and uncle served in Cuba's House before the family fled to the United States in 1959, the year of the revolution. The future congressman was 5 years old. His father's sister was married to Castro in the late 1940s and early 1950s, but they divorced and a falling-out between the families ensued. His father, Rafael Diaz-Balart, remained an exile leader of distinction. More than 1,000 people attended his funeral in Miami's Little Havana neighborhood in 2005 after he died of leukemia at age 79.

Diaz-Balart completed law school, then worked for a Miami legal services organization providing free legal help for the poor. He was a Dade County prosecutor in the early 1980s under Janet Reno, whom he frequently criticized during her time as attorney general under President Clinton.

A Democrat in his early days, Diaz-Balart was co-chairman of the Democrats for Reagan campaign in Florida in 1984 and switched to the GOP in 1985 along with his wife and brother. He easily won a state House seat the following year. He served three years in the House and three in the state Senate.

When the courts redrew Florida's congressional maps after the 1990 census, a second Hispanic-majority district was created. Diaz-Balart easily bested a fellow Cuban-American state senator in a two-way Republican primary. He drew no Democratic foe in November 1992, and did not face a serious challenge until 2008, from Democrat Raúl L. Martinez, a former mayor of Hialeah who sought to portray him as being in lockstep with Bush. But Diaz-Balart outraised Martinez and took 58 percent of the vote.

KEY VOTES

2008

No Delay consideration of Colombia free-trade agreement

Yes Override Bush veto of federal farm and nutrition programs reauthorization bill

Yes Overhaul surveillance laws and permit dismissal of suits against companies that conducted warrantless wiretapping

Yes Grant mortgage relief to homeowners and funding for Fannie Mae and Freddie Mac

No Approve initial $700 billion program to stabilize financial markets

No Approve final $700 billion program to stabilize financial markets

No Provide $14 billion in loans to automakers

2007

Yes Increase minimum wage by $2.10 an hour

No Approve $124.2 billion in emergency war spending and set goal for redeployment of troops from Iraq

Yes Reject federal contraceptive assistance to international family planning groups

Yes Override Bush veto of $23.2 billion water projects authorization bill

Yes Implement Peru free-trade agreement

Yes Approve energy policy overhaul with new fuel economy standards

Yes Clear $473.5 billion omnibus spending bill, including $70 billion for military operations

CQ VOTE STUDIES

	PARTY UNITY		PRESIDENTIAL SUPPORT	
	SUPPORT	OPPOSE	SUPPORT	OPPOSE
2008	80%	20%	41%	59%
2007	82%	18%	67%	33%
2006	90%	10%	87%	13%
2005	90%	10%	81%	19%
2004	90%	10%	91%	9%

INTEREST GROUPS

	AFL-CIO	ADA	CCUS	ACU
2008	60%	55%	82%	52%
2007	42%	25%	89%	60%
2006	21%	15%	93%	60%
2005	14%	5%	89%	87%
2004	7%	10%	84%	83%

FLORIDA 21

Southeast — most of Hialeah and Kendall

The Hispanic-majority 21st District is adjacent to the eastern edge of the Florida Everglades and includes middle-class suburbs in Miami-Dade County and a slice of Broward County, from parts of Pembroke Pines and Miramar in the north through most of Hialeah in its center and much of the Colombian-American area of Kendall to the south. It includes one-fourth of Miami-Dade's population.

Residents tend to commute from Hialeah — Florida's fifth-largest city by population and a blue-collar residential area filled with Cuban-Americans — to other parts of the Miami area for work. Miramar and Pembroke Pines host young professionals from Latin America, and the 21st has the nation's largest percentage (57 percent) of foreign-born residents.

Transportation-related businesses, including Carnival Cruise Lines, have facilities close to Miami International Airport in Fountainbleau, but as tourism revenue declines, the local economy is vulnerable. The airport — a major international hub that carries more than 33 million passengers annually, many of them to Latin America — is a key employment source

and economic driver in southern Florida.

Traditionally, the 21st's politics center around immigration issues and opposition to Fidel Castro, but these political norms are shifting and much of the local Cuban-American community no longer supports continuing the embargo against Cuba. Residents also hold moderate views on labor and social policy matters. The district's large, suburban Cuban-American community accounts for its GOP bent in statewide and federal elections. Few areas in Florida have been as heavily Republican as Hialeah, with its large base of elderly Cuban-American voters. Despite this historical GOP slant, Republican John McCain took only 51 percent of the district's 2008 presidential vote.

MAJOR INDUSTRY
Transportation, trade, small business

CITIES
Hialeah (pt.), 208,552; Kendall (unincorporated) (pt.), 59,676; Pembroke Pines (pt.), 54,246; Fountainbleau (unincorporated) (pt.), 52,244

NOTABLE
Amelia Earhart's final flight (1937) began in Hialeah; The Audubon Society has designated Hialeah Park Racetrack as a sanctuary for the American flamingo.

Rep. Ron Klein (D)

Elected 2006; 2nd term

CAPITOL OFFICE
225-3026
klein.house.gov
313 Cannon Bldg. 20515-0922; fax 225-8398

COMMITTEES
Financial Services
Foreign Affairs

RESIDENCE
Boca Raton

BORN
July 10, 1957; Cleveland, Ohio

RELIGION
Jewish

FAMILY
Wife, Dori Klein; two children

EDUCATION
Ohio State U., B.A. 1979 (political science);
Case Western Reserve U., J.D. 1982

CAREER
Lawyer; lobbyist

POLITICAL HIGHLIGHTS
Fla. House, 1992-96; Fla. Senate, 1996-2006
(minority leader, 2002-04)

ELECTION RESULTS

2008 GENERAL

Ron Klein (D)	169,041	54.7%
Allen West (R)	140,104	45.3%

2008 PRIMARY

Ron Klein (D)	20,507	85.1%
Paul Francis Renneisen (D)	3,603	14.9%

2006 GENERAL

Ron Klein (D)	108,688	50.9%
E. Clay Shaw Jr. (R)	100,663	47.1%
Neil Evangelista (X)	4,254	2.0%

Klein is a veteran of Florida politics who calls himself a "pro-business Democrat," but he also works on issues of concern to homeowners, teachers and military families. At the same time, he immerses himself in foreign policy and furthers his reputation as a prolific fundraiser.

His temperate manner contrasts with his friend from their days in the Florida Legislature, Debbie Wasserman Schultz, who represents a neighboring congressional district. "He feels passionately about his issues, but his style is unflappable," Wasserman Schultz said. "He doesn't swing from the chandeliers like I do."

But Klein is no pushover on the campaign trail. He helped Democrats capture the House in 2006 when he toppled 13-term Republican E. Clay Shaw Jr. in one of the year's nastiest and most expensive congressional races.

Once in Congress, Klein kept raising money aggressively, amassing a war chest of nearly $4 million during the 2007-08 cycle — seven times more than his opponent — and comfortably winning re-election.

He is a dependable Democratic vote, siding with his party in his first term on 95 percent of the votes in which a majority of the two parties opposed each other. He is a member of the centrist New Democrat Coalition and serves as co-chairman of its energy task force, where he has sought to make investments in alternative energy technologies as attractive as possible.

Klein is an active member of the Financial Services Committee. Representing a coastal district with many upscale beachfront homes often threatened by hurricanes, he is concerned about the cost of homeowners' insurance, an issue he also focused on as a state legislator. In August 2007, he introduced legislation with Tim Mahoney, another Florida Democrat on Financial Services, to create a national catastrophe fund aimed at lowering insurance prices. The bill, which would allow state insurance funds to join a national consortium in order to pool risks, was passed by the House in November 2007 but not taken up in the Senate. Klein won high marks for building support among conservatives who represent states prone to natural disasters.

He sponsored another bill that passed the House in July 2008 but did not advance in the Senate. It authorized $30 million in grants to a nonprofit organization that helps law enforcement with missing-persons cases.

Klein also introduced legislation to extend deductibility of state and local sales taxes as well as tax-free distributions from individual retirement accounts for charitable purposes. It also included a five-year extension of a tax cut targeting elementary and secondary school teachers. Portions of his bill were included in a $700 billion measure he supported in fall 2008 to aid the ailing financial services sector.

He also tried to push, unsuccessfully, a measure to permanently extend a provision allowing active-duty military to make penalty-free withdrawals from their retirement plans.

From his seat on the Foreign Affairs' Middle East and South Asia Subcommittee, Klein watches out for the interests of Israel, a country he has visited frequently. In May 2008 he joined Speaker Nancy Pelosi of California on a trip to celebrate Israel's 60th birthday and posted on his Web site a blog about his meetings with top Israeli officials.

He joined a bipartisan group of House members in December 2008 to pressure the U.S. Export-Import Bank to stop financing U.S. companies that indirectly abet trade with Iran. He also serves as co-chairman of the Congressional Task Force Against Anti-Semitism with conservative Mike Pence of

Indiana. As a state legislator, he saw enacted into law his legislation mandating Holocaust education in Florida schools.

Klein has pushed to require that all future U.S. assistance to Iraq for reconstruction, fuel and training costs be in the form of loans. "At a time when the Iraqi government is raking in billions of dollars in oil revenue, the American people are rightfully asking why we are continuing to foot the bill for their reconstruction," he said in 2008.

Klein's grandfather immigrated to the United States to escape the Holocaust, eventually opening a five-and-dime variety store in inner-city Cleveland. Klein's father later operated the shop while his mother raised Klein and his sister after leaving her job teaching elementary school.

Klein attended Ohio State University and law school at Case Western Reserve, getting his first exposure to politics as an intern for the Ohio General Assembly and Cincinnati congressman Tom Luken.

In 1985, he moved to Florida with his wife and 3-month-old son and worked as a lawyer in Boca Raton. But he found himself drawn back to politics, becoming involved in local Jewish community organizations. In 1992, he was elected to the state House, where he served two terms before winning election to the state Senate. He eventually rose to the position of Senate minority leader.

Democrats had urged Klein to run against Shaw, a conservative Republican who for 26 years represented a district that narrowly favored Massachusetts Sen. John Kerry for president in 2004. Shaw had won re-election over the years because he focused on issues relevant to the elderly, including the future of Social Security.

But Klein made headway by criticizing Shaw's support for establishing personal savings accounts in the Social Security program, a plan favored by President George W. Bush that drew little interest from Congress or the public. That fit into Klein's theme of tying Shaw closely to Bush. Shaw also was criticized for his support for the Iraq War. Both parties poured money into the race and enlisted high-profile surrogates, including former President Clinton. Klein won, taking 51 percent of the vote to Shaw's 47 percent.

He had an easier time in 2008. He ran up 85 percent of the vote in the Democratic primary against airline pilot Paul Francis Renneisen, who ran as an anti-war candidate. Klein's campaign coffers were then no match for Republican Allen West, an Iraq War veteran, and he won with nearly 55 percent.

In early 2009, Klein contemplated a bid for the seat being vacated in 2010 by retiring GOP Sen. Mel Martinez, though it would mean facing his Democratic colleague Kendrick Meek in a primary.

KEY VOTES

2008

Yes Delay consideration of Colombia free-trade agreement

Yes Override Bush veto of federal farm and nutrition programs reauthorization bill

Yes Overhaul surveillance laws and permit dismissal of suits against companies that conducted warrantless wiretapping

Yes Grant mortgage relief to homeowners and funding for Fannie Mae and Freddie Mac

Yes Approve initial $700 billion program to stabilize financial markets

Yes Approve final $700 billion program to stabilize financial markets

Yes Provide $14 billion in loans to automakers

2007

Yes Increase minimum wage by $2.10 an hour

Yes Approve $124.2 billion in emergency war spending and set goal for redeployment of troops from Iraq

No Reject federal contraceptive assistance to international family planning groups

Yes Override Bush veto of $23.2 billion water projects authorization bill

Yes Implement Peru free-trade agreement

Yes Approve energy policy overhaul with new fuel economy standards

No Clear $473.5 billion omnibus spending bill, including $70 billion for military operations

CQ VOTE STUDIES

	PARTY UNITY		PRESIDENTIAL SUPPORT	
	SUPPORT	OPPOSE	SUPPORT	OPPOSE
2008	98%	2%	17%	83%
2007	94%	6%	9%	91%

INTEREST GROUPS

	AFL-CIO	ADA	CCUS	ACU
2008	100%	95%	67%	4%
2007	96%	95%	67%	0%

FLORIDA 22

Southeast – coastal Broward and Palm Beach counties, parts of Fort Lauderdale and Boca Raton

The 22nd follows picturesque Route A1A down a sliver of Atlantic coastline from northern Palm Beach County to Fort Lauderdale in Broward County. Although its projections reach inland in places to pick up middle-class suburbs and gated communities, the district is recognized by its upscale beachfront areas, including parts of Boca Raton. Overwhelmingly white and mostly well-off, the 22nd has the highest median income in Florida and one of the nation's largest Jewish populations.

The district has a corporate presence and is home to major transportation centers — Fort Lauderdale/Hollywood International Airport, Port Everglades and the Port of Palm Beach. It boasts ritzy hotels and shopping centers, and the ports attract cruise line and shipping business. Economic downturns have stalled further development, and retail, construction and financial services sectors have seen widespread revenue losses and layoffs. The wealth of many district residents helps protect them from economic pressures, but the area depends heavily on tourism.

Several large hospitals and the local health care industry, serving a substantial elderly population and many military veterans, support the district's economy.

Social Security, the Middle East and port issues top the political agenda here. Residents also are concerned about roads, as urbanization and development have stretched the aging infrastructure and exacerbated heavy traffic problems. Republicans hold a slim voter registration edge in the 22nd, which is strongest in the district's portion of Palm Beach County, but the district is politically competitive. A shift toward the Democratic Party has grown since John Kerry won the district by 2 percentage points in the 2004 presidential election. Democratic Ron Klein solidified his hold on the U.S. House seat in 2008, and Barack Obama won here with 52 percent of the district's vote for president.

MAJOR INDUSTRY

Health care, tourism, shipping

CITIES

Fort Lauderdale (pt.), 61,509; Boca Raton (pt.), 55,946; Coral Springs (pt.), 43,354; Pompano Beach (pt.), 34,925; Palm Beach Gardens (pt.), 30,649

NOTABLE

The International Swimming Hall of Fame Museum is in Fort Lauderdale.

Rep. Alcee L. Hastings (D)

Elected 1992; 9th term

CAPITOL OFFICE
225-1313
alceehastings.house.gov
2353 Rayburn Bldg. 20515-0923; fax 225-1171

COMMITTEES
Rules
  (Legislative & Budget Process - chairman)
Select Intelligence

RESIDENCE
Miramar

BORN
Sept. 5, 1936; Altamonte Springs, Fla.

RELIGION
African Methodist Episcopal

FAMILY
Divorced; three children

EDUCATION
Fisk U., B.S. 1958 (zoology & botany); Howard U.,
attended 1958-60 (law); Florida A&M U., J.D. 1963

CAREER
Judge; lawyer

POLITICAL HIGHLIGHTS
Sought Democratic nomination for U.S. Senate,
1970; U.S. District Court judge, 1979-89; Democratic
nominee for Fla. secretary of state, 1990

ELECTION RESULTS

2008 GENERAL

Alcee L. Hastings (D)	172,835	82.2%
Marion D. Thorpe Jr. (R)	37,431	17.8%

2008 PRIMARY

Alcee L. Hastings (D)	31,182	88.7%
Ray Torres Sanchez (D)	4,235	11.3%

2006 GENERAL

Alcee L. Hastings (D)	unopposed

PREVIOUS WINNING PERCENTAGES
2004 (100%); 2002 (77%); 2000 (76%); 1998 (100%);
1996 (73%); 1994 (100%); 1992 (59%)

Hastings, now one of the senior members of Florida's congressional delegation, is a national leader in the area of human rights and an astute inside player in his party and state. Charismatic and partisan, he should be wielding even more influence now that his party rules the House, but he always runs into a roadblock: his impeachment as a federal judge.

The U.S. House impeached him in 1988 stemming from criminal charges related to an alleged bribery conspiracy; the Senate the following year removed him from office. He had been cleared of the charges before being removed from his seat, but the issue still rears its head, even as he has developed a proven track record in Congress.

Hastings was passed over as chairman of the Select Intelligence Committee at the start of the 110th Congress (2007-08) after Republicans raised the issue of the bribery case and his impeachment. When he saw trouble looming, Hastings told incoming Speaker Nancy Pelosi he would bow out. She "thanked me, and she hugged me," he said. Still, he felt bitter about the outcome. "No one ever cared that I was found not guilty in a court of law, that I was innocent of what I was charged with," he said.

He then shifted much of his attention from intelligence matters to foreign affairs. As consolation, Pelosi appointed him chairman of the U.S. Commission on Security and Cooperation in Europe, better known as the Helsinki Commission, an independent government agency that focuses on democracy and human rights. In 2009, he handed over the gavel to Sen. Benjamin L. Cardin of Maryland, assuming the role of co-chairman.

Hastings has a background in foreign affairs. In 2006, he had wrapped up a second one-year term as the first U.S. president of the Parliamentary Assembly of the Organization for Security and Cooperation in Europe, a 56-nation organization of mostly European nations that focuses on security issues, ranging from arms control to human rights. In that position, he visited nearly three dozen foreign countries, continuing his longtime interest in election monitoring in countries such as Azerbaijan, Ukraine and Belarus, where he led a group of 400 election monitors in March 2006.

As chairman of the Helsinki Commission, he scolded European governments at a June 2007 hearing on the future of the U.S. military detention center on the U.S. naval base at Guantánamo Bay, Cuba, complaining that they criticized the U.S. government but refused to take custody of more terror suspects. "Guantánamo has to be closed, over and out," Hastings said, as reported by the Miami Herald. "But if Europe isn't prepared to stand up and take their share, I believe they ought to mute some of their criticism."

Hastings sits on the powerful Rules Committee, where he chairs the Legislative and Budget Process Subcommittee. When the Republicans controlled the House, he used his Rules seat and his fiery oratorical style to protest the substance of Republican legislation as well as the floor procedures used by GOP leaders. He was a sharp critic of President George W. Bush's policies both at home and abroad. As a member of the Intelligence panel, Hastings regularly asked questions that were among the most pointed in the House about the veracity of the administration's intelligence assessments of Iraq's possession of weapons of mass destruction.

Hastings is also quite visible at home. He has long resisted what he sees as efforts by some white Florida Democrats to shift the state party to the right, diminishing the influence of black voters. He has several times urged African-Americans to consider voting for Republicans to send the Democratic Party a signal that it should not take their support for granted.

In 2007, Hastings and Florida's Democratic Sen. Bill Nelson sued the Democratic National Committee after it moved to strip Florida of its delegate votes at the August 2008 national convention. The committee said Florida violated party rules that set Feb. 5 as the first date on which most states could hold presidential nominating contests. The state legislature had moved up Florida's primary date to Jan. 29. (Michigan also violated the rules, holding a Jan. 15 contest.)

Hastings and Nelson said such penalties represented an unconstitutional infringement on Floridians' right to vote. "I would have hoped that we in Florida wouldn't still be talking about preserving one's right to vote 42 years after the passage of the Voting Rights Act," Hastings said. But a U.S. district judge ruled in favor of the Democratic committee, arguing the national party had a right to set its own rules. The dispute lingered until the eve of the convention, when the party relented and agreed to count all delegate votes from both states.

When Hastings arrived in the House in 1993, he was determined to impress the lawmakers who had impeached him five years before. "Succeeding is the best revenge," he once said. To that end, he has focused on issues of particular concern to his constituents — funding for Medicare, job training, Head Start and sugar subsidies. In the 109th Congress (2005-06), he criticized the administration's response to hurricanes that struck Florida in 2004 and 2005, and he has been pushing ever since to create a network of national emergency centers around the country to better prepare for disasters.

Hastings earned a degree in zoology and botany at Fisk University, and was accepted to medical school. He chose to pursue a law career instead. In 1979, President Carter nominated Hastings for a U.S. District Court seat in Miami, and he became the first black federal judge in Florida.

In 1983, a jury acquitted Hastings of charges that he solicited a $150,000 bribe in exchange for granting a lenient sentence, but a federal judicial panel later concluded he had lied and made up evidence to secure that verdict. The vote was 413-3 in the House to impeach him and 69-26 in the Senate to remove him from office. After losing a bid for Florida secretary of state in 1990, Hastings in 1992 won a House seat representing the new 23rd District, drawn for the 1990s with a slight black majority. State Rep. Lois Frankel, a liberal white Democrat, took 35 percent of the primary vote to his 28 percent, but Hastings prevailed in a primary runoff with 58 percent. He has coasted to re-election since then.

KEY VOTES

2008
Yes   Delay consideration of Colombia free-trade agreement
Yes   Override Bush veto of federal farm and nutrition programs reauthorization bill
Yes   Overhaul surveillance laws and permit dismissal of suits against companies that conducted warrantless wiretapping
Yes   Grant mortgage relief to homeowners and funding for Fannie Mae and Freddie Mac
Yes   Approve initial $700 billion program to stabilize financial markets
Yes   Approve final $700 billion program to stabilize financial markets
?   Provide $14 billion in loans to automakers

2007
Yes   Increase minimum wage by $2.10 an hour
Yes   Approve $124.2 billion in emergency war spending and set goal for redeployment of troops from Iraq
No   Reject federal contraceptive assistance to international family planning groups
Yes   Override Bush veto of $23.2 billion water projects authorization bill
No   Implement Peru free-trade agreement
?   Approve energy policy overhaul with new fuel economy standards
?   Clear $473.5 billion omnibus spending bill, including $70 billion for military operations

CQ VOTE STUDIES

	PARTY UNITY		PRESIDENTIAL SUPPORT	
	SUPPORT	OPPOSE	SUPPORT	OPPOSE
2008	99%	1%	13%	87%
2007	99%	1%	3%	97%
2006	94%	6%	31%	69%
2005	96%	4%	21%	79%
2004	97%	3%	23%	77%

INTEREST GROUPS

	AFL-CIO	ADA	CCUS	ACU
2008	100%	95%	65%	0%
2007	100%	90%	50%	0%
2006	100%	95%	33%	8%
2005	93%	90%	31%	4%
2004	92%	55%	21%	0%

FLORIDA 23

Southeast — parts of Fort Lauderdale, West Palm Beach and Lauderhill

One of two black-majority districts in the state, the heavily Democratic 23rd stretches southwest from working-class Fort Pierce to the eastern shores of Lake Okeechobee and back east toward coastal hubs such as West Palm Beach and Fort Lauderdale. Most residents live in Broward County, and much of the area west of the Florida Turnpike, including a significant portion of the Everglades, is rural. The eastern borders of the 23rd tend to be several blocks off the coast, with the neighboring 22nd taking in much of the prime beachfront property.

Most urban areas in the 23rd — such as Lauderhill, Lauderdale Lakes, Riviera Beach and portions of West Palm Beach — contain largely black neighborhoods and attract local government employees, educators and other middle-class professionals. The 23rd is growing more diverse, drawing in many Hispanic and Caribbean immigrants. Citrus, sugar cane and rice growers work the large but sparsely populated rural portions of the district, some of which were recently converted to conservation

land. The 23rd lacks a major employment sector, and the vulnerability of citrus crops to bad weather contributes to making it one of the poorest districts in the state. Ongoing recovery from significant property damage and home losses in Fort Lauderdale and towns bordering Lake Okeechobee after Hurricane Wilma in 2005 has been slow.

In the 23rd District Democrats outnumber Republicans by a ratio of nearly 5-to-1, and voters routinely give Democratic candidates more than 75 percent of the vote in competitive statewide elections. Indeed, many heavily black precincts — including some in western Fort Lauderdale and Lauderdale Lakes — give Democratic candidates more than 90 percent of the vote. Overall, the district gave Barack Obama 83 percent of its presidential vote in 2008.

MAJOR INDUSTRY
Agriculture, local government, service

CITIES
Fort Lauderdale (pt.), 57,387; West Palm Beach (pt.), 52,330; Lauderhill (pt.), 47,371; North Lauderdale, 32,264; Lauderdale Lakes (pt.), 30,895

NOTABLE
Lake Okeechobee, part of which is in the 23rd, is the second-largest freshwater lake contained wholly within the United States.

Rep. Suzanne M. Kosmas (D)

Elected 2008; 1st term

Kosmas brings to Capitol Hill a background as a successful real estate company owner and moderate Florida state legislator known for working with Republicans on education and budget issues. She is a fiscal conservative who belongs to the centrist New Democrat Coalition.

A member of the Financial Services Committee, Kosmas (KOSS-muss) is interested in stemming the tide of home foreclosures that has hit Florida especially hard. She touted provisions in a House-passed mortgage relief bill in March 2009 to require banks and homeowners to craft a loan modification before bankruptcy can be considered. "We need to help working families avoid bankruptcy, not push them into it," she said.

As a member of the Science and Technology Committee, she looks out for Kennedy Space Center, located in her district. One of her top priorities is the smooth transitions from the current space shuttle program to the new Constellation program. She supports including alternative energy and technological research among NASA's spaceflight initiatives.

Kosmas invited President Obama to attend a shuttle launch after he described himself as a "space guy" while returning aboard Air Force One from promoting his economic stimulus plan in her district in February 2009.

Her first act as a member of Congress was to cosponsor a bill that prevented a congressional pay raise. She said it was irresponsible to raise her own salary while her constituents were suffering from tough economic times. She supports pay-as-you-go budget rules that require offsets for any increases in spending and said she wants to "rein in wasteful spending and ensure accountability."

She came to office by toppling three-term incumbent Republican Tom Feeney with 57 percent of the vote. Feeney had been embroiled in controversy over his close ties to former House Majority Leader Tom DeLay of Texas and disgraced lobbyist Jack Abramoff. Kosmas' campaign was funded by a number of Democratic party heavyweights, as well as organizations such as Planned Parenthood and EMILY's List, which backs female Democratic candidates who support abortion rights.

CAPITOL OFFICE
225-2706
kosmas.house.gov
238 Cannon Bldg. 20515; fax 226-6299

COMMITTEES
Financial Services
Science & Technology

RESIDENCE
New Smyrna Beach

BORN
Feb. 25, 1944; Washington, D.C.

RELIGION
United Methodist

FAMILY
Divorced; four children

EDUCATION
Pennsylvania State U., attended 1961-63;
George Mason U., attended 1971-73; Stetson U.,
B.A. 1998 (political science)

CAREER
Real estate company owner; Realtor; homemaker

POLITICAL HIGHLIGHTS
Fla. House, 1996-2004

ELECTION RESULTS

2008 GENERAL

Suzanne M. Kosmas (D)	211,284	57.2%
Tom Feeney (R)	151,863	41.1%
Gaurav Bhola (X)	6,223	1.7%

2008 PRIMARY

Suzanne M. Kosmas (D)	18,672	72.3%
Clint Curtis (D)	7,137	27.6%

FLORIDA 24

East central — Orlando suburbs, part of Space Coast

The 24th includes nearly 60 miles of Atlantic coastline before it sweeps west to take in much of the area between the so-called Space Coast and the Orlando suburbs. It draws nearly equally from Orange, Seminole and Volusia counties, with just less than one-fifth of its population coming from its portion of Brevard County. It picks up several suburban areas north or east of Orlando, including most of Altamonte Springs and all of Oviedo.

The Kennedy Space Center is the region's economic engine. Residents are concerned about how the retirement of NASA's space shuttle program in 2010, as well as the proposed Orion replacement program set to launch in 2015, will impact the thousands of district jobs that rely on the aerospace and technology industries.

Tourism is another important pillar of the economy. Launches at Cape Canaveral are a huge draw, and the district's coastline and nature preserves attract eco-tourists and beach-goers. The 24th takes in one of Daytona Beach's jewels — Daytona International Speedway, home to NASCAR's Daytona 500 stock car race — as well as the city of Daytona Beach, most of which is in the neighboring 7th, and popular beach communities.

The 24th has a Republican lean but is politically competitive. In 2008, Democratic Rep. Suzanne M. Kosmas ousted incumbent Tom Feeney, but Republican John McCain took 51 percent of the district's presidential vote.

MAJOR INDUSTRY
Aerospace, tourism, technology

CITIES
Port Orange, 45,823; Titusville, 40,670; Altamonte Springs (pt.), 30,130; Oviedo, 26,316

NOTABLE
One Space Coast-region area code is 321, chosen to mimic the countdown to liftoff.

Rep. Mario Diaz-Balart (R)

Elected 2002; 4th term

CAPITOL OFFICE
225-2778
mariodiazbalart.house.gov
328 Cannon Bldg. 20515-0925; fax 226-0346

COMMITTEES
Budget
Science & Technology
Transportation & Infrastructure

RESIDENCE
Miami

BORN
Sept. 25, 1961; Fort Lauderdale, Fla.

RELIGION
Roman Catholic

FAMILY
Wife, Tia Diaz-Balart; one child

EDUCATION
U. of South Florida, attended 1979-82

CAREER
Marketing firm executive; mayoral aide

POLITICAL HIGHLIGHTS
Fla. House, 1988-92; Fla. Senate, 1992-2000; Fla. House, 2000-02

ELECTION RESULTS

2008 GENERAL

Mario Diaz-Balart (R)	130,891	53.0%
Joe Garcia (D)	115,820	46.9%

2008 PRIMARY

Mario Diaz-Balart (R)	unopposed

2006 GENERAL

Mario Diaz-Balart (R)	60,765	58.5%
Michael Calderin (D)	43,168	41.5%

PREVIOUS WINNING PERCENTAGES
2004 (100%); 2002 (65%)

Quick-talking and gregarious, Diaz-Balart maintains an unwavering hard line against Cuba's Castro regime. But like his brother, House Republican Lincoln Diaz-Balart, he recognizes that's no longer enough to get re-elected, so he talks up the federal funds he acquires to restore the Everglades and improve local highway and rail links.

Energy independence, he says, is just as important as regime change in Cuba. And, like his brother, his agenda includes more-liberal immigration policies than those advocated by the majority of his fellow Republicans.

Critics have dismissed him as "Lincoln Lite," but Mario Diaz-Balart (DEE-az ba-LART) differs from his older brother in several respects. While his brother was born in Cuba and lived there until Fidel Castro forced their family into exile, Mario was born in Fort Lauderdale. His district is less heavily Cuban than the two other Hispanic-majority districts in South Florida, represented by Lincoln and fellow Republican Ileana Ros-Lehtinen.

A large Colombian immigrant presence within his district explains why Diaz-Balart strongly backs a free-trade agreement with that nation. "It's a no-brainer for our economy; it's a no-brainer for national security," he said.

Diaz-Balart often disagrees with the majority of his fellow Republicans on immigration. In 2005, he voted with Democrats against a bill that tightened rules for immigrants trying to obtain asylum, and he sharply criticized GOP immigration legislation that would have made being an illegal immigrant a felony. Diaz-Balart said the idea was "offensive, excessive and demonized hard-working immigrants."

He was among a group of 40 Republicans who joined Democrats in early 2009 to pass an expansion of the State Children's Health Insurance Program, which covers children whose families do not qualify for Medicaid. He had voted against a similar expansion during the 110th Congress (2007-08), but said he changed his vote because the new bill included language to make clear that children of legal immigrants would be covered by the program.

A member of the Science and Technology Committee, Diaz-Balart is eager for a comprehensive energy policy that reduces the nation's reliance on foreign oil, even when gas prices are low. He said in the fall of 2008, "The fact that oil prices are down quite a bit does not mean we're out of this position where the United States in essence is subject to blackmail," he said.

He is also a member of the Budget Committee and says cutting waste and fraud in government spending is a priority. He opposed both versions of the George W. Bush administration's $700 billion plan in fall 2008 to aid the ailing financial services sector, calling it a "blank check" for the government. He also opposed a $787 billion economic stimulus bill signed into law in early 2009.

But he isn't shy about seeking federal money for Florida projects. Even though he voted against the stimulus bill, he joined his Florida colleagues in the House in a letter to the administration seeking a waiver so the state could qualify for $2.7 billion in education funding under the bill.

Diaz-Balart and his brother also voted against a $410 billion catchall spending bill for 2009, but did secure funding in it for a range of local projects. The bill also included millions for the Everglades restoration project, an important parochial project in his district, which includes vast tracts of Florida swamp and Everglades National Park. The U.S. Army Corps of Engineers project seeks to restore an ecosystem that has been destroyed by development; Diaz-Balart regularly pursues funding for the project as a member of the Transportation and Infrastructure Committee.

That committee will take up reauthorization of a massive 2005 surface transportation law, where he will get the opportunity to bring in more project funding. In the original law, he proudly trumpeted its authorization of $81.1 million for the expansion of Interstate 75 in southwest Florida.

While he focused on a range of issues in the 2008 campaign, Diaz-Balart said his election victory was a vindication of his approach to Cuba. "Cuban-Americans understand you should not give unilateral concessions to a regime that murders and imprisons people," he said. He is skeptical that Castro has relinquished power to his brother, Raúl.

Diaz-Balart's family is sometimes called the Cuban Kennedys. Florida International University's law school building was named in honor of Diaz-Balart's grandfather. School officials said that was a tribute to Mario Diaz-Balart, who supported the school while serving in the state legislature. His father, Rafael Diaz-Balart, was once majority leader of the Cuban House, and his aunt was Castro's first wife and mother of Castro's son. According to Ann Louise Bardach's book, "Cuba Confidential: Love and Vengeance in Miami and Havana," Fidel Castro used to jokingly boast to foreign guests about having two nephews serving in Congress, but he also has called the Diaz-Balarts his "most repulsive enemies." The Diaz-Balarts were a wealthy and politically prominent family under Cuban leader Fulgencio Batista, before Castro toppled Batista's government in 1959. Their home was looted and burned as the family vacationed in Paris.

The youngest of four brothers, Diaz-Balart dropped out of the University of South Florida to work for the campaign of Miami Mayor Xavier Suarez in 1985, the same year he and his brother switched from Democrat to Republican.

In 1988, he was elected to the Florida House, and four years later, to the state Senate. Forced out of the Senate by term limits in 2000, he ran successfully to return to the state House. When Florida got two new seats in Congress as a result of the census, Diaz-Balart was appointed by Florida House Speaker Tom Feeney to head the panel drawing a new congressional map. Diaz-Balart drew a Hispanic-majority district for himself and another GOP-leaning district in central Florida that Feeney ultimately won.

In the general election, Diaz-Balart outspent Annie Betancourt, a Democrat who is also Cuban-American, 6-to-1 and won with 65 percent of the vote. He was unopposed in 2004 and won easily in 2006.

In 2008, he faced a stronger challenger in Democrat Joe Garcia, the former head of the Cuban American National Foundation. Garcia labeled him a "one-trick pony" for his focus on Cuba, but Diaz-Balart prevailed with 53 percent of the vote.

KEY VOTES

2008
No Delay consideration of Colombia free-trade agreement
Yes Override Bush veto of federal farm and nutrition programs reauthorization bill
Yes Overhaul surveillance laws and permit dismissal of suits against companies that conducted warrantless wiretapping
Yes Grant mortgage relief to homeowners and funding for Fannie Mae and Freddie Mac
No Approve initial $700 billion program to stabilize financial markets
No Approve final $700 billion program to stabilize financial markets
No Provide $14 billion in loans to automakers

2007
Yes Increase minimum wage by $2.10 an hour
No Approve $124.2 billion in emergency war spending and set goal for redeployment of troops from Iraq
Yes Reject federal contraceptive assistance to international family planning groups
Yes Override Bush veto of $23.2 billion water projects authorization bill
Yes Implement Peru free-trade agreement
Yes Approve energy policy overhaul with new fuel economy standards
Yes Clear $473.5 billion omnibus spending bill, including $70 billion for military operations

CQ VOTE STUDIES

	PARTY UNITY		PRESIDENTIAL SUPPORT	
	SUPPORT	OPPOSE	SUPPORT	OPPOSE
2008	80%	20%	41%	59%
2007	84%	16%	68%	32%
2006	90%	10%	90%	10%
2005	94%	6%	87%	13%
2004	94%	6%	94%	6%

INTEREST GROUPS

	AFL-CIO	ADA	CCUS	ACU
2008	60%	55%	83%	52%
2007	42%	25%	89%	60%
2006	14%	15%	93%	64%
2005	8%	5%	96%	92%
2004	7%	5%	95%	96%

FLORIDA 25

South – western Miami-Dade County, the Everglades

The Hispanic-majority 25th takes in a broad swath of land covering the western portion of Miami-Dade County and almost all of Collier and Monroe counties' land area. Although geographically centered in Everglades National Park and Big Cypress National Preserve, nearly 90 percent of the population lives in Miami-Dade County, mostly on the western edge of the Miami region and in communities south of the city.

Although many residents commute to Miami for work, agriculture — especially the nursery and landscaping sector — is a mainstay for the local economy. Several years of only minor disruptions from hurricanes and other threats to the agriculture sector have allowed local winter vegetable, fruit and sugar cane crops to recover following severe damage from storms in 2005. Recent infrastructure development in Collier County may aid economic recovery in the area, as retail and construction downturns and housing market collapses in Collier and Miami-Dade have stalled development in the region.

National parks give the 25th an ecosystem and array of wildlife — from manatees to panthers — not commonly found in North America, and they are significant tourist draws. Restoration of the Everglades, oil drilling and the pace of development will remain contentious issues here.

A shift away from hard-line opposition to Fidel Castro-led Cuba has weakened Republican support after the GOP's longstanding alliance with southern Florida's large Cuban-American community. Republicans now hold only a very slight party registration edge over Democrats here, and the 25th has the state's highest percentage of independent voters. In the 2008 presidential election, Republican John McCain won the district by 1 percentage point.

MAJOR INDUSTRY
Agriculture, tourism

CITIES
Kendale Lakes (unincorporated), 56,901; Tamiami (unincorporated), 54,788; The Hammocks (unincorporated), 47,379

NOTABLE
Everglades National Park covers 1.5 million acres — which is just a small portion of the Everglades; The Coral Castle, located in Homestead, is a castle made from 1,100 tons of coral.

GEORGIA

Gov. Sonny Perdue (R)

First elected: 2002
Length of term: 4 years
Term expires: 1/11
Salary: $135,281
Phone: (404) 656-1776

Residence: Bonaire
Born: Dec. 20, 1946; Perry, Ga.
Religion: Baptist
Family: Wife, Mary Perdue; four children
Education: U. of Georgia, D.V.M. 1971
Military service: Air Force, 1971-74
Career: Fertilizer and grain business owner; veterinarian
Political highlights: Houston County Planning and Zoning Board, 1978-90; Ga. Senate, 1991-2001 (president pro tempore, 1997-99)

Election results:

2006 GENERAL
Sonny Perdue (R)	1,229,724	57.9%
Mark Taylor (D)	811,049	38.2%
G. Michael Hayes (LIBERT)	81,412	3.8%

Lt. Gov. Casey Cagle (R)

First elected: 2006
Length of term: 4 years
Term expires: 1/11
Salary: $88,941
Phone: (404) 656-5030

LEGISLATURE

General Assembly: January-March, limit of 40 days

Senate: 56 members, 2-year terms
2009 ratios: 34 R, 22 D; 51 men, 5 women
Salary: $17,342
Phone: (404) 656-0028

House: 180 members, 2-year terms
2009 ratios: 105 R, 75 D; 142 men, 38 women
Salary: $17,342
Phone: (404) 656-0305

TERM LIMITS

Governor: 2 terms
Senate: No
House: No

URBAN STATISTICS

CITY	POPULATION
Atlanta	416,474
Augusta-Richmond	199,775
Columbus	186,291
Savannah	131,510
Athens-Clarke	101,489

REGISTERED VOTERS

Voters do not register by party.

POPULATION

2008 population (est.)	9,685,744
2000 population	8,186,453
1990 population	6,478,216
Percent change (1990-2000)	+26.4%
Rank among states (2008)	9

Median age	33.4
Born in state	57.8%
Foreign born	7.1%
Violent crime rate	505/100,000
Poverty level	13%
Federal workers	93,207
Military	96,952

REDISTRICTING

A new 13-district map was signed in to law by Gov. Perdue on May 3, 2005.

ELECTIONS

STATE ELECTION OFFICIAL
(404) 656-2871
DEMOCRATIC PARTY
(404) 870-8201
REPUBLICAN PARTY
(404) 257-5559

MISCELLANEOUS

Web: www.georgia.gov
Capital: Atlanta

U.S. CONGRESS

Senate: 2 Republicans
House: 7 Republicans, 6 Democrat

2000 Census Statistics by District

DIST.	2008 VOTE FOR PRESIDENT OBAMA	MCCAIN	WHITE	BLACK	ASIAN	HISP	MEDIAN INCOME	WHITE COLLAR	BLUE COLLAR	SERVICE INDUSTRY	OVER 64	UNDER 18	COLLEGE EDUCATION	RURAL	SQ. MILES
1	37%	62%	69%	25%	1%	4%	$34,912	53%	32%	16%	11%	27%	17%	43%	11,406
2	54	45	48	48	1	3	$29,843	50	34	17	12	28	14	42	10,841
3	35	64	76	19	1	2	$47,553	58	30	12	10	27	21	44	4,112
4	79	20	30	53	5	11	$47,943	62	24	14	7	27	29	2	330
5	79	20	34	56	2	6	$37,802	67	18	16	10	22	37	0	246
6	35	63	81	7	4	6	$71,699	78	13	9	7	26	51	7	681
7	39	60	76	12	5	6	$60,450	69	21	10	6	29	32	13	972
8	43	56	63	32	1	3	$36,294	53	32	15	12	27	16	43	7,171
9	23	75	86	3	1	9	$41,116	51	37	11	11	26	16	53	4,334
10	37	62	74	20	2	3	$36,615	56	30	14	12	24	23	50	5,892
11	33	66	80	12	1	5	$45,710	58	30	12	9	27	22	30	2,693
12	54	45	51	45	1	3	$30,383	49	33	18	11	27	14	40	8,657
13	72	27	47	41	3	8	$46,477	61	26	13	7	28	23	4	572
STATE	47	52	63	28	2	5	$42,433	59	27	13	10	27	24	28	57,906
U.S.	53	46	69	12	4	13	$41,994	60	25	15	12	26	24	21	3,537,438

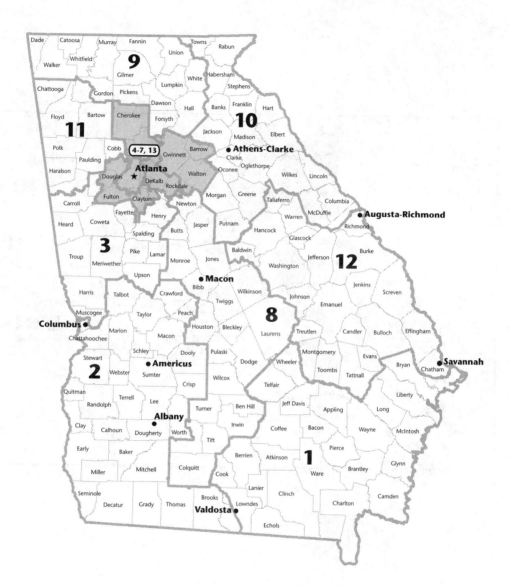

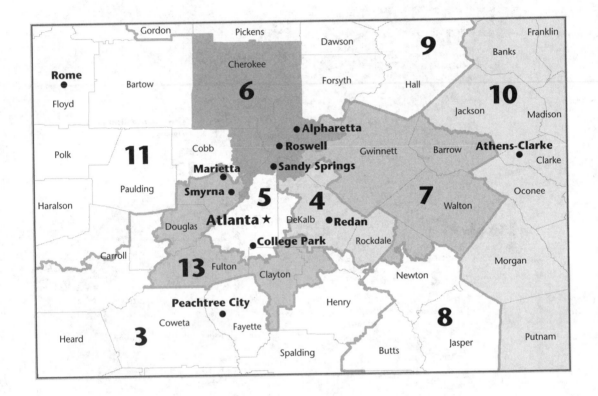

Sen. Saxby Chambliss (R)

Elected 2002; 2nd term

CAPITOL OFFICE
224-3521
chambliss.senate.gov
416 Russell Bldg. 20510-1005; fax 224-0103

COMMITTEES
Agriculture, Nutrition & Forestry - ranking member
Armed Services
Rules & Administration
Select Intelligence

RESIDENCE
Moultrie

BORN
Nov. 10, 1943; Warrenton, N.C.

RELIGION
Episcopalian

FAMILY
Wife, Julianne Chambliss; two children

EDUCATION
Louisiana Tech U., attended 1961-62;
U. of Georgia, B.B.A. 1966 (business
administration); U. of Tennessee, J.D. 1968

CAREER
Lawyer; hotel owner; firefighter; construction
worker

POLITICAL HIGHLIGHTS
Sought Republican nomination for U.S. House,
1992; U.S. House, 1995-2003

ELECTION RESULTS

2008 GENERAL RUNOFF

Saxby Chambliss (R)	1,228,033	57.4%
Jim Martin (D)	909,923	42.6%

2008 GENERAL

Saxby Chambliss (R)	1,867,090	49.8%
Jim Martin (D)	1,757,419	46.8%
Allen Buckley (LIBERT)	128,002	3.4%

2008 PRIMARY

Saxby Chambliss (R)	unopposed

PREVIOUS WINNING PERCENTAGES
2002 General (53%); 2000 House Election (59%);
1998 House Election (62%); 1996 House Election
(53%); 1994 House Election (63%)

Chambliss is a low-key, business-friendly conservative who focuses on state-specific issues, particularly those involving farmers and the military. Though hardly a high-profile ideologue, he is admired among Republicans — and deplored by Democrats — for his success in two elections: One highlighted the GOP's ability to paint their opponents as soft on terrorism, while the other slowed Democrats' shot at a 60-vote Senate majority.

Chambliss (full name: SAX-bee CHAM-bliss) is a consistent vote for his party; he took its side during George W. Bush's administration on 96 percent of the votes that pitted the parties against each other. He was a loyal foot soldier on the administration's conduct of the Iraq War and its $700 billion financial industry rescue bill in fall 2008. He also is a member of the Senate Republicans' whip team.

But Chambliss stood up to Bush in one noteworthy area — agriculture. As the ranking Republican on the Agriculture, Nutrition and Forestry Committee, he helped author a 2008 rewrite of farm programs that the president vetoed on grounds that it had too much unnecessary spending. Congress overrode the veto of the $289 billion measure, which significantly increased nutrition spending and preserved crop subsidies. Chambliss called it "a good bill not only for American agriculture, but for millions of needy Americans."

In February 2009, he led a group of Republicans and conservative Democrats in demanding that President Obama's Agriculture secretary, Tom Vilsack, follow the farm bill's liberalized intent regarding payment limit rules to farmers rather than more stringent proposals issued by the Bush administration. Chambliss also joined members of both parties who balked at Obama's budget proposal to phase out direct payments to farmers with more than $500,000 in sales revenue and to cap commodity supports at $250,000.

Chambliss watches out for his farm-dependent state, a major producer of peanuts, cotton and tobacco. Seeking to appease trading partners worldwide who have pressed for cuts in U.S. cotton subsidies, he and other Southern lawmakers agreed to terminate some cotton price supports in the farm bill. But their changes didn't go far enough to placate trading partners such as Brazil, which subsequently said it would seek penalties against the United States through the World Trade Organization.

Chambliss initially had hoped the farm legislation could greatly benefit Georgia's peanut farmers, whom he said were wronged in the previous farm bill in 2002. That measure ended the old peanut subsidy program and guaranteed farmers no more than coverage of their losses for five years. But the 2008 law continued the earlier version with only modest changes.

When a peanut processor failed to report tests showing salmonella-contaminated products at a Georgia plant in 2009, he called for the creation of a central data bank for information on outbreaks.

Chambliss served eight years in the House before joining the Senate, where he serves on three committees — Armed Services, Select Intelligence and Agriculture — that directly parallel his assignments in the House.

On Armed Services, he looks out for his state's military installations, which have thrived since World War II, thanks partly to the nearly continuous presence of a Georgian on the committee. He and Democratic Sen. Patty Murray of Washington have led congressional pleas to President Obama not to abandon production of the F-22 Raptor aircraft, which is made in Georgia.

Chambliss joined fellow Intelligence member Ron Wyden, an Oregon Democrat, in sponsoring legislation in 2007 to require a national intelligence estimate on U.S. energy security. The bill failed to make it out of committee. The following year, he teamed with Democrat Kent Conrad of North Dakota in leading a bipartisan coalition that unsuccessfully sought compromise energy legislation in 2008 to deal with rising gasoline prices.

The son of an Episcopal priest, Chambliss said his family's frequent moves when he was young made him learn to make friends quickly and prepared him for politics. When he was 5, his father was the announcer for the Rock Hill Chicks, a minor league baseball club in North Carolina. Chambliss dreamed of becoming a baseball star, and played second base on the University of Georgia baseball team. It was at college that he met Johnny Isakson, now his home-state Senate colleague. The two married members of the same sorority and are best friends.

In the years after graduation, Chambliss worked as a firefighter and construction worker to pay for law school. He spent much of his adult life before Congress as a small-town lawyer in rural southern Georgia, representing farmers who grew commodity crops like peanuts and cotton. He got to know federal farm laws inside out. "I just kind of backed into this," he says of his agri-legal expertise. "No one else in town wanted to take the time to read the regulations and study the law and figure out how the farm bill operates." He also coached YMCA basketball and Little League baseball. He owned a motel and was active in economic development efforts.

He lost his first bid for public office in 1992 when he sought the GOP nomination to challenge Democratic Rep. J. Roy Rowland. But when Rowland retired in 1994, Chambliss defeated Democrat Craig Mathis, becoming the first Republican since Reconstruction to represent the rural Georgia district.

He declined entreaties to run for the Senate against Democrat Zell Miller in 2000. Chambliss chose to stay in the House at the urging of Speaker J. Dennis Hastert, and expected to be rewarded with the chairmanship of the Budget Committee. When that prize went instead to Jim Nussle of Iowa, Chambliss again began thinking about the other chamber.

Three days after the Sept. 11 terrorist attacks in 2001, Chambliss' nascent challenge to Democratic Sen. Max Cleland got an important boost when Hastert picked Chambliss to chair a new Intelligence Subcommittee on Terrorism and Homeland Security. He made one slip that could have cost him the election had he not turned things around. In an offhand remark viewed as insensitive, he quipped that one route to security would be for local sheriffs to "arrest every Muslim that comes across the state line."

Chambliss went on the offensive against Cleland on the terrorism issue, alleging the incumbent had gone soft on defense by opposing portions of Bush's plans to create the Homeland Security Department. One Chambliss ad featured images of Osama bin Laden and Saddam Hussein; Democrats charged him with unfairly impugning the patriotism of Cleland, who lost both legs and an arm in the Vietnam War. But his focused campaign strategy, combined with a massive voter turnout effort, propelled him to a 7-point win.

In 2008, Democrats were eager to unseat Chambliss, especially because they were within reach of the 60 votes needed to thwart GOP filibusters. His opponent was Jim Martin, a former state representative who was the Democratic nominee for lieutenant governor in 2006. Chambliss came two-tenths of a percentage point short of an outright majority, forcing a December runoff.

With Democrats having picked up Senate seats in November, both parties focused intensely on the runoff. Chambliss' campaign brought in Alaska Gov. Sarah Palin — the party's vice presidential nominee and a favorite of conservatives — and other luminaries to argue a Chambliss win would serve as a crucial check against a Democratic Congress and White House. He ended up prevailing by nearly 15 percentage points in a victory he said could serve as a future GOP blueprint. "This is the first election of 2010," he said.

KEY VOTES

2008
Yes Prohibit discrimination based on genetic information
Yes Reauthorize farm and nutrition programs for five years
No Limit debate on "cap and trade" system for greenhouse gas emissions
No Allow lawsuits against companies that participated in warrantless wiretapping
Yes Limit debate on a bill to block a scheduled cut in Medicare payments to doctors
Yes Grant mortgage relief to homeowners and funding for Fannie Mae and Freddie Mac
Yes Approve a nuclear cooperation agreement with India
Yes Approve final $700 billion program to stabilize financial markets
No Allow consideration of a $14 billion auto industry loan package

2007
Yes Increase minimum wage by $2.10 an hour
No Limit debate on a comprehensive immigration bill
Yes Overhaul congressional lobbying and ethics rules for members and their staffs
No Limit debate on considering a bill to add House seats for the District of Columbia and Utah
? Limit debate on restoring habeas corpus rights to detainees
No Mandate minimum breaks for troops between deployments to Iraq or Afghanistan
Yes Override Bush veto of $23.2 billion water projects authorization bill
Yes Confirm Michael B. Mukasey as attorney general
No Limit debate on an energy policy overhaul containing $21.8 billion in tax incentives and reduced oil and gas subsidies

CQ VOTE STUDIES

	PARTY UNITY		PRESIDENTIAL SUPPORT	
	SUPPORT	OPPOSE	SUPPORT	OPPOSE
2008	95%	5%	72%	28%
2007	96%	4%	83%	17%
2006	94%	6%	93%	7%
2005	95%	5%	91%	9%
2004	99%	1%	100%	0%
2003	97%	3%	97%	3%
2002	98%	2%	90%	10%
2001	98%	2%	93%	7%
2000	95%	5%	24%	76%
1999	94%	6%	26%	74%

INTEREST GROUPS

	AFL-CIO	ADA	CCUS	ACU
2008	30%	25%	100%	76%
2007	11%	10%	82%	92%
2006	13%	0%	92%	96%
2005	21%	5%	94%	96%
2004	0%	5%	93%	96%
2003	15%	5%	91%	90%
2002	0%	0%	90%	100%
2001	17%	0%	95%	100%
2000	0%	0%	90%	91%
1999	33%	10%	80%	80%

Sen. Johnny Isakson (R)

Elected 2004; 1st term

CAPITOL OFFICE
224-3643
isakson.senate.gov
120 Russell Bldg. 20510-1006; fax 228-0724

COMMITTEES
Commerce, Science & Transportation
Foreign Relations
Health, Education, Labor & Pensions
Small Business & Entrepreneurship
Veterans' Affairs
Select Ethics - vice chairman

RESIDENCE
Marietta

BORN
Dec. 28, 1944; Atlanta, Ga.

RELIGION
Methodist

FAMILY
Wife, Dianne Isakson; three children

EDUCATION
U. of Georgia, B.B.A. 1966 (real estate)

MILITARY SERVICE
Ga. Air National Guard, 1966-72

CAREER
Real estate company president

POLITICAL HIGHLIGHTS
Candidate for Cobb County Commission, 1974;
Ga. House, 1977-90 (Republican leader, 1983-90);
Republican nominee for governor, 1990; Ga.
Senate, 1993-96; sought Republican nomination
for U.S. Senate, 1996; Ga. Board of Education
chairman, 1996-99; U.S. House, 1999-2005

ELECTION RESULTS

2004 GENERAL

Johnny Isakson (R)	1,864,202	57.9%
Denise L. Majette (D)	1,287,690	40.0%
Allen Buckley (LIBERT)	69,051	2.1%

2004 PRIMARY

Johnny Isakson (R)	346,670	53.2%
Herman Cain (R)	170,370	26.2%
Mac Collins (R)	133,952	20.6%

PREVIOUS WINNING PERCENTAGES
2002 House Election (80%); 2000 House Election
(75%); 1999 Special House Election (65%)

By the numbers, Isakson looks like a garden-variety conservative Republican. But numbers can deceive, and his consensus-seeking, results-oriented approach to legislating keeps the friendly, folksy Georgian in the thick of things on Capitol Hill.

"I try to be pragmatic on the issues and conservative in my philosophy," he said. "You can beat your chest all you want to, but if four is a majority, then three equals zero." He'd rather "try to make things happen" than maintain ideological purity and wind up with nothing.

His tactics have led to several successes during his Senate term and the nearly three House terms that preceded it, not to mention earlier in his career back home. And he doesn't fret about that changing just because Republicans are now in the minority. "For the 17 years I was in the Georgia legislature, I was in the minority," he said. "I pretty much developed my legislative skills in an environment where I was in the minority."

Isakson used those skills during debate on the economic stimulus package at the start of the 111th Congress (2009-10), winning Senate adoption of his amendment to offer homebuyers a $15,000 tax credit in order to spur housing sales. But after Isakson and all but three other Republicans refused to vote for the bill itself, the tax credit was halved in the final version.

He joined with Budget Chairman Kent Conrad of North Dakota in calling for a Financial Markets Commission, modeled after the bipartisan panel that investigated the Sept. 11 terrorist attacks, to delve into the causes of the economic crisis and make recommendations for future action.

Education reform has always been a top priority for Isakson. He was chairman of the Georgia Board of Education from 1996 to 1999, and as a member of the House he helped write the 2001 No Child Left Behind education law, working closely with Democratic Sen. Edward M. Kennedy of Massachusetts, among others. A member of the Health, Education, Labor and Pensions Committee, he is eager to revise and renew the law during the 111th Congress. He considers it a success, although he wants to allow greater flexibility in assessing and serving non-English-speaking children and those in special education.

Isakson also worked closely with Kennedy on two major issues in 2006 — an overhaul of the federal law governing private pension plans and a rewrite of mine safety standards. He labored successfully to ensure the final pension measure included provisions to give Atlanta-based Delta Air Lines and other financially strapped airlines extra time to fully fund their pension plans, which otherwise could have been dumped on the federal Pension Benefit Guaranty Corporation, shifting the burden to taxpayers.

Earlier in 2006, Isakson, then chairman of the Employment and Workplace Safety Subcommittee, went to West Virginia two days after an explosion at the Sago Mine killed a dozen coal miners. Isakson, Kennedy, West Virginia Democrat John D. Rockefeller IV and Wyoming Republican Michael B. Enzi talked to miners' families, the company and other experts. Within months, they had steered a new mine safety law to enactment.

Isakson had less success in tackling two high-profile issues during the 110th Congress (2007-08) — immigration and energy policy. He was part of small, bipartisan groups in the Senate that labored to produce middle-ground legislation on both topics, only to see their efforts crash and burn in the end.

Isakson, a multimillionaire former real estate executive, got his first taste of the business from his parents. "My father was a Greyhound bus driver, and on the side, he would buy houses, and my mother would fix them up and sell them. We lived in 12 houses the first five years of my life," he said.

Isakson also credits his dad, a high school dropout, for instilling his passion for education. After his older sister died as a young child, his father repeatedly told Isakson he was destined to be the first in the family to attend college. The elder Isakson bought season tickets to Georgia Tech football games, then deliberately parked 2 miles away so he could walk his son across the campus to the stadium. Isakson's father would point to the buildings and say, "One day you're going to go to a school like this."

Isakson began his focus on education early in his House career. Though he was the lowest-ranking Republican on the Education and the Workforce Committee in the 106th Congress (1999-2000), he was the driving force behind a proposal to help states pay for federally mandated school modernization costs such as asbestos removal and outfitting buildings for disabled students. Committee Republicans were resisting Democratic plans for the federal government to pay for the school repairs, but Isakson saw the potential political impact of the construction issue and convinced GOP leaders they would lose the debate without their own proposal.

Meanwhile, he kept an eye on district concerns. He promoted federal grants for programs like one in Dalton, Ga., that hired Mexican teachers to teach immigrant students who cannot speak English. He used his seat on the Transportation and Infrastructure panel to get more funds for traffic-clogged Atlanta. He also badgered Georgia officials to bring Atlanta into compliance with the Clean Air Act, a requirement for getting federal highway funds.

Isakson ranked among the top 10 Senate Republicans in the 109th Congress (2005-06) in his support of President George W. Bush and his loyalty to the Republican Party. In the 110th Congress, he was granted a seat on the Foreign Relations Committee, and in the 111th, he traded a seat on the Environment and Public Works Committee for one on the Commerce, Science and Transportation Committee. He also drew a less welcome assignment, as vice chairman of the Select Ethics Committee, and he sits on the Veterans' Affairs and Small Business committees.

Isakson is a fixture in Georgia politics. He was in the General Assembly for almost 17 years and was the GOP candidate for governor in 1990. He was defeated by Zell Miller, the Democratic lieutenant governor at the time. In 1996, he sought the Republican nomination for the U.S. Senate but lost. "I pretty much figured my political career was over," he said. But Miller fired the state school board members and asked Isakson to take the chairman's job.

When House Speaker Newt Gingrich resigned under an ethics cloud in 1999, Isakson ran for his congressional seat. Enjoying a huge advantage in name recognition and campaign funds, Isakson took 65 percent of the vote against five opponents in the special election. He easily cruised to re-election in 2000 and 2002.

Miller, meanwhile, had completed two terms as governor when he was appointed and then later elected to serve out the term of GOP Sen. Paul Coverdell, who died July 18, 2000. The conservative Democrat, who voted with Republicans more often than not, retired in 2004. Isakson jumped into the Senate race, challenged by two Republicans — businessman Herman Cain and 8th District Rep. Mac Collins. Isakson took 53 percent of the vote, avoiding a runoff, and defeated one-term Democratic Rep. Denise L. Majette with 58 percent.

He has wasted no time preparing for 2010, launching his campaign in early 2009 and piling up a war chest of more than $2 million by the time he announced his re-election bid. Given Georgia's pronounced GOP tilt, he is expected to encounter little trouble.

KEY VOTES

2008

Yes	Prohibit discrimination based on genetic information
Yes	Reauthorize farm and nutrition programs for five years
No	Limit debate on "cap and trade" system for greenhouse gas emissions
No	Allow lawsuits against companies that participated in warrantless wiretapping
Yes	Limit debate on a bill to block a scheduled cut in Medicare payments to doctors
Yes	Grant mortgage relief to homeowners and funding for Fannie Mae and Freddie Mac
Yes	Approve a nuclear cooperation agreement with India
Yes	Approve final $700 billion program to stabilize financial markets
No	Allow consideration of a $14 billion auto industry loan package

2007

Yes	Increase minimum wage by $2.10 an hour
No	Limit debate on a comprehensive immigration bill
Yes	Overhaul congressional lobbying and ethics rules for members and their staffs
No	Limit debate on considering a bill to add House seats for the District of Columbia and Utah
No	Limit debate on restoring habeas corpus rights to detainees
No	Mandate minimum breaks for troops between deployments to Iraq or Afghanistan
Yes	Override Bush veto of $23.2 billion water projects authorization bill
Yes	Confirm Michael B. Mukasey as attorney general
No	Limit debate on an energy policy overhaul containing $21.8 billion in tax incentives and reduced oil and gas subsidies

CQ VOTE STUDIES

	PARTY UNITY		PRESIDENTIAL SUPPORT	
	SUPPORT	OPPOSE	SUPPORT	OPPOSE
2008	94%	6%	72%	28%
2007	97%	3%	85%	15%
2006	97%	3%	93%	7%
2005	95%	5%	91%	9%
2004	99%	1%	89%	11%
2003	99%	1%	96%	4%
2002	94%	6%	85%	15%
2001	97%	3%	90%	10%
2000	91%	9%	30%	70%
1999	87%	13%	29%	71%

INTEREST GROUPS

	AFL-CIO	ADA	CCUS	ACU
2008	20%	25%	88%	76%
2007	11%	10%	82%	96%
2006	13%	0%	92%	96%
2005	21%	5%	94%	100%
2004	8%	5%	100%	95%
2003	0%	5%	100%	84%
2002	0%	5%	100%	96%
2001	9%	5%	100%	88%
2000	0%	5%	85%	72%
1999	13%	10%	91%	66%

Rep. Jack Kingston (R)

Elected 1992; 9th term

CAPITOL OFFICE
225-5831
kingston.house.gov
2368 Rayburn Bldg. 20515-1001; fax 226-2269

COMMITTEES
Appropriations

RESIDENCE
Savannah

BORN
April 24, 1955; Bryan, Texas

RELIGION
Episcopalian

FAMILY
Wife, Libby Kingston; four children

EDUCATION
U. of Georgia, B.A. 1978 (economics)

CAREER
Insurance broker

POLITICAL HIGHLIGHTS
Ga. House, 1984-92

ELECTION RESULTS

2008 GENERAL

Jack Kingston (R)	165,890	66.5%
Bill Gillespie (D)	83,444	33.5%

2008 PRIMARY

Jack Kingston (R)	unopposed

2006 GENERAL

Jack Kingston (R)	94,961	68.5%
Jim Nelson (D)	43,668	31.5%

PREVIOUS WINNING PERCENTAGES
2004 (100%); 2002 (72%); 2000 (69%); 1998 (100%);
1996 (68%); 1994 (77%); 1992 (58%)

One of Congress' most vocal fiscal conservatives, Kingston is a frequent and fierce critic of Democrats on a variety of issues, including their efforts to revive the ailing economy. But when the television cameras and microphones are turned off, his quick wit and easygoing manner keep him on friendly terms with colleagues across the aisle.

Kingston was elected two years before the GOP's historic class of 1994, but he shares with its firebrand members a bedrock belief in curtailing government's excesses. "There are very few things I dislike more than wasteful government spending," he said.

Kingston opposed all of the major economic recovery bills of 2008 — the tax rebates early in the year and the $700 billion financial industry rescue package later on — while also opposing emergency loans for domestic automakers. He likewise voted against President Obama's $787 billion stimulus package in early 2009. He warned that the bills mortgaged the country's future to foreign creditors and undermined free-market principles.

Kingston was one of just 28 Republicans to vote against the early 2008 law providing rebate checks to taxpayers. "If we want to create jobs, we need investment tax credits," he said. "This package gets an A+ for politics and an F for economics and jobs."

But unlike many of his conservative colleagues, Kingston, a member of the Appropriations Committee, does not condemn earmarks — funding set-asides for local projects that many Republicans oppose. Instead, Kingston does his best to protect Georgia's interests even when his home-state colleagues refuse to ask. In the fiscal 2009 catchall spending bill, for instance, he secured $9 million in earmarks for the University of Georgia, whose own Athens-area representative, Republican Paul Broun, declined to seek any. University officials said they regularly turn to Kingston for help.

Peanut and cotton crops help sustain his district's economy. On the Agriculture Appropriations Subcommittee, where he is the top Republican in the 111th Congress (2009-10), Kingston is sometimes at odds with fellow Republicans who view federal subsidy programs for crops such as peanuts as antithetical to free enterprise. Kingston and Democrat Sanford D. Bishop Jr. are the only Georgians on Appropriations. Kingston also serves on the Defense Subcommittee and previously chaired the Legislative Branch Subcommittee, which he used to demonstrate his fiscal conservatism. In 2004, Kingston produced one of the few spending bills that came close to honoring President George W. Bush's request for increases of less than 1 percent in spending — a point of pride for Kingston.

Kingston routinely sides with his fellow Republicans on votes that pit the two parties against each other, but on occasion he goes his own way. In addition to opposing 2008's rebate checks, he was one of just 47 Republicans to vote against a popular measure requiring insurers to provide mental health and addiction benefits equal to traditional medical benefits.

Kingston eschews the racial politics once prevalent in the South. In 2006, for example, he was the only Georgia Republican to vote in favor of renewing the 1965 Voting Rights Act, siding with leaders of both political parties. He credits the law with opening up the political process to Southern Republicans as well as African-Americans. "If not for the Voting Rights Act, I don't think I would be in Congress," he said. He was also a key Republican to sign on to Georgia Democratic Rep. John Lewis' proposal for an African-American museum on the National Mall, approved in 2003.

Kingston served as vice chairman of the House Republican Conference — which seeks to enhance the GOP's public image — during the 109th Congress (2005-06). But he fell short in a bid for the conference chairmanship in the 110th Congress (2007-08), losing to Adam H. Putnam of Florida by 100-91 on the third ballot.

Even though Kingston is no longer responsible for carrying the party's message, he has found other ways to publicize Republican viewpoints. He is ahead of many colleagues in using and appearing on alternative media, saying it is the best way to reach unaffiliated voters. Kingston was a regular guest on "Politically Incorrect," the old late-night ABC talk show with host Bill Maher, and he appears on Maher's new HBO show, "Real Time With Bill Maher." He was also the first congressman to go on "Better Know a District," a recurring segment on "The Colbert Report," comedian Stephen Colbert's satirical news show on Comedy Central. And he is a frequent guest on conservative mainstays such as Sean Hannity's show on Fox News Channel.

Kingston has embraced the new media world by blogging on his congressional Web site and producing podcasts (audio programs that can be downloaded) on which he discusses legislation and current events. His legislative interns produce an occasional amateur video documentary, "Journeys with Jack," and post it on YouTube. "Blogs are like political gasoline," Kingston said. "If you have a blog in place, when something happens you can react quickly and it's unfettered access."

Born in Texas, where his father was an art professor, Kingston and his family spent a few months in Ethiopia — his father was working with the Education Department to help set up schools in the African country — before settling in Georgia when Kingston was a toddler. He claims the Peach State as his native state, once joking, "If you're potty-trained in a state, I think that gives you native status." After earning an undergraduate degree in economics, Kingston moved to Savannah to sell insurance. He won election in 1984 to the state House, where he served for eight years. When Democrat Lindsay Thomas retired in 1992, Kingston was well-positioned to woo voters into the Republican column in a House race; many of them already had been voting Republican for president. Kingston drew minor primary opposition, then dispatched Democrat Barbara Christmas, a school principal. His 58 percent share of the vote that year remains his lowest election percentage.

Redistricting after the census put Kingston and GOP colleague Saxby Chambliss in the same House district in the 2002 election, but Chambliss opted for the Senate. The new 1st District had an even more GOP flavor, and Kingston has continued to win easily. He captured two-thirds of the vote in 2008.

KEY VOTES

2008
No Delay consideration of Colombia free-trade agreement
Yes Override Bush veto of federal farm and nutrition programs reauthorization bill
Yes Overhaul surveillance laws and permit dismissal of suits against companies that conducted warrantless wiretapping
No Grant mortgage relief to homeowners and funding for Fannie Mae and Freddie Mac
No Approve initial $700 billion program to stabilize financial markets
No Approve final $700 billion program to stabilize financial markets
No Provide $14 billion in loans to automakers

2007
No Increase minimum wage by $2.10 an hour
No Approve $124.2 billion in emergency war spending and set goal for redeployment of troops from Iraq
Yes Reject federal contraceptive assistance to international family planning groups
No Override Bush veto of $23.2 billion water projects authorization bill
Yes Implement Peru free-trade agreement
Yes Approve energy policy overhaul with new fuel economy standards
Yes Clear $473.5 billion omnibus spending bill, including $70 billion for military operations

CQ VOTE STUDIES

	PARTY UNITY		PRESIDENTIAL SUPPORT	
	SUPPORT	OPPOSE	SUPPORT	OPPOSE
2008	93%	7%	68%	32%
2007	95%	5%	90%	10%
2006	95%	5%	97%	3%
2005	98%	2%	85%	15%
2004	97%	3%	91%	9%

INTEREST GROUPS

	AFL-CIO	ADA	CCUS	ACU
2008	15%	10%	61%	96%
2007	8%	10%	65%	96%
2006	7%	5%	100%	92%
2005	15%	0%	92%	88%
2004	0%	0%	100%	96%

GEORGIA 1

Southeast — Valdosta, Savannah suburbs

As recently as two decades ago, the 1st was a Democratic stronghold of peanut and tobacco farmers. Today, the 1st still relies heavily on agriculture, but its voters now overwhelmingly favor Republicans. Spanning 25 counties in southeast Georgia, the 1st takes in all of the state's coastline, part of the border with Florida to the south, and primarily rural areas to the north and west.

The 1st's economy is wedded to agriculture — peanuts, cotton, carrots and blueberries are among the important crops here. Valdosta, almost all of which is in the 1st, is home to health care facilities, a state university and major retailers. Military influence is strong, with three of the state's major military bases in the 1st. The manufacturing sector retains a presence in the district despite layoffs by major employers.

Tourism is important here, as retirees and well-off visitors flock to a string of islands known for golf courses and resorts off the coast of Brunswick. Regional tourism hubs Savannah and Brunswick also have active ports (Savannah's is in the neighboring 12th). The district's ports and coastline make trade and coastal conservation dominant issues.

Redistricting prior to the 2006 elections had little effect on the district's political makeup. The 1st is reliably Republican, with GOP strength in Camden and Glynn counties on the coast and Chatham and Bryan counties near Savannah. Democrats can win, especially at the local level in some counties. In 2008, Rep. Jack Kingston won every county in the 1st except Liberty, which he narrowly lost. Liberty also supported Democrat Barack Obama in the presidential election, although Republican John McCain won 62 percent of the district's vote in 2008.

MAJOR INDUSTRY
Agriculture, military, manufacturing, tourism

MILITARY BASES
Fort Stewart (Army), 22,393 military, 2,536 civilian (2007) (shared with the 12th); Kings Bay Naval Submarine Base, 3,824 military, 1,762 civilian (2007); Moody Air Force Base, 3,763 military, 407 civilian (2007)

CITIES
Valdosta (pt.), 43,708; Hinesville, 30,392; Savannah (pt.), 20,894

NOTABLE
The Okefenokee Swamp — roughly 7,000 years old — covers 438,000 acres and is home to about 10,000 alligators and 233 species of birds.

Rep. Sanford D. Bishop Jr. (D)

Elected 1992; 9th term

CAPITOL OFFICE
225-3631
www.house.gov/bishop
2429 Rayburn Bldg. 20515-1002; fax 225-2203

COMMITTEES
Appropriations

RESIDENCE
Albany

BORN
Feb. 4, 1947; Mobile, Ala.

RELIGION
Baptist

FAMILY
Wife, Vivian Creighton Bishop; one stepchild

EDUCATION
Morehouse College, B.A. 1968 (political science);
Emory U., J.D. 1971

MILITARY SERVICE
Army, 1971

CAREER
Lawyer

POLITICAL HIGHLIGHTS
Ga. House, 1977-91; Ga. Senate, 1991-93

ELECTION RESULTS

2008 GENERAL

Sanford D. Bishop Jr. (D)	158,435	68.9%
Lee Ferrell (R)	71,351	31.0%

2008 PRIMARY

Sanford D. Bishop Jr. (D)	unopposed

2006 GENERAL

Sanford D. Bishop Jr. (D)	88,662	67.9%
Bradley C. Hughes (R)	41,967	32.1%

PREVIOUS WINNING PERCENTAGES
2004 (67%); 2002 (100%); 2000 (53%); 1998 (57%);
1996 (54%); 1994 (66%); 1992 (64%)

Bishop is a soft-spoken Southerner who has built a durable base of support back home by paying close heed to his district's agriculture and military interests through his powerful post on the Appropriations Committee.

He and fellow Georgia Democrat David Scott are the only black members of the coalition of roughly 50 fiscally conservative House Democrats known as the Blue Dogs. Bishop calls himself a "fiscally responsible Democrat" who also supports "social programs and policies that empower families and working Americans."

Bishop supported George W. Bush during his two terms as president more often than any other member of the Congressional Black Caucus. Bishop has earned relatively high marks from liberal groups and conservative ones, from unions and from business organizations.

Bishop expressed some early optimism about President Obama's legislative plans. He voted for Obama's $787 billion economic stimulus package, signed into law in February 2009, as well as a subsequent $410 billion catch-all spending bill for fiscal 2009. He also backed a $700 billion package to aid the financial sector in fall 2008. He didn't support Bush's 2001 and 2003 tax cuts, but in 2004, he was one of the first Democrats to indicate he would vote for a corporate tax overhaul bill.

Bishop is a successful practitioner of earmarking, the dedication of funding for special projects. He ranked 28th on the Taxpayers for Common Sense list of House members in terms of the value of earmarks obtained in fiscal 2008 spending bills. In the fiscal 2009 catchall spending bill, he obtained more than $20 million in earmarks. He doesn't apologize for that practice, saying he is looking out for his district.

But he came under scrutiny by Georgia investigators in 2009 for earmarks he steered to the Muscogee County Junior Marshal program based in Columbus, a program where he once worked and that provides mentoring for children before they enter high school. (In fiscal 2008, he steered $117,500 to the program.) News reports indicated Bishop's stepdaughter and her husband were employed by the program, and that paychecks were deposited directly to the account of Bishop's wife, the clerk of the county municipal court. Bishop denied having prior knowledge of the employment situation. "I have tried to be above that kind of innuendo," he told The Associated Press.

Bishop's assignments on Appropriations include the Defense, Military Construction-VA and Agriculture subcommittees. He supports a healthy defense budget and looks out for the interests of the 2nd District's military bases. The largest of these is Fort Benning, the Army's huge infantry training base. In the 2008 Defense spending law, he secured $116 million to upgrade facilities and services at the fort.

On the Iraq War, Bishop voted several times for setting a timetable for withdrawing U.S. troops but never agreed with those who preferred to end the U.S. military deployment to Iraq by terminating its funding. "Every dollar, every dime and every penny that the president's asking for Iraq is going to be provided — plus some," he said in March 2007 when public support for the war was near its nadir.

Agriculture is also central to Bishop's mission in Congress. More peanuts are grown in the 2nd District than in any other congressional district, and it produces more than a quarter of the nation's peanut output. Bishop served on the Agriculture Committee for his first decade in Congress, and there he played a crucial role in protecting peanut farmers when their subsidy program was overhauled in 2002. Bishop was mentioned as a possible choice for Agriculture secretary in the Obama administration, but the post went to the higher-profile Tom Vilsack, the former governor of Iowa.

One area where he comes closer to Republicans is on domestic energy production. In 2006 he was one of just 27 Democrats voting to permit oil drilling in Alaska's Arctic National Wildlife Refuge.

On social issues, too, he is often conservative. He was one of 34 in his own party who voted in 2006 for a proposed constitutional amendment to ban same-sex marriage. He has backed other conservative campaigns for constitutional amendments to require balanced federal budgets, to ban desecration of the flag, and to allow voluntary non-denominational prayer in schools. Still, he aligns with his fellow Democrats in supporting abortion rights.

Bishop also previously served on Select Intelligence, and had been in line to be the top-ranking Democrat in both the 107th (2001-02) and the 108th (2003-04) Congresses. But that position went to other lawmakers.

Bishop grew up in Mobile, Ala. His father was the president of a community college that is now named for him — Bishop State Community College. His mother was the college librarian.

While he was at Emory University Law School, Bishop spent a summer interning with the NAACP's Legal Defense Fund in New York. After earning his law degree, he practiced civil rights law in Columbus, Ga., representing inmates at a state prison whose 1972 lawsuit resulted in a Supreme Court decision ordering reforms at the overcrowded facility.

Bishop was elected to the state legislature in 1976, serving for 16 years. He was on the Reapportionment Committee that, with stern urging from the Justice Department, in 1992 drew new congressional district maps that made the 2nd District the state's third black-majority district. Columbus business leaders helped finance his challenge to white Democratic Rep. Charles Hatcher. Bishop won the nomination with 53 percent of the vote; in November, he coasted past Republican physician Jim Dudley.

In 1995, a federal court found the new district lines to be an unconstitutional "racial gerrymander" and handed down a revised map that put Columbus in the 3rd District. The black share of the population in the redrawn 2nd dropped from 51 percent to 39 percent. Bishop moved about 90 miles southeast to Albany, in the center of the 2nd. He weathered some tough races in his next three elections. But redistricting following the 2000 census put part of Muscogee County, his longtime home, back in the 2nd District and increased the black share of the population to 44 percent. He was unopposed in 2002 and has had little trouble since then.

KEY VOTES

2008

Yes Delay consideration of Colombia free-trade agreement

Yes Override Bush veto of federal farm and nutrition programs reauthorization bill

Yes Overhaul surveillance laws and permit dismissal of suits against companies that conducted warrantless wiretapping

\+ Grant mortgage relief to homeowners and funding for Fannie Mae and Freddie Mac

Yes Approve initial $700 billion program to stabilize financial markets

Yes Approve final $700 billion program to stabilize financial markets

Yes Provide $14 billion in loans to automakers

2007

Yes Increase minimum wage by $2.10 an hour

Yes Approve $124.2 billion in emergency war spending and set goal for redeployment of troops from Iraq

No Reject federal contraceptive assistance to international family planning groups

Yes Override Bush veto of $23.2 billion water projects authorization bill

Yes Implement Peru free-trade agreement

Yes Approve energy policy overhaul with new fuel economy standards

Yes Clear $473.5 billion omnibus spending bill, including $70 billion for military operations

CQ VOTE STUDIES

	PARTY UNITY		PRESIDENTIAL SUPPORT	
	SUPPORT	OPPOSE	SUPPORT	OPPOSE
2008	98%	2%	21%	79%
2007	95%	5%	10%	90%
2006	72%	28%	63%	37%
2005	77%	23%	47%	53%
2004	78%	22%	57%	43%

INTEREST GROUPS

	AFL-CIO	ADA	CCUS	ACU
2008	100%	90%	67%	4%
2007	96%	90%	70%	4%
2006	93%	65%	87%	64%
2005	80%	85%	74%	45%
2004	69%	55%	79%	35%

GEORGIA 2

Southwest — Albany, part of Columbus and Valdosta suburbs

The racially diverse and Democratic-leaning 2nd sits in southwestern Georgia, extending south from Talbot and Crawford counties and running along the Alabama border on the west before reaching the Florida line. Although mostly rural, the 2nd takes in the cities of Albany and Americus and more than half of Columbus.

The struggling farming industry is still the economic lifeline of the 2nd — more than 25 percent of the nation's peanuts are grown in the district. Farmers here also grow wheat, cotton, soybeans and tobacco, and a new $185 million ethanol plant in Mitchell County has opened, which is expected to produce up to 100 million gallons of ethanol annually.

Big-name manufacturers and retailers increasingly factor into the 2nd's economy, although an economic downturn may cost the district some jobs. The district's two military bases also play a vital role — Fort Benning (shared with the 3rd) and the Marine Corps base in Albany have

begun expanding operations as a result of the 2005 BRAC round.

Slightly less than half of the 2nd's population is black, and redistricting prior to the 2006 elections led to a stronger Democratic lean here. The 2nd gained Democratic Macon, Marion and Peach counties, and lost Turner, Tift and Colquitt counties, which all lean Republican. Pockets of GOP strength exist in centrally located Lee County, as well as in Thomasville and other southern parts of the district. Dougherty County, whose county seat is Albany, is the most populous county wholly in the district and is reliably Democratic. Barack Obama won the 2nd with 54 percent of the vote in the 2008 presidential election.

MAJOR INDUSTRY
Agriculture, military, manufacturing, health care

MILITARY BASES
Fort Benning (Army), 31,783 military, 3,422 civilian (shared with the 3rd); Marine Corps Logistics Base, 480 military, 2,720 civilian (2008)

CITIES
Columbus (pt.), 119,135; Albany, 76,939; Thomasville, 18,162

NOTABLE
Jackie Robinson, who broke baseball's color barrier in 1947, was born in Cairo; Sylvester hosts the annual Georgia Peanut Festival every October.

Rep. Lynn Westmoreland (R)

Elected 2004; 3rd term

CAPITOL OFFICE
225-5901
westmoreland.house.gov
1213 Longworth Bldg. 20515-1008; fax 225-2515

COMMITTEES
Oversight & Government Reform
Small Business
Transportation & Infrastructure

RESIDENCE
Grantville

BORN
April 2, 1950; Atlanta, Ga.

RELIGION
Southern Baptist

FAMILY
Wife, Joan Westmoreland; three children

EDUCATION
Georgia State U., attended 1969-70

CAREER
Construction company owner;
real estate developer

POLITICAL HIGHLIGHTS
Sought Republican nomination for Ga. Senate,
1988; Republican nominee for Ga. Senate, 1990;
Ga. House, 1993-2005 (minority leader, 2001-03)

ELECTION RESULTS

2008 GENERAL

Lynn Westmoreland (R)	225,055	65.7%
Stephen Camp (D)	117,522	34.3%

2008 PRIMARY

Lynn Westmoreland (R)	unopposed

2006 GENERAL

Lynn Westmoreland (R)	130,428	67.6%
Mike McGraw (D)	62,371	32.4%

PREVIOUS WINNING PERCENTAGES
2004 (76%)

Westmoreland is a steadfast conservative who rarely holds back from saying what's on his mind. Though his tart tongue has landed him in trouble, Republican leaders appreciate his loyalty and have rewarded him for it.

He disdains bipartisanship and said he doesn't "have a lot of confidence in Senate Republicans" because they're compromisers. "I'm not a bipartisan kind of guy," he once said. "I'm not saying if [the Democrats] didn't have a good idea, I wouldn't vote for it. I just haven't heard them have a good idea."

During his first two terms, Westmoreland took the GOP's side on 98 percent of the votes in that pitted Republicans against Democrats, and in the 111th Congress (2009-10), GOP leaders made him a deputy whip. That was his second time on the leadership ladder; in 2006 he lost his deputy whip title on his second day on the job for not supporting a leadership-backed rule governing debate on a bill, a violation of a GOP conference rule.

Westmoreland also was named one of five vice chairs of the National Republican Congressional Committee, the House GOP's campaign arm. He will oversee congressional redistricting efforts as states plan to redraw districts following the 2010 census.

He doesn't introduce much legislation; he sponsored just four bills in the 110th Congress (2007-08), one to designate a post office. But his voting record has won plaudits from conservatives back home and he has been mentioned as a possible candidate for governor in 2010.

Speculation about the governorship slowed in September 2008 when he called presidential candidate Barack Obama and his wife, Michelle, "uppity," a racially loaded word. Westmoreland later said he thought the word was an adjective for elitism and not a slur. "I think everyone knew I was being as sincere as I could be," he said of not knowing the word's connotation. "Sometimes it makes you look like a dumbass if you admit things like that. But if it makes me look like a dumbass, then I'm just a dumbass."

That wasn't the first time a racial issue put Westmoreland in the spotlight. In 2006, he battled with the leadership over the extension of the Voting Rights Act. He and other conservatives insisted one of the act's protections for minority voting rights was outmoded and should be dropped. "It doesn't make sense to subjugate Georgia to the whims of federal bureaucrats until 2031 based on turnout of an election featuring Barry Goldwater and Lyndon Johnson," Westmoreland wrote in the Atlanta Journal-Constitution.

In July 2007, Westmoreland was one of just two House members to oppose a bill, later enacted into law, requiring federal investigations into unsolved murder cases from the violent civil rights era, calling it a waste of money. Later that year, Hawaii Democrat Neil Abercrombie accused Westmoreland of blindsiding him in protesting as wasteful several provisions in another bill — included in a successful spending measure — that gave funds to native Hawaiians living in the state. "I am confining my remarks to the chair, because if I was saying it directly to [Westmoreland], he would know it a lot more physically," said Abercrombie in a floor speech.

Westmoreland is the only member of Georgia's House delegation on the Transportation and Infrastructure Committee, which is expected to take up a renewal of the 2005 surface transportation law, traditionally a vehicle for funding local projects. He said his chief priority is relieving congestion in Henry County, a growing suburban area southeast of Atlanta.

He vows to be a watchdog over Obama's administration from his spot on the Oversight and Government Reform Committee. In early 2009, he joined all House Republicans by opposing an economic stimulus bill Obama touted as a way to jump-start the nation's economy. Westmoreland lamented the lack of GOP input into the measure.

In fall 2008, he opposed two $700 billion measures — the second of which became law — intended to shore up the financial services industry. He considered both measures a waste of money. "Washington has a terrible habit of throwing money at problems, thinking they'll go away," he said.

A successful real estate builder and developer, Westmoreland uses his seat on the Small Business Committee to try to reduce government intervention. As ranking member of the Regulations and Health Care Subcommittee, he considers it his job to help members understand that small businesses are the backbone of the economy.

Westmoreland's hard-nosed opinions don't always please all factions of his party. In the 109th Congress (2005-06), then-Appropriations Chairman Jerry Lewis of California went after Westmoreland after he and a small group of Republican conservatives called for an end to earmark provisions, funding set-asides for projects in members' districts. Lewis' staff leaked to the press a list of earmarks Westmoreland and his allies had quietly requested.

Westmoreland hails from a family of Atlanta mill workers. His father was a firefighter in the Atlanta suburbs who died on the job while responding to an early-morning alarm at a warehouse fire in freezing cold weather. Westmoreland spent one year at Georgia State University, but left to work full time. He was married at the time and his father-in-law hired him in his home-building business. After a few years, he started his own construction business and later expanded into real estate development and sales in the late 1980s.

Westmoreland grew up in a family of conservative Democrats, but had little interest in politics until the mid-1980s, when he was inspired by another Georgian — Newt Gingrich, the fiery conservative who was emerging as a leader and later helped Republicans win majority control of Congress.

Westmoreland tried but failed twice to win a seat in the state legislature before prevailing in 1992. He was helped by a reapportionment that gave him a more favorable Republican state House district. He rose through the leadership ranks, and had the chance to become the first Republican Speaker of the Georgia House. But he decided instead to run for Congress in 2004.

He won a GOP primary runoff against a Gingrich-backed candidate, Dylan Glenn, a former White House and gubernatorial aide who sought to become the House's only black Republican. In 2006 and 2008, Westmoreland easily beat Democratic challengers by more than 30 percentage points.

KEY VOTES

2008

No Delay consideration of Colombia free-trade agreement

No Override Bush veto of federal farm and nutrition programs reauthorization bill

Yes Overhaul surveillance laws and permit dismissal of suits against companies that conducted warrantless wiretapping

No Grant mortgage relief to homeowners and funding for Fannie Mae and Freddie Mac

No Approve initial $700 billion program to stabilize financial markets

No Approve final $700 billion program to stabilize financial markets

No Provide $14 billion in loans to automakers

2007

No Increase minimum wage by $2.10 an hour

? Approve $124.2 billion in emergency war spending and set goal for redeployment of troops from Iraq

Yes Reject federal contraceptive assistance to international family planning groups

? Override Bush veto of $23.2 billion water projects authorization bill

Yes Implement Peru free-trade agreement

No Approve energy policy overhaul with new fuel economy standards

Yes Clear $473.5 billion omnibus spending bill, including $70 billion for military operations

CQ VOTE STUDIES

	PARTY UNITY		PRESIDENTIAL SUPPORT	
	SUPPORT	OPPOSE	SUPPORT	OPPOSE
2008	98%	2%	76%	24%
2007	99%	1%	91%	9%
2006	97%	3%	83%	17%
2005	98%	2%	90%	10%

INTEREST GROUPS

	AFL-CIO	ADA	CCUS	ACU
2008	80%	0%	67%	100%
2007	4%	0%	72%	100%
2006	14%	5%	100%	92%
2005	20%	5%	85%	96%

GEORGIA 3

West central — Atlanta and Columbus suburbs

Solidly Republican, the 3rd takes in all or part of 15 counties, beginning in overflow areas near Atlanta and ranging south and west through rural areas to reach the Alabama border and part of Columbus.

Atlanta suburbs in Fayette, Coweta and Henry counties accounted for growth in the northeastern part of the district, as new homes and subdivisions replaced previously rural areas. The population of Henry County (shared with the 13th) grew by more than 50 percent this decade, but as residents have left Atlanta to escape urban congestion, Henry has had to endure traffic problems of its own. Peachtree City in Fayette County is a planned community of more than 30,000 residents that is known for golf cart paths that snake through the city. Residents and officials in Henry and Fayette counties are concerned about rising unemployment rates.

In the 3rd's more rural counties, agriculture remains a mainstay. Textile and poultry processing plants dot the landscape, and the timber industry flourishes here. In Troup County, manufacturing is playing a larger role in LaGrange, which is nearly half black and was once famous for its textile

industry, and in West Point, home to a new Kia Motors plant. To the south, the 3rd's portion of Muscogee County includes part of Columbus, Fort Benning (shared with the 2nd and expanding as a result of the 2005 BRAC Commission process) and regional health care providers. The district's portion of Muscogee hosts many of Columbus' residential communities.

The 3rd is dependably Republican, despite being nearly one-fifth black. John McCain earned 64 percent of the 3rd's vote in the 2008 presidential election, and Republican Rep. Lynn Westmoreland carried the parts of each county wholly or partially in the 3rd.

MAJOR INDUSTRY
Agriculture, service, timber, poultry processing, manufacturing

MILITARY BASES
Fort Benning (Army), 31,783 military, 3,422 civilian (2008) (shared with the 2nd)

CITIES
Columbus (pt.), 67,156; Peachtree City, 31,580; LaGrange, 25,998

NOTABLE
Franklin D. Roosevelt died on April 12, 1945, at his Little White House in Warm Springs while posing for the "Unfinished Portrait," which is now on display in the home's museum.

Rep. Hank Johnson (D)

Elected 2006; 2nd term

For Johnson, serving in the House has meant a homecoming. He was born and raised in Washington, D.C., and still has many friends around town. He also is picking up friends among his Democratic colleagues, who have rewarded him with added responsibilities in relatively rapid fashion.

Johnson is soft-spoken and calm, with a judicious temperament he developed as a county judge. He and Democrat Mazie K. Hirono of Hawaii, another member of the Class of 2006, are the first two Buddhists to be elected to Congress. "My approach is not to jump out and make a big splash," he said, "but to get into the water like a crocodile — just kind of slide right in" and start swimming.

Though he didn't seek the job, his fellow Democrats named him a regional whip for the 111th Congress (2009-10), with responsibility for rounding up the votes of colleagues from Florida, Mississippi and Alabama in addition to his home state. He demonstrated his loyalty in his first term by siding with his party on 99 percent of the votes that pitted the parties against each other.

His only high-profile departure came in opposing two $700 billion measures — the second of which became law — to aid the ailing financial services industry in fall 2008. He said the legislation "further burdens the taxpayer and does nothing to address the economy from the bottom up."

Johnson serves on the Judiciary Committee, where he has put his legal training to good use. He believes the criminal justice system hurts minorities and the poor through such initiatives as mandatory minimum sentencing, which he calls "fundamentally unfair," and the death penalty, which he considers "immoral."

In January 2009 he became chairman of Judiciary's Courts and Competition Policy Subcommittee, which oversees such areas as antitrust law, monopolies and the administration of federal courts. He has examined the role of antitrust law in the consolidation of the banking industry as well as competition in the concert ticket business.

He scored a significant success in 2008 when Congress enacted his legislation to reauthorize the Byrne grant program, which supports state and local law enforcement. The George W. Bush administration repeatedly tried to consolidate or kill the program, but Congress refused. "We can't afford to deny local governments the resources that they so desperately need to fight and prevent crime," Johnson said.

In February 2009, he re-introduced a bill to ban pre-dispute mandatory arbitration clauses in consumer contracts, such as cell phone agreements and employee contracts, that can forbid people from filing lawsuits. Trial lawyers and other proponents say the measure is a response to the growing number of arbitration agreements buried in the fine print of contracts, but business interests strongly resist the idea.

Johnson also is a member of the Armed Services panel, where he worked with other Democrats in the 110th Congress (2007-08) to shift defense funds from big weapons systems of the future to the immediate needs of troops fighting the wars in Iraq and Afghanistan. "What motivates me is the question, do we move forward on a program that might work in 2015, or do we get equipment to an Army National Guard that has served the nation admirably and so desperately needs the equipment today?" he said in 2007.

Johnson's mother taught school in Arlington County, Va., a Washington suburb. His father was a high-level official with the federal Bureau of Prisons. He went south for college, first to his mother's alma mater, Clark College

CAPITOL OFFICE
225-1605
hankjohnson.house.gov
1133 Longworth Bldg. 20515-1004; fax 226-0691

COMMITTEES
Armed Services
Judiciary
(Courts & Competition Policy - chairman)

RESIDENCE
Lithonia

BORN
Oct. 2, 1954; Washington, D.C.

RELIGION
Buddhist

FAMILY
Wife, Mereda Davis Johnson; two children

EDUCATION
Clark College, B.A. 1976 (political science);
Texas Southern U., J.D. 1979

CAREER
Lawyer; county judge

POLITICAL HIGHLIGHTS
Sought Democratic nomination for Ga. House, 1986; DeKalb County Board of Commissioners, 2001-06

ELECTION RESULTS

2008 GENERAL

Hank Johnson (D)		unopposed

2008 PRIMARY

Hank Johnson (D)		unopposed

2006 GENERAL

Hank Johnson (D)	106,352	75.3%
Catherine Davis (R)	34,778	24.6%

(now known as Clark Atlanta University), and then to Texas Southern University for law school, where he met his wife, Mereda.

He attributes both his career choice and his political path to the influence of a much older cousin, Archibald "Tokey" Hill, who graduated from law school when Johnson was a young child. "When Tokey graduated from law school, I decided I wanted to be a lawyer," he said. His cousin moved to Oklahoma, eventually winning election to the state legislature.

Johnson, meanwhile, grew up reading The Washington Post aloud to his mother each day as she washed the dinner dishes. He also frequently passed the Capitol building. "Since I wanted to be an attorney, since I wanted to be a public official like my cousin Tokey, the only legislature that I knew was the United States Congress," he said. "So it was always kind of planted in the back of my head that I would be a member of Congress one day."

First, he set about building a legal career in Georgia. For nearly three decades he practiced law with his wife in Decatur, focusing on criminal and civil litigation. Along the way he spent 10 years as an associate judge in DeKalb County. He made one unsuccessful foray into politics, seeking the Democratic nomination for the Georgia House in 1986, then in 2000 won a seat on the DeKalb County Board of Commissioners. It was during that campaign that he began using the nickname "Hank" instead of Henry C. Johnson, his given name, because there were four other Johnsons in the race.

In 2005, Johnson decided to take on Democratic Rep. Cynthia A. McKinney, an often confrontational advocate for liberal causes, in the 2006 primary. Though once among her supporters, he said she became "ineffective and divisive." McKinney got into a highly publicized dust-up with the Capitol Police in 2006 when she tried to skirt a security checkpoint at the Capitol. She was not wearing her congressional identification pin, so the officer "reached out and grabbed her, and she turned around and hit him," according to Terrance W. Gainer, then chief of the Capitol Police. She insisted the officer should have recognized her and called herself a victim of "racial profiling."

Her response, Johnson said, "kind of caused people to take a second look at her." He held her to less than 50 percent of the vote in the July 2006 primary as a third Democrat in the race, John F. Coyne III, captured more than 8 percent of the vote. That pushed McKinney into a runoff with Johnson, who won the contest in August.

Winning the primary is tantamount to being elected in the strongly Democratic, black-majority 4th District. Johnson cruised in the general election, beating Republican Catherine Davis, a human resources manager, by more than 50 percentage points. He was unopposed in 2008.

KEY VOTES

2008

Yes Delay consideration of Colombia free-trade agreement

Yes Override Bush veto of federal farm and nutrition programs reauthorization bill

No Overhaul surveillance laws and permit dismissal of suits against companies that conducted warrantless wiretapping

Yes Grant mortgage relief to homeowners and funding for Fannie Mae and Freddie Mac

No Approve initial $700 billion program to stabilize financial markets

No Approve final $700 billion program to stabilize financial markets

Yes Provide $14 billion in loans to automakers

2007

Yes Increase minimum wage by $2.10 an hour

Yes Approve $124.2 billion in emergency war spending and set goal for redeployment of troops from Iraq

No Reject federal contraceptive assistance to international family planning groups

Yes Override Bush veto of $23.2 billion water projects authorization bill

No Implement Peru free-trade agreement

Yes Approve energy policy overhaul with new fuel economy standards

No Clear $473.5 billion omnibus spending bill, including $70 billion for military operations

CQ VOTE STUDIES

	PARTY UNITY		PRESIDENTIAL SUPPORT	
	SUPPORT	OPPOSE	SUPPORT	OPPOSE
2008	99%	1%	12%	88%
2007	99%	1%	4%	96%

INTEREST GROUPS

	AFL-CIO	ADA	CCUS	ACU
2008	100%	100%	47%	8%
2007	96%	100%	47%	0%

GEORGIA 4
Atlanta suburbs – most of DeKalb County

The Democratic, suburban DeKalb County-based 4th District grabs most of DeKalb, half of Rockdale and part of Gwinnett counties. One of Georgia's two black-majority districts, African-Americans make up 53 percent of residents here.

Like the rest of the Atlanta area, southern DeKalb and northern Rockdale experienced nearly two decades of explosive growth. Decatur (shared with the 5th) is fighting to retain its small-town feel but has filled up with condos and commuters. Residential development transformed previously unpopulated land from Lithonia east through Conyers, in Rockdale County. But, the collapse of the home construction sector and rising unemployment rates in the metropolitan area have slowed further growth and strained the local economy.

Many residents rely on jobs in Atlanta or work in service-oriented firms in the 4th. Emory University and the Centers for Disease Control and Prevention, both on the eastern edge of the 5th, employ many 4th District residents who commute in from the suburbs.

South DeKalb is home to some wealthy black communities. To the north, towns like Chamblee and Doraville (split with the 6th) are increasingly home to large foreign-born populations, and dozens of languages spoken in schools and at the cities' many ethnic restaurants and shops. As many as half of Clarkston's residents are refugees, and the 4th's part of Gwinnett has many Hispanic residents.

The 4th District is Democratic at all levels, and Barack Obama took his highest statewide percentage in the district in the 2008 presidential race. His 79 percent here was slightly higher than what he received in the neighboring 5th District. DeKalb is heavily Democratic, but some voters in the portions of Rockdale and Gwinnett, and in DeKalb's more white, affluent areas, favor the GOP.

MAJOR INDUSTRY

Service, health care, government

CITIES

Redan (unincorporated), 33,841; Candler-McAfee (unincorporated), 28,294; Tucker, 26,532

NOTABLE

Stone Mountain Park has a huge granite rock face onto which a sculpture of Robert E. Lee and other Confederate leaders is carved.

Rep. John Lewis (D)

Elected 1986; 12th term

An iconic figure in the Democratic Party, Lewis is the last surviving speaker from the 1963 civil rights march on Washington and Congress' most influential voice on race relations. He's a big-picture liberal who wants to end the Iraq War and recreate the energy of President Johnson's Great Society initiatives of the mid-1960s.

Lewis became famous as a leader of a March 7, 1965, protest march from Selma, Ala., to the state capitol at Montgomery. State and local police attacked the peaceful marchers on the Edmund Pettus Bridge at the start of their journey in what became known as "Bloody Sunday." The outrage sparked by images of the event inspired enactment of the landmark Voting Rights Act, which Johnson signed into law in August that year. Lewis shows visitors to his office the poster-sized pictures of himself being clubbed over the head by police, blows that left him with a severe concussion. He leads members of Congress on a pilgrimage each year to Selma and other major landmarks of the civil rights era.

Lewis speaks to groups of schoolchildren and voters around the country, reminding his listeners that voting now is nearly as easy as getting a glass of water. He was overcome by emotion at President Obama's inauguration as he gazed across the Mall from the Capitol's West Front. "And then my mind started reflecting back to the suffering, the struggles, the arrests, the jailings, the beatings, to the people who stood in an unmovable line, to Dr. King, to Robert Kennedy, to John Kennedy and to Lyndon Johnson," Lewis told CNN. "And I wish — I wish so much so that they all were here to witness what we all witnessed today here on the West Front of the United States Capitol."

Lewis is held in high regard by lawmakers of both parties. House Majority Leader Steny H. Hoyer once described him as "one of the most respected, if not the most respected" members of the House. Obama's Republican opponent, Arizona Sen. John McCain, in 2008 named Lewis one of three "wise men" to whom he would turn during a crisis.

During the presidential primary campaign, Lewis embodied the shift toward Obama among initially wary black lawmakers and voters. An early supporter of Sen. Hillary Rodham Clinton of New York, Lewis started wavering in late February after Obama easily won his Atlanta-based district in the Georgia primary. His endorsement of Obama dealt a serious blow to Clinton's campaign. It came less than two months after Lewis criticized Obama on Clinton's behalf, telling The Washington Post, "He is no Martin Luther King Jr."

He has advanced legislation related to his civil rights background, although that is by no means his only focus. His bill creating the National Museum of African American History and Culture was signed into law by President George W. Bush in 2003 after years of effort.

Lewis holds the appointive leadership post of senior chief deputy whip, and a plum spot on the Ways and Means Committee, where he is chairman of the Oversight panel. His top priority for the 111th Congress (2009-10) is securing universal health insurance, though he doesn't have a particular plan in mind; what matters, he said, is that it's universal.

On Ways and Means Lewis pushes for increased federal aid for hurricane-devastated areas. He has promoted bills to reduce racial disparities in health care, provide medical services for the poor and the uninsured, and prevent the IRS from using private firms to collect back taxes. With a phone call to the IRS commissioner, Lewis in 2008 helped Atlanta's struggling Grady Memorial Hospital to switch quickly from public to tax-exempt nonprofit status, allowing

CAPITOL OFFICE
225-3801
www.house.gov/johnlewis
343 Cannon Bldg. 20515-1005; fax 225-0351

COMMITTEES
Ways & Means
(Oversight - chairman)

RESIDENCE
Atlanta

BORN
Feb. 21, 1940; Troy, Ala.

RELIGION
Baptist

FAMILY
Wife, Lillian Lewis; one child

EDUCATION
American Baptist Theological Seminary, B.A. 1961 (theology); Fisk U., B.A. 1963 (religion & philosophy)

CAREER
Civil rights activist

POLITICAL HIGHLIGHTS
Sought Democratic nomination for U.S. House (special election), 1977; Atlanta City Council, 1982-86

ELECTION RESULTS

2008 GENERAL

John Lewis (D)	231,368	100.0%

2008 PRIMARY

John Lewis (D)	36,713	69.0%
Markel Hutchins (D)	8,287	15.6%
Mabel "Able" Thomas (D)	8,185	15.4%

2006 GENERAL

John Lewis (D)	122,380	100.0%

PREVIOUS WINNING PERCENTAGES
2004 (100%); 2002 (100%); 2000 (77%); 1998 (79%); 1996 (100%); 1994 (69%); 1992 (72%); 1990 (76%); 1988 (78%); 1986 (75%)

it to receive a $200 million grant from the city's largest foundation. When Congress approved new surveillance powers for law enforcement after the Sept. 11 terrorist attacks, Lewis voted no, saying he feared a return to the days when the government spied on him and other civil rights leaders.

In his 1998 autobiography, "Walking With the Wind," Lewis wrote, "I've never been the kind of person who naturally attracts the limelight. I'm not a handsome guy. I'm not flamboyant. I'm not what you would call elegant."

But activist groups and Democratic Party leaders call on him for everything from ribbon-cuttings to fundraising dinners. And his thundering preacher's voice is one of the House's most familiar. Mississippi Sen. Trent Lott, trying to salvage his job as Senate Republican leader, sought forgiveness from Lewis in 2002 after his off-the-cuff remarks praising Sen. Strom Thurmond's 1948 pro-segregation presidential campaign.

One of 10 children of sharecroppers, Lewis recalls he was shy as a boy attending segregated schools in rural Alabama. He was inspired by King's sermons on the radio and developed a sense of outrage at the brutal lynching of 15-year-old Emmett Till in Mississippi in 1955. Lewis was the same age as Till at the time. Later, as a student at the American Baptist Theological Seminary in Nashville, he attended workshops on non-violent resistance. He joined the Student Nonviolent Coordinating Committee, a youthful fulcrum of the civil rights movement that focused on civil disobedience.

As a Freedom Rider, Lewis sat in at segregated lunch counters and took dangerous bus rides through the Deep South. In 1963, with 24 arrests under his belt, he was chosen to be chairman of the SNCC. He led the group's effort for voting rights, including the Selma march. But a rift formed between Lewis' old guard, with its emphasis on non-violence, and newer, more confrontational activists led by Stokely Carmichael. In 1966, Lewis was replaced by Carmichael as chairman, and the SNCC's philosophy changed.

Lewis first ran for Congress in 1977, for the seat Andrew Young left to become U.N. ambassador, but lost to Wyche Fowler. He went to Washington to head the federal volunteer agency ACTION. Returning to Atlanta, he won a seat on the city council in 1981. He made his next bid for the House in 1986, when Fowler ran for the Senate. He beat state Sen. Julian Bond for the Democratic nomination, and breezed to victory by a 3-1 margin in November.

Lewis's initial reluctance to endorse Obama in 2008 led to a rare primary challenge against him by two Democratic candidates. He campaigned harder than at any time since his first election, mowing voters' lawns and dressing in a UPS uniform to deliver packages. He claimed victory with 69 percent of the vote, and was unopposed in November for the fourth straight election.

KEY VOTES

2008

Yes Delay consideration of Colombia free-trade agreement

Yes Override Bush veto of federal farm and nutrition programs reauthorization bill

No Overhaul surveillance laws and permit dismissal of suits against companies that conducted warrantless wiretapping

Yes Grant mortgage relief to homeowners and funding for Fannie Mae and Freddie Mac

No Approve initial $700 billion program to stabilize financial markets

Yes Approve final $700 billion program to stabilize financial markets

Yes Provide $14 billion in loans to automakers

2007

Yes Increase minimum wage by $2.10 an hour

No Approve $124.2 billion in emergency war spending and set goal for redeployment of troops from Iraq

No Reject federal contraceptive assistance to international family planning groups

Yes Override Bush veto of $23.2 billion water projects authorization bill

Yes Implement Peru free-trade agreement

Yes Approve energy policy overhaul with new fuel economy standards

No Clear $473.5 billion omnibus spending bill, including $70 billion for military operations

CQ VOTE STUDIES

	PARTY UNITY		PRESIDENTIAL SUPPORT	
	SUPPORT	OPPOSE	SUPPORT	OPPOSE
2008	99%	1%	15%	85%
2007	98%	2%	9%	91%
2006	99%	1%	15%	85%
2005	99%	1%	9%	91%
2004	98%	2%	18%	82%

INTEREST GROUPS

	AFL-CIO	ADA	CCUS	ACU
2008	100%	95%	50%	4%
2007	95%	85%	55%	0%
2006	85%	80%	10%	4%
2005	92%	100%	33%	0%
2004	100%	100%	10%	4%

GEORGIA 5

Atlanta

The heart of the 5th lies in Atlanta, the symbolic capital of the New South and the Southeast's commercial center. Black-majority and reliably Democratic, it takes in all of the city of Atlanta, much of surrounding Fulton County and slices of DeKalb and Clayton counties to the east and south.

Atlanta is a transportation hub, and Hartsfield-Jackson Atlanta International Airport has a more than $20 billion annual economic impact on the region. The loss of Delta Air Lines operations at the airport, the airline's primary hub, would cause substantial layoffs and other economic effects. Coca-Cola and CNN also have headquarters in the 5th.

Atlanta's cultural and entertainment sites — the Georgia World Congress Center, which includes Centennial Olympic Park and the Georgia Dome; Woodruff Arts Center; Turner Field, home of baseball's Braves; the World of Coca-Cola venue; and the Georgia Aquarium — are still popular tourist destinations. The 5th also hosts Emory University, Georgia State University and the Georgia Institute of Technology. Under 2005 BRAC Commission rules, Fort McPherson is slated to close by late 2011.

Renovation of the city's business and downtown districts fueled recent growth, but high foreclosure rates have stalled the economy in some neighborhoods. Falling real estate prices may not be sufficient to continue new construction, but many damaged structures were repaired following a tornado touchdown in 2008. Traffic congestion remains a problem, and officials are trying to expand mass transit lines.

Republicans have some luck in Atlanta's affluent outlying areas such as Buckhead, a mostly old-money neighborhood with trendy shops. Democrat Barack Obama took 79 percent of the 5th's 2008 presidential vote.

MAJOR INDUSTRY
Transportation, distribution, higher education

MILITARY BASES
Fort McPherson (Army), 1,673 military, 1,973 civilian (2007)

CITIES
Atlanta, 416,474; East Point, 39,595; Sandy Springs (pt.) (unincorporated), 27,359

NOTABLE
The Rev. Martin Luther King Jr.'s childhood home and the Ebenezer Baptist Church, where he was a pastor, are in the Sweet Auburn neighborhood.

Rep. Tom Price (R)

Elected 2004; 3rd term

Price, an articulate and fervent conservative, thrives on being in the minority as a leading mouthpiece for Republicans. Despite his affable nature, he is a thorn in the Democrats' side as chairman of the Republican Study Committee, the influential group of the most conservative House members.

Price's persona — which led The Washington Post to dub him a "Republican guerrilla warrior" — has earned him comparisons to former Speaker Newt Gingrich, whose wealthy suburban-Atlanta district Price now represents. Like Price, Gingrich made a name for himself with his repeated challenges to the Democratic majority. But Price, a physician, comes across more as a country-club Republican than a conservative firebrand. He told the Atlanta Journal-Constitution he has "a surgeon's mentality...Instead of creating controversy, I get things done."

One of Price's jobs is to ensure his like-minded colleagues remain upbeat; he told the Washington Times in February 2009 he considers it a "wonderful time" to be on the right because "this nation remains a common-sense, solutions-based conservative nation." He acknowledged his party's credibility with the public had waned, but promised to aggressively implement a series of alternatives to the plans of President Obama and the ruling Democratic majority in Congress.

He was a prominent critic of Obama's $787 billion economic stimulus bill in early 2009, joining Study Committee members in pushing a failed plan that relied chiefly on tax cuts. He also reaped a publicity windfall for alleging it contained $30 million to protect an endangered species of mouse in the San Francisco Bay Area, even waving a ball of fur from a pet store on the House floor to drive his point home. "Does that create jobs?" he asked of the provision. News media organizations, however, subsequently reported there were no specific funds for the mice in the measure.

Price frequently takes aim at the Democratic leadership. He helped organize fellow Republican members in August 2008 to prod Speaker Nancy Pelosi to call the House back into session in order to take up GOP energy legislation to expand oil and gas drilling. Price said Republicans were forced to take a stand against Pelosi, who "wouldn't allow the minority party to speak," and at one point he led the group in an a capella rendition of "God Bless America." He held a news conference outside Pelosi's office in February 2009 to criticize her work on the stimulus bill.

Price opposes abortion rights and would abolish the IRS and replace virtually all taxes — including income, corporate, dividend and capital gains — with a 23 percent national sales tax. In his first term, he introduced a bill requiring more public disclosure for earmarks, funding for special projects in members' districts. In January 2008, he announced that he wouldn't request any new earmarks until the earmarking system is overhauled.

On the Education and Labor Committee, Price was the only member of the nearly 50-member panel to vote against a bill that would expand the definition of the word "disabled." Price argued that the expanded definition was too broad. "If everyone is disabled, then nobody is actually disabled," he said. His fellow committee members, he said, were afraid to vote against the bill because of its title. "How can you vote against the Americans with Disabilities Act?" he said. "I didn't come here to pass horrendous legislation."

Price wants the United States to adopt a system of health courts to cut down on the number of malpractice suits, and he wants to use tax policy to provide incentives for every family to obtain health insurance. He has intro-

CAPITOL OFFICE
225-4501
tom.house.gov
424 Cannon Bldg. 20515-1006; fax 225-4656

COMMITTEES
Education & Labor
Financial Services

RESIDENCE
Roswell

BORN
Oct. 8, 1954; Lansing, Mich.

RELIGION
Presbyterian

FAMILY
Wife, Elizabeth Clark Price; one child

EDUCATION
U. of Michigan, B.A. 1976 (general studies),
M.D. 1979

CAREER
Surgeon

POLITICAL HIGHLIGHTS
Ga. Senate, 1997-2005 (minority whip, 1999-2002; majority leader, 2003)

ELECTION RESULTS

2008 GENERAL

Tom Price (R)	231,520	68.5%
Bill Jones (D)	106,551	31.5%

2008 PRIMARY

Tom Price (R)	unopposed

2006 GENERAL

Tom Price (R)	144,958	72.4%
Steve Sinton (D)	55,294	27.6%

PREVIOUS WINNING PERCENTAGES
2004 (100%)

duced legislation that would protect an employer's right to require that English be spoken at its workplace.

On the Financial Services Committee, Price frequently offers amendments to require legislation to comply with the House's pay-as-you-go budget rules, which require offsets for new tax cuts or increased mandatory spending. He strongly opposed the 2008 legislation to shore up the ailing financial services sector, calling the bill an "egregious proposal that undermines American ideals and puts taxpayers on the hook for $700 billion." Price said congressional leaders should have considered free-market alternatives.

As a freshman, Price rallied other GOP rookies to form a group called the Official Truth Squad. During the 109th Congress (2005-06), its members took to the floor just before adjournment for an hour of discussion on what Price called "the disinformation from our colleagues across the aisle."

Price grew up in Michigan, the son of a dairy farmer who decided to attend medical school at the age of 36 to become an emergency room doctor. During his childhood, he recalls going on rounds with his grandfather, who was also a doctor. He followed in their professional footsteps, though he left Michigan and moved to Atlanta for a residency in orthopedic surgery at Emory University and eventually settled in the area with his anesthesiologist wife.

Price was drawn to politics because he felt lawmakers wielded too much power over his actions as a doctor, and he is among the conservative doctors in Congress who believe the federal government should not make health care decisions for patients. "It is arrogant and irresponsible for us as a society — the federal government — to be making those [personal] decisions," he said. Price became increasingly involved in civic organizations like the Rotary Club and in Republican politics as an organizer and fundraiser. When a friend in the state Senate decided to retire in 1996, she urged Price to run. In the General Assembly, he was known as a quick study on the details of policy and the rules and mechanics of passing bills. Within two years, he was chosen for a leadership position, and when Republicans took control of the state Senate in 2003, he became the majority leader.

After Gingrich, who held the seat for 20 years and led the GOP takeover of Congress in 1994, resigned from Congress, Republican Johnny Isakson held the seat for almost three terms. When Isakson ran successfully for the Senate in 2004, it created an opening for Price. Price finished first in a seven-candidate primary, then went into a runoff against fellow GOP state Sen. Robert Lamutt. Lamutt got Gingrich's endorsement, but Price had the support of doctors and health care groups. He prevailed, 54 percent to 46 percent. He was unopposed in the general election and was easily re-elected in 2006 and 2008.

KEY VOTES

2008

No   Delay consideration of Colombia free-trade agreement

No   Override Bush veto of federal farm and nutrition programs reauthorization bill

Yes   Overhaul surveillance laws and permit dismissal of suits against companies that conducted warrantless wiretapping

No   Grant mortgage relief to homeowners and funding for Fannie Mae and Freddie Mac

No   Approve initial $700 billion program to stabilize financial markets

No   Approve final $700 billion program to stabilize financial markets

No   Provide $14 billion in loans to automakers

2007

No   Increase minimum wage by $2.10 an hour

No   Approve $124.2 billion in emergency war spending and set goal for redeployment of troops from Iraq

Yes   Reject federal contraceptive assistance to international family planning groups

Yes   Override Bush veto of $23.2 billion water projects authorization bill

Yes   Implement Peru free-trade agreement

No   Approve energy policy overhaul with new fuel economy standards

Yes   Clear $473.5 billion omnibus spending bill, including $70 billion for military operations

CQ VOTE STUDIES

	PARTY UNITY		PRESIDENTIAL SUPPORT	
	SUPPORT	OPPOSE	SUPPORT	OPPOSE
2008	99%	1%	76%	24%
2007	98%	2%	91%	9%
2006	96%	4%	97%	3%
2005	97%	3%	87%	13%

INTEREST GROUPS

	AFL-CIO	ADA	CCUS	ACU
2008	7%	10%	72%	100%
2007	4%	0%	80%	100%
2006	7%	0%	100%	92%
2005	13%	0%	93%	96%

GEORGIA 6

North Atlanta suburbs — Roswell, Alpharetta

Set in Atlanta's northern suburbs, the 6th takes in all of Cherokee County and parts of three other counties, and is home to corporate headquarters and Republican voters. The overwhelmingly white 6th is Georgia's most affluent and educated district. Office parks, malls, golf courses and housing subdivisions dominate most of the landscape, and the foothills of the Blue Ridge Mountains rise from northern Cherokee County.

Northern Fulton County, the center of the 6th, hosts UPS's corporate headquarters between Sandy Springs and Dunwoody, which is in adjacent DeKalb County. Alpharetta is a technology and telecommunications center, and is home to large offices for technology companies such as ADP. Roswell, formerly a cotton-milling center, is now a Fulton County bedroom community and home to the regional headquarters of the city's largest employer, Kimberly-Clark's biomedical manufacturing and marketing offices. Roswell's historic district lures visitors with historic landmarks, outdoor recreation, and shopping and dining venues.

While northern Cherokee County remains largely rural, the southern por-

tion of the county is becoming increasingly suburban. Despite job losses across the Atlanta area, towns in Cherokee are continuing with commercial development projects. Eastern Cobb County serves as a bedroom community for downtown Atlanta, but high unemployment rates have affected the largely white-collar, highly educated suburban workforce. GE Energy has its headquarters in the southern tip of the district.

The 6th has many fiscally conservative Republican voters, although the longtime GOP stronghold is trending more to the center. Northern DeKalb County is home to Atlanta's older, more traditional suburbs, and voters include more minorities and residents who tend to be socially moderate. John McCain won 63 percent of the district's 2008 presidential vote.

MAJOR INDUSTRY
Technology, distribution, finance, health care

CITIES
Roswell, 79,334; Sandy Springs (pt.) (unincorporated), 58,422; Alpharetta, 34,854; Dunwoody (unincorporated), 32,808

NOTABLE
The city of Mountain Park (Fulton County) is home to Indian Spring — Cherokee Indians would venture from the hills to the spring, believing the waters had healing powers.

Rep. John Linder (R)

Elected 1992; 9th term

CAPITOL OFFICE
225-4272
linder.house.gov
1026 Longworth Bldg. 20515-1007; fax 225-4696

COMMITTEES
Ways & Means

RESIDENCE
Duluth

BORN
Sept. 9, 1942; Deer River, Minn.

RELIGION
Presbyterian

FAMILY
Wife, Lynne Linder; two children

EDUCATION
U. of Minnesota, Duluth, B.S. 1963;
U. of Minnesota, D.D.S. 1967

MILITARY SERVICE
Air Force 1967-69

CAREER
Financial executive; dentist

POLITICAL HIGHLIGHTS
Ga. House, 1975-81; Republican nominee for
Ga. Senate, 1980; Ga. House, 1983-91; Republican
nominee for U.S. House, 1990

ELECTION RESULTS

2008 GENERAL

John Linder (R)	209,354	62.0%
Doug Heckman (D)	128,159	38.0%

2008 PRIMARY

John Linder (R)	unopposed

2006 GENERAL

John Linder (R)	130,561	70.9%
Allan Burns (D)	53,553	29.1%

PREVIOUS WINNING PERCENTAGES
2004 (100%); 2002 (79%); 2000 (100%); 1998 (69%);
1996 (64%); 1994 (58%); 1992 (51%)

Linder's conservatism is of the brand modeled after former GOP Speaker Newt Gingrich, who represented the neighboring 6th District for two decades until 1998. Linder is pro-business, favors tax cuts, opposes abortion and battles environmental regulation. Even with his party out of power and his attempts to regain a foot on the leadership ladder rebuffed, he is an unwavering party supporter.

A former entrepreneur, Linder has made himself known for his continued commitment to anti-tax conservative principles and, particularly, his relentless advocacy of a national sales tax — an idea that became the basis for a book he co-authored but that has gotten little traction in Congress.

Linder is on the tax-writing Ways and Means Committee and is the top-ranking Republican on its Income Security and Family Support panel. He argues that replacing all federal income, estate and payroll taxes with what he calls the FairTax would broaden the tax base, eliminate fraud and bureaucracy and solve long-term deficits in federal entitlement programs. Critics say a national sales tax is regressive and would largely hurt low-income people.

"The FairTax Book: Saying Goodbye to the Income Tax and the IRS," written by Linder and radio talk show host Neal Boortz, was published in 2005 and reached No. 1 on the New York Times' non-fiction best seller list. The Times' book reviewer was far less supportive, noting, "No reputable economist of any political stripe would support it." Yet millions of people bought the book, earning Linder several hundred thousand dollars in royalties.

In the 110th Congress (2007-08), Linder's legislation attracted 72 cosponsors, all but one of them a Republican. He reintroduced the bill during the first week of the 111th Congress (2009-10), seeking to capitalize on the country's financial woes. "You and I both know that our current income tax system has significantly contributed to our economic instability," he said in a letter to supporters. "While many in Congress on both sides of the aisle believe that change is necessary, they fear change as bold as the FairTax."

Linder introduced another measure popular with conservatives early in the 111th: a resolution calling for a restoration of diplomatic relations between the United States and Taiwan, an idea sharply opposed by mainland China's Communist regime. The measure calls for an end to the United States' "one China" policy and for Taiwan's full membership in international organizations.

Linder's standing among Republicans has fallen considerably since Gingrich's resignation following the 1998 elections in which the GOP lost five seats. The Speaker's departure cost Linder the chairmanship of the National Republican Congressional Committee, the organization that helps recruit and fund GOP candidates for the House. In 2008, Linder proposed making the NRCC position appointed by the Republican leader rather than elected by the caucus. His colleagues rejected the idea.

Linder was in line to chair the Rules Committee in the 109th Congress (2005-06). But Speaker J. Dennis Hastert granted a term-limit waiver to Chairman David Dreier of California, allowing him a fourth two-year stint at the helm. (Ironically, Linder had written the "Linder Rule," which set term limits on committee chairmanships.)

Yet Linder remains a loyal party member. Even though he pushed his own plan against the income tax, he supported President George W. Bush's tax proposals. He voted for the $70 billion, five-year tax cut extension of 2006 and the $137 billion corporate tax cut approved in 2004. He opposed the $700 billion financial industry rescue plan in 2008, as well as President Obama's $787 billion economic stimulus package in early 2009, which included funds for many infrastructure, environmental and health care projects. "Everybody likes to get gifts," he said. "Somebody has to pay for them."

Linder is also conservative socially. He opposes abortion and cosponsored a bill that became law in 2003 banning a procedure critics call "partial birth" abortion. He also supported Bush's 2006 veto of a bill to allow the use of federal funds for research on embryonic stem cells derived from surplus embryos at in vitro fertilization clinics. Linder has questioned whether humans are causing global warming. "The 4.5 billion-year-old planet has been heating or cooling every minute of its existence," Linder wrote in a 2007 opinion piece in The Washington Times. "The notion that humans have substantially changed the world which we inherited is just vanity." He supports offshore oil drilling.

Linder grew up in a small Minnesota town, the son of a car salesman. He worked his way through college at the University of Minnesota in Duluth, starting in pre-medicine but switching to dentistry. After dental school, he joined the Air Force, where he practiced dentistry in San Antonio. He and his wife then moved to suburban Atlanta, where he set up a dentistry practice.

He was increasingly interested in politics. Linder subscribed to the Congressional Record, a daily report of congressional floor activities, and also said he was moved by the writings of National Review founder William F. Buckley.

Linder ran successfully for a seat in the Georgia House in 1974 and served 14 years in the legislature, where he earned a reputation for battling the Democratic leadership. In 1977, he founded a lending institution specializing in providing assistance to small businesses. He eventually left dentistry and became a successful entrepreneur, building and selling a series of businesses, including an asbestos removal firm and an adhesives manufacturer.

Linder first ran for Congress in 1990, losing a tight battle with Democratic Rep. Ben Jones in the 4th District. Two years later, redistricting gave the district a more Republican tilt, and Linder narrowly edged out Democratic state Sen. Cathey Steinberg with 51 percent of the vote. After a Supreme Court decision invalidated Georgia's congressional map as racial gerrymandering, Linder in 1995 wound up representing a redrawn 11th District that included some Atlanta suburbs and rural areas.

He enjoyed easy re-elections until facing GOP Rep. Bob Barr — a fellow conservative with a higher national profile — in the 2002 primary in the newly drawn 7th District. Republican voters ultimately rejected Barr's acerbic style and polarizing politics in favor of the buttoned-down Linder, who prevailed by 29 percentage points. Linder went on to win in November with 79 percent of the vote. He was unopposed in 2004 and won easily in both 2006 and 2008.

KEY VOTES

2008

No Delay consideration of Colombia free-trade agreement

No Override Bush veto of federal farm and nutrition programs reauthorization bill

Yes Overhaul surveillance laws and permit dismissal of suits against companies that conducted warrantless wiretapping

No Grant mortgage relief to homeowners and funding for Fannie Mae and Freddie Mac

No Approve initial $700 billion program to stabilize financial markets

No Approve final $700 billion program to stabilize financial markets

No Provide $14 billion in loans to automakers

2007

No Increase minimum wage by $2.10 an hour

No Approve $124.2 billion in emergency war spending and set goal for redeployment of troops from Iraq

Yes Reject federal contraceptive assistance to international family planning groups

No Override Bush veto of $23.2 billion water projects authorization bill

Yes Implement Peru free-trade agreement

No Approve energy policy overhaul with new fuel economy standards

Yes Clear $473.5 billion omnibus spending bill, including $70 billion for military operations

CQ VOTE STUDIES

	PARTY UNITY		PRESIDENTIAL SUPPORT	
	SUPPORT	OPPOSE	SUPPORT	OPPOSE
2008	97%	3%	77%	23%
2007	97%	3%	92%	8%
2006	98%	2%	93%	7%
2005	97%	3%	89%	11%
2004	98%	2%	94%	6%

INTEREST GROUPS

	AFL-CIO	ADA	CCUS	ACU
2008	0%	0%	72%	100%
2007	4%	0%	75%	100%
2006	8%	0%	100%	96%
2005	13%	0%	93%	96%
2004	7%	0%	100%	100%

GEORGIA 7
East of Atlanta — outer Atlanta suburbs

A mix of eastern Atlanta suburbs and less-populous areas west of Athens, the solidly Republican 7th is centered in Gwinnett County (shared with the 4th), a growing and increasingly diverse county with a developing economy. The remainder of the 7th is split between suburban and rural areas, which include small parts of Newton and Forsyth counties and all of more sparsely populated Barrow and Walton counties. Despite their historically rural composition, western Walton, Barrow and Newton counties have also begun to fill up with bedroom communities.

Some district residents still commute to Atlanta for work, but jobs in Gwinnett County keep many locals here during the day. Gwinnett has an emerging science corridor along Interstate 85 that hosts several technology firms. Retail and service jobs have replaced manufacturing, but employment cuts in county government and the white-collar private sector have slowed the economy. Some construction jobs remain despite the economic downturn, particularly at the site of a new minor league baseball stadium and planned adjacent multi-use development.

Gwinnett, which accounts for more than three-fourths of the 7th's population, is transforming — almost one-fourth of residents were born abroad, and more Hispanics and Asians are registered to vote in Gwinnett than in any other Georgia county. The county's Hispanic population more than doubled during the last decade, and the international flavor is spicing up the school system, local businesses and politics. The Gwinnett Center's arena and performing arts center are the cultural hub.

Republican support in the 7th is anchored in Gwinnett County. The district's small portion of Newton County is more friendly to Democrats, but Gwinnett's Republican support keeps the district safely in the GOP corner. Changing demographics in Gwinnett, however, may alter the 7th's political makeup in the coming years. In the 2008 presidential election, Republican John McCain took 60 percent of the district's vote.

MAJOR INDUSTRY
Service, retail, technology, manufacturing, construction

CITIES
Lawrenceville, 22,397; Duluth, 22,122; Snellville, 15,351

NOTABLE
The town of Between, in Walton County, was named by a postmaster because of its location halfway between Loganville and Monroe.

Rep. Jim Marshall (D)

Elected 2002; 4th term

CAPITOL OFFICE
225-6531
jimmarshall.house.gov
504 Cannon Bldg. 20515-1003; fax 225-3013

COMMITTEES
Agriculture
Armed Services

RESIDENCE
Macon

BORN
March 31, 1948; Ithaca, N.Y.

RELIGION
Roman Catholic

FAMILY
Wife, Camille Hope; two children

EDUCATION
Princeton U., A.B. 1972 (politics); Boston U., J.D. 1977

MILITARY SERVICE
Army 1968-70

CAREER
Lawyer; professor; logging business owner

POLITICAL HIGHLIGHTS
Mayor of Macon, 1995-99; Democratic nominee for U.S. House, 2000

ELECTION RESULTS

2008 GENERAL

Jim Marshall (D)	157,241	57.2%
Rick Goddard (R)	117,446	42.8%

2008 PRIMARY

Jim Marshall (D)	44,211	85.7%
Robert Nowak (D)	7,396	14.3%

2006 GENERAL

Jim Marshall (D)	80,660	50.5%
Mac Collins (R)	78,908	49.4%

PREVIOUS WINNING PERCENTAGES
2004 (63%); 2002 (51%)

Marshall is a pointedly independent Democrat, keeping a closer eye on his district's desires than his leadership's goals. He frequently votes with Republicans on issues ranging from tax cuts to the Iraq War, following the interests of his conservative-leaning constituents. Only one House Democrat — Oklahoma's Dan Boren — sided more frequently with President George W. Bush on floor votes during the 110th Congress (2007-08).

His district is the home of Robins Air Force Base, which drives the area's economy, and Marshall focuses on military issues. A combat veteran who dropped out of Princeton to fight in Vietnam, Marshall is a member of the Armed Services Committee and a forceful advocate for veterans. He led the successful 2004 charge in Congress to phase out a rule that required disabled veterans' military pensions to be reduced by the amount of their disability payments.

Marshall has been a staunch opponent of any plan to withdraw U.S. forces from Iraq. The son and grandson of Army generals, he backed Bush's policy on the Iraq War long after others had left the president's side. He was one of only two Democrats in the House to vote "no" on the party's resolution opposing Bush's plan in 2007 to send more than 21,000 additional troops to Iraq. He also opposed Speaker Nancy Pelosi's call for congressional investigations of White House decision-making before the war. By early 2007, Marshall had visited the troops in Iraq 10 times since the war began in 2003. During a Thanksgiving 2005 trip, Marshall, Republican Tim Murphy of Pennsylvania and Democrat Ike Skelton of Missouri escaped serious injury when their military vehicle flipped over en route to the Baghdad airport.

Marshall's district also relies heavily on agriculture — cotton, peanuts, peaches, pecans and timber are harvested. As a member of the Agriculture Committee, he has been a spirited defender of crop subsidies. He obtained funds in the 2008 reauthorization of agriculture programs to aid peanut farmers who rotate their crops — a practice that helps resource conservation and prevents land erosion.

He had served on Financial Services until mid-2008, when he and others departed to make room for freshmen who had won special elections that year. One of his last acts on that committee was to secure passage of legislation to allow homeowners who have filed for bankruptcy to obtain mortgage loans insured by the Federal Housing Administration. He supported a $700 billion plan to rescue the financial services industry in fall 2008, but opposed a $14 billion bailout plan for the auto industry that December.

On other domestic issues, Marshall often defies his party. At the start of the 110th Congress, when Pelosi rushed the party's "Six for '06" campaign agenda to the floor, most Democrats voted for all six bills, which included an increase in the federal minimum wage and greater leverage for the government to negotiate prescription drug prices. Marshall was the only Democrat to vote against two of the six; he opposed easing restrictions on embryonic stem cell research, which uses discarded embryos created for in vitro fertilization, and a rollback of tax breaks and subsidies for oil and gas companies.

In 2007, he was one of only two Democrats to vote against overriding Bush's veto of a measure that would have expanded the State Children's Health Insurance Program, which covers children from low-income families that do not qualify for Medicaid. When Congress sent a similar bill to President Obama for his signature in early 2009, Marshall was one of just two House Democrats voting "no."

Marshall voted for the $787 billion economic stimulus package in February 2009, but he was one of 20 Democrats opposing the catchall $410 billion appropriations package for fiscal 2009 less than two weeks later.

Democratic leaders tolerate his independence, not wanting to endanger Marshall politically. A GOP-drawn district remap that took effect for the 2006 election renumbered his district as the 8th (from the 3rd) and excluded many of his old constituents. Marshall countered Republican efforts to cast him as a liberal by emphasizing his military background and his centrist voting record. He hung onto the seat by only 1,752 votes in one of the 10 closest House races of the year. He and Rep. John Barrow, another conservative who squeaked through in 2006, are Georgia's only two white Democrats.

Marshall was born in Ithaca, N.Y., but grew up on Army bases around the world. His family moved 22 times. He was a National Merit Scholar in high school in Mobile, Ala., before attending Princeton University. In 1968, he left school to become an Army ranger. Marshall says he felt it was wrong for him to sit out the war on an academic deferment. He was wounded twice in combat and earned a Purple Heart.

Marshall has survived several bouts of skin cancer, a condition he attributes to his exposure to the herbicide Agent Orange in Vietnam. In 2003, he had successful surgery to treat prostate cancer.

When his Army service ended in 1970, Marshall finished his degree in politics at Princeton and then worked a series of jobs, including as a wilderness instructor, a short-order cook, a welder and a high school economics teacher. He also owned and operated a small logging business in Idaho, during which time he was badly injured when a tree fell on his leg. While recovering, Marshall got a law degree from Boston University, where he met his wife, Camille, also a law student. (Her father, John Hope, a meteorologist, named Hurricane Camille for her.)

The two moved south and Marshall joined the faculty of Mercer University's law school in Macon. In 1995, at age 47, he won the race for mayor of Macon. In that role, he was credited with shoring up the city financially. A fitness buff and jogger, he earned local public affection in 1997 by chasing down a man who had broken into the women's locker room at his health club. Marshall overtook the suspect, who was later arrested.

Marshall ran for the House in 2000, challenging GOP Rep. Saxby Chambliss. He lost by 18 percentage points, but tried again in 2002 in a redrawn district. His Republican opponent was Calder Clay, a Macon city councilman. Marshall edged Clay by only 1,528 votes. Even including the close 2008 race, Marshall has won by wider margins since then.

KEY VOTES

2008

Yes Delay consideration of Colombia free-trade agreement
Yes Override Bush veto of federal farm and nutrition programs reauthorization bill
Yes Overhaul surveillance laws and permit dismissal of suits against companies that conducted warrantless wiretapping
Yes Grant mortgage relief to homeowners and funding for Fannie Mae and Freddie Mac
Yes Approve initial $700 billion program to stabilize financial markets
Yes Approve final $700 billion program to stabilize financial markets
No Provide $14 billion in loans to automakers

2007

Yes Increase minimum wage by $2.10 an hour
No Approve $124.2 billion in emergency war spending and set goal for redeployment of troops from Iraq
Yes Reject federal contraceptive assistance to international family planning groups
Yes Override Bush veto of $23.2 billion water projects authorization bill
No Implement Peru free-trade agreement
Yes Approve energy policy overhaul with new fuel economy standards
Yes Clear $473.5 billion omnibus spending bill, including $70 billion for military operations

CQ VOTE STUDIES

	PARTY UNITY		PRESIDENTIAL SUPPORT	
	SUPPORT	OPPOSE	SUPPORT	OPPOSE
2008	83%	17%	33%	67%
2007	75%	25%	37%	63%
2006	65%	35%	65%	35%
2005	67%	33%	59%	41%
2004	69%	31%	53%	47%

INTEREST GROUPS

	AFL-CIO	ADA	CCUS	ACU
2008	0%	70%	72%	28%
2007	76%	60%	53%	61%
2006	64%	35%	73%	72%
2005	67%	70%	63%	46%
2004	80%	55%	55%	48%

GEORGIA 8

Middle Georgia — Macon

The 8th, a long vertical strip in central Georgia, extends from outer Atlanta suburbs in Newton County south through Macon to Colquitt County near the Florida border. The district is politically, economically and racially diverse and includes urban, suburban and rural areas. About one-third of residents are black, and although the district is generally middle class, pockets of poverty dot the 8th.

Macon has a diverse economy — with regional distribution centers, a university and a hospital system — that serves central Georgia. The city's economy remained stable in recent years despite job loss after the 2006 closure of a large Brown & Williamson tobacco plant. South of Macon, Robins Air Force Base is the area's economic engine; the base employs more than 25,000 people, including military and civilian personnel and aerospace contractors and manufacturers.

In the 8th's north, growing Newton County serves as a bedroom community for Atlanta, and some of the old-line rural counties to the south of Newton also now house commuters. The 8th relies heavily on agriculture, especially in the southern tier of the district where cotton and peanuts are grown. Timber, peaches and pecans also are harvested in the 8th, and every county here has some agricultural production.

Many residents are traditional Southern "Yellow Dog" Democrats who still support Democrats at the local level but back the GOP in national races. Macon, more than 60 percent black, is a Democratic stronghold. Colquitt and Tift, in the southern tip, have become solidly GOP counties. While the district's portion of Newton is Republican, increases in black and younger residents are shifting it to the left. The 8th gave Republican candidate John McCain 56 percent of its presidential vote in 2008.

MAJOR INDUSTRY
Agriculture, aerospace, distribution, timber

MILITARY BASES
Robins Air Force Base, 5,216 military, 13,838 civilian (2007)

CITIES
Macon, 97,255; Warner Robins (pt.), 48,787; Dublin, 15,857

NOTABLE
Macon's Wesleyan College, one of the first degree-granting colleges for women, was founded in 1836.

Rep. Nathan Deal (R)

Elected 1992; 9th term

CAPITOL OFFICE
225-5211
www.house.gov/deal
2133 Rayburn Bldg. 20515-1010; fax 225-8272

COMMITTEES
Energy & Commerce

RESIDENCE
Gainesville

BORN
Aug. 25, 1942; Millen, Ga.

RELIGION
Baptist

FAMILY
Wife, Sandra Dunagan Deal; four children

EDUCATION
Mercer U., B.A. 1964, J.D. 1966

MILITARY SERVICE
Army, 1966-68

CAREER
Lawyer; state prosecutor

POLITICAL HIGHLIGHTS
Hall County Juvenile Court judge, 1971-72;
Hall County attorney, 1977-79; Ga. Senate, 1981-93
(served as a Democrat; president pro tempore,
1991-93)

ELECTION RESULTS

2008 GENERAL

Nathan Deal (R)	217,493	75.5%
Jeff Scott (D)	70,537	24.5%

2008 PRIMARY

Nathan Deal (R)	unopposed

2006 GENERAL

Nathan Deal (R)	128,685	76.6%
John D. Bradbury (D)	39,240	23.4%

PREVIOUS WINNING PERCENTAGES *
2004 (100%); 2002 (100%); 2000 (75%); 1998 (100%);
1996 (66%); 1994 (58%); 1992 (59%)
* Elected as a Democrat 1992-94

Deal is a onetime Democrat who switched parties but has always been thoroughly Southern in his conservative politics. His demeanor is low-key and approachable, a persona that dates at least as far back as his street-level, walk-in law practice at home in Gainesville, Ga.

For years, Deal's efforts were mostly behind the scenes, but he has taken on a higher profile in recent years as a senior member of the Energy and Commerce Committee, where he is ranking Republican on its health panel. And in 2009 he sought to boost his profile more as he set out on a bid for the governor's seat, pledging a focus on education and transportation.

Deal is among the influential conservatives willing to work with Democrats on expanding health care coverage, as long as "some basic principles we're concerned about are embodied in" any overhaul, he said in March 2009. "There has to be an element of the private sector that's still involved in the delivery system," he said.

At the same time, Deal doesn't hide his skepticism about trying to move too much too quickly. "The problem I think we have encountered is that we have known different ways to deal with this issue in small pieces over a long number of years, and we have failed to come to grips with dealing with those pieces," he said at a March 2009 hearing. "And now we are trying to deal with the system as a whole and talk about how bad the system is, even though we have not taken advantage of the opportunities to make it better incrementally."

Deal had been chairman of the Health Subcommittee for two years before Democrats took over the House and Senate in 2007. He acknowledged at the start of his tenure that he knew little about health care beyond what he had learned from his wife providing in-home care to his elderly in-laws. But as head of the subcommittee Deal managed to push a handful of substantial bills through the House. He won some changes in Medicaid — the country's main health care program for the poor — that gave states more flexibility, such as letting them set the amount of co-payments charged to patients.

Deal also supports the concept of Health Savings Accounts, which some people with high-deductible insurance plans use to pay for primary health care. And he joins with other Republicans seeking to make health care pricing information more transparent for patients.

Immigration is another national issue of great concern to Deal. He parted ways with President George W. Bush when it came to illegal immigration, regarding it as a drain on the nation's health care and other public services. When Bush proposed a law in the 110th Congress (2007-08) to allow illegal immigrants to embark on a path to citizenship, Deal was among the vocal critics in both parties who decried what they said was "amnesty" and helped pass a bill in the House rejecting this course.

His opposition to Bush's immigration plan was unusual for the conservative Deal. He supported Bush on the Iraq War, wants his tax cuts made permanent and generally votes with his party on such social issues as abortion rights and gun control. He is a critic of earmarks — the member-driven requests to fund pet projects in their districts — and has refused to seek any himself until a meaningful reform of the process is achieved. Such positions play well in his district, which gave Arizona Republican John McCain three-quarters of the vote in the 2008 presidential race — the highest total of any in the Peach State.

Deal watches out for his district's poultry processors; in 2003 he briefly found himself in the national spotlight when then-Speaker J. Dennis Hastert slipped a provision on his behalf into that year's catchall spending bill to give beef and poultry producers' animals non-organic feed and still label their meat as organic. Deal, who had sought the exemption on behalf of his district's Fieldale Farms, said the standards for organic producers were too strict. Amid an outcry from organic food producers, the provision was repealed.

Five years earlier, he also made headlines when actress and Atlanta resident Jane Fonda reportedly told a United Nations panel that North Georgia's living conditions were akin to those in some Third World countries. "If Fonda believes there are starving children in North Georgia," Deal said, "she should start feeding them instead of feeding buffalo in Montana," where Fonda and her then-husband Ted Turner had a ranch.

Deal was a Democrat who in his first term joined about 20 other freshman Democrats to form the Fiscal Caucus to pressure the Clinton administration to cut spending. That group was one of the forerunners of the Blue Dog Coalition, a Southern-dominated group of fiscally conservative House Democrats, which Deal helped found before he switched parties in 1995 shortly after Republicans took control of the House for the first time in four decades. He said at the time, "The Democratic Party's attitude wasn't in tune with me or my constituents' beliefs."

The switch enhanced Deal's political security. As a Democrat, he won his initial congressional election and re-election with slightly less than 60 percent of the vote. He has enjoyed easier victories since switching to the GOP, even running unopposed in two of the last four elections. He has served on Energy and Commerce since 1998.

Deal is the only child of two public school teachers (his wife is also a teacher), and although his parents were not active in politics, they impressed upon him the importance of being active in public life.

A successful high school and college debater, he proceeded to law school. He then joined the Army to fulfill his ROTC commitment, and served two years in the Judge Advocate General's Corps before opening a law practice in Gainesville. He served as a prosecutor and a juvenile court judge, then ran successfully for an open state Senate seat in 1980.

Deal had a string of effortless re-elections in the legislature by the time U.S. Rep. Ed Jenkins, a fellow conservative Democrat, announced his retirement in 1992. Deal overcame Republican Daniel Becker, who made abortion rights the focus of a "morality in government" campaign. In 2008, Deal again won easily with 76 percent of the vote. He announced in May 2009 he would not run for re-election, seeking instead a run for governor.

KEY VOTES

2008

No Delay consideration of Colombia free-trade agreement
No Override Bush veto of federal farm and nutrition programs reauthorization bill
Yes Overhaul surveillance laws and permit dismissal of suits against companies that conducted warrantless wiretapping
No Grant mortgage relief to homeowners and funding for Fannie Mae and Freddie Mac
No Approve initial $700 billion program to stabilize financial markets
No Approve final $700 billion program to stabilize financial markets
No Provide $14 billion in loans to automakers

2007

No Increase minimum wage by $2.10 an hour
No Approve $124.2 billion in emergency war spending and set goal for redeployment of troops from Iraq
Yes Reject federal contraceptive assistance to international family planning groups
No Override Bush veto of $23.2 billion water projects authorization bill
Yes Implement Peru free-trade agreement
No Approve energy policy overhaul with new fuel economy standards
Yes Clear $473.5 billion omnibus spending bill, including $70 billion for military operations

CQ VOTE STUDIES

	PARTY UNITY		PRESIDENTIAL SUPPORT	
	SUPPORT	OPPOSE	SUPPORT	OPPOSE
2008	99%	1%	74%	26%
2007	99%	1%	93%	7%
2006	97%	3%	80%	20%
2005	98%	2%	87%	13%
2004	100%	0%	87%	13%

INTEREST GROUPS

	AFL-CIO	ADA	CCUS	ACU
2008	7%	5%	83%	100%
2007	4%	0%	68%	100%
2006	15%	5%	92%	92%
2005	20%	5%	89%	96%
2004	7%	0%	94%	100%

GEORGIA 9

North — Dalton, Gainesville

Anchored by North Georgia's mountains, the 9th runs across most of the state's northern border. It includes Cloudland Canyon State Park, the man-made Lake Lanier, a chunk of the Chattahoochee National Forest and several Atlanta suburbs, as well as bedroom communities outside of Chattanooga, Tenn.

The 9th's economy long depended on poultry processing and carpet manufacturing industries rooted in Gainesville and Dalton. Downturns in the housing construction industry have put a strain on Dalton, and unemployment rates are high. The southern portions of Forsyth and Hall counties host suburbs full of Republicans and housing subdivisions.

As Atlanta expanded northward, the surge of new residents in the district's south brought white-collar and service sector jobs to the 9th and began to diversify the local economy. Gainesville is home to the Northeast Georgia Medical Center, a regional health care hub. Near the state's northwestern corner, Catoosa and Walker counties grew steadily as residents who commute to Chattanooga moved into new communities. In the northeast, mountainous Fannin, Union and White counties are popular destinations for tourists and retirees.

The district has the state's smallest proportion of black residents (3 percent), although its Hispanic population expanded when jobs were available in the blue-collar manufacturing and food processing industries. As a whole, the 9th's population is overwhelmingly white and strongly Republican, at both the national and local levels.

The GOP allegiance in some north-central counties dates to the Civil War. In redistricting prior to the 2006 election, the new 9th gained a few northeastern counties and shed some eastern Atlanta suburbs. Republican John McCain received 75 percent of the 9th's vote in the 2008 presidential election, his highest percentage statewide.

MAJOR INDUSTRY
Poultry processing, carpet manufacturing, service

CITIES
Dalton, 27,912; Gainesville, 25,578

NOTABLE
Springer Mountain is the southern terminus of the 2,175-mile Appalachian National Scenic Trail.

Rep. Paul Broun (R)

Elected July 2007; 1st full term

CAPITOL OFFICE
225-4101
broun.house.gov
325 Cannon Bldg. 20515-1009; fax 226-0776

COMMITTEES
Homeland Security
Natural Resources
Science & Technology

RESIDENCE
Athens

BORN
May 14, 1946; Atlanta, Ga.

RELIGION
Baptist

FAMILY
Wife, Niki Broun; three children

EDUCATION
U. of Georgia, B.S. 1967 (chemistry); Medical
College of Georgia, M.D. 1971

MILITARY SERVICE
Marine Corps Reserve, 1964-67; Naval Reserve,
1967-72; Ga. Air National Guard, 1972-73

CAREER
Physician

POLITICAL HIGHLIGHTS
Republican nominee for U.S. House, 1990;
sought Republican nomination for U.S. House,
1992; sought Republican nomination for U.S.
Senate, 1996

ELECTION RESULTS

2008 GENERAL

Paul Broun (R)	177,265	60.7%
Bobby Saxon (D)	114,638	39.3%

2008 PRIMARY

Paul Broun (R)	44,956	71.0%
Barry Fleming (R)	18,372	29.0%

2007 SPECIAL RUNOFF

Paul Broun (R)	23,529	50.4%
Jim Whitehead (R)	23,135	49.6%

Broun is an impassioned conservative with an affinity for colorful sound bites. He has compared himself to Texas Republican Rep. Ron Paul, a fellow physician who relies on the Constitution in taking iconoclastic and occasionally eyebrow-raising stands.

Broun (BROWN) drew attention for introducing a bill in 2008 to ban sales of Playboy and Penthouse at military bases. He drew further publicity for suggesting President-elect Obama might have socialist or Marxist tendencies, then for taking part in a religious ceremony to anoint with oil the Capitol passageway that Obama walked through to take the presidential oath of office.

A writer for an alternative newspaper in Augusta compared Broun to a class clown. An Atlanta Journal-Constitution columnist wrote, "He is the point at which the lunatic fringe and Republican officeholders intersect."

But Broun and his supporters on the Republican right say the congressman is a principled alternative to Congress' Democratic majority. His party's leaders at least partly share that view — in 2009 he became the top-ranking member on the Science and Technology Committee's Investigations and Oversight panel and deputy ranking member of the Homeland Security Committee's Intelligence panel.

His loyalty to the GOP agenda has helped. In 2008, Broun was the only House Republican to back his party on every issue in which a majority of Republicans voted against a majority of Democrats. He said he employs a four-way test to judge bills, taking into account their affordability, morality and necessity in addition to constitutionality.

His legislation regarding Playboy and Penthouse was aimed at amending a provision of a 1997 law banning sales of "sexually explicit material" on military bases. A Defense Department board determined that neither publication fit that definition, though it initially put Penthouse in that category. Broun's bill attracted 27 Republican cosponsors but didn't make it out of committee.

He defended his comments on Obama, saying the media should have focused on the Illinois Democrat's call during his campaign for a strong civilian force to protect citizens domestically and on Obama's support for a redistribution of wealth. "I do not apologize for stating the obvious: His socialist views are out of the mainstream of American political thought, and history shows that 'civilian national security forces' bode ill for citizens," Broun said in a statement.

Like other conservatives, Broun was deeply skeptical of Obama's $787 billion economic stimulus package in early 2009, calling it a "steamroll of socialism" that "economically enslaves people." He was just as quotably critical of two $700 billion proposals — the second of which became law — in fall 2008 to aid the ailing financial services sector. "This is a huge cow patty with a piece of marshmallow stuck in the middle," he said. "I'm not going to eat that cow patty."

Broun confounded conventional wisdom by winning a special election in 2007 to succeed the late Republican Rep. Charlie Norwood, who died of cancer that year. Broun edged out former state Sen. Jim Whitehead, a friend of Norwood's who had been viewed as the likely successor. Trying to build a political base, Broun spent his first few months in Congress attempting to heal remaining wounds from his bruising fight with Whitehead, who had been the best-known candidate and the only officeholder in a packed 10-person field to replace Norwood.

Instead of focusing on fundraising as many freshmen do, Broun set up district offices, including one in Augusta, Norwood's hometown and a city where Whitehead enjoyed an overwhelming advantage. Broun traveled extensively throughout the nearly 6,000-square-mile district, touting his conservatism and support for George W. Bush's policies in Iraq.

Broun said he believes the Iraq War is a piece of a worldwide war against "Islamic fascists." He said, "We need to find a way to cut the head off the snake that's trying to strike us." He also takes a hard-line stance on illegal immigration and opposes proposals to give legal status and a path to citizenship to the more than 11 million illegal immigrants in the United States. Broun strongly opposes abortion and supports gun rights.

From his seat on Homeland Security, Broun hopes to pull in federal dollars for biodefense research facilities back home. Just southeast of the district is South Carolina's Savannah River Site, a nuclear facility. Another one of his committee assignments is the Natural Resources panel.

The son of a tire dealership owner and stay-at-home mother, Broun was 16 when his father was elected to the Georgia Senate, where he served for nearly four decades. The same year, a peanut farmer from Plains named Jimmy Carter was elected to the same chamber. Broun's parents and the Carters became friends, and the future president would borrow Broun's bed for the night when visiting Athens.

In high school, Broun joined the ROTC. For much of the Vietnam War, he was in the Naval Reserves or the Georgia Air National Guard, while also attending medical school. Broun did not see active duty. He remained in Athens to go to college, earning a bachelor's degree from the University of Georgia in 1967, and four years later, a medical degree from the Medical College of Georgia in Augusta. Broun eventually opened a practice in his hometown and ran it with a personal touch, routinely making house calls.

In his mid-30s, Broun became an officer of the Safari Club International, a group that protects hunting rights and promotes wildlife conservation, and did unpaid lobbying for the group in Washington. He is still an avid sportsman. His Capitol Hill office is decorated with a stuffed warthog he hunted in Botswana and an Alaskan Kodiak bear he shot while visiting the Last Frontier State.

Broun's come-from-behind special-election victory over Whitehead in 2007 completed a quest he started nearly two decades earlier. He lost three bids for Congress. His narrow victory — attributed by some to Democratic crossover support in an election where no political designations were listed on the ballot — prompted a 2008 primary challenge from state Rep. Barry Fleming. But Broun trounced Fleming and coasted to victory in November over Iraq War veteran Bobby Saxon.

KEY VOTES

2008

No Delay consideration of Colombia free-trade agreement

No Override Bush veto of federal farm and nutrition programs reauthorization bill

Yes Overhaul surveillance laws and permit dismissal of suits against companies that conducted warrantless wiretapping

No Grant mortgage relief to homeowners and funding for Fannie Mae and Freddie Mac

No Approve initial $700 billion program to stabilize financial markets

No Approve final $700 billion program to stabilize financial markets

No Provide $14 billion in loans to automakers

2007

No Override Bush veto of $23.2 billion water projects authorization bill

Yes Implement Peru free-trade agreement

No Approve energy policy overhaul with new fuel economy standards

Yes Clear $473.5 billion omnibus spending bill, including $70 billion for military operations

CQ VOTE STUDIES

	PARTY UNITY		PRESIDENTIAL SUPPORT	
	SUPPORT	OPPOSE	SUPPORT	OPPOSE
2008	100%	0%	83%	17%
2007	99%	1%	93%	7%

INTEREST GROUPS

	AFL-CIO	ADA	CCUS	ACU
2008	0%	0%	67%	100%
2007	0%	–	64%	100%

GEORGIA 10
Northeast – Athens; part of Augusta

The Republican-leaning 10th takes in the state's mountainous northeastern corner and traces its eastern border to Augusta's GOP-heavy suburbs. In the west, Athens is home to the University of Georgia.

Higher-education jobs lend stability to the district's economy, which has been rocked by unemployment. The University of Georgia provides service and health care jobs, and a planned expansion of the Medical College of Georgia is expected to bring jobs. Agriculture remains an economic mainstay for many in the 10th: dairy, cattle, corn, soybeans and some cotton are produced in the district. The 10th's northern tier is largely rural, and the tourism-based economy near the Blue Ridge Mountains and a chain of lakes along the South Carolina border has slowed.

The 10th's southeastern arm takes in Augusta's northern and western suburbs in the district's portion of Richmond County and includes all of Columbia County, home to many Augusta commuters. Fort Gordon, mostly in Richmond and home to the Army Signal Center, was spared during the 2005 BRAC Commission's closures, although the smaller Navy Supply

Corps School in Athens is set to relocate to Rhode Island by 2011. The Savannah River Site, a nuclear facility located across the river in South Carolina, is still a key employer here despite losing thousands of jobs since the mid-1990s. Augusta is also a manufacturing and retail hub.

Most of the 10th's population lives in rural areas that support the GOP and the suburbs in Columbia County are also largely Republican. Rep. Paul Broun won every county in the 10th in 2008 except for Clarke, home to the liberal college town of Athens, and Richmond, which has a large black population. John McCain won the 10th with 62 percent of the vote in 2008.

MAJOR INDUSTRY
Higher education, service, agriculture, manufacturing

MILITARY BASES
Fort Gordon (Army), 9,490 military, 2,500 civilian (2007) (shared with the 12th); Navy Supply Corps School, 416 military, 174 civilian (2007)

CITIES
Athens-Clarke, 101,489; Augusta-Richmond (pt.), 79,910; Martinez (unincorporated), 27,749

NOTABLE
The annual Masters professional golf tournament is held at Augusta National Golf Club.

Rep. Phil Gingrey (R)

Elected 2002; 4th term

CAPITOL OFFICE
225-2931
www.house.gov/gingrey
119 Cannon Bldg. 20515-1011; fax 225-2944

COMMITTEES
Energy & Commerce

RESIDENCE
Marietta

BORN
July 10, 1942; Augusta, Ga.

RELIGION
Roman Catholic

FAMILY
Wife, Billie Gingrey; four children

EDUCATION
Georgia Institute of Technology, B.S. 1965
(chemistry); Medical College of Georgia, M.D. 1969

CAREER
Physician

POLITICAL HIGHLIGHTS
Marietta Board of Education, 1993-97
(chairman, 1994-97); Ga. Senate, 1999-2003

ELECTION RESULTS

2008 GENERAL

Phil Gingrey (R)	204,082	68.2%
Hugh "Bud" Gammon (D)	95,220	31.8%

2008 PRIMARY

Phil Gingrey (R)	unopposed

2006 GENERAL

Phil Gingrey (R)	118,524	71.1%
Patrick Samuel Pillion (D)	48,261	28.9%

PREVIOUS WINNING PERCENTAGES
2004 (57%); 2002 (52%)

Gingrey is dependably conservative: He has endorsed gun owners' rights, a constitutional ban on same-sex marriage, unfettered oil drilling in the United States and fiscal restraint. A member of the Republican Study Committee, a group of the most conservative House Republicans, his voting record puts him solidly in the ranks of lawmakers most loyal to the GOP leadership.

His medical background — he was an obstetrician before he was elected to Congress — has been a prominent part of his political life. He is one of the House's staunchest opponents of abortion, including in cases of rape or incest. And he drew unfavorable media attention during the 2005 congressional intervention in the case of Terri Schiavo, a Florida woman whose family fought in court over withdrawal of life support. He argued during a debate on the floor that Schiavo could improve "with proper treatment, now denied." He drew on his background as a doctor to justify intervention.

He is an opponent of requiring young girls to be vaccinated against human papilloma virus as a condition of attending school. And he favors government help to widen the use of information technology in the medical sector.

In 2009, Gingrey was granted a coveted seat on the powerful Energy and Commerce Committee and its Health Subcommittee, where he could have more influence on health care reform legislation. In early 2009, he was tapped to join 15 other House Republicans to craft a GOP health care overhaul proposal. In a letter in the Rome News-Tribune, he said he favors a market-driven approach to reducing health care costs, including an integrated online medical record system, tort reform and an expanded use of health savings accounts.

His desire to limit medical malpractice suits was one of his reasons for running for Congress. He said they drive up insurance premiums for doctors and have forced some to abandon their practices. The House in 2005 approved his legislation to cap punitive damage awards at $250,000, but the bill, like similar measures before it, died in the Senate.

In early 2009, he opposed a bill to expand the State Children's Health Insurance Program, which covers children whose families do not qualify for Medicaid. He and other Republicans worried the bill didn't focus on a limited group of low-income people. He said people carrying private health insurance "will drop it so they can get on the government dole," according to the International Herald Tribune.

Gingrey also is a member of the committee's trade panel. He has opposed several international free-trade agreements out of concern they would adversely affect the textile industry, an employer in his district. He did back President George W. Bush's Central America Free Trade Agreement in 2005, but the following year he voted against bills granting permanent normal trade relations to Vietnam, implementing a free-trade deal with Oman and giving trade breaks to Haiti.

Gingrey is generally a fiscal conservative — except when it comes to helping his district. In fall 2008, he joined many conservatives in voting against a $700 billion package — which became law — that infused funds into the financial services industry. Likewise, he opposed President Obama's economic stimulus package in early 2009. "This top-down approach...at printing money" to pay for increased government spending "is not going to work," he said. Gingrey backed a Republican alternative that included, among other things, more tax cuts, a repeal of the alternative minimum tax, a cut in the top corporate tax rate and spending cuts.

Subsequently, he opposed a $410 billion catchall spending bill for 2009, saying, "The road to a decreased deficit must start today." Yet Taxpayers for Common Sense noted he obtained more earmarks — funding set-asides for special projects — for Georgia in the bill than any other House member; he netted $36.3 million, mostly for water and infrastructure projects.

During the 110th Congress (2007-08), Gingrey used his seat on the Armed Services Committee to support the F-22 Raptor fighter, which is largely made at a Lockheed Martin plant in Marietta, in his district. He pressed the Obama administration in early 2009 to continue funding to keep the F-22 production lines humming.

In early 2009, Gingrey was the subject of numerous blogs and opinion pieces after he criticized conservative radio commentator Rush Limbaugh. He rebuked Limbaugh for saying he wanted Obama to fail, then subsequently apologized to the radio host for his comments.

Gingrey's mother was the daughter of Irish immigrants who grew up in Queens. His father, who grew up in South Carolina, owned a series of small businesses, including a drive-through restaurant, a liquor store and a motel in Augusta, Ga., none of which did particularly well. Gingrey worked his way through the Georgia Institute of Technology with a factory job. He intended to become an engineer, but after visiting an operating room with a family friend who was a neurosurgeon, he decided to go to medical school. Gingrey served about four years as Marietta school board chairman when his children were in school, then went on to two terms in the Georgia Senate while continuing with his medical practice. He became well-known for advocating tighter teen driving laws.

In 2001, he toyed with running against Democratic incumbent Sen. Max Cleland. But after redistricting gave Georgia two new House seats, he decided to run for that chamber. The 11th District was given a heavy Democratic tilt, so Republican Rep. Bob Barr, who represented a portion of it, chose to run in the 7th District primary against fellow Republican John Linder. With Barr out of the way, Gingrey jumped in and won the primary in the 11th. In November, he took 52 percent of the vote against Roger Kahn, a wealthy wholesale liquor distributor who lent his own campaign $2.5 million. Gingrey appealed to right-leaning and religious conservatives, and got help from the American Medical Association, which paid for polling and radio ads.

Mid-decade redistricting in 2005 was favorable to the GOP, and Gingrey won with 71 percent of the vote in 2006 and 68 percent in 2008.

He has faced some medical concerns of his own; in December 2002, he had double coronary bypass surgery.

KEY VOTES

2008

No Delay consideration of Colombia free-trade agreement
Yes Override Bush veto of federal farm and nutrition programs reauthorization bill
Yes Overhaul surveillance laws and permit dismissal of suits against companies that conducted warrantless wiretapping
No Grant mortgage relief to homeowners and funding for Fannie Mae and Freddie Mac
No Approve initial $700 billion program to stabilize financial markets
No Approve final $700 billion program to stabilize financial markets
No Provide $14 billion in loans to automakers

2007

No Increase minimum wage by $2.10 an hour
No Approve $124.2 billion in emergency war spending and set goal for redeployment of troops from Iraq
Yes Reject federal contraceptive assistance to international family planning groups
No Override Bush veto of $23.2 billion water projects authorization bill
Yes Implement Peru free-trade agreement
No Approve energy policy overhaul with new fuel economy standards
Yes Clear $473.5 billion omnibus spending bill, including $70 billion for military operations

CQ VOTE STUDIES

	PARTY UNITY		PRESIDENTIAL SUPPORT	
	SUPPORT	OPPOSE	SUPPORT	OPPOSE
2008	99%	1%	72%	28%
2007	98%	2%	92%	8%
2006	96%	4%	87%	13%
2005	97%	3%	87%	13%
2004	98%	2%	85%	15%

INTEREST GROUPS

	AFL-CIO	ADA	CCUS	ACU
2008	7%	10%	78%	96%
2007	4%	0%	75%	100%
2006	14%	5%	87%	92%
2005	13%	0%	89%	100%
2004	7%	5%	100%	96%

GEORGIA 11

Northwest — Rome, most of Marietta

Nestled against the Alabama border in northwest Georgia, the 11th runs south from Chattooga County into Carroll County and east into the western Atlanta suburbs in Cobb County. The conservative district takes in all of six counties and parts of three others, spanning rural areas in the west, small cities such as Rome and suburbs such as Marietta.

The 11th's chunk of Cobb hosts white-collar, middle-income suburbs and most of the city of Marietta (shared with the 13th and 6th districts), where the economy relies on aerospace and military jobs. Unemployment across non-defense-related jobs has hurt Cobb's economy. The local Lockheed Martin plant, next to a naval air station, builds cargo and fighter planes, although the air station is closing under 2005 BRAC Commission recommendations and continued funding for aerospace manufacturing at the plant is uncertain. Paulding County is filling up with residents who commute to Atlanta.

To the west, the string of rural counties along the Alabama border still depend on hay, cotton, corn and soybean farming. Haralson County

hosts Honda facilities, and Rome, in Floyd County, is home to three colleges, several medical centers and manufacturing plants — Pirelli Tires has expanded its large Rome factory. Textiles and carpet manufacturing remain important in the 11th's northern counties despite recent layoffs.

Safe territory for the GOP in federal and state elections, the district leans strongly Republican, although some conservative Southern Democrats in rural counties still vote for Democrats locally. The 11th's portion of Cobb, which accounts for roughly one-third of the district's population, remains a GOP stronghold, as does adjacent Paulding. Republican John McCain took 66 percent of the district's 2008 presidential vote, his second-highest percentage statewide.

MAJOR INDUSTRY
Defense, manufacturing, textiles, agriculture

MILITARY BASES
Naval Air Station Atlanta, 424 military, 444 civilian (2007)

CITIES
Marietta (pt.), 47,721; Rome, 34,980; Kennesaw, 21,675

NOTABLE
Like its Italian namesake, Rome is built on seven hills; A Kennesaw law requires each household to own a gun and the appropriate ammunition.

Rep. John Barrow (D)

Elected 2004; 3rd term

CAPITOL OFFICE
225-2823
barrow.house.gov
213 Cannon Bldg. 20515-1012; fax 225-3377

COMMITTEES
Energy & Commerce

RESIDENCE
Savannah

BORN
Oct. 31, 1955; Athens, Ga.

RELIGION
Baptist

FAMILY
Divorced; two children

EDUCATION
U. of Georgia, B.A. 1976 (history & political
science); Harvard U., J.D. 1979

CAREER
Lawyer

POLITICAL HIGHLIGHTS
Sought Democratic nomination for Ga. House
(special election), 1986; Athens-Clarke County
Commission, 1991-2005

ELECTION RESULTS

2008 GENERAL

John Barrow (D)	164,562	66.0%
John Stone (R)	84,773	34.0%

2008 PRIMARY

John Barrow (D)	45,235	76.4%
Regina D. Thomas (D)	13,955	23.6%

2006 GENERAL

John Barrow (D)	71,651	50.3%
Max Burns (R)	70,787	49.7%

PREVIOUS WINNING PERCENTAGES
2004 (52%)

Barrow is a fiscal conservative who breaks with the Democratic Party on votes more often than all but a handful of his colleagues. Party leaders happily accept and even reward his independence, knowing full well they are lucky just to have him in the House.

Barrow (BEAR-oh — rhymes with "arrow") won his first two elections by narrow margins — the second by a scant six-tenths of a point. He then cruised to victory in 2008 by 32 points, thanks to a plum seat on the powerful Energy and Commerce panel and special help from the party in his campaign. But he said he's not relaxing — "I don't think there's any such thing as a safe seat."

He credited his big win to his growing familiarity in his district; during 2007 and 2008, he said, he conducted 150 "town hall" meetings with his constituents.

He is a member of both the fiscally conservative Blue Dog Coalition and the New Democrat faction of the House Democratic Caucus. His positions on such matters as the budget, energy, immigration and many social issues are typically more in line with his district's views than with party leaders.

He voted against the Democrats' 2008 budget and against a $700 billion rescue of the financial services industry in fall 2008, but voted for a $14 billion bailout of the auto industry in December of that year. He said the banking bill was "essentially . . . a blank check to fund a program to be named later," while the auto bailout — which failed to move in the Senate — included specific plans for the industry and better oversight. Yet he was one of 17 Democrats to vote against a final $3.56 trillion budget blueprint for fiscal 2010.

But as concerns about the economy grew in early 2009, Barrow stuck with his party to support President Obama's $787 billion economic stimulus package, signed into law. "This job creation package will rebuild America, making us more globally competitive and energy independent, and transforming our economy for long-term growth," he said. He also lauded the law's provisions calling for greater transparency in how funds are spent. Subsequently, he supported a $410 billion catchall spending bill for 2009 and helped obtain nearly $4.3 million in earmarks — funding set-asides for special projects in his state.

From his seat on the Energy and Commerce Subcommittee on Energy and Environment, Barrow supports offshore drilling as one solution to the energy crisis. But when his party responded to GOP pressure in September 2008 to pass a bill to expand offshore drilling, he voted against it. "It didn't go far enough when it comes to responsible drilling for more of our own oil," he said. Shortly after House passage of the bill, a moratorium on offshore drilling was allowed to lapse. He is a co-leader of the Blue Dogs energy task force.

Barrow is tougher on the issue of immigration than many of his Democratic colleagues. In the 109th Congress, he joined Republicans in voting to authorize a 700-mile fence along the border with Mexico and to make it a felony to be in the United States without legal papers. He was one of 18 Democrats who voted to authorize the George W. Bush administration's warrantless electronic surveillance program and one of just four who supported an end to bilingual voting assistance.

Barrow also is a supporter of gun owners' rights, and voted in 2008 for a bill to end a ban on possession of firearms in the District of Columbia.

The son of two Army captains, Barrow is a big booster of the military and a strong supporter of the war in Iraq. He opposed a war spending bill that would have required the Pentagon to set deadlines for the withdrawal of troops from Iraq. He was one of just two Democrats voting early in 2007 to shift more than $500 million in a catchall spending bill from various domestic projects to military housing, anti-drug efforts and deficit reduction.

But as a member of the Commerce, Trade and Consumer Protection Sub-committee, Barrow is a supporter of labor. In early 2009, he supported two bills to combat wage discrimination. In 2007, he backed an increase in the minimum wage and legislation to make it easier for workers to organize a union at their workplace. He voted for the Peru free-trade deal, he said, because unions and business helped craft it and it included assurances for compliance with labor and environmental standards.

Barrow also is a member of the Health Subcommittee. He supported a bill that Obama signed into law to expand the State Children's Health Insurance Program, which covers children whose families do not qualify for Medicaid. He had supported similar bills during the 110th Congress (2007-08). He supports embryonic stem cell research.

Early in 2008, Barrow's district was hit by tragedy when an Imperial Sugar Co. refinery exploded and burned, killing 12 people. He and Democrat George Miller of California pushed a bill to require greater regulation of combustible dust in factories. Investigators concluded the blast at the Imperial plant was linked to sugar dust that had been allowed to accumulate. His bill passed the House but stalled in the Senate, and Barrow renewed the effort in 2009.

He has a strong interest in veterans' issues. The 12th is home to three large military installations. He has long sought to increase the amount veterans are reimbursed for their travel to Veterans Affairs hospitals for medical care.

Barrow is a native of Athens. His parents were civil rights advocates, serving in the 1960s as co-chairs of the local chapter of HOPE, which stood for Help Our Public Education, which fought for integration. After Harvard, Barrow returned to Athens to work as a trial lawyer. In 1986, he made a failed bid for the state House, losing by 30 votes in a special runoff. In 1990, he won a seat on the Athens-Clarke County Commission, where he served for 14 years.

In his first U.S. House race in 2004, he took 51 percent of the vote in a four-way primary and went on to oust GOP Rep. Max Burns by 7,904 votes — a 4-percentage-point margin — in a district that had been drawn to favor Democrats. But a 2005 redistricting by a GOP state legislature stripped away much of Barrow's Democratic base.

Burns set out to retake the seat, but Barrow moved to Savannah, at the heart of his new district, raised $2.5 million and built a centrist voting record that helped him withstand the challenge. He won by just 864 votes. In 2008, Barrow faced John Stone, a former aide to Burns and former Georgia Republican Rep. Charlie Norwood. Stone was unable to raise much money and was trounced at the polls.

KEY VOTES

2008

Yes Delay consideration of Colombia free-trade agreement

Yes Override Bush veto of federal farm and nutrition programs reauthorization bill

Yes Overhaul surveillance laws and permit dismissal of suits against companies that conducted warrantless wiretapping

Yes Grant mortgage relief to homeowners and funding for Fannie Mae and Freddie Mac

No Approve initial $700 billion program to stabilize financial markets

No Approve final $700 billion program to stabilize financial markets

Yes Provide $14 billion in loans to automakers

2007

Yes Increase minimum wage by $2.10 an hour

No Approve $124.2 billion in emergency war spending and set goal for redeployment of troops from Iraq

No Reject federal contraceptive assistance to international family planning groups

Yes Override Bush veto of $23.2 billion water projects authorization bill

Yes Implement Peru free-trade agreement

Yes Approve energy policy overhaul with new fuel economy standards

Yes Clear $473.5 billion omnibus spending bill, including $70 billion for military operations

CQ VOTE STUDIES

	PARTY UNITY		PRESIDENTIAL SUPPORT	
	SUPPORT	OPPOSE	SUPPORT	OPPOSE
2008	83%	17%	27%	73%
2007	70%	30%	24%	76%
2006	65%	35%	65%	35%
2005	78%	22%	47%	53%

INTEREST GROUPS

	AFL-CIO	ADA	CCUS	ACU
2008	87%	75%	67%	24%
2007	88%	70%	80%	24%
2006	64%	45%	87%	76%
2005	87%	75%	56%	40%

GEORGIA 12

East — most of Savannah and Augusta

The 12th reaches from Augusta to Savannah along the South Carolina border, taking in a string of sparsely populated counties on its western edge that were added during redistricting prior to the 2006 election. The politically competitive district includes urban Democratic strongholds, socially conservative rural counties and GOP-friendly suburbs.

Savannah's port, which continues to grow, fuels the 12th's economy, and Fort Stewart (shared with the 1st) and Hunter Army Airfield together employ tens of thousands of people. Savannah's downtown still has a solid tourism industry. Many in Richmond County (Augusta) work at Fort Gordon (shared with the 10th) or at the Energy Department's Savannah River Site, across the river in South Carolina. The local defense and aerospace manufacturing sector was dealt a blow with extensive layoffs at General Dynamics' Gulfstream facility.

Textile factories in the center of the district have shut down, and the rest of the 12th relies mainly on farming. Toombs County's Vidalia grows its famous sweet onion, and Bulloch and Emanuel counties produce timber.

Effingham County, north of Savannah, now hosts many white residents who have left urban areas of Chatham County (Savannah). GOP strength is rooted in Effingham and the southern counties of Toombs, Tattnall and Bulloch. The 12th's portions of Chatham and Richmond are reliably Democratic, as are Hancock and Washington counties. Hancock County, in the district's northwest, is one of Georgia's most heavily black counties and one of its poorest. Democratic John Barrow easily held the U.S. House seat in 2008, and Democrat Barack Obama took 54 percent of the district's presidential vote.

MAJOR INDUSTRY
Agriculture, manufacturing, timber

MILITARY BASES
Fort Stewart (Army), 22,393 military, 2,536 civilian (2007) (shared with the 1st); Fort Gordon (Army), 9,490 military, 2,500 civilian (2007) (shared with the 10th); Hunter Army Airfield, 7,000 military, 750 civilian (2008)

CITIES
Augusta-Richmond (pt.), 119,865; Savannah (pt.), 110,616; Statesboro, 22,698

NOTABLE
Vidalia onions were named the official state vegetable in 1990.

Rep. David Scott (D)

Elected 2002; 4th term

CAPITOL OFFICE
225-2939
davidscott.house.gov
225 Cannon Bldg. 20515-1013; fax 225-4628

COMMITTEES
Agriculture
 (Livestock, Dairy & Poultry - chairman)
Financial Services
Foreign Affairs

RESIDENCE
Atlanta

BORN
June 27, 1946; Aynor, S.C.

RELIGION
Baptist

FAMILY
Wife, Alfredia Scott; two children

EDUCATION
Florida A&M U., B.A. 1967 (English & speech);
U. of Pennsylvania, M.B.A. 1969

CAREER
Advertising agency owner; recruiting firm
executive; defense contracting company manager

POLITICAL HIGHLIGHTS
Ga. House, 1975-83; Ga. Senate, 1983-2003

ELECTION RESULTS

2008 GENERAL

David Scott (D)	205,919	69.0%
Deborah Honeycutt (R)	92,320	31.0%

2008 PRIMARY

David Scott (D)	30,719	63.7%
Donzella James (D)	17,526	36.3%

2006 GENERAL

David Scott (D)	103,019	69.2%
Deborah Honeycutt (R)	45,770	30.8%

PREVIOUS WINNING PERCENTAGES
2004 (100%); 2002 (60%)

House Democratic leaders' success, or lack thereof, depends greatly on persuading representatives like Scott, one of only two African-American members of the Blue Dog Coalition of roughly 50 fiscally conservative House Democrats. So far they're succeeding: Once a rebel who often parted ways with his party, Scott has become a much more reliable vote since becoming a member of the majority in 2007.

On votes that split the majority of Republicans and Democrats, Scott sided with his party 98 percent of the time in 2008, up more than 20 percentage points from his first year in the chamber, 2003, when the GOP reigned. During the 110th Congress (2007-08), he strayed on only three such votes. He voted with Republicans to grant immunity to telecommunications companies that assisted in the warrantless surveillance of terrorism suspects. He also voted in 2007 for a catchall spending bill that most House Democrats opposed because it included more war funding than they desired.

In the fall of 2008, he initially voted against President George W. Bush's $700 billion plan to help the ailing financial services industry. Scott called the bank rescue "totally unacceptable," but soon had a change of heart and helped secure the bill's passage when it came up a second time. He said the revised measure strengthened assistance to homeowners.

A member of the Financial Services Committee, Scott's support is crucial to President Obama's efforts to revive the flagging economy, and since his early defection on the bank bill, he's proved reliable. Scott in December 2008 supported an Obama-backed bill, which ultimately failed to move in the Senate, to provide loans to ailing automobile companies. And he stuck with his party to support Obama's economic stimulus bill that became law in February 2009.

But given Scott's past voting pattern, Democrats might have to work hard to maintain his loyalty. He was one of only seven Democrats to vote for Bush's 2003 tax cuts and, later that year, one of only 16 to back a Medicare prescription drug benefit that Bush supported but most Democrats felt wasn't generous enough. Later, he supported a GOP bill making it more difficult for individuals to declare bankruptcy and another providing for permanent repeal of the estate tax. He has supported a flat tax, long a dream of fiscal conservatives.

Scott's district nowadays is split along racial lines, with whites still holding a plurality. A component of Scott's appeal to white voters is his support for the military, which has a major presence in Georgia. He is a co-founder of the Democrats' national security study group, and he says Democrats can once again be the party associated with a strong military by returning to the hawkish defense postures of presidents Franklin D. Roosevelt and John F. Kennedy.

Scott opposed the Iraq War from the beginning and has since used his seat on the Foreign Affairs Committee to push for an end to the U.S. occupation.

That's not to say he ignores the concerns of black constituents. A member of the Agriculture Committee, Scott has long supported the efforts of black farmers to win compensation from the Agriculture Department for past discrimination. And during the debate over the 2008 reauthorization of agriculture and nutrition programs, Scott fought for increased food stamp benefits and funding for school lunch programs. He chairs the committee's Livestock, Dairy and Poultry Subcommittee.

The circumstances of Scott's first election permit him some independence from his party. Establishment Democrats in this suburban Atlanta district backed a rival in the 2002 primary when Scott, after more than 25 years in the Georgia General Assembly, decided to run for the new 13th District seat. Scott won the nomination over state Sen. Greg Hecht with strong support from affluent suburbanites, business leaders, doctors and big health care companies, and easily defeated businessman Clay Cox in the general election. His campaign featured ads by his wife's brother, baseball great Hank Aaron.

Over the years, Scott was closely associated with Atlanta's black and liberal leaders — former mayors Andrew Young and Maynard Jackson as well as Jimmy Carter, the governor who became president — but he calculated correctly that only a centrist could win the district.

Scott's background is a lesson in adaptation. Born in Aynor, S.C., an impoverished country town, he attended elementary school in Pennsylvania. When he was in sixth grade, his family moved to Scarsdale, N.Y., where his parents worked for a wealthy family as a chauffeur and a maid. An only child, Scott was also the only black student in his school. His classmates had money, while he lived in an apartment over the garage on the estate owned by his parents' employer. Civil rights protests raged across the country, and though Scott says he encountered little overt bigotry among Scarsdale's upper crust, his racial isolation was stressful. "I learned at a very young age how to have confidence in myself and how to get along with people who don't look like me," he said.

Scott finished high school in Daytona Beach, Fla., then attended Florida A&M University. During an internship in Washington with the Labor Department, Scott met George W. Taylor, a noted labor-management expert. Taylor suggested Scott apply to the University of Pennsylvania's Wharton School of Finance, where Taylor was on the faculty.

With a Wharton MBA in hand, in the early 1970s Scott was attracted to Atlanta and its emerging crop of black leaders. He was a volunteer with Young's campaign for the House in 1972. Two years later, Scott won his first election to the Georgia House, launching a 28-year career in the legislature. He chaired the state Senate Rules Committee.

A religious man who sees the hand of divine intervention in his career successes, Scott authored the Georgia law requiring a moment of silence at the beginning of the public school day. He has pushed a national version of the bill. He said the moment of silence has the effect of calming children and giving them "inner strength." He quotes liberally from both the Bible and Shakespeare.

In recent years, he has come under fire from ethics groups for, among other transgressions, failing to pay his taxes on time and putting family members on his campaign payroll. In June 2008, the Atlanta Journal-Constitution reported he had paid off all his personal local and state tax liens. The voters of the 13th District have continued to give him overwhelming majorities.

KEY VOTES

2008

Yes   Delay consideration of Colombia free-trade agreement

Yes   Override Bush veto of federal farm and nutrition programs reauthorization bill

Yes   Overhaul surveillance laws and permit dismissal of suits against companies that conducted warrantless wiretapping

Yes   Grant mortgage relief to homeowners and funding for Fannie Mae and Freddie Mac

No   Approve initial $700 billion program to stabilize financial markets

Yes   Approve final $700 billion program to stabilize financial markets

Yes   Provide $14 billion in loans to automakers

2007

Yes   Increase minimum wage by $2.10 an hour

Yes   Approve $124.2 billion in emergency war spending and set goal for redeployment of troops from Iraq

No   Reject federal contraceptive assistance to international family planning groups

Yes   Override Bush veto of $23.2 billion water projects authorization bill

No   Implement Peru free-trade agreement

Yes   Approve energy policy overhaul with new fuel economy standards

Yes   Clear $473.5 billion omnibus spending bill, including $70 billion for military operations

CQ VOTE STUDIES

	PARTY UNITY		PRESIDENTIAL SUPPORT	
	SUPPORT	OPPOSE	SUPPORT	OPPOSE
2008	98%	2%	18%	82%
2007	96%	4%	12%	88%
2006	85%	15%	45%	55%
2005	79%	21%	43%	57%
2004	79%	21%	47%	53%

INTEREST GROUPS

	AFL-CIO	ADA	CCUS	ACU
2008	100%	95%	67%	4%
2007	96%	90%	65%	4%
2006	86%	85%	60%	32%
2005	100%	80%	74%	38%
2004	86%	75%	78%	30%

GEORGIA 13

Atlanta suburbs — parts of Clayton, Cobb and Douglas counties

The 13th forms a crescent that cradles the southwest corner of Atlanta and takes in parts of six counties, including sizable chunks of Cobb and Douglas to the west and most of densely populated Clayton in the east.

The 13th includes a mix of middle-income urban, suburban and rural areas. A significant number of residents commute to Atlanta, where many district residents depend on jobs with major corporations. Regional health care providers are large employers in the 13th, as are universities nearby in the 5th (in Fulton County). The 13th experienced rapid growth over the past two decades, especially in southern Fulton and eastern Douglas counties, where working class families and retirees poured into once less-populated areas. Residents and local officials are concerned about high unemployment rates and a stalled local economy.

Cobb County accounts for about one-third of the district's population and has a growing black population. Some residents in southern Cobb work

in defense-related industries near Marietta. A national housing construction downturn forced layoffs at Home Depot, which has headquarters in the 13th and is a key employer here. South of Atlanta, Clayton County, which also has one-third of the population, has suffered from job losses and difficulties in the local education sector. Many commuters from Clayton still rely on transportation and warehousing jobs around the busy Hartsfield-Jackson Atlanta International Airport (in the 5th).

Minorities make up more than half of the 13th's population, although whites form a plurality, and the district is solidly Democratic. Republicans have some success in eastern Douglas, but Democrat Barack Obama easily won here with 72 percent of the district's 2008 presidential vote.

MAJOR INDUSTRY
Distribution, aerospace, health care, service

MILITARY BASES
Fort Gillem (Army), 408 military, 463 civilian (2007)

CITIES
Smyrna (pt.), 38,195; Mableton (unincorporated), 29,733

NOTABLE
Jonesboro was the setting for Tara, the plantation in Margaret Mitchell's novel "Gone With the Wind."

Gov. Linda Lingle (R)

First elected: 2002
Length of term: 4 years
Term expires: 12/10
Salary: $130,000
Phone: (808) 586-0034

Residence: Honolulu
Born: June 4, 1953; St. Louis, Mo.
Religion: Jewish
Family: Divorced
Education: California State U., Northridge, B.A. 1975 (journalism)
Career: Newspaper owner; journalist
Political highlights: Maui County Council, 1981-91; mayor of Maui, 1991-98; Republican nominee for governor, 1998; Hawaii Republican Party chairwoman, 1999-2002

Election results:

2006 GENERAL

Linda Lingle (R)	215,313	62.5%
Randy Iwase (D)	121,717	35.4%
Jim Brewer (GREEN)	5,435	1.6%

Lt. Gov. James "Duke" Aiona (R)

First elected: 2002
Length of term: 4 years
Term expires: 12/10
Salary: $120,444
Phone: (808) 586-0255

LEGISLATURE

Legislature: 60 days January-April

Senate: 25 members, 4-year terms
2009 ratios: 23 D, 2 R; 19 men, 6 women
Salary: $48,708
Phone: (808) 586-6720

House: 51 members, 2-year terms
2009 ratios: 45 D, 6 R; 33 men, 18 women
Salary: $48,708
Phone: (808) 586-6400

TERM LIMITS

Governor: 2 consecutive terms
Senate: No
House: No

URBAN STATISTICS

CITY	POPULATION
Honolulu	371,657
Hilo	40,759
Kailua	36,513
Kaneohe	34,970
Waipahu	33,108

REGISTERED VOTERS

Voters do not register by party.

POPULATION

2008 population (est.)	1,288,198
2000 population	1,211,537
1990 population	1,108,229
Percent change (1990-2000)	+9.3%
Rank among states (2008)	42

Median age	36.2
Born in state	56.9%
Foreign born	17.5%
Violent crime rate	244/100,000
Poverty level	10.7%
Federal workers	29,276
Military	53,632

ELECTIONS

STATE ELECTION OFFICIAL
(808) 453-8683
DEMOCRATIC PARTY
(808) 596-2980
REPUBLICAN PARTY
(808) 593-8180

MISCELLANEOUS

Web: www.hawaii.gov
Capital: Honolulu

U.S. CONGRESS

Senate: 2 Democrats
House: 2 Democrats

2000 Census Statistics by District

DIST.	2008 VOTE FOR PRESIDENT OBAMA	MCCAIN	WHITE	BLACK	ASIAN	HISP	MEDIAN INCOME	WHITE COLLAR	BLUE COLLAR	SERVICE INDUSTRY	OVER 64	UNDER 18	COLLEGE EDUCATION	RURAL	SQ. MILES
1	70%	28%	18%	2%	54%	5%	$50,798	64%	16%	20%	15%	22%	29%	1%	191
2	73	25	28	2	28	9	$48,686	57	21	22	11	27	23	16	6,232
STATE	72	27	23	2	41	7	$49,820	60	19	21	13	24	26	9	6,423
U.S.	53	46	69	12	4	13	$41,994	60	25	15	12	26	24	21	3,537,438

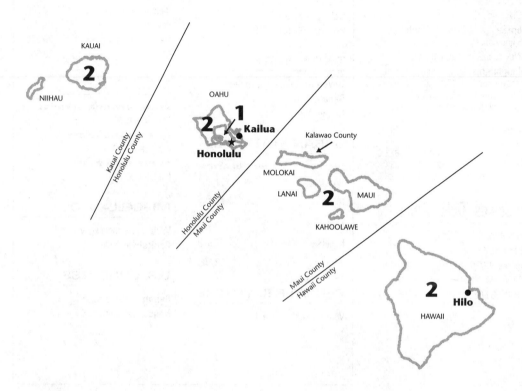

KAUAI

2

NIIHAU

Kauai County
Honolulu County

OAHU

2 **1**

Kailua

Honolulu

Kalawao County

MOLOKAI

LANAI

2

MAUI

KAHOOLAWE

Honolulu County
Maui County

Maui County
Hawaii County

2

Hilo

HAWAII

Sen. Daniel K. Inouye (D)

Elected 1962; 8th term

CAPITOL OFFICE
224-3934
inouye.senate.gov
722 Hart Bldg. 20510-1102; fax 224-6747

COMMITTEES
Appropriations - chairman
(Defense - chairman)
Commerce, Science & Transportation
Indian Affairs
Rules & Administration

RESIDENCE
Honolulu

BORN
Sept. 7, 1924; Honolulu, Hawaii

RELIGION
Methodist

FAMILY
Wife, Irene Hirano; one child

EDUCATION
U. of Hawaii, A.B. 1950 (government & economics);
George Washington U., J.D. 1952

MILITARY SERVICE
Army, 1943-47

CAREER
Lawyer; city prosecutor

POLITICAL HIGHLIGHTS
Hawaii Territorial House, 1954-58 (majority leader);
Hawaii Territorial Senate, 1958-59; U.S. House,
1959-63

ELECTION RESULTS

2004 GENERAL
Daniel K. Inouye (D)	313,629	75.5%
Cam Cavasso (R)	87,172	21.0%
Jim Brewer (NON)	9,269	2.2%
Lloyd J. "Jeff" Mallan (LIBERT)	5,277	1.3%

2004 PRIMARY
Daniel K. Inouye (D)	157,367	93.8%
Brian Evans (D)	8,051	4.8%
Eddie Yoon (D)	2,437	1.4%

PREVIOUS WINNING PERCENTAGES
1998 (79%); 1992 (57%); 1986 (74%); 1980 (78%);
1974 (83%); 1968 (83%); 1962 (69%); 1960 House
Election (74%); 1959 Special House Election (68%)

As chairman of the Appropriations Committee, Inouye commands a vital power center during one of the nation's most fiscally challenging periods. But the heightened public attention that comes with the gavel is somewhat uncomfortable for an intensely private man who prefers working behind the scenes.

Inouye's courteous, taciturn style also is a stark contrast to that of his brusque House counterpart, David R. Obey of Wisconsin. But he can be every bit as protective of his panel's prerogatives as Obey is. At the same time, he seeks to accommodate members' needs while ensuring his home state is well taken care of in annual spending bills.

Inouye (in-NO-ay) was elevated to the chairmanship after West Virginia Democrat Robert C. Byrd stepped down in November 2008 after a series of hospitalizations led senators in his party to question whether Byrd was up to maintaining the panel. Inouye also continues to lead the Defense Appropriations Subcommittee, a post from which he has guided the huge annual defense spending bill to passage, keeping it out of the stopgap measures and catchall funding bills that characterized the appropriations process in the 110th Congress (2007-08).

Driven by his notion of honor, Inouye is a throwback to an earlier political era, when collegiality was valued over partisan bombast and reverence for the Senate as an institution was the norm. He proudly notes that the décor in his ceremonial office gives no indication of which party he belongs to.

He does not give his word lightly, and once he does, he keeps it. Inouye declined to cast a tie-breaking vote for a Democratic amendment to President George W. Bush's 2001 tax bill in order to keep his promise to "pair" his votes that day with his best friend, former Sen. Ted Stevens, a Republican who would have voted the other way but was home in Alaska speaking at his granddaughter's high school graduation.

Inouye displayed his ironclad loyalty when Stevens was indicted in 2008 by a federal grand jury in Washington on seven felony counts of making false statements on his financial disclosure forms. Inouye, a character witness during the trial, told jurors that Stevens was an honorable man whom he could trust with his life. After Stevens was found guilty, Inouye stood by his friend. The Justice Department dropped the case in April 2009 after the judge criticized the trial prosecutors for failing to turn over documents to Stevens' defense lawyers.

In 1982, Inouye was the chief advocate on the Senate floor for New Jersey Democratic Sen. Harrison A. Williams, who was convicted of several felonies in connection with the FBI's so-called Abscam probe. Williams resigned before the Senate could complete the expulsion process.

In taking over the Appropriations panel, Inouye relinquished his chairmanship of the Commerce, Science and Transportation Committee, where Stevens served as ranking member. Referring to each other affectionately as "brother" and "co-chairman," they ran the panel in such unison that when they switched positions after Democrats took control of Congress at the beginning of the 110th, it was as if there had been no change at all.

On Appropriations, Inouye has secured billions of dollars for his state. His penchant for earmarks — funding set-asides for special projects — has drawn criticism from budget watchdog groups, but he defends his efforts. In fiscal 2008 spending bills, Inouye secured about $412 million in earmarks ranking him sixth among senators, according to Taxpayers for Common Sense. Indeed, when House Democratic leaders and Obama promised further restrictions on earmarks in early 2009, Inouye issued a statement noteworthy for its non-commital tone.

Inouye is a living link between Hawaii's past as a U.S. territory and its future as the nation's vibrant, multicultural bridge to the Pacific Rim. A member of the Indian Affairs Committee, he continues to push legislation that would grant sovereign status to Native Hawaiians, like that enjoyed by Alaska Natives and American Indians.

He has represented Hawaii in Congress since the archipelago joined the union in 1959 and is the fourth-longest-serving senator in history. Among current senators, only Byrd and Edward M. Kennedy of Massachusetts have been in the Senate longer.

In February 2008, Inouye became only the fourth senator in history to cast 15,000 roll call votes. After Senate leaders celebrated his milestone with lengthy and heartfelt floor speeches, Inouye — who has never called a news conference in a half-century in Washington — used just three sentences to express his thanks.

On the rare occasions when Inouye speaks out publicly, his words command attention. During the 2002 debate on whether to grant Bush authority to attack Iraq, Inouye made headlines when he took exception to a Bush comment that Democrats were not sufficiently concerned about national security. Inouye, who lost an arm while fighting Nazi Germany in World War II and who was awarded the Congressional Medal of Honor in 2000 for bravery, rose on the Senate floor to protest. "It grieves me when my president makes statements that would divide this nation," he said. "This is not a time for Democrats and Republicans to say, 'We got more medals than you, we've lost more limbs than you, we've shed more blood than you.'"

Inouye's colleagues rely on him to handle delicate tasks that require the appearance of impartiality and unquestioned probity. His 1987 appointment to chair the Senate committee investigating the Iran-Contra affair stemmed not only from his evenhanded manner but also from the esteem he won during the 1973 Watergate hearings that led to the resignation of President Nixon.

The first Japanese-American elected to Congress, Inouye is revered by Hawaii's large Japanese-American community. In 1943, as an 18-year-old pre-med student, he enlisted in the famed all-Nisei "Go for Broke" 442nd Regimental Combat Team and fought across Italy and France. When he advanced alone to take out a machine gun that had pinned down his men, he lost his right arm and spent 20 months in military hospitals.

At the Percy Jones Hospital in Michigan, he met another recuperating soldier — Bob Dole of Kansas, who later became Senate majority leader. Dole told Inouye he planned to be in Congress someday. Prevented by his injury from becoming a surgeon, Inouye decided he too would try politics.

He won his first election in 1954, to Hawaii's territorial House. He helped guide Hawaii to statehood in 1959 and was elected that year as its first U.S. House member. As a freshman, he wrote a note to Dole, playfully teasing him for not making it to Congress first.

Elected to the Senate in 1962, Inouye has been seriously threatened only once. In 1992, state Sen. Rick Reed, his GOP opponent, ran a radio ad featuring claims by Inouye's barber that Inouye had made unwanted sexual advances. Inouye called the accusation "unmitigated lies," and the Ethics Committee dropped a review of the charges. But the bad press likely contributed to the lowest vote percentage of his career in Congress: 57 percent.

He suffered a grievous loss in March 2006 when Maggie, his wife of almost 57 years, died of cancer. Always faithful to his duties, he was back at his Senate desk the day after her death to vote on amendments to the annual budget resolution. In May 2008, he married Irene Hirano, the president and CEO of the Japanese American National Museum in Los Angeles.

KEY VOTES

2008

Yes Prohibit discrimination based on genetic information

Yes Reauthorize farm and nutrition programs for five years

Yes Limit debate on "cap and trade" system for greenhouse gas emissions

No Allow lawsuits against companies that participated in warrantless wiretapping

Yes Limit debate on a bill to block a scheduled cut in Medicare payments to doctors

? Grant mortgage relief to homeowners and funding for Fannie Mae and Freddie Mac

Yes Approve a nuclear cooperation agreement with India

Yes Approve final $700 billion program to stabilize financial markets

Yes Allow consideration of a $14 billion auto industry loan package

2007

Yes Increase minimum wage by $2.10 an hour

Yes Limit debate on a comprehensive immigration bill

Yes Overhaul congressional lobbying and ethics rules for members and their staffs

Yes Limit debate on considering a bill to add House seats for the District of Columbia and Utah

Yes Limit debate on restoring habeas corpus rights to detainees

Yes Mandate minimum breaks for troops between deployments to Iraq or Afghanistan

Yes Override Bush veto of $23.2 billion water projects authorization bill

No Confirm Michael B. Mukasey as attorney general

Yes Limit debate on an energy policy overhaul containing $21.8 billion in tax incentives and reduced oil and gas subsidies

CQ VOTE STUDIES

	PARTY UNITY		PRESIDENTIAL SUPPORT	
	SUPPORT	OPPOSE	SUPPORT	OPPOSE
2008	83%	17%	46%	54%
2007	94%	6%	36%	64%
2006	90%	10%	56%	44%
2005	90%	10%	44%	56%
2004	95%	5%	59%	41%
2003	93%	7%	48%	52%
2002	90%	10%	76%	24%
2001	98%	2%	66%	34%
2000	91%	9%	94%	6%
1999	91%	9%	86%	14%

INTEREST GROUPS

	AFL-CIO	ADA	CCUS	ACU
2008	100%	85%	71%	0%
2007	94%	90%	45%	0%
2006	100%	95%	50%	8%
2005	100%	90%	44%	5%
2004	100%	100%	50%	8%
2003	100%	85%	40%	15%
2002	92%	80%	41%	0%
2001	100%	90%	43%	9%
2000	60%	60%	69%	23%
1999	88%	95%	50%	0%

Sen. Daniel K. Akaka (D)

Elected 1990; 3rd full term
Appointed April 1990

Akaka, with an unassuming, congenial attitude, is known more for giving everyone smiles and spreading what he calls the "spirit of Aloha" around the Capitol than holding forth on national policy. His demeanor is sometimes mistaken for passivity, but in recent years he has been quietly amassing a strong legislative record while forcefully advocating his home state's interests.

At 84, Akaka (uh-KAH-kuh) is among the oldest senators, and has long worked in close partnership with Hawaii's senior senator, Democrat Daniel K. Inouye, who has been in Congress 18 years longer. Inouye, now chairman of the powerful Appropriations Committee, has long overshadowed Akaka. But in recent years Akaka has emerged a bit from Inouye's shadow, having assumed the chairmanship of the Veterans' Affairs Committee in 2007. He also chairs the oversight subcommittee of the Homeland Security and Governmental Affairs Committee. And he sits on the Banking, Housing and Urban Affairs Committee, which will give him a voice in a planned overhaul of the nation's financial regulation system.

It is his role on Veterans' Affairs that is expected to become even more prominent during the 111th Congress (2009-10) as the Obama administration moves to bring troops home from Iraq and the Veterans Affairs Department attempts to improve its ability to provide medical, disability and housing benefits to hundreds of thousands of veterans and their families.

He set to work during the 110th Congress (2007-08) to address what he regarded as substandard care of troops returning from the Iraq War. His panel authorized the largest increase ever in funding for the VA in 2007. "For me, that's not enough," he said. "We need much more than that to take care of the needs of the veterans, which we are not fully doing."

Akaka has pressed for improvements in the handling of post-traumatic stress disorder and traumatic brain injuries. He successfully pushed to enactment a bill to implement regulations for notifying veterans who claim medical benefits about the status of their requests in simple terms. He also saw enacted a catchall measure addressing other concerns of returning troops, including housing, employment and access to courts. And after years of effort, he and Inouye won authorization in 2009 of lump-sum payments to aging Filipino World War II veterans who fought with the United States.

Akaka, who often recalls witnessing as a boy the Japanese attack on Pearl Harbor in 1941, likens the plight of the Filipino veterans to that of veterans from his home state of Hawaii. "Both Hawaii and the Philippines were U.S. possessions…Both were attacked that December," Akaka said. "For the duration of the Second World War, both Hawaii and the Philippines would send their children to battle under the command of the U.S. military."

As the only ethnic native Hawaiian ever to serve in the Senate — his mother was Hawaiian and his father was of Chinese and Hawaiian ancestry — Akaka lobbies on behalf of his people as a central focus of his career.

In 2009, he introduced the latest version of his signature legislation, known as the Akaka Bill, which would recognize ethnic Native Hawaiians as an indigenous group and give them a status similar to that held by Alaska Natives and American Indians. That would allow them to negotiate with the state and federal governments over land use. Conservative Republicans have consistently blocked the bill since 2000, arguing it could disrupt military operations and discriminate against Hawaiians of other ethnicities. The bill did pass the House in 2007, but it failed to move in the Senate after President George W. Bush threatened to veto it. Obama has expressed support for the bill.

CAPITOL OFFICE
224-6361
akaka.senate.gov
141 Hart Bldg. 20510-1103; fax 224-2126

COMMITTEES
Armed Services
Banking, Housing & Urban Affairs
Homeland Security & Governmental Affairs
(Oversight of Government Management -
chairman)
Indian Affairs
Veterans' Affairs - chairman

RESIDENCE
Honolulu

BORN
Sept. 11, 1924; Honolulu, Hawaii

RELIGION
Congregationalist

FAMILY
Wife, Millie Akaka; five children

EDUCATION
U. of Hawaii, B.Ed. 1952, M.Ed. 1966

MILITARY SERVICE
Army Corps of Engineers, 1945-47

CAREER
Gubernatorial aide; state economic grants official;
elementary school principal and teacher

POLITICAL HIGHLIGHTS
Sought Democratic nomination for lieutenant
governor, 1974; U.S. House, 1977-90

ELECTION RESULTS

2006 GENERAL

Daniel K. Akaka (D)	210,330	61.3%
Cynthia Thielen (R)	126,097	36.8%
Lloyd J. "Jeff" Mallan (LIBERT)	6,415	1.9%

2006 PRIMARY

Daniel K. Akaka (D)	129,158	54.6%
Ed Case (D)	107,163	45.3%

PREVIOUS WINNING PERCENTAGES
2000 (73%); 1994 (72%); 1990 Special Election (54%);
1988 House Election (89%); 1986 House Election
(76%); 1984 House Election (82%); 1982 House
Election (89%); 1980 House Election (90%); 1978
House Election (86%); 1976 House Election (80%)

Hawaii's last monarch, Queen Liliuokalani, was dethroned in 1893 in a rebellion led by the U.S. minister to Hawaii and supported by U.S.-owned business interests on the islands and the U.S. military. A century later, President Clinton signed a resolution sponsored by Akaka officially apologizing. An Akaka law enacted in 1995 compensates native Hawaiians by transferring federal land to a trust in return for lands seized by the United States during the state's territorial period.

Akaka was on the Energy and Natural Resources panel during the 110th, and secured a $5 million federal grant to establish a national marine renewable-energy center in Hawaii as part of the Democrats' 2007 energy bill. And he and Democratic Ron Wyden of Oregon successfully included provisions in a 2008 natural resources law that aim to protect natural resources at national parks.

One of only three remaining World War II veterans in the Senate, Akaka serves on the Armed Services Committee, where he often criticized the Bush administration's policies. "Due to the high operations tempo of our reserve forces, there is an appalling gap in readiness for homeland defense," Akaka warned Gen. David H. Petraeus, the top military commander in Iraq, during an April 2008 hearing.

As chairman of Homeland Security's oversight panel, he garnered Senate passage in December 2007 of a long-stalled bill aimed at closing loopholes in the Whistleblower Protection Act. He also joined Democratic efforts to restore some collective bargaining and appeals rights for federal workers as part of reforms to the government's National Security Personnel System. Those reforms became law as part of the fiscal 2008 defense authorization bill.

Akaka has used his seat on the Banking committee to advocate for mortgage holders and other affected by the economic crisis. In 2008 he called on credit companies and lenders to responsibly put money in the hands of the lower and middle class. That fall, he backed a $700 billion measure to shore up the nation's financial sector, saying the bill was "not perfect, but it includes accountability and it includes oversight to prevent abuse." He also backed the $787 billion economic stimulus package in 2009.

Akaka's career is a study in quiet perseverance. After graduating from the Kamehameha School for Boys, he served in the Army Corps of Engineers during World War II. Returning home, he got a degree in education from the University of Hawaii and became a teacher, then a principal. He rose through the Honolulu education bureaucracy and in 1976 prevailed in a tough primary contest for the 2nd District seat in the House. He rose to the middle tier of seniority on the House Appropriations Committee, where he concentrated almost entirely on parochial needs.

When Democratic Sen. Spark M. Matsunaga died in April 1990, Akaka was a logical choice to fill the vacancy. He was on good terms with Democratic Gov. John Waihee III, who made the appointment. He also was close to the state party leadership and had the support of Japanese-Americans.

But in the special election that fall to fill out Matsunaga's term, he faced a serious challenge from GOP Rep. Patricia F. Saiki. Akaka had been a sedate figure during his House career and was not readily identifiable to many Hawaiians. But he stressed his ability to deliver federal largess to Hawaii and prevailed with 54 percent of the vote. He won his next two Senate elections easily.

In 2006, Akaka drew his first serious political challenge in years when Rep. Ed Case, almost 30 years his junior, decided to take him on in the primary. While expressing respect and "the deepest aloha" for the incumbent, Case said it was time for "the next generation" of leadership. Akaka retorted that Hawaii benefited from his depth of experience, and his Senate colleagues rushed to his aid. So did the voters; he took 55 percent of the vote against Case in the primary and easily won re-election in November, although his 61 percent share of the general-election vote was his lowest since his initial Senate election.

KEY VOTES

2008

Yes   Prohibit discrimination based on genetic information
Yes   Reauthorize farm and nutrition programs for five years
Yes   Limit debate on "cap and trade" system for greenhouse gas emissions
Yes   Allow lawsuits against companies that participated in warrantless wiretapping
Yes   Limit debate on a bill to block a scheduled cut in Medicare payments to doctors
Yes   Grant mortgage relief to homeowners and funding for Fannie Mae and Freddie Mac
No   Approve a nuclear cooperation agreement with India
Yes   Approve final $700 billion program to stabilize financial markets
Yes   Allow consideration of a $14 billion auto industry loan package

2007

Yes   Increase minimum wage by $2.10 an hour
Yes   Limit debate on a comprehensive immigration bill
Yes   Overhaul congressional lobbying and ethics rules for members and their staffs
Yes   Limit debate on considering a bill to add House seats for the District of Columbia and Utah
Yes   Limit debate on restoring habeas corpus rights to detainees
Yes   Mandate minimum breaks for troops between deployments to Iraq or Afghanistan
Yes   Override Bush veto of $23.2 billion water projects authorization bill
No   Confirm Michael B. Mukasey as attorney general
Yes   Limit debate on an energy policy overhaul containing $21.8 billion in tax incentives and reduced oil and gas subsidies

CQ VOTE STUDIES

	PARTY UNITY		PRESIDENTIAL SUPPORT	
	SUPPORT	OPPOSE	SUPPORT	OPPOSE
2008	99%	1%	30%	70%
2007	95%	5%	40%	60%
2006	96%	4%	48%	52%
2005	96%	4%	40%	60%
2004	97%	3%	56%	44%
2003	97%	3%	51%	49%
2002	91%	9%	63%	37%
2001	98%	2%	70%	30%
2000	98%	2%	97%	3%
1999	96%	4%	89%	11%

INTEREST GROUPS

	AFL-CIO	ADA	CCUS	ACU
2008	100%	100%	50%	0%
2007	89%	95%	36%	0%
2006	93%	95%	30%	0%
2005	100%	95%	39%	8%
2004	100%	95%	29%	5%
2003	100%	90%	30%	11%
2002	100%	80%	53%	0%
2001	100%	95%	50%	13%
2000	86%	85%	46%	12%
1999	89%	100%	41%	4%

Rep. Neil Abercrombie (D)

Elected 1990; 10th full term
Also served Sept. 1986 – Jan. 1987

Irrepressibly loquacious and emotional, with a graying beard and long hair, Abercrombie stands out among his more conventionally combed colleagues.

When the maverick Abercrombie made his congressional debut in 1986, he seemed to have stepped out of a 1960s time capsule. His outspoken demeanor and appearance gave off verbal and visual cues of a lawmaker pushing the left edge of the ideological envelope at every turn. Minus a ponytail (it was shorn in 1997), Abercrombie retains much of his early intensity.

But he has not walked in lockstep with the left on every issue and is not timid about speaking his mind when it differs from the Democratic majority. Whether the subject is the war in Iraq or programs to benefit his Hawaiian constituents, Abercrombie considers himself not a liberal but a "radical conservative" and a "strict constitutionalist." He says his politics are based not on ideology, but rather on a determination "to go on offense for those who are being misused and mistreated."

Abercrombie hopes his approach can win him Hawaii's governorship in 2010, a job he called "the culmination of a lifetime of public service for me" in announcing his decision to run in March 2009. Like other Democratic candidates, he invoked Barack Obama's 2008 campaign message of hope and change, and said he would seek to build on the increased voter participation and involvement he believed has been stirred by President Obama, who grew up in Honolulu.

He has known the Obama family since the 1960s. In December 2006, he urged the Illinois senator in his first term that the timing was right for him to consider the White House. "There is going to be a great wave coming," he recalled telling Obama. "You either ride the wave or it'll roll over you."

For now, Abercrombie is preoccupied in Washington with his duties on the Armed Services Committee, where he chairs a subcommittee.

The one-time Vietnam War protester also is a member of the Out of Iraq Caucus. He sees no contradiction in his roles: He is a strong supporter of the U.S. military, which he feels has been severely overextended in Iraq and Afghanistan. Indeed, he is amused at the emphasis others put on his past, saying people assume "that you must have been against the military. And I wasn't, I never was. . . . I felt that the military was being misused for political purposes, and that always infuriated me."

He has the same objections on Iraq. He has consistently voted against spending measures and resolutions supporting the war, and has supported measures calling for a timetable for troop withdrawals. In a February 2007 floor speech opposing President George W. Bush's plan to send more than 21,00 additional U.S. troops to Iraq, he called the war "the greatest strategic foreign policy folly in our nation's history."

From his post as chairman of the Air and Land Forces Subcommittee, which authorizes most Army programs, he articulates his message that support for the troops does not mean support for the war or for certain top-dollar Pentagon programs. He repeatedly has proposed cutting the budget for the Army's next generation of equipment, the Future Combat Systems. He says the program, which would develop vehicles, aircraft and radios for tomorrow's Army, is based on questionable technology and is siphoning resources needed by soldiers in battle today.

Abercrombie also criticizes the toll the war has exacted on reserve and National Guard troops and their families, which he says is profoundly affecting whole communities.

CAPITOL OFFICE
225-2726
www.house.gov/abercrombie
1502 Longworth Bldg. 20515-1101; fax 225-4580

COMMITTEES
Armed Services
 (Air & Land Forces - chairman)
Natural Resources

RESIDENCE
Honolulu

BORN
June 26, 1938; Buffalo, N.Y.

RELIGION
Unspecified

FAMILY
Wife, Nancie Caraway

EDUCATION
Union College (N.Y.), B.A. 1959; U. of Hawaii, M.A. 1964, Ph.D. 1974 (American studies)

CAREER
Educator

POLITICAL HIGHLIGHTS
Sought Democratic nomination for U.S. Senate, 1970; Hawaii House, 1974-78; Hawaii Senate, 1978-86; U.S. House, 1986-87; defeated in primary for re-election to U.S. House, 1986; Honolulu City Council, 1988-90

ELECTION RESULTS

2008 GENERAL

Neil Abercrombie (D)	154,208	77.1%
Steve Tataii (R)	38,115	19.1%
Li Zhao (LIBERT)	7,594	3.8%

2008 PRIMARY

Neil Abercrombie (D)	unopposed

2006 GENERAL

Neil Abercrombie (D)	112,904	69.4%
Richard "Noah" Hough (R)	49,890	30.6%

PREVIOUS WINNING PERCENTAGES
2004 (63%); 2002 (73%); 2000 (69%); 1998 (62%); 1996 (50%); 1994 (54%); 1992 (73%); 1990 (61%); 1986 Special Election (30%)

He broke from most of his fellow Democrats in 2008 over whether to establish an outside body to oversee ethics investigations. He was one of only 23 Democrats to vote against the new House rule. "We cringe before our critics and turn over our obligation to govern ourselves to others," he said.

Despite his opposition to the Iraq War, Abercrombie counts among his proudest achievements the hundreds of millions he has procured for military research and construction at his district's numerous bases and installations, which include Pearl Harbor. His efforts have not gone unnoticed; in 2002, a new tugboat that services Navy vessels at Pearl Harbor was named after him.

Abercrombie also parts ways with his fellow Democrats on some tax policies important to the travel and tourism industries that account for a large share of his state's employment. He has pushed for legislation allowing a tax deduction for the full cost of business meals and entertainment as well as for travel costs of an accompanying spouse on a business trip. He also has backed GOP efforts to repeal the estate tax, which he says is harmful to Hawaii's many family-owned businesses.

A member of the Natural Resources Committee, Abecrombie has pushed legislation that would grant ethnic Native Hawaiians sovereign status similar to that held by American Indians and Alaskan Natives. He also has sought to broker political differences over oil and gas drilling; he and Pennsylvania Republican John E. Peterson unsuccessfully tried in September 2008 to repeal a moratorium on drilling in the Pacific and Atlantic oceans and the eastern Gulf of Mexico, while allowing states to restrict drilling 25 miles to 50 miles offshore.

He grew up in Buffalo, N.Y., went to Hawaii to attend graduate school and stayed. Along the way, he traveled widely and worked as a teaching assistant, a probation officer, a waiter and a custodian. Soon after he earned his Ph.D., he became a practitioner of protest politics, taking 13 percent of the 1970 Democratic primary vote for the U.S. Senate as an anti-Vietnam War candidate. Four years later, he won election to the state House.

After 11-plus years in the state legislature, Abercrombie won a special election for the U.S. House seat in 1986 to fill a vacancy and served briefly in the House. But he narrowly lost the primary election for a full term, which was held the same day. He got a second chance when the seat opened in 1990, winning the Democratic primary with 45 percent of the vote and cruising to an easy victory in November.

He faced difficult re-election battles in 1994 and 1996 and struggled to fend off charges he was an extreme liberal. But since then he has won by comfortable margins, carrying 69 percent of the vote in 2006 and 77 percent in 2008.

KEY VOTES

2008
Yes Delay consideration of Colombia free-trade agreement
Yes Override Bush veto of federal farm and nutrition programs reauthorization bill
No   Overhaul surveillance laws and permit dismissal of suits against companies that conducted warrantless wiretapping
Yes Grant mortgage relief to homeowners and funding for Fannie Mae and Freddie Mac
No   Approve initial $700 billion program to stabilize financial markets
Yes Approve final $700 billion program to stabilize financial markets
Yes Provide $14 billion in loans to automakers

2007
Yes Increase minimum wage by $2.10 an hour
Yes Approve $124.2 billion in emergency war spending and set goal for redeployment of troops from Iraq
No   Reject federal contraceptive assistance to international family planning groups
Yes Override Bush veto of $23.2 billion water projects authorization bill
No   Implement Peru free-trade agreement
Yes Approve energy policy overhaul with new fuel economy standards
No   Clear $473.5 billion omnibus spending bill, including $70 billion for military operations

CQ VOTE STUDIES

	PARTY UNITY		PRESIDENTIAL SUPPORT	
	SUPPORT	OPPOSE	SUPPORT	OPPOSE
2008	96%	4%	16%	84%
2007	97%	3%	6%	94%
2006	92%	8%	17%	83%
2005	92%	8%	15%	85%
2004	94%	6%	15%	85%

INTEREST GROUPS

	AFL-CIO	ADA	CCUS	ACU
2008	100%	95%	50%	8%
2007	96%	100%	53%	4%
2006	86%	90%	40%	12%
2005	100%	100%	42%	12%
2004	93%	85%	32%	0%

HAWAII 1
Oahu — Honolulu, Waipahu, Pearl City

On the southern coast of the island of Oahu, the compact 1st takes in a narrow plain that includes Honolulu — the engine that drives all of Hawaii — and Waipahu to the west. Rising above the plain to the north is part of the Koolau mountain range, and Keaiwa Heiau park's trails and campsites are north of Aiea. Manoa, Moiliili, Kaimuki and Kapahulu are neighborhoods east of downtown.

Honolulu, the state capital, hosts most of Hawaii's business and nearly one-third of its people, leading to pervasive traffic congestion. Waikiki to the east is the heart of tourism, the state's leading industry, and downtown Honolulu offers historical and cultural destinations. Although the industry regained its footing following Asia's mid-1990s economic crisis and the Sept. 11 attacks, a recent nationwide recession has taken its toll here. The legacy of World War II remains etched in the 1st's consciousness, as Pearl Harbor anchors a strong military presence in the district.

Democrats are entrenched in the 1st, and the district has elected only one Republican to Congress since Hawaii obtained two congressional districts in 1971. Democrats also do very well locally, although moderate Republican enclaves exist near Diamond Head and in Liliha and Ewa Beach. By far, the district has the highest percentage (54 percent) of Asian residents in the nation and a high percentage (17 percent) of multiethnic residents. Ethnic Native Hawaiians make up less than 7 percent of the population. In 2008, Honolulu-born Democrat Barack Obama took 70 percent of the district's presidential vote.

MAJOR INDUSTRY
Tourism, military, construction

MILITARY BASES
Naval Station Pearl Harbor, 13,700 military, 11,300 civilian (2009) (shared with the 2nd) Hickam Air Force Base, 4,436 military, 1,932 civilian (2007); Fort Shafter Army base, 1,719 military, 1,205 civilian (2007); Tripler Army Medical Center, 1,427 military, 1,642 civilian; Camp H.M. Smith Marine Corps installation, 1,020 military, 250 civilian (2007)

CITIES
Honolulu, 371,657; Waipahu, 33,108; Pearl City, 30,976; Waimalu, 29,371

NOTABLE
Iolani Palace in downtown Honolulu was the official residence of the Hawaiian Kingdom's last two monarchs.

Rep. Mazie K. Hirono (D)

Elected 2006; 2nd term

CAPITOL OFFICE
225-4906
hirono.house.gov
1524 Longworth Bldg. 20515-1102; fax 225-4987

COMMITTEES
Education & Labor
Transportation & Infrastructure

RESIDENCE
Honolulu

BORN
Nov. 3, 1947; Fukushima, Japan

RELIGION
Buddhist

FAMILY
Husband, Leighton Kim Oshima; one stepchild

EDUCATION
U. of Hawaii, B.A. 1970 (psychology);
Georgetown U., J.D. 1978

CAREER
Lawyer; campaign and state legislative aide

POLITICAL HIGHLIGHTS
Hawaii House, 1981-94; lieutenant governor,
1994-2002; Democratic nominee for governor, 2002

ELECTION RESULTS

2008 GENERAL

Mazie K. Hirono (D)	165,748	76.1%
Roger B. Evans (R)	44,425	20.4%
Shaun Stenshol (I)	4,042	1.8%
Lloyd J. "Jeff" Mallan (LIBERT)	3,699	1.7%

2008 PRIMARY

Mazie K. Hirono (D)	unopposed

2006 GENERAL

Mazie K. Hirono (D)	106,906	61.0%
Bob Hogue (R)	68,244	39.0%

Hirono is a Japanese native who sees herself as a successor to the late Hawaii Democratic Rep. Patsy T. Mink, the first non-Caucausian woman elected to Congress. Though less fiery in style than the famously temperamental Mink, she shares her predecessor's liberal views. "Patsy fought for working men and women and she fought for education," Hirono said. "Those are the issues that are really important to me."

Hirono (full name: may-ZEE hee-RO-no) sits on the Education and Labor Committee, where she is a vocal advocate for early-childhood education. In the 111th Congress (2009-10) she reintroduced a bill to provide grants to the neediest states to hire more educators, buy supplies and improve nutrition services in preschools. The committee approved her bill during the 110th Congress (2007-08), but it didn't reach the House floor. During the 110th, she also offered a bill to create a loan forgiveness program for the college expenses of early-childhood educators. The May 2007 reauthorization of the Head Start program included her provision ensuring preschool teacher training is conducted by people with expertise in infant and toddler development.

Hirono also serves on the Transportation and Infrastructure Committee, which she said is a good fit as traffic congestion is a growing concern on every island in the chain. She also wants federal money to come to Hawaii to improve the state's infrastructure.

A loyal Democrat, Hirono stuck with her party on major votes in the 110th Congress, voting to raise the minimum wage and to reduce the cost of college loans. She also agreed with most Democrats on reducing the U.S. commitment to the war in Iraq, voting to shift the mission from primarily combat to protecting U.S. soldiers, citizens and diplomats and providing limited support for Iraqi security forces.

She appears ready to be a loyal foot soldier for President Obama, who grew up in Honolulu. Hirono supported Obama's $787 billion economic stimulus bill in January 2009 as well as a $410 billion catchall spending bill for 2009, which were both signed into law. She lauded the latter measure's funding for educational, agricultural and infrastructure projects and programs in Hawaii.

Also in early 2009, Hirono supported a Democratic bill to expand the State Children's Health Insurance Program, which covers children whose families do not qualify for Medicaid.

Hirono served 14 years in the state legislature, was twice elected lieutenant governor and is one of the most prominent women in Hawaii politics after Republican Gov. Linda Lingle. She said she's proud to be among the small number of foreign-born members of Congress. "I think that I truly exemplify the American dream as an immigrant who came here with nothing, not speaking the language," she said.

Hirono was born in 1947 in Fukushima, Japan. She said she never really knew her father, an alcoholic and compulsive gambler. In 1955, her mother, Laura Chie Hirono, decided that life in rural Japan with an abusive husband was "no life for her family," and she moved to Hawaii. The move took covert plotting, but her mother managed to leave with Hirono and her oldest son. A year later, another son and Hirono's grandparents joined them.

Her mother worked various jobs to support the family, and slept sideways with the children on a single mattress. She relied on the children to help her learn English, and believed, Hirono recalls, that if she could learn to count from one to 100, she would somehow have made it in America. Her mother's struggle inspired Hirono's political career. "I know what it feels like to be discriminated against, to feel powerless, to have landlords who threaten to kick you out, and not having a place to go," she told the Honolulu Advertiser in 2002. "So, equality and fairness, equal opportunity, are very driving principles for me."

To succeed in her new country, she immersed herself in school and books, she said, and worked hard to learn the new language. She eventually graduated Phi Beta Kappa from the University of Hawaii and earned a law degree from Georgetown University.

At the University of Hawaii, Hirono majored in psychology, thinking she might want to be a social worker to "help people one by one." In college she met an antiwar protester named David Hagino, who in 1970 ran for the state House and asked Hirono to head his campaign. Hagino lost that race, but two years later, Hirono helped in the successful state House campaign of Democrat Anson Chong, and then went to work in Chong's legislative office.

After law school at Georgetown, Hirono returned to Hawaii and served as a deputy attorney general working on antitrust issues before winning a House seat of her own. In the Hawaii House, she focused on consumer protection issues, leading an effort to reform the state's no-fault car insurance laws, pushing for price caps on gasoline and sponsoring a bill to require drug companies to offer discounts to people with low incomes.

Hirono said she is most proud of her work on women's issues, including legislation to train prosecutors on how to handle rape cases and a bill to shield rape victims from being put on the witness stand. She also started a women's caucus so that the nine women in the House could better exert their influence.

She was elected lieutenant governor in 1994, and served for eight years. In 2002, Hirono was thwarted in her effort to move up to the governor's mansion by Lingle, whose victory ended 40 years of Democratic control of the governorship. Lingle's second term is up in 2010, and Hirono may try for the job again.

In 2006, Hirono leveraged her statewide name recognition to run for the 2nd District seat, which opened when Democrat Ed Case mounted an unsuccessful primary challenge to Sen. Daniel K. Akaka. Hirono competed against nine other Democrats in the September primary, and she gained an edge with support from EMILY's List, a national fundraising group for Democratic women. She placed first in the primary with 22 percent. She won the general election easily over GOP state Sen. Bob Hogue, with 61 percent of the tally. Hirono and Democrat Hank Johnson of Georgia also became the first Buddhists elected to Congress.

In 2008, she again won easily, taking 76 percent of the vote.

KEY VOTES

2008

Yes Delay consideration of Colombia free-trade agreement

Yes Override Bush veto of federal farm and nutrition programs reauthorization bill

No Overhaul surveillance laws and permit dismissal of suits against companies that conducted warrantless wiretapping

Yes Grant mortgage relief to homeowners and funding for Fannie Mae and Freddie Mac

No Approve initial $700 billion program to stabilize financial markets

Yes Approve final $700 billion program to stabilize financial markets

Yes Provide $14 billion in loans to automakers

2007

Yes Increase minimum wage by $2.10 an hour

Yes Approve $124.2 billion in emergency war spending and set goal for redeployment of troops from Iraq

No Reject federal contraceptive assistance to international family planning groups

Yes Override Bush veto of $23.2 billion water projects authorization bill

No Implement Peru free-trade agreement

Yes Approve energy policy overhaul with new fuel economy standards

No Clear $473.5 billion omnibus spending bill, including $70 billion for military operations

CQ VOTE STUDIES

	PARTY UNITY		PRESIDENTIAL SUPPORT	
	SUPPORT	OPPOSE	SUPPORT	OPPOSE
2008	99%	1%	13%	87%
2007	99%	1%	4%	96%

INTEREST GROUPS

	AFL-CIO	ADA	CCUS	ACU
2008	100%	100%	56%	4%
2007	96%	100%	45%	0%

HAWAII 2
Suburban and Outer Oahu; 'Neighbor Islands'

The 2nd is amazing in its geographic diversity, with sandy beaches, volcanoes, mountains, tropical rain forests and deserts, all inhabited by indigenous plants and animals unique to the district's islands. The district includes parts of Oahu and all of Hawaii's seven other major islands, as well as the Papahanaumokuakea Marine National Monument, which is larger than all U.S. national parks combined. The southernmost point of the 50 states is located in the district at Ka Lae on the island of Hawaii, also called the Big Island.

Tourism and agriculture, two of the 2nd's leading industries, struggled through the 1990s, and the closure of all but one of Hawaii's sugar plantations continues to hurt agricultural prospects. Growers have turned to macadamia nuts and coffee to counter the industry's recent job losses. Some farmers are working to bring pineapples back to a leading position in the industry, and the district's aquaculture sector also is growing.

Tourism rebounded in the last decade, but recent economic slowdowns nationwide have affected the number of visitors to the islands. Oahu, the island of Hawaii and Maui are the most-visited islands and have not been impacted by the downturn as much as Kauai, Molokai and Lanai.

The 2nd has the highest percentage of a multi-ethnic population in the nation (26 percent), a large Asian population (28 percent) and Native Hawaiians (12 percent). Economic problems offered the GOP an opening at the local level, but the 2nd remains Democratic. Every state legislative race in the district went to a Democrat in 2008, and Hawaii-born Barack Obama won more than 73 percent of the 2nd's 2008 presidential vote.

MAJOR INDUSTRY
Tourism, agriculture, military

MILITARY BASES
Schofield Barracks (Army), 17,714 military, 1,740 civilian; Naval Station Pearl Harbor, 13,700 military, 11,300 civilian (2009) (shared with the 1st); Marine Corps Base Hawaii, 7,500 military, 100 civilian (2009)

CITIES
Hilo, 40,759; Kailua, 36,513; Kaneohe, 34,970

NOTABLE
The Papahanaumokuakea Marine National Monument among the northwestern Hawaiian islands is, at more than 137,000 square miles, larger than all U.S. national parks combined.

Gov. C. L. "Butch" Otter (R)

First elected: 2006
Length of term: 4 years
Term expires: 1/11
Salary: $108,727
Phone: (208) 334-2100

Residence: Star
Born: May 3, 1942; Caldwell, Idaho
Religion: Roman Catholic
Family: Wife, Lori Otter; four children
Education: College of Idaho, B.A. 1967 (political science)
Military service: Idaho National Guard, 1967-73
Career: Agribusiness company executive; oil company partner
Political highlights: Idaho House, 1972-76; sought Republican nomination for governor, 1978; lieutenant governor, 1987-2001; U.S. House, 2001-07

Election results:
2006 GENERAL

C. L. "Butch" Otter (R)	237,437	52.7%
Jerry M. Brady (D)	198,845	44.1%
Marvin Richardson (CNSTP)	7,309	1.6%
Ted Dunlap (LIBERT)	7,241	1.6%

Lt. Gov. Brad Little (R)

Assumed office: 2009
Length of term: 4 years
Term expires: 1/11
Salary: $29,515
Phone: (208) 334-2200

LEGISLATURE

Legislature: January-March or April

Senate: 35 members, 2-year terms
2009 ratios: 28 R, 7 D; 27 men, 8 women
Salary: $16,116
Phone: (208) 332-1309

House: 70 members, 2-year terms
2009 ratios: 52 R, 18 D; 52 men, 18 women
Salary: $16,116
Phone: (208) 332-1140

TERM LIMITS

Governor: No
Senate: No
House: No

URBAN STATISTICS

CITY	POPULATION
Boise	185,787
Nampa	51,867
Pocatello	51,466
Idaho Falls	50,730
Meridian	34,919

REGISTERED VOTERS

Voters do not register by party.

POPULATION

2008 population (est.)	1,523,816
2000 population	1,293,953
1990 population	1,006,749
Percent change (1990-2000)	+28.5%
Rank among states (2008)	39

Median age	33.2
Born in state	47.2%
Foreign born	5%
Violent crime rate	253/100,000
Poverty level	11.8%
Federal workers	12,939
Military	9,730

ELECTIONS

STATE ELECTION OFFICIAL
(208) 334-2852
DEMOCRATIC PARTY
(208) 336-1815
REPUBLICAN PARTY
(208) 343-6405

MISCELLANEOUS

Web: www.idaho.gov
Capital: Boise

U.S. CONGRESS

Senate: 2 Republicans
House: 1 Democrat, 1 Republican

2000 Census Statistics by District

DIST.	2008 VOTE FOR PRESIDENT OBAMA	MCCAIN	WHITE	BLACK	ASIAN	HISP	MEDIAN INCOME	WHITE COLLAR	BLUE COLLAR	SERVICE INDUSTRY	OVER 64	UNDER 18	COLLEGE EDUCATION	RURAL	SQ. MILES
1	36%	62%	89%	0%	1%	7%	$38,364	56%	28%	15%	12%	28%	20%	34%	39,525
2	36	61	87	0	1	9	$36,934	57	27	16	11	29	23	33	43,222
STATE	36	62	88	0	1	8	$37,572	57	28	16	11	29	22	34	82,747
U.S.	53	46	69	12	4	13	$41,994	60	25	15	12	26	24	21	3,537,438

Sen. Michael D. Crapo (R)

Elected 1998; 2nd term

CAPITOL OFFICE
224-6142
crapo.senate.gov
239 Dirksen Bldg. 20510-1205; fax 228-1375

COMMITTEES
Banking, Housing & Urban Affairs
Budget
Environment & Public Works
Finance
Indian Affairs

RESIDENCE
Idaho Falls

BORN
May 20, 1951; Idaho Falls, Idaho

RELIGION
Mormon

FAMILY
Wife, Susan Crapo; five children

EDUCATION
Brigham Young U., B.A. 1973 (political science);
Harvard U., J.D. 1977

CAREER
Lawyer

POLITICAL HIGHLIGHTS
Idaho Senate, 1984-92 (president pro tempore,
1988-92); U.S. House, 1993-99

ELECTION RESULTS

2004 GENERAL

Michael D. Crapo (R)	499,796	99.2%

2004 PRIMARY

Michael D. Crapo (R)	unopposed

PREVIOUS WINNING PERCENTAGES
1998 (70%); 1996 House Election (69%); 1994 House
Election (75%); 1992 House Election (61%)

Unassuming and well-liked on Capitol Hill, Crapo's willingness to seek consensus serves him well. He has taken on a variety of behind-the-scenes tasks on behalf of Senate Republican leaders while juggling several important committee assignments.

It is no accident he is well-regarded. Crapo (CRAY-poe) said he learned as a freshman in high school that little gestures, such as making eye contact with people, can make a big difference in building relationships. Though conservative in philosophy, he is moderate in demeanor and doesn't have much of a thirst for attention. "He's not flamboyant, he's not seeking headlines, he is thoughtful, and he works," former Idaho GOP Sen. James A. McClure once told the Idaho Statesman newspaper. "That's a good combination."

Crapo rallies support for Senate GOP leadership priorities as a deputy whip. He also serves as chairman of the Committee on Committees party caucus, helping Minority Leader Mitch McConnell of Kentucky make Republican committee assignments. In the 110th Congress (2007-08), McConnell tapped Crapo for an internal panel on earmarks, though its recommendations on the funding set-asides for special projects did not advance.

At the same time, Crapo has sought opportunities for bipartisan legislative achievements. Among his proudest moments: passage of endangered species legislation as part of the 2008 law to reauthorize farm and nutrition programs. Among other things, the measure offers tax incentives to property owners who take steps to protect endangered species.

Crapo worked with environmental groups, property-rights advocates and Arkansas Democrat Blanche Lincoln before taking the proposal to Finance Chairman Max Baucus of Montana and top panel Republican Charles E. Grassley of Iowa. Said Crapo: "What we were able to do is go to them and say, 'We've got a good solution, for a big issue, which has consensus. And we have worked through the battles.'" He also led a bipartisan effort to loosen restrictions on guns in national parks.

From his seat on the Finance Committee, Crapo is well-positioned for the health care debate in the 111th Congress (2009-10). He was one of 16 senators who signed onto a bipartisan health care bill to repeal the tax exclusion on employer-provided health insurance, make some employers pay into a health care fund and require Americans to purchase coverage. He works to advance the GOP's tax-cutting agenda; he unsuccessfully pushed a proposal in January 2009 that would have permanently eliminated the capital gains tax.

Crapo also serves on the Banking, Housing and Urban Affairs panel, seemingly an unusual choice for a senator from a sparsely populated Western state. But, he said, his committees deal with issues critical to farmers.

He took the lead in 2006 on a wide-ranging banking regulation bill that became law to ease restrictions on banks, credit unions and other financial institutions. Crapo opposed a measure in October 2008 to aid the ailing financial services sector, contending it didn't do enough to protect taxpayers. But he joined Banking Chairman Christopher J. Dodd of Connecticut in March 2009 on a bill to raise the amount of money the Federal Deposit Insurance Corporation can borrow from the Treasury Department to pay off customers with deposits in banks that fail.

In 2009, Crapo rejoined the Environment and Public Works Committee, where he had served in his first term. He has worked on a new land-management plan for the Owyhee region of southwest Idaho, site of a long-running turf battle among conservationists, American Indians, the Air

Force, ranchers and off-road-vehicle groups. It was included in a major public lands bill the Senate passed in January 2009. He is one of three co-chairmen of the Senate Renewable Energy and Energy Efficiency Caucus, and seeks ways to advance nuclear energy as well as new technologies being developed at the Idaho National Laboratory.

Crapo's other committee assignments are Indian Affairs and Budget. He has joined Budget's top-ranking Republican, Judd Gregg of New Hampshire, in arguing for the need to control budget deficits. "There's this notion that you can spend your way to prosperity, but people forget there is a national debt, and it affects the economy, too," he said in January 2009.

Crapo's sunny demeanor belies an ambition that is fueled in part by his dedication to his oldest brother. An Idaho state legislator who was his mentor and law partner, Terry Crapo died just two weeks after being diagnosed with leukemia in 1982. Crapo faced his own trial when doctors diagnosed his prostate cancer in 2000 and operated. Early in 2005, the cancer returned and Crapo underwent radiation treatments while still working in the Senate. By early 2009, regular blood tests still indicated he was cancer-free.

Crapo sponsors regular prostate and breast cancer screening fairs in Idaho. He has pushed a bill to create an Office of Men's Health to coordinate and promote the status of men's health in the United States.

Wary of Canadian policies toward timber and agricultural trade with the U.S., as a House member he opposed legislation to implement both the 1993 North American Free Trade Agreement and the 1994 General Agreement on Tariffs and Trade. Since then, he voted to enact the 2000 law making permanent the normalized U.S.-China trade relationship and supported a 2007 trade deal with Peru, but he opposed the 2005 Central America Free Trade Agreement out of concern over its potential impact on Idaho sugar beet producers.

Crapo has voted against measures to limit medical malpractice awards, which would have pre-empted an Idaho law, and to provide tax incentives for charitable donations. He is among the minority of Senate Republicans who favor lifting the ban on travel to Cuba.

Crapo grew up in Idaho Falls, the youngest of six children of the local postmaster and his homemaker wife. His father also farmed 200 acres of potatoes, grain and pasture for cattle-grazing, and the children pitched in to help. The family farm expanded over the years and today is run by Crapo's uncles and cousins. He served as his high school's student body president.

At Brigham Young University, he earned a degree in political science and indulged a passion for dirt-bike racing. He then worked as a Washington intern for Idaho GOP Rep. Orval Hansen. He considered a career in medicine but changed his mind after gaining admission to Harvard Law School.

A cum laude graduate, Crapo returned to his hometown with his degree to practice law. He is a devout Mormon and said his experiences with the church, which gives its lay leaders considerable responsibilities in dealing with personal and community issues, helped prepare him for public office.

Crapo was elected to the Idaho Senate at age 33 and chosen as its president pro tempore just four years later. In 1992 he ran for the House seat being vacated by Democrat Richard Stallings, who ran unsuccessfully for the Senate. In the GOP-leaning 2nd District, Crapo was aided by President George Bush's presence on the ticket, and he defeated Democrat J.D. Williams by nearly 26 percentage points. In his first term he landed a sought-after seat on the Energy and Commerce Committee.

Crapo has never faced a tough election. When Republican Sen. Dirk Kempthorne ran for governor in 1998, Crapo quickly became the ordained front-runner to succeed him. Crapo's popularity and a strong Republican tide enabled him to crush Bill Mauk, a former Democratic state chairman, by more than 40 percentage points. He had token opposition in 2004.

KEY VOTES

2008
Yes Prohibit discrimination based on genetic information
Yes Reauthorize farm and nutrition programs for five years
No Limit debate on "cap and trade" system for greenhouse gas emissions
No Allow lawsuits against companies that participated in warrantless wiretapping
No Limit debate on a bill to block a scheduled cut in Medicare payments to doctors
Yes Grant mortgage relief to homeowners and funding for Fannie Mae and Freddie Mac
Yes Approve a nuclear cooperation agreement with India
No Approve final $700 billion program to stabilize financial markets
No Allow consideration of a $14 billion auto industry loan package

2007
Yes Increase minimum wage by $2.10 an hour
No Limit debate on a comprehensive immigration bill
No Overhaul congressional lobbying and ethics rules for members and their staffs
No Limit debate on considering a bill to add House seats for the District of Columbia and Utah
No Limit debate on restoring habeas corpus rights to detainees
No Mandate minimum breaks for troops between deployments to Iraq or Afghanistan
Yes Override Bush veto of $23.2 billion water projects authorization bill
Yes Confirm Michael B. Mukasey as attorney general
No Limit debate on an energy policy overhaul containing $21.8 billion in tax incentives and reduced oil and gas subsidies

CQ VOTE STUDIES

	PARTY UNITY		PRESIDENTIAL SUPPORT	
	SUPPORT	OPPOSE	SUPPORT	OPPOSE
2008	94%	6%	76%	24%
2007	92%	8%	81%	19%
2006	95%	5%	88%	12%
2005	95%	5%	84%	16%
2004	96%	4%	90%	10%
2003	98%	2%	97%	3%
2002	92%	8%	96%	4%
2001	94%	6%	96%	4%
2000	100%	0%	41%	59%
1999	97%	3%	30%	70%

INTEREST GROUPS

	AFL-CIO	ADA	CCUS	ACU
2008	20%	15%	75%	88%
2007	5%	15%	82%	88%
2006	7%	0%	83%	88%
2005	21%	10%	94%	100%
2004	8%	10%	94%	92%
2003	15%	5%	91%	89%
2002	9%	10%	94%	94%
2001	19%	10%	100%	92%
2000	0%	0%	93%	100%
1999	0%	0%	88%	100%

Sen. Jim Risch (R)

Elected 2008; 1st term

Tough, persistent and quick with a joke, Risch has long been one of the heaviest hitters in Idaho's GOP-centric politics. He ran the state Senate with an iron fist, served two terms as lieutenant governor and put in an eventful seven-month stint as governor. But as a U.S. Senate freshman, he's adjusting to being in the minority for the first time in his nearly four decades in politics.

Risch is a fiscal conservative who favors a balanced-budget amendment, aims to help make the 2001 and 2003 tax cuts permanent, and opposed the early economic measures of the Obama administration he viewed as too costly. And like many Western Republicans, he opposes granting illegal immigrants a path to citizenship and supports gun owners' rights.

He opposed confirming Eric H. Holder Jr. for attorney general in 2009 based on a disagreement over the interpretation of the Second Amendment. "He has argued its application is limited to states and militias, while I believe it means every individual has the 'right to keep and bear arms,'" he said. "Putting someone with that limited view of gun ownership in the role of chief law enforcement officer of the United States is simply a deal-breaker for me."

Risch followed the path of his two most recent predecessors — fellow Republicans Larry E. Craig and James A. McClure — by taking a seat on the Energy and Natural Resources Committee, where some of his views likely will clash with those of Democrats. The top Republican on the energy subcommittee, he advocates a comprehensive approach to energy that takes advantage of every option available to industry, including the promotion and use of solar, nuclear and geothermal energy. He also supports drilling in Alaska's Arctic National Wildlife Refuge and federal investment in "clean coal" technology.

Risch has significant experience in the stewardship of public lands, another of the committee's jurisdictions. He has a forestry degree, and negotiated a high-profile lands issue during his brief gubernatorial tenure. He spearheaded a deal on a proposal to protect millions of roadless acres in the state, an issue that had been debated to a stalemate before his arrival. In early 2009, he applauded an Interior Department announcement that gray wolves would be taken off the endangered species list — an issue Risch focused on as governor.

Risch also sits on the Foreign Relations Committee, where he is the ranking Republican on the Near Eastern and South and Central Asian Affairs Subcommittee. He also sits on the Select Ethics and Intelligence committees.

While Craig steered millions of federal dollars to Idaho and its national laboratory, Risch said he would "vote in a heartbeat to absolutely prohibit" earmarks. He said federal funding requests "need to go through the competitive process as opposed to just using political muscle."

In voting against President Obama's $787 billion economic stimulus law, he said, "This bill was not carefully crafted or deliberated in a bipartisan fashion. It was thrown together with pet project after pet project piled on." He likewise criticized a $410 billion catchall spending bill for fiscal 2009, even though it included earmarks for his state — nearly $45 million of which his predecessor Craig included in the bill when he was still in office.

Risch said he thought Obama should have banned earmarks outright. But he told the Idaho Statesman newspaper he would also continue to ask for earmarks for Idaho because "the system is in place, and I have no choice but to participate...I'm not happy about it."

Risch said he and Idaho Republican Sen. Michael D. Crapo would "operate as a team" in Washington. The two have been friends since the 1980s, beginning with Risch's decision to recruit Crapo for a slot on the state Sen-

CAPITOL OFFICE
224-2752
483 Russell Bldg. 20510; fax 228-1067

COMMITTEES
Energy & Natural Resources
Foreign Relations
Select Ethics
Select Intelligence
Joint Economic

RESIDENCE
Boise

BORN
May 3, 1943; Milwaukee, Wis.

RELIGION
Roman Catholic

FAMILY
Wife, Vicki Risch; three children

EDUCATION
U. of Wisconsin, Milwaukee, attended 1961-63;
U. of Idaho, B.S. 1965 (forest resources management), J.D. 1968

CAREER
Lawyer; rancher; trailer company owner; property management company owner; college instructor

POLITICAL HIGHLIGHTS
Ada County prosecuting attorney, 1970-74; Idaho Senate, 1974-89, 95-2003 (majority leader, 1976-82, 97-2003; president pro tempore, 1982-89); defeated for re-election to Idaho Senate, 1988; sought GOP nomination for Idaho Senate, 1994; lt. governor, 2003-06; governor, 2006; lt.governor, 2007-09

ELECTION RESULTS

2008 GENERAL

Jim Risch (R)	371,744	57.6%
Larry LaRocco (D)	219,903	34.1%
Rex Rammell (I)	34,510	5.4%
Kent A. Marmon (LIBERT)	9,958	1.5%
Pro-Life (I)	8,662	1.3%

2008 PRIMARY

Jim Risch (R)	80,743	65.3%
Soctt A. Syme (R)	16,660	13.5%
Richard Phennegar (R)	6,532	5.3%
Neal Thompson (R)	5,375	4.4%
Fred M. Adams (R)	4,987	4.0%
Bill Hunter (R)	4,280	3.5%
Brian E. Hefner (R)	2,915	2.4%
Hal James Styles (R)	2,082	1.7%

ate leadership. Crapo had encouraged Risch to run for the U.S. Senate seat when Craig announced he would not run for re-election. Craig pleaded guilty to a misdemeanor disorderly conduct charge after an undercover police officer in 2007 interpreted some of the senator's actions in an airport restroom as a solicitation for sex and arrested him.

Risch hails from Milwaukee, where his father climbed telephone polls for Wisconsin Bell and retired with a job in the company's accounting office. The nuns at the Catholic high school he attended thought he "needed some direction," so they gave him a career aptitude test. Risch was thrilled to learn he would make a fine forest ranger. After two years attending college in his hometown, Risch headed west to study forestry at the University of Idaho.

He fell in love with Idaho's mountains, but his interest in being a forest ranger faded. Five student deferments kept him out of the Vietnam War, and his attempt to enlist was denied due to an ulcer. After marrying his wife, Vicki, and graduating from law school, Risch was first elected to office in 1970, as prosecutor for Ada County. He thrived in the courtroom, but his efforts to crack down on narcotics almost cost him his life when leaders of a drug ring made a failed attempt to plant a bomb in his car.

After seeing a murderer he convicted go free after serving only 18 months of a life sentence, Risch decided to run for the state Senate. "The only way you could control the parole board was to get into the state Senate," Risch said. "I started rejecting all the appointments to the parole board real quick, and then the rest of them got mad and quit, and that was just fine by me."

Risch opened a private law practice that would make him wealthy. At the same time, he flourished in the state Senate, beating Craig for majority leader in 1976 and 1978. Risch wasn't afraid to make enemies as he mastered the inside political game. He carried an index card in his back pocket, one side listing the bills he wanted to pass and on the other those he wanted to kill. He lost his seat in 1988 after frequent clashes with the governor, but he returned to the state Senate in 1995 with a less aggressive style.

In 2002, Risch spent $360,000 of his own money on a successful run for lieutenant governor, a part-time job that paid $26,750 a year. He won another term and became Idaho's shortest-tenured governor when he filled out the seven-month term of Gov. Dirk Kempthorne, who had left the state in 2006 to be President George W. Bush's Interior secretary.

Before settling in as governor, Risch sat down with his wife and hashed out a lengthy list of legislative goals. "We've been married 40 years and we've been through 32 elections together," Risch said. "Everything we do is a partnership." In his brief but popular tenure, Risch overhauled the state's tax structure and made major inroads in the environmental community as an unexpected ally in the fight to keep Idaho's wild places pristine.

Risch did get some negative press in 2006 for comments he made following Hurricane Katrina's devastation. He told a British newspaper: "Here in Idaho, we couldn't understand how people could sit around on the curbs waiting for the federal government to come and do something. We had a dam break in 1976, but we didn't whine about it." The New Orleans Times-Picayune said in an editorial that Risch's "ignorance" of the storm's impact was "matched only by his smugness."

Risch, with Crapo as his campaign co-chairman, took on former Democratic Rep. Larry LaRocco in the 2008 Senate campaign. It was a re-match of sorts, as Risch beat LaRocco 58 percent to 39 percent in the 2006 race for lieutenant governor. The Senate campaign also drew Rex Rammell, an independent whose candidacy was triggered in part by a personal feud with Risch — as governor, Risch ordered state wildlife officials to shoot some untagged elk that had escaped from Rammell's ranch. Risch won easily, taking 58 percent of the vote.

Rep. Walt Minnick (D)

Elected 2008; 1st term

Minnick has a tough balancing act in the House, and party leaders are reluctant to come down too hard on him. He represents a solid Republican district, was once a Republican himself and still shares many of his district's social and fiscal concerns.

But in throwing off the GOP label to become a Democrat when he was in his 50s, he sought distance from the far-right social conservatives and "fiscal irresponsibility" of President George W. Bush, he told The Los Angeles Times. He also stands apart from liberals. "There's a whole lot of people now who want to remake America in their own image who I would not characterize as being in favor of limited government, or some of the values I hold," he said.

A member of the fiscally conservative Blue Dog Coalition, Minnick in February 2009 was one of just seven Democrats to oppose President Obama's $787 billion economic stimulus bill. He said he would have preferred "a much smaller bill" to create "private sector, spin-off jobs." He said he was never pressured by the White House to vote otherwise. He was one of 17 Democrats to vote against a $3.56 trillion budget blueprint for 2010.

On the Financial Services Committee, Minnick said he aims to bring common-sense business principles he learned from being an executive. He also serves on the Agriculture Committee. He grew up on a family wheat farm in Walla Walla, Wash. He teamed with fellow Idaho Republican Rep. Mike Simpson on a bill to overhaul how public lands in central Idaho can be used. An avid outdoorsman and hunter, Minnick said he has an interest in conservation and resource management.

After earning his law degree, he worked in the Defense Department before joining the Nixon White House, where he was involved in the creation of the Drug Enforcement Agency. He said he resigned after hearing of the Watergate break-in.

He landed in Idaho, where he ran a wood products company and later was a nursery company executive. In 2008, he took on outspoken freshman Republican Bill Sali, accusing him of being "out of touch," and won with just 51 percent of the vote, well above Obama's 36 percent of the district vote.

CAPITOL OFFICE
225-6611
minnick.house.gov
1517 Longworth Bldg. 20515-1201; fax 225-3029

COMMITTEES
Agriculture
Financial Services

RESIDENCE
Boise

BORN
Sept. 20, 1942; Walla Walla, Wash.

RELIGION
Unitarian

FAMILY
Wife, A.K. Minnick; four children

EDUCATION
Whitman College, B.A. 1964 (economics);
Harvard U., M.B.A. 1966, J.D. 1969

MILITARY SERVICE
Army, 1970-72

CAREER
Nursery company executive; wood products company executive; White House aide; lawyer

POLITICAL HIGHLIGHTS
Democratic nominee for U.S. Senate, 1996

ELECTION RESULTS

2008 GENERAL

Walt Minnick (D)	175,898	50.6%
Bill Sali (R)	171,687	49.4%

2008 PRIMARY

Walt Minnick (D)	unopposed

IDAHO 1

West – Nampa, Panhandle, part of Boise

From its smokestack-shaped panhandle that opens into British Columbia in the north, the 1st District travels 500 miles south to the Nevada state line, bordering both Washington and Oregon to the west. Rural and rugged, the 1st features rivers, canyons and the trails that Lewis and Clark traveled as they sought a route to the Pacific Ocean.

The most populated region of the rapidly growing district includes part of Boise, as well as suburban Meridian and Nampa, in Ada and Canyon counties. The Boise area has a diverse economy that includes technology, agriculture, manufacturing, construction and health services. Urbanization has brought the traffic congestion and environmental concerns common to other cities to this once pristine landscape.

Higher education jobs and the timber sector drive the midsize cities and heavily forested counties in the center of the district. In the northern part of the district, Coeur d'Alene runs on mining, call center and tourism jobs.

The traditionally Republican district's Democratic core is shifting from its former base near Coeur d'Alene south to Latah and Nez Perce counties, near Lewiston and the University of Idaho's main campus in Moscow. Only two Democrats have held the U.S. House seat since 1967, and Republican John McCain took 62 percent of the district's presidential vote in 2008, winning every county in the 1st except Latah.

MAJOR INDUSTRY
Technology, manufacturing, timber

CITIES
Boise City (pt.), 59,680; Nampa, 51,867; Meridian, 34,919; Coeur d'Alene, 34,514

NOTABLE
Near Riggins in Idaho County, Hells Canyon separates Idaho from Oregon and is the nation's deepest river gorge.

Rep. Mike Simpson (R)

Elected 1998; 6th term

CAPITOL OFFICE
225-5531
www.house.gov/simpson
2312 Rayburn Bldg. 20515-1202; fax 225-8216

COMMITTEES
Appropriations
Budget

RESIDENCE
Idaho Falls

BORN
Sept. 8, 1950; Burley, Idaho

RELIGION
Mormon

FAMILY
Wife, Kathy Simpson

EDUCATION
Utah State U., attended 1968-72 (pre-dentistry);
Washington U. (Mo.), D.M.D. 1977; Utah State U.,
B.S. 2002 (pre-dentistry)

CAREER
Dentist

POLITICAL HIGHLIGHTS
Blackfoot City Council, 1980-84; Idaho House,
1984-98 (Speaker, 1992-98)

ELECTION RESULTS

2008 GENERAL
Mike Simpson (R)	205,777	71.0%
Deborah Holmes (D)	83,878	29.0%

2008 PRIMARY
Mike Simpson (R)	49,586	85.2%
Jack Wayne Chappell (R)	4,900	8.4%
Gregory Nemitz (R)	3,747	6.4%

2006 GENERAL
Mike Simpson (R)	132,262	62.0%
Jim Hansen (D)	73,441	34.4%
Cameron Forth (I)	5,113	2.4%
Travis J. Hedrick (CNSTP)	2,516	1.2%

PREVIOUS WINNING PERCENTAGES
2004 (71%); 2002 (68%); 2000 (71%); 1998 (53%)

Simpson's deeply conservative leanings — he is anti-abortion, anti-regulation and anti-tax — are no obstacle to working with Democrats on the collegial Appropriations Committee. Rare are the hearings when he doesn't at least once let out a loud and deep laugh, either while talking to colleagues before getting started or in response to a remark during the meeting.

"I can sometimes work better with some of the Democrats than I could with some of the Republicans," Simpson said. With "most people in this body, if you are not too partisan, they don't get too partisan with you and they appreciate just being able to work with issues," he added. He estimates there are about 20 hard-liners on either side of the aisle who "just make the debates very partisan. I think that hurts the institution."

Simpson prefers to try to understand the point of view of those who differ with him. Since the days when he served in the Idaho House, Simpson has kept in his office a 12-point set of "Simpson's Rules," which include "hear both sides before judging" and "never, never make an enemy needlessly." In his quest to understand other viewpoints, he briefly joined the American Civil Liberties Union (ACLU) and the Idaho Conservation League, and he regularly attends meetings with environmental groups that disagree with him.

Simpson, who also serves on the Budget Committee, was one of 48 Republicans to vote for pay-as-you-go rules that Democrats set in 2007. Those rules require all tax cuts or new entitlement spending to be offset with equal tax increases or spending reductions to avoid adding to the deficit. Later that year, he joined Democrats in an unsuccessful effort to override George W. Bush's vetoes of the fiscal 2008 Labor, Health and Human Services, and Education spending bill and a bill to expand the State Children's Health Insurance Program, which covers children from low-income families that do not qualify for Medicaid — a measure he backed again in early 2009 when it became law.

He also broke with many conservatives to support two $700 billion proposals — the second of which became law — in fall 2008 to aid the ailing financial industry. "I am convinced that action is a necessary evil in order to keep small businesses afloat, keep retirees from losing their life savings and help end the growing credit crisis we now face," he said.

Nevertheless, in early 2009 he opposed a $410 billion catchall spending bill as well as President Obama's $787 billion economic stimulus bill. "I cannot support the astronomical amount of money that is being thrown at this problem with very little thought and no debate," he said of his stimulus vote.

Simpson is not apt to criticize his colleagues, but he will if he thinks they're out of line. At the start of the 110th Congress (2007-08), Republicans complained loudly as the Democrats created one big, unamendable package of the remaining fiscal 2007 spending bills that GOP leaders had left unfinished the year before. Simpson was the only Republican to vote for the rule governing debate of the legislation and one of a handful opposing procedural protest votes that Republicans forced. "I have a really hard time criticizing the Democrats in general when it's a result of our inability to pass the budget," he said.

Simpson originally won his seat on Appropriations in the 108th Congress (2003-04). In the 111th Congress (2009-10), Simpson is the ranking Republican on the Interior-Environment Appropriations Subcommittee and a member of the Energy and Water Development panel. He advocates an expansion of nuclear energy technologies and the development of a new generation of nuclear reactors.

Simpson will need all his consensus-building skills as he tries again to win enactment of legislation overhauling how public lands in central Idaho can be used. For years, he has been trying to push through a bill that would create three new wilderness areas while releasing other federal land for development. The House passed his measure in July 2006, but in December, at the end of the two-year Congress, it was removed at the last minute from a catchall tax bill as outgoing Speaker J. Dennis Hastert substituted some provisions aimed at helping his own state.

Simpson grew up in the eastern Idaho town of Blackfoot, where his father and uncle had a dental practice. He met his wife, Kathy, in high school. He was on the football team, and she was a cheerleader. They both attended Utah State University.

He received a dentistry degree from Washington University in St. Louis, but had left Utah State a few credits shy of his degree. Simpson finally collected his degree there in 2002, when a professor suggested he have some dental school credits transferred.

Returning to Blackfoot to join the family dental business, Simpson decided to run for a city council seat, a nonpartisan job, after he noticed that no one else was. He says his interest in politics was first sparked by a high school teacher who was a Democrat, but when he decided to run for the state legislature four years later, Simpson had to choose a party affiliation and concluded he was more comfortable with the GOP.

Simpson started out with a reputation as an occasionally angry maverick but mellowed and made a name for himself in Boise, rising through the ranks in the state House and serving as Speaker during his last six years there. He gave some thought to seeking the governorship in 1998 but decided against it when Republican Sen. Dirk Kempthorne chose to run. Republican Rep. Michael D. Crapo made a bid for Kempthorne's Senate seat, which created an opening for Simpson in the 2nd District. He won a four-way GOP primary despite criticism from social conservatives that he was insufficiently ardent on their issues.

During the campaign, Simpson was more worried about voters learning of his memberships in the ACLU and the Idaho Conservation League than of his use of marijuana in college 30 years earlier. He made no effort to hide that he is a lapsed Mormon who once smoked and still drinks occasionally, but these personal details seemed to have had little effect on the heavily Mormon, but also Republican, electorate. He went on to defeat conservative Democrat Richard Stallings, who had held the seat from 1985 to 1993, and has easily won re-election since.

KEY VOTES

2008

No Delay consideration of Colombia free-trade agreement

Yes Override Bush veto of federal farm and nutrition programs reauthorization bill

Yes Overhaul surveillance laws and permit dismissal of suits against companies that conducted warrantless wiretapping

No Grant mortgage relief to homeowners and funding for Fannie Mae and Freddie Mac

Yes Approve initial $700 billion program to stabilize financial markets

Yes Approve final $700 billion program to stabilize financial markets

No Provide $14 billion in loans to automakers

2007

Yes Increase minimum wage by $2.10 an hour

No Approve $124.2 billion in emergency war spending and set goal for redeployment of troops from Iraq

+ Reject federal contraceptive assistance to international family planning groups

Yes Override Bush veto of $23.2 billion water projects authorization bill

Yes Implement Peru free-trade agreement

Yes Approve energy policy overhaul with new fuel economy standards

Yes Clear $473.5 billion omnibus spending bill, including $70 billion for military operations

CQ VOTE STUDIES

	PARTY UNITY		PRESIDENTIAL SUPPORT	
	SUPPORT	OPPOSE	SUPPORT	OPPOSE
2008	92%	8%	62%	38%
2007	79%	21%	73%	27%
2006	95%	5%	89%	11%
2005	94%	6%	91%	9%
2004	94%	6%	79%	21%

INTEREST GROUPS

	AFL-CIO	ADA	CCUS	ACU
2008	27%	35%	94%	80%
2007	29%	20%	84%	72%
2006	21%	5%	93%	80%
2005	20%	10%	89%	92%
2004	7%	0%	95%	92%

IDAHO 2

East – Pocatello, Idaho Falls, part of Boise

Covering the Gem State's eastern and central portions, the 2nd includes most of Boise, a few midsize cities and a vast swath of agricultural land fed by the Snake River. The central and northern parts of the district are full of mountain ranges, rivers and fishing sites. Idaho's Sun Valley ski resort is located in the 2nd, and with natural wonders such as Shoshone Falls, the district attracts a steady stream of tourists. Waterfalls, snowmobile trails and spectacular views leave visitors with Idaho's motto, "Esto Perpetua" (Let it be perpetual), in mind.

Elmore County, in the district's west, is home to Mountain Home Air Force Base, but most of the district relies on agriculture — mainly potatoes, sugar beets and grain — and manufacturing and technology industries. Blackfoot, in Bingham County, is known as the potato-producing capital of the world, and eastern Idaho supplies about one-third of the nation's potato crop. The district also hosts technology firms, including Micron Technology, which is the state's largest private employer, and the Idaho National Laboratory nuclear research site near Idaho Falls.

Members of The Church of Jesus Christ of Latter-day Saints make up the district's largest religious group, and like most Mormon areas, the district is strongly conservative — eastern Idaho has been represented by a Mormon in the U.S. House since 1951. The district consistently supports Republicans in federal elections but can elect Democrats to the state legislature in the Boise area as well as in Blaine, Power and Bannock counties in the center of the 2nd. Blaine County, home to Sun Valley, is the only county to vote reliably for Democratic candidates in presidential elections. In 2008, Republican John McCain won the district with 61 percent of its presidential vote.

MAJOR INDUSTRY
Agriculture, food processing, tourism, technology

MILITARY BASES
Mountain Home Air Force Base, 4,173 military, 908 civilian (2009)

CITIES
Boise City (pt.), 126,107; Pocatello, 51,466; Idaho Falls, 50,730; Twin Falls, 34,469; Rexburg, 17,257

NOTABLE
Most of the commercial trout sold in the world are farmed in the Hagerman Valley near Twin Falls; Sun Valley was America's first ski resort.

Gov. Pat Quinn (D)

Assumed office: 2009
Length of term: 4 years
Term expires: 1/11
Salary: $156,091
Phone: (217) 782-0244

Residence: Chicago
Born: December 16, 1948; Chicago, Ill.
Religion: Roman Catholic
Family: Divorced; two children
Education: Georgetown U., B.A. 1971 (international economic affairs); Northwestern U., J.D. 1980
Career: Lawyer; college instructor; city government official; political activist; campaign and gubernatorial aide
Political highlights: Cook County Board of Tax Appeals, 1982-86; sought Democratic nomination for Ill. treasurer, 1986; Ill. treasurer, 1991-95; Democratic nominee for Ill. secretary of State, 1994; sought Democratic nomination for U.S. Senate, 1996; lieutenant governor, 2002-09

Recent election results:

2006 GENERAL

Rod R. Blagojevich (D)	1,736,731	49.8%
Judy Baar Topinka (R)	1,369,315	39.3%
Rich Whitney (GREEN)	361,336	10.4%

Lt. Gov. — Vacant *

* The attorney general is the next-highest ranking elected constitutional officer and would succeed Quinn in the case of a gubernatorial vacancy.

LEGISLATURE

General Assembly: January-May; meets in October or November to consider vetoes

Senate: 59 members, rotates between 2 and 4-year terms
2009 ratios: 37 D, 22 R; 46 men, 13 women
Salary: $67,836
Phone: (217) 782-5715

House: 118 members, 2-year terms
2009 ratios: 70 D, 48 R; 83 men, 35 women
Salary: $67,836
Phone: (217) 782-8223

TERM LIMITS

Governor: No
Senate: No
House: No

URBAN STATISTICS

CITY	POPULATION
Chicago	2,896,016
Rockford	150,115
Aurora	142,990
Naperville	128,358
Peoria	112,936

REGISTERED VOTERS

Voters do not register by party.

POPULATION

2008 population (est.)	12,901,563
2000 population	12,419,293
1990 population	11,430,602
Percent change (1990-2000)	+8.6%
Rank among states (2008)	5
Median age	34.7
Born in state	67.1%
Foreign born	12.3%
Violent crime rate	657/100,000
Poverty level	10.7%
Federal workers	91,284
Military	57,753

ELECTIONS

STATE ELECTION OFFICIAL
(217) 782-4141
DEMOCRATIC PARTY
(217) 546-7404
REPUBLICAN PARTY
(217) 525-0011

MISCELLANEOUS

Web: www.illinois.gov
Capital: Springfield

U.S. CONGRESS

Senate: 2 Democrats
House: 12 Democrats, 7 Republicans

2000 Census Statistics by District

DIST.	2008 VOTE FOR PRESIDENT OBAMA	MCCAIN	WHITE	BLACK	ASIAN	HISP	MEDIAN INCOME	WHITE COLLAR	BLUE COLLAR	SERVICE INDUSTRY	OVER 64	UNDER 18	COLLEGE EDUCATION	RURAL	SQ. MILES
1	87%	13%	27%	65%	1%	5%	$37,222	61%	22%	17%	13%	28%	19%	0%	98
2	90	10	26	62	1	10	$41,330	60	24	16	12	29	18	0	185
3	64	35	68	6	3	21	$48,048	58	28	14	14	26	21	0	124
4	85	13	18	4	7	74	$35,935	43	39	17	6	32	14	0	39
5	73	26	66	2	6	23	$48,531	65	22	14	12	20	34	0	57
6	56	43	75	3	8	12	$62,640	70	20	10	10	26	35	0	213
7	88	12	27	62	4	6	$40,361	71	16	14	10	27	32	0	56
8	56	43	79	3	6	11	$62,762	67	22	11	8	28	32	4	618
9	72	26	62	11	12	12	$46,531	70	16	14	16	21	40	0	75
10	61	38	75	5	6	12	$71,663	76	15	10	12	27	48	0	250
11	53	45	84	8	1	7	$47,800	55	30	15	12	27	19	22	4,241
12	56	43	80	16	1	2	$35,198	55	27	18	14	25	17	23	4,425
13	54	44	82	5	7	5	$71,686	75	16	9	9	28	42	1	355
14	55	44	74	5	2	18	$56,314	60	27	13	9	29	26	14	2,852
15	48	50	88	6	2	2	$38,583	58	27	15	14	23	23	36	10,072

2000 Census Statistics by District

DIST.	2008 VOTE FOR PRESIDENT OBAMA	MCCAIN	WHITE	BLACK	ASIAN	HISP	MEDIAN INCOME	WHITE COLLAR	BLUE COLLAR	SERVICE INDUSTRY	OVER 64	UNDER 18	COLLEGE EDUCATION	RURAL	SQ. MILES
16	53%	46%	86%	5%	1%	6%	$48,960	57%	30%	13%	12%	28%	21%	22%	4,098
17	56	42	87	7	1	4	$35,066	52	31	18	16	24	15	29	8,120
18	48	50	90	6	1	2	$41,934	59	25	15	15	24	21	32	8,186
19	44	54	94	3	0	1	$38,955	55	29	16	15	24	17	48	11,519
STATE	62	37	68	15	3	12	$46,590	62	24	14	12	26	26	12	55,584
U.S.	53	46	69	12	4	13	$41,994	60	25	15	12	26	24	21	3,537,438

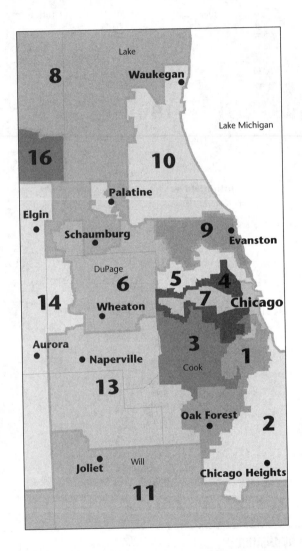

Sen. Richard J. Durbin (D)

Elected 1996; 3rd term

CAPITOL OFFICE
224-2152
durbin.senate.gov
309 Hart Bldg. 20510-1304; fax 228-0400

COMMITTEES
Appropriations
(Financial Services - chairman)
Judiciary
(Human Rights - chairman)
Rules & Administration
Joint Library

RESIDENCE
Springfield

BORN
Nov. 21, 1944; East St. Louis, Ill.

RELIGION
Roman Catholic

FAMILY
Wife, Loretta Durbin; three children
(one deceased)

EDUCATION
Georgetown U., B.S.F.S. 1966 (international affairs & economics), J.D. 1969

CAREER
Gubernatorial and state legislative aide; lawyer

POLITICAL HIGHLIGHTS
Democratic nominee for Ill. Senate, 1976;
Democratic nominee for lieutenant governor, 1978;
U.S. House, 1983-97

ELECTION RESULTS

2008 GENERAL

Richard J. Durbin (D)	3,615,844	67.8%
Steve Sauerberg (R)	1,520,621	28.5%
Kathy Cummings (GREEN)	119,135	2.2%

2008 PRIMARY

Richard J. Durbin (D)	unopposed

PREVIOUS WINNING PERCENTAGES
2002 (60%); 1996 (56%); 1994 House Election (55%); 1992 House Election (57%); 1990 House Election (66%); 1988 House Election (69%); 1986 House Election (68%); 1984 House Election (61%); 1982 House Election (50%)

As Senate majority whip, the savvy, industrious Durbin is one of the most powerful leaders in Congress. But he has been overshadowed in the public eye by Barack Obama, first his home-state colleague and now his commander in chief. Rather than resent the younger man's rapid political rise, Durbin has promoted it.

"I think everybody in their lives is going to be around others who have more talent or different talents," he told the Chicago Tribune in late 2007. "It may bother some, but it doesn't bother me. I've had a pretty good run here as the senior senator, smack-dab in the middle of the most important discussions in Congress."

In his party's No. 2 Senate leadership post, Durbin has often outshone his boss, Majority Leader Harry Reid of Nevada, a skilled inside player whose public persona is decidedly drab. Durbin has the build of a tenor and patented floor moves of a leading man. He almost always directly addresses a C-SPAN camera, speaking in conversational tones and swiveling periodically to play to the gallery with a sweep of his arms.

But he has a regular-guy manner, with a knack for matching his rhetoric to the occasion — catchy when the subject is broad political themes, detailed when it is the nuts and bolts of legislation. He can shift gears between the two in a way few other lawmakers can, using humor to spice up arcane arguments. "There is a provision I have in there which the mortgage bankers hate like the devil hates holy water," Durbin said in 2008 while pushing unsuccessfully to allow bankruptcy judges to modify the terms of a homeowner's mortgage.

Apart from his whip duties as a vote counter and sentry against GOP procedural ambushes, Durbin worked to drive Obama's priorities as both a White House aspirant and occupant. He attacked Obama's rival in the presidential race, Sen. John McCain of Arizona, as a clone of George W. Bush; "Sen. McCain's tax plan is George Bush's fiscal policy on steroids," Durbin gibed. And when Obama's economic initiatives met with sustained Republican opposition in early 2009, Durbin took the minority to task. "The Republicans have to decide if they want to be part of this discussion," he said. "If their idea is to say no to everything, then it will be very difficult to achieve the goals the American people want."

His friendship with Reid dates back to their early days as House freshmen in 1983. Durbin said he has an open invitation to attend any meetings Reid has with Democratic senators; Reid called his handpicked sidekick "one of the nicest and kindest members of the Senate."

Of course, nice guys don't always finish first on Capitol Hill. But Durbin's earnest, attentive style serves him well as a party leader, and his reputation for solving problems has helped make him a favorite to eventually succeed Reid, who is five years older and faces re-election in 2010. Durbin has refused to discuss his aspirations in ascending the leadership ladder." I don't think it's good for the caucus," he said.

Like Reid, Durbin can be combative, but he has a cool demeanor off the floor and often uses humor to disarm colleagues. He jokes about the "added burden" he endures living and working with a potential future leadership rival, Democratic Sen. Charles E. Schumer of New York. They share a Capitol Hill row house with two other veteran Democrats, Reps. Bill Delahunt of Massachusetts and George Miller of California. The décor, which Durbin compares to "a Goodwill store on drugs," is so notorious that it merited a New York Times write-up and visit from an ABC News TV crew in early 2007. Durbin proudly told ABC about the night he killed a large rat with a golf club. "I'm not a good golfer," he quipped. "I had to three-putt."

Durbin was a natural choice for whip when Reid moved up to replace Minority Leader Tom Daschle after the South Dakotan was defeated in the 2004 election. Liberals who dominate the Democratic caucus were initially wary of Reid, a Mormon who sometimes votes with Republicans on social issues. But they trusted Durbin as one of their own. He had honed his leadership skills under Daschle, heading a group of senators who met weekly to set the party's message.

Durbin's people skills, however, were tested by the furor surrounding Obama's replacement in the Senate. Illinois Democratic Gov. Rod R. Blagojevich appointed Roland W. Burris in late 2008 after the governor was accused of trying to sell the seat but before he was impeached and removed from office. Burris became the subject of an investigation by the Senate Committee on Ethics about whether he lied under oath about his contacts with Blagojevich before his appointment. Durbin said he was "disappointed" by Burris' conflicting statements and suggested in February 2009 that he resign.

Durbin looks out for Illinois' interests from his seat on the Appropriations Committee, where he chairs the Financial Services Subcommittee. He is well-positioned to weigh in on proposals to merge the Commodity Futures Trading Commission with the Securities Exchange Commission. The former has been criticized for being a weak regulator of traders for an important constituent, the CME Group, formed from the 2007 merger of the Chicago Mercantile Exchange and Chicago Board of Trade.

From his seat on the Judiciary Committee, Durbin has pushed for tighter oversight of temporary work visas and for a path to citizenship for the children of illegal immigrants who attend college or join the military. After Pennsylvania GOP Sen. Arlen Specter switched parties in 2009, Durbin agreed to let him chair the committee's panel on crime and drugs.

He led a successful push in the 110th Congress (2007-08) to cut interest rates on federal student loans and helped win enactment of tighter food safety regulations, a new countercyclical revenue safety net for farmers and broader authority for the Consumer Product Safety Commission to test toys and ban lead in children's products.

In the late 1980s, he led the successful effort to ban smoking on domestic airline flights. And in the 110th Congress he helped persuade the Rules Committee, on which he serves, to ban the sale of tobacco products in the Senate and to close two designated smoking rooms in Senate office buildings.

His concern is deeply personal. The youngest of three brothers raised in East St. Louis by an Irish-American father who was a railroad night watchman and a Lithuanian-born mother who was a switchboard operator, Durbin was just 14 years old when his chain-smoking father died of lung cancer. "I think it made me fight a little harder," he said.

Durbin caught the politics bug in college, when he was an intern for Democratic Sen. Paul Douglas, whose seat he now holds. He held long conversations with Douglas, who used to tell Durbin stories as the young intern handed him letters to sign. One of Durbin's sons is named after Douglas.

After law school, Durbin returned home and held a number of jobs in politics, including state Senate parliamentarian and aide to Lt. Gov. Paul Simon, who later became a senator and presidential candidate. In 1982, Durbin unseated 11-term GOP Rep. Paul N. Findley by 1,410 votes in a Springfield-based House district. He won re-election six times.

When his old mentor, Simon, announced he would not seek re-election in 1996, Durbin got into the race and won by 15 percentage points against conservative state Rep. Al Salvi. With Illinois tilting increasingly Democratic, Durbin coasted to a second term in 2002 and a third six years later.

KEY VOTES

2008
Yes Prohibit discrimination based on genetic information
Yes Reauthorize farm and nutrition programs for five years
Yes Limit debate on "cap and trade" system for greenhouse gas emissions
Yes Allow lawsuits against companies that participated in warrantless wiretapping
Yes Limit debate on a bill to block a scheduled cut in Medicare payments to doctors
Yes Grant mortgage relief to homeowners and funding for Fannie Mae and Freddie Mac
Yes Approve a nuclear cooperation agreement with India
Yes Approve final $700 billion program to stabilize financial markets
Yes Allow consideration of a $14 billion auto industry loan package

2007
Yes Increase minimum wage by $2.10 an hour
Yes Limit debate on a comprehensive immigration bill
Yes Overhaul congressional lobbying and ethics rules for members and their staffs
Yes Limit debate on considering a bill to add House seats for the District of Columbia and Utah
Yes Limit debate on restoring habeas corpus rights to detainees
Yes Mandate minimum breaks for troops between deployments to Iraq or Afghanistan
Yes Override Bush veto of $23.2 billion water projects authorization bill
No   Confirm Michael B. Mukasey as attorney general
Yes Limit debate on an energy policy overhaul containing $21.8 billion in tax incentives and reduced oil and gas subsidies

CQ VOTE STUDIES

	PARTY UNITY		PRESIDENTIAL SUPPORT	
	SUPPORT	OPPOSE	SUPPORT	OPPOSE
2008	98%	2%	31%	69%
2007	98%	2%	36%	64%
2006	98%	2%	47%	53%
2005	99%	1%	33%	67%
2004	96%	4%	54%	46%
2003	97%	3%	46%	54%
2002	97%	3%	67%	33%
2001	95%	5%	62%	38%
2000	99%	1%	97%	3%
1999	95%	5%	87%	13%

INTEREST GROUPS

	AFL-CIO	ADA	CCUS	ACU
2008	100%	100%	63%	4%
2007	100%	95%	45%	0%
2006	100%	100%	45%	4%
2005	100%	100%	28%	0%
2004	92%	95%	47%	4%
2003	85%	95%	35%	10%
2002	100%	95%	50%	0%
2001	94%	95%	31%	0%
2000	75%	95%	50%	4%
1999	89%	100%	35%	4%

Sen. Roland W. Burris (D)

Appointed January 2009; 1st term

CAPITOL OFFICE
224-2854
burris.senate.gov
387 Russell Bldg. 20510-1305; fax 228-4260

COMMITTEES
Armed Services
Homeland Security & Governmental Affairs
Veterans' Affairs

RESIDENCE
Chicago

BORN
Aug. 3, 1937; Centralia, Ill.

RELIGION
Baptist

FAMILY
Wife, Berlean M. Burris; two children

EDUCATION
Southern Illinois U., Carbondale, B.A. 1959
(government); Howard U., LL.B. 1963

CAREER
Lawyer; lobbyist; college instructor; civil rights
nonprofit director; bank executive

POLITICAL HIGHLIGHTS
Sought Democratic nomination for Ill. House,
1968; Department of General Services director,
1973-77; sought Democratic nomination for Ill.
comptroller, 1976; Ill. comptroller, 1979-91; sought
Democratic nomination for U.S. Senate, 1984;
Ill. attorney general, 1991-95; sought Democratic
nomination for governor, 1994; independent
candidate for mayor of Chicago, 1995; sought
Democratic nomination for governor, 1998, 2002

A self-assured longtime public official, Burris embarked on an unexpected second act in his political career when he was sworn in to fill President Obama's old Senate seat. Like his predecessor, Burris is the chamber's only African-American member. He aligns with the more liberal wing of the party and supported all of Obama's early legislative agenda. But Democrats aren't entirely comfortable with his presence.

His early months in office found him enmeshed in controversy surrounding his appointment by then-Illinois Democratic Gov. Rod R. Blagojevich, raising questions into whether — if Burris survived criminal and ethical investigations — he would have hope of making it through a 2010 election if he chooses to submit his name. Through it all, he remained undeterred, turning aside pleas from his own state colleagues to resign.

Blagojevich had appointed Burris to the seat just three weeks after the governor had been arrested and taken from his home in handcuffs, facing charges for alleged corrupt activities that included asking for fundraising and other favors in exchange for an appointment to the Senate seat. Blagojevich was subsequently impeached and removed from office, and a federal grand jury in April 2009 indicted him on 16 felony counts.

The entire Democratic caucus in the Senate asked Burris to refuse the appointment, but he ignored them. Though he had lost a slew of bids for higher office, Burris made it clear he viewed himself as worthy of the job. A former Illinois comptroller and attorney general, Burris described himself as "the most qualified person in the state of Illinois." He has never lacked self-confidence; he has built a large mausoleum for himself, carved with the words "Trail Blazer" and a list of his accomplishments.

Soon after being sworn in, however, another wave of controversy engulfed him. Reports revealed Burris had said under oath at a January 2009 hearing of the state House Impeachment Committee that he hadn't spoken to anyone associated with the governor about the seat. But in an affidavit released the next month, he acknowledged speaking repeatedly with the former governor's brother about fundraising. The Select Ethics Committee immediately began a preliminary inquiry — akin to a grand jury investigation — into discrepancies in his testimony.

Meanwhile, lawmakers learned the names of lobbying clients Burris declared to the state panel didn't match those on records he filed over the last decade with Illinois and Chicago agencies. Several of Burris' Illinois Democratic colleagues, including Sen. Richard J. Durbin and Gov. Pat Quinn — Blagojevich's replacement — issued calls for his resignation. Burris, however, maintained his innocence and pledged to cooperate with the committee and the inquiry of a county prosecutor in Illinois for possible perjury. He also asked the ethics committee in March 2009 for permission to create a legal defense fund to allow him to raise money, telling Durbin in private that his legal costs had already reached several hundred thousand dollars.

His appointment — and a subsequent controversial appointment by New York Democratic Gov. David A. Paterson to fill Sen. Hillary Rodham Clinton's old seat — led some lawmakers to consider banning governors from appointing senators.

He was given a seat on the Armed Services Committee; he told the Chicago Tribune he would support Obama's pledge to withdraw combat troops from Iraq while increasing the military presence in Afghanistan. His other assignments are Homeland Security and Governmental Affairs and Veterans' Affairs.

Burris also supports a ban on assault weapons and an expansion of O'Hare International Airport that has been controversial in the Chicago suburbs.

Burris supported Obama's early initiatives, including an expansion of the State Children's Health Insurance Program and a $787 billion economic stimulus law. He also backed a $410 billion catchall spending bill for fiscal 2009 and Obama's $3.56 trillion budget blueprint for fiscal 2010. After taking office, though, he said Obama should not rely on him to be a "rubber stamp."

Like other lawmakers, he repeatedly highlighted the release of funds from the stimulus bill that would aid projects in his state. He also went on a 10-city "economic tour" in early April, though it seemed to attract little media attention compared to the ongoing investigation of his appointment.

Burris' personal reputation was seen as free of controversy at the time he was appointed, though his accomplishments in Illinois were viewed as fairly undistinguished. His political base is in Chicago, where he enjoys support from the city's black voters in particular.

He was born in the small southern Illinois town of Centralia, and earned a degree in government from Southern Illinois University in Carbondale. He spent a year studying international law in Germany before moving to Washington to attend law school at Howard University.

After a stint as a federal bank examiner, Burris became a bank vice president in Illinois. He made a bid for the state House in 1968 in which he finished last. He later served in the Cabinet of Gov. Daniel Walker, who presided from 1973 to 1977. He made another failed bid for office in 1976, this time to be Illinois comptroller. He won the job two years later, becoming the first African-American elected to a statewide constitutional office in Illinois.

Hankering for higher office, he set his sights on Washington in 1984, entering the five-candidate Democratic primary for the seat of Republican Sen. Charles Percy. Burris did well among Chicago primary voters but performed poorly outside the city, finishing a distant second to Paul Simon, who went on to defeat Percy that November.

He was elected state attorney general in 1990 and served one term. But in 1994, 1998 and 2002, he was defeated in Democratic gubernatorial primaries (in the third try, he was aligned against Blagojevich), and he struggled each time to win enough votes outside of Chicago. He also waged an unsuccessful campaign, as an independent candidate, to unseat Democratic Chicago Mayor Richard M. Daley in 1995.

In 2002, Burris registered as a state-level lobbyist as chairman and chief executive officer of Burris & Lebed Consulting. The company also lobbies at the federal level for MicroSun Technologies on defense, manufacturing and science issues, but it fell out of compliance with federal lobbying rules requiring it to file quarterly reports on how much Burris and other principals were being paid. Burris' clients at the state level included Commonwealth Edison Co., Edusoft Corp. and the Council of Independent Tobacco Manufacturers of America.

Burris will have a short amount of time to prove himself if he decides to run in the 2010 election. When Illinois joined the "Super Tuesday" pileup of states that moved their 2008 presidential primaries up to Feb. 5, it also moved its primaries for other federal and state offices up to the first Tuesday in February.

That means Burris has only until the candidate filing deadline in November 2009 to persuade party officials he can win a full term — and to dissuade other Democrats from challenging him. He had jumped a line of political heavyweights who may or may not be willing to shelve their own Senate ambitions, including at least three other prominent African-Americans: Chicago-based Reps. Danny K. Davis and Jesse L. Jackson Jr. (although Jackson came under investigation for communications with Blagojevich) and state Senate President Emil Jones.

Rep. Bobby L. Rush (D)

Elected 1992; 9th term

CAPITOL OFFICE
225-4372
www.house.gov/rush
2416 Rayburn Bldg. 20515-1301; fax 226-0333

COMMITTEES
Energy & Commerce
(Commerce, Trade & Consumer Protection -
chairman)

RESIDENCE
Chicago

BORN
Nov. 23, 1946; Albany, Ga.

RELIGION
Protestant

FAMILY
Wife, Carolyn Rush; five children (one deceased)

EDUCATION
Roosevelt U., B.A. 1973 (political science);
U. of Illinois, Chicago, attended 1975-77 (political
science), M.A. 1994 (political science); McCormick
Seminary, M.A. 1998 (theological studies)

MILITARY SERVICE
Army, 1963-68

CAREER
Insurance broker; political activist

POLITICAL HIGHLIGHTS
Candidate for Chicago City Council, 1975;
sought Democratic nomination for Ill. House,
1978; Chicago City Council, 1983-93; candidate
for mayor of Chicago, 1999

ELECTION RESULTS

2008 GENERAL

Bobby L. Rush (D)	233,036	85.9%
Antoine Members (R)	38,361	14.1%

2008 PRIMARY

Bobby L. Rush (D)	134,343	87.5%
William Walls III (D)	19,272	12.5%

2006 GENERAL

Bobby L. Rush (D)	146,623	84.1%
Jason E. Tabor (R)	27,804	15.9%

PREVIOUS WINNING PERCENTAGES
2004 (85%); 2002 (81%); 2000 (88%); 1998 (87%);
1996 (86%); 1994 (76%); 1992 (83%)

Rush's life took numerous twists and turns before he landed in Congress, and it continues to do so. A former Black Panther and the only politician ever to defeat Barack Obama in an election, he is both an inspiring leader for liberal and low-income voters and a lightning rod for critics who accuse him of unfairly injecting race into politics.

Rush is among the most liberal House members, active in both the Progressive Caucus and the Congressional Black Caucus. His main goal in Congress, he says, is to better the lives of his South Side Chicago constituents, among the city's poorest residents. "These are difficult times, which require a strong and timely response to restore our ailing economy and help the unemployed and low-income families through this economic crisis," he said in January 2009 in supporting what became President Obama's $787 billion economic stimulus law.

He has worked assiduously to help consumers as chairman of the Energy and Commerce panel on Commerce, Trade and Consumer Protection. He has led the panel in debates on such varied topics as lead in children's toys, thoroughbred horse racing, computer "spyware," drug use in sports and the influence of explicit rap music. And he has put forward many of his own bills, including legislation to establish safety requirements for children's products and to modernize the Consumer Product Safety Commission (CPSC), which became law in 2008.

Rush was forced to step back from his work in February 2008 after learning he had a cancerous tumor on his salivary gland. The cancer was localized, and the tumor was surgically removed the next month. Subsequent radiation treatment and recovery kept him away from Capitol Hill for about five months. He returned just before Congress left on its August recess, in time to vote on the final version of the CPSC bill.

He missed more than 450 roll call votes on the House floor during his convalescence, but made efforts to stay involved. His staff inserted announcements in the Congressional Record about how he would have voted on most of the substantive votes he missed. When he returned, he urged Obama and his GOP presidential rival, Arizona Sen. John McCain, to make national health care a top priority. "I'm quite disappointed with the whole political scene, where neither of the candidates has shown [a] political commitment to nationalized health care," he said.

But the attention those comments received paled in comparison to the controversy he stoked following Obama's election to the presidency. Illinois Democratic Gov. Rod R. Blagojevich was subsequently impeached and removed from office for a series of alleged crimes that included allegedly trying to sell Obama's Senate seat, but not before the governor appointed former Illinois Attorney General Roland W. Burris.

Other Illinois lawmakers immediately called on Burris to refuse the appointment because of the allegations against the governor. But Rush became Burris' most outspoken defender, asking reporters not to "hang or lynch" the man who would be the Senate's only African-American. He later called the Senate "the last bastion of plantation politics." His invocation of race led Senate Democrats to back away from challenging Burris' appointment and provoked an outpouring of criticism; Illinois Democratic Sen. Richard J. Durbin said Rush's comments "were painful and hurtful."

Rush had served six months in prison for illegal possession of weapons when he was in his 20s. But in Congress he has been a strong advocate of strict controls on firearms — a position that was further strengthened when his son Huey (named after Black Panther leader Huey Newton) was shot and killed in a Chicago sidewalk robbery in 1999. Shortly before the assailants were convicted in 2002, Rush's nephew was charged with murder in what police said was a drug deal gone bad. "These kinds of stories have no winners, only losers, and occur far too often in our communities," Rush said.

He introduced a bill in January 2009 to set up a national handgun registry maintained by the Attorney General's Office. During his lengthy convalescence, Rush directed his staff to prepare brief tributes to gun victims, which were inserted in the Congressional Record every few days under the heading "The Daily 45," after the 45 people killed by guns on an average day in the United States. He also has spoken out against the death penalty, particularly in Illinois, where several people on death row subsequently were proved innocent.

Born in southern Georgia, Rush grew up in Chicago, where his mother moved when he was 7 after her marriage ended. She worked as a GOP activist because whites dominated the city's Democratic machine. Rush was a Boy Scout in an integrated troop and later volunteered for the Army. When he became disillusioned by a commanding officer he viewed as racist, he joined the Student Non-Violent Coordinating Committee, then went AWOL after the assassination of Martin Luther King Jr. (He was later honorably discharged.)

He joined the Black Panthers and soon founded the Illinois chapter. He coordinated a Panthers-run program that provided free breakfasts for children and a clinic that developed a mass screening effort for sickle cell anemia.

By 1974 Rush had quit the Panthers and earned a political science degree from Chicago's Roosevelt University. After graduation he sold insurance and entered politics. He won a 1983 election to the city council on the coattails of 1st District Democratic Rep. Harold Washington, who was elected in an upset as Chicago's first black mayor.

Rush ousted Democratic Rep. Charles A. Hayes in 1992. Since then, he has won every general election with ease. However, he had a poor showing when he sought to oust Democrat Richard M. Daley as mayor in 1999, receiving just 28 percent in the primary.

Following that defeat, Rush faced an emboldened field of primary challengers in 2000 but took 61 percent of the vote. Among the aspirants was Obama, then a state senator, who said at the time that Rush "exemplifies a politics that is reactive, that waits for crises to happen then holds a press conference, and hasn't been particularly effective at building broad-based coalitions." Rush dismissed Obama as an "educated fool" with an "ivory tower" outlook.

KEY VOTES

2008
+ Delay consideration of Colombia free-trade agreement
+ Override Bush veto of federal farm and nutrition programs reauthorization bill
− Overhaul surveillance laws and permit dismissal of suits against companies that conducted warrantless wiretapping
+ Grant mortgage relief to homeowners and funding for Fannie Mae and Freddie Mac
No Approve initial $700 billion program to stabilize financial markets
Yes Approve final $700 billion program to stabilize financial markets
Yes Provide $14 billion in loans to automakers

2007
Yes Increase minimum wage by $2.10 an hour
Yes Approve $124.2 billion in emergency war spending and set goal for redeployment of troops from Iraq
No Reject federal contraceptive assistance to international family planning groups
Yes Override Bush veto of $23.2 billion water projects authorization bill
No Implement Peru free-trade agreement
Yes Approve energy policy overhaul with new fuel economy standards
Yes Clear $473.5 billion omnibus spending bill, including $70 billion for military operations

CQ VOTE STUDIES

	PARTY UNITY		PRESIDENTIAL SUPPORT	
	SUPPORT	OPPOSE	SUPPORT	OPPOSE
2008	99%	1%	29%	71%
2007	98%	2%	5%	95%
2006	93%	7%	32%	68%
2005	97%	3%	20%	80%
2004	97%	3%	21%	79%

INTEREST GROUPS

	AFL-CIO	ADA	CCUS	ACU
2008	100%	30%	67%	13%
2007	100%	100%	60%	0%
2006	92%	80%	46%	9%
2005	100%	100%	44%	4%
2004	100%	100%	24%	0%

ILLINOIS 1

Chicago — South Side and southwest

The nation's first black-majority district, the 1st covers much of Chicago's South Side. Starting at 26th Street in the historic black hub, the district spreads out to the south and west through residential areas. It narrows through the southwestern neighborhoods of Washington Heights, Beverly and Morgan Park, then expands outside the city to scoop up close-in suburbs as it extends south to Cook County's border with Will County. About 70 percent of the 1st's residents live in Chicago.

The 1st has some of the city's largest subsidized housing projects, and roughly 20 percent of its population lives in poverty. Its median household income, at just more than $37,000, is one of the lowest in Illinois. Many people work in the service industry, and residents endure long commutes. Despite the presence of the University of Chicago in the Hyde Park neighborhood, only 19 percent of residents have a college education.

The district has several solidly middle-class black neighborhoods, including Chatham and Avalon Park. Bronzeville, in the district's north end, has attracted many black-owned businesses and young black professionals who move in and rehabilitate old houses instead of leaving the city. This has led to a shortage of available housing for poorer residents. The area is trying to use its rich history to attract tourism by refurbishing old buildings, investing in heritage sites and promoting its jazz and blues tradition.

The 1st, represented by black congressmen since 1929, has the nation's largest percentage of African-American residents at 65 percent. The district's Hispanic population is growing, and white voters are concentrated outside the city and in some southwest neighborhoods. In the 2008 presidential election, the strongly Democratic parts of the district within Chicago gave hometown candidate Barack Obama 98 percent of the vote, but he won relatively less support in parts of the 1st outside of the city (59 percent). Obama took 87 percent of the district's vote in 2008.

MAJOR INDUSTRY
Hospitals, higher education, manufacturing

CITIES
Chicago (pt.), 451,488; Oak Forest (pt.), 28,041; Orland Park (pt.), 27,342; Tinley Park (pt.), 23,863; Blue Island (pt.), 23,436

NOTABLE
The first self-sustaining nuclear reaction took place at the University of Chicago under the stands at Stagg Field in 1942.

Rep. Jesse L. Jackson Jr. (D)

Elected December 1995; 7th full term

CAPITOL OFFICE
225-0773
www.house.gov/jackson
2419 Rayburn Bldg. 20515-1302; fax 225-0899

COMMITTEES
Appropriations

RESIDENCE
Chicago

BORN
March 11, 1965; Greenville, S.C.

RELIGION
Baptist

FAMILY
Wife, Sandi Jackson; two children

EDUCATION
North Carolina A&T U., B.S. 1987 (business management); Chicago Theological Seminary, M.A. 1990 (theology); U. of Illinois, J.D. 1993

CAREER
Political activist

POLITICAL HIGHLIGHTS
No previous office

ELECTION RESULTS

2008 GENERAL

Jesse L. Jackson Jr. (D)	251,052	89.4%
Anthony W. Williams (R)	29,721	10.6%

2008 PRIMARY

Jesse L. Jackson Jr. (D)	unopposed

2006 GENERAL

Jesse L. Jackson Jr. (D)	146,347	84.8%
Robert Belin (R)	20,395	11.8%
Anthony W. Williams (LIBERT)	5,748	3.3%

PREVIOUS WINNING PERCENTAGES
2004 (88%); 2002 (82%); 2000 (90%); 1998 (89%); 1996 (94%); 1995 Special Election (76%)

The ambitious Jackson benefits from a unique combination of brains, connections and old-fashioned Chicago political clout. He is the son of a famous civil rights leader and a friend and political confidant of Barack Obama, serving as a national co-chairman of Obama's 2008 presidential campaign.

Jackson was considered a leading contender to replace Obama in the Senate in the 111th Congress (2009-10). But his ambitions were upended in December 2008 when Illinois Democratic Gov. Rod R. Blagojevich was indicted for allegedly trying to solicit bribes in return for the Senate appointment. The Justice Department's indictment mentioned a candidate No. 5 whom Blagojevich had said, in wiretapped conversations, was willing to raise money for him in exchange for the seat. Federal authorities later told reporters Jackson was that candidate.

Jackson immediately denied he offered Blagojevich anything and said he received assurances from federal investigators he wasn't a target of the probe. But it continues to cloud his future. "I'm fighting now for my character, and I'm also fighting for my life," Jackson told CNN in the midst of the uproar. "When the process is over, I profoundly hope that the people will give me my name back."

The Jackson family remains popular back home on the South Side of Chicago. Chicagoans have started referring to Jackson and his wife, Sandi, as "The Jackson Two" since she was elected alderman in Chicago's 7th Ward in 2007, defeating Darcel Beavers, the daughter of a local powerhouse, Cook County Board member William Beavers. In February 2008, Sandi Jackson ousted Beavers himself in the race for Democratic committeeman, a job that gives her a seat inside the councils of the vaunted Cook County party organization.

In Washington, Jackson rallied behind Obama's early efforts to revive the economy and advocated for liberal causes ranging from free health care for children to equal pay for women. He continues to hold considerable power on Capitol Hill via his seat on the Appropriations Committee, where he has helped fund a variety of projects in his South Side and suburban Chicago district. "If it doesn't immediately impact the people of the 2nd District, it's not what I wake up thinking about," he has said.

Over several years, he helped direct more than $148 million in federal funds to the Deep Tunnel Project, which is designed to improve flood protection and water quality for the Chicago metropolitan area.

But his efforts to boost construction of a third airport for the Chicago area, which he says will provide economic expansion for his district as well as relieve overcrowding at Chicago's O'Hare International Airport, have met with little success. Jackson and others want the new airport built on rural land outside of Peotone, just south of his district. It would aim to attract discount air carriers. But Chicago Mayor Richard M. Daley has backed a rival plan to expand O'Hare and has moved ahead with construction of a new runway and control tower.

Reflecting his family's civil rights heritage and his interest in history, Jackson has been active in promoting recognition of the contributions of African-Americans. In the 110th Congress (2007-08), he joined Republican Rep. Zach Wamp of Tennessee to pass legislation that named the main venue in the new Capitol Visitor Center "Emancipation Hall" in honor of the black slaves who played a major role in building the Capitol. He also shepherded through legislation to commission a $370,000 statue in the Capitol of civil rights pioneer Rosa Parks.

In October 2007, Jackson reacted to a study showing that House districts represented by white members on average garner twice as much in earmarks, funding set-asides for projects back home, as black-represented districts. He wanted the Congressional Black Caucus to propose allowing points of order that would throw out earmarks in bills in which minority districts were underfunded.

Jackson voted against the first version of the $700 billion financial industry rescue plan in September 2008, but voted for the revised version after a personal appeal from Obama. Jackson said Obama assured him that if elected president, he would use powers granted in the legislation to fight foreclosures and predatory lending in poor communities. "The bill isn't perfect. But it's a necessary start," Jackson said.

Jackson sits on the State-Foreign Operations Appropriations Subcommittee, where he has pushed aid for African nations, especially such troubled lands as Liberia and Sudan. He introduced a $225 million development aid proposal for Liberia.

He is a fitness buff who holds a black belt in tae kwon do. Jackson also frequently gets around Capitol Hill on his own Segway.

Although his family has Chicago roots, Jackson graduated from Washington, D.C.'s elite St. Albans School, and he has earned degrees in both theology and law. He followed in his father's footsteps, serving as vice president at-large of Operation PUSH (People United to Serve Humanity) and as national field director for the Rainbow Coalition.

But he rebuked his father in July 2008 after an open microphone picked up the elder Jackson whispering a crude criticism of Obama. He said his father was wrong to use "divisive and demeaning" language and "ugly rhetoric."

Jackson was first elected to Congress in a 1995 special election to replace Democrat Rep. Mel Reynolds, who resigned after being convicted of sexual misconduct. Jackson countered criticism that he was too young for the job by arguing that being the son of Jesse Jackson gave him a wealth of political experience.

After winning a hard-fought primary against state Sen. Emil Jones Jr., who later became Obama's political mentor in the state legislature, Jackson easily won the general election. He has sailed to re-election since then.

At one point in 2006, Jackson flirted with the idea of challenging Daley for a shot at running the Windy City. But once Democrats took over the House, Jackson dropped the idea, and Daley won re-election in a landslide.

KEY VOTES

2008
Yes Delay consideration of Colombia free-trade agreement
Yes Override Bush veto of federal farm and nutrition programs reauthorization bill
No   Overhaul surveillance laws and permit dismissal of suits against companies that conducted warrantless wiretapping
Yes Grant mortgage relief to homeowners and funding for Fannie Mae and Freddie Mac
No   Approve initial $700 billion program to stabilize financial markets
Yes Approve final $700 billion program to stabilize financial markets
Yes Provide $14 billion in loans to automakers

2007
Yes Increase minimum wage by $2.10 an hour
Yes Approve $124.2 billion in emergency war spending and set goal for redeployment of troops from Iraq
No   Reject federal contraceptive assistance to international family planning groups
Yes Override Bush veto of $23.2 billion water projects authorization bill
No   Implement Peru free-trade agreement
Yes Approve energy policy overhaul with new fuel economy standards
No   Clear $473.5 billion omnibus spending bill, including $70 billion for military operations

CQ VOTE STUDIES

	PARTY UNITY		PRESIDENTIAL SUPPORT	
	SUPPORT	OPPOSE	SUPPORT	OPPOSE
2008	99%	1%	14%	86%
2007	99%	1%	3%	97%
2006	98%	2%	23%	77%
2005	98%	2%	13%	87%
2004	98%	2%	15%	85%

INTEREST GROUPS

	AFL-CIO	ADA	CCUS	ACU
2008	100%	100%	61%	4%
2007	96%	100%	50%	0%
2006	100%	100%	27%	4%
2005	93%	100%	30%	0%
2004	100%	100%	14%	0%

ILLINOIS 2

Chicago — far South Side; Chicago Heights

The 2nd begins on Chicago's South Side along Lake Michigan and extends south along the Indiana border, as well as southwest, to take in Chicago Heights and other Cook County suburbs before reaching across the Will County line to grab University Park. The Chicago portion of the district starts in the Hyde Park area near the University of Chicago (located in the 1st) and takes in the South Shore, South Chicago, Roseland, Pullman and heavily Hispanic East Side neighborhoods. About 40 percent of the 2nd's residents live in the city.

The district once was built on the steel industry, but the industry's collapse in the late 1970s devastated the local economy. Ford Motor Co. is one of the few large manufacturing interests remaining here, with a stamping plant in Chicago Heights and an assembly plant north of Calumet City — the company's oldest operating facility in the world — but declining auto sales have caused layoffs.

Unemployment and foreclosure rates are high in the 2nd, and some more southern areas of the district are losing population as residents move into western suburbs. Previous plans by the Ho-Chunk Indian nation to build a casino and shopping complex in the district stalled, but a large parkland, commercial and residential development along the lakefront is planned. A proposed third Chicago-area airport in the neighboring 11th District near University Park could channel development and jobs through the 2nd District.

The district's suburbs are a mix of heavily black areas such as Harvey, Dolton and Ford Heights, and largely white areas like Homewood, Flossmoor and Thornton. Overall, the 2nd is more than 60 percent black and working-class. This staunchly Democratic base helped the district give Barack Obama his highest 2008 presidential vote percentage (90 percent) in the state and the sixth-highest in the nation.

MAJOR INDUSTRY
Automotive manufacturing, health care

CITIES
Chicago (pt.), 265,814; Calumet City, 39,071; Chicago Heights, 32,776

NOTABLE
Pullman, a factory town now part of Chicago that was built by the Pullman Palace Car Co. in the 1880s, was the first company-planned industrial town in the United States.

Rep. Daniel Lipinski (D)

Elected 2004; 3rd term

CAPITOL OFFICE
225-5701
www.house.gov/lipinski
1717 Longworth Bldg. 20515-1303; fax 225-1012

COMMITTEES
Science & Technology
  (Research & Science Education - chairman)
Small Business
Transportation & Infrastructure

RESIDENCE
Western Springs

BORN
July 15, 1966; Chicago, Ill.

RELIGION
Roman Catholic

FAMILY
Wife, Judy Lipinski

EDUCATION
Northwestern U., B.S. 1988 (mechanical engineering); Stanford U., M.S. 1989 (engineering-economic systems); Duke U., Ph.D. 1998 (political science)

CAREER
Professor; congressional and campaign aide

POLITICAL HIGHLIGHTS
No previous office

ELECTION RESULTS

2008 GENERAL

Daniel Lipinski (D)	172,581	73.3%
Michael Hawkins (R)	50,336	21.4%
Jerome Pohlen (GREEN)	12,607	5.4%

2008 PRIMARY

Daniel Lipinski (D)	62,439	53.8%
Mark N. Pera (D)	29,544	25.4%
Jim Capparelli (D)	13,312	11.4%
Jerry Bennett (D)	10,742	9.3%

2006 GENERAL

Daniel Lipinski (D)	127,768	77.1%
Raymond G. Wardingley (R)	37,954	22.9%

PREVIOUS WINNING PERCENTAGES
2004 (73%)

Lipinski espouses the same economic populist, socially conservative views that helped keep his predecessor and father, William O. Lipinski, in office for more than two decades. Like his father, Lipinski admires the policies of President Ronald Reagan, opposes free-trade legislation and works to help the Chicago area's transportation and manufacturing fields.

But there are generational differences between father and son. The elder Lipinski was an old-style urban pol who dropped out of college. His more analytically minded son earned engineering degrees from Northwestern and Stanford — plus a doctorate in political science from Duke — and has an avid interest in the science and environmental issues that are backbones of his party's current agenda.

Lipinski sits on the Transportation and Infrastructure Committee and is a member of the panels on aviation and railroads. He focuses on federal projects affecting Chicago's Midway Airport and the region's robust railroad sector.

With Congress expected to take up a reauthorization of the 2005 surface transportation law, Lipinski wants to continue funding for the Chicago Region Environmental and Transportation Efficiency program, a $1.5 billion partnership between the state, the city and its transit system, and freight railroads to improve rail infrastructure. He sees the program as an opportunity to address improvements that must occur if Chicago succeeds in its bid to host the 2016 Olympic Games. He also favors more funding for public transportation and bike paths. Early in 2009, Lipinski voted "present" on a $787 billion economic stimulus bill, which became law. He said it didn't include enough money for transportation.

On the Science and Technology Committee, where he chairs the Research and Science Education Subcommittee, Lipinski advocates policies that are both pro-business and environment-friendly. He cosponsored a successful amendment to the 2007 energy policy bill, requiring the use of energy-efficient light bulbs in Capitol buildings. He later won House approval of a bill to authorize $12 million annually for five years to make U.S. steel and other metals more efficient and environmentally sound.

Lipinski also teamed with South Carolina Republican Bob Inglis — the two lawmakers, both slender and silver-haired, are sometimes confused for one another — to win House approval of their bill to authorize $52 million over nine years to establish a national prize in hydrogen energy technology research.

Like his father, Lipinski is not hesitant to part ways with his party, especially on social issues. When Republicans controlled the House during his first term, he supported President George W. Bush nearly half the time on issues on which the president took a stand. That included voting against lifting Bush's restrictions on embryonic stem cell research funding and supporting a 700-mile fence on the U.S.-Mexico border.

Lipinski usually sticks with his Democratic colleagues on labor matters. He opposed the 2005 Central America Free Trade Agreement. Two years later, he opposed a free-trade agreement with Peru and supported legislation to place limits on how long employees must work each day. "We are still a country where we have a lot of people working in these blue-collar jobs," Lipinski said. "We need to make sure there is safety regulation and workers are being treated fairly." He backed an increase in the minimum wage in 2007.

In the fall of 2008, Lipinski opposed both versions of the Bush administration's proposal to shore up the failing financial sector. "Why are we writing a $700 billion blank check to the financial industry with no real accountability, no real oversight, and no real reform?" he asked.

His family connections have been both a help and a hindrance. The senior Lipinski all but assured that his son would succeed him. He first filed to run for re-election in 2004 and was unopposed in the March Democratic primary, but announced during the August recess that he would retire from the House after 11 terms. As permitted by state law, a committee of 3rd District Democrats, which included the senior Lipinski and several of his allies, unanimously selected Daniel to fill the vacated ballot slot. In November, the younger Lipinski defeated Republican political unknown Ryan Chlada by almost 3-to-1.

Some Democratic activists contended the selection process smacked of nepotism and remind Lipinski of it each time he faces re-election by backing other primary candidates. Lipinski defeated two candidates in the 2006 primary before coasting to re-election; in a primary two years later, he took 54 percent of the vote to easily best three challengers, including local prosecutor Mark N. Pera, who raised more campaign funds than the incumbent. He took the 2008 general election with more than 73 percent of the vote.

Lipinski has received criticism on other fronts. His father's current job is as a lobbyist for the Association of American Railroads, and a Washington Post story in 2007 raised questions as to whether he was hired to influence his son. Lipinski allowed his father to share a Chicago office with his district staff. And the Chicago Sun Times reported the elder Lipinski's charity, the All American Eagles Fund, gave $1,000 to the younger Lipinski in the 2008 election cycle.

Lipinski denied his father lobbies him or has acted improperly. "It is easy to talk about Bill and Dan Lipinski, and it is a simple story and doesn't require a lot of work," he said. "But I know how hard I work to get things done, and I know what I have been able to accomplish."

Lipinski was born and raised in the district, a working-class swath of the city and close-in suburbs. He later worked as an associate professor at the University of Tennessee in Knoxville. When he moved back to the Chicago area after 15 years for his first run for public office, he wasn't a total novice. He had worked on numerous Illinois campaigns, had served as a congressional aide to then Rep. Rod R. Blagojevich and served a fellowship in the office of House Minority Leader Richard A. Gephardt of Missouri.

His career in academia was devoted to politics as well. He has published several papers on how politicians communicate with constituents, including their increasing use of the Internet. At Duke the judge of his doctoral thesis was Democratic Rep. David E. Price of North Carolina, who was between congressional stints.

KEY VOTES

2008

Yes Delay consideration of Colombia free-trade agreement

Yes Override Bush veto of federal farm and nutrition programs reauthorization bill

Yes Overhaul surveillance laws and permit dismissal of suits against companies that conducted warrantless wiretapping

Yes Grant mortgage relief to homeowners and funding for Fannie Mae and Freddie Mac

No Approve initial $700 billion program to stabilize financial markets

No Approve final $700 billion program to stabilize financial markets

Yes Provide $14 billion in loans to automakers

2007

Yes Increase minimum wage by $2.10 an hour

Yes Approve $124.2 billion in emergency war spending and set goal for redeployment of troops from Iraq

Yes Reject federal contraceptive assistance to international family planning groups

Yes Override Bush veto of $23.2 billion water projects authorization bill

No Implement Peru free-trade agreement

Yes Approve energy policy overhaul with new fuel economy standards

No Clear $473.5 billion omnibus spending bill, including $70 billion for military operations

CQ VOTE STUDIES

	PARTY UNITY		PRESIDENTIAL SUPPORT	
	SUPPORT	OPPOSE	SUPPORT	OPPOSE
2008	97%	3%	16%	84%
2007	93%	7%	14%	86%
2006	86%	14%	49%	51%
2005	86%	14%	43%	57%

INTEREST GROUPS

	AFL-CIO	ADA	CCUS	ACU
2008	100%	90%	59%	8%
2007	96%	85%	55%	20%
2006	100%	70%	47%	33%
2005	87%	85%	46%	16%

ILLINOIS 3

Chicago — southwest side; south and west suburbs

The 3rd covers the southwest corner of Chicago and adjacent suburbs, part of a working-class region known as the Bungalow Belt that is stocked with voters of Eastern European, Italian and Irish descent.

Chicago residents make up about 40 percent of the district population. The 3rd includes the historically Irish neighborhood of Bridgeport, which is the political base of the powerful Daley family, and southwest Chicago neighborhoods such as Beverly, West Lawn, Clearing and Garfield Ridge, where Midway Airport is located. The largely Hispanic West Lawn and West Elsdon neighborhoods have experienced rapid growth.

Crisscrossed by highways, railroads and the Chicago Sanitary and Ship Canal, the 3rd has historically served as a manufacturing and distribution center. Canadian National's acquisition of the Elgin, Joliet & Eastern Railway Co. in late 2008 will shift to other suburban areas a significant amount of rail traffic from congested lines of the 3rd. The district also has relied on food processing — particularly candy and snacks — and distribution. Expansion at Midway in the early 2000s broadened the district's

retail and service base and created new jobs for district residents.

Southwest Airlines expanded operations at the airport to fill the void left by departures of other major carriers. A multibillion-dollar long-term lease between Midway and a private development company — the first of its kind nationwide — is expected to provide much-needed infrastructure funding to the area.

In national elections, the 3rd District typically votes Democratic, but not by the same wide margins as other Chicago-based districts — Barack Obama won 64 percent of the 2008 presidential vote here. Many working- and middle-class voters lean to the right on social issues, and there are Republican pockets in the district's more affluent western Cook County suburbs.

MAJOR INDUSTRY
Transportation, warehouses, manufacturing

CITIES
Chicago (pt.), 266,264; Oak Lawn, 55,245; Berwyn (pt.), 51,179

NOTABLE
Berwyn is home to the world's largest Laundromat, with roughly 300 washers and dryers combined, which runs on solar power.

Rep. Luis V. Gutierrez (D)

Elected 1992; 9th term

CAPITOL OFFICE
225-8203
luisgutierrez.house.gov
2266 Rayburn Bldg. 20515-1304; fax 225-7810

COMMITTEES
Financial Services
  (Financial Institutions & Consumer Credit -
  chairman)
Judiciary

RESIDENCE
Chicago

BORN
Dec. 10, 1953; Chicago, Ill.

RELIGION
Roman Catholic

FAMILY
Wife, Soraida Arocho Gutierrez; two children

EDUCATION
Northeastern Illinois U., B.A. 1975 (liberal arts)

CAREER
Mayoral aide; teacher; social worker

POLITICAL HIGHLIGHTS
Chicago City Council, 1986-93

ELECTION RESULTS

2008 GENERAL

Luis V. Gutierrez (D)	112,529	80.6%
Daniel Cunningham (R)	16,024	11.5%
Omar Lopez (GREEN)	11,053	7.9%

2008 PRIMARY

Luis V. Gutierrez (D)	unopposed

2006 GENERAL

Luis V. Gutierrez (D)	69,910	85.8%
Ann Melichar (R)	11,532	14.2%

PREVIOUS WINNING PERCENTAGES
2004 (84%); 2002 (80%); 2000 (89%); 1998 (82%);
1996 (94%); 1994 (75%); 1992 (78%)

Gutierrez represents one of the poorest, least-educated districts in the nation and he can be passionate in his defense of society's underdogs. The first Hispanic member of Congress from Illinois, he learned politics on the rough-and-tumble Chicago City Council, where his tenacity earned him the nickname "El Gallito," Spanish for "little fighting rooster." His style in Washington is much the same, but he can show a gentler side when he finds the need to bring in Republicans on his efforts.

His top priority has long been comprehensive immigration reform. He has been so frustrated by his failed attempts to pass a broad package of changes to U.S. law that he repeatedly has threatened to call it quits, only to change his mind. His on-again, off-again retirement announcements prompted criticism in the local press. A Chicago Sun Times columnist wrote in 2007 after one such abandoned threat, "Gutierrez has turned into the boy who cried wolf of Illinois politics."

Gutierrez (goo-tee-AIR-ez) holds two prime seats to look out for low-income families, minorities and small business: the Financial Services and Judiciary committees. On Financial Services, he has pushed for legislation aimed at protecting low-income and minority borrowers, pushed for greater disclosure from institutions selling high-interest "payday" loans and sponsored legislation to limit the use of credit scores in pricing insurance.

In 2009 he became chairman on the panel overseeing financial institutions and consumer credit. He supported a fall 2008 bill to aid the nation's struggling financial system, saying, "I refuse to stand idly by as the actions of Wall Street devastate the opportunities for families living on Division Street or the small businesses on 26th Street in Little Village."

As subcommittee chairman, he followed up with hearings about the difficulty of local small businesses to obtain loans from banks that had received help from the rescue. "We hear this story day in and day out, that the choking of credit" is causing thriving businesses to fail, he said.

Gutierrez also wants to address comprehensive mortgage lending reform.

But his primary focus remains immigration. Seventy-five percent of his constituent casework is related to the issue, and Gutierrez said that as of September 2008 his office had facilitated more than 50,500 citizenship applications. He made a 16-city tour in early 2009 to promote his plans. He favors what he calls a "holistic approach" that would create a guest worker program, improve enforcement of existing laws, enhance border security and make additional visas available in order to reunite families.

Though he was unsuccessful during the early years of George W. Bush's administration, his hopes were renewed with the Democratic takeover in the 110th Congress (2007-08), and he abandoned plans to run for mayor of Chicago against Richard M. Daley. Assigned to Judiciary and named vice chairman of its panel on immigration, Gutierrez and Arizona Republican Jeff Flake in early 2007 offered a bipartisan bill that would offer both a path toward citizenship for illegal immigrants and tougher border enforcement — stirring criticism from immigrant-rights advocates. But his plan again went nowhere and Democratic leaders focused on narrower measures. He complained that many Democrats "want to do what is easy and not exactly what is right."

He later voted against a 2008 initiative to make 20,000 green cards a year available for nurses because he preferred to achieve full reform rather than do a piecemeal approach. He did support a five-year reauthorization of E-Verify, a voluntary work-eligibility verification system.

Gutierrez's combative style has not always helped him. In March 2006 he argued on a CNBC broadcast with former Rep. Tom Tancredo, the Colorado Republican who led the opposition to a guest worker program. Their argument continued off-air and escalated into a shoving match, including charges of racism. I feel passionately about this and I lost my temper," Gutierrez said later of the incident. "It wasn't my best moment."

Yet he has courted the other side in gentler ways. He has appeared on CNN's "Moneyline," a platform for anchor Lou Dobbs' conservative views on immigration, and once invited Dobbs to a luncheon with 15 members of the Congressional Hispanic Caucus.

Gutierrez has repeatedly held out hope for progress on the issue. He had said in March 2007 he would retire, but by August he changed his mind. He said the improved chances for immigration reform under a Democratic president, and his wife's recovery from cancer, led him to reconsider.

Gutierrez, a friend and ally of Illinois Gov. Rod R. Blagojevich, was considered a potential successor to Obama in the Senate, and said he had discussions with the governor about the possibility. But many observers said he took himself out of the running by saying he only wanted to serve for two years and focus on getting comprehensive immigration legislation through the Senate rather than focus on a 2010 campaign.

Born in Chicago to Puerto Rican immigrants, Gutierrez went to high school in their home country and says he was nearly expelled for agitating for Puerto Rican independence. Later, at Northeastern Illinois University, he was part of a group of students who took over the university president's office to protest a lack of basic English language classes for incoming students.

Gutierrez worked for more than a decade as a teacher, social worker and community activist. In 1983, he joined the campaign of Democratic Rep. Harold Washington, who defeated incumbent Mayor Jane Byrne and Cook County State's Attorney Richard M. Daley, son of the longtime mayor, to become the city's first African-American mayor. That year, Gutierrez ran against Rep. Dan Rostenkowski, the powerful Democratic chairman of the House Ways and Means Committee, for ward boss for the 32nd Ward. He lost, then went to work for Washington. Three years later, he was elected to the City Council, where he spent nearly seven years.

After Washington died and Daley became mayor, he and Gutierrez reconciled. When the oddly shaped Hispanic-majority 4th District was created for the 1992 election, Daley backed Gutierrez for the seat. His support practically guaranteed Gutierrez the non-Hispanic white vote. He won easily in the heavily Democratic district and has won re-election easily since.

KEY VOTES

2008

Yes   Delay consideration of Colombia free-trade agreement

Yes   Override Bush veto of federal farm and nutrition programs reauthorization bill

Yes   Overhaul surveillance laws and permit dismissal of suits against companies that conducted warrantless wiretapping

Yes   Grant mortgage relief to homeowners and funding for Fannie Mae and Freddie Mac

Yes   Approve initial $700 billion program to stabilize financial markets

Yes   Approve final $700 billion program to stabilize financial markets

?   Provide $14 billion in loans to automakers

2007

Yes   Increase minimum wage by $2.10 an hour

Yes   Approve $124.2 billion in emergency war spending and set goal for redeployment of troops from Iraq

No   Reject federal contraceptive assistance to international family planning groups

Yes   Override Bush veto of $23.2 billion water projects authorization bill

No   Implement Peru free-trade agreement

Yes   Approve energy policy overhaul with new fuel economy standards

No   Clear $473.5 billion omnibus spending bill, including $70 billion for military operations

CQ VOTE STUDIES

	PARTY UNITY		PRESIDENTIAL SUPPORT	
	SUPPORT	OPPOSE	SUPPORT	OPPOSE
2008	99%	1%	16%	84%
2007	98%	2%	3%	97%
2006	97%	3%	23%	77%
2005	98%	2%	18%	82%
2004	99%	1%	24%	76%

INTEREST GROUPS

	AFL-CIO	ADA	CCUS	ACU
2008	100%	90%	56%	0%
2007	100%	100%	44%	0%
2006	100%	80%	31%	4%
2005	92%	100%	38%	0%
2004	100%	90%	22%	0%

ILLINOIS 4

Chicago — parts of North Side, southwest side

Surrounding the black-majority 7th District in the center of Chicago, the small, horseshoe-shaped 4th was drawn to unite the city's Hispanic neighborhoods into one voting bloc. Slightly less than 90 percent of district residents live in Chicago.

The district boasts the state's largest Hispanic population, and the nation's fifth-largest, at 74 percent. The 4th is largely young and poor, with the nation's fifth-lowest median age (27.2 years) and a median income slightly less than $36,000. Nearly half of the district's residents age 25 or older do not have a high school diploma. The 4th also has the state's largest percentage of blue-collar workers, many of whom are immigrants living in the district's Hispanic, Ukrainian and Polish neighborhoods. Most jobs in the district are in the transportation and manufacturing sectors, and the warehousing industry is strong.

A narrow strip of land about 10 miles in length — running along railroad tracks, highways and cemeteries — attaches the Puerto Rican neighborhood of Logan Square in the northern part of the 4th to Mexican-

American populations in Little Village and Pilsen in the southern portion. More than 90 percent of residents are Hispanic in these parts of the South Lawndale and Lower West Side communities around Cermak Road in the southern arm of the district. Close-in Chicago suburbs such as Cicero and Stone Park, formerly home to Slavic and Italian populations, respectively, also have seen rapid Hispanic growth. Artsy Wicker Park and Bucktown are growing areas with rising property values.

The district is plagued by low voter turnout, but is solidly Democratic and takes in left-leaning areas of Cicero as well as the gentrifying Wicker Park and Bucktown neighborhoods in Chicago. As a whole, Obama took 85 percent of the 2008 presidential vote in the 4th.

MAJOR INDUSTRY
Light manufacturing, transportation

CITIES
Chicago (pt.), 560,373; Cicero (pt.), 73,209; Melrose Park (pt.), 5,756

NOTABLE
Cermak Road is named for former Chicago Mayor Anton Cermak, who was killed in 1933 by a bullet meant for President-elect Franklin Delano Roosevelt; The Back of the Yards neighborhood in Chicago was the subject of Upton Sinclair's 1906 novel "The Jungle."

Rep. Mike Quigley (D)

Elected April 2009; 1st term

A former Cook County commissioner, Quigley follows the strict Democratic course charted by his predecessor, Rahm Emanuel, who resigned in January 2009 to become President Obama's chief of staff. Quigley advocates Obama's policies on issues ranging from climate change to tax policies to the Iraq War. He also said he will support abortion rights and federal efforts to expand access to medical care.

A member of the Oversight and Government Reform Committee, he is eager to promote administration policies to enhance government transparency and accountability by making federal records more readily available to the public. He promised to disclose even his smallest campaign donors and to forgo contributions from industries whose interests he's likely to vote against. "Reinventing, streamlining, restructuring, reforming ... this is my bread and butter," he said in March 2009.

Quigley also has a seat on the Judiciary Committee. He served as a criminal defense attorney for eight years and said he is a longtime advocate of civil rights.

Quigley took 60 percent of the vote in an April 2009 special election against Rosanna Pulido, the conservative Republican leader of an anti-immigration group. But his path to Congress was virtually assured after he won — with 22 percent of the vote — a March primary against other Democrats from all corners of local politics. His district, which stretches across Chicago's North Side and touches some adjacent suburbs, favored Obama with 73 percent of the vote in the 2008 presidential contest.

He was significantly outspent and somewhat less experienced than others in the primary field, among them a pair of state representatives and a veteran city councilman, but Quigley won by campaigning as both an insider with experience in elected office and an outsider "reformer" unafraid to fight the establishment on the county board.

As a board member, Quigley on occasion was the only Democrat to oppose tax increases. "I'm pretty well-known here in Chicago for dissenting when necessary," he said.

CAPITOL OFFICE
225-4061
quigley.house.gov
1319 Longworth Bldg. 20515-1305; fax 225-5603

COMMITTEES
Judiciary
Oversight & Government Reform

RESIDENCE
Chicago

BORN
October 17, 1958; Indianapolis, Ind.

RELIGION
Roman Catholic

FAMILY
Wife, Barbara Quigley

EDUCATION
Roosevelt U., B.A. 1981 (political science);
U. of Chicago, M.P.P 1985; Loyola U. (Chicago),
J.D. 1989

CAREER
College instructor; lawyer; legislative aide

POLITICAL HIGHLIGHTS
Candidate for Chicago City Council, 1991;
Cook County Board of Commissioners, 1998-2009

ELECTION RESULTS

2009 SPECIAL

Mike Quigley (D)	7,653	59.3%
Rosanna Pulido (R)	4,628	35.8%
Matt Reichel (GREEN)	635	4.9%

2009 PRIMARY SPECIAL

Mike Quigley (D)	12,118	22.0%
John A. Fritchey (D)	9,835	17.9%
Sara Feigenholtz (D)	9,194	16.7%
Victor A. Forys (D)	6,428	11.7%
Patrick J. O'Connor (D)	6,388	11.6%
Charles J. Wheelan (D)	3,681	6.7%
Tom Geoghegan (D)	3,342	6.1%
Paul J. Bryar (D)	1,111	2.0%
Jan H. Donatelli (D)	892	1.6%
Frank Annunzio (D)	755	1.4%
Cary Capparelli (D)	714	1.3%

ILLINOIS 5

Chicago — North Side

The 5th spans Chicago's North Side, stretching from Lake Michigan in the east to near O'Hare International Airport (located in the 6th) in the west. The district is home to one of the city's few remaining active industrial sectors, running through the middle of the 5th along the Chicago River's north branch.

DePaul University students and "lakefront liberals" inhabit wealthy east-side communities such as Lincoln Park. Areas such as Roscoe Village and Lakeview, which includes the gay community Boystown, have seen an influx of younger residents. Ethnic restaurants and entertainment spots in eastern parts of the district provide weekend and evening destinations for residents from other parts of the north side, the west side and suburbs.

The district's west covers part of the Bungalow Belt, a stretch of 1930s brick homes sep-arating the suburbs from downtown Chicago. The west's working-class base routinely supports populist-style Democrats, but far west-side areas and portions of the Bungalow Belt can support Republicans in local elections. Middle- and working-class neighborhoods and second- and third-generation German and Polish residents still dominate this part of town, but there is a growing number of Hispanic newcomers.

The combination of these voting habits makes for a largely Democratic constituency. The 5th supports Democrats in federal races, and Democratic statewide candidates also do well here. Barack Obama won 73 percent of the district's 2008 presidential vote.

MAJOR INDUSTRY
Manufacturing, warehousing and storage, electronics, health care

CITIES
Chicago (pt.), 549,762; Elmwood Park (pt.), 23,741

NOTABLE
Wrigley Field hosts baseball's Chicago Cubs.

Rep. Peter Roskam (R)

Elected 2006; 2nd term

CAPITOL OFFICE
225-4561
roskam.house.gov
507 Cannon Bldg. 20515-1306; fax 225-1166

COMMITTEES
Ways & Means

RESIDENCE
Wheaton

BORN
Sept. 13, 1961; Hinsdale, Ill.

RELIGION
Anglican

FAMILY
Wife, Elizabeth Roskam; four children

EDUCATION
U. of Illinois, B.A. 1983 (political science);
Illinois Institute of Technology, J.D. 1989

CAREER
Lawyer; nonprofit education scholarship
executive director; congressional aide; teacher

POLITICAL HIGHLIGHTS
Ill. House, 1993-99; sought Republican nomination
for U.S. House, 1998; Ill. Senate, 2000-07

ELECTION RESULTS

2008 GENERAL

Peter Roskam (R)	147,906	57.6%
Jill Morgenthaler (D)	109,007	42.4%

2008 PRIMARY

Peter Roskam (R)	unopposed

2006 GENERAL

Peter Roskam (R)	91,382	51.4%
Tammy Duckworth (D)	86,572	48.6%

Roskam has a conservative perspective similar to his predecessor, the formidable Republican Rep. Henry J. Hyde who served in the seat for 32 years, and is much in line with his mostly wealthy, white-collar constituency. He supports a smaller government and reduced regulation, backs the Iraq War and opposes abortion.

He says his philosophy of "less government is better" stems from his experiences working for Hyde as a legislative aide while in law school and on the staff of former GOP Rep. Tom DeLay of Texas in the mid-1980s.

Roskam's ambitions have helped him rise quickly in the House. In 2009, he won a coveted seat on the Ways and Means Committee, which oversees tax policy and health care and where he is expected to push back against the Democrats' agenda." In just his second term, he also serves as a deputy whip, one of the first rungs on the party leadership ladder.

And he already has his eye on the Senate; Roskam said he's weighing a run in 2010 for the seat now occupied by Democrat Roland W. Burris, who was appointed by former Illinois Democratic Gov. Rod R. Blagojevich after Burris' predecessor, Barack Obama, was elected president. "Any time a U.S. Senate seat comes up, any thinking person gives that a real long, slow look," he told the Chicago Sun Times in February 2009.

Roskam opposed Obama's early economic measures, including a stimulus bill and a catchall spending bill for 2009. He said of the $787 billion stimulus package, "The great need to revitalize our economy comes second to this Congress' insatiable appetite for pork barrel spending."

A member of the Financial Services Committee during the 110th Congress (2007-08), Roskam voted in the fall of 2008 against two versions of a $700 billion measure — the second of which became law — to shore up the struggling financial industry.

He said it would place too great a burden on taxpayers, while providing no guarantee of success. "You know when you're on the pitcher's mound and a batter spats a ball right at you and you have a split second to flinch one way or the other to get out of the way?" Roskam asked. "What the administration did on this is they flinched toward collectivism and going toward taxpayers. My district is one that says, 'Don't go that way first; flinch toward the marketplace.'"

In November 2007, he opposed a bill that would have tightened oversight of the mortgage-lending industry. He also opposed a huge 2008 housing bill, signed into law, to help borrowers get out from under loans they could not afford and to overhaul the mortgage giants Fannie Mae and Freddie Mac. Roskam said the bill would just increase the nation's debt.

One exception to Roskam's anti-regulatory zeal is in the area of food safety. After salmonella-tainted peanut products killed nine people in the United States, he teamed with fellow Illinois Republican Rep. Mark Steven Kirk on a bill in early 2009 to authorize the Food and Drug Administration to order mandatory recalls of bad food.

Like Hyde, Roskam is an unwavering supporter of the Iraq War. During the 110th, Roskam repeatedly denounced Democratic proposals to tie war funding to a timeline for withdrawal of U.S. troops from Iraq.

Also like his predecessor, Roskam opposes abortion. As a state senator, he led a fight against state funding for a procedure that opponents call "partial birth" abortion. He also opposed state funding of embryonic stem cell research. In the House, he's taken a similar line.

Roskam was born into a middle-class family from Glen Ellyn. His mother was a homemaker and later opened a nursery school; his father was a sales manager.

It was from his father that he learned the importance of charity. The elder Roskam dropped out of college because he was unable to afford it, but a gift from wealthy farmers enabled him to return. Years later, as a successful businessman, the elder Roskam started a nonprofit scholarship program, Education Assistance. During much of the 1990s, Roskam served as executive director of the program, which collects extra inventory from corporations and donates it to colleges. The colleges then grant scholarships in the amounts of the merchandise.

Roskam was a varsity gymnast in high school. His first foray into politics was a successful campaign for student senate president. He went on to earn a bachelor's degree in political science from the University of Illinois, then taught history and government in the U.S. Virgin Islands for a year. He moved to Washington in 1985 and worked for DeLay, who was then a freshman representative but went on to serve as House majority leader. Roskam worked for Hyde before graduating from law school in 1989.

Roskam won a state House seat in 1992 and served three terms before losing his first bid for the U.S. House. In that 1998 race in the 13th District, he lost in the Republican primary to Rep. Judy Biggert. He was appointed in 2000 to a state Senate seat, where he served until his successful 2006 bid for Congress in the 6th — one of the most hotly contested races of the year.

The race drew national attention as many saw it as a referendum on the Iraq War. Roskam's opponent, Democrat Tammy Duckworth, was a member of the Illinois Army National Guard who lost her legs when a rocket-propelled grenade hit her helicopter in Iraq. In the heyday of Hyde's long House career, GOP victory was a sure thing. But Roskam barely eked out a 3-percentage-point win. He faced another Iraq War veteran, retired Army Col. Jill Morgenthaler, in 2008, but defeated her by a more comfortable 15 percentage points.

Roskam, along with newly elected Democratic Rep. Debbie Halvorson, are the only members of Congress to have served with President Barack Obama when Obama served in the Illinois Senate. Roskam and Obama were regular rivals in the state Senate during the years they overlapped, 2000-04, but respected each other. In an effort to boost his 2008 campaign, Roskam started a Web site aimed at wooing Obama voters. The text began with an old Obama quotation: "I'm a member of the mutual admiration society with Sen. Roskam," Obama said in 2004. "He is always terrific."

KEY VOTES

2008

No Delay consideration of Colombia free-trade agreement
No Override Bush veto of federal farm and nutrition programs reauthorization bill
Yes Overhaul surveillance laws and permit dismissal of suits against companies that conducted warrantless wiretapping
No Grant mortgage relief to homeowners and funding for Fannie Mae and Freddie Mac
No Approve initial $700 billion program to stabilize financial markets
No Approve final $700 billion program to stabilize financial markets
No Provide $14 billion in loans to automakers

2007

No Increase minimum wage by $2.10 an hour
No Approve $124.2 billion in emergency war spending and set goal for redeployment of troops from Iraq
Yes Reject federal contraceptive assistance to international family planning groups
Yes Override Bush veto of $23.2 billion water projects authorization bill
Yes Implement Peru free-trade agreement
Yes Approve energy policy overhaul with new fuel economy standards
Yes Clear $473.5 billion omnibus spending bill, including $70 billion for military operations

CQ VOTE STUDIES

	PARTY UNITY		PRESIDENTIAL SUPPORT	
	SUPPORT	OPPOSE	SUPPORT	OPPOSE
2008	95%	5%	71%	29%
2007	95%	5%	77%	23%

INTEREST GROUPS

	AFL-CIO	ADA	CCUS	ACU
2008	13%	10%	94%	96%
2007	29%	10%	84%	96%

ILLINOIS 6

Northwest and west Chicago suburbs

Just west of Chicago, the 6th includes northern DuPage County and northwestern Cook County. Residents are mostly wealthy, white-collar workers who live in the older, mostly built-out suburbs along commuter rail lines that run into the city.

Residents here commute both to Chicago and to the booming northwest satellite cities. O'Hare International Airport (an extension of the city of Chicago and the district's eastern border) is one of the busiest airports in the world and is the center of the 6th's commercial district. Hotels and other travel-related businesses, and firms seeking close airport access, are located nearby.

Plans to modernize O'Hare have been met with mixed results: Construction is expected to generate local jobs, but expansion of the airport and surrounding expressways has been met with opposition from residents in Bensenville and Elk Grove Village, as Chicago acquires land west of the airport. United Airlines retains a major operations center in Elk Grove despite moving its headquarters to downtown Chicago in 2006.

Most workers in the 6th are professionals, and the district has the second-lowest percentage of service industry workers in Illinois. Overall, the 6th is one-eighth Hispanic, and areas in DuPage County, such as Addison, Bensenville and Glendale Heights, are becoming more racially diverse, and parts of Cook County are growing.

The district has a reputation as a Republican bastion, historically working in opposition to Chicago's Democrats. This is particularly true of DuPage, which accounts for three-fourths of the district's population, but the Cook County portions of the district traditionally also have a conservative lean. The district's conservatism has moderated in recent years, however, and the 6th supported Democrat Barack Obama in 2008, giving him 56 percent of its presidential vote.

MAJOR INDUSTRY
Airport, light manufacturing, health care

CITIES
Wheaton, 55,416; Elmhurst, 42,762; Lombard, 42,322; Carol Stream, 40,438; Addison, 35,914

NOTABLE
Barnes & Noble traces its beginnings to 1873, when Charles M. Barnes sold books from his home in Wheaton.

Rep. Danny K. Davis (D)

Elected 1996; 7th term

CAPITOL OFFICE
225-5006
www.house.gov/davis
2159 Rayburn Bldg. 20515-1307; fax 225-5641

COMMITTEES
Oversight & Government Reform
Ways & Means

RESIDENCE
Chicago

BORN
Sept. 6, 1941; Parkdale, Ark.

RELIGION
Baptist

FAMILY
Wife, Vera G. Davis; two children

EDUCATION
Arkansas AM&N College, B.A. 1961 (history &
education); Chicago State U., M.A. 1968 (guidance);
Union Institute, Ph.D. 1977 (public administration)

CAREER
Health care association executive; teacher;
postal clerk

POLITICAL HIGHLIGHTS
Chicago City Council, 1979-90; sought Democratic
nomination for U.S. House, 1984, 1986; Cook County
Commission, 1990-97; sought Democratic
nomination for mayor of Chicago, 1991

ELECTION RESULTS

2008 GENERAL

Danny K. Davis (D)	235,343	85.0%
Steve Miller (R)	41,474	15.0%

2008 PRIMARY

Danny K. Davis (D)	129,865	91.1%
Robert Dallas (D)	12,629	8.9%

2006 GENERAL

Danny K. Davis (D)	143,071	86.7%
Charles Hutchinson (R)	21,939	13.3%

PREVIOUS WINNING PERCENTAGES
2004 (86%); 2002 (83%); 2000 (86%); 1998 (93%);
1996 (82%)

A consistently liberal Democrat, Davis watches out for the downtrodden, minorities and the poor in his West Chicago district. Though he has eyed other jobs since coming to Congress, he is content for now to work on bolstering the federal commitment to housing, drug rehabilitation and other programs aimed at the underclass.

He was rewarded for 12 years of toil in the House in 2009 with a new post on the prestigious, tax-writing Ways and Means Committee that also has broad jurisdiction over Social Security, trade and health care legislation. Though his district takes in tonier parts of Chicago, including trendy new developments near the Loop, it is dominated by poor, drug-ravaged neighborhoods. "All of the issues associated with poverty are pronounced in my district," said Davis, who is given to impassioned speeches about the subject in his distinctive deep baritone.

He will have an ally in his longtime friend, New York's Charles B. Rangel, who chairs Ways and Means. Davis also can call in some chits with President Obama, whom he endorsed in the 2008 campaign. He helped Obama make inroads with union members when Obama was an Illinois state senator.

Davis found much to applaud in Obama's early economic measures. He backed a $787 billion stimulus plan in early 2009, saying it would "address the needs of low- and middle-class families hard hit by events out of their control." He also supported a bill, similar to legislation President George W. Bush twice vetoed, to expand the State Children's Health Insurance Program, which covers children from low-income families that do not qualify for Medicaid.

Davis retains his post on Oversight and Government Reform's postal service subcommittee, where he had been chairman. A former postal clerk, he has made his mark as a steady overseer of the civil service. Congress passed his bill in 2008 awarding back pay to Government Accountability Office analysts denied raises after a pay system overhaul at the agency. He also seeks to help more minorities win top civil service jobs. In June 2008, the House passed his bill ordering the Office of Personnel Management to set in motion a plan to boost minority representation in the senior executive ranks, but the bill stalled in the Senate.

Told time and again there aren't enough qualified minority candidates for the jobs, Davis also has tried to boost minority college attendance by pushing legislation to increase federal grants to low-income blacks. He credits his own education at the historically black University of Arkansas at Pine Bluff with helping him escape the fields where he toiled as a boy.

He is also an advocate for former criminals, many of whom end up settling in his district. Congress passed his bill in 2008 reauthorizing a grant program to help ex-offenders re-enter society. In 2009, he sponsored a bill that would reduce prison sentences for criminals who maintain a good record of conduct while in prison. A member of the Congressional Black Caucus, Davis also has pushed for a federal review of police brutality and racial profiling. He had found himself a victim of what he called "driving while being black," given a ticket in Chicago in 2007 for allegedly crossing over the center line. Davis fought the charge and was ultimately acquitted.

Davis was one of 11 children of sharecroppers who picked cotton in southeastern Arkansas. He and his siblings went to a segregated school four or five months of the year, spending the rest of the time doing farm work.

After graduating from college, he accepted $50 from his father and left Arkansas for California. He got as far as Chicago when his money ran out.

He stayed with an older sister, and got a job teaching language arts and social studies at a high school. He was also moonlighting at the post office.

Davis got involved in the community, and became president of the National Association of Community Health Centers. In 1979, he led a committee of neighborhood leaders looking for a candidate to challenge the Democratic machine in a Chicago City Council race, but he failed to turn up anyone. "So I said, 'What the hell,' and decided to run myself," he said.

On the council in the early 1980s, he was a close associate of Harold Washington, a former House member and the city's first black mayor, who also had challenged the mostly white Democratic machine. He made two unsuccessful attempts — in 1984 and 1986 — to unseat Democratic U.S. Rep. Cardiss Collins in the 7th District. And in 1991, he was the underdog in a Democratic primary campaign for mayor against the incumbent, Richard M. Daley.

He made another bid for the U.S. House when Collins announced plans to retire in 1996. Davis cleared through a crowded primary field and coasted to victory with 82 percent of the vote. He has had decisive wins ever since.

Before Democrats won the House in November 2006, Davis let it be known he was interested in becoming Cook County Board president, one of the most powerful jobs in Chicago politics, after President John Stroger suffered a debilitating stroke. But the Democratic party regulars chose the former board president's son, Todd Stroger.

In December 2008, Davis turned down a chance to take Obama's Senate seat — a post he would have loved to accept, but the offer came from Democratic Gov. Rod R. Blagojevich, who had been indicted (and later impeached) for allegedly trying to sell the seat to the highest bidder. (The Senate ultimately seated former Illinois Attorney General Roland W. Burris, appointed by Blagojevich.)

Davis' hopes of advancing often have been undermined by his 2004 appearance at an event in Washington honoring the controversial Sun Myung Moon, head of the Unification Church. Davis, clad in white gloves, carried one of the crowns with which Moon and his wife were crowned during a ceremony in a Senate office building. Moon went on to tell the crowd he was the messiah. Davis told the Chicago Tribune his involvement in the ceremony was intended as a "promotion of peace."

He also drew headlines in 2006 when he made a trip to Sri Lanka that was funded by an organization associated with the Tamil Tigers, which the State Department considers a terrorist group. He told the Tribune the trip was to investigate how the country was using post-tsunami reconstruction aid and that he thought the sponsor was a cultural group.

KEY VOTES

2008
Yes Delay consideration of Colombia free-trade agreement

Yes Override Bush veto of federal farm and nutrition programs reauthorization bill

No Overhaul surveillance laws and permit dismissal of suits against companies that conducted warrantless wiretapping

Yes Grant mortgage relief to homeowners and funding for Fannie Mae and Freddie Mac

Yes Approve initial $700 billion program to stabilize financial markets

Yes Approve final $700 billion program to stabilize financial markets

Yes Provide $14 billion in loans to automakers

2007
Yes Increase minimum wage by $2.10 an hour

Yes Approve $124.2 billion in emergency war spending and set goal for redeployment of troops from Iraq

No Reject federal contraceptive assistance to international family planning groups

Yes Override Bush veto of $23.2 billion water projects authorization bill

No Implement Peru free-trade agreement

? Approve energy policy overhaul with new fuel economy standards

No Clear $473.5 billion omnibus spending bill, including $70 billion for military operations

CQ VOTE STUDIES

	PARTY UNITY		PRESIDENTIAL SUPPORT	
	SUPPORT	OPPOSE	SUPPORT	OPPOSE
2008	99%	1%	16%	84%
2007	99%	1%	3%	97%
2006	97%	3%	25%	75%
2005	97%	3%	20%	80%
2004	98%	2%	16%	84%

INTEREST GROUPS

	AFL-CIO	ADA	CCUS	ACU
2008	100%	80%	56%	0%
2007	100%	90%	55%	0%
2006	100%	90%	40%	8%
2005	93%	100%	41%	4%
2004	87%	90%	30%	0%

ILLINOIS 7

Chicago – downtown, West Side; west suburbs

East to west, the 7th stretches from the Loop, Chicago's downtown business district, almost to the DuPage County line, taking in the well-to-do western suburbs of River Forest and Oak Park. North to south, the district runs from the upscale Lincoln Park neighborhood (shared with the 5th) to 57th Street on the South Side.

The eastern end of the 7th hosts some of Chicago's gems, including the Willis Tower (formerly known as the Sears Tower), newer skyscrapers and the plush high-rises of River North, several museums, and about a dozen colleges and universities. Chicago's "Magnificent Mile" includes high-end shops and first-rate hotels, but economic slowdowns have hurt revenue and occupancy rates along the famous stretch of Michigan Avenue. Most people employed in the 7th commute from nearby suburbs to the downtown headquarters of companies such as Boeing, United Airlines, Quaker and Hyatt, as well as to Chicago's financial center. The district also is home to most of Chicago's professional sports teams.

In contrast, most of the district lives in the poverty-stricken neighborhoods that stretch from the western Loop to the edge of the county. Except for a few communities of middle-class blacks, the West Side has had problems with gang violence, unemployment and crumbling infrastructure. The 7th is home to two-thirds of Chicago's public housing projects but improvements are ongoing, with some once-dilapidated areas now home to lofts and galleries.

The 7th fills with white commuters during the day, but more than 60 percent of district residents are black. A reliably Democratic district at all levels, the only genuine political contests in the 7th are the Democratic primaries. Barack Obama won 88 percent of the 7th's vote in the 2008 presidential election — his second-highest percentage in the state.

MAJOR INDUSTRY
Insurance, financial services, health care

CITIES
Chicago (pt.), 502,445; Oak Park, 52,524; Maywood (pt.), 24,895

NOTABLE
The Home Insurance Building, constructed in Chicago in 1885 and demolished in 1931, is considered the first skyscraper in the United States; The Grant Park Music Festival, held each year in Millennium Park, is a free outdoor classical music series.

Rep. Melissa Bean (D)

Elected 2004; 3rd term

CAPITOL OFFICE
225-3711
www.house.gov/bean
432 Cannon Bldg. 20515-1308; fax 225-7830

COMMITTEES
Financial Services
Small Business

RESIDENCE
Barrington

BORN
Jan. 22, 1962; Chicago, Ill.

RELIGION
Serbian Orthodox

FAMILY
Husband, Alan Bean; two children

EDUCATION
Oakton Community College, A.A. 1982 (business);
Roosevelt U., B.A. 2002 (political science)

CAREER
Technology consulting firm president;
telecommunications sales manager

POLITICAL HIGHLIGHTS
Democratic nominee for U.S. House, 2002

ELECTION RESULTS

2008 GENERAL

Melissa Bean (D)	179,444	60.7%
Steve Greenberg (R)	116,081	39.3%

2008 PRIMARY

Melissa Bean (D)	64,255	83.2%
Randi Scheurer (D)	12,968	16.8%

2006 GENERAL

Melissa Bean (D)	93,355	50.9%
David McSweeney (R)	80,720	44.0%
William C. Scheurer (X)	9,312	5.1%

PREVIOUS WINNING PERCENTAGES
2004 (52%)

Bean works assiduously to build credibility among her constituents in the far northern and northwest reaches of Chicago's vast suburbs by practicing fiscal conservatism and moderation on social issues. Her efforts pay off at the ballot box, and she has started to see some of her centrist legislative ideas make progress.

She came to politics after a 20-year business career, and she is vice chairwoman of the New Democrat Coalition, which bills itself as a moderate, pro-business, pro-growth faction in the Democratic Caucus. She describes her budget philosophy as "tough love."

Bean has voted for increased federal funding of embryonic stem cell research and against a constitutional ban on same-sex marriages. But she upset some liberals when she joined Republicans in 2005 to pass legislation limiting the legal liability of gun makers whose weapons are used in a crime. And she was one of just 14 Democrats in 2008 to vote to uphold President George W. Bush's veto of legislation reauthorizing farm programs. Bush said the $289 billion bill — which ultimately became law — contained too much unnecessary spending.

To stay attuned to suburban voters, she joined other Democratic House members — many of them, like her, from once-Republican suburban districts — to create the Democratic Middle Class Working Group in September 2008. The group offered a legislative agenda to address rising costs for college, health insurance, energy, care for children and aging parents, and to help foster small business. Based on her experience, Bean proposed offering employers a $500 tax credit for each employee's telecommuting equipment.

Bean is a member of the Financial Services Committee, where she serves on the subcommittee overseeing capital markets and insurance and a panel on financial institutions and consumer credit. She backed both versions of the $700 billion financial industry rescue package in 2008, the second of which became law.

She backed President Obama's $787 billion economic stimulus law in early 2009, but was one of 20 Democrats to oppose a $410 billion catchall spending bill for fiscal 2009, left over from the previous Congress, saying that it didn't represent fiscal responsibility. A member of the Small Business Committee and formerly chairwoman of its tax and finance panel, Bean and other New Democrat Coalition members met with Obama in March 2009 to urge him to include benefits for small business in his future economic proposals.

She wants to extend Federal Deposit Insurance Corporation (FDIC) protection to insurance companies by extending federal authority to regulate them, a power states currently hold. She believes such FDIC coverage would help stabilize insurers in a time of financial upheaval.

During the 110th Congress (2007-08), Bush signed legislation incorporating her proposal to create the first national Internet safety campaign for children, and a bill including her measure to increase investments in recycling by providing tax code incentives for companies to buy new, more efficient equipment.

She worked on two other bills related to children and the Internet, neither of which became law. One would have required convicted child predators to register their e-mail and instant message addresses with the National Sex Offender Registry in the same way they are required to register their physical addresses. The other aimed to help train law enforcement personnel to track down known sex offenders by following their online footprints.

Bean has been at the forefront of a major issue that arose out of consolidation of the railroad industry, which continues to make the Chicago area one of its key national hubs. The Canadian National Railway proposed buying most of the Elgin, Joliet & Eastern Railway Co., which owns freight track outside Chicago, and expanding it. Approval of the sale would allow Canadian National to bypass Chicago in moving cargo, easing the freight-rail bottleneck in the city.

Reflecting the anger of her constituents, Bean fought the plan, even though it was touted as environmentally sound because it would remove trucks from the clogged expressways around Chicago. Suburban communities said they would be swamped by more trains, traffic backed up at crossings and noise. She backed legislation offered by Minnesota Democrat James L. Oberstar, chairman of the Transportation and Infrastructure Committee, to require the Surface Transportation Board to consider the effect on safety, the environment and intercity passenger rail when weighing proposed railroad mergers. But her bill failed in the House in 2008 when opponents said it could limit future rail mergers, discourage investment and create additional litigation, and the purchase was finalized.

Bean was adopted as an infant into a Serbian-American family, where she was eventually the oldest of four children. She was raised in the Orthodox Church and surrounded by Serbian food, music and culture.

Her father ran an engineering and manufacturing firm, and Bean said that from an early age she knew she'd enter the business world herself. She earned college degrees in business and political science and worked part-time for Data Access Systems, a rapidly growing technology company. The company offered her full-time work, first in sales and then as a branch manager by the time she was 23. In 1995, she started her own technology consulting firm.

Along the way, she juggled work, education and parenthood, finishing one class just in time to give birth to her oldest daughter, Victoria, 10 days later.

Bean jumped into politics in 2002, taking 43 percent of the vote in a longshot bid against veteran incumbent GOP Rep. Philip M. Crane. That showing earned her more financial backing and support from national Democrats for her next run. In 2004 she ousted Crane, painting him as an out-of-touch congressman who had become more interested in traveling the globe than in representing northern Illinois.

In 2006, she held off a strong challenge from Republican David McSweeney, winning 51 percent of the vote. Two years later, the powerful Democratic tide in Illinois for Obama helped her breeze past Republican Steve Greenberg with 61 percent of the vote.

KEY VOTES

2008

No Delay consideration of Colombia free-trade agreement

No Override Bush veto of federal farm and nutrition programs reauthorization bill

Yes Overhaul surveillance laws and permit dismissal of suits against companies that conducted warrantless wiretapping

Yes Grant mortgage relief to homeowners and funding for Fannie Mae and Freddie Mac

Yes Approve initial $700 billion program to stabilize financial markets

Yes Approve final $700 billion program to stabilize financial markets

Yes Provide $14 billion in loans to automakers

2007

Yes Increase minimum wage by $2.10 an hour

Yes Approve $124.2 billion in emergency war spending and set goal for redeployment of troops from Iraq

No Reject federal contraceptive assistance to international family planning groups

Yes Override Bush veto of $23.2 billion water projects authorization bill

Yes Implement Peru free-trade agreement

Yes Approve energy policy overhaul with new fuel economy standards

Yes Clear $473.5 billion omnibus spending bill, including $70 billion for military operations

CQ VOTE STUDIES

	PARTY UNITY		PRESIDENTIAL SUPPORT	
	SUPPORT	OPPOSE	SUPPORT	OPPOSE
2008	88%	12%	33%	67%
2007	84%	16%	18%	82%
2006	76%	24%	50%	50%
2005	83%	17%	48%	52%

INTEREST GROUPS

	AFL-CIO	ADA	CCUS	ACU
2008	80%	65%	83%	20%
2007	83%	80%	70%	21%
2006	64%	60%	80%	48%
2005	73%	80%	73%	12%

ILLINOIS 8

Northwest Cook County – Schaumburg; part of Lake and McHenry counties

The 8th, located in the northeastern corner of the state, takes in northwestern Cook County and parts of Lake and McHenry counties. Most residents live in the affluent, well-established suburbs just northwest of Chicago or farther north through western Lake County and toward the Chain O' Lakes vacation communities near the Wisconsin border.

The district is home to many white-collar employers, including sales and health care companies. The 8th's range of industry provides varied employment and attracts residents to the area. As in other northwestern Chicago suburban districts, some of the 8th's cities, such as Palatine (shared with the 10th) and Schaumburg (a small part of which is in the 6th and 10th districts), have lured corporate headquarters.

A major shopping mall in Schaumburg draws business from across the northwest and west exurbs. Cook County benefits from its access to interstates and proximity to O'Hare International Airport (in the 6th), but Canadian National's acquisition of the Elgin, Joliet & Eastern Railway Co. may increase ground traffic congestion at the rail crossings in the district.

The 8th contains a significant portion of Lake County, where a slight majority of district residents live. This area is largely upscale and well-educated; in the southwest Lake villages of North Barrington and Kildeer, the median family income is more than $100,000. The northeastern part of McHenry County, which is west of Lake, is home to some sparsely populated, relatively affluent towns.

The northeast corner of Illinois sent Republicans to the U.S. House for more than a half century, but it's GOP lean has shifted and the 8th has supported Democratic Rep. Melissa Bean in three consecutive elections. Democrat Barack Obama won the district with 56 percent in 2008.

MAJOR INDUSTRY

Health care, insurance, retail, government

CITIES

Schaumburg (pt.), 71,577; Palatine (pt.), 47,077; Hoffman Estates (pt.), 39,568; Mundelein (pt.), 28,416

NOTABLE

The Volo Illinois Auto Museum features classic and celebrity cars.

Rep. Jan Schakowsky (D)

Elected 1998; 6th term

CAPITOL OFFICE
225-2111
www.house.gov/schakowsky
2367 Rayburn Bldg. 20515-1309; fax 226-6890

COMMITTEES
Energy & Commerce
Select Intelligence
   (Oversight & Investigations - chairwoman)

RESIDENCE
Evanston

BORN
May 26, 1944; Chicago, Ill.

RELIGION
Jewish

FAMILY
Husband, Robert Creamer; three children

EDUCATION
U. of Illinois, B.S. 1965 (elementary education)

CAREER
Senior citizens group director; consumer
advocate; teacher; homemaker

POLITICAL HIGHLIGHTS
Candidate for Cook County Commission, 1986;
Ill. House, 1991-99 (floor leader, 1994-99)

ELECTION RESULTS

2008 GENERAL

Jan Schakowsky (D)	181,948	74.7%
Michael Benjamin Younan (R)	53,593	22.0%
Morris Shanfield (GREEN)	8,140	3.3%

2008 PRIMARY

Jan Schakowsky (D)	98,374	87.9%
John Nocita (D)	13,485	12.1%

2006 GENERAL

Jan Schakowsky (D)	122,852	74.6%
Michael P. Shannon (R)	41,858	25.4%

PREVIOUS WINNING PERCENTAGES
2004 (76%); 2002 (70%); 2000 (76%); 1998 (75%)

Schakowsky is a tough-minded and ambitious liberal activist who has become a dependable ally of Speaker Nancy Pelosi of California. She is among the Democratic Party's most formidable fundraisers and grass-roots organizers as well as a top advocate for women's issues.

Schakowsky (shuh-KOW-ski) is close not only to Pelosi but to Henry A. Waxman of California, who chairs the Energy and Commerce Committee on which she serves. The two share similar views on a vigorous federal role in protecting consumers as well as on expanding access to health care. She also was an early supporter of Barack Obama's presidential bid and hopes to leverage their relationship to achieve her goals.

The liberal Nation magazine once described Schakowsky as "the truest heir to Paul Wellstone," the passionately left-leaning Minnesota Democratic senator who died in a 2002 plane crash. She has said she considers it important to be "a very clear, unapologetic progressive voice."

But she has split with fellow progressives when she fears their efforts could embarrass Democratic leaders. In April 2007, when a $124.2 billion emergency spending bill for the Iraq War and other purposes came to a vote, some progressives decided to buck Pelosi and voted against it because it did not set tough enough benchmarks leading to a withdrawal of U.S. troops. But Schakowsky's loyalty was to Pelosi; she voted for the bill.

In the 110th Congress (2007-08), Pelosi selected her to be a chief deputy whip, and she was given a spot on the Select Intelligence Committee, where she chairs the Subcommittee on Oversight and Investigations. Schakowsky retains her post on the Steering and Policy Committee, which makes Democratic committee assignments. She lost a bid to become vice chairwoman of the Democratic Caucus in 2006; she was among those mentioned for the job in 2008 but declined to run.

She co-chairs, with Oklahoma Republican Rep. Mary Fallin, the bipartisan Congressional Caucus for Women's Issues. Schakowsky has sought expanded funding and support for research and treatment in women's health matters, including heart disease. "Women face exceptional challenges and have a very personal stake in fixing our broken health care system — they understand we need to act now," she said in February 2009.

She continues to draw attention within Democratic circles for her fundraising prowess. With a safe seat, she raised more than $340,000 through her campaign committee for various party candidates and causes in the 2007-08 cycle. That included $260,000 for the Democratic Congressional Campaign Committee, the party's political arm in the House.

Schakowsky's post on Energy and Commerce enables her to continue the work she began more than three decades ago on behalf of consumers. In 2008, she pushed through Congress a bill, signed into law, requiring auto manufacturers to adopt safety measures to decrease the number of deaths and injuries resulting from children being backed over, strangled by power windows or killed when cars are inadvertently shifted into gear.

She also persuaded the House to pass legislation in 2007 that would require manufacturers of infant and toddler products to improve their product recall processes. Her inspiration was Daniel Keysar, a Chicago toddler who was strangled to death when his crib — which had been recalled five years earlier — collapsed. The bill did not advance in the Senate.

Though Schakowsky split with other House progressives on Iraq War spending, she's been a sharp critic of U.S. intervention in Iraq. And she has led efforts in the House to strengthen oversight of U.S. security contractors there. Her efforts gained momentum when Iraqi officials accused a State Department security contractor, Blackwater Worldwide, of killing Iraqi civilians. She applauded Secretary of State Hillary Rodham Clinton's decision in 2009 not to renew the company's contract.

A community activist for more than 25 years before entering Congress, Schakowsky and her husband, Robert Creamer, created a training program for political advocates that has been replicated nationwide. The program brought volunteers to Chicago to a "campaign school," where they were given instruction and political tools and then put to work on several House races.

Her husband was sentenced to prison for five months in 2006 for writing bad checks to generate cash for his failing nonprofit group, Illinois Public Action, and for failing to withhold taxes from employees' paychecks. Schakowsky stood by him, even as she acknowledged he made a mistake.

Schakowsky was a stay-at-home mother in the early 1970s when she helped launch a successful nationwide campaign to require freshness dates on food products. She said six women got together and decided they wanted to know how old the food was in their local grocery. "You would bring home cottage cheese and it would be green around the edges," she said. "We would find infant formula that was sometimes years beyond the [expiration] date." She continued as a community activist and was elected to the Illinois House in 1990. She rose to become chairwoman of the state House Labor and Commerce Committee and Democratic floor leader.

Liberal Democrat Sidney R. Yates held the 9th District seat for 48 years before retiring in 1998. Schakowsky bested state Sen. Howard W. Carroll and Hyatt hotel heir Jay "J.B." Pritzker in the primary and easily won the general election in the heavily Democratic district. She has won each election since with more than 70 percent of the vote.

Schakowsky had hoped to be appointed to Obama's Senate seat before federal prosecutors accused Illinois Democratic Gov. Rod R. Blagojevich in late 2008 of trying the sell the seat to the highest bidder. She was among the first lawmakers to call for Blagojevich's resignation.

She also called for the resignation of Democratic Sen. Roland W. Burris, whom Blagojevich appointed to the seat before the governor's impeachment and removal from office in 2009, because of allegedly conflicting statements Burris gave under oath about his contacts with Blagojevich prior to his appointment. She has left the door open to potentially challenging Burris or another Democrat in the 2010 Senate primary, though she suggested in February 2009 that a special election could be held before then.

KEY VOTES

2008

Yes Delay consideration of Colombia free-trade agreement
Yes Override Bush veto of federal farm and nutrition programs reauthorization bill
No Overhaul surveillance laws and permit dismissal of suits against companies that conducted warrantless wiretapping
Yes Grant mortgage relief to homeowners and funding for Fannie Mae and Freddie Mac
Yes Approve initial $700 billion program to stabilize financial markets
Yes Approve final $700 billion program to stabilize financial markets
Yes Provide $14 billion in loans to automakers

2007

Yes Increase minimum wage by $2.10 an hour
Yes Approve $124.2 billion in emergency war spending and set goal for redeployment of troops from Iraq
No Reject federal contraceptive assistance to international family planning groups
Yes Override Bush veto of $23.2 billion water projects authorization bill
No Implement Peru free-trade agreement
Yes Approve energy policy overhaul with new fuel economy standards
No Clear $473.5 billion omnibus spending bill, including $70 billion for military operations

CQ VOTE STUDIES

	PARTY UNITY		PRESIDENTIAL SUPPORT	
	SUPPORT	OPPOSE	SUPPORT	OPPOSE
2008	99%	1%	16%	84%
2007	99%	1%	3%	97%
2006	99%	1%	15%	85%
2005	99%	1%	9%	91%
2004	99%	1%	12%	88%

INTEREST GROUPS

	AFL-CIO	ADA	CCUS	ACU
2008	100%	100%	61%	0%
2007	100%	100%	50%	0%
2006	100%	95%	20%	0%
2005	100%	100%	29%	0%
2004	100%	100%	5%	0%

ILLINOIS 9
Chicago — North Side lakefront; Evanston

The 9th starts in upscale Wilmette (shared with the 10th), runs south through the liberal suburbs of Evanston and Skokie and Chicago's multi-ethnic North Side, and then drops into one of the city's most prosperous lakefront neighborhoods. It also extends west to blue-collar Des Plaines (shared with the 6th and 10th districts) and Rosemont (shared with the 6th), which is crisscrossed by expressways and has numerous hotels, entertainment venues and convention sites.

Slightly less than half of the district's population lives in Chicago. The neighborhoods of Uptown, Edgewater and Rogers Park — home to Loyola University Chicago — once housed Eastern European and Irish immigrants, but are now an eclectic mix of Asian, European and African immigrants. Uptown in particular has seen rapid gentrification, and residents are divided over redevelopment of what had been a working-class area. The 9th also has the state's largest percentage of Asian residents, and the district's suburbs, namely Skokie, contain a sizable Jewish population. The district includes a significant elderly population as well.

Young professionals have moved into the area near Wrigley Field (in the adjacent 5th), and most of the other Chicagoans in the 9th live in the far northwestern part of the city, near O'Hare International Airport (in the neighboring 6th). Some Park Ridge residents have opposed plans for the modernization of O'Hare because of expected air traffic noise increases.

Most jobs are concentrated in a few major industries. Northwestern University provides the bulk of jobs in Evanston, and health care also is a major employer as many residents work at several area hospitals.

The 9th ranges from the very wealthy to the very poor, but the mix of immigrants, affluent urbanites and college students make the 9th solidly Democratic. The district awarded Barack Obama 72 percent of its 2008 presidential vote — his sixth-best showing in the state.

MAJOR INDUSTRY
Health care, higher education, insurance, light manufacturing

CITIES
Chicago (pt.), 299,868; Evanston, 74,239; Skokie, 63,348; Des Plaines (pt.), 39,632; Park Ridge, 37,775; Niles, 30,068

NOTABLE
Tinkertoy sets were invented by an Evanston stonemason in 1913.

Rep. Mark Steven Kirk (R)

Elected 2000; 5th term

CAPITOL OFFICE
225-4835
www.house.gov/kirk
1030 Longworth Bldg. 20515-1310; fax 225-0837

COMMITTEES
Appropriations

RESIDENCE
Highland Park

BORN
Sept. 15, 1959; Champaign, Ill.

RELIGION
Congregationalist

FAMILY
Separated

EDUCATION
Cornell U., B.A. 1981 (history); London School of Economics, M.S. 1982; Georgetown U., J.D. 1992

MILITARY SERVICE
Naval Reserve, 1989-present

CAREER
Congressional aide; lawyer; U.S. State Department aide; World Bank officer

POLITICAL HIGHLIGHTS
No previous office

ELECTION RESULTS

2008 GENERAL

Mark Steven Kirk (R)	153,082	52.6%
Dan Seals (D)	138,176	47.4%

2008 PRIMARY

Mark Steven Kirk (R)	unopposed

2006 GENERAL

Mark Steven Kirk (R)	107,929	53.4%
Dan Seals (D)	94,278	46.6%

PREVIOUS WINNING PERCENTAGES
2004 (64%); 2002 (69%); 2000 (51%)

Kirk, one of a dwindling number of Republican House moderates, works to meet the concerns of his centrist-minded district in the Chicago suburbs by pushing for fiscal restraint while backing such liberal social measures as gun control, embryonic stem cell research and increases in the minimum wage. Democratic leaders often look to him for support, and he reaches out to like-minded conservatives in their party. Yet he still carries significant sway in the GOP, particularly as it seeks to solidify its ranks after severe losses in the previous two congressional elections.

Kirk doesn't have a high profile outside Illinois, but he attracted increasing attention after surviving strong Democratic challenges in both 2006 and 2008. He won by a comfortable margin against Democrat Dan Seals — an African-American marketing executive who drew comparisons to Barack Obama — even while 61 percent of the district turned out for Obama, their junior senator, for president in 2008. His success encouraged him in early 2009 to mull a bid for Obama's old Senate seat in 2010.

While he attributed his success at the polls to his support for more-centrist ideals — he frequently crossed party lines during the 110th Congress (2007-08) to support the Democratic agenda and oppose an increasingly unpopular President George W. Bush — in early 2009 he showed more solidarity with the Republican party than with the popular Obama. He stuck with his GOP colleagues to oppose all of Obama's early economic measures, including a stimulus package and a catchall spending bill for fiscal 2009. "We no longer have to worry about being blamed for all of the problems of the president and his administration," he said in February 2009. "Now, it's the moderate Democrats who have to worry about that."

Kirk has not faced any political fallout in the House from his voting record; he has been climbing through the ranks since his arrival in 2001. He won an Appropriations Committee seat after just one term, and former GOP Whip Roy Blunt of Missouri named him a deputy in the party's vote-gathering operations. He is a leader of the Tuesday Group of centrist Republicans and emphasizes the need for a balanced federal budget. But in 2008, he was unsuccessful in his efforts to encourage GOP leaders to get Republicans to agree to a one-year moratorium on earmarking, the practice by which individual members insert funds for specific projects into spending bills.

Also in 2008, he led the Tuesday Group in meetings with the Blue Dogs Coalition, a group of fiscally conservative Democrats. "Some of the ideas Blue Dogs have, we feel the Tuesday Group has, too," Kirk said. "I think it would be good to talk about the overlap."

Kirk champions his constituents' interests by spearheading an informal "suburban caucus" of Republican members that has devised proposals affecting swing voters in suburbs. The group focuses on such topics as fighting suburban drug gangs and increasing protections against child predators.

He has been a Naval Reserve intelligence officer since 1989 and serves on the Appropriations subcommittee that oversees the State Department and other foreign operations. He draws on his naval experience, which has included stints overseas in Bosnia, Iraq, Haiti and Panama.

In 2009, he led opposition to the nomination of Charles "Chas" Freeman to lead the National Intelligence Council; Freeman eventually withdrew from consideration. Critics complained that Freeman served on the board of directors of the China-owned Chinese National Offshore Oil Corp. and was president of the Middle East Policy Council, a think tank funded by the Saudi government. Many also were concerned about remarks he had made on China's actions during the 1989 Tiananmen Square protests and some of Israel's policies toward Palestinians. "There comes a point where somebody is mortally wounded and can't carry out their job," Kirk said of Freeman.

Back home, Kirk has fought to preserve the Veterans Administration hospital in North Chicago and helped secure funds to expand service on the North Central Line operated by Metra, the Chicago area's suburban commuter train system (the line opened in 1996 and was expanded in 2006). He is also a steady proponent of cleaning up the Great Lakes, especially the harbor area in Waukegan, the Lake County seat, where industrial PCBs (polychlorinated biphenyls) hinder redevelopment efforts.

For a deeply personal reason, Kirk has become involved in the fight against pulmonary fibrosis, an irreversible disease that causes lung scarring. In February 2008, his father, Francis, died of it, and Kirk has cosponsored a bill to create a patient registry for the disease.

His father was a telephone company executive, and Kirk grew up in Kenilworth, a wealthy suburb of Chicago. His near-death at age 16, when he almost drowned in a boating accident on Lake Michigan, convinced him to do something positive with his life. "To be given a second chance means it has to mean something," he told the Tribune. "For me, that means making a difference through public service."

He graduated from New Trier High School, long one of Illinois' top public high schools, and followed up with three university degrees, a stint in Mexico to learn Spanish and his career in military intelligence. He has traveled in more than 40 countries. One of his earliest jobs was as a legislative counsel for the House International Relations Committee. He also worked for several years on the staff of his predecessor, fellow GOP centrist Rep. John Edward Porter, and worked at the State Department and the World Bank.

When Porter announced his retirement before the 2000 election, Kirk ran in a primary field jammed with 10 other Republicans. Armed with Porter's backing, Kirk singled himself out by his grasp of policy questions. He won, beating his nearest rival by 16 percentage points. In the general election, he prevailed over Democratic state Rep. Lauren Beth Gash by 2 percentage points. He won with ease in 2002 and 2004 before facing tough battles with Seals in the last two elections, when he was a top target of the Democrats. In 2008, he won an endorsement from Planned Parenthood and was one of only six Republican congressional candidates endorsed by the Sierra Club. He raised more than $5 million, more than any other House member seeking re-election that year, and took 53 percent of the vote.

KEY VOTES

2008

No Delay consideration of Colombia free-trade agreement

No Override Bush veto of federal farm and nutrition programs reauthorization bill

Yes Overhaul surveillance laws and permit dismissal of suits against companies that conducted warrantless wiretapping

No Grant mortgage relief to homeowners and funding for Fannie Mae and Freddie Mac

Yes Approve initial $700 billion program to stabilize financial markets

Yes Approve final $700 billion program to stabilize financial markets

No Provide $14 billion in loans to automakers

2007

Yes Increase minimum wage by $2.10 an hour

No Approve $124.2 billion in emergency war spending and set goal for redeployment of troops from Iraq

No Reject federal contraceptive assistance to international family planning groups

Yes Override Bush veto of $23.2 billion water projects authorization bill

Yes Implement Peru free-trade agreement

Yes Approve energy policy overhaul with new fuel economy standards

Yes Clear $473.5 billion omnibus spending bill, including $70 billion for military operations

CQ VOTE STUDIES

	PARTY UNITY		PRESIDENTIAL SUPPORT	
	SUPPORT	OPPOSE	SUPPORT	OPPOSE
2008	73%	27%	53%	47%
2007	70%	30%	41%	59%
2006	79%	21%	80%	20%
2005	80%	20%	67%	33%
2004	84%	16%	63%	37%

INTEREST GROUPS

	AFL-CIO	ADA	CCUS	ACU
2008	47%	55%	83%	48%
2007	52%	40%	84%	40%
2006	36%	45%	80%	54%
2005	20%	30%	81%	36%
2004	29%	45%	90%	63%

ILLINOIS 10

North and northwest Chicago suburbs — Waukegan

The mostly upscale 10th hugs Lake Michigan, taking in southeast Lake County and northeast Cook County. Along the lakefront, Chicagoland's old-money elite live in tony areas such as Wilmette (shared with the 9th), Kenilworth and Winnetka.

The 10th has the state's highest percentage of college-educated (48 percent) and white-collar (76 percent) workers, and the wealth of the district's workforce mirrors the wealth of local industry. The 10th is home to several Fortune 500 companies, including Abbott Laboratories in North Chicago, Allstate Insurance in Northbrook and Walgreens in Deerfield, although a nationwide economic downturn is threatening jobs and revenues across many industries.

Most of the 10th's minorities live in the northern area between Highwood and Waukegan (a small part of which is in the 8th). That area also is home to the Great Lakes naval base, the nation's only naval recruit train-

ing command. Waukegan is roughly 45 percent Hispanic and 20 percent black, and North Chicago, just south of Waukegan, also has a minority majority. The 10th also has a large Jewish constituency.

Suburban white-collar workers and the more working-class residents of Waukegan combine to make the 10th fiscally conservative but socially liberal, especially on abortion rights and gun control. Its proximity to Lake Michigan makes environmental issues important here. While area residents have sent a Republican to the U.S. House for decades, the area generally supports Democratic presidential candidates, and backed Barack Obama in 2008 with 61 percent of its vote.

MAJOR INDUSTRY
Pharmaceutical research, insurance, military

MILITARY BASES
Naval Station Great Lakes, 3,685 military, 2,271 civilian (2008)

CITIES
Waukegan (pt.), 79,726; Arlington Heights (pt.), 69,414; Buffalo Grove, 42,909; North Chicago, 35,918; Wheeling, 34,496; Northbrook, 33,435

NOTABLE
The annual Ravinia Festival, held every summer in Highland Park, is the oldest outdoor music festival in North America.

Rep. Debbie Halvorson (D)

Elected 2008; 1st term

CAPITOL OFFICE
225-3635
halvorson.house.gov
1541 Longworth Bldg. 20515; fax 225-3521

COMMITTEES
Agriculture
Small Business
Veterans' Affairs

RESIDENCE
Crete

BORN
March 1, 1958; Chicago Heights, Ill.

RELIGION
Lutheran

FAMILY
Husband, Jim Bush; two children,
two stepchildren

EDUCATION
Prairie State College, A.G.S. 1998; Governors
State U., B.A. 2001 (Board of Governors), M.A.
2003 (communications and training)

CAREER
Cosmetics saleswoman; homemaker;
apartment property manager; driving instructor

POLITICAL HIGHLIGHTS
Crete Township clerk, 1993-96; Ill. Senate, 1997-
2009 (majority leader, 2005-09)

ELECTION RESULTS

2008 GENERAL

Debbie Halvorson (D)	185,652	58.4%
Marty Ozinga (R)	109,608	34.5%
Jason M. Wallace (GREEN)	22,635	7.1%

2008 PRIMARY

Debbie Halvorson (D)	unopposed

Halvorson is a former stay-at-home mom and cosmetics saleswoman who rose to majority leader of the Illinois Senate, where she served with President Obama. While she describes herself as a fiscal conservative and supporter of gun rights, she said she became a Democrat early in life because she believed "the average guy needed help."

Her background in Illinois helped her become one of just two freshmen named to the Democratic Steering and Policy Committee, an arm of the party's leadership, in 2009.

Overhauling health care is a top priority for Halvorson. When she was a child, her family didn't have health insurance, and her parents later scrambled to find coverage when her mother battled and survived breast cancer. "I saw the struggles and how we had to fight through her costs when we should have been able to fight the illness," she said. On the Veterans' Affairs Committee, Halvorson also focuses on expanding health coverage for veterans such as her stepson, a U.S. Army captain who was wounded while serving in Afghanistan.

From her seat on the Agriculture Committee, Halvorson promotes alternative energy programs that would help farmers in her district. She wants to make her district a major provider of "green jobs" to address unemployment and help reduce the nation's dependence on foreign oil.

The Small Business Committee is a natural fit for Halvorson; she owned a Mary Kay cosmetics business for 14 years. Her frank, rapid-fire style served her well with customers, who later made up her political base. Although she never won the pink Cadillac awarded to the company's top salespeople, she said she made a "very good living." While in the state Senate, Halvorson put herself through college and graduate school.

National and state Democrats urged Halvorson to run for the House in 2008 to replace retiring seven-term Republican Rep. Jerry Weller. After running unopposed in the primary, she beat Republican Marty Ozinga, a concrete company executive, with 58 percent of the vote — five points above Obama's showing in the district.

ILLINOIS 11

South Chicago exurbs — Joliet; part of Bloomington-Normal

Beginning south of Chicago in suburban Will County, the 11th heads west through the old industrial city of Joliet and into farm country, with a sliver making a southward turn in LaSalle County to run parallel to Interstate 39 as it heads to Bloomington-Normal.

Will County (shared mainly with the 13th) has seen an influx of families, and fast-growing Joliet's proximity to the Chicago metropolitan area has helped alleviate past economic troubles there. Many visitors to Joliet come to the Harrah's Casino and Hotel, the Rialto Square Theatre, and Silver Cross Field — home to the Joliet JackHammers independent baseball team.

Ongoing debate over construction of a third Chicago metro-area airport in Peotone, southeast of Joliet, pits residents in the 11th's northern areas, who say a new airport would bring an economic boost to the suburbs, against rural residents, who worry it would disrupt their way of life.

South of Will, the 11th includes Kankakee County, still in the ambit of Chicagoland, before assuming a more rural posture as it takes in a small corner of Livingston County, all of Grundy and LaSalle counties, and most of Bureau County. A jaunt south takes it to Bloomington-Normal (shared with the 15th). Illinois State University is here. The politically competitive 11th handed Democrat Barack Obama 53 percent of its 2008 presidential vote.

MAJOR INDUSTRY
Farm equipment manufacturing, agriculture, insurance

CITIES
Joliet (pt.), 105,052; Normal (pt.), 30,662; Bloomington (pt.), 30,298; Kankakee, 27,491

NOTABLE
The now-closed Joliet Correctional Center was featured in the TV show "Prison Break."

Rep. Jerry F. Costello (D)

Elected August 1988; 11th full term

CAPITOL OFFICE
225-5661
www.house.gov/costello
2408 Rayburn Bldg. 20515-1312; fax 225-0285

COMMITTEES
Science & Technology
Transportation & Infrastructure
   (Aviation - chairman)

RESIDENCE
Belleville

BORN
Sept. 25, 1949; East St. Louis, Ill.

RELIGION
Roman Catholic

FAMILY
Wife, Georgia Cockrum Costello; three children

EDUCATION
Belleville Area College, A.A. 1971; Maryville
College of the Sacred Heart, B.A. 1973

CAREER
Law enforcement official

POLITICAL HIGHLIGHTS
St. Clair County Board chairman, 1980-88

ELECTION RESULTS

2008 GENERAL

Jerry F. Costello (D)	213,270	71.4%
Timmy Jay Richardson Jr. (R)	74,634	25.0%
Roger W. Jennings (GREEN)	10,931	3.7%

2008 PRIMARY

Jerry F. Costello (D)	unopposed

2006 GENERAL

Jerry F. Costello (D)	unopposed

PREVIOUS WINNING PERCENTAGES
2004 (69%); 2002 (69%); 2000 (100%); 1998 (60%);
1996 (72%); 1994 (66%); 1992 (71%); 1990 (66%);
1988 (53%); 1988 Special Election (51%)

Costello has spent more than 20 years in the House quietly steering millions of federal dollars back home for light rail, bridges, housing and the district's local military base. He rarely speaks on the House floor, working diligently in committee and behind the scenes to push projects to boost economic prospects in his struggling hometown of East St. Louis, which was once a thriving steel industry town.

He has gained seniority during that time and now is the second-ranking Democrat on the Science and Technology Committee and the fourth-ranking on the Transportation and Infrastructure Committee, where he chairs the Aviation Subcommittee. Both seats put him in the center of high-profile national discussions as lawmakers look to fund infrastructure and technology projects in hopes of stemming the United States' economic crisis.

When his former colleague in the state delegation, Barack Obama, moved to the White House, he saw promise for some of his priorities that had been blocked by President George W. Bush. He immediately set out to include a range of infrastructure funds in Obama's economic stimulus package in early 2009. He obtained many of the funds, but failed to get approval for his request to include $1 billion for the construction of a clean-coal research facility known as FutureGen — a project the Bush administration had ultimately turned down but which he and Republican John Shimkus of the adjacent 19th District believe will help revive the area's sagging coal industry.

Nevertheless, Costello supported the final $787 billion stimulus plan, signed into law. "For the last six years, we have spent over $860 billion in Iraq and Afghanistan, billions of which have gone to rebuilding those countries, and it is time we made similar investments here at home," he said.

Transportation and Infrastructure is scheduled to rewrite the 2005 surface transportation law during the 111th Congress (2009-10), and Costello likely will seek further funding for local interests. He already has brought in millions of federal funding in the past, including $600 million for the MetroLink light rail that connects St. Louis with the district. In the 2005 law, Costello helped snag $239 million to pay part of the cost of building a new bridge across the Mississippi River between St. Louis and eastern Illinois.

Costello also won approval of legislation in 1999 to set aside federal land for a visitor center devoted to the journey of explorers Meriwether Lewis and William Clark, near where the expedition departed on its westward journey in 1804. And Costello looks out for Scott Air Force Base. He helped to protect it from the 2005 round of military base closings, and it subsequently was awarded new missions producing 800 new jobs. Costello and Shimkus obtained $34.6 million in 2006 for new facilities at the base.

On the Aviation Subcommittee, he works to restart the frequently stalled attempts to reauthorize the Federal Aviation Administration. Lawmakers approved a series of short-term extensions during the 110th Congress (2007-08), and approved another extension at the start of 2009. Costello aims to pass a bill to require airlines and airports to develop contingency plans for stranded passengers and raise aviation fuel taxes. From Science and Technology, Costello offered a bill early in the 110th to increase the use of coal as a fuel source in ethanol plants — a twofer for Illinois' coal and corn industries. But the bill didn't move.

Despite his propensity for sending dollars home, Costello calls himself a fiscal conservative. In 2007 he voted against a "patch" to limit the alternative minimum tax, which originally targeted wealthy taxpayers but was not indexed for inflation, because the patch lacked revenue-raising offsets. He also opposed two versions of a $700 billion plan to aid the financial sector in 2008 — the second of which became law. He also breaks with his party on many social issues, staying in line with his constituency's cultural conservatism. He opposes abortion and supports gun owners' rights. In 2006, he voted for a proposed constitutional amendment to ban same-sex marriage.

Costello has received his share of unfavorable publicity. Media reports in 2002 revealed Illinois Secretary of State Jesse White hired Costello's 26-year-old son for a $50,000-a-year job over a more experienced candidate after Costello called on his son's behalf. Costello described it as a routine reference call and attributed the flap, in part, to a long-running feud with his hometown newspaper, the Belleville News-Democrat.

In 1997, he was named an "unindicted co-conspirator" in the trial of his childhood friend and former business partner Amiel Cueto, who was convicted of trying to block the federal investigation of a convicted racketeer. Witnesses testified that Costello was a silent partner in two casino deals and that he helped pass a bill to aid an American Indian tribe that owned the land where one of the casinos was to be built. Costello denied wrongdoing, and the prosecutor later said he was not the target of the investigation.

Costello lived in East St. Louis until he was in high school. Then the family moved to nearby Belleville. His father had been elected county sheriff, and that job required him to live near the jail. While attending a local community college, Costello took a job as a bailiff. He eventually became administrator of the local court system. Costello entered local politics after he was frustrated in his efforts to push for expanding a juvenile-detention facility. In 1980, he was elected chairman of the St. Clair County Board, a job he held for eight years, during which time he developed a talent for snaring federal grants.

He ran his first race for the House in 1988, after elderly Democratic Rep. Melvin Price decided against seeking re-election. But in the primary, Madison County Auditor Pete Fields portrayed Costello as an old-style, hardball "boss" in the county Democratic Party. Costello survived because of a huge financial advantage but with only a 46 percent plurality.

When Price died in April, Costello squared off against Republican college official Robert H. Gaffner in a special election. Costello barely won the special election, then went on to win in November with 53 percent of the vote. In 1998, he faced Republican Bill Price, an orthopedic surgeon and son of the late Melvin Price. Costello overcame questions about his connections with Cueto and charged that Price represented a threat to Social Security and Medicare. Costello took 60 percent of the vote and has not dipped below 69 percent since.

KEY VOTES

2008

Yes Delay consideration of Colombia free-trade agreement

Yes Override Bush veto of federal farm and nutrition programs reauthorization bill

No Overhaul surveillance laws and permit dismissal of suits against companies that conducted warrantless wiretapping

Yes Grant mortgage relief to homeowners and funding for Fannie Mae and Freddie Mac

No Approve initial $700 billion program to stabilize financial markets

No Approve final $700 billion program to stabilize financial markets

Yes Provide $14 billion in loans to automakers

2007

Yes Increase minimum wage by $2.10 an hour

Yes Approve $124.2 billion in emergency war spending and set goal for redeployment of troops from Iraq

Yes Reject federal contraceptive assistance to international family planning groups

Yes Override Bush veto of $23.2 billion water projects authorization bill

No Implement Peru free-trade agreement

Yes Approve energy policy overhaul with new fuel economy standards

No Clear $473.5 billion omnibus spending bill, including $70 billion for military operations

CQ VOTE STUDIES

| | PARTY UNITY | | PRESIDENTIAL SUPPORT | |
	SUPPORT	OPPOSE	SUPPORT	OPPOSE
2008	96%	4%	15%	85%
2007	93%	7%	10%	90%
2006	87%	13%	37%	63%
2005	82%	18%	37%	63%
2004	82%	18%	41%	59%

INTEREST GROUPS

	AFL-CIO	ADA	CCUS	ACU
2008	100%	85%	50%	13%
2007	96%	95%	47%	16%
2006	93%	70%	40%	48%
2005	87%	80%	52%	40%
2004	93%	70%	38%	36%

ILLINOIS 12
Southwest — Belleville, East St. Louis, Carbondale

The 12th begins in the St. Louis suburbs along the Mississippi River and extends south along the river to Cairo at the southern tip of Illinois, where the Mississippi and Ohio rivers converge.

East St. Louis, an overwhelmingly black city in St. Clair County, has experienced declining population and some of the state's worst urban blight for years, and crime rates remain high. Federal and state aid, along with revenue from casino gambling, provide income for the city, but residents still face high unemployment and poverty rates.

Other cities in the 12th District also are attempting to overcome difficult economic situations. Alton is in the midst of a major revitalization aimed at providing jobs, growing industry and creating new tourism opportunities. The city, along with Clark Properties, converted the long-vacant Owens-Illinois Glass factory into usable warehouse and light industrial space. Belleville, largely dependent upon defense industry jobs, relies heavily on Scott Air Force Base, the area's major employer. Higher education remains one of the area's few steadfast employers, with Carbon-

dale's Southern Illinois University, and its 21,000 students, bolstering Jackson County's economy.

The district's economic anxiety and minority population (blacks make up 16 percent) make it solid Democratic turf. St. Clair County has voted Democratic in the past nine presidential elections, and gave Democrat Barack Obama his third-highest percentage statewide in the 2008 election. Despite only carrying St. Clair, Pulaski, Jackson and Alexander counties among the nine counties entirely in the 12th, Obama still captured 56 percent of the 12th's 2008 presidential vote.

MAJOR INDUSTRY
Manufacturing, higher education, casinos, agriculture

MILITARY BASES
Scott Air Force Base, 5,919 military, 3,211 civilian (2009)

CITIES
Belleville, 41,410; East St. Louis, 31,542; Granite City, 31,301; Alton, 30,496; O'Fallon, 21,910; Carbondale, 20,681

NOTABLE
Cahokia Mounds, a prehistoric civilization, was designated by the United Nations as a World Heritage Site in 1982; The Gateway Geyser, which stands at 600 feet, is a man-made fountain in East St. Louis.

Rep. Judy Biggert (R)

Elected 1998; 6th term

CAPITOL OFFICE
225-3515
www.house.gov/biggert
1034 Longworth Bldg. 20515-1313; fax 225-9420

COMMITTEES
Education & Labor
Financial Services
Science & Technology

RESIDENCE
Hinsdale

BORN
Aug. 15, 1937; Chicago, Ill.

RELIGION
Episcopalian

FAMILY
Husband, Rody Biggert; four children

EDUCATION
Stanford U., A.B. 1959 (international relations);
Northwestern U., J.D. 1963

CAREER
Lawyer

POLITICAL HIGHLIGHTS
Hinsdale Board of Education, 1982-85 (president,
1983-85); Village of Hinsdale Plan Commission,
1989-93; Ill. House, 1993-99

ELECTION RESULTS

2008 GENERAL

Judy Biggert (R)	180,888	53.6%
Scott Harper (D)	147,430	43.6%
Steve Alesch (GREEN)	9,402	2.8%

2008 PRIMARY

Judy Biggert (R)	58,533	77.3%
Sean O'Kane (R)	17,206	22.7%

2006 GENERAL

Judy Biggert (R)	119,720	58.3%
Joseph Shannon (D)	85,507	41.7%

PREVIOUS WINNING PERCENTAGES
2004 (65%); 2002 (70%); 2000 (66%); 1998 (61%)

Biggert's tendency to support federal involvement in areas such as education, low-income housing and health care puts her in the House's dwindling camp of Republican moderates. But she is comfortable working across the aisle and capable of getting things done. While that doesn't help her standing within her with own party, it does endear her to Democrats now in control of the House.

Her moderate bona fides makes her feel at home in the House GOP's Tuesday Group and the Republican Main Street Partnership, both middle-of-the-road organizations. She does vote with conservatives at times, particularly on labor issues and most recently on President Obama's economic agenda. But she is likely to continue to find more agreement with Democrats on her other high-priority items.

During the 110th Congress (2007-08), Biggert achieved a long-sought goal with the enactment of a law that bars employers or health insurers from basing enrollment or premium decisions on the results of genetic testing. Biggert had cosponsored the measure for eight years with Democrat Louise M. Slaughter of New York, never before mustering enough GOP backing to get it enacted. "I don't think people realize how important that is, and how it's really going to change health care," Biggert said. The promise of genetic research, she explained, will go unrealized if people are afraid to get tested for fear the results could be held against them.

A former school board president, Biggert focuses intently on education. From her seat on the Education and Labor Committee, she champions programs for homeless children. She has pushed a proposal to help homeless youth access student aid for colleges, which stalled during the years Republicans controlled the House. But a similar proposal became law in 2007 as part of Democratic legislation to cut student loan rates.

Biggert is likely to play a significant role during the 111th Congress (2009-10) on efforts to rewrite the No Child Left Behind Act, a law she helped draft in 2001. She believes the law, which ties federal aid for elementary and secondary education to improvement in student test scores, has brought about greater accountability. But she agrees with those who say the law also has "some real drawbacks" as currently structured and needs to allow state education officials more flexibility. "There's too much emphasis on the test. And we're losing some of the creativity and innovation in education that is so important," she said.

Another priority for Biggert is energy research — a vital issue for her district, where the Argonne National Laboratory, one of the Energy Department's largest facilities, is located. She uses her seat on the Science and Technology Committee to encourage the development of advanced technologies, especially hydrogen-fueled cars. The 2005 energy policy overhaul included her provisions to expand nuclear fuel reprocessing research at Argonne, plus $2 billion to put hydrogen fuel cell vehicles on the road by 2020, with much of that research also taking place at Argonne. She worries that Americans will repeat the mistakes of the 1970s, when they abandoned fuel-efficient vehicles and returned to gas guzzlers as soon as gasoline shortages ended.

A member of the Financial Services Committee, she strongly criticized Obama's economic agenda in 2009, even though she was one of 25 Republicans to switch their votes and support a 2008 bill, proposed by President George W. Bush, to spend $700 billion to shore up the financial services sector. With fellow Republicans, she introduced a bill in March 2009 to help struggling homeowners refinance their loans. She said the bill would exclude real estate speculators who'd made bad bets.

She rarely sides with Democrats on labor issues. In 2003, she sponsored "flex time" legislation to let employers offer compensatory time off instead of premium pay for overtime. She argued the change would help women juggle the competing demands of work and family. But the bill was scorned by women's groups and unions, who said too many companies would coerce employees to take comp time instead of extra pay.

When Biggert arrived in Congress in 1999, Fortune magazine identified her as one of the newcomers most likely to be a star. But her efforts to get into the leadership ranks were twice thwarted by conservatives who dominate the House GOP. She ran for Republican Conference secretary in 2001, reminding her colleagues she had been a prolific fundraiser for them, but lost to conservative Barbara Cubin of Wyoming. In 2002, Biggert tried again, but dropped out when she concluded conservative Californian John T. Doolittle had the election wrapped up.

Biggert is from a generation when career choices for women were limited. After earning her undergraduate degree at Stanford, Biggert applied to a master's degree program in business. She received a letter saying women weren't accepted, but that she was welcome to take a few night classes.

Instead, she enrolled at Northwestern to study law, and later clerked for a federal appeals court judge. After school, she and her husband Rody got offers from a Chicago law firm, but Biggert decided to start her own home-based law practice, specializing in real estate and estate planning. She worked at home for 20 years, while raising four children.

Biggert volunteered in civic groups, including a then-new federal program for at-risk children called Head Start. She served on the Hinsdale planning commission and the board of education, including a stint as board president from 1983 to 1985. Elected to the Illinois House in 1992, she focused on women's and children's issues and was elected assistant Republican leader after just one term.

Biggert was the hand-picked successor of Republican Harris W. Fawell when he retired in 1998. She defeated five men vying for the GOP nomination and went on to win the seat with 61 percent of the vote.

In 2004, she passed up entreaties to run for the Senate when GOP party leaders were desperate to replace a primary winner who withdrew amid a sex scandal, leaving the field open to an attractive newcomer, Obama. In 2008, she slipped by a well-funded challenger, who tried to tie her to the unpopular Bush, with just 54 percent of the vote.

KEY VOTES

2008
No Delay consideration of Colombia free-trade agreement
No Override Bush veto of federal farm and nutrition programs reauthorization bill
Yes Overhaul surveillance laws and permit dismissal of suits against companies that conducted warrantless wiretapping
Yes Grant mortgage relief to homeowners and funding for Fannie Mae and Freddie Mac
No Approve initial $700 billion program to stabilize financial markets
Yes Approve final $700 billion program to stabilize financial markets
No Provide $14 billion in loans to automakers

2007
Yes Increase minimum wage by $2.10 an hour
No Approve $124.2 billion in emergency war spending and set goal for redeployment of troops from Iraq
No Reject federal contraceptive assistance to international family planning groups
Yes Override Bush veto of $23.2 billion water projects authorization bill
Yes Implement Peru free-trade agreement
Yes Approve energy policy overhaul with new fuel economy standards
Yes Clear $473.5 billion omnibus spending bill, including $70 billion for military operations

CQ VOTE STUDIES

	PARTY UNITY		PRESIDENTIAL SUPPORT	
	SUPPORT	OPPOSE	SUPPORT	OPPOSE
2008	89%	11%	69%	31%
2007	83%	17%	66%	34%
2006	88%	12%	80%	20%
2005	87%	13%	72%	28%
2004	88%	12%	74%	26%

INTEREST GROUPS

	AFL-CIO	ADA	CCUS	ACU
2008	20%	35%	94%	84%
2007	42%	30%	85%	68%
2006	21%	30%	93%	64%
2005	13%	20%	89%	60%
2004	13%	35%	100%	64%

ILLINOIS 13

Southwest Chicago suburbs — Naperville

More than half of the suburban Chicago-based 13th's population lives in the district's southern part of DuPage County, an area that includes Naperville. Nearly one-third of district residents live in northern Will County communities such as Bolingbrook and Romeoville, with the rest living in the southwestern edge of Cook County.

Naperville, Downers Grove (a small part of which is in the 6th) and Oak Brook (shared with the 6th) have become leading suburban Chicago business centers, and companies such as OfficeMax, Sara Lee and McDonald's have corporate headquarters here. These large corporations and other high-paying employers have been attracted to the district by Chicago's busy O'Hare International Airport (nearby in the 6th) as well as the state's second-highest percentage of white-collar workers. The presence of these corporations has helped the 13th achieve the highest median income in the state, and one of the top 10 nationwide, at nearly $72,000.

The Argonne National Laboratory, in southeast DuPage, and the Fermi National Accelerator Laboratory, in the neighboring 14th, have made the area into a scientific research and technology hub. DePaul University also has a campus in Naperville.

The district's growth over the past decade has created serious traffic problems for its suburban residents. The national economic downturn is affecting cities in the district, some of which are experiencing rising unemployment rates and municipal budget shortfalls.

Voters in the 13th tend to be fiscally conservative and have a history of voting Republican in federal elections. But many residents here hold moderate views on social and environmental issues, and home-state Democrat Barack Obama won the 13th with 54 percent of the vote in the 2008 presidential election.

MAJOR INDUSTRY
Scientific research, health care, insurance

CITIES
Naperville, 128,358; Bolingbrook, 56,321; Downers Grove (pt.), 45,139

NOTABLE
The Millennium Carillon in Naperville is among the four largest such structures in the world, with a system of 72 bronze bells weighing up to 6 tons each.

Rep. Bill Foster (D)

CAPITOL OFFICE
225-2976
foster.house.gov
1339 Longworth Bldg. 20515-1314; fax 225-0697

COMMITTEES
Financial Services
Oversight & Government Reform

RESIDENCE
Batavia

BORN
Oct. 7, 1955; Madison, Wis.

RELIGION
Unspecified

FAMILY
Wife, Aesook Byon; two children

EDUCATION
U. of Wisconsin, B.A. 1976 (physics);
Harvard U., Ph.D. 1983 (experimental physics)

CAREER
Physicist; theater lighting company owner

POLITICAL HIGHLIGHTS
No previous office

ELECTION RESULTS

2008 GENERAL
Bill Foster (D)	185,404	57.7%
Jim Oberweis (R)	135,653	42.2%

2008 SPECIAL
Bill Foster (D)	52,205	52.5%
Jim Oberweis (R)	47,180	47.5%

2008 PRIMARY
Bill Foster (D)	32,410	42.4%
John Laesch (D)	32,012	41.9%
Joe Serra (D)	6,033	7.9%
Jotham Stein (D)	5,865	7.7%

2008 PRIMARY SPECIAL
Bill Foster (D)	32,982	49.6%
John Laesch (D)	28,433	42.8%
Jotham Stein (D)	5,082	7.6%

Elected March 2008; 1st full term

A former physicist, Foster has said he would like to see more facts and less partisan rhetoric in political debates. He gently prods for changes to legislation and maneuvers quietly through the House as he learns the ropes. But he takes every opportunity to publicize word of federal funds he's obtained for projects back home, where Republicans had held his seat for more than 30 years.

Foster won the seat in a stunning 2008 special election victory to replace Republican J. Dennis Hastert — a former House Speaker — who had resigned after more than 20 years. It was the first of three special-election victories that presaged the broad Democratic victories in the fall, when Foster won his first regular election by more than 15 percentage points.

Democratic leaders are eager for him to hold onto his seat and are expected to give Foster — a member of a group of moderates called the New Democrat Coalition — leeway on many votes. They also placed Foster, a former small businessman, on the Financial Services Committee, where he is in the center of discussions on how to address the nation's fiscal woes. His other assignment is the Oversight and Government Reform Committee.

He is in step with party leaders on most issues. In early 2009, he favored a series of bills backed by the Democratic leadership and President Obama, including a bill to expand the State Children's Health Insurance Program that covers children whose families don't qualify for Medicaid. He also voted for two measures to enable workers to combat wage discrimination, and legislation to allow bankruptcy judges to modify the terms of a mortgage.

Foster also backed Obama's $787 billion economic stimulus plan that became law in early 2009. He was among the Democrats highlighted in local press releases distributed by the U.S. Chamber of Commerce that applauded passage of the bill.

A few weeks later, Foster also voted for a $410 billion catchall spending bill for 2009, left over from the previous Congress. Foster had successfully included $4 million in federal funding for local projects, including funds for a proton therapy treatment and research center and for the Northern Illinois University Institute for Neutron Therapy at Fermilab, where he used to work, to provide information on the effectiveness of neutron therapy.

Foster may not always be loyal to his party, however. He was one of 14 Democrats who voted in May 2008 against his leadership's 2009 budget resolution because it didn't "lock the middle-class tax cuts" he campaigned on. He also introduced a bill to allow taxpayers to deduct some property taxes whether or not they itemized other deductions.

It is in science, though, where he may be most influential. He is one of three physicists in the House (the others are Michigan Republican Vernon J. Ehlers and New Jersey Democrat Rush D. Holt). In April 2008, Foster sponsored a bill aimed at improving the nation's nuclear forensics capability to help deter and respond to nuclear terrorism.

Foster comes from a family that was active in Democratic politics. His parents met while his mother was an aide to Democratic Illinois Sen. Paul H. Douglas and his father was an aide to Democratic Pennsylvania Sen. Francis J. Myers. His older sister's middle name is Adlai, after the former Illinois governor and two-time Democratic presidential nominee Adlai Stevenson.

The family settled in Madison, Wis., where Foster was born in 1955. His mother worked for the University of Wisconsin's administration office. His father, a trained chemist, was a law professor at the school while serving as a civil rights attorney. He wrote some of the landmark Civil Rights Act of 1964.

Foster was just 19 and a sophomore at Wisconsin when he and his younger brother Fred started Electronic Theatre Controls in their basement with $500 borrowed from their parents. The theater lighting equipment business now provides lighting for 70 percent of the country's theater and entertainment venues.

After earning a physics degree from Wisconsin in 1976, Foster worked with ETC for three years. He then went to Harvard and earned a Ph.D. in 1983 in experimental physics. He retained an advisory role on the company's board until 2007, when he sold his share of the company to prevent any conflict of interest.

He moved to the Chicago suburbs in the early 1980s and worked at Fermilab, a research lab for scientists studying high-energy physics. He was part of a small team that discovered the top quark, the heaviest known form of matter.

After nearly 25 years as a physicist, Foster took a leave of absence to step into politics. "I had gone through the experience that almost everyone has: You read the newspaper in the morning, you look at it and get angry at the way the government's being run and at the end you fold the newspaper and you go off to work," Foster says. "After 25 years of that, I decided that I should spend some of my life making a difference."

He volunteered for the successful campaign of Pennsylvania Rep. Patrick J. Murphy, who in 2006 defeated Republican Rep. Michael G. Fitzpatrick. And he volunteered in Murphy's Capitol Hill office, working for four months as an adviser on science and technology issues.

When Hastert announced in August 2007 he wasn't seeking a 12th term, Foster decided to run. A few months later, Hastert announced he would resign before the end of his term.

Foster's campaign themes touched on more federal incentives for research, tougher border security, flexibility on skilled-worker visas and funding for Illinois research laboratories. He also criticized the Bush administration's economic policy and its prosecution of the Iraq War.

In the February 2008 Democratic primary, he narrowly defeated Navy veteran John Laesch, who had run unsuccessfully against Hastert in 2006. One month later, Foster beat Republican Jim Oberweis by 5 percentage points in the special election. The two had spent a combined $8 million, more than $5 million of which came out of their own pockets. Foster contributed more than $2 million to his own campaign, which recorded $3.4 million in fundraising receipts. Although Republican officials criticized Oberweis as a flawed candidate after his March loss, he was again the party's nominee for the Nov. 4 election.

KEY VOTES

2008

Yes Delay consideration of Colombia free-trade agreement

Yes Override Bush veto of federal farm and nutrition programs reauthorization bill

No Overhaul surveillance laws and permit dismissal of suits against companies that conducted warrantless wiretapping

Yes Grant mortgage relief to homeowners and funding for Fannie Mae and Freddie Mac

Yes Approve initial $700 billion program to stabilize financial markets

Yes Approve final $700 billion program to stabilize financial markets

Yes Provide $14 billion in loans to automakers

CQ VOTE STUDIES

	PARTY UNITY		PRESIDENTIAL SUPPORT	
	SUPPORT	OPPOSE	SUPPORT	OPPOSE
2008	92%	8%	21%	79%

INTEREST GROUPS

	AFL-CIO	ADA	CCUS	ACU
2008	92%	65%	56%	13%

ILLINOIS 14
North central — Aurora, Elgin, DeKalb

The majority of the 14th's residents live in Kane County on the district's eastern side, in established towns along the Fox River Valley. West of the river, prairies and farms stretch to Henry County, nearly to the Mississippi River. Rich in soybeans and corn, the flat landscape is interrupted only by Northern Illinois University in DeKalb.

The district's population center in Kane County is on the outskirts of Chicago. Aurora (shared with the 13th) and neighboring cities in Kane are experiencing sprawl across the county line into Kendall County, one of the fastest-growing in the nation. Despite the city's increasingly residential feel, Aurora has a long history of manufacturing although heavy-equipment manufacturer Caterpillar, its key employer, has been forced into widespread layoffs as a result of stalling investment and plummeting demand in mining and infrastructure industries.

Aurora and Elgin (small parts of which are in the 8th and 6th) have benefited from job growth in nearby Naperville and Schaumburg, suburban cities that have emerged as Chicagoland business centers. Aurora and

Elgin also each host one of the state's nine riverboat casinos. Elgin and Aurora are about one-third Hispanic, and many of these residents are in the local blue-collar workforce. Only the Chicago-area 3rd, 4th and 5th districts have a greater Hispanic population than the 14th.

The district's minority influences as well as a willingness of voters in previously GOP-leaning areas to reject Republican candidates have helped Democrats. Areas in Kane, Kendall and DuPage counties supported Republicans, including former House Speaker J. Dennis Hastert, for decades but recently have shifted to the left at the federal level. Republican John McCain won only Lee County and the 14th's portions of Bureau and Henry counties here in the 2008 presidential election, and Barack Obama won the district overall with 55 percent of the vote.

MAJOR INDUSTRY
Farm machinery and other manufacturing, casinos, agriculture

CITIES
Aurora (pt.), 102,144; Elgin (pt.), 74,013; DeKalb, 39,018; Carpentersville, 30,586; St. Charles, 27,896; Batavia, 23,866; West Chicago (pt.), 23,449

NOTABLE
President Reagan's birthplace in Tampico and boyhood home in Dixon are operated as local museums.

Rep. Timothy V. Johnson (R)

Elected 2000; 5th term

CAPITOL OFFICE
225-2371
www.house.gov/timjohnson
1207 Longworth Bldg. 20515-1315; fax 226-0791

COMMITTEES
Agriculture
Transportation & Infrastructure

RESIDENCE
Urbana

BORN
July 23, 1946; Champaign, Ill.

RELIGION
Christian

FAMILY
Divorced; 10 children (one deceased)

EDUCATION
U.S. Military Academy, attended 1964;
U. of Illinois, B.A. 1969, J.D. 1972

CAREER
Lawyer; Realtor

POLITICAL HIGHLIGHTS
Urbana City Council, 1971-75; Ill. House, 1977-2000

ELECTION RESULTS

2008 GENERAL

Timothy V. Johnson (R)	187,121	64.2%
Steve Cox (D)	104,393	35.8%

2008 PRIMARY

Timothy V. Johnson (R)	unopposed

2006 GENERAL

Timothy V. Johnson (R)	116,810	57.6%
David Gill (D)	86,025	42.4%

PREVIOUS WINNING PERCENTAGES
2004 (61%); 2002 (65%); 2000 (53%)

Johnson, one of the most unconventional Republicans in the House, is also among the most independent. Throughout his career, he has been among the lawmakers most likely to buck his party's leadership.

During President George W. Bush's two terms, Johnson abandoned Republicans 24 percent of the time on votes that pitted the parties against each other; just five GOP House members in office at the time of Bush's departure bolted more often.

He was one of only 17 Republican House members in 2007 to vote against Bush's plan to send more than 21,000 additional U.S. troops into Iraq, though he opposed Democratic efforts to set a timetable for withdrawal from Iraq. Johnson also is against oil drilling in Alaska's Arctic National Wildlife Refuge, a stand that helps explain why in 2008 he was one of only six House Republicans to get Sierra Club backing.

Johnson continued his independent ways in the early months of President Obama's administration. He was one of only 10 Republicans to back a January 2009 bill putting the onus on employers to prove that pay differences between women and men doing the same jobs are the result of non-discriminatory business considerations. Current law requires the employee to prove that an employer intended to discriminate.

But he drew the line on Obama's $787 billion economic stimulus measure, joining all of his fellow House Republicans in opposition. He said it funded too many programs "that have little or nothing to do with job creation or getting our economy moving forward."

Johnson doesn't make many headlines, concentrating mainly on serving his constituents. Even so, he manages to distinguish himself on Capitol Hill. He is a familiar figure when the House is in session, walking purposefully through corridors with a cell phone held to his ear.

Johnson uses the most direct means possible to stay in touch with his constituents in a district spread across 22 mainly rural counties in eastern Illinois. He makes up to 200 calls a day to voters, asking them what's on their minds, and estimates that since coming to Congress in 2001, he has spoken to more than half of them.

"It really gives me grounding," Johnson said. "We lose sight that people on Main Street are thinking something different than we are. It keeps me aware of life beyond the Beltway."

The rail-thin, five-term former Illinois state assemblyman eats the same foods every day: fruit, rice cakes, granola, vitamin supplements, juice and farmer's cheese. He's also a fitness buff, devoting a chunk of every day to his House gym regimen, swimming laps or pounding out miles on a treadmill while catching up on reading.

The father of 10 and grandfather of 11, he generally supports efforts to restrict abortion, and he voted in 2005 against expanding federal funding for embryonic stem cell research, which uses cells harvested from surplus embryos at in vitro fertilization clinics. He also voted in 2004 for a constitutional amendment to ban same-sex marriage.

Johnson, whose district contains some 102,000 farms that concentrate on corn, soybeans and hogs, has a seat on the Agriculture Committee. He also serves on the Transportation and Infrastructure Committee. He has advocated the FutureGen project, a proposal to build the world's first coal-fueled, near-zero-emissions power plant in the town of Mattoon in his district. The project received a sharp setback in January 2008 when Energy Secretary

Samuel W. Bodman said the federal government was pulling out, citing rising costs. But Johnson and others in the Illinois delegation are still pushing the project.

On Agriculture, Johnson supported the successful override of Bush's veto of the $289 billion farm program reauthorization that included crop subsidies and food stamps. He said the legislation preserved a farmer's ability to produce, compete and contribute to "nutritional independence and energy independence."

Johnson also is active in the effort to ban methyl tertiary butyl ether (MBTE), a gasoline additive blamed for polluting groundwater. He advocates greater use of two MTBE rivals: ethanol, which is made from corn, and biodiesel, derived from soybeans. Both plants are grown in Johnson's district.

His voting behavior blends with his interest in building comity in the House. He bemoans the body's rancorous partisanship, telling the Bloomington's Pantagraph newspaper in 2004 that the lack of civility is "offensive to me" and that "both sides are guilty." Johnson and New York Democrat Steve Israel formed the Center Aisle Caucus in 2005 to encourage members to respect other points of view.

Johnson's mother and her parents were active in McLean County GOP politics. His father, originally a Democrat, became a Republican and served on the Urbana City Council. Johnson, who began passing out campaign literature when he was 3 or 4 years old, became a GOP precinct committee member at age 21 while still in college. By 24, he was on the Urbana City Council, and he was elected at 30 to the Illinois House, where he stayed for nearly 24 years. Johnson also worked in real estate and practiced law.

In 2000 he ran for the House when GOP Rep. Thomas W. Ewing retired. Johnson won 44 percent of the vote in a crowded four-man primary and later beat Democratic university instructor Mike Kelleher with 53 percent.

Johnson promised to limit himself to three two-year terms, but revoked that pledge right before the 2002 election. Redistricting that year put Democratic Rep. David Phelps' home in the 15th District, but Phelps ran in the 19th instead. Johnson cruised to a 2-1 victory over political novice Joshua T. Hartke. He has been easily re-elected since.

Johnson struck up a friendship with Boston Celtics basketball star Ray Allen when the Celtics visited the White House in September 2008. Allen said his son acquired Type 1 juvenile diabetes along with a cluster of other youths in Boston's affluent suburbs; Johnson's father is a diabetic. According to Boston magazine, Johnson promised to help have the Centers for Disease Control look into the matter.

KEY VOTES

2008
No Delay consideration of Colombia free-trade agreement
Yes Override Bush veto of federal farm and nutrition programs reauthorization bill
No Overhaul surveillance laws and permit dismissal of suits against companies that conducted warrantless wiretapping
No Grant mortgage relief to homeowners and funding for Fannie Mae and Freddie Mac
No Approve initial $700 billion program to stabilize financial markets
No Approve final $700 billion program to stabilize financial markets
No Provide $14 billion in loans to automakers

2007
Yes Increase minimum wage by $2.10 an hour
No Approve $124.2 billion in emergency war spending and set goal for redeployment of troops from Iraq
Yes Reject federal contraceptive assistance to international family planning groups
Yes Override Bush veto of $23.2 billion water projects authorization bill
Yes Implement Peru free-trade agreement
Yes Approve energy policy overhaul with new fuel economy standards
Yes Clear $473.5 billion omnibus spending bill, including $70 billion for military operations

CQ VOTE STUDIES

	PARTY UNITY		PRESIDENTIAL SUPPORT	
	SUPPORT	OPPOSE	SUPPORT	OPPOSE
2008	72%	28%	43%	57%
2007	69%	31%	43%	57%
2006	79%	21%	74%	26%
2005	77%	23%	54%	46%
2004	77%	23%	62%	38%

INTEREST GROUPS

	AFL-CIO	ADA	CCUS	ACU
2008	36%	50%	67%	68%
2007	68%	35%	84%	60%
2006	50%	20%	86%	76%
2005	33%	40%	70%	52%
2004	60%	40%	86%	64%

ILLINOIS 15

East central — Champaign, Bloomington, Danville

Agriculture is the dominant industry in the 15th, which takes in all or part of 22 counties, including Champaign — the district's main city. The 15th runs nearly 250 miles north to south, with a long, narrow appendage that hugs the Indiana border on the western bank of the Wabash River down to Gallatin County. The district's roughly 10,000 square miles encompass several population centers separated by expansive farmland.

Corn and soybean fields cover much of the territory, and the land both around Bloomington-Normal and in counties south of Champaign produces high crop yields. Both the district's family and commercial farms produce feed and raw material for food products manufactured just over the district border at Decatur-based worldwide distributor Archer Daniels Midland (in the 17th). The area food-processing industry served by the district remains steady in the face of nationwide economic downturns, rising transportation costs and falling commodities prices.

Scattered amid the farms are several midsize towns, including Danville, that are centered around agribusiness and manufacturing. Higher edu-

cation is big business in the 15th, with more than 40,000 students at the University of Illinois' flagship campus in Urbana-Champaign. Bloomington-Normal's Illinois State and Illinois Wesleyan universities are just outside the district (in the 11th). Bloomington, home to State Farm Insurance, leads downstate Illinois in insurance and finance.

The district has a GOP lean, and Republicans typically run strongest in counties north of Champaign, including Iroquois and Ford. Both counties gave Republican John McCain almost 65 percent of their vote in the 2008 presidential election. Champaign County's academic community keeps Democrats competitive in the county, and it gave Barack Obama 58 percent of the vote in 2008, his highest percentage in the district. Overall, McCain won the 15th with 50 percent of the vote.

MAJOR INDUSTRY
Agriculture, higher education, food processing, insurance

CITIES
Champaign, 67,518; Urbana, 36,395; Bloomington (pt.), 34,510; Danville, 33,904; Charleston, 21,039; Mattoon, 18,291

NOTABLE
The Lincoln Log Cabin State Historic Site in Coles County preserves the last home of Abraham Lincoln's father and stepmother.

Rep. Donald Manzullo (R)

Elected 1992; 9th term

CAPITOL OFFICE
225-5676
www.house.gov/manzullo
2228 Rayburn Bldg. 20515-1316; fax 225-5284

COMMITTEES
Financial Services
Foreign Affairs

RESIDENCE
Egan

BORN
March 24, 1944; Rockford, Ill.

RELIGION
Christian

FAMILY
Wife, Freda Manzullo; three children

EDUCATION
American U., B.A. 1967 (political science);
Marquette U., J.D. 1970

CAREER
Lawyer

POLITICAL HIGHLIGHTS
Sought Republican nomination for U.S. House,
1990

ELECTION RESULTS

2008 GENERAL

Donald Manzullo (R)	190,039	60.9%
Robert G. Abboud (D)	112,648	36.1%
Scott Summers (GREEN)	9,533	3.0%

2008 PRIMARY

Donald Manzullo (R)	unopposed

2006 GENERAL

Donald Manzullo (R)	125,951	63.6%
Richard D. Auman (D)	63,627	32.1%
General John Borling - write-in	8,523	4.3%

PREVIOUS WINNING PERCENTAGES
2004 (69%); 2002 (71%); 2000 (67%); 1998 (100%);
1996 (60%); 1994 (71%); 1992 (56%)

Manzullo is a persistent champion of the manufacturing industry and small business who often courts Democrats on issues he cares about. It was a practice that was seen as an affront to Republican leaders during GOP rule of the House. But with Democrats in charge of Congress and the White House, he considers such maneuvering necessary, even as he maintains his strong conservatism on social and fiscal issues.

Manzullo (man-ZOO-low) ranks among the top seven Republicans in seniority on both the Foreign Affairs and Financial Services committees, and by working across the aisle, he is able to promote some of his issues.

He worked with Democrats Brad Sherman of California and Joseph Crowley of New York in 2008 to successfully push through the House a bill to streamline federal licensing procedures for defense-related exports. Manzullo said the bill would help "U.S. companies sell more goods and services to our allies, creating more jobs." The Senate did not take up the bill.

His district is home to a Chrysler assembly plant, and he was one of just 32 Republicans to support a $14 billion bailout of the domestic auto industry in December 2008 that failed to advance in the Senate. He did complain the measure lacked provisions "to get people back in the showrooms to buy cars" — something he sought to remedy in 2009, when he unsuccessfully proposed that President Obama's $787 billion economic stimulus include a $5,000 voucher for all car buyers. He joined other House Republicans in opposing the stimulus, which was ultimately signed into law, because he said it didn't devote enough money to infrastructure.

Manzullo plays some aggressive defense when Democrats propose spending he finds excessive, but he is less successful. He opposed two $700 billion measures — the second of which became law — to aid the troubled financial services industry in fall 2008, partly because he didn't think lawmakers had enough time to review them. "I don't like somebody telling me that I have no alternative and push me against the wall without adequate time to read this thing and study it," he said.

Manzullo developed a reputation for combativeness during the years of Republican rule, refusing to compromise when he thought manufacturing interests were at risk. That was the case in the summer of 2005 when he led a highly unusual floor revolt against legislation by former Rep. Henry J. Hyde, a fellow Illinois Republican who headed the International Relations panel. Hyde's bill would have punished companies that illegally sold arms to China.

Manzullo feared the bill would hurt U.S. businesses that unknowingly sold illegal arms, including the Chicago-based Boeing Co. More than 60 lawmakers switched their votes on the bill, embarrassing GOP leaders trying to maintain discipline. The bill later passed, but with a revision making it clear that companies had to knowingly break U.S. law to be sanctioned; Manzullo proclaimed himself satisfied.

Manzullo's strong views on helping small business stem from his boyhood, when he lived with his family in a one-room apartment above their struggling grocery store in Rockford in the late 1940s. Manzullo's father, Frank, extended store credit to newly arrived immigrants from Poland, Latvia and Lithuania. In 1964, Manzullo's father started an Italian eatery and later brought Manzullo's brother into the business. The restaurant remained in operation for nearly four decades, until his brother was forced to close because of the high cost of providing health insurance to his employees. "He had to sell $70,000 of spaghetti in a year just to afford it for himself and his wife," said Manzullo, who has pushed several bills to help small businesses with the cost of health insurance — including one the House passed in 2005 allowing trade groups to sponsor plans for their members.

Every year, Manzullo leads the fight to convince Congress to adopt policies requiring the Pentagon to purchase only products that have at least 50 percent U.S.-made components. But lawmakers usually succumb to arguments that it is impractical because much of the technology the Pentagon buys is no longer made in the United States.

Unlike other friends of manufacturing in Congress, Manzullo is anti-protectionist and a defender of free trade. The way to help small firms survive competition with big companies and foreign rivals, he says, is to cut regulation and give them access to government contracts and foreign markets. Manzullo voted for the Peru free-trade deal in November 2007 and the Central America Free Trade Agreement in 2005.

Manzullo is a strong backer of the Export-Import Bank and the Overseas Private Investment Corporation, two government agencies that assist businesses in expanding exports. He says they are essential to counterbalance the help foreign governments give their business communities.

Manzullo has used his slot as top Republican on the Foreign Affairs Committee's Asia panel to lean on the Bush administration to pressure China to revalue its currency. Its strength against the dollar is widely blamed by manufacturers for the high trade deficit between the United States and China.

As an ardent social conservative, Manzullo early in his law career helped start pregnancy crisis centers in Rockford and picketed clinics that performed abortions. His wife, Freda, a microbiologist, taught their three children at home until eighth grade, when they went to a small Christian high school in suburban Washington. When the House is in recess, the family heads for their small beef cattle farm in Illinois.

Manzullo recalls deciding at age 4 he wanted to be a lawyer — and at 10, he decided he wanted to be in Congress. He spent 20 years practicing in Oregon, Ill., handling family cases, writing deeds and wills and advising small companies.

When Republican Rep. Lynn Martin decided to try for the Senate in 1990, Manzullo ran for her seat. He got a respectable 46 percent of the vote in the Republican primary, but Democrat John W. Cox Jr. won the general election. Two years later, Manzullo tried again, winning the primary with 56 percent of the vote. In November, the district reverted to its traditional Republican form and Manzullo ejected Cox by 12 percentage points. He has not had a serious challenge since.

KEY VOTES

2008
No Delay consideration of Colombia free-trade agreement
Yes Override Bush veto of federal farm and nutrition programs reauthorization bill
Yes Overhaul surveillance laws and permit dismissal of suits against companies that conducted warrantless wiretapping
No Grant mortgage relief to homeowners and funding for Fannie Mae and Freddie Mac
No Approve initial $700 billion program to stabilize financial markets
No Approve final $700 billion program to stabilize financial markets
Yes Provide $14 billion in loans to automakers

2007
No Increase minimum wage by $2.10 an hour
No Approve $124.2 billion in emergency war spending and set goal for redeployment of troops from Iraq
Yes Reject federal contraceptive assistance to international family planning groups
Yes Override Bush veto of $23.2 billion water projects authorization bill
Yes Implement Peru free-trade agreement
No Approve energy policy overhaul with new fuel economy standards
Yes Clear $473.5 billion omnibus spending bill, including $70 billion for military operations

CQ VOTE STUDIES

	PARTY UNITY		PRESIDENTIAL SUPPORT	
	SUPPORT	OPPOSE	SUPPORT	OPPOSE
2008	92%	8%	73%	27%
2007	95%	5%	81%	19%
2006	95%	5%	94%	6%
2005	94%	6%	70%	30%
2004	93%	7%	84%	16%

INTEREST GROUPS

	AFL-CIO	ADA	CCUS	ACU
2008	13%	20%	83%	92%
2007	13%	0%	80%	100%
2006	9%	10%	100%	91%
2005	13%	0%	93%	100%
2004	14%	5%	100%	100%

ILLINOIS 16

North — Rockford, part of McHenry County

The 16th spans most of the Illinois-Wisconsin border, taking in Rockford and covering the rolling northern prairie where family farmers grow corn and raise dairy cows. It includes all of six counties and parts of three others, including all of Winnebago and the majority of McHenry counties.

McHenry County (shared with the 8th) contains large expanses of farmland, and the proximity of Chicago draws many residents to the county's suburban enclaves. McHenry experienced several decades of growth, as did Boone County, to its west. Previously GOP strongholds, Boone and the 14th's portion of McHenry each gave a slight edge to Democrat Barack Obama in the 2008 presidential election.

Roughly one-fourth of the 16th's voters live in the industrial hub of Rockford in Winnebago County. At one time a major machine-tool manufacturing center, Rockford suffered a typical Rust Belt decline. Although the transition away from traditional manufacturing was difficult, the city upgraded to technology manufacturing. It is still one of the most densely populated manufacturing communities in the United States, but an

upswing in unemployment rates has hurt the city. Proposed construction of an aerospace manufacturing center may bring more high-tech jobs.

The 16th includes Illinois' leading dairy producers, and Jo Daviess County, in the northwest corner, is a state leader in raising beef cattle and producing hay. Galena, in the rolling hills of Jo Daviess near the Mississippi River, has a tourist-based economy.

Three-fourths of the district's black residents live in Rockford, giving the city a base of loyal Democrats. But the 16th overall covers historically conservative, Republican territory, and only once in the 20th century did voters here elect a Democrat to the House. Democrat Barack Obama won 53 percent of the district's vote in the 2008 presidential election.

MAJOR INDUSTRY
Manufacturing, aircraft and machine parts, agriculture, trade

CITIES
Rockford, 150,115; Crystal Lake (pt.), 37,740; Freeport, 26,443

NOTABLE
The Rockford Peaches, three-time winners of the league, were one of only two teams to play every season of the All-American Girls Professional Baseball League (1943-54).

Rep. Phil Hare (D)

Elected 2006; 2nd term

CAPITOL OFFICE
225-5905
hare.house.gov
428 Cannon Bldg. 20515-1317; fax 225-5396

COMMITTEES
Education & Labor
Transportation & Infrastructure

RESIDENCE
Rock Island

BORN
Feb. 21, 1949; Galesburg, Ill.

RELIGION
Roman Catholic

FAMILY
Wife, Beckie Hare; two children

EDUCATION
Alleman H.S., graduated 1967; Black Hawk College,
attended 1967-68, 74 (business administration &
accounting)

MILITARY SERVICE
Army Reserve, 1969-75

CAREER
Congressional district director; campaign aide;
clothing factory worker

POLITICAL HIGHLIGHTS
No previous office

ELECTION RESULTS

2008 GENERAL

Phil Hare (D)	220,961	99.8%

2008 PRIMARY

Phil Hare (D)	unopposed

2006 GENERAL

Phil Hare (D)	115,025	57.2%
Andrea Zinga (R)	86,161	42.8%

Hare is a candid and solidly pro-labor Democrat who often recalls his early days of working on the assembly line in a clothing factory in the 1970s, operating with one hand a circular, three-quarter-inch-thick electric cutter to slice through a stack of fabric he held down with his other hand. He eventually became a union leader, advocating for higher wages and better health care for his colleagues — something he still does.

He now also fights to stem any further damage to the economy in his district, which has seen the loss of many of those manufacturing jobs and numerous home foreclosures. He shares many of the same viewpoints of his predecessor and mentor Lane Evans, for whom he worked as district director for roughly 24 years.

During his first term, Hare was as reliable a Democratic vote as Evans. He backed his party 97 percent of the time on votes pitting most Democrats against most Republicans. He was rewarded with an appointment as a regional whip, securing votes among mostly Midwest lawmakers, and a plum spot on the Transportation and Infrastructure Committee, which must deal with a massive multi-year surface transportation bill in the 111th Congress (2009-10).

Hare wants to create jobs by providing passenger rail service between Chicago and the Quad Cities of Illinois and Iowa. He also seeks to bolster shipping on waterways. The Mississippi River forms the western border of his district, and he said its locks and dams are falling apart. "I went to a lock near Quincy, Ill., and hit it with my fist; chunks of concrete literally fell off," he said in a March 2009 statement to the Budget Committee. "It is of the utmost importance that the Army Corps of Engineers has sufficient funding to maintain and improve locks and dams throughout the Mississippi and Illinois rivers."

A member of the Education and Labor Committee, Hare ardently supported the 2007 increase in the minimum wage and said lawmakers should go even further by indexing it to keep pace with inflation. He also supports the Employee Free Choice Act, known as the "card check bill," that would enable workers to form unions by majority sign-up, as well as secret-ballot elections. The bill "is an economic stimulus package," he said in March 2009. "Giving workers the opportunity to join a union freely and fairly will strengthen the middle class and grow our economy."

Like Evans, Hare is a skeptic when it comes to trade deals. In November 2007, he was one of 116 Democrats who bucked party leaders and opposed the Peru free-trade agreement. When Colombia President Alvaro Uribe visited Washington in September 2008 to press for enactment of a free-trade agreement, Hare scoffed, "With our economy in shambles, I cannot think of a worse idea than passing another trade agreement destined to outsource more American jobs."

On education, Hare looks out for rural schools that he said have limited funds and difficulty in recruiting and training highly qualified teachers. He said some of the current federal funding formulas discriminate against small, rural districts, with some containing "an explicit bias" favoring districts with large concentrations of impoverished students.

In his first term, Hare took over Evans' work on the Veterans Affairs' Committee, trying to boost benefits for those who have served in uniform. He and other Democrats criticized the Veterans Affairs Department for improper care and treatment of veterans returning from combat, as well as underestimating budget needs. He was denied a waiver to continue on the panel when he got the Transportation seat.

Hare has spoken out on his state's political controversies surrounding Democratic Gov. Rod R. Blagojevich's appointment of Roland W. Burris to fill President Obama's Senate seat. Blagojevich was subsequently impeached and removed from office for allegedly soliciting bribes for the seat. Hare praised Burris but said the appointment should not stand. Later, when Burris became the subject of a Senate ethics investigation over his apparently conflicting statements about his contacts with Blagojevich before his appointment, Hare called for Burris to resign. "A cloud of corruption has hung over our state and its leaders for too long," he said in February 2009.

Hare is liberal on social issues. He voted for a measure to allow federal funding for embryonic stem cell research — an issue that hit close to home for Hare because Evans chose to retire due to an ongoing battle with Parkinson's disease. "He has a heart of a lion," Hare said. "If something happens to him, that will be very tough for me, for a long time."

Hare has had his own personal difficulties. He was in middle school when his father, a machinist, developed respiratory problems and was forced to go on disability. His mother then took a job at the local New York Store, one of Moline's major department stores, for $1 an hour. Hare, the only son of four children, worked as a paper boy. Unable to pay their mortgage, his parents lost their home to foreclosure. Hare said his father eventually "drank himself to death because he felt he let his family down." He said the first thing he does when receiving a paycheck is send in his house payment.

Hare's ties to the Democratic party and focus on labor issues stem from his parents' early influence. His father was a union leader and pressed the power of negotiation. "If it's not in that collective bargaining agreement, don't ask for it," Hare recalls his dad saying after he was elected steward. "If it is, don't take no for an answer." Hare's mother was Moline's Democratic chairwoman and hosted tea parties for Rose Kennedy, the mother of President Kennedy, when she visited the Quad Cities area.

Graduating from Alleman High School in 1967, Hare attended Moline Community College for two years before working at the Seaford Clothing factory for 13 years. His involvement in labor issues earned him connections in the political scene.

When Evans was elected in 1982, Hare became his district director until Evans announced his retirement in early 2006. He said the job prepared him well to step into Evans' shoes. Hare's knowledge of the district and his political connections enabled him to easily raise money, and he defeated Republican Andrea Zinga, a TV broadcaster, after raising more than twice as much as she did. He was unopposed in 2008.

KEY VOTES

2008

Yes Delay consideration of Colombia free-trade agreement

Yes Override Bush veto of federal farm and nutrition programs reauthorization bill

No Overhaul surveillance laws and permit dismissal of suits against companies that conducted warrantless wiretapping

+ Grant mortgage relief to homeowners and funding for Fannie Mae and Freddie Mac

Yes Approve initial $700 billion program to stabilize financial markets

Yes Approve final $700 billion program to stabilize financial markets

Yes Provide $14 billion in loans to automakers

2007

Yes Increase minimum wage by $2.10 an hour

Yes Approve $124.2 billion in emergency war spending and set goal for redeployment of troops from Iraq

No Reject federal contraceptive assistance to international family planning groups

Yes Override Bush veto of $23.2 billion water projects authorization bill

No Implement Peru free-trade agreement

Yes Approve energy policy overhaul with new fuel economy standards

No Clear $473.5 billion omnibus spending bill, including $70 billion for military operations

CQ VOTE STUDIES

	PARTY UNITY		PRESIDENTIAL SUPPORT	
	SUPPORT	OPPOSE	SUPPORT	OPPOSE
2008	99%	1%	12%	88%
2007	96%	4%	4%	96%

INTEREST GROUPS

	AFL-CIO	ADA	CCUS	ACU
2008	100%	100%	56%	0%
2007	96%	100%	55%	0%

ILLINOIS 17

West — Moline; parts of Decatur and Springfield

The 17th is one of the state's most expansive districts. Winding over nine full counties and parts of 14 others, it hugs much of the border along the Mississippi River and reaches its tentacle-like arms past Springfield as far inland as Decatur. The 17th includes rich farmland along the Mississippi, as well as Rock Island and Moline — Illinois' half of the industrial Quad Cities that straddle the river across from Iowa.

Moline is a retail hub for the Illinois Quad Cities, and the development of the John Deere Commons revitalized the city's downtown. It contains a visitors center with shopping, dining and lodging options. The cornerstone of the Commons is the 12,000-seat arena and convention center.

Corn, soybeans and hogs fuel most of the rest of the 17th's economy, and even the industrial sector here, which is dominated by John Deere and Archer Daniels Midland, depends on agriculture. Economic downturns have hurt agriculture-dependent economies and family farm profits, but the farm equipment manufacturer is still a key employer.

The Rock Island Arsenal has served as a major area employer, but commands have transferred out of the district and the installation has lost jobs as a result of the BRAC Commission reorganization.

The 17th has a Democratic tilt. With 62 percent support, Rock Island County gave Democrat Barack Obama his second-highest percentage statewide in the 2008 presidential election. Democratic votes in Rock Island, coupled with the strong lean in the 17th's parts of Springfield and Decatur and in Macoupin and Knox counties, are enough to overcome GOP tendencies in some rural areas. Obama captured 56 percent of the district's presidential vote here overall.

MAJOR INDUSTRY
Farm equipment manufacturing, agriculture, defense, food processing

MILITARY BASES
Rock Island Arsenal (Army), 271 military, 5,517 civilian (2007)

CITIES
Decatur (pt.), 58,701; Moline, 43,768; Quincy, 40,366; Rock Island, 39,684; Galesburg, 33,706; Springfield (pt.), 28,952; East Moline, 20,333

NOTABLE
Moline is known as the "Farm Implement Capital of the World."

Rep. Aaron Schock (R)

Elected 2008; 1st term

Both ambitious and precocious, Schock attracts attention. In his late 20s, he is the youngest member in Congress and is eager to push his ideas for a "traditional" conservative agenda that can rebuild the party.

Shortly after his February 2008 primary win, Schock started a "GOP Generation Y Fund" that donated thousands of dollars to fellow incoming freshmen, with hopes of getting a slot on the GOP Steering Committee, which makes committee assignments. He failed in that bid, but he did attract the attention of party leaders, who asked him to speak at the 2008 GOP convention.

Schock favors fiscal restraint and gun owners' rights. He opposed President Obama's $787 billion economic stimulus package, even after lobbying from the president. "I think all the president's men thought that the youngest member of Congress was the most impressionable member of Congress," he told an audience in East Peoria. When Caterpillar Inc., Peoria's largest employer, subsequently laid off about 900 employees, he said it was proof the stimulus wasn't working.

He is a member of the Transportation panel that will take up a renewal of a massive surface transportation bill. He also sits on the Oversight panel and, as a former business owner, is assigned to the Small Business panel. He successfully added language to a House bill governing the release of the second portion of the financial industry rescue funds approved in fall 2008. The amendment requires a database be created to track how money is spent.

He was born in Morris, Minn., but his family later moved to Peoria. In junior high, he started doing database management for a local bookstore. A few years later, he worked for an online ticket brokerage firm. He bought his first piece of real estate on his 18th birthday and, after graduating from Bradley University, started a home improvement firm.

Schock was elected to the Peoria board of education at 19 and served four years, then served in the Illinois state House before running for the U.S. House seat of retiring Republican Ray LaHood, who later became Transportation secretary. Schock cruised in a three-person primary and took 59 percent of the vote in November.

CAPITOL OFFICE
225-6201
schock.house.gov
509 Cannon Bldg. 20515-1318; fax 225-9249

COMMITTEES
Oversight & Government Reform
Small Business
Transportation & Infrastructure

RESIDENCE
Peoria

BORN
May 28, 1981; Morris, Minn.

RELIGION
Baptist

FAMILY
Single

EDUCATION
Illinois Central College, attended 1999-2002;
Bradley U., B.S. 2002 (finance)

CAREER
Real estate developer; home improvement company owner

POLITICAL HIGHLIGHTS
Board of Education of the City of Peoria, 2001-05 (president, 2004-05); Ill. House, 2005-09

ELECTION RESULTS

2008 GENERAL

Aaron Schock (R)	182,589	58.9%
Colleen Callahan (D)	117,642	37.9%
Sheldon Schafer (GREEN)	9,857	3.2%

2008 PRIMARY

Aaron Schock (R)	55,610	71.2%
Jim McConoughey (R)	13,363	17.1%
John D. Morris (R)	9,160	11.7%

ILLINOIS 18

Central – Peoria, parts of Springfield and Decatur

The 18th takes in all or part of 20 counties in central and western Illinois, with Peoria County making up nearly 30 percent of the population. In the south, it snags the northern part of Springfield (the state capital), some GOP-leaning suburbs north and west of the city, and rural turf that stretches west of the capital almost to the Mississippi River. In the southeast, it runs to northern Decatur.

Middle-class Peoria is the 18th's population center and hosts five hospitals, a University of Illinois medical campus and Bradley University. The downtown area works to remain vibrant, with continuing development of corporate, government, medical, convention and educational sites. Many of the city's residents live in high-rise condos, riverfront lofts or converted office and warehouse apartments.

In much of this predominately agricultural district, voters worry about crop prices, ethanol, free trade and estate taxes. The district's economic health still depends on Peoria-based heavy-equipment manufacturer Caterpillar, and recent layoffs by the company have unsettled many residents.

Peoria, with its strong manufacturing base, tends to vote Democratic, but the Republican lean of rural areas north of Springfield and in the district's west tips the 18th to the GOP. In the 2008 presidential election, Democrat Barack Obama won 60 percent of Peoria's vote, but Republican John McCain won the district overall with 50 percent.

MAJOR INDUSTRY
Manufacturing, ethanol and grain products, agriculture, health care

CITIES
Peoria, 112,936; Springfield (pt.), 57,209; Pekin, 33,857; East Peoria, 22,638

NOTABLE
Abraham Lincoln's tomb in Springfield is a state historic site.

Rep. John Shimkus (R)

Elected 1996; 7th term

CAPITOL OFFICE
225-5271
www.house.gov/shimkus
2452 Rayburn Bldg. 20515-1319; fax 225-5880

COMMITTEES
Energy & Commerce

RESIDENCE
Collinsville

BORN
Feb. 21, 1958; Collinsville, Ill.

RELIGION
Lutheran

FAMILY
Wife, Karen Muth Shimkus; three children

EDUCATION
U.S. Military Academy, B.S. 1980;
Southern Illinois U., M.B.A. 1997

MILITARY SERVICE
Army, 1980-86; Army Reserve, 1986-2008

CAREER
Teacher

POLITICAL HIGHLIGHTS
Candidate for Madison County Board, 1988;
Collinsville Township Board of Trustees, 1989-93;
Madison County treasurer, 1990-97; Republican
nominee for U.S. House, 1992

ELECTION RESULTS

2008 GENERAL

John Shimkus (R)	203,434	64.5%
Daniel Davis (D)	105,338	33.4%
Troy Dennis (GREEN)	6,817	2.2%

2008 PRIMARY

John Shimkus (R)	unopposed

2006 GENERAL

John Shimkus (R)	143,491	60.7%
Danny L. Stover (D)	92,861	39.3%

PREVIOUS WINNING PERCENTAGES
2004 (69%); 2002 (55%); 2000 (63%); 1998 (61%);
1996 (50%)

Shimkus often pitches for the Republicans in their annual charity baseball game against the Democrats and is a serious competitor whether he's on the field or the House floor. He brings forcefully conservative views to his role as a senior member of the Energy and Commerce Committee, where he seeks to counter Democratic positions he believes smack of too much regulation and could hurt businesses.

Shimkus (SHIM-kus) is a West Point graduate and retired Army Reserve lieutenant colonel who was an unwavering supporter of President George W. Bush's conduct of the Iraq War. He considers himself a "pro-life Christian" and typically backs his party, siding with Republicans 92 percent of the time on votes in which a majority of the two parties diverged during Bush's two terms.

Shimkus has been a member of Energy and Commerce since 1997. He gave up his seat as top-ranking Republican on the committee's Oversight and Investigations panel in 2009 to serve on three others dealing with major legislation: Health, Energy and Environment, and Communications, Technology and the Internet. "I hope to bring a point of view to these debates that do not cause increased energy prices for consumers or restrict health care access by adding government bureaucracy," he said.

In particular, Shimkus contends Democratic attempts to deal with global warming by capping industrial emissions could be "deadly" to oil, gas and coal companies. At a January 2009 hearing, he complained that the same financial services firms whose failings required government intervention could run the markets for trading what the industries are allowed to emit. "Let's develop a trading floor for U.S. emissions and let's let the big money folks at Goldman Sachs control it — what a great idea," he said sarcastically.

He supports opening Alaska's Arctic National Wildlife Refuge and the outer continental shelf to energy exploration. In mid-2008, when gas prices averaged $4 a gallon across the nation, Shimkus spoke almost daily on the House floor on the issue. "Let's explore for oil and gas, wind and solar," he said in June. "The great thing about the Republican policy is that we want everything, more of everything."

Shimkus generally favors easing environmental restrictions on refineries and power plants. In the 109th Congress (2005-06), he pushed legislation to give incentives to coal-to-liquid refineries that would benefit coal-producing areas. He has been one of the leading supporters of a revolutionary coal-fueled power plant in southern Illinois that would be virtually emissions-free. The so-called FutureGen plant suffered a setback at the start of 2008 when Energy Secretary Samuel W. Bodman pulled the plug on plans for it, but Shimkus and other lawmakers have urged the Obama administration to make a commitment to it.

He has been a staunch backer of nuclear energy. During a 2002 debate over Nevada's Yucca Mountain nuclear waste storage project, he brought onto the House floor a large poster of the Silver State's license plate featuring a mushroom cloud depicting one of its atomic bomb tests. "The state of Nevada can again fulfill its nuclear legacy and continue to aid this nation and our citizens" by accepting the storage site, he said. Nevada lawmakers who oppose the Yucca Mountain site said his comments were in poor taste, given that residents died during some of the tests.

On health care, Shimkus' concerns include portability — enabling insured workers to transfer coverage when changing jobs — as well as affordability and access. He has introduced legislation with his Illinois Democratic colleague Jerry F. Costello in January 2009 that seeks to improve the hiring process for doctors at Veterans Affairs Department facilities.

He has co-chaired the 50-member congressional E-911 Caucus that seeks to strengthen the nation's 911 emergency system. In July 2007 he helped secure first-time funding of $5 million for a Commerce Department agency to make matching grants to ensure that 911 call centers can locate emergency calls from mobile phones.

Despite his conservatism, he occasionally sides with Democrats on labor issues. He voted for a 2007 increase in the federal minimum wage. Three years earlier, he supported a proposal to extend unemployment insurance benefits, but voted against a similar bill in 2008.

Shimkus is of Lithuanian ancestry and grew up in Collinsville. His father worked at a local telephone company for 50 years and his mother was at home rearing seven children. In college, Shimkus played junior varsity baseball at West Point. He is still active, playing paddleball in the House gym in addition to pitching for the congressional baseball team. But he lost of lot of weight after open heart surgery in 2005.

He served in the Army from 1980 to 1986, then returned to Collinsville to teach high school history and government.

He won his first election in 1989 to the Collinsville Township Board of Trustees, and went on to be Madison County treasurer. In 1992, he challenged Democratic Rep. Richard J. Durbin, who had represented the 20th District for 10 years, and lost. When Durbin was elected to the Senate in 1996, Shimkus was ready to try again. In the general election, he faced state Rep. Jay C. Hoffman and won by 1,238 votes.

In 2002, reapportionment cost Illinois one of its House seats, and Shimkus and Democratic Rep. David Phelps ran against each other in the new 19th District. District demographics favored Shimkus, and he won the incumbent-vs.-incumbent matchup by almost 10 percentage points. He was re-elected in 2004 with more than two-thirds of the vote against businessman Tim Bagwell.

But his share of the vote dropped to 61 percent in 2006. The year before, he had broken his pledge to serve no more than six terms; also, as chairman of the three-member board that oversees the House's high school page program, he found himself in the middle of a 2006 uproar over sexually oriented electronic "instant messages" sent to male pages by Republican Rep. Mark Foley of Florida. The incident embarrassed Shimkus, forced Foley to resign and helped contribute to the Republicans' loss of the House. Nevertheless, Shimkus collected 64 percent of the vote in 2008.

KEY VOTES

2008

No   Delay consideration of Colombia free-trade agreement
Yes Override Bush veto of federal farm and nutrition programs reauthorization bill
Yes Overhaul surveillance laws and permit dismissal of suits against companies that conducted warrantless wiretapping
No   Grant mortgage relief to homeowners and funding for Fannie Mae and Freddie Mac
No   Approve initial $700 billion program to stabilize financial markets
No   Approve final $700 billion program to stabilize financial markets
No   Provide $14 billion in loans to automakers

2007

Yes Increase minimum wage by $2.10 an hour
No   Approve $124.2 billion in emergency war spending and set goal for redeployment of troops from Iraq
Yes Reject federal contraceptive assistance to international family planning groups
Yes Override Bush veto of $23.2 billion water projects authorization bill
Yes Implement Peru free-trade agreement
Yes Approve energy policy overhaul with new fuel economy standards
Yes Clear $473.5 billion omnibus spending bill, including $70 billion for military operations

CQ VOTE STUDIES

	PARTY UNITY		PRESIDENTIAL SUPPORT	
	SUPPORT	OPPOSE	SUPPORT	OPPOSE
2008	94%	6%	71%	29%
2007	89%	11%	70%	30%
2006	93%	7%	92%	8%
2005	92%	8%	80%	20%
2004	91%	9%	76%	24%

INTEREST GROUPS

	AFL-CIO	ADA	CCUS	ACU
2008	8%	20%	88%	91%
2007	38%	15%	85%	84%
2006	29%	0%	93%	83%
2005	27%	10%	89%	92%
2004	43%	20%	95%	88%

ILLINOIS 19

South — southern rural counties; part of Springfield

The 19th sprawls across southern Illinois, meandering over all or part of 30 counties to create the largest congressional district in the state. The district reaches from Springfield, in central Illinois, south to Metropolis, which borders Kentucky. In the east, it reaches from the Ohio River in Gallatin, Hardin, Pope and Massac counties across the state to the Mississippi River in Jersey and Madison counties.

The 19th's part of Madison County contains roughly 20 percent of the its population, and its portion of Sangamon County (Springfield) holds 10 percent. Everyone else is spread across the remaining counties. Pope County, the state's least populous, is partly within the Shawnee National Forest.

The northern counties cover typical Midwestern country — acres of corn and soybean fields dotted by small towns. The southern half, however, looks more like Appalachia than Midwestern prairie. The hilly, forested counties here once held rich deposits of coal and were one of the

nation's chief coal mining regions. Despite a 1990s uptick in mining, the economy now is driven by manufacturing and agriculture, with the 19th earning Illinois' top ranking in soybean yield and land used for farms.

Factory jobs account for most employment in Madison County's Edwardsville, Collinsville, Glen Carbon and Godfrey, but the county has suffered rising unemployment rates. Edwardsville hosts a Southern Illinois University campus, while state government, the University of Illinois-Springfield and the Southern Illinois University Medical School (in the nearby 17th) sustain the state capital of Springfield in Sangamon County.

The 19th has a historically conservative Democratic past but voted for the GOP candidate in the last three presidential elections. In 2008, Republican John McCain won a statewide-high 54 percent in the district, and only the 19th's portion of Gallatin County supported Barack Obama.

MAJOR INDUSTRY
Agriculture, manufacturing, food products

CITIES
Springfield (pt.), 25,293; Collinsville (pt.), 21,803; Edwardsville (pt.), 21,478

NOTABLE
Metropolis was declared the official hometown of Superman in 1972.

Gov. Mitch Daniels (R)

First elected: 2004
Length of term: 4 years
Term expires: 1/13
Salary: $95,000
Phone: (317) 232-4567

Residence: Indianapolis
Born: April 7, 1949;
Monongahela, Pa.
Religion: Presbyterian
Family: Wife, Cheri Daniels; four children
Education: Princeton U., A.B. 1971 (urban studies); Indiana U., attended 1975-76 (law); Georgetown U., J.D. 1979
Career: Pharmaceutical company executive; public policy institute executive; lawyer; White House aide; congressional and campaign aide; mayoral aide
Political highlights: U.S. Office of Management and Budget director, 2001-03

Election results:
2008 GENERAL
Mitch Daniels (R)	1,563,885	57.8%
Jill Long Thompson (D)	1,082,463	40.0%
Andy Horning (LIBERT)	57,376	2.1%

Lt. Gov. Rebecca Skillman (R)

First elected: 2004
Length of term: 4 years
Term expires: 1/13
Salary: $79,192
Phone: (317) 232-4545

LEGISLATURE

General Assembly: January-April in odd-numbered years; January-March in even-numbered years

Senate: 50 members, 4-year terms
2009 ratios: 33 R, 17 D; 37 men, 13 women
Salary: $22,616
Phone: (317) 232-9400

House: 100 members, 2-year terms
2009 ratios: 52 D, 48 R; 87 men, 13 women
Salary: $22,616
Phone: (317) 232-9600

TERM LIMITS

Governor: 2 terms
Senate: No
House: No

URBAN STATISTICS

CITY	POPULATION
Indianapolis	791,926
Fort Wayne	205,727
Evansville	121,582
South Bend	107,789
Gary	102,746

REGISTERED VOTERS

Voters do not register by party.

POPULATION

2008 population (est.)	6,376,792
2000 population	6,080,485
1990 population	5,544,159
Percent change (1990-2000)	+9.7%
Rank among states (2008)	16

Median age	35.2
Born in state	69.3%
Foreign born	3.1%
Violent crime rate	349/100,000
Poverty level	9.5%
Federal workers	37,567
Military	22,639

ELECTIONS

STATE ELECTION OFFICIAL
(317) 232-3939
DEMOCRATIC PARTY
(317) 231-7100
REPUBLICAN PARTY
(317) 635-7561

MISCELLANEOUS

Web: www.in.gov
Capital: Indianapolis

U.S. CONGRESS

Senate: 1 Democrat, 1 Republican
House: 5 Democrats, 4 Republicans

2000 Census Statistics by District

DIST.	2008 VOTE FOR PRESIDENT OBAMA	MCCAIN	WHITE	BLACK	ASIAN	HISP	MEDIAN INCOME	WHITE COLLAR	BLUE COLLAR	SERVICE INDUSTRY	OVER 64	UNDER 18	COLLEGE EDUCATION	RURAL	SQ. MILES
1	62%	37%	70%	18%	1%	10%	$44,087	53%	31%	15%	13%	27%	17%	13%	2,209
2	54	45	84	8	1	5	$40,381	51	35	14	13	26	17	27	3,679
3	43	56	88	6	1	4	$44,013	52	36	12	11	28	18	35	3,240
4	43	56	94	1	1	3	$45,947	57	30	13	11	26	22	32	4,016
5	40	59	93	3	1	2	$52,800	63	25	12	11	27	31	26	3,266
6	46	52	93	4	0	1	$39,002	50	35	15	14	25	15	41	5,550
7	71	28	63	29	1	4	$36,522	58	26	16	11	26	21	0	262
8	47	51	94	4	1	1	$36,732	52	32	16	14	24	16	42	7,042
9	48	50	94	2	1	2	$39,011	51	35	14	12	24	17	48	6,603
STATE	50	49	86	8	1	4	$41,567	54	32	14	12	26	19	29	35,867
U.S.	53	46	69	12	4	13	$41,994	60	25	15	12	26	24	21	3,537,438

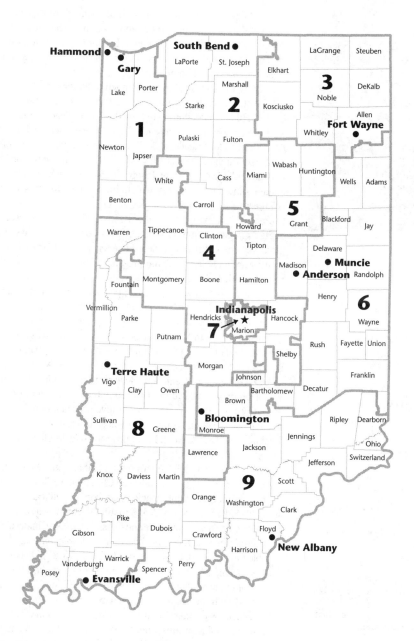

Hammond ●
● Gary
South Bend ●
LaPorte
St. Joseph
LaGrange
Steuben
Lake
Porter
Marshall
Elkhart
3
Noble
DeKalb
Starke
2
Kosciusko
Allen
Newton
Japser
Pulaski
Fulton
Whitley
Fort Wayne ●
1
White
Cass
Miami
Wabash
Huntington
Wells
Adams
Benton
Carroll
Warren
Tippecanoe
Howard
5
Grant
Blackford
Jay
Clinton
Tipton
Fountain
Montgomery
4
Boone
Hamilton
Delaware
Madison
● Muncie
● Anderson
Randolph
Vermillion
Parke
Putnam
Hendricks
Indianapolis
★
Marion
7
Hancock
Henry
6
Wayne
Rush
Fayette
Union
Shelby
● Terre Haute
Vigo
Clay
Owen
Morgan
Johnson
Bartholomew
Decatur
Franklin
Brown
Sullivan
8
Greene
● Bloomington
Monroe
Jennings
Ripley
Dearborn
Lawrence
Jackson
Jefferson
Ohio
Switzerland
Knox
Daviess
Martin
9
Scott
Orange
Washington
Clark
Pike
Dubois
Crawford
Floyd ●
New Albany
Gibson
Harrison
Vanderburgh
Warrick
Spencer
Perry
Posey
● Evansville

Sen. Richard G. Lugar (R)

Elected 1976; 6th term

The diligent and scholarly Lugar is the Senate's most senior Republican, commanding a level of respect and influence accorded few lawmakers. Regarded as a virtual icon in Indiana, he blends his image as an elder statesman on diplomatic and national security issues with a reputation for paying close attention to constituents.

Although Lugar failed to make much of an impact as a short-lived GOP presidential candidate in 1996, he has thrived in his three-plus decades on Capitol Hill. He was nominated for the Nobel Peace Prize in 2000 for his work on preventing the spread of nuclear weapons, and in 2008 the non-profit Council for Excellence in Government named him one of the 25 great public servants of the past 25 years. He was extremely close to President Obama and Vice President Joseph R. Biden Jr. when they served in the Senate, something Obama saw fit to highlight on the 2008 campaign trail.

Lugar's voting record is conservative, but he has shown both a willingness to break with his party and a knack for being ahead of the curve. As a member of the Agriculture, Nutrition and Forestry Committee, he has long advocated increased development of renewable energy, one of Obama's priorities. And on the Foreign Relations Committee, he pushed during the 1980s for democracy in South Africa and the Philippines — often against the wishes of President Reagan — and was a polite yet persistent critic of President George W. Bush's policy in Iraq well before public opinion turned against the war.

But he disdains showboating and regularly seeks bipartisan support. "I've learned how to work in the Senate to bring about as broad a consensus [as possible] on issues that I think are extremely important for our national security or for world security," Lugar told Gannett News Service in 2008.

Lugar's signature issue is nuclear non-proliferation. He teamed in 1991 with Democrat Sam Nunn of Georgia, then chairman of the Armed Services Committee, to create a cooperative program to help countries of the former Soviet Union secure and dispose of weapons of mass destruction. By the late 2000s, the Nunn-Lugar program had deactivated more than 7,500 Soviet nuclear warheads.

In the Obama administration's early months, Lugar showed his willingness to help his ex-colleague. He endorsed Christopher Hill as U.S. ambassador to Iraq in March 2009, blunting objections from Republicans who decried Hill's lack of Middle East experience. A month earlier, he was among nine Republicans who voted to reauthorize and expand the State Children's Health Insurance Program, which covers children from low-income families that are not eligible for Medicaid. But he opposed Obama's $787 billion economic stimulus law, calling it "a sprawling affair" that could provoke a trade war.

One of Lugar's main goals is renewing the START I nuclear-arms reduction treaty with Russia, which expires in December 2009. A trip to Russia in 2005 helped foster the relationship between Lugar and Obama, then a freshman senator. Obama subsequently worked with Lugar on nuclear weapons security, touting their efforts in a July 2008 campaign ad. Lugar returned the favor by giving a speech endorsing the Illinois Democrat's interest in talking with the leaders of U.S. enemies — a position that Obama's GOP rival, Arizona Sen. John McCain, had dismissed as naive.

Lugar allied with Biden when the Delaware senator was Foreign Relations' top Democrat; during Biden's abortive presidential bid, he said he would consider Lugar as his secretary of State. In the 110th Congress (2007-08), the pair helped steer into law a landmark civilian nuclear cooperation

CAPITOL OFFICE
224-4814
lugar.senate.gov
306 Hart Bldg. 20510-1401; fax 228-0360

COMMITTEES
Agriculture, Nutrition & Forestry
Foreign Relations - ranking member

RESIDENCE
Indianapolis

BORN
April 4, 1932; Indianapolis, Ind.

RELIGION
Methodist

FAMILY
Wife, Charlene Lugar; four children

EDUCATION
Denison U., B.A. 1954; Oxford U., M.A. 1956 (Rhodes scholar)

MILITARY SERVICE
Navy, 1957-60

CAREER
Farm manager; manufacturing company executive

POLITICAL HIGHLIGHTS
Indianapolis School Board, 1964-67; mayor of Indianapolis, 1968-75; Republican nominee for U.S. Senate, 1974; sought Republican nomination for president, 1996

ELECTION RESULTS

2006 GENERAL

Richard G. Lugar (R)	1,171,553	87.4%
Steve Osborne (LIBERT)	168,820	12.6%

2006 PRIMARY

Richard G. Lugar (R)	unopposed

PREVIOUS WINNING PERCENTAGES
2000 (67%); 1994 (67%); 1988 (68%); 1982 (54%); 1976 (59%)

agreement with India as well as a significant expansion in the efforts to fight AIDS, tuberculosis and malaria overseas. Earlier, they held dozens of oversight hearings on Iraq, probing the failures of U.S. efforts there even as Lugar backed Bush's refusal to set a timetable for troop withdrawal. In their 2006 book "The Broken Branch," political scholars Thomas E. Mann and Norman J. Ornstein called the senators' efforts "the single oasis in the desert of congressional obeisance" toward Bush's war policy at the time.

Lugar first chaired the Foreign Relations panel in 1985-86, when Republicans briefly controlled the Senate. In subsequent years, he was both the chairman and the top-ranking Republican on the Agriculture Committee.

His experience as a farmer helps shape policy on agriculture, a vital part of his state's economy. For more than half a century, he has run a 604-acre corn, soybean and walnut farm that belonged to his father. Critical of government safety nets, he helped steer to enactment in 1996 a sweeping reauthorization of agriculture programs that replaced New Deal-era crop subsidies and moved farmers toward a free-market system. But pressure from farmers prompted Congress in 2002 to undo most of the changes. Six years later, he was the only Senate conferee who did not sign the conference report reauthorizing the measure, agreeing with Bush that it had too much unneeded spending.

Lugar has cited the crop subsidies paid to U.S. and European farmers as a major contributor to the global food crisis and has called for the establishment of a "hunger czar" to coordinate domestic and international food aid.

When Congress began discussing ways to fight global warming in 2009, Lugar called for international assistance to help adapt to climate changes. He espoused the use of genetically modified crops. "An international fund for climate change adaptation that does not include cutting-edge advances in biotechnology will be unnecessarily limited," he said.

In recent years, Lugar has devoted increased time to energy issues, describing excessive U.S. reliance on foreign oil as "the albatross of national security." He has twice introduced a National Fuels Initiative designed to expand production of renewable fuels such as corn-based ethanol by 100 billion gallons a year by 2025 through a combination of regulatory mandates and tax credits. In February 2009, he called for a hike in the federal gasoline tax along with a decrease in payroll taxes.

Lugar was sickly as a child, plagued by allergies and ear infections. He passed much time reading biographies and publishing a family newspaper on a toy printing press. He learned piano and cello at his mother's urging, showing a flair for improvisation and composition.

Lugar was first in his class in high school and at Denison University, where he was student body co-president with his wife-to-be, Charlene Smeltzer. He later became a Rhodes scholar at Oxford and was a naval intelligence officer.

He first ran for office in 1963, winning a seat on the school board. He became mayor of Indianapolis in 1968 and went on to merge the city and surrounding Marion County into a single governmental unit. In 1974, running for the Senate in a Watergate-dominated year with a reputation as "Richard Nixon's favorite mayor," Lugar came within a respectable 75,000 votes of Democratic incumbent Birch Bayh (whose son, Evan, is now Indiana's junior senator). In 1976, he handily defeated Democratic incumbent Vance Hartke and has been re-elected five times since. In 2006 — which some political observers speculate may be his final race — he was the only senator granted a free ride to re-election, with only token opposition.

Briefly considered as a vice presidential prospect in 1980, Lugar was stung again eight years later when the No. 2 spot on the GOP ticket went to the less-experienced junior senator from Indiana, Dan Quayle. Lugar ran an abbreviated presidential campaign in 1996 but was doomed by his complex policy speeches on international affairs and a stiff campaign style.

KEY VOTES

2008
Yes   Prohibit discrimination based on genetic information
No   Reauthorize farm and nutrition programs for five years
No   Limit debate on "cap and trade" system for greenhouse gas emissions
No   Allow lawsuits against companies that participated in warrantless wiretapping
No   Limit debate on a bill to block a scheduled cut in Medicare payments to doctors
Yes   Grant mortgage relief to homeowners and funding for Fannie Mae and Freddie Mac
Yes   Approve a nuclear cooperation agreement with India
Yes   Approve final $700 billion program to stabilize financial markets
Yes   Allow consideration of a $14 billion auto industry loan package

2007
Yes   Increase minimum wage by $2.10 an hour
Yes   Limit debate on a comprehensive immigration bill
Yes   Overhaul congressional lobbying and ethics rules for members and their staffs
Yes   Limit debate on considering a bill to add House seats for the District of Columbia and Utah
Yes   Limit debate on restoring habeas corpus rights to detainees
No   Mandate minimum breaks for troops between deployments to Iraq or Afghanistan
Yes   Override Bush veto of $23.2 billion water projects authorization bill
Yes   Confirm Michael B. Mukasey as attorney general
Yes   Limit debate on an energy policy overhaul containing $21.8 billion in tax incentives and reduced oil and gas subsidies

CQ VOTE STUDIES

	PARTY UNITY		PRESIDENTIAL SUPPORT	
	SUPPORT	OPPOSE	SUPPORT	OPPOSE
2008	81%	19%	87%	13%
2007	67%	33%	78%	22%
2006	82%	18%	91%	9%
2005	84%	16%	84%	16%
2004	94%	6%	93%	7%
2003	97%	3%	98%	2%
2002	91%	9%	100%	0%
2001	92%	8%	100%	0%
2000	86%	14%	65%	35%
1999	88%	12%	40%	60%

INTEREST GROUPS

	AFL-CIO	ADA	CCUS	ACU
2008	20%	25%	100%	63%
2007	32%	45%	91%	60%
2006	20%	15%	100%	64%
2005	21%	10%	100%	88%
2004	8%	20%	100%	84%
2003	0%	10%	96%	80%
2002	31%	5%	95%	90%
2001	13%	15%	100%	92%
2000	0%	10%	100%	84%
1999	0%	5%	100%	88%

Sen. Evan Bayh (D)

Elected 1998; 2nd term

CAPITOL OFFICE
224-5623
bayh.senate.gov
131 Russell Bldg. 20510-1404; fax 228-1377

COMMITTEES
Armed Services
  (Readiness & Management Support - chairman)
Banking, Housing & Urban Affairs
  (Security & International Trade - chairman)
Energy & Natural Resources
Small Business & Entrepreneurship
Select Intelligence
Special Aging

RESIDENCE
Indianapolis

BORN
Dec. 26, 1955; Shirkieville, Ind.

RELIGION
Episcopalian

FAMILY
Wife, Susan Bayh; two children

EDUCATION
Indiana U., B.S. 1978 (business economics);
U. of Virginia, J.D. 1981

CAREER
Lawyer

POLITICAL HIGHLIGHTS
Ind. secretary of state, 1986-89; governor, 1989-97

ELECTION RESULTS

2004 GENERAL

Evan Bayh (D)	1,496,976	61.7%
Marvin B. Scott (R)	903,913	37.2%
Albert Barger (LIBERT)	27,344	1.1%

2004 PRIMARY

Evan Bayh (D)	unopposed

PREVIOUS WINNING PERCENTAGES
1998 (64%)

Bayh's family ties got him into politics, but his carefully centrist approach has helped him get ahead. The question that hangs over him is whether he has been too careful. He tends to inch ahead rather than rush forward on his legislative goals, and his floor speeches are rare and prosaic events, filled with calls for compromise and a reliance on "Hoosier values."

He's much the same in his attempts to accumulate political capital nationwide. Promoted as a potential presidential candidate from the moment he arrived in the Senate in 1999, Bayh (BY) briefly considered a 2004 race but concluded that his twin sons, born in November 1995, were too young to leave for a grueling campaign. He made a half-hearted stab at the Democratic nomination in 2008, only to pull back when he fared poorly in early polls. The last three Democratic presidential nominees — Al Gore in 2000, John Kerry in 2004 and Barack Obama in 2008 — considered him as a possible running mate but ultimately passed him over.

The son of Indiana Sen. Birch Bayh, a liberal Democrat who made a more sustained but unsuccessful run for president in 1976, Evan Bayh is a proven vote-getter in Indiana. He won two terms as governor, serving from 1989 to 1997. His 1992 re-election came by the largest margin of any governor in modern state history.

Although he supports much of President Obama's agenda, Bayh isn't a certain vote for his party, particularly on fiscal matters. He had concerns about Obama's economic stimulus package, and accompanied the president in early 2009 when Obama gave a speech in Elkhart, where the unemployment rate was more than 15 percent. Bayh said he told the president the package needed to have "safeguards to assure the money actually achieves the results that it's being spent for." But he ultimately supported the $787 billion bill, which was signed into law.

Bayh, a member of the Banking, Housing and Urban Affairs Committee, was one of eight Democrats who voted to block the release of the second half of the $700 billion approved in a fall 2008 law to bring stability to the financial markets. And he was one of three Democrats who voiced opposition to the $410 billion catchall spending plan for fiscal 2009. He was one of only two Senate Democrats to vote to strip out all earmarks from the underlying bill. "The bloated omnibus requires sacrifice from no one, least of all the government. It only exacerbates the problem and hastens the day of reckoning," he said.

He published an opinion piece in the Wall Street Journal criticizing the bill and calling on Obama to veto it. The article drew instant praise from Republican leaders, and Senate Minority Leader Mitch McConnell of Kentucky had it printed in the Congressional Record. But Bayh accepted the praise with caution: "Some of those who were agreeing with me need to look in the mirror themselves, because their record on fiscal issues is not very good, either," he told The Indianapolis Star.

In 2008, he was the only Senate Democrat to vote against his party's budget because of projections it would add $2 trillion to the national debt. He stuck to his guns even after more than 50 Indiana groups serving low-income families beseeched him to support the budget's added spending for social programs. He was one of three Democrats voting "no" on the next year's budget.

Bayh chairs the Security and International Trade Subcommittee of the Banking panel and often attacks China's trade practices and currency policies. In mid-2008, the Banking Committee wrote a big housing package that President George W. Bush signed into law. It carried a provision Bayh had pushed granting a one-time deduction of up to $1,000 per couple for property taxes to homeowners who do not itemize on their tax returns.

Bayh had earlier marred his standing with Democratic activists by cosponsoring and voting for the 2002 resolution authorizing Bush to use force against Iraq in a pre-emptive strike to stop Saddam Hussein from developing weapons of mass destruction. But by late 2004, Bayh said the administration had mishandled the war, and he called for the resignation of Defense Secretary Donald H. Rumsfeld. In 2008, he was part of a bipartisan Armed Services Committee group that drafted language in the fiscal 2009 defense authorization bill designed to force the U.S. government to shift some costs of the war to Iraq.

Bayh also sits on the Energy and Natural Resources Committee, where he plans to push for increased investment in energy-efficient technologies, such as hybrid vehicles, and the development of alternative fuels such as ethanol. He was part of a bipartisan "Gang of 20" in 2008 that supported expanded offshore drilling as part of a broader package that included an estimated $84 billion in investments in conservation and efficiency, offset by cutting tax breaks to oil and gas companies.

Bayh said he always looks for the center, because that is where deals are made, and he keeps in tune with the Hoosier State's conservative bent. From 2001 to 2005, he chaired the Democratic Leadership Council, the centrist party organization that Bill Clinton once led. He co-founded a Senate group in 2005 called the Third Way to generate middle-of-the-road legislative proposals. And in 2007, when Democrats regained control of the Senate after the 2006 elections, Bayh joined a bipartisan breakfast group of senators designed to get Republicans and Democrats talking to each other on issues of the day. Bayh sees the get-togethers as a way to push the Senate toward the center.

"If we govern in a sensible way and forge bipartisan compromises, then the progressive-center coalition will hold," he said early in 2008. "If not, we will allow the Republicans to come back." He formed yet another group in March 2009 of moderate Democrats focusing on fiscal matters.

Bayh's other committee assignments include Small Business and Entrepreneurship, Special Aging and Select Intelligence.

Bayh's full name is Birch Evan Bayh III, though he has always gone by his middle name. (One of his twin sons carries on the family name but goes by the nickname "Beau." The other boy is named Nicholas Harrison Bayh.)

Born in the small town of Shirkieville, Bayh moved to Washington at age 7, when his father was elected to the Senate. He attended the exclusive St. Albans School, and one of his baby sitters was Lynda Bird Johnson, the president's older daughter. Bayh met his wife, Susan, while she was a summer intern for the House Ways and Means Committee. In law school, he managed his father's losing campaign for a fourth term in 1980, when Birch Bayh was swept out in the Reagan landslide.

After clerking for a federal judge and practicing law, Bayh was elected Indiana secretary of state at age 30. Two years later, in 1989, he became the youngest governor in the nation and stayed popular for eight years, in part by riding the crest of a robust economy.

Term limits barred him from running for governor again, so Bayh prepared to challenge GOP incumbent Sen. Daniel R. Coats, who decided to retire in 1998 rather than face Bayh. In November, Bayh trounced Mayor Paul Helmke of Fort Wayne by a nearly 2-to-1 ratio. Bayh's movie-star good looks and cross-party appeal keep his ratings high in Indiana. He won re-election to the Senate in 2004 with 62 percent of the vote. Taking nothing for granted in 2010, in November 2008 he hired Democratic strategist Anita Dunn, one of Obama's chief strategists.

KEY VOTES

2008

Yes   Prohibit discrimination based on genetic information

Yes   Reauthorize farm and nutrition programs for five years

Yes   Limit debate on "cap and trade" system for greenhouse gas emissions

No   Allow lawsuits against companies that participated in warrantless wiretapping

Yes   Limit debate on a bill to block a scheduled cut in Medicare payments to doctors

Yes   Grant mortgage relief to homeowners and funding for Fannie Mae and Freddie Mac

Yes   Approve a nuclear cooperation agreement with India

Yes   Approve final $700 billion program to stabilize financial markets

Yes   Allow consideration of a $14 billion auto industry loan package

2007

Yes   Increase minimum wage by $2.10 an hour

No   Limit debate on a comprehensive immigration bill

Yes   Overhaul congressional lobbying and ethics rules for members and their staffs

Yes   Limit debate on considering a bill to add House seats for the District of Columbia and Utah

Yes   Limit debate on restoring habeas corpus rights to detainees

Yes   Mandate minimum breaks for troops between deployments to Iraq or Afghanistan

Yes   Override Bush veto of $23.2 billion water projects authorization bill

Yes   Confirm Michael B. Mukasey as attorney general

Yes   Limit debate on an energy policy overhaul containing $21.8 billion in tax incentives and reduced oil and gas subsidies

CQ VOTE STUDIES

	PARTY UNITY		PRESIDENTIAL SUPPORT	
	SUPPORT	OPPOSE	SUPPORT	OPPOSE
2008	65%	35%	47%	53%
2007	79%	21%	43%	57%
2006	89%	11%	58%	42%
2005	90%	10%	36%	64%
2004	78%	22%	64%	36%
2003	82%	18%	55%	45%
2002	70%	30%	79%	21%
2001	82%	18%	69%	31%
2000	92%	8%	98%	2%
1999	88%	12%	89%	11%

INTEREST GROUPS

	AFL-CIO	ADA	CCUS	ACU
2008	80%	70%	63%	29%
2007	100%	95%	64%	12%
2006	100%	85%	45%	16%
2005	100%	95%	56%	20%
2004	100%	90%	65%	20%
2003	85%	75%	43%	30%
2002	85%	70%	65%	30%
2001	100%	100%	50%	32%
2000	75%	80%	60%	16%
1999	89%	90%	59%	12%

Rep. Peter J. Visclosky (D)

Elected 1984; 13th term

CAPITOL OFFICE
225-2461
www.house.gov/visclosky
2256 Rayburn Bldg. 20515-1401; fax 225-2493

COMMITTEES
Appropriations
(Energy-Water - chairman)

RESIDENCE
Merrillville

BORN
Aug. 13, 1949; Gary, Ind.

RELIGION
Roman Catholic

FAMILY
Divorced; two children

EDUCATION
Indiana U. Northwest, B.S. 1970 (accounting);
U. of Notre Dame, J.D. 1973; Georgetown U.,
LL.M. 1982

CAREER
Congressional aide; lawyer

POLITICAL HIGHLIGHTS
No previous office

ELECTION RESULTS

2008 GENERAL

Peter J. Visclosky (D)	199,954	70.9%
Mark Leyva (R)	76,647	27.2%
Jeff Duensing (LIBERT)	5,421	1.9%

2008 PRIMARY

Peter J. Visclosky (D)	unopposed

2006 GENERAL

Peter J. Visclosky (D)	104,195	69.7%
Mark Leyva (R)	40,146	26.8%
Charles E. Barman (I)	5,266	3.5%

PREVIOUS WINNING PERCENTAGES
2004 (68%); 2002 (67%); 2000 (72%); 1998 (73%);
1996 (69%); 1994 (56%); 1992 (69%); 1990 (66%);
1988 (77%); 1986 (73%); 1984 (71%)

The hard-working Visclosky had one goal in mind when he first arrived in the House: a seat on the Appropriations Committee, where his predecessor and mentor had served. He made it onto the panel in October 1991 — six years, nine months and nine days after his first bid for the appointment, he later calculated — and has relished the job ever since. "I'm an appropriator," he said. "Money makes policy."

Since Democrats regained control of the House in 2007, Visclosky (vis-KLOSS-key) has been not only an appropriator but a "cardinal," as the panel's subcommittee chairmen are called. He heads the Energy and Water Development Subcommittee, which funds the Energy Department and politically popular water projects undertaken by the Army Corps of Engineers. He also sits on the powerful Defense Subcommittee, which provides funding for the Pentagon and Iraq War, and the Commerce-Justice-Science panel.

Visclosky has capitalized on his Appropriations post to set aside tens of millions of dollars for projects back home. During consideration of the fiscal 2008 spending bills, only four other House members — all appropriators with greater seniority — snagged more dollars than Visclosky. In just the Defense spending bill, he obtained $45 million in earmarks, according to Taxpayers for Common Sense. He also has sought millions of dollars for improvements to the Gary-Chicago International Airport to help make it a more viable alternative to the crowded O'Hare and Midway airports in Chicago.

But his proclivity for earmarking funds drew him unwelcome attention in early 2009 when news reports revealed Visclosky was the top recipient of contributions from the family of Paul Magliocchetti, founder of The PMA Group. The now-defunct lobbying group had specialized in earning its clients defense contracts but came under investigation for its campaign-contribution practices. Magliocchetti and nine of his relatives gave $138,500 to Visclosky's congressional campaign committee and his leadership political action committee, Calumet PAC, between 2000 and 2008. Magliocchetti is a former Appropriations aide who, when assembling his business, hired former top aides to Visclosky and Virginia Democrat James P. Moran.

Visclosky stayed quiet during the probe, although he did push back against Republican efforts to force the House ethics committee to conduct a probe into an alleged connection between PMA's campaign contributions and the earmarking process. He also said he would return the contributions, and as of late March 2009, he had given the U.S. Treasury $18,000. And after a federal grand jury subpoenaed records from Visclosky's congressional and campaign offices, he announced he would step down temporarily from the subcommittee chairmanship during consideration of its fiscal 2010 spending bill and allow the congressman next in line to take charge.

The controversy had thrown him into a spotlight he had worked assiduously to avoid. His floor speeches are typically brief tributes to individuals or groups, and his name seldom appears in the national news media. He acknowledged an aversion to publicity. "I try to avoid that like the plague," he said.

His low-key style shouldn't be confused with a lack of determination. He showed early on in his chairmanship that the Energy Department could expect a focused watchdog as its overseer. "Since the history of cost estimates is so incredibly rotten, how would you suggest Congress evaluate major projects?" he asked Energy Secretary Samuel W. Bodman at a March 2007 hearing.

As chairman, he worked to direct funds in the fiscal 2009 Energy-Water spending bill toward renewable-energy and water infrastructure programs, while pushing to sharply cut various nuclear weapons initiatives sought by President George W. Bush.

Visclosky also refused to go along with Bush's efforts to double the size of the Strategic Petroleum Reserve, and as gas prices soared in 2008, he joined other Democrats in calling on the president to start releasing oil from the stockpile in order to increase supplies and drive down prices.

Visclosky has battled with presidents — both Democratic and Republican — whom he believes haven't done enough to protect the domestic steel industry from unfair foreign competition. As the son of an ironworker and chairman of the Congressional Steel Caucus, he fights to revive the flagging domestic steel industry, the main industry of his northwestern Indiana district.

He supported efforts from the manufacturing industry to include in President Obama's $787 billion economic stimulus law provisions to "buy American." Although major U.S. exporters worried about protectionist retaliation, Visclosky said the provisions "are a common-sense way to focus U.S. taxpayer dollars on rapidly creating manufacturing jobs here in America, and not overseas."

Visclosky generally is a reliable vote for his party, but breaks with leadership on some budgetary matters; he said government has "a moral responsibility" to balance the budget. In fall 2008 he opposed both versions of the $700 billion legislation to aid the nation's ailing financial sector, calling it "in essence a blank check" with no concrete plan for how the money would be used. (He did back a subsequent failed proposal to bail out Detroit automakers.)

As a teenager, Visclosky aspired to the priesthood. But he dropped out of a Roman Catholic seminary at age 15. He went on to get degrees at two Catholic institutions, the University of Notre Dame and Georgetown University. Despite a passion for history, he made the practical decision to pursue an accounting degree as an undergraduate. After graduating from Notre Dame law school in 1973, he linked his fortunes to those of Adam Benjamin Jr., then a state senator and rising political star in Indiana. Visclosky coordinated Benjamin's successful campaign for Congress in 1976 and served as one of his top aides in Washington for nearly six years.

In 1984, Visclosky challenged Rep. Katie Hall, putting on dozens of $2 "dog and bean" dinners to attract the young, the elderly and the unemployed. His "Slovak kid" background helped, as did the memory that older voters had of his father, John Visclosky, who had served as Gary's comptroller in the 1950s and its mayor in 1962 and 1963. Visclosky bested Hall in the primary by 2 percentage points, then swamped Republican Joseph B. Grenchik, the mayor of Whiting, in November. He has won handily ever since.

KEY VOTES

2008

Yes Delay consideration of Colombia free-trade agreement

Yes Override Bush veto of federal farm and nutrition programs reauthorization bill

– Overhaul surveillance laws and permit dismissal of suits against companies that conducted warrantless wiretapping

Yes Grant mortgage relief to homeowners and funding for Fannie Mae and Freddie Mac

No Approve initial $700 billion program to stabilize financial markets

No Approve final $700 billion program to stabilize financial markets

Yes Provide $14 billion in loans to automakers

2007

Yes Increase minimum wage by $2.10 an hour

Yes Approve $124.2 billion in emergency war spending and set goal for redeployment of troops from Iraq

No Reject federal contraceptive assistance to international family planning groups

Yes Override Bush veto of $23.2 billion water projects authorization bill

No Implement Peru free-trade agreement

Yes Approve energy policy overhaul with new fuel economy standards

Yes Clear $473.5 billion omnibus spending bill, including $70 billion for military operations

CQ VOTE STUDIES

	PARTY UNITY		PRESIDENTIAL SUPPORT	
	SUPPORT	OPPOSE	SUPPORT	OPPOSE
2008	99%	1%	12%	88%
2007	98%	2%	4%	96%
2006	90%	10%	20%	80%
2005	91%	9%	26%	74%
2004	90%	10%	19%	81%

INTEREST GROUPS

	AFL-CIO	ADA	CCUS	ACU
2008	100%	80%	53%	8%
2007	96%	100%	50%	4%
2006	100%	100%	27%	12%
2005	93%	85%	37%	8%
2004	100%	95%	35%	4%

INDIANA 1
Northwest — Gary, Hammond

A Rust Belt district bordered by Lake Michigan to the north and Illinois to the west, the Democratic 1st is home to steelworkers, a large union presence and some large minority populations in Lake County. Most of the 1st's population is in Lake County, which includes Gary, where more than 80 percent of residents are black, and East Chicago, where more than half of the population is Hispanic. The 1st also is home to many Eastern European ethnic neighborhoods.

In contrast to the farming that dominates other Indiana districts, the steel industry has been a mainstay in the 1st District for decades. Competition in the global economy, however, has hindered recent production, and decreasing output and job loss in the industry continue. Nevertheless, there are still thousands of steelworkers residing in Gary, Hammond and East Chicago, and more steel is produced here than in any other district in the nation.

Residents in and around Gary still struggle with the effects of unemployment, high crime rates and a shrinking population, and local leaders now count on Lake Michigan-based tourism to lure people to the 1st. The region's lake boat gambling has brought in some jobs and attracted tourists, but has not countered the cutbacks and lower production in the steel industry and manufacturing. A stable health care sector may help prop up the region's economy as widespread job losses continue and the economy stalls.

The 1st generally supports Democratic candidates by large margins. There are GOP pockets in Lake County suburbs such as Crown Point and Merrillville, but the northern cities are mostly Democratic. Lake County gave Democrat Barack Obama 67 percent of its 2008 presidential vote — his best county statewide — and despite some Republican support in growing Porter County and in farming communities farther south, the 1st overall gave Obama 62 percent.

MAJOR INDUSTRY
Steel, health care, manufacturing, gambling

CITIES
Gary, 102,746; Hammond, 83,048; Portage, 33,496; East Chicago, 32,414; Merrillville, 30,560; Valparaiso (pt.), 27,362; Hobart, 25,363

NOTABLE
"A Christmas Story" is based on life in Hammond in the early 1940s.

Rep. Joe Donnelly (D)

Elected 2006; 2nd term

CAPITOL OFFICE
225-3915
donnelly.house.gov
1530 Longworth Bldg. 20515-1402; fax 225-6798

COMMITTEES
Financial Services
Veterans' Affairs

RESIDENCE
Granger

BORN
Sept. 29, 1955; Queens, N.Y.

RELIGION
Roman Catholic

FAMILY
Wife, Jill Donnelly; two children

EDUCATION
U. of Notre Dame, B.A. 1977 (government),
J.D. 1981

CAREER
Customized office products company owner;
lawyer

POLITICAL HIGHLIGHTS
Democratic nominee for Ind. Senate, 1990;
Democratic nominee for U.S. House, 2004

ELECTION RESULTS

2008 GENERAL

Joe Donnelly (D)	187,416	67.1%
Luke Puckett (R)	84,455	30.2%
Mark Vogel (LIBERT)	7,475	2.7%

2008 PRIMARY

Joe Donnelly (D)	unopposed

2006 GENERAL

Joe Donnelly (D)	103,561	54.0%
Chris Chocola (R)	88,300	46.0%

Donnelly is a centrist who is conservative on social and fiscal issues but a strong ally of organized labor. He hails from a manufacturing-oriented district where he is a searching for ways to revive the economy.

He is a member of the Blue Dog Coalition, a group of fiscally conservative Democrats. In his first term, he broke from his party on 22 percent of the votes in which a majority of Democrats voted against a majority of Republicans — more often than all but four House Democrats.

Donnelly put aside his concerns about soaring deficits to support President Obama's $787 billion economic stimulus plan in February 2009. Before its passage, Obama visited the city of Elkhart in Donnelly's district to tout the measure, and Donnelly succeeded in adding a last-minute provision to provide a tax break to recreational-vehicle manufacturers centered in the city, which had lost 8,000 jobs in a year. "RVs are the lifeblood of our area," he said. "This provision will help stimulate demand and put folks back to work."

A member of the Financial Services Committee, he also backed President George W. Bush's two $700 billion proposals — the second of which became law — to help the ailing financial services sector, as well as a subsequent failed $14 billion bailout for domestic automakers. He drew the line at a $410 billion fiscal 2009 catchall spending bill; he was one of just 20 House Democrats to vote no in February 2009.

In his first week in the House in 2007, Donnelly was one of four freshman Democrats to vote against a measure to lift restrictions on federally funded embryonic stem cell research, which uses discarded embryos created for in vitro fertilization. He also opposes gun control, abortion rights, amnesty for illegal immigrants and same-sex marriage.

"I grew up as a young man going to Catholic school, and that probably influenced me on the social issues like abortion," said Donnelly, who hails from a large Irish Catholic family that revered President John F. Kennedy and brother Robert F. Kennedy, the former attorney general.

Donnelly is more in step with his party on labor issues. He was a cosponsor of a successful Democratic measure in 2007 to increase the federal minimum wage from $5.15 an hour to $7.25. He opposed that year's Peru free-trade agreement and wants labor and environmental standards to be included in future trade agreements, a position favored by labor unions.

On energy, Donnelly favors a range of solutions, including nuclear power. He said exploring for more domestic oil should be a "bridge" to development of more efficient and renewable sources of energy.

Donnelly also sits on the Veterans' Affairs Committee. He introduced legislation that became the basis for a measure to modernize and improve the Veterans Affairs Department's disability claims process. That measure passed the House in 2008 but was never taken up in the Senate. He also joined with his Indiana colleague Mark Souder — a Republican and one of his best friends in Congress — to advocate for a medical clinic in Goshen that opened in 2007 to relieve the pressure on another clinic in South Bend. "There's an unwritten contract where we have an obligation to make sure that we've kept all our promises to our veterans," Donnelly said.

Donnelly grew up in Massapequa, N.Y., on Long Island, with one brother and three sisters. His mother died when he was 10, leaving his father to raise five children. His father was the manager of a printing shop in New York City, and his work ethic impressed his son. "My dad, for probably 50 years, got up in the morning, got on the train — hour and a half into work, hour and a half back from work — he worked like a dog every day. He set a wonderful example for his family and how a person should conduct themselves, and he let us know that we have an obligation to give back as well," he said.

He graduated from a Catholic high school, then went on to the University of Notre Dame for his undergraduate and law degrees. In college, he met his wife, Jill, and the two eventually settled in South Bend, Ind., where she grew up. Donnelly practiced law and became a member of the board for the Mishawaka Marian High School, a Catholic school, and later spent a year as its president.

His first stab at politics was in 1986, when he worked on the unsuccessful campaign of Democrat Thomas W. Ward, a candidate for what was then Indiana's 3rd District. He made an unsuccessful bid for Indiana attorney general in 1988 before becoming a member of the State Election Board for a year. In 1990, he was the Democratic nominee for an Indiana state Senate seat but lost.

Discouraged, Donnelly went back to earning a living and raising his two children. He coached their baseball and softball teams, and later opened an office supply business, splitting his time between his work as an attorney and developing his new business. "It was almost a blessing in disguise," he said of his losing streak in politics.

In 2004, Donnelly decided to try his hand again, saying he felt the country was headed in the wrong direction in economic policy and in the war in Iraq. He challenged Rep. Chris Chocola, a conservative Republican in a district roughly split between the two parties. Given the 2nd District's makeup, the race could have been competitive, but Donnelly was unable to come close to the incumbent in fundraising and lost by 10 percentage points.

Two years later, when Donnelly took on Chocola in a rematch, the political atmosphere in the district was strikingly different. Bush's job approval ratings had plunged, and Donnelly dwelled on the incumbent's frequent support for the president on House votes. Donnelly also was able to raise about twice as much money as he had two years earlier, and won the seat with 54 percent of the vote.

Upon taking office, Donnelly began holding "Congress at Your Corner" events at supermarkets and other locations to listen to constituent concerns. In 2008, he donated his 80,000 frequent-flyer miles from traveling between the district and Washington to the Hero Miles Program, which provides airfare for soldiers and family of wounded servicemembers.

He had little trouble winning re-election — he outraised GOP businessman Luke Puckett by a 6-to-1 margin and captured 67 percent of the vote in a district that Obama also easily carried over Republican Sen. John McCain of Arizona.

KEY VOTES

2008

Yes Delay consideration of Colombia free-trade agreement

Yes Override Bush veto of federal farm and nutrition programs reauthorization bill

Yes Overhaul surveillance laws and permit dismissal of suits against companies that conducted warrantless wiretapping

Yes Grant mortgage relief to homeowners and funding for Fannie Mae and Freddie Mac

Yes Approve initial $700 billion program to stabilize financial markets

Yes Approve final $700 billion program to stabilize financial markets

Yes Provide $14 billion in loans to automakers

2007

Yes Increase minimum wage by $2.10 an hour

Yes Approve $124.2 billion in emergency war spending and set goal for redeployment of troops from Iraq

Yes Reject federal contraceptive assistance to international family planning groups

Yes Override Bush veto of $23.2 billion water projects authorization bill

No   Implement Peru free-trade agreement

Yes Approve energy policy overhaul with new fuel economy standards

Yes Clear $473.5 billion omnibus spending bill, including $70 billion for military operations

CQ VOTE STUDIES

	PARTY UNITY		PRESIDENTIAL SUPPORT	
	SUPPORT	OPPOSE	SUPPORT	OPPOSE
2008	79%	21%	25%	75%
2007	77%	23%	19%	81%

INTEREST GROUPS

	AFL-CIO	ADA	CCUS	ACU
2008	87%	70%	72%	28%
2007	88%	85%	60%	44%

INDIANA 2

North central — South Bend, parts of Elkhart and Kokomo

The 2nd begins in Kokomo and moves north through small farming communities before reaching counties on the state's northern border, which include the cities of South Bend, Mishawaka and Elkhart and are home to nearly one-third of district residents.

South Bend, in St. Joseph County, is home to an ideologically and economically diverse population. The wealthy, white-collar, Catholic Notre Dame community that hosts faculty and professionals is joined by low-income, minority residents downtown, as well as blue-collar areas east of the city. Neighboring Mishawaka has grown as some South Bend residents have left downtown. Michigan City's steel manufacturers along the shores of Lake Michigan in the district's northwest have led to a strong northern Democratic-leaning region.

East of Mishawaka, communities in Elkhart County (shared with the 3rd) round out the 2nd's heavily populated northeast. Farming and business in

Elkhart create a faithful conservative constituency. But Elkhart, a national center for the manufactured housing industry, has experienced skyrocketing unemployment rates and the collapse of local manufacturing. Extended unemployment here has been coupled with a nationwide economic downturn that reduced demand for the recreational vehicles produced in the county. Kokomo (shared with the 5th) is another mainly white, blue-collar area; it relies on the struggling auto industry, and volatile markets have hurt key local employers Delphi and DaimlerChrysler.

The once Republican-leaning U.S. House seat flipped to Democratic control in 2006, and Rep. Joe Donnelly solidified his hold on the seat in 2008. LaPorte County gave Democrat Barack Obama fifth-highest statewide percentage in the 2008 presidential election, and Obama won the district with 54 percent.

MAJOR INDUSTRY
Manufacturing, higher education, agriculture

CITIES
South Bend, 107,789; Elkhart (pt.), 48,783; Mishawaka, 46,557; Michigan City, 32,900

NOTABLE
The World Whiffleball Championship is played every year in Mishawaka.

Rep. Mark Souder (R)

Elected 1994; 8th term

CAPITOL OFFICE
225-4436
souder.house.gov
2231 Rayburn Bldg. 20515-1403; fax 225-3479

COMMITTEES
Education & Labor
Homeland Security
Oversight & Government Reform

RESIDENCE
Fort Wayne

BORN
July 18, 1950; Fort Wayne, Ind.

RELIGION
Evangelical

FAMILY
Wife, Diane Souder; three children

EDUCATION
Indiana U., Fort Wayne, B.S. 1972 (business administration); U. of Notre Dame, M.B.A. 1974

CAREER
Congressional aide; furniture company executive; general store owner

POLITICAL HIGHLIGHTS
No previous office

ELECTION RESULTS

2008 GENERAL

Mark Souder (R)	155,693	55.0%
Michael Montagano (D)	112,309	39.7%
William Larsen (LIBERT)	14,877	5.3%

2008 PRIMARY

Mark Souder (R)	40,161	77.1%
Scott Wise (R)	11,946	22.9%

2006 GENERAL

Mark Souder (R)	95,421	54.3%
Thomas Hayhurst (D)	80,357	45.7%

PREVIOUS WINNING PERCENTAGES
2004 (69%); 2002 (63%); 2000 (62%); 1998 (63%); 1996 (58%); 1994 (55%)

Souder's socially conservative views are driven by his religious beliefs. He is a reliable party loyalist, but occasionally will cross the aisle when the issues are about helping those in need. Being a faith-based lawmaker, he said, isn't just about opposing abortion and homosexuality but is a "holistic" exercise in letting his beliefs guide him on all issues.

A former congressional aide, Souder (SOW — rhymes with "now" — dur) is friendly, talkative and wonkish. He likes to immerse himself in legislative detail and is rarely caught flat-footed on the facts. But his passion for policy has not yet translated into a leadership role, because he says he has no appetite for the year-round fundraising demanded of leaders. "I don't like to raise money, and I never will," Souder once said. "I'd much rather read a book, read a bill or sit through a three-hour hearing."

Souder walks a conservative path on most issues. He supports gun owners' rights and wants the government to build a fence along the Mexican border to keep illegal immigrants from crossing into the United States. He has pushed for tougher drug abuse policies and is the author of a 1998 law barring federal student loans to people convicted of selling or possessing illegal drugs. Congress modified the law in 2006 by making it apply only to people convicted of drug offenses while attending school.

He has been a leading proponent of spraying mycoherbicides — controversial weed killers made from toxic fungi — to eliminate the plants grown in South America that are made into drugs. "If proven to be successful, mycoherbicides could revolutionize our drug eradication efforts," he said in 2007.

Like every House Republican, he voted against Obama's stimulus package, telling The Associated Press that while the package had some "helpful provisions," he was seriously concerned that a "trillion dollars in new debt may cause a rise in interest rates that could prolong and deepen this recession."

Souder will sometimes support bills aimed at protecting the environment. He sided with Democrats in 2007 in voting for an energy bill, enacted into law, that included new fuel efficiency standards and emphasized conservation.

He sits on the Homeland Security Committee, where he is the top Republican on the Border, Maritime and Global Counterterrorism panel. He supported the shifting of $400 million in fiscal 2008 funding originally allocated for surveillance technology so it could be spent on the border fence. He urged the government to award contracts to build all 670 miles of the physical fencing before the George W. Bush administration left office, saying: "We have to go flat out and get as much as we can get," or risk losing the political momentum to complete the project as envisioned.

Souder's willingness to force his social policy views on the District of Columbia has made him unpopular with the city's leaders. The District's delegate in Congress, Democrat Eleanor Holmes Norton, has called him an "incorrigible extremist." Souder sits on the Oversight and Government Reform Committee, and on its panel that oversees the District.

He found himself playing defense on many issues related to the District after Democrats took the majority in 2007. That summer, he argued vociferously against efforts to lift a ban on a needle exchange program in the city that Congress had enacted under the Republicans. Souder said such programs "merely subsidize heroin use," but Democrats — hoping the programs would reduce transmission of HIV — dropped the ban anyway.

Souder again intervened after the Supreme Court struck down the District's ban on handguns in June 2008 and city officials replaced the ban with a highly restrictive law regulating gun ownership. He introduced legislation to repeal the District's ban on semiautomatic pistols and eliminate all registration requirements. Souder is unapologetic about his involvement in D.C. affairs. "We take large sums of money from our districts that then gets used in policies in our national capital," he told The Washington Post during the needle debate. "We do have some obligation to the taxpayers in our district and to our nation to supervise those funds."

A member of the Education and Labor panel, he unsuccessfully sought in 2007 to weaken a Democratic bill to protect gays and lesbians from discrimination. Democrats rejected his amendments before moving the bill to the floor. One would have removed language protecting people only perceived to be homosexual, while another would have deleted language prohibiting employers from requiring employees be married in states barring same-sex marriage.

When not working, Souder likes to visit national parks and follow his beloved Notre Dame football team and the Chicago White Sox. He is part of a tradition of Indianans adopting Chicago teams as their own.

The Souders were among the earliest settlers of Allen County with their arrival in the 1840s. The family's harness shop grew into a series of businesses in Grabill that made the Souder name well known. The modern-day Souders, many of them religious conservatives, for the most part avoided the gritty, temporal realm of politics. That changed the day Rep. Daniel R. Coats, a conservative Indiana Republican who later served in the Senate, dropped by the family store to buy some furniture and met Mark Souder. Coats' conservative beliefs appealed to Souder, and in 1985 he became Coats' staff director on the Select Committee on Children, Youth and Families. He later served as deputy chief of staff in Coats' Senate office.

Souder ran for Coats' former House seat in 1994. He won a six-candidate primary, then beat Democratic Rep. Jill L. Long by 11 percentage points.

In 1998, Souder declared his opposition to impeaching President Clinton, saying Clinton should be prosecuted as a private citizen. That stance earned him a serious primary opponent in 2000, but Souder eventually bested Allen County chief deputy prosecutor Michael Loomis.

After an easy win in 2004, Souder faced a tight general election in 2006, when three House Republicans from Indiana lost their seats. His 9-percentage-point margin over Democrat Thomas Hayhurst was his closest. A late infusion of cash from the GOP's House campaign committee helped Souder stave off a defeat. He faced another tough challenge in 2008 from 27-year-old lawyer Michael Montagano. Despite his distaste for fundraising, he brought in more than $1 million to Montagano's $854,000. Souder won 55 percent of the vote.

KEY VOTES

2008

No Delay consideration of Colombia free-trade agreement
Yes Override Bush veto of federal farm and nutrition programs reauthorization bill
Yes Overhaul surveillance laws and permit dismissal of suits against companies that conducted warrantless wiretapping
No Grant mortgage relief to homeowners and funding for Fannie Mae and Freddie Mac
Yes Approve initial $700 billion program to stabilize financial markets
Yes Approve final $700 billion program to stabilize financial markets
Yes Provide $14 billion in loans to automakers

2007

No Increase minimum wage by $2.10 an hour
No Approve $124.2 billion in emergency war spending and set goal for redeployment of troops from Iraq
Yes Reject federal contraceptive assistance to international family planning groups
Yes Override Bush veto of $23.2 billion water projects authorization bill
Yes Implement Peru free-trade agreement
Yes Approve energy policy overhaul with new fuel economy standards
Yes Clear $473.5 billion omnibus spending bill, including $70 billion for military operations

CQ VOTE STUDIES

	PARTY UNITY		PRESIDENTIAL SUPPORT	
	SUPPORT	OPPOSE	SUPPORT	OPPOSE
2008	92%	8%	64%	36%
2007	90%	10%	79%	21%
2006	94%	6%	92%	8%
2005	97%	3%	87%	13%
2004	94%	6%	79%	21%

INTEREST GROUPS

	AFL-CIO	ADA	CCUS	ACU
2008	29%	20%	94%	72%
2007	17%	10%	84%	92%
2006	21%	0%	100%	88%
2005	27%	5%	100%	96%
2004	13%	5%	100%	88%

INDIANA 3

Northeast – Fort Wayne

While the manufacturing center located around Fort Wayne may drive the 3rd's economy, it is conservative farmers living across the vast agricultural land who influence local politics and make the district Republican. Allen County (Fort Wayne) is the 3rd's population center, and nearly half of the district's population lives in the county.

Like other Midwestern cities, Fort Wayne has suffered from a downturn in the manufacturing industry, especially in the production of recreational vehicles and manufactured homes, which has been compounded by the nationwide economic crisis. Nevertheless, the 3rd remains a leading producer of orthopedic products, such as knee and hip replacement devices. Medical device manufacturing, health care technology and white-collar businesses, including financial services, have prevented the 3rd's economy from crumbling.

Fort Wayne has a rich entertainment history and attracts musical and theater performers to venues in the city. Educators and students visit Fort Wayne's Science Central, an interactive educational station that is rec-ognized statewide and designed to help Indiana become a leader in science and math. In the 3rd's northwest, particularly near Shipshewana, Indiana's Amish Country draws tourists each year. Various lakes throughout the district, including the state's deepest in Kosciusko County, become summer hotspots.

Despite union ties, social conservatism tends to have more influence over voters in the 3rd, and many district residents hold deep-rooted religious beliefs driven by traditional values. Rural voters, especially in Kosciusko County — which gave John McCain a statewide high of 68 percent in the 2008 presidential election — bolster the state's Republican leanings. McCain won the district as a whole with 56 percent.

MAJOR INDUSTRY
Manufacturing, agriculture, health care

CITIES
Fort Wayne (pt.), 202,769; Goshen (pt.), 26,611

NOTABLE
Author and naturalist Gene Stratton-Porter's former home is a state historical site on Sylvan Lake in Noble County; Warsaw, which calls itself the Orthopedic Manufacturing Capital of the World, was home to the first orthopedic device manufacturer, established in 1895.

Rep. Steve Buyer (R)

Elected 1992; 9th term

Buyer is a party loyalist and active legislator, but he is best known for his pugnacious demeanor that has put him variously at odds with President Bill Clinton, fellow Republicans, veterans' groups and, most recently, the equally combative chairman of the Veterans' Affairs Committee.

The conservative Hoosier energetically involves himself in both policy matters and political warfare. From his former seat on the Armed Services panel and now on the Energy and Commerce Committee, Buyer (BOO-yer) has played a key role in winning a much-expanded health care system for military retirees and has been involved in pharmaceutical and military personnel legislation. At the same time, he was eagerly involved in the impeachment proceedings against Clinton in 1998 and 1999 and participated in the 2000 presidential election vote-counting controversy in Florida. More recently, he has been engaged in long-running battles with California Democrat Bob Filner, Veterans' Affairs' current strong-willed chairman.

The two often have clashed bitterly, with tensions on display even on the House floor. "I wish that there were a collegial relationship between the chairman and the ranking member. It does not exist, unfortunately," Buyer said during a 2007 House debate on several veterans' bills. "The American people get to see the abuse of power that I have to deal with."

Buyer's relationship with veterans' organizations took a hit when, as committee chairman in 2006, he scrapped the traditional joint House-Senate hearing on the veterans' budget timed to coincide with the groups' annual D.C. conferences and traditionally packed with their supporters. Buyer said it made more sense to hold the hearings earlier in the federal budget process, but his decision angered veterans' groups.

He has cast a skeptical eye on President Obama's veterans-related moves. When Obama in March 2009 dropped his proposal to collect money from private insurance companies for treating veterans with service-connected disabilities at Veterans Affairs hospitals, Buyer said, "The administration should have recognized how outrageous the whole idea was that disabled veterans, who have sacrificed their bodies in defense of our freedom, should be responsible for paying for treatment of their injuries with their personal insurance coverage."

As a member of Energy and Commerce's Health Subcommittee, he is well placed to attend to the concerns of Indiana's health industry, his largest single campaign contributor. He authored an unsuccessful bill in 2008 to guard against imported counterfeit drugs finding their way into Americans' medicine cabinets. "Pharmaceutical counterfeiters are…the new drug lords of the world," Buyer told a subcommittee hearing that May.

Buyer broke with Energy and Commerce Chairman Joe L. Barton of Texas in 2005 to win adoption of an amendment that excluded mental health drugs from Medicaid cuts in a budget bill. Eli Lilly, the Indiana company that makes the antidepressant Prozac, stood to benefit, but Buyer bristled at media suggestions his amendment was aimed at helping the company. The amendment was later dropped in conference with the Senate.

Buyer also took a lead role in opposing Energy and Commerce efforts in early 2009 to give the Food and Drug Administration broad powers to regulate tobacco advertising and marketing. He offered half a dozen proposals to the Democrats' legislation when it passed out of committee, including a failed proposal to create a separate agency within the Health and Human Services Department to handle tobacco.

CAPITOL OFFICE
225-5037
stevebuyer.house.gov
2230 Rayburn Bldg. 20515-1404; fax 225-2267

COMMITTEES
Energy & Commerce
Veterans' Affairs - ranking member

RESIDENCE
Monticello

BORN
Nov. 26, 1958; Rensselaer, Ind.

RELIGION
Methodist

FAMILY
Wife, Joni Buyer; two children

EDUCATION
The Citadel, B.S. 1980 (business administration);
Valparaiso U., J.D. 1984

MILITARY SERVICE
Army Reserve, 1980-84; Army, 1984-87;
Army Reserve, 1987-present

CAREER
Lawyer; military prosecutor

POLITICAL HIGHLIGHTS
No previous office

ELECTION RESULTS

2008 GENERAL

Steve Buyer (R)	192,526	59.9%
Nels Ackerson (D)	129,038	40.1%

2008 PRIMARY

Steve Buyer (R)	45,538	71.6%
Mike Campbell (R)	9,541	15.0%
Firefighter LaRon Keith (R)	8,545	13.4%

2006 GENERAL

Steve Buyer (R)	111,057	62.4%
David Sanders (D)	66,986	37.6%

PREVIOUS WINNING PERCENTAGES
2004 (69%); 2002 (71%); 2000 (61%); 1998 (63%);
1996 (65%); 1994 (70%); 1992 (51%)

He introduced an unsuccessful bill in 2008 that encouraged domestic production of energy, including greater use of nuclear power and "clean" coal technology as well as expanded ethanol technologies. He has been critical of efforts to deal with global warming that would impact coal concerns.

Buyer voted against both versions of the $700 billion financial system rescue plan in the fall of 2008 despite appeals by President George W. Bush and leaders of both parties. "The legislation is an unprecedented intrusion of government power into the private financial sector," he said. He also opposed Obama's $787 billion economic stimulus law in early 2009, saying he didn't believe the government could spend its way out of a recession.

Buyer came to Congress fresh from duty in the Army Reserve in the Persian Gulf War, where he was a lawyer specializing in the treatment of prisoners, detained civilians and refugees. He remains a colonel in the reserve. When the United States invaded Iraq in 2003, he was notified he would again be called for active duty, but the Pentagon decided the presence of a congressman in the region would cause security problems.

During his tour of duty in the first Gulf War in 1991, Buyer was near an enemy munitions depot when it was destroyed by U.S. forces. He suffered a series of mysterious illnesses for years afterward, including breathing difficulty, kidney problems and two bouts of pneumonia. In 2000, the Defense Department told him he had likely been exposed to chemicals in the smoke cloud that drifted from the depot.

Buyer's father was a dentist who also operated a small farm along the banks of the Tippecanoe River in Indiana, where Buyer spent his childhood. He majored in business administration at The Citadel, the military college of South Carolina, then attended law school in Indiana. He worked his way through by painting fairgrounds, buildings and churches.

Buyer ran for Congress against three-term Democratic Rep. Jim Jontz. He criticized Jontz's vote in 1991 against giving President George Bush authority to commit troops to the Gulf and drew attention to Jontz's four overdrafts at the private House bank. Buyer's 4,500-vote win was among the biggest House upsets of 1992. He easily won his next four re-election bids.

Reapportionment after the 2000 census took one House seat away from Indiana, and Buyer's 5th District was parceled out among six districts. Only 3 percent of his former constituents were in the 4th, but his hometown was there, so Buyer decided to run for re-election there in 2002. To introduce himself to his new constituents, he staged a 260-mile run across the new district. He won the primary, cruised to a 45-percentage-point win in November and has enjoyed easy re-elections since then.

KEY VOTES

2008
? Delay consideration of Colombia free-trade agreement
Yes Override Bush veto of federal farm and nutrition programs reauthorization bill
Yes Overhaul surveillance laws and permit dismissal of suits against companies that conducted warrantless wiretapping
No Grant mortgage relief to homeowners and funding for Fannie Mae and Freddie Mac
No Approve initial $700 billion program to stabilize financial markets
No Approve final $700 billion program to stabilize financial markets
Yes Provide $14 billion in loans to automakers

2007
? Increase minimum wage by $2.10 an hour
No Approve $124.2 billion in emergency war spending and set goal for redeployment of troops from Iraq
Yes Reject federal contraceptive assistance to international family planning groups
? Override Bush veto of $23.2 billion water projects authorization bill
? Implement Peru free-trade agreement
Yes Approve energy policy overhaul with new fuel economy standards
Yes Clear $473.5 billion omnibus spending bill, including $70 billion for military operations

CQ VOTE STUDIES

	PARTY UNITY		PRESIDENTIAL SUPPORT	
	SUPPORT	OPPOSE	SUPPORT	OPPOSE
2008	93%	7%	66%	34%
2007	95%	5%	85%	15%
2006	97%	3%	90%	10%
2005	98%	2%	86%	14%
2004	96%	4%	87%	13%

INTEREST GROUPS

	AFL-CIO	ADA	CCUS	ACU
2008	29%	25%	81%	84%
2007	16%	10%	69%	90%
2006	33%	10%	87%	83%
2005	20%	0%	93%	96%
2004	13%	5%	100%	96%

INDIANA 4
West central — Indianapolis suburbs, Lafayette

Traversing the 4th by car requires a nearly 175-mile trip through a slender district that takes in a mixture of farmland, small towns and suburbs. It spans from White County, which is roughly halfway between Chicago and Indianapolis, south to Lawrence County, which is about halfway between Indianapolis and Louisville.

Tippecanoe County, just south of White, takes in the 4th's largest metropolitan area — Lafayette and West Lafayette. The latter is home to the main campus of Purdue University, and its enrollment of more than 39,000 students. Known for its engineering school, Purdue grooms students to lead the district's influential manufacturing industry. Beyond Purdue's campus, both the area's signature architecture and its historic neighborhoods make West Lafayette much more than a college town in the middle of expansive cornfields.

Montgomery, White (shared with the 2nd) and Boone counties, arrayed across the district's north near Tippecanoe, are some of the top Indiana counties in soybean production and are near the top in corn production.

Moving south and east, the 4th cuts into a western sliver of Marion County (Indianapolis) and takes in Hendricks County suburbs west of the city and Johnson County suburbs as it curves south of the city. Johnson is filling up with young, well-educated families.

The remaining southern counties of the 4th District consist of smaller farming communities similar to those found elsewhere across the state. The 4th's agriculture industry and rural areas make it Republican territory. Of the counties wholly in the 4th, only Tippecanoe supported Democrat Barack Obama in the 2008 presidential election — the county gave him 55 percent. John McCain won the 4th District in 2008, taking 56 percent of the vote.

MAJOR INDUSTRY
Higher education, agriculture, manufacturing

CITIES
Lafayette, 56,397; Indianapolis (pt.), 40,207; Greenwood, 36,037

NOTABLE
Tippecanoe Battlefield was where troops led by then-governor, and later president, William Henry Harrison fought off an American Indian attack in 1811; The first official U.S. airmail flight took off from Lafayette via balloon in 1859.

Rep. Dan Burton (R)

Elected 1982; 14th term

Burton's 14 terms in the House place him in the ranks of the most senior Republicans, but he is not popular among his colleagues. Though one of the House's most conservative members, his unpredictability has been a source of concern to some in his party and has made him a pariah among the Democrats who control the House.

Burton has faced criticism of being too dogmatic and more interested in playing golf than casting votes. Colleagues are wary of giving him a prominent post, fearing he might use it to make a spectacle of himself, as he has many times in the past. "Burton has proved time and again that if you give him a national stage, he will embarrass himself," an Indianapolis Star columnist wrote in 2008.

In 2008, Burton drew attention — mostly negative — for siding during a House hearing with retired Major League Baseball pitcher Roger Clemens, who was accused in a report by former Senate Majority Leader George J. Mitchell of Maine of abusing steroids. Burton derided Clemens' former trainer Brian McNamee, Mitchell's chief witness, for spreading "lies" and trying to ruin Clemens' reputation.

He also gained notice in early 2007 when he was the only House member of either party to vote against an ethics package that tightened gift and travel rules. He insisted the rules were too complicated and that full disclosure was the best way to prevent abuses by lawmakers.

Burton also has been at odds with Republicans on the Foreign Affairs Committee over his decision to back Pakistan in its dispute with India over the Kashmir region, and for years he was denied the party's top slot on Foreign Affairs' Middle East and South Asia Subcommittee because of it — until GOP leaders relented in 2009. Since 2005, he had held the top spot on the Western Hemisphere Subcommittee, where his agenda was least distressing to his colleagues.

Burton's most publicized recent departure from the party line involved a high-profile domestic issue: prescription drug prices. Despite the fact that thousands of employees of pharmaceutical giant Eli Lilly live in his district, Burton sides with Democrats in their efforts to force down prescription drug prices. His stance stems from the days when his first wife was battling breast cancer, which took her life in 2002, and he met other patients who could not afford their cancer-fighting drugs.

He was one of just 24 Republicans voting with Democrats in 2007 to require the government to negotiate prices for Medicare's prescription drug benefit. Four years earlier, Burton was among a minority of Republicans voting to allow imports of lower-priced prescription drugs from Canada.

Burton's crowning achievement is a 1996 law, on which he teamed with North Carolina GOP Sen. Jesse Helms, that codified the U.S. embargo against Cuba. But he is best known for his repeated investigations of President Bill Clinton in the late 1990s. As chairman of the Government Reform Committee at the time, he suggested that Clinton presidential counsel Vincent W. Foster Jr., who committed suicide in 1994, was murdered. He conducted his own investigation in his back yard assisted by a homicide detective, firing a gun into what he would describe only as "a head-like object" — reportedly a pumpkin or watermelon — to see whether the sound could be heard at a distance. It was during that time that Burton called his Democratic critics "squealing pigs" and Clinton a "scumbag."

Burton has a long-running feud with the Indianapolis Star, which was

CAPITOL OFFICE
225-2276
www.house.gov/burton
2308 Rayburn Bldg. 20515-1405; fax 225-0016

COMMITTEES
Foreign Affairs
Oversight & Government Reform

RESIDENCE
Indianapolis

BORN
June 21, 1938; Indianapolis, Ind.

RELIGION
Christian

FAMILY
Wife, Samia Burton; four children

EDUCATION
Indiana U., attended 1958-59; Cincinnati Bible College, attended 1959-60

MILITARY SERVICE
Army, 1956-57; Army Reserve, 1957-62

CAREER
Real estate and insurance agent

POLITICAL HIGHLIGHTS
Ind. House, 1967-69; Ind. Senate, 1969-71; Republican nominee for U.S. House, 1970; sought Republican nomination for U.S. House, 1972; Ind. House, 1977-81; Ind. Senate, 1981-83

ELECTION RESULTS

2008 GENERAL

Dan Burton (R)	234,705	65.5%
Mary Etta Ruley (D)	123,357	34.4%

2008 PRIMARY

Dan Burton (R)	45,682	51.8%
John McGoff (R)	39,701	45.0%
Clayton L. Alfred (R)	2,742	3.1%

2006 GENERAL

Dan Burton (R)	133,118	65.0%
Katherine Fox Carr (D)	64,362	31.4%
Sheri Conover Sharlow (LIBERT)	7,431	3.6%

PREVIOUS WINNING PERCENTAGES
2004 (72%); 2002 (72%); 2000 (70%); 1998 (72%); 1996 (75%); 1994 (77%); 1992 (72%); 1990 (63%); 1988 (73%); 1986 (68%); 1984 (73%); 1982 (65%)

among the media outlets to report in 1998 that he had fathered a son out of wedlock in the early 1980s. At the time of the disclosure, he was leading the House investigation of Clinton's attempts to cover up a sexual relationship.

In the past decade, Burton has doggedly pursued such issues as the reported link between childhood vaccines containing mercury and the rising incidence of autism (he has a grandchild with autism).

Burton was a co-founder in 1995 of the Conservative Action Team, now known as the Republican Study Committee, a group of the House's most conservative members. He continues to be a member, but is no longer one of its leaders.

Burton endured a difficult childhood. He said his father regularly beat both him and his mother and was eventually jailed for abuse. His family lived in hotels and trailer parks, and Burton had lived in 38 states, Mexico and Canada by the time he was 12. "I never stopped worrying that Dad would come back after he got out of jail," he told People magazine in 1994.

After a stint in the Army and a couple years of college, Burton worked as an insurance agent. At that time, he considered himself an independent but often voted Democratic. But in 1964 he read an interview with Norman Thomas, a socialist presidential candidate who said the Democratic Party was moving toward socialism. Burton read the Congressional Record and studied the legislation Democrats supported. Concluding Thomas was right, Burton called the local GOP and joined.

Two years later, at age 28, he won a seat in the state legislature as a Republican. He served 10 years there, interrupted by losing congressional bids in 1970 and 1972. In 1982, he won the House seat he had been seeking and has coasted to re-election since. His most serious election challenge came in the 2008 GOP primary against former Marion County coroner John McGoff. McGoff and the Star editorial page pilloried Burton for ignoring his legislative duties and relishing the perks of office. Among the behavior they criticized: Burton missing 19 votes in January 2007 to play in a charity golf tournament, skipping a March 2007 hearing on poor conditions at Walter Reed Army Medical Center in Washington, where many injured Iraq War veterans are treated, and leasing a Cadillac DeVille at taxpayer expense.

Burton responded not in the press — he despises the media and rarely grants interviews — but with a barrage of franked mail defending his record. He outspent McGoff by a ratio of more than 3-to-1 and won by 7 percentage points. He then crushed his Democratic opponent in the heavily Republican 5th. But GOP primary opponents began lining up in early 2009 to challenge Burton in 2010.

KEY VOTES

2008
No Delay consideration of Colombia free-trade agreement
No Override Bush veto of federal farm and nutrition programs reauthorization bill
Yes Overhaul surveillance laws and permit dismissal of suits against companies that conducted warrantless wiretapping
No Grant mortgage relief to homeowners and funding for Fannie Mae and Freddie Mac
No Approve initial $700 billion program to stabilize financial markets
No Approve final $700 billion program to stabilize financial markets
No Provide $14 billion in loans to automakers

2007
No Increase minimum wage by $2.10 an hour
No Approve $124.2 billion in emergency war spending and set goal for redeployment of troops from Iraq
Yes Reject federal contraceptive assistance to international family planning groups
No Override Bush veto of $23.2 billion water projects authorization bill
Yes Implement Peru free-trade agreement
No Approve energy policy overhaul with new fuel economy standards
Yes Clear $473.5 billion omnibus spending bill, including $70 billion for military operations

CQ VOTE STUDIES

| | PARTY UNITY | | PRESIDENTIAL SUPPORT | |
	SUPPORT	OPPOSE	SUPPORT	OPPOSE
2008	99%	1%	77%	23%
2007	98%	2%	85%	15%
2006	96%	4%	91%	9%
2005	97%	3%	89%	11%
2004	96%	4%	76%	24%

INTEREST GROUPS

	AFL-CIO	ADA	CCUS	ACU
2008	7%	10%	89%	100%
2007	17%	10%	75%	96%
2006	21%	0%	92%	88%
2005	13%	0%	92%	96%
2004	21%	0%	95%	100%

INDIANA 5
East central — part of Indianapolis and suburbs

Dominated by Indianapolis suburbanites and rural farmers, the 5th is Indiana's wealthiest district and is staunchly Republican turf. Although Hamilton, Hancock and the district's portion of Marion counties, which surround the state capital on three sides, make up a small percentage of the 5th's land area, half of the district's population lives there.

The 5th's most affluent residents live in northern Indianapolis (Marion County) and in the Hamilton County suburbs of Carmel, Fishers and Noblesville. Here, a growing white-collar workforce in electronics and financial services brings median incomes well above state and national averages. Hamilton and Hancock in particular used an increase in white-collar residents to boost income levels, but growth has stalled during a nationwide economic downturn. Southeast of Indianapolis, the 5th takes in most of Shelby County and a chunk of northeastern Johnson County.

The northern part of the 5th includes small cities that are closer to Fort Wayne than Indianapolis and are much different from the district's suburban southern portion. These residents earn modest incomes from the area's solid farming industry, based mostly in corn, and from operating small businesses. Half of the counties north of Hamilton lost population in the 1990s and five out of the six counties have lost residents thus far this decade. The 5th also takes in most of Howard County, including part of working-class Kokomo (shared with the 2nd), and all of Tipton County, where the manufacturing industry has struggled.

Suburban Indianapolis residents have made the 5th into the Hoosier state's most Republican district. While the rural communities are not as affluent as their suburban counterparts, they too solidly support GOP candidates. Republican John McCain captured 59 percent of the district's 2008 presidential vote — his best showing in the state.

MAJOR INDUSTRY
Financial services, electronics, agriculture

CITIES
Indianapolis (pt.), 131,892; Fishers, 37,835; Carmel, 37,733; Marion, 31,320

NOTABLE
The Elwood Haynes Museum in Kokomo honors the local inventor who was among the first to build a gasoline-powered car; The town of Fairmount hosts an annual James Dean Festival to honor their beloved rebel without a cause.

Rep. Mike Pence (R)

Elected 2000; 5th term

An articulate former radio talk show host, Pence has seen his influence on Capitol Hill catch up with his longtime clout among grass-roots conservative activists. He is chairman of the House Republican Conference — the third-ranking House GOP leadership post — and has the formidable job of ensuring his caucus' message isn't drowned out by those of the Obama administration and an expanded Democratic majority.

Pence has called himself "a Christian, a conservative and a Republican, in that order." He opposes abortion and embryonic stem cell research and was active in the debate to ban same-sex marriage. He is a popular figure within the right wing's blogosphere and among commentators. The conservative weekly Human Events named him its man of the year in 2005.

Pence ascended to the leadership following the November 2008 elections, in which his party saw its ranks shrink in the House. He wasted little time in outlining a communications strategy, including "tiger teams" to be dispatched daily to offer their takes on issues on television and radio talk shows. He also wants to increase the use of blogs, videos and other new media. And he took the unusual step in March 2009 of joining Senate Republicans in an attempt to mobilize opposition to President Obama's budget.

Pence plans to coach rank-and-file Republicans, especially new members, on how best to deal with the media to get their message out. He brushed aside House Democrats' criticism that he is among those hindering bipartisanship. "Bipartisanship should mean more than giving Republicans a chance to vote for Democrat bills," he said in February 2009.

Pence captured the conference chairman's job without opposition and with the backing of Minority Leader John A. Boehner of Ohio — a reversal of their earlier relationship. Pence had challenged Boehner for the top GOP position in late 2006, but was rejected by a lopsided 168-27. He failed to garner support from most of the large membership of the conservative Republican Study Committee, despite coming off a two-year stint as chairman. Some groused he had made them look bad before the election with his focus on the GOP majority's lack of restraint on spending.

But following that defeat, Pence maintained a cordial relationship with Boehner, who awarded Pence the top Republican slot on a six-member select committee set up in August 2007 to investigate a controversial floor vote in which Republicans charged Democrats with improperly changing the result. With Boehner's blessing, Pence also helped organize an elaborate 2008 protest by GOP members to focus attention on what they regarded as Democratic inaction on energy issues. The members held mock sessions on the House floor during the August congressional recess.

Pence is frequently in the face of appropriators, who sharply disagree with his belief in curbing federal spending. He unsuccessfully sought in 2008 to persuade House Republicans to fight for a one-year moratorium on earmarks, the special projects appropriators tuck into bills for their home districts.

When Republicans rejected Pence's plan, he took a pledge not to request any earmarks — a promise some civic leaders in his district urged him to reconsider. His stance became more awkward after tornadoes and flooding hit several counties in the district in June. But Pence refused to budge.

Pence led the charge in 2003 against a $400 billion-plus Medicare prescription drug bill as an unwarranted expansion of government. He also split with President George W. Bush on another signature initiative, the 2001 No Child Left Behind education law, because it would increase federal spending.

CAPITOL OFFICE
225-3021
mikepence.house.gov
1431 Longworth Bldg. 20515-1406; fax 225-3382

COMMITTEES
Foreign Affairs

RESIDENCE
Columbus

BORN
June 7, 1959; Columbus, Ind.

RELIGION
Christian

FAMILY
Wife, Karen Pence; three children

EDUCATION
Hanover College, B.A. 1981 (history);
Indiana U., J.D. 1986

CAREER
Radio and television broadcaster; think tank president; lawyer

POLITICAL HIGHLIGHTS
Republican nominee for U.S. House, 1988, 1990

ELECTION RESULTS

2008 GENERAL

Mike Pence (R)	180,608	64.0%
Barry A. Welsh (D)	94,265	33.4%
George Thomas Holland (LIBERT)	7,539	2.7%

2008 PRIMARY

Mike Pence (R)	unopposed

2006 GENERAL

Mike Pence (R)	115,266	60.0%
Barry A. Welsh (D)	76,812	40.0%

PREVIOUS WINNING PERCENTAGES
2004 (67%); 2002 (64%); 2000 (51%)

But Pence has bewildered conservatives at times. He proposed in 2006 a comprehensive immigration bill that would have required illegal immigrants to leave the country but would have allowed them to eventually return and become eligible for U.S. citizenship. Conservatives considered the move a capitulation to liberal demands for amnesty for illegal workers. Pence merely said the thrift and hard work of today's immigrants reminded him of his grandfather, who emigrated from Ireland and came to Ellis Island in 1923.

A member of the Foreign Affairs Committee, Pence takes a hard line against China's Communist government; he called the awarding of the 2008 Olympics to Beijing a "historic error." He put aside his usual fiscal concerns to support a sweeping reauthorization and expansion of global AIDS programs in April 2008, saying it was a moral obligation for the United States.

Pence grew up in Columbus, where his father ran a group of gas stations. The family was Irish Catholic and Democratic, and President John F. Kennedy was practically an icon. But Pence's views changed after he joined an evangelical fellowship group at Hanover College. His new religion pulled him to the right politically. He met his wife, Karen, at an evangelical church service, where she was playing the guitar.

In 1988, at age 29, Pence made a run for the House in a challenge to veteran Democratic Rep. Philip R. Sharp. He lost by 6 percentage points. Two years later, he tried again, this time losing by almost 19 points. In the latter race, Pence ran a harshly negative campaign against Sharp. Pence later repented with an article called "Confessions of a Negative Campaigner," in which he said, "Negative campaigning, I now know, is wrong."

It was during that period that conservative commentator Rush Limbaugh captured Pence's imagination. Pence's first radio show aired in 1989 in Rushville. He eventually built up a syndicated talk show that was heard on 18 stations across Indiana, sometimes as Limbaugh's "warm-up act."

His years as a radio broadcaster and host of a public affairs television show in Indianapolis kept his name before the public. When he decided in 2000 to run for the seat of GOP Rep. David M. McIntosh, who ran unsuccessfully for governor, Pence easily beat five opponents in the primary. He then topped Democratic lawyer Bob Rock by 12 percentage points in November.

Democrats who controlled the remapping process after the 2000 census sought to bolster vulnerable Democratic Rep. Baron P. Hill in the neighboring 9th District. In shaping the new 6th District, the Democrats gave Pence some of Hill's Republican-leaning rural territory in southeastern Indiana. Pence won easily in 2002 and in every election since. His success has led him to leave the door open for a future Senate run if a seat should open.

KEY VOTES

2008

No	Delay consideration of Colombia free-trade agreement
No	Override Bush veto of federal farm and nutrition programs reauthorization bill
Yes	Overhaul surveillance laws and permit dismissal of suits against companies that conducted warrantless wiretapping
No	Grant mortgage relief to homeowners and funding for Fannie Mae and Freddie Mac
No	Approve initial $700 billion program to stabilize financial markets
No	Approve final $700 billion program to stabilize financial markets
No	Provide $14 billion in loans to automakers

2007

No	Increase minimum wage by $2.10 an hour
No	Approve $124.2 billion in emergency war spending and set goal for redeployment of troops from Iraq
Yes	Reject federal contraceptive assistance to international family planning groups
No	Override Bush veto of $23.2 billion water projects authorization bill
Yes	Implement Peru free-trade agreement
No	Approve energy policy overhaul with new fuel economy standards
Yes	Clear $473.5 billion omnibus spending bill, including $70 billion for military operations

CQ VOTE STUDIES

	PARTY UNITY		PRESIDENTIAL SUPPORT	
	SUPPORT	OPPOSE	SUPPORT	OPPOSE
2008	99%	1%	88%	12%
2007	98%	2%	92%	8%
2006	96%	4%	90%	10%
2005	98%	2%	91%	9%
2004	99%	1%	94%	6%

INTEREST GROUPS

	AFL-CIO	ADA	CCUS	ACU
2008	0%	5%	81%	100%
2007	8%	5%	74%	96%
2006	8%	15%	100%	100%
2005	13%	0%	92%	100%
2004	0%	0%	100%	100%

INDIANA 6

East – Muncie, Anderson, Richmond

Covering most of Indiana's eastern border with Ohio, the 6th District combines a mix of farmland, midsize cities and suburban populations. The district's economy, anchored in Muncie, is driven by manufacturing, education and health care industries.

The auto industry has declined in the 6th District, and widespread layoffs in other manufacturing have in turn hurt the economies of the district's most populous cities — Muncie and Anderson. But there has been some positive news, as Honda opened a new automobile plant in Decatur County in Greensburg in late 2008 and international gear maker Brevini announced plans in to relocate its North American headquarters to Delaware County, by 2011.

The 6th District's largest cities also are its educational hubs. Muncie is home to Ball State University, and Anderson University is in nearby Anderson. The centerpiece of Anderson's revitalized downtown arts and culture center is the Paramount Theatre. South and east of Muncie and Anderson, the 6th takes in Wayne and Henry counties, where the per-

centage of residents over age 65 is among the highest in Indiana. This fertile land also hosts rich corn and soybean farms, as well as dairy silos and hog barns.

The 6th has a Democratic past that was fueled by its union population, but like most of rural Indiana, its residents now lean conservative, and the district is more Republican today. Democrat Barack Obama won Delaware (57 percent) and Madison (53 percent) counties, but Republican John McCain carried the other 17 counties wholly or partly in the 6th, earning 52 percent of the district's vote overall in 2008. Franklin County, in the district's south, and Wells County, near Fort Wayne, were among McCain's highest percentages statewide.

MAJOR INDUSTRY
Auto manufacturing, agriculture, light manufacturing

CITIES
Muncie, 67,430; Anderson, 59,734; Richmond, 39,124

NOTABLE
The Wilbur Wright Birthplace and Museum is in Millville; Ball State University alumni include late-night talk show host David Letterman and "Garfield" cartoonist Jim Davis; The Academy of Model Aeronautics is located in Muncie; The Indiana Basketball Hall of Fame is in New Castle.

Rep. André Carson (D)

Elected March 2008; 1st full term

CAPITOL OFFICE
225-4011
www.house.gov/carson
425 Cannon Bldg. 20515-1407; fax 225-5633

COMMITTEES
Financial Services

RESIDENCE
Indianapolis

BORN
Oct. 16, 1974; Indianapolis, Ind.

RELIGION
Muslim

FAMILY
Wife, Mariama Shaheed-Carson; one child

EDUCATION
Concordia U. Wisconsin, Indianapolis, B.A. 2003
(management of criminal justice); Indiana
Wesleyan U., M.S. 2005 (management)

CAREER
Marketing representative; state investigative
agency officer

POLITICAL HIGHLIGHTS
Indianapolis and Marion County City-County
Council, 2007-08

ELECTION RESULTS

2008 GENERAL

André Carson (D)	172,650	65.1%
Gabrielle Campo (R)	92,645	34.9%

2008 PRIMARY

André Carson (D)	66,659	46.5%
Woodrow A. "Woody" Myers Jr. (D)	33,683	23.5%
David Orentlicher (D)	29,231	20.4%
Carolene Mays (D)	11,011	7.7%

2008 SPECIAL

André Carson (D)	45,668	54.0%
Jon Elrod (R)	36,415	43.1%
Sean Shepard (LIBERT)	2,430	2.9%

Carson's liberal political philosophy mirrors that of his predecessor and grandmother, Julia Carson, who died of lung cancer in December 2007 during her 6th term in the House. She was one of Indiana's African-American political pioneers and an advocate for the poor and the disadvantaged.

Carson has allied himself with fellow African-American Democrats in the House, joining the Congressional Black Caucus (CBC). And he has proved an ally of labor unions, opposing a free-trade deal with Colombia a month after his special election win. He also was an early endorser of Barack Obama during his presidential primary race against Hillary Rodham Clinton. But Carson also expressed admiration for straight-arrow Indiana Republicans like Sen. Richard G. Lugar and said he wants to make friends on both sides of the aisle.

Carson sits on the Financial Services Committee, where his grandmother served and resisted GOP attempts to overhaul the federal public housing program. Carson will be involved in Democratic efforts to revive the ailing economy. In fall 2008, Carson defied his party and voted against a $700 billion plan to rescue the financial sector, saying he couldn't in good conscience give the George W. Bush administration such authority. When the bill came up a second time, however, he relented, calling the revised bill much improved. "I am voting to put the interests of those working Americans in my district first," he said, adding he thought the bill ultimately would help small businesses in his district. He was one of 13 CBC members to switch sides on the crucial vote, helping Democratic leaders and Bush secure a big victory. He's since toed the line, backing failed legislation to provide loans to domestic automakers as well as President Obama's 2009 $787 billion economic stimulus law.

Carson arrived in the House with far less political experience than his grandmother had prior to her 1996 election to Congress. She had served in local politics for two decades before running for the district seat; her grandson had served just several months on the Indianapolis and Marion County City-County Council before winning her seat.

Carson has an interest in education, and hopes to have a hand in the rewrite of the 2001 No Child Left Behind Act, which he believes has not received adequate funding and sets too many federal mandates for the states. Carson said the law has hurt the many low-income families in his district. His wife, Mariama Shaheed-Carson, is an assistant principal at an elementary school in Pike Township.

Carson cares deeply about the poor. He said he was born to a single mother who often neglected him, and he spent part of his preschool days in an Indianapolis homeless shelter before being taken in by Julia Carson, his maternal grandmother.

"The shelter experience resonated and really shook personal inclinations 'til this day of how I don't ever want to go back there," Carson said.

Raised a Baptist, Carson attended public and parochial schools in Indianapolis, spending his afternoons traversing the city with his grandmother. Julia made him start working for his keep at the age of 14, charging him a $50 monthly rent. "She had property that she would rent out, and the tenants were always late and she would give them a pass, but not me, a teenager," Carson jokes. "She was like the Godfather to me."

He considered entering the priesthood during his early teens, but was encouraged by a priest to study different faiths to be sure. He did so, reading

"The Autobiography of Malcolm X" among other things, and eventually converted to traditional Islam in the mid-1990s.

He is one of only two Muslims ever to serve in Congress, along with his House Democratic colleague from Minnesota, Keith Ellison.

As a young man, Carson also immersed himself in poetry, music and breakdancing to escape the crack epidemic sweeping across his Indianapolis neighborhood. "I watched friends get turned out and addicted to these drugs," he said. He performed at local variety shows, rapping under the stage name "Juggernaut," with dreams of becoming a professional singer after graduating from Arsenal Technical High School.

Despite serious attempts, his musical career didn't muster a major record deal. Carson eventually returned to school to study criminal justice while working as a state excise police officer, enforcing alcohol, tobacco and gambling laws. He graduated from the Indianapolis center of Concordia University Wisconsin in 2003. Three years later, he was assigned to be a liaison to the state's homeland security agency, traveling throughout Indiana working on such concerns as supremacist groups and threats of terrorism.

Carson said he "got his political feet wet" at age 9 when he attended the 1984 Democratic National Convention in San Francisco. "It was intense and a great experience," he says. His political career began in late 2007, when he was chosen to fill an open city-county seat for Indianapolis and Marion County. Less than seven months later, he faced an election to succeed his grandmother.

Carson spent the first few months of 2008 campaigning against Republican state Rep. Jon Elrod. Carson raised more than five times as much money and won by 11 percentage points in March. "People began to see me as my own man, as my own person," he said.

With fewer than two months under his belt, he faced the regular Democratic primary election for the next term. An inexperienced lawmaker, he ran against a large field that included state Reps. David Orentlicher and Carolene Mays, and Woodrow A. "Woody" Myers Jr., a former Indiana health commissioner. Myers, who also held privatesector positions as a health director for Ford Motor Co. and chief medical officer for WellPoint Inc., loaned his own campaign more than $1.6 million.

But Carson benefited from his popular last name and an endorsement from Obama. He won the primary with 47 percent of the vote, nearly double that of any challenger. In the general election race in November, Carson defeated crushed little-known Republican Gabrielle Campo with 65 percent of the vote.

KEY VOTES

2008

Yes Delay consideration of Colombia free-trade agreement

Yes Override Bush veto of federal farm and nutrition programs reauthorization bill

No Overhaul surveillance laws and permit dismissal of suits against companies that conducted warrantless wiretapping

Yes Grant mortgage relief to homeowners and funding for Fannie Mae and Freddie Mac

No Approve initial $700 billion program to stabilize financial markets

Yes Approve final $700 billion program to stabilize financial markets

Yes Provide $14 billion in loans to automakers

CQ VOTE STUDIES

	PARTY UNITY		PRESIDENTIAL SUPPORT	
	SUPPORT	OPPOSE	SUPPORT	OPPOSE
2008	99%	1%	12%	88%

INTEREST GROUPS

	AFL-CIO	ADA	CCUS	ACU
2008	100%	75%	53%	4%

INDIANA 7
Most of Indianapolis

The 7th, Indiana's smallest district in size, is the only one not to have a rural, farming identity. Despite its largely white-collar workforce, it has the state's lowest median income and is overwhelmingly Democratic. In a state where Democrat Barack Obama won only two districts in the 2008 presidential election, the 7th gave him 71 percent of its presidential vote, 9 percentage points higher than he took in the 1st District.

Almost four times bigger than Fort Wayne, the state's next-most-populous city, Indianapolis is the state's banking and commercial center. Manufacturing plays a role in the city's economy, with a few automotive plants hanging on despite industry downturns. The joint Indiana University-Purdue University at Indianapolis campus and Butler University make it a hub for higher education. Several large pharmaceutical and health care companies are located in Indianapolis, including Eli Lilly & Co., the district's largest employer.

Indianapolis also is home to the state's major professional sports teams: football's Colts and basketball's Pacers and Fever. Despite the teams'

local support, the 7th's biggest pro sport is auto racing — the Indianapolis Motor Speedway hosts the annual Indianapolis 500 race.

Indianapolis also is home to the national headquarters of The American Legion, the largest veterans organization in the world. The Soldiers' and Sailors' Monument, located in Monument Circle, complements a skyline graced by the state Capitol. The city has undergone considerable revitalization, particularly in the Fountain Square area.

Large minority populations in central Indianapolis — where some neighborhoods are up to 65 percent black — form the 7th's core and the base of its strong Democratic support. In the city's northern tier, white-collar residents are some of the wealthiest in the state and are more receptive to Republican candidates.

MAJOR INDUSTRY
Manufacturing, health care, higher education

CITIES
Indianapolis (pt.), 619,827; Lawrence (pt.), 28,086

NOTABLE
President Benjamin Harrison, poet James Whitcomb Riley, 3 vice presidents and 10 Indiana governors are buried in the Crown Hill cemetery.

Rep. Brad Ellsworth (D)

Elected 2006; 2nd term

CAPITOL OFFICE
225-4636
ellsworth.house.gov
513 Cannon Bldg. 20515-1408; fax 225-3284

COMMITTEES
Agriculture
Armed Services
Small Business

RESIDENCE
Evansville

BORN
Sept. 11, 1958; Jasper, Ind.

RELIGION
Roman Catholic

FAMILY
Wife, Beth Ellsworth; one child

EDUCATION
Indiana State U., Evansville, B.S. 1981 (sociology);
Indiana State U., M.S. 1993 (criminology)

CAREER
Police officer

POLITICAL HIGHLIGHTS
Vanderburgh County sheriff, 1999-2006

ELECTION RESULTS

2008 GENERAL

Brad Ellsworth (D)	188,693	64.7%
Greg Goode (R)	102,769	35.3%

2008 PRIMARY

Brad Ellsworth (D)	unopposed

2006 GENERAL

Brad Ellsworth (D)	131,019	61.0%
John Hostettler (R)	83,704	39.0%

Ellsworth is a popular former sheriff and conservative Democrat — opposed to abortion, in favor of gun owners' rights and fiscally tight-fisted — in the independent-minded mold of Hoosiers such as Sen. Evan Bayh and former Rep. Timothy J. Roemer. The fact that he shares Bayh's and Roemer's telegenic good looks hasn't hurt him, either.

In his first term, Ellsworth broke ranks with his party on 20 percent of the votes in which a majority of Democrats and Republicans diverged, more often than all but nine other Democrats. "I still believe Republicans have good ideas and Democrats have good ideas," he said. "If you're here for the right reasons, you should be able to push something forward and come to an agreement." That attitude, he added, mirrors his constituents: "Hoosiers are pretty independent thinkers."

Ellsworth will distance himself from his party on social issues such as expanding federal funding of embryonic stem cell research and classifying as hate crimes those offenses motivated by bias against homosexuals. But on major economic legislation, he generally has been loyal to his party. He supported both versions — the second of which became law — of a $700 billion measure to aid the ailing financial sector in fall 2008, as well as a $410 billion catchall spending bill in February 2009.

And though he opposed President Obama's economic stimulus package when the House passed it January 2009, he became one of five opposed Democrats to back the subsequent $787 billion measure that had been negotiated with the Senate. Obama courted him after his initial "no" vote, offering him a ride on Air Force One to a town hall meeting in Indiana, and listened to Ellsworth's insistence that the money needed to be spent more effectively than the George W. Bush administration's relief program for Hurricane Katrina or the first $350 billion devoted to the financial sector rescue. "I'm not willing to risk it and say we can sit back and let the market handle it, and we'll get through it, " he said in explaining his reversal.

A member of the Blue Dog Coalition of fiscally conservative Democrats, Ellsworth calls himself a "waste, fraud and abuse hawk." The House in April 2008 passed a bill he sponsored to prevent tax-delinquent companies from getting federal contracts or grants. He crafted the bill — which did not move in the Senate — in response to repeated reports from the Government Accountability Office showing that contractors with significant tax debts were continuing to get work from the federal government. Often, they would withhold taxes from employees' paychecks but would not send that money to the government, he said.

As a member of the Armed Services Committee, Ellsworth was assigned to a bipartisan panel in March 2009 to examine ways to improve the Defense Department's troubled procurement system. He also looks out for Martin County's Naval Surface Warfare Center, which is a major employer in his district. He has voted against setting an exact date for redeployment of troops from Iraq, but welcomed Obama's early 2009 pledge to remove combat forces by the end of August 2010. "It's time to cut the umbilical cord," he said in March 2009.

Ellsworth also sits on the Small Business Committee, where he promotes easing the expense for small businesses to provide competitive health care benefits to their employees by allowing multiple small businesses to pool their resources and thus enjoy the same buying power as larger companies.

From his seat on the Agriculture Committee, he protects the corn, soybean and wheat farmers whose fields line Highway 41, which stretches the length of his district.

Ellsworth was born in Jasper and spent his early years in Huntingburg. When he was 10 the family moved to Evansville, the state's third largest city, where he's lived ever since. Ellsworth says he didn't hear much about politics growing up. His father didn't have time to do much more than sleep at home while clocking 100-hour weeks as a crane operator at an Alcoa factory. His mother worked as a part-time secretary.

During college, Ellsworth lived at home and worked part-time jobs in the paint and hardware departments at a local Sears department store while attending the Evansville branch of Indiana State University (now the University of Southern Indiana). He flirted with a career in social work but ended up choosing law enforcement, and he earned a master's degree in criminology at Indiana State University.

Ellsworth was a policeman for 24 years at the local county sheriff's office. He said he became interested in politics when he watched the Democratic county councilmen fight to provide bulletproof vests for the police force. "Those were guys who were willing to put up county dollars," he said. "They cared about us."

During his time on the force, he was decorated twice for heroism in the line of duty. He was elected county sheriff in 1998 and served two terms, focusing on fighting local methamphetamine abuse and creating a Web site to track and monitor convicted sexual offenders. He also worked to build a new county jail to alleviate overcrowding.

His law enforcement background influences some of his votes in Congress; he was the only House member to oppose a bill in February 2009 aimed at reducing prisoner fatalities by requiring states to report details about deaths to the Justice Department.

National Democrats had frequently tried to talk him into running for Congress, reasoning that his law enforcement background and good looks would counterbalance GOP incumbent John Hostettler's support among Christian conservative groups. Ellsworth argued that Hostettler's views had fallen out of line with district residents. Hostettler returned fire, equating a vote for Ellsworth as a vote for California's Nancy Pelosi to be Speaker of the House. But 8th District voters weren't worried and Ellsworth won by 22 percentage points.

Two years later, he increased his margin of victory in handily defeating Republican Greg Goode, formerly Indiana State University's chief public and governmental affairs officer and a one-time congressional staffer.

KEY VOTES

2008
Yes Delay consideration of Colombia free-trade agreement
Yes Override Bush veto of federal farm and nutrition programs reauthorization bill
Yes Overhaul surveillance laws and permit dismissal of suits against companies that conducted warrantless wiretapping
Yes Grant mortgage relief to homeowners and funding for Fannie Mae and Freddie Mac
Yes Approve initial $700 billion program to stabilize financial markets
Yes Approve final $700 billion program to stabilize financial markets
Yes Provide $14 billion in loans to automakers

2007
Yes Increase minimum wage by $2.10 an hour
Yes Approve $124.2 billion in emergency war spending and set goal for redeployment of troops from Iraq
Yes Reject federal contraceptive assistance to international family planning groups
Yes Override Bush veto of $23.2 billion water projects authorization bill
Yes Implement Peru free-trade agreement
Yes Approve energy policy overhaul with new fuel economy standards
Yes Clear $473.5 billion omnibus spending bill, including $70 billion for military operations

CQ VOTE STUDIES

	PARTY UNITY		PRESIDENTIAL SUPPORT	
	SUPPORT	OPPOSE	SUPPORT	OPPOSE
2008	85%	15%	25%	75%
2007	78%	22%	19%	81%

INTEREST GROUPS

	AFL-CIO	ADA	CCUS	ACU
2008	87%	75%	72%	16%
2007	88%	75%	70%	36%

INDIANA 8

West – Evansville, Terre Haute

Indiana's southwest corner, formed by the converging Wabash and Ohio rivers, is home to the 8th, a district characterized by laborers and social conservatives. Evansville, an Ohio River port and the state's third-largest city, is southern Indiana's industrial center. It is located in Democratic-leaning Vanderburgh County, the district's most populous, and is home to the 8th's only substantial minority and liberal populations.

North of Evansville the 8th takes on a more rural and culturally conservative flavor. Gibson and Knox counties are among Indiana's top corn-producing areas. This region also grows soybeans, wheat and various fruits and vegetables. Daviess County has a large Amish population.

Terre Haute, farther north in generally Democratic Vigo County, is the district's other manufacturing center, and the 8th produces appliances, pharmaceuticals and automotive parts. Terre Haute gets some Democratic votes from Indiana State University's faculty and students, and Evansville is home to Southern Indiana and Evansville universities. Having refurbished its downtown, Evansville is trying to establish tourism

revenue despite far-ranging economic downturns, and the Casino Aztar is docked on the Ohio River.

Known in political circles as the "Bloody Eighth" for its aggressive and close races, the district's manufacturing base and history as a mining center long gave Democrats an edge. Cultural issues moved the district to the right, but local elections continue to be split between the two parties. McCain won 51 percent of the 8th's 2008 presidential vote overall, and took his second-highest percentage in the state in Daviess County. But, the district supported incumbent Rep. Brad Ellsworth in his first re-election run and he retained the U.S. House seat easily with 65 percent of the vote.

MAJOR INDUSTRY
Manufacturing, agriculture, higher education

MILITARY BASES
Naval Surface Warfare Center, Crane Division, 23 military, 3,618 civilian (2007)

CITES
Evansville, 121,582; Terre Haute, 59,614

NOTABLE
Vincennes is the oldest city in Indiana.

Rep. Baron P. Hill (D)

Elected 1998; 5th term
Did not serve 2005-07

CAPITOL OFFICE
225-5315
baronhill.house.gov
223 Cannon Bldg. 20515-1409; fax 226-6866

COMMITTEES
Energy & Commerce
Science & Technology
Joint Economic

RESIDENCE
Seymour

BORN
June 23, 1953; Seymour, Ind.

RELIGION
Methodist

FAMILY
Wife, Betty Hill; three children

EDUCATION
Furman U., B.A. 1975 (history)

CAREER
Financial adviser; state student assistance commission executive director; state legislative aide; insurance company manager

POLITICAL HIGHLIGHTS
Ind. House, 1982-90; Democratic nominee for U.S. Senate, 1990; defeated for re-election to U.S. House, 2004; U.S. House, 1995-2008

ELECTION RESULTS

2008 GENERAL

Baron P. Hill (D)	181,281	57.8%
Mike Sodrel (R)	120,529	38.4%
D. Eric Schansberg (LIBERT)	11,994	3.8%

2008 PRIMARY

Baron P. Hill (D)	99,332	67.6%
Gretchen Clearwater (D)	23,157	15.8%
John R. Bottorff (D)	18,963	12.9%
Lendall B. Terry (D)	5,429	3.7%

2006 GENERAL

Baron P. Hill (D)	110,454	50.0%
Mike Sodrel (R)	100,469	45.5%
D. Eric Schansberg (LIBERT)	9,893	4.5%

PREVIOUS WINNING PERCENTAGES
2002 (51%); 2000 (54%); 1998 (51%)

Hill is a conservative whose calls for fiscal restraint and views on some social policy issues are much in line with his largely rural constituency in southeastern Indiana. He is a staunch advocate of pay-as-you-go budget rules that require offsets for new entitlement spending or tax cuts. He supports gun owners' rights and splits his votes on abortion.

Hill has had to closely monitor the wishes of his constituents and can't afford to be seen as a tax-and-spend Democrat. His district has voted Republican in the last three presidential elections, and until 2008 he had never captured more than 55 percent of the vote. He has faced the same Republican opponent — Mike Sodrel — for four straight elections, and lost to him once, in 2004.

As one of three co-chairs of the Blue Dog Coalition, a group of fiscally conservative House Democrats, he helps direct the group's policy proposals. He said he used to have more in common with Republicans on fiscal issues, but then he criticized them for allowing federal budget deficits to soar while they were in control of Congress. He can be just as hard on his own party leaders. "My constituents have to live within a budget, and so should Congress," Hill said.

He did support the $787 billion economic stimulus and recovery package sought by Obama in early 2009, despite the fact that none of it was offset. But he was one of just 20 House Democrats to vote against a $410 billion catchall fiscal 2009 spending bill the following month. In 2008, he supported unsuccessful legislation to bail out the domestic auto industry but voted against two versions of a $700 billion plan to shore up the ailing financial services sector, the second of which became law.

In both 2007 and 2008, Hill voted against what has become an annual adjustment to prevent the alternative minimum tax, originally designed to target the wealthy, from expanding to hit millions of middle-class taxpayers. He did so because the cost was not offset. Most other House Democrats shared his objection, but gave in to the Senate in the end.

Hill sits on the Energy and Commerce Committee, where he will have a say on his top two priorities: health care reform and measures to spur renewable energy. In October 2007 he was part of an unsuccessful attempt to override President George W. Bush's veto of legislation that would have expanded a children's health insurance program by $35 billion over five years. He had opposed the plan in February 2007 and had been unsuccessful in amending it to ensure a more equitable distribution of the program's benefits. But he said the program was still vital to children in his district. He supported a similar bill that Obama signed into law in early 2009.

A member of the Energy and Environment Subcommittee, Hill encourages investment in renewable energies such as ethanol and biodiesel. In February 2008 he backed a multibillion-dollar tax incentive package that encouraged investment in renewable-energy technologies through provisions that would be paid for by cutting subsidies for five major oil and gas companies. But the Senate refused to act on the measure.

He is a member of the subcommittee on telecommunications and the Internet. In 2007 he voted for legislation to require the Federal Trade Commission to launch a $5 million Internet safety campaign.

Hill also serves on the Science and Technology Committee, where he can take part in discussions on investments in renewable-energy technologies and science education. He sits on the Space and Aeronautics Subcommittee.

When he first returned to Congress in 2007, Hill was among a group of freshmen pushing for stronger ethics rules. His bill, introduced in March 2007, would have set up an ethics commission consisting of 12 former House members. A year later, the House approved a plan by House Speaker Nancy Pelosi of California to set up an independent, six-person Office of Congressional Ethics to do the initial screening of ethics complaints.

Generally a social conservative, Hill has split with his party on some votes on abortion. He doesn't think the Supreme Court's landmark *Roe v. Wade* decision legalizing abortion should be overturned, but he has voted for laws requiring parental notification and consent for a minor seeking an abortion.

In the 107th Congress (2001-02), he went against party wishes when pushing for overseas trade markets he said would benefit his district's farmers and major shippers. In 2002, he was one of 25 Democrats to support legislation giving the president fast-track authority to negotiate trade agreements, which allows quick up-or-down votes on trade deals in Congress.

Hill is the youngest of seven children whose parents worked in a shoe factory. A basketball star at Seymour High School, he was inducted into the Indiana Basketball Hall of Fame in 2000, along with NBA legend Larry Bird.

He went to Furman University on a basketball scholarship. He picked up the political bug watching the Watergate hearings on television. He was fascinated by the process of government and the competitive aspect of politics, which reminded him of sports. He got a degree in history, returned to Seymour and ran an insurance and real estate business.

Elected to the Indiana House in 1982, he served there for eight years. He left the legislature in 1990 to wage an uphill battle for the U.S. Senate. Hill attracted some notice by walking the length of Indiana — from the Ohio River to Lake Michigan — where he celebrated by jumping into the 60-degree water. He lost to Republican Daniel R. Coats, who had been appointed to the seat two years earlier to replace Republican Dan Quayle, the party's vice presidential candidate that year. Hill did surprisingly well against Coats, capturing 46 percent of the vote.

He went to work as a financial analyst for Merrill Lynch, but returned to politics when Democratic Rep. Lee H. Hamilton let him know he'd be retiring from the 9th District seat in 1998 after 17 terms. He was still remembered for his high school basketball exploits, and he outspent state Sen. Jean Leising, $1 million to $650,000. He won by about 3 percentage points.

Republicans immediately targeted him, but Hill was able to stave off challenges until 2004, when Sodrel edged him by 1,425 votes in the second of their four election contests. In 2008, Hill racked up his biggest margin yet, winning with 58 percent of the vote.

KEY VOTES

2008

No Delay consideration of Colombia free-trade agreement

Yes Override Bush veto of federal farm and nutrition programs reauthorization bill

No Overhaul surveillance laws and permit dismissal of suits against companies that conducted warrantless wiretapping

Yes Grant mortgage relief to homeowners and funding for Fannie Mae and Freddie Mac

No Approve initial $700 billion program to stabilize financial markets

No Approve final $700 billion program to stabilize financial markets

Yes Provide $14 billion in loans to automakers

2007

Yes Increase minimum wage by $2.10 an hour

Yes Approve $124.2 billion in emergency war spending and set goal for redeployment of troops from Iraq

No Reject federal contraceptive assistance to international family planning groups

Yes Override Bush veto of $23.2 billion water projects authorization bill

Yes Implement Peru free-trade agreement

Yes Approve energy policy overhaul with new fuel economy standards

Yes Clear $473.5 billion omnibus spending bill, including $70 billion for military operations

CQ VOTE STUDIES

	PARTY UNITY		PRESIDENTIAL SUPPORT	
	SUPPORT	OPPOSE	SUPPORT	OPPOSE
2008	72%	28%	18%	82%
2007	82%	18%	11%	89%
2004	83%	17%	32%	68%
2003	38%	62%	83%	17%
2002	45%	55%	76%	24%

INTEREST GROUPS

	AFL-CIO	ADA	CCUS	ACU
2008	86%	75%	61%	20%
2007	88%	85%	70%	20%
2004	87%	85%	48%	20%
2003	80%	90%	53%	40%
2002	44%	70%	65%	28%

INDIANA 9

Southeast – Bloomington, New Albany

Bordering the Ohio River to the south, the 9th shares socially conservative roots and, more recently, competitive politics with Indiana's other river valley district (the 8th). Manufacturing forms the economic foundation, although agriculture and retail trade also are prevalent in Indiana's southeastern quadrant. The district extends as far north as Monroe County to take in almost all of Bloomington.

Residents from Cincinnati and Ohio suburbs moved into the 9th's northeastern counties, creating a slightly more suburban feel to the largely rural area. To the southwest, Clark and Floyd counties grow in parallel to growth in the Louisville metropolitan area — more of the 9th's residents live in Clark than in any of the district's other 19 counties. Manufacturing, retail jobs and the health care sector in these areas have helped these counties stave off high unemployment and poverty levels that run well above the state average in some of the 9th's other counties.

Elizabeth, in Harrison County west and south of Louisville, hosts a riverboat casino and resort that is a key employer in the region. Factories also provide jobs for residents of the small and midsize cities of the district, while corn and soybean fields occupy most of the rural landscape.

Bloomington is home to Indiana University and gives Monroe County a Democratic lean. While the university helps make Monroe one of Indiana's best-educated counties, the 9th as a whole is more blue-collar with a low percentage of college graduates. Despite the district's Democratic heritage, the area's social conservatism has propelled Republican candidates to victory in the last three presidential elections. In the 2008 presidential election, however, John McCain won the district with only 50 percent of the 9th's vote, significantly lower than the double-digit margin racked up here by George W. Bush in 2000 and 2004.

MAJOR INDUSTRY
Manufacturing, agriculture, retail

CITIES
Bloomington (pt.), 66,459; New Albany, 37,603; Jeffersonville, 27,362

NOTABLE
Larry Bird is from French Lick; "Breaking Away" features Bloomington's love for cycling, which is celebrated each October during the Hilly Hundred Bicycle Weekend; The movie "Hoosiers" was based on the state championship success of the 1954 Milan High School basketball team.

IOWA

Gov. Chet Culver (D)

First elected: 2006
Length of term: 4 years
Term expires: 1/11
Salary: $142,570
Phone: (515) 281-5211

Residence West
Des Moines
Born: Jan. 25, 1966;
Washington, D.C.
Religion: Presbyterian
Family: Wife, Mari Culver; two children
Education: Virginia Polytechnic Institute
and State U., B.A. 1988 (political science);
Drake U., M.A. 1994 (teaching)
Career: Teacher; state justice department
consumer and environmental analyst;
campaign aide; lobbyist
Political highlights: Iowa secretary
of state, 1999-2007

Election results:
2006 GENERAL

Chet Culver (D)	569,021	54.0%
Jim Nussle (R)	467,425	44.4%

Lt. Gov. Patty Judge (D)

First elected: 2006
Length of term: 4 years
Term expires: 1/11
Salary: $127,530
Phone: (515) 281-0225

LEGISLATURE

General Assembly: January-May

Senate: 50 members, 4-year terms
2009 ratios: 32 D, 18 R; 41 men,
9 women
Salary: $25,000
Phone: (515) 281-3371

House: 100 members, 2-year terms
2009 ratios: 56 D, 44 R; 76 men,
24 women
Salary: $25,000
Phone: (515) 281-3221

TERM LIMITS

Governor: No
Senate: No
House: No

URBAN STATISTICS

CITY	POPULATION
Des Moines	198,682
Cedar Rapids	120,758
Davenport	98,359
Sioux City	85,013
Waterloo	68,747

REGISTERED VOTERS

Others/unaffiliated	36%
Democrat	35%
Republican	29%

POPULATION

2008 population (est.)	3,002,555
2000 population	2,926,324
1990 population	2,776,755
Percent change (1990-2000)	+5.4%
Rank among states (2008)	30
Median age	36.6
Born in state	74.8%
Foreign born	3.1%
Violent crime rate	266/100,000
Poverty level	9.1%
Federal workers	18,928
Military	14,329

ELECTIONS

STATE ELECTION OFFICIAL
(515) 281-0145
DEMOCRATIC PARTY
(515) 244-7292
REPUBLICAN PARTY
(515) 282-8105

MISCELLANEOUS

Web: www.iowa.gov
Capital: Des Moines

U.S. CONGRESS

Senate: 1 Democrat, 1 Republican
House: 3 Democrats, 2 Republicans

2000 Census Statistics by District

DIST.	2008 VOTE FOR PRESIDENT OBAMA	MCCAIN	WHITE	BLACK	ASIAN	HISP	MEDIAN INCOME	WHITE COLLAR	BLUE COLLAR	SERVICE INDUSTRY	OVER 64	UNDER 18	COLLEGE EDUCATION	RURAL	SQ. MILES
1	58%	41%	92%	4%	1%	2%	$38,727	56%	29%	15%	14%	25%	20%	34%	7,217
2	60	39	92	2	2	3	$40,121	59	27	14	13	24	25	34	7,566
3	54	45	90	3	2	3	$43,176	62	24	14	13	26	25	27	6,979
4	53	46	95	1	1	3	$38,242	56	29	15	16	24	20	49	15,760
5	44	55	94	1	1	4	$36,773	53	31	16	17	26	16	51	18,348
STATE	54	45	93	2	1	3	$39,469	57	28	15	15	25	21	39	55,869
U.S.	53	46	69	12	4	13	$41,994	60	25	15	12	26	24	21	3,537,438

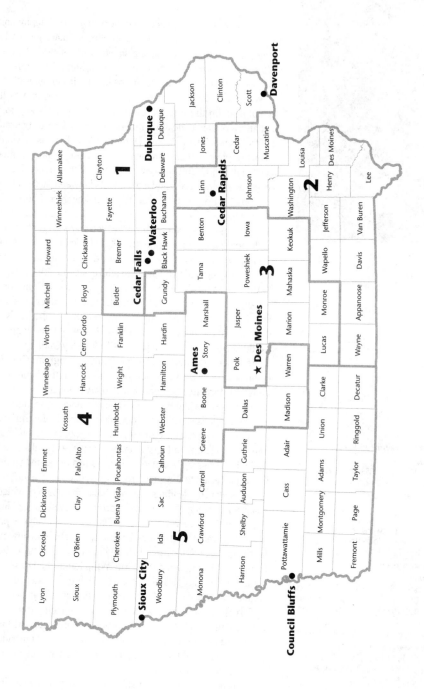

Sen. Charles E. Grassley (R)

Elected 1980; 5th term

CAPITOL OFFICE
224-3744
grassley.senate.gov
135 Hart Bldg. 20510; fax 224-6020

COMMITTEES
Agriculture, Nutrition & Forestry
Budget
Finance - ranking member
Judiciary
Joint Taxation

RESIDENCE
New Hartford

BORN
Sept. 17, 1933; New Hartford, Iowa

RELIGION
Baptist

FAMILY
Wife, Barbara Grassley; five children

EDUCATION
U. of Northern Iowa, B.A. 1955, M.A. 1956
(political science); U. of Iowa, attended 1957-58
(graduate studies)

CAREER
Farmer

POLITICAL HIGHLIGHTS
Republican nominee for Iowa House, 1956;
Iowa House, 1959-75; U.S. House, 1975-81

ELECTION RESULTS

2004 GENERAL

Charles E. Grassley (R)	1,038,175	70.2%
Arthur Small (D)	412,365	27.9%
Christy Welty (LIBERT)	15,218	1.0%

2004 PRIMARY

Charles E. Grassley (R)	78,819	99.7%

PREVIOUS WINNING PERCENTAGES
1998 (68%); 1992 (70%); 1986 (66%); 1980 (54%);
1978 House Election (75%); 1976 House Election
(57%); 1974 House Election (51%)

Grassley is an independent conservative who happily collaborates with Democrats to pass legislation, sometimes flustering his Republican colleagues. But he regards his legislative work as secondary to his oversight efforts: He has made a career of needling administrations both Republican and Democratic with investigations into their bureaucratic blunders.

With more than a quarter-century in Congress, and as the top-ranking Republican on the Finance Committee, Grassley is key to advancing any initiatives on taxes, health entitlements, Social Security, trade and welfare. He works hand-in-glove with Democrat Max Baucus of Montana, who took over the panel's chairmanship from Grassley when Democrats regained control in the 110th Congress (2007-08). The two men have swapped roles three times since 2001, and agreements between them helped clear the way for some of President George W. Bush's biggest victories, beginning with the 10-year, $1.35 trillion tax cut of 2001. They also were central to passage of 2002's fast-track trade authority, which allowed quick up-or-down votes on trade deals in Congress, and the 2003 Medicare prescription drug benefit.

Grassley and Baucus much prefer deal-cutting to partisan purity, a pattern they struggled to maintain in addressing health care reform during the 111th Congress (2009-10). When they have parted ways on major bills, it's usually been because their respective party leaders insisted they toe the line. But neither blames the other when that happens. "Not as much gets done out of the Finance Committee that would get done if the leadership would leave us to our own pursuits," Grassley said.

He expects results from the government programs Congress creates and compliance with the tax benefits that his committee hands out. His investigations have targeted the Food and Drug Administration, the Defense Department, nonprofits like the Nature Conservancy and Smithsonian Institution, and televangelists, which has displeased some in the Christian conservative movement. Oversight, Grassley says, is Congress' highest responsibility, more important than legislation, as it achieves results much more quickly. And it is necessary because "Congress has delegated so much power over the last 50 years to the executive branch of government," he said.

Grassley is the leading congressional champion of whistleblowers, both inside and out of government. His proudest legislative achievement is a 1986 update of the Civil War-era False Claims Act that allows private citizens to sue government contractors for fraud, and share in any money recovered for the government. He said the law has recouped more than $20 billion for taxpayers. He and Senate Majority Whip Richard J. Durbin, an Illinois Democrat, advanced legislation in early 2009 to broaden the law's reach and counter court decisions that Grassley said have weakened the powerful tool.

Perhaps no agency has received more scrutiny from Grassley than the FBI. A longtime member of the Judiciary Committee, he has criticized what he regards as the FBI's heavy-handed tactics and bureaucratic shortcomings and is known for sending letter after letter to its directors demanding they explain themselves.

His rebellious streak is cushioned by a disarming candor, the product of a lifetime in small-town Iowa, where he is quick to retreat when Congress is out of session. He grows corn and soybeans on 720 acres near New Hartford with his son and grandson, and to keep in touch with his staff, he tucks a cell phone set to vibrate under his cap while on a tractor. A veteran member of the Agriculture, Nutrition and Forestry Committee, he looks out for his state's many pork producers and corn growers with a farmer's eye for policy.

Grassley holds public hearings in all of Iowa's 99 counties every year, usually completing the tour by Labor Day. His devotion hasn't kept him away from Washington, however. He has the Senate's longest-running perfect attendance record; as of May 2009, the last roll call he missed was in July 1993.

Plain-spoken and blunt, Grassley delivers scathing speeches from the Senate floor against his opponents when crossed. In May 2008, he accused the Grocery Manufacturers Association of organizing a "smear campaign" against ethanol production from corn, which some blame for increasing the price of food.

In July, after House Ways and Means Chairman Charles B. Rangel of New York told him a relief package for Midwest flood victims would have to be offset by spending cuts or tax increases, Grassley took to the floor to note that similar relief programs for victims of Hurricane Katrina were not subject to the same requirement. "Why the double standard?" Grassley asked. "Is it because people aren't on rooftops complaining for helicopters to revive them and you see it on television for two months? We aren't doing that in Iowa; we're trying to help ourselves in Iowa. We have a can-do attitude."

For Grassley, the matter was personal: New Hartford was struck by both a massive tornado and the worst floods of Grassley's life. "It may never be the same," he said of his hometown. True to form, in one floor speech he criticized the owners of Kwik Star convenience stores for closing the only gas station in New Hartford after the floods.

The 110th Congress was a difficult one for Grassley legislatively as well. In 2007, he sided with Democrats to pass a $35 billion expansion of a health insurance program for children of low-income families, but Bush's veto of the legislation was upheld by congressional Republicans. In 2008, he sided with Bush to oppose a bill that averted a scheduled cut in Medicare payments to physicians and reduced payments to private insurers who participate in Medicare — a program championed by Bush and Grassley. Democrats were nonetheless able to pass the bill into law over Bush's veto.

Grassley is a social conservative who opposes abortion and gun control, and he votes the party line when it comes to approving conservative judges. On fiscal matters, he's not as conservative as some Republicans would like, but they can't argue with his personal thrift.

He refuses to buy the lunch offered at the party's weekly policy lunches — "I think they want $23 for it; that's ridiculous," he said. And a pet peeve of late is the large SUVs and sedans that idle around the Capitol, waiting to ferry high-ranking bureaucrats about Washington. Grassley sent a letter to Bush complaining in July 2008 about the fuel-wasting vehicles.

And he'll brook no idling by his own staff, either. "I had a staff person that was waiting for me, and the car was running, and I said, 'What's your car running for?' " Grassley recalled. The car was running, the staffer explained, so that the radio wouldn't run down the battery. Grassley reached into the car and turned off the ignition. "That's stupid," he said.

Grassley had dreamed of a career in politics since high school. After graduating from the University of Northern Iowa, he continued with graduate work there and at another Iowa university while working in a factory, where he was a Machinists union member. A few years later, he and his wife, Barbara, took over his family's grain and livestock operation.

He spent 16 years in the Iowa House and was elected to the U.S. House in 1974, succeeding H.R. Gross, a revered Republican figure in the state who retired. Six years later, he unseated liberal Democratic Sen. John C. Culver. He has won with ease ever since.

Now in his 70s, Grassley runs almost daily, usually 2 to 3 miles at a 9 ½ minute pace, a habit he adopted in 1999 as a New Year's resolution.

KEY VOTES

2008

Yes Prohibit discrimination based on genetic information

Yes Reauthorize farm and nutrition programs for five years

No Limit debate on "cap and trade" system for greenhouse gas emissions

No Allow lawsuits against companies that participated in warrantless wiretapping

No Limit debate on a bill to block a scheduled cut in Medicare payments to doctors

No Grant mortgage relief to homeowners and funding for Fannie Mae and Freddie Mac

Yes Approve a nuclear cooperation agreement with India

Yes Approve final $700 billion program to stabilize financial markets

No Allow consideration of a $14 billion auto industry loan package

2007

Yes Increase minimum wage by $2.10 an hour

No Limit debate on a comprehensive immigration bill

Yes Overhaul congressional lobbying and ethics rules for members and their staffs

No Limit debate on considering a bill to add House seats for the District of Columbia and Utah

No Limit debate on restoring habeas corpus rights to detainees

No Mandate minimum breaks for troops between deployments to Iraq or Afghanistan

Yes Override Bush veto of $23.2 billion water projects authorization bill

Yes Confirm Michael B. Mukasey as attorney general

Yes Limit debate on an energy policy overhaul containing $21.8 billion in tax incentives and reduced oil and gas subsidies

CQ VOTE STUDIES

	PARTY UNITY		PRESIDENTIAL SUPPORT	
	SUPPORT	OPPOSE	SUPPORT	OPPOSE
2008	93%	7%	72%	28%
2007	79%	21%	79%	21%
2006	93%	7%	87%	13%
2005	96%	4%	89%	11%
2004	97%	3%	94%	6%
2003	96%	4%	99%	1%
2002	88%	12%	95%	5%
2001	93%	7%	99%	1%
2000	94%	6%	42%	58%
1999	90%	10%	33%	67%

INTEREST GROUPS

	AFL-CIO	ADA	CCUS	ACU
2008	30%	25%	100%	76%
2007	32%	30%	64%	84%
2006	20%	5%	92%	88%
2005	14%	5%	100%	96%
2004	17%	20%	100%	96%
2003	0%	5%	100%	80%
2002	15%	10%	95%	95%
2001	13%	5%	100%	92%
2000	0%	0%	100%	96%
1999	0%	0%	94%	92%

Sen. Tom Harkin (D)

Elected 1984; 5th term

CAPITOL OFFICE
224-3254
harkin.senate.gov
731 Hart Bldg. 20510-1502; fax 224-9369

COMMITTEES
Agriculture, Nutrition & Forestry - chairman
Appropriations
(Labor-HHS-Education - chairman)
Health, Education, Labor & Pensions
Small Business & Entrepreneurship

RESIDENCE
Cumming

BORN
Nov. 19, 1939; Cumming, Iowa

RELIGION
Roman Catholic

FAMILY
Wife, Ruth Harkin; two children

EDUCATION
Iowa State U., B.S. 1962 (government & economics); Catholic U. of America, J.D. 1972

MILITARY SERVICE
Navy, 1962-67; Naval Reserve, 1968-74

CAREER
Lawyer; congressional aide

POLITICAL HIGHLIGHTS
Democratic nominee for U.S. House, 1972;
U.S. House, 1975-85; sought Democratic
nomination for president, 1992

ELECTION RESULTS

2008 GENERAL

Tom Harkin (D)	941,665	62.7%
Christopher Reed (R)	560,006	37.3%

2008 PRIMARY

Tom Harkin (D)	unopposed

PREVIOUS WINNING PERCENTAGES
2002 (54%); 1996 (52%); 1990 (54%); 1984 (56%);
1982 House Election (59%); 1980 House Election
(60%); 1978 House Election (59%); 1976 House
Election (65%); 1974 House Election (51%)

The longest-serving Senate Democrat in Iowa history, Harkin has survived on a populist streak and a good dose of pragmatism. He has long believed government should intervene to help the poor, the disabled and family farmers. With his party's majority in Congress further expanded, he is pushing hard to fulfill his liberal vision.

Harkin is proud of his old-school progressivism; during his 1992 presidential run, he proclaimed he was the "only Democrat in the race," tacking to the left of eventual winner Bill Clinton. His influence is felt on a wide range of issues, from health policy to farm subsidies, and he is adept at joining with moderates to strike deals.

Early in 2010, Harkin will have served in Congress for half of his life. His signature legislative achievement is the 1990 Americans With Disabilities Act, which extended broad civil rights protections to an estimated 54 million Americans with mental and physical disabilities. Harkin said he was inspired by his deaf brother, Frank, at the time of its passage and again in 2008, when President George W. Bush signed his bill expanding the number of people who qualify as disabled for purposes of the law's protections.

Harkin — the third-ranking Democrat on the Health, Education, Labor and Pensions Committee — gained a key role in crafting major health care reform legislation. The committee's ailing chairman, Edward M. Kennedy of Massachusetts, assigned Harkin in November 2008 to draft of the prevention and public health provisions of the bill. Harkin, also the chairman of the Appropriations panel's Labor, Health and Human Services and Education Subcommittee, quickly went to work. He convened a hearing the following month on the importance of wellness and prevention — "the key to transforming our sick care system." He subsequently proposed a range of ideas, including having government provide better food and more physical education in schools and reward doctors for keeping patients healthy. He also said he would favor higher insurance premiums for smokers and the obese.

Harkin's Appropriations panel oversees the largest of the 12 annual spending bills. He brings large sums of federal funding back home, which is one reason most Iowa newspapers endorse him for re-election. During debate on a $410 billion catchall spending bill in March 2009, he vehemently defended a $1.7 million provision for swine odor and manure management research. He challenged Republican Tom Coburn of Oklahoma, who criticized the provision, to visit pig farms to see the importance of odor control.

Harkin worked well with Pennsylvania's Arlen Specter when Specter was the panel's ranking Republican, and the two usually saw eye to eye on health care policy and increased funding for the National Institutes of Health. Harkin is also a champion of funding for special-education programs.

Specter and Harkin joined forces on another major health initiative, a bill to lift Bush's restrictions on federal funding of embryonic stem cell research, which uses discarded embryos created for in vitro fertilization and which some scientists say holds promise in the treatment of disease. After years of fruitless attempts, the pair saw the legislation pass in 2006 only to draw the first veto of Bush's presidency. An override attempt failed. When President Obama overturned the restrictions in March 2009, Harkin applauded the move.

As chairman of the Agriculture, Nutrition and Forestry Committee, Harkin oversaw the 2008 passage of a $289 billion bill reauthorizing agriculture and nutrition programs for five years, though he was occasionally frustrated and even undercut by party leaders. In the end, the legislation was the product of considerable compromise that resulted in the retention of controversial crop subsidies and the tightening of income requirements for farmers to qualify. The law also boosted funding for food stamps, conservation programs and ethanol production, a major priority for Iowa's corn farmers. Harkin proclaimed himself satisfied. Later that year, he successfully lobbied Obama to pick former Iowa Gov. Tom Vilsack as Agriculture secretary.

Harkin is a friend of organized labor, often drawing 100 percent ratings on the AFL-CIO's annual scorecard. He explained that his 2007 vote against ending debate on an immigration bill, which helped kill the measure, was a result of his concern that increased immigration could hurt Iowa wages.

But Harkin occasionally votes for free-trade agreements in deference to Iowa farmers eager to boost their exports. Also with his farmers in mind, he joined with agriculture-state Republicans in 2005 to win a provision in the energy bill requiring refiners to boost renewable fuels such as corn-based ethanol to 7.5 billion gallons by 2012, a move helped along by steep increases in gasoline prices at the time. Ethanol is key to Harkin's vision of making agriculture a vital component of the nation's energy security. To prove its safety for gas tanks, he once took a swig of it at a Senate hearing.

The son of a coal miner, Harkin grew up in a small, crowded house in Cumming. His life took a tragic turn when he turned 10 and lost his mother, a Slovenian immigrant. After working his way through college and law school, Harkin spent five years as a Navy pilot during the Vietnam War.

Though interested in politics since college — he was president of the Young Democrats at Iowa State — he stumbled into the field as a career. In 1968, out of the Navy and out of work, he was watching TV at a diner when President Lyndon B. Johnson startled him by announcing he would not seek another term. The next morning, a friend working for the Iowa Democratic Party offered him a job. "I thought, 'I'm going broke, I've got no prospects for the future. Why not?'" Harkin recalled.

In 1969, he was hired by Iowa Democratic Rep. Neal Smith as an aide on the House select committee investigating the U.S. military's progress in Vietnam. He made a name for himself with his discovery of South Vietnam's "tiger cages." Outwitting a government official on a guided tour of a prison camp, Harkin found, behind a hidden door, hundreds of people crammed into underground cells, with open grates on top through which guards poured skinsearing doses of the chemical lime. His photographs and story in Life magazine energized the anti-war movement and forced South Vietnam to shutter the tiger cages. The move cost the 30-year-old Harkin his Hill job.

Harkin ran for the House in 1972 against entrenched GOP incumbent William Scherle. He attracted publicity with his "work days," toiling alongside farmers, teachers and welfare caseworkers. He lost narrowly but tried again and toppled Scherle by a slim margin in 1974. In four House re-elections, he captured about 60 percent of the vote.

His Senate campaigns have been tougher. He won his seat in 1984 by ousting GOP Sen. Roger W. Jepsen with 56 percent of the vote. In 1990, his GOP challenger, Rep. Tom Tauke, accused Harkin of abusing congressional mailing privileges and voting for excessive spending. Harkin eventually won by 9 percentage points. He won a third term in 1996 by defeating GOP Rep. Jim Ross Lightfoot by 5 percentage points.

Enactment of the 2002 reauthorization of the farm bill just before the elections helped him stave off a tough challenge from Republican Rep. Greg Ganske. In 2008, Harkin eclipsed 60 percent for the first time as a senator. His five terms in the Senate far surpass the second-place Democrat in Iowa history — George W. Jones, who served more than 10 years (1848-59).

He takes advantage of his state's importance in the presidential election by hosting an influential "steak fry" each year for Democratic candidates.

KEY VOTES

2008

Yes Prohibit discrimination based on genetic information

Yes Reauthorize farm and nutrition programs for five years

Yes Limit debate on "cap and trade" system for greenhouse gas emissions

Yes Allow lawsuits against companies that participated in warrantless wiretapping

Yes Limit debate on a bill to block a scheduled cut in Medicare payments to doctors

? Grant mortgage relief to homeowners and funding for Fannie Mae and Freddie Mac

No Approve a nuclear cooperation agreement with India

Yes Approve final $700 billion program to stabilize financial markets

Yes Allow consideration of a $14 billion auto industry loan package

2007

Yes Increase minimum wage by $2.10 an hour

No Limit debate on a comprehensive immigration bill

Yes Overhaul congressional lobbying and ethics rules for members and their staffs

Yes Limit debate on considering a bill to add House seats for the District of Columbia and Utah

Yes Limit debate on restoring habeas corpus rights to detainees

Yes Mandate minimum breaks for troops between deployments to Iraq or Afghanistan

Yes Override Bush veto of $23.2 billion water projects authorization bill

No Confirm Michael B. Mukasey as attorney general

Yes Limit debate on an energy policy overhaul containing $21.8 billion in tax incentives and reduced oil and gas subsidies

CQ VOTE STUDIES

	PARTY UNITY		PRESIDENTIAL SUPPORT	
	SUPPORT	OPPOSE	SUPPORT	OPPOSE
2008	97%	3%	25%	75%
2007	96%	4%	35%	65%
2006	95%	5%	46%	54%
2005	98%	2%	27%	73%
2004	94%	6%	52%	48%
2003	98%	2%	46%	54%
2002	92%	8%	69%	31%
2001	97%	3%	63%	37%
2000	97%	3%	92%	8%
1999	97%	3%	91%	9%

INTEREST GROUPS

	AFL-CIO	ADA	CCUS	ACU
2008	100%	95%	50%	4%
2007	100%	95%	36%	8%
2006	100%	100%	36%	8%
2005	100%	100%	33%	4%
2004	100%	100%	59%	8%
2003	100%	95%	32%	15%
2002	100%	80%	45%	15%
2001	100%	100%	38%	8%
2000	75%	95%	57%	4%
1999	89%	100%	47%	4%

Rep. Bruce Braley (D)

Elected 2006; 2nd term

CAPITOL OFFICE
225-2911
braley.house.gov
1019 Longworth Bldg. 20515-1501; fax 226-5051

COMMITTEES
Energy & Commerce

RESIDENCE
Waterloo

BORN
Oct. 30, 1957; Grinnell, Iowa

RELIGION
Presbyterian

FAMILY
Wife, Carolyn Braley; three children

EDUCATION
Iowa State U., B.A. 1980 (political science);
U. of Iowa, J.D. 1983

CAREER
Lawyer

POLITICAL HIGHLIGHTS
No previous office

ELECTION RESULTS

2008 GENERAL

Bruce Braley (D)	186,991	64.6%
David Hartsuch (R)	102,439	35.4%

2008 PRIMARY

Bruce Braley (D)	unopposed

2006 GENERAL

Bruce Braley (D)	113,724	55.0%
Mike Whalen (R)	89,471	43.3%
James F. Hill (PIR)	2,184	1.1%

Braley's eloquent oratory easily reminds listeners of the two decades he spent in the courtroom as a trial lawyer. He uses his facility with language to espouse populist politics and is one of a declining number of Midwestern Democrats who are pro-union and liberal on social policy.

Though Braley initially opposed a $700 billion plan to shore up the financial services industry in fall 2008, he voted for a second version, which became law. He's also supported other Democratic efforts to revive the economy, but has felt restless about so much taxpayer money going to big companies and too little going to the middle class. So in February 2009, he became the founding chairman of a new populist caucus. "One of the things we've tried to do is try to bring more of a laser focus to these middle-class economic issues," he said.

But House Democratic leaders trust Braley, who rarely parted from the party line during his freshman term. In 2009 he was named vice chairman for candidate services of the Democratic Congressional Campaign Committee, responsible for House candidate recruitment, fundraising and candidate training. DCCC Chairman Chris Van Hollen of Maryland had earlier entrusted Braley in 2008 with Democrats' highly successful "Red to Blue" campaign program, which targeted seats held by Republicans.

House Democratic leaders also awarded Braley a plum spot on the Energy and Commerce Committee for the 111th Congress (2009-10). He's focused on rooting out waste in the government's stimulus spending while also railing against the "greedy crooks" at companies who have taken government money and then handed out bonuses to their executives.

During his first term, Braley won plaudits from liberals after a March 2007 Oversight and Government Reform Committee hearing when he was asked to lead Democratic debate and question Lurita Doan, administrator of the General Services Administration, during an investigation of improper political activity during George W. Bush White House meetings. Both Braley and then-committee Chairman Henry A. Waxman of California asked Doan if she recalled discussing 2008 Republican goals during a meeting between GSA officials and White House politicos. Democrats claimed there was a violation of the Hatch Act, which bars partisan activity in government offices.

"One of the difficult challenges that any committee member faces in any type of hearing is how you get meaningful information from a witness in five minutes," Braley said. "And I have the benefit of asking questions of people in all matter of circumstances and learning techniques that can encourage them to give you truthful answers and do it without wasting time."

Doan resigned at the end of April 2008. By that time, an Internet video of Braley — donning the persona of a trial lawyer — politely but relentlessly questioning Doan had attracted more than 100,000 viewers.

Despite his legal background, Braley doesn't enjoy the complexity of Washington's legislative process, especially its jargon. He pushed a bill in early 2008 to require federal government agencies to drop their use of bureaucratic writing style and use "plain language" instead. "This movement is going to catch fire," a passionate Braley said of his bill. "And there is absolutely no reason for people not to embrace it." The bill didn't go anywhere, but Braley said he will try again.

Sometimes Braley will part from liberal orthodoxy when it benefits his district. Despite his pro-union bona fides, he protested to Treasury Secretary Timothy F. Geithner in 2009 after Geithner pulled the plug on a program, despised by federal employee unions, that enlisted private collection companies in going after back taxes. One of the private firms was in his district.

Braley's family roots in Iowa date back 150 years, when his great-great-grandfather, George Washington Braley, walked from Vermont to the center of the state and set up a farm. The son of a grain elevator worker and a fourth-grade teacher, Braley says his blue-collar upbringing in the small town of Brooklyn made him a natural advocate for the Democratic Party. His interest in politics began during his adolescent years, when his father, a moderate Republican, and his mother, a Democrat, routinely talked about the daily news around the dinner table with their four children. He remembers discussing the Vietnam War and the Watergate scandal.

His first job, when he was in the third grade, was as a paper boy for the Des Moines Tribune. Later he tackled more labor-intensive jobs — baling hay, detasseling corn, working at a grain elevator and driving dump trucks. At BGM High School in Brooklyn he earned varsity letters in football, baseball, basketball, track and field and golf.

He has a passion for education stemming from his upbringing; his grandmother and great-grandmother also were teachers. When he was a child, his mother drove back and forth from their Brooklyn home to the University of Iowa's campus in Iowa City to get her four-year degree. His wife, Carolyn, teaches at Waterloo West High School, which all of their children attended.

Braley graduated in 1980 with a degree in political science from Iowa State University, where he also met his wife. After Braley earned a law degree from the University of Iowa, they settled in Waterloo, where Braley made a career as a plaintiffs' lawyer, typically representing employees on occupational safety issues and workers affected by corporate downsizing.

Braley made his bid for Congress in 2006 when GOP Rep. Jim Nussle left his Democratic-leaning district for an unsuccessful bid for governor. In the primary, Braley edged Rick Dickinson, a longtime Dubuque economic development official, 36 percent to 34 percent. Braley faced restaurant and hotel entrepreneur Mike Whalen in the general election. His campaign referred to Whalen as a "millionaire CEO," while Whalen described Braley as a "liberal trial lawyer" who would do more "suing" than "doing."

Braley often could be heard touting his populist message, specifically on the minimum wage. "What does it say about the values of our country when we refuse to raise the wages of the bottom segment of earners, however many they are?" he asked the Dubuque Telegraph Herald. The two political novices spent a combined $4.8 million, and Braley defeated Whalen by 12 percentage points. He handily defeated Iowa state Sen. David Hartsuch in 2008 for a second term.

KEY VOTES

2008
Yes Delay consideration of Colombia free-trade agreement
Yes Override Bush veto of federal farm and nutrition programs reauthorization bill
No Overhaul surveillance laws and permit dismissal of suits against companies that conducted warrantless wiretapping
Yes Grant mortgage relief to homeowners and funding for Fannie Mae and Freddie Mac
No Approve initial $700 billion program to stabilize financial markets
Yes Approve final $700 billion program to stabilize financial markets
Yes Provide $14 billion in loans to automakers

2007
Yes Increase minimum wage by $2.10 an hour
Yes Approve $124.2 billion in emergency war spending and set goal for redeployment of troops from Iraq
No Reject federal contraceptive assistance to international family planning groups
Yes Override Bush veto of $23.2 billion water projects authorization bill
? Implement Peru free-trade agreement
Yes Approve energy policy overhaul with new fuel economy standards
No Clear $473.5 billion omnibus spending bill, including $70 billion for military operations

CQ VOTE STUDIES

	PARTY UNITY		PRESIDENTIAL SUPPORT	
	SUPPORT	OPPOSE	SUPPORT	OPPOSE
2008	98%	2%	13%	87%
2007	96%	4%	6%	94%

INTEREST GROUPS

	AFL-CIO	ADA	CCUS	ACU
2008	100%	90%	56%	4%
2007	96%	90%	63%	0%

IOWA 1
East — Davenport, Waterloo, Dubuque

The 1st District takes in half of Iowa's Mississippi River counties as well as farmland to the west. The district is dominated by three midsize industrial cities: Dubuque and Davenport on the river, and Waterloo in inland Black Hawk County.

Located at the 1st's southern tip, Davenport and Bettendorf make up Iowa's half of the Quad Cities that straddle the Mississippi River into Illinois. Davenport is a district health care hub, and riverfront redevelopment projects are ongoing. Downtown boasts the area's minor league baseball team — the Quad Cities River Bandits — and a five-story high pedestrian sky bridge that offers visitors a sweeping view of the Mississippi River.

North of the Quad Cities and built against the bluffs facing the Mississippi River, Dubuque is Iowa's oldest city. Manufacturing and meatpacking, while still important, are not as dominant here as they once were. Recent layoffs at factories, such as heavy-equipment manufacturer John Deere, have been offset by overall growth in the local economy, particularly in

finance, insurance, health care and information technology sectors.

West along Route 20, Waterloo diversified its traditional meatpacking and farm implement industries to include finance and insurance businesses. Black Hawk County, which also includes Cedar Falls and the University of Northern Iowa, has a strong Democratic base from its academic and labor workforce.

There are many GOP voters in the rural farmland between the three main cities, but overall, the Democratic Party has a roughly 10-percentage-point voter registration edge. Democrat Barack Obama won 58 percent of the district's vote in the 2008 presidential election.

MAJOR INDUSTRY
Farm machinery, health care, agriculture, meatpacking

CITIES
Davenport, 98,359; Waterloo, 68,747; Dubuque, 57,686; Cedar Falls, 36,145

NOTABLE
Modern Woodmen Park, home of the River Bandits, has a cornfield in left field — players' entrances through the cornstalks during pre-game introductions resembles a scene from "Field of Dreams," which was filmed in Dyersville, 25 miles west of Dubuque.

Rep. Dave Loebsack (D)

Elected 2006; 2nd term

CAPITOL OFFICE
225-6576
loebsack.house.gov
1221 Longworth Bldg. 20515-1502; fax 226-0757

COMMITTEES
Armed Services
Education & Labor

RESIDENCE
Mount Vernon

BORN
Dec. 23, 1952; Sioux City, Iowa

RELIGION
Methodist

FAMILY
Wife, Teresa Loebsack; four children

EDUCATION
Iowa State U., B.S. 1974 (political science),
M.A. 1976 (political science); U. of California,
Davis, Ph.D. 1985 (political science)

CAREER
Professor

POLITICAL HIGHLIGHTS
No previous office

ELECTION RESULTS

2008 GENERAL

Dave Loebsack (D)	175,218	57.2%
Mariannette Miller-Meeks (R)	118,778	38.8%
Wendy Barth (GREEN)	6,664	2.2%
Brian White (X)	5,437	1.8%

2008 PRIMARY

Dave Loebsack (D)	unopposed

2006 GENERAL

Dave Loebsack (D)	107,683	51.3%
Jim Leach (R)	101,707	48.5%

Loebsack is a former college professor who has traveled extensively overseas — but he tries to emphasize that he doesn't see life from an ivory tower. The first sentence of his biography on his Web site says he "grew up in poverty and was raised by a single parent," and his background has informed his strong emphasis on using government to help others.

He is a faithful Democrat on a range of issues. He has backed an increase in the minimum wage, supported legislation to expand a health insurance program for children whose families don't qualify for Medicaid, supported embryonic stem cell research and worked for a measure banning job discrimination on the basis of sexual orientation. A former international relations professor at Iowa's Cornell College and the husband of a retired elementary school teacher, his primary interests are helping to make college affordable and bringing U.S. troops back from Iraq.

Loebsack (LOBE-sack) is a member of the Education and Labor Committee and is eager to help rewrite the 2001 No Child Left Behind education law. The law, which requires annual testing of public school students to assess their progress, has come under fire for lacking flexibility. "We need to reform it without punishing schools that are not meeting the standards or provide them with more resources so that they can succeed and not fail," he told the Iowa City Press-Citizen in May 2007.

Loebsack is also a strong believer in expanding federal student financial aid. Recalling his own experience relying on loans and grants to pay for his college education, he voted in July 2007 to cut interest rates for undergraduates with subsidized loans. "To me, there's nothing more important than providing each and every child a first-rate education, world-class education, starting in early childhood and continuing through adulthood," he said during a 2007 press conference of House freshmen.

In 2009, he backed President Obama's $787 billion economic stimulus package and from his seat on the labor committee helped draft an expansion of national service programs that Obama sought. The measure sped through the House with bipartisan support.

He also sits on Armed Services, where he is a vocal critic of the Iraq War. He has voted in favor of U.S. troop withdrawal deadlines and benchmarks. After President George W. Bush vetoed a war funding bill in 2007 that would have set a withdrawal goal of March 31, 2008, Loebsack voted against the second version, which lacked a timeline.

Loebsack and Democrat Elijah E. Cummings of Maryland successfully pushed an amendment to the fiscal 2008 defense authorization bill that requires the commander of multinational forces in Iraq and the U.S. ambassador to Iraq to report to Congress every six months on the war's progress. Loebsack said these reports would ensure the American people and Congress are regularly updated on the challenges facing U.S. troops in Iraq.

Iowa has one of the nation's largest percentages of elderly residents, and Loebsack wants to preserve Medicare and Social Security. He said the 2003 Medicare prescription drug law is confusing and must be simplified if not scrapped. He opposed the Bush administration's proposal to set up private accounts under Social Security.

Loebsack works to steer federal funds to his state and district. He joined others in the Iowa delegation in seeking federal aid of all types to help the state recover from devastating 2008 floods, and he worked with Iowa Republican Charles E. Grassley, the top Republican on the Senate Finance panel, to win tax relief later that year for victims of those floods. Loebsack then brought an IRS representative to his district to meet with taxpayers to explain the new law.

Loebsack also wants to ensure his constituents have an enjoyable experience when they visit the Capitol. In 2009, he joined Republican Rep. Mark Steven Kirk of Illinois in protesting tour restrictions instituted when the Capitol Visitor Center opened. In response, visitor center officials opened more slots for staff tours and said they would work to improve the process.

The son of a single mother who struggled with mental illness, Loebsack and his three siblings moved into his maternal grandmother's Sioux City home when he was in the fourth grade. "My grandmother was the rock in many ways," Loebsack said. "I made a decision that I would try to make something out of myself. I can't complain."

At 16, he started working at the Sioux City Waste Treatment Control Plant under a federally funded program providing employment opportunities for poor students.

To help pay for college he used student loans and Social Security survivor benefits from a father he hardly knew and who had died while he was in high school. He also worked during the summers as a janitor at his high school, Sioux City East. Loebsack said the principal offered him a job there so he would have money for college.

He entered Iowa State University thinking he would study meteorology, but eventually earned undergraduate and master's degrees in political science. He earned a doctorate from the University of California at Davis, then moved back to Iowa in 1982 to teach political science at Cornell College.

Loebsack decided to challenge 15-term GOP incumbent Jim Leach for the district seat in 2006. He failed to meet the technical requirements to qualify for the primary, but since no other Democrat filed to run, state law allowed the party to appoint Loebsack as the nominee.

Despite Leach's image as a GOP iconoclast, Loebsack convinced enough voters that a vote for Leach was tantamount to endorsing continued Republican control of Congress. It was one of the most civil campaigns of the mid-term election as both candidates refused to make personal attacks on each other. Loebsack's main argument in the campaign was that the difference between the two was that "he was a Democrat." Loebsack won with about 51 percent of the vote. In 2008, he took 57 percent.

His first piece of legislation after being sworn into the House for the 110th Congress (2007-08) was to rename the Davenport federal courthouse after Leach. While the measure stalled in the Senate, he reintroduced it early in the 111th (2009-10), and the House swiftly passed it again.

KEY VOTES

2008

Yes Delay consideration of Colombia free-trade agreement

Yes Override Bush veto of federal farm and nutrition programs reauthorization bill

No Overhaul surveillance laws and permit dismissal of suits against companies that conducted warrantless wiretapping

Yes Grant mortgage relief to homeowners and funding for Fannie Mae and Freddie Mac

Yes Approve initial $700 billion program to stabilize financial markets

Yes Approve final $700 billion program to stabilize financial markets

Yes Provide $14 billion in loans to automakers

2007

Yes Increase minimum wage by $2.10 an hour

Yes Approve $124.2 billion in emergency war spending and set goal for redeployment of troops from Iraq

No Reject federal contraceptive assistance to international family planning groups

Yes Override Bush veto of $23.2 billion water projects authorization bill

No Implement Peru free-trade agreement

Yes Approve energy policy overhaul with new fuel economy standards

No Clear $473.5 billion omnibus spending bill, including $70 billion for military operations

CQ VOTE STUDIES

	PARTY UNITY		PRESIDENTIAL SUPPORT	
	SUPPORT	OPPOSE	SUPPORT	OPPOSE
2008	97%	3%	13%	87%
2007	97%	3%	3%	97%

INTEREST GROUPS

	AFL-CIO	ADA	CCUS	ACU
2008	100%	90%	56%	0%
2007	96%	95%	58%	0%

IOWA 2

Southeast – Cedar Rapids, Iowa City

Shaped like a backward-facing L, the Democratic-leaning 2nd spreads across cornfields to take in 15 southeastern Iowa counties, bending from Cedar Rapids in its north to Wayne County in its southwest.

Cedar Rapids, in Linn County, is the state's second-most-populous city. Long a grain-processing center, the city now is home to a large Quaker Food and Snacks plant. The city was ravaged by a 500-year flood in 2008. Economic recovery is ongoing, and the city hopes to retain many key employers. A diversified local economy has insulated Cedar Rapids from the worst of nationwide economic downturns. The largest area employer is now a defense contractor, and technology, telecommunications equipment and energy are important sectors here.

About 25 miles south of Cedar Rapids is Iowa City, home to the University of Iowa. The university is by far the city's dominant employer while its hospital system is the second-largest job source. Technology companies and a strong health care industry support the local economy, and the academic community gives the city a strong liberal tilt.

The 2nd's other population center runs along the Mississippi River in the southeast, in Des Moines and Lee counties. Unions retain some influence in Burlington, a manufacturing hub, and riverboat casino-based tourism also contributes to the economy — a share of gaming revenues fund some local economic development. The land in the 2nd District's southwestern arm is predominately rural, depending mainly on corn and soybeans.

The 2nd has a decidedly Democratic tilt, anchored by strongholds in Linn (Cedar Rapids), Johnson (Iowa City), Lee, Des Moines (Burlington) and Wapello counties. Democrat Barack Obama took 60 percent of the 2nd's presidential vote in 2008, his highest percentage statewide.

MAJOR INDUSTRY

Technology, telecommunications, health care, grain processing, higher education

CITIES

Cedar Rapids, 120,758; Iowa City, 62,220; Burlington, 26,839; Marion, 26,294; Ottumwa, 24,998; Muscatine, 22,697

NOTABLE

The Cedar Rapids Museum of Art hosts the largest collection of art by "American Gothic" painter Grant Wood.

Rep. Leonard L. Boswell (D)

Elected 1996; 7th term

CAPITOL OFFICE
225-3806
boswell.house.gov
1427 Longworth Bldg. 20515-1503; fax 225-5608

COMMITTEES
Agriculture
(General Farm Commodities & Risk Management
- chairman)
Transportation & Infrastructure

RESIDENCE
Des Moines

BORN
Jan. 10, 1934; Harrison County, Mo.

RELIGION
Community of Christ

FAMILY
Wife, Dody Boswell; three children

EDUCATION
Graceland College, B.A. 1969 (business
administration)

MILITARY SERVICE
Army, 1956-76

CAREER
Farmer; Army officer

POLITICAL HIGHLIGHTS
Iowa Senate, 1985-97 (president, 1992-97); sought
Democratic nomination for U.S. House, 1986;
Iowa Democratic Central Committee, 1992-96;
Democratic nominee for lieutenant governor, 1994

ELECTION RESULTS

2008 GENERAL

Leonard L. Boswell (D)	176,904	56.4%
Kim Schmett (R)	132,136	42.1%
Frank V. Forrestal (SW)	4,599	1.5%

2008 PRIMARY

Leonard L. Boswell (D)	20,401	61.0%
Ed Fallon (D)	13,035	39.0%

2006 GENERAL

Leonard L. Boswell (D)	114,558	51.8%
Jeff Lamberti (R)	103,166	46.6%
Helen Meyers (SW)	3,426	1.5%

PREVIOUS WINNING PERCENTAGES
2004 (55%); 2002 (53%); 2000 (63%); 1998 (57%);
1996 (49%)

Boswell has long held the respect of his colleagues for his calm demeanor and varied career credentials. A livestock farmer, a Vietnam veteran and a longtime politician, Boswell has been sought by both parties for his expertise on a range of issues, and his tendency to stray has been tolerated by Democratic leaders.

Boswell had a reputation in the state legislature for seeking bipartisan solutions. During his first few terms in Congress, he was considered a moderate-to-conservative Democrat. A Republican majority and his loyalty to the Blue Dog Coalition, a group of fiscally conservative Democrats, fueled his independence from party leaders. He voted for several GOP spending and tax proposals and bills to ban flag desecration and to outlaw a procedure its opponents call "partial birth" abortion. But after he rebuffed an overture from the Republican Party during the 107th Congress (2001-02), he quickly moved closer to the party line — though he'll still go his own way to match his district's views.

He backed most of President Obama's early legislative efforts, voting for an expansion of the State Children's Health Insurance Program, which covers children whose families do not qualify for Medicaid. The bill, signed into law, was similar to two versions that President George W. Bush had vetoed.

Boswell also backed Obama's $787 billion economic stimulus package that became law in February 2009. He also praised Obama for overturning Bush's ban on federal funding for embryonic stem cell research.

A member of the Agriculture Committee since he entered Congress in 1997, Boswell is now chairman of its General Farm Commodities and Risk Management Subcommittee. He helped craft a portion of the Democrats' five-year farm bill reauthorization in 2008, including improvements and modernizations to the federal milk marketing order system and an extension to a program that helps dairy farmers pay for losses when the price of milk dips below a government target.

Concerned about unfair and costly arbitration of disputes with meatpackers, Boswell successfully inserted an amendment into the farm bill that limits mandatory arbitration agreements in livestock contracts and allows producers to settle disputes locally rather than in the jurisdiction of the company's headquarters. He had voted against the House farm bill in 2001 because it didn't include similar language, although he ultimately supported the final version negotiated with the Senate, declaring it the "best deal" possible for Iowa farmers.

He also uses his Agriculture seat to advocate the use of ethanol. Even before alternative fuels were part of the everyday vernacular, he championed research efforts in his home state to develop them from various crops, including corn.

As a member of the Transportation and Infrastructure Committee, Boswell will take part in a renewal of the 2005 surface transportation law. He said he will try to steer funds to areas in the Hawkeye State devastated by flooding and tornadoes in early 2008. "There is no way a community can pick up after something like that. But in a country like ours, they don't have to. We help," Boswell said after flying over the hard-hit areas in his personal plane. In June 2008, he supported a supplemental spending bill that included $2.7 billion for flood and tornado relief. From his Transportation seat, he has also sought to improve passenger aviation service to Des Moines, which like many midsize cities must deal with limited service options and high air fares.

A member of the Select Intelligence Committee until the 111th Congress (2009-10), he pushed in 2008 for the Senate rewrite of the Foreign Intelligence Surveillance Act to grant retroactive legal immunity to telecommunications companies that cooperated with warrantless government surveillance. "I don't see any point in going on a witch hunt against the telecommunications companies," Boswell said. He was one of 21 Democrats who sent a letter to Speaker Nancy Pelosi of California asking her to endorse the Senate version. The final version, which Bush signed into law in July 2008, effectively grants retroactive liability to the companies.

Boswell in 2002 had crossed party lines to support a resolution authorizing Bush to use force against Iraq. It is a vote Boswell later said he regretted. In early 2007, he opposed Bush's plan to send more than 21,000 additional U.S. combat troops to Iraq and supported an emergency war spending bill that set a goal for redeployment of troops from Iraq by March 2008.

Boswell understands the hardships created by combat. Drafted into the Army on his 22nd birthday, he served two one-year stints as an assault helicopter pilot in Vietnam. In 2007, he sponsored a suicide-prevention bill that mandated the screening of all veterans for suicide risk factors and the tracking of at-risk veterans at Veterans Affairs Department medical facilities.

In 2005, he spent 11 weeks recovering from a non-cancerous tumor in his stomach and lost 70 pounds. Three years later, he underwent surgery that "made some corrections" to the earlier procedure.

Raised in a farming family in southern Iowa, Boswell was destined to work in the state's rolling cornfields. But that path was derailed when he was drafted into the Army shortly after getting married in 1956. He would later go to officer training school and achieve the rank of lieutenant colonel.

Boswell eventually returned home to raise cattle on 475 acres in his native Decatur County, where he still raises about 140 cows a year. He also earned a degree in business administration and became involved in local politics, spending 12 years in the Iowa Senate and rising to become its president.

In 1996, he ran for the U.S. House, seeking the seat of Republican Jim Ross Lightfoot, who was running for the Senate. He won the primary easily. In the general election, he won the endorsement of the Iowa Farm Bureau and eked out a win against Mike Mahaffey, a county prosecutor and former state GOP chairman. At 63, he was the oldest House freshman in 1997.

Redistricting in 2002 compelled him to move to Des Moines, and he had to show his more liberal constituents he could serve their interests, too. He has since prevailed, albeit with less impressive margins for an incumbent. In 2004, he broke a pledge to serve only four terms by running for — and winning — a fifth, with 55 percent of the vote. He took 52 percent in 2006. In 2008, he won with 56 percent over Republican Kim Schmett, a former congressional aide.

KEY VOTES

2008

Yes Delay consideration of Colombia free-trade agreement

Yes Override Bush veto of federal farm and nutrition programs reauthorization bill

Yes Overhaul surveillance laws and permit dismissal of suits against companies that conducted warrantless wiretapping

?   Grant mortgage relief to homeowners and funding for Fannie Mae and Freddie Mac

Yes Approve initial $700 billion program to stabilize financial markets

Yes Approve final $700 billion program to stabilize financial markets

Yes Provide $14 billion in loans to automakers

2007

Yes Increase minimum wage by $2.10 an hour

Yes Approve $124.2 billion in emergency war spending and set goal for redeployment of troops from Iraq

No Reject federal contraceptive assistance to international family planning groups

Yes Override Bush veto of $23.2 billion water projects authorization bill

Yes Implement Peru free-trade agreement

Yes Approve energy policy overhaul with new fuel economy standards

No Clear $473.5 billion omnibus spending bill, including $70 billion for military operations

CQ VOTE STUDIES

	PARTY UNITY		PRESIDENTIAL SUPPORT	
	SUPPORT	OPPOSE	SUPPORT	OPPOSE
2008	98%	2%	17%	83%
2007	93%	7%	6%	94%
2006	78%	22%	47%	53%
2005	82%	18%	39%	61%
2004	83%	17%	39%	61%

INTEREST GROUPS

	AFL-CIO	ADA	CCUS	ACU
2008	100%	95%	61%	4%
2007	96%	90%	60%	8%
2006	86%	70%	67%	44%
2005	93%	60%	55%	32%
2004	87%	80%	55%	20%

IOWA 3
Central and east central — Des Moines

Squeezed between the state's other four districts, the 3rd is Iowa's only district not to border another state and is in some ways a microcosm of the Hawkeye State. It includes relatively well-off urban and suburban areas, as well as rural counties, industrial cities and scattered towns.

Almost two-thirds of the district's residents live in Des Moines or surrounding Polk County. Unlike the rest of Iowa's urban centers, the capital city is not dependent on agriculture and the economy is stable without it. Des Moines' economy experienced decades of growth, and the city is an anchor for insurance and financial companies. Some firms, such as Wells Fargo Financial, have headquarters in the city, and others have regional offices in the metropolitan area. Despite recent nationwide financial downturns, a bustling health care industry complements the smaller, but significant, manufacturing industry. The city's economy also is the hub of state government.

Des Moines' modern skyline includes the Iowa Events Center — a four-venue, multipurpose complex under one interconnected roof and home to the city's minor league basketball and hockey teams — which bolsters the area's economy. The city's 3 miles of skywalk allows residents to move quickly among new downtown developments, commercial centers and historical areas, such as East Village, where the state Capitol is located.

The rest of the 3rd takes on a more rural flavor, and no county outside of Polk has more than 40,000 residents. Des Moines' black and Hispanic residents help make the 3rd Iowa's most minority-populated district, although whites still comprise 90 percent of the district's population. The influence of Des Moines and surrounding Polk County gives the 3rd its slight Democratic lean overall. Democrat Barack Obama took 54 percent of the district's vote in the 2008 presidential election.

MAJOR INDUSTRY
Insurance, health care, government, agriculture, manufacturing

CITIES
Des Moines, 198,682; West Des Moines (pt.), 42,525; Urbandale (pt.), 28,745; Ankeny, 27,117; Newton, 15,579

NOTABLE
Each year, more than 1 million tourists visit the Amana Colonies, seven villages originally settled in 1855 by the Community of True Inspiration.

Rep. Tom Latham (R)

CAPITOL OFFICE
225-5476
www.house.gov/latham
2217 Rayburn Bldg. 20515-1504; fax 225-3301

COMMITTEES
Appropriations

RESIDENCE
Ames

BORN
July 14, 1948; Hampton, Iowa

RELIGION
Lutheran

FAMILY
Wife, Kathy Latham; three children

EDUCATION
Wartburg College, attended 1967; Iowa State U.,
attended 1967-70 (agriculture & business)

CAREER
Seed company executive; insurance agency
marketing representative; insurance agent;
bank teller

POLITICAL HIGHLIGHTS
Franklin County Republican Party chairman,
1984-91

ELECTION RESULTS

2008 GENERAL

Tom Latham (R)	185,458	60.6%
Becky Greenwald (D)	120,746	39.4%

2008 PRIMARY

Tom Latham (R)	unopposed

2006 GENERAL

Tom Latham (R)	120,984	57.2%
Selden E. Spencer (D)	90,359	42.8%

PREVIOUS WINNING PERCENTAGES
2004 (61%); 2002 (55%); 2000 (69%); 1998 (99%);
1996 (65%); 1994 (61%)

Elected 1994; 8th term

Latham spends much of each year in Washington, but his roots are deeply planted in the rich soil of Iowa, where he and his brothers own three farms and a seed company. He has spent his entire life in the Hawkeye State and assiduously looks out for its interests in Congress.

Now the dean of the five-member Iowa House delegation, he is a close friend and ally of House Minority Leader John A. Boehner of Ohio. Since the 1990s, the two have met regularly in an informal dinner club that includes two former GOP House members now in the Senate, Richard M. Burr of North Carolina and Saxby Chambliss of Georgia.

He typically supports the GOP agenda on national policy, but he doesn't hesitate to stray when his state's needs are at stake. With a good portion of his district dependent on agriculture, he voted to override President George W. Bush's veto of a new five-year farm bill in 2008, even though he disliked some of it. And unlike many in the GOP, he is an ardent and unapologetic advocate of earmarks, using his seat on the Appropriations Committee to go after funding set-asides for projects not just in his district, but his state as well. As the only Iowan on House Appropriations, Latham said he has "a tremendous amount of pressure from all five districts . . . to help out with their projects."

Latham also turned aside appeals by Boehner and other leaders in fall 2008 to support a $700 billion package to shore up the nation's financial services sector. In explaining his opposition to the measure, which became law, he quoted a constituent whom he said had called his office: "The people out here in the heartland see this bill and bailout as a result of Washington talking to Washington — and not talking and listening to the real people beyond the Beltway." He felt just as uncomfortable about an auto bailout bill offered that December. That bill died in the Senate.

Yet Latham, ranking Republican on Appropriations' Transportation, Housing and Urban Development Subcommittee, voted with his party to oppose President Obama's economic stimulus package, which directed billions in funding for "shovel-ready" transportation and infrastructure projects around the country. And while Democrats pushed for the bill to require money to be distributed quickly, Latham said, "We're asking our states to make hurried judgments."

Likewise, he voted against a $410 billion catchall spending bill for fiscal 2009, but faced criticism from Democrats for opposing the bill after helping to include more than $24.5 million for local projects. He also serves on the Appropriations subcommittee on agriculture. He flew into action in mid-2007 when rumors surfaced that panel Chairwoman Rosa DeLauro, a Connecticut Democrat, might cut earmarks for land-grant colleges by as much as 50 percent in her fiscal 2008 spending bill. Latham lives in Ames, home to Iowa State University, one of the nation's first land-grant schools, and he vowed to fight any funding cuts for the institutions. He wound up steering nearly $4 million to the university. Over the years, Latham also has directed millions of dollars to the National Animal Disease Center, a livestock health research facility in Ames. The facility tests for diseases such as mad cow and anthrax.

Although he makes no apologies for going after earmarks, Latham in August 2007 had to correct a March 15 letter to the Appropriations Committee seeking what became a $2 million earmark in the fiscal 2008 Defense spending bill to develop a monoclonal anthrax antibody. His request had mistakenly named Ervin Technical Associates, a boutique lobbying firm located on Capitol Hill, as the intended recipient of the earmark. But the money actually was intended for PharmAthene, which paid the lobbying firm $200,000 a year. Latham blamed a staff error and corrected the request after news reports surfaced about a colleague's similar error.

Iowa has one of the highest percentages of National Guard and reserve troops that have been deployed to Iraq, and Latham has fought for their interests. In 2005, he and Republican Sen. Lindsey Graham of South Carolina joined forces on a bill to give those troops the same health benefits as regular-duty soldiers. Critics said it was too costly, but after a heated debate, the House passed the bill as part of the annual defense authorization bill for fiscal 2006.

Latham grew up doing farm chores and helping in the family seed business. He attended Wartburg College about 50 miles east of his hometown of Alexander, then went to Iowa State University, about 60 miles south in Ames. He returned to Alexander, where he remained until moving to Ames in late 2006.

He said his interest in politics was sparked by a trip he took to Russia and Poland in 1990 as a member of a farm delegation. He was appalled at the primitive agricultural methods and machinery in the former communist countries. He remembers one Polish farmer who tearfully told him that farmers hadn't owned their land since the Nazis seized it in World War II.

In Iowa, Latham chaired the Franklin County Republican Party for seven years but rebuffed entreaties to run for the legislature because the seasonal nature of the seed business conflicted with legislative sessions. In 1994, however, when GOP Rep. Fred Grandy gave up the 5th District seat to seek the governorship, Latham decided to run. He breezed to election.

He was returned to the House easily in three subsequent elections, but in 2002 new district lines drafted by a nonpartisan state agency made the district more competitive. The new map put Latham's home in the 4th District, while more than half his constituents lived in the 5th.

Latham decided to run in the 4th anyway. He was well known to many of its residents, owing to his days as a traveling farm-seed salesman. He won by almost 12 percentage points against Democrat John Norris, a former state party chairman. He cruised to re-election in 2004, winning by almost 22 points and was re-elected by a still-comfortable margin of 14 percentage points in 2006. Latham was mentioned as a possible 2008 challenger to veteran Democratic Sen. Tom Harkin, but he opted to stay where he was in a year that did not look bright for Republicans. He sailed to an eighth term, taking 61 percent of the vote against Becky Greenwald, a Democratic activist who had worked in sales and marketing for seed companies and had support from EMILY's List and the national Democratic Party.

KEY VOTES

2008

No Delay consideration of Colombia free-trade agreement

Yes Override Bush veto of federal farm and nutrition programs reauthorization bill

Yes Overhaul surveillance laws and permit dismissal of suits against companies that conducted warrantless wiretapping

No Grant mortgage relief to homeowners and funding for Fannie Mae and Freddie Mac

No Approve initial $700 billion program to stabilize financial markets

No Approve final $700 billion program to stabilize financial markets

No Provide $14 billion in loans to automakers

2007

Yes Increase minimum wage by $2.10 an hour

No Approve $124.2 billion in emergency war spending and set goal for redeployment of troops from Iraq

Yes Reject federal contraceptive assistance to international family planning groups

Yes Override Bush veto of $23.2 billion water projects authorization bill

Yes Implement Peru free-trade agreement

Yes Approve energy policy overhaul with new fuel economy standards

Yes Clear $473.5 billion omnibus spending bill, including $70 billion for military operations

CQ VOTE STUDIES

	PARTY UNITY		PRESIDENTIAL SUPPORT	
	SUPPORT	OPPOSE	SUPPORT	OPPOSE
2008	90%	10%	63%	37%
2007	86%	14%	71%	29%
2006	95%	5%	97%	3%
2005	96%	4%	87%	13%
2004	92%	8%	88%	12%

INTEREST GROUPS

	AFL-CIO	ADA	CCUS	ACU
2008	20%	30%	89%	88%
2007	25%	20%	95%	84%
2006	21%	5%	100%	84%
2005	20%	5%	93%	84%
2004	20%	10%	100%	72%

IOWA 4
North and central — Ames, Mason City

The vast 4th District takes up most of the state's northern border and dips deeply south, hooking around the state capital of Des Moines (in the 3rd District), to reach Dallas, Madison and Warren counties.

Ames, nestled along Squaw Creek and the Skunk River, is about 30 miles north of the capital city and represents the district's largest population center. It is home to Iowa State University, and the university has become a renowned agricultural engineering institution. The university's influence gives Story County a strong Democratic lean.

Rural farming communities and smaller cities make up the rest of the 4th. Marshalltown, east of Ames, is home to a large meatpacking industry, which has brought Hispanic immigrants to the city. Mason City, the 4th's second-most-populous city, depends on manufacturing. Fort Dodge in Webster County is home to trucking firms, gypsum factories and veterinary pharmaceuticals. A rise in corn-based ethanol production brought business to the 4th, but deepening economic downturns nationwide and rising fuel costs concern local corn farmers.

Southwest of Ames, Dallas County is a big exception to Iowa's generally sluggish population growth. Suburban growth west of Des Moines fueled Dallas' sustained population increase since the 1990s, and the county has a median household income well above district and state averages.

The 4th District divides Republican-leaning western Iowa and Democratic-leaning eastern Iowa, and the two parties each hold sway among registered voters in half of the district's 28 counties. Recently, the 4th District has given less support to Republican presidential candidates — Democrat Barack Obama took 53 percent of the vote here in the 2008 presidential election four years after Republican George W. Bush won 51 percent of the presidential vote.

MAJOR INDUSTRY
Meatpacking, health care, veterinary pharmaceuticals, agriculture

CITIES
Ames, 50,731; Mason City, 29,172; Marshalltown, 26,009

NOTABLE
In 1959, Buddy Holly, Ritchie Valens and J.P. "The Big Bopper" Richardson died in a plane crash near Clear Lake; Madison County's covered bridges were popularized in Robert James Waller's book.

Rep. Steve King (R)

Elected 2002; 4th term

CAPITOL OFFICE
225-4426
www.house.gov/steveking
1131 Longworth Bldg. 20515-1505; fax 225-3193

COMMITTEES
Agriculture
Judiciary
Small Business

RESIDENCE
Kiron

BORN
May 28, 1949; Storm Lake, Iowa

RELIGION
Roman Catholic

FAMILY
Wife, Marilyn King; three children

EDUCATION
Northwest Missouri State U., attended 1967-70

CAREER
Construction company owner

POLITICAL HIGHLIGHTS
Iowa Senate, 1997-2002

ELECTION RESULTS

2008 GENERAL

Steve King (R)	159,430	59.8%
Rob Hubler (D)	99,601	37.4%
Victor Vara (I)	7,406	2.8%

2008 PRIMARY

Steve King (R)	unopposed

2006 GENERAL

Steve King (R)	105,712	58.4%
Joyce Schulte (D)	64,516	35.7%
Roy Nielsen (X)	8,194	4.5%
Cheryl L. Brodersen (X)	2,490	1.4%

PREVIOUS WINNING PERCENTAGES
2004 (63%); 2002 (62%)

King is one of the more boisterous members of his party's conservative wing. He attempts to stir up debates with his offbeat remarks, and agitates Democratic leaders by offering provacative legislation just to make his point. "I don't capitulate easy," he once said. "My job is to shake things up and move the political center to the right."

He has called former Communist-baiting Sen. Joseph R. McCarthy a hero and has questioned courts' authority when he doesn't agree with their decisions. During the 2008 campaign, he opined that terrorists would be "dancing in the streets" if Democratic Sen. Barack Obama of Illinois were to be elected president in part because he has an Arab-sounding middle name, Hussein.

King has been a consistent vote against President Obama's early legislative agenda, opposing a $787 billion economic stimulus measure and a $410 billion catchall spending bill for fiscal 2009. A strong supporter of the George W. Bush administration's policy in Iraq, he introduced a "Victory in Iraq" resolution in March 2009. He admitted it was an attempt to urge Obama not to pull U.S. troops out of the conflict too quickly. And when Obama issued an executive order to reinstate federal funding of embryonic stem cell research that month, King said, "President Obama has decided...that there will be no respect for conscientious objections from life-loving, tax-paying Americans."

King's antics are on most prominent display on the Judiciary Committee, where he is the top Republican on the immigration subcommittee and seeks to crack down on illegal immigration. He opposed a bill in May 2008 that would create a new visa category specifically for fashion models. "This bill should be called the Ugly American Act. It's based on the premise that there aren't enough attractive people in the United States," he said.

Later that year, he opposed a measure designed to help foreign nationals obtain legal residency when their U.S. citizen spouse or parent dies before their applications are cleared. King said he was worried about what might happen if, for example, a U.S. service member got married while intoxicated in Bangkok, and then died. That bill did not reach the House floor.

King is sometimes confused with his friend, former Colorado Republican Rep. Tom Tancredo, who ran for president in 2008 on his tough immigration views. King supported a 2006 law calling for construction of a 700-mile fence along the U.S. border with Mexico. In urging support, he built a small model out of wood and cardboard to demonstrate how it could be done.

King also has pushed for English to be the nation's official language. As an Iowa state senator he sponsored a successful bill making English the state's official language. In 2007, he sued Democratic Gov. Chet Culver and Secretary of State Michael Mauro, charging they violated the law by providing voter registration forms in other languages. His bill to make English the nation's official language has come to naught but he reintroduces it every Congress.

King is just as persistent in his battle on other issues. After the courts rebuffed Congress' attempt in March 2005 to intervene in the case of Terri Schiavo, a severely brain-damaged Florida woman being kept alive by a feeding tube, King asserted Congress had the power to retaliate against the courts that allowed the tube to be removed. "We have the constitutional authority to eliminate any and all inferior courts," he told The Washington Post, referring to district and circuit courts.

Supreme Court Justice Sandra Day O'Connor the following month invited King and a few other lawmakers to lunch, but he said the meeting didn't change his mind.

In July 2005, he proposed cutting the Supreme Court's budget by $1.5 million. He said the move, ultimately unsuccessful, was a symbolic protest against the "injustice done" by the court's ruling allowing the city of New London, Conn., to move on its plan to replace a faded residential neighborhood with offices for research and development, a conference hotel, new homes and a pedestrian "riverwalk."

King was once accused by a liberal Democrat of McCarthy-like tactics. He responded by praising the late senator from Wisconsin as a "hero for America," though McCarthy's outings of communists in the 1950s destroyed lives and careers.

King has had some luck with district-focused legislation. As an Agriculture Committee member, he inserted in a 2003 energy bill a provision granting a tax credit for small ethanol producers. It was aimed at making the half-dozen small producers in his district more competitive with ethanol giants Archer Daniels Midland and Cargill. On one of the few times he dissented from President Bush, King favored an override to Bush's 2008 veto of the reauthorization of the farm bill. He also sits on the Small Business Committee.

King has deep roots in the district. His maternal great-grandparents were among the original homesteaders after the Civil War.

In 1975, he started the King Construction Co., a small earth-moving firm that specialized in soil erosion solutions for farmers. His annual sales were about $700,000. (His son now runs the business.) He said he became increasingly angry at rising federal taxes, government regulations and Internal Revenue Service audits of his business. "After they picked my pocket, I went to work and sat there every day, thinking about how to get rid of them," he said.

In 1996, he won a seat in the Iowa Senate and became known for a culturally conservative agenda. His "God and Country" law requires Iowa public schools to teach that the United States has "derived its strength from biblical values." King fought an executive order in 2000 by Democratic Gov. Tom Vilsack banning discrimination against homosexuals in state jobs, arguing it gave preferential treatment to certain groups of people. He took the fight to the Iowa Supreme Court and won, overturning Vilsack's order.

Redistricting put 5th District Rep. Tom Latham's home in another district in 2002. In the 5th District King faced primary competition, but when no one got the required vote percentage the race was decided by a nominating convention. King prevailed and then won the general with 62 percent. He has been re-elected comfortably since, in spite of newspaper editorials strongly urging he be replaced. "There isn't enough space in this editorial to list all the times King has embarrassed Iowa," the Des Moines Register wrote in 2008.

KEY VOTES

2008

No	Delay consideration of Colombia free-trade agreement
Yes	Override Bush veto of federal farm and nutrition programs reauthorization bill
Yes	Overhaul surveillance laws and permit dismissal of suits against companies that conducted warrantless wiretapping
No	Grant mortgage relief to homeowners and funding for Fannie Mae and Freddie Mac
No	Approve initial $700 billion program to stabilize financial markets
No	Approve final $700 billion program to stabilize financial markets
No	Provide $14 billion in loans to automakers

2007

No	Increase minimum wage by $2.10 an hour
No	Approve $124.2 billion in emergency war spending and set goal for redeployment of troops from Iraq
Yes	Reject federal contraceptive assistance to international family planning groups
Yes	Override Bush veto of $23.2 billion water projects authorization bill
Yes	Implement Peru free-trade agreement
?	Approve energy policy overhaul with new fuel economy standards
Yes	Clear $473.5 billion omnibus spending bill, including $70 billion for military operations

CQ VOTE STUDIES

	PARTY UNITY		PRESIDENTIAL SUPPORT	
	SUPPORT	OPPOSE	SUPPORT	OPPOSE
2008	97%	3%	77%	23%
2007	99%	1%	89%	11%
2006	96%	4%	83%	17%
2005	98%	2%	87%	13%
2004	99%	1%	85%	15%

INTEREST GROUPS

	AFL-CIO	ADA	CCUS	ACU
2008	0%	5%	83%	96%
2007	4%	0%	75%	100%
2006	21%	15%	93%	100%
2005	13%	0%	93%	100%
2004	13%	5%	100%	96%

IOWA 5

West – Sioux City, Council Bluffs

The 32-county 5th takes in miles of fertile soil and gently undulating hills across the western part of the state. This bountiful land has allowed the region to remain more like the Iowa of old than any other part of the state. The 5th has the most farmland in Iowa and grows the most corn and soybeans in the state.

Sioux City is the district's largest metropolitan center and has a rich link to America's history — Lewis and Clark passed through it on their way to the Pacific Northwest. Bordering South Dakota and Nebraska to its west, Sioux City has become a major trading center for the tri-state area. Home of the original annual "Corn Palaces" in the late 19th century, Sioux City is now a distribution center for the state's primary crop and also for the local meatpacking industry, which is supported by livestock raised locally. Growth of alternative-fuel production was a boon for the area, and more than 30 ethanol plants operate within 90 miles of the city, but rising costs in the corn-based fuel industry and nationwide economic downturns have caused uncertainty here.

Council Bluffs, nicknamed "Iowa's Leading Edge," also is located on the state's western border, farther south along the Missouri River that divides it from Omaha, Neb. Public improvement projects underway since the mid-1990s attracted health care and distribution businesses to the city, but layoffs have affected all economic sectors. City officials plan to continue investment in infrastructure and riverfront development. Gaming became big business, and three of the city's major employers are casinos. Other residents commute across the river to work for Omaha businesses.

The Corn Belt farmland found in the rest of the 5th makes it Iowa's strongest Republican district. Twenty-five of the district's 32 counties favor the GOP, and Republican John McCain took 55 percent of the 2008 presidential vote in the 5th, the only Iowa district he won.

MAJOR INDUSTRY
Agriculture, meatpacking, distribution, gaming

CITIES
Sioux City, 85,013; Council Bluffs, 58,268; Spencer, 11,317

NOTABLE
The Lewis and Clark Interpretive Center is located in Sioux City; The Union Pacific Railroad Museum is located in Council Bluffs.

Gov. Mark Parkinson (D)

Assumed office: April 28, 2009, due to the appointment of Kathleen Sebelius, D, to be Health and Human Services secretary
Length of term: 4 years
Term expires: 1/11
Salary: $110,707
Phone: (785) 296-3232

Residence: Olathe
Born: June 24, 1957; Wichita, Kan.
Religion: Methodist
Family: Wife, Stacy Parkinson; three children
Education: Wichita State U., B.A. 1980 (secondary education – political science); U. of Kansas, J.D. 1984
Career: Lawyer; nursing home owner
Political highlights: Kan. House, 1991-93 (served as a Republican); Kan. Senate, 1993-97 (served as a Republican); Kan. Republican Party chairman, 1999-2003; lieutenant governor, 2007-09

Recent election results:
2006 GENERAL

Kathleen Sebelius (D)	491,993	57.9%
Jim Barnett (R)	343,586	40.4%
Carl Kramer (LIBERT)	8,896	1.0%

Lt. Gov. Troy Findley (D)

Assumed office: 2009
Length of term: 4 years
Term expires: 1/11
Salary: $31,313
Phone: (785) 296-2213

LEGISLATURE

Legislature: January to spring, limit of 90 days in even-numbered years

Senate: 40 members, 4-year terms
2009 ratios: 31 R, 9 D; 35 men, 5 women
Salary: $89/day in session; $109/day expenses
Phone: (785) 296-7344

House: 125 members, 2-year terms
2009 ratios: 77 R, 48 D; 91 men, 34 women
Salary: 89/day in session; $109/day expenses
Phone: (785) 296-7633

TERM LIMITS

Governor: 2 terms
Senate: No
House: No

URBAN STATISTICS

CITY	POPULATION
Wichita	344,284
Overland Park	149,080
Kansas City	146,866
Topeka	122,377

REGISTERED VOTERS

Republican	44%
Unaffiliated/others	28%
Democrat	28%

POPULATION

2008 population (est.)	2,802,134
2000 population	2,688,418
1990 population	2,477,574
Percent change (1990-2000)	+8.5%
Rank among states (2008)	33

Median age	35.2
Born in state	59.5%
Foreign born	5%
Violent crime rate	389/100,000
Poverty level	9.9%
Federal workers	25,639
Military	29,103

ELECTIONS

STATE ELECTION OFFICIAL
(785) 296-4561
DEMOCRATIC PARTY
(785) 234-0425
REPUBLICAN PARTY
(785) 234-3456

MISCELLANEOUS

Web: www.accesskansas.org
Capital: Topeka

U.S. CONGRESS

Senate: 2 Republicans
House: 3 Republicans, 1 Democrats

2000 Census Statistics by District

DIST.	2008 VOTE FOR PRESIDENT OBAMA	MCCAIN	WHITE	BLACK	ASIAN	HISP	MEDIAN INCOME	WHITE COLLAR	BLUE COLLAR	SERVICE INDUSTRY	OVER 64	UNDER 18	COLLEGE EDUCATION	RURAL	SQ. MILES
1	30%	69%	85%	2%	1%	11%	$34,869	53%	31%	16%	16%	26%	18%	48%	57,373
2	43	55	87	5	1	4	$37,855	58	27	16	14	25	23	40	14,134
3	51	48	80	9	3	7	$51,118	70	17	12	10	27	39	5	778
4	40	58	81	7	2	7	$40,917	57	29	14	13	28	23	21	9,531
STATE	42	57	83	6	2	7	$40,624	60	26	14	13	27	26	29	81,815
U.S.	53	46	69	12	4	13	$41,994	60	25	15	12	26	24	21	3,537,438

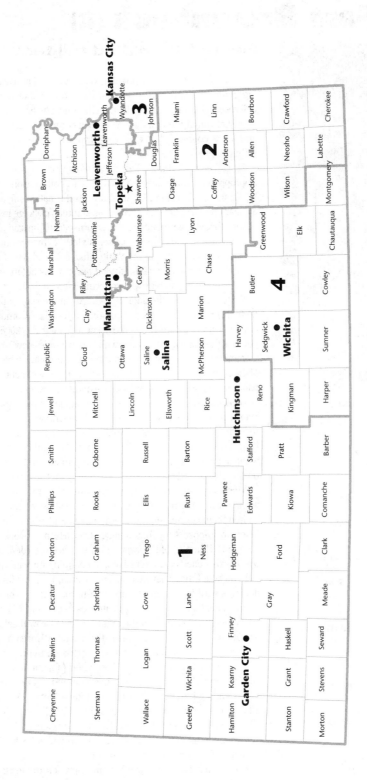

Sen. Sam Brownback (R)

Elected 1996; 2nd full term

A social conservative, Brownback has centered his career on an unswerving commitment to human rights. He opposes abortion, embryonic stem cell research and assisted suicide. His concerns branch into foreign policy; he rejects anything that doesn't offer a compassionate view of immigrants and wants countries like China and Iran held more accountable for human rights abuses.

He can be just as unbending about his fiscal conservatism. A member of the Appropriations Committee, he voted against both versions of President George W. Bush's $700 billion plan to shore up the nation's financial industry and against President Obama's economic stimulus package in early 2009. "I don't believe that we can spend our way to prosperity," he said of the stimulus.

Brownback had hoped his self-styled "compassionate conservatism" would earn him a shot at the White House, but his run for the 2008 Republican presidential nomination fizzled out months before the first votes were cast. He is sticking to his own two-term pledge and eyeing a run for governor.

With one foot out the door, Brownback at the start of the 111th Congress (2009-10) relinquished his position on the Judiciary Committee when Democrats became entitled to another seat following the 2008 elections. But he pursues the same agenda, even while he examines new issues serving on the Commerce, Science and Transportation Committee, which is rewriting part of the 2005 surface transportation law, and the Energy and Natural Resources panel, tasked with drafting global warming legislation.

Brownback considers politics a calling, and his religious beliefs inform everything he does. A former evangelical Christian who is now a Catholic, he is driven by a philosophy he calls "pro-life, whole life." His reverence for life goes well beyond opposing abortion. He said that "pro-life doesn't end when a child is born. It extends throughout life, and it extends everywhere on the planet, and it extends to everybody on the planet."

Many of Brownback's views run counter to those of Obama. But he worked with Obama in the Senate on several issues, including a call for the United States to condemn the genocide in Sudan's Darfur region and legislation to impose sanctions against Iran. He also worked with then-Sen. Joseph R. Biden Jr. of Delaware, now the vice president, in 2008 to expand a law Brownback co-authored in 2000 banning human trafficking.

Brownback has sharply criticized China, both for its business-as-usual dealings with Sudan and for its own human rights abuses. "China is the greatest enabler of human rights abuses in the world," he said in mid-2008.

To the consternation of the White House, Brownback also held up confirmation of a new U.S. ambassador to South Korea for months in 2008, criticizing the Bush administration's approach to six-party talks on North Korean nuclear disarmament. And when Obama nominated Christopher Hill in March 2009 to serve as ambassador to Iraq, Brownback accused Hill of misleading him when he was assistant secretary of State for East Asian affairs in promising to raise human rights in talks with North Korea.

When Obama picked Kansas Democratic Gov. Kathleen Sebelius as his Health and Human Services secretary, Brownback joined his Kansas GOP colleague Pat Roberts in praising her.

Brownback favors a more lenient approach to illegal immigrants than many in his party. He voted for a comprehensive immigration bill in 2006 even though most conservatives condemned it as amnesty for illegal immigrants. "They did not come here for handouts. Like us, they are looking for

CAPITOL OFFICE
224-6521
brownback.senate.gov
303 Hart Bldg. 20510-1604; fax 228-1265

COMMITTEES
Appropriations
Commerce, Science & Transportation
Energy & Natural Resources
Special Aging
Joint Economic - ranking member

RESIDENCE
Topeka

BORN
Sept. 12, 1956; Garnett, Kan.

RELIGION
Roman Catholic

FAMILY
Wife, Mary Brownback; five children

EDUCATION
Kansas State U., B.S. 1979 (agricultural economics); U. of Kansas, J.D. 1982

CAREER
College instructor; lawyer; White House fellow

POLITICAL HIGHLIGHTS
Kan. secretary of Agriculture, 1986-93;
U.S. House, 1995-96

ELECTION RESULTS

2004 GENERAL

Sam Brownback (R)	780,863	69.2%
Lee Jones (D)	310,337	27.5%
Steven A. Rosile (LIBERT)	21,842	1.9%
George Cook (REF)	15,980	1.4%

2004 PRIMARY

Sam Brownback (R)	286,839	87.0%
Arch Naramore (R)	42,880	13.0%

PREVIOUS WINNING PERCENTAGES
1998 (65%); 1996 Special Election (54%);
1994 House Election (66%)

the American dream," Brownback said. But he backed away from the measure two years later as GOP voters demanded a get-tough approach.

He also has been a strong supporter of prisoner rehabilitation programs. In the early days of his presidential campaign, he spent a weekend at the Louisiana State Penitentiary in Angola, La., spreading his message of faith to inmates. Early in 2009, when Obama made clear his decision to close the military detention facility on the U.S. naval base at Guantánamo Bay, Cuba, he lobbied the president not to relocate the prisoners to Fort Leavenworth in his state out of concern the detainees would harm the base's "educational mission," particularly for foreign students.

Although Brownback has supported the Iraq War, he initially spoke out against Bush's 2007 plan to send more than 21,000 additional U.S. combat troops to Iraq. Later he said, "I was wrong" about the surge.

His views usually are in line with the GOP right, especially on social issues. He is a leading critic of medical research using embryonic stem cells, which he equates with taking a human life. When Obama overturned Bush's restrictions on stem cell research in March 2009, Brownback was sharply critical. "If an embryo is a life, and I believe strongly that it is life, then no government has the right to sanction their destruction for research purposes," he said.

Every Congress he introduces the Unborn Child Pain Awareness Act, requiring women who seek an abortion after 20 weeks of pregnancy to sign a form saying they have been informed that a fetus can feel pain. He also has sponsored a bill to make human cloning a crime and championed a constitutional amendment to ban same-sex marriage.

When Brownback started his career in Congress, he was known as a small-government crusader and a leader of the young, change-minded Republicans in the watershed election of 1994. A doctor's diagnosis in 1995 of melanoma, which required two surgeries, launched Brownback on a spiritual odyssey. "I began to examine my life in a new light," he said. Brownback had been raised a Methodist, but he and his wife joined a nondenominational evangelical church. He converted to Catholicism in 2002 with the help of former Pennsylvania Republican Sen. Rick Santorum.

Brownback and his three siblings grew up in a white, one-story farmhouse in Parker, Kan., (population 280) where his family grew corn, wheat, soybean, cattle and hogs. His own economic standing changed dramatically when he married Mary Stauffer, heiress to a family media fortune that included the Topeka Capital-Journal and several TV stations. He regularly ranks as the Kansas delegation's wealthiest member, with publicly disclosed assets between $1.6 million and $7.2 million. The Brownbacks had three children and adopted two more, a girl from China and a boy from Guatemala.

Brownback was student body president at Kansas State University and a national officer of the Future Farmers of America. He was Kansas' secretary of agriculture, an appointed post, for about six years before running for office. In 1994 he ran for Democratic Rep. Jim Slattery's seat in the 2nd District when Slattery ran for governor. In that year's GOP tidal wave, Brownback easily defeated Democratic candidate John Carlin, a former two-term governor.

He declared for the Senate in 1996 the day after GOP presidential candidate Bob Dole announced his resignation. But GOP Gov. Bill Graves appointed Lt. Gov. Sheila Frahm to fill the seat until a special election. Brownback beat her in the primary by 13 percentage points, then took 54 percent in the special against Democrat Jill Docking. He was easily re-elected in 1998 and 2004.

He announced his presidential bid in January 2007, a year before the Iowa precinct caucuses, saying he believed Americans were hungry for a conservative in office. He dropped out 10 months later after pouring time and money into Iowa to little avail. The following month, he endorsed Arizona Sen. John McCain and became his national campaign co-chairman.

KEY VOTES

2008
Yes Prohibit discrimination based on genetic information
Yes Reauthorize farm and nutrition programs for five years
No Limit debate on "cap and trade" system for greenhouse gas emissions
No Allow lawsuits against companies that participated in warrantless wiretapping
No Limit debate on a bill to block a scheduled cut in Medicare payments to doctors
Yes Grant mortgage relief to homeowners and funding for Fannie Mae and Freddie Mac
Yes Approve a nuclear cooperation agreement with India
No Approve final $700 billion program to stabilize financial markets
Yes Allow consideration of a $14 billion auto industry loan package

2007
Yes Increase minimum wage by $2.10 an hour
No Limit debate on a comprehensive immigration bill
Yes Overhaul congressional lobbying and ethics rules for members and their staffs
No Limit debate on considering a bill to add House seats for the District of Columbia and Utah
No Limit debate on restoring habeas corpus rights to detainees
No Mandate minimum breaks for troops between deployments to Iraq or Afghanistan
No Override Bush veto of $23.2 billion water projects authorization bill
Yes Confirm Michael B. Mukasey as attorney general
No Limit debate on an energy policy overhaul containing $21.8 billion in tax incentives and reduced oil and gas subsidies

CQ VOTE STUDIES

	PARTY UNITY		PRESIDENTIAL SUPPORT	
	SUPPORT	OPPOSE	SUPPORT	OPPOSE
2008	94%	6%	78%	22%
2007	89%	11%	88%	12%
2006	83%	17%	92%	8%
2005	97%	3%	93%	7%
2004	98%	2%	98%	2%
2003	96%	4%	97%	3%
2002	94%	6%	98%	2%
2001	94%	6%	99%	1%
2000	98%	2%	40%	60%
1999	95%	5%	31%	69%

INTEREST GROUPS

	AFL-CIO	ADA	CCUS	ACU
2008	20%	20%	88%	76%
2007	8%	5%	86%	95%
2006	7%	5%	100%	87%
2005	14%	10%	89%	100%
2004	0%	15%	94%	96%
2003	0%	5%	100%	80%
2002	15%	5%	100%	100%
2001	19%	0%	93%	96%
2000	0%	0%	100%	100%
1999	0%	5%	94%	95%

Sen. Pat Roberts (R)

Elected 1996; 3rd term

CAPITOL OFFICE
224-4774
roberts.senate.gov
109 Hart Bldg. 20510-1605; fax 224-3514

COMMITTEES
Agriculture, Nutrition & Forestry
Finance
Health, Education, Labor & Pensions
Rules & Administration
Select Ethics

RESIDENCE
Dodge City

BORN
April 20, 1936; Topeka, Kan.

RELIGION
Methodist

FAMILY
Wife, Franki Roberts; three children

EDUCATION
Kansas State U., B.A. 1958 (journalism)

MILITARY SERVICE
Marine Corps, 1958-62

CAREER
Congressional aide; newspaper owner; reporter

POLITICAL HIGHLIGHTS
U.S. House, 1981-97

ELECTION RESULTS

2008 GENERAL

Pat Roberts (R)	727,121	60.1%
Jim Slattery (D)	441,399	36.5%
Randall L. Hodgkinson (LIBERT)	25,727	2.1%
Joseph L. Martin (REF)	16,443	1.4%

2008 PRIMARY

Pat Roberts (R)	unopposed

PREVIOUS WINNING PERCENTAGES
2002 (83%); 1996 (62%); 1994 House Election (77%);
1992 House Election (68%); 1990 House Election
(63%); 1988 House Election (100%); 1986 House
Election (77%); 1984 House Election (76%); 1982
House Election (68%); 1980 House Election (62%)

Roberts is conservative, but he has repeatedly bucked his party, especially in the year leading up to his 2008 re-election to a third term. That ability to blaze his own path, combined with a homespun and pithy style, has worked well for him during his nearly 30 years in Congress.

More than once, Washingtonian magazine's annual survey of congressional staff found him the "funniest senator." Lamenting his lack of input on the 2004 intelligence overhaul, Roberts said, "I'm like a one-legged chicken." In 2003, he said asking the federal agency that administers Medicare and Medicaid for help would be akin to "asking the Boston Strangler for a necklace." And when a reporter asked his position in 2007 on a minimum wage bill, he replied: "I think you need it."

While he is a reliable GOP vote on most issues, he often reaches across the aisle and is not afraid to defy party leaders. Indeed his support of his party on votes that pit a majority of Republicans against a majority of Democrats declined from a high of 97 percent in 2000 to 87 percent in 2008. Only seven Republican senators voted against President George W. Bush's position more often than Roberts in the 110th Congress (2007-08).

Rep. Barney Frank, a liberal Massachusetts Democrat, once told the Kansas City Star that Roberts was "not one of the impossible ideologues." In 2007, Roberts was one of 18 Republicans to defy Bush and vote to more than double spending over five years for the State Children's Health Insurance Program (SCHIP), which provides insurance for children from low-income families that do not qualify for Medicaid. In 2008, he was one of nearly two dozen Republican senators who opposed cutting fees for physicians who participate in the Medicare program. And he voted against Bush's $700 billion financial rescue plan in October 2008, saying it did not protect taxpayers and contained no meaningful oversight.

He was often in the headlines during his four years as Select Intelligence Committee chairman that began in 2003. He was regularly at war with John D. Rockefeller IV of West Virginia, the Intelligence panel's top Democrat. The two tussled repeatedly over a long-running investigation of prewar intelligence about Iraq and the uses made of it by top Bush administration policy-makers.

Though he does not tout the fact, few members have as good a claim as Roberts to foreseeing the threat of a terrorist attack before Sept. 11, 2001. As the first chairman of the Armed Services Subcommittee on Emerging Threats and Capabilities, which focuses on terrorism threats, Roberts in 1999 started pressing the Pentagon and Congress to get beyond a Cold War mentality and prepare for attacks that would use novel weapons. He urged preparedness for a gamut of possible terrorist assaults — attacks on civilian populations with nuclear, chemical or biological weapons and cyberattacks on critical computer networks.

Roberts' committee assignments shifted in 2007, as his attention moved homeward. Roberts seemed almost relieved when the 2006 Democratic electoral sweep stripped him of his Intelligence gavel. In fact, he left the panel altogether, opting for a less stressful spot as the lowest-ranking Republican on the Finance Committee. In that role, he not only was out front on the Medicare and SCHIP debates but also helped secure tax breaks for tornado victims in Kansas.

Roberts was ready for a break from the strain of dealing with national security issues while the United States was bogged down in wars in Iraq and Afghanistan and striving to prevent future terrorist attacks at home. During the Iraq intelligence investigation in 2004, he told a reporter, "My wife's getting tired of me leaving the house at 6:15 and coming in at midnight."

To take the Finance slot, he also had to give up his seat on Armed Services, though he has remained an outspoken defender of Kansas military installations and Boeing Co.'s attempt to secure a contract for U.S. military refueling planes, which would be built largely in Wichita.

Another issue that has always been high on his agenda is agriculture. A former House Agriculture Committee chairman, Roberts was a prime architect of the 1996 Freedom to Farm law, which replaced traditional crop subsidies with a system of fixed but declining payments to farmers. He voted against the 2002 farm bill, which undid a number of the changes he and other Republicans had earlier written into law.

He had the seniority to claim the top GOP slot at Senate Agriculture in the 110th Congress, when the committee drafted an overhaul of the nation's farm policy. Instead, he deferred to Saxby Chambliss of Georgia, declaring, "I intend to be his wingman." He supported the farm legislation that emerged, voting to override Bush's veto and enact the measure into law.

Roberts scored a coup for his farmland state in December 2008, when the Homeland Security Department recommended that Manhattan, Kan., become the home of the National Bio- and Agro-Defense Facility, a federal site for animal disease research and bioterrorism defense. Roberts had lobbied for the recommendation since 2005 and called the site's development "one of, if not the greatest, economic development initiatives in state history."

Since 1999, Roberts has been on the Select Ethics Committee, where he was the chairman from late 1999 to mid-2001. In 2002, he helped mete out the harshest punishment of a senator in years when Democrat Robert G. Torricelli was severely admonished for accepting gifts from a campaign donor.

A fourth-generation Kansan, Roberts earned a journalism degree from Kansas State University, intending to follow a family tradition in the news business. His great-grandfather, J.W. Roberts, founded the Oskaloosa Independent, the second-oldest newspaper in Kansas, after moving to the Kansas Territory from Ohio with "a Bible, a six-shooter and printing press in tow," according to a 1996 profile of Roberts in the Star. Politics ran in the family, too; Roberts' father, Wes, was chairman of the Republican National Committee under President Eisenhower.

After graduation, Roberts was drafted, so he joined the Marines, as his father had. The senator retains strong bonds to the corps. Indeed, Roberts' office is decorated with Marine regalia, though it has been more than 40 years since his service.

Returning home in 1962, he worked as a reporter and then co-owned a weekly newspaper in the Phoenix suburbs. He learned about zoning boards, city councils and boards of education, and developed, as he told the Star later, "a healthy respect and a degree of cynicism in a lot of federal programs."

He first came to Washington to work as a Senate aide and later ran the office of Republican Rep. Keith G. Sebelius of Kansas. When Sebelius announced his retirement in 1980, Roberts was ready. He cruised to victory in the general election, capitalizing on Sebelius' popularity and referring to "our record" so frequently that he sounded like an incumbent.

Roberts initially balked at making a Senate bid in 1996 when Republican Nancy Landon Kassebaum retired, saying he wanted to focus on shepherding the farm bill into law. But he eventually entered the race and handily won the GOP nod. Facing Democratic state Treasurer Sally Thompson in the fall, he won with 62 percent of the vote. In 2002, Democrats didn't field a candidate. Despite a Democratic tide nationally in 2008, he won again handily, with 60 percent, over former Democratic Rep. Jim Slattery, raising more than three times as much money as his challenger.

KEY VOTES

2008

Yes Prohibit discrimination based on genetic information

Yes Reauthorize farm and nutrition programs for five years

No Limit debate on "cap and trade" system for greenhouse gas emissions

No Allow lawsuits against companies that participated in warrantless wiretapping

Yes Limit debate on a bill to block a scheduled cut in Medicare payments to doctors

Yes Grant mortgage relief to homeowners and funding for Fannie Mae and Freddie Mac

Yes Approve a nuclear cooperation agreement with India

No Approve final $700 billion program to stabilize financial markets

No Allow consideration of a $14 billion auto industry loan package

2007

Yes Increase minimum wage by $2.10 an hour

No Limit debate on a comprehensive immigration bill

Yes Overhaul congressional lobbying and ethics rules for members and their staffs

No Limit debate on considering a bill to add House seats for the District of Columbia and Utah

No Limit debate on restoring habeas corpus rights to detainees

No Mandate minimum breaks for troops between deployments to Iraq or Afghanistan

Yes Override Bush veto of $23.2 billion water projects authorization bill

Yes Confirm Michael B. Mukasey as attorney general

No Limit debate on an energy policy overhaul containing $21.8 billion in tax incentives and reduced oil and gas subsidies

CQ VOTE STUDIES

	PARTY UNITY		PRESIDENTIAL SUPPORT	
	SUPPORT	OPPOSE	SUPPORT	OPPOSE
2008	87%	13%	65%	35%
2007	84%	16%	81%	19%
2006	94%	6%	88%	12%
2005	94%	6%	93%	7%
2004	99%	1%	92%	8%
2003	96%	4%	97%	3%
2002	96%	4%	96%	4%
2001	95%	5%	99%	1%
2000	97%	3%	38%	62%
1999	94%	6%	29%	71%

INTEREST GROUPS

	AFL-CIO	ADA	CCUS	ACU
2008	30%	20%	88%	72%
2007	26%	20%	73%	92%
2006	27%	5%	92%	84%
2005	8%	0%	100%	88%
2004	17%	15%	100%	92%
2003	0%	15%	100%	90%
2002	15%	0%	100%	100%
2001	13%	0%	93%	100%
2000	0%	0%	100%	92%
1999	0%	0%	94%	88%

Rep. Jerry Moran (R)

Elected 1996; 7th term

CAPITOL OFFICE
225-2715
www.jerrymoran.house.gov
2202 Rayburn Bldg. 20515-1601; fax 225-5124

COMMITTEES
Agriculture
Transportation & Infrastructure
Veterans' Affairs

RESIDENCE
Hays

BORN
May 29, 1954; Great Bend, Kan.

RELIGION
Methodist

FAMILY
Wife, Robba Moran; two children

EDUCATION
Fort Hays State U., attended 1972-73;
U. of Kansas, B.S. 1976 (economics), J.D. 1981

CAREER
Lawyer; banker

POLITICAL HIGHLIGHTS
Kan. Senate, 1989-97 (vice president, 1993-95; majority leader, 1995-97)

ELECTION RESULTS

2008 GENERAL

Jerry Moran (R)	214,549	81.9%
James Bordonaro (D)	34,771	13.3%
Kathleen M. Burton (REF)	7,145	2.7%
Jack Warner (LIBERT)	5,562	2.1%

2008 PRIMARY

Jerry Moran (R)	unopposed

2006 GENERAL

Jerry Moran (R)	156,728	78.6%
John Doll (D)	39,781	20.0%
Sylvester Cain (REF)	2,869	1.4%

PREVIOUS WINNING PERCENTAGES
2004 (91%); 2002 (91%); 2000 (89%); 1998 (81%); 1996 (73%)

Moran eschews political posturing in favor of pragmatism, often bucking his own party on major initiatives. And it's paid off — at the polls he has enjoyed some of the largest victory margins of any GOP House member.

Despite his distaste for political wrangling, he has had his sights on political office since he was a teenager, and his ambition still runs high. Moran in January 2009 filed to run for the Senate seat that Republican Sam Brownback will vacate in 2010 to comply with self-imposed term limits. Moran, who already had almost $3 million in campaign cash as of March 31, 2009, will face fellow Republican Rep. Todd Tiahrt in the primary. Kansas has not elected a Democrat to the Senate since 1932.

Moran's sizable electoral victories in years of Democratic gains stemmed in part from his ability to distance himself from George W. Bush's administration. In the 110th Congress (2007-08), Moran voted with President Bush only 70 percent of the time the administration staked out a position on legislation. "Even when in the majority, we lost sight of the one thing that we thought was to define Republicans, and that was limited government," Moran said.

He sounded a positive tone after President Obama took office, telling a Wichita audience the new president appeared to want to find "some level of common ground we can agree upon," rather than take part in partisan bickering. "It was about 'are you with me or against me' in the days of President Bush," Moran said.

Yet in early 2009, Moran joined his party in voting against Obama's final $787 billion economic stimulus plan in the House. He said his "no" vote was not due to partisanship, but a disagreement with details of the bill.

The vote was in keeping with his opposition in the fall of 2008 to two $700 billion measures — the second of which became law — aimed at helping the ailing financial industry. "I did not see the benefit to Kansans and was not convinced the administration had any concrete plan of how to turn the economy around despite being given $700 billion," Moran said.

Moran also had opposed Bush on other initiatives, including a 2003 Medicare prescription drug bill that became law, saying it was too costly and not good for his rural constituents. Though not naming Moran, then-GOP House Speaker J. Dennis Hastert complained in a 2004 autobiography about a fourth-term "Prairie State" member who "voted no, then ran and hid." Moran won plaudits from conservative and libertarian groups for his vote.

Moran has kept an eye out for Kansas' farmers from his perch on the Agriculture Committee and as ranking Republican on the General Farm Commodities and Risk Management Subcommittee. During debate in the 110th on the rewrite of the 2002 farm law, Moran said, he attended every field hearing the committee held, listening to "rice growers in California to catfish growers in Mississippi." Ultimately, Moran had little to say about the way the bill was written, though when debate bogged down, he introduced a bill to extend the previous farm law for one year. Moran opposed the final law, saying it failed to protect direct payments to farmers and maintain support for crop insurance.

Moran wants to create an energy policy that "develops America's own resources" and furthers research into renewable energy. He also supports creation of a presidential line-item spending veto.

He is a staunch proponent of easing restrictions on trade with Cuba, which he said work to the detriment of Kansas farmers. "When we don't sell them Kansas wheat, the Cubans buy French or Canadian wheat," he said. In 2007, he offered a provision to an appropriations bill to ease trade restrictions with Cuba, but House and Senate negotiators later stripped the provision.

Moran is a member of the Transportation and Infrastructure Committee, which is undertaking a reauthorization of the 2005 surface transportation law. Moran was involved in debate on that law, and helped obtain millions of federal dollars to build highways, roads and bridges in Kansas.

A member of the Veterans' Affairs Committee, Moran in 2008 saw the president sign into law his bill aimed at improving health care for veterans who live in rural areas. The law established a pilot program under which the Veterans Affairs Department must contract with local providers if a veteran lives a significant distance from a VA hospital. Moran said not a single VA hospital exists in his area. He became co-chairman of the Rural Health Care Coalition in 2009.

Moran is a native of the 1st District, which, at 57,373 square miles, is among the nation's largest and is known as the "Big First." He is the first in his family to attend college: his father was a laborer in the oil fields and his mother worked as a secretary at an electric utility. He was an avid reader, preferring biographies of historical figures and elected officials.

As a high school student government officer, Moran was in charge of inviting the local congressman, Republican Keith G. Sebelius, to speak at a fundraising dinner. In the summer of 1974, Moran went to Washington to work as an intern for Sebelius (father-in-law of President Obama's secretary of Health and Human Services, and former Kansas Gov. Kathleen Sebelius). That was at the height of the Watergate scandal, and Moran attended almost every House Judiciary Committee hearing concerning President Richard M. Nixon's impeachment.

After graduating from college with a degree in economics in 1976, Moran took a job as a banker. He earned his law degree five years later and opened his own practice in Hays, where he now lives.

He made a long-shot race for the state Senate in 1988 against an 18-year incumbent and won as a Republican in a historically Democratic district. Moran went on to become chairman of the state Senate Judiciary Committee, then ascended to majority leader in 1995.

He ran for Congress in 1996 when Republican Pat Roberts left the House to succeed Nancy Landon Kassebaum in the Senate. Moran rolled to an easy victory with 73 percent of the vote against John Divine, the former Salina mayor. In redistricting following the 2000 census, the Big First got even larger geographically to make up for population losses in many of the western and central counties. Yet Moran continued racking up decisive wins.

KANSAS 1

West – Salina, Hutchinson, Garden City, Emporia

In the 1960s, Truman Capote described western Kansas as a "lonesome area that other Kansans call 'out there.'" The fiscally conservative Big First takes in all of western Kansas and stretches as far east as Nemaha County in the north and the city of Emporia farther south, covering most of rural Kansas in the process. The district covers 70 percent of the state and has more land area than most U.S. states (including 25 of the 26 states east of the Mississippi River).

The 1st District's economy depends on agriculture, but several years of drought conditions have hurt the local wheat, sorghum and corn yields. Young people leaving the rural areas and an aging population have stalled growth — many counties have smaller populations now than they did a century ago.

The largest population center, Salina, is in the district's eastern portion and relies on agriculture and manufacturing. Food-related industry, manufacturing and health care jobs dominate Hutchinson, site of the annual Kansas State Fair. The return of the Army's Big Red One brigade to Fort

Riley (in the 2nd) has sparked a population boom in Junction City and the surrounding counties. In the west, towns such as Garden City and Dodge City rely on meatpacking and tourism. Despite suffering nationally, the cattle industry in Kansas remains relatively stable and has drawn large numbers of Mexican immigrants — over half of all schoolchildren in Garden City are Hispanic.

The 1st District is comfortably Republican and it overwhelmingly voted for John McCain in the 2008 presidential contest, giving him his highest percentage in the state with 69 percent of the vote. Republicans also dominates local offices, and many counties have no Democratic Party organizations.

MAJOR INDUSTRY
Agriculture, manufacturing, oil and gas

CITIES
Salina, 45,679; Hutchinson, 40,787; Garden City, 28,451; Emporia, 26,760; Dodge City, 25,176; Hays, 20,013; Liberal, 19,666; Junction City, 18,886

NOTABLE
Dwight D. Eisenhower's burial place and presidential library are in Abilene; The Kansas Cosmosphere in Hutchinson has a U.S. space artifact collection second only to the National Air and Space Museum's.

Rep. Lynn Jenkins (R)

Elected 2008; 1st term

Jenkins, a certified public accountant, spent six years as Kansas state treasurer "preaching to people" about the importance of fiscal responsibility, and she intends to do the same in Washington.

Jenkins has pledged that she will not vote for any tax increases and wants to abolish the federal estate tax, which she believes places burdens on Kansans who want to pass on family farms.

She hopes to communicate her thoughts on government fiscal responsibility from her seat on the Financial Services Committee. "We don't have the votes to legislate our ideas, so we really need to communicate," Jenkins said.

Alarmed by President Obama's plans to shut down the military detention facility on the U.S. naval base at Guantánamo Bay, Cuba, Jenkins wants to ensure that detainees held there are not sent to a federal prison at Fort Leavenworth. "It will be over my dead body that those detainees are sent to Leavenworth," she said. The first bill she introduced sought to block any such transfer.

Jenkins grew up on a dairy farm north of Topeka. She milked 100 cattle before and after school each day, and she grew up in a family that felt government should "get out of the way," save for national defense. As a child, she marched in the Jackson County 4-H Club State Parade wearing sandwich boards for Republican candidates. She served as student body president at her high school and went on to receive a degree in accounting from Weber State College in Ogden, Utah.

She later got involved in the local Republican Women's Club and when a state House vacancy opened up in 1997, she ran in a special election decided by party officials, but lost by a single vote. She ran again and won the following year. After two years in the Kansas House and two in the state Senate, she ran for state treasurer in 2002 and won with 56 percent of the vote.

In 2008, Jenkins edged former five-term GOP Rep. Jim Ryun in the primary, then faced first-term Democrat Nancy Boyda, who had ousted Ryun in 2006. She defeated Boyda by 4 percentage points in one of the year's few Republican takeaways.

CAPITOL OFFICE
225-6601
lynnjenkins.house.gov
130 Cannon Bldg. 20515-1602; fax 225-7986

COMMITTEES
Financial Services

RESIDENCE
Topeka

BORN
June 10, 1963; Topeka, Kan.

RELIGION
United Methodist

FAMILY
Divorced; two children

EDUCATION
Kansas State U., A.A. 1985 (business administration); Weber State College, B.S. 1985 (accounting)

CAREER
Accountant; homemaker

POLITICAL HIGHLIGHTS
Kan. House, 1999-2001; Kan. Senate, 2001-03; Kan. treasurer, 2003-09

ELECTION RESULTS

2008 GENERAL
Lynn Jenkins (R)	155,532	50.6%
Nancy Boyda (D)	142,013	46.2%
Leslie S. Martin (REF)	5,080	1.6%
Robert Garrard (LIBERT)	4,683	1.5%

2008 PRIMARY
Lynn Jenkins (R)	34,278	51.0%
Jim Ryun (R)	32,966	49.0%

KANSAS 2

East – Topeka, Manhattan, Leavenworth

The 2nd runs the length of east Kansas from Nebraska to Oklahoma, passing west of Kansas City. This district combines rural farm communities and urbanized areas, including the state capital of Topeka. One-fourth of the 2nd's residents live in Topeka or surrounding Shawnee County, where state government is the largest employer.

The 2nd enjoyed steady economic growth for decades, and construction of a new federal biodefense facility in Manhattan has brought jobs, but overall unemployment rates in the district have been rising recently.

Fort Riley and Fort Leavenworth are integral to the 2nd's economy. Revenue and new residents arrived in the district with the return of the Army's famed Big Red One infantry division to Fort Riley, in Manhattan. Rural areas rely on cattle, corn, soybeans and wheat, but farming, especially in the district's southeast, is vulnerable to droughts.

Rural areas in the district are mainly Republican, while Democrats find more success in Topeka, western Lawrence (the liberal University of Kansas is in the 3rd's portion of the city), the blue-collar southeast corner, and Manhattan, home to Kansas State University. The 2nd is conservative, but not overwhelmingly Republican, and gave John McCain 55 percent of its 2008 presidential vote.

MAJOR INDUSTRY
Agriculture, defense, higher education, government

MILITARY BASES
Fort Riley (Army), 16,000 military, 8,500 civilian (2008); Fort Leavenworth (Army), 2,838 military, 1,993 civilian (2007)

CITIES
Topeka, 122,377; Manhattan, 44,831; Leavenworth, 35,420; Lawrence (pt.), 25,768

NOTABLE
The Kansas Museum of History is in Topeka.

Rep. Dennis Moore (D)

Elected 1998; 6th term

CAPITOL OFFICE
225-2865
www.moore.house.gov
1727 Longworth Bldg. 20515-1603; fax 225-2807

COMMITTEES
Financial Services
(Oversight & Investigations - chairman)
Small Business

RESIDENCE
Lenexa

BORN
Nov. 8, 1945; Anthony, Kan.

RELIGION
Protestant

FAMILY
Wife, Stephene Moore; seven children

EDUCATION
Southern Methodist U., attended 1965;
U. of Kansas, B.A. 1967; Washburn U., J.D. 1970

MILITARY SERVICE
Army, 1970; Army Reserve, 1970-73

CAREER
Lawyer

POLITICAL HIGHLIGHTS
Johnson County district attorney, 1977-89;
Democratic nominee for Kan. attorney general,
1986

ELECTION RESULTS

2008 GENERAL

Dennis Moore (D)	202,541	56.4%
Nick Jordan (R)	142,307	39.7%
Joe Bellis (LIBERT)	10,073	2.8%
Roger D. Tucker (REF)	3,937	1.1%

2008 PRIMARY

Dennis Moore (D)	unopposed

2006 GENERAL

Dennis Moore (D)	153,105	64.6%
Chuck Ahner (R)	79,824	33.7%
Robert A. Conroy (REF)	4,051	1.7%

PREVIOUS WINNING PERCENTAGES
2004 (55%); 2002 (50%); 2000 (50%); 1998 (52%)

Moore, a centrist Democrat from a longstanding Republican-leaning district, insulates himself from tough challenges by focusing on constituent service — something that trumps any leadership ambitions — and preaching fiscal responsibility. He likes to show groups a chart detailing how tax dollars are spent along with a photo of his grandchildren to dramatize how future generations could be saddled with debt.

In his early years, Moore always had to sweat it out just to take 50 percent of the vote. But his reputation for responsiveness has helped increase his victory margins. "There is no one in Congress more diligent about constituent services than Dennis Moore," said The Johnson County Sun in its 2008 endorsement of Moore.

Moore belongs to the centrist New Democrat Coalition and has been a leader of the "Blue Dogs," a coalition of fiscally conservative House Democrats. He also is a member of the Center Aisle Caucus, a bipartisan group that works to establish a dialogue between the parties, and has urged the Democratic leadership to reinstate bipartisan retreats, the weekend events that usually include family members.

During President George W. Bush's administration, he initially sided with the GOP a tad more often than other Democrats. He supported Bush's decision to go to war with Iraq in 2002, and in 2005 he was one of only 15 Democrats who voted for the Central America Free Trade Agreement. But after his party regained control of Congress in 2007, he became a more reliable Democratic vote. He sided with Democrats on votes in which they diverged from Republicans 95 percent of the time in 2007 and 97 percent of the time in 2008.

One of Moore's chief goals is to write pay-as-you-go budget rules into law. The rules require new mandatory spending and tax cuts to be fully offset in an effort not to increase the deficit. He did set aside his qualms about deficits to support President Obama's economic stimulus in February 2009. Acknowledging "valid concerns" about the size of the $787 billion package, he nonetheless maintained it would put people back to work and increase consumer confidence.

A member of the Financial Services Committee, Moore in fall 2008 backed the $700 billion package, signed into law, intended to assist the ailing financial services industry. In January 2009, he was named chairman of the panel's Subcommittee on Oversight and Investigations, and he said he would put his background as a prosecutor to work in ensuring greater oversight and accountability for companies receiving funds. He also said he would help develop an improved structure to regulate financial institutions and transactions.

Moore's other committee assignment is Small Business. He has backed legislation aimed at making it easier for smaller companies to obtain investment capital and compete for federal contracts.

His slate of legislative accomplishments includes the passage of bills to address concerns raised by his constituents. In July 2008, he gained passage of a bill requiring portable gasoline containers to include child-resistant caps. Moore, who had pushed the bill for several years, frequently recounted stories of children with badly burned faces from gasoline fires. Another Moore-sponsored bill signed into law in 2008 commissioned a commemorative veterans coin to fund a memorial for disabled veterans near the Capitol.

In 2003, after listening to a National Public Radio report that troops on leave from Iraq and Afghanistan were being flown back to the East and West coasts for leave but had to fund their own travel home to locations like Kansas City, Kan., Moore sponsored a bill to reimburse the troops' travel all the way home. On his way to Bush's annual Christmas party, Moore tucked a "Dear Colleague" letter into his tuxedo jacket and handed it to then-Secretary of Defense Donald H. Rumsfeld at the party. The Defense Department later incorporated Moore's bill into its budget, retroactive to Sept. 11.

In the 111th Congress (2009-10), Moore plans to again push legislation to make it easier for government agencies to dispose of excess property. It passed the House in the 110th Congress (2007-08), but stalled in the Senate. Moore also hopes parts of a health information technology bill he sponsored will become part of a comprehensive health measure. His bill would allow patients to have their medical records electronically managed by health record trusts.

Moore grew up in Wichita, where his father, Warner Moore, was Sedgwick County attorney. He followed his father's career path by becoming a prosecuting attorney, and he is a Democrat because of his father. Warner, who died in 2006, twice ran unsuccessfully for the House, in 1958 and 1960.

In college, Moore joined the ROTC and was slated for two years in the service afterward. He went to Fort Benning, Ga., in 1970 for infantry officers basic training, expecting to be sent to Vietnam. But just before he graduated from law school, he got a letter saying the war was winding down and he could choose active duty or the reserves. He chose the reserves.

For a dozen years, Moore was the Johnson County district attorney, known for his personal touch. He took the lead in creating a county victims assistance program. In 1998, Moore unseated conservative Republican Rep. Vince Snowbarger after one term. Snowbarger had not raised much money, a mistake Moore was careful not to make. In his first re-election campaign, Moore raised $1.5 million to defeat state Rep. Phill Kline, another conservative.

Moore's 2002 race was tougher. The district had been redrawn to be slightly more Republican, and GOP nominee Adam Taff was more moderate than Moore's past challengers. Moore won with just 50 percent of the vote. He has won with wider margins of victory since. In 2008, he faced a strong challenge from state Sen. Nick Jordan, but Moore prevailed with 56 percent of the vote.

Moore loves to play guitar, and in his first campaign for Congress, he made an award-winning commercial in which he strummed and talked to voters. In 2006, he played and sang "This Land Is Your Land" for a group of 5th- and 6th-graders back in the district. One of them sent him a letter, which he has kept. It says, "If it didn't work out in Congress, you could have been a country singer."

KEY VOTES

2008

Yes Delay consideration of Colombia free-trade agreement
Yes Override Bush veto of federal farm and nutrition programs reauthorization bill
Yes Overhaul surveillance laws and permit dismissal of suits against companies that conducted warrantless wiretapping
Yes Grant mortgage relief to homeowners and funding for Fannie Mae and Freddie Mac
Yes Approve initial $700 billion program to stabilize financial markets
Yes Approve final $700 billion program to stabilize financial markets
Yes Provide $14 billion in loans to automakers

2007

Yes Increase minimum wage by $2.10 an hour
Yes Approve $124.2 billion in emergency war spending and set goal for redeployment of troops from Iraq
No   Reject federal contraceptive assistance to international family planning groups
Yes Override Bush veto of $23.2 billion water projects authorization bill
Yes Implement Peru free-trade agreement
Yes Approve energy policy overhaul with new fuel economy standards
Yes Clear $473.5 billion omnibus spending bill, including $70 billion for military operations

CQ VOTE STUDIES

	PARTY UNITY		PRESIDENTIAL SUPPORT	
	SUPPORT	OPPOSE	SUPPORT	OPPOSE
2008	97%	3%	22%	78%
2007	95%	5%	6%	94%
2006	87%	13%	37%	63%
2005	85%	15%	30%	70%
2004	83%	17%	38%	62%

INTEREST GROUPS

	AFL-CIO	ADA	CCUS	ACU
2008	100%	80%	71%	4%
2007	96%	90%	60%	4%
2006	92%	85%	60%	23%
2005	80%	80%	59%	16%
2004	87%	90%	62%	20%

KANSAS 3

Kansas City region – Overland Park, eastern Lawrence

Eastern Kansas' 3rd differs markedly from the state's other districts. Compact, it is almost entirely within the sphere of Kansas City, Mo., and roughly 90 percent of residents live either in Kansas City, Kan., or in its Johnson County suburbs. The district boasts Overland Park, Kansas City and Olathe, three of the state's most populous cities. Heading west, the 3rd takes in eastern Douglas County and most of Lawrence, Kansas' liberal bastion and home to the University of Kansas.

The district has a disparate economic character, containing both the state's richest and poorest counties. Poverty and unemployment are prevalent in Kansas City, Kan., and in surrounding Wyandotte County. But the Kansas Speedway, which opened in 2001 in western Wyandotte, fueled a renaissance in the area. Kansas City, an industrial town that has had its share of Rust Belt blues, has experienced more recent layoffs, although a growing bioscience sector may bring some white-collar jobs to the district.

Johnson County is the economic engine of Kansas — it is the state's richest county, with telecommunications company headquarters, suburban developments and a stable service sector. While Kansas City has lost population over the past decade, Johnson has grown, and its largest city, Overland Park, is now the second largest in the state. In the midst of economic slowdowns and declining property values, county government budget shortfalls concern residents and officials.

Populous, wealthy Johnson County tends to be strongly Republican, but socially moderate Republicans here often exhibit an independent streak. Democratic strength in Wyandotte and parts of Douglas keep the 3rd competitive. Democrat Barack Obama took 51 percent of the 2008 presidential vote in the 3rd, the only district in Kansas that he won.

MAJOR INDUSTRY
Telecommunications, auto manufacturing, service

CITIES
Overland Park, 149,080; Kansas City, 146,866; Olathe, 92,962; Lawrence (pt.), 54,330; Shawnee, 47,996; Lenexa, 40,238; Leawood, 27,656

NOTABLE
The Mahaffie Stagecoach Stop in Olathe is the last remaining Santa Fe Trail stagecoach stop that is still open to the public.

Rep. Todd Tiahrt (R)

Elected 1994; 8th term

CAPITOL OFFICE
225-6216
www.house.gov/tiahrt
2441 Rayburn Bldg. 20515; fax 225-3489

COMMITTEES
Appropriations

RESIDENCE
Goddard

BORN
June 15, 1951; Vermillion, S.D.

RELIGION
Assemblies of God

FAMILY
Wife, Vicki Tiahrt; three children (one deceased)

EDUCATION
South Dakota School of Mines and Technology, attended 1969-71; Evangel College, B.A. 1975 (business administration); Southwest Missouri State U., M.B.A. 1989 (marketing)

CAREER
College instructor; airline company project manager

POLITICAL HIGHLIGHTS
Republican nominee for Kan. House, 1990; Kan. Senate, 1993-95

ELECTION RESULTS

2008 GENERAL

Todd Tiahrt (R)	177,617	63.4%
Donald Betts Jr. (D)	90,706	32.4%
Susan G. Ducey (REF)	6,441	2.3%
Steven A. Rosile (LIBERT)	5,345	1.9%

2008 PRIMARY

Todd Tiahrt (R)	unopposed

2006 GENERAL

Todd Tiahrt (R)	116,386	63.5%
Garth J. McGinn (D)	62,166	33.9%
Joy R. Holt (REF)	4,655	2.5%

PREVIOUS WINNING PERCENTAGES
2004 (66%); 2002 (61%); 2000 (54%); 1998 (58%); 1996 (50%); 1994 (53%)

Tiahrt is a fiscal and social conservative whose religious convictions strongly influence his political views. His insistence on pursuing his agenda has sometimes puts him at odds with Republican leaders, and he has been thwarted in his efforts to join the GOP's leadership ranks.

A member of the groundbreaking Class of 1994 that propelled House Republicans into the majority after decades of Democratic rule, Tiahrt (TEE-hart) frequently tries to advance his conservative ideas by adding riders on issues such as abortion to the annual appropriations bills. He inserted a provision in one 2004 spending bill strictly limiting the disclosure of federally stored information about firearms that are used in crimes. Similar language has been included annually in spending bills.

Another of his signature policy amendments, banning use of tax dollars in the District of Columbia for needle-exchange programs, was repealed after Democrats took control in 2007. He also is an adamant defender of earmarks — funding set-asides for projects in member districts — and in November 2008 led the GOP caucus in defeating an earmark moratorium proposal by Minority Leader John A. Boehner of Ohio and Republican Eric Cantor of Virginia.

Early in 2009 Tiahrt announced he will run for the Senate in 2010, when Republican Sam Brownback will be stepping down in observance of his two-term pledge. But he will face fellow Rep. Jerry Moran in the GOP primary.

Life for Tiahrt sometimes can seem like all Boeing Co., all the time. A one-time contract manager with the aviation giant, he has always focused on issues affecting the aviation industry in Congress. It's no wonder: About half of all the general aviation aircraft sold in the world is produced in Wichita.

Tiahrt — a member of the powerful Appropriations Committee and its Defense Subcommittee — joined with other champions of Boeing to battle a February 2008 decision by the Air Force to award a $35 billion air tanker contract to a consortium made up of Northrop Grumman Corp. and the North American division of the European Aeronautic Defense and Space Co., the maker of Airbus, rather than Boeing. Tiahrt had cheered an earlier deal allowing the Air Force to lease 100 Boeing 767 aircraft for use as aerial refueling tankers. Work on the planes was to be done at Boeing's Wichita facility. But the Pentagon shelved the deal in 2004 after the $21 billion, no-bid contract came under fire from GOP Sen. John McCain of Arizona, and an Air Force procurement official admitted to illegally helping the company while negotiating a lucrative job offer.

Despite that scandal, Tiahrt in 2008 still thought Boeing should get the new tanker contract. "An American tanker should be built by an American company with American workers," he argued in a letter to President George W. Bush signed by 44 other House members. He took heart when the Government Accountability Office recommended the competition be done over — a recommendation Defense Secretary Robert M. Gates accepted.

Tiahrt has a strong relationship with Norm Dicks, a Democrat from Washington state who is another vocal supporter of Boeing.

In the 111th Congress (2009-10); in addition to his Defense post, Tiahrt is ranking Republican on the Labor, Health and Human Services, and Education Appropriations Subcommittee. He wants to help address rising health care costs, help create new jobs and find ways to help meet the "educational needs of a new workforce."

Tiahrt has been a rival of then-Republican Study Committee Chairman Jeb Hensarling of Texas, one of the strongest proponents of a ban on earmarks for all Republicans. Tiahrt had lost a bitter head-to-head race against Hensarling in late 2006 for the chairmanship of the RSC, a group of the most conservative House Republicans, on a 57-42 vote. Tiahrt later quit the group.

He had made an earlier attempt to break into the GOP leadership; in early 2006, he began campaigning for the job of Republican whip, then the third-ranking post among the majority House Republicans. But when Whip Roy Blunt of Missouri lost out to Boehner for the Republican leader post, Blunt decided to hang on to the whip's job, denying Tiahrt and other interested candidates the opportunity to replace him.

Born in South Dakota, Tiahrt grew up on a family farm in the southeastern part of the state. He learned to hunt and fish as a boy, and his father served on the local school board. Tiahrt played football in college, getting a scholarship to the South Dakota School of Mines and Technology. But a knee injury ended his sports career, and he lost the scholarship. He transferred to Evangel College in Springfield, Mo., a Christian institution run by the Assemblies of God church, of which Tiahrt is a member. A business administration major, he worked at a bank while in college.

After graduation, he worked as a project engineer for Zenith Electronics Corp., studying the assembly line process. One assignment was to determine how high boxes of televisions could be stacked. He later became a contract manager for Boeing, dealing mostly with Air Force contracts.

Tiahrt originally registered as a Democrat. His grandfather had impressed him with the story of how the federal government had helped with the purchase of the family farm during the Depression. But when he set out to run for the Kansas House in 1990, Tiahrt decided the Republican Party was a better match for his strong religious views.

Tiahrt lost that race for the state House, succumbing in a recount after initial tallies had shown him with a 24-vote lead. He remained active in local politics and two years later was elected to the state Senate, where he was best known for pushing legislation to allow people to carry concealed weapons.

Tiahrt waged a long-shot challenge in 1994 to popular nine-term Democratic Rep. Dan Glickman. He mobilized a grass-roots network that drew heavily from the ranks of the anti-abortion movement, in which his wife was active, and linked Glickman to the unpopular Clinton administration. He won by 6 percentage points. After a serious re-election battle in 1996, he has won subsequent elections by comfortable margins.

Tiahrt suffered a personal tragedy in 2004, when his 16-year-old son, Luke, committed suicide at the family's home in a Washington suburb.

KEY VOTES

2008
No   Delay consideration of Colombia free-trade agreement
?   Override Bush veto of federal farm and nutrition programs reauthorization bill
?   Overhaul surveillance laws and permit dismissal of suits against companies that conducted warrantless wiretapping
No   Grant mortgage relief to homeowners and funding for Fannie Mae and Freddie Mac
No   Approve initial $700 billion program to stabilize financial markets
No   Approve final $700 billion program to stabilize financial markets
No   Provide $14 billion in loans to automakers

2007
No   Increase minimum wage by $2.10 an hour
No   Approve $124.2 billion in emergency war spending and set goal for redeployment of troops from Iraq
Yes   Reject federal contraceptive assistance to international family planning groups
Yes   Override Bush veto of $23.2 billion water projects authorization bill
Yes   Implement Peru free-trade agreement
Yes   Approve energy policy overhaul with new fuel economy standards
Yes   Clear $473.5 billion omnibus spending bill, including $70 billion for military operations

CQ VOTE STUDIES

	PARTY UNITY		PRESIDENTIAL SUPPORT	
	SUPPORT	OPPOSE	SUPPORT	OPPOSE
2008	92%	8%	69%	31%
2007	91%	9%	78%	22%
2006	96%	4%	87%	13%
2005	97%	3%	91%	9%
2004	96%	4%	85%	15%

INTEREST GROUPS

	AFL-CIO	ADA	CCUS	ACU
2008	14%	15%	94%	91%
2007	13%	15%	90%	96%
2006	33%	5%	93%	84%
2005	13%	0%	93%	96%
2004	13%	5%	100%	92%

KANSAS 4

South central – Wichita

Wichita, the state's largest city, has long been known as the "Air Capital of the World" because general aviation aircraft production powered the district's economy. The moderately conservative 4th District is centered on Wichita and much of the rest of the district is farmland.

The aviation industry that Wichita and the district depend on suffered following the Sept. 11 terrorist attacks and during recent nationwide economic downturns. Cessna Aircraft, Raytheon Aircraft, Bombardier Aerospace, Boeing's Integrated Defense Systems and other airplane manufacturers have operations in the area. Aerostructures manufacturer Spirit AeroSystems also is headquartered in Wichita. But, volatility in the aerospace and commercial airline sectors have led to job loss here, and most local aviation employers have slowed production and cut employment.

City leaders hope that health care facilities and the area's universities can bolster the local economy. Although regional agricultural production has fed food manufacturing here, that sector has also shed jobs.

Sumner County, on the Oklahoma border, is Kansas' leading wheat-growing county. Harper and Kingman counties to the west also rely heavily on their wheat production. Sustained drought conditions, however, have diminished agricultural output. Cattle graze in sparsely populated Greenwood, Elk and Chautauqua counties to the east.

Republicans won the 4th's U.S. House seat in 1994 and have kept control of the GOP-leaning district since. Despite higher Republican voter registration, Democrats — aided by a strong union presence in Wichita — do capture some local offices. Republican John McCain took 58 percent of the district's 2008 presidential vote.

MAJOR INDUSTRY
Aviation, defense, agriculture, health care

MILITARY BASES
McConnell Air Force Base, 2,470 military, 397 civilian (2009)

CITIES
Wichita, 344,284; Derby, 17,807; Newton, 17,190

NOTABLE
Pizza Hut was founded in Wichita in 1958 by students at the University of Wichita (now called Wichita State University), and the original Pizza Hut restaurant has been moved onto the university's campus.

Gov. Steven L. Beshear (D)

First elected: 2007
Length of term: 4 years
Term expires: 1/12
Salary: $111,945
Phone: (502) 564-2611

Residence: Lexington
Born: September 21, 1944; Dawson Springs, Ky.
Religion: Disciples of Christ
Family: Wife, Jane Beshear; two children
Education: U. of Kentucky, B.A. 1966 (history), J.D. 1968
Military service: Army Reserve, 1969-75
Career: Lawyer
Political highlights: Ky. House, 1975-79; attorney general, 1979-83; lieutenant governor, 1983-87; sought Democratic nomination for governor, 1987; Democratic nominee for U.S. Senate, 1996

Election results:
2007 GENERAL

Steven L. Beshear (D)	619,552	58.7%
Ernie Fletcher (R)	435,773	41.3%

Lt. Gov. Daniel Mongiardo (D)

First elected: 2007
Length of term: 4 years
Term expires: 1/12
Salary: $91,437
Phone: (502) 564-2611

LEGISLATURE

General Assembly: January-April in even-numbered years, limit of 60 days; January-March in odd-numbered years, limit of 30 days

Senate: 38 members, 4-year terms
2009 ratios: 21 R, 16 D, 1 I; 32 men, 6 women
Salary: $187/day in session; $1,774/ month out of session
Phone: (502) 564-8100

House: 100 members, 2-year terms
2009 ratios: 65 D, 35 R; 85 men, 15 women
Salary: $187/day in session; $1,774/ month out of session
Phone: (502) 564-8100

TERM LIMITS

Governor: 2 terms
Senate: No
House: No

URBAN STATISTICS

CITY	POPULATION
Lexington-Fayette	260,512
Louisville Metro	674,032
Owensboro	54,067

REGISTERED VOTERS

Democrat	57%
Republican	36%
Others	7%

POPULATION

2008 population (est.)	4,269,245
2000 population	4,041,769
1990 population	3,685,296
Percent change (1990-2000)	+9.7%
Rank among states (2008)	26

Median age	35.9
Born in state	73.7%
Foreign born	2%
Violent crime rate	295/100,000
Poverty level	15.8%
Federal workers	36,234
Military	50,134

ELECTIONS

STATE ELECTION OFFICIAL
(502) 573-7100
DEMOCRATIC PARTY
(502) 695-4828
REPUBLICAN PARTY
(502) 875-5130

MISCELLANEOUS

Web: www.kentucky.gov
Capital: Frankfort

U.S. CONGRESS

Senate: 2 Republicans
House: 4 Republicans, 2 Democrats

2000 Census Statistics by District

DIST.	2008 VOTE FOR PRESIDENT OBAMA	MCCAIN	WHITE	BLACK	ASIAN	HISP	MEDIAN INCOME	WHITE COLLAR	BLUE COLLAR	SERVICE INDUSTRY	OVER 64	UNDER 18	COLLEGE EDUCATION	RURAL	SQ. MILES
1	37%	62%	90%	7%	0%	1%	$30,360	47%	39%	15%	15%	24%	12%	63%	11,683
2	38	61	91	6	1	2	$35,724	50	36	14	12	26	14	53	7,567
3	56	43	76	19	1	2	$39,468	62	24	14	14	24	25	2	367
4	38	60	95	2	0	1	$40,150	56	30	14	12	26	18	40	5,679
5	31	67	97	1	0	1	$21,915	48	36	15	12	25	10	79	10,676
6	43	55	87	8	1	2	$37,544	59	27	14	11	23	25	29	3,757
STATE	41	57	89	7	1	1	$33,672	54	32	14	13	25	17	44	39,728
U.S.	53	46	69	12	4	13	$41,994	60	25	15	12	26	24	21	3,537,438

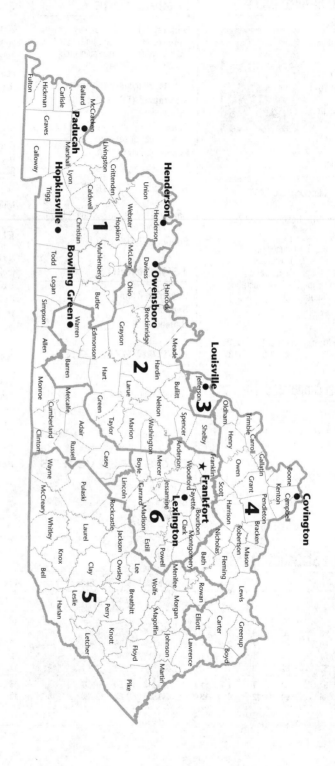

Sen. Mitch McConnell (R)

Elected 1984; 5th term

CAPITOL OFFICE
224-2541
mcconnell.senate.gov
361A Russell Bldg. 20510-1702; fax 224-2499

COMMITTEES
Agriculture, Nutrition & Forestry
Appropriations
Rules & Administration

RESIDENCE
Louisville

BORN
Feb. 20, 1942; Sheffield, Ala.

RELIGION
Baptist

FAMILY
Wife, Elaine L. Chao; three children

EDUCATION
U. of Louisville, B.A. 1964; U. of Kentucky,
J.D. 1967

CAREER
Lawyer; U.S. Justice Department official;
congressional aide

POLITICAL HIGHLIGHTS
Jefferson County judge-executive, 1978-85

ELECTION RESULTS

2008 GENERAL

Mitch McConnell (R)	953,816	53.0%
Bruce Lunsford (D)	847,005	47.0%

2008 PRIMARY

Mitch McConnell (R)	168,127	86.1%
Daniel Essek (R)	27,170	13.9%

PREVIOUS WINNING PERCENTAGES
2002 (65%); 1996 (55%); 1990 (52%); 1984 (50%)

McConnell is the GOP's highest-ranking elected official, a canny conservative who is a formidable backroom dealer and skilled parliamentarian. He sees his job as minority leader as keeping his party tightly unified to block Democratic initiatives while picking up the support of at least a few party moderates.

McConnell also seeks to rebuild his fallen party, albeit in a less flashy and attention-grabbing manner than many other national GOP figures employ. He wants to reach out to disaffected voters and carefully articulate the party's core values in "common-sense" language, such as using the phrase "light-switch tax" to describe what he regards as overly costly Democratic energy policies.

With his quarter-century of experience on Capitol Hill, McConnell knows how to barter and is willing to accept less than a full loaf to get a job done. "I'm a conservative Republican. On most issues, I would like to see a right-of-center result," he has said. "But I've also been in legislative politics long enough to know that rarely do you get exactly what you want. Our whole process is about accepting less than what you want in order to advance the ball."

He moves toward his goals in part by guiding his colleagues through persuasion rather than threats. "I start with the notion that everyone in the Senate is smart or they wouldn't have made it this far in politics. So I spend a lot of time listening," he said. That approach suits independent-minded moderates such as Maine's Olympia J. Snowe, with whom he frequently disagrees on policy. "He'll talk about maintaining cohesion in order to be able to assert minority rights ... Sometimes he would prefer you take a different position, but he will let you vote your conscience," she said. "There's always a good give-and-take."

McConnell has found his job can be anything but easy, especially in the early months of the 111th Congress (2009-10) when he had to deal with an expanded Senate majority intent on pushing President Obama's agenda through Congress. He was unable to thwart several major economic initiatives, including a $787 billion economic stimulus bill, a $410 billion catchall spending bill and a $3.56 trillion budget blueprint for fiscal 2010.

He did notch a few triumphs: He helped persuade Democrats to permit votes on GOP amendments more often than in the 110th Congress (2007-08), and his party was able to put many in the majority on the spot with an amendment to roll back the District of Columbia's gun restrictions. And he was able to pick up 12 Democratic votes in April 2009 to get the Senate to reject a proposal to give financially strapped homeowners flexibility in renegotiating mortgages, a process often referred to as "cramdown."

But he also faced discontent from within his own ranks. He tried, and failed, to dissuade Arizona Republican Sen. John McCain — whom he has often disagreed with over the years — from offering an alternative budget proposal, fearing it would detract from GOP criticism of the Democrats' plans. Meanwhile, McConnell's conservative Kentucky colleague Jim Bunning, whose erratic behavior led to speculation about his political future, fumed to reporters that the minority leader was responsible for the loss of Republican seats in the Senate. Of McConnell, Bunning said, "He wants to run everything."

As if that wasn't enough, McConnell and his party were dealt another crippling blow in April 2009: the switch of moderate Pennsylvania Sen. Arlen Specter to the Democratic side, putting Democrats on the cusp of a majority large enough to — in theory — block GOP filibusters aimed at derailing legislation. McConnell's reaction was to play down the message it sent about his party; he noted Specter had admitted he was switching parties because his pollster told him he couldn't win the Republican primary next year. McConnell declared, "This is not a national story. This is a Pennsylvania story."

Nevertheless, McConnell has been attuned to the Republicans' shortcomings. In a January 2009 speech to the Republican National Committee, he warned the GOP faced severe trouble if it couldn't expand its base beyond the South and parts of the Midwest. "The Republican Party seems to be slipping into a position of being more of a regional party than a national one," he said. "In politics, there's a name for a regional party: It's called a minority party. And I didn't sign up to be a member of a regional party."

He wasn't unyielding in his opposition to Obama; he said he generally supported the president's early 2009 approach to the wars in Iraq and Afghanistan, and told the Louisville Courier-Journal that the president "is impossible not to like — I do like him." But he found the president wanting in other ways on national security; McConnell was especially critical of Obama's decision to shut the military detention facility at the U.S. naval base at Cuba's Guantánamo Bay and constantly questioned where the detainees would be relocated.

In his first two years as his party's leader during the 110th Congress, when the Democratic majority was slightly narrower and a Republican was in the White House, McConnell repeatedly resorted to filibusters and parliamentary objections to block bills and conference negotiations. There were 112 votes to invoke cloture — or end debate — on Senate legislation, nearly double the previous record of 61 in the 107th Congress (2001-02).

During the summer of 2007, as GOP senators repeatedly objected to budget amendments relating to the Iraq War, Majority Leader Harry Reid of Nevada sent McConnell a letter chastising him for "partisan obstruction that I fear will make us less, not more, secure." But McConnell was unyielding. "The majority has the responsibility to set the agenda," he said. "If you set an overly partisan agenda, you get ... what they would argue is an overly partisan response."

In 2006, he managed to avert an embarrassing loss for President George W. Bush on a big budget bill. Faced with possible defections by Republicans who disagreed with Bush's spending priorities, McConnell secretly wooed a Democrat, Mary L. Landrieu of Louisiana, just days before a showdown Senate floor vote. McConnell persuaded then-Majority Leader Bill Frist of Tennessee to make an overture to Landrieu, and then, in his role as an Appropriations subcommittee chairman, he and other Republicans on the committee devised a package of recovery spending for Landrieu's state, heavily damaged by hurricanes the summer before. Landrieu's lone Democratic vote for Bush's budget gave political cover to wavering moderate Republicans, who fell in line behind the plan, providing a narrow but decisive 51-vote majority on the floor.

McConnell was intensely loyal to Bush; his wife, Elaine L. Chao, served as Bush's Labor secretary. His closeness put him in an awkward position at times when conservatives were at odds with the White House. During the 2007 debate on an immigration overhaul bill that Bush backed but conservatives abhorred, McConnell stayed out of the floor debate, not even helping to open the day's legislative proceedings or taking reporters' questions on the topic.

In October 2008, however, Reid and McConnell joined forces on pushing through the Bush administration's $700 billion plan to shore up the ailing financial services sector. The House rejected the initial measure, but Reid and McConnell got it through the Senate on the first try. "Mitch knows the Senate rules and Senate procedures...He has a feel for the institution," Reid said.

McConnell is devoted to tradition and constitutional principles. In 2006, he parted ways with most Republicans to oppose a constitutional amendment to allow Congress to ban flag burning. The measure failed by a single vote. He voted against it for the same reason he led the fight in 2002 against a major rewrite of campaign finance rules; McConnell, a self-described "First Amendment hawk," said both measures were violations of freedom of speech.

On campaign giving without restrictions:

"It is as American as apple pie. Not only is it the right thing for our people, it is the constitutionally protected thing for our country."
– February 1998

On Ronald Reagan:

"An ideal example of what a CEO the president ought to be: Somebody with a strong set of core convictions, but flexible enough and practical enough to understand that you are not going to get all of what you want."
– April 2006

On 'obstructionism':

"The majority has the responsibility to set the agenda. If you set an overly partisan agenda, you get...what they would argue is an overly partisan response."
– October 2007

On Republicans:

"As Republicans, we know that common-sense conservative principles aren't regional. But I think we have to admit that our sales job has been."
– January 2009

On Appropriations as well as the Agriculture, Nutrition and Forestry Committee, McConnell looks out for Kentucky's tobacco growers and other farming interests. Some Democrats accused him of hypocrisy in 2009 when he criticized their party as spending too much, but then he obtained numerous earmarks — funding for special-interest projects — in a $410 billion catchall spending law for fiscal 2009. His projects included $1.6 million for a forage animal production research laboratory in Lexington and nearly $1.1 million for an animal waste management research lab in Bowling Green. He defends such funding as crucial to diversifying his state's economy.

He also serves on the Rules and Administration Committee, which handles internal Senate housekeeping matters as well as campaign finance and election legislation. McConnell blocked a rewrite of campaign finance rules for 15 years, mounting more than 20 filibusters against various iterations of the legislation. When the measure finally was enacted in 2002, he assembled some of the nation's best legal minds and took the battle to the Supreme Court, which narrowly upheld the law in 2003. Government watchdog groups vilified him as chief defender of a corrupt status quo, but he was indifferent to the notoriety and made no apologies.

During his Senate career, McConnell has served in a variety of insider roles, some more pleasant than others. From 1999-2002, he chaired the Rules panel. He also chaired the Select Ethics Committee in 1995 when it voted to expel Oregon Republican Bob Packwood over charges of sexual misconduct. During the 1998 and 2000 election cycles, he chaired the National Republican Senatorial Committee, the party's Senate campaign arm.

An only child, McConnell was born in Alabama, lived in Georgia for part of his childhood and moved to Kentucky at age 13. His father, an Army officer who fought in World War II, became a civilian Army employee after the war and then a human resources director for DuPont in Louisville.

While the family was living in Alabama, McConnell, at age 2, was stricken with polio. His mother administered a physical therapy regimen and took him to specialists in nearby Warm Springs, Ga. At their urging, she kept him from walking until he was 4, a seemingly impossible task that saved him from permanent damage to his afflicted left leg. "She was a true saint," McConnell said. The episode, he added, taught him the value of "tenacity and discipline."

McConnell showed an early taste for politics. He was student body president in high school and college, and president of his law school class. After law school, he worked for GOP Sen. Marlow W. Cook of Kentucky, then served as a deputy assistant attorney general in the Ford administration. He served two terms as the chief executive of Jefferson County, now Louisville Metro, before waging his winning 1984 Senate race.

His campaign against two-term Democratic Sen. Walter D. Huddleston struggled until McConnell demonstrated the incumbent had limited influence and was often absent from committee meetings; McConnell aired TV ads showing bloodhounds sniffing around Washington in search of Huddleston. McConnell won by four-tenths of a percentage point, aided by President Reagan's re-election coattails. In 1990, McConnell advertised the fact that he was present and voted 99 percent of the time during his first term. He won with 52 percent of the vote. His victories stayed comfortable in his subsequent races.

In 2008, however, he faced a tough opponent in wealthy Democratic businessman Bruce Lunsford amid a hostile national political climate for the GOP. Lunsford highlighted McConnell's ties to Bush and said the minority leader deserved blame for the country's economic woes; Lunsford spent millions of his personal fortune on attack ads that helped pull him head-to-head in polls in the campaign's closing weeks. McConnell, however, played up his leadership status and Appropriations seat as assets in bringing home federal funds. He outspent Lunsford by a 2-to-1 margin, and captured 53 percent of the vote.

KEY VOTES

2008

Yes Prohibit discrimination based on genetic information
Yes Reauthorize farm and nutrition programs for five years
No Limit debate on "cap and trade" system for greenhouse gas emissions
No Allow lawsuits against companies that participated in warrantless wiretapping
No Limit debate on a bill to block a scheduled cut in Medicare payments to doctors
Yes Grant mortgage relief to homeowners and funding for Fannie Mae and Freddie Mac
Yes Approve a nuclear cooperation agreement with India
Yes Approve final $700 billion program to stabilize financial markets
No Allow consideration of a $14 billion auto industry loan package

2007

Yes Increase minimum wage by $2.10 an hour
No Limit debate on a comprehensive immigration bill
Yes Overhaul congressional lobbying and ethics rules for members and their staffs
No Limit debate on considering a bill to add House seats for the District of Columbia and Utah
No Limit debate on restoring habeas corpus rights to detainees
No Mandate minimum breaks for troops between deployments to Iraq or Afghanistan
No Override Bush veto of $23.2 billion water projects authorization bill
Yes Confirm Michael B. Mukasey as attorney general
No Limit debate on an energy policy overhaul containing $21.8 billion in tax incentives and reduced oil and gas subsidies

CQ VOTE STUDIES

	PARTY UNITY		PRESIDENTIAL SUPPORT	
	SUPPORT	OPPOSE	SUPPORT	OPPOSE
2008	97%	3%	76%	24%
2007	95%	5%	86%	14%
2006	96%	4%	91%	9%
2005	99%	1%	93%	7%
2004	99%	1%	98%	2%
2003	99%	1%	100%	0%
2002	97%	3%	96%	4%
2001	98%	2%	97%	3%
2000	99%	1%	42%	58%
1999	95%	5%	33%	67%

INTEREST GROUPS

	AFL-CIO	ADA	CCUS	ACU
2008	20%	20%	100%	80%
2007	11%	10%	82%	92%
2006	13%	5%	100%	84%
2005	14%	5%	94%	100%
2004	8%	15%	94%	96%
2003	0%	10%	100%	84%
2002	23%	0%	95%	100%
2001	6%	5%	93%	96%
2000	0%	5%	92%	100%
1999	0%	0%	88%	84%

Sen. Jim Bunning (R)

Elected 1998; 2nd term

CAPITOL OFFICE
224-4343
bunning.senate.gov
316 Hart Bldg. 20510-1703; fax 228-1373

COMMITTEES
Banking, Housing & Urban Affairs
Budget
Energy & Natural Resources
Finance

RESIDENCE
Southgate

BORN
Oct. 23, 1931; Southgate, Ky.

RELIGION
Roman Catholic

FAMILY
Wife, Mary Bunning; nine children

EDUCATION
Xavier U., B.S. 1953 (economics)

CAREER
Investment broker; sports agent; professional
baseball player

POLITICAL HIGHLIGHTS
Fort Thomas City Council, 1977-79; Ky. Senate,
1979-83; Republican nominee for governor, 1983;
U.S. House, 1987-99

ELECTION RESULTS

2004 GENERAL

Jim Bunning (R)	873,507	50.7%
Daniel Mongiardo (D)	850,855	49.3%

2004 PRIMARY

Jim Bunning (R)	96,545	84.0%
Barry Metcalf (R)	18,395	16.0%

PREVIOUS WINNING PERCENTAGES
1998 (50%); 1996 House Election (68%); 1994 House
Election (74%); 1992 House Election (62%); 1990
House Election (69%); 1988 House Election (74%);
1986 House Election (55%)

A Hall of Fame baseball pitcher known as a fierce competitor, Bunning has been one of the quirkier members in Congress since his arrival as a House member in 1987. His supporters say he has strong convictions and applaud his willingness to speak his mind. But detractors label him divisive, abrasive and short on major legislative accomplishments. What all agree on is that he is unafraid to go his own way.

Bunning — a member of the Finance and Banking, Housing and Urban Affairs committees — is one of the most outspoken supporters of a pure free-market philosophy. He even went against party leaders as they tried to help turn around the economy in late 2008. "Republican socialism," he thundered after two fellow Republicans, President George W. Bush and Treasury Secretary Henry M. Paulson Jr., unveiled their plans for a $700 billion package to rescue the financial industry, which was signed into law.

And during a March 2009 hearing after American International Group Inc. received its fourth infusion of funds from the financial rescue package and faced increasing criticism for giving out million-dollar bonuses to executives, Bunning warned against allowing the insurance giant to come back for more. "You will get the biggest 'no' you've ever gotten," warned Bunning, the top Republican on the Banking Subcommittee on Securities, Insurance and Investment. "I will hold the bill. I will do anything possible to stop you from wasting taxpayers' money on a lost cause, because that's what AIG is, a lost cause."

He was just as hard on President Obama's plans to turn around the economy. He joined Minority Whip Jon Kyl of Arizona in blocking the Finance Committee from moving ahead on a confirmation hearing for Timothy F. Geithner, Obama's choice for Treasury secretary, following revelations about problems with Geithner's tax returns. Geithner's nomination was eventually confirmed.

Bunning also opposed Obama's $787 billion economic stimulus proposal. "If we really want to stimulate the economy, we need to focus our attention on tax cuts for individuals, investment and businesses," he said on the Senate floor. He voted against the bill after the Senate rejected his proposal to allow individuals to deduct up to $15,000 in capital losses for 2009, up from the current $3,000 limit, and to remove a provision allowing corporations to apply tax credits against five year's prior tax payments and getting refunds.

With a degree in economics from Xavier University in Cincinnati and a seat on the Budget Committee, Bunning is generally well respected for his ability to discuss monetary policy. But he felt some heat after voting against federal help for the automakers. His paid appearance at a baseball card show in Michigan, the domestic auto industry's heartland, was canceled.

It wasn't the first time Bunning's comments had stirred a negative public reaction. During his 2004 bid for re-election to a second Senate term, Bunning told a joke to a home-state Republican audience in which he mockingly said his Italian-American Democratic opponent, little-known State Sen. Daniel Mongiardo, resembled one of Saddam Hussein's sons. Comments like that, as well as the senator's uncompromising views on a variety of topics and his refusal to debate Mongiardo face to face, helped turn a re-election campaign in which Bunning was initially the heavy favorite into a squeaker. He won by just 22,652 votes out of more than 1.7 million ballots cast.

His comments against the Bush administration raised questions regarding his ability to win re-election in 2010. And in January 2009, his absence from the Senate during consideration of a bill to release the second portion of the financial industry rescue funds and during discussions on the first of the Obama administration's Cabinet nominees raised further questions among political observers as to whether Bunning intends to seek re-election. Bunning told the Louisville Courier-Journal in mid-January he had been absent because he was fulfilling "a family commitment six months ago to do certain things, and I'm doing them."

Bunning continued to make headlines in the months that followed. He predicted that U.S. Supreme Court Justice Ruth Bader Ginsburg would die within a year of pancreatic cancer, prompting an apology to the liberal justice. A few weeks later, he apologized again for swearing at reporters when asked about the results of a campaign poll he had commissioned.

And he openly quarreled with his home-state GOP colleague, Minority Leader Mitch McConnell, and Texas' John Cornyn, chairman of the National Republican Senatorial Committee. Bunning contended in March 2009 that the two had sought someone to challenge him in the GOP primary, making it hard for him to raise money.

Such flare-ups only added to the Democrats' determination to make him a prime target for defeat in 2010. Just about every top Democratic officeholder in the state is mentioned as a possible opponent, including Mongiardo, who is now lieutenant governor.

Bunning had turned against Bush on several votes during the Republican administration. In 2006, he was one of only two senators to vote against Bush's nomination of Robert M. Gates to serve as Defense secretary. He also opposed Bush's nomination of Federal Reserve Chairman Ben S. Bernanke.

But he stood by Bush's Iraq War policy even as the United States got bogged down and as the American public turned against the war. "Failure in Iraq is not an option," Bunning said.

Bunning opposes abortion, gun control and same-sex marriage. But on occasion he reaches across the aisle to work with liberal Democrats on legislation. A member of the Energy and Natural Resources Committee, he joined with then-Illinois Sen. Barack Obama during the 109th Congress (2005-06) to cosponsor a bill to promote coal gasification as a way of boosting domestic energy production. Kentucky and Illinois are both big coal-producing states.

And Bunning, the father of nine children, worked with Nebraska Democrat Ben Nelson on legislation to make permanent tax incentives for adoption.

Bunning has been outspoken about the use of illegal steroids in professional sports, a topic Congress took up in 2005 and 2006. He denounced those who used the illegal substances to boost their performances. He said baseball sluggers such as Mark McGwire and Barry Bonds, both linked to steroid use, should be shunned by the sport.

He grew up in the Kentucky suburbs and after college played in the major leagues for 17 seasons, from 1955 to 1971, in both the American and National leagues. He was the first pitcher to score 100 wins and 1,000 strikeouts in both leagues. He ended his career with 224 wins and two no-hitters. One of them was a perfect game on June 21, 1964, when he pitched the Phillies to a victory over the New York Mets. He was voted into the Hall of Fame in 1996. After his playing days, he managed in the minor leagues, then became a sports agent.

Bunning began his political career in 1977, winning a seat on the city council in Fort Thomas. Two years later, he won a state Senate seat and rose to become Republican floor leader. In 1983, he ran an unsuccessful gubernatorial campaign against Democratic Lt. Gov. Martha Layne Collins. But he did unusually well for a Republican, getting 44 percent of the vote.

In 1986, Republican U.S. Rep. Gene Snyder retired from his seat in the 4th District. GOP leaders drafted Bunning, who won with 55 percent and was re-elected to the House five times. In 1998, he narrowly won the election to succeed retiring Democratic Sen. Wendell H. Ford, beating Democrat Scotty Baesler, a three-term House member, by fewer than 7,000 votes.

KEY VOTES

2008
Yes   Prohibit discrimination based on genetic information
Yes   Reauthorize farm and nutrition programs for five years
No   Limit debate on "cap and trade" system for greenhouse gas emissions
No   Allow lawsuits against companies that participated in warrantless wiretapping
No   Limit debate on a bill to block a scheduled cut in Medicare payments to doctors
–   Grant mortgage relief to homeowners and funding for Fannie Mae and Freddie Mac
Yes   Approve a nuclear cooperation agreement with India
No   Approve final $700 billion program to stabilize financial markets
No   Allow consideration of a $14 billion auto industry loan package

2007
Yes   Increase minimum wage by $2.10 an hour
No   Limit debate on a comprehensive immigration bill
Yes   Overhaul congressional lobbying and ethics rules for members and their staffs
No   Limit debate on considering a bill to add House seats for the District of Columbia and Utah
No   Limit debate on restoring habeas corpus rights to detainees
No   Mandate minimum breaks for troops between deployments to Iraq or Afghanistan
+   Override Bush veto of $23.2 billion water projects authorization bill
Yes   Confirm Michael B. Mukasey as attorney general
No   Limit debate on an energy policy overhaul containing $21.8 billion in tax incentives and reduced oil and gas subsidies

CQ VOTE STUDIES

	PARTY UNITY		PRESIDENTIAL SUPPORT	
	SUPPORT	OPPOSE	SUPPORT	OPPOSE
2008	95%	5%	79%	21%
2007	95%	5%	85%	15%
2006	97%	3%	90%	10%
2005	98%	2%	91%	9%
2004	98%	2%	94%	6%
2003	99%	1%	100%	0%
2002	97%	3%	96%	4%
2001	97%	3%	96%	4%
2000	98%	2%	33%	67%
1999	95%	5%	24%	76%

INTEREST GROUPS

	AFL-CIO	ADA	CCUS	ACU
2008	10%	5%	75%	88%
2007	5%	10%	80%	92%
2006	13%	0%	91%	96%
2005	14%	5%	94%	92%
2004	17%	15%	100%	100%
2003	0%	10%	100%	85%
2002	31%	0%	95%	100%
2001	13%	0%	93%	100%
2000	13%	5%	78%	100%
1999	11%	0%	82%	100%

Rep. Ed Whitfield (R)

Elected 1994; 8th term

CAPITOL OFFICE
225-3115
www.house.gov/whitfield
2411 Rayburn Bldg. 20515-1701; fax 225-3547

COMMITTEES
Energy & Commerce

RESIDENCE
Hopkinsville

BORN
May 25, 1943; Hopkinsville, Ky.

RELIGION
Methodist

FAMILY
Wife, Constance Whitfield; one child

EDUCATION
U. of Kentucky, B.S. 1965 (business);
Wesley Theological Seminary, attended 1966;
U. of Kentucky, J.D. 1969

MILITARY SERVICE
Army Reserve, 1967-73

CAREER
Lawyer; oil distributor; railroad executive

POLITICAL HIGHLIGHTS
Ky. House, 1974-75 (served as a Democrat)

ELECTION RESULTS

2008 GENERAL

Ed Whitfield (R)	178,107	64.3%
Heather A. Ryan (D)	98,674	35.6%

2008 PRIMARY

Ed Whitfield (R)	unopposed

2006 GENERAL

Ed Whitfield (R)	123,618	59.6%
Tom Barlow (D)	83,865	40.4%

PREVIOUS WINNING PERCENTAGES
2004 (67%); 2002 (65%); 2000 (58%); 1998 (55%);
1996 (54%); 1994 (51%)

Whitfield is an exceedingly polite, soft-spoken former Democrat who is a close ally of Senate Minority Leader Mitch McConnell, his state's dominant politician. He watches out for his region's coal and tobacco interests as he works behind the scenes on health, energy and other issues as a senior member of the Energy and Commerce Committee.

Whitfield generally takes his party's side, though he has been slightly more inclined to go his own way since becoming a member of the minority. During President George W. Bush's first six years in office, Whitfield backed the GOP at least 90 percent of the time on votes that pitted the two parties against each other. But after Democrats took control in 2007, his party support level dipped to 84 percent in 2007 and 89 percent in 2008.

He was among a minority of Republicans, for example, to vote for an increase in the minimum wage and for new pay-as-you-go budget rules and transparency in the process of approving earmarks — funds designated to specific projects in members' districts. And he was one of just 16 House Republicans to support a $410 billion catchall spending bill, for fiscal 2009.

Whitfield made a campaign pledge several years ago to ban the slaughter of horses. He and his wife ConstanceWhitfield — a senior adviser to the Humane Society of the United States — are horse lovers who have rescued several animals. The couple began working on the issue after being at a 2004 horse auction in Pennsylvania and witnessing a horse, too sick and feeble to travel, being loaded onto a trailer for a 1,500-mile trip to Texas for slaughter. The Whitfields felt euthanization would have been the humane approach.

Whitfield sponsored a bill in the 109th Congress (2005-06) to make it a crime to transport, sell or buy horses with the intent of killing them for human consumption. It passed the House overwhelmingly in 2006, but the Senate never took it up.

A federal appeals court ruled in 2007 that a 1949 Texas law prohibits the sale of horse meat there, forcing the state's two horse slaughter plants to close. That May, Illinois legislators voted to ban horse slaughter, shuttering the last remaining U.S. plant. Whitfield now is pushing legislation to bar the shipping of horses abroad for slaughter. "The problem now is that people are moving more of the horses to Mexico, where the slaughter process is even worse than it was in the U.S.," he told the Courier-Journal of Louisville.

Whitfield in 2008 added the care of race horses to his agenda after the second Kentucky Derby contender in three years had to be euthanized following a racing injury. He said he is planning to back legislation to ban the use of steroids in the sport.

Whitfield serves on Energy and Commerce's panels on Health and Energy and the Environment, affording him the opportunity to be a player on shaping major legislation in those areas. He has been an ardent supporter of the coal industry, a leading employer in his district, and said "clean" coal technology should become more widespread to reduce energy costs. Coal "is our most abundant resource, and expanding its use would give us the opportunity to compete and bring in more jobs," he said in October 2008.

Whitfield also has been active in shaping health care legislation. In 2005, Congress cleared his bill to allow electronic monitoring of prescription drugs, which discourages the overprescribing of medicines and "doctor shopping" by drug addicts. He also successfully pushed legislation in 2001 that compensated nuclear plant workers for the adverse health effects of exposure to radiation. The bill, signed into law, helped employees at the uranium enrichment plant in Paducah in his district.

He remains suspicious of government intrusion on health care providers. "We should be focusing on market-based reforms that modernize our regulatory structure and empower doctors and patients with information and options," he said in March 2009.

He was brought onto Energy and Commerce at the start of his first term, when the GOP took control of the House and an influential Republican colleague from another tobacco state, former Rep. Thomas J. Bliley Jr. of Virginia, became chairman and sought to bring friends of the industry onto the committee. Whitfield fought Clinton administration attempts in the latter half of the 1990s to sue tobacco companies for selling hazardous products. Later, in 2004, he pushed for provisions in a comprehensive corporate tax bill giving tobacco farmers a 10-year, $10 billion buyout. Congress passed the measure and Bush signed it.

Born in Hopkinsville, near the Tennessee border, Whitfield is the son of a railroad conductor. His mother worked in finance at a local hospital. Whitfield spent a year at Wesley Theological Seminary in Washington, D.C., before switching to law school.

Whitfield was a Democrat in those days, and served for two years in the state House as a member of that party shortly after law school. He switched parties during the Reagan revolution of the 1980s.

He spent much of his early career doing regulatory and legislative work for major railroads, including CSX Corp. He lived many of those years in Washington, and in the early 1990s was a lawyer for the Interstate Commerce Commission.

When Republicans sought to capture a majority in Congress in 1994, McConnell recruited Whitfield to challenge Democratic Rep. Tom Barlow. Whitfield had not lived in Kentucky for a dozen years; he moved from CSX headquarters in Jacksonville, Fla., to make the race. But efforts to paint him as a carpetbagger were offset by the strength of his family roots in the 1st District. His extended family had farmed in the area since 1799. Furthermore, Whitfield was a friend of Democrat Edward Breathitt, who was a Kentucky governor in the 1960s.

Whitfield won that race with 51 percent of the vote, becoming the first Republican to represent the district. He was threatened by the anti-Republican tide of the 2006 election, but ended up taking 60 percent of the vote in a rematch with Barlow, and won easily again in 2008.

KEY VOTES

2008

No Delay consideration of Colombia free-trade agreement

Yes Override Bush veto of federal farm and nutrition programs reauthorization bill

Yes Overhaul surveillance laws and permit dismissal of suits against companies that conducted warrantless wiretapping

No Grant mortgage relief to homeowners and funding for Fannie Mae and Freddie Mac

No Approve initial $700 billion program to stabilize financial markets

No Approve final $700 billion program to stabilize financial markets

No Provide $14 billion in loans to automakers

2007

Yes Increase minimum wage by $2.10 an hour

No Approve $124.2 billion in emergency war spending and set goal for redeployment of troops from Iraq

? Reject federal contraceptive assistance to international family planning groups

Yes Override Bush veto of $23.2 billion water projects authorization bill

Yes Implement Peru free-trade agreement

Yes Approve energy policy overhaul with new fuel economy standards

Yes Clear $473.5 billion omnibus spending bill, including $70 billion for military operations

CQ VOTE STUDIES

	PARTY UNITY		PRESIDENTIAL SUPPORT	
	SUPPORT	OPPOSE	SUPPORT	OPPOSE
2008	89%	11%	56%	44%
2007	84%	16%	69%	31%
2006	90%	10%	87%	13%
2005	94%	6%	87%	13%
2004	91%	9%	85%	15%

INTEREST GROUPS

	AFL-CIO	ADA	CCUS	ACU
2008	29%	35%	72%	78%
2007	26%	25%	90%	83%
2006	21%	0%	93%	76%
2005	21%	10%	85%	88%
2004	14%	5%	100%	88%

KENTUCKY 1

West – Hopkinsville, Henderson, Paducah

Located in the western part of the Bluegrass State, Kentucky's rural 1st is a hub of agricultural activity. Tobacco remains a major economic force, and the coal mining industry still contributes to the regional economy despite decades of decline. Volatility in agricultural and mining markets makes the district susceptible to high unemployment rates.

The Ohio River port of Paducah (McCracken County) traditionally has been western Kentucky's political and population center, although its population has been surpassed by both Henderson and Hopkinsville. Hopkinsville is an agricultural market center and has an ethanol plant that uses locally grown corn and produces 33 million gallons of fuel ethanol annually. The city also is heavily dependent on nearby Fort Campbell, much of which is in Tennessee.

Tobacco yields have increased in most of the 1st, but have decreased in the area around Paducah. The industry has faced uncertainty since the federal government's buyout of local tobacco farmers, which ended longstanding production quotas and price controls. The 1st also has an

abundance of coal, and the mining industry provides many jobs in the region, especially in Webster and Henderson counties. Tourism and recreation also play a role in the economy, especially near the 170,000-acre forested Land Between the Lakes area.

The 1st is no longer the Democratic stronghold that it once was, and the 1994 GOP wave sent the district's first Republican to Congress. Although there are nearly twice as many registered Democrats as registered Republicans in the 1st, John McCain took 62 percent of the district's presidential vote in 2008 and only lost one county (Henderson) here.

MAJOR INDUSTRY
Tobacco, agriculture, manufacturing, coal

MILITARY BASES
Fort Campbell, 30,178 military, 3,085 civilian (2009) (shared with Tennessee's 7th District))

CITIES
Hopkinsville, 30,089; Henderson, 27,373; Paducah, 26,307

NOTABLE
The Jefferson Davis Monument, located at his birthplace in Fairview, is a 351-foot obelisk; The nation's only plant that turns uranium into nuclear fuel is operated in Paducah by USEC, an energy company.

Rep. Brett Guthrie (R)

Elected 2008; 1st term

CAPITOL OFFICE
225-3501
guthrie.house.gov
510 Cannon Bldg. 20515; fax 226-2019

COMMITTEES
Education & Labor
Transportation & Infrastructure

RESIDENCE
Bowling Green

BORN
Feb. 18, 1964; Florence, Ala.

RELIGION
Church of Christ

FAMILY
Wife, Beth Guthrie; three children

EDUCATION
U.S. Military Academy, B.S. 1987 (mathematical economics); Yale U., M.P.P.M 1997

MILITARY SERVICE
Army, 1987-90; Army Reserve, 1990-2002

CAREER
Automotive supply company executive

POLITICAL HIGHLIGHTS
Ky. Senate, 1999-2009

ELECTION RESULTS

2008 GENERAL

Brett Guthrie (R)	158,936	52.6%
David E. Boswell (D)	143,379	47.4%

2008 PRIMARY

Brett Guthrie (R)	unopposed

Guthrie is a reliable conservative vote who says his experiences as a small businessman and nearly three-term state senator shaped his small-government approach, while his background as a West Point graduate and veteran of the 101st Airborne have made him staunchly pro-defense.

He is a member of the Republican Study Committee, the House's most conservative faction. Siding with all House Republicans, he opposed President Obama's $787 billion economic stimulus bill in February 2009, calling it a "partisan bill" that wouldn't stimulate the economy or create jobs. He criticized Democrats for not considering Republican input.

Guthrie is a former vice president of Trace Die Cast Inc. in Bowling Green, an automobile die-casting business founded by his father. The business began with a handful of workers but now has 500, and Guthrie says he wants to make use of his background as Congress deals with the ongoing financial crisis.

Guthrie sits on the Transportation and Infrastructure Committee, which plans to take up a renewal of the 2005 surface transportation bill. A former chairman of the state Senate Transportation Committee, Guthrie said he believes his past experience will give him a leg up. He hopes to fund local projects to help the district deal with the influx of up to 2,000 soldiers to the Fort Knox region that is expected by 2010.

Guthrie also serves on the Education and Labor Committee, where he is the top Republican on the Higher Education, Lifelong Learning and Competitiveness Subcommittee. He served on the education and labor panel during his service in the state legislature.

Fulfilling a campaign promise, Guthrie introduced a bill in February 2009 to maintain the health benefits of families of military members who die as a result of a combat-related injury.

In his race to succeed seven-term GOP Rep. Ron Lewis, who indicated his retirement the last filing day for the May 2008 primary, Guthrie was set for a battle against Lewis' chief of staff, Daniel London. London later withdrew. Guthrie's big test came in the general election, when he defeated state Sen. David E. Boswell with 53 percent of the vote.

KENTUCKY 2

West central — Owensboro, Bowling Green

The mostly rural 2nd District, anchored in Kentucky's west-central heartland, takes in some suburban areas near Louisville and the city of Owensboro, and runs through rolling tobacco country, ending in the river country to the west.

Tobacco remains a dominant crop in the district, despite the federal buyout of tobacco farms and the end of the production quota system. Coal and oil also provide some jobs throughout the district. An Amazon.com distribution center in Campbellsville has brought stability to an otherwise grim economy in the 2nd's rural areas, which have been subject to volatility in the coal industry. Bowling Green has been hurt by recent layoffs at its General Motors Corvette plant, and the district's manufacturing tradition is dwindling.

Tourism is a growing sector of the economy, and visitors tour the Mammoth Cave National Park in the southern part of the district, the barbecue joints of Daviess County in the northwest, and several of the distilleries on Kentucky's "Bourbon Trail" — the 2nd produces famous brands such as Jim Beam and Maker's Mark — to the east.

After a long period of Democratic dominance, 2nd District voters now side with the GOP in federal elections. In the 2008 presidential election, John McCain took 61 percent of the district's vote.

MAJOR INDUSTRY
Tobacco, coal, oil, tourism, manufacturing

MILITARY BASES
Fort Knox, 9,215 military, 5,406 civilian (2009)

CITIES
Owensboro, 54,067; Bowling Green, 49,296; Elizabethtown, 22,542; Radcliff, 21,961

NOTABLE
The U.S. Bullion Depository, or "Gold Vault," at Fort Knox houses the largest portion of the U.S. gold reserve.

Rep. John Yarmuth (D)

Elected 2006; 2nd term

CAPITOL OFFICE
225-5401
yarmuth.house.gov
435 Cannon Bldg. 20515-1703; fax 225-5776

COMMITTEES
Budget
Ways & Means

RESIDENCE
Louisville

BORN
Nov. 4, 1947; Louisville, Ky.

RELIGION
Jewish

FAMILY
Wife, Cathy Yarmuth; one child

EDUCATION
Yale U., B.A. 1969 (American studies);
Georgetown U. Law School, attended 1971-72

CAREER
Periodical publisher and columnist; television
commentator; public relations executive;
congressional aide; stockbroker

POLITICAL HIGHLIGHTS
Republican nominee for Louisville Board of
Alderman, 1975; Republican nominee for
Jefferson County Board of Commissioners, 1981

ELECTION RESULTS

2008 GENERAL

John Yarmuth (D)	203,843	59.4%
Anne M. Northup (R)	139,527	40.6%

2008 PRIMARY

John Yarmuth (D)	unopposed

2006 GENERAL

John Yarmuth (D)	122,489	50.6%
Anne M. Northup (R)	116,568	48.2%

A former columnist and talk radio host who started in politics as a Republican, Yarmuth has built a career on espousing his liberal views and believes his forceful communication skills can further the Democratic message. "Democrats like to be liked; they don't want to upset anybody," he said. "You can't be afraid of an argument."

Yarmuth is a faithful vote for his party, backing it during his first term on 97 percent of the votes in which a majority of Republicans and Democrats diverged. He was rewarded in 2009 with a slot on the choice Ways and Means Committee, where he seeks to address the needs of ordinary Americans on health care and tax policy. "Our government has made the rich and powerful its priority, and I think it is time that changed," he said.

He wants to work on implementing universal health care and providing other assistance to low-income families. He also hopes to have a chance to tackle the future solvency of entitlement programs. "When you talk about the long-range prospects for the country, virtually anything you want to do depends on us fixing Social Security and Medicare," he said.

Yarmuth makes clear — sometimes colorfully — his distaste for Republicans he believes are guilty of mismanagement. At an October 2008 hearing on the financial crisis, Yarmuth described the three GOP panelists — former Federal Reserve Chairman Alan Greenspan, former Treasury Secretary John W. Snow and Securities and Exchange Commission Chairman Christopher Cox — as "three Bill Buckners," a reference to the Boston Red Sox first baseman whose infamous fielding error helped cost his team the 1986 World Series. "All of you let the ball go through your legs," he told them.

He employs a variety of other methods to make his points. In October 2007, he began distributing tan lapel buttons emblazoned with "Article 1" of the Constitution — which invests legislative powers in the Congress — to House colleagues as a way to display their displeasure with what he calls "the imperial presidency." The House parliamentarian told him the buttons couldn't be worn while speaking on the floor because they violate rules against badges designed to convey a message. Yarmuth insisted they were no different than flag pins. Unsuccessful in pushing his point, he continued to distribute the buttons — just when he wasn't holding the floor.

He encourages constituents to submit their personal stories for him to read on the House floor. A note on his Web site says, "The stories of Louisvillians like you will remind other members of Congress just why we're here and who we work for." He tries to be accessible to them as well. "Ninety percent of this job is listening," he said during a February 2009 breakfast for African-American veterans.

From his seat on the Education and Labor Committee in the 110th Congress (2007-08), he emerged as a vocal critic of the mandatory testing standards imposed by the 2001 No Child Left Behind education law. He said his urban district has "very serious problems" with its reporting requirements and measurements of progress.

He has joined environmental groups in harshly criticizing the blasting away of mountaintops to remove coal, something done in parts of his state. He applauded the Obama administration when it announced in March 2009 plans to rein in the technique, and he said he supported forcing mining operators to find less harmful ways to dispose of byproducts of mountaintop removal.

Yarmuth in fall 2008 originally opposed the $700 billion bill to shore up the ailing U.S. financial services sector. But he supported the second version of the measure, which became law, after business owners in his district warned they might have to lay off workers or shut down because credit was drying up. "I finally said I'm not willing to roll the dice with the lives of my constituents," he said.

The product of a wealthy Kentucky family, Yarmuth is perhaps an unlikely populist. His father founded National Industries, which was at one time Kentucky's second-largest public company, with holdings in retail business, manufacturing, transportation, oil and services. His maternal grandfather was a prominent Louisville banker.

Though Yarmuth's political awakening came in 1960, when John F. Kennedy was elected president, he considered himself a Republican for years. His initial foray into politics came as a legislative aide to Kentucky Republican Sen. Marlow W. Cook from 1971 to 1974.

He ran unsuccessfully for office twice as a Republican, first for the Louisville Board of Aldermen in 1975 at age 27 and then for Jefferson County Board of Commissioners at the suggestion of a county judge named Mitch McConnell, who would go onto become a Kentucky senator and Republican leader.

Yarmuth's family fortune helped him begin a career in publishing. In 1976, Yarmuth founded Louisville Today magazine, publishing it until 1982, along with an alternative newspaper, City Paper. After a stint in public relations in the 1980s, he founded and edited the weekly Louisville Eccentric Observer in the 1990s and appeared as a radio and TV commentator.

It was not until 1985 that he became a Democrat, deciding the party more closely reflected his views. Nine years later, he financed his own TV ad attacking President George W. Bush's tax cuts.

He was a late entrant into the 2006 race and was not favored to win either the primary or general election. Enjoying a comfortable lifestyle, he was leaning against running, a position encouraged by prominent Democrats who cited his 15 years of columns that could be used against him. As predicted, some of his more extreme suggestions as a columnist — such as removing "under God" from the Pledge of Allegiance — provided fodder for his opponents' attack ads. But he won the primary handily and went on to edge out Republican Rep. Anne M. Northup by just 2 percentage points.

Northup came back for a rematch in 2008. The two covered much the same ground as in the earlier race, with Yarmuth tying her record to President Bush and Northup criticizing what she called her opponent's extreme positions. In the end, the Democratic tide — Yarmuth's district was the only one that Obama carried in Kentucky — proved too much for her, and Yarmuth won comfortably with 59 percent.

KEY VOTES

2008
Yes   Delay consideration of Colombia free-trade agreement

Yes   Override Bush veto of federal farm and nutrition programs reauthorization bill

Yes   Overhaul surveillance laws and permit dismissal of suits against companies that conducted warrantless wiretapping

Yes   Grant mortgage relief to homeowners and funding for Fannie Mae and Freddie Mac

No   Approve initial $700 billion program to stabilize financial markets

Yes   Approve final $700 billion program to stabilize financial markets

Yes   Provide $14 billion in loans to automakers

2007
Yes   Increase minimum wage by $2.10 an hour

Yes   Approve $124.2 billion in emergency war spending and set goal for redeployment of troops from Iraq

No   Reject federal contraceptive assistance to international family planning groups

?   Override Bush veto of $23.2 billion water projects authorization bill

No   Implement Peru free-trade agreement

Yes   Approve energy policy overhaul with new fuel economy standards

No   Clear $473.5 billion omnibus spending bill, including $70 billion for military operations

CQ VOTE STUDIES

	PARTY UNITY		PRESIDENTIAL SUPPORT	
	SUPPORT	OPPOSE	SUPPORT	OPPOSE
2008	98%	2%	13%	87%
2007	97%	3%	3%	97%

INTEREST GROUPS

	AFL-CIO	ADA	CCUS	ACU
2008	100%	95%	61%	4%
2007	96%	100%	53%	0%

KENTUCKY 3

Louisville Metro

With the Ohio River forming its western border, the 3rd District sprawls across ethnically and economically diverse neighborhoods of Louisville Metro. Compared to the rest of the state, Louisville has a sizable black population — nearly one-third of Kentucky's blacks live here.

Although tobacco, a statewide agricultural staple, still aids the 3rd's economy, other sectors now rival it. Local officials have focused on attracting new businesses to the area, and Louisville now hosts health care, financial services and insurance firms. Louisville's airport is an international hub for United Parcel Service, one of the area's largest private employers, although falling cargo traffic and rising fuel prices nationwide concern the tens of thousands of local UPS employees.

Manufacturing also retains a local presence: Two Ford assembly plants provide thousands of jobs, although many worry about widespread downturns in the domestic auto manufacturing industry. Despite some recent layoffs, General Electric Consumer & Industrial still employs roughly 5,000 at its Louisville plant. Tourism — centered around horse racing and downtown cultural attractions — is another contributor to the local economy, although economic slowdowns have hurt gaming revenue in the state.

The only district in the state won by Barack Obama in the 2008 presidential election, the 3rd is Kentucky's most Democratic district. Obama took only 56 percent of the district's presidential vote, but the party runs well at the local level, especially downtown. Labor strength runs deep among the blue-collar residents of the city's South End, despite job losses from industrial decline. Blacks living in the West End also back Democrats. Republicans near the river in the affluent East End, coupled with the growing number of white-collar suburbanites east of downtown, balance some of the left-leaning areas of the district.

MAJOR INDUSTRY
Service, trade, manufacturing, health care

CITIES
Louisville Metro, 674,032

NOTABLE
The Kentucky Derby, called "the greatest two minutes in sports," is held at Churchill Downs in south Louisville; The Louisville Slugger Museum & Factory is in downtown Louisville.

Rep. Geoff Davis (R)

Elected 2004; 3rd term

CAPITOL OFFICE
225-3465
www.house.gov/geoffdavis
1108 Longworth Bldg. 20515-1704; fax 225-0003

COMMITTEES
Ways & Means

RESIDENCE
Hebron

BORN
Oct. 26, 1958; Montreal, Canada

RELIGION
Christian

FAMILY
Wife, Pat Davis; six children

EDUCATION
U.S. Military Academy, B.S. 1981

MILITARY SERVICE
Army, 1976-87

CAREER
Manufacturing productivity consulting firm owner; aerospace technology consultant

POLITICAL HIGHLIGHTS
Republican nominee for U.S. House, 2002

ELECTION RESULTS

2008 GENERAL

Geoff Davis (R)	190,210	63.0%
Michael Kelley (D)	111,549	37.0%

2008 PRIMARY

Geoff Davis (R)	30,189	85.2%
Warren O. Stone (R)	2,831	8.0%
G. E. Puckett (R)	2,427	6.8%

2006 GENERAL

Geoff Davis (R)	105,845	51.7%
Ken Lucas (D)	88,822	43.4%
Brian Houillion (LIBERT)	10,100	4.9%

PREVIOUS WINNING PERCENTAGES
2004 (54%)

A business-oriented conservative with a military background, Davis has worked to solidify his control of what was once one of the country's most competitive districts. He appears to have gained the confidence of his constituents, despite occasional gaffes.

Davis is generally a reliable vote for his party. A West Point graduate and former Army flight commander with the 82nd Airborne, he has been supportive of the Iraq War. He holds conservative social views, which match his stance on fiscal issues. A member of the tax-writing Ways and Means Committee, he wants to extend the 2001 and 2003 tax cuts that President George W. Bush pushed. He also believes health care costs could be lowered by curbing lawsuits.

He does stray on occasion. He joined Democrats to support a 2007 increase in the minimum wage. Earlier in his career, he split with most House Republicans to support a 2005 ban on cruel or degrading treatment of U.S. detainees, requiring that interrogators stick to standards set forth in the Army Field Manual.

Davis strongly backed Bush's policy in the Iraq War. But in the run-up to his 2006 re-election, he faced stinging criticism for his answer in an October debate in which he badly underestimated the number of casualties in Iraq that month, one of the deadliest since the war began in March 2003. Davis said 17 U.S. military personnel had died, while the number was 71 on the day of the debate. Davis' campaign said he misspoke as a result of nervousness. But his Democratic opponent, former Rep. Ken Lucas, used the incident to paint Davis as out of touch with reality and beholden to the Bush administration.

Davis survived it, but he put his foot in his mouth again in April 2008, when he called Democratic presidential nominee Barack Obama a "boy" during a fundraising dinner in Hebron. Davis said he had taken part in a "highly classified, national security simulation" with Obama and come away unimpressed. "That boy's finger does not need to be on the button," Davis said. Davis hand-delivered a written apology to Obama's office shortly thereafter. (That November, however, 60 percent of his voting constituents backed Republican Sen. John McCain of Arizona in the presidential election.)

Davis remains committed to the war, but he's concerned about the strain on the military it has caused. He has called for an increase in the size of the U.S. military, pushing for about 100,000 more troops over five years to reduce the pressure on National Guard and reserve forces.

He also is attuned to the concerns of veterans in his district and was successful in amending the 2009 defense authorization bill to equalize disability payments to members of the reserves injured in combat with payments made to active-duty military.

From his seat on the Financial Services panel in the 109th Congress (2005-06), Davis sponsored legislation aimed at protecting members of the military from abusive or misleading sales practices by financial services companies. The legislation, enacted into law in 2006, gives state insurance regulators jurisdiction on military bases and prohibits the sale of certain products to members of the military.

The House in 2007 passed a bill he cosponsored lifting the limit on the number of reverse mortgages the government can insure. The mortgages are increasingly popular among house-rich, cash-poor seniors because they enable retirees to tap their home equity and remain in their homes.

A social conservative, Davis opposes abortion and efforts to restrict gun ownership. And he believes schools should be allowed to search students. He sponsored a bill, which the House passed in September 2006, to require local school systems to create policies that allow searches of students on "reasonable suspicion" that they might be carrying drugs or weapons. School systems that didn't create such policies would lose federal money for programs preventing drug use and violence, a provision that angered local school administrators and school boards. The measure died in the Senate.

Like many House conservatives, he broke with Bush on immigration. Davis said the battle to control the U.S. border is of paramount importance in dealing with terrorism. He supported erecting a 700-mile fence along the U.S.-Mexico border and opposed Bush's proposal to grant amnesty to many illegal immigrants. "The unfortunate fact is that we live in a time when terrorists want to hit us as hard as they can," Davis said. "And it is elementary that to defend ourselves against these determined and resourceful enemies, our border must be secure."

Davis once said limited government is desirable. But personal experiences have sensitized him to the help government can provide: Social Security survivor benefits enabled his family to make ends meet after his stepfather died, and a government-subsidized loan made it possible for his mother to buy a house. Davis worked as a janitor while in high school to help his family pay the bills.

After leaving the Army, Davis worked as an aerospace consultant before starting his own manufacturing and technology consulting firm.

Davis' military background has an appeal in his tradition-minded district. But old-fashioned politicking has helped Davis solidify his hold on the seat, too: He has been one of the top House users of the franking privilege — free use of the mail to communicate with constituents — even though he once criticized his predecessor, Lucas, for overusing that incumbent's prerogative. He also goes after earmarks for projects in his district, despite the attacks on such funding set-asides by many in the House GOP.

Davis first tried for the 4th District seat in 2002, losing to Lucas by just 3.5 percentage points. Lucas retired two years later, and Davis defeated actor George Clooney's father, longtime local newscaster and columnist Nick Clooney, to capture the seat in the 2004 general election. When Lucas tried for a comeback in 2006, Davis was ready, beating him by 8 percentage points.

Davis had an even easier time in 2008. He built up a large campaign war chest and took 63 percent of the vote against Oldham County physician Michael Kelley.

KEY VOTES

2008
No Delay consideration of Colombia free-trade agreement
Yes Override Bush veto of federal farm and nutrition programs reauthorization bill
Yes Overhaul surveillance laws and permit dismissal of suits against companies that conducted warrantless wiretapping
No Grant mortgage relief to homeowners and funding for Fannie Mae and Freddie Mac
No Approve initial $700 billion program to stabilize financial markets
No Approve final $700 billion program to stabilize financial markets
No Provide $14 billion in loans to automakers

2007
Yes Increase minimum wage by $2.10 an hour
No Approve $124.2 billion in emergency war spending and set goal for redeployment of troops from Iraq
Yes Reject federal contraceptive assistance to international family planning groups
No Override Bush veto of $23.2 billion water projects authorization bill
Yes Implement Peru free-trade agreement
No Approve energy policy overhaul with new fuel economy standards
Yes Clear $473.5 billion omnibus spending bill, including $70 billion for military operations

CQ VOTE STUDIES

	PARTY UNITY		PRESIDENTIAL SUPPORT	
	SUPPORT	OPPOSE	SUPPORT	OPPOSE
2008	95%	5%	73%	27%
2007	94%	6%	83%	17%
2006	94%	6%	95%	5%
2005	96%	4%	87%	13%

INTEREST GROUPS

	AFL-CIO	ADA	CCUS	ACU
2008	13%	15%	89%	96%
2007	17%	10%	83%	96%
2006	29%	5%	93%	84%
2005	13%	0%	93%	88%

KENTUCKY 4

North — Covington, Florence, Ashland

The 4th travels across northern Kentucky, from the industrial city of Ashland along the Ohio River, past tobacco farms and small towns and through the Ohio commuters' region before reaching the Oldham County suburbs northeast of Louisville Metro. Nearly half of district residents live in the Cincinnati suburbs.

After steady economic growth for over a decade, the city of Covington and other parts of northern Kentucky in Boone, Campbell and Kenton counties — which include Cincinnati suburbs — are experiencing sharp increases in unemployment rates. Located in Boone County, the Cincinnati-Northern Kentucky International Airport is the largest economic force in the region, but a decline in passenger travel and cargo traffic has forced furloughs and layoffs of pilots and airport employees.

Covington also serves as a regional processing center for the IRS, and federal government jobs provide some stability even as employers in the finance industry have been forced into widespread layoffs in the region. The economy in the eastern part of the district has struggled for years.

Ashland struggled to cope after businesses relocated and downsized in the late 1980s, and the city has declined as an industrial hub. Boyd County, which includes Ashland, was the only county in the 4th to lose population in the 1990s, and the county is still experiencing slow but steady population loss. Other regional jurisdictions, including those across the Ohio and Big Sandy rivers in Ohio and West Virginia, respectively, are cooperating to try to attract more industrial firms to this tri-state area, and Ashland officials are planning new development.

The 4th backs GOP presidential candidates, and Oldham joins counties in the Cincinnati area in voting reliably Republican. John McCain took 60 percent of the 4th's 2008 presidential vote and won every county wholly or partially in the district except for one. Elliott County has voted Democratic for president for nearly a century, and Barack Obama won 61 percent of the county's vote, his highest percentage statewide.

MAJOR INDUSTRY
Transportation, manufacturing, health care, service

CITIES
Covington, 43,370; Florence, 23,551; Ashland, 21,981

NOTABLE
The Kentucky Speedway racetrack is located near Sparta.

Rep. Harold Rogers (R)

Elected 1980; 15th term

CAPITOL OFFICE
225-4601
halrogers.house.gov
2406 Rayburn Bldg. 20515-1705; fax 225-0940

COMMITTEES
Appropriations

RESIDENCE
Somerset

BORN
Dec. 31, 1937; Barrier, Ky.

RELIGION
Baptist

FAMILY
Wife, Cynthia Doyle Rogers; three children

EDUCATION
Western Kentucky U., attended 1956-57;
U. of Kentucky, B.A. 1962, LL.B. 1964

MILITARY SERVICE
Ky. National Guard, 1956-57; N.C. National Guard,
1957-58; Ky. National Guard, 1958-63

CAREER
Lawyer

POLITICAL HIGHLIGHTS
Pulaski and Rockcastle counties commonwealth
attorney, 1969-80; Republican nominee for
lieutenant governor, 1979

ELECTION RESULTS

2008 GENERAL

Harold Rogers (R)	177,024	84.1%
Jim Holbert (I)	33,444	15.9%

2008 PRIMARY

Harold Rogers (R)	unopposed

2006 GENERAL

Harold Rogers (R)	147,201	73.8%
Kenneth Stepp (D)	52,367	26.2%

PREVIOUS WINNING PERCENTAGES
2004 (100%); 2002 (78%); 2000 (74%); 1998 (78%);
1996 (100%); 1994 (79%); 1992 (55%); 1990 (100%);
1988 (100%); 1986 (100%); 1984 (76%); 1982 (65%);
1980 (68%)

Rogers is a gregarious, old-style Republican who understands the art of cutting a legislative deal. Like other veteran appropriators, he enthusiastically steers as much money as he can to his district, even if his actions earn him extra scrutiny from the news media and barbs from watchdog groups.

"There are big slices of the country, like this, that are poor and without and having to fend for themselves, facing a transition from a coal industry to something else to try to make a living," he once said of his district.

He has arguably two of the best Republican seats in the House for the 111th Congress (2009-10). He landed a spot on the Defense Appropriations panel, which oversees more than $480 billion in annual funding. And he persuaded GOP leaders to waive a six-year term limit and give him another two years as the ranking member on the Homeland Security Appropriations Subcommittee, on which he has been the top Republican since the panel was formed in 2003.

The Homeland Security panel occupies much of Rogers' attention, and he said he plans to continue working to completely merge the 22 agencies within the department. He said he'll pay particular attention to border security and keeping the Transportation Security Administration in line.

Wielding the power that comes with being an appropriator is second nature to Rogers after more than a quarter-century in the House, although his tendency to use his power to reward friends and political supporters brings him unwanted attention at times. The Citizens for Responsibility and Ethics put Rogers on its 2007 list of the most corrupt members of Congress. News outlets in recent years documented his relationships with companies doing business with the Homeland Security Department, and chronicled expensive trips Rogers took to Hawaii, Palm Springs and Las Vegas paid for by private interests.

The Lexington Herald-Leader reported in 2005 that some of Rogers' allocations went to marginal projects, including $500,000 to pave a parking lot for Lee's Ford Marina Resort, owned by a campaign donor. The newspaper subsequently dubbed him the "Prince of Pork."

None of the attention, however, seems to have much diminished Rogers' popularity back home. First elected to the House in 1980, Rogers is the dean of the Kentucky delegation. Over the years, he has brought funding home for projects ranging from improving sanitation to Operation UNITE, a regional anti-drug initiative that has received more than $30 million since its founding in 2003, and the Center for Rural Development in his hometown of Somerset, locally called the "Taj MaHal," in reference to Rogers' nickname, Hal. While he opposed a $410 billion catchall spending bill, signed into law in March 2009, he subsequently distributed press releases touting the earmarks totalling more than $34 million that he obtained in the bill. Earmarks are funding set-asides for special projects.

Rogers continues his quest for the construction of Interstate 66, a new east-west highway stretching from eastern Kentucky's coal fields to the western region's corn fields. He also is an advocate for tobacco growers.

Rogers has been a reliable conservative vote, siding with his party on 95 percent of the votes on which it diverged from Democrats during the George W. Bush administration. But he's been willing to break with the party on trade matters. He opposed the North American Free Trade Agreement and has been against letting Chinese goods enter the United States under the same tariff rules as most other nations.

He speaks passionately against drug abuse, particularly that of the prescription painkiller Oxycontin. He said Congress has appropriated $34 million for the Harold Rogers Prescription Drug Monitoring Program, of which Kentucky has received $940,000 in grants. At a 2008 Appropriations hearing, he grilled Homeland Security Secretary Michael Chertoff about the drug war spilling out from Mexico. He reiterated his concerns during a March 2009 hearing, saying the government was not paying enough attention to drug-related violence just across the border. "I think we're conveniently burying our heads in the sands of Cancun beach," he said.

The 2002 law creating the Homeland Security Department settled a long-standing debate, in which Rogers played a leading role, over how to improve the performance of the Immigration and Naturalization Service. The agency was split in half, with one bureau to guard the nation's borders and another to process immigration paperwork. Both bureaus were placed in the new security department. Rogers had promoted such a plan, with little success, during the six years he was chairman of Appropriations' Commerce, Justice and State Subcommittee, which provided funding for the INS. Since then, Rogers has pressured the struggling department to shape up.

In 2005, angry that the Coast Guard hadn't done enough on its long-term modernization program called Deepwater, Rogers drafted a bill that provided $466 million less than the administration's request for the Guard. He relented in final talks on the bill, once he was satisfied with the service's progress.

His popularity with Appropriations colleagues didn't help him ascend to the chairmanship of the full committee in 2005. GOP leaders instead gave the gavel to Republican Jerry Lewis of California, whom they saw as more willing to let them curb the power of the Appropriations subcommittee chairmen.

Rogers said he believes in the adage "Plan your work, work your plan," and has offered this advice to agency officials at more than one hearing. His career in Congress has fulfilled at least one of his own ambitions. Rogers remembers how he had to leave home in search of work in Cincinnati after graduating from high school in rural Kentucky in 1955. Far from family and friends in an unfamiliar city, Rogers said he vowed then to try to bring jobs to Kentucky. He went home to earn undergraduate and law degrees at the University of Kentucky, and made a name for himself in the southeastern part of the state as a civic activist, promoting industrial development.

In 1969, he took over as the commonwealth's attorney in that part of the state and served as prosecutor for Pulaski and Rockcastle counties. He lost a 1979 campaign for lieutenant governor, but the name recognition he earned helped when he ran for the House in 1980 to succeed retiring Republican Tim Lee Carter. He won a 10-person GOP primary, then took 68 percent of the vote in November. It was the first in a long series of decisive victories.

KEY VOTES

2008
No Delay consideration of Colombia free-trade agreement
Yes Override Bush veto of federal farm and nutrition programs reauthorization bill
Yes Overhaul surveillance laws and permit dismissal of suits against companies that conducted warrantless wiretapping
No Grant mortgage relief to homeowners and funding for Fannie Mae and Freddie Mac
Yes Approve initial $700 billion program to stabilize financial markets
Yes Approve final $700 billion program to stabilize financial markets
No Provide $14 billion in loans to automakers

2007
Yes Increase minimum wage by $2.10 an hour
No Approve $124.2 billion in emergency war spending and set goal for redeployment of troops from Iraq
Yes Reject federal contraceptive assistance to international family planning groups
Yes Override Bush veto of $23.2 billion water projects authorization bill
Yes Implement Peru free-trade agreement
No Approve energy policy overhaul with new fuel economy standards
Yes Clear $473.5 billion omnibus spending bill, including $70 billion for military operations

CQ VOTE STUDIES

	PARTY UNITY		PRESIDENTIAL SUPPORT	
	SUPPORT	OPPOSE	SUPPORT	OPPOSE
2008	96%	4%	69%	31%
2007	91%	9%	77%	23%
2006	96%	4%	93%	7%
2005	96%	4%	91%	9%
2004	95%	5%	88%	12%

INTEREST GROUPS

	AFL-CIO	ADA	CCUS	ACU
2008	13%	20%	94%	84%
2007	17%	10%	90%	96%
2006	29%	10%	87%	80%
2005	13%	0%	93%	92%
2004	20%	0%	100%	88%

KENTUCKY 5

East and southeast – Somerset, Middlesboro

The rural 5th, which takes in eastern Kentucky's hardscrabble coal country, has struggled with poverty, undereducation and a lack of economic diversity. The district has the nation's highest percentage of white residents (97 percent) and its second-lowest median income.

Mining provides thousands of jobs in this sparsely populated Appalachian region, particularly in places such as Pike, Perry, Harlan and Knott counties, despite some increased demand due to exports and coal power generation. The region's coal industry has come under increased federal scrutiny regarding safety measures and the environmental impact of mountaintop removal, and these eastern counties are trying to diversify their economies. Some community leaders are trying to attract tourists by highlighting the area's country music heritage, building new arts centers and showcasing the area's coal history.

Population in the western portion of the district is concentrated in Pulaski and Laurel counties. Somerset, in Pulaski, relies heavily on tourism and recreation. Lake Cumberland is nearby, as is the Big South Fork National River and Recreation Area. The Daniel Boone National Forest extends from Rowan County in the north to the Tennessee border.

Methamphetamine abuse, a major problem in surrounding states, has become an issue in the 5th, but groups are attempting to improve local public awareness and drug enforcement efforts. Education also is a concern, as the 5th has the state's lowest percentage (10 percent) of residents with at least a bachelor's degree.

The 5th is secure GOP territory — no Democrat has represented the southeast Kentucky district since 1889. Republicans run particularly well in the more populous central and western areas. In 2008, John McCain carried the 5th with 67 percent of the presidential vote, his highest percentage statewide, and Jackson County was his best in the state.

MAJOR INDUSTRY
Coal, service, tourism

CITIES
Somerset, 11,352; Middlesborough, 10,384

NOTABLE
Colonel Harland Sanders began making what would later be known as Kentucky Fried Chicken at his service station in Corbin.

Rep. Ben Chandler (D)

Elected February 2004; 3rd full term

Chandler has learned to balance the demands of Democratic leaders with the desires of a district where voters show a willingness to split their vote between the parties on Election Day. He moves a bit to the right on certain social and economic issues, leans left on environmental protection and keeps his eye centered on ways to bring funds to his district.

He also has become adept at balancing his lawyerly intellect with an ability to connect with constituents and colleagues. "He's folksy and at ease with everybody he runs into, and that is a highly regarded skill in Washington," fellow Democrat Jim Cooper of Tennessee told the Lexington Herald-Leader.

Chandler, who flipped the district from the Republican column in 2004, is a member with Cooper of the Blue Dog Coalition, a group of fiscally conservative House Democrats, and holds a coveted spot on the Appropriations Committee.

Some of his maneuverings have been aided by a close working relationship he has developed with a home-state Republican who worked to defeat him in his first run for the House — Senate Minority Leader Mitch McConnell. The two collaborated in 2008 to secure at least $3 million in federal aid for science programs at Kentucky State University, in Chandler's district.

But early in the 111th Congress (2009-10), with a broader Democratic majority in the House and a Democratic president in the White House, Chandler was a ready vote on many Democratic initiatives. He had been an early supporter of Barack Obama in the 2008 presidential race. He acknowledged his decision would "go against the tide" in his district, which ultimately backed Republican John McCain with 55 percent of the vote. But he told the Louisville Courier-Journal at the time, "I believe that our country needs this kind of change; our country needs this kind of boldness."

Chandler in early 2009 backed the party's measure to expand the State Children's Health Insurance Program, which covers children whose families don't qualify for Medicaid, and supported two bills, ultimately signed into law, designed to strengthen the ability of workers to combat wage discrimination. He also backed Obama's $787 billion economic stimulus law and a $410 billion catchall spending measure for fiscal 2009.

He believes tax relief should be directed to middle- and lower-income taxpayers because "those are the very people who would have plugged it right back into the economy," he said. He voted against a 2006 bill to extend about $70 billion of President George W. Bush's 2001 and 2003 tax breaks over five years.

But his party loyalty isn't always a guarantee; he went against Democratic leaders' wishes and voted against a $700 billion plan to shore up the nation's financial sector in 2008. He also opposed successful bills in 2007 and 2008 to provide a one-year adjustment to prevent more than 20 million taxpayers from paying the alternative minimum tax on the previous year's income.

On social issues, Chandler opposes same-sex marriage and supports some curbs on abortion, though he opposes an outright ban. He backs gun owners' rights but has joined with most Democrats to support expanded federal funding for embryonic stem cell research, which uses cells harvested from surplus embryos at in vitro fertilization clinics.

Chandler sits on the Interior-Environment Appropriations Subcommittee and the Energy and Environment panel of the Science and Technology Committee. He considers environmental protection a priority and fairly brags

CAPITOL OFFICE
225-4706
chandler.house.gov
1504 Longworth Bldg. 20515; fax 225-2122

COMMITTEES
Appropriations
Science & Technology
Standards of Official Conduct

RESIDENCE
Versailles

BORN
Sept. 12, 1959; Versailles, Ky.

RELIGION
Presbyterian

FAMILY
Wife, Jennifer Chandler; three children

EDUCATION
U. of Kentucky, B.A. 1983 (history), J.D. 1986

CAREER
Lawyer

POLITICAL HIGHLIGHTS
Ky. auditor, 1992-96; Ky. attorney general, 1996-2004; Democratic nominee for governor, 2003

ELECTION RESULTS

2008 GENERAL

Ben Chandler (D)	203,764	64.7%
Jon Larson (R)	111,378	35.3%

2008 PRIMARY

Ben Chandler (D)	unopposed

2006 GENERAL

Ben Chandler (D)	158,765	85.5%
Paul Ard (LIBERT)	27,015	14.5%

PREVIOUS WINNING PERCENTAGES
2004 (59%); 2004 Special Election (55%)

about standing out as one of the greenest members of Kentucky's congressional delegation. The League of Conservation Voters, which helped bankroll his 2004 campaign, gave Chandler a perfect score on its legislative rankings for the 110th Congress (2007-08). He has pushed for funding for environmentally friendly school construction and modernization projects.

His seat on the Appropriations State-Foreign Operations Subcommittee is a good fit for him and his longtime interest in foreign affairs. As a college student, he served as an intern in the British Parliament, an experience he said gave him a global view of the world. Chandler also serves with 12 other members of Congress in the NATO Parliamentary Assembly, which aims to improve relationships among the NATO partners.

He also was given a seat in 2009 on the ethics committee, which immediately faced the task of deciding how to proceed with an investigation of New York Democrat Charles B. Rangel's fundraising and personal finances. Chandler was one of three Democrats assigned to the panel who had received campaign funds from the leadership PAC of the Ways and Means chairman; he got $10,000 in 2004.

Chandler lives in Woodford County on land that has been in his family since 1784, eight years before Kentucky became a state. He was born in Versailles, and he said he can trace his ancestors on his mother's side back to the second boat that arrived at Jamestown in 1609.

His grandfather and namesake, A.B. "Happy" Chandler, was a two-time governor and a U.S. senator and may be best remembered for his five-year stint as commissioner of Major League Baseball.

Chandler was elected Kentucky auditor in 1991. He then won elections for attorney general in 1995 and 1999. As Kentucky's top law enforcement officer, he oversaw the establishment of the state's "do not call" telemarketing list.

He ran for governor in 2003 but was defeated by Republican Rep. Ernie Fletcher. After his loss, Chandler ran in the special election for the House seat vacated by Fletcher. His race against GOP state Sen. Alice Forgy Kerr drew widespread attention. Both national parties recognized that the contest would be perceived as a bellwether and spent heavily on them. Chandler won by 12 percentage points. A little more than eight months later, he won election to a full term.

Chandler took more than 85 percent of the vote in 2006, and declared himself so happy with his work that he declined to take another stab at the governorship. But his 2008 win with nearly 65 percent of the vote encouraged him to contemplate a run for the U.S. Senate in 2010 for the seat of Republican Jim Bunning.

KEY VOTES

2008

Yes Delay consideration of Colombia free-trade agreement
Yes Override Bush veto of federal farm and nutrition programs reauthorization bill
Yes Overhaul surveillance laws and permit dismissal of suits against companies that conducted warrantless wiretapping
Yes Grant mortgage relief to homeowners and funding for Fannie Mae and Freddie Mac
No   Approve initial $700 billion program to stabilize financial markets
No   Approve final $700 billion program to stabilize financial markets
Yes Provide $14 billion in loans to automakers

2007

Yes Increase minimum wage by $2.10 an hour
Yes Approve $124.2 billion in emergency war spending and set goal for redeployment of troops from Iraq
No   Reject federal contraceptive assistance to international family planning groups
?   Override Bush veto of $23.2 billion water projects authorization bill
No   Implement Peru free-trade agreement
Yes Approve energy policy overhaul with new fuel economy standards
Yes Clear $473.5 billion omnibus spending bill, including $70 billion for military operations

CQ VOTE STUDIES

	PARTY UNITY		PRESIDENTIAL SUPPORT	
	SUPPORT	OPPOSE	SUPPORT	OPPOSE
2008	93%	7%	19%	81%
2007	93%	7%	9%	91%
2006	83%	17%	56%	44%
2005	80%	20%	50%	50%
2004	79%	21%	45%	55%

INTEREST GROUPS

	AFL-CIO	ADA	CCUS	ACU
2008	100%	85%	61%	12%
2007	96%	95%	47%	8%
2006	86%	60%	57%	50%
2005	87%	85%	52%	36%
2004	86%	70%	55%	32%

KENTUCKY 6

East central – Lexington, Frankfort

The 6th embodies the culture and economic pursuits that most outsiders associate with Kentucky. This is the heart of the Bluegrass region, which spawns Kentucky Derby champions and is host to considerable tobacco and liquor interests. The 6th is a patchwork of urban, suburban and rural communities.

Lexington has a strong equine industry and is known as the thoroughbred capital of the world. The city is home to the University of Kentucky, which is central Kentucky's largest employer. Just north of Lexington is Georgetown, where Toyota's first hybrid vehicle produced in the United States rolled off the line in 2006. But slowdowns in the domestic auto manufacturing sector have forced operating changes at the plant. The state capital, Frankfort, is located about 30 miles northwest of Lexington.

Tobacco, always a highly charged subject in this region, continues to be a strong economic force. The end of the quota system — which controlled the supply and price of tobacco — and the government's tobacco buyout have made the industry more competitive. Production also has generally shifted away from the 6th in favor of the state's western regions, although increasing demand for smokeless tobacco has benefitted local dark-tobacco growers.

The 6th is a politically competitive district, and voters here, who tend to be socially conservative, will support candidates from either party. The district re-elected Democrat Ben Chandler in 2008, but Barack Obama won only 43 percent of the presidential vote. Despite the primarily Democratic government workers of Frankfort, Republican presidential candidate John McCain eked out a slim victory in Franklin County in 2008. The GOP runs up big margins in the farmland south of Lexington, especially in Garrard and Jessamine counties and the 6th's portion of Lincoln County.

MAJOR INDUSTRY
Manufacturing, service, tobacco, retail

MILITARY BASES
Blue Grass Army Depot, 4 military, 1,200 civilian (2007)

CITIES
Lexington-Fayette, 260,512; Frankfort, 27,741; Richmond, 27,152

NOTABLE
Bourbon whiskey was named after Bourbon County.

LOUISIANA

Gov. Bobby Jindal (R)

Pronounced: JIN-dle
First elected: 2007
Length of term: 4 years
Term expires: 1/12
Salary: $130,000
Phone: (225) 342-7015

Residence: Kenner
Born: June 10, 1971; Baton Rouge, La.
Religion: Roman Catholic
Family: Wife, Supriya Jindal; three children
Education: Brown U., Sc.B. 1991 (biology & public policy); Oxford U., M.Litt. 1994 (Rhodes scholar)
Career: State university system president; management consultant
Political highlights: La. Health and Hospitals Department secretary, 1996-98; U.S. Health and Human Services assistant secretary for planning and evaluation, 2001-03; candidate for governor, 2003; U.S. House, 2005-08

Election results:

2007 GENERAL
Bobby Jindal (R)	699,275	53.9%
Walter J. Boasso (D)	226,476	17.5%
John Georges (X)	186,682	14.4%
Foster Campbell (D)	161,665	12.5%

Lt. Gov. Mitch Landrieu (D)

First elected: 2003
Length of term: 4 years
Term expires: 1/12
Salary: $115,000
Phone: (225) 342-7009

LEGISLATURE

Legislature: March-June in odd-numbered years; April-June in even-numbered years

Senate: 39 members, 4-year terms
2009 ratios: 23 D, 16 R; 31 men, 8 women
Salary: $16,800
Phone: (225) 342-2040

House: 105 members, 4-year terms
2009 ratios: 52 D, 50 R, 3 I; 91 men, 14 women
Salary: $16,800
Phone: (225) 342-6945

TERM LIMITS

Governor: 2 terms
Senate: 3 consecutive terms
House: 3 consecutive terms

URBAN STATISTICS

CITY	POPULATION
New Orleans	484,674
Baton Rouge	227,818
Shreveport	200,145
Lafayette	110,257
Lake Charles	71,757

REGISTERED VOTERS

Democrat	52%
Republican	26%
Unaffiliated/others	22%

POPULATION

2008 population (est.)	4,410,796
2000 population	4,468,976
1990 population	4,219,973
Percent change (1990-2000)	+5.9%
Rank among states (2008)	25

Median age	34
Born in state	79.4%
Foreign born	2.6%
Violent crime rate	681/100,000
Poverty level	19.6%
Federal workers	34,590
Military	41,392

ELECTIONS

STATE ELECTION OFFICIAL
(225) 922-0900
DEMOCRATIC PARTY
(225) 336-4155
REPUBLICAN PARTY
(225) 928-2998

MISCELLANEOUS

Web: www.louisiana.gov
Capital: Baton Rouge

U.S. CONGRESS

Senate: 1 Democrat, 1 Republican
House: 6 Republicans, 1 Democrats

2000 Census Statistics by District

DIST.	2008 VOTE FOR PRESIDENT OBAMA	MCCAIN	WHITE	BLACK	ASIAN	HISP	MEDIAN INCOME	WHITE COLLAR	BLUE COLLAR	SERVICE INDUSTRY	OVER 64	UNDER 18	COLLEGE EDUCATION	RURAL	SQ. MILES
1 *	26%	72%	80%	13%	2%	5%	$40,948	65%	21%	14%	13%	25%	27%	20%	2,402
2 *	75	23	28	64	3	4	$27,514	56	22	22	10	28	19	1	266
3 *	37	61	70	25	1	2	$34,463	50	35	15	11	29	11	27	7,010
4	40	59	62	33	1	2	$31,085	53	29	18	13	27	17	41	10,765
5	37	62	63	34	1	1	$27,453	54	29	18	13	27	16	47	13,775
6 *	41	57	63	33	1	2	$37,931	61	24	15	10	27	24	24	3,076
7 *	35	63	72	25	1	1	$31,453	55	29	17	12	28	17	31	6,268
STATE	40	59	63	32	1	2	$32,566	57	27	17	12	27	19	27	43,562
U.S.	53	46	69	12	4	13	$41,994	60	25	15	12	26	24	21	3,537,438

The districts with an asterisk in the above table experienced significant changes in population and demographics due to hurricanes Katrina and Rita in 2005. The statistics published here reflect information collected as part of the 2000 census. This information is the most recent comprehensive U.S. Census Bureau data broken down by congressional district.

Sen. Mary L. Landrieu (D)

Elected 1996; 3rd term

CAPITOL OFFICE
224-5824
landrieu.senate.gov
328 Hart Bldg. 20510-1804; fax 224-9735

COMMITTEES
Appropriations
Energy & Natural Resources
Homeland Security & Governmental Affairs
 (Disaster Recovery - chairwoman)
Small Business & Entrepreneurship - chairwoman

RESIDENCE
New Orleans

BORN
Nov. 23, 1955; Arlington, Va.

RELIGION
Roman Catholic

FAMILY
Husband, Frank Snellings; two children

EDUCATION
Louisiana State U., B.A. 1977 (sociology)

CAREER
Realtor

POLITICAL HIGHLIGHTS
La. House, 1980-88; La. treasurer, 1988-96;
candidate for governor, 1995

ELECTION RESULTS

2008 GENERAL

Mary L. Landrieu (D)	988,298	52.1%
John Kennedy (R)	867,177	45.7%

2008 PRIMARY

Mary L. Landrieu (D)	unopposed

PREVIOUS WINNING PERCENTAGES
2002 (52%); 1996 (50%)

Landrieu has undergone a political transformation: Once the Senate Democrat deemed most at risk of being unseated, she now chairs a committee and is the most powerful member of Louisiana's congressional delegation. Though her conservative leanings — along with her dogged pursuit of funds for her hurricane-ravaged state — can put her at odds with her caucus, they make her an active player on energy and economic issues.

Republican strategists had been confident they could thwart her quest for a third term in 2008, given her previous tight races and the overall difficulty Democrats face in the Deep South. But Landrieu (LAN-drew) had little trouble winning in a state where Republican John McCain easily prevailed over Barack Obama. The victory enabled her to take the helm of the Small Business and Entrepreneurship Committee and confirmed the clout she has in dealing with the Obama administration. "When the White House wants to make a key inquiry as to what's important for Louisiana, both as it pertains to politics and policy, she's going to be in the catbird seat," former Louisiana Democratic Sen. John B. Breaux told the Baton Rouge Advocate in January 2009.

She is the daughter of Moon Landrieu, who was New Orleans mayor for eight years and secretary of Housing and Urban Development under Carter. Her brother Mitch is the state's lieutenant governor. Despite her political lineage, Landrieu has more in common with Breaux and former Sen. J. Bennett Johnston Jr., both Bayou State centrists who were adept at reaching across the aisle while using their seniority to burnish their popularity back home.

Since Hurricane Katrina in 2005, Landrieu has pursued help for the battered Gulf Coast from any and all sources. She uses her seat on the Appropriations Committee as well as the chairmanship of the Homeland Security and Governmental Affairs Subcommittee on Disaster Recovery to make her case. Her efforts led her to rack up nearly $470 million in solo and combined earmarks, or funding set-asides for special projects, to spending bills in 2008 — a figure second only to Missouri Republican Thad Cochran in Congress, according to an analysis by Taxpayers for Common Sense.

As Small Business Committee chairwoman, Landrieu plans to try to help Gulf Coast companies still reeling from Katrina. She also hopes to remedy the shortfall in federal contracting for female-owned businesses and elevate the Small Business Administration to Cabinet-level status and boost its funding.

She and ranking Republican Olympia J. Snowe of Maine are the first female duo to lead a committee in either chamber. They previously teamed to lead a bipartisan group of senators that sprang from the "Gang of 14," an informal coalition that resolved a contentious impasse over judicial nominations in 2005. The Gang of 14 combined with members of the old Centrist Coalition to form a new Common Ground Coalition in January 2007.

But for all of her efforts at bipartisanship, Landrieu can be pugnacious. She is known to place legislative "holds" on nominations and bills as a way to seek leverage. When the Senate considered a bill to overhaul the flood insurance program in May 2008, Democrat Christopher J. Dodd of Connecticut sought to block an amendment package Landrieu and other Gulf Coast lawmakers had assembled. She threatened to delay the bill by reading aloud a litany of e-mail messages from constituents whose homes were destroyed by Katrina. Majority Leader Harry Reid of Nevada dissuaded her from doing so.

As Senate GOP leaders struggled in March 2006 to push through a budget, Landrieu cut a deal. She provided the final vote needed to pass the budget resolution, which called for subsequent legislation to open Alaska's Arctic

National Wildlife Refuge to oil drilling, a cause she had long supported. But she delivered her vote only after winning a provision to create a $10 billion Gulf Coast recovery fund that would draw some of the revenue from ANWR leases and offshore drilling. She was the only Democrat to vote for the resolution.

She subsequently helped shepherd into law in 2006 a measure to open new areas of the Gulf of Mexico to offshore drilling. The law is expected to provide Louisiana over the next three decades with at least $13 billion in royalties.

With energy policy among Obama's chief priorities, Landrieu will continue to advocate on behalf of her state's oil and gas industries. A member of the Energy and Natural Resources Committee, she has opposed rolling back tax breaks for oil companies and imposing a "windfall profits" tax on the largest of them. "I'm not going to spend my time beating up on the oil and gas companies," she said in July 2008. She also wants more investment in a new electrical grid and a greater focus on nuclear power.

Energy isn't the only issue that sets Landrieu apart from her caucus. During the George W. Bush administration, she broke ranks with her party on roughly one-quarter of the votes in which the majority of Democrats diverged from majority of Republicans. She has supported a constitutional amendment that would allow Congress to ban desecration of the American flag. And she was one of nine in her party to oppose a $700 billion rescue plan for the financial services industry in fall 2008 that became law.

But she stuck with her party to support a $787 billion economic stimulus plan, signed into law in early 2009, as well as a $410 billion catchall spending bill for fiscal 2009, in which she helped secure more than $332 million in earmarks — ranking third among senators in terms of funding obtained for special projects in their states.

Landrieu shares a strong bond with her female colleagues in the Senate. In 2000, she collaborated on a book about their rise, "Nine and Counting." She announced afterward she would not campaign against any of those women — Democrat or Republican. Her relationship with her home-state colleague, Republican David Vitter, is far less cordial. The two have openly feuded over the size and specifics of hurricane relief bills, and Vitter held up a public housing bill she sponsored in 2007.

With two adopted children at home, she has fought tirelessly to increase the adoption tax credit, reform the foster care system and ease international adoptions. She is co-chairwoman of the Congressional Coalition on Adoption.

Landrieu had a swift political rise. She was elected to the state House at age 23, went on to become state treasurer, then made an unsuccessful run for governor in 1995. A year later, in a contest to fill the seat of the retiring Johnston, she won by the slimmest margin ever in a Louisiana Senate race — 5,788 votes out of 1.7 million cast. The loser, conservative Louis "Woody" Jenkins, alleged voter fraud. The Senate Rules Committee, controlled by Republicans, conducted a divisive probe that dragged on for months after the election.

In 2002, she placed first with 46 percent in a nine-candidate field, which included prominent Republicans: state Elections Commissioner Suzanne Haik Terrell, Rep. John Cooksey and state Rep. Tony Perkins. But Landrieu fell short of the needed vote share to claim victory in Louisiana's nonpartisan race. In the runoff, she upped the size of her 1996 victory sevenfold, to 42,012 votes.

After Republicans put Landrieu's seat atop their 2008 incumbent wish list, they recruited State Treasurer John Kennedy, who switched parties from Democrat to Republican. But national Democrats ran ads labeling Kennedy a flip-flopper for campaigning as a conservative after running, and losing, a 2004 Senate race as a liberal Democrat and supporting Massachusetts Sen. John Kerry's presidential bid. Landrieu also received the backing of the U.S. Chamber of Commerce and some of the state's elected Republicans. She captured 52 percent of the vote.

KEY VOTES

2008
Yes Prohibit discrimination based on genetic information
Yes Reauthorize farm and nutrition programs for five years
No Limit debate on "cap and trade" system for greenhouse gas emissions
No Allow lawsuits against companies that participated in warrantless wiretapping
Yes Limit debate on a bill to block a scheduled cut in Medicare payments to doctors
Yes Grant mortgage relief to homeowners and funding for Fannie Mae and Freddie Mac
Yes Approve a nuclear cooperation agreement with India
No Approve final $700 billion program to stabilize financial markets
Yes Allow consideration of a $14 billion auto industry loan package

2007
Yes Increase minimum wage by $2.10 an hour
No Limit debate on a comprehensive immigration bill
Yes Overhaul congressional lobbying and ethics rules for members and their staffs
Yes Limit debate on considering a bill to add House seats for the District of Columbia and Utah
Yes Limit debate on restoring habeas corpus rights to detainees
Yes Mandate minimum breaks for troops between deployments to Iraq or Afghanistan
Yes Override Bush veto of $23.2 billion water projects authorization bill
Yes Confirm Michael B. Mukasey as attorney general
No Limit debate on an energy policy overhaul containing $21.8 billion in tax incentives and reduced oil and gas subsidies

CQ VOTE STUDIES

	PARTY UNITY		PRESIDENTIAL SUPPORT	
	SUPPORT	OPPOSE	SUPPORT	OPPOSE
2008	69%	31%	53%	47%
2007	78%	22%	47%	53%
2006	75%	25%	71%	29%
2005	76%	24%	64%	36%
2004	81%	19%	68%	32%
2003	78%	22%	58%	42%
2002	65%	35%	84%	16%
2001	81%	19%	74%	26%
2000	88%	12%	85%	15%
1999	81%	19%	86%	14%

INTEREST GROUPS

	AFL-CIO	ADA	CCUS	ACU
2008	100%	65%	75%	32%
2007	95%	80%	73%	40%
2006	73%	65%	75%	24%
2005	86%	95%	76%	44%
2004	100%	85%	71%	32%
2003	77%	60%	78%	20%
2002	83%	70%	84%	35%
2001	88%	85%	69%	28%
2000	63%	80%	73%	16%
1999	67%	95%	59%	4%

Sen. David Vitter (R)

Elected 2004; 1st term

Vitter is working to establish himself as one of the chamber's most unyielding conservatives. While he has skillfully worked to become a key player on high-profile issues such as immigration, drug reimportation and congressional ethics, he struggles to recapture career gains that have been overshadowed by a prostitute sex scandal that came to light in mid-2007.

Vitter's use of an escort service was exposed when Hustler magazine publisher Larry Flynt identified Vitter's telephone number in the records of "D.C. Madam" Deborah Jeane Palfrey after her arrest for allegedly running a prostitution ring. His phone number appeared five times between 1999 and 2001, when he was serving in the U.S. House.

With his wife, Wendy, at his side, Vitter held a news conference on July 16, 2007, in Metairie to offer "deep, sincere apologies to all of those I let down and disappointed with these actions from my past. I am completely responsible," he said. The Senate Select Ethics Committee dismissed the matter in May 2008 without reprimanding Vitter because the liaisons had occurred before he was elected to the Senate.

After the story broke, Vitter returned to Washington, apologized again at a closed luncheon of fellow Republican senators and tried to return to business. As if to demonstrate his resiliency, he immediately picked a fight with Majority Leader Harry Reid of Nevada on the floor. Vitter tried to amend a homeland security bill with his proposal to ease the importation of low-cost prescription drugs from Canada. When Reid objected, based on rules disallowing unrelated items on bills, Vitter first agreed to withdraw his amendment but then tried again to get it added to the bill. In an unusually harsh exchange between senators, Reid accused him of failing to keep his word, but Vitter's amendment prevailed.

The incident was reminiscent of Vitter's grit in earlier legislative battles, including his alliance with a group of conservatives who killed the George W. Bush administration's immigration bill in June 2007. They objected to provisions giving illegal aliens a chance to achieve legal status.

Vitter continues to be a thorn in the Democratic majority's side. He voted in December 2008 against helping out the ailing U.S. auto industry with $14 billion because the bill wasn't tough enough on the industry. He called the approach to the bailout "ass backwards."

In early 2009, he also opposed releasing the second half of a financial services industry rescue package signed into law in 2008. He said he was troubled by the use of such funds for the auto industry and an overall lack of accountability on spending. Vitter's joint resolution to withhold the money was defeated in the Senate in January 2009, allowing the new Obama administration to access it.

Vitter and South Carolina Republican Jim DeMint were the only senators to oppose New York Sen. Hillary Rodham Clinton's confirmation as secretary of State. Vitter voiced concern about President Clinton's overseas business and foundation dealings.

And Vitter made clear he intends to aggressively promote expanded oil and gas drilling as part of a broad energy policy while opposing what he considers Democrats' "extreme climate change policy that would have a big negative impact on our economy."

Vitter aligned himself with Bush and GOP leaders on the war in Iraq, tax policy and a wide range of issues important to social conservatives. But he also managed to stand out on a handful of issues.

CAPITOL OFFICE
224-4623
vitter.senate.gov
516 Hart Bldg. 20510-1803; fax 228-5061

COMMITTEES
Armed Services
Banking, Housing & Urban Affairs
Commerce, Science & Transportation
Environment & Public Works
Small Business & Entrepreneurship

RESIDENCE
Metairie

BORN
May 3, 1961; New Orleans, La.

RELIGION
Roman Catholic

FAMILY
Wife, Wendy Baldwin Vitter; four children

EDUCATION
Harvard U., A.B. 1983; Oxford U., B.A. 1985
(Rhodes scholar); Tulane U., J.D. 1988

CAREER
Lawyer; professor

POLITICAL HIGHLIGHTS
La. House, 1992-99; U.S. House, 1999-2005

ELECTION RESULTS

2004 GENERAL

David Vitter (R)	943,014	51.0%
Chris John (D)	542,150	29.3%
John Kennedy (D)	275,821	14.9%
Arthur A. Morrell (D)	47,222	2.6%

PREVIOUS WINNING PERCENTAGES
2002 House Election (81%); 2000 House Election (80%); 1999 Special Runoff House Election (51%)

Since 2005, Vitter has pushed his drug reimportation bill that was opposed by most GOP senators. His proposal would allow Americans to buy U.S.-made drugs from foreign countries, where they often can be purchased more cheaply than in the United States. Vitter says Americans without prescription drug coverage, including many in his home state, should have the option of buying drugs from Canada or other countries where they are cheaper.

Vitter has a cool personal relationship with his senior Louisiana colleague Democrat Mary L. Landrieu, and the two don't always work well together. After Hurricane Katrina devastated New Orleans and other Louisiana coastal areas in 2005, Vitter and Landrieu offered competing measures aimed at helping cash-strapped local governments pay essential workers. The conflict led to a confrontation on the Senate floor that ended only when Vitter walked out of the chamber. Then in 2007, Vitter blocked a bill backed by Landrieu and many local and state officials to reconstruct subsidized housing in New Orleans. Vitter claimed it would re-create the social problems, including high crime, that had plagued the housing developments before the storm.

No issue has dominated Vitter's agenda more than the impact of Katrina. He has been highly critical of the failure of governmental agencies at all levels, and was particularly hard on the Army Corps of Engineers, complaining the Corps had not moved quickly enough to repair the levees. Vitter grew up in New Orleans, the son of a petroleum engineer. But in recent years he hasn't enjoyed the same advantages as Landrieu, a member of the Senate's Democratic majority and the Appropriations Committee.

In the fall of 2007, Vitter's campaign committee was forced to pay $25,000 in fines for failing to include disclaimers on telephone bank calls during the 2004 Senate race. The committee spent $279,300 on two sets of phone bank calls to 490,000 voters that didn't identify his campaign as paying for the calls, the Federal Election Commission said.

These ethical and moral lapses were a stark turnabout for Vitter, who had modeled himself as a squeaky-clean reformer of Louisiana's notoriously corrupt politics. Vitter wrote in a Rhodes scholarship application that he aspired to change the reputation of cronyism and corruption typified by Huey Long Louisiana's legendary former governor. Vitter won the scholarship and was later elected to the U.S. House in 1999 at age 38.

Vitter ran in 2004 for the Senate seat of retiring Sen. John B. Breaux, a savvy Democrat known for working the backrooms of the Senate. Vitter had a tough opponent in Breaux's protégé, Democratic Rep. Chris John. Vitter was favored, but the question was whether his competitors would hold him to less than the required 50 percent of the vote and force a December runoff. Vitter won a rare outright victory by taking 51 percent of the votes. Louisiana had not had a Republican senator since Reconstruction.

Vitter has wasted little time demonstrating his commitment to getting reelected in 2010. On the first day of the 111th Congress (2009-10), he filed 34 bills and resolutions in a package the New Orleans Times-Picayune said "amounts to a political manifesto." Many of the measures were intended to appeal to Christian conservatives and addressed such topics as abortion, public prayer, home schooling, drugs, the death penalty and illegal immigration.

Political observers said Vitter could be trying to discourage any would-be GOP primary challengers who hope to make an issue of his behavior. But Vitter said his activity was nothing out of the ordinary and that he simply wants to make good on his promise after his scandal to work hard on his state's behalf. "I've told my constituents that it was an extremely serious mistake in my past that I have enormous regret for and that I will really spend the rest of my life trying to make up for it, first with my family but also everybody I represent," he said. "And the way I can do that…is to be an active, effective voice for them here in the Senate."

KEY VOTES

2008
Yes Prohibit discrimination based on genetic information
Yes Reauthorize farm and nutrition programs for five years
No Limit debate on "cap and trade" system for greenhouse gas emissions
No Allow lawsuits against companies that participated in warrantless wiretapping
No Limit debate on a bill to block a scheduled cut in Medicare payments to doctors
No Grant mortgage relief to homeowners and funding for Fannie Mae and Freddie Mac
Yes Approve a nuclear cooperation agreement with India
No Approve final $700 billion program to stabilize financial markets
No Allow consideration of a $14 billion auto industry loan package

2007
Yes Increase minimum wage by $2.10 an hour
No Limit debate on a comprehensive immigration bill
Yes Overhaul congressional lobbying and ethics rules for members and their staffs
No Limit debate on considering a bill to add House seats for the District of Columbia and Utah
No Limit debate on restoring habeas corpus rights to detainees
No Mandate minimum breaks for troops between deployments to Iraq or Afghanistan
Yes Override Bush veto of $23.2 billion water projects authorization bill
Yes Confirm Michael B. Mukasey as attorney general
No Limit debate on an energy policy overhaul containing $21.8 billion in tax incentives and reduced oil and gas subsidies

CQ VOTE STUDIES

	PARTY UNITY		PRESIDENTIAL SUPPORT	
	SUPPORT	OPPOSE	SUPPORT	OPPOSE
2008	98%	2%	76%	24%
2007	93%	7%	85%	15%
2006	94%	6%	87%	13%
2005	94%	6%	89%	11%
House Service:				
2004	98%	2%	94%	6%
2003	99%	1%	96%	4%
2002	99%	1%	85%	15%
2001	98%	2%	93%	7%
2000	92%	8%	25%	75%

INTEREST GROUPS

	AFL-CIO	ADA	CCUS	ACU
2008	20%	5%	88%	84%
2007	21%	10%	73%	96%
2006	20%	0%	92%	92%
2005	29%	15%	83%	96%
House Service:				
2004	7%	5%	100%	96%
2003	0%	10%	97%	88%
2002	11%	0%	95%	100%
2001	8%	0%	100%	100%
2000	0%	0%	85%	88%

Rep. Steve Scalise (R)

Elected May 2008; 1st full term

CAPITOL OFFICE
225-3015
scalise.house.gov
429 Cannon Bldg. 20515-1801; fax 226-0386

COMMITTEES
Energy & Commerce

RESIDENCE
Jefferson

BORN
Oct. 6, 1965; Baton Rouge, La.

RELIGION
Roman Catholic

FAMILY
Wife, Jennifer Scalise; two children

EDUCATION
Louisiana State U., B.S. 1989 (computer science)

CAREER
Software engineer; technology company marketing executive

POLITICAL HIGHLIGHTS
La. House, 1996-2008; La. Senate, 2008-08

ELECTION RESULTS

2008 GENERAL

Steve Scalise (R)	189,168	65.7%
Jim Harlan (D)	98,839	34.3%

2008 PRIMARY

Steve Scalise (R)	unopposed

2008 SPECIAL

Steve Scalise (R)	33,867	75.1%
Gilda Reed (D)	10,142	22.5%
R.A. "Skip" Galan (X)	786	1.7%

2008 PRIMARY RUNOFF

Steve Scalise (R)	19,338	58.1%
Tim Burns (R)	13,958	41.9%

Scalise holds tight to the same conservative principles that kept him in the Louisiana Legislature for 12 years and that his constituents have come to expect from their representative in Congress. He has staked his ground on a range of issues, from gun control to oil drilling, health care to fiscal policy. He likens his ideals to those of the late President Reagan, whom he professes to be his "political idol."

He loves the intricate details of policy and legislation, as well as the rigorous debate central to promoting his ideas. Former Democratic state Rep. Willie Hunter recalled to The Times-Picayune of New Orleans in 2008 several debates with his former colleague, particularly on raising the minimum wage and pay disparity issues. Hunter said Scalise wasn't a compromiser. "He wasn't one of these guys you call a lizard — today he's green and tomorrow he's brown," he said.

During a debate back home during the 2008 campaign, Scalise (skuh-LEASE) told constituents he "can work well with people of both parties to get things done," and later professed optimism about President Obama's early quest for bipartisanship. But Scalise, who was named an assistant Republican whip in January 2009, has shown little indication to veer toward the center since he won a May 2008 special election to succeed Republican Bobby Jindal, now Louisiana's governor.

A member of the powerful Energy and Commerce Committee and its Energy and Environment panel, he is part of ongoing debates on a broad energy plan for the United States. He supports offshore drilling for oil and wants to let Louisiana tap into funds made from drilling on new oil fields in the Gulf of Mexico and invest them in coastal restoration. "If you want to go fishing, the best fishing, probably in the world, is next to an oil rig in the Gulf of Mexico," he said to a small crowd in Elmwood, La., shortly after taking office.

Scalise portrays himself as a fiscal conservative. On one of his first votes in 2008, Scalise came out strongly against passage of a $289 billion law to reauthorize farm programs. He indicated he was concerned about an expansion of federal nutrition programs for the poor. "Unfortunately, this bill had little to do with helping hard-working Louisiana farmers and more to do with promoting the liberals' tax-and-spend agenda," he said. "We need to cut runaway welfare programs and rein in wasteful spending."

He voted in fall 2008 against a $700 billion package to shore up the financial services industry, advocating instead "a market-based approach that does not put taxpayer money at risk." While two other Louisianans changed their votes and supported a modified version that was signed into law, he remained firm.

He opposed all of Obama's early legislative measures, including a $787 billion economic stimulus measure in 2009. He said exchanging some new spending for tax cuts would "give us a better chance of turning around this economy."

"My daughter, Madison, who's 2 years old, will be inheriting more of this debt, thousands of dollars in national debt," he said on the House floor in March 2009. He said the bill, signed into law in February 2009, included new programs that weren't fully vetted and its infrastructure funding was limited.

Yet he pressed Obama to ensure continued federal assistance for hurricane recovery projects along the Gulf Coast, and helped obtain nearly $1.7 million, mostly for highway improvements, in the catchall spending bill signed into law in March 2009 — a bill he voted against.

Bringing in more funds to help his area recover from hurricanes Katrina and Rita was one of his campaign pledges. And when Hurricane Gustav was bearing down on the central Louisiana coast in August 2008, Scalise remained near the Mississippi River's southern end to monitor its effects rather than head north to St. Paul where the Republican National Convention was getting under way. He said he wanted to ensure the safety of his wife and young daughter, and make sure other people were taking care of their families.

He is unyielding on social issues. He voted against a 2009 bill to expand the State Children's Health Insurance Program, which provides coverage to children whose families don't qualify for Medicaid, after failing to get support for a provision to bar illegal immigrants from obtaining coverage. "I am disappointed that some members of Congress are attempting to make it the law of the land for illegal immigrants to receive federal health benefits," he said.

He is a supporter of gun owners' rights and a member of the National Rifle Association. As a state legislator he led a fight in 1999 against former New Orleans Democratic Mayor Marc Morial, who sued a group of gun manufacturers to reimburse the city for expenses related to its efforts to stem violent crime. Scalise drafted a bill that prohibited municipalities from suing companies for what customers did with the products. The Supreme Court upheld the legislation in 2000.

He is an opponent of abortion and the original sponsor of Louisiana's constitutional amendment, which voters approved in 2004, that defines marriage as a union between a man and a woman.

The middle of three children, Scalise grew up in Metairie, a suburb of New Orleans. His father sold real estate while his mother was a homemaker and an active volunteer in senior citizens' programs. As a child, Scalise roamed his local streets on a patriotic-bunted bicycle, speaking into a battery-powered microphone and encouraging his neighbors to visit the polls at election time. He became a registered Republican the day he turned 18.

After college, he worked in computer engineering while volunteering for several campaigns, including George H.W. Bush's successful 1988 run for president. Scalise was elected to the state House in 1995 and served 11 years before being elected to the state Senate in 2007.

He first considered running for the U.S. House in 1999, when a special election was held to replace GOP Rep. Robert L. Livingston. He changed his mind after party leaders favored Republican David Vitter, who won the seat. When Vitter vacated the seat for the Senate in 2004, Scalise was overlooked again, this time in favor of Jindal.

In the May 2008 special election to succeed Jindal, Scalise outran Democrat Gilda Reed, a psychologist, and two minor candidates. He took more than 65 percent of the vote that November election for a full term.

KEY VOTES

2008
No Override Bush veto of federal farm and nutrition programs reauthorization bill
Yes Overhaul surveillance laws and permit dismissal of suits against companies that conducted warrantless wiretapping
No Grant mortgage relief to homeowners and funding for Fannie Mae and Freddie Mac
No Approve initial $700 billion program to stabilize financial markets
No Approve final $700 billion program to stabilize financial markets
No Provide $14 billion in loans to automakers

CQ VOTE STUDIES

	PARTY UNITY		PRESIDENTIAL SUPPORT	
	SUPPORT	OPPOSE	SUPPORT	OPPOSE
2008	99%	1%	79%	21%

INTEREST GROUPS

	AFL-CIO	ADA	CCUS	ACU
2008	0%	5%	94%	100%

LOUISIANA 1
East – Metairie, part of Florida Parishes

A short distance from downtown New Orleans, the conservative 1st skims the edges of the city, heads north across the Lake Pontchartrain Causeway and reaches the Mississippi border. North of Lake Pontchartrain, the 1st includes three of the "Florida Parishes," so named because they were part of Spanish Florida until 1810.

Since Hurricane Katrina in 2005, a sizable segment of the population has spread from New Orleans and Jefferson Parish to neighborhoods on the lake's northern shore. Once a community of seasonal homes, the north shore is now a booming bedroom community, having experienced a population influx as residents from the rest of the state flocked to the relatively stable residential area. Slidell and other towns along the northern lakeshore faced rebuilding costs and infrastructure redevelopment from damage inflicted by the hurricane's high winds and flooding.

As with much of the Greater New Orleans area, local officials and residents north of the lake, as well as in Lakeview in western Orleans Parish and parts of historic Old Metairie in Jefferson Parish to the south, hope

that neighborhoods rebuilt since 2005 will retain their unique character and experience economic growth. A shortage of service industry workers, coupled with high workforce attrition, hindered growth for years, and prolonged national economic downturns have affected the area. But retail centers and residential development, particularly in St. Tammany and Tangipahoa parishes, have boosted the local economy. The petrochemicals and oil and gas industries have recovered, and Northrop Grumman provides thousands of jobs to district residents at its shipbuilding operations, based at the Avondale Shipyard in the 2nd District, and high-tech facilities in the 1st.

Residents warmly welcome the GOP on all levels, and John McCain won his highest percentage statewide here in the 2008 presidential election.

MAJOR INDUSTRY
Petrochemicals, oil

CITIES
Metairie (unincorporated) (pt.), 140,916; Kenner (pt.), 46,007; New Orleans (pt.), 37,451; Slidell, 25,695

NOTABLE
The Lake Pontchartrain Causeway is the world's longest highway bridge over water.

Rep. Anh "Joseph" Cao (R)

Elected 2008; 1st term

As a surprising victor over a flawed opponent in an overwhelmingly Democratic, black-majority district, Cao is a top Democratic target for 2010. But he contends that party affiliation isn't a big issue for a constituency that has so many pressing problems.

"I intend to work very hard and to convince the people that they can trust me, even though I'm Asian and even though I'm Republican," Cao (GOW) said days after his win over scandal-scarred Democratic Rep. William J. Jefferson.

His top aim is to secure as much federal assistance as possible for his district. "The rebuilding process has been very slow, and we are looking forward to speeding that up," Cao said of his efforts to help New Orleans recover from 2005's Hurricane Katrina. Cao serves on the Transportation and Infrastructure Committee, which is expected to take up a renewal of the 2005 surface transportation bill during the 111th Congress (2009-10). That will give him an opportunity to send federal funds home for highways, airports and other infrastructure improvements. He also serves on the Homeland Security panel.

Republicans, pleased to count the first Vietnamese-American member as one of their own, will help him as much as they can — and look the other way when he splits from the party line. He didn't wait long to do so. Cao was one of 40 Republicans to vote in early 2009 for an expansion of the State Children's Health Insurance Program, which covers children from low-income families that do not qualify for Medicaid.

Cao, the fifth of eight children, was 8 when he fled Vietnam with two siblings, three days after the 1975 fall of Saigon. He joined an uncle in Indiana. It was years before he saw his parents again. He learned English from some elderly neighbors and was strengthened by his Catholic faith. He spent six years as a Jesuit seminarian before becoming an immigration lawyer.

Ironically, Cao may owe his election victory in part to another big hurricane. The original primary election date was delayed because of Hurricane Gustav, pushing the general election to Dec. 6, 2008. With very low voter turnout, Jefferson, already weakened by an indictment on federal corruption charges, was unable to turn back his GOP challenger.

CAPITOL OFFICE
225-6636
josephcao.house.gov
2113 Rayburn Bldg. 20515-1802; fax 225-1988

COMMITTEES
Homeland Security
Transportation & Infrastructure

RESIDENCE
New Orleans

BORN
March 13, 1967; Ho Chi Minh City, Vietnam

RELIGION
Roman Catholic

FAMILY
Wife, Hieu "Kate" Hoang; two children

EDUCATION
Baylor U., B.S. 1990 (physics); Fordham U., M.A. 1995 (philosophical resources); Loyola U. (La.), J.D. 2000

CAREER
Lawyer

POLITICAL HIGHLIGHTS
Independent candidate for La. House, 2007

ELECTION RESULTS

2008 GENERAL

Anh "Joseph" Cao (R)	33,132	49.5%
William J. Jefferson (D)	31,318	46.8%
Malik Rahim (GREEN)	1,883	2.8%

2008 PRIMARY

Anh "Joseph" Cao (R)	unopposed

LOUISIANA 2

New Orleans

New Orleans suffered catastrophic damage in late 2005, as Hurricane Katrina devastated the below-sea-level city. The economy is fueled by post-hurricane construction and infrastructure redevelopment as locals attempt to restore the buildings and character of the "Big Easy." Despite ongoing economic recovery efforts, funding shortfalls and a national recession, the city's economy has become relatively stable.

Floods covered the 9th Ward, Gentilly and other low-lying areas, but higher-ground areas like the French Quarter and Uptown escaped most of the water. Famed for its food and jazz, the city continues to draw tourists to iconic events such as Mardi Gras and the Jazz & Heritage Festival.

The port, shipbuilding and petroleum sectors held steady after the storm despite losing some business to other Gulf cities. Northrop Grumman's Avondale Shipyard provides jobs, and the port's cargo and cruise facilities have rebounded.

New Orleans' population had already declined from its 1960 peak, and estimates put repopulation since the storm at only just more than 300,000. Despite a U.S. House seat flip to the GOP in 2008, the district retains a strongly Democratic tilt. The 2nd was the only district in the state won by Barack Obama in the 2008 presidential election, and he took 75 percent of the district's vote.

MAJOR INDUSTRY
Shipping, oil and gas, tourism, shipbuilding

MILITARY BASES
Naval Support Activity New Orleans, 1,265 military, 817 civilian (2009)

CITIES
New Orleans (pt.), 447,223; Marrero (unincorporated) (pt.), 35,796

NOTABLE
The National Shrine of Our Lady of Prompt Succor hosts a statue of the state's patron saint, who hears prayers in times of disaster.

Rep. Charlie Melancon (D)

Elected 2004; 3rd term

CAPITOL OFFICE
225-4031
melancon.house.gov
404 Cannon Bldg. 20515-1803; fax 226-3944

COMMITTEES
Budget
Energy & Commerce

RESIDENCE
Napoleonville

BORN
Oct. 3, 1947; Napoleonville, La.

RELIGION
Roman Catholic

FAMILY
Wife, Peachy Melancon; two children

EDUCATION
U. of Southwestern Louisiana, B.S. 1971
(agribusiness)

CAREER
Sugar cane trade group president; insurance
company owner; storage and housing rental
company owner; ice cream shop owner;
multi-county planning and development director

POLITICAL HIGHLIGHTS
Candidate for La. House, 1975; La. House, 1987-93

ELECTION RESULTS

2008 GENERAL

Charlie Melancon (D)		unopposed

2008 PRIMARY

Charlie Melancon (D)		unopposed

2006 GENERAL

Charlie Melancon (D)	75,023	55.0%
Craig Romero (R)	54,950	40.3%
Olangee "O.J." Breech (D)	4,190	3.1%
James Lee Blake (LIBERT)	2,168	1.6%

PREVIOUS WINNING PERCENTAGES
2004 (50%)

The lone remaining Democrat in Louisiana's seven-member House delegation, Melancon maintains an arm's-length relationship with his party's more liberal leaders. Folksy and unpretentious, he speaks out these days as one of three co-chairs of the influential Blue Dog Coalition of fiscally conservative Democrats.

Melancon (meh-LAW-sawn) and his fellow Blue Dogs want a return to the tough pay-as-you-go (PAYGO) budget rules that were in force during the 1990s and required funding offsets for new mandatory spending. And they want those constraints to be law, as they were until 2002, not just House rules. "We want to go back to something like the rules that were in effect during the Clinton administration," he said. "If you don't have PAYGO in effect in the Senate and in the White House, it's just not effective."

Melancon holds a seat on the Budget Committee, which strengthens his hand on deficit reduction. But his push for fiscal discipline hasn't diminished his pursuit of billions of dollars in federal funds, exempt from pay-as-you-go rules, to help his constituents recover from hurricanes Katrina and Rita, which tore through opposite ends of his southern Louisiana district in late August and September 2005, respectively. The district was again hard hit in 2008 by hurricanes Ike and Gustav.

After Katrina devastated St. Bernard and Plaquemines parishes, Melancon said the federal government had failed them. "As their congressman, it is painfully ironic that the help I have been able to give them has not been from the federal government at all," he said on the House floor. "I have had to work around the system, identifying needs and coordinating resources myself, much of it from private and unofficial sources."

He raised eyebrows shortly after Democrats took control of Congress in 2007 when he charged that his own leadership wasn't doing enough to address the recovery needs of the Gulf Coast. "I am disappointed that Speaker Pelosi hasn't lived up to her commitment to the people of Louisiana, Mississippi and the Gulf Coast," Melancon said in a February 2007 interview with the New Orleans Times-Picayune. "I've gotten past the point where I think it's just happenstance."

While his relationship with Pelosi remains cool, Melancon has nonetheless brought top House leaders and about two dozen other members to his district every summer since Katrina and Rita struck to see the recovery work firsthand. "I have said many times, people can't comprehend how widespread the destruction was, or how great the task of rebuilding still is, unless they see it for themselves," he said.

Melancon's distance from Democratic leaders is an electoral imperative. In 2004, he pulled off a rare feat in a Democratic takeback of a Southern district that had gone Republican, and managed to build his vote margin from 569 votes that year to more than 20,000 votes in 2006. By 2008, he ran unopposed. His success has national Democratic leaders eyeing him as a potential 2010 candidate to take on Republican Sen. David Vitter.

After Democrats captured the House in 2006, Melancon won assignment to the Energy and Commerce Committee, where his predecessor, Republican Billy Tauzin, had been chairman just a few years earlier. Even before he made it onto Energy and Commerce, he had a hand in the enactment of a major offshore drilling law in the 109th Congress (2005-06). The measure expanded oil and gas drilling in the Gulf of Mexico, and, for the first time, gave Louisiana and other Gulf Coast states a share of federal offshore drilling revenues. In the 110th Congress (2007-08), Melancon split with a majority of his fellow Democrats to support an end to a longstanding moratorium on drilling off the Atlantic and Pacific coasts.

Energy issues are not the only ones on which Melancon parts company with the more liberal majority of his party. He has voted to limit the scope of the Endangered Species Act, authorize the president's warrantless wiretapping program, impose stricter identification and asylum standards on immigrants, and build 700 miles of fencing along the U.S.-Mexico border.

Most of Melancon's constituents share his Roman Catholic faith, and he deviates from the party line on most social issues. In 2005, he voted to give the parents of Terri Schiavo, a brain-dead Florida woman, the right to appeal a court decision that eventually resulted in the removal of Schiavo's feeding tube. The following year, he voted to criminalize transporting minors across state lines to get abortions without parental notification. In 2007, he was one of 25 Democrats to vote against a bill to bar job discrimination based on sexual orientation.

But Melancon breaks with social conservatives over federal funding for embryonic stem cell research. He voted to expand federal support for such research in the 109th and 110th Congresses.

Melancon still lives in Napoleonville, the small town where his father was mayor and where he was born and raised. He made an unsuccessful bid for the state legislature in 1975, then went into the insurance business and opened Baskin Robbins ice cream stores. He also served as executive director of a regional planning and development commission. He won a special election to the state legislature in 1987, serving until 1993, when he became president of the American Sugar Cane League. He spent 11 years with the trade association, and when a law to reauthorize farm programs was enacted in the 110th Congress, Melancon helped secure provisions to protect the domestic sugar industry from imports.

It was members of the sugar industry who convinced Melancon to run for the House when Tauzin resigned in 2004. He beat Tauzin's son, Billy Tauzin III, in the closest election of the year by promising to maintain a conservative agenda. He drew only 24 percent of the first-round vote in November that year, but it was enough for second place in the first vote of a two-tiered election system and for a spot in the December runoff against Tauzin.

Melancon came into the 2006 election with a clear edge because of his profile as a conservative Democrat, his focus on hurricane repair and his well-funded campaign operation. And despite the district's conservative lean, he won with 55 percent of the vote over GOP state Sen. Craig Romero.

KEY VOTES

2008
Yes Delay consideration of Colombia free-trade agreement
Yes Override Bush veto of federal farm and nutrition programs reauthorization bill
Yes Overhaul surveillance laws and permit dismissal of suits against companies that conducted warrantless wiretapping
Yes Grant mortgage relief to homeowners and funding for Fannie Mae and Freddie Mac
Yes Approve initial $700 billion program to stabilize financial markets
Yes Approve final $700 billion program to stabilize financial markets
Yes Provide $14 billion in loans to automakers

2007
Yes Increase minimum wage by $2.10 an hour
Yes Approve $124.2 billion in emergency war spending and set goal for redeployment of troops from Iraq
Yes Reject federal contraceptive assistance to international family planning groups
Yes Override Bush veto of $23.2 billion water projects authorization bill
Yes Implement Peru free-trade agreement
Yes Approve energy policy overhaul with new fuel economy standards
Yes Clear $473.5 billion omnibus spending bill, including $70 billion for military operations

CQ VOTE STUDIES

	PARTY UNITY		PRESIDENTIAL SUPPORT	
	SUPPORT	OPPOSE	SUPPORT	OPPOSE
2008	93%	7%	27%	73%
2007	86%	14%	23%	77%
2006	62%	38%	72%	28%
2005	71%	29%	52%	48%

INTEREST GROUPS

	AFL-CIO	ADA	CCUS	ACU
2008	93%	80%	71%	12%
2007	96%	85%	75%	36%
2006	71%	40%	93%	76%
2005	93%	80%	67%	61%

LOUISIANA 3
South central — New Iberia, Houma, Chalmette

A maze of interconnected bayous, swamps and marshes, the 3rd runs along the coast of the Gulf of Mexico and takes in the Mississippi River delta and the eastern half of Acadiana, or Cajun country. The same geography that attracts commercial fishermen and sportsmen also leaves the area susceptible to significant hurricane damage. In 2005, Katrina and Rita destroyed or severely damaged towns and cities across the district. In 2008, flooding and high winds from Gustav and Ike affected agriculture, fishing and infrastructure.

Water submerged the mostly middle-class Plaquemines and St. Bernard parishes when levees failed in 2005, and these former bedroom communities still host only fractions of pre-storm populations. Some residents who remained in the area moved north into booming parts of the 1st, but federal- and state-funded construction and redevelopment projects have helped drive recovery efforts here. Residents are in favor of public transportation from rural areas of the 3rd — especially in St. John the Baptist and St. Charles parishes — to nearby cities and regional transit lines.

The 3rd long supported fishing, oystering and shrimping, but many small operations in Plaquemines and west along the coast have not gotten back on the water. West of Plaquemines, rural Lafourche and Terrebonne parishes grew sugar, rice and citrus, but agricultural production has suffered and ranchers have lost cattle. Oil and gas recovered from the storms, and the 3rd continues to support much of the regional offshore drilling economy.

Democrats dominated the region for most of a century, but the Catholic 3rd now trends Republican. The ability to bring federal and state aid to the district may largely determine future political success here. John McCain received 61 percent of the district's 2008 presidential vote.

MAJOR INDUSTRY
Oil and gas, petrochemicals, shipbuilding, agriculture

MILITARY BASES
Naval Air Station Joint Reserve Base New Orleans, 250 military, 170 civilian (2009)

CITIES
New Iberia, 32,623; Houma, 32,393; Chalmette (unincorporated), 32,069

NOTABLE
St. John the Baptist Parish holds its annual Andouille Festival in October.

Rep. John Fleming (R)

Elected 2008; 1st term

A physician and business owner who describes himself as a "Reagan Republican," Fleming wants to see the GOP become more conservative and hopes the party makes its small-government views felt on the economy, health care and a comprehensive energy plan.

"We need to return to conservative principles based upon less spending, balanced budgets and a lower tax burden," he said. "In this time of economic uncertainty, the last thing we need is to increase taxes, and Wall Street bailouts are not the solution to long-term stability."

He demonstrated his philosophy within the first few weeks of the 111th Congress (2009-10), when Fleming voted against what became President Obama's $787 billion economic stimulus law. Fleming said the legislation would result in $275,000 in spending per job created and that deficit spending wouldn't expand the economy.

A political newcomer who owns 30 Subway restaurant franchises as well as Fleming Expansions, a sub-franchisor of The UPS Store, Fleming said corporate taxes burden business and stifle economic development and that income taxes are overly complicated. He wants to abolish the IRS and favors replacing the federal income tax and all other federal taxes with a sales tax.

Fleming has seats on the Armed Services and Natural Resources committees. His district is home to Barksdale Air Force Base, Fort Polk and the Haynesville Shale, a source of natural gas. In the early months of the 111th, he gave several floor speeches attacking Obama's energy policies.

As a former Navy medical officer who maintains a medical practice in Minden, Fleming has firsthand experience as a health care practitioner. He opposes single-payer universal health care and wants to see more competition among private health insurers. He also is the author of the book, "Preventing Addiction: What Parents Must Know to Immunize Their Kids Against Drug and Alcohol Addiction."

In seeking to fill the seat held by retiring Republican Jim McCrery, Fleming loaned himself more than $1 million and was elected by a razor-thin margin of 350 votes against Democrat Paul J. Carmouche.

CAPITOL OFFICE
225-2777
fleming.house.gov
1023 Longworth Bldg. 20515-1804; fax 225-8039

COMMITTEES
Armed Services
Natural Resources

RESIDENCE
Minden

BORN
July 5, 1951; Meridian, Miss.

RELIGION
Baptist

FAMILY
Wife, Cindy Fleming; four children

EDUCATION
U. of Mississippi, B.S. 1973 (medicine), M.D. 1976

MILITARY SERVICE
Navy Medical Corps, 1976-82

CAREER
Physician; sandwich store owner

POLITICAL HIGHLIGHTS
Webster Parish coroner, 1996-2000

ELECTION RESULTS

2008 GENERAL

John Fleming (R)	44,501	48.1%
Paul J. Carmouche (D)	44,151	47.7%
Chester T. "Catfish" Kelley (X)	3,245	3.5%

LOUISIANA 4

Northwest and west — Shreveport, Bossier City

Covering most of western Louisiana, the conservative 4th takes in Shreveport in the north and wanders into timber country in Beauregard and Allen parishes in the south.

The Red River divides Shreveport and Bossier City geographically, but unites them economically. Riverboat casinos dock on the river, and gambling sites dot the shores. Service and retail jobs and riverfront renewal, including the Louisiana Boardwalk shopping and entertainment complex, help drive the economy in Bossier City.

Shreveport is a health care hub for northern Louisiana, eastern Texas and southern Arkansas, but production cutbacks at the city's General Motors plant have hurt the local economy. Barksdale Air Force Base near Bossier City is a key employer for both

cities, and base expansion is expected to bring construction, military and high-tech jobs. Natchitoches, the oldest permanent settlement in the former Louisiana Purchase territory, uses history to lure tourists. Besides Fort Polk in Vernon County, the rest of the 4th relies on cotton and forestry.

Registered Democrats outnumber Republicans and have enjoyed local success. Shreveport and Bossier City suburbs can back the GOP, and the 4th overall typically prefers a Republican in the White House. John McCain received 59 percent of the 2008 presidential vote here.

MAJOR INDUSTRY
Military, riverboat gambling, health care

MILITARY BASES
Fort Polk (Army), 9,297 military, 1,929 civilian (2009); Barksdale Air Force Base, 5,466 military, 1,181 civilian (2007)

CITIES
Shreveport, 200,145; Bossier City, 56,461

NOTABLE
Natchitoches has a yearly Meat Pie Festival.

Rep. Rodney Alexander (R)

Elected 2002; 4th term

CAPITOL OFFICE
225-8490
www.house.gov/alexander
316 Cannon Bldg. 20515-1805; fax 225-5639

COMMITTEES
Appropriations

RESIDENCE
Quitman

BORN
Dec. 5, 1946; Quitman, La.

RELIGION
Baptist

FAMILY
Wife, Nancy Alexander; three children

EDUCATION
Louisiana Tech U., attended 1965

MILITARY SERVICE
Air Force Reserve, 1965-71

CAREER
Insurance agent; road construction contractor

POLITICAL HIGHLIGHTS
Jackson Parish Police Jury, 1972-87
(president, 1980-87); La. House, 1988-2002
(served as a Democrat)

ELECTION RESULTS

2008 GENERAL

Rodney Alexander (R)		unopposed

2008 PRIMARY

Rodney Alexander (R)	27,819	89.6%
Andrew Clack (R)	3,213	10.4%

2006 GENERAL

Rodney Alexander (R)	78,211	68.3%
Gloria Williams Hearn (D)	33,233	29.0%
Brent Sanders (LIBERT)	1,876	1.6%
John Watts (X)	1,262	1.1%

PREVIOUS WINNING PERCENTAGES*
2004 (59%); 2002 (50%)
* Elected as a Democrat in 2002

One of the last conservative Dixiecrats to defect to the Republican Party, Alexander has fit in well with the socially conservative wing of the GOP since his 2004 party switch. He's won far fewer plaudits from fiscal conservatives in his party, due to his appetite for earmarks to aid his rural, low-income constituency.

"I think government's role at some level is to help those who can't help themselves," he said. And Alexander's constituents do need the help: His sprawling district has long been home to intractable poverty.

Alexander has used his seat on the Appropriations Committee to bring jobs home. He helped secure $129 million in the catchall spending bill for fiscal 2009, ranking him second among House members in terms of earmarks — funding set-asides for projects in member's districts — collected, according to the watchdog group Taxpayers for Common Sense. Included was funding for everything from termite research to sewer system improvements to work on a new airport terminal in Monroe. Alexander said all of it was worthwhile. "I have never requested money I was ashamed of," he said. "I have never made a request for anything that I wanted to be secret."

Alexander's seats on three Appropriations subcommittees in the 111th Congress (2009-10) — Agriculture; Energy and Water; and Labor, Health and Human Services and Education — should ensure the money keeps flowing. And despite alienating many Louisiana Democrats with his party switch, Alexander has found common cause with Louisiana's representative on the Senate Appropriations Committee, Democrat Mary L. Landrieu. Together, the two have proved a formidable team, and with the departure of several veteran Bayou State lawmakers, Alexander is now the senior member of the state's House delegation.

Alexander's enthusiasm for infrastructure spending likely will make him an early target of President Obama and congressional Democrats as they seek to win over Republican converts to their plans to stimulate the economy. But he refused to vote for a $787 billion Democratic stimulus bill in February 2009, which became law.

In 2007, Alexander did buck President George W. Bush in voting to override Bush's veto of a bill authorizing billions in water resources projects. In 2009, he was among a minority of House Republicans who voted for a massive authorization for water quality projects.

When Bush late in 2008 was pushing Congress to authorize $700 billion in spending to rescue the ailing financial services industry, Alexander — after initially opposing the plan — ultimately voted for it. "I've had so many calls from businesspeople throughout the state who have said that they're in such a financial crunch that not passing it would create a crisis," he said at the time.

During the 111th, Alexander said he will push for legislation to offer tax benefits to businesses who set up shop in rural areas, an idea that has won Democratic support in the past. He's also a potential ally for Democrats interested in lifting or modifying the economic embargo on Cuba. Alexander traveled to the island in 2007 and believes Cuba is a potential market for his state's rice farmers.

Unlike the typical politician, the easygoing Alexander is not someone who likes media attention, rarely making floor speeches. "I don't seek publicity," he said. One exception arose in 2006 when news reports revealed that a teenager he had sponsored as a congressional page had received inappropriate e-mail messages from Republican Rep. Mark Foley of Florida. Alexander handled the situation by informing the page's parents and the House Speaker. Still, the camera-shy Alexander ended up on cable networks such as Fox News and CNN as Foley was forced to resign.

Alexander's 2004 party switch, too, gained plenty of media attention. The move, which infuriated Democrats, came just minutes before the filing deadline for re-election, preventing Democrats from recruiting a strong challenger. Alexander sailed to an easy victory and Republicans rewarded him with a coveted seat on Appropriations starting in the 109th Congress (2005-06). He also served on the Budget Committee during the 110th Congress (2007-08) but was forced to relinquish that post after the Republicans lost seats in the 2008 election.

But Alexander said he didn't switch parties to win perks and that he has no regrets about his move, even though Democrats recaptured control of the House in the 2006 elections. "I'm pro-life, pro-family, pro-gun," he said. "That's why I was uncomfortable being a Democrat. I didn't change just to be in the majority."

Since his party switch, Alexander has voted with a majority of his fellow Republicans more than 90 percent of the time on votes pitting the parties against each other. But he does not consider himself partisan. In 2005, after Hurricane Katrina, he rose on the House floor — one of just three times he spoke on the floor that year — to defend Democratic Louisiana Gov. Kathleen Babineaux Blanco, who had come under criticism from many Republicans for her handling of the crisis.

"I served with the lady 20 years ago in the state legislature. She had some criticism for me when I changed parties last year, but I understand that. But she is a decent lady," Alexander said. "I would appreciate it if members would refrain from throwing stones at this particular time. We have some devastation down there and a lot of hurt people."

Alexander has since joined with state Democrats in seeking emergency funding to deal with Katrina's aftermath as well as more recent storms.

A former construction contractor who dropped out of Louisiana Tech University, Alexander has spent much of his adult life in politics. He was only 25 when he was first elected to the Jackson Parish Police Jury, the Louisiana equivalent of a county board of supervisors, and he later served 14 years in the state House before running for Congress.

Alexander won his first congressional race in 2002 by a mere 974 votes but has had no trouble winning re-election since then. He took 59 percent of the vote after his 2004 party switch and garnered 68 percent in 2006. In 2008, he ran unopposed.

KEY VOTES

2008
No Delay consideration of Colombia free-trade agreement
Yes Override Bush veto of federal farm and nutrition programs reauthorization bill
Yes Overhaul surveillance laws and permit dismissal of suits against companies that conducted warrantless wiretapping
No Grant mortgage relief to homeowners and funding for Fannie Mae and Freddie Mac
No Approve initial $700 billion program to stabilize financial markets
Yes Approve final $700 billion program to stabilize financial markets
No Provide $14 billion in loans to automakers

2007
Yes Increase minimum wage by $2.10 an hour
No Approve $124.2 billion in emergency war spending and set goal for redeployment of troops from Iraq
Yes Reject federal contraceptive assistance to international family planning groups
Yes Override Bush veto of $23.2 billion water projects authorization bill
Yes Implement Peru free-trade agreement
No Approve energy policy overhaul with new fuel economy standards
Yes Clear $473.5 billion omnibus spending bill, including $70 billion for military operations

CQ VOTE STUDIES

	PARTY UNITY		PRESIDENTIAL SUPPORT	
	SUPPORT	OPPOSE	SUPPORT	OPPOSE
2008	95%	5%	70%	30%
2007	87%	13%	74%	26%
2006	97%	3%	93%	7%
2005	97%	3%	89%	11%
2004	97%	3%	67%	33%

INTEREST GROUPS

	AFL-CIO	ADA	CCUS	ACU
2008	20%	25%	94%	84%
2007	29%	10%	90%	92%
2006	21%	5%	100%	80%
2005	13%	0%	93%	92%
2004	80%	40%	70%	48%

LOUISIANA 5

Northeast and central — Monroe, Alexandria

The 5th stretches south from the Arkansas border, with the Mississippi River delta parishes in its east and the national forests and midsize cities of central Louisiana in its west. It is conservative throughout and is plagued by pockets of poverty and unemployment despite numerous efforts to bring more economic opportunities to the area.

Although the rich, black soil along the Mississippi River produces much of the state's cotton and soybeans, poor education and transportation systems slow economic growth — the 5th is the eighth-poorest district in the country, with a median household income of just under $27,500.

The outlook is not entirely bleak, however. Monroe depends increasingly on health care, service and retail industries, and is home to a University of Louisiana campus and CenturyTel, a telecommunications company. Several development projects — including improvements to a Ouachita River port in West Monroe and the building of the NASCAR-affiliated Monroe Motor Speedway, which opened in 2008 — have brought jobs, tourism and revenue to the district.

The 5th's portion of central Louisiana is fueled by Alexandria in Rapides Parish, which is home to a Proctor & Gamble detergent manufacturing plant. In the district's northwest, Lincoln Parish hosts Louisiana Tech University in Ruston and the historically black Grambling State University in Grambling.

This historically Democratic district now leans Republican, but the 5th's voters still support conservatives of either party. Roughly one-third of the district's residents are black, and Democrats hold many local offices, although residents of Baptist- and Pentecostal-dominated northern Louisiana are more likely than the Catholics in the South to vote for Republicans. John McCain took 62 percent of the district's vote in the 2008 presidential election.

MAJOR INDUSTRY
Agriculture, health care, higher education

CITIES
Monroe, 53,107; Alexandria, 46,342; Ruston, 20,546

NOTABLE
Grambling State became the first Louisiana college or university to receive a visit from a sitting president when Bill Clinton gave the 1999 commencement address.

Rep. Bill Cassidy (R)

Elected 2008; 1st term

A former state lawmaker, Cassidy is a proponent of smaller government and lower taxes. He also supports expanded domestic oil drilling, an expansion of alternative energy and reduced government involvement in education.

His allegiance to fellow Republicans on key issues prompted party leaders to name him an assistant to the party's whip team and a member of the party's House Policy Committee in 2009. Cassidy also was granted a seat on the Education and Labor Committee. He has served on the education panel in the state Senate.

Cassidy also sits on the Natural Resources and Agriculture committees, where he said he will call for tax incentives for the production of hydrogen-fueled cars and alternative energy. And like his Republican colleagues from Louisiana, he plans to push for the state to receive a more immediate share of revenues from oil leases along the Gulf Coast.

Cassidy joined with his party in February 2009 to oppose a $787 million stimulus package, which was signed into law. He said passage of the legislation was "as if a patient came to [him] with heart trouble and [he] treated her for a broken leg."

A gastroenterologist, Cassidy hopes to also have a say in health care reform. He said any solution to the health care crisis must address access, cost and quality. In January 2009, he opposed an expansion of the State Children's Health Insurance Program, saying his state already does a good job enrolling the poor under the program.

Born in Highland Park, Ill., but raised in Baton Rouge, his interest in medicine was sparked during his senior year in high school, when doctors thought he had cancer and eventually diagnosed him with swollen lymph nodes. He earned a medical degree from Louisiana State University Medical School in New Orleans, where he met his wife, Laura, who also is a physician.

He won a 2006 special election for a state Senate seat. Aiming higher, he challenged incumbent Democratic U.S. Rep. Don Cazayoux in 2008 and won with 48 percent. Cassidy said he hopes to continue to work as a doctor in Louisiana because he believes it helps keep him informed and grounded.

CAPITOL OFFICE
225-3901
cassidy.house.gov
506 Cannon Bldg. 20515; fax 225-7313

COMMITTEES
Agriculture
Education & Labor
Natural Resources

RESIDENCE
Baton Rouge

BORN
Sept. 28, 1957; Highland Park, Ill.

RELIGION
Christian

FAMILY
Wife, Laura Layden Cassidy; three children

EDUCATION
Louisiana State U., B.S. 1979 (biochemistry),
M.D. 1983

CAREER
Physician

POLITICAL HIGHLIGHTS
La. Senate, 2006-08

ELECTION RESULTS

2008 GENERAL

Bill Cassidy (R)	150,332	48.1%
Don Cazayoux (D)	125,886	40.3%
Michael Jackson (X)	36,198	11.6%

2008 PRIMARY

Bill Cassidy (R)	unopposed

LOUISIANA 6
East central — Baton Rouge

Centered around Baton Rouge, the socially conservative 6th takes in a slew of petrochemical plants along the Mississippi River as well as rural parishes along the Mississippi border. Baton Rouge's economic stability has spurred population growth in neighboring parishes, which attract commuters with superior schools and lower crime rates.

Government is the primary employer in the state capital of Baton Rouge, and a strong construction sector based on redeveloping parts of the state hit hard by Hurricane Katrina in 2005 and other recent storms fuels job growth. Higher education also drives the economy, as Louisiana State University and Southern University are here. Casinos and other ventures, such as the new Shaw Center for the Arts, have helped Baton Rouge promote tourism. A proposed light-rail system connecting Baton Rouge to New

Orleans might help spur further growth, but implementation of those plans is still considered a long-term goal.

The Port of Greater Baton Rouge gives the area a boost and the petrochemical industry has rebounded in recent years, but agriculture fuels the 6th's rural parishes, with sugar cane in the west and paper mills and sweet potato farms in the northeast.

Socially conservative suburban and rural voters have shifted toward the GOP, but Baton Rouge's minority and blue-collar residents still vote Democratic. Republican John McCain won 57 percent of the 6th's 2008 presidential vote.

MAJOR INDUSTRY
Government, higher education, petrochemicals

CITIES
Baton Rouge, 227,818; Shenandoah (unincorporated), 17,070

NOTABLE
The state Capitol is the tallest in the nation.

Rep. Charles Boustany Jr. (R)

Elected 2004; 3rd term

CAPITOL OFFICE
225-2031
boustany.house.gov
1117 Longworth Bldg. 20515-1807; fax 225-5724

COMMITTEES
Ways & Means

RESIDENCE
Lafayette

BORN
Feb. 21, 1956; Lafayette, La.

RELIGION
Episcopalian

FAMILY
Wife, Bridget Boustany; two children

EDUCATION
U. of Southwestern Louisiana, B.S. 1978 (biology); Louisiana State U., M.D. 1982

CAREER
Surgeon

POLITICAL HIGHLIGHTS
No previous office

ELECTION RESULTS

2008 GENERAL

Charles Boustany Jr. (R)	177,173	61.9%
Donald "Don" Cravins Jr. (D)	98,280	34.3%
Peter Vidrine (X)	10,846	3.8%

2008 PRIMARY

Charles Boustany Jr. (R)	unopposed

2006 GENERAL

Charles Boustany Jr. (R)	113,720	70.7%
Mike Stagg (D)	47,133	29.3%

PREVIOUS WINNING PERCENTAGES
2004 (55%)

One of the few medical doctors in the House, Boustany sees politics more as an art than a science. He's willing to cut deals with Democrats when it serves his constituents, but won't bend on matters at the core of his socially and fiscally conservative philosophy.

Constituent service, in particular responding to hurricane devastation along the Louisiana coast, was his foremost preoccupation during his first two terms. Now Boustany (boo-STAN-knee) holds a coveted slot on the Ways and Means Committee and is stepping up to play a big role in formulating the GOP's response to Democratic efforts to overhaul the health care system.

He is the top-ranking Republican on the panel's Oversight Subcommittee during the 111th Congress (2009-10) and has used his seat there to criticize President Obama's efforts to revive the economy. Republican leaders also assigned Boustany to a GOP health care task force headed up by Missouri Rep. Roy Blunt. It is tasked with developing policy proposals to counter Democratic overhaul plans.

During two decades in the medical field — as a physician and heart surgeon — Boustany came to believe that the key to fixing the health care system is to empower the patient. He believes the government can do much to improve treatment outcomes, limit waste and reduce waiting times for medical services. But he rejects the single-payer model endorsed by many Democrats and is skeptical of other government-centric solutions that would cut costs by limiting treatments to those deemed most effective. Changes to the health care system have to be made in a "sustainable way that's responsible," he said.

Boustany wants Congress to allow Americans to carry health care insurance from job to job and to give self-employed workers the same tax break when they buy insurance that they would receive if they worked for a large company. He believes Congress could facilitate the creation of new purchasing-pool options that would cover more people and provide more choices for individuals and families. And he wants to make it legal for workers to buy health insurance across state lines in a national market.

Perhaps in a foreshadowing of larger health care fights to come, Boustany in early 2009 urged colleagues to oppose an expansion of a government-run health care program for poor children, eventually pushed through by Democrats and signed by President Obama, arguing it would do little to redirect the poor from emergency-room treatment to their own physicians.

On social issues — such as abortion — Boustany is almost always a doctrinaire conservative. But he did ally with Democrats in 2008 in moving a law expanding U.S. funding for global AIDS programs.

Boustany also joined with Democrats that July in voting for a new law aimed at helping homeowners struggling to pay their mortgages, an issue sure to resurface on Ways and Means' Income Security and Family Support Subcommittee, where Boustany holds a seat. Later that year, Boustany was one of 25 Republicans to switch his vote from "no" to "yes," helping President George W. Bush and Democratic leaders pass a $700 billion financial industry rescue package.

On trade issues, over which Ways and Means has jurisdiction, Boustany is unpredictable. He voted against the Central America Free Trade Agreement in 2005, saying it would hurt Louisiana farmers, but has supported similar deals with Colombia and Peru. He worked with Agriculture Chairman Collin C. Peterson, a Minnesota Democrat, in 2007 to direct sugar, which he feared Mexico was dumping on the U.S. market, into ethanol production as a way of protecting Louisiana sugar producers.

Boustany also has pushed colleagues to allow more seasonal immigrants to enter the country legally. He cited concerns about rice and sugar farmers and shrimp-peeling factories in his district that depend on the seasonal workers.

Boustany has found Democratic support to help Louisianans recover from a series of devastating hurricanes, from Katrina in 2005 to Gustav in 2008, his primary focus during his first two terms. Just nine months into office, Boustany won enactment of a bill in 2005 giving the Labor Department more flexibility in providing temporary work and training in disaster areas.

Boustany grew up in Lafayette, the son of Charles Boustany Sr., a long-time coroner for Lafayette Parish. His mother, a homemaker with 10 children, also did charitable work in the community. He is of Lebanese descent; he led a 2007 effort to increase aid to the Palestinian Authority to combat the anti-American influence of the rival group Hamas.

His family was staunchly Democratic, but Boustany as a young man was influenced by columnist George Will and other conservative thinkers. "It created friction," said Boustany of his political split with his father. Boustany's wife, Bridget, also is a former Democrat, in addition to being the niece of former Louisiana Democratic Gov. Edwin Edwards.

In 2001, Boustany developed severe arthritis in his neck and hands, forcing him to close his Lafayette medical practice. "It was devastating, because I was at the peak of my career," he said. He still lives with pain daily, following a physical-therapy routine to keep it at a "baseline" level.

As he pondered what to do with the rest of his life, Boustany began paying more attention to state politics. He wasn't pleased with what he saw. "That was an awakening," he said. "The common denominator here was a lack of good political leadership for the state." In 2004, after Democratic Rep. Chris John decided to run for the Senate, Boustany talked it over with his wife and decided to run for John's seat.

After finishing first with 39 percent of the vote in the Nov. 2 all-party primary, Boustany cruised to a comfortable 10-percentage-point win in the runoff with state Sen. Willie Landry Mount, a Democrat who'd run afoul of the area's sizable black community in defeating Democratic state Sen. Don Cravins to make the runoff. With Mount unable to galvanize support among blacks, Boustany made history as the first Republican to be elected from the area since 1884.

He was handily re-elected in 2006 and again in 2008, when he defeated Cravins' son, then-state Sen. Donald "Don" Cravins Jr.

KEY VOTES

2008

No — Delay consideration of Colombia free-trade agreement

Yes — Override Bush veto of federal farm and nutrition programs reauthorization bill

Yes — Overhaul surveillance laws and permit dismissal of suits against companies that conducted warrantless wiretapping

Yes — Grant mortgage relief to homeowners and funding for Fannie Mae and Freddie Mac

No — Approve initial $700 billion program to stabilize financial markets

Yes — Approve final $700 billion program to stabilize financial markets

No — Provide $14 billion in loans to automakers

2007

No — Increase minimum wage by $2.10 an hour

No — Approve $124.2 billion in emergency war spending and set goal for redeployment of troops from Iraq

Yes — Reject federal contraceptive assistance to international family planning groups

Yes — Override Bush veto of $23.2 billion water projects authorization bill

Yes — Implement Peru free-trade agreement

No — Approve energy policy overhaul with new fuel economy standards

Yes — Clear $473.5 billion omnibus spending bill, including $70 billion for military operations

CQ VOTE STUDIES

	PARTY UNITY		PRESIDENTIAL SUPPORT	
	SUPPORT	OPPOSE	SUPPORT	OPPOSE
2008	94%	6%	68%	32%
2007	87%	13%	80%	20%
2006	95%	5%	95%	5%
2005	96%	4%	86%	14%

INTEREST GROUPS

	AFL-CIO	ADA	CCUS	ACU
2008	8%	20%	94%	83%
2007	13%	5%	84%	100%
2006	21%	0%	100%	80%
2005	27%	15%	89%	96%

LOUISIANA 7

Southwest — Lafayette, Lake Charles

Anchored by blue-collar Lake Charles in the west, white-collar Lafayette in the east and the Gulf of Mexico to the south, the 7th boasts both coastal and city life.

Agriculture, along with oil and gas production, directs the 7th's economy, although in 2008 hurricanes Gustav and Ike destroyed soybean, sugar and hay crops, rice fields and thousands of cattle. In particular, the area's farmland continues to suffer the long-term effects of increased salinity, a result of hurricane flooding. Commercial fishing has also struggled, as the storms killed fish and vegetation. Cameron Parish, once a key port for the nation's commercial fishing industry, has lost a significant portion of its operating fleet.

Concerns about the age and effectiveness of waterway infrastructure worries local officials and Port of Lake Charles-based employers. Area construction and contracting jobs are expected to increase as hurricane-related repairs expand in the 7th, and federal funding for commercial and housing construction should bring more jobs.

While damage to New Orleans and southeastern Louisiana received considerable attention during the 2005 hurricane season, the 7th did not escape the storms unscathed. Hurricane Rita landed in Cameron Parish near Johnsons Bayou, flooded Lake Charles in Calcasieu Parish and demolished smaller towns such as Creole and Cameron. Farther east, Lafayette welcomed evacuees from other parts of the state.

The 7th's sizable Catholic population bolsters its socially conservative leanings. Despite this bent, the area sent a Democrat to Congress in every election from 1884 until 2004. The GOP solidified its hold on the district's vote for president — John McCain won 63 percent of the district's vote in 2008, 3 percentage points more than George W. Bush won here in 2004 — and Republican candidates find support in all of the 7th's parishes.

MAJOR INDUSTRY
Oil and gas, petrochemicals, agriculture, fishing

CITIES
Lafayette, 110,257; Lake Charles, 71,757; Opelousas, 22,860

NOTABLE
Southwest Louisiana Institute (now University of Louisiana at Lafayette) in 1954 was the first all-white state college in the South to desegregate.

Gov. John Baldacci (D)

Pronounced:
ball-DA-chee
First elected: 2002
Length of term: 4 years
Term expires: 1/11
Salary: $70,000
Phone: (207) 287-3531

Residence: Augusta
Born: Jan. 30, 1955; Bangor, Maine
Religion: Roman Catholic
Family: Wife, Karen Baldacci; one child
Education: U. of Maine, B.A. 1986 (history)
Career: Restaurant operator
Political highlights: Bangor City Council, 1978-81; Maine Senate, 1982-94; U.S. House, 1995-2003

Election results:

2006 GENERAL

John Baldacci (D)	209,927	38.1%
Chandler E. Woodcock (R)	166,425	30.2%
Barbara Merrill (IMC)	118,715	21.6%
Patricia H. LaMarche (GREEN)	52,690	9.6%

Senate President
Elizabeth H. Mitchell (D)

(no lieutenant governor)
Phone: (207) 287-1500

LEGISLATURE

Legislature: January-June in odd-numbered years; January-April in even-numbered years

Senate: 35 members, 2-year terms
2009 ratios: 20 D, 15 R; 27 men, 8 women
Salary: $23,400/2-year term
Phone: (207) 287-1540

House: 151 members, 2-year terms
2009 ratios: 95 D, 55 R,1 other; 104 men, 47 women
Salary: $23,400/2-year term
Phone: (207) 287-1400

TERM LIMITS

Governor: 2 consecutive terms
Senate: 4 consecutive terms
House: 4 consecutive terms

URBAN STATISTICS

CITY	POPULATION
Portland	64,249
Lewiston	35,690
Bangor	31,473
South Portland	23,325
Auburn	23,203

REGISTERED VOTERS

Unaffiliated/others	41%
Democrat	32%
Republican	27%

POPULATION

2008 population (est.)	1,316,456
2000 population	1,274,923
1990 population	1,227,928
Percent change (1990-2000)	+3.8%
Rank among states (2008)	40
Median age	38.6
Born in state	67.3%
Foreign born	2.9%
Violent crime rate	110/100,000
Poverty level	10.9%
Federal workers	13,542
Military	10,200

ELECTIONS

STATE ELECTION OFFICIAL
(207) 624-7736
DEMOCRATIC PARTY
(207) 622-6233
REPUBLICAN PARTY
(207) 622-6247

MISCELLANEOUS

Web: www.maine.gov
Capital: Augusta

U.S. CONGRESS

Senate: 2 Republicans
House: 2 Democrats

2000 Census Statistics by District

DIST.	2008 VOTE FOR PRESIDENT OBAMA	MCCAIN	WHITE	BLACK	ASIAN	HISP	MEDIAN INCOME	WHITE COLLAR	BLUE COLLAR	SERVICE INDUSTRY	OVER 64	UNDER 18	COLLEGE EDUCATION	RURAL	SQ. MILES
1	61%	38%	96%	1%	1%	1%	$42,044	61%	24%	14%	14%	24%	28%	51%	3,535
2	55	43	97	0	0	1	$32,678	53	31	16	15	23	18	71	27,244
STATE	58	40	96	1	1	1	$37,240	57	27	15	14	24	23	60	30,862
U.S.	53	46	69	12	4	13	$41,994	60	25	15	12	26	24	21	3,537,438

Sen. Olympia J. Snowe (R)

Elected 1994; 3rd term

CAPITOL OFFICE
224-5344
snowe.senate.gov
154 Russell Bldg. 20510-1903; fax 224-1946

COMMITTEES
Commerce, Science & Transportation
Finance
Small Business & Entrepreneurship - ranking
   member
Select Intelligence

RESIDENCE
Falmouth

BORN
Feb. 21, 1947; Augusta, Maine

RELIGION
Greek Orthodox

FAMILY
Husband, John R. McKernan Jr.

EDUCATION
U. of Maine, B.A. 1969 (political science)

CAREER
Congressional district aide; city employee

POLITICAL HIGHLIGHTS
Maine House, 1973-77; Maine Senate, 1977-79;
U.S. House, 1979-95

ELECTION RESULTS

2006 GENERAL

Olympia J. Snowe (R)	402,598	74.0%
Jean M. Hay Bright (D)	111,984	20.6%
William H. Slavick (I)	29,220	5.4%

2006 PRIMARY

Olympia J. Snowe (R)	58,979	98.9%
write-ins (R)	673	1.1%

PREVIOUS WINNING PERCENTAGES
2000 (69%); 1994 (60%); 1992 House Election (49%);
1990 House Election (51%); 1988 House Election
(66%); 1986 House Election (77%); 1984 House
Election (76%); 1982 House Election (67%); 1980
House Election (79%); 1978 House Election (51%)

Snowe exercises enormous clout as a moderate Republican dealmaker, something that inflames conservatives but keeps her popular among her state's stubbornly independent constituents. She doesn't allow GOP colleagues to bully her into blocking Democratic legislation and hews to what she sees as traditional GOP values — fiscal discipline, small government and individual rights.

Snowe works on a wide range of issues, placing a firm emphasis on practicality and disdaining partisanship. "The political center is essential to achieving results and concrete solutions," she said. "People don't look at ideology. It doesn't put food on the table."

Snowe can be even more of a centrist than her like-minded Maine GOP colleague Susan Collins. She broke ranks on more than three-quarters of the first 54 Senate votes in 2009 that pitted a majority of Democrats and Republicans against each other, while Collins did so on two-thirds. The conservative magazine Human Events derided Snowe as the No. 1 RINO (Republican In Name Only), noting that her 12 percent score from the American Conservative Union in 2008 was just one point higher than that of New York Democrat Hillary Rodham Clinton, as well as 4 percentage points below that of Majority Leader Harry Reid.

Snowe is an especially critical figure when Reid needs to persuade at least a few Republicans to help break the 60-vote barrier needed to overcome GOP parliamentary opposition on most legislation. Her seat on the Finance Committee also enhances her stature; she often is at the center of debates on financial and health care policy. And she provides Democrats entree to the Republican caucus as a member of Arizona Sen. Jon Kyl's whip team.

She was the subject of speculation as both a potential 2008 running mate for Republican presidential nominee John McCain and a possible Cabinet choice for President Obama. Her spokesman said the Obama administration approached her for an unspecified high-level job, but that she declined.

Snowe drew considerable attention for helping hand Obama his first significant legislative victory in February 2009. She joined Collins and Arlen Specter of Pennsylvania as the only three Republicans to back Obama's $787 billion economic stimulus bill, which became law. The three moderates agreed to support the measure after its size was scaled back to under $800 billion. "I always thought it was imperative to pass a stimulus," she told the Kennebec Journal. "The urgency directed by the times demanded that."

Snowe worked with Democrat Ron Wyden of Oregon on a provision to tax bonuses given out by financial institutions receiving money from the $700 billion financial sector rescue law passed in fall 2008. The language was dropped from the stimulus during House-Senate negotiations on the final agreement; when a political furor erupted the following month over $160 million in bonuses paid to failed insurance giant American International Group Inc., Snowe said their proposal could have averted the problem.

Snowe focuses on legislation she believes can make a difference to ordinary people, in Maine and across the country — home heating assistance for low-income families, an expansion of children's health insurance, tax breaks for small businesses and electronic medical records. She won enactment of legislation in 2008 banning discrimination in jobs and health insurance based on the results of genetic testing. She and Democratic Rep. Louise M. Slaughter of New York had pressed for the legislation for a decade. She calls its passage one of the "major satisfactions of my career here."

Snowe's biggest break with President George W. Bush was over his 2005 proposal to add private savings accounts to Social Security. She refused to support such accounts or the steep cuts in guaranteed benefits that would accompany them. She told Maine audiences she was proud of helping successfully obstruct the plan.

Snowe doesn't get everything she wants, but she often succeeds in slipping targeted provisions into final legislation, sometimes playing hardball to prevail. She blocked action in 2006 on a flood insurance bill until she was able to win $1 billion for the Low Income Home Energy Assistance Program, which helps poor families pay their heating bills.

Another local issue she watches closely as a member of the Commerce, Science and Transportation Committee is the reauthorization of the Magnuson-Stevens fisheries conservation law, important to Maine, with its 3,500 miles of coastline and robust fishing industry. She also looks out for the Bath Iron Works, the giant builder of Navy ships that is one of the state's largest employers. During the 2005 round of military base closings, she successfully fought a proposal to shut down the Portsmouth Naval Shipyard.

Snowe likes being a role model for younger generations entering politics. As top-ranking Republican on the Small Business and Entrepreneurship Committee, she encourages female entrepreneurs and is a close ally of the panel's chairwoman, Democratic moderate Mary L. Landrieu of Louisiana; the two are the first female duo to lead a Senate committee. Snowe has pressed Obama to elevate the Small Business Administration to Cabinet-level status as it was during the Clinton administration.

Snowe also serves on the Select Intelligence Committee. She has called for a "cyber czar" in the White House to coordinate computer activities across spy and civilian agencies. And she said in November 2008 that increased violence in Afghanistan demands more regional cooperation.

Snowe's father, Greek immigrant George Bouchles, and her mother, Georgia, operated the State Street Diner in Augusta, down the street from the state house. Georgia Bouchles loved politics, and the diner was a magnet for politicians, business people and journalists. In 1955, when Olympia was 8, her mother died of breast cancer. The next year, her father died of heart disease. Olympia was sent to St. Basil's Academy, a school for girls run by the Greek Orthodox Church in Garrison, N.Y. She spent summers in Auburn, Maine, with an uncle and his wife and their five children.

Snowe got through the University of Maine on student loans and with summer jobs at a Christmas ornament factory. After graduation, she married Peter Snowe, who, like her, was deeply interested in politics. Her husband was elected to the Maine Legislature, and she went to work as a district aide for GOP Rep. William S. Cohen, who later became a senator and secretary of Defense. In 1973, Peter Snowe was killed in an automobile accident during a snowstorm, and a still-grieving Olympia was elected to succeed him.

Three years later, in 1976, she won a seat in the Maine Senate. When Cohen made a winning race for the U.S. Senate in 1978, she captured his House seat. She later fell in love for the second time — with GOP Rep. John R. McKernan Jr., who represented the adjacent 1st District. They married in 1989, while he was serving the first of two terms as governor of Maine.

Snowe easily won re-election until 1990, when a deepening recession led to voter restlessness. She barely edged Democratic state Rep. Patrick K. McGowan, 51 percent to 49 percent. A 1992 rematch was even closer; she won with a 49 percent plurality. When Senate Democratic Leader George J. Mitchell retired in 1994, she ran for the seat and prevailed with 60 percent of the vote. In 2000 and 2006, she overwhelmed her Democratic opponents. She is so popular now that the town of Bethel, hoping for a record, built a 122-foot snowwoman in 2008 and named it "Olympia."

KEY VOTES

2008

Yes Prohibit discrimination based on genetic information

Yes Reauthorize farm and nutrition programs for five years

Yes Limit debate on "cap and trade" system for greenhouse gas emissions

No   Allow lawsuits against companies that participated in warrantless wiretapping

Yes Limit debate on a bill to block a scheduled cut in Medicare payments to doctors

Yes Grant mortgage relief to homeowners and funding for Fannie Mae and Freddie Mac

Yes Approve a nuclear cooperation agreement with India

Yes Approve final $700 billion program to stabilize financial markets

Yes Allow consideration of a $14 billion auto industry loan package

2007

Yes Increase minimum wage by $2.10 an hour

Yes Limit debate on a comprehensive immigration bill

Yes Overhaul congressional lobbying and ethics rules for members and their staffs

Yes Limit debate on considering a bill to add House seats for the District of Columbia and Utah

Yes Limit debate on restoring habeas corpus rights to detainees

Yes Mandate minimum breaks for troops between deployments to Iraq or Afghanistan

Yes Override Bush veto of $23.2 billion water projects authorization bill

Yes Confirm Michael B. Mukasey as attorney general

Yes Limit debate on an energy policy overhaul containing $21.8 billion in tax incentives and reduced oil and gas subsidies

CQ VOTE STUDIES

	PARTY UNITY		PRESIDENTIAL SUPPORT	
	SUPPORT	OPPOSE	SUPPORT	OPPOSE
2008	39%	61%	48%	52%
2007	44%	56%	57%	43%
2006	56%	44%	75%	25%
2005	56%	44%	67%	33%
2004	71%	29%	74%	26%
2003	75%	25%	82%	18%
2002	57%	43%	90%	10%
2001	64%	36%	84%	16%
2000	71%	29%	62%	38%
1999	69%	31%	49%	51%

INTEREST GROUPS

	AFL-CIO	ADA	CCUS	ACU
2008	100%	80%	71%	12%
2007	68%	60%	64%	28%
2006	47%	45%	75%	36%
2005	64%	65%	78%	32%
2004	67%	65%	71%	60%
2003	0%	55%	65%	45%
2002	31%	30%	85%	65%
2001	50%	40%	79%	60%
2000	0%	30%	73%	80%
1999	33%	45%	59%	60%

Sen. Susan Collins (R)

Elected 1996; 3rd term

CAPITOL OFFICE
224-2523
collins.senate.gov
413 Dirksen Bldg. 20510-1904; fax 224-2693

COMMITTEES
Appropriations
Armed Services
Homeland Security & Governmental Affairs -
    ranking member
Special Aging

RESIDENCE
Bangor

BORN
Dec. 7, 1952; Caribou, Maine

RELIGION
Roman Catholic

FAMILY
Single

EDUCATION
St. Lawrence U., B.A. 1975 (government)

CAREER
Business center director; congressional aide

POLITICAL HIGHLIGHTS
Maine Department of Professional and
Financial Regulation commissioner, 1987-91;
Small Business Administration official, 1992-93;
Maine deputy treasurer, 1993; Republican nominee
for governor, 1994

ELECTION RESULTS

2008 GENERAL

Susan Collins (R)	444,300	61.8%
Tom Allen (D)	279,510	38.2%

2008 PRIMARY

Susan Collins (R)	unopposed

2002 GENERAL

Susan Collins (R)	295,041	58.4%
Chellie Pingree (D)	209,858	41.6%

2002 PRIMARY

Susan Collins (R)	unopposed

PREVIOUS WINNING PERCENTAGES
1996 (49%)

Collins' style is soft-spoken and measured, but she is known as a demanding boss and fierce negotiator, with an appetite for combing the fine print of legislation. Her mentor is her former Senate boss, William S. Cohen, another moderate who served as secretary of Defense under President Clinton. Cohen said Collins "comes from that long lineage of Maine leaders who understand that most people live in the center of life — that you can't govern from the extremes."

Along with her like-minded Maine colleague Olympia J. Snowe, Collins is often a pivotal figure as Democrats seek Republican support on major legislation. She has joined many of the bipartisan working groups and "gangs" that have sprouted up to strike deals on judicial nominations, energy policy and other issues. She keeps her party's leaders from being too concerned about her by sometimes taking their side on fiscal and defense matters.

Collins joined the rest of the caucus in 2008 to oppose an amendment to the Foreign Intelligence Surveillance Act that would have allowed lawsuits against companies that participated in the National Security Agency's warrantless surveillance program. She also supported a $700 billion financial rescue package, signed into law, and a subsequent unsuccessful attempt to bail out U.S. automakers. In a rare break with Snowe that year, she voted against a $289 billion measure to reauthorize farm programs, which President George W. Bush had vetoed because he believed it contained excessive spending.

But she gave conservatives heartburn in 2009 when she joined Snowe and Pennsylvania's Arlen Specter as the only Republicans to support President Obama's $787 billion economic stimulus law, agreeing to the measure only after its cost was sliced to less than $800 billion. She also supported an expansion of the State Children's Health Insurance Program, which covers children from low-income families that do not qualify for Medicaid, and voting rights for the District of Columbia. She voted against a GOP effort to derail a $410 billion catchall spending bill.

She and Snowe have a cool relationship, though they do work closely together on issues affecting Maine. As the Homeland Security and Governmental Affairs Committee's top Republican, Collins has a more amicable relationship with the panel's chairman, Connecticut independent Joseph I. Lieberman. In the 111th Congress (2009-10), they plan to push legislation to allow the Department of Homeland Security to regulate laboratories dealing with dangerous pathogens. Such regulations are now handled by the departments of Agriculture and Health and Human Services. Collins also wants to look at computer security across the government.

Collins accumulated several accomplishments when she chaired the committee prior to the Democratic takeover in 2007. When the federal government was accused of poor response in the aftermath of Hurricane Katrina in 2005, she led calls for the Federal Emergency Management Agency to become independent of the department. She called the agency "a symbol of a bumbling bureaucracy." The proposal met with resistance from the Bush administration, but she succeeded in getting legislation into law the next year to clarify the federal chain of command during disasters. The agency was credited with more success in dealing with the 2007 California wildfires.

Her biggest victory was her work with Lieberman in the 108th Congress (2003-04) to rewrite the nation's intelligence laws to create a more centralized spy infrastructure — a key recommendation of the independent commission that investigated the Sept. 11 attacks. Senate leaders chose Collins, rather than the chief of either the Armed Services or Select Intelligence committees, to draft legislation. She then carefully navigated a series of turf battles among the Pentagon, Congress and the White House.

Collins serves on the Armed Services Committee, an assignment vital to one of Maine's largest industrial employers, Bath Iron Works. The shipyard builds destroyers that face perennial funding threats among defense priorities. She worked with Mississippi lawmakers in 2006 to block a proposed Navy strategy to build the ships in only one of the two states. And she has championed funding for a new coastal combat ship and a high-speed vessel program that Bath hopes to build as part of returning to a 313-ship Navy.

In 2008, Collins worked with Democrats Ben Nelson of Nebraska and Evan Bayh of Indiana on what she considered a major accomplishment — an amendment to the Defense Department authorization bill that requires Iraq to pay a greater share of its own reconstruction.

Collins also hopes to become involved in shaping health care legislation in the 111th. She helped create a grant program in 2002 to provide dental services in rural areas, which was extended in 2008 for another five years. She now wants to concentrate on the challenges of providing health care in a rural state lacking health care professionals.

Forestry is another major concern of Collins in a state where two of her brothers still operate a lumber company founded in 1844. In late 2008, she succeeded in including in the $700 billion financial services rescue a provision that created a $300 tax credit for buying a wood-burning stove. She sees burning wood products as an alternative source of energy. She also supports harnessing wood power.

Collins augmented her heavy committee workload by receiving a coveted assignment to the Appropriations Committee in January 2009.

Collins hails from a political family; each of her parents served as Caribou's mayor. She learned her steely competitiveness at an early age. As a 10-year-old, she and her older sister Nancy turned the dreary work of picking potatoes into a game by seeing who could toss more potatoes into the barrel behind a tractor that unearthed them before the ground froze. "I don't pretend that I was a champion picker, because I certainly was not. But I was a diligent one and a hard-working one," Collins recalled.

As a high school senior, Collins had a chance to meet former Maine GOP Sen. Margaret Chase Smith, who once went 13 straight years without missing a vote. Collins prides herself on a perfect voting record, surpassing Smith's record with 2,941 straight votes in November 2005.

After graduating from St. Lawrence University in 1975, Collins took her passion for politics to Washington and worked as an aide to Cohen, spending a dozen years on his staff. She then returned to Maine to serve as commissioner of the state's Department of Professional and Financial Regulation.

In 1994, Collins won the Republican nomination for governor but finished a disappointing third behind Democratic nominee Joseph E. Brennan, who finished second, and independent Angus King, who won the contest. But in 1996, when Cohen announced his retirement, Collins regrouped and took the race by 5 percentage points. She won handily in 2002, beating Democratic challenger Chellie Pingree, who was elected to a House seat in 2008.

In 2008, Collins faced an experienced opponent in Democratic Rep. Tom Allen, who had the backing of national Democrats. But she cruised to victory with 61 percent of the vote, even as Democratic presidential nominee Barack Obama carried the state. Collins said her win came from her reputation for working well with Democrats and that her party shouldn't draw sharp ideological lines if it wants to see its popularity return. "The people in my state are sick and tired of the hyperpartisanship and the gridlock that has blocked action on so many important issues that affect their lives directly," she said.

KEY VOTES

2008

Yes Prohibit discrimination based on genetic information

No Reauthorize farm and nutrition programs for five years

Yes Limit debate on "cap and trade" system for greenhouse gas emissions

No Allow lawsuits against companies that participated in warrantless wiretapping

Yes Limit debate on a bill to block a scheduled cut in Medicare payments to doctors

Yes Grant mortgage relief to homeowners and funding for Fannie Mae and Freddie Mac

Yes Approve a nuclear cooperation agreement with India

Yes Approve final $700 billion program to stabilize financial markets

Yes Allow consideration of a $14 billion auto industry loan package

2007

Yes Increase minimum wage by $2.10 an hour

No Limit debate on a comprehensive immigration bill

Yes Overhaul congressional lobbying and ethics rules for members and their staffs

Yes Limit debate on considering a bill to add House seats for the District of Columbia and Utah

No Limit debate on restoring habeas corpus rights to detainees

Yes Mandate minimum breaks for troops between deployments to Iraq or Afghanistan

Yes Override Bush veto of $23.2 billion water projects authorization bill

Yes Confirm Michael B. Mukasey as attorney general

Yes Limit debate on an energy policy overhaul containing $21.8 billion in tax incentives and reduced oil and gas subsidies

CQ VOTE STUDIES

	PARTY UNITY		PRESIDENTIAL SUPPORT	
	SUPPORT	OPPOSE	SUPPORT	OPPOSE
2008	46%	54%	59%	41%
2007	50%	50%	61%	39%
2006	66%	34%	79%	21%
2005	59%	41%	62%	38%
2004	78%	22%	82%	18%
2003	78%	22%	87%	13%
2002	57%	43%	88%	12%
2001	67%	33%	88%	12%
2000	74%	26%	57%	42%
1999	74%	26%	49%	51%

INTEREST GROUPS

	AFL-CIO	ADA	CCUS	ACU
2008	100%	75%	75%	20%
2007	68%	55%	64%	36%
2006	47%	45%	92%	48%
2005	64%	65%	78%	32%
2004	50%	45%	94%	68%
2003	31%	45%	78%	35%
2002	31%	35%	85%	55%
2001	50%	35%	79%	64%
2000	0%	25%	80%	76%
1999	11%	25%	76%	64%

Rep. Chellie Pingree (D)

Elected 2008; 1st term

CAPITOL OFFICE
225-6116
pingree.house.gov
1037 Longworth Bldg. 20515; fax 225-5590

COMMITTEES
Armed Services
Rules

RESIDENCE
North Haven

BORN
April 2, 1955; Minneapolis, Minn.

RELIGION
Lutheran

FAMILY
Divorced; three children

EDUCATION
U. of Southern Maine, attended 1973;
College of the Atlantic, B.A. 1979 (human ecology)

CAREER
Inn owner; Common Cause president; knitting
company owner; farmer

POLITICAL HIGHLIGHTS
North Haven Board of Assessors, 1981-87
(chairwoman, 1982-83, 1984-87); North Haven
Planning Board, 1981-91; Maine School
Administrative District #7 Board of Directors,
1990-93 (chairwoman, 1991-93); Maine Senate,
1992-2000 (majority leader, 1996-2000); Democratic
nominee for U.S. Senate, 2002

ELECTION RESULTS

2008 GENERAL

Chellie Pingree (D)	205,629	54.9%
Charlie Summers (R)	168,930	45.1%

2008 PRIMARY

Chellie Pingree (D)	24,324	43.9%
Adam Roland Cote (D)	15,706	28.4%
Michael F. Brennan (D)	6,040	10.9%
Ethan King Strimling (D)	5,833	10.5%
Mark W. Lawrence (D)	2,726	4.9%
Stephen J. Meister (D)	753	1.4%

Pingree has been working on political issues for decades, starting as a teenage anti-war protestor. She is a colorful former state Senate majority leader and past president of the nonpartisan lobbying group Common Cause. She said she has progressed into a "liberal, proactive, practical" legislator who is not afraid to get her hands dirty, "either in politics or on the farm."

House Speaker Nancy Pelosi asked Pingree (her first name is pronounced "Shelley") to serve on the Rules Committee, which sets terms for floor debate on bills. Pelosi cited Pingree's reputation in Maine for working across the aisle.

Pingree started her congressional career by managing a debate on a bill intended to make it easier for workers to challenge wage discrimination — the first measure of the 111th Congress (2009-10) that President Obama signed into law. She was a vocal supporter of Obama's $787 billion economic stimulus law, touting its benefits for her state's workers.

Pingree also serves on the Armed Services Committee — in the tradition of other Maine legislators — and is serving on the Oversight and Investigations and Seapower and Expeditionary Forces subcommittees.

Pingree wants to seek investment in renewable energy and continued development of wind resources in her state. She also intends to use her position to work on affordable health care and push for legislation to lower prescription drug prices — a cause she adopted after witnessing her brother's struggle with terminal cancer.

Pingree grew up in rural Minnesota and later moved to Maine to attend college. After graduating, she ran a small organic farm with her husband and later several small businesses in the area.

In 2008 she beat back five challengers in the Democratic primary to succeed Rep. Tom Allen, who lost a bid to topple GOP Sen. Susan Collins. Pingree then used her sizable financial edge of more than $1.5 million to defeat Republican Charlie Summers with 55 percent of the vote.

Pingree said she plans to continue to help manage her inn and restaurant in the small island town of North Haven, 14 miles off the coast of Rockland. She boasts she makes a "good backup bartender."

MAINE 1

South — Portland, Augusta

Covering Maine's southern tip, the 1st boasts both rural oceanfront property and high-paying jobs. Residents of the state's largest city, Portland, continue to move into outlying areas, bringing single-family homes to once-uninterrupted forests and farmland.

The technology boom that spread north from Boston during the 1990s slowed, but software jobs still offset manufacturing and textile plant closures. Health care, financial services and insurance firms are here, and Interstate 95 offers a straight shot between the district and Boston for both commuters and seasonal residents, who tend to live on the coast. Tourism is important in the lower part of the state, as residents from across New England and Canada head to popular beaches and shopping areas, including the L.L. Bean flagship store in Freeport.

The military's influence is strong in the 1st.

Portsmouth Naval Shipyard escaped the 2005 BRAC round, but Brunswick Naval Air Station will be ordered closed by 2011, and job losses will be staggered over several years.

The district's traditional Yankee Republican tendencies have given way to a solidly Democratic voting preference in federal elections. In 2008, the 1st favored Barack Obama by 23 percentage points. Republicans still find some support at the state and local levels, especially in York County towns.

MAJOR INDUSTRY
Military shipbuilding, financial services, technology, tourism

MILITARY BASES
Portsmouth Naval Shipyard, 95 military, 3,900 civilian (2007); Brunswick Naval Air Station, 1,526 military, 278 civilian (2007)

CITIES
Portland, 64,249; South Portland, 23,324

NOTABLE
The Wadsworth-Longfellow House museum is the oldest standing structure on the Portland peninsula.

Rep. Michael H. Michaud (D)

Elected 2002; 4th term

Confident and ambitious, Michaud doesn't hesitate to go after what he wants. He served two decades in the Maine Legislature seeking to clean up pollution caused in part by his former employer, Great Northern Paper Co. And in the House, he pushes to rectify past trade deals he believes led to the bankruptcy of such manufacturers.

He also is a strong proponent of federal funds for local economic development and a player in the fight for improved health care for veterans.

Michaud (ME-shoo) supported President Obama's $787 billion economic stimulus plan in early 2009, saying it would create or save up to 15,000 jobs in Maine. But he was less happy with the $700 billion measure Congress cleared and President George W. Bush signed into law in October 2008 to shore up the ailing financial services industry. Michaud said the measure failed to provide sufficient safeguards to protect taxpayers' investment.

Michaud has eagerly sought higher steps in political office. He seized the chance to run for Congress in 2002 as soon as Democrat John Baldacci gave up his House seat for a successful gubernatorial bid. After just two terms, Michaud made a bid for the chairmanship of the Veterans' Affairs Committee. He lost out to Californian Bob Filner, but the attempt did him no harm; he was given the gavel of the panel's Health Subcommittee.

Now, as Baldacci nears the end of the two terms allowed by Maine law, Michaud just might try to follow in his footsteps again. He said "lots of people" have approached him about running for governor in 2010.

If Michaud does decide to seek higher office, his unusual résumé could help him. Most members of Congress claim to be on the side of the working man in America, but Michaud has actually been one. He was a union-card-carrying paper mill worker for almost three decades before winning his House seat. While many of his House colleagues were pursuing college degrees, Michaud was punching a clock in Millinocket, Maine. The lunch bucket he carried to work each day now sits in his Capitol Hill office.

Three days after he was sworn in, Great Northern filed for bankruptcy protection and shuttered its two paper mills, including the one in East Millinocket where Michaud, his father, his grandfather and all five of his siblings had worked. Michaud blamed the 1993 North American Free Trade Agreement, and he has become one of the fiercest congressional critics of U.S. free-trade deals since then.

In 2008, Michaud and Ohio Democratic Sen. Sherrod Brown introduced legislation calling for a review and renegotiation of U.S. trade deals, including NAFTA. Their bill, which spells out labor, environment, food and product safety standards and other protections that they say should be included in trade pacts, did not advance in the 110th Congress (2007-08). But it is likely to get new attention in the 111th (2009-10). Meanwhile, Michaud fights to secure federal aid for workers in his district who continue to be displaced by trade deals. And he won enactment, as part of the 2008 reauthorization of farm programs, of his proposal to create a Northern Border Regional Commission to invest $30 million in federal funding annually in economic development and job creation projects in the most economically distressed areas of Maine, New Hampshire, Vermont and New York.

He also serves on the Transportation and Infrastructure Committee, where he will have a chance to steer highway funding to Maine as the panel starts work in 2009 on a new multi-year transportation law. He is especially interested in funding an east-west interstate highway from Calais to Watertown, N.Y.

CAPITOL OFFICE
225-6306
michaud.house.gov
1724 Longworth Bldg. 20515-1902; fax 225-2943

COMMITTEES
Small Business
Transportation & Infrastructure
Veterans' Affairs
 (Health - chairman)

RESIDENCE
East Millinocket

BORN
Jan. 18, 1955; Millinocket, Maine

RELIGION
Roman Catholic

FAMILY
Single

EDUCATION
Schenck H.S., graduated 1973

CAREER
Paper mill worker

POLITICAL HIGHLIGHTS
Maine House, 1981-94; Maine Senate, 1995-2002 (president, 2001)

ELECTION RESULTS

2008 GENERAL

Michael H. Michaud (D)	226,274	67.4%
John N. Frary (R)	109,268	32.6%

2008 PRIMARY

Michael H. Michaud (D)	unopposed

2006 GENERAL

Michael H. Michaud (D)	179,732	70.5%
Laurence S. D'Amboise (R)	75,146	29.5%

PREVIOUS WINNING PERCENTAGES
2004 (58%); 2002 (52%)

As chairman of the Veterans' Affairs Health Subcommittee, Michaud has championed measures to improve medical care for veterans returning from Iraq and Afghanistan. Several of his bills became law in 2008 as part of broad veterans' legislation, including one creating a pilot program to allow veterans who live in rural areas far from Veterans Health Administration facilities to receive covered care from private providers. Michaud also sits on the Small Business Committee.

Michaud is a critic of the Iraq War. He voted against war funding in 2008 and was one of 39 House members to oppose the defense authorization bill that paved the way for $68.6 billion in war spending in fiscal 2009.

Though he votes with Democrats most of the time, Michaud opposes abortion except to save the life of the woman. He is one of the few Northern Democrats to affiliate with the Blue Dogs, a coalition of about 50 fiscally conservative Democrats. He also criticized Democratic leaders in 2008 for refusing to allow amendments to energy bills that would open up more public lands for oil and gas drilling.

Michaud grew up in the small rural town of Medway, close to the Great Northern mill. After high school, he considered studying criminal justice to become a state trooper. But Great Northern beckoned with good wages and health benefits. He became a paper finisher, working on the final stages of papermaking. He remains a member of what is now United Steelworkers Local 4-00037.

Michaud decided to run for the state House because of his concern about pollution in the Penobscot River, to which Great Northern contributed. Elected in 1980, he took advantage of a clause in his union contract that allowed workers to keep their jobs while serving in the legislature. He worked at the mill when the legislature was not in session, and when it was, he chaired the Environment Committee and wrote bills to clean up the river. Sometimes he would put in a long day in Augusta, the state capital, then hurry back to the mill to work a midnight shift.

Michaud served seven terms in the state House, then ran for the Maine Senate in 1994. Two years later, he became chairman of the Appropriations Committee and in 2000 was elected state Senate president. At that point, he took a leave of absence from the mill.

In the 2002 race for Baldacci's U.S. House seat, support from organized labor helped Michaud eke out a narrow victory over Republican Kevin L. Raye, former chief of staff for Olympia J. Snowe, who held the 2nd District seat from 1979-95 and is now Maine's senior senator. Michaud has won re-election easily since.

KEY VOTES

2008

Yes	Delay consideration of Colombia free-trade agreement
Yes	Override Bush veto of federal farm and nutrition programs reauthorization bill
No	Overhaul surveillance laws and permit dismissal of suits against companies that conducted warrantless wiretapping
Yes	Grant mortgage relief to homeowners and funding for Fannie Mae and Freddie Mac
No	Approve initial $700 billion program to stabilize financial markets
No	Approve final $700 billion program to stabilize financial markets
Yes	Provide $14 billion in loans to automakers

2007

Yes	Increase minimum wage by $2.10 an hour
No	Approve $124.2 billion in emergency war spending and set goal for redeployment of troops from Iraq
No	Reject federal contraceptive assistance to international family planning groups
Yes	Override Bush veto of $23.2 billion water projects authorization bill
No	Implement Peru free-trade agreement
Yes	Approve energy policy overhaul with new fuel economy standards
No	Clear $473.5 billion omnibus spending bill, including $70 billion for military operations

CQ VOTE STUDIES

	PARTY UNITY		PRESIDENTIAL SUPPORT	
	SUPPORT	OPPOSE	SUPPORT	OPPOSE
2008	94%	6%	13%	87%
2007	96%	4%	8%	92%
2006	92%	8%	30%	70%
2005	92%	8%	18%	82%
2004	88%	12%	38%	62%

INTEREST GROUPS

	AFL-CIO	ADA	CCUS	ACU
2008	100%	90%	50%	12%
2007	92%	85%	55%	0%
2006	100%	90%	40%	12%
2005	93%	90%	48%	16%
2004	93%	90%	48%	20%

MAINE 2
North — Lewiston, Bangor, Presque Isle

Millions of acres of trees surround the small towns of northern Maine's 2nd. The largest district in a state east of the Mississippi, the 2nd attracts millions of visitors "from away" — local lingo for out of state — to Acadia National Park, Baxter State Park and Maine's many lakes and ski slopes. Development of the privately owned timber forests of the North Woods is a major issue, as resorts, single-family homes and immigration of residents from other states could permanently alter the landscape.

Lobstering dominates the coast, and the timber industry reigns inland. Farming is in decline in parts of the district, although the 2nd remains one of the nation's largest producers of potatoes and blueberries. Sparsely populated in parts, the region is less wealthy than the 1st, which has benefited from a more diverse employment base.

As the national economy has become more service-based, the 2nd has suffered. Manufacturing jobs, especially in shoes and textiles, have gone abroad, and some residents have headed south to find work. Business leaders and local officials have looked to green energy as a potential job source, and some residents have pushed for an east-west highway to promote economic growth, citing the district's easy access to Boston via Interstate 95.

A weak party system throughout the state and a higher proportion of rural voters have helped make the 2nd the more competitive of Maine's two congressional districts. Voters here gave 55 percent of the vote to Barack Obama in the 2008 presidential election — 6 percentage points less than he enjoyed in the 1st District. The 2nd's voters will support candidates from either major party, but the district has developed a Democratic lean, and overall Rep. Michael H. Michaud has enjoyed increasing margins of victory since his 2002 election.

MAJOR INDUSTRY
Logging, agriculture, fishing, tourism, textiles

CITIES
Lewiston, 35,690; Bangor, 31,473; Auburn, 23,203; Waterville, 15,605

NOTABLE
Established in 1919, Acadia National Park was the first national park east of the Mississippi River; Since 1992, Harrington-based Worcester Wreath has decorated, donated and delivered 5,000 wreaths every December for graveside ceremonies at Arlington National Cemetery.

Gov. Martin O'Malley (D)

First elected: 2006
Length of term: 4 years
Term expires: 1/11
Salary: $165,000
Phone: (410) 974-3901

Residence: Annapolis
Born: Jan. 18, 1963; Washington, D.C.
Religion: Roman Catholic
Family: Wife, Catherine Curran O'Malley; four children
Education: Catholic U., B.A. 1985 (political science); U. of Maryland, Baltimore, J.D. 1988
Career: Lawyer; city prosecutor; campaign aide
Political highlights: Democratic nominee for Md. Senate, 1990; Baltimore City Council, 1991-99; mayor of Baltimore, 1999-2007

Election results:

2006 GENERAL

Martin O'Malley (D)	942,279	52.7%
Robert L. Ehrlich Jr. (R)	825,464	46.2%

Lt. Gov. Anthony G. Brown (D)

First elected: 2006
Length of term: 4 years
Term expires: 1/11
Salary: $137,500
Phone: (410) 974-2804

LEGISLATURE

General Assembly: 90 days January-April

Senate: 47 members, 4-year terms
2009 ratios: 33 D, 14 R; 36 men, 11 women
Salary: $43,500
Phone: (410) 841-3700

House: 141 members, 4-year terms
2009 ratios: 104 D, 36 R, 1 I; 93 men, 48 women
Salary: $43,500
Phone: (410) 841-3800

TERM LIMITS

Governor: 2 consecutive terms
Senate: No
House: No

URBAN STATISTICS

CITY	POPULATION
Baltimore	651,154
Frederick	52,767
Gaithersburg	52,613
Bowie	50,269
Rockville	47,388

REGISTERED VOTERS

Democrat	57%
Republican	27%
Unaffiliated	14%
Others	2%

POPULATION

2008 population (est.)	5,633,597
2000 population	5,296,486
1990 population	4,781,468
Percent change (1990-2000)	+10.8%
Rank among states (2008)	19
Median age	36
Born in state	49.3%
Foreign born	9.8%
Violent crime rate	787/100,000
Poverty level	8.5%
Federal workers	151,044
Military	50,137

ELECTIONS

STATE ELECTION OFFICIAL
(410) 269-2840
DEMOCRATIC PARTY
(410) 269-8818
REPUBLICAN PARTY
(410) 263-2125

MISCELLANEOUS

Web: www.maryland.gov
Capital: Annapolis

U.S. CONGRESS

Senate: 2 Democrats
House: 7 Democrats, 1 Republican

2000 Census Statistics by District

DIST.	2008 VOTE FOR PRESIDENT OBAMA	MCCAIN	WHITE	BLACK	ASIAN	HISP	MEDIAN INCOME	WHITE COLLAR	BLUE COLLAR	SERVICE INDUSTRY	OVER 64	UNDER 18	COLLEGE EDUCATION	RURAL	SQ. MILES
1	40	58%	85%	11%	1%	2%	$51,918	63%	23%	14%	13%	25%	27%	36%	3,653
2	60	38	66	27	2	2	$44,309	61	23	15	12	26	20	2	355
3	59	39	76	16	3	3	$52,906	72	16	12	13	23	37	1	293
4	85	14	28	57	6	8	$57,727	71	15	14	7	28	33	2	315
5	65	33	60	30	4	3	$62,661	68	19	13	9	26	29	25	1,504
6	40	58	92	5	1	1	$50,957	61	24	14	12	26	24	39	3,062
7	79	20	34	59	4	2	$38,885	67	16	17	12	26	28	5	294
8	74	25	56	16	11	14	$68,306	77	11	12	12	24	54	1	297
STATE	62	37	62	28	4	4	$52,868	68	18	14	11	26	31	14	9,774
U.S.	53	46	69	12	4	13	$41,994	60	25	15	12	26	24	21	3,537,438

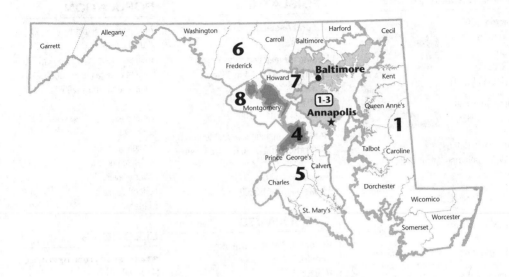

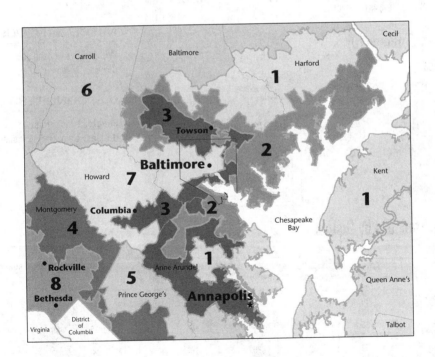

Sen. Barbara A. Mikulski (D)

Elected 1986; 4th term

CAPITOL OFFICE
224-4654
mikulski.senate.gov
503 Hart Bldg. 20510-2003; fax 224-8858

COMMITTEES
Appropriations
 (Commerce-Justice-Science - chairwoman)
Health, Education, Labor & Pensions
Select Intelligence

RESIDENCE
Baltimore

BORN
July 20, 1936; Baltimore, Md.

RELIGION
Roman Catholic

FAMILY
Single

EDUCATION
Mount Saint Agnes College, B.A. 1958 (sociology);
U. of Maryland, M.S.W. 1965

CAREER
Social worker

POLITICAL HIGHLIGHTS
Baltimore City Council, 1971-77; Democratic
nominee for U.S. Senate, 1974; U.S. House, 1977-87

ELECTION RESULTS

2004 GENERAL

Barbara A. Mikulski (D)	1,504,691	64.8%
E.J. Pipkin (R)	783,055	33.7%
Maria Allwine (GREEN)	24,816	1.1%

2004 PRIMARY

Barbara A. Mikulski (D)	408,848	89.9%
A. Robert Kaufman (D)	32,127	7.1%
Sidney Altman (D)	13,901	3.1%

PREVIOUS WINNING PERCENTAGES
1998 (71%); 1992 (71%); 1986 (61%); 1984 House
Election (68%); 1982 House Election (74%); 1980
House Election (76%); 1978 House Election (100%);
1976 House Election (75%)

Mikulski is a tough Democratic infighter who never shies from a legislative battle, nor from saying what she thinks. She prides herself on working hard; one of her guiding principles for her staff is, "We cannot always guarantee an outcome, but we can guarantee an effort."

The fourth-term Maryland senator is known on Capitol Hill for cutting off tongue-tied aides and reporters, brusquely demanding, "What's your question?" And she can be just as combative with her colleagues. During a 2008 lame-duck session, she tried to get the Senate to take up legislation to create an automobile sales tax and interest deduction as a way to help consumers and save auto industry jobs. But when New Hampshire Republican John E. Sununu — who had just been defeated for re-election — objected, Mikulski snapped, "Boy, am I sorry that is the last act of John Sununu in the Senate. I hope it is not the last thing." She then complained that "economic conservatives have their ostrich heads in the quicksand of our economy."

The auto bailout legislation stalled in Congress, but Mikulski remained committed to her idea. "We helped the sharks and we helped the whales," she said, referring to earlier measures to aid the troubled financial services industry. "Now it's time to help the minnows." Early in 2009, she won inclusion of an automobile purchase sales tax deduction in an economic stimulus bill.

Mikulski is a fierce advocate for Maryland's interests. She used every weapon in her arsenal in 2005 to wrestle through Congress a measure temporarily lifting a cap on temporary visas for seasonal workers needed by her state's crab processors and other small businesses. She pushed long after she was warned she was asking the impossible. "I promised small businesses they could count on me to keep fighting until we had a solution and they had the seasonal workers they needed to stay in business," she said. The cap expired in September 2007, but she continues to push for the seasonal worker visas.

Mikulski revels in her status as dean among Senate women. From the time she arrived in 1987 until 1992, Mikulski and Republican Nancy Landon Kassebaum of Kansas were the only female senators. As their ranks jumped to five in 1993 and to 17 in 2009, Mikulski offered the newcomers introductory seminars and dispensed advice on everything from organizing their offices to setting long-range goals. She served for a decade as Democratic caucus secretary, the No. 3 leadership post, before stepping down in 2004 to give another woman, Michigan's Debbie Stabenow, a boost onto the leadership ladder.

"I was at an initial disadvantage as a woman coming to the Senate, and it wasn't just that the gym was off-limits," Mikulski wrote in the 2000 book "Nine and Counting," a collaboration of the nine women then serving in the Senate. "I didn't come to politics by the traditional male route, being in a nice law firm or belonging to the right clubs. Like most of the women I've known in politics, I got involved because I saw a community need."

Mikulski is the most senior Democratic senator, besides Robert C. Byrd of West Virginia, who does not chair a full committee, but she has gained plenty of influence. She is a senior member of the Appropriations Committee and sits on the Health, Education, Labor and Pensions (HELP) Committee. In 2008, she stepped in for ailing Massachusetts Democratic Sen. Edward M. Kennedy to lead the HELP panel in the successful effort to pass major higher education legislation. And early in 2009, Mikulski spearheaded Senate passage of a bill to nullify a Supreme Court decision in a pay discrimination case. The high court had ruled that the statute of limitations for such a claim had expired.

She will be a major player in the 111th Congress (2009-10) on a health care overhaul effort; Kennedy tapped her to head up an informal task force that will focus on improving the quality of care.

Mikulski is the chairwoman of the Appropriations subcommittee that funds science programs as well as the departments of Commerce and Justice. In the 110th Congress (2007-08), she advocated more federal grants for state and local law enforcement against the George W. Bush administration's wishes, and moved to block its attempt to lower funding for a Justice Department office dedicated to fighting violence against women.

She is a longtime supporter of the National Aeronautics and Space Administration, which has a presence in Maryland at the Goddard Space Flight Center, a research facility that employs nearly 9,000 people. In 2008, Discover magazine named her one of the "50 Most Influential People in Science" because of her efforts to boost federal funding for science.

As a member of the Select Intelligence Committee, Mikulski looks out for the National Security Agency, the eavesdropping arm of the spy community whose headquarters are in her state.

Mikulski's roots are in working-class east Baltimore. Her parents ran a Baltimore grocery store called Willy's Market, across the street from their row house, opening early every morning so steel workers could buy lunch before their morning shift. Nearby, her Polish immigrant grandmother operated a bakery legendary for its jelly doughnuts and raisin bread.

She earned a master's degree in social work at the University of Maryland in 1965. When parts of her neighborhood were torched in anger after the 1968 assassination of the Rev. Martin Luther King Jr., social worker Mikulski delivered food to families during the riots, sometimes by riding atop a tank.

In the early 1970s, she jumped into a neighborhood battle to stop a highway project that would have leveled some Baltimore neighborhoods. At one point, she recalls, she jumped on a table and gave a fiery speech, saying, "The British couldn't take Fells Point, the termites couldn't take Fells Point and goddamn if we'll let the State Roads Commission take Fells Point!" to wild cheers from her audience. The battle against the highway project was successful, and Mikulski went on to win a city council seat in 1971 and become prominent in the feminist movement.

Mikulski seized on the public backlash against Republicans in the post-Watergate election of 1974 by challenging incumbent Sen. Charles McC. Mathias Jr. She lost, but got a respectable 43 percent of the vote. That positioned her for 1976, when Democrat Paul S. Sarbanes gave up his seat as Baltimore's congressman to run for the Senate. Mikulski won and went on to serve five terms in the House, becoming a champion of consumer causes from her seat on Energy and Commerce.

When Mathias retired in 1986, Mikulski won the race to succeed him, besting Republican Linda Chavez by 22 percentage points. She won her subsequent three re-elections by at least 30 points. She became Maryland's senior senator in the 110th, after Sarbanes retired, and given her popularity and Maryland's Democratic tilt is likely to remain in that position as long as she wants.

For years, Mikulski lived in a two-story Fells Point row house in Baltimore, commuting to the Capitol. In 1995, she was mugged as she walked from her car to her house, and the next year, she moved to a "maintenance free" condo near Johns Hopkins University. "I am changing my address, not changing my roots," she told constituents.

In 1996 and 1997, she joined with journalist Marylouise Oates to co-author two thrillers set in Washington. They feature a fictional female Pennsylvania senator, Norie Gorzack, who investigates murders — and who doesn't mind making enemies.

KEY VOTES

2008
Yes Prohibit discrimination based on genetic information

Yes Reauthorize farm and nutrition programs for five years

Yes Limit debate on "cap and trade" system for greenhouse gas emissions

No Allow lawsuits against companies that participated in warrantless wiretapping

Yes Limit debate on a bill to block a scheduled cut in Medicare payments to doctors

Yes Grant mortgage relief to homeowners and funding for Fannie Mae and Freddie Mac

Yes Approve a nuclear cooperation agreement with India

Yes Approve final $700 billion program to stabilize financial markets

Yes Allow consideration of a $14 billion auto industry loan package

2007
Yes Increase minimum wage by $2.10 an hour

Yes Limit debate on a comprehensive immigration bill

Yes Overhaul congressional lobbying and ethics rules for members and their staffs

Yes Limit debate on considering a bill to add House seats for the District of Columbia and Utah

Yes Limit debate on restoring habeas corpus rights to detainees

Yes Mandate minimum breaks for troops between deployments to Iraq or Afghanistan

Yes Override Bush veto of $23.2 billion water projects authorization bill

No Confirm Michael B. Mukasey as attorney general

Yes Limit debate on an energy policy overhaul containing $21.8 billion in tax incentives and reduced oil and gas subsidies

CQ VOTE STUDIES

	PARTY UNITY		PRESIDENTIAL SUPPORT	
	SUPPORT	OPPOSE	SUPPORT	OPPOSE
2008	88%	12%	42%	58%
2007	94%	6%	42%	58%
2006	96%	4%	49%	51%
2005	98%	2%	35%	65%
2004	96%	4%	61%	39%
2003	97%	3%	44%	56%
2002	96%	4%	68%	32%
2001	98%	2%	66%	34%
2000	97%	3%	92%	8%
1999	96%	4%	86%	14%

INTEREST GROUPS

	AFL-CIO	ADA	CCUS	ACU
2008	100%	90%	63%	0%
2007	94%	85%	55%	0%
2006	93%	100%	42%	0%
2005	100%	90%	41%	5%
2004	100%	100%	56%	8%
2003	100%	90%	39%	15%
2002	100%	100%	47%	0%
2001	100%	95%	43%	12%
2000	88%	95%	46%	8%
1999	89%	100%	59%	4%

Sen. Benjamin L. Cardin (D)

Elected 2006; 1st term

Cardin is a hard-working policy wonk whose regular-guy persona has enabled him to forge partnerships to develop consensus and maneuver his priorities through the Senate. He was named one of the "nicest senators" in Washingtonian magazine's annual survey of congressional staff in 2008.

With a thick Baltimore accent, he portrays in discussions of shaping legislation his deep reverence for the process. "This is an incredible place," he said of the Senate. "You can get a lot done here — every day, there are opportunities. Because you have a six-year term, you can be a bit more visionary."

Elected to the Senate in 2006, Cardin brought along nearly two decades of House experience. Long under GOP rule in the House, he has sought to make the most of his majority status. He has been active on issues ranging from climate change to foreign spying and hopes to become more of a player on health care and education.

His priorities fit with the general tenor of the Senate Democratic leadership: finding an exit strategy for Iraq, guiding the United States toward energy independence, lowering greenhouse gas emissions, training better teachers and providing more affordable health care.

Cardin sits on five committees: Foreign Relations, Judiciary, Environment and Public Works, Budget, and Small Business and Entrepreneurship. He also co-chairs the U.S. arm of the Commission on Security and Cooperation in Europe, known as the Helsinki Commission, the world's largest regional security organization.

During Senate debate on global warming legislation in 2008, Cardin added $171 million for public transportation, including funds for new rail transit systems, with the intent of curbing automobiles' greenhouse gas emissions and providing relief to the car-choked Washington, D.C., suburbs. He also added an amendment authorizing more money to implement climate change policies. But the bill was pulled from the floor before a final vote.

Cardin pays special attention to Chesapeake Bay, working with home-state colleague Barbara A. Mikulski to include funding in the 2008 multiyear rewrite of farm policy to improve water quality and farm viability in the region. At the start of 2009, he was named chairman of a newly created Environment and Public Works panel on water and wildlife.

From his seat on the Judiciary Committee, he introduced legislation in March 2009 aimed at providing a lifeline to the struggling newspaper industry by permitting papers to operate as nonprofits. That would allow advertising and subscription revenue to be tax-exempt, but newspapers could not make political endorsements. Some in the industry feared that would lead to government control of the news.

Cardin in late 2008 backed President-elect Obama's nomination of Eric J. Holder Jr. to be attorney general, saying, "We want to see the [next] attorney general take a leadership role in restoring the tradition of the Department of Justice" as a non-political agency. During the 110th Congress (2007-08), Democrats on the committee had given Cardin responsibility for keeping tabs on voting rights and the Justice Department's Civil Rights Division. Cardin took over in 2009 as chairman of the Terrorism and Homeland Security Subcommittee, which faced pressure from the FBI to renew intelligence-gathering provisions in the USA Patriot Act expected to expire at the end of the year.

From his seat on the Budget Committee, Cardin supported Obama's early legislative priorities, including an economic stimulus bill. He was among several Democrats who vowed to preserve Obama's priorities when

CAPITOL OFFICE
224-4524
509 Hart Bldg. 20510-2002; fax 224-1651

COMMITTEES
Budget
Environment & Public Works
    (Water & Wildlife - chairman)
Foreign Relations
Judiciary
    (Terrorism & Homeland Security - chairman)
Small Business & Entrepreneurship

RESIDENCE
Baltimore

BORN
Oct. 5, 1943; Baltimore, Md.

RELIGION
Jewish

FAMILY
Wife, Myrna Edelman Cardin; two children (one deceased)

EDUCATION
U. of Pittsburgh, B.A. 1964 (economics);
U. of Maryland, Baltimore, LL.B. 1967

CAREER
Lawyer

POLITICAL HIGHLIGHTS
Md. House, 1967-87 (Speaker, 1979-87);
U.S. House, 1987-2007

ELECTION RESULTS

2006 GENERAL

Benjamin L. Cardin (D)	965,477	54.2%
Michael S. Steele (R)	787,182	44.2%
Kevin Zeese (GREEN)	27,564	1.5%

2006 PRIMARY

Benjamin L. Cardin (D)	257,545	43.7%
Kweisi Mfume (D)	238,957	40.5%
Josh Rales (D)	30,737	5.2%
Dennis F. Rasmussen (D)	10,997	1.9%
Mike Schaefer (D)	7,773	1.3%

PREVIOUS WINNING PERCENTAGES
2004 House Election (63%); 2002 House Election (66%); 2000 House Election (76%); 1998 House Election (78%); 1996 House Election (67%); 1994 House Election (71%); 1992 House Election (74%); 1990 House Election (70%); 1988 House Election (73%); 1986 House Election (79%)

considering a 2010 budget exceeding $3.5 trillion during a tight economic environment. "I want to make sure we have in place money for health care and energy in particular," he said.

Cardin introduced health insurance legislation in 2007 that he hopes can be part of the debate on the issue in the 111th Congress (2009-10). It would require all uninsured Americans to enroll in a plan and would direct the Health and Human Services Department to work with insurance commissioners to develop low-cost options for poorer families.

As a Foreign Relations member, he has tried to be more skeptical about what briefers tell lawmakers. "I think prior to Iraq, the assumption always was that the piece of evidence we were receiving was substantiated," he said. "Now we're more likely to suggest that a specific piece of information may not lead to the conclusion that's in the document."

Though generally a dependable Democratic vote, Cardin takes pride in being a lawmaker willing to work across party lines to develop consensus. In 2008, he teamed with Maine Republican Sen. Olympia J. Snowe on a proposal to create a group of "master teachers" who would get a break on their federal income taxes in exchange for working in substandard schools.

On the Ways and Means Committee when he served in the House, Cardin developed a close relationship with Ohio Republican Rob Portman — the main conduit between the White House and GOP leaders during President George W. Bush's first term — who later became Bush's budget director. In the 108th Congress (2003-04), the two lawmakers developed an alternative to the president's plan to restructure Social Security and allow younger workers to divert a share of their payroll tax payments into personal retirement accounts.

Such endeavors didn't always sit well with House Democratic leaders. In 2006, Cardin was passed over for the top Democratic spot on the Ways and Means' Social Security Subcommittee after he said he was open to compromise on some GOP proposals for overhauling the program.

Cardin is a one-time "boy wonder" who entered the Maryland House of Delegates at age 23, before he had even graduated from the University of Maryland Law School. He was elected to a seat that had been held by his father and his uncle. Cardin went on to become the youngest House Speaker in Maryland in 100 years before being elected to his Baltimore-area House seat in 1986. His political hero is Theodore R. McKeldin, a GOP mayor of Baltimore and Maryland governor who helped build the city's urban and transportation infrastructure and who was among the first politicians to court the state's Jewish voters.

In 2006, after longtime Sen. Paul S. Sarbanes announced his retirement, Cardin ran in a primary against more than a dozen candidates. His chief competition was former Democratic Rep. Kweisi Mfume, a past NAACP president and longtime friend. Cardin narrowly won the race, 44 percent to 41 percent.

In the general election, he was up against another tough competitor — Republican Lt. Gov. Michael S. Steele, Maryland's first statewide black elected official. The Republican tailored his TV and radio ads to black voters and brought in endorsements from several prominent black Democrats. But Cardin succeeded in tying Steele to Bush and other prominent Republicans, and won with 54 percent of the vote.

Cardin's family is close-knit and shares his interests — Myrna, his wife of more than 40 years, is among his most trusted advisers. The couple endured a tragedy in 1998 when their son Michael, 30, who worked as a volunteer with low-income Baltimoreans, committed suicide. Cardin said his son's death has inspired his family to assist others even more. "I look at what he was able to accomplish in a few years as a challenge to all of us to make the most of what we have," he said. "Every now and then, we try to find some poor soul and help them and say, 'This is for Michael.'"

KEY VOTES

2008

Yes Prohibit discrimination based on genetic information

Yes Reauthorize farm and nutrition programs for five years

Yes Limit debate on "cap and trade" system for greenhouse gas emissions

Yes Allow lawsuits against companies that participated in warrantless wiretapping

Yes Limit debate on a bill to block a scheduled cut in Medicare payments to doctors

Yes Grant mortgage relief to homeowners and funding for Fannie Mae and Freddie Mac

Yes Approve a nuclear cooperation agreement with India

Yes Approve final $700 billion program to stabilize financial markets

Yes Allow consideration of a $14 billion auto industry loan package

2007

Yes Increase minimum wage by $2.10 an hour

Yes Limit debate on a comprehensive immigration bill

Yes Overhaul congressional lobbying and ethics rules for members and their staffs

Yes Limit debate on considering a bill to add House seats for the District of Columbia and Utah

Yes Limit debate on restoring habeas corpus rights to detainees

Yes Mandate minimum breaks for troops between deployments to Iraq or Afghanistan

Yes Override Bush veto of $23.2 billion water projects authorization bill

No Confirm Michael B. Mukasey as attorney general

Yes Limit debate on an energy policy overhaul containing $21.8 billion in tax incentives and reduced oil and gas subsidies

CQ VOTE STUDIES

	PARTY UNITY		PRESIDENTIAL SUPPORT	
	SUPPORT	OPPOSE	SUPPORT	OPPOSE
2008	97%	3%	31%	69%
2007	97%	3%	37%	63%
House Service:				
2006	95%	5%	25%	75%
2005	95%	5%	22%	78%
2004	94%	6%	35%	65%
2003	93%	7%	24%	76%
2002	90%	10%	35%	65%
2001	89%	11%	35%	65%
2000	92%	8%	94%	6%

INTEREST GROUPS

	AFL-CIO	ADA	CCUS	ACU
2008	100%	100%	63%	8%
2007	95%	95%	45%	0%
House Service:				
2006	100%	90%	40%	8%
2005	92%	95%	40%	0%
2004	100%	95%	43%	0%
2003	87%	90%	37%	20%
2002	100%	95%	55%	0%
2001	100%	100%	35%	4%
2000	90%	90%	42%	8%

Rep. Frank Kratovil Jr. (D)

Elected 2008; 1st term

Kratovil is a former prosecutor who can be as independent-minded as his predecessor, nine-term GOP Rep. Wayne T. Gilchrest. He is a staunch fiscal conservative and supports gun owners' rights — positions that are welcome in a district that gave Arizona Republican Sen. John McCain an 18-percent-age-point win over Barack Obama in the presidential race.

Gilchrest took the highly unusual step of endorsing Kratovil (KRAT-oh-vil) over his Republican opponent in 2008 after losing in the GOP primary, and Kratovil said they are like-minded in many respects. "We're not overwhelmed by the D.C. scene, and we're grounded in our constituents' views," he said.

He is a member of the Blue Dog Coalition, a group of fiscally conservative Democrats. He was one of just 20 Democrats to oppose a House-passed $410 billion catchall spending bill in February 2009. "In a time when we should be cutting back and focusing on priorities, this [legislation] doesn't fit either definition while increasing discretionary spending across the board," he said.

He also voted against the initial version of what became Obama's $787 billion economic stimulus package, saying he wasn't persuaded it would have a short-term impact. But he voted for the final version because it included money for renewable energy and other priorities.

He is a member of the Armed Services panel. Many of his constituents work at Fort George G. Meade and Aberdeen Proving Ground, located in a nearby district. Like Gilchrest he sits on the Natural Resources Committee, where he wants to improve environmental conditions in the Chesapeake Bay. And as a member of the Agriculture Committee, he wants to ease visa restrictions for immigrant workers in the seafood processing industry.

After winning a four-way primary in February 2008, Kratovil spent the next nine months seeking to highlight his differences with his Republican opponent, state Sen. Andy Harris. By winning every Eastern Shore county where Gilchrest was popular and staying competitive elsewhere in the district, Kratovil eked out a 2,852-vote win that was not decided until nearly a week after Election Day.

CAPITOL OFFICE
225-5311
kratovil.house.gov
314 Cannon Bldg. 20515-2001; fax 225-0254

COMMITTEES
Agriculture
Armed Services
Natural Resources

RESIDENCE
Stevensville

BORN
May 29, 1968; Lanham, Md.

RELIGION
Methodist

FAMILY
Wife, Kimberly Kratovil; four children

EDUCATION
Western Maryland College, B.A. 1990 (political science); U. of Baltimore, J.D. 1994

CAREER
Gubernatorial aide; county prosecutor

POLITICAL HIGHLIGHTS
Queen Anne's County state's attorney, 2003-09

ELECTION RESULTS

2008 GENERAL

Frank Kratovil Jr. (D)	177,065	49.1%
Andy Harris (R)	174,213	48.3%
Richard James Davis (LIBERT)	8,873	2.5%

2008 PRIMARY

Frank Kratovil Jr. (D)	28,566	40.2%
Christopher Robert Robinson (D)	21,892	30.8%
Steve Harper (D)	11,904	16.7%
Joseph Werner (D)	8,753	12.3%

MARYLAND 1

East – Eastern Shore, part of Anne Arundel County

The 1st includes the mostly rural Eastern Shore and some Anne Arundel County suburbs across the Chesapeake Bay. It crosses the Susquehanna River in northeastern Maryland and grabs chunks of Harford and Baltimore counties. The Eastern Shore, which holds about three-fifths of the district's population, has a steady agricultural base, relying mainly on vegetables, fruit and chicken breeding. Ocean City is a popular beach town on the Atlantic shore.

The central, more rural, part of the Eastern Shore is solidly Republican. The northern counties, closer to Baltimore and Philadelphia, and southern counties, with larger black and working-class populations, are more Democratic. Across the bay, the 1st includes some GOP-leaning parts of

Anne Arundel, including the predominately white, educated, upper-middle-class areas of Arnold, Severna Park and Millersville. Part of Baltimore's conservative northern suburbs also are included in the 1st.

Despite regional differences, all of the 1st's areas share a conservative bent that often benefits the GOP. Fiscally conservative Democrats can win, but the 1st supports Republicans for president. John McCain won 58 percent of the district's 2008 presidential vote.

MAJOR INDUSTRY
Agriculture, manufacturing, tourism

MILITARY BASES
U.S. Naval Academy/Naval Station Annapolis, 559 military, 1,075 civilian (2009) (shared with the 3rd District)

CITIES
Bel Air South (unincorporated) (pt.), 35,353; Severna Park (unincorporated) (pt.), 26,646; Bel Air North (unincorporated) (pt.), 25,372

NOTABLE
Wild ponies roam Assateague Island, a barrier island on the Atlantic Ocean.

Rep. C.A. Dutch Ruppersberger (D)

Elected 2002; 4th term

CAPITOL OFFICE
225-3061
dutch.house.gov
2453 Rayburn Bldg. 20515; fax 225-3094

COMMITTEES
Appropriations
Select Intelligence
   (Technical & Tactical Intelligence - chairman)

RESIDENCE
Cockeysville

BORN
Jan. 31, 1946; Baltimore, Md.

RELIGION
Methodist

FAMILY
Wife, Kay Ruppersberger; two children

EDUCATION
U. of Maryland, attended 1963-67;
U. of Baltimore, J.D. 1970

CAREER
Collection agency owner; county prosecutor;
lawyer

POLITICAL HIGHLIGHTS
Democratic nominee for Md. Senate, 1978;
Baltimore County Council, 1985-94; Baltimore
County executive, 1994-2002

ELECTION RESULTS

2008 GENERAL

C.A. Dutch Ruppersberger (D)	198,578	71.9%
Richard Pryce Matthews (R)	68,561	24.8%
Lorenzo Gaztanaga (LIBERT)	8,786	3.2%

2008 PRIMARY

C.A. Dutch Ruppersberger (D)	unopposed

2006 GENERAL

C.A. Dutch Ruppersberger (D)	135,818	69.2%
Jimmy Mathis (R)	60,195	30.7%

PREVIOUS WINNING PERCENTAGES
2004 (67%); 2002 (54%)

Ruppersberger, an affable former Baltimore County executive, concentrates on what he calls the "operations" side of government. He doesn't spend a lot of time discussing political ideology, preferring a results-oriented approach to issues.

"A lot of people are philosophical. I know how to count votes," Ruppersberger said. "When you come from local government, that's where the rubber meets the road." Managing a county with a bigger population than several states, "you are more project-oriented. You are getting things done. I like to see end-game results."

A member of both the Appropriations and Select Intelligence committees, Ruppersberger is willing to cross party lines to get things done in Congress. Republican Rep. Peter Hoekstra of Michigan, who chaired the Intelligence Committee when Ruppersberger joined it as a freshman, called him a "real consensus builder."

Ruppersberger joined Appropriations at the start of the 110th Congress (2007-08), taking the place of fellow Maryland Democrat Steny H. Hoyer, who relinquished the slot to serve as majority leader. Ruppersberger's twin assignments position him perfectly to look out for his district, which includes the National Security Agency (NSA) as well as Fort George G. Meade and the Aberdeen Proving Ground. "Appropriations allows you to take your agenda and follow through," he said.

He works to steer homeland security, defense and intelligence-related funds to his district. Baltimore is a major port city, less than an hour's drive from Washington, D.C., and is home to Baltimore/Washington International Thurgood Marshall Airport. He has championed more spending for first-responders — local fire, police and rescue squads. And as a former county prosecutor, Ruppersberger advocates increased funding for local law enforcement from his seat on the Commerce-Justice-Science Appropriations Subcommittee.

He votes with his party on most issues but doesn't hesitate to go his own way occasionally. He has consistently supported Iraq War funding bills despite his criticism of the George W. Bush administration's war policy, saying, "You must always support your troops." He also split with a majority of his party to support a 2008 overhaul of the Foreign Intelligence Surveillance Act, although he had opposed earlier FISA bills that contained fewer constraints on electronic spying.

"The NSA employees in my district need a clear law with a bright line between legal and illegal surveillance activities, and this bill provides that," Ruppersberger said.

He supported President Obama's early legislative efforts, voting for a bill to expand the State Children's Health Insurance Program, which covers children whose families are not eligible for Medicaid. Bush had twice vetoed a similar measure. Ruppersburger also voted for Obama's $787 billion economic stimulus bill, signed into law in February 2009.

Ruppersberger serves as chairman of the Intelligence Committee's Technical and Tactical Intelligence Subcommittee, which in 2008 issued a report warning that the nation's spy satellite programs are plagued by bad planning, poor coordination between agencies, inconsistent research and development funding, ambiguous demands on commercial companies and restrictive regulations.

Ruppersberger sponsors few bills, preferring to make his mark in the appropriations process. Nonetheless, the energy policy overhaul enacted in 2005 included his proposal to give tax incentives to drivers of hybrid vehicles. He and his wife both drive hybrids.

He was born Charles Albert Ruppersberger III, but goes by Dutch. The son of a Baltimore manufacturing salesman and a schoolteacher, he said the doctor who delivered him described him as a "big, blond Dutchman." (His hair has since turned black.) As practical a politician as they come, Ruppersberger later adopted the nickname legally when he realized his last name was too long for a bumper sticker.

A good athlete as a youth, he played lacrosse at the University of Maryland and made the U.S. team in 1967. During college summers, he was a lifeguard in Ocean City, Md., then worked his way through night school at the University of Baltimore Law School as an insurance claims adjuster.

Ruppersberger began his public career as a Baltimore County assistant state's attorney. While investigating a drug trafficking case in 1975, he was in a near-fatal car crash. He has said he devoted himself to public service thereafter at the urging of the doctor who saved his life at the University of Maryland's renowned Shock Trauma Center. He remains an avid supporter of the hospital, serving on the trauma center's board of visitors.

He lost a state Senate bid in 1978, but in 1985 he was appointed to finish a term on the Baltimore County Council, and was elected to the seat the following year. In 1994, he was elected county executive, and he steered the county to triple-A bond ratings while building new schools, roads and parks.

Ruppersberger planned to run for governor in 2002 but was dogged by events that took place two years earlier. In 2000, he had aggressively pushed legislation to allow the county to condemn private property for urban revitalization. People in the affected areas fought back with a referendum that passed by a 2-1 ratio, an embarrassing setback for the county executive. Then in November 2000, The Baltimore Sun reported he had steered government grants to an apartment rental firm with which he had personal business dealings. Ruppersberger called the report flawed and said he had broken no laws.

But he was too weakened politically to take on a primary fight against the well-financed Kathleen Townsend, daughter of Sen. Robert F. Kennedy. Hoyer urged him to run instead for the newly redrawn House 2nd District, which was 64 percent Democratic. Republicans put up popular former Rep. Helen Delich Bentley, who had represented the 2nd from 1985 to 1995, but Ruppersberger prevailed by almost 9 percentage points. He won re-election with more than two-thirds of the vote in the next three elections.

KEY VOTES

2008

Yes Delay consideration of Colombia free-trade agreement

Yes Override Bush veto of federal farm and nutrition programs reauthorization bill

Yes Overhaul surveillance laws and permit dismissal of suits against companies that conducted warrantless wiretapping

Yes Grant mortgage relief to homeowners and funding for Fannie Mae and Freddie Mac

Yes Approve initial $700 billion program to stabilize financial markets

Yes Approve final $700 billion program to stabilize financial markets

Yes Provide $14 billion in loans to automakers

2007

Yes Increase minimum wage by $2.10 an hour

Yes Approve $124.2 billion in emergency war spending and set goal for redeployment of troops from Iraq

No Reject federal contraceptive assistance to international family planning groups

Yes Override Bush veto of $23.2 billion water projects authorization bill

Yes Implement Peru free-trade agreement

Yes Approve energy policy overhaul with new fuel economy standards

Yes Clear $473.5 billion omnibus spending bill, including $70 billion for military operations

CQ VOTE STUDIES

	PARTY UNITY		PRESIDENTIAL SUPPORT	
	SUPPORT	OPPOSE	SUPPORT	OPPOSE
2008	97%	3%	21%	79%
2007	96%	4%	10%	90%
2006	85%	15%	46%	54%
2005	89%	11%	35%	65%
2004	88%	12%	44%	56%

INTEREST GROUPS

	AFL-CIO	ADA	CCUS	ACU
2008	100%	90%	67%	4%
2007	96%	90%	63%	8%
2006	93%	85%	67%	24%
2005	100%	95%	63%	20%
2004	86%	90%	55%	12%

MARYLAND 2

Part of Baltimore and suburbs —Dundalk, Essex

The 2nd includes parts of northern and eastern Baltimore, suburbs on most sides of the city and most of the land east of Interstate 95 between Baltimore and the Susquehanna River, along the Chesapeake Bay coastline of Baltimore and Harford counties.

The district's Anne Arundel County portion, south of Baltimore, includes the Baltimore/Washington International Thurgood Marshall Airport and Fort George G. Meade, home of the National Security Agency. Fort Meade was assigned thousands of jobs following the 2005 round of BRAC realignments, and construction projects to accommodate the arriving divisions already have begun.

In eastern Baltimore County, the blue-collar industrial sector, including Dundalk, has struggled. The Sparrows Point steel plant is still a key employer, but steelworkers and local officials worry about the impact foreign control of the industry may have on the Maryland economy. Multiple recent sales of the plant, possible further consolidations, job losses and health care and pension cuts are also concerns.

The district's northwest branch moves through the GOP-heavy northern suburbs but then hooks into largely African-American suburbs west of Baltimore, including Randallstown, which has a core commercial center along state Route 26. Blacks overall make up 27 percent of the 2nd's population.

Solidly Democratic voters in Baltimore County and Baltimore city, which together make up nearly three-fourths of the district's population, push the 2nd into the Democratic column. Democrat Barack Obama received 60 percent of the 2nd's vote in the 2008 presidential election.

MAJOR INDUSTRY
Manufacturing, defense, product distribution

MILITARY BASES
Fort George G. Meade (Army), 8,848 military, 19,528 civilian (2009); Aberdeen Proving Ground (Army), 3,437 military, 6,597 civilian (2007)

CITIES
Baltimore (pt.), 111,715; Dundalk (unincorporated), 62,306; Essex (unincorporated), 39,078; Randallstown (unincorporated) (pt.), 29,097

NOTABLE
Aberdeen is home to Cal Ripken Baseball, a youth division of the amateur Babe Ruth League.

Rep. John Sarbanes (D)

Elected 2006; 2nd term

CAPITOL OFFICE
225-4016
sarbanes.house.gov
426 Cannon Bldg. 20515-2003; fax 225-9219

COMMITTEES
Energy & Commerce
Natural Resources

RESIDENCE
Towson

BORN
May 22, 1962; Baltimore, Md.

RELIGION
Greek Orthodox

FAMILY
Wife, Dina Sarbanes; three children

EDUCATION
Princeton U., A.B. 1984 (public & international affairs); Harvard U., J.D. 1988

CAREER
Lawyer; state education consultant

POLITICAL HIGHLIGHTS
No previous office

ELECTION RESULTS

2008 GENERAL

John Sarbanes (D)	203,711	69.7%
Thomas E. "Pinkston" Harris (R)	87,971	30.1%

2008 PRIMARY

John Sarbanes (D)	86,598	89.1%
John M. Rea (D)	10,614	10.9%

2006 GENERAL

John Sarbanes (D)	150,142	64.0%
John White (R)	79,174	33.8%
Charles Curtis McPeek Sr. (LIBERT)	4,941	2.1%

Sarbanes shares the Ivy League pedigree and low-key style of his father, who retired from the Senate in 2006 after 36 years in Congress, including two terms in the seat his son now occupies. But while his father made his most lasting mark in financial regulation, the younger Sarbanes is trying to carve his own niche, primarily on health care and education.

And though his interests are different, he has proved to be just as loyal a Democrat as his father. He sided with the Democrats 99 percent of the time on votes that pitted majorities of the parties against each other during the 110th Congress (2007-08).

Sarbanes picked up a slot in 2009 on the Energy and Commerce Committee and its Health Subcommittee, which positions him well to help influence any debate on an overhaul of the nation's health care system. Sarbanes spent much of his legal career at Baltimore's prestigious Venable LLP law firm representing hospitals and other medical providers, and he spent the final six years there as the firm's health care practice chairman.

Sarbanes has advocated tinkering with the current system rather than "a grand plan" for drastic change. He has supported Democratic legislation to expand the State Children's Health Insurance Program, which covers children whose families are low-income but not poor enough to qualify for Medicaid.

He also has endorsed universal health care. "I have always been intrigued by the idea that you can insure six out of seven of your people and you are still a capitalist country, but somehow when you try to insure that last person to get to seven out of seven, you become socialist," he said. "That doesn't make any sense at all."

Energy and Commerce is expected to take up energy and climate change legislation. Like other Democrats, Sarbanes backs developing alternative sources and wants energy viewed outside a strictly domestic context. "Any discussion of our national energy policy must consider the international scope of this challenge," he said. He has endorsed proposals in Maryland to put cleaner cars on the roads to reduce greenhouse gas emissions.

To join Energy and Commerce, Sarbanes had to give up his seats on the Oversight and Government Reform panel and the Education and Labor Committee, where during his first term he focused on education issues; Sarbanes sponsored legislation aimed at encouraging research into what makes a good school administrator. That initiative was inspired by Sarbanes' own efforts to lure veteran suburban principals to help improve failing city schools during his seven-year, part-time stint as liaison for Maryland's superintendent of schools to Baltimore's troubled schools.

He has taken a middle-of-the-road approach to changing the 2001 No Child Left Behind Law, which ties federal funding to schools' performance on mandatory tests. Sarbanes is no fan of the law, but doesn't agree with other liberals espousing repeal. He said the federal government should have a role in imposing accountability on local schools, but he wants to move away from what he calls the law's "obsessive focus" on math and reading. He wants to encourage the study of science and the humanities by imposing additional mandates in those disciplines. "We see problems that need fixing, but don't want to throw the baby out with the bath water," he said.

He introduced legislation to establish grant programs for environmental education at all grade levels. Science classes would include a section on environmental protection and require teachers to integrate environmental awareness into their curricula. "The only way you can save the environment is by developing habits that millions of people exercise every day," he said. The House passed the bill but the Senate failed to take it up in the 110th Congress; he planned to reintroduce it in 2009.

As a member of the Natural Resources Committee, Sarbanes hopes to protect the nearby Chesapeake Bay. He has advocated legislation to permanently reauthorize and boost funding for the Chesapeake Bay Gateways Network, which helps the public learn more about the bay and its resources through a system of parks, refuges, museums, historic sites and trails.

He also hopes to address the growth in his district fueled by the Pentagon's plans to relocate thousands of military and civilian personnel to nearby Fort George G. Meade as part of a realignment of military bases. And he joined with his Maryland Democratic colleague C.A. Dutch Ruppersberger to lobby for the F-22 Raptor fighter aircraft, made by the state's Lockheed Martin Corp.

Sarbanes is a purebred Baltimorean. Some of his earliest memories are of attending Orioles games, which were played just a few blocks from his childhood home in the Guilford-Waverly neighborhood, a comfortable middle-class enclave. His father was elected to the state legislature when Sarbanes was 4 and entered Congress when his son was 8.

Like his father, Sarbanes was educated at Princeton University and Harvard Law School. The younger Sarbanes served as president of the Princeton University Democrats and co-chair of the Harvard Law School Democrats. It was at Harvard that he met his wife, Dina.

Sarbanes' father was a Rhodes Scholar at Oxford; the younger Sarbanes studied law and politics in Greece on a Fulbright scholarship. Before joining Venable, he clerked for U.S. District Court Judge J. Frederick Motz. For 15 years, he was a board member for the Public Justice Center, a Baltimore organization providing legal assistance to the economically disadvantaged.

Sarbanes got his shot at a House seat in 2006 when Democratic Rep. Benjamin L. Cardin launched his successful bid to succeed the senior Sarbanes, who was retiring that year from the Senate. There was intense interest in the seat, which has been the springboard for Maryland's three most recent senators — Sarbanes, Cardin, and Democrat Barbara A. Mikulski. Eight candidates vied in the primary. But the Sarbanes name trumped all; Sarbanes appeared alongside his father in ads and used his father's longtime motto of "fairness and opportunity" on his campaign literature.

In the November election, Sarbanes easily defeated Republican John White, an Annapolis marketing executive, with 64 percent of the vote. In 2008, he just as easily defeated Thomas E. "Pinkston" Harris, a little-known Republican teacher from Baltimore.

KEY VOTES

2008

Yes   Delay consideration of Colombia free-trade agreement
Yes   Override Bush veto of federal farm and nutrition programs reauthorization bill
No   Overhaul surveillance laws and permit dismissal of suits against companies that conducted warrantless wiretapping
Yes   Grant mortgage relief to homeowners and funding for Fannie Mae and Freddie Mac
Yes   Approve initial $700 billion program to stabilize financial markets
Yes   Approve final $700 billion program to stabilize financial markets
Yes   Provide $14 billion in loans to automakers

2007

Yes   Increase minimum wage by $2.10 an hour
Yes   Approve $124.2 billion in emergency war spending and set goal for redeployment of troops from Iraq
No   Reject federal contraceptive assistance to international family planning groups
Yes   Override Bush veto of $23.2 billion water projects authorization bill
No   Implement Peru free-trade agreement
Yes   Approve energy policy overhaul with new fuel economy standards
No   Clear $473.5 billion omnibus spending bill, including $70 billion for military operations

CQ VOTE STUDIES

	PARTY UNITY		PRESIDENTIAL SUPPORT	
	SUPPORT	OPPOSE	SUPPORT	OPPOSE
2008	99%	1%	16%	84%
2007	99%	1%	4%	96%

INTEREST GROUPS

	AFL-CIO	ADA	CCUS	ACU
2008	100%	100%	61%	0%
2007	96%	100%	50%	0%

MARYLAND 3

Part of Baltimore; eastern Columbia; Annapolis

Like a Z-shaped lightning bolt, the 3rd District flashes through three of Maryland's largest urban hubs — Baltimore, Columbia and Annapolis.

Starting in traditionally Jewish suburbs northwest of Baltimore, the 3rd District snakes east and south, grabbing northeastern suburbs and part of downtown by Fells Point and the stadiums for baseball's Orioles and football's Ravens. Many ethnic areas of eastern Baltimore are included in the district. The 3rd then twists south and west through suburban Arbutus, Linthicum Heights and Elkridge on its way to the eastern part of Columbia. Finally, the district moves southeast through Odenton and Crofton to Annapolis.

State and local governments provide jobs in Annapolis, which is both the state capital and the Anne Arundel County seat, although unemployment rates in the area are rising. Technology, financial services and health care push the economy of the Columbia area. Two key employers located in the neighboring 2nd District — Fort George G. Meade, near the 3rd's southwestern edge, and the Baltimore/Washington International

Thurgood Marshall Airport, in the Linthicum area — lure defense-related firms to the region and employ many residents of the 3rd. Financial trouble for the owners of the Pimlico Race Course in northwestern Baltimore has jeopardized Maryland's role as host of the Preakness Stakes, the second leg of horse racing's Triple Crown.

The district has some GOP-leaning areas in Anne Arundel and Baltimore counties, but overall the 3rd supports Democrats for federal office. Barack Obama won 59 percent of the district's 2008 presidential vote.

MAJOR INDUSTRY
Government, technology, defense

MILITARY BASES
U.S. Naval Academy/Naval Station Annapolis, 559 military, 1,075 civilian (2009) (shared with the 1st District)

CITIES
Baltimore (pt.), 168,687; Columbia (unincorporated) (pt.), 40,311; Annapolis, 35,838; Pikesville (unincorporated), 29,123

NOTABLE
The Annapolis Historic District takes in more than 100 buildings from the 18th century — including the campus of St. John's College, itself a National Historic Landmark — and the City Dock.

Rep. Donna Edwards (D)

Elected June 2008; 1st full term

CAPITOL OFFICE
225-8699
donnaedwards.house.gov
318 Cannon Bldg. 20515-2004; fax 225-8714

COMMITTEES
Science & Technology
Transportation & Infrastructure

RESIDENCE
Fort Washington

BORN
June 28, 1958; Yanceyville, N.C.

RELIGION
Baptist

FAMILY
Separated; one child

EDUCATION
Wake Forest U., B.A. 1980 (English);
Franklin Pierce Law Center, J.D. 1989

CAREER
Nonprofit executive director; lobbyist; lawyer;
aeronautical company project manager;
United Nations publication editor

POLITICAL HIGHLIGHTS
Sought Democratic nomination for U.S. House,
2006

ELECTION RESULTS

2008 GENERAL

Donna Edwards (D)	258,704	85.8%
Peter James (R)	38,739	12.8%
Thibeaux Lincecum (LIBERT)	3,384	1.1%

2008 SPECIAL

Donna Edwards (D)	16,481	80.5%
Peter James (R)	3,638	17.8%
Thibeaux Lincecum (LIBERT)	216	1.1%

2008 PRIMARY

Donna Edwards (D)	78,008	58.9%
Albert R. Wynn (D)	48,885	36.9%
George E. Mitchell (D)	1,737	1.3%
Michael Babula (D)	1,429	1.1%
Jason Jennings (D)	1,429	1.1%

Edwards is a former lawyer and activist whose impassioned liberalism plays well with her suburban district's overwhelmingly Democratic constituents. She came to office as a fierce Iraq War critic, but also works on expanding the area's job base while seeking to upgrade its roads and transportation systems.

Edwards is the first African-American woman elected from Maryland to the House. She won a June 2008 special election to succeed veteran Rep. Albert R. Wynn, whom she defeated in a primary four months earlier after pegging him as too moderate. Wynn — who had beaten Edwards in a primary two years earlier — had resigned from Congress in May to join the lobbying and law firm Dickstein Shapiro.

Edwards vowed to oppose any bill that included funding for the Iraq War. When President Obama announced in February 2009 he would draw down nearly two-thirds of U.S. forces there by August 2010, leaving behind as many as 50,000 troops, she continued to raise questions. "Many of us in Congress are going to be asking, you tell us what every single one of those troops who are left after the major withdrawal of the majority of the troops ... what they're doing," she told CNN.

But Edwards has appeared a rather dependable vote on most issues. She favors a national health care plan and repealing the No Child Left Behind law, a 2001 education law she said has been underfunded. She also supports tying increases of the minimum wage to inflation.

As a single mother at age 30, she was dependent on educational loans to get through law school. "People like me, who have had to work their way out of a hole to finally make it out, we don't want anybody feeling sorry for us," she told The Washington Post in 2008. "We just want public policy that works for us, that we get a few advantages every now and then."

She did break with her party's leaders in fall 2008 by joining other liberals in opposing a $700 billion measure to aid the ailing financial services sector. She told The Baltimore Sun that lawmakers were given "a false set of choices" and that the failed legislation needed more protections for taxpayers. Though she remained critical of a reworked version, she said she decided to switch her vote after receiving assurances from Obama — then an Illinois senator — that he would address her concerns if elected president. The measure passed the House and became law.

Edwards is a member of the Tom Lantos Human Rights Commission, a panel made up of members of Congress reviewing human rights issues that is named for the late chairman of the House Foreign Affairs Committee. At a January 2009 hearing on human rights in China, she said, "I've been deeply concerned about the high rate of suicide among women in China, forced labor conditions and the inability to organize in factories where a lot of U.S. products are made."

Edwards has a seat on the Transportation and Infrastructure Committee, which is expected to take up a renewal of the 2005 surface transportation law in the 111th Congress (2009-10). She will be in position to join other Washington-area lawmakers in getting mass transit funding for two of her priorities: the Purple Line, a proposed 16-mile rapid-transit line extending from Bethesda in Montgomery County to New Carrollton in Prince George's County; and a potential rail line across the Potomac River at the Woodrow Wilson Bridge.

Edwards also is a member of the Science and Technology Committee, drawing on her background as a project manager for Lockheed Martin Corp. at Goddard Space Flight Center, located in the neighboring 5th District. She supported legislation the committee passed in March 2009 to help communities facing water shortages.

Edwards is the second of six children raised by an Air Force officer and a stay-at-home mom. The family moved frequently around the world before settling in the Washington suburbs for her senior year in high school. She was elected class president when she attended high school in New Mexico, and campaigned for Janet Napolitano, who was running for governor of Girls State, a weeklong program about government. Napolitano is now the Homeland Security Department secretary.

Another friend from her days in New Mexico, Montgomery (Md.) County Council member Valerie Ervin, told the Post that Edwards "has always been very driven and very ambitious."

Edwards volunteered on the 1976 presidential campaign of Jimmy Carter and the 1984 and 1988 presidential runs of civil rights leader the Rev. Jesse Jackson. On the campaign trail, she often talked about being a resident adviser in college and aiding a woman who had been battered by her boyfriend. She later became a volunteer in domestic violence shelters and helped found the National Network to End Domestic Violence.

She graduated from Wake Forest University with a degree in English, then worked for a United Nations publication and Lockheed Martin before attending Franklin Pierce Law Center in Concord, N.H.

Edwards clerked for Wynn, a lawyer who then was a Maryland state senator, after her second year at law school. Edwards later also campaigned for one of Wynn's early congressional races. "I really supported him when he first ran," she told the Sun in 2006. "It's just been in recent years that I've been really, really disappointed."

After completing law school in 1989 and another clerkship for D.C. Superior Court Judge Stephen Eilperin, Edwards worked at Public Citizen, a nonprofit organization that lobbies for campaign finance reform. For the next 15 years, she worked for several nonprofit organizations such as the Center for New Democracy and the Arca Foundation.

After losing to Wynn by 3 percentage points in the 2006 primary, Edwards decided to challenge Wynn again in early 2008. She beat him by a 22-percentage-point margin and in the June special election to fill out the remainder of his term, Edwards handily defeated Republican Peter James, with roughly 80 percent of the vote. She boosted her total by getting 86 percent in their general election rematch.

KEY VOTES

2008

No Overhaul surveillance laws and permit dismissal of suits against companies that conducted warrantless wiretapping

Yes Grant mortgage relief to homeowners and funding for Fannie Mae and Freddie Mac

No Approve initial $700 billion program to stabilize financial markets

Yes Approve final $700 billion program to stabilize financial markets

Yes Provide $14 billion in loans to automakers

CQ VOTE STUDIES

	PARTY UNITY		PRESIDENTIAL SUPPORT	
	SUPPORT	OPPOSE	SUPPORT	OPPOSE
2008	99%	1%	17%	83%

INTEREST GROUPS

	AFL-CIO	ADA	CCUS	ACU
2008	100%	–	58%	7%

MARYLAND 4

Inner Prince George's County; part of Montgomery County

The first suburban district in the nation with a black majority, the 4th includes Washington's eastern suburbs in Prince George's County and a sizable swath of northern Montgomery County. Democrats have a strong hold on the district's largely middle-class, black population.

The 4th's economy is built on small business and the spillover of technology firms from Montgomery County and the Northern Virginia suburbs. With a mostly white-collar workforce, the district includes major Prince George's County aerospace engineering, biotech and nanotech employers. The 4th's technology industries are bolstered by the University of Maryland and NASA's Goddard Space Flight Center (both nearby in the 5th District).

Prince George's County is a national leader in black business formation, homeownership and education, but foreclosure and mortgage rates in the county have been rising. Many county residents are federal employees who have moved out of Washington. Although some of Prince George's County's low-income areas inside the Capital Beltway, which surrounds Washington, share the capital's problems of drug trafficking and violent crime, public safety in the county has improved in recent years.

Nearly 40 percent of the district's residents live in Montgomery County outer suburbs and exurbs, such as Burtonsville, Olney and Sandy Spring. The 4th's solid Democratic tendencies led voters to give Barack Obama 85 percent of the 2008 presidential vote here, his highest percentage in the state.

MAJOR INDUSTRY
Retail, computers, technology, recreation

MILITARY BASES
Andrews Air Force Base, 5,202 military, 4,798 civilian (2007); Adelphi Army Research Laboratory, 13 military, 617 civilian (2006)

CITIES
Silver Spring (unincorporated) (pt.), 46,910; Oxon Hill-Glassmanor (unincorporated), 35,355; Suitland-Silver Hill (unincorporated), 33,515

NOTABLE
Air Force One is kept at Andrews Air Force Base.

Rep. Steny H. Hoyer (D)

Elected May 1981; 14th full term

CAPITOL OFFICE
225-4131
hoyer.house.gov
1705 Longworth Bldg. 20515-2005; fax 225-4300

COMMITTEES
No committee assignments

RESIDENCE
Mechanicsville

BORN
June 14, 1939; Manhattan, N.Y.

RELIGION
Baptist

FAMILY
Widowed; three children

EDUCATION
U. of Maryland, B.S. 1963 (political science);
Georgetown U., J.D. 1966

CAREER
Lawyer

POLITICAL HIGHLIGHTS
Md. Senate, 1967-79 (president, 1975-79);
sought Democratic nomination for lieutenant
governor, 1978; Md. Board of Higher Education,
1978-81

ELECTION RESULTS

2008 GENERAL

Steny H. Hoyer (D)	253,854	73.6%
Collins Bailey (R)	82,631	24.0%
Darlene H. Nicholas (LIBERT)	7,829	2.3%

2008 PRIMARY

Steny H. Hoyer (D)	90,513	82.6%
James Patrick Cusick SR (D)	19,067	17.4%

2006 GENERAL

Steny H. Hoyer (D)	168,114	82.7%
Steve Warner (GREEN)	33,464	16.5%

PREVIOUS WINNING PERCENTAGES
2004 (69%); 2002 (69%); 2000 (65%); 1998 (65%);
1996 (57%); 1994 (59%); 1992 (53%); 1990 (81%);
1988 (79%); 1986 (82%); 1984 (72%); 1982 (80%);
1981 Special Election (55%)

Within the House Democratic leadership, the silver-haired, carefully coiffed Hoyer remains an independent force and is a popular figure among rank-and-file Democrats. He first won the majority leader's post over the opposition of Speaker Nancy Pelosi, and still sometimes differs with her behind the scenes in an effort to bring together varying factions.

Hoyer's successes in the No. 2 leadership post has solidified his image as a centrist conciliator. He has strong relationships with the fiscally conservative members of the Blue Dog Coalition, yet sometimes sides with more-liberal Democrats. At the same time, he knows how to work with Republicans and lend business executives a sympathetic ear.

Hoyer is a strong proponent of many traditional Democratic issues, several of which he has helped further. He was a longtime Appropriations Committee member who was skilled at putting together the annual spending bills. Pro-labor, he fought to increase the federal minimum wage, a goal Democrats achieved in 2007. And he is particularly proud of being an author of the 1990 Americans with Disabilities Act, which bars discrimination against people with disabilities. In 2008, he cosponsored successful legislation updating the act to counter several Supreme Court decisions over the preceding decade that had narrowed the scope of protections afforded by the original law.

His acumen at cultivating relationships helped implement Pelosi's "strong caucus" model to set the majority's leadership goals and develop consensus approaches to major legislation, rather than allowing individual committee chairmen complete purview over pieces of legislation. Hoyer and Pelosi used the approach to win passage of President Obama's early economic initiatives, including a $787 billion economic stimulus law and a $410 billion catchall spending bill.

Hoyer pursued an offshoot of the approach in spring 2009 when he met with the chairmen of three major committees — Ways and Means, Energy and Commerce and Education and Labor — and other pivotal players to plot strategy on a health care overhaul, another of Obama's top priorities. "Collective judgments are better than individual judgments — not in every instance, but over time," Hoyer said in April of that year.

Even though Hoyer has the luxury of being able to pass most bills without much GOP support — and even though House Republicans were united in opposing the stimulus and Obama's fiscal 2010 budget blueprint — he said he holds out hope for some semblance of bipartisanship. He promised in February 2009 to allow for more debate on issues and for amendments to be brought up on the floor. "I believe we could have been more open in the last Congress," he said.

As majority leader in the 110th Congress (2007-08), Hoyer played a key role in achieving and maintaining a high level of voting unity among Democrats. When the economy slowed in 2008, he became an outspoken advocate of increased spending to boost a troubled economy. He also served as his party's negotiator with House Republicans and the George W. Bush administration on such sticky issues as the $700 billion financial industry rescue law and legislation renewing domestic anti-terrorism surveillance programs.

Hoyer won the majority leader's post by beating John P. Murtha of Pennsylvania, Pelosi's pick, in a 149-86 secret-ballot vote after the 2006 elections. Pelosi vigorously supported Murtha, a decorated Marine veteran of the Vietnam War and her old friend whose 2005 conversion to the anti-Iraq War cause in Congress helped ignite legislative efforts to end the war. But Hoyer, who has raised millions of dollars for colleagues' campaigns and built a loyal following as he rose through the leadership ranks, trounced Murtha.

That vote was just one episode in a long-running Pelosi-Hoyer relationship that veers between cooperation and rivalry. The two are almost the same age. Pelosi, a Maryland native, first met Hoyer in the early 1960s when they both worked for their state's Democratic senator, Daniel B. Brewster.

Almost 40 years later, the San Francisco liberal defeated Hoyer for the Democratic whip post in 2001, his second try after losing a bid a decade earlier to another liberal, David E. Bonior of Michigan. After the first loss, Hoyer was elected in 1989 as caucus chairman, the fourth-highest-ranking job at that time among House Democrats. When Pelosi was elected minority leader after the 2002 elections, Hoyer won the whip's post.

Like Pelosi, who said her career in public service was inspired in good part by President Kennedy, Hoyer, a graduate of the University of Maryland who was selected "outstanding male graduate" in 1963, said he was driven by hearing Kennedy tell a college crowd that public service is a noble calling. But while Pelosi and other Kennedy acolytes moved to the left, Hoyer remained a centrist with a more muscular approach to foreign policy, as his support for the 1991 Gulf War and the 2002 Iraq War vote showed.

As the representative of a suburban district in southern Maryland that is home to thousands of federal employees, Hoyer regularly champions cost-of-living increases and other benefits for the federal workforce. He also has worked to locate federal facilities in his district.

Hoyer was born in New York City, the son of a Danish immigrant who abandoned his family when Hoyer was 9. His stepfather was in the Air Force, and his mother worked at the Navy Federal Credit Union. He spent much of his childhood in Florida. His stepfather's transfer to Andrews Air Force Base brought the family to Maryland when Hoyer was in high school.

In 1959, Hoyer was a struggling college public relations major when he heard then-Sen. Kennedy speak. He switched to political science, went to law school and landed the job with Brewster. In 1966, at age 27, he was elected to the Maryland Senate. Two terms later he became its youngest president ever.

Hoyer suffered defeat in 1978, when he ran for lieutenant governor on a ticket with acting Gov. Blair Lee III and the two lost the primary. Three years later, Hoyer revived his career by claiming the 5th District House seat after Rep. Gladys Noon Spellman fell ill and her seat was vacated. He held the seat easily until redistricting in the 1990s added a conservative swath of southern Maryland. He got 53 percent of the vote in 1992, but has since posted higher margins.

KEY VOTES

2008

Yes Delay consideration of Colombia free-trade agreement

Yes Override Bush veto of federal farm and nutrition programs reauthorization bill

Yes Overhaul surveillance laws and permit dismissal of suits against companies that conducted warrantless wiretapping

Yes Grant mortgage relief to homeowners and funding for Fannie Mae and Freddie Mac

Yes Approve initial $700 billion program to stabilize financial markets

Yes Approve final $700 billion program to stabilize financial markets

Yes Provide $14 billion in loans to automakers

2007

Yes Increase minimum wage by $2.10 an hour

Yes Approve $124.2 billion in emergency war spending and set goal for redeployment of troops from Iraq

No Reject federal contraceptive assistance to international family planning groups

Yes Override Bush veto of $23.2 billion water projects authorization bill

Yes Implement Peru free-trade agreement

Yes Approve energy policy overhaul with new fuel economy standards

Yes Clear $473.5 billion omnibus spending bill, including $70 billion for military operations

CQ VOTE STUDIES

	PARTY UNITY		PRESIDENTIAL SUPPORT	
	SUPPORT	OPPOSE	SUPPORT	OPPOSE
2008	99%	1%	18%	82%
2007	98%	2%	8%	92%
2006	92%	8%	27%	73%
2005	93%	7%	24%	76%
2004	95%	5%	24%	76%

INTEREST GROUPS

	AFL-CIO	ADA	CCUS	ACU
2008	100%	90%	67%	0%
2007	100%	90%	55%	4%
2006	100%	90%	40%	4%
2005	100%	95%	52%	12%
2004	100%	100%	38%	0%

MARYLAND 5

Outer Prince George's County; southern Maryland

The 5th includes part of Prince George's County, southern Anne Arundel County and all of the three growing southern counties of Charles, Calvert and St. Mary's. The mix of liberals in Prince George's County and conservative Democrats and Republicans throughout much of the rest of the district gives the 5th a broad array of political interests.

The district is enjoying a moderate amount of economic success based mainly around high-tech and government jobs, both in Prince George's County and in Southern Maryland. Its proximity to Washington gives the 5th the nation's second-highest percentage of government workers (29 percent), behind the neighboring 4th District.

Many residents and companies have migrated from the Washington metropolitan area to the southern counties, attracted by the abundance of land and the military presence. Population growth has led to traffic problems, as much of the workforce still commutes north to Washington. The tri-county area retains its Southern rural character, however, despite transitioning away from tobacco as a major crop.

Prince George's County, which accounts for half the district's population and nearly 60 percent of its registered Democrats, includes many liberal black communities as well as College Park, home of the University of Maryland's main campus. Republicans hold a slight registration edge among the 5th's Anne Arundel residents, but Democrats have the advantage elsewhere, and their statewide and federal candidates do well in the district. In the 2008 presidential election, Barack Obama won the district handily, taking 65 percent of the vote.

MAJOR INDUSTRY
Defense, agriculture, technology

MILITARY BASES
Naval Air Station Patuxent River, 3,100 military, 7,600 civilian (2007); Naval Surface Warfare Center, Indian Head Division, 6 military, 1,288 civilian

CITIES
Bowie (pt.), 47,714; St. Charles (unincorporated), 33,379; Clinton (unincorporated), 26,064; College Park, 24,657

NOTABLE
NASA Goddard Space Flight Center; The College Park Airport, established in 1909, is the world's oldest continuously operating airport.

Rep. Roscoe G. Bartlett (R)

Elected 1992; 9th term

CAPITOL OFFICE
225-2721
bartlett.house.gov
2412 Rayburn Bldg. 20515-2006; fax 225-2193

COMMITTEES
Armed Services
Science & Technology
Small Business

RESIDENCE
Frederick

BORN
June 3, 1926; Moreland, Ky.

RELIGION
Seventh-day Adventist

FAMILY
Wife, Ellen Bartlett; 10 children

EDUCATION
Columbia Union College, B.S. 1947 (theology
& biology); U. of Maryland, M.S. 1948 (physiology),
Ph.D. 1952 (physiology)

CAREER
Real estate developer; scientific research
company owner; farmer; biomedical engineer;
professor

POLITICAL HIGHLIGHTS
Sought Republican nomination for U.S. Senate,
1980; Republican nominee for U.S. House, 1982

ELECTION RESULTS

2008 GENERAL

Roscoe G. Bartlett (R)	190,926	57.8%
Jennifer P. Dougherty (D)	128,207	38.8%
Gary W. Hoover Sr. (LIBERT)	11,060	3.3%

2008 PRIMARY

Roscoe G. Bartlett (R)	51,635	77.6%
Joseph T. Krysztoforski (R)	5,686	8.6%
Tom Croft (R)	4,895	7.4%
John B. Kimble (R)	3,433	5.2%
Frank K. Nethken (R)	857	1.3%

2006 GENERAL

Roscoe G. Bartlett (R)	141,200	59.0%
Andrew Duck (D)	92,030	38.4%
Robert E. Kozak (GREEN)	6,095	2.5%

PREVIOUS WINNING PERCENTAGES
2004 (67%); 2002 (66%); 2000 (61%); 1998 (63%);
1996 (57%); 1994 (66%); 1992 (54%)

Bartlett is a conservative with a libertarian bent, making it sometimes hard to pigeonhole him. He is a member of the Republican Study Committee, a group of the most conservative members of the House GOP. But over his career, he has often strayed from his party's leadership, especially on energy policy and anti-terrorism measures.

Bartlett was 66 years old when he was first elected to the House in 1992, and his résumé includes a background as a scientist, inventor, teacher, businessman and farmer. The sole surviving Republican in Maryland's delegation, Bartlett has a laid-back, folksy manner. He styles himself as a citizen-legislator and he points to his strong religious beliefs and a strict reading of the Constitution as the basis for his political views.

His doctorate in physiology makes him one of the few scientists in Congress, and he applies his background assiduously as a member of the Science and Technology Committee. He wants to see more U.S. students specialize in math and science, and he annually donates scholarship money for residents of his district who major in math, science or engineering at colleges there.

His background in science informs his views on energy policy. Bartlett became a crusader on behalf of energy alternatives to petroleum long before oil prices soared and being "green" became fashionable. He was the first in Congress to drive a hybrid car, in which he commutes the 50 miles from his farmhouse in Frederick, which is heated by solar energy and a wood stove. His neighbors appear to share his mindset: BP's U.S. solar operations are based in Bartlett's district.

His knack for preparing for unforeseen crises extends beyond energy — indeed, it runs all the way to the bank. He has invested much of his personal wealth in gold instead of securities since the early 1990s, a move that looked particularly smart as financial markets imploded in late 2008.

Bartlett has often found himself alone in his energy crusade. He is often the first in the room to mention reducing consumption as a remedy for the energy crisis. He likes to cite the theory of "peak oil," to which he subscribes; it suggests the world is nearing a point at which global demand for oil will exceed production. Still, he supports expanded domestic oil and gas drilling. In 2007, for the first time since he came to the House, he sided with his fellow Republicans to support oil exploration in Alaska's Arctic National Wildlife Refuge as part of an "all of the above" approach to energy independence. Bartlett argued that he didn't actually change positions, telling The Baltimore Sun that he has always supported domestic drilling if oil revenues go toward investments in alternative energy.

A former small-business owner, Bartlett also sits on the Small Business Committee. He opposed President Obama's $787 billion economic stimulus bill early 2009, as well as President George W. Bush's $700 billion financial industry rescue package in fall 2008, saying tax breaks for small businesses would be more effective.

A member of the Armed Services Committee, and the top-ranking Republican on its Air and Land Forces panel, he is a staunch supporter of a muscular military. But Bartlett is not in lockstep with GOP orthodoxy on all national security matters. He regretted his 2001 vote for the anti-terrorism law known as the Patriot Act, which gave the government sweeping new powers to track, arrest and prosecute suspected terrorists. "Probably the least patriotic thing I've done since I got here," he lamented in an interview several months later. In 2005, he voted against reauthorization of the law.

Bartlett was also an early GOP critic of Bush's decision to detain alleged enemy combatants at the U.S. prison at Guantánamo Bay, Cuba. He said the facility, which Obama plans to close, has hurt America's image abroad.

Earlier in his career, Bartlett made headlines with his defense initiatives. He fought a 1994 Pentagon move to integrate men and women in housing and basic training, vowing to prevent a "powder puff" military. In 1996, he authored a provision to ban sale of "lascivious" materials, such as pornographic magazines, on military bases — a measure the courts later found unconstitutional.

And while there is a growing refrain against earmarks in the House — funding set-asides for projects in members' districts — Bartlett doesn't mind them. He said he has no problem working to bring money home to his district when it helps his constituents. He often boasts of getting awards for local defense contractors; in 2007, he touted getting $2 million for a hybrid vehicle powertrain research and development project that a major employer in his district worked on with the Air Force.

He was born on his grandfather's farm in Kentucky. His father worked as a tenant farmer in western Pennsylvania during the Depression, but refused to take any assistance from the government during those hard times — fostering Bartlett's own devotion to self-sufficiency. He intended to become a minister but instead pursued physiology at the University of Maryland. Bartlett continues to hold strong religious beliefs, displaying the Ten Commandments in his office beside a mural of the first prayer held in Congress.

Bartlett taught in California and Washington, D.C., and did research for the National Institutes of Health and the Navy's School of Aviation Medicine, where his mechanical skill led him into engineering. He holds 20 patents, including those for components found in breathing equipment used by pilots, astronauts and rescue workers. Bartlett was honored in 1999 for his lifetime achievements by the American Institute of Aeronautics and Astronautics.

In 1961, Bartlett moved to a dairy farm in Frederick County, which he operated while working at the Johns Hopkins Applied Physics Laboratory in Howard County. He later entered the homebuilding business.

Bartlett made an unsuccessful House bid in 1982 but a decade later narrowly won a three-way GOP primary. He expected to face conservative Democrat Beverly B. Byron, a seven-term incumbent who had defeated him almost 3-to-1 in that first bid. But Byron lost the Democratic primary to former state delegate Thomas H. Hattery, whom Bartlett then beat by 8 percentage points.

He has won re-election comfortably since, but retirement rumors dog him each election cycle. His most recent campaign was no different.

KEY VOTES

2008

No	Delay consideration of Colombia free-trade agreement
Yes	Override Bush veto of federal farm and nutrition programs reauthorization bill
Yes	Overhaul surveillance laws and permit dismissal of suits against companies that conducted warrantless wiretapping
No	Grant mortgage relief to homeowners and funding for Fannie Mae and Freddie Mac
No	Approve initial $700 billion program to stabilize financial markets
No	Approve final $700 billion program to stabilize financial markets
No	Provide $14 billion in loans to automakers

2007

No	Increase minimum wage by $2.10 an hour
No	Approve $124.2 billion in emergency war spending and set goal for redeployment of troops from Iraq
Yes	Reject federal contraceptive assistance to international family planning groups
Yes	Override Bush veto of $23.2 billion water projects authorization bill
Yes	Implement Peru free-trade agreement
No	Approve energy policy overhaul with new fuel economy standards
Yes	Clear $473.5 billion omnibus spending bill, including $70 billion for military operations

CQ VOTE STUDIES

	PARTY UNITY		PRESIDENTIAL SUPPORT	
	SUPPORT	OPPOSE	SUPPORT	OPPOSE
2008	94%	6%	65%	35%
2007	90%	10%	75%	25%
2006	85%	15%	77%	23%
2005	89%	11%	64%	36%
2004	93%	7%	76%	24%

INTEREST GROUPS

	AFL-CIO	ADA	CCUS	ACU
2008	0%	15%	78%	96%
2007	8%	15%	80%	88%
2006	14%	25%	80%	84%
2005	14%	5%	85%	84%
2004	20%	10%	90%	92%

MARYLAND 6
North and west — Frederick, Hagerstown

The 6th reaches across the northern tier of the state from Western Maryland to the Susquehanna River. It takes in all of Garrett, Allegany, Washington, Frederick and Carroll counties, as well as large portions of Baltimore and Harford counties and a small, exurban corner of Montgomery County. The 6th has a rural tradition and a conservative bent that benefits the GOP.

Frederick and Carroll counties grew economically over the last decade, as new residents escaped urban and inner suburban areas in Baltimore and Washington, D.C. Frederick County has military, government, education and manufacturing industries, but Carroll is still mainly agricultural. Unemployment in both counties is rising, particularly in construction and transportation sectors. A major BP Solar facility in Frederick has cut jobs and halted plans to complete a $100 million expansion project.

The three western counties are less populous and have a strong conservative bent. The decades-long demise of the old-line manufacturing industry harmed much of the Appalachian Mountain area, and prolonged national economic problems have resulted in job losses across Western Maryland. Hagerstown, the largest city in Washington County, serves as a junction of several highways, acting as a hub between the Appalachians and the highly populated Mid-Atlantic region. Nestled in the mountains, Allegany County is slightly more than two hours from Baltimore, Washington or Pittsburgh. Allegany and Garrett counties struggle and have become dependent on tourism as companies have closed their operations here.

The 6th also includes northern portions of Baltimore and Harford counties, where Republicans and conservative Democrats reign. The 6th gave John McCain 58 percent of its presidential vote in 2008.

MAJOR INDUSTRY
Technology, manufacturing, agriculture, tourism

MILITARY BASES
Fort Detrick (Army), 1,900 military, 7,700 civilian (2009)

CITIES
Frederick, 52,767; Hagerstown, 36,687; Eldersburg (unincorporated), 27,741; Cumberland, 21,518; Westminster, 16,731

NOTABLE
Camp David, the president's retreat, is located in Frederick County.

Rep. Elijah E. Cummings (D)

Elected April 1996; 7th full term

CAPITOL OFFICE
225-4741
www.house.gov/cummings
2235 Rayburn Bldg. 20515-2007; fax 225-3178

COMMITTEES
Oversight & Government Reform
Transportation & Infrastructure
  (Coast Guard & Maritime Transportation -
  chairman)
Joint Economic

RESIDENCE
Baltimore

BORN
Jan. 18, 1951; Baltimore, Md.

RELIGION
Baptist

FAMILY
Wife, Maya Rockeymoore Cummings;
three children

EDUCATION
Howard U., B.A. 1973 (political science);
U. of Maryland, J.D. 1976

CAREER
Lawyer

POLITICAL HIGHLIGHTS
Md. House, 1983-96 (Speaker pro tempore, 1995)

ELECTION RESULTS

2008 GENERAL

Elijah E. Cummings (D)	227,379	79.5%
Michael T. Hargadon (R)	53,147	18.6%
Ronald M. Owens-Bey (LIBERT)	5,214	1.8%

2008 PRIMARY

Elijah E. Cummings (D)	98,027	93.0%
Charles U. Smith (D)	7,322	7.0%

2006 GENERAL

Elijah E. Cummings (D)	158,830	98.1%
write-ins	3,147	1.9%

PREVIOUS WINNING PERCENTAGES
2004 (73%); 2002 (74%); 2000 (87%); 1998 (86%);
1996 (83%); 1996 Special Election (81%)

Cummings leaves no doubt about his priorities in Congress. He is there to look out for those with little voice and less influence, for the working poor and the poor without work.

He is the Marylander with perhaps the closest ties to President Obama, having chaired Obama's 2008 campaign in the state. But Cummings also created some havoc for the new president in early 2009 when he became one of the loudest critics of the government's efforts to resuscitate the moribund financial system.

Cummings, a member of the Oversight and Government Reform Committee as well as the Joint Economic Committee, has been always skeptical of using government funds to help Wall Street.

Late in 2008, when the George W. Bush administration asked Congress to support a $700 billion plan to rescue the faltering financial system, Cummings balked, saying the bill offered little to help his constituents. He lined up with a group of Democrats seeking an alternative. "What we've been trying to figure out," he said, "is how do we make sure that we take care of Wall Street, but also take care of Madison Avenue? And I'm not talking about Madison Avenue in New York; I'm talking about Madison Avenue in Baltimore, which is located in the inner city, by the way."

But Cummings switched his vote after receiving a plea from then-Democratic presidential nominee Obama. Cummings wasn't happy after the bill became law, grilling corporate executives and federal regulators at Oversight and Government Reform hearings about why the financial markets had veered off a cliff, as well as Obama administration officials about how they allowed some of the rescued firms to hand out generous bonuses.

Cummings was an early critic of bonuses and salaries at the company most caught up in that controversy, insurer American International Group Inc., and introduced legislation requiring companies that accept federal funds to post on a Web site lists of their spending on events, bonuses, corporate jet use and lobbying. He said the disclosure was reasonable because companies had come to Congress "on their knees begging for money" and then had continued "the partying on Wall Street with the corporate junkets and million-dollar bonuses" — behavior he described as "a slap in the face of the American taxpayers."

Cummings also played a big roll in 2008 in helping California Democrat Henry A. Waxman, a liberal, claim the chairmanship of the Energy and Commerce Committee away from the more senior, and more conservative, John D. Dingell of Michigan. Cummings argued Waxman's case before the House Democrats. Waxman's victory, which required him to surrender the chairmanship of the Oversight and Government Reform panel, allowed Cummings to move up there. But Cummings passed up an opportunity to run for chairman, instead endorsing the senior Edolphus Towns of New York.

Cummings also made a splash with his response to steroid abuse in professional sports in recent years. After New York Yankees baseball star Alex Rodriguez admitted to using steroids in 2009, for example, Cummings challenged him to come speak to Maryland school children about the dangers of steroid abuse. As co-founder of the Congressional Caucus on Drug Policy, he has participated heavily during the Oversight and Government Reform Committee's high-profile questioning of other Major League Baseball stars such as Mark McGwire, Rafael Palmeiro, Sammy Sosa and Roger Clemens. Cummings also works to improve relations among diverse groups in the Baltimore area, particularly between the black and Jewish communities. The Elijah Cummings Youth Program in Israel, launched in 1998, takes a dozen non-Jewish students from the 7th District to Israel for four weeks each summer.

Baltimore is a major port city, and Cummings displays his knowledge of maritime issues as chairman of the Transportation and Infrastructure Coast Guard and Maritime Transportation Subcommittee. In 2007, he won House passage of a bill to beef up the Coast Guard, overhaul its troubled Deepwater fleet modernization program and update efforts to prevent marine pollution. But the measure stalled in the Senate, so in 2008, he pushed through a narrower bill targeting only the Deepwater program.

In the 111th Congress (2009-10), Cummings wants to focus on Coast Guard safety programs, on rules governing cargo-carrying vessels on inland waterways and on preventing alien species from reaching U.S. inland waters from ships' ballast water.

The Coast Guard is a major player in the drug wars, intercepting and seizing massive amounts of cocaine and other illegal drugs every year, and Cummings wants that work to continue.

Born in Baltimore, Cummings was one of seven children of former sharecroppers who had migrated from South Carolina. As a child, he recalls, "We did not have many opportunities ... We did not play on grass. We played on asphalt." But he was set on a productive course by "two very strong parents," who scrimped and saved to buy their own home in a city neighborhood that was integrating.

He graduated Phi Beta Kappa from Howard University in Washington, D.C., where he was also student government president. He said his mother was hesitant about attending his graduation ceremony because she did not want to embarrass her son in front of "all those sophisticated people" at Howard. Cummings told her he would be honored to have her there.

He then earned a law degree from the University of Maryland and six years later was elected to the Maryland House. In 13 years there, he rose to the chamber's second-ranking position, at the time the highest Maryland office ever held by an African-American.

In 1996, he outpaced 26 other Democrats and five Republicans to replace Democrat Kweisi Mfume, who resigned his House seat early to become president of the NAACP. Since then, Cummings has won re-election overwhelmingly. He does not rule out a bid for higher office but isn't laying plans, either. He said he believes that "you have to go out there every day and give the best you've got, no matter what you are doing, and doors will open."

KEY VOTES

2008

Yes Delay consideration of Colombia free-trade agreement

Yes Override Bush veto of federal farm and nutrition programs reauthorization bill

No   Overhaul surveillance laws and permit dismissal of suits against companies that conducted warrantless wiretapping

Yes Grant mortgage relief to homeowners and funding for Fannie Mae and Freddie Mac

No   Approve initial $700 billion program to stabilize financial markets

Yes Approve final $700 billion program to stabilize financial markets

Yes Provide $14 billion in loans to automakers

2007

Yes Increase minimum wage by $2.10 an hour

Yes Approve $124.2 billion in emergency war spending and set goal for redeployment of troops from Iraq

No   Reject federal contraceptive assistance to international family planning groups

Yes Override Bush veto of $23.2 billion water projects authorization bill

No   Implement Peru free-trade agreement

Yes Approve energy policy overhaul with new fuel economy standards

No   Clear $473.5 billion omnibus spending bill, including $70 billion for military operations

CQ VOTE STUDIES

	PARTY UNITY		PRESIDENTIAL SUPPORT	
	SUPPORT	OPPOSE	SUPPORT	OPPOSE
2008	99%	1%	12%	88%
2007	98%	2%	3%	97%
2006	96%	4%	23%	77%
2005	97%	3%	17%	83%
2004	98%	2%	21%	79%

INTEREST GROUPS

	AFL-CIO	ADA	CCUS	ACU
2008	100%	100%	50%	5%
2007	96%	100%	50%	0%
2006	100%	100%	33%	8%
2005	93%	100%	41%	4%
2004	100%	100%	30%	0%

MARYLAND 7

Downtown Baltimore; part of Columbia

The 7th takes in both the largely poor neighborhoods of West Baltimore and much of downtown, with the bustling retail center of the Inner Harbor. The district then follows the black migration west to include Baltimore County's middle-class southwestern suburbs and the bulk of Howard County, including the western portion of Columbia, a liberal-leaning planned community between Baltimore and Washington.

Efforts to improve Baltimore's poor neighborhoods have been slow, and urban problems, such as crime, drug abuse, teen pregnancy and unemployment, prompted many of the city's middle-class residents to head to the suburbs. But the picture within the city is not all bleak. Many of Baltimore's most identifiable landmarks and businesses are in the 7th, and there are middle-class black communities along Liberty Heights Avenue in West Baltimore.

The 7th takes in the gentrified Mount Vernon area, home of the Walters Art Museum and the Peabody Institute, which is affiliated with Johns Hopkins University and is one of the nation's major academies for professionally trained musicians. Farther north are Johns Hopkins University and the Baltimore Museum of Art. West of the downtown hub, the old retail section around Lexington Market and the 1st Mariner Arena still survives. Just southwest of the city, the University of Maryland, Baltimore County campus and its adjacent research area are attracting technology firms. West of Baltimore County are sprawling suburbs in racially diverse and mainly wealthy, well-educated Howard County.

The 7th has the state's highest percentage of black residents and gives an edge to Democrats in national and local contests throughout most of the district, but the GOP can win locally in parts of Howard County. Barack Obama won 79 percent of the district's 2008 presidential vote.

MAJOR INDUSTRY
Health care, manufacturing, technology

CITIES
Baltimore (pt.), 370,752; Ellicott City (unincorporated) (pt.), 56,231; Columbia (unincorporated) (pt.), 47,943; Catonsville (unincorporated), 39,820; Woodlawn (unincorporated), 36,079

NOTABLE
The 7th's portion of Baltimore is home to NAACP national headquarters, author Edgar Allan Poe's gravesite and the National Aquarium.

Rep. Chris Van Hollen (D)

Elected 2002; 4th term

CAPITOL OFFICE
225-5341
vanhollen.house.gov
1707 Longworth Bldg. 20515-2008; fax 225-0375

COMMITTEES
Oversight & Government Reform
Ways & Means

RESIDENCE
Kensington

BORN
Jan. 10, 1959; Karachi, Pakistan

RELIGION
Episcopalian

FAMILY
Wife, Katherine Wilkens Van Hollen;
three children

EDUCATION
Swarthmore College, B.A. 1983 (philosophy);
Harvard U., M.P.P. 1985; Georgetown U., J.D. 1990

CAREER
Lawyer; gubernatorial aide; congressional aide

POLITICAL HIGHLIGHTS
Md. House, 1991-95; Md. Senate, 1995-2003

ELECTION RESULTS

2008 GENERAL

Chris Van Hollen (D)	229,740	75.1%
Steve Hudson (R)	66,351	21.7%
Gordon Clark (GREEN)	6,828	2.2%

2008 PRIMARY

Chris Van Hollen (D)	104,108	87.8%
Deborah A. Vollmer (D)	11,052	9.3%
Lih Young (D)	3,391	2.9%

2006 GENERAL

Chris Van Hollen (D)	168,872	76.5%
Jeffrey M. Stein (R)	48,324	21.9%
Gerard P. Giblin (GREEN)	3,298	1.5%

PREVIOUS WINNING PERCENTAGES
2004 (75%); 2002 (52%)

Van Hollen's swift rise to the House leadership's upper ranks has been fueled by a wonkish devotion to policy he developed as a Senate aide, as well as his considerable acumen at recruiting Democratic candidates and raising money for them. His calm, nice-guy demeanor and willingness to listen have helped him avoid tensions with others.

Admiring colleagues describe him as a future Speaker, senator or something else. "He has all of the skills that are necessary to be a national political figure," said fellow Democrat Artur Davis of Alabama, who told The Washington Times in January 2009 that the only potential obstacle to the presidency for Van Hollen could be his birth in Pakistan, where his father was posted as a diplomat.

It's no secret that Van Hollen has his eye on moving up — the only question is where. He very nearly ran for the Senate in 2006, when five-term Democrat Paul S. Sarbanes retired. But the party establishment favored veteran Rep. Benjamin L. Cardin. Van Hollen took a hard look at the situation and stood down; Cardin eventually won the seat.

For now, as chairman of the Democratic Congressional Campaign Committee, the House Democratic campaign unit, Van Hollen aims to continue to build on the party's successes in the 2006 and 2008 elections. He also serves as assistant to Speaker Nancy Pelosi of California with special responsibility as liaison to the Obama White House. He said the expanded responsibilities give him a hand in both politics and policy, a nexus he believes is essential to the primary goal of defending Democrats' newly expanded majority in 2010. "From my perspective, marrying the policy role and the political role is the best of both worlds," he said.

He had led candidate recruitment for the 2006 election, and his success led party leaders to name him DCCC chair for the 2008 elections. Van Hollen had considered making a run to be Democratic Caucus chairman in 2009, a job that would have placed him three slots from the speakership, but ultimately decided against it. That's when Pelosi asked him to stay on as DCCC chairman through the 2010 elections.

Van Hollen is a liberal on most big social issues, favoring abortion rights and restrictions on the availability of guns. He fought in vain to stop a bill shielding gun dealers and manufacturers from lawsuits by gun crime victims and another measure exempting gun sales statistics from public disclosure under the Freedom of Information Act.

Well-educated and well-traveled, Van Hollen is a good match for his district, a swath of demographically elite suburbs just outside Washington, D.C. Many of his constituents work for the federal government, its contractors or lobbyists; others are engaged in biomedical research, technology and other professions. Education is a priority for many of them and an issue Van Hollen continues to champion.

He has pressed for increased education funding, including for President George W. Bush's No Child Left Behind Act, which set tough new testing standards for public schools. He also has sought to give mandatory status to federal aid for special-needs students in order to boost it to the 40 percent level envisioned under the Individuals with Disabilities Education Act.

He also looks out for his district on the prestigious Ways and Means Committee, which deals with health care and tax-related legislation. He seeks to help his constituents by addressing the alternative minimum tax, which was originally intended to target only wealthy taxpayers but was not indexed for inflation. And he strongly advocated revoking the IRS's authority to hire private debt-collection companies to collect back taxes — a major concern of federal workers and unions. He applauded the Obama administration's decision in 2009 to halt the practice.

Van Hollen continues to serve on the Oversight and Government Reform Committee, where he looks out for the interests of the numerous federal employees in his district. He teams up with other local lawmakers to press for parity between military personnel and civilian workers when Congress sets annual cost-of-living adjustments.

During the 110th Congress (2007-08), Van Hollen joined other Maryland and Virginia lawmakers in successfully pressing for more funds to clean up the Chesapeake Bay in the 2008 five-year reauthorization of agriculture and nutrition programs.

The son of a Foreign Service officer, Van Hollen was born in Karachi and lived in Turkey, India and Sri Lanka, where his father was ambassador. His mother was an expert on Russia. He earned a graduate degree in public policy and national security studies from Harvard's Kennedy School of Government, where he met his wife, Katherine. He then joined the staff of Maryland Sen. Charles McC. Mathias Jr., a Republican moderate, as a legislative assistant for defense and foreign policy.

When Mathias retired in 1986, Van Hollen went to work for the Senate Foreign Relations Committee as an arms control and NATO specialist, while Katherine worked for the House Foreign Affairs Committee. "We got to compare notes at home," he once joked.

He won election to the Maryland House in 1990, and four years later went after a state Senate seat, taking on the incumbent Democrat in the primary, even though she had helped him win his House seat. Van Hollen won, and went on to serve eight years in the state Senate. He successfully championed a state law mandating trigger locks on guns, two cigarette tax increases opposed by the tobacco lobby and a big funding boost for Montgomery County schools.

He saw his chance to move up to Congress when redistricting after the 2000 census packed more Democrats into Maryland's 8th District, where liberal Republican Constance A. Morella regularly won re-election. First, he had to survive a four-way primary, narrowly edging out state Rep. Mark K. Shriver, a nephew of President Kennedy.

He and Morella then waged one of the costliest and most-watched contests of the 2002 election. Each spent about $3 million. Van Hollen eked out a 4-percentage-point win. He has sailed to re-election ever since.

KEY VOTES

2008

Yes Delay consideration of Colombia free-trade agreement

Yes Override Bush veto of federal farm and nutrition programs reauthorization bill

No Overhaul surveillance laws and permit dismissal of suits against companies that conducted warrantless wiretapping

Yes Grant mortgage relief to homeowners and funding for Fannie Mae and Freddie Mac

Yes Approve initial $700 billion program to stabilize financial markets

Yes Approve final $700 billion program to stabilize financial markets

Yes Provide $14 billion in loans to automakers

2007

Yes Increase minimum wage by $2.10 an hour

Yes Approve $124.2 billion in emergency war spending and set goal for redeployment of troops from Iraq

No Reject federal contraceptive assistance to international family planning groups

Yes Override Bush veto of $23.2 billion water projects authorization bill

Yes Implement Peru free-trade agreement

Yes Approve energy policy overhaul with new fuel economy standards

No Clear $473.5 billion omnibus spending bill, including $70 billion for military operations

CQ VOTE STUDIES

	PARTY UNITY		PRESIDENTIAL SUPPORT	
	SUPPORT	OPPOSE	SUPPORT	OPPOSE
2008	99%	1%	14%	86%
2007	98%	2%	6%	94%
2006	95%	5%	30%	70%
2005	99%	1%	15%	85%
2004	96%	4%	35%	65%

INTEREST GROUPS

	AFL-CIO	ADA	CCUS	ACU
2008	100%	100%	61%	0%
2007	96%	90%	55%	0%
2006	93%	90%	40%	4%
2005	93%	100%	37%	0%
2004	100%	100%	38%	4%

MARYLAND 8

Part of Montgomery County — Bethesda, Gaithersburg, Rockville

The 8th contains wealthy Montgomery County suburbs northwest of Washington, such as Bethesda, Chevy Chase and Potomac, along with less-affluent suburbs in eastern Montgomery and western Prince George's counties. It also includes the Interstate 270 technology corridor, a hotbed for high-tech and biotech companies that runs through Rockville and Gaithersburg. In the western part of the district, officials struggle to preserve an agricultural heritage, and traffic congestion plagues commuter routes and commercial centers elsewhere in the 8th.

Government dominates the 8th, where federal agencies, such as the National Institutes of Health and the Nuclear Regulatory Commission, abound and where federal employees who work in Washington reside. County and state government also provide jobs in Rockville, the Montgomery County seat. The large contingent of highly educated professionals supports an economy that is bolstered by a wide array of big-name business interests, including Lockheed Martin and Marriott.

The district has a strong Democratic lean, helped by liberal Takoma Park and heavily black and Hispanic neighborhoods in western Prince George's County. The 8th has the highest percentage of Asians (11 percent) and Hispanics (14 percent) of any Maryland district. Voters across the 8th supported Democrat Barack Obama in the 2008 presidential election — he took 74 percent here, his highest percentage among Maryland's six white-majority districts.

MAJOR INDUSTRY
Government, technology, service, retail

MILITARY BASES
National Naval Medical Center, 2,451 military, 2,506 civilian (2009); National Geospatial-Intelligence Agency, 45 military, 1,455 civilian; Naval Surface Warfare Center, Carderock Division, 3 military, 1,340 civilian (2007)

CITIES
Wheaton-Glenmont (unincorporated), 57,694; Bethesda (unincorporated), 55,277; Gaithersburg, 52,613; Rockville, 47,388

NOTABLE
Glen Echo Park has a working Dentzel Carousel in the menagerie style with handcrafted horses, rabbits and other animals that turns to the music of an original Wurlitzer band organ, one of only 11 that still exist.

MASSACHUSETTS

Gov. Deval Patrick (D)

Pronounced: DUH-vahl
First elected: 2006
Length of term: 4 years
Term expires: 1/11
Salary: $140,533
Phone: (617) 725-4005

Residence: Milton
Born: July 31, 1956; Chicago, Ill.
Religion: Presbyterian
Family: Wife, Diane Patrick; two children
Education: Harvard U., A.B. 1978 (English & American literature), J.D. 1982
Career: Lawyer; beverage company executive
Political highlights: Assistant attorney general, Civil Rights Division, 1994-1997

Election results:

2006 GENERAL
Deval Patrick (D)	1,234,984	55.6%
Kerry Healey (R)	784,342	35.3%
Christy Mihos (I)	154,628	7.0%
Grace Ross (GREEN)	43,193	1.9%

Lt. Gov. Timothy P. Murray (D)

First elected: 2006
Length of term: 4 years
Term expires: 1/11
Salary: $124,920
Phone: (617) 725-4005

LEGISLATURE

General Court: Usually year-round, but meeting time varies

Senate: 40 members, 2-year terms
2009 ratios: 35 D, 5 R; 28 men, 12 women
Salary: $61,440
Phone: (617) 722-1276

House: 160 members, 2-year terms
2009 ratios: 143 D, 16 R, 1 vacancy; 122 men, 37 women
Salary: $61,440
Phone: (617) 722-2356

TERM LIMITS

Governor: 2 terms
Senate: No
House: No

URBAN STATISTICS

CITY	POPULATION
Boston	589,141
Worcester	172,648
Springfield	152,082
Lowell	105,167
Cambridge	101,355

REGISTERED VOTERS

Unenrolled/others	51%
Democrat	37%
Republican	12%

POPULATION

2008 population (est.)	6,497,967
2000 population	6,349,097
1990 population	6,016,425
Percent change (1990-2000)	+5.5%
Rank among states (2008)	15
Median age	36.5
Born in state	66.1%
Foreign born	12.2%
Violent crime rate	476/100,000
Poverty level	9.3%
Federal workers	53,161
Military	23,516

ELECTIONS

STATE ELECTION OFFICIAL
(617) 727-2828
DEMOCRATIC PARTY
(617) 472-0637
REPUBLICAN PARTY
(617) 523-5005

MISCELLANEOUS

Web: www.mass.gov
Capital: Boston

U.S. CONGRESS

Senate: 2 Democrats
House: 10 Democrats

2000 Census Statistics by District

DIST.	2008 VOTE FOR PRESIDENT OBAMA	MCCAIN	WHITE	BLACK	ASIAN	HISP	MEDIAN INCOME	WHITE COLLAR	BLUE COLLAR	SERVICE INDUSTRY	OVER 64	UNDER 18	COLLEGE EDUCATION	RURAL	SQ. MILES
1	64%	33%	89%	2%	2%	6%	$42,570	60%	24%	16%	14%	24%	25%	31%	3,101
2	59	39	82	5	1	9	$44,386	61	24	15	14	26	23	15	922
3	58	39	86	3	3	6	$50,223	66	21	14	13	25	31	7	581
4	63	34	88	2	3	3	$53,169	68	20	13	14	24	37	12	732
5	59	39	80	2	5	12	$56,217	67	21	12	11	27	34	7	566
6	57	40	90	2	2	4	$57,826	70	18	13	14	24	35	5	480
7	65	33	84	3	6	5	$56,110	73	14	13	16	21	40	0	170
8	84	14	49	22	8	16	$39,300	71	13	17	9	18	40	0	41
9	60	38	79	8	4	5	$55,407	69	17	14	14	24	34	2	313
10	55	43	92	2	3	1	$51,928	67	18	15	17	23	34	8	934
STATE	62	36	82	5	4	7	$50,502	67	19	14	14	24	33	9	7,840
U.S.	53	46	69	12	4	13	$41,994	60	25	15	12	26	24	21	3,537,438

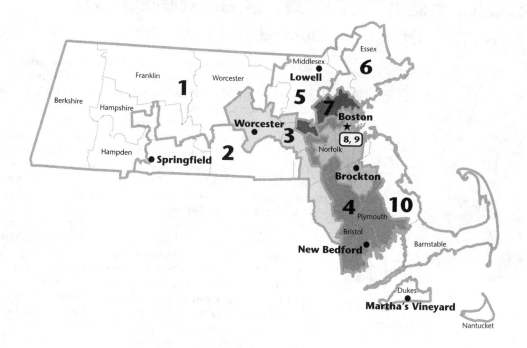

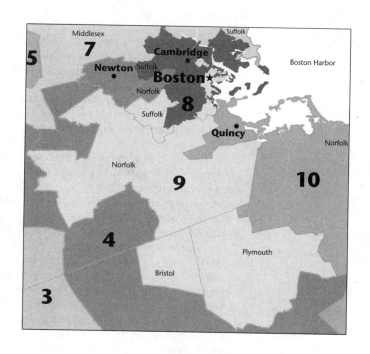

Sen. Edward M. Kennedy (D)

Elected 1962; 8th full term

CAPITOL OFFICE
224-4543
kennedy.senate.gov
317 Russell Bldg. 20510-2101; fax 224-2417

COMMITTEES
Armed Services
  (Seapower - chairman)
Health, Education, Labor & Pensions - chairman
Joint Economic

RESIDENCE
Hyannis Port

BORN
Feb. 22, 1932; Boston, Mass.

RELIGION
Roman Catholic

FAMILY
Wife, Victoria Reggie Kennedy; three children,
two stepchildren

EDUCATION
Harvard U., A.B. 1956 (government); International
Law School, The Hague (The Netherlands),
attended 1958; U. of Virginia, LL.B. 1959

MILITARY SERVICE
Army, 1951-53

CAREER
Lawyer

POLITICAL HIGHLIGHTS
Suffolk County assistant district attorney,
1961-62; sought Democratic nomination for
president, 1980

ELECTION RESULTS

2006 GENERAL
Edward M. Kennedy (D)	1,500,738	69.3%
Kenneth G. Chase (R)	661,532	30.5%

2006 PRIMARY
Edward M. Kennedy (D)	unopposed

PREVIOUS WINNING PERCENTAGES
2000 (73%); 1994 (58%); 1988 (65%); 1982 (61%);
1976 (69%); 1970 (62%); 1964 (74%); 1962 Special
Election (55%)

Kennedy's lineage, liberal views and legislative accomplishments ensure him a permanent place in the national consciousness. He is the last surviving son of Joseph P. Kennedy and the embodiment of his family's commitment to public service. He has endured numerous personal tragedies. And while past scandals limited him from advancing beyond the Senate, he has mastered the intricacies of the institution, fine-tuned the art of dealmaking and built tight bonds of friendship — all of which have helped him create and influence some of the landmark social legislation of modern times.

At the start of the 111th Congress (2009-10), Kennedy was second in seniority in the Senate — only to fellow Democrat Robert C. Byrd of West Virginia. And he is the third-longest-serving senator ever. He has been an anchor for his party's liberal base. Yet unlike many of his left-leaning colleagues, he has been more interested in making laws than staying on message, and will make a deal to get a bill passed. His Massachusetts Democratic colleague John Kerry said in 2008 of Kennedy's 46 years in the Senate: "Every major piece of legislation in that time, he's had an impact on one way or the other."

Queen Elizabeth II bestowed honorary knighthood on Kennedy in March 2009, an honor he called "moving and personal." But he can't be called "Sir Ted" — only British subjects are eligible for the formal designation.

Even into the 111th Congress, as his health remained touch-and-go since a May 2008 diagnosis of a malignant brain tumor, he kept atop discussions of major Democratic initiatives in Congress and the administration of Barack Obama, whose candidacy he had a strong hand in boosting with his endorsement. Kennedy retains the chairmanship of the Health, Education, Labor and Pensions (HELP) Committee, vowing to lead talks on health care reform legislation. He did, however, relinquish his longtime seat on the Judiciary panel in 2009. He remains the No. 2 Democrat on the Armed Services Committee.

Even before his cancer diagnosis, Kennedy had slowed physically and suffered chronic back pain. But few younger legislators can match his impact. "He's a bigger-than-life leader around this place, and I think he has tremendous gravitational pull for his party," former Oregon GOP Sen. Gordon H. Smith said in 2007. "If you want to get something, he's a great train to jump on."

Kennedy's policy portfolio is bursting. He has been at the forefront of recent efforts to promote faster adoption of electronic medical records, to lower the costs of prescription drugs and to allow students to get loans directly from the government. He has been a loud voice on behalf of organized labor, civil rights and environmental protection. He worked with the George W. Bush administration and Republicans to shape the education overhaul of 2001 and to create of a Medicare prescription drug benefit in 2003.

He helped push through the first overhaul of the nation's immigration laws in 1965 and a second in 1986. In 2006 and 2007, he led efforts, albeit unsuccessful, to combine border security measures with a new guest worker program and a pathway to citizenship for illegal immigrants currently in the country.

He was a leader of the fruitless Democratic effort to block Bush's Supreme Court nominations of John G. Roberts Jr. and Samuel A. Alito Jr. in the 109th Congress (2005-06). And he was one of just 23 senators who opposed the 2002 resolution authorizing the president to use military force in Iraq.

He sponsored a series of bills at the start of 2009 — to grant the Food and Drug Administration authority to regulate tobacco, to expand hate crimes law and to make it easier for unions to organize — but others had to lead debate during his absence while he struggled with his health. His bill to greatly expand national and community service programs was renamed in his honor before final passage. Kennedy, whose brother John F. Kennedy first issued a call to serve in his 1961 presidential inaugural address, has spent his career championing volunteer service.

But Kennedy didn't want to fully relinquish control of drafting health care reform legislation, which has long been among his priorities. He first introduced legislation to establish universal health care in 1969, and subsequently made repeated efforts at mandating employer coverage. In spring 2009, he worked in concert with Finance Chairman Max Baucus of Montana and Budget Chairman Kent Conrad of North Dakota on an expected wide-ranging initiative they planned to bring together on the Senate floor.

His presence on the Senate floor was infrequent in 2009, but in the past from his desk at the rear of the chamber, he often startled the somnolent with his thunderous roar, his face reddening and his voice needing no microphone. Republicans like to use him as a metaphor for the left, labeling Democrats at election time as "Ted Kennedy liberals." Behind the scenes, though, some of them nurture productive and friendly relationships with him.

Kennedy has won eight re-elections since his initial 1962 special-election win, only once dropping below 60 percent of the vote. His popularity back home stems not only from the tremendous influence he carries on national issues, but also for his attention to Massachusetts' needs. In 2005 he helped stop the planned closure of Otis Air Force Base on Cape Cod.

His public image has long been defined by family triumph, tragedy and scandal. He once had a penchant for reckless behavior. There was the 1969 auto accident at Chappaquiddick in which the passenger in his car, Mary Jo Kopechne, drowned; the long period of pub-crawling in the 1980s; and the 1991 revelry with his son, Democratic Rhode Island Rep. Patrick J. Kennedy, and nephew William Kennedy Smith at a Florida nightclub that ended with a woman accusing Smith of rape. (Smith was acquitted after a highly publicized trial.) Kennedy's personal life stabilized after 1992, when he married for the second time, to Washington attorney Victoria Reggie.

But doubts about his judgment fueled Republican hopes of defeating him in 1994, when venture capitalist Mitt Romney — later Massachusetts' governor and a 2008 GOP presidential candidate — tapped his personal fortune to mount a campaign tagging the senator as worn, used goods. Kennedy fought back, painting Romney as inexperienced. Bucking the year's GOP tide, Kennedy won with 58 percent of the vote. In 2000, he won his seventh full term with 73 percent against another wealthy businessman, Jack E. Robinson III.

The youngest of the nine children of Rose Fitzgerald, a congressman's daughter, and Joseph P. Kennedy, the first chairman of the Securities and Exchange Commission, Kennedy was elected in 1962, at age 30, to fill the remaining two years of President Kennedy's Senate term. At the time, Kennedy had little to show for himself; he had been kicked out of Harvard for cheating, and though he ultimately graduated after a stint in the Army and went on to earn a law degree, he had only held one full-time job as an assistant district attorney in Boston.

After John F. Kennedy was assassinated in 1963 and Sen. Robert F. Kennedy of New York was assassinated while seeking the Democratic presidential nomination in 1968, Kennedy felt intense pressure to take up his brothers' fallen banner. But when he challenged President Jimmy Carter in 1980, questions about Chappaquiddick exploded anew, and Kennedy failed to articulate a clear reason why he wanted to be president. For many, the most memorable moment of his campaign came at its finale, in his concession speech at the Democratic National Convention. "For all those whose cares have been our concern," Kennedy intoned, "the work goes on, the cause endures, the hope still lives, and the dream shall never die."

KEY VOTES

2008

Yes	Prohibit discrimination based on genetic information
?	Reauthorize farm and nutrition programs for five years
+	Limit debate on "cap and trade" system for greenhouse gas emissions
?	Allow lawsuits against companies that participated in warrantless wiretapping
Yes	Limit debate on a bill to block a scheduled cut in Medicare payments to doctors
?	Grant mortgage relief to homeowners and funding for Fannie Mae and Freddie Mac
?	Approve a nuclear cooperation agreement with India
?	Approve final $700 billion program to stabilize financial markets
?	Allow consideration of a $14 billion auto industry loan package

2007

Yes	Increase minimum wage by $2.10 an hour
Yes	Limit debate on a comprehensive immigration bill
Yes	Overhaul congressional lobbying and ethics rules for members and their staffs
Yes	Limit debate on considering a bill to add House seats for the District of Columbia and Utah
Yes	Limit debate on restoring habeas corpus rights to detainees
Yes	Mandate minimum breaks for troops between deployments to Iraq or Afghanistan
Yes	Override Bush veto of $23.2 billion water projects authorization bill
No	Confirm Michael B. Mukasey as attorney general
Yes	Limit debate on an energy policy overhaul containing $21.8 billion in tax incentives and reduced oil and gas subsidies

CQ VOTE STUDIES

	PARTY UNITY		PRESIDENTIAL SUPPORT	
	SUPPORT	OPPOSE	SUPPORT	OPPOSE
2008	99%	1%	18%	82%
2007	92%	8%	40%	60%
2006	99%	1%	48%	52%
2005	100%	0%	26%	74%
2004	98%	2%	59%	41%
2003	97%	3%	47%	53%
2002	97%	3%	64%	36%
2001	97%	3%	66%	34%
2000	98%	2%	94%	6%
1999	97%	3%	93%	7%

INTEREST GROUPS

	AFL-CIO	ADA	CCUS	ACU
2008	100%	60%	50%	0%
2007	87%	85%	64%	0%
2006	87%	100%	36%	0%
2005	93%	95%	28%	0%
2004	100%	100%	31%	0%
2003	100%	95%	26%	10%
2002	100%	100%	29%	0%
2001	100%	100%	38%	4%
2000	86%	90%	40%	12%
1999	88%	95%	47%	4%

Sen. John Kerry (D)

CAPITOL OFFICE
224-2742
kerry.senate.gov
218 Russell Bldg. 20510-2102; fax 224-8525

COMMITTEES
Commerce, Science & Transportation
  (Communications, Technology & the Internet
  - chairman)
Finance
Foreign Relations - chairman
Small Business & Entrepreneurship

RESIDENCE
Boston

BORN
Dec. 11, 1943; Denver, Colo.

RELIGION
Roman Catholic

FAMILY
Wife, Teresa Heinz Kerry; two children,
three stepchildren

EDUCATION
Yale U., B.A. 1966 (political science);
Boston College, J.D. 1976

MILITARY SERVICE
Navy, 1966-70

CAREER
Lawyer; county prosecutor

POLITICAL HIGHLIGHTS
Democratic nominee for U.S. House, 1972;
lieutenant governor, 1983-85; Democratic
nominee for president, 2004

ELECTION RESULTS

2008 GENERAL

John Kerry (D)	1,971,974	65.9%
Jeffrey K. Beatty (R)	926,044	31.0%
Robert J. Underwood (LIBERT)	93,713	3.1%

2008 PRIMARY

John Kerry (D)	342,446	68.9%
Edward J. O'Reilly (D)	154,395	31.1%

PREVIOUS WINNING PERCENTAGES
2002 (80%); 1996 (52%); 1990 (57%); 1984 (55%)

Elected 1984; 5th term

Kerry has carved out a powerful niche after a quarter-century in the Senate. He chairs the Foreign Relations Committee, giving him an influential voice on international affairs, and carries weight on such prominent domestic issues as global warming and the economy from his seats on two other powerful panels. Yet the 2004 presidential aspirant had to watch two of his former colleagues — one whose political ascension he helped propel — move to the White House, while another was chosen over him for a key Cabinet post.

Even among members of his party, Kerry has always struggled with an aloof, blue-blood image, something that hurt him in his bid to unseat President George W. Bush and something he has worked to overcome. Though he can boast of some legislative accomplishments, Democrats have embraced Kerry more warmly for his formidable fundraising ability.

As Foreign Relations chairman, Kerry seeks to work with President Obama, Vice President Joseph R. Biden Jr. and Secretary of State Hillary Rodham Clinton while still making his views distinct. He had expressed strong interest in the State job, but professed not to be bothered by his three ex-colleagues' advancement, citing the freedom he retains as a senator. "I am independent, call my shots," he told The New York Times in January 2009. "There are a lot of virtues, believe me."

He agrees with Obama on the need to emphasize diplomacy over military force in the Middle East. "Focusing on winning a war of ideas, as opposed to just killing terrorists, will not only enable us to defeat our enemies, it will also restore our ability to effect positive change in other arenas," Kerry told the Center for American Progress in July 2008. He supported a proposal Biden made, while serving as a senator, for conditioning military aid to Pakistan on efforts to fight al Qaeda and the Taliban. And he called for a rethinking of relations with Russia that includes deterring terrorism, approving new nuclear arms pacts and jointly restoring economic order to the world.

Kerry also hopes Russia and other nations can come together with the United States on combatting global warming, long one of his priorities. He warned in March 2009 that putting off action to curb greenhouse gases because of the global economic crisis amounted to "a mutual suicide pact," citing the seriousness of climate change.

Kerry is a member of the Finance Committee, where he seeks to increase the use of energy tax incentives as well as expand Medicaid. He also calls for shoring up the nation's infrastructure and included in Obama's $787 billion economic stimulus law a provision to allow transit projects to receive tax-exempt financing. He wants to explore how well tax treaties with other countries are working to fight tax evasion.

On the Commerce, Science and Transportation Committee, Kerry chairs the panel on Communications, Technology and the Internet. He seeks to work on such issues as promoting diversity in media ownership and improving communications networks for emergency-response workers.

A member and former chairman of the Small Business panel, Kerry teamed with Olympia J. Snowe of Maine, the panel's ranking Republican, on nanotechnology safety and energy legislation during the 110th Congress (2007-08).

It was at the Democratic convention to nominate Kerry for president in 2004 where Obama's keynote speech set in motion the Illinois senator's future in national politics. Kerry endorsed Obama in January 2008, just after Obama lost the New Hampshire primary to Clinton. Kerry subsequently took to the campaign trail to vigorously lambaste the Republican candidate, Arizona Sen.

John McCain, a friend and fellow Vietnam veteran whom he had considered as a potential running mate. Observers found his aggressiveness a stark contrast to his hesitance in countering GOP attacks in 2004. "If Kerry had conducted himself like this four years ago," Republican strategist John Weaver told The New Republic, "he might have been elected president."

Kerry lost his chance to topple Bush in a campaign that was marked by their frequent sparring over Iraq and the direction of U.S. foreign policy. Kerry ended up losing by 2.5 percentage points, receiving just over 59 million votes — 3 million fewer than Bush, but, as Kerry is fond of pointing out, 8 million more than Vice President Al Gore got in his 2000 race.

Kerry toyed with running again in 2008, but announced in January 2007 he would concentrate on pushing for an end to U.S. involvement in the Iraq War. The fact that Obama and Clinton topped early polls was a factor in his decision; another may have been an attempted joke a few months earlier about Bush that angry Republicans contended was an insult to U.S. troops. Kerry had stressed the importance of doing homework and studying hard: "If you don't, you get stuck in Iraq."

Kerry was pilloried by liberals for his 2002 vote in favor of authorizing the use of force in Iraq. But in the 110th he introduced several proposals to set a predetermined date for withdrawal.

As chairman of the Senate Select Committee on POW/MIA Affairs in the 102nd Congress (1991-92), he joined forces with McCain on a report that found no evidence that missing soldiers in Vietnam were still alive, helping pave the way for President Clinton to normalize diplomatic relations.

A former prosecutor, Kerry gained early prominence with his inquiry into the Bank of Credit and Commerce International scandal in the late 1980s. He was widely credited with spurring a federal investigation of BCCI officials, including Democratic power broker Clark Clifford.

Kerry has used his e-mail list to raise money for Democratic candidates throughout the country. Largely because of the inherited wealth of his wife, Teresa Heinz Kerry, he is one of Congress' richest members, with a net worth estimated by the Center for Responsive Politics of at least $284 million in 2007.

Kerry's immediate family was upper-middle class. His father was a Foreign Service officer and attorney. His mother was a nurse but also a member of the wealthy Forbes family. A relative paid for Kerry's education at elite prep schools in Switzerland and New England, and he subsequently attended Yale, where he delivered the class oration at graduation. He joined the Naval Reserve in college and entered active duty in 1966.

After rising to the rank of lieutenant in the Navy, Kerry became one of the nation's most prominent demonstrators against the Vietnam War when he returned to the United States. He got front-page coverage in 1971 when he asked the Foreign Relations Committee, "How do you ask a man to be the last man to die for a mistake?" He tried to exploit the publicity by moving to Lowell and running for an open House seat in 1972. He won the primary, but lost in the fall to Republican Paul Cronin.

After his defeat, he went to law school, then worked as an assistant district attorney in Middlesex County. He was elected lieutenant governor in a 1982 challenge to the Democratic establishment. Two years later, he beat Democratic Rep. James M. Shannon for the nomination to replace retiring Sen. Paul E. Tsongas. He won the general election over conservative businessman Raymond Shamie with 55 percent of the vote.

In 1996, he faced his toughest challenge from William F. Weld, then the state's popular GOP governor. But Kerry's late spending and solid performance in the debates carried him to victory. Republicans did not run a candidate against him in 2002, but in 2008 he easily dispatched lawyer Edward J. O'Reilly in the primary and coasted against Republican Jeffrey K. Beatty.

KEY VOTES

2008

Yes Prohibit discrimination based on genetic information
Yes Reauthorize farm and nutrition programs for five years
Yes Limit debate on "cap and trade" system for greenhouse gas emissions
Yes Allow lawsuits against companies that participated in warrantless wiretapping
Yes Limit debate on a bill to block a scheduled cut in Medicare payments to doctors
Yes Grant mortgage relief to homeowners and funding for Fannie Mae and Freddie Mac
Yes Approve a nuclear cooperation agreement with India
Yes Approve final $700 billion program to stabilize financial markets
+   Allow consideration of a $14 billion auto industry loan package

2007

Yes Increase minimum wage by $2.10 an hour
Yes Limit debate on a comprehensive immigration bill
Yes Overhaul congressional lobbying and ethics rules for members and their staffs
Yes Limit debate on considering a bill to add House seats for the District of Columbia and Utah
Yes Limit debate on restoring habeas corpus rights to detainees
Yes Mandate minimum breaks for troops between deployments to Iraq or Afghanistan
Yes Override Bush veto of $23.2 billion water projects authorization bill
No   Confirm Michael B. Mukasey as attorney general
Yes Limit debate on an energy policy overhaul containing $21.8 billion in tax incentives and reduced oil and gas subsidies

CQ VOTE STUDIES

	PARTY UNITY		PRESIDENTIAL SUPPORT	
	SUPPORT	OPPOSE	SUPPORT	OPPOSE
2008	98%	2%	30%	70%
2007	95%	5%	40%	60%
2006	95%	5%	51%	49%
2005	97%	3%	34%	66%
2004	100%	0%	50%	50%
2003	100%	0%	30%	70%
2002	92%	8%	72%	28%
2001	98%	2%	65%	35%
2000	96%	4%	97%	3%
1999	95%	5%	93%	7%

INTEREST GROUPS

	AFL-CIO	ADA	CCUS	ACU
2008	100%	95%	63%	4%
2007	95%	90%	50%	4%
2006	87%	95%	55%	12%
2005	93%	100%	33%	8%
2004	100%	25%	–	0%
2003	100%	85%	0%	13%
2002	92%	85%	55%	20%
2001	100%	95%	38%	4%
2000	75%	90%	53%	12%
1999	78%	95%	53%	0%

Rep. John W. Olver (D)

CAPITOL OFFICE
225-5335
www.house.gov/olver
1111 Longworth Bldg. 20515-2101; fax 226-1224

COMMITTEES
Appropriations
(Transportation-HUD - chairman)

RESIDENCE
Amherst

BORN
Sept. 3, 1936; Honesdale, Pa.

RELIGION
Unspecified

FAMILY
Wife, Rose Olver; one child

EDUCATION
Rensselaer Polytechnic Institute, B.S. 1955
(chemistry); Tufts U., M.S. 1956 (chemistry);
Massachusetts Institute of Technology, Ph.D.
1961 (chemistry)

CAREER
Professor

POLITICAL HIGHLIGHTS
Mass. House, 1969-73; Mass. Senate, 1973-91

ELECTION RESULTS

2008 GENERAL

John W. Olver (D)	215,696	72.8%
Nathan A. Bech (R)	80,067	27.0%

2008 PRIMARY

John W. Olver (D)	33,513	79.3%
Robert A. Feuer (D)	8,765	20.7%

2006 GENERAL

John W. Olver (D)	158,057	76.4%
William H. Szych (X)	48,574	23.5%

PREVIOUS WINNING PERCENTAGES
2004 (99%); 2002 (68%); 2000 (68%); 1998 (72%);
1996 (53%); 1994 (99%); 1992 (52%); 1991 Special
Election (50%)

Elected June 1991; 9th full term

Olver is a staunch liberal who prefers to yield the spotlight to other similarly ideological members. He may not be flashy, but he knows how the money flows: He is the only member of the Massachusetts delegation on the Appropriations Committee and uses his seat to direct dollars back home.

A solitary man, Olver enjoys perusing the details of spending bills. He believes it is the government's responsibility to solve society's problems and to play a part in economic development. "Better roads, bridges, airports, commuter rail systems and other public transit options are needed to connect people to educational centers, health and social services, and, perhaps most importantly, good jobs," he said in early 2007.

With that in mind, he supported President Obama's economic stimulus plan to help revive the nation's ailing economy. "We need a shock, an infusion of capital, to keep the economy from flat-lining," Olver said. And he supported a $410 billion catchall spending bill for fiscal 2009, which included nearly $44 million in earmarks — funding set-asides for special projects — that he helped secure for his district.

Securing earmarks is a common practice among appropriators, and Olver ranked among the most successful in 2008, directing $71.3 million toward 63 projects. The earmarks ranged from $705,000 for a telescope for the University of Massachusetts at Amherst, where he once taught chemistry, to $882,000 for a veterans' housing facility in Pittsfield.

Olver brushes off critics who call such parochial projects wasteful, noting earmarks are a tiny part of the overall budget and have their place in the process, especially in helping rural and less well-to-do regions. "We have a clearer idea of where the needs are in our districts," he said, comparing members' earmarks to grants given by federal agencies on a competitive basis, a process he said favors wealthier regions that can hire good grant writers.

He has not been as prolific as some in sponsoring legislation, he said, due to his responsibilities on Appropriations and as chairman of its panel on Transportation, Housing and Urban Development, where fights occur over funding for Amtrak and public housing. Olver also serves on the Appropriations Energy-Water Subcommittee and the panel funding the Interior Department.

Olver wants to increase federal funding for Amtrak, the national passenger rail system, and for public housing. A committed protector of Amtrak, he consistently opposed plans for the George W. Bush administration to end subsidies to the railroad absent congressional passage of a restructuring plan. Olver attracted attention when he refused to include money in a fiscal 2009 spending bill to help bail out the Highway Trust Fund, which was projected to run a $3.7 billion deficit. "This shortfall is not of this committee's making," he said.

A member of the Progressive Caucus, the most liberal faction of House Democrats, he opposed the war in Iraq from the start and sought to bar funding for the continued war effort. When Bush decided to boost the number of U.S. troops in Iraq by 21,000, Olver warned that the president "will be remembered for the deaths of many more American soldiers and Iraqi civilians."

At times, his passions can get the better of him. In 2007, Olver reportedly told liberal activists — when challenged about his refusal to endorse an impeachment resolution against Vice President Dick Cheney — that he believed the Bush administration might attack Iran and then use criticism of the attack as a pretext for canceling the 2008 presidential election. Olver later clarified, through a spokeswoman, that he did not mean his comments as any kind of prediction.

He also is outspoken on the issue of climate change, saying the nation must do more to reduce greenhouse gas emissions and to increase automobile fuel economy to help control global warming.

Olver was a founder of the House's Climate Change Caucus, whose members work to develop bipartisan agreements on climate issues. In the 110th Congress (2007-08), he pushed legislation to set caps on the amount of carbon dioxide emitted from the burning of fossil fuels and to create a market-based system that rewards companies for developing new technologies needed to combat climate change. In 2007, he also introduced a bill to create a market-driven system of greenhouse gas tradeable allowances to help reduce emissions.

Olver has a quiet personality, but he enjoys a challenge. Fit and trim in his early 70s, the 6-foot-4 inch Olver is an avid outdoorsman who still spends much of his free time hiking, rock climbing, wind surfing and cross-country skiing. He grew up on a farm in the Pocono area of Pennsylvania. His father ran the farm, which had 20 to 25 milking cows, and his mother tended their boardinghouse that welcomed young families who traveled by train from Philadelphia or New York. The Olver house fronted on a lake and had its own beach.

Olver attended a three-room schoolhouse, graduating at age 15. He finished college when he was 18 and earned a doctorate from the Massachusetts Institute of Technology at age 24. He taught chemistry at the University of Massachusetts' Amherst campus for eight years before making his first foray into politics, winning a state House race in 1968.

Four years later, he bucked the national GOP trend, unseating an incumbent Republican state senator. He stayed in the state Senate until 1991, when 17-term Silvio O. Conte, the liberal 1st District Republican, died in February. Olver won a 10-way Democratic primary with ease, then collected endorsements from his defeated rivals and from union members, environmentalists, women's groups and abortion rights supporters. He won the special election by fewer than 2,000 votes, marking the first time since 1892 that the area had sent a Democrat to the House.

He alternated close races in 1992 and 1996 (when he defeated Jane Swift, who would later serve as governor) with re-election romps in 1994 and 1998. His subsequent re-elections have been easy. In 2008, he easily fended off a primary challenge from Robert A. Feuer, then coasted to victory with 73 percent of the vote over Republican Nathan A. Bech, an Army veteran.

KEY VOTES

2008

Yes	Delay consideration of Colombia free-trade agreement
Yes	Override Bush veto of federal farm and nutrition programs reauthorization bill
No	Overhaul surveillance laws and permit dismissal of suits against companies that conducted warrantless wiretapping
Yes	Grant mortgage relief to homeowners and funding for Fannie Mae and Freddie Mac
Yes	Approve initial $700 billion program to stabilize financial markets
Yes	Approve final $700 billion program to stabilize financial markets
Yes	Provide $14 billion in loans to automakers

2007

Yes	Increase minimum wage by $2.10 an hour
Yes	Approve $124.2 billion in emergency war spending and set goal for redeployment of troops from Iraq
No	Reject federal contraceptive assistance to international family planning groups
Yes	Override Bush veto of $23.2 billion water projects authorization bill
No	Implement Peru free-trade agreement
Yes	Approve energy policy overhaul with new fuel economy standards
No	Clear $473.5 billion omnibus spending bill, including $70 billion for military operations

CQ VOTE STUDIES

	PARTY UNITY		PRESIDENTIAL SUPPORT	
	SUPPORT	OPPOSE	SUPPORT	OPPOSE
2008	100%	0%	14%	86%
2007	99%	1%	4%	96%
2006	96%	4%	15%	85%
2005	98%	2%	15%	85%
2004	98%	2%	21%	79%

INTEREST GROUPS

	AFL-CIO	ADA	CCUS	ACU
2008	100%	100%	56%	0%
2007	96%	90%	50%	0%
2006	100%	95%	40%	4%
2005	93%	95%	33%	0%
2004	100%	100%	19%	0%

MASSACHUSETTS 1

West – Pittsfield, Leominster, Westfield, Amherst

The oranges of autumn, the whites of winter and the greens of spring and summer attract vacationers to the 1st, which spans the western portion of the state. With three distinct geographical regions — the Berkshires, the Connecticut River Valley and the larger commuter towns to the northeast — the district embodies three vastly different population centers that rarely interact with one another.

Tourist areas include the kind of serene New England towns depicted in Norman Rockwell paintings. Tanglewood, the summer home of the Boston Symphony Orchestra, also attracts music fans to its outdoor theater in Lenox. The Yankee Candle Company, a large manufacturer of scented candles and a popular tourist attraction, is based in South Deerfield.

The region suffered heavy downsizing of its once-dominant textile mills, furniture manufacturing and plastics factories during a decades-long industry recession, with Pittsfield and Fitchburg suffering the most. Although Pittsfield's population loss has slowed after years of steady decline, the town's economy dipped again in 2009 with the closure of

hometown retail giant KB Toys. High foreclosure and unemployment rates in Fitchburg concern residents. A stable retail industry and an influx of Boston commuters may spur growth in Leominster, a western outgrowth of the Boston suburbs that sits at the junction of two major highways at the eastern edge of the district.

Once a Republican stronghold, the 1st still has some GOP-supporting, sparsely populated rural areas along the Connecticut border, but these last toeholds of Rockefeller Republicanism are overwhelmed by large numbers of Democratic union voters in the northeast, retirees in Berkshire County and university liberals around Amherst, where the state's flagship university is located. Barack Obama took 64 percent of the 2008 presidential vote here.

MAJOR INDUSTRY

Paper, tourism, higher education, plastics

CITIES

Pittsfield, 45,793; Leominster, 41,303; Westfield, 40,072; Holyoke, 39,838; Fitchburg, 39,102; West Springfield (unincorporated), 27,899

NOTABLE

William G. Morgan invented volleyball in 1895 in Holyoke, where the Volleyball Hall of Fame is currently located.

Rep. Richard E. Neal (D)

Elected 1988; 11th term

CAPITOL OFFICE
225-5601
www.house.gov/neal
2208 Rayburn Bldg. 20515; fax 225-8112

COMMITTEES
Ways & Means
 (Select Revenue Measures - chairman)

RESIDENCE
Springfield

BORN
Feb. 14, 1949; Worcester, Mass.

RELIGION
Roman Catholic

FAMILY
Wife, Maureen Neal; four children

EDUCATION
American International College, B.A. 1972
(political science); U. of Hartford, M.P.A. 1976

CAREER
College lecturer; teacher; mayoral aide

POLITICAL HIGHLIGHTS
Springfield City Council, 1978-84 (president, 1979);
mayor of Springfield, 1984-89

ELECTION RESULTS

2008 GENERAL

Richard E. Neal (D)	234,369	98.5%
write-ins	3,631	1.5%

2008 PRIMARY

Richard E. Neal (D)	unopposed

2006 GENERAL

Richard E. Neal (D)	164,939	98.7%
write-ins	2,254	1.3%

PREVIOUS WINNING PERCENTAGES
2004 (99%); 2002 (99%); 2000 (99%); 1998 (99%);
1996 (72%); 1994 (59%); 1992 (53%); 1990 (100%);
1988 (80%)

Neal, chairman of the Ways and Means tax-writing subcommittee, is positioning himself as one of the party's top figures on economic policy and a potential future chairman of the full committee. In his early 60s, he's among the youngest of the panel's senior members, but has proved his party loyalty and developed an in-depth knowledge of tax policy.

Chairman Charles B. Rangel of New York and four other Democrats sit between Neal and the gavel for the full committee, but even the youngest of those, John Lewis of Georgia, is nearly nine years older than Neal. Neal has been on Ways and Means for about 15 years, and has worked to close corporate tax loopholes, simplify the tax code and protect workers' pensions.

Admirers cite his ability to work with others. "He is a person who tries to accommodate everyone, and he does it with a tact and style that is appealing to everyone," Evan Dobelle, a former Carter administration and Democratic National Committee official, told The Republican of Springfield. Neal sees himself as a bipartisan legislator, and said he doesn't "have to be in the well of the House every day to explain how terrific I am." Nevertheless, he has difficulty breaking through decades of ideological deadlock over taxes.

As chairman of the Select Revenue Measures Subcommittee, he led his party's unsuccessful drive in 2007 to overhaul the alternative minimum tax, which threatens to hit millions of middle-income Americans, especially those who live in high-tax states or have big families. The tax was originally designed to ensure the richest people would have to pay some tax despite all the credits and deductions they might claim. But it was not indexed to inflation, and Congress has routinely enacted temporary "patches" to prevent it from growing.

Neal has championed the concept of automatically enrolling employees in an Individual Retirement Account, introducing a bill in the 110th Congress (2007-08) that applied to employers without a retirement plan. He lobbied President Obama on the idea and applauded when the president's first budget outline in March 2009 incorporated it. "It's clean, it's clear and it doesn't impose any onerous requirements on the employer," he said.

Another of Neal's priorities is to close tax loopholes. In the 110th he introduced legislation aimed at barring reduced-rate treatment of dividends from certain companies that avoid paying either U.S. or foreign income taxes, and he has continued to take aim at corporations that establish offshore operations to avoid U.S. taxation. His subcommittee also has held hearings on the tax treatment of derivatives and misclassification of workers as independent contractors.

But Neal also tries to protect the many financial services and insurance companies in his district. He has sponsored bills to make permanent a tax incentive that assists U.S. financial services companies with subsidiaries abroad. He wants to impose higher taxes on international re-insurance companies that compete with domestic firms.

The 2nd District residents of Springfield and its surrounding areas tend to be blue collar and Irish Catholic and are not as liberal as other voters in the state. Neal opposes federal funding of abortions and voted in favor of the 2003 ban on a procedure opponents call "partial-birth" abortion. He also voted in 2005 for a constitutional amendment allowing Congress to outlaw desecration of the U.S. flag. Yet in both 2004 and 2006, he voted against amending the Constitution to prohibit same-sex marriage.

In the past he has cast a swing vote on trade. Siding with labor and environment groups, he opposed the 2002 fast-track law giving the president author-ity to negotiate trade agreements without amendment by Congress. He voted for the 2007 Peru free-trade agreement that split Democrats but fit his belief the government should not stop globalization that can spur growth.

Neal has been a leader of congressional efforts to keep the United States involved in the search for peace in Northern Ireland. His paternal grand-parents are from Ireland, while his maternal grandparents are from North-ern Ireland; both sets were Irish nationalists.

Neal also is chairman of the congressional Friends of Ireland, and he has met on several occasions with leaders of both sides. They held a series of talks in March 2009 aimed at stopping a renewed burst of violence. Neal favors a power-sharing arrangement between factions that achieves a "par-ity of esteem."

As a former high school basketball player and the father of two boys who played at the college level, his passion for the game goes well beyond any sense of obligation he may feel as the representative of the city where bas-ketball was invented. His days on the court are rarer these days, but he's still a regular at the House gym.

Neal majored in political science in college and later was co-chairman of George McGovern's 1972 presidential campaign in western Massachusetts. After serving as an aide to Springfield Mayor William C. Sullivan, he won three elections to the city council. He also taught history and government at a high school and area colleges. In 1983, he won the first of three elections as Springfield mayor, drawing favorable notices for stimulating downtown rehabilitation. He still directs legislative efforts toward the city, securing funding for a new federal courthouse.

When Democrat Edward P. Boland announced his retirement in 1988 after 36 years in the House, Neal was quick off the mark. He won the nom-ination unopposed and crushed a weak GOP foe. He faced a couple of stiff challenges in the early 1990s — especially in 1994 when anti-incumbent fever was running high and Neal was being chastised for 87 overdrafts at the now-defunct private bank for House members. But Republicans have not fielded a challenger since 1996.

Even so, Neal has been a prolific fundraiser. He was among the top 10 House incumbents in early 2009 with the most campaign cash on hand, leading to speculation he was interested in a future Senate seat — some-thing his spokesman denied. The money could prove useful if Massachu-setts loses a House seat because of redistricting after the 2010 census, at which point he would be forced to run against another incumbent in 2012.

KEY VOTES

2008
Yes Delay consideration of Colombia free-trade agreement
Yes Override Bush veto of federal farm and nutrition programs reauthorization bill
No Overhaul surveillance laws and permit dismissal of suits against companies that conducted warrantless wiretapping
Yes Grant mortgage relief to homeowners and funding for Fannie Mae and Freddie Mac
Yes Approve initial $700 billion program to stabilize financial markets
Yes Approve final $700 billion program to stabilize financial markets
Yes Provide $14 billion in loans to automakers

2007
Yes Increase minimum wage by $2.10 an hour
Yes Approve $124.2 billion in emergency war spending and set goal for redeployment of troops from Iraq
No Reject federal contraceptive assistance to international family planning groups
Yes Override Bush veto of $23.2 billion water projects authorization bill
Yes Implement Peru free-trade agreement
Yes Approve energy policy overhaul with new fuel economy standards
No Clear $473.5 billion omnibus spending bill, including $70 billion for military operations

CQ VOTE STUDIES

	PARTY UNITY		PRESIDENTIAL SUPPORT	
	SUPPORT	OPPOSE	SUPPORT	OPPOSE
2008	100%	0%	14%	86%
2007	99%	1%	4%	96%
2006	96%	4%	18%	82%
2005	97%	3%	15%	85%
2004	98%	2%	24%	76%

INTEREST GROUPS

	AFL-CIO	ADA	CCUS	ACU
2008	100%	100%	61%	0%
2007	96%	95%	55%	0%
2006	100%	95%	36%	4%
2005	93%	85%	41%	0%
2004	100%	95%	33%	4%

MASSACHUSETTS 2

South central — Springfield, Chicopee, Northampton

The rolling hills and thick forests of the 2nd extend along the state's southern border from Springfield and Northampton in the west to Bellingham in the east. Springfield dwarfs all other communities in the 2nd; small, rural towns and intermittent farms fill out the rest of south-central Massachusetts.

The region's future rests with the insurance and health care industries — most notably MassMutual and Baystate Health System — which replaced some of Springfield's shrinking manufacturing base. Business parks are increasing commercial and industrial space, and service jobs and employment at Chicopee's Westover Air Reserve Base are also important to the area's economy.

The Basketball Hall of Fame and the recently restored MassMutual Center arena have brought more visitors to Springfield — a needed boost, as the city has experienced rising unemployment rates. New city programs and federal funds may prop up areas such as Old Hill, which have been hit hard by foreclosures.

Hispanics once gravitated to Springfield's North End but are now more dispersed through the city. Most blacks, although significantly fewer in number than Hispanics, live near the city's center. These two populations consist of well more than half of the city's total population, making Springfield the district's multicultural region.

Residents in and around Springfield, many of whom are blue-collar and Irish Catholic, vote Democratic and dominate the district's elections. Smith College, a large liberal arts college for women, produces a strongly liberal vote in Northampton. Despite this strong Democratic lean, some Republicans have been competitive, particularly among small-town and rural voters. In 2008, the 2nd gave Barack Obama 59 percent of its vote.

MAJOR INDUSTRY
Insurance, health care, higher education, tourism

CITIES
Springfield, 152,082; Chicopee, 54,653; Northampton, 28,978

NOTABLE
Theodor Geisel, better known as Dr. Seuss, was born in Springfield, where the Dr. Seuss National Memorial Sculpture Garden now sits at the Springfield Museums.

Rep. Jim McGovern (D)

Elected 1996; 7th term

CAPITOL OFFICE
225-6101
mcgovern.house.gov
438 Cannon Bldg. 20515-2103; fax 225-5759

COMMITTEES
Budget
Rules
  (Rules & the Organization of the House
  - chairman)

RESIDENCE
Worcester

BORN
Nov. 20, 1959; Worcester, Mass.

RELIGION
Roman Catholic

FAMILY
Wife, Lisa McGovern; two children

EDUCATION
American U., B.A. 1981 (history), M.P.A. 1984

CAREER
Congressional aide; campaign aide

POLITICAL HIGHLIGHTS
Sought Democratic nomination for
U.S. House, 1994

ELECTION RESULTS

2008 GENERAL

Jim McGovern (D)	227,619	98.5%
write-ins	3,488	1.5%

2008 PRIMARY

Jim McGovern (D)	unopposed

2006 GENERAL

Jim McGovern (D)	166,973	98.8%
write-ins	1,983	1.2%

PREVIOUS WINNING PERCENTAGES
2004 (71%); 2002 (99%); 2000 (99%); 1998 (57%);
1996 (53%)

McGovern is cut from the same liberal cloth as other more well-known Massachusetts public servants, such as Democratic Sens. Edward M. Kennedy and John Kerry and Rep. Barney Frank, chairman of the House Financial Services Committee. A thoughtful humanitarian, McGovern has a deep commitment to social and economic justice and is a vocal opponent of the Iraq War as well as continued U.S. military involvement in Afghanistan.

McGovern also has an encyclopedic knowledge of arcane House rules and procedures, a skill that serves him well from his seat on the Rules Committee, where he ranks just below Chairwoman Louise M. Slaughter of New York. He is an able bare-knuckle fighter in the committee's tartly partisan negotiations as it sets the parameters for floor debate, and he rejects GOP claims that Democrats are closing debate to Republicans. McGovern also has a seat on the Budget Committee.

Before his 1996 election, McGovern spent nearly two decades on Capitol Hill, first as an intern and campaign aide to South Dakota senator and presidential candidate George McGovern (no relation), and later on the staff of Joe Moakley, the Rules Committee chairman for five and a half years and dean of the Massachusetts House delegation until his death in 2001. "McGovern taught me it was OK to be an idealist," he told The Boston Globe. "Moakley taught me how to get things done."

McGovern recalls fondly his days working for the colorful Moakley, an old-fashioned, back-slapping pol who mentored him in politics. When Moakley died in 2001, McGovern moved quickly to get the vacancy on Rules. He said his goal is to follow Moakley as chairman.

McGovern was named co-chairman of the Congressional Human Rights Caucus in 2008, after the death of its longtime chairman, California Democrat Tom Lantos. Later that year, McGovern convinced House colleagues to pass a resolution creating a Tom Lantos Human Rights Commission to draw attention to human rights abuses and became its first chairman.

McGovern in early 2009 pursued legislation to limit the use of cluster bombs that are dropped from warplanes and are blamed in numerous civilian deaths.

The co-chairman of the House Hunger Caucus, McGovern also brings attention to the increasing problem of national and global hunger. He pledged to pursue legislation during the 111th Congress (2009-10) incorporating recommendations from international relief groups to require the Obama administration to appoint an international hunger coordinator in the White House and to restore the House Select Committee on Hunger, which was disbanded in 1994.

McGovern is not shy about taking his humanitarian beliefs out into the street. He was one of five House members arrested during a 2006 protest outside the Sudanese embassy in Washington, D.C., to protest the killing of civilians in Darfur.

"The Sudanese government will say it has nothing to do with the violence. They are liars," McGovern told students at the College of the Holy Cross during an April 2007 speech. "They cannot be counted on to keep their word." He also suggested the United States boycott the 2008 Olympics in China to protest China's friendly relations with Sudan.

McGovern has long held a keen interest in foreign affairs, particularly in Latin America. He came under criticism from conservatives in 2008 after he agreed to help the families of hostages held by leftist guerrillas in Colombia by interceding with the rebels, known as the FARC. McGovern rejected the criticism that he was aiding the rebels. "By caring about Americans and Colombians that are held hostage by the FARC, you somehow support the FARC? I've never heard anything so ludicrous in my life," he said.

He is also a strong voice against the Iraq War, introducing legislation in 2007 requiring complete withdrawal of U.S. forces within six months and pressing House leaders for a vote on it. He joined with a bipartisan group of anti-war House members in early 2009 to protest the continuing U.S. military presence in Afghanistan, as well as Obama's plan to expand it. "I have a sinking feeling that we are getting deeper and deeper into a war that has no end," he said.

McGovern backed all the major legislation aimed at bolstering the economy in 2008 and 2009, including bills aimed at rescuing struggling banks and auto makers and President Obama's stimulus legislation. He wrote the rule governing the floor debate for the $410 billion catchall spending bill for fiscal 2009. When voting for the bill, he said, "I believe that we need to do whatever humanly possible to get this economy back on track and to help the American people."

McGovern's parochial priorities have included providing improved commuter rail service in his district, more funding for open-space preservation and incentives for firms to develop renewable energy sources.

During his childhood in working-class Worcester — his father ran a liquor store and his mother taught dance — the McGoverns followed politics closely, especially where the Kennedy family was involved. He said that when Sen. Robert F. Kennedy was assassinated in 1968, "My father gathered us around the kitchen table and we wrote sympathy cards to Ethel," his wife.

He had his first brush with politics as a junior high school student in 1972, when he became involved in the campaign of presidential candidate McGovern. Later, as an American University student, he worked in McGovern's Senate office. In 1984, when the South Dakotan launched another presidential bid, McGovern was his campaign manager in Massachusetts and made the nominating speech at the Democratic National Convention. The elder McGovern returned the favor in 1996, campaigning for him in his House race.

McGovern had made an unsuccessful bid in 1994 for the 3rd District seat, but in 1996 he upset two-term Republican Peter I. Blute, and he has won easily since. During the 2004 presidential campaign, McGovern actively campaigned for John Kerry while many of his colleagues were gearing up to run for Kerry's Senate seat. McGovern was returning a favor; Kerry went out of his way to appear at a campaign event for him when few gave him much chance of beating Blute.

KEY VOTES

2008

Yes Delay consideration of Colombia free-trade agreement
Yes Override Bush veto of federal farm and nutrition programs reauthorization bill
No   Overhaul surveillance laws and permit dismissal of suits against companies that conducted warrantless wiretapping
Yes Grant mortgage relief to homeowners and funding for Fannie Mae and Freddie Mac
Yes Approve initial $700 billion program to stabilize financial markets
Yes Approve final $700 billion program to stabilize financial markets
Yes Provide $14 billion in loans to automakers

2007

Yes Increase minimum wage by $2.10 an hour
Yes Approve $124.2 billion in emergency war spending and set goal for redeployment of troops from Iraq
No   Reject federal contraceptive assistance to international family planning groups
Yes Override Bush veto of $23.2 billion water projects authorization bill
No   Implement Peru free-trade agreement
Yes Approve energy policy overhaul with new fuel economy standards
No   Clear $473.5 billion omnibus spending bill, including $70 billion for military operations

CQ VOTE STUDIES

	PARTY UNITY		PRESIDENTIAL SUPPORT	
	SUPPORT	OPPOSE	SUPPORT	OPPOSE
2008	99%	1%	13%	87%
2007	99%	1%	4%	96%
2006	98%	2%	23%	77%
2005	99%	1%	15%	85%
2004	98%	2%	21%	79%

INTEREST GROUPS

	AFL-CIO	ADA	CCUS	ACU
2008	100%	100%	50%	0%
2007	100%	95%	50%	0%
2006	100%	95%	40%	4%
2005	93%	100%	35%	0%
2004	93%	100%	38%	4%

MASSACHUSETTS 3

Central and south — Worcester, Attleboro, part of Fall River

The 3rd cuts a diagonal sliver from the mountains of Princeton to the fishing community of Fall River, winding its way from areas north and west of Boston almost to the Atlantic Ocean far south of the city.

Worcester, a city with working-class roots, is the 3rd District's population center. The city, which is the second-largest in the state after Boston, has a strong biotech industry and centralized its health care and research facilities into a medical center, spurring economic development and job growth. Worcester's emphasis on economic expansion and the presence of low housing costs relative to those in Boston were expected to draw residents to the area. With some of the highest foreclosure rates in the nation, however, Worcester's housing market has suffered recently. Local officials hope that planned revitalization projects for the downtown area will support continued development. Suburban communities outside of Worcester are home to commuters who work in Providence, R.I., and Boston.

At the district's southern tip, Fall River (shared with the 4th District) has long been a bastion of white, blue-collar, ethnic Democrats. The one-time textile hub has struggled for most of the past century during periods of high unemployment and shortages of affordable housing. Fall River had one of the state's highest unemployment rates in the 1990s before increased employment lowered the figure to roughly 5 percent in 2000. Early in 2009, the unemployment rate in Fall River exceeded 16 percent, nearly twice the state average.

Democratic dominance in Worcester and Fall River allows Democrats to overcome Republican support in the towns surrounding Worcester. Barack Obama took 67 percent of the 2008 presidential vote in Worcester, and he won in the district as a whole with 58 percent.

MAJOR INDUSTRY
Biotech, health care, heavy manufacturing, retail

CITIES
Worcester, 172,648; Fall River (pt.), 53,704; Attleboro, 42,068

NOTABLE
The Worcester Art Museum, home to an internationally recognized collection of paintings, sculptures, decorative arts, textiles and photography, boasts the nation's largest collection of Antiochian mosaics.

Rep. Barney Frank (D)

CAPITOL OFFICE
225-5931
www.house.gov/frank
2252 Rayburn Bldg. 20515-2104; fax 225-0182

COMMITTEES
Financial Services - chairman

RESIDENCE
Newton

BORN
March 31, 1940; Bayonne, N.J.

RELIGION
Jewish

FAMILY
Single

EDUCATION
Harvard U., A.B. 1962 (government), J.D. 1977

CAREER
Lawyer; mayoral and congressional aide

POLITICAL HIGHLIGHTS
Mass. House, 1973-81

ELECTION RESULTS

2008 GENERAL

Barney Frank (D)	203,032	68.0%
Earl Henry Sholley (R)	75,571	25.3%
Susan Allen (I)	19,848	6.6%

2008 PRIMARY

Barney Frank (D)	unopposed

2006 GENERAL

Barney Frank (D)	176,513	98.5%
write-ins	2,730	1.5%

PREVIOUS WINNING PERCENTAGES
2004 (78%); 2002 (99%); 2000 (75%); 1998 (98%);
1996 (72%); 1994 (99%); 1992 (68%); 1990 (66%);
1988 (70%); 1986 (89%); 1984 (74%); 1982 (60%);
1980 (52%)

Elected 1980; 15th term

Acerbic, fast-talking and famously impatient with those who ask foolish questions, Frank has cemented his standing as the House's leading expert on the financial world. His formidable intellect and zest for striking deals have won him respect from his party's leaders and Republicans, and he has become an increasingly familiar public figure — even as a parody target on "Saturday Night Live."

A passionate liberal, Frank deepened his influence in 2008 by guiding into law two pieces of legislation aimed at staving off another Great Depression. He has taken on an equally prominent role as he leads efforts to stem the economic crisis while seeking to overhaul the regulatory structure governing financial markets.

As chairman of the Financial Services Committee, Frank took the lead in reworking and steering to enactment the George W. Bush administration's $700 billion financial industry rescue plan. Not only did he work closely with Republicans behind the scenes, he regularly appeared before reporters to explain why the unpopular effort needed quick approval. Speaker Nancy Pelosi of California labeled him a "maestro" when the House passed the measure Oct. 3, four days after it rejected an earlier version.

Several Democrats attributed their decision to support the bill the second time around to Frank's considerable powers of persuasion. Fellow Massachusetts Democrat Stephen F. Lynch called the administration's original plan "a non-starter" and said "the only reason it got consideration was because of Barney Frank." Conservatives, however, remain distrustful of his activist approach. "Barney has a great deal of faith in government's ability to solve people's problems," New Jersey GOP Rep. Scott Garrett, a frequent Financial Services opponent of Frank's, told The New Yorker in January 2009. "The question is whether that faith is justified."

His alliance with Bush's Treasury secretary, Henry M. Paulson Jr., helped make the effort a reality. Several months earlier, the two combined forces on legislation to help 400,000 homeowners facing foreclosure and prevent troubled mortgage giants Fannie Mae and Freddie Mac from collapsing. "I thought it was remarkable when I came down here to find someone who had not been in the private sector and the capital markets who understood the capital markets as well as Barney Frank did," Paulson told The Washington Post.

Frank understands more than just capital markets. He has amassed an encyclopedic knowledge of public policy and parliamentary rules, which he employs with precision as one of the House's most adept debaters.

Frank delights in exploiting confusion in the Republican ranks. "The right hand doesn't know what the far right hand is doing," he once observed. When the first financial rescue bill failed to pass, GOP leaders said a dozen Republicans had been ready to support it but were turned off by a partisan Pelosi floor speech. Frank pounced. "Give me those 12 people's names," he said, "and I will go talk uncharacteristically nicely to them and tell them what wonderful people they are and maybe they'll now think about the country."

In the 111th Congress (2009-10), Frank plans to tackle a regulatory overhaul of the entire financial services industry, something he said was necessary to win support for further rescue efforts. He called for an entity to oversee a revamped regulatory system as well as legislation to outlaw certain credit card billing practices and some mortgage products.

Frank has not always been such an ardent advocate of regulation. Before the market collapse of 2008, he displayed a financial pragmatism grounded in the knowledge that a hands-off approach sometimes was the best choice when dealing with the economy and financial markets.

On the issue closest to his heart — affordable housing — Frank was the most potent critic of Bush's attempts to cut spending on rent assistance for low-income families. After years of infighting, he won inclusion in the 2008 housing legislation of provisions to establish an affordable-housing trust fund.

Until the 108th Congress (2003-04), when he became top Democrat on Financial Services, Frank also served on the Judiciary Committee. While on that panel he was a staunch advocate of civil rights and civil liberties.

Frank was the first House member to acknowledge his homosexuality and does not shy away from allusions to his personal life. He quipped to The New York Times in May 2008 that asking the Republican White House to support more government intervention was "like asking me to judge the Miss America contest — if your heart's not in it, you don't do a very good job."

He has been on the front line opposing Republican-led attempts to ban same-sex marriage, but he does not reflexively align with gay rights organizations. Several attacked him in 2007 for his decision to remove transgender people from a long-sought bill to protect gays, lesbians and bisexuals from job discrimination. He responded by warning against overreaching: "People who then denounce those who take reality into account…make it impossible to govern."

Frank's honesty about his homosexuality since he came out in 1987 helped him survive politically three years later when the House reprimanded him after a male prostitute revealed he'd had an affair with Frank and had run his business out of the lawmaker's Washington apartment. His mostly urban constituents took the scandal in stride: They re-elected him with 66 percent of the vote that year.

Frank grew up in Bayonne, N.J., the son of a truck stop operator on the New Jersey Turnpike. The Franks loved to discuss politics, and all four of the Frank children went on to careers tied to government service. Frank's sister is Ann Lewis, a longtime Democratic operative.

Frank graduated from Harvard and considered a life in academia. But he went to work instead as an aide to Boston Mayor Kevin White in 1967. He was a natural, though he did not fit the establishment mold. Still, he was elected to the Massachusetts House in 1972 and stayed for eight years. When Democratic Rep. Robert F. Drinan, a liberal Catholic priest, bowed to a papal prohibition on clergymen holding public office, Frank ran for his seat, winning in 1980 with 52 percent of the vote. He hasn't dropped below 60 percent of the vote since then.

KEY VOTES

2008

Yes Delay consideration of Colombia free-trade agreement
Yes Override Bush veto of federal farm and nutrition programs reauthorization bill
No Overhaul surveillance laws and permit dismissal of suits against companies that conducted warrantless wiretapping
Yes Grant mortgage relief to homeowners and funding for Fannie Mae and Freddie Mac
Yes Approve initial $700 billion program to stabilize financial markets
Yes Approve final $700 billion program to stabilize financial markets
Yes Provide $14 billion in loans to automakers

2007

Yes Increase minimum wage by $2.10 an hour
Yes Approve $124.2 billion in emergency war spending and set goal for redeployment of troops from Iraq
No Reject federal contraceptive assistance to international family planning groups
Yes Override Bush veto of $23.2 billion water projects authorization bill
Yes Implement Peru free-trade agreement
Yes Approve energy policy overhaul with new fuel economy standards
No Clear $473.5 billion omnibus spending bill, including $70 billion for military operations

CQ VOTE STUDIES

	PARTY UNITY		PRESIDENTIAL SUPPORT	
	SUPPORT	OPPOSE	SUPPORT	OPPOSE
2008	99%	1%	14%	86%
2007	99%	1%	4%	96%
2006	96%	4%	15%	85%
2005	96%	4%	15%	85%
2004	98%	2%	16%	84%

INTEREST GROUPS

	AFL-CIO	ADA	CCUS	ACU
2008	100%	100%	61%	0%
2007	96%	95%	60%	0%
2006	100%	95%	29%	12%
2005	93%	100%	33%	0%
2004	100%	100%	20%	4%

MASSACHUSETTS 4

New Bedford; Boston suburbs — Newton; Taunton; part of Fall River

Downtowns replete with 18th- and 19th-century town hall buildings dot the Yankee communities in the 4th, several of which have celebrated their 300th or 350th anniversaries. The district skips from thickly settled Boston suburbs south through rural cranberry bogs and encompasses urban New Bedford and parts of Fall River (shared with the 3rd District).

The economic health of the 4th reflects a split between the northern and southern tiers of the district. The economies of the northern well-to-do towns and Boston's commuter-settled suburbs benefited from the Route 128 technology corridor, although some high-tech jobs have moved closer in to Boston and Cambridge. The southern fishing and former textile mill communities, including Fall River and New Bedford, struggle to stave off double-digit unemployment rates, and these areas have felt the sting of recent economic downturns. Fishing remains an important industry and way of life here. In the 4th's center, the cranberry bogs in Middleborough and biotech firms farther north provide a strong economic base.

Other communities hit by rising unemployment, such as Taunton, hope that expansion of industrial parks and job creation programs will boost the local economy.

The blue-collar, immigrant-laden southern section of the district gives the 4th a strong Democratic lean. New Bedford, which has one of the lowest median household incomes in the state, and Fall River are heavily Portuguese and vote solidly Democratic. Westport, located south of Fall River and west of New Bedford, adds Democratic votes. The wealthy northwestern towns of Wellesley, Dover and Sherborn are more competitive, but the well-to-do and densely populated Newton and Brookline opt for liberal Democrats. The district gave Barack Obama 63 percent of its votes in the 2008 presidential election.

MAJOR INDUSTRY
Fishing, cranberries, health care

CITIES
New Bedford, 93,768; Newton, 83,829; Brookline (unincorp.), 57,107; Taunton, 55,976; Fall River (pt.), 38,234; Wellesley (unincorp.), 26,613

NOTABLE
Ocean Spray, the first producer of cranberry juice drinks, is headquartered in Lakeville-Middleborough.

Rep. Niki Tsongas (D)

Elected October 2007; 1st full term

CAPITOL OFFICE
225-3411
tsongas.house.gov
1607 Longworth Bldg. 20515-2105; fax 226-0771

COMMITTEES
Armed Services
Budget
Natural Resources

RESIDENCE
Lowell

BORN
April 26, 1946; Chico, Calif.

RELIGION
Episcopalian

FAMILY
Widowed; three children

EDUCATION
Michigan State U., attended 1964-65;
Smith College, B.A. 1968 (religion); Boston U.,
J.D. 1988

CAREER
College public affairs official; lawyer; homemaker;
paralegal; social worker

POLITICAL HIGHLIGHTS
No previous office

ELECTION RESULTS

2008 GENERAL

Niki Tsongas (D)	225,947	98.7%
write-ins	2,960	1.3%

2008 PRIMARY

Niki Tsongas (D)	unopposed

2007 SPECIAL

Niki Tsongas (D)	54,359	51.3%
Jim Ogonowski (R)	47,782	45.1%
Patrick Murphy (I)	2,175	2.0%
Kurt Hayes (I)	1,126	1.1%

Tsongas is the widow of a prominent national politician — Sen. Paul E. Tsongas — but keeps a relatively low profile on the Hill, preferring to focus on shoring up support at home. A staunch economic and social liberal, she said finding ways to help smaller cities and their low-income residents is a top goal.

As the first woman from Massachusetts to be elected to Congress in more than 25 years, Tsongas (SONG-us) works hard to retain the support of voters who first put her in office in a 2007 special election. She makes it a habit of holding office hours in local supermarkets, greeting constituents at a small table set up inside. She also visits libraries and post offices as part of her "Congress on Your Corner" sessions on Saturdays.

As the sole Massachusetts member on the House Armed Services Committee, Tsongas looks out for the fate of the next generation of Navy destroyers. Raytheon Co., which is building electronic and combat systems for the *Zumwalt*-class destroyer, is a local employer in the district and Tsongas has intensely questioned Navy officials about their future building plans.

She also has taken up the antiwar mantle on Armed Services from her Democratic predecessor, Martin T. Meehan. Tsongas has pressed for the withdrawal of U.S. troops from Iraq, which she compares to Vietnam. The first bill she introduced as a member of the House would have set deadlines for a military withdrawal.

She reacted to President Obama's February 2009 decision to draw down troops there by promising to ensure his plan was timely and would guarantee their safe return. "I believe it is critical that we continue to work to engage the international community to ensure political stability in the region," she told the Lowell Sun.

The daughter of an Air Force engineer and representative of a district with many veterans, Tsongas takes particular interest in her seat on the panel's Military Personnel Subcommittee. In early 2009, she pushed for passage of two bills aimed at improving mental health care for veterans. One would require the Department of Veterans Affairs to report vacancies in mental health professional positions at facilities on a quarterly basis. The other would create a pilot program to train counselors at higher education facilities to recognize the signs of post-traumatic stress disorder.

A member of the Budget Committee, she has backed efforts to revive the ailing U.S. economy, including Obama's $787 billion economic stimulus law, saying, "Inaction is not an option." She also supported a $700 billion plan in fall 2008 to shore up the nation's financial system. And she backed Obama's first budget blueprint, applauding its plans for health care reform and climate change and its funding for education.

But she also has joined with Democratic Chairman John M. Spratt Jr. of South Carolina to push pay-as-you-go budgeting, which requires all new tax cuts and increased mandatory spending to be offset by savings elsewhere in the budget. Tsongas also is a member of the Natural Resources Committee.

Her views on social issues are uniformly liberal. One of her first official actions in the House was to join her party in an unsuccessful attempt to override President George W. Bush's veto of legislation expanding the State Children's Health Insurance Program, which covers children from low-income families that do not qualify for Medicaid. She supported a nearly identical measure in early 2009 that Obama signed into law.

She also said she favored all six signature pieces of legislation Democrats steered to House passage in early 2007, including a minimum wage increase and a bill giving the government the authority to negotiate prescription drug prices on behalf of Medicare beneficiaries. She also opposes a ban on gay marriage and supports abortion rights. She supported two bills in early 2009 aimed at strengthening the ability of workers to combat wage discrimination.

Born in the foothills of California's Cascade Range, Tsongas lived for five years in Chico, but rarely stayed in place for long after that. Her father, who survived the attack on Pearl Harbor, moved frequently in his military job with stops in Germany, Japan, Texas and Virginia. Her mother was a painter and also worked as a copywriter. Tsongas was 14 when she got interested in politics. It was 1960, and she was with her grandmother aboard a military ship headed across the Pacific Ocean to Japan when presidential nominee John F. Kennedy gave his acceptance speech at the Democrats' national convention in Los Angeles. The two listened to the address over the radio.

During the summer between her junior and senior years at Smith College, she interned at a banking investment company in Washington, D.C., where she met her future husband, who was interning for former Republican Rep. F. Bradford Morse of Massachusetts.

In 1968, Tsongas became an activist for the "Get Clean for Gene" campaign of Minnesota Sen. Eugene McCarthy, an antiwar Democrat running an unsuccessful campaign for president. Tsongas helped her husband get elected in 1974 to the U.S. House, where he served two terms before winning a seat in the Senate. Tsongas was a stay-at-home mother until Paul was diagnosed with cancer and retired from Congress in 1985. For years she had attended law school at night and eventually earned a degree from Boston University in 1988. She then co-founded the first all-female law firm in Lowell.

Her husband made a brief return to politics in 1991, losing a bid for the Democratic presidential nomination. Suffering complications from his earlier cancer treatment, he died in 1997 at age 55.

Tsongas' name recognition helped in the race to succeed Meehan, an eight-term Democrat who resigned to become chancellor of the University of Massachusetts at Lowell. And she had the endorsements of some influential Democratic friends, including former President Clinton, House Speaker Nancy Pelosi of California and Massachusetts Sen. Edward M. Kennedy. But she had to spend heavily and was distracted by the death of her sister.

Her Republican opponent, Jim Ogonowski, a retired Air Force officer, drew attention and sympathy for his connection to the Sept. 11 tragedy. His brother was the pilot of the first airplane to be hijacked and flown into the World Trade Center. Nevertheless, Tsongas prevailed 51 percent to 45 percent. She ran unopposed in 2008.

KEY VOTES

2008
Yes Delay consideration of Colombia free-trade agreement
Yes Override Bush veto of federal farm and nutrition programs reauthorization bill
No Overhaul surveillance laws and permit dismissal of suits against companies that conducted warrantless wiretapping
Yes Grant mortgage relief to homeowners and funding for Fannie Mae and Freddie Mac
Yes Approve initial $700 billion program to stabilize financial markets
Yes Approve final $700 billion program to stabilize financial markets
Yes Provide $14 billion in loans to automakers

2007
Yes Override Bush veto of $23.2 billion water projects authorization bill
No Implement Peru free-trade agreement
Yes Approve energy policy overhaul with new fuel economy standards
No Clear $473.5 billion omnibus spending bill, including $70 billion for military operations

CQ VOTE STUDIES

	PARTY UNITY		PRESIDENTIAL SUPPORT	
	SUPPORT	OPPOSE	SUPPORT	OPPOSE
2008	99%	1%	15%	85%
2007	100%	0%	11%	89%

INTEREST GROUPS

	AFL-CIO	ADA	CCUS	ACU
2008	100%	100%	56%	0%
2007	100%	–	60%	0%

MASSACHUSETTS 5
North central — Lowell, Lawrence, Haverhill

More than a generation ago, billowing smokestacks put Lawrence and Lowell among the nation's leading industrial centers. Today, the cities remain blue-collar, strongly Democratic population hubs for the 5th, but the wealthy suburbs and rural communities — home to technology workers and some of the nation's most prestigious preparatory schools — give the district a more upscale flavor.

Manufacturing-based jobs are still vital to struggling Lawrence, where unemployment rates have risen to twice the statewide average. The town is no stranger to high unemployment: rates spiked in the early 1990s and again during recent nationwide economic downturns. Immigration has pushed Lawrence's growing Hispanic population, which is composed mostly of Dominicans and Puerto Ricans, into the majority and given Lawrence a Latin flavor, confirmed by the city's many ethnic restaurants.

Lowell and its surrounding suburbs largely succeeded in reinventing themselves following declines at once-major area employers. The retooled economic base attracted software firms and other technology companies, and previous economic upswings spurred growth in small towns where aging buildings that once housed textile mills and then defense contractors became homes for start-ups and financial services firms. But the area is now experiencing further economic struggles. Lowell — increasingly more diverse with a significant Cambodian population — has sought to become a cultural hub, and now boasts the nation's largest free folk festival.

The southern part of the 5th is generally wealthy, with Carlisle, Sudbury, Harvard and Bolton all registering six-figure median household incomes. Republican candidates can be competitive in these areas, but the district overall supports Democrats at the state and federal level. Barack Obama took the district with 59 percent of the vote in the 2008 presidential race.

MAJOR INDUSTRY
Computer software, defense manufacturing, light manufacturing

CITIES
Lowell, 105,167; Lawrence, 72,043; Haverhill, 58,969; Methuen, 43,789

NOTABLE
Concord was the site of the first day of fighting in the Revolutionary War on April 19, 1775 (now celebrated each year as Patriots Day).

Rep. John F. Tierney (D)

Elected 1996; 7th term

Tierney is an unwavering liberal with an interest in providing universal health care, publicly financing elections, improving public schools and creating more "green jobs" in the renewable-energy field. He can be persistent in pursuing his goals; if his bills don't pass in one Congress, he regularly re-introduces them in the next one, then the one after that.

For all of his interest in domestic issues, Tierney also makes his voice heard on foreign policy. He shares President Obama's commitment to engaging a wider number of nations and has pledged to help the administration define its goals abroad. As chairman of the Oversight and Government Reform Committee's National Security and Foreign Affairs panel, he will evaluate the administration's plan to bring stability to Afghanistan and its nuclear-armed neighbor, Pakistan. He also serves on the Select Intelligence Committee.

Tierney votes in lockstep with Massachusetts' all-Democratic House delegation, taking his party's side in every Congress on at least 95 percent of the votes that divide a majority of Democrats and Republicans. He has been overshadowed by his higher-profile Bay State colleagues, including Financial Services Chairman Barney Frank and Select Energy Independence and Global Warming Chairman Edward J. Markey. But he is close with Speaker Nancy Pelosi of California — Pelosi's daughter Christine was his chief of staff from 2001 to 2005 — and that relationship paid dividends when Democrats assumed control of the House in 2007.

That year, Pelosi granted Tierney a seat on the Democratic Steering Committee — which sets committee assignments — as well as the Select Intelligence and Education and Labor committees. From his Oversight and Government Reform post, he criticized the George W. Bush administration's policies on everything from defense contracting to its approach toward Pakistan and Iran. He gained notice for blasting Army officials early in 2007 after a Washington Post report about inadequate patient care at Walter Reed Army Medical Center, where injured soldiers from Iraq and Afghanistan and other veterans are treated.

But he wasn't just talk. In 2007, the House adopted his amendment to the State Department's spending bill providing $75 million to help Pakistan expand educational programs separate from the Islamic madrassas thought to encourage radicalism. He also asserted congressional authority to examine contracting decisions, leading a successful effort to create a Wartime Contracting Commission to audit contracts as part of the 2008 defense authorization bill.

Tierney also used his position on Education and Labor to raise his profile. In February 2008, the House passed a higher education bill, eventually signed by Bush, that incorporated Tierney's proposals requiring states to maintain their own funding levels for public universities even as federal aid increased. It also included his language to forgive federal student loans taken by graduates who work in certain public service professions.

He joined fellow liberal Hilda L. Solis of California — now Obama's secretary of Labor — in getting a provision in a 2007 energy law authorizing $125 million to establish state and national job training programs in the renewable-energy and energy efficiency fields. "An increase in green jobs would help to address job shortages, meet industry demand for a skilled work force, and boost America's global competitiveness," he said in 2008.

But Tierney can sometimes push moderates in his party too hard. A case in point came in May 2008 when he proposed an amendment to the 2009 defense authorization bill that would have stripped $1 billion in funding for

CAPITOL OFFICE
225-8020
www.house.gov/tierney
2238 Rayburn Bldg. 20515; fax 225-5915

COMMITTEES
Education & Labor
Oversight & Government Reform
  (National Security & Foreign Affairs - chairman)
Select Intelligence

RESIDENCE
Salem

BORN
Sept. 18, 1951; Salem, Mass.

RELIGION
Unspecified

FAMILY
Wife, Patrice Tierney

EDUCATION
Salem State College, B.A. 1973
(political science); Suffolk U., J.D. 1976

CAREER
Lawyer; chamber of commerce official

POLITICAL HIGHLIGHTS
Democratic nominee for U.S. House, 1994

ELECTION RESULTS

2008 GENERAL
John F. Tierney (D)	226,216	70.4%
Richard A. Baker (R)	94,845	29.5%

2008 PRIMARY
John F. Tierney (D)	unopposed

2006 GENERAL
John F. Tierney (D)	168,056	69.6%
Richard W. Barton (R)	72,997	30.2%

PREVIOUS WINNING PERCENTAGES
2004 (70%); 2002 (68%); 2000 (71%); 1998 (55%); 1996 (48%)

missile defense systems and redirected it to nuclear non-proliferation programs, destruction of chemical weapons and military suicide prevention efforts. "For far too long, Congress has funded missile defense in a way that is not commensurate with the threat our country faces from ballistic missiles," he said. But the vote split the Democrats down the middle, and opponents of the amendment joined with a united GOP to defeat it.

Another example is Tierney's longstanding push for a bill he calls "Clean Money, Clean Elections." It includes some politically difficult ideas pushed by government watchdog groups, such as public financing of elections, free broadcast time for candidates and limits on expenditures by political parties. A few provisions were included in the campaign finance law enacted in 2002, but the proposal has languished. He argues the momentum is shifting his way, and he has won the House Democratic Caucus' backing of public financing.

Tierney also been stymied in his push for universal health care, but figures to be a liberal voice in the health care debate. He offered legislation in the 110th Congress (2007-08) aimed at making it easier for states to win federal funding to experiment with new methods of expanding insurance coverage, but it didn't make it out of committee.

During the years Republicans controlled the House, Tierney often seemed frustrated and was mostly ineffectual as a legislator, unable or unwilling to compromise. He often accused Republicans of twisting facts to achieve their ends and putting wealthy corporate chiefs ahead of everyday people. Only with great reluctance did he switch his vote, in 2008, on the Bush administration's $700 billion rescue plan for Wall Street, finally siding with most Democrats in approving it after concluding, "The state of panic in the markets compels Congress to act."

Tierney first became interested in politics as a boy growing up in Salem. His uncle served as a ward councilor in Peabody, and Tierney used to campaign with him door to door. He worked to put himself through college, where he majored in political science. He obtained a law degree from Suffolk University and was a partner in the law firm of Tierney, Kalis and Lucas for more than 20 years, until his election to the House. Throughout his legal career, he was active in civic affairs in Salem, where he continues to reside.

Tierney launched his first campaign in 1994 and came within 4 percentage points of defeating freshman GOP Rep. Peter G. Torkildsen, who was aided by that year's Republican tide. He tried again in 1996, and with President Clinton sweeping the district by 28 percentage points, he managed a 371-vote win. Torkildsen was back for a rematch in 1998, but Tierney won by 12 points. His re-elections have been a breeze ever since.

KEY VOTES

2008

Yes	Delay consideration of Colombia free-trade agreement
Yes	Override Bush veto of federal farm and nutrition programs reauthorization bill
No	Overhaul surveillance laws and permit dismissal of suits against companies that conducted warrantless wiretapping
Yes	Grant mortgage relief to homeowners and funding for Fannie Mae and Freddie Mac
No	Approve initial $700 billion program to stabilize financial markets
Yes	Approve final $700 billion program to stabilize financial markets
Yes	Provide $14 billion in loans to automakers

2007

Yes	Increase minimum wage by $2.10 an hour
Yes	Approve $124.2 billion in emergency war spending and set goal for redeployment of troops from Iraq
No	Reject federal contraceptive assistance to international family planning groups
Yes	Override Bush veto of $23.2 billion water projects authorization bill
No	Implement Peru free-trade agreement
Yes	Approve energy policy overhaul with new fuel economy standards
No	Clear $473.5 billion omnibus spending bill, including $70 billion for military operations

CQ VOTE STUDIES

	PARTY UNITY		PRESIDENTIAL SUPPORT	
	SUPPORT	OPPOSE	SUPPORT	OPPOSE
2008	98%	2%	12%	88%
2007	99%	1%	4%	96%
2006	96%	4%	13%	87%
2005	98%	2%	13%	87%
2004	99%	1%	12%	88%

INTEREST GROUPS

	AFL-CIO	ADA	CCUS	ACU
2008	100%	95%	59%	4%
2007	92%	100%	50%	0%
2006	100%	100%	33%	8%
2005	93%	100%	30%	0%
2004	100%	100%	19%	0%

MASSACHUSETTS 6

North Shore — Lynn, Peabody

Pristine beaches line the cool ocean of Boston's North Shore, home to some of the state's largest homes. Country clubs, fox hunting and polo are popular diversions for residents of the northern inland, where the population is sparse but wealthy.

The population is denser along Route 128 in the southern part of the district, a high-tech center that developed when communities began to shift from manufacturing to an information-based economy in the 1990s. Lured in part by Boston's universities, technology firms have lined the corridor from Burlington to Gloucester, which hosts headquarters of semiconductor manufacturers and software companies. Gloucester's traditional fishing industry has declined, struggling to compensate for smaller catches and increasingly stringent federal regulations.

Urban dwellers are concentrated mostly in Lynn and Peabody, and provide blue-collar and minority votes for Democrats. Lynn is home to aerospace and defense contractors and hosts a General Electric jet engine plant. Other population centers include the adjacent coastal cities of

Beverly — which locals describe as the birthplace of the Navy because the first ship commissioned by the Continental Congress sailed from its harbor in 1775 — and major tourist destination Salem, with its rich history as the site of the 1692 witch trials. Salem is middle-class and has a Democratic slant, while Beverly is more politically independent.

Republicans can do well in upscale towns such as Boxford, Lynnfield, Topsfield and Wenham. While the 6th has a Democratic tilt, it is not overwhelming, and the GOP can win by attracting independent-minded "unenrolled" voters. In 2008, Barack Obama won 57 percent of the district's vote.

MAJOR INDUSTRY
Computer software, defense, fishing

MILITARY BASES
Hanscom Air Force Base, 1,400 military, 1,567 civilian (2008)

CITIES
Lynn, 89,050; Peabody, 48,129; Salem, 40,407; Beverly, 39,862; Gloucester, 30,273; Saugus (unincorporated), 26,078

NOTABLE
The 6th includes territory that spawned the original "gerrymander," a state legislative district named for Gov. Elbridge Gerry in 1812.

Rep. Edward J. Markey (D)

Elected 1976; 17th full term

CAPITOL OFFICE
225-2836
markey.house.gov
2108 Rayburn Bldg. 20515-2107; fax 226-0092

COMMITTEES
Energy & Commerce
  (Energy & Environment - chairman)
Natural Resources
Select Energy Independence & Global Warming
  - chairman

RESIDENCE
Malden

BORN
July 11, 1946; Malden, Mass.

RELIGION
Roman Catholic

FAMILY
Wife, Susan Blumenthal

EDUCATION
Boston College, B.A. 1968, J.D. 1972

MILITARY SERVICE
Army Reserve, 1968-73

CAREER
Lawyer

POLITICAL HIGHLIGHTS
Mass. House, 1973-77

ELECTION RESULTS

2008 GENERAL

Edward J. Markey (D)	212,304	75.6%
John Cunningham (R)	67,978	24.2%

2008 PRIMARY

Edward J. Markey (D)	unopposed

2006 GENERAL

Edward J. Markey (D)	171,902	98.3%
write-ins	2,889	1.7%

PREVIOUS WINNING PERCENTAGES
2004 (74%); 2002 (98%); 2000 (99%); 1998 (71%);
1996 (70%); 1994 (64%); 1992 (62%); 1990 (100%);
1988 (100%); 1986 (100%); 1984 (71%); 1982 (78%);
1980 (100%); 1978 (85%); 1976 Combined General &
Special Election (77%)

Markey is an idealist with a wry wit whose leftist views, formed during his initial foray into politics in the 1960s, have found a welcome home in a Democratic-controlled House and with the Obama White House. With a long record of advocacy for more-fuel efficient cars and against nuclear energy, along with a portfolio on innovative technology ideas and allies in the Democratic leadership, he has become a power player on a high-profile issue: climate change.

Markey shares many of the same environmental views as Speaker Nancy Pelosi and Energy and Commerce Chairman Henry A. Waxman, both of California. And he is a strong party loyalist. He backed his leadership on 99 percent of the votes that pitted most Democrats against most Republicans during the 110th Congress (2007-08). His record remained as strong in early 2009, as he backed President Obama's early economic initiatives. And his record on the fundraising circuit has the attention of the campaign arm of House Democrats. Before the end of the first quarter of 2009, he had already raised $200,000 of his $250,000 goal for the 2010 election cycle — ranking among the top 10 Democratic incumbents in fundraising for that time period.

He assumed the helm of the Energy and Commerce Committee's panel on Energy and the Environment in 2009. Previously named the Energy and Air Quality Subcommittee, the panel was expanded under Waxman to include drinking water and toxic waste sites, giving Markey even broader authority.

He also sits on the Natural Resources Committee and is chairman of the Select Committee on Energy Independence and Global Warming, created by Pelosi at the start of the 110th Congress. Markey immediately used the post to hold dozens of hearings on a wide range of climate and energy issues during the 110th and crafted a broad climate change bill in 2008, setting caps on greenhouse gas emissions that contribute to global warming. But the bill went nowhere in the face of opposition from the George W. Bush administration.

Markey and Waxman have the support of the Obama administration. But their difficulty remains gaining backing from industries and Democrats from coal-producing states and forming a bill that can win passage in the Senate. The pair introduced the outlines of a plan in March 2009 to set a cap on domestic emissions and create a market-based trading program of emissions credits for businesses to meet the cap. It also included Markey's proposal that 25 percent of electricity come from renewable sources by 2025. But the most contentious issue was left for further discussion: how to distribute emission allowances under a "cap and trade" program to address global warming.

Markey has long supported stricter fuel efficiency standards for vehicles, and in 2007 Congress enacted a new standard of 35 miles per gallon for cars and light trucks by 2022 in a broad energy bill. He opposes the expansion of oil and gas drilling to offshore areas, and in 2008 backed legislation aimed at encouraging companies to drill on lands they already lease.

He also opposes using nuclear power as a way to reduce carbon emissions, reflecting an anti-nuclear activism that goes back decades. During the Carter administration, Markey led a move to halt shipping of nuclear fuel to India, and he opposed the Bush administration's 2008 nuclear deal with that country. He once invoked a line from an old "Saturday Night Live" skit: "Nuclear power is like General Francisco Franco: It's still dead."

Energy and Commerce also is a forum for his interest in communications technology. In the 111th Congress (2009-10), he plans to push comprehensive electronic privacy legislation to address the use of tracking technology that enables advertisers to directly focus on users based on their Internet habits.

As chairman of the telecommunications panel during the 110th Congress, he led a push behind a "bill of rights" for the wireless communications community. His signature achievement remains the 1996 telecommunications overhaul that opened local phone markets to competition, set conditions for the powerful Bell companies to enter new markets and regulated competition between telephone and cable companies.

In 1992, he engineered the only veto override of President George Bush, leading the House to restore a bill he helped write that regulated the booming cable industry. But more recently Markey said government policies — or lack thereof — have undercut the 1996 act, leading to the country's loss of its pre-eminence in broadband Internet services. In November 2007, the House passed his bill requiring a nationwide map of broadband capabilities to guide future policies. The Senate never took up the measure.

Markey has ventured to the Internet himself. He conducted a hearing in April 2008 while his avatar, "EdMarkey Alter," conducted a virtual session focusing on the possibilities of Second Life, an interactive world on the Web where visitors use lifelike avatars to communicate.

Markey also has pushed for anti-terrorist security screening of cargo on passenger aircraft and on ships from foreign ports — provisions that became law in August 2007 after passage of a broader bill to implement more recommendations of the Sept. 11 commission.

Markey is admired for his quick quips. When news reports in March 2009 revealed employees at the troubled American International Group Inc. got bonuses through the government's financial rescue, he called it "complete March madness. You don't blow the big game and then still get a trophy."

The son of a milk truck driver, Markey was greatly influenced in his early years by another Irish Catholic from Massachusetts — President Kennedy. In 1968, the year Markey graduated from Boston College, he campaigned for liberal Democrat Eugene McCarthy.

After earning his law degree, Markey won a race for a state House seat and quickly became a thorn in the side of the old establishment Democrats. He picked a fight in 1976 with the party leaders over judicial reform, successfully pushing a bill to force judges to give up their law practices while in office. The Massachusetts bar endorsed the bill, but the Speaker kicked him off the Judiciary Committee. When he showed up for work the next day, his office was cleaned out. He went on to win an open U.S. House seat with the slogan, "The bosses can tell me where to sit, no one can tell me where to stand."

Markey has won elections by substantial margins; his biggest career frustration has been his inability to move up to the Senate.

KEY VOTES

2008

Yes Delay consideration of Colombia free-trade agreement

Yes Override Bush veto of federal farm and nutrition programs reauthorization bill

No Overhaul surveillance laws and permit dismissal of suits against companies that conducted warrantless wiretapping

Yes Grant mortgage relief to homeowners and funding for Fannie Mae and Freddie Mac

Yes Approve initial $700 billion program to stabilize financial markets

Yes Approve final $700 billion program to stabilize financial markets

Yes Provide $14 billion in loans to automakers

2007

Yes Increase minimum wage by $2.10 an hour

Yes Approve $124.2 billion in emergency war spending and set goal for redeployment of troops from Iraq

No Reject federal contraceptive assistance to international family planning groups

Yes Override Bush veto of $23.2 billion water projects authorization bill

No Implement Peru free-trade agreement

Yes Approve energy policy overhaul with new fuel economy standards

– Clear $473.5 billion omnibus spending bill, including $70 billion for military operations

CQ VOTE STUDIES

	PARTY UNITY		PRESIDENTIAL SUPPORT	
	SUPPORT	OPPOSE	SUPPORT	OPPOSE
2008	99%	1%	14%	86%
2007	99%	1%	3%	97%
2006	98%	2%	7%	93%
2005	98%	2%	15%	85%
2004	98%	2%	15%	85%

INTEREST GROUPS

	AFL-CIO	ADA	CCUS	ACU
2008	100%	100%	56%	0%
2007	96%	100%	58%	4%
2006	100%	100%	20%	4%
2005	93%	100%	30%	0%
2004	100%	100%	10%	0%

MASSACHUSETTS 7
Northwest Boston suburbs — Framingham

The affluent strip along eastern Massachusetts' technology corridor has shaped the 7th District's character, although some are looking to rebrand the tech industry's image in the post dot-com era. The district includes some of the state's most well-to-do communities as it jumps east from an urban retail center in Framingham to Route 128, which rings Boston, then through Medford and Malden to the middle-class coastal town of Revere. The area takes pride in its history: each year, Lexington re-enacts Paul Revere's ride and the first Revolutionary War battles (which took place in towns in the 7th and 5th districts) on Patriot's Day in April.

For decades, Revere has attracted vacationers to its beaches, but a stable software and Internet industry drives the 7th's economy, although economic downturns have caused job cuts and some municipal budget shortfalls. Many Medford and Malden residents commute to blue-collar jobs in Boston. Malden has a growing Asian community, and the 7th is home to the second-largest Asian population in the state, as well as numerous advocacy organizations for Asian-Americans.

The 7th's political roots are a mix of Protestant Yankee Republicans and Irish Democrats. The wealthy sections of the 7th vary from the moderate Weston to the liberal Lincoln. Democrats also draw votes from a blue-collar, middle-class base in Framingham and in the eastern part of the district, including Revere, Everett and Malden. But like all Massachusetts districts, the 7th votes Democratic in federal races. Barack Obama won 65 percent of the district's 2008 presidential vote.

MAJOR INDUSTRY
Computer software, telecommunications, defense

MILITARY BASES
Army Soldier Systems Center (Natick), 96 military, 1,184 civilian (2009)

CITIES
Framingham (unincorporated), 66,910; Waltham, 59,226; Malden, 56,340; Medford, 55,765; Revere, 47,283; Arlington (unincorporated), 42,389

NOTABLE
James Pierpont is said to have written "Jingle Bells" in 1850 while visiting Medford Square; The New England Confectionery Company (NECCO), the oldest multiline candy company in the United States, is located in Revere.

Rep. Michael E. Capuano (D)

Elected 1998; 6th term

CAPITOL OFFICE
225-5111
www.house.gov/capuano
1414 Longworth Bldg. 20515-2108; fax 225-9322

COMMITTEES
Financial Services
House Administration
(Capitol Security - chairman)
Transportation & Infrastructure
Joint Printing

RESIDENCE
Somerville

BORN
Jan. 9, 1952; Somerville, Mass.

RELIGION
Roman Catholic

FAMILY
Wife, Barbara Teebagy Capuano; two children

EDUCATION
Dartmouth College, B.A. 1973 (psychology);
Boston College, J.D. 1977

CAREER
Lawyer; state legislative aide

POLITICAL HIGHLIGHTS
Somerville Board of Aldermen, 1977-79;
candidate for mayor of Somerville, 1979, 1981;
Somerville Board of Aldermen, 1985-89; mayor
of Somerville, 1990-99; sought Democratic
nomination for Mass. secretary of state, 1994

ELECTION RESULTS

2008 GENERAL

Michael E. Capuano (D)	185,530	98.6%
write-ins	2,722	1.4%

2008 PRIMARY

Michael E. Capuano (D)	unopposed

2006 GENERAL

Michael E. Capuano (D)	125,515	90.7%
Laura Garza (SW)	12,449	9.0%

PREVIOUS WINNING PERCENTAGES
2004 (99%); 2002 (100%); 2000 (99%); 1998 (82%)

Capuano represents the historic Boston district that produced the Kennedy dynasty and former House Speaker Thomas P. "Tip" O'Neill Jr. A former alderman and mayor of the blue-collar Boston suburb of Somerville, Capuano fits the image of an old-time city pol. He's quick with a joke and a slap on the back and is well-attuned to the insider's game.

His views are as liberal as his better-known predecessors. A member of the Progressive Caucus, a group of left-leaning House Democrats, he is a leading voice on human rights issues. Capuano (KAP-you-AH-no) is co-chairman of the Congressional Caucus on Sudan and said the situation there is grave enough that he would support U.S. military deployments to Darfur, the region where the Sudanese government has committed genocide. "There's no other country in the world today that has such broad, widespread human rights abuses and such blatant violence that could be readily stopped," he said.

When President Obama named retired Air Force Maj. Gen. J. Scott Gration as United States Special Envoy to Sudan in March 2009, Capuano praised the choice and said it sent "a clear message" to Sudanese President Omar Hassan al Bashir "that the United States is deeply committed to bringing peace to the region and ending the atrocities there."

Yet his singular achievement as far as Bostonians are concerned has more to do with roads and bridges than with war and peace. As a member of the Transportation and Infrastructure Committee, he is credited with reversing the decline in grants to Massachusetts in reaction to the "Big Dig," the over-budget, scandal-ridden Boston tunnel project that had made many in Congress leery of the state's management of transportation funds.

When a concrete slab in a Big Dig tunnel fell and killed a motorist in 2006, Capuano led the state's congressional delegation in demanding a federal probe. His bill to establish a nationwide highway tunnel inspection program passed the House in January 2008.

Capuano proved adept at the horse trading that goes on behind the scenes in the stiff competition for earmarked federal grants, and he ultimately secured hundreds of millions of dollars for the state in 2005 as part of a reauthorization of the surface transportation law. He'll try to duplicate that feat as Congress moves to reauthorize its highway program again during the 111th Congress (2009-10). "We all have certain skills," he said. "I get along with these guys. I'm a compromiser when I need to be."

A tax attorney, Capuano also sits on the Financial Services panel. He voted for $700 billion legislation, signed into law in the fall of 2008, to aid the financial services sector, but he's been a big critic of its implementation since and has played a leading role in questioning corporate executives and Obama administration officials called before the panel.. When the House passed legislation in 2009 aimed at ensuring more congressional oversight of the financial rescue program, Capuano got language included to protect renters living in a foreclosed property from quick evictions.

He has earned the trust of Speaker Nancy Pelosi of California, who asked him to head the Democratic transition team after Democrats secured control of the House in the 2006 election. And at the start of the 110th Congress (2007-08), she asked Capuano to shoulder a task few lawmakers would relish — pushing for a rules change to allow outsiders to judge the ethical lapses of House members.

The Democratic leadership and Capuano reminded the rank and file, many of whom objected to the idea of outsiders judging their conduct, of past corruption cases that sent their colleagues to prison and contributed to the atmosphere that swept the Republicans out of office in 2006. "The public does not trust us on ethics issues at this point," Capuano said when his panel's recommendations were released. His committee's report was first delayed and then widely criticized, but a hard push by Pelosi in March 2008 secured passage of its key recommendation: the creation of an independent Office of Congressional Ethics.

Although he has an Ivy League education (Dartmouth University), Capuano likes to stress his roots in working-class Somerville, where he launched his political career in the 1970s as a city alderman. Capuano won the 8th District seat after Joseph P. Kennedy II, the son of Robert F. Kennedy and nephew of President John F. Kennedy, gave it up after six terms. The House seat has much of the original territory that it did when President Kennedy represented it for three terms, from 1947-53.

Capuano hails from a more modest political dynasty. His father was the first Italian-American elected to local office in Somerville. Although Capuano is half-Irish, his Italian-American name is a change of pace from the Irish identification of the Kennedys, former Gov. James Michael Curley and Speaker O'Neill.

Capuano must navigate a district where political tensions among various Democratic factions continually bubble to the surface. When he was mayor of Somerville, detractors called him "tyrannical" and said he managed the city like a ward boss, hiring friends and relatives and running enemies out of public agencies. Capuano, who won five elections and held the job for nearly a decade, dismissed the attacks on his leadership style, calling it "a sign of a good executive."

Capuano triumphed in a 10-person Democratic donnybrook created by Joseph Kennedy's unexpected 1998 retirement in the solidly Democratic district. The presumed front-runner was Raymond L. Flynn, a former Boston mayor and ambassador to the Vatican who had abandoned a flagging run for governor. But Capuano and others ganged up against Flynn and, although greatly outspent by two other candidates, Capuano was lifted to victory by a strong turnout in Somerville. He breezed by a Republican opponent that November, and the GOP has not fielded a candidate since.

He briefly eyed running for governor in 2006 but decided against it. "I am one of those guys who is absolutely shocked I'm a member of the House," Capuano said. "I still think they're going to tap me on the shoulder and say, 'We didn't mean you.' I still think of myself as just a Somerville kid hanging out around the corner."

KEY VOTES

2008
Yes Delay consideration of Colombia free-trade agreement
No   Override Bush veto of federal farm and nutrition programs reauthorization bill
No   Overhaul surveillance laws and permit dismissal of suits against companies that conducted warrantless wiretapping
Yes Grant mortgage relief to homeowners and funding for Fannie Mae and Freddie Mac
Yes Approve initial $700 billion program to stabilize financial markets
Yes Approve final $700 billion program to stabilize financial markets
Yes Provide $14 billion in loans to automakers

2007
Yes Increase minimum wage by $2.10 an hour
Yes Approve $124.2 billion in emergency war spending and set goal for redeployment of troops from Iraq
No   Reject federal contraceptive assistance to international family planning groups
Yes Override Bush veto of $23.2 billion water projects authorization bill
No   Implement Peru free-trade agreement
Yes Approve energy policy overhaul with new fuel economy standards
No   Clear $473.5 billion omnibus spending bill, including $70 billion for military operations

CQ VOTE STUDIES

	PARTY UNITY		PRESIDENTIAL SUPPORT	
	SUPPORT	OPPOSE	SUPPORT	OPPOSE
2008	99%	1%	22%	78%
2007	98%	2%	6%	94%
2006	96%	4%	25%	75%
2005	96%	4%	17%	83%
2004	96%	4%	24%	76%

INTEREST GROUPS

	AFL-CIO	ADA	CCUS	ACU
2008	100%	95%	67%	4%
2007	96%	95%	50%	0%
2006	100%	90%	40%	8%
2005	93%	95%	37%	4%
2004	93%	90%	19%	4%

MASSACHUSETTS 8

Part of Boston and suburbs — Cambridge, Somerville

The 8th combines Boston's historic Revolutionary War sites with neighborhoods that reflect its evolving future. It grabs approximately 70 percent of the city's population, almost all west of Interstate 93, picking up the Back Bay area, Chinatown and many largely black and Hispanic communities in areas like Roxbury, Dorchester and Jamaica Plain. The 8th is the state's only district where a majority of residents are minorities.

Among the 8th's many oft-visited Beantown sights are Bunker Hill, the Old North Church, the *USS Constitution* and Logan International Airport (shared with the 7th). In 2006, the Massachusetts Transit Authority completed its long-running "Big Dig" transportation project, most of which falls within the 8th, but structural deficiencies have caused continuing logistical problems.

Two of the world's most respected universities — Harvard and the Massachusetts Institute of Technology — lie across the Charles River from Boston in Cambridge. The district also takes in dozens of other colleges, which drive much of the economy, whether through blue-collar service employees who work at the schools and teaching hospitals or through biotech software firms that employ local talent.

Somerville, just north of Cambridge, has a thriving arts community, while Chelsea, with more-affordable housing and blue-collar jobs, has seen its Hispanic population expand to make up half the city's residents.

Typifying the district's monolithically liberal politics, Cambridge gave Republican George W. Bush just 13 percent of the vote in the 2000 and 2004 presidential elections, and Democrat Barack Obama received 84 percent of the district's presidential vote in 2008, his statewide high.

MAJOR INDUSTRY
Biotech, higher education, health care, tourism

CITIES
Boston (pt.), 420,922; Cambridge, 101,355; Somerville, 77,478

NOTABLE
The 8th is the descendant of the district once represented by John F. Kennedy (1947-53) and Thomas P. "Tip" O'Neill Jr. (1953-87); Fenway Park is home to baseball's Boston Red Sox.

Rep. Stephen F. Lynch (D)

Elected October 2001; 4th full term

CAPITOL OFFICE
225-8273
www.house.gov/lynch
221 Cannon Bldg. 20515-2109; fax 225-3984

COMMITTEES
Financial Services
Oversight & Government Reform
(Federal Workforce, Postal Service & the District
of Columbia - chairman)

RESIDENCE
Boston

BORN
March 31, 1955; Boston, Mass.

RELIGION
Roman Catholic

FAMILY
Wife, Margaret Lynch; two children

EDUCATION
Wentworth Institute of Technology, B.S. 1988
(construction management); Boston College,
J.D. 1991; Harvard U., M.A. 1998
(public administration)

CAREER
Lawyer; ironworker

POLITICAL HIGHLIGHTS
Mass. House, 1995-96; Mass. Senate, 1996-2001

ELECTION RESULTS

2008 GENERAL
Stephen F. Lynch (D)	242,166	98.7%
write-ins	3,128	1.3%

2008 PRIMARY
Stephen F. Lynch (D)	unopposed

2006 GENERAL
Stephen F. Lynch (D)	169,420	78.1%
Jack E. Robinson III (R)	47,114	21.7%

PREVIOUS WINNING PERCENTAGES
2004 (99%); 2002 (99%); 2001 Special Election (65%)

An ironworker turned lawyer, Lynch advocates for the working class while building his expertise in the international arena and on financial issues. In a Massachusetts delegation full of Democratic power brokers, he's still a junior partner, but he is gaining influence. And while he's not as predictable as most of his Democratic colleagues from the state — sometimes breaking from leadership on financial issues as well as social — he's persistent and direct, and attracts attention for his sharp tongue.

A member of the Financial Services Committee, Lynch can help his Bay State colleague, Chairman Barney Frank, move plans to fix the ailing U.S. economy and related mortgage meltdown. Lynch backed President Obama's economic stimulus in early 2009. And in August 2008, he backed a massive housing bill, signed into law, that aimed to shore up government-backed mortgage giants Fannie Mae and Freddie Mac and provide mortgage foreclosure relief. But he voted against two $700 billion measures, the second of which became law, aimed at helping the ailing financial services industry, saying that, among other things, he felt it was devised too quickly and wouldn't work.

And he, like other lawmakers, was incensed when American International Group (AIG) Inc. used some of that aid money to pay million-dollar executive bonuses. At a Financial Services subcommittee hearing in March 2009, he told Edward M. Liddy, chief executive officer of AIG, "This is like the captain and the crew of the ship reserving the lifeboats saying to hell with the passengers." When Liddy responded that he was offended, Lynch retorted, "Well, offense was intended. So you take it rightfully, sir."

Lynch also serves as chairman of the Oversight and Government Reform Committee panel overseeing the federal workforce, the Postal Service and the District of Columbia. He was critical when Postmaster General John E. Potter defended his $135,000 in bonuses while asking Lynch's panel to suspend the Postal Service's $2 billion annual payment to the retiree health fund in order to address the organization's financial problems. "Given today's environment, the whole situation with AIG bonuses...these difficult financial times, can we justify, can the Postal Service justify, your compensation package?" he asked.

From his seat on the Government Reform Committee in 2005, Lynch took on the role of inquisitor during hearings regarding the use of steroids in baseball. He aggressively questioned major league players suspected of steroid use and denounced the league's unwillingness to act. In the 110th Congress (2007-08), he introduced a bill to put human growth hormone on the same list of banned substances as anabolic steroids.

He also has traveled at least 10 times to Iraq since 2003, often leading congressional delegations looking for possible fraud and abuse in Iraq reconstruction projects. "We are spending about $10 billion every month here in Iraq and I'm concerned that a lot of that is being wasted," he said during a 2008 trip.

He often criticized the George W. Bush administration's handling of the war, but Lynch is not an anti-war Democrat. He has voted for spending bills that had money to continue the war and voted to authorize the war in 2002, although he later said he would have voted differently if he had "had all the facts at that moment." In another sign of his interest in international issues, Lynch also chairs the bipartisan Task Force on Terrorism Financing and Proliferation.

He's most proud of his work on a local project, the construction of Cushing House, now a 30-bed facility for adolescents with drug problems. Inspired by a spate of drug-related teen suicides in his district, Lynch secured federal funding for the facility, which was completed in 2005. He talked old union pals into donating labor and a factory owner into donating space. "There's already a waiting list," he said in 2006. "[It's] probably the best thing I've done."

A former labor leader, Lynch voted in 2003 to block Bush's plans to limit eligibility for overtime pay and more recently to raise the minimum wage and allow union organizers to bypass secret-ballot elections if a majority of eligible employees sign a petition in support of union formation.

Like many of his constituents, Lynch leans to the conservative side of the Democratic Party on social issues. A Roman Catholic, he opposes abortion and was one of just 47 Democrats to vote in 2005 with conservatives on congressional intervention in the case of Terri Schiavo, a severely brain-damaged Florida woman who was the subject of a major court battle over end-of-life medical decisions. But he has declined to join social conservatives in the battle over civil rights for homosexuals. He opposes a constitutional amendment to prohibit same-sex marriage and has expressed support for an extension of medical benefits to domestic partners. He voted for a bill in 2007 that would prohibit job discrimination based on sexual orientation.

Lynch came to the House after winning a special election in 2001 to replace a beloved longtime Democratic congressman, Joe Moakley, who died of leukemia. Lynch said in 2008, "I'd be lucky if I filled even one of Joe's shoes."

Lynch's father was an ironworker for 40 years, and his mother was a World War II welder who worked as a post office clerk. Lynch was an ironworker for 18 years, and at age 30 he was elected the youngest president ever of Ironworkers Local 7. He earned a law degree from Boston College and later a master's degree from Harvard, his tickets out of the unstable and dangerous trade. He joined a law firm and continued a practice he had begun in law school of representing housing-project residents for free.

In 1994, he unseated incumbent state Rep. Paul Gannon in the Massachusetts House; two years later, he won a special election for a state Senate seat. That gave him a solid launching pad to run for Congress when Moakley died.

Lynch was up against six other Democrats, several of whom criticized him for his opposition to abortion. Two of them raised questions about an incident from Lynch's attorney days, when he defended 14 white teenagers accused of harassing a white girl and her Hispanic boyfriend. But Lynch benefited from his up-by-the-bootstraps personal story, as well as from publicity over his decision to donate 60 percent of his liver to his brother-in-law, who had liver cancer.

Lynch won the primary with 39 percent of the vote and went on to defeat Republican state Sen. Jo Ann Sprague with 65 percent. He faced a Republican opponent in 2006, and took more than three-quarters of the vote, but in 2002, 2004 and 2008, no Republican challenged him for re-election.

KEY VOTES

2008

Yes Delay consideration of Colombia free-trade agreement

Yes Override Bush veto of federal farm and nutrition programs reauthorization bill

No Overhaul surveillance laws and permit dismissal of suits against companies that conducted warrantless wiretapping

Yes Grant mortgage relief to homeowners and funding for Fannie Mae and Freddie Mac

No Approve initial $700 billion program to stabilize financial markets

No Approve final $700 billion program to stabilize financial markets

Yes Provide $14 billion in loans to automakers

2007

Yes Increase minimum wage by $2.10 an hour

Yes Approve $124.2 billion in emergency war spending and set goal for redeployment of troops from Iraq

No Reject federal contraceptive assistance to international family planning groups

Yes Override Bush veto of $23.2 billion water projects authorization bill

Yes Implement Peru free-trade agreement

Yes Approve energy policy overhaul with new fuel economy standards

Yes Clear $473.5 billion omnibus spending bill, including $70 billion for military operations

CQ VOTE STUDIES

	PARTY UNITY		PRESIDENTIAL SUPPORT	
	SUPPORT	OPPOSE	SUPPORT	OPPOSE
2008	98%	2%	10%	90%
2007	96%	4%	5%	95%
2006	90%	10%	30%	70%
2005	92%	8%	16%	84%
2004	91%	9%	42%	58%

INTEREST GROUPS

	AFL-CIO	ADA	CCUS	ACU
2008	100%	95%	53%	8%
2007	96%	90%	60%	0%
2006	100%	90%	27%	20%
2005	93%	90%	37%	12%
2004	93%	85%	43%	28%

MASSACHUSETTS 9

Part of Boston; southern suburbs — Brockton, Braintree

The 9th begins with a central swath of downtown Boston, covering Beacon Hill, the West End and the financial district. The statehouse and brokerage houses — the 9th is home to one of the world's largest centers for mutual fund investing — dominate this part of Boston and share the area with sprawling Boston Common park and several of New England's major tourist attractions. Faneuil Hall Marketplace anchors a stable retail industry, but financial services job cuts concern some residents and local officials.

From central Boston the district hops the Fort Point Channel into South Boston, referred to as "Southie," and closely hugs Interstate 93 on its way into Milton. It connects through Dedham to West Roxbury, a mostly white suburban enclave in the southwestern part of Boston.

Some of the wealthiest neighborhoods in the state are along the Charles River, and the "Brahmin" homes of Beacon Hill are counterbalanced by

the poor and working-class neighborhoods of traditionally Irish Southie and middle-class suburban communities south and west of the city. Although solidly Democratic, Southie's political tradition is one of supporting pro-labor Democrats who are more socially conservative.

The 9th's areas outside of Boston are relatively conservative for Massachusetts. Although some of the district's suburbs helped elect GOP governors in the 1990s, Democratic Gov. Deval Patrick carried Randolph, Needham and Braintree in 2006. The district's mostly blue-collar base in Boston and Brockton keeps it solidly Democratic in federal elections, and Barack Obama won 60 percent of the district's 2008 presidential vote.

MAJOR INDUSTRY
Financial services, government, tourism

CITIES
Boston (pt.), 168,219; Brockton, 94,304; Braintree (unincorp.), 33,698; Randolph (unincorp.), 30,963; Needham (unincorp.), 28,911

NOTABLE
Patriots tossed boxes of tea into the Boston Harbor during the Boston Tea Party in 1773, a catalyst for the Revolutionary War; In the 1640s, Dedham authorized the nation's first solely taxpayer-funded school; The John F. Kennedy Library and Museum is in the 9th's portion of Boston.

Rep. Bill Delahunt (D)

Elected 1996; 7th term

Delahunt is a party loyalist who aims to revitalize what he considers America's soiled reputation in the world. His outspoken liberalism sometimes gets him in trouble with Republicans, but he has cultivated relationships across the ideological spectrum and has developed a knack for striking deals.

As chairman of the Foreign Affairs Subcommittee on International Organizations, Human Rights and Oversight, Delahunt (DELL-a-hunt) finds himself largely in sync with the Obama administration after years of warring with President George W. Bush, though his eagerness to investigate Bush's actions as president goes well beyond what President Obama supports.

Delahunt's panel held more than 50 hearings during the 110th Congress (2007-08), most of them aimed at exploring the damage he and other Democrats believe Bush caused to the nation's international image. He joined Judiciary Chairman John Conyers Jr. of Michigan in sponsoring a bill in early 2009 to set up a commission to investigate Bush's alleged abuses of power. Delahunt also cosponsored legislation to ban waterboarding, an interrogation technique that is widely considered torture but that the Bush administration refused to disavow. He applauded Obama's decision to ban torture, but said Congress must pass a law to bind future administrations.

And as co-chairman of the bipartisan Cuba Working Group, he has led efforts to open trade and travel with Cuba. His bill to make it easier for people with family in Cuba to visit there was included in a fiscal 2009 catch-all spending bill, and he has championed legislation to end all restrictions on travel. But supporters of the decades-old embargo continue to oppose loosening travel, arguing that opening Cuba to U.S. tourism would only increase revenue to prop up the Castro regime.

Delahunt has been accused of being too eager to deal with some foreign interests, to the extent of becoming too cozy with tyrants. He helped broker a much-publicized November 2005 deal for Venezuela's state-owned oil company Citgo to provide cut-rate heating oil to low-income Massachusetts residents. The conservative Wall Street Journal editorial page called the arrangement an attempt by Venezuelan President Hugo Chávez — a socialist and political adversary of the Bush administration — to buy friends in Washington. Delahunt defended it as a way of getting affordable fuel to people after Congress and the administration failed to help skyrocketing oil prices. "It's an embarrassment that we're forced to seek foreign assistance," he fired back.

He said he remains cordial with Chávez, but he took offense when the Venezuelan leader, in a speech at the United Nations in 2006, described the United States as "the greatest threat looming over our planet." Delahunt called the speech "an affront to the American people and unacceptable."

His fierce opinions also have landed him in controversy. A member of the Judiciary Committee, he tangled with former Vice President Dick Cheney's secretive top aide, David Addington, at a 2008 committee hearing after Addington told Delahunt he couldn't talk to him because "al Qaeda may watch C-SPAN." Delahunt responded: "I'm sure they are watching — and I'm glad they finally have a chance to see you…given your penchant for being unobtrusive." Republicans accused him of inviting terrorists to target Addington; Delahunt said he "meant no ill will" and was just being sarcastic.

Before Democrats took over Congress, Delahunt partnered with a few Republicans on law-and-order issues close to his heart. He and Republican Ray LaHood of Illinois — now Transportation secretary — won passage of a 2004 bill ensuring death row inmates have access to DNA evidence. In

CAPITOL OFFICE
225-3111
www.house.gov/delahunt
2454 Rayburn Bldg. 20515-2110; fax 225-5658

COMMITTEES
Foreign Affairs
(International Organizations, Human Rights
& Oversight - chairman)
Judiciary

RESIDENCE
Quincy

BORN
July 18, 1941; Quincy, Mass.

RELIGION
Roman Catholic

FAMILY
Divorced; two children

EDUCATION
Middlebury College, B.A. 1963;
Boston College, J.D. 1967

MILITARY SERVICE
Coast Guard, 1963; Coast Guard Reserve, 1963-71

CAREER
Lawyer

POLITICAL HIGHLIGHTS
Quincy City Council, 1971-73; Mass. House,
1973-75; Norfolk County district attorney, 1975-97

ELECTION RESULTS

2008 GENERAL

Bill Delahunt (D)	272,899	98.6%
write-ins	3,774	1.4%

2008 PRIMARY

Bill Delahunt (D)	unopposed

2006 GENERAL

Bill Delahunt (D)	171,812	64.3%
Jeffrey K. Beatty (R)	78,439	29.4%
Peter A. White (I)	16,808	6.3%

PREVIOUS WINNING PERCENTAGES
2004 (66%); 2002 (69%); 2000 (74%); 1998 (70%);
1996 (54%)

2005, Delahunt teamed with GOP Leader Tom DeLay to host a meeting of international relief groups, including UNICEF and the Red Cross, to discuss ways to crack down on international trafficking in women and children.

He mostly takes his party's side, but opposed two $700 billion measures, the second of which became law, in fall 2008 to aid the ailing financial services industry, citing a lack of help for people facing foreclosure and an unfair burden on taxpayers. He introduced a bill in 2009 to establish a rule-making entity to watch over financial products linked to predatory and deceptive practices.

Delahunt said he was inspired to enter politics by President Kennedy. While a student at Middlebury College, Delahunt was co-chairman of a group of Vermont college students supporting Kennedy. The other chairman was the late Ronald H. Brown, secretary of Commerce under President Clinton.

Delahunt spent more than 20 years working as a district attorney just south of Boston. During his tenure, he prosecuted John Salvi, who in 1994 killed two people at Brookline abortion clinics. Delahunt himself opposed abortion rights for many years but switched his position at the urging of his two grown daughters, Kara and Kristin.

Delahunt, who adopted Kara as an abandoned Vietnamese baby in 1975, has been a force behind legislation to ease overseas adoptions. In 2000 he won passage of his bill to grant automatic citizenship to children adopted from abroad, as well as to foreign-born children of U.S. parents.

Delahunt is a lifelong resident of Quincy, but while in Washington he rooms with three other Democrats — Sens. Charles E. Schumer of New York and Richard J. Durbin of Illinois and Rep. George Miller of California — in a storied house Miller owns on Capitol Hill. The place is so unkempt that Delahunt's chief of staff, Michele Jalbert, told the Boston Globe in 2007, "I'll do anything to avoid delivering something to this address."

Delahunt became a Quincy City Council member at age 30. Elected to the state House in 1972, he shared an office with a couple of other Beacon Hill rookies, Barney Frank and Edward J. Markey, both of whom preceded Delahunt in advancing to the House. Two years later, Gov. Michael S. Dukakis named Delahunt the district attorney for suburban Norfolk County.

When Democrat Gerry E. Studds announced his retirement in 1996, Delahunt was regarded as the Democratic front-runner from the start. After a hard-fought September primary that left him 300 votes behind state Rep. Phil Johnston, Delahunt went to court to charge that ballots that should have been counted for him had been counted as blank. A state judge concurred, and Delahunt was certified the primary winner. He went on to win the general election by 13 percentage points and has had no trouble retaining his seat.

KEY VOTES

2008

Yes	Delay consideration of Colombia free-trade agreement
Yes	Override Bush veto of federal farm and nutrition programs reauthorization bill
No	Overhaul surveillance laws and permit dismissal of suits against companies that conducted warrantless wiretapping
Yes	Grant mortgage relief to homeowners and funding for Fannie Mae and Freddie Mac
No	Approve initial $700 billion program to stabilize financial markets
No	Approve final $700 billion program to stabilize financial markets
?	Provide $14 billion in loans to automakers

2007

Yes	Increase minimum wage by $2.10 an hour
Yes	Approve $124.2 billion in emergency war spending and set goal for redeployment of troops from Iraq
No	Reject federal contraceptive assistance to international family planning groups
Yes	Override Bush veto of $23.2 billion water projects authorization bill
No	Implement Peru free-trade agreement
Yes	Approve energy policy overhaul with new fuel economy standards
No	Clear $473.5 billion omnibus spending bill, including $70 billion for military operations

CQ VOTE STUDIES

	PARTY UNITY		PRESIDENTIAL SUPPORT	
	SUPPORT	OPPOSE	SUPPORT	OPPOSE
2008	99%	1%	10%	90%
2007	98%	2%	3%	97%
2006	95%	5%	33%	67%
2005	99%	1%	9%	91%
2004	98%	2%	19%	81%

INTEREST GROUPS

	AFL-CIO	ADA	CCUS	ACU
2008	100%	95%	56%	10%
2007	96%	95%	50%	0%
2006	93%	90%	53%	12%
2005	92%	85%	35%	0%
2004	93%	95%	33%	0%

MASSACHUSETTS 10
South Shore – Quincy, Cape Cod, islands

Cool coastal breezes in the summer and warm ocean air in the winter attract retirees and tourists to the 10th, where most towns border the ocean. The area that spawned the nation's puritanical streak and the far Thanksgiving holiday still retains a Yankee flavor.

In contrast, the northern part of the 10th has attracted residents from Boston's neighborhoods and now boasts a strong ethnic flavor, as evidenced by the many varied restaurants and cultural celebrations in the area. Local officials hope that a planned $1 billion commercial and infrastructure redevelopment project for downtown Quincy will provide construction and retail jobs and boost municipal revenue.

With the exception of a handful of thriving cranberry bogs, the mainland coastal towns of the 10th, commonly referred to as the South Shore, consist mostly of bedroom communities for Boston's professionals or Quincy's blue-collar workers. The software industry helped the northern area recover from a recession in the early 1990s, and health care is now an important economic contributor.

On the Cape, tourism is dominant, but maritime technology and research are growing industries, especially in Woods Hole, home to world-renowned scientific institutions specializing in marine biology. Nantucket has been hit particularly hard by rising unemployment rates, but areas on Martha's Vineyard remain relatively stable.

The 10th tends to be more evenly split politically than any other districts in Massachusetts. While the state's most liberal population lives on the far end of Cape Cod, where Provincetown, a predominantly gay artists' colony and resort area, thrives, the district also includes one of the highest concentrations of Republicans in the state on the South Shore and in the wealthier towns on the Cape. As a result, the 10th was the state's least heavily Democratic district in the 2008 presidential election — Barack Obama took only 55 percent of the district's vote.

MAJOR INDUSTRY
Marine technology, biotechnology, health care, tourism

CITIES
Quincy, 88,025; Weymouth (unincorporated), 53,988; Barnstable, 47,821

NOTABLE
The John Alden House in Duxbury is named for the Pilgrim who sailed on the Mayflower.

Gov. Jennifer M. Granholm (D)

First elected: 2002
Length of term: 4 years
Term expires: 1/11
Salary: $177,000
Phone: (517) 373-3400

Residence: Lansing
Born: Feb. 5, 1959; Richmond, Canada
Religion: Roman Catholic
Family: Husband, Daniel G. Mulhern; three children
Education: U. of California, Berkeley, B.A. 1984 (political science & French); Harvard U., J.D. 1987
Career: Federal prosecutor; campaign aide; lawyer
Political highlights: Wayne County Corporation Counsel, 1994-98; Mich. attorney general, 1999-2003

Election results:

2006 GENERAL
Jennifer D. Granholm (D)	2,142,513	56.4%
Dick DeVos (R)	1,608,086	42.3%

Lt. Gov. John Cherry (D)

First elected: 2002
Length of term: 4 years
Term expires: 1/11
Salary: $123,900
Phone: (517) 373-3400

LEGISLATURE

Legislature: Year-round with recess

Senate: 38 members, 4-year terms
2009 ratios: 21 R, 16 D, 1 vacancy; 28 men, 9 women
Salary: $79,650
Phone: (517) 373-2400

House: 110 members, 2-year terms
2009 ratios: 67 D, 43 R; 83 men, 27 women
Salary: $79,650
Phone: (517) 373-0135

TERM LIMITS

Governor: 2 terms
Senate: 2 terms
House: 3 terms

URBAN STATISTICS

CITY	POPULATION
Detroit	951,270
Grand Rapids	197,800
Warren	138,247
Flint	124,943
Sterling Heights	124,471

REGISTERED VOTERS

Voters do not register by party.

POPULATION

2008 population (est.)	10,003,422
2000 population	9,938,444
1990 population	9,295,297
Percent change (1990-2000)	+6.9%
Rank among states (2008)	8
Median age	35.5
Born in state	75.4%
Foreign born	5.3%
Violent crime rate	555/100,000
Poverty level	10.5%
Federal workers	54,604
Military	21,833

ELECTIONS

STATE ELECTION OFFICIAL
(517) 373-2540
DEMOCRATIC PARTY
(517) 371-5410
REPUBLICAN PARTY
(517) 487-5413

MISCELLANEOUS

Web: www.michigan.gov
Capital: Lansing

U.S. CONGRESS

Senate: 2 Democrats
House: 8 Democrats, 7 Republicans

2000 Census Statistics by District

DIST.	2008 VOTE FOR PRESIDENT OBAMA	MCCAIN	WHITE	BLACK	ASIAN	HISP	MEDIAN INCOME	WHITE COLLAR	BLUE COLLAR	SERVICE INDUSTRY	OVER 64	UNDER 18	COLLEGE EDUCATION	RURAL	SQ. MILES
1	50%	48%	94%	1%	0%	1%	$34,076	51%	30%	19%	17%	23%	16%	67%	24,887
2	47	51	87	4	1	5	$42,589	51	34	15	12	28	18	44	5,365
3	49	49	82	8	2	6	$45,936	57	30	13	11	28	24	23	1,854
4	50	48	93	2	1	2	$39,020	54	29	17	14	25	19	59	7,451
5	64	35	75	18	1	4	$39,675	51	32	17	12	27	15	21	1,754
6	54	44	84	9	1	4	$40,943	53	32	15	12	26	21	42	3,331
7	52	46	88	6	1	3	$45,181	54	32	15	12	26	19	46	4,295
8	53	46	88	5	2	3	$52,510	63	23	14	9	26	29	30	2,254
9	56	43	81	8	6	3	$65,358	75	15	10	12	24	44	1	311
10	48	50	94	1	1	2	$52,690	55	32	13	11	27	17	34	3,549
11	54	45	90	4	3	2	$59,177	65	24	12	12	25	29	3	399
12	65	33	82	12	2	1	$46,784	60	27	14	16	23	20	0	160

2000 Census Statistics by District

DIST.	2008 VOTE FOR PRESIDENT OBAMA	MCCAIN	WHITE	BLACK	ASIAN	HISP	MEDIAN INCOME	WHITE COLLAR	BLUE COLLAR	SERVICE INDUSTRY	OVER 64	UNDER 18	COLLEGE EDUCATION	RURAL	SQ. MILES
13	85%	14%	29%	60%	1%	7%	$31,165	51%	29%	20%	11%	30%	14%	0%	108
14	86	13	32	61	1	2	$36,099	53	29	18	12	29	14	0	123
15	66	33	79	12	4	3	$48,963	59	26	14	10	25	28	12	961
STATE	57	41	79	14	2	3	$44,667	57	28	15	12	26	22	25	56,804
U.S.	53	46	69	12	4	13	$41,994	60	25	15	12	26	24	21	3,537,438

Sen. Carl Levin (D)

Elected 1978; 6th term

CAPITOL OFFICE
224-6221
levin.senate.gov
269 Russell Bldg. 20510-2202; fax 224-1388

COMMITTEES
Armed Services - chairman
Homeland Security & Governmental Affairs
  (Permanent Investigations - chairman)
Small Business & Entrepreneurship

RESIDENCE
Detroit

BORN
June 28, 1934; Detroit, Mich.

RELIGION
Jewish

FAMILY
Wife, Barbara Levin; three children

EDUCATION
Swarthmore College, B.A. 1956 (political science);
Harvard U., LL.B. 1959

CAREER
Lawyer

POLITICAL HIGHLIGHTS
Michigan Civil Rights Commission general counsel,
1964-67; Detroit chief appellate defender, 1968-69;
Detroit City Council, 1970-77 (president, 1974-77)

ELECTION RESULTS

2008 GENERAL

Carl Levin (D)	3,038,386	62.7%
Jack Hoogendyk Jr. (R)	1,641,070	33.8%
Scotty Boman (LIBERT)	76,347	1.6%

2008 PRIMARY

Carl Levin (D)	unopposed

2002 GENERAL

Carl Levin (D)	1,896,614	60.6%
Andrew Raczkowski (R)	1,185,545	37.9%

2002 PRIMARY

Carl Levin (D)	unopposed

PREVIOUS WINNING PERCENTAGES
1996 (58%); 1990 (57%); 1984 (52%); 1978 (52%)

As the Senate Democrats' leader on national security issues, the cerebral Levin has used his Armed Services Committee chairmanship to perform extensive oversight of the wars in Iraq and Afghanistan. He combines his dedication to military matters with a passion for his state, leading efforts to defend Michigan voting rights and fighting for help for its ailing auto industry.

Despite his rumpled suits and the reading glasses perched precariously on the tip of his nose, Levin is more pit bull than professor when it comes to pursuing his objectives. Whether he is probing offshore tax evasion or questioning Pentagon policy makers, he is unfailingly polite and utterly relentless, and after three decades in Washington shows few signs of slowing down.

After regaining the Armed Services chairmanship in 2007 (he had served as chairman from June 2001 to January 2003), Levin was determined to make up for the previous Republican leadership, which he saw as woefully deficient in steering war policy. His hearings on interrogation techniques, detainee treatment and the conduct of U.S. contractors in Iraq sought to increase Congress' influence in the conduct and direction of the war.

In his primary policy initiative, speeding the withdrawal of U.S. troops from Iraq, Levin's efforts included several attempts to attach withdrawal language to a host of defense bills. Each try contained successively fewer restrictive provisions aimed at drawing moderate Republicans toward a stance that would force President George W. Bush to begin lowering troop levels and changing the mission of U.S. forces there.

None of his amendments, co-written with committee colleague Jack Reed, a Rhode Island Democrat, ultimately became law. But Levin maintains that his campaign to end the war, along with his often-harsh criticisms of the Iraqi government, have had an effect. Bush eventually agreed with Iraqi leaders to a timetable for U.S. troop withdrawals in Iraq in a security agreement signed in November 2008.

Levin reacted to President Obama's decision in early 2009 to draw down troops — leaving behind as many as 50,000 soldiers in the war-torn country — by declaring that his own calculations showed a far smaller residual presence was feasible.

Meanwhile, he repeatedly criticized the Obama administration for supporting the notion that progress in Afghanistan was only achievable if Pakistan cracked down on extremists within its borders. He wants to make the Afghanistan conflict more Afghanistan's war than America's.

Levin's policy bills had a significant impact on the treatment of soldiers and veterans who had multiple overseas deployments, along with their families. His fiscal 2008 defense authorization bill contained the Wounded Warrior Act, a long list of provisions for veterans based on recommendations from a commission led by former Senate Majority Leader Bob Dole of Kansas and Donna Shalala, a former Health and Human Services secretary.

Levin has been critical, though ultimately supportive, of many expensive Defense Department programs, including the Army's Future Combat Systems and Bush administration plans to deploy a national missile defense system. He opposed beginning construction of U.S. missile defense sites in Poland and the Czech Republic until further testing could be done. He has called for developing a U.S.-Russian system to intercept missiles from Iran.

Levin's comprehension of the complicated issues he deals with is the foundation of his clout. He is a master of detail and is known for preparing for hours before questioning hostile witnesses in order to keep them from evading his questions. He is a dogged but genial interrogator in committee hearings and a tenacious negotiator in legislative drafting sessions.

As the chairman of the Homeland Security and Governmental Affairs panel's Permanent Subcommittee on Investigations, Levin branches out beyond defense issues to delve into such wide-ranging topics as energy-market manipulation and contractor abuses on projects in Iraq. He held hearings on such things as the IRS' failure to go after corporations that use loopholes to avoid paying dividend taxes. He also held hearings to expose the gap between accounting rules and tax laws for stock options, which he said allows companies to dodge further tax obligations.

And Levin devotes significant attention to Michigan. Toward the end of 2008, Levin led the call for $25 billion worth of loans for Detroit automakers. He complained of a "double standard" compared to the conditions imposed on the equally troubled financial services sector, but welcomed Obama's decision in March 2009 to take stringent action aimed at rescuing the automakers. Administration officials are "taking significant responsibility now for the future of the [auto] industry," he said.

When the Senate passed an energy policy overhaul in 2005, Levin thwarted efforts to increase statutory fuel efficiency standards for automobiles, arguing they are "both arbitrary and discriminatory" because they measure the fuel efficiency of an entire fleet of cars as opposed to individual models.

Levin also sits on the Small Business and Entrepreneurship Committee. He has called for expanding loan programs to small businesses and worked to provide such businesses disaster relief when they are affected by drought conditions in the Great Lakes and elsewhere.

During the 2008 presidential primary fight, he helped lead the successful effort to reseat Michigan's delegates following their disqualification after Michigan violated Democratic National Committee rules by holding its primary on Jan. 5. Michigan "succeeded in challenging the system," Levin said during the Democratic National Convention, where Michigan's delegates were restored full voting rights, well after the primary race had been effectively decided.

Levin and his older brother, Sander, who represents Michigan's 12th District in the House, have collaborated on trade issues, focusing particularly on relations with China. Although Carl Levin made it to the Senate four years before Sander M. Levin won his House seat, he says he has always looked up to his older brother. Both absorbed a passion for politics from their father, a lawyer active in social-justice causes in Detroit.

As a teenager, Levin worked the assembly line at a Chrysler DeSoto plant, and he still carries a fading United Auto Workers membership card in his wallet. Later, while in law school, Levin drove a taxicab, an experience he said helped him deal with people of all backgrounds.

In the 1960s, he was general counsel to the Michigan Civil Rights Commission. He had no plans to run for office until riots in 1967 ripped apart Detroit. In 1970, he was elected to the Detroit City Council and worked to rebuild a shattered city. He butted heads with federal housing officials, and he said he decided to run for the Senate in 1978 in part to try to make federal agents "more responsive to local communities."

Levin has an avuncular manner, but he can play political hardball. In 1984, he aired an ad showing his GOP opponent, Jack Lousma, telling an audience about the Toyota he owned — a faux pas in a state where the phrase "Japanese car" translates as joblessness. President Reagan carried Michigan with 59 percent of the vote that year, but Levin held on to win with 52 percent. In his four succeeding re-election efforts, Levin's margin of victory steadily improved. In 2008 he took almost 63 percent of the vote., nearly double that of his opponent, state Rep. Jack Hoogendyk Jr.

KEY VOTES

2008

Yes Prohibit discrimination based on genetic information

Yes Reauthorize farm and nutrition programs for five years

Yes Limit debate on "cap and trade" system for greenhouse gas emissions

Yes Allow lawsuits against companies that participated in warrantless wiretapping

Yes Limit debate on a bill to block a scheduled cut in Medicare payments to doctors

Yes Grant mortgage relief to homeowners and funding for Fannie Mae and Freddie Mac

Yes Approve a nuclear cooperation agreement with India

Yes Approve final $700 billion program to stabilize financial markets

Yes Allow consideration of a $14 billion auto industry loan package

2007

Yes Increase minimum wage by $2.10 an hour

Yes Limit debate on a comprehensive immigration bill

Yes Overhaul congressional lobbying and ethics rules for members and their staffs

Yes Limit debate on considering a bill to add House seats for the District of Columbia and Utah

Yes Limit debate on restoring habeas corpus rights to detainees

Yes Mandate minimum breaks for troops between deployments to Iraq or Afghanistan

Yes Override Bush veto of $23.2 billion water projects authorization bill

No Confirm Michael B. Mukasey as attorney general

Yes Limit debate on an energy policy overhaul containing $21.8 billion in tax incentives and reduced oil and gas subsidies

CQ VOTE STUDIES

	PARTY UNITY		PRESIDENTIAL SUPPORT	
	SUPPORT	OPPOSE	SUPPORT	OPPOSE
2008	97%	3%	31%	69%
2007	95%	5%	39%	61%
2006	94%	6%	56%	44%
2005	97%	3%	41%	59%
2004	96%	4%	60%	40%
2003	98%	2%	50%	50%
2002	95%	5%	66%	34%
2001	98%	2%	65%	35%
2000	97%	3%	92%	8%
1999	97%	3%	89%	11%

INTEREST GROUPS

	AFL-CIO	ADA	CCUS	ACU
2008	100%	100%	63%	0%
2007	100%	95%	45%	4%
2006	100%	100%	50%	8%
2005	93%	100%	39%	17%
2004	100%	100%	41%	0%
2003	85%	100%	39%	25%
2002	100%	95%	40%	0%
2001	100%	100%	36%	8%
2000	75%	90%	66%	12%
1999	89%	95%	53%	4%

Sen. Debbie Stabenow (D)

Elected 2000; 2nd term

CAPITOL OFFICE
224-4822
stabenow.senate.gov
133 Hart Bldg. 20510-2204; fax 228-0325

COMMITTEES
Agriculture, Nutrition & Forestry
Budget
Energy & Natural Resources
   (Water & Power - chairwoman)
Finance

RESIDENCE
Lansing

BORN
April 29, 1950; Clare, Mich.

RELIGION
United Methodist

FAMILY
Husband, Tom Athans; two children, one stepchild

EDUCATION
Michigan State U., B.A. 1972, M.S.W. 1975

CAREER
Leadership training consultant

POLITICAL HIGHLIGHTS
Ingham County Commission, 1975-78 (chairwoman,
1977-1978); Mich. House, 1979-91; Mich. Senate,
1991-94; sought Democratic nomination for
governor, 1994; Democratic nominee for lieutenant
governor, 1994; U.S. House, 1997-2001

ELECTION RESULTS

2006 GENERAL

Debbie Stabenow (D)	2,151,278	57.0%
Mike Bouchard (R)	1,559,597	41.4%

2006 PRIMARY

Debbie Stabenow (D)	unopposed

PREVIOUS WINNING PERCENTAGES
2000 (49%); 1998 House Election (57%); 1996 House
Election (54%)

Stabenow has a warm, maternal way about her that she maintains through the grittiest of political battles. She's a polished pol who has spent more than 30 years in politics at the local, state and federal levels, including a stint as Senate Democratic conference secretary — the fourth-ranking leadership job. She currently chairs the Senate Democratic Steering and Outreach Committee, which helps make committee assignments.

Stabenow (STAB-uh-now) has long sought to expand health care coverage to the uninsured, a goal she could help reach from her seat on the powerful Finance Committee. But she is often forced to spend more time on issues that have put Michigan at the epicenter of the faltering national economy, such as the state's ailing auto industry and the financial and foreclosure crises.

The daughter of an Oldsmobile dealer, she is a staunch ally of the many blue-collar workers she represents. She said Michigan's job losses are a product of past free-trade agreements. She opposed the Central America Free Trade Agreement in 2005, as well as the trade agreements with Panama, Peru and South Korea in 2007, despite Democratic leaders' efforts to secure long-sought labor and environmental standards. "There's a huge myth that we don't have to have manufacturing capability in this country anymore," Stabenow told the Detroit News in 2007. "You can't have an economy that continues to be successful if you don't make things and grow things."

Stabenow has worked with her Michigan Democratic colleague Carl Levin to try to rescue the state's Big Three auto companies, which pleaded that millions of industry-related jobs would be lost without federal help. "Do we care about 3 million people who have helped create the middle class of this country by making things for us in this country?" she asked the Banking Committee in November 2008. After that vote fell short in the Senate, she joined her state's delegation in successfully persuading White House officials to use funds from the $700 billion financial services sector rescue package on a short-term loan for the auto industry.

Stabenow had voted against that rescue package in October 2008 as she looked at high unemployment rates, the auto industry's struggles and financial and foreclosure woes across the state. She said she didn't see how the financial sector rescue helped middle-class families. When President Obama announced a stringent series of steps in March 2009 aimed at saving the Big Three automakers, she hailed it as "further evidence that the administration is taking seriously the need for a viable domestic auto industry to save the manufacturing base of this country and preserve jobs here at home."

She also serves on the Budget Committee, furthering her influence over fiscal policy. She backed Obama's early economic initiatives, including a $787 billion stimulus bill and an expansion of a state-federal program providing health coverage for children whose families don't qualify for Medicaid.

While Stabenow is typically a faithful Democrat, she stands apart on energy issues — in keeping with her concerns for not just the local auto industry, but the coal industry as well. She could pose several hurdles to President Obama's broad energy plan. A member of the Energy and Natural Resources Committee, and chairwoman of the Water and Power Subcommittee, she led a "Gang of 15" Democrats who raised concerns in early 2009 about Obama's plan for a "cap and trade" program. Such a plan would place increasingly strict caps on carbon dioxide emissions and allow companies that exceed their caps to buy emissions credits from ones that emit less. Rust Belt Democrats like Stabenow believe that would place a heavy burden on their state's industries.

In 2007, she was one of eight senators and the lone Democrat to vote against an energy policy overhaul that included new fuel efficiency standards for automobiles and emphasized energy conservation. At the time, Stabenow said she couldn't support the mandate without several incentives aimed at helping the auto industry meet the new standards.

A member of the Agriculture, Nutrition and Forestry Committee, Stabenow backed a successful 2008 override of President George W. Bush's veto of the bill reauthorizing agriculture and nutrition programs for five years, because it increased payments to specialty crop growers and included a provision of hers to require schools to purchase fruits and vegetables from local farmers when available. In the 2002 renewal, she won a provision that helped Michigan farmers by mandating a $200 million annual increase in expenditures on blueberries, cherries and other specialty crops for food programs for the poor.

Stabenow has spent her congressional career fighting to overhaul Medicare and to promote generic drugs over expensive brand-name prescription medicines, and she battled in vain to persuade the Bush administration to allow imports of cheaper drugs from Canada. In her first Senate campaign, she ushered busloads of Michigan senior citizens across the Canadian border to illustrate the plight of the elderly taking desperate measures to find affordable medicines.

Stabenow takes a traditional Democratic line on abortion rights, education funding and gun control. She championed a ban on oil and gas drilling in the Great Lakes, and in 2003 she fought for a year's delay of the allotment of $5 billion in rebuilding funds for Iraq, saying the money would be better spent on domestic issues such as school construction and veterans' health care. She sets an example for diversity in the workplace with a staff that is roughly two-thirds female and one-third racial minority.

Stabenow was born and raised in the small town of Clare, known as the gateway to Michigan's "Up North." The eldest of three children, she credits her parents with urging her to reach high. "In high school, I would hear 'nurse' or 'teacher' as career options," she told the Detroit News in 2005. "But dad would say, 'No, doctor or engineer.' He gave me confidence to take risks, to push limits."

After graduating from Michigan State University, she got involved in politics. A trained social worker, she was angered by the closing of a local nursing home. She successfully challenged an incumbent to win a seat on the Ingham County Commission in 1975, and went on to serve 12 years in the Michigan House and a term in the state Senate.

In 1994, she lost the Democratic gubernatorial primary to veteran Democratic Rep. Howard Wolpe and subsequently lost in the general election as Wolpe's lieutenant governor. But she made a comeback in 1996, ending Republican Rep. Dick Chrysler's one-term tenure in the politically competitive 8th District. She was easily re-elected to the seat in 1998.

That set up Stabenow's 2000 challenge to Sen. Spencer Abraham, a longtime GOP operative who started out with a big lead in the polls. But Stabenow and allied groups staged a counteroffensive. She had a campaign chest of $8 million and was the top recipient of funds from EMILY's List, a political action committee that backs Democratic women candidates who support abortion rights. Her campaign unleashed her war chest for an October advertisement blitz, and she won by less than 2 percentage points.

With a strong Democratic wind at her back in 2006, Stabenow handily defeated Oakland County Sheriff Mike Bouchard, winning with 57 percent. Her name briefly surfaced as a possible pick for Obama's secretary of Health and Human Services after former Senate Majority Leader Tom Daschle withdrew his name in light of his admission he had failed to pay some taxes.

KEY VOTES

2008

Yes Prohibit discrimination based on genetic information

Yes Reauthorize farm and nutrition programs for five years

Yes Limit debate on "cap and trade" system for greenhouse gas emissions

Yes Allow lawsuits against companies that participated in warrantless wiretapping

Yes Limit debate on a bill to block a scheduled cut in Medicare payments to doctors

Yes Grant mortgage relief to homeowners and funding for Fannie Mae and Freddie Mac

Yes Approve a nuclear cooperation agreement with India

No   Approve final $700 billion program to stabilize financial markets

Yes Allow consideration of a $14 billion auto industry loan package

2007

Yes Increase minimum wage by $2.10 an hour

No   Limit debate on a comprehensive immigration bill

Yes Overhaul congressional lobbying and ethics rules for members and their staffs

Yes Limit debate on considering a bill to add House seats for the District of Columbia and Utah

Yes Limit debate on restoring habeas corpus rights to detainees

Yes Mandate minimum breaks for troops between deployments to Iraq or Afghanistan

Yes Override Bush veto of $23.2 billion water projects authorization bill

No   Confirm Michael B. Mukasey as attorney general

Yes Limit debate on an energy policy overhaul containing $21.8 billion in tax incentives and reduced oil and gas subsidies

CQ VOTE STUDIES

	PARTY UNITY		PRESIDENTIAL SUPPORT	
	SUPPORT	OPPOSE	SUPPORT	OPPOSE
2008	98%	2%	31%	69%
2007	94%	6%	32%	68%
2006	88%	12%	51%	49%
2005	95%	5%	33%	67%
2004	96%	4%	58%	42%
2003	97%	3%	49%	51%
2002	95%	5%	66%	34%
2001	96%	4%	64%	36%
2000	82%	18%	74%	26%
1999	87%	13%	78%	22%

INTEREST GROUPS

	AFL-CIO	ADA	CCUS	ACU
2008	100%	100%	50%	4%
2007	100%	100%	27%	8%
2006	100%	90%	50%	16%
2005	93%	100%	44%	12%
2004	100%	100%	65%	8%
2003	85%	95%	39%	20%
2002	100%	95%	45%	0%
2001	100%	100%	43%	8%
2000	90%	90%	47%	16%
1999	78%	95%	44%	4%

Rep. Bart Stupak (D)

Elected 1992; 9th term

CAPITOL OFFICE
225-4735
www.house.gov/stupak
2268 Rayburn Bldg. 20515-2201; fax 225-4744

COMMITTEES
Energy & Commerce
(Oversight & Investigations - chairman)

RESIDENCE
Menominee

BORN
Feb. 29, 1952; Milwaukee, Wis.

RELIGION
Roman Catholic

FAMILY
Wife, Laurie Stupak; two children (one deceased)

EDUCATION
Northwestern Michigan Community College, A.A.
1972; Saginaw Valley State College, B.S. 1977
(criminal justice); Thomas M. Cooley Law School,
J.D. 1981

CAREER
Lawyer; state trooper; patrolman

POLITICAL HIGHLIGHTS
Mich. House, 1989-91; sought Democratic
nomination for Mich. Senate, 1990

ELECTION RESULTS

2008 GENERAL

Bart Stupak (D)	213,216	65.0%
Tom Casperson (R)	107,340	32.7%

2008 PRIMARY

Bart Stupak (D)	unopposed

2006 GENERAL

Bart Stupak (D)	180,448	69.4%
Don Hooper (R)	72,753	28.0%

PREVIOUS WINNING PERCENTAGES
2004 (66%); 2002 (68%); 2000 (58%); 1998 (59%);
1996 (71%); 1994 (57%); 1992 (54%)

Stupak is a dogged investigator of high-profile consumer issues, following in the footsteps of fellow Michigan Democrat John D. Dingell. A former police officer and state trooper, Stupak believes his law enforcement background makes him well suited for the job.

Stupak (STU-pack) is chairman of the House Energy and Commerce panel's Oversight and Investigations Subcommittee, which has a wide-ranging agenda, from nursing home management to nuclear proliferation issues. He lacks the hard-bitten approach of Dingell, whose intense interrogations made him a force to be reckoned with when he was chairman in the early 1990s. But Stupak shows the same willingness to dig deeply. And befitting someone from the frigid and self-reliant Upper Peninsula, Stupak is a Democrat who goes his own way often enough to preserve his standing back home as a centrist.

He teamed with Dingell in January 2009 to introduce a bill to overhaul the Food and Drug Administration (FDA). Energy and Commerce Chairman Henry A. Waxman — who had just taken the job from Dingell — said the bill would serve as the foundation of the committee's effort to revamp the nation's food safety laws. The measure would authorize new funding to increase inspections of food facilities and imposes stiff penalties on companies that violate safety standards.

Shortly after introducing the bill, in February 2009, Stupak confronted peanut industry executives after a salmonella outbreak at a peanut plant in Georgia was blamed in the deaths of nine people. Most alarming, Stupak said after the hearing, is the possibility "that there could be hundreds or even thousands of food processing facilities operating in this country that have never been inspected by the FDA."

During the 110th Congress (2007-08), Stupak led a series of investigations into foreign-origin drugs, including the blood-thinner heparin that has been linked to more than 80 deaths and hundreds of allergic reactions in the United States.

On a matter close to his heart, Stupak has for years pressed the FDA to impose tighter regulation on the acne medication Accutane, which he believes was the reason his son B.J. — a popular high school athlete and student leader — committed suicide at age 17 in 2000. Stupak instigated a two-year congressional investigation into the drug's effects, and in 2004 the FDA ordered doctors and pharmacies to inform patients about its risks and get their consent before dispensing it.

Stupak is also concerned about energy costs. As gasoline prices soared in 2007 and 2008 he fought alleged price gouging and excessive energy speculation that some blamed for driving up prices. His anti-gouging bill passed the House in May 2007 but died in the Senate. A revised bill also fell short a year later.

Stupak is the author of a consumer protection law, which President George W. Bush signed three months before he left office, to shut down rogue Internet pharmacies. The law, introduced in June 2008, is named for an 18-year-old Californian, Ryan Haight, who fatally overdosed in 2001 on narcotics that he had easily purchased on the Internet.

Stupak is willing to stray from his party when he deems it necessary. He voted for President Obama's stimulus legislation, aimed at reviving the ailing economy, in early 2009, but said he could not support another measure to allow bankruptcy court judges to rewrite the terms of mortgages to help struggling homeowners. Despite Stupak's defection and that of 24 other Democrats, it passed the House in March 2009. Stupak said he thought the bill would encourage more Americans to file for bankruptcy unnecessarily.

Stupak opposes abortion, which satisfies his district's many social conservatives. He is co-chairman of the House Pro-Life Caucus with New Jersey Republican Christopher H. Smith and votes with Republicans on bills aimed at restricting abortion.

He also is a supporter of gun owners' rights and won the endorsement of the National Rifle Association in 2008 thanks to his efforts to end local handgun control in the District of Columbia following a U.S. Supreme Court decision striking down the District's handgun ban as a violation of the Second Amendment.

But he is a steadfast ally of organized labor and opposes free-trade deals. He voted no on agreements the Bush administration had reached with Central American countries and Peru. Both passed anyway.

Stupak also keeps a close watch on issues affecting the Great Lakes. His vast district has a 1,600-mile shoreline on three of them. His proposal to ban oil drilling in the lakes became part of the 2005 energy law.

Law enforcement is also a natural priority for Stupak, who has a background in police work. In the 107th Congress (2001-02), he won enactment of a bill limiting public access to body armor, arguing it emboldens criminals to engage in shootouts with police. Since the 2001 terrorist attacks and the Sept. 11 commission's finding that local law enforcement often cannot communicate well with emergency services, Stupak has been a leading advocate of federal aid to improve first-responder communications systems.

As a lifelong resident of the Upper Peninsula (known by locals as the U.P.), Stupak prides himself on his "Yooper" background. While serving as an Escanaba police officer, he earned an undergraduate degree in criminal justice. He then earned a law degree while working as a trooper. He retired from the force in 1984 after injuring a knee while chasing a suspect on foot. Stupak practiced law and got involved in local politics. He won a state House seat in 1988 but gave it up after two years for a state Senate bid, in which he narrowly lost the Democratic primary.

Stupak's opportunity to try for Congress came in 1992, when Republican Rep. Robert W. Davis retired after seven terms. Stupak defeated former GOP Rep. Philip E. Ruppe with 54 percent of the vote. In subsequent elections in the 1990s, he only once polled more than 60 percent. But decennial redistricting for this decade created a slightly more Democratic 1st District, and Stupak's road to re-election has been easier since.

KEY VOTES

2008

Yes   Delay consideration of Colombia free-trade agreement

Yes   Override Bush veto of federal farm and nutrition programs reauthorization bill

Yes   Overhaul surveillance laws and permit dismissal of suits against companies that conducted warrantless wiretapping

Yes   Grant mortgage relief to homeowners and funding for Fannie Mae and Freddie Mac

No   Approve initial $700 billion program to stabilize financial markets

No   Approve final $700 billion program to stabilize financial markets

Yes   Provide $14 billion in loans to automakers

2007

Yes   Increase minimum wage by $2.10 an hour

Yes   Approve $124.2 billion in emergency war spending and set goal for redeployment of troops from Iraq

Yes   Reject federal contraceptive assistance to international family planning groups

Yes   Override Bush veto of $23.2 billion water projects authorization bill

No   Implement Peru free-trade agreement

Yes   Approve energy policy overhaul with new fuel economy standards

No   Clear $473.5 billion omnibus spending bill, including $70 billion for military operations

CQ VOTE STUDIES

	PARTY UNITY		PRESIDENTIAL SUPPORT	
	SUPPORT	OPPOSE	SUPPORT	OPPOSE
2008	94%	6%	15%	85%
2007	91%	9%	8%	92%
2006	90%	10%	37%	63%
2005	87%	13%	28%	72%
2004	91%	9%	41%	59%

INTEREST GROUPS

	AFL-CIO	ADA	CCUS	ACU
2008	100%	90%	56%	12%
2007	96%	95%	55%	12%
2006	100%	75%	33%	28%
2005	100%	80%	46%	25%
2004	93%	80%	38%	16%

MICHIGAN 1
Upper Peninsula; northern Lower Michigan

Beginning along the Saginaw Bay shore, the 1st stretches 25,000 square miles from Michigan's northern Lower Peninsula to take in the entire Upper Peninsula (U.P.). Full of rolling, forested hills, the rural 1st encompasses 44 percent of Michigan's land mass, but did not contain a single city with more than 20,000 residents at the time of the 2000 census.

Tourism is a major economic engine in the 1st, and many down-state residents head north to ski, hunt and fish. Touching three of the Great Lakes, the 1st has more freshwater shoreline than any other district in the continental United States. Mackinac Island, known for its Victorian-style lake houses, ban on cars and fudge, is a popular spot. Isle Royale, the state's northernmost outpost, plays host to wolves, elk and backpackers.

Self-proclaimed "Yoopers" from the U.P. are connected to the rest of the district in Northern Michigan only by the Mackinac Bridge. Despite being Michiganders, Yoopers, isolated from the rest of their state, tend to identify culturally with nearby Wisconsinites or Canadians. Although logging remains important, nearly tapped-out resources in the existing mining

industry now provide only modest incomes for district residents. Keweenaw County, once a booming copper mining center at the northern tip of the U.P., now has the highest unemployment rate in the state.

The district has suffered from recent national economic downturns, the continuing auto industry decline and steady population loss. Housing markets have crashed in Lower Peninsula lakefront towns such as Petoskey, Torch Lake and Charlevoix, established beach resort and second-home havens for residents of the state and visitors from across the upper Midwest.

There is a strong current of social conservatism in the 1st, particularly with regard to gun rights, although Democrats still dominate local politics. Democrat Barack Obama eked out a 2-percentage-point victory here in the 2008 presidential election.

MAJOR INDUSTRY
Tourism, logging, mining, auto parts

CITIES
Marquette, 19,661; Sault Ste. Marie, 16,542; Escanaba, 13,140

NOTABLE
The National Ski Hall of Fame is in Ishpeming.

Rep. Peter Hoekstra (R)

Elected 1992; 9th term

CAPITOL OFFICE
225-4401
hoekstra.house.gov
2234 Rayburn Bldg. 20515-2202; fax 226-0779

COMMITTEES
Appropriations Select Intelligence Oversight Panel
Education & Labor
Select Intelligence - ranking member

RESIDENCE
Holland

BORN
Oct. 30, 1953; Groningen, Netherlands

RELIGION
Christian Reformed Church

FAMILY
Wife, Diane Hoekstra; three children

EDUCATION
Hope College, B.A. 1975 (political science);
U. of Michigan, M.B.A. 1977

CAREER
Furniture company executive

POLITICAL HIGHLIGHTS
No previous office

ELECTION RESULTS

2008 GENERAL

Peter Hoekstra (R)	214,100	62.4%
Fred Johnson (D)	119,506	34.8%
Dan Johnson (LIBERT)	5,496	1.6%
Ronald E. Graeser (USTAX)	4,200	1.2%

2008 PRIMARY

Peter Hoekstra (R)	unopposed

2006 GENERAL

Peter Hoekstra (R)	183,006	66.5 %
Kimon Kotos (D)	86,950	31.6%

PREVIOUS WINNING PERCENTAGES
2004 (69%); 2002 (70%); 2000 (64%); 1998 (69%);
1996 (65%); 1994 (75%); 1992 (63%)

Hoekstra is a former business executive who shares conservative Republicans' general disdain for government's regulatory ways. And he has not been shy about making himself heard, both as the Select Intelligence Committee's top Republican and as a leading critic of mandatory student testing under the No Child Left Behind elementary and secondary education law.

Hoekstra (HOOK-struh) is reserved, even stolid, displaying the personal discipline that made him a success in business. He lives out of his office when Congress is in session, stowing his clothes, a sleeping bag and a pillow there; his wife and three children live in Michigan. He is conscious about how his party is perceived — he was the first member of Congress to call for Idaho Sen. Larry E. Craig's resignation after Craig was arrested for lewd conduct in a Minneapolis airport bathroom in August 2007.

But Hoekstra has had enough of Washington now that the GOP is mired in the minority. He launched a bid in March 2009 to become Michigan's next governor, hoping his corporate experience and relatively close ties to labor would help. He was expected to face plenty of competition in the primary election, but that didn't deter him. "We need to begin the process of rebuilding a strong Michigan," he said in announcing his candidacy.

Although best known in Washington for his work on the Intelligence Committee, Hoekstra is likely to focus more intently on education and labor issues as he shifts his political goals. At the beginning of the 110th Congress (2007-08), he reclaimed the seat on the Education and Labor Committee he had given up for two years while he chaired the Intelligence panel.

He is a sharp critic of the mandatory annual testing required under the No Child Left Behind Act, President George W. Bush's signature elementary and secondary education overhaul. He fought the testing mandate in vain in 2001. He champions an alternative that would let states determine how to measure school performance.

When Intelligence Chairman Porter J. Goss became CIA director in 2004, Speaker J. Dennis Hastert chose Hoekstra to replace Goss as chairman. He promptly helped steer to enactment a bipartisan bill to create a director of national intelligence (DNI) overseeing the CIA and other spy agencies. The position had been the main recommendation of the independent panel that investigated the Sept. 11 terrorist attacks.

But Hoekstra is disillusioned with the result. He said the DNI's office "has become a big bureaucracy" that has failed to make spy agencies work together smoothly and that the agencies are slower in providing analyses to lawmakers than they were before the office was set up. "I still firmly believe in the need for a DNI or centralized head of the community, but the bottom line is, it needs a radical makeover," he said.

Hoekstra supported the Bush administration's general approach to fighting terrorism, backing the view that the United States must go on the offense in Iraq and elsewhere to prevent future attacks at home. He is less impressed by President Obama's policies, although the two have found some areas of agreement. In a March 2009 speech discussing his strategy for Afghanistan and Pakistan, Obama urged Congress to pass a bipartisan bill cosponsored by Hoekstra to provide duty-free treatment to goods imported from "reconstruction opportunity zones" in the border region between the two countries to help develop their economies.

Because of his sworn-to-secrecy role as an Intelligence Committee member, Hoekstra got in some hot water in February 2009 when he told reporters about a high-level congressional delegation trip to Iraq and Afghanistan days before the group departed and then posted updates on the group's activities using the Twitter.com social network. "Just landed in Baghdad," Hoekstra told his followers. "Moved into Green Zone by helicopter. . . . Headed to new U.S. embassy." Lawmakers had been advised before the trip to keep it a secret, for security reasons, and the Pentagon began reviewing its communications with lawmakers after Hoekstra's "tweets."

A member of the conservative Republican Study Committee, Hoekstra sides with his party on most votes that divide the House along party lines — 95 percent of the time in the 110th Congress. But he has split with the GOP majority on occasion. After voting to defeat the initial version of the $700 billion financial rescue plan in fall 2008, he supported the final version, saying he feared the ongoing credit squeeze would harm businesses and employees throughout his state. He also voted to bail out the domestic auto industry, a plan that died in the Senate.

Hoekstra has enjoyed the endorsement of the Michigan Teamsters in his re-election races this decade, although he headed a probe of election corruption within the Teamsters while he chaired the Education and Labor panel's Oversight Subcommittee from 1995 to 2001. Democrats said he was seeking partisan advantage while Republicans objected he wasn't being political enough.

The child of immigrants from the Netherlands, Hoekstra was born Cornelius Peter Hoekstra, but Cornelius was dropped at the insistence of immigration officials who decreed it was not a familiar name in America. His family settled in the town of Holland in a heavily Dutch part of Michigan. Hoekstra's father ran a bakery shop for 25 years. The family spoke English and Dutch at home, but Hoekstra was encouraged to blend into his new surroundings.

After earning a master's degree in business administration from the University of Michigan, Hoekstra spent 15 years at the furniture design firm Herman Miller. He started as a project manager and rose to vice president for product management.

The House seat was his first attempt at public office. In the 1992 primary, he knocked off 13-term GOP Rep. Guy Vander Jagt, for whom he once had interned, accusing the incumbent of neglecting his constituents. He then took the general election with 63 percent of the vote. He promised to serve six terms and leave, but later revoked that pledge. Voters didn't seem to mind, re-electing him comfortably ever since.

KEY VOTES

2008

No Delay consideration of Colombia free-trade agreement
Yes Override Bush veto of federal farm and nutrition programs reauthorization bill
Yes Overhaul surveillance laws and permit dismissal of suits against companies that conducted warrantless wiretapping
No Grant mortgage relief to homeowners and funding for Fannie Mae and Freddie Mac
No Approve initial $700 billion program to stabilize financial markets
Yes Approve final $700 billion program to stabilize financial markets
Yes Provide $14 billion in loans to automakers

2007

No Increase minimum wage by $2.10 an hour
No Approve $124.2 billion in emergency war spending and set goal for redeployment of troops from Iraq
Yes Reject federal contraceptive assistance to international family planning groups
Yes Override Bush veto of $23.2 billion water projects authorization bill
No Implement Peru free-trade agreement
No Approve energy policy overhaul with new fuel economy standards
Yes Clear $473.5 billion omnibus spending bill, including $70 billion for military operations

CQ VOTE STUDIES

	PARTY UNITY		PRESIDENTIAL SUPPORT	
	SUPPORT	OPPOSE	SUPPORT	OPPOSE
2008	96%	4%	76%	24%
2007	95%	5%	82%	18%
2006	95%	5%	90%	10%
2005	96%	4%	91%	9%
2004	98%	2%	90%	10%

INTEREST GROUPS

	AFL-CIO	ADA	CCUS	ACU
2008	27%	20%	83%	88%
2007	17%	5%	68%	92%
2006	21%	5%	93%	92%
2005	13%	0%	89%	100%
2004	15%	5%	95%	96%

MICHIGAN 2
West — Muskegon, Holland

Stretching 160 miles along Lake Michigan on the western edge of the state's Lower Peninsula, the 2nd District is full of cherry trees, asparagus farms and sandy beaches that are bombarded every summer by vacationers hoping for at least one completely sunny day.

Most of the 2nd's land north of Muskegon, the district's largest city, consists of sparsely populated, smaller rural communities. Those small towns, once magnets for outdoor enthusiasts heading for the lakeshore dunes or to hunt and fish, are struggling as rising unemployment rates and energy costs keep would-be tourists at home.

Opportunities in the once-rich logging industry have been replaced by jobs at smaller manufacturing companies, which are mostly based in the district's south, although Muskegon has struggled to keep traditional manufacturing jobs. South of Muskegon, a decline in auto parts and furniture manufacturing has resulted in significant layoffs, but the southern part of the district still hosts several of the nation's top office furniture makers — including Herman Miller in Zeeland and Haworth in Holland.

The 2nd has the largest concentration of Dutch-Americans in the nation, and Holland is a conservative Dutch-settled port town that relies on tourism. Early 20th-century lifestyle is recreated in the Dutch Village Theme Park, which features traditional crafts and klompen dancers. Holland's annual tulip festival draws hundreds of thousands of visitors every May.

Increasingly politically competitive, the 2nd is still Michigan's most Republican district, primarily because of the traditional Dutch heritage in Ottawa County. It was John McCain's best county statewide in the 2008 presidential election. Republican presidential candidates have won their highest percentages statewide in the district in the last two elections: George W. Bush won 60 percent in 2004 and McCain took 51 percent here overall in 2008.

MAJOR INDUSTRY
Furniture, tourism, agriculture, manufacturing

CITIES
Muskegon, 40,105; Holland, 35,048; Norton Shores, 22,527

NOTABLE
Grand Haven, known as Coast Guard City USA, honors the men and women of the U.S. Coast Guard during its annual festival.

Rep. Vernon J. Ehlers (R)

Elected December 1993; 8th full term

CAPITOL OFFICE
225-3831
www.house.gov/ehlers
2182 Rayburn Bldg. 20515-2203; fax 225-5144

COMMITTEES
Education & Labor
Science & Technology
Transportation & Infrastructure

RESIDENCE
Grand Rapids

BORN
Feb. 6, 1934; Pipestone, Minn.

RELIGION
Christian Reformed Church

FAMILY
Wife, Jo Ehlers; four children

EDUCATION
Calvin College, attended 1952-55 (physics);
U. of California, Berkeley, A.B. 1956 (physics),
Ph.D. 1960 (physics)

CAREER
Professor; physicist

POLITICAL HIGHLIGHTS
Kent County Commission, 1975-83 (chairman, 1979-82); Mich. House, 1983-85; Mich. Senate, 1985-93 (president pro tempore, 1990-93)

ELECTION RESULTS

2008 GENERAL

Vernon J. Ehlers (R)	203,799	61.1%
Henry Sanchez (D)	117,961	35.4%
Erwin J. Haas (LIBERT)	11,758	3.5%

2008 PRIMARY

Vernon J. Ehlers (R)	unopposed

2006 GENERAL

Vernon J. Ehlers (R)	171,212	63.1%
James Rinck (D)	93,846	34.6%
Jeff A. Steinport (LIBERT)	3,702	1.4%

PREVIOUS WINNING PERCENTAGES
2004 (67%); 2002 (70%); 2000 (65%); 1998 (73%);
1996 (69%); 1994 (74%); 1993 Special Election (67%)

The first research physicist elected to Congress, Ehlers brings a scientist's analytical mind and a moderate's consensus-building approach to tackling science, transportation and other issues. "I'm a nonpartisan Republican," he said. "I'm a Republican in my heart and soul, but I'm interested in solutions."

His scholarly background and willingness to part ways with his party have elevated his influence on Capitol Hill, where Democrats tend to court his vote when they're in need of moderate Republican support.

During the 110th Congress (2007-08), Ehlers (AY-lurz) was among the Republicans most willing to side with the Democratic majority, voting with Democrats in favor of bills aimed at rescuing struggling automobile companies and banks, as well as for a measure that would have allowed the Food and Drug Administration to regulate tobacco as a drug. It passed the House but died in the Senate. In January 2009, he was among 40 Republicans to join Democrats in pushing through an expansion of a health care program for poor children.

Where Ehlers is most likely to find common cause with President Obama, though, is on the issue of science funding. As the ranking Republican on the Science and Technology Committee's panel on Research and Science Education, he has advocated relentlessly for the government to do more to expand scientific research, a goal Obama has also touted.

Specifically, Ehlers backs greater spending for NASA's earth science and aeronautics research programs as well as its more glamorous and costly mission-to-Mars effort. And he has repeatedly defended the National Science Foundation (NSF), which hands out about 20 percent of the federal money for research at U.S. universities. When the House passed a bill in May 2007 to reauthorize the foundation through fiscal 2010, Ehlers noted that it has funded research for 170 scientists who have gone on to win the Nobel Prize in science.

A member of the Education and Labor Committee, Ehlers successfully pushed through Congress in 2002 an NSF authorization measure that expanded the foundation's programs covering kindergarten through 12th grade. He also was able to get a provision in President George W. Bush's 2001 education policy overhaul that ensures students are tested on science as well as reading and math. In early 2009, he urged his colleagues to move quickly to reauthorize that law.

Ehlers travels extensively to schools and universities to promote science education and he said he's grown used to suspicion from non-scientists. "People are very happy to accept science that doesn't interfere with their basic world view or beliefs," he told U.S. News & World Report in December 2007. "Global warming is a good example. I often like to point out to people that in many cases, the opposite of rational is not irrational but emotional."

On the Transportation and Infrastructure Committee, Ehlers has had a longtime interest in technological upgrades to the nation's aging air traffic control system. And when the panel takes up a massive six-year reauthorization for highways and transit systems in the 111th Congress (2009-10), he hopes to convince colleagues to direct more federal funds to Michigan.

The white-haired, grandfatherly Ehlers briefly realized his goal of becoming a full committee chairman in 2006, heading the House Administration panel — which oversees the day-to-day operations of the Capitol — for a little less than a year before the Democratic takeover of the chamber. GOP leaders had appointed him to replace Bob Ney of Ohio, who was caught up in an influence-peddling scandal and eventually resigned. But with Democrats in control of the House, the Administration post lost much of its appeal. Ehlers stepped down before Republicans finalized committee selections for the 111th, saying he wanted to focus his attention on his other assignments.

Ehlers is among the Republican moderates who take a strong pro-environment stand. An environmental activist who launched his political career on green issues — he handed out spruce seedlings while campaigning door to door — Ehlers supports increased fuel efficiency standards for sport utility vehicles, an unpopular position in auto-centric Michigan. He chairs the House's Renewable Energy and Energy Efficiency Caucus.

Despite his record of reaching across the aisle, Ehlers occasionally has rankled Democrats. He told a National Academy of Sciences panel in 2004 that he considered it appropriate for presidential administrations to ask scientists about their voting records or party affiliation when considering them for advisory committees — a view that disappointed some Science Committee colleagues.

The son of a minister and a devout Christian himself, Ehlers keeps a Bible in his office, on a shelf next to his Basic Dictionary of Science.

A sickly child who suffered from severe asthma, Ehlers was schooled at home because his parents felt he would be less likely to catch colds from other children. His interest in science was sparked by his sister's subscription to Popular Science magazine. "I still remember doing some of those experiments at home," he said.

His father encouraged him to go to college, and Ehlers excelled academically, completing his doctorate in physics at the University of California at Berkeley at age 26. He stayed on as a research physicist for six years. In 1966, he left for the more conservative, religious atmosphere of Calvin College in Grand Rapids, which he had attended as an undergraduate.

In 1982, Ehlers won election to the state House, succeeding Republican Paul B. Henry, a former colleague at Calvin College who had moved to the state Senate. Over the next dozen years, Ehlers followed Henry up the political ladder, succeeding him in the state Senate and finally in Congress. Ehlers also served as president pro tempore of the Michigan Senate from 1990 to 1993.

Nearly 60 years old, he was looking for a new challenge and weighing a campaign for the Senate seat held by Democrat Donald W. Riegle Jr. But when Henry died of brain cancer that July, Ehlers launched a House bid. He won with 67 percent of the vote in the special election and has never faced a significant challenge to his re-election.

KEY VOTES

2008
No   Delay consideration of Colombia free-trade agreement
No   Override Bush veto of federal farm and nutrition programs reauthorization bill
Yes Overhaul surveillance laws and permit dismissal of suits against companies that conducted warrantless wiretapping
No   Grant mortgage relief to homeowners and funding for Fannie Mae and Freddie Mac
Yes Approve initial $700 billion program to stabilize financial markets
Yes Approve final $700 billion program to stabilize financial markets
Yes Provide $14 billion in loans to automakers

2007
Yes Increase minimum wage by $2.10 an hour
No   Approve $124.2 billion in emergency war spending and set goal for redeployment of troops from Iraq
Yes Reject federal contraceptive assistance to international family planning groups
Yes Override Bush veto of $23.2 billion water projects authorization bill
Yes Implement Peru free-trade agreement
Yes Approve energy policy overhaul with new fuel economy standards
Yes Clear $473.5 billion omnibus spending bill, including $70 billion for military operations

CQ VOTE STUDIES

	PARTY UNITY		PRESIDENTIAL SUPPORT	
	SUPPORT	OPPOSE	SUPPORT	OPPOSE
2008	81%	19%	64%	36%
2007	78%	22%	63%	37%
2006	84%	16%	95%	5%
2005	78%	22%	67%	33%
2004	86%	14%	79%	21%

INTEREST GROUPS

	AFL-CIO	ADA	CCUS	ACU
2008	33%	40%	100%	61%
2007	33%	20%	85%	68%
2006	21%	10%	80%	68%
2005	20%	15%	85%	64%
2004	27%	20%	100%	67%

MICHIGAN 3
West central — Grand Rapids

Nestled along the Grand River, Grand Rapids, Michigan's second-most-populous city, teems with auto plants and metals manufacturing, but it's a world away from Detroit. Conservative Dutch Republicans — not auto union Democrats — control the 3rd.

Also unlike Detroit, residents in the 3rd escaped complete dependence on the auto industry, and a majority of jobs in the metropolitan area are downtown and not in sprawling suburbs. The city is a leading producer of metal office furniture, in addition to avionics systems, tools and home appliances. Footwear manufacturer Wolverine World Wide, maker of brands such as Hush Puppies and Sebago, has headquarters in Rockford, north of Grand Rapids. One of the largest employers here, direct-sales company Alticor, based in Ada, markets personal- and home-care products. Grand Rapids' health care industry prompted Michigan State University to build a new medical school, to be completed by 2010.

Major efforts to revitalize downtown have attracted young professionals, who enjoy the 3rd's big-city amenities and close proximity to the Lake

Michigan shoreline. Downtown boasts new residential lofts, a convention center and numerous museums, all of which have contributed to rejuvenated business and entertainment districts. More than 80 percent of residents live in Kent County, which has experienced significant growth outside of Grand Rapids. The rest live in Ionia and Barry counties, located east and southeast of Kent, respectively.

Gerald R. Ford made his way to the U.S. House and then the Oval Office from Grand Rapids — area roads, buildings and an airport are named for the 38th president — and his brand of small-government Republicanism and fiscal restraint still holds sway in the 3rd District despite urban growth. George W. Bush won 59 percent of the district's presidential vote in 2004, but the 3rd favored Republican John McCain only by roughly 2,000 votes in 2008.

MAJOR INDUSTRY
Office furniture, auto parts, metals manufacturing, health care

CITIES
Grand Rapids, 197,800; Wyoming, 69,368; Kentwood, 45,255

NOTABLE
The Norton Mound Group, one of the best-preserved burial centers of the Hopewell culture, is in Grand Rapids.

Rep. Dave Camp (R)

Elected 1990; 10th term

CAPITOL OFFICE
225-3561
camp.house.gov
341 Cannon Bldg. 20515-2204; fax 225-9679

COMMITTEES
Ways & Means - ranking member
Joint Taxation - ranking member

RESIDENCE
Midland

BORN
July 9, 1953; Midland, Mich.

RELIGION
Roman Catholic

FAMILY
Wife, Nancy Camp; three children

EDUCATION
Albion College, B.A. 1975 (economics);
U. of San Diego, J.D. 1978

CAREER
Lawyer; congressional aide

POLITICAL HIGHLIGHTS
Mich. House, 1989-91

ELECTION RESULTS

2008 GENERAL

Dave Camp (R)	204,259	61.9%
Andrew D. Concannon (D)	117,665	35.7%
John Emerick (USTAX)	4,055	1.2%
Allitta Hren (LIBERT)	3,785	1.1%

2008 PRIMARY

Dave Camp (R)	unopposed

2006 GENERAL

Dave Camp (R)	160,041	60.6%
Mike Huckleberry (D)	100,260	37.9%

PREVIOUS WINNING PERCENTAGES
2004 (64%); 2002 (68%); 2000 (68%); 1998 (91%);
1996 (65%); 1994 (73%); 1992 (63%); 1990 (65%)

Camp is an unassuming policy wonk who diligently works behind the scenes to listen to others and find compromises. With his deep understanding of legislation and strong loyalty to party leaders, he has quietly ascended the GOP ranks to become the Michigan delegation's most powerful Republican.

Camp succeeded retiring Republican Jim McCrery of Louisiana in late 2008 for the top GOP slot on the Ways and Means Committee. Camp, who has served on the influential tax and trade panel for the last eight terms, prevailed over California's Wally Herger. Herger has more committee seniority, but Camp's ties to the House leadership and his fundraising prowess — he handed out nearly $900,000 from his campaign fund during the 2007-08 election cycle — gave him the edge.

Camp's challenge is balancing any desire to work with Democrats with remaining faithful to a Republican leadership that often prefers full-throated resistance. Further complicating matters for him is that two of the House GOP's leading conservative fiscal voices — Wisconsin's Paul D. Ryan and Minority Whip Eric Cantor of Virginia — also serve on Ways and Means.

Camp finds it useful to have "as many channels of communication as you can," including lawmakers from the era when Republicans controlled the House. He was spotted at the Capitol in January 2009 talking with former California Republican Rep. Bill Thomas, who served as Ways and Means chairman and is now a strategic adviser at a Washington law firm. "I'm the happy recipient of the advice he will share on issues and strategy," Camp said later.

Unlike the acerbic Thomas, Camp is well-liked in party circles. He is a member of both the conservative Republican Study Committee and the moderate Republican Main Street Partnership. "I'm a conservative on fiscal policy, but a moderate on some other issues," he said.

Michigan's dire economy — including his district, which had several counties mired in double-digit unemployment in early 2009 — occasionally spurs him to side with Democrats. He was one of three Republicans on Ways and Means to vote in favor of a Democratic measure in April 2008 to extend benefits for the nation's unemployed. And that December, he was one of 32 Republicans — including eight from Michigan — to approve a measure allowing up to $14 billion in loans to eligible domestic automakers. That legislation died in the Senate, although President George W. Bush later maneuvered to funnel loan funds to the auto industry from a $700 billion rescue package for the financial services industry, which cleared in fall 2008 with Camp's vote.

Reflecting his commitment to the Big Three automakers in his state, Camp voted against an energy bill in 2007 to require new fuel efficiency standards of 35 miles per gallon for cars and light trucks and 36 billion gallons of biofuels to be used annually by 2022. "We still want cars to be affordable for the American consumer," said Camp, who drives the same Pontiac he drove to Washington when first elected to Congress.

Camp has opposed a string of other Democratic initiatives, including a bill — which President Obama signed into law in early 2009 — to expand the State Children's Health Insurance Program, which provides coverage for children from low-income families ineligible for Medicaid. He said on the House floor that he supports the program. "The bill before us today, however, not only threatens the core mission of the program — providing health insurance for low-income children — but creates a new entitlement that will demand higher taxes on all Americans in just a few short years."

He also criticized Obama's $787 billion economic stimulus plan, signed into law in February 2009. Camp said it would "do more harm than good" and that he would have preferred a plan that reduced spending and included more tax cuts.

Camp's name was on a March 2009 fundraising letter, distributed by the campaign arm of House Republicans, which sought to benefit from public anger over the bonus payments made by American International Group Inc., which had benefited from the fall 2008 financial sector rescue law. The letter blamed Speaker Nancy Pelosi of California and Democrats for allowing the bonuses to happen. "While Republicans are fighting to ensure that you keep more of your own money, what do the Democrats continue to do? Vote to raise your taxes. And what will those taxes be used for? To pay Wall Street bonuses and bigger government," the letter states.

Camp has long promoted legislation to apply any lawmaker's unused office and staff funds to paying down the national debt, and during his tenure he has returned to the Treasury more than $1 million in unused office account money, though lawmakers aren't required to do so.

Camp has supported all the major trade agreements proposed by his party, and has been a leader in the GOP's quest to make permanent the package of tax cuts enacted in 2001.

During the 109th Congress (2005-06), he played a key role in a major pension overhaul bill that included significant new tax incentives for retirement savings. He was one of a handful of lawmakers from both chambers who spent months writing the final bill, which he said was among the most difficult issues he has tackled as a legislator.

Camp has drawn on his experience as a domestic-law attorney in Michigan to promote the adoption of children in foster care. In 2003, he won enactment of a bill to give states financial incentives to increase the number of adoptions each year, particularly of older children and those with special needs.

Camp's interest in politics began during law school, when he volunteered on the local judicial campaign of a lawyer for whom he was interning. He then got involved in GOP campaigns at the local and state levels. After practicing law for five years, Camp became chief of staff for Republican Rep. Bill Schuette, a childhood friend. He returned to Michigan in 1986 to manage Schuette's re-election campaign, and two years later Camp won an open state House seat based in Midland, his hometown.

When Schuette ran for the Senate against Democrat Carl Levin in 1990, Camp went after his mentor's congressional seat. With Schuette's endorsement, Camp eked out a primary victory. He went on to win the general election with 65 percent of the vote and has won re-election easily ever since.

KEY VOTES

2008

No	Delay consideration of Colombia free-trade agreement
Yes	Override Bush veto of federal farm and nutrition programs reauthorization bill
Yes	Overhaul surveillance laws and permit dismissal of suits against companies that conducted warrantless wiretapping
No	Grant mortgage relief to homeowners and funding for Fannie Mae and Freddie Mac
Yes	Approve initial $700 billion program to stabilize financial markets
Yes	Approve final $700 billion program to stabilize financial markets
Yes	Provide $14 billion in loans to automakers

2007

No	Increase minimum wage by $2.10 an hour
No	Approve $124.2 billion in emergency war spending and set goal for redeployment of troops from Iraq
Yes	Reject federal contraceptive assistance to international family planning groups
Yes	Override Bush veto of $23.2 billion water projects authorization bill
Yes	Implement Peru free-trade agreement
No	Approve energy policy overhaul with new fuel economy standards
Yes	Clear $473.5 billion omnibus spending bill, including $70 billion for military operations

CQ VOTE STUDIES

	PARTY UNITY		PRESIDENTIAL SUPPORT	
	SUPPORT	OPPOSE	SUPPORT	OPPOSE
2008	95%	5%	72%	28%
2007	95%	5%	77%	23%
2006	95%	5%	100%	0%
2005	95%	5%	83%	17%
2004	94%	6%	82%	18%

INTEREST GROUPS

	AFL-CIO	ADA	CCUS	ACU
2008	20%	20%	94%	83%
2007	17%	5%	90%	96%
2006	14%	0%	100%	84%
2005	21%	10%	89%	83%
2004	27%	10%	100%	88%

MICHIGAN 4
North central — Midland, Traverse City

Stretching from just west of Saginaw northwest to Leelanau Peninsula's lakeshore at the mouth of Grand Traverse Bay, bountiful forests, farms, vineyards and inland lakes cover much of the 14 central Michigan counties in the 4th District, Michigan's second-largest district in land area. The sparsely populated white pine forests northwest of Midland were once logging lands but now host summer cottages for vacationers and homes for retirees.

On the district's eastern border, Midland, the 4th's largest city, is home to Dow Chemical and Dow Corning, makers of chemicals, plastics and silicone products. The city benefits from the company's philanthropy, with churches, schools, libraries and a local minor league baseball stadium built by its fortune, but like other major employers in the state, Dow has cut jobs recently. A bright spot for the region is a $1 billion expansion of Hemlock Semiconductor, a Dow subsidiary, which makes components for solar panels and computer chips at its plant in Hemlock.

Thirty miles west of Midland, Mount Pleasant hosts Central Michigan

University's nearly 30,000 students. The area's growth in the education sector — which includes a new medical school expected to open in 2011 — has helped insulate it from economic downturns. Another key employer in Mount Pleasant is the Soaring Eagle Casino and Resort, although vulnerability in the gaming industry has forced some layoffs.

West and south of Midland and Mount Pleasant, the district turns agricultural. Farmers — who till fields of sugar beets, dry beans, corn, wheat and oats — worry about free trade, price supports and crop insurance. The number of farms and small towns throughout the 4th traditionally gives it a Republican edge, but a slim 2-percentage-point majority of voters in the district supported Democrat Barack Obama in the 2008 presidential election.

MAJOR INDUSTRY
Agriculture, chemical and plastics manufacturing, tourism

CITIES
Midland (pt.), 41,463; Mount Pleasant, 25,946

NOTABLE
Chesaning's Showboat Music Festival, which began during the Depression with hopes of aiding an ailing economy, has pumped millions of dollars into the community.

Rep. Dale E. Kildee (D)

Elected 1976; 17th term

CAPITOL OFFICE
225-3611
www.house.gov/kildee
2107 Rayburn Bldg. 20515-2205; fax 225-6393

COMMITTEES
Education & Labor
(Early Childhood, Elementary & Secondary
Education - chairman)
Natural Resources

RESIDENCE
Flint

BORN
Sept. 16, 1929; Flint, Mich.

RELIGION
Roman Catholic

FAMILY
Wife, Gayle Kildee; three children

EDUCATION
Sacred Heart Seminary, B.A. 1952; U. of Detroit,
attended 1954 (teaching certificate); U. of
Peshawar (Pakistan), attended 1958-59 (Rotary
fellowship); U. of Michigan, M.A. 1961 (history)

CAREER
Teacher

POLITICAL HIGHLIGHTS
Mich. House, 1965-75; Mich. Senate, 1975-77

ELECTION RESULTS

2008 GENERAL

Dale E. Kildee (D)	221,841	70.4%
Matt Sawicki (R)	85,017	27.0%
Leonard Schwartz (LIBERT)	4,293	1.4%
Ken Mathenia (GREEN)	4,144	1.3%

2008 PRIMARY

Dale E. Kildee (D)	unopposed

2006 GENERAL

Dale E. Kildee (D)	176,171	72.9%
Eric J. Klammer (R)	60,967	25.2%

PREVIOUS WINNING PERCENTAGES
2004 (67%); 2002 (92%); 2000 (61%); 1998 (56%);
1996 (59%); 1994 (51%); 1992 (54%); 1990 (68%);
1988 (76%); 1986 (80%); 1984 (93%); 1982 (75%);
1980 (93%); 1978 (77%); 1976 (70%)

Reserved and soft-spoken, Kildee rarely displays the kind of theatrics that put members on the front page of newspapers or get them mentioned in political blogs. He prefers to work quietly to protect the auto industry and labor unions, and provides a liberal vote on a range of social issues.

Kildee entered politics in the 1960s, the heyday of the civil rights movement and the Great Society war on poverty; his philosophy remains firmly rooted in that era. Though he was not a firebrand contributing to loud protests, he said he had a strong belief that "the government's role is to promote, protect, defend and enhance human dignity."

Kildee's concern for the auto industry and labor unions stems from his childhood, watching his father walk the 12 blocks from their Flint home to work on the assembly line at the General Motors Buick "40 plant." His father could never afford one of the cars when he started working at the plant, Kildee said, but thanks to the union's efforts on wages and pensions, he was able to buy a brand-new Buick when he retired in 1950. "That is what has made America successful," Kildee said.

So after President Obama took office and said he would allow the Environmental Protection Agency to reconsider a George W. Bush administration decision barring states from setting their own automobile emissions standards, Kildee protested, arguing it would overly burden the struggling industry. "A patchwork is going to make it fiscally and technologically difficult for the auto industry," he told Michigan's Saginaw News.

Kildee and Obama were on the same page, though, in late 2008 when Congress considered legislation, to grant emergency loans to near-bankrupt GM and Chrysler. Kildee and Obama, then an Illinois senator and presidential candidate, endorsed the legislation, which was passed by the House but stalled in the Senate. President Bush granted the loans anyway, using the wide discretion Congress gave him earlier in the year over a $700 billion fund meant to shore up ailing banks.

Kildee practices what he preaches. He requires his congressional employees who drive to work to do so in a car manufactured by members of the United Auto Workers. After all, he reasons, you would not expect to see Brazilian oranges in the office of a Florida lawmaker.

Kildee is the second-ranking Democrat on the Education and Labor panel, and holds that same spot on the Natural Resources Committee — good positions from which to press two of his other causes: education and protections for American Indians.

In 2001, he helped negotiate the No Child Left Behind education law, which increased federal funding for education but set strict accountability standards for states. With the law up for renewal during the 111th Congress (2009-10), Kildee has joined Democrats in pushing to loosen some of those strictures while providing even more funding.

Kildee was raised with a deep concern for the plight of American Indians. His grandparents, immigrants from Ireland, had frequent contact with Indians on the reservation near Traverse City and he recalled hearing his father say Indians were treated unfairly. In one of his suit pockets is a copy not only of the Constitution but also of the landmark 1832 Supreme Court decision that gave the federal government exclusive jurisdiction over Indian affairs.

On Natural Resources, Kildee has closely monitored a long-running class action lawsuit over alleged federal mismanagement of Indian trust funds. And when lawmakers in 1997 started talking about taxing Indian-run gambling operations, Kildee founded the Native American Caucus. In honor of his efforts, the Grand Traverse Band of Ottawa and Chippewa Indians in 1998 designated April 15 "Dale Kildee Day."

Kildee is liberal on most social policy issues but because of his strong Catholic faith he opposes abortion. A seminary graduate, he abandoned the path to the priesthood to become a Latin teacher.

Kildee's foreign policy outlook is shaped largely by his life experiences. As a young teacher, he won a Rotary Foundation Fellowship and studied at the University of Peshawar in Pakistan, which he said gave him great insight into the "real Islam" and helped him understand the divisions between Shiites and Sunnis that have roiled Iraq since the U.S.-led invasion there in 2003, which Kildee opposed.

Kildee takes the responsibility of House membership seriously. Starting in late 1985, he voted yes or no on more than 6,000 consecutive roll call votes on the House floor, the longest streak of any active member. The streak ended in June 1998, when he joined more than 60 lawmakers in voting "present" on a campaign finance bill. Kildee started a new streak from 2001 until April 2008, when he missed a vote to name a post office after the late Democratic Rep. Julia Carson of Indiana. Kildee keeps in one of his suit pockets a laminated sheet — routinely updated by his staff — that details how many consecutive votes he has cast and the number of votes he has missed since 1985.

Kildee is also frugal with his office budget and returns money from his allocation to the U.S. Treasury every year, with the total going beyond $1.4 million over his career.

He was a teacher at Flint Central High School when his political career began in 1964 with a successful bid for the state House. He won a state Senate seat in 1974, and two years later won election for an open U.S. House seat. He coasted through his re-election bids until 1992 and 1994, when Republican Megan O'Neill, who had worked in the White House under President George Bush, ran strong campaigns. In 1992, Kildee had become vulnerable after reports that he had 100 overdrafts at the private bank for House members. Plus redistricting for the 1990s had left him a redrawn district in which almost half the people were new to him.

After the redistricting by the GOP legislature, Kildee faced five-term incumbent Democrat James A. Barcia in a redrawn 5th District. But Barcia ran for the state Senate rather than take on Kildee in a 2002 primary, and Kildee locked up his seat once again. He took 70 percent of the vote in 2008 against Republican Matt Sawicki.

KEY VOTES

2008

Yes Delay consideration of Colombia free-trade agreement
Yes Override Bush veto of federal farm and nutrition programs reauthorization bill
Yes Overhaul surveillance laws and permit dismissal of suits against companies that conducted warrantless wiretapping
Yes Grant mortgage relief to homeowners and funding for Fannie Mae and Freddie Mac
Yes Approve initial $700 billion program to stabilize financial markets
Yes Approve final $700 billion program to stabilize financial markets
Yes Provide $14 billion in loans to automakers

2007

Yes Increase minimum wage by $2.10 an hour
Yes Approve $124.2 billion in emergency war spending and set goal for redeployment of troops from Iraq
Yes Reject federal contraceptive assistance to international family planning groups
Yes Override Bush veto of $23.2 billion water projects authorization bill
No Implement Peru free-trade agreement
Yes Approve energy policy overhaul with new fuel economy standards
Yes Clear $473.5 billion omnibus spending bill, including $70 billion for military operations

CQ VOTE STUDIES

	PARTY UNITY		PRESIDENTIAL SUPPORT	
	SUPPORT	OPPOSE	SUPPORT	OPPOSE
2008	99%	1%	15%	85%
2007	97%	3%	7%	93%
2006	96%	4%	33%	67%
2005	91%	9%	22%	78%
2004	93%	7%	35%	65%

INTEREST GROUPS

	AFL-CIO	ADA	CCUS	ACU
2008	100%	100%	61%	0%
2007	96%	100%	50%	4%
2006	100%	80%	27%	20%
2005	93%	80%	33%	20%
2004	100%	90%	38%	16%

MICHIGAN 5

East — Flint, Saginaw, Bay City

A thriving blue-collar tradition in the 5th has given way to Rust Belt deterioration and a workforce exodus. The vulnerable U.S. auto industry remains key to any economic stability here. The 5th's other staple is agriculture — in the northeastern part of the district that stretches across Tuscola County on Michigan's "Thumb" to Saginaw Bay, small towns thrive on family-owned farms and the sugar beet industry.

The auto industry in Flint and Saginaw, the district's most populous cities, employed well more than 100,000 people when manufacturing peaked in the late 1970s. Now, fewer than 15,000 district residents work in the industry. Widespread layoffs have led to population loss, which threatens school district viability and the housing market. Vacant homes in crumbling neighborhoods illustrate the distress in some residential areas of Saginaw, and municipal budget shortfalls in Flint have made it difficult for local government to provide public services.

Delphi and General Motors plant closings have stalled the auto parts manufacturing sector, but the industry still plays a role in the local econ-

omy, drawing suppliers and distributors to the 5th. And, engines for the new Chevy Volt will be built in Flint by 2010. Local officials hope to move away from the region's manufacturing past and develop education and health care hubs — Flint's University of Michigan campus and Kettering University continue to grow, and the aging population has required expansions to local hospitals.

The 5th District's blue-collar voters adhere to fiscal populism and social conservatism, and they tend to identify strongly with the Democratic Party. Genesee County (Flint), which accounts for two-thirds of the district's population, is strongly influenced by the United Auto Workers union and gave Barack Obama 66 percent of its vote in the 2008 presidential election. His Genesee tally was bolstered by a large African-American population.

MAJOR INDUSTRY
Auto parts manufacturing, agriculture, sugar processing, health care

CITIES
Flint, 124,943; Saginaw, 61,799; Bay City, 36,817; Burton, 30,308

NOTABLE
Michael Moore's 1989 documentary, "Roger & Me," chronicled the impact of GM's layoffs in the 1980s on Flint.

Rep. Fred Upton (R)

Elected 1986; 12th term

CAPITOL OFFICE
225-3761
www.house.gov/upton
2183 Rayburn Bldg. 20515-2206; fax 225-4986

COMMITTEES
Energy & Commerce

RESIDENCE
St. Joseph

BORN
April 23, 1953; St. Joseph, Mich.

RELIGION
Protestant

FAMILY
Wife, Amey Upton; two children

EDUCATION
U. of Michigan, B.A. 1975 (journalism)

CAREER
Congressional aide; White House budget analyst

POLITICAL HIGHLIGHTS
No previous office

ELECTION RESULTS

2008 GENERAL

Fred Upton (R)	188,157	58.9%
Don Cooney (D)	123,257	38.6%
Greg Merle (LIBERT)	4,720	1.5%
Edward Pinkney (GREEN)	3,512	1.1%

2008 PRIMARY

Fred Upton (R)	unopposed

2006 GENERAL

Fred Upton (R)	142,125	60.6%
Kim Clark (D)	88,978	37.9%
Kenneth E. Howe (LIBERT)	3,480	1.5%

PREVIOUS WINNING PERCENTAGES
2004 (65%); 2002 (69%); 2000 (68%); 1998 (70%);
1996 (68%); 1994 (73%); 1992 (62%); 1990 (58%);
1988 (71%); 1986 (62%)

Upton is moderately conservative, but goes his own way on issues ranging from the Iraq War and gun control to environmental and fiscal spending. Democrats often seek his vote — but that's not always a sure thing, either.

Boyish-looking and down-to-earth (he insists that everyone he meets calls him "Fred"), Upton considers himself a compromiser. "I'm not a rubber stamp and people know that," he said. "If you can convince me of the merits, you will have my vote every time."

During President George W. Bush's two terms, Upton declined to support the president on roughly a third of the votes in which Democrats deviated from Republicans. Only 22 House GOP lawmakers serving in Congress at the end of the Bush administration broke with the president more frequently. In 2008, Upton did back Bush's $700 billion plan to shore up the nation's financial services industry, saying foes of the plan would pay "a very heavy political price" if the companies fail.

And at the start of President Obama's administration, Upton indicated he wouldn't sway to Democrats' desires easily; he stuck with the 33-member, moderate Republican Main Street Partnership in opposing Obama's economic stimulus measure, despite heavy lobbying by the president. In a statement following his vote, Upton commended Obama for trying to open the process, but blamed Speaker Nancy Pelosi for closing the door to Republicans. He also complained Democrats quietly stripped out $10 billion that would have allowed taxpayers to deduct state sales taxes and car loan interest.

His views may be closer to Obama's on involvement in the Iraq War, which the new president has vowed to bring to a close. In February 2007, Upton was one of 17 Republicans who voted for a resolution disapproving of Bush's plan to increase troop strength in Iraq, although in 2002 he backed a resolution authorizing Bush to go to war. "Let's face it, this is civil war. It is a real anarchy," Upton said on the House floor. "And in fact, the Iraqis don't want us there."

And he was an enthusiastic supporter in early 2009 of a Democratic bill to expand the State Children's Health Insurance Program, which covers children from low-income families that do not qualify for Medicaid. Bush had twice vetoed similar bills.

Upton has typically aligned more closely with Democrats on some energy matters; he voted for the Democrats' 2007 energy policy overhaul that included new fuel economy standards and emphasized conservation. Many Michiganders saw his vote as an affront to the state's Big Three auto companies. Upton said he voted for the new standards because his district's economy is less reliant on the state's once robust auto industry. Upton chairs the Congressional Automotive Caucus with Michigan Democrat Dale E. Kildee, and in late 2008 supported a $14 billion loan for the auto industry, which passed the House but didn't move in the Senate.

Upton is the top-ranking Republican on the Energy and Commerce Subcommittee on Energy and Environment and has advocated increasing U.S. nuclear power production. He has been a leading backer of the proposed Yucca Mountain nuclear waste storage dump in Nevada, but said in 2008 that the nation should also look at recycling radioactive materials. In May 2008, he was one of 35 Republicans to favor a Democratic tax bill that includes an extension of tax credits to support research into alternative energy. During full-committee debate on the 2009 economic stimulus bill, Upton failed to get support for his proposal to extend loan guarantees for "zero emissions energy" produced by nuclear and "clean" coal power.

He warned the panel in March 2009 to be cautious about climate legislation that could overburden manufacturing and energy-intensive industries. "More often than not, the cost of energy is the difference between operating in the United States and shutting the doors to move overseas," Upton said.

He also serves on the Energy and Commerce Committee's panel on Communications, Technology and the Internet. He has pushed bills to raise broadcast indecency fines and allow telephone companies to compete with cable TV companies in the video market. After singer Janet Jackson's "wardrobe malfunction" during the 2004 Super Bowl halftime show, Upton sought to stiffen the fines the Federal Communications Commission could impose for broadcast indecency. Though he initially proposed increasing the maximum penalty for indecency violations from $32,500 to $500,000 per offense, he settled for an increase of $325,000 in 2006, saying the new cap would give the law some "teeth."

Upton and Democrat Edward J. Markey of Massachusetts in 2005 worked on a proposal to extend daylight-saving time for eight weeks. Congress ultimately cleared a version providing a one-month extension, beginning in 2007, which the pair said could help conserve energy used for lighting. Upton also cosponsored an amendment to the Democratic leadership's 2007 energy bill requiring the use of energy-efficient light bulbs in Capitol facilities. Later that year, he successfully pushed a House bill to criminalize the unauthorized distribution, possession or receipt of dextromethorphan, a primary ingredient in over-the-counter cough syrup. The bill didn't move in the Senate.

He comes from one of Michigan's wealthier families; his grandfather helped found Whirlpool Corp., which is based in Upton's district. After college, Upton worked on the 1976 congressional campaign of David A. Stockman, then worked for nearly a decade for Stockman on his congressional staff and at the Office of Management and Budget, where Stockman was President Reagan's budget director and Upton was the budget office's liaison to Capitol Hill.

In 1986, Upton ousted incumbent U.S. Rep. Mark D. Siljander, a Christian conservative activist, in a Republican primary. He won that November with 62 percent of the vote. His subsequent re-elections were relatively easy, except in 1990 when he garnered less than 60 percent of the vote. In Congress, Upton became a deputy to Newt Gingrich when Gingrich was elected GOP whip in 1989, and the next year joined Gingrich in castigating President George Bush for agreeing to raise taxes as part of a deal to reduce the deficit. But Upton resigned as a deputy whip in 1993 because he said he disliked Gingrich's confrontational style.

KEY VOTES

2008

No	Delay consideration of Colombia free-trade agreement
Yes	Override Bush veto of federal farm and nutrition programs reauthorization bill
Yes	Overhaul surveillance laws and permit dismissal of suits against companies that conducted warrantless wiretapping
No	Grant mortgage relief to homeowners and funding for Fannie Mae and Freddie Mac
Yes	Approve initial $700 billion program to stabilize financial markets
Yes	Approve final $700 billion program to stabilize financial markets
Yes	Provide $14 billion in loans to automakers

2007

Yes	Increase minimum wage by $2.10 an hour
No	Approve $124.2 billion in emergency war spending and set goal for redeployment of troops from Iraq
Yes	Reject federal contraceptive assistance to international family planning groups
Yes	Override Bush veto of $23.2 billion water projects authorization bill
Yes	Implement Peru free-trade agreement
Yes	Approve energy policy overhaul with new fuel economy standards
Yes	Clear $473.5 billion omnibus spending bill, including $70 billion for military operations

CQ VOTE STUDIES

	PARTY UNITY		PRESIDENTIAL SUPPORT	
	SUPPORT	OPPOSE	SUPPORT	OPPOSE
2008	84%	16%	47%	53%
2007	86%	14%	54%	46%
2006	81%	19%	80%	20%
2005	87%	13%	76%	24%
2004	88%	12%	82%	18%

INTEREST GROUPS

	AFL-CIO	ADA	CCUS	ACU
2008	73%	60%	89%	44%
2007	50%	40%	100%	56%
2006	36%	10%	100%	80%
2005	27%	10%	89%	80%
2004	47%	35%	90%	76%

MICHIGAN 6

Southwest – Kalamazoo, Portage, Benton Harbor

Forests, fertile soil and front-row seats to Lake Michigan in the state's southwestern corner make the 6th a prime spot for tourists in every season. Apples, blueberries and peaches grow in a fruit belt that extends north from St. Joseph and Benton Harbor through Van Buren County. The wooded shoreline north of the Indiana border boasts miles of sandy beaches where affluent Chicagoans keep second homes. Local vineyards produce a strong crop of juice grapes, and area wineries account for nearly half of the state's wine grapes.

Appliance manufacturer Whirlpool Corp., based in Benton Harbor, and orthopedic company Stryker, in Kalamazoo, make their headquarters in the 6th, although overall job losses in manufacturing have hurt the district. Despite repeated layoffs by pharmaceutical giant Pfizer, the district remains a regional hub for the state's health care industry. Local officials have encouraged growth of pharmaceutical start-ups, which provide some jobs for the science-based workforce.

Education is another pillar of the local economy. Western Michigan University is home, at least for most of the year, to roughly 25,000 students. The "Kalamazoo Promise," a scholarship program aimed at supporting Kalamazoo Public Schools graduates by offering to sponsor up to 100 percent of tuition to attend an in-state public college, has attracted families to the city, and the influx of residents has propped up property values in the area.

The 6th's conservative Dutch heritage, white-collar corporate managers and rural conservatives have made it a Republican-leaning district in the past. The district's Democratic centers are in working-class Kalamazoo and predominantly black Benton Harbor, balanced by conservative-leaning St. Joseph and Allegan counties. In the 2008 presidential election, Democrat Barack Obama took 54 percent of the district's vote.

MAJOR INDUSTRY
Manufacturing, agriculture, higher education, tourism, health care

CITIES
Kalamazoo, 77,145; Portage, 44,897; Niles, 12,204; Sturgis, 11,285

NOTABLE
The Berrien Springs courthouse, built in 1839 and now a museum, is the state's oldest courthouse; Colon, home to magic-trick manufacturers and an annual exposition, calls itself the "Magic Capital of the World."

Rep. Mark Schauer (D)

Elected 2008; 1st term

CAPITOL OFFICE
225-6276
schauer.house.gov
1408 Longworth Bldg. 20515-2207; fax 225-6281

COMMITTEES
Agriculture
Transportation & Infrastructure

RESIDENCE
Battle Creek

BORN
Oct. 2, 1961; Howell, Mich.

RELIGION
Methodist

FAMILY
Wife, Christine Schauer; three stepchildren

EDUCATION
Albion College, B.A. 1984 (Spanish & sociology);
Western Michigan U., M.P.A. 1986; Michigan
State U., M.A. 1996 (political science)

CAREER
Social services organization director; county
planner

POLITICAL HIGHLIGHTS
Candidate for Battle Creek City Commission,
1993; Battle Creek City Commission, 1994-97;
Mich. House, 1997-2003; Mich. Senate, 2003-09
(majority floor leader, 2003-06; minority leader,
2007-09)

ELECTION RESULTS

2008 GENERAL

Mark Schauer (D)	157,213	48.8%
Tim Walberg (R)	149,781	46.5%
Lynn Meadows (GREEN)	9,528	3.0%
Ken Proctor (LIBERT)	5,675	1.8%

2008 PRIMARY

Mark Schauer (D)	17,270	65.7%
Sharon Marie Renier (D)	9,034	34.3%

Schauer is a seasoned politician with more than 10 years of experience in the state legislature, where he served as his party's leader. Touting himself as a moderate Democrat, he defeated GOP Rep. Tim Walberg by painting him as too conservative and out of touch with voters. But Schauer will have to keep a close eye on his district, where voters show a tendency toward impatience.

Schauer's 2008 win was the second time the district turned out a freshman incumbent since 2006, and the first time in four elections a Democrat won the seat. He hopes to hold his ground by focusing on ways to help revitalize the economy. In early 2009 he made repeated visits back home to tout funds secured for local projects in President Obama's economic stimulus plan — ranging from sewer and wastewater treatment upgrades in Battle Creek to funds for energy efficiency improvement projects in Jackson County.

Schauer (SCHAU – rhymes with "now" –ur) is a member of the moderate New Democrat Coalition. He has pledged to seek trade policies "that level the playing field for Michigan businesses," making countries like China meet minimum labor and environmental standards. He supports labor, backing legislation in early 2009 to make it easier for unions to organize.

He opposed the release in early 2009 of the second portion of $700 billion to help the struggling financial services sector. He had criticized President George W. Bush for that plan in late 2008, yet applauded him when Bush secured funds from that package to aid the domestic automobile industry.

Schauer sits on the Transportation and Infrastructure panel, which will renew the 2005 surface transportation law. He backs a plan to expand high-speed rail service from Detroit to Chicago, through his district. He also sits on the Agriculture Committee. The agriculture industry is expected to take on a heightened role in Michigan's economic recovery as the nation increasingly moves toward alternative fuels made from crops such as switchgrass.

Schauer joined the Battle Creek City Commission in 1994. He jumped to the state House within a few years, and was elected to the state Senate in 2002. He and Walberg ran an expensive race; the two combined to spend nearly $4.5 million. Schauer won by 2 percentage points.

MICHIGAN 7

South central – Battle Creek, Jackson

The southern Michigan counties that make up the 7th take in small towns, farming communities and a few midsize cities. Kellogg's Tony the Tiger makes his home in Battle Creek, the district's largest city. The cereal giant is the city's largest employer, and its philanthropic organization donates generously to the Battle Creek area.

Auto parts manufacturing still drives many small-town economies, but suppliers have struggled in recent years along with the sagging auto industry. A General Motors factory opened in Delta Township in 2006, but plummeting auto sales have forced salary buy-outs and mass layoffs. Outside the cities and towns, expansive fields of soybeans and corn dominate the rest of the 7th, which is the state's leading producer of both crops.

Lenawee County is at the forefront of both soybean and corn harvesting for the region.

The farming counties of Branch and Hillsdale continue to be fertile ground for the GOP, but they are balanced by a more liberal Battle Creek to the west and the outskirts of heavily Democratic Ann Arbor (located in the neighboring 15th) in Washtenaw County to the east. In 2008, Democrat Barack Obama took 52 percent of the district's vote overall.

A Quaker tradition shaped the district's political and social culture. In 1854, Jackson's abolitionists selected anti-slavery candidates in a state convention that has become known as "Under the Oaks" and as the birth of the Republican Party.

MAJOR INDUSTRY
Agriculture, food processing, auto parts manufacturing, health care

CITIES
Battle Creek, 53,364; Jackson, 36,316

NOTABLE
Sojourner Truth lived in Battle Creek.

Rep. Mike Rogers (R)

Elected 2000; 5th term

CAPITOL OFFICE
225-4872
www.mikerogers.house.gov
133 Cannon Bldg. 20515-2208; fax 225-5820

COMMITTEES
Energy & Commerce
Select Intelligence

RESIDENCE
Howell

BORN
June 2, 1963; Livonia, Mich.

RELIGION
Methodist

FAMILY
Divorced; two children

EDUCATION
Adrian College, B.A. 1985 (sociology & criminal justice)

MILITARY SERVICE
Army, 1985-88

CAREER
Home construction company owner; FBI agent

POLITICAL HIGHLIGHTS
Mich. Senate, 1995-2000 (majority floor leader, 1999-2000)

ELECTION RESULTS

2008 GENERAL

Mike Rogers (R)	204,408	56.5%
Robert D. Alexander (D)	145,491	40.2%
Will Tyler White (LIBERT)	4,373	1.2%
Aaron Stuttman (GREEN)	3,836	1.1%

2008 PRIMARY

Mike Rogers (R)	unopposed

2006 GENERAL

Mike Rogers (R)	157,237	55.3%
Jim Marcinkowski (D)	122,107	42.9%

PREVIOUS WINNING PERCENTAGES
2004 (61%); 2002 (68%); 2000 (49%)

Rogers represents a divided district — part Democrat, part Republican — so he walks a fine line politically. While he backs his party on most issues, he fiercely protects the auto industry, a major employer in the 8th, and occasionally supports Democratic proposals.

His success at holding onto his seat can also be attributed to his aggressive fundraising skills. He regularly raises more than $1.3 million for his campaigns, and gives away vast amounts — more than $625,000 in the 2007-08 election cycle — to his colleagues, the Michigan Republican Party and the National Republican Congressional Committee. As finance chairman of the committee in 2004, he raised $16 million for colleagues in tough races.

District voters backed George W. Bush for president in 2000 and 2004, but supported Barack Obama in 2008. And Ingham County — home to Michigan State University and many pro-union automakers — is strongly Democratic.

When Democrats took control of the House after the 2006 elections, Rogers voted for two of their "Six for '06" priority measures — to cut interest rates on college student loans in half over five years, and to implement remaining recommendations of the independent Sept. 11 commission.

But after Obama took office, Rogers — a member of the Energy and Commerce Committee and its Health panel — voted against an expansion of the State Children's Health Insurance Program, which covers children whose families don't qualify for Medicaid. He criticized the final law, saying it didn't force states to locate uninsured children to make sure they are covered. He also opposed two bills designed to strengthen the ability of workers to combat wage discrimination. He likewise opposed several of Obama's early economic initiatives, including a $787 billion economic stimulus plan.

Yet Rogers has spent much time focusing on his state's sinking economy, repeatedly introducing a bill to give the Big Three auto companies up to $20 billion in federally backed loan guarantees to develop "green" technologies, such as hybrid engines and clean diesel fuel. And he joined others in the Michigan delegation in successfully urging President Bush to make an emergency loan to keep the auto industry afloat in late 2008 after the Senate failed to clear a loan bill the House had passed.

Rogers opposed a 2007 energy measure that toughened Corporate Average Fuel Economy (CAFE) standards to a combined 35 miles per gallon for cars and light trucks by 2020. "We're arguing over a regulation that was developed in the 1970s," he said of the CAFE standards. "We should have been talking about the innovation that makes CAFE irrelevant."

And he geared up in early 2009 to fight Obama's plan to combat global warming, which included a cap on permissible carbon dioxide emissions and a program allowing companies to sell their surplus allowances. Rogers said such a plan would raise prices at the pump and drive up electricity bills.

A former FBI agent, Rogers has served on the Select Intelligence Committee since 2005 and is now the ranking Republican on the terrorism subcommittee. Years before he was assigned to the panel, Rogers was asked for input as the Justice Department developed its anti-terrorism package — including proposals to broaden wiretap authority — just after the Sept. 11 attacks. As the so-called Patriot Act moved toward enactment, Rogers' colleagues sought his guidance on wiretapping and other law enforcement issues.

In the 110th Congress (2007-08), Rogers fought Democrats' efforts to rein in the executive branch's warrantless wiretapping as Congress struggled to rewrite the Foreign Intelligence Surveillance Act. He voted for the final 2008 overhaul, which permitted warrantless eavesdropping under certain circumstances and drew more votes from Republicans than from Democrats.

An Army veteran, Rogers initially urged a go-slow approach when Bush sought congressional authorization for war with Iraq. Once his concerns were satisfied, however, Rogers voted for the 2002 war resolution. He remained loyal to the war effort even as popular support plummeted. In early 2007, he opposed Bush's plan for a hefty troop buildup, but he voted against the Democrats' non-binding resolution opposing the plan.

As the House prepared to vote in March 2007 on a war supplemental funding bill setting a U.S. troop withdrawal deadline, Rogers' Lansing office was vandalized. The FBI investigated the vandalism, which included a sign in the front window that read, "Rogers: There Is Blood on Your Hands." Undaunted, he voted against the bill. "I'm an old FBI guy and you're not going to threaten me," he said. "You can't just do what I did for a living and be intimidated."

Rogers grew up in Livingston County, west of Detroit. His father was a high school vice principal and football coach, and a town supervisor. His mother ran the local Chamber of Commerce and served on the county commission. The youngest of five boys, Rogers said his mother would volunteer them for civic events. "I remember putting up Christmas light decorations for the city of Brighton. We used to call it forced family fun," he laughed. "My parents taught me that public service is an honorable thing."

Rogers knew as a teenager that he wanted to be an FBI agent. After graduating from college, he spent three years in the Army and then went to the FBI Academy, finishing first in his class. He got a coveted assignment to the Chicago field office, where he unraveled a major case involving public officials in the suburb of Cicero. Handcuffs and newspaper headlines from the case are framed in his Capitol Hill office.

In the 1990s, Rogers and his now ex-wife returned to Brighton to raise their family. With his father and brothers, he ran a modular home assembly company. He also entered state politics. When a longtime GOP incumbent retired from the state Senate, Rogers won the seat in the Republican district. Re-elected in 1998, he served as majority floor leader in his last term.

When Democrat Debbie Stabenow decided to give up her House seat to run for the Senate in 2000, Rogers made a bid and faced Democratic state Senate colleague Dianne Byrum in the general election. Rogers' 111-vote victory was not official until December, when Byrum conceded after a partial recount supported Rogers' slim lead. Redistricting for 2002 added thousands of GOP voters to the district and Rogers won with 68 percent of the vote. He has been returned safely to office, but his victory margins have decreased.

KEY VOTES

2008

No   Delay consideration of Colombia free-trade agreement

Yes   Override Bush veto of federal farm and nutrition programs reauthorization bill

Yes   Overhaul surveillance laws and permit dismissal of suits against companies that conducted warrantless wiretapping

No   Grant mortgage relief to homeowners and funding for Fannie Mae and Freddie Mac

No   Approve initial $700 billion program to stabilize financial markets

No   Approve final $700 billion program to stabilize financial markets

Yes   Provide $14 billion in loans to automakers

2007

No   Increase minimum wage by $2.10 an hour

No   Approve $124.2 billion in emergency war spending and set goal for redeployment of troops from Iraq

Yes   Reject federal contraceptive assistance to international family planning groups

Yes   Override Bush veto of $23.2 billion water projects authorization bill

Yes   Implement Peru free-trade agreement

No   Approve energy policy overhaul with new fuel economy standards

Yes   Clear $473.5 billion omnibus spending bill, including $70 billion for military operations

CQ VOTE STUDIES

	PARTY UNITY		PRESIDENTIAL SUPPORT	
	SUPPORT	OPPOSE	SUPPORT	OPPOSE
2008	91%	9%	68%	32%
2007	93%	7%	77%	23%
2006	95%	5%	90%	10%
2005	94%	6%	87%	13%
2004	95%	5%	97%	3%

INTEREST GROUPS

	AFL-CIO	ADA	CCUS	ACU
2008	33%	25%	89%	84%
2007	25%	5%	90%	100%
2006	21%	5%	93%	88%
2005	20%	5%	93%	92%
2004	20%	10%	100%	92%

MICHIGAN 8
Central — Lansing

Stamped with the state seal, the 8th — Michigan's capital district — used to be dominated by various manufacturing facilities of the influential auto industry. The district, once home to Olds Motor Vehicle Co., includes Lansing, East Lansing and various agricultural communities to the east, but is emerging from its agrarian and industrial tradition toward a suburban future.

Auto industry cutbacks have hurt the 8th: General Motors' Oldsmobile line was eliminated in 2004, and GM plants and auto parts suppliers have shut down or been forced to cut shifts and lay off workers. GM is now only the third-largest employer in the Lansing area, behind the state of Michigan and Michigan State University. Despite economic struggles, parts of Lansing are beginning to show signs of rebirth, especially around Oldsmobile Park, the minor league baseball stadium, and in the north side's quirky Old Town neighborhood. Health care is an important field in the capital region, as is a growing biotech sector.

Just down the road from the capital, East Lansing caters to one of the most liberal constituencies in the state, the Michigan State University community. The university, founded in 1855 and the nation's pioneer land grant college, is home to several top-ranked programs, including education and study abroad. The university was recently selected to develop an isotope accelerator that is expected to pump about $1 billion into the local economy and make the region a global hub for nuclear research.

Ingham County's Democratic lean is balanced by the 8th's powerful agricultural vote in Livingston and Shiawassee counties, which also are new commuter sanctuaries for residents who work in Lansing, Detroit and Flint. The remainder of the 8th's voters live in northern Oakland County, although the 8th's portion of the county remains the least developed. In 2008, Democrat Barack Obama won 53 percent of the district's presidential vote.

MAJOR INDUSTRY
State government, higher education, auto manufacturing

CITIES
Lansing (pt.), 114,321; East Lansing, 46,525; Okemos (unincorp.), 22,805

NOTABLE
The unincorporated hamlet of Hell, in Putnam Township, is a tourist stop that plays to its devilish name.

Rep. Gary Peters (D)

Elected 2008; 1st term

CAPITOL OFFICE
225-5802
peters.house.gov
1130 Longworth Bldg. 20515-2209; fax 226-2356

COMMITTEES
Financial Services
Science & Technology

RESIDENCE
Bloomfield Hills

BORN
Dec. 1, 1958; Pontiac, Mich.

RELIGION
Episcopalian

FAMILY
Wife, Colleen Ochoa Peters; three children

EDUCATION
Alma College, B.A. 1980 (political science);
U. of Detroit, M.B.A. 1984; Wayne State U., J.D.
1989; Michigan State U., M.A. 2007 (philosophy)

MILITARY SERVICE
Naval Reserve, 1993-2000, 01-05

CAREER
College instructor; investment firm branch
executive

POLITICAL HIGHLIGHTS
Democratic nominee for Mich. Senate, 1990;
Rochester Hills City Council, 1991-93; Mich.
Senate, 1995-2002; Democratic nominee for Mich.
attorney general, 2002; Mich. Lottery Bureau
commissioner, 2003-07

ELECTION RESULTS

2008 GENERAL

Gary Peters (D)	183,311	52.1%
Joe Knollenberg (R)	150,035	42.6%
Jack Kevorkian (X)	8,987	2.6%
Adam Goodman (LIBERT)	4,893	1.4%
Douglas Campbell (GREEN)	4,737	1.3%

2008 PRIMARY

Gary Peters (D)	unopposed

Peters touts himself as a fiscal conservative, pledging to cut wasteful government spending and promoting tax cuts for the middle class. He also is a supporter of labor, favors ending tax breaks for companies that ship jobs overseas and questions free trade. Peters is a member of the New Democrat Coalition, a group of centrist House Democrats.

A former assistant vice president at Merrill Lynch, Peters sits on the Financial Services Committee. He drew attention in March 2009 when the House swiftly passed his bill aimed at taxing bonuses distributed by insurance giant American International Group Inc., which had received funds from a $700 billion law, enacted in fall 2008, to rescue the financial services sector. Peters estimated the additional surtax imposed would allow the government to recoup nearly 100 percent of those bonuses. "Million-dollar bonuses for the very people who drove our economy into the ditch are simply unacceptable," he said.

Peters had voted for a bill in January 2009 to impose significant restrictions on the Obama administration's use of the second half of the rescue fund. But the following month he supported President Obama's $787 billion economic stimulus plan, saying it would fix infrastructure problems and create jobs.

Peters also sits on the Science and Technology Committee, where he hopes to help his state further develop industries in health care, engineering and auto manufacturing. "If we are going to have substantial growth, we have to invest in basic research and technology," he said.

Peters said his interest in politics was sparked when he interned as a college student for a local union organizer.

He later served on the Rochester Hills City Council and in the state Senate before losing a 2002 bid to be Michigan's attorney general. In 2003, Democratic Gov. Jennifer M. Granholm appointed him lottery commissioner.

He fought a tough campaign against GOP Rep. Joe Knollenberg in 2008. Peters' ability to tie his opponent to President George W. Bush, complemented by Obama's strong showing on the presidential ticket, led him to victory by roughly 9 percentage points.

MICHIGAN 9

Suburban Detroit – eastern Oakland County

Michigan's heavily suburban 9th is wholly contained in Oakland County, one of the nation's most affluent counties and home to the U.S. headquarters for Chrysler in Auburn Hills. Its economy has long revolved around the now-struggling auto industry, but unlike other suburban Detroit districts, the 9th has a more diverse economy.

Troy, in the 9th's southeastern corner, is a major office center and home to Michigan's banking and high-tech automotive research and design industries. The loss of Kmart in 2005 and recent auto industry slowdowns have caused local workforce job cuts and municipal budget shortfalls. North of Troy in Rochester, Oakland University is expanding, planning to open its William Beaumont School of Medicine by 2010 and a new

health care and research center by 2014.

Communities north of the northern Detroit border cut by 8 Mile Road form a corridor between Grand River Avenue and the Northwestern Highway that served as one of the key routes for whites' exodus from Detroit.

Traditionally Republican, upper-middle-class Bloomfield Township and Rochester Hills were competitive in the 2008 presidential race, and Democrats do well in Pontiac, where blacks have a plurality. Barack Obama won 87 percent of the city's vote and took the 9th overall with 56 percent, 7 points higher than John Kerry's percentage in 2004.

MAJOR INDUSTRY
Engineering, health care, auto manufacturing

CITIES
Farmington Hills, 82,111; Troy, 80,959; Rochester Hills, 68,825; Pontiac, 66,337; Waterford (unincorporated) (pt.), 66,316

NOTABLE
The first Holocaust museum built in the United States is in West Bloomfield.

Rep. Candice S. Miller (R)

Elected 2002; 4th term

Assertive and strong-willed, Miller displays a strong loyalty to her district's automobile industry and economy that typically keeps her in step with the GOP. But her concerns about health care and some traditionally liberal priorities, such as boosting the minimum wage, lead her to vote for some Democratic initiatives.

Her popularity remains high at home, where she has been viewed as a trailblazer for women in politics since being elected in 1994 as Michigan's first female secretary of state. She consistently wins with more than 66 percent of the vote in her re-election bids, even while her support of the Republican Party has continued to drop. In her first year of office, she backed the GOP in 96 percent of the votes that pitted most Republicans against most Democrats. That number dropped to 84 percent during the 110th Congress (2007-08).

Miller is not easily intimidated when it comes to parochial issues. She stands firmly behind Michigan's Big Three automakers; her daughter is a Ford assembly worker who belongs to the United Auto Workers. She backed a $14 billion loan to struggling domestic automakers in December 2008. When the bill failed in the Senate, she joined other members of Michigan's delegation in writing to President George W. Bush asking him to fund it. The Bush administration ultimately approved a loan through the $700 billion financial rescue law signed that fall. Miller had opposed that rescue bill.

When President Obama announced in March 2009 stringent conditions on further government aid to General Motors Corp. and Chrysler LLC, and forced the ouster of GM Chairman and CEO Richard Wagoner, Miller said Obama and his Auto Task Force were now "accountable for the jobs, accountable for the livelihoods of the families which are at stake and accountable for the survival of American manufacturing."

Her comments indicated her increasing challenge to some of Obama's initiatives. She had been an early supporter of the president's plan to stabilize the economy by investing in the nation's transportation and infrastructure. But two months later, she joined her party in opposing the final $787 billion economic stimulus law. Miller, a member of the Transportation and Infrastructure Committee, said she was disappointed it didn't focus on tax cuts and infrastructure spending, and that it scaled down, from $11 billion to $2 billion, an incentive to spur auto sales. She teamed with Democrat Betty Sutton of Ohio in March 2009 on a bill to offer a cash voucher to consumers for turning in aging vehicles and purchasing new, more fuel efficient models.

Miller, who sits on the Select Committee on Energy Independence and Global Warming, also protects her state's industry when it comes to environmental initiatives. In December 2007, she voted against a broad energy measure that included new fuel efficiency standards for vehicles, fearing it would bankrupt one of the automakers. She was particularly irritated when the choice of car to transport the bill from the U.S. Capitol to the White House for Bush's signature was a Toyota Prius, a hybrid car made in Japan.

When Michigan's Joe Knollenberg lost his re-election bid in 2008, she declined to seek his seat on the powerful Appropriations Committee, as it would have forced her to drop her seat on Transportation, where she felt she could better provide for her district. That committee takes up a renewal of the 2005 surface transportation law in the 111th Congress (2009-10).

Miller also is a member of the Homeland Security Committee. She wants the Selfridge Air National Guard Base to become the Midwest hub of the Homeland Security Department. Her husband, Donald Miller, is a circuit

CAPITOL OFFICE
225-2106
candicemiller.house.gov
228 Cannon Bldg. 20515-2210; fax 226-1169

COMMITTEES
Homeland Security
Select Energy Independence & Global Warming
Transportation & Infrastructure

RESIDENCE
Harrison Township

BORN
May 7, 1954; Detroit, Mich.

RELIGION
Presbyterian

FAMILY
Husband, Donald Miller; one child

EDUCATION
Macomb Community College, attended 1973-74;
Northwood Institute, attended 1974

CAREER
Boat saleswoman

POLITICAL HIGHLIGHTS
Harrison Township Board of Trustees, 1979-80;
Harrison Township supervisor, 1980-92;
Republican nominee for U.S. House, 1986;
Macomb County treasurer, 1993-95; Mich.
secretary of state, 1995-2002

ELECTION RESULTS

2008 GENERAL

Candice S. Miller (R)	230,471	66.3%
Robert Denison (D)	108,354	31.2%
Neil Kiernan Stephenson (LIBERT)	4,632	1.3%
Candace R. Caveny (GREEN)	4,146	1.2%

2008 PRIMARY

Candice S. Miller (R)	unopposed

2006 GENERAL

Candice S. Miller (R)	179,072	66.2%
Robert Denison (D)	84,689	31.3%
Mark Byrne (LIBERT)	2,875	1.1%

PREVIOUS WINNING PERCENTAGES
2004 (69%); 2002 (63%)

judge and former commander of the base. She has been a strong supporter of the war in Iraq.

Miller is a social conservative, but on many issues tends to side with labor. She supported a 2007 bill to increase the minimum wage, and in 2005 voted against a bill to implement the Central America Free Trade Agreement. But she did back a free-trade deal with Peru in 2007. She was one of only 35 Republicans who supported a bill that same year to prohibit job discrimination based on sexual orientation.

She also backed a 2009 measure to expand the State Children's Health Insurance Program, which covers children whose families don't qualify for Medicaid. The measure was similar to a version twice vetoed by Bush and which she supported.

Miller had an early stumble in her House career. She received a rebuke from the ethics committee in 2004 for threatening political retaliation against a fellow Republican who refused to support Bush's Medicare prescription drug plan. The ethics panel said Miller went too far when she cornered fellow Michigan Republican Nick Smith on the House floor and threatened to use her influence in his son's House race unless Smith supported the bill. At the time, Brad Smith was seeking to take his retiring father's place, a race he ultimately lost. The elder Smith complained to the ethics panel of pressure from Miller and Republican leaders.

Miller grew up in 1960s suburban Detroit, where her father owned a marina. Miller was a member of a high school boating crew. In 1970, she sailed as a member of the first all-woman crew to compete in a prestigious race across Lake Huron — but only after she and the other women beat back the local yacht club's effort to bar them.

Miller attended a community college but dropped out to sell boats for the family business. By 25, she was a divorced single mother with a toddler. (She later remarried.) When the local township board proposed a tax increase on marinas, she became a "noisy activist."

She was elected to the township board in 1979 and a year later unseated the Harrison Township supervisor, becoming the first woman to hold the job. In her two terms as secretary of state, she was recognized for making the office more efficient and for instituting fraud-proof driver's licenses. She made an unsuccessful bid to unseat Democratic Rep. David E. Bonior in 1986.

The Republican-controlled legislature redrew a congressional district in 2002 to include several GOP-leaning counties and Miller's base in Macomb County. She beat the county prosecutor, Carl J. Marlinga, with 63 percent of the vote. She has won easily since.

KEY VOTES

2008

No Delay consideration of Colombia free-trade agreement
Yes Override Bush veto of federal farm and nutrition programs reauthorization bill
Yes Overhaul surveillance laws and permit dismissal of suits against companies that conducted warrantless wiretapping
No Grant mortgage relief to homeowners and funding for Fannie Mae and Freddie Mac
No Approve initial $700 billion program to stabilize financial markets
No Approve final $700 billion program to stabilize financial markets
Yes Provide $14 billion in loans to automakers

2007

Yes Increase minimum wage by $2.10 an hour
No Approve $124.2 billion in emergency war spending and set goal for redeployment of troops from Iraq
Yes Reject federal contraceptive assistance to international family planning groups
Yes Override Bush veto of $23.2 billion water projects authorization bill
Yes Implement Peru free-trade agreement
No Approve energy policy overhaul with new fuel economy standards
Yes Clear $473.5 billion omnibus spending bill, including $70 billion for military operations

CQ VOTE STUDIES

	PARTY UNITY		PRESIDENTIAL SUPPORT	
	SUPPORT	OPPOSE	SUPPORT	OPPOSE
2008	83%	17%	44%	56%
2007	84%	16%	52%	48%
2006	89%	11%	94%	6%
2005	94%	6%	85%	15%
2004	93%	7%	85%	15%

INTEREST GROUPS

	AFL-CIO	ADA	CCUS	ACU
2008	67%	50%	78%	63%
2007	67%	30%	100%	72%
2006	25%	10%	93%	84%
2005	20%	5%	89%	84%
2004	27%	10%	100%	84%

MICHIGAN 10
Southeast – northern Macomb County, Port Huron, most of Michigan 'Thumb'

Stretching from Detroit's northern suburbs in Macomb County to the tip of Michigan's "Thumb," the 10th District combines suburban, lakefront and rural communities. Like most of Michigan, the district is enduring rising unemployment rates.

Macomb, where half of the 10th's population resides, retains a traditionally blue-collar "Reagan Democrat" feel despite growth in suburbs such as Harrison Township, Shelby and Sterling Heights (shared with the 12th). Macomb re-established its statewide bellwether status in the 2008 presidential election, favoring Democrat Barack Obama after supporting Republican George W. Bush four years earlier. Overall, Obama lost the 10th District by less than 6,000 votes.

Lapeer County, northwest of Macomb, has become a landing spot for upwardly mobile residents drifting farther away from decaying urban centers in Flint (to the west) and Detroit (to the south). Northeast of

Macomb is St. Clair County, a politically competitive region where one-fourth of district residents live. St. Clair's Port Huron, a source of blue-collar Democratic votes, is the U.S. terminus of the Blue Water bridges, which cross into Ontario, Canada. Bridge traffic into the United States stimulates the area's economy, as the weak dollar has prompted Canadian tourists to cross the border. Water-quality issues are important to local residents along Lake Huron and other district bays and rivers, and many small businesses rely on the tourism industry.

Elsewhere in the district, the 10th's rural communities depend on fruit, soybeans, corn, dairy and other crops. The 10th has the most productive sugar beet fields in the state, and the fertile soil of the Thumb is known for its navy bean fields. Huron County leads Michigan in milk production, with Sanilac County also in the top five.

MAJOR INDUSTRY
Auto manufacturing, agriculture, recreation

CITIES
Sterling Heights (pt.), 86,536; Shelby (unincorporated), 65,159; Port Huron, 32,338

NOTABLE
The U.S. Senate's famous navy bean soup uses only Michigan navy beans.

Rep. Thaddeus McCotter (R)

Elected 2002; 4th term

CAPITOL OFFICE
225-8171
mccotter.house.gov
1632 Longworth Bldg. 20515-2211; fax 225-2667

COMMITTEES
Financial Services

RESIDENCE
Livonia

BORN
Aug. 22, 1965; Detroit, Mich.

RELIGION
Roman Catholic

FAMILY
Wife, Rita McCotter; three children

EDUCATION
U. of Detroit, B.A. 1987 (political science),
J.D. 1990

CAREER
Lawyer

POLITICAL HIGHLIGHTS
Schoolcraft College Board of Trustees, 1989-92;
Wayne County Commission, 1993-98; Mich.
Senate, 1999-2002

ELECTION RESULTS

2008 GENERAL

Thaddeus McCotter (R)	177,461	51.4%
Joseph W. Larkin (D)	156,625	45.4%
John Tatar (LIBERT)	6,001	1.7%
Erik Shelley (GREEN)	5,072	1.5%

2008 PRIMARY

Thaddeus McCotter (R)	unopposed

2006 GENERAL

Thaddeus McCotter (R)	143,658	54.0%
Tony Trupiano (D)	114,248	43.0%
John Tatar (LIBERT)	4,340	1.6%
Charles E. Tackett (USTAX)	3,538	1.3%

PREVIOUS WINNING PERCENTAGES
2004 (57%); 2002 (57%)

McCotter chairs the House Republican Policy Committee, the GOP's in-house idea factory, but he's anything but a dull wonk. Quick-witted, quirky and quotable, he brings both deep conservative convictions and a love of rock 'n' roll to his work.

Thanks to McCotter, the Policy Committee's Web site has a downloadable copy of "Freedom Songs," in which House Republicans provide policy guidance texts packaged to resemble tunes such as "Tame the Tax Man." The group has issued position papers quoting Bob Dylan, and McCotter has compared the 1994 GOP "Contract with America" manifesto to The Beatles' acclaimed "Sgt. Pepper's Lonely Hearts Club Band" album.

He is among Republicans agitating for change since the election setbacks of 2006 and 2008. The GOP lost its way, he said, because of its endless thirst for campaign funds, leading to "a Beggar's Banquet at taxpayers' expense" — a reference to a Rolling Stones album. He wants the party to re-embrace the principles of limited government, lower taxes and expanded liberty.

McCotter denounced the George W. Bush administration's $700 billion financial system rescue plan in September 2008, making references to President Andrew Jackson and the battle over the Second Bank of the United States, along with "The Brothers Karamazov" and the 1917 Russian uprising. "In the Bolshevik Revolution, the slogan was 'Peace, land, and bread,'" he said. "Today you are being asked to choose between bread and freedom. I suggest the people on Main Street have said they prefer their freedom, and I am with them."

But two months later, McCotter — like others in the Michigan delegation — supported $14 billion in loans to failing domestic automakers, a measure that died in the Senate. And in March 2009, he criticized the Obama administration for forcing out General Motors' CEO, Rick Wagoner, saying Wagoner was being scapegoated while Wall Street executives clung to their jobs.

McCotter can be witheringly sarcastic in debate. He once took to the House floor with a series of charts on "speaking Democrat," with mock translations of "enhancing revenues" as raising taxes, "engage" as appease and "end the war" as lose it. When Democrats accused Republicans of spurning children during debate in October 2007 on expanding a children's health insurance program, McCotter retorted, "I assure you, Republicans like kids, and not just medium-rare with a side of fries."

He downplays his influence over his colleagues. "In a band, I'm happy being a rhythm guitar player," he said. McCotter actually does play in a band, or did at any rate, before retirements and the 2008 elections wiped out most of "The Second Amendments," a country-rock group. Now McCotter and Minnesota Democrat Collin C. Peterson are the only ones left. "We could become a duo like Simon and Garfunkel. But we've got to decide who plays Garfunkel," joked McCotter, who said the duo hoped to recruit new members.

McCotter is seldom without a cigarette; he has been known to smoke while fielding fly balls on the baseball diamond. He once got into a heated debate with a portly Republican state senator in Michigan who wanted to raise the dollar-a-pack tax on cigarettes. An angry McCotter threatened to propose a tax on candy and junk food. "I hate all taxes," he said to the man. "I don't care if it is on your snacks or beers or cigarettes. Government deals off cigarette tax revenue are wrong. You either make it illegal or leave it alone."

Despite his conservatism, McCotter has broken ranks with his party on occasion. In 2007 he joined Democrats in supporting an increase in the minimum wage, something he believed would help his economically struggling state. He also supported a Democratic a measure prohibiting job discrimination on the basis of a person's sexual orientation. He was critical of the GOP effort to eliminate spending earmarks — funding set-asides for projects in members' districts — though he announced in June 2008 he would not seek any.

Though most Republicans stayed mum as the Iraq War turned increasingly sour politically, McCotter in 2006 was one of six House Republicans to call for an independent, bipartisan commission to assess U.S. progress. In 2008, he said the 2007 "surge" of U.S. forces that sent more than 21,000 additional troops into Iraq "has fortunately been done in a manner that's allowed us to get closer to victory."

With a district near Detroit, McCotter champions the auto industry. He opposes tougher fuel efficiency standards for vehicles, saying they are "unfunded mandates" that would spur layoffs and disrupt the auto-dominated local economy. A self-described conservationist, he has signed on to numerous bills to clean up the Great Lakes and eliminate invasive species.

McCotter's parents were special-education teachers in the Detroit public schools. His mother, Joan, was elected to the Livonia City Council in 1985, a campaign he helped manage. In his youth, McCotter was a semi-professional musician playing guitar in several bands, including one called Sir Funk-a-Lot and the Knights of the Terrestrial Jam.

When stardom failed to materialize, McCotter attended the University of Detroit Law School and went into solo law practice. A friend persuaded him to get involved in the 1988 presidential campaign, and McCotter went to the Republican National Convention as a delegate pledged to George Bush.

In 1992, he won a seat on the Wayne County Commission, where he was the driving force behind a law requiring 60 percent voter approval for any tax increase. Elected to the state Senate in 1998, McCotter was vice chairman of the reapportionment committee that drew new congressional district maps after the 2000 census. That put him in position to draw the new 11th District, which happened to include his entire state Senate district.

In 2002, McCotter beat businessman David C. Hagerty in the primary and Democrat Kevin Kelley in the general election. Kelley, a township supervisor, had a long political résumé but got into the race late. McCotter got an infusion of $500,000 when George W. Bush headlined a fundraising dinner.

He has won re-election fairly easily ever since, though his margin shrank to 6 percentage points in the 2008 Democratic wave in which Obama carried the district by 9 percentage points.

KEY VOTES

2008

No Delay consideration of Colombia free-trade agreement

Yes Override Bush veto of federal farm and nutrition programs reauthorization bill

Yes Overhaul surveillance laws and permit dismissal of suits against companies that conducted warrantless wiretapping

No Grant mortgage relief to homeowners and funding for Fannie Mae and Freddie Mac

No Approve initial $700 billion program to stabilize financial markets

No Approve final $700 billion program to stabilize financial markets

Yes Provide $14 billion in loans to automakers

2007

Yes Increase minimum wage by $2.10 an hour

No Approve $124.2 billion in emergency war spending and set goal for redeployment of troops from Iraq

Yes Reject federal contraceptive assistance to international family planning groups

Yes Override Bush veto of $23.2 billion water projects authorization bill

Yes Implement Peru free-trade agreement

No Approve energy policy overhaul with new fuel economy standards

Yes Clear $473.5 billion omnibus spending bill, including $70 billion for military operations

CQ VOTE STUDIES

	PARTY UNITY		PRESIDENTIAL SUPPORT	
	SUPPORT	OPPOSE	SUPPORT	OPPOSE
2008	86%	14%	58%	42%
2007	87%	13%	66%	34%
2006	87%	13%	82%	18%
2005	89%	11%	78%	22%
2004	91%	9%	82%	18%

INTEREST GROUPS

	AFL-CIO	ADA	CCUS	ACU
2008	60%	40%	82%	72%
2007	50%	20%	75%	84%
2006	50%	15%	93%	83%
2005	40%	20%	81%	88%
2004	27%	15%	95%	88%

MICHIGAN 11
Southeast — Livonia, Westland, Novi

Carved from traditionally GOP-friendly suburbs north and west of Detroit, the 11th District has stood out in a region known for its support of pro-labor Democrats. But political shifts underway in the district led voters here to support Democrat Barack Obama with 54 percent of the district's presidential vote — 2 percentage points higher than Republican George W. Bush won here in 2004.

As in other Michigan districts that surround the Motor City, auto and auto parts manufacturing, and the economic troubles plaguing those sectors, play a dominant role in the district despite recent efforts to diversify the area's economy.

The district's population center is in northwestern Wayne County, where 70 percent of the district's residents live. This area is largely a collection of upper-middle-class communities such as politically competitive Livonia and liberal Redford Township, as well as growing Plymouth and Canton, which have seen success with downtown redevelopment efforts. Nearer to Detroit are Westland, Wayne and Garden City, Democratic

strongholds that have held fast to their blue-collar union roots.

The 11th also covers the more GOP-leaning southwestern Oakland County. Revitalization efforts in the 11th's smaller communities in Oakland are attracting younger residents. Novi has experienced steady population growth for two decades, and the city boasts a convention center that brings millions of visitors to the district each year.

While many areas such as Wixom were once almost entirely filled with auto workers, these communities have been affected by downsized or shuttered auto facilities. A recently passed state tax credit for filmmakers has spurred some development and may provide incentive for movie studios to occupy some of the abandoned factories. The rural northern part of the 11th's parcel of Oakland county is home to subdivisions.

MAJOR INDUSTRY
Auto manufacturing, engineering, health care

CITIES
Livonia, 100,545; Westland, 86,602; Canton (unincorporated), 76,366; Redford (unincorporated), 51,622; Novi, 47,386; Garden City, 30,047

NOTABLE
The Plymouth Ice Festival is North America's largest ice-carving festival.

Rep. Sander M. Levin (D)

Elected 1982; 14th term

CAPITOL OFFICE
225-4961
www.house.gov/levin
1236 Longworth Bldg. 20515-2212; fax 226-1033

COMMITTEES
Ways & Means
  (Trade - chairman)
Joint Taxation

RESIDENCE
Royal Oak

BORN
Sept. 6, 1931; Detroit, Mich.

RELIGION
Jewish

FAMILY
Widowed; four children

EDUCATION
U. of Chicago, B.A. 1952; Columbia U., M.A. 1954
(international relations); Harvard U., LL.B. 1957

CAREER
Lawyer; U.S. Agency for International
Development official

POLITICAL HIGHLIGHTS
Oakland Board of Supervisors, 1961-64;
Mich. Senate, 1965-71 (minority leader, 1969-70);
Mich. Democratic Party chairman, 1968-69;
Democratic nominee for governor, 1970, 1974

ELECTION RESULTS

2008 GENERAL

Sander M. Levin (D)	225,094	72.1%
Bert Copple (R)	74,565	23.9%
John Vico (LIBERT)	4,767	1.5%
Les Townsend (USTAX)	4,076	1.3%
William J. Opalicky (GREEN)	3,842	1.2%

2008 PRIMARY

Sander M. Levin (D)	unopposed

2006 GENERAL

Sander M. Levin (D)	168,494	70.2%
Randell J. Shafer (R)	62,689	26.1%
Andy Lecureaux (LIBERT)	3,259	1.4%

PREVIOUS WINNING PERCENTAGES
2004 (69%); 2002 (68%); 2000 (64%); 1998 (56%);
1996 (57%); 1994 (52%); 1992 (53%); 1990 (70%);
1988 (70%); 1986 (76%); 1984 (100%); 1982 (67%)

Levin is a faithful liberal Democrat who is considered his party's leading expert on trade. The continued resonance of trade and the schism it often causes within the party have kept Levin, a senior member of the Ways and Means Committee, in the spotlight. His goal as chairman of the Trade Subcommittee, he says, is a modern policy that doesn't try to stop globalization but tries to shape the course of trade to benefit workers.

Mild-mannered but tenacious, Levin has the look and speaking style of a distracted college professor. He is known for throwing his intellectual might into understanding the details of legislation and their practical implications, a trait that has earned him respect in the trade and tax worlds. By the end of lengthy hearings, he often looks so rumpled that he appears to be physically wrestling with the answers to his complex questions.

By raising concerns about poor labor laws in some Latin American countries, Levin helped lead the Democratic charge in 2005 against a free-trade agreement with Central America that passed the House by just two votes. Two years later, he and Ways and Means Chairman Charles B. Rangel of New York helped negotiate an agreement on a framework for trade agreements. The deal requires enforceable labor and environmental standards to be written into the pacts, which paved the way for the Peru free-trade agreement. Levin supported that agreement despite opposition from a majority of House Democrats.

Under Levin's watch on the Trade Subcommittee, the "fast-track" authority for the president to quickly negotiate trade deals — that Congress cannot amend — was allowed to lapse. Any new version of the authority must provide more opportunities for Congress to be involved in trade deals before the final vote, he argued.

He supported a February 2009 amendment to President Obama's $787 billion economic stimulus law expanding the Trade Adjustment Assistance program, which provides training, wage protections and unemployment assistance to workers struggling with competition from international business. But he wasn't interested in moving other trade deals. "Free-trade agreements must stand on their own merits as we continue to shape new trade policies with the Obama administration in an era of accelerated globalization," he said.

Levin also is a member of a commission that monitors China's behavior on human rights and compliance with trade rules. The panel was created under a 2000 law making China a permanent normal U.S. trading partner.

Earlier in his career, Levin often was able to find common ground with conservatives. He joined Ohio Republican Rob Portman on legislation to combat illegal drugs, including a bipartisan matching grant initiative. But he laments it is harder to find friendly Republicans. "There's much more polarization," he said.

Levin's influence on Ways and Means extends into the tax area. He led the 2007 effort to tax the "carried interest" earned by private equity fund managers as ordinary income instead of capital gains. The effort was blocked by Republicans and some Senate Democrats, but Levin said he will continue to pursue the issue of tax equity. He threw himself into the 2005 battle over Social Security and became a guiding force in the Democrats' successful effort to kill President George W. Bush's plan to create private accounts.

Levin represents Macomb County outside Detroit, where the term "Reagan Democrat" was coined and where the sagging auto industry is a major employer. During a Ways and Means debate on a bill extending unemployment insurance benefits, Levin read the personal stories of district residents struggling to get by without jobs.

When Obama announced a series of tough steps aimed at rescuing the domestic auto industry in March 2009, Levin expressed support but said the president's plan should include federal action to make technological advancements in new cars. He also urged the industry's creditors to "take their losses in a new framework for a viable auto industry" to stave off the automakers' bankruptcy.

His decades-long interest in changing the presidential nominating system was renewed by turmoil over the seating of Michigan's delegates to the 2008 Democratic National Convention because the state violated party rules by leapfrogging other primaries. He prefers a system he devised that would enable select states to vote on each of six primary days, with lotteries to allow different states to be early in the process in different years.

Levin, known as "Sandy," is the older half of a House-Senate sibling pair, but he was elected four years after Democratic Sen. Carl Levin. The two are close, getting together at least once a week to play squash, and often consult each other on policy. Both absorbed a passion for politics from their father, a lawyer active in social justice causes.

After four years as an appointed supervisor in Oakland County, Levin in 1964 won his first elective office, a state Senate seat. He was minority leader in Lansing, served as state Democratic Party chairman in the late 1960s, and was seen as a rising star as the party's gubernatorial nominee in 1970 and 1974. But his manner wasn't an asset, and he lost both times.

He worked as an assistant administrator in the U.S. Agency for International Development, then ran for the House seat of retiring Democratic Rep. William M. Brodhead in 1982. With his well-known surname and support from the party establishment, Levin overcame five primary opponents and went on to win the general election easily.

He had little trouble with re-election until redistricting after the 1990 census removed many metro Detroit Jewish voters from his district. In 1992, Republican challenger John Pappageorge held him to 53 percent of the vote. Levin won two rematches, in 1994 and 1996, with 52 percent and 57 percent. The GOP-led state legislature subsequently redrew Levin's district to make it more Democratic, and in 2002 Levin easily prevailed with 68 percent. He has won re-election easily since, though in early 2009 he was threatened with a primary challenge by a Democratic state senator.

He suffered a personal setback when his wife Victoria — a leader in federally funded research on the mental health and development of children and infants — died of breast cancer in September 2008.

KEY VOTES

2008

Yes Delay consideration of Colombia free-trade agreement

Yes Override Bush veto of federal farm and nutrition programs reauthorization bill

No Overhaul surveillance laws and permit dismissal of suits against companies that conducted warrantless wiretapping

Yes Grant mortgage relief to homeowners and funding for Fannie Mae and Freddie Mac

Yes Approve initial $700 billion program to stabilize financial markets

Yes Approve final $700 billion program to stabilize financial markets

Yes Provide $14 billion in loans to automakers

2007

Yes Increase minimum wage by $2.10 an hour

Yes Approve $124.2 billion in emergency war spending and set goal for redeployment of troops from Iraq

No Reject federal contraceptive assistance to international family planning groups

Yes Override Bush veto of $23.2 billion water projects authorization bill

Yes Implement Peru free-trade agreement

Yes Approve energy policy overhaul with new fuel economy standards

Yes Clear $473.5 billion omnibus spending bill, including $70 billion for military operations

CQ VOTE STUDIES

| | PARTY UNITY | | PRESIDENTIAL SUPPORT | |
	SUPPORT	OPPOSE	SUPPORT	OPPOSE
2008	99%	1%	16%	84%
2007	98%	2%	7%	93%
2006	93%	7%	25%	75%
2005	95%	5%	20%	80%
2004	95%	5%	26%	74%

INTEREST GROUPS

	AFL-CIO	ADA	CCUS	ACU
2008	100%	95%	59%	0%
2007	96%	90%	56%	0%
2006	100%	90%	40%	8%
2005	100%	95%	48%	4%
2004	100%	100%	38%	0%

MICHIGAN 12

Suburban Detroit – Warren, Clinton, Southfield

Heavily Democratic and dependent on the ailing auto manufacturing industry, the 12th is home to well-settled suburbs in Macomb and Oakland counties north of 8 Mile Road, Detroit's northern boundary. The shoe-shaped district borders Lake St. Clair at its heel and the city of Detroit at its instep before its toes extend to Southfield.

Nearly 70 percent of the 12th's residents live in Macomb in the district's eastern half. The county (shared with the 10th) supported Barack Obama with 53 percent of the vote in the 2008 presidential election. Warren, which is the district's most populous city, has been a traditional Democratic safe haven, and the city gave Barack Obama 59 percent of its presidential vote in 2008. Clinton Township, at slightly less than 100,000 people, claims to be the most populous township in Michigan. St. Clair Shores, the self-proclaimed "boat capital of Michigan," has more than 6 miles of waterfront.

To the west, the 12th takes in several southern Oakland County communities near the Detroit boundary that are heavily Democratic and have large black populations: Southfield, which has become a haven for black urban professionals escaping Detroit's crime, Lathrup Village and Oak Park. Other Oakland County communities in the 12th include Ferndale, Hazel Park and Madison Heights, which also are solidly Democratic but are overwhelmingly white.

The district is lined with auto manufacturing facilities, and Warren is home to the General Motors Technical Center design and engineering campus. The Army's Tank-automotive and Armaments Command and Chrysler's "Dodge City" complex are also in the 12th District. But layoffs have caused concern in the city and across the district, and municipal budget shortfalls have resulted in local governments raising taxes and cutting programs.

MAJOR INDUSTRY
Auto manufacturing, auto and tank research and design

CITIES
Warren, 138,247; Clinton (unincorporated), 95,648; Southfield, 78,296; St. Clair Shores, 63,096; Roseville, 48,129; Sterling Heights (pt.), 37,935

NOTABLE
The Detroit Zoo is in Royal Oak, which received its name in 1819 when Gov. Lewis Cass and his companions christened a large tree.

Rep. Carolyn Cheeks Kilpatrick (D)

Elected 1996; 7th term

CAPITOL OFFICE
225-2261
www.house.gov/kilpatrick
2264 Rayburn Bldg. 20515-2213; fax 225-5730

COMMITTEES
Appropriations

RESIDENCE
Detroit

BORN
June 25, 1945; Detroit, Mich.

RELIGION
African Methodist Episcopal

FAMILY
Divorced; two children

EDUCATION
Ferris State U., A.A. 1965; Western Michigan U., B.S. 1968 (education); U. of Michigan, M.A. 1972 (education)

CAREER
Teacher

POLITICAL HIGHLIGHTS
Mich. House, 1979-97; candidate for Detroit City Council, 1991; sought Democratic nomination for Mich. Senate, 1994

ELECTION RESULTS

2008 GENERAL

Carolyn Cheeks Kilpatrick (D)	167,481	74.1%
Edward J. Gubics (R)	43,098	19.1%
George L. Corsetti (GREEN)	9,579	4.2%
Gregory Creswell (LIBERT)	5,764	2.6%

2008 PRIMARY

Carolyn Cheeks Kilpatrick (D)	21,089	39.2%
Mary Waters (D)	19,303	35.8%
Martha G. Scott (D)	13,471	25.0%

2006 GENERAL

Carolyn Cheeks Kilpatrick (D)	unopposed

PREVIOUS WINNING PERCENTAGES
2004 (78%); 2002 (92%); 2000 (89%); 1998 (87%); 1996 (88%)

Kilpatrick seeks to address the problems facing her Detroit-based district: high infant mortality, high unemployment, significant school dropout rates, blighted neighborhoods, and substandard housing. She is well-positioned to help advance President Obama's priorities through her influential post on the Appropriations Committee.

Kilpatrick has more time to concentrate on her district after serving as chairwoman of the Congressional Black Caucus in the 110th Congress (2007-08). That job often put her in the spotlight, as did the multiple scandals involving her son and political protégé, Detroit Mayor Kwame Kilpatrick, whose career she tended to before he resigned and went to jail in 2008.

From her seat on the Appropriations Committee, Kilpatrick has been able to steer millions of dollars to her district, the poorest in the state. In the 111th Congress (2009-10), she serves on the Defense Appropriations Subcommittee and said she looks forward to bringing an end to the Iraq War. But she also made it clear to military leaders she wants to help them in their efforts to get more money. "I don't care what the OMB says," she told two of them at a March 2009 hearing, referring to the Office of Management and Budget, which helps the president prepare the federal budget. "You just have to let us know."

She also serves on the subcommittee funding the Transportation and Housing and Urban Development departments. She said she plans to push to secure jobs and homes for people in her district, as well as advocate for universal health care and a halt to high tuition increases at public universities. "We don't have a lot of time," she said in January 2009. "Children are suffering. People are hungry. The jobs are gone."

During her stint as head of the Black Caucus, its members played a pivotal role in the House passage of a host of bills, including funding for victims of Hurricane Katrina, a major multi-year rewrite of agriculture and nutrition programs and a minimum wage increase. The group vigorously backed an expansion of the State Children's Health Insurance Program, which covers children from low-income families that do not qualify for Medicaid. President George W. Bush twice vetoed an expansion, but the measure was reintroduced early in 2009 and was one of the first bills that Obama signed into law.

With the nation facing an economic crisis in September 2008, Kilpatrick opposed an initial $700 billion financial industry rescue package, unmoved by intense lobbying on the floor by Speaker Nancy Pelosi of California during the vote. Kilpatrick argued the bill didn't do enough to protect homeowners. But with the crisis deepening, she was one of 33 Democrats who switched their votes to support a revised version of the package. "If Congress does not do something soon, we possibly face an economic Armageddon the likes of which we have not seen since the Great Depression," she said.

The Wall Street meltdown, along with plummeting sales and scarce credit, left the Detroit-based automobile industry facing a potential collapse. Kilpatrick, whose district covers half of the city, supported a proposed rescue package for General Motors Corp., Chrysler LLC and Ford Motor Co. in late 2008, saying, "We've got to save the auto industry...We've got to make sure that we save those jobs." But Senate Republicans balked at the idea of loaning federal money to the automakers, and the measure died.

Although usually a loyal Democratic vote, Kilpatrick often broke from party ranks on the issue of fuel economy standards, which have long been anathema to the Big Three automakers. But in late 2008, she said the industry's resistance to such standards and clean-air vehicles have been "big mistakes."

Earlier in 2008, Kilpatrick, working with Democrat John Conyers Jr., who represents the other half of Detroit, was instrumental in blocking two bills by fellow Michigan Democrat John D. Dingell to allow American Indian casinos to be located in Port Huron and Romulus. Kilpatrick and Conyers said the legislation would threaten three Detroit casinos that are vital to the city's economy.

A native of Detroit, Kilpatrick holds a master's degree in education. She taught business and vocational classes in the public schools for eight years. She won the first of nine terms in the state House, a full-time job, in 1978. In Lansing, she was the first black woman to serve on the Appropriations Committee, and she once led a bipartisan coalition of lawmakers seeking to block a proposal by popular Republican Gov. John Engler to halt state funding for local transportation programs.

She lost a bid in 1991 for the Detroit City Council when questions arose about whether she was sufficiently independent from Mayor Coleman Young; and she also failed, after changing her mind several times, to win a spot on the 1994 state Senate ballot. In 1996, when Democratic U.S. Rep. Barbara-Rose Collins became the subject of investigations by the House ethics committee and the Justice Department into allegations of misconduct, Kilpatrick stepped forward to challenge her one-time political ally. Kilpatrick won a majority of the primary vote and beat Collins by 20 percentage points. The November outcome was a foregone conclusion in the heavily Democratic district.

Kilpatrick won re-election with ease until 2008, when she barely survived the primary against former state Rep. Mary Waters and state Sen. Martha G. Scott. A major element in the contest was a scandal ensnaring Kwame Kilpatrick, who was charged with eight felony counts, including charges of perjury for allegedly covering up a sexual affair with his former chief of staff. (In September, he resigned, pleaded guilty to charges related to the scandal and received a four-month jail sentence.)

Kilpatrick edged Waters by just 3 percentage points and won the 2008 general election with 74 percent of the vote, her smallest general election vote total ever. "It was by far my toughest election," she said. Ultimately, she said, "The people stuck with me because I deliver."

The Detroit Free Press, in endorsing Kilpatrick in the 2008 primary, said the primary "should serve as a needed wake-up call" for Kilpatrick, "who has been on cruise control for too long." The Detroit News backed Waters, saying Kilpatrick's seniority and influence had "paid too little dividends."

KEY VOTES

2008

Yes Delay consideration of Colombia free-trade agreement
Yes Override Bush veto of federal farm and nutrition programs reauthorization bill
No Overhaul surveillance laws and permit dismissal of suits against companies that conducted warrantless wiretapping
Yes Grant mortgage relief to homeowners and funding for Fannie Mae and Freddie Mac
No Approve initial $700 billion program to stabilize financial markets
Yes Approve final $700 billion program to stabilize financial markets
Yes Provide $14 billion in loans to automakers

2007

Yes Increase minimum wage by $2.10 an hour
Yes Approve $124.2 billion in emergency war spending and set goal for redeployment of troops from Iraq
No Reject federal contraceptive assistance to international family planning groups
Yes Override Bush veto of $23.2 billion water projects authorization bill
No Implement Peru free-trade agreement
Yes Approve energy policy overhaul with new fuel economy standards
No Clear $473.5 billion omnibus spending bill, including $70 billion for military operations

CQ VOTE STUDIES

| | PARTY UNITY | | PRESIDENTIAL SUPPORT | |
	SUPPORT	OPPOSE	SUPPORT	OPPOSE
2008	99%	1%	13%	87%
2007	99%	1%	4%	96%
2006	97%	3%	23%	77%
2005	96%	4%	17%	83%
2004	96%	4%	28%	72%

INTEREST GROUPS

	AFL-CIO	ADA	CCUS	ACU
2008	100%	95%	53%	4%
2007	96%	95%	63%	0%
2006	100%	100%	27%	4%
2005	93%	100%	32%	4%
2004	100%	95%	29%	4%

MICHIGAN 13
Part of Detroit; Lincoln Park; Wyandotte

The auto industry and Motown Records kept Detroit humming for decades before economic problems overwhelmed the city, which remains among the most crime-ridden in the nation. Detroit, divided between the 13th and 14th districts, still has a tough reputation and relatively high taxes, and many suburbs have become regional office centers that have lured companies away from the city.

A slightly larger share of Detroit's population lives in the black-majority 13th. A reputation for crime and a lack of available jobs — the city's unemployment rate topped 22 percent in early 2009 — have caused the city's population to plummet to less than half of what it was in 1950. Property values have cratered and homes here are, on average, worth less than they were in 2000. Future census figures are expected to show the city out of the top 10 most-populous U.S. cities for the first time since the late 19th century. Wealthy communities to the northeast, such as Grosse Pointe, also are losing population, although not as drastically.

Recent revitalization plans, however, are attempting to bring the roar back into the city, and the resurgent downtown is showing signs of life. A massive downtown entertainment complex includes two cornerstone sports stadiums — Comerica Park for baseball's Tigers and Ford Field for football's Lions — as well as the Fox Theater. The RiverWalk project, the first section of which opened in 2007, is aimed at promoting tourism along the Detroit River. Cobo Center hosts major cultural events and conventions, while Joe Louis Arena brings in the crowds for hockey's Red Wings. Three downtown casinos are a draw for gaming enthusiasts and General Motors has relocated its headquarters to the Renaissance Center on the waterfront.

Detroit remains overwhelmingly Democratic, and Barack Obama won the 13th District's portion of the city with 85 percent of the vote in the 2008 presidential election.

MAJOR INDUSTRY
Auto and auto parts manufacturing, government

CITIES
Detroit (pt.), 511,449; Lincoln Park, 40,008; Wyandotte, 28,006

NOTABLE
The headquarters of Michigan's famous Faygo "pop" is in the 13th; The Charles H. Wright Museum of African-American History.

Rep. John Conyers Jr. (D)

Elected 1964; 23rd term

CAPITOL OFFICE
225-5126
www.house.gov/conyers
2426 Rayburn Bldg. 20515-2214; fax 225-0072

COMMITTEES
Judiciary - chairman

RESIDENCE
Detroit

BORN
May 16, 1929; Detroit, Mich.

RELIGION
Baptist

FAMILY
Wife, Monica Conyers; two children

EDUCATION
Wayne State U., B.A. 1957, LL.B. 1958

MILITARY SERVICE
Mich. National Guard, 1948-50; Army, 1950-54;
Army Reserve, 1954-57

CAREER
Lawyer; congressional district aide

POLITICAL HIGHLIGHTS
Candidate for mayor of Detroit, 1989, 1993

ELECTION RESULTS

2008 GENERAL

John Conyers Jr. (D)	227,841	92.4%
Richard J. Secula (LIBERT)	10,732	4.4%
Clyde K. Shabazz (GREEN)	8,015	3.2%

2008 PRIMARY

John Conyers Jr. (D)	unopposed

2006 GENERAL

John Conyers Jr. (D)	158,755	85.3%
Chad Miles (R)	27,367	14.7%

PREVIOUS WINNING PERCENTAGES
2004 (84%); 2002 (83%); 2000 (89%); 1998 (87%);
1996 (86%); 1994 (81%); 1992 (82%); 1990 (89%);
1988 (91%); 1986 (89%); 1984 (89%); 1982 (97%);
1980 (95%); 1978 (93%); 1976 (92%); 1974 (91%);
1972 (88%); 1970 (88%); 1968 (100%); 1966 (84%);
1964 (84%)

Age and experience have infused Conyers with an easygoing manner that serves him well as chairman of the fractious Judiciary Committee. His low-key demeanor, however, masks fiercely partisan beliefs that have long made him one of Congress' most liberal members.

Conyers got his start as a lawmaker in the civil rights era. As a pioneering black politician, he would seem a natural ally for President Obama. But his uncompromising liberalism — which often antagonized George W. Bush's administration — could pose a challenge to Obama's intention to steer a bipartisan course.

Obama indicated in early 2009 that he was looking to cut a deal to overhaul the nation's health care system, but Conyers was sticking to his long-standing plan to create an entirely government-run system by expanding the Medicare program, anathema to Republicans. And early in the 111th Congress (2009-10) Conyers picked a fight with Obama over the president's plan to choose CNN correspondent Sanjay Gupta as surgeon general. Conyers called him unqualified; Gupta later avoided the confrontation by turning down the job offer.

Conyers was at the center of partisan controversy soon thereafter when he pushed legislation through the House to allow bankruptcy court judges to rewrite mortgage terms to help struggling homeowners. Several moderate Democrats rejected the plan for fear it would encourage people to file for bankruptcy. Conyers, who opposed legislation in 2008 aimed at rescuing ailing banks, said his bill was a better approach. "Unlike the hundreds of billions we have spent in recent months to bail out Wall Street banks, the mortgage modification provision in this legislation comes at no taxpayer expense," he said.

Meanwhile, Conyers refused to relinquish his goal of punishing the Bush administration for what he contends were its crimes in pursuing the Iraq War. Conyers said he wants to impanel a truth commission to examine the Bush record and repeatedly has tried to bring former Bush adviser Karl Rove before his committee. Obama has said he'd prefer to let the past remain in the past.

But Conyers also hopes to use his chairmanship during the 111th to move a major rewrite of federal patent law — an effort that stalled in the Senate after House passage in 2008. Conyers also is likely to face pressure from other panel Democrats to deal with such issues as disparity in federal criminal sentencing between crack and powder cocaine offenses.

Despite his partisan rhetoric, Conyers worked closely behind the scenes with Republican Judiciary Chairman F. James Sensenbrenner Jr. of Wisconsin when Democrats were in the minority in the House. And after assuming the chairmanship in 2007, Conyers forged a collegial relationship with top-ranking Republican Lamar Smith of Texas.

A co-founder of the Congressional Black Caucus, Conyers has championed the causes of civil rights, minorities and the poor. He introduced legislation to make the Rev. Martin Luther King Jr.'s birthday a national holiday just four days after the civil rights leader's assassination in 1968, and he pushed the bill until it was enacted in 1983. And he has long pursued legislation to establish a commission to see whether the government owes reparations to African-American descendants of slaves.

Conyers won the gratitude of other Democrats for his vociferous defense of President Clinton during the 1998 impeachment debate. He accused Republicans of a politically motivated attempt to remove a twice-elected president on trivial grounds related to his affair with a White House intern. By that time, Conyers was the only remaining Judiciary Committee member from 1974, when the panel had voted to impeach President Nixon for obstruction of justice and abuse of official powers.

Conyers argued that the Bush administration's sins in Iraq were far more grave when, in 2005, he called for impeachment proceedings. Conyers didn't press the issue, though, when House Democratic leaders made it clear they didn't want to move ahead. He did hold a single hearing in 2008, ostensibly on "executive power" rather than impeachment, after Ohio Democrat Dennis J. Kucinich pushed an impeachment resolution against Bush in the House.

In recent years, Conyers himself was under a cloud as the ethics committee investigated complaints he compelled his official staff to do campaign work and personal chores. The panel elicited a promise from Conyers in 2006 not to use his staff for campaign work.

Conyers has served in the House longer than all but fellow Michigan Democrat John D. Dingell. But in contrast to Dingell's hands-on style when he chaired the Energy and Commerce Committee, Conyers tends to delegate power to his subcommittee chairmen.

After serving in the Army in Korea, Conyers went home to Detroit and became involved in the Democratic Party apparatus while in law school there. The creation in 1964 of a second black-majority congressional district in the city provided an opening, and he won a primary race against accountant Richard H. Austin by 108 votes. He ran for Congress on a platform of "Equality, Jobs and Peace," pledging to strengthen the United Nations and to exempt low-income families from paying federal income tax. Among the qualifications Conyers cited for holding office were three years as a district aide to Dingell and service on a panel of lawyers picked by President Kennedy to look for ways of easing racial tensions in the South. He won the Democratic district in a rout that November and has not been seriously challenged for re-election since.

Despite his popularity in his district, Conyers twice was unable to translate it into a successful bid for mayor of Detroit. He finished last in 1989 and again four years later. His wife, Monica, is president of Detroit's City Council.

He has a deep interest in jazz and successfully sponsored a House resolution in 1987 declaring jazz a "rare and valuable national American treasure." He is also friends with liberal filmmaker and fellow Michigander Michael Moore and appeared in Moore's 2004 movie "Fahrenheit 9/11," where he acknowledged that lawmakers don't read most of the bills they vote on.

KEY VOTES

2008
Yes Delay consideration of Colombia free-trade agreement
Yes Override Bush veto of federal farm and nutrition programs reauthorization bill
No   Overhaul surveillance laws and permit dismissal of suits against companies that conducted warrantless wiretapping
Yes Grant mortgage relief to homeowners and funding for Fannie Mae and Freddie Mac
No   Approve initial $700 billion program to stabilize financial markets
No   Approve final $700 billion program to stabilize financial markets
Yes Provide $14 billion in loans to automakers

2007
Yes Increase minimum wage by $2.10 an hour
Yes Approve $124.2 billion in emergency war spending and set goal for redeployment of troops from Iraq
No   Reject federal contraceptive assistance to international family planning groups
Yes Override Bush veto of $23.2 billion water projects authorization bill
No   Implement Peru free-trade agreement
Yes Approve energy policy overhaul with new fuel economy standards
No   Clear $473.5 billion omnibus spending bill, including $70 billion for military operations

CQ VOTE STUDIES

	PARTY UNITY		PRESIDENTIAL SUPPORT	
	SUPPORT	OPPOSE	SUPPORT	OPPOSE
2008	98%	2%	12%	88%
2007	99%	1%	4%	96%
2006	98%	2%	8%	92%
2005	97%	3%	15%	85%
2004	98%	2%	7%	93%

INTEREST GROUPS

	AFL-CIO	ADA	CCUS	ACU
2008	100%	100%	50%	9%
2007	96%	95%	50%	0%
2006	93%	100%	20%	4%
2005	92%	95%	35%	13%
2004	100%	90%	11%	0%

MICHIGAN 14
Parts of Detroit and Dearborn

The first half of the 20th century brought great prosperity to Detroit, as General Motors helped make it the "Motor City." But race riots during the summer of 1967 and the oil crisis of the early 1970s sparked an exodus that is still occurring. In 1950, 1.85 million people lived in Detroit; in 2000, its population was 951,000, and more recent census estimates put its population at less than 900,000. Many residents have fled to the suburbs, and many domestic automakers have moved plants to Mexico while foreign-owned companies set up shop in non-union U.S. towns.

The 14th covers the residential neighborhoods that sprang up north of Detroit's auto plants. It includes slightly less than half of the city's residents (the rest are in the 13th), and Detroit accounts for two-thirds of the district's total population. Redevelopment efforts in the district have stalled, many properties sit vacant and the violent crime rates, while down in recent years, remain among the nation's highest. The city's finances also are in disarray — a potential problem in an area with a large public-sector workforce.

The 14th includes two-thirds of Dearborn, which is home to Ford Motor Co. and its Rouge Center factory. With 30 percent of the city's residents of Arab ancestry, Dearborn helps give the 14th the highest Arab-American population of any district in the nation. The district also includes two cities surrounded entirely by Detroit: Hamtramck, an ethnically diverse enclave originally settled by Polish immigrants, and Highland Park, an overwhelmingly black area plagued by high poverty rates. A new $146 million film studio in Allen Park is expected to create thousands of skilled jobs.

The 14th District has one of the country's highest percentages of black residents (61 percent) and is safely Democratic. In 2008, the 14th gave Barack Obama 86 percent of its presidential vote — his highest percentage in the state.

MAJOR INDUSTRY
Auto and auto parts manufacturing, health care

CITIES
Detroit (pt.), 439,821; Dearborn (pt), 64,759; Southgate, 30,136; Allen Park, 29,376; Hamtramck, 22,976

NOTABLE
Woodward Avenue, between 6 Mile and 7 Mile roads, was the nation's first paved road (1909); The Henry Ford museum in Dearborn.

Rep. John D. Dingell (D)

Elected December 1955; 27th full term

CAPITOL OFFICE
225-4071
www.house.gov/dingell
2328 Rayburn Bldg. 20515-2215; fax 226-0371

COMMITTEES
Energy & Commerce

RESIDENCE
Dearborn

BORN
July 8, 1926; Colorado Springs, Colo.

RELIGION
Roman Catholic

FAMILY
Wife, Debbie Dingell; four children

EDUCATION
Georgetown U., B.S. 1949 (chemistry), J.D. 1952

MILITARY SERVICE
Army, 1944-46

CAREER
County prosecutor

POLITICAL HIGHLIGHTS
No previous office

ELECTION RESULTS

2008 GENERAL

John D. Dingell (D)	231,784	70.7%
John J. Lynch (R)	81,802	25.0%
Aimee Smith (GREEN)	7,082	2.2%
Gregory Scott Stempfle (LIBERT)	4,002	1.2%

2008 PRIMARY

John D. Dingell (D)	unopposed

2006 GENERAL

John D. Dingell (D)	181,946	88.0%
Aimee Smith (GREEN)	9,447	4.6%
Gregory Scott Stempfle (LIBERT)	8,410	4.1%
Robert F. Czak (USTAX)	7,064	3.4%

PREVIOUS WINNING PERCENTAGES
2004 (71%); 2002 (72%); 2000 (71%); 1998 (67%);
1996 (62%); 1994 (59%); 1992 (65%); 1990 (67%);
1988 (97%); 1986 (78%); 1984 (64%); 1982 (74%);
1980 (70%); 1978 (77%); 1976 (76%); 1974 (78%);
1972 (68%); 1970 (79%); 1968 (74%); 1966 (63%);
1964 (73%); 1962 (83%); 1960 (79%); 1958 (79%);
1956 (74%); 1955 Special Election (76%)

Dingell once self-effacingly called himself "just a simple Polish lawyer from Detroit," but he is assured a spot in history books. Legendary for his tenacity and toughness, he has a career that has spanned more than half a century and given him a hand in transformational legislation, from the Civil Rights Act to the Endangered Species and Clean Air acts.

Dingell marked another achievement on Feb. 14, 2009, by becoming the longest-serving House member, surpassing Mississippi Democrat Jamie L. Whitten. But he was unable to celebrate that accomplishment while serving in the position that earned him his formidable reputation. In November 2008, his longtime rival Henry A. Waxman of California ousted him from the chairmanship of the Energy and Commerce Committee in a 137-122 vote of House Democrats, a move that upended the Democrats' tradition of seniority.

In challenging Dingell, Waxman stressed his ties to Barack Obama and his desire to implement an agenda on energy, climate and other issues unburdened by Dingell's uncompromising protection of his state's automobile industry. Though Dingell lined up support from moderate and conservative Democrats, along with many members of the Congressional Black Caucus, it was not enough. "I've had a good run," Dingell said in conceding defeat.

Dingell served as Energy and Commerce chairman from 1981 to 1995 and as top-ranking Democrat until 2007, when his party retook control of Congress and he regained the chairmanship. He built what scholars consider one of the most expansive congressional power centers of the post-World War II era, with jurisdiction on issues as diverse as energy, health care and telecommunications. "He will be remembered as one of the most influential members of Congress not to have served as president," said Texas Republican Joe L. Barton, who has served on the panel with Dingell for two decades.

Age has slowed Dingell. The tall, burly veteran walks slowly, leaning on a cane. In October 2008 he underwent knee replacement surgery, and a month later was hospitalized for what an aide called post-surgical complications.

It would be premature, however, to count out Dingell as a legislative force. Even without a chairmanship, he retains a thorough grasp of House rules and legislative detail. As he once famously said: "If you let me write procedure and I let you write substance, I'll screw you every time."

Dingell is especially knowledgeable and passionate about health care. It has been among his top issues since 1955, when, at age 29, he won a special election for the congressional seat left vacant when his father died unexpectedly in office. At the start of every Congress, he introduces a national health insurance bill that his father sponsored when he was a member.

And Dingell will be a primary player in the health care debate during the 111th Congress (2009-10). Setting aside differences, Waxman told Dingell he will be the lead sponsor of national health care legislation the committee will consider.

The announcement was a recognition of the great influence and power Dingell wields on the issue. He has made his mark on several initiatives. He helped write the law that created the Medicare program in 1965. In the first weeks of the 110th Congress (2007-08), the House passed and sent to the Senate a Dingell-sponsored bill to give the federal government negotiating leverage with prescription drug companies, something Republicans had blocked when they wrote the 2003 Medicare drug bill. Dingell wrote a bill to expand the State Children's Health Insurance Program, which covers children from low-income families ineligible for Medicaid, by $35 billion over five years. President George W. Bush successfully vetoed the measure, but Democrats revived it early in the 111th and rushed it to passage.

Waxman also let Dingell help draft food safety legislation in early 2009 that the chairman said would be the basis for what the panel considered. And Dingell will remain active on energy and climate change. He was a central player in the 2007 debate on the energy bill, in which he reversed decades of opposition to tougher fuel efficiency standards for automobiles. The bill included the first statutory increase in such standards in 32 years.

When Obama announced a tough series of steps for automakers in March 2009, Dingell vowed to do anything he could to help them avoid financial ruin. He thanked Obama "for laying out a clear path for us to follow" and added, "My sleeves are rolled up."

Dingell and his staff are celebrated for "Dingell-grams," lengthy letters full of detailed questions and document requests to federal agencies. An interrogation by a well-briefed and aggrieved Dingell during a congressional hearing can be brutal. In March 2007, he dragged all five members of the Federal Communications Commission before his committee to complain that they overstepped their authority in easing regulations for the cable industry.

Even in the minority, he was able to embarrass the Bush administration into responding to his requests, rather than dismissing them with form letters as they initially tried to do. Bush once called Dingell the "biggest pain in the ass" on Capitol Hill, according to the Detroit Free Press.

Dingell stands with liberal Democrats on most issues but opposes abortion rights and gun control. He inherited his political philosophy from his father, a New Deal Democrat who represented the Detroit-area district for 22 years. The younger Dingell grew up in Washington, was a congressional page and earned a law degree from Georgetown University.

He was an assistant county prosecutor in Dearborn, Mich., when his father died. Soon, his hero, Speaker Sam Rayburn of Texas, put him on what was then the Committee on Interstate and Foreign Commerce.

In 27 general elections, he drew less than 60 percent of the vote only once, when Republicans won control of Congress in 1994. But in 2002, after the GOP-controlled state legislature redrew boundaries to reflect Michigan's post-census loss of a House seat, Dingell was pitted in the primary against another incumbent Democrat, eight-year veteran Lynn Rivers. He won that primary with 59 percent of the vote. He ran without GOP opposition in 2006 and in 2008 took 71 percent of the vote.

KEY VOTES

2008

Yes Delay consideration of Colombia free-trade agreement

Yes Override Bush veto of federal farm and nutrition programs reauthorization bill

No Overhaul surveillance laws and permit dismissal of suits against companies that conducted warrantless wiretapping

Yes Grant mortgage relief to homeowners and funding for Fannie Mae and Freddie Mac

Yes Approve initial $700 billion program to stabilize financial markets

Yes Approve final $700 billion program to stabilize financial markets

Yes Provide $14 billion in loans to automakers

2007

Yes Increase minimum wage by $2.10 an hour

Yes Approve $124.2 billion in emergency war spending and set goal for redeployment of troops from Iraq

No Reject federal contraceptive assistance to international family planning groups

Yes Override Bush veto of $23.2 billion water projects authorization bill

Yes Implement Peru free-trade agreement

Yes Approve energy policy overhaul with new fuel economy standards

Yes Clear $473.5 billion omnibus spending bill, including $70 billion for military operations

CQ VOTE STUDIES

	PARTY UNITY		PRESIDENTIAL SUPPORT	
	SUPPORT	OPPOSE	SUPPORT	OPPOSE
2008	99%	1%	15%	85%
2007	97%	3%	6%	94%
2006	90%	10%	23%	77%
2005	92%	8%	26%	74%
2004	94%	6%	27%	73%

INTEREST GROUPS

	AFL-CIO	ADA	CCUS	ACU
2008	100%	90%	56%	4%
2007	96%	95%	65%	0%
2006	100%	95%	33%	13%
2005	100%	95%	52%	12%
2004	100%	95%	33%	4%

MICHIGAN 15

Southeast — Ann Arbor, Taylor, parts of Dearborn and Dearborn Heights, Ypsilanti

Situated in Michigan's southeast corner west and south of Detroit, the 15th's flat land contains a mix of academics, engineers and auto workers. GOP votes from the 15th's rural farming communities in the southwest are overshadowed by blue-collar strongholds in Wayne County's urban areas, as well as Ann Arbor, and Democrat Barack Obama carried the district with 66 percent of the 2008 presidential vote.

Home to the University of Michigan in the 15th's northwest corner in Washtenaw County, Ann Arbor is one of Michigan's most progressive cities and has remained stable in the face of significant economic pressure. A high standard of living, a strong medical research sector and a highly educated workforce make Ann Arbor a gem in an ailing state. Overall, the city gave Obama 82 percent in 2008. Despite some plant closings, Ann Arbor has avoided widespread job losses by relying on expansions at the university and in the private sector at employers such as Google's AdWords, a company advertising vehicle.

Ypsilanti, the working-class town southeast of Ann Arbor, is home to Eastern Michigan University and reliably backs Democrats. Engineering and robotics firms have emerged south and east of Ann Arbor, developing highly skilled and computerized auto manufacturing.

A little more than 40 percent of the 15th's residents live in the reliably Democratic Wayne County suburbs, including Taylor, located a few miles east of Detroit Metropolitan Wayne County Airport in Romulus. Local officials hope to spur job growth in developments between Metro Airport and nearby Willow Run Airport. Dearborn, the western third of which is in the 15th, Dearborn Heights (shared with the 11th) and Inkster form the district's northeast corner. Monroe County, south of Wayne and Washtenaw, abuts Lake Erie to the east and the Toledo area to the south.

MAJOR INDUSTRY
Auto and parts manufacturing, higher education, medical research, steel

CITIES
Ann Arbor, 114,024; Taylor, 65,868; Dearborn Heights (pt.), 44,694; Dearborn (pt.), 33,016; Inkster, 30,115; Romulus, 22,979; Ypsilanti, 22,362

NOTABLE
The National Oceanic and Atmospheric Administration's Great Lakes Environmental Research Laboratory is in Ann Arbor.

Gov. Tim Pawlenty (R)

First elected: 2002
Length of term: 4 years
Term expires: 1/11
Salary: $120,311
Phone: (651) 296-3391

Residence: Eagan
Born: Nov. 27, 1960;
South St. Paul, Minn.
Religion: Protestant
Family: Wife, Mary Pawlenty; two children
Education: U. of Minnesota, B.A. 1983
(political science), J.D. 1986
Career: Internet consulting firm
executive; lawyer
Political highlights: Eagan Planning
Commission, 1988-89; Eagan City Council,
1990-92; Minn. House, 1993-2003

Election results:
2006 GENERAL

Tim Pawlenty (R)	1,028,568	46.7%
Mike Hatch (D)	1,007,460	45.7%
Peter Hutchinson (I)	141,735	6.4%

Lt. Gov. Carol Molnau (R)

First elected: 2002
Length of term: 4 years
Term expires: 1/11
Salary: $78,196
Phone: (651) 296-3391

LEGISLATURE

Legislature: January-May in odd-numbered years; February-May in even-numbered years

Senate: 67 members, 4-year terms
2009 ratios: 46 D, 21 R; 40 men, 27 women
Salary: $31,141
Phone: (651) 296-0504

House: 134 members, 2-year terms
2009 ratios: 87 D, 47 R; 91 men, 43 women
Salary: $31,141
Phone: (651) 296-2146

TERM LIMITS

Governor: No
Senate: No
House: No

URBAN STATISTICS

CITY	POPULATION
Minneapolis	382,618
St. Paul	287,151
Duluth	86,918
Rochester	85,806
Bloomington	85,172

REGISTERED VOTERS

Voters do not register by party.

POPULATION

2008 population (est.)	5,220,393
2000 population	4,919,479
1990 population	4,375,099
Percent change (1990-2000)	+12.4%
Rank among states (2008)	21

Median age	35.4
Born in state	70.2%
Foreign born	5.3%
Violent crime rate	281/100,000
Poverty level	7.9%
Federal workers	32,833
Military	19,625

ELECTIONS

STATE ELECTION OFFICIAL
(651) 215-1440
DEMOCRATIC PARTY
(651) 293-1200
REPUBLICAN PARTY
(651) 222-0022

MISCELLANEOUS

Web: www.state.mn.us
Capital: St. Paul

U.S. CONGRESS

Senate: 1 Democrat, 1 vacancy
House: 5 Democrats, 3 Republicans

2000 Census Statistics by District

DIST.	2008 VOTE FOR PRESIDENT OBAMA	MCCAIN	WHITE	BLACK	ASIAN	HISP	MEDIAN INCOME	WHITE COLLAR	BLUE COLLAR	SERVICE INDUSTRY	OVER 64	UNDER 18	COLLEGE EDUCATION	RURAL	SQ. MILES
1	51%	47%	93%	1%	2%	3%	$40,941	57%	28%	15%	15%	25%	22%	44%	13,322
2	48	50	92	2	2	3	$61,344	65	23	12	8	30	31	20	3,035
3	52	46	89	4	4	2	$63,816	73	17	10	10	27	40	4	468
4	64	34	78	6	8	4	$46,811	67	19	14	12	26	33	0	202
5	74	24	71	13	5	6	$41,569	67	18	15	12	22	35	0	124
6	45	53	95	1	1	1	$56,862	60	27	12	8	29	25	36	3,081
7	47	50	93	0	1	3	$36,453	53	31	16	17	26	16	66	31,796
8	53	44	95	1	0	1	$37,911	53	30	17	16	25	18	63	27,583
STATE	54	44	88	3	3	3	$47,111	62	24	14	12	26	27	29	79,610
U.S.	53	46	69	12	4	13	$41,994	60	25	15	12	26	24	21	3,537,438

Sen. Amy Klobuchar (D)

Elected 2006; 1st term

CAPITOL OFFICE
224-3244
klobuchar.senate.gov
302 Hart Bldg. 20510-2305; fax 228-2186

COMMITTEES
Agriculture, Nutrition & Forestry
Commerce, Science & Transportation
  (Competitiveness, Innovation & Export
  Promotion - chairwoman)
Environment & Public Works
  (Children's Health - chairwoman)
Judiciary
Joint Economic

RESIDENCE
Minneapolis

BORN
May 25, 1960; Plymouth, Minn.

RELIGION
Congregationalist

FAMILY
Husband, John Bessler; one child

EDUCATION
Yale U., B.A. 1982 (political science);
U. of Chicago, J.D. 1985

CAREER
Lawyer; lobbyist

POLITICAL HIGHLIGHTS
Hennepin County attorney, 1999-2007

ELECTION RESULTS

2006 GENERAL

Amy Klobuchar (D)	1,278,849	58.1%
Mark Kennedy (R)	835,653	37.9%
Rob Fitzgerald (INDC)	71,194	3.2%

2006 PRIMARY

Amy Klobuchar (D)	294,671	92.5%
Darryl Stanton (D)	23,872	7.5%

Klobuchar has quickly built a reputation for forging bipartisan partnerships and being active on multiple legislative fronts. She calls herself "my own Democrat" and works on such traditional Republican issues as fiscal restraint and crime control, but also focuses on consumer safety matters and environmental concerns.

Klobuchar (KLO-buh-shar) generally backs her party; in her first two years, she voted with Democrats on 93 percent of the bills in which a majority of the two parties diverged. But she admires Olympia J. Snowe, a GOP moderate from Maine who was her assigned "mentor" as a freshman, for her ability to seek consensus. And she often works with Republicans on the five committees on which she serves: Agriculture, Nutrition and Forestry; Commerce, Science and Transportation; Environment and Public Works; Judiciary; and Joint Economic.

Protecting consumers is among her chief interests. As a member of Commerce, Klobuchar wrote provisions in a consumer safety bill that banned lead in all toys sold in the United States. The same bill, cleared by Congress in July 2008, included her provisions to ban industry-sponsored travel for Consumer Product Safety Commission members. But she is most proud of her crusade focused on pool drains. After a wading pool drain sucked out the intestines of a 6-year-old Minnesota girl — ultimately killing her — Klobuchar in 2007 quickly pushed through Congress legislation calling for tighter regulations.

From her seat on Agriculture, she joined a bipartisan group of senators in introducing a food safety bill in March 2009 in response to a nationwide salmonella outbreak blamed on contaminated peanuts. Around that time, she also lobbied Agriculture Secretary Tom Vilsack to assist her state's financially struggling dairy farmers.

During debate on the 2008 reauthorization of farm and nutrition programs, she pushed the Senate to provide incentives for farmers to grow perennial grasses and other biomass crops for cellulosic ethanol production. She also advocated increasing funds for research aimed at helping farmers find ways to store carbon in the soil. As gas prices soared and the country took an interest in alternative energy research, the ideas caught on; some form of nearly all the provisions made it into the final bill.

Klobuchar has been an ally of Environment and Public Works Chairwoman Barbara Boxer of California in efforts to combat climate change. Even in notoriously cold Minnesota, she said, the subject has been a recurring topic in talks with constituents. She joined Boxer, Snowe and California Democrat Dianne Feinstein in applauding the EPA's March 2009 decision to establish a registry to track greenhouse gas emissions; such a proposal was the first bill she introduced in Congress. She supports some version of a "cap and trade" system for limiting emissions, renewable-fuel content standards for cars and trucks, and strong standards for renewable electricity generation that make greater use of wind, solar and other alternative sources.

Shrinking the federal deficit and providing middle-class tax relief were cornerstones of her 2006 campaign, and she regularly shows signs of fiscal conservatism. During debate on a $410 billion catchall spending bill for fiscal 2009, she supported a failed GOP motion to set non-security spending at 2008 levels adjusted for inflation.

She put aside her concerns about deficits to back Obama's $787 billion economic stimulus law in early 2009. "Anyone in Minnesota can tell you, when it is 20 below, as it has been the last month, and your battery is dead and you need to get to work, your No. 1 priority is to get a jump-start right away, and not just stand around talking about it and debating and using the old ideas from the past," she said. "You need a jump-start, and that's what this economic recovery plan is about."

A chief prosecutor for Hennepin County for eight years, Klobuchar was grateful to land a seat on Judiciary in 2009. She swiftly won committee passage of a bill that would subject freight railroads to the same antitrust laws as most other industries, making it easier for shippers to sue the railroads for anti-competitive behavior. She also serves as Senate co-chair, with North Carolina Republican Richard M. Burr, of the Congressional E-911 Caucus, which seeks to improve emergency communications.

Klobuchar grew up in the Minneapolis suburb of Plymouth, the daughter of longtime Minneapolis Star Tribune newspaper columnist Jim Klobuchar. She attended Yale, where her senior thesis detailed the 10-year political debate over the building of the Hubert H. Humphrey Metrodome in Minneapolis. It was published as a book, "Uncovering the Dome," that has been used as a text in college courses.

After graduating from the University of Chicago's law school, Klobuchar returned to Minnesota to practice law and worked with former Vice President Walter Mondale, who provided her first Washington experience through an internship in his office.

She also helped her father recover from alcoholism, a battle he subsequently chronicled in a book, "Pursued by Grace: A Newspaperman's Own Story of Spiritual Recovery." The challenge gave her thick skin that came in handy during her Senate run. "Growing up with my dad being in the public eye was also very helpful," she said. His three DWI arrests "were all very prominent and well-known."

She first caught the political bug on her high school student council, but the catalyst that drove her into big-league politics came in 1995, when her daughter Abigail was born with a frozen palate that prevented her from swallowing. While the baby stayed at the hospital, Klobuchar was discharged after 24 hours because it was all her health plan would cover. Outraged, she lobbied state lawmakers successfully for a law to guarantee new mothers 48 hours at the hospital.

Klobuchar entered the Hennepin County attorney's race in 1998 and defeated former Republican Rep. Jim Ramstad's sister, Sheryl. Klobuchar focused on fighting violent crime, and was re-elected in 2002 without opposition.

When Mark Dayton announced his retirement from the Senate in early 2005, Klobuchar was recognized as an early favorite to secure the Democratic-Farmer-Labor Party nomination, and her three leading opponents dropped out of the race during the primary campaign.

In the general election, Klobuchar's main opponent was Republican Rep. Mark Kennedy, who represented the 6th District. She won with 58 percent of the vote to Kennedy's 38 percent and Independence Party candidate Robert Fitzgerald's 3 percent. She took all but eight of Minnesota's 87 counties, with the largest U.S. Senate election margin in the state since 1978.

Though a serious-minded legislator, Klobuchar has drawn attention for her wit. She won rave reviews as a speaker at the 2009 Washington Press Club Foundation's annual congressional dinner, where she joked about the many ticket-holders turned away from President Obama's inauguration: "So much for the Democrats being against torture."

Later, Klobuchar made light of her status as Minnesota's only senator during the protracted election battle involving her GOP colleague Norm Coleman and Democratic challenger Al Franken. "I never have any friction in my delegation," she told the St. Paul Pioneer Press. "There is not a lot of controversy among us."

KEY VOTES

2008

Yes Prohibit discrimination based on genetic information

Yes Reauthorize farm and nutrition programs for five years

Yes Limit debate on "cap and trade" system for greenhouse gas emissions

Yes Allow lawsuits against companies that participated in warrantless wiretapping

Yes Limit debate on a bill to block a scheduled cut in Medicare payments to doctors

Yes Grant mortgage relief to homeowners and funding for Fannie Mae and Freddie Mac

Yes Approve a nuclear cooperation agreement with India

Yes Approve final $700 billion program to stabilize financial markets

Yes Allow consideration of a $14 billion auto industry loan package

2007

Yes Increase minimum wage by $2.10 an hour

Yes Limit debate on a comprehensive immigration bill

+ Overhaul congressional lobbying and ethics rules for members and their staffs

Yes Limit debate on considering a bill to add House seats for the District of Columbia and Utah

Yes Limit debate on restoring habeas corpus rights to detainees

Yes Mandate minimum breaks for troops between deployments to Iraq or Afghanistan

Yes Override Bush veto of $23.2 billion water projects authorization bill

No Confirm Michael B. Mukasey as attorney general

Yes Limit debate on an energy policy overhaul containing $21.8 billion in tax incentives and reduced oil and gas subsidies

CQ VOTE STUDIES

	PARTY UNITY		PRESIDENTIAL SUPPORT	
	SUPPORT	OPPOSE	SUPPORT	OPPOSE
2008	94%	6%	31%	69%
2007	93%	7%	38%	62%

INTEREST GROUPS

	AFL-CIO	ADA	CCUS	ACU
2008	100%	100%	57%	16%
2007	95%	100%	45%	4%

Al Franken (D)

CAPITOL OFFICE
224-5641

RESIDENCE
Minneapolis

BORN
May 21, 1951; Manhattan, N.Y.

RELIGION
Jewish

FAMILY
Wife, Franni Franken; two children

EDUCATION
Harvard U., A.B. 1973 (general studies)

CAREER
Author; radio talk show host; screenwriter; comedian

POLITICAL HIGHLIGHTS
No previous office

ELECTION RESULTS

2008 UNOFFICIAL GENERAL

Al Franken (D)	1,212,629	41.5%
Norm Coleman (R)	1,212,317	41.5%
others	496,109	17.0%

2008 PRIMARY

Al Franken (D)	164,136	65.3%
Priscilla Lord Faris (D)	74,655	29.7%
Dick Franson (D)	3,923	1.6%
Bob Larson (D)	3,152	1.3%
Rob Fitzgerald (D)	3,095	1.2%

Sought 1st term in 2008

Few politicians have had as unconventional a career path as Franken, who went from cutting-edge late-night comedian to lacerating satirist of Republicans as a best-selling author and radio talk show host. And few have had as unusual an experience in seeking to serve in the Senate.

Franken challenged Republican Sen. Norm Coleman in November 2008 in an election whose outcome was so close it became ensnared in legal challenges for the better part of a year. A trial court declared Franken the winner by 312 votes out of 2.9 million cast, but Coleman continued efforts to prevent Franken from being seated. Franken, meanwhile, stayed out of the spotlight, refusing most national media interview requests while preparing for the job he hoped to assume. "I've been sort of keeping my head down in this period and trying to do the work," he told The New York Times in April 2009.

Franken wasn't always so restrained. As a writer and performer on NBC's "Saturday Night Live," he was known for pushing boundaries; he once conceived and acted in a skit lampooning network president Fred Silverman as a "total, unequivocal failure." His book "Rush Limbaugh is a Big Fat Idiot" not only attacked the popular talk-show host but took aim at then-House Speaker Newt Gingrich and ex-United Nations ambassador Jeane Kirkpatrick.

In a subsequent book, "Lies and the Lying Liars Who Tell Them," Franken blasted George W. Bush's administration and Fox News commentator Bill O'Reilly, among others. It so incensed O'Reilly that he got into a confrontation with Franken — calling him "vicious" — at a book convention. But Franken said he has long been irked by what he considers Republicans' hypocrisy and distortions of the truth. "What I do is jujitsu," he told the Minneapolis Star Tribune in October 2008. "They say something ridiculous and I subject them to scorn and ridicule."

Franken sought to be taken seriously as a political candidate, though. He portrayed himself as a successor to the legacy of Minnesota Sen. Paul Wellstone, a passionate champion of progressive causes who died in a 2002 plane crash. But unlike Wellstone, Franken has taken some centrist positions. Though he supports universal health care, he said states should be allowed to devise their own methods for expanding coverage rather than be subjected to a single federally mandated system. He also said he wants to work to establish a "green economy" that addresses global warming.

Franken grew up in Minnesota, where he moved from New York. His father owned a fabric factory and later worked as a printing salesman, while his mother sold real estate. After attending Harvard University, and a short stint in show business in Los Angeles, he was hired in 1975 for the new late-night TV show, "Saturday Night Live." He and his partner Tom Davis became among its most prolific writers. He would return to the show after another stint in show business in Los Angeles. He began dabbling in politics in 1988 as a political commentator, and he continued his career in comedy.

Franken in 2008 went in as an underdog against Coleman. But as the economy worsened and presidential candidate Barack Obama's campaign gained traction, Franken began climbing in the polls. After the recount following the election, Coleman challenged the results in court, questioning whether absentee ballots may have been improperly rejected or overlooked. Republicans took up his cause, further motivated in 2009 when Pennsylvania's Arlen Specter switched to the Democratic caucus. That meant if Franken won, he would be the 60th member of the caucus — a group large enough in theory to block GOP filibusters, a key weapon to block legislation.

Norm Coleman (R)

CAPITOL OFFICE
224-5641

110TH COMMITTEES
Agriculture, Nutrition & Forestry
Foreign Relations
Homeland Security & Governmental Affairs
Small Business & Entrepreneurship
Special Aging

RESIDENCE
St. Paul

BORN
August 17, 1949; Brooklyn, N.Y.

RELIGION
Jewish

FAMILY
Wife, Laurie Coleman; four children
(two deceased)

EDUCATION
Hofstra U., B.A. 1971 (political science);
Brooklyn Law School, attended 1972-74;
U. of Iowa, J.D. 1976

CAREER
Lawyer; state prosecutor and solicitor general;
city welfare aide

POLITICAL HIGHLIGHTS
Sought Democratic nomination for mayor of St.
Paul, 1989; mayor of St. Paul, 1994-02 (served as
a Democrat 1994-96); Republican nominee for
governor, 1998

ELECTION RESULTS

2008 UNOFFICIAL GENERAL

Al Franken (D)	1,212,629	41.5%
Norm Coleman (R)	1,212,317	41.5%
others	496,109	17.0%

2008 PRIMARY

Norm Coleman (R)	130,973	91.3%
Jack Shepard (R)	12,456	8.7%

PREVIOUS WINNING PERCENTAGES
2002 (50%)

Elected 2002; Sought 2nd term in 2008

Coleman is a former Democrat who aspires to be a moderating voice within the GOP, and during his first term was often an unpredictable vote on some key issues. Just as unpredictable was his 2008 re-election bid; after a disputed election and protracted court battle, Coleman fought for his political life for the better part of a year, leaving Minnesota with only one senator and Republicans with a nail-biting sense of frustration.

In the November election, Coleman initially edged Democrat Al Franken by 215 votes. But a mandatory recount flipped that result, leaving Franken ahead — first by 225 votes and then, after Coleman went into state court to contest the result and more ballots were counted, by 312 votes. The process dragged on so long that Coleman took a consulting job for the Republican Jewish Coalition, saying he needed to support his family.

More was at stake in Coleman's battle than his own career. With him in office for a second term, Republicans could count 41 senators, just enough to sustain a filibuster against the enlarged Democratic majority in the 111th Congress (2009-10). Without Coleman, they were potentially defenseless.

But Coleman has never sided with his party consistently. Some of this flexibility is necessary in the competitive world of Minnesota politics, and some of it is just Coleman. He parted ways with his fellow Republicans on 35 percent of the votes in the 110th Congress (2007-08) that pitted a majority of one party against a majority of the other, including a bill to expand the State Children's Health Insurance Program and an effort to mandate minimum intervals between troop deployments to the Iraq War. Earlier he voted several times against opening Alaska's Arctic National Wildlife Refuge to oil drilling.

With his New York accent, styled hair and glinting smile, Coleman seems an unlikely breadbasket politician. In his younger days, he went to the Woodstock music festival and was a roadie with the rock band Ten Years After.

A Brooklyn native, his high school classmate was New York Democratic Sen. Charles E. Schumer. While he was student body president at Hofstra University in Hempstead, N.Y., on Long Island, he led anti-war protests and organized a student strike in 1970 after protesters at Kent State University were shot by members of the Ohio National Guard.

After graduation, a mentor who had become a vice president at the University of Iowa's law school offered Coleman the chance to attend tuition-free by working as a graduate assistant. He earned his law degree. Then he was recruited by the Minnesota attorney general and became a prosecutor.

He entered politics as a member of Minnesota's Democratic-Farmer-Labor Party, winning election as mayor of St Paul in 1993. But he was uncomfortable in the DFL, and switched parties in December 1996, winning re-election the following year as a Republican. He opposes abortion and supports "pro-family" issues, he says, as a result of losing two of his four children in infancy to the incurable genetic disorder known as Zellweger syndrome. The deaths, he has said, gave him resolve to value every life.

As the GOP pick to take on Democratic Sen. Paul Wellstone, Coleman ran on his eight years as mayor, during which the city enjoyed job growth and downtown revitalization. The contest seemed deadlocked when Wellstone, his wife, daughter, three aides and two pilots died in the crash of their campaign plane in northern Minnesota. Democrats replaced Wellstone on the ballot with former Vice President Walter F. Mondale, the 1984 Democratic presidential nominee. But Coleman eked out a win by 2 percentage points and helped the GOP clinch control of the Senate.

Rep. Tim Walz (D)

CAPITOL OFFICE
225-2472
walz.house.gov
1722 Longworth Bldg. 20515-2301; fax 225-3433

COMMITTEES
Agriculture
Transportation & Infrastructure
Veterans' Affairs

RESIDENCE
Mankato

BORN
April 6, 1964; West Point, Neb.

RELIGION
Lutheran

FAMILY
Wife, Gwen Walz; two children

EDUCATION
Chadron State College, B.S. 1989 (social science education); Minnesota State U., Mankato, M.S. 2001 (educational leadership); Saint Mary's U. of Minnesota, attending

MILITARY SERVICE
Neb. National Guard, 1981-96; Minn. National Guard, 1996-2005

CAREER
Teacher; mortgage processor

POLITICAL HIGHLIGHTS
No previous office

ELECTION RESULTS

2008 GENERAL

Tim Walz (D)	207,753	62.5%
Brian J. Davis (R)	109,453	32.9%
Gregory Mikkelson (INDC)	14,904	4.5%

2008 PRIMARY

Tim Walz (D)	unopposed

2006 GENERAL

Tim Walz (D)	141,556	52.7%
Gil Gutknecht (R)	126,486	47.1%

Elected 2006; 2nd term

A plain-spoken, down-to-earth former high school teacher, Walz shows a dedication to the needs of his rural Minnesota district that impresses his constituents, who gave him a 30-percentage-point edge to win his first re-election bid in 2008.

Walz is a member of the House Democratic class of 2006, of which he was named president. Since defeating six-term Republican Gil Gutknecht, he has focused on constituent service, specifically securing federal funds for his district. That task is made easier by the influence of two state colleagues: Democrat Collin C. Peterson, chairman of the Agriculture Committee, and James L. Oberstar, chairman of the House Transportation and Infrastructure Committee. Walz (WALLS) sits on both panels.

In 2008, Walz helped Peterson move his bill updating federal farm programs through the House and eventually into law, saying the legislation would make it easier for southern Minnesota's farmers to enroll in conservation programs. Walz opposed an amendment to slash farm subsidies to the nation's richest farmers, though he has argued for revisions in the way such payments are doled out. With his district located in the Corn Belt, Walz is a champion of ethanol as an alternative to gasoline and supported a 2007 law that requires oil companies to double the amount of corn-based ethanol they blend with gasoline. He supports a combination of conservation, expansion of oil and gas drilling, and innovation for alternative fuels. "The thought of a new energy future means more jobs for small towns," Walz said.

Walz also uses his seat on Transportation and Infrastructure to steer attention to his district, backing the efforts of the high-profile Oberstar. When the Winona Interstate Bridge in his district closed in June 2008 for nearly two weeks after inspectors found structural problems — creating severe commuting problems and heavy transportation expenses for businesses — Walz brought Oberstar to see firsthand. It was nearly a year after the deadly collapse of an interstate highway bridge in Minneapolis, and Oberstar had introduced a bill aimed at improving the safety of the nation's bridges. Walz successfully attached an amendment to that bill to require the secretary of Transportation to report to Congress on the economic impacts and altered transportation patterns when a bridge is closed for emergency repairs. Oberstar's bill was passed by the House but didn't reach the Senate floor before the close of the 110th Congress (2007-08).

Walz will have an opportunity to bring more help to his district when the Transportation Committee takes up a renewal of the 2005 surface transportation law, traditionally a vehicle for funding local projects.

He is typically a dependable vote for his party, but he's also willing to go his own way, particularly on financial issues. He voted against a December 2007 bill that exempted 21 million additional taxpayers from the alternative minimum tax because he felt it was too expensive. And in the fall of 2008 he opposed two $700 billion measures — the second of which became law — that aimed to save the ailing financial services industry. Walz said the bills didn't do enough to protect homeowners from foreclosure. In December of that year, he was one of 20 Democrats to oppose a bill that would have provided emergency loans for the Big Three auto companies. It died in the Senate, though President George W. Bush later used existing executive authority to issue some loans.

Walz has been more willing to sign off on big spending bills now that President Obama is in the White House, backing both Obama's $787 billion economic stimulus law and a $410 billion catchall spending bill for fiscal 2009.

A military veteran and member of the Veterans' Affairs Committee, Walz advocates for improved health care for veterans and has opposed the Iraq War. He hailed the enactment of a war spending bill in 2008 that greatly expanded benefits under the GI Bill and granted equal veterans' education benefits to National Guard and reserve members who have served at least 20 months on active duty. "That is exactly why I ran for this job," Walz said in December 2008. "We have to do more than provide lip-service for these people."

In July 2008, the House passed his bill to require the Veterans Affairs Department to develop and implement a comprehensive policy on pain management services for veterans. That bill, incorporated into a larger veterans' health care measure, stalled in the Senate that year.

Walz grew up in a middle-class family from the sand hills of north-central Nebraska. His mother was a homemaker; his father was a school superintendent. Walz was in high school when his father was diagnosed with cancer. His mother and 8-year-old brother soon found themselves living off his father's Social Security survivor benefits. "If there wouldn't have been a safety net, it would have been different," he said.

At 17, Walz joined the Nebraska National Guard to help pay for his studies at Chardron State College. After college, Walz was part of the first government-sanctioned group of American educators to teach in China. He speaks Mandarin and is one of nine House members on the Congressional-Executive Commission on China, which monitors human rights abuses there.

After a teaching stint in Nebraska, Walz moved to Minnesota in 1996 to take a position at Mankato West High School, where he taught geography and coached football. His wife Gwen is the assessment coordinator for Mankato Public Schools.

Walz retired from the military in 2005 after more than two decades in the Army National Guard, including a deployment to Italy to oversee supply shipments to troops in Afghanistan. He rose to command sergeant major, making him the highest-ranking enlisted soldier ever to serve in Congress.

Walz's only venture into politics prior to his long-shot 2006 campaign consisted of some community organizing for Sen. John Kerry's 2004 presidential campaign. That lack of political experience turned out to be an asset when he challenged Gutknecht in 2006. Walz won with 53 percent of the vote.

Early in his first term, GOP operatives dubbed Walz "Twinkle Toes" because they felt he danced around the issues. He dismissed such criticism and, benefitting from the national Democratic tide and Bush's unpopularity, cruised to victory over oncologist Brian J. Davis.

KEY VOTES

2008
Yes Delay consideration of Colombia free-trade agreement
Yes Override Bush veto of federal farm and nutrition programs reauthorization bill
No Overhaul surveillance laws and permit dismissal of suits against companies that conducted warrantless wiretapping
Yes Grant mortgage relief to homeowners and funding for Fannie Mae and Freddie Mac
No Approve initial $700 billion program to stabilize financial markets
No Approve final $700 billion program to stabilize financial markets
No Provide $14 billion in loans to automakers

2007
Yes Increase minimum wage by $2.10 an hour
Yes Approve $124.2 billion in emergency war spending and set goal for redeployment of troops from Iraq
No Reject federal contraceptive assistance to international family planning groups
Yes Override Bush veto of $23.2 billion water projects authorization bill
No Implement Peru free-trade agreement
Yes Approve energy policy overhaul with new fuel economy standards
Yes Clear $473.5 billion omnibus spending bill, including $70 billion for military operations

CQ VOTE STUDIES

| | PARTY UNITY | | PRESIDENTIAL SUPPORT | |
	SUPPORT	OPPOSE	SUPPORT	OPPOSE
2008	96%	4%	14%	86%
2007	94%	6%	5%	95%

INTEREST GROUPS

	AFL-CIO	ADA	CCUS	ACU
2008	93%	85%	50%	20%
2007	96%	100%	60%	0%

MINNESOTA 1
South — Rochester, Mankato

Stretching from the flat plains at the South Dakota border to the towering bluffs overlooking the Mississippi River, the rural 1st is cut horizontally by Interstate 90 and vertically by Interstate 35. Rural areas continue to lose residents to the Twin Cities and elsewhere in the region, but cities like Mankato and Rochester, home to an IBM facility and the Mayo Clinic, remain stable. Agriculture and food processing still drive the economy.

Corn, soybeans, sugar beets, hogs and dairy are staples here. The 1st has one of the highest agricultural market values of any district in the country. Farming here is valued at roughly $3 billion and more than 20,000 farms dot the 1st's landscape. Food processing, from fresh turkey to canned soups, is prevalent throughout the area west of Rochester. West of Mankato, no town has more than 15,000 residents.

Rochester, the district's largest city and the third-largest city in Minnesota, is an overwhelmingly educated city: 38 percent of the city's residents hold at least a bachelor's degree and 16 percent hold a graduate degree. Declines in patient visiting at the Mayo Clinic, as a result of nationwide economic downturns, would affect service and hospitality industries here, as well. Rochester hosts the newest University of Minnesota campus, and Winona and Mankato both have state universities.

Although the 1st is still more than 90 percent white, Hispanic, Asian and black immigrants have come to the district to work in processing plants, in agriculture and at Rochester's hospitals. Worthington in particular has a large immigrant population and a significant proportion of non-English-speaking children enrolled in its schools.

The 1st is politically moderate, but it has leaned more Democratic in federal elections in recent years. Rep. Tim Walz was elected to his second term by a nearly 2-to-1 margin, and Barack Obama carried the district with 51 percent in the 2008 presidential election.

MAJOR INDUSTRY
Agriculture, food processing, health care

CITIES
Rochester, 85,806; Mankato, 32,427; Winona, 27,069; Austin, 23,314; Owatonna, 22,434

NOTABLE
The birthplace of SPAM, Austin is home to the SPAM Museum.

Rep. John Kline (R)

Elected 2002; 4th term

A faithful conservative, Kline has a straight-arrow military bearing befitting his 25 years in the Marine Corps, along with an easygoing charm that serves him in the political arena. Though he initially focused on defense work, he increasingly has become involved in health, labor and other issues.

Kline is a Vietnam veteran who later did a stint carrying the "football" — a briefcase containing the codes needed to launch a nuclear attack — for Presidents Carter and Reagan. He is now one of the few members of Congress with a child who has served in conflict. His son, John Daniel, is an Army Blackhawk helicopter pilot who served a yearlong tour in Iraq in 2006 and later was sent to Afghanistan. "I'm worried about him," Kline said. "But I'm worried about them all."

When it comes to both war fronts, Kline insists military leaders and not politicians should decide the proper course of action. A member of the Armed Services Committee, Kline throughout the 110th Congress (2007-08) denounced Democratic efforts to set a timeline for withdrawal from Iraq, a place he has visited several times since coming to Congress. He supports adding more troops in Afghanistan to control the spread of terrorism.

He successfully tucked a measure into the fiscal 2008 defense authorization law that nationalized a Minnesota National Guard initiative helping soldiers transition from combat to civilian life. The Yellow Ribbon Reintegration Program requires veterans to go through workshops on dealing with stress and substance abuse. "This isn't to harass them. We're not bringing them in to paint rocks," Kline said. "We're bringing them in to remind them what's available and to get a sense on how they are doing."

Kline's loyalty to the military has been matched by his loyalty to the GOP. From his arrival in Congress through the 110th Congress, he sided with Republicans on 97 percent of the votes that divided the two parties.

He belongs to the Republican Study Committee, the most conservative GOP bloc in the House, but he split with many in the group when he supported a $700 billion financial industry rescue bill enacted in October 2008. He said it would provide much-needed relief to Wall Street.

Like other committee members, Kline made a point during the 110th of spurning earmarks, funding set-asides for projects in member districts. His stance rankled some local officials in his district. He likewise did not seek earmarks in the $410 billion catchall spending bill for 2009 — a measure, signed into law, that spurred much criticism of Republicans who opposed the final bill even while touting funding for local projects.

Kline sparked an impassioned debate in July 2007 when he offered an amendment to a spending bill that sought to restore $2 million for the government's oversight of labor unions. Republicans accused Democrats of taking the funding out because they were too close to union bosses who helped get them elected. The amendment failed on a near-party-line vote. "I was outraged on what the other side had done," Kline said. "They added funding for every department, every agency and every office in the Department of Labor but one."

The top Republican on the Health, Employment, Labor and Pensions Subcommittee of the Education and Labor Committee, Kline was lead sponsor in early 2009 of the GOP alternative to a top legislative priority of organized labor — the so-called "card check" bill to allow unions to organize a workplace once a majority of employees sign a card requesting union representation. "No employee should be forced to tell his employer, his fellow

CAPITOL OFFICE
225-2271
kline.house.gov
1210 Longworth Bldg. 20515-2302; fax 225-2595

COMMITTEES
Armed Services
Education & Labor
Select Intelligence
Standards of Official Conduct

RESIDENCE
Lakeville

BORN
Sept. 6, 1947; Allentown, Pa.

RELIGION
Methodist

FAMILY
Wife, Vicky Kline; two children

EDUCATION
Rice U., B.A. 1969 (biology); Shippensburg U., M.S. 1988 (public administration)

MILITARY SERVICE
Marine Corps, 1969-94

CAREER
Think tank executive; farmer; management consultant; Marine officer

POLITICAL HIGHLIGHTS
Republican nominee for U.S. House, 1998, 2000

ELECTION RESULTS

2008 GENERAL
John Kline (R)	220,924	57.3%
Steve Sarvi (D)	164,093	42.5%

2008 PRIMARY
John Kline (R)	unopposed

2006 GENERAL
John Kline (R)	163,269	56.2%
Coleen Rowley (D)	116,343	40.0%
Douglas Williams (INDC)	10,802	3.7%

PREVIOUS WINNING PERCENTAGES
2004 (56%); 2002 (53%)

employees, his family, the union organizer and everybody else, what his position is or her position is on forming a union. They need the protection of the secret ballot," Kline told CNBC in March.

Earlier in his career on the committee, Kline served on the 2006 conference committee that negotiated a complex overhaul of the laws governing private pension plans — a plum for a relatively new lawmaker.

By his own admission, Kline has one of the most onerous jobs in Congress as a member of the House ethics committee. Members are appointed by party leaders and assigned the task of overseeing their colleagues and their staff. "It is a thankless committee to be on," he said. In 2007, he supported the Democrats' lobbying and ethics package that included new disclosure requirements for lobbyists and campaign committees.

Kline was born in Pennsylvania and as a young child moved to Corpus Christi, Texas, near where his father had purchased a small-town newspaper. His mother managed the Corpus Christi Symphony Orchestra for 40 years. He joined the ROTC at Rice University in Houston while earning a bachelor's degree in biology and later earned a master's degree in public administration from Shippensburg University in Pennsylvania.

During his military career, Kline piloted helicopters in Vietnam, commanded aviation forces in Somalia and flew the presidential helicopter, Marine One. He also worked at Marine Corps headquarters as a program development officer, responsible for developing a long-range spending plan. In 1994, he retired with the rank of colonel, settled in Lakeville, Minn., with his wife, and helped his father-in-law manage the family farm in Houston County, at the state's southeastern tip.

In 1998, contemplating a run for Congress, he sought advice from friend James A. Baker III, Reagan's former chief of staff, whom he met during his White House duty. Baker delivered a "dose of reality," telling him, "Well, you don't have your party's nomination, you are running against an incumbent and you don't have any money. Other than that, you're in good shape."

Kline got the GOP nomination that year at an old-fashioned, Minnesota-style convention, only to lose the general election to Democratic incumbent Rep. Bill Luther. He tried again in 2000, this time getting help from national Republican groups. He lost by just less than 5,500 votes. Then redistricting paired Luther with GOP Rep. Mark Kennedy in the new 6th District in 2002. Luther moved to the redrawn 2nd, which was far more Republican than before. Kline tried again. Luther tried to portray Kline as an "extremist," but Kline's message of lower taxes, smaller government and a strong military prevailed with voters. He has won with at least 56 percent since then.

KEY VOTES

2008

No Delay consideration of Colombia free-trade agreement

Yes Override Bush veto of federal farm and nutrition programs reauthorization bill

Yes Overhaul surveillance laws and permit dismissal of suits against companies that conducted warrantless wiretapping

No Grant mortgage relief to homeowners and funding for Fannie Mae and Freddie Mac

Yes Approve initial $700 billion program to stabilize financial markets

Yes Approve final $700 billion program to stabilize financial markets

No Provide $14 billion in loans to automakers

2007

No Increase minimum wage by $2.10 an hour

No Approve $124.2 billion in emergency war spending and set goal for redeployment of troops from Iraq

Yes Reject federal contraceptive assistance to international family planning groups

Yes Override Bush veto of $23.2 billion water projects authorization bill

Yes Implement Peru free-trade agreement

No Approve energy policy overhaul with new fuel economy standards

Yes Clear $473.5 billion omnibus spending bill, including $70 billion for military operations

CQ VOTE STUDIES

	PARTY UNITY		PRESIDENTIAL SUPPORT	
	SUPPORT	OPPOSE	SUPPORT	OPPOSE
2008	97%	3%	77%	23%
2007	98%	2%	86%	14%
2006	95%	5%	95%	5%
2005	97%	3%	89%	11%
2004	99%	1%	94%	6%

INTEREST GROUPS

	AFL-CIO	ADA	CCUS	ACU
2008	13%	15%	94%	88%
2007	8%	0%	80%	100%
2006	14%	0%	100%	88%
2005	13%	0%	93%	100%
2004	7%	5%	100%	96%

MINNESOTA 2
Southern Twin Cities suburbs

A blend of rural farmland in the south and a growing suburban north, the 2nd is tucked just south of the Minneapolis-St. Paul metropolitan area. The district includes all or part of seven counties and reflects what was more than a decade of population influx to the Twin Cities region. Interstate 35 provides easy access to Minneapolis' cultural and entertainment centers for residents from Scott and Dakota counties.

Increasingly suburban, the counties just south of the Twin Cities experienced rapid growth starting in the 1990s, and expensive housing developments underscored the area's high incomes. Carver, Scott and particularly Dakota (shared with the 4th) have become younger and wealthier, but a national housing market slowdown has left the local real estate market volatile. Affordable housing in the southern counties of Le Sueur, Rice and Goodhue attracted new residents, but this area still has fertile farmland, producing corn and soybeans, among other crops. Development encroached on some of the smaller family farms, although agricultural success here tends to rely on larger, incorporated farms.

Northwest Airlines, which has its headquarters in Eagan and merged with Delta Air Lines in September 2008, remains an economic linchpin for the region. Casinos are big business for the Shakopee Mdewakanton Sioux tribe in Prior Lake. Mystic Lake Casino in Shakopee is one of the country's largest Indian-owned casinos. Other key employers include Blue Cross/Blue Shield and Lockheed Martin — both in the 2nd's part of Dakota County — and 3M, headquartered in St. Paul (in the 4th District).

The district leans barely Republican, with GOP support in Scott and Carver counties, but many formerly Republican voters are trending left. Dakota County has some working-class Democratic-Farmer-Labor Party supporters, and the Rice County towns of Northfield — home to St. Olaf and Carleton colleges — and Faribault also provide Democratic votes. John McCain won here with 50 percent of the 2008 presidential vote.

MAJOR INDUSTRY
Manufacturing, casinos, aviation, agriculture

CITIES
Eagan, 63,557; Burnsville, 60,220; Apple Valley, 45,527; Lakeville, 43,128

NOTABLE
The late Sen. Paul Wellstone was a political science professor at Carleton College before beginning his political career.

Rep. Erik Paulsen (R)

Elected 2008; 1st term

Paulsen shares some of the fiscal and environmental views of his former boss and predecessor, nine-term GOP Rep. Jim Ramstad, who tended to oppose Republican leaders more often than his colleagues.

Paulsen gives the Republican Party much of the blame for the nation's fiscal deficit, yet wants to extend President George W. Bush's 2001 and 2003 tax cuts. A former business analyst for Target Corp. and a member of the Minnesota Legislature for 14 years, he sits on the Financial Services Committee, where he hopes to contribute to a long-term fiscal plan for the nation.

He sided with his party in opposing a $787 billion economic stimulus bill in February 2009, saying it didn't include enough tax relief or sufficient funding for infrastructure projects.

Like Ramstad, Paulsen has more-liberal views on environmental issues. After college, he worked at Yellowstone National Park, where he said he learned the importance of land preservation. He likely will join party moderates in efforts to battle Republicans who want to open Alaska's Arctic National Wildlife Refuge to oil drilling, although he does favor a broad GOP energy plan that would include expanding offshore drilling for oil and natural gas. He said it would be a viable way of reducing the nation's dependence on foreign oil.

Paulsen's stance on social issues may follow the centrist course of his predecessor as well. He sided with the majority of Democrats in early 2009 to pass a bill expanding the State Children's Health Insurance Program, which covers children from low-income families who do not qualify for Medicaid. As a state legislator, he supported bills that opposed using taxpayer money for stem cell research at the University of Minnesota.

Paulsen was born in Bakersfield, Calif., and his family moved about a year later to Chanhassen, a western Minneapolis suburb. He started in politics as Ramstad's legislative aide in Washington and later became Ramstad's district director. He parlayed that political connection into a state House seat, rising to majority leader. In the open race to succeed Ramstad, Paulsen faced Democrat Ashwin Madia, a former Republican and Iraq War veteran. He took 48 percent of the vote in a three-way race; Madia took 41 percent.

CAPITOL OFFICE
225-2871
paulsen.house.gov
126 Cannon Bldg. 20515-2303; fax 225-6351

COMMITTEES
Financial Services

RESIDENCE
Eden Prairie

BORN
May 14, 1965; Bakersfield, Calif.

RELIGION
Lutheran

FAMILY
Wife, Kelly Paulsen; four children

EDUCATION
St. Olaf College, B.A. 1987 (mathematics)

CAREER
Business strategies analyst; congressional aide

POLITICAL HIGHLIGHTS
Minn. House, 1995-2009 (majority leader, 2003-07)

ELECTION RESULTS

2008 GENERAL

Erik Paulsen (R)	178,932	48.5%
Ashwin Madia (D)	150,787	40.8%
David Dillon (INDC)	38,970	10.6%

2008 PRIMARY

Erik Paulsen (R)	unopposed

MINNESOTA 3

Hennepin County suburbs — Bloomington, Brooklyn Park, Plymouth

Lakes, stores and office parks dot the affluent 3rd. The district takes in Hennepin County's major suburbs north, west and south of Minneapolis. The primarily white-collar population is grounded in fiscal conservatism, adheres to moderate views on social issues and is known for its independent streak.

A classic picture of suburban living, the 3rd District boasts technology industries, white-collar workers in middle-class homes, excellent public schools, golf courses, and large indoor and outdoor shopping malls. The district also has the most-educated residents in the state, and several Fortune 500 corporations based in the district employ local residents, as do other large companies just outside the 3rd.

Traffic backups are increasingly common for commuters in the district, stretching from Maple Grove in the north to Bloomington in the south. Transportation and interstate highway upgrades are important issues here.

Blue-collar Brooklyn Park, Coon Rapids (a small part of which is in the 6th) and Brooklyn Center host conservative Democratic-Farmer-Labor Party voters, but the affluent, Republican south and west portions of the 3rd cast more votes. The 3rd split its vote in the 2008 election, supporting Democrat Barack Obama with 52 percent of its presidential vote and Republican Erik Paulsen with a 48 percent plurality in the U.S. House race.

MAJOR INDUSTRY
Electronics, manufacturing, transportation

CITIES
Bloomington, 85,172; Brooklyn Park, 67,388; Plymouth, 65,894; Coon Rapids (pt.), 58,396; Eden Prairie, 54,901; Minnetonka, 51,301

NOTABLE
Bloomington's Mall of America has 4.2 million square feet of retail and office space.

Rep. Betty McCollum (D)

Elected 2000; 5th term

A liberal with an interest in domestic and international issues, McCollum is an ally of Speaker Nancy Pelosi of California and a persistent voice for human rights and broader access to health care. Her views place her squarely on the left side of the Democratic Caucus, but they fit well at home in heavily Democratic St. Paul.

McCollum, the first woman to represent Minnesota in the House in more than 40 years, casts a dependable Democratic vote; she sided with her party 99 percent of the time in the 110th Congress (2007-08) on votes in which the two parties were in opposition. On the rare occasions when McCollum bucks party leaders, she usually thinks they aren't being progressive enough. She supports constitutional amendments to ban the death penalty and make health care a right for U.S. citizens, though neither effort has much chance of succeeding.

And from her seat on the Budget and Appropriations committees, she can be expected to fight to preserve President Obama's priorities for health care, energy and education in the annual spending bills. She backed Obama's $3.56 trillion budget blueprint for 2010 that contained these priorities. But she'll also pursue projects close to home, such as construction of new highways, a light-rail line and schools. She helped obtain more than $39 million in a catchall spending bill, cleared in March 2009, for a range of local projects, including several natural resource projects.

In September 2008, she was one of 19 Democrats to vote against a joint resolution — which ultimately passed — that banned almost any water transfer from the Great Lakes, as part of a broader regional compact for managing the lakes. "I could not in good conscience vote for [it] because the legislation has implications for generations to come and does not go far enough to protect against privatization, commercialization and exportation," she told a local newspaper.

McCollum, an early and ardent critic of the war in Iraq, was one of 126 Democrats who opposed the 2002 resolution sanctioning President George W. Bush's decision to go to war. After listening to administration officials make their case during several classified briefings that year, she came away convinced there was no need.

Interested in world diplomacy since she was a child, McCollum has been to Iraq to assess the war effort. In the 109th Congress (2005-06), she pressed without much success to force the International Affairs panel (now called the Foreign Affairs Committee) to hold oversight hearings on the war and to investigate the alleged disappearance of $1 billion from the Iraqi Ministry of Defense during the tenure of the U.S.-led interim government. She wants U.S. troops out of Iraq as soon as possible and, like President Obama, wants more attention paid to Afghanistan.

She supported the $700 billion financial sector rescue in late 2008, bringing a glossary of financial terms such as "warrants" and "asset managers" to a caucus meeting to help educate fellow members. She argued action was necessary to stabilize the economy, and she called for tighter regulation of the financial sector. "The Reagan era of deregulation for markets and labeling government as the problem is over."

On one of her signature issues, the global fight against AIDS, she believed that a compromise bill that ultimately became law fell short. House Democrats in 2008 had convinced Republicans to agree to a major expansion of the federal government's international AIDS program by dropping

CAPITOL OFFICE
225-6631
mccollum.house.gov
1714 Longworth Bldg. 20515-2304; fax 225-1968

COMMITTEES
Appropriations
Budget

RESIDENCE
St. Paul

BORN
July 12, 1954; Minneapolis, Minn.

RELIGION
Roman Catholic

FAMILY
Divorced; two children

EDUCATION
Inver Hills Community College, A.A. 1980; College of St. Catherine, B.A. 1987 (education)

CAREER
Teacher; retail saleswoman

POLITICAL HIGHLIGHTS
Candidate for North St. Paul City Council, 1984; North St. Paul City Council, 1987-92; Minn. House, 1993-2001

ELECTION RESULTS

2008 GENERAL

Betty McCollum (D)	216,267	68.4%
Ed Matthews (R)	98,936	31.3%

2008 PRIMARY

Betty McCollum (D)	unopposed

2006 GENERAL

Betty McCollum (D)	172,096	69.5%
Obi Sium (R)	74,797	30.2%

PREVIOUS WINNING PERCENTAGES
2004 (57%); 2002 (62%); 2000 (48%)

language that would have tied family-planning groups more closely to HIV/AIDS services. McCollum voted for the law even after failing to gain support for an amendment to benefit family-planning groups.

McCollum is the leading advocate of federal funding to aid in the resettlement of Hmong refugees from Laos in Minnesota, securing $19 million in the 2004 catchall spending bill. St. Paul is home to one of the highest concentrations of Hmong in the United States. She sponsored legislation in 2004 to normalize trade relations with Laos. The measure bitterly divided the Hmong community, with foes of the current regime in Laos arguing against rewarding the government with a trade pact. But McCollum said ending the isolation of Laos would give the United States more influence in the country's future, and trade relations were normalized by year's end.

Another major policy arena for McCollum is education, a key issue during her 2000 election campaign. From her perch on the Education Committee, where she served from 2001 to 2007, she criticized the Bush administration for underfunding the No Child Left Behind initiative, the overhaul of federal education policy that tied aid to performance on student achievement tests. McCollum was one of only six House Democrats in 2001 to vote against the final bill.

McCollum was born and raised in the Twin Cities area in what she describes as a frugal middle-class household. Family discussions often included world affairs and far-off places. "My father served in India and China during World War II, so we always had the atlas open at home, talking about countries and food and geography and culture and climate," she said.

She studied at a community college and worked as a sales clerk at JCPenney and Sears department stores and as a substitute teacher while raising two children. She got her bachelor's degree at 32, about the time she was venturing into politics. After being rebuffed by the city of North St. Paul in her quest to get immediate repairs at a local playground, McCollum ran for the city council. She lost that first bid but won in a second attempt. She moved to the state legislature six years later, beating two incumbents thrown into the same district by redistricting.

With 14 years in elective office under her belt, McCollum in 2000 jumped into the primary race for the House seat being vacated by Democrat Bruce M. Vento, who announced he had lung cancer and wouldn't run again. Although six other Democrats ran, McCollum gained an important edge when she was endorsed by the state Democratic Party. McCollum took 48 percent of the vote that November, outrunning Republican state Sen. Linda Runbeck and independent Tom Fole. She has been re-elected since with comfortable margins.

KEY VOTES

2008
Yes Delay consideration of Colombia free-trade agreement
Yes Override Bush veto of federal farm and nutrition programs reauthorization bill
No   Overhaul surveillance laws and permit dismissal of suits against companies that conducted warrantless wiretapping
Yes Grant mortgage relief to homeowners and funding for Fannie Mae and Freddie Mac
Yes Approve initial $700 billion program to stabilize financial markets
Yes Approve final $700 billion program to stabilize financial markets
Yes Provide $14 billion in loans to automakers

2007
Yes Increase minimum wage by $2.10 an hour
Yes Approve $124.2 billion in emergency war spending and set goal for redeployment of troops from Iraq
No   Reject federal contraceptive assistance to international family planning groups
Yes Override Bush veto of $23.2 billion water projects authorization bill
Yes Implement Peru free-trade agreement
Yes Approve energy policy overhaul with new fuel economy standards
No   Clear $473.5 billion omnibus spending bill, including $70 billion for military operations

CQ VOTE STUDIES

| | PARTY UNITY | | PRESIDENTIAL SUPPORT | |
	SUPPORT	OPPOSE	SUPPORT	OPPOSE
2008	99%	1%	13%	87%
2007	99%	1%	4%	96%
2006	96%	4%	20%	80%
2005	98%	2%	11%	89%
2004	97%	3%	21%	79%

INTEREST GROUPS

	AFL-CIO	ADA	CCUS	ACU
2008	100%	100%	56%	0%
2007	96%	90%	58%	0%
2006	93%	95%	33%	4%
2005	93%	95%	33%	0%
2004	93%	100%	24%	0%

MINNESOTA 4
Ramsey County – St. Paul and suburbs

St. Paul, the state capital and the heart of the 4th, is a collection of distinct neighborhoods, which include residential areas, liberal university communities, labor populations and state government. St. Paul developed as a major port and railroading center and still has a strong labor tradition.

For much of its history St. Paul was the upper Midwest's leading trade outpost, and the city had a strong manufacturing sector. For years, local leaders in St. Paul have aimed to fill the economic gaps caused by manufacturing downsizing with the growing renewable-energy and green building industries. More recently, city budget shortfalls and private-sector layoffs have concerned residents.

The 4th has a large percentage of white-collar workers who live in middle- and high-income neighborhoods and work at major companies based in the district or nearby in Minneapolis, and dairy producer Land O' Lakes is the leader of agribusiness in the area. St. Paul and surrounding areas are home to many colleges and universities, including the University of Minnesota's agriculture school and Macalester College.

The downtown Xcel Energy Center, which hosted the 2008 Republican National Convention, draws major sports events and concerts and is home to the NHL's Minnesota Wild and the state high school hockey tournament. The St. Paul Saints minor league baseball team draws crowds to Midway Stadium, and the Minnesota State Fair attracts more than 1.5 million visitors to St. Paul every August.

Represented in the U.S. House by a Democrat since 1949, voters in St. Paul, who make up nearly half of the current 4th District, consistently support the Democratic-Farmer-Labor Party at all levels. Today, blue-collar and growing black, Hispanic and Hmong communities — the city has one of the nation's largest Hmong populations — contribute to the overall Democratic flavor. Barack Obama garnered 64 percent of the 4th's 2008 presidential vote.

MAJOR INDUSTRY
State government, higher education, manufacturing

CITIES
St. Paul, 287,151; Maplewood, 34,947; Roseville, 33,690; Oakdale, 26,653

NOTABLE
In 2002, the area elected Mee Moua to the state Senate, making her the first Hmong state legislator in the United States.

Rep. Keith Ellison (D)

Elected 2006; 2nd term

CAPITOL OFFICE
225-4755
ellison.house.gov
1122 Longworth Bldg. 20515-2305; fax 225-4886

COMMITTEES
Financial Services
Foreign Affairs

RESIDENCE
Minneapolis

BORN
Aug. 4, 1963; Detroit, Mich.

RELIGION
Muslim

FAMILY
Wife, Kim Ellison; four children

EDUCATION
Wayne State U., B.A. 1986 (economics), attended
1986-87 (economics); U. of Minnesota, J.D. 1990

CAREER
Lawyer; nonprofit law firm executive director

POLITICAL HIGHLIGHTS
Minn. House, 2003-07

ELECTION RESULTS

2008 GENERAL

Keith Ellison (D)	228,776	70.9%
Barb Davis White (R)	71,020	22.0%
Bill McGaughey (INDC)	22,318	6.9%

2008 PRIMARY

Keith Ellison (D)	33,988	84.4%
Gregg A. Iverson (D)	6,251	15.5%

2006 GENERAL

Keith Ellison (D)	136,060	55.6%
Alan Fine (R)	52,263	21.3%
Tammy Lee (INDC)	51,456	21.0%
Jay Pond (GREEN)	4,792	2.0%

Ellison is outspoken about his liberal views; he is an advocate for universal health care and tougher environmental regulation and opposes trade deals. He said he most admires the ideology of Paul Wellstone, the former Democratic senator and firebrand from Minnesota whose picture adorns his office wall.

Ellison has attracted some of his own attention during his short time in the House. As the first Muslim to serve in Congress, he is a reluctant, but unwavering, defender of his faith and a strong voice for reconciliation between the United States and the Islamic world. Though he insists he is no "religious leader," He has not shied away from openly celebrating and defending his religion.

He used a Koran owned by Thomas Jefferson at a ceremonial swearing-in after he took the official oath in the House chamber in 2007. Subsequently, Republicans Bill Sali of Idaho and Virgil H. Goode Jr. of Virginia expressed misgivings. Ellison took the high road. "I just think it is a learning gap that we have to close," he said. In the end, Ellison got the last laugh; Sali and Goode were defeated in their 2008 re-election bids.

But Ellison still finds anti-Islamic views among his colleagues. He condemned GOP Sen. Jon Kyl of Arizona in 2009 for sponsoring the airing of what Ellison contended was an anti-Islamic film at the Capitol. The movie, "Fitna," was by the Dutch politician Geert Wilders, a critic of Islam who has called for the Koran to be banned.

Ellison proudly backed in 2007 the first congressional resolution recognizing the Muslim religious observance of Ramadan. And in 2008, he made a pilgrimage to Mecca, a holy obligation for Muslims, and told the Minneapolis Star Tribune he'd found the experience "transformative."

At the beginning of the 111th Congress (2009-10), House Democratic leaders gave Ellison a seat on the Foreign Affairs Committee, where he can play a greater role in pushing for better ties between Islamic countries and the United States. Ellison said he wanted to elevate "diplomacy and development" to their "proper place as instruments of peacemaking."

Pointing to the United States' image problems overseas, especially in the Middle East, Ellison said he's "willing to do whatever I can to make some friends for America." He wants to end the war in Iraq and was one of the first American officials to visit the Gaza Strip after military strikes by Israel on the Palestinian territory in early 2009. "I've always believed we need to resolve this thing by diplomacy," Ellison told the Star Tribune. "I'm even more convinced of that now."

Ellison is a member of the House Democracy Assistance Commission, a bipartisan, 20-member group organized to promote the development of democratic governments around the world, mainly through peer-to-peer partnerships. Returning from a 10-day journey to Africa in July 2008, Ellison said he was optimistic that the group's message was getting across and that he was pleased with new democracies in Africa. "In sub-Saharan Africa, America is still viewed as a country with a functioning parliament [Congress] that has some things to share," he told the Star Tribune.

Ellison aligns closely with his party's leadership. In his first term in office, he sided with Democrats nearly every time a vote pitted a majority of Republicans against a majority of Democrats.

From his seat on the Financial Services Committee, he has backed President Obama's efforts to bring the economy out of recession. He also supported legislation, pushed by President George W. Bush in 2008, that allowed the administration to use $700 billion to help the ailing financial services sector. But Ellison, a founding member of the House's Populist Caucus, is concerned such efforts aren't helping the most vulnerable citizens. So in early 2009, he introduced legislation aimed at preventing quick evictions of renters stuck in foreclosed properties and in barring some interest rate hikes by credit card companies.

Ellison is the third of five sons. His father was a psychiatrist; his mother was a social worker. Ellison said the importance of education was pressed upon him at an early age: he and three of his brothers are lawyers, while the other is a doctor.

After graduating from the University of Detroit High School, a Jesuit school on the city's northern edge, Ellison went to Wayne State University. It was there, while studying economics, that he converted to Islam at the age of 19. In the late 1980s, he moved to Minnesota for law school, graduating from the state's flagship public university in 1990.

Ellison remained in Minneapolis after law school, working on general commercial litigation before joining a nonprofit that specialized in the representation of indigent clients. He rose to become executive director of the Legal Rights Center.

He was elected to the Minnesota Legislature in 2002. His shot for a House seat opened four years later, when Democrat Martin Olav Sabo retired after representing the strongly Democratic Minneapolis-based 5th District for nearly three decades. Ellison won the party's primary, defeating longtime Sabo aide Mike Erlandson, who was also a former state party chairman, and former state Sen. Ember Reichgott Junge. Ellison won the nomination with 41 percent of the vote.

In November's general election, Republican candidate Alan Fine, a Jewish business consultant, criticized Ellison for several articles he had written as a law student. Ellison had defended Louis Farrakhan, the leader of the Nation of Islam, against allegations of anti-Semitism, but he denied personally ever having any anti-Semitic beliefs. In the end, Ellison received the endorsement of American Jewish World, Minnesota's Jewish newspaper, and took 56 percent of the vote, becoming the first African-American to represent Minnesota in Congress.

Ellison is one of a small handful of black lawmakers to represent districts with sizable white majorities: The 5th District's population is about 70 percent white and is the state's most racially diverse district. Ellison faced no serious opposition in 2008, winning re-election by nearly 50 points.

KEY VOTES

2008
Yes Delay consideration of Colombia free-trade agreement
Yes Override Bush veto of federal farm and nutrition programs reauthorization bill
No Overhaul surveillance laws and permit dismissal of suits against companies that conducted warrantless wiretapping
Yes Grant mortgage relief to homeowners and funding for Fannie Mae and Freddie Mac
Yes Approve initial $700 billion program to stabilize financial markets
Yes Approve final $700 billion program to stabilize financial markets
? Provide $14 billion in loans to automakers

2007
Yes Increase minimum wage by $2.10 an hour
Yes Approve $124.2 billion in emergency war spending and set goal for redeployment of troops from Iraq
No Reject federal contraceptive assistance to international family planning groups
Yes Override Bush veto of $23.2 billion water projects authorization bill
No Implement Peru free-trade agreement
Yes Approve energy policy overhaul with new fuel economy standards
No Clear $473.5 billion omnibus spending bill, including $70 billion for military operations

CQ VOTE STUDIES

	PARTY UNITY		PRESIDENTIAL SUPPORT	
	SUPPORT	OPPOSE	SUPPORT	OPPOSE
2008	99%	1%	13%	87%
2007	99%	1%	4%	96%

INTEREST GROUPS

	AFL-CIO	ADA	CCUS	ACU
2008	100%	100%	56%	0%
2007	91%	100%	50%	0%

MINNESOTA 5
Minneapolis and suburbs

Established at the northernmost navigable point on the Mississippi River, Minneapolis features skyscrapers, corporate headquarters and major sports venues. Minneapolis accounts for most of the 5th's residents, but population growth during the 1990s has contracted since 2000. Completion of the Hiawatha Line light rail in 2004 connecting southern suburbs to downtown has eased traffic congestion, which had been a problem during the decade of steady population growth, and the rail line will continue to expand both in the suburbs and downtown.

Minneapolis, which attracted well-educated, white-collar workers in the 1990s, is home to large corporations, including Target, U.S. Bancorp and General Mills, as well as Best Buy in nearby Richfield. Recent widespread layoffs have hit the economy hard, however, and local financial institutions and housing markets are vulnerable.

The University of Minnesota, the Guthrie Theater and the Walker Art Center anchor the city's art and theater community — Minneapolis currently has the second-most theaters per capita, trailing only New York City. Downtown Minneapolis also hosts four professional sports teams: basketball's Timberwolves and Lynx, baseball's Twins, and football's Vikings. The Minnesota Twins are scheduled to open a new baseball stadium here in 2010, but the University of Minnesota football team is moving from Minneapolis' Metrodome into St. Paul (in the 4th) in 2009.

Although Minneapolis is known for its Scandinavian heritage, the 5th is the state's most racially diverse district. Hmong, Tibetans and blacks — including a sizable Somali population — add to the Democratic-Farmer-Labor Party voter rolls and help shape the district's traditionally liberal politics, as do large American Indian communities and many members of the white-collar workforce. In the 2008 presidential election, Barack Obama carried the district with 74 percent of the vote, his highest percentage in the state.

MAJOR INDUSTRY
Corporate offices, banking, higher education

CITIES
Minneapolis, 382,618; St. Louis Park, 44,126

NOTABLE
Minneapolis features the world's largest skyway system, which covers 80 blocks in an effort to protect pedestrians from harsh winter weather.

Rep. Michele Bachmann (R)

Elected 2006; 2nd term

CAPITOL OFFICE
225-2331
bachmann.house.gov
107 Cannon Bldg. 20515-2306; fax 225-6475

COMMITTEES
Financial Services

RESIDENCE
Woodbury

BORN
April 6, 1956; Waterloo, Iowa

RELIGION
Evangelical Lutheran

FAMILY
Husband, Marcus Bachmann; five children

EDUCATION
Winona State U., B.A. 1978 (political science & English); Oral Roberts U., J.D. 1986; College of William and Mary, LL.M. 1988 (tax law)

CAREER
Homemaker; U.S. Treasury Department lawyer

POLITICAL HIGHLIGHTS
Candidate for Stillwater Area School District Board, 1999; Minn. Senate, 2001-07

ELECTION RESULTS

2008 GENERAL

Michele Bachmann (R)	187,817	46.4%
El Tinklenberg (D)	175,786	43.4%
Bob Anderson (INDC)	40,643	10.0%

2008 PRIMARY

Michele Bachmann (R)	19,127	85.9%
Aubrey Immelman (R)	3,134	14.1%

2006 GENERAL

Michele Bachmann (R)	151,248	50.1%
Patty Wetterling (D)	127,144	42.1%
John Paul Binkowski (INDC)	23,557	7.8%

Bachmann is an ardent social conservative who quickly has become one of the far right's most visible standard-bearers and one of the left-wing blogosphere's most vilified figures. Her uncompromising views and incendiary rhetoric have made her a regular on the TV talk-show circuit — but nearly jeopardized her re-election in a solidly Republican district.

Bachmann (BOCK-man) is sometimes compared to Alaska Gov. Sarah Palin, another high-profile female conservative who elicits strong reactions across the political spectrum. The congresswoman's admirers laud her for speaking on behalf of like-minded Americans disenchanted with Democratic control of Congress and the White House. Critics call her divisive and take her to task for what they say are her frequent factual distortions.

Bachmann, who was in much the same position in her earlier stint as a state senator, takes the controversy she generates in stride. "I have strong views; I am not a waffling personality," she told the St. Paul Pioneer Press in 2008.

Elected in 2006, it didn't take Bachmann long to distinguish herself among her fellow freshmen. She became a YouTube sensation after she was videotaped clinging to President George W. Bush after his 2007 State of the Union address. The clip ended up being among the most-viewed videos ever on the Web site for KSTP-TV in St. Paul — so much so that it stalled the servers. "In that particular point in [Bush's] presidency, the one thing he could use was a pat on the back. And I think I supplied that for him," Bachmann later quipped.

A month later, she made headlines when she said she knew of an Iranian plan to partition Iraq. She later clarified the statement in an opinion piece posted on the Minneapolis Star Tribune's Web site. "I said that an agreement had already been made to divide Iraq and create a safe haven for terrorists," she wrote. "Rather, I meant that America's adversaries are in agreement that a divided Iraq benefits their objective to expel America from the region, resulting in Iraq being a safe haven for terrorists."

But the attention those incidents brought Bachmann paled in comparison to her October 2008 appearance on MSNBC's "Hardball." Discussing Barack Obama's connections to 1960s radical Bill Ayers, she said, "I'm very concerned that [Obama] may have anti-American views." She expressed regret in the days that followed for the term "anti-American" and said she didn't question Obama's patriotism. But her double-digit lead in the polls over Democratic challenger El Tinklenberg vanished, and he raised more than $1 million in four days. She made a furious fundraising push of her own, though, and was able to eke out a 3-percentage-point win in a district that Arizona GOP Sen. John McCain carried by 8 percentage points in the presidential election.

She remained a visible figure in the months that followed. She said that because of Democratic policies, "We are headed down the lane of economic Marxism." She said on Fox News that she spurned earmarks, the member-generated spending requests to benefit their districts — only to have bloggers and TV pundits note she had sought $3.8 million for her district. She later clarified she did take earmarks in the past. And when black Republican National Committee Chairman Michael L. Steele spoke at a conservative conference at which she was the emcee, she told him, "You be da man!"

She also contended Obama's $787 billion economic stimulus law — a measure she strongly opposed — directed money away from GOP districts and included a "national rationing board" that would prevent doctors from making health care decisions. Her comments prompted Minnesota Democratic-Farmer-Labor Chairman Brian Melendez to respond that Bachmann "long ago showed that she'll say anything to anyone, even if it's totally untrue, so long as it grabs her a headline."

Bachmann displays her fiscal-conservative tendencies on the Financial Services Committee. She said she considers the tax code an "albatross for American families." Along with Minnesota Republican John Kline, she voted no on an end-of-the-year spending bill in 2007 that included money for repairing a Minnesota bridge that collapsed in August 2007 and killed 13 people. Bachmann criticized the bill for including thousands of earmarks.

Bachmann strays from her party only when she advocates a more conservative stance or reduced government control. She opposed Bush's guest worker proposal for illegal immigrants and favors repealing No Child Left Behind, the 2001 rewrite of the elementary and secondary education law. She introduced a bill in March 2008 to repeal the nationwide phase-out of conventional light bulbs, arguing the government has no right telling consumers what kind of light bulbs to buy.

Bachmann was born in Waterloo, Iowa. Her mother worked in a factory before staying home to raise four children; her father was an engineer.

When Bachmann was a teenager, her father accepted a job with Honeywell in the Twin Cities. A few years later her parents divorced.

Bachmann met her husband, Marcus, at Winona State University. After working for Jimmy Carter's 1976 campaign, Bachmann made her first trek to Washington to attend Carter's inaugural. While reading Gore Vidal's "Burr" during the train ride home, she realized she was no longer a Democrat. She said she thought the book — a novel about Aaron Burr, a Revolutionary War hero and suspected traitor — was mocking the founding fathers. In 1978 Bachmann married Marcus, a clinical therapist. They later settled in Minnesota, where Bachmann was a federal tax litigation attorney in St. Paul.

She became a local activist after objecting to the state's performance-based Profile of Learning program; she favors local control of schools. She was encouraged to enter politics, but lost a race in 1999 for the Stillwater Area School District Board. A year later, she won a campaign to unseat 28-year Republican incumbent Gary Laidig in the state Senate.

When Republican Rep. Mark Kennedy decided to run for the U.S. Senate, Bachmann entered the race and defeated two other well-known legislators in the primary. In the general election, Bachmann called herself a "woman on a mission" against Democrat Patty Wetterling, who gained prominence as a child-safety advocate after the 1989 abduction of her 11-year-old son, who never was found. Bachmann won by 8 percentage points. She is likely to be among the Democrats' top 2010 GOP targets.

KEY VOTES

2008

No   Delay consideration of Colombia free-trade agreement

No   Override Bush veto of federal farm and nutrition programs reauthorization bill

Yes   Overhaul surveillance laws and permit dismissal of suits against companies that conducted warrantless wiretapping

No   Grant mortgage relief to homeowners and funding for Fannie Mae and Freddie Mac

No   Approve initial $700 billion program to stabilize financial markets

No   Approve final $700 billion program to stabilize financial markets

No   Provide $14 billion in loans to automakers

2007

No   Increase minimum wage by $2.10 an hour

No   Approve $124.2 billion in emergency war spending and set goal for redeployment of troops from Iraq

Yes   Reject federal contraceptive assistance to international family planning groups

Yes   Override Bush veto of $23.2 billion water projects authorization bill

Yes   Implement Peru free-trade agreement

No   Approve energy policy overhaul with new fuel economy standards

Yes   Clear $473.5 billion omnibus spending bill, including $70 billion for military operations

CQ VOTE STUDIES

	PARTY UNITY		PRESIDENTIAL SUPPORT	
	SUPPORT	OPPOSE	SUPPORT	OPPOSE
2008	96%	4%	75%	25%
2007	98%	2%	89%	11%

INTEREST GROUPS

	AFL-CIO	ADA	CCUS	ACU
2008	7%	0%	94%	100%
2007	8%	0%	75%	100%

MINNESOTA 6

North and east Twin Cities suburbs; St. Cloud

One of Minnesota's three largely suburban districts, the 6th hooks counterclockwise from eastern Twin Cities suburbs through conservative areas northwest of Hennepin County to the former granite-quarrying city of St. Cloud, the 6th's only major urban center.

Home to the second-largest college in Minnesota — St. Cloud State University — St. Cloud has a strong college town atmosphere. Development has not yet made the fast-growing city, in heavily Catholic Stearns County, a Twin Cities suburb. North Star Commuter Rail, a commuter train line linking Sherburne County with the Twin Cities, is expected to open in late 2009 and will likely help alleviate traffic problems along Interstate 94.

Anoka and Wright counties, to the north and west of Minneapolis and its first-ring suburbs, had boasted new, wealthy suburban developments. But the effects of a nationwide housing market downturn are evident in Wright, where declining real estate values, high foreclosure rates and an increasing number of empty homes concern local officials, while Anoka County's budget is suffering. Washington County, to the east and north of

St. Paul, includes other towns, such as Woodbury (a small part of which is in the 2nd), that experienced explosive population growth and now are vulnerable to economic slowdowns, and the small town of Stillwater on the St. Croix River, which marks the Wisconsin border.

The 6th District traditionally supports the GOP. The 6th District gave Republican John McCain his largest victory in the state with 53 percent of its vote in the 2008 presidential race. The young, high-income families that fueled the region's growth tend to favor fiscal conservatism, but are not necessarily conservative on social issues such as public safety and education. Blue-collar communities in the suburbs of Anoka and Washington counties are faithful Democratic-Farmer-Labor Party supporters, but Sherburne provided McCain with his third-highest percentage of any county statewide.

MAJOR INDUSTRY
Corporate administration, manufacturing

CITIES
St. Cloud, 59,107; Blaine, 44,942; Woodbury (pt.), 44,767; Andover, 26,588; Ramsey, 18,510

NOTABLE
Writer and radio show host Garrison Keillor was born in Anoka.

Rep. Collin C. Peterson (D)

Elected 1990; 10th term

CAPITOL OFFICE
225-2165
collinpeterson.house.gov
2211 Rayburn Bldg. 20515-2307; fax 225-1593

COMMITTEES
Agriculture - chairman

RESIDENCE
Detroit Lakes

BORN
June 29, 1944; Fargo, N.D.

RELIGION
Lutheran

FAMILY
Divorced; three children

EDUCATION
Moorhead State U., B.A. 1966 (accounting)

MILITARY SERVICE
Minn. National Guard, 1963-69

CAREER
Accountant

POLITICAL HIGHLIGHTS
Minn. Senate, 1977-87; sought Democratic
nomination for U.S. House, 1982; Democratic
nominee for U.S. House, 1984, 1986; sought
Democratic nomination for U.S. House, 1988

ELECTION RESULTS

2008 GENERAL

Glen Menze (R)	227,187	72.2%
Collin C. Peterson (D)	87,062	27.7%

2008 PRIMARY

Collin C. Peterson (D)	unopposed

2006 GENERAL

Collin C. Peterson (D)	179,164	69.7%
Michael J. Barrett (R)	74,557	29.0%
Ken Lucier (CNSTP)	3,303	1.3%

PREVIOUS WINNING PERCENTAGES
2004 (66%); 2002 (65%); 2000 (69%); 1998 (72%);
1996 (68%); 1994 (51%); 1992 (50%); 1990 (54%)

Peterson is one of the more conservative House Democrats, looking to pull in the reins on most aspects of the federal budget, opposing abortion and supporting gun owners' rights. But he remains a Democrat, he said, because the party does "a better job of standing up for ordinary people."

His primary concern has been looking out for his district's farmers, and he has shown he can work to find compromise and achieve his goals. As chairman of the Agriculture Committee, he shepherded into law in 2008 a major rewrite of U.S. farm policy — winning much of what he wanted, including billions of dollars in federal subsidies to farmers — and has set an ambitious agenda moving forward.

Peterson's success on the farm bill quieted the grumbling among more-liberal Democrats when he ascended to the party's top spot on the committee in 2005. Peterson is a founding member of the fiscally conservative Blue Dog Coalition and in the past has split with his party considerably more often than the typical Democrat. He voted in 2007 to maintain a ban on the use of federal funds to support international family planning programs. He also sided with Republicans in voting to continue President George W. Bush's program of warrantless wiretapping of suspected terrorists.

Outside of farm programs, Peterson has maintained a fiscally conservative stance. He opposed a $700 billion financial rescue plan, signed into law in October 2008, and opposed Bush's second round of tax cuts in 2003 because he thought they would lead to deficits. He was just as hard on President Obama, joining six other Democrats to oppose the new president's $787 billion economic stimulus bill in early 2009. "While I understand the desire for a quick fix, I cannot support those in Congress who are rushing to meet an artificial deadline that will result in more unrestrained spending in the hope that it will solve all our problems," he said. And he was one of 20 Democrats to oppose a $410 billion catchall spending bill for fiscal 2009, left over from the 110th Congress (2007-08).

A strong supporter of labor, Peterson voted for two Democratic bills in early 2009 designed to strengthen the ability of workers to combat wage discrimination. And he is no fan of free trade. He opposed the Bush administration's trade deal with Peru in 2007 and voted against the 2005 Central America Free Trade Agreement.

Yet perhaps in a nod to the need to build allies for the farm bill fight, Peterson displayed his highest level of party support ever during the 110th; he sided with fellow Democrats on 88 percent of the votes that separated a majority of Democrats and Republicans.

Peterson's priority on the farm bill was to maintain subsidies for the major staple crops, such as wheat, corn and soybeans, grown in the Midwest. But conservatives and Bush deemed such subsidies wasteful, while budget pressures required Peterson to find cuts or revenue for any new spending. Peterson also had his sights set on creating a new disaster fund to help farmers in the wake of severe droughts and floods. Peterson had to appease West Coast lawmakers who wanted funding for fruit and vegetable growers, and Southerners worried about his proposal to eliminate subsidy payments for large farms in order to create the disaster fund and add other spending.

Peterson undercut conservative opposition with language barring farmers with particularly high incomes from collecting subsidies, and he appeased Southerners, many with larger farms, by lifting limits on short-term loans. His bill also included mandatory country-of-origin labeling for meat starting in September 2008, subsidies for California fruit and vegetable farmers, and his disaster fund, all while maintaining most subsidies. The final product, Peterson joked, would "make everybody equally angry."

Much of his handiwork remained intact when the $289 billion measure cleared Congress in May 2008. Bush vetoed it, saying its subsidies were too generous, but the House and Senate voted overwhelmingly to override him.

When Obama, in his 2010 budget, proposed phasing out direct payments to farmers with more than $500,000 in sales revenue and capping commodity supports at $250,000, Peterson pushed back. "We just passed a fiscally responsible farm bill that made cuts to farm programs, so now is not the time to reopen it," he said.

Looking ahead, Peterson wants to tighten regulation of commodities trading and restructure the Agriculture Department bureaucracy, which he said has grown top-heavy. He also wants to overhaul federal food inspection practices after several costly produce recalls in 2007 and 2008 but expects jurisdictional disputes with other committees over those plans. He supports a mandatory national livestock identification system and a system to trace food-borne illnesses to farm commodities.

He has earned high marks from the National Rifle Association and is an avid sportsman. He once boasted he has "more dead animals on my wall than anybody in this Congress, except for [Alaska Republican] Don Young." He also is a pilot who for years has flown his own plane to and from Washington.

Peterson gets along so well with the GOP opposition that he was long the lone Democrat in a five-member country rock band he fronted called "The Second Amendments," which performed for U.S. troops overseas. Retirements and 2008 election defeats left him with only one backup man: Michigan Republican Thaddeus McCotter. The two sought new recruits in 2009.

Peterson grew up on his family's farm near the North Dakota border and learned self-sufficiency at an early age. He used the money he made working on the farm to buy a guitar. At 16, he joined a touring band. But he gave up his dream of stardom when it became clear he'd have to quit college to pursue it. He made a practical choice of accounting as a career.

He got his start in politics with 10 years in the state Senate. In the 1980s, he made four unsuccessful bids for a U.S. House seat; in two attempts, he failed to get even the Democratic nomination.

He decided to run again in 1990 when GOP Rep. Arlan Stangeland was weakened by revelations he had used his House credit card to charge calls to or from the phone of a female lobbyist. Peterson won with 54 percent. After scratching out close re-election wins in 1992 and 1994, he has since won easily.

KEY VOTES

2008
Yes Delay consideration of Colombia free-trade agreement
Yes Override Bush veto of federal farm and nutrition programs reauthorization bill
Yes Overhaul surveillance laws and permit dismissal of suits against companies that conducted warrantless wiretapping
Yes Grant mortgage relief to homeowners and funding for Fannie Mae and Freddie Mac
No   Approve initial $700 billion program to stabilize financial markets
No   Approve final $700 billion program to stabilize financial markets
No   Provide $14 billion in loans to automakers

2007
Yes Increase minimum wage by $2.10 an hour
Yes Approve $124.2 billion in emergency war spending and set goal for redeployment of troops from Iraq
Yes Reject federal contraceptive assistance to international family planning groups
Yes Override Bush veto of $23.2 billion water projects authorization bill
No   Implement Peru free-trade agreement
Yes Approve energy policy overhaul with new fuel economy standards
Yes Clear $473.5 billion omnibus spending bill, including $70 billion for military operations

CQ VOTE STUDIES

	PARTY UNITY		PRESIDENTIAL SUPPORT	
	SUPPORT	OPPOSE	SUPPORT	OPPOSE
2008	91%	9%	21%	79%
2007	87%	13%	14%	86%
2006	63%	37%	60%	40%
2005	64%	36%	54%	46%
2004	63%	37%	50%	50%

INTEREST GROUPS

	AFL-CIO	ADA	CCUS	ACU
2008	80%	80%	50%	20%
2007	96%	85%	60%	33%
2006	79%	35%	73%	72%
2005	80%	65%	70%	56%
2004	80%	55%	76%	52%

MINNESOTA 7
West – Moorhead, Willmar

Stretching 330 miles from north to south, the vast 7th District spans almost the entire western third of Minnesota. The landscape varies from flat prairie in the west to hills, lakes and heavy forests in the middle of the state. Apart from Willmar in the south, the 7th's main population centers — Moorhead and East Grand Forks — are on the Red River, which forms the border between Minnesota and North Dakota. Both locales have much larger companion cities across the river in North Dakota.

The 7th's agricultural production includes sugar beets, soybeans, wheat, corn and sunflower seeds. The district relies on poultry raising and processing. Willmar is home to the headquarters of turkey processor Jennie-O Turkey Store, and Schwan Food is based in Marshall. Floods and droughts are perpetual problems to the northwest, and recent major flooding of the Red River has threatened infrastructure as well as crop yields. Reductions in harvests have forced some farmers to supplement their livelihood with part-time work in other industries and have sent younger residents fleeing to the Twin Cities area or out of the state.

Western Minnesota's economy now includes renewable- and alternative-energy production. Another significant employer is Appleton's Prairie Correctional Facility, a private prison with inmates from out of state. The 7th's manufacturing sector — producing hockey sticks, windows, snowmobiles and skis — is vulnerable to widespread economic slowdowns.

The district tends to be socially conservative and fiscally moderate, but it has supported candidates from both parties. The 7th supported Republican John McCain in the 2008 presidential election, giving him 50 percent of its vote. Many of the more highly populated counties in the district and areas to the southeast provided McCain his best support. Midsize Sibley County gave him 58 percent, his second-best percentage in the state. Democrat Barack Obama won several counties here, including all but one of the counties along the Red River.

MAJOR INDUSTRY
Agriculture, poultry processing, light manufacturing, recreation

CITIES
Moorhead, 32,177; Willmar, 18,351; Fergus Falls, 13,471

NOTABLE
Writer Sinclair Lewis, who was the first American to win the Nobel Prize in Literature, grew up in Sauk Centre.

Rep. James L. Oberstar (D)

Elected 1974; 18th term

CAPITOL OFFICE
225-6211
oberstar.house.gov
2365 Rayburn Bldg. 20515-2308; fax 225-0699

COMMITTEES
Transportation & Infrastructure - chairman

RESIDENCE
Chisholm

BORN
Sept. 10, 1934; Chisholm, Minn.

RELIGION
Roman Catholic

FAMILY
Wife, Jean Oberstar; six children

EDUCATION
College of St. Thomas, B.A. 1956 (French
& political science); College of Europe (Belgium),
M.A. 1957 (comparative government)

CAREER
Language teacher; congressional aide

POLITICAL HIGHLIGHTS
Sought Democratic nomination for U.S. Senate,
1984

ELECTION RESULTS

2008 GENERAL

James L. Oberstar (D)	241,831	67.7%
Michael Cummins (R)	114,871	32.2%

2008 PRIMARY

James L. Oberstar (D)	unopposed

2006 GENERAL

James L. Oberstar (D)	180,670	63.6%
Rod Grams (R)	97,683	34.4%
Harry Robb Welty (UNT)	5,508	1.9%

PREVIOUS WINNING PERCENTAGES
2004 (65%); 2002 (69%); 2000 (68%); 1998 (66%);
1996 (67%); 1994 (66%); 1992 (59%); 1990 (73%);
1988 (75%); 1986 (73%); 1984 (67%); 1982 (77%);
1980 (70%); 1978 (87%); 1976 (100%); 1974 (62%)

Oberstar is a workaholic who gets fidgety when there's even a small gap in his daybook. He insists that his staff leave no space in it even for lunch. And he uses his carefully conserved time, as chairman of the Transportation and Infrastructure Committee, to keep close tabs on everything his committee does, attending nearly every subcommittee hearing and asking pointed, detailed questions of witnesses.

He is now eighth in seniority among House Democrats — one of just four "Watergate babies" elected in 1974 still serving in the House, where seniority is almost synonymous with power. He wields that power effectively yet fairly, seeking bipartisanship even when the lure of money for member districts can't push a bill through. Fellow Democratic committee member Nick J. Rahall II of West Virginia once described him as "the true builder of America."

Oberstar has a strong working relationship with John L. Mica of Florida, his panel's top Republican, and the two brokered a deal in 2008 to reauthorize funding for Amtrak for the first time in 11 years. Previous attempts had failed due to partisan differences.

Like his mentor and predecessor, Democrat John A. Blatnik, who chaired what was then called the Public Works Committee, Oberstar firmly believes generous federal spending on transportation and infrastructure is vital to maintaining America's global competitiveness. When Congress tackled President Obama's economic stimulus plan in early 2009, Oberstar proposed $85 billion in new highway, transit and environmental infrastructure funding that he said would create or sustain more than 2.4 million jobs. He had to settle for a little more than half that much in funding.

Oberstar had supported the $700 billion package to assist the ailing financial services sector in fall 2008 but, like other Democrats, said it wasn't enough. "We are facing a worldwide economic, financial meltdown," he told Time magazine in January 2009. "And these measures taken so far by Treasury to stabilize the bank system itself, free up credit, are either not working or working so slowly that there is no trust in the credit system. And you need something much bigger. You need to put people to work." But Oberstar also believes the government can't just freely hand out money — something he said he learned more than 45 years ago as an aide to Blatnick, when the Kennedy administration attempted a similar plan for boosting the economy.

In the 111th Congress (2009-10), Oberstar's committee plans to reauthorize the 2005 surface transportation law that governs spending on highways and mass transit. He faces a daunting challenge, as revenues in the Highway Trust Fund have been declining as federal gasoline tax receipts fall. When the I-35W bridge in Minneapolis collapsed in 2007, Oberstar lobbied for a 5-cent increase to the gas tax to pay for repairs of broken bridges nationwide. Resistance from the White House and lawmakers killed its chances.

Oberstar and Mica bristled when Obama, in his first budget, suggested subjecting highway and aviation funding to the annual appropriations process, ending their protected trust funds. The House pair, along with their Senate counterparts, brusquely dismissed that idea as "ill-advised."

Oberstar is wrestling with thorny financing questions in aviation as well, where a dispute over how to pay for a much-needed modernization of the air traffic control system has delayed action on a reauthorization of the Federal Aviation Administration. His panel approved a rewrite in March 2009.

After serving as the Transportation panel's top Democrat during 12 years of GOP rule, Oberstar wasted no time in the 110th Congress

(2007-08), pushing a series of measures into law. Among them was a 2007 bill authorizing $23.2 billion in water resources projects. President George W. Bush vetoed the measure, calling it too expensive, but both chambers voted overwhelmingly to override the veto. Oberstar is a fierce ally of unions. His father was a union official and an iron ore miner who worked in both underground mine shafts and open pits, where Oberstar also labored as a teenager. His mother worked in a shirt factory. He repeatedly sought ways to help airline workers laid off in the aftermath of the Sept. 11 terrorist attacks.

In 2007, he pushed a wastewater treatment bill through the House that applied Davis-Bacon prevailing-wage laws to state and local projects funded with federal grants authorized by the bill. The bill died in the Senate, but Oberstar guided a new version through the House in early 2009.

A bicyclist, Oberstar included in the 1998 transportation law many provisions to encourage biking and enhance bicycle safety. He protected those measures when the law was renewed in 2005. Though he sides with his party on most votes that split Republicans from Democrats, Oberstar strays on abortion and gun owners' rights. In 2008 he voted to nullify a District of Columbia law restricting handgun ownership. And in 2007, he was one of 25 Democrats voting to maintain a ban on federal funding for international organizations that perform abortions. A devout Roman Catholic, he has proposed a constitutional amendment to ban abortion except when the woman's life is in danger.

In 2006, he was one of 14 House Democrats voting to sustain Bush's veto of a bill expanding federal funding of embryonic stem cell research. In the 111th Congress is expected to try to cement President Obama's expansive stem cell research policy into law.

He adopted his oldest child and co-chairs the Congressional Coalition on Adoption. He also seeks more federal funding for breast cancer research. His first wife died after a long battle with the disease, and he has since married a woman who lost her first spouse to cancer. He has pushed to provide financial relief, including a tax credit, to caregivers of sick family members.

A policy wonk with a dry sense of humor, he can converse in six languages, including French and Creole, which he taught to U.S. Navy personnel in Haiti in the early 1960s. Oberstar sometimes speaks fluent French during hearings, and when the French ambassador hosted a reception in 2005 for the Congressional French Caucus, which Oberstar co-chairs, Oberstar delivered a speech in English and French. He has a graduate degree from a college in Belgium, and also speaks some Spanish, Italian, Slovenian and Serbo-Croatian.

Oberstar served as Blatnik's chief aide for 11 years. He was elected to succeed Blatnik in 1974 and has won re-election easily since.

KEY VOTES

2008

Yes Delay consideration of Colombia free-trade agreement

Yes Override Bush veto of federal farm and nutrition programs reauthorization bill

No Overhaul surveillance laws and permit dismissal of suits against companies that conducted warrantless wiretapping

Yes Grant mortgage relief to homeowners and funding for Fannie Mae and Freddie Mac

Yes Approve initial $700 billion program to stabilize financial markets

Yes Approve final $700 billion program to stabilize financial markets

Yes Provide $14 billion in loans to automakers

2007

Yes Increase minimum wage by $2.10 an hour

Yes Approve $124.2 billion in emergency war spending and set goal for redeployment of troops from Iraq

Yes Reject federal contraceptive assistance to international family planning groups

? Override Bush veto of $23.2 billion water projects authorization bill

? Implement Peru free-trade agreement

Yes Approve energy policy overhaul with new fuel economy standards

No Clear $473.5 billion omnibus spending bill, including $70 billion for military operations

CQ VOTE STUDIES

	PARTY UNITY		PRESIDENTIAL SUPPORT	
	SUPPORT	OPPOSE	SUPPORT	OPPOSE
2008	99%	1%	15%	85%
2007	95%	5%	8%	92%
2006	88%	12%	35%	65%
2005	93%	7%	23%	77%
2004	91%	9%	27%	73%

INTEREST GROUPS

	AFL-CIO	ADA	CCUS	ACU
2008	100%	80%	56%	4%
2007	95%	75%	56%	13%
2006	100%	80%	27%	22%
2005	100%	90%	31%	20%
2004	93%	75%	14%	12%

MINNESOTA 8

Northeast — Duluth, Iron Range

The expansive 8th District covers Minnesota's northeast quadrant, including Duluth and the Iron Range — taconite-mining communities that stretch across the middle of the state through Cass, Crow Wing and St. Louis counties. The district has the most varied terrain in the state, from farms in the south and west through the Iron Range and a watery northern border near International Falls.

Timber and mining, traditional economic mainstays here, still serve as a solid base for the region. Duluth, on Lake Superior, is the shipping point for much of the grain from the Plains states and is the westernmost deep-sea port to the Atlantic. The University of Minnesota has a regional campus in Duluth that serves more than 11,000 students. Northwest of Duluth, in Chisolm, there is a reservations center for Northwest Airlines, which was recently bought by Delta Air Lines, that provides nearly 500 jobs.

Resorts and casinos near the Canadian border traditionally draw both local and out-of-state tourists, supporting the local economy, but nationwide economic slowdowns have limited the number of tourists venturing to the gambling spots. The 8th District takes in the 61-mile Superior National Forest Scenic Byway, and winter sport tourism, fishing, canoeing and camping can also draw visitors. Huge tracts of land in the district are designated as state and national forests, and the Boundary Waters Canoe Area Wilderness along the Canadian border is noted for its motor-free beauty.

Blue-collar workers with strong ties to labor cement the 8th's long affiliation with the Democratic-Farmer-Labor Party. Voters here favor a hands-off approach to federal land management and tend to oppose gun control and abortion. The district is Democratic, and northeastern Minnesota has not been represented by a Republican in the U.S. House since 1947. Although Republican John McCain won many counties along the district's southern and western edges in the 2008 presidential election, Barack Obama took 53 percent of the district's vote overall.

MAJOR INDUSTRY
Mining, timber, recreation

CITIES
Duluth, 86,918; Hibbing, 17,071; Brainerd, 13,178

NOTABLE
The U.S. Hockey Hall of Fame is in Eveleth.

MISSISSIPPI

Gov. Haley Barbour (R)

First elected: 2003
Length of term: 4 years
Term expires: 1/12
Salary: $122,160
Phone: (601) 359-3150

Residence: Yazoo City
Born: Oct. 21, 1947; Yazoo City, Miss.
Religion: Presbyterian
Family: Wife, Marsha Barbour; two children
Education: U. of Mississippi, attended 1965-69 (political science), J.D. 1973
Career: Lobbyist; lawyer; White House aide; party official
Political highlights: Republican nominee for U.S. Senate, 1982; Republican National Committee chairman, 1993-97

Election results:
2007 GENERAL
Haley Barbour (R)	430,807	57.9%
John Eaves (D)	313,232	42.1%

Lt. Gov. Phil Bryant (R)

First elected: 2007
Length of term: 4 years
Term expires: 1/12
Salary: $60,000
Phone: (601) 359-3200

LEGISLATURE

Legislature: 90 days January-April
Senate: 52 members, 4-year terms
2009 ratios: 27 D, 25 R, 48 men, 4 women
Salary: $10,000
Phone: (601) 359-3202

House: 122 members, 4-year terms
2009 ratios: 73 D, 48 R, 1 vacancy; 100 men, 21 women
Salary: $10,000
Phone: (601) 359-3360

TERM LIMITS

Governor: 2 terms
Senate: No
House: No

URBAN STATISTICS

CITY	POPULATION
Jackson	184,256
Gulfport	71,127
Biloxi	50,644
Hattiesburg	44,779
Greenville	41,633

REGISTERED VOTERS

Voters do not register by party.

POPULATION

2008 population (est.)	2,938,618
2000 population	2,844,658
1990 population	2,573,216
Percent change (1990-2000)	+10.5%
Rank among states (2008)	31

Median age	33.8
Born in state	74.3%
Foreign born	1.4%
Violent crime rate	361/100,000
Poverty level	19.9%
Federal workers	25,318
Military	35,850

ELECTIONS

STATE ELECTION OFFICIAL
(601) 359-6357
DEMOCRATIC PARTY
(601) 969-2913
REPUBLICAN PARTY
(601) 948-5191

MISCELLANEOUS

Web: www.ms.gov
Capital: Jackson

U.S. CONGRESS

Senate: 2 Republicans
House: 3 Democrats, 1 Republicans

2000 Census Statistics by District

DIST.	2008 VOTE FOR PRESIDENT OBAMA	MCCAIN	WHITE	BLACK	ASIAN	HISP	MEDIAN INCOME	WHITE COLLAR	BLUE COLLAR	SERVICE INDUSTRY	OVER 64	UNDER 18	COLLEGE EDUCATION	RURAL	SQ. MILES
1	37%	62%	71%	26%	0%	1%	$32,535	49%	39%	12%	12%	27%	14%	62%	11,413
2	66	33	35	63	0	1	$26,894	52	31	17	11	29	17	37	13,625
3	39	61	64	33	1	1	$31,907	57	30	13	13	26	20	60	13,168
4	32	67	73	22	1	2	$33,023	52	31	17	12	27	17	46	8,701
STATE	43	56	61	36	1	1	$31,330	52	33	15	12	27	17	51	46,907
U.S.	53	46	69	12	4	13	$41,994	60	25	15	12	26	24	21	3,537,438

Sen. Thad Cochran (R)

Elected 1978; 6th term

CAPITOL OFFICE
224-5054
cochran.senate.gov
113 Dirksen Bldg. 20510-2402; fax 224-9450

COMMITTEES
Agriculture, Nutrition & Forestry
Appropriations - ranking member
Rules & Administration
Joint Library

RESIDENCE
Oxford

BORN
Dec. 7, 1937; Pontotoc, Miss.

RELIGION
Baptist

FAMILY
Wife, Rose Cochran; two children

EDUCATION
U. of Mississippi, B.A. 1959 (psychology);
Trinity College (U. of Dublin, Ireland), attended
1963-64 (international law); U. of Mississippi,
J.D. 1965

MILITARY SERVICE
Navy, 1959-61

CAREER
Lawyer

POLITICAL HIGHLIGHTS
U.S. House, 1973-78

ELECTION RESULTS

2008 GENERAL

Thad Cochran (R)	766,111	61.4%
Erik Fleming (D)	480,915	38.6%

2008 PRIMARY

Thad Cochran (R)	unopposed

PREVIOUS WINNING PERCENTAGES
2002 (85%); 1996 (71%); 1990 (100%); 1984 (61%);
1978 (45%); 1976 House Election (76%); 1974 House
Election (70%); 1972 House Election (48%)

Cochran is the archetypal appropriator. He operates behind the scenes to achieve his objectives, which center on sending prodigious sums of money to his state, with a minimum of fuss. He is a stickler for Senate procedure and works cordially with like-minded lawmakers regardless of their political beliefs.

As the Appropriations Committee's top Republican, Cochran sees himself as a necessary restraint against potential Democratic excesses in the 111th Congress (2009-10). "There are a lot of people coming in with a lot of enthusiasm," he said in November 2008. "We need some people with a little gray hair to help be a calming influence."

An easygoing Southern gentleman who is seldom without a smile, Cochran generally refrains from criticizing others. Nevertheless, the most attention he drew in the 110th Congress (2007-08) came from an unusually blunt remark to a Boston Globe reporter in January 2008 about his colleague John McCain of Arizona. "The thought of his being president sends a cold chill down my spine," Cochran said of McCain. "He is erratic. He is hotheaded. He loses his temper, and he worries me."

The comment became fodder for Democrats eager to build a case against McCain's candidacy. The two senators patched up their differences, with Cochran throwing his support behind McCain the following month when it appeared the Arizonan had wrapped up the nomination. But the incident showed how protective Cochran can be of the member-driven earmarks — funding set-asides for special projects in appropriations bills — that McCain has spent much of his career attacking as pork barrel spending.

Cochran was the most prolific member of Congress at earmarking in fiscal 2008 spending bills, according to the watchdog group Taxpayers for Common Sense. He accumulated $837 million either by himself or working with other members — far ahead of the runner-up, Louisiana Democratic Sen. Mary L. Landrieu, who was responsible for nearly $470 million. He also had the highest earmark total — $474 million — in the fiscal 2009 catchall spending bill.

Like other veteran appropriators, Cochran says there is nothing untoward about his efforts. He says the earmarks always receive his colleagues' blessing and greatly benefit his poor, rural state. Among the chief recipients of his largesse have been universities conducting scientific research and communities ravaged by Hurricane Katrina and other storms. He also has made sure that Mississippi's cotton, peanut, rice and sugar farmers get emergency relief when they ask for it. But he casts a wide net — the fiscal 2008 catchall spending bill included $131,000 to create a national repository for music of all genres at the University of Mississippi.

Cochran was Appropriations chairman in the 109th Congress (2005-06), having waited his turn for decades. An institutionalist at heart, he made a priority of getting all of the appropriations bills through the Senate in his first year at the helm, after several years in which the Republican majority had to rely on eleventh-hour omnibus bills to fund the government. As a member of the minority during the 110th, he often lamented Democrats' inability to follow suit and their tendency to include their priorities in stimulus spending bills. "If [Democrats] were serious about funding for local law enforcement grants or medical research, they would have worked to move across the House and Senate floors the annual appropriations bills that fund these programs," he said in September 2008.

In mid-2008, Cochran took over for colleague Ted Stevens of Alaska as top-ranking Republican on the Defense Appropriations Subcommittee when

Stevens became caught in an ethics controversy and was forced to relinquish the post. Cochran has long obtained money for Northrop Grumman Corp.'s naval shipyard in Pascagoula and the state's other military installations. He previously was top Republican on the Homeland Security Appropriations Subcommittee, where he worked to bolster spending for the Federal Emergency Management Agency and the Coast Guard.

Cochran also serves on the Agriculture, Nutrition and Forestry Committee. In 2002, he was a major player in the rewrite of the law that authorizes federal agriculture subsidies and conservation and nutrition programs. But his 2003-04 stint as Agriculture chairman was uneventful. He held few meetings to debate bills, in part to prevent Iowa Republican Charles E. Grassley, a panel member, from offering amendments to reduce the maximum federal payments a farmer could receive. Grassley wanted to free money for other farm programs, while Cochran opposed lower payment limits.

On the Rules and Administration panel, which handles election laws, Cochran played a pivotal role in the drive to curb large individual donations to campaigns, called soft money. His 2001 announcement that he would support a McCain-sponsored bill that GOP leaders opposed began an erosion of Republican opposition. The law was enacted 14 months later.

Cochran's voting record is conservative; over the past decade he has led the push to deploy a nationwide antimissile defense system, one of the GOP's signature defense issues. Yet his thoughtful persona enables him to work with colleagues across the ideological spectrum. In 2008, he teamed with liberal Democrats Edward M. Kennedy of Massachusetts and Christopher J. Dodd of Connecticut on legislation aimed at enhancing national service; he joined Dodd on a 2009 measure to promote geography literacy among students.

Cochran's father was a school principal, his mother a math teacher. He was a standout in high school: valedictorian of his class; a Boy Scout leader; a member of the 4-H Club; and an athlete, lettering in football, basketball, baseball and tennis. Another legacy of his childhood is musical talent. A baby grand piano sits in his Senate office, transferred there when he moved into a Capitol Hill apartment that lacked room for it.

At Ole Miss, Cochran was a fraternity president and cheerleader who was four years ahead of Trent Lott, later his congressional colleague and sometime rival. In his first year of law school, Cochran posted the highest scholastic average and later got a Rotary fellowship to study international law at Trinity College in Dublin. He joined a Jackson law firm after graduation, and he made partner in less than three years.

Cochran was active in local party politics during his law career and a key state figure in Richard Nixon's 1968 presidential campaign. In 1972, when Democratic Rep. Charles H. Griffin retired, Cochran narrowly won the open seat. Lott was elected to the House the same year, and the two soon led warring factions within the state party. The pragmatists, led by Cochran, and the ideologues, led by Lott, feuded with increasing intensity for nearly two decades.

Cochran became Mississippi's first GOP senator in a century when long-serving Democrat James O. Eastland retired from the Senate in 1978. Cochran won with 45 percent of the vote, as an independent black candidate drew much of the black vote away from Democrat Maurice Dantin, a former Columbia mayor. All of Cochran's Senate re-elections have been cakewalks. Democrats didn't field a challenger in 1990 or 2002, and he took 62 percent of the vote in 2008. He said beforehand it would be his last election.

Cochran won election to the Senate a decade before Lott. But by 1995, Lott had zipped ahead of Cochran to become GOP whip. When Majority Leader Bob Dole resigned to focus on his 1996 presidential campaign, the two Mississippians battled one another for the job; Lott won easily, 44-8.

KEY VOTES

2008
Yes   Prohibit discrimination based on genetic information
Yes   Reauthorize farm and nutrition programs for five years
No   Limit debate on "cap and trade" system for greenhouse gas emissions
No   Allow lawsuits against companies that participated in warrantless wiretapping
No   Limit debate on a bill to block a scheduled cut in Medicare payments to doctors
Yes   Grant mortgage relief to homeowners and funding for Fannie Mae and Freddie Mac
Yes   Approve a nuclear cooperation agreement with India
No   Approve final $700 billion program to stabilize financial markets
No   Allow consideration of a $14 billion auto industry loan package

2007
Yes   Increase minimum wage by $2.10 an hour
No   Limit debate on a comprehensive immigration bill
No   Overhaul congressional lobbying and ethics rules for members and their staffs
No   Limit debate on considering a bill to add House seats for the District of Columbia and Utah
No   Limit debate on restoring habeas corpus rights to detainees
No   Mandate minimum breaks for troops between deployments to Iraq or Afghanistan
Yes   Override Bush veto of $23.2 billion water projects authorization bill
Yes   Confirm Michael B. Mukasey as attorney general
No   Limit debate on an energy policy overhaul containing $21.8 billion in tax incentives and reduced oil and gas subsidies

CQ VOTE STUDIES

	PARTY UNITY		PRESIDENTIAL SUPPORT	
	SUPPORT	OPPOSE	SUPPORT	OPPOSE
2008	85%	15%	74%	26%
2007	85%	15%	82%	18%
2006	87%	13%	89%	11%
2005	97%	3%	96%	4%
2004	98%	2%	92%	8%
2003	98%	2%	98%	2%
2002	86%	14%	96%	4%
2001	84%	16%	96%	4%
2000	98%	2%	45%	55%
1999	94%	6%	38%	62%

INTEREST GROUPS

	AFL-CIO	ADA	CCUS	ACU
2008	10%	15%	88%	68%
2007	11%	15%	82%	83%
2006	15%	10%	92%	67%
2005	21%	0%	100%	88%
2004	8%	15%	100%	92%
2003	0%	5%	100%	85%
2002	23%	25%	100%	90%
2001	25%	15%	86%	88%
2000	0%	0%	100%	92%
1999	0%	0%	88%	84%

Sen. Roger Wicker (R)

Appointed December 2007; 1st term

CAPITOL OFFICE
224-6253
wicker.senate.gov
555 Dirksen Bldg. 20510-2403; fax 228-0378

COMMITTEES
Armed Services
Commerce, Science & Transportation
Foreign Relations
Small Business & Entrepreneurship
Veterans' Affairs

RESIDENCE
Tupelo

BORN
July 5, 1951; Pontotoc, Miss.

RELIGION
Southern Baptist

FAMILY
Wife, Gayle Wicker; three children

EDUCATION
U. of Mississippi, B.A. 1973 (political science
& journalism), J.D. 1975

MILITARY SERVICE
Air Force, 1976-80; Air Force Reserve, 1980-2004

CAREER
County public defender; lawyer; military
prosecutor; congressional aide

POLITICAL HIGHLIGHTS
Miss. Senate, 1988-94; U.S. House, 1995-2007

ELECTION RESULTS

2008 GENERAL

Roger Wicker (R)	683,409	55.0%
Ronnie Musgrove (D)	560,064	45.0%

PREVIOUS WINNING PERCENTAGES
2006 House Election (66%); 2004 House Election
(79%); 2002 House Election (71%); 2000 House
Election (70%); 1998 House Election (67%); 1996
House Election (68%); 1994 House Election (63%)

Wicker envisions his role, primarily, as that of a provider of federal funds to his home state, even while he expresses conservative views on fiscal as well as social issues. But after becoming a comfortable insider during 13 years in the House, he's found it's not as easy to get things done in the Senate. He has nonetheless set out to master the chamber's idiosyncrasies as well as his predecessor, former Senate Majority Leader Trent Lott, did during his nearly two-decade career.

"If both houses were like the House of Representatives, we would have to invent something to put the brakes on legislation," said Wicker, who was appointed to the seat by Mississippi Republican Gov. Haley Barbour on New Year's Eve of 2007, two weeks after Lott resigned to become a lobbyist. Wicker wasn't used to the Senate's slow debate, but figured out his way around well enough to secure the support of his constituents, who in November 2008 granted him a 10-point win over former Democratic Gov. Ronnie Musgrove — who once roomed with Wicker when both were in the state Senate.

During his first year as a senator, Wicker focused his efforts on helping to reconstruct areas of his state that were hard-hit by hurricanes in 2005. He talked to Lott almost weekly and made several trips to the state's southern edge. He tried to bring money home to help his constituents with the efforts. He sponsored legislation to give $5,000 tax credits to hurricane victims; the bill went nowhere but Wicker did manage to push through an extension of legislation, passed in the wake of Hurricane Katrina, which provides tax incentives to developers who build in the devastated regions of Mississippi and Louisiana.

Wicker picked up where he left off when the 111th Congress (2009-10) convened in January 2009. He was one of just eight Republican senators to support a $410 billion catchall spending bill for fiscal 2009. The bill included nearly $400 million secured by Wicker for earmarks — funding set-asides for special projects. Wicker's proficiency as a purveyor of such funding placed him second only to his home-state colleague, GOP Sen. Thad Cochran for that bill.

Wicker developed a knack for appropriations while in the House, where he grew to enjoy the often behind-the-scenes, but highly collaborative, work of the Appropriations Committee. Members on that panel are known for providing something for everyone at the end of the day, regardless of party affiliation. Wicker's position on the clubby panel allowed him an easy transition when Democrats took control of Congress in the 110th Congress (2007-08). In the fiscal 2008 budget, he earmarked more money for projects in his state than any other House member.

In the Senate, Wicker's seats on the Armed Services, Veterans' Affairs and Commerce, Science and Transportation panels will be essential to continuing the efforts he began while serving on House Appropriations to turn his impoverished state into a magnet for high-tech defense jobs. As an appropriator Wicker had managed, with Lott's help, to send millions of dollars back home to encourage research, provide tax breaks and build infrastructure.

Wicker also was a member of the House Appropriations subcommittee that funds health, education and labor programs for six terms and took a special interest in beefing up spending on medical research. He was active in efforts to double the budget for the National Institutes of Health, and he pressed for more spending to fight polio and muscular dystrophy.

The funds he and other Mississippians in Washington have procured routinely put the state among the top 10 recipients of "pork per capita," according to the watchdog group Citizens Against Government Waste, but

Wicker nonetheless regards himself as a fiscal conservative willing to rein in federal spending in other areas.

He opposed President Obama's $787 billion economic stimulus bill, which became law in early 2009. He said it called for too much spending. And arguing that it would add too much to the national debt, he voted against President George W. Bush's $700 billion plan in fall 2008 to rescue the financial sector. That plan also became law. In late 2008, Wicker helped sink a bill providing emergency loans for near-bankrupt automobile companies.

Wicker is equally conservative on social issues and adamantly opposed to abortion. He sought to offer an amendment to the fiscal 2009 spending bill that would have stopped $50 million from going to the United Nations Population Fund, an organization that he charged supports China's "immoral" one-child policy as well as coercive abortion and sterilization.

He also serves on the Foreign Relations Committee and joined Majority Whip Richard J. Durbin of Illinois in sponsoring a bill in 2009 to encourage low-income students and those attending community college to spend part of their undergraduate careers studying abroad to to help them understand the world. His other assignment is Small Business and Entrepreneurship.

He is proud to have been a leader of the Republican class of 1994 and attended a 10th anniversary reunion intended to rekindle some of the intellectual fires of that election. But Wicker said he never viewed taking control of the House for the first time in 40 years as a revolution. "I didn't come to Washington to burn all the buildings down. We were all unfairly painted with the same brush," he said in 1998.

Wicker scored one of his biggest legislative victories in the 108th Congress (2003-04). Appalled by the poor understanding most high school students have of American history, he joined with Republican Sen. Lamar Alexander of Tennessee in a two-year effort to create special academies to teach history to high school students and teachers. Bush signed the bill in 2004.

The grandson of sharecroppers from Benton, Wicker said his father's humble upbringing makes his ascension to Congress "a pretty powerful statement of the American Dream." His father lived in a small farmhouse with his parents and four siblings before graduating from law school and becoming a county attorney, a state senator and then a circuit judge for 20 years. Wicker organized the local teenage Republican club in high school. Although his father was a Democrat — as was virtually every officeholder in the South in those days — Wicker said, "There's not a dime's worth of difference in his philosophy of government and mine."

He was the first Republican ever to be elected student body president at Ole Miss. While still in college, he was a delegate to the 1972 Republican National Convention; he became acquainted with a young Trent Lott as Lott was making his first run for Congress. Wicker was in the Air Force ROTC and after law school served four years on active duty as both a prosecutor and defense counsel before going to work for Lott in Washington in 1980. He came home to practice law and, in 1987, won a state Senate seat. In Jackson, he helped write Mississippi's strict abortion law and pushed through an education overhaul that included a controversial school-choice provision.

When Democratic Rep. Jamie L. Whitten retired in 1994 after 53 years in the House — the longest service in the chamber's history at the time — the conservative-minded 1st District was ripe for GOP picking. Wicker emphasized his legislative experience and edged out Grant Fox, a former Senate aide, for the Republican nomination. In November, he won with 63 percent of the vote, and was never seriously challenged for his remaining House terms.

His accession to the Senate marked the first time in nearly 20 years that Mississippi does not have a senator from the southern half of the state, as Cochran hails from Jackson.

KEY VOTES

2008

Yes Prohibit discrimination based on genetic information

Yes Reauthorize farm and nutrition programs for five years

No Limit debate on "cap and trade" system for greenhouse gas emissions

No Allow lawsuits against companies that participated in warrantless wiretapping

No Limit debate on a bill to block a scheduled cut in Medicare payments to doctors

Yes Grant mortgage relief to homeowners and funding for Fannie Mae and Freddie Mac

Yes Approve a nuclear cooperation agreement with India

No Approve final $700 billion program to stabilize financial markets

No Allow consideration of a $14 billion auto industry loan package

House Service:

2007

No Increase minimum wage by $2.10 an hour

No Approve $124.2 billion in emergency war spending and set goal for redeployment of troops from Iraq

Yes Reject federal contraceptive assistance to international family planning groups

Yes Override Bush veto of $23.2 billion water projects authorization bill

Yes Implement Peru free-trade agreement

No Approve energy policy overhaul with new fuel economy standards

Yes Clear $473.5 billion omnibus spending bill, including $70 billion for military operations

CQ VOTE STUDIES

| | PARTY UNITY | | PRESIDENTIAL SUPPORT | |
	SUPPORT	OPPOSE	SUPPORT	OPPOSE
2008	94%	6%	70%	30%
House Service:				
2007	89%	11%	81%	19%
2006	97%	3%	97%	3%
2005	97%	3%	84%	16%
2004	95%	5%	86%	14%
2003	97%	3%	96%	4%
2002	99%	1%	85%	15%
2001	99%	1%	95%	5%
2000	93%	7%	22%	78%

INTEREST GROUPS

	AFL-CIO	ADA	CCUS	ACU
2008	20%	10%	88%	80%
House Service:				
2007	%	5%	84%	96%
2006	7%	0%	100%	88%
2005	20%	5%	93%	96%
2004	8%	0%	100%	87%
2003	0%	10%	97%	88%
2002	11%	0%	90%	100%
2001	8%	0%	96%	96%
2000	0%	0%	85%	84%

Rep. Travis W. Childers (D)

Elected May 2008; 1st full term

CAPITOL OFFICE
225-4306
childers.house.gov
1708 Longworth Bldg. 20515-2401; fax 225-3549

COMMITTEES
Agriculture
Financial Services

RESIDENCE
Booneville

BORN
March 29, 1958; Booneville, Miss.

RELIGION
Baptist

FAMILY
Wife, Tami Childers; two children

EDUCATION
Northeast Mississippi Junior College,
A.A. 1978 (business administration);
U. of Mississippi, B.A. 1980

CAREER
Realtor; retirement and nursing home owner

POLITICAL HIGHLIGHTS
Prentiss County chancery clerk, 1992-2008

ELECTION RESULTS

2008 GENERAL

Travis W. Childers (D)	185,959	54.5%
Greg Davis (R)	149,818	43.9%
Wally Pang (I)	3,736	1.1%

2008 SPECIAL RUNOFF

Travis W. Childers (D)	58,037	53.8%
Greg Davis (R)	49,877	46.2%

2008 SPECIAL

Travis W. Childers (D)	33,304	49.4%
Greg Davis (R)	31,177	46.3%
Glenn L. McCullough (R)	968	1.4%
Steve Holland (D)	789	1.2%
Wally Pang (I)	725	1.1%

2008 PRIMARY RUNOFF

Travis W. Childers (D)	20,797	56.6%
Steve Holland (D)	15,958	43.4%

A devout Baptist, Childers is a social and fiscal conservative whose views align with those of many rural Democrats and moderates in his area, even if they stray far from the wishes of his party's leaders. He opposes abortion, same-sex marriage and gun control. In his first seven months in office, he split with his party almost one-third of the time on votes pitting most Democrats against most Republicans.

Democratic leaders don't hold a grudge, though. Childers (CHILL-ders) votes with them on some key issues like education and health care — more than his predecessor, Republican Roger Wicker, did. Childers won a special election in May 2008 to replace Wicker, who had been appointed to the Senate in late 2007 after serving in the House since 1995. Dismissing accusations that he is more Republican than Democrat, Childers said he's a member of the party because it "believes that everyone should have an opportunity."

Childers is a member of the Blue Dog Coalition, a group of fiscally conservative House Democrats that backed his campaign. He said he's more in line with his political idol, Jamie L. Whitten, a Democrat who represented the same area from 1941 to 1995. Whitten was a conservative appropriator who later turned against President Reagan's economic and fiscal policies. During the 111th Congress (2009-10), Blue Dogs quickly served notice they will keep a close watch on the Obama administration's expected spending on initiatives ranging from health care to the environment.

Childers did stick with his party to help pass Obama's economic stimulus plan in early 2009, even though he was one of two Democrats who voted for the Republican alternative first. (That version relied almost entirely on tax cuts, not spending.) "While it is not a perfect piece of legislation, it is necessary for uplifting hard-working families and getting our faltering economy back on track by putting Americans back to work," he said.

Childers also voted to expand the State Children's Health Insurance Program, which covers children from low-income families that do not qualify for Medicaid, helping enact a bill nearly identical to a measure President George W. Bush twice vetoed. But in January 2009, he was one of just five Democrats to oppose a measure that cleared Congress to make it easier for workers to challenge wage discrimination. And he was one of 20 Democrats to vote against a catchall $410 billion fiscal 2009 spending bill, saying its funding was "excessive under the nation's current economic crisis."

Childers sits on the Financial Services Committee, where he can work on housing legislation that benefits the rural communities scattered throughout his district. A realtor by trade, he supported a 2008 law that was intended to help 400,000 homeowners facing foreclosure and prevent troubled mortgage giants Fannie Mae and Freddie Mac from collapsing. In the fall of 2008, however, Childers opposed two $700 billion measures — the second of which became law — intended to help the ailing financial industry. He also opposed a bailout for the auto industry that failed to clear Congress.

Childers also is a member of the Agriculture Committee. The grandson of sharecroppers from Prentiss County, he said he understands the difficulties farmers have in his district. He voted for a successful override of Bush's veto of the 2008 farm bill, saying he supported its loan guarantee programs and updated farm subsidies.

A quiet back-bencher learning the ropes on Capitol Hill, Childers drew attention in September 2008 when he sponsored a proposal to roll back the District of Columbia's weapons regulations to comply with a recent Supreme

Court decision that voided the city's handgun ban. The proposal, offered as an amendment to a narrower bill by D.C. Del. Eleanor Holmes Norton, easily passed the House but stalled in the Senate. Childers was back the next year with a gun amendment to legislation to grant the District voting representation in the House. Flustered Democratic leaders yanked the bill off the floor to figure out how to deal with his proposal.

Born and raised in Booneville, Childers draws on his longtime connection to the district. He said his family has lived in the area for five generations.

Childers was 16 when his father died. He worked nights and weekends at a Booneville convenience store while in high school to help supplement his mother's income as a textile factory worker and waitress. He continued to contribute financially by working during college.

After attending Northeast Mississippi Junior College, he received a degree in business administration from the University of Mississippi in 1980 and continued work as a realtor, a license he maintains today. He and his wife, Tami, also own a nursing home and a retirement facility.

In 1991, Childers was elected Prentiss County chancery clerk, a position that encompasses many duties, including auditor and treasurer. When Wicker was appointed to replace Republican Sen. Trent Lott, Childers saw an opening to pursue higher ambitions. The GOP rolled out every big gun it could: Prominent Mississippi Republicans such as Gov. Haley Barbour, Sen. Thad Cochran and Lott supported Republican Greg Davis, and Vice President Dick Cheney also stumped on his behalf.

Democrats went to bat for Childers; the party's House campaign committee spent $2 million in independent expenditures to help him capture the seat. Childers said many members of the Blue Dogs, especially Tennessee Rep. John Tanner, also helped him across the finish line. He beat Davis by 8 percentage points. In November 2008, he expanded that margin to 11 points.

"They threw everything at me that you can throw at a human being," Childers said of the GOP. "I have operated my whole life under a pretty simple philosophy that to build myself up I never had to tear someone down."

Childers benefited from political geography. He comes from the largely rural eastern part of the district, where many voters looked askance at Davis' roots in the northwestern part of the district that has been absorbed into metropolitan Memphis.

Childers' first victory gave the Democrats their third special-election takeover victory in 2008, which marked the first time in 30 years a party had overtaken three seats from the opposing party in special elections during a single session of Congress.

KEY VOTES

2008

Yes Override Bush veto of federal farm and nutrition programs reauthorization bill

Yes Overhaul surveillance laws and permit dismissal of suits against companies that conducted warrantless wiretapping

Yes Grant mortgage relief to homeowners and funding for Fannie Mae and Freddie Mac

No Approve initial $700 billion program to stabilize financial markets

No Approve final $700 billion program to stabilize financial markets

No Provide $14 billion in loans to automakers

CQ VOTE STUDIES

	PARTY UNITY		PRESIDENTIAL SUPPORT	
	SUPPORT	OPPOSE	SUPPORT	OPPOSE
2008	68%	32%	26%	74%

INTEREST GROUPS

	AFL-CIO	ADA	CCUS	ACU
2008	83%	–	64%	41%

MISSISSIPPI 1
North — Tupelo, Southaven, Columbus

The northeastern Hill Country and rich farmland on the edge of the Delta region in northwestern Mississippi support an agricultural economy in the 1st, while manufacturing dominates in Lee County (Tupelo) and surrounding areas. Tupelo is a major producer of upholstered furniture, Columbus has some steel manufacturing and Oxford is home to the University of Mississippi.

The visitors center for the 444-mile Natchez Trace Parkway is in Tupelo. The district also includes Mississippi's entire portion of the soon-to-be-completed Interstate 22 (currently Highway 78), which will connect Memphis and Birmingham through Tupelo. In addition to infrastructure development, the area received good news when Toyota announced a new Prius plant northwest of Tupelo, but the expected 2010 opening has been pushed back as the auto industry continues to struggle. The city's status as the birthplace of Elvis Presley attracts hundreds of thousands of visitors each year and generates millions of dollars in revenue.

Desoto County, the district's most populous and Mississippi's fastest-growing, is becoming a haven for residents who commute from the 1st's northwestern corner into Memphis over the Tennessee border. Southaven and Olive Branch, both located in Desoto County, have evolved into major distribution hubs for large manufacturing companies. To the east, Marshall and Benton counties are home to many of the district's African-Americans, a group that makes up more than one-fourth of the 1st District's population.

Democrats occupied the northeastern Mississippi U.S. House seat for more than a century until Republicans took it over in 1994. Conservative Democrats can still win here, as did Rep. Travis W. Childers in 2008, but district voters now support Republicans in presidential races. John McCain took 62 percent of the 1st's 2008 presidential vote.

MAJOR INDUSTRY
Furniture, manufacturing, agriculture

MILITARY BASES
Columbus Air Force Base, 1,440 military, 399 civilian (2009)

CITIES
Tupelo, 34,211; Southaven, 28,977; Columbus, 25,944; Olive Branch, 21,054

NOTABLE
Columbus lures visitors to its historic antebellum home tours.

Rep. Bennie Thompson (D)

Elected April 1993; 8th full term

CAPITOL OFFICE
225-5876
benniethompson.house.gov
2432 Rayburn Bldg. 20515-2402; fax 225-5898

COMMITTEES
Homeland Security - chairman

RESIDENCE
Bolton

BORN
Jan. 28, 1948; Bolton, Miss.

RELIGION
United Methodist

FAMILY
Wife, London Thompson; one child

EDUCATION
Tougaloo College, B.A. 1968 (political science);
Jackson State College, M.S. 1972 (educational
administration)

CAREER
Teacher

POLITICAL HIGHLIGHTS
Bolton Board of Aldermen, 1969-73; mayor
of Bolton, 1973-79; Hinds County Board
of Supervisors, 1980-93

ELECTION RESULTS

2008 GENERAL

Bennie Thompson (D)	201,606	69.0%
Richard Cook (R)	90,364	31.0%

2008 PRIMARY

Bennie Thompson (D)	111,077	86.2%
Dorothy "Dot" Benford (D)	17,824	13.8%

2006 GENERAL

Bennie Thompson (D)	100,160	64.3%
Yvonne E. Brown (R)	55,672	35.7%

PREVIOUS WINNING PERCENTAGES
2004 (58%); 2002 (55%); 2000 (65%); 1998 (71%);
1996 (60%); 1994 (54%); 1993 Special Runoff Election
(55%)

Thompson's early experiences as a black politician in Mississippi and the makeup of his constituency — largely black, rural and poor — helped him fashion a career as a champion of civil rights and rural development. Those experiences also made him an expert at maximizing opportunities.

Although his poor Deep South district may seem an unlikely terrorist target, he is chairman of the Homeland Security Committee, having snared the senior Democratic slot on the committee when it was created in 2005. He is a staunch liberal yet runs the committee with an even-keeled temperament and willingness to listen to all sides to address a range of safety issues. All the while, he staves off competitors back home by maintaining six district offices — more than the norm — and bringing home money for special projects.

Thompson's position on Homeland brings a greater voice for Gulf Coast states, which were highly critical of the Federal Emergency Management Agency's response to hurricanes Katrina and Rita. Thompson wants to maintain oversight of the agency and has lobbied the Obama administration not to heed the wishes of House Transportation and Infrastructure Chairman James L. Oberstar and remove it from the Department of Homeland Security (DHS). "At its core, FEMA is the nucleus of preparedness and response at the department — its removal would be senseless and detrimental to our nation's security," he said in February 2009. "Let's stop wasting time debating a move that would likely set FEMA and the department back years and, instead, focus on FEMA's progress since [Hurricane Katrina in 2005] and start building on it."

Thompson also works to give his committee more clout. About 100 committees and subcommittees can claim oversight over DHS, but Thompson at the start of the 111th Congress (2009-10) persuaded House Democrats to ensure more legislation is referred to his committee than in years past.

He also started off the 111th with a strong focus on drug-related violence along the border of Mexico. He has made several visits to the region, including one in spring 2009, after which he reported progress in border security but called for more resources to bar the violence from flowing into the United States. He applauded a March 2009 plan by the Obama administration to deploy additional personnel to the border.

Another of his priorities is the Visa Waiver Program, which allows nationals from participating countries to travel to the United States without visas. His panel will oversee implementation of an electronic exit system to record and confirm the departure of each traveler who entered under the program.

Thompson also hopes to continue to push chemical plant security legislation, an effort that has drawn objections from interest groups such as the American Chemistry Council which say current regulations should be met first. Thompson said he has tried to be patient and consider all views.

Thompson overcame similar opposition from agriculture and business lobbyists to push through legislation to regulate the purchase and sale of ammonium nitrate, a fertilizer chemical that can be used in bomb-making. The lobbyists call the regulation unnecessary; Thompson ultimately pushed it into law by attaching it to a catchall fiscal 2008 spending bill that members were disinclined to oppose. "Those industries can't say that they did not have an opportunity to work with committee staff and others to work out concerns they had," Thompson said.

Early in the 110th Congress (2007-08), he pushed through the House a bill calling for new regulations, and authorizing more than $6.1 billion over four years, for rail and mass transit security. And he quickly saw House passage of his bill to implement recommendations of the Sept. 11 commission, though he was immediately criticized for not including more funding details in his rush to get the bill through. His response: "We'll work it out."

He wants to boost overall spending for homeland security, especially for local and state first-responders, and to restructure the way the Homeland Security Department contracts for goods and services.

Thompson also hopes to secure more federal funding to improve his district's infrastructure, rural housing and health care. He has called for aggressive federal action to combat discrimination, particularly in the Agriculture Department's administration of federal farm and loan programs.

He is a dependable vote, siding with his party more than 94 percent of the time on votes that pitted a majority of each party against the other during the George W. Bush administration. He opposed both versions of the administration's $700 billion proposal to aid the ailing financial services industry in fall 2008. "I know the people who, as they say, live on Main Street or Martin Luther King Boulevard, and they have not seen any measurable change in their lives since the bailout was passed," he said two months after its enactment.

He is a stronger proponent of Obama's measures to turn around the economy, backing a $787 billion economic stimulus bill. And he has a closer working relationship with Obama than he did with Bush, whom he said he never talked to during his first two years as chairman.

Born in 1948, Thompson was educated in segregated elementary and secondary schools. His father, a mechanic, died when Thompson was in the 10th grade. At Tougaloo College, he met civil rights activist Fannie Lou Hamer, who inspired him to pursue politics. He graduated in 1968, the year he made his first run for public office and, at age 20, was elected alderman in his hometown of Bolton. The town's whites didn't want a black man on the board, so they barred him from City Hall. He got a court order forcing them to back down and let him claim his seat.

Four years later he was elected mayor. Then at 32, he was elected to the board of supervisors for Hinds County, which includes the capital city, Jackson. President Clinton named Thompson as one of 100 "unsung African-Americans" at the 2004 opening of his presidential library.

He ran for the House in a 1993 special election after Rep. Mike Espy resigned to become Clinton's Agriculture secretary. Thompson triumphed in a runoff, with 55 percent of the vote. One of the candidates he defeated was Clarksdale Mayor Henry Espy, Mike Espy's brother. In his 1994 bid for a full term, he won by 15 percentage points, and his subsequent re-elections have been by comfortable margins.

KEY VOTES

2008
Yes Delay consideration of Colombia free-trade agreement
Yes Override Bush veto of federal farm and nutrition programs reauthorization bill
Yes Overhaul surveillance laws and permit dismissal of suits against companies that conducted warrantless wiretapping
Yes Grant mortgage relief to homeowners and funding for Fannie Mae and Freddie Mac
No Approve initial $700 billion program to stabilize financial markets
No Approve final $700 billion program to stabilize financial markets
Yes Provide $14 billion in loans to automakers

2007
Yes Increase minimum wage by $2.10 an hour
Yes Approve $124.2 billion in emergency war spending and set goal for redeployment of troops from Iraq
No Reject federal contraceptive assistance to international family planning groups
Yes Override Bush veto of $23.2 billion water projects authorization bill
No Implement Peru free-trade agreement
Yes Approve energy policy overhaul with new fuel economy standards
No Clear $473.5 billion omnibus spending bill, including $70 billion for military operations

CQ VOTE STUDIES

	PARTY UNITY		PRESIDENTIAL SUPPORT	
	SUPPORT	OPPOSE	SUPPORT	OPPOSE
2008	99%	1%	13%	87%
2007	98%	2%	5%	95%
2006	90%	10%	41%	59%
2005	93%	7%	17%	83%
2004	92%	8%	33%	67%

INTEREST GROUPS

	AFL-CIO	ADA	CCUS	ACU
2008	100%	90%	50%	8%
2007	88%	100%	50%	0%
2006	100%	90%	60%	30%
2005	87%	95%	52%	12%
2004	87%	85%	45%	8%

MISSISSIPPI 2

West central – Jackson, Mississippi Delta

Lying mostly west of Interstate 55 and north of Interstate 20, the 2nd combines most of Jackson, the state's capital and largest city, with Vicksburg and the nutrient-rich flatlands of the Mississippi Delta. North of Vicksburg, the road drops 15 feet in Issaquena County, marking the start of the Delta.

Agriculture is important both to the state and the district, and the 2nd supports catfish-raising and other aquaculture, cotton, rice and soybeans. The Delta's agricultural economy has promoted landowner/tenant relationships that have made the 2nd one of the nation's poorest districts, with a median household income of slightly less than $27,000.

Aside from agriculture, the 2nd's economy relies on a variety of sources. Successes include Vicksburg, where a mixture of tourism, casinos and a Mississippi River port have fostered some local prosperity. A new ethanol plant that produces more than 50 million gallons annually, one of the largest plants in the South, also calls Vicksburg home.

Outside Canton, a Nissan assembly plant north of Jackson employs about 3,400 workers, and the company plans a $118 million expansion to the facility despite job cuts and revenue losses in the auto industry.

Government, service and small-scale manufacturing jobs long kept unemployment in check in Jackson, although recent nationwide economic downturns have hurt the capital. The city is working to revitalize its downtown and recently opened a new convention center. Jackson also hosts the State Fair and annual rodeo.

Although some low-income white residents live in the 2nd, it is the only black-majority district in a state with the highest percentage of black residents in the nation. Despite a GOP foothold in some areas near Jackson and to the northeast, the 2nd was the state's only district to favor Barack Obama in the 2008 presidential election, giving him 66 percent of its vote.

MAJOR INDUSTRY
Agriculture, government, casinos

CITIES
Jackson (pt.), 152,424; Greenville, 41,633; Vicksburg, 26,407

NOTABLE
Norris Bookbinding, based in Greenwood, is the largest Bible rebinding plant in the nation.

Rep. Gregg Harper (R)

Elected 2008; 1st term

CAPITOL OFFICE
225-5031
harper.house.gov
307 Cannon Bldg. 20515-2403; fax 225-5797

COMMITTEES
Budget
House Administration
Judiciary
Joint Library

RESIDENCE
Pearl

BORN
June 1, 1956; Jackson, Miss.

RELIGION
Southern Baptist

FAMILY
Wife, Sidney Harper; two children

EDUCATION
Mississippi College, B.S. 1978 (chemistry);
U. of Mississippi, J.D. 1981

CAREER
City prosecutor; lawyer

POLITICAL HIGHLIGHTS
Rankin County Republican Party chairman,
2000-07

ELECTION RESULTS

2008 GENERAL

Gregg Harper (R)	213,171	62.5%
Joel L. Gill (D)	127,698	37.5%

2008 PRIMARY RUNOFF

Gregg Harper (R)	29,321	57.0%
Charlie Ross (R)	22,178	43.0%

2008 PRIMARY

Charlie Ross (R)	22,254	33.4%
Gregg Harper (R)	18,892	28.3%
David Landrum (R)	17,082	25.6%
John Rounsaville (R)	6,949	10.4%
Gregory W. Hatcher (R)	748	1.1%

An avid conservative, Harper never held elected office before coming to Washington. But his behind-the-scenes work in politics caught the eye of his party's leaders, who have assigned him plenty of tasks.

Harper is a former county Republican Party chairman and volunteered on a series of campaigns. He served as an observer in the recount battle in Florida following the 2000 presidential election and as a legal volunteer for President George W. Bush's 2004 re-election campaign in Ohio.

A member of the Republican Steering Committee charged with making committee assignments, he is the only freshman on the House Administration panel, which controls the House's operations. And he serves on a task force created by Minority Leader John A. Boehner to try to ensure nonpartisanship in the 2010 census, which will form the basis of how congressional districts are redrawn.

Harper ran his campaign on faith and family values and opposes abortion rights and gay marriage. He intends to push fiscal conservatism as a member of the Budget Committee. He blames the economic crisis in part on an energy policy that he said has not helped small businesses; he supports increased domestic oil drilling as well as expanded coal and nuclear power. "It's inexcusable for us not to get our natural resources," he said.

A former prosecutor, Harper also serves on the Judiciary Committee, where he plans to oppose any legislation that would allow illegal immigrants a path to citizenship. He supports efforts to tighten border security and to make English the country's official language.

Harper wants to promote research on the genetic syndrome Fragile X, which causes mental impairment and often autism. His son has Fragile X, and Harper says advocating for parents of special-needs children is particularly significant for him.

Once considered a long shot, Harper put together a strong grass-roots campaign and prevailed in a Republican primary and runoff to succeed retiring six-term GOP Rep. Charles W. "Chip" Pickering Jr. He then easily defeated Democrat Joe L. Gill to represent the largely conservative district.

MISSISSIPPI 3

East central to southwest — Jackson suburbs

The strongly Republican 3rd picks up Jackson's northeast corner and some of its mostly white northern and eastern suburbs as it sprawls across 28 counties, moving from Oktibbeha and Noxubee counties in the east central part of the state to the Mississippi River in the southwestern corner.

Timber is dominant here, but health care and defense also are key industries. Meridian is home to medical centers, a Naval Air Station and Peavey Electronics, one of the world's largest guitar and amplifier manufacturers. The district's white-collar workers provide economic stability.

Elsewhere in the district poultry and dairy farms are prevalent, and Rankin County's growth over the past two decades has been spurred by an influx of nearby Jackson resi-

dents moving to the suburbs. Pearl's minor league baseball stadium and a nearby Bass Pro Shop outdoor store anchor an entertainment complex. Natchez, on the Mississippi River, relies on tourism and attracts nearly 700,000 visitors annually to its antebellum homes and dockside casinos. Mississippi State University (MSU), the state's largest university, is located in Starkville at the district's northeastern tip.

Republicans dominate the federal politics of the 3rd, as Democrats did for most of the 20th century, and John McCain took 61 percent of the district's 2008 presidential vote.

MAJOR INDUSTRY
Timber, poultry, agriculture, defense

MILITARY BASES
Naval Air Station Meridian, 2,200 military, 1,500 civilian (2009)

CITIES
Meridian, 39,968; Jackson (pt.), 31,832

NOTABLE
MSU hosts a collection of papers from author and alumnus John Grisham.

Rep. Gene Taylor (D)

Elected October 1989; 10th full term

After two decades in the House, Taylor still has the swagger and tenacity of a young firebrand. A fiercely independent-minded Democrat known for his staunch advocacy for the military, he can be a fun-loving guy — but he also doesn't shy away from a fight.

Taylor has kept his seat in his deeply conservative district — Arizona Republican Sen. John McCain carried it by a 2-to-1 margin over Barack Obama in the 2008 presidential race — by protecting its vital shipbuilding industry as chairman of Armed Services' Seapower and Expeditionary Forces panel. He also wins plaudits for breaking with his party more often than just about every other House Democrat.

A member of the Blue Dog Coalition of fiscally conservative Democrats, Taylor is especially prone to go his own way on economic matters. He was one of just seven House members in his party to oppose President Obama's $787 billion economic stimulus package, and one of 20 to oppose a $410 billion catchall spending bill for fiscal 2009. He also was one of 17 opposing the Democrats' $3.56 trillion budget blueprint for fiscal 2010. When Obama unveiled his budget, Taylor scoffed, "Change is not running up even bigger deficits than George Bush did."

Similarly, he opposed two $700 billion measures — the second of which became law — in fall 2008 to aid the ailing financial services sector, comparing warnings about the economy's imminent collapse to inaccurate predictions about Iraq's pre-war military might. "Where have I heard this before? The Iraqis have weapons of mass destruction and they're ready to use them,'" Taylor said sarcastically. "I'm in no rush to do this."

Taylor also often sides with Republicans on energy issues, favoring a policy that includes oil drilling off the nation's coastlines, including Mississippi's Gulf Coast. And he is equally conservative on social policy: He was the only Democrat in 1998 who voted in favor of all House articles of impeachment against President Clinton, and eight years later the only Democrat to vote for four amendments that Southern Republicans offered to a bill extending the landmark 1965 Voting Rights Act. He also voted for constitutional amendments to ban same-sex marriage and flag desecration.

On Armed Services, Taylor is a strong proponent of powering new submarines, aircraft carriers and large surface combat ships through nuclear power. He also has called on the Obama administration to make sweeping changes to Navy programs to build the next generation of destroyers and small, speedy fighting vessels, saying the programs were financially crippled during President George W. Bush's tenure.

No issue involving Bush, however, angered Taylor as much as the aftermath and cleanup from Hurricane Katrina. Ever since the August 2005 storm ravaged his district, he has railed against the insurance industry and tangled with the Federal Emergency Management Agency — most memorably with the agency's chief, Michael D. Brown, who resigned in September 2005 in the wake of intense public criticism. During a hearing shortly after Katrina, Taylor accused Brown of being ignorant of the situation and woefully unprepared to respond. "You get an F-minus in my book," he said.

Katrina has had an immeasurable impact on Taylor. His coastal home, more than 100 years old and 14 feet above sea level, and his neighborhood were washed away. Working mostly on the weekends, he rebuilt the house, which now sits on pylons and is about one-third the size of the original.

Taylor has been a scourge of the insurance industry, which refused to

CAPITOL OFFICE
225-5772
www.house.gov/genetaylor
2269 Rayburn Bldg. 20515-2404; fax 225-7074

COMMITTEES
Armed Services
  (Seapower & Expeditionary Forces - chairman)
Transportation & Infrastructure

RESIDENCE
Bay St. Louis

BORN
Sept. 17, 1953; New Orleans, La.

RELIGION
Roman Catholic

FAMILY
Wife, Margaret Taylor; three children

EDUCATION
Tulane U., B.A. 1976 (history & political science); U. of Southern Mississippi, Gulf Park, attended 1978-80 (business & economics)

MILITARY SERVICE
Coast Guard Reserve, 1971-84

CAREER
Box company sales representative

POLITICAL HIGHLIGHTS
Bay St. Louis City Council, 1981-83; Miss. Senate, 1983-89; Democratic nominee for U.S. House, 1988

ELECTION RESULTS

2008 GENERAL

Gene Taylor (D)	216,542	74.5%
John McCay III (R)	73,977	25.5%

2008 PRIMARY

Gene Taylor (D)	unopposed

2006 GENERAL

Gene Taylor (D)	110,996	79.8%
Randy McDonnell (R)	28,117	20.2%

PREVIOUS WINNING PERCENTAGES
2004 (64%); 2002 (75%); 2000 (79%); 1998 (78%); 1996 (58%); 1994 (60%); 1992 (63%); 1990 (81%); 1989 Special Election Runoff (65%)

cover damage to thousands of Gulf Coast homes, including Taylor's, claiming that flooding — not wind — was responsible. And like many of his constituents, Taylor sued his insurer, State Farm, for denying his wind damage claim. "They told me I had not $1 worth [of wind damage] in a place that had eight hours of up to 100-mile-per-hour winds," he said.

On his list of priorities, improving disaster insurance coverage "would be numbers one through five as far as my constituents are concerned," he said. In 2006, he won adoption of an amendment to a flood insurance bill mandating a federal investigation into whether insurers inappropriately ascribed Katrina damages to flooding instead of excessive wind. The following year, he pushed to allow individuals and business owners to purchase optional "multi-peril" coverage against wind damage through the National Flood Insurance Program. While the House passed an overhaul of the program that included Taylor's multi-peril language, the Senate balked. He reintroduced his legislation in early 2009.

A populist who argues that working people are hurt by trade liberalization while the wealthy benefit, Taylor typically sides with his party on trade issues. He has voted against every major trade law enacted during his tenure, including the 2005 Central America Free Trade Agreement and a 2007 trade pact with Peru.

Despite his serious mien, Taylor has an easygoing side and enjoys kidding around with reporters. He once owned a gorilla costume, which he lost to the Katrina flooding, and enthusiastically celebrates Mardi Gras in Washington.

A devout Catholic, Taylor remembers the nuns at his school wheeling in a television set so students could watch the inauguration of the first Catholic president, John F. Kennedy. He was 7, he recalls, and that moment triggered his interest in politics. His father served with John D. Dingell in the Panama Canal Zone during World War II, and Dingell — now the most senior House member — later supported Taylor's first House campaign.

After graduating from Tulane in New Orleans, Taylor became a salesman for a box company. With his customers providing his political base, he won a seat on the Bay St. Louis City Council in 1981. Two years later he began a six-year turn in the state Senate.

The national Democratic Party had little interest in Taylor when he sought the seat Republican Trent Lott left open in 1988 to run for the Senate. But he surprised them with a strong, 45 percent showing against Republican Larkin Smith. Less than a year later, Smith died in a plane crash. In the special election, Taylor prevailed over Lott's longtime aide Tom Anderson Jr. and Democratic Attorney General Mike Moore. He has won with ease since.

KEY VOTES

2008

Yes Delay consideration of Colombia free-trade agreement

Yes Override Bush veto of federal farm and nutrition programs reauthorization bill

Yes Overhaul surveillance laws and permit dismissal of suits against companies that conducted warrantless wiretapping

Yes Grant mortgage relief to homeowners and funding for Fannie Mae and Freddie Mac

No Approve initial $700 billion program to stabilize financial markets

No Approve final $700 billion program to stabilize financial markets

Yes Provide $14 billion in loans to automakers

2007

Yes Increase minimum wage by $2.10 an hour

No Approve $124.2 billion in emergency war spending and set goal for redeployment of troops from Iraq

Yes Reject federal contraceptive assistance to international family planning groups

Yes Override Bush veto of $23.2 billion water projects authorization bill

No Implement Peru free-trade agreement

Yes Approve energy policy overhaul with new fuel economy standards

Yes Clear $473.5 billion omnibus spending bill, including $70 billion for military operations

CQ VOTE STUDIES

	PARTY UNITY		PRESIDENTIAL SUPPORT	
	SUPPORT	OPPOSE	SUPPORT	OPPOSE
2008	88%	12%	17%	83%
2007	74%	26%	28%	72%
2006	73%	27%	60%	40%
2005	65%	35%	45%	55%
2004	67%	33%	45%	55%

INTEREST GROUPS

	AFL-CIO	ADA	CCUS	ACU
2008	93%	75%	56%	24%
2007	48%	65%	60%	72%
2006	71%	40%	53%	68%
2005	54%	60%	59%	60%
2004	67%	60%	52%	54%

MISSISSIPPI 4

Southeast — Gulf Coast, Hattiesburg

Mississippi's only Gulf Coast district, the conservative 4th relies on shipbuilding, casinos, petrochemicals and defense-related government jobs to propel the economy in Hancock, Harrison and Jackson counties. The University of Southern Mississippi and Camp Shelby, a large military reserves training facility, bring thousands of people to Hattiesburg. Rural communities to the north support a thriving poultry industry.

The district's coastal counties suffered catastrophic damage in 2005 when Hurricane Katrina displaced 100,000 residents and left more than one-fifth of the region's population unemployed. Billions of dollars in federal recovery assistance supported homebuilding, infrastructure redevelopment and job creation, and the coastal population has returned to near pre-Katrina levels.

Northrop Grumman Ship Systems employs more than 12,000 Jackson County residents. Mississippi's Gulf Coast has blossomed into a major hub for the U.S. aerospace industry, and NASA's John C. Stennis Space Center in Hancock is a rocket propulsion testing site that hosts Lockheed

Martin, Pratt & Whitney Rocketdyne and federal agency facilities.

Harrison County, the nation's third-largest gaming destination, draws tourists to its 11 casinos, which have fully recovered since Hurricane Katrina forced closures in 2005. Gulfport, the district's largest city, has planned a $12 million project to restore 80 downtown buildings, and construction is underway on a new $700 million casino in Biloxi.

A Democrat holds the 4th's U.S. House seat, and residents will support conservatives of either party. In the 2008 presidential election, John McCain took 67 percent of the vote, his best showing statewide.

MAJOR INDUSTRY
Military, shipbuilding, casinos

MILITARY BASES
Keesler Air Force Base, 6,900 military, 3,300 civilian (2008); Naval Construction Training Center Gulfport, 3,664 military, 799 civilian (2008); Naval Oceanographic Office, 59 military, 941 civilian (2008)

CITIES
Gulfport, 71,127; Biloxi, 50,644; Hattiesburg, 44,779; Pascagoula, 26,200

NOTABLE
Black Creek is the state's only National Scenic River.

MISSOURI

Gov. Jay Nixon (D)

First elected: 2008
Length of term: 4 years
Term expires: 1/13
Salary: $120,087
Phone: (573) 751-3222

Residence: Jefferson City
Born: February 13, 1956; DeSoto, Mo.
Religion: Methodist
Family: Wife, Georganne Wheeler Nixon; two children
Education: U. of Missouri, B.A. 1978 (political science); J.D. 1981
Career: Lawyer
Political highlights: Mo. Senate, 1987-93; Democratic nominee for U.S. Senate, 1988; Mo. attorney general, 1993-2009; Democratic nominee for U.S. Senate, 1998

Election results:

2008 GENERAL
Jay Nixon (D)	1,680,611	58.4%
Kenny Hulshof (R)	1,136,364	39.5%
Andrew W. Finkenstadt (LIBERT)	31,850	1.1%
Gregory E. Thompson (CNSTP)	28,941	1.0%

Lt. Gov. Peter Kinder (R)

First elected: 2004
Length of term: 4 years
Term expires: 1/13
Salary: $77,184
Phone: (573) 751-4727

LEGISLATURE

General Assembly: January-May

Senate: 34 members, 4-year terms
2009 ratios: 23 R, 11 D; 26 men, 8 women
Salary: $35,915
Phone: (573) 751-3766

House: 163 members, 2-year terms
2009 ratios: 89 R, 74 D; 130 men, 33 women
Salary: $35,915
Phone: (573) 751-3659

TERM LIMITS

Governor: 2 terms
Senate: 2 terms
House: 4 terms

URBAN STATISTICS

CITY	POPULATION
Kansas City	441,545
St. Louis	348,189
Springfield	151,580
Independence	113,288
Columbia	84,531

REGISTERED VOTERS

Voters do not register by party.

POPULATION

2008 population (est.)	5,911,605
2000 population	5,595,211
1990 population	5,117,073
Percent change (1990-2000)	+9.3%
Rank among states (2008)	18

Median age	36.1
Born in state	67.8%
Foreign born	2.7%
Violent crime rate	490/100,000
Poverty level	11.7%
Federal workers	57,783
Military	38,091

ELECTIONS

STATE ELECTION OFFICIAL
(573) 751-2301
DEMOCRATIC PARTY
(573) 636-5241
REPUBLICAN PARTY
(573) 636-3146

MISCELLANEOUS

Web: www..mo.gov
Capital: Jefferson City

U.S. CONGRESS

Senate: 1 Democrat, 1 Republican
House: 5 Republicans, 4 Democrats

2000 Census Statistics by District

DIST.	2008 VOTE FOR PRESIDENT OBAMA	MCCAIN	WHITE	BLACK	ASIAN	HISP	MEDIAN INCOME	WHITE COLLAR	BLUE COLLAR	SERVICE INDUSTRY	OVER 64	UNDER 18	COLLEGE EDUCATION	RURAL	SQ. MILES
1	80%	19%	46%	50%	2%	1%	$36,314	62%	21%	17%	14%	26%	22%	1%	217
2	44	55	93	2	2	1	$61,416	71	18	11	11	27	38	8	1,248
3	60	39	86	9	2	2	$41,091	60	24	15	13	25	23	13	1,247
4	38	61	92	3	1	2	$34,541	51	33	16	14	25	16	60	14,544
5	63	36	66	24	1	6	$38,311	62	23	15	13	26	23	4	512
6	45	54	92	3	1	2	$41,225	59	27	15	13	25	21	34	13,032
7	35	63	93	1	1	3	$32,929	55	29	16	14	24	19	41	5,480
8	36	62	92	4	0	1	$27,865	48	36	16	16	25	12	60	18,681
9	44	55	93	4	1	1	$36,693	54	31	15	13	25	20	54	13,925
STATE	49.3	49.4	84	11	1	2	$37,934	58	27	15	14	26	22	31	68,886
U.S.	53	46	69	12	4	13	$41,994	60	25	15	12	26	24	21	3,537,438

Sen. Christopher S. Bond (R)

Elected 1986; 4th term

CAPITOL OFFICE
224-5721
bond.senate.gov
274 Russell Bldg. 20510-2503; fax 224-8149

COMMITTEES
Appropriations
Environment & Public Works
Small Business & Entrepreneurship
Select Intelligence - vice chairman

RESIDENCE
Mexico

BORN
March 6, 1939; St. Louis, Mo.

RELIGION
Presbyterian

FAMILY
Wife, Linda Bond; one child

EDUCATION
Princeton U., A.B. 1960; U. of Virginia, LL.B. 1963

CAREER
Lawyer

POLITICAL HIGHLIGHTS
Republican nominee for U.S. House, 1968;
Mo. auditor, 1971-73; governor, 1973-77;
defeated for re-election as governor, 1976;
governor, 1981-85

ELECTION RESULTS

2004 GENERAL

Christopher S. Bond (R)	1,518,089	56.1%
Nancy Farmer (D)	1,158,261	42.8%

2004 PRIMARY

Christopher S. Bond (R)	541,998	88.1%
Mike Steger (R)	73,354	11.9%

PREVIOUS WINNING PERCENTAGES
1998 (53%); 1992 (52%); 1986 (53%)

Bond navigates two different worlds. As the Select Intelligence Committee's top Republican, he is an unwavering supporter of overseas military efforts and a critic of Democratic initiatives he considers insufficient in fighting terrorism. But as a senior member of the Appropriations Committee, the collegial, cigar-puffing Bond happily cuts deals across the aisle.

Bond — known by his nickname, "Kit" — has established himself so proficiently in each arena that some of his closest supporters were startled in January 2009 when he announced he wouldn't seek a fifth term in 2010. That decision will bring to a close a 40-year career that has made him his state's pre-eminent GOP power broker. "In 1972, I became Missouri's youngest governor," he said. "I do not aspire to become Missouri's oldest senator."

He showed his dual persona in the weeks that followed his retirement announcement. Bond called on Democrats not to forget the lessons of the Sept. 11 terrorist attacks and denounced President Obama's decision to close the controversial detention facility at Guantánamo Bay, Cuba. Meanwhile, he joined most Senate Republicans in opposing Obama's $787 billion economic stimulus bill — but not before backing a Democratic amendment to boost highway spending and joining three Democrats to add tax breaks for motorcycle buyers.

During the latter years of George W. Bush's administration, Bond had served as Senate point man for its efforts in Iraq and was a staunch defender of the administration's secret warrantless surveillance program. He was a fierce critic of Iraq's former leader Saddam Hussein, causing a stir in 1998 by proposing repeal of an executive branch policy barring U.S. intelligence agencies from sponsoring or carrying out political assassinations.

During the 110th Congress (2007-08), he often sparred with Intelligence Chairman John D. Rockefeller IV of West Virginia. When Rockefeller and other Democrats issued a report in June 2008 accusing President Bush of making claims about the case for war that intelligence reports couldn't substantiate, Bond and other Republicans accused Democrats of politicizing their work, shielding Democrats' own statements from scrutiny and shifting the focus of their investigation. He and Rockefeller were unable to get into law an annual bill authorizing spy programs. With the committee's support, Bond backed an unspecified "technology demonstration program" in the field of "imagery" — spy satellites — in 2008, only to meet with strong resistance from the Bush administration.

The war and issues related to gathering intelligence are personal for Bond. His only child, Sam, is a Marine Corps intelligence officer who deployed to Iraq for a second time in 2007.

Bond's high profile on spy issues is a leap from his former focus on the parochial concerns of Missouri and the work that had previously consumed him on Appropriations. He is known for the amount of money he sends to Missouri, particularly for roads, highways and water projects, often over the objections of budget conservatives in his party.

When critics in 2008 attacked such projects as "pork barrel spending," he quipped, "In the next batch, I'll bring my own barbecue sauce." In fiscal 2008, his earmark total of $454.6 million ranked him fourth among senators, according to Taxpayers for Common Sense.

He is the top Republican on the Appropriations panel on housing and highway spending. And he sits on the Environment and Public Works Committee, which will be working on a renewal of the 2005 surface transportation bill. He led a pack of Senate Republicans who locked horns with the White House over the 2005 version, pushing for a more expensive alternative.

Though typically a conservative, Bond is a moderate on some spending issues. He fought Bush's attempts to cut Community Development Block Grants in the 2006 budget and opposed a plan to gut HOPE, a housing program Bond helped create in 1990 that provides money to demolish blighted public housing. He was a chief sponsor of legislation that created the 1993 Family and Medical Leave Act.

Bond's efforts have endeared him to some Democrats. Fellow appropriator Barbara A. Mikulski of Maryland once described him as "very concerned about people who need extra help." He regularly dines with his Missouri colleague Claire McCaskill, even though he campaigned on her opponent's behalf in 2006.

Though sometimes gruff, Bond tries to stay on good terms with journalists; after the St. Louis Post-Dispatch published a story about Missouri chestnuts in 2008, he sent the reporter a bag of them from his farm.

A booster of the National Guard, Bond in 2006 joined Vermont Democrat Patrick J. Leahy in winning approval of almost $3 billion in a Defense spending bill to replenish Guard equipment used or destroyed in Iraq and Afghanistan and to buy new gear. Two years later, he and Leahy blasted an expert commission's recommendation to subordinate leaders of the Army National Guard and Air National Guard to their respective chiefs of staff; they argued it would undermine the Guard's power.

In 2002, the divorced Bond made GOP political consultant Linda Pell his second wife. The pair share a comfortable existence in a $2.2 million house they purchased in an exclusive section of Washington in 2005.

He has a reputation as energetic and strongly pro-business — he once chaired the Small Business and Entrepreneurship Committee and still serves on the panel — yet has been unable to translate his efforts into a leadership post. He lost three attempts to chair the Senate GOP caucus.

When Congress overhauled election laws in 2002, the bill contained his provision requiring voters to show proof of residence before casting a ballot. It was intended to fix problems like those found in 2000 in St. Louis, where thousands of voters had registered in more than one place. But some saw it as a racist impediment to minority voters. Bond negotiated with Democrats for six months on a compromise.

Bond was born into an affluent family that made its fortune in brick manufacturing. For college, it was Princeton, and after that, the University of Virginia for law school, where he graduated first in his class.

He won his first statewide race, for auditor, in 1970 at age 31. Two years later, he became Missouri's first Republican governor since World War II. In his first term, Democrats in the legislature found him aloof, and Republicans chafed at his efforts to abolish patronage jobs. He lost his bid for re-election in 1976 to Democrat Joseph P. Teasdale. But in 1980, Bond came back and avenged that loss, helped by President Reagan's coattails.

He faced Democratic Lt. Gov. Harriett Woods in a bitter 1986 contest for the Senate seat being vacated by Democrat Thomas F. Eagleton. Bond ran as a budget-conscious conservative and won with 53 percent of the vote. His victory margins in his next three re-election races were more comfortable.

In announcing his decision to retire from the Senate, Bond denied ethical concerns were a factor. In 2008, a government watchdog group filed an ethics complaint against him in the wake of a Justice Department report contending Bond's staff was behind the 2006 removal of a Missouri federal prosecutor. Two months later, a former aide to Bond and Missouri GOP Rep. Roy Blunt who also worked for disgraced lobbyist Jack Abramoff, pleaded guilty to failing to report thousands of dollars in illegal gifts from lobbyists.

KEY VOTES

2008

Yes Prohibit discrimination based on genetic information
Yes Reauthorize farm and nutrition programs for five years
No   Limit debate on "cap and trade" system for greenhouse gas emissions
No   Allow lawsuits against companies that participated in warrantless wiretapping
No   Limit debate on a bill to block a scheduled cut in Medicare payments to doctors
?   Grant mortgage relief to homeowners and funding for Fannie Mae and Freddie Mac
Yes Approve a nuclear cooperation agreement with India
Yes Approve final $700 billion program to stabilize financial markets
Yes Allow consideration of a $14 billion auto industry loan package

2007

Yes Increase minimum wage by $2.10 an hour
No   Limit debate on a comprehensive immigration bill
Yes Overhaul congressional lobbying and ethics rules for members and their staffs
No   Limit debate on considering a bill to add House seats for the District of Columbia and Utah
No   Limit debate on restoring habeas corpus rights to detainees
No   Mandate minimum breaks for troops between deployments to Iraq or Afghanistan
Yes Override Bush veto of $23.2 billion water projects authorization bill
Yes Confirm Michael B. Mukasey as attorney general
No   Limit debate on an energy policy overhaul containing $21.8 billion in tax incentives and reduced oil and gas subsidies

CQ VOTE STUDIES

	PARTY UNITY		PRESIDENTIAL SUPPORT	
	SUPPORT	OPPOSE	SUPPORT	OPPOSE
2008	92%	8%	78%	22%
2007	82%	18%	80%	20%
2006	91%	9%	89%	11%
2005	94%	6%	93%	7%
2004	94%	6%	92%	8%
2003	97%	3%	97%	3%
2002	89%	11%	98%	2%
2001	94%	6%	99%	1%
2000	96%	4%	46%	54%
1999	93%	7%	34%	66%

INTEREST GROUPS

	AFL-CIO	ADA	CCUS	ACU
2008	33%	20%	100%	75%
2007	21%	25%	100%	83%
2006	7%	5%	92%	80%
2005	21%	0%	100%	88%
2004	42%	20%	100%	96%
2003	8%	5%	100%	80%
2002	15%	10%	100%	84%
2001	19%	10%	93%	88%
2000	0%	0%	100%	92%
1999	0%	0%	94%	84%

Sen. Claire McCaskill (D)

Elected 2006; 1st term

CAPITOL OFFICE
224-6154
mccaskill.senate.gov
717 Hart Bldg. 20510-2505; fax 228-6326

COMMITTEES
Armed Services
Commerce, Science & Transportation
Homeland Security & Governmental Affairs
(Contracting Oversight - chairwoman)
Special Aging

RESIDENCE
Kirkwood

BORN
July 24, 1953; Rolla, Mo.

RELIGION
Roman Catholic

FAMILY
Husband, Joseph Shepard; seven children

EDUCATION
U. of Missouri, B.A. 1975 (political science),
J.D. 1978

CAREER
Lawyer; city prosecutor

POLITICAL HIGHLIGHTS
Mo. House, 1983-89; sought Democratic
nomination for Jackson County prosecutor, 1988;
Jackson County Legislature, 1991-93; Jackson
County prosecutor, 1993-99; Mo. auditor, 1999-2007;
Democratic nominee for governor, 2004

ELECTION RESULTS

2006 GENERAL

Claire McCaskill (D)	1,055,255	49.6%
Jim Talent (R)	1,006,941	47.3%
Frank Gilmour (LIBERT)	47,792	2.2%

2006 PRIMARY

Claire McCaskill (D)	282,767	80.8%
Bill Clinton Young (D)	67,173	19.2%

McCaskill is a centrist who has earned a reputation as a white-hat sheriff of the Senate, focusing on oversight and ethical issues and writing laws that aim to increase transparency and accountability in government. It is a passion she shares with a good friend who's gone on to bigger things.

As a freshman senator, Illinois Democrat Barack Obama made several trips to Missouri in 2006 to help McCaskill win her uphill Senate battle against GOP incumbent Jim Talent. It was then that she first urged Obama to run for president. They became close Senate colleagues — working together on ethics reform and correcting problems at Walter Reed Army Medical Center — and eventually she gave Obama a pivotal endorsement, becoming the first Democratic woman in the Senate to back him in the primaries against then-New York Sen. Hillary Rodham Clinton. She has been an adviser and confidante to both the president and his wife, Michelle, serving as their surrogate and defender on talk shows and at campaign events.

McCaskill was mentioned as a possibility in the vice presidential and Cabinet nomination guessing games, but demurred. "I'm the first one of my partisan stripe in a long time to serve in the United States Senate from Missouri," she told the St. Louis Post-Dispatch in late 2008. "I feel a special obligation to continue in the Senate."

That isn't likely to diminish her newfound clout. "There are very few people who are closer to me, who I have relied on more for counsel or advice," Obama told the Post-Dispatch in June 2008. "Should I be successful, she will be somebody who has the utmost access to the Obama administration."

On the other hand, McCaskill isn't afraid to buck Obama. When the new president waived his own ethics rules to nominate William Lynn, a former lobbyist for defense contractor Raytheon Co., as deputy secretary of Defense, McCaskill cast the only Democratic vote against Lynn's confirmation. A former auditor and prosecutor, she has pursued accountability and transparency on two high-profile committees: Armed Services and Homeland Security and Governmental Affairs, where she works as easily with Republicans as with Democrats. In the 111th Congress (2009-10), Homeland Security Chairman Joseph I. Lieberman, a Connecticut independent, put her in charge of a new panel on contracting oversight that he created to examine a half-trillion dollars a year in federal contracts across the entire government.

McCaskill was already deeply involved in the pursuit of fraud and abuse in war-related contracting. With fellow freshman Democrat Jim Webb of Virginia, she secured in 2007 an amendment to the fiscal 2008 defense authorization act that created a latter-day version of the Truman Committee, which uncovered profiteering during World War II. Joined by Webb and Republican Susan Collins of Maine, McCaskill in February 2009 attended the inaugural meeting of the Commission on Wartime Contracting to urge an aggressive investigation of what she called a "massive failure" of accountability.

Collaborating with Collins, the top Republican on the Homeland Security panel, McCaskill helped shepherd into law in 2008 a measure designed to insulate the federal government's inspectors general from political influence. It required the president to alert Congress of the reasons for any dismissals of inspectors general, and it increased their autonomy.

She persuaded the Armed Services Committee to make its earmarks and their authors public in reports published with the defense policy bill. She was among the minority of senators who renounced earmarks — funding set-asides for special projects — and espoused a one-year freeze on all earmarking.

And when the committee voted in favor of several of President George W. Bush's nominees for senior military posts in the 110th Congress (2007-08), it was over the objection of McCaskill, defying the customary deference senators show presidents on all but their most controversial nominees. She alone voted against Gen. Duncan J. McNabb to head U.S. Transportation Command because of her concerns about his reported role in the Air Force's spending of counterterrorism funds on amenities for generals' jetliners.

As a red-state Democrat, McCaskill split with her party more often in the 110th than all but three other Democrats on votes that divided the two parties. She has emerged as a key centrist on economic issues, pushing her party and her president to compromise with Republicans. She has maintained a skeptical approach to federal spending.

She voted in 2008 for the $700 billion rescue package for the financial sector, but only reluctantly. "This bill stinks," she said on her Web site, "but the alternative is much worse." Early the next year, she was one of two Democrats voting for a GOP amendment to the $410 billion catchall fiscal 2009 appropriations bill that would have frozen spending at prior-year levels. And she joined other centrists in both parties to trim more than $100 billion from what ultimately became a $787 billion economic stimulus package.

McCaskill also sits on the Commerce, Science and Transportation Committee, a post she uses to look out for consumer interest. And she serves on the Special Aging Committee — a good fit, as her state has a large senior population. She works on improving hospital care for veterans and easing the senior population's transition from analog to digital television. In 2007, she supported a House-passed bill that would have allowed the government to negotiate prescription drug prices for seniors.

McCaskill comes from a politically active family. Her father served as state insurance director, and her mother was the first woman to serve on the Columbia City Council. She recalls going to political events wearing sashes and "those obnoxious foam little bowler hats" to advertise candidates' campaigns. She caught the political bug, particularly after a teacher urged her to become a lawyer, noting she was better at arguing than she was at subjects that had obvious right and wrong answers.

After graduating from the University of Missouri and its law school, she clerked for the Missouri Court of Appeals and soon got a job as an assistant prosecutor in Kansas City, specializing in sex crime, homicide and arson cases. In 1982, she won a seat in the Missouri House, where she wrote the state's first minimum-sentencing law for repeat offenders. McCaskill was elected Jackson County prosecutor on her second try in 1992, becoming the first woman to hold the office. She focused on punishing domestic violence and created a drug court to help non-violent offenders seek treatment. Six years later, she was elected state auditor, where she examined waste — such as a stash of $1 million worth of state-owned computers that had never been used — and ineffective programs, such as the state's troubled foster care system.

In 2004, McCaskill took on the Democratic Party establishment by defeating the incumbent governor, Bob Holden, in the primary. She lost the general election to Republican Matt Blunt, the son of then-House Minority Whip Roy Blunt, by just less than 3 percentage points.

Party leaders urged McCaskill to make one more run for higher office in 2006, this time against incumbent Talent. She campaigned hard to win over the rural voters she had lost in the governor's race, and she criticized Talent relentlessly for failing to ask tough questions of the Bush administration on the Iraq War. She also was aided by the popularity of a ballot initiative to expand embryonic stem cell research, which she supported and Talent opposed. McCaskill won by a little more than 2 percentage points, helping Democrats gain control of the Senate.

KEY VOTES

2008
Yes Prohibit discrimination based on genetic information
Yes Reauthorize farm and nutrition programs for five years
Yes Limit debate on "cap and trade" system for greenhouse gas emissions
No Allow lawsuits against companies that participated in warrantless wiretapping
Yes Limit debate on a bill to block a scheduled cut in Medicare payments to doctors
Yes Grant mortgage relief to homeowners and funding for Fannie Mae and Freddie Mac
Yes Approve a nuclear cooperation agreement with India
Yes Approve final $700 billion program to stabilize financial markets
Yes Allow consideration of a $14 billion auto industry loan package

2007
Yes Increase minimum wage by $2.10 an hour
No Limit debate on a comprehensive immigration bill
Yes Overhaul congressional lobbying and ethics rules for members and their staffs
Yes Limit debate on considering a bill to add House seats for the District of Columbia and Utah
Yes Limit debate on restoring habeas corpus rights to detainees
Yes Mandate minimum breaks for troops between deployments to Iraq or Afghanistan
No Override Bush veto of $23.2 billion water projects authorization bill
No Confirm Michael B. Mukasey as attorney general
Yes Limit debate on an energy policy overhaul containing $21.8 billion in tax incentives and reduced oil and gas subsidies

CQ VOTE STUDIES

	PARTY UNITY		PRESIDENTIAL SUPPORT	
	SUPPORT	OPPOSE	SUPPORT	OPPOSE
2008	81%	19%	45%	55%
2007	81%	19%	41%	59%

INTEREST GROUPS

	AFL-CIO	ADA	CCUS	ACU
2008	90%	80%	75%	20%
2007	95%	90%	9%	8%

Rep. William Lacy Clay (D)

Elected 2000; 5th term

CAPITOL OFFICE
225-2406
lacyclay.house.gov
2418 Rayburn Bldg. 20515-2501; fax 225-1725

COMMITTEES
Financial Services
Oversight & Government Reform
  (Information Policy, Census & National Archives
  - chairman)

RESIDENCE
St. Louis

BORN
July 27, 1956; St. Louis, Mo.

RELIGION
Roman Catholic

FAMILY
Separated; two children

EDUCATION
U. of Maryland, B.S. 1983 (government & politics)

CAREER
Paralegal; real estate agent; congressional aide

POLITICAL HIGHLIGHTS
Mo. House, 1983-91; Mo. Senate, 1991-2000

ELECTION RESULTS

2008 GENERAL

William Lacy Clay (D)	242,570	86.9%
Robb E. Cunningham (LIBERT)	36,700	13.1%

2008 PRIMARY

William Lacy Clay (D)	unopposed

2006 GENERAL

William Lacy Clay (D)	141,574	72.9%
Mark J. Byrne (R)	47,893	24.7%
Robb E. Cunningham (LIBERT)	4,768	2.5%

PREVIOUS WINNING PERCENTAGES
2004 (75%); 2002 (70%); 2000 (75%)

A second-generation congressman from St. Louis, Clay shares the liberal views of his father, William L. Clay — an African-American political pioneer who served in the House for 32 years — but strongly touts his independence. He has devoted considerable energy to opening the public's access to government documents, and is at the forefront of congressional efforts to oversee the 2010 census.

In his fifth term, Clay never has dipped below 94 percent in voting with Democrats on legislation in which a majority of the party diverged from Republicans. He has been amenable to President Obama's legislative plans, backing Obama's $787 billion economic stimulus legislation in January 2009 as well as a subsequent $410 billion catchall spending bill for fiscal 2009. "This is the most serious economic emergency since the Great Depression, and the American people expect us to act without delay," Clay said in supporting the stimulus.

But his independent streak was clear in the fall of 2008 when he turned aside a personal appeal from Obama, then the Democratic presidential nominee, and voted against a $700 billion financial rescue plan for Wall Street. His constituents "don't think it's right. They have paid their bills on time. They haven't gotten into risky mortgages," said Clay, a Financial Services Committee member. In March 2009 he criticized the program set up under the law "for largely failing to unfreeze the credit market and allow credit-worthy businesses to access credit on reasonable terms."

Clay also has occasionally deviated from Democratic orthodoxy on free trade, supporting a 2007 deal with Peru, even after he voted against a similar pact with Central American countries in 2005. And as Democrats took charge of the House in 2007, he was one of just 21 in his party to vote against their leaders' lobbying and ethics overhaul package. He said the bill, which became law, would "mandate unprecedented levels of record-keeping and disclosure that are more burdensome than productive."

In his role as chairman of the Oversight and Government Reform panel on public information and the census, Clay has aggressively pushed the executive branch to adopt open-government policies, the issue on which he has done his most-successful legislating.

Over the objections of the George W. Bush administration, Clay won House passage in March 2007 of legislation to stop former presidents and vice presidents from shielding their records from the public. The legislation would have upended Bush's executive order of 2001, aimed at protecting some of his father's records, that allowed former Oval Office occupants and their successors to keep certain documents secret.

Another House-passed bill that emerged from Clay's subcommittee would require presidential libraries to disclose the identities of big donors. Both measures stalled in the Senate. Undeterred, Clay pushed them through the House again in early 2009; Obama also reversed the 2001 order one day into his presidency.

Clay's persistence on open government paid off late in 2007 when Bush agreed to tighten the timeline by which executive branch agencies must respond to Freedom of Information Act requests. In the past, requestors from the public or media had sometimes waited years for responses. The law now requires agencies to respond to such requests within 20 business days and to establish a system for tracking the requests. "Nothing undermines public confidence as much as obstruction and obsessive secrecy," Clay said.

The census is Clay's foremost concern during the 111th Congress (2009-10). He believes the Census Bureau routinely leaves poor people and minorities out of its count and has vowed to ensure that it never happens again. An accurate count is crucial because it determines the number of representatives each state has in the House as well as funding levels for a variety of federal programs. Clay began the 111th with a series of hearings examining the bureau's strategy for getting the count right, while pressuring the bureau to expand its outreach campaign to minority communities.

Clay has been active in an effort among African-American members to get more earmarks — funding set-asides for special projects in their districts or home states — in response to data that showed minority representatives lagged in receiving such federal money. He has worked for economic development in urban St. Louis County, where crime, the loss of manufacturing jobs and troubled public schools have led to a steady population loss.

Clay is an avid cook and a golf fanatic, but his mother told a local newspaper that politics "has been his life. That's the only thing he knows." He was 12 when his father was elected to Congress, and he spent his teenage years in suburban Maryland, attending high school in Silver Spring and college at the University of Maryland. To pay for college, Clay was a House doorman for six years. The hours he spent watching the action from the cloakrooms and the Speaker's Lobby gave him ample insight into the ways of Congress.

He was starting law school when an opening in the Missouri House led him back to St. Louis to run in a special election. He spent 17 years in the General Assembly, serving eight years in the House before winning a 1991 special election for a state Senate vacancy. He supplemented his part-time legislator's salary by working in real estate and as a paralegal.

In Jefferson City, Clay helped push through measures benefiting welfare recipients, imposing penalties for hate crimes, and creating tax breaks for those saving for education and homeownership. When the Ku Klux Klan said its members would "adopt" a stretch of Interstate 55 to keep it clean, Clay orchestrated legislative action to name that segment of the road after civil rights icon Rosa Parks.

Clay was the presumed heir to the 1st District seat from the moment his father announced his retirement in 1999. The younger Clay both embraced his father and declared his independence when he entered the race to succeed him. He won election easily in 2000 with 75 percent of the vote. Even after the district was altered some in decennial redistricting, he has had no problems winning re-election. Clay won his first re-election with 70 percent in 2002 and took 87 percent in 2008.

KEY VOTES

2008

Yes Delay consideration of Colombia free-trade agreement

Yes Override Bush veto of federal farm and nutrition programs reauthorization bill

No Overhaul surveillance laws and permit dismissal of suits against companies that conducted warrantless wiretapping

Yes Grant mortgage relief to homeowners and funding for Fannie Mae and Freddie Mac

No Approve initial $700 billion program to stabilize financial markets

No Approve final $700 billion program to stabilize financial markets

Yes Provide $14 billion in loans to automakers

2007

Yes Increase minimum wage by $2.10 an hour

Yes Approve $124.2 billion in emergency war spending and set goal for redeployment of troops from Iraq

No Reject federal contraceptive assistance to international family planning groups

Yes Override Bush veto of $23.2 billion water projects authorization bill

Yes Implement Peru free-trade agreement

Yes Approve energy policy overhaul with new fuel economy standards

No Clear $473.5 billion omnibus spending bill, including $70 billion for military operations

CQ VOTE STUDIES

	PARTY UNITY		PRESIDENTIAL SUPPORT	
	SUPPORT	OPPOSE	SUPPORT	OPPOSE
2008	97%	3%	11%	89%
2007	99%	1%	4%	96%
2006	94%	6%	28%	72%
2005	96%	4%	16%	84%
2004	97%	3%	24%	76%

INTEREST GROUPS

	AFL-CIO	ADA	CCUS	ACU
2008	100%	100%	47%	8%
2007	100%	95%	61%	4%
2006	93%	90%	67%	16%
2005	92%	85%	44%	21%
2004	87%	100%	35%	8%

MISSOURI 1

North St. Louis; northeast St. Louis County

Flanked by the Mississippi and Missouri rivers, the heavily Democratic, St. Louis-based 1st is a mixture of poor urban neighborhoods, middle-class suburbs and a business district that once was the center of one of the five largest cities in the United States.

The 1st takes in the northern half of St. Louis, including many of the city's popular attractions, such as the Gateway Arch and Forest Park, which attracts more than 12 million visitors a year and is about 500 acres larger than New York's Central Park. Major area employers, such as Boeing, BJC HealthCare — one of the largest nonprofit health care organizations in the nation — and Monsanto, are scattered throughout the 1st.

Suburbs in St. Louis County include the region's main airport. Once one of the nation's 10 busiest, Lambert International Airport's ranking has dropped significantly in the last decade. A Ford SUV assembly plant in Hazelwood closed in 2006, eliminating nearly 1,500 local jobs, but local officials hope to begin developing the land into a commercial and light-industrial business park by mid-2009.

By far the state's most heavily Democratic district, the 1st gave Barack Obama 80 percent of its vote in the 2008 presidential election. Roughly half of the district's population is black, and local and state contests almost always favor Democrats.

St. Louis hemorrhaged 60 percent of its population between 1950 and 2006. Frustrated by failing schools and aging housing stock, residents were lured to suburbia, where seemingly endless acres were converted from farmland. But revival in downtown neighborhoods and population growth outpacing that of the metropolitan area as a whole indicate at least some success by the developers and lawmakers who have poured billions of dollars into downtown redevelopment projects, including a new stadium for baseball's St. Louis Cardinals.

MAJOR INDUSTRY
Aircraft and other manufacturing, health care, higher education

CITIES
St. Louis (pt.), 163,020; Florissant, 50,497; Hazelwood, 26,206; University City (pt.), 24,075; Ferguson, 22,406

NOTABLE
The first suit filed by Dred Scott was tried in St Louis' historic Old Courthouse, now part of Jefferson National Expansion Memorial Park.

Rep. Todd Akin (R)

Elected 2000; 5th term

Akin's conservatism takes him to the far right of his party. And with an expanded Democratic majority in Congress and a Democrat in the White House, he doesn't plan on changing direction — he remains a loyal Republican with no signs of giving an inch on fiscal, social or military issues.

A member of the Republican Study Committee, the coalition of the House's most conservative members, Akin sides nearly all of the time with his party on votes that split a majority of Democrats against Republicans. His departures come when he thinks party leaders aren't conservative enough, such as on federal funding.

In a January 2009 Washington Times opinion column, he thanked departing President George W. Bush for "outstanding decision-making on a number of essential issues," including a foreign policy that "blended the soft partnership of daring to dream of a better world with the muscular condemnation and opposition of evil." He was among the cosponsors of a 2005 effort to put Ronald Reagan's likeness on the $50 bill.

Akin voted against a February 2009 bill, signed into law by President Obama, to expand the State Children's Health Insurance Program, which that provides health care to children from low-income families that do not qualify for Medicaid. He then voted twice against Obama's economic stimulus plan, which became law later that month.

Before the initial vote on the bill, which included funding for a range of infrastructure projects as well as health care and environmental programs, Akin said on the House floor: "So basically what you're doing is, you're taking these entitlement programs and you're inflating them and you're increasing the rate at which essentially the government is going to grow beyond the ability of the American taxpayer or the economy to finance it." He said it all smacked of "socialism" to him.

Akin also opposed Bush's $700 billion measure, which became law in the fall of 2008, aimed at helping the ailing financial services industry. A member of the Small Business Committee, Akin said the plan would do nothing to help small-business owners. Later that year, he opposed a $14 billion bill to aid struggling U.S. automakers — a measure that stalled in the Senate, though Bush later granted some emergency loans.

His positions on social policy are consistent: He favors restricting abortion and toughening enforcement of obscenity laws, and he steadfastly opposes same-sex marriage and gun control. His six children have been home-schooled and he wants to give parents more choice in the schools their children attend.

Akin is a staunch defender of the Iraq War, where his oldest son, Marine Lt. Perry Akin, served two stints as a combat engineer. "I pray every night for the troops," Akin told the St. Louis Post-Dispatch in July 2007. "But there's a little motivation to pray extra hard when it's your son."

But Akin was not blindly supportive of the Bush administration's war policy. As the top-ranking Republican on the Oversight and Investigations panel of the Armed Services Committee during the 110th Congress (2007-08), he criticized his own party for not overseeing the war effectively. He also said the administration had conducted the war "on the cheap." Shifting off of the investigations panel in 2009, Akin is now top-ranking Republican on Armed Services' Seapower and Expeditionary Forces Subcommittee, where he plans to protect military spending.

The defense budget is the only area where Akin, a former Army lieutenant, supports increased funding. He tried unsuccessfully in 2007 and 2008

CAPITOL OFFICE
225-2561
www.house.gov/akin
117 Cannon Bldg. 20515-2502; fax 225-2563

COMMITTEES
Armed Services
Science & Technology
Small Business

RESIDENCE
Town & Country

BORN
July 5, 1947; Manhattan, N.Y.

RELIGION
Christian

FAMILY
Wife, Lulli Akin; six children

EDUCATION
Worcester Polytechnic Institute, B.S. 1971 (engineering); Covenant Theological Seminary, M.Div. 1985;

MILITARY SERVICE
Army, 1972; Army Reserve, 1972-80

CAREER
University lecturer; steel company manager; computer company marketing executive

POLITICAL HIGHLIGHTS
Mo. House, 1989-2000

ELECTION RESULTS

2008 GENERAL

Todd Akin (R)	232,276	62.3%
William C. "Bill" Haas (D)	132,068	35.4%
Thomas L. Knapp (LIBERT)	8,628	2.3%

2008 PRIMARY

Todd Akin (R)	unopposed

2006 GENERAL

Todd Akin (R)	176,452	61.3%
George D. "Boots" Weber (D)	105,242	36.6%
Tamara A. Millay (LIBERT)	5,923	2.1%

PREVIOUS WINNING PERCENTAGES
2004 (65%); 2002 (67%); 2000 (55%)

to amend defense authorization bills that called for cuts to the Army's Future Combat Systems, the service's main modernization program. Boeing Co.'s Integrated Defense Systems, which is a prime contractor on the program, is headquartered in Akin's district. In 2004, Akin helped ensure the defense authorization bill included $357 million in funding for research on Boeing's new electronic attack aircraft.

Akin is known for his efforts to protect the Pledge of Allegiance. In recent years he has pushed legislation to bar federal courts, including the U.S. Supreme Court, from hearing constitutional challenges to the pledge. Many conservatives were incensed by a 2002 U.S. Court of Appeals ruling that the phrase "under God" in the pledge was an unconstitutional endorsement of religion. The Supreme Court struck down the appeals court decision in June 2004 on technical, not constitutional, grounds, and Akin has pressed for legislation to prevent further rulings against the pledge. The House has twice passed his bill, but the Senate has ignored it.

Akin also serves on the Science and Technology Committee. He blasted Obama's decision in early 2009 to lift Bush's restrictions on federal funding of embryonic stem cell research, saying, "The fact that non-embryonic stem cell research is producing superior results makes the decision to issue such an executive order appear more politically than scientifically significant."

Akin's great-grandfather founded the Laclede Steel Co. of St. Louis, and his father worked there as well. Akin grew up in the St. Louis area and studied engineering at Massachusetts' Worcester Polytechnic Institute, where he joined the Army ROTC. After serving as an Army combat engineer, Akin sold computers for IBM in Massachusetts, where he met his wife, Lulli. After four years, he returned to Missouri and worked at Laclede Steel before entering state politics.

During his 12-year tenure in the Missouri House, he unsuccessfully sued the state after the legislature approved a schools bill with $310 million in tax increases. He also brought suit against the state's approval of riverboat casino licenses, which led to a state referendum that permitted the licenses yet resulted in stricter state regulation of the industry.

Akin's reputation as a doctrinaire state legislator spurred opponents to label him ideologically isolated when he launched his campaign for the House seat vacated by Republican Jim Talent, who ran for governor in 2000. But grassroots support enabled Akin to narrowly prevail in a five-way primary; he defeated former St. Louis County Executive Gene McNary by just 56 votes. He went on to defeat Democratic state Sen. Ted House by 13 percentage points and has won with more than 60 percent of the vote since.

KEY VOTES

2008

No	Delay consideration of Colombia free-trade agreement
No	Override Bush veto of federal farm and nutrition programs reauthorization bill
Yes	Overhaul surveillance laws and permit dismissal of suits against companies that conducted warrantless wiretapping
No	Grant mortgage relief to homeowners and funding for Fannie Mae and Freddie Mac
No	Approve initial $700 billion program to stabilize financial markets
No	Approve final $700 billion program to stabilize financial markets
No	Provide $14 billion in loans to automakers

2007

No	Increase minimum wage by $2.10 an hour
No	Approve $124.2 billion in emergency war spending and set goal for redeployment of troops from Iraq
Yes	Reject federal contraceptive assistance to international family planning groups
Yes	Override Bush veto of $23.2 billion water projects authorization bill
Yes	Implement Peru free-trade agreement
No	Approve energy policy overhaul with new fuel economy standards
Yes	Clear $473.5 billion omnibus spending bill, including $70 billion for military operations

CQ VOTE STUDIES

	PARTY UNITY		PRESIDENTIAL SUPPORT	
	SUPPORT	OPPOSE	SUPPORT	OPPOSE
2008	99%	1%	81%	19%
2007	98%	2%	88%	12%
2006	97%	3%	95%	5%
2005	99%	1%	91%	9%
2004	99%	1%	94%	6%

INTEREST GROUPS

	AFL-CIO	ADA	CCUS	ACU
2008	0%	10%	89%	96%
2007	8%	0%	80%	100%
2006	14%	0%	100%	92%
2005	14%	0%	89%	100%
2004	7%	0%	95%	100%

MISSOURI 2

West St. Louis County; north and east St. Charles County— St. Charles

Composed mostly of upper-middle-class white suburbanites, the 2nd is the state's richest district. The district's population swelled as a result of decades of residential and commercial migration out of St. Louis.

As economic downturns take a toll on home construction and retail sectors, growth has slowed in St. Charles County, one of Missouri's fastest-growing overall since the 2000 census. Traffic into the St. Louis business district from the county remains heavy, and officials are trying to ease congestion. Plans for a $535 million reconstruction and improvement project for Interstate 64 in St. Louis County (shared with 1st) should improve the drive for commuters after its completion in 2010. Also, many local residents have solved their traffic problems by finding jobs away from downtown, and officials hope to mitigate rising unemployment rates by luring white-collar employers to the 2nd, which has the state's highest percentage of residents who have at least a bachelor's degree.

Boeing Co., with plants in the 2nd and on the outskirts of St. Louis (in the 1st) is a key employer, as are financial services and biotech companies. Production slowdowns and job cuts at the General Motors plant in Wentzville and the likely closure of a Chrysler plant in Fenton worry local officials and residents.

The 2nd District's dwindling but diverse agricultural industry supports the northern fringes of the Mississippi-Missouri river junction. Lincoln County, located in the district's northwest, is still heavily dependent on both manufacturing and agriculture. The district's wealthier communities and the strong white-collar vote favors Republicans at nearly all levels. It gave Republican John McCain 55 percent of its vote in the 2008 presidential race.

MAJOR INDUSTRY
Manufacturing, biotechnology, agriculture

CITIES
St. Charles, 60,321; St. Peters (pt.), 50,001; Chesterfield, 46,802; O'Fallon (pt.), 44,949; Wildwood, 32,884; Ballwin, 31,283

NOTABLE
St. Charles was the last established U.S. town that explorers Lewis and Clark visited as they embarked on their journey.

Rep. Russ Carnahan (D)

Elected 2004; 3rd term

CAPITOL OFFICE
225-2671
www.house.gov/carnahan
1710 Longworth Bldg. 20515-2503; fax 225-7452

COMMITTEES
Foreign Affairs
Science & Technology
Transportation & Infrastructure

RESIDENCE
St. Louis

BORN
July 10, 1958; Columbia, Mo.

RELIGION
Methodist

FAMILY
Wife, Debra Carnahan; two children

EDUCATION
U. of Missouri, B.S. 1979 (public administration),
J.D. 1983

CAREER
Lawyer; campaign aide; state legislative aide

POLITICAL HIGHLIGHTS
Democratic nominee for U.S. House, 1990;
Mo. House, 2001-05

ELECTION RESULTS

2008 GENERAL

Russ Carnahan (D)	202,470	66.4%
Chris Sander (R)	92,759	30.4%
Kevin C. Babcock (LIBERT)	5,518	1.8%
Cynthia "Cindy" Redburn (CNSTP)	4,324	1.4%

2008 PRIMARY

Russ Carnahan (D)	unopposed

2006 GENERAL

Russ Carnahan (D)	145,219	65.6%
David Bertelsen (R)	70,189	31.7%
R. Christophel (LIBERT)	4,213	1.9%

PREVIOUS WINNING PERCENTAGES
2004 (53%)

Carnahan is slowly emerging from the long shadow cast by his family, a multi-generational force in Missouri Democratic politics. He is active on foreign policy, environmental and health care issues, and he focuses on his district's transportation needs.

His Washington office doubles as a museum for his family's history. On the wall hangs the congressional license plate of his grandfather, A.S.J. Carnahan, who served in the House in the 1940s and 1950s. Also on display, under a glass-topped coffee table, are campaign buttons for his late father, Mel, a former Missouri governor.

Mel Carnahan died in a plane crash while campaigning for the Senate in 2000. When he posthumously won the race against Republican John Ashcroft, his widow and Russ Carnahan's mother, Jean, was appointed to the seat and served two years before losing her bid for a full term to Republican Jim Talent. Russ Carnahan's sister Robin is Missouri's secretary of state and a leading candidate for the Senate seat being vacated by Republican Christopher S. Bond in 2010.

As in other families with deep political roots, Russ Carnahan said he feels like he has always been in politics because it was a family project. He said his surname helps voters notice him but also leads some of them to judge him too quickly. "It's a two-edged sword," he said shortly after his election to Congress in 2004. "Some people will agree with you or disagree with you based on the name."

Carnahan followed his forebears in building a solid Democratic voting record. He is not as liberal as his predecessor, Richard A. Gephardt, the former Democratic House leader; he voted in favor of a constitutional amendment to ban flag desecration in 2005, and supported renewing the controversial USA Patriot Act anti-terrorism legislation. But he is loyal to his party. During the 110th Congress (2007-08), he sided with fellow Democrats on 97 percent of the votes in which the two parties were divided.

Health care is a primary concern for Carnahan, and as a member of the Foreign Affairs Committee he worked on a 2008 measure that reauthorized funding for foreign countries hit hard by AIDS. Carnahan said a trip President George W. Bush took to Africa, which has been especially ravaged by AIDS, "convinced [Bush] that it was a little more worthwhile to be broad-minded." Carnahan said he sees improving the U.S. image abroad as one of the committee's main tasks in the 111th Congress (2009-10).

Carnahan has been an active traveler since joining the Foreign Affairs panel. During the 110th, as a member of Foreign Affairs' International Organizations, Human Rights and Oversight Subcommittee, he accepted nearly $50,000 worth of trips provided by nonprofit groups allowed to provide free travel to members of Congress, an amount that ranked him fifth among all House members.

Transportation will be another priority for Carnahan as a member of the Transportation and Infrastructure Committee, which will take up a multi-year reauthorization of surface transportation programs during the 111th. He has advocated the expansion and widening of several roads as well as construction of a light-rail system in his district's fast-growing suburban areas.

A committed environmentalist, he introduced legislation in 2009 to require the Transportation Department to study the feasibility of making asphalt from plants. And Carnahan is proud of the fact that he receives high marks from the League of Conservation Voters in its annual vote ratings.

Carnahan also brings an environmentalist's perspective to the Science and Technology panel, where he promotes alternative-energy programs and fighting global warming. He joined Illinois Republican Mark Steven Kirk in introducing a resolution in April 2007 expressing the need for the United States to participate in international agreements on climate change. While it did not pass, Carnahan is confident that the Obama administration is more attuned to working with foreign governments on the issue.

Carnahan was one of the rare freshmen to get a bill passed in the House in his first term. But the legislation, which increased funding for embryonic stem cell research, became the first bill vetoed by Bush. Less than three years later, Carnahan praised President Obama for lifting Bush's ban on expanding federal funding for much of that research early in 2009.

Before politics, Carnahan was an attorney for nine years for the St. Louis-based health care provider BJC Healthcare. He backs the importation of prescription drugs from Canada and an expansion of government medical services to the uninsured. He also has pushed for more money for multiple sclerosis research and co-founded a congressional caucus on the disease.

Carnahan remembers packing into the family's Pontiac station wagon at age 8 for the "Caravan for Carnahan" during his father's 1966 campaign for the state legislature. Led by a flatbed truck with a piano on the back and loudspeakers, the caravan traveled to small towns, where the family handed out campaign fliers as a piano player belted out tunes.

Carnahan's first job after graduating in 1979 from the University of Missouri was driving an old Chevy van to take his father to every county as he campaigned for state treasurer. He attended law school, also at Missouri, where he met his wife, Debra, now a judge in St. Louis' municipal court and a member of the national board of Planned Parenthood. After earning his law degree, he worked as a legislative aide for the Missouri House Speaker.

He worked at a St. Louis law firm before launching his first bid for elective office at age 31. In 1990 he posed an unsuccessful challenge to veteran Republican Rep. Bill Emerson. But in 2000 he was elected to the Missouri House and stayed for two terms.

Despite his name recognition and four years in the state legislature, his election was hardly a sure thing when he ran to succeed Gephardt in 2004. Carnahan narrowly beat out a crowded field of nine other candidates in the primary. In the general election, he faced Republican Bill Federer, an author. Carnahan won with 53 percent of the vote. Despite concerns among Democrats that he might be vulnerable in 2006, he won re-election with 66 percent and matched that in 2008.

KEY VOTES

2008
Yes Delay consideration of Colombia free-trade agreement
Yes Override Bush veto of federal farm and nutrition programs reauthorization bill
No   Overhaul surveillance laws and permit dismissal of suits against companies that conducted warrantless wiretapping
Yes Grant mortgage relief to homeowners and funding for Fannie Mae and Freddie Mac
Yes Approve initial $700 billion program to stabilize financial markets
Yes Approve final $700 billion program to stabilize financial markets
Yes Provide $14 billion in loans to automakers

2007
Yes Increase minimum wage by $2.10 an hour
Yes Approve $124.2 billion in emergency war spending and set goal for redeployment of troops from Iraq
No   Reject federal contraceptive assistance to international family planning groups
Yes Override Bush veto of $23.2 billion water projects authorization bill
No   Implement Peru free-trade agreement
Yes Approve energy policy overhaul with new fuel economy standards
No   Clear $473.5 billion omnibus spending bill, including $70 billion for military operations

CQ VOTE STUDIES

	PARTY UNITY		PRESIDENTIAL SUPPORT	
	SUPPORT	OPPOSE	SUPPORT	OPPOSE
2008	99%	1%	16%	84%
2007	97%	3%	4%	96%
2006	91%	9%	40%	60%
2005	94%	6%	22%	78%

INTEREST GROUPS

	AFL-CIO	ADA	CCUS	ACU
2008	100%	90%	61%	0%
2007	96%	100%	55%	4%
2006	100%	90%	53%	12%
2005	93%	95%	41%	0%

MISSOURI 3

South St. Louis; southeast St. Louis County; Jefferson and Ste. Genevieve counties

Bordered on the east by the Mississippi River, the 3rd includes the southern half of St. Louis, as well as older, established suburbs and newer, sprawling ones. Most of the district's suburban middle-class residents commute to St. Louis County's business district, although there are traces of small-scale farming, manufacturing and river trading.

Whereas St. Louis as a whole (shared with the 1st District) has declined in population, immigrant communities continue to bolster south St. Louis' residential areas. Traditionally the German Bevo and Tower Grove neighborhoods now host a large Vietnamese community, as well as one of the nation's largest Bosnian populations. To the south, Jefferson County has been one of the state's fastest-growing areas and has gained national attention for its methamphetamine problem.

Many suburban residents work outside the 3rd District, but Anheuser-Busch, headquartered in the 3rd's portion of St. Louis, is a major provider of jobs to the region. The brewery is a St. Louis icon, and thousands of tourists visit its historical center each year. The 2008 merger of Anheuser-Busch and Belgian InBev resulted in massive layoffs across the metropolitan area. The district's other large employers include a National Geospatial-Intelligence Agency defense facility and the St. Louis VA Medical Center-Jefferson Barracks Division, which provides medical assistance for veterans. Farther south, on the fringes of Ste. Genevieve County, small farming complements a sizable trading industry along the Mississippi River.

The district's blue-collar base favors Democrats, although the GOP finds some support in middle-class communities. The 3rd gave Barack Obama 60 percent of its vote in the 2008 presidential election.

MAJOR INDUSTRY
Beer manufacturing, defense, health care

CITIES
St. Louis (pt.), 185,169; Oakville (unincorporated), 35,309

NOTABLE
The 1904 Olympics — the first to award gold, silver and bronze medals for first, second and third places, respectively — were held at Washington University's Francis Field.

Rep. Ike Skelton (D)

Elected 1976; 17th term

Skelton is a moderate-to-conservative Democrat who chairs the Armed Services Committee in relatively bipartisan fashion. Born Isaac Newton Skelton, the dean of the Missouri delegation has a certain gravity about him. He is serious, practical and homespun. He can also be cantankerous and curt.

His consistent refrain to the Clinton and George W. Bush administrations was the need to ensure military readiness for all potential missions, and in recent years he has criticized the Iraq War in part because of its effect on that goal. Showing prescience, Skelton also urged greater emphasis on the conflict in Afghanistan, which he called "the forgotten war," even before President Obama took up the cause.

He has long been a supporter of robust defense budgets, though he also has been outspoken about the need to reform the military acquisition system to curb ballooning costs. In April 2009, he called Defense Secretary Robert M. Gates' first budget outline for Obama a "good-faith effort" on that score, but pointedly added that "the buck stops with Congress, which has the critical constitutional responsibility to decide whether to support these proposals." Skelton had already created a special panel to examine ways to improve the Pentagon's troubled procurement system.

Skelton's other priorities include improving military recruiting and retention, curbing the spread of nuclear weapons, and improving cooperation among agencies that deploy abroad in post-war scenarios. He also wants to assess how national security is affected by the economic crisis and climate change, two of Obama's key concerns. He warned in March 2009 that the global economic crisis could destabilize countries around the world and might increase demand "for our national defense capabilities."

Skelton took over Armed Services in 2007 after eight years as the panel's ranking minority member. He hit the Bush administration hard on the wars in Iraq and Afghanistan, but also worked with Republicans in authorizing funds for troop needs. Although he favored a timetable for withdrawing troops from Iraq, he kept such a provision out of his committee's annual defense authorization measure for fear the debate could sink the whole bill.

He voted in 2002 to give the president authority to wage the Iraq War, but even before it began, Skelton worried about its aftermath, warning President Bush in a letter that the challenge would not be toppling Saddam Hussein so much as stabilizing the country afterward. "Like the proverbial dog chasing the car," Skelton wrote, "we must consider what we would do after we caught it."

Skelton is known for taking particular care of the military facilities in his district: Fort Leonard Wood Army base, Whiteman Air Force Base and the Missouri National Guard headquarters. The fiscal 2009 defense authorization bill that he shepherded through the House contained $97.8 million for those installations.

Skelton also took issue with the Bush administration's approach to the treatment of detainees in U.S. government custody. He voted in 2005 to ban cruel, inhuman and degrading treatment of prisoners. And he helped write legislation in 2007 to guarantee detainees in U.S. military prisons access to federal courts through habeas corpus petitions. The bill did not advance after being approved by a House Judiciary panel.

Skelton has shown little interest in burnishing his public image. He avoids TV talk show appearances and frequently brushes off reporters with a tight-lipped answer that is generally along the lines of "we'll see."

CAPITOL OFFICE
225-2876
www.house.gov/skelton
2206 Rayburn Bldg. 20515-2504; fax 225-2695

COMMITTEES
Armed Services - chairman

RESIDENCE
Lexington

BORN
Dec. 20, 1931; Lexington, Mo.

RELIGION
Christian Church

FAMILY
Engaged, Patty Martin; three children

EDUCATION
Wentworth Military Academy, A.A. 1951;
U. of Edinburgh (United Kingdom), attended 1953;
U. of Missouri, A.B. 1953 (history), LL.B. 1956

CAREER
Lawyer; state prosecutor

POLITICAL HIGHLIGHTS
Lafayette County prosecuting attorney, 1957-60;
Mo. Senate, 1971-77

ELECTION RESULTS

2008 GENERAL

Ike Skelton (D)	200,009	65.9%
Jeff Parnell (R)	103,446	34.1%

2008 PRIMARY

Ike Skelton (D)	unopposed

2006 GENERAL

Ike Skelton (D)	159,303	67.6%
James A. "Jim" Noland Jr. (R)	69,254	29.4%
Bryce Holthouse (LIBERT)	4,479	1.9%
Melinda "Mel" Ivey (PRO)	2,459	1.0%

PREVIOUS WINNING PERCENTAGES
2004 (66%); 2002 (68%); 2000 (67%); 1998 (71%);
1996 (64%); 1994 (68%); 1992 (70%); 1990 (62%);
1988 (72%); 1986 (100%); 1984 (67%); 1982 (55%);
1980 (68%); 1978 (73%); 1976 (56%)

Polio kept Skelton out of the service, but he has never lost his fascination with military history. His Web site has a "History Matters!" page and a list of his favorite national security books.

Skelton has always taken a long view of national security. He helped write the Goldwater-Nichols law in 1986 that institutionalized greater cooperation among the services. He is looking today at whether a similar reorganization is needed on a governmentwide level.

Politically, Skelton is hard to pigeonhole. His interest group ratings and degree of party loyalty have fluctuated from year to year. On most social issues, Skelton is in tune with his constituents and at odds with his more-liberal Democratic colleagues. He has opposed abortion in most cases, voted to repeal the ban on certain semiautomatic assault-style weapons and supported amending the Constitution to bar same-sex marriage. Skelton also split with many Democrats to back free-trade agreements such as the one with Peru in 2007 and the Central America Free Trade Agreement in 2005.

Skelton was a high school sophomore when he contracted polio, dashing his dream of attending the U.S. Military Academy at West Point. He became a patient at Warm Springs, Ga., where President Franklin D. Roosevelt went for treatment. He learned there to get on with his life, avoiding self-pity. He worked tirelessly to regain strength and joined the school track team as a 2-miler. "He proved there really were no limitations," a teammate told the St. Louis Post-Dispatch in 2007.

Skelton's father, a friend of Harry S Truman, took his son to Washington for the 1949 inauguration. Truman played a central role in Skelton's political life. He asked Skelton to run for Congress in 1962 against Democratic Rep. Bill Randall, whom the former president disliked. But Skelton opted against it; he was a young lawyer who had only recently married. His wife, Susie, died in August 2005; they raised three sons.

In August 2008, he became engaged to Patty Martin, a widowed school counselor in Lexington, Mo., whom he had known for years.

After serving six years in the state Senate, Skelton did run in 1976 when Randall retired. Skelton was endorsed by Truman's widow, and he won with 56 percent of the vote. He chaired a joint session of Congress on the day it observed Truman's 100th birthday, and he fought a Smithsonian exhibit on the dropping of the first atomic bomb that he viewed as unfairly questioning Truman's motives.

In his recent electoral wins, he has taken about two-thirds of the vote — including 2008, a year in which Arizona GOP Sen. John McCain carried Skelton's district over Obama by 23 percentage points.

KEY VOTES

2008

Yes Delay consideration of Colombia free-trade agreement

Yes Override Bush veto of federal farm and nutrition programs reauthorization bill

Yes Overhaul surveillance laws and permit dismissal of suits against companies that conducted warrantless wiretapping

Yes Grant mortgage relief to homeowners and funding for Fannie Mae and Freddie Mac

Yes Approve initial $700 billion program to stabilize financial markets

Yes Approve final $700 billion program to stabilize financial markets

Yes Provide $14 billion in loans to automakers

2007

Yes Increase minimum wage by $2.10 an hour

Yes Approve $124.2 billion in emergency war spending and set goal for redeployment of troops from Iraq

Yes Reject federal contraceptive assistance to international family planning groups

Yes Override Bush veto of $23.2 billion water projects authorization bill

Yes Implement Peru free-trade agreement

Yes Approve energy policy overhaul with new fuel economy standards

Yes Clear $473.5 billion omnibus spending bill, including $70 billion for military operations

CQ VOTE STUDIES

	PARTY UNITY		PRESIDENTIAL SUPPORT	
	SUPPORT	OPPOSE	SUPPORT	OPPOSE
2008	97%	3%	20%	80%
2007	92%	8%	13%	87%
2006	75%	25%	60%	40%
2005	76%	24%	61%	39%
2004	80%	20%	68%	32%

INTEREST GROUPS

	AFL-CIO	ADA	CCUS	ACU
2008	100%	85%	61%	4%
2007	96%	85%	72%	25%
2006	86%	55%	80%	50%
2005	79%	75%	70%	38%
2004	93%	65%	60%	48%

MISSOURI 4

West central — Kansas City suburbs, Jefferson City

Laden with lakes, rivers and farmland, the 4th's northern border is formed in part by the Missouri River. With the exception of some southeast Kansas City suburbs, the state capital of Jefferson City and midsize Sedalia, the district typifies rural and small-town Missouri.

Agriculture has been an economic mainstay here for decades. Most residents work at small-scale farming, mainly row crops, with soybeans, corn and wheat, or livestock. Others work for moderate-size manufacturers of household goods. Tourism helps in the rural areas. With miles of shoreline, modern hotels and retail outlets, the Lake of the Ozarks region (shared with the 9th) attracts boaters and shoppers. The lake areas also draw retirees and professionals looking to set up second homes.

The 4th's piece of the Kansas City suburbs has not grown as fast as the area north of the city (in the 6th), and the suburbs are not as affluent, but they do provide some blue-collar manufacturing jobs. Moving east, the district picks up the smaller cities of Warrensburg and Sedalia, where the Scott Joplin Ragtime Festival is held each June. State government employs more than 15,000 people in Jefferson City, all but a very small sliver of which is located in the 4th.

Voters in some of the western counties favor Democrats in congressional elections, but GOP state legislators heavily outnumber their Democratic counterparts in the 4th District. Republican John McCain took 61 percent of the 2008 presidential election vote here, winning 24 of the 25 counties in the district — Barton and Dade counties, which are sparsely populated and also voted for GOP gubernatorial candidate Kenny Hulshof in the 2008 election, gave McCain his highest (74) and third-highest (70) percentages statewide.

MAJOR INDUSTRY
Government, defense, agriculture, manufacturing

MILITARY BASES
Fort Leonard Wood, 7,200 military, 3,500 civilian (2008); Whiteman Air Force Base, 3,352 military, 774 civilian (2008)

CITIES
Jefferson City (pt.), 39,611; Sedalia, 20,339; Warrensburg, 16,340

NOTABLE
President Harry S Truman was born in Lamar; The restored home of George Caleb Bingham in Arrow Rock honors the American artist.

Rep. Emanuel Cleaver II (D)

Elected 2004; 3rd term

An ordained Methodist minister and former Kansas City mayor, Cleaver seeks to minimize the roles of race and religion in politics. In that respect, he has more in common with President Obama than some of his peers in the Congressional Black Caucus, whose identities are more intertwined with their priorities.

Since his election to Congress in 2004, Cleaver has held to a simple rule: "What you're trying to do is not get people to think about race." After Obama's election, he warned African-Americans to keep their expectations in check. "Obama will fall short of fulfilling the considerable hopes and dreams of the minorities who supported him, just as we could not fulfill those of ours," Cleaver wrote in The Washington Post, recalling the high expectations he faced as the first black Kansas City mayor in the 1990s.

Cleaver also disdains efforts by his colleagues to promote certain religious beliefs. In his first term, he was one of 22 House members, all Democrats, who voted against a House resolution expressing support for Christmas. He still calls the effort "one of the low moments" for Congress.

Cleaver is equally unusual in his frankness about legislative matters. A member of the Financial Services Committee, he joined colleagues in March 2009 in voting to heavily tax bonuses given to executives of the insurance firm American International Group Inc.

The government had rescued AIG the year before from bankruptcy, and many in Congress were incensed about the bonuses. But shortly thereafter, Cleaver told a crowd of Missourians gathered on Capitol Hill that he had erred. "I joined the cowards," Cleaver said, adding that his vote "was the only time since I've been in Congress that I was embarrassed to go home." He said the tax, which later got held up in the Senate, was meaningless populism.

But Cleaver was nearly as emotional in the fall of 2008, when he was one of 32 Democrats to switch their votes and approve a $700 billion rescue plan for the ailing financial services sector. "It's a lose-lose," Cleaver told the Kansas City Star. "As an elected official, you never receive appreciation for the things that don't happen. If we don't go under, people will say, 'See, there was nothing wrong.' And if we do go under, people will say, 'You had more information than I had, so why didn't you do the right thing?'"

While such internal struggles might hurt another politician, Cleaver's constituents chalk it up to his religious background and say they appreciate his honesty. It was Cleaver's credibility among religious leaders that led Speaker Nancy Pelosi of California to appoint him in 2007 to a panel on energy independence and global warming with the specific charge to reach out to his fellow ministers.

To prove his environmental bona fides, Cleaver uses a 1998 Ford Econoline van, converted to run on vegetable oil, as an office-on-wheels in his district. In 2007, he inserted a provision in an energy law barring House members from leasing vehicles through their office budgets that emit high levels of greenhouse gases, forcing many of them to turn in the keys for the luxury sedans and SUVs they had been driving.

Cleaver is a loyal Democrat but has occasionally deviated from party orthodoxy on trade, supporting a 2007 deal with Peru, for example. And as a member of the Homeland Security Committee, he voted in 2008 to provide immunity for telecommunications firms who'd helped the George W. Bush administration eavesdrop on conversations between suspected terrorists and Americans. The bill narrowly divided Democrats and ultimately passed.

CAPITOL OFFICE
225-4535
www.house.gov/cleaver
1027 Longworth Bldg. 20515-2505; fax 225-4403

COMMITTEES
Financial Services
Homeland Security
Select Energy Independence & Global Warming

RESIDENCE
Kansas City

BORN
Oct. 26, 1944; Waxahachie, Texas

RELIGION
Methodist

FAMILY
Wife, Dianne Cleaver; four children

EDUCATION
Murray State College (Okla.), attended 1963-64; Prairie View A&M College, B.S. 1972 (sociology); Saint Paul School of Theology, M.Div. 1974

CAREER
Minister; radio talk show host; civil rights group chapter founder; charitable group manager; car wash owner

POLITICAL HIGHLIGHTS
Sought Democratic nomination for Mo. House, 1970; sought Democratic nomination for Kansas City Council, 1975; Kansas City Council, 1979-91; mayor of Kansas City, 1991-99

ELECTION RESULTS

2008 GENERAL

Emanuel Cleaver II (D)	197,249	64.4%
Jacob Turk (R)	109,166	35.6%

2008 PRIMARY

Emanuel Cleaver II (D)	unopposed

2006 GENERAL

Emanuel Cleaver II (D)	136,149	64.2%
Jacob Turk (R)	68,456	32.3%
Randall D. Langkraehr (LIBERT)	7,314	3.5%

PREVIOUS WINNING PERCENTAGES
2004 (55%)

Cleaver is the first vice chairman of the Congressional Black Caucus during the 111th Congress (2009-10). But as one of the few members of the caucus who represents a white-majority district, Cleaver will go his own way. Unlike most caucus members, he backed then-New York Sen. Hillary Rodham Clinton — now Secretary of State — over Obama in the Democratic presidential primaries.

The most prominent item in Cleaver's congressional office is a framed photo of the shack in which he grew up with his father, mother and three sisters in Waxahachie, Texas. The dwelling, which Cleaver calls a "slave shanty," housed slaves in the 1800s.

Cleaver lived there until he was almost eight years old, when the family moved to public housing. Eventually, Cleaver's father — a maître d' at an exclusive club — saved enough to buy a home in a predominately white part of town. But rampant racism there forced them to move to the black district on the east side.

He has served as a pastor at St. James United Methodist Church in Kansas City since 1972, when it was a 25-member congregation. Now it counts 2,000 members, including Cleaver's son, who became a co-pastor in 2008. Cleaver still delivers occasional sermons.

For 18 years, Cleaver and the rabbi of a prominent Kansas City synagogue preached to each other's congregations. Cleaver also founded Harmony in a World of Difference, an organization that seeks to promote interfaith dialogue.

Cleaver was elected to the Kansas City Council in 1979 and became the city's mayor in 1991. In eight years in office, he helped bring new firms to the region and oversaw the rejuvenation of the historic 18th and Vine jazz district as part of his frequently stated goal of making it a "world-class city." But he said he was most proud of averting strife at a time when racial disturbances occurred in other urban areas.

Cleaver sought in 2004 to succeed retiring Democratic Rep. Karen McCarthy. He faced Republican businesswoman Jeanne Patterson, who spent more than $2.8 million of her own money — much of it on ads questioning Cleaver's professional and personal ethics. Cleaver denied Patterson's charges and accused her of trying to buy the seat. Emphasizing his mayoral record, he defeated Patterson by a comfortable 13 percentage points. But the next year, according to The Associated Press, he paid back taxes on a car wash business.

He easily won re-election in 2006 against Republican Jacob Turk with 64 percent of the vote and matched that percentage in a rematch in 2008.

KEY VOTES

2008

Yes Delay consideration of Colombia free-trade agreement

Yes Override Bush veto of federal farm and nutrition programs reauthorization bill

Yes Overhaul surveillance laws and permit dismissal of suits against companies that conducted warrantless wiretapping

Yes Grant mortgage relief to homeowners and funding for Fannie Mae and Freddie Mac

No Approve initial $700 billion program to stabilize financial markets

Yes Approve final $700 billion program to stabilize financial markets

Yes Provide $14 billion in loans to automakers

2007

Yes Increase minimum wage by $2.10 an hour

Yes Approve $124.2 billion in emergency war spending and set goal for redeployment of troops from Iraq

No Reject federal contraceptive assistance to international family planning groups

Yes Override Bush veto of $23.2 billion water projects authorization bill

Yes Implement Peru free-trade agreement

Yes Approve energy policy overhaul with new fuel economy standards

No Clear $473.5 billion omnibus spending bill, including $70 billion for military operations

CQ VOTE STUDIES

	PARTY UNITY		PRESIDENTIAL SUPPORT	
	SUPPORT	OPPOSE	SUPPORT	OPPOSE
2008	99%	1%	13%	87%
2007	99%	1%	4%	96%
2006	93%	7%	32%	68%
2005	96%	4%	22%	78%

INTEREST GROUPS

	AFL-CIO	ADA	CCUS	ACU
2008	100%	90%	61%	4%
2007	96%	95%	55%	0%
2006	100%	95%	50%	8%
2005	93%	100%	48%	8%

MISSOURI 5

Kansas City and suburbs

Kansas City long has been known for its blues style of jazz and its barbecue grilling. The Democratic 5th takes in some of the city's minority, lower-income communities and some suburban middle-class areas in Jackson and Cass counties. Today, Kansas City is the nation's second-largest rail hub, and a resurgence in high-end loft communities has lured younger, well-to-do residents to the city.

Most of the 5th's residents live in northern Jackson County cities, with 70 percent of the district's population either in Kansas City (shared with the 6th) or Independence (a small part of which is in the 6th). Overall, the 5th is almost two-thirds white-collar, with tax preparation and personal finance company H&R Block and Hallmark Cards both headquartered in the district. A diverse economic base helped the district grow into a transportation and telecommunications hub, and the area is still home to a number of call centers and other electronic-based businesses. Some other residents still commute out of the 5th to companies such as Sprint Nextel, in Kansas, but widespread layoffs at white-collar employers have strained the economy and municipal budgets.

Despite national declines in demand for steel products — especially for the struggling domestic auto industry— the Kansas City area's steel and auto assembly plants still employ thousands of local residents. The federal government is a key employer in Kansas City, although the city's Marine Corps Support Activity base closed as part of the 2005 BRAC round of realignments. The southern communities depend on agriculture: Despite economic diversification, the 5th is still a viable market for winter wheat.

With nearly all of Kansas City's black neighborhoods, the 5th is roughly one-fourth black, the district is reliably Democratic and socially moderate. Democrats have held the Kansas City seat since 1949, and Barack Obama took 63 percent of the district's 2008 presidential vote.

MAJOR INDUSTRY
Transportation, auto manufacturing, agriculture, telecommunications

CITIES
Kansas City (pt.), 322,910; Independence (pt.), 110,822; Lee's Summit (pt.), 65,498; Raytown, 30,388

NOTABLE
The Negro Leagues Baseball Museum is in Kansas City.

Rep. Sam Graves (R)

Elected 2000; 5th term

CAPITOL OFFICE
225-7041
www.house.gov/graves
1415 Longworth Bldg. 20515-2506; fax 225-8221

COMMITTEES
Agriculture
Small Business - ranking member
Transportation & Infrastructure

RESIDENCE
Tarkio

BORN
Nov. 7, 1963; Fairfax, Mo.

RELIGION
Baptist

FAMILY
Wife, Lesley Graves; three children

EDUCATION
U. of Missouri, B.S. 1986 (agronomy)

CAREER
Farmer

POLITICAL HIGHLIGHTS
Mo. House, 1993-95; Mo. Senate, 1995-2000

ELECTION RESULTS

2008 GENERAL

Sam Graves (R)	196,526	59.4%
Kay Barnes (D)	121,894	36.9%
Dave Browning (LIBERT)	12,279	3.7%

2008 PRIMARY

Sam Graves (R)	unopposed

2006 GENERAL

Sam Graves (R)	150,882	61.6%
Mary Jo Shettles (D)	87,477	35.7%
Erik Buck (LIBERT)	4,757	1.9%

PREVIOUS WINNING PERCENTAGES
2004 (64%); 2002 (63%); 2000 (51%)

Graves' priorities and governing philosophy are tailored to the needs of his rural northwest Missouri district. In other words, he favors minimal government intervention except in the case of farm policy. And he is not given to half-measures in his conservative views.

He has called for a halt in all immigration until foreigners already here are accounted for. He sponsored a bill to terminate the federal income tax code, and wants the federal government to stop acquiring land for national parks and forests. In fall 2008, Graves voted against a $700 billion measure — which became law — to shore up the nation's financial system, saying it amounted to a "blank check with no real safeguard for taxpayers, investors and retirees." He also opposed President Obama's $787 billion economic stimulus law in February 2009, saying, "I am appalled that Congress has passed along billions of dollars of debt to our children."

One of the rare places Graves sees a proper role for the federal government is in helping farmers like himself. Graves, a sixth-generation farmer, argues that farmers are at the mercy of factors beyond their control — including the imperative of providing low-cost food to consumers — so government involvement is essential.

From his seat on the Agriculture Committee, Graves had a hand in a major rewrite of farm and nutrition programs in the 110th Congress (2007-08). He authored language in the bill that bars people convicted of defrauding an Agriculture Department program from future eligibility for the program. Graves then voted to override President George W. Bush's veto of the legislation, saying it "works for Missouri." He said the veto "only hurt our ability to provide the country with the food it needs."

Graves is the top-ranking Republican of the Small Business Committee in the 111th Congress (2009-10), and he wasted no time making his views known. Most small-business advocates, including his Senate counterpart, Republican Olympia J. Snowe of Maine, hailed the Obama administration's plans to purchase up to $15 billion in securities backed by Small Business Administration loans in order to spur new lending. Graves objected, calling it "one more step into the federal government doing everything."

Earlier in his career, Graves once proposed exemptions to a billboard ban under Lady Bird Johnson's Highway Beautification Act of 1965 in order to allow businesses to advertise where they wanted. It was an example of what he views as government meddling. "If we continue to take away billboards because someone in Washington decides what is pretty to look at, small businesses will continue to suffer," he said.

A member of the Transportation and Infrastructure Committee, Graves will have a hand in writing the next federal highway bill. He successfully amended the 2005 version to ban vicarious liability, a legal avenue for people injured by drivers of rental cars to sue the rental car company as well as the driver. The trial lawyer lobby defended vicarious liability.

Graves' wife, Lesley, is an elementary school teacher, and Graves is active on education issues. Two of his proposals were included in the 2002 No Child Left Behind education law, which is up for reauthorization in the 111th Congress. One requires that 95 percent of federal education dollars be spent in the classroom, and the other protects teachers from frivolous lawsuits arising from disciplining students. Graves joined Democrats Phil Hare of Illinois and Earl Pomeroy of North Dakota in forming the House Rural Education Caucus in 2009.

A lifelong resident of tiny Tarkio, Graves returned to the family farm after graduating with a degree in agronomy from the University of Missouri in 1986. The following year, NBC's "Today" show featured him as an example of a young person willing to stay on the land and farm. He said on the show that he wanted to preserve his family's heritage.

Now, his younger brother Danny and his father, Sam Graves run the farm, raising corn, soybeans and cattle. He still will wax rhapsodic about the many uses of baling wire and his memories of climbing up on the 1968 John Deere 4020 tractor that his grandfather bought new. When he's in his home district, Graves sometimes helps out. "If I'm out on the combine all day by myself, I take a tape recorder and it clears my head," he said.

Graves' involvement in politics was a natural fit, given his family's long history in northwest Missouri politics. Graves' great-grandfather, also named Sam, was a Democrat who served on the Atchison County Commission. And Graves' brother Todd was appointed by Bush to be the U.S. attorney for western Missouri. According to a 2008 Justice Department inspector general's report, aides to Missouri Republican Sen. Christopher S. Bond engineered Todd Graves' removal from that post because he would not help resolve "discord" between the Missouri staffs of the two lawmakers.

Graves became involved in politics through the Missouri Farm Bureau, and once he was named the national organization's outstanding young farmer. He spent two years in the Missouri House and roughly six in the state Senate. He once staged a filibuster threatening a school desegregation bill that he thought did not contain enough for rural districts.

Six months before the 2000 election, when the popular Democratic Rep. Pat Danner unexpectedly announced her retirement after four terms, Graves jumped into the primary contest and quickly overshadowed several less-known Republican hopefuls.

The Democrats nominated the congresswoman's son, Steve Danner. But Graves' assertive campaign and conservative politics gave him momentum and the win. Though historically Democratic, the district had become competitive, and is now considered Republican.

Graves has won re-election easily since. In 2008, he won a fifth term with 59 percent of the vote against Kay Barnes, a former Democratic mayor of Kansas City, after emphasizing his deep Missouri roots and painting Barnes as a free-spending liberal politician. He outran Republican presidential nominee Arizona Sen. John McCain by 5 percentage points in the district.

Barnes is one of a number of pilots in Congress. He enjoys flying his 1967 Piper Cub airplane.

MISSOURI 6

Northwest — St. Joseph, part of Kansas City

In Missouri's northwest, the 6th is bordered by Iowa to the north and the Missouri River to the west and much of the south. Rich farmland continues to drive the district's economy, while suburban areas surrounding Kansas City and St. Joseph — both located on the Missouri River — provide a solid middle-class workforce for the area's shipping and manufacturing industries.

Platte, Clay and eastern Jackson counties surround Kansas City (shared with the 5th). Platte County's Kansas City International Airport, a major hub for Southwest Airlines, provides many district jobs. Layoffs at a Ford plant in Claycomo, American Airlines and a Harley-Davidson plant, among other employers, have hurt the local workforce. The state's largest city north of Kansas City — about an hour's drive — is St. Joseph, which was a Pony Express terminus for riders carrying mail to and from California in the early 1860s. Today, it remains a distribution center and a district economic hub.

Outside of the two metropolitan areas, farmland spreads for miles. Corn

KEY VOTES

2008

No Delay consideration of Colombia free-trade agreement
Yes Override Bush veto of federal farm and nutrition programs reauthorization bill
Yes Overhaul surveillance laws and permit dismissal of suits against companies that conducted warrantless wiretapping
No Grant mortgage relief to homeowners and funding for Fannie Mae and Freddie Mac
No Approve initial $700 billion program to stabilize financial markets
No Approve final $700 billion program to stabilize financial markets
No Provide $14 billion in loans to automakers

2007

No Increase minimum wage by $2.10 an hour
No Approve $124.2 billion in emergency war spending and set goal for redeployment of troops from Iraq
Yes Reject federal contraceptive assistance to international family planning groups
Yes Override Bush veto of $23.2 billion water projects authorization bill
Yes Implement Peru free-trade agreement
Yes Approve energy policy overhaul with new fuel economy standards
Yes Clear $473.5 billion omnibus spending bill, including $70 billion for military operations

CQ VOTE STUDIES

	PARTY UNITY		PRESIDENTIAL SUPPORT	
	SUPPORT	OPPOSE	SUPPORT	OPPOSE
2008	89%	11%	54%	46%
2007	92%	8%	69%	31%
2006	98%	2%	95%	5%
2005	95%	5%	86%	14%
2004	93%	7%	79%	21%

INTEREST GROUPS

	AFL-CIO	ADA	CCUS	ACU
2008	47%	40%	83%	88%
2007	42%	15%	95%	82%
2006	15%	0%	100%	88%
2005	13%	0%	93%	92%
2004	20%	10%	100%	92%

and livestock are prevalent here, and processing plants have created a growing market for soybeans as well. Craig, in Holt County, is home to the Golden Triangle ethanol plant, and wind energy production is increasing as turbines pop up across the landscape.

Although historically Democratic, the 6th became politically competitive during the last quarter of the 20th century before moving into the GOP column this decade. John McCain won all but two of the 26 counties wholly or partly in the district — and only lost in Buchanan County by fewer than 100 votes — in the 2008 presidential election, earning him 54 percent of the 6th's vote. Republicans seeking state office also have fared better recently, especially in the northern, rural areas.

MAJOR INDUSTRY
Agriculture, international shipping, manufacturing

CITIES
Kansas City (pt.), 118,635; St. Joseph, 73,990; Blue Springs (pt.), 39,698; Gladstone, 26,365; Liberty, 26,232

NOTABLE
The Jesse James Home in St. Joseph was where the outlaw was shot and killed in 1882; The Camden Point Baptist Church Cemetery is the oldest Confederate cemetery west of the Mississippi River.

Rep. Roy Blunt (R)

Elected 1996; 7th term

Not long ago, Blunt was talked about as a future Speaker of the House. His business-friendly conservatism, willingness to do favors for colleagues and reputation for staying cool under fire made him one of his party's senior leaders. These days, though, he no longer is in the leadership and must content himself with heading GOP task forces to devise alternatives to the Democratic majority's proposals.

Given his diminished stature, it was unsurprising when Blunt announced in February 2009 he would run for the seat of retiring GOP Sen. Christopher S. Bond in 2010. His bid will test whether Republicans can begin to politically surmount the unpopular administration of George W. Bush and problems of a House GOP leadership that promoted many of Bush's policies during the six years of his presidency in which the party held the House majority.

As majority whip, the No. 3 leadership post under GOP rule, Blunt was instrumental in ensuring the Bush White House and the House were in sync — an arrangement he now acknowledges should have had more distance. "I think you can argue that our leadership was too close to President Bush," Blunt said in March 2009. "One of our mistakes that harmed our majority and President Bush was not being willing to have more veto fights with him."

Republicans' poor electoral showings in November 2008 and shaky ties to conservatives led Blunt to step down from his whip post for the 111th Congress (2009-10). Announcing his decision two days after the election, he said he was "tired of asking members to do something they don't want to do."

The pressures on Blunt as the House GOP's chief vote-counter came to a head that fall, when he took heat for the House's initial rejection of a $700 billion package aimed at shoring up the financial services industry. Democrats blamed Blunt and Minority Leader John A. Boehner for finding just 65 GOP "yes" votes, while some Republicans criticized the lack of sweeteners, such as a hike in the federal deposit insurance cap, that were added to the later version that passed and was signed into law. Blunt defended his work as a negotiator: "I was asked to serve by Mr. Boehner. It was a job that had to be done."

Blunt shared Boehner's "big tent" GOP vision but also earned a reputation as a deal-cutter with ties to Majority Leader Steny H. Hoyer. Blunt and Hoyer worked on an electronic surveillance overhaul in 2008 that gave telecommunications providers aiding the government a virtual waiver from liability suits.

Boehner named Blunt to the Select Intelligence Committee in 2009. He also tapped him to head a group of 16 Republicans to craft a GOP health care overhaul. Blunt said he had told President Obama it was possible to write legislation that could draw support from 70 percent to 80 percent of Congress. But he said a host of issues likely would cost his vote, starting with the proposed creation of a government health plan to compete with private insurers. "I'm a big believer that a government-organized system would be much more effective than a government-operated system," he said in March 2009.

Blunt also chaired a GOP task force on energy in the 110th Congress (2007-08), leading a push for more oil and gas drilling and incentives for alternative energy to attack high gasoline prices and stimulate the economy. After former Speaker J. Dennis Hastert retired in 2007, Blunt took Hastert's seat on the Energy and Air Quality panel (now Energy and the Environment) of the Energy and Commerce Committee. He helped push for a spending measure that allowed the offshore oil-drilling moratorium to expire in the fall of 2008.

Blunt still looks for bipartisan solutions, such as his collaboration with Hoyer on a 2008 clarification of the Americans with Disabilities Act. Yet he

CAPITOL OFFICE
225-6536
blunt.house.gov
2229 Rayburn Bldg. 20515-2507; fax 225-5604

COMMITTEES
Energy & Commerce
Select Intelligence

RESIDENCE
Strafford

BORN
Jan. 10, 1950; Niangua, Mo.

RELIGION
Baptist

FAMILY
Wife, Abigail Blunt; four children

EDUCATION
Southwest Baptist U., B.A. 1970 (history);
Southwest Missouri State U., M.A. 1972
(history & government)

CAREER
University president; teacher

POLITICAL HIGHLIGHTS
Greene County clerk, 1973-84; Republican nominee for lieutenant governor, 1980; Mo. secretary of state, 1985-93; sought Republican nomination for governor, 1992

ELECTION RESULTS

2008 GENERAL

Roy Blunt (R)	219,016	67.8%
Richard Monroe (D)	91,010	28.2%
Kevin Craig (LIBERT)	6,971	2.2%
Travis Maddox (CNSTP)	6,166	1.9%

2008 PRIMARY

Roy Blunt (R)	unopposed

2006 GENERAL

Roy Blunt (R)	160,942	66.7%
Jack Truman (D)	72,592	30.1%
Kevin Craig (LIBERT)	7,566	3.1%

PREVIOUS WINNING PERCENTAGES
2004 (70%); 2002 (75%); 2000 (74%); 1998 (73%);
1996 (65%)

took a hard line in procedural fights and endorsed symbolic gestures like voting "present" to embarrass Democrats by defeating, 141-149, an Iraq War funding amendment in May 2008.

As whip, Blunt earned a reputation for using favors and persuasion, not threats. He remained a force in Missouri politics, backing Rep. Kenny Hulshof's unsuccessful bid to succeed his son, Missouri Gov. Matt Blunt, who opted not to run for re-election in 2008, amid low poll ratings.

Blunt once seemed a shoo-in to succeed Majority Leader Tom DeLay of Texas. But he lost traction after DeLay left under an ethics cloud. In February 2006, Blunt fell shy of a majority needed to win a first-ballot caucus race and lost the second round to Boehner, who attracted backers of a third candidate, Arizona's John Shadegg. Instead of stepping aside as whip, Blunt kept that job. After the GOP lost its majority in the 2006 elections, Boehner and Blunt prevailed against conservative challengers.

A network of allies on both ends of Pennsylvania Avenue and on K Street helped Blunt win close votes, such as passage of the Central America Free Trade Agreement in 2005 and the Medicare prescription drug benefit in 2003. It also helped him to survive ethics queries about ties to lobbyists. In 2002, he tried to slip a provision benefiting Philip Morris USA into a homeland security bill at a time he was romantically involved with a Philip Morris lobbyist, Abigail Perlman, whom he later married after divorcing his first wife of 35 years.

He rose through the ranks quickly with the help of DeLay, who appointed him chief deputy whip in the 106th Congress (1999-2000). He won election as whip after the 2002 elections, broadening his base by working on GOP campaigns. His Rely on Your Own Beliefs political action committee donated $1.6 million to candidates in the 2008 cycle and $1.2 million in 2006.

The son of a dairy farmer and a state legislator, Blunt was raised on a farm near Springfield. He still lives on a farm near there. After college, he became a high school government and history teacher. But he was active in politics at an early age, working in 1972 on an unsuccessful congressional bid by Republican John Ashcroft, who later became governor, senator and then U.S. attorney general. A year later, Blunt was appointed Greene County clerk by Bond, who was then Missouri's governor.

Blunt won the first of two terms as Missouri secretary of state in 1984. That set the stage for his campaign for governor in 1992. After losing the GOP primary, Blunt accepted the presidency of his alma mater, Southwest Baptist University. But he jumped back into public life when GOP Rep. Mel Hancock announced his retirement in 1996. Blunt cruised to victory with 65 percent of the vote, and has been easily re-elected since.

KEY VOTES

2008
No   Delay consideration of Colombia free-trade agreement
Yes   Override Bush veto of federal farm and nutrition programs reauthorization bill
Yes   Overhaul surveillance laws and permit dismissal of suits against companies that conducted warrantless wiretapping
No   Grant mortgage relief to homeowners and funding for Fannie Mae and Freddie Mac
Yes   Approve initial $700 billion program to stabilize financial markets
Yes   Approve final $700 billion program to stabilize financial markets
No   Provide $14 billion in loans to automakers

2007
No   Increase minimum wage by $2.10 an hour
No   Approve $124.2 billion in emergency war spending and set goal for redeployment of troops from Iraq
Yes   Reject federal contraceptive assistance to international family planning groups
No   Override Bush veto of $23.2 billion water projects authorization bill
Yes   Implement Peru free-trade agreement
Yes   Approve energy policy overhaul with new fuel economy standards
Yes   Clear $473.5 billion omnibus spending bill, including $70 billion for military operations

CQ VOTE STUDIES

	PARTY UNITY		PRESIDENTIAL SUPPORT	
	SUPPORT	OPPOSE	SUPPORT	OPPOSE
2008	97%	3%	80%	20%
2007	98%	2%	90%	10%
2006	98%	2%	97%	3%
2005	98%	2%	91%	9%
2004	97%	3%	100%	0%

INTEREST GROUPS

	AFL-CIO	ADA	CCUS	ACU
2008	7%	15%	83%	88%
2007	13%	10%	79%	96%
2006	7%	0%	100%	88%
2005	14%	0%	93%	96%
2004	7%	0%	100%	96%

MISSOURI 7
Southwest – Springfield, Joplin

The 7th sits nestled in the state's southwestern corner. Springfield is the region's industrial and commercial center, while Branson leads the 7th's thriving tourism industry. This part of the "Show Me State," where unpredictable weather reigns, retains a strong agricultural foundation.

Springfield, in Greene County, has a solid manufacturing hub and is also home to some large national retail chains like O'Reilly Auto Parts and Bass Pro Shops. But economic downturns have forced job cuts, especially within Bass Pro Shops' boat-making division. Nearly 50 percent of district residents live in either Greene or neighboring Christian County on the 7th's eastern edge. The district's other population center, Joplin, is across the district in Jasper County. Once a lead and zinc mining town, Joplin is now a manufacturing and trucking center. Despite relative economic stability in Joplin, ties to manufacturing have resulted in some lost jobs.

A family-friendly entertainment destination, Branson is a magnet for country music fans. This town of 6,000 draws more than 7 million visitors a year, and Branson Airport, the first privately developed and operated

commercial service airport in the country, is expected to bring in even more tourists after it opens in 2009. Overall, the area relies on the city's more than 40 theaters — including the Andy Williams Moon River, Mel Tillis and Dick Clark's American Bandstand theaters — and the resort industry around Taneycomo and Table Rock lakes.

The southwestern corner of the district supports beef and dairy cattle, along with poultry farming. Expansion along U.S. Highway 71, which runs from Kansas City into Arkansas, has improved area accessibility.

The 7th ong has been a GOP bastion. The Assemblies of God, based in Springfield, is among the active religious groups that reflect the area's devout, conservative population. In 2008, John McCain won the district with 63 percent of the presidential vote, his best showing in the state.

MAJOR INDUSTRY
Agriculture, tourism, manufacturing

CITIES
Springfield, 151,580; Joplin, 45,504; Carthage, 12,668

NOTABLE
George Washington Carver's boyhood home in Diamond (Newton County) is a national monument.

Rep. Jo Ann Emerson (R)

Elected 1996; 7th full term

CAPITOL OFFICE
225-4404
www.house.gov/emerson
2440 Rayburn Bldg. 20515-2508; fax 226-0326

COMMITTEES
Appropriations

RESIDENCE
Cape Girardeau

BORN
Sept. 16, 1950; Washington, D.C.

RELIGION
Presbyterian

FAMILY
Husband, Ron Gladney; two children,
six stepchildren

EDUCATION
Ohio Wesleyan U., B.A. 1972 (political science)

CAREER
Public affairs executive; lobbyist

POLITICAL HIGHLIGHTS
No previous office

ELECTION RESULTS

2008 GENERAL

Jo Ann Emerson (R)	198,798	71.4%
Joe Allen (D)	72,790	26.2%
Branden C. McCullough (LIBERT)	4,443	1.6%

2008 PRIMARY

Jo Ann Emerson (R)	unopposed

2006 GENERAL

Jo Ann Emerson (R)	156,164	71.6%
Veronica J. Hambacker (D)	57,557	26.4%
Branden C. McCullough (LIBERT)	4,268	2.0%

PREVIOUS WINNING PERCENTAGES*
2004 (72%); 2002 (72%); 2000 (69%); 1998 (63%);
1996 (50%); 1996 Special Election (63%)
*Elected as an independent in 1996 general election

Emerson is a moderate willing to ally with Democrats on issues affecting her district's working poor: hunger, health care and, more recently, the economy. She typically makes more headway with Democrats than she did with her own party when it was in power, a reflection of the skills she cultivated as a campaign staffer and lobbyist — and congressman's spouse — before she came to Congress.

Her Appropriations Committee seat has put her in a good position to help direct federal dollars to her centerpiece issues. And as ranking member on the committee's panel on Financial Services during the 111th Congress (2009-10), she has a voice in continued discussions on the economy and the ailing financial services industry. In fall 2008, she supported a $700 billion measure aimed at rescuing ailing financial institutions, saying it would protect the "paychecks, jobs and retirement savings" of her constituents. She also voted for a measure to bail out automakers that the Senate defeated in December 2008.

Though she joined GOP colleagues in opposing President Obama's $787 billion economic stimulus law, Emerson broke from her party on other issues in early 2009. She was one of just 16 House Republicans to support a $410 billion catchall spending bill for fiscal 2009 and one of 40 voting to expand the State Children's Health Insurance Program, which covers children from low-income families that do not qualify for Medicaid. She also was one of 38 in the GOP who refused to back the House Republicans' alternative fiscal 2010 budget proposal, although she stuck with her party and voted against the Democrats' $3.56 trillion resolution.

Emerson was steeped in politics from an early age. She grew up in suburban Washington, while her father, Ab Hermann, was executive director of the Republican National Committee. She says her father taught her to get along with Democrats, including family friend Hale Boggs, the powerful Louisiana representative who rose to majority leader before disappearing on a plane flight in Alaska in 1972. "The model that I was given and grew up with was that you reach across the aisle and try to find solutions as opposed to throw bombs," she said.

Like Boggs' widow, Lindy, Emerson followed her husband, Bill Emerson, to the House after he died of cancer in 1996 while seeking his ninth term. She has passionately taken up his cause of combating hunger. During the 110th Congress (2007-08), she sponsored legislation — a version of which became law — to encourage federal agencies to donate leftover food to soup kitchens.

Emerson co-chairs the Congressional Hunger Center, which carries on her husband's legacy by awarding fellowships in his name to individuals interested in receiving training to help fight hunger at home and abroad. "We're the richest country in the world, and we have the means by which to get every person in this country nutrition and food, but somehow there are people who are just falling through the cracks," she said. A member of the Agriculture Appropriations Subcommittee, she is among the proponents of creating an executive branch "food czar" to oversee food safety.

She also is deeply involved in health care issues. In January 2009, she was one of four original cosponsors of a measure to provide assistance to rural hospitals by increasing their Medicare payments. She plans to push for legislation to make it easier for Americans to gain access to cheaper medications imported from Canada and to expedite the approval process for generic drugs.

Emerson is often blunt and direct when talking about the issues she cares about most. With drug prices soaring, she said lawmakers needed to "stop listening to the scare tactics of drug companies" and pay more attention to average citizens. She refuses to allow drug company lobbyists into her office.

In arguing for allowing Medicare to negotiate lower, bulk prices, she said, "The Department of Defense isn't forced to buy bullets one at a time and we shouldn't force Medicare to buy medicines one pill at a time."

Emerson's conservatism comes through on social issues. Although she supports embryonic stem cell research, which uses discarded embryos created for in vitro fertilization, she opposes abortion and same-sex marriage. During the 110th, she stuck by fellow Republicans in voting against a bill to bar employment discrimination against gays and lesbians, and in voting for another measure maintaining the prohibition on federal aid to international groups that perform abortions.

The Iraq War is a tough issue for her. She voted in 2002 to authorize the war. Her stepdaughter Jessica, an Army captain, did a tour in Iraq, something Emerson says she is very proud of. But she has since wavered. In 2007, she told the St. Louis Post-Dispatch she was "totally against" President George W. Bush's plan to send more than 20,000 additional troops to Iraq; nevertheless, she voted against a Democratic resolution in opposition, saying it "is not going to change one thing." When Democrats tried in April of that year to set a withdrawal date as a non-binding goal, she was among only a few Republicans to not oppose it, voting present instead.

Farming is a mainstay in Emerson's district, and she has become a self-taught expert on agriculture policy. Her first choice for an Appropriations subcommittee ranking member seat in January 2009 was the Agriculture panel. She had also been rumored to be considered for secretary of Agriculture in the Obama administration.

Emerson knows the importance of delivering federal dollars to her district, as symbolized by her husband's legacy, a $100 million Mississippi River bridge linking Missouri and Illinois that bears his name.

After graduating from Ohio Wesleyan, she worked for the National Republican Congressional Committee and then as a lobbyist. In Washington, she met Bill Emerson, who was also a lobbyist, and they married. Bill Emerson was elected to the House in 1980. When he died in 1996, Jo Ann Emerson ran as an independent in the general-election race to succeed him because the partisan filing deadline had passed. She won with 50 percent of the vote, finishing 13 percentage points ahead of Democrat Emily Firebaugh and 39 points ahead of the official GOP candidate, Richard A. Kline. She has not faced a serious challenge since. In 2000, she married a Democrat, St. Louis labor lawyer Ron Gladney.

KEY VOTES

2008

No Delay consideration of Colombia free-trade agreement

Yes Override Bush veto of federal farm and nutrition programs reauthorization bill

Yes Overhaul surveillance laws and permit dismissal of suits against companies that conducted warrantless wiretapping

No Grant mortgage relief to homeowners and funding for Fannie Mae and Freddie Mac

Yes Approve initial $700 billion program to stabilize financial markets

Yes Approve final $700 billion program to stabilize financial markets

Yes Provide $14 billion in loans to automakers

2007

Yes Increase minimum wage by $2.10 an hour

P Approve $124.2 billion in emergency war spending and set goal for redeployment of troops from Iraq

Yes Reject federal contraceptive assistance to international family planning groups

Yes Override Bush veto of $23.2 billion water projects authorization bill

Yes Implement Peru free-trade agreement

Yes Approve energy policy overhaul with new fuel economy standards

Yes Clear $473.5 billion omnibus spending bill, including $70 billion for military operations

CQ VOTE STUDIES

	PARTY UNITY		PRESIDENTIAL SUPPORT	
	SUPPORT	OPPOSE	SUPPORT	OPPOSE
2008	86%	14%	53%	47%
2007	76%	24%	46%	54%
2006	89%	11%	74%	26%
2005	90%	10%	68%	32%
2004	89%	11%	61%	39%

INTEREST GROUPS

	AFL-CIO	ADA	CCUS	ACU
2008	60%	65%	83%	56%
2007	71%	50%	85%	60%
2006	50%	15%	93%	72%
2005	27%	15%	89%	88%
2004	50%	20%	86%	76%

MISSOURI 8

Southeast – Cape Girardeau, Ozark Plateau

The 8th is Missouri's largest district in size, and some of the state's most bountiful farmland can be found here alongside mountains, forests and Mississippi Valley towns. The district has the state's lowest median income (less than $28,000), and only 12 percent — Missouri's smallest percentage — of the 8th's residents have at least a bachelor's degree.

Agriculture and lead mining fuel the central counties, while the southeast area, dubbed the boot heel because of its shape, is a former wheat-growing region that now produces soybeans, corn, cotton and rice. A slowdown in home construction across the country has put lumber jobs, which have featured heavily in the 8th, at risk. Rising unemployment rates across all sectors are straining the economy.

The northern counties of Phelps and St. Francois, which had relied on light manufacturing and defense subcontracting firms, hope to boost employment and revenue through infrastructure projects. Located on the Mississippi River, Cape Girardeau is the district's most populous city and is a regional hub for education, commerce and health care.

The district includes four-fifths of the 1.5 million-acre Mark Twain National Forest that dots the countryside of southern Missouri. Frequent flooding and earthquakes from the New Madrid fault line that runs through the eastern portion of the district make the 8th a disaster-prone region, and the strength of levees and highways concern local officials and residents. Preparation for smaller floods along the Mississippi is still an annual spring ritual in the border towns.

The 8th District spans the political spectrum from solidly Republican counties in the west and in the northeast along the Mississippi River to "Yellow Dog" Democratic territory in the boot heel. Voters tend to be conservative on social issues such as abortion and gun control. Republican John McCain carried the district with 62 percent of the district's 2008 presidential vote.

MAJOR INDUSTRY
Agriculture, lead mining, lumber

CITIES
Cape Girardeau, 35,349; Sikeston, 16,992; Poplar Bluff, 16,651; Rolla, 16,367

NOTABLE
The Laura Ingalls Wilder Historic Home and Museum is in Mansfield, where the author wrote her "Little House" series.

Rep. Blaine Luetkemeyer (R)

Elected 2008; 1st term

CAPITOL OFFICE
225-2956
luetkemeyer.house.gov
1118 Longworth Bldg. 20515-2509; fax 225-5712

COMMITTEES
Agriculture
Small Business

RESIDENCE
St. Elizabeth

BORN
May 7, 1952; Jefferson City, Mo.

RELIGION
Roman Catholic

FAMILY
Wife, Jackie Luetkemeyer; three children

EDUCATION
Lincoln U. (Mo.), B.A. 1974 (political science)

CAREER
Insurance agency owner; rancher; banker;
state finance examiner

POLITICAL HIGHLIGHTS
Village of St. Elizabeth Board of Trustees,
1978-87; Mo. House, 1999-2005; sought
Republican nomination for Mo. treasurer, 2004;
Mo. Tourism Commission director, 2006-08

ELECTION RESULTS

2008 GENERAL

Blaine Luetkemeyer (R)	161,031	50.0%
Judy Baker (D)	152,956	47.5%
Tamara A. Millay (LIBERT)	8,108	2.5%

2008 PRIMARY

Blaine Luetkemeyer (R)	21,543	39.7%
Bob Onder (R)	15,752	29.0%
Danielle "Danie" Moore (R)	10,609	19.5%
Brock Olivo (R)	5,501	10.1%
Dan Bishir (R)	890	1.6%

Luetkemeyer spent six years in the Missouri House, where he chaired the Financial Services Committee as well as the Republican caucus. He earned a reputation as a serious legislator uninterested in scoring political points. "He's not a grandstander," Bob Johnson, a former GOP colleague, told the St. Louis Post-Dispatch.

Luetkemeyer (LUTE-ka-myer) also wouldn't mind if constituents don't see much difference between him and his predecessor, six-term Republican Kenny Hulshof. "Kenny and I are very much alike in our basic philosophy," he said.

An ardent social and fiscal conservative, Luetkemeyer seeks to further Hulshof's work of in looking out for — and actively listening to — his district's farmers and small businesses. "Folks back home in Missouri have made it clear to me if they have to balance their checkbooks, then so does Washington," he said in blasting President Obama's fiscal 2010 budget proposal.

Luetkemeyer said his career in state government and as a banking regulator gives him the experience to deal with economic matters as a member of the Small Business panel. The first bill he introduced seeks to improve the Small Business Administration's entrepreneurial development programs by creating planning standards and a national task force to examine the programs.

His farming background benefits him on the Agriculture Committee; his family still owns and operates his great-grandfather's farm.

His work in Congress also is shaped by his religious views. Raised in a family with strong Catholic values, he taught Sunday school and served on the board of St. Lawrence Catholic Church. "At the end of day, you put your hand in the Good Lord's hand," he said in discussing his future goals.

Luetkemeyer affiliates himself with the Republican Study Committee, the House's most conservative Republicans.

Using $1.8 million of his own money, Luetkemeyer won a narrow victory over Democratic state Rep. Judy Baker for the seat left vacant by Hulshof, who left to wage an unsuccessful bid for governor. His nearly 3-percentage-point victory was far short of the 11-point margin posted by GOP presidential candidate Arizona Sen. John McCain.

MISSOURI 9

Northeast — Columbia, St. Louis exurbs

Bordering Iowa, Illinois and five other Missouri districts, the 9th picks up small towns scattered among the farmland of northeastern and central Missouri. Columbia, the 9th's lone large city, and some western St. Louis suburbs are the only population centers.

The 9th splits suburban St. Charles County with the 2nd and encompasses all of adjacent Warren and Franklin counties. General Motors has cut jobs in the area, although many residents still work at Boeing plants in nearby districts. Small businesses, recently a source of economic growth, have take a hit during the nationwide recession. Nestled along the district's portion of the Missouri River Valley, residents of Gasconade and surrounding counties boast a wine industry that dates back to the 19th century. In other rural

areas, the district's economy still thrives on cattle, soybeans, corn and winter wheat.

About halfway between St. Louis and Kansas City, Columbia is a mostly middle-class city. State revenue shortfalls have affected the 9th's primary economic engine and the state's largest public research university: University of Missouri flagship campus. The city hosts the Harry S Truman Memorial Veterans Hospital and is a regional hub for companies in the insurance industry.

Historically Democratic, the 9th has swayed increasingly Republican over the past two decades with the rise of white-collar GOP voters. John McCain won 55 percent of the district's 2008 presidential vote.

MAJOR INDUSTRY
Higher education, agriculture, health care

CITIES
Columbia, 84,531; Hannibal, 17,757

NOTABLE
Samuel Clemens (Mark Twain) was born in Monroe County and grew up in Hannibal.

Gov. Brian Schweitzer (D)

First elected: 2004
Length of term: 4 years
Term expires: 1/13
Salary: $100,121
Phone: (406) 444-3111

Residence: Helena
Born: Sept. 4, 1955; Havre, Mont.
Religion: Roman Catholic
Family: Wife, Nancy Schweitzer; three children
Education: Colorado State U., B.S. 1978 (international agronomy); Montana State U., Bozeman, M.S. 1980 (soil science)
Career: Farmer; rancher; agronomist
Political highlights: Democratic nominee for U.S. Senate, 2000

Election results:
2008 GENERAL

Brian Schweitzer (D)	318,670	65.5%
Roy Brown (R)	58,268	32.5%
Stan Jones (LIBERT)	9,796	2.0%

Lt. Gov. John Bohlinger (R)

First elected: 2004
Length of term: 4 years
Term expires: 1/13
Salary: $79,007
Phone: (406) 444-3111

LEGISLATURE

Legislature: January-April in odd-numbered years, limit of 90 days

Senate: 50 members, 4-year terms
2009 ratios: 27 R, 23 D; 40 men, 10 women
Salary: $83/day in session; $104/day in session allowance
Phone: (406) 444-4880

House: 100 members, 2-year terms
2009 ratios: 50 D, 50 R; 71 men, 29 women
Salary: $83/day in session; $104/day in session allowance
Phone: (406) 444-4819

TERM LIMITS

Governor: 2 terms in a 16-year period
Senate: 2 terms in a 16-year period
House: 4 terms in a 16-year period

URBAN STATISTICS

CITY	POPULATION
Billings	89,847
Missoula	57,053
Great Falls	56,690
Butte-Silver Bow	34,606
Bozeman	27,509

REGISTERED VOTERS

Voters do not register by party.

POPULATION

2008 population (est.)	967,440
2000 population	902,195
1990 population	799,065
Percent change (1990-2000)	+12.9%
Rank among states (2008)	44

Median age	37.5
Born in state	56.1%
Foreign born	1.8%
Violent crime rate	241/100,000
Poverty level	14.6%
Federal workers	13,044
Military	8,349

ELECTIONS

STATE ELECTION OFFICIAL
(406) 444-4732
DEMOCRATIC PARTY
(406) 442-9520
REPUBLICAN PARTY
(406) 442-6469

MISCELLANEOUS

Web: www.mt.gov
Capital: Helena

U.S. CONGRESS

Senate: 2 Democrats
House: 1 Republican

2000 Census Statistics by District

DIST.	2008 VOTE FOR PRESIDENT OBAMA	MCCAIN	WHITE	BLACK	ASIAN	HISP	MEDIAN INCOME	WHITE COLLAR	BLUE COLLAR	SERVICE INDUSTRY	OVER 64	UNDER 18	COLLEGE EDUCATION	RURAL	SQ. MILES
AL	47%	50%	90%	0%	1%	2%	$33,024	59%	24%	17%	13%	26%	24%	46%	145,552
STATE	47	50	90	0	1	2	$33,024	59	24	17	13	26	24	46	145,552
U.S.	53	46	69	12	4	13	$41,994	60	25	15	12	26	24	21	3,537,438

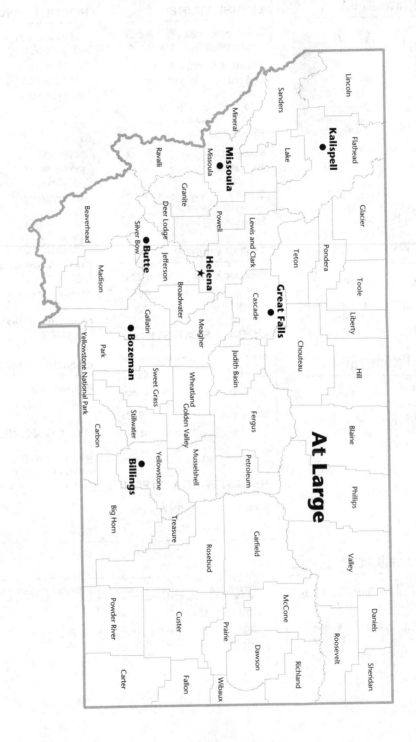

Sen. Max Baucus (D)

Elected 1978; 6th term

CAPITOL OFFICE
224-2651
baucus.senate.gov
511 Hart Bldg. 20510-2602; fax 224-0515

COMMITTEES
Agriculture, Nutrition & Forestry
Environment & Public Works
  (Transportation & Infrastructure - chairman)
Finance - chairman
Joint Taxation - vice-chairman

RESIDENCE
Helena

BORN
Dec. 11, 1941; Helena, Mont.

RELIGION
Protestant

FAMILY
Divorced; one child

EDUCATION
Stanford U., A.B. 1964 (economics), LL.B. 1967

CAREER
Lawyer

POLITICAL HIGHLIGHTS
Mont. House, 1973-75; U.S. House, 1975-78

ELECTION RESULTS

2008 GENERAL

Max Baucus (D)	348,289	72.9%
Bob Kelleher (R)	129,369	27.1%

2008 PRIMARY

Max Baucus (D)	unopposed

PREVIOUS WINNING PERCENTAGES
2002 (63%); 1996 (50%); 1990 (68%); 1984 (57%); 1978 (56%); 1976 House Election (66%); 1974 House Election (55%)

The highly practical Baucus has an influential role shaping fiscal policy as chairman of the powerful Finance Committee. He can be a forceful advocate for the party line, but has long been one of the centrist Democrats that Republicans look to on taxes, trade and even Medicare. He has served on Finance since 1979; if he completes his current term, he will have been on the panel longer than any senator in history, eclipsing legendary Louisiana Democrat Russell Long, a former chairman and Finance member for 34 years.

Stylistically, Baucus stands in contrast to his high-profile predecessors, such as Republican Bob Dole of Kansas and Democrats Lloyd Bentsen of Texas and Daniel Patrick Moynihan of New York. Neither a glad-handing dealmaker nor a fixture on the TV talk show circuit, he can be standoffish. Though no slouch intellectually, he is not known as one of his party's visionary thinkers.

But Baucus continues the committee's tradition of bipartisanship. He has an unusually strong working relationship — even by the clubby Senate's standards — with ranking Republican Charles E. Grassley of Iowa, who also has taken turns as Finance chairman. Both come from rural states, and they share many of the same concerns. "I tend to think we don't wear our egos on our sleeves, like some others do," Baucus told The American Prospect. "That makes it easier for us to work together."

He broke from his party to back President George W. Bush's signature 2001 tax cuts, although he voted against the 2003 follow-up that cut taxes on capital gains and dividends. Baucus was one of just two Democrats that Republicans allowed to participate in drafting the final 2003 Medicare prescription drug law, enraging liberals who thought the result favored insurers and short-changed seniors. The Nation magazine dubbed Baucus "K Street's favorite Democrat."

In the 110th Congress (2007-08), Baucus split with his party's majority more often than all but a half-dozen other Senate Democrats on votes that divided the two parties. But on most issues, he is a loyalist. He helped kill Bush's 2005 push to create private investment accounts in Social Security, and helped President Obama win enactment of a $787 billion economic stimulus bill early in his presidency. He also dismayed Grassley by helping Democrats clear a 2009 expansion of the State Children's Health Insurance Program that was more generous than a 2008 version that Grassley had helped negotiate. The program covers children from low-income families that do not qualify for Medicaid.

Baucus is in agreement with Obama's call for universal access to health care. But he laid out his own health care reform plan in November 2008, before the new administration or new Congress were even sworn in. His proposal incorporated several elements Obama had called for during his campaign, but also staked out a ground independent from the president — including, for example, an individual mandate to buy coverage. And Baucus objected to using fast-track budget procedures to advance a health care bill, preferring to strike a deal with Republicans to maximize support.

Baucus also sits on the Environment and Public Works and Agriculture, Nutrition and Forestry committees, where he must balance competing interests in his state. As a member of the Environment panel for more than 15 years, and as its chairman in the early 1990s, he was a key player on several major environmental laws, including the Safe Drinking Water Act, the Clean Water Act and the superfund law governing cleanup of hazardous-waste sites. Yet over the years he has drawn the ire of environmentalists for seeking to protect miners and ranchers in his state from tough regulations.

Baucus can be pugnacious, a tendency that was on display as he staked out a key role in the financial industry rescue package. He demanded the administration accept taxpayer protections during late-night negotiations with Treasury Secretary Henry M. Paulson Jr. Then, after the bill failed on the House floor — sparking a record drop in the stock market — Baucus led the charge to add controversial "sweeteners" to the package. The House and Senate had deadlocked for much of the 110th Congress over business and energy tax cut extensions, as well as a "patch" to keep the alternative minimum tax, which was originally intended to target only wealthy taxpayers but was not indexed for inflation, from hitting millions more families. House Democrats demanded such provisions be fully offset with revenue-raisers; the Senate balked. Adding the extensions to the rescue bill, without full offsets, helped secure the Republican votes needed for final passage of the measure.

The move further aggravated Baucus' already rocky relationship with his House counterpart, liberal Ways and Means Chairman Charles B. Rangel of New York. But Baucus and Rangel share some priorities, including trade liberalization and tax benefits for the working poor. Baucus generally supports proposals intended to relax trade constraints and votes to approve bilateral trade agreements.

Baucus is an ardent champion of Montana beef producers. He wants Japan to open its markets to U.S. beef, and he supported a 2006 bill to impose economic sanctions if the Japanese government did not lift its ban on U.S. beef imports. A negotiator on the 2008 law reauthorizing farm programs, he and North Dakota Democrat Kent Conrad won inclusion of a $3.8 billion disaster relief fund for farmers hit by drought and other natural disasters. The law also tightened country-of-origin meat labeling requirements popular with Western ranchers.

Now entering his late 60s, Baucus attempts physical feats that men half his age wouldn't contemplate. In recent years, he has suffered a motorcycle accident, a major head injury when he fell during a 50-mile ultramarathon (the latter required an operation in which two small holes were drilled into his skull) and heart surgery to implant a pacemaker.

Baucus' family emigrated from Germany in the late 1800s and eventually settled in Montana. His great-grandfather Henry Sieben was named to the Cowboy Hall of Fame. Baucus' brother and sister-in-law now run the sprawling Sieben Ranch north of Helena. Of the ranch, Baucus said, "It's my blood. It's the soil. It's the earth. It's my family."

Baucus spent part of his junior year in college at an exchange program in France. He then went to England, where he traveled with some Gypsies. He left England and journeyed across Europe, the Middle East and Africa. He was in the Belgian Congo, he said, when he had an "epiphany" that he should undertake a career in public service.

After finishing Stanford Law School in 1967, he was an attorney for the Securities and Exchange Commission for three years. He returned to Montana in 1971 to coordinate the state's constitutional convention, and in 1972 he won a seat in the state legislature. He captured a U.S. House seat in the post-Watergate election of 1974, ousting a two-term GOP incumbent. Four years later, he arrived in the Senate. Although he had just won a six-year term starting in January 1979, he was appointed to the seat in December 1978 after Democrat Paul Hatfield resigned. Hatfield had been appointed earlier in the year upon the death of Sen. Lee Metcalf, who had served in Congress for 25 years. But Baucus defeated him in the Democratic primary.

Re-election has not always been easy in a state that has been solidly Republican; in 1996 Baucus won by fewer than 20,000 votes over Republican Denny Rehberg, then the lieutenant governor and now Montana's sole House member. But since then, Baucus has cruised.

KEY VOTES

2008

Yes Prohibit discrimination based on genetic information

Yes Reauthorize farm and nutrition programs for five years

Yes Limit debate on "cap and trade" system for greenhouse gas emissions

Yes Allow lawsuits against companies that participated in warrantless wiretapping

Yes Limit debate on a bill to block a scheduled cut in Medicare payments to doctors

Yes Grant mortgage relief to homeowners and funding for Fannie Mae and Freddie Mac

Yes Approve a nuclear cooperation agreement with India

Yes Approve final $700 billion program to stabilize financial markets

No Allow consideration of a $14 billion auto industry loan package

2007

Yes Increase minimum wage by $2.10 an hour

No Limit debate on a comprehensive immigration bill

Yes Overhaul congressional lobbying and ethics rules for members and their staffs

No Limit debate on considering a bill to add House seats for the District of Columbia and Utah

Yes Limit debate on restoring habeas corpus rights to detainees

Yes Mandate minimum breaks for troops between deployments to Iraq or Afghanistan

Yes Override Bush veto of $23.2 billion water projects authorization bill

No Confirm Michael B. Mukasey as attorney general

Yes Limit debate on an energy policy overhaul containing $21.8 billion in tax incentives and reduced oil and gas subsidies

CQ VOTE STUDIES

	PARTY UNITY		PRESIDENTIAL SUPPORT	
	SUPPORT	OPPOSE	SUPPORT	OPPOSE
2008	89%	11%	35%	65%
2007	83%	17%	41%	59%
2006	79%	21%	61%	39%
2005	74%	26%	45%	55%
2004	72%	28%	57%	43%
2003	74%	26%	54%	46%
2002	67%	33%	88%	12%
2001	67%	33%	71%	29%
2000	88%	12%	97%	3%
1999	87%	13%	81%	19%

INTEREST GROUPS

	AFL-CIO	ADA	CCUS	ACU
2008	90%	80%	75%	8%
2007	89%	80%	55%	20%
2006	71%	70%	70%	8%
2005	85%	95%	71%	24%
2004	92%	85%	71%	29%
2003	62%	85%	74%	15%
2002	69%	75%	70%	37%
2001	81%	80%	71%	28%
2000	75%	85%	46%	16%
1999	78%	95%	59%	4%

Sen. Jon Tester (D)

CAPITOL OFFICE
224-2644
tester.senate.gov
724 Hart Bldg. 20510-2603; fax 224-8594

COMMITTEES
Appropriations
Banking, Housing & Urban Affairs
Homeland Security & Governmental Affairs
Indian Affairs
Veterans' Affairs

RESIDENCE
Big Sandy

BORN
Aug. 21, 1956; Havre, Mont.

RELIGION
Church of God

FAMILY
Wife, Sharla Tester; two children

EDUCATION
College of Great Falls, B.A. 1978 (music
education & secondary education)

CAREER
Farmer; teacher

POLITICAL HIGHLIGHTS
Big Sandy School Board of Trustees, 1983-92
(chairman, 1986-91); Mont. Senate, 1999-2007
(minority whip, 2001-03; minority leader, 2003-05;
president, 2005-07)

ELECTION RESULTS

2006 GENERAL

Jon Tester (D)	199,845	49.2%
Conrad Burns (R)	196,283	48.3%
Stan Jones (LIBERT)	10,377	2.6%

2006 PRIMARY

Jon Tester (D)	65,757	60.8%
John Morrison (D)	38,394	35.5%
Paul Richards (D)	1,636	1.5%
Robert Candee (D)	1,471	1.4%

Elected 2006; 1st term

Tester's plain-spoken, independent and transparent approach appeals to his constituency. In defiance of his party, he supports expanding disclosure of spending earmarks while opposing legislation to rescue struggling banks and automakers. He also posts his daily schedule on his Web site, listing all his appointments and activities. The postings name names — and affiliations.

With Democrats holding nearly enough Senate seats to stave off Republican filibusters, Tester — a first-term Democrat in a conservative state — will face pressure to stay in line during the 111th Congress (2009-10). His party's leaders are striving to keep him happy; in January 2009 they awarded him a plum spot on the Appropriations Committee. Majority Leader Harry Reid of Nevada had promised him the assignment "as soon as possible" after Tester helped Democrats win control of the Senate in 2006.

During his first two years, Tester declined to back his party on 14 percent of the votes that split a majority of Republicans from a majority of Democrats; only eight other Democrats did so more often during that period.

In the closing days of the 110th Congress (2007-08), as lawmakers struggled with how to fix the ailing economy, Tester opposed the $700 billion financial rescue plan. He said it didn't "require the common-sense regulations needed to prevent this mess from happening again." He also balked at loans to bail out struggling U.S. automakers, criticizing them for not coming up with a credible business plan to escape bankruptcy.

In doing so, Tester — a burly third-generation Montana farmer who strides the Capitol in cowboy boots and a 1950s-style flat-top haircut — stuck with what works for Democrats in the conservative West: populism. Handouts for wealthy industrialists and financiers just don't fly in Montana.

When senators debated President Obama's economic stimulus proposal in February 2009, Tester showed up with a photo of a Montanan holding a sign reading: "Work Needed." He explained his support for the bill and his refusal to call it a stimulus. "The word 'stimulus' is a Washington, D.C., word that doesn't mean much in my book," he said. "That's why, from Day One, I have called this the jobs bill. Because that's exactly what it is. You're either for jobs or you're against jobs...Now some D.C. politicians say we don't need to pass a jobs bill because the current recession is only temporary. I ask you to tell that to this guy standing on the street in Whitefish, Montana"

Tester's populism also emerges on immigration issues. He was among a small minority of Democrats to vote to kill a 2007 bill that aimed to provide illegal immigrants with a path to citizenship. He said he simply didn't think it would work. And he won't budge on the issue of gun rights. He signed a court brief in 2008 asking the Supreme Court to overturn a restrictive District of Columbia law banning citizens from owning handguns. The court eventually agreed. In 2009, he and Democrat Max Baucus, Montana's senior senator, wrote to Attorney General Eric H. Holder Jr. warning they would oppose any gun restrictions the administration might propose.

Tester uses his seat on the Veterans' Affairs Committee to help his state's relatively large veteran population. He sponsored 2007 legislation, which eventually was signed into law, to increase the mileage reimbursement rate for veterans traveling to Veterans Affairs Department health clinics, a big issue in a state as spread-out as Montana.

Though not on the Agriculture panel — Baucus holds the state's seat there — Tester keeps a close eye on farm issues. During the 2008 debate to reauthorize farm and nutrition programs, he teamed with Baucus to push to include federal subsidies for Montana growers of camelina, a grain well-suited for use as a biofuel. Both senators also favor a bigger exclusion and lower rate for the estate tax than Obama wants, in part to help their state's family farmers and ranchers.

Tester also sits on the Indian Affairs Committee. He introduced legislation in the 110th Congress to finalize a water rights agreement among the Crow Nation, Montana and the federal government that stalled after clearing the committee. His other committee assignment is Homeland Security and Governmental Affairs, where he has sought to raise the profile of northern border security.

Growing up on an 1,800-acre farm near Big Sandy, population 703, Tester and his brothers were put to work at an early age. The labor came at a price. Grinding meat as a child, he severed three fingers on his left hand. But Tester relishes farm work nonetheless, calling his long rides on his tractor during breaks back home ideal times to think through the issues facing Congress.

He had an early interest in politics and got involved in student government during high school. After graduating from college, he taught music for a couple of years at his hometown elementary school. He gave up teaching to concentrate on the farm, where the family also operated a custom butcher shop his parents had started in the 1960s. They went organic in 1987 and now grow wheat, barley, lentils, peas, millet, buckwheat, alfalfa and hay. In 2007, Tester's daughter and son-in-law moved back to the farm to run the place in his absence.

He served as chairman of the Big Sandy school board and of the local Soil Conservation Service Committee before winning election to the Montana Senate, a seat he went after in 1998 because he was infuriated by the soaring rates that followed electricity deregulation approved by a Republican-controlled legislature.

He rose to minority whip and minority leader before becoming president of the state Senate in 2005, after Democrats gained control of the chamber. He championed legislation requiring public utilities in the state to use more renewable energy and supported tax credits for companies that generate wind power in the state.

After two four-year terms, Tester was reaching his state term limit. Democrat Brian Schweitzer, a rancher and friend with a political profile much like his, had been elected governor of Montana in 2004. Sentiment in the state was swinging against Republicans, and Tester entered the Senate race after traveling with his wife to see whether they could imagine living in the nation's capital. They decided they could.

The first test was the primary, and Tester trounced state Auditor John Morrison, a better-known, better-funded candidate backed by the Democratic establishment. Morrison was leading in initial polls but lost support after revelations emerged that he'd had an affair and allegations surfaced that he had allowed the relationship to influence his official conduct. With Democrats eager to beat three-term GOP Sen. Conrad Burns on ethics, they wanted a candidate with a spotless reputation.

That November, Tester beat Burns, attacking him for excessive coziness with lobbyists. Burns had accepted $150,000 from disgraced lobbyist Jack Abramoff, his firm or his clients. Burns later gave the money to charities, but Tester rode the issue hard and, since his election, has made sure to steer clear of any similar associations with Washington's business advocates.

Tester also spoke out strongly against the war in Iraq, saying President George W. Bush had failed to develop a plan for ending it. Burns suffered from a series of gaffes such as scolding firefighters for a "piss-poor job" fighting a huge fire in eastern Montana. Tester won by 3,562 votes, getting 49 percent of the total cast in 2006. He'll surely be one of the GOP's top targets in 2012.

KEY VOTES

2008

Yes Prohibit discrimination based on genetic information
Yes Reauthorize farm and nutrition programs for five years
Yes Limit debate on "cap and trade" system for greenhouse gas emissions
Yes Allow lawsuits against companies that participated in warrantless wiretapping
Yes Limit debate on a bill to block a scheduled cut in Medicare payments to doctors
Yes Grant mortgage relief to homeowners and funding for Fannie Mae and Freddie Mac
Yes Approve a nuclear cooperation agreement with India
No   Approve final $700 billion program to stabilize financial markets
No   Allow consideration of a $14 billion auto industry loan package

2007

Yes Increase minimum wage by $2.10 an hour
No   Limit debate on a comprehensive immigration bill
Yes Overhaul congressional lobbying and ethics rules for members and their staffs
Yes Limit debate on considering a bill to add House seats for the District of Columbia and Utah
Yes Limit debate on restoring habeas corpus rights to detainees
Yes Mandate minimum breaks for troops between deployments to Iraq or Afghanistan
Yes Override Bush veto of $23.2 billion water projects authorization bill
No   Confirm Michael B. Mukasey as attorney general
Yes Limit debate on an energy policy overhaul containing $21.8 billion in tax incentives and reduced oil and gas subsidies

CQ VOTE STUDIES

	PARTY UNITY		PRESIDENTIAL SUPPORT	
	SUPPORT	OPPOSE	SUPPORT	OPPOSE
2008	92%	8%	30%	70%
2007	84%	16%	37%	63%

INTEREST GROUPS

	AFL-CIO	ADA	CCUS	ACU
2008	90%	85%	63%	16%
2007	95%	95%	30%	16%

Rep. Denny Rehberg (R)

Elected 2000; 5th term

CAPITOL OFFICE
225-3211
www.house.gov/rehberg
2448 Rayburn Bldg. 20515-2601; fax 225-5687

COMMITTEES
Appropriations

RESIDENCE
Billings

BORN
Oct. 5, 1955; Billings, Mont.

RELIGION
Episcopalian

FAMILY
Wife, Janice Lenhardt Rehberg; three children

EDUCATION
Montana State U., attended 1973-74;
Washington State U., B.A. 1977 (political science)

CAREER
Rancher; congressional aide; Realtor

POLITICAL HIGHLIGHTS
Mont. House, 1985-91; lieutenant governor,
1991-97; Republican nominee for U.S. Senate, 1996

ELECTION RESULTS

2008 GENERAL

Denny Rehberg (R)	307,177	64.2%
John Driscoll (D)	154,710	32.4%
Mike Fellows (LIBERT)	16,282	3.4%

2008 PRIMARY

Denny Rehberg (R)	unopposed

2006 GENERAL

Denny Rehberg (R)	239,124	58.9%
Monica Lindeen (D)	158,916	39.1%
Mike Fellows (LIBERT)	8,085	2.0%

PREVIOUS WINNING PERCENTAGES
2004 (64%); 2002 (65%); 2000 (52%)

A former real estate agent, Rehberg is a fiscal and social conservative who likes to criticize Democrats for charging toward a broad social spending agenda. But clad in dark jeans, black cowboy boots and an open-collared, starched white shirt, he also likes to remind his colleagues he represents ranchers, rural families and American Indians, and he's willing to take an occasional step across party lines if their interests are at stake.

Rehberg, a rancher, is one of the wealthiest members of Congress; he was worth at least $6.9 million in 2007, according to the Center for Responsive Politics. Nevertheless, he sleeps on his Capitol Hill office couch for "efficiency" reasons, and flies home nearly every weekend.

During the George W. Bush administration, Rehberg proved to be a loyal party player, supporting his party on 93 percent of the votes that pitted Republicans against Democrats. But toward the end of Bush's second term, Rehberg began to put some distance between himself and an increasingly unpopular administration and national Republican party.

A member of the Appropriations Committee, Rehberg in fall 2008 opposed two $700 billion measures — the second of which became law — aimed at shoring up the ailing financial services industry. He even rejected Vice President Dick Cheney's pleas to vote for the bill. "I have to look at the long term and not just the short term," he told the Flathead Beacon newspaper. "Ultimately, Americans and Montanans will judge us on how well we solve the problem, not how fast we solve the problem." He said the legislation wouldn't prevent a future economic collapse and wouldn't do enough to help small commercial banks in states like his.

He was highly critical of President Obama's final $787 economic stimulus bill that became law in February 2009, contending Democrats didn't work hard enough to seek consensus with Republicans. He told an audience in Flathead, according to the Beacon, that Congress used the crisis "to further a social agenda." His vote prompted at least one potential challenge in the 2010 election. In early 2009, Montana Democratic Party Chairman Dennis McDonald filed paperwork in preparation for a run, according to The Associated Press.

In voting against the measure, Rehberg was at odds with his Democratic counterparts from Montana, senators Max Baucus — a former political opponent of his — and Jon Tester, who argued for quick action. On other issues, however, Rehberg seeks to find consensus with the two, particularly when it comes to such issues as health care, education and agriculture. "I need their help in a Democratic-controlled Congress," Rehberg said.

Rehberg was one of 40 Republicans who backed a Baucus-authored bill in early 2009 to expand funding for the State Children's Health Insurance Program, which covers children from low-income families that do not qualify for Medicaid, by $32.8 billion over the next five years. The bill, similar to a measure that Bush twice vetoed, was signed into law by Obama, and Rehberg was invited to the signing ceremony. "Washington spends a lot of money on stupid things," Rehberg told The Western News, "but providing health insurance for kids isn't one of them."

Rehberg also will cross party lines if he sees a threat to his state's agriculture sector. He was one of just 27 Republicans who voted against the Central America Free Trade Agreement in 2005. He similarly opposed Australia trade legislation in the 108th Congress (2003-04), because he feared more beef imports would threaten the livelihood of Montana ranchers. In 2005, he sought to include language in the agricultural spending bill to speed up implementation of a country-of-origin labeling law that would distinguish U.S.-produced beef from imports.

As a member of Appropriations since 2005, Rehberg likes having a seat at the table during discussions of every issue affecting his state. He sits on the Energy-Water Appropriations Subcommittee, where he consistently puts the need for greater energy production ahead of environmental concerns. He believes federal regulation is the biggest obstacle to expanding the nation's energy policy. For example, he said federal rules have made hydroelectric power in Montana expensive and time-consuming.

Rehberg protects Montana's military installations. He voted to delay the scheduled 2005 round of base closures and pushed to keep all 200 Minuteman III intercontinental ballistic missiles in silos at Malmstrom Air Force Base in Great Falls, although the Pentagon eliminated 50 of them by July 2008.

Rehberg grew up on his family's beef cattle and cashmere goat ranch, competing in gymnastics and playing the drums. His mother taught elementary school, and his father, Jack, ran the ranch and worked other jobs to help support the family. Jack Rehberg was the GOP nominee for a House seat in 1970, but took just 36 percent of the vote against the incumbent, Democrat John Melcher. The elder Rehberg also served in the state legislature.

After earning a degree in political science, Rehberg worked as an intern in the Montana Senate, sold real estate for two years, then moved to Washington in 1979 to join the staff of GOP Rep. Ron Marlenee of Montana. He returned to the family ranch three years later and ended up serving six years in the state House. He managed political campaigns for Marlenee in 1986 and Republican Conrad Burns in his successful Senate bid in 1988.

Rehberg was appointed lieutenant governor in 1991 when Allen Kolstad quit to join the administration of President George Bush. Rehberg was elected to a four-year term in 1992. In 1996, he came within 5 percentage points of defeating Baucus for a Senate seat, though Baucus outspent him almost 3-to-1.

In 2000, he was unopposed for the House nomination when GOP Rep. Rick Hill retired after two House terms, citing poor health. He then beat Democratic state school superintendent Nancy Keenan by 5 percentage points. During that race, Rehberg removed himself from the management of the family ranch by arranging to move its 600 goats to the Baucus family ranch. The two families now share the profits from the operation.

In 2008, the Democrats' early favorite to challenge Rehberg dropped out of the race, citing health reasons, and some speculated McDonald would run. Rehberg ultimately faced former Montana House Speaker John Driscoll, who raised no money and proved to be a weak challenger.

KEY VOTES

2008

No Delay consideration of Colombia free-trade agreement

Yes Override Bush veto of federal farm and nutrition programs reauthorization bill

Yes Overhaul surveillance laws and permit dismissal of suits against companies that conducted warrantless wiretapping

No Grant mortgage relief to homeowners and funding for Fannie Mae and Freddie Mac

No Approve initial $700 billion program to stabilize financial markets

No Approve final $700 billion program to stabilize financial markets

No Provide $14 billion in loans to automakers

2007

No Increase minimum wage by $2.10 an hour

No Approve $124.2 billion in emergency war spending and set goal for redeployment of troops from Iraq

Yes Reject federal contraceptive assistance to international family planning groups

Yes Override Bush veto of $23.2 billion water projects authorization bill

Yes Implement Peru free-trade agreement

Yes Approve energy policy overhaul with new fuel economy standards

Yes Clear $473.5 billion omnibus spending bill, including $70 billion for military operations

CQ VOTE STUDIES

	PARTY UNITY		PRESIDENTIAL SUPPORT	
	SUPPORT	OPPOSE	SUPPORT	OPPOSE
2008	93%	7%	65%	35%
2007	88%	12%	68%	32%
2006	97%	3%	95%	5%
2005	95%	5%	83%	17%
2004	96%	4%	76%	24%

INTEREST GROUPS

	AFL-CIO	ADA	CCUS	ACU
2008	33%	40%	89%	84%
2007	33%	20%	90%	88%
2006	29%	0%	100%	83%
2005	27%	10%	89%	92%
2004	13%	5%	95%	96%

MONTANA

At Large

Montana's Big Sky country has long been a place where pioneers traveled to strike it rich. Once explored by Lewis and Clark and later by fur trappers and gold seekers, Montana is now a prime destination for celebrities and telecommuters who want to purchase their own small piece of the frontier.

The economy is supported by natural resources, forcing Montana to find a balance between exploiting its terrain and protecting it, especially in the face of increased global demand for energy resources. Some of the more populated counties are experiencing rising unemployment, but the statewide economy remains stable. Butte, the site of years of copper mining, is the site of a massive superfund cleanup effort. The economy also relies on tourism, with three of the five entrances to Yellowstone National Park in southern Montana and Glacier National Park located in the northwestern part of the state.

The district combines the state's two politically independent halves into an unpredictable voting bloc. The western, mountainous half of the state leans Democratic, with an environmental base and a union tradition in mining and lumber mills. The area has been shifting to support more natural-resources-based development in recent years. It also is home to the state's university community in Missoula. Most of the eastern half, a flat plain where wheat and cattle are raised, follows a tradition of rural Republicanism.

Voters here will support both parties. In 2008, 13 of the state's 56 counties voted Democratic in the presidential election, and John McCain narrowly won the state with 50 percent of the vote. Many voters split their tickets as Democratic Sen. Max Baucus was re-elected with 73 percent of the vote.

MAJOR INDUSTRY
Agriculture, tourism, forestry

MILITARY BASES
Malmstrom Air Force Base, 3,407 military, 567 civilian (2007)

CITIES
Billings, 89,847; Missoula, 57,053; Great Falls, 56,690; Butte-Silver Bow, 34,606; Bozeman, 27,509; Helena, 25,780

NOTABLE
Montana elected Jeannette Rankin, the first woman in Congress, in 1916.

Gov. Dave Heineman (R)

First elected: 2006; assumed office Jan. 20, 2005, due to appointment of Mike Johanns, R, to be Agriculture secretary
Length of term: 4 years
Term expires: 1/11
Salary: $105,000
Phone: (402) 471-2244

Residence: Lincoln
Born: May 12, 1945; Falls City, Neb.
Religion: Eastern Orthodox
Family: Wife, Sally Ganem; one child
Education: U.S. Military Academy, B.S. 1970 (economics)
Military service: Army, 1970-75
Career: Congressional aide; health and beauty products company salesman
Political highlights: Neb. Republican Party executive director, 1979-81; Fremont City Council, 1990-94; Neb. treasurer, 1995-2001; lieutenant governor, 2001-05

Election results:
2006 GENERAL

Dave Heineman (R)	435,507	73.4%
David Hahn (D)	145,115	24.5%
Barry Richards (NEB)	8,953	1.5%

Lt. Gov. Rick Sheehy (R)

First elected: 2006; assumed office Jan. 24, 2005, due to Heineman's ascension to governor
Length of term: 4 years
Term expires: 1/11
Salary: $75,000
Phone: (402) 471-2256

LEGISLATURE

Unicameral Legislature: 90 days in odd-numbered years; 60 days in even-numbered years

Legislature: 49 nonpartisan members, 4-year terms
2009 ratios: 39 men, 10 women
Salary: $12,000
Phone: (402) 471-2271

TERM LIMITS

Governor: 2 consecutive terms
Legislature: 2 consecutive terms

URBAN STATISTICS

CITY	POPULATION
Omaha	390,007
Lincoln	225,581
Bellevue	44,382
Grand Island	42,940
Kearney	27,431

REGISTERED VOTERS

Republican	48%
Democrat	34%
Nonpartisan/others	18%

POPULATION

2008 population (est.)	1,783,432
2000 population	1,711,263
1990 population	1,578,385
Percent change (1990-2000)	+8.4%
Rank among states (2008)	38
Median age	35.3
Born in state	67.1%
Foreign born	4.4%
Violent crime rate	328/100,000
Poverty level	9.7%
Federal workers	15,620
Military	15,040

ELECTIONS

STATE ELECTION OFFICIAL
(402) 471-2555
DEMOCRATIC PARTY
(402) 434-2180
REPUBLICAN PARTY
(402) 475-2122

MISCELLANEOUS

Web: www.nebraska.gov
Capital: Lincoln

U.S. CONGRESS

Senate: 1 Democrat, 1 Republican
House: 3 Republicans

2000 Census Statistics by District

DIST.	2008 VOTE FOR PRESIDENT OBAMA	MCCAIN	WHITE	BLACK	ASIAN	HISP	MEDIAN INCOME	WHITE COLLAR	BLUE COLLAR	SERVICE INDUSTRY	OVER 64	UNDER 18	COLLEGE EDUCATION	RURAL	SQ. MILES
1	44%	54%	91%	1%	2%	4%	$40,021	58%	27%	15%	13%	25%	24%	35%	11,951
2	50	49	80	10	2	6	$45,235	67	20	13	10	27	31	2	411
3	30	69	92	0	0	6	$33,866	54	31	15	17	26	17	54	64,511
STATE	42	57	87	4	1	6	$39,250	59	26	15	14	26	24	30	76,872
U.S.	53	46	69	12	4	13	$41,994	60	25	15	12	26	24	21	3,537,438

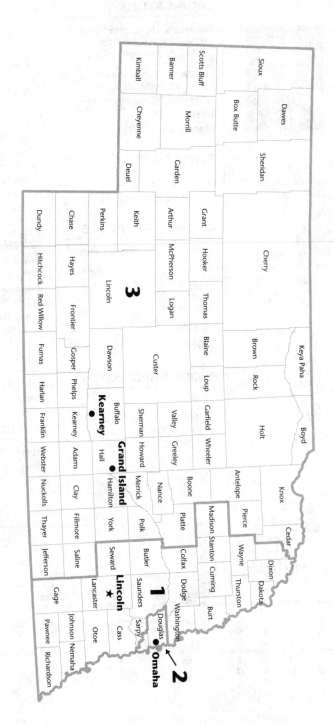

Sen. Ben Nelson (D)

CAPITOL OFFICE
224-6551
bennelson.senate.gov
720 Hart Bldg. 20510-2706; fax 228-0012

COMMITTEES
Agriculture, Nutrition & Forestry
Appropriations
 (Legislative Branch - chairman)
Armed Services
 (Personnel - chairman)
Rules & Administration

RESIDENCE
Omaha

BORN
May 17, 1941; McCook, Neb.

RELIGION
Methodist

FAMILY
Wife, Diane Nelson; four children

EDUCATION
U. of Nebraska, B.A. 1963 (philosophy), M.A. 1965
(philosophy), J.D. 1970

CAREER
Lawyer; insurance company executive

POLITICAL HIGHLIGHTS
Neb. director of insurance, 1975-76; governor,
1991-99; Democratic nominee for U.S. Senate, 1996

ELECTION RESULTS

2006 GENERAL
Ben Nelson (D)	378,388	63.9%
Pete Ricketts (R)	213,928	36.1%

2006 PRIMARY
Ben Nelson (D)	unopposed

PREVIOUS WINNING PERCENTAGES
2000 (51%)

Elected 2000; 2nd term

Nelson is the Senate's most conservative Democrat. He has remained anchored to the right of his colleagues on both fiscal and social policy even after comfortably winning a second term in his Republican-leaning state. He also is quick to join the bipartisan "gangs" that have sprung up in recent years to find a middle ground on contentious issues.

During the 110th Congress (2007-08), Nelson broke from Democrats on 30 percent of the votes that divided the parties — well ahead of runners-up Sens. Evan Bayh of Indiana and Mary L. Landrieu of Louisiana, who both tied with 25 percent.

Despite frequently crossing the aisle, Nelson insists he feels most comfortable among Democrats, who he says are on the proper side on issues such as civil rights, Medicare and Social Security. "While I have had overtures from Republicans [to switch parties], I've concluded that I'm very comfortable where I am," he said.

President George W. Bush lavished attention on Nelson, keeping in regular touch and bestowing several nicknames on him. (Nelson preferred the more macho "Benator" to "Nelly" or "Benny.") President Obama may skip the pet names, but he can't afford to pay any less attention to Nelson at a time when moderates are still critical to passing major legislation despite the strong Democratic majority. And Nelson wasted no time showing the new president both his appetite for centrist dealmaking and his determination to keep a rein on federal spending.

In the early months of the 111th Congress (2009-10), Nelson and moderate Republican Susan Collins of Maine took the lead in hammering out and passing through the Senate a compromise economic stimulus bill that shaved more than $100 billion from the original proposal. Then, during debate on the fiscal 2010 budget resolution, Nelson repeatedly broke with his party to support GOP amendments aimed at cutting spending. He was one of just three Democrats to vote against the $3.56 trillion blueprint.

He learned his penny-pinching ways early on. He grew up in McCook, a small town in south-central Nebraska where his mother started a taxpayers' watchdog group. Her attention to how tax revenue was spent wasn't lost on her son. "Watching the purse strings is the most important basic thing you can do in government," he said.

Nelson has been outspoken on Iraq and Afghanistan from his seat on the Armed Services Committee. In the 110th Congress, he said Iraq needed to pay a greater share of its reconstruction costs. "The blank-check policy must end," Nelson said, "and the Iraqis need to invest — really invest — in their own future by repaying the United States for future reconstruction funds." In 2009, he called for clear benchmarks to measure U.S. progress in Afghanistan — a concept that Obama embraced.

Nelson solidified his credentials as a negotiator in 2005, when he helped lead a bipartisan group of senators who wanted to avert a potentially damaging Senate showdown over judicial nominees. Seven Democrats and seven Republicans, known as the "Gang of 14," spent weeks hammering out a deal that stopped Tennessee Republican Bill Frist, the majority leader at the time, from using a parliamentary maneuver to do away with filibusters of nominees to the federal bench. The group agreed to allow some previously filibustered nominees through and to block future nominees only under "extraordinary circumstances."

Nelson joined a less successful bipartisan group in 2008 that attempted to draft comprehensive energy legislation that would have expanded both spending on renewable energy and offshore drilling.

Nelson is one of a small but growing number of Senate Democrats who oppose abortion rights in most cases. In the 109th Congress (2005-06), he supported a bill that would criminalize the transport of a minor across state lines to get an abortion, and he voted in 2003 to ban a medical procedure opponents call "partial birth" abortion, unless it is necessary to save the woman's life. In 2006 he was the only Senate Democrat to vote against expanding federal funding for embryonic stem cell research, which uses discarded embryos created for in vitro fertilization.

Nelson shows his Democratic stripes, though, when the Senate considers anti-discrimination measures or changes to Social Security, Medicare or farm programs. He joined his party in July 2008 to enact legislation over Bush's objections to prevent a scheduled cut in Medicare payments to physicians. In early 2009, he supported a successful measure to make it easier for workers to advance wage discrimination claims in court. And he backed a large expansion of a children's health insurance program that Obama signed into law.

As a member of the Agriculture, Nutrition and Forestry Committee, Nelson worked with other lawmakers to override Bush's veto of a 2008 reauthorization of farm programs that the president considered too costly. He urged caution in the consideration of Obama's 2009 efforts to scale back some of its subsidies.

On the Appropriations Committee, Nelson is an unabashed advocate of earmarks for Nebraska, which he calls "just doing my job." But in 2007, he dropped his request for a $7.5 million earmark for an Omaha defense company where his son worked. Nelson's also serves on Rules and Administration, which oversees election matters.

Nelson enjoys being a practical joker. As governor, he participated in a segment of the TV show "Candid Camera" in which he told visitors to his office he was planning to change the state's name to "something much more modern … something like Zenmar or Quentron." He also held a party for others named Ben Nelson. Twelve people from Nebraska, 10 from other states and one dog attended. (The senator goes by his middle name; his first name is actually Earl.)

Nelson has yearned for statewide office since age 17, when he was elected governor of a model Nebraska high school legislature. The election of his high school superintendent and debate coach, Ralph Brooks, to be Nebraska's governor convinced Nelson "you didn't have to be from a big city to have an opportunity in politics."

He considered joining the ministry while at the University of Nebraska and would later serve as a lay minister in the Disciples of Christ. But Nelson eventually opted for law school and, upon graduation, began a long career in insurance. He ran an insurance company, headed a national association of insurance regulators and directed his state's insurance department. He launched his first statewide bid for office in 1990, surviving the Democratic primary for governor by just 42 votes. He went on to defeat the incumbent, Republican Kay Orr, by 4,000 votes.

After eight years as governor, he returned in 1999 to his law firm, Kaufman-Nelson-Pattee. There he helped states develop Washington lobbying strategies, though he notes he was never a lobbyist himself. When Democratic Sen. Bob Kerrey announced he would retire the next year, Nelson was a shoo-in for the party's nomination. He then defeated Republican Attorney General Don Stenberg by 2 percentage points in the closest Senate election in Nebraska history. His second win — against a self-funded candidate who dramatically outspent Nelson — was by 28 percentage points.

KEY VOTES

2008

Yes	Prohibit discrimination based on genetic information
Yes	Reauthorize farm and nutrition programs for five years
Yes	Limit debate on "cap and trade" system for greenhouse gas emissions
No	Allow lawsuits against companies that participated in warrantless wiretapping
Yes	Limit debate on a bill to block a scheduled cut in Medicare payments to doctors
Yes	Grant mortgage relief to homeowners and funding for Fannie Mae and Freddie Mac
Yes	Approve a nuclear cooperation agreement with India
Yes	Approve final $700 billion program to stabilize financial markets
Yes	Allow consideration of a $14 billion auto industry loan package

2007

Yes	Increase minimum wage by $2.10 an hour
No	Limit debate on a comprehensive immigration bill
Yes	Overhaul congressional lobbying and ethics rules for members and their staffs
Yes	Limit debate on considering a bill to add House seats for the District of Columbia and Utah
Yes	Limit debate on restoring habeas corpus rights to detainees
Yes	Mandate minimum breaks for troops between deployments to Iraq or Afghanistan
Yes	Override Bush veto of $23.2 billion water projects authorization bill
Yes	Confirm Michael B. Mukasey as attorney general
Yes	Limit debate on an energy policy overhaul containing $21.8 billion in tax incentives and reduced oil and gas subsidies

CQ VOTE STUDIES

	PARTY UNITY		PRESIDENTIAL SUPPORT	
	SUPPORT	OPPOSE	SUPPORT	OPPOSE
2008	72%	28%	48%	52%
2007	70%	30%	49%	51%
2006	36%	64%	76%	24%
2005	46%	54%	76%	24%
2004	52%	48%	82%	18%
2003	57%	43%	80%	20%
2002	51%	49%	91%	9%
2001	58%	42%	74%	26%

INTEREST GROUPS

	AFL-CIO	ADA	CCUS	ACU
2008	100%	75%	71%	16%
2007	95%	75%	64%	32%
2006	47%	35%	83%	64%
2005	71%	55%	94%	60%
2004	82%	65%	81%	52%
2003	62%	45%	86%	42%
2002	62%	50%	63%	55%
2001	81%	70%	71%	56%

Sen. Mike Johanns (R)

Elected 2008; 1st term

Johanns' quiet temperament masks an iron-willed discipline that once led him to kick a two- to three-pack-a-day smoking habit and has served him well as a mayor, governor and Cabinet secretary. A steadfast conservative, he is a reliable but not reflexive Republican vote in the Senate, where he leverages his experience and existing relationships in Washington, especially on agriculture, energy and federal spending.

From his boyhood spent tending to his family's cows to his nearly three-year tenure as Agriculture secretary, Johanns (JOE-hannes — rhymes with "cans") cultivated a mastery of rural issues to match his self-professed love for life on the farm. As head of the Agriculture Department, he was President George W. Bush's point man on a five-year reauthorization of farm programs. He won praise from congressional leaders for his directness and willingness to listen to all sides. "I always found him pleasant to work with, and I was very impressed by how involved he was in this farm bill process," said Iowa Democrat Tom Harkin, chairman of the Agriculture, Nutrition and Forestry Committee.

Johanns' listening skills were honed during six years as Nebraska's governor, and he frequently alludes to his efforts as chief executive to hear from all those affected by government policies. "I just think listening is always a good thing," he said at an early 2009 Indian Affairs Committee hearing.

Johanns resigned from Bush's Cabinet in September 2007 to launch his candidacy for the Senate seat being vacated by Republican Chuck Hagel. Johanns drew some criticism for leaving the Agriculture Department before the $289 billion farm measure was completed. "It is completely irresponsible for the Agriculture secretary to leave his post right in the middle of negotiations in Congress over the next farm bill," said Sen. Kent Conrad, a North Dakota Democrat who worked extensively with Harkin on the legislation.

Before leaving Washington, Johanns led efforts to reopen foreign markets that had banned U.S. beef imports after a case of mad cow disease and pushed to prevent huge corporate farms from receiving federal funding. As Nebraska's governor, Johanns had sought emergency drought relief for states. But as Agriculture secretary, he opposed a permanent disaster fund — something included in the farm bill enacted over Bush's veto in 2008.

Johanns supports trade pacts as a way to open overseas markets to Nebraska's farm products, noting that about 25 percent of his state's farm income is tied to trade. He participated in World Trade Organization negotiations as Agriculture secretary and played an integral role in building congressional support for a 2005 free-trade agreement among the United States and nations in Central America.

Johanns also promoted alternative and renewable fuels as Agriculture secretary and will continue that advocacy from his seat on the Agriculture Committee. "I just fundamentally believe that so much dependence on foreign oil is dangerous," he said. He supports research and development of cellulosic ethanol — a biofuel derived from wood, grasses and plants — as well as an expansion of nuclear power and domestic oil drilling.

He opposes President Obama's "cap and trade" plan to curb carbon dioxide emissions, warning it could "mean a $3,000 energy tax" on families annually and drive up crop production costs in his state from $40 to $80 per acre. During debate on the Senate's fiscal 2010 budget resolution, Johanns won adoption of an amendment to bar use of the fast-track, filibuster-proof "reconciliation" process to advance any climate change legislation.

CAPITOL OFFICE
224-4224
johanns.senate.gov
404 Russell Bldg. 20510; fax 224-5213

COMMITTEES
Agriculture, Nutrition & Forestry
Banking, Housing & Urban Affairs
Commerce, Science & Transportation
Indian Affairs
Veterans' Affairs

RESIDENCE
Omaha

BORN
June 18, 1950; Osage, Iowa

RELIGION
Roman Catholic

FAMILY
Wife, Stephanie Johanns; two children

EDUCATION
St. Mary's College (Minn.), B.A. 1971
(communication arts); Creighton U., J.D. 1974

CAREER
Lawyer

POLITICAL HIGHLIGHTS
Lancaster County Board of Commissioners, 1983-87; Lincoln City Council, 1989-91; mayor of Lincoln, 1991-98; governor, 1999-2005; Agriculture secretary, 2005-07

ELECTION RESULTS

2008 GENERAL

Mike Johanns (R)	455,854	57.5%
Scott Kleeb (D)	317,456	40.1%
Kelly Renee Rosberg (NEB)	11,438	1.4%
Steven R. Larrick (GREEN)	7,763	1.0%

2008 PRIMARY

Mike Johanns (R)	112,191	78.0%
Pat Flynn (R)	31,560	22.0%

During his nearly two terms as governor, state law compelled Johanns to balance budgets. He wants Obama to give a higher priority to deficit reduction. He joined other Republicans in voting against the $787 billion economic recovery bill in 2009 and criticized Obama's first budget for "massive overspending."

Johanns has a good relationship with Nebraska's Democratic Sen. Ben Nelson, whose independent streak often leads him to vote with Republicans. Like Nelson and Hagel, Johanns has no qualms about breaking from his party when he sees fit. Although he served in Bush's Cabinet, Johanns opposed the administration's initial version of the $700 billion financial sector stabilization bill in the fall of 2008 because he said it gave too much power to the Treasury secretary. As a member of the Banking, Housing and Urban Affairs Committee, he plunged into oversight of the law and preparations for a broad financial system regulatory overhaul.

Johanns was raised on a dairy farm in Osage, Iowa, just south of the Minnesota border. He inherited his parents' work ethic and devout Catholicism. Although his parents were not much interested in politics, the family living room displayed pictures of the pope and President Kennedy.

As teenagers, Johanns and his brother raised hogs when they weren't helping their father on the family's farm. They began their small venture with a handshake agreement with a local minister who had some unused land and kept it going throughout high school. It made Johanns just enough money to pay for some of his college education. Johanns still has the hand-painted sign that advertised their business.

Johanns loved farming and considered making a career of it, but his parents encouraged him to continue his education and keep his options open. He graduated from college in 1971 and later earned a law degree from Creighton University in Omaha. He worked as a lawyer before starting his political career in 1983 on the Lancaster County board.

On Christmas Eve 1986, Johanns married his wife, Stephanie, whom he met while the two served together on the county board. Soon after, he gave up smoking, left politics and switched his party affiliation from Democrat to Republican, as he had become an admirer of Ronald Reagan. But it didn't take long for him to jump back into the political fray. In 1989 he was elected to the city council in Lincoln. He was elected mayor two years later and won re-election to that post without opposition in 1995.

Johanns' low-key demeanor belies his strong campaign skills and competitiveness. During his 1998 run as an underdog candidate for governor, he visited each of Nebraska's 93 counties, racking up more than 140,000 miles on his Chevrolet Corsica. Four years later, he became the first Republican governor in Nebraska to win re-election since 1956. He resigned in January 2005, midway through his second four-year term, after Bush tapped him as Agriculture secretary. No Nebraska governor had resigned from office since 1901.

Hagel's September 2007 announcement of his retirement led Johanns to take a shot at the Senate. Johanns' Democratic opponent was Scott Kleeb, a Yale-educated rancher and educator who in 2006 took a respectable 45 percent against Republican Rep. Adrian Smith in the sprawling and overwhelmingly Republican 3rd District. The Omaha World-Herald endorsed Johanns, praising his fiscal discipline as governor and saying he "displayed steadiness, energy and sound judgment" as Agriculture secretary. Although the Democrats surged nationwide, Johanns coasted past Kleeb with 58 percent of the vote.

His old smoking habit, 20 years in the past, came back to scare him in March 2009, when he underwent surgery to investigate a suspicious spot on one lung. "When I went into surgery, I thought I did have cancer," Johanns later told KETV-7 in Omaha. He didn't, and with enormous relief, soon returned to work in the Senate — finally settling into a permanent office and leaving the double-wide trailer he and his staff had occupied for three months.

Rep. Jeff Fortenberry (R)

Elected 2004; 3rd term

CAPITOL OFFICE
225-4806
fortenberry.house.gov
1535 Longworth Bldg. 20515-2701; fax 225-5686

COMMITTEES
Agriculture
Foreign Affairs
Oversight & Government Reform

RESIDENCE
Lincoln

BORN
Dec. 27, 1960; Baton Rouge, La.

RELIGION
Roman Catholic

FAMILY
Wife, Celeste Fortenberry; five children

EDUCATION
Louisiana State U., B.A. 1982 (economics);
Georgetown U., M.P.P. 1986; Franciscan U. of
Steubenville, M.Div. 1996 (theology)

CAREER
Publishing firm public relations manager and sales
representative; economist; congressional aide

POLITICAL HIGHLIGHTS
Lincoln City Council, 1997-2001

ELECTION RESULTS

2008 GENERAL

Jeff Fortenberry (R)	184,923	70.4%
Max Yashirin (D)	77,897	29.6%

2008 PRIMARY

Jeff Fortenberry (R)	unopposed

2006 GENERAL

Jeff Fortenberry (R)	121,015	58.4%
Maxine Moul (D)	86,360	41.6%

PREVIOUS WINNING PERCENTAGES
2004 (54%)

Fortenberry tends to the farm-related interests of his constituents, but that work shares the stage with his longstanding involvement in foreign affairs. That may seem unconventional for a Nebraska lawmaker, but Fortenberry is simply following in the footsteps of his predecessor, Doug Bereuter, who was regarded as one of the House GOP's most influential leaders on international issues.

Fortenberry is conservative on both social and economic matters but has shown a willingness in the minority to sometimes vote with Democrats. He is a member of the Republican Study Committee, an organization of the most conservative House Republicans, but in recent years has been among the least loyal members of that group, as measured by the frequency with which he has voted against the majority of his party.

He broke with fellow Republicans in April 2009, for example, in voting to authorize the Food and Drug Administration to regulate tobacco products. The previous year, he sided with Democrats in voting to expand funding aimed at combatting AIDS overseas. "If it's right, or has enough right things in it, I think it's reasonable to justify voting yes," he said. Otherwise, he added, "the constant lining up of legislation along party lines…leads to that stagnation."

That's not to say Fortenberry is a pushover. He stood by fellow Republicans late in 2008 and early in 2009 in voting against every major piece of legislation aimed at reviving the economy, from President George W. Bush's financial industry rescue to President Obama's $787 billion stimulus. Fortenberry said the new laws were too expensive and would leave "an unfair debt burden on our children and generations of Americans to come." He pledged to use his seat on the Oversight and Government Reform Committee to push for more accountability.

He cares deeply about international humanitarian issues. After meeting former child soldiers in Liberia, he sponsored a 2007 bill to prohibit U.S. assistance for governments whose armed forces use children as fighters, calling the practice "one of the most egregious human rights violations of our times." Provisions from Fortenberry's bill eventually were signed into law by Bush.

Fortenberry is also concerned about nuclear security, and in September 2008 he was one of only 10 House Republicans to vote against a nuclear cooperation agreement with India. The legislation "could open a floodgate for worldwide nuclear commerce that…could significantly damage the stability and integrity of U.S. and international nuclear non-proliferation efforts," he said.

Fortenberry serves on the Middle East and South Asia Subcommittee of the Foreign Affairs Committee and his views of the region are more nuanced than those of many lawmakers. They were influenced, he says, by his travels to Egypt as a college student, when he immersed himself in Arab history, culture and religion.

Fortenberry backed the war in Iraq but sought to mitigate its toll. In 2007, he played a key role in promoting legislation, ultimately passed into law, to allow Iraqis who worked for the U.S. government as translators — and therefore were in danger of reprisals — access to more special immigrant visas to allow them to move to the United States.

From his seat on the Agriculture Committee, where he is the top-ranking Republican on the Operations, Oversight, Nutrition and Forestry Subcommittee during the 111th Congress (2009-10), Fortenberry tries to help small farmers. He added an amendment to the 2008 multi-year reauthorization of farm and nutrition programs to help schools purchase locally grown food, which he says is more nutritious. "I think there's a growing movement in society to want to reconnect the urban with the rural, the family to the farm," he said.

Fortenberry also promotes alternative energy sources in rural communities. He is a strong supporter of ethanol and wind power. He added a provision in the 2008 farm bill to promote renewable energy sources and supported the 2007 energy overhaul that required 36 billion gallons of biofuels to be produced domestically by 2022.

Fortenberry was born and raised in Baton Rouge, La. His father died in a car accident when Fortenberry was 12; he says that instilled in him a feeling of responsibility. He was interested in politics from a young age. He remembers that in the fifth grade he wrote a letter to President Nixon about Nixon's 1972 trip to China.

At 17, Fortenberry served as a page to a Democratic Louisiana state senator. He switched parties in 1982, he says, because of the influence of President Reagan, whom he felt better reflected his conservative values than Democrats of that time.

After earning a master's degree in public policy at Georgetown University, Fortenberry interned for the U.S. Department of Agriculture and then worked for a Senate subcommittee, where he studied falling land prices in Nebraska, the state he would later call home. But he felt something was missing. "I had a real deep nagging of the heart to really go into the deeper questions of life," Fortenberry told the Lincoln Journal Star in 2006.

He enrolled in the Franciscan University of Steubenville, in Ohio, where he earned a master's in theology and met his wife, Celeste. The couple headed west after graduation to Lincoln, where Fortenberry became the public relations director for what is now Sandhill Publishing. (His interest in publishing surfaced in 2009 when he introduced legislation to exempt libraries from testing books for lead under consumer safety laws, something public libraries said they could not afford.) He also landed a seat on the Lincoln City Council, serving from 1997 to 2001.

After Bereuter retired from the House seat he'd held for nearly 26 years, a free-for-all ensued in the 2004 Republican primary. Fortenberry campaigned hard, shaking every hand he could find. In the seven-candidate field, he won with 39 percent of the vote and went on to triumph by 11 percentage points that November in the solidly Republican 1st District. He has not faced a serious re-election challenge since.

KEY VOTES

2008
No Delay consideration of Colombia free-trade agreement
Yes Override Bush veto of federal farm and nutrition programs reauthorization bill
Yes Overhaul surveillance laws and permit dismissal of suits against companies that conducted warrantless wiretapping
No Grant mortgage relief to homeowners and funding for Fannie Mae and Freddie Mac
No Approve initial $700 billion program to stabilize financial markets
No Approve final $700 billion program to stabilize financial markets
No Provide $14 billion in loans to automakers

2007
No Increase minimum wage by $2.10 an hour
No Approve $124.2 billion in emergency war spending and set goal for redeployment of troops from Iraq
Yes Reject federal contraceptive assistance to international family planning groups
Yes Override Bush veto of $23.2 billion water projects authorization bill
Yes Implement Peru free-trade agreement
Yes Approve energy policy overhaul with new fuel economy standards
Yes Clear $473.5 billion omnibus spending bill, including $70 billion for military operations

CQ VOTE STUDIES

	PARTY UNITY		PRESIDENTIAL SUPPORT	
	SUPPORT	OPPOSE	SUPPORT	OPPOSE
2008	82%	18%	56%	44%
2007	81%	19%	65%	35%
2006	89%	11%	87%	13%
2005	95%	5%	87%	13%

INTEREST GROUPS

	AFL-CIO	ADA	CCUS	ACU
2008	27%	40%	72%	84%
2007	21%	15%	90%	88%
2006	21%	5%	93%	84%
2005	20%	5%	93%	92%

NEBRASKA 1

East – Lincoln, Fremont

The 1st takes in eastern Nebraska, excluding Omaha and its suburbs. The district includes the state's capital, Lincoln, and the University of Nebraska's Memorial Stadium, which could qualify as the state's third-largest city when filled to its 81,000-seat capacity. Despite the small-town, rural feel, economic diversification in Lincoln, Norfolk and South Sioux City is helping to make the eastern part of the state more urban.

Lincoln's economy — stabilized by state and city government jobs, health care and university sectors, and agricultural production — has remained relatively strong during economic slowdowns, but unemployment has affected many industries here. The University of Nebraska Technology Park, a joint venture between the university and private investors, has attempted to expand the area's economy with high-tech jobs. The park is located in a northwestern section of the city that had been declared blighted, and local officials hope that the park's growth will boost redevelopment efforts. Banking and insurance firms in Lincoln have felt the effects of the national financial crisis.

The region is still heavily dependent on agriculture, and traditional crop and hog farming is supplemented by other agribusiness, such as meat processing, food packaging and fertilizer production. Polling and telemarketing call centers add white-collar jobs, but layoffs by small employers have hit residents in rural areas particularly hard.

Although the 1st District was home to populist William Jennings Bryan and many of his supporters at the turn of the 20th century, the 1st now votes consistently Republican at all levels. Voter registration favors Republicans in both the city of Lincoln and surrounding Lancaster County, but Democrat Barack Obama won the county in the 2008 presidential election despite losing the district overall. The 1st District's strongest Democratic areas are in the northeast, especially in Thurston County, which is made up entirely of the Omaha and Winnebago American Indian reservations.

MAJOR INDUSTRY
Agriculture, higher education, technology, health care, government

CITIES
Lincoln, 225,581; Fremont, 25,174; Norfolk, 23,516

NOTABLE
Johnny Carson, the late host of "The Tonight Show," grew up in Norfolk.

Rep. Lee Terry (R)

Elected 1998; 6th term

CAPITOL OFFICE
225-4155
leeterry.house.gov
2331 Rayburn Bldg. 20515-2702; fax 226-5452

COMMITTEES
Energy & Commerce

RESIDENCE
Omaha

BORN
Jan. 29, 1962; Omaha, Neb.

RELIGION
Protestant

FAMILY
Wife, Robyn Terry; three children

EDUCATION
U. of Nebraska, B.S. 1984 (political science);
Creighton U., J.D. 1987

CAREER
Lawyer

POLITICAL HIGHLIGHTS
Omaha City Council, 1991-99 (president, 1994-95)

ELECTION RESULTS

2008 GENERAL

Lee Terry (R)	142,473	51.9%
Jim Esch (D)	131,901	48.1%

2008 PRIMARY

Lee Terry (R)	23,146	84.4%
Steven Laird (R)	4,288	15.6%

2006 GENERAL

Lee Terry (R)	99,475	54.7%
Jim Esch (D)	82,504	45.3%

PREVIOUS WINNING PERCENTAGES
2004 (61%); 2002 (63%); 2000 (66%); 1998 (66%)

Terry is a modest Midwesterner who prefers quiet dealmaking to overt salesmanship, something that has forced him to work harder at the polls in recent years. Though usually a loyal conservative, he isn't afraid to go his own way when it suits him. He focuses on energy and technology, believing that hooking up rural areas with faster Internet access, as well as expanded use of biofuels, will help Nebraska's farmers.

Terry is a reliable social conservative. He opposed expanded federal funding for embryonic stem cell research, which uses discarded embryos created for in vitro fertilization, and supported a constitutional amendment to ban same-sex marriage. But he tries to pick his legislative battles. "I want to fight the good fight on abortion, but that doesn't mean I drag down an appropriations bill," Terry told the Omaha World-Herald.

A member of the Energy and Commerce Committee, Terry has a good spot from which to advance his signature issue — promoting the use of corn-based ethanol as fuel for cars. An increase in demand for ethanol would be a boon for both Nebraska's corn farms and its small towns, with their ethanol processing plants.

Terry worked to include a provision in major energy legislation, which passed in December 2007, to accelerate deployment of E85, a blend of 85 percent ethanol and 15 percent gasoline. He introduced a bill in 2008 that sought to improve access to ethanol at the pump as well as provide other renewable-energy incentives, but it did not move.

Another priority for Terry is getting broadband Internet service to rural areas. He wants to require telecommunications companies to provide broadband connections. "Competitiveness in the 21st century is about moving data and information," he said. He has worked on the issue with fellow Energy and Commerce member Rick Boucher of Virginia, a Democrat who shares his interest in making his rural district as wired as possible.

Terry was the subject of a spurt of media attention in 2003 as one of just eight lawmakers to vote against creation of a federal "do not call" list for telemarketers. He explained later that 39,000 people in his district are employed, directly or indirectly, by telemarketers.

He also drew some attention for his temper in July 2007. During debate on an agriculture spending bill, he participated in a profanity-laced exchange with Illinois Democrat Jesse L. Jackson Jr. Terry said Jackson shouted at him, "They [Republicans] can't be trusted." Terry shouted back, "Shut up!" Other lawmakers separated the two men. Terry later apologized when he learned it was another Democrat — Anthony Weiner of New York — who shouted the initial, "They can't be trusted."

Despite that blowup, Terry occasionally joins with Democrats on high-profile legislation. He backed a bill granting the Food and Drug Administration the authority to regulate tobacco products in 2009, and in fall 2008 was one of just 25 Republicans to switch his initial vote "no" to "yes" on two versions of a $700 billion plan to aid the ailing financial services sector — the second of which became law. In both cases, he was among a minority of his GOP colleagues.

In addition, he helped Democrats move a 2008 bill that averted a cut in physicians' reimbursement rates in Medicare and another that required insurers to pay for psychiatric treatments in the same way they reimburse other medical costs.

Terry belongs to a small group of lawmakers who save money by living in their offices during the workweek, using the House gym to shave and shower and commuting home on weekends. He spent the first several years sleeping on leaky air mattresses. "The major problem is they're not very durable," he says. "Lots of holes and a lot of time patching and a lot of time on flat mattresses." Terry's nighttime ordeals ended when his wife bought him a rollaway cot.

Terry was raised in Omaha, where his father was a news anchor with a political talk show. Terry would sometimes go to work with him to watch interviews with congressmen, senators and other local celebrities. He had two autographs on his bedroom wall: one from Evel Knievel and the other from conservative Nebraska Sen. Roman Hruska.

When he was in eighth grade, Terry handed out pamphlets for his father's unsuccessful run for the House in 1976 — the seat Terry himself won two decades later. In college, Terry planned a career in politics. After getting his law degree, he was elected to the Omaha City Council, where he served for eight years.

In 1998, his position on the city council made him the front-runner for the House seat that Republican Jon Christensen vacated to make a failed run for governor. Terry won the five-way primary by 10 percentage points and then triumphed by 31 points in November over an underfunded Democrat, newscaster Michael Scott.

When he first ran for Congress, Terry had pledged to serve no more than three terms, but later backed away from that promise. He said he quickly realized when he got to Washington the benefits that come with seniority.

Voters didn't seem to mind, and Terry coasted to easy re-election wins until 2006. That year, with Republicans facing a nationwide backlash from voters upset over ethical scandals on Capitol Hill and the war in Iraq, Terry was forced to spend nearly $1 million to hold off Jim Esch, a young, underfunded lawyer and Chamber of Commerce official. Terry's tally fell to 55 percent of the vote, and in an attempt to raise his profile, he put up pictures of himself on 17 large billboards in and around Omaha. The billboards said, "Thank you for your trust."

Esch tried again in 2008, questioning Terry's accomplishments on Capitol Hill while Terry argued that Esch was too liberal for the district, especially on social issues. Terry pulled out the win as Barack Obama carried the district over Republican Arizona Sen. John McCain, but his margin tightened again. Terry said he'd simply done a poor job informing his constituents of his accomplishments. "It's my fault," he told the World-Herald. "I've done a poor job of selling myself. It's not part of my personality. I don't like to brag."

KEY VOTES

2008
No   Delay consideration of Colombia free-trade agreement

No   Override Bush veto of federal farm and nutrition programs reauthorization bill

Yes   Overhaul surveillance laws and permit dismissal of suits against companies that conducted warrantless wiretapping

No   Grant mortgage relief to homeowners and funding for Fannie Mae and Freddie Mac

No   Approve initial $700 billion program to stabilize financial markets

Yes   Approve final $700 billion program to stabilize financial markets

No   Provide $14 billion in loans to automakers

2007
No   Increase minimum wage by $2.10 an hour

No   Approve $124.2 billion in emergency war spending and set goal for redeployment of troops from Iraq

Yes   Reject federal contraceptive assistance to international family planning groups

Yes   Override Bush veto of $23.2 billion water projects authorization bill

Yes   Implement Peru free-trade agreement

Yes   Approve energy policy overhaul with new fuel economy standards

Yes   Clear $473.5 billion omnibus spending bill, including $70 billion for military operations

CQ VOTE STUDIES

	PARTY UNITY		PRESIDENTIAL SUPPORT	
	SUPPORT	OPPOSE	SUPPORT	OPPOSE
2008	90%	10%	68%	32%
2007	93%	7%	76%	24%
2006	97%	3%	97%	3%
2005	94%	6%	85%	15%
2004	93%	7%	88%	12%

INTEREST GROUPS

	AFL-CIO	ADA	CCUS	ACU
2008	13%	15%	100%	92%
2007	21%	10%	90%	88%
2006	14%	0%	100%	92%
2005	13%	0%	89%	92%
2004	29%	0%	90%	92%

NEBRASKA 2

East – Omaha and suburbs

Formerly the eastern terminus of the Union Pacific Railroad, Omaha is the heart of the 2nd District. Omaha grew up as a blue-collar city: a railroad junction, a Missouri River port and a place where cattle became steaks. To outsiders, this broad-shouldered, gritty image remains. But the city has become mainly a place of downtown office buildings and white-collar jobs in agriculture and insurance businesses. It also is known as the nation's 1-800 capital, thanks to a glut of call centers for telemarketing, customer service and credit processing operations.

Omaha's economy grew steadily for the past decade, and although its sturdiest industries did not completely insulate the local workforce from the current national recession, Omaha remains stable. Residents here still enjoy a relatively low cost of living. Local officials continue economic diversification efforts, but even the city's four Fortune 500 companies have experienced downturns. Building on the success of an earlier downtown redevelopment plan, the city has implemented a new plan to guide revitalization of the northern section of downtown. Omaha continues to expand outward, and officials from the city and surrounding Douglas County have considered merging into a single municipality. Offutt Air Force Base, the district's largest employer, contributes billions of dollars to the local economy annually.

Traditionally a reliably Republican district, the 2nd supported Democrat Barack Obama with a slim 1-percentage-point margin in the 2008 presidential election. Omaha's dwindling blue-collar base and its university and African-American populations support Democrats. Obama became the first Democratic candidate to carry Douglas County, home to more than 80 percent of district residents, since Lyndon B. Johnson in 1964.

MAJOR INDUSTRY
Phone service centers, military, agriculture, insurance

MILITARY BASES
Offutt Air Force Base, 5,741 military, 1,985 civilian (2009)

CITIES
Omaha, 390,007; Bellevue, 44,382; Papillion, 16,363

NOTABLE
Billionaire investor Warren Buffett lives in Omaha — his father, Republican Howard Buffett, represented Omaha in the House from 1943-49 and 1951-53.

Rep. Adrian Smith (R)

Elected 2006; 2nd term

CAPITOL OFFICE
225-6435
adriansmith.house.gov
503 Cannon Bldg. 20515-2703; fax 225-0207

COMMITTEES
Agriculture
Natural Resources
Science & Technology

RESIDENCE
Gering

BORN
Dec. 19, 1970; Scottsbluff, Neb.

RELIGION
Christian

FAMILY
Single

EDUCATION
Liberty U. , attended 1989-90; U. of Nebraska,
B.S. 1993 (secondary education)

CAREER
Storage company owner; Realtor; education
workshop coordinator; substitute teacher

POLITICAL HIGHLIGHTS
Gering City Council, 1994-98; Neb. Legislature,
1999-2006

ELECTION RESULTS

2008 GENERAL

Adrian Smith (R)	183,117	76.9%
Jay C. Stoddard (D)	55,087	23.1%

2008 PRIMARY

Adrian Smith (R)	55,225	87.4%
Jeremiah Ellison (R)	7,947	12.6%

2006 GENERAL

Adrian Smith (R)	113,687	55.0%
Scott Kleeb (D)	93,046	45.0%

Smith is one of the youngest Republicans in the House, but he has ample political experience. He served four years on the Gering City Council and nearly eight years in the Nebraska Legislature, where he was known as an anti-abortion, anti-bureaucracy, Christian conservative — a reputation he has furthered on Capitol Hill. When the conservative Heritage Foundation think tank asked what makes him happy, Smith said, "Having the freedom to pursue opportunities relating to my faith while upholding the ideals of our Founding Fathers."

His party's leaders have taken notice. In 2009 they granted him a slot on the GOP Steering Committee, which makes committee assignments. They also gave him, in only his second term, the top Republican seat on the Science and Technology Committee's Technology and Innovation panel.

He quickly affirmed his political lean in Washington, voting with the GOP on 98 percent of the votes pitting most Republicans against most Democrats in his first term. He opposed President Obama's early efforts to revive the economy, saying Obama's $787 billion economic stimulus legislation was too expensive. "The scale of this bill is breathtaking," he said, calling it a "wish list of big government spending." He later opposed a $410 billion catchall spending bill funding most government agencies on the same grounds. The previous year, he gave similar reasons in voting against President George W. Bush's plans to rescue ailing banks and automakers.

But on the Agriculture Committee, Smith is not afraid to stray from party leaders when it benefits his district. In July 2007, he was one of 19 Republicans to vote for the Democrats' five-year rewrite of farm and nutrition policy. Some Republicans objected to a tax provision targeting foreign-owned companies that was included to help offset the cost of the bill. He also was among a narrow majority of his party that, a year later, voted to override Bush's veto of the bill. He has condemned Obama for trying to phase out federal subsidies for wealthy farmers.

A proud advocate for his state's cattle and meatpacking industries, Smith was successful early in 2009 in convincing the Food and Drug Administration to delay new rules aimed at preventing the spread of mad cow disease by limiting the use of cattle as feed for other animals. He argued that existing protections were working and that the rules would make disposing of dead cattle nearly impossible.

Meanwhile, he was an easy choice for a top post on the Science subcommittee. When talking about the committee's agenda, Smith is much like a giddy elementary school student showing off his first science fair project. He enjoys delving into issues like space exploration and NASA aeronautic and research programs. He also hopes to deal with "the 'brain drain' in rural America."

From his seat on the Natural Resources Committee, Smith joins fellow Republicans in pushing for greater use of domestic oil, by drilling offshore or in protected regions. In September 2008 he criticized Democratic energy legislation offered in response to soaring gasoline prices as both "ineffective" and "counterproductive" and blasted Democrats for not letting GOP members of his committee have a hand in drafting it.

Reared in Nebraska's western tier, Smith was an only child. His father still sells general insurance. His mother is a retired schoolteacher and now owns a store selling school supplies. He attended a small grade school in Wildcat Hills, where he was one of just six students in his eighth-grade class. He was a percussion player for Gering High School and a member of the school's choir. He prefers listening to contemporary Christian and country music.

Smith's interest in politics stems from conversations with his maternal grandfather, a supporter of President Carter, who lost to Ronald Reagan in 1980. "My parents told me the differences and I figured I was for Reagan," Smith laughed. He decided he was a Republican while in the fourth grade. Almost three decades later, his Capitol Hill office is adorned with posters and memorabilia of Reagan.

His father eventually served as the Scotts Bluff County GOP chair and his mother is the secretary of the Nebraska Republican Party. "I am probably more responsible for their political involvement than they are for mine," Smith said.

After high school, Smith attended Liberty University in Lynchburg, Va., which was founded and run by the Rev. Jerry Falwell until the Moral Majority founder's death in 2007. But Smith became homesick and, after a year and a half, returned to his home state and enrolled at the University of Nebraska, where he became active in the College Republicans. He bought an apartment, which became a second home a few years later when he made the 400-plus-mile commute from Gering to Lincoln as a member of the state's unique unicameral legislature.

After earning a degree in secondary education, he returned to western Nebraska and briefly worked as a substitute teacher. But envisioning a political future, Smith settled on a career in real estate, which gave him a more flexible schedule.

At 23, he was elected to the Gering City Council, and four years later he won a seat in the Nebraska Legislature. In that 1998 campaign, he touted his conservative anti-abortion agenda and defeated Democratic incumbent Joyce Hillman, for whom he worked part-time during college. He said his proudest state legislative accomplishment was securing $650,000 to expand the Western Nebraska Veterans Home in Scottsbluff. He may be best known, though, for his failures: He made several unsuccessful attempts to repeal Nebraska's mandatory motorcycle helmet law and ban casino gambling.

Smith's path to the House opened when Republican Rep. Tom Osborne made a failed bid for governor in 2006. Smith entered the race to replace him, outpacing four rivals for the Republican nomination. Despite a difficult year for Republican candidates, Smith coasted to a 10-percentage-point win in the heavily Republican district that November. He trumped that in 2008 by crushing his Democratic opponent Jay C. Stoddard by 54 percentage points, bettering Arizona GOP Sen. John McCain's showing over Obama in the district by 8 percentage points.

KEY VOTES

2008
No Delay consideration of Colombia free-trade agreement
Yes Override Bush veto of federal farm and nutrition programs reauthorization bill
Yes Overhaul surveillance laws and permit dismissal of suits against companies that conducted warrantless wiretapping
No Grant mortgage relief to homeowners and funding for Fannie Mae and Freddie Mac
No Approve initial $700 billion program to stabilize financial markets
No Approve final $700 billion program to stabilize financial markets
No Provide $14 billion in loans to automakers

2007
No Increase minimum wage by $2.10 an hour
No Approve $124.2 billion in emergency war spending and set goal for redeployment of troops from Iraq
Yes Reject federal contraceptive assistance to international family planning groups
Yes Override Bush veto of $23.2 billion water projects authorization bill
Yes Implement Peru free-trade agreement
Yes Approve energy policy overhaul with new fuel economy standards
Yes Clear $473.5 billion omnibus spending bill, including $70 billion for military operations

CQ VOTE STUDIES

	PARTY UNITY		PRESIDENTIAL SUPPORT	
	SUPPORT	OPPOSE	SUPPORT	OPPOSE
2008	98%	2%	74%	26%
2007	98%	2%	83%	17%

INTEREST GROUPS

	AFL-CIO	ADA	CCUS	ACU
2008	7%	15%	89%	96%
2007	4%	10%	95%	96%

NEBRASKA 3

West – Grand Island, North Platte, Scottsbluff

Scouting what would later become the Oregon Trail, early 19th-century explorers described this section of the country as the "Great American Desert." Most of the 3rd's land is arid, and most of the district's population lives along the Platte River.

Grand Island, North Platte and Scottsbluff each serve as regional centers for the retail and health care needs of the surrounding counties, while Kearney, Columbus and Hastings cater to industry and manufacturing. Hastings in particular has been preparing to transition from traditional manufacturing jobs to more high-tech processes, but the effects of a national recession have forced layoffs across the industry.

The rest of the land in the district's 69 counties is left to cattle ranchers and sugar beet, soybean and wheat farmers. The extensive Union Pacific railroad network, one of Nebraska's most prominent industries, brings crops from isolated areas to larger markets, but economic slowdowns have forced the railroad to idle tens of thousands of cars.

The 3rd's agrarian economy is susceptible to changes in the region's weather, and water is a precious commodity here. A decade of drought conditions has hurt grazing operations and caused poor crop yields. Every county in the 3rd was designated as a drought disaster area in 2006, with the western portion taking an especially hard hit. Stabilized water levels have relieved some of the concern, but droughts remain a matter of particular urgency to residents in the 3rd, as it contains several of the nation's poorest counties.

The 3rd overall is conservative and strongly favors GOP candidates, but there are Democratic pockets in Greeley and Sherman counties. Democrat Barack Obama won Saline County in the 2008 presidential election, but Republican John McCain easily won the district overall with 69 percent of the 3rd's vote.

MAJOR INDUSTRY
Agriculture, food processing, transportation

CITIES
Grand Island, 42,940; Kearney, 27,431

NOTABLE
Union Pacific's Bailey Yard in North Platte is the world's largest railroad classification yard.

Gov. Jim Gibbons (R)

First elected: 2006
Length of term: 4 years
Term expires: 1/11
Salary: $141,000
Phone: (775) 684-5670

Residence: Carson City
Born: Dec. 16, 1944; Sparks, Nev.
Religion: Mormon
Family: Separated; three children
Education: U. of Nevada, Reno, B.S. 1967 (geology), M.S. 1973 (mining geology); Southwestern U., J.D. 1979
Military service: Air Force, 1967-71; Nev. Air National Guard, 1975-95
Career: Airline pilot; lawyer; geologist
Political highlights: Nev. Assembly, 1989-94 (minority whip, 1993); Republican nominee for governor, 1994, U.S. House, 1997-2007

Election results:

2006 GENERAL

Jim Gibbons (R)	279,003	47.9%
Dina Titus (D)	255,684	43.9%
None of these candidates	20,699	3.6%
Christopher H. Hansen (IA)	20,019	3.4%
Craig Bergland (GREEN)	6,753	1.2%

Lt. Gov. Brian R. Krolicki (R)

First elected: 2006
Length of term: 4 years
Term expires: 1/11
Salary: $60,000
Phone: (775) 684-5637

LEGISLATURE

Legislature: February-June in odd-numbered years, limit of 120 days

Senate: 21 members, 4-year terms
2009 ratios: 12 D, 9 R; 14 men, 7 women
Salary: $146/day in session; $167/day allowance
Phone: (775) 684-1402

Assembly: 42 members, 2-year terms
2009 ratios: 28 D, 14 R; 29 men, 13 women
Salary: $146/day in session; $167/day allowance
Phone: (775) 684-8555

TERM LIMITS

Governor: 2 terms
Senate: 3 terms
Assembly: 6 terms

URBAN STATISTICS

CITY	POPULATION
Las Vegas	478,434
Reno	180,480
Henderson	175,381
North Las Vegas	115,488

REGISTERED VOTERS

Democrat	44%
Republican	36%
Nonpartisan/others	20%

POPULATION

2008 population (est.)	2,600,167
2000 population	1,998,257
1990 population	1,201,833
Percent change (1990-2000)	+66.3%
Rank among states (2008)	35

Median age	35
Born in state	21.3%
Foreign born	15.8%
Violent crime rate	524/100,000
Poverty level	10.5%
Federal workers	14,701
Military	11,932

ELECTIONS

STATE ELECTION OFFICIAL
(775) 684-5705
DEMOCRATIC PARTY
(702) 737-8683
REPUBLICAN PARTY
(702) 258-9182

MISCELLANEOUS

Web: www.nv.gov
Capital: Carson City

U.S. CONGRESS

Senate: 1 Democrat, 1 Republican
House: 2 Democrats, 1 Republican

2000 Census Statistics by District

DIST.	2008 VOTE FOR PRESIDENT OBAMA	MCCAIN	WHITE	BLACK	ASIAN	HISP	MEDIAN INCOME	WHITE COLLAR	BLUE COLLAR	SERVICE INDUSTRY	OVER 64	UNDER 18	COLLEGE EDUCATION	RURAL	SQ. MILES
1	64%	34%	52%	12%	5%	28%	$39,480	48%	23%	29%	10%	27%	15%	0%	177
2	49	49	75	2	3	15	$43,879	55	25	20	11	26	19	21	105,079
3	55	43	69	5	6	16	$50,749	57	18	25	12	24	20	4	4,570
STATE	55	43	65	7	4	20	$44,581	53	22	25	11	26	18	8	109,826
U.S.	53	46	69	12	4	13	$41,994	60	25	15	12	26	24	21	3,537,438

Sen. Harry Reid (D)

Elected 1986; 4th term

CAPITOL OFFICE
224-3542
reid.senate.gov
522 Hart Bldg. 20510-2803; fax 224-7327

COMMITTEES
No committee assignments

RESIDENCE
Searchlight

BORN
Dec. 2, 1939; Searchlight, Nev.

RELIGION
Mormon

FAMILY
Wife, Landra Reid; five children

EDUCATION
Southern Utah State College, A.S. 1959;
Utah State U., B.A. 1961 (history & political
science); George Washington U., J.D. 1964;
U. of Nevada, Las Vegas, attended 1969-70

CAREER
Lawyer

POLITICAL HIGHLIGHTS
Nev. Assembly, 1969-71; lieutenant governor,
1971-75; Democratic nominee for U.S. Senate,
1974; candidate for mayor of Las Vegas, 1975;
Nevada Gaming Commission chairman, 1977-81;
U.S. House, 1983-87

ELECTION RESULTS

2004 GENERAL

Harry Reid (D)	494,805	61.1%
Richard Ziser (R)	284,640	35.1%
None of these candidates	12,968	1.6%
Thomas L. Hurst (LIBERT)	9,559	1.2%

2004 PRIMARY

Harry Reid (D)	unopposed

PREVIOUS WINNING PERCENTAGES
1998 (48%); 1992 (51%); 1986 (50%); 1984 House
Election (56%); 1982 House Election (58%)

Reid carries considerable influence as Senate majority leader, but that can be tough to discern by watching him. He shuns self-promotion and avoids the social circuit; he once passed up a White House state dinner honoring Queen Elizabeth II to stay home with his wife. He can be taciturn, even dour, on television and often speaks in such a whisper that he made a New Year's resolution for 2008: "I'm going to try to talk louder." But he more than makes up for any stylistic shortcomings by being the consummate inside player and dealmaker.

Reid, an ex-boxer, called his 2008 autobiography "The Good Fight," a reference to his willingness to enter a tussle. As leader of the Senate Democrats, Reid no longer regularly scraps with the White House the way he did when it was in Republican hands, plus he enjoys an expanded base of Democrats that gives him greater leeway to operate. But he isn't assured of a totally peaceful life.

He is under pressure to push the Obama administration's ambitious agenda through a chamber in which every senator can boast of some leverage. He often needs to corral his party's independent-minded moderates while fending off criticism from its liberal base. And he deals with a conservative-leaning GOP caucus keen on embarrassing him tactically and defeating him at the polls in 2010. "He has the toughest job here, no matter what the numbers are," Oklahoma Republican Tom Coburn, a frequent foe of Reid's, told The Washington Post in January 2009.

Well-liked by colleagues, Reid can be persuasive behind closed doors. He was instrumental in talking former Vermont Sen. James M. Jeffords into leaving the Republican caucus in 2001, handing Democrats a majority until 2003. He also ensured Connecticut independent Joseph I. Lieberman wasn't booted from the Democratic caucus late in 2008 for enthusiastically supporting Arizona Republican Sen. John McCain's presidential bid. And he helped pull moderate Pennsylvanian Arlen Specter into the Democrats' camp in April 2009, even after earlier dismissing the idea because of Specter's opposition to "card check" legislation aimed at easing union organizing rules.

Reid has a respectful relationship with Kentucky Republican Mitch McConnell, his savvy rival as minority leader. As longtime appropriators, Reid and McConnell became well acquainted early in their Senate career and mastered the art of horse trading and greasing bills with earmarks — funding for specific projects added to spending bills. They have worked together on various shared objectives, but both are fierce partisans as well. Reid also has had close ties to his Nevada GOP colleague John Ensign since an acrimonious 1998 Senate race in which Reid barely edged out Ensign.

Reid promotes bedrock Democratic values, but is apt to consult with conservatives with whom he shares some beliefs on social issues. A practicing Mormon, he often votes with Republicans in favor of restrictions on abortion. And he was among the Democrats who crossed party lines in 2004 to vote against renewing the 10-year federal ban on assault weapons, and again five years later to codify a Supreme Court ruling that struck down the District of Columbia's ban on gun ownership.

Such positions occasionally inflame liberals who yearn for a more dynamic and dependable figure at the Senate's helm. They also chastise him for being overly cautious, such as when he refused to quickly push through President Obama's nomination of Dawn Johnsen to head the Justice Department's Office of Legal Counsel in May 2009. But Reid doesn't care. "We cannot and must not govern in a way that merely demonstrates to the world that we can behave just as arrogantly as the Republicans did when they held the majority in Congress," he wrote in a 2009 epilogue to "The Good Fight."

Reid doesn't just focus on national issues; he also takes pains to focus on Nevada matters, especially when the two intersect. He has devoted most of his quarter-century in Congress to leading the opposition to the proposed Yucca Mountain nuclear waste repository in his state, an issue that unites Nevada politicians. Reid helped move up Nevada's Democratic presidential primary to January 2008, essentially pushing the crowded field of candidates to take a public stand against the repository. Obama complied and after becoming president proposed to stop the repository's funding while a blue-ribbon panel explores other alternatives for waste disposal from the nation's nuclear power plants.

Reid said that in early 2007 he encouraged Obama — then a freshman senator from Illinois — to seek the presidency, praising his oratorical and political gifts. He worked to hand the new president several significant successes in his early months at the White House, including a $787 billion economic stimulus law. Reid had labored for weeks to appease House members wanting more-traditional Democratic priorities — such as school modernization funding — and a handful of reluctant Senate moderates from both parties. He succeeded in securing $8 billion in the law for high-speed rail — among Obama's priorities — that he hoped could one day help lead to an ultra-fast railroad from Los Angeles to Las Vegas.

But Reid also has sought to establish that he works with Obama, not for him. When the president proposed curbs on earmarks in March, Reid issued a joint statement with other Senate Democratic leaders that stopped short of endorsing the president's specific changes. He also put some distance between himself and Obama on the issue of the Iraq War when he initially expressed concerns over the president's plans to keep 50,000 troops in the country, though he subsequently praised the plans as "sound and measured."

When Reid ascended to majority leader in the 110th Congress (2007-08), he was quick to lay out an agenda tracking the issues Democrats used to oust Republican incumbents in the 2006 election. By the end of the session, he could point to several accomplishments, including an increase in the minimum wage, increased funding for veterans' programs, new lobbying rules, an energy bill, a farm bill and economic recovery packages for the housing and financial services sectors.

But Reid and other Democrats had just as long a list of legislation they were unable to bring to fruition, including an end to the Iraq War. With Republicans often relying on filibusters to block legislation, Reid resorted to parliamentary moves to keep GOP amendments from being ruled in order. (In the early months of 2009 he showed a greater inclination to allow votes on Republican proposals.)

Reid is routinely critical of the GOP's tactics, displaying a sharp edge that sometimes lands him in trouble. In May 2005, he had to apologize for calling President George W. Bush a "loser" in remarks to Las Vegas high school students. His autobiography is laden with criticism of the president he calls "King George." (He said in January 2009, however, that he had mended fences with Bush as the president left office.) And in 2007, he declared that the war in Iraq "is lost," a pronouncement some Democrats thought went too far.

He is just as forthright on other matters. Even the opening of the Capitol Visitor Center in December 2008 brought Reid headlines; he mentioned at a ceremony that he wouldn't miss the hot days when "you could literally smell the tourists" around the Senate chambers. He makes no apologies, though, for his bluntness or anything else. "I believe something to be right and I do it. And then I don't worry about it," he wrote in his autobiography.

On his approach:

"I believe something to be right and I do it. And then I don't worry about it. This has not always necessarily served me well, but it is who I am."
– 2008

On the public side of the job:

"I don't enjoy banquets, parades or press conferences."
– March 2000

On being in the majority:

"We cannot and must not govern in a way that merely demonstrates to the world that we can behave just as arrogantly as the Republicans did when they held the majority in Congress."
– 2009

On Republicans:

"We have reached out to the Republicans every way we know how. I have to believe that the message going out to the American people is that Republicans want to continue to be the party of 'no.'"
– April 2009

Before being elected leader, Reid was the party's second-in-command as the whip for six years under Tom Daschle of South Dakota. When Daschle was defeated for re-election in 2004, Reid in a matter of hours lined up the votes he needed to move up.

When Democrats won control in 2006, there was no question Reid would make the transition from minority to majority leader. In the previous two years, he had held Democrats together to prevent then-Majority Leader Bill Frist of Tennessee from passing a reduction in the estate tax and rallied his troops to stop Frist from taking away the minority's power to filibuster judicial nominations. A bipartisan group of senators, known as the Gang of 14, struck a deal to keep the GOP leadership from permanently altering Senate tradition.

Reid grew up in a cabin without indoor plumbing in the tiny mining town of Searchlight on the edge of the Mojave Desert. His mother was a high school dropout who took in laundry to support the family; his father was an alcoholic miner who killed himself at 58.

As a young man, Reid was an amateur middleweight boxer who sometimes sparred with pros in exhibition fights. (He still does 120 push-ups and 200 sit-ups each day.) But he wanted out of Searchlight and a boxer's hardscrabble life. Reid applied himself to his studies, boarding with families 40 miles away in Henderson to attend high school, where he became student body president.

History teacher Donald O'Callaghan, also the local Democratic chairman, took notice and helped arrange a scholarship for Reid at Utah State University. He earned a law degree at George Washington University while moonlighting as a U.S. Capitol Police officer.

Reid returned to Henderson and, at age 28, won election to the Nevada Assembly. When O'Callaghan became governor in 1970, Reid was elected the youngest lieutenant governor in state history. He made a bid for the U.S. Senate in 1974 but lost to Republican Paul Laxalt. A few years later, O'Callaghan appointed Reid chairman of the Nevada Gaming Commission, giving him oversight of the state's top industry at a time it was tainted by organized crime. Reid later told the Las Vegas Review-Journal, "They put bombs on my car, there were threatening phone calls at night, people tried to bribe me and went to jail."

In 1982, Reid won his first of two terms in the U.S. House. He tried again for the Senate in 1986 and won with 50 percent of the vote over Republican Rep. Jim Santini. He has had a few close calls since. In 1992, Democrat Charles Woods, a wealthy broadcast executive, held Reid to 53 percent in the primary. In the general election, Reid outspent GOP rancher Demar Dahl 5-to-1 to prevail with 51 percent of the vote.

In his 1998 campaign, Reid won by only 428 votes over Ensign, then a House member from Las Vegas, in a bitter contest. Reid called Ensign "an embarrassment to the state," and Ensign described Reid as an "old card shark." The two reconciled after Ensign was elected in 2000 to the state's other Senate seat; Reid has described them as "soul mates."

Reid coasted in 2004 over Republican Richard Ziser, an activist against same-sex marriage. Mindful of Daschle's defeat that year when Daschle was Democratic leader, Reid wasted little time in preparing for a serious challenge in 2010; by the end of March 2009 he had $5.1 million in the bank. Republicans pointed to early polls showing low approval ratings in his home state as evidence that he could be ripe for ouster. But he has become enough of a fixture in the Silver State — which Obama easily won after Bush carried it twice — that Republicans will not have an easy time unseating him.

His focus on his campaign came as his son Rory — who is chairman of Nevada's Clark County Commission — considered a run for the state's governorship in 2010.

KEY VOTES

2008

Yes	Prohibit discrimination based on genetic information
Yes	Reauthorize farm and nutrition programs for five years
Yes	Limit debate on "cap and trade" system for greenhouse gas emissions
Yes	Allow lawsuits against companies that participated in warrantless wiretapping
Yes	Limit debate on a bill to block a scheduled cut in Medicare payments to doctors
Yes	Grant mortgage relief to homeowners and funding for Fannie Mae and Freddie Mac
Yes	Approve a nuclear cooperation agreement with India
Yes	Approve final $700 billion program to stabilize financial markets
No	Allow consideration of a $14 billion auto industry loan package

2007

Yes	Increase minimum wage by $2.10 an hour
Yes	Limit debate on a comprehensive immigration bill
Yes	Overhaul congressional lobbying and ethics rules for members and their staffs
Yes	Limit debate on considering a bill to add House seats for the District of Columbia and Utah
Yes	Limit debate on restoring habeas corpus rights to detainees
Yes	Mandate minimum breaks for troops between deployments to Iraq or Afghanistan
Yes	Override Bush veto of $23.2 billion water projects authorization bill
No	Confirm Michael B. Mukasey as attorney general
Yes	Limit debate on an energy policy overhaul containing $21.8 billion in tax incentives and reduced oil and gas subsidies

CQ VOTE STUDIES

	PARTY UNITY		PRESIDENTIAL SUPPORT	
	SUPPORT	OPPOSE	SUPPORT	OPPOSE
2008	84%	16%	43%	57%
2007	95%	5%	39%	61%
2006	93%	7%	57%	43%
2005	92%	8%	38%	62%
2004	83%	17%	61%	39%
2003	95%	5%	53%	47%
2002	94%	6%	71%	29%
2001	96%	4%	65%	35%
2000	94%	6%	92%	8%
1999	92%	8%	82%	18%

INTEREST GROUPS

	AFL-CIO	ADA	CCUS	ACU
2008	50%	70%	75%	16%
2007	89%	85%	45%	0%
2006	93%	90%	50%	12%
2005	93%	100%	50%	4%
2004	100%	90%	53%	21%
2003	100%	70%	35%	21%
2002	100%	85%	45%	10%
2001	100%	100%	43%	20%
2000	88%	90%	40%	12%
1999	100%	90%	35%	12%

Sen. John Ensign (R)

Elected 2000; 2nd term

CAPITOL OFFICE
224-6244
ensign.senate.gov
119 Russell Bldg. 20510-2805; fax 228-2193

COMMITTEES
Budget
Commerce, Science & Transportation
Finance
Homeland Security & Governmental Affairs
Rules & Administration

RESIDENCE
Las Vegas

BORN
March 25, 1958; Roseville, Calif.

RELIGION
Christian

FAMILY
Wife, Darlene Ensign; three children

EDUCATION
U. of Nevada, Las Vegas, attended 1976-79;
Oregon State U., B.S. 1981; Colorado State U.,
D.V.M. 1985

CAREER
Veterinarian; casino manager

POLITICAL HIGHLIGHTS
U.S. House, 1995-99; sought Republican
nomination for U.S. Senate, 1998

ELECTION RESULTS

2006 GENERAL

John Ensign (R)	322,501	55.4%
Jack Carter (D)	238,796	41.0%
None of these candidates	8,232	1.4%
David K. Schumann (IA)	7,774	1.3%

2006 PRIMARY

John Ensign (R)	127,023	90.4%
None of these candidates	6,754	4.8%
Ed Hamilton (R)	6,649	4.7%

PREVIOUS WINNING PERCENTAGES
2000 (55%); 1996 House Election (50%); 1994 House
Election (48%)

Ensign has several qualities that make him a rising star in Republican circles: He is deeply competitive, well-versed in technology and tax policy, and a prolific fundraiser. A perpetual tan and a mane of silver hair that looks like a senatorial coif from central casting haven't hurt him, either.

But none of those attributes was of much use to Ensign in the 110th Congress (2007-08) as chairman of the National Republican Senatorial Committee, the Senate Republicans' fundraising arm. His efforts didn't prevent his party from losing several seats. But his colleagues — recognizing the difficulty of that job — kept him in the leadership by subsequently making him chairman of the Republican Policy Committee, where he shapes his party's message as a counterweight to the Democratically-controlled White House and Congress.

Ensign has a reputation as a ferocious competitor, whether he's on the golf course, running track or working on Capitol Hill. Friends say he turns everyday tasks into head-to-head contests. "If you walk with him in the airport, he wants to beat you and be first at the gate," said Pete Ernaut, a Republican political consultant and former Ensign campaign manager.

Ensign came to Congress as part of the Republican takeover in 1995, and adheres to the fiscal conservatism that distinguished many of the newcomers in that watershed political year. A member of the Budget Committee, he disdains government spending. He was sharply critical of President Obama's $787 billion economic stimulus law in early 2009, arguing it would lead states to overspend. "Not only do we have them not make the tough cuts they should be making, we actually encourage them to spend more because to be able to get the money, they have to spend more," he said. He also offered an unsuccessful amendment to a $410 billion catchall spending bill for fiscal 2009 that would have frozen spending at 2008 levels.

In 2008, Ensign was one of 15 senators to oppose a $289 billion, five-year reauthorization of farm programs and one of 13 to vote against a housing finance package extending relief to struggling mortgage giants Fannie Mae and Freddie Mac. He did support the $700 billion rescue of the nation's financial sector that fall, saying something should be done to aid Wall Street.

Ensign has been just as conservative on social policy. He has sought to limit benefits for illegal immigrants and sponsored a 2006 initiative, passed by the Senate but stalled in negotiations with the House, to make it a crime to help a minor circumvent parental notification laws by crossing state lines to obtain an abortion. And he angered supporters of voting rights for the District of Columbia in the Senate in 2009 when he successfully added an amendment aimed at complicating passage of a voting-rights bill for the District. His proposal would repeal restrictions on certain semiautomatic weapons and bar registration requirements in the nation's capital for most guns.

From his seat on the powerful Finance Committee, Ensign tries to help solar, wind and other renewable-energy industries. He held up consideration of the housing package by insisting on attaching an $8.2 billion package of energy-related tax breaks. Democratic leaders rebuffed his attempts.

Ensign has long had an interest in technology issues. He is the top-ranking Republican on the Commerce, Science and Transportation Committee's panel on Communications, Technology and the Internet. In the 109th Congress (2005-06), he chaired the GOP's High Tech Task Force.

Ensign also sits on the Rules and Administration Committee, where he has tangled with Democrats over proposed legislation to require incumbents and Senate candidates to file campaign finance reports electronically. He said he backs the idea but wants to add language to force groups filing complaints with the Select Ethics Committee to disclose their contributors. In the 111th Congress (2009-10), he picked up a seat on the Homeland Security and Governmental Affairs panel.

Ensign has an unusually close relationship with Nevada's senior senator, Democrat Harry Reid, the chamber's majority leader. The two work together so closely on state-specific legislation that Nevada political commentator Jon Ralston has referred to them as "Harry Ensign." Their relationship is remarkable because Reid defeated Ensign in an acrimonious 1998 race. "I wish other people had the same non-aggression pact we have," Reid once said. Though Republicans would dearly love to unseat Reid in 2010, Ensign has promised not to serve as an attack dog.

Ensign and Reid have fought vigorously to stop the establishment of a nuclear waste storage facility at Yucca Mountain, 100 miles northwest of Las Vegas. They have called for a national commission to study alternatives to burying spent fuel there from commercial nuclear power plants.

Ensign is equally forceful in his efforts to protect Nevada's gaming industry. From his seat on the Commerce panel, he fights against legislation outlawing gambling on college sports, which is legal in Nevada, and works to limit Internet gambling that can cut into casinos' revenues. He joins other Nevada lawmakers in urging colleagues not to bad-mouth Las Vegas and jeopardize its tourism business.

As the Senate GOP's campaign chairman, Ensign worked hard to put his stamp on the job. He used his political action committee to give hundreds of thousands of dollars to more than two dozen candidates, turning to his Las Vegas business contacts to assist them as well. After Democratic senators far outpaced Republicans in contributing to their colleagues, he took the audacious step in August 2008 of issuing a statement blasting his fellow lawmakers for their inactivity. "The hardest thing, by far, is trying to get your colleagues to do things," he lamented later. Several of his GOP colleagues' retirements and a strong national Democratic tide in 2008 only made his task more difficult.

Ensign got an early glimpse of the gambling world. His mother, who raised Ensign and his two siblings by herself, worked a $12-a-day job at Harrah's casino as a "change girl," doling out quarters to slot-machine players. During the 1995 debate on welfare overhaul, he pointed to his mother's refusal to accept government assistance as an example for others. "We were brought up in a family where you just don't take things," he said. "Welfare was for people who couldn't work, not for people who wouldn't work."

His mother eventually remarried, to a man who rose to become chairman and chief executive officer of the Mandalay Resort Group. Ensign worked in casinos and became a general manager at two of them in Las Vegas, but decided to follow his interest in animals and became a veterinarian.

GOP leaders urged him to run for the House in 1994, and though he was a political novice, Ensign assembled an organization of volunteers and embarked on an energetic precinct-walking effort. In the Republican sweep that year, he overcame a large Democratic registration advantage to squeeze past four-term Democrat James Bilbray in the Las Vegas-based 1st District by just 1,436 votes.

As a freshman on the Ways and Means Committee, he participated in overhauling the nation's welfare system. He left the House to challenge Reid in 1998, losing by just 428 votes. Then, in early 1999, Democrat Richard H. Bryan announced he wouldn't seek a third Senate term. Ensign spent twice as much money as Democratic attorney Ed Bernstein, and won with 55 percent of the vote in 2000. In 2006, he drew opposition from Jack Carter, eldest son of former President Carter, who campaigned on a platform critical of Republicans on the Iraq War. He outspent Carter heavily, and won with 55 percent.

KEY VOTES

2008

Yes Prohibit discrimination based on genetic information

No Reauthorize farm and nutrition programs for five years

No Limit debate on "cap and trade" system for greenhouse gas emissions

No Allow lawsuits against companies that participated in warrantless wiretapping

No Limit debate on a bill to block a scheduled cut in Medicare payments to doctors

No Grant mortgage relief to homeowners and funding for Fannie Mae and Freddie Mac

Yes Approve a nuclear cooperation agreement with India

Yes Approve final $700 billion program to stabilize financial markets

No Allow consideration of a $14 billion auto industry loan package

2007

Yes Increase minimum wage by $2.10 an hour

No Limit debate on a comprehensive immigration bill

No Overhaul congressional lobbying and ethics rules for members and their staffs

No Limit debate on considering a bill to add House seats for the District of Columbia and Utah

No Limit debate on restoring habeas corpus rights to detainees

No Mandate minimum breaks for troops between deployments to Iraq or Afghanistan

No Override Bush veto of $23.2 billion water projects authorization bill

Yes Confirm Michael B. Mukasey as attorney general

No Limit debate on an energy policy overhaul containing $21.8 billion in tax incentives and reduced oil and gas subsidies

CQ VOTE STUDIES

	PARTY UNITY		PRESIDENTIAL SUPPORT	
	SUPPORT	OPPOSE	SUPPORT	OPPOSE
2008	100%	0%	83%	17%
2007	97%	3%	89%	11%
2006	91%	9%	90%	10%
2005	94%	6%	89%	11%
2004	90%	10%	100%	0%
2003	95%	5%	98%	2%
2002	90%	10%	96%	4%
2001	88%	12%	97%	3%

INTEREST GROUPS

	AFL-CIO	ADA	CCUS	ACU
2008	10%	0%	88%	92%
2007	5%	0%	56%	91%
2006	20%	5%	92%	100%
2005	15%	5%	88%	100%
2004	9%	15%	75%	92%
2003	0%	10%	91%	100%
2002	15%	15%	95%	85%
2001	19%	20%	93%	84%

Rep. Shelley Berkley (D)

Elected 1998; 6th term

CAPITOL OFFICE
225-5965
www.berkley.house.gov
405 Cannon Bldg. 20515-2801; fax 225-3119

COMMITTEES
Foreign Affairs
Ways & Means

RESIDENCE
Las Vegas

BORN
Jan. 20, 1951; Manhattan, N.Y.

RELIGION
Jewish

FAMILY
Husband, Larry Lehrner; two children,
two stepchildren

EDUCATION
U. of Nevada, Las Vegas, B.A. 1972 (political
science); U. of San Diego, J.D. 1976

CAREER
Lawyer; casino executive

POLITICAL HIGHLIGHTS
Nev. Assembly, 1983-85; University and
Community College System of Nevada Board
of Regents, 1990-98

ELECTION RESULTS

2008 GENERAL

Shelley Berkley (D)	154,860	67.6%
Kenneth Wegner (R)	64,837	28.3%
Caren Alexander (IA)	4,697	2.0%
Jim Duensing (LIBERT)	4,528	2.0%

2008 PRIMARY

Shelley Berkley (D)	19,444	89.7%
Mark John Budetich Jr. (D)	2,222	10.3%

2006 GENERAL

Shelley Berkley (D)	85,025	64.8%
Kenneth Wegner (R)	40,917	31.2%
Jim Duensing (LIBERT)	2,843	2.2%
Darnell Roberts (IA)	2,339	1.8%

PREVIOUS WINNING PERCENTAGES
2004 (66%); 2002 (54%); 2000 (52%); 1998 (49%)

In a chamber full of pastel personalities, Berkley stands out like a splash of neon. She is a proud product of Sin City who sees no reason to turn down the wattage just because she's a member of Congress. But she also seeks to convey that she's a serious-minded legislator.

Her Capitol Hill office is adorned with photos of the Vegas skyline and decorated with slot machines. Her purse is full of poker chips that read, "Bet on Berkley," and during an impassioned March 2009 floor speech in which she promoted tourism in her city she announced, "I am wearing roulette earrings right now. So I take this very seriously."

In 2005, she cheerfully told her local newspaper she was still "black and blue" after cosmetic surgery. Shortly after her election in 1998, she appeared at a news conference in high-heeled tennis shoes. And in 1999, she was married at Bally's casino with 19 bridesmaids to attend to her — among them Dina Titus, who became her Democratic House colleague in 2009.

Berkley's fundraising skills — she contributed more than $1 million to Democratic candidates and causes from her campaign committee between 2005 and 2008 — helped her win a seat on the influential Ways and Means Committee in 2007. Although Nevada Republican Dean Heller also sits on the tax-writing panel, Berkley is in a better position to help her state's hospitality and gambling interests with Democrats in charge. Her business experience — she is a former casino company executive — makes her somewhat more sympathetic to business concerns than the average Democrat. And with the 2001 and 2003 income tax cuts of the George W. Bush era set to expire in 2010, she will be thrust into the middle of some of the most complex and contentious debates in Congress.

During her initial two years on the panel, Berkley pushed for an extension of tax credits for investments in renewable energy sources such as solar, wind and geothermal power. She told her colleagues that construction of such projects takes years, and their developers need certainty. Renewable-energy tax credits were added to a $700 billion proposal in fall 2008 aimed at shoring up the ailing financial services industry. After voting against the initial legislation, Berkley supported a second version that became law. In addition to the inclusion of the tax credits, she said the nation's fast-mounting financial troubles warranted her reconsideration. "I hate this like poison, but I think relief is necessary," she told the Las Vegas Sun.

Berkley was loyal to President Obama's economic agenda in the early months of his term, strongly backing legislation signed into law to expand a children's health insurance program that President Bush had vetoed, as well as Obama's $787 billion economic stimulus plan. When Nevada Republican Gov. Jim Gibbons expressed reluctance to accept unemployment money that was part of the stimulus law, saying it would require expanding a state program once the money was gone, Berkley scoffed. "We will be so foolish" if Nevada doesn't take the money, she said in March 2009.

But she bristled when Obama said that companies shouldn't take trips to Las Vegas at taxpayers' expense. Berkley led the charge in imploring the president and other lawmakers to refrain from making comments that could hurt Nevada's business.

Helping Nevada also means helping the gaming industry, which wants to get into Internet gambling, now controlled by offshore companies. Congress in 2006 barred online gambling businesses from accepting credit cards or electronic transfers for the purpose of betting, except for wagers made on horse races. Berkley fought that law, and in 2007 she introduced legislation calling for the National Academy of Sciences to study online gambling, hoping to lay the groundwork for future modifications. "An estimated 10 million Americans are still wagering online on poker alone, and they are doing so without the benefit of the protections afforded by effective regulatory oversight," she said at a 2007 Judiciary Committee hearing.

Nevada's biggest political battle has been against the proposed nuclear waste repository at Yucca Mountain, about 100 miles northwest of Las Vegas. Berkley has joined the rest of the state's congressional delegation in trying to slash funding for the project.

On the Foreign Affairs Committee, Berkley serves on the Middle East and Central Asia Subcommittee, allowing her to pursue her avid interest in Israel. In the 110th Congress (2007-08) she gave up her seat on Foreign Affairs to serve on Ways and Means, but returned for the 111th Congress (2009-10). In March 2009, she urged Secretary of State Hillary Rodham Clinton to condition $900 million in promised aid for the Palestinians on an end to rocket attacks on Israel from Gaza and the release of a captured Israeli soldier.

Berkley's parents came to the U.S. from Eastern Europe and moved to Las Vegas when she was 6 years old. She attended the University of Nevada at Las Vegas, where she served as student body president before graduating with a political science degree. After earning a law degree from the University of San Diego, Berkley returned to Las Vegas to start a career. She did a stint as in-house counsel for Southwest Gas and served as vice president of government and legal affairs for the Sands Hotel, and as board chairwoman of the Nevada Hotel and Motel Association. She served in the Nevada Assembly from 1983-85 but became better-known as a state university regent. She was appointed to the board of regents in 1990 and served two four-year terms.

Berkley first won election to the House in 1998 when Republican Rep. John Ensign gave up his 1st District seat to run for the Senate. He was narrowly defeated by Democrat Harry Reid, now the Senate majority leader. (Ensign won election to the other Senate seat in 2000.) Berkley squeaked by Republican Don Chairez, a former county judge, by just 3 percentage points after battling ethics questions involving memos she had written several years earlier in which she advised a legal client to make campaign contributions to judges as a way to curry favor.

In 2000, fending off the same ethics questions, Berkley defeated GOP Rep. Jon Porter, then a state senator, by 8 percentage points. Redistricting following the 2000 census left her with a more urban, Democratic constituency, and Berkley has won ever since by wide margins.

KEY VOTES

2008

Yes Delay consideration of Colombia free-trade agreement

Yes Override Bush veto of federal farm and nutrition programs reauthorization bill

Yes Overhaul surveillance laws and permit dismissal of suits against companies that conducted warrantless wiretapping

Yes Grant mortgage relief to homeowners and funding for Fannie Mae and Freddie Mac

No Approve initial $700 billion program to stabilize financial markets

Yes Approve final $700 billion program to stabilize financial markets

Yes Provide $14 billion in loans to automakers

2007

Yes Increase minimum wage by $2.10 an hour

Yes Approve $124.2 billion in emergency war spending and set goal for redeployment of troops from Iraq

No Reject federal contraceptive assistance to international family planning groups

Yes Override Bush veto of $23.2 billion water projects authorization bill

No Implement Peru free-trade agreement

Yes Approve energy policy overhaul with new fuel economy standards

Yes Clear $473.5 billion omnibus spending bill, including $70 billion for military operations

CQ VOTE STUDIES

	PARTY UNITY		PRESIDENTIAL SUPPORT	
	SUPPORT	OPPOSE	SUPPORT	OPPOSE
2008	97%	3%	18%	82%
2007	95%	5%	12%	88%
2006	90%	10%	32%	68%
2005	92%	8%	28%	72%
2004	93%	7%	41%	59%

INTEREST GROUPS

	AFL-CIO	ADA	CCUS	ACU
2008	100%	85%	67%	4%
2007	96%	85%	58%	8%
2006	100%	80%	54%	13%
2005	93%	90%	54%	13%
2004	93%	95%	60%	8%

NEVADA 1

Las Vegas

Neon lights along the "Strip" and the chance of easy money still lure some pleasure seekers into the 1st, which includes Las Vegas and its immediate environs, but a housing market collapse, declining gaming revenue and municipal budget shortfalls have led to layoffs and commercial construction stoppages.

The increasingly urbanized district experienced decades of explosive growth and skyrocketing home values, and it depends largely on its hospitality-based economy, which has been hit hard by national economic downturns. Foreign visitors armed with an advantageous exchange rate picked up some of the slack as early signs of the recession appeared, but a contracting airline industry and fewer convention guests arriving in Las Vegas may prolong the damage. Even if casino-based revenues rebound, a decade of diversification of the city's non-gaming economy may slow recovery as retail, restaurant and nightlife sectors struggle.

A few luxury resorts and casinos have continued planned development, but many projects have halted, slashing labor and service industry jobs,

and loan defaults by large developers have extended the crisis into the financial sector. Local cultural centers have scaled back events, but cuts by health care providers are of much greater concern to residents.

Federal funding to support real estate market stabilization here — an area recognized as the hardest hit by the foreclosure crisis — is expected to keep a large number of residential properties from falling into blight even as unemployment rates and mortgage payments continue to rise.

Although pockets of Republicans live here, the 1st has a strong Democratic base in unionized service workers and does not include most of the GOP-leaning suburbs. In 2008, Democrat Barack Obama won the district with 64 percent of its presidential vote.

MAJOR INDUSTRY
Tourism, gambling, conventions

CITIES
Las Vegas (pt.), 362,908; North Las Vegas, 115,488; Paradise (unincorporated) (pt.), 77,893; Sunrise Manor (unincorporated) (pt.), 68,288

NOTABLE
The Little White Wedding Chapel on Las Vegas Boulevard has a drive-through window for weddings.

Rep. Dean Heller (R)

Elected 2006; 2nd term

CAPITOL OFFICE
225-6155
heller.house.gov
125 Cannon Bldg. 20515-2802; fax 225-5679

COMMITTEES
Ways & Means

RESIDENCE
Carson City

BORN
May 10, 1960; Castro Valley, Calif.

RELIGION
Mormon

FAMILY
Wife, Lynne Heller; four children

EDUCATION
U. of Southern California, B.S. 1985
(business administration)

CAREER
Commercial banker; chief deputy state
treasurer; stockbroker

POLITICAL HIGHLIGHTS
Nev. Assembly, 1990-94; Nev. secretary of state,
1995-2007

ELECTION RESULTS

2008 GENERAL

Dean Heller (R)	170,771	51.8%
Jill Derby (D)	136,548	41.4%
John Everhart (IA)	11,179	3.4%
Sean Patrick Morse (LIBERT)	5,740	1.7%
Craig Bergland (GREEN)	5,282	1.6%

2008 PRIMARY

Dean Heller (R)	43,112	86.0%
James W. Smack (R)	7,009	14.0%

2006 GENERAL

Dean Heller (R)	117,168	50.3%
Jill Derby (D)	104,593	44.9%
Daniel Rosen (I)	5,524	2.4%
James C. Kroshus (IA)	5,439	2.3%

Heller has a commitment to conservative economic principles and a willingness to speak and vote his mind, even if it irritates Republican colleagues. He draws on his background as a former stockbroker to preach against what he considers excessive government interference in financial markets.

An upbringing in the self-reliant West and a chance meeting with supply-side tax-cutting pioneer Jack F. Kemp helped shape Heller's beliefs. In the mid-1980s, Heller met Kemp at a friend's wedding, and the two discussed economics. "He probably doesn't even remember it," Heller recalled with a laugh about the former New York GOP congressman and 1996 vice presidential nominee. "But it was part of developing my view of the world."

Heller has a chance to espouse his laissez faire agenda as a member of the powerful Ways and Means Committee, which has jurisdiction over taxes, trade and entitlement programs. He joins his Democratic Nevada colleague Shelley Berkley on the panel, giving their state's gambling industry added political clout.

Heller served on the Financial Services Committee in his first term. He voted against both versions of the $700 billion effort to shore up the ailing financial services industry in fall 2008, the second of which became law. "That is Wall Street arrogance," he told the Las Vegas Review-Journal. "They created their problems and they want someone else to bail them out."

He expressed confidence the market "will work itself out" without the need to put taxpayers on the hook. Instead of government intervention, he would like to see lower corporate tax rates and the elimination of deficit spending.

Heller occasionally shows an independent streak. During his second week in office in 2007, he was the only GOP House freshman to back a bill expanding federal funding for medical research on embryonic stem cells. "It's not necessarily pro-choice or pro-stem cells," he said. "It's just, get the government out of the way."

Heller angered some in the GOP in 2008 when he told the Review-Journal the Republican Party needed to "clean house...The next couple of election cycles are going to do that." He said some of the Republicans who helped their party take control of Congress in 1994 "came to change Washington and Washington changed them."

However, Heller doesn't typically wander far from the party line. He sided with fellow Republicans on 94 percent of the votes splitting the parties in the 110th Congress (2007-08). He strongly backs gun owners' rights and espouses a tough line on immigration-related issues. He opposed Democratic legislation to expand the State Children's Health Insurance Program, which covers children whose families have low incomes but are not poor enough to qualify for Medicaid. And in 2009 he voted against the $787 billion economic stimulus package, arguing it "will not create jobs, nor will it help our ailing economy."

A member of the Natural Resources Committee during the start of the 110th, Heller vigorously opposed legislation that would have forced the hard-rock mining industry to pay royalties on minerals extracted from public lands. He warned that the measure "hurts, perhaps even kills, the domestic mining industry and with it the towns and communities in western Nevada and rural America."

Heller also joins the rest of Nevada's congressional delegation in fighting the proposed nuclear waste repository at Yucca Mountain, 100 miles northwest of Las Vegas. He joined with Berkley and fellow Nevada Republican

Jon Porter in 2007 in an unsuccessful quest to to slash funding for the project by $200 million.

Heller is a product of the parochial state capital of Carson City, the son of an auto mechanic whose customers included a number of state legislators. As a boy, he rode his bike from his father's shop to play with the children of Paul Laxalt, the Nevada governor who went on to become a U.S. senator.

Heller was a star basketball player at Carson High School. As an adult, he played 17 consecutive years in the same recreational basketball league in Carson City. He also enjoys stock car racing, a hobby he shares with his father, and competes in several races each year in Nevada and California.

At the University of Southern California in Los Angeles, Heller studied business administration, specializing in finance and securities analysis. He put himself through college by working on the Pacific Stock Exchange. After graduation, he worked as a stockbroker and as a trader in Los Angeles. "Watching the market and watching a specific stock going up and down, you always know it is affected by taxes and the government," he said.

In 1989, Heller returned to Carson City to become the deputy to Nevada Treasurer Ken Santor, a Republican. On Heller's first day on the job, Santor had a falling-out with the Nevada Assembly's powerful Ways and Means Committee chairman, and Heller was asked to substitute for his boss at committee meetings. The minority leader, a Republican, took notice and suggested Heller run for public office himself. The following year, he was elected to the Assembly, with the help of his father and his father's reputation.

Heller was elected secretary of state in 1994. In his three terms, he became known for making Nevada the first state to implement an auditable paper trail for electronic voting machines. In 2006, as five-term Republican Rep. Jim Gibbons launched his successful campaign for governor, Heller was hitting his term limit as secretary of state. He went after the open House seat but had to compete with four others, including Gibbons' wife, a state legislator, in the GOP primary. Heller edged out Assemblywoman Sharron E. Angle by a scant 421 votes in the primary. Conservative activists had supported Angle, viewing Heller as too moderate. They now profess themselves "pleasantly surprised" by his record in Congress.

That November, he beat Democrat Jill Derby, a member of the Nevada System of Higher Education Board of Regents, by just 5 percentage points in the GOP-leaning district. Heller prevailed again in a 2008 rematch, this time by double digits. Heller harbors ambitions of running for governor of Nevada. For the 2010 cycle, however, he is assisting with the House Republicans' incumbent retention efforts.

KEY VOTES

2008

No   Delay consideration of Colombia free-trade agreement

No   Override Bush veto of federal farm and nutrition programs reauthorization bill

Yes   Overhaul surveillance laws and permit dismissal of suits against companies that conducted warrantless wiretapping

Yes   Grant mortgage relief to homeowners and funding for Fannie Mae and Freddie Mac

No   Approve initial $700 billion program to stabilize financial markets

No   Approve final $700 billion program to stabilize financial markets

No   Provide $14 billion in loans to automakers

2007

No   Increase minimum wage by $2.10 an hour

No   Approve $124.2 billion in emergency war spending and set goal for redeployment of troops from Iraq

Yes   Reject federal contraceptive assistance to international family planning groups

Yes   Override Bush veto of $23.2 billion water projects authorization bill

Yes   Implement Peru free-trade agreement

No   Approve energy policy overhaul with new fuel economy standards

Yes   Clear $473.5 billion omnibus spending bill, including $70 billion for military operations

CQ VOTE STUDIES

	PARTY UNITY		PRESIDENTIAL SUPPORT	
	SUPPORT	OPPOSE	SUPPORT	OPPOSE
2008	92%	8%	68%	32%
2007	94%	6%	75%	25%

INTEREST GROUPS

	AFL-CIO	ADA	CCUS	ACU
2008	36%	25%	89%	80%
2007	13%	15%	80%	96%

NEVADA 2
Reno, Carson City and the 'Cow Counties'

The 2nd takes in everything outside of Las Vegas and its suburbs, including almost all of the state's vast rural areas. Reno and the capital, Carson City, anchor the district in the west. In the "Cow Counties," agriculture, mining and ranching dominate. Nearly 90 percent of the district's land is federally owned. The 2nd also dips into two areas of Clark County in the southern part of the state, taking in Nellis Air Force Base and much of the northern part of Clark, as well as a few suburban communities in the county's southwest.

Several counties in the district were among the hardest hit by Nevada's housing market collapse. Lyon, Nye and Washoe counties saw high rates of mortgage defaults, and Clark — shared by the 1st and 3rd — will have to recover from oversupply in the condominium market.

The gold rush attracted fortune hunters to Reno in the 1800s, and casinos drew them in for decades in the 20th century, making gambling and tourism big business here. But Washoe County has suffered prolonged declines in gambling revenue, and fewer tourists are heading to Lake

Tahoe resorts to the south. Officials in the gambling industry are also concerned that Indian reservation casinos in California will continue to lure visitors away from Washoe. Diversification of the non-gaming economy through public and private development of other entertainment sectors and outdoor attractions may prop up western Nevada.

The 2nd votes mostly Republican in local elections, and John McCain won handily in some of the district's rural counties in the 2008 presidential election. But left-leaning Carson City, Reno and Clark County residents favored Democrat Barack Obama, and McCain only barely edged out a win in the district overall by fractions of a percentage point.

MAJOR INDUSTRY
Gambling, mining, manufacturing

MILITARY BASES
Nellis Air Force Base, 8,636 military, 3,748 civilian (2008); Naval Air Station Fallon, 923 military, 418 civilian (2008)

CITIES
Reno, 180,480; Sparks, 66,346; Carson City, 52,457; Pahrump (unincorporated), 24,631

NOTABLE
Reno's National Bowling Stadium hosts championship tournaments.

Rep. Dina Titus (D)

Elected 2008; 1st term

Titus has experience in both the theoretical and practical applications of political science, with more than 30 years as a college political science professor and 20 years as a state legislator under her belt.

During her two decades in the Nevada Senate, the last 16 as the minority leader, Titus was known as a policy wonk who looked to solve problems through compromise. She formed a coalition to help protect Red Rock Canyon from encroaching development and championed legislation to provide tax breaks for renewable-energy development and require utilities to boost use of "green" energy.

With her professional background in mind, Democrats gave Titus a seat on the Education and Labor Committee. Her goals include increasing federal support to the states and to local school districts. From her seat on the higher education subcommittee, Titus will be an ally of public universities looking for federal aid so they can curb tuition increases.

She supported the $787 billion economic stimulus package that Congress enacted in early 2009; it included more than $500 million for Nevada education programs and nearly $300 million for transportation projects in the state. Titus said she'll be pushing for more federal dollars on such projects from her assignment on the Transportation and Infrastructure Committee.

Titus, born in Georgia and educated in the South (her Southern drawl remains), moved to Nevada in 1977 to take a teaching post at the University of Nevada, Las Vegas. After teaching political science and government there for more than a decade, she won a 1988 race for the Nevada Senate, where she developed a pro-business, pro-environment record. The Nevada Legislature is a part-time job, and she continued to teach at the university.

After losing a 2006 race for governor by 4 percentage points to Jim Gibbons, Titus was hesitant to wage another high-profile campaign. But she eventually entered the House race in May 2008, giving Republican incumbent Jon Porter a big money-raising edge. But voters knew her from her years in the state Senate and from the 2006 race and she took advantage of increased Democratic voter registration. She prevailed by 5 points.

CAPITOL OFFICE
225-3252
titus.house.gov
319 Cannon Bldg. 20515-2803; fax 225-2185

COMMITTEES
Education & Labor
Homeland Security
Transportation & Infrastructure

RESIDENCE
Las Vegas

BORN
May 23, 1950; Thomasville, Ga.

RELIGION
Greek Orthodox

FAMILY
Husband, Thomas C. Wright

EDUCATION
College of William & Mary, A.B. 1970 (government); U. of Georgia, M.A. 1973 (political science); Florida State U., Ph.D. 1976 (political science)

CAREER
Professor

POLITICAL HIGHLIGHTS
Nev. Senate, 1989-2009 (minority leader, 1993-2009); Democratic nominee for governor, 2006

ELECTION RESULTS

2008 GENERAL

Dina Titus (D)	165,912	47.4%
Jon Porter (R)	147,940	42.3%
Jeffrey C. Reeves (I)	14,922	4.3%
Joseph P. Silvestri (LIBERT)	10,164	2.9%
Floyd Fitzgibbons (IA)	6,937	2.0%
Bob Giaquinta (GREEN)	3,937	1.1%

2008 PRIMARY

Dina Titus (D)	22,232	84.7%
Barry Michaels (D)	2,312	8.8%
Anna Nevenich (D)	1,114	4.2%
Carlo "Tex" Poliak (D)	587	2.2%

NEVADA 3
Las Vegas suburbs

The pinwheel-shaped 3rd is located in Clark County and saw explosive population growth, suburban expansion and an influx of white-collar workers in past decades. But recent double-digit unemployment rates, a housing crisis and declining gaming revenue have hampered economic progress.

The district includes a chunk of Las Vegas but is mainly composed of the city's suburbs. Although most area casinos are in the urban 1st, southward expansion of the Las Vegas "Strip" has brought some large resorts into the 3rd. The district is home to many who work in the gaming industry and are part of the area's strong union structure.

Most of the 3rd's population lives in suburbs such as Henderson, Spring Valley and Paradise. Summerlin, to the west, is a massive planned community along the western rim of Las Vegas Valley. To the east, the population is largely Mormon. In the south, the 3rd contains lightly populated mining communities near Laughlin. Small ranching communities are in the district's western reaches. The demand on the Colorado River for fresh water, a valuable commodity in the 3rd District's hot, desert communities, is a perennial issue here.

Despite the presence of conservative-leaning new arrivals to the state, as well as one of the fastest-growing elderly populations in the country, the 3rd now is politically competitive. Barack Obama won with 55 percent of the 2008 presidential vote.

MAJOR INDUSTRY
Gambling, mining, ranching

CITIES
Henderson, 175,381; Spring Valley (unincorporated), 117,390; Las Vegas (pt.), 115,526; Paradise (unincorporated) (pt.), 108,177

NOTABLE
The Hoover Dam, about 30 miles southeast of Las Vegas, often is called one of the greatest engineering works in history.

Gov. John Lynch (D)

First elected: 2004
Length of term: 2 years
Term expires: 1/11
Salary: $108,990
Phone: (603) 271-2121

Residence: Hopkinton
Born: Nov. 25, 1952; Waltham, Mass.
Religion: Roman Catholic
Family: Wife, Susan Lynch; three children
Education: U. of New Hampshire, B.A. 1974 (English); Harvard U., M.B.A. 1979; Georgetown U., J.D. 1984
Career: Business consulting firm owner; furniture manufacturing company president; college admissions director; state party executive director
Political highlights: No previous office

Election results:
2008 GENERAL

John Lynch (D)	479,042	70.2%
Joe Kenney (R)	188,555	27.6%
Susan M. Newell (LIBERT)	14,987	2.2%

Senate President Sylvia B. Larsen (D)

(no lieutenant governor)
Phone: (603) 271-2111

LEGISLATURE

General Court: January-June

Senate: 24 members, 2-year terms
2009 ratios: 14 D, 10 R; 11 men, 13 women
Salary: $200/2-year term
Phone: (603) 271-2111

House: 400 members, 2-year terms
2009 ratios: 222 D, 176 R, 2 vacancies; 255 men, 143 women
Salary: $200/2-year term
Phone: (603) 271-3315

TERM LIMITS

Governor: No
Senate: No
House: No

URBAN STATISTICS

CITY	POPULATION
Manchester	107,006
Nashua	86,605
Concord	40,687
Derry	34,021
Rochester	28,461

REGISTERED VOTERS

Unaffiliated	38%
Republican	31%
Democrat	31%

POPULATION

2008 population (est.)	1,315,809
2000 population	1,235,786
1990 population	1,109,252
Percent change (1990-2000)	+11.4%
Rank among states (2008)	41

Median age	37.1
Born in state	43.3%
Foreign born	4.4%
Violent crime rate	175/100,000
Poverty level	6.5%
Federal workers	7,933
Military	4,435

ELECTIONS

STATE ELECTION OFFICIAL
(603) 271-3242
DEMOCRATIC PARTY
(603) 225-6899
REPUBLICAN PARTY
(603) 225-9341

MISCELLANEOUS

Web: www.nh.gov
Capital: Concord

U.S. CONGRESS

Senate: 1 Democrat, 1 Republican
House: 2 Democrats

2000 Census Statistics by District

DIST.	2008 VOTE FOR PRESIDENT BUSH	MCCAIN	WHITE	BLACK	ASIAN	HISP	MEDIAN INCOME	WHITE COLLAR	BLUE COLLAR	SERVICE INDUSTRY	OVER 64	UNDER 18	COLLEGE EDUCATION	RURAL	SQ. MILES
1	53%	46%	95%	1%	1%	2%	$50,135	63%	24%	13%	12%	25%	29%	33%	2,449
2	56	43	95	1	1	2	$48,762	62	25	13	12	25	29	48	6,519
STATE	54	45	95	1	1	2	$49,467	62	25	13	12	25	29	41	8,968
U.S.	53	46	69	12	4	13	$41,994	60	25	15	12	26	24	21	3,537,438

Coos

Grafton

Carroll

2

1

Belknap

Strafford

Sullivan

Merrimack

Rochester ●

Concord ★

Dover ●

Portsmouth ●

Cheshire

Manchester ●

Rockingham

Hillsborough

Nashua ●

Sen. Judd Gregg (R)

Elected 1992; 3rd term

CAPITOL OFFICE
224-3324
gregg.senate.gov
201 Russell Bldg. 20510-2904; fax 224-4952

COMMITTEES
Appropriations
Budget - ranking member
Health, Education, Labor & Pensions

RESIDENCE
Rye Beach

BORN
Feb. 14, 1947; Nashua, N.H.

RELIGION
Congregationalist

FAMILY
Wife, Kathleen MacLellan Gregg; three children

EDUCATION
Columbia U., A.B. 1969; Boston U., J.D. 1972,
LL.M. 1975

CAREER
Lawyer

POLITICAL HIGHLIGHTS
N.H. Governor's Executive Council, 1979-81;
U.S. House, 1981-89; governor, 1989-93

ELECTION RESULTS

2004 GENERAL

Judd Gregg (R)	434,847	66.2%
Doris "Granny D" Haddock (D)	221,549	33.7%

2004 PRIMARY

Judd Gregg (R)	60,597	91.6%
Tom Alciere (R)	2,682	4.0%
Michael Tipa (R)	2,563	3.9%

PREVIOUS WINNING PERCENTAGES
1998 (68%); 1992 (48%); 1986 House Election (74%);
1984 House Election (76%); 1982 House Election
(71%); 1980 House Election (64%)

A conservative Yankee with an understated style, Gregg can work with members across the aisle as well as throw a partisan punch. He is the Budget Committee's senior Republican and one of Congress' few consistent spending hawks.

But as President Obama discovered in February 2009, Gregg's bipartisanship has its limits. Obama nominated him to serve as secretary of Commerce, which would have made him one of three Republicans in the Cabinet. He focused on Gregg's long résumé on business, budget and policy issues.

Eight days later, however, Gregg withdrew. He cited "irresolvable conflicts" on such issues as the president's economic stimulus — which only three Senate Republicans had supported — and the 2010 census. "Unfortunately, we did not adequately focus on these concerns," he said. "We are functioning from a different set of views on many critical items of policy."

His Senate GOP colleagues warmly welcomed him back to the fold. He is respected by the chamber's Republican brain trust on economic and fiscal issues, where he focuses much of his energy, and attends leadership meetings even though he does not have a formal position. He announced soon after that he would retire at the end of the 111th Congress (2009-10), forgoing a time-consuming re-election battle in a state that has become increasingly Democratic.

Gregg won praise from from both parties in 2008 when he served as the Senate GOP's point man during negotiations on the $700 billion plan to shore up the nation's ailing financial sector. He was not the obvious choice — the legislation was in the purview of the Banking, Housing and Urban Affairs Committee, a panel on which Gregg does not serve. But Banking's chief Republican, Alabama's Richard C. Shelby, did not want to be part of the negotiations because he disagreed with the George W. Bush administration's proposal, prompting Minority Leader Mitch McConnell of Kentucky to tap Gregg.

His role on the bill showed Gregg's ability to compromise, but he more often serves as a fierce critic of Democrats' economic and budget proposals. During debates, he paces the Senate floor while firing one-liners like "fudge-it budget," "Swiss-cheese-go" to describe the Democrats' anti-deficit "pay-as-you-go" rule, and "Obama-spend-o-rama" — Gregg's 2008 critique of the Democratic presidential candidate's policy proposals.

Within weeks of his decision not to join Obama's Cabinet, Gregg took up the task of blasting the president's $3.56 trillion budget proposal for fiscal 2010. He dismissed it as "a missed opportunity for American taxpayers" that would implement large spending increases and fail to address the soaring budget deficit. But he joined GOP leaders in declining to offer an alternative budget proposal, preferring to offer amendments — most of which were rejected, including one that would create a point of order and require 60 votes to waive any budget resolution that would double the public debt over 11 years.

In recent years, Gregg has been most vocal about Congress' need to address the unsustainable growth of Social Security, Medicare and Medicaid. On this issue, he takes the attitude that compromise is necessary because inaction is the far less appealing option. "I have never believed you could move on major issues that affect all Americans that are just hugely political…without doing it in a bipartisan way because the American people will not accept one party moving forward in this area," Gregg said.

He has joined Budget Chairman Kent Conrad of North Dakota in proposing a task force of members of Congress and administration officials who would draw up policy proposals to deal with the sustainability of large entitlement programs. The idea hit a snag in April 2009 when Gregg proposed a requirement that any recommendations from the proposed panel have the backing of a majority of the members from each party; Conrad called Gregg's proposed change unfair.

Gregg was Budget chairman from 2005 to 2007 and never was able to advance proposals to rein in the debt. He also was a major supporter of the 2001 and 2003 tax cuts that many say have contributed to the red ink. Gregg maintains the tax cuts remain good policy and that the real culprit has been too much spending. He is quick to note that in 2003, he voted against the GOP's costly Medicare prescription drug benefit bill. "There is no question as a party that we did not discipline spending," he said.

Gregg also has spent a good part of his career on the Appropriations Committee, and is the ranking member on the State-Foreign Operations Subcommittee. He said in March 2009 it is "probably necessary" to double foreign aid, given U.S. commitments to fighting terrorism and other overseas needs.

Gregg sits on the Health, Education, Labor and Pensions Committee, where he forged a solid working relationship with Democrat Edward M. Kennedy, a fellow New Englander with diametrically opposite views on most social policy issues and a far different temperament. During the 108th Congress (2003-04), the two men worked to enact legislation of mutual concern: a rewrite of the law governing special education for disabled students.

A conservative on social issues, Gregg has battled legislation to ban job discrimination against homosexuals, saying a federal law should not overturn state rulings. He also has been a longtime ally of anti-abortion forces.

Gregg in 2004 supported a constitutional ban on same-sex marriage, but during the 109th Congress (2005-06) he made an about-face and voted no. Gregg credited his change of heart to the fact that the 2003 Massachusetts Supreme Court ruling declaring such bans unconstitutional did not lead to judicial imposition of gay marriage across the country, as he had feared.

Outside Congress, Gregg saw the end of a disturbing personal chapter in summer 2005 when two men who kidnapped his wife in 2003 were sentenced to long jail terms. The men broke into Gregg's home in McLean, Va., held Kathleen Gregg down and threatened to rape and kill her while they ransacked the house. She persuaded the men to take her to the bank, which they did at knifepoint. She managed to escape after giving them money.

Not long after the sentencing, Gregg got more welcome news. He bought about $20 worth of tickets in the Powerball lottery at a gas station and ended up matching five of six numbers, winning $853,492. "Even senators can be lucky," he joked to reporters after picking up his check.

The son of a former GOP governor of New Hampshire — Hugh Gregg, who served from 1953-55 — Gregg has spent most of his life in public service. He practiced law only a short time before launching his political career in 1978, when he unseated a Republican incumbent to join the five-member state executive council. Two years later, he won the House seat of retiring Republican James C. Cleveland. His training as a tax attorney helped win him a seat on the Ways and Means Committee. After four terms he left Congress for a pair of two-year terms as governor.

When Gregg sought to return to Washington in 1992, he ran into stiff opposition. New Hampshire's economic woes fired up an angry electorate, putting pro-business Democrat John Rauh in a position to give Gregg his toughest electoral fight. Bill Clinton captured the state in the presidential race, and Gregg lost most of the counties in his old congressional district on the western side of New Hampshire. But he carried the populous southeast corner and the GOP "North Country" and prevailed by 3 percentage points. In 1998 and 2004, he won with at least 66 percent of the vote.

KEY VOTES

2008

? Prohibit discrimination based on genetic information

No Reauthorize farm and nutrition programs for five years

? Limit debate on "cap and trade" system for greenhouse gas emissions

No Allow lawsuits against companies that participated in warrantless wiretapping

No Limit debate on a bill to block a scheduled cut in Medicare payments to doctors

Yes Grant mortgage relief to homeowners and funding for Fannie Mae and Freddie Mac

Yes Approve a nuclear cooperation agreement with India

Yes Approve final $700 billion program to stabilize financial markets

No Allow consideration of a $14 billion auto industry loan package

2007

Yes Increase minimum wage by $2.10 an hour

Yes Limit debate on a comprehensive immigration bill

Yes Overhaul congressional lobbying and ethics rules for members and their staffs

No Limit debate on considering a bill to add House seats for the District of Columbia and Utah

No Limit debate on restoring habeas corpus rights to detainees

No Mandate minimum breaks for troops between deployments to Iraq or Afghanistan

No Override Bush veto of $23.2 billion water projects authorization bill

Yes Confirm Michael B. Mukasey as attorney general

No Limit debate on an energy policy overhaul containing $21.8 billion in tax incentives and reduced oil and gas subsidies

CQ VOTE STUDIES

	PARTY UNITY		PRESIDENTIAL SUPPORT	
	SUPPORT	OPPOSE	SUPPORT	OPPOSE
2008	95%	5%	82%	18%
2007	86%	14%	90%	10%
2006	90%	10%	93%	7%
2005	91%	9%	82%	18%
2004	94%	6%	98%	2%
2003	92%	8%	93%	7%
2002	81%	19%	96%	4%
2001	96%	4%	100%	0%
2000	98%	2%	38%	62%
1999	94%	6%	33%	67%

INTEREST GROUPS

	AFL-CIO	ADA	CCUS	ACU
2008	20%	15%	86%	83%
2007	0%	10%	82%	72%
2006	7%	15%	100%	72%
2005	7%	5%	72%	72%
2004	0%	15%	88%	88%
2003	0%	15%	78%	85%
2002	15%	10%	100%	85%
2001	13%	0%	100%	88%
2000	0%	0%	86%	100%
1999	0%	0%	76%	91%

Sen. Jeanne Shaheen (D)

Elected 2008; 1st term

Shaheen is a seasoned politician whose pragmatism and resourcefulness — learned from decades on the campaign trail and in state office — will be crucial as she pursues her key legislative priorities: education, health care and energy policy. "New Hampshire is a very independent state — it's fiscally conservative, but it's a state that is socially progressive," she said. "I not only believe in those values, I intend to reflect them in the Senate."

Shaheen worked for decades on political campaigns in New Hampshire. She served roughly seven years in the state legislature and six more as governor. During a foray into academia in 2003, she taught a university course on how to govern in a partisan environment, drawing on her experience as a Democratic governor with a Republican legislature.

Upon joining the Senate, Shaheen quickly joined a group of 15 Democratic moderates who hope to build bipartisan coalitions on key issues. She told MSNBC in a March 2009 interview that issues such as health care and climate change often divide along geographic, not partisan, lines. "And so, it's important for us to be able to build those bridges and relationships so we can bring everybody along" to get legislation passed, she said. She said she particularly admires Maine Republican Sens. Olympia J. Snowe and Susan Collins, two of the chamber's most active moderates.

Shaheen has a strong commitment to public education. She attended public schools and universities, then taught language arts at a newly integrated high school in Mississippi to help put her husband through law school. In her 1996 gubernatorial race, Shaheen called for expanded access to kindergarten. As governor, she instituted a kindergarten initiative and increased state assistance for public schools and the state's university system.

In the Senate, she supports more investment in early childhood education, an overhaul of the 2001 No Child Left Behind education law and measures to ensure that students have access to college. In 1996, Shaheen campaigned for governor in part on the need to expand access to kindergarten. As governor, she instituted a kindergarten initiative and increased state assistance for public schools and the state's university system.

Shaheen is a vocal supporter of the State Children's Health Insurance Program (SCHIP), which covers children from low-income families that do not qualify for Medicaid. As governor, Shaheen launched her state's program, and obtained funds from a local foundation when the state's Republican legislature refused to fund New Hampshire's half of the federal SCHIP law. "For me, children's health insurance was a no-brainer in terms of what can we do to better prepare children," she said. She voted for the 2009 expansion of SCHIP's federal funding.

Shaheen, whose eldest granddaughter, Ellie, has juvenile diabetes, called the George W. Bush administration's limits on federally funded embryonic stem cell research "unconscionable." She hailed President Obama's March 2009 executive order lifting those restrictions, calling it "a major step in restoring America's role as a leader in science and medicine." Her daughter Stefany and Ellie attended the announcement ceremony at the White House.

As governor, Shaheen signed the first state law in the country to require power plants to reduce emissions of carbon dioxide, sulfur dioxide, nitrogen oxides and mercury. She is likely to be an active participant in the debate over climate change legislation in the 111th Congress (2009-10). As a member of the Energy and Natural Resources Committee, she also wants refundable tax credits for winter heating fuels and argues for redirecting oil sub-

CAPITOL OFFICE
224-2841
shaheen.senate.gov
520 Hart Bldg. 20510-3102; fax 228-4131

COMMITTEES
Energy & Natural Resources
Foreign Relations
    (European Affairs - chairwoman)
Small Business & Entrepreneurship

RESIDENCE
Madbury

BORN
Jan. 28, 1947; St. Charles, Mo.

RELIGION
Protestant

FAMILY
Husband, Bill Shaheen; three children

EDUCATION
Shippensburg State College, B.A. 1969 (English);
U. of Mississippi, M.S.S. 1973 (political science)

CAREER
University public affairs institute director;
campaign aide; jewelry store owner; teacher

POLITICAL HIGHLIGHTS
Democratic nominee for N.H. Senate, 1978;
Madbury Zoning Board of Adjustment, 1983-96
(chairwoman, 1987-96); N.H. Senate, 1990-96;
governor, 1997-2003; Democratic nominee for
U.S. Senate, 2002

ELECTION RESULTS

2008 GENERAL

Jeanne Shaheen (D)	358,438	51.6%
John E. Sununu (R)	314,403	45.3%
Ken Blevens (LIBERT)	21,516	3.1%

2008 PRIMARY

Jeanne Shaheen (D)	42,968	88.3%
Raymond Stebbins (D)	5,281	10.8%

sidies into tax credits for alternative energy and energy efficiency.

Shaheen also serves on the Foreign Relations and Small Business and Entrepreneurship committees. The latter is a particularly good fit for her; she and her husband ran a family business for eight years after they first married, selling jewelry. On Foreign Relations, she chairs the Subcommittee on European Affairs — the same panel that Obama chaired as a senator.

Shaheen grew up in various small towns across Missouri. Her father worked in the shoe manufacturing business and her mother was a church secretary. The family attended Methodist church each week and was solidly Republican. Her father traces his Republican ties back to the Civil War, when his family fed potatoes to the Union troops in Missouri. And it was her father who first fueled Shaheen's penchant for politics by quizzing his three daughters about current events at the dinner table. Shaheen got involved in student government both in high school and college.

When she was in her teens, Shaheen's family moved to Pennsylvania, where she attended Shippensburg State College. In 1968, Shaheen cast her first presidential vote for Richard Nixon, but then migrated to the Democratic Party after being frustrated with the Vietnam War and inspired by the civil rights movement.

Shaheen's future in New Hampshire politics was born when she worked at a lobster pound in Maine the summer after graduating from college. It was there that she met her husband, Bill Shaheen, a second-generation Lebanese-American who grew up in New Hampshire. After he completed law school and she finished a master's in political science, the couple settled in New Hampshire, where she signed up to be a regional organizer for Jimmy Carter's 1976 campaign. Shaheen went on to serve as Carter's state coordinator in 1980 and as Gary Hart's campaign's state director in 1984. She also worked on several state and local campaigns through the 1980s.

In 1990, she was elected to the state Senate, and in 1997 became the state's first elected female governor. "When I first ran for governor, I was referred to in the newspaper as 'Betty Crocker,'" Shaheen said during a "Women, Power and Politics" PBS feature. "And that was meant as a compliment!"

Shaheen said her campaigns have always been family affairs: Her husband left a judgeship in 1996 when she ran for governor, her eldest daughter took a term off from college to work on the campaign and her youngest daughter worked full-time on her mother's 2008 Senate bid, running a blog called "On the Road With Govy," the pet name Shaheen's children have for her.

Shaheen first made a bid for the U.S. Senate seat in 2002, challenging John E. Sununu, then a GOP House member. Though her popularity helped make it a close race, Sununu pulled out a 4-percentage-point victory.

After her defeat, Shaheen became a fellow at Harvard's Kennedy School of Government and taught a course at Tufts University, but she couldn't stay away from politics. She served as national chairwoman for Massachusetts Sen. John Kerry's 2004 presidential campaign, and she and her husband were largely credited with Kerry's clinching of the Democratic nomination. In 2005, she became director of the Kennedy School's Institute of Politics.

Shaheen entered the fray again, in September 2007, after a University of New Hampshire poll showed Sununu trailing her by 16 points in a hypothetical matchup. Shaheen said she wasn't planning to run, but thought about what she would say to her grandchildren in 10 years if they were to ask why she hadn't run when she had a chance to change the country's direction. "I realized it really just wasn't good enough to say I wasn't willing to step up, I wanted my weekends off," Shaheen said at a campaign fundraiser.

She benefitted from an environment that had shifted markedly toward the Democrats in the six years since her first Senate try, both nationally and in New Hampshire. She won her rematch with Sununu by 6 percentage points.

Rep. Carol Shea-Porter (D)

Elected 2006; 2nd term

CAPITOL OFFICE
225-5456
shea-porter.house.gov
1330 Longworth Bldg. 20515-2901; fax 225-5822

COMMITTEES
Armed Services
Education & Labor
Natural Resources

RESIDENCE
Rochester

BORN
December 1952; Brooklyn, N.Y.

RELIGION
Roman Catholic

FAMILY
Husband, Gene Porter; two children

EDUCATION
U. of New Hampshire, B.A. 1975 (social services),
M.P.A. 1979

CAREER
Community college instructor; social worker

POLITICAL HIGHLIGHTS
No previous office

ELECTION RESULTS

2008 GENERAL

Carol Shea-Porter (D)	176,435	51.7%
Jeb Bradley (R)	156,338	45.8%
Robert Kingsbury (LIBERT)	8,100	2.4%

2008 PRIMARY

Carol Shea-Porter (D)	20,839	98.2%
write-ins (D)	378	1.8%

2006 GENERAL

Carol Shea-Porter (D)	100,691	51.3%
Jeb Bradley (R)	95,527	48.6%

Shea-Porter is a liberal anti-war activist who won election in 2006 more because of New Hampshire's frustration with the situation in Iraq than her own accomplishments. But she has begun to win her constituents' respect by broadening her focus on middle-class issues such as education and health care.

After Barack Obama assumed the presidency, Shea-Porter supported his early efforts to revive the economy, including new infrastructure spending and middle-class tax cuts. But she also joined 20 Democratic colleagues in forming a new Populist Caucus, which she said would work to ensure Congress and the Obama administration keep their focus on the middle class.

She has supported legislation increasing the minimum wage and equal pay for women and routinely opposes trade deals on the grounds that they hurt American workers. "I'm a populist and proud to be one," she told the Boston Globe. "I try to speak up for what I always call 'the bottom 99 percent.'"

A former social worker and community college instructor, Shea-Porter cited her own pedigree as her rationale, in 2008, for voting against a $700 billion rescue plan for Wall Street that most Democrats supported. "The lack of oversight and accountability on Wall Street has been devastating to both the health of our financial system and the security of the middle class," she said.

Later that year, Shea-Porter backed a plan to grant emergency loans to near-bankrupt U.S. automakers. But she wrote a letter to House Speaker Nancy Pelosi of California and House Financial Services Committee Chairman Barney Frank of Massachusetts, asking them to "ensure that any funds provided to automakers incentivize that industry to keep and bring jobs back to this country."

Shea-Porter has used her seat on the Education and Labor Committee to try to cut college costs. She supported a September 2007 bill that reduced government subsidies to student loan firms by about $20 billion and redirected most of the money to aid for students. In 2008, she backed a reauthorization of the Higher Education Act that sought increases in federal financial aid programs.

Shea-Porter also supports universal health care coverage and in early 2009 voted for a bill to expand the State Children's Health Insurance Program, which covers children from low-income families that do not qualify for Medicaid. In 2009, she offered legislation to protect $250,000 of the value of the home of an individual facing a financial crisis due to a medical catastrophe.

From her seat on the Armed Services Committee, Shea-Porter has looked out for the needs of soldiers, veterans and their families even as she has vociferously opposed the Iraq War, saying she still supports a robust military. She introduced legislation early in 2009 that would ensure veterans throughout the continental United States can access health care easily through the Veterans Affairs Department. Her husband, Gene Porter, is a retired army officer, and she has fought for the construction in her district of a full-service hospital for veterans or local access to equivalent medical care. New Hampshire currently is the only state without either.

She also has sought to take care of Portsmouth Naval Shipyard, saying in 2008 that it had not received the money it has deserved in recent years.

Shea-Porter picked up a seat on the Natural Resources Committee in 2009. The assignment enables her to become more involved in debates over combating climate change, promoting energy development and protecting endangered species.

Shea-Porter was born in Brooklyn, N.Y., and moved to Durham as a teenager. Her parents were Republican. Her father was a lawyer and her mother watched over a household that included her six siblings, a great-uncle and a grandmother.

She graduated from Durham's Oyster River High School before earning her bachelor's and master's degrees from the University of New Hampshire. After college, she worked as a social worker. She later taught current affairs and American history at a community college in Maryland. She and her husband returned to New Hampshire in the 1990s.

Shea-Porter said she decided to seek elected office after making two visits as a volunteer to New Orleans after it was hit by Hurricane Katrina in August 2005. She said she was concerned about the slow federal response to assist victims. But it was her activism against the Iraq War that gained her the most attention in her district.

Shea-Porter's 2006 election was a surprise, the result of the huge Democratic wave that swept the GOP out of power that year. Former Democratic National Committee Chairman Howard Dean stumbled to pronounce her name the day after she defeated two-term incumbent Republican Jeb Bradley. But Shea-Porter had wooed the right people, grass-roots activists increasingly angry over the Iraq War. "Americans have spent billions on this unnecessary war only to see tragedy, fraud and waste," she said.

In the September 2006 primary, she trounced state House Democratic leader Jim Craig, the choice of the party establishment. Two months later, she edged Bradley by 3 percentage points.

Facing a rematch with Bradley in the next election, Shea-Porter had to prove her mettle. She declined to accept money from the Democratic Party but she did take more than $500,000 from the political action committees of unions, liberal groups and other Democratic politicians, raising more than $1.5 million overall. That was more than 15 times what Shea-Porter raised for her 2006 race.

Obama's showing in the district — he carried it with nearly 53 percent of the vote — provided her with a boost, and Shea-Porter, who boasted to constituents of her success in winning federal funding for home state projects, increased her victory margin to 6 percentage points.

After initially considering a Senate bid for the seat being vacated by Republican Judd Gregg in 2010, Shea-Porter decided to stay put, avoiding a potential primary fight with her Democratic House colleague Paul W. Hodes. But she has been mentioned as a possible replacement whenever New Hampshire Gov. John Lynch, a fellow Democrat, decides to step aside.

KEY VOTES

2008

Yes Delay consideration of Colombia free-trade agreement
Yes Override Bush veto of federal farm and nutrition programs reauthorization bill
No Overhaul surveillance laws and permit dismissal of suits against companies that conducted warrantless wiretapping
Yes Grant mortgage relief to homeowners and funding for Fannie Mae and Freddie Mac
No Approve initial $700 billion program to stabilize financial markets
No Approve final $700 billion program to stabilize financial markets
Yes Provide $14 billion in loans to automakers

2007

Yes Increase minimum wage by $2.10 an hour
Yes Approve $124.2 billion in emergency war spending and set goal for redeployment of troops from Iraq
No Reject federal contraceptive assistance to international family planning groups
Yes Override Bush veto of $23.2 billion water projects authorization bill
No Implement Peru free-trade agreement
Yes Approve energy policy overhaul with new fuel economy standards
No Clear $473.5 billion omnibus spending bill, including $70 billion for military operations

CQ VOTE STUDIES

	PARTY UNITY		PRESIDENTIAL SUPPORT	
	SUPPORT	OPPOSE	SUPPORT	OPPOSE
2008	97%	3%	14%	86%
2007	98%	2%	5%	95%

INTEREST GROUPS

	AFL-CIO	ADA	CCUS	ACU
2008	100%	90%	50%	12%
2007	96%	95%	50%	0%

NEW HAMPSHIRE 1

East — Manchester, Rochester, Dover

The 1st District covers about one-fourth of New Hampshire's land, mainly in the southeast, yet contains most of its larger communities, including the state's most populous, Manchester. Many residents of southeastern towns in the 1st, especially Dover, Hampton and Exeter, still commute to work in Massachusetts. Farther north along the Maine border, Carroll County relies primarily on tourism and farming.

Manchester has hosted technology and manufacturing companies, and has a large, but vulnerable, health care sector. A decade of diversification helped stabilize the city's economy after years of slow growth, but recent job losses have affected all areas of the economy. Manchester's housing market took a hit recently, and Bedford to the southwest also has seen home values drop and retail stores shuttered, although redevelopment of some commercial areas is planned.

The Portsmouth Naval Shipyard, across the state line in Kittery, Maine, employs many district residents and serves as an economic anchor in the eastern part of the district. Portsmouth has lost population over the past two decades, but expansion at the shipyard is expected to boost the economy. Other cities on the coast, such as Seabrook near the Massachusetts border, are struggling as nationwide economic downturns hurt the local construction and manufacturing sectors.

Despite strong GOP roots, the 1st has become increasingly competitive in recent years. Throughout the district and the state, the majority of voters identify as Independents. Strafford County, which includes Durham (home to the University of New Hampshire) and Dover, gives Democrats healthy margins at the polls. Republicans do well in midsize and smaller towns, but the GOP no longer dominates population centers such as Manchester, although voters there did oust their Democratic mayor in 2005. Barack Obama won the 1st with 53 percent of its vote in the 2008 presidential election.

MAJOR INDUSTRY

Health care, computer manufacturing

CITIES

Manchester, 107,006; Rochester, 28,461; Dover, 26,884; Derry (unincorporated), 22,661

NOTABLE

Robert Frost operated a farm in Derry that is now a state historic site.

Rep. Paul W. Hodes (D)

Elected 2006; 2nd term

CAPITOL OFFICE
225-5206
hodes.house.gov
1317 Longworth Bldg. 20515-2902; fax 225-2946

COMMITTEES
Financial Services
Oversight & Government Reform

RESIDENCE
Concord

BORN
March 21, 1951; Manhattan, N.Y.

RELIGION
Jewish

FAMILY
Wife, Peggo Horstmann Hodes; two children

EDUCATION
Dartmouth College, A.B. 1972 (French & drama);
Boston College, J.D. 1978

CAREER
Lawyer; musician; state prosecutor

POLITICAL HIGHLIGHTS
Democratic nominee for U.S. House, 2004

ELECTION RESULTS

2008 GENERAL

Paul W. Hodes (D)	188,332	56.4%
Jennifer M. Horn (R)	138,222	41.4%
Chester L. Lapointe II (LIBERT)	7,121	2.1%

2008 PRIMARY

Paul W. Hodes (D)	22,638	98.6%
write-ins (D)	330	1.4%

2006 GENERAL

Paul W. Hodes (D)	108,743	52.7%
Charles Bass (R)	94,088	45.6%
Ken Blevens (LIBERT)	3,305	1.6%

Hodes is a lawyer with a background in music and theater and a natural performer whose wit has made him popular among his colleagues. A liberal in a state where registered independents outnumber Republicans and Democrats, he positions himself as a champion of the little guy and congressional ethics reform.

Describing the new Democratic majority in 2007, Hodes (rhymes with "roads") told an audience, "It's sort of like the 'Lord of the Rings,' and the Hobbits have risen up!" He proceeded to back his party on 98 percent of the votes that pitted a majority of Democrats against a majority of Republicans during the 110th Congress (2007-08). But he is likely to pick his shots carefully as he sets his sights on the U.S. Senate. In February 2009, he announced he would seek the seat held by Republican Sen. Judd Gregg, who said he wouldn't seek a fourth term.

Hodes is a member of the Financial Services Committee, which helps him position himself as a champion of the little guy. He supported a massive 2008 bill, signed into law, that granted mortgage relief to homeowners and provided financing to mortgage giants Fannie Mae and Freddie Mac. But in the fall of that year, he opposed a $700 billion rescue package for the financial services industry, saying it wouldn't help Main Street. He came up with a zinger when word got out in early 2009 that American International Group Inc., the recipient of more than $180 billion in federal aid from that law, had paid out $165 million in bonuses to executives and top-tier employees. "AIG now stands for arrogance, incompetence and greed," he said.

Hodes supported President Obama's $787 billion economic stimulus package in early 2009, saying it would provide millions of infrastructure dollars and thousands of jobs for his state. Yet he failed in his attempt to add an amendment to give cold-weather states like New Hampshire additional time to build roads using money provided under the bill.

Hodes notched several legislative victories during his first term. He was among the lawmakers who included language in the 2008 reauthorization of agriculture and nutrition programs to create a Northern Border Regional Commission. The group, modeled after the Appalachian Regional Commission, authorizes economic assistance to communities in Maine, New Hampshire, New York and Vermont near the U.S.-Canada border.

Hodes also won praise locally for getting a measure signed into law that allows college students to remain covered by their family health insurance if they take a medical leave of up to one year from school. His bill was named for New Hampshire student Michelle Morse, who was diagnosed with cancer in 2003 while in college and stayed in school full time — against her doctors' advice — in order to maintain coverage under her parents' insurance. Six months after graduation, she died at age 22.

As freshman class president in the 110th, Hodes spent months pushing for a new ethics system. In March 2008, the House created the Office of Congressional Ethics to add some arm's-length objectivity to reviews traditionally handled exclusively by sitting members.

But Hodes' efforts during his first term didn't escape criticism. Various news outlets reported him spending more than $235,000 and sending out more than 1 million pieces of mass mail through the franking privilege — an amount some state GOP leaders and newspaper editorials called excessive. Hodes said the mailings give him a way to stay in touch with his constituents. A member of the Oversight and Government Reform Committee,

Hodes vows to be a watchdog over the White House.

Hodes is mindful of the weight on his shoulders. He said he sometimes draws inspiration from talking to the statues of distinguished figures lining the Capitol corridors, particularly Daniel Webster, who represented New Hampshire in the House. "Sometimes, I [visit them] early in the morning," he said. "I'll be walking through all alone, and I'll say, 'Hello, gentlemen.' Just a quiet joke between the statues and I."

Hodes was raised in New York City. His father was a lawyer and his mother worked in the home, caring for Hodes and his younger brother, Tony. He was in college when Tony, then 15, died of Hodgkin's disease, a cancer of the lymph nodes. Hodes said he spent a lot of time alone, taking refuge in music. "[Music] helped me deal with what was a difficult personal time," he said.

After high school, he studied theater and French at Dartmouth College, graduating in 1972 and setting out for New York to be an actor, musician and playwright. He spent three years working in the entertainment business, including a stint on a radio show, work on two documentaries and a role in an off-Broadway comedy about the Nixon era called "What's a Nice Country Like You Doing in a State Like This?"

His first love continues to be music and theater. He and his wife, Peggo, founded a musical group called "Peggosus." They have recorded six children's albums, which have earned several Parents' Choice Awards. Their music has been described as "Jefferson Airplane for kids."

But Hodes also took his grandmother's advice and enrolled in law school at Boston College so he would have another career to fall back on. As a newly minted attorney in 1978, he became a prosecutor under then-New Hampshire Attorney General David H. Souter, now a Supreme Court justice. Hodes prosecuted homicides and white-collar crimes and won the state's first criminal case against an environmental polluter.

He joined the politically connected law firm of Shaheen and Gordon in 1996, working for Bill Shaheen, the husband of Sen. Jeanne Shaheen, who was New Hampshire's Democratic governor from 1997 to 2003. During that time, a friend asked him to serve as chairman of the Capitol Center for the Arts in Concord. He oversaw the restoration of an old vaudeville hall into a modern performing arts center, and credits the experience with giving him a taste for public life.

He ran for Congress in 2004 against 2nd District Rep. Charles Bass, a Republican, and lost by 20 percentage points. Two years later, Hodes was much better organized and better funded. He won 53 percent of the vote. In 2008, he defeated GOP radio talk show host Jennifer M. Horn with 56 percent.

KEY VOTES

2008

Yes Delay consideration of Colombia free-trade agreement

Yes Override Bush veto of federal farm and nutrition programs reauthorization bill

No Overhaul surveillance laws and permit dismissal of suits against companies that conducted warrantless wiretapping

Yes Grant mortgage relief to homeowners and funding for Fannie Mae and Freddie Mac

No Approve initial $700 billion program to stabilize financial markets

No Approve final $700 billion program to stabilize financial markets

Yes Provide $14 billion in loans to automakers

2007

Yes Increase minimum wage by $2.10 an hour

Yes Approve $124.2 billion in emergency war spending and set goal for redeployment of troops from Iraq

No Reject federal contraceptive assistance to international family planning groups

Yes Override Bush veto of $23.2 billion water projects authorization bill

No Implement Peru free-trade agreement

Yes Approve energy policy overhaul with new fuel economy standards

No Clear $473.5 billion omnibus spending bill, including $70 billion for military operations

CQ VOTE STUDIES

	PARTY UNITY		PRESIDENTIAL SUPPORT	
	SUPPORT	OPPOSE	SUPPORT	OPPOSE
2008	97%	3%	15%	85%
2007	98%	2%	4%	96%

INTEREST GROUPS

	AFL-CIO	ADA	CCUS	ACU
2008	100%	90%	56%	12%
2007	96%	100%	50%	0%

NEW HAMPSHIRE 2
West – Nashua, Concord

The 2nd District encompasses the entire western half of New Hampshire and most of the state's southern border with Massachusetts, extending from white-collar territory in the southern tier to the mountains and forests of the sparsely populated "North Country."

The district has an economy as varied as its population. Many former Massachusetts residents who fled higher tax rates live along the 2nd's populous southern tier in places such as Salem, Windham and Atkinson, but still work across the state line. Nashua, the 2nd's most populous city, remains deeply involved in the computer and defense electronics industries. A nascent green-technology sector is expected to bolster a generally flagging economy, and Nashua's housing market has remained stable.

The economy of the heavily forested North Country is closely tied to paper manufacturing and wood products. Local officials hope that diversification of the wood products manufacturing industry and developing renewable-energy interests in Coos County will boost the struggling economy here. In the far northern reaches of the state, about 20 miles from the border with Quebec, is tiny Dixville Notch, where residents cast the nation's first votes at the stroke of midnight on Election Day.

Between the Massachusetts border and the North Country lie many smaller blue-collar towns that depend on tourism revenue from lake visitors and skiers. In addition to its small towns, Grafton County hosts technology firms and Dartmouth College.

Once rock-ribbed Republican, the 2nd has shifted to the left recently. In the 2008 presidential election, Democrat Barack Obama won the district with 56 percent of its vote. Nashua leans Democratic, and the liberalism of the college towns of Hanover and Keene, as well as of the state capital of Concord, add Democratic votes. Other population centers, such as Salem, Atkinson and Milford, are politically competitive.

MAJOR INDUSTRY

High-tech, manufacturing

CITIES

Nashua, 86,605; Concord, 40,687; Keene, 22,563; Claremont, 13,151

NOTABLE

The State House in Concord is the oldest U.S. legislative building in which both houses continue to sit in their original chambers.

Gov. Jon Corzine (D)

Pronounced: COR-zyne
First elected: 2005
Length of term: 4 years
Term expires: 1/10
Salary: $175,000
Phone: (609) 777-2500

Residence: Hoboken
Born: Jan. 1, 1947; Taylorville, Ill.
Religion: Christian non-denominational
Family: Divorced; three children
Education: U. of Illinois, B.A. 1969; U. of Chicago, M.B.A. 1973
Military service: Marine Corps Reserve, 1969-75
Career: Investment bank CEO, manager; bond trader
Political highlights: U.S. Senate, 2001-06

Election results:

2005 GENERAL
Jon Corzine (D)	1,224,551	53.5%
Doug Forrester (R)	985,271	43.0%
Hector L. Castillo (ENC)	29,452	1.3%

Senate President Richard J. Codey (D)

(no lieutenant governor)
Phone: (609) 292-5213

LEGISLATURE

Legislature: Year-round with recess

Senate: 40 members, 4-year terms
2009 ratios: 23 D, 17 R; 33 men, 7 women
Salary: $49,000
Phone: (609) 292-4840

Assembly: 80 members, 2-year terms
2009 ratios: 48 D, 32 R; 53 men, 27 women
Salary: $49,000
Phone: (609) 292-4840

TERM LIMITS

Governor: 2 consecutive terms
Senate: No
Assembly: No

URBAN STATISTICS

CITY	POPULATION
Newark	273,546
Jersey City	240,055
Paterson	149,222
Elizabeth	120,568
Edison	97,687

REGISTERED VOTERS

Unaffiliated	47%
Democrat	33%
Republican	20%

POPULATION

2008 population (est.)	8,682,661
2000 population	8,414,350
1990 population	7,730,188
Percent change (1990-2000)	+8.9%
Rank among states (2008)	11

Median age	36.7
Born in state	53.4%
Foreign born	17.5%
Violent crime rate	384/100,000
Poverty level	8.5%
Federal workers	64,174
Military	27,982

ELECTIONS

STATE ELECTION OFFICIAL
(609) 292-3760
DEMOCRATIC PARTY
(609) 392-3367
REPUBLICAN PARTY
(609) 989-7300

MISCELLANEOUS

Web: www.nj.gov
Capital: Trenton

U.S. CONGRESS

Senate: 2 Democrats
House: 8 Democrats, 5 Republicans

2000 Census Statistics by District

DIST.	2008 VOTE FOR PRESIDENT OBAMA	MCCAIN	WHITE	BLACK	ASIAN	HISP	MEDIAN INCOME	WHITE COLLAR	BLUE COLLAR	SERVICE INDUSTRY	OVER 64	UNDER 18	COLLEGE EDUCATION	RURAL	SQ. MILES
1	65%	34%	71%	16%	3%	8%	$47,473	62%	23%	15%	12%	27%	21%	1%	335
2	54	45	72	14	2	10	$44,173	54	24	23	14	25	18	21	1,982
3	52	47	83	9	3	4	$55,282	68	19	14	17	24	27	4	926
4	47	52	81	8	2	8	$54,073	65	20	14	16	25	25	7	719
5	45	54	86	1	7	4	$72,781	73	16	11	13	26	39	17	1,099
6	61	38	62	16	8	12	$55,681	66	20	14	12	24	30	0	196
7	50	49	79	4	8	7	$74,823	74	16	10	13	25	42	10	595
8	63	36	54	13	5	26	$51,954	64	23	13	13	25	28	0	107
9	61	38	61	7	11	19	$52,437	67	20	13	15	21	30	0	93
10	87	13	21	57	4	15	$38,177	58	24	18	11	27	18	0	66
11	45	54	83	3	6	7	$79,009	76	14	10	12	25	45	7	610
12	58	41	72	11	9	5	$69,668	76	14	10	13	25	42	7	633
13	75	24	32	11	6	48	$37,129	56	28	16	11	23	21	0	57
STATE	57	42	66	13	6	13	$55,146	66	20	14	13	25	30	6	7,417
U.S.	53	46	69	12	4	13	$41,994	60	25	15	12	26	24	21	3,537,438

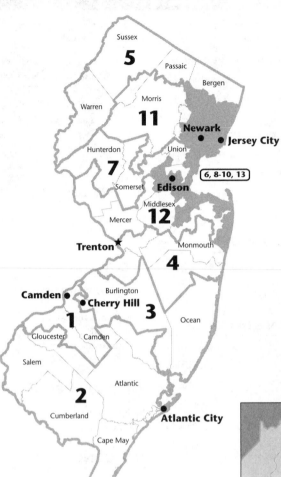

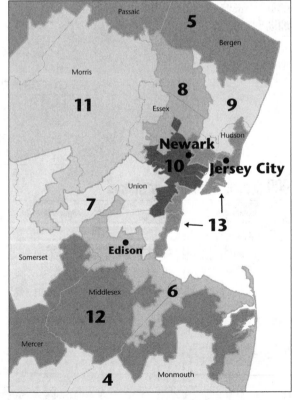

Sen. Frank R. Lautenberg (D)

Elected 1982; 5th term
Did not serve 2001-2003

CAPITOL OFFICE
224-3224
lautenberg.senate.gov
324 Hart Bldg. 20510-3003; fax 228-4054

COMMITTEES
Appropriations
Commerce, Science & Transportation
(Surface Transportation and Merchant Marine
- chairman)
Environment & Public Works
(Superfund, Toxics & Environmental Health
- chairman)

RESIDENCE
Cliffside Park

BORN
Jan. 23, 1924; Paterson, N.J.

RELIGION
Jewish

FAMILY
Wife, Bonnie Lautenberg; four children

EDUCATION
Columbia U., B.S. 1949 (economics)

MILITARY SERVICE
Army, 1942-46

CAREER
Paycheck processing firm founder

POLITICAL HIGHLIGHTS
No previous office

ELECTION RESULTS

2008 GENERAL

Frank R. Lautenberg (D)	1,951,218	56.0%
Dick Zimmer (R)	1,461,025	42.0%

2008 PRIMARY

Frank R. Lautenberg (D)	203,012	58.9%
Robert E. Andrews (D)	121,777	35.3%
Donald Cresitello (D)	19,743	5.7%

PREVIOUS WINNING PERCENTAGES
2002 (54%); 1994 (50%); 1988 (54%); 1982 (51%)

In his mid-80s, Lautenberg is one of the Senate's oldest members and the only New Jersey senator ever elected to five terms. He is an unabashed liberal who maintains an active agenda on environmental and transportation issues, fending off critics who suggest he make way for someone younger.

With his enviable combination of years of experience and few political concerns, he is free to bash Republicans whenever he pleases. With Democrats in the majority, he has tried to adjust to the responsibility of being in charge instead of simply being on the attack. But he can't resist a few jabs from time to time. When he and President Obama won their November 2008 elections, Lautenberg said, "We're going to give our country back to its rightful owners."

Lautenberg serves on the Appropriations Committee, where he spent 15 years before his brief retirement from the Senate from 2001 to 2003 and where he focuses on his state's many mass transit systems and projects. One of them, a giant rail station in Secaucus, was named for him in 2003.

Transportation also is a concern of Lautenberg's on both the Commerce, Science and Transportation and the Environment and Public Works committees. As chairman of Commerce's Surface Transportation and Merchant Marine Subcommittee, he has led efforts to boost Amtrak. He shepherded into law in 2008 a bipartisan bill authorizing $14.4 billion over five years for the struggling national passenger railroad. He presses Obama administration officials to ensure they follow through with providing money.

He also urged colleagues in March 2009 to pay more attention to mass transit in an upcoming reauthorization of highway and transportation programs. "Our future needs call for a true surface transportation bill that encompasses all modes of transportation," he said.

Lautenberg chairs the Environment panel on Superfund, Toxins and Environmental Health — a position enabling him to work closely with EPA Administrator Lisa P. Jackson, a former New Jersey environmental protection commissioner.

When the full Environment Committee took up global warming legislation in 2007, Lautenberg held out for last-minute changes intended to strengthen the measure. To satisfy Lautenberg, sponsor Joseph I. Lieberman of Connecticut, expanded its scope to include limits by 2012 on all greenhouse gases emitted from natural gas use, including the heating of commercial and residential buildings. The bill never made it through the Senate.

Lautenberg also championed a measure signed into law in June 2008 that required states to change their laws so repeat drunk drivers will have ignition interlocks installed on their vehicles. The devices prevent a car from starting if a tube connected to a sensor detects alcohol on the driver's breath.

He introduced a comprehensive sex-education bill in March 2009 that called for discussions of condoms, contraceptives and AIDS prevention with children of appropriate ages. "Our bill will treat sexual education like the serious public health issue it is," he said.

Nevertheless, a Quinnipiac University poll in July 2007 found a narrow majority of respondents — and nearly half of the Democrats — felt Lautenberg was "too old to effectively serve another six-year term." He drew a Democratic opponent in 2008 — Rep. Robert E. Andrews, who had long been known to harbor ambitions for statewide office. But in the June primary, Lautenberg defeated Andrews with 59 percent of the vote and breezed past former GOP Rep. Dick Zimmer in the general election.

Lautenberg had retired from the Senate at the end of 2000 but was summoned back when New Jersey Democratic Sen. Robert G. Torricelli was forced to abandon his 2002 re-election bid amid revelations of improper dealings with a campaign donor. It was just five weeks before the election. The party furiously courted replacement candidates, but they declined, and Democrats feared losing the seat to GOP businessman Doug Forrester.

Age 78 at the time, Lautenberg was perhaps an older candidate than party leaders would have preferred, but he was widely known and still popular. The race ended in a rout, with Lautenberg winning by 10 percentage points. Democrats were grateful for his return but didn't restore the seniority he had accrued during his first stint in the Senate.

Upon his return, Lautenberg quickly drew attention for his stinging sound bites. He stunned some colleagues in 2004 after mocking Republican Vice President Dick Cheney as a "chicken hawk," saying the vice president — who did not serve in Vietnam — was among the Republicans who had no business questioning Democratic presidential candidate John Kerry's military record.

During his first Senate tenure, Lautenberg took on two of Washington's most influential forces: the tobacco and gun lobbies. A former two-pack-a-day smoker, he was the driving force in the Senate behind the 1989 law barring smoking on domestic airline flights. And he led the crusade to restrict smoking in federal buildings. In the 110th Congress (2007-08), Lautenberg sponsored legislation to change how tobacco companies market and sell cigarettes, stopping them from labeling their brands as "light" and "low-tar" cigarettes.

Lautenberg pushed through language in 1997 barring anyone convicted of domestic violence from possessing a firearm. And he won a Senate vote in 1999 to require background checks on all people who buy firearms at gun shows.

Born in Paterson, Lautenberg is the son of Polish and Russian immigrants. His parents moved their family a dozen times in their constant search for work. His father, Sam, worked in silk mills, sold coal and once ran a tavern. When his father died of cancer, Lautenberg, then a teenager, worked nights and weekends to help the family stay afloat.

After high school, Lautenberg enlisted and served in the Army Signal Corps in Europe during World War II. When he returned, he enrolled in Columbia University on the GI Bill, graduating with an economics degree in 1949. With two boyhood friends from his old neighborhood, he started a payroll services company, Automatic Data Processing, and turned it into one of the world's largest computing services companies.

Lautenberg also dabbled in politics as a Democratic activist and fundraiser. His $90,000 contribution to George McGovern's 1972 campaign earned him a place on President Nixon's enemies list. In 1982, he ran for the open New Jersey Senate seat after Democratic incumbent Harrison A. Williams Jr. was convicted in the Abscam corruption probe. Spending $4 million of his own money, Lautenberg took 51 percent of the vote to defeat GOP Rep. Millicent Fenwick.

In 1988, he beat back an aggressive challenge from Republican Peter M. Dawkins, once the Army's youngest brigadier general. Lautenberg survived the 1994 GOP tide with a 3-percentage-point victory over conservative state Assembly Speaker Garabed "Chuck" Haytaian.

Lautenberg is one of the wealthiest members of Congress, with at least $53 million in assets in 2007, according to the Center for Responsive Politics. His private family foundation had invested $7.3 million with financier Bernard Madoff, who confessed in 2008 to running a Ponzi scheme that lost investors more than $50 billion. In February 2009 the foundation sued Madoff's brother, Peter, who worked with Bernard.

KEY VOTES

2008
Yes Prohibit discrimination based on genetic information
Yes Reauthorize farm and nutrition programs for five years
Yes Limit debate on "cap and trade" system for greenhouse gas emissions
Yes Allow lawsuits against companies that participated in warrantless wiretapping
Yes Limit debate on a bill to block a scheduled cut in Medicare payments to doctors
Yes Grant mortgage relief to homeowners and funding for Fannie Mae and Freddie Mac
Yes Approve a nuclear cooperation agreement with India
Yes Approve final $700 billion program to stabilize financial markets
Yes Allow consideration of a $14 billion auto industry loan package

2007
Yes Increase minimum wage by $2.10 an hour
Yes Limit debate on a comprehensive immigration bill
Yes Overhaul congressional lobbying and ethics rules for members and their staffs
Yes Limit debate on considering a bill to add House seats for the District of Columbia and Utah
Yes Limit debate on restoring habeas corpus rights to detainees
Yes Mandate minimum breaks for troops between deployments to Iraq or Afghanistan
Yes Override Bush veto of $23.2 billion water projects authorization bill
No   Confirm Michael B. Mukasey as attorney general
Yes Limit debate on an energy policy overhaul containing $21.8 billion in tax incentives and reduced oil and gas subsidies

CQ VOTE STUDIES

	PARTY UNITY		PRESIDENTIAL SUPPORT	
	SUPPORT	OPPOSE	SUPPORT	OPPOSE
2008	99%	1%	30%	70%
2007	98%	2%	37%	63%
2006	97%	3%	46%	54%
2005	98%	2%	27%	73%
2004	96%	4%	57%	43%
2003	97%	3%	44%	56%
2000	98%	2%	98%	2%
1999	96%	4%	93%	7%
1998	97%	3%	90%	10%
1997	94%	6%	87%	13%

INTEREST GROUPS

	AFL-CIO	ADA	CCUS	ACU
2008	100%	100%	63%	4%
2007	100%	90%	55%	0%
2006	93%	100%	42%	0%
2005	93%	100%	29%	0%
2004	100%	100%	38%	0%
2003	100%	95%	26%	15%
2000	75%	90%	46%	4%
1999	78%	100%	44%	0%
1998	88%	95%	50%	4%
1997	71%	95%	60%	0%

Sen. Robert Menendez (D)

Elected 2006; 1st full term
Appointed January 2006

CAPITOL OFFICE
224-4744
menendez.senate.gov
528 Hart Bldg. 20510-3004; fax 228-2197

COMMITTEES
Banking, Housing & Urban Affairs
  (Housing, Transportation & Community
  Development - chairman)
Budget
Energy & Natural Resources
Finance
Foreign Relations
  (International Development - chairman)

RESIDENCE
Hoboken

BORN
Jan. 1, 1954; Manhattan, N.Y.

RELIGION
Roman Catholic

FAMILY
Divorced; two children

EDUCATION
Saint Peter's College, B.A. 1976 (political science
& urban studies); Rutgers U., J.D. 1979

CAREER
Lawyer

POLITICAL HIGHLIGHTS
Union City Board of Education, 1974-82;
mayor of Union City, 1986-92; N.J. Assembly,
1987-91; N.J. Senate, 1991-93; U.S. House,
1993-2006

ELECTION RESULTS

2006 GENERAL
Robert Menendez (D)	1,200,843	53.4%
Thomas H. Kean Jr. (R)	997,775	44.3%

2006 PRIMARY
Robert Menendez (D)	159,604	84.0%
James D. Kelly Jr. (D)	30,340	16.0%

PREVIOUS WINNING PERCENTAGES
2004 House Election (76%); 2002 House Election
(78%); 2000 House Election (79%); 1998 House
Election (80%); 1996 House Election (79%); 1994
House Election (71%); 1992 House Election (64%)

One of two Hispanics in the Senate, Menendez is a fiercely partisan lawmaker and strategist who always seems to be in the middle of the latest political challenge, whether in D.C. or back home. Articulate and aggressive, he drives particularly hard to protect the rights of Hispanics and immigrants.

His political acumen and fundraising skills have helped to quickly heighten his influence since his arrival on Capitol Hill. He was the first Hispanic of either party elected to a top leadership post in Congress when he served as House Democratic Caucus chairman before his appointment to the Senate in 2006. He co-chaired the 2008 Democratic presidential campaign of former Sen. Hillary Rodham Clinton of New York and was mentioned as a possible running mate. And he became chairman of the Democratic Senatorial Campaign Committee in 2009, stepping up from vice chairman to take the reins from New York's Charles E. Schumer, who had helped the party gain at least 13 Senate seats over the previous two elections. In its first two months with Menendez in charge, the DSCC raised $5.4 million, outperforming its GOP counterpart, which raised $4.7 million.

He also gained a seat on the influential Finance Committee at the start of 2009, an assignment that dovetails with his seats on the Banking, Housing and Urban Affairs Committee and the Budget Committee. He had successfully included in a 2008 housing law provisions calling for education on home financing for prospective homeowners. He and Democrat Edward M. Kennedy of Massachusetts also designed a fund to help homeless students stay in their schools. Menendez supported the $700 billion measure in fall 2008 to shore up the nation's financial services system, although he complained it would do little to further help struggling homeowners. "I think it's ironic that we can keep a CEO in the office, but we can't keep a family in their home," he said.

The Finance Committee also expects during the 111th Congress (2009-10) to take up legislation on health care and taxes. When it comes to tax policy, Menendez wants to clearly define "middle class." He called President George W. Bush "uncompassionate" in 2007 for vetoing bills to expand the State Children's Health Insurance Program, which covers children from low-income families that do not qualify for Medicaid. He applauded President Obama for signing a nearly identical bill.

As a member of the Energy and Natural Resources Committee, Menendez has opposed offshore drilling and railed against rising oil company profits. He supports extending renewable-energy tax credits to combat global warming and has backed energy efficiency block grants for cities.

But it is his work on the Foreign Relations Committee, where he is chairman of the International Development Subcommittee, that has consumed much of his time. He takes a tough line on U.S. relations with the Castro regime in Cuba. Menendez's parents moved to New York from Cuba in 1953 because of their opposition to the Batista government. He was sharply critical of provisions in a catchall spending bill for fiscal 2009 that would loosen rules on travel and imports of food and medicine to Cuba. He supported the bill after the administration said the provisions would be interpreted narrowly. But he expressed displeasure when Obama soon after announced his policy easing travel restrictions along with permission for unlimited cash transfers to family members in Cuba. He also helps guide policy and aid for housing, health care and education in Latin America.

He is particularly sensitive to the concerns of Hispanic immigrants. In the 110th Congress (2007-08), he bitterly pushed back against Republicans who referred to Latinos as "those people." He participated in bipartisan talks on a proposed immigration overhaul bill in 2007, but stepped out when he viewed the draft as too draconian, opting instead to offer amendments on the floor.

Menendez was piqued by a proposed merit-based system for awarding green cards that valued highly skilled workers over applicants seeking family reunification. He pushed to give legal permanent resident status to parents, spouses or children of military servicemembers who served in active duty. And underscoring his opposition to a fence along the Mexican border, Menendez suggested that some of the $3 billion for the project also be used to build a barrier along the Canadian border. Judiciary Chairman Patrick J. Leahy of Vermont swatted down the idea with a parliamentary move.

For the most part, Menendez's proposals were called "poison pills" and were defeated. He was part of the mostly-Republican majority that blocked final Senate action on the bill.

In 2008, Menendez introduced a measure requiring basic health care for immigration detainees and protested the unlawful detention of U.S. citizens and permanent residents. "The legitimate desire to get control over our borders has too often turned into a witch hunt against Hispanic-Americans and other people of color," he complained on the Senate floor. He also blocked reauthorization of E-Verify, an online system employers can use to confirm the employment eligibility of new hires, until Senate leaders agreed to a provision allowing for recapture of unused green card allocations dating back to 1992.

A strong union ally, Menendez argues for better wages, health and retirement benefits, and extensions of unemployment benefits. He helped negotiate the hiring of the Senate food service vendor, keeping an eye on proposed benefits, salaries and job security for workers.

Among his home state pet projects are pollution cleanup and protection of New Jersey's beaches, renewal of federal terrorism risk insurance, and tighter chemical plant security. New Jersey has more than 110 chemical facilities.

Menendez grew up in Union City, where his family lived in a tenement. When he was a high school senior, his teachers nominated him for the honors program. The invitation to join came with a cost of $200 for extra books — money that his family lacked. "I created such a ruckus that they gave me the books, told me to shut up and put me in the honors program," he recalled.

But his desire to help others in similar circumstances helped set him on a path to public office. He initiated a successful referendum to replace the appointed school board with an elected body. At 20, while attending St. Peter's College in Jersey City, Menendez was elected to the board.

He was elected mayor of Union City in 1986 and to the state legislature in 1987, serving in both offices simultaneously. In 1991, he was named to fill a vacancy in the state Senate, where he served until winning a U.S. House seat in a district that saw its Hispanic population nearly double after redistricting in 1992. Menendez outmaneuvered fellow New Jersey House Democrats to win appointment to the Senate in 2006 for the seat vacated by Democrat Jon Corzine, who was elected governor in November 2005. "Is he aggressive? Yeah," Corzine told The Bergen Record in defending his decision. "But I believe in competency and people who get things done, and Bob is one of those people."

His campaign for a full six-year term to the Senate in 2006 was marked by a federal probe into charges by opponents that he steered federal funds to a nonprofit group that rented property from him. As the election campaign heated up, his Republican opponent, state Sen. Thomas H. Kean Jr., repeatedly called him a "Hudson County political boss" and reminded voters of several past reports questioning Menendez's ethics. Menendez denied any wrongdoing and struck back hard, countering that Kean — the son of a popular former governor — had ethics problems of his own. Raising nearly $12 million to Kean's $7.9 million, he won by 9 percentage points.

KEY VOTES

2008

Yes Prohibit discrimination based on genetic information
Yes Reauthorize farm and nutrition programs for five years
Yes Limit debate on "cap and trade" system for greenhouse gas emissions
Yes Allow lawsuits against companies that participated in warrantless wiretapping
Yes Limit debate on a bill to block a scheduled cut in Medicare payments to doctors
Yes Grant mortgage relief to homeowners and funding for Fannie Mae and Freddie Mac
Yes Approve a nuclear cooperation agreement with India
Yes Approve final $700 billion program to stabilize financial markets
Yes Allow consideration of a $14 billion auto industry loan package

2007

Yes Increase minimum wage by $2.10 an hour
Yes Limit debate on a comprehensive immigration bill
Yes Overhaul congressional lobbying and ethics rules for members and their staffs
Yes Limit debate on considering a bill to add House seats for the District of Columbia and Utah
Yes Limit debate on restoring habeas corpus rights to detainees
Yes Mandate minimum breaks for troops between deployments to Iraq or Afghanistan
Yes Override Bush veto of $23.2 billion water projects authorization bill
No   Confirm Michael B. Mukasey as attorney general
Yes Limit debate on an energy policy overhaul containing $21.8 billion in tax incentives and reduced oil and gas subsidies

CQ VOTE STUDIES

	PARTY UNITY		PRESIDENTIAL SUPPORT	
	SUPPORT	OPPOSE	SUPPORT	OPPOSE
2008	98%	2%	28%	72%
2007	97%	3%	38%	62%
2006	95%	5%	50%	50%
House Service:				
2005	93%	7%	24%	76%
2004	93%	8%	34%	66%
2003	93%	7%	24%	76%
2002	87%	13%	28%	72%
2001	89%	11%	30%	70%
2000	91%	9%	78%	22%

INTEREST GROUPS

	AFL-CIO	ADA	CCUS	ACU
2008	100%	100%	63%	4%
2007	95%	95%	55%	0%
2006	93%	90%	55%	4%
House Service:				
2005	93%	100%	40%	4%
2004	93%	85%	35%	8%
2003	93%	90%	37%	20%
2002	89%	95%	42%	8%
2001	100%	95%	35%	16%
2000	100%	95%	38%	8%

Rep. Robert E. Andrews (D)

Elected 1990; 10th full term

CAPITOL OFFICE
225-6501
www.house.gov/andrews
2265 Rayburn Bldg. 20515-3001; fax 225-6583

COMMITTEES
Armed Services
 (Defense Acquisition Reform - chairman)
Budget
Education & Labor
 (Health, Employment, Labor & Pensions
 - chairman)

RESIDENCE
Haddon Heights

BORN
Aug. 4, 1957; Camden, N.J.

RELIGION
Episcopalian

FAMILY
Wife, Camille Spinello Andrews; two children

EDUCATION
Bucknell U., B.A. 1979 (political science);
Cornell U., J.D. 1982

CAREER
Professor; lawyer

POLITICAL HIGHLIGHTS
Camden County Board of Freeholders, 1987-90
(director, 1988-90); sought Democratic nomination
for governor, 1997; sought Democratic nomination
for U.S. Senate, 2008

ELECTION RESULTS

2008 GENERAL

Robert E. Andrews (D)	206,453	72.4%
Dale M. Glading (R)	74,001	26.0%

2006 GENERAL

Robert E. Andrews (D)	unopposed

PREVIOUS WINNING PERCENTAGES
2004 (75%); 2002 (93%); 2000 (76%); 1998 (73%);
1996 (76%); 1994 (72%); 1992 (67%); 1990 (54%);
1990 Special Election (55%)

Andrews is an ambitious, articulate Democrat who is active on some of his party's core priorities, including pensions and education. He has carved out a comfortable niche in the House — so comfortable, in fact, that he chose to disregard his initial plans to leave politics following a humiliating loss in a 2008 Senate primary.

After losing to incumbent Democratic Sen. Frank R. Lautenberg by 24 percentage points — in his second statewide race — Andrews talked with the investment banking firm Goldman Sachs. But he ultimately turned down a job offer to seek re-election. "I changed my mind because my heart told me to do so," said Andrews, who won a 10th full term with ease.

Andrews returned to the chairmanship of the Education and Labor Committee's Health, Employment, Labor and Pensions Subcommittee. He hopes to work with the Obama administration on expanding and protecting retirement benefits and on its health care overhaul effort.

During the 109th Congress (2005-06), he helped write legislation to overhaul federal regulation of the private pension system. A member of the team of House and Senate negotiators charged with drafting the final bill, he fought to protect worker benefits while giving corporations relief from excessive paperwork. He also worked to ensure older workers weren't disadvantaged when their employers switched from a traditional defined-benefit pension plan to a "cash-balance" plan. In the end, however, House Republican leaders abandoned the negotiating process and brought another pension bill up for a vote. Andrews voted against that measure, objecting to the tactic and to the final bill's treatment of Continental Airlines, a major employer in New Jersey.

The son and grandson of shipyard workers, Andrews generally takes the side of organized labor, opposing free-trade agreements he said could cost U.S. workers their jobs. In early 2009, Andrews backed a bill sponsored by Education and Labor Chairman George Miller of California that aimed to make it easier for unions to organize by allowing employees to sign authorization cards rather than requiring secret-ballot elections, which have proved disadvantageous to organized labor.

Earlier in his career, Andrews helped negotiate the final version of No Child Left Behind, President George W. Bush's signature education law. Andrews has sought to make the law more flexible and improve provisions addressing special education, English-language learners and the use of supplemental services to help students and schools.

Andrews also is a member of the Budget Committee and supports reversing Bush's 2001 and 2003 tax cuts that reduced income tax and capital gains tax rates. He suggests using the money to pay for health insurance and to reduce the budget deficit. In early 2009, he was assigned to chair a new Armed Services Committee panel to examine ways to improve the Defense Department's procurement system. The Defense Acquisition Reform Panel was charged with addressing the Pentagon's problems in acquiring goods and services on time and on budget. The Government Accountability Office had reported that the estimated cost of major U.S. defense programs in fiscal 2007 exceeded initial estimates by about $295 billion.

He is somewhat hawkish on foreign policy, and supported the U.S. invasion of Iraq. But in early 2007, Andrews came out against Bush's plan to send more than 21,000 additional combat troops to Iraq. He told The Star-Ledger of Newark in May 2008 that he considered the war a "fiasco."

He is a fairly conventional Northeastern Democrat, supporting environmental protection, abortion rights and gun control. In 2008, he was one of seven House Democrats to support his party on every bill in which a majority of Democrats voted against a majority of Republicans.

When Andrews was 14, he went to work for the Suburban Newspaper Group, a local newspaper chain, hoping to cover basketball and football. Instead, he was assigned to report on local government, for $6 an article. "The experience covering government and what went on in the local scene made me want to be a part of it," he said. The first in his family to go to college, Andrews was a teaching assistant in his senior year at Bucknell University and wrote this question to serve as the entire final exam for an introductory political science class: "Politics is everything. Explain."

After six years practicing law, Andrews at age 29 won a seat on the Camden County governing board. Two years later he was chosen to head the board.

He was a protégé of liberal Democratic Rep. James Florio. After Florio was elected governor in 1989, Andrews took his place in the House, winning a 1990 special election (and a full term the same day) despite voter anger at Florio over a large state tax increase that year. Among his campaign staffers was a young opposition researcher named Rahm Emanuel, who later would become a House colleague and White House chief of staff.

In 1997, Andrews ran for governor and narrowly lost in the Democratic primary to James E. McGreevey, who later was forced to resign following a personal scandal. Andrews was again disappointed in 2005, when newly elected Gov. Jon Corzine chose House Democrat Robert Menendez for the Senate seat that Corzine gave up when he was elected governor. But Andrews came away with Corzine's endorsement for a 2008 race if Lautenberg retired.

Even though Lautenberg chose to run, Andrews decided he couldn't wait any longer and — against the wishes of numerous state party leaders — challenged the then-84-year-old senator. He won the endorsement of The Star-Ledger, the state's largest newspaper, and sought to make an issue of his opponent's age, but picked up little support outside his South Jersey base.

Andrews' subsequent decision to seek to keep his House seat — his wife, Camille, had won the Democratic primary to replace him, but then stepped aside for her husband — was met with criticism from his GOP opponent, Dale M. Glading. But the district's strong Democratic makeup — Barack Obama prevailed there by almost a 2-to-1 margin — ensured him an easy victory.

At night, Andrews usually takes the 2 1/2-hour train trip from Washington home to Haddon Heights, south of Camden, to be with his wife and two school-age daughters, whom he credits with making him less of a workaholic.

KEY VOTES

2008

? Delay consideration of Colombia free-trade agreement

Yes Override Bush veto of federal farm and nutrition programs reauthorization bill

No Overhaul surveillance laws and permit dismissal of suits against companies that conducted warrantless wiretapping

Yes Grant mortgage relief to homeowners and funding for Fannie Mae and Freddie Mac

Yes Approve initial $700 billion program to stabilize financial markets

Yes Approve final $700 billion program to stabilize financial markets

Yes Provide $14 billion in loans to automakers

2007

Yes Increase minimum wage by $2.10 an hour

Yes Approve $124.2 billion in emergency war spending and set goal for redeployment of troops from Iraq

No Reject federal contraceptive assistance to international family planning groups

Yes Override Bush veto of $23.2 billion water projects authorization bill

No Implement Peru free-trade agreement

Yes Approve energy policy overhaul with new fuel economy standards

No Clear $473.5 billion omnibus spending bill, including $70 billion for military operations

CQ VOTE STUDIES

	PARTY UNITY		PRESIDENTIAL SUPPORT	
	SUPPORT	OPPOSE	SUPPORT	OPPOSE
2008	100%	0%	17%	83%
2007	97%	3%	6%	94%
2006	94%	6%	35%	65%
2005	92%	8%	23%	77%
2004	94%	6%	26%	74%

INTEREST GROUPS

	AFL-CIO	ADA	CCUS	ACU
2008	100%	85%	63%	0%
2007	96%	100%	50%	0%
2006	86%	85%	40%	16%
2005	92%	95%	42%	8%
2004	93%	95%	24%	0%

NEW JERSEY 1
Southwest — Camden, Pennsauken

The 1st is a Democratic stronghold in southwestern New Jersey across the Delaware River from Philadelphia. Its largest concentration of residents lives in the troubled city of Camden, one of the poorest in the nation. Almost two-thirds of the district's population lives in Camden County, with most of the rest in Gloucester County and a handful on the western edge of Burlington County.

Camden has been plagued by the departure of residents and businesses, a shrinking tax base, surging unemployment and crime — particularly drug trafficking. Nearly a decade after the state assumed control of the city's finances and approved a $175 million plan to redevelop and revitalize the area, construction and infrastructure improvements continue. An aquarium and a 25,000-seat outdoor amphitheater have attracted more tourists to the waterfront, which is starting to generate interest from corporations, thanks in part to tax incentives set up by the state. The city's port, a joint facility shared with Philadelphia, provides a revenue source for major projects, and an EPA-funded industrial waste clean-up program is underway. Camden also is home to the Campbell Soup Company, which recently pledged $10 million to assist in the city's revitalization.

As distressed as the city is, some of its suburbs are developing, and Bridgeport, in northern Gloucester County, is home to a large industrial park, while a new cargo port is scheduled to open in 2009 in Paulsboro, a refinery town on the Delaware River. The district also takes in the Rutgers University-Camden campus and Glassboro's Rowan University.

Blacks and Hispanics form an overwhelming majority of the population in Camden, while many whites live in the surrounding suburbs. Overall, blacks and Hispanics combined total one-fourth of the district's population. The 1st has a large working-class contingent, and Barack Obama took 65 percent of the 2008 presidential vote here. In Camden, which historically has low voter turnout, Obama received 94 percent.

MAJOR INDUSTRY
Shipping, manufacturing, health care, education

CITIES
Camden, 79,904; Pennsauken (unincorporated), 35,737; Glassboro, 19,068

NOTABLE
Poet Walt Whitman lived in Camden at the time of his death.

Rep. Frank A. LoBiondo (R)

Elected 1994; 8th term

CAPITOL OFFICE
225-6572
www.house.gov/lobiondo
2427 Rayburn Bldg. 20515-3002; fax 225-3318

COMMITTEES
Armed Services
Transportation & Infrastructure

RESIDENCE
Ventnor

BORN
May 12, 1946; Bridgeton, N.J.

RELIGION
Roman Catholic

FAMILY
Wife, Tina Ercole; two children

EDUCATION
Saint Joseph's U., B.S. 1968 (business administration)

CAREER
Trucking company operations manager

POLITICAL HIGHLIGHTS
Cumberland County Board of Freeholders, 1985-87; N.J. Assembly, 1988-94; Republican nominee for U.S. House, 1992

ELECTION RESULTS

2008 GENERAL

Frank A. LoBiondo (R)	167,701	59.1%
David Kurkowski (D)	110,990	39.1%

2008 PRIMARY

Frank A. LoBiondo (R)	16,026	88.8%
Donna M. Ward (R)	2,025	11.2%

2006 GENERAL

Frank A. LoBiondo (R)	111,245	61.6%
Viola Thomas-Hughes (D)	64,279	35.6%
Robert E. Mullock (PGS)	3,071	1.7%

PREVIOUS WINNING PERCENTAGES
2004 (65%); 2002 (69%); 2000 (66%); 1998 (66%); 1996 (60%); 1994 (65%)

The low-key LoBiondo has managed to thrive as a Republican in the increasingly Democratic Northeast by compiling a strong pro-union and pro-environment record — he receives much of his campaign money from labor groups and regularly gets the Sierra Club's endorsement — while sticking with his party's conservatives on most other issues.

LoBiondo (lo-bee-ON-dough) prefers to work behind the scenes. He seldom speaks on the House floor and is rarely quoted in the national media. He introduced just 11 measures in the 110th Congress (2007-08).

During the 110th, only two Republicans split with the GOP more often than LoBiondo on votes where the two parties diverged. He continued that pattern as the 111th Congress (2009-10) got under way, departing from the GOP line early in 2009 to support major expansions of the State Children's Health Insurance Program and of national service programs, as well as a bill granting varying degrees of protection to millions of acres of public land across the country, including 2 million acres designated as wilderness.

He focuses on legislation that directly affects his district, which covers the lower third of New Jersey and is surrounded on three sides by water. He strongly opposes oil drilling off the state's coast, fearing spills that could despoil local beaches and fishing. He has introduced legislation to block any such exploration in every Congress of the past decade. "We want gambling in Atlantic City; we don't want gambling in our environment," he said.

After 250,000 gallons of partially treated sewage leaked from an Asbury Park treatment plant into the Atlantic Ocean in 2007, he joined with New York Democrat Timothy H. Bishop on a measure to mandate monitoring and public notification of sewer overflows. The House passed their bill in June 2008, but it stalled in the Senate. A new version passed the House in March 2009 as part of a broad water quality package.

LoBiondo was one of only eight House Republicans to get the Sierra Club's backing in 2006 and one of only six in 2008.

LoBiondo also has earned the admiration of labor unions; he led a group of GOP moderates in 2006 who pressured their leaders to permit a vote on increasing the minimum wage. In 2007, he joined House Democratic leaders in supporting the unionization of Government Accountability Office employees and worked to increase funding for the National Labor Relations Board. Organized labor PACs are his largest single source of campaign contributions, giving more than two and a half times that of any other industry.

The son of the owner of a small trucking company, he helped run the business for years, often acting as the family's chief labor negotiator, working out union disputes with dock workers, drivers and mechanics. He still has a commercial driver's license.

Still, GOP conservatives can typically count on LoBiondo when it comes to votes related to fiscal policy and gun control (the National Rifle Association has backed all of his House races). He opposed both versions of the measure in fall 2008 to shore up the nation's ailing financial sector. "There was little justification to support the bill, with its $700 billion price tag, when a return on the taxpayers' investment was far from certain," he said. He also opposed President Obama's $787 billion economic stimulus package in 2009, saying it was insufficiently targeted on job creation. But he was one of just 16 House Republicans voting for a $410 billion catchall fiscal 2009 appropriations package that included funding for a number of projects in his district.

A member of the Armed Services Committee, he supported the 2002 resolution authorizing the war in Iraq, and in early 2007 he voted against a House war supplemental funding bill that included a timeline for withdrawal of U.S. troops from Iraq. He looks out for the New Jersey National Guard's 177th Fighter Wing, based in Atlantic City, which protects the skies over New York, Washington, D.C., and Philadelphia. After a May 2007 fire closed its Warren Grove Gunnery Range, LoBiondo petitioned Gov. Jon Corzine three times to reopen the range until the governor did so.

LoBiondo is one of two New Jersey members on the Transportation and Infrastructure Committee, which will have a major hand in crafting a new comprehensive surface transportation bill in the 111th Congress.

He has served since 2001 on the panel's Coast Guard and Maritime Transportation Subcommittee, where he is now the top-ranking Republican. As chairman of the panel from 2001 through 2006, he pushed for more money for the Coast Guard, including its long-term fleet modernization effort, Deepwater.

A member of the historic House GOP class of 1994, LoBiondo initially joined many Republican candidates of that year in vowing to serve no more than six terms. But as he reaped the benefits of seniority in Congress, LoBiondo backed off. "I didn't fully understand what personal relationships and seniority could mean to the district," he told The Associated Press in 2003. Voters didn't mind; they re-elected him in 2004 by a wide margin.

LoBiondo's grandparents came to southern New Jersey from Sicily and established a vegetable farm, on which he grew up. In the 1920s, when Atlantic City's hospitality industry was booming, his father bought a used truck to take his produce to market himself. His father was soon doing the same for the neighbors, and the enterprise grew into LoBiondo Brothers Motor Express Inc., where LoBiondo worked for 26 years. He credits his father with kick-starting his political career. His father was mayor of rural Deerfield Township, president of the school board, an active member of the Kiwanis and founder of the local fire department. "He would say it was a tremendous opportunity for him to be able to come to this country," LoBiondo recalled. "Basically, the philosophy was, 'You give back.'"

The younger LoBiondo was elected to a county office in 1984, not intending to go further. But the state assemblyman from the district, who was retiring because he had cancer, urged LoBiondo to run for the seat. He won and served in the statehouse for almost seven years.

In 1992, he challenged Democratic Rep. William J. Hughes and lost. Two years later, Hughes retired and LoBiondo tried again, winning with 65 percent of the vote. He has won with ease ever since.

KEY VOTES

2008

No Delay consideration of Colombia free-trade agreement
No Override Bush veto of federal farm and nutrition programs reauthorization bill
Yes Overhaul surveillance laws and permit dismissal of suits against companies that conducted warrantless wiretapping
No Grant mortgage relief to homeowners and funding for Fannie Mae and Freddie Mac
No Approve initial $700 billion program to stabilize financial markets
No Approve final $700 billion program to stabilize financial markets
No Provide $14 billion in loans to automakers

2007

Yes Increase minimum wage by $2.10 an hour
No Approve $124.2 billion in emergency war spending and set goal for redeployment of troops from Iraq
Yes Reject federal contraceptive assistance to international family planning groups
Yes Override Bush veto of $23.2 billion water projects authorization bill
No Implement Peru free-trade agreement
Yes Approve energy policy overhaul with new fuel economy standards
Yes Clear $473.5 billion omnibus spending bill, including $70 billion for military operations

CQ VOTE STUDIES

	PARTY UNITY		PRESIDENTIAL SUPPORT	
	SUPPORT	OPPOSE	SUPPORT	OPPOSE
2008	73%	27%	39%	61%
2007	64%	36%	38%	62%
2006	73%	27%	73%	27%
2005	81%	19%	70%	30%
2004	82%	18%	68%	32%

INTEREST GROUPS

	AFL-CIO	ADA	CCUS	ACU
2008	67%	60%	72%	52%
2007	79%	50%	63%	44%
2006	50%	25%	73%	68%
2005	47%	30%	70%	60%
2004	60%	30%	76%	60%

NEW JERSEY 2
South — Atlantic City, Vineland

One of the state's most politically and economically diverse districts, the 2nd stretches from the Philadelphia suburbs in Gloucester County to the beach communities of Ocean City and Cape May, taking in much of the southern tier of the state.

The western corner of the 2nd is largely rural Salem County, home to a nuclear energy plant run by PSEG. The district's center includes Cumberland and Atlantic counties, where farmers' markets and small agrarian communities grow peaches, blueberries, cranberries, tomatoes and soybeans. To the south, Cumberland County is the 2nd's most industrial area, although local officials hope to shift the economy from a reliance on glass and plastics manufacturing to service industries and construction. Cumberland County houses one federal prison and three state prisons.

The 2nd includes one of the nation's most well-known gambling resort destinations, Atlantic City. Hotels and casinos have created jobs, but the poorer parts of the city are ravaged by crime and urban blight. Nationwide economic downturns have resulted in fewer visitors to the gambling mecca, and several casinos struggle with crippling debt.

Tourism is the cash crop in shore communities on the eastern side of the district. Boating and commercial and sport fishing do well on the Delaware Bay and on the Atlantic Ocean along the Cape May County coastline. The area is a leading state producer of clams, and the bay is the focus of a major oyster revitalization project. The Delaware River's busy port also contributes to the economy.

A GOP-leaning district, locals often support smaller government and oppose gun control. In statewide races, Democrats do well in parts of Atlantic and Cumberland counties and in some of the 2nd's industrial towns. Democrat Barack Obama took 54 percent in the 2008 race.

MAJOR INDUSTRY
Gambling, tourism, agriculture, petroleum, manufacturing

CITIES
Vineland, 56,271; Atlantic City, 40,517; Millville, 26,847; Bridgeton, 22,771

NOTABLE
The main federal air marshal training facility is in Pomona at Atlantic City International Airport; The U.S. Coast Guard Training Center in Cape May is the nation's only Coast Guard recruit training center.

Rep. John Adler (D)

Elected 2008; 1st term

As a Democrat representing a south-central New Jersey district long held by Republicans, Adler is regarded as one of his party's most vulnerable freshmen. Nevertheless, he began his tenure in Congress in 2009 by casting dependably Democratic votes on government spending, worker protections, the environment and health care.

On the latter issue, Adler is particularly sensitive: When he was a child, his father, who owned a dry cleaning establishment, had a series of heart attacks, and inadequate insurance and inability to work eventually cost him the business. When his father died in 1976, Adler and his mother had to rely on Social Security. "I have enormous regard for a government that helps people to help themselves," Adler told the Cherry Hill Courier-Post.

Among those he hopes to help are senior citizens and veterans. The first bill he introduced called for a one-time, $500 tax payment to retired or unemployed seniors and veterans.

Adler sits on the Veterans' Affairs Committee. The 3rd District is home to the Joint Base McGuire-Dix-Lakehurst and a large number of veterans. He also received a seat on the Financial Services Committee. He is a member of the New Democrat Coalition, a group of pro-business party moderates.

Adler grew up in Haddonfield. He was in junior high when his father suffered his first heart attack. After graduating from Harvard Law School, he returned to New Jersey and worked in private practice. He was elected to the Cherry Hill Township Council in 1987. After losing a 1990 House race to GOP Rep. H. James Saxton, Adler won a state Senate seat in 1991 — a year in which he was the only Democrat in the state to beat a GOP incumbent in the legislature. As chairman of the state Senate's Judiciary Committee, he was known for grilling executives and judicial nominees, no matter their party affiliation.

In the race to succeed the retiring moderate Saxton, Adler faced Republican Medford Mayor Chris Myers. Despite raising more than double the campaign funds, Adler won with just 52 percent of the vote. The Democratic Congressional Campaign Committee immediately designated Adler for extra help to bolster his 2010 re-election prospects.

CAPITOL OFFICE
225-4765
adler.house.gov
1223 Longworth Bldg. 20515-3003; fax 225-0778

COMMITTEES
Financial Services
Veterans' Affairs

RESIDENCE
Cherry Hill

BORN
Aug. 23, 1959; Philadelphia, Pa.

RELIGION
Jewish

FAMILY
Wife, Shelley Adler; four children

EDUCATION
Harvard U., A.B. 1981 (government), J.D. 1984

CAREER
Lawyer

POLITICAL HIGHLIGHTS
Cherry Hill Township Council, 1988-91;
Democratic nominee for U.S. House, 1990;
N.J. Senate, 1992-2009

ELECTION RESULTS

2008 GENERAL

John Adler (D)	166,390	52.1%
Chris Myers (R)	153,122	47.9%

2008 PRIMARY

John Adler (D)	unopposed

NEW JERSEY 3

South central – Cherry Hill, Toms River

The 3rd crosses New Jersey's south-central section and takes in its entire political spectrum, from the solidly Republican shores of Ocean County to the staunchly Democratic Cherry Hill area in Camden County.

The 2005 BRAC round integrated McGuire Air Force Base, Fort Dix and the Lakehurst naval station into a realigned "mega-base" that will host additional personnel and aircraft. The presence of the joint base (shared with the 4th) makes national defense a salient issue here.

Communities around Toms River are concerned that offshore waste disposal may affect their beach tourist industry, and local officials, who mostly are Republicans, emphasize their "green" credentials. Burlington County, most of which is in the 3rd, is one of the largest cranberry-producing counties in the nation. The district has a lot of wealthy elderly voters, many living in retirement communities along Route 70. Municipal and school budgets, as well as tax rates, are among the lowest in the state.

While Burlington County leans Republican, Democrats can combine with the 3rd's small share of Camden County to make elections competitive. In 2008, Barack Obama took 52 percent of the district's presidential vote, and the U.S. House seat flipped to Democratic control by a slim margin.

MAJOR INDUSTRY
Retail, health care, agriculture, defense

MILITARY BASES
Joint Base McGuire-Dix-Lakehurst (shared with the 4th), 5,724 military, 4,435 civilian (2009)

CITIES
Toms River (unincorporated), 86,327;
Springdale (unincorporated), 14,409

NOTABLE
NFL Films is based in Mt. Laurel.

Rep. Christopher H. Smith (R)

Elected 1980; 15th term

Smith has earned a reputation as a tenacious pursuer of his priorities, many of which — especially his vehement opposition to abortion — stem from his deep Roman Catholic faith. With his party out of power and his anti-abortion agenda stalled, he has shifted his focus to international human rights, an area where he finds common ground with Democrats. But he also pours some energy into other causes, including veterans' health care and the global battle against AIDS.

His willingness to regularly devote 12-hour days to his work, one of the House's most effective constituent-service operations and a reputation untarnished by scandal have kept him popular in a solidly Democratic state. In 2008, a year in which Republicans were drubbed at the polls in New Jersey and his district saw a surge in Democratic registrations, Smith won re-election by a 2-to-1 margin.

Smith prides himself on reaching across the aisle. "Some people just put bills in; I put bills in and they pass," he told The Times of Trenton. "It's all about work product." He did get several measures through the House during the 110th Congress (2007-08), but none survived the Senate.

One 2007 measure sought to block increases in non-humanitarian aid to Vietnam unless the government improved its human rights record. A resolution that year urged then-Russian President Vladimir Putin to authorize cooperation with investigators in solving the killings of journalists in Russia.

And in March 2009, the House passed his bill demanding that Brazil's government return an 8-year-old New Jersey boy to his father under the Hague Convention, a treaty that provides for the recovery of a child from one nation to another. The boy's father, David Goldman, had been fighting for custody of his son since his Brazilian wife first took the boy out of the country to her home in 2004, ignoring a court order to return. Smith traveled down to Brazil with Goldman and helped reunite him with his son in February 2009.

Smith has been frustrated by what he considers a lack of attention by both parties to China's human rights record. He called on President George W. Bush to boycott the opening ceremonies of the 2008 Olympics in Beijing to protest China's treatment of political and religious dissidents.

He introduced a bill in the 110th Congress to punish U.S. Internet companies that share users' personal information with foreign governments that restrict online access. Smith first introduced the measure in 2006 after hearing news accounts that companies including Yahoo were conforming to restrictions demanded by China. He said the Internet is "increasingly being used as a tool for oppression." In 2008, Smith revealed that hackers based in China partially disabled computers used by his aides who deal with human rights.

Smith's dogged attention to his priorities has not always gone over well with party leaders. He was unceremoniously stripped of the Veterans' Affairs Committee chairmanship at the start of the 109th Congress (2005-06) and left the panel after serving on it for 24 years. Speaker J. Dennis Hastert took away his gavel after Smith battled to increase veterans' health care funding in the face of demands by Bush and GOP leaders for leaner budgets. Smith said the 2007 disclosures of severe problems at Walter Reed Army Medical Center in Washington and veterans' hospitals around the country vindicated his stance. "Health care cannot be provided on the cheap," he wrote in an opinion piece for the Asbury Park Press.

In the 110th, Smith bolted from his party on 36 percent of the votes in

CAPITOL OFFICE
225-3765
www.house.gov/chrissmith
2373 Rayburn Bldg. 20515-3004; fax 225-7768

COMMITTEES
Foreign Affairs

RESIDENCE
Hamilton

BORN
March 4, 1953; Rahway, N.J.

RELIGION
Roman Catholic

FAMILY
Wife, Marie Smith; four children

EDUCATION
Trenton State College, B.A. 1975 (business)

CAREER
Sporting goods executive; state anti-abortion group director

POLITICAL HIGHLIGHTS
Republican nominee for U.S. House, 1978

ELECTION RESULTS

2008 GENERAL

Christopher H. Smith (R)	202,972	66.2%
Joshua M. Zeitz (D)	100,036	32.6%
Steven Welzer (GREEN)	3,543	1.2%

2008 PRIMARY

Christopher H. Smith (R)	unopposed

2006 GENERAL

Christopher H. Smith (R)	124,482	65.7%
Carol E. Gay (D)	62,905	33.2%

PREVIOUS WINNING PERCENTAGES
2004 (67%); 2002 (66%); 2000 (63%); 1998 (62%);
1996 (64%); 1994 (68%); 1992 (62%); 1990 (63%);
1988 (66%); 1986 (61%); 1984 (61%); 1982 (53%);
1980 (57%)

which majorities of the two parties diverged, a level second only to Maryland's Wayne T. Gilchrest among House GOP members.

But Smith has long been among the vanguard of abortion opponents, pushing to prevent federal funds from paying for the abortions of poor women, to stop foreign aid to agencies that counsel women about abortion or to protect the legal rights of abortion protesters. In the 108th Congress (2003-04), Smith spearheaded the drive that led to enactment of a ban on a procedure that anti-abortion groups call "partial birth" abortion.

He blasted President Obama's executive order in March 2009 lifting Bush's restrictions on federal funding of embryonic stem cell research, which uses discarded embryos created for in vitro fertilization. Smith argued such research is unnecessary because of advances using stem cells extracted harmlessly from adults and from amniotic fluid. "At a time when highly significant — even historic — breakthroughs in adult stem cell research have become almost daily occurrences...President Obama has chosen to turn back the clock and, starting today, will force taxpayers to subsidize the unethical over the ethical, the unworkable over what works, and hype and hyperbole over hope," he said.

Smith has a strong interest in the rights of children and has sponsored legislation to monitor child labor conditions abroad and crack down on abuses. He often refers in conversation to his own four children, whose photographs are prominently displayed in his congressional office. In 2000, he won enactment of a law to combat trafficking in women and children, who are often forced into prostitution. In 2006, Bush signed Smith's bill toughening anti-trafficking measures and calling for $361 million in funding over two years.

Smith, whose parents owned a New Jersey wholesale sporting goods business, told the Times he first became interested in the issue of abortion as a 19-year-old student at Trenton State College when he read a newspaper article about a fetus that had survived an abortion. "It got the wheels turning about where were those child's rights," he said.

After an internship with a state senator, he was hooked on politics. He ran someone else's unsuccessful Democratic Senate campaign in 1976 and then lost his own race for the House two years later.

He was executive director of the New Jersey Right to Life Committee before winning election to Congress at age 27. He defeated 13-term Democrat Frank Thompson, who had been tainted by a bribery scandal. He faced a stiff challenge in his first re-election battle, taking just 53 percent of the vote, but hasn't fallen below 60 percent since.

KEY VOTES

2008

No Delay consideration of Colombia free-trade agreement

No Override Bush veto of federal farm and nutrition programs reauthorization bill

Yes Overhaul surveillance laws and permit dismissal of suits against companies that conducted warrantless wiretapping

Yes Grant mortgage relief to homeowners and funding for Fannie Mae and Freddie Mac

No Approve initial $700 billion program to stabilize financial markets

No Approve final $700 billion program to stabilize financial markets

Yes Provide $14 billion in loans to automakers

2007

Yes Increase minimum wage by $2.10 an hour

No Approve $124.2 billion in emergency war spending and set goal for redeployment of troops from Iraq

Yes Reject federal contraceptive assistance to international family planning groups

Yes Override Bush veto of $23.2 billion water projects authorization bill

No Implement Peru free-trade agreement

Yes Approve energy policy overhaul with new fuel economy standards

Yes Clear $473.5 billion omnibus spending bill, including $70 billion for military operations

CQ VOTE STUDIES

	PARTY UNITY		PRESIDENTIAL SUPPORT	
	SUPPORT	OPPOSE	SUPPORT	OPPOSE
2008	68%	32%	32%	68%
2007	62%	38%	37%	63%
2006	72%	28%	67%	33%
2005	79%	21%	60%	40%
2004	77%	23%	67%	33%

INTEREST GROUPS

	AFL-CIO	ADA	CCUS	ACU
2008	80%	65%	67%	28%
2007	79%	55%	70%	44%
2006	50%	30%	67%	68%
2005	60%	30%	70%	60%
2004	67%	40%	76%	54%

NEW JERSEY 4
Central — part of Trenton, Lakewood

The 4th spreads across the center of the state, where the Garden State begins its transition from South to North Jersey, extending from Trenton and the Delaware River to the Jersey Shore and coastal communities such as Point Pleasant and Spring Lake.

The district includes much of the southern and eastern portions of Trenton, the state capital. While these areas vote Democratic, they do not lean quite as strongly as other parts of the city which are contained in the 12th District to the north. Most of Trenton's white residents live in the 4th, which includes the historically Italian neighborhood of Chambersburg. But the area is not without diversity — more than 25 percent of the 4th's portion of Trenton is black and 30 percent is Hispanic.

The area's major multi-branch military base is important to the economy, but the district does not rely solely on defense. Trenton and its suburbs have a diverse range of businesses, and the towns along the shore in Ocean and Monmouth counties depend heavily on tourism. The 4th also includes rural territory dotted with horse and agricultural farms, in areas

such as Colts Neck. Like much of central and southern New Jersey, the 4th is loaded with small towns, such as Hightstown and Manasquan in Mercer and Monmouth counties, and the district takes in a chunk of Burlington County, a growing area outside of Philadelphia. Burlington Coat Factory, a clothing retail chain, is headquartered in Burlington.

Ocean and Monmouth counties dominate the 4th's geography and give the district its GOP lean. Lakewood Township, in Ocean County, has a large Orthodox Jewish population. Republican John McCain did 10 percentage points better in the 4th (52 percent) than he did statewide in the 2008 presidential election.

MAJOR INDUSTRY
State government, tourism, manufacturing, defense

MILITARY BASES
Joint Base McGuire-Dix-Lakehurst (shared with the 3rd), 5,724 military, 4,435 civilian (2009)

CITIES
Trenton (pt.), 37,745; Lakewood (unincorporated), 36,065

NOTABLE
Trenton, a Revolutionary War battleground, was temporarily the U.S. capital; Bruce Springsteen hails from Freehold.

Rep. Scott Garrett (R)

Elected 2002; 4th term

While the GOP's conservative faction draws much of its strength from the South and West, Garrett serves as one of its anchors in a region where the party has a shrinking foothold: the Northeast. A born-again Christian, he spends Saturday mornings in a Bible study breakfast group. He favors prohibitions on same-sex marriage, embryonic stem cell research and abortion.

One of the last three House Republicans in the New York metropolitan area (New York's Peter T. King and New Jersey's Rodney Frelinghuysen are the others), Garrett argues against trying to revive the GOP's moderate wing. Instead, he calls for drawing clear political lines. "When a party is too much like the other party, people go with what they're familiar with — and in New Jersey, that's the Democratic Party...It will be conservative principles that get us back into the majority," he said.

To underscore his message, he sometimes takes a lead role for the conservative Republican Study Committee in trying to curb the growth of domestic spending and to kill earmarks — funding set-asides for special projects in members' districts. In one high-profile tussle in 2007, Garrett won applause from fellow conservatives for attempting to cut funding for an Alaska Native education program and weathering a tough rebuke by the program's champion, Republican Don Young of Alaska. "Too many members of Congress see the dollars that we appropriate here not as the taxpayers' dollar, but see it as their very own personal checking account." Garrett said in a thinly veiled slap at Young.

Garrett continues to climb the ladder on the Financial Services Committee. He belongs to a cadre of vocal Study Committee members on the panel who sometimes work with Financial Services Chairman Barney Frank, a liberal Massachusetts Democrat, on routine bills but who often take opposing sides on measures that would expand the scope of government programs. Garrett worked with Frank on a bipartisan House-passed measure in the 110th Congress (2007-08) that would phase out flood insurance subsidies for some homes built before 1974, but it stalled in the Senate.

As a founder of the Constitution Caucus, Garrett often refers to the reserve clause of the Constitution when arguing against funding for programs that weren't mentioned or envisioned by the framers. "When we look at the vast scope of the federal government today, it's clear that Congress has overstepped these constitutional boundaries," he said in 2007.

He called for tough oversight of the $700 billion financial sector rescue law of 2008, which he opposed, and attacked plans to bail out troubled automakers. He told constituents in an open letter that lawmakers should "stand against this commitment of your money with little or no government oversight."

He wasted little time becoming a critic of the Obama administration's approach to the financial crisis. "What are the markets looking for? They're looking for confidence and consistency," he said on MSNBC in 2009. "We have not gotten that out of this administration for the three months that they've been in. They've been coming out with plans or saying they're going to come out with plans. And they come out with plans and there's no details to them."

But he breaks ranks with his party on some issues. He voted against the Medicare prescription drug benefit in 2003; five years later, he said other Republicans felt "buyer's remorse" for supporting that initiative instead of sticking to the GOP's traditional opposition to new government mandates.

On the Budget Committee, he works closely with Paul D. Ryan of Wisconsin and another Study Committee ally, Jeb Hensarling of Texas. Garrett took

CAPITOL OFFICE
225-4465
garrett.house.gov
137 Cannon Bldg. 20515-3005; fax 225-9048

COMMITTEES
Budget
Financial Services

RESIDENCE
Wantage

BORN
July 9, 1959; Englewood, N.J.

RELIGION
Protestant

FAMILY
Wife, Mary Ellen Garrett; two children

EDUCATION
Montclair State College, B.A. 1981 (political science); Rutgers U., J.D. 1984;

CAREER
Lawyer

POLITICAL HIGHLIGHTS
N.J. Assembly, 1990-2003; sought Republican nomination for U.S. House, 1998, 2000

ELECTION RESULTS

2008 GENERAL

Scott Garrett (R)	172,653	55.9%
Dennis Shulman (D)	131,033	42.4%
Ed Fanning (GREEN)	5,321	1.7%

2008 PRIMARY

Scott Garrett (R)	unopposed

2006 GENERAL

Scott Garrett (R)	112,142	54.9%
Paul Aronsohn (D)	89,503	43.8%
R. Matthew Fretz (AIV)	2,597	1.3%

PREVIOUS WINNING PERCENTAGES
2004 (58%); 2002 (59%)

the lead on a committee-backed economic growth proposal in 2008 that would have slashed the corporate tax rate from 35 percent to 25 percent and provided for expensing of buildings and other business assets. He also called for capping federal spending at 20 percent of the gross domestic product.

The son of a Uniroyal executive, Garrett represents a district that encompasses Wall Street commuters and family farm operators. As a youth, his family moved from Bergen County's suburbs to a 100-acre farm in Wantage, where they grew greenhouse tomatoes, Yorkshire pigs and Christmas trees.

Garrett's farm roots attracted unwanted publicity in 2008, when his opponent accused him of omitting a 10-acre plot of land — on which his family claimed a tax break as farmland — from financial disclosure forms. Garrett argued the tax break was justified and said the property was exempt from disclosure because he lived there and had no stake in his brother's separate Christmas tree business.

Garrett is a lawyer with an interest in environmental law and occasionally tilts to the center on conservation-related themes. He pushed for the 2006 law that designated parts of the Musconetcong River for protection as a wild and scenic river. "One of the main reasons why I got involved in government was to try to preserve open space," he said.

He took an early interest in civics, publishing an alternative high school newspaper that questioned the school administration's spending practices and getting elected student government treasurer. After getting his law degree, he worked in insurance and jumped into politics. He served more than a decade in the New Jersey Legislature, where he belonged to a group of maverick, conservative Republicans called the "mountain men."

In 1998, Garrett launched his campaign to unseat his moderate predecessor, Marge Roukema. Although he lost the primary, he captured the attention of national conservative groups like the Club for Growth, an influential anti-tax group that spent more than $250,000 in his behalf two years later. He lost again, but by only 2,000 votes. By 2002, Roukema had lost a bid to chair Financial Services and was ready to retire, paving the way for Garrett.

He won the primary against two moderate rivals, who split the large moderate vote in Bergen County. In the general he garnered 59 percent of the vote in defeating Democratic ophthalmologist Anne Sumers, with help from attack ads sponsored by the National Republican Congressional Committee. In 2008, New York City Mayor Michael Bloomberg endorsed his Democratic rival, Dennis Shulman, a psychologist and ordained rabbi. But Garrett had support from former New York City Mayor Rudy Giuliani; he outraised Shulman and won with 56 percent.

KEY VOTES

2008

No Delay consideration of Colombia free-trade agreement

No Override Bush veto of federal farm and nutrition programs reauthorization bill

Yes Overhaul surveillance laws and permit dismissal of suits against companies that conducted warrantless wiretapping

No Grant mortgage relief to homeowners and funding for Fannie Mae and Freddie Mac

No Approve initial $700 billion program to stabilize financial markets

No Approve final $700 billion program to stabilize financial markets

No Provide $14 billion in loans to automakers

2007

No Increase minimum wage by $2.10 an hour

No Approve $124.2 billion in emergency war spending and set goal for redeployment of troops from Iraq

Yes Reject federal contraceptive assistance to international family planning groups

No Override Bush veto of $23.2 billion water projects authorization bill

Yes Implement Peru free-trade agreement

No Approve energy policy overhaul with new fuel economy standards

Yes Clear $473.5 billion omnibus spending bill, including $70 billion for military operations

CQ VOTE STUDIES

	PARTY UNITY		PRESIDENTIAL SUPPORT	
	SUPPORT	OPPOSE	SUPPORT	OPPOSE
2008	97%	3%	77%	23%
2007	97%	3%	86%	14%
2006	89%	11%	83%	17%
2005	98%	2%	84%	16%
2004	98%	2%	88%	12%

INTEREST GROUPS

	AFL-CIO	ADA	CCUS	ACU
2008	0%	5%	78%	100%
2007	4%	0%	70%	100%
2006	14%	20%	87%	100%
2005	20%	5%	85%	100%
2004	7%	5%	95%	100%

NEW JERSEY 5

North and west — Bergenfield, Paramus

Although the 5th District stretches across northern New Jersey, three-fifths of its population is packed into northern Bergen County, which is home to affluent voters, many of whom commute into New York City. The rest of the district is scenic and hilly and includes the state's small portion of the Appalachian Trail. No municipality here has more than 30,000 residents. The 5th also has the smallest minority population of any New Jersey district.

Despite declining home prices, the 5th's property values and income levels are still among the highest in the state. Saddle River, in wealthy Bergen County, has been known for its multimillion-dollar homes, but foreclosures may impact the area. Bergen County's tony suburbs contrast with a more rural feel in the 5th's portion of Passaic County to the west, which includes the New Jersey Botanical Garden and attractions dating back to the colonial era.

The scenic back country of Sussex and Warren counties traditionally has been a mix of farmland and small towns, but both counties have

started to change as young professionals from New York City move into the area. Warren County's population has increased by 20 percent since 1990, and the county is experiencing ongoing housing development, but local officials and residents remain committed to preserving an agricultural heritage across the county.

Although most voters register as independents, the 5th tends to vote Republican. Democrats are successful in some areas, including Tenafly in Bergen County and Phillipsburg in south Warren County, the only county to lie entirely within the district's boundaries. John McCain captured 54 percent of the 5th's vote in the 2008 presidential election. The Bergen County portion of the district favored McCain with a slim majority, but his margin was wider in the 5th's part of the three outlying counties.

MAJOR INDUSTRY

Pharmaceuticals, electronics, shipping, agriculture

CITIES

West Milford (unincorporated), 26,410; Bergenfield, 26,247; Paramus, 25,737; Ridgewood, 24,936

NOTABLE

Hackettstown hosts the Mars Snackfood US national office and an M&M's brand manufacturing plant.

Rep. Frank Pallone Jr. (D)

Elected 1988; 11th full term

CAPITOL OFFICE
225-4671
www.house.gov/pallone
237 Cannon Bldg. 20515-3006; fax 225-9665

COMMITTEES
Energy & Commerce
(Health - chairman)
Natural Resources

RESIDENCE
Long Branch

BORN
Oct. 30, 1951; Long Branch, N.J.

RELIGION
Roman Catholic

FAMILY
Wife, Sarah Pallone; three children

EDUCATION
Middlebury College, B.A. 1973 (history & French);
Tufts U., M.A. 1974 (international relations);
Rutgers U., J.D. 1978

CAREER
Lawyer

POLITICAL HIGHLIGHTS
Long Branch City Council, 1982-88;
N.J. Senate, 1984-88

ELECTION RESULTS

2008 GENERAL

Frank Pallone Jr. (D)	164,077	66.9%
Robert McLeod (R)	77,469	31.6%
Herb Tarbous (I)	3,531	1.4%

2008 PRIMARY

Frank Pallone Jr. (D)	unopposed

2006 GENERAL

Frank Pallone Jr. (D)	98,615	68.6%
Leigh-Ann Bellew (R)	43,539	30.3%
Herb Tarbous (DIS)	1,619	1.1%

PREVIOUS WINNING PERCENTAGES
2004 (67%); 2002 (66%); 2000 (68%); 1998 (57%);
1996 (61%); 1994 (60%); 1992 (52%); 1990 (49%);
1988 (52%); 1988 Special Election (52%)

The ambitious Pallone has long been at the forefront of putting out the Democratic message on the environment, energy and, more recently, health care. But he now tempers his aggressive partisanship as he tries to prove he can effectively legislate as chairman of the Energy and Commerce Subcommittee on Health.

But after more than two years at the helm, he still sits in the shadow of more powerful personalities on the full committee. Henry A. Waxman of California, who chaired the Health panel when Democrats ran Congress before the 1994 Republican takeover, took the gavel of the full committee at the start of 2009. Former committee chairman John D. Dingell of Michigan, the chamber's longest-serving member, has had a hand in virtually every major health care debate over the past half-century and still wields great power in such discussions, despite being toppled by Waxman.

Waxman and Dingell largely agree when it comes to health care issues, and some said Dingell was going to attempt to take the chairmanship of the subcommittee from Pallone, who had strongly backed Waxman's bid for Dingell's chair in late 2008. But Dingell was satisfied when Waxman gave him the lead in developing national health care legislation for the 111th Congress (2009-10).

Pallone (puh-LOAN) knew little of the details of health policy before the 110th Congress (2007-08), when his seniority status put him in position to take over the panel. But after helping Dingell shepherd through legislation on the FDA, Medicare, and Medicaid, he began to demonstrate a growing knowledge and became a regular at meetings with leadership when health care was at the top of the docket. He sponsored the bill in early 2009 to expand a state-federal children's health insurance program, which Obama signed into law; the bill was similar to two versions that President George W. Bush vetoed.

And while he catches up on the subject matter, he is trying to learn to work with House Republicans and the Senate. Under GOP rule in the House, he had served as the Democrats' partisan, liberal voice in his role as communications chairman of the Democratic Steering and Policy Committee. "My ideology hasn't moved — I still consider myself a liberal and progressive," Pallone said in 2008. But, he added, "I want to get things done, so from a practical point of view that means having to work with the more conservative Democrats and also with the Republicans."

His seat on Energy and Commerce, as well as the Natural Resources Committee, also allows him to continue his focus on environment and energy policies of interest to his coastline district. He speaks passionately about renewable energy and the cleanup of New Jersey's pollution sites.

A member of the Energy and Environment Subcommittee of Energy and Commerce, Pallone opposes offshore drilling for oil and gas. He also has opposed the siting of a liquefied natural gas importation facility off the New Jersey coast. He backs a national requirement for electricity suppliers to step up production from wind, solar and other renewable sources. New Jersey is among more than 20 states that already have such a rule.

From his seat on the Natural Resources Committee's oceans subcommittee, he tends to the needs of recreational fishing interests in his state, where boaters — more than half of them fishing enthusiasts — spend more than $2 billion a year. He also supports the designation of Atlantic striped bass as a game fish and offered a bill in 2007 to put the fish off-limits to commercial fishing in coastal waters. He pushes to bring more flexibility into the 2007 Magnuson-Stevens Fishery Conservation and Management Act to rebuild fish stocks.

In April 2008 he saw House passage of his bill to require the EPA to develop rapid testing procedures to detect water contamination in six hours or less so beaches can be quickly closed to swimming. (The measure stalled in the Senate.) He has promoted continuation of the federal program to bulk up beaches with additional sand. But he has opposed plans to mine sand and gravel in the Atlantic, arguing it would hurt marine life.

Pallone has opposed all major trade laws, in part because of his concerns about environmental damage from expanded global trade. He also watches out for the interests of the sizable Indian-American community in the 6th District; he is a founder of the House Caucus on India and Indian-Americans. He supported the 2006 U.S.-India nuclear pact allowing shipments of civilian nuclear fuel to India, saying it would help keep the country a strategic ally in the increasingly unstable region.

He has taken a special interest in Armenian issues because of a large district presence and a longtime curiosity about the area. As co-chairman of the House Armenian Caucus, he cosponsored a resolution condemning as genocide the mass killings of Armenians in Ottoman Turkey in 1915. Pallone and other members backed off the idea amid administration warnings it would damage U.S. relations with its ally.

His father, who sparked his interest in politics, was a police officer in Long Branch and a longtime activist in local Democratic affairs, including the campaigns of former Rep. James J. Howard. After graduating from Middlebury College in Vermont, he enrolled at Tufts University's Fletcher School in Massachusetts to study international relations. He was accepted into an exchange program that would have allowed him to spend a year studying in Switzerland, a common track to a State Department job. But Pallone said he realized he preferred Jersey politics and chose to attend law school at Rutgers, where he later taught.

Howard urged Pallone to run for the Long Branch City Council in 1982. One year later, Pallone won a state Senate seat. In 1988, Howard died of a heart attack and many Democratic insiders, including Howard's widow, lined up behind Pallone. In November, he won two races on the same day — a special election to fill the vacancy and a full term in his own right, each by only 5 percentage points. He has faced several other challenges since then, the closest of which came in 1990 when he squeaked by with a margin of just 4,258 votes.

New Jersey lost a House seat in reapportionment in the 1990s, and Pallone had to scramble to hold his redrawn district. But redistricting after the 2000 census made his subsequent re-elections easier. He has been among the most eager of New Jersey's House Democrats to move to the Senate.

KEY VOTES

2008

Yes Delay consideration of Colombia free-trade agreement
Yes Override Bush veto of federal farm and nutrition programs reauthorization bill
No Overhaul surveillance laws and permit dismissal of suits against companies that conducted warrantless wiretapping
Yes Grant mortgage relief to homeowners and funding for Fannie Mae and Freddie Mac
Yes Approve initial $700 billion program to stabilize financial markets
Yes Approve final $700 billion program to stabilize financial markets
Yes Provide $14 billion in loans to automakers

2007

Yes Increase minimum wage by $2.10 an hour
Yes Approve $124.2 billion in emergency war spending and set goal for redeployment of troops from Iraq
No Reject federal contraceptive assistance to international family planning groups
Yes Override Bush veto of $23.2 billion water projects authorization bill
No Implement Peru free-trade agreement
Yes Approve energy policy overhaul with new fuel economy standards
No Clear $473.5 billion omnibus spending bill, including $70 billion for military operations

CQ VOTE STUDIES

	PARTY UNITY		PRESIDENTIAL SUPPORT	
	SUPPORT	OPPOSE	SUPPORT	OPPOSE
2008	99%	1%	17%	83%
2007	99%	1%	4%	96%
2006	97%	3%	23%	77%
2005	97%	3%	17%	83%
2004	96%	4%	18%	82%

INTEREST GROUPS

	AFL-CIO	ADA	CCUS	ACU
2008	100%	100%	67%	0%
2007	100%	100%	45%	0%
2006	100%	100%	27%	4%
2005	93%	100%	30%	4%
2004	93%	95%	24%	4%

NEW JERSEY 6

East central — New Brunswick, Plainfield, part of Edison

Wedged in the heart of suburbs south of New York and Newark, the 6th combines industrial communities in Middlesex County with a long, thin stretch that incorporates beach towns in Monmouth County.

Like much of the state, the 6th previously was politically competitive, but has shifted toward Democratic candidates in recent years. Heavily Democratic Plainfield in Union County and part of Somerset in Somerset County have added to the leftward pull of the 6th. Barack Obama took 61 percent of the district's presidential vote in 2008.

East of Somerset, New Brunswick consolidates two Democratic voting blocs — students from Rutgers University (shared with the 12th District) and minorities. Nearby Piscataway, Highland Park and Metuchen also favor Democrats. Upper-middle-class and independent-voting residents cluster around Edison (shared with the 7th), which is home to some corporate offices and manufacturing. The 6th District includes residents

with various ethnic backgrounds, ranging from the Irish and Polish who populate South Amboy in Middlesex County to the Italians who are prevalent in Long Branch in Monmouth County. Edison also has an established Indian community.

In Monmouth County, the problems of Asbury Park, a vacation site made famous by rocker Bruce Springsteen, are an exception to the area's generally sunny outlook. Yet hope exists here, thanks to a 10-year, $1.25 billion waterfront redevelopment plan that broke ground in 2004, and some success in reducing the city's narcotics trade. Other shore communities in the district include Deal, a summer enclave for Syrian Jews, and Atlantic Highlands, where many area residents catch a ferry to jobs in New York City.

MAJOR INDUSTRY
Higher education, technology, pharmaceuticals, manufacturing

CITIES
Edison (unincorporated) (pt.), 65,782; New Brunswick, 48,573; Plainfield, 47,829; Sayreville, 40,377; Long Branch, 31,340

NOTABLE
The Sandy Hook Light, opened in 1764, is the nation's oldest standing lighthouse.

Rep. Leonard Lance (R)

Elected 2008; 1st term

Lance is a political throwback to a time when centrist Northeastern Republicans flourished in the GOP. A self-professed "Eisenhower Republican," Lance met the former president as a child and studied under presidential historian and Eisenhower scholar Fred Greenstein at Princeton University. "Eisenhower was a moderate who brought people together," Lance said.

Lance is a fiscal conservative, pledging to oppose all tax increases and to fight to repeal the estate and alternative minimum taxes. But in contrast to his socially conservative predecessor, Republican Mike Ferguson, he is pro-choice, supports embryonic stem cell research and seeks to promote conservation by increasing incentives for hybrid vehicles and renewable energy.

As a member of the Financial Services Committee, Lance held with his party in early 2009 in opposing President Obama's economic stimulus plan, saying it contained "wasteful spending."

He led a group of GOP freshmen in introducing a bill in March 2009 calling on Treasury to recoup within two weeks bonuses paid to employees by the troubled insurer American International Group Inc., which received funds through the 2008 financial sector law. He opposed a Democratic bill, which the House ultimately approved, aimed at curbing employee bonuses at companies receiving such funds. Lance said the bill was too broad.

When he served in the New Jersey Assembly, Lance was one of a handful of Republicans to oppose GOP Gov. Christine Todd Whitman's plan to borrow billions of dollars for the public employee pension system. As punishment, he lost the chairmanship of the Budget Committee.

Lance was the third generation in his family — which has lived in Hunterdon County since 1710 — to serve in the state legislature. "We were an adult-centered, not child-centered, household," he said.

His Democratic opponent in his 2008 campaign for the U.S. House, state Rep. Linda Stender, had come within a percentage point of defeating Ferguson in 2006 and had a 4-to-1 spending advantage. But in 2008 Lance was endorsed by many of the district's major papers. He won by 8 percentage points.

CAPITOL OFFICE
225-5361
lance.house.gov
114 Cannon Bldg. 20515-3007; fax 225-9460

COMMITTEES
Financial Services

RESIDENCE
Lebanon

BORN
June 25, 1952; Easton, Pa.

RELIGION
Roman Catholic

FAMILY
Wife, Heidi A. Rohrbach; one stepchild

EDUCATION
Lehigh U., B.A. 1974 (American studies);
Vanderbilt U., JD 1977; Princeton U., M.P.A. 1982

CAREER
Lawyer; gubernatorial aide

POLITICAL HIGHLIGHTS
N.J. Assembly, 1991-2002; sought Republican nomination for U.S. House, 1996; N.J. Senate, 2002-09 (minority leader, 2004-09)

ELECTION RESULTS

2008 GENERAL

Leonard Lance (R)	148,461	50.2%
Linda Stender (D)	124,818	42.2%
Michael P. Hsing (HFC)	16,419	5.6%
Dean Greco (ADBP)	3,259	1.1%

2008 PRIMARY

Leonard Lance (R)	10,094	39.5%
Kate Whitman (R)	5,052	19.8%
P. Kelly Hatfield (R)	3,902	15.3%
Martin Marks (R)	3,211	12.6%
Tom Roughneen (R)	1,845	7.2%
Darren Young (R)	1,232	4.8%

NEW JERSEY 7

North central – Woodbridge Township

The 7th District, which is centered in bedroom communities for residents commuting to Newark and New York City, zigzags across north-central New Jersey from the Delaware River to Woodbridge.

Drug manufacturers fuel the economy, led by Whitehouse Station's Merck & Co., which will merge with Schering-Plough in 2009. Roche Molecular Systems in Branchburg is a key employer. Plummeting sales and revenue at international telecommunications company Alcatel-Lucent in Murray Hill (Union County) have led to major layoffs.

The district has several of New Jersey's superfund toxic waste sites, and residents tend to be environmentally conscious. Other important local issues include aircraft noise from nearby Newark Liberty International Airport (in the 10th and 13th districts) and

money for infrastructure. Amtrak's Metropark station, the only stop in the 7th for north-central New Jersey residents headed up or down the East Coast, is in Iselin.

And although the western areas of the district are less densely populated, office parks and shopping malls have sprouted in parts of Somerset and Hunterdon counties once dotted by horse farms.

The 7th District contains some wealthy, heavily Republican areas in Somerset and Hunterdon counties and contains a large chunk of Democratic Union County. The district is highly competitive overall. Barack Obama narrowly won the 7th's 2008 presidential vote.

MAJOR INDUSTRY
Pharmaceuticals, manufacturing

CITIES
Edison (unincorp.) (pt.), 31,905; Westfield, 29,644; Union (unincorp.) (pt.), 27,066

NOTABLE
The U.S. equestrian team's headquarters is in Gladstone.

Rep. Bill Pascrell Jr. (D)

Elected 1996; 7th term

CAPITOL OFFICE
225-5751
pascrell.house.gov
2464 Rayburn Bldg. 20515-3008; fax 225-5782

COMMITTEES
Homeland Security
Ways & Means

RESIDENCE
Paterson

BORN
Jan. 25, 1937; Paterson, N.J.

RELIGION
Roman Catholic

FAMILY
Wife, Elsie Marie Pascrell; three children

EDUCATION
Fordham U., B.A. 1959 (journalism), M.A. 1961
(philosophy)

MILITARY SERVICE
Army, 1961; Army Reserve, 1962-67

CAREER
City official; teacher

POLITICAL HIGHLIGHTS
Paterson Board of Education, 1977-81
(president, 1981); N.J. Assembly, 1988-97;
mayor of Paterson, 1990-97

ELECTION RESULTS

2008 GENERAL

Bill Pascrell Jr. (D)	159,279	71.1%
Roland Straten (R)	63,107	28.2%

2008 PRIMARY

Bill Pascrell Jr. (D)	unopposed

2006 GENERAL

Bill Pascrell Jr. (D)	97,568	70.9%
Jose M. Sandoval (R)	39,053	28.4%

PREVIOUS WINNING PERCENTAGES
2004 (69%); 2002 (67%); 2000 (67%); 1998 (62%);
1996 (51%)

Pascrell prides himself on being a "neighborhood guy" who hasn't strayed from his blue-collar roots. Working-class Paterson is the heart of the territory he represents and where his Italian immigrant grandparents settled. It is where he served as head of the school board, mayor and a state legislator. And it is where he still has his home, a modest house in a middle-class neighborhood.

He uses his prized seat on the Ways and Means panel to look out for his district, and he is a party loyalist, rarely splitting from other House Democrats. In the 110th Congress (2007-08), he sided with his party 98 percent of the time on votes that pitted most Democrats against most Republicans.

Pascrell (pass-KRELL) is proud of a tax credit for first-time homebuyers that he championed as part of a 2008 law intended to stabilize the battered housing sector. The $7,500 tax credit was boosted to $8,000 as part of the 2009 economic recovery and stimulus package. He said the tax credit will motivate new homebuyers who have been afraid to enter the market.

Pascrell is especially proud of a tax credit for first-time homebuyers that he championed as part of a 2008 law intended to stabilize the battered housing sector. The $7,500 tax credit was boosted to $8,000 as part of the 2009 economic recovery and stimulus package. Pascrell said the tax credit will motivate new homebuyers who have been afraid to enter the market.

He has opposed most recent trade pacts, saying they hurt U.S. manufacturers, a view shared by many of his constituents. But in 2007, he supported a free-trade agreement with Peru; Paterson has a sizeable Peruvian community.

Pascrell got the coveted Ways and Means seat at the start of the 110th Congress in part because of his outspoken support of Pennsylvania Democrat John P. Murtha for majority leader. Murtha had been Nancy Pelosi's candidate, and the Speaker rewarded Pascrell even after Maryland Democrat Steny H. Hoyer defeated Murtha for majority leader. Pascrell is a close friend of Murtha, the chairman of the Defense Appropriations Subcommittee and one of the most vocal opponents of the war in Iraq. Although Pascrell voted in 2002 to authorize the use of force in Iraq, he supported Murtha's 2005 resolution calling for the withdrawal and redeployment of all U.S. forces stationed there. Afghanistan and Pakistan, not Iraq, "are really the epicenter of terrorism," he said.

Another friend is Hawaii Democrat Neil Abercrombie, who was the subject of a Pascrell-penned poem titled "The Ghost of Abercrombie." Connecticut Democrat John B. Larson liked the tribute — which honored their colleague for having "bragged sincerely of life and death long before the funeral chant" — so much that he added it to the Congressional Record. "I love writing poetry," he said. "I believe it's a beautiful thing. What the hell, I can't paint."

Ways and Means members usually may not serve on other committees, but Pelosi granted a waiver to allow Pascrell to sit on the Homeland Security Committee. On that panel, he champions more funding for firefighters and other emergency personnel. He shepherded through Congress in 2000 a bill creating a federal program to direct hundreds of millions of dollars to hire, train and equip local firefighters. He and other Democrats fought off George W. Bush administration efforts to curtail grants to first-responders, and Pascrell has urged the Obama administration to keep those funds flowing.

Before joining Ways and Means, Pascrell served on the Transportation and Infrastructure Committee; he made sure the surface transportation bill passed by the House in the 109th Congress (2005-06) contained funding for road, bridge and mass transit projects in his district.

Another longstanding cause has been to improve research on and treatment of brain injuries. Inspired by the plight of a constituent, Pascrell was a co-founder in 2001 of the Congressional Brain Injury Task Force. In April 2008, he helped steer into law the reauthorization of a traumatic-brain-injury treatment program that offers research and rehabilitation grants to states.

In 2009 he won a bittersweet victory with the enactment, as part of an omnibus lands package, of a bill he had promoted for years to include the Great Falls in Paterson in the national park system. As a catcher on his school baseball team, he always walked by the falls with his mother on their way home from games; it was a place both cherished. But Pascrell's 95-year-old mother, Roffie, died two days before President Obama signed the lands bill into law.

He generally backs his party's positions things like gun control and education funding. But he has voted for tougher penalties for juvenile offenders, a GOP-written overhaul of the nation's public housing system and a ban on the medical procedure described by its opponents as "partial birth" abortion.

Pascrell, whose father worked for the railroad, was the first member of his family to go to high school, and his neighborhood pals razzed him when he went off to college. He worked his way through Fordham University, earning a bachelor's degree in journalism and a master's in philosophy. He then embarked on a 12-year career as a high school teacher in neighboring Paramus, and along the way did a stint in the Army. In 1974, he became the director of public works for the city of Paterson, and then headed up the planning and development office. At the same time, he worked as a campaign volunteer for Democratic Rep. Robert A. Roe and others. He was appointed to the Paterson Board of Education and later was elected its president.

He won a seat in the state Assembly in 1987 and also served as mayor of Paterson beginning in 1990. As mayor, he promoted tough law enforcement measures, particularly in drug trafficking. To make it more difficult for dealers to communicate with their customers, he personally ripped out the lines and receivers of pay telephones that had not been issued a city permit. In 1996, his New Jersey mayoral colleagues of both parties elected him "mayor of the year."

Pascrell was his party's choice to take on Rep. Bill Martini in 1996, two years after Martini's narrow win had ended 34 years of Democratic hegemony in the district. The national party gave Pascrell a boost, inviting him to speak at the Democratic National Convention. The AFL-CIO targeted the race as a key labor battlefield. Pascrell needed every bit of help he could get: He toppled Martini by just 6,200 votes. Acknowledging his tenuous hold on the seat, he quickly began amassing a war chest for 1998, which dissuaded Martini from running. Since then, his re-election contests have been routine.

KEY VOTES

2008

Yes Delay consideration of Colombia free-trade agreement

Yes Override Bush veto of federal farm and nutrition programs reauthorization bill

No Overhaul surveillance laws and permit dismissal of suits against companies that conducted warrantless wiretapping

Yes Grant mortgage relief to homeowners and funding for Fannie Mae and Freddie Mac

No Approve initial $700 billion program to stabilize financial markets

Yes Approve final $700 billion program to stabilize financial markets

Yes Provide $14 billion in loans to automakers

2007

Yes Increase minimum wage by $2.10 an hour

Yes Approve $124.2 billion in emergency war spending and set goal for redeployment of troops from Iraq

No Reject federal contraceptive assistance to international family planning groups

Yes Override Bush veto of $23.2 billion water projects authorization bill

Yes Implement Peru free-trade agreement

Yes Approve energy policy overhaul with new fuel economy standards

No Clear $473.5 billion omnibus spending bill, including $70 billion for military operations

CQ VOTE STUDIES

	PARTY UNITY		PRESIDENTIAL SUPPORT	
	SUPPORT	OPPOSE	SUPPORT	OPPOSE
2008	99%	1%	13%	87%
2007	98%	2%	6%	94%
2006	95%	5%	25%	75%
2005	93%	7%	15%	85%
2004	94%	6%	31%	69%

INTEREST GROUPS

	AFL-CIO	ADA	CCUS	ACU
2008	100%	95%	56%	4%
2007	100%	95%	55%	0%
2006	100%	95%	27%	12%
2005	93%	100%	37%	0%
2004	100%	90%	40%	4%

NEW JERSEY 8
Northeast — Paterson, Clifton, Passaic

The 8th is a diverse combination of urban centers and suburban towns that begins in Pompton Lakes and moves south through the southern portion of Passaic County into northern Essex County, extending into parts of Livingston, West Orange and South Orange, just to the west of Newark. It includes Paterson, the state's third-largest city, as well as Clifton and Passaic.

Paterson was once known for silk mills that made it a leading textile producer in the late 19th century. But after labor strife and the introduction of rayon and other materials, the city experienced a serious economic downturn from which it never fully recovered. Yet there may be some light at the end of the tunnel: Center City, a major development project in downtown Paterson, is expected to be completed by mid-2009.

The 8th District also includes some less populated areas, which have more of a small-town feel but still battle the frequent nemesis of North Jersey residents — traffic. Wayne is mostly residential, but is perhaps best known as the home of a retail power center: Willowbrook Mall. The district is a melting pot of cultures with dozens of ethnic groups, from a large Peruvian community in Paterson to an enclave of Italian and Polish residents in Clifton.

The 8th's slice of Passaic County has given Democrats a solid base in recent years — especially Paterson, with its deep-seated labor tradition. Overall, the district is more than one-fourth Hispanic and 13 percent black. Barack Obama received 63 percent of the presidential vote in 2008.

Republicans fare slightly better in the district's Essex County portion, which is mostly suburban and includes wealthy Livingston (shared with the 11th) and the middle-class towns of Nutley and Belleville. Many residents here commute to Newark or New York.

MAJOR INDUSTRY
Pharmaceuticals, manufacturing, communications, education

CITIES
Paterson, 149,222; Clifton, 78,672; Passaic, 67,861; Wayne (unincorporated), 54,069; Bloomfield (unincorporated), 47,683

NOTABLE
Lifestyle guru Martha Stewart and Sen. Frank R. Lautenberg graduated from Nutley High School.

Rep. Steven R. Rothman (D)

Elected 1996; 7th term

An ambitious and keen politician, Rothman works to secure federal dollars for highway and mass transit projects in his densely populated district of commuter suburbs of New York City. He has snagged federal aid for rail service in the Northeast Corridor, highway improvements to ease congestion throughout the district, and downtown Newark revitalization projects.

Rothman cut his teeth on local Democratic politics, and he keeps a tight connection with local party officials as he watches for a chance to run for the Senate upon the retirement of Sen. Frank R. Lautenberg, now in his mid-80s. In January 2009 — reacting to some intraparty wrangling over Lautenberg's 2008 bid for a fifth term that portends a future battle for that seat — Rothman secured the endorsement of newly elected Bergen County Democratic Chairman Michael Kasparian.

He also keeps money flowing to his Democratic colleagues; he contributed $186,000 to other candidates in the 2008 election cycle. And he spent more than a year and a half fundraising for Barack Obama's presidential bid as the campaign's Northeast co-chairman.

But primarily he keeps money flowing to his district and the rest of New Jersey from his seat on the Appropriations Committee. As the 111th Congress (2009-10) got under way, Rothman worked to from his seat on Appropriatons to bring home some of the $787 billion that President Obama and Congress agreed to spend in an effort to stimulate the economy.

His haul included a $47.6 million project to upgrade two bridges on Route 46 in Lodi and improve drainage on flood-prone Main Street beneath the bridges. He also touted $10 million for energy efficiency projects and $13 million for housing projects in the district, among other plums. With a new seat on the Homeland Security Appropriations Subcommittee for the 111th Congress, Rothman hopes to secure more money to protect his district from terrorist threats. He also serves on the Defense and State-Foreign Operations subcommittees.

Rothman is a dependable vote for his party. In the 110th Congress (2007-08), he stuck with his party 98 percent of the time when the majority of Democrats and Republicans squared off on an issue. He sides with his party on abortion rights, environmental protection, gun control and health care. He does, however, make an occasional foray into Republican territory. A former Bergen County Surrogate Court judge, he sometimes votes with the GOP for tougher punishments for violent offenders, and he supports the death penalty.

Rothman did not support the $700 billion financial sector rescue package in late 2008. "I won't be steamrolled into spending hundreds of billions of dollars of taxpayer money on an approach that will not solve the economic problems we face," he said. But in January 2009, he supported a successful bill that allowed release of the second half of those funds, with some conditions.

Rothman believes one of his greatest legacies in the House is the Secure Our Schools Act, which he sponsored with GOP Rep. Henry J. Hyde of Illinois in 2000. He said the bill was a response to letters he received from middle school students who felt unsafe in their schools because of fellow students who brought weapons to school. "I'll never forget one young girl who said, 'Isn't this what you congressmen are supposed to do? Protect us kids?' " said Rothman. The law created a program to provide grants to schools for security devices such as cameras and metal detectors. In the 110th, the House passed a Rothman-sponsored bill to increase the amount of funding authorized and expand the list of uses for the grants. The mea-

CAPITOL OFFICE
225-5061
www.house.gov/rothman
2303 Rayburn Bldg. 20515; fax 225-5851

COMMITTEES
Appropriations
Science & Technology

RESIDENCE
Fair Lawn

BORN
Oct. 14, 1952; Englewood, N.J.

RELIGION
Jewish

FAMILY
Wife, Jennifer Rothman; five children

EDUCATION
Syracuse U., B.A. 1974 (political philosophy);
Washington U., J.D. 1977

CAREER
Lawyer

POLITICAL HIGHLIGHTS
Mayor of Englewood, 1983-89; Democratic nominee for Bergen County Board of Freeholders, 1989; Bergen County Surrogate Court judge, 1993-96

ELECTION RESULTS

2008 GENERAL
Steven R. Rothman (D)	151,182	67.5%
Vincent Micco (R)	69,503	31.0%
Michael Perrone Jr. (PRO)	3,200	1.4%

2008 PRIMARY
Steven R. Rothman (D)	unopposed

2006 GENERAL
Steven R. Rothman (D)	105,853	71.5%
Vincent Micco (R)	40,879	27.6%

PREVIOUS WINNING PERCENTAGES
2004 (68%); 2002 (70%); 2000 (68%); 1998 (65%); 1996 (56%)

sure stalled in the Senate, but Rothman vowed to continue to purse it.

Even though Rothman left the Transportation Appropriations panel in 2007, he continues to look out for New Jersey interests. He is the Washington point man for an intense local battle over noise and congestion at bustling Teterboro Airport, a general-aviation facility convenient to Manhattan. In 2006 Rothman brokered a deal to eliminate the loudest jets at the airport, impose a curfew on late-night flights, and keep heavy planes from operating there.

Since entering Congress, he also has fought to preserve the remaining 8,400 acres of undeveloped land in the Meadowlands, where a large sports complex is located. He also sits on the Science and Technology panel.

Rothman was born in Englewood. His grandparents came through Ellis Island as Jewish immigrants from Russia, Poland and Austria. His father was a tool-and-die maker until a moonlighting venture building houses with a friend evolved into an industrial real estate business.

After graduating from high school, Rothman landed a summer internship with a local state senator, Democrat Matthew Feldman. As mayor of Teaneck in the early 1960s, Feldman had led that city's racial integration of neighborhoods and public schools and was a strong supporter of the creation of the state of Israel. Feldman became Rothman's role model.

At Syracuse University, Rothman majored in political philosophy, then obtained a law degree from Washington University in St. Louis and fulfilled his dream of becoming a trial lawyer. He opened his practice in 1978 and got involved in local Democratic Party politics, where he stuffed envelopes, worked at phone banks and solicited votes door-to-door for local politicians. In 1983, he was elected Englewood mayor. "I was the candidate of the Black Clergy Council and the cops — it was the first time those groups had endorsed the same candidate for mayor," Rothman said. He later made an unsuccessful bid for Bergen County freeholder, or councilman, but won his next campaign, for the court judgeship, in 1993.

In 1996, he ran for the House when Robert G. Torricelli gave up his seat to run successfully for the Senate. Rothman took 80 percent of the primary vote and 56 percent in the general election. He has won re-election easily ever since, although after the 2008 election he did receive some criticism in the local press when a report indicated he had spent $59,000 of his campaign funds on a hybrid SUV and $150,000 for a party during the Democratic convention in Denver.

His personal life took a happy turn in 2005. As a divorced father of two, Rothman employed an online dating service for Jewish singles called JDate.com. He met and eventually married Jennifer Anne Beckenstein.

KEY VOTES

2008
Yes Delay consideration of Colombia free-trade agreement
Yes Override Bush veto of federal farm and nutrition programs reauthorization bill
No Overhaul surveillance laws and permit dismissal of suits against companies that conducted warrantless wiretapping
Yes Grant mortgage relief to homeowners and funding for Fannie Mae and Freddie Mac
No Approve initial $700 billion program to stabilize financial markets
No Approve final $700 billion program to stabilize financial markets
Yes Provide $14 billion in loans to automakers

2007
Yes Increase minimum wage by $2.10 an hour
Yes Approve $124.2 billion in emergency war spending and set goal for redeployment of troops from Iraq
No Reject federal contraceptive assistance to international family planning groups
Yes Override Bush veto of $23.2 billion water projects authorization bill
? Implement Peru free-trade agreement
Yes Approve energy policy overhaul with new fuel economy standards
No Clear $473.5 billion omnibus spending bill, including $70 billion for military operations

CQ VOTE STUDIES

	PARTY UNITY		PRESIDENTIAL SUPPORT	
	SUPPORT	OPPOSE	SUPPORT	OPPOSE
2008	98%	2%	14%	86%
2007	98%	2%	7%	93%
2006	98%	2%	9%	91%
2005	93%	7%	29%	71%
2004	94%	6%	31%	69%

INTEREST GROUPS

	AFL-CIO	ADA	CCUS	ACU
2008	100%	100%	56%	8%
2007	96%	95%	44%	0%
2006	100%	90%	27%	8%
2005	87%	95%	48%	5%
2004	93%	95%	30%	5%

NEW JERSEY 9
Northeast — Hackensack, part of Jersey City

Across the Hudson from northern Manhattan, the 9th is an overwhelmingly Democratic district that takes in southeast Bergen County before dipping into parts of Hudson County and suburbs adjacent to Newark. Prestigious areas lie in the north, including Englewood Cliffs and Fort Lee; the district becomes more blue-collar and middle-class as it runs south into Lyndhurst and parts of Jersey City.

The district is a mix of tightly packed neighborhoods in areas such as Leonia and Ridgefield and more-commercial parts such as Secaucus. As New York City apartment prices have climbed, many commuters have moved to the 9th's Hudson River towns, like Edgewater. In its northwestern sliver, the district's small section of Passaic County consists entirely of Hawthorne, an older bedroom community.

Anchored by East Rutherford's Meadowlands Sports Complex, the southern part of the 9th District has seen some new commercial and residential development. Football's Jets' and Giants' are expected to move into their new joint stadium at the complex by 2010, and light-rail

connections to the stadium site will link East Rutherford to Manhattan, Hoboken and Newark. But the collapse of financial markets and retail sectors have delayed the opening of the $2 billion shopping and entertainment portion of the Meadowlands Xanadu project. Hockey's Devils have moved south to Newark, and soccer's Red Bulls are preparing to move to Harrison.

The 9th District's part of Bergen is Democratic — Hackensack, Englewood and Teaneck all gave Barack Obama more than 70 percent of their vote in the 2008 presidential election. Hispanics around Jersey City (shared with the 10th and 13th districts) and sizable proportions of black, Jewish and Asian voters add to Democratic strength here. Overall Obama won 61 percent of the 9th's vote.

MAJOR INDUSTRY
Manufacturing, health care, shipping, stadium events

CITIES
Jersey City (pt.), 58,129; Hackensack, 42,677; Teaneck (unincorporated), 39,260; Kearny (pt.), 38,250; Fort Lee, 35,461; Fair Lawn, 31,637

NOTABLE
Teterboro Airport is home to the Aviation Hall of Fame and Museum of New Jersey.

Rep. Donald M. Payne (D)

Elected 1988; 11th term

CAPITOL OFFICE
225-3436
www.house.gov/payne
2310 Rayburn Bldg. 20515-3010; fax 225-4160

COMMITTEES
Education & Labor
Foreign Affairs
(Africa & Global Health - chairman)

RESIDENCE
Newark

BORN
July 16, 1934; Newark, N.J.

RELIGION
Baptist

FAMILY
Widowed; three children

EDUCATION
Seton Hall U., B.A. 1957 (social studies)

CAREER
Computer forms company executive;
company community affairs director; teacher

POLITICAL HIGHLIGHTS
Essex County Board of Freeholders, 1972-78;
sought Democratic nomination for Essex County
executive, 1978; sought Democratic nomination
for U.S. House, 1980; Newark Municipal Council,
1982-88; sought Democratic nomination for U.S.
House, 1986

ELECTION RESULTS

2008 GENERAL

Donald M. Payne (D)	169,945	98.9%
Michael Taber (SW)	1,848	1.1%

2008 PRIMARY

Donald M. Payne (D)	unopposed

2006 GENERAL

Donald M. Payne (D)	unopposed

PREVIOUS WINNING PERCENTAGES
2004 (97%); 2002 (84%); 2000 (88%); 1998 (84%);
1996 (84%); 1994 (76%); 1992 (78%); 1990 (81%);
1988 (77%)

Payne is a quiet operator on Capitol Hill, which belies the political power he traditionally enjoyed in Newark. One of the most liberal House members, he defends traditional Democratic priorities and presses his concern for human rights abroad and closer to home. He is best known for his commitment to the plight of Africa, but also advocates for the impoverished in the United States.

Payne first visited Africa more than 30 years ago, and since arriving in Congress in 1989, he has served on the Foreign Affairs Committee's Africa and Global Health panel, where he is now chairman. He still travels to the continent regularly, and African sculptures, masks and artifacts fill his office. The job is not without its perils; on an April 2009 trip to Somalia, insurgents fired mortar shells near Mogadishu's airport as his plane took off safely there.

Payne is a member of the board of Discovery Channel's Global Education Partnership, which provides television and educational videos to Nigeria, Angola, South Africa and Venezuela. "The people back in Newark aren't always aware of what I'm doing in foreign affairs," he told The Star-Ledger of Newark in March 2009. "That's all right. I don't make an issue out of it."

Payne has pushed each administration to provide more aid to Africa. His influence reached a high point in 1998 when he persuaded President Bill Clinton to travel there. Two years later, he helped facilitate negotiations that led to enactment of a law expanding trade with sub-Saharan Africa. Payne enjoyed less clout with George W. Bush's administration, though Bush did twice appoint Payne as a congressional delegate to the United Nations. However, Payne was pleased with Bush's efforts to boost funding for AIDS relief. "He went beyond what any other president has done," he said of Bush.

Payne is equally committed to holding Africa's worst human rights abusers accountable. He says Ethiopia's role as a key ally in the volatile Horn of Africa and in the fight against terrorism shouldn't excuse its disregard for human rights. "That doesn't help the tarnished image of the USA at all," he said.

In 2007, he gained House passage of a bill to condition U.S. military assistance to Ethiopia on the release of political prisoners, punishment of those involved in the killing of demonstrators and prisoners, and an independent judiciary. The White House could waive the restrictions, but it nevertheless opposed the bill, saying it would tie its hands and could disturb fragile negotiations for the release of prisoners.

Payne leads efforts to sanction the government of Sudan for the murder, rape and plunder of black Africans in Darfur, the country's western region. The atrocities have been attributed to mostly Arab militias backed by the government. He was a founder of the Sudan Caucus, and in 2001, Payne took an uncharacteristically public step to push his case: He chained himself to the gates of the Sudanese Embassy and was arrested. "Ending the suffering in Darfur is critical," he said in March 2009. "However, we cannot afford to ignore the south and other parts of Sudan." His concern for human rights has also led him to oppose a bilateral free-trade agreement with Colombia.

From his seat on the Education and Labor Committee, Payne fights to bring federal funds to low-income school districts. He says it is time to "stop the apartheid we see in education — one side is black or Hispanic and poor, the other side is affluent and predominately white." He is a member of the elementary and secondary education panel, which in 2009 is set to take up a rewrite of Bush's signature No Child Left Behind law that imposed new testing requirements on students to measure the effectiveness of schools. He was one of 10 Democrats who voted against the law in 2001.

He ardently supports reforming the health care system, touting steps in early 2009 to expand the State Children's Health Insurance Program, which covers children whose families do not qualify for Medicaid, and provide $20 billion in President Obama's economic stimulus for health information technology. "We want to see these moves continue," he said.

In fall 2008, Payne voted against a $700 billion package to shore up the nation's struggling financial system. He said he would have preferred direct assistance to homeowners facing foreclosure, an economic stimulus package and provisions to prevent a future financial crisis.

A member of the Congressional Black Caucus, Payne served a term as its chairman starting in 1995, just as the GOP took control of the House and cut off funding for such groups. He helped raise money privately to maintain caucus operations.

Born in Newark, Payne grew up poor during the Depression. His mother died when he was 7, and he went to live with his grandmother because his father worked long hours on the docks. He took his first job at age 9, delivering the Star-Ledger. He credits his rise in life to an organization called The Leaguers and its founders, Reynold and Mary Burch, both leaders of Newark's black community. Burch used her contacts with Seton Hall University to help Payne win a four-year scholarship.

Payne was a high school history teacher and football coach after college, and he ran a "storefront YMCA" in Newark in the late 1950s. He was the first black president of the National Council of YMCAs in 1970, served as chairman of the YMCA's International Committee on Refugees and is on the board of the Newark YMCA. In 1963, he became community affairs director for the Newark-based Prudential Insurance Co. and was vice president of a computer forms company founded by his brother. At the same time, the widowed Payne was raising his three children and building his political career. He served six years as an Essex County freeholder, akin to a county councilman, and another six on the Newark Municipal Council.

He made unsuccessful attempts in 1980 and 1986 to win the U.S. House seat in the black-majority 10th District. Blocking his path was Democrat Peter W. Rodino Jr., who had held the seat since 1949 and led the 1974 impeachment proceedings against President Nixon. When Rodino decided to retire in 1988, party officials got behind Payne. He easily defeated city council colleague Ralph T. Grant Jr. in the primary, and his November victory was a formality in the overwhelmingly Democratic district. He became the first black representative from New Jersey and has won easily ever since; he has not taken less than 75 percent of the vote in any general election.

KEY VOTES

2008
Yes   Delay consideration of Colombia free-trade agreement
Yes   Override Bush veto of federal farm and nutrition programs reauthorization bill
No   Overhaul surveillance laws and permit dismissal of suits against companies that conducted warrantless wiretapping
Yes   Grant mortgage relief to homeowners and funding for Fannie Mae and Freddie Mac
No   Approve initial $700 billion program to stabilize financial markets
No   Approve final $700 billion program to stabilize financial markets
Yes   Provide $14 billion in loans to automakers

2007
Yes   Increase minimum wage by $2.10 an hour
Yes   Approve $124.2 billion in emergency war spending and set goal for redeployment of troops from Iraq
No   Reject federal contraceptive assistance to international family planning groups
?   Override Bush veto of $23.2 billion water projects authorization bill
No   Implement Peru free-trade agreement
Yes   Approve energy policy overhaul with new fuel economy standards
No   Clear $473.5 billion omnibus spending bill, including $70 billion for military operations

CQ VOTE STUDIES

| | PARTY UNITY | | PRESIDENTIAL SUPPORT | |
	SUPPORT	OPPOSE	SUPPORT	OPPOSE
2008	99%	1%	13%	87%
2007	99%	1%	4%	96%
2006	99%	1%	5%	95%
2005	99%	1%	7%	93%
2004	99%	1%	9%	91%

INTEREST GROUPS

	AFL-CIO	ADA	CCUS	ACU
2008	100%	95%	47%	8%
2007	100%	100%	42%	0%
2006	100%	85%	14%	4%
2005	100%	85%	29%	0%
2004	100%	95%	5%	0%

NEW JERSEY 10
Northeast – parts of Newark and Jersey City

Covering a multiracial, urban region centered in Newark, the black-majority 10th provides a solid base for Democrats. Outside Newark (which is shared with the 13th), the district extends into Essex County's working-class suburbs of Irvington, East Orange and Orange. It also takes in portions of Jersey City (shared with the 9th and 13th districts) and Elizabeth (shared with the 13th).

The 10th's portion of Newark is made up of the largely black central, south and west wards of the city. Although deep poverty continues to be a problem in some spots, efforts to revitalize the area have had some success. The area is home to University Heights Science Park, a collaboration between three universities and start-up technology companies. The New Jersey Institute of Technology completed an $83.5 million plan to transform its generally commuter-based Newark campus into a residential location. A performing arts center has also helped.

Newark Liberty International Airport (some of which is in the 13th) is a transportation center for travelers to New York City, as well as a hub for

Continental Airlines, which is struggling through nationwide economic downturns. Newark Penn Station is the state's busiest transit location, with connections to Amtrak, PATH and New Jersey Transit rail and bus service. Port Newark-Elizabeth (partly in the 13th District) also provides jobs for the region.

The 10th District votes consistently Democratic at all levels, although Millburn, a wealthy enclave shared with the 11th District, and Rahway host some Republicans. Democrat Barack Obama posted his highest percentage in the state here in the 2008 presidential election, winning 87 percent of the district's vote.

MAJOR INDUSTRY
Aviation, shipping, insurance, higher education, pharmaceuticals

CITIES
Newark (pt.), 155,413; Elizabeth (pt.), 74,984; East Orange, 69,824; Jersey City (pt.), 63,725; Irvington (unincorporated), 60,695; Orange (unincorporated), 32,868; Linden (pt.), 30,356

NOTABLE
Economist Milton Friedman grew up in Rahway; The University of Medicine and Dentistry of New Jersey, headquartered in Newark, is the nation's largest public university of the health sciences.

Rep. Rodney Frelinghuysen (R)

Elected 1994; 8th term

CAPITOL OFFICE
225-5034
frelinghuysen.house.gov
2442 Rayburn Bldg. 20515-3011; fax 225-3186

COMMITTEES
Appropriations

RESIDENCE
Harding

BORN
April 29, 1946; Manhattan, N.Y.

RELIGION
Episcopalian

FAMILY
Wife, Virginia T. Frelinghuysen; two children

EDUCATION
Hobart College, B.A. 1969; Trinity College (Conn.),
attended 1971 (American history)

MILITARY SERVICE
Army, 1969-71

CAREER
County board aide

POLITICAL HIGHLIGHTS
Morris County Board of Freeholders, 1974-83
(director, 1980); sought Republican nomination for
U.S. House, 1982; N.J. Assembly, 1983-94; sought
Republican nomination for U.S. House, 1990

ELECTION RESULTS

2008 GENERAL

Rodney Frelinghuysen (R)	189,696	62.4%
Tom Wyka (D)	113,510	37.3%

2008 PRIMARY

Rodney Frelinghuysen (R)	24,304	86.7%
Kate Erber (R)	3,731	13.3%

2006 GENERAL

Rodney Frelinghuysen (R)	126,085	71.6%
Tom Wyka (D)	47,414	26.9%

PREVIOUS WINNING PERCENTAGES
2004 (68%); 2002 (72%); 2000 (68%); 1998 (68%);
1996 (66%); 1994 (71%)

Frelinghuysen is a low-key Republican who quietly takes care of his upscale, suburban district through his seat on the Appropriations Committee. While he splits with his party on social issues, he hews to conservative orthodoxy on tax cuts, the Iraq War and cracking down on illegal immigration.

Frelinghuysen (FREE-ling-high-zen) is the sixth member of his family to serve the state in Congress, a fact that is reflected throughout northern New Jersey. There's the Frelinghuysen Arboretum in Morris Township and the Frelinghuysen Middle School in Morristown, as well as Rutgers University's Frelinghuysen Hall. The first Frelinghuysen served in the Continental Congress; another was a senator and secretary of State; another was Henry Clay's vice presidential running mate on the losing Whig ticket in 1844. Frelinghuysen's father, Peter H. Frelinghuysen, served in the House for 22 years, until 1975.

The current Frelinghuysen has said he had been aware of his family's singular role, and his place in it, from age 6, when his father first ran for Congress. "A lot of what you do in life is the direct result of those who bring you up. It either drives you toward this life or drives you away," he said.

Frelinghuysen was elected as part of the 73-member Republican class of 1994, a group that inaugurated 12 years of GOP House control. But he was less of an angry outsider than were many of his classmates, a difference due to his family background and personal fortune. He is among the wealthiest members of Congress, with at least $22 million in assets in 2007, according to the Center for Responsive Politics.

He patiently accrued seniority on Appropriations in the years of GOP control, becoming a subcommittee chairman, or "cardinal," in 2003. But in 2005, his gavel was yanked when Majority Leader Tom DeLay pushed through an Appropriations Committee reorganization that cut the number of subcommittees from 13 to 10. As the most junior cardinal, Frelinghuysen lost out.

For the 111th Congress (2009-10), Frelinghuysen is the top-ranking Republican on the Energy-Water Appropriations Subcommittee. Although a moderate on environmental issues, he faced criticism in August 2008 when the group Environment New Jersey ranked the state's 13 House members based on 13 key votes. His rating was 54 percent, the second-lowest.

He also serves on the Defense Appropriations Subcommittee and said that during the 111th he hopes to ensure U.S. troops engaged in wars in Iraq and Afghanistan are adequately funded.

Frelinghuysen tends to side with his party on taxes; he supported the George W. Bush administration's 2001 and 2003 tax cuts and voted for ending the federal estate tax. He opposed the initial $700 billion proposal to shore up the financial services industry in fall 2008 but switched his vote to back the second one, in part, he said, because the revised version included a provision to prevent the alternative minimum tax from hitting millions more Americans. He also was one of 32 House Republicans voting for emergency loans to bail out the U.S. automakers, a proposal that died in the Senate.

As an appropriator, he takes his share of earmarks — funding set-asides for projects in members' districts. He ranks first among New Jersey's 13 House members in terms of securing earmarks, despite his minority status. He defends the practice, saying in a June 2008 interview that "legislators should have control of the budget, not the administration." His stance earned him the top spot among House Republicans in Citizens Against Government Waste's "2008 Congressional Pig Book."

One of New Jersey's leading newspapers, The Bergen Record, reported in June 2008 that the congressman had obtained earmarks for nine private companies and nine nonprofit groups. Seven of the companies and the heads of at least three of the nonprofits had contributed money to his campaigns.

His local focus extends beyond earmarks. He has fought the Federal Aviation Administration over its plans for redesigning airspace management over New Jersey and New York. When New York City Mayor Michael Bloomberg proposed charging drivers congestion-pricing fees, Frelinghuysen, looking out for his constituents who drive into the city, proposed a bill "to prohibit a state from imposing discriminatory commuter taxes on non-residents." Bloomberg's proposal died.

He has long worked to preserve scenic areas of his district. He pushed for expansion of the Morristown National Historic Park and the Great Swamp Wildlife Refuge, and he secured funds to clean up superfund sites, protect the state's coast and help protect against floods. He also has worked to preserve the Highland — mountainous and scenic watershed lands in northern New Jersey, New York, Pennsylvania and Connecticut. In 2004, he won enactment of a bill that authorized funds for land conservation partnerships in the four-state region. He also helped arrange for the federal purchase of lands in the Sterling Forest in 1996.

Frelinghuysen received a burst of attention in May 2007 when he was mugged in his Georgetown neighborhood and chased his perpetrators down the street, holding one of them until police arrived. Other New Jersey lawmakers weren't surprised. "No one takes advantage of him," said former GOP Gov. Christine Todd Whitman. Democratic Rep. Bill Pascrell Jr. said: "I want him on my side when I go into a fight."

Frelinghuysen entered politics after college and Army service in Vietnam. He went to work for Dean Gallo, a Republican Morris County freeholder who later was elected to the House. Frelinghuysen became a freeholder, akin to a county councilman, in 1974. He lost a Republican primary for the 12th District House seat in 1982 but won a state Assembly seat the next year. In 1990 he lost again in a race for the 12th District nomination, running third in the primary.

He eventually won his House seat in 1994, but the victory was bittersweet because he took the seat of his mentor and friend Gallo, who had become ill. Gallo designated Frelinghuysen, who was managing the re-election effort, as his successor. Frelinghuysen coasted to victory in what is now one of the handful of solidly Republican districts in New Jersey. He has been re-elected handily since, drawing 62 percent of the vote in 2008.

KEY VOTES

2008

No Delay consideration of Colombia free-trade agreement

No Override Bush veto of federal farm and nutrition programs reauthorization bill

Yes Overhaul surveillance laws and permit dismissal of suits against companies that conducted warrantless wiretapping

No Grant mortgage relief to homeowners and funding for Fannie Mae and Freddie Mac

No Approve initial $700 billion program to stabilize financial markets

Yes Approve final $700 billion program to stabilize financial markets

Yes Provide $14 billion in loans to automakers

2007

Yes Increase minimum wage by $2.10 an hour

No Approve $124.2 billion in emergency war spending and set goal for redeployment of troops from Iraq

No Reject federal contraceptive assistance to international family planning groups

Yes Override Bush veto of $23.2 billion water projects authorization bill

Yes Implement Peru free-trade agreement

Yes Approve energy policy overhaul with new fuel economy standards

Yes Clear $473.5 billion omnibus spending bill, including $70 billion for military operations

CQ VOTE STUDIES

	PARTY UNITY		PRESIDENTIAL SUPPORT	
	SUPPORT	OPPOSE	SUPPORT	OPPOSE
2008	87%	13%	73%	27%
2007	79%	21%	63%	37%
2006	87%	13%	83%	17%
2005	89%	11%	83%	17%
2004	88%	12%	79%	21%

INTEREST GROUPS

	AFL-CIO	ADA	CCUS	ACU
2008	13%	15%	100%	80%
2007	25%	30%	80%	56%
2006	29%	25%	80%	60%
2005	13%	15%	89%	60%
2004	20%	25%	100%	67%

NEW JERSEY 11

North central — Morris County

Exclusive, pastoral estates and Fortune 500 firms make the 11th one of the most privileged districts in the nation. Located in northern New Jersey and centered in Morris County, the district has the nation's second-highest median income.

Residents here live mainly in small to midsize bedroom communities connected by a number of interstate highways and state routes. The district has experienced some population growth as couples and families move here to get away from large cities, and suburban sprawl has become a major issue.

While the 11th is loaded with commuters making trips to New York, it also hosts its own large, white-collar firms. The corporate presence in the district includes giants like Nabisco (Kraft Foods) in East Hanover and Honeywell's headquarters in Morristown, but widespread economic downturns have hurt business. Uncertainty in the pharmaceutical sector may lead to restructuring and layoffs at Morris Plains-based Pfizer and Madison's Wyeth. Novartis, in East Hanover, has also cut jobs. Although

relatively low, the unemployment rate in Morris County is rising as layoffs continue across all economic sectors.

Morris County officials also hope to lure tourists to historic parks, dwellings and other sites. In addition to all of Morris, the 11th takes in chunks of Essex County in the east, Somerset County in the south, Sussex County in the northwest and a sliver of Passaic County in the northeast.

The area's voters have been economically conservative for some time, and the 11th is one of the most solidly Republican districts in the northeast. John McCain captured 54 percent of the vote here in the 2008 presidential election, his highest percentage in New Jersey.

MAJOR INDUSTRY
Pharmaceuticals, finance, telecommunications, manufacturing

MILITARY BASES
Picatinny Arsenal (Army), 65 military, 2,792 civilian (2009)

CITIES
Morristown, 18,544; Dover, 18,188; Madison, 16,530

NOTABLE
Morris County was considered the "Military Capital of the American Revolution" because of its repeated use by Gen. George Washington.

Rep. Rush D. Holt (D)

Elected 1998; 6th term

CAPITOL OFFICE
225-5801
holt.house.gov
1214 Longworth Bldg. 20515-3012; fax 225-6025

COMMITTEES
Appropriations Select Intelligence Oversight Panel
 - chairman
Education & Labor
Natural Resources
Select Intelligence

RESIDENCE
Hopewell

BORN
Oct. 15, 1948; Weston, W.Va.

RELIGION
Quaker

FAMILY
Wife, Margaret Lancefield; three children

EDUCATION
Carleton College, B.A. 1970 (physics);
New York U., M.S. 1980 (physics), Ph.D. 1981
(physics)

CAREER
University research assistant director;
physics professor

POLITICAL HIGHLIGHTS
Sought Democratic nomination for U.S. House,
1996

ELECTION RESULTS

2008 GENERAL

Rush D. Holt (D)	193,732	63.1%
Alan R. Bateman (R)	108,400	35.3%
David Corsi (CS)	4,802	1.6%

2008 PRIMARY

Rush D. Holt (D)	unopposed

2006 GENERAL

Rush D. Holt (D)	125,468	65.7%
Joseph S. Sinagra (R)	65,509	34.3%

PREVIOUS WINNING PERCENTAGES
2004 (59%); 2002 (61%); 2000 (49%); 1998 (50%)

A former research physicist and "Jeopardy" champion, Holt has the thoughtful, intellectual demeanor of a college professor. He is a loyal Democrat, yet shuns polarizing rhetoric, preferring to focus on the specific details of the topic at hand.

Holt has been given the chance to apply his brainpower to a variety of issues. He sits on four committees, including an Appropriations subcommittee charged with overseeing spending on intelligence programs, which dovetails with his work on the Select Intelligence Committee. The subcommittee, which he chairs, was established at the start of the 110th Congress (2007-08) in response to a recommendation from the independent commission that investigated the Sept. 11 attacks.

Holt said the panel has made a difference in scrutinizing spy agencies' budgets and that it has not met resistance from either Intelligence Committee members or appropriators. He pledged several hearings during the 111th Congress (2009-10) following the release of a report that indicated the Office of the Director of National Intelligence needs to better manage problems such as reducing intelligence agency turf battles and establishing rules for protecting the privacy of U.S. citizens.

Holt also wants to boost the foreign language skills at the CIA and other agencies. He has pushed proposals to increase funds for universities to establish programs in critical languages such as Arabic, Farsi and Pashto and to provide scholarships to language students in exchange for federal service.

"The problem is not only in the area of national defense," he wrote in a September 2008 blog opinion posting. "Our companies lose international contracts to competitors, our scientists miss important collaborations, international assistance organizations fail to understand local customs critical to advancing America's interests and average Americans are deprived of a cultural enrichment in their lives."

He introduced a bill in early 2009 to create a commission to investigate the 2001 anthrax attacks and the federal government's response. One of the anthrax-laden letters was mailed from his district.

On the Education and Labor Committee, Holt promotes math and science education. A measure to reauthorize a higher education program, enacted in 2008, included several of Holt's proposals, including a program providing grants and loan forgiveness to math and science students committing to serve in a related field after graduation. In early 2009, he helped boost funding — to $22 billion — for research and other scientific activities in President Obama's $787 billion economic stimulus law.

Holt has applied his interest in education to his work on the Natural Resources Committee. A House-passed bill in 2008 included a proposal by Holt and Republican Mark Souder of Indiana to encourage schools to take advantage of federal lands as a tool for teaching children about the environment. He also has worked to replenish the Land and Water Conservation Fund.

At home, Holt has been at the forefront of trying to slow suburban sprawl. He noted his district is among the few left in New Jersey with some open space.

Another of his priorities is election reform. He has pressed for legislation to overhaul the electronic voting machines introduced in many states after the 2000 presidential election uncovered voting irregularities in Florida.

Holt's voting record during President George W. Bush's two terms showed loyalty to the Democratic Party. And he applauded Obama's early initiatives, including expanding a state-federal children's health insurance program and an executive order lifting a ban on federal funding for embryonic stem cell research.

Holt, who hands out bumper stickers proclaiming, "My congressman IS a rocket scientist!" said he developed his interest in science at an early age from his mother, who earned a master's degree in zoology and taught science at a junior college. He also learned politics at home. His mother was a West Virginia state legislator and secretary of state. His father, Rush Dew Holt, was elected to the U.S. Senate from West Virginia at age 29. He had to wait six months to take office because under the Constitution senators must be at least 30 years old. Holt's father died when Holt was in first grade, and he and his mother later moved to Washington, D.C., where he went to high school and she worked for the Department of Housing and Urban Development.

Holt earned a Ph.D. in physics after completing a doctoral dissertation about the outer layer of the sun. He holds a patent for improving the efficiency of solar ponds, a source of thermal energy.

After school, he worked at the State Department on arms control and space activities, then became assistant director of Princeton's Plasma Physics Laboratory. While living in Princeton, N.J., he became interested in running for office. He told The Star-Ledger of Newark that his motivation was a distaste for the "shortsightedness and mean-spiritedness" of the GOP-led Congress.

He ran for a U.S. House seat in 1996, losing in the Democratic primary to David N. Del Vecchio, who in turn lost a close race to Republican Michael Pappas. Two years later, Holt portrayed socially conservative Pappas as too far to the right for the district and won.

His 5,000-vote victory made Holt one of the GOP's most-targeted incumbents in 2000. His campaign against moderate Republican Dick Zimmer, who had held the House seat for three terms ending in 1996, was bitter, and the outcome was in doubt for three weeks after Election Day. Holt was eventually declared the victor by 651 votes.

The GOP kept the 12th District on its target list for 2002 and offered up a formidable candidate, DeForest "Buster" Soaries, an African-American Baptist minister who had served as New Jersey's secretary of state. Holt took 61 percent of the vote, and has won easily since. He has expressed interest in running for the Senate one day. "You can accomplish more in that position, and I truly believe I would be the strongest candidate for statewide office," he told a Star-Ledger columnist in March 2009.

Holt is a five-time winner on the TV quiz show "Jeopardy" and is amused by the attention that it brings. Given the reaction he gets from journalists covering his campaigns, he once said, "It must be the most significant thing I've done."

KEY VOTES

2008

Yes Delay consideration of Colombia free-trade agreement

Yes Override Bush veto of federal farm and nutrition programs reauthorization bill

No Overhaul surveillance laws and permit dismissal of suits against companies that conducted warrantless wiretapping

Yes Grant mortgage relief to homeowners and funding for Fannie Mae and Freddie Mac

Yes Approve initial $700 billion program to stabilize financial markets

Yes Approve final $700 billion program to stabilize financial markets

Yes Provide $14 billion in loans to automakers

2007

Yes Increase minimum wage by $2.10 an hour

Yes Approve $124.2 billion in emergency war spending and set goal for redeployment of troops from Iraq

No Reject federal contraceptive assistance to international family planning groups

Yes Override Bush veto of $23.2 billion water projects authorization bill

No Implement Peru free-trade agreement

Yes Approve energy policy overhaul with new fuel economy standards

No Clear $473.5 billion omnibus spending bill, including $70 billion for military operations

CQ VOTE STUDIES

	PARTY UNITY		PRESIDENTIAL SUPPORT	
	SUPPORT	OPPOSE	SUPPORT	OPPOSE
2008	98%	2%	15%	85%
2007	98%	2%	6%	94%
2006	97%	3%	15%	85%
2005	97%	3%	11%	89%
2004	98%	2%	26%	74%

INTEREST GROUPS

	AFL-CIO	ADA	CCUS	ACU
2008	100%	100%	61%	0%
2007	96%	90%	50%	0%
2006	100%	95%	20%	5%
2005	93%	100%	33%	0%
2004	93%	95%	19%	4%

NEW JERSEY 12

Central — part of Trenton, East Brunswick, Princeton

Set in the middle of the state, the 12th begins in Hunterdon County, slides south to hit ethnically diverse Trenton (shared with the 4th) and then picks up East Brunswick as it winds east to Monmouth County. It ends just short of the Atlantic Ocean in shore communities such as Rumson.

Despite its jagged shape, many of the district's towns are similar. Office parks dominate the landscape in these affluent and white communities. But there are pockets of blue-collar diversity, such as in the state capital, Trenton, with its black-majority population. Plainsboro in Middlesex County is among the areas with large Asian populations.

The 12th benefited from economic growth, although midsize communities such as Ewing in Mercer County contend with the side effects of suburban sprawl. In addition to the Capitol, the district also boasts the governor's official residence, the stately and imposing Drumthwacket in Princeton. Delaware River towns, such as Frenchtown and Lambertville in Hunterdon County, offer quaint antiques shops and bed-and-breakfasts. The 2005 BRAC round dealt the 12th a blow, as Fort Monmouth made the closure list and must be shut down by late 2011.

A solidly Democratic constituency in Mercer County is anchored by Princeton's academics, and an influx of independents and the northeast's rising Democratic wave in national elections have shifted the district's politics away from its historical old money and suburban-based GOP lean. Republican John McCain carried the 12th's portion of Monmouth County and eked out a plurality in its part of Hunterdon in the 2008 presidential race, but Barack Obama took 58 percent of the 12th District's vote overall.

MAJOR INDUSTRY
Higher education, military, pharmaceuticals

MILITARY BASES
Fort Monmouth (Army), 467 military, 5,088 civilian (2007)

CITIES
Trenton (pt.), 47,658; East Brunswick (unincorporated), 46,756; North Brunswick (unincorporated), 36,287; Ewing (unincorporated), 35,707

NOTABLE
The New Jersey Vietnam Veterans' Memorial is on the grounds of the PNC Bank Arts Center, a 17,500-seat concert venue in Holmdel.

Rep. Albio Sires (D)

Elected 2006; 2nd full term

Sires is an easy figure to spot on Capitol Hill: He is a burly 6-foot-4-inch Cuban-American who gives interviews in Spanish to Hispanic reporters. He uses his presence to press two issues of importance to him — maintaining a hard line against Cuba's Castro regime and seeking funds for his district's transportation projects and low-income residents.

Sires (SEAR-eez — like "series") works on both tasks from his seats on the Foreign Affairs and Transportation and Infrastructure committees. "I am in a good position for New Jersey and my district," he told The Star-Ledger of Newark in February 2009.

A loyal Democrat, he supported his party on 98 percent of the votes on which Republicans and Democrats diverged in the 110th Congress (2007-08). Party leaders in early 2009 named him one of three vice chairs for the Democratic Congressional Campaign Committee for the 2010 election cycle; as leader of member participation and outreach, he coordinates activities for Democratic incumbents representing GOP-leaning districts and Democrats challenging Republican incumbents in Democrat-tilting areas.

However, Sires has shown a knack for connecting with people across political divides. In his first year in the House, he teamed up with Republican Judy Biggert of Illinois to sponsor legislation that would crack down on companies that fraudulently represent their ties to the Federal Deposit Insurance Corporation. The House passed their bill in July 2007, though it stalled in the Senate.

Another of his first moves as a freshman was to forge an alliance with Cuban-born Republican Lincoln Diaz-Balart and his brother, Republican Mario Diaz-Balart, who like Sires are both fervent critics of Fidel Castro and his brother Raúl. In August 2007, Sires and the Diaz-Balarts, of Florida, traveled to the Czech Republic, Hungary and Poland to meet with former dissidents to discuss democratization for Cuba.

Since then, Sires has joined his New Jersey Democratic colleague, Sen. Robert Menendez, who also is of Cuban heritage, in fighting colleagues' attempts to loosen travel and trade restrictions to the island nation. They say it remains a human-rights violator whose jails hold multitudes of political prisoners. "We need to get some concessions from these people," Sires said in April 2009, referring to the Castros. "We do from every other country, so why not Cuba?"

On the Transportation panel, Sires worked to include more than $56 million for his district's local projects in the fiscal 2009 catchall spending bill, including initiatives to ease traffic by building a new rail tunnel under the Hudson River from New Jersey to New York's Penn Station. He also wants to use a multi-year surface transportation bill in the 111th Congress (2009-10) to increase light-rail service linking cities of the Hudson River waterfront.

Sires has been a political player in New Jersey's Hudson County for nearly three decades, with a reputation as a favorite son of the Cuban community in West New York. He was born in Bejucal, Cuba, not long before Castro's Communist regime seized power. "I remember when the government came in and took all of the history books out of the town and replaced them with the Russian version of history," he said. When Sires and his schoolmates weren't marching in formation, they were being taught how to handle a Czechoslovakian machine gun.

In January 1962, Sires and his family fled Cuba and settled in the predominately Italian town of West New York. Sires' father worked in a foam

CAPITOL OFFICE
225-7919
www.house.gov/sires
1024 Longworth Bldg. 20515-3013; fax 226-0792

COMMITTEES
Foreign Affairs
Transportation & Infrastructure

RESIDENCE
West New York

BORN
Jan. 26, 1951; Bejucal, Cuba

RELIGION
Roman Catholic

FAMILY
Wife, Adrienne Sires; one stepchild

EDUCATION
Saint Peter's College, B.A. 1974 (Spanish & marketing); Middlebury College, M.A. 1985 (Spanish)

CAREER
Property title insurance firm owner; state community affairs agency aide; teacher

POLITICAL HIGHLIGHTS
Candidate for West New York Town Commission, 1983; Republican nominee for U.S. House, 1986; Republican nominee for Hudson County Board of Chosen Freeholders, 1987; candidate for West New York Town Commission, 1991; candidate for West New York Town Commission (recall election), 1993; West New York Town Commission, 1995-2006 (mayor, 1995-2006); N.J. Assembly, 2000-2006 (Speaker, 2002-06)

ELECTION RESULTS

2008 GENERAL

Albio Sires (D)	120,382	75.4%
Joseph Turula (R)	34,735	21.7%
Julio V. Fernandez (X)	3,661	2.3%

2008 PRIMARY

Albio Sires (D)	unopposed

2006 GENERAL

Albio Sires (D)	77,238	77.5%
John J. Guarini (R)	19,284	19.4%
Brian Williams (SW)	1,049	1.0%
Herbert H. Shaw (PAC)	998	1.0%

PREVIOUS WINNING PERCENTAGES
2006 (97%)

rubber factory making $1.39 an hour, and his mother was a seamstress. Little by little, the family saved enough money to move out of his aunt's house and into a $45-a-month cold-water flat.

Just 11 years old, Sires struggled to learn English and was left back following his first year in his new school. In time, playing basketball helped him make friends. As an All-State point guard for West New York's Memorial High School, he became a local celebrity and earned a scholarship to Saint Peter's College. After graduating from there, he decided to return to his high school to teach Spanish and coach basketball. By then, West New York had seen a dramatic influx of Cuban refugees.

Ethnic differences boiled over into the local politics, which were controlled in the 1980s by a Democratic political machine headed by Anthony DeFino, West New York's longtime mayor. DeFino worked to crush Sires' bid for the city commission. Having been locked out of a future in the local Democratic party, Sires switched his affiliation to Republican.

In 1986, he ran as the GOP candidate for the House seat held by longtime incumbent and Hudson County Democrat Frank J. Guarini. Sires lost badly, getting less than 30 percent of the vote. (Once in office, though, Sires had a post office in Jersey City named in honor of Guarini, with whom he'd developed a friendship.)

No longer teaching and once again on the losing end of a campaign, Sires spent a year coordinating outreach to the Hispanic community for Republican Gov. Thomas H. Kean. Although Sires ultimately left the Republican Party, he still considers Kean an important mentor.

Sires started his own title insurance business and lost two bids for local office as an independent. When DeFino opted not to run for re-election in 1995, Sires jumped into the race and won. In 1999, he was overwhelmingly re-elected and rejoined the Democratic Party to run for the New Jersey Assembly.

He was just two years into his career in the legislature when Governor-elect James E. McGreevey backed Sires to serve as Speaker, the third-highest position in New Jersey government. He spent almost four years as Speaker, then turned his attention to the U.S. House seat being vacated by Menendez, who was tapped by newly elected Gov. Jon Corzine in 2006 to fill his Senate seat.

Benefiting from his Hudson County ties, Sires posted a landslide victory in the 2006 Democratic primary against state Rep. Joseph Vas. That win in the Democratic stronghold sewed up his election in November against Republican John J. Guarini, a second cousin to Frank J. Guarini. Sires breezed to re-election in 2008.

KEY VOTES

2008

?   Delay consideration of Colombia free-trade agreement

Yes Override Bush veto of federal farm and nutrition programs reauthorization bill

Yes Overhaul surveillance laws and permit dismissal of suits against companies that conducted warrantless wiretapping

Yes Grant mortgage relief to homeowners and funding for Fannie Mae and Freddie Mac

Yes Approve initial $700 billion program to stabilize financial markets

Yes Approve final $700 billion program to stabilize financial markets

Yes Provide $14 billion in loans to automakers

2007

Yes Increase minimum wage by $2.10 an hour

Yes Approve $124.2 billion in emergency war spending and set goal for redeployment of troops from Iraq

No   Reject federal contraceptive assistance to international family planning groups

Yes Override Bush veto of $23.2 billion water projects authorization bill

Yes Implement Peru free-trade agreement

Yes Approve energy policy overhaul with new fuel economy standards

No   Clear $473.5 billion omnibus spending bill, including $70 billion for military operations

CQ VOTE STUDIES

	PARTY UNITY		PRESIDENTIAL SUPPORT	
	SUPPORT	OPPOSE	SUPPORT	OPPOSE
2008	99%	1%	16%	84%
2007	97%	3%	7%	93%
2006	100%	0%	40%	60%

INTEREST GROUPS

	AFL-CIO	ADA	CCUS	ACU
2008	100%	90%	71%	0%
2007	96%	95%	55%	0%
2006	0%	10%	0%	%

NEW JERSEY 13

Northeast — parts of Jersey City and Newark

Within sight of the Statue of Liberty and Manhattan's skyscrapers, the 13th District covers a long, thin swath from part of North Bergen to Perth Amboy along the Hudson River, Newark Bay and Arthur Kill. The 13th takes in parts of Jersey City and Newark, linking together Hispanic areas to create a Hispanic plurality (48 percent).

A transportation hub, the 13th includes parts of Port Newark-Elizabeth and Newark Liberty International Airport, both of which are shared with the 10th. Several lines carry commuters across the district, and PATH trains, ferries and tunnels bring passengers to and from New York. There is a sizable manufacturing sector in areas such as Kearny (shared with 9th) and Carteret.

Young professionals and financial companies moved across the river from Manhattan to Hoboken as industrial sites were converted into condominiums and office space. Although Hoboken's retail sector is stable and new restaurants are popping up, municipal budget shortfalls worry local officials and residents. A waterfront redevelopment initiative in Hoboken continues to transform former shipping piers into parks. Hoboken is also home to Stevens Institute of Technology.

Officials spent decades turning long-suffering Jersey City, which is shared with the 9th and 10th districts, into "Wall Street West," but the worldwide financial market meltdowns have caused uncertainty in the district's insurance and banking industries. Northwest of Jersey City, soccer's Red Bulls hope to move into a new 25,000-seat stadium in Harrison by 2010, part of a billion-dollar mixed-use redevelopment plan.

Portuguese, Indian, Irish and Puerto Rican communities add to the district's diversity and its overwhelming Democratic vote. A Middle Eastern community is growing, and much of the Cuban population is based in West New York and Union City. Barack Obama won 75 percent of the 13th's 2008 presidential vote.

MAJOR INDUSTRY
Transportation, health care, retail, finance

CITIES
Jersey City (pt.), 118,201; Newark (pt.), 118,133; Union City, 67,088

NOTABLE
Frank Sinatra was born in Hoboken.

Gov. Bill Richardson (D)

First elected: 2002
Length of term: 4 years
Term expires: 1/11
Salary: $110,000
Phone: (505) 476-2200

Residence: Santa Fe
Born: Nov. 15, 1947; Pasadena, Calif.
Religion: Roman Catholic
Family: Wife, Barbara Richardson
Education: Tufts U., B.A. 1970 (political science & French), M.A. 1971 (international relations)
Career: International trade consultant; state party official; congressional aide
Political highlights: Democratic nominee for U.S. House, 1980; U.S. House, 1983-97; United Nations ambassador, 1997-98; Energy secretary, 1998-2001

Election results:
2006 GENERAL

Bill Richardson (D)	384,806	68.8%
John Dendahl (R)	174,364	31.2%

Lt. Gov. Diane Denish (D)

First elected: 2002
Length of term: 4 years
Term expires: 1/11
Salary: $85,000
Phone: (505) 476-2250

LEGISLATURE

Legislature: 60 days January-March in odd-numbered years; 30 days January-February in even-numbered years

Senate: 42 members, 4-year terms
2009 ratios: 27 D, 15 R; 31 men, 11 women
Salary: $144/day per diem
Phone: (505) 986-4714

House: 70 members, 2-year terms
2009 ratios: 45 D, 25 R; 47 men, 23 women
Salary: $144/day per diem
Phone: (505) 986-4751

TERM LIMITS

Governor: 2 consecutive terms
Senate: No
House: No

URBAN STATISTICS

CITY	POPULATION
Albuquerque	448,607
Las Cruces	74,267
Santa Fe	62,203
Rio Rancho	51,765
Roswell	45,293

REGISTERED VOTERS

Democrat	51%
Republican	31%
Unaffiliated/others	18%

POPULATION

2008 population (est.)	1,984,356
2000 population	1,819,046
1990 population	1,515,069
Percent change (1990-2000)	+20.1%
Rank among states (2008)	36

Median age	34.6
Born in state	51.5%
Foreign born	8.2%
Violent crime rate	758/100,000
Poverty level	18.4%
Federal workers	28,772
Military	17,163

ELECTIONS

STATE ELECTION OFFICIAL
(505) 827-3600
DEMOCRATIC PARTY
(505) 830-3650
REPUBLICAN PARTY
(505) 298-3662

MISCELLANEOUS

Web: www.newmexico.gov
Capital: Santa Fe

U.S. CONGRESS

Senate: 2 Democrats
House: 3 Democrats

2000 Census Statistics by District

DIST.	2008 VOTE FOR PRESIDENT OBAMA	MCCAIN	WHITE	BLACK	ASIAN	HISP	MEDIAN INCOME	WHITE COLLAR	BLUE COLLAR	SERVICE INDUSTRY	OVER 64	UNDER 18	COLLEGE EDUCATION	RURAL	SQ. MILES
1	60%	39%	49%	2%	2%	43%	$38,413	65%	19%	16%	11%	26%	30%	9%	4,717
2	49	50	44	2	1	47	$29,269	53	29	18	13	29	17	29	69,493
3	61	38	41	1	1	36	$35,058	60	23	17	11	29	24	37	47,146
STATE	57	42	45	2	1	42	$34,133	60	23	17	12	28	24	25	121,356
U.S.	53	46	69	12	4	13	$41,994	60	25	15	12	26	24	21	3,537,438

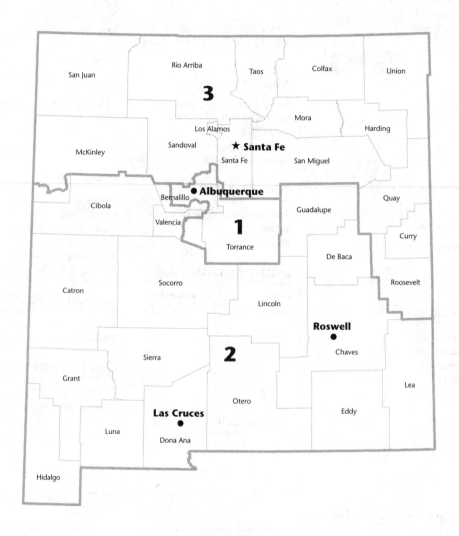

Sen. Jeff Bingaman (D)

Elected 1982; 5th term

CAPITOL OFFICE
224-5521
bingaman.senate.gov
703 Hart Bldg. 20510-3102; fax 224-2852

COMMITTEES
Energy & Natural Resources - chairman
Finance
(Energy, Natural Resources & Infrastructure -
chairman)
Health, Education, Labor & Pensions
Joint Economic

RESIDENCE
Santa Fe

BORN
Oct. 3, 1943; El Paso, Texas

RELIGION
Methodist

FAMILY
Wife, Anne Bingaman; one child

EDUCATION
Harvard U., A.B. 1965 (government);
Stanford U., J.D. 1968

MILITARY SERVICE
Army Reserve, 1968-74

CAREER
Lawyer

POLITICAL HIGHLIGHTS
N.M. attorney general, 1979-83

ELECTION RESULTS

2006 GENERAL
Jeff Bingaman (D)	394,365	70.6%
Allen W. McCulloch (R)	163,826	29.3%

2006 PRIMARY
Jeff Bingaman (D)	unopposed

PREVIOUS WINNING PERCENTAGES
2000 (62%); 1994 (54%); 1988 (63%); 1982 (54%)

The laconic Bingaman rarely makes headlines, but his work behind the scenes as Energy and Natural Resources Committee chairman has made him one of the Senate's most respected Democrats. He deploys his legislative acumen and ability to cooperate with Republicans on a variety of initiatives he doggedly pursues.

Bingaman puts the intricacies of policy above the fervor of politics. He often defers to others — including, for many years, his more publicity-minded New Mexico colleague, Pete V. Domenici — when it comes to taking credit for legislative accomplishments, avoids the talk-show circuit and seldom holds news conferences. His mastery of unglamorous topics such as technology sharing between government and industry has furthered his obscurity. "Some of the things I've worked on may be a little too down in the weeds to interest a lot of folks," he said.

But with energy policy on the Obama administration's front burner, Bingaman's work stirs plenty of interest. He is a centrist on energy; he backs more domestic oil drilling and increased conservation. He favors more widespread use of wind, solar and other renewable sources, but supports some expansion of nuclear power, an idea many environmentalists abhor.

In the waning days of the 110th Congress (2007-08), he began soliciting colleagues for ideas on a bill tackling six challenges: making wider use of technology through renewable energy; improving energy efficiency; producing more oil and gas; increasing innovation; improving oversight of energy markets to prevent huge gasoline price spikes; and protecting the environment. He began moving legislation in spring 2009, putting the most popular measures first — a strategy intended to give Bingaman and top-ranking Energy Committee Republican Lisa Murkowski of Alaska time to agree on two controversial ideas: creating a mandate for renewable-electricity generation and authorizing the federal government to site thousands of miles of new transmission lines to move the renewable power.

The mandate has long been among Bingaman's top priorities. President Obama backs the idea, but it has drawn opposition from Southern lawmakers who argue their states lack enough wind power to make it economically feasible. Bingaman championed it as part of a comprehensive 2007 energy bill, but Senate leaders jettisoned it along with a package of tax incentives for alternative energy to win passage of the bill and avoid a presidential veto.

His close relationship with Domenici helped shape that bill, which set the first statutory increase in vehicle fuel efficiency standards in 32 years and mandated wider use of ethanol and other biofuels by 2022. Two years earlier, the two worked together in steering a separate energy bill to enactment.

Bingaman also wants a hand in combating global warming in the 111th Congress (2009-10). He said previous bills — including one he introduced in 2007 with Pennsylvania's Arlen Specter — have tried to accomplish too much apart from their original goal of limiting greenhouse gases. "The resulting excessive complexity may have hurt the cause of climate legislation more than it has helped," he said.

Bingaman's legislation was seen as more industry-friendly than the global warming measure Environment and Public Works Chairwoman Barbara Boxer of California moved to the floor without success in 2008. While both bills would have capped carbon emissions and allowed polluters to trade emissions allowances, his plan included a "safety valve" if the price of the allowances rose too high.

In an effort to ensure passage of legislation, Bingaman often writes amendments designed to win broad bipartisan support. During the contentious 2007 debate on immigration, he secured 74 votes on a successful amendment to reduce the number of work visas allowed under President George W. Bush's proposed guest worker program from at least 400,000 a year to 200,000. He contended the program was untested.

Bingaman usually votes with Democrats, but carefully picks his spots to break ranks. He was one of just 12 Democrats to oppose a U.S.-India nuclear agreement in October 2008, saying India's failure to sign the Nuclear Non-Proliferation Treaty alarmed him.

From his seat on the Health, Education, Labor and Pensions Committee, Bingaman has introduced legislation aimed at reducing obesity among children and adolescents. And with Democrat Edward M. Kennedy of Massachusetts and Republican Richard M. Burr of North Carolina, he sponsored a measure in 2007 aimed at reforming "dropout factories," schools where high percentages of students never graduate.

He also is interested in improving dental care for children and finding ways to avoid bringing in doctors and other health care providers from developing countries. "I don't think it's good policy to be taking the best and brightest that India or the Philippines can produce and leaving [the countries] high and dry," he said. He also wants to shorten the waiting period that people who are deemed too sick to work face before they can qualify for Medicare.

As a member of the powerful Finance Committee, Bingaman supported some Bush administration free-trade agreements that other Democrats assailed on grounds they lacked adequate labor and environmental protections. He was one of just 10 Democrats to support the 2005 Central America Free Trade Agreement, and voted for a free-trade pact with Peru in 2007.

Bingaman has taken on a variety of unheralded assignments in the Senate. In the late 1990s he served on task forces studying Social Security and the settlement between tobacco companies and the states. At the request of Democratic leader Harry Reid of Nevada, Bingaman helped lead a 2005 effort to ensure that all the top-ranking Democrats on committees worked together smoothly. And he sits on the Democratic Steering and Outreach Committee, which helps make committee assignments.

Bingaman grew up in the mining town of Silver City. His father was a science professor at Western New Mexico University and his mother taught elementary school. As a boy, he had a paper route and was active in the Boy Scouts, earning the rank of Eagle Scout. His uncle John Bingaman was a confidant of the state's 24-year Democratic senator, Clinton Anderson.

While at Stanford Law School, Bingaman worked for Democratic Sen. Robert F. Kennedy's 1968 presidential campaign. He also met and later married a fellow law student, Anne Kovacovich. Returning to New Mexico, he served as counsel to the 1969 state constitutional convention, joined a politically connected law firm and was elected attorney general in 1978. (Bingaman's wife served as assistant attorney general for antitrust law in the Clinton administration.)

When Bingaman ran for the Senate in 1982, he was little-known outside the political and legal communities, but also was politically unscarred. He won 54 percent of the vote to topple incumbent GOP Sen. Harrison H. Schmitt, a former Apollo astronaut.

Only one re-election race since has featured a serious challenger — Colin McMillan, a former Pentagon official who used much of his own money in 1994 to criticize Bingaman for his stance on fees for grazing on public lands and his support for President Clinton's budget policy. But Bingaman prevailed with 54 percent of the vote. In 2006, he coasted with 71 percent.

KEY VOTES

2008

Yes	Prohibit discrimination based on genetic information
Yes	Reauthorize farm and nutrition programs for five years
Yes	Limit debate on "cap and trade" system for greenhouse gas emissions
Yes	Allow lawsuits against companies that participated in warrantless wiretapping
Yes	Limit debate on a bill to block a scheduled cut in Medicare payments to doctors
Yes	Grant mortgage relief to homeowners and funding for Fannie Mae and Freddie Mac
No	Approve a nuclear cooperation agreement with India
Yes	Approve final $700 billion program to stabilize financial markets
Yes	Allow consideration of a $14 billion auto industry loan package

2007

Yes	Increase minimum wage by $2.10 an hour
No	Limit debate on a comprehensive immigration bill
Yes	Overhaul congressional lobbying and ethics rules for members and their staffs
Yes	Limit debate on considering a bill to add House seats for the District of Columbia and Utah
Yes	Limit debate on restoring habeas corpus rights to detainees
Yes	Mandate minimum breaks for troops between deployments to Iraq or Afghanistan
Yes	Override Bush veto of $23.2 billion water projects authorization bill
No	Confirm Michael B. Mukasey as attorney general
Yes	Limit debate on an energy policy overhaul containing $21.8 billion in tax incentives and reduced oil and gas subsidies

CQ VOTE STUDIES

	PARTY UNITY		PRESIDENTIAL SUPPORT	
	SUPPORT	OPPOSE	SUPPORT	OPPOSE
2008	99%	1%	28%	72%
2007	95%	5%	40%	60%
2006	94%	6%	51%	49%
2005	85%	15%	43%	57%
2004	90%	10%	64%	36%
2003	91%	9%	50%	50%
2002	78%	22%	79%	21%
2001	91%	9%	68%	32%
2000	87%	13%	95%	5%
1999	88%	12%	84%	16%

INTEREST GROUPS

	AFL-CIO	ADA	CCUS	ACU
2008	100%	100%	50%	0%
2007	94%	90%	45%	4%
2006	93%	100%	36%	8%
2005	86%	95%	72%	13%
2004	92%	90%	71%	12%
2003	85%	95%	48%	10%
2002	92%	90%	60%	17%
2001	100%	90%	50%	29%
2000	75%	85%	64%	16%
1999	78%	100%	59%	4%

Sen. Tom Udall (D)

CAPITOL OFFICE
224-6621
tomudall.senate.gov
110 Hart Bldg. 20510; fax 228-0900

COMMITTEES
Commerce, Science & Transportation
Environment & Public Works
Indian Affairs
Rules & Administration
Joint Printing

RESIDENCE
Santa Fe

BORN
May 18, 1948; Tucson, Ariz.

RELIGION
Mormon

FAMILY
Wife, Jill Z. Cooper; one child

EDUCATION
Prescott College, B.A. 1970 (government
& political science); Cambridge U., B.L.L. 1975;
U. of New Mexico, J.D. 1977

CAREER
Lawyer; congressional aide

POLITICAL HIGHLIGHTS
Assistant U.S. attorney, 1978-81; sought
Democratic nomination for U.S. House, 1982;
Democratic nominee for U.S. House, 1988; N.M.
attorney general, 1991-99; U.S. House, 1999-2009

ELECTION RESULTS

2008 GENERAL

Tom Udall (D)	505,128	61.3%
Steve Pearce (R)	318,522	38.7%

2008 PRIMARY

Tom Udall (D)	unopposed

PREVIOUS WINNING PERCENTAGES
2006 House Election (75%); 2004 House Election
(69%); 2002 House Election (100%); 2000 House
Election (67%); 1998 House Election (53%)

Elected 2008; 1st term

Udall maintains the strong focus on energy and the environment that has given his family a reputation as serious stewards of the West's natural resources. Affable and well-liked among his colleagues, he was a near-automatic vote for his party during 10 years in the House and is likely to remain so in the Senate.

Udall has a political bloodline beyond almost any lawmaker whose last name isn't Kennedy. His father, Stewart L. Udall, was an Arizona congressman and secretary of Interior under presidents Kennedy and Johnson. His uncle, Morris K. Udall, succeeded his brother Stewart in the House in 1961 and was a well-known leader on environmental protection for 30 years in addition to running for president in 1976. "From the time I was 6, I heard my father and uncle talk about public service," he said.

Udall has an added family connection: He was elected to the House — and later the Senate — at the same time as his cousin Mark, a Democrat from neighboring Colorado. Tom Udall's voting record is a tad more liberal than his cousin's; he sided with his party 98 percent of the time in the 110th Congress (2007-08) on votes that divided a majority of Republicans against a majority of Democrats, compared with Mark's 94 percent. But he said they share the same philosophy. "I don't know that there are that many differences between us," he said. "We've always worked well with each other."

The two Udalls, in fact, plan to assist each other from their differing committees during their Senate terms. While Mark Udall was given seats on the Armed Services, Energy and Natural Resources and Special Aging committees, his cousin was assigned to serve on Environment and Public Works, Indian Affairs, Rules and Administration and Commerce, Science and Transportation. "We will have covered the whole range of issues," Tom Udall said.

On the Environment panel, he expects to be deeply involved in global warming legislation, one of President Obama's priorities. Though some lawmakers have balked at enacting laws that could hurt industries financially in a depressed economy, he said he favors action to curb greenhouse gases as well as on comprehensive energy legislation. "We need to be talking about sacrifice to the American people," he said. "We can knuckle down, but we need everyone involved."

In the House, Udall was a leading proponent of legislation to require states to obtain a certain portion of their electricity from solar, wind or other renewable sources. In August 2007, the House voted, 220-190, to adopt his language for a 15 percent national mandate for retail electricity production from renewable sources by 2020 as part of a comprehensive energy package. But the proposal died in the Senate, as Southern lawmakers expressed concerns that their states lacked the wind capacity to meet the requirement.

He resurrected the measure in slightly altered form as soon as he took his seat in the Senate, where he has the support of his New Mexico colleague Jeff Bingaman, who chairs Energy and Natural Resources. "We need to send a price signal in the market to move us forward on this green revolution," Udall said.

Udall also shares Bingaman's desire to have New Mexico's two national laboratories, Los Alamos and Sandia, play a greater role in developing new energy technologies as they seek to diversify their missions beyond nuclear weapons research. He said the labs and local small businesses could have stronger connections.

As a member of Commerce, Udall plans to work on consumer protection issues, an area he specialized in when he served as New Mexico's attorney general during the 1990s. He also wants to expand Internet and broadband access into rural areas and help the beleaguered U.S. railroad industry. "We should be bringing back the railroads; they're 10 times more efficient than cars and trucks," he said. He introduced a bill in March 2009 to require airlines to train employees and gate attendants on recognizing and dealing with drunk and belligerent passengers.

Udall's other priorities include universal health care coverage, with a greater emphasis on preventing illness. He supports allowing uninsured Americans over age 55 to buy into Medicare at a fixed cost. Small businesses should be allowed to buy into the federal employee benefit package that applies to members of Congress, he said. On education, he wants the government to pay for two years of college for each year that a person spends in national service.

Udall was loyal to his party's leaders as a House member. Speaker Nancy Pelosi of California gave him a coveted spot on the Appropriations Committee in the 110th Congress. But in a rare departure from the party line, he opposed the $700 billion effort in October 2008 to aid the ailing financial services sector, saying it didn't do enough to help homeowners and did nothing to prevent a repeat of future mistakes.

In early 2009, he also was among 22 Democrats — most of them from Western or conservative-leaning states — who backed an amendment by Nevada Republican John Ensign to codify a 2008 Supreme Court ruling striking down a District of Columbia gun ownership ban. The amendment was offered to legislation to grant District residents a representative with full voting rights in the House.

Udall was born in Tucson, Ariz., the state where the Udall clan is centered. After earning degrees from both Prescott College and England's Cambridge University, he entered law school at the University of New Mexico, graduating in 1977. He stayed on in the state as an appeals court law clerk, then worked as an assistant U.S. attorney and chief counsel to the state Department of Health and Environment before going into private practice.

He also worked with his father on behalf of Navajo Indians who had been exposed to radiation while mining uranium for use in weapons work and southern Utah residents living downwind of bomb fallout from the Nevada Test Site.

During this period, Udall twice ran for Congress unsuccessfully: He lost the 1982 primary to Democrat Bill Richardson, who is now governor, and the 1988 election to Republican Rep. Steven H. Schiff before getting the attorney general post in 1990.

Udall made a third try for the House in 1998, winning an eight-candidate Democratic primary, then handily beating incumbent Bill Redmond, a conservative Republican minister. He regularly won re-election with at least two-thirds of the vote and seemed a natural favorite to replace Pete V. Domenici when the veteran Republican senator announced in 2007 that he would not seek a seventh term because of health problems.

But Udall initially turned down a chance to run, citing his seat on Appropriations as his best opportunity to serve his constituents. He eventually bowed to pressure from the national Democratic Party and entered the race.

His opponent was his House colleague Steve Pearce, a conservative from the state's southeast corner who prevailed over the delegation's other House member, Heather A. Wilson, in a bitter GOP primary battle. Pearce sought to portray Udall as too liberal for New Mexico, but it was an ill-timed message in a state that gave Barack Obama 57 percent of the vote after President George W. Bush carried it four years earlier. Udall won easily with 61 percent of the vote.

KEY VOTES

House Service:

2008

Yes Delay consideration of Colombia free-trade agreement

Yes Override Bush veto of federal farm and nutrition programs reauthorization bill

No Overhaul surveillance laws and permit dismissal of suits against companies that conducted warrantless wiretapping

Yes Grant mortgage relief to homeowners and funding for Fannie Mae and Freddie Mac

No Approve initial $700 billion program to stabilize financial markets

No Approve final $700 billion program to stabilize financial markets

Yes Provide $14 billion in loans to automakers

2007

Yes Increase minimum wage by $2.10 an hour

Yes Approve $124.2 billion in emergency war spending and set goal for redeployment of troops from Iraq

No Reject federal contraceptive assistance to international family planning groups

Yes Override Bush veto of $23.2 billion water projects authorization bill

No Implement Peru free-trade agreement

Yes Approve energy policy overhaul with new fuel economy standards

No Clear $473.5 billion omnibus spending bill, including $70 billion for military operations

CQ VOTE STUDIES

House Service:

	PARTY UNITY		PRESIDENTIAL SUPPORT	
	SUPPORT	OPPOSE	SUPPORT	OPPOSE
2008	96%	4%	14%	86%
2007	98%	2%	3%	97%
2006	96%	4%	10%	90%
2005	97%	3%	11%	89%
2004	95%	5%	21%	79%
2003	97%	3%	18%	82%
2002	98%	2%	20%	80%
2001	96%	4%	23%	77%
2000	91%	9%	77%	23%
1999	92%	8%	78%	22%

INTEREST GROUPS

House Service:

	AFL-CIO	ADA	CCUS	ACU
2008	100%	90%	47%	12%
2007	96%	100%	47%	0%
2006	100%	95%	29%	4%
2005	100%	95%	41%	0%
2004	93%	100%	29%	8%
2003	100%	100%	23%	12%
2002	89%	100%	35%	0%
2001	100%	100%	30%	4%
2000	90%	80%	35%	9%
1999	100%	95%	24%	0%

Rep. Martin Heinrich (D)

Elected 2008; 1st term

Youthful and ambitious, Heinrich has the background and platform that made him a favorite of environmental interests during his congressional bid. A former Albuquerque City Council president, he served as his state's natural resources director and as executive director of a foundation dedicated to educating young people about wilderness.

A member of the Natural Resources Committee, Heinrich (HINE-rick) has proposed an "Apollo Project" for energy independence, reminiscent of President Kennedy's 1960s space exploration initiative. Heinrich's plan rejects a slow, incremental approach and opts for what he calls an "everything" agenda that would utilize the collective energy of government, industry, labor, nonprofits and academics.

He also sponsored legislation to require a percentage of electricity sold to be generated from renewable sources — a top priority for his state's two Democratic senators, Tom Udall and Jeff Bingaman.

Heinrich strongly backed President Obama's legislative efforts in early 2009 to revive the economy and said he was confident they would trickle down to his chronically poor and federally dependent state. "I come from a working-class background and know well that economic hardship is nothing new either to rural areas of the state or the inner city in New Mexico," he said.

On the Armed Services panel, Heinrich advocates for his district's Kirtland Air Force Base and Sandia National Laboratories, which conducts military- and energy-related research for the government. He criticized a proposal in early 2009 to transfer control of Sandia and other national labs from the Energy Department to the Pentagon, contending it could threaten jobs there.

Heinrich's district is regarded as one of the nation's most competitive swing districts, but he easily dispatched Republican Darren White for the seat left vacant by GOP Rep. Heather A. Wilson, who unsuccessfully sought to move to the Senate. He hit the ground running in the 111th Congress (2009-10), winning the title of freshman class president to serve the first of four six-month rotations.

CAPITOL OFFICE
225-6316
heinrich.house.gov
1505 Longworth Bldg. 20515-3101; fax 225-4975

COMMITTEES
Armed Services
Natural Resources

RESIDENCE
Albuquerque

BORN
Oct. 17, 1971; Fallon, Nev.

RELIGION
Lutheran

FAMILY
Wife, Julie Heinrich; two children

EDUCATION
U. of Missouri, B.S. 1995 (mechanical engineering);
U. of New Mexico, attended 2001-02

CAREER
State natural resources director; community advocacy consultant; outdoor education nonprofit director; mechanical engineering draftsman

POLITICAL HIGHLIGHTS
Albuquerque City Council, 2003-07 (president, 2005-06)

ELECTION RESULTS

2008 GENERAL

Martin Heinrich (D)	166,271	55.6%
Darren White (R)	132,485	44.3%

2008 PRIMARY

Martin Heinrich (D)	22,341	43.5%
Rebecca D. Vigil-Giron (D)	12,660	24.7%
Michelle Lujan Grisham (D)	12,074	23.5%
Robert L. Pidcock (D)	4,273	8.3%

NEW MEXICO 1

Central — Albuquerque

Built around Albuquerque, the 1st is the only urban district in a sparsely populated desert state. Since the Manhattan Project set the region on a technology-driven course in the 1940s, still-expanding Albuquerque has grown from 35,000 people before WWII to more than the 440,000 counted in 2000.

Sandia National Laboratories is the basis for a steady defense industry, and its success has contributed to a surge in computer, laser and other technology firms here, including Emcore and Intel. Sandia, the University of New Mexico and the Air Force Research Laboratory at Kirtland Air Force Base coordinate to conduct energy and defense research.

Statewide commitments to renewable- and alternative-energy research, and state laws that require utilities to invest in alternative energy, benefit local companies such as

Advent Solar and Sacred Power, a Native American-owned solar power company.

In the highly competitive 1st, Democrats hold most local offices, and the GOP lost its hold on the U.S. House seat here for the first time since its creation in 1968. Much of the GOP vote comes from the mainly white, upper-middle-class Northeast Heights section of Albuquerque, but the large government workforce and predominately Hispanic South Valley provide Democrats with an overall edge.

MAJOR INDUSTRY
Higher education, scientific research, defense, government

MILITARY BASES
Kirtland Air Force Base, 3,057 military, 2,791 civilian (2008)

CITIES
Albuquerque (pt.), 442,365; South Valley (unincorporated), 39,060

NOTABLE
The National Museum of Nuclear Science & History is in Albuquerque.

Rep. Harry Teague (D)

Elected 2008; 1st term

CAPITOL OFFICE
225-2365
teague.house.gov
1007 Longworth Bldg. 20515-3102; fax 225-9599

COMMITTEES
Transportation & Infrastructure
Veterans' Affairs

RESIDENCE
Hobbs

BORN
June 29, 1949; Gracemont, Okla.

RELIGION
Baptist

FAMILY
Wife, Nancy Teague; two children

EDUCATION
Hobbs H.S., attended 1964-66

CAREER
Oil well services company owner

POLITICAL HIGHLIGHTS
Lea County Board of Commissioners, 1999-2006
(chairman, 2003-06)

ELECTION RESULTS

2008 GENERAL

Harry Teague (D)	129,572	56.0%
Ed Tinsley (R)	101,980	44.0%

2008 PRIMARY

Harry Teague (D)	20,281	52.2%
Bill McCamley (D)	18,597	47.8%

As the only member of Congress who didn't graduate from high school, Teague believes he brings a working-class sensibility to the job. "I think it's important we have somebody to represent working people," he said. "When you look at the background of representatives and senators, there aren't many ones that come from a working background."

Teague is more than two decades older than his fellow New Mexico Democratic freshman colleagues, Ben Ray Luján and Martin Heinrich, and a bit more conservative than both. He declined to support President Obama's fiscal 2010 budget proposal, and while he shares his colleagues' strong interest in alternative energy, he sees a place for oil and gas as well.

He had some early success changing the country's energy policies: A bill he sponsored to extend renewable-energy production credits for two years was added to Obama's $787 billion economic recovery law in early 2009.

Teague serves on the Veterans' Affairs Committee. His district, which encompasses much of the southern part of the state, is home to two military facilities, and veterans are more than 15 percent of the population.

He also serves on the Transportation and Infrastructure Committee, where he said his business background will be of use.

The son of farmers, Teague was born in Caddo County, Okla., where his family lived without running water. The family moved to Hobbs when Teague was 9; he dropped out of high school at 17 to work in the oil fields, earning $1.50 an hour. Since then, Teague has worked various jobs related to oil and gas and in 2000 formed Teaco Energy Services, an oil well servicing company.

Later, as chairman of the Lea County Board of Commissioners, Teague spearheaded an effort to build a uranium enrichment facility in the county. He is a former member of the New Mexico Transportation Commission.

The 2008 election marked Teague's first foray into national politics. He won by 12 percentage points even though Arizona GOP Sen. John McCain narrowly carried the district over Obama. Because of the district's Republican lean, Teague is likely to be among the GOP's top 2010 targets.

NEW MEXICO 2

South – Las Cruces, Roswell, Little Texas

Before hosting the first atomic bomb explosion in 1945, the mostly rural 2nd, covering the southern half of the state, looked like the old American West. Since then, the area has attracted nuclear research and waste facilities to the remote Chihuahua Desert and its deep salt beds.

Towns in the 2nd have built a stable economy on traditional Western industries: copper and lead mining in the Mexican Highlands along the Arizona border; and oil and gas, as well as cattle and sheep ranching, in the southeastern corner of the state. Severe water shortages prevent large-scale industrial development and larger corporate farming. New Mexico's strong military presence is evident in the 2nd, home of Holloman Air Force Base and White Sands Missile Range.

New Mexico State University, based in Las Cruces and known for agricultural research, now uses a 64,000-acre section of its ranch as a proving ground for new border security technologies developed by government contractors.

Democrats hold the vast majority of local offices, although some voters still support GOP candidates at the federal level. In 2008, Republican John McCain won 50 percent of the 2nd's presidential vote, but the U.S. House seat flipped to Democratic control.

MAJOR INDUSTRY
Agriculture, mining, oil and gas, defense

MILITARY BASES
Holloman Air Force Base, 2,779 military, 1,041 civilian (2008); White Sands Missile Range, 434 military, 6,158 civilian (2006)

CITIES
Las Cruces, 74,267; Roswell, 45,293; Alamogordo, 35,582; Hobbs, 28,657

NOTABLE
Roswell hosts an annual UFO festival near the site where a UFO allegedly crashed in 1947.

Rep. Ben Ray Luján (D)

Elected 2008; 1st term

Luján follows in the active environmentalist mold of his predecessor, Democrat Tom Udall, who moved over to the Senate. In addition to collecting campaign endorsements from the Sierra Club and other green groups, he won praise from Udall's father — former Interior Secretary Stewart L. Udall, who served under presidents Kennedy and Johnson — for being "right, in my opinion, on all the big issues."

Luján's own father is a well-known New Mexico figure; he is Speaker of the state House. While the junior Luján (loo-HAHN) isn't a veteran dealmaker like his father, he has picked up a few traits — one of the state's newspapers observed he "excels at old-fashioned retail politics" and that he's "adept at responding to questions with answers that sound as polished as those in his press releases."

Luján did not officially enter politics until 2002, when he began a stint as deputy state treasurer. Two years later, he was elected to the state's public regulation commission, which oversees utilities, telecommunications, motor carriers and insurance companies. By 2005, he became its chairman.

He takes that experience to the Science and Technology Committee, where he advocates for more robust investment in technologies for renewable and alternative energy sources, such as wind and solar. He serves as vice chairman of Science's Technology and Innovation panel.

Luján, whose district includes large rural areas, also is an advocate for expanding high-speed Internet access in rural communities. To accommodate such an expansion, he said, lawmakers should consider tapping the Universal Service Fund, which is used primarily to pay for traditional telephone infrastructure in rural areas.

He also serves on the Homeland Security Committee, where he looks out for his district's Los Alamos National Laboratory in seeking to broaden its portfolio beyond nuclear weapons work.

Luján easily beat five other candidates in the Democratic primary to succeed Udall, a victory that all but ensured his election in November 2008 in the heavily Democratic district.

CAPITOL OFFICE
225-6190
lujan.house.gov
502 Cannon Bldg. 20515-3103; fax 226-1331

COMMITTEES
Homeland Security
Science & Technology

RESIDENCE
Nambé

BORN
June 7, 1972; Santa Fe, N.M.

RELIGION
Roman Catholic

FAMILY
Single

EDUCATION
U. of New Mexico, attended 1990-95;
New Mexico Highlands U., B.B.A. 2007
(business administration)

CAREER
State government aide; human resources manager; legislative publication marketing director; casino services supervisor

POLITICAL HIGHLIGHTS
N.M. Public Regulation Commission, 2005-09
(chairman, 2005-07)

ELECTION RESULTS

2008 GENERAL
Ben Ray Luján (D)	161,292	56.7%
Daniel K. East (R)	86,618	30.5%
Carol Miller (I)	36,348	12.8%

2008 PRIMARY
Ben Ray Luján (D)	26,775	41.5%
Donald H. Wiviott (D)	16,497	25.6%
Benny J. Shendo Jr. (D)	10,148	15.7%
Harry B. Montoya (D)	7,234	11.2%
Jon Adams (D)	1,979	3.1%
Rudy Martin (D)	1,845	2.9%

NEW MEXICO 3
North – Santa Fe, Rio Rancho, Farmington

For nearly a century, the 3rd's landscape and unique Spanish and American Indian heritage have attracted thousands of artists and tourists. Galleries and ski resorts still lure visitors from around the world, while an influx of retirees has made the area one of the fastest-growing parts of the state.

But the 3rd is a district of extremes. Luxury resorts and the bountiful art trade exist beside extraordinary poverty. Gallup, in McKinley County, boasts millionaires, while the county itself remains one of the nation's poorest. Large American Indian populations in the northwest struggle with modest farming and ranching ventures, while the same area provides lofty incomes for oil and gas producers. Many western reservations are plagued with alcoholism and drug abuse.

Cannon Air Force Base, near Clovis, escaped a recommendation of closure in the 2005 BRAC round, but the commission voted to transfer the base's F-16 squadrons and required a complete overhaul of base activity. Cannon is expanding to accommodate new aircraft fleets and military personnel.

GOP pockets exist in Rio Rancho, home to a large Intel site; near Los Alamos National Laboratory; and among energy producers in San Juan County. But Hispanics, American Indians and Santa Fe's wealthy liberals give Democrats an edge. Barack Obama won 61 percent of the 3rd's 2008 presidential vote.

MAJOR INDUSTRY
State government, ranching, defense

MILITARY BASES
Cannon Air Force Base, 2,517 military, 565 civilian (2009)

CITIES
Santa Fe, 62,203; Rio Rancho (pt.), 46,701; Farmington, 37,844; Clovis, 32,667

NOTABLE
The Aztec Ruins National Monument.

NEW YORK

Gov. David A. Paterson (D)

Assumed office: March 17, 2008, due to the resignation of Eliot Spitzer, D.

Length of term: 4 years

Term expires: 1/11

Salary: $179,000

Phone: (518) 474-8390

Residence: Manhattan

Born: May 20, 1954; Brooklyn, N.Y.

Religion: Roman Catholic

Family: Wife, Michelle Paige Paterson; two children

Education: Columbia U., B.A. 1977 (history); Hofstra U., J.D. 1983

Career: College instructor; campaign aide

Political highlights: N.Y. Senate, 1986-2006; candidate for New York City public advocate, 1993; lieutenant governor, 2007-08

Recent election results:

2006 GENERAL

Eliot Spitzer (D)	3,086,709	69.6%
John J. Faso (R)	1,274,335	28.7%
Malachy McCourt (GREEN)	42,166	1.0%

Lt. Gov. – Vacant *

* The position of temporary president of the Senate fullfils the duties of lieutenant governor.

LEGISLATURE

Legislature: Officially year-round; main session January-June

Senate: 62 members, 2-year terms

2009 ratios: 30 R, 32 D; 52 men, 10 women

Salary: $79,500

Phone: (518) 455-3216

Assembly: 150 members, 2-year terms

2009 ratios: 107 D, 41 R, 2 vacancies; 107 men, 41 women

Salary: $79,500

Phone: (518) 455-4218

TERM LIMITS

Governor: No

Senate: No

Assembly: No

URBAN STATISTICS

CITY	POPULATION
New York City	8,008,278
Buffalo	292,648
Rochester	219,773
Yonkers	196,086
Syracuse	147,306

REGISTERED VOTERS

Democrat	50%
Republican	25%
Unaffiliated/others	25%

POPULATION

2008 population (est.)	19,490,297
2000 population	18,976,457
1990 population	17,990,455
Percent change (1990-2000)	+5.5%
Rank among states (2008)	3

Median age	35.9
Born in state	65.3%
Foreign born	20.4%
Violent crime rate	554/100,000
Poverty level	14.6%
Federal workers	133,980
Military	57,987

ELECTIONS

STATE ELECTION OFFICIAL
(518) 474-6220

DEMOCRATIC PARTY
(212) 725-8825

REPUBLICAN PARTY
(518) 462-2601

MISCELLANEOUS

Web: www.state.ny.us

Capital: Albany

U.S. CONGRESS

Senate: 2 Democrats

House: 26 Democrats, 3 Republicans

2000 Census Statistics by District

DIST.	2008 VOTE FOR PRESIDENT OBAMA	MCCAIN	WHITE	BLACK	ASIAN	HISP	MEDIAN INCOME	WHITE COLLAR	BLUE COLLAR	SERVICE INDUSTRY	OVER 64	UNDER 18	COLLEGE EDUCATION	RURAL	SQ. MILES
1	51%	48%	84%	4%	2%	8%	$61,884	64%	21%	15%	12%	26%	27%	6%	646
2	56	43	72	10	3	14	$71,147	66	20	14	12	27	31	0	239
3	47	52	87	2	3	7	$70,561	69	17	14	15	24	31	0	183
4	58	41	62	18	4	14	$66,799	68	17	15	14	25	31	0	90
5	63	36	44	5	24	23	$51,156	65	18	17	15	22	34	0	66
6	89	11	13	52	9	17	$43,546	57	21	22	11	27	18	0	40
7	79	20	28	17	13	40	$36,990	57	21	22	13	24	20	0	26
8	74	25	69	5	11	12	$47,061	79	10	11	14	18	48	0	15
9	55	44	64	4	15	14	$45,426	68	18	14	17	21	31	0	37
10	91	9	16	60	3	17	$30,212	60	18	22	10	30	18	0	18
11	90	9	21	59	4	12	$34,082	61	16	23	9	27	25	0	12
12	86	13	23	9	16	49	$29,195	51	28	21	9	26	17	0	19
13	49	51	71	6	9	11	$50,092	65	18	17	13	24	24	0	65
14	78	21	66	5	11	14	$57,152	82	8	10	13	13	57	0	13
15	93	6	16	31	3	48	$27,934	64	15	21	11	24	25	0	10

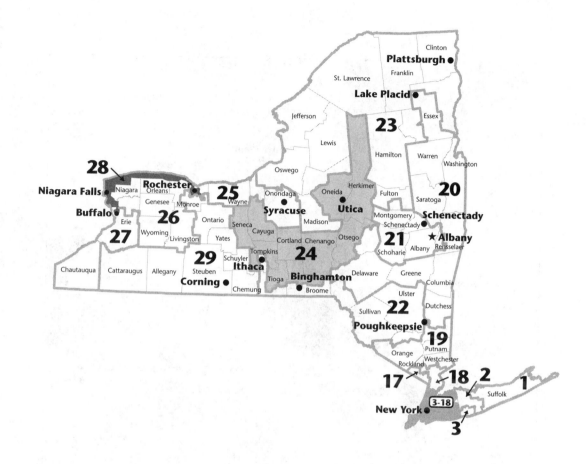

2000 Census Statistics by District

DIST.	2008 VOTE FOR PRESIDENT OBAMA	MCCAIN	WHITE	BLACK	ASIAN	HISP	MEDIAN INCOME	WHITE COLLAR	BLUE COLLAR	SERVICE INDUSTRY	OVER 64	UNDER 18	COLLEGE EDUCATION	RURAL	SQ. MILES
16	95%	5%	3%	30%	2%	63%	$19,311	46%	24%	30%	7%	35%	8%	0%	12
17	72	28	41	30	5	20	$44,868	65	16	19	13	27	29	0	127
18	62	38	67	9	5	16	$68,887	73	13	14	14	25	44	1	222
19	51	48	84	5	2	8	$64,337	67	19	14	11	27	32	21	1,401
20	51	48	93	2	1	2	$44,239	61	24	15	14	24	25	55	7,018
21	58	40	85	7	2	3	$40,254	66	19	15	15	23	27	16	1,935
22	59	39	80	8	3	8	$38,586	61	22	17	14	24	24	32	3,246
23	52	47	93	3	1	2	$35,434	52	29	19	12	25	16	65	13,235
24	50	48	92	3	1	2	$36,082	57	25	17	15	24	19	49	6,164
25	56	43	87	7	2	2	$43,188	65	21	14	14	26	28	21	1,620
26	46	52	92	3	2	2	$46,653	62	24	14	14	25	26	29	2,731
27	54	44	89	4	1	5	$36,884	58	26	16	16	24	20	18	1,830
28	68	30	62	29	1	6	$31,751	58	23	18	14	26	21	7	534
29	48	50	93	3	2	1	$41,875	61	24	15	14	25	26	42	5,660
STATE	**63**	**36**	**62**	**15**	**5**	**15**	**$43,393**	**64**	**20**	**17**	**13**	**25**	**27**	**13**	**47,214**
U.S.	**53**	**46**	**69**	**12**	**4**	**13**	**$41,994**	**60**	**25**	**15**	**12**	**26**	**24**	**21**	**3,537,438**

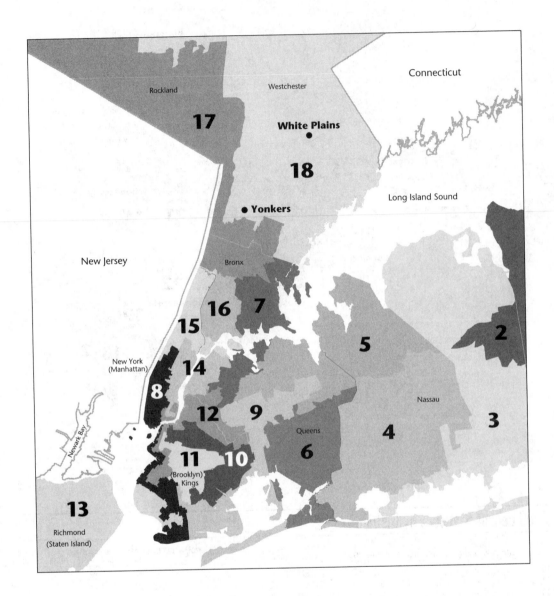

Connecticut

Rockland

Westchester

17

White Plains
●

18

Long Island Sound

New Jersey

● **Yonkers**

Bronx

16 **7**

15

5

2

New York
(Manhattan)

14

8

12 **9**

Nassau

Queens

6

4

3

11

10

(Brooklyn)
Kings

Newark Bay

13

Richmond
(Staten Island)

Sen. Charles E. Schumer (D)

Elected 1998; 2nd term

CAPITOL OFFICE
224-6542
schumer.senate.gov
313 Hart Bldg. 20510-3203; fax 228-1218

COMMITTEES
Banking, Housing & Urban Affairs
Finance
Judiciary
(Immigration, Refugees & Border Security
- chairman)
Rules & Administration - chairman
Joint Economic - vice chairman
Joint Library - vice chairman
Joint Printing - chairman

RESIDENCE
Brooklyn

BORN
Nov. 23, 1950; Brooklyn, N.Y.

RELIGION
Jewish

FAMILY
Wife, Iris Weinshall; two children

EDUCATION
Harvard U., A.B. 1971, J.D. 1974

CAREER
Lawyer

POLITICAL HIGHLIGHTS
N.Y. Assembly, 1975-81; U.S. House, 1981-99

ELECTION RESULTS

2004 GENERAL

C. Schumer (D, INDC, WFM)	4,769,824	71.2%
Howard Mills (R)	1,625,069	24.2%
Marilyn F. O'Grady (C)	220,960	3.3%

2004 PRIMARY

Charles E. Schumer (D)	unopposed

PREVIOUS WINNING PERCENTAGES
1998 (55%); 1996 House Election (75%); 1994
House Election (73%); 1992 House Election (89%);
1990 House Election (80%); 1988 House Election
(78%); 1986 House Election (93%); 1984 House
Election (72%); 1982 House Election (79%); 1980
House Election (77%)

As the Senate's third-ranking Democratic leader, Schumer carries the title of caucus vice chairman. But he functions more like a one-man conglomerate: policy strategist, fundraising rainmaker and maestro of his party's daily message.

His portfolio includes a new title as Rules and Administration Committee chairman in the 111th Congress (2009-10), with purview over elections protocol and his colleagues' office space, including prized private Capitol hideaways. He's a highly active member of the Finance, Judiciary, and Banking, Housing and Urban Affairs committees. And he's vice chairman of the Joint Economic Committee.

Schumer speaks with authority on a wide range of subjects via frequent TV appearances, clever quotes and an incessant stream of news releases. He jumps into any issue that strikes his fancy and has been known to put in 17-hour workdays. "God has blessed me with a lot of energy," he said.

He is high on the short list of potential successors to Majority Leader Harry Reid of Nevada. For now, he bides his time one rung below Majority Whip Richard J. Durbin of Illinois, with whom he shares a rented Capitol Hill house along with two House members. Schumer offers advice on politics and policy to Reid and Durbin, both master parliamentarians.

Schumer was overshadowed on the national stage by former New York Sen. Hillary Rodham Clinton. But he is back before the microphones and cameras at every turn. Sometimes his taste for the limelight draws controversy; he released a letter to regulators in June 2008 warning that IndyMac Bancorp Inc. "could face a failure" because of bad mortgages. That led bank employees to ask California Attorney General Edmund G. Brown Jr. to investigate whether Schumer's statements had triggered the bank's demise, a request Brown denied.

Generally, though, Schumer is adept at seizing his share of a story. When Bruce Springsteen fans complained in February 2009 that online concert ticket seller Ticketmaster sold tickets for more than face value, Schumer joined New Jersey Rep. Bill Pascrell Jr. in calling for the Federal Trade Commission to investigate. He subsequently introduced a bill aimed at improving fans' chances of getting tickets at face value — promising to try to pass it in time for New York Mets and Yankees baseball fans to get their playoff seats.

Schumer initially supported Clinton in the 2008 presidential primaries, but he stumped for Barack Obama among Jewish voters once the Illinois senator had bested her. After Obama's election, he argued against giving him a blank check, calling for pragmatic deals to help Democrats in the 2010 midterm elections, when the party in power traditionally has lost seats. "Domestic policy should be more collaborative," Schumer said.

As chairman of the Democratic Senatorial Campaign Committee, Schumer helped Democrats regain the Senate majority in 2006 and expand it two years later. He was a relentless fundraiser — he brought in $121 million in the 2005-06 cycle to the GOP's $89 million — and recruited moderates whose ideologies did not always mesh with those of Democratic interest groups. He relinquished the chairmanship in November 2008 to New Jersey's Robert Menendez, another aggressive fundraiser, but is on call as an adviser.

Schumer wants to help build a durable Democratic majority. As part of that vision, he argues for focusing on the middle class. His reference point is an imaginary Long Island couple, Joe and Eileen Bailey, whom he envisions when thinking about policy. The Baileys, he said, earn a combined $75,000 a year and believe politicians devote too much attention to either the very wealthy or very poor. "Too often, the Democratic Party ignored them; I make it my mission not to," he wrote in his 2007 book, "Positively American."

On Rules, Schumer has purview over the mechanics of elections. He took aim in the 110th Congress (2007-08) at new measures to prevent election fraud, such as a bill he introduced with Obama to make it a crime to disseminate false information about the time and place of elections, voter eligibility and candidate endorsements.

Schumer served as chairman of the Joint Economic Committee in the 110th, and more than a year before the financial sector meltdown occurred, began Joint Economic hearings on subprime mortgages. When crisis hit, he was well positioned to push in 2008 for several key elements in the final $700 billion rescue package, including a proposal to divide the money into two installments. He helped Democrats derail a resolution in 2009 that would have blocked release of the second half of the funds.

On Judiciary, Schumer weighs in on high-profile issues from abortion to the war on terrorism and is poised to help his fellow Harvard Law School alumnus, Obama, in confirming Democratic judicial nominees. He was a leading critic of President George W. Bush's choices for the Supreme Court. As chairman of the subcommittee on immigration, he will be in the thick of what could be one of the most contentious fights of the 111th Congress.

From his seats on Finance and Banking, Housing and Urban Affairs, he keeps an eye out for Wall Street and tends to home-state requirements such as his proposal to raise the monthly tax-free mass transit benefit that employers can provide from $115 to $220.

As a House member, Schumer brokered deals on several landmark bills, including the 1994 anti-crime law that put 100,000 new police officers on the beat, banned 19 kinds of assault weapons and created a "three strikes" mandatory life sentence for repeat violent offenders. An ardent gun-control advocate, he was the chief sponsor of the 1993 Brady law requiring background checks for handgun buyers and a 2006 bill requiring that stolen guns be reported in every state. When the National Rifle Association called him "the criminal's best friend," Schumer shot back, "I wear this like a badge of honor."

Schumer was born and raised in the Kings Highway section of Brooklyn. His father, Abe, owned a pest extermination business and his mother, Selma, stayed at home with Schumer and his two siblings. He said he "didn't have a political bone" in his body until he worked on Eugene McCarthy's presidential primary campaign in his freshman year at Harvard. Schumer decided to become a lawyer with the goal of getting into politics.

After law school, he decided to decline a job at a prominent law firm and run for the state Assembly. His parents argued with him, but he was steadfast. Schumer won the seat at age 23. "My first election night, in September 1974, was probably the hardest of my career," he wrote in "Positively American." "When the polls closed, I had no idea what was going to happen, in part because my mother had told all her friends to vote against me!" Six years later, Schumer easily won the Brooklyn-based House seat of Democrat Elizabeth Holtzman, who was running for the Senate.

In 1998, after 18 years in the House, Schumer took aim at Republican Sen. Alfonse D'Amato, winning the Democratic nomination with 51 percent of the vote against former Rep. Geraldine A. Ferraro, the 1984 vice presidential nominee, and New York City Public Advocate Mark Green. Schumer pointed to his anti-crime and gun control efforts in the House and recounted D'Amato's ethics problems, and won with 55 percent of the vote.

In 2004, he lost in only one New York county — Hamilton County in the northern part of the state. He has at times been rumored to have his eye on the governorship, but passed up a 2006 gubernatorial primary.

KEY VOTES

2008
Yes Prohibit discrimination based on genetic information
Yes Reauthorize farm and nutrition programs for five years
Yes Limit debate on "cap and trade" system for greenhouse gas emissions
Yes Allow lawsuits against companies that participated in warrantless wiretapping
Yes Limit debate on a bill to block a scheduled cut in Medicare payments to doctors
Yes Grant mortgage relief to homeowners and funding for Fannie Mae and Freddie Mac
Yes Approve a nuclear cooperation agreement with India
Yes Approve final $700 billion program to stabilize financial markets
Yes Allow consideration of a $14 billion auto industry loan package

2007
?   Increase minimum wage by $2.10 an hour
Yes Limit debate on a comprehensive immigration bill
Yes Overhaul congressional lobbying and ethics rules for members and their staffs
Yes Limit debate on considering a bill to add House seats for the District of Columbia and Utah
Yes Limit debate on restoring habeas corpus rights to detainees
Yes Mandate minimum breaks for troops between deployments to Iraq or Afghanistan
Yes Override Bush veto of $23.2 billion water projects authorization bill
Yes Confirm Michael B. Mukasey as attorney general
Yes Limit debate on an energy policy overhaul containing $21.8 billion in tax incentives and reduced oil and gas subsidies

CQ VOTE STUDIES

	PARTY UNITY		PRESIDENTIAL SUPPORT	
	SUPPORT	OPPOSE	SUPPORT	OPPOSE
2008	98%	2%	30%	70%
2007	97%	3%	35%	65%
2006	93%	7%	52%	48%
2005	93%	7%	31%	69%
2004	91%	9%	62%	38%
2003	96%	4%	47%	53%
2002	95%	5%	68%	32%
2001	92%	8%	65%	35%
2000	97%	3%	98%	2%
1999	94%	6%	91%	9%

INTEREST GROUPS

	AFL-CIO	ADA	CCUS	ACU
2008	100%	100%	63%	4%
2007	100%	90%	55%	0%
2006	100%	100%	64%	4%
2005	86%	100%	39%	8%
2004	100%	100%	65%	12%
2003	85%	95%	39%	10%
2002	92%	85%	50%	10%
2001	100%	95%	43%	16%
2000	75%	95%	53%	12%
1999	89%	100%	53%	4%

Sen. Kirsten Gillibrand (D)

Appointed Jan. 2009; 1st term

In just a short time in Congress, Gillibrand has earned a reputation as someone willing to go her own way. She has tended to have more-conservative views than most Northeastern Democrats, particularly on gun owners' rights and economic issues.

Gillibrand (full name: KEER-sten JILL-uh-brand) combines her centrist views with a driven and disciplined persona. She is a formidable fundraiser, and some friends predict she could someday be a Cabinet official or even a presidential candidate.

She has faced close scrutiny in left-leaning New York since Gov. David A. Paterson appointed her in January 2009 over other more experienced Democrats to fill the seat vacated by Hillary Rodham Clinton, who became secretary of State. Many Democrats lined up to run against her in the 2010 special-election primary to fill out the remainder of Clinton's term, which expires in 2012. She lined up her offense, launching an aggressive fundraising effort that brought in $2.3 million in her first two months in the Senate. She also exercised some caution on certain votes and began making visits around the state.

Her fiscal conservatism led her to vote in the House against both versions of the $700 billion proposal in the fall of 2008 to shore up the ailing financial services industry, the second of which became law. She said the plan lacked enough protection for taxpayers and that she wants to be involved in ensuring there is tighter regulation over the industry. Yet she backed President Obama's $787 billion economic stimulus measure in early 2009 in one of her first Senate floor votes. She called it a "good deal for New York" that would create jobs. She also supported his fiscal 2010 budget blueprint.

Gillibrand grew up in a family of hunters and has opposed measures to curtail gun ownership; she supported legislation in 2008 to repeal the District of Columbia's gun laws and received a 100 percent score from the National Rifle Association. But in February 2009 she voted against a GOP amendment to repeal the District's restrictions on most semiautomatic weapons. She said the amendment, which passed as part of a D.C. voting rights bill, would threaten "some of the common-sense regulations and laws that actually can crack down on the criminals getting access to the weapons."

She said her vote doesn't reflect a change in position: "I feel very strongly that I'm going to fight against gun violence in our communities and keep guns out of the hands of criminals, and I'm also going to protect the Second Amendment. I think those two views are not mutually exclusive."

Gillibrand intends to continue to focus on constituent service — something she does in a different manner than most of her colleagues. She posts her daily schedule on the Internet so constituents can see which lobbyists she's meeting with and which fundraisers she's attending each day. "I can defend anything I spend congressional time doing," she said. "If an opponent uses it against me, so be it. This is what I do, this is whom I met with, and it's important that my constituents know." She was one of the first to post online a list of all earmarks — funding set-asides for special projects — that she requested. She said she wants to look out for her district and give everyone equal opportunity to solicit federal dollars. "I don't like earmarks, but I'm not going to disadvantage my district, so I'm going to put my requests up online," she said.

Her staff objected, but she allowed a New York Times reporter to sit in on a 2007 meeting where she sorted out which earmark requests to prioritize. During that budget cycle, she secured nearly $24 million in earmarks.

Gillibrand sits on the Environment and Public Works Committee, where

CAPITOL OFFICE
224-4451
gillibrand.senate.gov
478 Russell Bldg. 20510-3204; fax 228-0282

COMMITTEES
Agriculture, Nutrition & Forestry
Environment & Public Works
Foreign Relations
Special Aging

RESIDENCE
Greenport

BORN
Dec. 9, 1966; Albany, N.Y.

RELIGION
Roman Catholic

FAMILY
Husband, Jonathan Gillibrand; two children

EDUCATION
Dartmouth College, A.B. 1988 (Asian studies);
U. of California, Los Angeles, J.D. 1991

CAREER
Lawyer; U.S. Housing and Urban Development Department aide

POLITICAL HIGHLIGHTS
U.S. House, 2007-09

ELECTION RESULTS

2008 HOUSE GENERAL

Kirsten Gillibrand (D, WFM)	193,651	62.1%
Sandy Treadwell (R, INDC, C)	118,031	37.9%

2008 HOUSE PRIMARY

Kirsten Gillibrand (D, WFM)	unopposed

PREVIOUS WINNING PERCENTAGES
2006 House Election (53%)

she can take part in discussions on global warming legislation. She supports reducing carbon emissions by 80 percent by the year 2050 and calls for investments in renewable energy production and energy-efficient technology.

She also sits on the Agriculture, Nutrition and Forestry Committee, where she continues work she started on the same committee in the House. Her old House district, the 20th, takes in part of the Hudson River Valley and is home to many fruit and dairy farms. In 2007, she and fellow New York Democrat Michael Arcuri offered an amendment to the Democratic farm bill that would require the Milk Income Loss Contract program to take feed and fuel costs into account when setting price supports. She supported a successful override of President George W. Bush's veto of the farm bill in May 2008, which included a version of that amendment.

Gillibrand also sits on the Foreign Relations Committee, where her degree in Asian studies and fluency in Chinese may prove useful. She studied abroad in China and Taiwan, and during her senior year at Dartmouth College she spent a month in India on a fellowship where she interviewed the Dalai Lama and Tibetan refugees for a senior project.

As a lawyer for Davis, Polk & Wardwell during the 1990s, Gillibrand spent five years representing tobacco giant Philip Morris as it endured civil lawsuits and criminal investigations. She told the Albany Times-Union that her work focused on assembling information sought by federal investigators checking out claims that the company was involved in crimes against consumers. In her last two campaign cycles, she received at least $26,500 from the company and its executives, according to FEC records analyzed by CQ MoneyLine.

She backed a measure in July 2008 to allow the FDA to regulate tobacco. Philip Morris, which would prefer no regulation, nevertheless backed the bill, which could give it a competitive edge against smaller companies. But Gillibrand has insisted her past work doesn't influence her votes. She told the Times-Union in October 2008: "I don't think clients you represented as an associate are relevant," she said. "I think how you vote is relevant."

Gillibrand was reared in New York's capital of Albany. Her father is a prominent Democratic lobbyist; her mother is a lawyer who has pushed for women's rights in the workforce. As a young girl, Gillibrand canvassed door-to-door with her grandmother, who founded the first women's Democratic club in Albany.

She worked in the office of New York GOP Sen. Alfonse M. D'Amato while in college. She then attended law school and worked as an attorney, concentrating on securities litigation. She recalled listening to Clinton's 1995 speech in Beijing when the first lady declared that women's rights are human rights. "It really shook me at the time, and I thought, 'What am I doing? I should be doing something more meaningful than I'm doing now,'" she recalled.

During the end of the Clinton administration, she served as special counsel to the secretary of Housing and Urban Development, Andrew Cuomo.

In 2006, she challenged four-term Republican Rep. John E. Sweeney, questioning his ties to lobbying groups. Republicans attempted to turn the tables on Gillibrand over the investments of her husband, a financial consultant, but she capitalized on allegations that Sweeney tried to gloss over a past drunken-driving incident. She also proved to be one of the year's strongest non-incumbent fundraisers. Her libertarian viewpoints and her own ethics pledge helped her win by about 6 percentage points.

Two years later, she faced Sandy Treadwell, a former state GOP chairman and secretary of state. Treadwell sought to tie Gillilbrand to liberal Speaker Nancy Pelosi of California, but she answered by describing her voting record as "one of the most conservative in the state." In the end, she coasted to victory with 62 percent of the vote — more than 11 points ahead of Obama, who took the district despite its history of Republicanism. In May 2008, Gillibrand became the sixth woman to give birth while in Congress.

KEY VOTES

House Service:

2008

Yes	Delay consideration of Colombia free-trade agreement
?	Override Bush veto of federal farm and nutrition programs reauthorization bill
Yes	Overhaul surveillance laws and permit dismissal of suits against companies that conducted warrantless wiretapping
Yes	Grant mortgage relief to homeowners and funding for Fannie Mae and Freddie Mac
No	Approve initial $700 billion program to stabilize financial markets
No	Approve final $700 billion program to stabilize financial markets
Yes	Provide $14 billion in loans to automakers

2007

Yes	Increase minimum wage by $2.10 an hour
Yes	Approve $124.2 billion in emergency war spending and set goal for redeployment of troops from Iraq
No	Reject federal contraceptive assistance to international family planning groups
Yes	Override Bush veto of $23.2 billion water projects authorization bill
Yes	Implement Peru free-trade agreement
Yes	Approve energy policy overhaul with new fuel economy standards
Yes	Clear $473.5 billion omnibus spending bill, including $70 billion for military operations

CQ VOTE STUDIES

House Service:

	PARTY UNITY		PRESIDENTIAL SUPPORT	
	SUPPORT	OPPOSE	SUPPORT	OPPOSE
2008	91%	9%	22%	78%
2007	90%	10%	6%	94%

INTEREST GROUPS

House Service:

	AFL-CIO	ADA	CCUS	ACU
2008	100%	70%	69%	23%
2007	96%	95%	60%	8%

Rep. Timothy H. Bishop (D)

Elected 2002; 4th term

CAPITOL OFFICE
225-3826
www.house.gov/timbishop
306 Cannon Bldg. 20515-3201; fax 225-3143

COMMITTEES
Budget
Education & Labor
Transportation & Infrastructure

RESIDENCE
Southampton

BORN
June 1, 1950; Southampton, N.Y.

RELIGION
Roman Catholic

FAMILY
Wife, Kathryn Bishop; two children

EDUCATION
College of the Holy Cross, A.B. 1972;
Long Island U., M.P.A. 1981

CAREER
College provost and administrator

POLITICAL HIGHLIGHTS
No previous office

ELECTION RESULTS

2008 GENERAL

Timothy H. Bishop (D, INDC, WFM)	162,083	58.4%
Lee M. Zeldin (R, C)	115,545	41.6%

2008 PRIMARY

Timothy H. Bishop (D, WFM)	unopposed

2006 GENERAL

Timothy H. Bishop (D, INDC, WFM)	104,360	62.2%
Italo A. Zanzi (R, C)	63,328	37.8%

PREVIOUS WINNING PERCENTAGES
2004 (56%); 2002 (50%)

Bishop calls himself a "left-of-center guy" in a district that's "decidedly right of center," and that dynamic shapes his approach to the job. Even as he remains a reliable vote for the Democrats' national priorities, the former college administrator works on issues that have wide bipartisan appeal and resonate locally, such as beach improvements, wastewater treatment and open-space preservation.

He jumped into politics relatively late in life and without a long political résumé, but the career shift wasn't as abrupt as it seems. "My experience running a college was enormously helpful and, I think, the perfect preparation for what I do now," Bishop said in late 2008. "You lead on a college campus by forming alliances, by building consensus, by finding commonality of either idea or purpose. And that's how you get things done here."

Democratic leaders can count on Bishop to support them on social and economic policy, and he voted with the party 99 percent of the time in the 110th Congress (2007-08) on votes that pitted Democrats against Republicans. He supported the leadership's position on major issues of the year, voting for the $700 billion rescue of the financial services sector, the Democrats' Medicare doctor-payments bill, regulation of tobacco by the Food and Drug Administration and a bailout of domestic auto manufacturers.

Several of his legislative initiatives involve fixing what he sees as quirks in the law. As a member of the Education and Labor Committee, Bishop in 2008 pushed a bill through the House to amend the 1993 federal family-leave law to cover airline flight crews, who currently cannot qualify because of the way their work hours are calculated. Though the bill did not advance in the Senate, Bishop started over in the 111th Congress (2009-10), steering it through the House early in 2009.

He also came back in the 111th with a bill to change tax law to make it easier for landowners to sell the development rights to their properties without incurring a severe tax hit, which he said is a particular problem on Long Island. And, with New Jersey Republican Frank A. LoBiondo, he won House passage in 2009 of legislation to require public notification after sewage spills.

But his primary focus is education. A mid-ranking Democrat on the Education committee, he aspires to chair the panel on higher education. As a member of that subcommittee in the 111th, he wants to expand federal resources for colleges, universities and students while keeping higher education affordable. "I am viewed as a go-to guy by various higher education groups," he said. "I speak their language. I worked with these issues for close to 30 years." He supports President Obama's plan to replace subsidized private loans with direct government loans to college students, using the savings to boost Pell grants for low-income students. He was a forceful advocate in 2007 for a successful Democratic initiative that cut interest rates on college loans.

He also pushes to prioritize funding for education and infrastructure from his seat on the Budget Committee. He supports more federal funds to help schools adapt to the 2001 No Child Left Behind Law.

The son of a telephone lineman, Bishop is a friend of organized labor. In his first term in the House, he pushed a proposal to increase the minimum wage from $5.15 to $7 an hour and another to require company pension boards to have employee representation. He actively opposed the George W. Bush administration's plan to scale back worker protections for overtime pay. During debate, Bishop described how his father worked more than 80 hours a week and depended on overtime wages to put five children through college.

Bishop also sits on the Transportation and Infrastructure Committee, which plans to take up a five-year surface transportation law reauthorization. He said he plans to work with Long Island's other four representatives to agree on a "game changer" project for the region, such as direct train access to Manhattan's east side or a track project that would allow for easier reverse commuting from New York City to Long Island.

He has been trying to strike a careful balance on proposed changes to the Plum Island Animal Disease Center in his district to prevent it from becoming a home to more dangerous research but also to prevent the facility from closing. Also close to home, Bishop wants to build consensus around a long-delayed study of improvements to the Long Island shoreline.

Bishop has deep roots in the district. His father's family came to Southampton from Southampton, England, in 1643, and his great-great-grandfather was mayor of the town. He still lives a block from the house where he grew up. His mother's relatives were potato farmers, and Bishop has warm memories of weekends helping out during harvest time.

In 1973, Bishop took a job as an admissions counselor at Southampton College and worked his way up to dean of enrollment and director of financial aid. He earned a master's degree in public administration along the way and eventually became provost of the school.

When he decided to take on incumbent Felix J. Grucci Jr. in 2002, Bishop's only political experience was a stint as chairman of the Southampton Town Board of Ethics. Grucci, former president of Fireworks by Grucci, was well-known, well-financed and a Republican in a district where the GOP enjoyed a 3-2 edge over Democrats. But Bishop had some advantages, especially a 30-year friendship with entertainment mogul Robert F.X. Sillerman, who had a home in the Hamptons. Sillerman was Bishop's campaign chairman and tapped Hollywood and Hamptons money circles to help him.

During the campaign, Grucci ran an ad wrongly accusing Bishop of covering up a student rape while he was provost, a charge based on an old, discredited article in a student newspaper. Bishop won public sympathy as a result. He also was able to hurt Grucci by publicizing a county health department report identifying the Grucci fireworks factory in Yaphank as a likely source of pollution in local drinking water wells. He squeaked through with just 50 percent of the vote.

The one blemish on his first term was a media revelation he had accepted a gift from Sillerman of $21,000 for college costs for his daughter, Meghan. Bishop said his friend has never asked for a legislative favor. He won his next three re-elections with relative ease.

KEY VOTES

2008

+ Delay consideration of Colombia free-trade agreement
Yes Override Bush veto of federal farm and nutrition programs reauthorization bill
Yes Overhaul surveillance laws and permit dismissal of suits against companies that conducted warrantless wiretapping
Yes Grant mortgage relief to homeowners and funding for Fannie Mae and Freddie Mac
Yes Approve initial $700 billion program to stabilize financial markets
Yes Approve final $700 billion program to stabilize financial markets
Yes Provide $14 billion in loans to automakers

2007

Yes Increase minimum wage by $2.10 an hour
Yes Approve $124.2 billion in emergency war spending and set goal for redeployment of troops from Iraq
No Reject federal contraceptive assistance to international family planning groups
Yes Override Bush veto of $23.2 billion water projects authorization bill
Yes Implement Peru free-trade agreement
Yes Approve energy policy overhaul with new fuel economy standards
No Clear $473.5 billion omnibus spending bill, including $70 billion for military operations

CQ VOTE STUDIES

	PARTY UNITY		PRESIDENTIAL SUPPORT	
	SUPPORT	OPPOSE	SUPPORT	OPPOSE
2008	99%	1%	16%	84%
2007	99%	1%	4%	96%
2006	97%	3%	31%	69%
2005	95%	5%	15%	85%
2004	95%	5%	32%	68%

INTEREST GROUPS

	AFL-CIO	ADA	CCUS	ACU
2008	100%	85%	71%	0%
2007	96%	95%	55%	0%
2006	100%	85%	40%	16%
2005	93%	95%	41%	0%
2004	100%	100%	48%	4%

NEW YORK 1

Eastern Suffolk County — Hamptons, Smithtown, Brookhaven

Covering the eastern two-thirds of Long Island's Suffolk County, the 1st reaches out into the Atlantic Ocean. Its western edge is home to small communities that have grown alongside the district's research facilities, while its eastern end takes in second homes for some of New York's wealthiest in the Hamptons and Shelter Island. Villages and hamlets line Route 27 on the way to Montauk at the rural end of the island, which retains its pastoral character with scattered fishing villages and farms.

Scientific research, attracted by local colleges and Brookhaven National Laboratory, dominates the district's economy. The education and health care sectors have provided jobs in the region, even during an economic downturn. Stony Brook University Medical Center is a renowned teaching hospital, and Brookhaven has produced six Nobel Prize recipients. On a smaller economic scale, Suffolk County brings in the most agriculture money of any county in the state, and the 1st's portion of Long Island's wine industry also has a significant presence. In 35 years, the

industry has grown from one vineyard to 60 wineries and more than 4,000 acres. Instability in the retail and real estate sectors of the über-elite Hamptons concern residents and local officials.

The 1st takes in some blue-collar towns and areas that depend on fishing and tourism, where environmental issues rank high. The 1st's lingering rural temperament and small-town feel make it more likely to lean to the right than many other districts near New York City. As many liberal-leaning homeowners reside primarily in New York, voter registration favors the GOP. Republicans win at the local level, but Democrats make the 1st competitive at the federal level — Democrat Barack Obama secured a slim majority of 51 percent in the 2008 presidential election four years after Republican George W. Bush won a narrow plurality here.

MAJOR INDUSTRY
Higher education, research, health care, tourism

CITIES
Coram (unincorporated), 34,923; Centereach (unincorporated), 27,285; Shirley (unincorporated), 25,395; Medford (unincorporated), 21,985

NOTABLE
The Montauk Point Lighthouse, built in 1796, was the first lighthouse in New York State.

Rep. Steve Israel (D)

Elected 2000; 5th term

The gregarious Israel's liberal bent and focus on energy and middle-class economic issues have raised his stature in New York Democratic circles and among his party's leaders, but he doesn't turn away from working with Republicans. He is a powerhouse fundraiser who has his eye on higher office in the future.

Israel is generally a reliable vote for his party; in the 110th Congress (2007-08), he sided 98 percent of the time with Democrats on issues that pitted a majority of each party against each other. In early 2009 he was put in charge of leading the Democratic Congressional Campaign Committee's candidate recruiting efforts for the 2010 election cycle — a formidable task given that the party in power historically tends to lose seats in midterms.

Israel can be a determined dealmaker. He once buttonholed President George W. Bush to talk about prescription drug coverage for seniors when Bush stopped by the Capitol to pass along holiday greetings one December. "I just planted myself at the center of the room — he was going to have to knock me down to get past," he later told The New York Times.

He and six House colleagues in September 2008 announced the formation of the Democratic Middle Class Working Group, which pushes an agenda that includes college affordability (he has two daughters in college), better care for the elderly and retirement savings. He joined several House members in April 2009 in introducing a bill to adjust income tax brackets for the cost of living. "All federal policy that is intended to address middle-class economics starts off on the wrong assumption," he said. "Nobody's defined what the middle class is, because no one works into the calculation that actual cost of living that middle-class families confront."

Israel's tendency to reach for the center is an asset in his job on the powerful Appropriations Committee, which controls the federal purse strings. As a member of the panel's Energy-Water Subcommittee, he hopes to work with the Obama administration to boost funding for energy and advanced technology initiatives, some of which could provide jobs in his district.

Inspired by President Kennedy's 1962 call to put a man on the moon, Israel has developed an ambitious blueprint for energy issues. It includes expanded tax credits for families to offset the costs of alternative fuel and energy-efficient technologies and a broad range of tax and investment incentives for businesses to encourage more wind, solar and other renewable-energy sources. He also joined Democrat Betty Sutton of Ohio in sponsoring a bill in 2009 to create a "cash for clunkers" program to encourage consumers to trade in older cars for more fuel-efficient models.

Much of Israel's thinking on energy was shaped by his work on the Armed Services Committee, where he served before moving to Appropriations. From his seat on that panel, he championed legislation to equip commercial planes with anti-missile technology, which was prompted by a shoulder-fired missile that just missed an Israeli plane as it took off from Kenya in 2002.

Another of Israel's top concerns is health care. He has pushed to beef up the Food and Drug Administration's ability to crack down on counterfeit drugs. He also has worked for the availability of affordable housing, an issue of concern to his suburban constituents.

The co-founder of a bipartisan group called the Center Aisle Caucus, Israel regularly dines with GOP colleagues at a Chinese restaurant on Capitol Hill to discuss areas of mutual agreement — a ritual he said has proved instructive. He started the group after a busy day in 2005, when he was racing to

CAPITOL OFFICE
225-3335
www.house.gov/israel
2457 Rayburn Bldg. 20515-3202; fax 225-4669

COMMITTEES
Appropriations

RESIDENCE
Huntington

BORN
May 30, 1958; Brooklyn, N.Y.

RELIGION
Jewish

FAMILY
Wife, Marlene Budd; two children

EDUCATION
Nassau Community College, A.A. 1978 (liberal arts); Syracuse U., attended 1978-79; George Washington U., B.A. 1982 (political science)

CAREER
Public relations and marketing firm manager; assistant county executive; university fundraising director; Jewish advocacy group county director; congressional aide

POLITICAL HIGHLIGHTS
Democratic nominee for Suffolk County Legislature, 1987; Huntington Town Board, 1993-2001 (majority leader, 1997-2001)

ELECTION RESULTS

2008 GENERAL

Steve Israel (D, INDC, WFM)	161,279	66.9%
Frank J. Stalzer (R, C)	79,641	33.1%

2008 PRIMARY

Steve Israel (D, INDC, WFM)	unopposed

2006 GENERAL

Steve Israel (D, INDC, WFM)	105,276	70.4%
John W. Bugler (R, C)	44,212	29.6%

PREVIOUS WINNING PERCENTAGES
2004 (67%); 2002 (58%); 2000 (48%)

catch a flight home and flung open a House door with such force it struck the guy in front of him, Rep. Timothy V. Johnson, an Illinois Republican. The two had not met before, so Israel introduced himself. The two lawmakers are the caucus' co-founders.

Israel was mentioned as a possibility for the Senate seat vacated by Hillary Rodham Clinton before New York Democratic Gov. David A. Paterson chose his colleague Kirsten Gillibrand to fill it. He was among those mulling a 2010 primary challenge to Gillibrand and had more year-end fundraising receipts for 2008 — almost $500,000 — than any other House member. But in what he called a "tough, heartfelt decision," he backed off in May 2009 after President Obama discouraged him from running.

Israel became interested in politics at an early age. He started reading newspapers in elementary school, after hearing the news in school one day that Sen. Robert F. Kennedy, a New York Democrat and the late president's brother, had been assassinated. "I was thinking, at fourth grade, 'Why would someone get killed for what they believed in?' " he said.

In high school, he rode his bicycle after school to the campaign headquarters of Democrat Franklin Ornstein, who in 1974 waged an unsuccessful challenge to GOP Rep. Norman F. Lent. As a political science student at George Washington University, Israel worked part time for California Democratic Rep. Robert T. Matsui and then spent three years with Rep. Richard L. Ottinger, a New York Democrat. He returned to Long Island in 1983, where he worked as a fundraiser for Touro College, a Jewish-sponsored institution. In 1987, he lost a bid for the Suffolk County Legislature.

Israel formed his own fundraising and public relations firm, and was the director of the Institute on the Holocaust and the Law, which is affiliated with Touro and the American Jewish Congress. He stayed active in local politics, winning a seat on the Huntington Town Board in a 1993 special election. During his roughly seven years on the board, Israel worked with Republicans to put the town on a sound financial footing.

During his years in Long Island politics, Israel said, he always had in mind a return to Washington. His chance came in 2000 when Republican New York Mayor Rudy Giuliani announced that he had prostate cancer and was giving up his bid for the Senate. The 2nd District's four-term congressman, Republican Rick A. Lazio, stepped in to take the Senate nomination and Israel immediately launched a campaign for the open seat. He narrowly beat out Suffolk County legislator David Bishop for the Democratic nod and went on to win in the general election. Israel's subsequent races have resulted in easy victories.

KEY VOTES

2008

Yes Delay consideration of Colombia free-trade agreement

Yes Override Bush veto of federal farm and nutrition programs reauthorization bill

No Overhaul surveillance laws and permit dismissal of suits against companies that conducted warrantless wiretapping

Yes Grant mortgage relief to homeowners and funding for Fannie Mae and Freddie Mac

Yes Approve initial $700 billion program to stabilize financial markets

Yes Approve final $700 billion program to stabilize financial markets

Yes Provide $14 billion in loans to automakers

2007

Yes Increase minimum wage by $2.10 an hour

Yes Approve $124.2 billion in emergency war spending and set goal for redeployment of troops from Iraq

No Reject federal contraceptive assistance to international family planning groups

Yes Override Bush veto of $23.2 billion water projects authorization bill

Yes Implement Peru free-trade agreement

Yes Approve energy policy overhaul with new fuel economy standards

No Clear $473.5 billion omnibus spending bill, including $70 billion for military operations

CQ VOTE STUDIES

| | PARTY UNITY | | PRESIDENTIAL SUPPORT | |
	SUPPORT	OPPOSE	SUPPORT	OPPOSE
2008	99%	1%	15%	85%
2007	98%	2%	4%	96%
2006	93%	7%	28%	72%
2005	94%	6%	24%	76%
2004	92%	8%	30%	70%

INTEREST GROUPS

	AFL-CIO	ADA	CCUS	ACU
2008	100%	95%	61%	0%
2007	95%	85%	58%	0%
2006	100%	90%	50%	12%
2005	87%	90%	52%	8%
2004	93%	100%	47%	13%

NEW YORK 2
Long Island — Brentwood, Commack

Covering most of western Suffolk County and a small part of east-central Nassau County on Long Island, the 2nd is full of upper-middle-class suburban communities. Many residents who do not commute to New York City also contribute to the district's large white-collar workforce by working at technology firms in the 2nd.

The economy in the 2nd's portion of Nassau County, which includes Jericho, Old Bethpage, Plainview and Woodbury, remains stable. The district, once dependent on the defense industry, now hosts many computer and technology companies. Recent layoffs by key employers in manufacturing and the financial sector, and a slowdown in the real estate market, have hurt the 2nd. A large computer and electronics presence remains despite job cuts — Arrow Electronics and Audiovox both have headquarters in the district.

The 2nd hosts a relatively diverse population, mixing well-to-do communities such as the district's Nassau County portion and Dix Hills with solidly middle- and working-class neighborhoods. During the summer, many

New Yorkers flock to the district's communities along the Atlantic Ocean in the south. Some residents in the coastal areas still make modest incomes in the fishing industry, but Fire Island (shared with the 3rd) relies on tourism.

With a nearly 30 percent minority population, a significant Jewish community and a blue-collar base, the 2nd has a substantial, but not overwhelming, Democratic vote. Moderate Republicans can do well in local races, but the district favors Democratic candidates in federal elections. Registered Democrats outnumber Republicans here by 7 percentage points, and Barack Obama captured 56 percent of the district's vote in the 2008 presidential election.

MAJOR INDUSTRY
Computers, electronics, service

CITIES
Brentwood (unincorp.), 53,917; Commack (unincorp.), 36,363; Central Islip (unincorp.), 31,950; Huntington Station (unincorp.), 29,910

NOTABLE
The Walt Whitman Birthplace State Historic Site and Interpretive Center is in West Hills (South Huntington); Ocean Beach, a village on the Fire Island National Seashore, prohibits eating and drinking on the beach.

Rep. Peter T. King (R)

Elected 1992; 9th term

King is a longtime GOP maverick with a reputation as a colorful quipster. He seeks to prove he can reach across the aisle to get things done as the senior Republican on the Homeland Security Committee, just as he did when he chaired the panel.

Outspoken and brusque, King once dismissed then-Speaker Newt Gingrich as "roadkill on the highway of American politics" and labeled France a "third-rate country," suggesting in 2003 that French leaders go to Baghdad "to instruct the Iraqis in how to surrender."

But when King was made Homeland Security chairman in September 2005 after campaigning hard for the job, he was keen to show he could do more than just toss out lively sound bites. He guided the committee to a series of impressive accomplishments, including a $2 billion port security law to screen millions of containers that enter the United States each year. He also had a hand in restructuring the Federal Emergency Management Agency after its bungling of the 2005 Hurricane Katrina crisis.

As a member of the minority since the 110th Congress (2007-08), he had to relinquish the chairmanship to Mississippi Democrat Bennie Thompson. Nevertheless, King remained active in shaping legislation. He authored and piloted through the House a bill to set up an office within the Homeland Security Department to promote international cooperation in developing technology to fight terrorists. The legislation was rolled into a bill to adopt the recommendations of the Sept. 11 commission, which became law. He also guided through the House a separate proposal to create an office within the department to prevent terrorist bombing attacks, a bill he advanced again in 2009.

King is frustrated his committee still must share jurisdiction over the department with other panels, despite the Sept. 11 commission's recommendations for consolidating oversight. He noted in a November 2008 letter to Speaker Nancy Pelosi of California that DHS reports to 108 committees and subcommittees. "I don't want to come across as one of these turf-crazy ranking members or committee chairmen that just want everything for his committee...I just feel very strongly as a matter of policy that homeland security has to be much more consolidated than it is now," he said in an interview.

The son of a New York City police officer, King supports close coordination between the federal government and local police and firefighters in combating terrorism. He thinks Congress should try to make the public more vigilant about preventing terrorism. "Too many have forgotten the lessons of 9/11," he said in 2009.

As a member of the Financial Services Committee, King championed a bill that extended for seven years the Terrorism Risk Insurance Act, which obligates the government to help pay for financial losses from future attacks. The measure was signed into law in December 2007.

He also supported both versions — the second of which became law — of legislation in fall 2008 to shore up the ailing financial services industry, along with a subsequent failed effort to assist struggling U.S. automakers.

King is just enough of a GOP maverick to frequently get his name into the newspapers and on the air, and he's just enough of a conservative to keep himself in the good graces of the Republican leadership. He's one of the few members of Congress to have pictures on his wall of himself with both Bill Clinton and George W. Bush.

King votes with his party on most fiscal and social issues, supporting expanded trade opportunities and private-school vouchers while opposing

CAPITOL OFFICE
225-7896
www.house.gov/king
339 Cannon Bldg. 20515-3203; fax 226-2279

COMMITTEES
Financial Services
Homeland Security - ranking member

RESIDENCE
Seaford

BORN
April 5, 1944; Manhattan, N.Y.

RELIGION
Roman Catholic

FAMILY
Wife, Rosemary King; two children

EDUCATION
St. Francis College, B.A. 1965 (history);
U. of Notre Dame, J.D. 1968

MILITARY SERVICE
N.Y. National Guard, 1968-73

CAREER
Lawyer

POLITICAL HIGHLIGHTS
Hempstead Town Council, 1978-81; Nassau County comptroller, 1981-93; Republican nominee for N.Y. attorney general, 1986

ELECTION RESULTS

2008 GENERAL

Peter T. King (R, INDC, C)	172,774	63.9%
Graham E. Long (D, WFM)	97,525	36.1%

2008 PRIMARY

Peter T. King (R)	6,847	88.4%
Robert Previdi (R)	897	11.6%

2006 GENERAL

Peter T. King (R, INDC, C)	101,787	56.0%
David L. Mejias (D, WFM)	79,843	44.0%

PREVIOUS WINNING PERCENTAGES
2004 (63%); 2002 (72%); 2000 (60%); 1998 (64%); 1996 (55%); 1994 (59%); 1992 (50%)

abortion. But he also supports labor unions' efforts to raise the minimum wage and expand worker protections.

King has had an important role in promoting peace efforts in Northern Ireland. He has made several trips there and has a close relationship with Gerry Adams, the leader of Sinn Fein, the political wing of the Irish Republican Army (IRA). Nevertheless, in 2005, frustrated with increasing criminal behavior in the IRA, King called for it to disband, a major step for one of Sinn Fein's biggest backers in Congress.

King draws on his experiences to fuel his pastime: fiction writing. In his 2004 novel "Vale of Tears," the congressman protagonist faces radical Islamists in cahoots with the IRA. In the earlier "Deliver Us From Evil," another thinly disguised congressman character seeks an end to fighting in Northern Ireland. And in "Terrible Beauty," he chronicled a housewife's involvement with the IRA after her husband is wrongfully jailed for murder.

His interest in Irish affairs — three of his grandparents are from Ireland — brought King close to former Democratic Sen. Hillary Rodham Clinton, now secretary of State. King worked closely with her husband's administration on a 1998 peace accord and flew to Ireland on Air Force One for the celebration. The same year, King argued against impeaching the president, and was one of four Republicans to vote against all four impeachment articles.

King grew up in a blue-collar Queens neighborhood, which proved good training for his future in neighboring Nassau County's rough-and-tumble politics. Neighborhood kids were as likely to be boxing fans as baseball fans. "This is the one sport where you are out there on your own," King, who boxes for exercise, told Newsday.

He borrowed money to attend Notre Dame's law school. Afterward he interned (along with Rudy Giuliani, who later became mayor of New York) at Richard Nixon's New York law firm. He entered public life in 1972 as a deputy Nassau County attorney and eventually became the county comptroller, serving three terms. During his tenure, King lost a 1986 run for New York attorney general.

When veteran GOP Rep. Norman F. Lent stepped down in 1992, King moved quickly to claim the seat. After coasting through the primary, he edged the better-funded Democrat, Steve A. Orlins. He won re-election easily until 2006, when the anti-GOP tide held him to 56 percent of the vote.

King said in mid-2008 he was toying with running for New York governor in 2010, but by early 2009, he appeared to be more interested in a potential 2010 challenge to Democrat Kirsten Gillibrand, who was appointed to Clinton's Senate seat.

KEY VOTES

2008
No Delay consideration of Colombia free-trade agreement
No Override Bush veto of federal farm and nutrition programs reauthorization bill
Yes Overhaul surveillance laws and permit dismissal of suits against companies that conducted warrantless wiretapping
Yes Grant mortgage relief to homeowners and funding for Fannie Mae and Freddie Mac
Yes Approve initial $700 billion program to stabilize financial markets
Yes Approve final $700 billion program to stabilize financial markets
Yes Provide $14 billion in loans to automakers

2007
Yes Increase minimum wage by $2.10 an hour
No Approve $124.2 billion in emergency war spending and set goal for redeployment of troops from Iraq
Yes Reject federal contraceptive assistance to international family planning groups
Yes Override Bush veto of $23.2 billion water projects authorization bill
Yes Implement Peru free-trade agreement
Yes Approve energy policy overhaul with new fuel economy standards
Yes Clear $473.5 billion omnibus spending bill, including $70 billion for military operations

CQ VOTE STUDIES

	PARTY UNITY		PRESIDENTIAL SUPPORT	
	SUPPORT	OPPOSE	SUPPORT	OPPOSE
2008	87%	13%	67%	33%
2007	80%	20%	63%	37%
2006	89%	11%	95%	5%
2005	89%	11%	83%	17%
2004	83%	17%	77%	23%

INTEREST GROUPS

	AFL-CIO	ADA	CCUS	ACU
2008	53%	45%	94%	50%
2007	57%	30%	90%	68%
2006	36%	5%	100%	76%
2005	20%	0%	89%	83%
2004	50%	25%	80%	71%

NEW YORK 3

Long Island – Levittown, Hicksville, Long Beach

Most of Long Island's eastern Nassau County and the south shore of western Suffolk County make up the 3rd, where extravagant estates mix with some of the nation's oldest middle-class suburbs. The district boasts New York state's second-highest median income and is overwhelmingly white, with the lowest percentage of black residents (2 percent) in the state and the lowest percentage of Hispanics (7 percent) in the New York City area.

Aircraft manufacturing giant Northrop Grumman, once a major local employer, still employs thousands but plays a reduced role in the 3rd's economy. Information technology companies have spread throughout the 3rd and neighboring Long Island districts, diversifying the local economy. Rising foreclosure rates in suburbs such as Levittown concern residents, as do job cuts across blue- and white-collar industries.

Tourism helps the district's economy, as thousands of visitors flock to summer paradises like Freeport's "Nautical Mile" and to beautiful golf courses, including Bethpage State Park, home to the 2009 U.S. Open

Championship. The 3rd boasts a variety of beautiful south shore beaches, including Long Beach and Jones Beach, which hosts an outdoor summer concert series. Other visitors travel to President Theodore Roosevelt's Sagamore Hill estate in Oyster Bay and his nearby grave in Youngs Memorial Cemetery.

The district tends to favor Republican candidates, but a significant labor presence from construction and professional unions gives Democrats some areas of strength. Democrats also have made gains in Nassau County, but John McCain won 52 percent of the district's vote overall in the 2008 election.

MAJOR INDUSTRY
Higher education, information technology, service

CITIES
Levittown (unincorporated), 53,067; Hicksville (unincorporated) (pt.), 39,670; Long Beach, 35,462; West Islip (unincorporated) (pt.), 27,171; Lindenhurst (pt.), 27,162; Glen Cove, 26,622

NOTABLE
The C.W. Post Campus of Long Island University, named for the breakfast cereal and food company founder, is located on the grounds of the former Brookville estate of the magnate's daughter.

Rep. Carolyn McCarthy (D)

Elected 1996; 7th term

CAPITOL OFFICE
225-5516
carolynmccarthy.house.gov
2346 Rayburn Bldg. 20515-3204; fax 225-5758

COMMITTEES
Education & Labor
(Healthy Families & Communities - chairwoman)
Financial Services

RESIDENCE
Mineola

BORN
Jan. 5, 1944; Brooklyn, N.Y.

RELIGION
Roman Catholic

FAMILY
Widowed; one child

EDUCATION
Glen Cove Nursing School, L.P.N. 1964

CAREER
Nurse

POLITICAL HIGHLIGHTS
No previous office

ELECTION RESULTS

2008 GENERAL

Carolyn McCarthy (D, INDC, WFM)	164,028	64.0%
Jack M. Martins (R, C)	92,242	36.0%

2008 PRIMARY

Carolyn McCarthy (D)	unopposed

2006 GENERAL

Carolyn McCarthy (D, INDC, WFM)	101,861	64.9%
Martin W. Blessinger (R, C)	55,050	35.1%

PREVIOUS WINNING PERCENTAGES
2004 (63%); 2002 (56%); 2000 (61%); 1998 (53%);
1996 (57%)

McCarthy has dealt with a series of tragedies in her life that have shaped her views, most strongly on gun control. But she brings the same determination to other issues on her plate, including education, health care, and more recently financial matters as she seeks to help constituents weather the nation's economic downturn.

She is a steady friend of labor and supports legislation to promote abortion rights and environmental protection. But she can sometimes tilt toward conservatism: She has backed constitutional amendments to ban desecration of the U.S. flag and to require a two-thirds congressional majority to raise federal taxes. She also has voted to repeal the estate tax, though she opposed President George W. Bush's 2003 tax cuts.

McCarthy first ran for Congress after a deranged gunman shot and killed her husband, Dennis, and seriously wounded her adult son, Kevin, on a Long Island commuter train in December 1993. She said she accepts that she will always be identified with the tragedy. "I've come to peace with the fact that that will be in my obituary," she told The Associated Press. And it has been the basis of much of her work in the House.

The killing of 32 students and faculty members by a student at Virginia Tech University in an April 2007 shooting spree gave her the political momentum to push to strengthen crime laws. A 1968 gun control law prohibits people "adjudicated as a mental defective" from purchasing guns, but states had never systematically turned over records of mentally ill people for inclusion in the FBI's National Instant Criminal Background Check System. The Virginia Tech shooter, Seung-Hui Cho, had been treated for mental illness involuntarily in 2005 and should have been on the list.

After the shootings, the National Rifle Association — despite opposition from some gun rights advocates — backed McCarthy's legislation to require states to turn over mental health records to the FBI. The House passed it unanimously in June 2007 and it was signed by Bush in January 2008. Later that year, Bush signed into law a bill reauthorizing higher education programs, which included language drafted by McCarthy — a member of the Education and Labor Committee — that requires universities to develop plans to inform students of on-campus emergencies. Many criticized Virginia Tech for failing to notify students after Cho killed two students hours before he massacred 30 more people.

McCarthy still can't find enough votes to extend an assault weapons ban that expired in 2004. And in June 2008, the Supreme Court appeared to further complicate her efforts when it struck down a District of Columbia law banning handguns and declared for the first time that the Second Amendment includes an individual right to bear arms. She was disappointed when the House passed, as an amendment to a D.C. voting rights bill, a provision codifying the high court's ruling. "Local municipalities and cities have the right to make their own laws," she said.

The issue of guns also led McCarthy to mull a 2010 primary challenge to Democrat Kirsten Gillibrand, whom Democratic Gov. David A. Paterson named to the Senate to replace Hillary Rodham Clinton after Clinton became secretary of State. McCarthy strongly criticized Gillibrand's positions protecting gun control while she served in the House.

Having struggled with dyslexia, McCarthy has a special interest in education and has been active on Education and Labor. As chairwoman of the Healthy Families and Communities Subcommittee, she has pushed to provide tax credits for purchasing hearing aids and to reverse funding cuts for mammograms and other medical imaging services. She also has focused on school nutrition programs. While she backed President Obama's $787 billion economic stimulus law in early 2009, she was disappointed funds weren't set aside for school modernization.

She played an active role when the Education panel drafted No Child Left Behind, an education law Bush signed in 2002. McCarthy joined forces with Michigan Democrat Dale E. Kildee and Indiana Republican Mark Souder to defeat an attempt to consolidate drug-abuse prevention and after-school programs into a single block grant.

McCarthy also sits on the Financial Services Committee. She was a reluctant supporter of the $700 billion law, signed in fall 2008, to help the nation's ailing financial services sector. She said she supported it because many workers in her district rely on Manhattan's banks for employment. The following spring she harshly criticized American International Group Inc. for providing million-dollar bonuses to company executives: "This is the height of irresponsibility, arrogance and hypocrisy."

A massive 2008 housing law includes her provision directing funding to organizations that provide early outreach and counseling to people at risk of foreclosure. A 2007 law to reduce college costs includes her proposal to provide federal loan forgiveness to people who go into nursing, teaching or other public service work. She pushed through Congress in early 2009 a bill to expand national and community service programs.

She was born in Brooklyn and her family moved to Mineola, Long Island, when she was 8. She and her husband later bought her childhood home from her parents. Twenty-seven years later, McCarthy held his funeral reception there. Her kitchen is full of plates with Norman Rockwell paintings on them.

As a high school student, McCarthy planned on being a gym teacher. Then her boyfriend was involved in a serious car accident. She watched as a private-duty nurse cared for him and as he died of his injuries a few days later. "I came home that day and applied to nursing school," she told Good Housekeeping magazine. She worked as a nurse for more than 30 years, caring for terminally ill patients. After McCarthy married, she and her stockbroker husband lived in Mineola, where they raised their son. After the shootings, her son was paralyzed and not expected to walk again, but with McCarthy's care, he was able to resume his commute to Manhattan to work.

Since her initial race in 1996, McCarthy has won re-election with ease, with the exception of her second contest. In 1998, eight-term state Rep. Gregory R. Becker held her to a 6-percentage-point margin.

KEY VOTES

2008
Yes Delay consideration of Colombia free-trade agreement
Yes Override Bush veto of federal farm and nutrition programs reauthorization bill
Yes Overhaul surveillance laws and permit dismissal of suits against companies that conducted warrantless wiretapping
Yes Grant mortgage relief to homeowners and funding for Fannie Mae and Freddie Mac
Yes Approve initial $700 billion program to stabilize financial markets
Yes Approve final $700 billion program to stabilize financial markets
Yes Provide $14 billion in loans to automakers

2007
Yes Increase minimum wage by $2.10 an hour
Yes Approve $124.2 billion in emergency war spending and set goal for redeployment of troops from Iraq
No Reject federal contraceptive assistance to international family planning groups
Yes Override Bush veto of $23.2 billion water projects authorization bill
Yes Implement Peru free-trade agreement
Yes Approve energy policy overhaul with new fuel economy standards
No Clear $473.5 billion omnibus spending bill, including $70 billion for military operations

CQ VOTE STUDIES

	PARTY UNITY		PRESIDENTIAL SUPPORT	
	SUPPORT	OPPOSE	SUPPORT	OPPOSE
2008	99%	1%	16%	84%
2007	98%	2%	5%	95%
2006	92%	8%	30%	70%
2005	93%	7%	22%	78%
2004	94%	6%	32%	68%

INTEREST GROUPS

	AFL-CIO	ADA	CCUS	ACU
2008	100%	95%	65%	0%
2007	96%	90%	58%	0%
2006	100%	90%	47%	20%
2005	93%	90%	50%	8%
2004	93%	100%	45%	12%

NEW YORK 4
Southwest Nassau County – Hempstead

The Long Island-based 4th extends east from the Queens border to take in southwest and west-central Nassau County. The district combines wealthy white-collar suburbanites, some of whom still commute to Wall Street, with some low- and middle-income residents.

Bordered roughly by Interstate 495 in the north, the 4th picks up numerous midsize communities and includes a small portion of Long Island's Atlantic Ocean coastline in Atlantic Beach. Hempstead is home to Hofstra University's 240-acre campus, which continues to drive Hempstead's economy. Construction of a new medical school expected to open in 2011 will bring jobs and boost the college's impact. Many local officials and residents hope that major redevelopment of the area surrounding the Nassau Veterans Memorial Coliseum, home of hockey's New York Islanders, will bring jobs without exacerbating traffic issues.

Despite a decline in the defense industry that began two decades ago, defense technology companies still provide jobs here. A number of working-class residents are employed by John F. Kennedy International

Airport (located nearby in the 6th District), Belmont Park race track or large shopping centers such as Garden City's Roosevelt Field Mall. Hospitals and health care facilities throughout the district also employ many area residents. Job losses affecting residents who commute to Manhattan's financial sector have hurt the local economy.

The 4th has the largest minority population of Long Island's four congressional districts and has a Democratic base, particularly in Hempstead and Uniondale, which include large black and Hispanic communities. The largely Jewish "Five Towns" (Inwood, Lawrence, Cedarhurst, Woodmere and Hewlett), in the 4th's southwestern corner, also lean Democratic. In local elections, the 4th favors some moderate Republicans, but Democrats win in federal and statewide races. Barack Obama took 58 percent of the district's 2008 presidential vote.

MAJOR INDUSTRY
Health care, technology, higher education

CITIES
Hempstead, 56,554; East Meadow (unincorporated), 37,461; Valley Stream, 36,368; Freeport (pt.), 34,958; Elmont (unincorporated), 32,657

NOTABLE
In 1957, Adelphi University hosted the first National Wheelchair Games.

Rep. Gary L. Ackerman (D)

Elected March 1983; 13th full term

CAPITOL OFFICE
225-2601
www.house.gov/ackerman
2243 Rayburn Bldg. 20515-3205; fax 225-1589

COMMITTEES
Financial Services
Foreign Affairs
   (Middle East & South Asia - chairman)

RESIDENCE
Roslyn Heights

BORN
Nov. 19, 1942; Brooklyn, N.Y.

RELIGION
Jewish

FAMILY
Wife, Rita Ackerman; three children

EDUCATION
Queens College, B.A. 1965

CAREER
Teacher; newspaper publisher and editor;
advertising executive

POLITICAL HIGHLIGHTS
Sought Democratic nomination for New York
City Council at large, 1977; N.Y. Senate, 1979-83

ELECTION RESULTS

2008 GENERAL

Gary L. Ackerman (D, INDC, WFM)	112,724	71.0%
Elizabeth Berney (R)	43,039	27.1%
Jun Policarpio (C)	3,010	1.9%

2008 PRIMARY

Gary L. Ackerman (D)	unopposed

2006 GENERAL

Gary L. Ackerman (D, INDC, WFM)	unopposed

PREVIOUS WINNING PERCENTAGES
2004 (71%); 2002 (92%); 2000 (68%); 1998 (65%);
1996 (64%); 1994 (55%); 1992 (52%); 1990 (100%);
1988 (100%); 1986 (77%); 1984 (69%); 1983 Special
Election (50%)

One of the House's most colorful characters, Ackerman is an old-school New Yorker: irreverent, quirky and more than willing to push hard on issues that concern him — national security, tougher financial regulation, the U.S. image abroad — while protecting his district's interests.

Ackerman's funny and unorthodox views have made him an occasional guest on radio shock jock Howard Stern's program. He is a liberal on most issues, yet at times spars with progressive activists and some in his own party because of his uncompromising defense of Israel and other Middle East issues.

In May 2008, when many liberal activists feared the George W. Bush administration was considering a military strike against Iran to disrupt its alleged nuclear weapons program, Ackerman introduced a resolution declaring that preventing Iran from acquiring the weapons is vital to U.S. national security. That summer, 15 activists from the anti-war group Code Pink — aboard three canoes and an inflatable raft — surrounded Ackerman's houseboat on the Potomac River, his home while he's in Washington. (He calls his houseboat the Unsinkable II — the first Unsinkable wasn't.)

The protestors blew sirens, banged on drums and chanted through megaphones demanding that Ackerman withdraw his resolution, which they contended would mark a first step toward war. Ackerman emerged and planted a kiss on one of the activists. But he declined to withdraw his resolution.

As chairman of the Foreign Affairs panel's Middle East and South Asia Subcommittee, Ackerman is a close ally of Foreign Affairs Chairman Howard L. Berman of California. Like Berman, Ackerman voted to authorize war with Iraq but now says he wants "a prudent withdrawal at earliest opportune moment." Ackerman also shares Berman's desire for a new Pakistan policy focused on demonstrating support for democracy.

During the 110th Congress (2007-08), Ackerman used his subcommittee post to secure non-binding resolutions expressing the sense of the House on various foreign policy matters, the Iran resolution being a primary example. In early 2007, just after the end of Israel's war with Lebanon, the House endorsed his resolution calling for the immediate and unconditional release of Israeli soldiers held by the terrorist groups Hamas and Hezbollah. A year later, Ackerman sponsored the resolution condemning the assassination of former Pakistani Prime Minister Benazir Bhutto.

As a senior member of the Financial Services Committee, Ackerman helped steer to enactment a 2007 bill that renewed for seven years a federal program to backstop insurance companies in the event of a catastrophic terrorist attack. Ackerman argued the terrorism risk insurance law was necessary to allow New York City to rebuild at the site of the former World Trade Center, destroyed in the 2001 terrorist attacks.

Ackerman supported the $700 billion financial sector rescue plan enacted in October 2008. During the 111th Congress (2009-10) he was pushing to toughen rules governing how credit rating agencies evaluate products such as the mortgage-backed securities that were at the heart of the financial crisis and economic meltdown that followed.

Ackerman had constituents who fell victim to investment scam artist Bernard Madoff, arrested in late 2008 for what was described as the biggest Ponzi scheme in history. He excoriated Securities and Exchange Commission officials for failing to act against Madoff when they were warned he was up to no good. "Your mission, you said, was to protect investors and detect fraud quickly," he angrily told the SEC's enforcement chief at a 2009 hearing. "How'd that work out?…You couldn't find your backside with two hands if the lights were on."

At a hearing in February 2007 with Secretary of State Condoleezza Rice, Ackerman criticized the Pentagon for firing linguists fluent in Arabic and Farsi because they are homosexual. "For some reason, the military seems more afraid of gay people than they are of terrorists," he said. "And if the terrorists ever got a hold of this information, they would get a platoon of lesbians to chase us out of Baghdad."

He carefully tends to the parochial concerns of his diverse 5th District. He saved the U.S. Coast Guard station at Eatons Neck from threatened closure; he pushed for resolution of the 1994 Long Island Rail Road strike; and he lobbies relentlessly for funds to clean up Long Island Sound.

He sports a white carnation boutonniere daily, a habit he picked up more than 30 years ago as a New York public school teacher. One morning, he stopped at a florist, added a flower to his lapel, and told his students, who assumed incorrectly that it was his birthday, "Every day is special."

Ackerman was born in Brooklyn and grew up in a Queens housing project with his parents and a brother. His mother was a Polish immigrant. He trusted his cabbie father for a sense of what people in New York were thinking, later calling him his "pollster" and "always right on the money."

After college, Ackerman was a social studies teacher. In 1969, as a new father, he successfully sued the New York City Board of Education for the right of a father to receive unpaid leave to care for newborns, at a time when the benefit was offered only to women. He later left teaching to launch his own community newspaper in Queens, and subsequently had run-ins with the local Democratic machine. He is still on the board of managers of Tribco LLC, publisher of the Queens Tribune and nine other weekly newspapers.

Ackerman was elected to the state Senate in 1978. After 7th District Democratic Rep. Benjamin S. Rosenthal died in 1983, Ackerman persuaded Democratic leaders to support him in the special election. He won with 50 percent of the vote, then cruised through four re-elections.

In redistricting for the 1992 election, some of Ackerman's base in Queens was replaced with conservative, suburban areas in Nassau and Suffolk counties, throwing him into Long Island's 5th District. He was hurt by revelations he had 111 overdrafts at the House members' bank, but he prevailed by 7 percentage points. Further changes to the boundaries before the 2002 election made the 5th more Democratic, and Ackerman has taken each re-election since with ease.

KEY VOTES

2008
Yes Delay consideration of Colombia free-trade agreement
Yes Override Bush veto of federal farm and nutrition programs reauthorization bill
Yes Overhaul surveillance laws and permit dismissal of suits against companies that conducted warrantless wiretapping
Yes Grant mortgage relief to homeowners and funding for Fannie Mae and Freddie Mac
Yes Approve initial $700 billion program to stabilize financial markets
Yes Approve final $700 billion program to stabilize financial markets
Yes Provide $14 billion in loans to automakers

2007
Yes Increase minimum wage by $2.10 an hour
Yes Approve $124.2 billion in emergency war spending and set goal for redeployment of troops from Iraq
No   Reject federal contraceptive assistance to international family planning groups
Yes Override Bush veto of $23.2 billion water projects authorization bill
Yes Implement Peru free-trade agreement
Yes Approve energy policy overhaul with new fuel economy standards
No   Clear $473.5 billion omnibus spending bill, including $70 billion for military operations

CQ VOTE STUDIES

| | PARTY UNITY | | PRESIDENTIAL SUPPORT | |
	SUPPORT	OPPOSE	SUPPORT	OPPOSE
2008	99%	1%	15%	85%
2007	99%	1%	7%	93%
2006	95%	5%	33%	67%
2005	98%	3%	24%	76%
2004	99%	1%	30%	70%

INTEREST GROUPS

	AFL-CIO	ADA	CCUS	ACU
2008	100%	100%	67%	0%
2007	96%	90%	55%	0%
2006	93%	95%	47%	8%
2005	93%	95%	37%	4%
2004	93%	95%	41%	4%

NEW YORK 5
Northeast Queens; northwest Nassau County

The 5th stretches east from south of LaGuardia Airport in Queens into northwestern Nassau County, reaching Roslyn and East Hills. Almost 80 percent of the Democratic-leaning 5th's residents live in Queens.

Just under half of New York City's Asians live in Queens, especially in downtown Flushing, which has the second-largest Chinatown in New York. The district has the largest Asian population of any congressional district outside Hawaii or California. The neighborhoods in Corona have a strong Hispanic influence.

The 5th's economy, especially in Flushing, is supported both by small businesses and national chains. The economy here also is heavily driven by white-collar jobs located outside the district and is boosted by the U.S. Merchant Marine Academy at Kings Point. Sports fans and tourists visit major sporting venues Citi Field in Flushing, the new home of baseball's Mets, and the USTA National Tennis Center in Flushing Meadows-Corona Park, where the U.S. Open tennis tournament is held each year. Planned residential and retail development in Flushing aims to

transform waterfront and former industrial sites.

Although pockets of low-income neighborhoods exist in the 5th, northeastern Queens has affluent areas such as Douglaston and Little Neck. Before fanning eastward into Nassau, the district buttonhooks to the south and west along the Grand Central Parkway to take in some communities in north Jamaica. Residents along Long Island's "Gold Coast" in Nassau County areas such as Roslyn Estates enjoy some of the nation's highest incomes and a generally rich lifestyle.

The district's portion of Nassau tends to be more politically competitive than its strongly Democratic section of Queens. Democrat Barack Obama won the parts of both counties that are in the district, and he took 63 percent overall in the district in the 2008 presidential election.

MAJOR INDUSTRY
Higher education, health care, small business

CITIES
New York (pt.), 517,889; Port Washington (unincorporated), 15,215

NOTABLE
Trumpet virtuoso Louis Armstrong is buried at Flushing Cemetery; The Queens County Farm Museum is New York City's largest tract of farmland.

Rep. Gregory W. Meeks (D)

Elected February 1998; 6th full term

CAPITOL OFFICE
225-3461
www.house.gov/meeks
2342 Rayburn Bldg. 20515-3206; fax 226-4169

COMMITTEES
Financial Services
  (International Monetary Policy & Trade
  - chairman)
Foreign Affairs

RESIDENCE
Queens

BORN
Sept. 25, 1953; Harlem, N.Y.

RELIGION
African Methodist Espiscopal

FAMILY
Wife, Simone-Marie Meeks; three children

EDUCATION
Adelphi U., B.A. 1975; Howard U., J.D. 1978

CAREER
Workers' compensation board judge; lawyer; city
prosecutor

POLITICAL HIGHLIGHTS
N.Y. Assembly, 1993-98

ELECTION RESULTS

2008 GENERAL
Gregory W. Meeks (D)   unopposed
2008 PRIMARY
Gregory W. Meeks (D)   unopposed
2006 GENERAL
Gregory W. Meeks (D)   unopposed
PREVIOUS WINNING PERCENTAGES
2004 (100%); 2002 (97%); 2000 (100%); 1998 (100%);
1998 Special Election (56%)

Meeks typifies the new breed of pro-business black politician that has emerged since the civil rights movement. He is a member of both the New Democrat Coalition and the Democratic Leadership Council, which advance politically moderate policies. "I'm one who understands that, particularly in the African-American community, the key is now economic," he once said. "We have to move toward the economic redistribution of our community more than we have in the past. That's what I'm about."

Meeks represents a middle-class, largely black district in Queens and chairs the Congressional Black Caucus' economic security task force. He uses his seat on the Financial Services Committee to focus on modernizing rules for Wall Street and helping cash-strapped homeowners. As chairman of the panel's International Monetary Policy and Trade Subcommittee and a member of the Foreign Affairs Committee, he advocates economic and trade policies that will help poor nations.

His district is home to the John F. Kennedy International Airport, and he has advocated trade to help boost cargo traffic at the airport. He said he supported the U.S.-Colombia trade agreement in 2008, which had languished because of Democratic concerns about violence toward union organizers and other human rights issues. He also backed the 2005 Central America Free Trade Agreement, drawing the ire of labor groups. He pushes for debate over trade to also include consideration of poor nations, arguing the so-called "global economy" ignores most of sub-Saharan Africa as well as parts of Asia, the Pacific and the Middle East.

"U.S. trade policy needs to help these regions on the outside, through reform of the U.S. textile tariffs, European and Japanese farm quotas and Indian and Chinese import limits, which tilt world trade policies against the outsiders," he said in a Miami Herald opinion column he co-authored in 2007.

When President Obama in early 2009 pledged to help boost International Monetary Fund resources to help other economies in crisis — a proposal that drew some concerns in Congress about another bailout — Meeks said the fund "has to play a big role" in helping poorer countries.

But much of his work focuses closer to home. He used his seat on Financial Services during the 110th Congress (2007-08) to oppose increased regulation of mortgage giants Fannie Mae and Freddie Mac, urging instead that they increase homeownership. But as the financial crisis worsened, he supported Congress' attempt to rescue them in July 2008. He also backed a subsequent $700 billion initiative to shore up the ailing financial services sector, saying frozen credit markets could make it impossible for his district's small businesses and nonprofit groups to keep operating.

He followed up to ensure such businesses, many of them minority-owned, could be approved for the rescue funds. He also said he wanted the funds to help cash-strapped homeowners, maintaining the government can use leverage over financial services firms and banks and force them to renegotiate individual mortgages. Meeks wants to increase the power of regulators and possibly create an agency to effectively oversee more-exotic financial instruments, such as credit default swaps, which contributed to the financial crisis.

Meeks chairs the Democratic Leadership Council's Global Economy Project, which is intended to develop policies aimed at preserving U.S. economic leadership and helping workers take advantage of opportunities. One crucial way to accomplish that and compete on a global level, he believes, is to improve public education. "Otherwise, we're going to lose," he said.

He is interested in airline issues and introduced a bill in 2008 aimed at blocking an administration plan to auction takeoff and landing slots at New York airports to reduce congestion. He argued it favored bigger, wealthier airlines.

He is active on civil rights and was arrested for protesting the under-representation of minority law clerks at the Supreme Court. And after four New York City police officers shot and killed Guinean immigrant Amadou Diallo in 1999, he joined other black leaders in protesting police violence against minorities.

Raised in public housing in East Harlem, Meeks traces his interest in public affairs to his mother, who resumed her education when her four children were in their teens and frequently got her kids involved in community improvement projects. As a youth, his idol was legendary civil rights attorney and Supreme Court Justice Thurgood Marshall. "From the time that I could remember, I wanted to be a lawyer," Meeks told Newsday. "I always admired Thurgood Marshall, and I learned from my parents what he was doing to make life better for people of color."

After graduating from Howard University Law School, Meeks began his career as a Queens County assistant district attorney and narcotics crime prosecutor. After a brief stint on the state Commission of Investigation, which probes wrongdoing by state officials and organized crime, Meeks was appointed as a state workers' compensation judge. During those years, Meeks became involved in a variety of community projects — neighborhood clean-ups, street repairs, traffic problems and street safety — in the working-class neighborhood of Far Rockaway, where his parents eventually moved.

Meeks said he always thought his involvement in politics would be behind the scenes, but in 1992 he ran for and won the first of three terms to the state Assembly. In his years in Albany, he had seats on panels that oversaw state codes, the judiciary, insurance, small business and government operations.

When Democrat Floyd H. Flake resigned from the House in late 1997 to lead an influential African Methodist Episcopal church in Jamaica, Queens, he endorsed Meeks as his successor. Meeks also got the backing of local Democratic leaders in the February 1998 special election, helping him capture 56 percent of the vote in a five-way contest. He was unopposed for a full term in November and has not drawn Republican opposition in subsequent elections.

Early in 2008, Meeks agreed to pay a $63,000 fine and to reimburse his campaign committee after a 2006 Federal Election Commission finding that he had illegally used campaign cash from the 2004 election for a personal trainer and leased cars for personal use. Meeks blamed the problems on sloppy bookkeeping by his then-treasurer, who he said owned a gym. Meeks said he didn't know the treasurer was paying the trainer to work with him.

KEY VOTES

2008

Yes   Delay consideration of Colombia free-trade agreement

Yes   Override Bush veto of federal farm and nutrition programs reauthorization bill

Yes   Overhaul surveillance laws and permit dismissal of suits against companies that conducted warrantless wiretapping

Yes   Grant mortgage relief to homeowners and funding for Fannie Mae and Freddie Mac

Yes   Approve initial $700 billion program to stabilize financial markets

Yes   Approve final $700 billion program to stabilize financial markets

Yes   Provide $14 billion in loans to automakers

2007

Yes   Increase minimum wage by $2.10 an hour

Yes   Approve $124.2 billion in emergency war spending and set goal for redeployment of troops from Iraq

No   Reject federal contraceptive assistance to international family planning groups

Yes   Override Bush veto of $23.2 billion water projects authorization bill

Yes   Implement Peru free-trade agreement

Yes   Approve energy policy overhaul with new fuel economy standards

No   Clear $473.5 billion omnibus spending bill, including $70 billion for military operations

CQ VOTE STUDIES

	PARTY UNITY		PRESIDENTIAL SUPPORT	
	SUPPORT	OPPOSE	SUPPORT	OPPOSE
2008	99%	1%	19%	81%
2007	98%	2%	6%	94%
2006	88%	12%	41%	59%
2005	93%	7%	32%	68%
2004	94%	6%	37%	63%

INTEREST GROUPS

	AFL-CIO	ADA	CCUS	ACU
2008	100%	90%	65%	0%
2007	96%	95%	58%	0%
2006	86%	90%	57%	8%
2005	92%	90%	59%	12%
2004	93%	75%	55%	9%

NEW YORK 6

Southeast Queens – Jamaica, St. Albans

The black-majority, mostly middle-class 6th is economically focused around John F. Kennedy International Airport on Jamaica Bay in southeastern Queens. It is the only district wholly within the 2.2 million-resident borough of Queens.

The 6th is bound roughly by Cross Bay Boulevard to the west, Grand Central Parkway to the north and the Nassau County line to the east. South of the airport, across Jamaica Bay, the 6th takes in part of Rockaway, including Edgemere and Far Rockaway. Included in the 6th's boundaries are St. John's University, located in the far north, and Aqueduct Racetrack, in the far west.

More than a generation ago, communities such as Springfield Gardens and and St. Albans were settled by an Irish and Italian Catholic middle class. The demographics have completely changed today, and the district is one of the nation's most economically sound black-majority districts. Nevertheless, some areas, such as South Jamaica, still suffer from high foreclosure and crime rates. JFK Airport, the 6th's largest employer, provides a steady job base and is New York City's busiest and largest airport as well as the top international arrivals gateway into the United States. Airport-based jobs, complemented by employment in health care, municipal government and residential construction, give the 6th a strong union constituency. Nearly 90 percent of residents work in the service industry, and district residents have the nation's longest average travel time to work — 46 minutes.

With a sizable Hispanic constituency to go along with its black majority, the district is overwhelmingly Democratic — registered Democrats outnumber Republicans nearly 10-to-1 in the 6th. Barack Obama won 89 percent of the district's presidential vote in 2008.

MAJOR INDUSTRY
Airport, health care, education

CITIES
New York (pt.), 654,361

NOTABLE
On Feb. 7, 1964, what would become known as "Beatlemania" began at JFK Airport as the Beatles held their first U.S. press conference; King Park in Jamaica was the farm of Rufus King, a delegate to the Constitutional Convention and later a Federalist senator from New York.

Rep. Joseph Crowley (D)

Elected 1998; 6th term

CAPITOL OFFICE
225-3965
crowley.house.gov
2404 Rayburn Bldg. 20515-3207; fax 225-1909

COMMITTEES
Foreign Affairs
Ways & Means

RESIDENCE
Queens

BORN
March 16, 1962; Queens, N.Y.

RELIGION
Roman Catholic

FAMILY
Wife, Kasey Crowley; three children

EDUCATION
Queens College, B.A. 1985 (communications
& political science)

CAREER
State legislator

POLITICAL HIGHLIGHTS
N.Y. Assembly, 1987-99

ELECTION RESULTS

2008 GENERAL

Joseph Crowley (D, WFM)	118,459	84.6%
William E. Britt Jr. (R, C)	21,477	15.3%

2008 PRIMARY

Joseph Crowley (D, WFM)	unopposed

2006 GENERAL

Joseph Crowley (D, WFM)	63,997	84.0%
Kevin Brawley (R, C)	12,220	16.0%

PREVIOUS WINNING PERCENTAGES
2004 (81%); 2002 (73%); 2000 (72%); 1998 (69%)

An Irishman with the gift of gab and an occasional fondness for singing in public, Crowley has one of the House's most prominent personalities. He uses his burly, 6-foot-4 inch frame and New York City bluntness to advocate business-friendly policies and position himself for a potential future move into the chamber's leadership.

Crowley (KRAU-lee) has been in politics for much of his life; he won a state House seat at the age of 24 and served in the New York Assembly until entering Congress in 1999 at the age of 37. The son of a cop, he doesn't give up without a good fight — making him a suitable pick as one of the nine chief deputy whips who help round up votes and enforce party discipline.

In fall 2008, Crowley helped rally support for a $700 billion economic rescue package. As the first version of the legislation failed in the House, Crowley screamed, "The Dow just dropped 600 points!" across the chamber at Republicans, in a last-ditch effort to sway their votes. Months later, Crowley recalled his frustration and the Republican reaction to his outburst: "There was just silence. They were just kind of looking at me, like deer in the headlights."

Crowley has twice lost bids for a higher leadership post in the Democratic Party, but he cannot be counted out as a future contender. He is one of the leaders of the moderate New Democrat Coalition, owns a prized spot on the Ways and Means Committee, and, due to a waiver from leadership, also holds a seat on the Foreign Affairs panel. He also is an impressive fundraiser for the party, serving as the Democratic Congressional Campaign Committee's vice chairman of finance, and sits on the leadership-run Steering and Policy Committee, which makes committee assignments. Crowley holds significant power back home too, as head of the Queens Democratic Party, the most powerful political machine in New York.

On Ways and Means, Crowley often is in the thick of debate on tax issues. Although he supports the Democrats' overall approach to tilting the tax code toward the middle class, Crowley also tries to help certain industries, particularly the financial services sector that employs so many New Yorkers. In the 110th Congress (2007-08), he pushed targeted provisions helping accountants, real estate investment trusts and the shoe industry.

He joined fellow New York Democrat Anthony Weiner in early 2009 in asking the IRS to clarify regulations concerning tax payments made on what turned out for thousands of investors to be "phantom income" derived from Ponzi schemes such as the one run by financier Bernard Madoff.

Crowley said he wants to be a voice "for reasonable, fair trade agreements" that incorporate labor and environmental standards. He supported Speaker Nancy Pelosi's decision to delay a vote on a Colombia trade deal because of concerns of treatment of union organizers. In the 109th Congress (2005-06), Crowley joined a bipartisan group of lawmakers who called on the George W. Bush administration to renegotiate the Central America Free Trade Agreement.

Crowley is not categorically opposed to global trade deals, however. He split with his party to back free-trade pacts with Chile and Singapore in 2003, and in 2006 he cosponsored legislation to establish permanent normal trade relations with Vietnam. He also joined many Democrats in voting in 2007 for an agreement with Peru.

Crowley uses his Foreign Affairs seat to build alliances with the home countries of many of his constituents, including India and Bangladesh. He was one of the most active House members in driving a nuclear agreement with India through Congress, deciding that it was important enough to pass even though it meant giving President a victory.

Crowley failed in his first two efforts to join the leadership. In February 2006, he made a bid for the vice chairmanship of the Democratic Caucus, the lowest rung on the elected leadership ladder, but lost to John B. Larson of Connecticut. Crowley was on the shortlist in 2005 to chair the Democratic Congressional Campaign Committee, an appointive post, but the job went to another rising star, Rahm Emanuel of Illinois. In 2008, he thought about running for the vice chairmanship again, but deferred to Xavier Becerra of California.

Crowley comes from a close-knit family. Today he, his siblings and his mother all live within 3 miles of one another in Queens, where Crowley was born and raised. His mother emigrated from County Armagh in Northern Ireland as a young girl. His father, a first-generation Irish-American, was a city police officer who earned a law degree at night.

Crowley inherited his political thirst from his father as well as from his uncle, Walter Crowley, a well-known local politician who served on the New York City Council. But Crowley truly flourished under the mentorship of Democrat Thomas J. Manton, his predecessor in the House, whom he once considered an enemy. In 1984, Manton beat Crowley's beloved uncle in a four-way primary for the House seat. Then in 1986, Manton tapped him on the shoulder at an Irish dinner dance and asked whether he'd thought about running for the local assembly seat, which had unexpectedly opened up.

Crowley went on to win the seat at the age of 24, just one year out of Queen's College. He spent 12 years in Albany, and developed a close friendship with Manton. In 1998, Manton picked Crowley as his successor in the U.S. House by announcing his retirement several days after the filing deadline and then joining with other party officials in nominating him. Crowley swamped the Republican candidate, corporate security manager James J. Dillon, in the general election. Manton's tactics angered other Democrats, but Crowley successfully defended his seat in 2000. He has won his last four elections with ease.

A guitar player, Crowley does a decent imitation of rocker Van Morrison singing "Wild Night." He occasionally sings in public and once belted out the national anthem before a New York Knicks basketball game. He inserted a provision in a 2009 bill that cleared Congress to create a Musicians and Artists Corps sending entertainers to low-income communities, schools and other areas to lead music and arts engagement programs.

KEY VOTES

2008
Yes Delay consideration of Colombia free-trade agreement
Yes Override Bush veto of federal farm and nutrition programs reauthorization bill
Yes Overhaul surveillance laws and permit dismissal of suits against companies that conducted warrantless wiretapping
Yes Grant mortgage relief to homeowners and funding for Fannie Mae and Freddie Mac
Yes Approve initial $700 billion program to stabilize financial markets
Yes Approve final $700 billion program to stabilize financial markets
Yes Provide $14 billion in loans to automakers

2007
Yes Increase minimum wage by $2.10 an hour
Yes Approve $124.2 billion in emergency war spending and set goal for redeployment of troops from Iraq
No   Reject federal contraceptive assistance to international family planning groups
Yes Override Bush veto of $23.2 billion water projects authorization bill
Yes Implement Peru free-trade agreement
Yes Approve energy policy overhaul with new fuel economy standards
No   Clear $473.5 billion omnibus spending bill, including $70 billion for military operations

CQ VOTE STUDIES

	PARTY UNITY		PRESIDENTIAL SUPPORT	
	SUPPORT	OPPOSE	SUPPORT	OPPOSE
2008	98%	2%	19%	81%
2007	98%	2%	6%	94%
2006	89%	11%	35%	65%
2005	97%	3%	15%	85%
2004	93%	7%	30%	70%

INTEREST GROUPS

	AFL-CIO	ADA	CCUS	ACU
2008	100%	100%	67%	0%
2007	96%	95%	60%	0%
2006	93%	95%	57%	8%
2005	93%	95%	44%	8%
2004	93%	90%	55%	9%

NEW YORK 7
Parts of Queens and the Bronx

Few districts in the nation are as ethnically and racially diverse as the 7th, which takes in part of northern Queens and the eastern part of the Bronx. Blacks, Hispanics and Asians each make up more than 10 percent of the population, with Hispanics a clear plurality at 40 percent.

A majority of the 7th's residents live in the district's northern tier in the Bronx. This area reaches as far west as the Bronx Zoo and the New York Botanical Garden and as far north as Co-op City, which houses more than 15,000 apartments, and the Westchester County line. The Bronx portion also includes Morris Park, Pelham Bay and City Island, and the borough's half of the Throgs Neck Bridge. While portions of the Bronx struggle economically, the areas around Eastchester Bay have some of the borough's highest incomes. The health care industry and small retailers are major employers in the Bronx.

The district's southern portion climbs northeast from near the intersection of the Brooklyn-Queens and Long Island expressways (in the neighboring 12th) to take in Woodside, Jackson Heights, Elmhurst and LaGuar-

dia Airport. This fast-growing area is heavily Hispanic and contributed to Queens' population boom during the 1990s. Jackson Heights also has a significant Indian population. LaGuardia provides thousands of jobs here and, along with nearby JFK Airport (in the 6th), makes Queens a major transportation hub. East of the airport, the district also includes most of Flushing Bay, College Point and the Whitestone Bridge, and a small part of Flushing.

Like most New York City districts, the 7th strongly supports Democrats, although a bit less uniformly. It is generally middle-class with some lower-income sections. Barack Obama easily carried the district in the 2008 presidential election with 79 percent of the vote.

MAJOR INDUSTRY
Airport, health care, service

CITIES
New York (pt.), 654,360

NOTABLE
The Maritime Industry Museum and SUNY Maritime College are at Fort Schuyler in Throgs Neck, where the East River hits Long Island Sound; The Bronx Zoo is the largest urban wildlife conservation facility in the nation.

Rep. Jerrold Nadler (D)

Elected 1992; 9th full term

CAPITOL OFFICE
225-5635
www.house.gov/nadler
2334 Rayburn Bldg. 20515-3208; fax 225-6923

COMMITTEES
Judiciary
   (Constitution, Civil Rights & Civil Liberties
   - chairman)
Transportation & Infrastructure

RESIDENCE
Manhattan

BORN
June 13, 1947; Brooklyn, N.Y.

RELIGION
Jewish

FAMILY
Wife, Joyce L. Miller; one child

EDUCATION
Columbia U., A.B. 1969 (government);
Fordham U., J.D. 1978

CAREER
State legislative aide; lawyer

POLITICAL HIGHLIGHTS
N.Y. Assembly, 1976-92; candidate for
Manhattan borough president, 1985;
candidate for New York City comptroller, 1989

ELECTION RESULTS

2008 GENERAL

Jerrold Nadler (D, WFM)	160,730	80.4%
Grace Lin (R, C)	39,047	19.5%

2008 PRIMARY

Jerrold Nadler (D, WFM)	unopposed

2006 GENERAL

Jerrold Nadler (D, WFM)	108,536	85.0%
Eleanor Friedman (R)	17,413	13.6%
Dennis E. Adornato (C)	1,673	1.3%

PREVIOUS WINNING PERCENTAGES
2004 (81%); 2002 (76%); 2000 (81%); 1998 (86%);
1996 (82%); 1994 (82%); 1992 (81%); 1992 Special
Election (100%)

Nadler is a passionate liberal who is always at the ready in a partisan debate, particularly when it comes to civil liberties and the concerns of his constituents. His district, which stretches from Manhattan through Greenwich Village and into Brooklyn, is home to one of the largest concentrations of liberal Jewish voters and gay and lesbian political activists in the country, and he vehemently defends their views.

His district also was home to the World Trade Center, and he still works to help his district heal from the Sept. 11 attacks. Yet as chairman of the Judiciary Committee's panel on the Constitution, Civil Rights and Civil Liberties, Nadler (NAD-ler) also seeks to constrain what he sees as an exorbitant growth of presidential power under the guise of national security. He accused the George W. Bush administration of "making claims of power that nobody's ever made." He has pursued his investigation into curbing such power even with a Democrat in the White House.

Nadler contended Bush committed potentially impeachable offenses with his Iraq and counterterrorism policies and held a series of hearings in 2008 to explore what he described as abuses of executive power. But he eventually conceded that, as a practical matter, Democrats could not have removed Bush from office through impeachment. "You don't impeach somebody if you can't get a consensus in the nation," he said.

He also fought against giving retroactive legal immunity to telecommunications firms that aided warrantless government surveillance for several years after the terrorist attacks, but the House eventually passed legislation, which became law, granting the immunity. He said he found that outcome "very frustrating."

Republicans accused him of playing politics at the expense of national security — a notion he dismissed. "I'm not interested in protecting terrorists," he said. "I'm interested in protecting people maybe accused of being terrorists."

After President Obama took office, Nadler resumed his efforts to check executive power. He introduced bills early in 2009 to circumscribe the government's use of the "state secrets" privilege to thwart lawsuits, and to set procedural protections for the use of so-called national security letters to obtain information. To counteract "midnight rules" promulgated by presidents just before they leave office, he introduced legislation to freeze such regulations until a new president's agency chiefs have a chance to review and reverse them, if desired. He also wants to establish a special prosecutor to investigate potential crimes by mid- and high-level executive branch officials that "endanger liberty" and is considering proposing a constitutional amendment to limit the president's pardon power.

He also held a joint hearing with the Judiciary panel's immigration subcommittee into allegations of racial profiling by immigration enforcement officials. "It appears that, in their zeal to enforce our immigration laws, some local law enforcement officials have gone far afield, violating our civil rights laws, the Constitution, and rights of U.S. citizens and non-citizens who are here legally. That's not law enforcement, that's a subversion of the law."

Nadler is a supporter of gay rights. In 2006 he was a vocal opponent of a constitutional amendment — ultimately rejected by the House — barring same-sex marriage, which he said was motivated by political expediency. Also in 2006, he led the opposition to a Republican-sponsored measure making it difficult and more expensive to sue government officials over public expressions of religion.

He sits on the Transportation and Infrastructure Committee, where he hopes to secure funds in the next surface transportation bill for a freight rail tunnel under New York Harbor to connect Brooklyn with Bayonne, N.J. The Brooklyn terminus of the proposed tunnel would be in the 8th District. He said the tunnel would foster economic development, reduce air pollution and lower consumer costs in the city. He also wants to foster high-speed rail and find ways to fund highway and bridge improvements other than with the gasoline tax.

Nadler took on a more personal struggle in 2002 when he decided to undergo gastric bypass surgery to tackle obesity issues that had the 5-foot-4-inch lawmaker weighing 338 pounds. Years later, the weight loss is still "significant," as are the health benefits, according to his staff.

Nadler has sought to help his constituents cope with the aftermath of Sept. 11. In 2008 he cosponsored legislation with other New York lawmakers to provide medical monitoring to people exposed to dust and debris after the attacks and reopen a federal victims' compensation fund to aid people sickened from exposure to toxic materials. And he released a Government Accountability Office report that showed the government still did not have a detailed plan for protecting the health and safety of emergency responders.

Born in Brooklyn, Nadler spent his early years on a New Jersey poultry farm. He said that he was drawn to public service, in part, after watching his father rail against President Eisenhower and Agriculture Secretary Ezra Taft Benson, blaming them for federal government policies that made it impossible for Nadler's family to keep the farm.

His family moved back to New York City after the farm failed. He stayed in the city to pursue his education, earning a degree in government from Columbia University and a law degree from Fordham University, which he attended at night while working at an off-track betting office during the day.

Nadler organized a group of Columbia students, dubbed the "West Side Kids," to advance a liberal agenda in New York politics. He was an aide to a New York state senator, and he campaigned for liberal Democrat Ted Weiss' election to Congress. In 1976, Nadler won a seat in the state Assembly.

When Weiss died on the eve of the 1992 Democratic primary, voters renominated him anyway, giving party officials the right to pick a successor. That set off a scramble among Democratic activists, with six candidates jumping into the frenetic nine-day race for the nomination. While other aspirants, such as former Rep. Bella S. Abzug, were better known to the public, Nadler had longstanding ties to the insiders who cast the votes. He got the nomination and went on to win the special election as well as the general election for a full term on the same day. He has since won re-election with ease.

KEY VOTES

2008
Yes Delay consideration of Colombia free-trade agreement
Yes Override Bush veto of federal farm and nutrition programs reauthorization bill
No   Overhaul surveillance laws and permit dismissal of suits against companies that conducted warrantless wiretapping
Yes Grant mortgage relief to homeowners and funding for Fannie Mae and Freddie Mac
Yes Approve initial $700 billion program to stabilize financial markets
Yes Approve final $700 billion program to stabilize financial markets
Yes Provide $14 billion in loans to automakers

2007
Yes Increase minimum wage by $2.10 an hour
Yes Approve $124.2 billion in emergency war spending and set goal for redeployment of troops from Iraq
No   Reject federal contraceptive assistance to international family planning groups
Yes Override Bush veto of $23.2 billion water projects authorization bill
No   Implement Peru free-trade agreement
Yes Approve energy policy overhaul with new fuel economy standards
No   Clear $473.5 billion omnibus spending bill, including $70 billion for military operations

CQ VOTE STUDIES

	PARTY UNITY		PRESIDENTIAL SUPPORT	
	SUPPORT	OPPOSE	SUPPORT	OPPOSE
2008	99%	1%	14%	86%
2007	99%	1%	4%	96%
2006	99%	1%	15%	85%
2005	98%	2%	13%	87%
2004	99%	1%	18%	82%

INTEREST GROUPS

	AFL-CIO	ADA	CCUS	ACU
2008	100%	95%	53%	0%
2007	96%	95%	47%	0%
2006	100%	100%	27%	4%
2005	93%	100%	35%	0%
2004	100%	100%	29%	0%

NEW YORK 8

West Side of Manhattan; Borough Park; Coney Island

Starting west of Central Park, the 8th travels through Manhattan's West Side from 89th Street south to Wall Street and Battery Park, taking in part of the Theater District and Times Square, Chelsea, Greenwich Village, SoHo and TriBeCa. At Manhattan's southern tip, it slips through the Brooklyn-Battery Tunnel to skim Brooklyn's western waterfront. It includes some working-class areas, much of Brighton Beach and some of Brooklyn's southern coastline, including Coney Island.

At the center of the 8th's portion of Brooklyn is Borough Park, with large Hasidic and Orthodox Jewish populations. Many of Brooklyn's quirky shops, eclectic restaurants and vibrant nightlife hot spots have struggled during the recent recession. Redevelopment plans for the once-popular urban resort spot Coney Island remain in limbo.

Manhattan's finance industry, at the center of the international economic crisis, has shed tens of thousands of jobs but remains the district's economic touchstone. In lower Manhattan, rebuilding efforts at the World Trade Center are underway. The new skyscrapers will offer office and retail space, and the complex will include a memorial and museum, residential property and an extensive transportation hub.

Manhattan's heavily Democratic West Side, with politically active gay, minority, artistic and academic communities, has sent liberal representatives to Congress for decades and overwhelmingly supported Democratic presidential candidates. There are GOP-leaning middle-class neighborhoods in Brooklyn, and Republican John McCain won the 8th's portion of the borough with 55 percent of the 2008 presidential vote. The 8th's conservative Jewish voters back pro-Israel candidates, but conservative voters in Brooklyn are outnumbered at the polls by the district's liberal bloc. In 2008, Barack Obama won 74 percent of the district's vote.

MAJOR INDUSTRY
Finance, retail, tourism, small business

CITIES
New York (pt.), 654,360

NOTABLE
Home of the Statue of Liberty, Empire State Building, American Museum of Natural History, Penn Station, Madison Square Garden and City Hall.

Rep. Anthony Weiner (D)

Elected 1998; 6th term

CAPITOL OFFICE
225-6616
www.house.gov/weiner
2104 Rayburn Bldg. 20515-3209; fax 226-7253

COMMITTEES
Energy & Commerce
Judiciary

RESIDENCE
Queens

BORN
Sept. 4, 1964; Brooklyn, N.Y.

RELIGION
Jewish

FAMILY
Single

EDUCATION
State U. of New York, Plattsburgh, B.A. 1985
(political science)

CAREER
Congressional aide

POLITICAL HIGHLIGHTS
New York City Council, 1992-99; sought Democratic
nomination for mayor of New York, 2005

ELECTION RESULTS

2008 GENERAL

Anthony Weiner (D, WFM)	112,205	93.0%
Alfred F. Donohue (C)	8,378	6.9%

2008 PRIMARY

Anthony Weiner (D, WFM)	unopposed

2006 GENERAL

Anthony Weiner (D, WFM)	unopposed

PREVIOUS WINNING PERCENTAGES
2004 (71%); 2002 (66%); 2000 (68%); 1998 (66%)

Weiner is the quintessential New Yorker: a brash and close-in brawler who regularly is at the front of partisan fights on national and international issues. But his motivation for almost all his legislating goes directly back to New York.

He voted for the $700 billion financial rescue plan in the fall of 2008 because he said it was especially critical to the city that is home of Wall Street. Weiner (WEE-ner) has fought against black-market cigarettes that he said fund terrorist groups who have targeted New York. And he has opposed weapons sales to Saudi Arabia, which he said has threatened peace in the Middle East. "That's how I look at my job in Congress," Weiner said. "Yes, I fight against funding for the Saudis. But when I get up in the morning, I'm thinking about the five boroughs."

He focused on keeping open a troubled Queens hospital in early 2009 and highlighted how President Obama's economic stimulus law would aid his city. And he joined fellow New York Democrat Joseph Crowley in asking the IRS to clarify regulations concerning tax payments on what turned out for thousands of investors to be "phantom income" derived from Ponzi schemes such as the one run by financier Bernard Madoff.

During debate over the financial bailout, Weiner also appeared regularly on television to talk about the disproportionate impact the crisis had on his city — not just on bankers and traders, but also on the people working in the service industries that support Wall Street. "When the financial community catches cold, New York gets pneumonia," he said. "It's the secondary and tertiary jobs, the guys who measure the suits, the guys who run the catering carts that also are hurt."

Since the Sept. 11 attacks, terrorism and security issues also have been a top priority for Weiner. He serves on the Judiciary Committee and its crime and terrorism panel. The House passed his bill in 2008 to crack down on tobacco smugglers and illicit tobacco sales over the Internet, in part to reduce black-market funds used to fund terrorist organizations such as Hezbollah; the Senate did not act on it.

He is a strong proponent of the Community Oriented Policing Services, a federal program that helps states and localities hire more police officers. The program was designed to reduce street crime, but after Sept. 11 it became a tool to fund first-responder programs and emergency-response equipment. He helped secure $1 billion in the 2009 economic stimulus law to hire more than 5,000 additional police officers.

The terrorist attacks also deepened Weiner's activism on issues relating to the Middle East. Weiner, who is Jewish, serves a heavily Jewish constituency and is an unwavering advocate for Israel. When Hamas, a militant Islamic party that has called for the destruction of Israel, won a majority of seats in 2006 Palestinian parliamentary elections, Weiner called for an immediate halt to U.S. aid. Weiner also led efforts in 2008 to oppose a move by President George W. Bush to sell weapons guidance systems to Saudi Arabia, which he accused of not doing enough to stop terrorist activity in the Middle East.

He also has fought to reopen the Statue of Liberty, which was closed after the Sept. 11 attacks. The monument's pedestal was reopened in 2004, but visitors continued to be prohibited from climbing to the crown. The Obama administration intends to fully reopen the monument on July Fourth.

A member of Judiciary's immigration panel, Weiner also hopes Obama will successfully lead an overhaul of immigration laws. Weiner used his seat on that panel in 2008 to push for a bill to make it easier for international fashion models to get work visas in the United States. While the tabloids chided the unmarried Weiner for trying to "increase his dating pool," he said the bill promoted economic development. The full committee approved the bill, but it was never taken up by the full House.

On the Energy and Commerce panel, he pushes to improve New York's health care system and economy. He led an investigation showing Brooklyn women had the longest wait time for mammography screenings — 7.4 weeks — in the entire New York City area. He also released a report that found that while the number of banks in wealthy New York neighborhoods was increasing, poor neighborhoods were being left behind. He called for stronger regulations and greater incentives to increase the number of banks in poor areas.

Weiner weighed a run for mayor of the Big Apple in 2009. He narrowly lost the 2005 Democratic primary contest to challenge incumbent GOP Mayor Michael Bloomberg. Though Bloomberg had been prohibited under New York term limits from running for a third term, in 2008 he announced plans to extend the limits and quickly launched an aggressive campaign. Weiner said he wouldn't be daunted. "The middle class and those struggling to make it in this city deserve to have a voice," he said. But he also expressed concern about needing to focus on his job in Washington.

New York tabloids delight in describing Weiner as a "political hot dog" and pronouncing, "Weiner on a roll!" He not only doesn't mind the wordplay, he uses it himself. For a student government campaign in college, he used the slogan, "Vote for Weiner. He'll be frank." He regularly drives across his district in a self-described "Weinermobile," a hybrid SUV, to meet with constituents.

The middle son of a lawyer father and a schoolteacher mother, Weiner grew up on a tree-lined street in the Park Slope section of Brooklyn, going to public schools. He attended the State University of New York at Plattsburgh because of its prowess in his sport, ice hockey. His professors noticed his gift for making a cogent argument for any position and a tenacity for driving it home. As a political science major, Weiner decided he wanted to be in Congress someday.

After graduation, he spent six years as an aide to Democrat Charles E. Schumer, then in the House. In 1991, at age 27, Weiner became the youngest person at the time ever elected to the New York City Council. Seven years later, after Schumer left the House seat open for a successful Senate run, Weiner won a tight four-way primary by 489 votes. He coasted in the strongly Democratic district in November and in every election since.

Weiner is a close friend of "Daily Show" comedian Jon Stewart, with whom he shared a beach house in 1987. "It's odd that we get along," Stewart told New York magazine. "I'm pretty cynical; he really believes in this stuff."

KEY VOTES

2008
Yes Delay consideration of Colombia free-trade agreement
Yes Override Bush veto of federal farm and nutrition programs reauthorization bill
No Overhaul surveillance laws and permit dismissal of suits against companies that conducted warrantless wiretapping
Yes Grant mortgage relief to homeowners and funding for Fannie Mae and Freddie Mac
Yes Approve initial $700 billion program to stabilize financial markets
Yes Approve final $700 billion program to stabilize financial markets
Yes Provide $14 billion in loans to automakers

2007
Yes Increase minimum wage by $2.10 an hour
Yes Approve $124.2 billion in emergency war spending and set goal for redeployment of troops from Iraq
? Reject federal contraceptive assistance to international family planning groups
Yes Override Bush veto of $23.2 billion water projects authorization bill
Yes Implement Peru free-trade agreement
Yes Approve energy policy overhaul with new fuel economy standards
No Clear $473.5 billion omnibus spending bill, including $70 billion for military operations

CQ VOTE STUDIES

	PARTY UNITY		PRESIDENTIAL SUPPORT	
	SUPPORT	OPPOSE	SUPPORT	OPPOSE
2008	99%	1%	15%	85%
2007	97%	3%	6%	94%
2006	96%	4%	23%	77%
2005	99%	1%	15%	85%
2004	99%	1%	30%	70%

INTEREST GROUPS

	AFL-CIO	ADA	CCUS	ACU
2008	100%	100%	59%	0%
2007	96%	90%	60%	0%
2006	100%	95%	40%	8%
2005	93%	95%	37%	0%
2004	100%	100%	38%	4%

NEW YORK 9

Parts of Brooklyn and Queens — Forest Hills, Rockaway, Sheepshead Bay

The Democratic-leaning, predominately white 9th takes in north-central and western Queens and slides along the Jamaica Bay coastline into southeastern Brooklyn. Almost 70 percent of residents live in Queens.

The 9th District extends westward from near Nassau County at the edge of Oakland Gardens through Fresh Meadows and Hillcrest to Forest Hills. There are some wealthy communities in Queens in the northern arm of the district.

The 9th narrows and runs south from Forest Park — the third-largest park in Queens and home to free Queens Symphony Orchestra concerts each summer — to take in part of the Woodhaven, Ozone Park and Lindenwood neighborhoods. In these areas, Hispanics now outnumber whites, and the Asian population is rapidly expanding.

The district also takes in much of the Rockaway area in far southwestern Queens along the Atlantic Ocean. Breezy Point, a tight-knit private com-munity at the tip of the Rockaways, has the nation's highest concentration of Irish-Americans (60 percent) according to the 2000 census. In Brooklyn, the district includes Floyd Bennett Field, which was New York City's first municipal airport, and much of the Gateway National Recreation Area on Jamaica Bay. Farther west, Sheepshead Bay, a popular area fishing spot, has seen an influx of Russian immigrants.

Previously a Democratic stronghold, the 9th, particularly its Brooklyn portion, moved right in the aftermath of the Sept. 11 terrorist attacks. Republican John McCain won the Brooklyn part with 57 percent of the 2008 presidential vote. The 9th was the only New York City district in which Democrat Barack Obama did not improve on John Kerry's 2004 presidential vote percentage, and Obama was held to his second-lowest percentage (55 percent) of any New York City district.

MAJOR INDUSTRY
Service, finance, insurance

CITIES
New York (pt.), 654,360

NOTABLE
Howard Hughes' historic 1938 around-the-world flight started and ended at Floyd Bennett Field.

Rep. Edolphus Towns (D)

Elected 1982; 14th term

CAPITOL OFFICE
225-5936
www.house.gov/towns
2232 Rayburn Bldg. 20515-3210; fax 225-1018

COMMITTEES
Oversight & Government Reform - chairman

RESIDENCE
Brooklyn

BORN
July 21, 1934; Chadbourn, N.C.

RELIGION
Baptist

FAMILY
Wife, Gwendolyn Towns; two children

EDUCATION
North Carolina A&T State U., B.S. 1956;
Adelphi U., M.S.W. 1973

MILITARY SERVICE
Army, 1956-58

CAREER
Professor; hospital administrator

POLITICAL HIGHLIGHTS
Brooklyn Borough deputy president, 1976-82

ELECTION RESULTS

2008 GENERAL

Edolphus Towns (D)	155,090	94.2%
Salvatore Grupico (R, C)	9,565	5.8%

2008 PRIMARY

Edolphus Towns (D)	24,405	67.8%
Kevin Powell (D)	11,558	32.1%

2006 GENERAL

Edolphus Towns (D)	72,171	92.2%
Jonathan H. Anderson (R)	4,666	6.0%
Ernest Johnson (C)	1,470	1.9%

PREVIOUS WINNING PERCENTAGES
2004 (92%); 2002 (98%); 2000 (90%); 1998 (92%);
1996 (91%); 1994 (89%); 1992 (96%); 1990 (93%);
1988 (89%); 1986 (89%); 1984 (85%); 1982 (84%)

Towns is a veteran liberal who displays an independent streak that sometimes puts him at odds with key constituencies and Democratic leaders, notably on the hot-button issue of trade. He shuns self-promotion and prefers to work quietly — so quietly he has drawn unsuccessful primary challengers who have accused him of not advocating aggressively enough for his district.

Such qualities stand in marked contrast to California's Henry A. Waxman, Towns' predecessor as chairman of the Oversight and Government Reform Committee. Not only is the combative Waxman loyal to his party's leadership, he is adept at drawing publicity. But Towns began taking steps in 2009 to raise his profile, using his new committee role to look into the Obama administration's response to the financial crisis.

Towns and Oversight and Government Reform's top-ranking Republican, Darrell Issa of California, held multiple hearings to grill administration officials about their enforcement of the $700 billion financial sector rescue law enacted in 2008. Towns didn't hold back in criticizing officials from his own party; he said in March 2009 that the Treasury Department "just does not know what Wall Street is doing with government funds — in fact, I don't think they even know how much they don't know."

Towns looked at Treasury's dealings with American International Group Inc., the insurance giant that paid bonuses to employees after receiving billions in federal aid. At the same time, he got his name on several pieces of legislation. He sponsored two House-passed bills aimed at strengthening oversight of the White House and making the records of former presidents more accessible. And a House-passed bill to regulate tobacco included his proposal to make up for a shortfall in excise tax revenue from an anticipated drop in sales of tobacco products.

All of the activity was something of a departure for Towns, who developed a reputation for missing hearings when Waxman chaired the Oversight panel. USA Today reported in December 2008 that Towns was present at just 12 of the 74 hearings the panel held in the 110th Congress (2007-08). Towns blamed his absences partly on conflicts with his other seat on Energy and Commerce, which he gave up when he took the Oversight chair.

It was Towns' 2005 vote in favor of the Central America Free Trade Agreement (CAFTA) that set him apart from his Democratic colleagues, angered labor leaders in New York and led Democratic leader Nancy Pelosi of California to threaten to boot him off Energy and Commerce for not voting often enough with his party. His vote helped give the GOP a 217-215 win. Pelosi was also angry that Towns was one of two Democrats who missed a vote on a Republican budget bill that squeaked through the House during the 109th Congress (2005-06).

He has maintained his prerogative to vote as he sees fit. Towns joined with a minority of House Democrats in 2007 to vote for a free-trade agreement with Peru that U.S. labor groups were cool toward. In another show of independence, Towns was one of only 25 Democrats to vote in November 2007 against legislation to prohibit job discrimination against gays, lesbians and bisexuals.

Towns, in his mid-70s, can look back on a career with some notable successes. But those are rarely news in a town full of more-prominent and self-promoting lawmakers. "I should jump out and push and get in front of the cameras, but that's just not my nature," he said.

He helped bring considerable largess to his Brooklyn district — including $153 million for a federal courthouse and a $150 million reconstruction bond for the borough's Interfaith Hospital — and built a political base that could someday be useful to his son, New York Assemblyman Darryl Towns, if he decides to run for Congress.

Towns wants the federal government to increase educational opportunities, improve health services and spur economic development to help his district's low-income and working-class residents.

He won inclusion of a provision in the 1996 Telecommunications Act that allowed small businesses and minority- and women-owned businesses to put money from a new Telecommunications Development Fund into interest-bearing accounts with the fund. In 2006, he worked with New Jersey Republican Mike Ferguson to gain approval of a proposal authorizing $30 million to expand the use of electronic medical records to better coordinate care for low-income and uninsured patients. The provision was included in a broader Energy and Commerce bill, but Congress failed to act on a final measure.

Towns' major legislative accomplishment was the 1990 passage of the Student Right to Know Act requiring colleges to report the graduation rates of their scholarship athletes.

Towns was born in southeastern North Carolina and graduated from historically black North Carolina A&T in Greensboro. After a two-year stint in the Army, he worked as a teacher and hospital administrator and earned a master's degree in social work from Adelphi University. In 1976, he was appointed Brooklyn Borough deputy president.

His chance to run for the House came in 1982 after redistricting gave the 11th District an almost even split of blacks and Hispanics. With support from party regulars, he fended off two Hispanic primary contenders to win the nomination with 50 percent of the vote, then won easily in November. Redistricting in 1992 put him in a newly drawn but just as Democratic 10th District, where he has faced tough primary battles several times. But he took 89 percent of the vote in the 1994 general election, and has garnered at least 90 percent of the vote in every general election since.

In 2006, two Democratic contenders used his CAFTA vote against him; Towns won by a narrower margin than would be expected of a 12-term veteran from New York City. Two years later, he again faced a Democratic opponent, writer and activist Kevin Powell, who accused him of a lackluster legislative record and accepting excessive contributions from business interests regulated by Energy and Commerce. Towns campaigned vigorously and won with ease.

KEY VOTES

2008
Yes Delay consideration of Colombia free-trade agreement
Yes Override Bush veto of federal farm and nutrition programs reauthorization bill
No   Overhaul surveillance laws and permit dismissal of suits against companies that conducted warrantless wiretapping
Yes Grant mortgage relief to homeowners and funding for Fannie Mae and Freddie Mac
Yes Approve initial $700 billion program to stabilize financial markets
Yes Approve final $700 billion program to stabilize financial markets
Yes Provide $14 billion in loans to automakers

2007
Yes Increase minimum wage by $2.10 an hour
Yes Approve $124.2 billion in emergency war spending and set goal for redeployment of troops from Iraq
No   Reject federal contraceptive assistance to international family planning groups
Yes Override Bush veto of $23.2 billion water projects authorization bill
Yes Implement Peru free-trade agreement
Yes Approve energy policy overhaul with new fuel economy standards
No   Clear $473.5 billion omnibus spending bill, including $70 billion for military operations

CQ VOTE STUDIES

	PARTY UNITY		PRESIDENTIAL SUPPORT	
	SUPPORT	OPPOSE	SUPPORT	OPPOSE
2008	99%	1%	13%	87%
2007	98%	2%	7%	93%
2006	94%	6%	30%	70%
2005	93%	7%	33%	67%
2004	96%	4%	15%	85%

INTEREST GROUPS

	AFL-CIO	ADA	CCUS	ACU
2008	100%	100%	56%	0%
2007	96%	90%	65%	0%
2006	100%	95%	53%	8%
2005	86%	70%	60%	14%
2004	100%	90%	33%	0%

NEW YORK 10

Part of Brooklyn — Bedford-Stuyvesant, Canarsie, Downtown Brooklyn, East New York

The boomerang-shaped 10th begins just inland of Brooklyn's industrial waterfront in Downtown Brooklyn and heads east, bounding back southwest after reaching the Queens border. The solidly Democratic district contains New York City's highest percentage of black residents.

In south-central Brooklyn, the 10th scoops up a chunk west of Flatbush Avenue that includes part of Midwood. East of this area, the 10th takes in Georgetown and Canarsie, bordering Jamaica Bay. Canarsie's racial mix has changed dramatically, as neighborhoods that were once largely white now host many blacks of Caribbean descent. Many families here are solidly middle-class, an exception for most of the 10th. In the elbow of the boomerang is East New York, home to the Gateway Center, a large suburban-style retail project that spurred affordable housing in the area.

Farther north and west, the 10th includes Bedford-Stuyvesant. Once beset by crime and poverty, the neighborhood is experiencing ongoing revitalization as "Bed-Stuy" natives work to aid the rebirth while minimizing displacement of residents. In its northwestern corner, the district takes in Fort Greene and part of Williamsburg. Previously home to black artistic populations, the areas are transforming into hipster enclaves.

The 10th's declining manufacturing base has caused unemployment, and a landmark Pfizer plant closed in 2008. Government jobs in Downtown Brooklyn and education jobs at the 10th's colleges — such as Brooklyn College, Long Island University-Brooklyn and New York City College of Technology — aid the economy.

GOP candidates have found some small pockets of support from Jewish voters in Williamsburg, but they pale in comparison with the overwhelmingly Democratic voting patterns of the rest of the 10th. Barack Obama was able to secure 91 percent of the district's presidential vote in 2008.

MAJOR INDUSTRY
Government, higher education, small business, retail

CITIES
New York (pt.), 654,361

NOTABLE
A Spike Lee film, "Do the Right Thing," was set in Bedford-Stuyvesant.

Rep. Yvette D. Clarke (D)

Elected 2006; 2nd term

CAPITOL OFFICE
225-6231
clarke.house.gov
1029 Longworth Bldg. 20515-3211; fax 226-0112

COMMITTEES
Education & Labor
Homeland Security
(Emerging Threats - chairwoman)
Small Business

RESIDENCE
Brooklyn

BORN
Nov. 21, 1964; Brooklyn, N.Y.

RELIGION
Christian

FAMILY
Single

EDUCATION
Oberlin College, attended 1982-86 (Black studies)

CAREER
Local economic development director; day care
and youth program coordinator; state agency and
legislative aide

POLITICAL HIGHLIGHTS
New York City Council, 2002-07; sought
Democratic nomination for U.S. House, 2004

ELECTION RESULTS

2008 GENERAL

Yvette D. Clarke (D, WFM)	168,562	92.8%
Hugh C. Carr (R)	11,644	6.4%

2008 PRIMARY

Yvette D. Clarke (D, WFM)	unopposed

2006 GENERAL

Yvette D. Clarke (D, WFM)	88,334	90.0%
Stephen Finger (R, LIBERT)	7,447	7.6%
Mariana Blume (C)	1,325	1.4%
Ollie M. McClean (FDM)	996	1.0%

A staunch liberal, Clarke draws inspiration from two sources to guide her in Congress: her roots as a Caribbean-American and her service — along with that of her mother Una — on the New York City Council. Those experiences still influence her work on such issues as homeland security, immigration and education.

Clarke focuses much of her legislative work on the Homeland Security Committee, where she brings her experience from chairing a city committee charged with rebuilding the New York Fire Department's infrastructure after the Sept. 11 terrorist attacks. She chairs the Subcommittee on Emerging Threats, putting her at the center of a range of looming security concerns. The assignment led Clarke in February 2009 to quip to a New York radio host, "Just call me Jackie Bauer," a reference to the terrorist-fighting Jack Bauer character on the Fox TV show "24."

But Clarke is serious about her work on the panel. She was a strong critic of President George W. Bush's response to the threat of terrorism, and has sought to ease the effects of his administration's terrorism laws on innocent citizens. "We have to become more forward-thinking in how we're going to regulate our lives as a result of 9/11, but we can't live in the shadow of it," she said.

In 2008, the House passed her bill to order the Homeland Security Department to create a comprehensive list of people cleared of allegations of connections to terrorism. She said it would cut down the hassle for travelers subjected to repeat searches because they share a name or other identifying feature with someone on the terrorist watch list. Though the Senate did not take up the measure, the House passed it again in February 2009.

Clarke also has echoed other Democrats in criticizing what they see as low morale at Homeland Security, saying the department needs a substantive change that includes an increase in staffing stability. And she has cited a need for tighter protections on personal credit card information than the security controls used by much of the private sector.

Clarke sought the seat on Homeland Security not only because she wanted to add to New York's voice on the panel but also because she wanted to take part in the immigration debate. Born to Caribbean immigrant parents, Clarke is a strong proponent of the value of immigrants as a workforce, particularly in the growing renewable-energy and infrastructure repair sectors, and wants to ease the process for immigration.

She has also observed the hardships of the Pakistani community in her district, a community she said often has to cope with Immigration and Customs Enforcement raids. Her first bill, introduced just shy of a year after her election, aimed to reduce the backlog in processing requests made by immigration officials to the FBI.

Clarke also takes an interest in issues affecting the Caribbean. She has called for a collaborative relationship between the United States and the islands, saying they have useful resources in terms of labor and natural gas and oil. She has referred to the islands as "an extension of the homeland."

She said her Caribbean roots have made her especially sensitive to the malnutrition, famine and poverty rampant in Haiti, and she traveled there with the Congressional Black Caucus in 2007. She said the U.S. government has a moral obligation to keep lines of communication and support with Haiti open, and that if the situation there gets worse, it could become "a breeding ground for terrorists."

Clarke became the Black Caucus' whip in 2009 and has joined its members in seeking influence on the federal agencies responsible for dealing with the economic crisis. When Federal Reserve Chairman Ben S. Bernanke addressed a Black Caucus conference in March 2009, she said the outreach "seemed to be a continuation of the status quo."

With her city council background, she considers her memberships on the Education and Labor and Small Business committees to be a natural fit. On the Education panel, she backed in 2008 an overhaul of the law governing federal aid to education. The measure, which was enacted into law, focuses on limiting the cost of college. She backed a provision granting the forgiveness of loans for teachers.

She applauds the No Child Left Behind law, Bush's signature education program, for ensuring that more qualified teachers are in the classroom and for helping pinpoint subject areas where more attention is needed. But she said there should be ways other than testing to determine students' progress, and she calls for full funding of the law's mandates.

Clarke was born in Brooklyn and attended Oberlin College, where she majored in black studies. She then served as the first business development director for the Bronx Empowerment Zone and the Bronx branch of the New York City Empowerment Zone.

She took over her mother's seat on the New York City Council after a term limit forced Una Clarke to step down in 2001, and she was re-elected twice. While on the council, Clarke won adoption of an ordinance requiring city government buildings to have twice as many restroom stalls for women as for men. In Congress, she cosponsored a bill by her New York Democratic colleague, Edolphus Towns, that would apply the same requirement to bathrooms in federal buildings.

In 2000, Una Clarke lost a primary contest to the incumbent Democrat, Rep. Major R. Owens. Four years later, Clarke herself took her turn against Owens and lost, drawing 29 percent of the vote in a four-way primary, enabling Owens to limp to renomination with a plurality of the vote.

When Owens announced his retirement in 2006, after 12 terms, the younger Clarke decided to try again. She bested a trio of other hopefuls, including the congressman's son, political activist Chris Owens, to claim the nomination. That was tantamount to election in the heavily Democratic district. She sailed to re-election in 2008.

When not working, Clarke tries to find time for dancing, no matter what style. "I can go from salsa to merengue to reggae to dancehall," she told a New York political newspaper. "I love to dance."

KEY VOTES

2008
Yes Delay consideration of Colombia free-trade agreement
Yes Override Bush veto of federal farm and nutrition programs reauthorization bill
No   Overhaul surveillance laws and permit dismissal of suits against companies that conducted warrantless wiretapping
Yes Grant mortgage relief to homeowners and funding for Fannie Mae and Freddie Mac
Yes Approve initial $700 billion program to stabilize financial markets
Yes Approve final $700 billion program to stabilize financial markets
Yes Provide $14 billion in loans to automakers

2007
Yes Increase minimum wage by $2.10 an hour
Yes Approve $124.2 billion in emergency war spending and set goal for redeployment of troops from Iraq
No   Reject federal contraceptive assistance to international family planning groups
Yes Override Bush veto of $23.2 billion water projects authorization bill
Yes Implement Peru free-trade agreement
Yes Approve energy policy overhaul with new fuel economy standards
No   Clear $473.5 billion omnibus spending bill, including $70 billion for military operations

CQ VOTE STUDIES

	PARTY UNITY		PRESIDENTIAL SUPPORT	
	SUPPORT	OPPOSE	SUPPORT	OPPOSE
2008	99%	1%	16%	84%
2007	99%	1%	6%	94%

INTEREST GROUPS

	AFL-CIO	ADA	CCUS	ACU
2008	100%	100%	56%	0%
2007	100%	75%	64%	0%

NEW YORK 11

Part of Brooklyn — Flatbush, Crown Heights, Brownsville, Park Slope

The ethnically diverse 11th District, nestled in central Brooklyn, is home to a large black population (59 percent); minorities overall make up almost four-fifths of the district's population.

At the heart of the 11th is Flatbush, a working-class neighborhood with a "country in the city" atmosphere that is home to many black and Hispanic residents as well as Caribbean immigrants. In the district's far south, Midwood, traditionally an Orthodox Jewish center, has recently experienced an influx of diverse immigrant populations. Brownsville to the far east is heavily black. The 11th extends northwest through Crown Heights, home to the world headquarters of the Chabad-Lubavitch Hasidic Jews as well as a sizable black population. Like areas to the north (in the 10th), this area has seen recent gentrification, and some native residents have been priced out of their homes.

To the northwest, Prospect Park attracts more than 8 million visitors each year, and residents and visitors head to nearby Brooklyn Botanic Garden and the Brooklyn Museum of Art, which lures enthusiasts to its Egyptology collection. Further west, the 11th includes affluent pockets in Park Slope, Carroll Gardens, Cobble Hill and Brooklyn Heights.

Many residents work at the 11th's medical facilities, including Kings County Hospital Center and the State University of New York Downstate Medical Center. Dramatic increases in the number of eclectic small businesses and restaurants supported the local economy for much of the last decade, but the economic downturn has hurt Brooklyn's retail sector.

The 11th's GOP pockets have a minimal effect on elections: Barack Obama won more than 90 percent of the district's 2008 presidential vote.

MAJOR INDUSTRY
Health care, retail

CITIES
New York (pt.), 654,361

NOTABLE
Ebbets Field, where the Brooklyn Dodgers played from 1913 to 1957, was demolished in 1960 and is now a housing complex; The West Indian Day Carnival Parade attracts millions of visitors each year on Labor Day.

Rep. Nydia M. Velázquez (D)

Elected 1992; 9th term

CAPITOL OFFICE
225-2361
www.house.gov/velazquez
2466 Rayburn Bldg. 20515-3212; fax 226-0327

COMMITTEES
Financial Services
Small Business - chairwoman

RESIDENCE
Brooklyn

BORN
March 28, 1953; Yabucoa, P.R.

RELIGION
Roman Catholic

FAMILY
Husband, Paul Bader

EDUCATION
U. of Puerto Rico, B.A. 1974 (political science);
New York U., M.A. 1976 (political science)

CAREER
Puerto Rican Community Affairs Department
director; professor; congressional aide

POLITICAL HIGHLIGHTS
New York City Council, 1984-85; defeated
for election to New York City Council, 1984

ELECTION RESULTS

2008 GENERAL

Nydia M. Velázquez (D, WFM)	123,046	90.0%
Allan E. Romaguera (R, C)	13,747	10.0%

2008 PRIMARY

Nydia M. Velázquez (D, WFM)	unopposed

2006 GENERAL

Nydia M. Velázquez (D, WFM)	62,847	89.7%
Allan E. Romaguera (R, C)	7,182	10.3%

PREVIOUS WINNING PERCENTAGES
2004 (86%); 2002 (96%); 2000 (86%); 1998 (84%);
1996 (85%); 1994 (92%); 1992 (77%)

A native of Puerto Rico who moved to New York more than 30 years ago, Velázquez is a passionate — and increasingly prominent — advocate of equal rights for minorities, women, immigrants and the poor. She persistently calls for improved health care, affordable housing and aid for struggling entrepreneurs.

In more than 15 years in the House, Velázquez (full name: NID-ee-uh veh-LASS-kez) has forged a trail that has positioned her to contribute from a variety of angles to the debate on the economic crisis during the 111th Congress (2009-10). She chairs the Small Business Committee, holds a seat on the Financial Services Committee and leads the Congressional Hispanic Caucus. She is the first Hispanic woman to chair a full House committee and the youngest person to do so in the current Congress.

She seeks to raise the profile of the Small Business Committee, which has long been relegated to second-tier status, and intends to ensure it has a prominent role in addressing the current economic slump and the effect of the tight credit markets on small companies. She was pleased to see tax incentives for small businesses in the 2009 economic stimulus law, but pressed the IRS to cut red tape so entrepreneurs could benefit quickly from those provisions.

In 2008, she led the committee in several hearings on the effects of the financial crisis on small business. The panel urged expansion of unemployment benefits, food stamps and capital projects to help small businesses.

She seeks to promote economic development and increase government contracts for minorities, women and veterans. She also tries to increase small businesses' access to capital, technology, trade, farm and energy programs. Entrepreneur magazine in 2008 named her one of 25 "Influencers" in business, along with Federal Reserve Chairman Ben S. Bernanke and Oprah Winfrey.

In her first year at the helm, she oversaw House passage of 17 bills that took steps to restore Small Business Administration (SBA) funding to pre-2001 levels, before President George W. Bush cut the funding in half. But efforts to enact a comprehensive overhaul of the SBA fell short, leaving the agency to operate under a series of short-term reauthorizations. "Extending these programs is important, but we must not lose sight of a larger goal," Velázquez said when an extension cleared in March 2009. "Later this Congress we will pass legislation to modernize the SBA and change the agency's culture. In these difficult economic times, we will need an SBA that can respond effectively."

Velázquez said curbing health care costs is also vital to small businesses. "Until that roadblock is cleared, these businesses will be unable to grow, and unable to help lead the path to economic recovery," she said. In 2003, she backed the Bush administration's association health plan proposal, which would have streamlined regulations for small businesses that pool their money to buy health insurance. In 2009, with bipartisan support, she introduced a modified version of that plan that included refundable tax credits for businesses that join purchasing cooperatives.

Medical records privacy is intensely personal for Velázquez. Her records detailing a 1991 suicide attempt with sleeping pills and vodka were leaked to the news media in 1992, shortly after she had defeated veteran Democratic Rep. Stephen J. Solarz in the Democratic primary. In 1994, Velázquez sued the hospital for failing to protect her privacy.

Her efforts to look out for the disadvantaged carry over to her work on Financial Services, where she is the No. 2 Democrat on the Housing and Community Opportunity Subcommittee. She supported the $700 billion law in 2008 to aid the financial services sector. She said it would help "keep New Yorkers in their homes and assist small-business owners." And when the panel earlier in 2008 wrote a bill to stem housing foreclosures, Velázquez included $35 million in grants for legal counseling services for low-income homeowners in the hardest-hit areas.

In 2007, she introduced a bill to let local governments purchase buildings owned by the Department of Housing and Urban Development and slated for foreclosure, to use as affordable housing for low-income families.

As chairwoman of the Hispanic Caucus, she is working to heal divisions caused by California's Joe Baca, whose leadership alienated some female members. Among her first priorities is ensuring the caucus plays a role in debate on the economic crisis. "The current environment poses many challenges for Latinos, from the foreclosure crisis and immigration to accessing quality health care and education," she said in November 2008. She also traveled with President Obama in April 2009 to the Summit of the Americas in Trinidad and Tobago. "Our relations with Latin America could not be more important than they are in today's economic and political climate," she said.

She has long been an immigrant rights activist. In 2006, she joined in demonstrations protesting GOP proposals to criminalize undocumented immigrants. From 1986 until 1992, when she was elected as the first Puerto Rican congresswoman, she worked as a liaison between the Puerto Rican government and Latino communities in the United States. She once led 50 members of Congress in filing a court brief against an "English only" law in Arizona.

Velázquez was raised in the sugar cane region in southeastern Puerto Rico with her twin sister and seven other siblings. Her father cut cane and her mother helped make ends meet by selling food to other cane workers. Her father also made cinder blocks and, according to The New York Times, owned a cockfighting pit. He had only a third-grade education, but was a community leader and founded a political party in their hometown of Yabucoa.

She was the first in her family to receive a college diploma, graduating from the University of Puerto Rico with a political science degree. She went to New York City for graduate school and taught Puerto Rican studies at Hunter College. She then became a special assistant to Democratic Rep. Edolphus Towns, and served on the New York City Council.

Before running for Congress, Velázquez ran a Hispanic voter registration drive financed by the Puerto Rican government. Her biggest obstacle in the 1992 Democratic primary was nine-term incumbent Solarz, but Velázquez beat him by a 5-percentage-point margin, then won the general election with 77 percent of the vote. She has won re-election by solid margins ever since.

KEY VOTES

2008
Yes Delay consideration of Colombia free-trade agreement
Yes Override Bush veto of federal farm and nutrition programs reauthorization bill
No Overhaul surveillance laws and permit dismissal of suits against companies that conducted warrantless wiretapping
Yes Grant mortgage relief to homeowners and funding for Fannie Mae and Freddie Mac
Yes Approve initial $700 billion program to stabilize financial markets
Yes Approve final $700 billion program to stabilize financial markets
Yes Provide $14 billion in loans to automakers

2007
Yes Increase minimum wage by $2.10 an hour
Yes Approve $124.2 billion in emergency war spending and set goal for redeployment of troops from Iraq
No Reject federal contraceptive assistance to international family planning groups
Yes Override Bush veto of $23.2 billion water projects authorization bill
No Implement Peru free-trade agreement
Yes Approve energy policy overhaul with new fuel economy standards
No Clear $473.5 billion omnibus spending bill, including $70 billion for military operations

CQ VOTE STUDIES

	PARTY UNITY		PRESIDENTIAL SUPPORT	
	SUPPORT	OPPOSE	SUPPORT	OPPOSE
2008	100%	0%	14%	86%
2007	99%	1%	4%	96%
2006	99%	1%	10%	90%
2005	98%	2%	18%	82%
2004	96%	4%	15%	85%

INTEREST GROUPS

	AFL-CIO	ADA	CCUS	ACU
2008	100%	100%	50%	0%
2007	96%	95%	60%	0%
2006	93%	100%	27%	4%
2005	80%	100%	48%	0%
2004	87%	100%	32%	8%

NEW YORK 12

Lower East Side of Manhattan; parts of Brooklyn and Queens

The 12th combines part of Manhattan's Lower East Side with portions of Brooklyn and Queens. Minorities make up more than three-fourths of the population of this working-class Democratic bastion, which has a Hispanic plurality (49 percent). The 12th's economy, anchored by the health care sector, also has a blue-collar workforce affiliated with industries along the East River. Barack Obama won 86 percent of the district's 2008 presidential vote.

Nearly two-thirds of the 12th's residents live in Brooklyn. In its southwestern corner, the district begins in Sunset Park, home to large Hispanic and Chinese populations. The district takes in part of Park Slope and Red Hook and then narrows along Brooklyn's waterfront before enveloping the Brooklyn Navy Yard. It also includes part of Williamsburg and Greenpoint, which has a large Polish population. New high-rises in the Greenpoint and Williamsburg industrial waterfront areas may replace historic factories and port facilities, and local residents hope to keep

vibrant commercial corridors and residential areas from being dwarfed by new construction. The 12th also moves southeast, along the Brooklyn-Queens border, to the heavily Hispanic neighborhoods of Bushwick, Cypress Hills and City Line.

On the Queens side of the border, the district takes in parts of the Sunnyside and Woodside neighborhoods. Originally a heavily Irish area, the 12th District's part of Queens now includes residents with a diverse mix of ethnic backgrounds, including a growing Hispanic population from many different countries. The district also includes the Brooklyn, Manhattan and Williamsburg bridges, and it crosses the East River into Manhattan to take in Chinatown, most of Little Italy, Alphabet City and the Lower East Side.

MAJOR INDUSTRY
Health care, service

CITIES
New York (pt.), 654,360

NOTABLE
Brooklyn's Green-Wood Cemetery, where the more than 560,000 interred include Leonard Bernstein, Horace Greeley and notorious 19th-century New York politician William M. "Boss" Tweed.

Rep. Michael E. McMahon (D)

Elected 2008; 1st term

McMahon is the first Democrat to win the conservative-leaning 13th District since 1981 and plans to follow a centrist course. He was the beneficiary of Republican disarray after his GOP predecessor, Vito J. Fossella, decided in the spring of 2008 not to seek a seventh term following a drunk driving arrest and the revelation that he had a 3-year-old daughter from an extramarital affair.

A former New York City Council member, McMahon doesn't believe his win is solely attributable to his predecessor's mistakes. "I believe I was elected because of my activist approach to community issues and local government," he said.

McMahon, who serves on the Transportation and Infrastructure Committee, was instrumental as a city council member in helping convene a traffic mitigation task force to address growing congestion throughout the city's five boroughs. He backed Republican New York Mayor Michael Bloomberg's unsuccessful attempt to reduce traffic by increasing the cost of driving into the most overcrowded areas.

He also was responsible for a bill that increased ferry service to and from Staten Island. And he successfully fought to permanently close the borough's massive Fresh Kills Landfill, once the largest in the world. The site is being redeveloped as a 2,200-acre public park.

McMahon also sits on the Foreign Affairs Committee, where he hopes to address issues that are relevant to his district's many immigrants. He also was named freshman majority whip.

After Fossella announced his retirement, GOP leaders initially tapped Frank Powers, a well-liked Metropolitan Transportation Authority board member and retired Wall Street executive. But midway through the campaign, Powers died of a sudden heart attack. Robert A. Straniere, next to receive the endorsement, was dogged throughout the campaign by ethical, legal, and financial problems, including accusations that he didn't live in the district he hoped to represent, as required by law.

McMahon took 61 percent of the vote, even as Republican John McCain carried the district over Democrat Barack Obama in the presidential race.

CAPITOL OFFICE
225-3371
mcmahon.house.gov
323 Cannon Bldg. 20515-3213; fax 226-1272

COMMITTEES
Foreign Affairs
Transportation & Infrastructure

RESIDENCE
Staten Island

BORN
Sept. 12, 1957; Staten Island, N.Y.

RELIGION
Roman Catholic

FAMILY
Wife, Judith McMahon; two children

EDUCATION
New York U., B.A. 1980 (politics); Heidelberg U. (Germany), A.A. 1982 (German); New York Law School, J.D. 1985

CAREER
Lawyer; state legislative aide

POLITICAL HIGHLIGHTS
New York City Council, 2002-09

ELECTION RESULTS

2008 GENERAL

Michael E. McMahon (D, WFM)	114,219	60.9%
Robert A. Straniere (R)	62,441	33.3%
Timothy J. Cochrane (C)	5,799	3.1%
Carmine A. Morano (INDC)	4,947	2.6%

2008 PRIMARY

Michael E. McMahon (D)	unopposed

NEW YORK 13

Staten Island; part of southwest Brooklyn

The 13th includes all of Staten Island (Richmond County) and a small portion of southwestern Brooklyn across the Verrazano-Narrows Bridge. Two-thirds of the district's white, upper-middle-class population lives on Staten Island.

The 13th has the nation's largest Italian-American population, and the predominantly Catholic community gives the district a socially conservative edge. Although a Republican stronghold for 30 years, residents sent a Democrat to the U.S. House in 2008. John McCain won a slim 51 percent of the 2008 presidential vote in the 13th, the only New York City district he carried.

Staten Island is the least ethnically diverse of New York's five boroughs and is 78 percent white. Hispanic and black populations live mostly in the borough's northeast. There is an Asian presence in some mid-island neighborhoods, and the 13th has the second-most residents of Arab descent in the nation. Staten Island University Hospital is a key employer, and retail, finance and insurance jobs provide work.

The Brooklyn part of the 13th extends from the Verrazano into Bay Ridge, Dyker Heights and part of Bensonhurst, before buttonhooking south of Cropsey Avenue and moving east to take in part of Gravesend, home to many new middle-class immigrants, particularly Russians.

MAJOR INDUSTRY
Health care, retail, communications

MILITARY BASES
Fort Hamilton (Army), 970 military, 925 civilian (2007)

CITIES
New York (pt.), 654,361

NOTABLE
The 1977 disco movie "Saturday Night Fever" was set in Bay Ridge.

Rep. Carolyn B. Maloney (D)

Elected 1992; 9th term

CAPITOL OFFICE
225-7944
maloney.house.gov
2332 Rayburn Bldg. 20515-3214; fax 225-4709

COMMITTEES
Financial Services
Oversight & Government Reform
Joint Economic - chairwoman

RESIDENCE
Manhattan

BORN
Feb. 19, 1948; Greensboro, N.C.

RELIGION
Presbyterian

FAMILY
Husband, Clifton H.W. Maloney; two children

EDUCATION
Greensboro College, A.B. 1968

CAREER
State legislative aide; teacher

POLITICAL HIGHLIGHTS
New York City Council, 1982-93

ELECTION RESULTS

2008 GENERAL

Carolyn B. Maloney (D, WFM)	183,190	79.9%
Robert G. Heim (R)	43,365	18.9%
Isiah Matos (LIBERT)	2,659	1.2%

2008 PRIMARY

Carolyn B. Maloney (D, WFM)	unopposed

2006 GENERAL

Carolyn B. Maloney (D, INDC, WFM)	119,582	84.5%
Danniel Maio (R)	21,969	15.5%

PREVIOUS WINNING PERCENTAGES
2004 (81%); 2002 (75%); 2000 (74%); 1998 (77%);
1996 (72%); 1994 (64%); 1992 (50%)

A hard-charging liberal, Maloney is a dervish of activity on behalf of the causes she most cares about, including national security, consumer credit protections and women's rights. She ranks among the top legislators in volume of bills introduced.

Since her election in 1992, she has supported abortion rights, advocated for an equal-rights constitutional amendment and paid leave for working parents, and lamented the plight of women worldwide. She also has helped overhaul the U.S. intelligence community and sought health benefits for victims of and responders to the Sept. 11 terrorist attacks. But most recently, her attention has turned to the financial crisis.

As a member of the Financial Services Subcommittee on Financial Institutions and Consumer Credit and chairwoman of the Joint Economic Committee, Maloney is immersed in discussions regarding the mortgage crisis and lending practices. She helped negotiate in fall 2008 an emergency $700 billion package to shore up the nation's financial system. Speaking on the House floor that September, Maloney said, "A wholesale failure of the banking system would be the financial equivalent of an economic heart attack."

She joined other Democrats in early 2009 in seeking to recoup funds from the financial rescue law that were paid out in million-dollar bonuses to executives at American International Group Inc. "It would be both morally reprehensible and fiscally irresponsible for us to quietly hand over millions to those who have cost this country billions," she said.

An equally important priority for her on Financial Services is addressing credit card billing practices she said hurt consumers. "As we are helping Wall Street, we also need to help Main Street," she said. In 2008, She claimed a personal victory when the House passed her measure to curb practices such as retroactively increasing interest rates. The bill was vigorously opposed by the credit industry and many Republicans. The Senate didn't take it up. But she resumed her efforts in early 2009, and her legislation cleared Congress and was signed into law. She also continued to push legislation intended to help consumers better manage bank overdraft fees.

Maloney, who wears a silver bracelet with 9-11-01 engraved on it, has been tireless in her efforts on behalf of survivors of the 2001 terrorist attacks and the first-responders who fought to save them. She was in her Capitol Hill office when a friend from New York called and told her a plane had crashed into the World Trade Center. After watching the news, she drove to New York and headed straight for the disaster scene. Discovering responders needed phones, she called Florida Republican C.W. Bill Young, then the chairman of the Appropriations Committee. The next morning, the phones arrived.

From her seat on the Oversight and Government Reform panel, she helped win enactment in 2004 of a sweeping bill to reorganize U.S. intelligence operations and create a national intelligence director in response to the recommendations of the bipartisan panel that investigated the attacks. She called it the "most important work I've done in Congress."

The following year, she and New York Republican Peter T. King secured $75 million for the Centers for Disease Control and Prevention to screen, monitor and treat those injured or sickened in the attacks and their aftermath. A law enacted in early 2006 carried a provision by Maloney granting federal military retirement credit to all National Guard soldiers who were on active duty in the affected areas of New York and Virginia in the year after the attacks.

Republicans in the 110th Congress (2007-08) blocked her bill to allow 19

www.cqpress.com

immigrants with family members who died in the attack to become permanent legal residents. But she authored a law revamping the government's process for scrutinizing the national security risks posed by foreign investments.

Maloney, a member and former co-chairwoman of the Caucus for Women's Issues, has long been concerned about the rights of women. She published a book in May 2008 on the status of women, "Rumors of Our Progress Have Been Greatly Exaggerated." She told an audience: "In this period of economic downturn, there's one area where we have achieved equality — job loss."

Maloney sought to demonstrate the plight of Afghan women under the Taliban by coming to the House floor in October 2001 in a head-to-toe blue burqa. And she condemned President George W. Bush over his decision to bar U.S. contributions to the U.N. Population Fund, which helps deliver birth control information and services to women in Third World nations. President Obama overturned that ban after he took office.

Maloney repeatedly pushes without success an equal-rights constitutional amendment. She has had more success with other measures. In 1999, her legislation to permit breast-feeding on federal property became law. And in 2006, she and Republican Rep. Deborah Pryce of Ohio saw their bill to address sex trafficking enacted as part of a broader measure.

Congress passed Maloney's bill in 2008 reauthorizing for five years a grant program aimed at reducing a backlog of DNA evidence awaiting analysis. Maloney had first introduced legislation creating the grant program in 2001 (it was enacted in 2004), after a rape victim whose attacker was later identified through DNA analysis testified before a House committee.

She continued in 2009 to press legislation requiring federal employees to be granted four weeks of paid parental leave; the House passed her bill in 2008 but it failed to become law.

Maloney hails from Greensboro, N.C. She visited New York City in her early 20s and decided to stay, eventually teaching adult education in East Harlem and joining the city's vast educational bureaucracy. She said she realized government had a greater impact than any teacher on the education of the city's youth, and so she moved to Albany to work for the state legislature. Five years later, Maloney was elected to the New York City Council, where she served about 10 years and was a watchdog against government waste.

When Maloney ran against seven-term GOP Rep. Bill Green in 1992, media hype about the "Year of the Woman" lent momentum to her underdog challenge. She also benefited from redistricting, which forced Green to campaign on some unfamiliar turf. She beat him narrowly with 50 percent of the vote. Her election victories since then have been runaways.

KEY VOTES

2008

Yes	Delay consideration of Colombia free-trade agreement
Yes	Override Bush veto of federal farm and nutrition programs reauthorization bill
No	Overhaul surveillance laws and permit dismissal of suits against companies that conducted warrantless wiretapping
Yes	Grant mortgage relief to homeowners and funding for Fannie Mae and Freddie Mac
Yes	Approve initial $700 billion program to stabilize financial markets
Yes	Approve final $700 billion program to stabilize financial markets
Yes	Provide $14 billion in loans to automakers

2007

Yes	Increase minimum wage by $2.10 an hour
Yes	Approve $124.2 billion in emergency war spending and set goal for redeployment of troops from Iraq
No	Reject federal contraceptive assistance to international family planning groups
Yes	Override Bush veto of $23.2 billion water projects authorization bill
Yes	Implement Peru free-trade agreement
Yes	Approve energy policy overhaul with new fuel economy standards
No	Clear $473.5 billion omnibus spending bill, including $70 billion for military operations

CQ VOTE STUDIES

	PARTY UNITY		PRESIDENTIAL SUPPORT	
	SUPPORT	OPPOSE	SUPPORT	OPPOSE
2008	99%	1%	17%	83%
2007	99%	1%	4%	96%
2006	94%	6%	33%	67%
2005	98%	2%	17%	83%
2004	97%	3%	28%	72%

INTEREST GROUPS

	AFL-CIO	ADA	CCUS	ACU
2008	100%	95%	65%	0%
2007	95%	90%	58%	0%
2006	93%	85%	43%	8%
2005	93%	100%	37%	0%
2004	100%	100%	45%	4%

NEW YORK 14

East Side of Manhattan; western Queens

Home to New York City's wealthy high-society, the 14th's traditional old-money elite has been partially displaced by young, professional "limousine liberals," many of whom are in white-collar industries vulnerable to nationwide economic downturns. The 14th has the nation's highest percentage of residents with at least a bachelor's degree (57 percent) and the country's highest percentage of people who walk to work (22 percent).

Taking in all of Central Park in the district's northwest corner, the 14th's western edge then roughly follows Broadway south toward Union Square before narrowing to reach the Lower East Side. Landmarks include Carnegie Hall, Rockefeller Center, Grand Central Terminal, the United Nations, the Chrysler Building and Fifth Avenue's Museum Mile, which includes the Metropolitan Museum of Art.

But the tony neighborhoods of Manhattan's East Side do not tell the whole story of a district that crosses Roosevelt Island to pick up ethnic working-class sections of Queens, such as Astoria, which is still the city's Greek hub despite an influx of other ethnic groups. The 14th is both economically and geographically diverse — 40 percent of the district's population speaks a language other than English at home. Long Island City, once an industrial powerhouse, experienced decline but is seeing a resurgence through commercial development and the construction of waterfront luxury apartments. A burgeoning arts community has taken advantage of affordable housing in the area. Queens residents make up 31 percent of the district.

Republicans generally are unable to compete against the overwhelming Democratic presence in this district: Barack Obama won 78 percent of the 14th's presidential vote in 2008. Extremely active politically, district residents are known for making some of the largest campaign contributions in the nation.

MAJOR INDUSTRY
Finance, health care, tourism, communications, advertising, publishing

CITIES
New York (pt.), 654,361

NOTABLE
Gracie Mansion, in Carl Schurz Park, is the official residence of New York's mayor; The Museum of the Moving Image is in Astoria.

Rep. Charles B. Rangel (D)

Elected 1970; 20th term

CAPITOL OFFICE
225-4365
www.house.gov/rangel
2354 Rayburn Bldg. 20515-3215; fax 225-0816

COMMITTEES
Ways & Means - chairman
Joint Taxation - chairman

RESIDENCE
Manhattan

BORN
June 11, 1930; Manhattan, N.Y.

RELIGION
Roman Catholic

FAMILY
Wife, Alma Rangel; two children

EDUCATION
New York U., B.S. 1957; St. John's U., LL.B. 1960

MILITARY SERVICE
Army, 1948-52

CAREER
Lawyer

POLITICAL HIGHLIGHTS
Assistant U.S. attorney, 1961-62; N.Y. Assembly, 1967-71; sought Democratic nomination for N.Y. City Council president, 1969

ELECTION RESULTS

2008 GENERAL

Charles B. Rangel (D, WFM)	177,060	89.2%
Edward Daniels (R)	15,668	7.9%
Craig Schley (VPC)	3,706	1.9%
Martin Koppel (SW)	2,141	1.1%

2008 PRIMARY

Charles B. Rangel (D, WFM)	unopposed

2006 GENERAL

Charles B. Rangel (D, WFM)	103,916	94.0%
Edward Daniels (R)	6,592	6.0%

PREVIOUS WINNING PERCENTAGES
2004 (91%); 2002 (88%); 2000 (92%); 1998 (93%); 1996 (91%); 1994 (97%); 1992 (95%); 1990 (97%); 1988 (97%); 1986 (96%); 1984 (97%); 1982 (97%); 1980 (96%); 1978 (96%); 1976 (97%); 1974 (97%); 1972 (96%); 1970 (87%)

After nearly four decades and countless raspy-voiced wisecracks, Rangel has reached the pinnacle of his career — which appears, at times, to be a precipice. As the crafty, combative chairman of the powerful Ways and Means Committee, he has put his dealmaking prowess to frequent use but endured close scrutiny of his personal finances and political dealings.

Rangel spent much of 2008 mired in three separate controversies. First, news reports revealed he had multiple rent-stabilized apartments in his Harlem building, including one used as a campaign office. Then he came under attack for using a congressional letterhead as part of a fundraising campaign for a college center that will be named for him. Finally, and most damaging to the leader of the tax-writing committee, Rangel acknowledged he had underreported rental income from a villa in the Dominican Republic and began trying to correct discrepancies in his financial disclosure statements.

Rangel referred all of the matters to the House ethics committee, which was investigating, but Republicans repeatedly called for him to step down from the Ways and Means chairmanship, an idea that Rangel rebuffed. "I really don't believe that making mistakes means that you have to give up your career," he said in September 2008. Even as the ethics probe resumed in the 111th Congress (2009-10), House Democratic leaders rallied to Rangel's side, preferring to keep the focus on the economic stimulus bill they were rushing to President Obama's desk and plans for massive health care legislation.

Rangel is well-liked by his colleagues, and many Democrats have benefited from his fundraising talent. During the 2008 election cycle, his campaign and political committees contributed $2.5 million to 197 Democratic candidates and party organizations, according to an analysis of Federal Election Commission records by CQ MoneyLine.

Rangel defies easy classification. At first, he seems like an old-school liberal as he supports gun control, opposes the Iraq War and wants to redistribute wealth from top to bottom. He can be unyielding and defiant in partisan fights, displaying a sharp-tongued wit. Interviewed by a New York television station in 2005, Rangel was asked his view of President George W. Bush. "Well," he said, "I really think he shatters the myth of white supremacy once and for all. It shows that, in this great country, anyone can become president."

But business lobbyists and many Republicans know a different Rangel, one not always wedded to ideology. When he took charge of Ways and Means in 2007, Rangel tried to change the tone within the committee, which had soured under abrasive Republican Bill Thomas of California, who had just retired after six years as chairman. At the start of the 110th Congress (2007-08), he worked with the new top Republican, Jim McCrery of Louisiana, to advance legislation providing small-business tax breaks, added relief for Hurricane Katrina victims, taxpayer identity protections and a ban on genetic discrimination by health insurers — all before the 2007 spring recess.

Rangel struck several other important agreements later in the 110th. He negotiated a trade framework with the Bush administration that strengthened labor and environmental standards, allowing a free-trade deal with Peru to become law. He paired a minimum wage increase with tax breaks, satisfying Republicans who wanted to soften the blow for businesses. Working with the administration and GOP leaders, he pushed an economic stimulus package through Congress that gave tax rebates to consumers and provided investment incentives to businesses.

www.cqpress.com

With McCrery's retirement, Rangel has a new GOP counterpart in Michigan's Dave Camp, who in his desire to reach across the aisle has tried to straddle his leaders' desire to oust Rangel from his chairmanship.

Because of his position, Rangel's influence stretches into almost every policy area. Pay-as-you-go rules adopted when Democrats took control in 2007 require that tax cuts or mandatory spending increases get paired with revenue increases or spending cuts. Committee chairmen whose bills had financial holes came to view Rangel as their banker, and he rationed money to them, allowing significant farm and energy legislation to become law.

On April 10, 2008, Rangel and Pete Stark of California, the No. 2 Democrat on Ways and Means, marked 12,500 days of service on the panel — the longest tenure in the committee's 220-year history. Together, they surpassed the record set earlier by Arkansas Democrat Wilbur D. Mills, who retired in 1977.

Over his long career, the Harlem-based Rangel has had his greatest legislative success with efforts to spur economic development in underserved neighborhoods. He wrote the 1993 "empowerment zones" law providing tax credits to businesses that move into blighted areas and the 1986 tax credit for developers of low-income housing. He is also one of the House's leading advocates of expanded trade with Caribbean countries, the home region for many of his upper-Manhattan constituents.

Rangel was a passionate critic of the 1996 law ending welfare's status as an entitlement. After the U.S. invasion of Iraq in 2003, Rangel spoke out against it and proposed legislation to reinstate the military draft. He argued that the all-volunteer military relied too heavily on poor and working-class enlistees who needed jobs and education benefits.

His long tenure has not been without setbacks, even before his recent troubles. He was among the members swept up in the House bank scandal in the early 1990s, and in 1999 he was entangled in a financial scandal at Harlem's historic Apollo Theater. The state of New York later dropped a lawsuit against Rangel and others on the theater board, saying they acted in good faith.

Raised by his seamstress mother and her family in Harlem, Rangel dropped out of high school at 16, joined the Army and won a Purple Heart and Bronze Star in the Korean War, surviving firefights that claimed much of his unit. The harrowing experience provided the title of his autobiography: "And I Haven't Had a Bad Day Since." Once back home, he finished high school and college, then landed an internship in the local district attorney's office.

After four years in the state Assembly, he ousted Rep. Adam Clayton Powell Jr. in the 1970 Democratic House primary. He won his first general election with 87 percent of the vote and has amassed even larger wins ever since.

KEY VOTES

2008

Yes Delay consideration of Colombia free-trade agreement

Yes Override Bush veto of federal farm and nutrition programs reauthorization bill

No Overhaul surveillance laws and permit dismissal of suits against companies that conducted warrantless wiretapping

Yes Grant mortgage relief to homeowners and funding for Fannie Mae and Freddie Mac

Yes Approve initial $700 billion program to stabilize financial markets

Yes Approve final $700 billion program to stabilize financial markets

Yes Provide $14 billion in loans to automakers

2007

Yes Increase minimum wage by $2.10 an hour

Yes Approve $124.2 billion in emergency war spending and set goal for redeployment of troops from Iraq

No Reject federal contraceptive assistance to international family planning groups

Yes Override Bush veto of $23.2 billion water projects authorization bill

Yes Implement Peru free-trade agreement

Yes Approve energy policy overhaul with new fuel economy standards

No Clear $473.5 billion omnibus spending bill, including $70 billion for military operations

CQ VOTE STUDIES

	PARTY UNITY		PRESIDENTIAL SUPPORT	
	SUPPORT	OPPOSE	SUPPORT	OPPOSE
2008	100%	0%	16%	84%
2007	98%	2%	6%	94%
2006	96%	4%	27%	73%
2005	98%	2%	16%	84%
2004	98%	2%	19%	81%

INTEREST GROUPS

	AFL-CIO	ADA	CCUS	ACU
2008	100%	85%	61%	0%
2007	95%	95%	60%	0%
2006	100%	95%	40%	4%
2005	93%	100%	38%	0%
2004	93%	95%	30%	0%

NEW YORK 15

Northern Manhattan — Harlem, Washington Heights

The 15th takes in Upper Manhattan's Harlem and Washington Heights, stretching to Inwood at its tip, and picks up Marble Hill north of the Harlem River. East of Manhattan, it includes Randalls, Wards and Rikers islands, and a small industrial area of Queens. At only 10 square miles in size, the 15th is the nation's smallest district in area.

The past two decades have brought substantial change to the district, with Puerto Rican and Dominican immigrants — primarily in East Harlem and Washington Heights — supplanting the 15th's African-American majority. Hispanics now far outnumber non-Hispanic blacks, but low voter participation among Hispanics means the smaller black population (31 percent) continues to dominate the district's politics.

North Manhattan's 1994 designation as a federal empowerment zone resulted in an economic resurgence. Refurbished brownstones, new restaurants, national retail chains and prominent corporations have moved into the area. Washington Heights is experiencing a similar rebirth.

The district's hospitals and colleges, along with its retail establishments, provide much of the employment, although many jobs are out of reach to less-educated residents, and economic slowdowns have hurt small businesses. Among the 15th's universities is Columbia in Morningside Heights, and the area's health care industry hosts major research and teaching hospitals, including parts of New York Presbyterian Hospital. Many residents also are employed on Rikers Island, the New York City correctional facility in the East River that has roughly 17,000 inmates and is officially part of the Bronx, but is connected to Queens by a bridge.

Since its creation in 1944, the decidedly liberal 15th District seat has been held by two black Democrats: Adam Clayton Powell Jr. and Charles B. Rangel. In the 2008 presidential race, the district gave Barack Obama 93 percent, his second-highest percentage in the nation.

MAJOR INDUSTRY
Health care, higher education, retail, city government

CITIES
New York (pt.), 654,361

NOTABLE
Legendary venues such as the Cotton Club and the Apollo Theater.

Rep. José E. Serrano (D)

Elected March 1990; 10th full term

CAPITOL OFFICE
225-4361
serrano.house.gov
2227 Rayburn Bldg. 20515-3216; fax 225-6001

COMMITTEES
Appropriations
(Financial Services - chairman)

RESIDENCE
Bronx

BORN
Oct. 24, 1943; Mayaguez, P.R.

RELIGION
Roman Catholic

FAMILY
Divorced; five children

EDUCATION
Dodge Vocational H.S., graduated 1961;
Lehman College, attended 1979-80

MILITARY SERVICE
Army Medical Corps, 1964-66

CAREER
School district administrator; banker

POLITICAL HIGHLIGHTS
N.Y. Assembly, 1975-90; sought Democratic
nomination for Bronx borough president, 1985

ELECTION RESULTS

2008 GENERAL

José E. Serrano (D, WFM)	127,179	96.6%
Ali Mohamed (R, C)	4,488	3.4%

2008 PRIMARY

José E. Serrano (D, WFM)	unopposed

2006 GENERAL

José E. Serrano (D, WFM)	56,124	95.3%
Ali Mohamed (R, C)	2,759	4.7%

PREVIOUS WINNING PERCENTAGES
2004 (95%); 2002 (92%); 2000 (96%); 1998 (95%);
1996 (96%); 1994 (96%); 1992 (91%); 1990 (93%);
1990 Special Election (92%)

One of 12 "cardinals" who chair Appropriations subcommittees in the House, the gregarious Serrano moves easily through the halls of Congress, always ready with a quip or a joke. But he maintains that despite his loquaciousness, he is a serious-minded liberal.

Sporting a thick black mustache, Serrano is one of the most noticeable — and humorous — members of Congress. Constantly referencing his home in New York's South Bronx and his Puerto Rican roots, Serrano (full name: ho-ZAY sa-RAH-no, with a rolled 'R') keeps his colleagues and constituents laughing. Attending a tree-planting ceremony in New York in April 2009, he presented Mayor Michael Bloomberg with two new quarters honoring Puerto Rico and said: "I paid for these myself...I give you two so you can rub them together and see what you can make of it. This is the only country in the world where a guy who was born in a one-room flat with a latrine, grew up in public housing, is giving Michael Bloomberg two quarters."

Serrano has been chairman of the Financial Services Appropriations Subcommittee since Democrats took control of the House in 2007. He shepherds the bills responsible for the funding of a wide array of federal agencies and government operations, including the Treasury Department. His panel drafted a portion of the 2009 economic stimulus law that directed funds to the Small Business Administration and the General Services Administration. He called the final measure a "bold move" to help turn around the economy.

Yet Serrano opposed the $700 billion package to shore up the financial services industry in fall 2008. "I was speaking for the people in the Bronx and people across the nation who are stuck without any help from our government," he said. "I was speaking against bailing out the very people who caused this mess. I was speaking for fairness in our economic policies."

Serrano also serves on the Homeland Security and Commerce-Justice-Science Appropriations subcommittees. His role as an appropriator gives him ample opportunity to bring money home. He helped obtain federal money to clean up the Bronx River, plant trees in the borough and reduce air pollution from trucks, which is believed to be a contributing factor in the high incidence of asthma among his constituents. He proudly notes that a beaver was spotted in 2007 living in the Bronx River for the first time in two centuries. Biologists named it José, in Serrano's honor. In 2008, Serrano obtained $700,000 for the river. In a catchall spending measure for fiscal 2009, he helped obtain more than $11.4 million in earmarks — funding set-asides for special projects.

Serrano has long been an advocate of easing trade and travel restrictions to Cuba. The 2009 catchall spending law included his provision to allow Americans with family members living in Cuba more expansive travel rights. The move garnered sharp protest from several members, including Democrat Debbie Wasserman Schultz, whose Florida district is home to a number of Cuban-Americans. "There is no reason to place harsh restrictions on those who simply wish to visit close family members," Serrano said. He added that his efforts to shake up Cuban sanctions are not politically motivated.

Serrano regularly weighs in on issues of importance to the island of his birth. Nearly 200,000 of Serrano's constituents are of Puerto Rican descent, and he believes citizens of the island should be allowed to decide whether it is granted statehood or independence. In 2007, he sponsored a bill calling for a plebiscite for Puerto Ricans to choose between the status quo or a change to either statehood or independence. The Natural Resources Committee approved the legislation in October 2007, but the bill didn't go further.

In 2000, Serrano was arrested outside the White House for protesting the Navy's continued use of the island of Vieques, off the coast of Puerto Rico, for training exercises using live bombs. On the Vieques issue and others, Serrano has aligned with black activist Al Sharpton, and he endorsed Sharpton's 2004 bid in the Democratic presidential primaries.

Serrano's voting record is solidly Democratic; he supported his party 99 percent of the time during the 110th Congress (2007-08). He raised more than a few eyebrows in 2007 when he signed on to a bill by Democrat Jim McGovern of Massachusetts to require the withdrawal of U.S. troops from Iraq within six months and cut off funding for the war thereafter. Serrano was among three Democratic appropriators, including Barbara Lee of California and John W. Olver of Massachusetts, to join the measure, which went further in calling for an end to the war than other Democratic resolutions that year.

The baseball-crazed nature of his native Puerto Rico has rubbed off on Serrano. The congressman, whose district is home to the New York Yankees, has long offered legislation and ideas regarding the state of the game. He lobbied the commissioner of Major League Baseball on the draft status of Puerto Ricans and pushed for the league to retire the number of Puerto Rican legend Roberto Clemente. He introduced a bill in early 2009 to ease prohibitions on Cubans coming to the United States to play professional baseball.

Serrano grew up in the Millbrook Houses, a public housing project in the Bronx. His parents had emigrated from Puerto Rico when he was 7, and Serrano said he learned English by listening to the Frank Sinatra records his father brought back from the Army. Serrano became a big fan, amassing a large collection of Sinatra records and sponsoring the 1997 measure that awarded Sinatra a Congressional Gold Medal. In 2008, he helped the U.S. Postal Service introduce a commemorative Sinatra stamp.

Serrano graduated from a vocational high school, served in the Army, took a job in a New York City bank and began making political contacts, which helped him win a state Assembly seat in 1974. His tenure in Albany made him a fixture in New York Hispanic politics. His son, José Marco Serrano, was elected in 2001 to the New York City Council and in 2004 to the state Senate, where he still serves.

When Democratic Rep. Robert Garcia resigned his seat in 1990 after he was convicted of defense contract extortion, Serrano moved quickly to stake his claim. He breezed to victory with 92 percent of the vote in the special election and won a full term with 93 percent that November. He has won subsequent re-elections with at least 91 percent.

KEY VOTES

2008

Yes Delay consideration of Colombia free-trade agreement

Yes Override Bush veto of federal farm and nutrition programs reauthorization bill

No Overhaul surveillance laws and permit dismissal of suits against companies that conducted warrantless wiretapping

Yes Grant mortgage relief to homeowners and funding for Fannie Mae and Freddie Mac

No Approve initial $700 billion program to stabilize financial markets

No Approve final $700 billion program to stabilize financial markets

Yes Provide $14 billion in loans to automakers

2007

Yes Increase minimum wage by $2.10 an hour

Yes Approve $124.2 billion in emergency war spending and set goal for redeployment of troops from Iraq

No Reject federal contraceptive assistance to international family planning groups

Yes Override Bush veto of $23.2 billion water projects authorization bill

No Implement Peru free-trade agreement

Yes Approve energy policy overhaul with new fuel economy standards

No Clear $473.5 billion omnibus spending bill, including $70 billion for military operations

CQ VOTE STUDIES

	PARTY UNITY		PRESIDENTIAL SUPPORT	
	SUPPORT	OPPOSE	SUPPORT	OPPOSE
2008	99%	1%	13%	87%
2007	98%	2%	5%	95%
2006	96%	4%	16%	84%
2005	96%	4%	9%	91%
2004	98%	2%	12%	88%

INTEREST GROUPS

	AFL-CIO	ADA	CCUS	ACU
2008	100%	100%	39%	8%
2007	91%	95%	55%	0%
2006	100%	90%	15%	4%
2005	93%	100%	33%	4%
2004	100%	100%	30%	0%

NEW YORK 16

South Bronx

The 16th, which covers the distressed neighborhoods of the South Bronx, is the nation's poorest district in terms of median income and is one of the least educated. One-third of families live on a household income of less than $10,000, and the area is plagued by urban ills and low rates of home ownership. Some South Bronx neighborhoods have begun to turn around, thanks to grass-roots community work, federal funding and commercial redevelopment efforts.

The South Bronx, overtaken by a post-World War II influx of Hispanics to New York City, has elected men of Puerto Rican origin to the House since 1970. The 16th's strong Puerto Rican influence is complemented by African and South and Central American immigrant communities. The district's 3 percent non-Hispanic white population is the nation's lowest.

Subsidized economic development organizations have built several downtown developments of single-family and low-rise housing on vacant lots. Light manufacturing firms also have set up shop, replacing some of the heavy industry that moved out decades ago. The Fulton Fish Market, which moved from Lower Manhattan to Hunts Point, is the nation's largest grouping of seafood wholesalers.

The new, $1.5 billion Yankee Stadium opened in 2009 and replaced one of New York City's iconic landmarks. Local businesses rely on the economic benefit of hosting the oft-visited "Bronx Bombers" and hope that fans continue to arrive in droves despite nationwide economic slowdowns. And local residents hope that promised redevelopment of community and park space occurs as part of the stadium construction plan. Fordham University also is in the 16th.

The 16th is one of the nation's most strongly Democratic districts — it gave Barack Obama his highest percentage in the 2008 presidential election (95 percent) — but like many districts with large minority and immigrant populations, voter turnout tends to be low.

MAJOR INDUSTRY
Health care, light manufacturing, seafood distribution

CITIES
New York (pt.), 654,360

NOTABLE
The Edgar Allan Poe Cottage (the writer's last home) is owned by the city.

Rep. Eliot L. Engel (D)

Elected 1988; 11th term

CAPITOL OFFICE
225-2464
www.house.gov/engel
2161 Rayburn Bldg. 20515-3217; fax 225-5513

COMMITTEES
Energy & Commerce
Foreign Affairs
  (Western Hemisphere - chairman)

RESIDENCE
Bronx

BORN
Feb. 18, 1947; Bronx, N.Y.

RELIGION
Jewish

FAMILY
Wife, Patricia Ennis Engel; three children

EDUCATION
Hunter-Lehman College, B.A. 1969 (history);
City U. of New York, Lehman College, M.A. 1973
(guidance & counseling); New York Law School,
J.D. 1987

CAREER
Teacher; guidance counselor

POLITICAL HIGHLIGHTS
Bronx Democratic district leader, 1974-77; N.Y.
Assembly, 1977-88

ELECTION RESULTS

2008 GENERAL

Eliot L. Engel (D, INDC, WFM)	161,594	79.9%
Robert Goodman (R, C)	40,707	20.1%

2008 PRIMARY

Eliot L. Engel (D, INDC, WFM)	unopposed

2006 GENERAL

Eliot L. Engel (D, WFM)	93,614	76.4%
Jim Faulkner (R, INDC, C)	28,842	23.6%

PREVIOUS WINNING PERCENTAGES
2004 (76%); 2002 (63%); 2000 (90%); 1998 (88%);
1996 (85%); 1994 (78%); 1992 (80%); 1990 (61%);
1988 (56%)

Engel has always paid close attention to detail. As a boy fascinated with politics, he memorized the names of all 100 senators. He still recalls, to the penny, the monthly rents his parents paid over the years in their Bronx walk-up apartment. And he has kept himself in Congress for two decades by ensuring his constituents can get help on any problem, big or small.

Engel is among the few white lawmakers representing a majority-minority district, and its ethnic diversity has led him to be active on the Foreign Affairs Committee as well as on health and consumer issues. But his attentiveness to his constituents is his hallmark; he keeps more staff in New York than in Washington to handle complaints on everything from cable fare increases to broken traffic lights. "Even if someone disagrees with how I vote, if they know I am hardworking and available to them, they're going to vote for me," he said.

Engel is chairman of the Foreign Affairs' Western Hemisphere Subcommittee, a position he was granted in 2007 in recognition of his district's immigrant communities from Latin America and the Caribbean. He has used the position to encourage assistance for Haiti to address food shortages and hurricane damage. He also supported a provision in 2007 authorizing aid to Mexico and Latin America to fight illegal drugs. He applauded the Obama administration for its March 2009 announcement that it would boost law enforcement along the border with Mexico to help stem the drug-related violence that threatened to flow into the United States.

Engel has long supported U.S. involvement on international humanitarian issues. He was an early proponent of U.S. intervention in Yugoslavia's civil war, and in 1993 he urged the Clinton administration to side against the Bosnian Serbs, who were accused of forcing the removal of Muslims.

He opposed granting China normal trade status in 2000 because of the country's human rights abuses. "Are we only for the almighty dollar, or are we for morality and doing what's right?" he asked.

Despite his visibility on Foreign Affairs, Engel's recent legislative victories came from his work on the Energy and Commerce Committee, where he focuses on health and communications. Though a staunch Democrat — during the 110th Congress (2007-08) he supported his party 98 percent of the time on votes in which the majority of Democrats and Republicans divided — he steered several bills through the House with bipartisan support.

Among them were two pieces of health-related legislation. One provided for research on muscular dystrophy, and the other established a national registry to study data on amyotrophic lateral sclerosis (ALS), a disease Engel said took his grandmother's life. Both bills sailed through Congress and were signed into law in October 2008.

Engel also has raised concerns about tuberculosis, calling it "the greatest curable infectious killer on this planet." In 2007, the House passed his bill to make fighting the disease globally a goal of the U.S. foreign assistance program, but the Senate did not act on it.

Engel's district includes significant foreign-born and lower-income populations, and he is quick to fight back when he feels his constituents are being mistreated. In 2007, he sponsored a House-passed bill to require calling card companies to clearly disclose terms and fees. Engel said the cards, which are used by people making frequent overseas calls or those who cannot afford long-distance service, often fail to provide the services advertised. The Senate didn't take up the bill.

Another local battle for him is a proposed airspace redesign that would dramatically increase air traffic over Rockland County. Under such a plan, the noise would be "unbelievable" for the communities below, Engel said: "It's a perfect example of government riding roughshod over people who they are ostensibly there to protect."

In line with his liberal district, Engel supports labor unions, rejects punitive immigration measures and opposes limiting civil liberties in the name of fighting terrorism. However, he has found a conservative ally on energy issues in Republican Jack Kingston of Georgia, with whom he worked to promote tax incentives for hybrid vehicles in the 2007 energy overhaul law. Engel said that if he had known how "incompetent" the George W. Bush administration would be in executing the Iraq War, he wouldn't have voted in 2002 to authorize it — even if the intelligence about weapons of mass destruction had turned out to be right. In 2008, he voted against funding for the wars in Afghanistan and Iraq and in favor of an amendment that would require troop withdrawal.

However, Engel was among the pro-Israel lawmakers who persuaded House Democratic leaders to drop a provision from a March 2007 war funding bill that would have barred the president from taking military action against Iran without congressional authorization. He argued Bush needed maximum flexibility to pressure Iran to end its nuclear program and its support of radical Islamic groups that foment violence against Israel.

He also sees Syria as a threat to Israel and the broader Middle East. During the 108th Congress (2003-04), he teamed up with Republican Ileana Ros-Lehtinen of Florida to win passage of a sanctions bill targeting Syria.

One of Engel's most noticeable quirks is that he always arrives early for the annual State of the Union address to grab an aisle seat in the House chamber, where he can greet the president and renew acquaintances with a number of ambassadors. "The constituents love it," he once explained. "And as long as they love it, I love it."

Engel grew up in the Democratic clubs of the Bronx and walked the picket lines with his father, a welder who was active in his union. "He had a very strong sense of social justice and doing what was right for working people," Engel said. He attended New York City public schools, where he later worked as a teacher and guidance counselor. He was elected to the state Assembly in 1976, where he worked on housing and substance abuse issues. In 1988, he successfully challenged Democratic Rep. Mario Biaggi, who was convicted of bribery, conspiracy and extortion. He easily rebuffed a Biaggi comeback attempt in his 1992 election, and has faced minimal opposition since then.

KEY VOTES

2008

Yes Delay consideration of Colombia free-trade agreement

Yes Override Bush veto of federal farm and nutrition programs reauthorization bill

Yes Overhaul surveillance laws and permit dismissal of suits against companies that conducted warrantless wiretapping

Yes Grant mortgage relief to homeowners and funding for Fannie Mae and Freddie Mac

Yes Approve initial $700 billion program to stabilize financial markets

Yes Approve final $700 billion program to stabilize financial markets

Yes Provide $14 billion in loans to automakers

2007

Yes Increase minimum wage by $2.10 an hour

Yes Approve $124.2 billion in emergency war spending and set goal for redeployment of troops from Iraq

No Reject federal contraceptive assistance to international family planning groups

Yes Override Bush veto of $23.2 billion water projects authorization bill

Yes Implement Peru free-trade agreement

Yes Approve energy policy overhaul with new fuel economy standards

No Clear $473.5 billion omnibus spending bill, including $70 billion for military operations

CQ VOTE STUDIES

	PARTY UNITY		PRESIDENTIAL SUPPORT	
	SUPPORT	OPPOSE	SUPPORT	OPPOSE
2008	98%	2%	17%	83%
2007	98%	2%	6%	94%
2006	95%	5%	34%	66%
2005	93%	7%	26%	74%
2004	96%	4%	36%	64%

INTEREST GROUPS

	AFL-CIO	ADA	CCUS	ACU
2008	100%	95%	65%	0%
2007	95%	80%	53%	0%
2006	100%	95%	36%	4%
2005	93%	95%	41%	0%
2004	93%	90%	35%	4%

NEW YORK 17

North Bronx; part of Westchester and Rockland counties — Mount Vernon, part of Yonkers

The 17th takes in the northwestern part of the Bronx and parts of Westchester and Rockland counties just north of New York City. Blacks and Hispanics together constitute a majority of residents in the district, which is ethnically, racially and economically diverse territory.

Riverdale, a heavily Jewish neighborhood, sits at the western edge of the Bronx and is one of New York City's most affluent areas. It is home to numerous college preparatory schools, medical facilities and new apartment buildings. East of Riverdale, on the other side of Van Cortlandt Park and Woodlawn Cemetery, there is a large black population. The 17th reaches almost as far east as the huge Co-op City apartment complex (in the 7th). About 45 percent of district residents live in the Bronx.

In Westchester County, home to one-fourth of the 17th's residents, the district takes in all of heavily black Mount Vernon, which hosts commercial industries and some notable health care facilities, including Mount

Vernon Hospital. Other black and Hispanic communities are found in southwestern Yonkers, and there are predominately white areas, many with residents of Italian and Irish descent, in the southeastern part of the city. In 2007, Yonkers' portion of the Hudson River waterfront became a terminus for water taxis moving commuters to and from Manhattan.

The 17th narrows in northern Yonkers, wandering north along Route 9 and the Hudson River to cross the Tappan Zee Bridge into Rockland County, where the rest of the 17th's population lives. The mostly suburban area is loaded with commuters and also has a number of pharmaceutical manufacturing facilities and an Avon Products research and development site.

Barack Obama took 72 percent of the 17th's 2008 presidential vote — tallying 87 percent of the vote in the district's portion of the Bronx.

MAJOR INDUSTRY
Health care, higher education, city government

CITIES
New York (pt.), 292,423; Yonkers (pt.), 87,617; Mount Vernon, 68,381

NOTABLE
Duke Ellington, Elizabeth Cady Stanton, F.W. Woolworth, Nellie Bly and "Bat" Masterson are among those buried in Woodlawn Cemetery.

Rep. Nita M. Lowey (D)

Elected 1988; 11th term

CAPITOL OFFICE
225-6506
www.house.gov/lowey
2329 Rayburn Bldg. 20515-3218; fax 225-0546

COMMITTEES
Appropriations
(State-Foreign Operations - chairwoman)

RESIDENCE
Harrison

BORN
July 5, 1937; Bronx, N.Y.

RELIGION
Jewish

FAMILY
Husband, Stephen Lowey; three children

EDUCATION
Mount Holyoke College, B.A. 1959 (political science)

CAREER
State government aide; homemaker

POLITICAL HIGHLIGHTS
N.Y. assistant secretary of state, 1985-87

ELECTION RESULTS

2008 GENERAL

Nita M. Lowey (D, WFM)	174,791	68.5%
Jim Russell (R, C)	80,498	31.5%

2008 PRIMARY

Nita M. Lowey (D, WFM)	unopposed

2006 GENERAL

Nita M. Lowey (D, WFM)	124,256	70.7%
Richard A. Hoffman (R, C)	51,450	29.3%

PREVIOUS WINNING PERCENTAGES
2004 (70%); 2002 (92%); 2000 (67%); 1998 (83%); 1996 (64%); 1994 (57%); 1992 (56%); 1990 (63%); 1988 (50%)

Lowey is chatty and approachable and can seem more like a grandmother — which she is — than a veteran politician. But she is a savvy politician who presses her priority issues affecting women and health care and brings home millions of federal dollars for her relatively wealthy district. And she holds the gavel of the Appropriations subcommittee that doles out foreign aid, which gives her powerful influence over the nation's international reputation.

Lowey is also one of her party's better fundraisers. She helped raise $6 million for House Democrats' efforts to recruit and elect women candidates in 2000. Two years later, picked by party leaders to head the Democratic Congressional Campaign Committee, she set fundraising records. She then served as a "Hillraiser" — a fundraiser who brings in more than $100,000 — for Hillary Rodham Clinton's 2008 presidential campaign and doled out more than $360,000 in contributions to colleagues and Democratic causes from her campaign fund during the 2007-08 election cycle.

Lowey (LO-ee) had hoped to advance to the Senate in 2000, but her hopes were dashed when Clinton moved to New York — to Lowey's district, in fact — for her successful run for the seat of retiring Democratic Sen. Daniel Patrick Moynihan. Lowey, who bowed out gracefully, has since developed strong ties to the Clintons and teamed up in 2004 and 2006 with Sen. Clinton on a bill to make basic education for children worldwide a goal of U.S. foreign policy.

When President Obama nominated Clinton for secretary of State, speculation arose that Lowey would be appointed to Clinton's Senate seat, but Lowey again removed herself from consideration. She said she much preferred having control over the budget of Clinton's future agency. "It makes no sense for me to give up my seniority in the House," she said.

She relishes being one of the 12 "cardinals," as Appropriations subcommittee chairpersons are known, and uses her position on the State-Foreign Operations panel to deliver ample federal funding to her white-collar district. She is also the second-ranking Democrat on the panel funding the Labor, Health and Human Services, and Education departments, and she is a member of the Homeland Security Appropriations Subcommittee.

Lowey is expected to work well with Texas' Kay Granger, the top-ranking Republican member on the State-Foreign Operations panel, who shares her concerns for women's rights issues.

Lowey pushes for bigger aid packages to both Israel and the Arab world. And she has helped secure funding increases to provide basic education in developing countries, from $98 million in 2001 to $700 million in 2008. But while she is a proponent of boosting federal aid, she warned in January 2009 that helping President Obama meet his broad campaign pledges — such as doubling U.S. foreign assistance spending to $50 billion a year by 2012 and allocating $50 billion to combat global AIDS and HIV by 2013 — would be unlikely considering the economic downturn. "We are confident that he can deliver the new direction he has promised Americans. I am not as confident that he'll be doubling the foreign aid budget, but I'm confident he'll lead us in a new direction," Lowey said.

Lowey is a strong defender of abortion rights and applauded Obama for overturning, in January 2009, President George W. Bush's 2001 executive order barring the use of U.S. foreign aid funds for family planning programs abroad that perform or counsel about abortion.

Other issues affecting women and health care also are important to Lowey. She won a major victory in October 2008, when a measure she had sponsored was signed into law to concentrate federal research on the links between breast cancer and the environment. Another one of her achievements in recent years was a law passed in 2004 requiring the food industry to more clearly label products that contain the eight most common allergens: milk, eggs, fish, shellfish, tree nuts, peanuts, wheat and soybeans. And in 1998, she got the government to agree to cover contraception for federal workers.

Lowey also has brought home funds to directly benefit her district, including money for a ferry system to run from Rockland County through Yonkers to lower Manhattan; the ferry began operations in 2007. She secured $8.6 million to curb flooding in the Hudson Valley in a 2007 war spending bill.

From her seat on the Homeland Security Committee during the 110th Congress (2007-08), she pushed to establish a threat-based formula for localities getting federal homeland security grants, which in effect would help New York get a larger share of the funds. In 2008, the House passed her bill to prevent investigators from tipping off airport screeners to covert audits of their security practices. She was unsuccessful, though, at winning passage of legislation to grant collective bargaining rights to Transportation Security Administration employees, which she thinks would stem the agency's high turnover.

Lowey got her start in politics more than 30 years ago. She was a homemaker in Queens when she volunteered in a neighbor's 1974 campaign for lieutenant governor. The neighbor was Mario Cuomo. Though Cuomo lost the primary race, new Democratic Gov. Hugh L. Carey appointed him secretary of state, and Cuomo hired Lowey to work in the anti-poverty division.

By the mid-1980s, Cuomo was governor and Lowey was the top aide to new Secretary of State Gail Shaffer. Lowey made an impressive debut in electoral politics in 1988 to unseat two-term GOP Rep. Joseph J. DioGuardi in the then-20th District. She survived a primary against Hamilton Fish III, publisher of The Nation magazine and son of a GOP House member, and against businessman Dennis Mehiel. And she raised $1.3 million, a huge sum for a challenger at the time.

Yet in the general election, DioGuardi outspent her. His campaign was damaged by a newspaper account of a scheme involving a New Rochelle auto dealer funneling $57,000 in corporate contributions to DioGuardi's campaign. Lowey won narrowly. DioGuardi returned for a rematch in 1992, but Lowey won decisively. Since then, she has outdistanced all competition.

Lowey is one of the wealthiest members of Congress, with a net worth in 2007 of at least $16.9 million, according to the Center for Responsive Politics.

KEY VOTES

2008

Yes	Delay consideration of Colombia free-trade agreement
Yes	Override Bush veto of federal farm and nutrition programs reauthorization bill
Yes	Overhaul surveillance laws and permit dismissal of suits against companies that conducted warrantless wiretapping
Yes	Grant mortgage relief to homeowners and funding for Fannie Mae and Freddie Mac
Yes	Approve initial $700 billion program to stabilize financial markets
Yes	Approve final $700 billion program to stabilize financial markets
Yes	Provide $14 billion in loans to automakers

2007

Yes	Increase minimum wage by $2.10 an hour
Yes	Approve $124.2 billion in emergency war spending and set goal for redeployment of troops from Iraq
No	Reject federal contraceptive assistance to international family planning groups
Yes	Override Bush veto of $23.2 billion water projects authorization bill
Yes	Implement Peru free-trade agreement
Yes	Approve energy policy overhaul with new fuel economy standards
No	Clear $473.5 billion omnibus spending bill, including $70 billion for military operations

CQ VOTE STUDIES

	PARTY UNITY		PRESIDENTIAL SUPPORT	
	SUPPORT	OPPOSE	SUPPORT	OPPOSE
2008	99%	1%	14%	86%
2007	99%	1%	5%	95%
2006	98%	2%	23%	77%
2005	98%	2%	13%	87%
2004	95%	5%	35%	65%

INTEREST GROUPS

	AFL-CIO	ADA	CCUS	ACU
2008	100%	100%	67%	0%
2007	96%	95%	56%	0%
2006	100%	95%	40%	4%
2005	93%	95%	41%	0%
2004	100%	100%	47%	4%

NEW YORK 18

Most of Westchester County — New Rochelle, most of Yonkers

The 18th takes in large portions of southern and central Westchester County before hopping the Hudson River to pick up most of New City and Congers and all of Haverstraw in Rockland County. Mostly white-collar, the district is home to wealthy, educated suburbanites employed in health care, higher education and technology sectors, in Westchester County or via an easy commute into Manhattan or Connecticut.

The district includes a mix of residential and commercial territory in northern and central Yonkers, which has seen recent downtown revitalization. Much of the 18th's portion of Yonkers is middle class but it also includes a few wealthier neighborhoods such as Crestwood. The 18th also includes Ossining, site of Sing Sing prison — its location north of the city on the Hudson River led New Yorkers to refer to prison-bound criminals as being "sent up the river."

The 18th also has working-class areas, such as parts of Sleepy Hollow,

Port Chester and urban portions of White Plains and New Rochelle. White Plains is home to Westchester County's largest retail hub and boasts the City Center complex and Renaissance Square hotel, shopping, and residential buildings. Both White Plains and New Rochelle are home to several colleges. The 18th hosts headquarters for PepsiCo in Purchase and defense contractor ITT in White Plains. The district also includes areas facing widespread layoffs and economic slowdowns.

Some areas in Westchester County have been friendly to Republican candidates, but the working-class communities, coupled with some affluent Democratic areas, are more than enough to offset the GOP base. For many years, the district has had a sizable Jewish population, but the Hispanic population is growing, mainly in Yonkers. Barack Obama carried the 18th overall with 62 percent of its vote in 2008.

MAJOR INDUSTRY
Health care, higher education, retail

CITIES
Yonkers (pt.), 108,469; New Rochelle, 72,182; White Plains, 53,077

NOTABLE
North Tarrytown was renamed Sleepy Hollow in honor of the Washington Irving story set there.

Rep. John Hall (D)

Elected 2006; 2nd term

The former lead singer of the pop band Orleans in the 1970s, Hall had a claim on fame before launching a second career in politics, writing and recording the hit "Still the One." He was incensed when President George W. Bush and Arizona Republican John McCain tried to use the song in their 2004 and 2008 presidential campaigns, because he said those men advanced agendas he adamantly opposes: conservative economic policies, expanded nuclear power and a continuation of the Iraq War.

Hall has supported President Obama's economic agenda, has been involved in the environmental movement since the 1970s and laments the human cost of a war he said never should have been fought. He works to make his views known and to serve his constituents, knowing he can't rely on his musical celebrity to help him fend off challenges from the Republican Party, which is eager to regain a seat it had held for decades prior to 2006.

Hall focuses on solidifying his grasp on his district via constituent service and addressing local concerns from his seats on the Veterans' Affairs and Transportation and Infrastructure committees. As chairman of the disability subcommittee, Hall has become an advocate for reforming the system of disability assistance. He obtained House support in 2008 for a bill, which later stalled, aimed at modernizing the disability benefits claims processing system of the Veterans Affairs Department.

He also pushed a bill to shorten the time it takes for wounded soldiers to begin receiving veterans' benefits after leaving duty. And he introduced legislation in February 2009 aimed at making it easier for veterans with post-traumatic stress disorder to receive disability benefits and treatment.

Hall does have some ties to the military: The U.S. Military Academy at West Point is located in his district and his father-in-law and brother-in-law are West Point graduates. He backed federal employees in early 2009 at the Military Academy who protested a federal job efficiency study initiated by the Bush administration in 2006 and completed in March. The study forced West Point's directorate of public works to bid against private contractors, according to the Hudson Valley's Times Herald-Record. Hall and fellow New York Democrat Maurice D. Hinchey said they would push legislation to block the study's recommendations from being implemented if Defense Secretary Robert M. Gates doesn't disregard them.

His seat on Transportation gives him an avenue to send money home. The panel is expected during the 111th Congress (2009-10) to take up a reauthorization of the 2005 surface transportation bill, and he said he'll seek to improve highways and rail service to Stewart International Airport and add air traffic controllers. In fiscal 2008 spending bills, he obtained nearly $21 million for local projects.

And he supported a $410 billion catchall spending bill for fiscal 2009, in which he obtained $10 million for local projects, including $1.3 million for the Newburgh-Beacon Ferry.

Hall also supported Obama's $787 economic stimulus bill, saying it would create thousands of jobs for New Yorkers, and in fall 2008 he supported both versions — the second of which became law — of a $700 billion measure to aid the ailing financial services sector.

Hall also holds a seat on the Select Committee on Energy Independence and Global Warming, which provides him an avenue to help shape legislation addressing global warming and the nation's energy policy. He supported a 2007 energy policy overhaul that included new fuel economy standards.

CAPITOL OFFICE
225-5441
johnhall.house.gov
1217 Longworth Bldg. 20515-3219; fax 225-3289

COMMITTEES
Transportation & Infrastructure
Veterans' Affairs
    (Disability Assistance & Memorial Affairs - chairman)
Select Energy Independence & Global Warming

RESIDENCE
Dover Plains

BORN
July 23, 1948; Baltimore, Md.

RELIGION
Christian

FAMILY
Wife, Pamela Bingham Hall; one child

EDUCATION
U. of Notre Dame, attended 1964-65 (physics);
Loyola College (Md.), attended 1965-66 (English)

CAREER
Songwriter and musician; ski instructor

POLITICAL HIGHLIGHTS
Ulster County Legislature, 1990-91; Saugerties Central School District Board of Education, 1996-98 (president, 1998)

ELECTION RESULTS

2008 GENERAL

John Hall (D, INDC, WFM)	164,859	58.7%
Kieran Michael Lalor (R, C)	116,120	41.3%

2008 PRIMARY

John Hall (D, INDC, WFM)	unopposed

2006 GENERAL

John Hall (D)	100,119	51.2%
Sue W. Kelly (R, INDC, C)	95,359	48.8%

Hall has lived the better part of his adult life in the 19th District. He said he was first drawn to the Hudson Valley by the music and arts festival known as Woodstock in Bethel in 1969, and later settled in nearby Saugerties.

He was born in Baltimore in 1948 but grew up in Elmira, N.Y., a small town along the Pennsylvania border. He started playing piano at 4 and took lessons for 11 years and French horn for six. But he eventually rebelled from his classical music training by teaching himself the guitar.

Hall attended Notre Dame University, where he studied physics, then transferred to Loyola College before dropping out to start his music career. He began as a songwriter, and got his break writing songs for Broadway shows and then for blues rocker Janis Joplin. Joplin recorded "Half Moon," a song Hall wrote for her "Pearl" album, two days before she died of a drug overdose. "It established me in other people's eyes in the business as a song-writer," Hall said. To this day, he makes a substantial portion of his income from music royalties. Despite refusing to let Bush and McCain use "Still the One," he has said he didn't balk when former New York Democratic senator and current Secretary of State Hillary Rodham Clinton — whose views are more to his liking — played it before ending her own presidential bid.

Hall formed the band Orleans in 1972 with musicians Wells Kelly and brothers Larry and Lance Hoppen. The band went on to record 18 albums. In 1979, he joined the coalition Musicians United for Safe Energy, which put on a series of "No Nukes" concerts in 1979 and 1980 that raised more than $1 million. "The advantage to being a performer is that I've always been the product — I'm used to getting up in front of people and selling myself and my ideas," Hall told The Associated Press.

In 1989, he was spurred to run for the Ulster County Legislature to stop the last undeveloped farm in his town from being turned into a solid-waste dump and incinerator. He accomplished that during his one two-year term. His next foray into public service was in the late 1990s, when he was elected to the Saugerties school board. He eventually became board president.

Hinchey, who had known Hall since a 1970s citizens' campaign to stop construction of nuclear power plants in the valley, convinced Hall to run for the U.S. House in 2005. He easily won the primary, surprising national Democrats who had backed his rival, Judith Aydelott. In the general election against six-term incumbent GOP Rep. Sue W. Kelly, he ran as an anti-war, pro-environment candidate, knocking Kelly for her consistent backing of the Bush agenda. In an election year that saw a GOP backlash across the board, Hall upended Kelly, 51 percent to 49 percent. In 2008, he easily defeated Peekskill Republican Kieran Michael Lalor.

KEY VOTES

2008

Yes   Delay consideration of Colombia free-trade agreement

Yes   Override Bush veto of federal farm and nutrition programs reauthorization bill

No   Overhaul surveillance laws and permit dismissal of suits against companies that conducted warrantless wiretapping

Yes   Grant mortgage relief to homeowners and funding for Fannie Mae and Freddie Mac

Yes   Approve initial $700 billion program to stabilize financial markets

Yes   Approve final $700 billion program to stabilize financial markets

Yes   Provide $14 billion in loans to automakers

2007

Yes   Increase minimum wage by $2.10 an hour

Yes   Approve $124.2 billion in emergency war spending and set goal for redeployment of troops from Iraq

No   Reject federal contraceptive assistance to international family planning groups

Yes   Override Bush veto of $23.2 billion water projects authorization bill

No   Implement Peru free-trade agreement

Yes   Approve energy policy overhaul with new fuel economy standards

No   Clear $473.5 billion omnibus spending bill, including $70 billion for military operations

CQ VOTE STUDIES

	PARTY UNITY		PRESIDENTIAL SUPPORT	
	SUPPORT	OPPOSE	SUPPORT	OPPOSE
2008	99%	1%	14%	86%
2007	96%	4%	3%	97%

INTEREST GROUPS

	AFL-CIO	ADA	CCUS	ACU
2008	100%	95%	56%	0%
2007	96%	100%	50%	0%

NEW YORK 19

Hudson Valley — Peekskill, West Point

Wedged between Connecticut and New Jersey, the 19th links New York City suburbs to upstate New York. The Hudson River flows through the center of the district, along which lie some of the state's richest communities in the south and technology and research firms in the north. East and west of the river are rural towns and vegetable farms.

The southeastern, Westchester County portion of the district is known for elegant exurban homes that lure celebrities and wealthy commuters from Manhattan. Although the median family income has approached $200,000 in some places, residents have been faced with corporate lay-offs and rising foreclosure rates. Growing Peekskill, with a working- and middle-class base, has a strong cultural and arts center, and a major hospital in nearby Cortlandt Manor is undergoing expansion.

Both sides of the river have steep embankments in the Hudson Highlands north of Peekskill. The U.S. Military Academy is here, and just north of West Point in Dutchess County is Beacon, which faces Newburgh (in the 22nd) and New Windsor across the Hudson River.

Technology and research firms continue to move into the mid-Hudson region south of Poughkeepsie, and there is a small but growing "green" job market. Rail commuter lots fill early each day as 19th District residents commute to white-collar and public-sector jobs in New York City or southern Westchester County. Health care is an important industry in Orange County, which ranges from farms and small towns in the west to suburbia in the east.

The wealth in the 19th's south and the rural character of its western reaches, which extend to the foothills of the Catskill Mountains, help make the district politically competitive. Barack Obama won the district by only 3 percentage points in the 2008 presidential race.

MAJOR INDUSTRY
Computers, telecommunications, agriculture

MILITARY BASES
U.S. Military Academy, 1,165 military, 2,735 civilian (2009)

CITIES
Peekskill, 22,441; Jefferson Valley-Yorktown (unincorporated), 14,891

NOTABLE
The home and farm of John Jay, first chief justice of the United States, is in Katonah.

Rep. Scott Murphy (D)

Elected March 2009; 1st term

CAPITOL OFFICE
225-56147
scottmurphy.house.gov
120 Cannon Bldg. 20515-2507; fax 225-1168

COMMITTEES
Agriculture
Armed Services

RESIDENCE
Glens Falls

BORN
Jan. 26, 1970; Columbia, Mo.

RELIGION
Roman Catholic

FAMILY
Wife, Jen Murphy; three children

EDUCATION
Harvard U., A.B. 1992 (social studies)

CAREER
Investment firm executive; lobbyist; gubernatorial aide; Internet company owner

POLITICAL HIGHLIGHTS
No previous office

ELECTION RESULTS

2009 SPECIAL
Scott Murphy (D, INDC, WFM)	80,833	50.2%
Jim Tedisco (R, C)	80,107	49.8%

Murphy campaigned on a platform of job creation and an allegiance to President Obama's economic agenda. Despite being a political neophyte, he touts his experience creating jobs as the founder of several Internet companies and as a venture capitalist.

Like his predecessor, Kirsten Gillibrand, who moved to the Senate to replace Secretary of State Hillary Rodham Clinton, Murphy strikes a moderate tone on social issues as he seeks to represent a largely suburban and rural population that has shown Republican and independent leanings, although Obama narrowly won the district in 2008. Murphy has worked to portray himself as focused on solutions rather than partisanship.

A member of the Agriculture Committee, he said he embraces renewable energy and new technology as ways to move the district away from its traditional reliance on manufacturing and toward a 21st-century high-tech economy. He also sits on the Armed Services Committee.

Murphy's first dose of professional politics came in his home state of Missouri, where he served as an aide to two Democratic governors, Mel Carnahan and Roger Wilson, from 1993 to 2001. He was Wilson's deputy chief of staff beginning in 2000.

He moved from Missouri to the upper Hudson Valley in Glens Falls this decade so his family could be closer to his wife's relatives, who are dairy farmers.

Republicans attempted to paint Murphy as more liberal than he let on during the special-election campaign, highlighting his opposition to the death penalty, even for the terrorists who attacked the United States on Sept. 11. They also noted his criticism of military recruiting on campus, pointing to college editorials he wrote as a Harvard undergraduate in the early 1990s.

The March 2009 special election between Murphy and Republican state lawmaker Jim Tedisco dragged on almost after polls closed due to its closeness and the lengthy process of counting and litigation of absentee ballots. Tedisco eventually conceded. Together the candidates spent almost $3.8 million on the race.

NEW YORK 20

North Hudson Valley — Saratoga Springs, Glens Falls

Running along the state's eastern border, the politically competitive 20th starts just outside Poughkeepsie and roughly follows Interstate 87 north into the scenic Adirondack Mountains and the resort areas of Lake George and Essex County. Lake Placid, in Essex County, is at the district's northern tip.

The 20th covers much of the residential Hudson River Valley, where apple farms are the core of its agriculture industry. Although Albany, Schenectady and Troy are all in the 21st, the 20th claims most of their suburbs, helping fuel a population boom in southern Saratoga County. Saratoga Springs attracts tourists during the summer. Malta's Saratoga Technology + Energy Park and Saratoga Springs' Luther Forest Technology Campus add technology manufacturing and alternative energy jobs.

The 20th's western end is made up of mainly rural and rugged land and dairy farms from the Hudson River through Greene County, picking up parts of Delaware and Otsego counties. Much of this area hosts fishing, camping and other recreational sites.

Saratoga County sets the tone politically for the district. The presence of unionized state workers outside Albany makes labor an important constituency, but farmers and small-town voters tend to favor the GOP. The 20th, which has the state's lowest minority percentage, gave Barack Obama 51 percent of its 2008 presidential vote, but Republican John McCain did well in Greene County and eked out wins in the district's parts of Delaware, Ostego and Rensselaer counties.

MAJOR INDUSTRY
Agriculture, tourism, manufacturing

CITIES
Saratoga Springs, 26,186; Glens Falls, 14,354

NOTABLE
The National Bottle Museum in Ballston Spa celebrates the history of glass bottle-making.

Rep. Paul Tonko (D)

Elected 2008; 1st term

Tonko is a loyal Democrat with an energy-related background he accrued as a public official at the local and state levels. He chaired the Energy Committee in the New York State Assembly for 15 years and later led a state agency focused on energy efficiency and affordability.

On the Science and Technology Committee, he said he hopes to push development of a "green-collar workforce" that can work with local universities to better promote conservation and environmental management. "The longer we delay, the more difficult and expensive the outcome," he said of investing in energy innovation.

He also advocates a comprehensive energy plan that would include increased fuel efficiency standards for vehicles, funding for renewable-energy research and a "cap and trade" system to limit carbon emissions. As a state legislator, Tonko sponsored one of the first laws in the country mandating a statewide renewable-energy requirement.

Tonko also sits on the Education and Labor Committee, where he hopes to expand the nanotechnology industry in New York's capital region. He said his expertise has allowed him to "plant seeds" in technology issues such as superconductive cable and renewable manufacturing.

He added an amendment in March 2009 to committee-passed legislation — which subsequently passed the House — expanding volunteer service programs to establish a Social Innovation Fund providing seed money for individuals and nonprofit groups carrying out private sector initiatives for tackling social problems.

Tonko supports a universal, single-payer health care system and backs the rights of same-sex couples to marry. He also is "firmly pro-choice." While in the state Assembly, he spearheaded an effort that required health insurers to cover mental health treatment.

In his race to replace retiring 10-term Democratic Rep. Michael R. McNulty, Tonko defeated four other Democrats in the September 2008 primary. He breezed past GOP Scotia businessman James Buhrmaster in the general election with 62 percent of the vote.

CAPITOL OFFICE
225-5076
tonko.house.gov
128 Cannon Bldg. 20515-3221; fax 225-5077

COMMITTEES
Education & Labor
Science & Technology

RESIDENCE
Amsterdam

BORN
June 18, 1949; Amsterdam, N.Y.

RELIGION
Roman Catholic

FAMILY
Single

EDUCATION
Clarkson U., B.S. 1971 (mechanical and industrial engineering)

CAREER
State public works engineer;
state transportation agency employee

POLITICAL HIGHLIGHTS
Montgomery County Board of Supervisors, 1976-83 (chairman, 1981); N.Y. Assembly, 1983-2007; New York State Energy Research Development Authority president, 2007-08

ELECTION RESULTS

2008 GENERAL

Paul Tonko (D, WFM)	171,286	62.1%
James Buhrmaster (R, C)	96,599	35.0%
Phillip G. Steck (INDC)	7,965	2.9%

2008 PRIMARY

Paul Tonko (D)	15,932	39.5%
Tracey Brooks (D)	12,166	30.2%
Phillip G. Steck (D)	7,498	18.6%
Darius Shahinfar (D)	4,002	9.9%
Joseph P. Sullivan (D)	738	1.8%

NEW YORK 21

Capital District – Albany, Schenectady, Troy

As the terminus of the Erie Canal linking the Great Lakes to the Hudson River, New York's Capital District was one of the state's earliest industrial centers. Blue-collar workers and state employees give the Albany-Schenectady-Troy area a substantial union population and a solidly Democratic vote.

Government jobs are at risk in Albany, home to the state capital, as state budget shortfalls lead to massive layoffs. Albany's College of Nanoscale Science and Engineering, which works exclusively on nanotech research and development, and other local colleges make Albany a regional technology industry hub. The Egg performing arts complex is a centerpiece of Albany's skyline.

Despite large-scale, decades-long industrial losses, manufacturing remains important in the district. But the region has diversified, hosting research and development, alternative energy, and technology firms.

Local officials in Schenectady and Troy hope to attract white-collar employers and use commercial projects to revitalize the economy. The rest of the 21st includes rolling farm fields in the west and a gateway to the Adirondack Mountains in its north.

The 21st's Democrats are not self-described liberals, but Barack Obama won the district with 58 percent of its 2008 presidential vote.

MAJOR INDUSTRY
Government, technology, manufacturing

MILITARY BASES
Watervliet Arsenal (Army), 163 military, 879 civilian (2009)

CITIES
Albany, 95,658; Schenectady, 61,821; Troy, 49,170

NOTABLE
Samuel Wilson is believed to be the inspiration for "Uncle Sam" and is buried in Troy.

Rep. Maurice D. Hinchey (D)

Elected 1992; 9th term

CAPITOL OFFICE
225-6335
www.house.gov/hinchey
2431 Rayburn Bldg. 20515-3222; fax 226-0774

COMMITTEES
Appropriations
Natural Resources
Joint Economic

RESIDENCE
Hurley

BORN
Oct. 27, 1938; Manhattan, N.Y.

RELIGION
Roman Catholic

FAMILY
Wife, Allison Lee; three children

EDUCATION
State U. of New York, New Paltz, B.S. 1968
(political science & English), M.A. 1970 (English)

MILITARY SERVICE
Navy, 1956-59

CAREER
State education department aide; state highway
toll collector; cement and paper mill equipment
operator

POLITICAL HIGHLIGHTS
Democratic nominee for N.Y. Assembly, 1972;
N.Y. Assembly, 1975-93

ELECTION RESULTS

2008 GENERAL

Hinchey (D, INDC, WFM)	168,558	66.4%
George K. Phillips (R, C)	85,126	33.6%

2008 PRIMARY

Maurice D. Hinchey (D, INDC, WFM)	unopposed

2006 GENERAL

Maurice D. Hinchey (D, INDC, WFM)	unopposed

PREVIOUS WINNING PERCENTAGES
2004 (67%); 2002 (64%); 2000 (62%); 1998 (62%);
1996 (55%); 1994 (49%); 1992 (50%)

Hinchey earned a reputation in his younger days for standing up to bullies in New York City and throwing a few punches along the way. Now typically attired in pinstripe suits and silk ties, he fights on a different level but with as much persistence as he seeks to protect jobs in his district, promote alternative energy and protection of wilderness areas, and oversee management of the Food and Drug Administration.

Hinchey was one of the harshest critics of President George W. Bush — whom he called "the bully in the White House" — mostly notably for his Iraq War policy and promotion of offshore oil drilling. Hinchey hailed President Obama in February 2009 as "the leader who can help guide us out of trouble." But from his seat on the Appropriations Committee, he indicated early on he wouldn't easily let Obama off the hook; he harshly criticized the administration when it proposed defense cuts that could cost jobs in his district, home to Lockheed Martin Corp. and Stewart Air National Guard Base.

Hinchey supported Obama's early initiatives to jump-start the economy, including a $787 billion stimulus law that Hinchey said "wisely invests in all of America rather than just the elite." He also said he backed Obama's pledge to cut government waste and ensure taxpayers' dollars are spent wisely.

But Hinchey, a member of the Defense Appropriations Subcommittee, drew the line at certain Defense spending cuts, including a proposal to eliminate a program, contracted mainly to Lockheed Martin, to replace a fleet of Marine One presidential helicopters. Hinchey said the program to provide the president safer and more-secure aircraft, initiated after the Sept. 11 terrorist attacks, "is too important to be derailed by politics." But he also expressed to local press his desire to save hundreds of jobs related to the program.

Environmental policies have long been his passion, and he serves on both the Interior-Environment and Agriculture Appropriations subcommittees. A fight in the 1970s over the development of a large power plant on the Hudson River was the primary reason for his entry into electoral politics. Thirty-some years later, he sponsored an amendment to the fiscal 2008 Energy-Water spending bill that effectively would have barred the government from designating more National Interest Electric Transmission Corridors, which allow the construction of power lines in rural areas to serve urban centers. Hinchey also has steered millions of dollars to his district to help create a "Green Valley" — an alternative-energy hub similar to the technology area in California's Silicon Valley.

From his seat on the Natural Resources Committee, he has long pushed a bill designating millions of acres as wilderness. He took the issue over from former Utah Democrat Wayne Owens, who left the House in 1993. Former Utah Republican Chris Cannon opposed it so strongly he went to Hinchey's district in 1997 and held a news conference to push Hinchey to delay the proposal. That only provoked Hinchey to go ahead and introduce it, and he's done so every Congress with Democratic Sen. Richard J. Durbin of Illinois.

Hinchey pushed legislation in 2004 and 2005 to require sellers of ammonium nitrate, a fertilizer chemical used in the 1995 Oklahoma City bombing, to be licensed and purchasers to obtain permits. The bills failed to pass, but after Democrats took over in 2007, Homeland Security Chairman Bennie Thompson of Mississippi pushed into law a provision requiring anyone who owns or purchases the chemical to register with the Homeland Security Department.

Hinchey repeatedly fought the Bush administration on the issue of expanded oil drilling. He also assailed the management of the FDA, and has attempted to reform the agency to end alleged inappropriate relationships with the drug industry. He won enactment of a law in 2005 requiring members of FDA advisory groups to disclose potential conflicts of interest.

A typically reliable vote for party leaders, Hinchey can deviate on gun issues. In 1996, he was the only New York Democrat to vote to repeal a ban on certain semiautomatic assault-style weapons. Still, he supported the 1993 Brady bill, which calls for a five-day waiting period for handgun purchases. In 2004, he voted against repealing the District of Columbia's gun control law.

He drew unwelcome attention during his first term when he was charged with carrying a loaded handgun in his baggage at Ronald Reagan Washington National Airport. He pleaded no contest and was given a suspended sentence. He drew attention again in 2008 when he faced a second-degree harassment charge for allegedly swatting a National Rifle Association representative on the head at a street fair. He denied the charge and a judge dismissed it.

Hinchey comes from a working-class background. Born in Manhattan, he spent most of his childhood in Greenwich Village. His family moved upstate, to Saugerties; when he was a teenager, he split his time between his new home and his old haunts in New York City.

His father worked at a factory, while his mother raised their five children. Hinchey, the oldest, still talks in the tough cadence of a city boy who used to rough it up in street gangs. "My instinct as a kid was to try to not have other people be oppressed and not have other kids pushed around from bullies," he said. He joined the Navy after high school, serving aboard a destroyer in the Pacific. After his discharge, he returned home and worked in various jobs for five years, including at the local cement plant where his father had worked. He later enrolled at the State University of New York and paid his way by collecting tolls on the New York State Thruway from 10:30 p.m. to 6:30 a.m. He asked for the "graveyard" shift so he could do his studying during quiet periods.

Hinchey's parents had been active in local party politics, and after college he got involved in behind-the-scenes political activities while starting a career in education. He lost his first bid for the state Assembly in 1972, but won two years later to begin an 18-year tenure in Albany.

In 1992, when nine-term Democratic Rep. Matthew F. McHugh retired, Hinchey went after the seat. He started as the Democratic primary underdog, but prevailed against Binghamton Mayor Juanita M. Crabb by pushing a plan to revitalize the economy of the recession-hit region. He then edged Republican Bob Moppert, a six-year county legislator, by 8,819 votes. He survived a 1994 rematch by an even closer margin of slightly more than 1,200 votes. Since then, however, he has rolled up more-comfortable margins.

KEY VOTES

2008

Yes	Delay consideration of Colombia free-trade agreement
Yes	Override Bush veto of federal farm and nutrition programs reauthorization bill
No	Overhaul surveillance laws and permit dismissal of suits against companies that conducted warrantless wiretapping
Yes	Grant mortgage relief to homeowners and funding for Fannie Mae and Freddie Mac
No	Approve initial $700 billion program to stabilize financial markets
No	Approve final $700 billion program to stabilize financial markets
Yes	Provide $14 billion in loans to automakers

2007

Yes	Increase minimum wage by $2.10 an hour
Yes	Approve $124.2 billion in emergency war spending and set goal for redeployment of troops from Iraq
No	Reject federal contraceptive assistance to international family planning groups
Yes	Override Bush veto of $23.2 billion water projects authorization bill
No	Implement Peru free-trade agreement
Yes	Approve energy policy overhaul with new fuel economy standards
No	Clear $473.5 billion omnibus spending bill, including $70 billion for military operations

CQ VOTE STUDIES

	PARTY UNITY		PRESIDENTIAL SUPPORT	
	SUPPORT	OPPOSE	SUPPORT	OPPOSE
2008	98%	2%	15%	85%
2007	99%	1%	3%	97%
2006	98%	2%	7%	93%
2005	98%	2%	11%	89%
2004	99%	1%	20%	80%

INTEREST GROUPS

	AFL-CIO	ADA	CCUS	ACU
2008	100%	95%	50%	12%
2007	96%	100%	45%	0%
2006	100%	100%	27%	4%
2005	93%	100%	30%	4%
2004	100%	95%	25%	0%

NEW YORK 22

South central — Binghamton, Poughkeepsie, Ithaca

The scenic 22nd reaches from the hills above Cayuga Lake to the east bank of the Hudson River. Most residents are found at those extremes: Ithaca and Binghamton in the west and the Hudson Valley region, including Poughkeepsie, Newburgh and Kingston, in the east.

Ithaca, at the district's northwestern tip, is home to Cornell University, Ithaca College and a corps of liberal activists, and the city remains one of the few expanding economies in the 22nd.

The district then extends south from Ithaca to the Pennsylvania border, before turning east and stretching along the border from Tioga County to Sullivan County, taking in Broome County's Tri-Cities — Binghamton, Johnson City and Endicott. The 22nd then widens in Sullivan to head for Hudson River population centers in Orange, Ulster and Duchess counties.

Manufacturing jobs in the 22nd have declined, and many local officials are working to recruit more technology companies to the area as some employers are cutting jobs. Defense firms Lockheed Martin Corp. and

BAE Systems are still key local employers, but the loss of federal contracts for major projects will impact their revenues and workforce. IBM continues to reduce operations in the area. Officials hope to use the state university in Binghamton as an anchor for economic development.

In general, the 22nd is rural, with a large portion of the Catskill Mountains in the center and many apple and dairy farms throughout. The Catskills' Borscht Belt, a prominent Jewish resort area, declined as tourists began vacationing in more-exotic locales, but officials are hoping to reinvigorate the hospitality industry here.

The district's mixture of cities and farmland creates a politically diverse environment, although the region's blue-collar history and the liberal areas surrounding the 22nd's universities give Democrats an edge. Barack Obama took 59 percent of the district's 2008 presidential vote.

MAJOR INDUSTRY
Higher education, agriculture, technology

CITIES
Binghamton, 47,380; Poughkeepsie, 29,871; Ithaca, 29,287

NOTABLE
Bethel was the site of the marathon Woodstock rock concert in 1969.

Rep. John M. McHugh (R)

Elected 1992; 9th term

CAPITOL OFFICE
225-4611
mchugh.house.gov
2366 Rayburn Bldg. 20515-3223; fax 226-0621

COMMITTEES
Armed Services - ranking member
Oversight & Government Reform

RESIDENCE
Pierrepont Manor

BORN
Sept. 29, 1948; Watertown, N.Y.

RELIGION
Roman Catholic

FAMILY
Divorced

EDUCATION
Utica College of Syracuse U., B.A. 1970
(political science); State U. of New York,
Albany, M.P.A. 1977

CAREER
State legislative aide; city official;
insurance broker

POLITICAL HIGHLIGHTS
N.Y. Senate, 1985-93

ELECTION RESULTS

2008 GENERAL

John M. McHugh (R, INDC, C)	143,029	65.3%
Michael P. Oot (D, WFM)	75,871	34.7%

2008 PRIMARY

John M. McHugh (R, C, INDC)	unopposed

2006 GENERAL

John M. McHugh (R, INDC, C)	106,781	63.1%
Robert J. Johnson (D, WFM)	62,318	36.9%

PREVIOUS WINNING PERCENTAGES
2004 (71%); 2002 (100%); 2000 (74%); 1998 (79%);
1996 (71%); 1994 (79%); 1992 (61%)

As one of the few remaining Republicans from the increasingly Democratic Northeast, McHugh expresses views that often are out of sync with those of his party. But his political skills, put to use in Capitol committee rooms and hallways rather than in front of television cameras, have earned him the confidence of GOP colleagues, who admire his sharp focus and collegiality.

Among those noticing his talents was President Obama, who in June 2009 announced his intention to nominate McHugh as secretary of the Army under Defense Secretary Robert M. Gates, another Republican. Obama singled out McHugh's "pragmatism that has won him respect on both sides of the aisle."

McHugh had become ranking Republican on the Armed Services Committee in 2009, expressing a desire to closely scrutinize the Obama administration's moves in Iraq and Afghanistan and its proposal to scale back purchases of large weapons projects. But in readily accepting Obama's offer for the Army post, McHugh told reporters, "The Army's always had a special place in my heart." He had been bracing for a congressional redistricting that could affect his seat after the 2010 census and he was the subject of speculation in New York media outlets in 2008 that he was interested in running for the state Senate.

He had supported several of Obama's early initiatives; he was one of only seven House GOP lawmakers to vote for legislation allowing bankruptcy judges to modify mortgage terms for troubled homeowners, an issue often referred to as "cramdown." And he backed an extension of the State Children's Health Insurance Program that President George W. Bush had vetoed twice. During the 110th Congress (2007-08), McHugh broke ranks with his party on 26 percent of the votes in which a majority of Democrats and Republicans diverged — a level exceeded by just 10 other House Republicans.

Unlike Republicans who openly chafe at their minority status, McHugh has accepted the adjustment to life in a Democrat-controlled House. "I went out of my way when I was in the majority to treat people fairly — at the end of the day, people are people," he told Syracuse's Post-Standard in October 2008. "And now, people are inclined to treat me the same way."

McHugh spent six years as chairman of the Armed Services personnel subcommittee before the Democrats took control in 2007. Though not a veteran himself — he said a childhood bout with rheumatic fever made him ineligible when he tried to enlist in the Air Force — he is closely attuned to the needs of Fort Drum in his district. McHugh has directed funding to maintain Fort Drum's standing as one of the Army's most modern bases on the East Coast.

McHugh is wary of Pentagon efforts to drastically slash spending on weapons programs given the current economic crisis. "When you begin cutbacks in the name of so-called budget efficiencies, what you're doing is laying people off," he said in January 2009. He also was critical of Gates' proposed reductions in missile defense spending and expressed skepticism about predictions that a weakened global economy would lead U.S. adversaries to cut their defense budgets. "In fact, it can be argued the opposite is more plausible," he said in March 2009. "Faced with fiscal constraints, will Iran double down on its ballistic-missile program?"

Although he supported a 2002 resolution authorizing Bush to go to war in Iraq and in late 2007 voted for a broad spending bill that included funds for the war, he pushed Bush to ensure the Iraqis were doing their part to bring peace to the country. In early 2007, McHugh introduced his own version of a supplemental spending bill that asserted that future spending requests be predicated on the achievement of a series of benchmarks for handing control of Iraq to the Iraqis. However, McHugh wouldn't go as far as Democrats, who were demanding a timeline for withdrawal.

In January 2009, McHugh joined with Financial Services Chairman Barney Frank, a Massachusetts Democrat, on a bill to exempt laid-off workers from having to pay federal taxes on up to $40,000 in severance pay. He also collaborated with New York Democratic Sen. Charles E. Schumer on legislation to boost maple syrup production — a key agricultural activity in their state — and introduced another measure to slash sulfur, nitrogen and mercury emissions from coal-fired power plants as a way to curb global warming.

McHugh also serves on the Oversight and Government Reform Committee. A former chairman of its panel overseeing postal issues, he won a glamourless, decade long battle to restructure the Postal Service in the 109th Congress (2005-06), perhaps most impressive for its success in keeping the government's mail-delivery system solvent and competitive in an era of instant communication. He brought together a diverse array of stakeholders, including unions, Postal Service competitors such as FedEx and UPS, and postal-dependent businesses. "I think I'm most proud of that," he said.

McHugh's path to politics was circumspect. After graduating from college, he abandoned plans to earn a law degree and worked for his father's insurance business. He didn't like the work and eventually landed a job as the assistant city manager in his hometown of Watertown.

When he decided he needed a graduate degree after five years, he enrolled in the public affairs school at the State University of New York at Albany, which required him to become an intern in a government office. That in turn led him to state Sen. H. Douglas Barclay, who paid him for the internship and offered him a job when he graduated. When Barclay retired nearly a decade later, he cleared the field for McHugh to succeed him.

In 1992, Republican Rep. David O'Brien Martin decided to retire after 12 years in the House, and McHugh jumped into the race. He won the primary over a more conservative opponent, Morrison J. Hosley Jr. That was tantamount to winning election in the historically Republican region; he won his first term with 61 percent of the vote and has done better than that ever since. Even when his party lost control of the neighboring 20th and 24th districts in 2006, McHugh cruised to re-election with 63 percent of the vote.

He improved his showing to 65 percent in 2008, even as Obama carried his district. He dismissed speculation circulating in New York media outlets that he was ready to leave Washington and would instead seek a state Senate seat enabling him to be closer to home.

KEY VOTES

2008
No Delay consideration of Colombia free-trade agreement
Yes Override Bush veto of federal farm and nutrition programs reauthorization bill
Yes Overhaul surveillance laws and permit dismissal of suits against companies that conducted warrantless wiretapping
Yes Grant mortgage relief to homeowners and funding for Fannie Mae and Freddie Mac
Yes Approve initial $700 billion program to stabilize financial markets
Yes Approve final $700 billion program to stabilize financial markets
Yes Provide $14 billion in loans to automakers

2007
Yes Increase minimum wage by $2.10 an hour
No Approve $124.2 billion in emergency war spending and set goal for redeployment of troops from Iraq
Yes Reject federal contraceptive assistance to international family planning groups
Yes Override Bush veto of $23.2 billion water projects authorization bill
No Implement Peru free-trade agreement
Yes Approve energy policy overhaul with new fuel economy standards
Yes Clear $473.5 billion omnibus spending bill, including $70 billion for military operations

CQ VOTE STUDIES

	PARTY UNITY		PRESIDENTIAL SUPPORT	
	SUPPORT	OPPOSE	SUPPORT	OPPOSE
2008	81%	19%	51%	49%
2007	70%	30%	45%	55%
2006	84%	16%	85%	15%
2005	89%	11%	78%	22%
2004	87%	13%	76%	24%

INTEREST GROUPS

	AFL-CIO	ADA	CCUS	ACU
2008	73%	60%	83%	40%
2007	74%	45%	78%	60%
2006	57%	15%	86%	75%
2005	47%	20%	81%	80%
2004	50%	20%	90%	64%

NEW YORK 23
North — Watertown, Plattsburgh, Oswego

The vast 23rd covers more than one-fourth of the state, bordering Lake Champlain, the St. Lawrence Seaway and Lake Ontario. The waterways provide an inexpensive source of electricity, which has lured some heavy industry to the district. But most of the district is rural, full of small towns, dairy farms, maple syrup producers and colleges. It reaches south to Oneida Lake and Madison County.

Fort Drum (near Watertown, the district's largest city) is one of the largest and most modern Army facilities on the East Coast. It thus far has been safe from post-Cold War base closures, and consists of 107,000 acres and trains almost 80,000 troops annually. Roughly 30 miles from Ontario, Watertown's economy relies on Canadian visitors. The proximity to waterways and forests made paper production a major industry in the district, but many mills have been forced to close their doors.

Unemployment remains a problem throughout the 23rd, as harsh winters and high transportation costs make attracting jobs difficult. The North Country took a hit in 2009 when General Motors closed a plant in Mas-

sena in St. Lawrence County. State correctional facilities are an economic driver in the 23rd, but with the state's budget woes, at least one of them is expected to close in 2009. Bright spots include seasonal tourism — the 23rd covers much of the Adirondack Mountains, where winter weather caters to snowmobile riders and ice fishers, and long summers attract visitors to regional festivals and seasonal-use cottages.

The northeastern corner of the state has sent Republicans to the U.S. House since the 1872 election. Despite Republicans holding a voter registration edge in the district, Barack Obama won 52 percent of the 23rd's 2008 presidential vote. In 2008, John McCain's highest percentage in any county statewide was in sparsely populated Hamilton (63 percent).

MAJOR INDUSTRY
Agriculture, manufacturing, tourism, defense

MILITARY BASES
Fort Drum, 16,950 military, 3,960 civilian (2007)

CITIES
Watertown, 26,705; Plattsburgh, 18,816; Oswego, 17,954

NOTABLE
Little Trees air fresheners were invented in Watertown, home to the headquarters and a manufacturing plant of Car-Freshner Corp.

Rep. Michael Arcuri (D)

Elected 2006; 2nd term

CAPITOL OFFICE
225-3665
arcuri.house.gov
127 Cannon Bldg. 20515-3224; fax 225-1891

COMMITTEES
Rules
Transportation & Infrastructure

RESIDENCE
Utica

BORN
June 11, 1959; Utica, N.Y.

RELIGION
Roman Catholic

FAMILY
Wife, Sabrina Arcuri; three children

EDUCATION
State U. of New York, Albany, B.A. 1981
(history); New York Law School, J.D. 1984

CAREER
Lawyer; college instructor

POLITICAL HIGHLIGHTS
Oneida County district attorney, 1994-2007

ELECTION RESULTS

2008 GENERAL

Michael Arcuri (D, WFM)	130,799	52.0%
Richard Hanna (R, INDC, C)	120,880	48.0%

2008 PRIMARY

Michael Arcuri (D, WFM)	unopposed

2006 GENERAL

Michael Arcuri (D, INDC, WFM)	109,686	53.9%
Ray Meier (R, C)	91,504	45.0%
Michael J. Sylvia III (LIBERT)	2,134	1.0%

Arcuri describes his district as fiscally conservative and socially moderate-to-liberal, and that's the image he tries to project in Congress — much like his popular predecessor, Republican Sherwood L. Boehlert. His definition of family values is "minimum wage, health care and preserving Social Security."

The first Democrat elected to represent the area since the Truman administration, Arcuri (are-CURE-ee) was a political novice when he arrived in Congress but has quickly learned the ropes from his seat on the Rules Committee. He also is a member of the Blue Dog Coalition, a group of about 50 fiscally conservative Democrats that provides a counterpoint to the dominant liberals in the House Democratic Caucus. And he is a member of the business-oriented New Democrat Coalition and vice chairman of the new Populist Caucus, which is focused on issues of concern to the middle class.

Arcuri was a county district attorney before he was elected to the House. His initial experiences in Washington were not what he expected, he acknowledged in a 2007 interview with Syracuse's Post-Standard: "As a D.A., you're really in an executive position, so you decided what you wanted to achieve, and…it's just a question of whether you're able to achieve it." Dealing with the legislative necessity of building a consensus and forging majority support, he added, was "significantly more difficult."

But he has benefited from a crash course in the legislative process from his seat on Rules. "It has given me an opportunity to learn about every bill that has come through…and, equally important, you learn the process extremely quickly," he said. "Being from a non-legislative background, it has been a great equalizer for me."

He's learned that politics counts as much as process. He and other upstate New York lawmakers have waged a furious battle against a planned 190-mile New York Regional Interconnect (NYRI) power line from his district south toward New York City. In 2007, Arcuri offered a floor amendment to energy legislation to prevent power companies from using federal eminent domain authority to seize private property for the transmission line. The amendment failed.

He told the Syracuse newspaper that colleagues he considered friends told him, "Mike, sorry, I can't help you out, you know, our power companies are dead set against this, and they employ too many people, I can't be with you on this." That was an epiphany for him, he said. "After I lost that vote, I was really annoyed…I went home a few days after, and it occurred to me that people really need to vote on issues based on their constituents. It's not personal. They just have to vote based on their constituency."

As a member of Rules, Arcuri takes his turn on the House floor explaining the rules that govern debate on bills, allowing him to build chits with Democratic leaders for undertaking an "inside baseball" assignment.

Arcuri addresses his constituents' needs from his seat on the Transportation and Infrastructure panel, where he played a role in legislation to reauthorize Amtrak. He won House approval of provisions aimed at improving upstate New York Amtrak service, which he said had suffered because needed track maintenance had been deferred. Later, he was named as a conferee to write the final bill that was enacted in 2008.

He applauded President Obama's $787 billion economic stimulus law in March 2009 for providing more than $7 million for his district's local transit systems. "Better transit is the first step to rebuilding our downtowns and creating jobs and economic opportunity," he said.

Arcuri was born into politics. His grandfather sat on Oneida County's Democratic Committee, and his parents met during a campaign event. Arcuri's father worked for economic-development organizations for years, eventually becoming the general manager of the Utica Transit Authority. His mother was a stenographer for the state of New York.

A collection of campaign buttons, started by his father, adorns a wall in his Capitol Hill office. It includes buttons from almost every presidential candidate since the 1900 election. Arcuri is missing only 1904 Democratic candidate Alton B. Parker, who suffered a landslide defeat at the hands of incumbent President Theodore Roosevelt.

Arcuri's first taste of Washington came as a high school sophomore when he accompanied his father on a business trip, during which they met the district's GOP congressman, Rep. Donald J. Mitchell, and his staffer, Boehlert, who would become Mitchell's successor.

Arcuri majored in history and became a Division III All-American center playing football for the State University of New York at Albany. Some 30 years later, he is a runner and competes in road races for fun. He also holds a black belt in tae kwon do.

After earning a law degree from New York Law School, Arcuri moved back to Utica to open a practice. In 1993, he defeated a GOP incumbent to be elected Oneida County's first Democratic district attorney in more than 40 years. During three terms, he helped implement the county's Drug Treatment Alternative-to-Prison program and created a victim's advocate position. In 2003, he was elected president of the New York State District Attorneys Association.

Democrats had predicted for years that they could win the 24th District seat once Boehlert retired, and Arcuri's successful run as district attorney made him their logical candidate. He had no 2006 primary challenger.

The Republican nominee, state Sen. Ray Meier, sought to brand Arcuri as just another tax-and-spend Democrat. And the National Republican Congressional Committee, which supports GOP House campaigns, produced an ad accusing Arcuri of seeking taxpayer reimbursement for a phone-sex call.

The tactic didn't work. Arcuri's swift response, including evidence the number was called accidentally when an aide misdialed, allowed him to make the case that the Republicans were distorting the truth, though the ad never aired. Arcuri outspent Meier and won by 9 percentage points.

Arcuri took 52 percent of the vote in 2008 to defeat Republican businessman Richard Hanna — a surprisingly close result given the strong national Democratic tide, his incumbency and success in outraising Hanna. The national GOP will be keen on toppling him in 2010.

KEY VOTES

2008

Yes   Delay consideration of Colombia free-trade agreement

Yes   Override Bush veto of federal farm and nutrition programs reauthorization bill

Yes   Overhaul surveillance laws and permit dismissal of suits against companies that conducted warrantless wiretapping

Yes   Grant mortgage relief to homeowners and funding for Fannie Mae and Freddie Mac

Yes   Approve initial $700 billion program to stabilize financial markets

Yes   Approve final $700 billion program to stabilize financial markets

Yes   Provide $14 billion in loans to automakers

2007

Yes   Increase minimum wage by $2.10 an hour

Yes   Approve $124.2 billion in emergency war spending and set goal for redeployment of troops from Iraq

No   Reject federal contraceptive assistance to international family planning groups

Yes   Override Bush veto of $23.2 billion water projects authorization bill

No   Implement Peru free-trade agreement

Yes   Approve energy policy overhaul with new fuel economy standards

No   Clear $473.5 billion omnibus spending bill, including $70 billion for military operations

CQ VOTE STUDIES

	PARTY UNITY		PRESIDENTIAL SUPPORT	
	SUPPORT	OPPOSE	SUPPORT	OPPOSE
2008	96%	4%	20%	80%
2007	96%	4%	5%	95%

INTEREST GROUPS

	AFL-CIO	ADA	CCUS	ACU
2008	100%	90%	67%	4%
2007	96%	100%	55%	0%

NEW YORK 24

Central — Utica, Rome, Auburn

The J-shaped 24th starts at the western edge of the Adirondack Mountains, sweeps through the central part of the state — south of Syracuse and north of Binghamton — and extends into the Finger Lakes region. In the heart of the Leatherstocking Region made famous by James Fenimore Cooper, the area is known for its rich history and depends on dairy farming and local colleges.

Much of the 24th's central region is full of small-size towns that face harsh winters and enjoy mild summers and whose economies are influenced by the farming seasons. These areas become crowded each fall, as visitors embark on foliage tours and trips to the region's cider mills. The district is home to the Oneida Indian Nation's Turning Stone Casino in Verona, where economic woes have employees bracing for layoffs. The 24th also boasts several halls of fame, including the National Baseball Hall of Fame in Cooperstown, the National Soccer Hall of Fame in Oneonta and the National Distance Running Hall of Fame in Utica.

In the west, the 24th is home to other historical gems, including the site of

the 1848 Women's Rights Convention and the National Women's Hall of Fame in Seneca Falls. This area is a gateway to the Finger Lakes, which, among other things, attract wine connoisseurs to dozens of wineries.

The 24th's main population center is in Oneida County. Oneida's Utica and Rome are aging industrial cities on the Mohawk River that suffered as manufacturing jobs have left the state. Local officials have attempted to diversify the economic base in order to withstand widespread layoffs.

Although the 24th's natural beauty makes earth-friendly policies important here, voters are Yankee Republicans. Despite a GOP voter registration edge in the district, Democrat Barack Obama narrowly won the 24th's 2008 presidential vote (50 percent). Democratic pockets in Utica and along college campuses provide just enough support to keep Michael Arcuri in the U.S. House seat.

MAJOR INDUSTRY
Agriculture, tourism, manufacturing, service

CITIES
Utica, 60,651; Rome, 34,950; Auburn, 28,574

NOTABLE
Francis Bellamy, author of the Pledge of Allegiance, is buried in Rome.

Rep. Dan Maffei (D)

Elected 2008; 1st term

A former congressional staffer, Maffei hails from his district's urban center, Syracuse, and fervently hopes to put the struggling city "back on the map economically." But he says he's prepared to represent rural interests, too — he notes that some of his relatives were farmers.

Maffei (muh-FAY) campaigned on using alternative energy technology to create jobs while forging public-private partnerships to add workers in health care. He also pledged to work on ending tax breaks that reward companies for moving jobs overseas. Another idea — shared with other upstate New York lawmakers — is to bring high-speed rail or similar upgrades to the region. "It's been 50 years since we had any new infrastructure" upstate, he said. "We are sort of cut off...We need a 21st-century Erie Canal."

A member of the Financial Services Committee, Maffei cosponsored 2009 legislation to crack down on abusive credit card practices. He also serves on the Judiciary panel, where he will have influence over bankruptcy law. "I am committed to using my position and power through the Judiciary Committee to fight for regular people who are facing this recession," he said.

Maffei began his career as a journalist. "I liked the excitement of TV, the immediacy of it," he said, but he became restless, yearning to be more of an advocate. So he shifted gears, working for Democratic Sens. Bill Bradley of New Jersey and Daniel Patrick Moynihan of New York. He also worked on the House Ways and Means Committee staff.

In 2006, he ran for the House against nine-term GOP Rep. James T. Walsh, losing by 3,417 votes. Two years later, with Walsh retiring, Maffei tried again, facing Republican Dale A. Sweetland. Maffei raised more than $2.3 million, a record for the 25th District, and won by 13 percentage points.

His past work as an aide has given him a leg up on other freshmen, particularly in understanding legislative rules, but it didn't prepare Maffei for everything. "What's very different is the things members do," he said. "Committee selection. Figuring out how to balance different constituent groups when you decide how to vote. That's as new to me as it would be to anyone else."

CAPITOL OFFICE
225-3701
maffei.house.gov
1630 Longworth Bldg. 20515-3225; fax 225-4042

COMMITTEES
Financial Services
Judiciary

RESIDENCE
DeWitt

BORN
July 4, 1968; Syracuse, N.Y.

RELIGION
Roman Catholic

FAMILY
Wife, Abby Davidson Maffei

EDUCATION
Brown U., B.A. 1990 (history); Columbia U.,
M.S. 1991 (journalism); Harvard U., M.P.P. 1995

CAREER
Investment firm executive; political consultant;
congressional aide; television reporter and
producer

POLITICAL HIGHLIGHTS
Democratic nominee for U.S. House, 2006

ELECTION RESULTS

2008 GENERAL
Dan Maffei (D, WFM)	157,375	54.8%
Dale A. Sweetland (R, C)	120,217	41.9%
Howie Hawkins (GRP)	9,483	3.3%

2008 PRIMARY
Dan Maffei (D, WFM)	unopposed

NEW YORK 25

North central — Syracuse, most of Irondequoit

Syracuse, in the district's east, is the 25th's only major city and its economic hub. The district stretches west, roughly along Lake Ontario in the north and the Erie Canal in the south, from Onondaga County to reach most of Irondequoit in the Rochester suburbs. Syracuse and the Rochester area are home to diverse economies that rely on educational institutions to spur other industries. Small towns and farms fill much of the land between the two cities.

More than two-thirds of the 25th's residents live in Onondaga County, which is home to Syracuse. Syracuse University drives the city's economy. Syracuse University and the State University of New York Upstate Medical University, both located in the city on University Hill, are the county's top two employers.

South of Syracuse, dairy and produce farms dot the landscape. The district also includes coastal and inland farming-based towns stretching from Moon Beach in the east to the banks of the Genesee River in the west. Many Rochester-area residents work in white-collar industries.

Minorities and blue-collar workers contribute to the Democratic vote in Syracuse, while GOP candidates get votes from conservatives scattered throughout the 25th, particularly in more lightly populated Wayne County, which voted for John McCain by a 10-percentage-point margin in the 2008 presidential election. The district as a whole gave 56 percent to Barack Obama in 2008.

MAJOR INDUSTRY
Higher education, agriculture, health care

CITIES
Syracuse, 147,306; Irondequoit (unincorporated) (pt.), 32,661

NOTABLE
Syracuse University's Carrier Dome is the nation's largest on-campus domed stadium.

Rep. Christopher Lee (R)

CAPITOL OFFICE
225-5265
chrislee.house.gov
1711 Longworth Bldg. 20515-3226; fax 225-5910

COMMITTEES
Financial Services

RESIDENCE
Clarence

BORN
April 1, 1964; Kenmore, N.Y.

RELIGION
Protestant

FAMILY
Wife, Michele Lee; one child

EDUCATION
U. of Rochester, B.A. 1987 (economics);
Chapman U., M.B.A. 1997

CAREER
Motion control technologies company executive;
computer company sales manager

POLITICAL HIGHLIGHTS
No previous office

ELECTION RESULTS

2008 GENERAL

Christopher Lee (R, INDC, C)	148,607	55.0%
Alice Kryzan (D)	109,615	40.5%
Jonathan P. Powers (WFM)	12,104	4.5%

2008 PRIMARY

Christopher Lee (R)	unopposed

Elected 2008; 1st term

A strict fiscal conservative, Lee is new to Congress but has been familiar with the institution since the early 1990s. His father, Patrick, was finance director for Republican Jack Quinn, who represented a neighboring western New York district. "I always admired him," Lee said of Quinn, who was a strong champion of organized labor. "He was always very in touch with his constituents."

Lee said his experience working for his family's company gives him a perspective on two issues important to constituents: job creation and taxes. "When you've had to meet a payroll and you've been inundated with the regulations that Albany and Washington impose upon business, you understand what needs to get changed," he said.

He holds a seat on the Financial Services Committee, which plays a central role in tackling the nation's economic crisis. A member of the conservative Republican Study Committee, he advocates extending President George W. Bush's 2001 and 2003 tax cuts — laws that Quinn supported. He also has advocated a $5,000 tax credit to refinance homeowners' mortgages.

He has strong opinions about trade policy. He said U.S. firms need to follow the lead of the manufacturing firm he headed, which aggressively went after foreign markets. "You can't pretend we're not in a global economy," he said.

Lee grew up in Western New York and attended college at the University of Rochester. He took a job at Microtek Laboratories in California in 1990 and was promoted to its director of sales. Five years later, he began working from the West Coast for an arm of his family's business, Enidine Incorporated, a collection of companies that produced actuators, shock absorbers, motors and other motion technologies. After earning his MBA, Lee in 1998 returned to the Buffalo area, eventually becoming president of the company's automation group.

Lee raised about $2.2 million for his 2008 campaign to succeed retiring Republican Thomas M. Reynolds — about half of which was self-funded — and took 55 percent of the vote in one of the four New York districts that Arizona GOP Sen. John McCain carried over Barack Obama.

NEW YORK 26

Suburban Buffalo and Rochester; rural west

Stretching from suburban Buffalo to the Rochester suburbs, the Republican-leaning 26th scoops up miles of farmland between and to the south of the two cities. Slightly less than half the district's residents live in Niagara and Erie counties, and manufacturing drives their local economies. Abundant dairy farms and apple orchards shape the rural regions.

The population is anchored in the district's portion of Erie County, particularly in Amherst. The north campus of the state university at Buffalo, which houses most of the university's programs, and corporate office parks are Amherst mainstays.

The 26th District's share of Niagara County includes Lockport and North Tonawanda, which becomes a tourist hotspot each summer. Visitors are attracted to North Tonawanda's Gateway Harbor Park, the last spot before the Erie Canal joins the Niagara River and part of development efforts along the waterfront.

The 26th has a noticeable GOP lean, but voting habits differ across the 26th's seven counties. The district's portions of the politically competitive population centers of Erie and Niagara counties have a slight Democratic edge, while Monroe County outside of Rochester and Livingston to the south have more Republican voters. Agricultural Wyoming, Genesse and Orleans counties are solidly Republican. Overall, the 26th gave John McCain 52 percent of its vote in the 2008 presidential election.

MAJOR INDUSTRY
Manufacturing, agriculture, service

CITIES
North Tonawanda, 33,262; Lockport, 22,279

NOTABLE
The Herschell Carrousel Factory Museum is in North Tonawanda.

Rep. Brian Higgins (D)

Elected 2004; 3rd term

CAPITOL OFFICE
225-3306
www.house.gov/higgins
431 Cannon Bldg. 20515-3227; fax 226-0347

COMMITTEES
Ways & Means

RESIDENCE
Buffalo

BORN
Oct. 6, 1959; Buffalo, N.Y.

RELIGION
Roman Catholic

FAMILY
Wife, Mary Jane Hannon; two children

EDUCATION
State U. of New York, Buffalo State, B.A.
1984 (political science), M.A. 1985 (history);
Harvard U., M.P.A. 1996

CAREER
State and county legislative aide

POLITICAL HIGHLIGHTS
Buffalo Common Council, 1988-94; Democratic
nominee for Erie County comptroller, 1993;
N.Y. Assembly, 1999-2004

ELECTION RESULTS

2008 GENERAL

Brian Higgins (D, WFM)	185,713	74.4%
Daniel J. Humiston (R, INDC)	56,354	22.6%
Harold W. Schroeder (C)	7,478	3.0%

2008 PRIMARY

Brian Higgins (D, WFM)	unopposed

2006 GENERAL

Brian Higgins (D, INDC, WFM)	140,027	79.3%
Michael J. McHale (R)	36,614	20.7%

PREVIOUS WINNING PERCENTAGES
2004 (51%)

With an unassuming demeanor, Higgins tends to the many challenges facing his economically distressed Buffalo-based district, typically focusing on narrow issues away from Congress' high-profile and often partisan debates. But his seat on the powerful Ways and Means Committee could put him in the spotlight as the interests of his district and the nation converge on the issues of tax, trade, energy and health care in the midst of the economic crisis.

Higgins' dedication to his constituents has made him popular at home, where he has won his past two re-elections with 74 percent of the vote or better. He's a loyal Democrat, voting with his party 98 percent of the time during the 110th Congress (2007-08) on issues that pitted Democrats against Republicans.

During debate on President Obama's economic stimulus bill in early 2009, Higgins kept tabs on the details of the tax relief, health care support and infrastructure funding directed to his district. A former member of the Transportation and Infrastructure Committee, and the end of a line of generations of bricklayers, he believes strongly in boosting investment in infrastructure and was disappointed to see funding for certain projects in his district dwindle as negotiations proceeded. Erie and Niagara counties would receive less than other New York counties for highway, energy, sewer, water and community development projects, according to the Buffalo News.

Yet Higgins voted for the final version, lauding the bill's provisions for, among other things, tax credits and first-time homebuyer credits, and funding for two major transportation projects in Chautauqua County and schools there and in Erie County.

Ways and Means also is expected to take up portions of broad health care legislation during the 111th Congress (2009-10). Higgins favors a universal health care plan, calling it a linchpin to solving the problems of access and availability to services. He also routinely talks about the need to increase funding for the National Cancer Institute, the federal government's principal agency for cancer research and training. In January 2009, he supported an expansion of the State Children's Health Insurance Program, which covers children from low-income families that do not qualify for Medicaid, calling it "an important step toward improving economic security and quality of life for American families." But he added, "Our work to repair America's broken health care system…is far from complete."

An ally of labor unions, Higgins is skeptical of free-trade deals. He voted against the Central America Free Trade Agreement in 2005 and two years later opposed a trade agreement with Peru. "Free trade is not necessarily fair trade" when finding a balance between the economic and environmental needs of his district, he said.

To take a seat on Ways and Means, Higgins had to give up his seat on the Transportation and Infrastructure panel, where he helped steer $42 million to his district in the 2005 surface transportation bill. In 2005, he took the lead in negotiations with the State Power Authority, demanding it help finance waterfront development in exchange for the right to operate the Niagara Power Project for a $391 million deal over the next 50 years. And at the behest of Transportation Chairman James L. Oberstar of Minnesota, Higgins and Ohio Republican Michael R. Turner helped start a task force on revitalizing older cities.

In the 110th Congress, Higgins also sat on the Oversight and Government Reform Committee. He criticized the George W. Bush administration's handling of the Iraq War and opposed a requirement that travelers show passports for U.S.-Canada border crossings, saying it would have a negative economic impact on his area.

Higgins is a reliable Democrat when it comes to social issues. He voted in 2008 to prohibit job discrimination based on sexual preference. In 2006, he voted against a bill that would make it a crime to transport a minor across state lines to obtain an abortion, and he voted to override President Bush's veto of a bill to expand federal funding for embryonic stem cell research, which uses surplus embryos from in vitro fertilization.

Higgins made local headlines in 2007 when, during a Sunday mass in the church where he was baptized and married, a lay deacon rebuked him for supporting federal funding of embryonic stem cell research. Higgins walked out of the service and later got an apology from the pastor.

The Higgins family has been in Buffalo since his grandfather emigrated from Ireland as a 12-year-old orphan. His grandfather was a bricklayer, a trade he handed down to Higgins' father and uncles. Higgins and all four siblings helped lay bricks. His father served on the Buffalo Common Council and later was a commissioner of the state workers' compensation board.

Higgins earned an undergraduate degree in political science from Buffalo State in 1984, followed by a master's degree in history a year later. He was elected to the Buffalo Common Council in 1987 at the age of 28.

After losing a 1993 bid for Erie County comptroller, he left upstate New York to get a master's degree at Harvard's Kennedy School of Government. He then returned home and worked as a legislative aide for the Erie County legislature and gave lectures at his alma mater, where he focused on the rise and fall of Buffalo as what he calls "one of the great industrial centers" of the United States. He was elected to the New York State Assembly in 1998, where he focused on local economic development.

When Republican Rep. Jack Quinn ended his 12-year run in Washington in 2004, Higgins jumped into the race and emerged the winner in a five-way Democratic primary. In the general election, he won by only 3,774 votes, ending years of frustration for Democrats during the long tenure of Quinn, a moderate with a pro-labor voting record.

In late 2008, he was among the names considered to fill the Senate seat of New York Democrat Hillary Rodham Clinton, who became secretary of State. Leonard Lenihan, the Democratic chairman in Erie County, which includes Buffalo, advocated for Higgins, saying it would blunt criticism that state Democrats are too New York City-centric. Ultimately, New York Democratic Gov. David A. Paterson went for an even newer face — Rep. Kirsten Gillibrand, who had just won her first re-election.

KEY VOTES

2008

Yes Delay consideration of Colombia free-trade agreement

Yes Override Bush veto of federal farm and nutrition programs reauthorization bill

Yes Overhaul surveillance laws and permit dismissal of suits against companies that conducted warrantless wiretapping

Yes Grant mortgage relief to homeowners and funding for Fannie Mae and Freddie Mac

Yes Approve initial $700 billion program to stabilize financial markets

Yes Approve final $700 billion program to stabilize financial markets

Yes Provide $14 billion in loans to automakers

2007

Yes Increase minimum wage by $2.10 an hour

Yes Approve $124.2 billion in emergency war spending and set goal for redeployment of troops from Iraq

No Reject federal contraceptive assistance to international family planning groups

Yes Override Bush veto of $23.2 billion water projects authorization bill

No Implement Peru free-trade agreement

Yes Approve energy policy overhaul with new fuel economy standards

No Clear $473.5 billion omnibus spending bill, including $70 billion for military operations

CQ VOTE STUDIES

	PARTY UNITY		PRESIDENTIAL SUPPORT	
	SUPPORT	OPPOSE	SUPPORT	OPPOSE
2008	99%	1%	20%	80%
2007	98%	2%	7%	93%
2006	89%	11%	33%	67%
2005	89%	11%	29%	71%

INTEREST GROUPS

	AFL-CIO	ADA	CCUS	ACU
2008	100%	80%	65%	4%
2007	96%	95%	50%	0%
2006	100%	85%	43%	20%
2005	87%	95%	52%	16%

NEW YORK 27

West — most of Buffalo; south and east suburbs

Tucked along the shores of Lake Erie in western New York, the 27th contains all of Erie County south of Buffalo and all but the northeastern corner of the city itself (which is in the 28th). Most of Buffalo's minority residents live in the 28th's portion of the city.

Nationwide economic downturns and a shrinking domestic auto market have hurt Buffalo's manufacturing base. The city's large blue-collar workforce used to rely on auto manufacturing, and shipping and cargo transportation were key to economic stability. Diversification into white-collar finance, insurance and real estate industries — growth driven mostly by two banks: HSBC and M&T, which provide thousands of area jobs and have remained stable during the international financial crisis — bolstered the economy, but layoffs have touched service and retail jobs. Health research facilities also are important in the Buffalo area.

Local leaders continue to see the waterfront as the core of Buffalo's renaissance effort. Development along the inner harbor is ongoing, and many officials believe the outer harbor presents a valuable opportunity to create both public space and commercial developments. The local professional sports teams, particularly football's Bills and hockey's Sabres, are a source of pride in the city. South of Buffalo, the 27th follows the New York State Thruway to the southwest to take in all of Chautauqua County, which borders Lake Erie on the north and Pennsylvania on the south and west. This area is mainly made up of small communities that depend on agriculture and a robust grape-growing industry.

While these mostly rural areas south of Buffalo in both Erie and Chautauqua counties tend to support Republicans, they cannot match the city's strong union ties: Barack Obama's 76 percent of the vote in Buffalo helped him win 54 percent of the 2008 presidential vote in the 27th.

MAJOR INDUSTRY

Auto manufacturing, government, agriculture, tourism

CITIES

Buffalo (pt.), 163,179; Cheektowaga (unincorporated), 79,988; West Seneca (unincorporated), 45,943; Jamestown, 31,730

NOTABLE

Westfield, home to a Welch's plant, calls itself the "Grape Juice Capital of the World."

Rep. Louise M. Slaughter (D)

Elected 1986; 12th term

CAPITOL OFFICE
225-3615
louise.house.gov
2469 Rayburn Bldg. 20515-3228; fax 225-7822

COMMITTEES
Rules - chairwoman

RESIDENCE
Fairport

BORN
Aug. 14, 1929; Harlan County, Ky.

RELIGION
Episcopalian

FAMILY
Husband, Robert Slaughter; three children

EDUCATION
U. of Kentucky, B.S. 1951 (bacteriology),
M.P.H. 1953

CAREER
State government aide; market researcher;
microbiologist

POLITICAL HIGHLIGHTS
Monroe County Legislature, 1975-79;
N.Y. Assembly, 1983-87

ELECTION RESULTS

2008 GENERAL

Slaughter (D, INDC, WFM)	172,655	78.0%
David W. Crimmen (R, C)	48,690	22.0%

2008 PRIMARY

Louise M. Slaughter (D, INDC, WFM)	unopposed

2006 GENERAL

Slaughter (D, INDC, WFM)	111,386	73.2%
John E. Donnelly (R, C)	40,844	26.8%

PREVIOUS WINNING PERCENTAGES
2004 (73%); 2002 (62%); 2000 (66%); 1998 (65%);
1996 (57%); 1994 (57%); 1992 (55%); 1990 (59%);
1988 (57%); 1986 (51%)

With a frequent smile, Slaughter uses her sharp wit and no-nonsense approach to run the Rules Committee. Poised and energetic, the oldest woman in Congress guides the Democratic leadership's agenda onto the House floor and brushes off GOP cries of partisanship. Outgunned Republicans chide the Democrats for failing to live up to the pledge to be more accommodating to the minority, but she deflects the criticism as "all sound and fury."

And she finds time for her own legislative priorities. With degrees in bacteriology and public health, many of her concerns focus on specific health care issues, such as genetic discrimination. She also is a strong advocate of the arts.

As a party loyalist, Slaughter was hand-picked by Speaker Nancy Pelosi of California to head Rules. And she adeptly engages in the classic committee dance, talking about bipartisanship and openness while moving her party's bills with few opportunities for amendment. She smoothly pushed President Obama's economic stimulus bill through the House in early 2009 by whittling down the number of amendments from 206 to 11, focusing on three criteria: if they were relevant, had a stimulative effect on the economy and didn't increase the overall price tag. She did let through a proposal for another $3 billion in transit spending that Democrats favored.

Republicans balk when she bars amendments. But she casts the blame on the Senate; she said it's hard enough to get bills through that chamber without extraneous changes. "The more changes we make, the less likely we are going to get it passed," she said.

The committee in January 2009 adopted a package of ethics rules changes that, among other things, eliminate term limits for committee chairpersons, make it easier to avoid pay-as-you-go requirements for offsets for new tax cuts or increased mandatory spending, and restrict the minority's ability to derail legislation. The panel's top-ranking Republican, David Dreier of California, accused Democrats of undermining Obama's pledge for a new era of bipartisanship. But Slaughter insisted the new rules would allow the House to "function more effectively."

While she usually does the bidding of the Democratic leadership, in 2007 she jumped out ahead of Pelosi on ethics rules changes. She proposed the hiring of an inspector general to monitor Congress and an independent board to investigate ethics complaints. Slaughter eventually compromised and agreed to accept a six-member board of outsiders as the new Office of Congressional Ethics.

She was more successful on a long-running priority — a ban on genetic discrimination, which was signed into law in 2008. That measure prohibits insurers from basing coverage or premium decisions on the results of genetic tests and bars employers from using the same information in personnel decisions. Slaughter called the bill "the most important thing I've done in my life."

Slaughter has used her medical expertise to reap other legislative successes, including the establishment of a national task force to ensure children get proper care in the event of a terrorist attack, and a bill to increase education about the health risks of the anti-miscarriage drug DES, which has caused cancer and abnormalities in some children of women who took the drug. She is a longtime advocate of women's issues, and cheered, "Hallelujah!" from the presiding officer's chair when the House passed a wage discrimination bill in 2008. The outburst got her pulled from the dais, but, she said, "I didn't have to go to the basement and get in that cell or anything." That bill, which would make it easier for women who are paid less than their male counterparts to bring lawsuits against their employers and be compensated, stalled that year but became law in 2009.

As a backer of the arts, she worked to boost spending for the National Endowment for the Arts in 2004. She also was once a leading proponent of reinstating the Fairness Doctrine, a Cold War-era policy requiring radio and TV stations to provide equal time for opposing viewpoints on matters of public interest — a move that has drawn opposition from conservatives who regard it as a Democratic attempt to shut down right-wing talk radio. Obama and other Democrats have taken a dim view of the idea.

She also tends to the interests of major employers in her district. She fought against the Western Hemisphere Travel Initiative that would require Canadians entering the U.S. to show national identification, saying it would harm her border district's economy by slowing traffic. She brings a skeptical eye to debates over international trade, pointing to what she sees as the devastating effects of the North American Free Trade Agreement on her constituents.

Slaughter has lived most of her adult life in a suburb of Rochester, but she grew up as a coal miner's daughter — and descendant of famous frontiersman Daniel Boone — in the mountains of Kentucky's Harlan County (and still speaks with a slight twang native to the area). When she came to Congress, Democratic leaders took a liking to her warmth, grit and liberal views. They gave her a seat on Rules in 1989 and on the Budget Committee in 1991. She was granted the top minority spot on Rules in the 109th Congress (2005-06).

Slaughter moved with her husband to New York in the 1950s. Her first brush with public policy came in 1971, when she joined neighbors to try to save a stand of trees from development. "I thought in my best Kentucky fashion that if I would put on my best dress and go and be very nice and polite and ask them to save this forest that they would say, 'Well, why not?' " she later told The Associated Press. "And they just handed me my hat."

The episode sparked an interest in politics. She served as a Monroe County legislator and as an assistant to Mario Cuomo, New York's secretary of state at that time. In 1982, she ousted a Republican incumbent to move to the state Assembly, where she served four years before winning her seat in the House with 51 percent of the vote against conservative first-term Republican Fred J. Eckert. Actor Richard Gere, with whom she shared an interest in Central American issues, campaigned door-to-door with her.

Not until 1998, in her seventh House race, did Slaughter begin to draw better than 60 percent. Reapportionment after the 2000 census forced her into the same district as 14-term Democrat John J. LaFalce, who then retired. Slaughter won by 25 percentage points in 2002 and has won handily ever since.

KEY VOTES

2008
Yes Delay consideration of Colombia free-trade agreement
Yes Override Bush veto of federal farm and nutrition programs reauthorization bill
No Overhaul surveillance laws and permit dismissal of suits against companies that conducted warrantless wiretapping
Yes Grant mortgage relief to homeowners and funding for Fannie Mae and Freddie Mac
Yes Approve initial $700 billion program to stabilize financial markets
Yes Approve final $700 billion program to stabilize financial markets
Yes Provide $14 billion in loans to automakers

2007
Yes Increase minimum wage by $2.10 an hour
Yes Approve $124.2 billion in emergency war spending and set goal for redeployment of troops from Iraq
No Reject federal contraceptive assistance to international family planning groups
Yes Override Bush veto of $23.2 billion water projects authorization bill
No Implement Peru free-trade agreement
Yes Approve energy policy overhaul with new fuel economy standards
No Clear $473.5 billion omnibus spending bill, including $70 billion for military operations

CQ VOTE STUDIES

	PARTY UNITY		PRESIDENTIAL SUPPORT	
	SUPPORT	OPPOSE	SUPPORT	OPPOSE
2008	100%	0%	12%	88%
2007	99%	1%	4%	96%
2006	99%	1%	14%	86%
2005	97%	3%	14%	86%
2004	98%	2%	24%	76%

INTEREST GROUPS

	AFL-CIO	ADA	CCUS	ACU
2008	100%	95%	47%	0%
2007	100%	100%	47%	0%
2006	100%	85%	29%	9%
2005	100%	100%	41%	4%
2004	100%	95%	44%	0%

NEW YORK 28
Northwest — Rochester, part of Buffalo

A small strip of land along Lake Ontario connects the ends — Buffalo and Rochester — of the telephone-receiver-shaped 28th. The district encompasses the northeastern portion of Buffalo, all of Niagara Falls and almost all of Rochester, giving the 28th most of the Democratic-rich voting areas in western New York.

Both Buffalo and Rochester are trying to recover from recent economic declines. Job losses in the manufacturing sector largely were offset by service industries, but lower salaries have exacerbated the problems of Rochester's low-income residents who are vulnerable to layoffs.

The optic and imaging manufacturing firms and tech companies that have helped drive Rochester's economy are concerned about the impact of layoffs at two of the area's major corporations, Eastman Kodak and Xerox. The University of Rochester is a top employer, and its optics institute is highly ranked, while the Rochester Institute of Technology has one of the nation's best imaging science departments. Work at the Roswell Park Cancer Institute and the Hauptman-Woodward Medical Research Institute has helped transform the Buffalo region into a health care hub.

Niagara Falls attracts millions of tourists from around the world, although many of those visitors travel to the Canadian side of the border rather than the 28th's side. Local officials hope revitalization efforts including the Seneca Niagara Casino, which opened in 2002, will draw more visitors to the U.S. shore.

Between Rochester and Buffalo, the 28th is home to rural communities that farm fruit and favor the GOP. Minorities total 38 percent of the 28th's population, giving it a far higher proportion of minority residents than any other New York district north of Westchester County. Combined with a blue-collar workforce, minorities helped Barack Obama win 68 percent of the district's 2008 presidential vote.

MAJOR INDUSTRY
Service, tourism, higher education, research, manufacturing

CITIES
Rochester (pt.), 219,729; Buffalo (pt.), 129,469; Niagara Falls, 55,593

NOTABLE
Women's rights activist Susan B. Anthony and abolitionist Frederick Douglass are both buried in Rochester's Mount Hope Cemetery.

Rep. Eric Massa (D)

CAPITOL OFFICE
225-3161
massa.house.gov
1208 Longworth Bldg. 20515-3229; fax 226-6599

COMMITTEES
Agriculture
Armed Services
Homeland Security

RESIDENCE
Corning

BORN
Sept. 16, 1959; Charleston, S.C.

RELIGION
Christian

FAMILY
Wife, Beverly Massa; three children

EDUCATION
U.S. Naval Academy, B.S. 1981 (engineering)

MILITARY SERVICE
Navy, 1981-2001

CAREER
Navy officer; defense firm consultant; campaign and congressional aide; photonics engineer

POLITICAL HIGHLIGHTS
Democratic nominee for U.S. House, 2006

ELECTION RESULTS

2008 GENERAL

Eric Massa (D, WFM)	140,529	51.0%
John R. "Randy" Kuhl Jr. (R, INDC, C)	135,199	49.0%

2008 PRIMARY

Eric Massa (D, WFM)	unoppposed

Elected 2008; 1st term

Massa's background prepares him for almost anything. He served in the Navy for two decades, worked at a manufacturing company before being laid off, overcame cancer and served briefly as a staffer for the Armed Services Committee while it was controlled by the GOP.

"It means I can't be intimidated politically, and when people say, 'You have to vote on this,' I say, 'No, my vote is mine and what are you going to do to me?'" Massa (MASS-uh) said of his varied life experiences.

He now serves on the committee where he once was an aide. He said he was forced out of that staff job for opposing "the flawed strategy being set forth" by former Defense Secretary Donald H. Rumsfeld and his GOP allies in the run-up to the Iraq War. He supports President Obama's moves to beef up U.S. troop strength in Afghanistan but still frets about strains on the military.

Massa also sits on the Homeland Security and Agriculture committees. In March 2009, he came out against Obama's fiscal 2010 budget proposal to phase out subsidies to farmers whose sales exceed $500,000 a year, saying "this proposal ignores completely the production costs required to create that level of sales."

Massa retired from the Navy in 2001 after a diagnosis of terminal non-Hodgkin's lymphoma, undergoing aggressive treatment and eventually becoming cancer-free. He worked as an engineer at Corning before being laid off because of what he calls "unfair free-trade agreements."

Massa said his battle with cancer convinced him the nation's health care system needs a massive overhaul. "I believe to the core of my soul that all Americans should have access to the same medical care that I had access to 10 years ago," he said.

During his Navy career, Massa was a special assistant to Gen. Wesley K. Clark, the NATO commander in Europe, during the Bosnian conflict. He later signed on as an adviser to Clark's failed bid for the 2004 Democratic presidential nomination. In 2006, he ventured into politics himself, losing to incumbent GOP Rep. John R. "Randy" Kuhl Jr. by less than 3 percentage points. In their 2008 rematch, Massa edged Kuhl by 2 percentage points.

NEW YORK 29

Southern Tier – Elmira, Corning; Rochester suburbs

The 29th blankets much of the southwestern portion of New York known as the Southern Tier, taking in a mix of forests, lakes, farms and small towns. It also reaches north to take in the western portion of the Finger Lakes region and some of Rochester's suburbs.

Agriculture helps drive the economy, mostly through farms and wineries. The Finger Lakes and surrounding parks draw thousands of visitors annually, and the Finger Lakes region is the largest wine-producing area by volume outside of California.

In the north, the 29th takes in southern parts of Monroe County outside Rochester, where a plurality of the district's residents live. The 29th's westernmost point is Cattaraugus County, a rural area that includes Allegany State Park and St. Bonaventure University.

To the east, Steuben County hosts a thriving tourism industry as well as Corning, one of the better-known U.S. company towns due to its glass products and costly crystal pieces. Nearby Elmira, located in Chemung County, is home to manufacturing plants. Olean, in Cattaraugus, hosts the headquarters of kitchen cutlery maker CUTCO.

Republicans hold an edge over Democrats in voter registration here despite the district's large presence of blue-collar workers. Republican John McCain eked out a win with a slim 50 percent majority in the 2008 presidential election. The 29th also has the lowest percentage of Hispanic residents (1 percent) in any New York district.

MAJOR INDUSTRY
Agriculture, manufacturing, tourism

CITIES
Elmira, 30,940; Brighton (unincorp.) (pt.), 25,869

NOTABLE
Watkins Glen International race track ("The Glen") is just south of Seneca Lake.

Gov. Bev Perdue (D)

First elected: 2008
Length of term: 4 years
Term expires: 1/13
Salary: $130,629
Phone: (919) 733-4240

Residence: New Bern
Born: January 14, 1947; Grundy, Va.
Religion: Episcopalian
Family: Husband, Bob Eaves; two children, two stepchildren
Education: U. of Kentucky, B.A. 1969 (history); U. of Florida, M.Ed. 1974 (educational administration), Ph.D. 1976, (educational administration)
Career: Geriatric health care specialist; teacher
Political highlights: N.C. House, 1987-90; N.C. Senate, 1991-2000; lieutenant governor, 2001-09

Election results:
2008 GENERAL

Beverly Perdue (D	2,146,189	50.3%
Pat McCrory (R)	2,001,168	46.9%
Michael C. Munger (LIBERT)	121,584	2.8%

Lt. Gov. Walter Dalton (D)

First elected: 2008
Length of term: 4 years
Term expires: 1/13
Salary: $115,289
Phone: (919) 733-7350

LEGISLATURE

General Assembly: January-June

Senate: 50 members, 2-year terms
2009 ratios: 30 D, 20 R; 44 men, 6 women
Salary: $13,951
Phone: (919) 733-4111

House: 120 members, 2-year terms
2009 ratios: 68 D, 52 R; 83 men, 37 women
Salary: $13,951
Phone: (919) 733-4111

TERM LIMITS

Governor: 2 consecutive terms
Senate: No
House: No

URBAN STATISTICS

CITY	POPULATION
Charlotte	540,828
Raleigh	276,093
Greensboro	223,891
Durham	187,035
Winston-Salem	185,776

REGISTERED VOTERS

Democrat	46%
Republican	32%
Unaffiliated	22%

POPULATION

2008 population (est.)	9,222,414
2000 population	8,049,313
1990 population	6,628,637
Percent change (1990-2000)	+21.4%
Rank among states (2008)	10

Median age	35.3
Born in state	63%
Foreign born	5.3%
Violent crime rate	498/100,000
Poverty level	12.3%
Federal workers	60,331
Military	118,281

ELECTIONS

STATE ELECTION OFFICIAL
(919) 733-7173
DEMOCRATIC PARTY
(919) 821-2777
REPUBLICAN PARTY
(919) 828-6423

MISCELLANEOUS

Web: www.ncgov.com
Capital: Raleigh

U.S. CONGRESS

Senate: 1 Democrat, 1 Republicans
House: 8 Democrats, 5 Republicans

2000 Census Statistics by District

DIST.	2008 VOTE FOR PRESIDENT OBAMA	MCCAIN	WHITE	BLACK	ASIAN	HISP	MEDIAN INCOME	WHITE COLLAR	BLUE COLLAR	SERVICE INDUSTRY	OVER 64	UNDER 18	COLLEGE EDUCATION	RURAL	SQ. MILES
1	63%	37%	44%	50%	0%	3%	$28,410	46%	37%	18%	14%	26%	12%	52%	7,199
2	52	47	59	30	1	8	$36,510	52	34	14	10	26	16	50	3,956
3	38	61	76	17	1	4	$37,510	56	29	15	12	24	20	47	6,192
4	62	37	69	21	4	5	$53,847	75	14	11	8	25	48	17	1,253
5	38	61	88	7	1	4	$39,710	54	34	12	13	23	20	57	4,402
6	36	63	85	9	1	4	$43,503	56	33	11	14	24	23	48	2,944
7	47	52	63	23	0	4	$33,998	50	34	16	13	25	18	55	6,087
8	52	47	62	27	2	7	$38,390	53	33	14	11	26	18	31	3,283
9	45	55	83	10	2	4	$55,059	69	20	10	10	25	36	16	991
10	36	63	85	9	1	3	$37,649	45	42	12	13	24	14	50	3,302
11	47	52	90	5	0	3	$34,720	52	32	16	18	21	21	56	6,025
12	71	29	45	45	2	7	$35,775	52	32	16	11	26	19	11	821
13	59	40	63	27	2	6	$41,060	60	26	13	11	23	27	26	2,256
STATE	50	49	70	21	1	5	$39,184	56	31	14	12	24	23	40	48,711
U.S.	53	46	69	12	4	13	$41,994	60	25	15	12	26	24	21	3,537,438

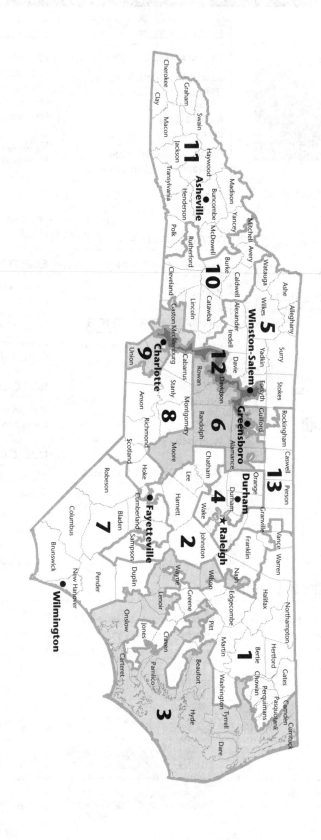

Sen. Richard M. Burr (R)

Elected 2004; 1st term

A minister's son, Burr is a serious-minded conservative who has won attention from his party's leaders and in GOP circles for his diligent work on terrorism, health care and veterans' issues. But he aims to broaden his appeal by trying to help low-income voters and satisfy other constituencies in a state that was once solidly Republican but has become increasingly Democratic.

Burr's adherence to the Republican agenda — he sided with the GOP on 98 percent of the votes in the 110th Congress (2007-08) in which a majority of the two parties diverged — helped him earn the title of chief deputy whip in 2009. Although he is unbending on issues where his state's interests are at stake, such as tobacco regulation, he can make a deal. He initially blocked legislation to expand funding for the global fight against AIDS and other diseases, then helped hammer out a compromise enacted in 2008.

Democrats marked Burr as one of their top targets for defeat in 2010, seeking to capitalize on his low approval rating in polls — in the mid-30 percent range in early 2009 — that they said reflected his inability to connect with voters. They hoped to replicate their experience with his former Senate GOP colleague Elizabeth Dole, whom they defeated in 2008 after criticizing her for devoting too little time to helping North Carolinians. Burr vowed not to fall into that trap. "I tend to be more of a policy guy than I am a guy who shows up on the 24-hour talk shows or a guy who goes to the floor and speaks," he told The Charlotte Observer in April 2009. "Listen, I know I am going to have to raise my profile in the next 18 months."

To that end, Burr sought to strengthen ties to black voters, a source of just 12 percent of his support in his 2004 election. He introduced legislation in February 2009 aimed at boosting graduation rates for low-income and minority students. He also is involved in efforts to combat sickle cell disease and to reauthorize the Healthy Start program, which is designed to reduce infant mortality and the number of babies born at low weights. Both issues disproportionately affect African-Americans.

Burr drew unwanted attention with a remark that he ordered his wife to withdraw money from an automatic teller machine during the 2008 banking crisis. He said he only did what many other people did, but liberal MSNBC commentator Rachel Maddow dubbed him "Bank-run Burr."

As a North Carolina lawmaker, Burr is a champion for tobacco companies, including Reynolds American Inc., a big employer in his hometown of Winston-Salem. He opposes legislation directing the Food and Drug Administration (FDA) to regulate tobacco. He argued in a 2008 opinion column in USA Today that giving the FDA control over tobacco would "severely impede the FDA's core mission" by taking the agency's focus away from existing problems such as drug and food safety. He joined Democratic Sen. Kay Hagan of North Carolina in April 2009 on a less stringent alternative that still would impose limits on marketing tobacco. He also helped win passage in 2004 of a popular tobacco buyout that steered $3.8 billion to his state's farmers. Personally, however, Burr is anti-tobacco. He quit smoking cigarettes in 1998 after making a televised vow to do so.

In September 2007, Burr took over as the top Republican on the Veterans' Affairs panel. He worked closely with the George W. Bush administration to protect GOP priorities when Democrats moved in 2008 to expand education benefits for veterans under the GI Bill. He helped win inclusion of Bush's proposal to allow veterans to transfer unused benefits to family members.

But he didn't always succeed. He sought to strip a provision in a 2008 veter-

CAPITOL OFFICE
224-3154
burr.senate.gov
217 Russell Bldg. 20510-3306; fax 228-2981

COMMITTEES
Armed Services
Energy & Natural Resources
Health, Education, Labor & Pensions
Veterans' Affairs - ranking member
Select Intelligence

RESIDENCE
Winston-Salem

BORN
Nov. 30, 1955; Charlottesville, Va.

RELIGION
Methodist

FAMILY
Wife, Brooke Burr; two children

EDUCATION
Wake Forest U., B.A. 1978 (communications)

CAREER
Marketing manager; kitchen appliance salesman

POLITICAL HIGHLIGHTS
Republican nominee for U.S. House, 1992;
U.S. House, 1995-2005

ELECTION RESULTS

2004 GENERAL

Richard M. Burr (R)	1,791,450	51.6%
Erskine Bowles (D)	1,632,527	47.0%
Tom Bailey (LIBERT)	47,743	1.4%

2004 PRIMARY

Richard M. Burr (R)	302,319	87.9%
John Ross Hendrix (R)	25,971	7.6%
Albert Lee Wiley Jr. (R)	15,585	4.5%

PREVIOUS WINNING PERCENTAGES
2002 House Election (70%); 2000 House Election (93%); 1998 House Election (68%); 1996 House Election (62%); 1994 House Election (57%)

ans' bill that would replace compensation payments to surviving Filipino soldiers who fought in World War II with housing and car grants for American veterans. "Is this the right priority at a time of war when the needs of our men and women serving in Iraq and Afghanistan are so great?" he asked. Several senators who served in the war objected to his attempt, and it was defeated.

A member of the Health, Education, Labor and Pensions Committee, Burr was chairman of its Bioterrorism and Public Health Preparedness Subcommittee in the 109th Congress (2005-06). He won enactment in late 2006 of his bill aimed at boosting the nation's preparedness for a bioterror attack or major disease outbreak. That was the culmination of Burr's two-year effort in the Senate to renew and update a 2002 law that strengthened national defenses against biological or chemical attack in the aftermath of the Sept. 11 terrorist attacks. Burr had been a chief negotiator in drafting the original law.

He also sits on the Armed Services and Select Intelligence panels. In 2005, the Defense spending bill included his provision to shield drug manufacturers from lawsuits involving vaccines and drugs for treating or preventing disease outbreaks or bioterror attacks. He and Democrat Bob Casey of Pennsylvania formed a caucus on terrorism and weapons of mass destruction in February 2009.

On the Energy and Natural Resources Committee, Burr supports increased domestic oil drilling along with expanding renewable energy. He also touts nuclear power, which provides almost one-third of his state's electricity.

Close ties to Republican Sen. John McCain of Arizona, his party's presidential nominee, led to Burr's inclusion on some early lists of potential vice presidential nominees in 2008. Burr played down such rumors, avowing no interest in following Aaron Burr, a distant relative who was a New York senator and vice president under Thomas Jefferson. He did serve as co-chairman of the GOP platform committee during the party's 2008 national convention.

Burr also made a bid for Republican Conference chairman when the No. 3 leadership post opened up in late 2007, but lost to Lamar Alexander of Tennessee by a vote of 31-16. Burr said he thought the leadership could use a younger voice to "move forward with a new generation of voters."

Born in Virginia, Burr moved with his family to Winston-Salem when he was 6. His father, head of the city's 3,000-member First Presbyterian Church, was often gone, ministering to his large flock. After college, Burr took a job with Carswell Distributing, selling appliances and teaching housewives how to cook with their newfangled microwave ovens. He rose to national sales manager. He also became active politically in the growing conservative anti-tax movement, co-chairing North Carolina Taxpayers United.

Burr came home from his job one day in 1991 and surprised his wife by announcing he wanted to run for Congress, even though he had no political experience and no clue what a congressman earned. He lost his first bid in 1992, got back in the fray two years later and won with 57 percent of the vote against state Sen. A.P. "Sandy" Sands. He arrived as part of the House GOP's ideals-driven Class of '94, but soon proved to be more pragmatic than many of the newcomers. He played a large role in winning passage in 1997 of legislation to speed FDA approval of new drugs and medical devices.

Encouraged by state party officials to run for governor in 2000, Burr declined, saying the job was too administrative for him. He wanted to run for an open Senate seat in 2002, but deferred to Dole, who was the Bush administration's choice. He began preparing to run for Democrat John Edwards' Senate seat more than a year in advance of the 2004 election, even before Edwards announced he would not seek re-election. Burr then weathered criticism for an initially lackluster campaign against Democrat Erskine Bowles, former chief of staff to President Clinton. But aided by Bush's strong showing, Burr won with 52 percent of the vote to Bowles' 47 percent.

KEY VOTES

2008
Yes Prohibit discrimination based on genetic information
Yes Reauthorize farm and nutrition programs for five years
No   Limit debate on "cap and trade" system for greenhouse gas emissions
No   Allow lawsuits against companies that participated in warrantless wiretapping
No   Limit debate on a bill to block a scheduled cut in Medicare payments to doctors
?   Grant mortgage relief to homeowners and funding for Fannie Mae and Freddie Mac
Yes Approve a nuclear cooperation agreement with India
Yes Approve final $700 billion program to stabilize financial markets
No   Allow consideration of a $14 billion auto industry loan package

2007
Yes Increase minimum wage by $2.10 an hour
No   Limit debate on a comprehensive immigration bill
No   Overhaul congressional lobbying and ethics rules for members and their staffs
No   Limit debate on considering a bill to add House seats for the District of Columbia and Utah
No   Limit debate on restoring habeas corpus rights to detainees
No   Mandate minimum breaks for troops between deployments to Iraq or Afghanistan
No   Override Bush veto of $23.2 billion water projects authorization bill
Yes Confirm Michael B. Mukasey as attorney general
No   Limit debate on an energy policy overhaul containing $21.8 billion in tax incentives and reduced oil and gas subsidies

CQ VOTE STUDIES

	PARTY UNITY		PRESIDENTIAL SUPPORT	
	SUPPORT	OPPOSE	SUPPORT	OPPOSE
2008	99%	1%	81%	19%
2007	97%	3%	89%	11%
2006	94%	6%	88%	12%
2005	95%	5%	89%	11%
2004	92%	8%	79%	21%
2003	94%	6%	96%	4%
2002	95%	5%	92%	8%
2001	95%	5%	93%	7%
2000	92%	8%	22%	78%
1999	93%	7%	17%	83%

INTEREST GROUPS

	AFL-CIO	ADA	CCUS	ACU
2008	10%	5%	100%	79%
2007	5%	0%	73%	92%
2006	20%	10%	67%	92%
2005	29%	5%	94%	92%
2004	33%	10%	94%	87%
2003	27%	15%	93%	84%
2002	11%	0%	100%	96%
2001	17%	10%	96%	88%
2000	10%	5%	80%	88%
1999	33%	5%	84%	87%

Sen. Kay Hagan (D)

Elected 2008; 1st term

Hagan can be hard to peg. She has described herself as "pragmatic" and a "realist," and indicated that she intends to continue on the centrist course she followed during a decade in the North Carolina Senate. But some critics at home said she never distinguished herself from the state Democratic political machine; the Raleigh News and Observer in October 2008 described her record as "difficult to separate" from that of the state senate's Democratic leaders. Meanwhile, a 2008 primary opponent accused her of being "essentially a Republican state senator."

On social issues, Hagan's views often are in line with Democrats. She supports abortion rights; in the state Senate backed increased pay for teachers and an increase in the minimum wage; and she was a proponent of comprehensive sex education. But she also supports gun owners' rights — her House Web site describes gun ownership as "part of the fabric of North Carolina" — and voted to eliminate a needle exchange program. She also has some fiscal conservative views; back home, she supported lower taxes for businesses and cuts to Medicaid even as some Democrats deplored the move as a give-away to wealthy corporate interests and a punishment for the poor.

A member of the Moderate Dems Working Group, she also supports pay-as-you-go rules to balance the federal budget, which require new spending to be offset. She advocates paying for new spending by improved enforcement of tax laws to claims billions in uncollected taxes. And she wants to end tax breaks for companies that outsource jobs overseas.

Hagan is a member of the Health, Education, Labor and Pensions Committee, where in early in 2009 she displayed her willingness to cross party lines; she joined with her North Carolina colleague, Republican Richard M. Burr, in offering an alternative to a main Democratic bill to regulate tobacco. While the bill backed by most Democrats aimed to give the Food and Drug Administration (FDA) authority to regulate nicotine levels in cigarettes and other products, Hagan and Burr's proposal aimed to create a separate regulatory entity that could only test for nicotine levels and require that products be labeled accordingly. "I will not stand idly by while the FDA is put in charge of such a critical industry to North Carolina," Hagan said.

Her campaign was not heavily funded by tobacco interests, but she has a connection to tobacco farmers; she spent summers as a child helping to harvest the crop at her grandparents' farm.

Hagan also intends to push for trade agreements to better protect middle-class workers and proposes establishing a post at the Justice Department to enforce the pacts. And she supports boosting the creation of renewable-energy jobs, contending that was one promise from President Obama's economic stimulus plan in early 2009 that she also backed. "With green industry jobs, there's a huge sector of jobs in the U.S. I want to be sure North Carolina is the leader in renewable energy," she told the Watauga Democrat while touring the Appalachian State University campus to view its renewable-energy projects in April 2009. Hagan, a member of the Small Business and Entrepreneurship Committee, said savings in energy also would help new businesses be successful.

Hagan that April also supported the Senate's $3.56 trillion version of Obama's budget, although she lamented the Budget Committee had reduced funding in the blueprint for crop subsidies by $350 million. "This not only threatens the domestic supply of food and fiber

CAPITOL OFFICE
224-6342
hagan.senate.gov
521 Dirksen Bldg. 20510-1904; fax 224-1100

COMMITTEES
Armed Services
Health, Education, Labor & Pensions
Small Business & Entrepreneurship

RESIDENCE
Greensboro

BORN
May 26, 1953; Shelby, N.C.

RELIGION
Presbyterian

FAMILY
Husband, Chip Hagan; three children

EDUCATION
Florida State U., B.A. 1975 (American studies);
Wake Forest U., J.D. 1978

CAREER
Homemaker; bank executive

POLITICAL HIGHLIGHTS
N.C. Senate, 1999-2009

ELECTION RESULTS

2008 GENERAL

Kay Hagan (D)	2,249,311	52.6%
Elizabeth Dole (R)	1,887,510	44.2%
Christopher Cole (LIBERT)	133,430	3.1%

2008 PRIMARY

Kay Hagan (D)	801,920	60.1%
Jim Neal (D)	239,623	17.9%
Marcus W. Williams (D)	170,970	12.8%
Duskin C. Lassiter (D)	62,136	4.6%
Howard Staley (D)	60,403	4.5%

that Americans depend upon, it further undermines our rural communities already in crisis," she stated.

Hagan also sits on the Armed Services Committee, a pivotal position for a state with several large military bases.

Hagan promotes that she oversaw balanced budgets from her positions on the state Senate budget panel. But she also well understands the power of earmarks — funding set asides for special projects —having used that position to shower Greensboro and High Point with cash. She flowed funds to Greensboro for a controversial civil rights museum — a critical project for the city's black community — and for an expensive downtown park, while High Point won state funding to bolster its annual furniture market, which is threatened by new competition in Las Vegas.

She said she is conscientious of her constituents' desires, even when they conflict with her own views. She supported establishing a lottery in North Carolina, which polls indicated was the popular position in the state. But she told the Greensboro News and Record, "I'm not crazy about it at all." She voted for a death penalty moratorium, though she supports the death penalty, and against an amendment to the state constitution banning gay marriage, though she supports existing state law banning the marriages.

Hagan was born in Shelby and later her family moved to Lakeland, Fla., when her father became the city's mayor. She attended college in the state, then returned to North Carolina for law school, where she met her husband. The couple settled in Greensboro and raised three children.

Hagan, a niece of former Democratic Florida Gov. and Sen. Lawton Chiles, was recruited into politics by former Democratic North Carolina Gov. Jim Hunt. Hunt selected Hagan — a former banker — to lead his Guilford County organization in his 1992 and 1996 campaigns. Then in 1998, Hunt and state Sen. Marc Basnight recruited Hagan to challenge a local Republican state senator.

Hagan told the News & Record she approached the party as early as 2005 about running for the U.S. Senate. But she demonstrated uncertainty about the campaign in 2007, at first saying in October she wouldn't run, then changing her mind a few weeks later. She won the Democratic primary with more than 60 percent of the vote. During the general election against Elizabeth Dole, Hagan was at first overlooked as a serious contender, but she blanketed the state with campaign appearances as the national Democratic Party did likewise on the airwaves with advertisements.

She criticized Dole for her vote against an expansion of the State Children's Health Insurance Program, which covers children from low-income families that don't qualify for Medicaid. She also emphasized her North Carolina roots, frequently jabbing Dole — wife of former Senate majority leader and 1996 GOP presidential nominee Bob Dole — for a life spent largely in Kansas and Washington, D.C. One ad by the Democratic Senatorial Campaign Committee featured two elderly men in rocking chairs, debating whether Dole was 93 or 92. The numbers referred to a ranking of her effectiveness among the 100 senators and the percent of votes in which she was loyal to President George W. Bush, respectively. But the ad also subtly mocked Dole's age; she was 72 at the time.

Hagan also benefitted from a strong national Democratic tide that helped Barack Obama edge out GOP nominee John McCain to carry North Carolina. Bush had easily won the state in 2000 and 2004.

Late in the campaign, as polls began to indicate a Hagan victory, Dole ran TV ads suggesting Hagan was an atheist. Hagan, a Sunday school teacher and elder at her church, fired back both in an ad, declaring "I believe in God," and a lawsuit, charging Dole with defamation. Hagan withdrew the lawsuit after her victory by 8 percentage points.

Rep. G.K. Butterfield (D)

Elected July 2004; 3rd full term

CAPITOL OFFICE
225-3101
www.house.gov/butterfield
413 Cannon Bldg. 20515-3301; fax 225-3354

COMMITTEES
Energy & Commerce
Standards of Official Conduct

RESIDENCE
Wilson

BORN
April 27, 1947; Wilson, N.C.

RELIGION
Baptist

FAMILY
Divorced; two children

EDUCATION
North Carolina Central U., B.A. 1971
(political science & sociology), J.D. 1974

MILITARY SERVICE
Army, 1968-70

CAREER
Lawyer; child care center owner

POLITICAL HIGHLIGHTS
Candidate for Wilson City Council, 1976;
N.C. Superior Court judge, 1989-2001; N.C.
Supreme Court, 2001-02; defeated for election
to N.C. Supreme Court, 2002; N.C. Superior Court
judge, 2003-04

ELECTION RESULTS

2008 GENERAL

G.K. Butterfield (D)	192,765	70.3%
Dean Stephens (R)	81,506	29.7%

2008 PRIMARY

G.K. Butterfield (D)	unopposed

2006 GENERAL

G.K. Butterfield (D)	unopposed

PREVIOUS WINNING PERCENTAGES
2004 (64%); 2004 Special Election (71%)

Representing one of the nation's poorest districts, Butterfield focuses on helping his constituents improve their lot in life. He wants a new war on poverty declared, but with a different emphasis from the 1960s version; he believes the Lyndon B. Johnson program relied too heavily on subsidies and giveaways. In his model, he said, "You train and retrain people, you provide jobs, you build infrastructure, you invest in education."

A descendant of slaves, Butterfield is a former state judge who maintains a relatively low profile on Capitol Hill. He doesn't speak up often in committee or at party meetings, preferring to operate quietly. "I can say in two minutes what some people say in 20. And I say it just as well," he said.

Party leaders have recognized his behind-the-scenes efforts. He secured a coveted seat on the Energy and Commerce Committee in the 110th Congress (2007-08). He was helped by the fact he sits on the leadership-run Steering and Policy Committee, which makes committee assignments. In another measure of his standing in his party, in 2007 he was named one of the nine chief deputy whips. Two years later, Speaker Nancy Pelosi put him on the House ethics panel. He also serves as secretary for the Congressional Black Caucus.

Butterfield is faithful to his party in casting votes, regularly keeping in mind those with low incomes. He strongly endorsed President Obama's $787 billion economic stimulus law, noting in January 2009 that five of his district's counties suffered from double-digit unemployment. In addition to extending and increasing unemployment benefits, he said, the measure would offset cuts in local law enforcement.

But the next month, he urged Obama — for whom he campaigned ardently in the presidential race — to protect working families from effects of legislation intended to curb greenhouse gas emissions. "When climate change legislation is enacted, poor people could be forced to bear a disproportionate share of the pain" through higher utility costs passed on to consumers, he said. "We have an obligation to avoid this." He proposed that 35 percent of the money collected from credits or taxes on carbon dioxide be used to pay the electricity bills of the poorest customers.

Although his district has a heavy concentration of tobacco farmers, Butterfield backed legislation in 2008 and 2009 to authorize the Food and Drug Administration to regulate tobacco. He praised it for protecting tobacco farmers. Butterfield also supported Democratic legislation to expand the State Children's Health Insurance Program — which covers children whose families don't qualify for Medicaid — even though its costs would be covered by a big increase in the federal cigarette tax.

He is an advocate of efforts to bring high-tech training and equipment to poor rural areas like his district. In 2008, the House passed his bill to require donation of surplus federal electronic equipment, including computers, fax machines and printers, to schools in such areas. But the measure didn't advance in the Senate.

As a member of the ethics panel, Butterfield was tasked with helping investigate the fundraising practices and personal finances of New York Democrat Charles B. Rangel, chairman of the Ways and Means Committee. Butterfield was one of three Democrats on the panel who had received contributions from political action committees Rangel controlled. Though some watchdog groups called on the lawmakers to return the money or recuse themselves, Butterfield's spokesman said the most recent contribution of $1,000 came before his boss joined the panel and that it would have no effect on his decision-making.

Butterfield grew up in Wilson. His great-grandfather was a white slave-holder who conceived a child with one of his slaves. The child, Butterfield's grandfather, was born in the final days of slavery and became a minister. Butterfield's mother was a schoolteacher. His father, George Kenneth Butterfield, for whom Butterfield is named, was a native of Bermuda who came to the United States at age 16. A decade later, he opened a dental office and practiced for 50 years.

His father became a civic leader, and the all-white political establishment granted him the right to vote as a "favor," said Butterfield. The elder Butterfield began encouraging other blacks to register to vote but stopped under pressure from white leaders. He resumed the effort after the Depression. When literacy tests were introduced to discourage blacks from voting, Butterfield's father began teaching people to read. He then ran for the city council, winning narrowly in 1953.

In 1957, while the family was vacationing in New York, town officials substituted at-large elections for ward-by-ward elections, which had allowed the elder Butterfield to win among a black-majority constituency. That eliminated the chance for any black candidate to succeed. "I saw how the political system was manipulated to obtain an unfair result," Butterfield said. "Having seen that injustice has made me want to be involved politically."

Those childhood events spurred Butterfield to study law. Ultimately, he got the last word in his father's long fight by handling several voting-rights lawsuits in eastern North Carolina counties, resulting in the court-ordered implementation of district elections for local officials.

On April 4, 1968, Butterfield was expecting to meet with the Rev. Martin Luther King Jr. at a voter registration rally in his hometown of Wilson. King was planning to visit North Carolina to help a friend's campaign. Instead, he went to Memphis to support striking sanitation workers and was assassinated.

Butterfield's first try for elective office was a losing city council bid in 1976. But he was elected a Superior Court judge in 1988 and held that job until Democratic Gov. Michael F. Easley elevated him to the state Supreme Court in 2001. After Butterfield lost a 2002 election for the seat in his own right, Easley reinstated him on the lower court.

In 2004, when Democratic Rep. Frank W. Ballance Jr. gave up his seat midterm due to illness, party officials tapped Butterfield to succeed him. He defeated Republican security consultant Greg Dority in the special election by 44 percentage points. In a repeat matchup for a full term that November, Butterfield won by 28 points. In 2006, he was unopposed; two years later he coasted with 70 percent of the vote.

KEY VOTES

2008
Yes Delay consideration of Colombia free-trade agreement
Yes Override Bush veto of federal farm and nutrition programs reauthorization bill
Yes Overhaul surveillance laws and permit dismissal of suits against companies that conducted warrantless wiretapping
Yes Grant mortgage relief to homeowners and funding for Fannie Mae and Freddie Mac
No Approve initial $700 billion program to stabilize financial markets
No Approve final $700 billion program to stabilize financial markets
No Provide $14 billion in loans to automakers

2007
Yes Increase minimum wage by $2.10 an hour
Yes Approve $124.2 billion in emergency war spending and set goal for redeployment of troops from Iraq
No Reject federal contraceptive assistance to international family planning groups
? Override Bush veto of $23.2 billion water projects authorization bill
Yes Implement Peru free-trade agreement
Yes Approve energy policy overhaul with new fuel economy standards
No Clear $473.5 billion omnibus spending bill, including $70 billion for military operations

CQ VOTE STUDIES

	PARTY UNITY		PRESIDENTIAL SUPPORT	
	SUPPORT	OPPOSE	SUPPORT	OPPOSE
2008	98%	2%	11%	89%
2007	97%	3%	5%	95%
2006	89%	11%	37%	63%
2005	93%	7%	30%	70%
2004	87%	13%	27%	73%

INTEREST GROUPS

	AFL-CIO	ADA	CCUS	ACU
2008	93%	100%	56%	12%
2007	100%	95%	58%	0%
2006	93%	95%	47%	16%
2005	93%	85%	56%	12%
2004	–	35%	57%	0%

NORTH CAROLINA 1

Northeast — part of Goldsboro, Rocky Mount and Greenville

Situated among eastern North Carolina tobacco fields and Baptist churches, the 1st is a poor, rural Democratic stronghold. It has the lowest education and income levels of any congressional district in the state.

The 1st, which takes in all of 13 counties and parts of 10 others, is the only black-majority district in the state — 50 percent of residents are black. The main body of the district sits along the Virginia border, with appendages winding south to take in parts of several of the region's manufacturing centers — Rocky Mount, Wilson and Greenville, which shares East Carolina University with the adjacent 3rd District. Cotton and peanut fields prevail in the northern counties, while tobacco, hogs and poultry dominate farther south. Manufacturers are scattered throughout the 1st, producing textiles, pharmaceuticals and machinery.

Nationwide economic downturns that forced the state's unemployment rate into double digits have also caused widespread job losses in the dis-trict's rural counties. Health care and local government jobs prop up areas in Pitt and Greene counties, but areas such as Rocky Mount that have less-diversified economies struggle as tobacco and cotton profits have fallen. Local officials in western counties hope to attract new jobs.

Registered Democrats outnumber Republicans by nearly 4-to-1 in the 1st, and Democrats generally dominate. However, unaffiliated white voters can support Republican candidates in coastal areas such as Perquimans and Chowan counties. Overall, the 1st gave Barack Obama his second-biggest win in the state with 63 percent of the vote.

MAJOR INDUSTRY
Agriculture, health care, manufacturing

MILITARY BASES
Marine Corps Air Station Cherry Point, 8,684 military, 4,743 civilian (2008); Seymour Johnson Air Force Base, 5,233 military, 533 civilian (2008)

CITIES
Goldsboro (pt.), 36,187; Rocky Mount (pt.), 32,062; Wilson (pt.), 25,068; Greenville (pt.), 22,028

NOTABLE
Caleb Bradham started selling "Brad's Drink" in 1898 at his New Bern drug store — the beverage is now known as Pepsi-Cola.

Rep. Bob Etheridge (D)

Elected 1996; 7th term

CAPITOL OFFICE
225-4531
www.house.gov/etheridge
1533 Longworth Bldg. 20515-3302; fax 225-5662

COMMITTEES
Budget
Ways & Means

RESIDENCE
Lillington

BORN
Aug. 7, 1941; Sampson County, N.C.

RELIGION
Presbyterian

FAMILY
Wife, Faye Cameron Etheridge; three children

EDUCATION
Campbell College, B.S. 1965 (business administration)

MILITARY SERVICE
Army, 1965-67

CAREER
Hardware store owner; tobacco farmer

POLITICAL HIGHLIGHTS
Harnett County Commission, 1973-77 (chairman, 1975-77); N.C. House, 1979-88; N.C. superintendent of Public Instruction, 1989-96

ELECTION RESULTS

2008 GENERAL

Bob Etheridge (D)	199,730	66.9%
Dan Mansell (R)	93,323	31.3%
Will Adkins (LIBERT)	5,377	1.8%

2008 PRIMARY

Bob Etheridge (D)	unopposed

2006 GENERAL

Bob Etheridge (D)	85,993	66.5%
Dan Mansell (R)	43,271	33.5%

PREVIOUS WINNING PERCENTAGES
2004 (62%); 2002 (65%); 2000 (58%); 1998 (57%); 1996 (53%)

Whether in Washington or in North Carolina, Etheridge's style is down-home and warm. A Presbyterian Sunday school teacher, he gets along with conservatives as well as some of the most liberal members of his own party as he carefully navigates the political center.

A member of the moderate, pro-business New Democrat Coalition, Etheridge has kept attuned to the strong Republican presence in his district while building an expertise on agriculture, energy and education. While he tends to follow Democratic leaders as he goes after funding to benefit his constituents, he also fiercely protects businesspeople back home, whether they be farmers or entrepreneurs. He will have to navigate just as carefully from his seats on the Ways and Means Committee and Budget committees as they address trade, tax and health care issues in a declining economic environment.

Etheridge stuck with his party to support President Obama's $787 billion economic stimulus bill — a measure which House Republicans united to oppose. He was pleased the package included tax-free school construction bonds, a priority of his since he came to Congress in 1997. He also supported both versions — the second of which became law — of a $700 billion plan in fall 2008 to shore up the financial services sector. But in early 2009, he voted for a House bill to reclaim employee bonuses paid out by American International Group Inc. which had received funding from the rescue law.

He worked hard back home in spring 2009 to explain to constituents his support of Obama's more than $3.56 trillion budget blueprint for fiscal 2010. He scheduled a dozen visits throughout his district to explain his belief that the budget's investments in education, health care reform and energy independence would further stimulate the economy, save money and still cut taxes. "As we come out of this downturn, we have got to get our financial house in order for the long haul, and this budget does that," Etheridge told the Rocky Mount Telegram.

Etheridge tends to side more with Republicans when it comes to trade issues. He voted in 2002 to give George W. Bush fast-track trade negotiating authority, which limits Congress' role in trade agreements. That angered the state's textile lobby, but Etheridge has been more concerned with attracting technology firms to the Raleigh area and satisfying his district's farmers. He backed pacts with Chile, Singapore, Australia, Oman and Peru. But he did vote against the Central America Free Trade Agreement in 2005.

When Etheridge won the seat on Ways and Means for the 111th Congress (2009-10), he was forced to relinquish his posts on the Agriculture and Homeland Security committees.

He has been attentive to farmers' needs; he is a part-time farmer himself, growing soybeans and grains, and one of his sons still farms in the district. His greatest pleasure on weekends, he has said, is to "get on the tractor. It takes me back." During election season, he is likely to spend more time swapping tales with residents about experiences with cows escaping from fenced farmland than handing out campaign buttons.

As chairman of the Agriculture commodities subcommittee during the 110th Congress (2007-08), he helped craft the 2008 farm law, ensuring it provides conservation payments for farmers who set aside part of their land as well as subsidies to producers of various commodities. North Carolina universities were pleased it calls for the creation of an institute to send money to agricultural researchers through competitive grants. Etheridge also tucked into the bill provisions to help textile mills modernize equipment.

Etheridge secured passage of separate legislation in 2008 to protect small farmers. That law, signed by Bush in the waning days of the session, suspended for a year rules put forward by the Agriculture Department requiring producers to farm at least 10 acres to receive program benefits.

Etheridge was a part-time tobacco farmer when Congress in 2004 enacted a buyout for tobacco farmers as part of a corporate tax cut bill. The deal meant $3.8 billion for farmers in his state, including him; he was one of eight members of Congress to benefit from the deal.

When the House voted to give the Food and Drug Administration (FDA) authority to regulate tobacco products in 2009, Etheridge supported a GOP alternative to put tobacco regulation not under the FDA, but in a new "tobacco harm reduction center" in the Department of Health and Human Services. That proposal failed. Etheridge voted for the final bill only after sponsor Henry A. Waxman of California assured him the bill wouldn't affect tobacco growers, only manufacturers of tobacco products.

He championed a bill in 2008 to curb skyrocketing energy prices. It sought to control excessive speculation in the futures market for specified commodities, including oil. It passed the House but didn't get through the Senate.

Before coming to Congress, he ran the state's public school system and has spoken at length of his desire to "build on what is working well in our public schools, rather than scapegoating public school principals, teachers, parents and children." He supported the No Child Left Behind Act, signed into law in 2002, but said its mandatory testing and standards shouldn't be enforced until the federal government provides all the funds authorized.

As a member of the Homeland Security Committee from its creation in 2003 through 2008, he touts the 2006 implementation of his bill granting federal survivor benefits to the families of firefighters, police and emergency personnel who die in the line of duty from heart attacks or strokes. He credits one of his constituents for inspiring the law.

Born, raised and educated in east-central North Carolina, Etheridge spent his childhood on the family farm. When he went off to nearby Campbell College (now a university), he spent most of his time on the basketball court. He got a full basketball scholarship and became team captain.

Etheridge entered politics in 1972, winning election to the Harnett County Commission, and by 1978 was elected to the state House, where he rose to chair the Appropriations Committee. After four terms, he served as state school superintendent for about eight years. In 1996, he took on Republican U.S. Rep. David Funderburk and won with 53 percent of the vote. Etheridge's share of the vote has exceeded 60 percent in the last four elections.

KEY VOTES

2008
Yes   Delay consideration of Colombia free-trade agreement
Yes   Override Bush veto of federal farm and nutrition programs reauthorization bill
Yes   Overhaul surveillance laws and permit dismissal of suits against companies that conducted warrantless wiretapping
Yes   Grant mortgage relief to homeowners and funding for Fannie Mae and Freddie Mac
Yes   Approve initial $700 billion program to stabilize financial markets
Yes   Approve final $700 billion program to stabilize financial markets
Yes   Provide $14 billion in loans to automakers

2007
Yes   Increase minimum wage by $2.10 an hour
Yes   Approve $124.2 billion in emergency war spending and set goal for redeployment of troops from Iraq
No   Reject federal contraceptive assistance to international family planning groups
Yes   Override Bush veto of $23.2 billion water projects authorization bill
Yes   Implement Peru free-trade agreement
Yes   Approve energy policy overhaul with new fuel economy standards
Yes   Clear $473.5 billion omnibus spending bill, including $70 billion for military operations

CQ VOTE STUDIES

	PARTY UNITY		PRESIDENTIAL SUPPORT	
	SUPPORT	OPPOSE	SUPPORT	OPPOSE
2008	98%	2%	20%	80%
2007	95%	5%	13%	87%
2006	84%	16%	50%	50%
2005	88%	12%	24%	76%
2004	85%	15%	47%	53%

INTEREST GROUPS

	AFL-CIO	ADA	CCUS	ACU
2008	100%	85%	67%	0%
2007	92%	90%	65%	8%
2006	93%	80%	60%	44%
2005	100%	95%	52%	16%
2004	87%	85%	52%	20%

NORTH CAROLINA 2
Central — parts of Raleigh and Fayetteville

From the state capital of Raleigh, the 2nd pinwheels east, north and south to take in several surrounding rural counties and part of Fayetteville. While the high-tech Research Triangle Park, the area's economic hub, lies in the neighboring 4th, its influence radiates through the low hills of this eastern Piedmont district and largely has insulated the district from recent statewide and national economic downturns.

Research Triangle techies, university academics and government employees live in Raleigh (shared with the 4th and 13th districts) and form the basis of the district's Democratic tilt. Much of the region consists of growing and increasingly urban bedroom communities such as Garner. Sprawl has begun to infiltrate surrounding counties as well, but they still rely primarily on tobacco farming (especially in Johnston and Harnett counties) and blue-collar manufacturing jobs.

The district's strong military presence is centered around Pope Air Force Base and part of Fort Bragg (shared with the 7th and 8th) at the southwestern edge of the district. The 2005 BRAC round realignment of

Pope into an Army airfield, to be completed by 2011, is under way, and growth at Fort Bragg will accommodate thousands of new personnel.

A 20-percentage-point voter registration advantage exaggerates the Democratic Party's strength across the 2nd. Federal and statewide Republican candidates run well in areas such as Johnston and Harnett despite a Democratic registration edge in the counties. The district's Democratic lean is aided by the presence of a black-majority section of Fayetteville, and the district also contains the mostly black and strongly Democratic southeastern part of Raleigh. Democrat Barack Obama won the 2nd with 52 percent of the district's 2008 presidential vote.

MAJOR INDUSTRY
Technology, government, military, agriculture, manufacturing

MILITARY BASES
Fort Bragg (Army), 45,650 military, 5,941 civilian (2008) (shared with the 7th and 8th); Pope Air Force Base, 5,152 military, 512 civilian (2007)

CITIES
Fayetteville (pt.), 49,899; Raleigh (pt.), 45,368; Fort Bragg (unincorporated), 29,183; Sanford, 23,220

NOTABLE
A sign — made of brick — near Sanford names it the U.S. brick capital.

Rep. Walter B. Jones (R)

Elected 1994; 8th term

CAPITOL OFFICE
225-3415
jones.house.gov
2333 Rayburn Bldg. 20515-3303; fax 225-3286

COMMITTEES
Armed Services
Financial Services

RESIDENCE
Farmville

BORN
Feb. 10, 1943; Farmville, N.C.

RELIGION
Roman Catholic

FAMILY
Wife, Joe Anne Jones; one child

EDUCATION
North Carolina State U., attended 1962-65 (history);
Atlantic Christian College, B.A. 1968 (history)

MILITARY SERVICE
N.C. National Guard, 1967-71

CAREER
Lighting company executive; insurance benefits
company executive; office supply company
executive

POLITICAL HIGHLIGHTS
N.C. House, 1983-92 (served as a Democrat);
sought Democratic nomination for U.S. House,
1992

ELECTION RESULTS

2008 GENERAL

Walter B. Jones (R)	201,686	65.9%
Craig Weber (D)	104,364	34.1%

2008 PRIMARY

Walter B. Jones (R)	23,699	59.0%
Joe McLaughlin (R)	16,491	41.0%

2006 GENERAL

Walter B. Jones (R)	99,519	68.6%
Craig Weber (D)	45,458	31.4%

PREVIOUS WINNING PERCENTAGES
2004 (71%); 2002 (91%); 2000 (61%); 1998 (62%);
1996 (63%); 1994 (53%)

Jones is a Southern gentleman who says his decisions as a member of Congress are driven by his perception of God's will. His faith and strength of purpose often cause him to travel a separate, and sometimes lonely, road from the rest of his party. "My heart dictates my thinking many, many times," he said.

His voting record defies simple characterization. A former Democrat, he is fiercely conservative on social and fiscal matters and quit the Republican Study Committee — the caucus of the House's most conservative members — in 2006 after its leader at the time announced a compromise position on illegal immigration, an issue of which he takes an unyielding hard line. But he became one of the GOP's most passionate critics of the Iraq War after initially supporting it.

Jones serves on the Financial Services Committee, where he criticized government intervention to help the struggling banking and automobile industries. He joined fellow conservative Todd Tiahrt of Kansas in sponsoring a March 2009 resolution opposing any taxpayer-funded relief. "Instead of driving economic growth, these bailouts have done nothing but fuel public anger over how these institutions are spending the taxpayers' money," he said. That month, he was among just 10 Republicans who supported a Democratic bill to limit bonus payments to employees of companies receiving federal assistance.

Jones also joined Minnesota Republican Michele Bachmann in sponsoring a resolution to prohibit the Obama administration from doing away with the dollar in favor of a multinational currency. Bachmann and other conservative activists charged that Treasury Secretary Timothy F. Geithner was open to considering the idea, but news media outlets and Democratic bloggers subsequently dismissed it as a distortion of Geithner's comments.

Jones does support a voluntary public-financing system for political campaigns. He cosponsored Democratic legislation in 2009 to provide federal grants to candidates who agreed to accept no more than $100 per contributor for each election and meet certain fundraising targets. That would relieve candidates of the need to raise millions of dollars for the typical Senate race and hundreds of thousands of dollars for a House race, advocates said.

As a member of the Armed Services Committee, Jones takes an avid interest in the Marine Corps. His district is home to Camp Lejeune, the Marines' East Coast headquarters, and he introduced a bill in January 2009 to officially rename the Department of the Navy the "Department of the Navy and Marine Corps" in recognition of their longtime operation as a single entity.

Jones voted in 2002 to authorize President George W. Bush to use force in Iraq. In fact, it was Jones who popularized the term "freedom fries" as a replacement for French fries in the House cafeteria, a protest of France's lack of support for the war. His support for the president's war policy was upended in 2005, however, when Jones had a spiritual awakening at the funeral of a young Marine named Michael Bitz. After that, he decided the war was wrong. Jones was one of 24 Republicans voting in June 2008 to send to the Judiciary Committee a privileged resolution by Ohio Democrat Dennis J. Kucinich to bring impeachment articles against Bush for "high crimes and misdemeanors."

For Jones, the war is personal. His office writes every family that has lost someone in Iraq or Afghanistan, sending off more than 8,150 letters as of mid-March 2009. His office is filled with photos, letters and military paraphernalia from the casualties' families. But he says he cannot read their letters, because he becomes too emotional. He intends to write a book about the letters because, he says, "God wants me to."

When President Obama announced plans early in his administration to move troops out of Iraq and add forces in Afghanistan, Jones called for Obama to reconsider. He pointed to the Soviet Union's earlier failure in Afghanistan and the United States' pressing economic problems. "Let us know what we're going to do before we begin this escalation, because it will be too late if we're talking about this one year from now," he said in March 2009.

His opposition to the Iraq War has come with a political price back home. It met with hostility from Marines stationed at Camp Lejeune. When Bush made a public appearance in Fayetteville, not far from Jones' district, Jones was not invited to share the stage with the president. Some local Republicans also disapproved: In 2006, Jones headed off the prospect of a primary challenge from some of them by holding town hall meetings at which he explained his position. He won that election with nearly 70 percent of the vote. In 2008, however, he was challenged in the GOP primary for the first time since his 1994 election. But Jones fended off his challenger, Joe McLaughlin, by netting 59 percent of the vote.

Outside of his votes on the war and social issues, Jones's voting record is an ideological hodgepodge. He was one of 27 Republicans to vote against the Central America Free Trade Agreement in 2005, a sensitive issue in his textile-producing state. And he usually joins Democrats in voting against offshore oil and gas drilling when state officials oppose it. He seeks to protect the Outer Banks beaches in his district, an important tourist area.

Jones grew up around politics and government. His father was Democratic Rep. Walter B. Jones Sr., a pragmatist who was a bit more liberal than his son. Jones attended Virginia's Hargrave Military Academy, which emphasized Christian values; he became a standout basketball player there. He graduated from Atlantic Christian College in 1968, did a stint in the National Guard and then took a job as a wine broker with a region covering North Carolina and Virginia. Raised a Baptist, he converted to Catholicism when he was 29.

Jones was almost 40 when he followed his father into politics. In 1982, the local Democratic Party asked him to finish the term of a state assemblyman who had died in office. Jones wound up staying for a decade.

In 1992, the senior Jones fell ill and retired from the House. Jones ran for his father's 1st District seat as a Democrat, but lost a primary runoff. The next year, he registered as a Republican, feeling he had more in common with the GOP philosophically, including his opposition to abortion. He ran in the 3rd District in 1994, and was swept into office by the strong GOP tide that year.

KEY VOTES

2008

Yes   Delay consideration of Colombia free-trade agreement

Yes   Override Bush veto of federal farm and nutrition programs reauthorization bill

?   Overhaul surveillance laws and permit dismissal of suits against companies that conducted warrantless wiretapping

No   Grant mortgage relief to homeowners and funding for Fannie Mae and Freddie Mac

No   Approve initial $700 billion program to stabilize financial markets

No   Approve final $700 billion program to stabilize financial markets

No   Provide $14 billion in loans to automakers

2007

Yes   Increase minimum wage by $2.10 an hour

Yes   Approve $124.2 billion in emergency war spending and set goal for redeployment of troops from Iraq

Yes   Reject federal contraceptive assistance to international family planning groups

Yes   Override Bush veto of $23.2 billion water projects authorization bill

No   Implement Peru free-trade agreement

Yes   Approve energy policy overhaul with new fuel economy standards

Yes   Clear $473.5 billion omnibus spending bill, including $70 billion for military operations

CQ VOTE STUDIES

	PARTY UNITY		PRESIDENTIAL SUPPORT	
	SUPPORT	OPPOSE	SUPPORT	OPPOSE
2008	77%	23%	37%	63%
2007	71%	29%	43%	57%
2006	64%	36%	53%	47%
2005	81%	19%	61%	39%
2004	86%	14%	75%	25%

INTEREST GROUPS

	AFL-CIO	ADA	CCUS	ACU
2008	53%	50%	59%	58%
2007	26%	50%	79%	71%
2006	62%	45%	50%	79%
2005	17%	45%	58%	80%
2004	36%	30%	70%	79%

NORTH CAROLINA 3

East – Jacksonville, part of Greenville, Outer Banks

The 3rd runs along the eastern shore from the Virginia border to north of Wilmington, sweeping from the fragile barrier islands of the Outer Banks to the tobacco and peanut fields of the coastal plain. It is a large swath of rural land inlaid with waterways, affluent vacation towns and military facilities; the closest thing to skyscrapers here are historic lighthouses that dot the shoreline.

Many residents earn their living through fishing, farming and tourism. The 3rd's military bases have a large impact on the economy, particularly the expansive Camp Lejeune, which contributes roughly $3 billion annually. From the southernmost coast, two fingers of land reach northwest, taking in turkey, hog and wheat farms.

The western leg of the 3rd stretches from Onslow County in the south, where Jacksonville and Camp Lejeune are located, all the way north to Nash County, including western Rocky Mount. Another leg stretches

northwest to Greenville in Pitt County. Prolonged economic downturns in manufacturing and agricultural production have hurt these areas, but local leaders hope the presence of Greenville's East Carolina University (shared with the 1st) will bolster the economy.

Although registered Democrats outnumber Republicans here by more than 7 percentage points, the 3rd has a conservative bent and supports GOP candidates on the federal level. John McCain took 61 percent of the 2008 presidential vote.

MAJOR INDUSTRY
Military, agriculture, tourism

MILITARY BASES
Camp Lejeune Marine Corps Base, 38,798 military, 1,019 civilian (2007); New River Marine Corps Air Station, 6,646 military, 162 civilian (2009)

CITIES
Jacksonville, 66,715; Greenville (pt.), 38,448; Wilson (pt.), 19,337

NOTABLE
Dare County is named for Virginia Dare, the first child born of English parents in America (1587); Kitty Hawk is where Wilbur and Orville Wright made their first flight; The infamous pirate Edward Teach, better known as Blackbeard, lived in Hammock House in Beaufort.

Rep. David E. Price (D)

Elected 1986; 11th term
Did not serve 1995–97

A former political science professor, Price likes to analyze, assess and reassess the funding that comes under his purview as chairman of the Homeland Security Appropriations Subcommittee. He displays a strong commitment to education and science — important to his district encompassing North Carolina's Research Triangle — and a thoughtful approach to determining how to combat terrorism. His appreciation for the complexities of legislation and the political process earns respect from colleagues on both sides of the aisle.

He is as careful in his examination of all measures, pursuing a centrist course on politically charged home-state issues such as tobacco regulation. But he generally votes with the majority of his party; he consistently backs abortion rights and environmental protection measures and was a vocal opponent of President George W. Bush's 2001 tax cut. He supported both versions of the $700 billion measure — the second of which became law — in fall 2008 to assist the ailing financial services industry, as well as President Obama's $787 billion economic stimulus law in February 2009. He is an advocate of free trade, but was skeptical of the deals negotiated by the Bush administration, only supporting the Peru free-trade agreement in 2007 because it included labor and environmental standards.

The soft-spoken Price said in 2008 that overseeing homeland security funding was not what he envisioned when he first arrived in Congress more than two decades ago. He gained a seat on Appropriations during his third term and largely focused on education and science. He landed a seat on the Homeland Security Subcommittee after the formation of the Homeland Security Department in 2003. Minnesota Democrat Martin Olav Sabo's retirement and the Democratic takeover of Congress in 2006 propelled him to the panel's top slot.

When he picked up the subcommittee gavel in 2007, Price quickly sought a broad assessment of the state of the five-year-old department. He held two multiday hearings and brought in experts from the Sept. 11 commission, Rand Corp., the Government Accountability Office and the DHS's inspector general. Price sought their guidance on how to think about the long term, rather than focus on one-year chunks of time, as appropriators tend to do.

Price then sought to improve border security by providing funding for additional border patrol officers and to improve the Federal Emergency Management Agency's responsiveness and reassess the way in which grants are made to state and local responders. As drug-cartel related violence raged along the border of Mexico into 2009, he questioned how various agencies worked together on the gunrunning issue when their jurisdictions cross. He requested that the Homeland Security Department provide data on the scope of the gun smuggling issue, including the types of weapons being trafficked, along with lists of relevant agencies, laws and regulations involved with enforcement.

During much of 2008, Price shepherded through the House a $41.1 billion spending bill that included his provision requiring enhanced privacy and civil liberties standards as a prerequisite for funding intelligence-gathering projects. The bill also aimed to promote accountability by freezing funding on numerous department programs until cost-benefit analyses have been conducted. Republicans objected, arguing it would hold up funding needed to build the 2,000-mile border fence between the United States and Mexico that was approved in 2006. But he was able to shepherd the bill into law — one of the few to provide full-year funding for its agency at a time when many other spending bills were folded into a short-term continuing resolution. It included $4.2 billion — nearly double Bush's request — for state and local grants that

CAPITOL OFFICE
225-1784
price.house.gov
2162 Rayburn Bldg. 20515-3304; fax 225-2014

COMMITTEES
Appropriations
  (Homeland Security - chairman)

RESIDENCE
Chapel Hill

BORN
Aug. 17, 1940; Erwin, Tenn.

RELIGION
Baptist

FAMILY
Wife, Lisa Price; two children

EDUCATION
Mars Hill College, attended 1957-59; U. of North Carolina, B.A. 1961 (American history & math); Yale U., B.D. 1964 (theology), Ph.D. 1969 (political science)

CAREER
Professor

POLITICAL HIGHLIGHTS
N.C. Democratic Party chairman, 1983-84; U.S. House, 1987-95; defeated for re-election to U.S. House, 1994

ELECTION RESULTS

2008 GENERAL
David E. Price (D)	265,751	63.3%
William "B.J." Lawson (R)	153,947	36.7%

2008 PRIMARY
David E. Price (D)	unopposed

2006 GENERAL
David E. Price (D)	127,340	65.0%
Steve Acuff (R)	68,599	35.0%

PREVIOUS WINNING PERCENTAGES
2004 (64%); 2002 (61%); 2000 (62%); 1998 (57%); 1996 (54%); 1992 (65%); 1990 (58%); 1988 (58%); 1986 (56%)

help governments prepare for and respond to terrorist attacks.

For many years, Price has used his Appropriations seat to tend to the needs of his district, which has several private research and technology companies, as well as 11 colleges and universities. He has snagged tens of millions of dollars annually for many of the research centers. In fiscal 2009 spending bills, he helped obtain about $82 million worth of earmarks — funding set-asides for special projects — including $208,000 for a beaver management program, which quickly became fodder for Arizona Republican Sen. John McCain's attack on earmarks. State officials said the program to trap the creatures and destroy their dams helps save millions of dollars in potential flood damage. "Maybe you should ask him how much he knows about this and why he picked it out for ridicule," Price told The News and Observer in Raleigh. "We know why he chose this — because it sounds funny."

In 1993, Price's bill was enacted to create the Advanced Technology Education Program to provide technical education and training programs for community college students via the National Science Foundation. Congress passed his 1997 bill making interest on student loans tax deductible and permitting penalty-free withdrawals from IRA accounts for education expenses. He has tried to push through Congress legislation that would provide college scholarships to students who agree to become public school teachers.

Price was born and raised in the town of Erwin in eastern Tennessee. His father was the local high school principal, while his mother was an English teacher. He earned an undergraduate degree from the University of North Carolina, then went to Yale University for graduate study, earning political science and divinity degrees. As a political science professor in the 1970s, he became heavily involved in state Democratic politics. He served as chairman of the state party in 1983 and 1984, and in 1985 he was a founding member of the national Democratic Leadership Council.

The contacts Price made in his party work helped him raise money and attract supporters for a successful House race in 1986. He beat out three opponents for the Democratic nomination, then ousted freshman GOP Rep. Bill Cobey Jr. by 12 percentage points. He won re-election three times by comfortable margins but lost to former Raleigh Police Chief Fred Heineman by 1,215 votes in the GOP landslide of 1994.

Price avenged that defeat in 1996, waging an aggressive campaign that emphasized door-to-door canvassing. He won by almost 11 percentage points and has prevailed easily in subsequent elections. In a district made more comfortably Democratic after the last reapportionment, Price has not dipped below 60 percent in the past five elections, winning 63 percent in 2008.

KEY VOTES

2008
Yes Delay consideration of Colombia free-trade agreement
Yes Override Bush veto of federal farm and nutrition programs reauthorization bill
No   Overhaul surveillance laws and permit dismissal of suits against companies that conducted warrantless wiretapping
Yes Grant mortgage relief to homeowners and funding for Fannie Mae and Freddie Mac
Yes Approve initial $700 billion program to stabilize financial markets
Yes Approve final $700 billion program to stabilize financial markets
Yes Provide $14 billion in loans to automakers

2007
Yes Increase minimum wage by $2.10 an hour
Yes Approve $124.2 billion in emergency war spending and set goal for redeployment of troops from Iraq
No   Reject federal contraceptive assistance to international family planning groups
Yes Override Bush veto of $23.2 billion water projects authorization bill
Yes Implement Peru free-trade agreement
Yes Approve energy policy overhaul with new fuel economy standards
No   Clear $473.5 billion omnibus spending bill, including $70 billion for military operations

CQ VOTE STUDIES

	PARTY UNITY		PRESIDENTIAL SUPPORT	
	SUPPORT	OPPOSE	SUPPORT	OPPOSE
2008	99%	1%	14%	86%
2007	99%	1%	4%	96%
2006	92%	8%	33%	67%
2005	96%	4%	16%	84%
2004	90%	10%	41%	59%

INTEREST GROUPS

	AFL-CIO	ADA	CCUS	ACU
2008	100%	100%	61%	0%
2007	100%	95%	55%	0%
2006	100%	95%	47%	4%
2005	93%	100%	48%	4%
2004	87%	95%	52%	12%

NORTH CAROLINA 4
Central — Durham, Chapel Hill, part of Raleigh

The 4th revolves around Research Triangle Park and the three major universities at the vertices of the triangle. The medical and technological research park was created in the 1950s by a group of academics, politicians and businessmen who saw a need to diversify the state's economy beyond the traditional tobacco and textile industries. While based primarily in the Triangle, the 4th also passes through the rolling hills and evergreen forests of the Piedmont region.

Duke University in Durham represents the northern point of the triangle, while the University of North Carolina at Chapel Hill takes up the western point and North Carolina State University in Raleigh (shared with the 2nd and 13th districts) is the southeastern point. A strong university and research presence gives the 4th the state's highest education rate, with nearly half of the residents age 25 and older holding a college degree.

As the Research Triangle grew, especially in the 1980s, the Durham of James B. Duke's Lucky Strike cigarettes largely disappeared, and developers began converting tobacco warehouses into apartment buildings.

The region's educational and technological strengths have helped the Raleigh-Durham area land on the Forbes list of the 10 best places for business and careers for six years in a row. While the 4th has not been immune to national economic downturns and several major employers have cut jobs, its diversified economy creates stability in the region.

The 4th is a Democratic stronghold, with the party drawing support not only from the large black population in Durham but also from the liberal atmosphere surrounding the university in Chapel Hill. A Democrat has held the district's U.S. House seat for all but four years since 1969, but the area's highly educated voters — one in five holds a postgraduate or professional degree — can be independent-minded. Durham County gave Democrat Barack Obama his highest percentage of any county statewide (76 percent), and he took the district with 62 percent overall.

MAJOR INDUSTRY
Technology research, higher education

CITIES
Durham, 187,035; Cary (pt.), 83,478; Chapel Hill, 48,715; Raleigh (pt.), 38,149

NOTABLE
Universities in the 4th have won eight of the last 28 NCAA Division I men's basketball championships.

Rep. Virginia Foxx (R)

Elected 2004; 3rd term

CAPITOL OFFICE
225-2071
www.foxx.house.gov
1230 Longworth Bldg. 20515-3305; fax 225-2995

COMMITTEES
Rules

RESIDENCE
Watauga County

BORN
June 29, 1943; Bronx, N.Y.

RELIGION
Roman Catholic

FAMILY
Husband, Tom Foxx; one child

EDUCATION
Lees-McRae College, attended 1961;
Appalachian State Teachers' College, attended
1962-63; U. of North Carolina, B.A. 1968 (English),
M.A.C.T. 1972 (sociology); U. of North Carolina,
Greensboro, Ed.D. 1985 (curriculum and
teaching/higher education)

CAREER
Community college president; nursery and
landscaping company owner; state government
official; professor; secretary

POLITICAL HIGHLIGHTS
Candidate for Watauga County Board of
Education, 1974; Watauga County Board of
Education, 1977-89; N.C. Senate, 1995-2004

ELECTION RESULTS

2008 GENERAL

Virginia Foxx (R)	190,820	58.4%
Roy Carter (D)	136,103	41.6%

2008 PRIMARY

Virginia Foxx (R)	unopposed

2006 GENERAL

Virginia Foxx (R)	96,138	57.2%
Roger Sharpe (D)	72,061	42.8%

PREVIOUS WINNING PERCENTAGES
2004 (59%)

Foxx is a do-it-yourself person. In an era of image-conscious politicians surrounded by consultants and fundraisers, she writes her own letters, makes her own phone calls and chooses her own path. She wants to know what her constituents think, but she makes up her own mind.

A former college administrator and state legislator, she got where she is by unrelenting hard work to overcome a hardscrabble upbringing in the mountain hollows of Western North Carolina. She grew up in a house that didn't have running water or electricity until she was 14 years old. "I'm the eldest child of a very poor family, and I take everything I do seriously," she said.

Foxx has compiled a staunchly conservative record, touting her 100 percent approval rating from the American Conservative Union in 2007 and 2008 and her inclusion on its "Best and Brightest" list of 61 members in August 2008. Although typically a party loyalist ("I see myself as a team player," she said), she can go her own way at times.

Foxx stuck out like a sore thumb in 2005 when she opposed a popular bill funding the emergency spending needed after Hurricane Katrina, one of just 11 House members to do so. She also was one of 27 Republicans to vote against the Central America Free Trade Agreement, a major George W. Bush administration priority that passed the House by just two votes in 2005.

While GOP leaders dragooned a number of Republicans from states hardhit by manufacturing job losses into voting for CAFTA, Foxx was immovable. She told Bush in person she was not going to vote for the bill, and she held fast despite calls from Vice President Dick Cheney, Secretary of State Condoleezza Rice and U.S. Trade Representative Rob Portman during the debate. "I made a promise during the campaign," Foxx said. "It was pivotal in terms of testing whether or not I would do what I promised."

In 2007, Hanesbrands Inc. announced the closing of its fabrics plant in Winston-Salem as it pursued lower-cost production in the Caribbean and Central America. Foxx told constituents that was why she voted against CAFTA.

While serving on the Agriculture Committee in the 110th Congress (2007-08), she voted against the five-year law reauthorizing farm and nutrition programs enacted in 2008 over Bush's veto. Foxx also served on the House-Senate conference committee in 2008 that drafted the final version of the first complete overhaul of the Higher Education Act in a decade. She was the only House member to vote against the bill in the conference committee, and she did so again on the floor, one of just 49 members (all Republicans) to oppose the popular measure.

House Republicans put her on the Rules Committee in 2009, a job that indulges her penchant for attacking the Democratic majority in speeches. Foxx often targets the newly elected Democratic freshmen on the House floor as part of a Republican effort to catch them off guard and make them appear flustered.

Shortly after joining the panel, she sponsored a resolution of disapproval designed to block release of the second half of the $700 billion fund set up in late 2008 to rescue ailing financial firms. Though the House approved the bill, it had no substantive effect because the Senate rejected a similar resolution. "What is particularly troublesome is that President Obama was elected on the promise of bringing change, but another $350 billion is not change," she said.

She also could not stop legislation intended to help victims of wage discrimination file lawsuits, a bill that became the first Obama signed into law.

Foxx objected to Democrats' decision not to allow any amendments and said the bill would invite a wave of lawsuits. "The majority is very happy to discriminate against us," she said, "while they lead the charge against discrimination of other people."

She generated some controversy in April 2009 when she blasted Democrats for their plan to ban bonuses for executives of corporations that took financial rescue money. She said, "I thought about just a common-sense way to describe this to people: The Democrats have a tar baby on their hands and they simply can't get away from it." Democrats called her comments racially insensitive.

First elected to the House at age 61, she was one of the oldest members of the freshman class of 2004. She quickly drew on her decade in the North Carolina Legislature as she maneuvered her way through Congress. She was the first freshman to get a bill passed by the House in 2005, a measure allowing military personnel to put their combat pay into tax-deferred Individual Retirement Accounts. Colleagues warned Foxx that as a new member, she would never get her bill through unscathed. She proved them wrong; Bush signed her bill into law in 2006.

She grew up poor as the granddaughter of Italian immigrants. In her teens, she was the janitor at her high school as part of an after-school job. As she was sweeping floors one day, a teacher told her she was smart and needed to go to college, marry a college man and get out of town.

She did all three. She earned her bachelor's and advanced degrees from the University of North Carolina. A small-town girl, she briefly tried New York City in the mid-1960s, where she worked as a typist on Wall Street. But she returned to the mountains of North Carolina and married Tom Foxx, who came from similarly humble beginnings. (He lived out of a school bus his final years in high school.) They settled in Watauga County and started a successful nursery and landscaping business.

She says her husband influenced her political views. She became a strong backer of the Republican Party, even though her parents were Democrats.

She got her start in politics during a dozen years on the Watauga County Board of Education and then served for a decade in the state Senate. When 5th District Republican Rep. Richard M. Burr decided to run for the Senate in 2004, Foxx prevailed over seven other Republicans in the primary and went on to best Democrat Jim A. Harrell Jr. in November.

In 2006, she was unopposed in the primary and prevailed against Democrat Roger Sharpe, taking 57 percent of the vote. Two years later, she improved slightly on that showing in winning re-election.

KEY VOTES

2008
No   Delay consideration of Colombia free-trade agreement
No   Override Bush veto of federal farm and nutrition programs reauthorization bill
Yes   Overhaul surveillance laws and permit dismissal of suits against companies that conducted warrantless wiretapping
No   Grant mortgage relief to homeowners and funding for Fannie Mae and Freddie Mac
No   Approve initial $700 billion program to stabilize financial markets
No   Approve final $700 billion program to stabilize financial markets
No   Provide $14 billion in loans to automakers

2007
No   Increase minimum wage by $2.10 an hour
No   Approve $124.2 billion in emergency war spending and set goal for redeployment of troops from Iraq
Yes   Reject federal contraceptive assistance to international family planning groups
No   Override Bush veto of $23.2 billion water projects authorization bill
Yes   Implement Peru free-trade agreement
No   Approve energy policy overhaul with new fuel economy standards
Yes   Clear $473.5 billion omnibus spending bill, including $70 billion for military operations

CQ VOTE STUDIES

	PARTY UNITY		PRESIDENTIAL SUPPORT	
	SUPPORT	OPPOSE	SUPPORT	OPPOSE
2008	97%	3%	84%	16%
2007	98%	2%	91%	9%
2006	97%	3%	83%	17%
2005	99%	1%	87%	13%

INTEREST GROUPS

	AFL-CIO	ADA	CCUS	ACU
2008	7%	5%	78%	100%
2007	4%	0%	70%	100%
2006	14%	5%	93%	96%
2005	20%	5%	78%	100%

NORTH CAROLINA 5
Northwest — part of Winston-Salem

This northern Piedmont district stretches west from Winston-Salem through rolling hills and rural towns to the Tennessee border. Its northern counties, which run along the Virginia border, are filled with small rural towns such as Mount Airy, the childhood home of Andy Griffith and the inspiration for the fictional setting of his 1960s television series.

The district's major population center is in Winston-Salem and surrounding Forsyth County, home to R.J. Reynolds Tobacco. The company's corporate headquarters is in the 12th District (which has most of Winston-Salem), but its largest plant is in the 5th, in the aptly named town of Tobaccoville. Forsyth's economy has veered away from tobacco and textiles. Tobacco production is still important, but it now ranks second to health care, partly because of Wake Forest University's medical center.

With the decline of the tobacco industry, many tobacco producers have converted their farms into vineyards and wineries. The Yadkin Valley wine region, most of which is in the district, has become a tourist destination. The 5th also hosts the Krispy Kreme Doughnuts headquarters, a

BB&T division headquarters and a Tyson Foods division, Wilkes County's largest employer. Despite a decade of job growth, the 5th has shared in statewide economic downturns — Winston-Salem's unemployment rate hit double digits in early 2009. Layoffs by key employers, such as a Dell manufacturing site, concern local officials and residents.

Textile and blue-collar work still prevail in other counties, and grazing cattle wander over Surry County's low, rolling hills. The solidly GOP 5th is the state's most rural district, and the party dominates Davie and Yadkin counties, west of Winston-Salem. John McCain took his highest percentage statewide in Yadkin in the 2008 presidential election. The 5th's share of the largely Democratic Forsyth County leans Republican, as most of Winston-Salem's sizable black population is in the 12th.

MAJOR INDUSTRY
Health care, tobacco, agriculture, textiles

CITIES
Winston-Salem (pt.), 69,790; Statesville (pt.), 23,280; Kernersville, 17,126

NOTABLE
First organized in 1924, Union Grove's Old Time Fiddlers' Convention (now called the Ole Time Fiddler's and Bluegrass Festival) is the nation's longest-running bluegrass festival.

Rep. Howard Coble (R)

Elected 1984; 13th term

CAPITOL OFFICE
225-3065
coble.house.gov
2468 Rayburn Bldg. 20515-3306; fax 225-8611

COMMITTEES
Judiciary
Transportation & Infrastructure

RESIDENCE
Greensboro

BORN
March 18, 1931; Greensboro, N.C.

RELIGION
Presbyterian

FAMILY
Single

EDUCATION
Appalachian State Teachers' College, attended 1949-50 (history); Guilford College, A.B. 1958 (history); U. of North Carolina, J.D. 1962

MILITARY SERVICE
Coast Guard, 1952-56; Coast Guard Reserve, 1960-82; Coast Guard, 1977-78

CAREER
Lawyer; insurance claims supervisor

POLITICAL HIGHLIGHTS
N.C. House, 1969-70; assistant U.S. attorney, 1969-73; N.C. Department of Revenue secretary, 1973-77; Republican nominee for N.C. treasurer, 1976; N.C. House, 1979-84

ELECTION RESULTS

2008 GENERAL

Howard Coble (R)	221,018	67.0%
Teresa Sue Bratton (D)	108,873	33.0%

2008 PRIMARY

Howard Coble (R)	unopposed

2006 GENERAL

Howard Coble (R)	108,433	70.8%
Rory Blake (D)	44,661	29.2%

PREVIOUS WINNING PERCENTAGES
2004 (73%); 2002 (90%); 2000 (91%); 1998 (89%); 1996 (73%); 1994 (100%); 1992 (71%); 1990 (67%); 1988 (62%); 1986 (50%); 1984 (51%)

Coble is a plain-spoken former prosecutor whose fierce independent streak often puts him at odds with Republican leaders on economic policy and certain social policy issues such as stem cell research. It has even cost him the ranking slot on the Judiciary Committee. But he keeps constituents satisfied as he hews to his ideals of fiscal responsibility and his district's needs. "I've never been a real good rubber stamp," Coble said in 2008.

Coble generally tries to keep a low profile in Washington, even if he sometimes gets attention for his go-it-alone ways. But he is often seen back home in Greensboro. A regular on the local parade circuit, he reaches out to those he represents and prides himself on being one of them.

Some of his views may be closer in line with President Obama than they were with Obama's predecessor — such as a desire to bring troops home from Iraq and to allow federal funding of stem cell research. But Coble indicated he is just as willing to go against the new president and speak up when he disagrees. He voted against the economic stimulus bill, which he said few in Congress had read. The Lexington Dispatch reported him as saying to a local retirement community in April 2009: "We're pushing legislation in too hurriedly that has not been examined, hadn't been diagnosed, debated or dialogue." He blamed both parties for the economic downturn, however.

In fall 2008, he originally voted against a $700 billion measure to rescue the nation's ailing financial services sector, then switched his vote to support a slightly altered version. "It may be politically damaging," he said as he announced his switch. "The political sky may fall on my head, but I feel the limited access to credit or no access to capital may affect us all." But in early 2009 he voted against releasing the second half of that money.

In the 110th Congress (2007-08), Coble was one of only 35 House members and the sole member of the North Carolina delegation to vote against an economic stimulus bill in January 2008, calling it "deficit spending at its worst."

And he was an early skeptic of President George W. Bush's policy in Iraq. He was among 17 Republicans who backed a Democratic resolution in early 2007 opposing Bush's call for more than 21,000 additional troops. He voted against the administration's requests to fund the war in 2005 and 2006. But in 2007 he voted for a $555 billion catchall spending bill that included $70 billion for military operations in Iraq and Afghanistan. "When I voted against funding...I did it symbolically to send the message," he said. "But it's tough to vote against the troops."

Coble also tangled with Republican leaders and the administration on the Central America Free Trade Agreement (CAFTA), which he considered a sensitive issue personally and for his state, home to many of the nation's remaining textile factories. His mother sewed pockets onto overalls in a North Carolina textile factory in the days before air conditioning. Coble told Bush during a White House visit, "When I go into these plants and have employees plead with me to vote no, that's my mama talking to me." He was one of only 27 Republicans to vote against CAFTA in 2005, although he did support the 2007 trade agreement with Peru.

And while Coble generally votes conservatively on social matters, he has consistently supported federal funding for stem cell research, despite holding staunchly anti-abortion views. "Some of my Republican colleagues, and some Democrats, too, concluded that it was an abortion-rights issue, and I never did believe that," he explained.

It is just that kind of independent behavior that cost him the seat of top-ranking Republican on the Judiciary Committee at the start of the 110th. He was next in line for the spot, but leaders instead chose Lamar Smith of Texas, a more reliable backer of the party's priorities.

Coble is the top-ranking member of the Judiciary Subcommittee on Courts, and Competition Policy, and he chaired a similar panel from 1997 to 2002. He co-authored the Digital Millennium Copyright Act in 1998, which bans any computer program or device that circumvents the software that encrypts digital movies and music to prevent unauthorized reproduction During the 110th, he helped subcommittee Chairman Howard L. Berman of California push through the House a bill to improve intellectual property protections. He also helped gain House support for a bill to overhaul the nation's patent laws, but it stalled in the Senate.

Coble prides himself on returning leftover office funds to the federal coffers each year. He is one of the few lawmakers who declines to participate in the congressional pension program, calling it "a taxpayer rip-off."

But from his seat on the Transportation and Infrastructure Committee, he unapologetically steers funds to his district. In 2008 he helped tap $10 million to fund runway construction at his district's airport, and in 2005 he secured $50 million for his district in the surface transportation bill. "Those of us on the Transportation Committee usually do pretty well, and I have no problem with that," he said. "I think your own committee should take care of you."

In spring 2009, he voted against a bill to grant the Food and Drug Administration power to regulate tobacco. "I don't believe the FDA needs to insert its oars in the tobacco water," he said, adding that it doesn't have the resources.

Coble was born in rural Guilford County to parents who had little formal education. His father spent 44 years working at the Belk department store chain, starting as a floor sweeper and working his way up to manager of the Greensboro store. His mother worked in the textile factories.

Coble built a career as a federal prosecutor before being appointed as North Carolina's chief tax collector in the mid-1970s. After four years as a state representative, in 1984 he became the GOP's candidate against freshman Democratic Rep. Robin Britt after winning the primary by 164 votes. Coble stressed his fiscal conservatism while painting Britt as an extravagant liberal who had voted against President Reagan on two of every three votes in 1983. Tapping into the votes of conservative Democrats who crossed party lines in Reagan's re-election landslide that year, Coble won by 2,662 votes.

Britt plotted a comeback, and in 1986 only 79 votes separated him from Coble. Britt challenged the election results but was unsuccessful. Coble has had little to worry about since.

KEY VOTES

2008
No Delay consideration of Colombia free-trade agreement
Yes Override Bush veto of federal farm and nutrition programs reauthorization bill
Yes Overhaul surveillance laws and permit dismissal of suits against companies that conducted warrantless wiretapping
No Grant mortgage relief to homeowners and funding for Fannie Mae and Freddie Mac
No Approve initial $700 billion program to stabilize financial markets
Yes Approve final $700 billion program to stabilize financial markets
No Provide $14 billion in loans to automakers

2007
No Increase minimum wage by $2.10 an hour
No Approve $124.2 billion in emergency war spending and set goal for redeployment of troops from Iraq
Yes Reject federal contraceptive assistance to international family planning groups
Yes Override Bush veto of $23.2 billion water projects authorization bill
Yes Implement Peru free-trade agreement
Yes Approve energy policy overhaul with new fuel economy standards
Yes Clear $473.5 billion omnibus spending bill, including $70 billion for military operations

CQ VOTE STUDIES

	PARTY UNITY		PRESIDENTIAL SUPPORT	
	SUPPORT	OPPOSE	SUPPORT	OPPOSE
2008	96%	4%	65%	35%
2007	94%	6%	80%	20%
2006	94%	6%	73%	27%
2005	94%	6%	78%	22%
2004	94%	6%	71%	29%

INTEREST GROUPS

	AFL-CIO	ADA	CCUS	ACU
2008	13%	20%	89%	88%
2007	4%	10%	88%	83%
2006	15%	10%	93%	92%
2005	20%	10%	78%	84%
2004	13%	5%	95%	88%

NORTH CAROLINA 6
Central – parts of Greensboro and High Point

Located in the heart of the state, the 6th takes in part of the city of Greensboro and surrounding Guilford County, then spreads south to Moore County to pick up the upscale golf and retirement centers of Southern Pines and Pinehurst — host to two men's U.S. Open Championships in the last decade — near Fort Bragg. Solid GOP turf, the district gave John McCain 63 percent in the 2008 presidential race.

The 6th takes in two large chunks of Guilford County that are connected at a single point, on the Reedy Fork Creek in the northern part of the county. The Guilford portions surround Greensboro, although most of the city's more diverse and Democratic-leaning population resides in the 12th and 13th districts. The rural part of the 6th is tobacco country: more than 1,600 residents are employed in factories for two brands owned by Lorillard Tobacco Company, which is based in the 13th.

Greensboro is home to a blend of manufacturing and service companies, particularly in the textile, furniture and insurance industries. It also hosts the North American headquarters of Volvo Trucks, which will be joined by manufacturing and information technology operations of Volvo-affiliated Mack Trucks, and a major office of the VF Corp. (Wrangler Jeans). An American Express regional credit card service center and six colleges and universities have helped to diversify Greensboro's economy. FedEx expects to operate out of a new regional hub at Greensboro's Piedmont-Triad International Airport, but economic slowdowns have forced the company to scale back plans.

Like much of North Carolina, economic recession has hit all business sectors in the district. Trade issues also loom large here, particularly in the textile and furniture industries. Nearby High Point is a national furniture manufacturing hub, and its market draws 85,000 people annually. Attempts by Las Vegas officials to lure furniture trade shows to their new convention center, in addition to foreign competition from Asia and elsewhere, threaten High Point's dominance.

MAJOR INDUSTRY
Tobacco, textiles, furniture manufacturing

CITIES
Greensboro (pt.), 59,010; High Point (pt.), 33,404; Asheboro, 21,672

NOTABLE
The Richard Petty Museum in Randleman honors the NASCAR legend.

Rep. Mike McIntyre (D)

Elected 1996; 7th term

CAPITOL OFFICE
225-2731
www.house.gov/mcintyre
2437 Rayburn Bldg. 20515-3307; fax 225-5773

COMMITTEES
Agriculture
(Rural Development, Biotechnology, Specialty Crops & Foreign Agriculture - chairman)
Armed Services

RESIDENCE
Lumberton

BORN
Aug. 6, 1956; Lumberton, N.C.

RELIGION
Presbyterian

FAMILY
Wife, Dee McIntyre; two children

EDUCATION
U. of North Carolina, B.A. 1978 (political science), J.D. 1981

CAREER
Lawyer

POLITICAL HIGHLIGHTS
No previous office

ELECTION RESULTS

2008 GENERAL

Mike McIntyre (D)	215,383	68.8%
Will Breazeale (R)	97,472	31.2%

2008 PRIMARY

Mike McIntyre (D)	unopposed

2006 GENERAL

Mike McIntyre (D)	101,787	72.8%
Shirley Davis (R)	38,033	27.2%

PREVIOUS WINNING PERCENTAGES
2004 (73%); 2002 (71%); 2000 (70%); 1998 (91%); 1996 (53%)

McIntyre wants to use the federal government to help his rural constituents start businesses and access government services, and he will vote the way he sees best to make that happen. He is one of the most conservative House Democrats and often finds himself at odds with party leaders.

He is a member of the Blue Dog Coalition of about 50 fiscally conservative Democrats. McIntyre splits with the majority of his party on social issues and certain fiscal policy votes, and he opposes expansions of free trade that he thinks hurt the state's textile industry. Voters back home like where he stands and have given him at least 68 percent of the vote in every re-election.

In 2008 he was one of four Democrats who voted for a budget alternative proposed by Republicans. That October, he was one of 63 Democrats to oppose a $700 billion plan to shore up the nation's financial sector. "We needed a clean bill that would help American families and small businesses, not foreign investors and foreign banks," he said. "We also needed a bill that was not loaded down with extra spending that increases the national debt even more."

He supported President Obama's $787 billion economic stimulus law in February 2009, but only after urging that sufficient funds be directed to rural areas to address such needs as water, wastewater and community facilities projects. "The challenge is to make sure that, once again, rural America isn't overlooked," McIntyre said during debate on the measure.

That is a common refrain as he chairs the Agriculture Committee's panel on specialty crops and rural development. Even while Vice President Joseph R. Biden Jr. visited eastern North Carolina to announce $1.2 billion in stimulus funds to help rural communities, McIntyre led his panel in a series of hearings to further investigate the impact of the stimulus on such areas. "Even with this infusion of funds...rural areas still face a tough struggle," he said.

During debate on a major rewrite of farm and nutrition programs in 2007, he used the opportunity to enact an idea that had been languishing for years: creating the Southeast Regional Crescent Commission to advance rural economic development and worker training in seven states, including North Carolina. He also advanced provisions to improve access to education and medical services for rural residents.

During the 110th Congress (2007-08), McIntyre also advanced a bill to provide federal recognition for the Lumbee tribe of American Indians and allow them to receive federal funding for the first time. In a concession and with the blessing of tribal leaders, McIntyre inserted a provision into the bill saying the Lumbees would not build a casino. McIntyre sees Lumbee recognition as a way to provide assistance to an economically struggling area and as a moral issue. "This was done," he said, "to give them the dignity that they have been fighting for for 100 years." The bill passed the House but stalled in the Senate.

For years, McIntyre was a stout defender of the federal tobacco program, which he said was essential to preserving small family farms in his state. But in the early 2000s, declaring it "time for a new approach," he developed a controversial plan to buy out tobacco growers. From 2003 through 2006, he was the top-ranking Democrat on the Agriculture panel overseeing tobacco programs, and he helped push a $10 billion tobacco buyout bill to passage in 2004 as part of a corporate tax measure. But he opposed a bill in spring 2009 to give the Food and Drug Administration power to regulate tobacco: "The last thing we want is for government bureaucrats to be coming on the farm."

He also initially fought against the use of tobacco taxes to pay for an expansion of the State Children's Health Insurance Program, which covers children whose families are not eligible for Medicaid. In 2007, he was one of eight Democrats who voted against such a bill, arguing that tobacco is an all-too-convenient "whipping boy." Then, less than a month later, he reversed course and voted to override President George W. Bush's veto. McIntyre said he changed his mind because of his long support for family and children's issues and because "there were amplifiers above our head" that made the politics around the bill solely about children. Those amplifiers, he said, were his own party's leaders. He supported a similar version of the bill in January 2009 that Obama signed into law.

McIntyre also has shifted his position on offshore drilling. As late as July 2008, he opposed allowing oil exploration off North Carolina's coast. But as gas prices rose, he changed his position, voting for a bill in September he said would have allowed limited drilling in a way that would have brought revenue to coastal communities.

He also sits on the Armed Services Committee, where he can represent the large military establishment in his district. Fort Bragg employs many of his constituents, while Camp Lejeune is just over the 3rd District line to the east. He has worked to increase the number of veterans' health clinics in the district and in 2007 moved a bill through the House to expand outreach efforts to veterans.

McIntyre was raised in Lumberton; his father was an optometrist and his mother was a bank branch manager. He was chairman of the Teen Democrats in high school and spent the summer after his junior year at a congressional seminar program in Washington. When he was 16, his father, a city council member in Lumberton, took him to a 1972 victory party for newly elected Rep. Charlie Rose. And he was standing at the back of the room on the day White House lawyer John Dean testified before the Senate Watergate Committee, which was chaired by North Carolina's legendary Sam J. Ervin Jr.

The next summer, he worked as an intern in Rose's office. At the University of North Carolina, he majored in political science and was vice president of the campus chapter of college Democrats. He later was an organizer of the Robeson County Young Democrats. After graduating from law school at the University of North Carolina, he was involved in dozens of community, church, civic and professional activities as he built a law practice in Lumberton.

When Rose announced his retirement in 1996, McIntyre was one of seven Democratic primary entrants. He took 23 percent of the vote, then faced Bill Caster, a Republican New Hanover County commissioner and retired Coast Guard officer. McIntyre's conservative stance on most issues helped blunt GOP attacks, and he won with 53 percent.

KEY VOTES

2008
Yes Delay consideration of Colombia free-trade agreement
Yes Override Bush veto of federal farm and nutrition programs reauthorization bill
Yes Overhaul surveillance laws and permit dismissal of suits against companies that conducted warrantless wiretapping
Yes Grant mortgage relief to homeowners and funding for Fannie Mae and Freddie Mac
No   Approve initial $700 billion program to stabilize financial markets
No   Approve final $700 billion program to stabilize financial markets
No   Provide $14 billion in loans to automakers

2007
Yes Increase minimum wage by $2.10 an hour
Yes Approve $124.2 billion in emergency war spending and set goal for redeployment of troops from Iraq
Yes Reject federal contraceptive assistance to international family planning groups
Yes Override Bush veto of $23.2 billion water projects authorization bill
No   Implement Peru free-trade agreement
Yes Approve energy policy overhaul with new fuel economy standards
Yes Clear $473.5 billion omnibus spending bill, including $70 billion for military operations

CQ VOTE STUDIES

	PARTY UNITY		PRESIDENTIAL SUPPORT	
	SUPPORT	OPPOSE	SUPPORT	OPPOSE
2008	89%	11%	17%	83%
2007	86%	14%	22%	78%
2006	74%	26%	63%	37%
2005	71%	29%	57%	43%
2004	74%	26%	59%	41%

INTEREST GROUPS

	AFL-CIO	ADA	CCUS	ACU
2008	93%	85%	61%	32%
2007	88%	85%	65%	44%
2006	79%	50%	73%	64%
2005	80%	70%	62%	48%
2004	80%	60%	60%	60%

NORTH CAROLINA 7
Southeast — Wilmington, part of Fayetteville

The 7th stretches from the well-off historic port city of Wilmington in the southeast to the military-fueled commercial hub of Fayetteville in the north. In between lie tobacco fields, hog farms and manufacturing plants.

A sliver of Fort Bragg, the huge military base that will be adding thousands of personnel as a result of the 2005 BRAC round, is on the edge of the 7th's portion of Fayetteville and is integral to the area. Tobacco, textiles and agriculture also drive the local economy, although textile declines have led to high unemployment in some counties. Free-trade agreements are viewed with suspicion here. Like Fayetteville (shared with the 2nd and 8th), Wilmington's growth is reflected in its expanding medical center and emerging biotech industry. The city also has become a desirable retirement community, and the area's Atlantic beaches have made the district a tourist spot. Economic slowdowns, however, have hurt retail and tourism sectors.

The region's poor farmers, Lumbee Indians (mainly in Robeson County) and a cohesive black community in Fayetteville and rural Bladen County

provide a slight Democratic lean. But wealthy condominium-dwellers in Wilmington and surrounding New Hanover County, as well as voters in adjacent Brunswick County, exert a rightward influence in presidential elections. The 7th District gave Republican John McCain 52 percent in the 2008 presidential election.

Due in part to Robeson County, the 7th has the fifth-largest percentage of American Indians of any district in the nation, and the largest percentage of any district east of the Mississippi River. Almost 19 percent of Duplin County (shared with the 3rd) is Hispanic, and 15 percent of the population there speaks a language other than English at home.

MAJOR INDUSTRY
Agriculture, military, manufacturing, tourism

MILITARY BASES
Fort Bragg (Army), 45,650 military, 5,941 civilian (2008) (shared with the 7th and 8th)

CITIES
Wilmington, 75,838; Lumberton, 20,795; Fayetteville (pt.), 19,418

NOTABLE
Wilmington has a strong film and television industry, with movies and shows such as "The Secret Life of Bees" and "One Tree Hill" filmed there.

Rep. Larry Kissell (D)

Elected 2008; 1st term

A former textile worker, Kissell hopes to boost economic development in his district and change trade policies that he blames for the loss of jobs like his old one. At the same time, he plans to protect rural areas and farmers.

His fight against free-trade agreements was the center of his 2008 campaign against five-term Republican Robin Hayes. It was a rematch of a 2006 race that Kissell lost by just 329 votes; he won this time by more than 10 percentage points. Kissell (KISS-ell) campaigned with a goat named CAFTA (after the Central America Free Trade Agreement) and called American textile jobs the "sacrificial lamb" of free-trade agreements. He even subsidized gas for motorists at $1.22 a gallon, the price at the pump when Hayes was first elected.

In his first month in Congress, he successfully included in the $787 billion stimulus law a provision requiring the Homeland Security Department to buy U.S.-made uniforms for the Transportation Security Administration.

He also showed a willingness to depart from the party line, telling C-SPAN that "you've got to remember the people you represent and that you're there to speak for them and their interest and not the interest of the political party." He was one of only six Democrats to oppose a bill that would have heavily taxed the executive bonuses paid by American International Group Inc. after it received funds from the $700 billion financial sector rescue law of 2008. And he was one of only 23 Democrats to oppose a bill to expand homeowners' access to bankruptcy.

A member of the Agriculture Committee, Kissell was one of eight Democrats who voted against a bill in April 2009 to empower the Food and Drug Administration to regulate tobacco products. He supported a failed Republican alternative to create a new entity within the Health and Human Services Department to study the issue. He also sits on the Armed Services Committee, where he can look out for Fort Bragg, part of which resides in his district.

In 2008, Kissell outraised Hayes by a more than 2-to-1 margin and took a higher percentage of the vote in his district than President Obama. However, Republicans hope to regain the seat in 2010, and began the attack early.

CAPITOL OFFICE
225-3715
kissell.house.gov
512 Cannon Bldg. 20515-3308; fax 225-4036

COMMITTEES
Agriculture
Armed Services

RESIDENCE
Biscoe

BORN
Jan. 31, 1951; Pinehurst, N.C.

RELIGION
Baptist

FAMILY
Wife, Tina Kissell; two children

EDUCATION
Wake Forest U., B.A. 1973 (economics)

CAREER
Teacher; textile mill supervisor; chemical company foreman

POLITICAL HIGHLIGHTS
Democratic nominee for U.S. House, 2006

ELECTION RESULTS

2008 GENERAL

Larry Kissell (D)	157,185	55.4%
Robin Hayes (R)	126,634	44.6%

2008 PRIMARY

Larry Kissell (D)	unopposed

NORTH CAROLINA 8

South central — parts of Charlotte, Fayetteville, Concord and Kannapolis

The 8th stretches from Charlotte in the west to military-dominated Fayetteville in the east. Charlotte adds an urban component to an otherwise suburban and rural district.

Cabarrus, a fast-growing, largely white and Republican county north of Charlotte, and Cumberland, which includes the 8th's share of Fayetteville, are the district's most populous counties. In Mecklenburg County, the district almost reaches downtown Charlotte, heading as far west as Memorial Stadium. The 8th's share of the city has a sizable black population, giving the district's portion of Mecklenburg a decidedly Democratic lean.

Textile-based economies along Interstate 85, notably Concord and Kannapolis, have suffered major losses as manufacturing jobs headed overseas. In the east, the 8th becomes poorer and more rural. Fort Bragg (shared with the 2nd and 7th) in Hoke and Cumberland counties in the Sandhills part of the district lends a strong military flavor.

The 8th is politically competitive, with Democrats accounting for a plurality of registered voters. In 2008, Democrat Larry Kissell took 55 percent of the vote over incumbent Robin Hayes two years after losing to Hayes in the nation's second-closest congressional race. Barack Obama won 52 percent of the 2008 presidential vote here.

MAJOR INDUSTRY
Military, manufacturing, agriculture, livestock

MILITARY BASES
Fort Bragg (Army), 45,650 military, 5,941 civilian (2008) (shared with the 7th and 8th)

CITIES
Charlotte (pt.), 100,756; Concord (pt.), 55,938; Fayetteville (pt.), 51,698

NOTABLE
Lowe's Motor Speedway in Concord can draw 180,000 people to NASCAR races.

Rep. Sue Myrick (R)

CAPITOL OFFICE
225-1976
myrick.house.gov
230 Cannon Bldg. 20515-3309; fax 225-3389

COMMITTEES
Energy & Commerce
Select Intelligence

RESIDENCE
Charlotte

BORN
Aug. 1, 1941; Tiffin, Ohio

RELIGION
Evangelical Methodist

FAMILY
Husband, Ed Myrick; two children,
three stepchildren

EDUCATION
Heidelberg College, attended 1959-60
(elementary education)

CAREER
Advertising executive; secretary

POLITICAL HIGHLIGHTS
Candidate for Charlotte City Council, 1981;
Charlotte City Council, 1983-85; sought
Republican nomination for mayor of Charlotte,
1985; mayor of Charlotte, 1987-91; sought
Republican nomination for U.S. Senate, 1992

ELECTION RESULTS

2008 GENERAL

Sue Myrick (R)	241,053	62.4%
Harry Taylor (D)	138,719	35.9%
Andy Grum (LIBERT)	6,711	1.7%

2008 PRIMARY

Sue Myrick (R)	51,402	92.2%
Jack Stratton (R)	4,370	7.8%

2006 GENERAL

Sue Myrick (R)	106,206	66.5%
Bill Glass (D)	53,437	33.5%

PREVIOUS WINNING PERCENTAGES
2004 (70%); 2002 (72%); 2000 (69%); 1998 (69%);
1996 (63%); 1994 (65%)

Elected 1994; 8th term

Myrick is in a constant fight against breast cancer, illegal immigration and radical Islamic terrorism, mixing hard-edged conservatism with a personal quest.

A former chairwoman of the conservative Republican Study Committee, she typically votes with the majority of her party, breaking away only occasionally on parochial issues such as free-trade deals that threaten the textile manufacturers in her district. And in 2008, Myrick, whose district includes the headquarters of Bank of America Corp. and Wachovia (before its sale), was one of 25 Republicans who voted against the first version of a $700 billion rescue bill for the financial sector and switched their vote on the next version that became law. She she said she was swayed by conversations at home. "I talked to people I trust…good, solid businesses," she said. "They could not get credit."

Her biggest legislative victories have come from her personal battle with breast cancer. She underwent surgery in late 1999 and received treatments for about six months. She kept up with floor votes by wearing a pink surgical mask to reduce the risk of infection. In 2000, she shepherded into law a measure that provides treatment for low-income women diagnosed with breast or cervical cancer. Six years later, she steered through the House a bill reauthorizing early-detection programs, though it stalled short of enactment. And in 2008, she and New York Democrat Nita M. Lowey wrote a law creating an interagency breast cancer research committee.

A member of the Energy and Commerce Committee and its Health Subcommittee, she also advocates congressional action on mental health issues, in part because she has a granddaughter with bipolar disorder. But, Myrick said, she sometimes finds herself philosophically opposed to Democratic legislation on the issue, such as the initial version of a bill in the 110th Congress (2007-08) to require insurers to treat mental and physical diseases equally. "I just hate mandates, which they had in there," she said. The measure passed as part of the financial sector rescue bill.

On energy issues, Myrick in 2007 voted for an energy bill that included new fuel economy standards and emphasized conservation. And as gas prices soared in 2008, she introduced a bill to encourage offshore drilling on the outer continental shelf.

A member of the Commerce, Trade and Consumer Protection Subcommittee, she has been a skeptic of some trade deals that could further threaten jobs in her state. But in 2002 she did vote to grant President George W. Bush fast-track trade negotiating authority after Bush pledged to look out for the textile industry. And she voted for the 2005 Central America Free Trade Agreement and the Peru Free Trade Agreement in 2007.

Another of Myrick's priorities is pushing for a crackdown on illegal immigration. She has sponsored a bevy of bills on the subject, including one to deny highway aid to states that accept taxpayer identification numbers in lieu of Social Security numbers in issuing drivers' licenses. Her state, Myrick said, had become a destination for illegal immigrants who discovered that the taxpayer ID numbers were easier to obtain.

She has been particularly troubled by a recent string of car collisions involving illegal immigrants driving under the influence. "Culturally," she said, "there's a difference between the countries south of the border and us, relative to drinking and driving." In the 110th, she sponsored a bill to deny funding to colleges and universities that admit illegal immigrants. In 2009, she introduced for the third time "The 10k Run for the Border Act" to increase penalties for employing illegal immigrants.

She is also deeply troubled by Islamic terrorism, though she said she isn't sure how to halt the spread of an ideology. She introduced a "Wake Up, America" agenda in April 2008, calling for investigations of the nonprofit status of the Council on American-Islamic Relations and the process for selecting government Arabic translators, as well as the canceling of student scholarship visa programs with Saudi Arabia.

In 2009, Myrick was named the top-ranking member of the Intelligence Community Management panel of the Select Intelligence Committee. She also serves on the terrorism subcommittee.

Her ardent conservatism and her distinct status as the only Southern Republican woman in the GOP's takeover class of 1994 caught the attention of party leaders when she first arrived in Congress. She got a seat on the Budget Committee in her first term and a post on the Rules panel in her second.

But in 1997 she joined a small group of disgruntled conservatives who, impatient with the pace of the "Republican revolution," plotted to depose Newt Gingrich as Speaker. The coup was foiled, and Myrick's influence in the House waned; she lost a race for secretary of the Republican Conference to Deborah Pryce of Ohio. She has, however, been a deputy whip since 2003.

Born in Tiffin, Ohio, Myrick was reared on a farm where her parents grew peaches but they later switched to growing nursery stock used in landscaping. As a child, she got 50 cents an hour for staffing the family's snack stand, which sold sandwiches and drinks.

She attended Heidelberg College in her hometown for a year before her parents decided their limited financial resources should be used for her three brothers' higher education. They figured "I'd just get married," Myrick said. She took a secretarial job at an army depot.

Myrick had no political aspirations until the early 1980s, when she and her husband sparred with the Charlotte City Council over the purchase of a property for use as a combination home and business. She ran for the city council in 1981 and lost, but she was victorious two years later. She lost a bid to become mayor of Charlotte in 1985, but she won the office in 1987, ousting Harvey B. Gantt. She was re-elected in 1989.

After five-term GOP Rep. Alex McMillan announced his retirement in 1994, Myrick's political experience gave her wide name recognition in a five-way Republican primary. Still, she struggled to win the nomination, prevailing only when news broke that her principal opponent, state House Minority Leader David Balmer, had falsified his résumé. That November, she met only modest Democratic resistance. She has easily won re-election since then.

KEY VOTES

2008
No Delay consideration of Colombia free-trade agreement
No Override Bush veto of federal farm and nutrition programs reauthorization bill
Yes Overhaul surveillance laws and permit dismissal of suits against companies that conducted warrantless wiretapping
No Grant mortgage relief to homeowners and funding for Fannie Mae and Freddie Mac
No Approve initial $700 billion program to stabilize financial markets
Yes Approve final $700 billion program to stabilize financial markets
No Provide $14 billion in loans to automakers

2007
No Increase minimum wage by $2.10 an hour
No Approve $124.2 billion in emergency war spending and set goal for redeployment of troops from Iraq
Yes Reject federal contraceptive assistance to international family planning groups
No Override Bush veto of $23.2 billion water projects authorization bill
Yes Implement Peru free-trade agreement
Yes Approve energy policy overhaul with new fuel economy standards
Yes Clear $473.5 billion omnibus spending bill, including $70 billion for military operations

CQ VOTE STUDIES

	PARTY UNITY		PRESIDENTIAL SUPPORT	
	SUPPORT	OPPOSE	SUPPORT	OPPOSE
2008	99%	1%	79%	21%
2007	97%	3%	89%	11%
2006	96%	4%	92%	8%
2005	97%	3%	89%	11%
2004	99%	1%	91%	9%

INTEREST GROUPS

	AFL-CIO	ADA	CCUS	ACU
2008	14%	10%	94%	91%
2007	4%	10%	74%	96%
2006	14%	0%	100%	92%
2005	17%	0%	87%	96%
2004	0%	0%	95%	100%

NORTH CAROLINA 9

South central — parts of Charlotte and Gastonia

The predominately Republican 9th centers around Charlotte, the largest metropolitan area in the state. Nearly 40 percent of district residents live within the city's limits, and nearly 60 percent live in Mecklenburg County, which includes Charlotte.

The primarily white suburbs on the southern side of Charlotte provide the city with many of its bankers, brokers, accountants, health care professionals and other white-collar workers. Most of Charlotte's black residents live in the 8th or 12th districts. The 9th has the highest median household income in North Carolina, due to upper-middle-class areas such as Huntersville, in northern Mecklenburg County.

Charlotte, the nation's biggest banking center after New York since the banking-industry consolidation in the 1990s, has been hit hard by the nationwide credit and investment brokerage collapse. Job losses, instability at Bank of America and the acquisition of Wachovia by San Francisco-based Wells Fargo have created uncertainty in the community. The region's growth over the last two decades brought the traffic con-

gestion, shopping malls and higher home values that usually accompany suburban sprawl, but real estate market declines, high foreclosure rates, retail sector struggles and rising unemployment concern residents.

To the west, Gastonia and surrounding towns have been hit by continuing declines in the textile industry. The 9th, however, lessened its dependence on manufacturing and textiles, and the population of Gastonia continues to grow. Union County, a suburban bedroom community located southeast of Charlotte, is the fastest-growing county in the state.

Republicans hold an 11-percentage-point registration edge and dominate elections in the 9th. Republican John McCain won 55 percent of the district's 2008 presidential vote. Since the 9th became a Charlotte-based district prior to the 1968 election, it has been represented in the U.S. House only by Republicans.

MAJOR INDUSTRY
Finance, service, retail, manufacturing

CITIES
Charlotte (pt.), 243,947; Gastonia (pt.), 60,498; Huntersville, 24,960

NOTABLE
Pineville hosts the James K. Polk State Historic Site.

Rep. Patrick T. McHenry (R)

Elected 2004; 3rd term

CAPITOL OFFICE
225-2576
mchenry.house.gov
224 Cannon Bldg. 20515-3310; fax 225-0316

COMMITTEES
Budget
Financial Services
Oversight & Government Reform

RESIDENCE
Cherryville

BORN
Oct. 22, 1975; Charlotte, N.C.

RELIGION
Roman Catholic

FAMILY
Single

EDUCATION
North Carolina State U., attended 1994-97;
Belmont Abbey College, B.A. 2000 (history)

CAREER
Real estate broker; U.S. Labor Department
special assistant; campaign aide

POLITICAL HIGHLIGHTS
Republican nominee for N.C. House, 1998;
N.C. House, 2003-04

ELECTION RESULTS

2008 GENERAL

Patrick T. McHenry (R)	171,774	57.6%
Daniel Johnson (D)	126,699	42.4%

2008 PRIMARY

Patrick T. McHenry (R)	34,457	67.1%
Lance Sigmon (R)	16,892	32.9%

2006 GENERAL

Patrick T. McHenry (R)	94,179	61.8%
Richard Carsner (D)	58,214	38.2%

PREVIOUS WINNING PERCENTAGES
2004 (64%)

McHenry is at the vanguard of the young, pugnacious House conservatives constantly spoiling for a fight. His quick-witted jabs at the Democratic leadership, which draw applause from Republicans and scoffs from Democrats, make him well-suited for life in the minority and spots on TV talk shows.

McHenry is not a prolific author of legislation, sponsoring just four bills in the 110th Congress (2007-08). But he is a reliable vote against almost anything Democratic Speaker Nancy Pelosi of California wants to do, and he makes sure everyone knows exactly how misguided he thinks she is. "I truly believe Nancy Pelosi's liberal agenda will harm the country," he said in 2008. "Pelosi's style is combative and inflammatory."

When Democrats promoted bicycle use as part of an energy bill, McHenry shot back, mocking them for "promoting 19th-century solutions to 21st-century problems. If you don't like it, ride a bike. If you don't like the prices at the pumps, ride a bike. Stay tuned for the next big idea by the Democrats: improving energy efficiency by riding the horse-and-buggy."

As a deputy whip, McHenry will try to help leaders keep Republicans together on legislation. But there's also the bigger goal of helping the team take back seats after two years of losses to Democrats at the polls. "This is a longer-term comeback we are trying to make now," he told the Charlotte Observer in February 2009. "And so in many respects it's a marathon, an endurance competition."

McHenry holds seats on three key committees from which to oversee the Republican attack on the Democratic agenda: Financial Services, Budget, and Oversight and Government Reform.

In an opinion piece posted on LincolnTribune.com in early February 2009, McHenry called the Democrats' economic stimulus plan a "massive spending bill" created in "a secretive, hasty and partisan process that clearly demonstrates the Democrat majority's disregard for America's desire for bipartisan cooperation in this time of crisis." He criticized Democrats for not offering enough tax relief for working families and small businesses.

He is fearless on the House floor, even engaging in repartee with legendary debater Barney Frank. When the Massachusetts Democrat sat in the Speaker's chair during consideration of embryonic stem cell research legislation in 2007, Frank shot down McHenry's repeated "parliamentary inquiries" as political statements, not inquiries. That prompted Republican Joe L. Barton of Texas to object that Frank had engaged in the same tactics as McHenry when he was in the minority.

McHenry and Frank also spar on the Financial Services Committee, where the chairman barely tolerates McHenry's frequent partisan amendments and inflammatory statements. "To be a bomb-thrower, you have to be able to hit your target," Frank said. "He's not strategic. He has contributed to an impression in which people are often dismissive of him, almost at the outset."

He was at the forefront of an effort in the 110th to use a House procedure called the "motion to recommit" to win last-minute adoption of GOP-favored amendments to Democratic-written bills. He also joined Republican Tom Price of Georgia and several other GOP panel members in urging President George W. Bush to veto in 2008 an initial mortgage rescue plan aimed at easing the subprime crisis on individuals. He said the bill was a complete bailout for lenders and borrowers who should be punished for their poor decision-making.

McHenry that year also opposed the $700 billion plan, which became law, to rescue the ailing financial services industry. "I continue to believe that action is needed to stabilize our financial markets but this is not the right approach," he said. "The U.S. Treasury has bailed out a number of financial institutions and yet the problem persists."

As top-ranking member of the Oversight subcommittee on the census, McHenry strongly criticized President Obama when a senior administration official said in early 2009 that the Census Bureau director would report directly to the White House rather than to the Commerce secretary. McHenry called it a blatant attempt to seek a partisan advantage.

McHenry rarely departs from the conservative line. He supports offshore drilling and gun owners' rights, opposes gay marriage and stem cell research, and calls himself a "family values" man. A fiscal conservative, McHenry once said, "I have never voted for a tax increase on western North Carolina families and never will." But many western North Carolina residents blame trade liberalization laws for job losses, and he was one of 27 Republicans to vote against the Central America Free Trade Agreement in 2005.

Until the 111th Congress (2009-10), McHenry was the youngest member of the House, and in some ways, he was not far removed from his days as a College Republican. Just months into his first year in the House, his appetite for hardball politics put him at the center of a khakis-and-blazer electoral controversy. During a nasty fight in 2005 for the presidency of the College Republican National Committee, McHenry made phone calls to North Carolina College Republicans urging them to change their votes and help elect his friend Paul Gourley, who won. McHenry was accused of threatening retribution, a charge he denied.

McHenry had served as chairman of the state College Republicans and as treasurer for the national College Republicans in the late 1990s. He also had worked on several campaigns, including fellow North Carolina Republican Rep. Robin Hayes' failed 1996 gubernatorial bid and Bush's successful 2000 presidential race, as well as his own contests for the state legislature.

When veteran GOP Rep. Cass Ballenger announced his retirement in 2004, McHenry battled through a four-way Republican primary, combating criticism he wasn't ready for the job. His second-place finish put him in a runoff against David Huffman, a well-known local sheriff. With a financial boost from the Club for Growth, a Washington-based group that supports fiscally conservative candidates, he won by a scant 85 votes. In the general he defeated little-known Democratic Party activist Anne N. Fischer by more than 28 percentage points in the overwhelmingly Republican district. He cruised to re-election in 2006 with 62 percent of the vote, and got 58 percent against former prosecutor and Navy veteran Daniel Johnson in 2008.

KEY VOTES

2008

No Delay consideration of Colombia free-trade agreement
No Override Bush veto of federal farm and nutrition programs reauthorization bill
Yes Overhaul surveillance laws and permit dismissal of suits against companies that conducted warrantless wiretapping
No Grant mortgage relief to homeowners and funding for Fannie Mae and Freddie Mac
No Approve initial $700 billion program to stabilize financial markets
No Approve final $700 billion program to stabilize financial markets
No Provide $14 billion in loans to automakers

2007

No Increase minimum wage by $2.10 an hour
No Approve $124.2 billion in emergency war spending and set goal for redeployment of troops from Iraq
Yes Reject federal contraceptive assistance to international family planning groups
No Override Bush veto of $23.2 billion water projects authorization bill
Yes Implement Peru free-trade agreement
No Approve energy policy overhaul with new fuel economy standards
Yes Clear $473.5 billion omnibus spending bill, including $70 billion for military operations

CQ VOTE STUDIES

	PARTY UNITY		PRESIDENTIAL SUPPORT	
	SUPPORT	OPPOSE	SUPPORT	OPPOSE
2008	98%	2%	78%	22%
2007	99%	1%	92%	8%
2006	98%	2%	83%	17%
2005	99%	1%	87%	13%

INTEREST GROUPS

	AFL-CIO	ADA	CCUS	ACU
2008	13%	10%	78%	100%
2007	8%	0%	75%	100%
2006	7%	10%	93%	92%
2005	20%	5%	89%	100%

NORTH CAROLINA 10

West – Hickory

Set among the small towns of the western part of the state, the 10th has a rustic, small-business and conservative flavor. A solidly Republican district, the 10th has sent a GOP lawmaker to the U.S. House for 40 years, and many residents who consider themselves conservative Democrats will support Republicans in federal races.

While the 10th includes some suburban communities near Charlotte, it is mostly rural — only one town, Hickory, has a population of more than 30,000. Suburban sprawl has reached the eastern and southern edges of the 10th. In Hickory and other areas along U.S. Route 321, the furniture industry employs a large part of the workforce. Historically, the economy of the southern counties was based largely on textile and furniture manufacturing, with cotton-growing areas in Cleveland County. In the north, there are Christmas tree growers, and tourists visit the mountains near the Tennessee border and ski in areas like Banner Elk.

The 10th has the state's highest percentage of blue-collar workers, and the district's relies on factory jobs. Employment gaps in textile and furni-ture manufacturing have been compounded by job losses at key technology manufacturing employers. Fiber-optic giant Corning Cable Systems has announced a plant closure, although the company plans to maintain other facilities in the district. Google recently built a data center in Lenoir, but its continued expansion is uncertain.

In the 2008 presidential election, Republican John McCain won the district with more than 63 percent of its vote — his highest percentage statewide. Every county wholly or partly in the 10th voted for McCain, and rural Avery (72 percent) and Mitchell (70 percent) counties along the Tennessee border gave McCain his second- and fourth-highest percentages in the state.

MAJOR INDUSTRY
Manufacturing, agriculture

CITIES
Hickory, 37,222; Shelby, 19,477; Mooresville (pt.), 18,782

NOTABLE
The Elliott-Carnegie Public Library in Hickory was the last U.S. public library to receive a grant from the Carnegie Foundation (in 1917); Despite the 10th's Republican slant, the longest-serving congressman from North Carolina, Democrat Bob Doughton, represented the 10th for 42 years.

Rep. Heath Shuler (D)

Elected 2006; 2nd term

CAPITOL OFFICE
225-6401
shuler.house.gov
422 Cannon Bldg. 20515; fax 226-6422

COMMITTEES
Small Business
 (Rural Development, Entrepreneurship & Trade -
 chairman)
Transportation & Infrastructure

RESIDENCE
Waynesville

BORN
Dec. 31, 1971; Bryson City, N.C.

RELIGION
Baptist

FAMILY
Wife, Nikol Shuler; two children

EDUCATION
U. of Tennessee, B.A. 2001 (psychology)

CAREER
Real estate company owner; medical record
smart card company president; professional
football player

POLITICAL HIGHLIGHTS
No previous office

ELECTION RESULTS

2008 GENERAL

Heath Shuler (D)	211,112	62.0%
Carl Mumpower (R)	122,087	35.8%
Keith Smith (LIBERT)	7,517	2.2%

2008 PRIMARY

Heath Shuler (D)	unopposed

2006 GENERAL

Heath Shuler (D)	124,972	53.8%
Charles H. Taylor (R)	107,342	46.2%

One of the most socially and fiscally conservative Democrats in the House, Shuler has drawn attention for his close relationship with Republicans on such high-profile issues as immigration. A former pro football quarterback and a devout Christian, he cherishes his independence. "I am pretty stubborn," he said. "You could me back in the corner and I wouldn't budge for nothing."

Shuler (SHOO-lur) holds many positions that appear more in line with the GOP: He opposes abortion, gun control and same-sex marriage. In his first term, he departed from his party on 22 percent of votes pitting most Democrats against most Republicans, bucking party leaders more often than all but four Democrats. Oklahoma Republican Tom Cole, who chaired the House GOP's campaign committee in 2008, pointed admiringly to Shuler as an example of how Democrats found candidates well-suited to win rural districts. Shuler, Cole told The New York Times, is "to the right of Genghis Khan."

An influential member of the Blue Dog Coalition, a group of fiscally conservative House Democrats that backed his campaign, Shuler started his congressional career by cutting one of his credit cards in half. "If you start overspending, one of the first things you need to do at home is cut your credit cards up. That is what we should do [in the government]," he said. "We can't live above our means."

In late 2008, Shuler twice voted against a $700 billion measure to shore up the nation's financial system. He said that taxpayers should not be "responsible for the bad business decisions made on Wall Street."

He continued to display his fiscal conservatism in the early months of President Obama's administration by being one of seven House Democrats to oppose Obama's $787 billion economic stimulus proposal. He said it didn't contain enough for infrastructure, pointing to its inclusion of $5.5 million for transportation in Buncombe County. "That won't quite build a bridge in Buncombe," he said.

Shuler did, however, support the fiscal 2010 budget resolution; he called it "an ugly budget, but it's an honest assessment of where we are."

Among the first issues Shuler tended to in the 110th Congress (2007-08) was overhauling immigration. He wants to beef up border security and opposes a new guest worker program that includes ways for illegal immigrants to earn citizenship. When debate on the issue stalled in 2007, he offered a bill that would have mandated employers participate in a government-sponsored employee verification system. The Republican-dominated, pro-enforcement House Immigration Reform Caucus — and other advocates of strong border security — quickly rallied around the bill, which also would have permanently authorized the program along with additional Border Patrol agents. But the chamber ultimately passed a five-year renewal of the program that calls for voluntary participation.

Despite various policy differences, Shuler said he joined the Democrats "because the party helps those who can't help themselves." From his seats on the Small Business and Transportation and Infrastructure committees, he tends to the concerns of a rural district struggling to protect its resources and renew its economy after the loss of manufacturing jobs.

In the 111th Congress (2009-10), the Transportation Committee is expected to take up a renewal of a massive surface transportation bill — typically an opportunity for members to bring attention and funds to specific projects in their districts. He opposes building a 34-mile "road to nowhere" through the heart of the Great Smoky Mountains National Park. Discussion for the road began more than 60 years ago, but a $600 million-plus tab and environmental concerns have prevented construction. Shuler favors a monetary settlement between the park service and local residents.

Shuler opposes offshore oil and gas drilling and calls for the development and production of forms of renewable energy to reduce global warming and end reliance on foreign fuel. As chairman of the Rural Development, Entrepreneurship and Trade Subcommittee, he shepherded through Congress a bill that allows small businesses to get tax credits for investing in the production of alternative sources and energy-efficient technology.

Shuler was the only freshman to participate in House and Senate negotiations on a bill in the 110th to reauthorize farm and nutrition programs, which he backed for its provisions on conservation and funding for renewable energy and economic development.

Born Joseph Heath Shuler, he took up his middle name so he wouldn't be known as "Joe Junior." His father, Joseph Shuler, was a mail carrier in Bryson City, a gateway community to the Smokies. His mother helped run the town's youth baseball and football programs. He was in the fifth grade when he fell in love with football. As starting quarterback, he led Swain County High School to back-to-back state football championships before having a standout career at the University of Tennessee; he was the runner-up for the Heisman Trophy in 1993.

The Washington Redskins chose him third overall in the NFL draft in 1994. Yet his career failed to achieve the success expected. Nagged by injuries, Shuler retired after five years. In 1998, he returned to Knoxville and started a real estate company with his younger brother Benjie. Their company grew to more than 200 agents. Shuler later sold his share to his brother and moved to Waynesville.

In 2006, Rahm Emanuel of Illinois, the chairman of the Democratic Congressional Campaign Committee, asked him to challenge GOP Rep. Charles H. Taylor. It was a tough battle, but Shuler received a boost in October of that year when the Wall Street Journal published a story questioning whether Taylor used his seat on the Appropriations Committee to benefit himself and business partners. The story came on the heels of several national stories on corruption scandals in Congress. Taylor spent more than twice Shuler's $1.8 million, but it didn't matter; Shuler won by 8 percentage points.

In 2008 Shuler faced Republican Carl Mumpower, a psychologist, conservative activist and Asheville city councilman. Shuler raised more than $1.6 million for the contest and was easily re-elected.

KEY VOTES

2008

Yes Delay consideration of Colombia free-trade agreement

Yes Override Bush veto of federal farm and nutrition programs reauthorization bill

Yes Overhaul surveillance laws and permit dismissal of suits against companies that conducted warrantless wiretapping

Yes Grant mortgage relief to homeowners and funding for Fannie Mae and Freddie Mac

No Approve initial $700 billion program to stabilize financial markets

No Approve final $700 billion program to stabilize financial markets

No Provide $14 billion in loans to automakers

2007

Yes Increase minimum wage by $2.10 an hour

Yes Approve $124.2 billion in emergency war spending and set goal for redeployment of troops from Iraq

Yes Reject federal contraceptive assistance to international family planning groups

Yes Override Bush veto of $23.2 billion water projects authorization bill

No Implement Peru free-trade agreement

Yes Approve energy policy overhaul with new fuel economy standards

Yes Clear $473.5 billion omnibus spending bill, including $70 billion for military operations

CQ VOTE STUDIES

	PARTY UNITY		PRESIDENTIAL SUPPORT	
	SUPPORT	OPPOSE	SUPPORT	OPPOSE
2008	83%	17%	18%	82%
2007	76%	24%	19%	81%

INTEREST GROUPS

	AFL-CIO	ADA	CCUS	ACU
2008	87%	75%	56%	24%
2007	88%	80%	55%	44%

NORTH CAROLINA 11

West — Asheville

Based in the Great Smoky Mountains of Appalachia, the 11th is a largely rural district dotted with tree farms, wood mills and campgrounds. Agriculture and forestry long played a major role in the region's economy. Widespread layoffs have restricted economic opportunity in the westernmost counties of the 11th, some of which have the highest unemployment rates in the state. Metropolitan Asheville will depend on the growth of high-tech manufacturing to counter declines in traditional manufacturing, retail and construction sectors.

Asheville and surrounding Buncombe County take in nearly one-third of the district's residents. The blend of small-town, mountain remoteness and the city's urban amenities still draw young professionals and retirees to Asheville. Downtown condos and lofts have continued to sell despite a bleak national housing market. People flock to the area's ski slopes, as well as to hiking trails in parks, forests and on Mount Mitchell (the highest peak east of the Mississippi River). More than 1 million tourists each year enjoy the Biltmore Estate, the nation's largest privately owned home.

The 11th has the highest median age and the smallest black population of any North Carolina district, and the Eastern Band of Cherokee Indians' reservation gives the district a larger-than-average American Indian population. Many of the state's Cherokee Indians are descendants of the Cherokees who hid in the western North Carolina mountains to avoid forced migration to Oklahoma.

While Democrats hold a slight lead in voter registration, the district traditionally leans Republican. Henderson County is solidly GOP territory, and the district overall gave Republican John McCain 52 percent in the 2008 presidential race. Democrat Barack Obama took a 14-percentage-point win in Buncombe County, and Jackson County — which George W. Bush won in 2004 — supported Obama with 52 percent.

MAJOR INDUSTRY
Retail, forest products, health care, tourism

CITIES
Asheville, 68,889; Hendersonville, 10,420

NOTABLE
The National Climatic Data Center, the world's largest archive of weather data, is located in Asheville.

Rep. Melvin Watt (D)

Elected 1992; 9th term

CAPITOL OFFICE
225-1510
www.house.gov/watt
2304 Rayburn Bldg. 20515-3312; fax 225-1512

COMMITTEES
Financial Services
  (Domestic Monetary Policy & Technology -
  chairman)
Judiciary

RESIDENCE
Charlotte

BORN
Aug. 26, 1945; Charlotte, N.C.

RELIGION
Presbyterian

FAMILY
Wife, Eulada Watt; two children

EDUCATION
U. of North Carolina, B.S. 1967 (business
administration); Yale U., J.D. 1970

CAREER
Nursing home owner; campaign aide; lawyer

POLITICAL HIGHLIGHTS
N.C. Senate, 1985-86

ELECTION RESULTS

2008 GENERAL

Melvin Watt (D)	215,908	71.6%
Ty Cobb Jr. (R)	85,814	28.4%

2008 PRIMARY

Melvin Watt (D)	unopposed

2006 GENERAL

Melvin Watt (D)	71,345	67.0%
Ada M. Fisher (R)	35,127	33.0%

PREVIOUS WINNING PERCENTAGES
2004 (67%); 2002 (65%); 2000 (65%); 1998 (56%);
1996 (71%); 1994 (66%); 1992 (70%)

Watt is a Yale-educated lawyer whose intellect and liberal politics comple-ment like-minded Massachusetts Democrat Barney Frank. Watt sits on the Financial Services Committee, which Frank chairs. But unlike the voluble Frank, Watt — whose political experience includes a behind-the-scenes stint as a campaign manager — is often measured and reserved in public.

Watt has long advocated on behalf of African-Americans and once chaired the Congressional Black Caucus, whose members can be among the most liberal of Democrats, but he also is on cordial terms with the business and financial community. Watt's district includes part of Charlotte, the country's No. 2 banking hub behind New York, and he is chairman of the Domestic Monetary Policy and Technology Subcommittee. As such, he has become one of Frank's chief lieutenants.

When legislation to aid the struggling housing industry became law in July 2008, Watt joined Frank and several other panel Democrats in calling on mortgage holders to postpone foreclosing on any homes until the law went into effect. He urged colleagues to support a bill in early 2009 to permit bankruptcy judges to write down the principal and interest rate of loans for people whose mortgages are higher than the value of their homes. "They have to have that sledgehammer in their back pocket," he said. "You want few people to actually use it, but you still want them to have access to it."

Financial services companies credit Watt with giving their views a fair hearing, and he occasionally agrees with them. He opposed, for example, proposals to raise the $100,000 ceiling on federally insured deposits. "Try-ing to walk the balance between the banker interests and the consumer interests is very difficult," he once said. He has backed legislation to ban several credit card billing practices, siding with consumer groups over Wachovia and Bank of America, two of his district's largest employers.

Watt did not play much of a public role in late 2008 on the $700 billion effort to shore up the financial services industry. He supported the pro-posal despite objections from some of his constituents, saying he believed there was ample evidence it could avert greater crises. But he will be heav-ily involved in the panel's deliberations on how best to restructure and regulate the financial system.

As a member of the Judiciary Committee, Watt is known for his meticu-lous attention to legislative detail. He was the chief Democratic negotiator in 2006 on a measure to extend the 1965 Voting Rights Act. He produced a bipartisan bill that was praised by both then-Chairman F. James Sensen-brenner Jr. of Wisconsin and senior panel Democrat John Conyers Jr. of Michigan. Watt and Sensenbrenner are usually at opposite poles on issues. Watt said he got heavily involved because the bill dealt with redistricting. "I've been the poster child of redistricting. My district was changed five times in a 10-year period, so people knew that I understood that issue," he said.

He had less success in his effort to stop the renewal of the Patriot Act, a law passed after the Sept. 11 terrorist attacks giving law enforcement broad powers to investigate terrorism suspects. Watt believes the law tramples on civil liberties and gives police too much power to monitor the activities of the innocent. He voted against renewing the act in 2005, and failed in his efforts to attach an amendment requiring the government to disclose infor-mation about library record searches.

As Congressional Black Caucus chairman in the 109th Congress (2005-06), Watt was embroiled in several high-profile issues. He objected to his party's treatment of former Louisiana Democratic Rep. William J. Jefferson, who was the target of a federal corruption probe, but had not yet been indicted. When the House voted in 2006 to remove Jefferson from the Ways and Means Committee, Watt argued that the Democratic Caucus used a double standard because Jefferson is black. There is no House rule calling for removal of a rank-and-file member not charged with a crime.

Underpinning Watt's success is the determination he developed during a difficult early life. He grew up in rural Mecklenburg County in a tin-roofed shack that lacked running water and electricity. His mother raised him and his two brothers while working as a maid, and he earned money by shining shoes at a barbershop where he could not get his hair cut until night.

"People look at you in a suit as a member of Congress, and they think you've always been in a suit and always been a member of Congress," he once said. "I came out of a different kind of history."

After attending a segregated high school, he went on to graduate Phi Beta Kappa from the University of North Carolina, posting the highest academic average in the business school. He then earned his law degree from Yale.

Watt worked for several years as an attorney for a firm specializing in civil rights law. He interrupted his practice for a brief stint as an appointed state senator and to manage the 1990 Senate campaign of Democrat Harvey Gantt, who nearly upset GOP incumbent Jesse Helms that year.

In 1992, when a widely meandering black-majority district was created, Watt won it with relative ease and became one of the first African-Americans to represent North Carolina in Congress. But the boundaries of Watt's district were challenged in court through the 1990s, and the 12th District's lines were redrawn twice during the decade in response to lawsuits alleging unconstitutional racial gerrymandering.

The state's map was redrawn again in 2001 when North Carolina received another House seat because of population gains. The Democrats in charge of the process made sure to give Watt electorally safe territory. But the changing shape of his district has proved more of a distraction than a political threat: He consistently wins with at least 65 percent of the vote.

Watt, a good athlete, runs, plays tennis and has been the Democrats' pitcher in the annual charity baseball game with GOP lawmakers. (He was the Democrats' most valuable player in the 1995 and 1996 games, and was the winning pitcher and co-MVP in 2000.)

He is also a fan of NASCAR racing and promotes the hiring of more minorities for management and marketing jobs in the industry, as well as for jobs as drivers and in pit crews.

KEY VOTES

2008
Yes   Delay consideration of Colombia free-trade agreement
Yes   Override Bush veto of federal farm and nutrition programs reauthorization bill
No   Overhaul surveillance laws and permit dismissal of suits against companies that conducted warrantless wiretapping
Yes   Grant mortgage relief to homeowners and funding for Fannie Mae and Freddie Mac
Yes   Approve initial $700 billion program to stabilize financial markets
Yes   Approve final $700 billion program to stabilize financial markets
Yes   Provide $14 billion in loans to automakers

2007
Yes   Increase minimum wage by $2.10 an hour
Yes   Approve $124.2 billion in emergency war spending and set goal for redeployment of troops from Iraq
No   Reject federal contraceptive assistance to international family planning groups
Yes   Override Bush veto of $23.2 billion water projects authorization bill
Yes   Implement Peru free-trade agreement
Yes   Approve energy policy overhaul with new fuel economy standards
No   Clear $473.5 billion omnibus spending bill, including $70 billion for military operations

CQ VOTE STUDIES

	PARTY UNITY		PRESIDENTIAL SUPPORT	
	SUPPORT	OPPOSE	SUPPORT	OPPOSE
2008	99%	1%	15%	85%
2007	98%	2%	4%	96%
2006	97%	3%	17%	83%
2005	98%	2%	16%	84%
2004	97%	3%	26%	74%

INTEREST GROUPS

	AFL-CIO	ADA	CCUS	ACU
2008	100%	100%	61%	0%
2007	96%	90%	55%	0%
2006	100%	95%	47%	4%
2005	93%	100%	35%	0%
2004	93%	95%	29%	0%

NORTH CAROLINA 12

Central — parts of Charlotte, Winston-Salem and Greensboro

The Democratic 12th winds north from Charlotte to the Triad area of Greensboro, Winston-Salem and High Point. The district became known as the mother of all racial gerrymanders when it was originally drawn for the 1992 elections. Struck down by the courts and widely ridiculed for a serpentine shape that aimed to maximize the black population, the 12th was redrawn twice in the 1990s. The current 12th is 45 percent black and has a massive Democratic tilt. In the last three presidential elections, the district has given the Democratic nominee his best showing in the state.

While not as contorted as its 1990s predecessors, the current 12th zig-zags from Charlotte along Interstate 85 north and east to take in part of Salisbury, and then scoops up large black populations in Winston-Salem, High Point and Greensboro. The district takes in about one-third of Charlotte's population but two-thirds of its black residents, and 60 percent of Winston-Salem's population but nearly 90 percent of its black residents. Most of the 12th's black residents are lower- to middle-class.

Nearly one-third of the 12th's residents live in Charlotte, home to the nation's biggest banking center outside of New York. Volatility in the banking and investment sectors, however, has cast doubt over continued economic growth in the region. The Biddleville neighborhood, west of the business district, hosts the predominately black Johnson C. Smith University and is a hub of the black community. But the city's downtown — known as "uptown" — has its share of poverty and crime.

Highway infrastructure in the Triad area, including the junction of three interstates, couples with the Charlotte airport to create a stable base for trade. The vulnerable furniture manufacturing industry is vital to High Point's local economy.

MAJOR INDUSTRY
Finance, transportation, health care

CITIES
Charlotte (pt.), 196,125; Winston-Salem (pt.), 115,986; Greensboro (pt.), 62,075; High Point (pt.), 52,429; Salisbury (pt.), 26,399

NOTABLE
A Woolworth's lunch counter in Greensboro was the site of the first major civil rights sit-in in 1960.

Rep. Brad Miller (D)

Elected 2002; 4th term

CAPITOL OFFICE
225-3032
www.house.gov/bradmiller
1127 Longworth Bldg. 20515-3313; fax 225-0181

COMMITTEES
Financial Services
Foreign Affairs
Science & Technology
(Investigations & Oversight - chairman)

RESIDENCE
Raleigh

BORN
May 19, 1953; Fayetteville, N.C.

RELIGION
Episcopalian

FAMILY
Wife, Esther Hall

EDUCATION
U. of North Carolina, B.A. 1975 (political science);
London School of Economics, M.S.C. 1978
(comparative government); Columbia U., J.D. 1979

CAREER
Lawyer

POLITICAL HIGHLIGHTS
Wake County Democratic Party chairman,
1985-87; Sought Democratic nomination for
N.C. secretary of state, 1988; N.C. House, 1993-94;
defeated for re-election to N.C. House, 1994;
N.C. Senate, 1997-2002

ELECTION RESULTS

2008 GENERAL

Brad Miller (D)	221,379	65.9%
Hugh Webster (R)	114,383	34.1%

2008 PRIMARY

Brad Miller (D)	113,254	88.5%
Derald Hafner (D)	14,744	11.5%

2006 GENERAL

Brad Miller (D)	98,540	63.7%
Vernon L. Robinson (R)	56,120	36.3%

PREVIOUS WINNING PERCENTAGES
2004 (59%); 2002 (55%)

Miller is a rarity: a white Southern Democrat who doesn't avoid the "liberal" label. An occasional contributor to the Daily Kos blog that's popular among progressives, he seeks to help struggling homeowners, conduct tough oversight of corporations and end the Iraq War. "I went to college in the early '70s, so everyone was liberal," he said. "But I didn't get over it like some others did; I never grew out of it."

Miller's views reflect the political makeup of North Carolina's northern tier. It is more urban than many Southern districts, and the technology and biotechnology firms in the Research Triangle around Raleigh have drawn thousands of well-educated transplants. The district also takes in sizable black neighborhoods, University of North Carolina at Greensboro students and faculty, and blue-collar textile workers, all Democratic-leaning constituencies.

A member of the Financial Services Committee, Miller seeks ambitious changes to housing laws. A collapse in the nation's real estate market and the subsequent credit crisis helped him and other Democrats enact a law in 2008 to revamp the nation's mortgage regulations and eliminate some of the more exotic loans consumers had received.

While federal regulators are moving ahead with similar mortgage overhaul efforts, Miller wants to go one step further and move legislation to change the bankruptcy code. He said changing the code to allow bankruptcy judges to rewrite primary residence mortgages would be the best way to help beleaguered homeowners still facing the loss of their homes. He backed legislation, passed by the House in March 2009, that included such a provision.

At the same time, he continues to push for legislation to reduce predatory lending, change the way mortgage brokers are paid and increase regulation of credit rating agencies, a business he likened to "astrology." The House passed his bill in 2007, but it was never taken up by the Senate. He introduced a similar bill with tougher standards in 2009, confident the timing was right. He also said the landscape was right for legislation, offered by Massachusetts Democrat Bill Delahunt in early 2009, to create a Financial Product Safety Commission.

Miller's focus on housing issues brings him in line with a large Democratic bloc in Congress, including the Congressional Black Caucus, which argues that lawmakers need to do more to help struggling homeowners. He supports other key Democratic priorities, including strengthened consumer protection and public education.

Miller also serves on the Science and Technology Committee, where he chairs its Investigations and Oversight Subcommittee. He wants to strengthen the government's role in overseeing regulations governing toxic chemicals. He said he enjoys his task on the panel: "There are two reasons people enter politics — one is to comfort the afflicted, the other is to afflict the comfortable. The second…has suited me pretty well in an oversight role."

A member the Foreign Affairs Committee, he has long called for an end to U.S. involvement in Iraq. He expressed support for President Obama's plan to draw down troops over 18 months, but questioned the intention to leave up to 50,000 in place until the end of 2011 to train Iraqi forces and protect U.S. contractors. Miller expressed concern about whether the troops would be in danger and "how much humor the Iraqi people will show for continued presence."

Miller got the political bug early in life; he often cites an inspirational visit to the U.S. Capitol as a 9-year-old. Yet reaching his goal of working there wasn't easy. His father, the manager of the local post office in Fayetteville, died of a heart attack when Miller was 12. He and his siblings were raised by their mother, a school cafeteria bookkeeper. She pushed her children to go to college — something she and her husband had aspired to but never had the financial means to accomplish.

Miller graduated from the University of North Carolina and later got a law degree from Columbia University in New York City. Between those degrees, he decided to broaden his experience by getting a master's degree in comparative government at the London School of Economics. He clerked for a year for a federal appellate judge in Chapel Hill, then moved to Raleigh to work as a litigator at private firms. He became chairman of the Wake County Democratic Party and waited for an opportunity to run for office.

In 1988, he lost a Democratic primary for secretary of state. He was primed to run for the state legislature in 1992 after redistricting created a new House district that included his neighborhood. He won the seat but lost it two years later in the GOP surge of 1994.

He got even two years later by unseating a Republican in the state Senate, where he served three terms. While in the legislature, Miller wrote North Carolina's safe-gun-storage law, one of the first of its kind. He also cosponsored a law ending the state sales tax on food and pushed for higher teacher salaries and smaller class sizes.

When reapportionment after the 2000 census gave North Carolina a new House seat, Miller, as chairman of the state Senate redistricting committee, helped draw the new 13th District for himself, giving it a Democratic voter registration advantage and including much of his political base. In a fierce general election race, Miller defeated GOP businesswoman Carolyn W. Grant by 12 percentage points. He outspent Grant and benefited from endorsements from labor unions, teachers and environmentalists. Grant charged Miller with voting for $1 billion in new taxes and giving state lawmakers a big pay raise.

Since then, Miller's voting record has provoked more challenges from the right. In 2004, GOP Speaker J. Dennis Hastert and Republican Sen. Elizabeth Dole of North Carolina campaigned for his opponent, lawyer and former Hill aide Virginia Johnson, but Miller won with 59 percent of the vote. Republican Vernon L. Robinson — calling himself the "black Jesse Helms," after the state's notoriously conservative former senator — ran a sharply negative campaign in 2006, dubbing Miller a "San Francisco liberal." But Miller beat Robinson by a ratio of nearly 2-to-1 and duplicated that total two years later in trouncing Republican Hugh Webster.

KEY VOTES

2008
- Yes Delay consideration of Colombia free-trade agreement
- Yes Override Bush veto of federal farm and nutrition programs reauthorization bill
- No   Overhaul surveillance laws and permit dismissal of suits against companies that conducted warrantless wiretapping
- Yes Grant mortgage relief to homeowners and funding for Fannie Mae and Freddie Mac
- Yes Approve initial $700 billion program to stabilize financial markets
- Yes Approve final $700 billion program to stabilize financial markets
- Yes Provide $14 billion in loans to automakers

2007
- Yes Increase minimum wage by $2.10 an hour
- Yes Approve $124.2 billion in emergency war spending and set goal for redeployment of troops from Iraq
- No   Reject federal contraceptive assistance to international family planning groups
- Yes Override Bush veto of $23.2 billion water projects authorization bill
- No   Implement Peru free-trade agreement
- Yes Approve energy policy overhaul with new fuel economy standards
- No   Clear $473.5 billion omnibus spending bill, including $70 billion for military operations

CQ VOTE STUDIES

	PARTY UNITY		PRESIDENTIAL SUPPORT	
	SUPPORT	OPPOSE	SUPPORT	OPPOSE
2008	99%	1%	15%	85%
2007	97%	3%	6%	94%
2006	90%	10%	38%	62%
2005	93%	7%	26%	74%
2004	89%	11%	38%	62%

INTEREST GROUPS

	AFL-CIO	ADA	CCUS	ACU
2008	100%	100%	61%	0%
2007	96%	100%	47%	0%
2006	100%	90%	47%	17%
2005	93%	100%	41%	0%
2004	87%	90%	43%	8%

NORTH CAROLINA 13
North central — parts of Raleigh and Greensboro

The 13th is defined by its urban anchors of Greensboro and Raleigh, which are connected by several rural counties along the Virginia border. Almost half of the district's population lives in Wake County (Raleigh), including a large number of government employees and recent arrivals from out of state.

The district encompasses northern and central Raleigh, an area that falls into the Research Triangle and is built around an economy of technology, biotech and financial services. The 13th takes in about 70 percent of Raleigh's residents (the city is shared with the 2nd and 4th), and its slice of the city includes most of downtown and the state Capitol. In Greensboro, the state's third-most-populous city, tobacco processing long was the city's economic backbone, and Lorillard Tobacco, the nation's third-largest tobacco company, is still important to the region. Tobacco's influence on the economy, however, has decreased.

Raleigh and Greensboro have grown rapidly and feature diverse economies, but there have been widespread layoffs in both cities. The north-

ern, rural areas of Rockingham, Caswell, Person and Granville counties, on the Virginia border, and Alamance County, south of Caswell and shared with the 6th, still rely heavily on farming and manufacturing, particularly tobacco and a waning textile sector. The 13th dips into Alamance to reach Burlington.

The 13th has an overall Democratic lean, in part because of a sizable black population and a number of white moderates and liberals in the urban areas. Registered Democrats outnumber Republicans by more than 20 percentage points, but the actual Democratic advantage at the polls is smaller. The potential for swing voting exists in both the cities and suburbs, but the 13th moved to the left in the last presidential election, giving Barack Obama 59 percent in 2008. Obama won solidly in the district's portion of Guilford and Wake counties, but he lost in Person and Rockingham counties.

MAJOR INDUSTRY
Technology, financial services, state government, agriculture

CITIES
Raleigh (pt.), 192,576; Greensboro (pt.), 102,806; Burlington (pt.), 23,836

NOTABLE
Caswell County has one of the largest Amish communities in the South.

Gov. John Hoeven (R)

Residence: HO-ven
First elected: 2000
Length of term: 4 years
Term expires: 12/12
Salary: $96,183
Phone: (701) 328-2200

Residence: Bismarck
Born: March 13, 1957; Bismarck, N.D.
Religion: Roman Catholic
Family: Wife, Mikey Hoeven; two children
Education: Dartmouth College, B.A. 1979 (history & economics); Northwestern U., M.B.A. 1981
Career: Bank CEO
Political highlights: No previous office

Election results:
2008 GENERAL

John Hoeven (R)	235,009	74.4%
Tim Mathern (D)	74,279	23.5%
DuWayne Hendrickson (I)	6,404	2.0%

Lt. Gov. Jack Dalrymple (R)

First elected: 2000
Length of term: 4 years
Term expires: 12/12
Salary: $74,668
Phone: (701) 328-2200

LEGISLATURE

Legislative Assembly: January-April in odd-numbered years

Senate: 47 members, 4-year terms
2009 ratios: 26 R, 21 D; 41 men, 6 women
Salary: $141/day in session
Phone: (701) 328-2916

House: 94 members, 4-year terms
2009 ratios: 58 R, 36 D; 78 men, 16 women
Salary: $141/day in session
Phone: (701) 328-2916

TERM LIMITS

Governor: No
Senate: No
House: No

URBAN STATISTICS

CITY	POPULATION
Fargo	90,599
Bismarck	55,532
Grand Forks	49,321
Minot	36,567
Mandan	16,718

REGISTERED VOTERS

Voters do not register by party.

POPULATION

2008 population (est.)	641,481
2000 population	642,200
1990 population	638,800
Percent change (1990-2000)	+0.5%
Rank among states (2008)	48

Median age	36.2
Born in state	72.5%
Foreign born	1.9%
Violent crime rate	81/100,000
Poverty level	11.9%
Federal workers	9,656
Military	12,479

ELECTIONS

STATE ELECTION OFFICIAL
(701) 328-4146
DEMOCRATIC PARTY
(701) 255-0460
REPUBLICAN PARTY
(701) 255-0030

MISCELLANEOUS

Web: www.nd.gov
Capital: Bismarck

U.S. CONGRESS

Senate: 2 Democrats
House: 1 Democrat

2000 Census Statistics by District

DIST.	2008 VOTE FOR PRESIDENT OBAMA	MCCAIN	WHITE	BLACK	ASIAN	HISP	MEDIAN INCOME	WHITE COLLAR	BLUE COLLAR	SERVICE INDUSTRY	OVER 64	UNDER 18	COLLEGE EDUCATION	RURAL	SQ. MILES
AL	45%	53%	92%	1%	1%	1%	$34,604	59%	24%	17%	15%	25%	22%	44%	68,976
STATE	45	53	92	1	1	1	$34,604	59	24	17	15	25	22	44	68,976
U.S.	53	46	69	12	4	13	$41,994	60	25	15	12	26	24	21	3,537,438

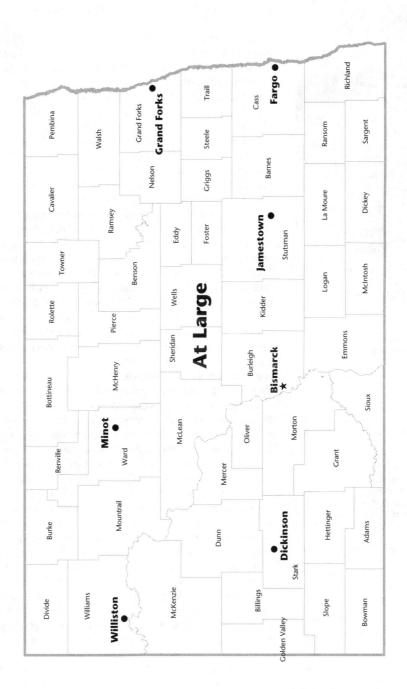

Pembina

Walsh

Grand Forks

Grand Forks

Traill

Cass

Fargo ●

Richland

Cavalier

Ramsey

Nelson

Steele

Ransom

Sargent

Griggs

Barnes

La Moure

Dickey

Towner

Benson

Eddy

Foster

Jamestown ●

Stutsman

Rolette

Pierce

Wells

Logan

McIntosh

Sheridan

Kidder

Bottineau

McHenry

At Large

Burleigh

Bismarck ★

Emmons

Sioux

Renville

Minot ●

Ward

McLean

Oliver

Morton

Grant

Burke

Mountrail

Dunn

Mercer

Dickinson ●

Hettinger

Adams

Divide

Williams

Williston ●

McKenzie

Stark

Billings

Slope

Bowman

Golden Valley

Sen. Kent Conrad (D)

Elected 1986; 4th full term

CAPITOL OFFICE
224-2043
conrad.senate.gov
530 Hart Bldg. 20510-3403; fax 224-7776

COMMITTEES
Agriculture, Nutrition & Forestry
Budget - chairman
Finance
   (Taxation, IRS Oversight & Long-Term
   Growth - chairman)
Indian Affairs
Joint Taxation

RESIDENCE
Bismarck

BORN
March 12, 1948; Bismarck, N.D.

RELIGION
Unitarian

FAMILY
Wife, Lucy Calautti; one child

EDUCATION
U. of Missouri, attended 1967; Stanford U.,
A.B. 1971 (government & political science);
George Washington U., M.B.A. 1975

CAREER
Management and personnel director

POLITICAL HIGHLIGHTS
Candidate for N.D. auditor, 1976; N.D. tax
commissioner, 1981-87

ELECTION RESULTS

2006 GENERAL

Kent Conrad (D)	150,146	68.8%
Dwight Grotberg (R)	64,417	29.5%
Roland Riemers (I)	2,194	1.0%

2006 PRIMARY

Kent Conrad (D)	unopposed

PREVIOUS WINNING PERCENTAGES
2000 (62%); 1994 (58%); 1992 Special Election (63%);
1986 (50%)

A policy wonk from a prairie state, Conrad has proved adept at looking after North Dakota's interests while forging a reputation as a fiscal hawk who decries Washington's inability to tackle the soaring levels of government debt.

As chairman of the Budget Committee, Conrad has the opportunity to be more than just a vocal scold. Righting the government's fiscal imbalances is a cause he genuinely embraces —"the debt is the threat" is a favorite phrase — but he has found it vexing to press his colleagues.

In the 110th Congress (2007-08), he teamed with his friend and frequent sparring partner Judd Gregg of New Hampshire, Budget's top-ranking Republican, to introduce legislation to create a task force charged with crafting policy proposals for dealing with the long-term budget problems. Conrad said he would have his committee vote on the plan, but it never did; he later said he feared damaging the proposal by moving it too quickly. In 2009, although the two Budget leaders still favored the notion, they disagreed on the details. Nevertheless, Conrad said, "It is going to take some special structure to deal with these long-term deficits and debt threats."

The fiscal 2010 budget plan that Conrad steered to Senate passage in April 2009 gave President Obama most of what he wanted. He did have to scale back some of Obama's proposals to show debt and deficit levels lower than those contained in an assessment of the president's proposal by the CBO.

Conrad achieved one of his priorities soon after Democrats took control of Congress in 2007: the restoration of the pay-as-you-go budget rule, which requires offsets for new tax cuts or increased mandatory spending. Democrats were critical of Republicans for letting the rule lapse in 2002. But Congress' record of following the rule since its return has been spotty at best.

Conrad does not fit the stereotype of a rugged Westerner; he looks more like a bookish "Jeopardy!" contestant. But he can be relentless when dealing with his state's issues. That is especially true when it comes to farmers and their communities, even when his efforts conflict with his fiscal sensibilities.

In 2009, just as he was taking the floor for the budget debate, Conrad also was keeping a close eye on rising flood waters, aggravated by heavy snowfall, that threatened his state. He agreed with a radio interviewer that simultaneous flooding and blizzards created an apt metaphor for the nation's financial situation. "It's my worst nightmare," he said. But he did express satisfaction that the federal response to the floods was prompt.

A member of the Agriculture, Nutrition and Forestry panel, he emerged as a major player on the 2008 reauthorization of agriculture and nutrition programs, sometimes appearing to overshadow Chairman Tom Harkin of Iowa. He secured a long-sought goal: a disaster relief fund for farmers and ranchers. His influence was also felt in 2002, when he played a central role in rewriting a GOP-drafted 1996 farm law that sought to phase out traditional crop subsidies and replace them with fixed but declining payments. The rewrite substantially expanded subsidies.

Conrad also has pressed for millions of dollars in improvements to the Air Force bases in Grand Forks and Minot and is a defender of funding for the state National Guard's 119th Fighter Wing. He has worked to make health care more accessible in his rural state, through such initiatives as a program that allows foreign-born, U.S.-trained doctors to stay in the country longer if they work in areas lacking physicians.

Conrad is known for his prodigious use of charts during floor debates. In 2001, the Rules and Administration Committee gave Conrad his own printing equipment because he was running off more charts than all of his colleagues combined. His charts sometimes tread between whimsical and corny; one depicted all the presidents preceding George W. Bush on one side, and Bush on the other, to make the point that the nation's debt had almost doubled during the 43rd president's term.

On the Finance Committee, he has focused on shrinking the "tax gap" — the difference between what is paid and owed — and cracking down on tax avoidance as a way of bringing in more revenue without raising tax rates. He is fond of showing a picture of a five-story building in the Cayman Islands that he says more than 12,000 businesses claim as their home to avoid paying taxes.

Conrad's clean-cut image took a hit in 2008 when he became involved in a controversy over whether he and Connecticut Democrat Christopher J. Dodd received favorable mortgages from Countrywide Financial. Portfolio magazine reported that in 2004, Countrywide waived a 1-percentage-point fee when Conrad refinanced a Delaware beach house loan, saving him $10,700.

Both Conrad and Dodd denied any knowledge of special treatment and pointed out the rates they received from Countrywide were market value at the time. Conrad also donated $10,700 to a Habitat for Humanity chapter in Bismarck and gave repeated interviews to discuss the issue.

On most social issues, Conrad's positions reflect the more conservative side of the prairie populist tradition from which he hails. In 2004, he voted to make it a criminal offense to injure or kill a fetus during the commission of a violent crime. He waded into the debate over energy policy in 2008. He joined Georgia Republican Saxby Chambliss in leading a bipartisan group of centrist senators who tried unsuccessfully to end the impasse over how Congress should respond to rising gas prices.

Another one of Conrad's committee assignments is Indian Affairs, where he has worked with his home-state colleague, Chairman Byron L. Dorgan, on health care. On the wall in Conrad's office in Bismarck hangs a prized gift from the state's Standing Rock American Indian Tribe: a framed resolution bearing his honorary Sioux name, Namni Sni, or Never Turns Back.

Conrad's early years were marked by the death of his parents in an automobile accident when he was 5. He and his brothers were raised by his grandparents, who moved into the family home in Bismarck. He attended high school at a U.S. military base in Libya, where he lived with family friends. The experience shaped his views on Iraq and the Middle East. "Anybody who knows the history of that part of the world knows that whoever has gone in there, whatever their intentions, have quickly been seen as occupiers rather than liberators, and almost without exception it has ended badly," he said.

Upon his return to North Dakota, he headed a statewide campaign — while still a teenager — to grant voting rights to 19-year-olds. The effort failed, but his engagement in politics continued. He was elected state tax commissioner in 1980, and gained popularity by vigorously auditing out-of-state corporations. Then, in 1986, the troubles besetting North Dakota's farms and small towns gave Conrad an opening against Republican Sen. Mark Andrews. Conrad defeated Andrews by 2,000 votes.

During that first campaign, Conrad pledged he wouldn't seek re-election unless the trade and budget deficits were significantly reduced during his term. In April 1992, he kept his promise by announcing his retirement. But in September of that year, North Dakota's senior senator, Democrat Quentin N. Burdick, died at age 84. Democrats persuaded Conrad to run in a special election the following December, and he defeated Republican state Rep. Jack Dalrymple. He has sailed to re-election since then.

Both Conrad and his wife, Lucy Calautti, are avid baseball fans. She has been a lobbyist for Major League Baseball since 2000 after having worked for Dorgan; he has been known to bring his glove along to games.

KEY VOTES

2008

Yes Prohibit discrimination based on genetic information
Yes Reauthorize farm and nutrition programs for five years
? Limit debate on "cap and trade" system for greenhouse gas emissions
No Allow lawsuits against companies that participated in warrantless wiretapping
Yes Limit debate on a bill to block a scheduled cut in Medicare payments to doctors
Yes Grant mortgage relief to homeowners and funding for Fannie Mae and Freddie Mac
No Approve a nuclear cooperation agreement with India
Yes Approve final $700 billion program to stabilize financial markets
Yes Allow consideration of a $14 billion auto industry loan package

2007

Yes Increase minimum wage by $2.10 an hour
Yes Limit debate on a comprehensive immigration bill
Yes Overhaul congressional lobbying and ethics rules for members and their staffs
Yes Limit debate on considering a bill to add House seats for the District of Columbia and Utah
Yes Limit debate on restoring habeas corpus rights to detainees
Yes Mandate minimum breaks for troops between deployments to Iraq or Afghanistan
Yes Override Bush veto of $23.2 billion water projects authorization bill
No Confirm Michael B. Mukasey as attorney general
Yes Limit debate on an energy policy overhaul containing $21.8 billion in tax incentives and reduced oil and gas subsidies

CQ VOTE STUDIES

| | PARTY UNITY | | PRESIDENTIAL SUPPORT | |
	SUPPORT	OPPOSE	SUPPORT	OPPOSE
2008	91%	9%	40%	60%
2007	87%	13%	44%	56%
2006	78%	22%	52%	48%
2005	76%	24%	48%	52%
2004	81%	19%	62%	38%
2003	85%	15%	58%	42%
2002	86%	14%	66%	34%
2001	90%	10%	66%	34%
2000	87%	13%	90%	10%
1999	87%	13%	73%	27%

INTEREST GROUPS

	AFL-CIO	ADA	CCUS	ACU
2008	100%	90%	57%	0%
2007	89%	80%	45%	12%
2006	93%	85%	45%	33%
2005	85%	85%	69%	21%
2004	100%	90%	53%	20%
2003	77%	80%	70%	15%
2002	100%	95%	45%	10%
2001	94%	85%	50%	36%
2000	71%	85%	42%	29%
1999	89%	90%	53%	16%

Sen. Byron L. Dorgan (D)

Elected 1992; 3rd term

CAPITOL OFFICE
224-2551
dorgan.senate.gov
322 Hart Bldg. 20510; fax 224-1193

COMMITTEES
Appropriations
(Energy-Water - chairman)
Commerce, Science & Transportation
(Aviation Operations, Safety & Security -
chairman)
Energy & Natural Resources
Indian Affairs - chairman

RESIDENCE
Bismarck

BORN
May 14, 1942; Dickinson, N.D.

RELIGION
Lutheran

FAMILY
Wife, Kim Dorgan; four children (one deceased)

EDUCATION
U. of North Dakota, B.S. 1965; U. of Denver,
M.B.A. 1966

CAREER
Aerospace company management trainer

POLITICAL HIGHLIGHTS
N.D. tax commissioner, 1969-80; Democratic
nominee for U.S. House, 1974; U.S. House, 1981-92

ELECTION RESULTS

2004 GENERAL

Byron L. Dorgan (D)	211,843	68.3%
Mike Liffrig (R)	98,553	31.8%

2004 PRIMARY

Byron L. Dorgan (D)	unopposed

PREVIOUS WINNING PERCENTAGES
1998 (63%); 1992 (59%); 1990 House Election (65%);
1988 House Election (71%); 1986 House Election
(76%); 1984 House Election (79%); 1982 House
Election (72%); 1980 House Election (57%)

Dorgan has devoted his more than a quarter-century in Congress to railing against Big Business and Big Government when he feels they are neglecting or trampling on ordinary Americans. But he has augmented his crusades by securing a comfortable spot for himself within his party's leadership.

With impeccably neat hair, glasses and polite Midwestern manners, Dorgan is an MBA-holding former state tax official who comes to his battles steeped in details. While he denounces perceived injustices in vivid and combative language, he also uses humor to make his point. Appearing on comedian Stephen Colbert's TV show, Dorgan once said, "If somebody says, 'You want to have Mexican food?' then buy Fig Newton cookies. They're made in Monterrey."

Trade agreements are perennial targets for Dorgan, who in 2005 published a book, "Take This Job and Ship It: How Corporate Greed and Brain-Dead Politics Are Selling Out America." An admitted "prairie populist," Dorgan often seeks ways to protect U.S. workers.

Dorgan is particularly critical of the financial services sector. He voted against a $700 billion rescue package for the ailing industry in fall 2008 and later joined Arizona Republican John McCain in calling for a select Senate committee to investigate what led to its problems. He won belated praise from liberal activists for his arguments in 1999 against a law that repealed part of the 1933 Glass-Steagall Act and opened up competition among banks, securities companies and insurance companies. "I think we will, in 10 years' time, look back and say we should not have done that," he predicted at the time.

Dorgan has shown a bit of an independent streak since he arrived in the House in 1981 — not surprising for a Democrat whose state has supported Republican presidential candidates since 1968. He joined Republicans in supporting the 1996 welfare overhaul. He was in the minority of Democrats who voted in 2002 to authorize the use of force in Iraq. In 2003, he supported a ban on a procedure that opponents call "partial birth" abortion. In 2007, he joined Republicans in blocking an immigration overhaul measure.

As a member of the Energy and Natural Resources Committee and chairman of the Appropriations Committee's Energy and Water panel, Dorgan pushes for increased federal support of research into cleaner and renewable fuels. Touting his state as the "Saudi Arabia of wind" (he says North Dakota has the largest wind power potential of any state), Dorgan wants to advance a plan to build a nationwide distribution grid for wind- and solar-produced electricity.

Since taking the helm of the Indian Affairs Committee in 2007, Dorgan has been on a quest to get the federal government to improve health care, housing and police protection for some of the poorest Americans — those who live on reservations. In 2008, he was a key mover in legislation to renew an American Indian housing program that also would assist in the building of day-care centers, Laundromats and community centers as well as homes.

Dorgan also serves on the Commerce, Science and Transportation Committee, where in 2009 he took the gavel of its panel on aviation. He has pushed for faster modernization of air traffic control systems while seeking to boost air service and aviation-related spending in his state.

He has shown the most creativity as chairman of the Democratic Policy Committee. During George W. Bush's administration, he turned the committee into perhaps the most aggressive Senate examiner of fraud and waste in Iraq. Even without subpoena power, the party panel delved into matters

www.cqpress.com

ranging from complaints about poor electric work and plumbing by contractors endangering soldiers to reports of diversions of ice meant for troops fighting in the desert. Dorgan said he expects to continue these inquiries.

The Policy Committee post puts Dorgan on a middle rung of the Democratic leadership ladder. He had yearned to move up to the top tier but has been stymied by other ambitious Democrats. In 2004, Dorgan considered running for the No. 2 job of party whip. He bowed out days later when Richard J. Durbin of Illinois claimed enough votes to prevail.

When Dorgan served as the top-ranking minority member on Indian Affairs, he worked with then-Chairman McCain to investigate activities of convicted lobbyist Jack Abramoff, suspected of bilking American Indian tribes with casino operations. In 2006, McCain and Dorgan teamed up on legislation to tighten federal regulation of Indian gaming.

Another Republican, Lindsey Graham of South Carolina, worked with Dorgan in a 2006 bid to revoke China's permanent normal trade status. Dorgan had supported a 2000 law granting permanent normal relations with China, hoping for a huge new market for U.S. farm commodities. He later charged that artificially low wages for China's workers and other abuses had created an uneven playing field for U.S. farmers.

Agriculture is North Dakota's major industry, with much of the state comprised of farmland. Although he generally opposed the Bush administration's efforts to scale back the 2002 farm law, he strongly supported its failed proposal to put a $250,000 limit on federal farm payments. Dorgan believes federal payments should go to family farms, not agribusiness. When President Obama proposed in 2009 to end payments exceeding $250,000, Dorgan praised the idea. The next day, though, his office said Dorgan didn't support another Obama-proposed limitation that would phase out direct payments to some farmers based "simply on a gross income test."

Although Dorgan is a shade to the left of Democrat Kent Conrad, his North Dakota partner in the Senate, the two seem in harmony both politically and personally. When Dorgan first ran for Congress in 1974, Conrad was his campaign manager. When Dorgan won a House seat six years later, his successor as state tax commissioner was Conrad. Lucy Calautti, Conrad's wife, was Dorgan's chief of staff for 10 years.

Dorgan was raised in the wheat-growing and ranching community of Regent, where, he likes to say, he graduated in the top 10 of his high school class. "There were nine of us," Dorgan jokes. In Regent — latest population estimate: 211 in the 2000 census — his father was in the petroleum business. His parents also raised horses and were active in the Farmers Union.

Other than a brief stint with a Denver-based aerospace firm, Dorgan has spent virtually his entire career in government. While Dorgan was still in graduate school, Democratic Gov. William Guy recruited him to be deputy tax commissioner. In 1969, when the commissioner died, Dorgan took his place, becoming, at 26, the youngest constitutional officer in North Dakota's history. He made a name for himself by suing out-of-state corporations for unpaid taxes.

Dorgan took on GOP Rep. Mark Andrews in 1974, holding him to 56 percent of the vote. When Andrews ran for the Senate in 1980, Dorgan captured the at-large House seat. He won five re-elections with ease and became a leading opponent on the Ways and Means Committee of tax cuts pushed by presidents Reagan and George Bush.

He won election to the Senate with 59 percent of the vote in 1992, after Conrad announced he was retiring to fulfill a campaign pledge to leave the Senate that year unless the deficit was reduced. (Conrad won a Senate seat that year anyway, after Sen. Quentin N. Burdick died.) He was easily re-elected in 1998 and 2004.

KEY VOTES

2008

Yes	Prohibit discrimination based on genetic information
Yes	Reauthorize farm and nutrition programs for five years
No	Limit debate on "cap and trade" system for greenhouse gas emissions
Yes	Allow lawsuits against companies that participated in warrantless wiretapping
Yes	Limit debate on a bill to block a scheduled cut in Medicare payments to doctors
Yes	Grant mortgage relief to homeowners and funding for Fannie Mae and Freddie Mac
No	Approve a nuclear cooperation agreement with India
No	Approve final $700 billion program to stabilize financial markets
Yes	Allow consideration of a $14 billion auto industry loan package

2007

Yes	Increase minimum wage by $2.10 an hour
No	Limit debate on a comprehensive immigration bill
Yes	Overhaul congressional lobbying and ethics rules for members and their staffs
Yes	Limit debate on considering a bill to add House seats for the District of Columbia and Utah
Yes	Limit debate on restoring habeas corpus rights to detainees
Yes	Mandate minimum breaks for troops between deployments to Iraq or Afghanistan
Yes	Override Bush veto of $23.2 billion water projects authorization bill
No	Confirm Michael B. Mukasey as attorney general
Yes	Limit debate on an energy policy overhaul containing $21.8 billion in tax incentives and reduced oil and gas subsidies

CQ VOTE STUDIES

	PARTY UNITY		PRESIDENTIAL SUPPORT	
	SUPPORT	OPPOSE	SUPPORT	OPPOSE
2008	92%	8%	30%	70%
2007	86%	14%	37%	63%
2006	80%	20%	46%	54%
2005	88%	12%	40%	60%
2004	84%	16%	62%	38%
2003	90%	10%	55%	45%
2002	88%	12%	70%	30%
2001	91%	9%	68%	32%
2000	90%	10%	90%	10%
1999	88%	12%	73%	27%

INTEREST GROUPS

	AFL-CIO	ADA	CCUS	ACU
2008	100%	90%	50%	8%
2007	89%	85%	27%	12%
2006	93%	95%	33%	12%
2005	86%	100%	33%	17%
2004	100%	95%	50%	20%
2003	92%	80%	61%	10%
2002	100%	90%	50%	20%
2001	94%	85%	50%	36%
2000	75%	90%	46%	16%
1999	100%	95%	35%	12%

Rep. Earl Pomeroy (D)

Elected 1992; 9th term

CAPITOL OFFICE
225-2611
www.pomeroy.house.gov
1501 Longworth Bldg. 20515-3401; fax 226-0893

COMMITTEES
Agriculture
Ways & Means

RESIDENCE
Bismark

BORN
Sept. 2, 1952; Valley City, N.D.

RELIGION
Presbyterian

FAMILY
Divorced; two children

EDUCATION
Valley City State U., attended 1970-71;
U. of North Dakota, B.A. 1974 (political science);
U. of Durham (United Kingdom), attended 1975
(legal history); U. of North Dakota, J.D. 1979

CAREER
Lawyer

POLITICAL HIGHLIGHTS
N.D. House, 1981-85; N.D. insurance
commissioner, 1985-93

ELECTION RESULTS

2008 GENERAL

Earl Pomeroy (D)	194,577	62.0%
Duane Sand (R)	119,388	38.0%

2008 PRIMARY

Earl Pomeroy (D)	unopposed

2006 GENERAL

Earl Pomeroy (D)	142,934	65.7%
Matt Mechtel (R)	74,687	34.3%

PREVIOUS WINNING PERCENTAGES
2004 (60%); 2002 (52%); 2000 (53%); 1998 (56%);
1996 (55%); 1994 (52%); 1992 (57%)

Pomeroy is an easygoing Midwesterner who has become known for his expertise on complex financial issues, particularly insurance and pension law. He tends toward the ideals of fiscal conservative policy, but also looks for any chance to helps his rural state when it comes to business or health care.

A member of both the Ways and Means and Agriculture committees, Pomeroy looks out for farmers in North Dakota whose business has been severely weakened in recent years by harsh weather conditions and foreign competition. He supports government subsidies for the farmers and opposes most free-trade deals. But he also balances his social-welfare bent and party loyalty with his state's conservative leanings. He supports gun ownership rights and pushes to ban child pornography and obscenity on the Internet.

Pomeroy took a lead role in negotiations on the farm bill in the 110th Congress (2007-08). He worked with Agriculture Chairman Collin C. Peterson of Minnesota, whose district borders Pomeroy's state, to secure a permanent disaster relief fund to aid farmers in North Dakota facing crop losses due to unpredictable weather. Pomeroy also used his seat on Agriculture to fight President George W. Bush's attempts to reopen the border to Canadian beef cattle imports during the 109th Congress (2005-06) and pass a free-trade agreement with Australia during the 108th (2003-04).

He's skeptical of the reputed benefits of free-trade deals in general. "Those deals haven't opened up markets," he once said. He voted against the North American Free Trade Agreement in 1993 and the Central America Free Trade Agreement in 2005. But in 2007, he supported an agreement with Peru that included labor and environmental standards negotiated between the administration and congressional Democrats.

On Ways and Means, Pomeroy — who served eight years as North Dakota's insurance commissioner — has worked with members of both parties on private pension issues, and once added a proposal to pension overhaul legislation to make it easier for workers to transfer their retirement savings to a new job. He has a particular interest in shoring up the Social Security program; his family relied on the program's survivor benefits to put him through college after his father died.

Like other members of the Blue Dog Coalition of fiscally conservative Democrats, Pomeroy advocates pay-as-you-go budgeting rules that compel new spending not to add to the federal deficit. He backed the $700 billion law in fall 2008 to shore up the nation's financial services sector, along with President Obama's $787 billion economic stimulus law in February 2009, despite their increasing the deficit. He hailed the stimulus package for extending a tax credit for wind energy — a booming industry in his state — and providing infrastructure investment as well as funding for health information technology. But when American International Group Inc. paid out bonuses to executives after receiving funds from the financial services rescue law, he backed a House measure to set a 90 percent tax on the bonuses. "You disgust us," he said to AIG executives. "By any measure, you are disgraced professional losers. And, by the way, give us our money back."

Pomeroy has long taken an interest in health issues, particularly those affecting the elderly. In 2007, he sponsored a bipartisan bill that would allow workers to use pre-tax dollars to pay for long-term care insurance. He supported legislation to expand the State Children's Health Insurance Program, which covers children whose families do not qualify for Medicaid. It was signed into law by Obama in early 2009.

Pomeroy's interests extend internationally: He and his now-ex-wife adopted two Korean children, and he helped reunite a family separated in the Kosovo War. He helped an Iraqi family immigrate to North Dakota in 2005 after the father was killed assisting National Guard soldiers from the state.

Pomeroy has voted to limit access to abortion and says tax dollars should not be used to pay for the procedure. But he has supported federal funding of embryonic stem cell research, which uses discarded embryos created for in vitro fertilization. North Dakota has a high incidence of Type 1 juvenile diabetes and Parkinson's disease, and advocates hope stem cell research will yield treatments.

Pomeroy has been close to North Dakota's two Democratic senators, Kent Conrad and Byron L. Dorgan, since the 1970s. Just a year out of college, Pomeroy drove Dorgan around the state in an unsuccessful campaign for the House. Conrad was Dorgan's campaign manager. "They're like brothers to me," he said. "We trust each other, we see the world the same way." The friends work closely on state-specific issues such as disaster aid for farmers.

Pomeroy grew up in a small North Dakota town where his father ran a feed and fertilizer store. He and his brother raised chickens on the family's small farm to make a few extra dollars. As a young man, he traveled with his church to Mississippi to work in the civil rights battle and helped mentally disabled people in his hometown. During college, Pomeroy won a Rotary Foundation award to study legal history at the University of Durham in the United Kingdom. When he returned to the United States, he was inspired to enter law school, a result of his overseas studies and television. "All my life, I loved watching those lawyer shows on TV," he said. "The lawyers on those shows were always fighting for great causes."

While in law school, he managed his brother Glenn's campaign for the state legislature. In 1980, Pomeroy won his own seat. "In North Dakota, there are no waiting lines for political participation," he said. "You don't have to be wealthy and you don't have to be a third- or fourth-generation politician."

In 1992, Pomeroy and his wife decided to join the Peace Corps and move to Russia. But at that year's state Democratic convention, Conrad announced his retirement due to a campaign promise not to seek re-election unless the deficit was reduced (though he later ran for the state's other Senate seat that year). A political scramble ensued. Then-Rep. Dorgan went after Conrad's Senate seat, while a party delegate urged Pomeroy to consider a run for the House. Pomeroy agreed to run just hours before the nominations. He won by 17 percentage points. In his subsequent re-elections he was held to less than 60 percent of the vote, but he won easily in 2006 and 2008.

KEY VOTES

2008
Yes	Delay consideration of Colombia free-trade agreement
Yes	Override Bush veto of federal farm and nutrition programs reauthorization bill
Yes	Overhaul surveillance laws and permit dismissal of suits against companies that conducted warrantless wiretapping
Yes	Grant mortgage relief to homeowners and funding for Fannie Mae and Freddie Mac
Yes	Approve initial $700 billion program to stabilize financial markets
Yes	Approve final $700 billion program to stabilize financial markets
Yes	Provide $14 billion in loans to automakers

2007
Yes	Increase minimum wage by $2.10 an hour
Yes	Approve $124.2 billion in emergency war spending and set goal for redeployment of troops from Iraq
No	Reject federal contraceptive assistance to international family planning groups
Yes	Override Bush veto of $23.2 billion water projects authorization bill
Yes	Implement Peru free-trade agreement
Yes	Approve energy policy overhaul with new fuel economy standards
Yes	Clear $473.5 billion omnibus spending bill, including $70 billion for military operations

CQ VOTE STUDIES

	PARTY UNITY		PRESIDENTIAL SUPPORT	
	SUPPORT	OPPOSE	SUPPORT	OPPOSE
2008	97%	3%	20%	80%
2007	93%	7%	10%	90%
2006	81%	19%	47%	53%
2005	80%	20%	41%	59%
2004	82%	18%	47%	53%

INTEREST GROUPS

	AFL-CIO	ADA	CCUS	ACU
2008	100%	85%	61%	4%
2007	96%	85%	60%	4%
2006	100%	80%	50%	38%
2005	93%	90%	67%	36%
2004	93%	85%	67%	28%

NORTH DAKOTA
At Large

North Dakota includes fertile eastern Red River farmlands, wheat-covered plains, arid grasslands farther west and Teddy Roosevelt's beloved ranches near the western border.

The state's agriculture-based economy must withstand extreme weather conditions, including severe droughts in the northwestern and southwestern corners and flooding along the Red River. The climate, foreign competition and a reduction in federal support systems have shaken the state's agricultural foundation. The energy industry — wind energy, biofuel, coal, gas and oil — is growing in the western part of the state, helping to offset the agricultural downturn. Technology has emerged as a significant economic contributor in the eastern part of the state, with Fargo hosting a Microsoft campus, but manufacturing losses hurt the statewide economy.

Economic trends have intensified migration of the state's young people away from rural farming communities and into the cities of Fargo and Grand Forks, where a diversified economy, health care facilities and

several universities provide greater job choice. Many residents continue to move out of state in search of work. Local lawmakers have supported legislation that would encourage people, through tax breaks and other incentives, to live and work in scarcely populated, rural areas.

North Dakota's entire congressional delegation has been Democratic for two decades. Republicans are more numerous and unwavering in the western part of the state, while eastern communities and American Indian reservations are more supportive of Democrats. But Republican roots are strong throughout the state — the state legislature and governorship are GOP-controlled, and John McCain carried the state with 53 percent of the vote in the 2008 presidential election.

MAJOR INDUSTRY
Agriculture, energy, technology, health care, higher education

MILITARY BASES
Minot Air Force Base, 4,435 military, 1,303 civilian (2008); Grand Forks Air Force Base, 1,986 military, 366 civilian (2008)

CITIES
Fargo, 90,599; Bismarck, 55,532; Grand Forks, 49,321; Minot, 36,567

NOTABLE
The National Buffalo Museum is in Jamestown.

Gov. Ted Strickland (D)

First elected: 2006
Length of term: 4 years
Term expires: 1/11
Salary: $144,833
Phone: (614) 466-3555

Residence: Bexley
Born: Aug. 4, 1941; Lucasville, Ohio
Religion: Methodist
Family: Wife, Frances Smith Strickland
Education: Asbury College, B.A. 1963 (history); U. of Kentucky, M.A. 1966 (guidance counseling); Asbury Theological Seminary, M.A. 1967 (divinity); U. of Kentucky, Ph.D. 1980 (counseling psychology)
Career: Professor; psychologist; minister
Political highlights: Democratic nominee for U.S. House, 1976, 1978, 1980; U.S. House, 1993-95; defeated for re-election to U.S. House, 1994; U.S. House, 1997-2007

Election results:
2006 GENERAL

Ted Strickland (D)	2,435,384	60.5%
J. Kenneth Blackwell (R)	1,474,285	36.6%
William S. Peirce (X)	71,468	1.8%
Robert Fitrakis (X)	40,965	1.0%

Lt. Gov. Lee Fisher (D)

First Elected: 2006
Length of term: 4 years
Term expires: 1/11
Salary: $75,916
Phone: (614) 466-0990

LEGISLATURE

General Assembly: January-June in odd-numbered years; January-July in even-numbered years

Senate: 33 members, 4-year terms
2009 ratios: 21 R, 12 D; 27 men, 6 women
Salary: $60,584
Phone: (614) 466-4900

House: 99 members, 2-year terms
2009 ratios: 53 R, 46 D; 78 men, 21 women
Salary: $60,584
Phone: (614) 466-3357

TERM LIMITS

Governor: 2 terms
Senate: 2 consecutive terms
House: 4 consecutive terms

URBAN STATISTICS

CITY	POPULATION
Columbus	711,470
Cleveland	478,403
Cincinnati	331,285
Toledo	313,619
Akron	217,074

REGISTERED VOTERS

Democrat	66%
Republican	32%
Unaffiliated	2%

POPULATION

2008 population (est.)	11,485,910
2000 population	11,353,140
1990 population	10,847,115
Percent change (1990-2000)	+4.7%
Rank among states (2008)	7

Median age	36.2
Born in state	74.7%
Foreign born	3%
Violent crime rate	334/100,000
Poverty level	10.6%
Federal workers	80,445
Military	36,713

ELECTIONS

STATE ELECTION OFFICIAL
(614) 466-2585
DEMOCRATIC PARTY
(614) 221-6563
REPUBLICAN PARTY
(614) 228-2481

MISCELLANEOUS

Web: www.ohio.gov
Capital: Columbus

U.S. CONGRESS

Senate: 1 Democrat, 1 Republican
House: 10 Democrats, 8 Republicans

2000 Census Statistics by District

DIST.	2008 VOTE FOR PRESIDENT OBAMA	MCCAIN	WHITE	BLACK	ASIAN	HISP	MEDIAN INCOME	WHITE COLLAR	BLUE COLLAR	SERVICE INDUSTRY	OVER 64	UNDER 18	COLLEGE EDUCATION	RURAL	SQ. MILES
1	55%	44%	69%	27%	1%	1%	$37,414	60%	23%	16%	13%	26%	22%	5%	416
2	40	59	92	5	1	1	$46,813	64	23	13	12	26	29	27	2,612
3	47	51	79	17	1	1	$41,591	60	26	14	14	25	23	15	1,595
4	38	60	92	5	1	1	$40,100	47	38	15	14	26	13	41	4,620
5	45	53	94	1	0	4	$41,701	46	40	14	13	26	15	51	6,128
6	48	50	95	2	0	1	$32,888	52	32	16	15	23	14	50	5,198
7	45	54	89	7	1	1	$43,248	57	28	14	12	25	19	29	2,848
8	38	61	92	4	1	1	$43,753	56	30	14	12	26	19	22	2,014
9	62	36	80	14	1	4	$40,265	55	29	16	14	26	20	14	1,102
10	59	39	87	4	2	5	$41,841	63	23	14	16	23	23	1	195
11	85	14	39	56	2	2	$31,998	61	21	17	15	26	23	0	135
12	54	44	72	22	2	2	$47,289	68	18	13	10	27	32	12	1,016
13	57	42	82	12	1	4	$44,524	59	27	14	14	26	22	7	531
14	49	49	94	2	1	1	$51,304	62	25	12	13	26	27	26	1,797
15	54	45	85	7	3	2	$43,885	66	20	14	10	23	32	9	1,178

2000 Census Statistics by District

DIST.	2008 VOTE FOR PRESIDENT OBAMA	MCCAIN	WHITE	BLACK	ASIAN	HISP	MEDIAN INCOME	WHITE COLLAR	BLUE COLLAR	SERVICE INDUSTRY	OVER 64	UNDER 18	COLLEGE EDUCATION	RURAL	SQ. MILES
16	48%	50%	92%	5%	1%	1%	$41,801	55%	31%	14%	14%	26%	19%	26%	1,732
17	62	36	85	12	1	2	$36,705	52	32	16	15	24	16	16	1,006
18	45	53	96	2	0	1	$34,462	46	38	16	14	26	11	57	6,826
STATE	52	47	84	11	1	2	$40,956	57	28	15	13	25	21	23	40,948
U.S.	53	46	69	12	4	13	$41,994	60	25	15	12	26	24	21	3,537,438

Sen. George V. Voinovich (R)

Elected 1998; 2nd term

CAPITOL OFFICE
224-3353
voinovich.senate.gov
524 Hart Bldg. 20510-3504; fax 228-1382

COMMITTEES
Appropriations
Environment & Public Works
Homeland Security & Governmental Affairs

RESIDENCE
Cleveland

BORN
July 15, 1936; Cleveland, Ohio

RELIGION
Roman Catholic

FAMILY
Wife, Janet Voinovich; four children
(one deceased)

EDUCATION
Ohio U., B.A. 1958 (government); Ohio State U.,
J.D. 1961

CAREER
Lawyer; state prosecutor

POLITICAL HIGHLIGHTS
Ohio House, 1967-71; Cuyahoga County auditor,
1971-76; Cuyahoga County Commission, 1977-78;
lieutenant governor, 1979; mayor of Cleveland,
1979-89; Republican nominee for U.S. Senate,
1988; governor, 1991-99

ELECTION RESULTS

2004 GENERAL

George V. Voinovich (R)	3,464,356	63.9%
Eric D. Fingerhut (D)	1,961,171	36.2%

2004 PRIMARY

George V. Voinovich (R)	640,082	76.6%
John R. Mitchel (R)	195,476	23.4%

PREVIOUS WINNING PERCENTAGES
1998 (56%)

Voinovich is a low-wattage, middle-of-the-road Republican with a deep commitment to fiscal restraint and an abiding interest in foreign policy. Popular at home, he often draws on his more than four decades of government experience that includes stints as mayor of Cleveland and Ohio's governor.

Now in his 70s, Voinovich (VOY-no-vitch) announced in January 2009 that he would not seek a third Senate term in 2010. He said he wanted to dedicate himself to confronting fiscal and national security challenges that he described as unparalleled since the Great Depression and World War II. "These next two years in office, for me, will be the most important years that I have served in my entire political career," he said. "I must devote my full time, energy and focus to the job I was elected to do, the job in front of me, which seeking a third term — with the money-raising and campaigning that it would require — would not allow me to do."

Voinovich has a long history of political independence. He has voted against GOP tax cuts and was one of the first members of his party to call for a withdrawal from Iraq, a position that prompted a near brawl with fellow Republican John McCain of Arizona during one closed-door meeting in 2007. During the 110th Congress (2007-08), he sided with his caucus on 68 percent of the votes in which it diverged from Democrats; only five other GOP senators broke from the party more frequently.

In late 2008, Voinovich joined a bipartisan group of senators from states with significant domestic auto production in pressing for an automaker bailout, which ultimately failed. He had earlier voted in favor of a $700 billion package to shore up the ailing financial services industry. His votes on those issues were a departure from his normal tight-fisted view of federal spending. He quickly reverted to his norm in the 111th Congress (2009-10), voting against a costly expansion of a joint federal-state children's health insurance program and against the $787 billion economic stimulus package.

He also spoke out against the $410 billion fiscal 2009 catchall appropriations bill, although he was a newly minted member of the Appropriations Committee. "The stimulus and omnibus has caused everyone who paid attention to say: 'My God, we have to do something to get back on firm fiscal footing.' They know that unless we fix our tax and entitlement system we might as well be flying a kamikaze plane," he said on the Senate floor.

Voinovich has spent most of his Senate career warning about exploding budget deficits due to the combined strains of Iraq War funding, soaring Social Security and Medicare costs, and reduced tax revenues. A fierce proponent of pay-as-you-go budgeting, which requires offsets for new tax cuts or increased mandatory spending, he said: "I think everybody is playing games. If we were responsible right now, we would have a temporary tax. We're putting everything on the credit card for our children."

Voinovich was one of the few Republicans to express buyer's remorse after voting for President George W. Bush's tax cuts in 2001 and 2003. He was one of three Senate Republicans to vote against an extension of the reduced tax rates for capital gains and dividends in 2006. Also that year, Voinovich was one of two Republicans to vote against permanently repealing of the estate tax, which failed. "I don't like the estate tax," he explained, "but I think doing away with it is bad. We've got to raise revenue to pay for expenses."

Voinovich is friendlier to labor and its causes than many Republicans. As mayor of Cleveland in the 1980s, he worked closely with public employee unions to rescue the city from insolvency. He said he weighs labor issues one by one: "Some I support, others I don't."

In 2002, as the Senate worked on legislation to create the Department of Homeland Security, Voinovich's colleagues often called on his knowledge of government personnel issues. But he was not included in the inner circle of GOP negotiators. His historically good working relations with government employee unions gave other Republicans pause.

He has positioned himself as a defender of Ohio's declining manufacturing base. That explains why he opposed legislation aimed at curbing global warming that the Environment and Public Works Committee took up in 2008. He drafted an alternative measure that would have imposed limits on greenhouse gas more gradually. In the 111th Congress, he will again be looking out for his state's industrial base as the panel takes up climate change legislation. He is the top Republican on the subcommittee that will draft a new surface transportation bill, and he is likely to be deeply involved in that effort as well.

Voinovich's experience has frequently led him to argue for more local control in deciding how to spend federal funds. He applauded the 1999 "Ed-Flex" law that gave states the flexibility to spend federal education money with fewer strings attached. But in 2001, he cast one of only three GOP votes in the Senate against the No Child Left Behind legislation, a major rewrite of education policy that tied federal aid to performance on student achievement tests. Voinovich called it an "all-out assault on local control."

Of Serbian and Slovenian ancestry, Voinovich in his first year as a senator took a politically risky stance as a vocal opponent of the NATO military action in Kosovo that involved U.S. forces. He advocated continued diplomatic negotiations with Serb leader Slobodan Milosevic, but refused to go to Serbia as long as Milosevic was in control. He also played a leading Senate role in the 2002 expansion of NATO that brought in Slovenia, Romania and the Baltic states, and looks forward to the Balkan nations such as Macedonia, Croatia and Albania joining the alliance in the future.

While he retains an abiding interest in foreign policy, Voinovich relinquished his seat on the Foreign Relations Committee to take the Appropriations slot at the beginning of the 111th Congress.

The grandson of immigrants reared on Cleveland's east side, where he still lives, Voinovich is the oldest of six children. His father was an architect, his mother a schoolteacher. Until Voinovich was 16, he wanted to be a doctor. But, he said, "sciences and I didn't get along, and I like other stuff better — like Boy Scouts." He became president of his high school class and was voted most likely to succeed. Friends from that era tell him he predicted even then that he would someday be mayor and governor.

He made it, and then some. After an early political career that included four years in the state House and four more as Cuyahoga County auditor, he was elected lieutenant governor in 1978. The next year, he unseated Cleveland Mayor Dennis J. Kucinich, now a Democratic Ohio congressman, after the city went into financial default on Kucinich's watch. With the help of a financial control board, Voinovich reversed some of the city's problems.

He lost a 1988 race against former Democratic Sen. Howard M. Metzenbaum, by 14 percentage points. "I was damaged goods," he said. "But we have a tradition in Ohio. You can't win statewide until you run and lose."

Voinovich rebounded two years later, winning the governorship. During his two terms, he won acclaim for putting the state on solid financial footing. In 1998, when Democratic Sen. John Glenn retired after four terms, Voinovich was instantly his presumptive successor. He was not seriously challenged for the GOP nomination and won the general election easily over Democrat Mary O. Boyle, a former Cuyahoga County commissioner. His 2004 re-election was a breeze; he won by almost 28 percentage points.

KEY VOTES

2008
Yes Prohibit discrimination based on genetic information

No Reauthorize farm and nutrition programs for five years

No Limit debate on "cap and trade" system for greenhouse gas emissions

No Allow lawsuits against companies that participated in warrantless wiretapping

Yes Limit debate on a bill to block a scheduled cut in Medicare payments to doctors

Yes Grant mortgage relief to homeowners and funding for Fannie Mae and Freddie Mac

Yes Approve a nuclear cooperation agreement with India

Yes Approve final $700 billion program to stabilize financial markets

Yes Allow consideration of a $14 billion auto industry loan package

2007
Yes Increase minimum wage by $2.10 an hour

No Limit debate on a comprehensive immigration bill

Yes Overhaul congressional lobbying and ethics rules for members and their staffs

Yes Limit debate on considering a bill to add House seats for the District of Columbia and Utah

No Limit debate on restoring habeas corpus rights to detainees

No Mandate minimum breaks for troops between deployments to Iraq or Afghanistan

Yes Override Bush veto of $23.2 billion water projects authorization bill

Yes Confirm Michael B. Mukasey as attorney general

No Limit debate on an energy policy overhaul containing $21.8 billion in tax incentives and reduced oil and gas subsidies

CQ VOTE STUDIES

	PARTY UNITY		PRESIDENTIAL SUPPORT	
	SUPPORT	OPPOSE	SUPPORT	OPPOSE
2008	67%	33%	74%	26%
2007	69%	31%	80%	20%
2006	77%	23%	89%	11%
2005	84%	16%	87%	13%
2004	88%	12%	90%	10%
2003	93%	7%	95%	5%
2002	88%	12%	96%	4%
2001	92%	8%	95%	5%
2000	78%	22%	59%	41%
1999	87%	13%	45%	55%

INTEREST GROUPS

	AFL-CIO	ADA	CCUS	ACU
2008	30%	25%	88%	52%
2007	33%	25%	82%	48%
2006	40%	20%	75%	56%
2005	29%	15%	100%	68%
2004	42%	30%	94%	76%
2003	15%	15%	100%	83%
2002	33%	5%	95%	90%
2001	13%	15%	93%	83%
2000	13%	10%	80%	64%
1999	33%	20%	82%	88%

Sen. Sherrod Brown (D)

Elected 2006; 1st term

CAPITOL OFFICE
224-2315
brown.senate.gov
713 Hart Bldg. 20510-3503; fax 228-6321

COMMITTEES
Agriculture, Nutrition & Forestry
Banking, Housing & Urban Affairs
  (Economic Policy - chairman)
Health, Education, Labor & Pensions
Veterans' Affairs
Select Ethics

RESIDENCE
Avon

BORN
Nov. 9, 1952; Mansfield, Ohio

RELIGION
Lutheran

FAMILY
Wife, Connie Schultz; two children, two
stepchildren

EDUCATION
Yale U., B.A. 1974 (Russian & East European
studies); Ohio State U., M.A. 1979 (education)
M.A. 1981 (public administration)

CAREER
College instructor

POLITICAL HIGHLIGHTS
Ohio House, 1975-83; Ohio secretary of state,
1983-91; defeated for re-election as Ohio
secretary of state, 1990; U.S. House, 1993-2007

ELECTION RESULTS

2006 GENERAL

Sherrod Brown (D)	2,257,369	56.2%
Mike DeWine (R)	1,761,037	43.8%

2006 PRIMARY

Sherrod Brown (D)	583,776	78.1%
Merrill Samuel Keiser (D)	163,628	21.9%

PREVIOUS WINNING PERCENTAGES
2004 House Election (67%); 2002 House Election
(69%); 2000 House Election (65%); 1998 House Election (62%); 1996 House Election (60%); 1994 House
Election (49%); 1992 House Election (53%)

Brown lacks the national profile of Rep. Dennis J. Kucinich but shares with his Ohio Democratic colleague a fierce passion for progressive causes. With his occasionally unruly mop of hair, love of baseball and predilection for mentioning his state's localities in floor speeches, he conveys a regular-guy persona that resonates with his working-class constituents.

He is also an intellectual. He holds two master's degrees and wrote a 2004 book on one of the topics about which he cares fervently — problems with free trade. With a Democratic presidential administration joining his party's majority in Congress, he is eager to wield more influence.

Brown made his mark during his 14-year tenure in the House with his vigorous opposition to treaties such as the North American and Central American free-trade agreements, which he said have harmed the manufacturing industry in his state and across the nation and exacerbated the nation's trade deficit. He said he would revamp trade pacts with incentives for corporations to create jobs in this country rather than outsource them. "There's nothing I feel stronger about than how this country has sold out the middle class on trade issues," said Brown, a member of the Health, Education, Labor and Pensions (HELP) Committee.

His attitude toward trade has led him to be a staunch supporter of organized labor. In 10 of his 14 years in the House, and in his first two years in the Senate, Brown received a 100 percent score from the AFL-CIO. He wears his allegiance on his chest: A lapel pin depicting a canary in a cage serves as a reminder that miners a century ago brought canaries into shafts to determine whether toxic gases were present.

Brown calls the inability of workers to receive a fair share of the wealth they help to create "the most fundamental problem in our economy." He often says he wants to make Ohio the Silicon Valley of jobs in the alternative-energy sector to offset the heavy manufacturing losses.

He believes in the need to fight global warming, introducing a bill in 2009 to give grants and loans to manufacturers to adopt energy-efficient technologies that reduce greenhouse gas emissions. But he was one of four Democrats to vote in June 2008 against limiting debate on legislation to cap greenhouse gas emissions because, he said, it could needlessly hurt his state's economy. He said an expansion of nuclear power should be considered as part of the effort — a position at odds with that of most liberal Democrats.

A member of the Banking, Housing and Urban Affairs Committee, Brown took a prominent role in trying to pass bailout legislation in late 2008 on behalf of the Big Three U.S. automakers, which employ more than 30,000 workers in Ohio. The measure couldn't get through the Senate, but the outgoing George W. Bush administration subsequently agreed to provide some relief. When President Obama announced a get-tough policy in March 2009 in which he urged the United Auto Workers to make concessions, Brown called on investors holding General Motors' corporate debt to "come to the table so debt can be restructured to manageable levels."

Brown did back a successful $700 billion law in fall 2008 to assist the ailing financial services industry. He said a failure to help the industry would greatly harm average Americans. But he said his support shouldn't be construed as being more supportive of giant banking and investment institutions. "I'm always skeptical of the upper-class accent that they use on Wall Street," he said.

Health care is another of Brown's passions. The son of a doctor, he has sponsored several bills on the subject, including measures intended to improve drug labeling, improve care for diabetes and give health care to workers at nuclear facilities. He worked with HELP Chairman Edward M. Kennedy of Massachusetts and Texas Republican Kay Bailey Hutchison on a measure, signed into law in 2008, to improve detection and treatment of tuberculosis. Though supportive of a single-payer system, he said it is politically unfeasible and backs a mix between private and public health coverage.

Brown also serves on the Agriculture, Nutrition and Forestry Committee, where he sought the input of his state's farmers in working on the reauthorization of farm programs in the 110th Congress (2007-08). One farmer's suggestion led him to propose a change to the bill — which made it into the law — to replace subsidies based on declining crop prices with an alternative intended to protect against drops in yield or prices.

During the 111th Congress (2009-10), Brown has the responsibility of helping to police the conduct of his colleagues from his seat on the Select Ethics panel. He also serves on the Veterans' Affairs panel.

Brown's liberalism extends to social issues and infuses both his public and private life. Long divorced, he had become an enthusiastic reader of a local newspaper writer's columns about Cleveland's neglected and needy. Brown sent an admiring e-mail to the writer, future Pulitzer Prize-winner Connie Schultz. E-mail led to a meeting and quickly to romance; less than a year after their first date in 2003, they were married.

To avoid a conflict of interest, Schultz gave up her column once Brown's Senate campaign got under way. She did, however, pen a 2007 book about her experience working for Brown's Senate campaign in which she detailed the demands it placed on the couple, including instances of political operatives rifling through the family's garbage.

Raised in Mansfield, in the north-central part of the state, Brown's first taste of elective office came as student council president in high school. His interest in politics was sparked by the Vietnam War, the civil rights movement and the 1968 presidential candidacy of Robert F. Kennedy.

Brown was 21 when he was elected to the Ohio House in 1974 — the same year he earned a degree in Russian studies from Yale University. He served in the state legislature for eight years, followed by an eight-year stint as Ohio secretary of state. He was defeated for re-election in 1990 by Republican Bob Taft, who would later serve two terms as governor.

In 1992, Brown won the open seat in the 13th District, which lies west of Cleveland, overcoming criticism that he moved into the district to run for Congress. He won a coveted seat on the Energy and Commerce Committee and focused on trade issues and his strong opposition to the North American Free Trade Agreement, which President Clinton supported.

Brown was nearly defeated for re-election in 1994, a strong Republican year. But he won subsequent elections with ease and in the process amassed a huge campaign treasury to prepare for a bid for governor or senator.

Brown originally said he wouldn't challenge incumbent Republican Mike DeWine, but reversed himself in October 2005. DeWine hammered Brown's positions on tax policy and national security issues. But Brown won by 12 percentage points, racking up large percentages in the counties around Cleveland and Mahoning Valley — traditionally the most unionized part of Ohio.

An avid, statistics-spouting baseball fan, Brown used his hobby to help win his seat on House Energy and Commerce. He gave a favored baseball card — that of 1950s Boston Red Sox outfielder Jimmy Piersall, who suffered from mental illness — to influential California Democrat Vic Fazio, with the note: "Don't be crazy. Vote for Sherrod Brown for Energy and Commerce." Years later, upon seeing New York GOP Rep. Sherwood Boehlert, Brown told a reporter, "He's a Republican, but I like him. How could I not? He represents Cooperstown" — home of baseball's Hall of Fame.

KEY VOTES

2008

Yes Prohibit discrimination based on genetic information
Yes Reauthorize farm and nutrition programs for five years
No Limit debate on "cap and trade" system for greenhouse gas emissions
Yes Allow lawsuits against companies that participated in warrantless wiretapping
Yes Limit debate on a bill to block a scheduled cut in Medicare payments to doctors
Yes Grant mortgage relief to homeowners and funding for Fannie Mae and Freddie Mac
No Approve a nuclear cooperation agreement with India
Yes Approve final $700 billion program to stabilize financial markets
Yes Allow consideration of a $14 billion auto industry loan package

2007

Yes Increase minimum wage by $2.10 an hour
No Limit debate on a comprehensive immigration bill
Yes Overhaul congressional lobbying and ethics rules for members and their staffs
Yes Limit debate on considering a bill to add House seats for the District of Columbia and Utah
Yes Limit debate on restoring habeas corpus rights to detainees
Yes Mandate minimum breaks for troops between deployments to Iraq or Afghanistan
Yes Override Bush veto of $23.2 billion water projects authorization bill
No Confirm Michael B. Mukasey as attorney general
Yes Limit debate on an energy policy overhaul containing $21.8 billion in tax incentives and reduced oil and gas subsidies

CQ VOTE STUDIES

	PARTY UNITY		PRESIDENTIAL SUPPORT	
	SUPPORT	OPPOSE	SUPPORT	OPPOSE
2008	97%	3%	30%	70%
2007	97%	3%	35%	65%
House Service:				
2006	92%	8%	36%	64%
2005	97%	3%	7%	93%
2004	98%	2%	26%	74%
2003	99%	1%	11%	89%
2002	98%	2%	22%	78%
2001	98%	2%	12%	88%
2000	97%	3%	81%	19%

INTEREST GROUPS

	AFL-CIO	ADA	CCUS	ACU
2008	100%	95%	63%	8%
2007	100%	95%	36%	0%
House Service:				
2006	93%	75%	40%	25%
2005	93%	100%	33%	4%
2004	100%	95%	24%	4%
2003	100%	100%	25%	16%
2002	100%	95%	25%	4%
2001	100%	95%	22%	4%
2000	100%	90%	25%	4%

Rep. Steve Driehaus (D)

Elected 2008; 1st term

Driehaus is a fiscal conservative who said he hopes to build on his earlier work in the Ohio state House in improving accountability in government. He seeks to provide "more-dynamic leadership" for his district, describing leadership as "getting your hands dirty, getting into the neighborhoods, working with leaders when it's boring, when it's not exciting…to get stuff done."

As a member of the Oversight and Government Reform Committee, Driehaus (DREE-house) pushed a bill through the House in March 2009 that directs federal agencies to make unclassified information more widely accessible. It directs the archivist of the United States to issue regulations preventing agencies from designating information with labels that are more restrictive than merited. The federal government uses more than 100 "information control designations."

Driehaus also serves on the Financial Services Committee, where he supported President Obama's $787 billion economic stimulus law in early 2009 for its emphasis on upgrading local roads, bridges and other eroding infrastructure. But Driehaus was one of just 20 House Democrats to oppose a subsequent $410 billion catchall spending measure for fiscal 2009; although he said he supported many of the bill's programs, he opposed the overall spending level.

During his eight years in the Ohio legislature, where he served as minority whip for two years, Driehaus focused on housing issues. He urged Democratic Gov. Ted Strickland to create foreclosure prevention task forces and said he would continue to focus on the issue in Congress.

Born into a large and politically influential Ohio family, he said his first experience in politics came at age 2, when his father unsuccessfully campaigned for the seat he now holds. He said that as a youth, while his friends went camping, he went door-to-door with his brothers and sisters, passing out leaflets and pounding in yard signs.

He ousted seven-term Republican incumbent Steve Chabot with 52 percent of the vote in 2008, benefitting from the Democratic tide that enabled Barack Obama to carry the district four years after George W. Bush won it.

CAPITOL OFFICE
225-2216
driehaus.house.gov
408 Cannon Bldg. 20515-3501; fax 225-3012

COMMITTEES
Financial Services
Oversight & Government Reform

RESIDENCE
Cincinnati

BORN
June 24, 1966; Cincinnati, Ohio

RELIGION
Roman Catholic

FAMILY
Wife, Lucienne Driehaus; three children

EDUCATION
Miami U. (Ohio), B.A. 1988 (political science & diplomacy and foreign affairs); Indiana U., M.P.A. 1995

CAREER
Community outreach program director; city council and congressional district aide; Peace Corps volunteer

POLITICAL HIGHLIGHTS
Ohio House, 2001-08 (minority whip, 2005-07)

ELECTION RESULTS

2008 GENERAL

Steve Driehaus (D)	155,455	52.5%
Steve Chabot (R)	140,683	47.5%

2008 PRIMARY

Steve Driehaus (D)	unopposed

OHIO 1

Western Cincinnati and suburbs

Nestled in Ohio's southwestern corner, the 1st takes in more than three-fourths of Cincinnati's residents. Traditional German Catholic conservatives in the city and a growing suburban base are crucial to Republicans, while Cincinnati's 43-percent-black population is key to Democrats.

A diverse economy, with research firms, corporate headquarters and a manufacturing base, has fortified Cincinnati against previous economic downturns, but layoffs in construction and finance sectors have slowed growth. Ohio River access earned the city a reputation as a commercial hub. Manufacturing still provides blue-collar jobs, and General Electric's aircraft engine branch is headquartered in the city.

Corporate headquarters in Cincinnati, including Procter & Gamble, Macy's Inc. and Kroger, prop up the retail industry and have

lured consumer market research and development companies. Cincinnati also is a cultural and entertainment hub. Among other locations, the 1st District hosts the Museum Center at Union Terminal, Carew Tower (the city's tallest building) and Paul Brown Stadium — the home field of football's Bengals.

Cincinnati's heavily black neighborhoods, including Over-the-Rhine, Avondale and Bond Hill, vote dependably Democratic. Outside of Cincinnati, Hamilton County is becoming slightly more Democratic as the county's Republican base moves farther north. In 2008, Democrat Barack Obama carried the 1st District with 55 percent of its presidential vote.

MAJOR INDUSTRY
Consumer products, service

CITIES
Cincinnati (pt.), 257,122; Norwood, 21,675

NOTABLE
The National Underground Railroad Freedom Center is in Cincinnati.

Rep. Jean Schmidt (R)

Elected August 2005; 2nd full term

Schmidt, a fervent conservative who runs several miles and attends Mass before work each morning, has had to fight tooth and nail to hold on to her seat in a solid GOP district. But she appears to be cementing her grip on the job.

She seldom speaks on the House floor, is sparing in offering legislation and issues few news releases (the only one she issued in 2008 urged the United States to pursue offshore oil and gas drilling opportunities). What she does is make sure her votes reflect the values and interests of her constituents. And in 2008, they rewarded her at the polls with her biggest margin of victory yet — 8 percentage points.

Her congressional career got off to a rough start in November 2005 when, less than three months after she had narrowly won a special election, Schmidt described a prominent congressman and decorated Marine veteran as a "coward." When her comments sparked boos from other lawmakers in the chamber, Schmidt withdrew her words immediately. She later told reporters that she did not know Pennsylvania Democrat John P. Murtha was a Marine and a war veteran. She wrote him a note of apology, which he accepted, but that did not end the fallout for Schmidt. The Cincinnati Enquirer called her remarks "way out of line," and Murtha has since campaigned vigorously for her Democratic opponent.

Schmidt has steered relatively clear of the House floor since. In 2008, she spoke on the floor about issues or legislation less than a half-dozen times. The incident, though, reinforced her reputation among critics back in Ohio as "Mean Jean." While Schmidt doesn't care for the nickname, she is proud of her toughness. "You have to be in this environment," Schmidt said. "Politics is not for the faint of heart."

Her toughness was put to the test in October 2008 when a car hit her as she was jogging and threw her off the road. She initially shook it off but later had to scrap a trip to Afghanistan when the pain worsened and she realized she had broken ribs and vertebrae.

Schmidt, a longtime anti-abortion activist, said she is a Republican because the GOP is the only party to recognize that life begins at conception. Before being elected to the House, she was president of the Cincinnati-area Right to Life organization and campaigned on a promise to "uphold the moral values that this district holds so dear." She opposes abortion in all cases, opposes the death penalty and supports a constitutional amendment banning same-sex marriage.

She introduced legislation in 2009 to authorize post-placement counseling services to women who put their babies up for adoption. She also plans to fight to keep longstanding policy language in various appropriations bills barring use of taxpayer funds to perform or advocate abortion.

Schmidt sayid her pro-life views "extend beyond the child in the womb," and she noted an amendment she sponsored to the farm bill in 2008 that authorized states to provide nutrition education programs.

Schmidt mostly matches her views on social issues with right-of-center economic policy positions. She supports making President George W. Bush's 2001 and 2003 tax cuts permanent and favors a flat tax rather than the existing graduated income tax system. She initially voted against the $700 billion financial sector rescue plan in the fall of 2008, but she voted for the modified version when it came up for a vote less than a week later. "I could see that the financial markets were collapsing before us and felt that we needed to do something in order to stall this credit freeze," Schmidt said.

CAPITOL OFFICE
225-3164
www.house.gov/schmidt
418 Cannon Bldg. 20515-3502; fax 225-1992

COMMITTEES
Agriculture
Transportation & Infrastructure

RESIDENCE
Miami Township

BORN
Nov. 29, 1951; Cincinnati, Ohio

RELIGION
Roman Catholic

FAMILY
Husband, Peter Schmidt; one child

EDUCATION
U. of Cincinnati, B.A. 1974 (political science)

CAREER
Teacher; homemaker

POLITICAL HIGHLIGHTS
Miami Township trustee, 1990-2000; Clermont County Republican Party chairwoman, 1996-98; Ohio House, 2001-04; sought Republican nomination for Ohio Senate, 2004

ELECTION RESULTS

2008 GENERAL

Jean Schmidt (R)	148,671	44.8%
Victoria Wulsin (D)	124,213	37.5%
David Krikorian (I)	58,710	17.7%

2008 PRIMARY

Jean Schmidt (R)	41,987	57.5%
Tom Brinkman Jr. (R)	28,897	39.6%
Nathan W. Bailey (R)	2,126	2.9%

2006 GENERAL

Jean Schmidt (R)	120,112	50.5%
Victoria Wulsin (D)	117,595	49.4%

PREVIOUS WINNING PERCENTAGES
2005 Special Election (52%)

Schmidt grew up on a farm in Clermont County in southern Ohio, where her father, Gus Hoffman, is the owner of a sprint car racing team, Hoffman Auto Racing, started in 1929. She said the "best day of my life" was May 8, 1974, when her father's car qualified for the Indianapolis 500. By the late 1970s, she and her twin sister worked some races for her dad's team. "All of us got the racing bug," said Schmidt, who occasionally throws the green flag to start car races in her district. Growing up on the family farm with two older brothers, Schmidt learned how to shoot a gun, and she still regularly carries a Bersa semiautomatic handgun that her stockbroker husband gave her as a present.

Schmidt traces her interest in politics back to the Kennedy-Nixon debates, which she watched as an 8-year-old with her parents. "I liked the sound of Nixon, I liked the sound of Republican. I decided when I grew up, I wanted to be a Republican," said Schmidt, whose grandfather was vice chairman of the Hamilton County Democratic Party.

After graduating from the University of Cincinnati in 1974 with a degree in political science, Schmidt worked as a bank manager and fitness instructor and got involved in local party politics. In 1978, she took up running after giving birth to her daughter and suffering postpartum depression. She began with a half-mile run. As of April 2009, Schmidt had run in 76 marathons, including many Boston Marathons.

After a decade as township trustee, Schmidt went on to serve four years in the Ohio House. Following a loss for the state Senate, she became president of the anti-abortion group. When Republican Rob Portman left Congress in early 2005 to become U.S. trade representative, Schmidt entered a crowded field of better-known Republicans, including former Rep. Bob McEwen and Pat DeWine, a county commissioner and son of then-Sen. Mike DeWine. She won and then focused on social issues to beat Democrat Paul Hackett by 3 percentage points.

In 2006, Schmidt staved off a primary challenge by McEwen before eking out a 2,517-vote victory over Democratic challenger Victoria Wulsin, a physician who ran a nonprofit AIDS prevention organization. The race was so close that Wulsin didn't concede until late November.

Schmidt faced a rematch with Wulsin in 2008, along with independent David Krikorian. Political analyst Stuart Rothenberg called the contest the worst congressional race he has ever witnessed. After a nasty campaign, many voters said they were not pleased with either of the major-party candidates, but Schmidt emerged 8 percentage points ahead. That victory, particularly the margin, was a pleasant surprise to the GOP.

KEY VOTES

2008
No Delay consideration of Colombia free-trade agreement
No Override Bush veto of federal farm and nutrition programs reauthorization bill
Yes Overhaul surveillance laws and permit dismissal of suits against companies that conducted warrantless wiretapping
No Grant mortgage relief to homeowners and funding for Fannie Mae and Freddie Mac
No Approve initial $700 billion program to stabilize financial markets
Yes Approve final $700 billion program to stabilize financial markets
No Provide $14 billion in loans to automakers

2007
Yes Increase minimum wage by $2.10 an hour
No Approve $124.2 billion in emergency war spending and set goal for redeployment of troops from Iraq
Yes Reject federal contraceptive assistance to international family planning groups
Yes Override Bush veto of $23.2 billion water projects authorization bill
Yes Implement Peru free-trade agreement
Yes Approve energy policy overhaul with new fuel economy standards
Yes Clear $473.5 billion omnibus spending bill, including $70 billion for military operations

CQ VOTE STUDIES

	PARTY UNITY		PRESIDENTIAL SUPPORT	
	SUPPORT	OPPOSE	SUPPORT	OPPOSE
2008	95%	5%	72%	28%
2007	96%	4%	80%	20%
2006	96%	4%	97%	3%
2005	98%	2%	87%	13%

INTEREST GROUPS

	AFL-CIO	ADA	CCUS	ACU
2008	21%	15%	94%	87%
2007	17%	15%	89%	92%
2006	14%	0%	100%	88%
2005	0%	0%	82%	88%

OHIO 2
Eastern Cincinnati and suburbs; Portsmouth

The 2nd stretches from some of wealthy areas in eastern Cincinnati and Hamilton County in the state's southwest to struggling rural communities in southern Ohio. A distinct split between its suburban and rural elements defines the district.

The district's economy had revolved around light manufacturing and the retail and service industries, but a home and commercial construction market collapse and job cuts at local manufacturing firms have stalled the economy in the Cincinnati area. The 2nd takes in less than one-fourth of Cincinnati's residents, including upscale neighborhoods of Hyde Park and Mount Lookout. Nearly 40 percent of the population lives in Hamilton County, including the well-to-do areas of Madeira, Mariemont, Blue Ash and the Village of Indian Hill.

To the east, once-undeveloped Clermont County has attracted some business growth and residential development, in large part due to its low taxes. To the north, Warren County has experienced sizable residential growth as well-off families move in from Hamilton County. As more sub-urban residents have moved in, Warren County has begun to shed its agricultural tradition.

In the district's east, Brown, Adams, Pike and Scioto counties are all struggling economically. Pike and Scioto depend mainly on corn and soybeans, while tobacco is still big in Brown and Adams counties. Unemployment rates in some of the district's rural Appalachian counties have reached 15 percent; local officials hope to spur growth here by investing in infrastructure projects and broadband Internet access.

The 2nd is reliably Republican at the presidential level, and John McCain took the 2nd overall with 59 percent of its presidential vote in 2008. The district's portion of Hamilton, however, supported Democrat Victoria Wulsin in the U.S. House race, and generally Democratic-voting Scioto and Pike also voted for the Democratic challenger.

MAJOR INDUSTRY
Manufacturing, service, retail, agriculture

CITIES
Cincinnati (pt.), 74,163; Portsmouth, 20,909

NOTABLE
Ulysses S. Grant's birthplace in Point Pleasant is a state historical site.

Rep. Michael R. Turner (R)

Elected 2002; 4th term

CAPITOL OFFICE
225-6465
www.house.gov/miketurner
1740 Longworth Bldg. 20515-3503; fax 225-6754

COMMITTEES
Armed Services
Oversight & Government Reform

RESIDENCE
Centerville

BORN
Jan. 11, 1960; Dayton, Ohio

RELIGION
Protestant

FAMILY
Wife, Lori Turner; two children

EDUCATION
Ohio Northern U., B.A. 1982 (political science);
Case Western Reserve U., J.D. 1985; U. of Dayton,
M.B.A. 1992

CAREER
Real estate developer; lawyer

POLITICAL HIGHLIGHTS
Mayor of Dayton, 1994-2002; defeated for
re-election as mayor of Dayton, 2001

ELECTION RESULTS

2008 GENERAL

Michael R. Turner (R)	200,204	63.3%
Jane Mitakides (D)	115,976	36.7%

2008 PRIMARY

Michael R. Turner (R)	unopposed

2006 GENERAL

Michael R. Turner (R)	127,978	58.5%
Richard Chema (D)	90,650	41.5%

PREVIOUS WINNING PERCENTAGES
2004 (62%); 2002 (59%)

For Turner, a former mayor of Dayton with blue-collar roots and a keen interest in urban issues, Democratic control of Congress is not nearly as traumatic as it is for many of his GOP colleagues. He has had a chance to support issues that many in the Republican Party had overlooked while teaming with Democrats on economic and historic preservation matters.

During his first four years in office, Turner voted at least 91 percent of the time with his GOP colleagues on issues on which majorities of the two parties diverged. That percentage fell to 83 percent in the 110th Congress (2007-08), as he joined Democrats on issues ranging from children's health insurance to raising the minimum wage. He said that "with the shift in leadership in the House…we've had the opportunity to vote on matters that I've had an interest in, that the Bush administration does not."

He continued that pattern in the early months of President Obama's administration. He supported a bill to expand a children's health insurance program — a measure President George W. Bush vetoed twice but which Obama signed into law — and in recognition of his state's foreclosure woes, was one of just seven House Republicans to back a bill allowing bankruptcy judges to modify mortgage terms for troubled homeowners, an issue often called "cramdown." He refused, however, to back Obama's $787 billion economic stimulus law or a $410 billion catchall spending bill for fiscal 2009.

Turner has emerged as an authority on urban issues. He presses for federal initiatives to promote public-private partnerships, and defended Community Development Block Grants, beloved by mayors, against the Bush administration's attempts to eliminate them.

In his first year in Congress in 2003, Turner was appointed by Speaker J. Dennis Hastert as chairman of a 24-member working group called Saving America's Cities, later subsumed into a broader House GOP task force. He is vice chairman of the Congressional Urban Caucus, led by Pennsylvania Democrat Chaka Fattah, who represents Philadelphia. And he and North Carolina Democrat Brad Miller co-founded the Historic Preservation Caucus. His highest urban priority, he said, is legislation that would provide tax credits to companies that clean up polluted former industrial sites.

Redevelopment of the sites, known as brownfields, was a priority for Turner as Dayton's mayor from 1994 to 2002. He is credited with reversing the city's downtown decline with programs that built a new arts center and a minor league baseball stadium and restored a riverfront. A project he dubbed "Rehabarama," a public-private partnership to restore historic houses, was recognized by the National Trust for Historic Preservation.

But Turner also has strong socially conservative views. He is outspoken in his opposition to same-sex marriage and abortion, and was especially involved in pushing a GOP bill recognizing a fetus as a legal victim when the fetus is injured or killed in an attack on the mother.

He takes a traditional Republican view of national security matters as a member of the Armed Services Committee, where he is the top-ranking GOP member on the Strategic Forces panel. He joined the committee's top Republican, John M. McHugh of New York, in early 2009 in arguing against Obama's efforts to cut spending for national missile defense. One of his major parochial preoccupations is looking out for Wright-Patterson Air Force Base, a big winner in the most recent round of base realignments. Dayton expects 1,000 new jobs as a result of the base's expansion.

Turner has joined California Democrat Jane Harman on legislation to develop a comprehensive system to prevent sexual assaults in the military. The prosecution of rape cases in the armed forces is well below that of the rest of the country.

Turner keeps a fairly low profile, rarely speaking on the House floor. He did earn a bit of national notoriety in 2007, after a constituent complained that the acting Architect of the Capitol had refused to include the word "God" in a certificate accompanying a flag flown over the Capitol in honor of the constituent's grandfather. Turner collected more than 160 signatures on a letter to Speaker Nancy Pelosi of California demanding a change in the policy. The architect relented.

Turner was raised in Dayton and attended public schools. His father, Ray, worked for more than 40 years at a General Motors plant and was a member of the electrical workers union. His mother, Vivian, was an elementary school teacher. His father had dropped out of school at age 16 to work at the GM plant. But after putting his wife through school and pushing Turner toward college, his father decided he did not want to be the only one in the family without a high school diploma, so he belatedly got one. Today, Turner considers education an American prerogative.

Turner practiced law before winning his first term as mayor in 1993. He had become involved in nonprofit groups in Dayton dealing with low-income housing, homelessness and community development and decided to try to tackle those problems from City Hall.

He lost his bid for a third term to a popular Democratic state senator. But his bipartisan appeal caught the eye of GOP recruiters. When Bush tapped 12-term Democratic Rep. Tony P. Hall to serve as ambassador to a trio of world hunger relief organizations, Turner became a party favorite to run for the seat. He first beat back a primary challenge from newspaper publisher Roy Brown, then took 59 percent of the vote to defeat Democrat Rick Carne, Hall's former chief of staff. Turner was easily re-elected in 2004 and 2006.

His 2008 campaign found Turner embroiled in an ethics controversy: The Dayton Development Coalition, which is a clearinghouse for federal ear- marks — funding set-asides for special projects — and aid requests for Turner's district, hired his wife's public relations firm for a marketing cam- paign, netting her business more than $300,000 in profit.

The issue drew criticism from government watchdog groups. Turner said the council itself does not receive federal money, and that he and his wife are careful to avoid ethics issues. In the end, he outraised Democratic advertising executive Jane Mitakides by nearly a 3-to-1 margin and won a fourth term with 63 percent of the vote.

KEY VOTES

2008
No Delay consideration of Colombia free-trade agreement
Yes Override Bush veto of federal farm and nutrition programs reauthorization bill
Yes Overhaul surveillance laws and permit dismissal of suits against companies that conducted warrantless wiretapping
Yes Grant mortgage relief to homeowners and funding for Fannie Mae and Freddie Mac
No Approve initial $700 billion program to stabilize financial markets
No Approve final $700 billion program to stabilize financial markets
No Provide $14 billion in loans to automakers

2007
Yes Increase minimum wage by $2.10 an hour
No Approve $124.2 billion in emergency war spending and set goal for redeployment of troops from Iraq
Yes Reject federal contraceptive assistance to international family planning groups
Yes Override Bush veto of $23.2 billion water projects authorization bill
Yes Implement Peru free-trade agreement
No Approve energy policy overhaul with new fuel economy standards
Yes Clear $473.5 billion omnibus spending bill, including $70 billion for military operations

CQ VOTE STUDIES

	PARTY UNITY		PRESIDENTIAL SUPPORT	
	SUPPORT	OPPOSE	SUPPORT	OPPOSE
2008	85%	15%	58%	42%
2007	82%	18%	62%	38%
2006	91%	9%	90%	10%
2005	92%	8%	85%	15%
2004	92%	8%	88%	12%

INTEREST GROUPS

	AFL-CIO	ADA	CCUS	ACU
2008	57%	55%	81%	63%
2007	54%	25%	100%	80%
2006	29%	5%	93%	80%
2005	27%	5%	96%	80%
2004	33%	5%	100%	88%

OHIO 3
Southwest — most of Dayton, Kettering

Dayton, once one of the state's most successful manufacturing centers, has suffered economic setbacks and a torrent of departures that dis- placed its manufacturing base. The city has struggled to diversify what has become an increasingly service-oriented economy.

Montgomery County, which surrounds Dayton, dominates the 3rd. Mid- way between Cincinnati and Dayton, fast-growing Warren County (shared with the 2nd) has bedroom communities for both cities. Clinton and Highland counties to the east are more rural but increasingly devel- oped, and the loss of key employers hurts growth. Although Warren is still growing, Montgomery, which accounts for nearly three-fourths of the district's residents, has lost population over the past decade.

Tied to manufacturing for generations, the Dayton area will struggle as more plants close; in Moraine, the closure of a General Motors SUV plant will result in the loss of thousands of area jobs, at the plant and among suppliers, and reduce to a small fraction a GM-based workforce in the Dayton area that had still been as large as 19,000 employees a

decade ago. Despite general economic setbacks, the area's defense industry has had some success in attracting aerospace, medical research and information technology companies to the area around Wright-Patterson Air Force Base (shared with the 7th). A "Tech Town" district in eastern Dayton (shared with the 8th) is under construction.

The urban vote — driven by Dayton's ample black population and blue- collar workforce — makes Montgomery slightly Democratic. Dayton's southern suburbs include GOP-inclined, white-collar areas, and the counties outside of Montgomery give the 3rd its GOP lean. John McCain won 51 percent of the 3rd's 2008 presidential vote.

MAJOR INDUSTRY
Defense, service, manufacturing

MILITARY BASES
Wright-Patterson Air Force Base, 10,166 military, 10,332 civilian (2005) (shared with the 7th District)

CITIES
Dayton (pt.), 137,180; Kettering, 57,502; Trotwood, 27,420

NOTABLE
The National Museum of the United States Air Force (at Wright-Patter- son) is the world's largest and oldest military aviation museum.

Rep. Jim Jordan (R)

Elected 2006; 2nd term

Jordan was a champion wrestler in high school and college and has transferred his competitive ferocity on the mat to Capitol Hill. His unwavering criticism of Democrats' "big federal government approach" and "fiscal irresponsibility" — honed during a dozen years as a state legislator — has helped him rise in the GOP ranks and kept him popular at home.

Jordan is a member of the Republican Study Committee, a group of the most conservative House GOP lawmakers, and is chairman of its budget and spending task force. He wants to use the position to build support for his proposal to have budget watchdogs identify wasteful spending to be cut. "I am convinced that unless we change our course and begin exercising some fiscal restraint, the debt facing our kids and grandkids will soon be insurmountable," said Jordan, who sits on the Budget Committee.

Despite his district's dependence on automobile manufacturing, Jordan's concerns about debt led him to strongly oppose the George W. Bush administration's proposed $14 billion bailout of U.S. automakers in late 2008 that failed to become law. The administration had said it might appoint a "car czar" or senior official to negotiate between automakers and other parties. "The same government that has given us record deficits and debt should not attempt to tell the auto industry how to run its business with concepts like 'car czar,' " Jordan said.

He said the lack of coherent energy policy has hurt his area's auto industry. He supports a policy that permits new oil and gas drilling and expanded refinery capacity, as well as more incentives for renewable and alternative fuels. He is critical of raising vehicle fuel efficiency standards because he said it leads to reducing vehicles' size and weight, something he worries raises traffic fatalities while forcing companies to stop making larger and sturdier cars.

Jordan harshly condemned President Obama's $787 billion economic stimulus bill that became law in February 2009 without any House GOP support. He had joined other Republicans in proposing their own stimulus plan that relied more heavily on tax cuts and said he was deeply skeptical Obama's plan would work. "The federal government almost never does anything well," he told The Lima News.

He has another forum for his views as he serves as the top-ranking Republican on the Oversight and Government Reform's Subcommittee on Domestic Policy. The subcommittee is chaired by Democrat Dennis J. Kucinich, a fellow Ohioan whose liberal views are diametrically opposite Jordan's, but Jordan in February 2009 said he hopes the two can find common ground. He said both have agreed to seek out government waste, as well as investigate high salaries for non-political executive branch employees.

His other committee assignment is Judiciary, where he has fought proposals from the panel's liberal Democrats. He also has used his seat to promote a crackdown on illegal immigration; he supports strengthening border security and penalizing businesses that knowingly employ illegal immigrants.

He is a strong opponent of abortion, except to save the life of the pregnant woman. He led a bipartisan coalition of 180 lawmakers in February 2009 urging Obama to support longstanding anti-abortion policies in spending bills. Two years earlier he sponsored an amendment, which the Judiciary Committee rejected, to add an anti-abortion provision to a bill intended to expand access to a program that provides money to combat methamphetamine. He said his stance on abortion stems from his Christian faith. As a state legislator, Jordan sponsored legislation that created Ohio's "Choose

CAPITOL OFFICE
225-2676
jordan.house.gov
515 Cannon Bldg. 20515-3504; fax 226-0577

COMMITTEES
Budget
Judiciary
Oversight & Government Reform

RESIDENCE
Urbana

BORN
Feb. 17, 1964; Troy, Ohio

RELIGION
Christian

FAMILY
Wife, Polly Jordan; four children

EDUCATION
U. of Wisconsin, B.S. 1986 (economics);
Ohio State U., M.A. 1991 (education);
Capital U., J.D. 2001

CAREER
College wrestling coach

POLITICAL HIGHLIGHTS
Ohio House, 1995-2000; Ohio Senate, 2001-06

ELECTION RESULTS

2008 GENERAL

Jim Jordan (R)	186,154	65.2%
Mike Carroll (D)	99,499	34.8%

2008 PRIMARY

Jim Jordan (R)	unopposed

2006 GENERAL

Jim Jordan (R)	129,958	60.0%
Richard E. Siferd (D)	86,678	40.0%

Life" license plates, the proceeds from which go to nonprofit organizations that counsel pregnant women about adoption.

Jordan grew up in the small rural community of St. Paris, about an hour's drive west of Columbus. His father worked at the local General Motors automobile plant from his teens until he retired. His mother, who cared for Jordan and two younger siblings, supplemented the family income by running a cleaning business.

In junior high school, Jordan took a keen interest in wrestling, influenced by several of his relatives who were amateur wrestlers. After school, Jordan frequently could be found behind the house in a wrestling room that his father built for practicing. "I think about the sacrifices that my parents made so [my siblings and I] could go compete across the country, so we could get better," he said. "They did what parents always do, and frankly it's that concept that makes America great — moms and dads willing to sacrifice so their kids and grandkids can have life a little bit better than they had."

Jordan became a four-time state wrestling champion at Graham High School, where he lost only one match, and parlayed that success into a wrestling scholarship at the University of Wisconsin at Madison. Moving from his GOP-leaning part of central Ohio, he found himself a fish out of water in notoriously liberal Madison. As a member of the university's wrestling squad, he won two national championships. In 2005, he was elected to the University of Wisconsin Athletics Hall of Fame.

Between his junior and senior years, Jordan married his high school sweetheart. He returned to Ohio, where he went to graduate school at Ohio State University. There he began a career in coaching. His wife had just given birth to their fourth child in 1994 when Jordan decided to get into the contest to succeed a longtime GOP incumbent in the Ohio House. In a heated primary, Jordan defeated two better-known Republicans and went on to win the general election. While serving in the state legislature, he attended Capital University and earned a law degree in 2001. During his six years in the state House and six more in the state Senate, Jordan routinely bucked Republican leaders, often voting against proposals he felt weren't conservative enough.

When Republican Rep. Michael G. Oxley of Ohio retired in 2006, Jordan's time in the legislature was his calling card in a six-candidate Republican primary field; he took more than 50 percent of the primary vote. In November, he cruised to victory over Democratic lawyer Richard E. Siferd. Despite the Democratic tide that helped Obama carry Ohio two years later, the strong GOP tilt of Jordan's district won him nearly two-thirds of the vote.

KEY VOTES

2008

No Delay consideration of Colombia free-trade agreement

No Override Bush veto of federal farm and nutrition programs reauthorization bill

Yes Overhaul surveillance laws and permit dismissal of suits against companies that conducted warrantless wiretapping

No Grant mortgage relief to homeowners and funding for Fannie Mae and Freddie Mac

No Approve initial $700 billion program to stabilize financial markets

No Approve final $700 billion program to stabilize financial markets

No Provide $14 billion in loans to automakers

2007

No Increase minimum wage by $2.10 an hour

No Approve $124.2 billion in emergency war spending and set goal for redeployment of troops from Iraq

Yes Reject federal contraceptive assistance to international family planning groups

No Override Bush veto of $23.2 billion water projects authorization bill

Yes Implement Peru free-trade agreement

No Approve energy policy overhaul with new fuel economy standards

Yes Clear $473.5 billion omnibus spending bill, including $70 billion for military operations

CQ VOTE STUDIES

	PARTY UNITY		PRESIDENTIAL SUPPORT	
	SUPPORT	OPPOSE	SUPPORT	OPPOSE
2008	95%	5%	85%	15%
2007	99%	1%	91%	9%

INTEREST GROUPS

	AFL-CIO	ADA	CCUS	ACU
2008	0%	0%	83%	100%
2007	4%	0%	70%	100%

OHIO 4
West central — Mansfield, Lima, Findlay

The 4th, a solid block of Ohio Corn Belt counties, supports soybeans, corn, livestock and Republicans. Not one of the 11 counties in the 4th has backed a Democratic presidential candidate since 1964, and John McCain swept the counties again in 2008. Two of the three most populous, Allen and Hancock counties, last voted Democratic in the Roosevelt-Landon contest of 1936.

Corn and soybeans are integral to the 4th's economy, and ethanol plants and a strong agricultural base have stabilized it during decades of decline in the auto manufacturing sector. A food processing plant has relocated to Lima, lured to the new Gateway Commerce Park at the junction of several highways and rail cargo transit lines. An army tank plant in Lima that builds the Abrams tank increased production after emerging safely from the 2005 round of BRAC closings and is a leading job provider in the area.

Although health care is the leading industry in Lima, manufacturing remains important as the 4th tries to maintain its roots: Small industrial companies and large auto plants continue to aid the economy. A Ford

engine plant in Lima is expecting permanent layoffs as lower demand in the domestic auto industry results in decreased production. A Honda facility in East Liberty has also cut jobs.

Other manufacturing interests in the 4th include a large Whirlpool dishwasher plant in Findlay, as well as Cooper Tire & Rubber facilities in the city. Findlay also hosts a Marathon Petroleum production site. Budget shortfalls in several counties in the district endanger government jobs.

Democrats have few pockets of support, but they can normally count on votes in Mansfield, which is one-fifth black. While those votes help Democrats locally, they barely make a dent in the district's underlying Republican lean. In the 2008 presidential election, McCain won 60 percent of the 4th's vote, his second best showing in Ohio.

MAJOR INDUSTRY
Agriculture, manufacturing, food processing, oil

CITIES
Mansfield, 49,346; Lima, 40,081; Findlay, 38,967; Marion, 35,318

NOTABLE
Astronaut Neil Armstrong's hometown of Wapakoneta has a museum in his honor.

Rep. Bob Latta (R)

Elected December 2007; 1st full term

CAPITOL OFFICE
225-6405
latta.house.gov
1531 Longworth Bldg. 20515-3505; fax 225-1985

COMMITTEES
Agriculture
Budget
Transportation & Infrastructure

RESIDENCE
Bowling Green

BORN
April 18, 1956; Bluffton, Ohio

RELIGION
Roman Catholic

FAMILY
Wife, Marcia Latta; two children

EDUCATION
Ohio Northern U., 1974-75; Bowling Green
State U., B.A. 1978 (history); Ohio Northern U.,
1978-79; U. of Toledo, J.D. 1981

CAREER
Lawyer

POLITICAL HIGHLIGHTS
Ohio Republican Central Committee, 1986-88;
sought Republican nomination for U.S. House,
1988; Ohio Republican Central Committee, 1990-92;
Wood County Commission, 1990-96; Ohio Senate,
1997-2000; Ohio House, 2001-07

ELECTION RESULTS

2008 GENERAL
Bob Latta (R)	188,905	64.1%
George Mays (D)	105,840	35.9%

2008 PRIMARY
Bob Latta (R)	54,093	74.8%
Scott B. Radcliffe (R)	12,347	17.1%
Michael L. Reynolds (R)	5,873	8.1%

2007 SPECIAL
Bob Latta (R)	56,114	57.0%
Robin Weirauch (D)	42,229	42.9%

2007 PRIMARY SPECIAL
Bob Latta (R)	32,392	43.7%
Steve Buehrer (R)	29,850	40.2%
Mark Hollenbaugh (R)	4,955	6.7%
Fred Pieper (R)	4,252	5.7%
Michael Smitley (R)	2,742	3.7%

Latta is a loyal conservative who is typically unwilling to bend his principles supporting business and small government — unless it's for the benefit of his district's wheat, soybean and corn growers. More often than not he emphatically opposes Democratic ideas, calling them a form of "socialism," and often jokes when someone asks if he's interested in a compromise.

Many of his views are in line with those of his father, Delbert L. Latta, a budget hawk who held the same seat for 30 years before retiring in 1989. Yet while the Toledo Blade credited the elder Latta for being someone "who listened and responded to the needs of his district, turning constituent service into a fine art," the newspaper criticized his son just days before the 2008 election, saying he was "far to the political right of the father." Nevertheless, Latta took 64 percent of the vote in his first election for a full term.

An assistant House Republican whip and member of the Budget Committee, Latta supports a balanced-budget constitutional amendment and giving presidents a line-item veto. He joined his party in February 2009 in opposing President Obama's $787 billion stimulus law. "If you want government to take everything, if you want government to take more and more over with the banks, more of the industries, all of a sudden you're going to have a government auto czar, right there, right down the line, that's socialism," he told the Blade.

He also opposed at the start of the 111th Congress (2009-10) a $410 billion catchall spending bill for fiscal 2009 and an expansion to the State Children's Health Insurance Program, which covers children from families who don't qualify for Medicaid. Latta said in 2008, during debate on a similar measure, that an expansion of the program makes a step toward government-run health care.

Latta also sides with most Republicans in criticizing Obama's announcement to institute a plan, commonly called "cap and trade," that would set a limit on greenhouse gases and create a market-based trading program for emissions credits. "I think what it will end up being is a cap and tax," Latta told the Tiffin Advertiser-Tribune in March 2009.

He laughed when some Democrats in early 2009 wanted to reinstate the Fairness Doctrine, a Cold War-era policy requiring radio and TV stations to provide equal time on matters of public interest. He considered the idea another way for Democrats to tell Americans what to listen to and a way to shut down right-wing talk radio.

Republican leaders couldn't persuade him to back a $700 billion rescue measure for the final services industry, backed by President George W. Bush in fall 2008. He opposed two versions of the bill — the second of which became law — even after heavy lobbying from Minority Leader John A. Boehner, a fellow Ohio Republican. He said the price tag was too large to support. Soon after the second vote, he assured Boehner it wasn't personal: "I like John. This is not a referendum on John."

The following December, Latta also opposed a bill aimed at bailing out the U.S. auto industry. He said he couldn't support a bill that failed to "provide accountability on American taxpayers' investments, security to the millions employed by the automotive industry." That bill stalled in the Senate before Bush granted the industry a loan through the financial rescue.

But as a member of the Agriculture Committee, Latta did support a successful override of Bush's veto of the Democrats' farm bill in 2008, saying the legislation would keep Ohio farmers employed and thereby benefit the nation's economy. Bush opposed the $289 billion price tag on the reauthorization, which included crop subsidies and food stamps, as well as conservation, rural development and agricultural trade programs.

From his seat on the Transportation and Infrastructure Committee, Latta also plans to try to push federal dollars to his district and state when debate begins on the renewal of the 2005 surface transportation law in the 111th Congress.

Latta said he learned the importance of constituent service from his father. "It's not the big things you do in life for people; it's the little things," he told the Blade. "People expect the big things, not the little things."

Latta was 2 when his father won a seat in Congress in 1958. The family split time between residences in Bowling Green and Washington. When he entered the fifth grade, he was enrolled in Virginia schools full-time, though he later returned to Ohio for high school.

He often spent days off from school with his father on Capitol Hill. When his father served on the Rules Committee, which governs floor debate on legislation, the younger Latta often sat behind Massachusetts Democrat Thomas P. "Tip" O'Neill Jr., who later became Speaker.

As a teenager, Latta helped his father by answering phone calls from local residents and taking shifts driving his father to and from local airports. "During campaign season, he would spend the weekends with cousins preparing mailing pamphlets and yard signs for his father.

He earned a history degree from Bowling Green State University in 1978 while working for a local Wood County judge. Three years later, he earned a law degree from the University of Toledo. He worked for a corporate firm and dabbled in private practice before joining the Toledo Bank Trust Company.

Latta made a run for his father's seat in 1988, but lost to Paul E. Gillmor in the Republican primary by 27 votes. In 1990, he ran a successful race for commissioner in Wood County, defeating a Democratic incumbent. Six years later, he was elected to the Ohio legislature and served four years in the Senate and six in the House. He was a chief proponent of eliminating Ohio's estate tax and was instrumental in passing a bill, which became law, that requires DNA testing of all convicted felons and other criminals.

When Gillmor passed away in September 2007, Latta made another run for Congress and took the primary after an often unruly campaign in which Latta and his chief primary opponent, state Sen. Steve Buehrer, accused each other of lying about their respective legislative records. He then defeated Democrat Robin Weirauch with 57 percent of the vote in the December 2007 special election.

KEY VOTES

2008

No   Delay consideration of Colombia free-trade agreement

Yes   Override Bush veto of federal farm and nutrition programs reauthorization bill

Yes   Overhaul surveillance laws and permit dismissal of suits against companies that conducted warrantless wiretapping

No   Grant mortgage relief to homeowners and funding for Fannie Mae and Freddie Mac

No   Approve initial $700 billion program to stabilize financial markets

No   Approve final $700 billion program to stabilize financial markets

No   Provide $14 billion in loans to automakers

2007

No   Approve energy policy overhaul with new fuel economy standards

Yes   Clear $473.5 billion omnibus spending bill, including $70 billion for military operations

CQ VOTE STUDIES

	PARTY UNITY		PRESIDENTIAL SUPPORT	
	SUPPORT	OPPOSE	SUPPORT	OPPOSE
2008	99%	1%	73%	27%
2007	100%	0%	60%	40%

INTEREST GROUPS

	AFL-CIO	ADA	CCUS	ACU
2008	7%	15%	89%	96%

OHIO 5

Northwest – Bowling Green, Tiffin, Fremont

Bordering Indiana and Michigan in the northwestern corner of the state, the 5th cuts south of Toledo into the north-central portion of Ohio. Flat farmland born out of the once-impervious Great Black Swamp covers the middle of Ohio's second-largest district in land area. The district's largest jurisdiction is centrally located Wood County, with the rest of the population spread evenly between counties east and west of Wood.

The largest city in Wood County, and in the district, is Bowling Green. The city is heavily dependent on Bowling Green State University, but local officials hope the city's Innovative Technology Park will help diversify its economy and attract jobs in a region struggling with layoffs.

North of Wood, across the Maumee River, the 5th picks up GOP-leaning southern suburbs in Toledo-dominated Lucas County (most of which is in the 9th). Wheat, tomatoes, soybeans and corn dominate most of Wood. Many of the remaining counties form the heart of Ohio's wheat-growing country, and rely almost exclusively on agriculture and food packaging. The 5th leads Ohio in wheat, soybean and corn production.

East and west of Wood, migrant-worker Hispanic populations boost the district's Hispanic population to 4 percent, double the state's average. Manufacturing is important here, with a Heinz ketchup plant in Fremont, an Arm & Hammer Baking Soda site in Old Fort, and a large Whirlpool washing machine production facility in Clyde. Five of Ohio's 10 counties with the highest unemployment rates are wholly or partly in the 5th — Huron County's rate is higher than 17 percent.

The 5th is strong GOP territory. Mercer (shared with the 8th) and Putnam counties were John McCain's best counties statewide in the 2008 presidential election. Despite the strong GOP slant, Barack Obama won 45 percent of the 5th's vote in 2008, 7 percentage points more than Democrat John Kerry took here in 2004.

MAJOR INDUSTRY
Agriculture, manufacturing

CITIES
Bowling Green, 29,636; Tiffin, 18,135; Fremont, 17,345

NOTABLE
Perrysburg, named to honor Commodore Oliver Perry's victory over the British in the 1813 Battle of Lake Erie, is one of only two U.S. cities to have been planned by the federal government.

Rep. Charlie Wilson (D)

Elected 2006; 2nd term

CAPITOL OFFICE
225-5705
charliewilson.house.gov
226 Cannon Bldg. 20515-3506; fax 225-5907

COMMITTEES
Financial Services
Science & Technology

RESIDENCE
St. Clairsville

BORN
Jan. 18, 1943; Martins Ferry, Ohio

RELIGION
Roman Catholic

FAMILY
Divorced; four children

EDUCATION
Ohio U., B.G.S. 1980 (general studies)

CAREER
Real estate company owner; funeral home
and furniture company owner; auto worker

POLITICAL HIGHLIGHTS
Ohio House, 1997-2004 (assistant minority
leader, 2000-04); Ohio Senate, 2005-06

ELECTION RESULTS

2008 GENERAL

Charlie Wilson (D)	176,330	62.3%
Richard Stobbs (R)	92,968	32.8%
Dennis Spisak (GREEN)	13,812	4.9%

2008 PRIMARY

Charlie Wilson (D)	unopposed

2006 GENERAL

Charlie Wilson (D)	135,628	62.1%
Chuck Blasdel (R)	82,848	37.9%

Wilson reflects the conservative social values and blue-collar priorities of his economically distressed district straddling Appalachia. A former auto worker and union member, he resists free-trade agreements he believes threaten U.S. manufacturers — including Ohio's steelmakers — and embraces "clean coal" technology as a way to bring in new jobs.

Many Democrats share those concerns, but Wilson tends to diverge when it comes to social issues. He has voted for legislation to repeal gun control laws in Washington, D.C. A member of the National Rifle Association representing a region where hunting and fishing are popular, Wilson said he doesn't see gun control as a party issue, but as a "city and rural contrast." He also said he opposes abortion except in cases of rape and incest and to save the life of the mother. He has voted against expanding federal funding for embryonic stem cell research, which uses discarded embryos created for in vitro fertilization.

Still, Wilson's record from his first term in the House shows him to be a dependable Democrat, having sided with his party 93 percent of the time on votes pitting most Democrats against most Republicans. And in early 2009, he backed a bill to expand the State Children's Health Insurance Program, which covers children from low-income families that do not qualify for Medicaid. President Obama signed that bill into law.

He also supported Obama's $787 billion economic stimulus plan, saying it would provide his district more than $40 million in funds for schools, bring in 7,200 jobs and prevent many home foreclosures. "Our choice was action vs. inaction. I voted for action," Wilson said in a statement. "Who would stand by and do nothing while their community, their country falls off a cliff?"

A member of the Blue Dog Coalition, a group of fiscally conservative House Democrats, he also voted in fall 2008 for two $700 billion measures — the second of which became law — to help the ailing financial sector. He said "it was not a gift to Wall Street." He also backed a measure that would have granted $14 billion in loans to the struggling U.S. auto industry. That bill stalled in the Senate.

From his seat on the Financial Services Committee, Wilson set an early focus on predatory lending, which often threatens families with foreclosure. In 2007, he introduced a bill to specify unacceptable lending practices and put in place a system that randomly selects appraisers to reduce the risk of influence-peddling. But the bill didn't move during the 110th Congress (2007-08). He had pushed similar legislation through the Ohio Senate, where he served for two years before being elected to Congress.

Wilson also served eight years in the Ohio House, about half that time as the Democratic assistant leader. During his tenure in the General Assembly, he was a strong advocate for public education.

Representing a district suffering from high unemployment in slumping industries such as coal mining and steel manufacturing, Wilson voted against free-trade agreements with Peru in 2007 and Colombia in 2008, which he said lacked adequate labor standards. "Free trade is not really fair trade," he once said. "We need to keep our steel mills functional in the event we need them, rather than be dependent on offshore steel."

Wilson serves on the Science and Technology Committee and supports the development of domestic energy sources. To help jump-start the coal industry, Wilson supported during the 110th Congress a bill — which the House did not act on — to provide loan guarantees to plants that produce coal-based fuels, the first of which is scheduled to be built in his district in the town of Wellsville.

Wilson opposed the presence of U.S. military forces in Iraq, and joined liberal Democrats in 2007 in calling for withdrawing troops from Iraq altogether. But he was among 59 Democrats who voted against legislation in May 2007 that would have required the withdrawal of U.S. troops from Iraq. After a visit to Iraq in September 2007, he told the Athens News, "I don't think we should just drop out and take everything away, and then lose what gains have been made, whatever they are. But I think it's time for redeployment, and it's time for redeployment in a big way." He was pleased when Obama announced a plan in early 2009 to draw down troop levels over 18 months. He said the administration had "clearly signaled that the war will responsibly come to an end and that Iraq's own security forces will be the major force behind securing Iraq."

He grew up in Bridgeport, which is near the border of West Virginia and is home to about 2,000 people, many of whom Wilson knew by name. His family roots in eastern Ohio date back 108 years, when his ancestors emigrated from Germany. His family owned a funeral parlor and a furniture store. He played football for Dillonvale High School, where he also was voted class president.

After high school, Wilson worked as a welder and painter on an auto assembly line in Lorain building Ford Falcons and Comets. He later took over the family businesses and opened his own real estate firm.

In 2006, he made a bid for the 6th District seat being vacated by Democratic Rep. Ted Strickland, who ran successfully for governor.

Given his long service in the state legislature, Wilson was by then a seasoned politician. But his campaign manager — his son, who succeeded him in the state Senate — failed to collect the 50 valid signatures needed to qualify for the primary, requiring Wilson to run as a write-in candidate, often an insurmountable hurdle in a contested election.

He ran a tireless primary campaign against two lesser-known opponents, using his own money to hire door-to-door canvassers armed with hand-held computers. A stray beagle named Write-in was his companion as he traveled throughout the district. Wilson ultimately sunk nearly $553,000 of his own money into the campaign. He also got help from the national Democratic Party.

On primary day, supporters came out to the polls with 4-foot-long pencils that had "Write-in Charlie Wilson for Congress" on them. He won nearly two-thirds of the votes cast in the primary, then breezed to victory over Republican state Rep. Chuck Blasdel in the general election. The devoted pooch Write-in, after helping him to victory, was adopted by a Wilson staff member and renamed Charlotte. His 2008 re-election was far easier — he handily defeated Republican Richard Stobbs, a former Belmont County sheriff.

KEY VOTES

2008

Yes Delay consideration of Colombia free-trade agreement

Yes Override Bush veto of federal farm and nutrition programs reauthorization bill

Yes Overhaul surveillance laws and permit dismissal of suits against companies that conducted warrantless wiretapping

Yes Grant mortgage relief to homeowners and funding for Fannie Mae and Freddie Mac

Yes Approve initial $700 billion program to stabilize financial markets

Yes Approve final $700 billion program to stabilize financial markets

Yes Provide $14 billion in loans to automakers

2007

Yes Increase minimum wage by $2.10 an hour

Yes Approve $124.2 billion in emergency war spending and set goal for redeployment of troops from Iraq

Yes Reject federal contraceptive assistance to international family planning groups

Yes Override Bush veto of $23.2 billion water projects authorization bill

No Implement Peru free-trade agreement

Yes Approve energy policy overhaul with new fuel economy standards

Yes Clear $473.5 billion omnibus spending bill, including $70 billion for military operations

CQ VOTE STUDIES

	PARTY UNITY		PRESIDENTIAL SUPPORT	
	SUPPORT	OPPOSE	SUPPORT	OPPOSE
2008	97%	3%	22%	78%
2007	91%	9%	14%	86%

INTEREST GROUPS

	AFL-CIO	ADA	CCUS	ACU
2008	100%	80%	67%	4%
2007	96%	85%	63%	21%

OHIO 6
South and east – Boardman, Athens, Steubenville

The 6th parallels the Ohio River for nearly 300 miles, bordering three states and taking in hardscrabble areas from Ohio's Appalachia to the Mahoning Valley near Youngstown.

As of the 2000 census, one-third of residents lived in the district's north in Mahoning and Columbiana counties, which still rely on waning steel, coal, retail and manufacturing sectors. But the counties have been losing population steadily for decades. Jefferson County has lost population in each of the past four censuses and has Ohio's highest proportion of elderly residents. Several counties in the 6th's old coal mining areas have high rates of low household incomes, difficulty retaining younger residents and high unemployment rates — Meigs County's unemployment has reached 15 percent. Lawrence, Athens (shared with the 18th), Scioto (shared with the 2nd) and Meigs counties have some of the lowest incomes in the state.

The 6th has a Democratic orientation, but it leans conservative on social issues and is highly competitive in presidential elections. Athens, in Athens County, is home to Ohio University and has a liberal slant. Meigs and the southern counties have tended to blend populist fiscal policy with social conservatism. Washington County will support Democrats at the local and congressional levels but favors GOP presidential candidates.

North of Washington, the 6th tilts Democratic, with Monroe, Belmont and Jefferson counties strongly Democratic, especially in local races — Monroe and Belmont counties voted for Democrat Barack Obama in the 2008 presidential election. The 6th's share of Mahoning takes in Boardman and Poland and is more competitive than the solidly Democratic part of the county in the 17th. Republicans George W. Bush and John McCain each won seven of the district's 12 counties en route to narrow wins here in the last three presidential elections. McCain took 50 percent of the district's vote overall in 2008.

MAJOR INDUSTRY
Service, manufacturing

CITIES
Boardman (unincorporated), 37,215; Athens, 21,342; Steubenville, 19,015

NOTABLE
Gallipolis, in Gallia County, was founded in 1790 by a group of 500 French immigrants.

Rep. Steve Austria (R)

Elected 2008; 1st term

Austria is former financial planner who advocates reduced government and looks out for small business. From his seat on the Budget Committee, he intends to battle Democratic spending proposals he views as too costly.

His conservative views also extend to social policy; as a state legislator, he backed laws to strengthen penalties against violent pedophiles, protect children from sex offenders on the Internet and make it a crime to drive while under the influence of illegal drugs.

His fellow freshmen elected him class president in 2009, which will enable him to forge closer ties with Minority Leader John A. Boehner, who represents an adjacent district.

Austria opposed the $787 billion economic stimulus bill President Obama signed into law in 2009, saying it "contained too much wasteful borrowing and spending." He made national headlines after an interview with the Columbus Dispatch, which quoted him comparing the stimulus plan to President Franklin D. Roosevelt's approach to spending. Roosevelt "tried to borrow and spend, he tried to use the Keynesian approach, and our country ended up in a Great Depression," Austria said. "That's just history." He later withdrew his statements, saying he never intended to blame Roosevelt for the Depression.

In early 2009 he showed some willingness to cross party lines; he was one of 40 Republicans to back expansion of the State Children's Health Insurance Program, which covers children whose families don't qualify for Medicaid.

From his seat on the Homeland Security panel, Austria can look out for Wright-Patterson Air Force Base, one of the district's largest employers. He said he wants Miami Valley to take the lead in developing the nation's strategy on tackling cybersecurity through a partnership among local universities, hospitals and the private sector.

Austria grew up in Xenia as the oldest of nine children. His mother was a nurse; his father was a doctor and preceded him on the central committee of Greene County Republicans. In the campaign to replace retiring Republican David L. Hobson, he defeated three Republicans before facing attorney Sharen Neuhardt in the general election. He won with 58 percent of the vote.

CAPITOL OFFICE
225-4324
austria.house.gov
1641 Longworth Bldg. 20515-3507; fax 225-1984

COMMITTEES
Budget
Homeland Security

RESIDENCE
Beavercreek

BORN
Oct. 12, 1958; Cincinnati, Ohio

RELIGION
Roman Catholic

FAMILY
Wife, Eileen Austria; three children

EDUCATION
Marquette U., B.A. 1982 (political science)

CAREER
Financial services firm owner;
state legislative aide

POLITICAL HIGHLIGHTS
Ohio House, 1999-2001; Ohio Senate, 2001-08 (majority whip, 2005-07)

ELECTION RESULTS

2008 GENERAL

Steve Austria (R)	174,915	58.2%
Sharen Neuhardt (D)	125,547	41.8%

2008 PRIMARY

Steve Austria (R)	42,499	55.0%
Ron Hood (R)	25,984	33.6%
Dan Harkins (R)	4,817	6.2%
John R. Mitchel (R)	4,030	5.2%

OHIO 7

Central — Springfield, Lancaster, part of Columbus

The GOP-leaning 7th is a diverse swath of land in south-central Ohio that includes urban, suburban and rural areas.

The district's two most-populous counties, Greene and Clark, form the 7th's western arm. The Air Force base, which anchors Greene, is Ohio's largest single-site employer. The county also has several colleges and universities. Clark and its county seat, Springfield, have hosted auto plants and technology companies, but unemployment rates have climbed over the past decade.

Residential growth near Columbus, a sliver of which is in the 7th, has spurred Fairfield County, now a white-collar commuter area. Pickaway County has suffered declines in manufacturing. Cargo hub Rickenbacker International Airport is key to Franklin County

just north of Pickaway. Residents in Fayette, the 7th's least-populous county, breed horses. Perry County relies on manufacturing and agriculture but has struggled with very high unemployment. Overall, the district supports corn, wheat and soybeans.

The 7th is politically disparate. Clark and Perry counties are competitive. Pickaway tends to favor the GOP. Fairfield, Fayette and Green are solid GOP counties. John McCain won 54 percent of the 7th's presidential vote.

MAJOR INDUSTRY
Military, technology research, agriculture

MILITARY BASES
Wright-Patterson Air Force Base, 10,166 military, 10,332 civilian (2005) (shared with the 3rd District)

CITIES
Springfield, 65,358; Columbus (pt.), 51,097; Beavercreek, 37,984; Lancaster, 35,335

NOTABLE
The modern combine, invented in Springfield, helped revolutionize the agriculture industry.

Rep. John A. Boehner (R)

Elected 1990; 10th term

CAPITOL OFFICE
225-6205
johnboehner.house.gov
1011 Longworth Bldg. 20515-3508; fax 225-0704

COMMITTEES
No committee assignments

RESIDENCE
West Chester Township

BORN
Nov. 17, 1949; Cincinnati, Ohio

RELIGION
Roman Catholic

FAMILY
Wife, Debbie Boehner; two children

EDUCATION
Xavier U., B.S. 1977

MILITARY SERVICE
Navy, 1968

CAREER
Plastics and packaging executive

POLITICAL HIGHLIGHTS
Union Township Board of Trustees, 1982-84;
Ohio House, 1985-91

ELECTION RESULTS

2008 GENERAL

John A. Boehner (R)	202,063	67.9%
Nicholas von Stein (D)	95,510	32.1%

2008 PRIMARY

John A. Boehner (R)	unopposed

2006 GENERAL

John A. Boehner (R)	136,863	63.8%
Mort Meier (D)	77,640	36.2%

PREVIOUS WINNING PERCENTAGES
2004 (69%); 2002 (71%); 2000 (71%); 1998 (71%);
1996 (70%); 1994 (100%); 1992 (74%); 1990 (61%)

As leader of the House's Republicans, Boehner is a crafty strategist who practices an accommodating style with Republican colleagues as he fights uphill battles against a commanding Democratic majority. He is more of a creature of the institution than his younger lieutenants, but matches their conservatism in his voting habits — and is just as caustic in his criticism of President Obama and his House colleagues across the aisle.

Boehner (BAY-ner) has a laid-back leadership manner and encourages input, both positive and negative, from colleagues. He makes way for his ambitious GOP whip, Virginia's Eric Cantor, to increasingly serve as a national face of the party. Boehner has formed Republican task forces on earmarks — funding set-asides for projects in member districts — in addition to health care and other issues that can divide his fractious caucus.

In 2007, he convened a group of allies to work on "branding" his party's image in the hope of better relaying the Republican message to the public, and has remained focused on the task. "If we articulate ideas and do a better job of connecting with the American people on their terms and advocating solutions to the serious challenges they face, we will build a majority coalition by winning the issues, one at a time," he said in January 2009.

He is a unique presence on Capitol Hill. Always tanned, his complexion led Obama to joke at the 2009 White House Correspondents' Dinner that Boehner was a fellow "person of color," though "not a color found in nature." He chain-smokes Barclay cigarettes and delivers his statements in a booming baritone that resonates throughout a hearing room. When a fellow member or a reporter asks a difficult question, he responds with the "Boehner shrug," a stiff, unquotable raising of the shoulders that encourages the questioner to drop the subject.

Boehner is a case study in political survival. He ascended to the top GOP leadership post in the House in 2006 after a disastrous midterm election in which his party lost the majority in both the House and Senate. The victory completed his transformation from youthful rebel to has-been power broker to savvy legislator. He had earlier risen to become GOP Conference chairman after Republicans gained control in 1994, but was dumped when they lost seats in the 1998 elections and narrowed their majority margin. Undaunted, he spent five years as chairman of the Education and the Workforce Committee and displayed his skill as a bipartisan deal-cutter on President George W. Bush's 2001 No Child Left Behind education law and other measures.

After his party lost more than 20 seats in the 2008 elections, he retained his role as leader, making him one of just a few influential House Republicans to emerge intact from Bush's presidency. Republican Mike Pence of Indiana, who had lost overwhelmingly to Boehner in the bid for the leader's job two years earlier, praised the Ohioan for providing "consistent, conservative leadership."

After an early flirtation with bipartisan cooperation with Obama, Boehner became a consistent and outspoken critic of almost all of the new president's major initiatives. He contended that although Obama invited Republicans to the White House to get their input on a massive economic stimulus plan, the measure passed without sufficient GOP input. "That's when it became apparent to me that all the talk of a post-partisan atmosphere was a ruse," he said in April 2009. Boehner's GOP colleagues also unanimously refused to back Obama's $3.56 trillion budget blueprint for fiscal 2010. The minority leader blasted the stimulus, the budget and a $410 billion catchall spending bill for fiscal 2009 as "one big down payment on a new American socialist experiment."

Seeking to avoid being criticized as representing a "Party of No," he issued an alternative budget plan, which Democrats pounced on for containing no spending numbers or specifics. When the Republican Study Committee (RSC), the coalition of the House's most conservative members, brought its own alternative budget weighted heavily toward tax cuts to the floor in April 2009, Boehner broke from Cantor and his party's other leaders and voted against it.

In general, though, Boehner sets an example for his caucus by toeing the party line. He was one of 15 House Republicans in the 110th Congress (2007-08) to side with a majority of the GOP on 99 percent of the votes that pitted Republicans against Democrats. Through 2008, he had a lifetime rating of nearly 94 percent from the American Conservative Union.

Boehner was supportive of Obama's plans in early 2009 to step up the U.S. military presence in Afghanistan. Just as he opposed benchmarks when Democrats sought to impose them on Bush's Iraq War policy, Boehner said in May 2009 he opposed placing them on the Obama administration as it tried to redirect the conflict away from Iraq.

On most issues, he has sought to reach out to the Study Committee, whose members sought a more confrontational leadership style in the early months of Democratic rule. Boehner added planks it backed to the House GOP Conference agenda, including the flat tax and measures to help small businesses cover health care costs. In 2008, he assembled a new team of allies, including Cantor, who helped provide a seal of approval on issues important to the RSC. At Boehner's request, Cantor made a surprise appearance in June 2008 at a pair of decisive bipartisan summit meetings on a spending package for the Iraq War.

Boehner also agreed to conservatives' demands to aggressively call attention to high gas prices in the summer of 2008. He lambasted Speaker Nancy Pelosi of California for adjourning Congress for the August recess without holding a vote on offshore drilling. Pelosi and other Democrats eventually acquiesced and allowed the drilling ban to expire. He vowed in 2009 to fight Democratic energy legislation that he said would unduly burden businesses and consumers. And he demanded that Pelosi provide proof of her allegation that the CIA misled her about terrorism-related interrogation tactics or apologize for her accusations.

Boehner has resisted the RSC's call for Republicans to voluntarily refrain from requesting spending earmarks, saying that while he likes the idea, it lacks broad GOP support. Nor has he attempted to use a "nuclear option" suggested by former Speaker Newt Gingrich of Georgia that would involve uniting Republicans and moderate Democrats to challenge rulings on the House floor that have blocked GOP amendments.

The pressures on Boehner were never more evident than in September 2008 and the House vote on the $700 billion financial rescue law. Boehner, with his close ties to the Bush White House, was inclined to support its plan — even though he described it as a "crap sandwich." But conservatives began fighting the plan soon after it was announced. Boehner reversed course, quietly appointing a group led by Cantor to develop an alternative. And he was quickly forced to replace his chief negotiator, Spencer Bachus of Alabama, with then-Minority Whip Roy Blunt of Missouri.

When a vote on an initial measure came up short, Boehner found himself the target of criticism from all sides. Democrats accused him of being unable to control his caucus and derided his suggestion that a partisan pre-vote speech by Pelosi cost the proposal some GOP votes. Meanwhile, some conservatives viewed his support of both the first version and a reworked plan that became law as a betrayal. "The incompetence of Boehner and Blunt and their team is beyond belief," longtime GOP activist Richard Viguerie told Time magazine in October 2008 after the reworked plan passed.

On his upbringing:

"I'm the only one in my family ever to attempt to go to college, let alone graduate."

– February 1995

On the financial rescue plan he backed:

"A crap sandwich."

– September 2008

On House Republicans:

"During the 111th Congress, Republicans will strive not to be the party of 'opposition,' but the party of better solutions."

– January 2009

On Democrats:

"They're laying the groundwork for everything in these bills — expanded welfare, government-run health care, green jobs, the works. They even want to pay irresponsible neighbors' mortgages off for them. All this is being done on the backs of our kids and our grandkids."

– February 2009

Boehner's crisp, expensive suits and patrician bearing belie his blue-collar upbringing in western Ohio's Rust Belt, where he was the second of 12 children. As a kid, he rose at 5 a.m. to help his father, Earl, sort bottles and mop floors at Andy's Cafe restaurant and bar. He worked his way through Xavier College as a janitor, one of only two people in his family to earn a college degree. "I just decided I had to go to college," Boehner recalled. "It was never talked about in our house because, I think, my parents never saw it as a possibility, and there was no reason to raise false expectations."

After school, he and a partner bought a small plastics and packaging firm, Nucite Sales Inc., and built it into a multimillion-dollar business. His first political race brought him a seat on the sleepy local township board. "He was good-looking and sharp as a tack, and that doesn't hurt in politics," recalled Patricia William, the longtime township treasurer.

Boehner went on to serve six years in the Ohio House, then in 1990 jumped into the primary against Rep. Donald E. "Buz" Lukens, who had been convicted of having sex with a teenage girl. Boehner outspent the front-runner, former Rep. Thomas N. Kindness, and won the primary with 49 percent of the vote. In November, he bested former Democratic Mayor Gregory V. Jolivette of Hamilton and has had easy re-elections ever since.

Boehner came to Congress in 1991 as a young Republican bent on changing the congressional culture at a time his party was frozen out of power. He was one of the freshmen who railed against the excesses of incumbents and pushed for full disclosure during the 1992 scandal involving members who overdrew their House checking accounts without being penalized.

His zeal made him a favorite of the new breed of confrontational Republicans led by Gingrich, and four years later he became Republican Conference chairman, the No. 4 leader who handled message and communications. Boehner later lost his leadership post after being suspected of participating in a secret, failed effort among a handful of leaders to oust Gingrich, whose popularity had tumbled.

Before losing the leadership post, Boehner found himself in an unusual public spat with Democratic Rep. Jim McDermott of Washington. He sued McDermott in 1998, accusing him of leaking the contents of a conference call that a Florida couple had illegally taped from Boehner's cell phone two years earlier. A federal judge in March 2008 ordered McDermott to pay more than $1 million in attorney's fees awarded to Boehner.

Boehner is known for his devotion to golf — The Plain Dealer of Cleveland reported in March 2009 his handicap was seven — and has worked the sport into his political fundraisers.

KEY VOTES

2008

No   Delay consideration of Colombia free-trade agreement

No   Override Bush veto of federal farm and nutrition programs reauthorization bill

Yes   Overhaul surveillance laws and permit dismissal of suits against companies that conducted warrantless wiretapping

No   Grant mortgage relief to homeowners and funding for Fannie Mae and Freddie Mac

Yes   Approve initial $700 billion program to stabilize financial markets

Yes   Approve final $700 billion program to stabilize financial markets

No   Provide $14 billion in loans to automakers

2007

No   Increase minimum wage by $2.10 an hour

No   Approve $124.2 billion in emergency war spending and set goal for redeployment of troops from Iraq

Yes   Reject federal contraceptive assistance to international family planning groups

No   Override Bush veto of $23.2 billion water projects authorization bill

Yes   Implement Peru free-trade agreement

No   Approve energy policy overhaul with new fuel economy standards

Yes   Clear $473.5 billion omnibus spending bill, including $70 billion for military operations

CQ VOTE STUDIES

	PARTY UNITY		PRESIDENTIAL SUPPORT	
	SUPPORT	OPPOSE	SUPPORT	OPPOSE
2008	99%	1%	85%	15%
2007	99%	1%	93%	7%
2006	96%	4%	100%	0%
2005	97%	3%	91%	9%
2004	97%	3%	100%	0%

INTEREST GROUPS

	AFL-CIO	ADA	CCUS	ACU
2008	0%	0%	94%	92%
2007	4%	5%	79%	100%
2006	14%	5%	100%	88%
2005	13%	0%	88%	100%
2004	7%	0%	100%	100%

OHIO 8
Southwest — Hamilton, most of Middletown

Hugging the state's western border, the 8th is fertile GOP ground that is steered economically and politically by Butler County, home to the district's two largest cities, Hamilton and Middletown. The district's solid Republican tilt is anchored in Butler, which has long voted Republican — the county has been known for electing some of Ohio's more conservative state and congressional legislators.

Butler and Miami counties propelled the district's growth through residential construction and commercial development. West Chester Township, in Butler, is one of the state's fastest-growing suburbs, and many residents commute to Cincinnati or Dayton. The 8th's manufacturing base, grounded in the steel industry, and a healthy agricultural sector have helped keep the district's economy relatively stable as unemployment rates rise. The presence of Miami University in Oxford bolsters the local economy, and the university is investing in development of its regional campuses, all three of which are in the district.

The 8th also encompasses a slice of Montgomery County, including

parts of northeast Dayton near Wright-Patterson Air Force Base, which is in the 3rd and 7th districts.

About one-fifth of the 8th's residents live outside Butler in a string of fertile Corn Belt counties — Mercer (shared with 5th), Darke and Preble. Corn and soybeans are the major cash crops here, and poultry and livestock also are moneymakers. Darke and Mercer are the two largest agricultural counties in the state, and Mercer is the top county in agricultural sales.

Republican John McCain won his highest percentage statewide here in the 2008 presidential election. He took 61 percent of the district's vote as he won Darke and Preble counties easily, and Miami County, the district's second-most-populous, gave McCain 63 percent of its vote. Exceptions to the GOP dominance in the district are Oxford and the urban portion of Montgomery in the 8th.

MAJOR INDUSTRY
Agriculture, manufacturing, higher education

CITIES
Hamilton (pt.), 60,675; Middletown (pt.), 49,574; Fairfield, 42,097

NOTABLE
The Voice of America Park is in West Chester Township.

Rep. Marcy Kaptur (D)

Elected 1982; 14th term

CAPITOL OFFICE
225-4146
www.house.gov/kaptur
2186 Rayburn Bldg. 20515-3509; fax 225-7711

COMMITTEES
Appropriations
Budget
Oversight & Government Reform

RESIDENCE
Toledo

BORN
June 17, 1946; Toledo, Ohio

RELIGION
Roman Catholic

FAMILY
Single

EDUCATION
U. of Wisconsin, B.A. 1968 (history);
U. of Michigan, M.U.P. 1974 (urban planning);
Massachusetts Institute of Technology,
attended 1981 (urban planning)

CAREER
White House aide; urban planner

POLITICAL HIGHLIGHTS
No previous office

ELECTION RESULTS

2008 GENERAL

Marcy Kaptur (D)	222,054	74.4%
Bradley Leavitt (R)	76,512	25.6%

2008 PRIMARY

Marcy Kaptur (D)	unopposed

2006 GENERAL

Marcy Kaptur (D)	153,880	73.6%
Bradley Leavitt (R)	55,119	26.4%

PREVIOUS WINNING PERCENTAGES
2004 (68%); 2002 (74%); 2000 (75%); 1998 (81%);
1996 (77%); 1994 (75%); 1992 (74%); 1990 (78%);
1988 (81%); 1986 (78%); 1984 (55%); 1982 (58%)

Kaptur has been in Congress for more than a quarter of a century but sticks to her ethnic, blue-collar Toledo roots. She champions the working class, organized labor and farmers, and makes it her job to provide them with federal funds.

She considers herself a proud member of the Democratic Party — not the "Democrat Party," as she scolded Texas GOP Rep. Jeb Hensarling in a March 2009 exchange that drew cheers from liberal activists. "The party that you were referring to doesn't even exist, and I would just appreciate the courtesy when you refer to our party, if you're referring to the Democratic Party, to refer to it as such," she told him at a hearing after he invoked a Republican custom of derogatorily dropping the last two letters. "We wouldn't say Republic Party in the instance of the party that you belong to, and I think that that really was unnecessary." Hensarling tried to respond, but Kaptur cut him off.

Kaptur is the most senior female Democrat in the House, yet doesn't chair a committee or hold an elected leadership post. She made a bid for Democratic Caucus vice chairwoman in November 2008, noting that all of the House's leaders were from either the East or West coasts. "I felt we needed a voice from the heartland," she said. Nevertheless, she lost to California's Xavier Becerra in the party's only contested race.

She has opted not to make the sacrifices usually required of those seeking to advance. Most weekends, she returns to the small house she grew up in and attends Mass at the same church where she was baptized. She grows vegetables in her garden, makes Polish coffee cakes and sausages at the holidays, and paints watercolors — activities she prefers to fundraising.

Kaptur opposed both versions of a $700 billion measure in fall 2008 — the second of which became law — to aid the ailing financial services sector. She drew attention when she advocated that homeowners threatened with foreclosure refuse to leave their houses because the loans they received may have been illegal. "I say to the American people, 'You be squatters in your own homes,'" she said in a January 2009 floor speech.

Kaptur once worked as an auto worker to help pay for college and serves as vice chairwoman of the Congressional Automotive Caucus. She strongly backed a House-passed bailout for domestic automakers in December 2008 that failed to make it through the Senate, though the outgoing George W. Bush administration put parts of it into practice administratively. "People are asking, 'Why will Congress help Wall Street and let the real wealth creators go without?'" she said at the time.

Kaptur serves on the Appropriations and Budget committees. She has used her seat on the Defense Appropriations Subcommittee to look out for an Ohio Air National Guard fighter wing based at Toledo's airport and to criticize the war in Iraq, which she has opposed from the outset.

She opposed all of Bush's major trade expansion initiatives — just as she opposed those of President Clinton — which she blames for devastating Ohio's manufacturing base. "Free trade isn't really free," Kaptur said. "It's hollowing out critical sectors of our economy, and the casualties are profound."

Kaptur has always looked out for her district's farmers; she still serves on the Agriculture Appropriations Subcommittee. She backs most agricultural subsidies, saying it is only fair to help U.S. industries survive when they have to comply with labor, environmental and health standards that are higher than in other nations.

Kaptur said she believes the country needs to gain energy independence and find new power sources. She displays a roll of solar panel roofing in her office, a reminder of her district's burgeoning solar and wind research efforts, for which she obtained a $3.2 million earmark for her district in the 2008 Defense spending bill.

Her legislative achievements include the development of the $182 million World War II Memorial on the National Mall, opened in 2004 after a 17-year political and legislative effort. The project was sparked by the request of a constituent who wondered why there was no Washington monument honoring World War II soldiers.

A member of the Oversight and Government Reform Committee and a supporter of campaign finance reform, Kaptur said her party's emphasis on fundraising has caused it to lose its historical focus on the working class. In 2002, she challenged Californian Nancy Pelosi for minority leader simply to make that point. Once she gave her speech, she withdrew her name.

Kaptur is more socially conservative than many in her party. In 2007, she voted against additional federal funding for embryonic stem cell research and opposed a bill allowing the federal government to provide donated contraceptives to international family planning groups. Her views match those of her ethnic blue-collar constituents — Germans, Irish, Poles, Hungarians and Hispanics — who share the Roman Catholic Church's opposition to abortion.

Kaptur is of the same stock; her father's parents were from western Poland and her mother's were from eastern Poland, in an area now part of Ukraine.

Her father, Stephen, ran a grocery store in Rossford, just south of Toledo, where he was known for giving credit to people who couldn't afford food for the week. After the 1997 death of her mother, Anastasia, Kaptur and her brother founded the nonprofit Anastasia Fund, which has helped support democracy movements in Ukraine, China and Mexico. Kaptur also has established the Kaptur Community Fund, which makes charitable donations in Toledo; she regularly contributes her congressional pay raise to the fund.

After college, she worked as a city planner, helping to create community development corporations to revitalize low-income areas of Toledo. That led to a job in the Carter administration as an adviser on urban policy.

Kaptur was studying for her doctorate in urban planning at the Massachusetts Institute of Technology when she was recruited to challenge first-term GOP Rep. Ed Weber in 1982. With northwestern Ohio in a deep recession, Weber's support for President Ronald Reagan's economic policies proved politically fatal; Kaptur won by 19 percentage points. She was held to 55 percent of the vote in 1984 but has won by overwhelming margins since.

KEY VOTES

2008

Yes Delay consideration of Colombia free-trade agreement

Yes Override Bush veto of federal farm and nutrition programs reauthorization bill

No Overhaul surveillance laws and permit dismissal of suits against companies that conducted warrantless wiretapping

No Grant mortgage relief to homeowners and funding for Fannie Mae and Freddie Mac

No Approve initial $700 billion program to stabilize financial markets

No Approve final $700 billion program to stabilize financial markets

Yes Provide $14 billion in loans to automakers

2007

Yes Increase minimum wage by $2.10 an hour

Yes Approve $124.2 billion in emergency war spending and set goal for redeployment of troops from Iraq

Yes Reject federal contraceptive assistance to international family planning groups

Yes Override Bush veto of $23.2 billion water projects authorization bill

No Implement Peru free-trade agreement

Yes Approve energy policy overhaul with new fuel economy standards

No Clear $473.5 billion omnibus spending bill, including $70 billion for military operations

CQ VOTE STUDIES

	PARTY UNITY		PRESIDENTIAL SUPPORT	
	SUPPORT	OPPOSE	SUPPORT	OPPOSE
2008	95%	5%	9%	91%
2007	96%	4%	8%	92%
2006	88%	12%	27%	73%
2005	93%	7%	23%	77%
2004	97%	3%	33%	67%

INTEREST GROUPS

	AFL-CIO	ADA	CCUS	ACU
2008	100%	100%	47%	13%
2007	100%	95%	47%	8%
2006	100%	85%	33%	21%
2005	93%	95%	41%	21%
2004	100%	95%	33%	8%

OHIO 9

North — Toledo, Sandusky

Along nearly 80 miles of Lake Erie's shoreline, the strongly Democratic 9th moves east from Lucas County and Toledo into Cleveland's orbit in Lorain County. More than two-thirds of the district's population resides in Lucas. Outside of that county, farmland and vacation spots contribute to the local economy.

At the mouth of the Maumee River, the largest river flowing into the Great Lakes, Toledo accounts for about half of the 9th's residents. Once nicknamed the "Glass City" because of its history in that industry, Toledo relied on auto manufacturing for decades. The city's blue-collar industries now struggle to provide enough jobs. Chrysler and General Motors employed thousands of district residents, but bankruptcy and production stoppages have forced several of the manufacturing plants to close. The city's health care sector has grown, especially with the merger of the University of Toledo and the Medical University of Ohio, which resulted in Ohio's third-largest public university operating budget.

Agriculture is important to the 9th, with greenhouse and fruit production

leading the way, but tourism is a key secondary economy. Sandusky's Cedar Point Amusement Park attracts more than 3 million visitors annually to its 364-acre park and resort: Cedar Point claims the most rides (75) and roller coasters (17) of any park in the world. In addition, millions of visitors travel to Lake Erie's Bass Islands each year.

Toledo's large concentrations of ethnic blue-collar workers — Germans, Irish, Poles, Hungarians and Hispanics — make it a lonely Democratic outpost in rural, Republican northwestern Ohio. The 9th's easternmost county of Lorain (shared with the 13th) leans Democratic and takes in the strongly liberal area around Oberlin College. The district's Republicans tend to live in the affluent suburbs on Toledo's west side, but are not enough to sway the district's vote at the federal level. Overall, the 9th gave Barack Obama 62 percent of the vote in the 2008 presidential election.

MAJOR INDUSTRY

Agriculture, health care, tourism

CITIES

Toledo, 313,619; Sandusky, 27,844; Oregon, 19,355; Sylvania, 18,670

NOTABLE

Oberlin College, founded in 1833, was the first co-educational institution of higher learning in the United States.

Rep. Dennis J. Kucinich (D)
Elected 1996; 7th term

CAPITOL OFFICE
225-5871
www.house.gov/kucinich
2445 Rayburn Bldg. 20515-3510; fax 225-5745

COMMITTEES
Education & Labor
Oversight & Government Reform
(Domestic Policy - chairman)

RESIDENCE
Cleveland

BORN
Oct. 8, 1946; Cleveland, Ohio

RELIGION
Roman Catholic

FAMILY
Wife, Elizabeth Kucinich; one child

EDUCATION
Case Western Reserve U., B.A., M.A. 1973
(speech communications)

CAREER
Video producer; public power consultant; sportswriter

POLITICAL HIGHLIGHTS
Cleveland City Council, 1969-75; Democratic
nominee for U.S. House, 1972; independent
candidate for U.S. House, 1974; mayor of
Cleveland, 1977-79; defeated for re-election as
mayor of Cleveland, 1979; Cleveland City Council,
1983-85; sought Democratic nomination for U.S.
House, 1988, 1992; Ohio Senate, 1995-97; sought
Democratic nomination for president, 2004, 2008

ELECTION RESULTS

2008 GENERAL

Dennis J. Kucinich (D)	157,268	57.0%
Jim Trakas (R)	107,918	39.1%
Paul Conroy (LIBERT)	10,623	3.8%

2008 PRIMARY

Dennis J. Kucinich (D)	72,646	50.3%
Joe Cimperman (D)	50,760	35.1%
Barbara Anne Ferris (D)	9,362	6.5%
Thomas E. O'Grady (D)	7,264	5.0%
Rosemary A. Palmer (D)	4,339	3.0%

2006 GENERAL

Dennis J. Kucinich (D)	138,393	66.4%
Michael D. Dovilla (R)	69,996	33.6%

PREVIOUS WINNING PERCENTAGES
2004 (60%); 2002 (74%); 2000 (75%); 1998 (67%);
1996 (49%)

Kucinich is a scrappy pro-labor, anti-war Midwestern populist who doesn't let an absence of support from his party's leadership blunt his drive to infuse the Democratic Party, and the country at large, with a large dose of liberalism. Among the mementos he keeps in his office is a script from the play "Man of La Mancha" — fitting for a lawmaker who engages in many quixotic quests.

Kucinich (ku-SIN-itch) is an occasional target of right-wing ridicule for his views, which include the creation of a Department of Peace, and for his lifestyle. He meditates, is a practicing vegan and enjoys a New Age crowd of admirers that includes actress Shirley MacLaine. But his stands on labor issues help keep him popular in his district, which includes the western part of Cleveland and some of its suburbs.

His abortive runs for president in 2004 and 2008, and a marriage in between to a much younger British activist, have broadened his fan base well beyond that of other lawmakers. What remains to be seen is how successfully Kucinich sustains that base with a Democratic president who won strong support from liberals instead of a Republican unpopular with them.

Kucinich backed most of President Obama's early legislative initiatives, but he was critical of Obama's plans to withdraw combat forces from Iraq by 2010 while sending more to Afghanistan. "We're accelerating a war there instead of getting out," he told MSNBC in April 2009. "I think it's very dangerous." He was one of 17 Democrats to oppose the fiscal 2010 budget proposal, objecting to its funding for the wars.

Kucinich serves on the Oversight and Government Reform Committee, where he chairs the Domestic Policy Subcommittee. His panel has held hearings on topics as diverse as the possible links between cell phone use and tumors and the $700 billion financial services industry rescue — a measure he opposed in fall 2008. The Treasury Department's management of the rescue program "has perpetuated business as usual," he complained in March 2009. "It defers to the judgment of the same corporate management in many cases that led to the crisis we are embroiled in."

As a member of the Education and Labor Committee, Kucinich has scored some legislative wins. In 2007, he won the inclusion of worker protection provisions in a NASA reauthorization bill. He authored provisions in a 2008 energy bill aimed at establishing jobs and training programs for people to evaluate the energy efficiency of buildings.

Kucinich championed a single-payer health care system and the withdrawal of U.S. troops from Iraq during each of his White House runs. "I'm kind of the Seabiscuit of this campaign," he said in 2007, referring to the legendary racehorse who improbably became a champion. After garnering little support in the early nominating contests in Iowa and New Hampshire, however, Kucinich dropped his second bid for the presidency in January 2008 in order to defend his House seat against four challengers in a Democratic primary battle. He ended up winning the nomination by a comfortable margin and cruised to re-election in November.

Kucinich distinguishes himself not only by his perseverance but also by his rhetorical flourishes and self-deprecating wit. When he arrived in Congress, he handed out trading cards featuring himself as a 4-foot-9-inch, 97-pound backup high school quarterback in 1960. At a 2007 Democratic presidential debate, he quipped, "We need to make sure that the next president was right about Iraq, was right about the Patriot Act. You can have a president like that, who was right about Iraq, who voted against it from the beginning and against the funding. You can have a president against — who was for a single-payer, not-for-profit health care system, one who will stop the Patriot Act…or you can have a president who's tall."

Kucinich fought the 2002 resolution authorizing President George W. Bush to launch a pre-emptive military strike on Iraq — a vote he took pains to highlight during his presidential runs. Kucinich's proposal for a delay received 101 votes on the House floor. He and five other Democrats then sued to bar Bush from attacking without a specific congressional declaration of war. A federal appeals court tossed out the suit in March 2003.

Kucinich also launched long-shot efforts in 2007 and 2008 to impeach Vice President Dick Cheney and Bush on various grounds, including the conduct of the war, warrantless surveillance and the response to Hurricane Katrina. He kept at it despite the aversion of Democratic leaders to an impeachment inquiry. In June 2008, he spent more than four hours on the House floor, reading the entire text of an impeachment resolution against Bush.

In August 2005, after 18 years of bachelorhood, Kucinich married Elizabeth Harper, a British consultant for a monetary think tank, who is 30 years his junior. The congressman, who is twice-divorced, said they are a perfect match: "I'm happier than I've ever been. I have a real partnership."

The son of a truck driver who was often out of work, Kucinich and his six siblings moved frequently and sometimes slept in the family car for weeks at a time. He worked two jobs to put himself through college, getting a master's degree in speech communications and launching a career as a copy editor, sportswriter and political commentator — jobs that taught him to reduce complicated public policy disagreements to easily understood terms. Kucinich also has been a hospital orderly and a teacher.

Elected mayor of Cleveland at 31, he served a single term, during which the city fell into financial default after Kucinich refused to sell off the city's power company, Muny Light, as a condition of getting bank credit. His popularity sank so low he wore a bulletproof vest to throw out the first pitch of the Cleveland Indians' 1978 season. Later that year, he barely survived a recall vote, and the next year lost to Republican George V. Voinovich, now Ohio's senior senator.

But later Kucinich won praise for not selling Muny Light and, bucking the GOP tide in 1994, he seized a state Senate seat from a Republican incumbent. Two years later, he toppled two-term Republican Rep. Martin R. Hoke on his fifth try for Congress, a quest he began as an anti-Vietnam War candidate in 1972. His subsequent elections have been easy.

KEY VOTES

2008

Yes Delay consideration of Colombia free-trade agreement

Yes Override Bush veto of federal farm and nutrition programs reauthorization bill

No Overhaul surveillance laws and permit dismissal of suits against companies that conducted warrantless wiretapping

Yes Grant mortgage relief to homeowners and funding for Fannie Mae and Freddie Mac

No Approve initial $700 billion program to stabilize financial markets

No Approve final $700 billion program to stabilize financial markets

Yes Provide $14 billion in loans to automakers

2007

Yes Increase minimum wage by $2.10 an hour

No Approve $124.2 billion in emergency war spending and set goal for redeployment of troops from Iraq

No Reject federal contraceptive assistance to international family planning groups

Yes Override Bush veto of $23.2 billion water projects authorization bill

No Implement Peru free-trade agreement

Yes Approve energy policy overhaul with new fuel economy standards

? Clear $473.5 billion omnibus spending bill, including $70 billion for military operations

CQ VOTE STUDIES

	PARTY UNITY		PRESIDENTIAL SUPPORT	
	SUPPORT	OPPOSE	SUPPORT	OPPOSE
2008	91%	9%	20%	80%
2007	94%	6%	14%	86%
2006	97%	3%	13%	87%
2005	98%	2%	11%	89%
2004	96%	4%	22%	78%

INTEREST GROUPS

	AFL-CIO	ADA	CCUS	ACU
2008	93%	95%	39%	8%
2007	89%	70%	35%	4%
2006	93%	100%	20%	4%
2005	93%	100%	30%	0%
2004	100%	90%	6%	0%

OHIO 10
Cleveland — West Side and suburbs

Taking in the western portion of Cleveland, the 10th follows the migration of its ethnic residents into the western and southern suburbs. The line between the 10th and 11th districts generally divides Cleveland's white and black neighborhoods. The 10th contains large concentrations of ethnic voters, including Poles and immigrants from a multitude of other Eastern European countries.

Once solely dependent on manufacturing, this Democratic district has gradually made the transition to a service economy, with growth in the banking and financial services sectors as well. Although manufacturing is still the backbone of the city's economy, the 10th has attracted smaller technology companies, and Cleveland has undergone a decades-long downtown restoration, with such projects as the Euclid Corridor Transportation Project making the area more accessible. The 10th also is home to Cleveland Hopkins International Airport.

The immediate suburbs have a strong union presence and a Democratic lean. Traditionally Democratic-leaning, middle-income communities that abut western Cleveland, such as Brooklyn and Lakewood, are losing population. A blue-collar tradition in Brook Park makes that city decidedly Democratic. Brook Park's Ford auto plant has been repeatedly shut down and re-opened, but the latest re-opening will have the plant building "greener" engines for a new line of cars, and residents hope that the auto industry, once a regional economic driver, will continue to provide employment. Farther west, incomes rise, as does the level of Republicanism: Bay Village, Westlake and Rocky River residents have above-average incomes.

The strong Democratic tendencies of Cleveland — matched up against the GOP lean of some of Cleveland's western and southern suburbs — give the 10th a decided but not overwhelming Democratic tilt. Barack Obama won 59 percent of the district's presidential vote in 2008.

MAJOR INDUSTRY
Manufacturing, banking, technology

CITIES
Cleveland (pt.), 190,224; Parma, 85,655; Lakewood, 56,646; North Olmsted, 34,113; Westlake, 31,719

NOTABLE
Cleveland is home to NASA's Glenn Research Center.

Rep. Marcia L. Fudge (D)

Elected 2008; 1st full term

Fudge brings a hard-working, problem-solving persona — honed as mayor of a Cleveland suburb — to the task of creating jobs and improving health care in her economically distressed district. She tends to avoid the spotlight, unlike her more outgoing predecessor, Democrat Stephanie Tubbs Jones.

Like Tubbs Jones, though, Fudge is a committed liberal voter who believes in using government as much as possible to assist those in need. "We have the same heart about people," Fudge said of her friend and mentor, whose death in 2008 led to Fudge's election. "We believe very strongly about service and helping people."

Fudge represents one of the two-dozen districts nationwide with a black-majority population; it has the lowest median income of Ohio's 18 congressional districts, according to the 2000 census. Her goals include attacking predatory lending practices and helping laid-off workers who lose pensions when their employers go bankrupt. She said President Obama's economic stimulus law, signed in early 2009, was a welcome initial lifeline. "The people of Ohio are crying for relief, and this package begins to address our areas of need," she said before its passage.

As mayor of Warrensville Heights, Fudge was credited with helping the city build 200 new homes and shore up a sagging retail base. Former Cleveland Mayor Jane Campbell described her to The Plain Dealer of Cleveland as "absolutely the hardest worker you have ever seen."

With a seat on the Education and Labor Committee, Fudge hopes to elevate Cleveland's struggling public schools. She supported the stimulus in part because her district was expected to receive tens of millions of dollars for technology and updating aging infrastructure. As a member of the panel's Higher Education, Lifelong Learning and Competitiveness Subcommittee, Fudge looks for ways to aid research at Case Western Reserve University.

Fudge also sits on the Health, Employment, Labor and Pensions Subcommittee and is a strong backer of organized labor. Her mother, Marian Saffold, worked as a lab technician at a now-defunct Cleveland hospital and was among the first black women to act as union organizers for the American Federation of State, County and Municipal Employees. In early 2009, Fudge supported a Democratic bill, signed into law, that makes it easier for workers to challenge wage discrimination.

Like many Democrats in the Rust Belt manufacturing region, Fudge opposes free-trade deals, saying they have moved thousands of jobs overseas. She aligned with the rest of her state's Democratic delegation in backing a December 2008 bill to loan $14 billion to domestic automakers. Though the measure passed the House, it failed in the Senate. "More than 130,000 people work for the auto industry in the state of Ohio. It was an easy vote for me," Fudge said. "When people send you to do a job, they expect you to protect their interests."

Fudge also sits on the Science and Technology Committee — an important seat for an area with a robust aerospace industry, including the NASA Glenn Research Center in the nearby 10th District. She said her job is to ensure continued growth for the area's biotech and bioscience industries. She cited NASA Glenn's goals of using space technology to improve quality of life, such as a program that detects cataracts — the leading cause of vision loss — before they occur.

She joins many in her party seeking to tackle global warming, but she hopes industries aren't forced to do too much at the outset through a proposed system of trading credits to cap greenhouse gas emissions. "We must

CAPITOL OFFICE
225-7032
fudge.house.gov
1513 Longworth Bldg. 20515; fax 225-1339

COMMITTEES
Education & Labor
Science & Technology

RESIDENCE
Warrensville Heights

BORN
Oct. 29, 1952; Cleveland, Ohio

RELIGION
Baptist

FAMILY
Single

EDUCATION
Ohio State U., B.S. 1975 (business administration);
Cleveland State U., J.D. 1983

CAREER
Congressional aide; county government finance administrator; aw clerk; sales and marketing representative

POLITICAL HIGHLIGHTS
Mayor of Warrensville Heights, 2000-08

ELECTION RESULTS

2008 SPECIAL

Marcia L. Fudge (D)		unopposed

2008 GENERAL

Marcia L. Fudge (D)	212,667	85.2%
Thomas Pekarek (R)	36,708	14.7%

2008 PRIMARY SPECIAL

Marcia L. Fudge (D)	10,753	74.3%
Jeffrey Johnson (D)	2,028	14.0%
Carolyn Johnson (D)	690	4.8%
Sean Ryan (D)	241	1.7%
Thomas Wheeler (D)	175	1.2%
Isaac Powell (D)	162	1.1%
Frank Rives (D)	155	1.1%

be aggressive enough to safeguard the environment, but not so overzealous that businesses cannot participate," Fudge told Investor's Business Daily in February 2009.

She credits her mother and maternal grandmother for getting her active in public service. When she was 10, Fudge went with a neighbor to the capital to see the Rev. Martin Luther King Jr.'s 1963 march on Washington. And as a teenager she worked on the 1967 Cleveland mayoral bid of Carl Stokes, who became the first black mayor of a major U.S. city.

In high school she lettered in several sports and was named best female athlete of her class. She earned a business administration degree from Ohio State University in 1975 and eight years later earned a law degree from Cleveland State University.

In conversation, Fudge often talks about her allegiance to Delta Sigma Theta, a sorority of predominately black college-educated women. It was through its Cleveland chapter that she met Tubbs Jones, who was known on Capitol Hill for wearing Delta Sigma Theta red. Fudge became a national president of the organization and even thanked her fellow members upon being sworn in to Congress.

Her relationship with her predecessor blossomed in the early 1990s, when she worked under Tubbs Jones, who was then Cuyahoga County prosecutor. When Tubbs Jones was elected to Congress, Fudge became her chief of staff. She then won a 2000 mayoral race for Warrensville Heights, becoming its first black executive.

When Tubbs Jones died in August 2008 after suffering an aneurysm, Fudge emerged as the front-runner to replace her. She won the backing of Cleveland Mayor Frank Jackson and former Ohio Democratic Rep. Louis Stokes as well as Tubbs Jones' sister Barbara Tubbs Walker, who told The Plain Dealer she saw Fudge as "very talented and diverse and inclusive — she can bring the district together."

Tubbs Jones had died after winning the Democratic nomination for the seat, so the Cuyahoga County Democratic Party's executive committee was charged with choosing her replacement for the November ballot. Fudge finished with 175 of the 280 committee members' votes in September, well ahead of runner-up C.J. Prentiss, a former Ohio Senate minority leader.

Fudge also won the primary special election to finish out the final weeks of Tubbs Jones' term, handily defeating nine other challengers with 74 percent of the vote, and was unopposed in the special election. In the November general election for her own two-year term, she trounced her GOP opponent, retired naval reservist Thomas Pekarek.

KEY VOTES

2008
Yes   Provide $14 billion in loans to automakers

CQ VOTE STUDIES

	PARTY UNITY		PRESIDENTIAL SUPPORT	
	SUPPORT	OPPOSE	SUPPORT	OPPOSE
2008	100%	0%	100%	0%

INTEREST GROUPS

	AFL-CIO	ADA	CCUS	ACU
2008	100%	–	–	0%

OHIO 11
Cleveland — East Side and suburbs

The 11th is a diverse district economically and ethnically. In addition to its African-American majority, the district also includes a substantial Jewish population. The district takes in poor, inner-city areas of Cleveland's East Side, as well as the city's downtown destinations, and extends out to the east to take in various historic neighborhoods such as Little Italy and upper-middle-class suburbs. The district's black majority and liberal suburbanites combine to make it very Democratic.

Driving a staunch Democratic bent here is a 60 percent share of Cleveland. Much of the 11th's black majority lives in poverty-riddled inner-city neighborhoods, and the district has Ohio's lowest median income. The 11th has lost population over the last decade and many areas were hit particularly hard by Cleveland's recent housing market collapse.

Although suburban growth has lured many businesses and residents outside the city, the 11th is gradually making itself a medical, biotech and banking hub. Cleveland's cultural center, located in University Circle, is home to Case Western Reserve University, the Cleveland Orchestra and the Cleveland Museum of Art. The Circle also is the face of Cleveland's health care industry; the University Hospitals of Cleveland, Cleveland Clinic and Louis Stokes Veterans Affairs Medical Center are all located here. Driving west along historic Euclid Avenue, the city's geographic center includes the Rock and Roll Hall of Fame, the city's sports stadiums and Public Square.

The upper-middle-class suburbs of Cleveland Heights, Shaker Heights, University Heights and Beachwood are home to large communities of Jews and young professionals, forming some of Ohio's most liberal and racially integrated areas. Farther east, the 11th takes in areas such as Mayfield Heights, Richmond Heights, Lyndhurst and Pepper Pike, which has one of Ohio's highest income levels.

MAJOR INDUSTRY
Health care, manufacturing, utilities, education

CITIES
Cleveland (pt.), 288,179; Euclid, 52,717; Cleveland Heights, 49,958; Shaker Heights, 29,405; East Cleveland, 27,217; Maple Heights, 26,156

NOTABLE
A landmark 1926 case brought by the city of Euclid was the first U.S. Supreme Court decision to uphold city zoning ordinances.

Rep. Pat Tiberi (R)

Elected 2000; 5th term

Tiberi grew up in a Democratic household with an immigrant father who lost his blue-collar job, a background that gives him a different perspective on labor and pension issues from that of the typical Republican. But even though he'll work across the aisle on some matters, he's a GOP loyalist with close ties to Minority Leader John A. Boehner.

Tiberi (TEA-berry) and Boehner not only hail from the same state, they also worked together on the Education and Labor Committee, which Boehner chaired until 2006. Tiberi helped Boehner defeat Missouri Republican Roy Blunt in a tense intraparty fight for the No. 2 GOP leadership post in 2006, and backed Boehner again as he defeated conservative Mike Pence of Indiana to become minority leader in the 110th Congress (2007-08).

With friends in high places, Tiberi in the 110th got the seat he had coveted on the Ways and Means Committee. With Republicans in the minority, though, he's been unable to press his tax-cutting agenda; instead, he finds himself battling Democratic proposals to raise taxes on wealthy Americans.

Tiberi has expressed frustration at the Democrats' tight partisan control of the legislative process. He is anxious to have a hand in tackling broad health care and tax issues as the top Republican on Ways and Means' Select Revenue Measures Subcommittee.

In his first two terms, Tiberi was a dependable supporter of President George W. Bush, but that changed as Bush's popularity dropped and Tiberi faced stiffer challenges at home. In the 109th Congress (2005-06), he expressed skepticism about Bush's proposal to create private investment accounts in Social Security, and voted to prohibit cruel or degrading treatment of U.S. detainees.

During the 110th Congress, he voted for several major Democratic bills, including a measure to boost vehicle fuel efficiency standards, one version of an expanded children's health insurance program, and legislation to combat foreclosures and stabilize Fannie Mae and Freddie Mac. He was one of 35 House Republicans to support a bill that sought to outlaw employment discrimination based on sexual orientation. He followed through in 2009, becoming one of 40 House Republicans to support the children's health insurance expansion that President Obama signed early in his term.

Yet Tiberi has been there when GOP leaders needed him on tough votes. He voted for the 2005 Central America Free Trade Agreement, which squeaked through, 217-215. He also was one of 25 Republicans who opposed the initial $700 billion bill to aid the ailing financial services sector in fall 2008, but he voted for the final version after fervent pleas from Boehner and the Bush administration.

One of Tiberi's main legislative accomplishments was a bipartisan effort in the 109th that renewed the law governing social services for senior citizens through fiscal 2011. Called the Older Americans Act, the law was part of President Johnson's 1965 Great Society agenda and calls for about $1.8 billion in annual spending. Rubén Hinojosa, a Texas Democrat who worked with Tiberi on the legislation, said he was "fair and is willing to find a way to make things work."

Tiberi is the eldest of three children of Italian immigrants who arrived in the United States three years before he was born. His mother was a seamstress; his father was a machinist who lost his job and his pension when his company restructured. Tiberi was the first in his family to go to college.

He met his wife at a Northland High School marching band alumni gather-

CAPITOL OFFICE
225-5355
www.house.gov/tiberi
113 Cannon Bldg. 20515-3512; fax 226-4523

COMMITTEES
Ways & Means

RESIDENCE
Genoa Township

BORN
Oct. 21, 1962; Columbus, Ohio

RELIGION
Roman Catholic

FAMILY
Wife, Denice Tiberi; four children

EDUCATION
Ohio State U., B.A. 1985 (journalism)

CAREER
Realtor; congressional district aide

POLITICAL HIGHLIGHTS
Ohio House, 1993-2001 (majority leader, 1999-2001)

ELECTION RESULTS

2008 GENERAL
Pat Tiberi (R)	197,447	54.8%
David Robinson (D)	152,234	42.2%
Steven Linnabary (LIBERT)	10,707	3.0%

2008 PRIMARY
Pat Tiberi (R)	63,450	90.5%
David Ryon (R)	6,681	9.5%

2006 GENERAL
Pat Tiberi (R)	145,943	57.3%
Bob Shamansky (D)	108,746	42.7%

PREVIOUS WINNING PERCENTAGES
2004 (62%); 2002 (64%); 2000 (53%)

ing. He played trumpet; she played flute. Tiberi, who was senior class president, says he had no interest in politics as a career until a political science class at Ohio State University led to an internship in the Columbus office of Republican Rep. John R. Kasich. At that point, he became a Republican.

He spent eight years handling constituent casework for Kasich. In 1992, state legislative district remapping created an open seat in his neighborhood. He won that election and spent four terms in the state House, rising to majority leader in 1999 and earning a reputation as a conservative willing to work with Democrats. He established a DNA database to track violent criminals and was a prime mover behind a state law that, for a time, limited large jury awards but later was ruled unconstitutional.

Barred by Ohio term limits from seeking re-election to the General Assembly in 2000, Tiberi was considering a career change when Kasich announced he was leaving the House. Kasich's support — and Boehner's backing — helped Tiberi cruise to an easy primary victory over three rivals. Democrats put up Columbus City Councilwoman Maryellen O'Shaughnessy, but Tiberi racked up big margins in the suburban GOP strongholds of Delaware and Licking counties and won by 9 percentage points.

Some of Kasich's staff, who had been Tiberi's supervisors and co-workers in the 1980s, now work for him — an unusual display of staff longevity and loyalty.

In 2005, Tiberi helped Ohio Republicans defeat a ballot initiative that would have changed the state's redistricting process in a way that could have cost the GOP seats in the next election. As a token of gratitude, Rep. Thomas M. Reynolds of New York, then chairman of the National Republican Congressional Committee, gave Tiberi a framed map of the state signed by Ohio's GOP lawmakers. Every Ohio Republican incumbent on the November ballot won re-election in 2006.

Tiberi took 57 percent of the vote that year, defeating Bob Shamansky, a former one-term House member. Tiberi credited his victory to his constant presence in the district and his deep roots there. As a local newspaper columnist once said, "Every groundbreaking, every parade, every ribbon-cutting with a pair of scissors to spare ... is likely to find Pat Tiberi." He won again easily in 2008, despite Obama carrying his district by 10 percentage points.

Before he dug in for the 111th Congress, Tiberi took a few days off in January 2009, missing Obama's inauguration. He had a good excuse: His wife, Denice, gave birth to triplets, doubling the size of their family in one day. The three new girls joined 5-year-old Angelina.

KEY VOTES

2008
No Delay consideration of Colombia free-trade agreement
No Override Bush veto of federal farm and nutrition programs reauthorization bill
Yes Overhaul surveillance laws and permit dismissal of suits against companies that conducted warrantless wiretapping
Yes Grant mortgage relief to homeowners and funding for Fannie Mae and Freddie Mac
No Approve initial $700 billion program to stabilize financial markets
Yes Approve final $700 billion program to stabilize financial markets
No Provide $14 billion in loans to automakers

2007
No Increase minimum wage by $2.10 an hour
No Approve $124.2 billion in emergency war spending and set goal for redeployment of troops from Iraq
Yes Reject federal contraceptive assistance to international family planning groups
No Override Bush veto of $23.2 billion water projects authorization bill
Yes Implement Peru free-trade agreement
Yes Approve energy policy overhaul with new fuel economy standards
Yes Clear $473.5 billion omnibus spending bill, including $70 billion for military operations

CQ VOTE STUDIES

	PARTY UNITY		PRESIDENTIAL SUPPORT	
	SUPPORT	OPPOSE	SUPPORT	OPPOSE
2008	92%	8%	60%	40%
2007	91%	9%	77%	23%
2006	92%	8%	87%	13%
2005	95%	5%	71%	29%
2004	92%	8%	82%	18%

INTEREST GROUPS

	AFL-CIO	ADA	CCUS	ACU
2008	40%	35%	94%	72%
2007	29%	20%	85%	88%
2006	36%	0%	100%	84%
2005	27%	5%	96%	88%
2004	13%	10%	100%	96%

OHIO 12
Central – Eastern Columbus and suburbs

The 12th includes the eastern half of Columbus in Franklin County and suburban counties to the north and east of the city. The district has a slight Republican lean, with a strong GOP influence in the 12th's suburbs balancing a Democratic tilt in Columbus.

The 12th's economy relies heavily on Columbus' business sector, parts of which have been hit hard by layoffs at major employers. The city hosts headquarters for several national chains, and despite losses, the city's primarily white-collar economy remains relatively stable. The service economy has led to significant growth in both the city and its adjacent areas over the past two decades.

Democrats find support in the urban, predominately black part of the district in Franklin County. Within Franklin County, but outside Columbus, the 12th includes Dublin, an upscale, solidly GOP suburb in the northwest part of the county known to many as the headquarters of Wendy's. Dublin also is home to health care manufacturer Cardinal Health, which has been forced to cut jobs.

In Franklin County, Westerville, Gahanna and Reynoldsburg — traditionally Republican areas outside Columbus — show signs of increasing Democratic support. North of Franklin, Delaware County has experienced explosive growth — its population more than doubled over the past 15 years — and it has the state's lowest unemployment and highest household income. Offsetting the Democrats in Franklin County are Republicans in Delaware and western Licking County, whose numbers are swelling due to the overall growth.

John McCain took 59 percent of the 2008 presidential vote in Delaware County and 56 percent in Licking (shared with the 18th). But a strong showing in Franklin County was enough for Democrat Barack Obama to win the district's overall vote with 54 percent.

MAJOR INDUSTRY
Financial services, government, manufacturing, service

CITIES
Columbus (pt.), 275,882; Westerville, 35,318; Gahanna, 32,636; Reynoldsburg, 32,069; Dublin (pt.), 31,370; Delaware, 25,243

NOTABLE
The Anti-Saloon League, which lobbied successfully for Prohibition, was based in Westerville beginning in 1909.

Rep. Betty Sutton (D)

Elected 2006; 2nd term

A former labor lawyer, Sutton fights to protect her Rust Belt district, which has been hard hit by a loss of manufacturing jobs. She opposes free-trade agreements she views as unfair and seeks ways to protect the local auto parts industry. A proponent of ending the U.S. involvement in the Iraq War, she also has sought to protect the benefits of soldiers and presses for accountability and honesty in government.

At the start of 2009 she joined a new Populist Caucus, chaired by Iowa Democrat Bruce Braley, with the intent to focus on middle-class values. Sutton, raised in a blue-collar community, said on the House floor in March: "With health care costs rising, with insurance not available to all, with pensions a little shaky out there…the promise of the middle class is slipping away from far too many." She blamed the George W. Bush administration for pushing through "economic policies that benefited the wealthy and the well-connected …at the expense of the rest of us."

Sutton learned the procedures of the House from a seat on the Rules Committee during her first term. She now sits on the powerful Energy and Commerce Committee, where she has backed President Obama's early efforts to revive the economy, including the struggling automobile industry.

She supported Obama's $787 billion economic stimulus law in February 2009, saying, "This legislation is aimed squarely at restoring the promise of the middle class to our families." She also backed a provision calling for all stimulus-funded projects to make use of only U.S.-made steel, iron, concrete and other manufactured products.

She subsequently proposed a measure to give car buyers a cash voucher of $3,000 to $5,000 when they trade in a car or truck at least eight years old for a new, more fuel-efficient vehicle made in North America. The bill would grant larger vouchers for new cars with higher gas mileage. And cars made in the United States would qualify for larger incentives than those from Canada or Mexico. "It's good for Detroit and good for America," Sutton said. "There is a sense of urgency with car sales slumping." She added that higher sales could keep jobs in the United States. Obama endorsed the idea.

She had supported a bill in late 2008 to rescue the auto industry, and when that bill stalled in the Senate, backed President Bush's move to use funds from a financial rescue law signed earlier in the year. Sutton had originally opposed that rescue measure — which provided $700 billion to shore up the nation's financial services sector — but supported it on a second vote.

As state legislator, Sutton criticized what she saw as attempts by insurance companies to assume too much control over health care. She now seeks to make prescription drugs more affordable under Medicare and allow for reimportation of federally approved drugs from Canada and other countries.

Sutton also is concerned about potentially unfair trade deals. "We want trade, but we want it to work for our folks, not against them," she said. She voted against the implementation of a free-trade agreement with Peru, saying she was concerned about the enforceability of labor and safety standards in the bill and about the United States' growing trade deficit.

Sutton during the 110th Congress (2007-08) strongly pushed setting a timeline for withdrawal of U.S. troops from Iraq. Then, concerned about soldiers kept on active duty after their enlistment period ends, she secured passage of a bill to ensure financial compensation for the soldiers. She said instead of forcing soldiers to serve, the military should improve its recruitment efforts. Her measure became law as part of a fiscal 2009 spending bill.

CAPITOL OFFICE
225-3401
sutton.house.gov
1721 Longworth Bldg. 20515-3513; fax 225-2266

COMMITTEES
Energy & Commerce

RESIDENCE
Copley Township

BORN
July 31, 1963; Barberton, Ohio

RELIGION
Methodist

FAMILY
Husband, Doug Corwon; two stepchildren

EDUCATION
Kent State U., B.A. 1985 (political science);
U. of Akron, J.D. 1990

CAREER
Lawyer; campaign aide; modeling school administrator

POLITICAL HIGHLIGHTS
Barberton City Council, 1990-91; Summit County Council, 1991-92 (vice president, 1992); Ohio House, 1993-2000

ELECTION RESULTS

2008 GENERAL

Betty Sutton (D)	192,593	64.7%
David Potter (R)	105,050	35.3%

2008 PRIMARY

Betty Sutton (D)	unopposed

2006 GENERAL

Betty Sutton (D)	135,639	61.2%
Craig Foltin (R)	85,922	38.8%

Defense Secretary Robert M. Gates announced in March 2009 the department would end the practice of extending soldiers' duty.

The youngest in a family of six children, Sutton was reared in Barberton, a suburb of Akron. Her mother was clerk-treasurer for the city library, while her father worked in a boilermaker factory despite having earned a teaching degree in history.

Sutton's father died of lung cancer during her first year of law school at the University of Akron. The next year, she ran an impressive door-to-door campaign and won a seat on the Barberton City Council. She then moved to the Summit County Council and later ran successfully for a seat in the Ohio House.

In Columbus, Sutton was known to alert the press of closed-door gatherings between lobbyists and legislators. When ethics became a campaign theme for Democrats in 2006, Sutton quickly touted her record. And while pushing two state domestic violence bills in the 1990s, she testified before the state legislature about her own history of being in an abusive first marriage. "There were people who said, 'If you deal with domestic violence, they will pigeonhole you.' I said, 'The fact I know about this means I have to do it.'" Sutton has since married a retired firefighter, and her Capitol Hill office is adorned with firefighter memorabilia.

In the race to replace Democrat Sherrod Brown, now Ohio's junior senator, Sutton was one of 17 candidates, eight of them Democrats. She earned her party's nod by defeating former Rep. Tom Sawyer, shopping mall heiress Capri S. Cafaro and Gary J. Kucinich, a former Cleveland city councilman and brother of 10th District Democratic Rep. Dennis J. Kucinich.

Throughout the campaign she criticized Sawyer's support for the 1993 North American Free Trade Agreement. Taking 31 percent of the vote, Sutton wound up winning the primary, which was a major victory for EMILY's List, the group that backs Democratic women candidates who support abortion rights.

In the general election, Sutton continued to campaign on a six-point anticorruption platform against her GOP opponent, Lorain Mayor Craig Foltin, who had a record of winning on Democratic turf. Foltin could not overcome the poor environment for the GOP nationwide, however, especially in a state where former Republican Rep. Bob Ney had pleaded guilty in 2006 to federal corruption charges stemming from his association with convicted lobbyist Jack Abramoff.

In a watershed election year that heavily favored her party, Sutton posted a 22-percentage-point victory over Foltin. Two years later, she easily defeated Republican David Potter, a medical devices salesman.

KEY VOTES

2008

Yes   Delay consideration of Colombia free-trade agreement

Yes   Override Bush veto of federal farm and nutrition programs reauthorization bill

No   Overhaul surveillance laws and permit dismissal of suits against companies that conducted warrantless wiretapping

Yes   Grant mortgage relief to homeowners and funding for Fannie Mae and Freddie Mac

No   Approve initial $700 billion program to stabilize financial markets

Yes   Approve final $700 billion program to stabilize financial markets

Yes   Provide $14 billion in loans to automakers

2007

Yes   Increase minimum wage by $2.10 an hour

Yes   Approve $124.2 billion in emergency war spending and set goal for redeployment of troops from Iraq

No   Reject federal contraceptive assistance to international family planning groups

Yes   Override Bush veto of $23.2 billion water projects authorization bill

No   Implement Peru free-trade agreement

Yes   Approve energy policy overhaul with new fuel economy standards

No   Clear $473.5 billion omnibus spending bill, including $70 billion for military operations

CQ VOTE STUDIES

	PARTY UNITY		PRESIDENTIAL SUPPORT	
	SUPPORT	OPPOSE	SUPPORT	OPPOSE
2008	99%	1%	13%	87%
2007	98%	2%	4%	96%

INTEREST GROUPS

	AFL-CIO	ADA	CCUS	ACU
2008	100%	100%	61%	4%
2007	96%	100%	55%	0%

OHIO 13

Northeast — parts of Akron and suburbs, Cleveland suburbs

The lightning-bolt-shaped 13th runs from the shores of Lake Erie west of Cleveland, southeast through the city's mostly middle-class suburbs to Akron (shared with 17th). Summit is the most populous county in the 13th, making up 44 percent of the population.

Many tire factories have left Akron, once known as the world's rubber capital, auto plants in the area have been closing and corporate headquarters have faced layoffs. Despite double-digit unemployment rates in the area, Akron remains a scientific research hub, and the University of Akron's College of Polymer Science and Polymer Engineering is located here. The National Inventors Hall of Fame in Akron expects to complete construction of a specialized math, science and technology middle school on its campus. The city also hosts some of Ohio's leading health care providers, such as the Akron Children's Hospital.

The 13th includes 60 percent of Akron's residents, including much of its black population. Blue-collar workers, together with blacks, ethnic whites and the University of Akron community, help the city retain its Democratic character.

Bordering Lake Erie at the 13th's other end is Lorain County, which relied on large steel and medical device plants. But layoffs by U.S. Steel have hurt the local economy. The 13th's part of Lorain County include staunchly Democratic Lorain and Sheffield Lake and Democratic-leaning Elyria. Both Avon and Avon Lake are upper-middle-class and GOP-friendly.

In the district's middle are some GOP-leaning communities in southern Cuyahoga County and northern Medina County. But Summit and Lorain's dominance gives the 13th a decided Democratic tilt. Barack Obama received 57 percent of the district's presidential vote in 2008.

MAJOR INDUSTRY
Polymer research, steel, health care

CITIES
Akron (pt.), 129,298; Lorain, 68,652; Elyria, 55,953; Cuyahoga Falls (pt.), 39,051; Brunswick, 33,388; Strongsville, 29,715; North Royalton, 28,648

NOTABLE
The American Toy Marble Museum is in Akron.

Rep. Steven C. LaTourette (R)

Elected 1994; 8th term

CAPITOL OFFICE
225-5731
www.house.gov/latourette
2371 Rayburn Bldg. 20515-3514; fax 225-3307

COMMITTEES
Appropriations

RESIDENCE
Bainbridge Township

BORN
July 22, 1954; Cleveland, Ohio

RELIGION
Methodist

FAMILY
Wife, Jennifer LaTourette; five children

EDUCATION
U. of Michigan, B.A. 1976 (history);
Cleveland State U., J.D. 1979

CAREER
Lawyer

POLITICAL HIGHLIGHTS
Candidate for Lake County prosecutor, 1984;
Lake County prosecutor, 1989-94

ELECTION RESULTS

2008 GENERAL

Steven C. LaTourette (R)	188,488	58.3%
Bill O'Neill (D)	125,214	38.7%
David Macko (LIBERT)	9,511	2.9%

2008 PRIMARY

Steven C. LaTourette (R)	unopposed

2006 GENERAL

Steven C. LaTourette (R)	144,069	57.6%
Lewis R. Katz (D)	97,753	39.1%
Werner J. Lange (X)	8,500	3.4%

PREVIOUS WINNING PERCENTAGES
2004 (63%); 2002 (72%); 2000 (65%); 1998 (66%);
1996 (55%); 1994 (48%)

LaTourette has honed a reputation for taking moderate, independent stands on issues involving health care and social services. A former prosecutor and public defender, he is a longtime ally of fellow Ohioan and Minority Leader John A. Boehner and sometimes takes on tough jobs for the leadership that require his skills as a negotiator and investigator.

He sits on three Appropriations subcommittees: Interior-Environment, Legislative Branch, and Transportation-HUD. His district expects him to bring in plenty of federal funding.

LaTourette (la-tuh-RHETT) is a strong proponent of earmarks and frequently played up the financial wins he made for his region from his former seat on the Transportation and Infrastructure Committee, including grants for fire departments and funds for the Route 8 freeway project and for road work throughout the district.

He looks to promote a new high-speed rail corridor connecting Cleveland and Chicago, and he advocates dedicating a good portion of the revenue President Obama hopes to earn from charging polluters for carbon dioxide emissions to be allocated to energy-efficient transportation projects.

With his beard and spectacles, LaTourette looks like a college professor and employs the smooth, persuasive style of a lawyer making his closing argument on the floor. He has earned a reputation for leading after-hours member groups; he is a co-chairman, with Democrat James L. Oberstar of Minnesota, of the Northeast-Midwest Coalition and was a co-founder of a new Caucus on the Middle Class in 2008.

He often emphasizes his dissents with the GOP leadership, which plays well back home. As a member of the Financial Services Committee during the 110th Congress (2007-08), he served as one of the leaders of the opposition in the fall of 2008 to the $700 billion financial rescue package. He called for a smaller package of $250 billion, criticized tax breaks for makers of rum and children's wooden arrows, and argued for tax incentives to encourage companies to buy troubled investments from banks. "I'd rather have rich guys in three-piece suits buy up this bad mortgage debt and get a tax break for doing so than have taxpayers foot the bill," he said.

In late 2008, he fought a proposed acquisition of Cleveland-based National City Corp. by a beneficiary of the financial rescue law, Pittsburgh-based PNC Financial Services Group Inc. "It is not what Congress intended nor what Congress should stand for," LaTourette said.

He tilts to the center on some Democratic initiatives on education and social programs and on union-backed priorities, such as a 2007 minimum wage hike and a House-passed "card check" proposal to permit unions to organize workplaces with petition drives instead of full-blown elections. When the House in 2009 took up a bill to authorize wastewater treatment grants and loans, he said he would favor the application of the Davis-Bacon Law, which would require contractors to pay prevailing wages on projects. Most Republicans had opposed such a provision.

As a social conservative, LaTourette opposes abortion and voted in 2004 and 2006 to amend the Constitution to outlaw same-sex marriage. But he backs expanded research on stem cells from discarded embryos created for in vitro fertilization. And while LaTourette voted in 2002 to authorize the war in Iraq and backs funding for the war, he was one of 17 Republicans to vote with Democrats in early 2007 to disapprove of Bush's decision to deploy an additional 21,000 troops there.

Now in his eighth term, LaTourette has twice broken a term-limit pledge. While stressing the importance of his seniority in delivering projects to Ohio, he survived a nasty 2004 re-election battle in which his personal life became an issue. The Akron Beacon Journal charged at the time that he had "cheated on and left his wife for a woman who now lobbies one of his committees." LaTourette's ex-wife backed his Democratic opponent, shopping mall heiress Capri S. Cafaro. The state Democratic Party asked the Justice Department to investigate LaTourette's relationship with the lobbyist, Jennifer Laptook, his former chief of staff.

The congressman told The Plain Dealer of Cleveland he had broken no laws or ethics rules. "I am a divorced person who has stayed overnight at her home," he said of his former aide. "I am involved in a serious personal relationship." LaTourette and Laptook married in February 2005. (After LaTourette was named to Appropriations, his wife announced she was severing connections to Northeast Ohio clients to bar any perceptions of conflict of interest.)

In early 2005, GOP leaders removed LaTourette and other Republican members from the ethics committee for being too quick to admonish former Majority Leader Tom DeLay of Texas for ethical lapses.

LaTourette was raised in a politically active home. His mother and grandmother volunteered for the Cleveland area's longtime GOP congresswoman, Frances Payne Bolton. His grandmother inspired one of his legislative efforts, a bill requiring sweepstakes mailers to disclose the slim odds of winning. In her mid-80s, she had subscribed to Field and Stream magazine thinking it would boost her chances of winning.

Even as a youth, LaTourette wasn't afraid to rock the boat. In high school, he led a petition drive to permit students to wear jeans and grow facial hair. He has sported a beard since he was 18 "because I've always thought my face looked better that way." Early in his House career, he allowed humor columnist Dave Barry to work as a volunteer press assistant for him and delivered a speech that Barry wrote on tort reform: "As a lawyer, I am the last person to suggest that everybody in my profession is a money-grubbing, scum-sucking toad. The actual figure is only about 73 percent."

LaTourette was in his second term as Lake County prosecutor when he decided to run for Congress in 1994. Dubbing Democratic freshman Rep. Eric Fingerhut an out-of-touch liberal, LaTourette won by 5 percentage points. He has been re-elected by comfortable margins since then; even as Barack Obama carried Ohio in 2008, LaTourette easily beat former state appeals court judge Bill O'Neill.

KEY VOTES

2008

No Delay consideration of Colombia free-trade agreement

Yes Override Bush veto of federal farm and nutrition programs reauthorization bill

Yes Overhaul surveillance laws and permit dismissal of suits against companies that conducted warrantless wiretapping

Yes Grant mortgage relief to homeowners and funding for Fannie Mae and Freddie Mac

No Approve initial $700 billion program to stabilize financial markets

No Approve final $700 billion program to stabilize financial markets

Yes Provide $14 billion in loans to automakers

2007

Yes Increase minimum wage by $2.10 an hour

No Approve $124.2 billion in emergency war spending and set goal for redeployment of troops from Iraq

Yes Reject federal contraceptive assistance to international family planning groups

Yes Override Bush veto of $23.2 billion water projects authorization bill

No Implement Peru free-trade agreement

Yes Approve energy policy overhaul with new fuel economy standards

Yes Clear $473.5 billion omnibus spending bill, including $70 billion for military operations

CQ VOTE STUDIES

	PARTY UNITY		PRESIDENTIAL SUPPORT	
	SUPPORT	OPPOSE	SUPPORT	OPPOSE
2008	82%	18%	46%	54%
2007	71%	29%	44%	56%
2006	82%	18%	73%	27%
2005	86%	14%	71%	29%
2004	86%	14%	82%	18%

INTEREST GROUPS

	AFL-CIO	ADA	CCUS	ACU
2008	73%	60%	76%	52%
2007	83%	55%	65%	52%
2006	50%	20%	93%	72%
2005	50%	15%	78%	71%
2004	47%	15%	86%	71%

OHIO 14

Northeast – Cleveland and Akron suburbs

The 14th District moves eastward along the Lake Erie shoreline from just outside Cleveland to the Pennsylvania border in the state's northeastern corner. The depressed far northeastern communities remain reliant on the ailing steel, chemical and auto manufacturing industries, but have seen some new life from an influx of former Cleveland residents moving here from the city. Wealthy suburban residents help give the district the state's highest median income.

The 14th's portion of Cuyahoga County includes the upscale villages of Bentleyville and Moreland Hills in the east, while Progressive Insurance is based in Mayfield Village. The district's lakeshore region, which takes in Lake and Ashtabula counties, is home to fruit farms and much of Ohio's wine grape acreage. South of Lake, the district takes in all of Geauga County — a GOP-leaning, affluent, well-educated area — and northern Portage County. The 14th also includes northern Trumbull County and northeastern Summit County, taking in Stow and Twinsburg, where auto manufacturing job losses have kept unemployment rates relatively high.

Despite being Ohio's smallest county in land area, Lake has more than one-third of the district's residents. Chemical company Lubrizol has headquarters in Wickliffe, which also is a manufacturing site for ABB, a power and automation technologies company. In Geauga County, the KraftMaid Cabinetry corporate headquarters is in Middlefield. Counties across the 14th have faced widespread layoffs in manufacturing and white-collar sectors.

In Lake, Republicans generally perform well in areas south of Mentor, such as Kirtland and Kirtland Hills, which are overwhelmingly wealthy and white. Democrats do well in Painesville, where more than half of Lake's blacks and Hispanics reside. The 14th District's Republican tendencies was just enough to give John McCain the district's presidential vote in the 2008 election — McCain won the 14th by less than 1 percentage point.

MAJOR INDUSTRY
Health care, chemicals, manufacturing

CITIES
Mentor, 50,278; Stow, 32,139; Willoughby, 22,621; Hudson, 22,439

NOTABLE
Twinsburg calls its annual August gathering of twins the world's largest.

Rep. Mary Jo Kilroy (D)

Elected 2008; 1st term

Kilroy's central Ohio district has been hit by the economic crisis and a wave of home foreclosures. She said her first priority in Congress is to "get our economy going in the right direction."

She favors stronger oversight of the financial services industry, as well as a moratorium on home foreclosures — objectives she plans to pursue from her seat on the Financial Services Committee.

Education also is a priority for Kilroy, who worked her way through college and later served two terms on the Columbus Board of Education. Her district includes Ohio State University, and Kilroy has outlined a middle-class tax proposal that includes a $5,000 tax credit to help families offset educational expenses.

Kilroy was elected a Franklin County commissioner in 2000 and re-elected in 2004. She served as president of the county board of commissioners from 2005 to 2007. In that post, she said, she worked on "a lot of federal programs that the county administers. That gives me, I think, a unique perspective as well, taking that kind of experience to Washington."

She can apply her expertise in intergovernmental relations as a member of the Homeland Security Committee, which oversees programs steering federal funds to local first responders.

Kilroy — who was diagnosed with multiple sclerosis in 2003 — is a strong advocate of a comprehensive health care overhaul. Many of the bills she cosponsored in her first few months in Congress were health-related, including a successful expansion of the State Children's Health Insurance Program and a bill to authorize federal funding of embryonic stem cell research.

Kilroy grew up in a working-class home; her father was a pipefitter, while her stay-at-home mother looked after her and her four siblings. "We weren't deprived," she said. "But we didn't have a lot of stuff either."

Kilroy narrowly lost an initial bid for her current congressional seat in 2006 against Republican incumbent Deborah Pryce by 1,062 votes. Her 2008 campaign was also a cliffhanger; she won by 2,312 votes. That close margin made her an instant target for Republicans in 2010.

CAPITOL OFFICE
225-2015
kilroy.house.gov
1237 Longworth Bldg. 20515-3515; fax 225-3529

COMMITTEES
Financial Services
Homeland Security

RESIDENCE
Columbus

BORN
April 30, 1949; Cleveland, Ohio

RELIGION
Roman Catholic

FAMILY
Husband, Robert Handelman; two children, one stepchild

EDUCATION
Cleveland State U., B.A. 1977 (political science); Ohio State U., J.D. 1980

CAREER
Lawyer

POLITICAL HIGHLIGHTS
Columbus Board of Education, 1992-99 (president, 1999); Democratic nominee for Ohio Senate, 1996; Franklin County Board of Commissioners, 2001-09 (president, 2005-07); Democratic nominee for U.S. House, 2006

ELECTION RESULTS

2008 GENERAL

Mary Jo Kilroy (D)	139,584	45.9%
Steve Stivers (R)	137,272	45.2%
Mark Noble (LIBERT)	14,061	4.6%
Don Eckhart (I)	12,915	4.2%

2008 PRIMARY

Mary Jo Kilroy (D)	unopposed

OHIO 15

Western Columbus and suburbs

The 15th is centered in Franklin County and on Columbus, the state's centrally located capital. It takes in most of Columbus, including all of the city that lies west of High Street, a major north-south thoroughfare.

Ohio State University, one of the nation's largest universities and a major regional employer and research hub, is located in the 15th's portion of Columbus, as are the Capitol and City Hall. Columbus is not known as a tourist destination, but large crowds descend for Ohio State home football games. Franklin County's technology and research centers have aided the 15th's economy. Columbus serves as the home for corporate headquarters, but there have been layoffs at major white-collar employers, such as Nationwide Mutual Insurance.

West of Franklin, Madison County is a major corn- and soybean-producing area. Marysville, in Union County, is home to soybean fields, livestock and Honda auto plants that have been threatened by stalling demand.

The politically competitive 15th's portion of Franklin, where nearly 90 percent of district residents live, leans left. Ohio State's academic community and areas in the west side of Columbus support Democrats, but Republicans are strong in the suburbs. In 2008, Barack Obama won the 15th, despite John McCain's strong showing in rural, and dependably Republican, Madison and Union counties. Union County last voted for a Democratic presidential candidate in 1932.

MAJOR INDUSTRY
Government, health care, higher education

CITIES
Columbus (pt.), 384,491; Upper Arlington, 33,686

NOTABLE
A full-scale replica of Christopher Columbus' ship, the *Santa Maria*, is in Columbus.

Rep. John Boccieri (D)

Elected 2008; 1st term

A Democrat representing a traditionally Republican district, Boccieri aims to transition the area from a manufacturing to a service-oriented economy to address the area's heavy job loss, which he blames on corporate outsourcing and unfair trade policies. He favors "clean coal" technologies and nuclear power and has called for a program to transition away from oil as a primary energy source.

Boccieri (bo-CHAIR-ee) plans to promote broadening the country's energy options as a member of the Agriculture Committee's Conservation, Credit, Energy and Research panel. He also sits on the Transportation and Infrastructure Committee, where he will be able to target funds for local projects when the panel takes up a reauthorization of the 2005 surface transportation law.

He voted in favor of President Obama's $787 billion stimulus bill in 2009, saying, "This bill is about creating jobs. It's about investing in our people, our country and our future." He had opposed the release of the second half of $700 billion from a 2008 law aimed at aiding the financial services sector. He cited a lack of accountability, and cosponsored a bill to empower the Treasury Department to limit the luxury expenses of companies receiving funding from it.

Like his GOP predecessor Ralph Regula, Boccieri served in the military during a time of war — including four tours in Iraq and Afghanistan — and has a strong interest in looking out for veterans. A major in the Air Force Reserve, he was chosen by Democratic leaders to give the response to President George W. Bush's Memorial Day radio address in 2008. Referring to veterans, he said, "The best way to honor their service and sacrifice is to ensure they have the benefits they deserve and the resources they need to succeed when they come home." He promoted issues important to veterans during his eight years in the Ohio legislature.

In the Democratic primary to replace Regula, Boccieri gained the endorsement of Gov. Ted Strickland and cruised to victory with 64 percent. In the general election, Boccieri outraised fellow state Sen. Kirk Schuring, in part thanks to help from Democratic incumbents. Boccieri won by 11 percentage points, but the GOP began targeting his seat in early 2009.

CAPITOL OFFICE
225-3876
boccieri.house.gov
1516 Longworth Bldg. 20515-3516; fax 225-3059

COMMITTEES
Agriculture
Transportation & Infrastructure

RESIDENCE
Alliance

BORN
Oct. 5, 1969; Youngstown, Ohio

RELIGION
Roman Catholic

FAMILY
Wife, Stacey Boccieri; 4 children

EDUCATION
St. Bonaventure U., B.S. 1992 (economics); Webster U., Little Rock, M.A. 1996 (business), M.P.A. 1996

MILITARY SERVICE
Air Force, 1994-98; Ohio Air National Guard, 1998-2000; Air Force Reserve, 2000-present

CAREER
State legislative aide

POLITICAL HIGHLIGHTS
Ohio House, 2001-07; Ohio Senate, 2007-08

ELECTION RESULTS

2008 GENERAL
John Boccieri (D)	169,044	55.4%
Kirk Schuring (R)	136,293	44.6%

2008 PRIMARY
John Boccieri (D)	71,038	63.7%
Mary M. Cirelli (D)	40,429	36.3%

OHIO 16
Northeast – Canton

Settled in the northeast quadrant of Ohio, the 16th features a contrast between rural areas, which make up roughly one-quarter of the district's land, and urban Canton.

Canton, with a manufacturing and steel-producing history, has retained a high-skill manufacturing base despite industry employment declines. To overcome manufacturing job losses, city officials have supported a transition to retail and service-based employment. Major employers include Aultman Hospital and Timken, which manufactures bearings. Outside Canton, the district hosts several colleges and universities.

As Canton's population continues its nearly 60-year decline — it now accounts for just one-fifth of Stark County's population — the city's blue-collar Democratic base has become less important to the 16th's overall political picture. Massillon and Alliance, the county's next-most-populous cities, however, also lean Democratic.

As a whole, the 16th leans Republican primarily because of rural conservative areas west of Stark County, although northern Stark County is upper-middle-class and GOP-leaning as well. Wayne County, a top state producer of oats, hay and dairy products, is politically competitive. The 16th also takes in most of Ashland County, which leans conservative. While Canton's political role has dimmed, the GOP margin in the 16th is not overwhelming. Republican John McCain won only 50 percent of the district's presidential vote in 2008.

MAJOR INDUSTRY
Steel, health care, higher education

CITIES
Canton, 80,806; Massillon, 31,325; Medina, 25,139; Wooster, 24,811

NOTABLE
The Professional Football Hall of Fame and William McKinley's tomb are in Canton.

Rep. Tim Ryan (D)

Elected 2002; 4th term

CAPITOL OFFICE
225-5261
timryan.house.gov
1421 Longworth Bldg. 20515-3517; fax 225-3719

COMMITTEES
Appropriations

RESIDENCE
Niles

BORN
July 16, 1973; Niles, Ohio

RELIGION
Roman Catholic

FAMILY
Divorced

EDUCATION
Youngstown State U., attended 1991-92;
Bowling Green State U., B.A. 1995 (political
science); Franklin Pierce Law Center, J.D. 2000

CAREER
Congressional aide

POLITICAL HIGHLIGHTS
Ohio Senate, 2001-02

ELECTION RESULTS

2008 GENERAL

Tim Ryan (D)	218,896	78.1%
Duane Grassell (R)	61,216	21.8%

2008 PRIMARY

Tim Ryan (D)	unopposed

2006 GENERAL

Tim Ryan (D)	170,369	80.2%
Don Manning II (R)	41,925	19.7%

PREVIOUS WINNING PERCENTAGES
2004 (77%); 2002 (51%)

One of the youngest Democrats in the House, Ryan pairs a decidedly old-fashioned attitude toward earmarks with a more modern, skeptical view of free-trade deals. As an appropriator, he fiercely defends the practice of sending money back home where foreign competition opened by such trade agreements has battered manufacturers. "I'll be damned if I'm going to let somebody come in and tell us that somehow we're wasting money," Ryan once said.

Ryan is the regional recruitment chairman for the Democratic Congressional Campaign Committee and a reliable party vote on most issues. But, like many of his colleagues from socially conservative working-class districts, he opposes abortion and supports gun ownership rights. After Democratic losses in 2004, he said the party suffered from unreasonable absolutism on social issues. When Barack Obama took the White House in 2009 — alongside expanded Democratic majorities in Congress — he said he was encouraged by the new president's vow to steer clear of cultural and religious battles that had bogged down such national debates.

Another of Obama's priorities was to cut down on earmarks — funding set-asides for projects in member districts. But Ryan showed little inclination to follow along. As the Appropriations Committee prepared to take up spending bills for fiscal 2010, he, like other appropriators, put a notice on his Web site detailing his requests and soliciting others from local organizations. "Significant developments are made possible by bringing much-needed federal dollars to a project that would otherwise be impossible to complete," the notice said. Ryan steered nearly $44 million to local projects in fiscal 2009 spending bills. About $14 million of the earmarked money was directed toward defense-related projects. He also directed millions of dollars in both fiscal 2008 and fiscal 2009 toward industrial research and development, including in the areas of alternative energy and transportation.

Ryan said he wants to build new jobs in his district to replace lost manufacturing jobs. "Our guys in Youngstown and Akron now should be making solar panels, not talking about making solar panels," said Ryan, who sits on the Energy-Water Appropriations panel. "If they got laid off because of [the North American Free Trade Agreement] from a steel mill or a manufacturing plant, boom, right over to the solar panel, because we, as a country, made that investment." Ryan also keeps a close eye on trade. His skepticism of new deals includes a concern for human rights and the environment. "Our trade needs to represent our values as a country," he said. He voted against the Central America Free Trade Agreement in 2005. He also opposed the trade agreements with Peru and Panama in 2007 that followed a Democratic agreement with the George W. Bush administration requiring enforceable labor and environmental standards.

He supported Obama's $787 billion economic stimulus measure in 2009 and was a strong advocate of its provision requiring any projects funded from the bill to make use of U.S.-made steel, iron, concrete and other manufactured products. The provision stirred much debate, drawing opposition from some companies and groups who feared it could set off trade battles with Canada, the European Union and other trading partners. Ryan responded: "That these companies would oppose buying American iron and steel shows just how far removed they are from the country that gave them their start." The final version of the stimulus said the provision would apply only if it doesn't violate U.S. obligations at the World Trade Organization.

Ryan also serves on the panel that funds the Labor, Health and Human Services, and Education departments. He backed legislation Obama signed into law in 2009 to expand the State Children's Health Insurance Program, which covers children from low-income families that don't qualify for Medicaid.

He has repeatedly teamed with liberal Democrat Rosa DeLauro of Connecticut to push a bill that seeks to reduce abortions. It includes provisions aimed at preventing unintended pregnancies as well as strengthening alternatives to abortion, such as adoption tax credits and help — food stamps and child care subsidies, for example — for poor mothers. He said in early 2009 the political timing was right to push the bill harder. "[A] lot of people are coming in moderate on this issue, not extreme one way or the other. There is a good chance we can have some common ground," he said.

Ryan bucked strong sentiment in his district when he voted in 2003 — and in 2005 — against a constitutional amendment to ban flag burning. He said he feared civil liberties were under assault. He twice has voted against amending the Constitution to ban same-sex marriage. He did vote for a 2007 bill — which didn't make it through the Senate — to ban job discrimination based on sexual orientation.

Ryan also sits on the Democratic Steering and Policy Committee, which makes committee assignments, and is co-chair of the Manufacturing Caucus, which he founded in his first term with Illinois Republican Donald Manzullo.

Ryan's parents divorced when he was in grade school, and he and his older brother were raised by their mother and grandparents. His mother was, and still is, a chief deputy clerk of Trumbull County. His grandmother worked for the county clerk of courts, his grandfather was a steelworker and both were union members. Ryan was a football player in high school and college until he ruined his knee.

In the mid-1990s, he worked as a congressional aide to the colorful Democratic Rep. James A. Traficant Jr. He won election to the Ohio Senate in 2000, the year he completed law school. In 2002, with Traficant facing jail on bribery and racketeering charges (he was eventually expelled from the House), Ryan entered a competitive primary for the seat. He faced eight-term Rep. Tom Sawyer, who was thrown into the district by reapportionment. Sawyer outspent him 10-to-1, but Ryan prevailed and went on to easily defeat GOP state Sen. Ann Womer Benjamin.

He has won re-election with ease. In early 2009 he briefly considered a 2010 run for retiring Ohio Republican Sen. George V. Voinovich's seat. He was later mentioned as a possible running mate for Gov. Ted Strickland in that year's race, but he ultimately decided to run for re-election.

KEY VOTES

2008
Yes Delay consideration of Colombia free-trade agreement
Yes Override Bush veto of federal farm and nutrition programs reauthorization bill
No Overhaul surveillance laws and permit dismissal of suits against companies that conducted warrantless wiretapping
Yes Grant mortgage relief to homeowners and funding for Fannie Mae and Freddie Mac
Yes Approve initial $700 billion program to stabilize financial markets
Yes Approve final $700 billion program to stabilize financial markets
Yes Provide $14 billion in loans to automakers

2007
Yes Increase minimum wage by $2.10 an hour
Yes Approve $124.2 billion in emergency war spending and set goal for redeployment of troops from Iraq
No Reject federal contraceptive assistance to international family planning groups
Yes Override Bush veto of $23.2 billion water projects authorization bill
No Implement Peru free-trade agreement
Yes Approve energy policy overhaul with new fuel economy standards
No Clear $473.5 billion omnibus spending bill, including $70 billion for military operations

CQ VOTE STUDIES

	PARTY UNITY		PRESIDENTIAL SUPPORT	
	SUPPORT	OPPOSE	SUPPORT	OPPOSE
2008	98%	2%	20%	80%
2007	97%	3%	4%	96%
2006	90%	10%	37%	63%
2005	91%	9%	30%	70%
2004	95%	5%	30%	70%

INTEREST GROUPS

	AFL-CIO	ADA	CCUS	ACU
2008	100%	90%	61%	4%
2007	96%	95%	55%	0%
2006	92%	80%	47%	28%
2005	100%	95%	48%	25%
2004	100%	80%	35%	17%

OHIO 17

Northeast — Youngstown, Warren, part of Akron

Bordering Pennsylvania in part of northeastern Ohio's Mahoning Valley, including Youngstown, the 17th is a Democratic bastion. Once a leading steel producer, the valley now symbolizes industrial decline; most of the mills that have not been torn down are either silent or abandoned.

A plurality of district residents lives in Trumbull County (shared with the 14th). Sustained economic downturns hit the area hard. Manufacturing jobs recently employed as much as one-fourth of Trumbull's workforce, but unemployment here is now above 14 percent as auto assembly and parts manufacturing plants have shut down. Despite some economic diversification, young people searching for jobs look elsewhere.

The population of Youngstown, in Mahoning County, hovered around 170,000 from the 1930s to the 1960s; the 2000 census found just 82,000 people living in the city, a number that is still dropping precipitously. The city has been hit again by recent layoffs — Youngstown's economic devastation and decades of population loss have forced local officials to plan for a smaller city, converting vacant homes and commercial and industrial sites into open space, eventually abandoning some outer neighborhoods and demolishing some infrastructure.

The 17th's share of Mahoning County is solidly Democratic, and the county overall last voted for a GOP presidential candidate in 1972. Warren, Trumbull County's most populous city, propels the county's staunch Democratic lean. Parts of Summit and Portage counties to the west are less solidly Democratic, although they still supported Democrat Barack Obama in the 2008 presidential election. The Summit portion includes the eastern half of Akron, a city that once produced 90 percent of the nation's tires and is still home to Goodyear Tire & Rubber despite layoffs and a declining auto industry. The Portage portion includes Kent, where Kent State University is located. Overall, Obama took 62 percent of the vote districtwide, which made the 17th his third-best district in Ohio.

MAJOR INDUSTRY
Service, manufacturing

CITIES
Akron (pt.), 87,776; Youngstown, 82,026; Warren, 46,832

NOTABLE
The Butler Institute of American Art, dedicated in 1919, was one of the first museums to display only American art.

Rep. Zack Space (D)

Elected 2006; 2nd term

CAPITOL OFFICE
225-6265
space.house.gov
315 Cannon Bldg. 20515-3518; fax 225-3394

COMMITTEES
Energy & Commerce
Veterans' Affairs

RESIDENCE
Dover

BORN
Jan. 27, 1961; Dover, Ohio

RELIGION
Greek Orthodox

FAMILY
Wife, Mary Space; two children

EDUCATION
Kenyon College, B.A. 1983 (political science);
Ohio State U., J.D. 1986

CAREER
Lawyer; county public defender

POLITICAL HIGHLIGHTS
Sought Democratic nomination for Ohio House,
1990; Dover law director, 2000-06

ELECTION RESULTS

2008 GENERAL

Zack Space (D)	164,187	59.9%
Fred Dailey (R)	110,031	40.1%

2008 PRIMARY

Zack Space (D)	87,503	84.6%
Mark Pitrone (D)	15,980	15.4%

2006 GENERAL

Zack Space (D)	129,646	62.1%
Joy Padgett (R)	79,259	37.9%

Space is a hard-working moderate and vigorous fundraiser who seeks to use his small-town charm and affability to revitalize a seat tarnished by his predecessor in the House. He pays close heed to the needs of his Republican-leaning and economically struggling district, devoting special attention to improving its technology.

As a freshman in 2006, Space was often referred to as "the guy from Ney's district," in reference to his predecessor, Republican Bob Ney, who pleaded guilty that year to federal corruption charges stemming from his association with disgraced lobbyist Jack Abramoff. But Space has since forged his own identity, and party leaders rewarded him in 2009 with a plum spot on the Energy and Commerce Committee.

Space focuses on bringing high-speed Internet access to rural areas of Appalachia. He noted in March 2009 that the unemployment rate in his district's Morgan County exceeded 16 percent. "As our national economy has become more global in scale, places like Morgan County and other regions I represent have largely been left behind because they simply do not have the resources to remain competitive or to attract new business investments," he said.

Space helped push into law in 2008 a bill to authorize funding for the Appalachian Regional Commission, which oversees grant programs to assist a 13-state area. He added a provision allowing $65 million over five years to promote energy efficiency and renewable resources, particularly biomass, and support technologies to reduce greenhouse gas emissions. "Alternative-energy production will breathe life into the struggling rural regions of Appalachia," he said.

His district's economy also has long been reliant on coal, and Space supports "clean coal" technologies that he said would provide employment opportunities and help wean the nation from foreign energy sources.

Space considers himself a centrist. In the 110th Congress (2007-08), he sided with his party 89 percent of the time on votes pitting most Democrats against most Republicans. He was one of 10 Democrats, seven of them freshmen, who supported a permanent repeal of the estate tax. He supports gun owners' rights and is a member of the Blue Dog Coalition, a group of fiscally conservative Democrats.

But he has stuck with his party on several high-profile votes, including President Obama's $787 billion economic stimulus law. Space supported all of the Democrats' six signature pieces of legislation in early 2007, including an issue that hits close to home for him: expanding federal funding for medical research on stem cells taken from surplus embryos at in vitro fertilization clinics.

His youngest son, Nicholas, was diagnosed with juvenile diabetes at age 6. In a speech on the House floor, Space described how his son, now in high school, has undergone thousands of injections and blood tests. When Obama overturned the George W. Bush administration's funding curbs on embryonic stem cell research in March 2009, Space hailed the move as "long overdue."

On the Veterans' Affairs Committee, Space voices concerns related to the war in Iraq and funding for veterans' health care, especially for those returning from Iraq and Afghanistan. He joined fellow freshman Democrats Tim Walz of Minnesota and Jason Altmire of Pennsylvania in 2008 in urging expanded funding for eye injuries sustained during combat.

Space has hit a few minor bumps since coming to Capitol Hill. He was criticized in November 2007 for taking a taxpayer-funded trip to Greece and Cyprus; he defended it as important for economic development and diplomatic reasons, but local Republicans and news media outlets labeled it a junket. He was issued a citation in March 2009 for the minor misdemeanor of driving a vehicle without a valid license; he said he forgot to renew his driver's license and paid a fine.

A former Dover High School football player, Space feels most comfortable in his hometown, where he spends many Friday nights cheering on his alma mater. "I come here to [Washington] and just feel lost," Space said. "I love my job, but back home when you walk down main street, you say 'hi' or smile and everyone does it. If you do that here, you are going to get thrown in jail, they think you're crazy. I much prefer being at home."

One of three children, Space was reared by a close-knit Greek family in north-central Ohio. His father, a lawyer named Socrates, was active in the Democratic Party and served as chairman of the Tuscarawas County Democrats. After graduating high school, Space got a scholarship to Kenyon College, where he started on the offensive line of the football team and earned a bachelor's degree in political science.

Space attended law school at Ohio State University, then worked part-time for the Tuscarawas County public defenders office, where he met his future wife, Mary, also an attorney. He then worked at his father's general practice for about 15 years before receiving what he calls his "big political break" by mistake. In 2000, a close friend, who at the time was Dover's chief city attorney, died in an auto accident. Space was soon appointed to the position held by his friend. The highly visible job gave him enough name identification when he decided to run for Congress.

Buoyed by a strong showing in his home county, Space came from behind to win the four-candidate May 2008 Democratic primary. That summer, Ney relinquished the GOP nomination and was replaced on the ballot by state Sen. Joy Padgett, who was burdened by her ties to unpopular Republican Gov. Bob Taft and to Ney (who pleaded guilty that October and resigned just four days before the November election). Space coasted with 62 percent of the vote; two years later, he won with 60 percent even though Arizona GOP Sen. John McCain carried the district over Barack Obama.

Space's impressive showing led him to flirt with running for the Senate seat in 2010 being vacated by Ohio GOP Sen. George V. Voinovich's retirement. Drawing on a network of fellow Greek-Americans nationwide, he raised more than $410,000 during the first three months of 2009.

KEY VOTES

2008

Yes Delay consideration of Colombia free-trade agreement
Yes Override Bush veto of federal farm and nutrition programs reauthorization bill
Yes Overhaul surveillance laws and permit dismissal of suits against companies that conducted warrantless wiretapping
Yes Grant mortgage relief to homeowners and funding for Fannie Mae and Freddie Mac
Yes Approve initial $700 billion program to stabilize financial markets
Yes Approve final $700 billion program to stabilize financial markets
Yes Provide $14 billion in loans to automakers

2007

Yes Increase minimum wage by $2.10 an hour
Yes Approve $124.2 billion in emergency war spending and set goal for redeployment of troops from Iraq
No Reject federal contraceptive assistance to international family planning groups
Yes Override Bush veto of $23.2 billion water projects authorization bill
No Implement Peru free-trade agreement
Yes Approve energy policy overhaul with new fuel economy standards
Yes Clear $473.5 billion omnibus spending bill, including $70 billion for military operations

CQ VOTE STUDIES

	PARTY UNITY		PRESIDENTIAL SUPPORT	
	SUPPORT	OPPOSE	SUPPORT	OPPOSE
2008	94%	6%	23%	77%
2007	86%	14%	12%	88%

INTEREST GROUPS

	AFL-CIO	ADA	CCUS	ACU
2008	100%	80%	61%	12%
2007	96%	95%	58%	20%

OHIO 18

East – Zanesville, Chillicothe

Ohio's most geographically vast district, the 18th envelops 12 whole counties and parts of four others in eastern and southern Ohio. Beginning in the north, the 18th takes in the rolling hills south of Canton and runs southwest to rugged areas of Appalachia. The socially conservative district, which roughly parallels but does not touch the Ohio River, depends on steel and coal jobs and includes a large Catholic population of ethnic Eastern Europeans and Greeks.

The 18th's most-populous county is Tuscarawas, which relies on agriculture — particularly dairy and beef cattle production — and a stalling manufacturing sector. Newark (shared with the 12th) in Licking County is slowly becoming a research and manufacturing center, and unemployment in the county remains below the state average.

South of Muskingum County (Zanesville), where unemployment rates remain high, the district narrows as it takes in struggling Morgan County and northwestern Athens County, although Ohio University and Athens are in the adjacent 6th District. Moving westward, the 18th remains rural

as it crosses forests to take in most of Ross County, including Chillicothe.

The blue-collar 18th leans Republican at the federal level, although Tuscarawas tends to be more Democratic and can push a Democrat to victory here. Holmes County, to Tuscarawas' west, is Amish country and is heavily Republican: John McCain took 69 percent of the county's 2008 presidential vote. Coshocton County, south of Holmes, also generally supports Republicans.

McCain took 53 percent of the 18th's presidential vote and won every county that is wholly within the district except for Tuscarawas, where Barack Obama eked out a 50 percent majority. Democrat Zack Space won Tuscarawas with 70 percent of its vote in his 2008 re-election race.

MAJOR INDUSTRY
Steel, manufacturing, agriculture, coal

CITIES
Zanesville, 25,586; Chillicothe, 21,796

NOTABLE
Aviator Amelia Earhart called Zanesville "the most recognizable city in the country" from the air because of its Y-shaped bridge across the Muskingum and Licking rivers.

Gov. Brad Henry (D)

First elected: 2002
Length of term: 4 years
Term expires: 1/11
Salary: $147,000
Phone: (405) 521-2342

Residence: Shawnee
Born: July 10, 1963; Shawnee, Okla.
Religion: Baptist
Family: Wife, Kim Henry; three children
Education: U. of Oklahoma, B.A. 1985 (economics), J.D. 1988
Career: Lawyer
Political highlights: Okla. Senate, 1993-2002

Election results:

2006 GENERAL
Brad Henry (D)	616,135	66.5%
Ernest Istook (R)	310,327	33.5%

Lt. Gov. Jari Askins (D)

First elected: 2006
Length of term: 4 years
Term expires: 1/11
Salary: $109,250
Phone: (405) 521-2161

LEGISLATURE

Legislature: February-May

Senate: 48 members, 4-year terms
2009 ratios: 26 R, 22 D; 44 men, 4 women
Salary: $38,400
Phone: (405) 524-0126

House: 101 members, 2-year terms
2009 ratios: 61 R, 40 D; 89 men, 12 women
Salary: $38,400
Phone: (405) 521-2711

TERM LIMITS

Governor: 2 terms
Senate: No more than 12 years combined
House: No more than 12 years combined

URBAN STATISTICS

CITY	POPULATION
Oklahoma City	506,132
Tulsa	393,049
Norman	95,694
Lawton	92,757
Broken Arrow	74,859

REGISTERED VOTERS

Democrat	49%
Republican	39%
Unaffiliated	11%

POPULATION

2008 population (est.)	3,642,361
2000 population	3,450,654
1990 population	3,145,585
Percent change (1990-2000)	+9.7%
Rank among states (2008)	28

Median age	35.5
Born in state	62.6%
Foreign born	3.8%
Violent crime rate	498/100,000
Poverty level	14.7%
Federal workers	44,984
Military	41,575

ELECTIONS

STATE ELECTION OFFICIAL
(405) 521-2391
DEMOCRATIC PARTY
(405) 427-3366
REPUBLICAN PARTY
(405) 528-3501

MISCELLANEOUS

Web: www.ok.gov
Capital: Oklahoma City

U.S. CONGRESS

Senate: 2 Republican
House: 4 Republicans, 1 Democrat

2000 Census Statistics by District

DIST.	2008 VOTE FOR PRESIDENT OBAMA	MCCAIN	WHITE	BLACK	ASIAN	HISP	MEDIAN INCOME	WHITE COLLAR	BLUE COLLAR	SERVICE INDUSTRY	OVER 64	UNDER 18	COLLEGE EDUCATION	RURAL	SQ. MILES
1	36%	64%	74%	9%	1%	5%	$38,610	63%	23%	14%	12%	26%	26%	10%	1,737
2	34	66	70	4	0	2	$27,885	48	35	17	15	26	13	64	20,563
3	27	73	81	4	1	5	$32,098	54	30	16	14	26	18	49	34,089
4	34	66	78	7	2	5	$35,510	57	27	16	12	26	20	37	10,212
5	41	59	68	14	3	8	$33,893	61	24	15	13	26	25	12	2,067
STATE	34	66	74	7	1	5	$33,400	57	28	16	13	26	20	35	68,667
U.S.	53	46	69	12	4	13	$41,994	60	25	15	12	26	24	21	3,537,438

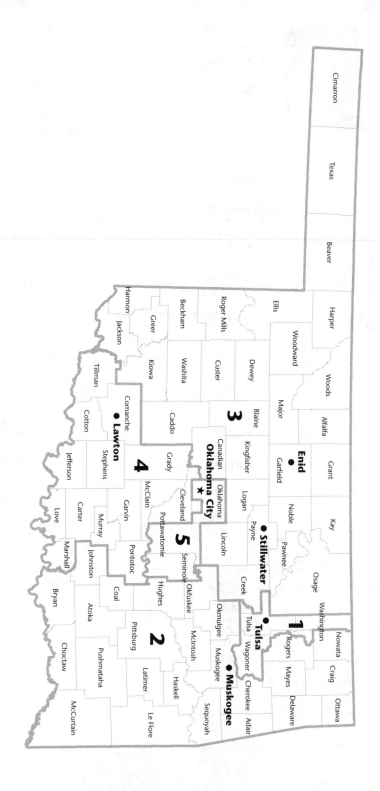

Sen. James M. Inhofe (R)

Elected 1994; 3rd full term

CAPITOL OFFICE
224-4721
inhofe.senate.gov
453 Russell Bldg. 20510-3603; fax 228-0380

COMMITTEES
Armed Services
Environment & Public Works - ranking member

RESIDENCE
Tulsa

BORN
Nov. 17, 1934; Des Moines, Iowa

RELIGION
Presbyterian

FAMILY
Wife, Kay Inhofe; four children

EDUCATION
U. of Tulsa, B.A. 1973

MILITARY SERVICE
Army, 1957-58

CAREER
Real estate developer; insurance executive

POLITICAL HIGHLIGHTS
Okla. House, 1967-69; Okla. Senate, 1969-77;
Republican nominee for governor, 1974;
Republican nominee for U.S. House, 1976;
mayor of Tulsa, 1978-84; defeated for re-election
as mayor of Tulsa, 1984; U.S. House, 1987-94

ELECTION RESULTS

2008 GENERAL

James M. Inhofe (R)	763,375	56.7%
Andrew Rice (D)	527,736	39.2%
Stephen P. Wallace (I)	55,708	4.1%

2008 PRIMARY

James M. Inhofe (R)	116,371	84.2%
Evelyn L. Rogers (R)	10,770	7.8%
Ted Ryals (R)	7,306	5.3%
Dennis Lopez (R)	3,800	2.7%

PREVIOUS WINNING PERCENTAGES
2002 (57%); 1996 (57%); 1994 Special Election (55%);
1992 House Election (53%); 1990 House Election
(56%); 1988 House Election (53%); 1986 House
Election (55%)

Brash and direct, Inhofe relishes playing the role of conservative contrarian. He is the leading congressional skeptic of human-caused global warming and a vocal critic of other Democratic initiatives, a job that keeps him busy with both a Democratic Congress and White House.

For years, Inhofe (IN-hoff) has kept a framed document in his office, an interest group's assessment describing him as the Senate's most conservative member. He makes a point of ensuring visitors take note of it. "Yes, I'm a little extreme. I am conservative. Some people don't like that idea," he told Oklahoma's Stillwater NewsPress in 2008. But "they don't have any doubt where I'm going to vote."

Inhofe is well positioned to hold up the Republicans' agenda as the top-ranking Republican on the Environment and Public Works Committee and the second-highest-ranking GOP member on the Armed Services Committee, behind Arizona's John McCain. He shares many of the same views as his home-state GOP colleague Tom Coburn, the Senate's most frequent blocker of Democratic legislation.

But one area on which the two Oklahomans disagree — and where Inhofe is a far more conventional Washington politician than Coburn — is the federal government's role in building infrastructure. While Coburn condemns such funding, Inhofe strongly supports it. Exploiting his seniority in the Senate, he has brought millions of dollars back to Oklahoma to fund roads, bridges and military bases — a practice Coburn strongly criticizes, believing such projects should be paid for by states and localities.

Inhofe found much to criticize in the early months of President Obama's administration: its $787 billion economic stimulus law; its proposed cuts in defense and plans to withdraw troops from Iraq; a call to ratify a decade-old treaty to control illegal weapons across the border; the United Nations Convention on the Law of the Sea governing international seafaring; and its efforts to distribute funding under the $700 billion financial rescue law of 2008, which he had opposed. On the latter, he proposed an accounting of where all funds were distributed and charged that "fringe organizations" received some of the money. "We were lied to," he said in April 2009.

He also locked horns with Democratic senators, getting into a fierce debate with West Virginia's John D. Rockefeller IV in February 2009 over Inhofe's efforts to prevent the transfer of prisoners at the military detention facility on the naval base at Guantánamo Bay, Cuba, to U.S. prisons. In a rare departure from Senate protocol, Rockefeller refused to acknowledge Inhofe for a rebuttal, a move that incensed the Oklahoman.

Inhofe wasn't afraid to tangle with George W. Bush's administration, either. In 2007, he guided a $23.2 billion authorization bill for water resources projects through the Senate and to the president's desk. He successfully included $30 million in the bill to complete the ongoing buyout at the Tar Creek superfund site in northeastern Oklahoma, allowing local residents to move at government expense — funding Inhofe had once strongly opposed. When Bush vetoed the measure, Inhofe said the president's decision was "stupid" and "deceitful." The Senate overwhelmingly voted to override the veto.

Inhofe has been the leading critic of global warming legislation since 2003, when, as chairman of the Environment panel, he said on the Senate floor, "With all of the hysteria, all of the fear, all of the phony science, could it be that man-made global warming is the greatest hoax ever perpetrated on the American people?"

He hasn't backed down a bit since. When TV networks went looking for someone to rebut former Democratic Vice President Al Gore and his movie "An Inconvenient Truth" in 2006, they frequently booked Inhofe on their shows. "The political agenda of extremists must not dictate our efforts to provide common-sense protections that are based on science," Inhofe said. When Gore testified before the committee in March 2007, Inhofe called him an "alarmist" who would damage the U.S. economy.

And when the Environmental Protection Agency declared in April 2009 that carbon dioxide posed a health hazard and the agency would consider enforcing its discharge, Inhofe blasted the decision as "the beginning of a regulatory barrage that will destroy jobs, raise energy prices for consumers and undermine America's global competitiveness."

Inhofe also has contempt for what he sees as the political correctness of coastal liberals. He has a lifetime "A+" grade from the National Rifle Association and tells a story about an incident that occurred in 1982, while he was Tulsa's mayor, to bolster his pro-gun credentials. When a group of activists seeking to resettle Cuban refugees came to Inhofe's home to protest, Inhofe said he chased them off, saying, "I have guns in my house. If you're not off my property in one minute, I'll kill all of you." News accounts from the time confirm the confrontation, but not the threat.

Even so, Tulsa's conservative voters love his combativeness. And the rest of the state also appreciates his prowess at bringing home federal funds — a prime reason he won the endorsement of both of the state's major newspapers in 2008, including the Tulsa World, with which he has occasionally feuded.

Besides keeping the region's military bases well funded, Inhofe has used his Armed Services Committee seat to support a national missile defense system and improve the military's readiness for combat. Drafted into the Army in 1957, he credits the service with teaching him discipline and an appreciation for getting an education. Inhofe was stationed in Fort Chaffee, Ark., and Fort Lee, Va.

Inhofe was born in Des Moines, Iowa, but his parents moved in 1942 to Tulsa in search of jobs in the insurance industry. Inhofe inherited their penchant for business; at 15, he worked as a door-to-door salesman. He lives in a house just three houses away from the one in which he was raised.

Inhofe has about 50 years of experience as a pilot. He's never lost his love of flying, despite nearly losing his life on more than one occasion. In September 2006, his TV-8 single-engine stunt plane spun out of control on landing in Tulsa, an incident he attributed to a malfunctioning rudder. While flying to Oklahoma City in 1999, his private plane lost a propeller, forcing him to make an emergency high-speed landing.

After his stint in the service, Inhofe followed his parents into insurance, then became a real estate developer. As a businessman, he became frustrated with an "over-regulated society," which launched him into a 10-year career in the Oklahoma Legislature.

While a state senator, Inhofe lost a 1974 campaign for governor to Democrat David L. Boren. Elected mayor of Tulsa in 1978, he was defeated for re-election in 1984. He bounced back two years later and picked up a House seat, taking 55 percent of the vote to succeed Democrat James R. Jones. He never cracked 56 percent in four elections, despite being in the state's most Republican district. In 1988, his campaign was complicated when he sued his brother over a stock sale involving the family insurance business.

In 1994, when Boren decided to leave in the middle of his term, Inhofe made a run for the seat, facing Rep. Dave McCurdy, a pro-business Democrat favored to win. But McCurdy became closely associated with President Clinton, whom he introduced at the 1992 Democratic National Convention. Inhofe won by 15 percentage points, and he hasn't had a tough race since.

KEY VOTES

2008
Yes Prohibit discrimination based on genetic information
Yes Reauthorize farm and nutrition programs for five years
No Limit debate on "cap and trade" system for greenhouse gas emissions
No Allow lawsuits against companies that participated in warrantless wiretapping
No Limit debate on a bill to block a scheduled cut in Medicare payments to doctors
? Grant mortgage relief to homeowners and funding for Fannie Mae and Freddie Mac
Yes Approve a nuclear cooperation agreement with India
No Approve final $700 billion program to stabilize financial markets
No Allow consideration of a $14 billion auto industry loan package

2007
- Increase minimum wage by $2.10 an hour
No Limit debate on a comprehensive immigration bill
No Overhaul congressional lobbying and ethics rules for members and their staffs
No Limit debate on considering a bill to add House seats for the District of Columbia and Utah
No Limit debate on restoring habeas corpus rights to detainees
No Mandate minimum breaks for troops between deployments to Iraq or Afghanistan
Yes Override Bush veto of $23.2 billion water projects authorization bill
Yes Confirm Michael B. Mukasey as attorney general
No Limit debate on an energy policy overhaul containing $21.8 billion in tax incentives and reduced oil and gas subsidies

CQ VOTE STUDIES

	PARTY UNITY		PRESIDENTIAL SUPPORT	
	SUPPORT	OPPOSE	SUPPORT	OPPOSE
2008	99%	1%	75%	25%
2007	98%	2%	87%	13%
2006	94%	6%	88%	12%
2005	94%	6%	91%	9%
2004	98%	2%	92%	8%
2003	98%	2%	97%	3%
2002	96%	4%	96%	4%
2001	96%	4%	95%	5%
2000	100%	0%	30%	70%
1999	95%	5%	23%	77%

INTEREST GROUPS

	AFL-CIO	ADA	CCUS	ACU
2008	22%	5%	63%	96%
2007	5%	10%	80%	100%
2006	20%	0%	91%	100%
2005	21%	5%	83%	100%
2004	17%	10%	100%	100%
2003	0%	5%	100%	84%
2002	17%	10%	100%	100%
2001	25%	10%	93%	96%
2000	13%	5%	85%	100%
1999	11%	0%	94%	100%

Sen. Tom Coburn (R)

Elected 2004; 1st term

CAPITOL OFFICE
224-5754
coburn.senate.gov
172 Russell Bldg. 20510-3602; fax 224-6008

COMMITTEES
Health, Education, Labor & Pensions
Homeland Security & Governmental Affairs
Indian Affairs
Judiciary
Select Intelligence

RESIDENCE
Muskogee

BORN
March 14, 1948; Casper, Wyo.

RELIGION
Baptist

FAMILY
Wife, Carolyn Coburn; three children

EDUCATION
Oklahoma State U., B.S. 1970 (accounting);
U. of Oklahoma, M.D. 1983

CAREER
Physician; optical firm manager

POLITICAL HIGHLIGHTS
U.S. House, 1995-2001

ELECTION RESULTS

2004 GENERAL

Tom Coburn (R)	763,433	52.8%
Brad Carson (D)	596,750	41.3%
Sheila Bilyeu (I)	86,663	6.0%

2004 PRIMARY

Tom Coburn (R)	145,974	61.2%
Kirk Humphreys (R)	59,877	25.1%
Bob Anthony (R)	29,596	12.4%
Jay Richard Hunt (R)	2,944	1.2%

PREVIOUS WINNING PERCENTAGES
1998 House Election (58%); 1996 House Election
(55%); 1994 House Election (52%)

A practicing obstetrician and proud obstructionist, Coburn has established himself in his first Senate term as a veritable human dam in an institution that prides itself on collegiality. His propensity for leveraging the power of a single senator to halt legislative action frustrates members on both sides.

Coburn came to Congress as part of the rebellious House Republican class of 1994, and the trademark pugnacity he brought to that chamber has continued in the Senate. He rails against the incumbency mind-set that he says puts staying in power ahead of passing conservative legislation. He revels in challenging the status quo, and if he has to step on his colleagues' toes along the way, so be it. "I didn't come here with delusions about making a lot of friends, and I haven't been disappointed," he said in 2008.

With Democrats controlling both the White House and Congress, he shows few signs of tempering his style. Coburn — one of the few non-lawyers on the Judiciary Committee — opposed the nomination of Attorney General Eric H. Holder Jr., whom he accused of trampling on gun owners' rights. He told a town hall meeting in his state that Holder "doesn't believe in the Second Amendment."

Coburn also ardently opposed President Obama's early economic initiatives. Nevertheless, he is more accommodating than other conservatives to Obama, who had forged a relationship with Coburn when he served in the Senate. Coburn told Fox News in April 2009 that while he opposes the president's domestic agenda, he supports his multilateral approach to international issues. "That's one area where I compliment the president," said Coburn, a Select Intelligence Committee member. "I think his outreach in terms of foreign policy has been tremendously positive."

An unwavering fiscal conservative, Coburn has waged war against members' earmarks, funding for pet projects that lawmakers slip into spending bills. One of his rare victories on that front came in late 2006, when he teamed with Obama on a bill establishing a searchable online database listing the recipients of all federal spending. Their bill passed after bloggers publicized the names of Alaska Republican Ted Stevens and West Virginia Democrat Robert C. Byrd, who had put a secret anonymous "hold" on it.

In a break from his normal course, Coburn supported a $700 billion financial plan in 2008 aimed at rescuing the nation's faltering financial services sector, saying, "We will face a financial catastrophe if we do nothing." To alleviate the fiscal crisis, he called on lawmakers to put their earmarks "on the chopping block."

Coburn often places holds on legislation, ranging from the major to the mundane. He keeps a list of bills he's tracking on cards that he carries in the pocket of his suit jacket. "What I'm trying to do is create the expectation among my peers in the Senate that if you've got something that doesn't pass the smell test, I'm going to be challenging it, and if you really want it, then you got to come to the floor and debate me on it, on why we ought to do it," he told C-SPAN in 2007.

Coburn's approach has pitted him in a protracted battle with Majority Leader Harry Reid of Nevada. Reid, who has called Coburn's maneuvering "obstruction on steroids," retaliated in 2008 by assembling a $10 billion bill, known as the "Tomnibus," that included more than 30 unrelated measures Coburn had blocked. The bill stalled in the Senate, but it included some measures that were eventually enacted separately after Coburn's concerns were addressed.

In April 2007, the House passed a bill prohibiting employers and health insurers from discriminating on the basis of genetic information, but Coburn stalled the measure for a year, arguing it would expose companies and insurers to undue risk of lawsuits. One year after the House action, leaders and bill sponsors — who had worked for 13 years to enact the discrimination ban — began intense negotiations with Coburn and the George W. Bush administration. Coburn dropped his hold, and the bill cleared soon after.

In 2005, Coburn tried to overrule the Select Ethics Committee when it refused to modify a longstanding ban on outside payment for professional services. But he fell nine votes short of the 60 votes he needed. A champion of anti-abortion measures and other conservative social policies, Coburn wanted to keep collecting just enough fees from his obstetrics practice in Muskogee to cover his costs. The House had allowed him to do so; the Senate did not. He has continued seeing patients anyway, practicing for free and covering the costs himself.

A member of the Health, Education, Labor and Pensions Committee, Coburn often opposes legislation that directs funding to research for specific diseases, arguing such allocations should be decided by the National Institutes of Health. On Homeland Security and Governmental Affairs, he has joined other conservatives in denouncing as "amnesty" measures to provide illegal immigrants with a path to citizenship.

In 2009 he became the top-ranking Republican on Judiciary's Subcommittee on Human Rights and the Law and on Homeland Security's Subcommittee on Permanent Investigations. The latter panel is considered very powerful, having jurisdiction to investigate almost any aspect of the federal government.

His other committee assignment is Indian Affairs, where he has pushed for an overhaul of the Indian Health Service. He angered tribes when he said during his Senate campaign that many residents on the Cherokee reservation in his former House district "aren't Indians."

Coburn was born in Casper, Wyo., but grew up in Muskogee, which is still his hometown. He had a strained relationship with his father, an alcoholic who founded a successful optical business. (They reconciled six months before his father's death.) His father's company made equipment to process optical lenses and eventually became Muskogee's biggest employer.

After his junior year at Oklahoma State, Coburn married Carolyn Denton, a former Miss Oklahoma he'd had a crush on since elementary school. He went to work for his father at age 22 and for several years managed a branch of the business in Virginia, Coburn Optical Products. He built it into a $40 million venture, which Revlon bought in 1975.

Coburn moved back to Oklahoma, and at 31, decided to go to medical school. He credits his career change to his experience with cancer. A doctor diagnosed him with a malignant melanoma, a deadly form of skin cancer, when he was just 23. Coburn spent the next two years in treatment. He still has a pronounced scar on his neck. He fought a second battle against cancer, this time colon cancer, shortly before he decided to run for the Senate in 2004.

Coburn was a first-time candidate for public office when he ran for the House in 1994, a year of voter disgruntlement with incumbents and a favorable one for neophytes. Democratic Rep. Mike Synar, the incumbent, lost in the primary, and Coburn went on to beat Synar's Democratic replacement, a 71-year-old retired middle school teacher.

Unlike many lawmakers elected in the GOP takeover, Coburn stuck to his term limits pledge, serving three terms in the House and then leaving. But he missed the fray, and in 2004 ran for the seat of retiring GOP Sen. Don Nickles. His opponent was Democrat Brad Carson, a moderate House member.Despite a gaffe-prone campaign, Coburn won by more than 11 percentage points.

KEY VOTES

2008

Yes Prohibit discrimination based on genetic information

No Reauthorize farm and nutrition programs for five years

No Limit debate on "cap and trade" system for greenhouse gas emissions

No Allow lawsuits against companies that participated in warrantless wiretapping

No Limit debate on a bill to block a scheduled cut in Medicare payments to doctors

No Grant mortgage relief to homeowners and funding for Fannie Mae and Freddie Mac

Yes Approve a nuclear cooperation agreement with India

Yes Approve final $700 billion program to stabilize financial markets

No Allow consideration of a $14 billion auto industry loan package

2007

No Increase minimum wage by $2.10 an hour

No Limit debate on a comprehensive immigration bill

No Overhaul congressional lobbying and ethics rules for members and their staffs

No Limit debate on considering a bill to add House seats for the District of Columbia and Utah

No Limit debate on restoring habeas corpus rights to detainees

No Mandate minimum breaks for troops between deployments to Iraq or Afghanistan

No Override Bush veto of $23.2 billion water projects authorization bill

Yes Confirm Michael B. Mukasey as attorney general

No Limit debate on an energy policy overhaul containing $21.8 billion in tax incentives and reduced oil and gas subsidies

CQ VOTE STUDIES

	PARTY UNITY		PRESIDENTIAL SUPPORT	
	SUPPORT	OPPOSE	SUPPORT	OPPOSE
2008	99%	1%	85%	15%
2007	96%	4%	89%	11%
2006	92%	8%	88%	12%
2005	93%	7%	91%	9%
House Service:				
2000	91%	9%	23%	77%
1999	90%	10%	14%	86%
1998	94%	6%	16%	84%
1997	93%	7%	24%	76%
1996	91%	9%	29%	71%

INTEREST GROUPS

	AFL-CIO	ADA	CCUS	ACU
2008	0%	0%	75%	96%
2007	17%	5%	50%	100%
2006	27%	5%	64%	100%
2005	21%	5%	89%	100%
House Service:				
2000	20%	15%	63%	95%
1999	38%	10%	67%	100%
1998	22%	5%	71%	100%
1997	0%	5%	78%	95%
1996	9%	10%	80%	89%

Rep. John Sullivan (R)

Elected January 2002; 4th full term

CAPITOL OFFICE
225-2211
sullivan.house.gov
434 Cannon Bldg. 20515-3601; fax 225-9187

COMMITTEES
Energy & Commerce
Select Energy Independence & Global Warming

RESIDENCE
Tulsa

BORN
Jan. 1, 1965; Tulsa, Okla.

RELIGION
Roman Catholic

FAMILY
Wife, Judy Sullivan; five children
(one deceased)

EDUCATION
Northeastern State U., B.B.A 1992 (marketing)

CAREER
Petroleum marketing executive;
real estate broker

POLITICAL HIGHLIGHTS
Okla. House, 1995-2002

ELECTION RESULTS

2008 GENERAL

John Sullivan (R)	193,404	66.2%
Georgianna W. Oliver (D)	98,890	33.8%

2008 PRIMARY

John Sullivan (R)	33,563	91.7%
Fran Moghaddam (R)	3,025	8.3%

2006 GENERAL

John Sullivan (R)	116,920	63.6%
Alan Gentges (D)	56,724	30.9%
Bill Wortman (I)	10,085	5.5%

PREVIOUS WINNING PERCENTAGES
2004 (60%); 2002 (56%); 2002 Special Election (54%)

In an era when many Republicans are losing support, Sullivan is strengthening his grip on his district. As his rising re-election percentages show, his constituents appreciate his brand of conservatism, in which he frequently fights the growth of government.

Sullivan sums up his political philosophy this way: "If it's in the Yellow Pages, government shouldn't be doing it." He is serious about his right-wing views, takes a hard tack against Democratic proposals he sees as unnecessarily expensive and pushes hard for stringent immigration control. But he makes some exceptions in his philosophy in order to protect private enterprise and boost jobs in his district.

He loves to trumpet his success snagging funding for special projects. But as a member of the conservative Republican Study Committee, he is a fierce critic of other kinds of spending. He was among those urging spending cuts in other programs to offset the billions of dollars Congress appropriated in 2005 and 2006 to help the Gulf Coast recover from a devastating hurricane season. In March 2009, he opposed passage of President Obama's $3.56 trillion budget blueprint for fiscal 2010, saying, "This Democrat budget proposal spends too much, taxes too much and borrows too much."

He also opposed a bill in early 2009 that would allow bankruptcy judges to renegotiate mortgages. He called it "another massive bailout that rewards irresponsible homebuyers." And he opposed a $787 billion economic stimulus bill Obama signed into law in 2009, saying it was the "largest spending bill in our nation's history." In 2008, he voted against an effort to override President George W. Bush's veto of a massive farm bill that provides generous subsidies to Oklahoma farmers. He did, however, support in fall 2008 a $700 billion effort to stabilize the financial services industry. "This is for the well-being of our country, not for political popularity," Sullivan said.

He had long sought to station Immigration and Customs Enforcement agents in Tulsa, and in September 2008 the agency announced it would base a "fugitive operations team" in the city. Previously, the closest office in the state was in Oklahoma City, more than 100 miles away. He was instrumental in increasing its staffing from four to 12. He opposes efforts to create a path to citizenship for illegal immigrants. He lamented in 2008 that the rhetoric on both sides of the immigration debate had become overly inflamed. "We need to put all of that aside and have a good debate on it," he told the Tulsa World.

A former petroleum marketing executive, he serves on the Energy and Commerce Committee and a select panel on energy independence. He also was named to a Republican energy task force in 2009 to help draft legislation. He has been one of the GOP's strongest supporters of increased domestic production of fossil fuels and said he wants to focus on an "all-of-the-above strategy" for energy, including oil, gas, nuclear energy and conservation. But he criticized Obama's outline in his 2010 budget to set a cap on greenhouse emissions and create a market-based emissions trading program. Sullivan said it would result in a tax on every American and would be "a jobs killer."

On health care, Sullivan remains hopeful Congress will adopt part of the GOP's approach in developing legislation allowing people to get their own policies, preferably through tax credits. He also wants more emphasis on prevention of health problems. He voted against a bill to expand the State Children's Health Insurance Program, which provides coverage for children whose families don't qualify for Medicaid; Bush had twice vetoed versions of the bill, but Obama signed it into law in early 2009.

Sullivan first found the spotlight in July 2003 when he defied a doctor's orders and went to the House floor in a wheelchair to cast the deciding vote on a bill to significantly change the Head Start early education program. He had been injured two days before when a security barrier at a Capitol parking lot malfunctioned and hit his car, setting off the air bag. The bill ultimately died in the Senate.

Sullivan said his interest in politics was sparked when, as a kid walking to kindergarten, he saw yard signs for presidential candidates Richard Nixon and George McGovern. Not knowing what they meant, he asked his parents if they could get one. That touched off an argument between his Democratic mother and Republican father that ended with his mother flinging a glass of orange juice at his dad. Ultimately, it was his father's political leanings that swayed the boy. He trailed along as his father worked to elect Henry Bellmon, Oklahoma's first Republican governor. In college, Sullivan initially majored in political science, but after his father died he switched to marketing. He worked as a real estate broker and in petroleum marketing while running a political memorabilia business. He also worked on several GOP campaigns. He ran for an open state House seat in 1994 and won. During seven years in the legislature, he battled to reduce sales taxes and estate taxes.

In 2001, he entered a five-way primary for the seat of Republican Rep. Steve Largent, who was resigning to run for governor. Sullivan bested Cathy Keating, wife of GOP Gov. Frank Keating, in that race and then Democrat and former Tulsa School Board member Doug Dodd in the special election. Sullivan's district had been redrawn to be more Republican for the 2002 general election, and he beat Dodd in a rematch.

His re-election in 2004 came after a tough campaign. Past supporters, including an earlier political consultant to Sullivan who accused his former boss of cheating him out of nearly $20,000 in fees, backed GOP businessman Bill Wortman in the primary. Sullivan's office later acknowledged his aides used phony names to telephone call-in radio shows and posed easy questions to their boss. Wortman seized on that and on two cases in which he said Sullivan lied about his police record. Yet Sullivan beat Wortman and prevailed over Dodd with 60 percent of the vote.

Sullivan has long acknowledged a rocky youth in which careless drinking led to several arrests, including one for assault. He has spoken about the dangers of alcohol consumption to high school students. Voters were untroubled, and in 2006, he won with 64 percent of the vote. He took 66 percent in 2008, 2 percentage points above Arizona GOP Sen. John McCain's showing in the district.

KEY VOTES

2008
No   Delay consideration of Colombia free-trade agreement
No   Override Bush veto of federal farm and nutrition programs reauthorization bill
Yes Overhaul surveillance laws and permit dismissal of suits against companies that conducted warrantless wiretapping
No   Grant mortgage relief to homeowners and funding for Fannie Mae and Freddie Mac
No   Approve initial $700 billion program to stabilize financial markets
Yes Approve final $700 billion program to stabilize financial markets
No   Provide $14 billion in loans to automakers

2007
No   Increase minimum wage by $2.10 an hour
No   Approve $124.2 billion in emergency war spending and set goal for redeployment of troops from Iraq
+   Reject federal contraceptive assistance to international family planning groups
Yes Override Bush veto of $23.2 billion water projects authorization bill
Yes Implement Peru free-trade agreement
No   Approve energy policy overhaul with new fuel economy standards
Yes Clear $473.5 billion omnibus spending bill, including $70 billion for military operations

CQ VOTE STUDIES

	PARTY UNITY		PRESIDENTIAL SUPPORT	
	SUPPORT	OPPOSE	SUPPORT	OPPOSE
2008	97%	3%	69%	31%
2007	98%	2%	83%	17%
2006	97%	3%	95%	5%
2005	97%	3%	89%	11%
2004	97%	3%	85%	15%

INTEREST GROUPS

	AFL-CIO	ADA	CCUS	ACU
2008	13%	20%	100%	92%
2007	13%	5%	71%	100%
2006	15%	5%	100%	92%
2005	13%	5%	85%	100%
2004	7%	0%	100%	100%

OKLAHOMA 1
Tulsa; Wagoner and Washington counties

Wooden homes on small plots of land in the city's outskirts contrast with the skyscrapers of downtown Tulsa, the heart of the 1st and one of the most solidly Republican enclaves in Oklahoma. Tulsa and Oklahoma City, the two main metropolitan areas in the state, have a friendly rivalry. Tulsa is more insular and tied to old money than Oklahoma City and the rest of the state, and Tulsans like to distinguish themselves from the "dust-on-their-boots" stereotype of the rest of Oklahoma.

Once the "oil capital of the world," Tulsa thrived on drilling until the market dried up in the 1980s; after a recent revival it again relies on the energy sector. Dramatic fluctuations in the demand and price for oil in the last decade, however, have affected the downtown office real estate market. The city is still actively seeking to diversify its economic identity, and efforts that began two decades ago are now paying off. Tulsa has become a manufacturing hub for flight simulators, and while aviation and aerospace production remains profitable, financial services and telecommunications sectors have prolonged growth.

Real estate prices rose here even while falling elsewhere across the country, and Tulsa and its neighboring cities seem to have escaped the worst of the recession. Young professionals are moving into the city's center. South Tulsa is sprinkled with luxury homes, and subdivisions are springing up in the fast-growing suburbs of Broken Arrow, Jenks and Owasso, which has more than doubled in population since 1990.

Democrats can win local elections in the northern half of Tulsa, but Republicans dominate at the federal level. The region has voted for a Democratic presidential candidate only twice since 1920. Socially conservative issues play well in the district, which is the home of Oral Roberts University.

MAJOR INDUSTRY
Oil, aerospace, telecommunications, financial services, defense manufacturing

CITIES
Tulsa (pt.), 387,419; Broken Arrow, 74,859; Bartlesville, 34,746; Owasso, 18,502; Sand Springs (pt.), 17,172

NOTABLE
Oral Roberts University is known for its 200-foot Prayer Tower and the "Praying Hands" sculpture at the campus' main entrance.

Rep. Dan Boren (D)

Elected 2004; 3rd term

CAPITOL OFFICE
225-2701
www.house.gov/boren
216 Cannon Bldg. 20515-3602; fax 225-3038

COMMITTEES
Armed Services
Natural Resources
Select Intelligence

RESIDENCE
Muskogee

BORN
Aug. 2, 1973; Shawnee, Okla.

RELIGION
Methodist

FAMILY
Wife, Andrea Boren; one child

EDUCATION
Texas Christian U., B.A. 1997 (economics);
U. of Oklahoma, M.B.A. 2001

CAREER
College fundraiser; congressional district
aide; bank teller; state utility regulation
commission aide

POLITICAL HIGHLIGHTS
Okla. House, 2002-04

ELECTION RESULTS

2008 GENERAL

Dan Boren (D)	173,757	70.5%
Raymond J. Wickson (R)	72,815	29.5%

2008 PRIMARY

Dan Boren (D)	66,041	85.2%
Kevin Coleman (D)	11,438	14.8%

2006 GENERAL

Dan Boren (D)	122,347	72.7%
Patrick K. Miller (R)	45,861	27.3%

PREVIOUS WINNING PERCENTAGES
2004 (66%)

Following in the footsteps of his forebears, Boren is one of the House's most conservative Democrats. He describes himself as a "pro-gun, pro-business" Democrat. Staking out that position is a matter of survival in a district that backed Republican John McCain by nearly a 2-to-1 ratio in the 2008 presidential election.

Boren voted with President George W. Bush 36 percent of the time in the 110th Congress (2007-08), the highest level among House Democrats who served a full two-year term. "My district will not re-elect me if I go to the left," Boren once told the Tulsa World newspaper.

He is the third generation of Borens to serve in the U.S. Congress from Oklahoma. His father is David L. Boren, a Democratic senator who resigned his seat in 1994 to become president of the University of Oklahoma. His grandfather Lyle Boren served in the House from 1937 to 1947. The 2nd District of today includes about half the area Boren's grandfather once represented.

Boren sees his mission as ensuring his party doesn't go too far to the left; he said doing so could jeopardize its hold on power. "It's my hope that we can moderate our caucus and pass legislation that will, frankly, keep the Democratic Party in control," he said.

He has pressed for more conservatism from Democrats for some time. Just after the 2006 election, when the party was celebrating the historic rise of Nancy Pelosi of California as incoming House Speaker, Boren declined to endorse the California liberal until he met her to ask for assurances that she was willing to include Republicans and conservative Democrats in legislative dealmaking. When the Obama administration kept silent on the issue of gun control in early 2009, Boren told Newsweek: "The Democratic Party understands this is a losing issue…It's a dead loser. It's one of the reasons they lost the Congress in 1994 and Al Gore was not elected president in 2000."

He is decidedly in favor of gun ownership. He is on the National Rifle Association's board of directors and co-chairs the Congressional Sportsmen's Caucus. His office walls are covered with the fruits of his hunting trips: stuffed deer heads, a wild turkey and a bearskin.

It is on fiscal matters that Boren is most clearly conservative. He is a leader in the group of about 50 Democratic budget hawks called the "Blue Dogs," which frequently plays a pivotal role in legislative outcomes. He said he fundamentally agrees with the Democratic goal of "giving opportunity to all" on issues such as education and health care, but he has often come out against his party on taxes. He was one of 20 House Democrats who voted against Obama's $3.56 trillion budget for 2010, saying "it increased taxes in a time of economic uncertainty and added trillions of dollars in spending that will burden our children and grandchildren." He supported the $787 billion economic stimulus law Obama signed in early 2009. But he did so reluctantly, all the while insisting the largesse be temporary and that the government stop deficit spending and pay down its debt.

But Boren has not repudiated earmarks — money funding special-interest projects added to spending bills. "I've asked for money for roads and for our universities, and I'm proud of it," he told the World in 2006. "If the money is not spent here, it's going to be spent somewhere else."

He has backed the GOP on other issues. In his first term, he supported the GOP's immigration plan cracking down on illegal immigrants. He was the only Democrat to side with Republicans by voting in favor of giving the FBI access to records about books people check out of libraries and buy in bookstores.

He joined seven other Democrats in voting for a GOP-crafted lobbying and ethics bill in 2006, and was one of only two Democrats in 2007 to vote against a bill to make it easier for unions to establish themselves in the workplace.

But Boren drew the line against cooperating with Republicans on Social Security, opposing Bush's plan to privatize part of the program by letting individuals invest some of their savings on their own. And he switched his position on the State Children's Health Insurance Program, eventually supporting a bill — which Obama signed into law in February 2009 — to expand the program, which covers children from families that don't qualify for Medicaid. He originally opposed it due to concerns over a tobacco tax that would help pay for it.

He was granted a seat on the Select Intelligence Committee in 2009, an assignment he described as "something that I've worked toward my entire career." His father chaired the Senate Select Intelligence panel and was a confidant of CIA Director George J. Tenet, who served under presidents Clinton and George W. Bush. The younger Boren said one of his priorities will be examining U.S. efforts in Africa and the potential for terrorist activity there.

Boren also sits on the National Resources panel, where he looks out for the interests of American Indians, who make up nearly one-fifth of his constituency. He counts among his proudest accomplishments securing passage of a bill honoring "code talkers" who, by speaking in their native tongues on military radios during World Wars I and II, enabled U.S. forces to discuss operations confidentially. He also looks out for the oil, gas and timber industries, which employ many of his constituents. In 2009, he sponsored a bill aimed at expanding the use of natural gas as an alternative to conventional transportation fuel and authorize grants to help develop natural gas vehicles.

Boren's father became governor of Oklahoma two years after Boren was born. His parents later divorced, and he split his time between living in Oklahoma with his mother, the late Janna L. Robbins, and in Washington with his father. After college, he worked as an aide to Denise Bode, who headed the Oklahoma utility regulatory agency and once worked in his father's Senate office. In 2002, at 29, he beat an incumbent for an Oklahoma House seat. In the legislature, he was a proponent of tax cuts and of efforts to make it more difficult for trial lawyers to press what he termed frivolous lawsuits. A year into his term, a U.S. House seat opened when Democrat Brad Carson left for an ultimately unsuccessful Senate bid. Boren didn't hesitate to go for it.

His name recognition helped him beat local District Attorney Kalyn Free, a member of the Cherokee Nation, in the primary. He sprinted past Republican Wayland Smalley, a horse breeder, in the general election, and had little trouble winning re-election in 2006 and 2008.

KEY VOTES

2008

No Delay consideration of Colombia free-trade agreement

Yes Override Bush veto of federal farm and nutrition programs reauthorization bill

Yes Overhaul surveillance laws and permit dismissal of suits against companies that conducted warrantless wiretapping

Yes Grant mortgage relief to homeowners and funding for Fannie Mae and Freddie Mac

Yes Approve initial $700 billion program to stabilize financial markets

Yes Approve final $700 billion program to stabilize financial markets

Yes Provide $14 billion in loans to automakers

2007

Yes Increase minimum wage by $2.10 an hour

No Approve $124.2 billion in emergency war spending and set goal for redeployment of troops from Iraq

Yes Reject federal contraceptive assistance to international family planning groups

Yes Override Bush veto of $23.2 billion water projects authorization bill

? Implement Peru free-trade agreement

Yes Approve energy policy overhaul with new fuel economy standards

Yes Clear $473.5 billion omnibus spending bill, including $70 billion for military operations

CQ VOTE STUDIES

	PARTY UNITY		PRESIDENTIAL SUPPORT	
	SUPPORT	OPPOSE	SUPPORT	OPPOSE
2008	91%	9%	36%	64%
2007	79%	21%	36%	64%
2006	54%	46%	85%	15%
2005	59%	41%	65%	35%

INTEREST GROUPS

	AFL-CIO	ADA	CCUS	ACU
2008	73%	65%	78%	24%
2007	59%	50%	94%	57%
2006	57%	25%	100%	72%
2005	60%	55%	81%	64%

OKLAHOMA 2
East — Muskogee, 'Little Dixie'

The 2nd's overall Democratic lean does not disguise a cultural split between the district's regions. Running from Kansas to Texas in eastern Oklahoma, the 2nd takes in outlying areas of Tulsa to the north and the "Little Dixie" region in the south. Farming and die-hard "Yellow Dog" Democrats typify southeastern Oklahoma, while northeastern residents are more liberal, at least by Oklahoma's standards. Still, both areas support Republicans in presidential races.

The district, especially Little Dixie, suffers from a high susceptibility to severe drought conditions. Southeast Oklahoma has been particularly hard-hit by long-term drought conditions that have escalated since 2005. Threats of fire, crop failures and reduced grazing options for livestock are concerns for farmers in a district that relies on ranching and agriculture. In addition to raising beef and poultry, farmers here cultivate peanuts and wheat.

Other natural resources also bolster the region's economy. The number of small oil and natural gas wells has grown to meet recent increased industry demands. The timber industry in rocky southeastern McCurtain County supports paper mills, saw mills and other secondary industries. Pittsburg County hosts McAlester Army Ammunition Plant, a high-capacity ordnance storage facility.

Farther north, the forested section in the foothills of the Ozark Mountains is a poor rural area with Democratic sympathies. Lakes and waterways — including Lake Eufaula, the state's largest lake — attract tourists. The remote locations here also appeal to the elderly: The 2nd has Oklahoma's greatest proportion of people age 65 or older. The 2nd also has the nation's third-largest district share of American Indians (17 percent), and includes Tahlequah, the Cherokee Nation's capital.

MAJOR INDUSTRY
Ranching, timber, oil and gas, agriculture

MILITARY BASES
McAlester Army Ammunition Plant, 1 military, 1,400 civilian (2009)

CITIES
Muskogee, 38,310; McAlester, 17,783; Claremore, 15,873

NOTABLE
The American Indian "Trail of Tears" of 1838-39 ended in Tahlequah — about one-quarter of the Cherokee Nation died en route.

Rep. Frank D. Lucas (R)

Elected May 1994; 8th full term

CAPITOL OFFICE
225-5565
www.house.gov/lucas
2311 Rayburn Bldg. 20515-3603; fax 225-8698

COMMITTEES
Agriculture - ranking member
Financial Services
Science & Technology

RESIDENCE
Cheyenne

BORN
Jan. 6, 1960; Cheyenne, Okla.

RELIGION
Baptist

FAMILY
Wife, Lynda Lucas; three children

EDUCATION
Oklahoma State U., B.S. 1982
(agricultual economics)

CAREER
Farmer; rancher

POLITICAL HIGHLIGHTS
Republican nominee for Okla. House, 1984, 1986;
Okla. House, 1989-94

ELECTION RESULTS

2008 GENERAL

Frank D. Lucas (R)	184,306	69.7%
Frankie Robbins (D)	62,297	23.6%
Forrest Michael (I)	17,756	6.7%

2008 PRIMARY

Frank D. Lucas (R)	unopposed

2006 GENERAL

Frank D. Lucas (R)	128,042	67.5%
Sue Barton (D)	61,749	32.5%

PREVIOUS WINNING PERCENTAGES
2004 (82%); 2002 (76%); 2000 (59%); 1998 (65%);
1996 (64%); 1994 (70%); 1994 Special Election (54%)

Lucas describes his political philosophy as "old-style conservative Republicanism." He advocates a limited role for the federal government, except when it comes to business development and innovation, farm policy, infrastructure and what he considers "fair" taxation — all popular in a district that Arizona GOP Sen. John McCain carried by 46 percentage points over Barack Obama in 2008.

Lucas has deep roots in Oklahoma. He was born and raised on a farm that his family has owned since the turn of the 20th century. He has held on to it even while many of his neighbors have moved to towns and cities. That steady emptying of rural Oklahoma is an underlying factor in much of his legislative agenda and his close attention to serving constituents in his district, which encompasses almost half the geographic area of the state. While he tends to such duties from his seat as ranking Republican on the Agriculture Committee, his wife runs their beef cattle and wheat operation back home.

With Democrats controlling the White House and Congress, Oklahoma's mostly GOP delegation has lost much of the clout it once had. To Lucas, being in the minority demands extra hours of work. "I think it means the Republican members of the delegation have to work even harder," he told the Daily Oklahoman in December 2008.

He presses hard for benefits and disaster assistance for farmers, which was included in the 2008 reauthorization of farm and nutrition programs that he had a hand in drafting. He aims to ensure the Obama administration carries out the farm law in a way that benefits farmers.

When Obama proposed a budget for fiscal 2010 that aimed to repeal certain farm subsidies and cap direct payments to high-income producers, Lucas accused him of veering from the farm bill "in a direction that has been rejected by policy makers in the past." Lucas wrote a letter to Agriculture Secretary Tom Vilsack charging that it "seems clear that during an economic crisis, this administration is intent on helping everyone but those who live and work in rural America."

Lucas, who also serves on the Science and Technology Committee, is a big supporter of alternative fuels such as ethanol, since his state has plenty of the switch grass and corn used to make it. Lucas also is a promoter of wind and solar power, and during the 110th Congress (2007-08) he introduced legislation to provide tax breaks to farmers who install wind turbines on their land. Oklahoma is one of the country's top producers of wind power.

But he was concerned that farmers would be stuck with unnecessary fees and balked when the Environmental Protection Agency in 2009 indicated it plans to establish a nationwide system for reporting greenhouse gas emissions, which would include animal-feed operations. He proposed legislation to bar the program from requiring livestock farmers to obtain an operating permit under the Clean Air Act.

His environmental interests are often in line with those of Democratic leaders, but he is likely to be far less accommodating on the Financial Services Committee as the panel seeks to help revive the struggling economy. In late 2008, he opposed both versions of a $700 billion measure — the second of which became law — aimed at rescuing the financial services sector.

Subsequently, despite intense pressure from the George W. Bush administration, he voted against an unsuccessful measure aimed at preventing major car manufacturers from going bankrupt. He said the initiatives would have amounted to unjust favoritism for certain industries. When Oklahoma's agricultural and energy companies have suffered in the past, he argued, "the government did not help us."

He also opposed Obama's $787 billion economic stimulus law in early 2009. He said he would prefer to focus on short-term stimulus spending and reduce the capital gains rate.

Lucas' district is also home to Altus Air Force Base and Vance Air Force Base, and he sits on Science and Technology's Space and Aeronautics panel.

Lucas is also a social conservative and supports efforts to ban abortion and prohibit same-sex marriage and stem cell research. He helped pass a bill in 2006 that would keep the words "Under God" in the Pledge of Allegiance.

A rare break with party orthodoxy came in 2006, when he voted against a renewal of the USA Patriot Act that granted the government more powers to investigate suspected terrorists.

When he was first elected, Lucas spent much of his time working on legislation stemming from the April 1995 bombing in downtown Oklahoma City that destroyed the Alfred P. Murrah Federal Building and killed 168 people. The federal building was in Lucas' old district, the 6th. In the years after the bombing, Lucas helped secure more than $100 million in federal funds for relief, recovery and rebuilding the area. He also won passage of a measure to establish a national memorial on the bombing site.

Lucas regularly introduces bills relating to his hobby of collecting coins. He has offered legislation to bar the government from claiming possession of coins minted before 1993, and to replace the nickel with a half-dime. He said his favorite coin is a 1971 Eisenhower dollar.

As a child, Lucas accompanied his Republican father (his mother was a Texas Democrat) to local political events. At Oklahoma State University, he became a student senator and president of the College Republicans and volunteered in local campaigns. But he majored in agricultural economics and always came home to the family farm.

He subsequently made two unsuccessful bids for a state House seat in what was then a mostly Democratic area, then captured a state House seat in a sprawling rural district in 1988.

Lucas made his first bid for Congress when 10-term Democratic Rep. Glenn English resigned in early 1994. He won the nomination over four other Republicans. By stressing his work in agriculture and his lifelong residency in the district, he won with 54 percent of the vote in the special election against Democrat Dan Webber Jr., a former aide to Oklahoma Democratic Sen. David L. Boren. That was Lucas' closest election and he has won handily since.

KEY VOTES

2008

No Delay consideration of Colombia free-trade agreement

Yes Override Bush veto of federal farm and nutrition programs reauthorization bill

Yes Overhaul surveillance laws and permit dismissal of suits against companies that conducted warrantless wiretapping

No Grant mortgage relief to homeowners and funding for Fannie Mae and Freddie Mac

No Approve initial $700 billion program to stabilize financial markets

No Approve final $700 billion program to stabilize financial markets

No Provide $14 billion in loans to automakers

2007

No Increase minimum wage by $2.10 an hour

No Approve $124.2 billion in emergency war spending and set goal for redeployment of troops from Iraq

Yes Reject federal contraceptive assistance to international family planning groups

Yes Override Bush veto of $23.2 billion water projects authorization bill

Yes Implement Peru free-trade agreement

No Approve energy policy overhaul with new fuel economy standards

Yes Clear $473.5 billion omnibus spending bill, including $70 billion for military operations

CQ VOTE STUDIES

	PARTY UNITY		PRESIDENTIAL SUPPORT	
	SUPPORT	OPPOSE	SUPPORT	OPPOSE
2008	96%	4%	66%	34%
2007	91%	9%	80%	20%
2006	98%	2%	95%	5%
2005	97%	3%	87%	13%
2004	94%	6%	87%	13%

INTEREST GROUPS

	AFL-CIO	ADA	CCUS	ACU
2008	14%	15%	89%	96%
2007	4%	10%	85%	100%
2006	7%	5%	93%	88%
2005	13%	0%	92%	92%
2004	17%	0%	95%	96%

OKLAHOMA 3

Panhandle; west and north-central Oklahoma

Nothing stops the constant wind that forces its way across the 3rd's flat plains in western and north-central Oklahoma, an area that was devastated by the Dust Bowl in the 1930s. Few areas have suffered the vacillations of the oil industry more than the 3rd, and oil busts chased residents from the area over the years. Skyrocketing oil prices this decade made the small drilling operations that dot the landscape profitable.

Recent demand for domestic petroleum had revived oil exploration and industry demand for workers, although economic slowdowns have begun to limit growth. High-paying jobs and royalties for landowners who allow drilling have boosted the economy. Renewable-energy interests, such as grains for biofuel processing and wind farms, are also important.

The 3rd also depends on crops and livestock, and the district, the state's largest, leads Oklahoma in hogs, cattle, wheat, sorghum and sunflower seeds. The average farm and ranch size here has grown markedly, as agricultural sustainability now requires larger operations than in the past. Always thriving Stillwater, home to Oklahoma State University,

brings droves to Boone Pickens Stadium to watch Big 12 football.

Bible Belt conservatism typifies the eastern plains areas north and west of Oklahoma City, while the southern part of the district is home to conservative Democrats who support Democrats for state office. Cimarron, Texas and Beaver counties on the panhandle are some of the most heavily Republican-voting counties in the state, and John McCain topped 85 percent in each of these counties in the 2008 presidential election. Overall, the 3rd gave McCain 73 percent of its vote, his highest percentage statewide, and the 16 counties that gave McCain his highest percentage margins in the state are wholly in the 3rd.

MAJOR INDUSTRY
Oil, agriculture, military, higher education

MILITARY BASES
Altus Air Force Base, 2,089 military, 1,255 civilian (2007); Vance Air Force Base, 1,337 military, 1,300 civilian (2009)

CITIES
Enid, 47,045; Stillwater, 39,065; Ponca City, 25,919; Altus, 21,447

NOTABLE
Roger Mills County, on the western border, was named in 1892 by referendum in honor of then-U.S. Rep. Roger Q. Mills from Texas.

Rep. Tom Cole (R)

Elected 2002; 4th term

CAPITOL OFFICE
225-6165
www.house.gov/cole
2458 Rayburn Bldg. 20515-3604; fax 225-3512

COMMITTEES
Appropriations

RESIDENCE
Moore

BORN
April 28, 1949; Shreveport, La.

RELIGION
Methodist

FAMILY
Wife, Ellen Cole; one child

EDUCATION
Grinnell College, B.A. 1971 (history); Yale U.,
M.A. 1974 (British history); U. of Oklahoma,
Ph.D. 1984 (19th Century British history)

CAREER
Political consultant; party official;
congressional district director; professor

POLITICAL HIGHLIGHTS
Okla. Republican Party chairman, 1985-89;
Okla. Senate, 1989-91; Okla. secretary of state,
1995-99

ELECTION RESULTS

2008 GENERAL

Tom Cole (R)	180,080	66.0%
Blake Cummings (D)	79,674	29.2%
David E. Joyce (I)	13,027	4.8%

2008 PRIMARY

Tom Cole (R)	unopposed

2006 GENERAL

Tom Cole (R)	118,266	64.6%
Hal Spake (D)	64,775	35.4%

PREVIOUS WINNING PERCENTAGES
2004 (78%); 2002 (54%)

Cole is an ambitious conservative who doesn't stray far from the party line. But he is collegial enough to have once been the only Republican invited to speak at a charity roast of Illinois' Rahm Emanuel, then one of the House's hardest-driving Democrats and now the White House chief of staff.

Relationships have been the building blocks for Cole's entire political career. As a longtime Republican operative, he became known in Oklahoma political circles and then at a national level, running successful campaigns for others in the party before finally becoming a candidate himself. He now concentrates on developing good relations among colleagues on the famously clubby Appropriations Committee to steer money to his state.

Serving on Appropriations is far easier for Cole than his challenging stint in the 110th Congress (2007-08) as the head of the National Republican Congressional Committee (NRCC), the campaign arm of House Republicans. In that job, he endured accounting scandals, lackluster fundraising and a rash of retirements that — along with the national Democratic electoral tide — further entrenched his party's minority status in November 2008.

Cole expressed opposition in early 2009 to President Obama's proposed cuts in the defense budget, some of which affected his state's military contractors. He also joined others in his party in criticizing Obama's $787 billion economic stimulus law and a subsequent budget plan for fiscal 2010. "This unprecedented growth in the size and expense of the federal government is truly stunning," he said in March 2009.

Cole did put aside his concerns over government spending to support the $700 billion law in fall 2008 to rescue the nation's ailing financial sector. He said that at the time of the vote, the nation's economic crisis required swift action. But when populist anger boiled over in March 2009 at the hefty bonuses paid to employees of American International Group Inc. with rescue funds, Cole called on Treasury Secretary Timothy F. Geithner to resign for not stopping the payments. "Simply put, it is clear that Secretary Geithner is in over his head," he said.

Cole's no-nonsense yet wry demeanor, along with his ties to the American Indian community — he is part Chickasaw and the only American Indian in Congress — have helped him connect with his district. Yet his low-key manner belies a sharp intellect and worldliness; he was a Fulbright scholar at the University of London and earned a doctorate in British history.

Cole has long been a major booster of tribal interests, consistently taking their side in disagreements with the federal government. He opposed the George W. Bush administration's proposal to cut American Indian programs to pay some $7 million in legal fees as part of a 1996 lawsuit seeking to force the Interior Department to account for funds in individual Indian trust accounts. He cosponsored legislation that became law in the 110th Congress to protect the water rights of the Soboba Band of Luisena Indians in California.

He also looked out for his state's military facilities as a member of the Armed Services panel in the 110th. Early in 2008, he expressed interest in succeeding Mississippi Republican Roger Wicker on the Appropriations Committee when Wicker moved to the Senate. But he said he ended up withdrawing his name from consideration at the request of Minority Leader John A. Boehner of Ohio after Boehner agreed to back him for the next open spot on the committee in the 111th Congress (2009-10).

Cole won the NRCC position in November 2006, thanks in part to his demonstrated fundraising abilities. His task was to rebuild the party's

House election prospects after the disastrous 2006 election saw the GOP lose 30 seats and control of Congress. But it gradually became apparent the 2008 election was not destined to be much more successful. "Tom was dealt an almost unwinnable hand," Republican consultant Rich Bond told The New York Times.

Cole places much of the blame for the party committee's struggles on organizational failings. When he started at the NRCC, "The place was really just basically broken," he said. "There were nine staff people, $18 million in debt and bills…a great place to start."

The first six months of 2008 were particularly rocky. In February, NRCC administrators discovered their treasurer had embezzled more than $725,000 from the committee since 2001. A series of stinging special-election losses of previously Republican-held seats in the spring did not help.

Restless House Republicans began calling for Cole's ouster in May, but Boehner refused. The minority leader did, however, take on a bigger role in overseeing the committee's operations as the campaign committee's troubles worsened.

Cole's earliest political experiences were with the campaigns of his late mother, Helen, who was a state legislator. He said he got hooked on the thrill of winning a political race, a feeling akin to being in a locker room after a football victory.

He later served as state party chairman, as a state senator and as Oklahoma secretary of state. He was a founding partner of Cole, Hargrave, Snodgrass & Associates, a political consulting firm. In 1994, he ran the successful campaign of friend J.C. Watts Jr. for the 4th District.

When Watts retired in 2002, Cole jumped into the race for the seat and defeated former Democratic state Sen. Darryl Roberts with 54 percent of the vote. By the time he got to the House as a freshman, Cole was well acquainted with the top GOP leaders, including Speaker J. Dennis Hastert. It didn't take him long to climb to deputy whip, helping GOP leaders round up votes for important bills. And when Hastert decided to clean house at the ethics committee in 2005 after the panel admonished his close ally, Majority Leader Tom DeLay, he tapped Cole as one of the replacements.

In 2004, Cole faced no Democratic opposition and won with 78 percent. He was easily re-elected in his two subsequent races.

Although he said he thought "long and hard" about running for Oklahoma governor in 2010, he announced his desire to stay put in the House. He said he could contribute more to the state through his position on the Appropriations Committee.

KEY VOTES

2008

No Delay consideration of Colombia free-trade agreement

Yes Override Bush veto of federal farm and nutrition programs reauthorization bill

Yes Overhaul surveillance laws and permit dismissal of suits against companies that conducted warrantless wiretapping

No Grant mortgage relief to homeowners and funding for Fannie Mae and Freddie Mac

Yes Approve initial $700 billion program to stabilize financial markets

Yes Approve final $700 billion program to stabilize financial markets

No Provide $14 billion in loans to automakers

2007

No Increase minimum wage by $2.10 an hour

No Approve $124.2 billion in emergency war spending and set goal for redeployment of troops from Iraq

Yes Reject federal contraceptive assistance to international family planning groups

Yes Override Bush veto of $23.2 billion water projects authorization bill

Yes Implement Peru free-trade agreement

No Approve energy policy overhaul with new fuel economy standards

Yes Clear $473.5 billion omnibus spending bill, including $70 billion for military operations

CQ VOTE STUDIES

| | PARTY UNITY | | PRESIDENTIAL SUPPORT | |
	SUPPORT	OPPOSE	SUPPORT	OPPOSE
2008	95%	5%	73%	27%
2007	92%	8%	78%	22%
2006	96%	4%	95%	5%
2005	98%	2%	91%	9%
2004	97%	3%	91%	9%

INTEREST GROUPS

	AFL-CIO	ADA	CCUS	ACU
2008	7%	10%	94%	88%
2007	13%	10%	84%	100%
2006	21%	0%	100%	84%
2005	14%	0%	96%	100%
2004	20%	0%	100%	96%

OKLAHOMA 4

South central — Norman, Lawton, part of Oklahoma City

Home to the state's largest university and two military bases, the 4th covers part of Oklahoma City, its Southern suburbs, and the western edges of "Little Dixie," so named for its southern influence. Oklahomans flock to Norman for Sooner football games at the University of Oklahoma, whose stadium can hold nearly every resident who lives in the city.

Military jobs in the 4th expanded during the 1990s, increasing the area's population and enhancing its defense presence. The 2002 Crusader artillery system cancellation hurt Fort Sill and the city of Lawton, which is heavily dependent on the base, but the 2005 BRAC round eased worries about the base's future. The fort expects 10,000 new residents by 2011, some of whom have already begun to arrive.

The 4th's economy suffered from low oil prices a decade ago, and long-term drought conditions have decimated the region. Still, the oil industry enjoyed recent price increases in the middle of this decade, and agriculture remains an essential economic cog. Farms here grow soybeans, cotton, peanuts and wheat.

The 4th echoes the state's GOP preference in national elections. Although once confined to presidential races, the tendency now extends to congressional candidates and state legislators. Democrats remain competitive, especially in the district's rural, southern areas and around the university, although Republicans find strength in other parts of Norman. Overall, John McCain received 66 percent of the 4th's vote in the 2008 presidential election.

MAJOR INDUSTRY
Military, higher education, oil, agriculture

MILITARY BASES
Fort Sill (Army), 16,500 military, 7,500 civilian (2009); Tinker Air Force Base, 5,700 military, 12,200 civilian (2009)

CITIES
Norman, 95,694; Lawton, 92,757; Oklahoma City (pt.), 70,896; Midwest City (pt.), 45,044; Moore, 41,138

NOTABLE
The National Oceanic and Atmospheric Administration's National Weather Service Storm Prediction Center is located in Norman.

Rep. Mary Fallin (R)

Elected 2006; 2nd term

CAPITOL OFFICE
225-2132
fallin.house.gov
1432 Longworth Bldg. 20515-3605; fax 226-1463

COMMITTEES
Armed Services
Small Business
Transportation & Infrastructure

RESIDENCE
Edmond

BORN
Dec. 9, 1954; Warrensburg, Mo.

RELIGION
Christian non-denominational

FAMILY
Divorced; two children

EDUCATION
Oklahoma Baptist U., attended 1973-75;
Oklahoma State U., B.S. 1977 (family relations
and child development); U. of Central Oklahoma,
attended 1979-81 (business administration)

CAREER
Real estate broker; hotel properties manager;
state tourism agency official

POLITICAL HIGHLIGHTS
Okla. House, 1990-94; lieutenant governor,
1995-2007

ELECTION RESULTS

2008 GENERAL

Mary Fallin (R)	171,925	65.9%
Steven L. Perry (D)	88,996	34.1%

2008 PRIMARY

Mary Fallin (R)	unopposed

2006 GENERAL

Mary Fallin (R)	108,936	60.4%
David Hunter (D)	67,293	37.3%
Matthew Horton Woodson (I)	4,196	2.3%

Fallin hails from one of the nation's most reliably conservative states, and her politics and her voting record reflect it. She initially sought election to the House with the slogan "Faith, Family, Freedom." Although she defends the practice of seeking funding for specific projects back home, she touts herself as a fiscal conservative and proponent of small government. She is also a traditional social conservative, fiercely opposing abortion and supporting gun owners' rights

Fallin (FAL-in — rhymes with "Allen") is also ambitious. She was a state legislator and Oklahoma's first female lieutenant governor before joining Congress. In early 2009, shortly after she was named communications chairwoman for the conservative Republican Study Committee and co-chairwoman for the Congressional Caucus on Women's Issues, she announced she would run for governor in 2010.

She began the 111th Congress (2009-10) strongly denouncing President Obama and the Democratic majority. When Obama signed an executive order reversing George W. Bush administration policy and allowing more federal funding for embryonic stem cell research, she said it was akin to "ordering taxpayers to foot the bill for research that many, including myself, find morally repugnant." When the House took up a housing bill that included a provision to allow bankruptcy judges to renegotiate homeowner mortgages, she fumed, "Obama said himself we need a bill that does not reward that neighbor down the street who bought a house he could never hope to afford. Unfortunately, this bill does reward that neighbor."

And she likened the new president's $787 billion economic stimulus law to a "big Christmas tree" with gifts for nearly everyone underneath. Yet she fought for Oklahoma's share of the funding after passage of the bill. "No matter what someone's position was on the stimulus…the fact is that it's done, it's law," Fallin told Oklahoma City's Journal Record. "And now our responsibility should be to make sure that it is spent on priorities …that the money is used in efficient ways."

But she has on occasion gone astray of party wishes and her own principle of limited government. When the House took up a bill to grant the Food and Drug Administration expanded power to regulate tobacco, she broke from a majority of her party to support it. She said her vote was influenced by the death of her parents to smoking-related illnesses. Fallin won approval for two earmarks — funding set-asides for local projects — in a water resources bill during the 110th Congress (2007-08). She voted to pass that bill into law over Bush's veto. Fallin initially went against Bush's wishes and voted in fall 2008 against an initial version of a $700 billion measure to rescue the financial services industry. But she voted for a second version that was signed into law, saying it was "a less bitter pill to swallow." She also said she changed her vote because she was increasingly concerned about state employee pension funds.

Fallin sits on the Armed Services Committee, where she can to look out for Tinker Air Force Base in the adjacent 4th District. She raised concerns in early 2009 when the Obama administration proposed cuts to defense spending, and toured military bases throughout the state, including Camp Gruber, the McAlester Army Ammunition Plant and Altus Air Force Base. During a visit to Altus in April, she said, "The unwillingness of this administration to adequately fund the military is especially striking given the record deficits it has racked up in the last three months alone." She also introduced a bill to prohibit spending federal funds to move prisoners from the military detention facility at the U.S. naval base at Guantánamo Bay, Cuba, to Oklahoma.

From her seat on the Transportation and Infrastructure Committee, she plans to seek funding for Oklahoma's highways, railroads and waterways when members rewrite the 2005 surface transportation law. She calls her state a Midwest "crossroads" and has noted that it has a high number of structurally deficient bridges.

She also serves on the Small Business Committee. She won House passage of a bill during the 110th to bolster federally funded women's business centers, though the measure stalled in the Senate.

Fallin has spent the majority of her life in and around the state capital. Her mother was a social worker and her father worked in unemployment security. Her parents were conservative Democrats, and her father was not pleased when young Mary registered as a Republican. Her mother and grandmother later switched their party registrations in order to vote for her.

Fallin got her first taste of politics when her father ran for mayor of Tecumseh — and lost. She helped him campaign the second time, and he won. When he died of heart failure at 56, Fallin's mother was appointed to serve as mayor and later won re-election.

After college, Fallin worked for the Oklahoma Securities Commission and the Department of Tourism before moving to the private sector, taking jobs with an oil company, Marriott hotels and in real estate. She married in 1984 (they divorced in 1998). Two months after launching her first campaign for the state House in 1989, Fallin discovered she was pregnant with her second child. She recalls standing on street corners in the Oklahoma heat that summer, nearly eight months pregnant, holding two signs, one with a campaign slogan and the other reading, "Yes, I am married."

In the state legislature, she drew notice from the staff of Republican Sen. James M. Inhofe of Oklahoma for attacking President Clinton's 1993 health care overhaul plan. At a local debate, an aide to Inhofe took her aside and suggested she run for lieutenant governor. She won the post in 1994 and held it for a dozen years. She had been lieutenant governor for 101 days when Timothy McVeigh, Terry Nichols and Michael Fortier blew up the Oklahoma City federal building.

Fallin had planned to run for re-election as lieutenant governor until seven-term Republican Ernest Istook announced he would run for governor in 2006. She won the party's nomination for his seat in a runoff, then handily defeated Democratic surgeon David Hunter. In 2008, she won re-election with 66 percent of the vote.

KEY VOTES

2008

No Delay consideration of Colombia free-trade agreement

Yes Override Bush veto of federal farm and nutrition programs reauthorization bill

Yes Overhaul surveillance laws and permit dismissal of suits against companies that conducted warrantless wiretapping

No Grant mortgage relief to homeowners and funding for Fannie Mae and Freddie Mac

No Approve initial $700 billion program to stabilize financial markets

Yes Approve final $700 billion program to stabilize financial markets

No Provide $14 billion in loans to automakers

2007

No Increase minimum wage by $2.10 an hour

No Approve $124.2 billion in emergency war spending and set goal for redeployment of troops from Iraq

Yes Reject federal contraceptive assistance to international family planning groups

Yes Override Bush veto of $23.2 billion water projects authorization bill

Yes Implement Peru free-trade agreement

No Approve energy policy overhaul with new fuel economy standards

Yes Clear $473.5 billion omnibus spending bill, including $70 billion for military operations

CQ VOTE STUDIES

	PARTY UNITY		PRESIDENTIAL SUPPORT	
	SUPPORT	OPPOSE	SUPPORT	OPPOSE
2008	95%	5%	67%	33%
2007	95%	5%	83%	17%

INTEREST GROUPS

	AFL-CIO	ADA	CCUS	ACU
2008	13%	15%	94%	92%
2007	8%	5%	85%	100%

OKLAHOMA 5

Most of Oklahoma City; Pottawatomie and Seminole counties

The 5th contains all of downtown Oklahoma City, including the governor's mansion and state Capitol, and is home to several colleges and universities. Oil and gas, along with some agriculture, make up a large chunk of the district's economy. An oil price collapse roughly 20 years ago caused residents to leave the area and forced the city to diversify. A decade of spikes and drops in oil prices have made the energy sector vulnerable.

Local manufacturing has taken hits — Bridgestone/Firestone and General Motors closed plants in 2006 — but job growth exists in the science and technology fields. Dell Computers opened a customer service center in 2004, but prolonged revenue losses may lead to layoffs in the area. The biosciences sector now employs tens of thousands in the region. The 5th shares some of those jobs with the 3rd and 4th districts, as it does with jobs associated with Tinker Air Force Base (in the 4th).

The Ford Center arena, which hosts the NBA's Oklahoma City Thunder, is part of the first phase of a decade of downtown revitalization efforts. Restaurants and apartments add to the vibrant feel of the city, and the Bricktown neighborhood, once filled with abandoned warehouses, is now a staple of the urban nightlife. Local officials hope that infrastructure redevelopment along Interstate 40 will promote commercial and residential growth between downtown areas and the Oklahoma River to the south. And waterfront redevelopment is expected to include condominiums, pedestrian-accessible retail and office space, and the American Indian Cultural Center & Museum.

The GOP dominates the 5th. The towns of Shawnee and Seminole, both home to large Indian populations, and the largely black northeastern portion of Oklahoma City, aren't enough to threaten the GOP's hold. John McCain took 59 percent of the 5th's vote in the 2008 presidential race.

MAJOR INDUSTRY
Oil, technology, bioscience, government, higher education, agriculture

CITIES
Oklahoma City (pt.), 420,387; Edmond, 68,315

NOTABLE
Seminole County is the historic Seminole Nation territory, accepted by the tribes in exchange for their departure from the Florida Territory.

OREGON

Gov. Theodore R. Kulongoski (D)

Pronounced:
koo-long-GOSS-ski
First elected: 2002
Length of term: 4 years
Term expires: 1/11
Salary: $99,600
Phone: (503) 378-3111

Residence: Salem
Born: Nov. 5, 1940; Missouri
Religion: Roman Catholic
Family: Wife, Mary Oberst; three children
Education: U. of Missouri, B.A. 1967
(political science & public administration),
J.D. 1970
Military service: Marine Corps, 1960-63
Career: Lawyer
Political highlights: Ore. House, 1975-79;
Ore. Senate, 1979-81; Democratic nominee
for U.S. Senate, 1980; Democratic nominee
for governor, 1982; Ore. insurance
commissioner, 1987-91; Ore. attorney
general, 1993-97; Ore. Supreme Court, 1997-
2001

Election results:
2006 GENERAL
Theodore R. Kulongoski (D)	699,786	50.7%
Ron Saxton (R)	589,748	42.8%
Mary Starrette (CNSTP)	50,229	3.6%
Joe Keating (GREEN)	20,030	1.5%
Richard Morley (LIBERT)	16,798	1.2%

Secretary of State
Kate Brown (D)

(no lieutenant governor)
Phone: (503) 986-1523

LEGISLATURE

Legislative Assembly: January-
June in odd-numbered years

Senate: 30 members, 4-year terms
2009 ratios: 18 D, 12 R; 19 men,
11 women
Salary: $21,612
Phone: (503) 986-1187

House: 60 members, 2-year terms
2009 ratios: 36 D, 24 R; 46 men,
14 women
Salary: $21,612
Phone: (503) 986-1187

TERM LIMITS

Governor: 2 terms
Senate: No
House: No

URBAN STATISTICS

CITY	POPULATION
Portland	529,121
Eugene	137,893
Salem	136,924
Gresham	90,205

REGISTERED VOTERS

Democrat	43%
Republican	32%
Unaffiliated	20%
Others	4%

POPULATION

2008 population (est.)	3,790,060
2000 population	3,421,399
1990 population	2,842,321
Percent change (1990-2000)	+20.4
Rank among states (2008)	27
Median age	36.3
Born in state	45.3%
Foreign born	8.5%
Violent crime rate	351/100,000
Poverty level	11.6%
Federal workers	29,090
Military	12,984

ELECTIONS

STATE ELECTION OFFICIAL
(503) 986-1518
DEMOCRATIC PARTY
(503) 224-8200
REPUBLICAN PARTY
(503) 587-9233

MISCELLANEOUS

Web: www.oregon.gov
Capital: Salem

U.S. CONGRESS

Senate: 2 Democrats
House: 4 Democrats, 1 Republican

2000 Census Statistics by District

DIST.	2008 VOTE FOR PRESIDENT OBAMA	MCCAIN	WHITE	BLACK	ASIAN	HISP	MEDIAN INCOME	WHITE COLLAR	BLUE COLLAR	SERVICE INDUSTRY	OVER 64	UNDER 18	COLLEGE EDUCATION	RURAL	SQ. MILES
1	61%	36%	81%	1%	5%	9%	$48,464	65%	22%	13%	10%	25%	33%	13%	2,941
2	43	54	86	0	1	9	$35,600	54	29	17	15	26	19	36	69,491
3	71	26	77	5	5	8	$42,063	59	25	16	11	24	25	7	1,021
4	54	43	90	1	2	4	$35,796	55	28	17	15	23	21	31	17,181
5	54	43	84	1	2	10	$44,409	61	25	15	13	26	27	20	5,362
STATE	**57**	**40**	**84**	**2**	**3**	**8**	**$40,916**	**59**	**26**	**15**	**13**	**25**	**25**	**21**	**95,997**
U.S.	**53**	**46**	**69**	**12**	**4**	**13**	**$41,994**	**60**	**25**	**15**	**12**	**26**	**24**	**21**	**3,537,438**

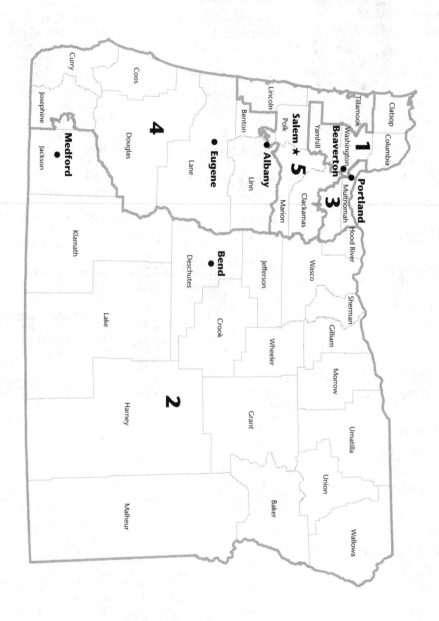

Sen. Ron Wyden (D)

Elected January 1996; 2nd full term

Wyden is a workhorse who likes to operate collaboratively and in almost nonpartisan fashion, a style that enabled him to settle into political security long before his party came to dominate Oregon politics. The son of a librarian, he approaches issues as a student, mastering the complexities of health care and technology policy; he can hold forth expansively on those issues as well as on almost any other subject that stirs his interest.

But Wyden professes no interest in a leadership post or advancement on the national stage. Referring to the strong desire among many of his colleagues to eventually advance to the White House, he once said, "I'll be the Senate's designated driver, so that if everybody's out running and folks get a little intoxicated, I can take them home."

Such a deliberate approach has enabled Wyden — who chairs no full Senate committee and is only fifth in seniority among Democrats on the Finance Committee's Health Care Subcommittee — to be at the center of debates over health care. He developed an expertise on the subject while serving in the House, where he had a seat on the Energy and Commerce Committee, and carried over his interest to the Senate. Wyden was an advocate of expanding Medicare to cover seniors' prescription drug costs well before the 2003 law was passed.

In recent years Wyden has lined up cosponsors behind a health insurance overhaul bill he touts as the first truly bipartisan "universal coverage" measure in Senate history. Utah Republican Robert F. Bennett is his chief ally on the bill, which the two say is the product of collaboration with both labor and business leaders. The bill would upend the nation's existing system of employer-based health insurance, providing subsidies for Americans to buy coverage directly from private insurers instead, while eventually reducing the deficit.

The bill is not the first time Wyden has cultivated allies from both ends of the political spectrum. For years, he has teamed with conservative Republican Charles E. Grassley of Iowa to try to force senators who place secret "holds" that block legislation to identify themselves. A member of the Budget Committee, he also has worked with that panel's top Republican, New Hampshire's Judd Gregg, on a proposal that would mirror the landmark 1986 tax code overhaul, with lower marginal rates and fewer deductions and credits.

Wyden helped negotiate a compromise version of President George W. Bush's so-called Healthy Forests legislation in 2003 to combat wildfires. The next year, Wyden worked with former Republican George Allen of Virginia to extend a ban on state taxation of Internet access through October 2007. Congress extended the ban for seven more years that month.

Wyden is a foe of the tobacco industry, garnering wide TV coverage in 1994 when, as a House member, he asked a panel of tobacco executive witnesses whether they considered tobacco addictive. Under oath, they all denied that it is. He repeated the question in 1998 during Senate Commerce hearings, and four of the five CEOs recanted.

There is one health-related issue unique to Oregon: It is the only state in the country with a law permitting physician-assisted suicide. When Republicans were in the majority, Wyden devoted much time and energy to defending the law, scouring legislation to ensure no one slipped in provisions that would gut it.

Oregon is also the only state in the nation to conduct all of its elections by mail. Wyden successfully protected the mail-ballot system from changes when a federal law overhauling voting procedures was enacted at the end

CAPITOL OFFICE
224-5244
wyden.senate.gov
223 Dirksen Bldg. 20510-3703; fax 228-2717

COMMITTEES
Budget
Energy & Natural Resources
(Public Lands & Forests - chairman)
Finance
(International Trade, Customs & Global
Competitiveness - chairman)
Judiciary
Select Intelligence
Special Aging

RESIDENCE
Portland

BORN
May 3, 1949; Wichita, Kan.

RELIGION
Jewish

FAMILY
Wife, Nancy Bass-Wyden; four children

EDUCATION
U. of California, Santa Barbara, attended 1967-69;
Stanford U., A.B. 1971 (political science);
U. of Oregon, J.D. 1974

CAREER
Senior citizen advocacy group state director;
lawyer; professor

POLITICAL HIGHLIGHTS
U.S. House, 1981-96

ELECTION RESULTS

2004 GENERAL

Ron Wyden (D)	1,128,728	63.4%
Al King (R)	565,254	31.8%
Teresa Keane (I)	43,053	2.4%
Dan Fitzgerald (LIBERT)	29,582	1.7%

2004 PRIMARY

Ron Wyden (D)	unopposed

PREVIOUS WINNING PERCENTAGES
1998 (61%); 1996 Special Election (48%); 1994
House Election (73%); 1992 House Election (77%);
1990 House Election (81%); 1988 House Election
(99%); 1986 House Election (86%); 1984 House
Election (72%); 1982 House Election (78%); 1980
House Election (72%)

of 2002. He introduced an unsuccessful bill in 2007 to create an $18 million grant program to help other states transition to a vote-by-mail system.

Oregon's vast forests and many parks are also of high interest to Wyden as chairman of the Energy and Natural Resources Committee's Public Lands and Forests Subcommittee. After a long battle with Republicans, he and the rest of his state's congressional delegation scored a significant victory in 2009 when their measure protecting wilderness around Mount Hood and other areas of the state was signed into law.

Logging's decline in the Pacific Northwest has damaged the economy of many of Oregon's rural communities, and Wyden has successfully sought more federal funding for them as compensation. In 2008, he proposed a compromise between environmentalists and timber companies to allow expanded logging of Oregon's overgrown forests. Wyden's plan would allow more trees to be cut, but it would preserve "old growth" trees and forbid clear-cutting.

Wyden chairs Finance's Subcommittee on International Trade, Customs and Global Competitiveness. He has been a strong advocate of using tax credit bonds — with which the federal government pays a tax credit to the bondholder in lieu of the issuer paying interest — to finance the nation's infrastructure needs.

From his seat on the Judiciary Committee, he has worked on boosting information technology funding for the FBI. He also has sought to protect consumers, advocating a five-star rating system for credit cards.

Wyden has worked for greater openness as a member of the Select Intelligence panel, pushing to declassify the amount of spending on spy programs. He also led the charge in 2003 against the Bush administration's short-lived Total Information Awareness program, a domestic intelligence-gathering effort that he said would lead to spying on law-abiding citizens. "You go on this committee because you want to handle extraordinarily important questions that are about our Constitution and our freedoms and are particularly trying, in very difficult times," he told The Oregonian in April 2009. "You try to strike the right balance between collective security and individual liberty. I really do compare it to a constitutional teeter-totter."

Born in Wichita, Kan., Wyden steadily moved west as his father's journalism career advanced. He attended college on a basketball scholarship but abandoned his dream of playing professionally and instead went to law school. After receiving his bachelor's degree from Stanford in 1971, he followed a girlfriend to Oregon and earned a law degree at University of Oregon in 1974. "I was smitten with the state immediately," he recalled. "Independent people, open, seemed very receptive to new ideas, fresh thinking, just seemed like a perfect fit."

Wyden was Oregon executive director for the Gray Panthers, an organization promoting senior citizens' interests, when he first ran for the House in 1980. (He now attends to their needs as a member of the Special Aging panel.) He ousted Democratic Rep. Robert B. Duncan in the primary and won with 72 percent in November of that year in a Democratic Portland-based district.

When Republican Sen. Bob Packwood resigned in disgrace in 1995 after a sexual-harassment controversy, Wyden jumped into the special-election race. He edged out fellow Democratic Rep. Peter A. DeFazio in the primary, then narrowly defeated conservative Republican Gordon H. Smith by portraying himself as a reasonable-minded alternative. Smith subsequently won election to Oregon's other Senate seat and became an extremely close ally of Wyden's before his 2008 defeat. Wyden won two re-elections with ease and is considered a shoo-in in 2010.

In 2005, Wyden married Nancy Bass, whose family owns the voluminous Strand bookstore in New York City. Two years later, the couple had twins. Wyden also has two children from a previous marriage.

KEY VOTES

2008
Yes Prohibit discrimination based on genetic information
Yes Reauthorize farm and nutrition programs for five years
Yes Limit debate on "cap and trade" system for greenhouse gas emissions
Yes Allow lawsuits against companies that participated in warrantless wiretapping
Yes Limit debate on a bill to block a scheduled cut in Medicare payments to doctors
Yes Grant mortgage relief to homeowners and funding for Fannie Mae and Freddie Mac
Yes Approve a nuclear cooperation agreement with India
No Approve final $700 billion program to stabilize financial markets
+ Allow consideration of a $14 billion auto industry loan package

2007
Yes Increase minimum wage by $2.10 an hour
Yes Limit debate on a comprehensive immigration bill
Yes Overhaul congressional lobbying and ethics rules for members and their staffs
Yes Limit debate on considering a bill to add House seats for the District of Columbia and Utah
Yes Limit debate on restoring habeas corpus rights to detainees
Yes Mandate minimum breaks for troops between deployments to Iraq or Afghanistan
Yes Override Bush veto of $23.2 billion water projects authorization bill
No Confirm Michael B. Mukasey as attorney general
Yes Limit debate on an energy policy overhaul containing $21.8 billion in tax incentives and reduced oil and gas subsidies

CQ VOTE STUDIES

	PARTY UNITY		PRESIDENTIAL SUPPORT	
	SUPPORT	OPPOSE	SUPPORT	OPPOSE
2008	97%	3%	28%	72%
2007	95%	5%	39%	61%
2006	94%	6%	51%	49%
2005	94%	6%	26%	74%
2004	93%	7%	62%	38%
2003	93%	7%	47%	53%
2002	87%	13%	74%	26%
2001	90%	10%	64%	36%
2000	97%	3%	95%	5%
1999	91%	9%	91%	9%

INTEREST GROUPS

	AFL-CIO	ADA	CCUS	ACU
2008	100%	95%	50%	8%
2007	94%	95%	55%	4%
2006	100%	100%	42%	8%
2005	79%	95%	33%	4%
2004	100%	100%	59%	4%
2003	92%	90%	43%	15%
2002	85%	85%	60%	15%
2001	100%	95%	43%	8%
2000	63%	90%	60%	8%
1999	78%	100%	59%	4%

Sen. Jeff Merkley (D)

CAPITOL OFFICE
224-3753
merkley.senate.gov
107 Russell Bldg. 20510; fax 228-3997

COMMITTEES
Banking, Housing & Urban Affairs
Budget
Environment & Public Works
Health, Education, Labor & Pensions

RESIDENCE
Portland

BORN
Oct. 24, 1956; Eugene, Ore.

RELIGION
Lutheran

FAMILY
Wife, Mary Sorteberg

EDUCATION
Stanford U., B.A. 1979 (international relations);
Princeton U., M.P.A. 1982

CAREER
Nonprofit executive; computer repair company
owner; Congressional Budget Office analyst

POLITICAL HIGHLIGHTS
Ore. House, 1999-2009 (minority leader, 2003-07;
Speaker, 2007-09)

ELECTION RESULTS

2008 GENERAL

Jeff Merkley (D)	864,392	48.9%
Gordon H. Smith (R)	805,159	45.6%
David Brownlow (CNSTP)	92,565	5.2%

2008 PRIMARY

Jeff Merkley (D)	246,482	44.8%
Steve Novick (D)	230,889	42.0%
Candy Neville (D)	38,367	7.0%
Roger S. Obrist (D)	12,647	2.3%
Pavel Goberman (D)	12,056	2.2%
David Loera (D)	6,127	1.1%

Elected 2008; 1st term

As a young intern in the 1970s, Merkley got an insider's look at how Congress operated from a legendary GOP senator whose seat he now occupies: Mark O. Hatfield. But Merkley makes clear he doesn't share the centrist views of his former boss or of the like-minded Republican he ousted in the 2008 election, Gordon H. Smith. He sees himself as more in line with President Obama; both developed a devotion to Democratic causes while working as community activists and advocates for affordable housing.

Merkley said Democrats must not miss their chance to move on liberal priorities. "There are times when you need to move boldly," he said in early 2009. "That's exactly where our nation is at. It's not a time to tinker with the system. We have major problems." But as a former Congressional Budget Office (CBO) analyst who focused on defense issues, he also can be a cautious wonk. "It's valuable to lay out policy options, think through the options and think about how they reverberate in complex ways," he said.

Former Oregon state Rep. Deborah Kafoury, who served with Merkley in the state House, told The Oregonian in 2008 that Merkley calls to mind some of the intense students she knew in college. "We used to call them 'heavy, deep and real,' " she said.

Merkley supported Obama's early initiatives, and in many areas suggested additional concerns or new approaches. A member of the Budget and Environment and Public Works committees, he supported the 2009 economic stimulus law after pushing successfully for several energy-related provisions, including infrastructure improvements to modernize the nation's electricity grid and a program to upgrade schools and other public facilities to make them more energy efficient.

He hailed the president's 2010 budget blueprint, noting in particular its proposal for a program to cap greenhouse gas emissions and create a market-based industry trading program. And in April 2009, he applauded the Environmental Protection Agency's finding that greenhouse gases contribute to air pollution — a reversal of the George W. Bush administration's pronouncement. Merkley has called for a 25 percent renewable-energy requirement for utilities by 2025, and wants more emphasis on conservation and solar energy as alternatives to nuclear power.

He also sits on the Health, Education, Labor and Pensions Committee. He favored a bill in 2009 that aimed to make it easier for employees to unionize. "When workers are able to band together to improve their workplaces and wages, we strengthen the middle class," he said.

In a signal that he's willing to seek deals, he backed a bipartisan proposal by his state's senior senator, Democrat Ron Wyden, to convert employer-provided health benefits into higher wages to pay for regulated private health care plans. "We should be open to common-sense ideas," he said. From his seat on the Banking, Housing and Urban Affairs Committee, he targets ways to help families and workers during the economic downturn. He supported a bill introduced by Chairman Christopher J. Dodd of Connecticut in early 2009 to set new regulations on the credit card industry and rein in so-called predatory practices. "At a time of economic turmoil, workers shouldn't be worried they are carrying a fiscal time bomb in their wallet," he said.

As a candidate in 2008, he spoke out against the $700 billion law aimed at rescuing the financial services industry, citing a lack of adequate oversight and accountability provisions. After taking office, he wrote Treasury Secretary Timothy F. Geithner urging him to press other nations to contribute aid to the financial markets since foreign banks were receiving rescue funds, and to help recover bonuses paid employees by firms who received rescue funds. "When U.S. taxpayer money is flowing to foreign institutions, the American people have a right to expect countries whose institutions benefit to share the burden," he said.

Despite his ties to Obama, Merkley has indicated he is willing to break ranks with his party's leadership. On some issues, he tilts further to the left than Obama. For example, he has called for ending an electronic surveillance overhaul that expanded the use of wiretapping without warrants. He takes a liberal stand on abortion rights, but leans to the center in defending gun ownership rights.

Drawing on his expertise on military issues, he proposed a plan to end U.S. involvement in the Iraq War that would redeploy all combat troops within a year, eliminate permanent U.S. military bases in Iraq and remove all American contractors from the country, replacing them with Iraqi contractors. He applauded Obama's desire to bring home U.S. forces, but questioned the president's February 2009 plan for a 18-month schedule to draw down forces and leave in place up to 50,000 troops. He said "the remaining force would still be too great."

Merkley spent part of his youth in rural southwestern Oregon, where his father worked in a wood mill. But troubles in the timber industry prompted the family to move to Portland, where his father worked as an equipment mechanic and Merkley attended high school. He still lives in a three-bedroom ranch-style house in a working-class neighborhood in East Portland, near his boyhood home.

He cites his father's nightly dinner table talks as his inspiration to enter public service. "He would come home from work and watch the news and provide a commentary about what we could do to make things better," he said.

In the 1980s, Merkley worked as a presidential fellow at the Pentagon. Then, as a CBO analyst, he wrote reports on weapons systems — including his 1988 opus, "The B-1B Bomber and Options for Enhancements."

While in Washington, Merkley met his future wife, Mary Sorteberg, who was working for the Lutheran Volunteer Corps at a homeless shelter, N Street Village. Merkley also bought a house in the city, which he still owns and which serves as the Lutheran group's headquarters. After returning to Oregon, he served as director of Portland's Habitat for Humanity and became executive director of the World Affairs Council, an education group focused on international politics and culture.

He began his five terms as a state legislator in 1999 and moved up the ladder rapidly. As Speaker from 2007 to 2009, he won enactment of a cap on consumer loan interest rates, a ban on junk food in schools and new civil contracts, called domestic partnerships, to lock in legal rights for same-sex couples.

In 2008, Merkley gave up a safe seat as speaker to take on Smith, while potential rivals like Reps. Peter A. DeFazio and Earl Blumenauer took a pass. His campaign got off to a rough start; he survived an accident when a Toyota Prius he was riding in rolled over on an icy highway.

He took a $250,000 mortgage out on his Washington house (he owns four other properties in the Portland area) to finance his campaign and edged out Steve Novick, a Portland lawyer and political consultant, in the primary. In the general election, Merkley criticized the moderate Smith for neutralizing the liberal votes of Wyden. He also attacked Smith for supporting Bush's economic policies and for coming late to the campaign to end the Iraq War.

Smith raised $9.2 million for his campaign, about a third more than Merkley's $6.4 million, but the challenger got help from an ad blitz by the Democratic Senatorial Campaign Committee. Merkley won 49 percent of the vote, edging Smith by 3 percentage points.

Rep. David Wu (D)

Elected 1998; 6th term

CAPITOL OFFICE
225-0855
www.house.gov/wu
2338 Rayburn Bldg. 20515-3701; fax 225-9497

COMMITTEES
Education & Labor
Science & Technology
(Technology & Innovation - chairman)

RESIDENCE
Portland

BORN
April 8, 1955; Hsinchu, Taiwan

RELIGION
Presbyterian

FAMILY
Wife, Michelle Wu; two children

EDUCATION
Stanford U., B.S. 1977; Harvard Medical School,
attended 1978; Yale U., J.D. 1982

CAREER
Lawyer

POLITICAL HIGHLIGHTS
No previous office

ELECTION RESULTS

2008 GENERAL

David Wu (D)	237,567	71.5%
Joel Haugen (I)	58,279	17.5%
Scott Semrau (CNSTP)	14,172	4.3%
H. Joe Tabor (LIBERT)	10,992	3.3%
Chris Henry (PACGRN)	7,128	2.1%
write-ins	4,110	1.2%

2008 PRIMARY

David Wu (D)	91,466	77.9%
Will Hobbs (D)	19,659	16.7%
Mark Welyczko (D)	5,982	5.1%

2006 GENERAL

David Wu (D)	169,409	62.8%
Derrick Kitts (R)	90,904	33.7%
Drake Davis (LIBERT)	4,497	1.7%
Dean Wolf (CNSTP)	4,370	1.6%

PREVIOUS WINNING PERCENTAGES
2004 (58%); 2002 (63%); 2000 (58%); 1998 (50%)

The son of Chinese scientists who immigrated to the United States, Wu's priorities on Capitol Hill reflect his parents' struggles and triumphs. He is an advocate of scientific research, a strong believer in the power of education to improve lives, and a defender of human rights and free speech.

Wu — the first person of full Chinese ancestry to serve in Congress — works quietly behind the scenes to craft legislation to meet his goals. And while he describes his politics as fiscally conservative and socially liberal, he almost always sides with Democratic leaders on votes that split the parties.

As chairman of the Science and Technology panel on Technology and Innovation, Wu in early 2009 commended President Obama for indicating he would protect scientific investigations across the federal government from political influences — a strong allegation against the George W. Bush administration and its consideration of the influences of climate change. "We now have a president who believes that, like oil and water, good science and political influence do not mix," Wu said.

Wu is a strong proponent of scientific research and education, following in his parents' footsteps; his father is a metallurgist and his mother is a chemical engineer. He backed provisions in the economic stimulus law, signed in February 2009, to provide funding for health information technology and training. He also obtained funding in the catchall spending bill for fiscal 2009 for local projects, including millions for science research and education.

From his seat on the Education and Labor Committee during the 110th Congress (2007-08), he played a role in the reauthorization of a law funding higher education programs in 2008. It includes a provision by Wu aimed at aiding institutions serving Asian-American populations. He continues to advocate for education, backing provisions for funding in the stimulus law for local schools but lamenting that others for higher education were eliminated.

Wu also applauded Obama's economic stimulus law in 2009 for providing money to upgrade schools, highways and bridges, and to develop renewable-energy technology.

Wu's rare splits from his party included his vote initially opposing 2008 legislation granting the Bush administration authority to aid ailing financial institutions. Under intense pressure from party leaders who feared the bill's failure would cause credit markets to seize up, Wu voted for a slightly revised version of the $700 billion bill that was signed into law. He said the first bill was considered too hastily but "the risk of doing nothing" was "too great."

In 2003, Wu cast the last vote during the nearly three-hour roll call in which the House passed the final version of the GOP-drafted bill to add a prescription drug benefit to Medicare. Only after Republican leaders had engineered a victory by switching four GOP votes did Wu cast his ballot in favor of the measure. He was one of just 16 Democrats to vote for the bill. Yet in early 2007, he voted with his entire party in favor of a measure requiring the federal government to negotiate with drug companies on the prices of drugs covered under Medicare.

Wu has long kept an eye on U.S. relations with China, including its record on human rights. He supported a GOP-sponsored resolution during the 109th Congress (2005-06) that sanctioned countries that sell arms or defense-related technology to China. In 2000, he voted against a law granting trade preferences to China, despite intense pressure from the Oregon business community to vote for it. Wu's decision so angered the athletic shoe giant Nike Inc., which is based in Wu's district, that it gave money to his opponent that year.

Domestically, Wu fights government intrusions on civil liberties, a stance he attributes to his parents' experience in China. He voted against 2001's Patriot Act anti-terrorism legislation, as well as against warrantless wiretapping in 2006 and 2008.

Wu had a spate of bad publicity during the 109th and 110th Congresses. He generated some unwelcome headlines when he intervened with the U.S. Bureau of Prisons in the case of an imprisoned Portland executive, Andrew Wiederhorn, whom he called a "friend and constituent." Wiederhorn, who had donated thousands of dollars to Wu's campaign, had pleaded guilty to taking part in a scheme to conceal massive investment losses from clients and to filing a false tax return.

In 2007, talk-radio host Rush Limbaugh criticized Wu for comparing the Bush administration to "Star Trek" characters. Wu opposed a troop increase in Iraq and referred to "Rise of the Vulcans," a book about the influence of neoconservatives on Bush's war policy.

Wu's parents' early years were shaped by war. They met after his father fled his home near Shanghai following the Japanese invasion. The couple moved to Taiwan to seek work, but the Chinese civil war that followed prevented them from returning to the mainland. His father then left Taiwan, six years before the rest of the family, to study in America.

Wu, who was born in Hsinchu, Taiwan, was 6 when he and his sisters and mother arrived in the United States. The family settled in Latham, N.Y., where his father was working, and two years later moved to Southern California.

Wu attended Stanford University for his undergraduate studies and went on to Harvard University for medical school, where he roomed with future GOP Senate Majority Leader Bill Frist of Tennessee. But deciding medicine wasn't for him, he went to Yale University to earn a law degree.

After law school, he worked for a year as a clerk for a federal judge in Portland, then worked briefly with a law firm in Palo Alto, Calif., before working on Gary Hart's 1984 presidential campaign. After Hart was defeated in the primaries, Wu worked to support the Democratic nominee, Walter Mondale, in Portland. He stayed in Portland after the election, working for a law firm for four years before starting his own firm, specializing in intellectual property and technology law.

Wu made a run for the U.S. House when Democrat Elizabeth Furse announced her retirement in 1998. He edged past Washington County Commission Chairwoman Linda Peters in the primary. In the general election, he won a 3-percentage-point victory over public relations consultant Molly Bordonaro. He's won re-election with ease since then.

KEY VOTES

2008

Yes	Delay consideration of Colombia free-trade agreement
Yes	Override Bush veto of federal farm and nutrition programs reauthorization bill
No	Overhaul surveillance laws and permit dismissal of suits against companies that conducted warrantless wiretapping
Yes	Grant mortgage relief to homeowners and funding for Fannie Mae and Freddie Mac
No	Approve initial $700 billion program to stabilize financial markets
Yes	Approve final $700 billion program to stabilize financial markets
Yes	Provide $14 billion in loans to automakers

2007

Yes	Increase minimum wage by $2.10 an hour
Yes	Approve $124.2 billion in emergency war spending and set goal for redeployment of troops from Iraq
No	Reject federal contraceptive assistance to international family planning groups
Yes	Override Bush veto of $23.2 billion water projects authorization bill
No	Implement Peru free-trade agreement
Yes	Approve energy policy overhaul with new fuel economy standards
No	Clear $473.5 billion omnibus spending bill, including $70 billion for military operations

CQ VOTE STUDIES

	PARTY UNITY		PRESIDENTIAL SUPPORT	
	SUPPORT	OPPOSE	SUPPORT	OPPOSE
2008	97%	3%	13%	87%
2007	96%	4%	3%	97%
2006	92%	8%	23%	77%
2005	92%	8%	29%	71%
2004	90%	10%	38%	62%

INTEREST GROUPS

	AFL-CIO	ADA	CCUS	ACU
2008	100%	90%	50%	4%
2007	96%	100%	50%	0%
2006	100%	90%	33%	12%
2005	93%	100%	50%	8%
2004	87%	90%	55%	12%

OREGON 1

Western Portland and suburbs; Beaverton

Nestled on the western bank of the Willamette River, the 1st combines three distinct parts: western Portland suburbs; a northern section that follows the Columbia River to the Pacific Ocean and relies on traditional outdoor industries; and a southern branch that takes in all of Yamhill County and its part of the Willamette Valley wine region. Although the area west of Portland is still referred to as the "Silicon Forest," the high-tech economy has been wilting for years, and 2008 brought widespread layoffs and closures at several local technology firms.

Washington County, which accounts for 65 percent of the district's population, has a highly educated workforce. The economic engine of the 1st for two decades, the county is facing budget shortfalls, falling housing prices and rising unemployment. The populations of Hillsboro, Beaverton and the western suburbs exploded after 1990. Aided by a light-rail line that reaches Hillsboro, towns that were once bedroom communities turned into satellite cities with their own commuter streams.

East of Washington County, the 1st's portion of Portland includes the

Pearl District neighborhood, where old warehouses were turned into retail shops, art galleries, offices and condos, and new development has sprung up. The southern edge of the Pearl District is Burnside Street, home to the famous Powell's City of Books.

Outside the Portland metro area, the 1st struggles to keep traditional logging and fishing industries intact despite declining forestry revenue and dwindling salmon stocks. State officials hope to transition the workforce in both fields to emerging industries in electronics and agriculture. International trade is a hot issue for the number of large businesses.

Democrats do well in Multnomah, Clatsop and Columbia counties, while the GOP has a small edge in Yamhill and races in Washington County are close. Democrat Barack Obama won the 1st with 61 percent of the vote.

MAJOR INDUSTRY
Electronics, computer manufacturing, wine production, nurseries

CITIES
Beaverton, 76,129; Portland (pt.), 74,097; Hillsboro, 70,186; Aloha (unincorporated), 41,741; Tigard, 41,223

NOTABLE
Nike's headquarters are in Beaverton.

Rep. Greg Walden (R)

Elected 1998; 6th term

CAPITOL OFFICE
225-6730
www.walden.house.gov
2352 Rayburn Bldg. 20515-3702; fax 225-5774

COMMITTEES
Energy & Commerce

RESIDENCE
Hood River

BORN
Jan. 10, 1957; The Dalles, Ore.

RELIGION
Episcopalian

FAMILY
Wife, Mylene Walden; two children
(one deceased)

EDUCATION
U. of Alaska, attended 1974-75; U. of Oregon,
B.S. 1981 (journalism)

CAREER
Radio station owner; congressional aide

POLITICAL HIGHLIGHTS
Ore. House, 1989-95 (majority leader, 1991-93);
Ore. Senate, 1995-97 (assistant majority leader,
1995-97)

ELECTION RESULTS

2008 GENERAL

Greg Walden (R)	236,560	69.5%
Noah Lemas (D)	87,649	25.8%
Tristin Mock (PACGRN)	9,668	2.8%
Richard D. Hake (CNSTP)	5,817	1.7%

2008 PRIMARY

Greg Walden (R)	83,087	99.1%

2006 GENERAL

Greg Walden (R)	181,529	66.8%
Carol Voisin (D)	82,484	30.4%
Jack Alan Brown (CNSTP)	7,193	2.6%

PREVIOUS WINNING PERCENTAGES
2004 (72%); 2002 (72%); 2000 (74%); 1998 (61%)

The only Republican in Oregon's delegation, Walden's low-key, consensus-seeking approach helps him make some headway on his priorities, though he admits it's harder with Democrats in charge. He does not vote a straight GOP line, but he is loyal enough to have gained prominence in his party. In addition to his seat on the powerful Energy and Commerce Committee, he is deputy chairman of the National Republican Congressional Committee (NRCC), the party's fundraising arm for elections, albeit a tough job as the party must recover from bruising losses in the last two election cycles.

His district includes at least part of 10 national forests and shares his constituents' dislike of federal intrusion into land use and environmental management, but aims for bipartisan partnerships to seek solutions for limiting wildfires and helping rural counties hurt by federal cutbacks in logging.

A member of the Energy and Environment Subcommittee of Energy and Commerce, Walden said he supports a comprehensive energy plan, but opposes proposals for a cap on greenhouse gas emissions matched with a market-based industry trading program. And like many in his party, he supports drilling for gas and oil off the nation's coasts.

Walden was one of just 38 Republicans to join the majority of Democrats to pass a land conservation bill in early 2009 designating millions of acres in nine states for preservation. Walden had helped ensure the measure protects a vast swath in the Mount Hood National Forest. He and Oregon Democrat Earl Blumenauer, who launched efforts to protect the area during the 109th Congress (2005-06), backpacked around Mount Hood — covering 41 miles, climbing and descending 9,000 feet in four days and three nights.

At the ceremony when President Obama signed the bill into law, Walden handed the president a letter urging him to allow more timber to be cut in national forests to prevent future forest fires. Walden believes speeding up forest management action in his district would curb high unemployment rates and help the health of the current forest. That issue was at the heart of why he favored a 2008 law to help the ailing financial services industry; the measure included an extension to the program that pays rural counties hurt by federal logging cutbacks.

Walden won enactment in 2003 of a Healthy Forests law that reversed decades of environmental policy and authorized logging and other steps to thin forests on public lands to reduce the threat of wildfires. The measure had been stymied for years by opposition from environmentalists and some Democrats. But Walden teamed with Oregon's senior senator, Democrat Ron Wyden, and helped address bug infestations and other concerns.

He was not as successful with another forestry bill to accelerate salvage logging and cleanup of federal lands hit by wildfires, hurricanes and natural disasters. The House passed the bill during the 109th, but it died in the Senate.

Walden continues to push Congress to pass legislation to restore a 2000 law that provided a formula for so-called timber or county payments, which the government makes to compensate rural counties that encompass U.S. Forest Service and Bureau of Land Management lands. The payments are to compensate the counties for property tax money they don't collect for government-owned land. Walden in the past has paired with Oregon Democrat Peter A. DeFazio in the cause, but in the 110th Congress (2007-08), they disagreed on how to pay for it.

From his seat on the Energy Committee's panel on Communications, Technology and the Internet, Walden opposed the 2009 economic stimulus law, because he believed it directed a larger portion of funding for Internet build-out in suburban and urban areas than for rural areas.

Walden also serves as ranking member of the committee's Oversight and Investigations panel. He gained national media attention in February 2009 during a committee hearing on the recall of contaminated peanut products. He held up a jar filled with recalled peanut products and wrapped in crime scene tape and asked Stewart Parnell, owner of Peanut Corp. of America, if he would be willing to eat the food.

He is an advocate for press freedoms. He earned a degree in journalism from the University of Oregon and worked at his father's radio station in Hood River as both a disc jockey and a talk show host. He and his wife later bought the business, and their company, Columbia Gorge Broadcasters Inc., operated five radio stations. In October 2007, he backed a bill to protect journalists from having to disclose their confidential sources.

He opposes gun control laws, but he has adopted a middle-ground position on abortion. He opposes federal funding for abortions and voted to outlaw a procedure its opponents call "partial birth" abortion. But he doesn't support a reversal of the Supreme Court's *Roe v. Wade* decision establishing a woman's right to an abortion, saying the decision of whether to have an abortion should be left to the individual. He said his views on the issue were shaped when he and his wife considered but rejected aborting a fetus diagnosed with a congenital heart defect. The baby boy was born prematurely and died.

His judgment was called into question in the 110th over allegations of false accounting by a former treasurer of the NRCC during Walden's tenure as head of its audit committee. NRCC officials said hundreds of thousands of dollars in unauthorized wire transfers were sent to committees and accounts controlled by the former official, who was fired in January 2008. Walden said he had studied the audits and they seemed authentic. But state Democrats said the phony accounting scheme happened because of Walden's lax oversight.

Walden was raised on an 80-acre cherry orchard property east of Portland. His father served in the Oregon legislature and his mother volunteered for the Red Cross. He worked as an aide to Oregon GOP Rep. Denny Smith for about five years in the 1980s. He then served eight years in the legislature, including three as House majority leader and two as assistant Senate majority leader.

When GOP Rep. Bob Smith decided to retire in 1998, Walden easily bested Democrat Kevin M. Campbell, a former county judge. His closest race since was in 2006, when he took 67 percent of the vote to defeat Democrat Carol Voisin, a college instructor. Democratic Gov. Theodore R. Kulongoski is term-limited, and in early 2009, Walden considered a 2010 run for governor.

KEY VOTES

2008
No   Delay consideration of Colombia free-trade agreement
Yes   Override Bush veto of federal farm and nutrition programs reauthorization bill
Yes   Overhaul surveillance laws and permit dismissal of suits against companies that conducted warrantless wiretapping
No   Grant mortgage relief to homeowners and funding for Fannie Mae and Freddie Mac
Yes   Approve initial $700 billion program to stabilize financial markets
Yes   Approve final $700 billion program to stabilize financial markets
No   Provide $14 billion in loans to automakers

2007
Yes   Increase minimum wage by $2.10 an hour
No   Approve $124.2 billion in emergency war spending and set goal for redeployment of troops from Iraq
No   Reject federal contraceptive assistance to international family planning groups
Yes   Override Bush veto of $23.2 billion water projects authorization bill
Yes   Implement Peru free-trade agreement
Yes   Approve energy policy overhaul with new fuel economy standards
Yes   Clear $473.5 billion omnibus spending bill, including $70 billion for military operations

CQ VOTE STUDIES

	PARTY UNITY		PRESIDENTIAL SUPPORT	
	SUPPORT	OPPOSE	SUPPORT	OPPOSE
2008	93%	7%	63%	37%
2007	82%	18%	62%	38%
2006	93%	7%	87%	13%
2005	92%	8%	80%	20%
2004	93%	7%	82%	18%

INTEREST GROUPS

	AFL-CIO	ADA	CCUS	ACU
2008	20%	30%	89%	75%
2007	42%	30%	90%	68%
2006	31%	15%	100%	80%
2005	20%	20%	93%	76%
2004	27%	15%	100%	80%

OREGON 2
East and southwest – Medford, Bend

The rural and sometimes rugged 2nd is Oregon's most reliably Republican district. It encompasses the eastern two-thirds of the state, taking in all of 19 counties and part of one other, and borders Washington, Idaho, Nevada and California. The federal government owns most of the land, which has fertile fields, towering mountains and protected forests.

The strength of the local agriculture industry lies in its diversity. Ranchers in the district's southeast raise livestock, while farmers in the north harvest more wheat than anywhere else in Oregon. From the district's northwest near Mount Hood south to the Rogue River Valley is a rich fruit belt: Almost all of the state's pears are grown either in Jackson County or Hood River County, which leads the nation in pear production. Cherries and apples are grown here as well, and Central Oregon hosts breweries. A downturn in the timber and fishing industries drove people away from Eastern Oregon in the 1980s, but an influx of retirees and a growing tourism industry attracted newcomers.

In Deschutes County in Central Oregon, Bend's skyrocketing cost of living paralleled recent growth, but a housing market collapse has hurt the local economy. Adjacent to Deschutes, Crook County has suffered spiking unemployment rates as the regional home construction sector diminished. To the southwest, health care facilities in Medford, in Jackson County, provide jobs. Southeast of Medford is Ashland, which has hosted the Oregon Shakespeare Festival since 1935. Harney County farther east is vast, arid and rural. The county is losing population and suffers rising unemployment rates, but there may be economic growth with construction of wind-energy facilities, and wind turbines already spin energy along the Columbia River Gorge on the 2nd's northern border.

An independent streak, the legacy of a farming and ranching, remains throughout the 2nd, and growing pockets of Democrats in Bend and Ashland are still too few to swing the district. John McCain took 54 percent of the 2008 presidential vote here, the only Oregon district he won.

MAJOR INDUSTRY
Agriculture, forestry, tourism

CITIES
Medford, 63,154; Bend, 52,029; Grants Pass, 23,003

NOTABLE
Crater Lake is the deepest lake in the United States.

Rep. Earl Blumenauer (D)

Elected May 1996; 7th full term

CAPITOL OFFICE
225-4811
blumenauer.house.gov
2267 Rayburn Bldg. 20515; fax 225-8941

COMMITTEES
Budget
Select Energy Independence & Global Warming
Ways & Means

RESIDENCE
Portland

BORN
Aug. 16, 1948; Portland, Ore.

RELIGION
Unspecified

FAMILY
Wife, Margaret Kirkpatrick; two children,
two stepchildren

EDUCATION
Lewis and Clark College, B.A. 1970
(political science), J.D. 1976

CAREER
Public official

POLITICAL HIGHLIGHTS
Ore. House, 1973-77; Multnomah County
Commission, 1978-86; candidate for Portland
City Council, 1980; Portland City Council, 1986-96;
candidate for mayor of Portland, 1992

ELECTION RESULTS

2008 GENERAL

Earl Blumenauer (D)	254,235	74.5%
Delia Lopez (R)	71,063	20.8%
Michael Meo (PACGRN)	15,063	4.4%

2008 PRIMARY

Earl Blumenauer (D)	121,176	86.7%
John Sweeney (D)	9,389	6.7%
Joseph Walsh (D)	8,783	6.3%

2006 GENERAL

Earl Blumenauer (D)	186,380	73.5%
Bruce Broussard (R)	59,529	23.5%
David Brownlow (CNSTP)	7,003	2.8%

PREVIOUS WINNING PERCENTAGES
2004 (71%); 2002 (67%); 2000 (67%); 1998 (84%);
1996 (67%); 1996 Special Election (70%)

The bicycle-riding, bow-tie-wearing Blumenauer stands poised to see a number of his key interests reach the top of the congressional agenda, including increased attention to renewable energy and the environment. It also helps that he was one of the earliest supporters of President Obama's presidential campaign, and that he sits on the powerful Ways and Means Committee.

Despite a solidly liberal voting record, Blumenauer (BLUE-men-hour) shows a willingness to avoid the shrill partisanship that often stymies consensus. He has displayed a canny ability to work with Republicans to steer legislative proposals through Congress. On Ways and Means, where he sits on the Select Revenue Measures panel, he has shown patience regarding the overhaul of the George W. Bush administration's 2001 and 2003 tax cuts. He said in late 2008 it would make sense for Congress to take time to examine issues such as business taxation, the treatment of investment income and the progressiveness of the tax structure.

When it comes to protecting the environment and addressing climate change, he practices what he preaches. He commutes on a burnt-orange Trek bike from his Capitol Hill apartment to his office and rides it to meetings at the White House. Blumenauer has long sought to increase the nation's use of bicycles. In the 110th Congress (2007-08), he proposed new tax benefits for commuters who ride bicycles to work. In 2007, he designed a "bike to work" program for congressional employees as part of a Democratic initiative to make the Capitol more environmentally friendly.

Blumenauer, who cycles everywhere when he is home in Portland, created a bike caucus as one of his first acts when he entered Congress in 1996. He used the caucus, and his seat on the Transportation and Infrastructure Committee from 1997 to 2006, to help shepherd to his district millions of dollars for bicycle trails, pedestrian facilities and mass transit systems. The now 170-plus member caucus of cycling legislators, many of whom wear bicycle pins on their lapels, may be a force to be reckoned with when the Congress considers reauthorizing the 2005 surface transportation bill.

Blumenauer is also an advocate for mass transit, and secured federal money for Portland to build a 5.8-mile Interstate Max light-rail line extension, which opened in 2004, between downtown and the Columbia River. He successfully pressed in 2007 to block federal rules that gave cities seeking funds for buses an advantage over those like Portland that have sought to expand the use of streetcars.

He is the second-ranking Democrat on the Select Committee on Energy Independence and Global Warming, which looks at ways to reduce the nation's contribution to greenhouse gases that contribute to global warming. He introduced a bill in 2009 to require 10 percent of revenue from a "cap and trade" program of trading greenhouse gas emissions credits to be spent on energy-efficient transportation projects.

He told The New York Times in early 2009 that the global financial collapse is "perhaps the best opportunity we will ever see" to build environmental sustainability into the nation's infrastructure, with urban streetcar systems, bike and pedestrian paths, more-efficient energy transmission, and conversion of the federal government's 600,000-vehicle fleet to alternative fuels.

Blumenauer worked for years to protect Mount Hood, 50 miles southeast of Portland. He got a provision into a massive public-lands bill that was signed into law in 2009 to designate almost 127,000 acres around it as federally protected wilderness.

Though he typically backs his party, Blumenauer refused to support the $700 billion law in fall 2008 to assist the nation's ailing financial services sector. A member of the Budget Committee, he said he wanted greater protection for individual homeowners facing foreclosure.

Blumenauer chooses his path carefully when it comes to trade issues. He seeks to protect the labor interests in his district while recognizing that international trade provides many jobs in his port city. His votes in favor of free-trade agreements have come under attack from some liberal activists. Blumenauer argues free trade can help promote labor and environmental progress. But in 2007 he angered local activists — including four who were arrested in a protest in his office — when he voted for the Peru free-trade agreement, noting the pact's protections against illegal logging.

He opposed the Iraq War from the start, but he feels strongly that the U.S. government must not abandon the Iraqi refugees. He voted for the 2009 defense authorization bill that includes provisions calling for the administration to aid Iraqi refugees, but he distinguishes that legislation from spending bills that actually appropriate money for the war.

An activist since his teens, Blumenauer was just one year out of college in 1971 when he testified before Congress in support of a constitutional amendment to lower the voting age to 18.

Elected to the state House at 24, in four years he rose to chair the Revenue Committee, where he says he first developed an interest in tax policy. He then spent eight years on the Multnomah County Commission, followed by 10 years on the Portland City Council, where he was instrumental in establishing Portland's ambitious land-use planning procedures to control metropolitan sprawl.

He ran unsuccessfully for mayor of Portland in 1992, but won a 1996 special election to the U.S. House. The 3rd District seat was vacant after Democrat Ron Wyden won a special Senate election to replace Republican Bob Packwood, who had resigned the previous fall. Blumenauer easily took the primary and special election and has cruised to re-election ever since. He was discussed as a contender for GOP Sen. Gordon H. Smith's Senate seat but announced in 2007 he would not launch a challenge. Blumenauer won with 75 percent of the vote in 2008.

Despite his comfortable political situation, Blumenauer is a prolific fundraiser and generous donor to his colleagues. Of the nearly $1.2 million he collected in the 2008 election cycle, Blumenauer gave nearly half to fellow Democrats. He has already sent $100,000 from his coffers to the party's campaign arm in 2009.

KEY VOTES

2008

Yes	Delay consideration of Colombia free-trade agreement
No	Override Bush veto of federal farm and nutrition programs reauthorization bill
No	Overhaul surveillance laws and permit dismissal of suits against companies that conducted warrantless wiretapping
Yes	Grant mortgage relief to homeowners and funding for Fannie Mae and Freddie Mac
No	Approve initial $700 billion program to stabilize financial markets
No	Approve final $700 billion program to stabilize financial markets
Yes	Provide $14 billion in loans to automakers

2007

Yes	Increase minimum wage by $2.10 an hour
Yes	Approve $124.2 billion in emergency war spending and set goal for redeployment of troops from Iraq
No	Reject federal contraceptive assistance to international family planning groups
Yes	Override Bush veto of $23.2 billion water projects authorization bill
Yes	Implement Peru free-trade agreement
Yes	Approve energy policy overhaul with new fuel economy standards
No	Clear $473.5 billion omnibus spending bill, including $70 billion for military operations

CQ VOTE STUDIES

	PARTY UNITY		PRESIDENTIAL SUPPORT	
	SUPPORT	OPPOSE	SUPPORT	OPPOSE
2008	98%	2%	15%	85%
2007	97%	3%	6%	94%
2006	97%	3%	8%	92%
2005	97%	3%	11%	89%
2004	93%	7%	23%	77%

INTEREST GROUPS

	AFL-CIO	ADA	CCUS	ACU
2008	100%	95%	53%	12%
2007	96%	85%	50%	0%
2006	93%	90%	27%	8%
2005	93%	100%	37%	4%
2004	93%	95%	26%	9%

OREGON 3

North and east Portland; eastern suburbs

Split by the Willamette River, the city of Portland has two personalities. The eastern portion, covered by the 3rd, still depends on the blue-collar economy that made the city a thriving international port for lumber and fruit. The Port of Portland and Portland International Airport make the city a center of trade and distribution. Computer chips and cappuccino drive the city's western side (in the 1st and 5th districts). Rising unemployment and foreclosure rates and a stalling home construction sector, an economic staple here for decades, have hurt the Portland area.

Area sports fans watch basketball's Trailblazers at the Rose Garden arena on the eastern side of the Willamette, and Portland's many breweries are havens for beer enthusiasts. The 3rd's portion of Portland takes in the University of Portland, Reed College and several hospitals.

Compared with the rest of Portland, the 3rd is a multicultural haven. There is a large black population in precincts just east of the Willamette River, near Interstate 5 and Martin Luther King Jr. Blvd. A sizable Hispanic population resides in northeastern Portland and in Gresham and Wood Village

east of the city. Asians are numerous in east-central Portland, near 82nd Avenue and Interstate 205. The district's second-largest city, Gresham, was once a thriving farm community. It is now the easternmost stop on Portland's light-rail system and hopes to continue attracting new large-scale business investments to its downtown area. Beyond the Portland metropolitan area, the district quickly turns rural. Its far eastern border reaches Mount Hood — Oregon's highest peak at 11,239 feet — and the Mount Hood National Forest in the western part of the Cascade Range.

Although there are politically competitive portions of rural Clackamas County, Portland's liberal leanings make the 3rd Oregon's most staunchly Democratic district. In the 2008 presidential election, Barack Obama won the 3rd with 71 percent of the vote, his highest percentage statewide.

MAJOR INDUSTRY
Wholesale trade and distribution, health care, education

CITIES
Portland (pt.), 432,388; Gresham, 90,205; Milwaukie, 20,490

NOTABLE
"The Simpsons" creator Matt Groening grew up in Portland — perhaps coincidentally, many of his characters share the names of local streets.

Rep. Peter A. DeFazio (D)

Elected 1986; 12th term

CAPITOL OFFICE
225-6416
www.house.gov/defazio
2134 Rayburn Bldg. 20515-3704; fax 225-0032

COMMITTEES
Homeland Security
Natural Resources
Transportation & Infrastructure
(Highways & Transit - chairman)

RESIDENCE
Springfield

BORN
May 27, 1947; Needham, Mass.

RELIGION
Roman Catholic

FAMILY
Wife, Myrnie L. Daut

EDUCATION
Tufts U., B.A. 1969 (economics & political science);
U. of Oregon, attended 1969-71 (international
studies), M.S. 1977 (public administration
& gerontology)

MILITARY SERVICE
Air Force, 1967-71

CAREER
Congressional aide

POLITICAL HIGHLIGHTS
Lane County Commission, 1982-86; sought
Democratic nomination for U.S. Senate
(special election), 1996

ELECTION RESULTS

2008 GENERAL

Peter A. DeFazio (D)	275,143	82.3%
Jaynee Germond (CNSTP)	43,133	12.9%
Mike Beilstein (PACGRN)	13,162	3.9%

2008 PRIMARY

Peter A. DeFazio (D)	119,366	99.2%

2006 GENERAL

Peter A. DeFazio (D)	180,607	62.2%
Jim Feldkamp (R)	109,105	37.6%

PREVIOUS WINNING PERCENTAGES
2004 (61%); 2002 (64%); 2000 (68%); 1998 (70%);
1996 (66%); 1994 (67%); 1992 (71%); 1990 (86%);
1988 (72%); 1986 (54%)

DeFazio has pushed a liberal, populist agenda since he arrived in Congress more than two decades years ago. He is loud, persistent and viewed by his critics as a smart aleck, but he also is a savvy lawmaker who is adept at securing federal funds for his district.

DeFazio (da-FAH-zee-o) loves to hector Republicans; he did so regularly when the GOP ran the House and hasn't stopped with Democrats in control of Congress and the White House. When House Republicans unveiled an alternative to President Obama's budget plan in March 2009, he scoffed at one of the GOP's most frequently proposed fiscal prescriptions. "Tax cuts — tax cuts solve all problems," he said sarcastically on MSNBC. "I mean, we are pretty soon going to fill in potholes with tax cuts — collapsing bridges, health care. Everything comes from tax cuts."

Despite his fondness for baiting his opponents, DeFazio doesn't always march in lockstep with his party. He was one of just seven House Democrats to oppose President Obama's $787 billion economic stimulus law in early 2009 and the only one of the seven who represented a district that Obama had carried. He said the plan's tax cuts were too large and it didn't include enough spending on infrastructure.

Obama took notice. During a subsequent meeting with House Democrats, DeFazio asked him about putting more infrastructure money in his fiscal 2010 budget. The president responded, "I know you think we need more for that because you voted against [the stimulus]. Don't think we're not keeping score, brother." A satisfied DeFazio — who supported the budget — said later, "At least I got his attention."

DeFazio has much to say on the subject of infrastructure spending. He chairs the Highways and Transit panel of the Transportation and Infrastructure Committee, which has responsibility for drafting a massive reauthorization of highway and surface transportation programs in the 111th Congress (2009-10). DeFazio passed up a chance to challenge Oregon Republican Sen. Gordon H. Smith in 2008 because he preferred to hold on to that subcommittee gavel instead.

DeFazio has been especially outspoken in opposing free-trade agreements. He voted against normalizing trade relations with China in 2000 and a free-trade pact with five Central American countries in 2005. He asserts such pacts lead to shuttered factories and jobless workers. "Our trade policy's a disaster, plain and simple," he said. "How are you going to be a great nation if you don't make things anymore?"

DeFazio is also engaged on the Natural Resources Committee, where he often faces a juggling act on forest issues. His constituency includes two groups with conflicting interests on those issues: Loggers, who oppose curbs on timber cutting, and environmentalists, who want restrictions.

The competing pressures were evident in 2003, when DeFazio first opposed a sweeping forest-thinning measure championed by Oregon Republican Greg Walden, then voted for a final version of the legislation that included significant changes made by the Senate at Oregon Democrat Ron Wyden's insistence.

DeFazio often teams up with Walden to protect Oregon's interests on public-lands issues. The two represent most of the state outside of the populated northwest corner and even though Walden is the sole Republican in Oregon's House delegation, they work well together. DeFazio and Walden fought efforts by the George W. Bush administration to force the federally owned Bonneville Power Administration, headquartered in Portland, to charge higher rates for its electricity as a deficit-trimming step.

He and Walden formed the House Small Brewers Caucus in 2007 to promote the interests of the microbrewery industry. A year later, though, the two diverged when Walden proposed opening up more offshore territory to oil drilling and using the lease revenue to replace timber subsidies.

DeFazio is active on security issues from his seat on the Homeland Security Committee. After the Sept. 11 terrorist attacks, he led the House Democrats' campaign against GOP efforts to retain private contract workers as airport screeners. The aviation security law that was ultimately enacted not only federalized the baggage screeners but also made a number of other security changes DeFazio had sought for years.

He made headlines himself in March 2009 after he reportedly became angry when pulled aside at Portland's airport for a random security check. He denied causing a scene with the Transportation Security Administration, telling The Oregonian, "I went over there, I put my bag down and I said, 'You know, this is stupid. You know, I helped to create the TSA. You know, I'm an expert on security.'…I didn't say, 'You can't look through my bag.'"

DeFazio refuses to keep congressional pay raises beyond the rate of Social Security cost-of-living increases as long as government spending is in the red. Instead, he uses the money to fund two scholarships at each of five community colleges in his district. He established the scholarships for displaced timber workers, and expanded them to include displaced workers in general, and then to include veterans of the wars in Iraq and Afghanistan. DeFazio establishes the scholarship criteria, and a state agency administers the scholarships.

After growing up in Massachusetts, DeFazio moved to Oregon to attend the University of Oregon. While a student there, he established an employment program for seniors that is still in existence. After earning a graduate degree in gerontology, he ran a senior citizens' program for a time, then landed a job as a specialist on elder issues with former Democratic Rep. James Weaver, a hot-tempered populist.

In 1982, DeFazio struck out on his own, getting elected to the Lane County Commission. He earned a reputation for aggressiveness by suing to nullify contracts between Oregon utilities and the Washington Public Power Supply System, whose failed nuclear projects resulted in rate increases.

When Weaver announced he would not seek re-election in 1986, DeFazio stepped in. Casting himself as heir to Weaver's populist mantle, he squeaked by in the primary, won the seat with 54 percent and has held it safely since.

KEY VOTES

2008

Yes Delay consideration of Colombia free-trade agreement

Yes Override Bush veto of federal farm and nutrition programs reauthorization bill

No Overhaul surveillance laws and permit dismissal of suits against companies that conducted warrantless wiretapping

No Grant mortgage relief to homeowners and funding for Fannie Mae and Freddie Mac

No Approve initial $700 billion program to stabilize financial markets

No Approve final $700 billion program to stabilize financial markets

Yes Provide $14 billion in loans to automakers

2007

Yes Increase minimum wage by $2.10 an hour

Yes Approve $124.2 billion in emergency war spending and set goal for redeployment of troops from Iraq

No Reject federal contraceptive assistance to international family planning groups

Yes Override Bush veto of $23.2 billion water projects authorization bill

No Implement Peru free-trade agreement

No Approve energy policy overhaul with new fuel economy standards

No Clear $473.5 billion omnibus spending bill, including $70 billion for military operations

CQ VOTE STUDIES

	PARTY UNITY		PRESIDENTIAL SUPPORT	
	SUPPORT	OPPOSE	SUPPORT	OPPOSE
2008	93%	7%	13%	87%
2007	95%	5%	1%	99%
2006	91%	9%	17%	83%
2005	91%	9%	17%	83%
2004	90%	10%	27%	73%

INTEREST GROUPS

	AFL-CIO	ADA	CCUS	ACU
2008	100%	90%	50%	20%
2007	96%	90%	37%	4%
2006	93%	90%	47%	28%
2005	87%	100%	37%	12%
2004	100%	95%	43%	16%

OREGON 4

Southwest — Eugene, Springfield, part of Corvallis

Taking in the southern half of Oregon's Pacific coast and parts of the Cascade Mountains, the 4th's economy is dependent on the district's natural resources. Environmentalists, loggers and fishermen combine to give the 4th a potentially combustible political mix.

A steady decline in the forestry and fishing industries started a pattern of layoffs over the past several decades, stunting the 4th's population growth. Agriculture in the 4th is based in the fertile valley between the Cascade and Coast mountain ranges. Although other areas now dominate Oregon's wine industry, the state's wine grape growing began in the Umpqua Valley in the early 1960s. The region continues to provide rich soil for that industry as well as for a variety of field crops.

Unemployment rates have climbed across the 4th, with rural southwestern Josephine County and more developed Douglas County hit particularly hard. Fishing towns in Coos and Curry counties are struggling. Lane County's Eugene and Springfield, the district's most populous cities, have lost jobs in white-collar, construction and retail sectors.

Research at the University of Oregon in Eugene, still a hotbed of environmentalism, lured technology companies. Computer manufacturers and software developers still drive the area's economy despite some layoffs. Eugene, the self-proclaimed "Track Town U.S.A.," also is the center of the Oregon running culture.

The electoral success of liberal Peter A. DeFazio belies the 4th District's political competitiveness. Eugene and Springfield make Lane County reliably Democratic. Linn and Douglas counties vote solidly Republican, and Coos and Curry counties lean toward Republicans. Barack Obama took 54 percent of the vote here in the 2008 presidential election, 5 percentage points higher than Democrat John Kerry's plurality win in the district in the 2004 race.

MAJOR INDUSTRY
Forestry, agriculture, fishing, technology, tourism

CITIES
Eugene, 137,893; Springfield, 52,864; Albany (pt.), 36,950; Corvallis (pt.), 32,076; Roseburg, 20,017; Coos Bay, 15,374

NOTABLE
Much of the movie "Animal House" was filmed at the University of Oregon and nearby Cottage Grove.

Rep. Kurt Schrader (D)

CAPITOL OFFICE
225-5711
schrader.house.gov
1419 Longworth Bldg. 20515-3705; fax 225-5699

COMMITTEES
Agriculture
Budget
Small Business
(Finance & Tax - chairman)

RESIDENCE
Canby

BORN
Oct. 19, 1951; Bridgeport, Conn.

RELIGION
Episcopalian

FAMILY
Wife, Martha Schrader; four children

EDUCATION
Cornell U., B.A. 1973 (government); U. of Illinois,
B.S. 1975 (veterinary medicine), D.V.M. 1977

CAREER
Veterinarian; farmer

POLITICAL HIGHLIGHTS
Democratic nominee for Ore. House, 1994;
Ore. House, 1997-2003; Ore. Senate, 2003-08

ELECTION RESULTS

2008 GENERAL

Kurt Schrader (D)	181,577	54.2%
Mike Erickson (R)	128,297	38.3%
Sean Bates (I)	6,830	2.0%
Douglas Patterson (CNSTP)	6,558	2.0%
Alex Polikoff (PACGRN)	5,272	1.6%
Steve Milligan (LIBERT)	4,814	1.4%

2008 PRIMARY

Kurt Schrader (D)	51,980	53.8%
Nancy Moran (D)	18,597	19.3%
Steve Marks (D)	17,643	18.3%
Andrew Foster (D)	6,104	6.3%
Richard Nathe (D)	1,748	1.8%

Elected 2008; 1st term

Schrader is a moderate Democrat who earned a reputation as a fiscal conservative during his more than 12 years in the Oregon legislature. As co-chairman of its Joint Ways and Means Committee, he was nicknamed "Darth Schrader" by colleagues.

He is expected to target the same ideals of budgetary restraint from his seat on the Budget Committee. He backs rules to require new spending or tax increases to be offset if they increase the deficit. But at the same time he advocates more funding for education and health care. And he supported President Obama's $3.56 trillion budget blueprint for fiscal 2010, a $410 billion catchall spending bill for fiscal 2009, and a $787 billion economic stimulus law. After passage of the stimulus law, Schrader successfully urged House and Senate negotiators to ensure the education funds were released immediately in order to prevent drastic cuts to local school budgets.

In the Oregon legislature, Schrader made an unsuccessful effort to overhaul the state tax system and create a business tax to help pay for K-12 education.

An organic fruit and vegetable farmer and member of the Agriculture Committee, he also advocates investment in renewable-energy sources and supports a federal program that compensates rural counties for the loss of timber revenue on government-owned land. Many local governments in his district rely on such payments.

A former veterinary clinic owner who still maintains his license, Schrader also sits on the Small Business Committee.

Schrader's background gives him an interest in health care. He supports expanding prescription drug coverage for seniors, and in early 2009 he voted for an expansion of the State Children's Health Insurance Program, which provides coverage for children whose families don't qualify for Medicaid.

Schrader served as a member of the Canby Planning Commission in Oregon from 1981 until 1996 before taking a seat in the state legislature. He made a bid for the U.S. House when Democratic Rep. Darlene Hooley decided to retire in 2008. He bested Republican businessman Mike Erickson, whose campaign was hobbled by controversy.

OREGON 5

Willamette Valley – Salem, parts of Portland and Corvallis

The 5th takes in the northern part of the Willamette Valley and the state capital of Salem, then spills over the Coast Range to cover two Pacific counties, Tillamook and Lincoln. It also includes a small part of Portland (shared with the 1st and 3rd districts).

Clackamas, Marion and Polk counties are at the heart of the Willamette Valley, Oregon's most fertile farmland. The valley is the center of the state's trade in greenhouse crops, seeds and berries. Hops from Marion and Clackamas counties go into some of the nation's finest beers. Polk County grows cherries and wine grapes; wineries dot Polk and Marion counties.

Once exclusively reliant on agriculture and timber, the 5th's economy has diversified and now supports environmental research and technology manufacturing. Salem and surrounding Marion County host government workers and a food processing industry. Budget shortfalls have hurt Clackamas County Portland suburbs such as Oregon City and Lake Oswego.

Marion, the district's most populous jurisdiction, is competitive in statewide races. Strong Democratic areas include Corvallis (shared with the 4th), which is home to Oregon State University, and southwestern Multnomah County, which hosts some affluent liberals around Lewis & Clark College. Overall, Barack Obama won 54 percent of the 5th's 2008 presidential vote.

MAJOR INDUSTRY
Agriculture, timber, food processing, manufacturing, state government

CITIES
Salem, 136,924; Lake Oswego (pt.), 35,263; Keizer, 32,203

NOTABLE
Salem's Willamette University, established in 1842, was the first university in the West.

PENNSYLVANIA

Gov. Edward G. Rendell (D)

First elected: 2002
Length of term: 4 years
Term expires: 1/11
Salary: $174,914
Phone: (717) 787-2500

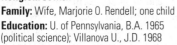

Residence: Philadelphia
Born: Jan. 5, 1944;
New York, N.Y.
Religion: Jewish
Family: Wife, Marjorie O. Rendell; one child
Education: U. of Pennsylvania, B.A. 1965
(political science); Villanova U., J.D. 1968
Military service: Army Reserve, 1968-74
Career: Lawyer; city prosecutor
Political highlights: Philadelphia district
attorney, 1978-86; sought Democratic
nomination for governor, 1986; sought
Democratic nomination for mayor of
Philadelphia, 1987; mayor of Philadelphia,
1992-2000; Democratic National Committee
chairman, 1999-2001

Election results:

2006 GENERAL

Edward G. Rendell (D)	2,470,517	60.4%
Lynn Swann (R)	1,622,135	39.6%

Lt. Gov. Joe Scarnati (D)

Assumed office: 2008
Length of term: 4 years
Term expires: 1/11
Salary: $146,926
Phone: (717) 787-3300

LEGISLATURE

General Assembly: Year-round with
recess

Senate: 50 members, 4-year terms
2009 ratios: 30 R, 20 D; 40 men,
10 women
Salary: $78,315
Phone: (717) 787-5920

House: 203 members, 2-year terms
2009 ratios: 104 D, 99 R; 176 men, 27
women
Salary: $78,315
Phone: (717) 787-2372

TERM LIMITS

Governor: 2 consecutive terms
Senate: No
House: No

URBAN STATISTICS

CITY	POPULATION
Philadelphia	1,517,550
Pittsburgh	334,563
Allentown	106,632
Erie	103,717
Upper Darby	81,821

REGISTERED VOTERS

Democrat	51%
Republican	37%
Others	12%

POPULATION

2008 population (est.)	12,448,279
2000 population	12,281,054
1990 population	11,881,643
Percent change (1990-2000)	+3.4%
Rank among states (2008)	6

Median age	38
Born in state	77.7%
Foreign born	4.1%
Violent crime rate	420/100,000
Poverty level	11%
Federal workers	105,903
Military	43,271

ELECTIONS

STATE ELECTION OFFICIAL
(717) 787-5280
DEMOCRATIC PARTY
(717) 920-8470
REPUBLICAN PARTY
(717) 234-4901

MISCELLANEOUS

Web: www.pa.gov
Capital: Harrisburg

U.S. CONGRESS

Senate: 2 Democrats
House: 12 Democrats, 7 Republican

2000 Census Statistics by District

DIST.	2008 VOTE FOR PRESIDENT OBAMA	MCCAIN	WHITE	BLACK	ASIAN	HISP	MEDIAN INCOME	WHITE COLLAR	BLUE COLLAR	SERVICE INDUSTRY	OVER 64	UNDER 18	COLLEGE EDUCATION	RURAL	SQ. MILES
1	88%	12%	33%	45%	5%	15%	$28,261	57%	21%	22%	12%	28%	14%	0%	59
2	90	10	30	61	4	3	$30,646	66	15	19	14	24	24	0	59
3	49	49	94	3	0	1	$35,884	52	31	16	15	24	18	42	3,969
4	44	55	94	3	1	1	$43,547	64	23	14	17	24	27	22	1,302
5	44	55	96	1	1	1	$33,254	51	33	15	15	22	17	54	11,042
6	58	41	86	7	4	2	$55,611	68	20	12	14	25	34	14	813
7	56	43	88	5	4	1	$56,126	73	16	11	15	24	36	1	290
8	54	45	91	3	2	2	$59,207	68	21	11	13	26	31	9	619
9	35	63	96	2	0	1	$34,910	49	36	16	16	24	13	59	7,160
10	45	54	95	2	0	1	$35,996	53	32	15	17	23	17	55	6,558
11	57	42	93	2	1	3	$34,979	54	30	16	18	22	16	27	2,218
12	49	49	95	3	0	1	$30,612	51	31	18	19	21	14	38	2,752
13	59	41	86	6	4	3	$49,319	68	19	12	17	23	29	2	255
14	70	29	73	23	2	1	$30,139	62	19	20	18	21	21	0	162
15	56	43	86	3	2	8	$45,330	59	27	14	16	24	22	13	845

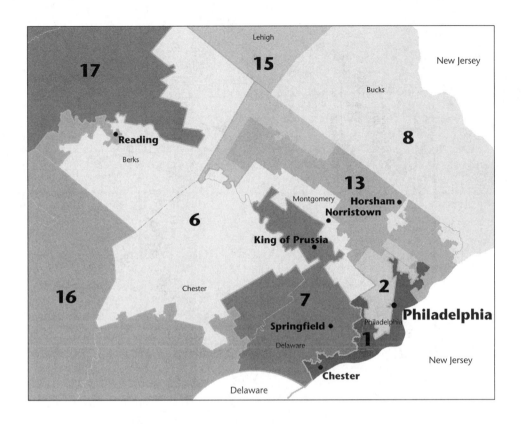

2000 Census Statistics by District

DIST.	2008 VOTE FOR PRESIDENT OBAMA	MCCAIN	WHITE	BLACK	ASIAN	HISP	MEDIAN INCOME	WHITE COLLAR	BLUE COLLAR	SERVICE INDUSTRY	OVER 64	UNDER 18	COLLEGE EDUCATION	RURAL	SQ. MILES
16	48%	51%	85%	4%	1%	9%	$45,934	54%	31%	14%	13%	27%	23%	24%	1,290
17	48	51	87	7	1	3	$40,473	55	31	14	16	23	17	31	2,335
18	44	55	95	2	1	1	$44,938	66	20	14	18	22	29	16	1,432
19	43	56	92	3	1	3	$45,345	57	30	13	14	24	21	29	1,658
STATE	55	44	84	10	2	3	$40,106	60	26	15	16	24	22	23	44,817
U.S.	53	46	69	12	4	13	$41,994	60	25	15	12	26	24	21	3,537,438

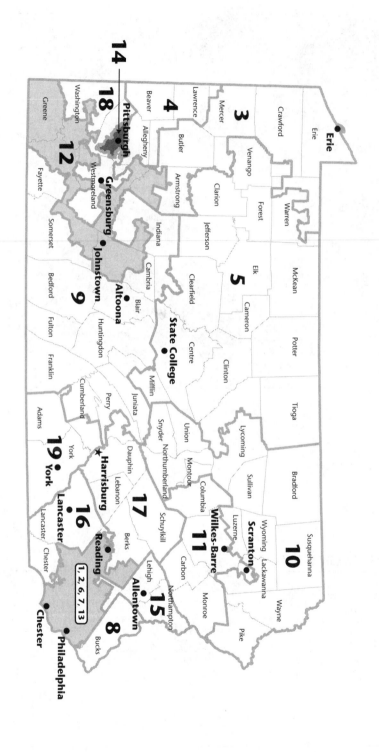

Sen. Arlen Specter (D)

Elected 1980; 5th term

CAPITOL OFFICE
224-4254
specter.senate.gov
711 Hart Bldg. 20510-3802; fax 228-1229

COMMITTEES
Appropriations
Environment & Public Works
Judiciary
   (Crime & Drugs - chairman)
Veterans' Affairs
Special Aging

RESIDENCE
Philadelphia

BORN
Feb. 12, 1930; Wichita, Kan.

RELIGION
Jewish

FAMILY
Wife, Joan Specter; two children

EDUCATION
U. of Pennsylvania, B.A. 1951
(international relations); Yale U., LL.B. 1956

MILITARY SERVICE
Air Force, 1951-53

CAREER
Lawyer; professor

POLITICAL HIGHLIGHTS
Philadelphia district attorney, 1966-74 (elected as
Republican); Republican nominee for mayor of
Philadelphia, 1967; defeated for re-election as
Philadelphia district attorney, 1973; sought
Republican nomination for U.S. Senate, 1976;
sought Republican nomination for governor, 1978

ELECTION RESULTS

2004 GENERAL

Arlen Specter (R)	2,925,080	52.6%
Joseph M. Hoeffel (D)	2,334,126	42.0%
James N. Clymer (CNSTP)	220,056	4.0%
Betsy Summers (LIBERT)	79,263	1.4%

2004 PRIMARY

Arlen Specter (R)	530,839	50.8%
Patrick J. Toomey (R)	513,693	49.2%

PREVIOUS WINNING PERCENTAGES*
1998 (61%); 1992 (49%); 1986 (56%); 1980 (50%)
*Elected as a Republican 1980-2004

Quick-witted and notoriously blunt, Specter is also self-assured to the point of cockiness. He has alternately irritated and impressed Republicans and Democrats alike for more than four decades, first as Philadelphia's district attorney and now as Pennsylvania's longtime senior senator.

His standing among Democrats, and enmity toward him from GOP conservatives, took a quantum leap in April 2009. Specter announced that — after years of considering doing so — he would switch parties and run as a Democrat for re-election to a sixth term in 2010. Since his first election to the Senate in 1980, "the Republican Party has moved far to the right," he said. "Last year, more than 200,000 Republicans in Pennsylvania changed their registration to become Democrats. I now find my political philosophy more in line with Democrats than Republicans."

Two months before announcing his decision to change parties, Specter had earned Democrats' gratitude by being one of just three Republicans to back President Obama's $787 billion economic stimulus bill. That vote triggered intense criticism among Republicans and helped spur his 2004 primary opponent, former Rep. Patrick J. Toomey, to announce a 2010 rematch — a move that political observers said put Specter in deep political trouble.

However, after the stimulus vote, Specter subsequently infuriated Democrats by announcing he would vote against limiting debate on one of their major priorities — so-called "card check" legislation that would ease union organizing rules. Specter said in announcing his party switch that his position on that issue wouldn't change. And as a newly minted Democrat, he continued his independence on other issues, voting against both Obama's $3.56 trillion budget blueprint for fiscal 2010 and an amendment to housing legislation that allowed bankruptcy judges to set new terms for home mortgages, a process referred to as "cramdown."

Before Specter's party switch, Majority Leader Harry Reid of Nevada had complained that — despite Specter's strong maverick streak — he usually sided with his fellow Republicans in do-or-die battles. Specter "is always with us when we don't need him," Reid groused in his 2008 book "The Good Fight."

But when Specter joined his caucus, Reid said the Pennsylvanian's seniority would be set as if he had been a Democrat when first elected in 1980. That led some Democrats to express concerns about Specter leapfrogging them on committee rosters, and Reid backed off. He then accepted Majority Whip Richard J. Durbin's offer to step aside as chairman of Judiciary's Crime and Drugs Subcommittee and allow Specter to assume that post. If Specter is re-elected in 2010, Democrats will revisit the seniority issue in the next Congress.

When the GOP ran the Senate, Specter held the gavel of the full Judiciary Committee for the 109th Congress (2005-06), but was put on a short leash. Republican leaders made him promise to advance President George W. Bush's judicial nominees to the full Senate regardless of his own views, and he complied.

There was a reason for the leaders' demands. He had enraged conservatives when he opposed the nomination of Robert H. Bork to the Supreme Court in 1987. He angered liberals four years later by defending conservative nominee Clarence Thomas against sexual harassment charges by Anita Hill. Specter's aggressive grilling of Hill during the Thomas confirmation hearings infuriated many women. During President Clinton's 1999 impeachment trial, he invoked Scottish law by voting "Not proven, therefore not guilty," instead of "guilty" or "not guilty."

And he was sharply critical when the Bush administration's use of warrantless surveillance of Americans in terrorism investigations became public in 2006. He sponsored a bill compelling the president to get approval from a special court created for that purpose. Most Republicans sided with Bush, who insisted he had constitutional authority for the wiretaps. Specter was so eager to be a central player that he rewrote his bill, capitulating on his initial demand for court review, but the legislation was not enacted.

In recent years, Specter has maintained an energetic and combative attitude in the Senate despite his ongoing battle with cancer. He was diagnosed with advanced Hodgkin's disease — which affects the lymphatic system — in February 2005. He underwent chemotherapy while, as Judiciary chairman, he was managing the grueling confirmation proceedings for Chief Justice John G. Roberts Jr. and Justice Samuel A. Alito Jr. The treatments left him gaunt and completely bald. He eventually went into complete remission for three years. In 2008, he announced he had been diagnosed with a recurrence of the disease and underwent weekly chemotherapy treatments.

He has battled other health problems; in the 1990s, he survived a brain tumor and heart problems that led to bypass surgery. He credits his squash regimen — he said in 2008 he had continued to play nearly every day since October 1970 — with helping him stay healthy enough to survive his medical setbacks. "The tougher the battle, the sweeter the victory," he said in his 2008 book, "Never Give In." "The key factor is to keep working and keep fighting."

Before announcing his party switch, Specter had been top-ranking Republican on the Appropriations subcommittee that funds the departments of Labor, Health and Human Services, and Education. He has used his seat on that panel to dramatically increase funding for the National Institutes of Health, more than doubling it between 1995 and 2006. He also sits on the Environment and Public Works, Veterans' Affairs and Special Aging panels.

The son of a Jewish peddler who immigrated from Ukraine, Specter grew up mostly in Kansas, though Harry Specter moved the family from place to place, selling blankets to Nebraska farmers in the winter and melons to Midwestern housewives in the summer. The family later settled in Philadelphia.

Specter grew up listening to his father talk about government and politics. "My father's obsession with politics and my own youthful addiction to baseball combined to instill in me a sense of history," Specter wrote in his 2000 autobiography, "Passion for Truth." "Since I could not hit or field but was born on Lincoln's birthday, I gravitated toward politics."

He began to make a name for himself as an aide to the Warren Commission, helping to devise the "single bullet" theory that a lone gunman was responsible for the 1963 assassination of President Kennedy.

Specter was a Democrat until 1965, when he ran on the Republican ticket for district attorney in Philadelphia against a Democratic incumbent whom he saw as controlled by the city's Democratic machine. Specter won the election, and officially changed his party registration to Republican.

He lost a mayoral race in 1967, but was re-elected district attorney in 1969. He then suffered a series of political setbacks: He was defeated for re-election to a third term as district attorney in 1973; he lost his first primary bid for a Senate seat in 1976; he lost his bid for the Republican gubernatorial nomination in 1978. His political luck changed when he ran for the Senate in 1980, defeating Pittsburgh Mayor Peter Flaherty for an open seat.

In the 1992 election, Democratic challenger Lynn Yeakel made an issue of his treatment of Hill, and she held Specter to a 3-percentage-point win. He had another close call in 2004, when Toomey, a conservative GOP congressman, challenged him in the Republican primary. Specter narrowly won with 51 percent of the vote, then defeated Democratic Rep. Joseph M. Hoeffel in November with 53 percent.

KEY VOTES

2008

Yes	Prohibit discrimination based on genetic information
Yes	Reauthorize farm and nutrition programs for five years
?	Limit debate on "cap and trade" system for greenhouse gas emissions
No	Allow lawsuits against companies that participated in warrantless wiretapping
Yes	Limit debate on a bill to block a scheduled cut in Medicare payments to doctors
Yes	Grant mortgage relief to homeowners and funding for Fannie Mae and Freddie Mac
Yes	Approve a nuclear cooperation agreement with India
Yes	Approve final $700 billion program to stabilize financial markets
Yes	Allow consideration of a $14 billion auto industry loan package

2007

Yes	Increase minimum wage by $2.10 an hour
Yes	Limit debate on a comprehensive immigration bill
Yes	Overhaul congressional lobbying and ethics rules for members and their staffs
Yes	Limit debate on considering a bill to add House seats for the District of Columbia and Utah
Yes	Limit debate on restoring habeas corpus rights to detainees
No	Mandate minimum breaks for troops between deployments to Iraq or Afghanistan
Yes	Override Bush veto of $23.2 billion water projects authorization bill
Yes	Confirm Michael B. Mukasey as attorney general
No	Limit debate on an energy policy overhaul containing $21.8 billion in tax incentives and reduced oil and gas subsidies

CQ VOTE STUDIES

	PARTY UNITY		PRESIDENTIAL SUPPORT	
	SUPPORT	OPPOSE	SUPPORT	OPPOSE
2008	62%	38%	58%	42%
2007	49%	51%	63%	37%
2006	61%	39%	76%	24%
2005	69%	31%	85%	15%
2004	70%	30%	88%	12%
2003	84%	16%	89%	11%
2002	60%	40%	89%	11%
2001	60%	40%	87%	13%
2000	67%	33%	59%	41%
1999	64%	36%	53%	47%

INTEREST GROUPS

	AFL-CIO	ADA	CCUS	ACU
2008	70%	45%	86%	42%
2007	68%	60%	82%	40%
2006	31%	30%	100%	43%
2005	54%	45%	88%	63%
2004	64%	45%	87%	75%
2003	16%	25%	87%	65%
2002	46%	35%	85%	50%
2001	63%	40%	79%	56%
2000	50%	40%	53%	62%
1999	44%	40%	47%	48%

Sen. Bob Casey (D)

Elected 2006; 1st term

CAPITOL OFFICE
224-6324
casey.senate.gov
393 Russell Bldg. 20510-3804; fax 228-0604

COMMITTEES
Agriculture, Nutrition & Forestry
Foreign Relations
   (Near Eastern & South & Central Asian Affairs
   - chairman)
Health, Education, Labor & Pensions
Special Aging
Joint Economic

RESIDENCE
Scranton

BORN
April 13, 1960; Scranton, Pa.

RELIGION
Roman Catholic

FAMILY
Wife, Terese Casey; four children

EDUCATION
College of the Holy Cross, A.B. 1982 (English);
Catholic U. of America, J.D. 1988

CAREER
Lawyer; campaign aide

POLITICAL HIGHLIGHTS
Pa. auditor general, 1997-2005; sought
Democratic nomination for governor, 2002;
Pa. treasurer, 2005-07

ELECTION RESULTS

2006 GENERAL

Bob Casey (D)	2,392,984	58.7%
Rick Santorum (R)	1,684,778	41.3%

2006 PRIMARY

Bob Casey (D)	629,271	84.6%
Chuck Pennacchio (D)	66,364	8.9%
Alan Sandals (D)	48,113	6.5%

In his initial years in the Senate, Casey has shown himself to be a staunch advocate for his state — hard-hit by the economic decline — and a Democratic loyalist on most issues. His prominent opposition to abortion has been one area that has put him at odds with his party, but his enthusiastic embrace of Barack Obama's successful presidential candidacy in 2008 could pay off for his state as well as his own political future.

On many issues, the low-key Casey shares the same views as his father, who served as governor of Pennsylvania from 1987 to 1995. The Caseys are Catholic, and liberal on almost every score except abortion rights and gun control — part of their appeal to the state's crossover voters. As leader of the anti-abortion wing of the Democratic Party, the elder Casey famously feuded in 1992 with presidential nominee Bill Clinton and was denied a speaking role at that year's convention.

But Sen. Casey endorsed Obama in March 2008, before the Illinois senator had locked up his bitter primary fight against Sen. Hillary Rodham Clinton of New York. He became a key Obama surrogate in the general-election campaign in his crucial swing state, and won the limelight his father was denied. "The fact that I'm speaking here tonight is testament to Barack's ability to show respect for the views of people who may disagree with him," Casey told the Democratic convention crowd in Denver in August 2008.

Casey sits on the Health, Education, Labor and Pensions (HELP) Committee, where he can pursue some of his top priorities — expanding access to child care and pre-kindergarten education. He introduced legislation early in 2009 to award grants to states that establish or expand high-quality, full-day pre-kindergarten programs. Under the bill, which is similar to one Casey introduced in the 110th Congress (2007-08), the federal government would provide half the funding for pre-kindergarten. A relentless pitchman for the cause, Casey — at a White House Super Bowl party in 2009 — interrupted his cheering of the victorious Pittsburgh Steelers to lobby Obama to support his bill.

To take the HELP Committee seat, Casey gave up a slot on the Banking, Housing and Urban Affairs panel, where he weighed in on the Bush administration's $700 billion financial system rescue plan in 2008. He backed a modified version of that proposal, but criticized the Treasury Department for not doing more to help struggling homeowners renegotiate their mortgages.

As a member of the Agriculture, Nutrition and Forestry Committee, Casey worked to help his state's dairy farmers in the 2008 reauthorization of farm programs.

He also serves on the Foreign Relations Committee, and with ranking Republican Richard G. Lugar of Indiana, has proposed creating a so-called hunger czar at the White House to pump up agriculture development aid abroad and coordinate aid policy across domestic and foreign policy agencies. "You want to be able to help in the short term but also to build the long-term facility that the developing world should have to feed their people with their own infrastructure," Casey said.

Working with another Republican, Richard M. Burr of North Carolina, Casey in 2009 formed a new bipartisan caucus on weapons of mass destruction and terrorism, seeking to provide a forum for senators and staff from disparate committees to discuss the risks and solutions of that volatile combination.

Despite acknowledging public criticism of funding earmarks, Casey defends seeking money for special projects in his state. "If there's a dollar that's available to the people of Pennsylvania, I don't want it to go to some other state, and I don't want some bureaucrat making that decision," he said. It helps that Casey has forged a good relationship with his state's senior senator, Arlen Specter, who is a senior member of the Appropriations Committee.

After an Army staff sergeant and Pittsburgh native, Ryan D. Maseth, was accidentally electrocuted and killed while serving in Iraq, Casey took the lead in pressing the Defense Department for answers and action against contractors accused of negligence. It was a cause he continued to press in 2009, as the deaths and injuries from electrocutions mounted. "It's a continuing outrage. And it's about time that the Army and the Pentagon and this new administration now…takes a fresh look at this," Casey said. He was pressing for specific actions by the military to prevent future accidents, as well as sanctions against the contractors who supervised shoddy work in Iraq.

Casey lives with his wife and four daughters in Scranton, where the Caseys have their political base. Scranton was showered with electoral attention in 2008 as the birthplace of Casey's colleague and Obama's running mate, then-Sen. Joseph R. Biden Jr. of Delaware.

Growing up in working-class Scranton, Casey was the fourth of eight children and the first son. His grandfather worked in the coal mines; his father became a lawyer. The family's finances were sometimes volatile, given his father's numerous political campaigns and the vicissitudes of his employment, but Casey recalls a happy upbringing. "With that many children, it's hard to convey a sense that everyone's equal, and that each parent loves each child as much as the other. And they did that," he said. All of the Casey children, except two brothers who practice law in Philadelphia, still live within 10 miles of one another.

As Casey would later, his father lost elections for governor. But unlike Casey, his father ultimately prevailed — after 20 years of attempts. "He won when I was 26," said Casey, who has the same distinguishing bushy eyebrows as his dad. Another trait he shares with his father is a genetic history, one that puts him at risk for the same disease — amyloidosis, a genetic condition in which proteins turn against the body and destroy internal organs — that took the elder Casey's life in 2000 at age 68.

He graduated from the College of the Holy Cross in 1982, then spent a year teaching fifth grade in Philadelphia with the Jesuits. Like his father, he got his law degree and practiced in Scranton until he won his first election as state auditor general in 1996. During two terms, he conducted a hard-hitting audit of nursing homes that led to the resignation of the state's top health official.

In 2004, Casey ran for state treasurer and won, attracting the attention of Democrats in Washington, who were gearing up for a challenge to Rick Santorum, then the Senate's third-ranking GOP leader. The conservative senator was viewed as vulnerable in a state that had voted Democratic in four previous presidential elections. Sen. Charles E. Schumer of New York, then chairman of the Senate Democrats' campaign organization, recruited Casey.

Casey blew by two lesser-known candidates to secure the Democratic nomination, then prepared for what was widely anticipated to be a titanic and close contest. Santorum and fellow Republicans ridiculed Casey as non-committal on important issues, weak on fighting terrorism and dealing with illegal immigration, and unwilling to meet the energetic Santorum in a long series of debates. But Santorum's eagerness to debate was a sign of his underdog status. And Casey's conservative social positions took away a typical line of GOP attack. Casey raised plenty of money, and the political wind was in the Democrats' direction. Casey defeated Santorum by a landslide 17 percentage points. He led Santorum even outside the state's traditional Democratic bastions of Philadelphia and Allegheny County, which includes Pittsburgh.

KEY VOTES

2008

Yes Prohibit discrimination based on genetic information

Yes Reauthorize farm and nutrition programs for five years

Yes Limit debate on "cap and trade" system for greenhouse gas emissions

Yes Allow lawsuits against companies that participated in warrantless wiretapping

Yes Limit debate on a bill to block a scheduled cut in Medicare payments to doctors

Yes Grant mortgage relief to homeowners and funding for Fannie Mae and Freddie Mac

Yes Approve a nuclear cooperation agreement with India

Yes Approve final $700 billion program to stabilize financial markets

Yes Allow consideration of a $14 billion auto industry loan package

2007

Yes Increase minimum wage by $2.10 an hour

Yes Limit debate on a comprehensive immigration bill

Yes Overhaul congressional lobbying and ethics rules for members and their staffs

Yes Limit debate on considering a bill to add House seats for the District of Columbia and Utah

Yes Limit debate on restoring habeas corpus rights to detainees

Yes Mandate minimum breaks for troops between deployments to Iraq or Afghanistan

Yes Override Bush veto of $23.2 billion water projects authorization bill

No Confirm Michael B. Mukasey as attorney general

Yes Limit debate on an energy policy overhaul containing $21.8 billion in tax incentives and reduced oil and gas subsidies

CQ VOTE STUDIES

	PARTY UNITY		PRESIDENTIAL SUPPORT	
	SUPPORT	OPPOSE	SUPPORT	OPPOSE
2008	93%	7%	35%	65%
2007	93%	7%	44%	56%

INTEREST GROUPS

	AFL-CIO	ADA	CCUS	ACU
2008	100%	90%	63%	8%
2007	100%	100%	36%	8%

Rep. Robert A. Brady (D)

Elected May 1998; 6th full term

CAPITOL OFFICE
225-4731
www.house.gov/robertbrady
206 Cannon Bldg. 20515-3801; fax 225-0088

COMMITTEES
Armed Services
House Administration - chairman
Joint Library - chairman
Joint Printing - vice chairman

RESIDENCE
Philadelphia

BORN
April 7, 1945; Philadelphia, Pa.

RELIGION
Roman Catholic

FAMILY
Wife, Debra Brady; two children

EDUCATION
St. Thomas More H.S., graduated 1963

CAREER
Union lobbyist; local government official;
carpenter

POLITICAL HIGHLIGHTS
34th Ward Democratic Executive Committee,
1967-present (leader, 1980-present); candidate
for Philadelphia City Council, 1983; Philadelphia
Democratic Party chairman, 1986-present;
sought Democratic nomination for mayor of
Philadelphia, 2007

ELECTION RESULTS

2008 GENERAL

Robert A. Brady (D)	242,799	90.8%
Mike Muhammed (R)	24,714	9.2%

2008 PRIMARY

Robert A. Brady (D)	unopposed

2006 GENERAL

Robert A. Brady (D)	unopposed

PREVIOUS WINNING PERCENTAGES
2004 (86%); 2002 (86%); 2000 (88%); 1998 (81%);
1998 Special Election (74%)

At 6 feet 2 inches and 250 pounds, Brady is a bear of a man. In Philadelphia politics, he's a grizzly. For more than 20 years, he's chaired the city Democratic Party. He has a thick Philly accent, a city native's street credibility and a penchant for bringing home federal funds, all of which has helped him unify a city party long stricken with racial strife, a big reason why his majority-black constituency re-elects him overwhelmingly.

Brady was, until recently, far less influential in Washington than at home. He's not known for his lawmaking. But with the help of a home-state power broker, Democratic Rep. John P. Murtha, he secured the chairmanship of the House Administration Committee in 2007, becoming the unofficial mayor of Capitol Hill with responsibility for overseeing nearly $1 billion in federal spending. He also manages the House complex and doling out office spaces and parking spots. It's a post that suits an old-school machine politician like Brady.

The committee also monitors efforts by the states to make voting procedures more sound and oversees management of the $621 million Capitol Visitor Center, the new entrance point to the Capitol for an estimated 3 million tourists each year. In March 2008, Brady's bill establishing a management structure for the new facility passed the House. President George W. Bush signed it into law later that year.

In Philadelphia, Brady has an uncanny ability to settle disputes among warring tribes. "Nobody can do better than me in my relationships with colleagues," Brady told the Philadelphia Inquirer in 2007. "I have a history of putting people together." In perhaps his most notable mediation, Brady literally talked City Councilman Rick Mariano off the brink in 2005, after Mariano had gone to the top of City Hall in a highly publicized suicide scare just before he was to be indicted.

As a former union man — Brady worked as a carpenter before getting into politics — he has particular credibility in negotiating labor disputes. It's a skill that translates well in his new job. Soon after taking over the House Administration Committee, he settled a four-year-old debate by moving legislation to merge the previously separate Library of Congress and U.S. Capitol police forces. A member of the House Armed Services Committee, Brady is also pushing to employ more wounded veterans in administrative and support positions in the House complex.

Though Brady has taken well to the role of House mayor, what he really wanted was to be Philadelphia's mayor. He ran in the 2007 Democratic primary for the job and was an early frontrunner. But a spitting match ensued between Brady and one rival, wealthy former insurance executive Tom Knox. The negative publicity cost both of them the win; former City Councilman Michael Nutter won the seat.

Brady grew up in Philadelphia's Overbrook section and still lives there with his second wife, a former cheerleader for the Philadelphia Eagles. Catholic and white when Brady was a child, the neighborhood is now mostly black.

Only by securing African-American support has Brady managed to survive. It's a task he's taken on with gusto, giving endorsements and patronage appointments without regard to race. In Congress, he's cosponsored a resolution apologizing for slavery and published a book through the Administration Committee about African-Americans who've served in Congress. He calls Georgia Democratic Rep. John Lewis, the civil rights leader beaten during the 1965 march on Selma, Ala., his hero.

While Brady has a strong party allegiance — he almost never deviates from party orthodoxy when Republicans and Democrats are divided — he has even stronger ties to Murtha, who chairs Appropriations' Defense Subcommittee. "Jack always tells me where to go, what to do, where I should be," he said.

With Murtha's help, Brady is a prolific provider of earmarked federal funding for local projects. During his mayoral campaign, he said he'd secured more than $2 billion in such funds, often derided in Washington as pork barrel spending. But Brady makes no apologies. "It is what it is, I am what I am, I do what I do," Brady told the Inquirer in 2007. "I deliver money. I just don't present checks and write press releases."

Brady's loyalty to organized labor reflects his working-class roots. He does occasionally part with Democratic colleagues on union matters. In 2001, Brady infuriated some longtime allies in the environmental lobby by supporting Bush's proposal to allow oil drilling in Alaska's Arctic National Wildlife Refuge, an idea backed by the Teamsters Union and the AFL-CIO's building trades division as part of a push for domestic energy jobs.

An athlete in his younger days, Brady once teamed up with Wilt Chamberlain in a neighborhood pickup basketball game and sparred with Muhammad Ali. The son of a cop who died young and a supermarket checker, Brady had college scholarship offers but went to work as a carpenter instead to help support his family. After 12 years in the trade, he moved into a full-time post with the carpenters' union. Brady still carries a union card and has a lifetime score of 100 percent in the AFL-CIO's rating of congressional voting records.

He credits his decision to get into politics to a broken streetlight. Brady was worried about his mother walking home from her food market job at night, so he asked his local Democratic ward boss to fix it. When the committeeman failed to follow through, Brady ran for a local party post and won.

Once in the party organization, Brady hit it off with then-City Council President George X. Schwartz, securing his patronage by fixing up Schwartz's basement, gratis. When Schwartz was convicted in the 1980 Abscam scandal, in which undercover FBI agents offered money to members of Congress and some local and state officials for government contracts, Schwartz cleared the way for Brady to succeed him as the local Democratic ward leader. Brady made an unsuccessful bid for the city council in 1983 but continued to be a key player in city politics. He has been chairman of the city Democratic Party since 1986.

When Democratic Rep. Thomas M. Foglietta resigned, Brady won a 1998 special election to succeed him, with 74 percent of the vote, and has rolled up even bigger tallies since then, even following his loss in the mayoral race; he won re-election in 2008 with 91 percent of the vote.

KEY VOTES

2008

Yes Delay consideration of Colombia free-trade agreement

Yes Override Bush veto of federal farm and nutrition programs reauthorization bill

No Overhaul surveillance laws and permit dismissal of suits against companies that conducted warrantless wiretapping

Yes Grant mortgage relief to homeowners and funding for Fannie Mae and Freddie Mac

Yes Approve initial $700 billion program to stabilize financial markets

Yes Approve final $700 billion program to stabilize financial markets

Yes Provide $14 billion in loans to automakers

2007

Yes Increase minimum wage by $2.10 an hour

Yes Approve $124.2 billion in emergency war spending and set goal for redeployment of troops from Iraq

No Reject federal contraceptive assistance to international family planning groups

? Override Bush veto of $23.2 billion water projects authorization bill

No Implement Peru free-trade agreement

Yes Approve energy policy overhaul with new fuel economy standards

No Clear $473.5 billion omnibus spending bill, including $70 billion for military operations

CQ VOTE STUDIES

	PARTY UNITY		PRESIDENTIAL SUPPORT	
	SUPPORT	OPPOSE	SUPPORT	OPPOSE
2008	99%	1%	14%	86%
2007	99%	1%	5%	95%
2006	92%	8%	30%	70%
2005	93%	7%	18%	82%
2004	96%	4%	18%	82%

INTEREST GROUPS

	AFL-CIO	ADA	CCUS	ACU
2008	100%	100%	56%	0%
2007	100%	85%	44%	0%
2006	100%	95%	53%	16%
2005	100%	100%	35%	4%
2004	100%	95%	19%	4%

PENNSYLVANIA 1

South and central Philadelphia; Chester

The birthplace of the Constitution, the 1st boasts many recognizable icons, such as the Liberty Bell and the Philly cheesesteak. With 90 percent of its population in Philadelphia, the W-shaped 1st is the state's most racially and ethnically diverse district. The rest of the 1st falls in a working-class slice of Delaware County.

Beyond the historical streets, much of the 1st has a bleak economic landscape. The district has the state's lowest median income, and less than one-fifth of the population has a college education. Jobs at Aker Philadelphia Shipyard have helped stabilize the blue-collar workforce, but earlier factory losses are now compounded by a construction sector downturn and some layoffs in the usually solid government, education and health care arenas. Philadelphia International Airport has seen its two major commercial carriers lose passenger traffic and revenue.

Football's Eagles, baseball's Phillies, basketball's 76ers and hockey's Flyers play in arenas and stadiums on Broad Street in South Philadelphia. Local officials hope the sports complex can revitalize nearby

neighborhoods, which are still recovering from past economic losses. Developers hope to build two casinos in the city, and farther south, a stadium for soccer's new Philadelphia Union franchise and a waterfront complex in Chester are expected to be complete by 2010.

Blacks represent the largest population bloc in the 1st, at 45 percent, and whites make up one-third of the district's population. The district also has a large Asian presence, concentrated in Philadelphia's Chinatown, and nearly three-fourths of Philadelphia's Hispanic population resides in the 1st. The district's Italian-American population supports a famous food market, which is the oldest and largest outdoor market in the United States. The 1st's strong union presence and substantial minority population make it a slam-dunk for Democratic candidates. Barack Obama took 88 percent of the 2008 presidential vote here.

MAJOR INDUSTRY
Government, health care, service, shipbuilding, airport

CITIES
Philadelphia (pt.), 571,130; Chester, 36,854

NOTABLE
Eastern State Penitentiary, now a museum, was the most expensive prison upon its opening in 1829 and held gangster Al Capone.

Rep. Chaka Fattah (D)

Elected 1994; 8th term

CAPITOL OFFICE
225-4001
www.house.gov/fattah
2301 Rayburn Bldg. 20515-3802; fax 225-5392

COMMITTEES
Appropriations

RESIDENCE
Philadelphia

BORN
Nov. 21, 1956; Philadelphia, Pa.

RELIGION
Baptist

FAMILY
Wife, Renee Chenault-Fattah; four children

EDUCATION
Community College of Philadelphia, attended
1976 (political science); U. of Pennsylvania,
M.A. 1986 (government administration)

CAREER
Public official

POLITICAL HIGHLIGHTS
Democratic candidate for Philadelphia City
Commission, 1978; Pa. House, 1983-89; Pa. Senate,
1989-95; Consumer Party nominee for U.S. House
(special election), 1991; sought Democratic
nomination for mayor of Philadelphia, 2007

ELECTION RESULTS

2008 GENERAL

Chaka Fattah (D)	276,870	88.9%
Adam A. Lang (R)	34,466	11.1%

2008 PRIMARY

Chaka Fattah (D)	unopposed

2006 GENERAL

Chaka Fattah (D)	165,867	88.6%
Michael Gessner (R)	17,291	9.2%
David G. Baker (GREEN)	4,125	2.2%

PREVIOUS WINNING PERCENTAGES
2004 (88%); 2002 (88%); 2000 (98%); 1998 (87%);
1996 (88%); 1994 (86%)

Fattah is a savvy liberal who presses an urban-oriented policy agenda, including education, child welfare and — more recently — alternative-energy projects. Since arriving in Congress, he has kept his focus on helping his hometown of Philadelphia in surmounting poverty, gang violence and other problems.

Given his druthers, Fattah (full name: SHOCK-ah fa-TAH) would prefer to be running Philadelphia from City Hall; he lost in the 2007 mayoral election. But he remains well-positioned to help determine priorities back home as a member of the powerful Appropriations Committee. He also has stood up for the city as chairman of the Congressional Urban Caucus, which consists of members representing the nation's largest metropolitan areas and focuses on such issues as housing, job training and education.

He sits on Appropriations' Energy and Water and Financial Services panels, which give him avenues to address his main concerns. Like other Congressional Black Caucus members, he said that some funding in the $700 billion financial sector rescue law and President Obama's subsequent $787 billion economic stimulus law should be geared toward helping inner-city residents.

Fattah also sits on the Commerce-Justice-Science Appropriations panel. He gained national attention in 2009 when he said NASA should uphold rules in an online contest that allowed Internet users to name a new room in the International Space Station after TV talk-show comedian Stephen Colbert. But NASA officials — who said they always reserved the right to make the final decision — chose second-place winner "Serenity" and named a new space station treadmill after Colbert instead.

Although he gave up his seat on the Education and Labor panel when he joined Appropriations, Fattah still views education as his top legislative priority and the key to helping low-income Americans escape poverty. In 2008, Congress cleared a major overhaul of the Higher Education Act that included an update of the GEAR UP program, which Fattah considers his most significant legislative achievement. The grant program, which encourages low-income youths to set their sights on college, became law in 1998 after Fattah joined with conservative Republican Mark Souder of Indiana and won support from the Clinton administration. The program underwrites tutoring, mentoring and counseling for students as early as sixth grade and gives schools incentives to offer college preparatory classes. The 2008 revisions included a new effort to reach foster children, whose needs are of special concern to Fattah.

Fattah continues to press a second major education initiative: a student bill of rights that would require states to ensure that students in urban areas have the same access to quality education as their suburban counterparts. And in 2009, he introduced a bill to replace the current tax code with a fee on transactions over $500, which he said would offer money for investment in infrastructure, health care and schools.

He also promoted education outside of Congress, as a founder of and active fundraiser for CORE Philly, a nonprofit program providing scholarships to help Philadelphia high school graduates attend select Pennsylvania colleges. He announced in November 2008 that he was closing CORE due to budget constraints on Philadelphia's city government, one of its main donors.

Fattah has pressed interests in child welfare issues, backing a bill the House passed in June 2008 that would reduce the number of children in foster care and improve the quality of those services. He also has pushed to revive a White House conference on children initiated by President Theodore Roosevelt.

Fattah's own academic career was decidedly unconventional. He dropped out of high school in early 1974 and got a General Equivalency Diploma later that year. He took undergraduate classes at a Philadelphia community college, but never graduated. Later, as a state lawmaker, he obtained a master's degree in 1986 from the University of Pennsylvania.

Born Arthur Davenport, one of six boys in a household headed by his widowed mother, his name changed when his mother married community activist David Fattah. According to a Philadelphia Inquirer profile long displayed on his office wall, his mother named him "Chaka" in honor of a Zulu warrior. While he was growing up, Fattah met Democratic Rep. William H. Gray III and worked on one of his campaigns. At age 21, he made his own try for elective office, finishing fourth in a run for a municipal office. Four years later, he took on a Democratic Party-backed incumbent and won a state House seat and became, at 25, the youngest person ever elected to the state legislature. It was the first time — but by no means the last — that he challenged the party establishment and won.

After six years in the state House and six in the state Senate, Fattah entered the 1991 special-election race to succeed Gray, who had resigned to become president of the United Negro College Fund. But the Democratic Party backed longtime City Councilman Lucien E. Blackwell, so Fattah temporarily quit the party to run on the Consumer Party ticket. He lost.

Redistricting in 1992 — in which Fattah had a hand as a member of the state Senate — reduced the percentage of African-Americans in the 2nd District from 80 percent to 62 percent. That undercut Blackwell, who had his base among West Philly's poor and working-class blacks. Fattah went after the incumbent in 1994, outworking him and claiming victory in the Democratic primary. It was his last close contest for the House. In the overwhelmingly Democratic 2nd, Fattah has not been seriously challenged since.

Fattah jumped into the Philadelphia mayoral race in the fall of 2006, saying the job offered a more direct opportunity than Congress to make a difference on the issues he cares about. He outlined what the Philadelphia Daily News called a "wildly ambitious" agenda for overhauling the public schools, curbing gun violence and slashing the city's poverty rate. But the job went to Michael Nutter, a former city councilman who focused on everyday concerns of voters. Fattah came in fourth in the Democratic primary, just behind Democrat Robert A. Brady, who represents the 1st District, also based in Philadelphia. Neither had to give up his House seat to run.

KEY VOTES

2008
Yes Delay consideration of Colombia free-trade agreement
Yes Override Bush veto of federal farm and nutrition programs reauthorization bill
No Overhaul surveillance laws and permit dismissal of suits against companies that conducted warrantless wiretapping
Yes Grant mortgage relief to homeowners and funding for Fannie Mae and Freddie Mac
Yes Approve initial $700 billion program to stabilize financial markets
Yes Approve final $700 billion program to stabilize financial markets
Yes Provide $14 billion in loans to automakers

2007
Yes Increase minimum wage by $2.10 an hour
Yes Approve $124.2 billion in emergency war spending and set goal for redeployment of troops from Iraq
No Reject federal contraceptive assistance to international family planning groups
Yes Override Bush veto of $23.2 billion water projects authorization bill
Yes Implement Peru free-trade agreement
Yes Approve energy policy overhaul with new fuel economy standards
No Clear $473.5 billion omnibus spending bill, including $70 billion for military operations

CQ VOTE STUDIES

	PARTY UNITY		PRESIDENTIAL SUPPORT	
	SUPPORT	OPPOSE	SUPPORT	OPPOSE
2008	99%	1%	13%	87%
2007	99%	1%	6%	94%
2006	96%	4%	28%	72%
2005	96%	4%	11%	89%
2004	99%	1%	20%	80%

INTEREST GROUPS

	AFL-CIO	ADA	CCUS	ACU
2008	100%	95%	53%	0%
2007	96%	75%	55%	0%
2006	100%	100%	40%	8%
2005	92%	95%	40%	4%
2004	100%	85%	22%	0%

PENNSYLVANIA 2
West Philadelphia; Chestnut Hill; Cheltenham

From the vantage point of the William Penn statue atop City Hall, one can see the 2nd stretching west and north over some of Philadelphia's long-established neighborhoods. The district encompasses Center City skyscrapers, then moves west across the Schuylkill River past the University of Pennsylvania and Drexel University. West Philadelphia, once Irish, Greek and Jewish, is now nearly all black and features pockets of middle-class and poor communities. Overall, more than three-fifths of the 2nd's residents are African-American.

Except for the Montgomery County township of Cheltenham, the 2nd is within Philadelphia. The district includes the affluent city neighborhoods of Rittenhouse Square, one of five squares Penn designed in his original plan of the city, and Chestnut Hill, in the city's northwest corner. Fairmount Park, which flanks the Schuylkill River, houses the city's art museum, zoo and "Boathouse Row," and runs north along diverse, middle-class neighborhoods such as Brewerytown and Manayunk, ending in Chestnut Hill.

Areas just north of downtown and Temple University (shared with the 1st) have some of the city's lowest family incomes. Home values have plummeted in West Philadelphia and University City, Center City and Fairmount neighborhoods, but partnerships with local businesses provide some relief to poor areas. As part of the University of Pennsylvania's "Penn Compact," the school works with communities to improve education, public health, economic and job development, quality of life and the landscape of West Philadelphia and nearby areas. And UPenn's medical school complements the 2nd's health care industry.

The 2nd's blue-collar workforce and large minority population give it an overwhelming Democratic majority. In the 2008 presidential election, Barack Obama had his best showing in the state here, taking 90 percent of the district's vote.

MAJOR INDUSTRY
Higher education, health care, tourism

CITIES
Philadelphia (pt.), 609,480; Glenside (unincorporated) (pt.), 3,093

NOTABLE
The steps of the Philadelphia Museum of Art were immortalized in the movie "Rocky"; The 30th Street Station is in West Philadelphia.

Rep. Kathy Dahlkemper (D)

Elected 2008; 1st term

Dahlkemper supports most of her party's fiscal policies while reflecting her district's conservative social bent with an opposition to abortion and gun control. Though a political newcomer, she said the quarter-century she spent in the health field and the decade-plus she was a small-business owner qualify her to address several issues.

As Congress deals with health care, she said her past as a dietician will lead her to advocate for disease prevention and against childhood obesity, as well as reducing overall health costs. And from her seat on the Agriculture Committee she hopes to help the public understand the links between farming and the economy.

Meanwhile, she said her more recent job at a landscaping company started by her father-in-law is beneficial to her on the Small Business Committee, where she chairs the Regulations and Healthcare Subcommittee. She said she was responsible for human resources and health care coverage at the company, learning firsthand the difficulties of providing coverage to employees.

Dahlkemper also serves on the Science and Technology Committee. She plans to work on diversifying her area's declining manufacturing-driven base by encouraging investment in energy technology and "green job" creation. "We had a depressed economy before the rest of the nation was really suffering as they are right now," she said at a March 2009 panel hearing.

Dahlkemper backed most of President Obama's early economic initiatives, including a $787 billion economic stimulus law that she said would help create jobs and spur growth. But she was one of just 24 House Democrats — eight of them freshmen from competitive swing districts — to vote against a measure allowing federal bankruptcy judges to modify the terms of a home mortgage in some cases to prevent foreclosure, a procedure known as "cramdown."

Campaigning as a Washington outsider, Dahlkemper ousted seven-term Republican Phil English in 2008 with 51 percent of the vote. She got campaign help from former President Bill Clinton, but her district's support for Arizona GOP Sen. John McCain in the 2008 presidential race makes her a Republican target for 2010.

CAPITOL OFFICE
225-5406
dahlkemper.house.gov
516 Cannon Bldg. 20515-3803; fax 225-3103

COMMITTEES
Agriculture
Science & Technology
Small Business
(Regulations & Healthcare - chairwoman)

RESIDENCE
Erie

BORN
Dec. 10, 1957; Erie, Pa.

RELIGION
Roman Catholic

FAMILY
Husband, Dan Dahlkemper; five children

EDUCATION
Edinboro State College, Erie, B.S. 1982 (dietetics)

CAREER
Landscaping company owner; dietician

POLITICAL HIGHLIGHTS
No previous office

ELECTION RESULTS

2008 GENERAL

Kathy Dahlkemper (D)	146,846	51.2%
Phil English (R)	139,757	48.8%

2008 PRIMARY

Kathy Dahlkemper (D)	43,858	44.9%
Kyle W. Foust (D)	24,672	25.3%
Tom Myers (D)	18,584	19.0%
Mike Waltner (D)	10,532	10.8%

PENNSYLVANIA 3

Northwest — Erie

Nestled in the state's northwestern corner, the 3rd takes in all of Erie County — Pennsylvania's only Lake Erie coastline — and parts of six other counties. The economy of this Rust Belt, historically blue-collar area centers around the city of Erie's port.

Erie County, where roughly 45 percent of the district's residents live, has retained an industrial feel despite decades of decline. Manufacturing still makes up nearly one-fourth of the county's workforce, but job opportunities in the service sector and health care industry have expanded in the last 20 years. There are several high-tech companies here, and the city also attracts visitors to the public beaches and Presque Isle State Park during the warmer months.

Outside of Erie, no city has more than 17,000 residents. These communities rely on small business and scores of tooling and machine shops, especially in Crawford County. Mercer County (a portion of which is in the 4th) still has some steel mills. Butler County in the south is dominated by manufacturing, but it also hosts Slippery Rock University.

The city of Erie's median household income is well below state and national averages, while surrounding areas are above the median. Pockets of black residents in northern and central Erie help give the county a Democratic lean. These Democratic tendencies are mostly offset by the GOP lean in Butler and Crawford counties. In 2008, Republican presidential candidate John McCain eked out a 49 percent victory by 17 votes in the 3rd, but incumbent Phil English was ousted by Democrat Kathy Dahlkemper.

MAJOR INDUSTRY
Manufacturing, service

CITIES
Erie, 103,717; Sharon, 16,328; Butler, 15,121

NOTABLE
The rebuilt *U.S. Brig Niagara*, a fighting ship from the War of 1812, is docked in Erie.

Rep. Jason Altmire (D)

Elected 2006; 2nd term

Altmire is a former congressional aide and lobbyist who likes to quietly find ways to compromise. He hews a careful middle path and tacks rightward on some social issues, yet strongly supports his party on core concerns like education and health care.

In his first term, Altmire bucked his party 20 percent of the time on votes pitting most Democrats against most Republicans, a level only nine House Democrats exceeded. He supported a Republican bill to reject federal contraceptive assistance to international family planning groups and another to repeal the District of Columbia's law prohibiting firearm possession.

He also refused to back two $700 billion proposals in fall 2008 — the second of which became law — to assist the ailing financial services sector, calling the legislation fundamentally flawed. He did, however, support a subsequent $14 billion bailout of U.S. automakers, which stalled in the Senate, as well as President Obama's $787 billion stimulus package that became law, hailing the latter as a "targeted and transparent economic recovery plan."

But Altmire, a member of the fiscally conservative Blue Dog Coalition, was among a group of Democrats who cautioned the new president and Democratic leaders not to pursue an overambitious agenda that could result in favoring more affluent areas and not the heartland. "I'm not saying don't do big things. But maybe we should wait until we get the economy stabilized, in a year or so," he said.

Altmire also takes a more conservative stance on immigration. He wants to beef up border security and target employers who knowingly hire illegal immigrants. A member of the Republican-dominated House Immigration Reform Caucus, he opposes creating a path to citizenship for illegal immigrants.

The son of a former schoolteacher, Altmire sits on the Education and Labor Committee. He favors revising the 2001 No Child Left Behind national education law, which he said has been drastically underfunded. In 2007, he supported the first reauthorization of Head Start, an early-childhood development program for low-income preschoolers, in almost a decade. And despite being a social conservative, he voted against an amendment that would have allowed faith-based Head Start providers to take religion into account when hiring.

Altmire is a former hospital association executive and was part of a congressional task force on health care during President Bill Clinton's unsuccessful push in 1993 for a new national policy. Altmire still has set his heart on helping to shape an overhaul, though he has learned the lessons of the earlier effort's failure. "My view is I don't want to do something that pushes the envelope too far," Altmire said. "I want to take an evolutionary approach, not a revolutionary one."

He wants to allow the importation of prescription drugs from Canada and Western Europe and supports a move toward letting younger people buy their way into Medicare coverage. And he said he supports federal funding for embryonic stem cell research, which uses discarded embryos created during in vitro fertilization, because he saw its benefits while working for the University of Pittsburgh Medical Center.

Altmire has a seat on the Transportation and Infrastructure Committee. When the panel takes up a reauthorization of the 2005 surface transportation law, he hopes to secure funding for the future Allegheny Valley Commuter Rail and for completing the designation of the future I-376 corridor, which is expected to spur economic development in Allegheny County and points north.

CAPITOL OFFICE
225-2565
altmire.house.gov
332 Cannon Bldg. 20515-3804; fax 226-2274

COMMITTEES
Education & Labor
Small Business
(Investigations & Oversight - chairman)
Transportation & Infrastructure

RESIDENCE
McCandless

BORN
March 7, 1968; Kittanning, Pa.

RELIGION
Roman Catholic

FAMILY
Wife, Kelly Altmire; two children

EDUCATION
Florida State U., B.S. 1990 (political science);
George Washington U., M.H.S.A. 1998
(health services administration)

CAREER
Hospital association executive; lobbyist;
congressional aide

POLITICAL HIGHLIGHTS
No previous office

ELECTION RESULTS

2008 GENERAL

Jason Altmire (D)	186,536	55.9%
Melissa A. Hart (R)	147,411	44.1%

2008 PRIMARY

Jason Altmire (D)	unopposed

2006 GENERAL

Jason Altmire (D)	131,847	51.9%
Melissa A. Hart (R)	122,049	48.1%

Altmire's other committee assignment is Small Business, where he chairs the Investigations and Oversight Subcommittee. He has held hearings to review the effect of rising gas prices on small businesses and the impact of federal regulations on small home medical suppliers. He authored a bill during the 110th Congress (2007-08) to allow a business to keep the "small" classification even if it partners with a large private investor. That measure passed the House, but didn't move in the Senate.

With the 4th District's large veterans population in mind, Altmire also has been a supporter of increasing benefits to former soldiers. In his first term, he won enactment of a measure allowing the military to let members of the armed forces keep their sign-up bonuses even if injuries force them to leave the service.

Altmire's independence stretches to energy, where he supports a comprehensive plan that includes nuclear power and increased domestic oil drilling. He also favors developing alternative resources such as coal-to-liquids — important issues for the former coal and steel towns of western Pennsylvania looking to spur economic growth. But he said in April 2009 he would vote against any energy plan that included a cap on greenhouse gas emissions coupled with a market-based emissions trading system — a proposal advocated by Obama. "I'm not interested in the politics," he said. "I just think cap and trade is bad policy."

Altmire grew up in a working-class neighborhood of Lower Burrell. He was the only child of a single parent. His mother taught special education to high school students; he never knew his father.

He lettered in two sports in high school and was a football player at Florida State. As a political science major, he helped former Florida Democratic Rep. Pete Peterson on his 1990 campaign. Altmire subsequently was offered a job on Capitol Hill, where he worked for several years as Peterson's congressional aide and went to school at night, earning a master's degree in health services administration from George Washington University. He ended up working for the Federation of American Hospitals and then the University of Pittsburgh Medical Center.

Altmire said he decided to run against GOP incumbent Melissa A. Hart because he couldn't understand how the district could be represented by someone with "such a right-of-center voting record." After besting local businesswoman Georgia Berner in the primary, he linked Hart to President George W. Bush and the GOP congressional leadership, and won with 52 percent of the vote. In a tense rematch two years later, Altmire defeated Hart with 56 percent.

KEY VOTES

2008

Yes Delay consideration of Colombia free-trade agreement

Yes Override Bush veto of federal farm and nutrition programs reauthorization bill

Yes Overhaul surveillance laws and permit dismissal of suits against companies that conducted warrantless wiretapping

Yes Grant mortgage relief to homeowners and funding for Fannie Mae and Freddie Mac

No Approve initial $700 billion program to stabilize financial markets

No Approve final $700 billion program to stabilize financial markets

Yes Provide $14 billion in loans to automakers

2007

Yes Increase minimum wage by $2.10 an hour

Yes Approve $124.2 billion in emergency war spending and set goal for redeployment of troops from Iraq

Yes Reject federal contraceptive assistance to international family planning groups

Yes Override Bush veto of $23.2 billion water projects authorization bill

No Implement Peru free-trade agreement

Yes Approve energy policy overhaul with new fuel economy standards

Yes Clear $473.5 billion omnibus spending bill, including $70 billion for military operations

CQ VOTE STUDIES

	PARTY UNITY		PRESIDENTIAL SUPPORT	
	SUPPORT	OPPOSE	SUPPORT	OPPOSE
2008	84%	16%	24%	76%
2007	77%	23%	15%	85%

INTEREST GROUPS

	AFL-CIO	ADA	CCUS	ACU
2008	100%	80%	61%	24%
2007	96%	95%	55%	28%

PENNSYLVANIA 4

West – Pittsburgh suburbs

The 4th District begins in the southwestern corner of Mercer County and runs down the state's western border before heading east to wrap around the northern and eastern sides of Pittsburgh. Once a top steel producer, this traditionally blue-collar district has yet to fully recover from economic hardships and has been battered by recent downturns.

The area's major highways and its proximity to Pittsburgh make the 4th attractive to commuters as well as to new and expanding companies. Although abandoned steel mills still line the rivers here, other job sectors are beginning to develop. The 4th's health care industry is a major employer, as are a growing number of computer firms. Larger companies, such as Philips Respironics in Murrysville and TRACO in Cranberry Township bring jobs to the area, although a weak national homebuilding market has hurt Aliquippa-based wallboard manufacturer USG.

The district has yet to regain the population it had during its booming steel days, but some areas, including parts of southern Butler County, are experiencing residential growth and host a growing white-collar,

well-educated workforce. Outside of Pittsburgh's exurbs, smaller communities produce numerous agricultural products, including corn, soybeans, dairy and winter wheat.

Although union tradition has kept the district Democratic at the local level, Republicans can break the Democratic grip. The 4th's GOP base is found mainly in small farming communities and wealthy Pittsburgh suburbs such as Franklin Park, Fox Chapel and Marshall Township. In 2006, Democrats recaptured the 4th after six years of GOP control. Democrat Jason Altmire easily won re-election in 2008 even though Republican presidential candidate John McCain took 55 percent of the district's presidential vote.

MAJOR INDUSTRY
Health care, steel, manufacturing

CITIES
Ross Township, 32,551; Shaler Township, 29,757; McCandless Township, 29,022; Plum, 26,940; New Castle, 26,309

NOTABLE
Oliver B. Shallenberger invented the electric meter, which indicated the amount of electrical energy dispensed or applied, in Rochester; New Castle calls itself the fireworks capital of the United States.

Rep. Glenn Thompson (R)

Elected 2008; 1st term

A former school board member and health services manager, Thompson hopes to end a reliance on standardized education testing and to improve health care. He also favors the development of new energy resources, but watches out for how new regulations impact industries and small businesses.

He is outspoken in his opposition to the Democratic agenda. When President Obama issued an executive order reinstituting federal funding for embryonic stem cell research, Thompson said he was disturbed Obama "deemed it appropriate to use taxpayer dollars for the destruction of human embryos." When House Speaker Nancy Pelosi of California indicated Democrats were devising climate change legislation that likely would include a cap on greenhouse gases and a market-based trading system for emissions, his office put out a news release titled, "How 'Bout that San Francisco Treat!"

A member of the Agriculture Committee and its panel on energy and research, Thompson said, "Ramming climate change legislation through the House to appease the radical environmental movement will devastate an already ailing economy." He is a member of the GOP's American Energy Solutions Group, which was asked to craft a GOP alternative to the energy bill.

A member of the Small Business Committee, he opposed Obama's $787 billion economic stimulus measure, saying it would, among other things, boost taxes that would hurt small business. He also intends to use his seat on the panel to boost health care payments to rural doctors. He opposes government-backed universal health care, but did support an expansion of the State Children's Health Insurance Program, which provides coverage for children from low-income families that don't qualify for Medicaid.

As a member of the Education and Labor Committee, he criticized Democratic legislation that would allow workers to organize by majority sign-up, instead of being limited by employers to secret-ballot elections. And he said he would support efforts to rescind the 2001 No Child Left Behind law, which relies on standardized testing.

In 2008, he easily bested Democrat Mark B. McCracken with 57 percent of the vote to succeed Republican John E. Peterson, who retired.

CAPITOL OFFICE
225-5121
thompson.house.gov
124 Cannon Bldg. 20515-3805; fax 225-5796

COMMITTEES
Agriculture
Education & Labor
Small Business

RESIDENCE
Howard

BORN
July 27, 1959; Bellefonte, Pa.

RELIGION
Protestant

FAMILY
Wife, Penny Thompson; three children

EDUCATION
Pennsylvania State U., B.S. 1981 (recreation & parks); Temple U., M.Ed. 1998 (sports management & leisure studies)

CAREER
Rehabilitation therapist

POLITICAL HIGHLIGHTS
Bald Eagle Area School Board, 1990-95;
Republican nominee for Pa. House, 1998, 2000;
Centre County Republican Party chairman, 2002-08

ELECTION RESULTS

2008 GENERAL

Glenn Thompson (R)	155,513	56.7%
Mark B. McCracken (D)	112,509	41.0%
James Fryman (LIBERT)	6,155	2.2%

2008 PRIMARY

Glenn Thompson (R)	13,988	19.2%
Derek A. Walker (R)	13,153	18.0%
Matt Shaner (R)	12,860	17.6%
Jeffrey J. Stroehmann (R)	9,921	13.6%
Keith Richardson (R)	7,094	9.7%
Lou Radkowski (R)	5,083	7.0%
John Rea Stroup (R)	4,550	6.2%
Chris Exarchos (R)	4,376	6.0%
John T. Krupa (R)	1,916	2.6%

PENNSYLVANIA 5

North central — State College

The sprawling 5th covers one-fourth of the state's land area and takes in all or part of 17 counties in north-central Pennsylvania. The district's small towns are spread among state and national parks and forests.

State College, known by locals as "Happy Valley," is the 5th's most populated city and hosts Pennsylvania State University. Despite some job cuts in traditional manufacturing sectors, Centre County has one of the state's lowest unemployment rates and has attracted electronics and computer firms. The global headquarters of AccuWeather is located just outside State College. The county also relies on small businesses.

The 5th's other counties remain tied to timber production, manufacturing, oil refining and tourism. In 2004, parts of the 5th's western region — which has experienced massive population loss in recent years — were des-ignated as the Oil Region National Heritage Area. Many tourists who visit the district travel through the Allegheny National Forest. In the east, the roughly 160,000 acres of the Tioga State Forest include the Grand Canyon of Pennsylvania. In southern Jefferson County, Punxsutawney, home of the famous groundhog Phil, draws national attention each February.

Much of the 5th — particularly the northern counties — votes Republican. Penn State keeps Centre County competitive for Democrats, but John McCain won 55 percent of the district's 2008 presidential vote.

MAJOR INDUSTRY
Higher education, timber, tourism, manufacturing

CITIES
State College, 38,420; St. Marys, 14,502

NOTABLE
Drake's Well, the birthplace of the modern petroleum industry, is located on the banks of Oil Creek near Titusville; South Williamsport hosts the Little League World Series.

Rep. Jim Gerlach (R)

Elected 2002; 4th term

Gerlach is one of a vanishing breed of centrist House Republicans who are more interested in fostering compromise than picking fights. His politics have helped him fight off aggressive Democratic challenges in each of his election bids — albeit narrowly — leading him to explore whether his appeal can translate statewide.

Gerlach's (GUR-lock) voting record is peppered with high-profile stands against President George W. Bush and the House GOP leadership on issues ranging from same-sex marriage to oil drilling in wilderness areas. Only 10 House Republicans broke from their party on floor votes more often during the 110th Congress (2007-08). His record practically mirrored the decline in Bush's approval ratings: In 2003, Gerlach backed the president's position 91 percent of the time, but in 2008 that figure plummeted to 44 percent. When President Obama took office, he stuck with his party on major economic votes, but found some issues to support in the early agenda of the Democratic president, whom his district had strongly supported at the polls in 2008.

Gerlach represents a classic swing suburban district that was redrawn after the 2000 census with a slight Republican edge. He has won most of his elections by less than 3 percentage points. In the 110th, Gerlach was one of just eight House Republicans from districts that Bush did not win in the 2004 election. The GOP leadership is understanding, therefore, when he drifts from party positions. The leaders also have helped him raise his visibility by giving him seats on the Transportation and Infrastructure and Financial Services Committees. The former lets him steer highway projects to his district; the latter is a magnet for contributions from banking and insurance firms.

He voted against the first version of a $700 billion bill to shore up the financial services sector in 2008, after concluding the bill's defeat would spur improvements to it. Gerlach said the bill's opponents "thought if it went down the first time, we'd get a better bill in the process, which is what happened." He voted for a revised version that included, among other provisions, a boost in the federal deposit insurance limit and language curtailing the reach of the alternative minimum tax, which was originally intended to target only wealthy taxpayers but was not indexed for inflation.

After Obama took office, Gerlach was regarded as a potential supporter of the president's economic recovery proposal. But he joined other House Republicans in opposing the $787 billion package; he told the Norristown Times-Herald in February 2009 he considered it a "spending orgy" of programs that wouldn't achieve the desired effect of jump-starting the economy. He subsequently called on Democratic Gov. Edward G. Rendell to create a bipartisan panel to oversee spending of the stimulus funds in Pennsylvania. And he opposed Obama's $3.56 trillion budget blueprint for fiscal 2010.

He did back Democratic proposals to reauthorize and expand the State Children's Health Insurance Program, which covers children from low-income families that do not qualify for Medicaid, and to require employers seeking to justify unequal pay for male and female workers to prove such disparities are job-related.

Also in February, Gerlach filed paperwork to form an exploratory committee to seek Pennsylvania's governorship in 2010. Two-term Democratic incumbent Rendell is forced to retire because of a term limit law. Gerlach issued a statement saying he would take the next few months to "speak with political, business and community leaders, help our 2009 statewide judicial candidates, conduct polling and determine if there is a clear path to victory."

CAPITOL OFFICE
225-4315
www.house.gov/gerlach
308 Cannon Bldg. 20515-3806; fax 225-8440

COMMITTEES
Financial Services
Transportation & Infrastructure

RESIDENCE
West Pikeland Township

BORN
Feb. 25, 1955; Ellwood City, Pa.

RELIGION
Protestant

FAMILY
Wife, Karen Gerlach; three children, three stepchildren

EDUCATION
Dickinson College, B.A. 1977 (political science); Dickinson School of Law, J.D. 1980

CAREER
Lawyer

POLITICAL HIGHLIGHTS
Republican nominee for Pa. House, 1986; Pa. House, 1991-95; Pa. Senate, 1995-2003

ELECTION RESULTS

2008 GENERAL

Jim Gerlach (R)	179,423	52.1%
Bob Roggio (D)	164,952	47.9%

2008 PRIMARY

Jim Gerlach (R)	unopposed

2006 GENERAL

Jim Gerlach (R)	121,047	50.7%
Lois Murphy (D)	117,892	49.3%

PREVIOUS WINNING PERCENTAGES
2004 (51%); 2002 (51%)

From his seat on Transportation and Infrastructure, Gerlach will seek to secure funds for his district when Congress takes up a rewrite of the 2005 surface transportation law. A co-founder of the House Land Trust Caucus, now called the Land Conservation Caucus, Gerlach also will continue to concentrate on farmland and land preservation issues, which he has championed since his days as a state legislator.

Gerlach has collaborated with Democrat Joe Sestak, who also represents a suburban Philadelphia district. The pair has proposed creating an Office of Public Advocate within the Justice Department to deal with natural gas pipeline projects considered by the Federal Energy Regulatory Commission.

He wants the House to change its rules to foster more bipartisanship. He said proposed amendments to legislation with both a Democratic and Republican sponsor should be debated and voted upon. "What has been frustrating to me is the lack of efforts to bring together good ideas," Gerlach said, adding that although both parties have been heavy-handed in their rule of the House, "I think we've got to figure out, from an institutional standpoint, how to break through that partisanship."

Gerlach was born and raised in Ellwood City, a small steel town north of Pittsburgh. His mother, who raised Gerlach and his two sisters on her own after his father was killed by a drunk driver when Gerlach was 5, "was just a terrific role model," he said. Before coming to Congress, Gerlach spent 12 years as a state legislator. He was the prime sponsor of Pennsylvania's 1996 welfare law overhaul. He also championed legislation to combat suburban sprawl and mediated disputes among local authorities.

Though Pennsylvania lost two House seats in post-2000 census reapportionment, Gerlach's colleagues in the Republican-dominated General Assembly redrew the congressional map with him in mind. No House incumbent chose to run in the redrawn 6th District — which had a close partisan split, but overlapped with much of Gerlach's state Senate territory — and he was unopposed for the GOP nod in 2002. That November, he won by 5,520 votes over Democratic lawyer Dan Wofford, the son of former U.S. Sen. Harris Wofford. His three subsequent re-elections were also difficult, but in 2008 he won re-election by 4 percentage points, his largest margin to date.

Early in 2007, the Federal Election Commission fined his campaign $120,000 — one of the largest fines ever — for inaccurate campaign finance reports in 2004 and 2005. Gerlach and the commission agreed a clerical error was to blame; his treasurer erroneously reported the entire amount of campaign funds raised in the cycle on a line calling for the amount of funds raised in just the last part of the year.

KEY VOTES

2008

No   Delay consideration of Colombia free-trade agreement

Yes   Override Bush veto of federal farm and nutrition programs reauthorization bill

Yes   Overhaul surveillance laws and permit dismissal of suits against companies that conducted warrantless wiretapping

No   Grant mortgage relief to homeowners and funding for Fannie Mae and Freddie Mac

No   Approve initial $700 billion program to stabilize financial markets

Yes   Approve final $700 billion program to stabilize financial markets

No   Provide $14 billion in loans to automakers

2007

Yes   Increase minimum wage by $2.10 an hour

No   Approve $124.2 billion in emergency war spending and set goal for redeployment of troops from Iraq

Yes   Reject federal contraceptive assistance to international family planning groups

Yes   Override Bush veto of $23.2 billion water projects authorization bill

Yes   Implement Peru free-trade agreement

Yes   Approve energy policy overhaul with new fuel economy standards

Yes   Clear $473.5 billion omnibus spending bill, including $70 billion for military operations

CQ VOTE STUDIES

	PARTY UNITY		PRESIDENTIAL SUPPORT	
	SUPPORT	OPPOSE	SUPPORT	OPPOSE
2008	75%	25%	44%	56%
2007	74%	26%	45%	55%
2006	70%	30%	69%	31%
2005	82%	18%	69%	31%
2004	84%	16%	76%	24%

INTEREST GROUPS

	AFL-CIO	ADA	CCUS	ACU
2008	64%	60%	81%	48%
2007	67%	40%	90%	52%
2006	57%	45%	79%	62%
2005	40%	35%	81%	56%
2004	14%	20%	100%	68%

PENNSYLVANIA 6

Southeast — parts of Berks and Chester Counties, Philadelphia suburbs

The 6th takes in urban, suburban and rural communities stretching from a slice of Montgomery County in the Philadelphia area, including the county seat of Norristown, through northern Chester County and southern and eastern portions of Berks County, including part of Reading and all of Kutztown. Most of the 6th spreads through sparsely populated towns.

Manufacturing remains the 6th's largest industry, and factories are found throughout, especially in areas such as Coatesville, which, like other aging towns, hopes to revitalize its core downtown area. Vanguard, an investment management company, is based in the district, and a food processing sector should help stabilize the 6th's economy as it copes with rising unemployment rates in both Berks and Chester counties. Once known for its railroads and industrial prowess, the economy of Berks now includes service and retail jobs. Reading has moved away from its industrial image, becoming an entertainment and shopping hub outside of Philadelphia, but widespread layoffs have reached jobs at the

Reading Hospital and Medical Center, Berks County's largest employer. With its share of historical sites and untouched land, the 6th enjoys a modest tourism industry. The district is home to covered bridges, old mill towns and Pennsylvania Dutch communities. It also is home to both the Hopewell Furnace National Historic Site in Elverson and Valley Forge National Historical Park (shared with the 7th), where George Washington trained Continental Army soldiers during the Revolutionary War.

The generally competitive 6th backed Barack Obama by 17 percentage points in the 2008 presidential election despite supporting Republican Jim Gerlach in the U.S. House race. Growth and water-use issues dominate much of the political discussion in the region, which is mostly situated in the area triangulated by Philadelphia, Reading and Lancaster.

MAJOR INDUSTRY
Manufacturing, tourism, retail

CITIES
Reading (pt.), 36,911; Norristown, 31,282; Pottstown, 21,859

NOTABLE
The largest quilt sale in the United States takes places each year at the Kutztown Pennsylvania German Festival.

Rep. Joe Sestak (D)

Elected 2006; 2nd term

A retired admiral, Sestak is the highest-ranking former military officer ever to serve in the House. But his passion for shaping national security policy is dwarfed by his strong feelings about ensuring all Americans have access to health care.

Colleagues describe Sestak (SESS-tack) as a brilliant and demanding leader. He campaigned in 2006 on the Naval Academy's tenet of "Don't lie, don't steal, don't cheat" — a theme that helped him topple 10-term Republican Curt Weldon after Weldon was accused of using his post to get contracts for his daughter's lobbying firm.

Sestak's deep beliefs about health care emerged from personal experience. His daughter is one of three children in the country to have lived at least three years with a particularly virulent kind of brain cancer, Sestak said. She underwent surgery at the age of 4. At the time, she shared a hospital room with a 2-year-old boy with leukemia whose family lacked health insurance.

To Sestak, watching the boy's family struggle with paying for care was a radicalizing experience that motivated him to seek public office. "Everybody thinks I got in for Iraq; I did not. I got in for health care," he said. "This is payback time."

Although he has not been able to win the seat he coveted on the Energy and Commerce Committee, which has a leading role in health policy, he made sure his subcommittee assignments included health-related posts on the committees on Education and Labor and Small Business.

The wars in Iraq and Afghanistan, of course, also are near the top of his agenda. As a former admiral and new Democratic congressman, Sestak got a lot of attention early in his first term, when the war seemed to be going poorly for the United States and its allies. He appeared on NBC's "Meet the Press" after two months on the job, and has since become a frequent guest on TV talk shows, demonstrating a pronounced zest for rhetorical combat in some interviews by conservative hosts.

Sestak's military background, passion for health care reform and formidable campaign fundraising skills pushed him to the forefront of Democrats mentioned as potential 2010 contenders for the Senate seat of veteran Arlen Specter. By the end of March 2009, Sestak had a war chest exceeding $3 million. When Specter switched parties and became a Democrat in April 2009, Sestak remained critical of him and did not immediately rule out a primary challenge.

In his first term Sestak toiled in relative obscurity on arcane provisions in the Armed Services Committee's defense authorization bill, including measures to improve the Pentagon's procurement system, such as requiring a study of aircraft mishap rates and urging greater use of commercial software in military systems. His focus on procurement issues suddenly took on prominence in the 111th Congress (2009-10), as President Obama and Defense Secretary Robert M. Gates took aim at wasteful Pentagon spending and outdated weapons system priorities.

In March 2009, Armed Services leaders named Sestak to a new panel on defense acquisition reform created to address fundamental issues behind the Pentagon's continuing problems in acquiring goods and services on time and on budget. The Government Accountability Office in 2008 found that the estimated costs of major U.S. defense programs it studied exceeded initial estimates by about $295 billion.

CAPITOL OFFICE
225-2011
sestak.house.gov
1022 Longworth Bldg. 20515-3807; fax 226-0280

COMMITTEES
Armed Services
Education & Labor
Small Business

RESIDENCE
Edgmont

BORN
Dec. 12, 1951; Secane, Pa.

RELIGION
Roman Catholic

FAMILY
Wife, Susan Clark-Sestak; one child

EDUCATION
U.S. Naval Academy, B.S. 1974 (American political systems); Harvard U., M.P.A. 1980, Ph.D. 1984 (political economy & government)

MILITARY SERVICE
Navy, 1974-2005

CAREER
Navy officer

POLITICAL HIGHLIGHTS
No previous office

ELECTION RESULTS

2008 GENERAL

Joe Sestak (D)	209,955	59.6%
W. Craig Williams (R)	142,362	40.4%

2008 PRIMARY

Joe Sestak (D)	unopposed

2006 GENERAL

Joe Sestak (D)	147,898	56.4%
Curt Weldon (R)	114,426	43.6%

A month later, Gates targeted several major weapons systems for proposed cuts, delays or caps, including the F-22 fighter, the VH-71 presidential helicopter, the Navy's DDG-1000 *Zumwalt*-class destroyer and a new Air Force bomber. As lawmakers from both parties scrambled to protect their home-state interests, Sestak was a staunch public defender of the secretary's proposals — even though one of them would affect a combat search-and-rescue aircraft system in his district. "That's the problem," he said on MSNBC. "Let's be upfront about it. People tend to go to the Armed Services committees because they have districts that happen to have defense industries in them…The fight's going to be a tough, tough battle. And it's a shame. If there's a transformation needed, it's now."

Around the same time, Sestak found himself in the spotlight when Somali pirates briefly seized a U.S. ship and took its captain hostage. He said such incidents posed a new test. "If this change to a transformative Navy able to address these challenges that are different at sea isn't made, it will begin to harm the primacy of the United States Navy," he told CNN in April 2009.

Sestak's father, an immigrant from Slovakia, served 22 years in the Navy, having attended the Naval Academy and fought in World War II. His mother raised eight children, including six girls, and then taught math. "I made up my mind to go to the Navy in the third grade," Sestak said.

He followed his father's path, graduating second in his class at the Naval Academy and then earning master's and doctorate degrees from Harvard University. During 31 years in the Navy, he held a series of posts culminating in command of the *George Washington* aircraft carrier battle group of 30 U.S. and allied ships.

Sestak also served as director for defense policy on President Bill Clinton's National Security Council. After the Sept. 11 terrorist attacks, he became the first director of "Deep Blue," the Navy's anti-terrorism unit.

With his credentials and the anti-incumbent tide against the GOP in 2006, Sestak had little trouble unseating Weldon, and two years later he won re-election comfortably. Soon after taking office, though, Sestak found the position demanding, with thousands of requests from constituents for help. He went through staffers at a rapid clip, earning his office a reputation as an unpleasant place to work. It wasn't the first time; Sestak was reassigned from a top Navy post in 2005 amid reports that morale in his command was not high.

He says the Navy reassignment was the product of differences of opinion over shipbuilding policies, not questions about his leadership. And while he acknowledges the hard-driving nature of his office, he said: "I don't apologize at all. There was a lot to do to set it all up and get it all going."

KEY VOTES

2008

Yes Delay consideration of Colombia free-trade agreement

Yes Override Bush veto of federal farm and nutrition programs reauthorization bill

Yes Overhaul surveillance laws and permit dismissal of suits against companies that conducted warrantless wiretapping

Yes Grant mortgage relief to homeowners and funding for Fannie Mae and Freddie Mac

Yes Approve initial $700 billion program to stabilize financial markets

Yes Approve final $700 billion program to stabilize financial markets

Yes Provide $14 billion in loans to automakers

2007

Yes Increase minimum wage by $2.10 an hour

Yes Approve $124.2 billion in emergency war spending and set goal for redeployment of troops from Iraq

No Reject federal contraceptive assistance to international family planning groups

Yes Override Bush veto of $23.2 billion water projects authorization bill

Yes Implement Peru free-trade agreement

Yes Approve energy policy overhaul with new fuel economy standards

Yes Clear $473.5 billion omnibus spending bill, including $70 billion for military operations

CQ VOTE STUDIES

	PARTY UNITY		PRESIDENTIAL SUPPORT	
	SUPPORT	OPPOSE	SUPPORT	OPPOSE
2008	97%	3%	18%	82%
2007	95%	5%	8%	92%

INTEREST GROUPS

	AFL-CIO	ADA	CCUS	ACU
2008	100%	90%	61%	0%
2007	96%	95%	60%	0%

PENNSYLVANIA 7

Suburban Philadelphia — most of Delaware County

Anchored in the suburbs south and west of Philadelphia, the politically competitive 7th takes in heavily populated unincorporated townships in vast tracts of middle-class suburbia, including most of Delaware County, the district's population center, as well as southwestern Montgomery and eastern Chester counties.

Older suburbs in Delaware County such as Norwood, Ridley Park, Media and Upper Darby are mostly white and working-class. Oil refineries and chemical facilities drive the economy around the Delaware River communities of Marcus Hook and Trainer, but these mainstays of employment have seen recent job cuts. Upper Merion Township in Montgomery County has been expanding rapidly since the 1990s opening of the Blue Route (Interstate 476), which links Interstate 95 along the Delaware River with the Schuylkill Expressway near King of Prussia, home of a gigantic shopping mall complex.

A Boeing's helicopter facility in Ridley Park and Lockheed Martin's plant in King of Prussia provide jobs, as do the district's pharmaceutical and technology sectors. The growth of white-collar jobs gave the 7th the state's most educated workforce, but layoffs have hurt some sectors. New residential developments, many of which have sprung up in less-populated areas of Chester County, are attracting city residents.

Either major party can win here, with Democrats making inroads in previously Republican Delaware County. In 1988, Delaware County supported Republican George Bush in the presidential election by 21 percentage points; two decades later in 2008, Democrat Barack Obama won by the same margin.

Overall, Obama took 56 percent of the 7th District's vote in the 2008 presidential election, and voters here re-elected Democrat Joe Sestak to his second term in 2008 with nearly 60 percent of the vote.

MAJOR INDUSTRY
Pharmaceuticals, defense, health care

CITIES
Radnor Township, 30,878; Drexel Hill (unincorporated), 29,364

NOTABLE
Villanova University hosts the largest student-organized Special Olympics festival.

Rep. Patrick J. Murphy (D)

Elected 2006; 2nd term

CAPITOL OFFICE
225-4276
patrickmurphy.house.gov
1609 Longworth Bldg. 20515-3808; fax 225-9511

COMMITTEES
Armed Services
Select Intelligence

RESIDENCE
Bristol Township

BORN
Oct. 19, 1973; Philadelphia, Pa.

RELIGION
Roman Catholic

FAMILY
Wife, Jenni Murphy; one child

EDUCATION
Bucks County Community College, attended
1991-92; King's College (Pa.), B.S. 1996
(psychology & human resources); Widener U.,
Harrisburg, J.D. 1999

MILITARY SERVICE
Army, 1996-2004; Army Reserve, 2004-07

CAREER
Lawyer; military prosecutor; college instructor

POLITICAL HIGHLIGHTS
No previous office

ELECTION RESULTS

2008 GENERAL

Patrick J. Murphy (D)	197,869	56.8%
Tom Manion (R)	145,103	41.6%
Tom Lingenfelter (I)	5,543	1.6%

2008 PRIMARY

Patrick J. Murphy (D)	unopposed

2006 GENERAL

Patrick J. Murphy (D)	125,656	50.3%
Michael G. Fitzpatrick (R)	124,138	49.7%

Murphy has leveraged his visibility as the first Iraq War veteran in Congress into powerful friends, money for home projects and full campaign coffers. He also keeps alive a slight independent streak designed to appeal to his moderate but diverse constituency.

On the House floor, Murphy usually can be found in the southeast corner of the chamber, manning his post as a confidant of Defense Appropriations Chairman John P. Murtha,who quickly became Murphy's primary mentor and benefactor. Both are from Pennsylvania and each was the first veteran of their respective wars (the Vietnam War for Murtha) to enter Congress. Their association has given Murphy pull with the leadership and has helped him reap millions of dollars in earmarks, funding set-asides for projects back home. Murphy, in turn, has sought to mentor other Iraq and Afghanistan war veterans who are trying to enter politics.

Murphy had never held public office and had few local political ties before he ousted Rep. Michael G. Fitzpatrick by 1,518 votes in one of the tightest races of the 2006 elections. He was then immediately embraced by Democratic leaders, who granted him seats on the Armed Services and Select Intelligence panels and relied on him heavily during their push to end the war.

But Murphy doesn't always toe the Democratic line. In the 110th Congress (2007-08), he split with his fellow Democrats on one out of every 10 votes that pitted a majority of one party against the other, placing him in the bottom fifth in party unity among his caucus. He joined the fiscally conservative coalition of "Blue Dog" Democrats and voted against the Democratic budget in March 2007, saying it didn't do enough to guarantee middle-class tax breaks or rein in government spending.

In 2009, however, with the economy in a deep recession, Murphy backed not only his party's budget, but also a $787 billion economic stimulus law and a $410 billion fiscal 2009 catchall spending bill. He also supports his party on some social issues; he voted in 2007 for legislation to bar job discrimination based on sexual preference, has backed measures to permit the Food and Drug Administration to regulate tobacco, and supports federal funding of embryonic stem cell research.

Despite being courted by Sen. Hillary Rodham Clinton of New York, in August 2007 Murphy was the first member of Pennsylvania's Democratic delegation to support Illinois Sen. Barack Obama's presidential bid, bucking the conventional wisdom of his party at the time and parting ways with Murtha, who was firmly in Clinton's camp.

Murphy and Obama have shared a desire to bring U.S. troops back from Iraq. The two, with California Democrat Mike Thompson, had tried to push legislation in 2007 to halt troop escalation and set a timeline for withdrawal, but were unsuccessful. In an impassioned speech on the House floor during debate on a war funding bill for fiscal 2007, Murphy said: "For the last four years, this Republican Congress followed lock step as my fellow soldiers continued to die in Iraq without a clear mission, without benchmarks to determine success, without a clear timeline for coming home." He strongly commended Obama's plan in February 2009 to draw down troops over 18 months.

Murphy did not express doubts about the U.S. mission in Afghanistan. When President Obama in March 2009 announced plans to deploy additional combat troops to that country, including 4,000 from Murphy's old unit, the 82nd Airborne, he hailed the decision "to send my fellow paratroopers to do what they do best — take the fight to the enemies of the United States."

From his seat on Armed Services, he saw his bill mandating stricter oversight and clear rules of engagement for private contractors operating in Iraq added to the fiscal 2008 defense authorization bill and subsequently signed into law. He also has backed several bills to improve benefits for war veterans and carries in his wallet a picture of Michael Levin, a Bucks County resident killed while serving as a paratrooper in Iraq.

Murphy sponsored a bill during the 110th Congress (2007-08) condemning a boycott of Israeli academia, and he often speaks out on issues important to the Jewish community, which makes up a substantial part of his constituency.

Murphy grew up in a working-class Catholic family in Northeast Philadelphia, the son of a police officer and a deeply religious mother. He joined ROTC at King's College and signed up for active duty with the Army immediately upon graduation. Military service was in his blood — his father and multiple uncles had served. Murphy was named after a friend of his mother's who was killed in Vietnam.

Murphy earned a law degree from Widener University in 1999. While working as a prosecutor later, he was asked to teach a constitutional law class at West Point, which made him the youngest professor there at the time. But soon after taking that position came the attacks of Sept. 11, and Murphy volunteered to fight in Iraq, partly to avenge the deaths of two family members of his childhood best friend.

After a short stint with the U.N. peacekeeping mission in Bosnia, Murphy joined the 82nd Airborne Division and was deployed to Iraq in 2003. He felt uneasy about the war even at that time, but he threw himself into the mission and was awarded a Bronze Star. He lost 19 members of his unit in combat. "You have to execute the orders that you are given, but there was something in my stomach that just didn't feel right," he recalled.

Upon returning from Iraq, he became determined to work to bring the troops home and volunteered in Democrat John Kerry's 2004 presidential campaign. Following Kerry's defeat, Murphy decided to forgo a lucrative legal career to take on incumbent Fitzpatrick through a huge grass-roots effort that enlisted more than 1,000 young volunteers.

When he entered the race, he hadn't lived in the district for years and had no roots in the local political community. The 8th had long been dominated by a strong Bucks County GOP organization. But district voters, who had elected Republicans since 1992, were fed up with the war and ready for a change.

Murphy won his first re-election in 2008 by 15 percentage points over Republican Tom Manion, a retired Marine Corps colonel whose son died in 2007 while serving in Iraq.

KEY VOTES

2008

Yes Delay consideration of Colombia free-trade agreement

Yes Override Bush veto of federal farm and nutrition programs reauthorization bill

Yes Overhaul surveillance laws and permit dismissal of suits against companies that conducted warrantless wiretapping

Yes Grant mortgage relief to homeowners and funding for Fannie Mae and Freddie Mac

Yes Approve initial $700 billion program to stabilize financial markets

Yes Approve final $700 billion program to stabilize financial markets

Yes Provide $14 billion in loans to automakers

2007

Yes Increase minimum wage by $2.10 an hour

Yes Approve $124.2 billion in emergency war spending and set goal for redeployment of troops from Iraq

No Reject federal contraceptive assistance to international family planning groups

Yes Override Bush veto of $23.2 billion water projects authorization bill

No Implement Peru free-trade agreement

Yes Approve energy policy overhaul with new fuel economy standards

No Clear $473.5 billion omnibus spending bill, including $70 billion for military operations

CQ VOTE STUDIES

	PARTY UNITY		PRESIDENTIAL SUPPORT	
	SUPPORT	OPPOSE	SUPPORT	OPPOSE
2008	95%	5%	20%	80%
2007	87%	13%	9%	91%

INTEREST GROUPS

	AFL-CIO	ADA	CCUS	ACU
2008	93%	85%	67%	12%
2007	92%	95%	55%	4%

PENNSYLVANIA 8

Northern Philadelphia suburbs – Bucks County

North of Philadelphia, the 8th takes in all of Bucks County, a small part of Montgomery County and a slice of Northeast Philadelphia. Founded in 1682 as one of the state's three original counties, Bucks' stately mansions, scenery and charm have attracted wealthy, white-collar residents. Development began in the 1950s with the opening of Levittown, one of the earliest planned U.S. suburbs.

Steel, once a major employer in Bucks, caused long-term job losses in the blue-collar sector, and a shuttered U.S. Steel plant in Fairless Hills was redeveloped to lure varied heavy industry. Recent layoffs at a wind turbine plant there have cost the district further factory jobs, although the company will continue to produce turbine parts at the plant.

Propping up the economy are small businesses and several hospitals. A deep-water port makes the 8th something of a distribution and warehouse center. One of the state's first racetrack and casino enterprises opened in the county in 2006, and Philadelphia Park Casino and Racetrack draws visitors and revenue. But that economic diversity has not

insulated the county from rising unemployment rates and cutbacks in social services.

Voters in the 8th tend to be fiscally conservative but support environmentalism and hold above moderate stances on some social issues. Upper Bucks leans Republican, and the GOP also does well in wealthy Upper and Lower Makefield townships. Although the GOP dominates local elections in the 8th, Democrats compete in statewide and federal elections and are strong in southeastern Bucks and in the Pennsylvania suburbs of Trenton, N.J. Democrat Patrick J. Murphy won Bucks in his 2008 re-election run, after narrowly losing it in 2006. Murphy's gains in Bucks, coupled with 70 percent of the vote in Montgomery County, were enough for him to win the district comfortably. Democrat Barack Obama won the district with 54 percent in the 2008 presidential election.

MAJOR INDUSTRY
Health care, wholesale and retail trade

CITIES
Levittown (unincorporated), 53,966; Philadelphia (pt.), 30,938

NOTABLE
George Washington's Delaware River crossing is re-enacted in Washington Crossing each Christmas Day.

Rep. Bill Shuster (R)

Elected May 2001; 4th full term

CAPITOL OFFICE
225-2431
www.house.gov/shuster
204 Cannon Bldg. 20515-3809; fax 225-2486

COMMITTEES
Armed Services
Natural Resources
Transportation & Infrastructure

RESIDENCE
Hollidaysburg

BORN
Jan. 10, 1961; McKeesport, Pa.

RELIGION
Lutheran

FAMILY
Wife, Rebecca Shuster; two children

EDUCATION
Dickinson College, B.A. 1983 (political science
& history); American U., M.B.A. 1987

CAREER
Car dealer; tire company manager

POLITICAL HIGHLIGHTS
No previous office

ELECTION RESULTS

2008 GENERAL
Bill Shuster (R)	174,951	63.9%
Tony Barr (D)	98,735	36.1%

2008 PRIMARY
Bill Shuster (R)	unopposed

2006 GENERAL
Bill Shuster (R)	121,069	60.3%
Tony Barr (D)	79,610	39.7%

PREVIOUS WINNING PERCENTAGES
2004 (70%); 2002 (71%); 2001 Special Election (52%)

Most Republicans from the Northeast have at least some moderate tendencies, but not Shuster. Representing one of the region's most unabashedly red districts, he combines a conservative philosophy with a record of steering home federal funds for economic development and public works improvements.

A loyal Republican on both fiscal and social policy, Shuster rarely opposes his party's leaders. Since his arrival in 2001, Shuster has sided with Republicans on roughly 95 percent of the votes in which a majority of the two parties diverged.

That philosophy is popular in a district where two-thirds of voters backed George W. Bush in 2004 and 63 percent supported Arizona Republican Sen. John McCain in 2008; both were the highest percentages of any district in the Northeast. His loyalty to Republican leadership earned him the post of deputy GOP whip in 2007.

In delivering funds to the district, Shuster proudly continues in the tradition of his father, GOP Rep. Bud Shuster, known as the "King of Asphalt" during his six-year reign as the chairman of the Transportation and Infrastructure Committee. Bud Shuster resigned in 2001, citing health concerns, a year after the House ethics committee reprimanded him for his relationship with a longtime aide who had become a lobbyist.

By waiting to resign until he was sworn in for a 15th term, Bud Shuster paved the way for his son to run for his seat in an abbreviated special election. Bill Shuster not only won, he also followed his father onto Transportation and Infrastructure, where GOP leaders held a seat open for him.

The younger Shuster has grown accustomed to comparisons with his father. "That never bothers me," he said. "He's been a great teacher and a mentor; I ask for his advice on issues. People still occasionally call me Bud."

The elder Shuster was hired as a railroad lobbyist in 2007, the same year his son became ranking Republican on Transportation's Subcommittee on Railroads, Pipelines and Hazardous Materials. Government watchdog groups say such arrangements among relatives are troubling, but Bill Shuster said his father never lobbies him and doesn't need to — his father has close relationships with more-senior committee members.

With Congress set to take up a massive surface transportation authorization in the 111th Congress (2009-10), Shuster will have plenty of opportunities to find new ways to pave and otherwise spruce up his district, which is comprised of small towns. "We've got to make sure that rural America gets improvements to the highway system," he said.

Shuster opposed President Obama's early economic initiatives, including a $787 billion economic stimulus law and a $410 billion catchall spending bill. "The American people know we can't borrow and spend our way back to prosperity," he said in an April 2009 newspaper opinion column. Nevertheless, he saw no conflict when he held photo opportunities to hand out funds for firefighters' radios, downtown improvements and other projects. He said getting earmarks — the special-interest funds steered to specific districts — is a key part of his job.

As a member of the Armed Services Committee, Shuster strongly backed Bush's Iraq policy while looking out for Letterkenny Army Depot, an Army missile facility in Chambersburg. He has joined other Republicans on the panel in arguing against cuts for missile defense in the face of threats from North Korea and other nations.

Shuster's district includes Shanksville, where United Airlines Flight 93 crashed after passengers fought hijackers trying to fly the plane to Washington, D.C., on Sept. 11, 2001. In 2007, Shuster introduced legislation to posthumously award a Congressional Gold Medal to the passengers and crew members; a year later, he secured $4.9 million to build a memorial at the crash site.

In the fall of 2008, Shuster initially joined other conservatives in opposing the Bush administration's proposed $700 billion rescue package for the financial services sector. He voted for a reworked version a week later because he said it contained tougher oversight of the troubled industry.

But Shuster, who used to own an auto dealership in East Freedom, refused to back a subsequent plan to bail out domestic automakers. He said that to get his support, the proposal would have required more concessions from the United Auto Workers union, which he contends is partly responsible for the automakers' downfall.

From his seat on the Natural Resources Committee, Shuster has lobbied for more domestic oil and natural gas drilling. The production of wind energy has been growing in his district and coal mining is still relevant.

Bill Shuster was not the first of Bud Shuster's sons to seek a House seat. Bill's brother, Bob, ran in 1996 to succeed retiring nine-term GOP Rep. William F. Clinger in the 5th District, which borders the 9th. He lost the Republican primary to John E. Peterson, who went on to win and hold the seat. Bob Shuster was mentioned as a possible 9th District candidate after his father's resignation, but Bill emerged as the Shuster of choice.

Bill Shuster had no prior experience in elective office. Despite his family ties, his special-election victory in May 2001 was closer than expected. He appeared to be hindered by the hard feelings among some Republicans who felt he had been given the nomination unfairly, and about a dozen Republicans emerged as contenders. But at a special convention GOP officials tapped Shuster, who defeated Democrat Scott Conklin, a Centre County commissioner, with 52 percent of the vote.

After an easy re-election in 2002, Shuster had another tough campaign in 2004, during which one of his congressional aides was accused of spying on his political opponent at his home and at fundraising events. Shuster said the aide was acting independently, but the aide said Shuster had ordered the spying. His opponent, Republican Michael DelGrosso, a financial consultant, came within 2 percentage points of defeating Shuster, who went on to win in November with 70 percent of the vote. He won re-election easily in 2006 and 2008.

KEY VOTES

2008

No Delay consideration of Colombia free-trade agreement

Yes Override Bush veto of federal farm and nutrition programs reauthorization bill

Yes Overhaul surveillance laws and permit dismissal of suits against companies that conducted warrantless wiretapping

No Grant mortgage relief to homeowners and funding for Fannie Mae and Freddie Mac

No Approve initial $700 billion program to stabilize financial markets

Yes Approve final $700 billion program to stabilize financial markets

No Provide $14 billion in loans to automakers

2007

No Increase minimum wage by $2.10 an hour

No Approve $124.2 billion in emergency war spending and set goal for redeployment of troops from Iraq

Yes Reject federal contraceptive assistance to international family planning groups

Yes Override Bush veto of $23.2 billion water projects authorization bill

Yes Implement Peru free-trade agreement

Yes Approve energy policy overhaul with new fuel economy standards

Yes Clear $473.5 billion omnibus spending bill, including $70 billion for military operations

CQ VOTE STUDIES

	PARTY UNITY		PRESIDENTIAL SUPPORT	
	SUPPORT	OPPOSE	SUPPORT	OPPOSE
2008	94%	6%	67%	33%
2007	93%	7%	83%	17%
2006	97%	3%	93%	7%
2005	98%	2%	87%	13%
2004	96%	4%	82%	18%

INTEREST GROUPS

	AFL-CIO	ADA	CCUS	ACU
2008	13%	20%	94%	92%
2007	17%	10%	89%	96%
2006	14%	0%	100%	84%
2005	20%	5%	93%	100%
2004	15%	5%	100%	96%

PENNSYLVANIA 9
South central – Altoona

Situated in the south-central part of Pennsylvania, the 9th District contains no booming metropolis — Altoona, the largest city, is tucked into the Allegheny Mountains and maintains a small-town feel. Most of the 9th's towns have populations numbering less than 5,000, making this one of the nation's 20 most rural districts.

Altoona's early growth was due to the Pennsylvania Railroad; its Horseshoe Curve permitted completion of a trans-Pennsylvania rail line. Dependent on transportation industries for centuries — first rail and later interstate highway — Altoona has focused economic development efforts on manufacturing interests and office parks. The city also has been working to repair neighborhoods and reduce blight and drug-related crime. South of Altoona, Breezewood, the self-proclaimed "Traveler's Oasis," continues to lure road-weary travelers to hotels and fast-food restaurants with its garish display of signs at the Pennsylvania Turnpike interchange with southbound Interstate 70.

Still, the bulk of the district's land is rural and depends on agriculture. But

that rural land is producing more than crops. Since 2001, there are more of the towering windmills that rise above farms in Somerset and Fayette counties (shared with 12th), and the output capacity of these utility- and small-scale windmills is increasing.

Most voters in the 9th oppose gun control and "big government" policies. Its small-business owners and farmers also tend to be fiscally conservative, and the district solidly backs Republicans at all levels. In the 2008 presidential election, John McCain's two highest percentages statewide were in Fulton and Bedford counties, where he took 74 percent and 72 percent, respectively. He won 63 percent of the district's vote overall — his best showing in the state.

MAJOR INDUSTRY
Agriculture, manufacturing, service

MILITARY BASES
Letterkenny Army Depot, 77 military, 1,500 civilian (2009)

CITIES
Altoona, 49,523; Chambersburg, 17,862; Waynesboro, 9,614

NOTABLE
A memorial to United Airlines Flight 93 is in Shanksville, where the hijacked airplane crashed in a field Sept. 11, 2001.

Rep. Christopher Carney (D)

Elected 2006; 2nd term

CAPITOL OFFICE
225-3731
carney.house.gov
416 Cannon Bldg. 20515-3810; fax 225-9594

COMMITTEES
Homeland Security
  (Management & Oversight - chairman)
Transportation & Infrastructure

RESIDENCE
Dimock Township

BORN
March 2, 1959; Cedar Rapids, Iowa

RELIGION
Roman Catholic

FAMILY
Wife, Jennifer Carney; five children

EDUCATION
Cornell College, B.S.S. 1981 (environmental
studies & history); U. of Wyoming, M.A. 1983
(international relations); U. of Nebraska, Ph.D.
1993 (political science)

MILITARY SERVICE
Naval Reserve, 1995-present

CAREER
U.S. Defense Department counterterrorism
consultant; professor

POLITICAL HIGHLIGHTS
No previous office

ELECTION RESULTS

2008 GENERAL

Christopher Carney (D)	160,837	56.3%
Chris Hackett (R)	124,681	43.7%

2008 PRIMARY

Christopher Carney (D)	unopposed

2006 GENERAL

Christopher Carney (D)	110,115	52.9%
Don Sherwood (R)	97,862	47.1%

Carney was initially propelled into office in 2006 by the news of sex scandals of his predecessor, four-term Republican Don Sherwood. To keep his seat in a traditionally Republican district, party leaders give him leeway to stray from the party line on certain social and fiscal issues. And they appreciate his expertise in counterterrorism, allowing him the chairmanship of a Homeland Security subcommittee.

Carney has supported his party on several social issues, including expansion of the State Children's Health Insurance Program, which covers children from families that don't qualify for Medicaid, and prohibiting job discrimination based on sexual orientation. As a cancer survivor, he also supports expanding federal funding for embryonic stem cell research. But he takes a more conservative stance than most Democrats on immigration, advocating efforts to beef up border security and opposing pathways for illegal immigrants to earn citizenship. He also opposes gun control laws. Carney said he weighs many factors when it comes to voting. "If I make bad decisions, the voters will speak," he once said. "I won't be back."

Some voters spoke up when he supported President Obama's $787 billion economic stimulus law in early 2009. Lewisburg residents who attended a meeting with Carney in April questioned why he voted for the measure. "You voted for the largest budget deficit in our nation's history. Aren't you worried about your own children?" a Union Township resident asked. Carney, a member of the fiscally conservative Blue Dog Coalition, maintained that he voted for the bill because money would be funneled to education and to job creation.

He also backed the president's $3.56 trillion fiscal 2010 budget blueprint and is much in line with the party's view on the Iraq War. As a counterterrorism consultant to the Defense Department before Congress, he briefed key intelligence officials on a possible ties between Iraq and al Qaeda in the months before the war began. He has since opposed the war and said he favors Obama's plan of withdrawing all U.S. combat troops by mid-2010.

As chairman of the Homeland Security Committee's oversight panel, he has looked into the Department of Homeland Security's procurement policies, employee morale and preparation for handling a catastrophe. Carney is a former college professor, and his questions are often pointed and direct. In the 110th Congress (2007-08), he grilled DHS officials on whether they were setting benchmarks and had tangible evidence and whether they had learned lessons from the poor federal response to Hurricane Katrina. In one such hearing, he asked Wayne Parent, DHS deputy director of the Office of Operations Coordination, to pretend it was Aug. 26, 2005, three days before Katrina hit the Gulf Coast. "What are you doing to advise the secretary and his senior leaders, including what concrete action should be taken, and how does this differ from what actually was done?"

Carney in 2008 supported an overhaul of the Foreign Intelligence Surveillance Act that effectively granted retroactive immunity for telecommunications companies that had assisted in a warrantless surveillance program.

He also sits on the Transportation and Infrastructure panel, which is expected to take up a reauthorization of the 2005 surface transportation law. He hopes for construction of a rail line to cater to commuters living in the 10th's eastern edge and working in New Jersey and New York. He also wants funding for the Central Susquehanna Valley Thruway project, which is intended to ease traffic congestion on U.S. Routes 11 and 15 in Snyder County and state Route 147 in Northumberland County.

He sided with his party 81 percent of the time in his first term on votes pitting most Democrats against most Republicans, bucking party leaders more often than all but 11 Democrats. He was one of six Democrats who voted against a bill to give the District of Columbia full voting representation in the House and supported a bill to repeal D.C. laws prohibiting firearm possession.

His opposition to gun control is firm. In March 2009, after the fatal shooting of three Pittsburgh police officers, he joined 64 other House Democrats in a letter to Attorney General Eric H. Holder Jr. stating their opposition to reinstating a federal assault weapons ban, contending it doesn't reduce crime rates.

Carney, who has five children, got a provision into a bill signed into law in 2008 to make it easier for the Justice Department to prosecute people who produce and repeatedly view child pornography — something he called "a serious issue."

Carney grew up in Coggon, Iowa. His father was a schoolteacher; his mother was a dietician at a local hospital. He often jokes about coming from a "broken home," where his father was a Democrat and his mother was a Republican (she registered as an independent once Carney decided to run for Congress). To help pay for college, Carney worked as an EMT in nearby Cedar Rapids. He then earned a master's degree from Wyoming University, where he met his wife, Jennifer. After earning his doctorate, he took a job at Penn State University's Scranton campus.

Carney had been a professor for 12 years, and a member of the Naval Reserve for 10, when he decided to run for Congress. He was driving from the Pentagon to his home in Dimock Township when he saw Sherwood at a Sheetz gas station in Gettysburg. Sherwood was traveling to Washington to vote on a measure to allow the parents of Terry Schaivo, a brain-damaged woman whose husband wanted to let her die, to contest in federal court the removal of a feeding tube. "I knew where he was going," Carney said. "The more I thought about it, the more agitated I became. I said, 'All right, damn it. I am going to run for Congress. We can do better.'"

In his first run for public office, Carney benefited from his moderate policy stands, a strong grass-roots campaign and a national mood that had soured on Republicans. But it also didn't hurt that Sherwood was involved in a sex scandal with a younger woman who claimed Sherwood had tried to strangle her. Sherwood later admitted to a lengthy extramarital affair.

He defeated Sherwood with 53 percent of the vote. Two years later, the Republican Party amassed a heavy campaign to retake the seat, and Shavertown businessman Chris Hackett raised more than $2.5 million. But Carney took in more than $2.3 million and won with 56 percent of the vote.

KEY VOTES

2008

Yes Delay consideration of Colombia free-trade agreement

Yes Override Bush veto of federal farm and nutrition programs reauthorization bill

Yes Overhaul surveillance laws and permit dismissal of suits against companies that conducted warrantless wiretapping

Yes Grant mortgage relief to homeowners and funding for Fannie Mae and Freddie Mac

No Approve initial $700 billion program to stabilize financial markets

No Approve final $700 billion program to stabilize financial markets

Yes Provide $14 billion in loans to automakers

2007

Yes Increase minimum wage by $2.10 an hour

Yes Approve $124.2 billion in emergency war spending and set goal for redeployment of troops from Iraq

No Reject federal contraceptive assistance to international family planning groups

Yes Override Bush veto of $23.2 billion water projects authorization bill

No Implement Peru free-trade agreement

Yes Approve energy policy overhaul with new fuel economy standards

Yes Clear $473.5 billion omnibus spending bill, including $70 billion for military operations

CQ VOTE STUDIES

	PARTY UNITY		PRESIDENTIAL SUPPORT	
	SUPPORT	OPPOSE	SUPPORT	OPPOSE
2008	83%	17%	26%	74%
2007	81%	19%	16%	84%

INTEREST GROUPS

	AFL-CIO	ADA	CCUS	ACU
2008	100%	85%	59%	20%
2007	92%	85%	53%	28%

PENNSYLVANIA 10
Northeast – Central Susquehanna Valley

Situated in the northeastern corner of Pennsylvania, the 10th is home to a portion of the Pocono Mountains region, a retreat known for its skiing, fishing and golfing. The district's southern arm dips into the Central Susquehanna Valley.

The four Central Susquehanna Valley counties of Northumberland, Union, Snyder and Montour account for 30 percent of the population and contribute to the 10th's manufacturing, retail and service industries, although widespread layoffs have contributed to rising unemployment rates. Northumberland has many manufacturers, but closures of some plants in Milton's industrial park concern local officials and residents. Montour is home to the Geisinger Health System and Danville State Hospital, which employ many residents.

The 10th includes some of the state's best areas for lumber and agriculture. Dairy farming is particularly prominent in Bradford County, although the industry has been hurt by falling prices, and a contracting home construction market has hurt timber values. Tourism remains strong, especially during summer, when visitors come for the scenery in the district's east and for the Little League World Series, played annually in South Williamsport (in the neighboring 5th), in its western reaches. Booming Pike County on the district's eastern border hosts many commuters to New Jersey and New York City who prefer its small-town setting, cheaper land and access to main highways. Pike has experienced the state's fastest population growth since 2000, and officials are considering transportation projects to ease travel.

The 10th has large swaths of rural, socially conservative heartland, although Democrats crop up in Carbondale and Archbald in Lackawanna County and in parts of Northumberland County. In the 2008 presidential election, John McCain won 54 percent of the district's vote.

MAJOR INDUSTRY
Agriculture, tourism, manufacturing, timber

CITIES
Williamsport, 30,706

NOTABLE
The mammoth Starrucca Viaduct has carried trains across Lanesboro since 1848; Thomas Edison first demonstrated his electrical lighting system in 1883 by wiring the Sunbury Hotel (now named the Edison Hotel).

Rep. Paul E. Kanjorski (D)

Elected 1984; 13th term

CAPITOL OFFICE
225-6511
kanjorski.house.gov
2188 Rayburn Bldg. 20515-3811; fax 225-0764

COMMITTEES
Financial Services
    (Capital Markets, Insurance & GSEs - chairman)
Oversight & Government Reform

RESIDENCE
Nanticoke

BORN
April 2, 1937; Nanticoke, Pa.

RELIGION
Roman Catholic

FAMILY
Wife, Nancy Kanjorski; one child

EDUCATION
Temple U., attended 1957-62; Dickinson
School of Law, attended 1962-65

MILITARY SERVICE
Army, 1960-61

CAREER
Lawyer

POLITICAL HIGHLIGHTS
Sought Democratic nomination for U.S. House
(special election), 1980; sought Democratic
nomination for U.S. House, 1980

ELECTION RESULTS

2008 GENERAL

Paul E. Kanjorski (D)	146,379	51.6%
Lou Barletta (R)	137,151	48.4%

2008 PRIMARY

Paul E. Kanjorski (D)	unopposed

2006 GENERAL

Paul E. Kanjorski (D)	134,340	72.5%
Joseph F. Leonardi (R)	51,033	27.5%

PREVIOUS WINNING PERCENTAGES
2004 (94%); 2002 (56%); 2000 (66%); 1998 (67%);
1996 (68%); 1994 (67%); 1992 (67%); 1990 (100%);
1988 (100%); 1986 (71%); 1984 (59%)

Kanjorski is a loyal Democrat on fiscal matters and an ally to labor unions. But his socially conservative views reflect the concerns of the white, working-class people who still dominate politics in his part of Pennsylvania. He balances serving those constituents while wrestling with national economic concerns.

Kanjorski knows a good deal about House practices and procedures and has proved his mettle in a range of tough circumstances. Serving as a House page in 1954, he narrowly missed becoming a casualty when Puerto Rican terrorists sprayed gunfire on the chamber from the visitors' gallery. More recently, he eked out a win in one of the nation's most closely watched elections in 2008, coming from behind in the polls to defeat a GOP challenger he had easily beaten six years earlier. That came a year after a triple bypass operation that led some observers to wonder if he was ready to retire.

Kanjorski is the Financial Services Committee's second-ranking Democrat and chairs its panel on Capital Markets, Insurance and Government Sponsored Enterprises. The job puts him at the center of efforts to stem the financial crisis, an area in which he seeks a well-thought-out response even as other Democrats press for quick action. When Treasury Secretary Timothy F. Geithner outlined his plans for overhauling regulation of the financial system in March 2009, Kanjorski preached caution. "The gravity of this situation requires that the Congress deliberate and exercise patience so that we lay a thoughtful regulatory structure that will establish the basis for a strong economy for many years to come," he said.

One of Kanjorski's desires is to improve mark-to-market rules, which require firms to value assets based on their current market price. As the financial crisis has worsened, banks and businesses have increasingly complained the rules have forced them to report huge and unneccessary losses on assets, even if the losses haven't actually been realized. Kanjorski said he wants to find a way to provide investors with information needed to make decisions without burdening financial institutions.

His subcommittee also began looking in early 2009 at the multibillion-dollar Ponzi scheme pulled off by disgraced financier Bernard L. Madoff. Kanjorski said he was upset securities regulators missed opportunities to uncover such schemes. "Clearly, our regulatory system has failed miserably, and we must rebuild it now," he said.

At the outset of the 110th Congress (2007-08), he had planned to work on a longtime goal — overhauling Freddie Mac and Fannie Mae, the two financial behemoths that are the foundation of the U.S. housing market. Kanjorski had supported an overhaul measure that Chairman Barney Frank of Massachusetts brokered with the Treasury Department in early 2007.

But the financial crisis precluded action on that measure and left him explaining to angry voters why he hadn't acted sooner to forestall the problems. Large donations from the two companies further complicated his re-election bid, as Republicans painted him as being in bed with the companies he should have been regulating.

The crisis did, however, give him a national spotlight in its resolution. Kanjorski pushed several new regulatory schemes and helped influence the way Frank and the Democratic majority crafted responses to the crises. At the same time, he protected two key local employers — student loan companies Sallie Mae and the Pennsylvania Higher Education Assistance Agency — by pushing the Federal Reserve and the Education Department to give the companies, which were battered by the financial crisis, some degree of a lifeline from the government.

Kanjorski is also the No. 2 Democrat on the Oversight and Government Reform Committee. In the 105th Congress (1997-98) he was one of the leading critics of Chairman Dan Burton, an Indiana Republican, when Burton led a probe of Democratic fundraising activities.

A Polish-American Catholic, Kanjorski opposes abortion rights and gun control and supports school prayer. But in 2004 and 2006, he voted against a constitutional amendment to ban same-sex marriage. A supporter of organized labor and a loyal Democrat on fiscal matters, he repeatedly weighed in against President George W. Bush's tax cuts.

Kanjorski supports tight restrictions on illegal immigration and calls for strong enforcement of current laws. He supports making English the official language, opposes amnesty for illegal immigrants and supports increasing fines for employers who hire them.

But fervent anti-immigration sentiment in his district in 2008 put him in his closest race ever, even though Kanjorski and his Republican challenger, Lou Barletta, held similar views. Barletta got a boost from a 2006 ordinance he pushed as Hazleton mayor to deny business permits to firms employing illegal immigrants and fine landlords who rent to them. Barletta led throughout much of the campaign, but the race tightened after Kanjorski brought in such luminaries as former President Bill Clinton and Democratic vice presidential candidate Joseph R. Biden Jr. Kanjorski won with 52 percent of the vote in a district Barack Obama carried with 57 percent.

Barletta had aggressively challenged Kanjorski in 2002, when the congressman was the subject of news reports that the FBI was looking into allegations he had steered federal grants to businesses connected to his family. The FBI never confirmed or denied the reports, and Kanjorski prevailed by 13 percentage points.

Kanjorski was born and raised in Nanticoke, just southwest of Wilkes-Barre. He attended Temple University and the Dickinson School of Law but didn't graduate from either. He became a lawyer and worked as an attorney in Northeast Pennsylvania for almost 20 years. He was an administrative law judge for workers' compensation cases and served as the unpaid assistant city solicitor for Nanticoke for more than a decade.

After two unsuccessful House campaigns in 1980 (one in a special election), Kanjorski ousted Democratic Rep. Frank Harrison in the 1984 primary and that November defeated Republican Robert P. Hudock with 59 percent of the vote.

KEY VOTES

2008
Yes Delay consideration of Colombia free-trade agreement
Yes Override Bush veto of federal farm and nutrition programs reauthorization bill
Yes Overhaul surveillance laws and permit dismissal of suits against companies that conducted warrantless wiretapping
Yes Grant mortgage relief to homeowners and funding for Fannie Mae and Freddie Mac
Yes Approve initial $700 billion program to stabilize financial markets
Yes Approve final $700 billion program to stabilize financial markets
Yes Provide $14 billion in loans to automakers

2007
Yes Increase minimum wage by $2.10 an hour
Yes Approve $124.2 billion in emergency war spending and set goal for redeployment of troops from Iraq
Yes Reject federal contraceptive assistance to international family planning groups
Yes Override Bush veto of $23.2 billion water projects authorization bill
No   Implement Peru free-trade agreement
Yes Approve energy policy overhaul with new fuel economy standards
Yes Clear $473.5 billion omnibus spending bill, including $70 billion for military operations

CQ VOTE STUDIES

	PARTY UNITY		PRESIDENTIAL SUPPORT	
	SUPPORT	OPPOSE	SUPPORT	OPPOSE
2008	96%	4%	23%	77%
2007	94%	6%	10%	90%
2006	83%	17%	36%	64%
2005	80%	20%	39%	61%
2004	88%	12%	27%	73%

INTEREST GROUPS

	AFL-CIO	ADA	CCUS	ACU
2008	93%	80%	67%	12%
2007	92%	90%	45%	17%
2006	100%	70%	43%	29%
2005	93%	80%	48%	24%
2004	100%	80%	30%	21%

PENNSYLVANIA 11
Northeast — Scranton, Wilkes-Barre

In the 20th century, the health of northeastern Pennsylvania's 11th was inextricably linked to the production, manufacturing and sale of coal. The industry virtually disappeared in the 1960s, and the loss significantly altered the economy of the Wyoming Valley.

Regional revitalization efforts are ongoing, including recent expansions to Wilkes-Barre/Scranton International Airport and the Wilkes-Barre VA Medical Center. There also are long-term proposals to restore passenger and freight rail service from Scranton to New York City. Development of a trail along Scranton's Lackawanna riverfront is under way. To the southwest, the Wyoming Valley has received millions of dollars to repair levees originally damaged by Hurricane Agnes in 1972 and to prevent future damage. A portion of the funds was allocated for a riverfront project in Wilkes-Barre to create new landing areas and piers, a performance amphitheater, and walking trails.

Carbon County, bridging the northern part of the Lehigh Valley and the Poconos region, has struggled with high unemployment rates. Rural Monroe and Columbia counties, growing areas in the Poconos where many residents commute via Interstate 80 to their jobs in New Jersey and New York, have also seen job losses.

The 11th has a decided but not absolute Democratic lean, the result of a large Irish population and a strong union tradition. Democrats do well in Scranton and Luzerne County, with strong showings in Wilkes-Barre and in smaller cities to the north and east. In the 2008 presidential election, Democrat Barack Obama also carried both Carbon and Monroe counties. John McCain won 52 percent in rural Columbia County, but Obama took 57 percent of the 11th's overall presidential vote.

MAJOR INDUSTRY
Manufacturing, retail trade, tourism

MILITARY BASES
Tobyhanna Army Depot, 23 military, 4,602 civilian (2008)

CITIES
Scranton, 76,415; Wilkes-Barre, 43,123; Hazleton, 23,329

NOTABLE
Scranton's Houdini Museum and Psychic Theater honors the magician's legacy and explores elements of the paranormal, such as séances, in stage performances.

Rep. John P. Murtha (D)

Elected February 1974; 18th full term

CAPITOL OFFICE
225-2065
www.house.gov/murtha
2423 Rayburn Bldg. 20515-3812; fax 225-5709

COMMITTEES
Appropriations
  (Defense - chairman)

RESIDENCE
Johnstown

BORN
June 17, 1932; New Martinsville, W.Va.

RELIGION
Roman Catholic

FAMILY
Wife, Joyce Murtha; three children

EDUCATION
U. of Pittsburgh, B.A. 1962 (economics)

MILITARY SERVICE
Marine Corps, 1952-55, 1966-67; Marine Corps
Reserve, 1967-90

CAREER
Car wash owner and operator

POLITICAL HIGHLIGHTS
Democratic nominee for U.S. House, 1968;
Pa. House, 1969-74

ELECTION RESULTS

2008 GENERAL

John P. Murtha (D)	155,268	57.8%
William Russell (R)	113,120	42.1%

2008 PRIMARY

John P. Murtha (D)	unopposed

2006 GENERAL

John P. Murtha (D)	123,472	60.8%
Diana Irey (R)	79,612	39.2%

PREVIOUS WINNING PERCENTAGES
2004 (100%); 2002 (73%); 2000 (71%); 1998 (68%);
1996 (70%); 1994 (69%); 1992 (100%); 1990 (62%);
1988 (100%); 1986 (67%); 1984 (69%); 1982 (61%);
1980 (59%); 1978 (69%); 1976 (68%); 1974 (58%);
1974 Special Election (50%)

An ex-Marine who can be both salty and passionate, Murtha is a back-room dealmaker who is nonetheless a nationally known figure. Though his outspoken challenge to the George W. Bush administration's Iraq policy first gained him wide notice, he continues to draw attention as a target for lawmakers and watchdog groups who decry his methods of doing business.

A decorated Vietnam combat veteran, he retired in 1990 as a colonel in the reserves after 37 years in the military. Whatever position he is defending — his right to steer appropriations toward constituents or the immorality of the Iraq War — Murtha is not shy. As chairman of the Defense Appropriations Subcommittee, he wields his clout unapologetically, even arrogantly. Asked once whether the Pentagon was stonewalling his panel on Iraq information, he responded that officials knew better than to do that, because if they did, they would get their genitals "cut off."

A key aspect of Murtha's leadership of the subcommittee, whether as chairman or ranking member, is his dogged pursuit of earmarks — funding set-asides for special projects. Taxpayer groups consistently criticize Murtha for directing spending toward his district. In fiscal 2008, he secured $159.1 million for 73 projects, according to Taxpayers for Common Sense.

Murtha's earmarking ways brought him plenty of other unwelcome headlines during the early months of 2009. Federal investigators raided the offices of The PMA Group, a now defunct Virginia-based lobbying firm with close ties to Murtha. The firm closed its political action committee amid reports the FBI was investigating possibly illegal campaign contributions to Murtha and other lawmakers.

Subsequent news stories said federal agents had raided Kuchera Industries, a Johnstown company whose owners held a fundraiser for Murtha on their private game ranch. They also said the Justice Department was investigating Concurrent Technologies Corp., a nonprofit government contractor based in Johnstown that was founded by Murtha.

Murtha brushed off the controversies with characteristic bluntness. "If I'm corrupt, it is because I take care of my district," he told the Pittsburgh Post-Gazette. But his situation stirred considerable unease among his colleagues. Republicans clamored for an ethics investigation; some Democrats agreed. A fellow Appropriations member, New York Democrat Steve Israel, said he would no longer seek earmarks for private companies. Other Democrats introduced a bill to ban lawmakers from taking contributions from companies, executives or lobbyists for whom they secured earmarks.

All of the attention came as Murtha sought to work with the new Obama administration on its defense priorities. When Defense Secretary Robert M. Gates proposed an array of major changes to the Pentagon's spending priorities, including the termination of some of the U.S. military's highest-profile weapons programs, Murtha was supportive in principle but noncommittal on the details. And when President Obama announced he would remove troops from Iraq and build up forces in Afghanistan, Murtha said in March 2009 it would take about 600,000 troops to fully quell violence in that country. He also said he was uncomfortable with Obama's decision to increase the number of troops in Afghanistan by 17,000 before a goal was clearly defined.

Murtha was a strong supporter of the 2002 measure authorizing President Bush to use force against Iraq. But by late 2005, he had concluded the operation was headed in the wrong direction. "You can't sustain a war with the small force that we have," he said.

Republicans called Murtha unpatriotic but had a tough time making it stick. In the remaining years of Bush's term, Murtha repeatedly wrote defense spending legislation requiring a withdrawal of most U.S. troops from Iraq and setting conditions on war funding. Ever persistent, he was occasionally successful in getting these provisions through the House. But he could never get them enacted.

Impatient with the PowerPoint presentations favored by the Pentagon brass, Murtha travels without fanfare to deployments in far-off regions to assess U.S. progress. His Iraq decision was informed by frequent visits to injured soldiers at military hospitals in the Washington area. "Generals, they have to talk the party line, but the troops…give me a lot of information about what's going on that I can't get almost anyplace else," he said.

Murtha's combination of charm and muscle wasn't enough in 2007 to win him the position of House majority leader over Maryland's Steny H. Hoyer, despite his close relationship with Speaker Nancy Pelosi of California. Murtha had chaired Pelosi's campaign for minority leader in 2002, and she often consults with him in the "Pennsylvania corner," in the chamber's southeast corner, where Murtha conducts much of his business.

Murtha grew up in Mt. Pleasant in a family with a long tradition of military service. His mother's ancestors fought in the Revolutionary War. His father, who ran a gas station and car wash, served in World War II. Murtha left college to join the Marines in 1952. After a three-year hitch, he returned and helped run the family gas station, but remained in the Marine Reserves. In 1966, with the Vietnam conflict under way, Murtha voluntarily returned to active duty, ultimately earning a Bronze Star and two Purple Hearts.

Murtha started out in the state legislature. Cambria County Democrats urged him to aim higher when longtime GOP Rep. John P. Saylor died in 1973. Murtha won narrowly over Harry M. Fox, a former Saylor aide, in a 1974 special election that focused on the GOP's Watergate problems.

In the early 1980s, he was an unprosecuted co-conspirator and witness for prosecutors in the FBI bribery probe known as Abscam, which resulted in convictions of one senator and several House members. But he rarely encountered political trouble until 2008, when he described his district as "racist" in an interview. Though he apologized, he told a TV interviewer a few days later the region had been "really redneck" for years.

Challenger William Russell, a retired Army lieutenant colonel, got more than $400,000 from the RNC, which also ran TV ads replaying Murtha's remarks. Democrats, along with defense contractors and lobbyists, poured money into the race in the final days, and Murtha won with 58 percent.

KEY VOTES

2008

Yes   Delay consideration of Colombia free-trade agreement

Yes   Override Bush veto of federal farm and nutrition programs reauthorization bill

Yes   Overhaul surveillance laws and permit dismissal of suits against companies that conducted warrantless wiretapping

Yes   Grant mortgage relief to homeowners and funding for Fannie Mae and Freddie Mac

Yes   Approve initial $700 billion program to stabilize financial markets

Yes   Approve final $700 billion program to stabilize financial markets

Yes   Provide $14 billion in loans to automakers

2007

Yes   Increase minimum wage by $2.10 an hour

Yes   Approve $124.2 billion in emergency war spending and set goal for redeployment of troops from Iraq

Yes   Reject federal contraceptive assistance to international family planning groups

Yes   Override Bush veto of $23.2 billion water projects authorization bill

Yes   Implement Peru free-trade agreement

Yes   Approve energy policy overhaul with new fuel economy standards

Yes   Clear $473.5 billion omnibus spending bill, including $70 billion for military operations

CQ VOTE STUDIES

	PARTY UNITY		PRESIDENTIAL SUPPORT	
	SUPPORT	OPPOSE	SUPPORT	OPPOSE
2008	97%	3%	23%	77%
2007	96%	4%	10%	90%
2006	76%	24%	43%	57%
2005	76%	24%	38%	62%
2004	80%	20%	34%	66%

INTEREST GROUPS

	AFL-CIO	ADA	CCUS	ACU
2008	100%	85%	65%	4%
2007	100%	95%	50%	8%
2006	100%	65%	50%	28%
2005	100%	75%	62%	40%
2004	93%	50%	48%	30%

PENNSYLVANIA 12
Southwest – Johnstown

The oddly contorted 12th hopscotches across nine southwestern Pennsylvania counties, eight of which are shared with other districts. Once a booming center of coal, steel and iron production, this area is attempting to diversify in order to escape economic distress and industrial loss.

Johnstown, the district's most populous city, was once an industrial center, but floods, recession, coal and steel industry decline, and scarce opportunities in manufacturing left the region with skyrocketing unemployment by the late 1980s. The city and district have partly bounced back by attracting new biomedical research and health care companies, such as specialized care provider Conemaugh Health System, and a number of defense and research firms, such as KDH Defense Systems. Capitalizing on past hardships, the Johnstown Flood Museum also draws tourists to the area, and tourism now contributes nearly $150 million to the region each year. Despite these new industries, recent nationwide economic downturns have forced local businesses to cut jobs.

On the other side of the district in the state's southwestern corner, residents of rural Greene County — which borders West Virginia to its west and south and is the only county entirely within the 12th — continue to suffer. Just north of Greene, Washington County's city of Washington took a hit in 2009 when a bankrupt title insurance company left its namesake office building at the center of a $100 million downtown revitalization project that included a new amphitheater, a hotel and a parking garage. The district also includes Washington and Jefferson College and has a small agriculture industry, producing corn, wheat and cattle.

The 12th has been a Democratic stronghold since the New Deal. Like other Pennsylvania towns with an industrial past and aging residents, Johnstown is more socially conservative than the national Democratic Party and wants federal help. At the presidential level, Republican candidates can compete, and John McCain won the district with 49 percent of its vote in 2008.

MAJOR INDUSTRY
Manufacturing, service, health care, tourism

CITIES
Johnstown, 23,906; Washington, 15,268; New Kensington, 14,701

NOTABLE
The National Drug Intelligence Center in Johnstown tracks illegal drugs.

Rep. Allyson Y. Schwartz (D)

Elected 2004; 3rd term

CAPITOL OFFICE
225-6111
schwartz.house.gov
330 Cannon Bldg. 20515-3813; fax 226-0611

COMMITTEES
Budget
Ways & Means

RESIDENCE
Jenkintown

BORN
Oct. 3, 1948; Queens, N.Y.

RELIGION
Jewish

FAMILY
Husband, David Schwartz; two children

EDUCATION
Simmons College, B.A. 1970 (sociology);
Bryn Mawr College, M.S.W. 1972

CAREER
Municipal child and elderly welfare official;
women's health center founder; nonprofit health
plan assistant director

POLITICAL HIGHLIGHTS
Pa. Senate, 1991-2004; sought Democratic
nomination for U.S. Senate, 2000

ELECTION RESULTS

2008 GENERAL

Allyson Y. Schwartz (D)	196,868	62.8%
Marina Kats (R)	108,271	34.5%
John P. McDermott (CNSTP)	8,374	2.7%

2008 PRIMARY

Allyson Y. Schwartz (D)	unopposed

2006 GENERAL

Allyson Y. Schwartz (D)	147,368	66.1%
Raj Peter Bhakta (R)	75,492	33.9%

PREVIOUS WINNING PERCENTAGES
2004 (56%)

Schwartz has established herself as a health care expert, a formidable fundraiser and an influential force within her party. Though she generally takes Democrats' side on floor votes, she is well-regarded enough to develop good working relationships with colleagues across the aisle.

She holds a coveted seat on the Ways and Means Committee, which provides her a platform to push her health care priorities while beginning to delve into tax questions. And she has furthered her prominence by serving as vice chairwoman of both the Budget Committee and the moderate New Democrat Coalition, where she looks carefully at the impact of issues on both businesses and the economy.

Schwartz also heads the Democratic Congressional Campaign Committee's Women LEAD program, an outreach effort aimed at involving women in politics and getting more of them elected to the House. She has been a generous contributor to her party's causes and colleagues, donating more than $385,000 from her campaign committee during the 2007-08 election cycle.

She realized a major goal when President Obama signed into law the reauthorization of the State Children's Health Insurance Program, expanding a program to cover more than 10 million children whose families don't qualify for Medicaid. Schwartz took a special interest in the bill because it was built on a state initiative she helped start in the Pennsylvania legislature in the early 1990s. She said she was disappointed by President George W. Bush's two vetoes of the bill. "As we work to reverse the economic downturn, we can and should ensure that our children's health will be protected, now and in the future," she said in January 2009.

The children's health initiative exemplifies the incremental approach of Schwartz and other New Democrats to expanding health insurance. She sees the country heading toward a "uniquely American" solution, as opposed to a national health care plan. Ultimately, she said, employers still will offer insurance to their workers, while the government will expand coverage to include all children and encourage small businesses to pool together to improve coverage for their employees.

She was part of a bipartisan group in April 2009 that introduced legislation to expand access to long-term care insurance by enabling people to pay premiums using pre-tax dollars. A month earlier, she added a provision to a House-passed water quality bill to study the presence of pharmaceuticals in water supplies.

Schwartz also pushes for expansion of information technology throughout the health care sector, even while aiming to contain costs and improve outcomes. She worked to help ensure $19 billion for health IT was included in Obama's $787 billion economic stimulus law in early 2009.

Schwartz also has used her Ways and Means seat to tout a tax break for companies hiring veterans of the wars in Iraq and Afghanistan, an initiative inspired by her father's experience as a Korean War veteran. It passed as part of a 2007 minimum wage package that was tucked into a huge spending bill.

As a freshman in 2005, she made her first House floor speech during a commemoration of the 60th anniversary of the liberation of the Nazis' Auschwitz death camp in Poland. She described her mother's escape from Austria to America as a teenager in the early days of World War II. "Those who survived the Holocaust could not hide their gratitude and love for this country, relishing the opportunity and freedom granted to them as new Americans," Schwartz said. "My own love and respect for our country and my belief in our responsibility to each other stems in great part from this strong sense of patriotism."

Although Schwartz was born and raised in Flushing, in Queens, N.Y., her parents met in Philadelphia, where her father was a dental student and her mother had been sent by a group helping Jewish refugees. Her maternal grandmother committed suicide shortly before Schwartz's mother, as a teenager, escaped to the United States. "My mother was very clear that painful experiences in childhood don't necessarily make you stronger, which is maybe where my interest in children and family comes from," she said. Schwartz's mother could not overcome the pain; she committed suicide herself when Schwartz was 26. "These experiences stay with you. You just don't get past them by saying so," she said of her mother's traumas.

Schwartz moved to Philadelphia in the 1970s so her husband, David, now a cardiologist, could attend Jefferson Medical College. She earned her graduate degree in social work at Bryn Mawr.

Schwartz entered the public eye in 1975 as the co-founder and first director of a women's health clinic. She had spent a year at the Philadelphia Health Department as a graduate student, then worked for a fledgling HMO for three years before helping to start the Elizabeth Blackwell women's clinic, which offered a full range of health services, including abortions. She and her partners took out a bank loan to launch the clinic.

In 1983, Schwartz wrote health care position papers for Wilson Goode, who was in the midst of a successful campaign for mayor. During Goode's second term, she became a deputy commissioner of Philadelphia's Department of Human Services, serving until her 1990 election to the state Senate. She defeated a 12-year incumbent to claim that seat, then stayed for 14 years.

Schwartz in 2000 entered the Democratic primary to run against GOP Sen. Rick Santorum. She demonstrated impressive fundraising skills, but came in second in a six-way primary, behind Rep. Ron Klink, who lost to Santorum that November.

A long-shot bid by 13th District Democrat Joseph M. Hoeffel to unseat Sen. Arlen Specter in 2004 gave Schwartz an opening for a second try at Congress. She won a hard-fought primary. Then, calling on her solid political base and campaign bankroll, she won by more than 14 percentage points — trouncing ophthalmologist Melissa Brown, a three-time GOP candidate for the House. She was easily re-elected in 2006 and 2008.

Schwartz had been mentioned as a potential Senate contender in 2010 before Specter's decision to run as a Democrat. In the spring of 2009 she had amassed a campaign war chest of more than $2 million.

KEY VOTES

2008
Yes Delay consideration of Colombia free-trade agreement
Yes Override Bush veto of federal farm and nutrition programs reauthorization bill
No Overhaul surveillance laws and permit dismissal of suits against companies that conducted warrantless wiretapping
Yes Grant mortgage relief to homeowners and funding for Fannie Mae and Freddie Mac
Yes Approve initial $700 billion program to stabilize financial markets
Yes Approve final $700 billion program to stabilize financial markets
Yes Provide $14 billion in loans to automakers

2007
Yes Increase minimum wage by $2.10 an hour
Yes Approve $124.2 billion in emergency war spending and set goal for redeployment of troops from Iraq
No Reject federal contraceptive assistance to international family planning groups
Yes Override Bush veto of $23.2 billion water projects authorization bill
Yes Implement Peru free-trade agreement
Yes Approve energy policy overhaul with new fuel economy standards
Yes Clear $473.5 billion omnibus spending bill, including $70 billion for military operations

CQ VOTE STUDIES

	PARTY UNITY		PRESIDENTIAL SUPPORT	
	SUPPORT	OPPOSE	SUPPORT	OPPOSE
2008	99%	1%	15%	85%
2007	96%	4%	8%	92%
2006	91%	9%	27%	73%
2005	92%	8%	17%	83%

INTEREST GROUPS

	AFL-CIO	ADA	CCUS	ACU
2008	100%	90%	56%	0%
2007	96%	90%	55%	4%
2006	100%	85%	47%	16%
2005	93%	90%	44%	4%

PENNSYLVANIA 13

East – northeast Philadelphia, part of Montgomery County

With its residents nearly evenly divided between Montgomery County and Northeast Philadelphia, the 13th combines white-collar suburbia with a portion of the city known for its blue-collar grit. The district extends northwest from the Delaware River in the city into northern Montgomery County suburbs and eventually out into rural areas near the county's western border.

Prescription drugs and health care are big issues in the district, thanks to a large senior citizen population in Northeast Philadelphia. Education also draws attention, as Philadelphia public schools are in worse shape than Montgomery County schools. Public housing, home values and energy issues also are of concern to residents.

Many shopping centers, strip malls, health care and pharmaceutical firms and small businesses are found throughout Northeast Philadelphia. But that diversification has not insulated the area from layoffs in the city

and more affluent Montgomery County. The 2005 BRAC round ordered Naval Air Station Willow Grove closed by 2011, but the state will redevelop at least part of the base into a homeland security and emergency preparedness facility and maintain an operating airfield at the site. The 13th also includes Philadelphia Northeast Airport, a general aviation airport.

Democratic candidates in recent statewide and federal races have enjoyed an advantage in Montgomery County, while local races tend to be more competitive. Overall, Democrat Barack Obama took 59 percent of the district's 2008 presidential vote.

MAJOR INDUSTRY
Health and business services, chemicals

MILITARY BASES
Naval Air Station Willow Grove, 1,500 military, 365 civilian (2009)

CITIES
Philadelphia (pt.), 306,002; Lansdale, 16,071

NOTABLE
Pennypack Park, known as the green heart of Northeast Philadelphia, is home to the Pennypack Bridge — a stone bridge that has been in use since 1697.

Rep. Mike Doyle (D)

Elected 1994; 8th term

CAPITOL OFFICE
225-2135
www.house.gov/doyle
401 Cannon Bldg. 20515-3814; fax 225-3084

COMMITTEES
Energy & Commerce

RESIDENCE
Forest Hills

BORN
Aug. 5, 1953; Pittsburgh, Pa.

RELIGION
Roman Catholic

FAMILY
Wife, Susan Doyle; four children

EDUCATION
Pennsylvania State U., B.S. 1975
(community development)

CAREER
Insurance company executive;
state legislative aide

POLITICAL HIGHLIGHTS
Swissvale Borough Council, 1977-81
(served as a Republican)

ELECTION RESULTS

2008 GENERAL

Mike Doyle (D)	242,326	91.3%
Titus North (GREEN)	23,214	8.7%

2008 PRIMARY

Mike Doyle (D)	unopposed

2006 GENERAL

Mike Doyle (D)	161,075	90.1%
Titus North (GREEN)	17,720	9.9%

PREVIOUS WINNING PERCENTAGES
2004 (100%); 2002 (100%); 2000 (69%); 1998 (68%);
1996 (56%); 1994 (55%)

A former steelworker and strong labor supporter, Doyle wants to preserve the relics of Pittsburgh's once-mighty steel industry for posterity while diversifying the area's economy by bringing in more high-tech industries. His seat on the powerful Energy and Commerce Committee enables him to battle what he views as unfair trade agreements, boost opportunities for energy and technology companies and monitor the impact of new regulations on business.

Doyle has over time become more of a party loyalist — apart from his opposition to abortion — and has aligned with some influential players, such as Pennsylvania's John P. Murtha, the Defense Appropriations panel chairman, who have helped him garner millions of dollars for his district each year.

Although the mills have long been silent, Doyle wants to incorporate their historic remains into the National Park system, making them eligible for federal funding as a national historic site. In the 110th Congress (2007-08), he tried unsuccessfully to gain passage of a bill to include in the park system the site of the 1892 Battle of Homestead, a bloody clash between striking Homestead Works steelworkers and company guards.

Doyle also champions the interests of local industry. He opposed the Central America Free Trade Agreement in 2005 and the Peru free-trade agreement in 2007, arguing that the agreements were unfair because other countries aren't hampered by labor and environmental laws as stringent as those in the United States.

Meanwhile, he has sought ways to turn the region's manufacturing base to other technologies. He secured several million dollars in government funds in 2003 to establish in Pittsburgh the Doyle Center for Manufacturing Technology, a federally funded nonprofit group he said would revitalize the region's economy "by providing small local manufacturers with the tools they need to participate in military contracts with big defense contractors like Boeing, Lockheed Martin and Raytheon." But he took much ribbing for his high number of earmarks — funding set-asides for projects in member districts — and later tried to remove his name from the center. He succeeded in fall 2008 in changing the name to DSN Innovations.

From his seat on the Energy and the Environment Subcommittee, Doyle pushes to reduce U.S. reliance on foreign oil and urges the development of alternative energy such as fuel cells. In spring 2009, he resisted GOP entreaties to oppose any climate change legislation that included a "cap and trade" system for greenhouse gas emissions, instead working with Democratic colleagues in hopes of drafting a bill that would have minimal impact on steel and coal industries and utility customers.

Doyle and California Republican Mary Bono Mack during the 110th pushed legislation calling for "green" federal buildings that meet energy conservation standards. Its provisions were expanded to include encouragement of green building construction in the private sector and became part of a sweeping energy bill that cleared Congress in December 2007.

From his seat on the committee's Communications, Technology and the Internet panel, he has called for universal and open access to Internet service. Among his most popular legislative successes was enactment of his bill in February 2008 to bar any expiration date for telephone numbers listed on the "do not call" registry maintained by the Federal Trade Commission to curb unwanted telemarketing. He also has pushed legislation to pave the way for hundreds of new low-power FM radio stations to sprout around the country.

Doyle is a mid-ranking member of the Energy and Commerce panel, holds no leadership position or gavel and doesn't even sit on Appropriations; all that would make it seem unlikely for him to win such an outsize share of earmarked dollars. But he collected $34 million in earmarks for fiscal 2009, $15 million from the Defense spending bill alone, according to Taxpayers for Common Sense. The group reported that in fiscal 2008 bills he had garnered $18 million, a level higher than 22 Democrats on the Appropriations panel.

A passionate advocate in the fight against autism, Doyle co-chairs the Coalition on Autism Research and Education and helped obtain $8 million in a fiscal 2009 spending bill for continued autism research at the Defense Department. He had obtained the same appropriation for fiscal 2007.

Doyle also has been teased for his role as a co-chairman of the Congressional Robotics Caucus, which he formed with Tennessee Republican Zach Wamp in 2007 to look out for the industry. "We've been portrayed as latecomers to the issue and parrots of Bill Gates — and those are the positive reviews," Doyle said. "We've also been reviled for revealing the fact that all politicians are actually robots rather than just acting like them."

He has long used campaign money to pay his wife, Susan, a salary for various campaign fundraising duties. The practice is not illegal, but California Democrat Adam B. Schiff in 2007 sought, unsuccessfully, to end it for Doyle and other members. Doyle comes from a family of steelworkers; his grandfather and father were steelworkers, and he worked summers in the mills. He earned a degree in community development from Penn State, then returned to his hometown of Swissvale where he entered the insurance business, became involved in community affairs and was elected to the borough council.

For many years, Doyle worked for Republican state Sen. Frank A. Pecora, switching to the GOP out of deference to his boss. He switched back to the Democratic label when Pecora changed parties in 1992 to mount an unsuccessful challenge to Republican Rick Santorum, who was seeking a second House term. When Santorum ran for the Senate in 1994, Doyle ran in the open 18th District, taking a seven-person primary with 20 percent of the vote. He won the following November by 10 percentage points. He won the next three elections with ease.

Redistricting after the 2000 census pushed him into the 14th District of fellow Democrat William J. Coyne, who then retired. Since 2002 the GOP has declined to field a candidate against him, but in his last two elections he easily defeated Green Party candidate Titus North.

Doyle has managed the Democrats' team for the annual congressional charity baseball game. Nicknamed "Mad Dog," he won't let lawmakers cut practice.

KEY VOTES

2008

Yes Delay consideration of Colombia free-trade agreement

Yes Override Bush veto of federal farm and nutrition programs reauthorization bill

No Overhaul surveillance laws and permit dismissal of suits against companies that conducted warrantless wiretapping

Yes Grant mortgage relief to homeowners and funding for Fannie Mae and Freddie Mac

Yes Approve initial $700 billion program to stabilize financial markets

Yes Approve final $700 billion program to stabilize financial markets

Yes Provide $14 billion in loans to automakers

2007

Yes Increase minimum wage by $2.10 an hour

Yes Approve $124.2 billion in emergency war spending and set goal for redeployment of troops from Iraq

No Reject federal contraceptive assistance to international family planning groups

Yes Override Bush veto of $23.2 billion water projects authorization bill

No Implement Peru free-trade agreement

Yes Approve energy policy overhaul with new fuel economy standards

No Clear $473.5 billion omnibus spending bill, including $70 billion for military operations

CQ VOTE STUDIES

	PARTY UNITY		PRESIDENTIAL SUPPORT	
	SUPPORT	OPPOSE	SUPPORT	OPPOSE
2008	99%	1%	16%	84%
2007	98%	2%	5%	95%
2006	91%	9%	35%	65%
2005	90%	10%	28%	72%
2004	93%	7%	29%	71%

INTEREST GROUPS

	AFL-CIO	ADA	CCUS	ACU
2008	100%	95%	56%	0%
2007	96%	95%	53%	4%
2006	100%	85%	47%	12%
2005	100%	95%	44%	16%
2004	100%	80%	48%	12%

PENNSYLVANIA 14

Pittsburgh and some close-in suburbs

The 14th includes all of Pittsburgh and some of its close-in suburbs. The city's economic transformation from "steel capital" into the region's banking and health care hub has made it a great success story in an otherwise suffering Rust Belt.

Medical centers and universities, parks, skyscrapers and technology firms have replaced the steel industry's smokestacks that once rose between and along the Allegheny, Monongahela and Ohio rivers. A thriving, corporate downtown has grown up in the "Golden Triangle," where the three rivers meet — six Fortune 500 companies maintain their corporate headquarters in downtown Pittsburgh. Baseball's Pirates, at PNC Park, and football's Steelers, at Heinz Field, both play in modern stadiums just across the Allegheny from downtown, where hockey's Penguins play in Mellon Arena. Local officials have cleaned up, or "redd up" in Pittsburghese, the city, which for years had one of the lowest crime rates among the nation's largest metropolitan areas. Health care and high-tech companies are establishing relationships with the many local colleges, but widespread layoffs concern officials and residents.

Areas such as Monroeville and Penn Hills (both shared with the 18th) have attracted development and some tech jobs, while other areas have languished. Many of Pittsburgh's neighborhoods, such as Bloomfield and Lawrenceville, retain their ethnic roots – German, Italian, Irish and Polish. Squirrel Hill long has been the center of the city's Jewish population.

Even with the diversification of the 14th's economy, the district retains strong Democratic roots. Union strength translates into lopsided margins, and Democrats far outnumber Republicans, whose regional outposts are in neighboring, suburban districts. Pittsburgh's staunch Democratic support helped Barack Obama take 70 percent of the 14th's vote in the 2008 presidential election.

MAJOR INDUSTRY
Banking, government, health care, higher education

CITIES
Pittsburgh, 334,563; Penn Hills (unincorporated) (pt.), 35,864; McKeesport, 24,040; West Mifflin, 22,464; Wilkinsburg, 19,196

NOTABLE
The Andy Warhol Museum celebrates Pittsburgh's native son.

Rep. Charlie Dent (R)

Elected 2004; 3rd term

CAPITOL OFFICE
225-6411
dent.house.gov
1009 Longworth Bldg. 20515-3815; fax 226-0778

COMMITTEES
Homeland Security
Standards of Official Conduct
Transportation & Infrastructure

RESIDENCE
Allentown

BORN
May 24, 1960; Allentown, Pa.

RELIGION
Presbyterian

FAMILY
Wife, Pamela Dent; three children

EDUCATION
Pennsylvania State U., B.A. 1982
(foreign service & international politics);
Lehigh U., M.P.A. 1993

CAREER
College fundraiser; electronics salesman; hotel
clerk; congressional aide

POLITICAL HIGHLIGHTS
Pa. House, 1991-99; Pa. Senate, 1999-2005

ELECTION RESULTS

2008 GENERAL

Charlie Dent (R)	181,433	58.6%
Sam Bennett (D)	128,333	41.4%

2008 PRIMARY

Charlie Dent (R)	unopposed

2006 GENERAL

Charlie Dent (R)	106,153	53.6%
Charles Dertinger (D)	86,186	43.5%
Greta Browne (GREEN)	5,802	2.9%

PREVIOUS WINNING PERCENTAGES
2004 (59%)

Dent walks around with a political target on his back. He's one of a half-dozen moderate House Republicans representing a district that Democrats John Kerry and Barack Obama carried in the last two presidential elections. As a result, he chooses his positions with deliberation and seeks to build alliances with a wide range of colleagues.

The task is nothing new to Dent, who staked out middle-ground positions during 14 years in the Pennsylvania General Assembly and Senate before coming to Capitol Hill in 2005. He co-chairs the Tuesday Group, a dwindling band of House GOP centrists, with Mark Steven Kirk of Illinois, and he refuses to be bullied by either political extreme. "In this environment, both parties seem to be appealing to their bases. Centrists must carefully weigh each issue," he said in February 2009.

Dent is against illegal immigration and favors tough law enforcement to protect the homeland from terrorism. He tends to side with industry on environmental issues, but he's much more liberal than most Republicans when it comes to issues like abortion and gay rights.

Dent opposed several of President Obama's early economic initiatives, including a $787 billion economic stimulus law and the fiscal 2010 budget blueprint. But he did back a $410 billion catchall spending bill that just 15 other GOP lawmakers supported; he also voted in favor of an extension of the State Children's Health Insurance Program, which covers children from low-income families that don't qualify for Medicaid. The measure was similar to legislation President George W. Bush had vetoed twice.

He originally opposed the Bush administration's $700 billion financial rescue bill in 2008, but switched his vote to enable a second version to become law. He said he wasn't enthusiastic about the that version, but it was "vastly improved." He refused, however, to support a subsequent attempt to bail out the domestic auto industry that passed the House but stalled in the Senate.

Dent is one of seven Pennsylvania lawmakers with a seat on the Transportation and Infrastructure Committee, where he plans to fight for his district's share of funding in a massive reauthorization of highway and surface transportation programs during the 111th Congress (2009-10). A member of the panel's Aviation Subcommittee, he guided a bill through the full committee in April 2009 that sought an examination of how the Civil Air Patrol — the Air Force's civilian auxiliary — can support homeland security missions.

Dent also works on such issues as a member of the Homeland Security Committee, where he serves as ranking Republican on the panel on Transportation Security and Infrastructure Protection. On terrorism-related issues, he spares no criticism of Democrats. He delivered a national radio address in March 2008 accusing Democrats of blocking legislation to allow the Bush administration to more easily use electronic surveillance to track foreign terrorists. Democrats contended the bill threatened civil liberties.

Dent is also well within the Republican mainstream on environmental issues. During debate on the Democrats' energy policy overhaul in 2007, he voted against amendments to require utilities to produce more energy from renewable sources and to raise taxes on oil and gas companies. In the end, though, he voted for the law, which did include controversial new fuel economy mandates. A year later, he joined a conservative-led protest of perceived Democratic inaction on high gasoline prices during the August recess.

But Dent tends to side more often with liberal Democrats on social issues. In 2007, he was one of just 12 Republicans to reject an amendment to bar federal funding for international family planning groups that perform abortions. A liberal perspective on abortion runs in Dent's family: His aunt, Mary Dent Crisp, his father's sister and a longtime GOP activist in Arizona, resigned her post as co-chairwoman of the Republican National Convention in 1980 to protest the party's anti-abortion platform. And he reacted favorably when Obama overturned Bush's restrictions on federally funded embryonic stem cell research.

House GOP leaders in 2009 assigned Dent to the ethics committee, an assignment he readily acknowledged was "at times difficult and unpleasant."

A lifelong resident of Allentown, Dent has deep roots in his district. His family has been in Pennsylvania since colonial times. His great-grandfather started a well-known hardware business in the district; his father worked at Bethlehem Steel in the human resources department, and his mother was a high school teacher.

Dent says his political awakening came in high school, when he took a class on the Cold War. He majored in foreign service and international politics at Penn State, then interned with one of his predecessors in Congress, former GOP Rep. Don Ritter. He went on to work as a salesman in the electronics industry and as a development officer for Lehigh University.

Dent says his experience at the university sparked his interest in running for office. In 1990, he ran for the Pennsylvania House, defeating a Democratic incumbent. He credits his upset win to knocking "on over 20,000 doors" and running a "door-to-door, grass-roots, shoe-leather campaign." Eight years later, he won an open state Senate seat, serving there for six years.

He decided to run for Congress in 2004 when conservative GOP Rep. Patrick J. Toomey retired and launched an unsuccessful primary challenge to Arlen Specter, then a Republican. Dent won easily with nearly 59 percent.

His bid for a second term in 2006 was expected to be a cakewalk. But Northampton County Councilman Charles Dertinger made a race of it despite a severe fundraising deficit — he raised $90,000 to Dent's $1.3 million — and little support from national Democrats. Playing off the party's national themes, Dertinger attempted to link Dent to Bush. Dent pulled out a victory, but his 54 percent share of the vote was a relatively close call.

Two years later, Allentown Democratic Party activist Sam Bennett challenged Dent. Bennett quickly took up the national Democratic Party themes, condemning the Iraq War and urging change. But her slow fundraising gave Dent some reassurance, and he touted his "much stronger crossover appeal" among voters. He won with nearly 59 percent of the vote in a district that gave Obama 56 percent.

KEY VOTES

2008
No   Delay consideration of Colombia free-trade agreement
No   Override Bush veto of federal farm and nutrition programs reauthorization bill
Yes Overhaul surveillance laws and permit dismissal of suits against companies that conducted warrantless wiretapping
No   Grant mortgage relief to homeowners and funding for Fannie Mae and Freddie Mac
No   Approve initial $700 billion program to stabilize financial markets
Yes Approve final $700 billion program to stabilize financial markets
No   Provide $14 billion in loans to automakers

2007
Yes Increase minimum wage by $2.10 an hour
No   Approve $124.2 billion in emergency war spending and set goal for redeployment of troops from Iraq
No   Reject federal contraceptive assistance to international family planning groups
Yes Override Bush veto of $23.2 billion water projects authorization bill
Yes Implement Peru free-trade agreement
Yes Approve energy policy overhaul with new fuel economy standards
Yes Clear $473.5 billion omnibus spending bill, including $70 billion for military operations

CQ VOTE STUDIES

	PARTY UNITY		PRESIDENTIAL SUPPORT	
	SUPPORT	OPPOSE	SUPPORT	OPPOSE
2008	78%	22%	49%	51%
2007	75%	25%	49%	51%
2006	81%	19%	80%	20%
2005	89%	11%	78%	22%

INTEREST GROUPS

	AFL-CIO	ADA	CCUS	ACU
2008	60%	55%	83%	56%
2007	42%	45%	100%	52%
2006	43%	30%	93%	72%
2005	27%	25%	89%	76%

PENNSYLVANIA 15
East – Allentown, Bethlehem

Centered in the Lehigh Valley about 60 miles north of Philadelphia and abutting the Delaware River, the 15th takes in Allentown, Bethlehem and Easton — historically known as steel and coal industry strongholds.

The region once suffered from the Rust Belt blues that singer Billy Joel enshrined in his 1982 song, "Allentown," and recent layoffs include the announced departure of the corporate headquarters and assembly jobs of Mack Trucks. But the area's economy has diversified over the past several decades: health care employers and warehouse and distribution industries provide jobs, and small businesses now dot a landscape where factories and small farms once were mainstays.

Local leaders hope the transformation of the former Bethlehem Steel factory — once the Lehigh Valley's largest employer and one of the world's largest steel manufacturers — into the Sands Casino Resort Bethlehem gaming, hotel and restaurant venue will churn out revenue. Olympus America moved its headquarters to the 15th in 2006, and other key employers include the Lehigh Valley Hospital complex, electric utility

PPL, and technology company LSI Corp. Emmaus-based Rodale Press has been forced to cut jobs.

Many of the district's towns, some with well-established Pennsylvania Dutch heritages, date to colonial times. But the 250-year-old German influence has been diluted by a century of immigration and steady migration from New Jersey and New York commuters. White-collar commuters have brought higher incomes to the area, and there has been an influx of lower-income residents as well, making the Lehigh Valley one of the fastest-growing areas in the Northeast. Blue-collar, ethnic workers provide a dwindling yet still-powerful base for Democrats, and Barack Obama won 56 percent of the 15th's 2008 presidential vote. But an increasing white-collar core and a socially conservative streak among blue-collar voters have helped the GOP win House races here.

MAJOR INDUSTRY
Technology, health care, warehousing, manufacturing

CITIES
Allentown, 106,632; Bethlehem, 71,329; Easton, 26,263

NOTABLE
The Valley Preferred Cycling Center, a premier site for track cycling, has hosted Olympic trial, Junior World Championship and World Cup races.

Rep. Joe Pitts (R)

CAPITOL OFFICE
225-2411
www.house.gov/pitts
420 Cannon Bldg. 20515-3816; fax 225-2013

COMMITTEES
Energy & Commerce

RESIDENCE
Kennett Square

BORN
Oct. 10, 1939; Lexington, Ky.

RELIGION
Protestant

FAMILY
Wife, Virginia M. "Ginny" Pitts; three children

EDUCATION
Asbury College, A.B. 1961 (philosophy & religion);
West Chester State College, M.Ed. 1972
(comprehensive sciences)

MILITARY SERVICE
Air Force, 1963-69

CAREER
Nursery and landscaping business owner; teacher

POLITICAL HIGHLIGHTS
Pa. House, 1973-97

ELECTION RESULTS

2008 GENERAL

Joe Pitts (R)	170,329	55.8%
Bruce A. Slater (D)	120,193	39.4%
John A. Murphy (I)	11,768	3.9%

2008 PRIMARY

Joe Pitts (R)	unopposed

2006 GENERAL

Joe Pitts (R)	115,741	56.6%
Lois K. Herr (D)	80,915	39.5%
John A. Murphy (I)	7,958	3.9%

PREVIOUS WINNING PERCENTAGES
2004 (64%); 2002 (88%); 2000 (67%); 1998 (71%);
1996 (59%)

Elected 1996; 7th term

During more than 35 years in politics — in the state legislature and in Congress — Pitts has followed the same road, advocating cutting taxes and limiting the scope of the federal government while fervently opposing abortion. While he has had to put many of his social conservative priorities on the back burner with Democrats in control, he hasn't forgotten them.

Pitts has tried to adapt to life in the minority by making bipartisan issues such as energy, open space preservation and health care his top priorities from his seat on the powerful Energy and Commerce Committee. But he doesn't hesitate to go after Democrats for the directions they take. Lamenting early initiatives of the Obama administration and the 111th Congress (2009-10), Pitts said in April 2009, "We are going down the road toward European socialism."

Pitts voted in fall 2008 against the $700 billion law to aid the ailing financial services sector. He said he believed recovery from the economic crisis would come only from market-based solutions. He likewise opposed a $14 billion auto industry bailout — which stalled in the Senate later that year — and blamed the industry's problems on poor management and the United Auto Workers.

He also opposed President Obama's $787 billion economic stimulus package in early 2009, saying "it was full of big government, special-interest spending and has little hope of accomplishing the job creation that our economy so desperately needs to get back on track."

He had no sympathy as lawmakers cried foul when American International Group Inc., which received funds from the rescue law, distributed employee bonuses. He voted against a measure to impose a 90 percent tax on the bonuses, but asked, "For a politician that used the term 'exit strategy' to great effect during the election, I ask the president, where is your exit strategy to remove the American taxpayer from the mess called AIG?" The "exit strategy" Pitts referred to was Obama's plan for pulling troops out of Iraq.

Perhaps his greatest criticism came when Obama signed an executive order reinstating federal funding for embryonic stem cell research. Pitts, who leads the Values Action Team — a group of about 70 social conservatives — said he was disappointed "Obama has chosen to force American taxpayers to fund research that destroys human life against the objections of their conscience."

Primarily, though, Pitts laments that House GOP leaders don't push his team's priorities harder. In July 2008, in hopes of reviving efforts, the team came up with its own Values Agenda that addresses banning abortion, outlawing same-sex marriage, allowing prayer in public schools, banning flag burning and protecting the Pledge of Allegiance.

But he has also sought to be a player on other high-profile issues. A member of Energy's panel on Energy and the Environment, he said he favors a market-oriented and competition-based course when tackling climate change legislation. From that post, he fiercely opposes regulations affecting the coal industry. He criticized Democratic leaders in early 2009 when they proposed "cap and trade" legislation, saying it would kill jobs. He also pushes legislation to increase U.S. oil refinery capacity by building three new refineries on military bases that are slated for closure by the Base Realignment and Closure Commission.

A member of the Health Subcommittee, Pitts favors a consumer-driven health care system and advocates a policy to give individuals tax credits similar to those given to employers to purchase health coverage with pre-tax dollars. During the 110th Congress (2007-08), he sponsored legislation to increase the availability of advanced medical imaging services.

Pitts also tries to protect his district's agricultural areas that are constantly pressured by development by seeking to exempt farmers from paying federal capital gains taxes on profits made from selling off development rights. His intent is to provide an incentive to farmers to preserve their land permanently.

And he has formed the Land Conservation Caucus with fellow Pennsylvania Republican Jim Gerlach and Democrat Christopher S. Murphy of Connecticut to promote and support land preservation measures. He also works to defends the rights and the simple, rural lifestyle of Lancaster's insular Amish community and fought for an expansion of child labor laws to ensure Amish teenagers can enter apprenticeships once their formal education is complete. The proposal was included in a catchall spending law in 2004.

From his seat on the commerce and trade subcommittee, Pitts consistently sides with the majority of his party on trade deals.

Pitts' highest-profile stand against President George W. Bush was on the No Child Left Behind Act of 2001. A former educator, Pitts fears the law's stringent testing requirements force teachers to ignore materials that are not on standardized exams.

He has a strong interest in foreign policy and humanitarian work stemming from his childhood living in the backcountry in the Philippines as, the son of missionaries. Every year, he invites ambassadors from 195 countries to his district to tour businesses and cultural historic sites.

In the aftermath of the Sept. 11 terrorist attacks, Pitts and a handful of other lawmakers formed the Silk Road Caucus to promote greater contact between the United States and Central Asia. He has organized equipment drives for hospitals in Pakistan and is active in several human rights organizations.

While Pitts spent much of his youth in the Philippines, he returned to his native Kentucky, where he married and earned a degree in philosophy and religion. Pitts and his wife then embarked on teaching careers. He later joined the Air Force for more than five years, including three stints in Southeast Asia.

The family then moved to Pennsylvania, and Pitts returned to teaching high school math and science, and eventually started his own landscaping firm. In 1972, colleagues persuaded him to make a bid for an open state House seat. He served there for 24 years, including eight years as chairman of the Appropriations Committee.

When Republican Robert S. Walker decided to retire in 1996, Pitts won a hard-fought five-way primary race and won easily in November. In the 2008 election he substantially outraised Democrat Bruce Slater and won with 56 percent of the vote.

KEY VOTES

2008
No   Delay consideration of Colombia free-trade agreement
No   Override Bush veto of federal farm and nutrition programs reauthorization bill
Yes Overhaul surveillance laws and permit dismissal of suits against companies that conducted warrantless wiretapping
No   Grant mortgage relief to homeowners and funding for Fannie Mae and Freddie Mac
No   Approve initial $700 billion program to stabilize financial markets
No   Approve final $700 billion program to stabilize financial markets
No   Provide $14 billion in loans to automakers

2007
No   Increase minimum wage by $2.10 an hour
No   Approve $124.2 billion in emergency war spending and set goal for redeployment of troops from Iraq
Yes Reject federal contraceptive assistance to international family planning groups
No   Override Bush veto of $23.2 billion water projects authorization bill
Yes Implement Peru free-trade agreement
No   Approve energy policy overhaul with new fuel economy standards
Yes Clear $473.5 billion omnibus spending bill, including $70 billion for military operations

CQ VOTE STUDIES

	PARTY UNITY		PRESIDENTIAL SUPPORT	
	SUPPORT	OPPOSE	SUPPORT	OPPOSE
2008	98%	2%	76%	24%
2007	98%	2%	94%	6%
2006	95%	5%	84%	16%
2005	97%	3%	85%	15%
2004	97%	3%	91%	9%

INTEREST GROUPS

	AFL-CIO	ADA	CCUS	ACU
2008	0%	5%	88%	100%
2007	8%	0%	75%	100%
2006	8%	5%	92%	86%
2005	7%	0%	88%	100%
2004	13%	5%	95%	100%

PENNSYLVANIA 16
Southeast – Lancaster, part of Reading

Located in southeastern Pennsylvania and bordering Delaware and Maryland, the 16th includes all of Lancaster County, the southern half of Chester County and portions of southwest Berks County, including part of Reading. The predominately white and mainly white-collar district also includes much of Pennsylvania Dutch Country.

The strong work ethic of the local labor force and the district's proximity to major roadways attract companies to the area, which is central to the mid-Atlantic's major markets. Economic expansion attracted new residents for several decades, and some of the area's farmland has been built over with tract housing. Rolling and pastoral Chester County (shared with the 6th and 7th districts) has grown by more than 28 percent since the 1990s. The Kennett Square area produces one of the nation's largest mushroom crops.

Farm preservation remains a major concern, especially in Lancaster County, which has a diverse agricultural economy, produces more farm-based revenue than any other county in the state and is a national leader

in poultry and livestock raising. Tourism also adds to the diversity of the 16th's economy. An estimated 8 million visitors annually flock to Dutch Country to gaze at Amish horse-drawn carriages, browse at quilt shops and dine in family-style restaurants.

Since the dawn of the Civil War, the areas of the 16th favored the GOP at all levels, but Republican John McCain eked out only a slim, 51 percent majority in the 2008 presidential election. Lancaster County, which accounts for more than 70 percent of the district population, has traditionally set the district's conservative political tone with its Amish heritage. But McCain took 56 percent of the county's vote in 2008, 10 percentage points lower than George W. Bush won four years earlier. Barack Obama won votes in the more socially moderate Chester County, although he lost the district by three percentage points overall.

MAJOR INDUSTRY
Agriculture, tourism, manufacturing

CITIES
Lancaster, 56,348; Reading (pt.), 44,296; West Chester, 17,861

NOTABLE
The original five-and-dime store that started the Woolworth chain opened in Lancaster in 1879.

Rep. Tim Holden (D)

Elected 1992; 9th term

A former sheriff, Holden looks out for the constituents in his working-class district in central Pennsylvania even when their interests lead him astray of the wishes of Democratic leaders. An easygoing and affable man — his constituents call him Timmy — he seeks to protect their jobs and their guns, and brings home federal money for projects to boost the local economy.

But he makes little effort to seek the limelight, on the floor or elsewhere. "The last thing Congress needs is another prima donna looking for C-SPAN time," he once said. The Harrisburg Patriot News, in endorsing him in 2008, noted that Holden "works toward practical solutions on whatever problem he confronts."

A member of the fiscally conservative Blue Dog Coalition, Holden supported President Obama's $787 billion economic stimulus law in February 2009, saying it would bring $1.3 billion to his state for highways, bridges and mass transit. He indicated less willingness to support Obama's $3.56 trillion fiscal 2010 budget blueprint, saying it was too large, but he reluctantly supported the House bill.

Holden typically sides with Democrats and organized labor on economic issues such as the minimum wage and an extension of unemployment benefits, and he opposes most trade agreements. In early 2009, he supported a pair of bills designed to strengthen the ability of workers to combat wage discrimination.

But he has crossed the aisle on other votes; he supported a GOP energy policy overhaul in 2005, as well as Republican bills to limit class action lawsuits and to cap damages in medical malpractice cases, and in 2006 backed a tough border security bill that most House Democrats opposed. He once opposed funding for embryonic stem cell research, but later altered his position after talking with researchers and patients who might benefit. And he was among a group of lawmakers who urged Attorney General Eric H. Holder Jr. in 2009 not to reinstate the expired ban on assault weapons.

Holden is the party's second-most-senior member of the Agriculture Committee and chairman of its panel on Conservation, Credit, Energy and Research. He advocates the creation of a second generation of alternative fuel sources, such as switchgrass, and pushes to create such crops on the fertile ground of abandoned strip mines. During debate on the 2008 farm law, he had to rein in efforts by subcommittee members to tack on new programs that couldn't be financed under the bill's restricted funding. But his panel did include new incentives for alternative energy, as well as provisions that provide credit for conservation programs to benefit state farmers, authorize $440 million for water quality conservation in the Chesapeake Bay watershed and extend a program that compensates dairy farmers when milk prices fall.

Holden also sits on the Transportation and Infrastructure Committee, where he has touted his successes in securing funding for local highway and transit projects in the 1998 and 2005 surface transportation laws, which will be renewed during the 111th Congress (2009-10). He has teamed with neighboring Pennsylvania Republican Joe Pitts in pushing for a commuter rail link between Harrisburg and Lancaster; the two obtained more than $11 million in the fiscal 2009 budget for the project.

Another pet project is working to make the 17th District's coal reserves more marketable by spurring researchers to develop technology to burn the fuel more cleanly.

Holden aggressively seeks federal funding for a wide array of projects

CAPITOL OFFICE
225-5546
www.holden.house.gov
2417 Rayburn Bldg. 20515-3817; fax 226-0996

COMMITTEES
Agriculture
(Conservation, Credit, Energy & Research
- chairman)
Transportation & Infrastructure

RESIDENCE
St. Clair

BORN
March 5, 1957; St. Clair, Pa.

RELIGION
Roman Catholic

FAMILY
Wife, Gwen Holden

EDUCATION
U. of Richmond, attended 1976-77;
Bloomsburg U., B.A. 1980 (sociology);

CAREER
Probation officer; insurance broker; Realtor

POLITICAL HIGHLIGHTS
Schuylkill County sheriff, 1985-93

ELECTION RESULTS

2008 GENERAL

Tim Holden (D)	192,699	63.7%
Toni Gilhooley (R)	109,909	36.3%

2008 PRIMARY

Tim Holden (D)	unopposed

2006 GENERAL

Tim Holden (D)	137,253	64.5%
Matthew A. Wertz (R)	75,455	35.5%

PREVIOUS WINNING PERCENTAGES
2004 (59%); 2002 (51%); 2000 (66%); 1998 (61%);
1996 (59%); 1994 (57%); 1992 (52%)

back home. He obtained $17.3 million in earmarks in fiscal 2009 spending bills, and $36.4 million for fiscal 2008.

Many of his earmarks are obtained thanks to his allegiance to fellow Pennsylvania Democrat John P. Murtha, chairman of the Defense Appropriations subcommittee. He is among a group of Murtha's protégés who typically congregate in the southeast corner of the House chamber. But the association and subsequent earmarks have also earned Holden some unwanted national attention.

News media outlets reported in 2007 on a $3.2 million defense contract for Fidelity Technologies, a Pennsylvania firm that had at that point donated $10,550 to his re-election campaigns. Holden defended the earmark: "Who is going to contribute to your campaign, people you don't help?" he asked the Allentown Morning Call newspaper. In early 2009, the controversy continued when Holden's name was associated with Murtha's as the FBI investigated possible illegal campaign contributions to Murtha and others for their close ties to a now defunct lobbying firm, The PMA Group. Holden is among the top 20 recipients of PMA campaign dollars since 2001.

Holden's great-grandfather John Siney founded the Miner's Benevolent Association, the forerunner of the United Mine Workers. His father, Joseph "Sox" Holden, was a Schuylkill County commissioner for almost two decades and a catcher for the Philadelphia Phillies from 1934 to 1936. Holden keeps his dad's #10 jersey framed in his office and takes the field in the same position at the annual congressional charity baseball game.

Holden started college in Virginia on a football scholarship but returned home after a year to recuperate from a bout of tuberculosis and then stayed close by to finish school. He earned an insurance license and a real estate broker license, and worked in both fields part time to make ends meet while he served as a probation officer; sergeant at arms in the Pennsylvania House; and Schuylkill County sheriff, a post he won at age 28.

When Democratic Rep. Gus Yatron retired in 1992, Holden won by 4 percentage points in what was then the 6th District. He won re-election with increasing margins until 2002, when his margin narrowed in a race against 20-year veteran GOP incumbent Rep. George W. Gekas in the newly drawn 17th District.

In 2004, Scott Paterno, son of legendary Penn State football coach Joe Paterno, raised more than $1 million to try to unseat Holden. But Holden won by more than 20 percentage points. Two years later, Republican Matthew A. Wertz, citing health and personal reasons, suspended his campaign in the fall and Holden won by 29 percentage points. He took 64 percent in 2008.

KEY VOTES

2008
Yes Delay consideration of Colombia free-trade agreement
Yes Override Bush veto of federal farm and nutrition programs reauthorization bill
Yes Overhaul surveillance laws and permit dismissal of suits against companies that conducted warrantless wiretapping
Yes Grant mortgage relief to homeowners and funding for Fannie Mae and Freddie Mac
No Approve initial $700 billion program to stabilize financial markets
No Approve final $700 billion program to stabilize financial markets
Yes Provide $14 billion in loans to automakers

2007
Yes Increase minimum wage by $2.10 an hour
Yes Approve $124.2 billion in emergency war spending and set goal for redeployment of troops from Iraq
Yes Reject federal contraceptive assistance to international family planning groups
Yes Override Bush veto of $23.2 billion water projects authorization bill
No Implement Peru free-trade agreement
Yes Approve energy policy overhaul with new fuel economy standards
Yes Clear $473.5 billion omnibus spending bill, including $70 billion for military operations

CQ VOTE STUDIES

	PARTY UNITY		PRESIDENTIAL SUPPORT	
	SUPPORT	OPPOSE	SUPPORT	OPPOSE
2008	95%	5%	20%	80%
2007	92%	8%	13%	87%
2006	79%	21%	56%	44%
2005	75%	25%	52%	48%
2004	76%	24%	48%	52%

INTEREST GROUPS

	AFL-CIO	ADA	CCUS	ACU
2008	100%	85%	61%	16%
2007	92%	80%	45%	16%
2006	100%	60%	53%	64%
2005	93%	80%	63%	40%
2004	93%	70%	67%	48%

PENNSYLVANIA 17
East central — Harrisburg, Lebanon, Pottsville

Anchored in the eastern part of south-central Pennsylvania, the 17th is home to Harrisburg, the state capital, which sits 100 miles west of Philadelphia and 200 miles east of Pittsburgh. The 17th has two distinct zones: a stretch of agricultural lands along the Susquehanna River in the west, and industrial areas in Schuylkill and Berks counties in the east. Here, in GOP-minded central Pennsylvania, state government and manufacturing remain key sources of employment.

Harrisburg's skyline is dominated by the Capitol, with a dome inspired by St. Peter's Basilica in Rome. With many government employees and a black majority, the city typically votes Democratic. Visitors wanting a real taste of Dauphin County skip Harrisburg and go to Hershey, also known as "the sweetest place on Earth," where even the streetlights are shaped like Hershey's Kisses. The chocolate factory stands in the center of town, emitting the most pleasant of industrial odors.

The economy in Dauphin and Lebanon counties relies on health care, education and government jobs. There have been layoffs at computer

and electrical components manufacturers in the area, and municipal budget shortfalls have caused concern. Harrisburg, in Dauphin, is a key distribution hub for metropolitan markets in the mid-Atlantic region, and it hosts the Penn State Milton S. Hershey Medical Center.

The 17th has a distinct Republican lean, but moderate Democrats can play here due to the district's mix of agrarian and industrial communities. The GOP is strong in Lebanon County and in the areas of Dauphin outside of Harrisburg, but the city's concentration of Democratic voters outweighs the county's conservative areas. Democrats are competitive in Schuylkill County, long a coal mining powerhouse, with comfortable margins at the state and U.S. House levels in Shenandoah, Pottsville and Mahanoy, although GOP presidential candidate John McCain won areas in Pottsville and 54 percent of the vote in the county as a whole in 2008. Overall, McCain won 51 percent of the 17th's presidential vote.

MAJOR INDUSTRY
Government, service, manufacturing, tourism, agriculture, biotech

CITIES
Harrisburg, 48,950; Lebanon, 24,461; Pottsville, 15,549

NOTABLE
Pottsville is home to Yuengling, America's oldest active brewery.

Rep. Tim Murphy (R)

Elected 2002; 4th term

CAPITOL OFFICE
225-2301
murphy.house.gov
322 Cannon Bldg. 20515-3818; fax 225-1844

COMMITTEES
Energy & Commerce

RESIDENCE
Upper St. Clair

BORN
Sept. 11, 1952; Cleveland, Ohio

RELIGION
Roman Catholic

FAMILY
Wife, Nan Murphy; one child

EDUCATION
Wheeling College, B.S. 1974 (psychology);
Cleveland State U., M.A. 1976 (psychology);
U. of Pittsburgh, Ph.D. 1979 (psychology)

CAREER
Psychologist; professor

POLITICAL HIGHLIGHTS
Pa. Senate, 1997-2003

ELECTION RESULTS

2008 GENERAL

Tim Murphy (R)	213,349	64.1%
Steve O'Donnell (D)	119,661	35.9%

2008 PRIMARY

Tim Murphy (R)	unopposed

2006 GENERAL

Tim Murphy (R)	144,632	57.8%
Chad Kluko (D)	105,419	42.2%

PREVIOUS WINNING PERCENTAGES
2004 (63%); 2002 (60%)

Murphy shares many of the socially conservative views of his constituents in the Pittsburgh suburbs; he opposes abortion and federal funding for embryonic stem cell research, has voted against legislation to ban job discrimination based on sexual orientation, and supported bills to allow faith-based Head Start providers to take religion into account when hiring. But on his pet issue — health care — he has increasingly aligned with Democrats.

Since Democrats took control of the House, Murphy has been less inclined to take the GOP's side on votes in which the majority of the two parties diverge. Though the shift has come on a few fiscal votes, it has been primarily on health care matters as he seeks to align himself with Democrats on the Energy and Commerce Committee. Even so, former GOP House Speaker Newt Gingrich of Georgia has cited him as someone to watch, praising his work on health issues.

Murphy wants to improve health care information technology to help reduce medical errors that lead to increased health care costs. In early 2009, he was named to a GOP group charged with coming up with a Republican alternative health care plan.

A psychologist by trade, Murphy has pushed bills to provide liability protection to doctors volunteering at community health centers and to promote the use of electronic prescriptions and medical record-keeping to track every aspect of a patient's care.

In 2008, he supported passage of a measure requiring insurers to offer mental health benefits equal in scope to other health benefits, despite GOP resistance. He also teamed with then-Energy and Commerce Chairman John D. Dingell of Michigan on a bill, later incorporated into a supplemental funding law for the war in Iraq, which prevented the George W. Bush administration from shifting Medicaid costs to the states. And in defiance of most of his GOP colleagues, he supported a new law reauthorizing U.S. efforts to combat HIV and AIDS overseas.

He also supported legislation in early 2009 to expand the State Children Health's Insurance Program, which Obama signed into law. It provides coverage to children of low-income families ineligible for Medicaid. He had supported similar legislation that Bush had twice vetoed.

Murphy also tends to side with Democrats on labor issues. In 2007, he voted to increase the federal minimum wage and opposed a free-trade deal with Peru that labor unions opposed. He did, however, provide a crucial vote in favor of the Central America Free Trade Agreement in 2005. Labor unions have forgiven that vote and the Pennsylvania AFL-CIO continues to support him.

Murphy played to populist sentiment in the fall of 2008 when he opposed a law providing $700 billion to rescue ailing financial institutions. He has also shored up support in his district by attacking trade with China and by winning federal funding for local projects. He has funneled millions of dollars back home for hospitals, roads and the Pittsburgh airport.

He opposed Obama's $787 billion economic stimulus law in early 2009, although the final version included "Buy America" provisions he had pushed to ensure any infrastructure projects completed with stimulus funds be made with U.S. steel and iron. But he backed the Democrats' $410 billion catchall spending bill for fiscal 2009, which included about $7.8 million in earmarks — funding set-asides for special projects — he had helped obtain.

Murphy does not, however, line up with Democrats on energy issues. He supports increased use of nuclear power and more domestic oil drilling. And he said during a hearing in April 2009 that he believes a cap on greenhouse gas emissions coupled with a market-based trading system for emissions would not reduce pollution and would send jobs to China, Brazil and India.

Murphy's biggest legislative success came in 2006, when the House passed his bill making it illegal for callers to "spoof" caller-ID devices. The bill was prompted by election-season phone calls critical of Murphy that had been rigged to appear as though they originated in his own offices. The bill died in the Senate; House Democrats passed a similar measure early in the 110th Congress (2007-08) with Murphy as a cosponsor that also stalled.

Growing up as one of 11 children, Murphy paid his way through school by cleaning out horse stalls and digging graves. He supports vouchers and other programs that could allow low-income families to send their children to private or parochial schools.

Murphy, who taught himself to play guitar, performed in acoustic bands in high school, college and graduate school. The bands played in coffeehouses and once opened in Cleveland for banjo legend Earl Scruggs.

He earned a doctorate in psychology and worked in several hospitals in Western Pennsylvania. He eventually opened his own practice, taught at the University of Pittsburgh and gave medical advice as "Dr. Tim" on Pittsburgh radio and television.

He was motivated to run for elective office by a desire to address problems in managed care and won a state Senate seat in 1996. He pushed through the legislature a Patients' Bill of Rights. In 2001, Murphy co-wrote a book titled, "The Angry Child: Regaining Control When Your Child Is Out of Control." The book explored the sources of anger in children and recommended ways parents could respond.

Pennsylvania lost a pair of House seats in reapportionment after the 2000 census. But the Republican-controlled General Assembly drew an 18th District south of Pittsburgh configured to favor Murphy, who had become the presumptive heir to the seat when four-term Democrat Frank R. Mascara decided to mount what proved to be an unsuccessful primary challenge to Democratic Rep. John P. Murtha in the 12th District.

He took 60 percent of the vote to defeat Democrat Jack M. Machek in 2002, and two years later won with 63 percent over political newcomer Mark G. Boles, after having raised almost 10 times more money than his opponent.

Questions about ethics have arisen prior to both of Murphy's most recent re-elections, specifically allegations that Murphy used his House staff for political purposes and overused his House franking privilege. But Democrats have struggled to put up viable challengers, and Murphy cruised to victory.

KEY VOTES

2008
No Delay consideration of Colombia free-trade agreement
Yes Override Bush veto of federal farm and nutrition programs reauthorization bill
Yes Overhaul surveillance laws and permit dismissal of suits against companies that conducted warrantless wiretapping
Yes Grant mortgage relief to homeowners and funding for Fannie Mae and Freddie Mac
No Approve initial $700 billion program to stabilize financial markets
No Approve final $700 billion program to stabilize financial markets
Yes Provide $14 billion in loans to automakers

2007
Yes Increase minimum wage by $2.10 an hour
No Approve $124.2 billion in emergency war spending and set goal for redeployment of troops from Iraq
Yes Reject federal contraceptive assistance to international family planning groups
Yes Override Bush veto of $23.2 billion water projects authorization bill
No Implement Peru free-trade agreement
Yes Approve energy policy overhaul with new fuel economy standards
Yes Clear $473.5 billion omnibus spending bill, including $70 billion for military operations

CQ VOTE STUDIES

| | PARTY UNITY | | PRESIDENTIAL SUPPORT | |
	SUPPORT	OPPOSE	SUPPORT	OPPOSE
2008	76%	24%	45%	55%
2007	74%	26%	48%	52%
2006	91%	9%	87%	13%
2005	91%	9%	80%	20%
2004	92%	8%	84%	16%

INTEREST GROUPS

	AFL-CIO	ADA	CCUS	ACU
2008	73%	60%	81%	48%
2007	71%	40%	85%	68%
2006	43%	10%	93%	80%
2005	21%	15%	92%	84%
2004	36%	20%	95%	92%

PENNSYLVANIA 18

West – Pittsburgh suburbs, part of Washington and Westmoreland counties

Taking in suburbs of Pittsburgh on three sides of the city, the socially conservative 18th moves east from Washington County through parts of southern Allegheny County into Westmoreland County. Access to major waterways made the first half of the 20th century prosperous for parts of the district, which was once a prodigious steel producer. Now, many areas outside the Pittsburgh suburbs, especially in southwestern Washington and southeastern Westmoreland, are struggling economically.

Roughly 55 percent of the 18th's residents live in Allegheny County, which is dominated by Pittsburgh, located in the 14th District. The 18th's share of the suburbs includes well-off areas in southwestern Allegheny such as Upper St. Clair and Mount Lebanon, as well as middle- and working-class Democratic enclaves like blue-collar Carnegie and Dormont, which are just southwest of Pittsburgh.

The district's universities and hospitals have lured some technology companies to the area, as has the 18th's high percentage of residents with a college degree (29 percent). In the district's northwest, thousands of area jobs are provided by Pittsburgh International Airport, and the new headquarters for Dick's Sporting Goods provides hundreds more. Economic downturns have forced layoffs in the health care sector and at the airport, which has lost most of the traffic from its one-time primary carrier, US Airways.

The 18th includes most of Westmoreland County, which is a former Democratic bastion that has moved to the right, supporting Republican John McCain by nearly 17 percentage points in the 2008 presidential election. Overall, McCain captured 55 percent of the 18th's vote in 2008.

MAJOR INDUSTRY
Health care, technology, manufacturing, steel

CITIES
Bethel Park, 33,556; Mount Lebanon (unincorporated), 33,017; Monroeville (pt.), 24,294

NOTABLE
Andy Warhol is buried in Bethel Park; The Meadowcroft Village at the Museum of Rural Life, near Avella in Washington County, preserves the history of mid-19th-century rural life in western Pennsylvania.

Rep. Todd R. Platts (R)

Elected 2000; 5th term

CAPITOL OFFICE
225-5836
www.house.gov/platts
2455 Rayburn Bldg. 20515-3819; fax 226-1000

COMMITTEES
Education & Labor
Oversight & Government Reform
Transportation & Infrastructure

RESIDENCE
York

BORN
March 5, 1962; York, Pa.

RELIGION
Episcopalian

FAMILY
Wife, Leslie Platts; two children

EDUCATION
Shippensburg U., B.S. 1984 (public administration);
Pepperdine U., J.D. 1991

CAREER
Lawyer; gubernatorial and state legislative aide

POLITICAL HIGHLIGHTS
Pa. House, 1993-2000; sought Republican
nomination for York County Commission, 1995

ELECTION RESULTS

2008 GENERAL

Todd R. Platts (R)	218,862	66.6%
Philip J. Avillo Jr. (D)	109,533	33.4%

2008 PRIMARY

Todd R. Platts (R)	unopposed

2006 GENERAL

Todd R. Platts (R)	142,512	64.0%
Philip J. Avillo Jr. (D)	74,625	33.5%
Derf W. Maitland (GREEN)	5,640	2.5%

PREVIOUS WINNING PERCENTAGES
2004 (92%); 2002 (91%); 2000 (73%)

Platts is a proudly iconoclastic Republican who takes no campaign contributions from corporations, interest groups or his own party's leaders and has never run a television campaign advertisement. He votes his own way, even if his interests don't align with House GOP leaders' wishes — and sometimes they don't.

He tends to take a conservative stance on most major fiscal measures. But he has opposed his leadership on votes ranging from campaign finance reform to increasing the minimum wage to federal funding of embryonic stem cell research. He said there have been no repercussions. "I've worked hard to have very good relations with my leadership," he said. Honesty helps a lot, he added. His positions are "never going to be a secret — they're going to know whether I'm voting against them or with them and why."

He stuck with his party in early 2009 to oppose President Obama's $787 billion economic stimulus law. And in the fall of 2008, he stood against the leaders of both parties and voted against a $700 billion plan to rescue the financial sector, which became law. Earlier in the year, he opposed a Democratic measure aimed at providing home mortgage relief and giving a lifeline to the giant mortgage financing companies Fannie Mae and Freddie Mac.

But Platts supported a measure to expand the State Children's Health Insurance Program, which provides coverage to kids whose families don't qualify for Medicaid. And he joined with Democrat Edward J. Markey of Massachusetts on a measure calling for 25 percent of the nation's electricity to be generated from renewable sources like wind, solar and geothermal energy by 2025.

During the 110th Congress (2007-08), he was one of only three Republicans who voted for all six bills that Democratic leaders brought to the House floor as part of their "first 100 hours" agenda. That included an increase in the federal minimum wage, allowing expanded federal funding for embryonic stem cell research and empowering the government to negotiate lower prices for Medicare's drug benefit. He also voted for a Democratic energy policy bill that raised fuel efficiency standards for cars and trucks and for a bill renewing generous subsidies to farmers.

In his first term, he was one of 20 Republicans who signed a discharge petition forcing the GOP leadership to bring campaign finance legislation to a vote. He was one of the 41 Republicans to vote for the bill that became law in 2002.

Good government is an obsession for Platts, down to the "Mr. Smith Goes to Washington" poster in his office — a gift from his brother when he first won office. A member of the Oversight and Government Reform panel, he takes no political action committee (PAC) money, and wonders why the government's books are not as tidy as his own finances. "If my checkbook is off by 10 cents, I'll stay up all night until I find that 10 cents," Platts once lectured a NASA official appearing before a subcommittee. "Your checkbook is off by $2 billion."

His reputation for trying to keep government on the straight and narrow dates to his days as a member of the Pennsylvania House, where he aggravated colleagues by being unbending and going after their perquisites of office. The York Daily Record newspaper once dubbed him the "King of Clean."

Platts thinks PAC contributions undermine the public's trust in government, though he doesn't think the money compromises many of his colleagues. "If I took a PAC contribution, or even the individual contributions I get, it's not going to change my vote," he said. "But it will certainly change the perception of the public of what guides my votes and will diminish their trust."

He said he wouldn't take PAC contributions even if he faced a well-funded candidate; he has his staff write "void" on the PAC checks he sometimes receives unsolicited and return them to their senders with a note of thanks.

Platts said he may have picked up his stubborn tendencies from his father, who with his mother bucked the local Little League establishment by insisting every child who showed up at practice should play. His parents argued so vociferously to league officials that they implemented a rule requiring every child who practiced to receive playing time during games.

Platts also goes to great lengths not to be a creature of Washington. He drives back and forth to Capitol Hill from his home in York every day, about two hours each way, and he said he hasn't spent a night in the District since 2005. Daily involvement with his family and constituents, he said, is more important than a good night's sleep.

He also sits on the Transportation and Infrastructure Committee. When the panel takes up a renewal of the 2005 surface transportation law, Platts said, he'll rely on local leaders to recommend highway projects to him.

A member of the Education and Labor Committee, Platts tries to work across the aisle. He once wrote an early childhood education bill with George Miller of California, a liberal Democrat who is now chairman of the committee, that sought to boost the pay and improve the training of child care workers. Unlike many Republicans, Platts opposes vouchers for private schools and says the federal government should keep its longstanding promise to pay its full share of the costs of educating disabled students under the Individuals With Disabilities Education Act. He voted for President George W. Bush's 2001 education overhaul known as No Child Left Behind but now believes the law needs major revisions to give more flexibility to state and local school officials.

Platts said being a member of Congress has been his ambition since he was a teenager. He worked for Republican Gov. Dick Thornburgh and served as a legislative committee staff member and assistant finance director for the state Republican Party. In 1992, he won election to the state legislature. He made an unsuccessful run for the York County Commission in 1995, then went on to win two more state House terms.

In early 1999, when Republican Rep. William F. Goodling announced his plan to retire in 2000, Platts was the first to jump into the race. Though greatly outspent in the GOP primary, he won with 33 percent of the vote. He defeated college professor Jeff Sanders in November and didn't face another Democratic opponent until 2006, when another professor, Phillip J. Avillo Jr., took barely 34 percent of the vote. Avillo tried again in 2008. Platts raised a mere $211,000 for his campaign, more than enough to swamp the underfunded Avillo, who spent a paltry $64,000. Platts took two-thirds of the vote.

KEY VOTES

2008

No Delay consideration of Colombia free-trade agreement

Yes Override Bush veto of federal farm and nutrition programs reauthorization bill

Yes Overhaul surveillance laws and permit dismissal of suits against companies that conducted warrantless wiretapping

No Grant mortgage relief to homeowners and funding for Fannie Mae and Freddie Mac

No Approve initial $700 billion program to stabilize financial markets

No Approve final $700 billion program to stabilize financial markets

No Provide $14 billion in loans to automakers

2007

Yes Increase minimum wage by $2.10 an hour

No Approve $124.2 billion in emergency war spending and set goal for redeployment of troops from Iraq

Yes Reject federal contraceptive assistance to international family planning groups

No Override Bush veto of $23.2 billion water projects authorization bill

Yes Implement Peru free-trade agreement

Yes Approve energy policy overhaul with new fuel economy standards

Yes Clear $473.5 billion omnibus spending bill, including $70 billion for military operations

CQ VOTE STUDIES

	PARTY UNITY		PRESIDENTIAL SUPPORT	
	SUPPORT	OPPOSE	SUPPORT	OPPOSE
2008	80%	20%	49%	51%
2007	77%	23%	54%	46%
2006	72%	28%	80%	20%
2005	84%	16%	80%	20%
2004	88%	12%	85%	15%

INTEREST GROUPS

	AFL-CIO	ADA	CCUS	ACU
2008	47%	55%	78%	68%
2007	42%	45%	70%	64%
2006	50%	25%	93%	72%
2005	33%	25%	85%	67%
2004	33%	20%	95%	84%

PENNSYLVANIA 19

South central — York, Gettysburg

Situated west of the Susquehanna River, mostly east of the South Mountain ridge and mostly south of Harrisburg (in the neighboring 17th District), the 19th's historic landscape has a Republican-leaning constituency and major agricultural and manufacturing industries.

Located along several major highways, the district is a prime location for manufacturing and distribution centers, including depots and logistical support facilities for the Defense Department, and York County serves as the 19th's industrial hub. Residential growth, a more recent trend, also can be attributed to the district's location — many Marylanders have moved here for lower taxes and affordable real estate. Adams, York and Cumberland counties have all seen rapid growth since 1990.

Tourism also plays a major role in the district's economy. Nearly 2 million visitors each year come to see the site of the 1863 Battle of Gettysburg in Adams County, now a largely fruit-growing area. Many come for the annual re-enactment of one of the Civil War's most significant battles and to see monuments, military grave sites, historic markers and the site of Abraham Lincoln's Gettysburg Address. The new Gettysburg National Military Park Museum and Visitor Center opened in 2008, and the David Wills House, where Lincoln stayed while at Gettysburg, opened as a museum on the bicentennial of the president's birthday in February 2009.

John McCain won 56 percent of the district's 2008 presidential vote. Adams County gave him 59 percent, while the more populated Cumberland (shared with the 9th) and York counties each gave him 56 percent. Democrats find more strength in the city of York, where blacks and Hispanics combined make up more than 40 percent of the population, and Gettysburg, which has a large college-age population.

MAJOR INDUSTRY
Agriculture, manufacturing, distribution, defense, tourism

MILITARY BASES
Carlisle Barracks, 435 military, 647 civilian (2008); Defense Distribution Depot Susquehanna, 296 military, 1,047 civilian (2004)

CITIES
York, 40,862; Carlisle, 17,970; Hanover, 14,535

NOTABLE
York served as the first U.S. Capital from 1777-78 while the British occupied Philadelphia.

RHODE ISLAND

Gov. Donald L. Carcieri (R)

Pronounced:
CAR-cheery
First elected: 2002
Length of term: 4 years
Term expires: 1/11
Salary: $119,817
Phone: (401) 222-2080

Residence:
East Greenwich
Born: Dec. 16, 1942; East Greenwich, R.I.
Religion: Roman Catholic
Family: Wife, Sue Carcieri; four children
Education: Brown U., A.B. 1965
(international relations)
Career: Manufacturing company executive;
aid relief worker; bank executive; teacher
Political highlights: No previous office

Election results:
2006 GENERAL
Donald L. Carcieri (R)	197,306	51.0%
Charles J. Fogarty (D)	189,503	49.0%

Lt. Gov. Elizabeth Roberts (D)

First elected: 2006
Length of term: 4 years
Term expires: 1/11
Salary: $99,214
Phone: (401) 222-2371

LEGISLATURE

General Assembly: January-June

Senate: 38 members, 2-year terms
2009 ratios: 34 D, 4 R; 30 men,
8 women
Salary: $14,089
Phone: (401) 222-6655

House: 75 members, 2-year terms
2009 ratios: 69 D, 6 R; 58 men,
17 women
Salary: $14,089
Phone: (401) 222-2466

TERM LIMITS

Governor: 2 terms
Senate: No
House: No

URBAN STATISTICS

CITY	POPULATION
Providence	173,618
Warwick	85,808
Cranston	79,269
Pawtucket	72,958
East Providence	48,688

REGISTERED VOTERS

Unaffiliated	47%
Democrat	43%
Republican	11%

POPULATION

2008 population (est.)	1,050,788
2000 population	1,048,319
1990 population	1,003,464
Percent change (1990-2000)	+4.5%
Rank among states (2008)	43
Median age	36.7
Born in state	61.4%
Foreign born	11.4%
Violent crime rate	298/100,000
Poverty level	11.9%
Federal workers	10,207
Military	9,161

ELECTIONS

STATE ELECTION OFFICIAL
(401) 222-2345
DEMOCRATIC PARTY
(401) 721-9900
REPUBLICAN PARTY
(401) 732-8282

MISCELLANEOUS

Web: www.ri.gov
Capital: Providence

U.S. CONGRESS

Senate: 2 Democrats
House: 2 Democrats

2000 Census Statistics by District

DIST.	2008 VOTE FOR PRESIDENT OBAMA	MCCAIN	WHITE	BLACK	ASIAN	HISP	MEDIAN INCOME	WHITE COLLAR	BLUE COLLAR	SERVICE INDUSTRY	OVER 64	UNDER 18	COLLEGE EDUCATION	RURAL	SQ. MILES
1	65%	34%	83%	4%	2%	7%	$40,616	61%	23%	15%	15%	23%	26%	4%	325
2	62	37	81	4	3	10	$44,129	61	23	16	14	25	25	14	720
STATE	63	35	82	4	2	9	$42,090	61	23	16	15	24	26	9	1,045
U.S.	53	46	69	12	4	13	$41,994	60	25	15	12	26	24	21	3,537,438

Sen. Jack Reed (D)

Elected 1996; 3rd term

CAPITOL OFFICE
224-4642
reed.senate.gov
728 Hart Bldg. 20510-3903; fax 224-4680

COMMITTEES
Appropriations
Armed Services
(Emerging Threats & Capabilities - chairman)
Banking, Housing & Urban Affairs
(Securities, Insurance & Investment - chairman)
Health, Education, Labor & Pensions

RESIDENCE
Jamestown

BORN
Nov. 12, 1949; Providence, R.I.

RELIGION
Roman Catholic

FAMILY
Wife, Julia Reed; one child

EDUCATION
U.S. Military Academy, B.S. 1971 (engineering);
Harvard U., M.P.P. 1973, J.D. 1982

MILITARY SERVICE
Army, 1971-79; Army Reserve, 1979-91

CAREER
Lawyer

POLITICAL HIGHLIGHTS
R.I. Senate, 1985-91; U.S. House, 1991-97

ELECTION RESULTS

2008 GENERAL

Jack Reed (D)	320,644	73.4%
Robert G. Tingle (R)	116,174	26.6%

2008 PRIMARY

Jack Reed (D)	48,038	86.8%
Christopher F. Young (D)	7,277	13.2%

PREVIOUS WINNING PERCENTAGES
2002 (78%); 1996 (63%); 1994 House Election (68%);
1992 House Election (71%); 1990 House Election
(59%)

The serious-minded Reed has secured a place for himself as a leader among Senate Democrats, particularly on defense issues, and earned respect on both sides of the aisle as well as in the Obama administration's upper ranks. The Providence Journal, in endorsing him for re-election in 2008, hailed him as "thoughtful, hard-working, very disciplined and scandal-free."

As a West Point graduate and former Army paratrooper, Reed was a leading voice of the opposition to the Iraq War and an advocate of shifting more U.S. military resources to the deteriorating situation in Afghanistan. But he has extended his influence beyond military matters into finance, health and education — all while sending money back to his state as a member of the Appropriations Committee.

Several of the top military leaders in Iraq and Afghanistan were his contemporaries at West Point, and Reed and Gen. John P. Abizaid, the former head of the U.S. Central Command, were in the same parachute brigade in the 82nd Airborne Division. Though Reed never served in combat, he said his training and service give him an appreciation for the military's power — and its limits. "It's very impressive when you're lighting up the night sky pretty quickly," he once said. "But decisive action usually involves political, economic, social and cultural action as well."

As a member of the Armed Services Committee, Reed joined forces with Chairman Carl Levin of Michigan on the Democrats' central rejoinder to the George W. Bush administration's conduct of the war in Iraq: a bill that would require a withdrawal of U.S. combat forces, except for a vestigial force dedicated to more-limited missions. They were never able to advance it, largely because they were short of the votes needed to overcome a Republican-led filibuster.

After President Obama took office and announced a drawdown of troops in Iraq with a corresponding buildup in Afghanistan, Reed called for the administration to establish benchmarks to gauge the Afghan government's progress. He said during a subsequent April 2009 visit to the region that he was extremely troubled Pakistan had relinquished control of an area bordering Afghanistan to a Taliban-like group.

Reed gets to the Middle East more often than most of his colleagues — his April trip was his 13th to Iraq. In July 2008, he joined Obama, then an Illinois senator and presidential contender, on a high-profile tour of the war zones. The trip fueled speculation about Reed's place in a possible Obama administration as a running mate or as Defense secretary. Reed insisted he wasn't interested in being vice president.

Reed has been a tough questioner of Defense Department witnesses at committee hearings. And serving on the panel allows Reed to push for support for the Rhode Island-based Naval Undersea Warfare Center and Naval Education Training Center, in addition to funding that goes to Rhode Island contractors including Textron Systems and Raytheon Co.

He also works to protect federal contracts for the building of attack submarines at the General Dynamics Electric Boat Corp., which employs roughly 10,000 workers in its Rhode Island and nearby Groton, Conn., facilities. In 2007, he was able to secure a provision in the Senate's fiscal 2008 defense authorization bill for $1.2 billion for a new attack sub.

In addition to defense, Reed has devoted his energies to affordable housing and education. He takes pride in having worked to pass a bill in 2008 that would require mortgage giants Fannie Mae and Freddie Mac to shift a portion of their earnings to a fund that would help build, preserve and rehabilitate rental housing for low-income families. On education, Reed is pleased to have written a provision that would simplify the application form for federal student aid.

He joined Missouri Republican Christopher S. Bond in introducing a bill in April 2009 aimed at consolidating homeless assistance programs at the Department of Housing and Urban Development. The measure would authorize a new emergency grants program to serve people at risk of homelessness. "If we combine federal dollars with the right incentives to local communities, we can prevent and end long-term homelessness," Reed said.

As a member of the Banking, Housing and Urban Affairs Committee, Reed makes his opinions on the economic crisis clear at committee hearings. In early 2009, he suggested the Federal Reserve's penchant for keeping its reviews confidential may have prevented it from acting before it did. "There might have been earlier, prompter and more-effective action to deal with some of these issues that are bedeviling us at the moment," he said.

He also added an amendment to the fiscal 2010 budget blueprint that essentially reasserted that funds provided by the 2008 financial rescue law should be spent directly to help consumers by saving homes, shoring up small businesses and expanding credit, among other purposes.

As a member of the Health, Education, Labor and Pensions Committee, he has made oversight of the Food and Drug Administration one of his priorities, working for stronger regulation of products such as cigarettes and tanning beds.

Reed is a dependable liberal on most social issues. In 2004, he voted to extend the assault weapons ban for another 10 years. Despite being a devout Roman Catholic, in recent years he voted against banning a procedure its opponents call "partial birth" abortion. He also opposed amending the Constitution to prohibit same-sex marriage.

Reed grew up in a working-class family in Cranston, where his father, Joseph Reed, was a school custodian and his mother, Mary Monahan, a factory worker. At age 12, Reed told his parents he wanted to go to a military service academy. He finished second in his class at his Catholic prep school, where he was an overachieving, 124-pound defensive back.

His parents had his teeth straightened after learning he needed good teeth to qualify for West Point. Reed was admitted, barely meeting the minimum height requirement. After graduation, the Army put him through a master's program at the John F. Kennedy School of Government at Harvard University. Reed then commanded a company of the Army's 82nd Airborne Division and taught at West Point.

After attaining the rank of captain, he left the Army at age 29 to attend Harvard Law School. He returned home to a job in Rhode Island's biggest corporate law firm. In 1984, he won a seat in the state Senate. Six years later, Reed took 59 percent of the vote to win the 2nd District House seat that Republican Claudine Schneider gave up to run, unsuccessfully, for the Senate.

When Democratic Sen. Claiborne Pell decided to retire in 1996 after 36 years in office, Reed was well-prepared to run. He overcame a vigorous negative advertising campaign paid for by the National Republican Senatorial Committee, which portrayed him as a tax-and-spend liberal. He won with 63 percent of the vote against Republican state Treasurer Nancy J. Mayer. Reed won handily in his first re-election in 2002 with 78 percent, and six years later took 73 percent.

In 2005, at age 55, Reed married. He and Julia Hart, then 39, an employee of the Senate office that arranges international travel for senators, wed in West Point's Catholic chapel, a first marriage for both. In January 2007, their daughter was born. "I'm told that's probably a more demanding job than most of the things I have done in my life," Reed said of fatherhood.

KEY VOTES

2008

Yes Prohibit discrimination based on genetic information

No   Reauthorize farm and nutrition programs for five years

Yes Limit debate on "cap and trade" system for greenhouse gas emissions

Yes Allow lawsuits against companies that participated in warrantless wiretapping

Yes Limit debate on a bill to block a scheduled cut in Medicare payments to doctors

Yes Grant mortgage relief to homeowners and funding for Fannie Mae and Freddie Mac

No   Approve a nuclear cooperation agreement with India

Yes Approve final $700 billion program to stabilize financial markets

Yes Allow consideration of a $14 billion auto industry loan package

2007

Yes Increase minimum wage by $2.10 an hour

Yes Limit debate on a comprehensive immigration bill

Yes Overhaul congressional lobbying and ethics rules for members and their staffs

Yes Limit debate on considering a bill to add House seats for the District of Columbia and Utah

Yes Limit debate on restoring habeas corpus rights to detainees

Yes Mandate minimum breaks for troops between deployments to Iraq or Afghanistan

Yes Override Bush veto of $23.2 billion water projects authorization bill

No   Confirm Michael B. Mukasey as attorney general

Yes Limit debate on an energy policy overhaul containing $21.8 billion in tax incentives and reduced oil and gas subsidies

CQ VOTE STUDIES

	PARTY UNITY		PRESIDENTIAL SUPPORT	
	SUPPORT	OPPOSE	SUPPORT	OPPOSE
2008	99%	1%	35%	65%
2007	97%	3%	41%	59%
2006	96%	4%	53%	47%
2005	98%	2%	29%	71%
2004	98%	2%	60%	40%
2003	98%	2%	45%	55%
2002	98%	2%	66%	34%
2001	99%	1%	64%	36%
2000	97%	3%	95%	5%
1999	96%	4%	89%	11%

INTEREST GROUPS

	AFL-CIO	ADA	CCUS	ACU
2008	100%	95%	50%	4%
2007	100%	95%	40%	0%
2006	100%	100%	42%	4%
2005	93%	100%	33%	0%
2004	100%	100%	35%	0%
2003	100%	100%	26%	20%
2002	100%	100%	40%	0%
2001	100%	100%	36%	4%
2000	75%	95%	46%	12%
1999	100%	100%	47%	4%

Sen. Sheldon Whitehouse (D)

Elected 2006; 1st term

CAPITOL OFFICE
224-2921
whitehouse.senate.gov
502 Hart Bldg. 20510-3904; fax 228-6362

COMMITTEES
Budget
Environment & Public Works
(Oversight - chairman)
Health, Education, Labor & Pensions
Judiciary
(Administrative Oversight & the Courts
- chairman)
Select Intelligence
Special Aging

RESIDENCE
Newport

BORN
Oct. 20, 1955; Manhattan, N.Y.

RELIGION
Episcopalian

FAMILY
Wife, Sandra Whitehouse; two children

EDUCATION
Yale U., B.A. 1978 (architecture);
U. of Virginia, J.D. 1982

CAREER
Lawyer; gubernatorial aide

POLITICAL HIGHLIGHTS
R.I. Department of Business Regulation director,
1992-94; U.S. attorney, 1994-98; R.I. attorney
general, 1999-2003; sought Democratic
nomination for governor, 2002

ELECTION RESULTS

2006 GENERAL

Sheldon Whitehouse (D)	206,043	53.5%
Lincoln Chafee (R)	178,950	46.5%

2006 PRIMARY

Sheldon Whitehouse (D)	69,290	81.5%
Christopher F. Young (D)	8,939	10.5%
Carl L. Sheeler (D)	6,755	7.9%

Whitehouse urges action to tackle climate change, advocates for universal health care and supports federal funding for embryonic stem cell research and extra spending to revive a dragging economy. All are views and aspirations much in line with President Obama's, and as a member of the Budget Committee, Whitehouse works to obtain financial support for all of them.

Those goals also ran counter to the agenda of the George W. Bush administration, which he routinely challenged. Using his extensive legal background and prosecutorial talents, Whitehouse primarily gained recognition during his first two years in the Senate by challenging that administration's sweeping assertions of executive power — and he hasn't stopped doing so. From his seats on the Judiciary and Select Intelligence committees, the former U.S. attorney and Rhode Island attorney general focuses on Bush's approval of the use of harsh interrogation tactics against terrorism suspects.

When Select Intelligence Chairwoman Dianne Feinstein of California announced in March 2009 the committee would launch an investigation into the Bush administration's detention and interrogation practices, Whitehouse said, "This inquiry will be a powerful step towards correcting America's tragic trespass into the dark side."

"Our country is turning away from this dark moment," he said. "But we cannot afford to leave it behind until we fully understand what went wrong, and do what we can to ensure that America never again loses sight of its most sacred principles." He told The Providence Journal that the public needs "a lot more hard information" about detainee treatment, from the formulation of the interrogation policy by the administration to its execution in the field.

His concern about the interrogation practices led him in 2007 to oppose the nomination of Michael B. Mukasey as attorney general. During a confirmation hearing, Whitehouse asked the former federal judge carefully phrased, pointed questions about the use of "waterboarding," or simulated drowning, against terrorism suspects. Whitehouse initially intended to support Mukasey's nomination, but said he was appalled by Mukasey's refusal to denounce waterboarding as torture. He later said he couldn't support someone who would not "draw that bright line at what we all know in our hearts and minds to be abhorrent to our Constitution and our values."

Whitehouse was the sponsor of an amendment to the fiscal 2008 intelligence authorization bill that limited CIA and other executive branch interrogation tactics to those contained in the 2006 Army field manual, which banned waterboarding and other harsh tactics. A slightly modified version made it into the final bill, drawing a veto from Bush.

Whitehouse also was a vocal critic of the warrantless electronic surveillance program Bush launched after the Sept. 11 terrorist attacks. Whitehouse won the declassification of the legal opinions the administration had relied on in pursuing its broad surveillance activities. He then picked them apart. He helped draft an overhaul of the 1978 Foreign Intelligence Surveillance Act that tightened the rules for such spying, especially when the government intercepts the communications of U.S. citizens.

But Whitehouse parted company with many in his party to support the administration's successful demand for retroactive legal immunity for telecommunications companies that had cooperated with the warrantless surveillance program. "I've been a prosecutor. I've run wiretap investigations," he said. "I've come to recognize the importance of cooperation with the private sector. I've come to learn how valuable, in any investigation, that [surveillance] authority can be."

That wasn't the only time he parted company with his fellow Democrats. When the Senate voted in 2007 to pass a one-year "patch" that kept the alternative minimum tax from hitting millions more families, Whitehouse cast one of five "no" votes. And he joined fellow Rhode Island Democrat Jack Reed in opposing the five-year overhaul of farm policy that was enacted in 2008 over Bush's veto. They were the only Democrats to oppose the override.

Such splits from his party are rare. He backed Obama's early 2009 agenda, including the president's executive order to lift restrictions on federal funding for embryonic stem cell research put in place by the Bush administration; the research uses discarded embryos created for in vitro fertilization. "Politics should never trump science, especially when our environment and public health are at stake," he said. "But for eight years, science has been overrun by political ideology, at great cost to our government's ability to protect Americans' health and well-being."

He supported Obama's $3.56 trillion budget blueprint for fiscal 2010. Whitehouse told the Journal in April that if the federal deficit worsens, Congress may have to scale back Obama's plans in the areas of health care, education and the environment. But he said the prospects for mounting debt would have to be really bad for that to happen.

A member of the Environment and Public Works Committee, he supports Obama's plan for a "cap and trade" program to limit greenhouse gas emissions, and has been active on climate change issues on the panel. In mid-2008, he took the lead in seeking a Justice Department investigation into whether EPA Administrator Stephen L. Johnson had made false or misleading statements in testimony regarding a 2007 decision to block California from regulating greenhouse gases from motor vehicles. Whitehouse and other committee Democrats called for Johnson's resignation.

Whitehouse is the son of a wealthy ambassador, Charles S. Whitehouse, who worked first for the CIA and then for the State Department. (The elder Whitehouse roomed with John H. Chafee, who later became a Republican senator and was the father of Lincoln Chafee, the GOP senator Whitehouse defeated in 2006.) Whitehouse's grandfather also was a career diplomat. Whitehouse was educated at St. Paul's, a boarding school in New Hampshire, and lived part of the time with his parents in Cambodia, France, Laos, South Africa and Vietnam. As a young man, he taught for awhile in Vietnam.

Fellow Democrats often rib Whitehouse about his blueblood upbringing and his button-down ways. At a roast of Whitehouse in 2002, then-Lt. Gov. Charles J. Fogarty offered him a can of "Stiff Begone," as a cure for "the uptight WASP."

After law school, he clerked for the West Virginia Supreme Court, then worked in the Rhode Island attorney general's office for five years.

President Clinton appointed him U.S. attorney in 1994, and in that role he secured the largest fine in state history for an oil spill off the coast that wiped out millions of lobsters, fish and birds. He also launched a public corruption investigation of Buddy Cianci, the Providence mayor who wound up going to prison.

Whitehouse was elected Rhode Island attorney general in 1998, and in 2002 made an ill-fated bid for governor.

In 2006 he challenged an already weakened Lincoln Chafee, who originally had been appointed to the seat when his father died in office in 1999. Whitehouse campaigned against the Republicans at large, rather than Chafee's record, which many voters had no problem with, and won with 54 percent of the vote. He was one of six Democratic challengers to unseat a Republican senator in 2006.

KEY VOTES

2008

Yes Prohibit discrimination based on genetic information

No Reauthorize farm and nutrition programs for five years

Yes Limit debate on "cap and trade" system for greenhouse gas emissions

Yes Allow lawsuits against companies that participated in warrantless wiretapping

Yes Limit debate on a bill to block a scheduled cut in Medicare payments to doctors

Yes Grant mortgage relief to homeowners and funding for Fannie Mae and Freddie Mac

No Approve a nuclear cooperation agreement with India

Yes Approve final $700 billion program to stabilize financial markets

Yes Allow consideration of a $14 billion auto industry loan package

2007

Yes Increase minimum wage by $2.10 an hour

Yes Limit debate on a comprehensive immigration bill

Yes Overhaul congressional lobbying and ethics rules for members and their staffs

Yes Limit debate on considering a bill to add House seats for the District of Columbia and Utah

Yes Limit debate on restoring habeas corpus rights to detainees

Yes Mandate minimum breaks for troops between deployments to Iraq or Afghanistan

Yes Override Bush veto of $23.2 billion water projects authorization bill

No Confirm Michael B. Mukasey as attorney general

Yes Limit debate on an energy policy overhaul containing $21.8 billion in tax incentives and reduced oil and gas subsidies

CQ VOTE STUDIES

	PARTY UNITY		PRESIDENTIAL SUPPORT	
	SUPPORT	OPPOSE	SUPPORT	OPPOSE
2008	95%	5%	41%	59%
2007	98%	2%	35%	65%

INTEREST GROUPS

	AFL-CIO	ADA	CCUS	ACU
2008	100%	90%	50%	8%
2007	100%	95%	36%	0%

Rep. Patrick J. Kennedy (D)
Elected 1994; 8th term

CAPITOL OFFICE
225-4911
www.patrickkennedy.house.gov
407 Cannon Bldg. 20515-3901; fax 225-3290

COMMITTEES
Appropriations
Oversight & Government Reform

RESIDENCE
Portsmouth

BORN
July 14, 1967; Brighton, Mass.

RELIGION
Roman Catholic

FAMILY
Single

EDUCATION
Providence College, B.A. 1991 (social science)

CAREER
Public official

POLITICAL HIGHLIGHTS
R.I. House, 1989-95

ELECTION RESULTS

2008 GENERAL

Patrick J. Kennedy (D)	145,254	68.6%
Jonathan P. Scott (R)	51,340	24.2%
Kenneth A. Capalbo (I)	15,108	7.1%

2008 PRIMARY

Patrick J. Kennedy (D)	unopposed

2006 GENERAL

Patrick J. Kennedy (D)	124,634	69.2%
Jonathan P. Scott (R)	41,836	23.2%
Kenneth A. Capalbo (I)	13,634	7.6%

PREVIOUS WINNING PERCENTAGES
2004 (64%); 2002 (60%); 2000 (67%); 1998 (67%);
1996 (69%); 1994 (54%)

Kennedy is not as outspokenly liberal as his famous father, Sen. Edward M. Kennedy of Massachusetts, though he has also weathered his fair share of scandal. These days, however, he appears to be on his way to rebuilding his reputation as an influential heir to the Kennedy political dynasty.

Moving from pinnacle to pitfall and back, Kennedy in 2008 completed the greatest achievement of his legislative career: passage of a bill requiring insurers to treat mental and physical illnesses equally. The success came less than three years after a drug-related car crash that landed him in the headlines and led him to seek rehabilitation treatment at the Mayo Clinic.

Kennedy advanced the mental-health parity bill with the help of Jim Ramstad, a former Minnesota Republican whom he did not know well until the older man became his Alcoholics Anonymous sponsor in 2006. The pair worked tirelessly on the issue, rallying support in the House, navigating conflicts with Kennedy's father — who pushed a watered-down version to get it through the Senate — and watching the issue get dragged into unrelated fights.

Their bill eventually became the legislative vehicle for the $700 billion measure to rescue the ailing financial services sector.

Kennedy continues to press for more attention to mental-health and substance-abuse issues, introducing bills in 2009 to address eating disorders and juveniles and to create a national neurotechnology program. And he can use his seat on the Appropriations Committee to boost funding for screening and treatment of post-traumatic stress disorder and other mental illnesses in soldiers returning from Iraq. "We've passed parity, but we're a long ways off from ever integrating mental health into the overall health care system," he said.

Kennedy also uses the Appropriations seat to guide defense industry funding back to his district, including billions of dollars for a destroyer project that supports 500 jobs at a Raytheon Co. facility in Portsmouth.

In 2009, he took a seat on the Oversight and Government Reform Committee, where he vowed to work on uncovering bureaucratic fraud and abuse.

In his biggest political split with his father, the younger Kennedy voted in 2002 to authorize President George W. Bush to wage war in Iraq; he was the only member of the Rhode Island delegation to do so. His father, from the start, was one of the sharpest opponents of the war. By 2007, however, the congressman had also turned against the conflict.

Apart from that issue, Kennedy has been a strong supporter of the Democratic leadership, backing a range of legislation to ensure equal rights, supporting labor unions and backing the party's fiscal measures — including President Obama's early economic agenda. But other than his success on the mental-health parity law, his activity on Capitol Hill falls much under the radar while his personal ordeals make the news.

Kennedy has struggled with drug abuse, depression and bipolar disorder since he was a teenager. A member of one of America's most famous political dynasties, the man also known as "Patches" has often talked of the burdens of the family name and the stresses that come with it. His mother, Joan, has struggled with addiction as well.

He was back in the headlines in 2006 after crashing his car into a Capitol security barrier. The accident was his second within a month. The first, a two-car crash back home, drew less attention; local police said he was at fault, but they found no evidence of intoxication or impairment.

The early-morning May 4 incident at the Capitol was different. The congressman told Capitol Police he was on his way to a House vote, but the House wasn't in session. The police report said Kennedy was unsteady on his feet and had slurred speech and red, watery eyes. Kennedy blamed a mix of prescription drugs; he later said he was addicted to the painkiller OxyContin.

He entered a monthlong rehabilitation program at Mayo, then pleaded guilty to driving under the influence of prescription drugs and was sentenced to drug treatment, a year's probation and a $350 fine. The day after the accident, The New York Times later reported, Kennedy got a phone call — and a lifeline — from Ramstad.

His late uncles were President Kennedy and Sen. Robert F. Kennedy of New York. A grandfather, Joseph P. Kennedy, was the first Securities and Exchange Commission chairman and an ambassador to Great Britain. A great-grandfather, John Francis Fitzgerald, represented Boston in the House at the end of the 19th century. A cousin, Joseph P. Kennedy II, represented Boston in the House a century later, from 1987 to 1999.

Patrick J. Kennedy's political ascent began early. He decided to run for office during a month-long recovery from back surgery during college. As a 21-year-old student at Providence College, he won election to the state House in 1988. It wasn't a natural profession for the soft-spoken, introverted Kennedy. "Some people have the innate major personality that makes them natural pols," he said. "Because I didn't, politics was a great kind of bridge to me to get out where I wouldn't have otherwise gotten out because of the nature of my way."

Six years later, he went to Washington, one of just 13 Democrats elected to the House during the 1994 Republican tide that year.

At the start of his third term, Kennedy was appointed chairman of the Democratic Congressional Campaign Committee (DCCC), a leadership role that put him in charge of raising money for Democratic House candidates. He pulled in almost $100 million for the 2000 campaigns, a record that was more than double what had been raised by the committee in 1998.

At times, he runs from the burden of the famous family; he didn't consult his father before his first political campaign. And he has passed up opportunities to run for the Senate, citing concerns about being overshadowed.

But he also appears to enjoy the perks and privileges of being a Kennedy. He frequents his father's prime hideaway on the Capitol's third floor, with its National Mall view and comfy couches. And, when he was DCCC chairman, he noted that the name helped get his calls returned.

Republicans have tried to capitalize on Kennedy's personal troubles, but his re-election bids have never drawn less than 60 percent of the vote. In 2008, he won 69 percent in a district that Obama carried with 65 percent.

KEY VOTES

2008

Yes   Delay consideration of Colombia free-trade agreement

?   Override Bush veto of federal farm and nutrition programs reauthorization bill

No   Overhaul surveillance laws and permit dismissal of suits against companies that conducted warrantless wiretapping

Yes   Grant mortgage relief to homeowners and funding for Fannie Mae and Freddie Mac

Yes   Approve initial $700 billion program to stabilize financial markets

Yes   Approve final $700 billion program to stabilize financial markets

Yes   Provide $14 billion in loans to automakers

2007

Yes   Increase minimum wage by $2.10 an hour

Yes   Approve $124.2 billion in emergency war spending and set goal for redeployment of troops from Iraq

No   Reject federal contraceptive assistance to international family planning groups

Yes   Override Bush veto of $23.2 billion water projects authorization bill

No   Implement Peru free-trade agreement

Yes   Approve energy policy overhaul with new fuel economy standards

No   Clear $473.5 billion omnibus spending bill, including $70 billion for military operations

CQ VOTE STUDIES

	PARTY UNITY		PRESIDENTIAL SUPPORT	
	SUPPORT	OPPOSE	SUPPORT	OPPOSE
2008	99%	1%	14%	86%
2007	99%	1%	5%	95%
2006	96%	4%	21%	79%
2005	96%	4%	22%	78%
2004	95%	5%	35%	65%

INTEREST GROUPS

	AFL-CIO	ADA	CCUS	ACU
2008	100%	100%	59%	0%
2007	96%	100%	50%	0%
2006	100%	85%	31%	10%
2005	93%	95%	37%	4%
2004	93%	95%	40%	8%

RHODE ISLAND 1

East – Pawtucket, part of Providence, Newport

The Democratic 1st includes Rhode Island's entire border with Massachusetts, both to the north and east, and takes in industrial towns in the Blackstone Valley, before moving south to scoop up Pawtucket and the northeastern part of Providence, the state capital. It then runs south along the east bank of Narragansett Bay to pick up the scenic coastal town of Newport and the southeast island communities.

Eastern Rhode Island has not transformed its economy from its manufacturing past — the nation's first successful textile mill was in Pawtucket. Decades-long attempts to lure banking, biotech and health care jobs have not insulated the 1st from the current national recession. The mainly industrial workforce has been hit hard, and employers such as drugstore chain CVS, based in Woonsocket, and Hasbro, a toy and game manufacturer based in Pawtucket, have struggled. A financial-sector collapse affected many area white-collar jobs, and economic declines also have created municipal budget shortfalls.

A maritime defense industry along the coast south of Providence has

provided some stability. Portsmouth-based defense contractors and a large naval base and training center in Newport fuel the industry. Visitors to Newport and Providence make tourism key to the economy.

The 1st's share of Providence includes the state Capitol, the affluent and picturesque East Side neighborhood and several colleges, including Brown University and Providence College. Democrats dominate the district, bolstered by students, government workers and minority voters. Some small, wealthy coastal towns support the GOP, but larger towns lean Democratic. In 2008, Democrat Barack Obama took 65 percent of the district's presidential vote.

MAJOR INDUSTRY
Health care, government, education, tourism, defense, manufacturing

MILITARY BASES
Naval Station Newport, 2,199 military, 1,132 civilian (2008)

CITIES
Pawtucket, 72,958; Providence (pt.), 72,102; East Providence, 48,688; Woonsocket, 43,224; North Providence (unincorporated), 32,411

NOTABLE
Touro Synagogue in Newport, designed by colonial architect Peter Harrison and dedicated in 1762, is the oldest synagogue in the nation.

Rep. Jim Langevin (D)

Elected 2000; 5th term

The first quadriplegic to serve in the House, Langevin's story is a testament to the power of perseverance — something he hopes can pay off legislatively as well, now that a Democrat is in the White House.

His priorities include a universal health insurance system, greatly increased funding for the National Institutes of Health and upgraded security measures to protect against terrorist attacks. His personal standing as a disabled person who has overcome many obstacles, and his committee assignments — which include seats on Budget and Armed Services — give him a place at the table on those issues.

At 16, Langevin (LAN-juh-vin) was accidentally shot while working with the Warwick police as part of a Boy Scout Explorer program. The bullet severed his spinal cord, paralyzing him from the waist down and leaving him only minimal use of his arms and hands. After the injury, he and his family were amazed at the hundreds of strangers who pitched in to help. Langevin resolved to somehow repay them and soon decided public service and politics was the way he could do that.

In the House, Langevin has been a loyal Democrat and an enthusiastic supporter of President Obama's early initiatives. He hailed the $787 billion economic stimulus law of 2009 for including funds for military construction projects, veterans, state Medicaid programs, health benefits for the unemployed, and health information technology. And he supported Obama's $3.5 trillion budget blueprint for fiscal 2010.

He also supported a 2009 law to expand the State Children's Health Insurance Program. He has said the nation's fiscal woes can largely be addressed by bringing health care costs under control. He also wants to provide universal coverage and has pushed legislation to make available to every American the type of health care afforded to federal employees.

Langevin has been an outspoken advocate of embryonic stem cell research. When Obama signed an executive order expanding federal funding for embryonic stem cell research, Langevin said it "sends a clear signal around the world that our nation supports research based on science, not politics." A Roman Catholic and sometime abortion opponent, Langevin tried to help House Democrats in their 2007 attempt to expand funding for the research, serving as the ambassador to anti-abortion members of their freshman class. The Roman Catholic Church strongly opposes the research on the grounds it requires the destruction of a human embryo. "Being pro-life isn't just about protecting life in the womb," he told the freshmen. "It has to be about protecting and extending the quality of life for people who are living among us."

The research is thought to hold promise for the treatment of a wide range of diseases such as Parkinson's, Alzheimer's and diabetes. He said in 2008, "I recognize that I can be a visible symbol of the promise of stem cell research. But it goes far beyond Jim Langevin and spinal cord injuries. It's also about the millions of other people whose lives could be extended or improved as a result of stem cell research."

He also pressed for legislation to enhance research on paralysis. The measure — named for the late actor Christopher Reeve, who was paralyzed in an equestrian accident — became law in early 2009 as part of an omnibus public lands bill. In the 109th Congress (2005-06), he helped win enactment of a bill authorizing federal grants to agencies that recruit and train people to provide a respite to families caring for disabled patients at home. He continually pushes for increased funding for the program.

CAPITOL OFFICE
225-2735
www.house.gov/langevin
109 Cannon Bldg. 20515; fax 225-5976

COMMITTEES
Armed Services
Budget
Select Intelligence

RESIDENCE
Warwick

BORN
April 22, 1964; Warwick, R.I.

RELIGION
Roman Catholic

FAMILY
Single

EDUCATION
Rhode Island College, B.A. 1990
(political science & public administration);
Harvard U., M.P.A. 1994

CAREER
Public official

POLITICAL HIGHLIGHTS
R.I. House, 1989-95; R.I. secretary of state,
1995-2001

ELECTION RESULTS

2008 GENERAL

Jim Langevin (D)	158,416	70.1%
Mark S. Zaccaria (R)	67,433	29.9%

2008 PRIMARY

Jim Langevin (D)	unopposed

2006 GENERAL

Jim Langevin (D)	140,315	72.7%
Rodney D. Driver (I)	52,729	27.3%

PREVIOUS WINNING PERCENTAGES
2004 (75%); 2002 (76%); 2000 (62%)

Though Langevin describes himself as pro-life, he has fallen out of favor with anti-abortion groups for his advocacy on behalf of stem cell research. In 2007, he angered the National Right to Life Committee by voting to allow federal funding of international family planning groups that provide abortions.

Langevin takes a liberal view on most other social issues. For example, he voted in 2007 to bar workplace discrimination based on sexual orientation and has opposed efforts to amend the Constitution to ban same sex marriage.

As a member of the Homeland Security Committee during the 110th Congress (2007-08), Langevin was a leading voice for protecting government computer systems against cyber-attacks. He pushed through the House legislation to require the Homeland Security Department to ramp up its efforts against computer hackers, but the Senate didn't act. He and Texas Republican Michael McCaul were co-chairmen of a Commission on Cyber Security for the 44th Presidency, and the commission's report, completed in December 2008, was the basis of 2009 legislation to put a "cyber czar" in the White House.

Langevin also focuses on terrorism through his seat on the Armed Services Committee's panel on terrorism and unconventional threats.

He originally hoped to enforce laws, not write them. As a boy, he dreamed of being a police officer or an FBI agent. He enrolled in a police department cadet program in his hometown of Warwick, riding along with officers and getting to know the daily police routine. On Aug. 22, 1980, his life and ambitions changed forever when he was in the police locker room with two members of the SWAT team and one of them inadvertently pulled the trigger of a loaded gun. The bullet ricocheted off a locker and hit Langevin in the neck.

Four years later, Langevin volunteered in Frank Flaherty's campaign for mayor of Warwick, and Flaherty recalls being amazed at Langevin's tenacity, making phone calls and stuffing envelopes despite his injury.

At age 21, while still a college student, Langevin was elected as a delegate to the Rhode Island Constitutional Convention. In 1988, he won the first of three terms in the Rhode Island House. In 1994, he was elected secretary of state and six years later, when 2nd District Democratic Rep. Bob Weygand decided to run for the Senate, Langevin made a bid for his seat and took 62 percent of the vote. He has won at least 70 percent of the vote since then.

Because of his disability, an aide helps Langevin with domestic chores, and he uses a motorized wheelchair. Congressional leaders gave him a ground-floor office and renovated access to the House chamber to ensure he could move around there readily. Langevin has said he is convinced he will walk again one day.

KEY VOTES

2008
Yes Delay consideration of Colombia free-trade agreement
Yes Override Bush veto of federal farm and nutrition programs reauthorization bill
Yes Overhaul surveillance laws and permit dismissal of suits against companies that conducted warrantless wiretapping
Yes Grant mortgage relief to homeowners and funding for Fannie Mae and Freddie Mac
Yes Approve initial $700 billion program to stabilize financial markets
Yes Approve final $700 billion program to stabilize financial markets
Yes Provide $14 billion in loans to automakers

2007
Yes Increase minimum wage by $2.10 an hour
Yes Approve $124.2 billion in emergency war spending and set goal for redeployment of troops from Iraq
No   Reject federal contraceptive assistance to international family planning groups
Yes Override Bush veto of $23.2 billion water projects authorization bill
No   Implement Peru free-trade agreement
Yes Approve energy policy overhaul with new fuel economy standards
No   Clear $473.5 billion omnibus spending bill, including $70 billion for military operations

CQ VOTE STUDIES

	PARTY UNITY		PRESIDENTIAL SUPPORT	
	SUPPORT	OPPOSE	SUPPORT	OPPOSE
2008	99%	1%	15%	85%
2007	98%	2%	5%	95%
2006	94%	6%	30%	70%
2005	92%	8%	20%	80%
2004	91%	9%	42%	58%

INTEREST GROUPS

	AFL-CIO	ADA	CCUS	ACU
2008	100%	100%	61%	0%
2007	96%	100%	50%	0%
2006	93%	75%	33%	16%
2005	93%	85%	44%	8%
2004	93%	85%	45%	25%

RHODE ISLAND 2
West – part of Providence, Warwick, Cranston

The 2nd takes in an eclectic mix of countryside, city life and shoreline that makes up the western two-thirds of the nation's smallest state. Bordering Connecticut on one side and the Narragansett Bay on the other, it covers rolling hills in the north, as well as most of the metropolitan area around Providence (shared with the 1st). In the south, Washington County's idyllic beaches and lakes attract tourists and residents alike.

As manufacturing continues a decades-long decline, the 2nd is attempting to transition from a blue-collar to a white-collar economy. A heavy statewide investment in developing the the service economy had helped stabilize the area, and the 2nd enjoyed some growth in the technology, financial services and health care industries. Maritime defense contractors here, including General Dynamics' Electric Boat submarine facility at Quonset Point, depend on major military manufacturing projects, some of which face funding obstacles. Aviation company Textron Systems has cut jobs at its corporate headquarters in the 2nd's part of Providence, and former textile mills in the city remain abandoned. Local officials hope to team

firms in the emerging medical, life-science and alternative energy sectors with the area's several major colleges, including Johnson & Wales University, Rhode Island College and the University of Rhode Island.

Economic pressures here are causing population shifts, and residents are leaving Providence to find jobs. As white residents have departed the Providence area, more blacks and Hispanics have moved in, increasing the city's already Democratic tendency.

The 2nd is home to many working- and middle-class towns that have a substantial and Democratic-leaning union presence, although the large Catholic population makes abortion a key issue that can impact electoral outcomes. No Republican presidential candidate has carried the district since 1984, and Barack Obama won with 62 percent in 2008.

MAJOR INDUSTRY
Service, defense, higher education, banking, health care

CITIES
Providence (pt.), 101,516; Warwick, 85,808; Cranston, 79,269

NOTABLE
Block Island, 12 miles off the southern coast, is a scenic vacation spot that has 17 miles of beaches and 365 fresh water ponds.

SOUTH CAROLINA

Gov. Mark Sanford (R)

First elected: 2002
Length of term: 4 years
Term expires: 1/11
Salary: $106,078
Phone: (803) 734-2100

Residence:
Sullivan's Island
Born: May 28, 1960;
Fort Lauderdale, Fla.
Religion: Episcopalian
Family: Wife, Jenny Sanford; four children
Education: Furman U., B.A. 1983 (business administration); U. of Virginia, M.B.A. 1988
Military service: Air Force Reserve, 2002-present
Career: Real estate investor; investment banker
Political highlights: U.S. House, 1995-2001

Election results:
2006 GENERAL

Mark Sanford (R)	601,868	55.1%
Tommy Moore (D)	489,076	44.8%

Lt. Gov. André Bauer (R)

First elected: 2002
Length of term: 4 years
Term expires: 1/11
Salary: $46,545
Phone: (803) 734-2080

LEGISLATURE

General Assembly: January-June

Senate: 46 members, 4-year terms
2009 ratios: 26 R, 20 D; 45 men, 1 woman
Salary: $10,400
Phone: (803) 212-6200

House: 124 members, 2-year terms
2009 ratios: 72 R, 52 D; 107 men, 17 women
Salary: $10,400
Phone: (803) 734-2010

TERM LIMITS

Governor: 2 consecutive terms
Senate: No
House: No

URBAN STATISTICS

CITY	POPULATION
Columbia	116,278
Charleston	96,650
North Charleston	79,641
Greenville	56,002
Rock Hill	49,765

REGISTERED VOTERS

Voters do not register by party.

POPULATION

2008 population (est.)	4,479,800
2000 population	4,012,012
1990 population	3,486,703
Percent change (1990-2000)	+15.1%
Rank among states (2008)	24

Median age	35.4
Born in state	64%
Foreign born	2.9%
Violent crime rate	805/100,000
Poverty level	14.1%
Federal workers	27,923
Military	57,585

ELECTIONS

STATE ELECTION OFFICIAL
(803) 734-9060
DEMOCRATIC PARTY
(803) 799-7798
REPUBLICAN PARTY
(803) 988-8440

MISCELLANEOUS

Web: www.sc.gov
Capital: Columbia

U.S. CONGRESS

Senate: 2 Republicans
House: 4 Republicans, 2 Democrats

2000 Census Statistics by District

DIST.	2008 VOTE FOR PRESIDENT OBAMA	MCCAIN	WHITE	BLACK	ASIAN	HISP	MEDIAN INCOME	WHITE COLLAR	BLUE COLLAR	SERVICE INDUSTRY	OVER 64	UNDER 18	COLLEGE EDUCATION	RURAL	SQ. MILES
1	42%	56%	74%	21%	1%	3%	$40,713	60%	23%	17%	12%	24%	25%	22%	2,645
2	45	54	68	26	1	3	$42,915	63	23	14	11	25	29	34	4,767
3	35	64	76	21	1	2	$36,092	49	37	14	13	24	17	50	5,392
4	38	60	75	20	1	3	$39,417	56	31	13	12	25	22	26	2,151
5	46	53	64	32	1	2	$35,416	48	38	13	12	26	15	53	7,035
6	64	35	40	57	1	1	$28,967	48	34	18	12	26	14	52	8,120
STATE	45	54	66	29	1	2	$37,082	54	31	15	12	25	20	40	30,109
U.S.	53	46	69	12	4	13	$41,994	60	25	15	12	26	24	21	3,537,438

Sen. Lindsey Graham (R)

Elected 2002; 2nd term

CAPITOL OFFICE
224-5972
lgraham.senate.gov
290 Russell Bldg. 20510-4001; fax 224-3808

COMMITTEES
Armed Services
Budget
Homeland Security & Governmental Affairs
Judiciary
Veterans' Affairs
Special Aging

RESIDENCE
Seneca

BORN
July 9, 1955; Seneca, S.C.

RELIGION
Southern Baptist

FAMILY
Single

EDUCATION
U. of South Carolina, B.A. 1977 (psychology),
attended 1977-78 (public administration),
J.D. 1981

MILITARY SERVICE
Air Force, 1982-88, 1990; S.C. Air National Guard,
1989-94; Air Force Reserve, 1995-present

CAREER
Lawyer; military prosecutor

POLITICAL HIGHLIGHTS
S.C. House, 1993-95; U.S. House, 1995-2003

ELECTION RESULTS

2008 GENERAL

Lindsey Graham (R)	1,014,396	57.6%
Bob Conley (D)	742,362	42.2%

2008 PRIMARY

Lindsey Graham (R)	187,736	66.8%
Buddy Witherspoon (R)	93,125	33.2%

PREVIOUS WINNING PERCENTAGES
2002 (54%); 2000 House Election (68%); 1998 House
Election (100%); 1996 House Election (60%); 1994
House Election (60%)

Graham has a friendly demeanor that masks a keen legal mind and solidly conservative instincts. His intellectual gifts and willingness to work with Democrats make him a closely watched lawmaker in many of Congress' major battles.

He is a more genteel version of his close friend, the more prominent and earthier Republican Sen. John McCain of Arizona. Like McCain, Graham has a tendency to buck his party leaders and go his own way, often staking out positions with widespread popular appeal. He sometimes comes under fire in his solidly Republican state for his willingness to work with Democrats, but he downplays the criticism. "People at home expect me to be conservative, but they like the fact that I'm trying to solve problems," he said.

Graham is an active member of the Judiciary Committee. During George W. Bush's administration, Graham was a dealmaker on several major issues, including the battle over judicial nominations and the debate over the government's treatment of terrorism suspects. He was part of a GOP troika, with McCain and former Sen. John W. Warner of Virginia, that forced Bush to back down on tough measures for the treatment of suspected terrorists.

Graham's background as a former military prosecutor gave him credibility on the issue. But he blasted a 2008 Supreme Court decision that detainees held at the U.S. naval base at Guantánamo Bay, Cuba, have a constitutional right to mount habeas corpus challenges to their detentions as "a tremendously dangerous and irresponsible ruling." Graham said terrorists should be tried in the military justice system, either by military commission, court-martial or a hybrid of the two systems.

He showed his tendencies toward both combativeness and compromise in the early months of President Obama's administration. A member of the Budget Committee, he blasted the president's economic policies, calling his $3.56 trillion fiscal 2010 budget blueprint "a road map to disaster that will bankrupt this country" and criticizing the $787 billion economic stimulus law for failing to help small businesses and create jobs. As a member of the Armed Services panel, he attacked the administration for proposing to cut the defense budget.

At the same time, though, he refused to join other conservatives in opposing the nominations of Treasury Secretary Timothy F. Geithner and Attorney General Eric H. Holder Jr. He expressed a desire to work with the administration to equalize federal sentences for offenses involving crack and powdered cocaine. Reacting to Obama's proposal to build up troops in Afghanistan, he said he wanted to avoid the confrontational stance that led to a lack of cooperation between the parties when making decisions about Iraq.

Graham took the lead in the 109th Congress (2005-06) in an effort to overhaul Social Security, even though he did not hold any committee memberships or leadership positions that would have afforded him a natural power base. He held a series of bipartisan sessions for lawmakers in an effort to develop a proposal. He floated the idea of raising the payroll tax cap, as well as changing the formula for calculating benefits that was projected to halve the program's long-term deficit by giving smaller payouts to wealthier retirees.

The effort collapsed in the face of fierce Democratic opposition. But Graham vows to keep working on Social Security. "I'm going to try to use my time up here to be a vehicle to find a middle ground," he said.

Graham's search for the productive middle in politics marks an evolution from his early days on Capitol Hill. He arrived with the rambunctious House

GOP class of 1994 and was one of the leaders of a 1997 effort by conservatives to oust GOP Speaker Newt Gingrich of Georgia because they felt he was increasingly ineffective and too willing to compromise with President Bill Clinton. Gingrich put down the insurrection, and Graham ended up not suffering any political consequences.

Later in 1998, Graham was one of the 13 House managers in the impeachment case against Clinton. He was more restrained stylistically than other conservatives condemning the president for a sexual affair with a White House intern. "Is this Watergate or Peyton Place?" he said.

Once elected to the Senate in 2002, Graham continued his contrarian ways, breaking with most Republicans to Bush's Medicare overhaul creating a prescription drug benefit, which he called costly and ineffective.

For all his headline-grabbing defections from the fold, though, Graham is a conservative at heart. He stuck with his fellow Republicans in partisan Senate votes more than 92 percent of the time for all but one of his first six years in the chamber. Graham once joined an effort to shut down the National Endowment for the Arts and typically favors limiting the scope of the federal government. He is an opponent of gun control, and he has voted to amend the Constitution to outlaw flag desecration and ban same-sex marriage. Graham has backed legislation to make it a federal crime to harm a fetus in the course of committing any one of 68 federal offenses.

Graham's other committee assignments are Homeland Security and Governmental Affairs, Veterans' Affairs, and Special Aging.

He takes an interest in energy issues. With gas prices at more than $4 per gallon in 2008, Graham changed his mind about opposing oil exploration off South Carolina's coast. According to the Charlotte Observer, he said that "we have to make sure it's done in an environmentally sensitive way…I don't want people on the coast of South Carolina to look at a bunch of oil rigs." In 2009, he introduced a bill calling for the government to rebate more than $30 billion in fees paid by electricity customers from nuclear power if the Yucca Mountain waste dump in Nevada is not used to store spent radioactive fuel.

Graham is the son of a tavern owner and grew up racking billiards in his parents' bar in the textile town of Central. The death of both parents from illness when he was not yet out of college left him to care for his 13-year-old sister, Darline, whom he legally adopted. "It changes your world and you have to grow up a lot quicker," Graham said.

After law school, he joined the Air Force and later transferred to Germany as a prosecutor. Graham served on active duty in both the 1991 Persian Gulf War and, in 2007, the U.S. occupation of Iraq.

Graham won a state House seat in 1992. He saw an opportunity for advancement early in 1994, when 10-term Democratic Rep. Butler Derrick decided to retire from the U.S. House. Graham won easily that fall, beating Democratic state Sen. James Bryan with 60 percent of the vote to become the first Republican to represent his district since 1877.

He won three more terms with relative ease and began planning for a Senate run after longtime South Carolina GOP Sen. Strom Thurmond made it clear his seventh full term would be his last. By 2002, Graham was unopposed for his party's nomination. He easily beat Democrat Alex Sanders, a quick-witted former president of the College of Charleston, by repeatedly portraying Sanders as a party loyalist who would vote with "Washington liberals."

In 2008, Graham bested orthodontist Buddy Witherspoon in the GOP primary by 34 points and easily won re-election with nearly 58 percent over Democrat Bob Conley, a North Myrtle Beach engineer. He spent much of his time tagging along with McCain on the presidential campaign trail and helped his friend win South Carolina's Republican presidential primary, a key early contest.

KEY VOTES

2008

Yes	Prohibit discrimination based on genetic information
Yes	Reauthorize farm and nutrition programs for five years
?	Limit debate on "cap and trade" system for greenhouse gas emissions
No	Allow lawsuits against companies that participated in warrantless wiretapping
No	Limit debate on a bill to block a scheduled cut in Medicare payments to doctors
?	Grant mortgage relief to homeowners and funding for Fannie Mae and Freddie Mac
Yes	Approve a nuclear cooperation agreement with India
Yes	Approve final $700 billion program to stabilize financial markets
–	Allow consideration of a $14 billion auto industry loan package

2007

Yes	Increase minimum wage by $2.10 an hour
Yes	Limit debate on a comprehensive immigration bill
No	Overhaul congressional lobbying and ethics rules for members and their staffs
No	Limit debate on considering a bill to add House seats for the District of Columbia and Utah
No	Limit debate on restoring habeas corpus rights to detainees
No	Mandate minimum breaks for troops between deployments to Iraq or Afghanistan
Yes	Override Bush veto of $23.2 billion water projects authorization bill
Yes	Confirm Michael B. Mukasey as attorney general
No	Limit debate on an energy policy overhaul containing $21.8 billion in tax incentives and reduced oil and gas subsidies

CQ VOTE STUDIES

	PARTY UNITY		PRESIDENTIAL SUPPORT	
	SUPPORT	OPPOSE	SUPPORT	OPPOSE
2008	97%	3%	72%	28%
2007	92%	8%	87%	13%
2006	82%	18%	91%	9%
2005	92%	8%	89%	11%
2004	92%	8%	92%	8%
2003	96%	4%	95%	5%
House Service:				
2002	89%	11%	82%	18%
2001	93%	7%	84%	16%
2000	98%	2%	17%	83%

INTEREST GROUPS

	AFL-CIO	ADA	CCUS	ACU
2008	14%	15%	100%	82%
2007	0%	20%	100%	88%
2006	7%	0%	92%	83%
2005	29%	20%	83%	96%
2004	8%	25%	88%	92%
2003	17%	15%	83%	90%
House Service:				
2002	22%	15%	70%	83%
2001	17%	15%	78%	88%
2000	10%	5%	70%	100%

Sen. Jim DeMint (R)

Elected 2004; 1st term

DeMint's genial demeanor masks his rapid rise as one of the Senate's most aggressively conservative insurgents. Bucking traditional notions of freshmen as deferential, he has held up bipartisan legislation on everything from highway spending to combating AIDS in the name of fiscal discipline, all while causing headaches for his Republican colleagues in other ways.

He uses his background in advertising and market research to put his beliefs before the public. Long before other lawmakers adapted to the Internet, he was sending "Freedom Alerts" to constituents. He illustrated his call to scrap the tax code in 2000 by scattering all 17,000 pages of the Internal Revenue Code from a hot air balloon over his hometown of Greenville. And in 2008, he unveiled a Web site, completethefencenow.com, to communicate with bloggers about construction of a border fence and to provide them with research and related topics such as sex and drug trafficking along the U.S.-Mexican border. That year, he co-authored a book, "Why We Whisper: Restoring Our Right to Say It's Wrong," in an attempt to push back against what he decries as the secularization of American values.

His efforts have won him praise from his home state's media as well as the political right, but he hasn't always endeared himself to his fellow GOP colleagues. As chairman of the Republican Steering Committee, the Senate's caucus of conservative lawmakers, he irritated fellow Republicans in 2007 with proposals to rewrite caucus rules and abolish seniority as the basis for choosing committee chairmen and ranking members.

In April 2009, he approached moderate Republican Sen. Arlen Specter of Pennsylvania and told him he would be backing Specter's conservative GOP primary opponent in 2010, former Rep. Patrick J. Toomey. Five days later, Specter announced he was becoming a Democrat, partly because the GOP had moved too far to the right for him. DeMint was unmoved. "We don't have to be purists…but there have to be core principles, or there's no way for us to be a party," he said. "Maybe we could sign a pledge or something. Limited government, free markets and personal freedom."

His conservative views on both social and fiscal issues pervade his work on all his committee assignments: Banking, Housing and Urban Affairs; Foreign Relations; Commerce, Science and Transportation; and Joint Economic. And they have fueled a continuous stream of rhetoric against President Obama's agenda and his Cabinet picks.

DeMint said former Democratic Rep. Hilda L. Solis of California, who was eventually confirmed as Labor secretary, was too close to unions and would oppose secret-ballot elections in the workplace, and he said Democratic Kansas Gov. Kathleen Sebelius, eventually confirmed as secretary of Health and Human Services, had a record of vetoing legislation aimed at limiting abortion. "Americans remain divided on abortion, but in recent years we've made bipartisan progress to protect life. That national consensus is being threatened by President Obama's pro-abortion agenda and his choice for HHS secretary," DeMint said. As for former Democratic New York Sen. Hillary Rodham Clinton, later confirmed as secretary of State, he said he was worried about a conflict of interest with her husband's foundation.

DeMint adamantly opposes abortion and federal funding of embryonic stem cell research. When Obama announced he would reinstate funding for the research, DeMint said it showed "that America is willing to kill innocent human life for unproven scientific goals."

He opposed Obama's spending plans in early 2009. He said the $3.56 trillion

CAPITOL OFFICE
224-6121
demint.senate.gov
340 Russell Bldg. 20510-4002; fax 228-5143

COMMITTEES
Banking, Housing & Urban Affairs
Commerce, Science & Transportation
Foreign Relations
Joint Economic

RESIDENCE
Greenville

BORN
Sept. 2, 1951; Greenville, S.C.

RELIGION
Presbyterian

FAMILY
Wife, Debbie DeMint; four children

EDUCATION
U. of Tennessee, B.S. 1973 (communications);
Clemson U., M.B.A. 1981

CAREER
Market research company owner;
advertising and sales representative

POLITICAL HIGHLIGHTS
U.S. House, 1999-2005

ELECTION RESULTS

2004 GENERAL

Jim DeMint (R)	857,167	53.7%
Inez Tenenbaum (D)	704,384	44.1%

2004 PRIMARY RUNOFF

Jim DeMint (R)	154,644	59.2%
David Beasley (R)	106,480	40.8%

PREVIOUS WINNING PERCENTAGES
2002 House Election (69%); 2000 House Election (80%); 1998 House Election (58%)

budget blueprint for fiscal 2010 "focused on growing government, not growing jobs. We cannot tax our way out of recession, spend our way to prosperity or borrow our way out of debt." And he suggested that health care provisions in the budget would lead to "socialized medicine." He likewise criticized Obama's economic stimulus plan, saying, "It's temporary and it's wasteful."

In many of DeMint's heated comments on Obama's budgeting he asserted the president showed a lack of commitment to his own pledge to reforming earmarks, funding set-asides for special projects. He had challenged Obama to veto a $410 billion catchall spending bill for fiscal 2009 that DeMint said carried thousands of earmarks. When the president didn't comply, he said Obama "did what politicians always do; he spoke loudly but refused to lead by example. He kicked the can down Pennsylvania Avenue and naively asked earmark addicts to police themselves."

DeMint, with Oklahoma Republican Tom Coburn, has waged a strong war against earmarks. The pair even introduced their own "2008 Conservative Agenda to Secure America's Future" that included proposals for permanent tax cuts and withholding dues to the United Nations in addition to an earmark ban. Despite Democratic leaders' attempts to stop him, DeMint successfully included in a broad ethics and lobbying overhaul bill, which passed the Senate in 2007, an amendment requiring the identification of the sponsor and recipient of each earmark. When the broader reform effort stalled, he continued his assault, offering amendments to strip specific earmarks from several bills. He lost almost every time, accomplishing little except annoying his colleagues.

While in the House, DeMint was a leader among the ultraconservative lawmakers. But he also liked to emphasize his work on bipartisan legislation. He gathered more than 280 cosponsorships in 2001 on legislation to double the adoption tax credit to $10,000. The credit was included in the $1.35 trillion, 10-year tax cut enacted that year. DeMint is no fan of the federal income tax system and would like to see it replaced by a tax on the consumption of goods and services.

His loyalty to a pro-business agenda has gotten DeMint into trouble at home on occasion, especially for his pro-trade stances. In the House, he was derided in 2002 for joining the razor-thin majority that helped enact a law reviving the president's authority to negotiate treaties Congress must approve or reject without amendment. His vote infuriated the state's powerful textile interests, and it became the key issue when DeMint sought re-election to the House in 2002. But he nevertheless won easily.

Raised by a single mother who operated a dance school out of their home, DeMint and his three siblings grew up quickly, handling household chores at a young age. Yet DeMint sparked controversy during his Senate campaign when he asserted during a debate that unwed mothers with live-in boyfriends should not teach in public schools. He also said a "practicing homosexual" should be similarly barred. He later apologized, saying it was up to states to decide who is fit to teach.

DeMint entered politics in 1992 as an unpaid adviser to his predecessor in the House, Republican Bob Inglis. Six years later, when Inglis gave up the seat for an unsuccessful Senate bid, DeMint won the GOP nomination against state Sen. Mike Fair, who had the backing of the Christian Coalition. DeMint went on to win the general election by 18 percentage points.

Facing a self-imposed six-year term limit in the House in 2004, DeMint ran for the Senate. Veteran Sen. Ernest F. Hollings announced his retirement that year, and DeMint easily defeated former Gov. David Beasley in a GOP primary runoff before beating Inez Tenenbaum, the state education superintendent, that November. His victory gave South Carolina two Republican senators for the first time since Reconstruction.

KEY VOTES

2008
? Prohibit discrimination based on genetic information
No Reauthorize farm and nutrition programs for five years
? Limit debate on "cap and trade" system for greenhouse gas emissions
No Allow lawsuits against companies that participated in warrantless wiretapping
No Limit debate on a bill to block a scheduled cut in Medicare payments to doctors
No Grant mortgage relief to homeowners and funding for Fannie Mae and Freddie Mac
Yes Approve a nuclear cooperation agreement with India
No Approve final $700 billion program to stabilize financial markets
No Allow consideration of a $14 billion auto industry loan package

2007
No Increase minimum wage by $2.10 an hour
No Limit debate on a comprehensive immigration bill
No Overhaul congressional lobbying and ethics rules for members and their staffs
No Limit debate on considering a bill to add House seats for the District of Columbia and Utah
No Limit debate on restoring habeas corpus rights to detainees
No Mandate minimum breaks for troops between deployments to Iraq or Afghanistan
No Override Bush veto of $23.2 billion water projects authorization bill
Yes Confirm Michael B. Mukasey as attorney general
No Limit debate on an energy policy overhaul containing $21.8 billion in tax incentives and reduced oil and gas subsidies

CQ VOTE STUDIES

	PARTY UNITY		PRESIDENTIAL SUPPORT	
	SUPPORT	OPPOSE	SUPPORT	OPPOSE
2008	100%	0%	84%	16%
2007	98%	2%	90%	10%
2006	97%	3%	90%	10%
2005	96%	4%	91%	9%
House Service:				
2004	98%	2%	92%	8%
2003	98%	2%	89%	11%
2002	97%	3%	85%	15%
2001	98%	2%	95%	5%
2000	98%	2%	22%	78%

INTEREST GROUPS

	AFL-CIO	ADA	CCUS	ACU
2008	0%	0%	57%	100%
2007	5%	0%	55%	100%
2006	13%	0%	92%	100%
2005	21%	5%	89%	96%
House Service:				
2004	0%	0%	92%	100%
2003	7%	20%	93%	96%
2002	11%	0%	90%	100%
2001	0%	0%	96%	100%
2000	0%	0%	90%	100%

Rep. Henry E. Brown Jr. (R)

Elected 2000; 5th term

CAPITOL OFFICE
225-3176
brown.house.gov
103 Cannon Bldg. 20515-4001; fax 225-3407

COMMITTEES
Natural Resources
Transportation & Infrastructure
Veterans' Affairs

RESIDENCE
Hanahan

BORN
Dec. 20, 1935; Bishopville, S.C.

RELIGION
Baptist

FAMILY
Wife, Billye Brown; three children
(one deceased)

EDUCATION
Berkeley H.S., graduated 1953

MILITARY SERVICE
S.C. National Guard, 1953-62

CAREER
Grocery chain executive; grocery store data
processor; shipyard worker

POLITICAL HIGHLIGHTS
Hanahan City Council, 1981-85; S.C. House,
1985-2000

ELECTION RESULTS

2008 GENERAL

Henry E. Brown Jr. (R)	177,540	51.9%
Linda Ketner (D)	163,724	47.9%

2008 PRIMARY

Henry E. Brown Jr. (R)	42,588	70.0%
Katherine Jenerette (R)	11,488	18.9%
Paul V. Norris (R)	6,718	11.0%

2006 GENERAL

Henry E. Brown Jr. (R)	115,766	59.7%
Randy Maatta (D, WFM)	73,218	37.7%
James E. Dunn (GREEN)	4,875	2.5%

PREVIOUS WINNING PERCENTAGES
2004 (88%); 2002 (89%); 2000 (60%)

Brown once expressed an overriding aspiration: "to be really conservative." He has easily fulfilled that goal, though he also looks for common ground with Democrats on a few environmental and transportation-related matters.

Brown, who commutes home from Washington every weekend, focuses on funding local projects. He says parochial matters suit him, describing himself as a "backseat guy'" who tries "not to make a big splash." His penchant for pursuing tax dollars for his district irks some of the state's more avid fiscal conservatives; Republican Gov. Mark Sanford, who was Brown's predecessor in the House, groused to The State newspaper of Columbia in January 2009: "Henry Brown has been anything but a guardian of the taxpayer."

In fiscal 2008 appropriations bills, Brown secured more than $35.7 million in earmarks, the member-driven spending items for their districts, according to Taxpayers for Common Sense. In a catchall spending measure for fiscal 2009, he obtained more than $14.1 million. Both totals were higher than those of any of the state's three other GOP House members.

As a member of the Transportation and Infrastructure Committee, he will have an opportunity to obtain more federal funding for his area when the panel takes up a rewrite of the 2005 surface transportation law. In the earlier version of the bill, he worked with other South Carolina delegation members to include $81 million for an extension of Interstate 73 leading to Myrtle Beach, the vacation hot spot in the 1st District.

Brown also is a member of the Natural Resources Committee, where he backs increased offshore exploration for oil and gas, including off South Carolina's coast. "I think we must maintain some level of the economy that we can all have a good quality of life," he said at a February 2009 hearing on offshore drilling. "You know, I'm not willing to give up my automobile… I mean, I like riding bicycles and this sort of stuff, but I think it's going to be a long time coming."

Brown is the top-ranking Republican on the Natural Resources panel on Insular Affairs, Oceans and Wildlife. He introduced a pair of bills in 2009 that drew bipartisan support: One sought to reauthorize a 2004 law to protect endangered marine turtles, while the other called for the issuance of a stamp depicting the turtles along with African and Asian animals, with revenues from the stamps going to conservation funds.

Brown riled some voters in 2008 when he introduced a bill to remove an undeveloped spit of land on Kiawah Island from a program aimed at discouraging development in coastal areas. Environmentalists and other skeptics flooded his office with phone calls and e-mails. Brown announced in August 2008 he would kill the bill: "Our constituents spoke, and we listened," he told The Post and Courier of Charleston.

From his seat on the Veterans' Affairs Committee, Brown has sought to expand veterans' benefits. He pushed for legislation signed into law at the end of the 109th Congress (2005-06) that expanded eligibility for educational help for veterans' survivors and dependents as well as established health care research and clinical centers for Parkinson's and other diseases. In 2008 he introduced a bill to establish amyotrophic lateral sclerosis, or Lou Gehrig's disease, as a service-connected disability; the Veterans Affairs Department subsequently announced it would do so.

During Brown's first six years in Congress, he sided with his party at least 95 percent of the time each year on votes in which majorities of Democrats and Republicans diverged. After Democrats assumed the majority in

2007, those numbers dipped to 90 percent in 2007 and 92 percent in 2008 — still high but below the state's three other Republican House members. He was the only one of the four in 2008 to support a Democratic bill, signed into law, to create an independent regulator for mortgage giants Fannie Mae and Freddie Mac and offer relief to homeowners.

Brown drew headlines in December 2007 when it was reported his office frequently spent tax dollars on mailings to constituents. He sent 1.3 million pieces of mail in 2006, more than any other House member, and his overall cost of free or "franked" mail that year — $177,705 — was among the highest, according to an Associated Press analysis.

The findings provoked criticism from government watchdog groups that regard the mailings as a waste of money. But Brown defended the practice and promised to continue the mailings, saying they are a practical way to keep in touch with his district's growing population and that voters' responses indicate they are happy with his efforts to help his district.

Brown grew up on a farm about 25 miles north of Charleston. After high school, he entered the National Guard and got a job in North Charleston with the local electric company, where he was among the early workers in the emerging information technology field. Later, he went to work at the Charleston Naval Shipyard. He then began a long career with Piggly Wiggly Carolina Co., the South Carolina franchise of the Southern grocery chain, eventually becoming a vice president of the firm's computer operations.

Brown was active in civic affairs in the town of Hanahan, north of Charleston; he served on the planning board and in 1981 won a seat on the nonpartisan city council. By 1985, he was serving in the state legislature, where he spent nearly 16 years.

In his first bid for Congress in 2000, he sought to stand out in a crowd of five other Republicans by mailing 20,000 Oh Henry! candy bars to voters. He finished first in the primary and prevailed in a runoff election. In November, he easily outpaced former Democratic Senate aide Andy Brack.

He had little trouble in subsequent elections and was initially expected to win easily in 2008, but ended up in a tight race against Democrat Linda Ketner, a wealthy philanthropist and affordable-housing advocate whose father started the Food Lion grocery chain. She poured $700,000 of her own money into the campaign and drew support from the national Democratic campaign arm, running a series of hard-hitting advertisements that depicted Brown as out of touch. He fought back, portraying the native North Carolinian as a liberal outsider, and won with just 52 percent of the vote, his closest margin ever.

KEY VOTES

2008

No Delay consideration of Colombia free-trade agreement
Yes Override Bush veto of federal farm and nutrition programs reauthorization bill
Yes Overhaul surveillance laws and permit dismissal of suits against companies that conducted warrantless wiretapping
Yes Grant mortgage relief to homeowners and funding for Fannie Mae and Freddie Mac
Yes Approve initial $700 billion program to stabilize financial markets
Yes Approve final $700 billion program to stabilize financial markets
No Provide $14 billion in loans to automakers

2007

No Increase minimum wage by $2.10 an hour
No Approve $124.2 billion in emergency war spending and set goal for redeployment of troops from Iraq
Yes Reject federal contraceptive assistance to international family planning groups
Yes Override Bush veto of $23.2 billion water projects authorization bill
Yes Implement Peru free-trade agreement
Yes Approve energy policy overhaul with new fuel economy standards
Yes Clear $473.5 billion omnibus spending bill, including $70 billion for military operations

CQ VOTE STUDIES

	PARTY UNITY		PRESIDENTIAL SUPPORT	
	SUPPORT	OPPOSE	SUPPORT	OPPOSE
2008	92%	8%	69%	31%
2007	90%	10%	82%	18%
2006	97%	3%	95%	5%
2005	96%	4%	83%	17%
2004	97%	3%	91%	9%

INTEREST GROUPS

	AFL-CIO	ADA	CCUS	ACU
2008	14%	20%	94%	83%
2007	4%	10%	90%	96%
2006	7%	0%	100%	84%
2005	13%	0%	93%	96%
2004	20%	0%	100%	96%

SOUTH CAROLINA 1
East — part of Charleston, Myrtle Beach

Taking in most of the state's coastline, the 1st is marked by two of South Carolina's landmark tourist destinations: Charleston and Myrtle Beach. Horry County, which includes Myrtle Beach, still has plenty of farmland but grew quickly in the last decade. The 1st's tourism-based economy is stuttering amid national economic downturns, and agricultural production has not been able to pick up the slack. The 1st tends to favor the GOP, although John McCain won only 56 percent of the 2008 presidential vote here and the U.S. House race was decided by 4 percentage points.

Eighty percent of Charleston's residents live in the 1st. The city is still one of the nation's busiest ports, and shipping is a staple of the local economy. There is a strong military presence here: Charleston Air Force Base provides troop, equipment and medical supply airlift operations, and Naval Weapons Station Charleston is a training and logistics center. The city also is home to the Medical University of South Carolina. Although an icon of the New South, the city is surrounded by reminders of its antebellum history. The church steeples marking its skyline lend Charleston its nickname, the "Holy City," and city officials hope to lure tourists back to the homes and boulevards of the city's large historic district.

Moving north, tobacco farming has long been prominent in inland areas, but rising cigarette taxes and a national decline in demand have cut into revenues. The Myrtle Beach area is as popular for its championship golf courses as for its beaches, but economic declines have hurt municipal budgets and the housing market. Continuing conservation efforts are directed at mitigating congestion, pollution, wetlands destruction and beach erosion following decades of residential and commercial growth.

MAJOR INDUSTRY
Shipping, tourism, agriculture, military

MILITARY BASES
Charleston Air Force Base, 3,553 military, 962 civilian (2009); Naval Weapons Station Charleston, 195 military, 411 civilian (2006)

CITIES
Charleston (pt.), 77,434; Mount Pleasant, 47,609; North Charleston (pt.), 45,530; Goose Creek, 29,208; Summerville, 27,752; Myrtle Beach, 22,759

NOTABLE
Charleston Harbor is home to Fort Sumter, where the first battle of the Civil War took place in 1861.

Rep. Joe Wilson (R)

Elected December 2001; 4th full term

CAPITOL OFFICE
225-2452
www.joewilson.house.gov
212 Cannon Bldg. 20515-4002; fax 225-2455

COMMITTEES
Armed Services
Education & Labor
Foreign Affairs

RESIDENCE
Springdale

BORN
July 31, 1947; Charleston, S.C.

RELIGION
Presbyterian

FAMILY
Wife, Roxanne Wilson; four children

EDUCATION
Washington and Lee U., B.A. 1969 (political science); U. of South Carolina, J.D. 1972

MILITARY SERVICE
Army Reserve, 1972-75;
S.C. National Guard, 1975-2003

CAREER
Lawyer; campaign aide;
U.S. Energy Department official

POLITICAL HIGHLIGHTS
Pine Ridge town judge, 1974-76; Republican nominee for S.C. Senate, 1976; Springdale town judge, 1977-80; S.C. Senate, 1985-2001

ELECTION RESULTS

2008 GENERAL

Joe Wilson (R)	184,583	53.7%
Rob Miller (D)	158,627	46.2%

2008 PRIMARY

Joe Wilson (R)	44,783	85.1%
Phil Black (R)	7,831	14.9%

2006 GENERAL

Joe Wilson (R)	127,811	62.6%
Michael Ray Ellisor (D)	76,090	37.3%

PREVIOUS WINNING PERCENTAGES
2004 (65%); 2002 (84%); 2001 Special Election (73%)

A conservative Republican who believes in a robust defense and limited government, Wilson pursues his causes with boundless energy, rushing back and forth across Capitol Hill and delivering hundreds of one-minute speeches on the House floor. "He is like the Energizer Bunny," Florida Republican Jeff Miller once told The State newspaper of Columbia. "If he's invited to 10 meetings a day, he will go to those 10 meetings — and set up five more."

Wilson is the only Republican to sit on both the Armed Services and Foreign Affairs committees and is well-positioned to press his goals of improving benefits for soldiers and reservists and fighting the global war on terrorism. Though he had a student deferment during the Vietnam War that kept him out of the conflict, he speaks with a certain authority on defense issues; He was in the South Carolina National Guard for close to three decades, retiring as a colonel, and served in the Army Reserve for three years. His four sons, all Eagle Scouts, followed him into the service.

He has never wavered in his support of the war in Iraq. In 2007, he adamantly opposed a Democratic-sponsored resolution denouncing President George W. Bush's decision to send more troops to Iraq and suggesting a timeline for U.S. troop withdrawal. "For me, a timeline is determined by both sides," Wilson said. "And since the other side has determined that this is the center front for the global war on terror, timetables can't be established."

He co-founded the Victory in Iraq Caucus in 2004 and has remained an active member. When President Obama outlined his plan in February 2009 to withdraw combat troops from Iraq over 18 months, Wilson said it was "thanks to the tremendous courage and professionalism of our military and their leadership" that such a drawdown could even begin. But he warned, "Any decision made regarding the size and nature of our forces in Iraq or any theater of combat must be made deliberately and cautiously."

When the South Carolina National Guard's 218th Brigade, his old unit, shipped out to Afghanistan, Wilson visited the troops every three months during their January 2007 to April 2008 deployment.

As the top-ranking Republican on Armed Services' Military Personnel Subcommittee, Wilson in early 2009 pushed legislation to enable National Guard and reservists to obtain retirement pay earlier, and he has advocated for military pay increases. He also spoke out against fee and co-payment increases for the military health care system, the fastest-growing portion of the defense budget.

Wilson vigorously supported two other Bush administration priorities during the 110th Congress (2007-08): expanding U.S. support for the global effort to combat AIDS and passing legislation to endorse a U.S.-India nuclear cooperation agreement, which he called "a giant step forward in strengthening our nation's partnership with the people of India."

A member of the Education and Labor Committee, Wilson is no fan of the 2001 No Child Left Behind law, which mandates national student testing standards. He opposes federal involvement in local school decisions. "I represent some of the wealthiest communities in North America and some of the poorest communities in North America," he said. "So what works in one community won't work in another." In 2004, Wilson saw enactment of his measure to expand a loan-forgiveness program for teachers in poverty-stricken public schools.

From his seat on the Workforce Protections Subcommittee, Wilson said in early 2009 he opposes legislation to make it easier for unions to organize by majority sign-up or secret-ballot elections. And he regularly resists Democratic proposals to tighten workplace safety standards.

Wilson also opposed Obama's early economic initiatives, including a $787 billion economic stimulus law. "Congress does not have to choose between a big spending agenda and no action," he said. "We can create jobs while holding the line on spending."

Wilson upset some of his constituents in 2008 when he announced he wouldn't seek any earmarks — funding set-asides for projects in his district. A member of the conservative Republican Study Committee, he said the importance of revamping the system justified his self-imposed earmark abstinence. He kept to his pledge for the fiscal 2009 spending cycle, but listed on his Web site nearly $118 million in earmarks for fiscal 2010.

Wilson delivered tough "yes" votes for GOP leaders on two high-profile issues — the 2005 Central America Free Trade Agreement and the 2008 law to aid the nation's financial sector. His support of the trade deal was especially tough, given concerns about his state's textile industry.

Though he goes by Joe, Wilson's full name is Addison Graves Wilson. His mother was a Democrat, but Wilson, an admirer of President Eisenhower, always thought he might be a Republican. He made the transition as a high school student in the early 1960s. He met his wife at a camp for Republican teenagers where she was a camper and he was a counselor.

While in college, Wilson interned for GOP Sen. Strom Thurmond. He joined the staff of Rep. Floyd D. Spence while he was in law school. He managed five of Spence's re-election campaigns and was involved in numerous statewide GOP campaigns in the 1980s and 1990s while working as a real estate lawyer.

Wilson came up short in a contest for the state Senate in 1976, losing after a recount. After a two-year stint with the Department of Energy in Washington, he successfully challenged a GOP incumbent in 1984 for the first of four terms in the state Senate.

When Spence died in 2001, Wilson said he had his deathbed endorsement. While Wilson's claim rankled some of his rivals, it was backed up by Spence's widow. He won the five-way GOP primary with 76 percent of the vote and cruised to a 48-percentage-point win. Wilson immediately claimed a seat on Armed Services, which Spence had chaired from 1995 to 2001.

Democrats did not even challenge him in 2002. In 2004 and 2006, he beat Democratic attorney Michael Ray Ellisor with more than 60 percent of the vote. He faced a better-financed Democratic challenger in 2008, Iraq War veteran Rob Miller, who kept him to 54 percent of the vote.

KEY VOTES

2008

No   Delay consideration of Colombia free-trade agreement

No   Override Bush veto of federal farm and nutrition programs reauthorization bill

Yes Overhaul surveillance laws and permit dismissal of suits against companies that conducted warrantless wiretapping

No   Grant mortgage relief to homeowners and funding for Fannie Mae and Freddie Mac

Yes Approve initial $700 billion program to stabilize financial markets

Yes Approve final $700 billion program to stabilize financial markets

No   Provide $14 billion in loans to automakers

2007

No   Increase minimum wage by $2.10 an hour

No   Approve $124.2 billion in emergency war spending and set goal for redeployment of troops from Iraq

Yes Reject federal contraceptive assistance to international family planning groups

No   Override Bush veto of $23.2 billion water projects authorization bill

Yes Implement Peru free-trade agreement

Yes Approve energy policy overhaul with new fuel economy standards

Yes Clear $473.5 billion omnibus spending bill, including $70 billion for military operations

CQ VOTE STUDIES

	PARTY UNITY		PRESIDENTIAL SUPPORT	
	SUPPORT	OPPOSE	SUPPORT	OPPOSE
2008	98%	2%	82%	18%
2007	98%	2%	90%	10%
2006	97%	3%	92%	8%
2005	97%	3%	91%	9%
2004	99%	1%	91%	9%

INTEREST GROUPS

	AFL-CIO	ADA	CCUS	ACU
2008	7%	10%	100%	92%
2007	8%	10%	65%	96%
2006	7%	5%	91%	91%
2005	13%	0%	93%	100%
2004	13%	0%	100%	96%

SOUTH CAROLINA 2

Central and south — part of Columbia and suburbs, Hilton Head Island

The 2nd runs from the coast up the Georgia border and into central South Carolina, button-hooking north around Columbia to scoop up some of the capital city. The district's two ends take in wealthy areas — Columbia suburbs in Richland and Lexington counties, and Beaufort and Hilton Head Island in the south.

Government jobs remain the Columbia area's largest employment base. Ongoing private sector economic diversification, especially in health care, has not insulated the area from rising unemployment rates. On the Georgia border, the Department of Energy's Savannah River Site nuclear complex (shared with the 3rd) still provides jobs. Considerably poorer smaller towns and rural areas dot the land between Columbia and Hilton Head, a destination for retirees and tourists. Military issues are important here — just up the shore from swank resorts, recruits sweat at the Parris Island Marine Corps Recruitment camp. Growing Fort Jackson in Richland County in the north and Beaufort Marine Corps Air Station add

to the 2nd's heavy military presence.

Many families in heavily black Allendale, Barnwell, Hampton and Jasper counties live below the poverty line, relying on tenant farming and sharecropping. That area favored Barack Obama in the 2008 presidential election but makes up only a small portion of the 2nd's total vote. Overall, wealthy white-collar professionals in the north and along the coast push the district into the Republican column. John McCain won 68 percent of the 2008 presidential vote in Lexington County, the 2nd's most populous, and he took 54 percent of the overall district vote.

MAJOR INDUSTRY
Government, military, tourism, health care, agriculture

MILITARY BASES
Fort Jackson (Army), 11,768 military, 2,390 civilian (2008); Beaufort Marine Corps Air Station, 3,710 military, 647 civilian (2008); Marine Corps Recruitment Depot (Parris Island), 2,142 military, 865 civilian (2009)

CITIES
Columbia (pt.), 59,771; Hilton Head Island, 33,862

NOTABLE
Mitchelville, established on Hilton Head Island during the Civil War, was the first U.S. town founded specifically for freed black slaves.

Rep. J. Gresham Barrett (R)

Elected 2002; 4th term

CAPITOL OFFICE
225-5301
www.house.gov/barrett
439 Cannon Bldg. 20515-4003; fax 225-3216

COMMITTEES
Financial Services
Foreign Affairs
Standards of Official Conduct

RESIDENCE
Westminster

BORN
Feb. 14, 1961; Westminster, S.C.

RELIGION
Baptist

FAMILY
Wife, Natalie Barrett; three children

EDUCATION
The Citadel, B.S. 1983 (business administration)

MILITARY SERVICE
Army, 1983-87

CAREER
Furniture store owner

POLITICAL HIGHLIGHTS
S.C. House, 1997-2002

ELECTION RESULTS

2008 GENERAL

J. Gresham Barrett (R)	186,799	64.7%
Jane Ballard Dyer (D)	101,724	35.2%

2008 PRIMARY

J. Gresham Barrett (R)	unopposed

2006 GENERAL

J. Gresham Barrett (R)	111,882	62.9%
Lee Ballenger (D, WFM)	66,039	37.1%

PREVIOUS WINNING PERCENTAGES
2004 (100%); 2002 (67%)

Barrett is one of the youthful, confident and maximally conservative lawmakers that give the House Republican caucus its rightward bent. He describes himself as "a real country boy"; he boasts he had never visited Washington, D.C., until he was running for Congress and had never flown on an airplane before jumping out of one during his Army training.

With the House under Democratic control, his ardent conservatism has led his influence to wane, so it was unsurprising when Barrett announced in March 2009 that he would seek South Carolina's governorship in 2010. He promised to focus on economic development in the state. "These are uncertain times and I think I bring some certain qualities to the race," Barrett said, referring to his military background and House service. "I can bring people together. Bring the legislature together, bring the business people, bring the laypeople."

But Barrett soon found that bringing people together might not always be easy. Appearing in his state at one of the April 2009 "tea party" rallies held around the country to protest high taxes under President Obama, Barrett was drowned out in boos from a group in the audience angered by his decision in fall 2008 to switch his initial "no" vote on a $700 billion financial industry rescue package to "yes" on the slightly modified final version.

Barrett was one of 26 Republicans who changed their votes after urgent pleas from GOP leaders and the George W. Bush administration. A member of the Financial Services Committee, whose leaders helped craft the final rescue bill, Barrett called the votes shortly after final passage "the most difficult I have taken thus far." He said that while "in a vacuum" he would have preferred no government involvement, "in reality, we face extremely volatile markets and frozen credit with companies throughout my district and state — large and small — days or weeks away from not being able to make payroll."

During the 110th Congress (2007-08), Barrett backed his party on 99 percent of the votes that pitted a majority of one party against the other. His infrequent breaks with his party leaders typically come when they take positions he doesn't consider conservative enough.

He was one of only 33 House members, and the only South Carolina Republican, to vote against a renewal of the landmark 1965 Voting Rights Act in 2006. He objected to the provision in the law requiring states with a history of discrimination to get approval from the Justice Department before making changes to their voting procedures. South Carolina is one of nine states affected.

In 2003, he voted against the GOP bill to add a prescription drug benefit to Medicare, a top priority for President Bush and so important to Republican leaders that they kept the House in session all night until they had the votes to pass the measure. Barrett said the bill would do more harm than good, telling the Columbia State newspaper, "What we did today was take a 30-year loan out on an old broken-down boat, slapped some patches on it and stuck it back in the water."

Barrett frequently calls for more fiscal discipline. He was part of a House GOP "stimulus quick-response team" that opposed President Obama's $787 billion law in early 2009. He said he had found the new president "very charming and very sincere," but that Speaker Nancy Pelosi of California hadn't allowed Republican lawmakers much input into the bill. "What the president is saying and what the Speaker of the House is implementing are two separate things," he said.

As a member of the Foreign Affairs Committee, Barrett was one of Bush's most fervent supporters on the Iraq War. He said he was "deeply troubled" by Obama's decision in January 2009 to close the military detention facility on the U.S. naval base Guantánamo Bay, Cuba. Barrett also sits on the ethics committee.

He is friends with another ambitious young conservative, Indiana's Mike Pence, who chairs the House Republican Caucus. Barrett and Pence met at a prayer breakfast, and Barrett says that on the topics of religion, politics and family, the two think alike. Barrett has criticized judges who authorize same-sex marriages.

Since entering Congress, Barrett has looked out for the Energy Department's Savannah River Site, a sprawling nuclear weapons complex located mostly in his district that has been seeking new missions since the end of the Cold War. A champion of nuclear power, he promotes building a new reactor at the site and calls for expanding the use of nuclear power nationwide. He dismisses environmentalists' fears about nuclear power, saying, "The difference between 35 years ago and today is like the space shuttle versus Orville and Wilbur" Wright.

Like other South Carolina lawmakers, Barrett tries to help the state's beleaguered textile industry. He voted for the Central America Free Trade Agreement in 2005 — which squeaked through the House by 217-215 — only after provisions were added to address the concerns of his state's textile manufacturers. "It took a lot of wheeling and dealing," Barrett said. "At the end, our textile guys said this is something we can live with and this is something we honestly think will make our industry stronger."

Barrett entered the Army after graduating from The Citadel military academy, and he spent four years as a field artillery officer. He left the military with the rank of captain to manage the family furniture business, which closed in 2004.

His conservative credentials were forged in the state House, where he served three terms. And his involvement in Bush's 2000 South Carolina presidential primary campaign helped him build a strong organization that he put to good use in his 2002 bid for the House, after Republican Lindsey Graham gave up the 3rd District seat to run successfully for the Senate.

Barrett won the Republican nod over five rivals, then claimed the general-election win by better than 2-to-1 over George Brightharp, a high school guidance counselor. In 2004, bowing to the district's strong conservative leanings, Democrats did not field a candidate. Though he was challenged in 2006 and 2008, he won with ease.

KEY VOTES

2008

No Delay consideration of Colombia free-trade agreement
No Override Bush veto of federal farm and nutrition programs reauthorization bill
Yes Overhaul surveillance laws and permit dismissal of suits against companies that conducted warrantless wiretapping
No Grant mortgage relief to homeowners and funding for Fannie Mae and Freddie Mac
No Approve initial $700 billion program to stabilize financial markets
Yes Approve final $700 billion program to stabilize financial markets
No Provide $14 billion in loans to automakers

2007

No Increase minimum wage by $2.10 an hour
No Approve $124.2 billion in emergency war spending and set goal for redeployment of troops from Iraq
Yes Reject federal contraceptive assistance to international family planning groups
No Override Bush veto of $23.2 billion water projects authorization bill
Yes Implement Peru free-trade agreement
No Approve energy policy overhaul with new fuel economy standards
Yes Clear $473.5 billion omnibus spending bill, including $70 billion for military operations

CQ VOTE STUDIES

	PARTY UNITY		PRESIDENTIAL SUPPORT	
	SUPPORT	OPPOSE	SUPPORT	OPPOSE
2008	98%	2%	83%	17%
2007	99%	1%	92%	8%
2006	96%	4%	90%	10%
2005	99%	1%	93%	7%
2004	99%	1%	85%	15%

INTEREST GROUPS

	AFL-CIO	ADA	CCUS	ACU
2008	0%	5%	94%	96%
2007	4%	0%	70%	100%
2006	7%	10%	93%	96%
2005	14%	0%	85%	100%
2004	0%	0%	100%	100%

SOUTH CAROLINA 3

West – Anderson, Aiken, Greenwood

The largely rural, conservative 3rd District, on the eastern bank of the Savannah River, takes in South Carolina's hilly northwestern corner and the state's highest peaks. Many voters here are converts to the Republican Party, having shifted over from a "Yellow Dog" Democratic past.

At the district's southern tip, an engineering base surrounding the Energy Department's Savannah River Site nuclear complex, which is shared with the neighboring 2nd District and keeps the regional economy relatively stable, helped attract Fortune 500 firms and several U.S. divisions of foreign companies to the area. Fujifilm's manufacturing and research facility in Greenwood now employs more than 1,000 people in the area.

Farther north, Anderson's industrial economy relies on high-tech and automotive parts manufacturing, and many plants in a diminishing textile market have shifted to high-tech fiber manufacturing. The county, like most of the state, has been slammed with widespread layoffs — textile and fiber mills and manufacturing plants are facing slowdowns and job cuts. The gem of Pickens County remains Clemson University, which pro-

vides the economic and social nexus for the 3rd's northern tip.

Agriculture is a significant part of the 3rd's economy, especially in southern areas: Aiken (shared with the 2nd), Edgefield and Saluda counties are among the state's top peach-producing counties. Cotton is another important crop here.

The district votes solidly Republican in federal and statewide races. The 3rd's most populous voting jurisdictions — Anderson, Aiken and Pickens counties — are heavily Republican. The less populous counties in the 3rd's midsection, including black-majority McCormick County, are more rural and less GOP-leaning. The 3rd gave John McCain his highest percentage statewide (64 percent) in the 2008 presidential election.

MAJOR INDUSTRY

Nuclear research, manufacturing, textiles, agriculture

CITIES

Anderson, 25,514; Aiken (pt.), 22,810; Greenwood, 22,071; Easley, 17,754

NOTABLE

The 70,000-acre Lake Thurmond, previously known as Clarks Hill Lake, was renamed for former GOP Sen. Strom Thurmond, the oldest person ever to serve in the Senate.

Rep. Bob Inglis (R)

Elected 2004; 6th term
Also served 1993-99

CAPITOL OFFICE
225-6030
inglis.house.gov
100 Cannon Bldg. 20515-4004; fax 226-1177

COMMITTEES
Foreign Affairs
Science & Technology

RESIDENCE
Travelers Rest

BORN
Oct. 11, 1959; Savannah, Ga.

RELIGION
Presbyterian

FAMILY
Wife, Mary Anne Inglis; five children

EDUCATION
Duke U., B.A. 1981 (political science);
U. of Virginia, J.D. 1984

CAREER
Lawyer

POLITICAL HIGHLIGHTS
U.S. House, 1993-99; Republican nominee
for U.S. Senate, 1998

ELECTION RESULTS

2008 GENERAL

Bob Inglis (R)	184,440	60.1%
Paul Corden (D)	113,291	36.9%
C. Faye Walters (GREEN)	7,332	2.4%

2008 PRIMARY

Bob Inglis (R)	37,571	67.0%
Charles Jeter (R)	18,545	33.0%

2006 GENERAL

Bob Inglis (R)	115,553	64.2%
William Griff Griffith (D)	57,490	32.0%
John Cobin (LIBERT)	4,467	2.5%
C. Faye Walters (GREEN)	2,336	1.3%

PREVIOUS WINNING PERCENTAGES
2004 (70%); 1996 (71%); 1994 (73%); 1992 (50%)

Inglis is on a more temperate path compared with his first tenure in the 1990s, when he declared himself a soldier in a "culture war to determine whose set of values rule." He's toned down his self-righteousness, embraced funding earmarks he once eschewed and abandoned the idea of term limits he once fervently promoted. And he displays an independent streak that puts him at odds with party leaders on such issues as the environment.

Inglis (ING-lis) first represented the 4th from 1993 until 1999, when he reached his self-imposed limit of three terms and made an unsuccessful bid for the Senate. Since his return in 2005, he has supported his party on most issues. During the 110th Congress (2007-08), he joined with Republicans on 94 percent of the votes that pitted a majority of each party against each other.

He is still conservative on most social issues, blasting President Obama in March 2009 for lifting President George W. Bush's restrictions on federal funding of embryonic stem cell research, which uses discarded embryos created for in vitro fertilization. "Utilitarianism beat down human dignity in the stroke of President Obama's pen," he fumed.

Inglis went against conservative orthodoxy, though, in April 2009 when he said GOP leaders have failed to take a decisive stand against climate change and have offered insufficient alternative proposals to reduce carbon emissions. "Global warming is not a matter of belief. It's a matter of facts," he said. "We don't want to be a party of deniers."

Inglis, who is the top-ranking Republican on the Science and Technology panel's Energy and Environment Subcommittee, reached his conclusions about climate change after trips to Greenland and Antarctica, where in January 2008 he checked progress on the National Science Foundation's analysis of the ice layers and fluctuations in carbon dioxide levels over time.

He also worked in 2009 with Arizona Republican Jeff Flake — another conservative who is fond of going his own way — on legislation to impose a carbon tax of $15 a ton on producers of carbon-based fuels such as oil, natural gas and coal.

Inglis has shown a willingness to step across the aisle to push his environmental priorities. He says that during his six-year absence, he realized lawmakers spend too much time vying for partisan advantage.

He was once at odds with Illinois Democrat Daniel Lipinski, but the two began to make their mark as a bipartisan team during the 110th Congress. They pushed through the House a proposal to provide $50 million over 10 years to the Energy Department to pay for cash awards for successful research programs dealing with hydrogen energy technologies. The two also paired with California Democrat Jane Harman and Michigan Republican Fred Upton to successfully push an amendment to a spending bill to require the use of energy-efficient light bulbs in Capitol buildings.

Inglis, a member of the Foreign Affairs Committee, also strayed from the party line on Iraq. He was not in Congress for the 2002 vote authorizing Bush to go to war. But at the start of the 110th Congress, Inglis joined 16 other Republicans in voting for a Democratic resolution disapproving of Bush's plan to send more than 21,000 additional combat troops to Iraq — a move that nearly prompted a rebuke from local Republican Party leaders.

With Obama's decision to draw down troops in Iraq, Inglis turned his attention to other international issues in early 2009. He joined other Republicans in protesting cuts in missile defense, saying, "This is not time to go wobbly on missile defense." He also criticized Secretary of State Hillary

Rodham Clinton for not condemning China's human rights and abortion policies when she visited there.

Inglis once labeled appropriators "big hogs" and scorned earmarks — money set aside for special projects in member districts. But gone is the white sign that used to adorn his office door: "Notice to all PACs: Remember, you didn't give me a dime and I don't owe you a thing." In fiscal 2008 he netted nearly $14 million in earmarks. Among them was $3 million for the design of a cold-weather clothing system, which drew him some unwanted attention as he listed the earmark as going to Cassidy Associates, a lobbying firm that specializes in obtaining earmarks for clients. It was intended for a Spartanburg textile firm operated by Roger Milliken, an Inglis campaign donor.

Inglis was born in Savannah, Ga., and grew up in the small town of Bluffton, population 825. He developed an interest in politics as a high school student during the 1976 presidential campaign. Inglis was inspired by Republican candidate Ronald Reagan after hearing him speak in Charleston.

At Duke University, Inglis was a fraternity boy who regularly attended Bible study. After graduating from the University of Virginia's law school, he went on to become the youngest partner, at 31, in one of Greenville's most prestigious law firms.

In 1992, he saw a chance to defeat incumbent Democratic Rep. Liz J. Patterson. He advertised himself as a Washington outsider — "unbought and not for sale." He won 50 percent of the vote and went on to rack up higher totals in the next two elections.

With his three-term limit approaching, Inglis decided to challenge Democratic Sen. Ernest F. Hollings in 1998. He rejected political action committee donations and was outspent more than 2-to-1 by Hollings. He lost the race 53 percent to 46 percent.

Inglis returned to his Greenville law firm, toyed with running for lieutenant governor and never lost his yen for the Senate. But when Hollings retired in 2004, GOP Rep. Jim DeMint decided to run for the seat, sidelining Inglis. He then opted to run for DeMint's seat — the one he had held before. His still-familiar name and the district's overwhelming GOP leanings enabled Inglis to cruise through a comeback campaign in 2004. He won handily again in 2006 and 2008 — though by spring 2009 his independence had drawn him challenges from four GOP primary opponents for the next election.

Inglis has abandoned the self-imposed limit that ended his first stretch in the House in 1998. Term limits, he said in 2008, are a form of "unilateral disarmament."

KEY VOTES

2008

No   Delay consideration of Colombia free-trade agreement

No   Override Bush veto of federal farm and nutrition programs reauthorization bill

Yes Overhaul surveillance laws and permit dismissal of suits against companies that conducted warrantless wiretapping

No   Grant mortgage relief to homeowners and funding for Fannie Mae and Freddie Mac

Yes Approve initial $700 billion program to stabilize financial markets

Yes Approve final $700 billion program to stabilize financial markets

No   Provide $14 billion in loans to automakers

2007

No   Increase minimum wage by $2.10 an hour

No   Approve $124.2 billion in emergency war spending and set goal for redeployment of troops from Iraq

Yes Reject federal contraceptive assistance to international family planning groups

No   Override Bush veto of $23.2 billion water projects authorization bill

Yes Implement Peru free-trade agreement

Yes Approve energy policy overhaul with new fuel economy standards

Yes Clear $473.5 billion omnibus spending bill, including $70 billion for military operations

CQ VOTE STUDIES

	PARTY UNITY		PRESIDENTIAL SUPPORT	
	SUPPORT	OPPOSE	SUPPORT	OPPOSE
2008	93%	7%	79%	21%
2007	94%	6%	86%	14%
2006	89%	11%	90%	10%
2005	93%	7%	76%	24%

INTEREST GROUPS

	AFL-CIO	ADA	CCUS	ACU
2008	7%	5%	89%	84%
2007	13%	5%	80%	88%
2006	7%	15%	87%	84%
2005	13%	5%	85%	80%

SOUTH CAROLINA 4
Northwest — Greenville, Spartanburg

Nestled in the "upstate" region, the 4th is the state's most compact district and is centered on Greenville County, the state's most-populous. Greenville and Spartanburg counties together account for 95 percent of the district population. The 4th also takes in the northernmost tip of Laurens County and Union County, a heavily forested and lightly populated area.

Once known only for its textile mills, the area is now home to diversified manufacturing and warehousing industries, and more than 80 internationally owned companies employ district residents. The cities of Greenville and Spartanburg have been able to avoid the skyrocketing unemployment rates plaguing other areas in the state, but residents and officials still worry about job losses. Michelin's North American base is in Greenville, and Spartanburg's BMW plant is the exclusive producer of the X5 and X6 models but has cut more than 1,000 jobs.

The area is no longer textile capital of the world, but trade issues are still important here. The 4th retains a textile presence, although industry giant Milliken & Co. — which is headquartered in Spartanburg — has been

forced to cut hundreds of jobs nationwide. Agriculture also plays a role around Spartanburg, and the county's orchards yield large peach crops.

Greenville has become a research hub and is building the 250-acre International Center for Automotive Research, a public-private venture with Clemson University. The adjacent Millennium Campus is a 150-acre office park that is recruiting corporate headquarters.

The combination of business-oriented conservatives and social conservatives focused around Greenville-based Bob Jones University keeps the 4th solidly Republican. In the 2008 presidential election, both Greenville and Spartanburg counties favored Republican John McCain, and he took 60 percent of the district's overall vote.

MAJOR INDUSTRY
Manufacturing, agriculture, textiles

CITIES
Greenville, 56,002; Spartanburg, 39,673; Wade Hampton (unincorporated), 20,458; Taylors (unincorporated), 20,125; Greer, 16,843

NOTABLE
Spartanburg was named for the local "Spartan Rifles" militia unit of the Revolutionary War.

Rep. John M. Spratt Jr. (D)

Elected 1982; 14th term

CAPITOL OFFICE
225-5501
www.house.gov/spratt
1401 Longworth Bldg. 20515-4005; fax 225-0464

COMMITTEES
Armed Services
Budget - chairman

RESIDENCE
York

BORN
Nov. 1, 1942; Charlotte, N.C.

RELIGION
Presbyterian

FAMILY
Wife, Jane Spratt; three children

EDUCATION
Davidson College, A.B. 1964 (history); Oxford U.,
M.A. 1966 (philosophy, politics & economics;
Marshall scholar); Yale U., LL.B. 1969

MILITARY SERVICE
Army, 1969-71

CAREER
Banker; insurance agency owner; lawyer

POLITICAL HIGHLIGHTS
No previous office

ELECTION RESULTS

2008 GENERAL

John M. Spratt Jr. (D)	188,785	61.6%
Albert F. Spencer (R)	113,282	37.0%
Frank Waggoner (CNSTP)	4,093	1.3%

2008 PRIMARY

John M. Spratt Jr. (D)	unopposed

2006 GENERAL

John M. Spratt Jr. (D)	99,669	56.9%
Ralph Norman (R)	75,422	43.1%

PREVIOUS WINNING PERCENTAGES
2004 (63%); 2002 (86%); 2000 (59%); 1998 (58%);
1996 (54%); 1994 (52%); 1992 (61%); 1990 (100%);
1988 (70%); 1986 (100%); 1984 (92%); 1982 (68%)

Spratt is the personification of an old-line Southern Democrat — fiscally and socially moderate-to-conservative, strongly pro-defense and always a gentleman.

As chairman of the Budget Committee, Spratt has a front-row seat to politics at its most partisan. But there is nothing fire-breathing about the calm South Carolinian, who has the air of a professor more at home with his books than giving lectures. He never hesitates to make the Democratic case when it comes to tax and spending policies, but he is far more interested in the policy debate than in scoring political points.

He also has a civility that harks back to an earlier time on Capitol Hill. When President George W. Bush nominated former Iowa Rep. Jim Nussle, Spratt's Republican predecessor as committee chairman, to be White House budget director in 2007, many Democrats balked at the choice, charging that Nussle was a hard-edged partisan. But Spratt spoke on Nussle's behalf during a Senate confirmation hearing. "I thought that I should stick up for somebody with whom I had a decent working relationship," he said.

Spratt in early 2009 was forced to shelve his usual message of fiscal restraint to help the Obama administration address the economic crisis through expanded federal spending. "I'm supposed to be the guy who reminds everyone we have a deficit," he lamented to the Charlotte Observer in January of that year. He said his goal is to try to ensure any investments are done in ways that don't hurt the country's financial health in the decades ahead.

Spratt joined his similarly deficit-minded counterpart on the Senate Budget Committee, North Dakota's Kent Conrad, in turning aside Obama's initial 10-year budget intended to show the longer-term implications of his proposals. Both their plans covered only five years because they said the uncertain economy made it difficult to do projections further into the future.

After Spratt shopped Obama's early budget ideas around with his colleagues, he found the biggest resistance was on energy issues, leading him to pare down some of the details in that area and let the president fight those battles further down the line. Then, as he guided the budget through the House, Spratt scoffed at a Republican alternative. "It calls for some substantial cuts that are so enormous that they strain credulity," he said in April 2009.

Spratt acknowledged Congress still must address the rising cost of health care and determine how to handle the strain on Medicare, Medicaid and Social Security. Many of Spratt's like-minded fiscal hawks have called for a commission to produce policy proposals for Congress to consider. But he prefers to address such issues through the regular committee process and bipartisan negotiations like the 1997 summit that led to the balanced-budget deal between President Clinton and the GOP-run Congress.

Spratt was a lead negotiator in that summit and called it "the biggest achievement that I can lay any claim on." The pact turned big deficits into a budget surplus by the time Bush replaced Clinton in 2001, but a lapse in the pay-as-you-go rules, which require offsets for new tax cuts or increased mandatory spending, after the Sept. 11 terrorist attacks and during the Iraq War have brought the budget back into the red.

The war brought into focus Spratt's knowledge of both the budget and national security issues. As the No. 2 Democrat on the Armed Services Committee, he is pro-defense but with an eye toward fiscal consequences. He voted in 2002 for the resolution giving Bush authority to invade Iraq — but he also commissioned the Congressional Budget Office to study the costs and consistently criticized the ad hoc way in which the Bush administration budgeted for operations in Iraq.

Spratt joined a group of House and Senate defense leaders in introducing a bill in March 2009 to reform Pentagon acquisition programs to avoid unreasonable cost estimates and other problems. "There's huge room for improvement in defense procurement," he said.

As a Democrat from a district that favors Republicans, Spratt treads carefully when it comes to social issues. In both 2004 and 2006, he supported a constitutional amendment to ban same-sex marriage. Spratt also must be mindful of the effects of foreign trade policies on his district, where empty textile factories serve as a reminder of the jobs that have gone overseas.

Spratt often has had to work to convince his conservative-leaning constituents that he understands and defends their interests. With his lofty academic credentials — he holds degrees from Davidson, Oxford and Yale — and his background as a lawyer, banker and insurance agency owner, Spratt is not the obvious choice to represent voters from poor textile towns.

He has been a leading advocate for the textile industry, which helps fuel the 5th District's economy. He voted for the North American Free Trade Agreement in 1993 — "the toughest vote I ever took" — but has since been even more circumspect of trade agreements. He opposed the 2005 Central America Free Trade Agreement, for instance, as well as a handful of subsequent bilateral trade agreements.

Spratt said his interest in politics was sparked by his father, "an old kind of Rooseveltian New Dealer," who was active in local races. His father was a lawyer and owned a small bank in Fort Mill. His older sister married Hugh L. McColl Jr., who later became chairman and chief executive officer of Bank of America. Spratt views his brother-in-law, who retired from the bank in 2001, as a mentor.

Spratt attended Yale Law School then served two years in the Army, working in the comptroller's office at the Pentagon with Henry M. Paulson Jr., who later became Bush's Treasury secretary. He then returned to South Carolina, joined his father's law firm and became president of his bank.

He won his first House race in 1982 by arguing his work with small-town law clients and bank depositors helped him understand their circumstances. He trounced a longtime friend and legal client, Republican John Wilkerson, by 36 percentage points, and won re-election with ease throughout the 1980s. He survived the GOP sweep of 1994 by just 4 percentage points and did not win more than 60 percent of the vote in the next three elections. But after winning with just 57 percent in 2006, he took 62 percent in 2008.

KEY VOTES

2008

Yes Delay consideration of Colombia free-trade agreement

Yes Override Bush veto of federal farm and nutrition programs reauthorization bill

Yes Overhaul surveillance laws and permit dismissal of suits against companies that conducted warrantless wiretapping

Yes Grant mortgage relief to homeowners and funding for Fannie Mae and Freddie Mac

Yes Approve initial $700 billion program to stabilize financial markets

Yes Approve final $700 billion program to stabilize financial markets

Yes Provide $14 billion in loans to automakers

2007

Yes Increase minimum wage by $2.10 an hour

Yes Approve $124.2 billion in emergency war spending and set goal for redeployment of troops from Iraq

No Reject federal contraceptive assistance to international family planning groups

Yes Override Bush veto of $23.2 billion water projects authorization bill

No Implement Peru free-trade agreement

Yes Approve energy policy overhaul with new fuel economy standards

Yes Clear $473.5 billion omnibus spending bill, including $70 billion for military operations

CQ VOTE STUDIES

	PARTY UNITY		PRESIDENTIAL SUPPORT	
	SUPPORT	OPPOSE	SUPPORT	OPPOSE
2008	98%	2%	20%	80%
2007	94%	6%	8%	92%
2006	84%	16%	44%	56%
2005	88%	12%	27%	73%
2004	86%	14%	41%	59%

INTEREST GROUPS

	AFL-CIO	ADA	CCUS	ACU
2008	100%	85%	61%	4%
2007	96%	95%	55%	4%
2006	100%	75%	50%	44%
2005	100%	90%	52%	12%
2004	93%	80%	48%	20%

SOUTH CAROLINA 5
North central — Rock Hill

The expansive 5th covers all or part of 14 mostly rural counties in the north-central part of the state, stretching from near Charlotte, N.C., to the Columbia suburbs, while also spreading west to Newberry County and east to Dillon County. Tobacco farmers, white-collar Charlotte commuters and textile workers make this a conservative district, although it still clings to traditional Southern Democrat roots.

Lee, Darlington, Marlboro and Dillon counties grow wheat, as well as cotton for the textile mills that historically dominated the region's economy. Labor costs forced many companies to downsize or close textile plants in the area, which faces unemployment rates above the national average. During sustained economic downturns, local officials struggle to keep existing textile jobs while expanding the local economy. Darlington and Dillon also depend heavily on tobacco farming.

The city of Sumter, which once was the center of an agricultural landscape, is trying to diversify its economy to combat manufacturing layoffs. Seven miles west, Shaw Air Force Base supports a large portion

of the area's economy, and more jobs are expected to move to the base by 2011 as part of the 2005 BRAC round. In York County to the north, Rock Hill now hosts white-collar commuters who work in Charlotte and Winthrop University. Development of a redesigned downtown known as the "Textile Corridor" and the city's $600 million River Falls industrial park has stalled.

The 5th tends to favor Republicans slightly in federal races, but conservative Democratic candidates who appeal to the district's numerous poor and rural residents can win here. Democrats also are helped by the district's 32-percent-black population, the largest of any South Carolina district except the black-majority 6th.

MAJOR INDUSTRY
Agriculture, military, tobacco, textiles

MILITARY BASES
Shaw Air Force Base, 4,777 military, 589 civilian (2008)

CITIES
Rock Hill, 49,765; Sumter (pt.), 20,518; Gaffney, 12,968

NOTABLE
The Lee County Cotton Festival and Agricultural Fair, held every October, celebrates the agricultural history of "King Cotton."

Rep. James E. Clyburn (D)

Elected 1992; 9th term

CAPITOL OFFICE
225-3315
clyburn.house.gov
2135 Rayburn Bldg. 20515-4006; fax 225-2313

COMMITTEES
No committee assignments

RESIDENCE
Columbia

BORN
July 21, 1940; Sumter, S.C.

RELIGION
African Methodist Episcopal

FAMILY
Wife, Emily Clyburn; three children

EDUCATION
South Carolina State College, B.A. 1962
(social studies)

CAREER
State agency official; teacher

POLITICAL HIGHLIGHTS
Candidate for S.C. House, 1970; S.C. human
affairs commissioner, 1974-92; sought Democratic
nomination for S.C. secretary of state, 1978, 1986

ELECTION RESULTS

2008 GENERAL

James E. Clyburn (D)	193,378	67.5%
Nancy Harrelson (R)	93,059	32.5%

2008 PRIMARY

James E. Clyburn (D)	unopposed

2006 GENERAL

James E. Clyburn (D)	100,213	64.4%
Gary McLeod (R)	53,181	34.2%
Antonio Williams (GREEN)	2,224	1.4%

PREVIOUS WINNING PERCENTAGES
2004 (67%); 2002 (67%); 2000 (72%); 1998 (73%);
1996 (69%); 1994 (64%); 1992 (65%)

The House's highest-ranking African-American, Clyburn has a knack for cultivating ties to the chamber's diverse factions that helps him succeed as majority whip and clinch victories for the leadership. He often chats up members on the floor, relying on persuasion rather than pressure to round up votes. "The whip is on my wall in a case. I don't plan to crack it at all," he said.

Some colleagues contend Clyburn's non-threatening style is a counterbalance to Speaker Nancy Pelosi's arm-twisting ways. But they say he can be firm when necessary; at a caucus meeting in early 2009, he chided several Democrats for not voting the way they had promised. "I don't like to be surprised," Clyburn said he informed the lawmakers.

He seeks to help colleagues in other ways. In the 2007-08 election cycle, his political action committee, Bridge PAC, doled out nearly $1 million to Democratic candidates and causes, according to CQ MoneyLine. A minister's son and a 1960s civil rights activist, he also serves as a key player in his party's drive to woo evangelical Christians and expand its base.

Clyburn has had some close calls on votes, but he often finds enough allies to make the difference on tough measures like spending bills and the 2007 lobbying overhaul. "If the distance between me and the other person is five steps, I don't mind taking three of them," he said.

Thanks to their comfortable majority, House Democrats were able to swiftly pass some of President Obama's early measures, including a $787 billion economic stimulus, an expansion of the State Children's Health Insurance Program and a $410 billion catchall spending bill for fiscal 2009.

But Obama's budget blueprint for fiscal 2010 was expected to be a tough sell within the caucus, pitting fiscal hawks critical of higher spending and taxes against more-liberal factions clamoring for more programs.

In the end, it was primarily the conservatives he lost in the 17 departures from the party line. He had aimed for 225 Democratic votes and garnered 233 on the final $3.56 trillion resolution. But the blueprint also set up a series of priorities for the leadership that could prove cumbersome for Clyburn if they reach the floor, including measures to reform health care and address climate change.

Perhaps his toughest challenge as whip came in the fall of 2008, when the House twice voted on a $700 billion rescue plan for the teetering financial services sector. Among those resisting the leadership's plea for support were 21 of 39 voting members of the Congressional Black Caucus, who saw nothing in the initial package to help their constituents. After it failed, Clyburn helped win over 13 caucus members who opposed the first bill to help ensure passage of the slightly different second version. Democratic presidential nominee Barack Obama also wooed those vote-switchers.

In the 2008 primary season, Clyburn stayed neutral in his state's Democratic primary contest but later sharply admonished former President Clinton to tone down his criticism of Obama. And when the primary season drew to a close, Clyburn was the first member of the House Democratic leadership team to endorse Obama. As Democrats gathered in Denver to make the nomination official, Clyburn was overcome by emotion. "I thought it would happen one day, but I never thought I would live to see it," he said. "It will be a great thing to have lived to see it."

Clyburn was unopposed for his leadership post at the start of the 110th Congress (2007-08) after a potential rival, Rahm Emanuel of Illinois, backed off, settling for Clyburn's old post as House Democratic Caucus chairman

(Emanuel is now White House chief of staff). Clyburn professes no interest in going elsewhere. "Any future I have will be in the House," he said in 2008.

A former appropriator, Clyburn calls earmarks for projects back home "an important part of my job" to serve poor families and rural communities. He stepped down as board chairman of a planned International African American Museum in Charleston after critics questioned several related earmarks. Clyburn said his resignation would avoid a potential conflict involving a nephew who worked as a project architect.

Clyburn casts an occasional conservative vote. He has voted for constitutional amendments to require a balanced federal budget, to set congressional term limits and to allow Congress to ban desecration of the flag.

He made news in 2008 by hiring a new district office employee: John "Rick" Rickenbacker, a former Orangeburg County Council chairman who had pleaded guilty to bribery in an FBI investigation. "Everyone deserves a second chance," said Clyburn, who has worked to encourage prisoner rehabilitation.

Clyburn moved up steadily after arriving in the House in 1993, becoming an appropriator and Congressional Black Caucus chairman in 1999. Four years later, he became vice chairman of the Democratic Caucus, then became chairman in 2006. Clyburn is the first African-American elected to Congress from South Carolina since his great-uncle, George Washington Murray, served in the House during Reconstruction. An uncle served in the state legislature and a cousin was a U.S. attorney.

As a youth, Clyburn attended an all-black boarding school called Mather Academy. He read books about his hero, Harry S Truman, but his family belonged to the GOP — the party of Abraham Lincoln — until the mid-1960s. As a young man, Clyburn jumped into the civil rights movement, becoming an early member of the Student Nonviolent Coordinating Committee, affiliated with the Rev. Martin Luther King Jr.'s Southern Christian Leadership Conference. He was arrested several times and once spent four days in jail. The U.S. Supreme Court overturned a state court that convicted him and others of "breach of peace" for demonstrating against segregation.

After college, Clyburn became the state employment commission's lone black employee. In 1971, Democratic Gov. John West named him a special assistant for human resources, and in 1974 he became human affairs commissioner. In 1978 and 1986, he unsuccessfully sought the Democratic nomination for secretary of state. When 1992 redistricting created the black-majority 6th District, he saw his opening. White Democratic Rep. Robin Tallon chose not to seek re-election. Clyburn defeated four other black Democrats in the primary, won the general and has cruised to re-election since.

KEY VOTES

2008

Yes   Delay consideration of Colombia free-trade agreement

Yes   Override Bush veto of federal farm and nutrition programs reauthorization bill

Yes   Overhaul surveillance laws and permit dismissal of suits against companies that conducted warrantless wiretapping

Yes   Grant mortgage relief to homeowners and funding for Fannie Mae and Freddie Mac

Yes   Approve initial $700 billion program to stabilize financial markets

Yes   Approve final $700 billion program to stabilize financial markets

Yes   Provide $14 billion in loans to automakers

2007

Yes   Increase minimum wage by $2.10 an hour

Yes   Approve $124.2 billion in emergency war spending and set goal for redeployment of troops from Iraq

No   Reject federal contraceptive assistance to international family planning groups

Yes   Override Bush veto of $23.2 billion water projects authorization bill

Yes   Implement Peru free-trade agreement

Yes   Approve energy policy overhaul with new fuel economy standards

Yes   Clear $473.5 billion omnibus spending bill, including $70 billion for military operations

CQ VOTE STUDIES

| | PARTY UNITY | | PRESIDENTIAL SUPPORT | |
	SUPPORT	OPPOSE	SUPPORT	OPPOSE
2008	99%	1%	18%	82%
2007	98%	2%	6%	94%
2006	94%	6%	35%	65%
2005	92%	8%	25%	75%
2004	93%	7%	30%	70%

INTEREST GROUPS

	AFL-CIO	ADA	CCUS	ACU
2008	100%	95%	56%	0%
2007	100%	95%	68%	0%
2006	100%	95%	50%	12%
2005	93%	85%	48%	9%
2004	86%	90%	45%	13%

SOUTH CAROLINA 6

Central and east — parts of Columbia, Florence and Charleston

A black-majority district designed to take in black areas in Columbia, Charleston and elsewhere in the state, the 6th includes all or part of 15 eastern counties, starting near the North Carolina border and reaching the southeastern coast. With five of the state's six poorest counties, the 6th has the state's lowest median household income, although it also includes historically black South Carolina State University.

In the rural portions of the district, many families depend on tobacco, corn, cotton and related agribusiness. These regions have low education levels and double-digit unemployment rates. Economic downturns have further hurt mainstay employment sources, such as the textile industry. Slowdowns also have hurt mostly middle-class Florence (shared with the 5th), which depends on industries like plastics, pharmaceuticals, textiles and paperboard manufacturing. The city did receive some good news when Monster Worldwide, an online job recruitment and career resources firm, and H.J. Heinz announced new facilities in Florence that

are expected to add more than 1,000 jobs. But there have been layoffs and production stoppages at two nearby Honda plants in Timmonsville that make all-terrain vehicles and personal watercraft.

The 6th's portion of Columbia includes the state Capitol complex, and the state's flagship university, the University of South Carolina. State and local government agencies provide area jobs, while private sector employment in the health care sector has expanded. In the coastal parts of the 6th, maritime industries and tourism support the economy.

The 6th supports Democratic candidates at all levels. Its black-majority areas — including its shares of Columbia and North Charleston, which are more than two-thirds black — make the 6th a Democratic lock.

MAJOR INDUSTRY
Agriculture, government, higher education, tourism, textiles

CITIES
Columbia (pt.), 56,507; North Charleston (pt.), 34,111; Florence (pt.), 26,623; Charleston (pt.), 19,216; Sumter (pt.), 19,125

NOTABLE
Clarendon County (pop. 32,502) can claim five South Carolina governors, all related to each other.

Gov. Michael Rounds (R)

First elected: 2002
Length of term: 4 years
Term expires: 1/11
Salary: $115,331
Phone: (605) 773-3212

Residence: Pierre
Born: Oct. 24, 1954; Pierre, S.D.
Religion: Roman Catholic
Family: Wife, Jean Rounds; four children
Education: South Dakota State U., B.S. 1977 (political science)
Career: Insurance and real estate executive; insurance agent; campaign aide
Political highlights: S.D. Senate, 1991-2000 (majority leader, 1995-2000)

Election results:

2006 GENERAL

Michael Rounds (R)	206,990	61.7%
Jack Billion (D)	121,226	36.1%
Steve Willis (CNSTP)	4,010	1.2%
Tom Gerber (LIBERT)	3,282	1.0%

Lt. Gov. Dennis Daugaard (R)

First elected: 2002
Length of term: 4 years
Term expires: 1/11
Salary: $17,699
Phone: (605) 773-3661

LEGISLATURE

Legislature: 40 days in odd-numbered years starting in January; 35 days in even-numbered years, starting in January

Senate: 35 members, 2-year terms
2009 ratios: 21 R, 14 D; 28 men, 7 women
Salary: $12,000/2-year-term
Phone: (605) 773-3821

House: 70 members, 2-year terms
2009 ratios: 46 R, 24 D; 57 men, 13 women
Salary: $12,000/2-year-term
Phone: (605) 773-3851

TERM LIMITS

Governor: 2 consecutive terms
Senate: 2 consecutive terms
House: 4 consecutive terms

URBAN STATISTICS

CITY	POPULATION
Sioux Falls	123,975
Rapid City	59,607
Aberdeen	24,658

REGISTERED VOTERS

Republican	46%
Democrat	38%
Others	15%

POPULATION

2008 population (est.)	804,194
2000 population	754,844
1990 population	696,004
Percent change (1990-2000)	+8.5%
Rank among states (2008)	46
Median age	35.6
Born in state	68.1%
Foreign born	1.8%
Violent crime rate	167/100,000
Poverty level	13.2%
Federal workers	10,803
Military	8,489

ELECTIONS

STATE ELECTION OFFICIAL
(605) 773-3537
DEMOCRATIC PARTY
(605) 271-5405
REPUBLICAN PARTY
(605) 224-7347

MISCELLANEOUS

Web: www.sd.gov
Capital: Pierre

U.S. CONGRESS

Senate: 1 Democrat, 1 Republican
House: 1 Democrat

2000 Census Statistics by District

DIST.	2008 VOTE FOR PRESIDENT OBAMA	MCCAIN	WHITE	BLACK	ASIAN	HISP	MEDIAN INCOME	WHITE COLLAR	BLUE COLLAR	SERVICE INDUSTRY	OVER 64	UNDER 18	COLLEGE EDUCATION	RURAL	SQ. MILES
AL	45%	53%	88%	1%	1%	1%	$35,282	59%	25%	16%	14%	27%	22%	48%	75,885
STATE	45	53	88	1	1	1	$35,282	59	25	16	14	27	22	48	75,885
U.S.	53	46	69	12	4	13	$41,994	60	25	15	12	26	24	21	3,537,438

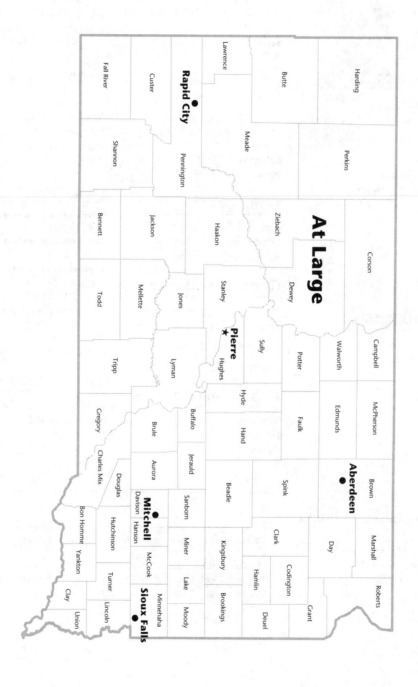

Sen. Tim Johnson (D)

Elected 1996; 3rd term

CAPITOL OFFICE
224-5842
johnson.senate.gov
136 Hart Bldg. 20510; fax 228-5765

COMMITTEES
Appropriations
    (Military Construction-VA - chairman)
Banking, Housing & Urban Affairs
    (Financial Institutions - chairman)
Energy & Natural Resources
Indian Affairs

RESIDENCE
Vermillion

BORN
Dec. 28, 1946; Canton, S.D.

RELIGION
Lutheran

FAMILY
Wife, Barbara Johnson; three children

EDUCATION
U. of South Dakota, B.A. 1969 (government),
M.A. 1970 (government); Michigan State U.,
attended 1970-71 (political science);
U. of South Dakota, J.D. 1975

CAREER
Lawyer; county prosecutor; state legislative aide

POLITICAL HIGHLIGHTS
S.D. House, 1979-83; S.D. Senate, 1983-87;
U.S. House, 1987-97

ELECTION RESULTS

2008 GENERAL

Tim Johnson (D)	237,889	62.5%
Joel Dykstra (R)	142,784	37.5%

2008 PRIMARY

Tim Johnson (D)	unopposed

PREVIOUS WINNING PERCENTAGES
2002 (50%); 1996 (51%); 1994 House Election (60%);
1992 House Election (69%); 1990 House Election
(68%); 1988 House Election (72%); 1986 House
Election (59%)

A fourth-generation South Dakotan, Johnson is a classic prairie populist who looks out for his state's miners, ranchers and farmers. He is known for his deliberate approach, whether obtaining money for his rural state's needs or surviving a major health scare that overshadowed the end of his second term in the Senate.

His interests tend to center on farm policy, renewable energy, American Indian affairs and veterans' needs. But he's been deeply immersed in banking and financial industry issues as chairman of the Banking, Housing and Urban Affairs Subcommittee on Financial Institutions. The panel will be in the midst of ongoing efforts to stabilize the teetering U.S. financial system and get credit markets working normally again.

He signaled in 2008 that he won't necessarily go along with the crowd; he was one of just nine Senate Democrats to vote against the $700 billion rescue plan for the financial services industry. And in April 2009, he joined Republicans on the full Banking Committee to oppose legislation aimed at barring what critics call predatory practices by the credit card industry.

Johnson has been South Dakota's senior senator since the 2004 defeat of former Democratic leader Tom Daschle. He was close to Daschle, but has developed a comfortable working relationship with his successor, Republican John Thune, who had almost unseated Johnson in 2002. The two charter planes together for the long trips home and team up on issues important to their largely rural state.

Johnson also votes with Thune, and most Senate Republicans, on selected issues, part of the balancing act required of a Democrat from a Republican-leaning state. In 2008, he was one of four Democrats to vote against limiting debate on a climate change bill, which he saw as a threat to his state's coal industry. In 2005, Johnson was one of just two Democrats who voted to cut off a filibuster against renewing the 2001 anti-terrorism law known as the Patriot Act. Earlier that year, he helped Republicans to victories on laws to shield gun manufacturers, dealers and importers from lawsuits. The National Rifle Association endorsed him in 2008 for the first time in his Senate career.

He stuck with his party, however, in backing much of President Obama's agenda in early 2009. A member of the Appropriations Committee, Johnson voted for a bill, signed into law, to expand the State Children's Health Insurance Program, which provides coverage for children whose families don't qualify for Medicaid. He also backed a $787 billion economic stimulus law and a $3.56 trillion budget blueprint for fiscal 2010. But his allegiance may be further tested as lawmakers move on Obama's priorities as outlined in that budget.

He uses his seat on Appropriations — and his chairmanship of the panel on Military Construction and Veterans Affairs — to direct funds to an array of areas in his state, particularly those aimed at helping veterans and American Indians, many of whom live in poverty on reservations. He also applauded Obama's plans to increase funding for "Priority 8" veterans, those with no service-connected disabilities who generally earn more than $30,000 a year.

He has looked out for his constituents in other ways. A member of the Energy and Natural Resources Committee, Johnson has a keen interest in expanding the use of ethanol and soy-based biodiesel as alternative fuels that can bolster his state's economy. He also seeks to expand the energy uses of wind, something else South Dakota has in abundance.

He wrote a provision in the 2002 farm bill that required mandatory country-of-origin labels on fruit, vegetables and meat — helpful to the ranchers in his state — and then fought for years to get the provision implemented. He was repeatedly thwarted by congressional Republicans and the George W. Bush administration, but the labeling requirement was part of a 2008 rewrite of the farm bill and finally took effect that year. Johnson has some concerns about the implementation guidelines, but he's pleased with the progress.

Johnson spent the first part of the 110th Congress (2007-08) recovering from emergency brain surgery. In December 2006, he suffered from a congenital arteriovenous malformation that caused bleeding in his brain and produced stroke-like symptoms. Even before the session convened in January 2007, the Senate held its collective breath; Democrats had won the Senate the previous November by the narrowest of margins, gaining effective control of 51 seats to 49 for Republicans.

He was hospitalized for months and slowly regained strength, speech and mobility. He returned to work at the Capitol in September 2007 — a month after joking to a Sioux Falls crowd, "I will promise you that when my speech is back to normal, I will not act like a typical politician and overuse the gift." His wife, Barbara, said he was "extremely determined" to recover. "How he's gotten through this and maintained an even balance I will never understand, because I cannot maintain the balance that Tim maintains," she told ABC News.

Johnson has long valued family time and advocated its importance. He introduced legislation in the 108th Congress (2003-04) to bar telemarketers from calling between 5:30 p.m. and 7:30 p.m. as a way of keeping family dinner hours "sacred." He said he regularly advises new senators to bring their families to Washington so that they can attend school meetings and their children's athletic activities, as he did.

When Johnson was elected to the House in 1986, his wife gave up her tenured position as a University of South Dakota social work professor to move the family to Washington, where she became a public school social worker. All three Johnson children went to school in Virginia but returned to South Dakota for college. Their son Brooks served with the Army in Iraq and Afghanistan.

Family issues almost stopped Johnson from running for the Senate even though he had a good shot at unseating GOP incumbent Larry Pressler in 1996. In the middle of the campaign, Johnson's wife learned she had breast cancer, the first of two bouts with the disease she has suffered. But she encouraged him to stay in and he went on to win the race.

Johnson himself is a cancer survivor, having had successful surgery for prostate cancer in 2004. He also is deaf in his left ear as a result of surgery to remove a benign tumor found on his eardrum when he underwent a physical for and was refused admission to the U.S. military during the Vietnam War.

Johnson won a seat in the state legislature in 1978, then ran for Congress in 1986 when Daschle gave up the House seat for a Senate race. After a narrow primary win, Johnson easily won the general election. When he took on Pressler in 1996, he won by just 8,600 votes, the only challenger to defeat a sitting senator that year.

Six years later, his re-election bid sparked a titanic showdown between the two political parties. Thune was personally recruited by President Bush to take on Johnson, while Daschle jumped in full throttle to defend Johnson. The state's 760,000 inhabitants were bombarded with TV ads, and both candidates broke all previous records for spending. Throughout the campaign, Johnson's quiet style was compared with that of the more gregarious and handsome Thune. In the end, it was Johnson who prevailed by 524 votes.

Johnson ran for re-election again in 2008, despite his health problems. His colleagues jumped in early to raise campaign funds while he was still hospitalized. Republicans, uncertain whether they would face Johnson or another Democratic candidate, struggled to recruit a high-profile challenger. Johnson handily defeated the eventual GOP nominee, state Rep. Joel Dykstra.

KEY VOTES

2008

Yes Prohibit discrimination based on genetic information

Yes Reauthorize farm and nutrition programs for five years

No Limit debate on "cap and trade" system for greenhouse gas emissions

No Allow lawsuits against companies that participated in warrantless wiretapping

Yes Limit debate on a bill to block a scheduled cut in Medicare payments to doctors

Yes Grant mortgage relief to homeowners and funding for Fannie Mae and Freddie Mac

Yes Approve a nuclear cooperation agreement with India

No Approve final $700 billion program to stabilize financial markets

Yes Allow consideration of a $14 billion auto industry loan package

2007

? Increase minimum wage by $2.10 an hour

? Limit debate on a comprehensive immigration bill

? Overhaul congressional lobbying and ethics rules for members and their staffs

Yes Limit debate on considering a bill to add House seats for the District of Columbia and Utah

Yes Limit debate on restoring habeas corpus rights to detainees

Yes Mandate minimum breaks for troops between deployments to Iraq or Afghanistan

Yes Override Bush veto of $23.2 billion water projects authorization bill

No Confirm Michael B. Mukasey as attorney general

Yes Limit debate on an energy policy overhaul containing $21.8 billion in tax incentives and reduced oil and gas subsidies

CQ VOTE STUDIES

	PARTY UNITY		PRESIDENTIAL SUPPORT	
	SUPPORT	OPPOSE	SUPPORT	OPPOSE
2008	80%	20%	44%	56%
2007	88%	12%	29%	71%
2006	83%	17%	57%	43%
2005	83%	17%	45%	55%
2004	90%	10%	60%	40%
2003	93%	7%	50%	50%
2002	85%	15%	68%	32%
2001	87%	13%	71%	29%
2000	91%	9%	98%	2%
1999	93%	7%	78%	22%

INTEREST GROUPS

	AFL-CIO	ADA	CCUS	ACU
2008	100%	80%	75%	12%
2007	89%	40%	80%	0%
2006	87%	85%	50%	12%
2005	86%	95%	60%	13%
2004	100%	85%	59%	11%
2003	100%	80%	39%	15%
2002	100%	90%	53%	15%
2001	94%	85%	64%	32%
2000	75%	80%	60%	16%
1999	89%	95%	47%	8%

Sen. John Thune (R)

Elected 2004; 1st term

CAPITOL OFFICE
224-2321
thune.senate.gov
493 Russell Bldg. 20510-4103; fax 228-5429

COMMITTEES
Agriculture, Nutrition & Forestry
Armed Services
Commerce, Science & Transportation
Small Business & Entrepreneurship

RESIDENCE
Sioux Falls

BORN
Jan. 7, 1961; Pierre, S.D.

RELIGION
Protestant

FAMILY
Wife, Kimberley Thune; two children

EDUCATION
Biola U., B.S. 1983 (business administration);
U. of South Dakota, M.B.A. 1984

CAREER
Lobbyist; local governments association
executive; U. S. Small Business Administration
official; congressional aide

POLITICAL HIGHLIGHTS
S.D. Republican Party executive director,
1989-91; S.D. railroad director, 1991-93;
U.S. House, 1997-2003; Republican nominee
for U.S. Senate, 2002

ELECTION RESULTS

2004 GENERAL

John Thune (R)	197,848	50.6%
Tom Daschle (D)	193,340	49.4%

2004 PRIMARY

John Thune (R)	unopposed

PREVIOUS WINNING PERCENTAGES
2000 House Election (73%); 1998 House Election
(75%); 1996 House Election (58%)

Thune's laid-back, affable demeanor belies savvy political skills that have made him a valued deal-broker for Senate Republicans and a capable watchdog for his state's agricultural interests.

As the GOP Conference vice chairman, he works to put out the party message and to keep moderates and more -mainstream conservative colleagues on the same page in order to thwart Democratic initiatives. "You try to point out why it's important to get a result, why it's important to the team," he said.

Tall and lean, Thune (THOON) has telegenic looks that help him snare coveted invitations from Sunday political talk shows and have stoked speculation he could one day be a candidate for president or vice president. For now, he has his sights set on the 2010 election, when his and several other Republican seats are up for grabs. With that in mind, he works to bolster the GOP image both on and off Capitol Hill.

Early in the Obama administration, he said the president would have to seek bipartisan compromise, despite strengthened Democratic majorities in the Senate. He expressed some optimism when Republicans were allowed to offer amendments to the president's economic stimulus measure. But as he saw his and dozens of other GOP amendments rejected, Thune said he would be "inclined" to use procedural tactics to stall the bill. The measure eventually became law with a bare minimum of support from Senate Republicans.

The day Obama marked his first 100 days in office, Thune remained somewhat optimistic of his party's role: "We are defining the debate and drawing contrasts and hopefully in most cases putting forward positive alternatives," he told The New York Times. But he acknowledged it's tough. He said Obama "is riding a wave of popularity, and the Democrats in Congress have a lot of running room with the American public."

To top it off, Sen. Arlen Specter of Pennsylvania moved from the Republican Party into the Democratic caucus on that same day. Thune said Specter's switch moves Washington toward one-party rule in which Democrats could run "roughshod" over the minority party. But he plans to do what he can to keep the other side in check.

Thune and House Minority Whip Eric Cantor of Virginia announced the formation of a bicameral group to track how the administration spends the stimulus funds. "We believe that when you are shoveling that amount of money out the door, it's a recipe for waste, fraud and abuse," Thune said.

Thune won the role of Conference vice chairman after John Cornyn of Texas moved up to become chairman of the National Republican Senatorial Committee. During the 110th Congress (2007-08), Thune served as the party's chief deputy whip, where he proved his mettle at making deals. For example, he cut a deal with supporters of a $50 billion global AIDS bill to redirect $2 billion of the sum to American Indian programs. The compromise satisfied Republicans concerned that $50 billion for global health was too much, and it addressed the health care needs of a traditionally underserved community that includes tribes in Thune's home state.

Thune has a strong religious faith that keeps him in the conservative wing in the party, although he tends to stay out of the fray when the chamber debates such high-profile "values issues" as abortion or bans on gay marriage. He favors a constitutional amendment to ban gay marriage, opposes embryonic stem cell research and supports gun owners' rights.

But he breaks with his caucus on some parochial issues. When the Agriculture, Nutrition and Forestry Committee took up a major rewrite of farm policy in 2008, he collaborated with North Dakota Democrats Byron L. Dorgan and Kent Conrad to restore a permanent disaster aid section that authorizes mandatory spending when an agricultural disaster is declared. The 1990 version of the farm law included such a section, but Republicans stripped it in 1996, preferring to provide disaster relief through spending bills.

And looking out for South Dakota corn growers and ethanol producers, he backed the farm bill's extension of the tariff on ethanol imports.

Thune also sits on the Commerce, Science and Transportation Committee. He opposes a plan to cap greenhouse gas emissions and impose a market-based emissions credit trading program, calling such a proposal a "national energy sales tax." He said he would prefer market-based incentives to expand the use of solar, wind and other alternative energy sources. He also supports expanded drilling for oil and gas.

He looks out for the train industry in South Dakota. In early 2007, he spearheaded an effort to increase funding for transportation by "unfreezing" about $4 billion in highway and transit funding increases under the 2005 highway law.

From his seat on Armed Services, he has been a strong supporter of the Iraq War. When Obama opened the door to potential prosecution of George W. Bush administration officials for the use of torture during interrogation of terrorism suspects, Thune said on MSNBC: "I think, at this point, the goal should be . . . what steps can we take to keep the country safer and not what steps can the president take to make the left wing of his party happy."

Thune seeks to protect Ellsworth Air Force Base. He stood up to the Bush administration to lobby for the base just five months into his first year in the Senate, when the base was slated to be closed by the Base Realignment and Closure Commission. He opposed the confirmation of Bush's embattled nominee for United Nations ambassador, John R. Bolton, and refused to budge for three months, holding up consideration of a defense authorization bill. Ultimately, Ellsworth was removed from the closure list.

Thune grew up in the small town of Murdo, about 40 miles south of Pierre. He comes from a family of New Deal Democrats, but was won over by Ronald Reagan's policies and world view.

He aspired to become a professional basketball player but said he was thwarted from reaching his NBA dreams by a "lack of leaping." But his aptitude on the court helped him break into politics. Impressed with Thune's performance in a game during his freshman year in high school, South Dakota Rep. James Abdnor, who played high school basketball against Thune's father, struck up a conversation with the young man, and they stayed in touch over the years. After graduate school, Thune worked for then-Sen. Abdnor. After Abdnor was defeated for re-election in 1986, Thune followed him to the Small Business Administration, where Abdnor served as administrator.

In 1989, Thune served a few months as deputy staff director of the Senate Small Business Committee and then returned to South Dakota, where he was executive director of the state Republican Party and then state railroad director. In 1993, he was named executive director of the South Dakota Municipal League, an association of local governments.

Three years later, Thune vied for the state's lone House seat, vacated by Democrat Tim Johnson. He defeated Lt. Gov. Carole Hillard in the GOP primary, then handily defeated Rick Weiland, a longtime aide to former Sen. Tom Daschle, by 21 percentage points in the general election. He was re-elected by impressive margins in 1998 and 2000.

In 2004, he eked out a victory over Daschle by just more than 1 percentage point. Thune successfully turned the election into a referendum on Daschle's role as leader of his party, which, he argued, was centered around thwarting President Bush.

KEY VOTES

2008

Yes Prohibit discrimination based on genetic information

Yes Reauthorize farm and nutrition programs for five years

No Limit debate on "cap and trade" system for greenhouse gas emissions

No Allow lawsuits against companies that participated in warrantless wiretapping

No Limit debate on a bill to block a scheduled cut in Medicare payments to doctors

No Grant mortgage relief to homeowners and funding for Fannie Mae and Freddie Mac

Yes Approve a nuclear cooperation agreement with India

Yes Approve final $700 billion program to stabilize financial markets

No Allow consideration of a $14 billion auto industry loan package

2007

Yes Increase minimum wage by $2.10 an hour

No Limit debate on a comprehensive immigration bill

Yes Overhaul congressional lobbying and ethics rules for members and their staffs

No Limit debate on considering a bill to add House seats for the District of Columbia and Utah

No Limit debate on restoring habeas corpus rights to detainees

No Mandate minimum breaks for troops between deployments to Iraq or Afghanistan

Yes Override Bush veto of $23.2 billion water projects authorization bill

Yes Confirm Michael B. Mukasey as attorney general

Yes Limit debate on an energy policy overhaul containing $21.8 billion in tax incentives and reduced oil and gas subsidies

CQ VOTE STUDIES

	PARTY UNITY		PRESIDENTIAL SUPPORT	
	SUPPORT	OPPOSE	SUPPORT	OPPOSE
2008	95%	5%	76%	24%
2007	88%	12%	82%	18%
2006	95%	5%	87%	13%
2005	87%	13%	86%	14%
House Service:				
2002	83%	17%	82%	18%
2001	92%	8%	81%	19%
2000	91%	9%	29%	71%
1999	91%	9%	22%	78%
1998	95%	5%	23%	77%

INTEREST GROUPS

	AFL-CIO	ADA	CCUS	ACU
2008	30%	10%	100%	84%
2007	16%	20%	55%	88%
2006	20%	0%	92%	100%
2005	21%	10%	93%	92%
House Service:				
2002	13%	10%	90%	88%
2001	33%	10%	91%	80%
2000	10%	5%	85%	76%
1999	11%	10%	92%	80%
1998	0%	5%	100%	92%

Rep. Stephanie Herseth Sandlin (D)

Elected June 2004; 3rd full term

CAPITOL OFFICE
225-2801
hersethsandlin.house.gov
331 Cannon Bldg. 20515-4101; fax 225-5823

COMMITTEES
Agriculture
Natural Resources
Veterans' Affairs
(Economic Opportunity - chairwoman)
Select Energy Independence & Global Warming

RESIDENCE
Brookings

BORN
Dec. 3, 1970; Aberdeen, S.D.

RELIGION
Lutheran

FAMILY
Husband, Max Sandlin; one child

EDUCATION
Georgetown U., B.A. 1993 (government),
M.A. 1996 (government), J.D. 1996

CAREER
Farm union official; lawyer; professor

POLITICAL HIGHLIGHTS
Democratic nominee for U.S. House, 2002

ELECTION RESULTS

2008 GENERAL

Stephanie Herseth Sandlin (D)	256,041	67.6%
Chris Lien (R)	122,966	32.4%

2008 PRIMARY

Stephanie Herseth Sandlin (D)	unopposed

2006 GENERAL

Stephanie Herseth Sandlin (D)	230,468	69.1%
Bruce W. Whalen (R)	97,864	29.3%
Larry Rudebusch (LIBERT)	5,230	1.6%

PREVIOUS WINNING PERCENTAGES
2004 (53%); 2004 Special Election (51%)

A youthful Democrat representing a largely Republican state, Herseth Sandlin strives to be a pragmatic consensus-builder. She is one of three co-chairpersons of the fiscally conservative Blue Dog Coalition, which has the numbers and influence to resist the most liberal whims of Democratic leaders but also has been forced to relax its usual allegiance to balanced budgets to help shore up the nation's dire economy.

She has shown a strong willingness to vote her own way. Herseth Sandlin in 2008 opposed a $700 billion law to prop up ailing financial institutions, saying it was a rushed solution without enough safeguards to protect tax-payers. And she bucked her party that year to support a 2008 law permitting the surveillance of foreign intelligence targets.

She has also supported stronger border security and immigration enforcement. Unlike many Democrats, she backs a proposed constitutional amendment to ban same-sex marriage, but supports abortion rights and embryonic stem cell research.

She was among three Blue Dogs — Baron P. Hill of Indiana and Heath Shuler of North Carolina were the other two — who wrote to House Speak-er Nancy Pelosi of California in February 2009 to warn that she would lose votes if Obama's $819.5 billion economic stimulus package wasn't pared down. The final version was trimmed down to $787 billion, and Herseth Sandlin voted for it, saying it would have a "strongly stimulative effect on our economy through tax cuts, job creation and infrastructure investment." She also supported Obama's $3.56 trillion budget blueprint for fiscal 2010, although 13 other Blue Dogs opposed it.

A member of the Natural Resources Committee, she is a champion of ethanol as an alternative to gasoline and was a chief sponsor of a 2007 law that requires oil companies to double the amount of corn-based ethanol they blend with gasoline. As a member of the Select Committee on Energy Inde-pendence and Global Warming, she has advocated for expansion of offshore drilling for oil and natural gas, along with nuclear energy, "clean coal" tech-nology, biofuels and wind power.

She sees such development as an economic opportunity and a chance to create new jobs. "No one wants to miss that opportunity, because the econ-omy is struggling so much," she said.

She said she wants to make sure her state's interests are taken into account as Democrats and the Obama administration move forward on a plan to cap greenhouse gas emissions and set up a market-based trading system for emissions credits.

From her seat on the Agriculture Committee, Herseth Sandlin pushed for mandatory country-of-origin labeling for meat products — a priority for South Dakota ranchers — in the 2008 farm law. She also successfully worked with Democrat Tim Walz of Minnesota to insert language to help beginning and socially disadvantaged farmers and ranchers by increasing farm ownership loans. She also added bison to the definition of livestock and inserted an amendment to the farm law that sets aside federal funds to help public television stations in rural areas upgrade equipment.

As chairwoman of the Veterans' Affairs Committee's panel on Economic Opportunity, she has focused on ways to help soldiers transition to civilian life. She sponsored a 2008 bill to increase educational benefits for returning Iraq and Afghanistan veterans. But it faltered in the face of a more generous Senate plan. Herseth Sandlin ultimately acquiesced when the House approved the far more expensive Senate version. But she was praised by colleagues on both sides of the aisle for her efforts.

Her political roots in South Dakota run deep. Her grandfather, Ralph E. Herseth, was the Democratic governor from 1959 to 1961. Her grandmother, Lorna B. Herseth, was South Dakota secretary of state from 1973 to 1979. And her father, Lars Herseth, spent 20 years in the legislature and was an unsuccessful gubernatorial nominee in 1986. After that campaign, her parents divorced.

Herseth Sandlin grew up on her family's farm and ranch near Houghton, in the northeast part of the state. She then headed to Washington, D.C., to attend college at Georgetown University, where she also obtained a law degree. She then worked on energy and telecommunications issues for the South Dakota Public Utilities Commission in Pierre, organizing meetings with tribal leaders on utility regulation. She was also executive director of the South Dakota Farmers Union Foundation.

Herseth Sandlin first ran for the U.S. House in 2002 to take the seat vacated by Republican John Thune, who was running for the Senate. She received 46 percent of the vote but lost to Republican Gov. Bill Janklow. But Janklow's career was effectively ended when he killed a motorcyclist with his car in August 2003 after running a stop sign at high speed. Convicted of second-degree manslaughter, Janklow resigned in January 2004.

In the June special election, Herseth Sandlin won with 51 percent of the vote over former Republican state Sen. Larry Diedrich. In the general election, Herseth Sandlin, then 33, won her first full term by a margin of more than 7 percentage points — defeating Diedrich again.

Her win was aided by the national focus on the Senate race, in which Thune ultimately toppled Democratic leader Tom Daschle.

Herseth Sandlin is the first woman from South Dakota to win a general election to Congress, though two Republican women briefly served in the Senate — Gladys Pyle, who came to Washington for two months after winning a special election in 1938, and Vera C. Bushfield, who was appointed in 1948 to complete the term of her husband when he died in office.

Herseth Sandlin has easily won re-election since 2004 and was touted as a possible Democratic candidate in the 2010 governor's race, when GOP Gov. Mike Rounds is forced to step aside due to term limits. She also is a potential challenger to Thune, who is up for re-election in 2010.

In March 2007, she married former Rep. Max Sandlin, a Texas Democrat 18 years her senior whom she met during her failed 2002 campaign against Janklow. They had a boy in December 2008.

KEY VOTES

2008

Yes Delay consideration of Colombia free-trade agreement

Yes Override Bush veto of federal farm and nutrition programs reauthorization bill

Yes Overhaul surveillance laws and permit dismissal of suits against companies that conducted warrantless wiretapping

Yes Grant mortgage relief to homeowners and funding for Fannie Mae and Freddie Mac

No Approve initial $700 billion program to stabilize financial markets

No Approve final $700 billion program to stabilize financial markets

No Provide $14 billion in loans to automakers

2007

Yes Increase minimum wage by $2.10 an hour

Yes Approve $124.2 billion in emergency war spending and set goal for redeployment of troops from Iraq

No Reject federal contraceptive assistance to international family planning groups

Yes Override Bush veto of $23.2 billion water projects authorization bill

Yes Implement Peru free-trade agreement

Yes Approve energy policy overhaul with new fuel economy standards

Yes Clear $473.5 billion omnibus spending bill, including $70 billion for military operations

CQ VOTE STUDIES

| | PARTY UNITY | | PRESIDENTIAL SUPPORT | |
	SUPPORT	OPPOSE	SUPPORT	OPPOSE
2008	91%	9%	22%	78%
2007	89%	11%	13%	87%
2006	76%	24%	50%	50%
2005	79%	21%	39%	61%
2004	76%	24%	45%	55%

INTEREST GROUPS

	AFL-CIO	ADA	CCUS	ACU
2008	80%	70%	56%	28%
2007	96%	90%	65%	12%
2006	86%	65%	80%	60%
2005	87%	85%	63%	33%
2004	63%	55%	50%	31%

SOUTH DAKOTA

At Large

South Dakota's agriculture-based economy had largely recovered from low crop prices a decade ago when farmland values fell and corn production for ethanol plants dropped. Uncertainty in the agriculture industry has contributed to a steady migration to the state's cities, where finance, computers and health care have become primary industries.

Lower taxes and wages lured some national corporations, but employers in the banking industry have been forced to cut jobs. In the west, away from the most populated areas, the arid, hilly portion of the state relies on ranching, mining and tourism. The Badlands, along with Mount Rushmore and other Black Hills attractions, are here.

South Dakota has one of the nation's highest percentages of American Indians, at just more than 8 percent of the population. All nine of the state's Indian reservations grew in population over the past two decades, and eight of the nine operate casinos. While gaming has been an economic bright spot, it has failed to eliminate the poverty conditions on reservations. Buffalo County, home to part of the Crow Creek Indian Reservation, and Shannon County, entirely within the Pine Ridge Indian Reservation, are among the nation's poorest counties.

The Missouri River, which splits the state, sometimes is considered a political divide as well — western ranching Republicans edge out eastern urban and farming Democrats at the polls. Overall, an 8-percentage-point GOP voter registration advantage helped John McCain take 53 percent of the state's 2008 presidential vote. Although South Dakotans often vote Republican at the local level, they will support Democrats in some federal races: Democrats have won elections to Congress, but the state has not supported a Democratic presidential candidate since 1964.

MAJOR INDUSTRY
Agriculture, finance, tourism

MILITARY BASES
Ellsworth Air Force Base, 3,144 military, 451 civilian (2007)

CITIES
Sioux Falls, 123,975; Rapid City, 59,607; Aberdeen, 24,658

NOTABLE
More than 200 Sioux were massacred in one day at Wounded Knee in 1890; The largest and most complete fossil of a Tyrannosaurus Rex ever found was uncovered near Faith in 1990.

TENNESSEE

Gov. Phil Bredesen (D)

Pronounced:
BREAD-eh-sen
First elected: 2002
Length of term: 4 years
Term expires: 1/11
Salary: $159,960
Phone: (615) 741-2001

Residence: Nashville
Born: Nov. 21, 1943; Oceanport, N.J.
Religion: Presbyterian
Family: Wife, Andrea Conte; one child
Education: Harvard U., S.B. 1967 (physics)
Career: Health insurance company founder; health care executive; computer programmer
Political highlights: Candidate for Mass. Senate, 1970; candidate for mayor of Nashville, 1987; sought Democratic nomination for U.S. House, 1987; mayor of Nashville, 1991-99

Election results:
2006 GENERAL

Phil Bredesen (D)	1,247,491	68.6%
Jim Bryson (R)	540,853	29.7%

Lt. Gov. Ronald L. Ramsey (R)

First elected: 2007*
Length of term: 2 years
Term expires: 1/11
Salary: $54,372
Phone: (615) 741-2368
*Elected by the Senate

LEGISLATURE

General Assembly: 90 days over 2 years starting in January

Senate: 33 members, 4-year terms
2009 ratios: 19 R, 14 D; 24 men, 9 women
Salary: $19,009
Phone: (615) 741-2730

House: 99 members, 2-year terms
2009 ratios: 50 D, 49 R; 83 men, 16 women
Salary: $19,009
Phone: (615) 741-2901

TERM LIMITS

Governor: 2 terms
Senate: No
House: No

URBAN STATISTICS

CITY	POPULATION
Memphis	650,100
Nashville-Davidson	569,891
Knoxville	173,890
Chattanooga	155,554
Clarksville	103,455

REGISTERED VOTERS

Voters do not register by party.

POPULATION

2008 population (est.)	6,214,888
2000 population	5,689,283
1990 population	4,877,185
Percent change (1990-2000)	+16.7%
Rank among states (2008)	17

Median age	35.9
Born in state	64.7%
Foreign born	2.8%
Violent crime rate	707/100,000
Poverty level	13.5%
Federal workers	50,140
Military	25,585

ELECTIONS

STATE ELECTION OFFICIAL
(615) 741-7956
DEMOCRATIC PARTY
(615) 327-9779
REPUBLICAN PARTY
(615) 269-4260

MISCELLANEOUS

Web: www.tn.gov
Capital: Nashville

U.S. CONGRESS

Senate: 2 Republicans
House: 5 Democrats, 4 Republicans

2000 Census Statistics by District

DIST.	2008 VOTE FOR PRESIDENT OBAMA	MCCAIN	WHITE	BLACK	ASIAN	HISP	MEDIAN INCOME	WHITE COLLAR	BLUE COLLAR	SERVICE INDUSTRY	OVER 64	UNDER 18	COLLEGE EDUCATION	RURAL	SQ. MILES
1	29%	70%	95%	2%	0%	1%	$31,228	50%	35%	15%	15%	22%	15%	45%	4,093
2	34	64	90	6	1	1	$36,796	60	26	14	13	23	23	29	2,427
3	37	62	85	11	1	2	$35,434	54	32	14	14	23	19	36	3,411
4	34	64	93	4	0	2	$31,645	45	42	13	14	24	11	68	10,038
5	56	43	68	23	2	4	$40,419	64	22	14	11	23	28	11	894
6	37	62	89	6	1	3	$39,721	53	35	12	11	25	16	47	5,480
7	34	65	83	11	1	2	$50,090	64	24	12	10	27	29	39	6,292
8	43	56	74	22	0	2	$33,001	48	38	15	13	26	13	53	8,262
9	77	23	35	59	2	3	$33,806	60	24	15	11	27	22	0	321
STATE	42	57	79	16	1	2	$36,360	56	31	14	12	25	20	36	41,217
U.S.	53	46	69	12	4	13	$41,994	60	25	15	12	26	24	21	3,537,438

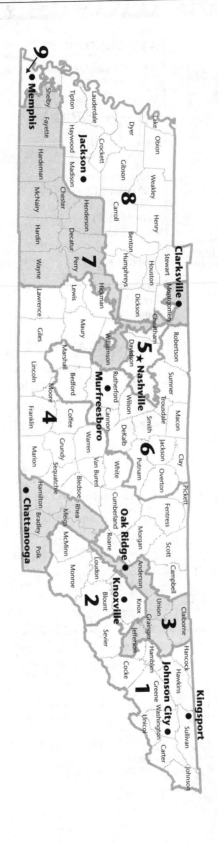

Sen. Lamar Alexander (R)

Elected 2002; 2nd term

CAPITOL OFFICE
224-4944
alexander.senate.gov
455 Dirksen Bldg. 20510-4204; fax 228-3398

COMMITTEES
Appropriations
Budget
Environment & Public Works
Health, Education, Labor & Pensions
Rules & Administration

RESIDENCE
Walland

BORN
July 3, 1940; Maryville, Tenn.

RELIGION
Presbyterian

FAMILY
Wife, Honey Alexander; four children

EDUCATION
Vanderbilt U., B.A. 1962 (Latin American history);
New York U., J.D. 1965

CAREER
Education consulting firm chairman; lobbyist;
university president; White House and
congressional aide; lawyer

POLITICAL HIGHLIGHTS
Republican nominee for governor, 1974;
governor, 1979-87; Education secretary,
1991-93; sought Republican nomination for
president, 1996, 2000

ELECTION RESULTS

2008 GENERAL

Lamar Alexander (R)	1,579,477	65.1%
Robert D. Tuke (D)	767,236	31.6%
Edward L. Buck (I)	31,631	1.3%

2008 PRIMARY

Lamar Alexander (R)	unopposed

PREVIOUS WINNING PERCENTAGES
2002 (54%)

Alexander portrayed himself as a folksy Washington outsider during his two unsuccessful presidential campaigns, but he is now in the thick of setting the Republican legislative agenda as Senate Republican Conference chairman. He seeks to develop consensus among his colleagues and then communicate their message — no small tasks in an age when Democrats control Congress and the terms of debate.

Alexander believes Republicans must cooperate with Democrats on areas of mutual agreement while outlining how they would do things differently if they were in the majority. To that end, he unveiled a multipronged GOP agenda in 2008 that included promoting universal access to health care, normally a Democratic plank. He also wants his party to be a player on the environment, and repeatedly calls for a "new Manhattan Project" centered on research and development of a raft of low-carbon energy initiatives, as well as an expansion of nuclear power.

Alexander's approach pleases his moderate colleagues. But some hardline conservatives have privately grumbled it can downplay some of the more defining (and divisive) issues on the GOP agenda — such as tax cuts, border security and curbs on earmarking federal funds for specific projects — that often energize the party's base. To mollify those lawmakers, Alexander seeks to let their voices be heard. North Carolina's Richard M. Burr, his rival for the conference chairmanship, was assigned to manage promotion of the GOP health care plan. And Oklahoma's James M. Inhofe was given time at a party caucus to explain his opposition to climate change legislation.

Alexander also took a hard line against President Obama's economic initiatives in early 2009, complaining his party had no input into Obama's $787 billion economic stimulus law. Despite the new president's meetings with GOP lawmakers, Alexander said Obama would have to do more than engage in "a nice social visit." He added: "If this administration wants to get 20 Republicans, he's going to have to lose 10 Democrats."

Alexander subsequently helped GOP leaders ensure that no members of their party backed Obama's fiscal 2010 budget. And he led an effort to maintain a student lending program that the administration proposed ending.

Alexander was elected to the conference chairmanship in December 2007, after Senate GOP Whip Trent Lott's announcement of his resignation from Congress. Conference Chairman Jon Kyl of Arizona moved into the whip's job, putting Alexander in a race with the younger and more conservative Burr. He trounced Burr by a vote of 31-16, drawing support from many of his older colleagues as well as younger moderates.

For Alexander, the post represents a long-sought opportunity to apply the experience and knowledge he accumulated as governor of Tennessee and as secretary of Education. He went after the whip post — the No. 2 leadership position — shortly after entering the Senate in 2003, campaigning as an optimistic, pragmatic conservative. But he couldn't fight off a last-minute challenge from Lott, a former majority leader who pulled off a stunning one-vote victory in November 2006.

As a consolation prize of sorts, GOP leader Mitch McConnell of Kentucky named Alexander to a coveted seat on the Appropriations Committee. The assignment enables him to have a direct say in funding of the education, energy and environmental issues on which he spends most of his time.

Alexander carefully looks after the interests of the Tennessee Valley Authority, a power wholesaler, and his state's Oak Ridge National Laboratory while pushing an agenda that would greatly boost the amount of money spent on physical sciences. He tries to build support for advanced computing initiatives at Oak Ridge, which has been involved in developing high-end supercomputers.

Alexander also sits on the Rules and Administration Committee as well as the Environment and Public Works panel. He joined Delaware Democrat Thomas R. Carper on a 2009 bill to impose stiffer controls on sulfur, nitrogen and mercury emissions from coal-fired power plants. Though he supports a "cap and trade" plan to reduce carbon emissions that contribute to global warming, he said any new revenues from an emissions credit funding trading program "ought to be given directly back to the American people and not put into some massive slush fund in Washington for politicians to spend."

Alexander, who served two terms as Tennessee's governor, has emerged as one of the most ardent advocates for state and local governments in Washington. During debate on the overhaul of the Higher Education Act in 2008, he joined state legislators who unsuccessfully sought to block a provision to penalize states that diminish their overall higher education funding.

Alexander once served a stint as president of the University of Tennessee and as secretary of Education, making the Health, Education, Labor and Pensions Committee a natural fit. One of his proudest accomplishments is a bipartisan law aimed at maintaining U.S. leadership in science and technology by boosting funding for research and education in those fields. Although he called the measure "the most important piece of legislation in this session for our country's future," he lamented that it drew little attention when President George W. Bush signed it into law in 2007.

A seventh-generation Tennessean, Alexander was born and raised in the state's mountainous east. He worked his way through Vanderbilt University, where, as a student newspaper editor, he led a campaign to desegregate the school. After graduating with a degree in Latin American history, he earned a law degree at New York University. An accomplished musician, he played trombone, tuba and washboard at a Bourbon Street nightclub while clerking for a federal judge in New Orleans.

His first run for office, at age 34, was an unsuccessful 1974 bid for governor against Democrat Roy Blanton. Four years later, with the help and advice of his mentor and friend, Senate GOP leader Howard H. Baker Jr. of Tennessee, Alexander ran again. This time, he gained national attention by traversing the state on foot — he is a lifelong hiker — in what would become his trademark red-and-black plaid shirt. Voters liked it, electing him with 56 percent of the vote.

During eight years as governor, Alexander built a reputation as a pragmatist who lured businesses to Tennessee and pushed a major education package through a Democratic-controlled General Assembly. He then spent more than three years as the chief executive of Tennessee's state university system. He joined President George Bush's Cabinet in 1991, serving as secretary of Education for two years.

Alexander geared up for the 1996 presidential election, but his campaign foundered when he had a hard time coming up with memorable campaign themes. He dropped out soon after finishing third behind Kansas Sen. Robert Dole and Patrick J. Buchanan in the New Hampshire primary. He set his sights on the 2000 nomination but stopped campaigning in the summer of 1999, when George W. Bush had become the clear front-runner.

Two years later, when Fred Thompson announced he was retiring after eight years in the Senate, Republicans looked to Alexander to take his place. In a bitter race against then-Rep. Bob Clement, Alexander won by 10 percentage points. He had an even easier time in 2008 prevailing over Robert D. Tuke, a former state Democratic Party chairman.

KEY VOTES

2008
Yes Prohibit discrimination based on genetic information
Yes Reauthorize farm and nutrition programs for five years
No Limit debate on "cap and trade" system for greenhouse gas emissions
No Allow lawsuits against companies that participated in warrantless wiretapping
Yes Limit debate on a bill to block a scheduled cut in Medicare payments to doctors
Yes Grant mortgage relief to homeowners and funding for Fannie Mae and Freddie Mac
Yes Approve a nuclear cooperation agreement with India
Yes Approve final $700 billion program to stabilize financial markets
 – Allow consideration of a $14 billion auto industry loan package

2007
Yes Increase minimum wage by $2.10 an hour
No Limit debate on a comprehensive immigration bill
Yes Overhaul congressional lobbying and ethics rules for members and their staffs
No Limit debate on considering a bill to add House seats for the District of Columbia and Utah
No Limit debate on restoring habeas corpus rights to detainees
No Mandate minimum breaks for troops between deployments to Iraq or Afghanistan
Yes Override Bush veto of $23.2 billion water projects authorization bill
 + Confirm Michael B. Mukasey as attorney general
No Limit debate on an energy policy overhaul containing $21.8 billion in tax incentives and reduced oil and gas subsidies

CQ VOTE STUDIES

	PARTY UNITY		PRESIDENTIAL SUPPORT	
	SUPPORT	OPPOSE	SUPPORT	OPPOSE
2008	92%	8%	77%	23%
2007	84%	16%	79%	21%
2006	94%	6%	93%	7%
2005	92%	8%	88%	12%
2004	95%	5%	98%	2%
2003	98%	2%	98%	2%

INTEREST GROUPS

	AFL-CIO	ADA	CCUS	ACU
2008	11%	25%	75%	72%
2007	21%	20%	82%	76%
2006	20%	5%	92%	72%
2005	21%	5%	100%	88%
2004	0%	15%	94%	92%
2003	0%	10%	100%	85%

Sen. Bob Corker (R)

Elected 2006; 1st term

CAPITOL OFFICE
224-3344
corker.senate.gov
185 Dirksen Bldg. 20510-4205; fax 228-0566

COMMITTEES
Banking, Housing & Urban Affairs
Energy & Natural Resources
Foreign Relations
Special Aging

RESIDENCE
Chattanooga

BORN
Aug. 24, 1952; Orangeburg, S.C.

RELIGION
Protestant

FAMILY
Wife, Elizabeth Corker; two children

EDUCATION
U. of Tennessee, B.S. 1974
(industrial management)

CAREER
Commercial real estate developer;
construction company owner

POLITICAL HIGHLIGHTS
Sought Republican nomination for U.S. Senate,
1994; Tenn. Finance and Administration
Department commissioner, 1995-96;
mayor of Chattanooga, 2001-05

ELECTION RESULTS

2006 GENERAL

Bob Corker (R)	929,911	50.7%
Harold E. Ford Jr. (D)	879,976	48.0%

2006 PRIMARY

Bob Corker (R)	231,541	48.1%
Ed Bryant (R)	161,189	33.5%
Van Hilleary (R)	83,078	17.3%
Tate Harrison (R)	5,309	1.1%

In his first term, Corker has proved to be a hard-working, serious legislator who has won respect from senior lawmakers of both parties. Even though Republicans have lost clout, Corker has positioned himself as a dealmaker and swing vote on issues from financial regulation to health care and energy.

Corker is a workaholic; in the mid-1990s, he sometimes started his workdays as Tennessee's finance commissioner at 4 a.m. "Now, I wake up and begin cramming. I delve into policy as much as I can," he said in 2008. "I'm being a student so I can influence the outcome." Still, he finds his new job frustrating at times, especially after spending four years as mayor of Chattanooga. "Being mayor, you're able to create a vision and make it real," he said. "It's like being CEO of a company. Being in the Senate is like being on the board of directors. You don't see that immediate impact."

As a freshman Republican on the Banking, Housing and Urban Affairs Committee, the wealthy former real estate developer played a central role in two major debates of 2008. He helped write the $700 billion financial sector rescue package, and he was the GOP negotiator on a failed bill to help ailing U.S. automakers. Banking Chairman Christopher J. Dodd, a Connecticut Democrat who had invited Corker to participate in the financial rescue negotiations, called him "knowledgeable, thoughtful [and] pragmatic."

Corker pressed for the $700 billion to be doled out in installments, an idea that became part of the law. But when Congress voted in 2009 to release the second half of the funds, Corker voted no, saying the Obama administration had failed to provide specifics on how the money would be used. Corker and Democrat Mark Pryor of Arkansas introduced legislation to require the Treasury Department to provide greater detail about how banks were using the taxpayer dollars they received.

On the auto bailout bill, Corker offered a last-ditch proposal that would have required deep concessions from General Motors Corp. and Chrysler LLC bondholders and the United Auto Workers. The legislation ultimately failed, but Corker's conditions were adopted by outgoing President George W. Bush when he provided $13.4 billion in emergency loans to GM and Chrysler to keep them operating into 2009.

Corker brought his bipartisan approach to energy policy as an original member of the "Gang of 10," a group of five Democrats and five Republicans who pushed unsuccessfully for an energy plan during the 110th Congress (2007-08) that included oil drilling, coal-to-liquid production and energy conservation. In the 111th Congress (2009-10), he is seen as a pivotal vote when the Senate addresses climate change legislation. "We have to do something, when we do it, that drives our economy, that adds to our GDP, that makes us more energy-secure and deals with climate at the same time," he said.

Corker generally supports his party; in his first two years, he sided with the GOP 88 percent of the time on votes in which most of the party diverged from the majority of Democrats. But he and fellow Tennessee Republican Lamar Alexander split with their GOP colleagues early in 2009 to support an expansion of the State Children's Health Insurance Program that carried a long-sought provision to allow a Memphis regional hospital to be reimbursed by Arkansas and Mississippi for treating uninsured patients from those states.

While he is a fiscal conservative, Corker doesn't shy away from seeking funds for his state, such as a $60 million grant for supercomputing that he and Alexander got for the University of Tennessee in 2007. "It's a very interesting balance," Corker said. "To the extent that you don't make requests for your state — all of ours have been real tangible — everyone knows it just goes to another state."

Corker, who was born in South Carolina, moved to Chattanooga when he was 11 after his father, a DuPont engineer, was transferred there. He adjusted quickly and was president of his senior class in high school. He worked a variety of jobs as a teenager, earned a college degree in industrial management, then took a job as a construction superintendent. He loved being outdoors and working with his hands. College friends with coat-and-tie jobs were shocked when they would visit him on a job site. "I might not have shaved. I was drinking day-old coffee," he said. "I had mud all over me."

After four years, he started his own construction company with a pickup truck and $8,000 in savings. By the time he sold the company in 1990, it was operating in 18 states, with projects ranging from strip malls to apartments. He also owned Corker Group, a successful real estate development company, which he sold in 2006, retaining just two properties.

Corker's views on public policy were shaped by his work experience and his religion. In business, he felt a light hand from government was best. A church mission to Haiti in the 1980s opened his eyes to poverty and led him on an internal debate about whether he could make a bigger difference in public service or in the private sector. He began working weekends back home to revitalize inner-city neighborhoods, then started a nonprofit organization to help families secure affordable housing.

Corker first ran for the Senate in 1994, losing the primary to Bill Frist, who went on to become the Senate Republican leader. Corker had initially planned to run for governor that year but deferred to GOP Rep. Don Sundquist, who won the election and made him state finance commissioner. During his 1995-96 stint in that job, Corker spent about 80 percent of his time on health care, developing expertise he is likely to build on in the Senate.

Elected mayor of Chattanooga in 2001, Corker launched a successful $120 million effort to transform the city's waterfront with a new park, a river walk, museum expansions and other features. Three years into his mayoral service, he was invited to join Frist and the senator's two young sons on their annual hike. Along the way, the GOP leader convinced Corker that he should consider running for the Senate, as Frist was retiring.

Corker entered the primary as an underdog against two former GOP congressmen — Van Hilleary and Ed Bryant. They painted him as a moderate who had been inconsistent on abortion, which they strongly opposed. But Corker poured his own money into the race, and his branding as the only "non-career politician" in the field helped him. Corker won handily.

Democrats had cleared a path for Rep. Harold Ford Jr., a five-term centrist from Memphis who was seeking to become the first popularly elected African-American senator from the South. Corker emphasized his faith and his conservative values and made a pitch for votes from ordinary Tennesseans, including Democrats, by talking about his days "pouring concrete."

The race turned nasty with a late October television ad by the Republican National Committee satirizing Ford's supposed attendance at a Super Bowl party sponsored by Playboy. The ad closed with a white woman winking and saying, "Harold, call me." Democrats and civil rights groups erupted in anger, calling the ad racist. Corker's campaign denounced the ad and asked the RNC to yank the commercial, but had no authority to do anything.

The election contest went down to the wire, with late polls often in conflict about who was ahead and by how much. When the votes were counted, Corker had won by just under 3 percentage points. The first bill Corker introduced in the Senate was a measure to, among other things, give a candidate control over campaign ads on his behalf.

KEY VOTES

2008

Yes Prohibit discrimination based on genetic information

Yes Reauthorize farm and nutrition programs for five years

No Limit debate on "cap and trade" system for greenhouse gas emissions

No Allow lawsuits against companies that participated in warrantless wiretapping

Yes Limit debate on a bill to block a scheduled cut in Medicare payments to doctors

No Grant mortgage relief to homeowners and funding for Fannie Mae and Freddie Mac

Yes Approve a nuclear cooperation agreement with India

Yes Approve final $700 billion program to stabilize financial markets

No Allow consideration of a $14 billion auto industry loan package

2007

Yes Increase minimum wage by $2.10 an hour

No Limit debate on a comprehensive immigration bill

Yes Overhaul congressional lobbying and ethics rules for members and their staffs

No Limit debate on considering a bill to add House seats for the District of Columbia and Utah

No Limit debate on restoring habeas corpus rights to detainees

No Mandate minimum breaks for troops between deployments to Iraq or Afghanistan

Yes Override Bush veto of $23.2 billion water projects authorization bill

Yes Confirm Michael B. Mukasey as attorney general

No Limit debate on an energy policy overhaul containing $21.8 billion in tax incentives and reduced oil and gas subsidies

CQ VOTE STUDIES

	PARTY UNITY		PRESIDENTIAL SUPPORT	
	SUPPORT	OPPOSE	SUPPORT	OPPOSE
2008	90%	10%	72%	28%
2007	87%	13%	83%	17%

INTEREST GROUPS

	AFL-CIO	ADA	CCUS	ACU
2008	10%	20%	75%	83%
2007	26%	20%	82%	83%

Rep. Phil Roe (R)

Elected 2008; 1st term

An obstetrician who served in the Army Medical Corps, Roe was the first candidate in Tennessee in 42 years to defeat an incumbent congressman in a primary. He casts himself as a principled but pragmatic conservative who seeks to balance the federal budget but also invest in infrastructure that benefits his district.

Roe is a member of the Republican Study Committee, the coalition of the most conservative House Republicans, and opposed President Obama's early economic initiatives. Roe told a local audience in February 2009 that the federal government could not keep up with money paid out from the $700 billion financial industry rescue passed in fall 2008. "If I sent my kids to McDonald's with a $100 bill and they bought a couple hamburgers, I'd want to know where the change is…Right now, we don't know where the [financial rescue] change is," he said.

Roe retired after practicing medicine for more than three decades. A member of the Education and Labor Committee, he said he wants to draw attention to risks such as obesity and smoking and improve health care access without adding government paperwork or rules.

Roe also serves on the Veterans' Affairs Committee, where he is the top Republican on the Oversight and Investigations panel. He said he wants to work to ensure generous treatment of those returning from war. His other committee assignment is Agriculture.

Roe's political career began in 2003 when he was elected to the Johnson City Board of Commissioners, where after four years he was elected by the commission to serve as mayor. As both a commissioner and mayor, Roe boasts of passing six balanced budgets while cutting spending and not increasing taxes.

Roe first competed in the GOP primary in 2006 to replace retiring Republican Rep. Bill Jenkins, but came in fourth, losing to David Davis, who won the seat. Roe ran again two years later, attacking Davis for earmarks — funding set-asides for member districts — and ties to oil companies. He won the primary by only 482 votes before winning easily in November.

CAPITOL OFFICE
225-6356
roe.house.gov
419 Cannon Bldg. 20515-4201; fax 225-5714

COMMITTEES
Agriculture
Education & Labor
Veterans' Affairs

RESIDENCE
Johnson City

BORN
July 21, 1945; Clarksville, Tenn.

RELIGION
Methodist

FAMILY
Wife, Pam Roe; three children

EDUCATION
Austin Peay State U., B.S. 1967 (biology);
U. of Tennessee, M.D. 1973

MILITARY SERVICE
Army Medical Corps, 1973-74

CAREER
Physician

POLITICAL HIGHLIGHTS
Johnson City Board of Commissioners, 2003-09
(mayor, 2007-09); sought Republican nomination
for U.S. House, 2006

ELECTION RESULTS

2008 GENERAL

Phil Roe (R)	168,343	71.8%
Rob Russell (D)	57,525	24.5%
Joel Goodman (I)	3,988	1.7%
James W. Reeves (I)	2,544	1.1%

2008 PRIMARY

Phil Roe (R)	25,993	50.1%
David Davis (R)	25,511	49.2%

TENNESSEE 1

Northeast – Tri-cities, Morristown

Rolling hills and mountains cover the 1st, which combines a manufacturing sector to the east with smaller agricultural and tourism centers to the west and south.

Near Virginia, the Tri-Cities of Kingsport, Johnson City and Bristol anchor the district's economy. They focus their energies on chemicals, auto parts and drug manufacturing, although recent layoffs and retail sales slowdowns have hurt economic growth in the region. East Tennessee State University in Johnson City is a key employer and a medical hub for much of this part of Appalachia. To the northwest, Hancock County is severely impoverished. Farmers in Washington, Cocke and Greene counties raise livestock, tobacco and fruit, providing one of the only sources of economic stability here.

Hamblen County offers outdoor recreation, and Morristown, which is known for its Civil War heritage, also has popular watersports sites. Farther south, tourists visit the Great Smoky Mountains National Park and the excursion circuit of outlet shopping malls and neon-lit amusement parks. Gatlinburg's Star Cars Museum houses famous cars from movies, and the Dollywood theme park in Pigeon Forge lures millions of tourists.

East Tennessee's strong GOP lean dates to the Civil War. In 2008, John McCain won the district with 70 percent of its presidential vote, his highest percentage statewide, and he did not take less than 65 percent of the vote in any of the 1st's dozen counties.

MAJOR INDUSTRY
Tourism, health care, manufacturing, farming

CITIES
Johnson City, 55,469; Kingsport, 44,905; Morristown, 24,965; Bristol, 24,821

NOTABLE
Jonesborough, the state's oldest settlement, is home to the National Storytelling Festival.

Rep. John J. "Jimmy" Duncan Jr. (R)

Elected 1988; 11th full term

CAPITOL OFFICE
225-5435
www.house.gov/duncan
2207 Rayburn Bldg. 20515-4202; fax 225-6440

COMMITTEES
Natural Resources
Oversight & Government Reform
Transportation & Infrastructure

RESIDENCE
Knoxville

BORN
July 21, 1947; Lebanon, Tenn.

RELIGION
Presbyterian

FAMILY
Wife, Lynn Duncan; four children

EDUCATION
U. of Tennessee, B.S. 1969 (journalism);
George Washington U., J.D. 1973

MILITARY SERVICE
Tenn. National Guard and Army Reserve, 1970-87

CAREER
Judge; lawyer

POLITICAL HIGHLIGHTS
Knox County Criminal Court judge, 1981-88

ELECTION RESULTS

2008 GENERAL

John J. "Jimmy" Duncan Jr. (R)	227,120	78.1%
Bob Scott (D)	63,639	21.9%

2008 PRIMARY

John J. "Jimmy" Duncan Jr. (R)	unopposed

2006 GENERAL

John J. "Jimmy" Duncan Jr. (R)	157,095	77.7%
John Greene (D)	45,025	22.3%

PREVIOUS WINNING PERCENTAGES
2004 (79%); 2002 (79%); 2000 (89%); 1998 (89%);
1996 (71%); 1994 (90%); 1992 (72%); 1990 (81%);
1988 (56%); 1988 Special Election (56%)

Duncan is an old-fashioned lawmaker who eschews cell phones, e-mail and the sort of party discipline that's a prerequisite for advancement in the House GOP caucus. He was an early skeptic about the war in Iraq and has regularly chastised both parties for overspending, including on defense and homeland security.

He has found that his advancement has been thwarted by his own failure to be a loyal Republican foot soldier. "I do have an independent, contrarian streak in me," said Duncan, who insists that, like him, many natives of East Tennessee "march to the beat of a different drummer."

GOP leaders in 2007 passed over Duncan and three others on the seniority ladder for top Republican spot on the Transportation and Infrastructure Committee in favor of John L. Mica of Florida, a party loyalist. He previously was bypassed for the chairmanship of the Resources Committee at the start of the 108th Congress (2003-04). And in the 111th Congress (2009-10), he remains the fourth-ranking Republican on that panel, now called the Natural Resources Committee. Despite the move of Alaska's Don Young from the top Republican spot, Duncan failed to even move up the ladder. Young's spot went to Washington state's Doc Hastings, a more reliable party man.

But as the top-ranking Republican on the Transportation and Infrastructure Committee's Highways and Transit panel, Duncan could still play a major role in helping craft a new highway and surface transportation bill in the 111th.

He has charted his path in Congress using as a guide the experience of his father, John J. Duncan, who held the eastern Tennessee seat for more than 23 years before he did. When Republicans took control of Congress in 1994, Duncan passed up a seat on the Ways and Means Committee, where his father served for two decades without ever being a chairman, because he thought he'd have a better shot at a top slot on Transportation and Infrastructure.

His independence was evident when Duncan was one of just six Republicans to vote in 2002 against authorizing President George W. Bush to go to war against Iraq and one of 17 in his party to vote in 2007 to oppose the president's decision to send more than 21,000 additional U.S. troops to the area. Ron Paul of Texas is the only other Republican still in the House who voted the same way on both occasions. In 2003, angry the administration wasn't pushing Iraq to pick up some of the reconstruction tab, Duncan was one of five GOP House members to vote against a war funding bill.

And in April 2009, he was one of 10 Republicans to vote in favor of the Democrats' bill to curb employee bonuses at companies receiving federal money from the 2008 law to rescue the financial services industry.

A fiscal conservative, Duncan voted against that $700 billion law, as he did a subsequent bill — which ultimately failed — to bail out the auto industry. "We would come out of our economic problems much sooner if we let the free market work," he said.

He often votes against spending bills he regards as bloated — including President Obama's $787 billion economic stimulus law and his $3.56 trillion budget blueprint for 2010. Duncan voted no on a catchall fiscal 2009 spending bill even though it included more than $10.3 million for projects and programs he sought for his district. In 1997, he voted to abolish crop insurance subsidies for tobacco, even though it was the largest cash crop grown by East Tennessee farmers.

There's something else Duncan doesn't spend much money on: communications technology. He doesn't carry a BlackBerry, rarely uses a cell phone and said he considers computers "the biggest time-wasters in the world."

As chairman of the Transportation Subcommittee on Water Resources and Environment during the 109th Congress (2005-06), he was unable to win enactment of a huge water resources bill, which stalled in conference with the Senate. In April 2007, the committee's Democratic leaders quickly pushed through the House a revised version that included $45 million in projects in Duncan's district that hadn't been in the previous measure.

Duncan earlier chaired the Aviation Subcommittee and helped write the aviation security law enacted two months after the Sept. 11 terrorist attacks. The measure required tighter screening at airports, better equipment to detect explosives and stronger cockpit doors.

From his Natural Resources panel seat, Duncan contends out-of-control conservationists "will absolutely destroy our standard of living. Unfortunately, we cannot turn our entire nation into a giant tourist attraction." He supports opening Alaska's Arctic National Wildlife Refuge to oil drilling and ending a moratorium on most offshore oil and gas exploration.

Duncan also serves on the Oversight and Government Reform Committee. In early 2007, he cheered passage of legislation requiring public disclosure of big-dollar donors to presidential libraries. He had been trying to win passage of similar legislation since the 106th Congress (1999-2000), inspired by what he considered questionable contributions to the library of President Clinton. Duncan felt vindicated when Clinton released in 2008 details of his donor rolls that included many foreign governments and business interests.

Previously a supporter of free-trade agreements, he said he has become increasingly concerned about domestic job losses to overseas manufacturers. He voted against the 2007 Peru free-trade agreement.

Duncan's father was part of a business group that brought minor league baseball to Knoxville in 1956. Young Duncan spent five and a half happy seasons as the Smokies' batboy and was the public address announcer during his first year in college. Then his father switched to politics, and Jimmy Duncan followed in his footsteps.

The younger Duncan served seven years as a criminal court judge in Knox County, helping build a reputation to run for office in his own right when his father, in failing health, announced that the 100th Congress (1987-88) would be his last. His father died in 1988, shortly after that announcement.

In his first House race, Duncan campaigned primarily as his father's successor, even appearing on the ballot as John J. Duncan, though he goes by Jimmy. He won 56 percent of the vote in both the special and general elections that year and has not been seriously challenged since.

KEY VOTES

2008

No Delay consideration of Colombia free-trade agreement

No Override Bush veto of federal farm and nutrition programs reauthorization bill

Yes Overhaul surveillance laws and permit dismissal of suits against companies that conducted warrantless wiretapping

No Grant mortgage relief to homeowners and funding for Fannie Mae and Freddie Mac

No Approve initial $700 billion program to stabilize financial markets

No Approve final $700 billion program to stabilize financial markets

No Provide $14 billion in loans to automakers

2007

Yes Increase minimum wage by $2.10 an hour

No Approve $124.2 billion in emergency war spending and set goal for redeployment of troops from Iraq

Yes Reject federal contraceptive assistance to international family planning groups

Yes Override Bush veto of $23.2 billion water projects authorization bill

No Implement Peru free-trade agreement

No Approve energy policy overhaul with new fuel economy standards

No Clear $473.5 billion omnibus spending bill, including $70 billion for military operations

CQ VOTE STUDIES

	PARTY UNITY		PRESIDENTIAL SUPPORT	
	SUPPORT	OPPOSE	SUPPORT	OPPOSE
2008	94%	6%	67%	33%
2007	94%	6%	73%	27%
2006	89%	11%	74%	26%
2005	93%	7%	72%	28%
2004	92%	8%	82%	18%

INTEREST GROUPS

	AFL-CIO	ADA	CCUS	ACU
2008	0%	15%	72%	84%
2007	13%	20%	70%	84%
2006	14%	10%	87%	88%
2005	20%	5%	81%	92%
2004	20%	5%	90%	88%

TENNESSEE 2
East – Knoxville

Nestled in the valley of the Great Smoky Mountains at the mouth of the Tennessee River, the 2nd envelops Knoxville and stretches south and west to include several conservative, rural counties. The district's economy is almost solely determined by the success of Knoxville, while surrounding areas are full of small towns and forests, lakes and parks.

State budget shortfalls have threatened government- and state-funded higher education jobs, a sector that area residents have relied on for economic stability despite their criticisms of big government year after year. Restaurants, hotels and other businesses in the district still depend on revenue from the influx of people who attend sporting events at the University of Tennessee, which is located in Knoxville. In fact, on football game days, the university's Neyland Stadium surpasses the population of the state's sixth-largest city, holding more than 104,000 orange-and-white-clad fans. The university's basketball arena and the Women's Basketball Hall of Fame also draw significant crowds.

Knoxville had struggled for years to revitalize its downtown, but state and private medical facilities have spurred some economic growth, and redevelopment plans continue. Rejuvenated areas of the city, such as historic Market Street, now attract many tourists. The district's less-populous rural regions provide a tourist destination outside of Knoxville's orbit and continue to lure visitors to mountain locales.

Like all of East Tennessee, the 2nd has a long history of voting Republican, and the district has not sent a Democrat to the U.S. House since before the Civil War. Downtown Knoxville, which includes much of the city's black population and is the only real Democratic pocket, could not prevent John McCain from taking surrounding Knox County by 23 percentage points in the 2008 presidential election. He exceeded his Knox County percentage in each of the 2nd's other counties.

MAJOR INDUSTRY
Higher education, medical services, tourism, government

CITIES
Knoxville, 173,890; Maryville, 23,120; Farragut, 17,720; Athens, 13,220

NOTABLE
A statue in Haley Heritage Square honors "Roots" author Alex Haley; The town of Alcoa is named after the company whose plant there produces enough aluminum every minute to make 75,000 beverage cans.

Rep. Zach Wamp (R)

Elected 1994; 8th term

CAPITOL OFFICE
225-3271
www.house.gov/wamp
1436 Longworth Bldg. 20515-4203; fax 225-3494

COMMITTEES
Appropriations

RESIDENCE
Chattanooga

BORN
Oct. 28, 1957; Fort Benning, Ga.

RELIGION
Baptist

FAMILY
Wife, Kim Wamp; two children

EDUCATION
U. of North Carolina, attended 1977-78
(industrial relations); U. of Tennessee, attended
1978-79; U. of North Carolina, attended 1979-80
(political science)

CAREER
Real estate broker

POLITICAL HIGHLIGHTS
Republican nominee for U.S. House, 1992

ELECTION RESULTS

2008 GENERAL

Zach Wamp (R)	184,964	69.4%
Doug Vandagriff (D)	73,059	27.4%
Jean Howard-Hill (I)	4,848	1.8%
Ed Choate (I)	3,750	1.4%

2008 PRIMARY

Zach Wamp (R)	31,782	91.0%
Teresa Sheppard (R)	3,125	9.0%

2006 GENERAL

Zach Wamp (R)	130,791	65.7%
Brent Benedict (D)	68,324	34.3%

PREVIOUS WINNING PERCENTAGES
2004 (65%); 2002 (65%); 2000 (64%); 1998 (66%);
1996 (56%); 1994 (52%)

Wamp is an independent-minded conservative with an active agenda on energy, government reform and other issues. Though his rebellious ways once angered GOP leaders, he has seen a rebound in his popularity and influence.

Wamp hopes to translate that rebound into a bid for Tennessee's governorship in 2010. He announced his intentions in early January 2009 following a decision by former Republican Senate Majority Leader Bill Frist — a better-known figure statewide — not to run. Current Democratic Gov. Phil Bredesen is term-limited and cannot run again.

Wamp came to Congress as one of the "Contract With America" Republicans elected in 1994, and during his career he has shown flashes of the old revolutionary spirit. He drew the line after House Republicans voted in November 2004 to change their ethics rules in a way that could have allowed then-Majority Leader Tom DeLay to retain his leadership post if indicted in his home state of Texas. Wamp warned he and other Republicans might break ranks on one of the first votes of the 109th Congress (2005-06). DeLay and other GOP leaders backed off.

Wamp had a history of challenging DeLay on other matters and paid a stiff price. "You almost have to be me every day to feel it and see it and know they're not going to help you and you're not going to get advanced and the staff is all told that Zach Wamp's a rebel and he's not always with the team ... It took me a while to recover," he said in 2008.

Not that Wamp has become a conformist. He was among 61 Republicans supporting a Democratic measure in July 2008 aimed at curbing oil speculators who were blamed for driving up energy costs. The bill fell short of the two-thirds majority needed to pass. GOP leaders had opposed any bill that didn't allow oil drilling, but Wamp said they couldn't claim to back "all of the above" solutions without heeding the other side of the aisle. "Frankly, I think my party is starting to hurt our own position because if you're not going to vote for these Democratic proposals, then you can't say you're for all of the above," he told the Chattanooga Times Free Press.

He looks out for the Tennessee Valley Authority and Oak Ridge National Laboratory in his district. Since 2001, he has co-chaired the Renewable Energy and Energy Efficiency Caucus. Many of his ideas to provide tax incentives for wind, solar and other sources were included in the 2005 energy law.

He is among the few members of the conservative Republican Study Committee (RSC) to also sit on the Appropriations Committee, where he is the top Republican on the Military Construction-VA Subcommittee and a member of the Energy-Water panel. Some RSC members grouse at appropriators for being too free-spending, but Wamp takes the opposite view; he lamented in September 2008 that many bills for fiscal 2009 were funded at "flat spending levels."

Wamp joined 10 other RSC members in opposing the initial $700 billion proposal to shore up the ailing financial services industry in fall 2008, calling it a political "stink bomb." But he supported a reworked version that passed and was subsequently signed into law, saying he saw a serious threat to the nation's economy through continued inaction. In December of that year, he voted against a $14 billion plan to bail out the auto industry, saying he preferred a Republican alternative that he said "would establish firm benchmarks and a tight timeline for the Detroit automakers to restructure."

In early 2009, Wamp stuck with his party to oppose a $787 billion economic stimulus law and President Obama's $3.56 trillion budget blueprint for fiscal 2010. To address one of the RSC's biggest priorities, in December 2008 he joined a special GOP committee to curb earmarks — funding set-asides for projects in members' districts. But Wamp said he's not against all earmarking. Total elimination would "require some kind of constitutional challenge," he said.

Wamp regularly collaborates with Democrats. He worked with Illinois' Jesse L. Jackson Jr. on a 2007 law to name the Capitol's largest space Emancipation Hall. He and fellow Tennessean John Tanner introduced a bill to turn the redistricting process over to commissions, instead of state legislatures, in order to stem the practice of gerrymandering. And he worked with Minnesota's Keith Ellison to push through the House in 2008 a bill to promote an interfaith dialogue among Christian, Jewish and Muslim leaders.

Religion has played a big role in Wamp's life since 1984, when he was addicted to cocaine and alcohol and his life appeared to be headed nowhere. He attended a rehabilitation clinic and became a "spiritual man" in both his personal life and career. He is devoted to the House Prayer Breakfast, where several dozen members from both parties meet weekly to sing hymns, discuss their problems and pray.

His interests and voting record put him in the heart of the conservative mainstream. He belongs to the House Pro-Life Caucus and is a reliable vote for tax cuts. He voted in both 2004 and 2006 in favor of a constitutional amendment to prohibit same-sex marriage.

He is an avid believer in physical fitness and is the co-founder, along with Colorado Democratic Sen. Mark Udall, of the Congressional Fitness Caucus. He runs five to seven miles four days a week, but has cut down on basketball and football due to shoulder and hand injuries.

Wamp was raised in a Democratic family with deep roots in Southern politics. His great-great-great-grandfather spent 40 years in the Alabama legislature, and his great-uncle was a leader in the Alabama General Assembly. Wamp voted for Jimmy Carter in 1976 but entered the GOP fold four years later, concluding Ronald Reagan offered a "breath of hope and optimism for America" in the depths of the Iran hostage crisis.

Wamp won his first election in high school, as student body president. At 26, he became the youth coordinator for a victorious Chattanooga mayoral candidate. Four years later, he chaired his local GOP organization. Community leaders and his wife encouraged Wamp, a real estate broker, to run for office. He came within 3,000 votes of unseating Democratic Rep. Marilyn Lloyd in 1992. When Lloyd retired in 1994, Wamp won with 52 percent of the vote. He has won each re-election since with ease.

KEY VOTES

2008

No	Delay consideration of Colombia free-trade agreement
No	Override Bush veto of federal farm and nutrition programs reauthorization bill
Yes	Overhaul surveillance laws and permit dismissal of suits against companies that conducted warrantless wiretapping
No	Grant mortgage relief to homeowners and funding for Fannie Mae and Freddie Mac
No	Approve initial $700 billion program to stabilize financial markets
Yes	Approve final $700 billion program to stabilize financial markets
No	Provide $14 billion in loans to automakers

2007

Yes	Increase minimum wage by $2.10 an hour
No	Approve $124.2 billion in emergency war spending and set goal for redeployment of troops from Iraq
Yes	Reject federal contraceptive assistance to international family planning groups
Yes	Override Bush veto of $23.2 billion water projects authorization bill
Yes	Implement Peru free-trade agreement
Yes	Approve energy policy overhaul with new fuel economy standards
Yes	Clear $473.5 billion omnibus spending bill, including $70 billion for military operations

CQ VOTE STUDIES

	PARTY UNITY		PRESIDENTIAL SUPPORT	
	SUPPORT	OPPOSE	SUPPORT	OPPOSE
2008	96%	4%	70%	30%
2007	93%	7%	80%	20%
2006	95%	5%	87%	13%
2005	94%	6%	87%	13%
2004	93%	7%	79%	21%

INTEREST GROUPS

	AFL-CIO	ADA	CCUS	ACU
2008	7%	15%	100%	96%
2007	17%	20%	75%	92%
2006	14%	5%	87%	88%
2005	20%	0%	88%	88%
2004	13%	0%	100%	88%

TENNESSEE 3

East — Chattanooga, Oak Ridge

From the borders of Kentucky and Virginia to its north and Georgia and North Carolina to its south, the 3rd spans the height of Tennessee. Chattanooga, the district's largest city, has attracted technology and manufacturing jobs to the region.

The 3rd's geographic center falls near Oak Ridge, where multi-disciplinary high-tech national research facilities sprawl over parts of Anderson and Roane counties. Once solely dependent on federal dollars, Oak Ridge has begun to promote its "Secret City" history and selection as one site of the Manhattan Project.

Half of the 3rd's population resides in Hamilton County, which includes Chattanooga and abuts Georgia. With the city as its anchor, the 3rd is becoming the "Technology Corridor" of the state, modeling its growth on Research Triangle Park in North Carolina. Volkswagen recently broke ground on a $1 billion auto assembly plant in Chattanooga, bringing thousands of jobs to the area, but regional auto parts suppliers are still struggling through declines in the domestic auto industry.

Complementing Chattanooga's beautiful scenery, the city has injected life into its downtown over the past several decades through renewal projects such as the Tennessee Aquarium, a rejuvenated waterfront and programs at a local University of Tennessee campus. Just east of Chattanooga, Bradley — including the city of Cleveland — and Polk counties offer tours of the Cherokee National Forest and a rich history of the Cherokee Indians.

District residents support low-tax fiscal policies and hold conservative views on social issues, making the 3rd a Republican-leaning district. In 2008, John McCain took 55 percent of Hamilton County's presidential vote, but he did even better in the district overall (62 percent) and took 74 percent of the vote in Bradley County, his best county statewide.

MAJOR INDUSTRY
Nuclear and high-tech research, technology, higher education

CITIES
Chattanooga, 155,554; Cleveland, 37,192; Oak Ridge, 27,387

NOTABLE
Ruby Falls in Chattanooga is the nation's largest underground waterfall; The 1925 Scopes "Monkey" Trial in Dayton (Rhea County) upheld a law making it illegal to teach evolution.

Rep. Lincoln Davis (D)

Elected 2002; 4th term

A devout Baptist, Davis was among the forerunners of his party's increasingly successful strategy of co-opting traditionally Republican positions on social issues in conservative districts. But he is also a down-to-earth populist who focuses on economic aid for constituents in his mostly poor and rural slice of central Tennessee.

A member of the Blue Dog Coalition, a group of fiscally conservative House Democrats, he also has a desire for fiscal restraint and intends to use his seat on the Appropriations Committee to watch the flow of money into the Obama administration's priorities for health care, energy and education, all while Congress and the administration work to address an economic crisis. But that means he also has a direct line into funding for his own district.

Davis put aside his fiscal conservatism when it came to President Obama's early economic agenda, including a $787 billion stimulus plan and a $3.56 trillion budget blueprint for fiscal 2010. But the Blue Dogs obtained promises from House Speaker Nancy Pelosi of California that the party would eventually push to reduce the national deficit.

Davis may have a harder time following the party line as it moves on social issues such as embryonic stem cell research. Shortly after taking office, Obama issued an executive order to reinstate federal funding of the research, which had been limited by George W. Bush's administration. Davis had voted in 2006 against an override of President Bush's veto of a bill to expand federal funding for the research. To fulfill Obama's order, funding will have to go through Appropriations.

His conservative positioning on such social issues is what originally helped him wrest back — and hold — his district from the Republican Party, which had gained it in a 1994 nationwide election sweep. His successful 2002 campaign included the pledge that no candidate would "outgun me, outpray me or outdaddy me." National Democratic Party types didn't understand the potency of the "values" issue and thought it was the wrong tactic. But in the years since, a similar strategy has been followed at least in part by several other conservative Democrats.

Davis has strayed on other issues. He was one of only 25 Democrats to vote against a bill prohibiting job discrimination on the basis of sexual orientation, and he has twice voted for a proposed constitutional amendment to ban same-sex marriage. He also voted for the 2003 law that banned a procedure opponents call "partial birth" abortion. (In the state Senate, Davis had sponsored a similar Tennessee law.) And he pushes legislation intended to encourage more women to carry pregnancies to term. Such a measure would provide grants to support teens and college students who are pregnant or have children, increase the adoption tax credit and allow the State Children's Health Insurance Program to cover pregnant women and their "unborn children." And he supported a 2009 bill to expand the program, which currently covers children from low-income families that do not qualify for Medicaid.

Davis also is a member of the Science and Technology Committee and has parted ways with most Democrats on environmental issues. He has supported opening Alaska's Arctic National Wildlife Refuge to oil and gas drilling, lifting a moratorium on most offshore oil drilling and easing environmental reviews in order to speed construction of new refineries.

But he supported the Democrats' $289 billion farm law of 2008, which provided generous subsidies to farmers. The bill was reviled by conservative Republicans and budget watchdog groups for its largesse, but Davis

CAPITOL OFFICE
225-6831
www.house.gov/lincolndavis
410 Cannon Bldg. 20515-4204; fax 226-5172

COMMITTEES
Appropriations
Science & Technology

RESIDENCE
Pall Mall

BORN
Sept. 13, 1943; Pall Mall, Tenn.

RELIGION
Baptist

FAMILY
Wife, Lynda Davis; three children

EDUCATION
Tennessee Technological U., B.S. 1966 (agronomy)

CAREER
Farmer; construction company owner; U.S. Agriculture Department official

POLITICAL HIGHLIGHTS
Mayor of Byrdstown, 1979-83; Tenn. House, 1981-85; sought Democratic nomination for U.S. House, 1984, 1994; Tenn. Senate, 1997-2003

ELECTION RESULTS

2008 GENERAL

Lincoln Davis (D)	146,776	58.8%
Monty J. Lankford (R)	94,447	37.8%
James Anthony Gray (I)	4,869	1.9%
Kevin Ragsdale (I)	3,713	1.5%

2008 PRIMARY

Lincoln Davis (D)	30,487	90.4%
Bert Mason (D)	3,233	9.6%

2006 GENERAL

Lincoln Davis (D)	123,666	66.4%
Kenneth Martin (R)	62,449	33.6%

PREVIOUS WINNING PERCENTAGES
2004 (55%); 2002 (52%)

called it "an investment in our farmers, rural infrastructure and homegrown, renewable energy." He noted that about three-quarters of the funding would go to food aid — an attractive feature for his district, where 16 percent of the population lives below the poverty line.

As a member of the Financial Services Committee during the 110th Congress (2007-08), he sponsored a 2007 bill to add five counties in his district — Giles, Hickman, Lawrence, Lewis and Lincoln — to the area officially designated as the Appalachian Region, making them eligible for federal economic development assistance from the Appalachian Regional Commission.

Tennessee is home to thousands of Kurds, and Nashville served as one of the voting precincts for the 2005 Iraqi national elections. Davis co-founded the Kurdish-American Caucus with Republican Joe Wilson of South Carolina in June 2008 to give voice to what he calls a "deeply oppressed" people. But he said he doesn't support an independent Kurdish state.

Raised on a farm, Davis didn't have electricity in his home until his teenage years, when his family and their neighbors strung their own power lines. Davis, who started a construction business before launching his political career, said he dug the water lines for his house himself. He earned a degree in agronomy from Tennessee Technological University and worked for the Agriculture Department as a soil tester and land assessor. He continues to farm with his brother Charlie, who he said "does all the work." He owns three mules and rode one of them, Pete, in Columbia's Mule Day parade in 2008.

He served in the Tennessee House from 1981 to 1985 and in the state Senate from 1997 to 2003. In between were two failed attempts in the Democratic primaries for open House seats before his 2002 win. He had worked with the state House in the redistricting process to increase Democratic strength in the 4th District before running for the seat left open by Republican Van Hilleary's gubernatorial bid.

Davis won the primary with 57 percent of the vote against Fran F. Marchum, a well-funded opponent running to his left, then defeated Republican Janice H. Bowling, a former top aide to Hilleary, by 6 percentage points. He won a 2004 rematch against Bowling by 11 points and took 66 percent of the vote in 2006. In 2008, he took 59 percent of the vote in an election in which Arizona Republican Sen. John McCain trounced Obama by 30 points.

He is considered a potential candidate to succeed Tennessee's Democratic governor, Phil Bredesen, who will be term-limited in 2010. Davis got a look at what's involved in a statewide race in 2006, when he served as chairman of the unsuccessful Senate campaign of former Democratic Rep. Harold E. Ford Jr. If Davis chooses to run for governor, Ford could be among his opponents.

KEY VOTES

2008

Yes Delay consideration of Colombia free-trade agreement

Yes Override Bush veto of federal farm and nutrition programs reauthorization bill

Yes Overhaul surveillance laws and permit dismissal of suits against companies that conducted warrantless wiretapping

Yes Grant mortgage relief to homeowners and funding for Fannie Mae and Freddie Mac

No Approve initial $700 billion program to stabilize financial markets

No Approve final $700 billion program to stabilize financial markets

Yes Provide $14 billion in loans to automakers

2007

Yes Increase minimum wage by $2.10 an hour

No Approve $124.2 billion in emergency war spending and set goal for redeployment of troops from Iraq

Yes Reject federal contraceptive assistance to international family planning groups

Yes Override Bush veto of $23.2 billion water projects authorization bill

Yes Implement Peru free-trade agreement

Yes Approve energy policy overhaul with new fuel economy standards

Yes Clear $473.5 billion omnibus spending bill, including $70 billion for military operations

CQ VOTE STUDIES

	PARTY UNITY		PRESIDENTIAL SUPPORT	
	SUPPORT	OPPOSE	SUPPORT	OPPOSE
2008	93%	7%	24%	76%
2007	87%	13%	22%	78%
2006	67%	33%	70%	30%
2005	67%	33%	65%	35%
2004	68%	32%	59%	41%

INTEREST GROUPS

	AFL-CIO	ADA	CCUS	ACU
2008	93%	80%	61%	12%
2007	96%	75%	68%	38%
2006	79%	35%	93%	80%
2005	67%	70%	78%	64%
2004	67%	60%	86%	56%

TENNESSEE 4

Middle Tennessee — northeast and south

Stretching across more than 10,000 square miles and touching Tennessee's borders with Kentucky in the north and Alabama and Georgia in the south, the 4th is the state's most geographically vast district. It is a melting pot of Tennessee's three regions, as plains turn east into rolling hills that merge with the Cumberland Plateau and eventually the Appalachian Mountains.

While the 4th falls in the orbits of Oak Ridge and Chattanooga in the east and Nashville in the west, it is overwhelmingly rural. Columbia, with just 33,000 residents, is the district's most populous city. No one major media market serves all of the 4th, forcing coverage to be shared with larger ones from Oak Ridge, Chattanooga, Nashville and Huntsville, Ala. The district's median income is below that of the state, and its constituency has the lowest level of formal education of any Tennessee district.

The 4th includes tobacco farms and light industry in the south. Spring Hill, in Maury County, faces economic uncertainty as General Motors closed its original Saturn plant and is determining the future of its other

brands' operations in the city. Proximity to Nashville is one reason the populations of Maury and next-door Williamson County (shared with the 7th) continue to grow. Although tourism plays only a small role in the district's economy overall, the northern region of the 4th does attract visitors to the Big South Fork National River and Recreation Area in Fentress, Pickett and Scott counties.

Although the 4th has an ancestrally Democratic lean, underlying social conservatism — manifested in opposition to abortion and gun control measures — gives the 4th a Republican edge in federal contests. In 2008, Republican John McCain won the 4th by 30 percentage points, taking all 24 counties that are wholly or partly in the district.

MAJOR INDUSTRY
Agriculture, auto parts, manufacturing, tobacco

MILITARY BASES
Arnold Air Force Base, 54 military, 2,674 civilian (2009)

CITIES
Columbia, 33,055; Tullahoma, 17,994

NOTABLE
The Jack Daniel's sour mash whiskey distillery in Lynchburg is located in dry Moore County.

Rep. Jim Cooper (D)

Elected 2002; 10th term
Also served 1983-95

Cooper has his niche among the Blue Dog Coalition of fiscally conservative House Democrats: "I'm the nerd; I usually know the details of things." He applies his knowledge and penchant for detail to a range of complicated issues, including the budget deficit, health care and national security.

Cooper is among his party's most experienced fiscal experts, having logged more than a decade in Congress and then eight years in the financial world before he returned to Capitol Hill in 2003 for a second tour of duty. But he is also independent-minded and doesn't mind rankling his party's more liberal leaders with his tart and candid remarks.

Cooper initially voted against President Obama's $787 billion economic stimulus law in early 2009, but supported the final conference report even though he believed it was rushed through too quickly. "I got into terrible trouble with our leadership because they don't care what's in the bill; they just want it to pass and they want it to be unanimous," he told a Nashville radio program. "We're just treated like mushrooms most of the time."

He has proposed creating a commission to tackle the government's long-term budget problems. Cooper and his cosponsor, Virginia Republican Frank R. Wolf, said the panel is necessary to determine how to control growth in entitlement spending. The Appropriations Committee in 2008 narrowly defeated an amendment to attach the proposal to a financial services spending bill.

A related pet cause of Cooper's is to change the method of calculating the federal budget. He argues that accrual accounting — rather than the cash accounting basis that reflects current expenditures and revenues only — which recognizes statutory commitments to future spending, such as Social Security and Medicare obligations, can show the true condition of the federal budget. The use of accrual accounting, he said, would add at least $200 billion to the deficit. Making such a change "would do wonders to help citizens and policy makers understand our current fiscal plight," he said.

Cooper has promoted what he regards as other common-sense budget approaches, including a return to pay-as-you-go budget rules requiring both tax cuts and mandatory spending increases to be offset. He joined other Blue Dogs in objecting to several pieces of legislation they said violated the House's pay-as-you-go rules, including the 2008 rewrite of farm policy. He said in April 2009 he was pleased to win a written promise from House Democratic leaders and Obama to push for a law mandating pay-as-you-go in exchange for support of the president's fiscal 2010 budget.

He also set aside his usual concerns to support a $700 billion measure in fall 2008 aimed at aiding the financial services sector, warning that the economy faced dire consequences if Congress didn't act. "It's not every day you get a chance to save your country," he said at the time.

Cooper splits with his party on a variety of issues ranging from trade to gun control. Early in 2007, he even split with most Blue Dogs when he was unable to get their backing for a budget plan that called for the extension of some soon-to-expire tax breaks and cuts in some entitlement programs. He wound up casting the lone Democratic vote for a competing GOP budget plan to cut entitlements and freeze other domestic spending.

Cooper cooperates with Republicans on many issues. Among them was his leadership of an ad hoc Armed Services panel that examined the changing responsibilities of the military services. Cooper worked closely with the panel's top ranking Republican, Georgia's Phil Gingrey, to issue a report in 2008 that looked not only at the Pentagon but intelligence agencies and the

CAPITOL OFFICE
225-4311
cooper.house.gov
1536 Longworth Bldg. 20515-4205; fax 226-1035

COMMITTEES
Armed Services
Oversight & Government Reform

RESIDENCE
Nashville

BORN
June 19, 1954; Nashville, Tenn.

RELIGION
Episcopalian

FAMILY
Wife, Martha Hayes Cooper; three children

EDUCATION
U. of North Carolina, B.A. 1975 (history & economics); Oxford U., B.A., M.A. 1977 (Rhodes scholar); Harvard U., J.D. 1980

CAREER
Investment firm owner; investment bank managing director; lawyer

POLITICAL HIGHLIGHTS
U.S. House, 1983-95; Democratic nominee for U.S. Senate, 1994

ELECTION RESULTS

2008 GENERAL
Jim Cooper (D)	181,467	65.8%
Gerard Donovan (R)	85,471	31.0%
Jon Jackson (I)	5,464	2.0%
John P. Miglietta (I)	3,196	1.2%

2008 PRIMARY
Jim Cooper (D)	unopposed

2006 GENERAL
Jim Cooper (D)	122,919	69.0%
Thomas F. Kovach (R)	49,702	27.9%
Ginny Welsch (I)	3,766	2.1%

PREVIOUS WINNING PERCENTAGES
2004 (69%); 2002 (64%); 1992 (66%); 1990 (69%); 1988 (100%); 1986 (100%); 1984 (75%); 1982 (66%)

State Department in highlighting such problems as interagency coordination. In 2009, he was named to another panel to look at ways to improve the Pentagon's troubled procurement system.

Cooper is avidly interested in health care. He is among those championing a bipartisan approach drafted by Oregon Democratic Sen. Ron Wyden that would upend the nation's existing system of employer-based health insurance, providing subsidies for Americans to buy coverage directly from private insurers instead, while eventually reducing the deficit.

Cooper also is a member of the Oversight and Government Reform Committee, where his interests have included the electric cooperative industry. He said in a 2008 article published in the Harvard Journal on Legislation that too many co-ops have "taken on deeply troubling anti-consumer behaviors." He drew adverse notice in 2008 when it was revealed he entered a members-only Web site run by a trade group for the cooperatives, leading the group to hire a computer crime expert who approached the FBI about investigating the congressman's activities. Cooper dismissed the notion he had done anything wrong as "completely ridiculous" and said the industry was only trying to shift attention away from itself.

Cooper has long had an affection for government. His father, Prentice, was Tennessee's governor in the 1960s. He made it through the University of North Carolina in just three years, attended Oxford as a Rhodes Scholar, then picked up a law degree from Harvard. After practicing law for two years, he ran for an open House seat in 1982 against then-Senate Majority Leader Howard H. Baker Jr.'s daughter, Cissy, and won easily, becoming at age 28 the youngest member of the House.

Despite his youthfulness, Cooper developed a reputation as a skilled dealmaker and was a key player on issues ranging from health care to telecommunications policy to clean air. But when he ran for the Senate in 1994, he was trounced by actor and attorney Fred Thompson.

Cooper then took a break from politics. He entered the investment banking world and taught business at the Owen Graduate School of Management at Vanderbilt University; he said those experiences helped him as a politician.

When a House seat in Tennessee opened up in 2002 after Democrat Bob Clement decided to run for the Senate, Cooper jumped at the chance for a comeback. Despite surgery in June 2002 to remove a tumor from his colon — doctors said the cancer had not spread — Cooper won the August primary with 47 percent of the vote to 24 percent for his closest competitor. He captured 64 percent that November against businessman Robert Duvall and has had no trouble holding the seat since then.

KEY VOTES

2008

No	Delay consideration of Colombia free-trade agreement
No	Override Bush veto of federal farm and nutrition programs reauthorization bill
Yes	Overhaul surveillance laws and permit dismissal of suits against companies that conducted warrantless wiretapping
Yes	Grant mortgage relief to homeowners and funding for Fannie Mae and Freddie Mac
Yes	Approve initial $700 billion program to stabilize financial markets
Yes	Approve final $700 billion program to stabilize financial markets
No	Provide $14 billion in loans to automakers

2007

Yes	Increase minimum wage by $2.10 an hour
Yes	Approve $124.2 billion in emergency war spending and set goal for redeployment of troops from Iraq
No	Reject federal contraceptive assistance to international family planning groups
Yes	Override Bush veto of $23.2 billion water projects authorization bill
Yes	Implement Peru free-trade agreement
Yes	Approve energy policy overhaul with new fuel economy standards
Yes	Clear $473.5 billion omnibus spending bill, including $70 billion for military operations

CQ VOTE STUDIES

	PARTY UNITY		PRESIDENTIAL SUPPORT	
	SUPPORT	OPPOSE	SUPPORT	OPPOSE
2008	92%	8%	28%	72%
2007	88%	12%	16%	84%
2006	82%	18%	37%	63%
2005	80%	20%	38%	62%
2004	82%	18%	35%	65%

INTEREST GROUPS

	AFL-CIO	ADA	CCUS	ACU
2008	79%	60%	72%	20%
2007	88%	85%	75%	16%
2006	79%	70%	53%	40%
2005	67%	80%	59%	24%
2004	79%	85%	57%	13%

TENNESSEE 5

Nashville

Home of the Grand Ole Opry and the Country Music Hall of Fame and Museum, the 5th's Nashville long has been known for its place in country music history. The state capital, however, has left behind that one-dimensional image to become a cosmopolitan mecca for tourism, culture and higher education. With many buildings in the classical style, Nashville proclaims itself the "Athens of the South."

Although the district is most famous for its rich music tradition, state government is the top employer, and Nashville is a higher education hub for the Volunteer State. The 5th also is a health care center, and the city hosts several research facilities, including the Vanderbilt University Medical Center. Budget shortfalls and the potential for widespread layoffs concern local officials and residents. Nashville's Printers Alley is now an entertainment hotspot, but the name gives credence to the district's once-thriving publishing sector.

Two large sports arenas — the homes of football's Titans and hockey's Predators — enhance the district's entertainment sector. Events at auto

racing's Nashville Superspeedway, located just outside the district in the adjacent 6th's portion of Lebanon, also are major draws. Meanwhile, area suburbs still rely on tourists and locals to support the retail and service economies based around bargain stores and other attractions.

The Nashville area's economic growth, which spread across most of the 5th, attracted young, Republican-leaning, upper-class couples to the neighborhoods of Bellevue and Hermitage. The strongly Democratic city core of government employees, academics and unions, however, negates almost any chance that the district could fall into Republican hands. No Republican won Nashville's congressional seat during the 20th century, and Barack Obama took 60 percent of the Davidson County vote and 56 percent of the district's vote in the 2008 presidential race.

MAJOR INDUSTRY
Government, music, higher education, publishing, health care, tourism

CITIES
Nashville-Davidson (pt.), 524,339; Lebanon (pt.), 12,718

NOTABLE
"The Hermitage" was the home of Andrew Jackson; A full-scale reproduction of the Parthenon was built in 1897 and stands in Nashville's Centennial Park.

Rep. Bart Gordon (D)

CAPITOL OFFICE
225-4231
gordon.house.gov
2306 Rayburn Bldg. 20515-4206; fax 225-6887

COMMITTEES
Energy & Commerce
Science & Technology - chairman

RESIDENCE
Murfreesboro

BORN
Jan. 24, 1949; Murfreesboro, Tenn.

RELIGION
Methodist

FAMILY
Wife, Leslie Gordon; one child

EDUCATION
Middle Tennessee State U., B.S. 1971;
U. of Tennessee, J.D. 1973

MILITARY SERVICE
Army Reserve, 1971-72

CAREER
Lawyer; state party official

POLITICAL HIGHLIGHTS
Tenn. Democratic Party chairman, 1981-83

ELECTION RESULTS

2008 GENERAL

Bart Gordon (D)	194,264	74.4%
Chris Baker (I)	66,764	25.6%

2008 PRIMARY

Bart Gordon (D)	unopposed

2006 GENERAL

Bart Gordon (D)	129,069	67.1%
David R. Davis (R)	60,392	31.4%
Robert L. Garrison (I)	2,035	1.1%

PREVIOUS WINNING PERCENTAGES
2004 (64%); 2002 (66%); 2000 (62%); 1998 (55%);
1996 (54%); 1994 (51%); 1992 (57%); 1990 (67%);
1988 (76%); 1986 (77%); 1984 (63%)

Elected 1984; 13th term

Tennessee has grown more Republican over the years, and Gordon, who is now in his third decade in the House, has stayed in tune with his voters. A member of the fiscally conservative Blue Dog Coalition, he supports tax cuts and gun owners' rights and takes a hard line on immigration. Yet he is among the lawmakers the Obama administration works with on proposals for developing renewable sources of energy and addressing other technology needs.

Gordon is known in Washington more for his foot speed than his swiftness in getting legislation into law: In 2009 he outpaced his congressional colleagues in the annual Capitol Challenge Charity Race for a 20th year, beating a lawmaker less than half his age. But as chairman of the Science and Technology Committee and a member of the Energy and Commerce Committee, he hopes President Obama's avid interest in those issues can elevate his role in reviving the nation's economy while improving the environment.

One of Gordon's chief concerns is boosting science and education. He cites the Soviet Union's 1957 launch of the Sputnik satellite — a move that led an embarrassed United States to begin the space race — as an example of what the nation faces as it loses ground to other nations. "As the father of a 7-year-old daughter, I fear that today's children will be the first generation of Americans that does not inherit a standard of living better than their parents," he said in 2008. "Today, with the rapid economic and technological advances of other countries, I fear we are now on the cusp of another Sputnik moment."

The Science and Technology panel has never been one of Congress' highest-profile committees, but it has a recent tradition of bipartisanship that Gordon has sought to maintain. In addition to getting along with panel Republicans, he works closely with Tennessee's senior senator, Republican Lamar Alexander, who shares Gordon's interest in science and energy. The two sponsored legislation in 2009 to ban foreign nuclear waste from coming to the United States.

Gordon is already shaping the alternative-energy research agenda and points to accomplishments of the 110th Congress (2007-08) as ideas for boosting the economy. He steered through legislation calling for establishment of an Advanced Research Projects Agency at the Energy Department (ARPA-E), modeled on the Defense Advanced Research Projects Agency (DARPA) within the Pentagon, which helped develop the Internet. The agency received $400 million from the 2009 economic stimulus law.

The new ARPA-E agency was just one element of a larger Gordon "competitiveness" measure that authorized significantly more federal funding for math and science research and education. He has called on scientists to do their part to stimulate interest. "You have to help us make the public understand that science is about jobs and the quality of life," he said at the American Association for the Advancement of Science's public policy conference in April 2009.

He has sought a stronger federal financial commitment to science and space exploration. During the 110th, he won enactment of a NASA reauthorization that called for $2.6 billion more than President George W. Bush originally proposed, including $1 billion to accelerate development of a replacement for the current shuttle fleet. The committee will give the Obama administration time to decide whether to continue with plans to retire the space shuttle fleet in 2010.

Gordon's positions on social policy vary. In 2007, he was he was one of 25 Democrats who voted against a bill banning employment discrimination based on sexual orientation. And in 2004, he sided with other social conservatives in supporting a constitutional ban on same-sex marriage. But he supported a vote to override Bush's veto of a bill to expand federal funding for embryonic stem cell research, which uses discarded embryos created for in vitro fertilization.

He is more conservative on immigration. He was one of 46 Democrats to cosponsor a bill by North Carolina Democrat Heath Shuler to require employers to verify the legal status of all workers and to add thousands of new Border Patrol agents. He supported a 2006 repeal of bilingual voting assistance requirements and voted to authorize construction of a 700-mile fence along the U.S.-Mexico border. In 2007, the House passed his bill — which was subsequently enacted into law — to require the EPA to create guidelines for the cleanup of illegal methamphetamine labs.

Despite his conservative views on some issues, Gordon has become more loyal to his party. During the 109th Congress (2005-06) he voted with his party on 74 percent of the votes that pitted a majority of one party against the other; that figure increased to 90 percent during the 110th.

Gordon grew up in Murfreesboro, where he still lives. His father was a farmer and his mother a schoolteacher. He became interested in politics through his grandfather, a county commissioner, and his father, who started the local farm bureau. He spent four years in the Army ROTC and was commissioned for the Vietnam War, but suffered from an ulcer and was honorably discharged. He then opened a law practice in Murfreesboro. "I had murders and dog bites — everything a small-town lawyer does," he said.

Gordon worked in the unsuccessful 1968 congressional campaign of Democratic state Rep. John Bragg. After law school, he won a seat on the state Democratic Executive Committee, and in 1979 he became the party's executive director. Two years later, he won the party chairmanship.

When Al Gore gave up his House seat in 1984 to run for the Senate, Gordon was ready. He prevailed in a six-way primary and won all but two counties on Election Day. He generally won re-election by comfortable margins until 1994, the year Republicans took over Congress, when he was held to 51 percent of the vote. His next three re-election victories were also comparatively close.

When the Democratic state legislature did redistricting for this decade, it added two Democratic-leaning counties to the district and took away some heavily GOP territory in suburban Nashville. Gordon trounced Robert L. Garrison, a libertarian GOP gadfly, by 34 percentage points in 2002. He won easily in 2004 and 2006 and had no GOP challenger in 2008.

KEY VOTES

2008

Yes Delay consideration of Colombia free-trade agreement

Yes Override Bush veto of federal farm and nutrition programs reauthorization bill

Yes Overhaul surveillance laws and permit dismissal of suits against companies that conducted warrantless wiretapping

Yes Grant mortgage relief to homeowners and funding for Fannie Mae and Freddie Mac

Yes Approve initial $700 billion program to stabilize financial markets

Yes Approve final $700 billion program to stabilize financial markets

+ Provide $14 billion in loans to automakers

2007

Yes Increase minimum wage by $2.10 an hour

Yes Approve $124.2 billion in emergency war spending and set goal for redeployment of troops from Iraq

No Reject federal contraceptive assistance to international family planning groups

Yes Override Bush veto of $23.2 billion water projects authorization bill

Yes Implement Peru free-trade agreement

Yes Approve energy policy overhaul with new fuel economy standards

Yes Clear $473.5 billion omnibus spending bill, including $70 billion for military operations

CQ VOTE STUDIES

	PARTY UNITY		PRESIDENTIAL SUPPORT	
	SUPPORT	OPPOSE	SUPPORT	OPPOSE
2008	93%	7%	21%	79%
2007	88%	12%	11%	89%
2006	74%	26%	63%	37%
2005	74%	26%	46%	54%
2004	72%	28%	55%	45%

INTEREST GROUPS

	AFL-CIO	ADA	CCUS	ACU
2008	100%	80%	67%	4%
2007	96%	85%	70%	20%
2006	79%	50%	80%	60%
2005	80%	90%	74%	40%
2004	87%	75%	75%	42%

TENNESSEE 6

Middle Tennessee — Murfreesboro

Nashville's population boom continues to spill into much of the 6th, which forms a sideways V-shape around Tennessee's capital city clockwise from the north to the south. The hilly countryside includes two notable college communities — Middle Tennessee State University in Murfreesboro, and Tennessee Tech University in Cookeville — establishing a top-tier industry for the district's economy.

A well-developed highway system eases the commute into the neighboring 5th District's Nashville from Murfreesboro for those 6th District residents who have state government jobs. Most residents, however, have relied more on automobile manufacturing jobs in the 6th itself. Nissan's primary American plant in Smyrna has seen recent cutbacks, but the company plans to expand future production here, and local auto parts manufacturers have supplied other plants located around the state. Despite tobacco revenue losses in some of the 6th's farming communities, Robertson County is still the state's top tobacco producer. Book, video and music distribution also is big business in the district.

Rutherford County, which surrounds Murfreesboro, grew by more than 50 percent in the 1990s and has been targeted as a center for retail-sector revitalization. The planned commercial sites are expected to complement the already preserved areas commemorating the Civil War.

In recent presidential elections, Republican candidates have benefited from the presence of newly arrived suburbanites in the historically Democratic 6th. Republican John McCain won the district by 25 percentage points in the 2008 election and won easily in the district's most populous counties of Rutherford and Sumner. Unionized conservative Democrats are losing their clout as socially conservative tendencies launch local Republicans into public office.

MAJOR INDUSTRY
Distribution, higher education, tobacco, auto manufacturing

CITIES
Murfreesboro, 68,816; Hendersonville, 40,620; Smyrna, 25,569; Cookeville, 23,923; Gallatin, 23,230

NOTABLE
Former Rep. Joe L. Evins' idea for a fiddler jamboree in Smithville succeeded, and the event now attracts hundreds of thousands of visitors annually; Shelbyville is the heart of Tennessee Walking Horse country.

Rep. Marsha Blackburn (R)

Elected 2002; 4th term

CAPITOL OFFICE
225-2811
www.house.gov/blackburn
217 Cannon Bldg. 20515-4207; fax 225-3004

COMMITTEES
Energy & Commerce
Select Energy Independence & Global Warming

RESIDENCE
Brentwood

BORN
June 6, 1952; Laurel, Miss.

RELIGION
Presbyterian

FAMILY
Husband, Chuck Blackburn; two children

EDUCATION
Mississippi State U., B.S. 1973
(home economics)

CAREER
Retail marketing company owner;
state economic development official;
sales manager

POLITICAL HIGHLIGHTS
Williamson County Republican Party
chairwoman, 1989-91; Republican nominee
for U.S. House, 1992; Tenn. Senate, 1999-2002

ELECTION RESULTS

2008 GENERAL

Marsha Blackburn (R)	217,332	68.6%
Randy G. Morris (D)	99,549	31.4%

2008 PRIMARY

Marsha Blackburn (R)	30,997	62.0%
Tom Leatherwood (R)	19,025	38.0%

2006 GENERAL

Marsha Blackburn (R)	152,288	66.0%
Bill Morrison (D)	73,369	31.8%

PREVIOUS WINNING PERCENTAGES
2004 (100%); 2002 (71%)

Blackburn is about as loyal a Republican as can be found in the House. Her political action committee is called Wedge PAC; the name reflects her maiden name, Wedgeworth, and "wedge issues," such as same-sex marriage, abortion and gun rights, about which she feels strongly.

She hectors the Democratic majority from the right on the range of issues as a member of the GOP's whip team and the Republican Study Committee, the conservative core of the House GOP caucus. In the 110th Congress (2007-08), she scored near the top in party loyalty, siding with a majority of her fellow Republicans on 99 percent of all votes pitting the parties against each other.

Republican leaders in 2005 rewarded her for her loyalty with a coveted assignment to the Energy and Commerce Committee. She was bumped from the panel briefly when the Republicans lost their majority, but regained the seat soon after the February 2007 death of panel member Charlie Norwood of Georgia.

She was an enthusiastic participant in Republicans' 2008 attempts to turn public anxiety over high gasoline prices against Democrats. Blackburn also was given a seat on the Select Committee on Energy Independence and Global Warming, where she has been wary of any proposals that could burden businesses.

Blackburn was known as a firebrand in the Tennessee Senate, particularly for her relentless and ultimately successful crusade against a state income tax. She displays a gold-plated ax with the words "Ax the Tax" in her House office as a reminder. In the House, she cosponsored legislation to allow residents of Tennessee and the eight other states without broadly based income taxes to deduct state sales taxes when calculating their federal tax liability, a provision that became law in 2004 and was renewed in 2006 and 2008.

Blackburn has fought any and all proposed tax increases, instead urging cuts in domestic spending to offset even emergency spending for disaster relief following Hurricane Katrina in 2005. Blackburn and 20 fellow members of the Study Committee wrote President George W. Bush on Sept. 15 that year, calling for offsetting cuts in other domestic spending.

Her zeal sometimes gets her in over her head. At an April 2009 hearing on global warming, Blackburn grilled fellow Tennesseean and former Vice President Al Gore about "your motives" in pressing for climate change legislation, noting his partnership in a venture capital firm with investments in companies that might benefit from a "cap and trade" system to control carbon emissions. Gore said that "every penny that I have made I have put right into a nonprofit, the Alliance for Climate Protection, to spread awareness of why we have to take on this challenge." And he added tartly, "If you believe that the reason I have been working on this issue for 30 years is because of greed, you don't know me."

Blackburn helped steer through a 2006 law gradually removing long-standing restrictions preventing Southwest Airlines from flying nonstop between Dallas' Love Field and most states. Southwest flies more than five times the passengers through Nashville than the next-busiest carrier.

Blackburn is a co-founder of the Congressional Songwriters Caucus and a staunch advocate of copyright protections — an important issue in music cities Nashville and Memphis, located in neighboring districts. She plays guitar, piano and ukulele, and loves listening to Bach.

Born in rural Mississippi, Blackburn learned civic involvement from her family. Her mother was active in the local 4-H clubs, and Blackburn went to llege on a 4-H scholarship. Her father instilled a sense of frugality. "It ally has an impact watching your parents and uncles and seeing how ugal they are and how hard they work," she said.

Blackburn worked in a series of business and government jobs before ming to Congress. She paid her way through college selling books door--door for the Nashville-based Southwestern Co. and worked there after llege as well. She got her start in politics as Republican Party chairwom- in Williamson County. She first ran for Congress in 1992 against Demo- atic Rep. Bart Gordon, drawing 41 percent of the vote. In the mid-1990s, e served a stint as executive director of Tennessee's Film, Entertainment d Music Commission before winning a state Senate seat in 1998.

In 2002, she leveraged the income tax issue and her base in the Memphis d Nashville suburbs to prevail in a crowded 7th District primary field after ur-term Republican Rep. Ed Bryant made an unsuccessful Senate bid. She as the first woman from Tennessee to be elected in her own right and mains the lone woman in the state's delegation. She made explicit her avid pport of gun owners' rights; in one of her campaign ads, she cited not just er support of the right to bear arms, but her perfect score on a marksman- hip test with her Smith & Wesson .38.

She was unopposed in both the primary and general elections in 2004. uring her 2006 campaign, she was unscathed by a Memphis Commercial ppeal article reporting that her campaign committee and political action ommittee had given $123,000 to a company run by her lobbyist son-in-law.

Blackburn looked hard at the race to succeed Bill Frist, the Senate GOP ader who retired at the end of the 109th Congress (2005-06). But in early 005, she decided against a bid and instead easily won re-election to the ouse in both 2006 and 2008.

Blackburn was one of four Republicans — and the lone woman — vying chair the GOP Conference in the 110th Congress. She and two other ontenders were members of the Republican Study Committee. But the inner, on the third ballot, was establishment candidate Adam H. Putnam Florida, who led all the way.

Blackburn has been mentioned as a potential candidate for governor in 010, when term-limited Democrat Phil Bredesen will be wrapping up his enure. But her fellow Tennessee Republican, Rep. Zach Wamp, jumped into e primary field early in 2009, as did other contenders, and Blackburn cked questions about the topic. "I always say my job isn't to chart my ath, that's God's job," Blackburn said in mid-2008. "My job is to be ready hen doors open."

KEY VOTES

2008

No	Delay consideration of Colombia free-trade agreement
Yes	Override Bush veto of federal farm and nutrition programs reauthorization bill
Yes	Overhaul surveillance laws and permit dismissal of suits against companies that conducted warrantless wiretapping
No	Grant mortgage relief to homeowners and funding for Fannie Mae and Freddie Mac
No	Approve initial $700 billion program to stabilize financial markets
No	Approve final $700 billion program to stabilize financial markets
No	Provide $14 billion in loans to automakers

2007

No	Increase minimum wage by $2.10 an hour
No	Approve $124.2 billion in emergency war spending and set goal for redeployment of troops from Iraq
Yes	Reject federal contraceptive assistance to international family planning groups
No	Override Bush veto of $23.2 billion water projects authorization bill
Yes	Implement Peru free-trade agreement
No	Approve energy policy overhaul with new fuel economy standards
Yes	Clear $473.5 billion omnibus spending bill, including $70 billion for military operations

CQ VOTE STUDIES

	PARTY UNITY		PRESIDENTIAL SUPPORT	
	SUPPORT	OPPOSE	SUPPORT	OPPOSE
2008	99%	1%	78%	22%
2007	99%	1%	91%	9%
2006	98%	2%	89%	11%
2005	99%	1%	93%	7%
2004	99%	1%	91%	9%

INTEREST GROUPS

	AFL-CIO	ADA	CCUS	ACU
2008	0%	10%	83%	96%
2007	4%	5%	72%	100%
2006	14%	0%	100%	96%
2005	13%	0%	89%	100%
2004	7%	0%	100%	100%

ENNESSEE 7

astern Memphis suburbs; southern Nashville uburbs; most of Clarksville

tailor-made, meandering district, the 7th touches five other Tennessee 'stricts and borders Kentucky to the north and Mississippi and Alabama the south. The 7th's population centers fall at both ends of the district, ear Memphis in the southwest and near Nashville in the east.

lmost one-third of district voters live in Shelby County suburbs outside 1emphis, giving the 7th a strongly anti-tax and socially conservative ent despite a Democratic past. Shelby has experienced growth as mid- e-class residents migrate from downtown Memphis (in the 9th) to the utskirts of the county, a trend that helps explain the 7th's GOP shift.

/illiamson County, outside Nashville, mirrors Shelby in its growth and epublican leanings. The relocation of Nissan's North American regional eadquarters to Franklin, near what has been the company's primary orth American manufacturing plant in Smyrna (in the 6th), included onstruction of a $100 million facility. Nissan has announced plans to

produce electric vehicles in Tennessee by 2010 and has consolidated its North and South American regional operations in Franklin.

The bulk of the area between Shelby and Williamson sweeps over vast farming regions that produce corn, cotton and hogs. Northwest of Williamson, the district ambles northward along the Cumberland River to take in most of Clarksville. The Clarksville area has benefited from diverse manufacturing, a robust education sector around Austin Peay State University (nearby in the 8th) and expansions at Fort Campbell — which straddles the Tennessee-Kentucky line. John McCain won the district by 31 percentage points in the 2008 presidential election.

MAJOR INDUSTRY
Agriculture, manufacturing

MILITARY BASES
Fort Campbell, 30,178 military, 3,085 civilian (2009) (shared with Kentucky's 1st District)

CITIES
Clarksville (pt.), 83,680; Bartlett (pt.), 40,409; Germantown (pt.), 34,200

NOTABLE
Shiloh National Military Park memorializes the soldiers who died in one of the bloodiest battles of the Civil War.

Rep. John Tanner (D)

CAPITOL OFFICE
225-4714
www.house.gov/tanner
1226 Longworth Bldg. 20515-4208; fax 225-1765

COMMITTEES
Foreign Affairs
Ways & Means
(Social Security - chairman)

RESIDENCE
Union City

BORN
Sept. 22, 1944; Halls, Tenn.

RELIGION
Disciples of Christ

FAMILY
Wife, Betty Ann Tanner; two children

EDUCATION
U. of Tennessee, B.S. 1966 (business), J.D. 1968

MILITARY SERVICE
Navy, 1968-72; Tenn. National Guard, 1974-2000

CAREER
Lawyer; insurance company owner

POLITICAL HIGHLIGHTS
Tenn. House, 1977-89

ELECTION RESULTS

2008 GENERAL
John Tanner (D)	180,465	100.0%

2008 PRIMARY
John Tanner (D)	unopposed

2006 GENERAL
John Tanner (D)	129,610	73.2%
John Farmer (R)	47,492	26.8%

PREVIOUS WINNING PERCENTAGES
2004 (74%); 2002 (70%); 2000 (72%); 1998 (100%);
1996 (67%); 1994 (64%); 1992 (84%); 1990 (100%);
1988 (62%)

Elected 1988; 11th term

A founder of the Blue Dog Coalition who is also a chief deputy whip, Tanner serves as a bridge between the often-rebellious faction of fiscally conservative Democrats and more-liberal party leaders. It is not always a comfortable position, but it is one he has handled deftly.

A retired National Guard colonel with close-cropped steel-gray hair, Tanner has the easygoing manner of a country lawyer. On the floor, he can usually be found offering advice and trading gossip with fellow Blue Dogs in their back-center rows. The group, which has about 50 members in the 111th Congress (2009-10), is a growing force within the House Democratic Caucus. Tanner serves a dual role with the Blue Dogs, pushing their position in leadership meetings while sometimes wooing them to accept leadership-backed bills.

Tanner helped engineer the Blue Dogs' signature victory in the 110th Congress (2007-08) — a new House pay-as-you-go rule requiring offsets for new entitlement spending or tax cuts. But he also helped the leadership pass some economic stimulus and supplemental spending bills as emergency measures exempt from the offset requirement.

In the 111th, the Blue Dogs won a commitment from House Democratic leaders to strengthen pay-as-you go requirements, even as Congress adopted a fiscal 2010 budget resolution with a huge deficit. Tanner warned, "If we don't get our own fiscal house in order, our international creditors will do it for us, and we will lose our economic freedom." He keeps a running tally of the national debt on his House Web site, along with a "your share" calculation.

He won't bless many exceptions to the budget rule. He was one of 64 Democrats, most of them Blue Dogs, who voted against a 2007 bill to prevent the alternative minimum tax from hitting millions more families. But in 2009, with the economy in a severe recession, Tanner reluctantly backed President Obama's $787 economic stimulus package. "I would not support this package if I did not believe that our country's future hung in the balance," he said.

A member of the powerful Ways and Means Committee and a staunch free-trade advocate, Tanner pushed for a contested Colombia free-trade agreement in 2008. He backed the Peru trade pact in 2007 and was one of just 15 Democrats who voted for the Central America Free Trade Agreement in 2005. He also voted for the 2002 bill giving the president fast-track authority to enter into trade deals that can't be amended by Congress.

Tanner chairs Ways and Means' Social Security panel. He has been among a bipartisan group of lawmakers calling for an independent commission to study how to deal with the long-term instability of Social Security and Medicare, which are expected to become financially insolvent in the future.

He has spent his congressional career railing against the national debt, which he deems a deadly threat. "Foreign ownership of U.S. debt is a potential threat to national security and the U.S. economy," Tanner said in a Ways and Means hearing in 2008.

While Blue Dogs, like Republicans, spurn most tax increases, Tanner in 2008 helped persuade many of them to support a tax hike for the wealthy, dubbed the "millionaires' surtax," to finance expanded education benefits for veterans. "If we cannot have those who earn the most give a little more to those who give the most to this country, what has become of patriotism?" Tanner asked. Although the surtax was later dropped, the campaign aligned Blue Dogs with a call by party leaders to raise taxes on the rich to pay for other priorities, including extensions of middle-class tax cuts in the 111th Congress.

Tanner splits with a majority of his fellow Democrats on a number of topics. In 2008, he joined a centrist push to repeal restrictions on offshore oil drilling and helped pressure Speaker Nancy Pelosi of California to cut a deal on an overhaul of federal wiretapping authority by signing a letter with more than 20 Democrats to back a liability waiver for telecommunications companies. He also championed a proposal to roll back District of Columbia municipal gun control laws after the Supreme Court voided the city's handgun ban. He supports the drive for a constitutional amendment banning same-sex marriage and voted to outlaw a procedure opponents call "partial birth" abortion.

Earlier in his career, after Republicans took control of Congress in 1995, Tanner worked with moderate Republican Michael N. Castle of Delaware on a bipartisan bill overhauling the welfare system. President Clinton endorsed the Tanner-Castle measure, and elements of their bill eventually became part of the landmark law enacted in 1996.

From his seat on Foreign Affairs in the 110th, Tanner called for reinforcing the international peacekeeping mission in Afghanistan. "The United States and NATO are more or less joined at the hip. We must make a success of Afghanistan," Tanner said in 2007. He was designated by Pelosi to chair the House delegation to the NATO Parliamentary Assembly and was elected in November 2008 to a two-year term as president of that international group of legislators. "At this crucial time, it is imperative that we begin to rebuild our alliances with other NATO nations, especially given the role NATO is playing in Afghanistan in the global fight against radical fundamentalism," Tanner said.

Tanner's father was a farmer who also worked in the insurance business. His mother ran a dress shop. After earning his undergraduate and law degrees at the University of Tennessee, Tanner spent four years prosecuting courts-martial in the Navy. He then joined a private practice in his home-town of Union City. In 1976, he ran for the state House at the urging of colleagues in the American Legion, where he was a state officer. He won and served in the General Assembly for 12 years.

In 1988, when Democratic Rep. Ed Jones, a longtime family friend, retired, Tanner was fast out of the blocks. His relaxed, good-old-boy style helped him win over rural and small-town voters. He took 62 percent of the vote against Republican Ed Bryant, a Jackson lawyer, and has rolled to re-election ever since. After Al Gore was elected vice president in 1992, the Tennessee governor, Ned McWherter, had to appoint an interim replacement to fill Gore's seat in the Senate. The job was said to be Tanner's for the asking, but he told McWherter he preferred to stay in the House.

KEY VOTES

2008
P Delay consideration of Colombia free-trade agreement
Yes Override Bush veto of federal farm and nutrition programs reauthorization bill
Yes Overhaul surveillance laws and permit dismissal of suits against companies that conducted warrantless wiretapping
Yes Grant mortgage relief to homeowners and funding for Fannie Mae and Freddie Mac
Yes Approve initial $700 billion program to stabilize financial markets
Yes Approve final $700 billion program to stabilize financial markets
Yes Provide $14 billion in loans to automakers

2007
Yes Increase minimum wage by $2.10 an hour
Yes Approve $124.2 billion in emergency war spending and set goal for redeployment of troops from Iraq
No Reject federal contraceptive assistance to international family planning groups
Yes Override Bush veto of $23.2 billion water projects authorization bill
Yes Implement Peru free-trade agreement
Yes Approve energy policy overhaul with new fuel economy standards
Yes Clear $473.5 billion omnibus spending bill, including $70 billion for military operations

CQ VOTE STUDIES

	PARTY UNITY		PRESIDENTIAL SUPPORT	
	SUPPORT	OPPOSE	SUPPORT	OPPOSE
2008	95%	5%	22%	78%
2007	85%	15%	19%	81%
2006	74%	26%	66%	34%
2005	74%	26%	38%	62%
2004	74%	26%	39%	61%

INTEREST GROUPS

	AFL-CIO	ADA	CCUS	ACU
2008	100%	80%	71%	13%
2007	88%	80%	65%	21%
2006	71%	55%	86%	58%
2005	73%	75%	70%	50%
2004	69%	60%	56%	43%

TENNESSEE 8

West – Jackson; parts of Memphis and Clarksville

The mighty Mississippi to the west and the Tennessee and Cumberland rivers to the east frame the rolling hills and flat farmland that make up the predominately rural 8th. As residents flood to Memphis' northern sub-urbs and Nashville's western outposts, this once Democratic-leaning district shows growing Republican ties.

In the 2008 presidential election, suburban areas outside of the state's two most populous cities helped Republican John McCain defeat Barack Obama by 13 percentage points in the 8th. Large black populations in Haywood County helped Obama win there, and he also won in rural and generally poor Houston County. Conservative-leaning Democrats have held the area's U.S. House seat since Reconstruction.

The 8th is poor, but stable manufacturing in the Jackson area protects the economy from further decline. A Pringles potato chip facility in Jackson, the only Pringles plant in North America, employs many district residents. Tire, auto parts and chicken processing plants dot less-populous areas. Mechanization hurt factory employment, but it improved productivity on the district's many small cotton and soybean farms.

Two state prisons provide much-needed government jobs, and a naval air station has rebounded after previous downsizing. In the north, Clarksville's population has risen due to military growth and the expansion of Austin Peay State University.

The Tennessee River feeds into Kentucky Lake in the northeast, where conservationists journey each summer. The waterways of the Tennessee Valley Authority dams and power plants attract many avid hunters and fishermen to the district. Thousands of birdwatchers flock to Reelfoot Lake in the northwest each winter to view bald eagle migration.

MAJOR INDUSTRY
Manufacturing, agriculture, government

MILITARY BASES
Naval Support Activity Mid-South, 2,091 military, 1,195 civilian (2008)

CITIES
Jackson, 59,643; Memphis (pt.), 53,080; Clarksville (pt.), 19,775

NOTABLE
A 60-foot tall replica of the Eiffel Tower is in Paris, which is also home to the World's Biggest Fish Fry.

Rep. Steve Cohen (D)

Elected 2006; 2nd term

As a white House member with a large percentage of black constituents in his district, Cohen tries to make it clear where his loyalty lies. Shortly after his 2006 election, he sought to be the first Caucasian member of the Congressional Black Caucus — a bid that was unsuccessful yet emblematic of how he strives to stay in touch with his constituency.

Cohen — who represented a Memphis district in the state Senate for roughly 24 years — has since continued to try to further measures that keep him connected to his district, where about three-fifths of residents are black and just more than one-third are white. He works on legislation to help low-income constituents, and in February 2009 touted his 90 percent score and "A" rating from the NAACP as the highest in the Tennessee delegation.

He is a member of the Progressive Caucus and a firm liberal, supporting his party 98 percent of the time in the 110th Congress (2007-08) on votes in which majorities of the two parties diverged. But he said he recognizes the nation's many problems could temper a progressive agenda. "In politics, you have to move the ball forward, sometimes a little at a time. You make progress evolutionarily, not revolutionarily," he said in November 2008.

His greatest success came when the House approved his resolution offering a formal apology for slavery and for the segregationist policies of the Jim Crow era that ended with the civil rights laws of the 1960s. Such an apology had long been discussed in Congress, but it was only acted on when Cohen, a member of the Judiciary Committee, started pushing the idea in early 2007. The House adopted the resolution just a few days before Cohen faced his Memphis district Democratic voters in an Aug. 7, 2008, primary in which he faced two black challengers, including attorney Nikki Tinker, who ran second to him in the 2006 primary.

Cohen denied the primary had anything to do with the timing of the floor vote on his resolution, which was adopted by voice vote. But observers noted it was a bit strange that the resolution came up even though the Judiciary panel had never considered it.

Cohen, who supports the idea of a study for possibly making reparations to the millions of African-American descendants of slaves, said on the House floor that approval of his resolution was long overdue. He also was the author of a successful resolution honoring Memphis' role as a soul music center and another measure honoring the pre-integration-era Negro baseball leagues.

Cohen became chairman of Judiciary's Subcommittee on Commercial and Administrative Law in 2009, pledging to work on ways to let homeowners have their mortgages modified under bankruptcy court protection. He also joined Judiciary Chairman John Conyers Jr. of Michigan in introducing a bill in March 2009 to study racial disparities in the criminal justice system.

A member of the Transportation and Infrastructure Committee, Cohen also has brought home federal grants for institutions in his district, including Memphis International Airport, St. Jude Children's Research Hospital and the University of Tennessee's biocontainment laboratory.

Cohen is a fourth-generation member of a Jewish family in Memphis. His father was a pediatrician and his mother was a housewife. He contracted polio when he was 5 years old and still walks with a noticeable limp. But his physical limitations indirectly led to his liberal political outlook. As a child in the 1950s, his father took him to an exhibition Major League Baseball game in Memphis, and Cohen got to go down near the field to ask for play-

CAPITOL OFFICE
225-3265
cohen.house.gov
1005 Longworth Bldg. 20515-4209; fax 225-5663

COMMITTEES
Judiciary
 (Commercial & Administrative Law - chairman)
Transportation & Infrastructure

RESIDENCE
Memphis

BORN
May 24, 1949; Memphis, Tenn.

RELIGION
Jewish

FAMILY
Single

EDUCATION
Vanderbilt U., B.A. 1971 (history);
Memphis State U., J.D. 1973

CAREER
Lawyer

POLITICAL HIGHLIGHTS
Democratic nominee for Tenn. House, 1970;
Tenn. Constitutional Convention, 1977-78
(vice president, 1977-78); Shelby County
Commission, 1978-80; Shelby County General
Sessions Court, 1980-80; defeated for election
to Shelby County General Sessions Court, 1981;
Tenn. Senate, 1983-2006; sought Democratic
nomination for governor, 1994; sought
Democratic nomination for U.S. House, 1996

ELECTION RESULTS

2008 GENERAL

Steve Cohen (D)	198,798	87.8%
Jake Ford (I)	11,003	4.9%
Dewey Clark (I)	10,047	4.4%
Mary "Taylor Shelby" Wright (I)	6,434	2.8%

2008 PRIMARY

Steve Cohen (D)	50,306	79.4%
Nikki Tinker (D)	11,817	18.6%
Joe Towns Jr. (D)	914	1.4%

2006 GENERAL

Steve Cohen (D)	103,341	59.9%
Jake Ford (I)	38,243	22.2%
Mark White (R)	31,002	18.0%

rs' autographs. One of his idols was Minnie Minoso, a speedy black Cuban utfielder for the Chicago White Sox. He handed Minoso a program to sign, ut instead of handing it back to the boy, Minoso gave it to a white player tanding next to him to pass on to Cohen.

Cohen asked his father why his idol couldn't hand him the autograph irectly, and was told some of the realities of life in the segregated South. ohen, who has a picture of Minoso on his office wall, said he never forgot e incident, or Minoso. Cohen still leads an effort to get Minoso enshrined baseball's Hall of Fame in Cooperstown, N.Y.

Cohen graduated from Vanderbilt University, where he served as the chool's "Mr. Commodore" mascot and then came home to get a law degree om Memphis State University. He said he knew even as a youth that poli- cs and public service were for him. "I never really considered anything lse," he said.

He first ran for office at 21, undertaking a losing bid for the Tennessee Iouse. Seven few years later he was elected vice president of the Tennessee onstitutional Convention. A stint as a Shelby County commissioner fol- wed, and in 1983 he was elected to the state Senate. Cohen became known s the "father of Tennessee's lottery" for his longtime advocacy of the idea. he winding road to enactment included a fight to amend the state Consti- ution, followed by a successful public referendum.

When Harold E. Ford Jr. announced in 2006 he was giving up the U.S. Iouse seat he had taken over from his father, Cohen jumped into the con- est. He survived a 15-candidate primary in which Cohen's race was a major ssue, winning 31 percent of the vote. He coasted to victory that November.

In 2008, he faced a primary challenge from a field that again included inker. Cohen was endorsed by some Black Caucus members, while others ent for Tinker. Cohen raised far more money than his opponents and onfidently predicted an easy victory, but political analysts insisted the pri- ary would be competitive.

Racial issues again surfaced, especially in the last few days before the aug. 7 primary, when the Tinker campaign ran TV spots criticizing Cohen or coming to "our churches" in search of votes and for voting against an ffort to remove the name of Ku Klux Klan founder Nathan Bedford Forrest rom a Memphis park. Cohen said he had opposed the renaming because t would be divisive and because Forrest, his wife and Confederate veterans re buried in the park, and renaming would have involved the expensive rocess of relocating the graves. In the end, Cohen took the primary and on easily in November.

TENNESSEE 9
Memphis

he 9th takes in most of the state's largest city, Memphis, which sits atop e bluffs of the Mississippi River. Memphis is 60 percent African- merican, and counts more black residents than any Southern city utside of Texas. Traditional GOP voters gravitated out of the district to e outskirts of Shelby County, making the 9th the most comfortably emocratic district in Tennessee.

he area first sent an African-American to Congress in 1974, initiating a eign of Democratic black political power in Memphis. Although local lections still tend to be decided along racial lines, residents historically ote for Democrats in federal races. The 9th has favored Democratic andidates in U.S. House races with at least 60 percent of the vote for ecades. In 2008, Barack Obama took 77 percent of the district's vote for resident, by far his highest percentage in the state.

Memphis is the most populous city along the Mississippi and uses its entral location between St. Louis and New Orleans, as well as Memphis International Airport, to thrive as a distribution center. The

world's busiest cargo airport, it hosts FedEx's global hub. FedEx and the presence of several passenger carriers based at the airport have boosted the region's economy, although recent widespread layoffs at airline and freight carriers have hurt the district. And AutoZone, the nation's largest auto parts retailer, has headquarters in the 9th. The district also depends on St. Jude Children's Research Hospital and a local health care industry.

Renewal efforts have paved the way for inner-city economic development and new residential communities downtown. Tourism is a mainstay for the 9th, and both the FedExForum and Liberty Bowl Memorial Stadium draw audiences. Music-minded Memphis visitors take in Beale Street, and tourists flock here to honor two icons — Elvis Presley and Martin Luther King Jr. In 1968, King was assassinated at the Lorraine Motel, which is now a civil rights museum.

MAJOR INDUSTRY
Distribution, health care, tourism

CITIES
Memphis (pt.), 571,661

NOTABLE
Graceland was the home of Elvis Presley.

www.cq.com

2008
Yes Delay consideration of Colombia free-trade agreement
Yes Override Bush veto of federal farm and nutrition programs reauthorization bill
No   Overhaul surveillance laws and permit dismissal of suits against companies that conducted warrantless wiretapping
Yes Grant mortgage relief to homeowners and funding for Fannie Mae and Freddie Mac
Yes Approve initial $700 billion program to stabilize financial markets
Yes Approve final $700 billion program to stabilize financial markets
Yes Provide $14 billion in loans to automakers

2007
Yes Increase minimum wage by $2.10 an hour
Yes Approve $124.2 billion in emergency war spending and set goal for redeployment of troops from Iraq
No   Reject federal contraceptive assistance to international family planning groups
Yes Override Bush veto of $23.2 billion water projects authorization bill
No   Implement Peru free-trade agreement
Yes Approve energy policy overhaul with new fuel economy standards
No   Clear $473.5 billion omnibus spending bill, including $70 billion for military operations

CQ VOTE STUDIES

	PARTY UNITY		PRESIDENTIAL SUPPORT	
	SUPPORT	OPPOSE	SUPPORT	OPPOSE
2008	99%	1%	14%	86%
2007	97%	3%	4%	96%

INTEREST GROUPS

	AFL-CIO	ADA	CCUS	ACU
2008	100%	100%	61%	0%
2007	96%	100%	50%	0%

947

Gov. Rick Perry (R)

First elected: 2002; assumed office Dec. 21, 2000, following the resignation of George W. Bush, R, to become president
Length of term: 4 years
Term expires: 1/11
Salary: $150,000
Phone: (512) 463-2000

Residence: Austin
Born: March 4, 1950; Paint Creek, Texas
Religion: Methodist
Family: Wife, Anita Perry; two children
Education: Texas A&M U., B.S. 1972 (animal science)
Military service: Air Force, 1972-77
Career: Farmer; rancher
Political highlights: Texas House, 1984-90; Texas department of Agriculture commissioner, 1990-98; lieutenant governor, 1999-2000

Election results:
2006 GENERAL
Rick Perry (R)	1,716,792	39.0%
Chris Bell (D)	1,310,337	29.8%
Carole Keeton Strayhorn (I)	796,851	18.1%
Richard S. "Kinky" Friedman (I)	547,674	12.4%

Lt. Gov. David Dewhurst (R)

First elected: 2002
Length of term: 4 years
Term expires: 1/11
Salary: $7,200
Phone: (512) 463-0001

LEGISLATURE

Legislature: January-May in odd-numbered years
Senate: 31 members, 4-year terms
2009 ratios: 19 R, 12 D; 25 men, 6 women
Salary: $7,200
Phone: (512) 463-0001

House: 150 members, 2-year terms
2009 ratios: 76 R, 74 D; 113 men, 37 women
Salary: $7,200
Phone: (512) 463-0845

TERM LIMITS

Governor: No
Senate: No
House: No

URBAN STATISTICS

CITY	POPULATION
Houston	1,953,631
Dallas	1,188,580
San Antonio	1,144,646
Austin	656,562
El Paso	563,662

REGISTERED VOTERS

Voters do not register by party.

MISCELLANEOUS

Web: www.tx.gov
Capital: Austin

POPULATION

2008 population (est.)	24,326,974
2000 population	20,851,820
1990 population	16,986,510
Percent change (1990-2000)	+22.8%
Rank among states (2008)	2

Median age	32.3
Born in state	62.2%
Foreign born	13.9%
Violent crime rate	545/100,000
Poverty level	15.4%
Federal workers	173,367
Military	170,659

REDISTRICTING

The U.S. Supreme Court on June 28, 2006, invalidated part of the map that was used in the 2004 election. The U.S. District Court for the Eastern District of Texas on August 4, 2006, issued a new map that reconfigured five of Texas' 32 districts.

ELECTIONS

STATE ELECTION OFFICIAL
(512) 463-5650
DEMOCRATIC PARTY
(512) 478-9800
REPUBLICAN PARTY
(512) 477-9821

U.S. CONGRESS

Senate: 2 Republicans
House: 20 Republicans, 12 Democrats

2000 Census Statistics by District

DIST.	2008 VOTE FOR PRESIDENT OBAMA	MCCAIN	WHITE	BLACK	ASIAN	HISP	MEDIAN INCOME	WHITE COLLAR	BLUE COLLAR	SERVICE INDUSTRY	OVER 64	UNDER 18	COLLEGE EDUCATION	RURAL	SQ. MILES
1	30%	69%	71%	18%	1%	9%	$33,461	53%	31%	15%	14%	26%	18%	49%	8,508
2	40	60	64	19	3	13	$47,029	63	24	13	10	27	23	11	1,937
3	42	57	63	9	8	17	$60,878	75	15	10	5	29	41	1	265
4	30	69	79	10	1	8	$38,276	56	29	14	13	27	18	50	9,534
5	36	63	72	12	2	13	$41,007	60	27	14	12	27	19	32	5,429
6	40	60	66	13	3	16	$45,857	62	24	13	9	28	24	20	6,198
7	41	58	67	6	7	18	$57,846	79	11	9	9	24	50	0	198
8	26	74	80	9	1	9	$40,459	56	30	15	11	27	18	50	8,150
9	77	23	17	37	11	33	$34,870	58	23	19	6	30	24	0	154
10	44	55	66	9	4	19	$52,465	70	19	11	8	28	35	19	3,803
11	24	75	65	4	1	30	$32,711	55	28	17	15	27	17	29	34,995
12	36	63	67	6	2	24	$41,735	58	28	14	10	28	21	17	2,168
13	23	76	74	6	1	18	$33,501	53	29	18	14	26	17	30	40,197
14	33	66	62	10	2	25	$41,335	56	29	15	11	28	19	29	7,095
15	60	40	20	2	1	78	$26,840	52	28	19	11	32	13	18	10,717

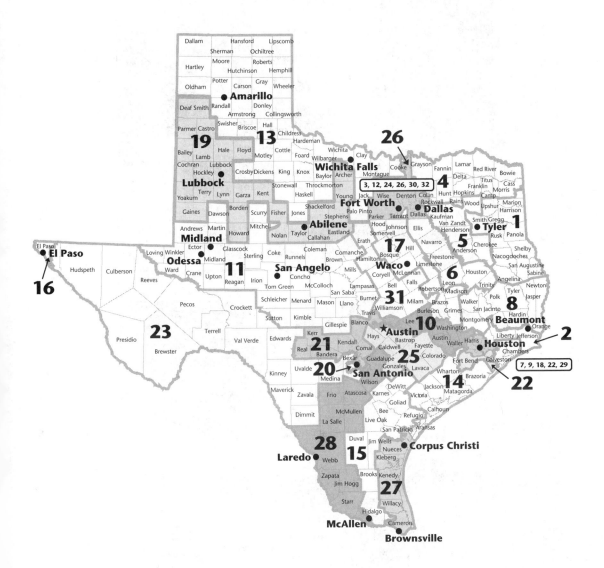

2000 Census Statistics by District

DIST.	2008 VOTE FOR PRESIDENT OBAMA	MCCAIN	WHITE	BLACK	ASIAN	HISP	MEDIAN INCOME	WHITE COLLAR	BLUE COLLAR	SERVICE INDUSTRY	OVER 64	UNDER 18	COLLEGE EDUCATION	RURAL	SQ. MILES
16	66%	33%	17%	3%	1%	78%	$31,245	58%	25%	17%	10%	32%	17%	2%	581
17	32	67	71	10	1	15	$35,253	57	27	16	12	25	20	36	7,691
18	77	22	20	40	3	36	$31,291	52	30	18	8	29	14	0	227
19	27	72	64	5	1	29	$31,575	57	26	17	13	27	19	26	25,268
20	64	36	23	7	1	67	$31,937	57	24	19	10	29	15	0	184
21	41	58	68	6	3	21	$49,036	73	15	12	12	24	37	19	5,130
22	41	58	61	9	8	20	$57,932	69	20	11	7	29	32	5	971
23	51	48	30	3	1	65	$33,574	56	27	17	10	31	18	24	48,456
24	44	55	64	10	6	18	$56,098	73	17	10	6	27	36	1	334
25	59	40	53	10	2	34	$39,794	61	23	15	9	25	28	25	6,146

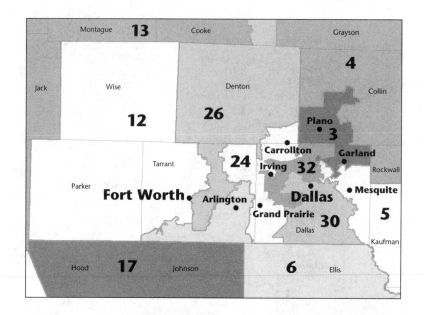

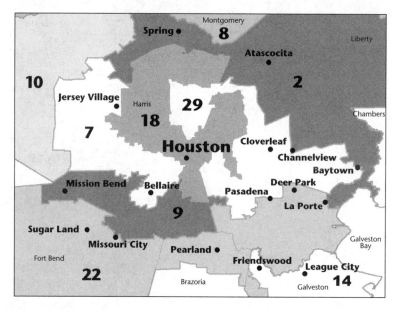

2000 Census Statistics by District

DIST.	2008 VOTE FOR PRESIDENT OBAMA	MCCAIN	WHITE	BLACK	ASIAN	HISP	MEDIAN INCOME	WHITE COLLAR	BLUE COLLAR	SERVICE INDUSTRY	OVER 64	UNDER 18	COLLEGE EDUCATION	RURAL	SQ. MILES
26	41%	58%	66%	15%	2%	14%	$48,714	64%	22%	13%	8%	29%	27%	9%	1,292
27	53	46	28	2	1	68	$31,327	55	26	18	11	31	16	11	4,720
28	56	44	20	1	0	78	$28,866	51	31	18	9	34	13	21	13,600
29	62	38	22	10	1	66	$31,751	40	43	16	7	33	6	1	236
30	82	18	22	41	1	34	$33,505	52	31	17	8	30	16	1	317
31	41	57	66	13	2	16	$43,381	63	23	14	9	29	24	22	7,134
32	46	53	50	8	4	36	$45,725	66	21	13	9	25	36	0	160
STATE	44	56	52	11	3	32	$39,927	61	25	15	10	28	23	17	261,797
U.S.	53	46	69	12	4	13	$41,994	60	25	15	12	26	24	21	3,537,438

Sen. Kay Bailey Hutchison (R)

Elected June 1993; 3rd full term

A trailblazing woman in the rough-and-tumble world of Texas politics, Hutchison is well-regarded in her home state. Her name is rarely attached to major legislation, and she has allowed Texas' junior senator, Republican John Cornyn, to step out front on most national issues. But while the one-time cheerleader doesn't play to the galleries, she works behind the scenes to fund Lone Star State projects and safeguard her constituents' pocketbooks.

Hutchison has a strongly conservative voting record, but is considered a bit wishy-washy on the issue of abortion by some of those to the right of her in Texas. Though she usually votes with her anti-abortion colleagues, she has supported federal funding for embryonic stem cell research, which uses discarded embryos created for in vitro fertilization, and dodged questions on whether she would like to see the Supreme Court's 1973 *Roe v. Wade* decision legalizing abortion overturned.

After Pennsylvania Sen. Arlen Specter broke from the GOP to join the Democrats in April 2009, a Texas Monthly writer suggested Hutchison consider doing the same. She shot back an e-mail: "I was a proud Republican even when we could hold our gatherings in a phone booth. Having helped make the GOP the dominant party in Texas in the late '90s, I am committed to helping us get back on track both here in Texas and in the nation."

She's hoping her popularity will carry over into a run for governor in 2010. In December 2008, she set up an exploratory committee for a bid to unseat incumbent Republican Rick Perry. While Hutchison is, by and large, a stalwart partisan in Washington, she'll be cast as the moderate against Perry.

First elected to the GOP Senate leadership team in 2000, breaking an all-male glass ceiling, Hutchison dropped a planned bid for the third-ranking post of conference chairman in late 2007, when Mississippi Sen. Trent Lott retired, because of opposition from conservatives in the caucus.

That move, along with her decision in 2006 to back off a run against Perry, has raised questions about whether she can handle a tough fight, after years of easy elections. But it's a "bad rap," she told the Dallas Morning News: "If I'm committed to doing something, I'm a fighter." Win or lose, Hutchison said, she will not pursue a fourth full Senate term in 2012. She stepped down from her chairmanship of the GOP Policy Committee in November 2008 to prepare for the gubernatorial run.

Hutchison has shown her mettle in her occasional breaks with her party. She tried to forge a deal in 2007 on legislation aimed at helping young illegal immigrants to stay in the country if they have earned a U.S. high school diploma or been admitted to a higher education program in the United States. Most Republicans opposed the bill, and it ultimately failed to win enough votes to make it to the floor. Later that year, she wrote a provision in a major spending bill to provide the Homeland Security Department with more flexibility in designing and building a Southwest border fence, prompting some immigration hard-liners to deride her as soft on illegal immigration.

She also parted with Republicans in early 2007 when she expressed lukewarm feelings about President George W. Bush's decision to send more than 21,000 additional troops to Iraq. Instead she joined Senate Foreign Relations Chairman Joseph R. Biden Jr. of Delaware — now the vice president — in pushing to partition Iraq along ethnic and religious lines.

In 2009 she backed an expansion of the State Children's Health Insurance Program, which provides coverage to children whose families don't qualify for Medicaid; Bush had vetoed earlier versions. A member of the Banking,

CAPITOL OFFICE
4-5922
tchison.senate.gov
4 Russell Bldg. 20510-4304; fax 224-0776

COMMITTEES
propriations
anking, Housing & Urban Affairs
mmerce, Science & Transportation
- ranking member
les & Administration

RESIDENCE
allas

BORN
ly 22, 1943; Galveston, Texas

RELIGION
iscopalian

FAMILY
usband, Ray Hutchison; two children

EDUCATION
of Texas, B.A. 1992, J.D. 1967

CAREER
oadcast journalist; lawyer; banking executive;
ndy company owner

POLITICAL HIGHLIGHTS
xas House, 1973-76; National Transportation
afety Board, 1976-78; sought Republican
mination for U.S. House, 1982; Texas treasurer,
91-93

ELECTION RESULTS

2006 GENERAL
ay Bailey Hutchison (R)	2,661,789	61.7%
arbara Ann Radnofsky (D)	1,555,202	36.0%
cott Lanier Jameson (LIBERT)	97,672	2.3%

2006 PRIMARY
ay Bailey Hutchison (R) unopposed

PREVIOUS WINNING PERCENTAGES
00 (65%); 1994 (61%); 1993 Special Runoff
ection (67%)

Housing and Urban Affairs Committee, she supported the 2008 law to rescue the ailing financial services sector.

Hutchison has brought home billions in federal funding, much in the form of earmarks — funding set-asides for special projects — she secures via her seat on the Appropriations panel. She has fought to ensure that Texans can continue to deduct the sales tax they pay from their federal taxes, a crucial issue there because Texas does not have a state income tax, which is a big federal deduction for most taxpayers. She has also fought to keep tolls off the state's highways and to allow Texas to withdraw from the federal government's system for funding new road construction, to which Texas has in the past contributed more than it has received in return. This has added in no small part to her success and to the overwhelming support she gets at the ballot box. She breezed to a full third term in 2006 with 62 percent of the vote.

Hutchison also sits on the Rules and Administration Committee and is the top Republican on the Commerce, Science and Transportation Committee. As the top Republican on Commerce's subcommittee on aviation during the 110th Congress (2007-08), she worked to help airlines based in her states.

During the 2008 reauthorization of the Federal Aviation Administration, Hutchison fought to remove an accounting section in the bill aimed at securing airline pension plans that she feared would put Dallas-based American Airlines and Houston-based Continental Airlines at a competitive disadvantage. In 2006, Hutchison was instrumental in helping to resolve a dispute that raged for decades between American and Southwest Airlines over the use of Dallas' Love Field, which is Southwest's headquarters.

Her solid career and leadership experience have quieted critics who used to portray her as superficial. When she was Texas state treasurer, the late liberal newspaper columnist Molly Ivins dubbed her "the Breck Girl," after an old shampoo commercial featuring a woman tossing her long tresses.

But Hutchison is well aware of her role as a model for younger women, and in 2007 she published "Leading Ladies: American Trailblazers" with biographies of successful women across a range of fields. Hutchison was the first, and so far only, woman elected to the Senate from Texas.

She graduated in 1967 from the University of Texas School of Law, one of only five women in a class of 500. She found law firms weren't willing to hire women, assuming they would get married and quit or move away. Instead, Hutchison took a job as a legal correspondent for a television station.

She grew up in La Marque, a small town on the Gulf Coast. Her great-great-grandfather, Charles S. Taylor, was a signer of the Texas Declaration of Independence. In a school diary, Hutchison once penciled, "I want to be president of the United States." But she says she never had any real political ambitions until a local GOP leader urged her to run for the state House. She did and was elected in 1972, a time when most women in Texas politics were Democrats.

In 1976, President Ford appointed her to the National Transportation Safety Board. Hutchison moved to Dallas in 1978 and married for a second time, to attorney Ray Hutchison, a former colleague in the state House. She unsuccessfully sought the GOP nomination for an open U.S. House seat in 1982. Hutchison spent a good chunk of the 1980s in the business world, as a banking executive and owner of a candy-manufacturing company.

Returning to politics in 1990, she was elected state treasurer. In 1993, she won a special Senate election called after President Clinton chose longtime Democratic Sen. Lloyd Bentsen to be his Treasury secretary. Democratic Gov. Ann W. Richards appointed Bob Krueger, a former House member, to the seat. Hutchison challenged him in the state's open primary, also competing against Republican Reps. Joe L. Barton and Jack Fields. Krueger and Hutchison tied with 29 percent of the vote; she won the runoff with 67 percent. She has won easily ever since.

KEY VOTES

2008

Yes	Prohibit discrimination based on genetic information
Yes	Reauthorize farm and nutrition programs for five years
No	Limit debate on "cap and trade" system for greenhouse gas emissions
No	Allow lawsuits against companies that participated in warrantless wiretapping
Yes	Limit debate on a bill to block a scheduled cut in Medicare payments to doctors
No	Grant mortgage relief to homeowners and funding for Fannie Mae and Freddie Mac
Yes	Approve a nuclear cooperation agreement with India
Yes	Approve final $700 billion program to stabilize financial markets
No	Allow consideration of a $14 billion auto industry loan package

2007

Yes	Increase minimum wage by $2.10 an hour
No	Limit debate on a comprehensive immigration bill
Yes	Overhaul congressional lobbying and ethics rules for members and their staffs
No	Limit debate on considering a bill to add House seats for the District of Columbia and Utah
No	Limit debate on restoring habeas corpus rights to detainees
No	Mandate minimum breaks for troops between deployments to Iraq or Afghanistan
Yes	Override Bush veto of $23.2 billion water projects authorization bill
Yes	Confirm Michael B. Mukasey as attorney general
No	Limit debate on an energy policy overhaul containing $21.8 billion in tax incentives and reduced oil and gas subsidies

CQ VOTE STUDIES

	PARTY UNITY		PRESIDENTIAL SUPPORT	
	SUPPORT	OPPOSE	SUPPORT	OPPOSE
2008	94%	6%	67%	33%
2007	88%	12%	80%	20%
2006	91%	9%	84%	16%
2005	90%	10%	96%	4%
2004	89%	11%	94%	6%
2003	94%	6%	96%	4%
2002	92%	8%	96%	4%
2001	90%	10%	96%	4%
2000	96%	4%	45%	55%
1999	90%	10%	29%	71%

INTEREST GROUPS

	AFL-CIO	ADA	CCUS	ACU
2008	20%	20%	100%	76%
2007	26%	20%	90%	88%
2006	20%	5%	92%	84%
2005	14%	15%	94%	92%
2004	8%	25%	94%	84%
2003	0%	10%	100%	75%
2002	23%	5%	95%	100%
2001	19%	10%	85%	96%
2000	0%	0%	93%	96%
1999	0%	0%	94%	88%

Sen. John Cornyn (R)

Elected 2002; 2nd term

Ambitious and well-respected by colleagues, Cornyn hopes to succeed where former President George W. Bush — his good friend and fellow Texan — failed. He wants to combat an ascendant Democratic Party and re-establish the conservative brand with voters, while giving his own national profile a lift in the process.

Cornyn (CORE-nin) is far less brash and more formal than Bush, but just as disdainful of many Democratic ideas. He also shares a willingness to play up his Lone Star ties. He wears cowboy boots emblazoned with "United States Senate Texas" along with his business suits. And he recorded a campaign video in 2008 as cowboy-hatted, fringe-jacketed "Big Bad John," a takeoff on the 1960s hit song of the same name. The video became popular on YouTube; it included the lyrics "He rose to the top in just one term, kept Texas in power, made lesser states squirm."

At the start of his second term in 2009, Cornyn took over as chairman of the National Republican Senatorial Committee, the Senate GOP's recruiting and fundraising arm. (He had previously served as vice chairman of the Senate Republican Conference.) He faces the task of trying to recapture control of the Senate when nearly half the seats his minority party now holds will be on the ballot in 2010. The job puts him at the fulcrum of the competing pressures within his party, either to strengthen ideological purity in order to shore up the base, or to relax its orthodoxy in an effort to expand that base.

Cornyn's response in the early months of the 111th Congress (2009-10) was aggressive rhetoric and tough tactics. He criticized and briefly held up the nominations of Hillary Rodham Clinton and Eric H. Holder Jr. as President Obama's secretary of State and attorney general. He also objected to the seating of Democratic senatorial contender Al Franken of Minnesota, who edged ahead of Republican incumbent Norm Coleman in the final recount of the November 2008 election. He served notice he would target Democratic senators politically for backing what he considers excessive spending.

While acknowledging the early enthusiasm for Obama as a "phenomenon," he said it didn't mean his party should be accommodating. "If you talked to any pollster after the election, they would say this was an election based on personalities," he said. "This is still a center-right country ideologically."

Cornyn plans to upgrade the NRSC's fundraising structure, which took in $93 million during the 2007-08 election cycle — more than $60 million behind the Democrats' campaign organization. He vowed to help the party compete more vigorously in adopting voter outreach based on technological tools such as social networking sites, text messaging and online fundraising.

Taking the NRSC post enabled Cornyn to give up a thankless job on the Select Ethics Committee, where he served as vice chairman in the 110th Congress (2007-08). He also relinquished his seat on the Armed Services Committee. In its place, he acquired a coveted slot on the Finance Committee, where he is expected to be a key proponent of making permanent the Bush tax cuts of 2001 and 2003. He also will figure in resisting Democratic efforts to enact broad-ranging health care; he fears a government-run system could lead to rationing of services and fewer alternatives for individuals.

Cornyn retained his seat on the Budget Committee. In fall 2008, he backed the $700 billion law to shore up the ailing financial services industry but sharply criticized Obama's early economic initiatives, including a $787 billion economic stimulus law he said was "not bipartisan."

Cornyn loyally supported Bush in his floor votes, but parted company

CAPITOL OFFICE
224-2934
cornyn.senate.gov
517 Hart Bldg. 20510-4302; fax 228-2856

COMMITTEES
Budget
Finance
Judiciary

RESIDENCE
San Antonio

BORN
Feb. 2, 1952; Houston, Texas

RELIGION
Church of Christ

FAMILY
Wife, Sandy Cornyn; two children

EDUCATION
Trinity U., B.A. 1973 (journalism);
St. Mary's U. (Texas), J.D. 1977; U. of Virginia, LL.M. 1995

CAREER
Lawyer; real estate agent

POLITICAL HIGHLIGHTS
Texas District Court judge, 1985-91; Texas Supreme Court, 1991-97; Texas attorney general, 1999-2002

ELECTION RESULTS

2008 GENERAL

John Cornyn (R)	4,337,469	54.8%
Richard J. "Rick" Noriega (D)	3,389,365	42.8%
Yvonne Adams Schick (LIBERT)	185,241	2.3%

2008 PRIMARY

John Cornyn (R)	997,216	81.5%
Larry Kilgore (R)	226,649	18.5%

PREVIOUS WINNING PERCENTAGES
2002 (55%)

with him on immigration. A member of the Judiciary Committee, he rejected a comprehensive approach favored by Bush and passed by the Senate in 2006 because it included a path to eventual U.S. citizenship for most illegal immigrants. Instead, he offered his own bill, with Republican Jon Kyl of Arizona, to require immigrants to return home before they could apply for temporary guest worker status that didn't include eventual citizenship. He tried again in 2009, seeking to prod Obama to lead the effort as he worked with New York Democrat Charles E. Schumer.

As chairman of the Judiciary Subcommittee on the Constitution in the 108th Congress (2003-04), Cornyn spearheaded efforts to pass proposed constitutional amendments banning same-sex marriage and flag burning. None of the proposals made it through the Senate.

A former Texas attorney general, district court judge and state Supreme Court judge, Cornyn chafes at many judicial rulings on social issues. In 2005, he suggested in a Senate floor speech that public anger over politically charged decisions might be responsible for several instances of violence against judges. He returned to the floor a day later to say, "There is no possible justification for courthouse violence."

Cornyn also backed Bush's decision to wage war in Iraq and to deploy a national missile defense system. In 2005, he was one of just nine senators — all Republicans — to vote against an amendment banning cruel, inhumane or degrading treatment of prisoners captured in the fight against terrorism.

Cornyn, who once considered a career in journalism, is a strong proponent of more openness in government. He is a forceful advocate of the Freedom of Information Act, steering a bill through the Senate in 2005 to require Congress to tell the public when it exempts information from FOIA disclosures. In 2006, and again in 2007, he helped guide legislation through Judiciary to permit applicants to track the progress of their requests for information.

Cornyn's career in state government was characterized primarily by a pro-business, limited-government philosophy. He favored strict restrictions on medical malpractice lawsuits, and while on the state Supreme Court, he joined a ruling allowing cigarette companies to partially escape responsibility for smoking-related health claims.

Cornyn is the son of a World War II B-17 pilot. His family eventually settled in San Antonio, where his father became an Air Force pathologist. A wrestler in high school and college, Cornyn majored in journalism at Texas' Trinity University. He waited tables while earning his real estate license. When that career faltered in a sagging economy, he went to law school. He later practiced in San Antonio, specializing in defending doctors against medical malpractice suits.

In 1984, some Republican friends — looking to crack the Democrats' longstanding hold on Texas' judicial elections — asked him to run for a state district court seat. He did, and he won. Six years later, he was elected to the state Supreme Court. In 1998, he won a bruising attorney general's race against Democrat Jim Mattox.

As attorney general, Cornyn chaired a commission tasked with proposing new political boundaries to the state legislature after the 2000 census. He presented a redistricting plan that could have resulted in major Republican gains. The courts eventually imposed a less partisan map.

When Texas GOP Sen. Phil Gramm decided to retire in 2002, Cornyn ran for the seat and won a GOP primary against four little-known opponents. In the November race against former Dallas Mayor Ron Kirk, now the U.S. trade representative, Cornyn ran on his loyalty to Bush and won with 55 percent. Six years later, Cornyn's opponent was Richard J. "Rick" Noriega, a Democratic state representative from Houston. Cornyn swamped him in fundraising and won with 55 percent of the vote.

KEY VOTES

2008

Yes   Prohibit discrimination based on genetic information

Yes   Reauthorize farm and nutrition programs for five years

?   Limit debate on "cap and trade" system for greenhouse gas emissions

No   Allow lawsuits against companies that participated in warrantless wiretapping

Yes   Limit debate on a bill to block a scheduled cut in Medicare payments to doctors

No   Grant mortgage relief to homeowners and funding for Fannie Mae and Freddie Mac

Yes   Approve a nuclear cooperation agreement with India

Yes   Approve final $700 billion program to stabilize financial markets

–   Allow consideration of a $14 billion auto industry loan package

2007

Yes   Increase minimum wage by $2.10 an hour

No   Limit debate on a comprehensive immigration bill

No   Overhaul congressional lobbying and ethics rules for members and their staffs

No   Limit debate on considering a bill to add House seats for the District of Columbia and Utah

No   Limit debate on restoring habeas corpus rights to detainees

No   Mandate minimum breaks for troops between deployments to Iraq or Afghanistan

+   Override Bush veto of $23.2 billion water projects authorization bill

+   Confirm Michael B. Mukasey as attorney general

No   Limit debate on an energy policy overhaul containing $21.8 billion in tax incentives and reduced oil and gas subsidies

CQ VOTE STUDIES

	PARTY UNITY		PRESIDENTIAL SUPPORT	
	SUPPORT	OPPOSE	SUPPORT	OPPOSE
2008	97%	3%	73%	27%
2007	98%	2%	91%	9%
2006	97%	3%	91%	9%
2005	95%	5%	98%	2%
2004	97%	3%	96%	4%
2003	99%	1%	98%	2%

INTEREST GROUPS

	AFL-CIO	ADA	CCUS	ACU
2008	11%	20%	100%	79%
2007	0%	15%	80%	96%
2006	13%	0%	83%	96%
2005	14%	10%	89%	96%
2004	8%	5%	100%	100%
2003	0%	10%	100%	85%

Rep. Louie Gohmert (R)

Elected 2004; 3rd term

CAPITOL OFFICE
225-3035
www.house.gov/gohmert
511 Cannon Bldg. 20515-4301; fax 226-1230

COMMITTEES
Judiciary
Natural Resources
Small Business

RESIDENCE
Tyler

BORN
Aug. 18, 1953; Pittsburg, Texas

RELIGION
Baptist

FAMILY
Wife, Kathy Gohmert; three children

EDUCATION
Texas A&M U., B.A. 1975 (history);
Baylor U., J.D. 1977

MILITARY SERVICE
Army, 1978-82

CAREER
Lawyer; state prosecutor

POLITICAL HIGHLIGHTS
Smith County District Court judge, 1993-2002;
Texas Court of Appeals chief justice, 2002-03

ELECTION RESULTS

2008 GENERAL

Louie Gohmert (R)	189,012	87.6%
Roger L. Owen (I)	26,814	12.4%

2008 PRIMARY

Louie Gohmert (R)	unopposed

2006 GENERAL

Louie Gohmert (R)	104,099	68.0%
Roger L. Owen (D)	46,303	30.2%
Donald Perkison (LIBERT)	2,668	1.7%

PREVIOUS WINNING PERCENTAGES
2004 (61%)

A former judge, Gohmert is a conservative provocateur, wielding a sharp tongue and comic timing to stand out from the meeker members of the minority. He uses a combination of persistence, logic and humor — including sarcasm and facetious gestures — to make his points, even if that approach sometimes backfires or brings him unwanted attention.

Gohmert rages against spending bills he views as too costly, including bills to rescue the ailing economy. And he has been a dogged conservative voice on his committees, using his Natural Resources seat to push for more domestic energy production and using his Judiciary post to advance his socially conservative agenda.

Gohmert was one of the loudest voices arguing against the $700 billion financial sector rescue measure in the fall of 2008. On the morning of the first vote, as leaders were hoping to pass the bill and leave town by midday, Gohmert offered a delaying tactic that irritated his colleagues. "I motion to adjourn," he said, "so we don't do this terrible thing to America." The motion got only eight votes, and one lawmaker called him an "SOB," but Gohmert was unrepentant. After the bailout was approved a few days later, Gohmert said Congress should rescind it and instead suspend income taxes and Social Security taxes for the first two months of 2009.

Gohmert also railed against President Obama's $787 billion economic stimulus law in 2009, offering his own alternative: a two-month holiday for wage earners from all payroll and income taxes.

But he was one of just 34 House members who voted against a package of tax rebates in early 2008, objecting to the fact that payments could go to workers who earned too little to owe income taxes. He took advantage of a quick chat with President George W. Bush to needle him on the subject. "There was $40 billion in there dedicated as rebates to people who did not pay tax," Gohmert said later. "So I asked the president there at the State of the Union, how do you give a rebate to people who didn't put any 'bate' in?"

Gohmert also opposes annual increases in federal spending to compensate for inflation. But when Hurricane Rita hit his district in 2005, he said the federal government wasn't doing enough to reimburse "the many communities, faith-based entities and the state of Texas," which had "drained [their] assets to save lives," The Washington Post reported.

In the 110th Congress (2007-08), he was particularly vocal on the treatment of terrorism suspects, flustering Attorney General Michael B. Mukasey by asking during a Judiciary hearing whether Mukasey would be willing to prosecute Gohmert's Army drill sergeant for committing acts of torture during basic training. Gohmert was using a ridiculous question to make a point: "It just occurs to me that we have people in uniform of our own country that go through worse so-called torture by drill instructors than those that are being defended in Congress at this time who want to destroy our country," he said. To make his point, he introduced a bill to move detainees from the U.S. naval base at Guantánamo Bay, Cuba, to the grounds of the U.S. Supreme Court so the justices can "more effectively micromanage" them.

Gohmert's experience as a judge is reflected in the legislation he introduced in his first term to increase criminal penalties against people who threaten or attack judges and prosecutors. He said it was prompted by the 2005 murder in Chicago of U.S. District Judge Joan Lefkow's husband and mother by a litigant she ruled against in a medical malpractice suit. Another incident occurred in Gohmert's hometown of Tyler; in February 2005, an armed man killed his ex-wife and wounded his son and several police officers right outside the Smith County courthouse where Gohmert had presided. Gohmert said he has been threatened many times by defendants and people he put in jail.

In his first term, he strained the patience of both Democrats and Republicans during a Judiciary debate on a measure aimed at reducing recidivism rates of newly released prisoners. Gohmert tried nine times over three hours to add language expressly stating that faith-based organizations would be eligible for funds under the bill. All of his attempts were rejected.

He was similarly persistent during a 2007 debate on a bill to help former inmates adjust to life after imprisonment. He tried at two separate Judiciary panel meetings to strike the phrase "creed and religion" from an amendment prohibiting religious groups from discriminating against employees. Gohmert angered Jewish Democrats when he suggested that not allowing religious groups to hire only employees of like faith could force Jewish organizations to hire Nazis. "I said nothing inappropriate and nothing that should have been taken out of context. I meant what I said," Gohmert recalled. "You would be forced to hire people who wanted to work against what you wanted to do."

Gohmert grew up in Mount Pleasant, an East Texas town of 8,000 where his father worked as an architect and his mother taught eighth-grade English. He worked a variety of jobs while growing up, including hauling hay, pumping gas and working at a construction site. He first won elective office as class president of his junior high school. He followed his father in attending Texas A&M University, where he was given an ROTC scholarship and rose to the rank of brigade commander in the school's Corps of Cadets.

Gohmert attended law school, then worked as a state assistant district attorney for three East Texas counties while waiting for his call to active military duty. He served four years as an Army lawyer at Fort Benning, Ga.

Returning to Texas in 1982, he worked as a civil litigator on mostly contract and insurance cases. His mother's death in 1991 prompted him to consider her advice to become a judge. He ran in 1992 after he was unable to find anyone willing to challenge the Smith County District Court incumbent. He served for the next 10 years, then was appointed by the governor to the Texas Court of Appeals.

After former House Majority Leader Tom DeLay's success in pushing through the Texas redistricting plan, Gohmert unseated four-term Democratic Rep. Max Sandlin in 2004 by almost 24 percentage points. Gohmert won easily in 2006 and 2008.

KEY VOTES

2008

No Delay consideration of Colombia free-trade agreement
Yes Override Bush veto of federal farm and nutrition programs reauthorization bill
? Overhaul surveillance laws and permit dismissal of suits against companies that conducted warrantless wiretapping
? Grant mortgage relief to homeowners and funding for Fannie Mae and Freddie Mac
No Approve initial $700 billion program to stabilize financial markets
No Approve final $700 billion program to stabilize financial markets
No Provide $14 billion in loans to automakers

2007

No Increase minimum wage by $2.10 an hour
No Approve $124.2 billion in emergency war spending and set goal for redeployment of troops from Iraq
Yes Reject federal contraceptive assistance to international family planning groups
No Override Bush veto of $23.2 billion water projects authorization bill
Yes Implement Peru free-trade agreement
No Approve energy policy overhaul with new fuel economy standards
Yes Clear $473.5 billion omnibus spending bill, including $70 billion for military operations

CQ VOTE STUDIES

	PARTY UNITY		PRESIDENTIAL SUPPORT	
	SUPPORT	OPPOSE	SUPPORT	OPPOSE
2008	92%	8%	63%	37%
2007	97%	3%	82%	18%
2006	93%	7%	78%	22%
2005	95%	5%	88%	12%

INTEREST GROUPS

	AFL-CIO	ADA	CCUS	ACU
2008	7%	10%	75%	96%
2007	9%	10%	80%	100%
2006	18%	5%	100%	96%
2005	15%	0%	85%	96%

TEXAS 1
Northeast – Tyler, Longview

In this lush portion of East Texas, tree-covered hills and cypress swamps share space with what remains of the once-prominent oil centers in Longview and Tyler and Nacogdoches County. Slower population growth in comparison to the rest of the state and miles of forests and farmland are hallmarks of the 1st, which runs roughly 140 miles along the Louisiana border and takes in the Toledo Bend Reservoir. The district shares more traits with its traditionally laid-back Cajun neighbors than with the fast-paced urban life of nearby Dallas and its suburbs.

Timber is still central to the economy of the southern part of the 1st, complemented by poultry, dairy and beef cattle operations. But timber has faced stiff competition from companies in China and South America, where wage and energy costs are lower. After Hurricane Rita caused severe wind damage to the local timber crop in 2005, Hurricane Ike hit parts of the 1st with high winds and flooding again in 2008. Although unemployment rates have spiked in timber-dependent Sabine County, retirees moving in have kept the housing market relatively stable.

In Smith County, the 1st's western edge, Tyler's economy is growing. It has stable timber, natural gas and health care industries, with some hospital systems based in the city. The area, however, has struggled with massive layoffs at major manufacturing employers Eastman Chemical in Longview and Carrier and Trane facilities in Tyler. SYSCO has a regional distribution center in Longview.

Residents tend to be conservative, even among Democrats, and the region associates itself with the Bible Belt that stretches through much of the South. The 1st has one of the state's highest percentages of elderly residents, which makes health care access an important issue in rural areas. Many of the district's largest and most-populated counties — Nacogdoches, Rusk, Gregg and Smith — reliably favor Republicans. John McCain won 69 percent of the district's vote in the 2008 presidential election.

MAJOR INDUSTRY
Timber, agriculture, manufacturing, steel, oil and gas

CITIES
Tyler, 83,650; Longview, 73,344; Lufkin, 32,709; Nacogdoches, 29,914

NOTABLE
Tyler boasts the nation's largest public rose garden, with 40,000 roses.

Rep. Ted Poe (R)

CAPITOL OFFICE
225-6565
poe.house.gov
430 Cannon Bldg. 20515-4302; fax 225-5547

COMMITTEES
Foreign Affairs
Judiciary

RESIDENCE
Humble

BORN
Sept. 10, 1948; Temple, Texas

RELIGION
United Church of Christ

FAMILY
Wife, Carol Poe; four children

EDUCATION
Abilene Christian College, B.A. 1970
(political science); U. of Houston, J.D. 1973

MILITARY SERVICE
Air Force Reserve, 1970-76

CAREER
County prosecutor; college instructor

POLITICAL HIGHLIGHTS
Harris County District Court judge, 1981-2003

ELECTION RESULTS

2008 GENERAL

Ted Poe (R)	175,101	88.9%
Craig Wolfe (LIBERT)	21,813	11.1%

2008 PRIMARY

Ted Poe (R)	unopposed

2006 GENERAL

Ted Poe (R)	90,490	65.6%
Gary E. Binderim (D)	45,080	32.7%
Justo J. Perez (LIBERT)	2,295	1.7%

PREVIOUS WINNING PERCENTAGES
2004 (56%)

Elected 2004; 3rd term

Poe says he was shy as a child, but now he can be found almost daily on the House floor, delivering pithy one-minute speeches espousing his fervently conservative views before the C-SPAN cameras. "I'm still shy," he said. "But when it comes to getting down in the mud and the blood and the beer with people, I usually have a position and I tell them what I think." What he thinks is never in doubt. And neither is he, ending every speech with the same sign-off: "And that's just the way it is."

Poe likes to say he is a conservative first and a Republican second, and nowhere is that more true than in his unbending views on crime and punishment. A former county prosecutor who spent 22 years as a judge in Houston, he made it a point to publicly shame convicts in what became known as "Poe-etic justice." He now propounds his get-tough stance as a member of the Judiciary and Foreign Affairs committees.

Not surprisingly, President Obama's administration is one of his favorite targets. In a speech marking the 100th day of Obama's presidency, Poe said, "The question to be asked is, 'Is America safer today than a hundred days ago?'" He then listed a litany of grievances, from Obama's decision to close the prison for terrorist detainees at the U.S. naval base at Cuba's Guantánamo Bay to "the little fellow from Iran" — President Mahmoud Ahmadinejad — pursuing nuclear weapons to destroy Israel.

Poe became something of a sensation on YouTube with a May 2008 floor speech blasting provisions of a 2007 law that phases out use of incandescent bulbs in favor of more-energy-efficient compact fluorescent lights. The video drew more than 5.7 million hits within the first 90 days of its posting. "You want to go down in history as giving a speech like the Gettysburg Address as a politician, and then you get known for light bulbs," Poe observed ruefully to his hometown newspaper, the Humble Observer. Though he is loathed and mocked in the liberal blogosphere, a grass-roots group of his admirers launched a Web site trying to draft Poe to run for Texas' governorship in 2010.

He regularly assails illegal immigration, which he casts as an "invasion" and a threat to national security. He was upset when President George W. Bush pressed in 2006 for a comprehensive immigration overhaul that would have combined tighter border enforcement with a path to eventual citizenship for illegal immigrants living in the United States, a plan Poe and other conservatives denounced as "amnesty." His approach? Seal the border, jail employers who hire illegal immigrants and deport those already here.

"The border with Mexico is violent. The border is porous, and the border is being invaded," he said in June 2008. "The most powerful nation in the history of the world can stop the secret invasion if it, first, had the moral resolve to do so, and second, the courage to do whatever is necessary to stop the onslaught of invaders. Maybe we should even use the National Guard or returning troops from Iraq on our southern border."

When drug-related violence in Mexico flared in 2009, Mexican President Felipe Calderón called on U.S. officials to reconsider renewing the expired ban on military-style assault weapons that have flowed across the border. Poe was unmoved. "It is not our responsibility to keep guns out of Mexico — and reviving the ban will not affect the way Mexico protects its border," he told The Houston Chronicle.

Poe also looks out for the economic interests of his suburban Houston district, such as energy production and Gulf Coast shipping. Topping his priorities is a project to widen and deepen the Sabine-Neches Waterway, where 20 percent to 30 percent of the nation's commercial jet fuel is produced and shipped. Poe won inclusion in a 2007 water resources development law of language to fast track studies needed before the project can be built. When Bush vetoed the bill, Poe joined other lawmakers of both parties in a successful override of the veto.

He also parts company with others on the far right in embracing earmarks, the funding set-asides for pet projects that lawmakers add to spending bills. The boot-wearing lawmaker is a proud Texan. Born in Temple and raised in Houston, Poe has filled his Capitol Hill office with photographs of the Texas countryside that he personally has snapped. He said a major turning point in his life came in the ninth grade. "I was shy so my daddy made me take speech class so that I would talk more. I've been talking ever since, I guess," he said. He often delivers motivational speeches to law enforcement groups.

Poe was deeply influenced by his grandmother, a "Yellow Dog Democrat," who died at the age of 99. "She never forgave me for being a Republican. She told me once, 'I'm not sure you can go to Heaven being a Republican.' She might have meant it too," Poe chuckled.

He said he was also affected by the story of William Barrett Travis, the Texas commander at the Battle of the Alamo. Posted at the door of Poe's personal office is a framed copy of Travis' Letter from the Alamo, which Poe often quotes in his speeches.

Poe earned a political science degree from Abilene Christian College and a law degree from the University of Houston. He served in the U.S. Air Force Reserve. He was an assistant district attorney and chief felony prosecutor for eight years and never lost a jury trial.

He said he became a Republican when Gov. William Clements named him to the bench. One of Poe's more famous punishments required an auto thief to serve jail time — and to hand over the keys to his Trans Am to his victim, a 75-year-old grandmother, who drove the car until her stolen vehicle was recovered and repaired. He also once made a burglar stand on a sidewalk wearing a sign that read, "I stole from this store."

In 2004, Poe entered the race for the 2nd District, which had been redrawn by his fellow Texas Republican, Majority Leader Tom DeLay, to favor the GOP. The district included almost half the former 9th District constituent base represented by four-term Democrat Nick Lampson. Poe ousted Lampson with 56 percent of the vote. He won again easily in 2006 — as Lampson captured DeLay's old seat in the 22nd District after DeLay resigned — and in 2008.

KEY VOTES

2008

No   Delay consideration of Colombia free-trade agreement

Yes Override Bush veto of federal farm and nutrition programs reauthorization bill

Yes Overhaul surveillance laws and permit dismissal of suits against companies that conducted warrantless wiretapping

No   Grant mortgage relief to homeowners and funding for Fannie Mae and Freddie Mac

No   Approve initial $700 billion program to stabilize financial markets

No   Approve final $700 billion program to stabilize financial markets

No   Provide $14 billion in loans to automakers

2007

Yes Increase minimum wage by $2.10 an hour

No   Approve $124.2 billion in emergency war spending and set goal for redeployment of troops from Iraq

Yes Reject federal contraceptive assistance to international family planning groups

Yes Override Bush veto of $23.2 billion water projects authorization bill

?   Implement Peru free-trade agreement

No   Approve energy policy overhaul with new fuel economy standards

Yes Clear $473.5 billion omnibus spending bill, including $70 billion for military operations

CQ VOTE STUDIES

	PARTY UNITY		PRESIDENTIAL SUPPORT	
	SUPPORT	OPPOSE	SUPPORT	OPPOSE
2008	94%	6%	68%	32%
2007	95%	5%	79%	21%
2006	90%	10%	85%	15%
2005	94%	6%	81%	19%

INTEREST GROUPS

	AFL-CIO	ADA	CCUS	ACU
2008	7%	10%	56%	96%
2007	25%	5%	72%	96%
2006	21%	10%	87%	84%
2005	20%	0%	89%	92%

TEXAS 2

East — Beaumont, Port Arthur, part of Houston and northern and eastern suburbs

The 2nd stretches 100 miles from Louisiana and the Gulf of Mexico west to some of Houston's more affluent northern suburbs. In the east are Beaumont, an oil city on the Neches River, and Port Arthur, 15 miles away on Sabine Lake, and the two cities anchor the 2nd's robust shipping-based economy. In late 2005, Hurricane Rita made landfall along the Sabine River, the border between Texas and Louisiana. In 2008, Hurricane Ike hit just south of the district along the Bolivar Peninsula, and rebuilding efforts continue in areas such as Sea Rim State Park.

Petrochemical manufacturing dominates the area between Beaumont and Port Arthur. Major manufacturing sites here include an ExxonMobil Chemical plant in Beaumont and a Flint Hills Resources facility in Port Arthur, but falling prices have forced layoffs and plant idling. The 2nd has a large rural portion, with unpopulated areas in Jefferson and Liberty counties. Liberty County's population continues to grow, and many residents make the long commute into Houston.

A southern branch dips into Houston's eastern suburbs and takes in part of Baytown, a petrochemical city. The rest of the 2nd's portion of Harris County, near Lake Houston and to its west, is suburban. Many residents work at George Bush Intercontinental Airport (in the adjacent 18th). The 2nd hosts several large companies in traditional blue-collar industries and a growing white-collar employment sector, but a lack of economic diversification has hurt the district, spurring high unemployment rates.

Mostly white with a growing Hispanic population, the 2nd tends to vote like Texas overall — mostly conservative and Republican — but not overwhelmingly enough to shut out Democrats. Harris County provides candidates with a solid Republican base, but the Beaumont area tends to favor moderate to conservative Democrats. The district still gave John McCain 60 percent of its vote in the 2008 presidential election.

MAJOR INDUSTRY
Petrochemicals, shipping, service

CITIES
Beaumont, 113,866; Port Arthur, 57,755; Houston (pt.), 57,580

NOTABLE
South of Beaumont, the Spindletop-Gladys City Boomtown Museum is located on the site of the 1901 gusher that began Texas' oil boom.

Rep. Sam Johnson (R)

Elected May 1991; 9th full term

CAPITOL OFFICE
225-4201
samjohnson.house.gov
1211 Longworth Bldg. 20515-4303; fax 225-1485

COMMITTEES
Ways & Means

RESIDENCE
Plano

BORN
Oct. 11, 1930; San Antonio, Texas

RELIGION
Methodist

FAMILY
Wife, Shirley Johnson; three children

EDUCATION
Southern Methodist U., B.B.A. 1951; George
Washington U., M.S.I.A. 1974 (international affairs)

MILITARY SERVICE
Air Force, 1951-79

CAREER
Home builder; Top Gun flight school director;
Air Force pilot

POLITICAL HIGHLIGHTS
Texas House, 1985-91

ELECTION RESULTS

2008 GENERAL

Sam Johnson (R)	170,742	59.7%
Tom Daley (D)	108,693	38.0%
Christopher J. Claytor (LIBERT)	6,348	2.2%

2008 PRIMARY

Sam Johnson (R)	36,050	86.9%
Harry Pierce (R)	3,466	8.4%
Wayne Avellanet (R)	1,952	4.7%

2006 GENERAL

Sam Johnson (R)	88,690	62.5%
Dan Dodd (D)	49,529	34.9%
Christopher J. Claytor (LIBERT)	3,662	2.6%

PREVIOUS WINNING PERCENTAGES
2004 (86%); 2002 (74%); 2000 (72%); 1998 (91%);
1996 (73%); 1994 (91%); 1992 (86%); 1991 Special
Runoff Election (53%)

A founder of the Republican Study Committee, the caucus of the House's most conservative members, Johnson is a fierce champion of limited government. Though he is best-known for his defense of U.S. involvement in the Iraq War, his legislative energies increasingly focus on tax and health policy.

Johnson has a prominent platform for his stringent views on the Ways and Means Committee, where he is the ranking Republican on the Social Security panel. He eschewed a bid for the top GOP slot on the full committee in 2009. Deferring to two Republicans above him on the ladder, Johnson explained, "I believe in seniority, and I didn't want to muddy the water."

Johnson has long pushed for legislation to make it easier for small businesses to band together to purchase health insurance through association health plans exempt from state laws mandating coverage for specific conditions and treatments. The House passed his bill in July 2005, when Republicans controlled the chamber, but the measure died in the Senate. With Democrats in control, there is little chance the legislation will advance without significant modifications, although both parties agree on the need to spur more small businesses to provide health insurance to their workers.

Johnson shares his party's aversion to tax increases, but he can swallow his distaste on occasion if the interests of his constituents are at stake. In 2008, Ways and Means considered Democratic-sponsored legislation to revive or renew a slew of tax breaks for individuals and businesses — including a popular sales tax deduction in states such as Texas that have no state income tax. Although the bill included other tax increases to offset the cost of the tax breaks, Johnson voted for the measure. He was one of just three Republicans to do so.

Johnson is a stalwart defender of the military and its involvement in Iraq. A career Air Force pilot — he once was the director of the Air Force's "Top Gun" fighter pilot school — he spent seven years as a prisoner of war in Vietnam, half of it in solitary confinement. He once roomed with Republican Sen. John McCain of Arizona during their shared time as POWs. He says he decided to become active in politics during those years. "You can sit there and shoot bullets at the government all day, but unless you get personally involved, you can't get a lot done," he said in his slow Texas drawl.

When President Obama announced in February 2009 his plan to withdraw the bulk of U.S. forces in Iraq by August 2010, Johnson hailed the move as proof of the troops' success. "Y'all did your jobs no matter what the critics in Congress and your country said ... I am optimistic about today's news and look forward to hearing even more good reports from Iraq," he said.

When the House narrowly passed a $124.2 billion war supplemental in March 2007 that aimed to set a timetable for the withdrawal of U.S. troops from Iraq, Johnson brought a hush to the House when he described the last days of the war in Vietnam. "Just think back to the dark day in history when we saw visions of American Marines airlifting Vietnamese out of the U.S. Embassy," he said. "Do you remember that? That's what happens when America makes a commitment, Congress cuts the funding, and we go home with our tails between our legs." He voted against the bill.

One of four founders of the Study Committee, originally known as the Conservative Action Team, Johnson doesn't often stray from his party. In the 110th Congress (2007-08), he stuck with the GOP on 99 percent of the votes that pitted a majority of Republicans against a majority of Democrats — higher than any other House member from the Lone Star State.

He did vote against President George W. Bush's position on a 2006 measure to grant permanent normal trade relations to Vietnam. The bill, which failed in the House, later became law as part of a broader trade package. Johnson said, "I still think Vietnam is communist, and they don't have a government of the people, by the people and for the people."

Johnson also split with Bush over immigration policy, upset by the president's efforts to combine tighter border controls with legalization options for illegal immigrants already living and working in the United States. Although his district, which includes parts of Dallas and its suburbs, is 400 miles from Mexico, Johnson has pushed for a crackdown at the border and introduced legislation designed to force employers to check the legal status of all new workers they hire.

Johnson did not plan on a military career. He said participation in the ROTC was mandatory when he went to high school. He was aiming for a career in business and law when the Korean War intervened and his entire ROTC class at Southern Methodist University was called to duty. Accepted into flight training school, he soon fell in love with flying and was sold on a career in the Air Force. In addition to his combat missions over Korea and Vietnam, Johnson was a member of the Thunderbirds precision flying team for two years.

Johnson does not talk much about his days as a POW, but he did write a book about his experience, "Captive Warriors." Upon his release in 1973, he had three operations on his right hand, including a tendon transplant, and then he resumed flying.

Like McCain, Johnson has paid a physical price for his years as a prisoner of war. He attributes a number of joint problems to that time, when he was held in leg chains for two years. In the summer of 2006, he had his right knee replaced, and in July 2007 he underwent hip replacement surgery.

Despite his experience, Johnson was slow to embrace McCain's presidential ambitions. He went to South Carolina in 2000 to campaign for Bush — McCain was also seeking the presidential nomination — during the GOP primary and did not formally endorse the Arizona senator on his second try until March 2008, when it was clear McCain had clinched the nomination.

After retiring from the Air Force in 1979 as a colonel, Johnson went into the homebuilding business in Dallas. He got into local Republican Party affairs and, in 1984, won a seat in the Texas House. When GOP Rep. Steve Bartlett resigned in March 1991 to run for mayor of Dallas, Johnson overcame a tough scramble to win his party's nomination. He's had no trouble since then in the wealthy, solidly Republican district.

KEY VOTES

2008

No Delay consideration of Colombia free-trade agreement

No Override Bush veto of federal farm and nutrition programs reauthorization bill

Yes Overhaul surveillance laws and permit dismissal of suits against companies that conducted warrantless wiretapping

No Grant mortgage relief to homeowners and funding for Fannie Mae and Freddie Mac

No Approve initial $700 billion program to stabilize financial markets

No Approve final $700 billion program to stabilize financial markets

No Provide $14 billion in loans to automakers

2007

No Increase minimum wage by $2.10 an hour

No Approve $124.2 billion in emergency war spending and set goal for redeployment of troops from Iraq

Yes Reject federal contraceptive assistance to international family planning groups

? Override Bush veto of $23.2 billion water projects authorization bill

Yes Implement Peru free-trade agreement

No Approve energy policy overhaul with new fuel economy standards

Yes Clear $473.5 billion omnibus spending bill, including $70 billion for military operations

CQ VOTE STUDIES

	PARTY UNITY		PRESIDENTIAL SUPPORT	
	SUPPORT	OPPOSE	SUPPORT	OPPOSE
2008	99%	1%	81%	19%
2007	99%	1%	92%	8%
2006	98%	2%	82%	18%
2005	98%	2%	93%	7%
2004	99%	1%	93%	7%

INTEREST GROUPS

	AFL-CIO	ADA	CCUS	ACU
2008	0%	0%	83%	96%
2007	5%	0%	79%	100%
2006	17%	5%	91%	90%
2005	8%	0%	88%	96%
2004	0%	0%	100%	100%

TEXAS 3

Part of Dallas and northeast suburbs — Plano, part of Garland and McKinney

The rapidly expanding Dallas suburbs of Plano, McKinney, Frisco and Allen in Collin County form the heart of the 3rd, which also takes in part of Dallas itself and most of Garland and Rowlett in northeastern Dallas County. The 3rd's residents are overwhelmingly white and Republican and they have the state's highest median income. The 3rd also has the state's highest number of residents who have attained a bachelor's degree or higher. Many residents rely on jobs in the vulnerable, but historically lucrative, banking, telecommunications and defense industries.

Many corporate headquarters have moved into the Plano area, where majority of the district's residents live, and wealthy executives have been building expensive homes in Frisco and the surrounding areas for years. But the national housing crisis caused slowdowns in residential and commercial development, and municipal budget shortfalls in the region worry local officials.

Major companies among the concentration of telecommunications and electronics firms along the U.S. Highway 75 "Telecom Corridor," including Electronic Data Systems and Texas Instruments, have shed thousands of jobs recently. Richardson benefited from technology firms and expanding banking and financial services industries in the past decade, but continued layoffs concern residents. Although downtown Dallas is in the 30th, many white-collar workers commute to the city from residential areas in the 3rd.

Collin County, which has experienced explosive growth since 1990, is filled with upwardly mobile professionals and is strongly Republican. Forty percent of the district's residents live in the northeastern corner of Dallas County. The district overall gave John McCain 57 percent of its vote in the 2008 presidential election, 9 percentage points fewer than George W. Bush won here in 2004.

MAJOR INDUSTRY

Telecommunications, transportation, banking, defense

CITIES

Plano, 219,890; Garland (pt.), 142,379; Dallas (pt.), 128,651

NOTABLE

Seven-time Tour de France winner Lance Armstrong grew up in Plano.

Rep. Ralph M. Hall (R)

Elected 1980; 15th term

The grandfatherly Hall is the oldest member of the House, using his status as top Republican on the Science and Technology Committee and membership on the Energy and Commerce panel to advocate domestic energy production and funding for space exploration.

Hall, one of just five World War II veterans left in Congress, could be much more powerful had he not switched parties in 2004, becoming a Republican just two years before the party lost control of the House. Then again, Hall's shift from renegade Democrat to solid Republican helped prolong his career, because it allowed him to survive in a reconfigured district. And his folksy humor and sharp political acumen help him gain the attention and admiration of lawmakers in both parties.

Among Hall's top priorities is finding money to continue space shuttle flights beyond their scheduled end in 2010 and to speed up the completion of a new U.S. space vehicle to replace the shuttle, which is being retired. After the shuttle is gone, but before a new vehicle is ready, astronauts will have to hitch rides with Russians to reach the space station. Hall senses a can't-do attitude within NASA, arguing that agency officials need to take a lesson from World War II Admiral Chester Nimitz's determination to get the battle-damaged *USS Yorktown* ready for the Battle of Midway.

Hall also supported the George W. Bush administration's plan to send a man to Mars, as it held the potential to bring new missions to the Johnson Space Center in Houston. As a booster of NASA, Hall has championed the space agency's biomedical and basic science programs. After the 2003 loss of the space shuttle *Columbia*, Hall pressed for a greater focus on safety, adding an amendment to the annual NASA funding bill directing the agency to conduct studies on improving space shuttle crew survivability. In the 110th Congress (2007-08), he helped pass legislation to improve math and science education and increase funding for basic science research.

Stylistically, Hall is anything but a firebrand. He introduced just 11 bills in the 110th, preferring to look after Texas' oil and gas industry quietly from his seat on the Energy and Commerce panel. He supports government action to fight climate change, but Hall said he wants to achieve that through enhanced research and new technology rather than government regulation. He is frustrated with Democrats' reluctance to direct money and support to coal-to-liquid and other coal-based technologies, and has said he believes a "cap and trade" program for greenhouse gas emissions would weaken U.S. competitiveness. In early 2009, the House passed his bill promoting research on ways to purify and reuse brackish water produced when oil, gas and coal-bed methane are extracted from the ground.

Hall strongly supports additional oil drilling on federal land and off the coastlines, and especially in Alaska's Arctic National Wildlife Refuge. He sponsored a bill in 2008 that would have allowed Alaska to make that decision for itself. He said he unsuccessfully tried to talk to Speaker Nancy Pelosi of California about why she supports giving California and Florida the right to block drilling off their coasts but opposes Alaska's ability to use its own resources.

He has other interests as well. In 2008, he was the GOP cosponsor of legislation directing the Department of Health and Human Services to take steps to reduce falls by elderly people. A companion Senate version became law.

From his rural East Texas district, Hall has been involved in developing an early-warning system for droughts, sponsoring a measure in 2006 with Democrat Mark Udall of Colorado that authorized $81 million for such a system.

CAPITOL OFFICE
225-6673
2405 Rayburn Bldg. 20515-4304; fax 225-3332

COMMITTEES
Energy & Commerce
Science & Technology - ranking member

RESIDENCE
Rockwall

BORN
May 3, 1923; Fate, Texas

RELIGION
Methodist

FAMILY
Widowed; three children

EDUCATION
Texas Christian U., attended 1943; U. of Texas, attended 1946-47; Southern Methodist U., LL.B. 1951

MILITARY SERVICE
Navy, 1942-45

CAREER
Lawyer; aluminum company president

POLITICAL HIGHLIGHTS
Rockwall County judge, 1951-63; Texas Senate, 1963-73 (president pro tempore, 1968-69; served as a Democrat); sought Democratic nomination for lieutenant governor, 1972

ELECTION RESULTS

2008 GENERAL

Ralph M. Hall (R)	206,906	68.8%
Glenn Melancon (D)	88,067	29.3%
Fred Annett (LIBERT)	5,771	1.9%

2008 PRIMARY

Ralph M. Hall (R)	41,764	73.4%
Kathy Seei (R)	5,835	10.2%
Gene Christensen (R)	5,492	9.6%
Kevin George (R)	2,965	5.2%
Joshua Kowert (R)	852	1.5%

2006 GENERAL

Ralph M. Hall (R)	106,495	64.4%
Glenn Melancon (D)	55,278	33.4%
Kurt G. Helm (LIBERT)	3,496	2.1%

PREVIOUS WINNING PERCENTAGES*
2004 (68%); 2002 (58%); 2000 (60%); 1998 (58%); 1996 (64%); 1994 (59%); 1992 (58%); 1990 (100%); 1988 (66%); 1986 (72%); 1984 (58%); 1982 (74%); 1980 (52%) * Elected as a Democrat 1980-2002

A fiscal conservative, Hall favors scrapping most of the existing tax code and replacing it with a flat tax or a national sales tax. He opposed President Obama's early legislative agenda, including his $787 billion economic stimulus law and a $3.56 trillion budget blueprint for 2010. He stands with the right on social issues as well, opposing abortion and same-sex marriage.

His flagging allegiance to Democrats was evident for years before he switched parties. In 1985, he voted "present" rather than support the re-election of liberal Democrat Thomas P. "Tip" O'Neill Jr. of Massachusetts as Speaker. In 1998, he was one of only five Democrats to support the impeachment of President Clinton on the critical first charge of lying to a federal grand jury. In 2000, he publicly championed the presidential candidacy of Bush, then Texas' Republican governor. After the 2002 election, Hall told GOP leaders he might back Republican J. Dennis Hastert of Illinois for Speaker if his vote were the deciding one.

He consistently strayed from the party line more often than any other House member in the early 2000s. Some speculated he would leave the Democratic Party after the GOP took over Congress in 1994. Instead, he helped start the Blue Dog Coalition, a group of fiscally conservative House Democrats.

In 2003, the GOP-controlled Texas Legislature drew a new congressional map and created a new, Republican-leaning 4th District with only about a third of Hall's constituents. Facing a tough re-election, he registered as a Republican just before the state candidate filing deadline in January 2004.

Hall briefly made headlines in 2007, when the watchdog group Citizens for Responsibility and Ethics in Washington said in a report that he was among the 72 House members who used campaign funds to pay relatives or their relatives' employers. Hall told USA Today he hired his daughter-in-law because he trusts her: "I'm not sure that it's a good thing to do, but it's a safe thing to do."

Hall got an early start in politics. He was elected as county judge, or chief executive, of Rockwall County in 1950 while still attending law school in nearby Dallas. Twelve years later, he moved up to the state Senate and spent a decade there, rising to become president pro tempore.

After finishing fourth in the Democratic primary for lieutenant governor in 1972, he left public life for a time. But when 4th District Democrat Ray Roberts announced his retirement in 1980, Hall took the seat with 52 percent of the vote. He won by comfortable margins as a Democrat through 2002. In 2004, Hall won the general election with more than two-thirds of the vote. He won with similar ease in 2006 and 2008, earning his 15th term just months after the death of Mary Ellen Hall, his wife of more than 63 years.

KEY VOTES

2008

No Delay consideration of Colombia free-trade agreement

Yes Override Bush veto of federal farm and nutrition programs reauthorization bill

Yes Overhaul surveillance laws and permit dismissal of suits against companies that conducted warrantless wiretapping

No Grant mortgage relief to homeowners and funding for Fannie Mae and Freddie Mac

No Approve initial $700 billion program to stabilize financial markets

No Approve final $700 billion program to stabilize financial markets

No Provide $14 billion in loans to automakers

2007

No Increase minimum wage by $2.10 an hour

No Approve $124.2 billion in emergency war spending and set goal for redeployment of troops from Iraq

Yes Reject federal contraceptive assistance to international family planning groups

Yes Override Bush veto of $23.2 billion water projects authorization bill

Yes Implement Peru free-trade agreement

No Approve energy policy overhaul with new fuel economy standards

Yes Clear $473.5 billion omnibus spending bill, including $70 billion for military operations

CQ VOTE STUDIES

	PARTY UNITY		PRESIDENTIAL SUPPORT	
	SUPPORT	OPPOSE	SUPPORT	OPPOSE
2008	96%	4%	65%	35%
2007	92%	8%	80%	20%
2006	93%	7%	85%	15%
2005	96%	4%	84%	16%
2004	92%	8%	82%	18%

INTEREST GROUPS

	AFL-CIO	ADA	CCUS	ACU
2008	33%	30%	83%	84%
2007	8%	10%	90%	96%
2006	21%	5%	93%	84%
2005	20%	5%	92%	92%
2004	13%	5%	100%	84%

TEXAS 4

Northeast – Sherman, Texarkana, Paris

The 4th begins in Dallas' eastern and northern suburbs before moving east to less-populated and rural areas in the northeastern corner of the state. The district extends along the Oklahoma and Arkansas borders, taking in Texarkana, but its four western counties contain about half of the population. It has Texas' second-highest percentage of white residents (79 percent) and lowest percentage of Hispanics (8 percent).

The district includes a mix of suburban and rural communities, with no city having more than 40,000 residents. In the east, timber, oil and natural gas are big industries, while Dallas commuters and other white-collar workers populate the growing western counties, especially Collin. This area hosts soccer's FC Dallas at Pizza Hut Park, Frisco's regional sports complex that also is used as a retail center and entertainment venue.

Manufacturing and small businesses drive much of the economy in the 4th. Food processing giants Pilgrim's Pride chicken, headquartered in Pittsburg, and a Tyson Foods meat production plant in Sherman have cut jobs and struggled with rising costs. The Texarkana-area economy nar-rowly avoided a hit when the BRAC Commission reversed a 2005 Defense Department recommendation to close the Red River Army Depot. The district struggles, as does the rest of the state, with finding adequate water supplies for its growing communities. Transportation development is also an issue for most of East Texas, as the area is poised for both passenger and commercial rail development.

Associated with the Bible Belt that stretches through much of the South, the 4th is fertile territory for the GOP. Even Democrats, who can win local races in the east, tend to be conservative here. Every county in the 4th voted for the Republican presidential candidate in 2004 and 2008, and John McCain won 69 percent of the district's vote overall in 2008.

MAJOR INDUSTRY
Manufacturing, agriculture, retail, health care

MILITARY BASES
Red River Army Depot, 3 military, 2,500 civilian (2006)

CITIES
Sherman, 35,082; Texarkana, 34,782; Paris, 25,898; Greenville, 23,960

NOTABLE
Former House Speaker Sam Rayburn hailed from Bonham, now home of the Sam Rayburn Library and Museum.

Rep. Jeb Hensarling (R)

Elected 2002; 4th term

CAPITOL OFFICE
225-3484
www.house.gov/hensarling
129 Cannon Bldg. 20515-4305; fax 226-4888

COMMITTEES
Budget
Financial Services

RESIDENCE
Dallas

BORN
May 29, 1957; Stephenville, Texas

RELIGION
Episcopalian

FAMILY
Wife, Melissa Hensarling; two children

EDUCATION
Texas A&M U., B.A. 1979 (economics);
U. of Texas, J.D. 1982

CAREER
Child support collection software firm owner;
energy company communications executive;
senatorial campaign committee executive
director; congressional district and
campaign aide; lawyer

POLITICAL HIGHLIGHTS
No previous office

ELECTION RESULTS

2008 GENERAL

Jeb Hensarling (R)	162,894	83.6%
Ken Ashby (LIBERT)	31,967	16.4%

2008 PRIMARY

Jeb Hensarling (R)	unopposed

2006 GENERAL

Jeb Hensarling (R)	88,478	61.8%
Charlie Thompson (D)	50,983	35.6%
Mike Nelson (LIBERT)	3,791	2.6%

PREVIOUS WINNING PERCENTAGES
2004 (64%); 2002 (58%)

Hensarling has earned a reputation for passionate, unbending stands on almost everything as a senior member of the Republican Study Committee (RSC), the most conservative bloc and dominant force within the House GOP. He regularly assails federal spending, regulation and government involvement in the marketplace.

With trademark cowboy boots and a boyish mop of hair, Hensarling (HENN-sur-ling) is a political and ideological heir — part strategist and part policy wonk — to once-powerful GOP leaders from the Lone Star State like former Majority Leader Dick Armey, whom he counts as a mentor, and former Sen. Phil Gramm, for whom he once worked as a Senate aide.

"I believe that faith and family are the genius of America," he says. "The government does a lot in a poor or mediocre fashion."

Instead of cutting deals with Democrats, Hensarling believes Republicans should highlight their differences with the majority party. He contends that his party's free-spending ways contributed to its defeats in the 2006 elections that turned control of the House over to the Democrats. "We must be true to our conservative roots and principles," he said. "We've got to be bigger and bolder in order to let American people know the difference between the parties."

He can be doctrinaire and humorless in drawing those lines, but he doesn't much care who likes him or doesn't. "I didn't come to Washington to make friends, and I haven't been disappointed," he said. "For all the flak I've received in Washington, it's amazing how many people in my district cheer me on and slap me on my back."

He is one of five members of a congressionally established oversight board that monitors the Troubled Asset Relief Program created in late 2008 to rescue the floundering financial sector. Hensarling voted against the $700 billion plan, calling it a "step down the slippery slope to socialism." From his oversight post, he has sharply criticized implementation of the law.

Though he is a strong party loyalist, when he breaks from the lines it is usually further to the right. In 2008, he split with President George W. Bush and Arizona Sen. John McCain, then on his way to winning his party's presidential nomination, to oppose a bipartisan housing rescue proposal allowing the government to extend credit and buy stock in mortgage financiers Fannie Mae and Freddie Mac. "The bottom line: The taxpayer is about to be big loser here…I came here to protect free enterprise, not big banks," Hensarling said.

In the 110th Congress (2007-08), Hensarling joined Jeff Flake of Arizona and Mike Pence of Indiana in an all-out assault on earmarks — funding setasides for member projects back home. In early 2008, the trio urged that Republicans adopt a self-imposed moratorium on seeking earmarks. Party leaders demurred, saying there was no consensus behind the plan. That point was underscored late in the year, when a majority of Republicans voted against even a temporary moratorium on GOP earmark requests. As a sop, Majority Leader John A. Boehner of Ohio named both Flake and Hensarling to a 10-member group charged with "thoughtfully examining the way Washington spends taxpayer dollars and recommending the next steps for reform."

Hensarling isn't giving up. And he thinks Republican defenders of earmarks are a dwindling breed. "It's kind of like turning a battleship…The battleship is turning in the right direction. There are fewer Republicans and there are more conservatives," he said.

He was RSC chairman in the 110th, having defeated a more senior rival, Kansas appropriator Todd Tiahrt, for the post. Hensarling helped draw media attention to RSC causes through splashy shows like the parade of GOP speakers who took to an empty House chamber during the 2008 summer recess to denounce Democrats on energy policy and blame them for high gas prices.

He was one of the loudest critics of President Obama's $787 billion stimulus package and the two measures that followed it in 2009, a $410 billion catchall law and a $3.56 trillion fiscal 2010 budget resolution. "I cannot remember a time in American history where so few voted so fast to spend so much that our children and grandchildren will pay for," he complained.

Hensarling, who is a lawyer, had a varied career in business that included a stint as vice president of Austin-based Green Mountain Energy Co., a provider of electricity from wind and solar power.

After hours, Hensarling often works with outside conservative groups such as the Club for Growth to build support for his priorities. "There's an inside game and an outside game," he said. In 2008, he helped raise $8 million for the House GOP as chairman of the annual President's Dinner attended by Bush.

Hensarling is a social conservative. He voted in both 2004 and 2006 for a constitutional amendment to ban same-sex marriage, and he opposes abortion, voting in 2006 to make it a felony to take a minor across state lines for an abortion. In 2009, he voted against legislation to expand federal hate crime law to cover offenses based on sexual orientation.

He was born in Stephenville. His father and grandfather were poultry farmers, but Hensarling decided early that he wouldn't enter the family business. His first taste of politics came in 1964, when his Republican parents had him knocking on doors for Barry Goldwater. He started a Republican Club at his high school, and acted as a GOP precinct captain at Texas A&M University, where he took a money and banking class from Gramm.

Three years out of law school, Hensarling was hired in 1985 to oversee Gramm's field offices in Texas. When Gramm became chairman of the National Republican Senatorial Committee in the run-up to the 1992 election, he made Hensarling its executive director. Running the committee helped Hensarling build a network of political friends on Capitol Hill.

He took a break from government to go home to Texas to start his own business, a firm that made computer software to help single parents collect child support payments. Then in 2002, the 5th District was reconfigured after Texas gained two seats in post-2000 census reapportionment. Republican Pete Sessions, who had represented the 5th for four terms, decided to run in the new 32nd District. Hensarling won a five-way primary for the nomination and bested Democrat Ron Chapman, a Dallas-area judge, by 18 percentage points in the general election. He has coasted since.

KEY VOTES

2008

No Delay consideration of Colombia free-trade agreement

No Override Bush veto of federal farm and nutrition programs reauthorization bill

Yes Overhaul surveillance laws and permit dismissal of suits against companies that conducted warrantless wiretapping

No Grant mortgage relief to homeowners and funding for Fannie Mae and Freddie Mac

No Approve initial $700 billion program to stabilize financial markets

No Approve final $700 billion program to stabilize financial markets

No Provide $14 billion in loans to automakers

2007

No Increase minimum wage by $2.10 an hour

No Approve $124.2 billion in emergency war spending and set goal for redeployment of troops from Iraq

Yes Reject federal contraceptive assistance to international family planning groups

No Override Bush veto of $23.2 billion water projects authorization bill

Yes Implement Peru free-trade agreement

No Approve energy policy overhaul with new fuel economy standards

Yes Clear $473.5 billion omnibus spending bill, including $70 billion for military operations

CQ VOTE STUDIES

	PARTY UNITY		PRESIDENTIAL SUPPORT	
	SUPPORT	OPPOSE	SUPPORT	OPPOSE
2008	99%	1%	87%	13%
2007	98%	2%	92%	8%
2006	96%	4%	85%	15%
2005	98%	2%	93%	7%
2004	98%	2%	100%	0%

INTEREST GROUPS

	AFL-CIO	ADA	CCUS	ACU
2008	0%	5%	78%	100%
2007	4%	0%	70%	100%
2006	7%	10%	93%	100%
2005	13%	0%	81%	100%
2004	8%	0%	95%	100%

TEXAS 5

Part of Dallas and east suburbs – Mesquite, part of Garland; Palestine

The 5th winds east and southeast from eastern Dallas through Dallas County suburbs and six other counties. Only 14 percent of Dallas County's population is here, but it is home to almost half of the 5th's residents.

The 5th's part of Dallas differs from the glitz characterizing the portion in the neighboring 32nd. The 5th takes in eastern and northeastern Dallas, which have more of a working-class flavor and are home to many small businesses. Areas near White Rock Lake, such as Old Lake Highlands, however, are upper-middle class. Mesquite, a suburb east of the city, is another population center. Located in far eastern Dallas County, its economic landscape continues to diversify, as manufacturing developments complement recreational and tourism projects. Union Pacific Railroad operates a distribution facility in the city's Skyline Industrial Park, a regional industrial center east of the Dallas-Fort Worth Metroplex.

Many of the district's suburbs have growing populations and provide easy access to a bustling metropolis while supplying the benefits of small-town life. Southeast of Dallas, the district moves from flat prairies into the forest region of East Texas. Prisons are key employers in rural parts of the 5th District, and cattle, natural gas and coal are important industries as well. Long-term plans by the city of Dallas to create a reservoir using water from the Upper Neches River in Anderson and Cherokee counties to supply its expanding suburbs have met with environmental opposition.

The 5th generally favors Republicans. GOP areas abound in northeastern Dallas and in Anderson and Henderson counties well southeast of the city. Some heavily Hispanic areas in Dallas County's southeastern precincts tend to vote more Democratic, and Mesquite often is politically competitive. Republican presidential candidate John McCain garnered 63 percent of the district's vote overall in 2008.

MAJOR INDUSTRY
Small business, technology, prisons, ranching

CITIES
Mesquite, 124,523; Dallas (pt.), 95,286; Garland (pt.), 73,389

NOTABLE
Resistol Arena is home to the Mesquite Championship Rodeo.

Rep. Joe L. Barton (R)

Elected 1984; 13th term

APITOL OFFICE
5-2002
barton.house.gov
09 Rayburn Bldg. 20515-4306; fax 225-3052

OMMITTEES
ergy & Commerce - ranking member

SIDENCE
nis

ORN
pt. 15, 1949; Waco, Texas

ELIGION
ethodist

MILY
fe, Terri Barton; four children

DUCATION
xas A&M U., B.S. 1972 (industrial engineering);
rdue U., M.S. 1973 (industrial administration)

AREER
gineering consultant

OLITICAL HIGHLIGHTS
ught Republican nomination for U.S. Senate
ecial election), 1993

ECTION RESULTS

08 GENERAL
e L. Barton (R)   174,008   62.0%
dwig Otto (D)   99,919   35.6%
ax W. Koch III (LIBERT)   6,655   2.4%

08 PRIMARY
e L. Barton (R)   unopposed

06 GENERAL
e L. Barton (R)   91,927   60.5%
vid T. Harris (D)   56,369   37.1%
rl Nulsen (LIBERT)   3,740   2.5%

EVIOUS WINNING PERCENTAGES
04 (66%); 2002 (70%); 2000 (88%); 1998 (73%);
96 (77%); 1994 (76%); 1992 (72%); 1990 (66%);
88 (68%); 1986 (56%); 1984 (57%)

Barton is a strong-willed conservative who often is reluctant to compromise on issues if it means creating more government regulation. As top Republican on the Energy and Commerce Committee, he has positioned himself as the watchdog over what he perceives as any Democratic tendencies to railroad bills through too quickly.

Barton has been around long enough to be savvy about the political complexities of passing major legislation, though he hasn't always been able to close the deal. At times he shows a willingness to work with Democrats — such as on health care and food safety legislation — but he often employs a take-it-or-leave-it approach, whether he's in the chairman's seat or not.

Barton is the House's leading skeptic of the science behind the proposition that human activities related to the emission of greenhouse gases, mostly carbon dioxide, are partly responsible for Earth's rising temperatures. In a policy statement posted on his Web site, Barton said the theory that human actions are responsible for changes in global temperatures is worthy of continued research, but adds that it doesn't "warrant the immediate and draconian measures called for by some segments of the environmental community."

He strongly opposes "cap and trade" legislation to impose a limit on greenhouse gas emissions and set up a market-based trading system for emissions credits — a stance that led Democrats in early 2009 to shut him and other conservatives out of negotiations on broad climate change legislation. When President Obama's fiscal 2010 blueprint outlined such a plan, Barton said, "A money machine posing as planetary salvation may help the rookie White House staff write their first budget, but it seems unlikely to stop global warming and sure to help impoverish Americans." He instead proposed requiring federal regulations to lower emissions from new electric power plants.

A former oil company engineering consultant, Barton has long been the go-to guy in the House for the oil and gas industries, keystones of the Texas economy. They trust him to shield them from what they see as potentially drastic new rules, and he relies on them for political cash; they are among his top contributors. He joined his GOP colleagues in voting against Obama's economic stimulus law in February 2009, even though Energy and Commerce had approved billions for energy projects under the measure.

He was a leader in a successful fight to end a 26-year-old moratorium on oil and gas drilling off the Atlantic and Pacific coasts when gasoline prices were averaging $4 a gallon in the summer of 2008. The Obama administration, however, in early 2009 put a hold on letting that drilling go forward.

When Democrats proposed to ban certain plastic softeners in children's products in 2008 as part of a bill to toughen consumer safety, citing health concerns, Barton objected. He joined manufacturers of the plasticizers in contending the scientific evidence didn't support a ban of the softeners, known as phthalates. Lawmakers eventually agreed to outlaw three phthalates outright and temporarily bar three others pending further study.

Barton is among a group of 16 Republicans tapped by Minority Leader John A. Boehner in 2009 to devise a GOP plan for a health care overhaul. The group is likely to avoid an expansion of government programs such as Medicaid and Medicare, a key element of many Democratic health care proposals. Barton is critical of what he calls "made-in-Washington health care." Even so, he holds out hope the two parties can find common ground. Before a March 2009 White House summit on health care, Barton released a statement: "Not all of the Democrats' ideas are objectionable. Just nearly all."

He opposed the 2009 law to expand the State Children's Health Insurance Program, saying it didn't set strict enough limits on income level for participation nor ensure access was barred for illegal immigrants.

Barton has shown some interest in bipartisanship, saying in early 2009 he saw promise in finding a bipartisan deal on food safety regulation. He also generated some enthusiasm on both sides of the aisle — particularly from Obama — for his 2009 bill to regulate how college football picks its best team. His measure would change out the computerized Bowl Championship Series in favor of a more traditional playoff race.

A player in telecommunications policy, Barton in 2005 pushed through a requirement that television broadcasters switch from analog to digital transmission signals by early 2009. But Congress cleared a bill delaying the switch by four months when it became clear in February 2009 that more than 3 million people were waiting for the $40 government subsidy for a converter box to keep their old analog TVs working. Barton tried unsuccessfully to push legislation to help keep the switch on schedule.

Barton portrays himself as a churchgoing conservative. He supports amending the Constitution to ban same-sex marriage. A reliable anti-abortion vote, he nonetheless has supported legislation to expand federally supported stem cell research. He said he was influenced by his father's death from complications of diabetes and by the death of his brother, Texas District Judge Jon Barton, who succumbed to liver cancer in 2000 at age 44.

Born in Waco, Barton is the son of an agribusiness salesman and a schoolteacher. His father in his later years was a plant geneticist, breeding new strains of cotton. Barton studied industrial engineering at Texas A&M University, then earned a master's degree from Purdue University. He moved to Ennis and became an engineering consultant for Atlantic Richfield Co.

In 1981, Barton was a White House fellow at the Energy Department when he got the government bug. His made a successful 1984 bid for the House seat of Republican Phil Gramm, who moved to the Senate. In the general election, Barton linked Democrat Dan Kubiak, a former state representative, to liberal Democratic presidential nominee Walter F. Mondale, whose positions were unpopular in the district. He was also aided by Ronald Reagan's coattails.

He made an unsuccessful bid for the Senate when Democrat Lloyd Bentsen left in 1993 to be President Clinton's Treasury secretary. He mulled a second bid for the Senate when Gramm retired in 2002, but the George W. Bush White House endorsed Republican John Cornyn, the former Texas attorney general who was then appointed to fill out the remainder of Gramm's term. Barton has easily won re-election.

KEY VOTES

2008

No Delay consideration of Colombia free-trade agreement

No Override Bush veto of federal farm and nutrition programs reauthorization bill

Yes Overhaul surveillance laws and permit dismissal of suits against companies that conducted warrantless wiretapping

No Grant mortgage relief to homeowners and funding for Fannie Mae and Freddie Mac

No Approve initial $700 billion program to stabilize financial markets

No Approve final $700 billion program to stabilize financial markets

Yes Provide $14 billion in loans to automakers

2007

No Increase minimum wage by $2.10 an hour

No Approve $124.2 billion in emergency war spending and set goal for redeployment of troops from Iraq

Yes Reject federal contraceptive assistance to international family planning groups

Yes Override Bush veto of $23.2 billion water projects authorization bill

Yes Implement Peru free-trade agreement

No Approve energy policy overhaul with new fuel economy standards

Yes Clear $473.5 billion omnibus spending bill, including $70 billion for military operations

CQ VOTE STUDIES

	PARTY UNITY		PRESIDENTIAL SUPPORT	
	SUPPORT	OPPOSE	SUPPORT	OPPOSE
2008	98%	2%	82%	18%
2007	95%	5%	88%	12%
2006	95%	5%	87%	13%
2005	96%	4%	87%	13%
2004	97%	3%	94%	6%

INTEREST GROUPS

	AFL-CIO	ADA	CCUS	ACU
2008	14%	10%	94%	96%
2007	4%	10%	85%	96%
2006	7%	15%	93%	88%
2005	14%	0%	92%	92%
2004	7%	0%	100%	96%

TEXAS 6

Suburban Dallas – Arlington; part of Fort Worth and Mansfield; Corsicana

The overwhelming majority of the 6th's land area is a boot-shaped band of counties that extends southeast from Ellis County, but nearly two-thirds of the district's population lives just north of Ellis in eastern or southern Tarrant County. This suburban-rural district takes in a sliver of Fort Worth and all of Arlington in the Dallas-Fort Worth Metroplex before stretching southeast along Interstate 45, where it becomes more rural and its economy more reliant on agriculture.

Arlington has mainly shed its blue-collar image, and the General Motors assembly plant that used to employ thousands has been hit by heavy losses. Today, the University of Texas at Arlington is among the city's top employers, and the school has been an incubator for the city's growing technology sector. In addition, hundreds of thousands of people travel to Arlington each summer to visit the Six Flags Over Texas amusement park, while others head to the Rangers' ballpark for baseball. The new Cowboys Stadium is scheduled to open here in September 2009.

South of Tarrant, most of the rest of the 6th District's residents are located in Ellis and Navarro counties. Ellis, which includes Waxahachie and Ennis, used to be dependent on cotton farming, but the cement industry has taken hold here. Farther south, Freestone and Leon counties are rural, less-populous and sustained by oil, ranching and farming. Houston County and northern Trinity County, east of Leon, have a fairly large timber industry.

The 6th is heavily Republican. Most of the Tarrant precincts are aligned with the GOP, although there is some Democratic strength in southern Fort Worth and eastern Arlington, where the population is more diverse. Ellis' overwhelming Republican support makes the 6th a safe haven for GOP candidates — John McCain took 60 percent of the district's vote in the 2008 presidential election.

MAJOR INDUSTRY
Transportation, home building, technology, agriculture

CITIES
Arlington, 332,968; Mansfield (pt.), 27,409; Fort Worth (pt.), 26,709

NOTABLE
Squeeze-box melodies and traditional Czech culture on display at the National Polka Festival have lured visitors to Ennis for over 40 years.

Rep. John Culberson (R)

Elected 2000; 5th term

CAPITOL OFFICE
225-2571
www.culberson.house.gov
1514 Longworth Bldg. 20515-4307; fax 225-4381

COMMITTEES
Appropriations

RESIDENCE
Houston

BORN
Aug. 24, 1956; Houston, Texas

RELIGION
Methodist

FAMILY
Wife, Belinda Culberson; one child

EDUCATION
Southern Methodist U., B.A. 1981 (history);
South Texas College of Law, J.D. 1988

CAREER
Lawyer; political advertising agency employee;
oil rig mud logger

POLITICAL HIGHLIGHTS
Texas House, 1987-2001

ELECTION RESULTS

2008 GENERAL

John Culberson (R)	162,635	55.9%
Michael Skelly (D)	123,242	42.4%
Drew Parks (LIBERT)	5,057	1.7%

2008 PRIMARY

John Culberson (R)	unopposed

2006 GENERAL

John Culberson (R)	99,318	59.2%
Jim Henley (D)	64,514	38.5%
Drew Parks (LIBERT)	3,953	2.4%

PREVIOUS WINNING PERCENTAGES
2004 (64%); 2002 (89%); 2000 (74%)

Culberson lives by the adage that all politics is local. A self-styled "Jeffersonian Republican" — he has several portraits of the third president on his office walls, including one set precisely at Jefferson's height of 6 feet 2 1/2 inches — he believes most decisions are best left to the states.

An assistant GOP whip, the bespectacled Texan uses his Web savvy to help round up support for the party's initiatives and put out the Republican message calling for more-limited government and reduced spending. But from his seat on the powerful Appropriations Committee, he also works to obtain federal funds to enable his district to pursue such projects as roads and medical and scientific research at local universities. He also tries to influence debate on immigration, a top concern of his Houston-based district.

Like many conservatives, Culberson believed former President George W. Bush's policies were too lax, which likely will put him at odds with the Obama administration. He wants to boost border enforcement and opposes a path to citizenship for illegal immigrants that he considers amnesty. He carries in his suit pocket a machine gun bullet he said he found on a tour at the International Bridge in Laredo, which he uses to illustrate his oft-repeated point: "We will either have law and order on the border or *plata o plomo*," which translates to "silver or lead," a threat referring to drug lords either bribing or killing.

From his seat on Appropriations, he closely questioned Bush administration officials during hearings in a style that is marked by polite persistence with a dash of hyperactive energy. But he failed to persuade those officials to his point of view on many occasions, whether it was his contention that drug couriers are not being prosecuted or a plan to create armed civilian militias to help local police along the Mexican border.

He also tries to amend spending bills that would affect immigration policies, but often withdraws the amendments after being allowed to make his point. And he championed the cause of two Border Patrol agents who were sentenced to prison in 2006 for shooting a fleeing Mexican drug trafficker and hiding evidence, saying that it was an "unjust criminal prosecution of two officers who were protecting our borders from criminals and terrorists." Before leaving office, Bush commuted the prison sentences of the two officers.

Culberson primarily uses his post on Appropriations to keep his district stocked with federal money for new highways and flood control projects. And from his seat on the subcommittee responsible for NASA funding, he protects dollars for the Houston-based space program. In the 110th Congress (2007-08), he joined the GOP push for a re-evaluation of the earmarking process, but that didn't stop him from requesting funding for his own proposals. He helped obtain nearly $45 million in the fiscal 2009 spending bills.

But in early 2009 he harshly criticized Democrats for spending too heavily on Obama's early spending initiatives. When Obama's economic stimulus plan was unveiled, Culberson said: "This stimulus is really a Trojan horse. It's part of a plan that would turn the United States into France." He ultimately voted against the $787 billion law.

In his first term, Culberson was put on the Republican Steering Committee and won over colleagues by selflessly focusing on securing good appointments for other freshmen. In 2005, party leaders rewarded him with an appointment to Appropriations.

Culberson has embraced new technology as way to get out his message on immigration and a range of issues. "My ultimate goal is to become a real-time representative," he said. In August 2008 he joined fellow Republicans on the House floor during a congressional recess to protest the lack of a vote on expanding oil and gas drilling. While his fellow Republicans shouted their message from a lectern with the microphone off, Culberson posted messages on Twitter.com and video cell phone interviews with Republicans on Qik.com. A few months later, he posted video streams on Qik of President Obama's inauguration from his choice vantage point on the Capitol's congressional viewing platform. Subsequently, he got on Twitter to criticize Obama's address to Congress.

Culberson is an amateur fossil collector and initially led opposition to an omnibus lands bill in early 2009 because it included a provision that would set heavy penalties for taking any paleontological resource from federal lands without a permit. Ultimately, Oklahoma Republican Sen. Tom Coburn won approval to modify the language to forestall criminal prosecution of visitors who remove a few stones containing fossils.

The third of four children, Culberson was born in Houston and is a lifelong resident of the district. His father was a political consultant and graphic designer who worked on GOP Sen. John Tower's re-election in 1966, when Culberson was 10. He recalls going with his father on campaign trips.

He was campus chairman at Southern Methodist University for the 1980 presidential campaign of George Bush. (Culberson represents Bush's old House district.) After college, Culberson worked with his father while getting his law degree. At age 30, he won a seat in the Texas House and stayed for 14 years while also practicing civil defense law.

In the state House, Culberson waged an ultimately successful 11-year campaign to return control of the troubled Texas prison system to the state from the supervision of federal Judge William Wayne Justice. One of his goals is a constitutional amendment to give state legislatures the right to approve federal judges every 10 years.

In his office is a refurbished mahogany roll-top desk that he bought at an antiques store when he discovered that it had once belonged to his great-great-uncle, Charles Culberson, who was governor of Texas from 1895 to 1899 and a U.S. senator from 1899 to 1923.

When Rep. Bill Archer decided to retire in 2000, Culberson entered a crowded primary and won an expensive runoff, ensuring his election in the solidly Republican district. His elections have gotten tougher recently. He was re-elected in 2008 with 56 percent of the vote, his closest contest yet, after Democratic challenger Michael Skelly raised more than $3 million — including $1 million of his own money — to Culberson's $1.7 million.

KEY VOTES

2008

No Delay consideration of Colombia free-trade agreement
No Override Bush veto of federal farm and nutrition programs reauthorization bill
Yes Overhaul surveillance laws and permit dismissal of suits against companies that conducted warrantless wiretapping
No Grant mortgage relief to homeowners and funding for Fannie Mae and Freddie Mac
No Approve initial $700 billion program to stabilize financial markets
No Approve final $700 billion program to stabilize financial markets
No Provide $14 billion in loans to automakers

2007

No Increase minimum wage by $2.10 an hour
No Approve $124.2 billion in emergency war spending and set goal for redeployment of troops from Iraq
Yes Reject federal contraceptive assistance to international family planning groups
Yes Override Bush veto of $23.2 billion water projects authorization bill
Yes Implement Peru free-trade agreement
No Approve energy policy overhaul with new fuel economy standards
Yes Clear $473.5 billion omnibus spending bill, including $70 billion for military operations

CQ VOTE STUDIES

	PARTY UNITY		PRESIDENTIAL SUPPORT	
	SUPPORT	OPPOSE	SUPPORT	OPPOSE
2008	97%	3%	77%	23%
2007	97%	3%	89%	11%
2006	97%	3%	95%	5%
2005	98%	2%	93%	7%
2004	97%	3%	90%	10%

INTEREST GROUPS

	AFL-CIO	ADA	CCUS	ACU
2008	7%	5%	88%	100%
2007	4%	0%	79%	100%
2006	14%	10%	93%	88%
2005	14%	0%	88%	92%
2004	0%	0%	100%	96%

TEXAS 7

Western Houston and suburbs — Bellaire, West University Place, Jersey Village

Situated in western Houston, the 7th starts inside the Interstate 610 loop at Main Street south of downtown before moving through the city's western outposts and into the suburbs. White-collar executives, good schools and religious conservatism characterize much of the 7th, and John McCain took 58 percent of the 2008 presidential vote here.

The 7th includes some of Houston's oil and gas industry, as well as much of the Texas Medical Center, Houston's museum district (both of which are shared with the 9th and 18th districts), and the Galleria shopping and corporate complex. The medical center, which collaborates with area universities, employs tens of thousands of area residents. Rice University, which is adjacent to the medical center, focuses on nanotech and other applied sciences. An emphasis on attracting technology firms and corporate headquarters has enabled the 7th to enjoy decades of economic growth despite periodic national economic downturns.

Three-fifths of district residents live in Houston, and the 7th's share of the city is mostly middle class. Minorities, mainly Hispanics, make up one-third of the 7th's population. Northwest Houston has a large Hispanic population, and there are sizable black and Asian populations in southwest Houston. Much of the city's gay and lesbian community is centered around the Montrose neighborhood to the east.

Close ties to the oil and gas and health care industries make the 7th one of the state's wealthiest districts. Tony villages Piney Point, Bunker Hill and Hunters Creek, which are near Interstate 10 and surrounded on all sides by Houston, bring up the median income. The 7th also is one of the nation's top 10 most-educated districts, with half of its residents age 25 years or older having a bachelor's degree.

MAJOR INDUSTRY
Energy, health care, education and research, retail

CITIES
Houston (pt.), 390,922; Bellaire, 15,642; West University Place, 14,211

NOTABLE
On Sept. 12, 1962, during a speech at Rice University Stadium, President John F. Kennedy famously proclaimed that an American would reach the moon before the end of that decade.

Rep. Kevin Brady (R)

Elected December 1996; 7th term

CAPITOL OFFICE
225-4901
www.house.gov/brady
301 Cannon Bldg. 20515-4308; fax 225-5524

COMMITTEES
Ways & Means
Joint Economic

RESIDENCE
The Woodlands

BORN
April 11, 1955; Vermillion, S.D.

RELIGION
Roman Catholic

FAMILY
Wife, Cathy Brady; two children

EDUCATION
U. of South Dakota, B.S. 1990
(mass communication)

CAREER
Chamber of commerce executive

POLITICAL HIGHLIGHTS
Texas House, 1991-96

ELECTION RESULTS

2008 GENERAL

Kevin Brady (R)	207,128	72.6%
Kent Hargett (D)	70,758	24.8%
Brian Stevens (LIBERT)	7,565	2.6%

2008 PRIMARY

Kevin Brady (R)	unopposed

2006 GENERAL

Kevin Brady (R)	105,665	67.3%
James "Jim" Wright (D)	51,393	32.7%

PREVIOUS WINNING PERCENTAGES
2004 (69%); 2002 (93%); 2000 (92%); 1998 (93%);
1996 General Election Runoff (59%)

Brady, a reliable pro-business conservative, has long pressed for free trade, spending restraint and tax relief. He helped lead the way on those priorities during much of the George W. Bush administration, but finds it harder to make headway with Democrats in charge of Congress and the White House.

Yet he has a safe seat and growing seniority; he has climbed the Republican ranks on the Ways and Means Committee to become fourth in seniority and the top-ranking Republican on the Trade Subcommittee. He comes from a Democratic family, but his allegiance to his party leaders remains strong, including on most social issues.

When Republicans were in the majority, party leaders tapped Brady to lead the drive to pass implementing legislation for the Central America Free Trade Agreement. He helped keep the Bush administration up to date on the latest vote count and counseled trade officials on the timing of sending the legislation to Congress. The bill squeaked through in 2005.

He strongly supported passage in 2007 of a free-trade deal with Peru. But he said in 2008 that it has been "frustrating" to carry the free-trade banner under Democrats, who have been hostile to most trade pacts in recent years, including an agreement with Panama that lawmakers may consider during the 111th Congress (2009-10).

The senior House Republican on the Joint Economic Committee, Brady supported a $700 billion law in 2008 to aid the ailing financial services sector. But he opposed President Obama's early economic initiatives for their high spending and tax levels, including a $3.56 trillion budget blueprint for fiscal 2010. He pointed to testimony from businesses that taxes proposed on independent energy producers could cost hundreds of thousands of jobs in oil drilling. He also criticized the size of the spending plan.

In early 2009, he joined with colleagues to form the House-Senate Fiscal Responsibility Working Group to oversee spending through the $787 billion economic stimulus law signed in February. He also was named in 2008 to a GOP panel charged with devising a way to end the practice of earmarking — setting aside funds in spending bills for special projects. He said in 2009 a majority of GOP lawmakers want to curtail a practice that House leaders use to prod lawmakers to vote for bad legislation. "Earmarks are the tools of whoever is in the majority," Brady said. "It is the sugar that sweetens unhealthy bills."

But Brady has worked for years to secure disaster relief and recovery funds for his district in the wake of the devastating 2005 Gulf Coast hurricanes. His district, close to the Louisiana border, was among the first to take in Katrina evacuees. Hurricane Rita later damaged 70,000 homes in the area and destroyed $1 billion in timber. He again helped push for federal assistance to respond to hurricanes in 2008.

In 2004, he won enactment of a tax provision allowing residents of Texas and other states that have no state income tax to take a federal deduction for sales taxes instead. The deduction was renewed in 2006, but efforts to extend it stalled in the 110th Congress (2007-08).

Brady also wants to get more involved in the health care debate. Beginning in the summer of 2007, he began soliciting new approaches through town hall sessions and telephone conferences in his district, headlined "50 Ideas to Improve Health Care."

Concerned about stemming the flow of illegal immigrants, Brady worked on legislation with his Texas Republican colleague Sam Johnson to require all employers to take part in a new employee verification system to ensure legal status of their workers.

Transforming government is a Brady theme. He routinely sponsors legislation to set expiration dates for each federal agency, department and program unless they are affirmatively renewed. The proposal is similar to a law he won in Texas that has eliminated 52 agencies.

No one questions Brady's loyalty to the Republican Party, but visitors to his Capitol Hill office sometimes do a double-take when they see a photograph of the late Ann W. Richards, a famously tart-tongued Democratic governor of Texas. What they are looking at is a snapshot of his roots.

Pictured with Richards is Brady's mother, Nancy, a big fan of the salty Texan. "They look like they could be sisters … They both have big white hair," Brady noted. The two women had something else in common, too: unswerving allegiance to the Democratic Party. It's Brady who changed parties. His uncle was a Democratic state senator, his father — a Korean War veteran — was a county party official in South Dakota, where the congressman was born.

Brady for a while split with his party on the issue of gun rights. When he was 12 years old, his father, a lawyer, was shot and killed in a South Dakota courtroom by the deranged spouse of a client, and the incident shaped his outlook on gun control. As a state representative in Texas — where he moved at age 26 to take a job with the Chamber of Commerce in Beaumont — Brady was one of just two Republicans to oppose a bill allowing Texans to carry concealed weapons. But more recently he said the law has not been abused and has protected many individuals and small businesses "in tough areas." In April 2009, he warned against "potential overreaction to the Mexican drug violence" that could lead to curbing gun owners' rights.

He attended the University of South Dakota but left in 1978 without graduating because he had neglected to complete the paperwork for a work-study class. After an opponent in his first Texas House race in 1990 unearthed Brady's lack of a degree, Brady cleared up the incomplete grade. He went on to serve six years in the state legislature.

When Republican Jack Fields announced he wouldn't seek re-election in the 8th District in 1996, Brady had to face several primary races and runoffs before defeating wealthy Republican physician Gene Fontenot. But then a three-judge federal panel redrew the 8th as well as 12 other Texas congressional districts in response to a Supreme Court ruling that found illegal "racial gerrymandering" in the Texas map. The court ordered new elections and the two were forced into another runoff; Brady prevailed with 59 percent of the vote. He has been safely ensconced in Congress ever since.

KEY VOTES

2008
No Delay consideration of Colombia free-trade agreement
Yes Override Bush veto of federal farm and nutrition programs reauthorization bill
Yes Overhaul surveillance laws and permit dismissal of suits against companies that conducted warrantless wiretapping
No Grant mortgage relief to homeowners and funding for Fannie Mae and Freddie Mac
Yes Approve initial $700 billion program to stabilize financial markets
Yes Approve final $700 billion program to stabilize financial markets
No Provide $14 billion in loans to automakers

2007
No Increase minimum wage by $2.10 an hour
No Approve $124.2 billion in emergency war spending and set goal for redeployment of troops from Iraq
Yes Reject federal contraceptive assistance to international family planning groups
No Override Bush veto of $23.2 billion water projects authorization bill
Yes Implement Peru free-trade agreement
No Approve energy policy overhaul with new fuel economy standards
Yes Clear $473.5 billion omnibus spending bill, including $70 billion for military operations

CQ VOTE STUDIES

	PARTY UNITY		PRESIDENTIAL SUPPORT	
	SUPPORT	OPPOSE	SUPPORT	OPPOSE
2008	94%	6%	77%	23%
2007	95%	5%	86%	14%
2006	96%	4%	97%	3%
2005	98%	2%	91%	9%
2004	98%	2%	94%	6%

INTEREST GROUPS

	AFL-CIO	ADA	CCUS	ACU
2008	7%	10%	88%	86%
2007	4%	5%	75%	100%
2006	7%	5%	100%	88%
2005	13%	0%	89%	96%
2004	7%	0%	100%	100%

TEXAS 8
East central – The Woodlands, Conroe

A Republican stronghold, the 8th begins in Houston's rapidly growing Montgomery County suburbs north of the city and moves east through rural areas to the Louisiana border. More than four-fifths of district residents are white, the highest percentage of white residents in any Texas district. The district gave John McCain 74 percent of its vote in the 2008 presidential election, and he won easily in every county in the district.

Located about 30 miles north of downtown Houston, The Woodlands — a large planned community that gets its name from its proximity to Sam Houston National Forest — is an exclusive area filled with large houses and some of the state's highest-rated schools. The area is a corporate and business center, and several petroleum and biotechnology companies have made their homes here.

The timber industry and some cattle ranches populate the northern part of Montgomery County, although much of the county is turning into suburbanized bedroom communities for Houston, and the residents in the district have some of the longest commutes in the state. Conroe has one of the largest lakes in the area and many wealthy lakefront homeowners. Lake Conroe also offers golf courses, resorts and marinas, and some of the 8th's lakes provide drinking water to Houston and are a magnet for retirees. Farther north are Livingston and Huntsville, where the Texas State Penitentiary houses the state's death row and is a major employer. High winds and flooding during Hurricane Ike, and the subsequent loss of electricity and running water, damaged residential areas in the 8th, as well as the forests and cattle ranches. More than 10,000 acres of timber in Montgomery County sustained damage from the 2008 storm.

In the southeastern part of the 8th, the economy relies on petrochemical production and on ship repair in Orange County and nearby Beaumont and Port Arthur (both in the 2nd District). Abundant pine forests in the district's east still support a vulnerable timber industry.

MAJOR INDUSTRY
Petrochemicals, shipping, timber, education, prisons

CITIES
The Woodlands (unincorporated), 55,649; Conroe, 36,811; Huntsville, 35,078

NOTABLE
Texas' Lone Star flag was designed in Montgomery County in 1839.

Rep. Al Green (D)

Elected 2004; 3rd term

A former civil rights leader, Green speaks passionately about his belief that the federal government should provide for the poor and disadvantaged. He pushes for more affordable housing, improved health care, better wages and job security. Green is always seen wearing a lapel pin that reads, "God is Good All the Time."

His district is one of the most racially diverse, and he sits on both the Congressional Black Caucus and the Asian Pacific American Caucus. Green said he feels comfortable moving in both circles, partially because he isn't entirely sure about his own ethnic background. "I don't know what I am," he said. As such, he advocates for all minorities and anyone he views as disadvantaged.

"The richest country in the world, the country where one out of every 110 persons is a millionaire, how does it treat persons who are among the least, the last and the lost who have suffered as a result of a natural disaster?" Green said on the House floor in 2007 when pressing for continued federal assistance for refugees of hurricanes Katrina and Rita. More than 20,000 hurricane victims came to his district. "Americans of goodwill want to see that no American … is left behind."

In 2007, he pushed through the House a proposal to extend a temporary housing voucher program run by the Federal Emergency Management Agency until the end of the year. During a hearing on FEMA's slow response to provide housing, Green noted the families of Sept. 11 victims received an average of $3.1 million in compensation. "We cannot treat the people of New York better than we treat people in New Orleans," said Green, who was born in the Crescent City.

He has used his seat on the Homeland Security Committee to push for assistance for hurricane victims. When Hurricane Ike blew through Houston in September 2008, Green took to the streets of his district, speaking through a bullhorn and urging his constituents to remain calm. He backed the passage of $22.9 billion in disaster relief as part of a catchall spending bill Congress cleared later that month. He also keeps tabs on rail and cargo security as well as border enforcement. Green is not as intent on closing America's borders as helping those immigrants who are already here.

He advocates for a national affordable health care system, saying, "I don't think people ought to receive good health care by virtue of their station in life." And he pushes legislation that would index the minimum wage to ensure full-time workers remain above the federal poverty line.

He backed President Obama's $3.56 trillion budget blueprint for fiscal 2010, saying it "will get our economy moving again, without losing sight of the long-term challenges that our country faces, such as achieving quality, universal health care, securing our energy independence, providing our children with quality education that is unparalleled elsewhere and getting our budget deficit under control."

From his seat on the Financial Services Committee, Green pays particular attention to housing, insurance and lender practices that hurt low- to moderate-income neighborhoods. He successfully included in a 2009 national service law a provision encouraging volunteers to work on behalf of affordable housing for economically disadvantaged individuals.

Green initially opposed a $700 billion plan to aid the nation's troubled financial system in fall 2008. "We cannot give the perception that we're willing to help Wall Street but not take care of the people on Home Street," he

CAPITOL OFFICE
225-7508
www.house.gov/algreen
236 Cannon Bldg. 20515-4309; fax 225-2947

COMMITTEES
Financial Services
Homeland Security

RESIDENCE
Houston

BORN
Sept. 1, 1947; New Orleans, La.

RELIGION
Christian

FAMILY
Divorced

EDUCATION
Florida A&M U., attended 1966-71;
Tuskegee Institute of Technology, attended;
Texas Southern U., J.D. 1973

CAREER
Lawyer; NAACP chapter president

POLITICAL HIGHLIGHTS
Harris County Justice of the Peace Court judge, 1977-2004; candidate for mayor of Houston, 1981

ELECTION RESULTS

2008 GENERAL

Al Green (D)	143,868	93.6%
Brad Walters (LIBERT)	9,760	6.4%

2008 PRIMARY

Al Green (D)	unopposed

2006 GENERAL

Al Green (D)	unopposed

PREVIOUS WINNING PERCENTAGES
2004 (72%)

told The Houston Chronicle. But he supported a slightly revised version that was signed into law.

He was one of a dozen lawmakers who discussed with Federal Reserve Chairman Ben S. Bernanke in early 2009 the idea of making Fed programs more available to minority-owned businesses.

He backed a 2008 housing finance package intended to stabilize financial markets and the battered housing sector. The bill, signed into law, includes a $300 billion expansion of the Federal Housing Administration's loan insurance programs aimed at helping borrowers avoid foreclosure. It also includes language Green helped draft to increase funding for legal assistance related to home ownership preservation and home foreclosure prevention. But the bill eliminated a program that allowed sellers to provide down payment assistance for mortgages backed by the FHA, a move Green said would disproportionately hurt minorities.

Green said he is most proud of legislation he introduced to provide $200 million in transitional housing assistance and 20,000 housing rental vouchers to low-income veterans. The House passed the bill in July 2008, but it became the subject of political maneuvering between the two parties. The Democratic presidential nominee, Sen. Barack Obama of Illinois, sponsored the Senate's version, but the George W. Bush administration threatened to veto it, saying it would duplicate existing programs.

Green was born in New Orleans, the son of an auto mechanic and a maid. He grew up in Florida, where his maternal grandfather was a Methodist minister. He attended Florida A&M University and the Tuskegee Institute of Technology through work-study and grant programs. He didn't earn an undergraduate degree but eventually gained a law degree from the Thurgood Marshall School of Law at Texas Southern University. He then co-founded a law practice that included criminal defense. One of his adversaries in the courtroom, who became a good friend, was then-prosecutor Ted Poe — a Republican elected to represent the 2nd District in 2004.

Green served 26 years as a justice of the peace. During the 1980s and early 1990s, he was president of the local chapter of the NAACP. He took advantage of the GOP-inspired remapping of Texas congressional districts prior to the 2004 election, which significantly altered the demographics of the 9th District and enabled him to score a crushing primary victory over Democratic Rep. Chris Bell. He then won the general election with even greater ease. He faced no major party opposition in 2006 or 2008.

He shares the same name as the famous soul singer, which he said can be a disadvantage because "people often ask me to sing." Occasionally he obliges.

KEY VOTES

2008

Yes Delay consideration of Colombia free-trade agreement
Yes Override Bush veto of federal farm and nutrition programs reauthorization bill
Yes Overhaul surveillance laws and permit dismissal of suits against companies that conducted warrantless wiretapping
Yes Grant mortgage relief to homeowners and funding for Fannie Mae and Freddie Mac
No Approve initial $700 billion program to stabilize financial markets
Yes Approve final $700 billion program to stabilize financial markets
Yes Provide $14 billion in loans to automakers

2007

Yes Increase minimum wage by $2.10 an hour
Yes Approve $124.2 billion in emergency war spending and set goal for redeployment of troops from Iraq
No Reject federal contraceptive assistance to international family planning groups
Yes Override Bush veto of $23.2 billion water projects authorization bill
No Implement Peru free-trade agreement
Yes Approve energy policy overhaul with new fuel economy standards
No Clear $473.5 billion omnibus spending bill, including $70 billion for military operations

CQ VOTE STUDIES

	PARTY UNITY		PRESIDENTIAL SUPPORT	
	SUPPORT	OPPOSE	SUPPORT	OPPOSE
2008	99%	1%	14%	86%
2007	98%	2%	3%	97%
2006	94%	6%	30%	70%
2005	93%	7%	20%	80%

INTEREST GROUPS

	AFL-CIO	ADA	CCUS	ACU
2008	100%	100%	67%	4%
2007	100%	100%	50%	4%
2006	100%	95%	60%	20%
2005	100%	100%	48%	16%

TEXAS 9

Southern Houston and suburbs — Mission Bend, part of Missouri City

The 9th takes in southern Houston and a few suburbs to the west. It is Texas' smallest district in area, but its most ethnically diverse — blacks are 37 percent of residents, Hispanics one-third and Asians 11 percent.

The district's eastern edge takes in largely black communities such as Sunnyside, which is one of the oldest black communities in Houston. As the 9th stretches west, it picks up the entertainment complex Reliant Park. Among other venues, the park is home to Reliant Stadium, which is the home field for football's Texans, and the historic Astrodome. Local officials have discussed turning the multi-use Astrodome into a convention hotel or other new facility.

The 9th's western portion takes in much of Houston's Asian community, with Chinese, Korean and Japanese enclaves as well as several South Asian immigrant communities. Almost one-third of district residents are foreign-born, the highest percentage in the state. Retail dominates here, and stores spring up with signs in both English and Asian languages.

Leading the local health care sector, part of the Texas Medical Center falls in the 9th in the Hermann Park area (shared with the 7th and 18th districts). Its portion of the center includes the Houston Academy of Medicine and the Michael E. Debakey VA Medical Center. Job creation is a high priority among the area's many poor residents. Some of the "super neighborhoods," communities created by residents in order to better connect local needs to the city government, have focused on safety and housing issues. In 2008, although Hurricane Ike hit the coastal areas of Texas with more force, parts of the 9th suffered wind and flood damage.

The 9th strongly supports Democrats, and gave Barack Obama his third-highest percentage statewide in the 2008 presidential election.

MAJOR INDUSTRY
Retail, health care, entertainment

CITIES
Houston (pt.), 551,793; Mission Bend (unincorporated), 30,831

NOTABLE
The Chinatown area boasts the Hong Kong City Mall, one of the nation's largest Asian-themed malls.

Rep. Michael McCaul (R)

Elected 2004; 3rd term

A former prosecutor and counterterrorism official, McCaul is seen by his peers and Republican leaders as a man on the move. He was elected freshman class liaison to the leadership when he arrived in 2005; he became a member of the GOP whip's vote-counting operation in 2007 and is now the top Republican on the Homeland Security Subcommittee on Intelligence, Information Sharing and Terrorism Risk Assessment.

He also is a member of the conservative Republican Study Committee. McCaul votes against most spending bills in the name of fiscal restraint while fighting to protect the interests of oil companies, and he hews to the party line on such social issues as abortion and embryonic stem cell research. Like most Texas Republicans, he sees illegal immigration as a major national security issue and has backed plans for tougher border security enforcement.

During the 110th Congress (2007-08), he hosted meetings in his district between local law enforcement authorities and representatives of Homeland Security's Immigration and Customs Enforcement agency in an effort to speed deportation of undocumented immigrants arrested for alleged criminal activity. As violence stemming from the drug war in Mexico threatened to spill over the border in early 2009, McCaul urged the administration to increase funding to boost border security.

He also backed legislation in 2009 offered by Texas Republican Lamar Smith to bar inmates from a terrorist detention center at Guantánamo Bay, Cuba, from being brought into the United States. "Our objective in the war on terror has always been to keep terrorists off of U.S. soil and away from our cities and Americans they intend to harm," McCaul told the Brenham Banner-Press.

A member of the Foreign Affairs Committee. McCaul has repeatedly expressed an interest in the concept of the U.S. government fomenting internal resistance to the Iranian government, particularly through the MEK — a group listed by the State Department as a foreign terrorist organization. At a hearing in January 2007, he asked Secretary of State Condoleezza Rice what the U.S. government was doing to assist any internal resistance and whether the MEK could be removed from the list of terrorist groups.

One of his proudest accomplishments in the international arena came in an unofficial capacity. During a trip to Pakistan in summer 2008, he successfully urged Pervez Musharraf, then president of Pakistan, to order the release of two American teenagers who were being held against their will at a fundamentalist Islamic religious school in Pakistan's tribal areas. "Within days, the boys were coming home. That's a memory that will stay with me," he recalled.

McCaul also sits on the Science and Technology Committee, which oversees the NASA policies important to constituents involved in the work of the Johnson Space Center in Houston. He introduced bills in the 109th Congress (2005-06) to promote high-risk, high-reward research and to integrate education and research. In 2006, he pushed through legislation to advance graduate education in "green" technology and building practices.

His sense of institutional duty led him in 2007 to accept one of the most thankless jobs in Congress: an assignment to the Committee on Standards of Official Conduct, better known as the ethics committee. The following year he was named top Republican on a subcommittee to investigate Republican Rick Renzi of Arizona, who had been indicted on extortion, money-laundering and conspiracy charges in connection with a land-swap deal. The panel eventually suspended its probe at the request of the Justice Department to avoid

CAPITOL OFFICE
225-2401
www.house.gov/mccaul
131 Cannon Bldg. 20515-4310; fax 225-5955

COMMITTEES
Foreign Affairs
Homeland Security
Science & Technology

RESIDENCE
Austin

BORN
Jan. 14, 1962; Dallas, Texas

RELIGION
Roman Catholic

FAMILY
Wife, Linda McCaul; five children

EDUCATION
Trinity U., B.A. 1984 (business & history);
St. Mary's U. (Texas), J.D. 1987

CAREER
U.S. Justice Department official; state and federal prosecutor; lawyer

POLITICAL HIGHLIGHTS
No previous office

ELECTION RESULTS

2008 GENERAL

Michael McCaul (R)	179,493	53.9%
Larry Joe Doherty (D)	143,719	43.1%
Matt Finkel (LIBERT)	9,871	3.0%

2008 PRIMARY

Michael McCaul (R)	unopposed

2006 GENERAL

Michael McCaul (R)	97,726	55.3%
Ted Ankrum (D)	71,415	40.4%
Michael Badnarik (LIBERT)	7,614	4.3%

PREVIOUS WINNING PERCENTAGES
2004 (79%)

interfering with the criminal case. McCaul left the panel in 2009.

The role of ethics investigator is a familiar one for McCaul, who was a prosecutor in the Justice Department's public integrity section early in his career before becoming deputy to current GOP Sen. John Cornyn, who was then the Texas attorney general. McCaul later was chief of counterterrorism and national security in the U.S. attorney's office in Austin and led its Joint Terrorism Task Force.

In line with his desire for fiscal restraint, he introduced a bill in January 2009 to extend and expand a 2008 law he authored that barred, through March 2009, federal spending on projects named after members of Congress. The next month he voted against the $787 billion economic stimulus package. He had told News 8 in Austin that "the bill did too much spending and not enough creating jobs and stimulating." He voted against the $700 billion financial sector rescue law in the fall of 2008, resisting entreaties of GOP leaders.

McCaul typically votes with other Republicans to promote domestic oil and gas drilling and combat Democratic proposals for higher taxes on oil companies. But in 2007, he voted for a Democratic energy bill that increased fuel efficiency standards for vehicles and set a requirement for the production and use of biofuels. He opposed an earlier version of the legislation because it would have rolled back tax breaks for oil and gas companies to pay for new renewable-energy incentives.

McCaul attributes his career in public service to the example set by his father, a B-17 pilot during World War II, and his education at the Jesuit College Preparatory Academy of Dallas. He is one of the wealthiest members of Congress, with a minimum net worth of $23 million in 2007, according to the Center for Responsive Politics. His wife, Linda, is the daughter of Clear Channel Communications CEO Lowry Mays, and McCaul spent nearly $2 million to win his first campaign.

The 2004 GOP primary that marked McCaul's political debut was an eight-candidate free-for-all. He amassed support from Republican insiders and won the runoff with 63 percent of the vote. Democrats didn't field a candidate in November, and McCaul took 79 percent of the vote in a newly drawn district.

In 2006, a bad year for Republicans, McCaul won at the polls against former NASA official Ted Ankrum with just 55 percent of the vote. In 2008, he faced trial attorney Larry Joe Doherty and won with close to 54 percent. In early 2009, McCaul briefly contemplated a 2010 bid for state attorney general, but told the Austin American-Statesman in April that he had decided to run for re-election "because the challenges we face in Washington have never been greater."

KEY VOTES

2008
No Delay consideration of Colombia free-trade agreement
Yes Override Bush veto of federal farm and nutrition programs reauthorization bill
Yes Overhaul surveillance laws and permit dismissal of suits against companies that conducted warrantless wiretapping
No Grant mortgage relief to homeowners and funding for Fannie Mae and Freddie Mac
No Approve initial $700 billion program to stabilize financial markets
No Approve final $700 billion program to stabilize financial markets
No Provide $14 billion in loans to automakers

2007
No Increase minimum wage by $2.10 an hour
No Approve $124.2 billion in emergency war spending and set goal for redeployment of troops from Iraq
Yes Reject federal contraceptive assistance to international family planning groups
Yes Override Bush veto of $23.2 billion water projects authorization bill
Yes Implement Peru free-trade agreement
Yes Approve energy policy overhaul with new fuel economy standards
Yes Clear $473.5 billion omnibus spending bill, including $70 billion for military operations

CQ VOTE STUDIES

	PARTY UNITY		PRESIDENTIAL SUPPORT	
	SUPPORT	OPPOSE	SUPPORT	OPPOSE
2008	95%	5%	68%	32%
2007	94%	6%	81%	19%
2006	94%	6%	90%	10%
2005	96%	4%	85%	15%

INTEREST GROUPS

	AFL-CIO	ADA	CCUS	ACU
2008	13%	25%	89%	96%
2007	9%	15%	85%	96%
2006	21%	0%	100%	83%
2005	20%	5%	93%	96%

TEXAS 10

East central — eastern Austin and western Houston suburbs, Brenham

The 10th mimics a drive that many University of Texas students from the Houston area know well as they travel back and forth to school in Austin. The district stretches west from the northern Houston suburbs and follows U.S. Highway 290 to Austin, where it hugs downtown as it wraps around the city's northwestern edge. Along its 150-mile journey, the 10th picks up affluent suburbs, a technology belt and a chunk of farmland.

Narrowly missing the Democratic stronghold of Hyde Park and the University of Texas in Austin, the 10th instead takes in the more upscale areas of the Arboretum, Far West and the neighborhood of West Lake. It also reaches up to Pflugerville and the northern suburbs, which host many of Austin's tech firms. IBM and Samsung have facilities in the city, and Dell is based in Round Rock just across the district line in the 31st, but the local tech sector has struggled with widespread layoffs. Although the majority of the University of Texas flagship campus is in the adjacent 21st, the 10th takes in the university's J.J. Pickle Research Campus.

As the 10th District moves east away from Austin, it becomes increasingly rural, and takes in the towns of Elgin, Giddings, Hempstead and Prairie View. This area also includes Brenham, which is home to ice cream maker Blue Bell Creameries. The district then dips into suburbs in northwestern Harris County, including Tomball and part of Spring, which has gotten bigger as people moved farther from downtown Houston. Most residents commute, which makes transportation and infrastructure policies important issues here.

The district, as a whole, is two-thirds white and has a growing Hispanic presence, although areas such as Prairie View are predominately black. The more-rural areas of the district struggle with high levels of poverty. Although the 10th includes vastly different urban, suburban and rural areas, it is reliably Republican. John McCain captured 55 percent of the vote here in the 2008 presidential election.

MAJOR INDUSTRY
Software, technology, agriculture

CITIES
Austin (pt.), 209,200; Pflugerville, 16,335

NOTABLE
Serbin's annual "Wendish Fest" honors the area's link to Slavic culture.

Rep. K. Michael Conaway (R)

Elected 2004; 3rd term

CAPITOL OFFICE
225-3605
conaway.house.gov
1527 Longworth Bldg. 20515-4311; fax 225-1783

COMMITTEES
Agriculture
Armed Services
Standards of Official Conduct
Select Intelligence

RESIDENCE
Midland

BORN
June 11, 1948; Borger, Texas

RELIGION
Baptist

FAMILY
Wife, Suzanne Conaway; four children

EDUCATION
East Texas State U., B.B.A. 1970 (accounting)

MILITARY SERVICE
Army, 1970-72

CAREER
Accountant; bank chief financial officer;
oil and gas exploration company
chief financial officer

POLITICAL HIGHLIGHTS
Midland school board, 1985-88; candidate
for U.S. House (special election), 2003

ELECTION RESULTS

2008 GENERAL

K. Michael Conaway (R)	189,625	88.3%
James R. Strohm (LIBERT)	25,051	11.7%

2008 PRIMARY

K. Michael Conaway (R)	unopposed

2006 GENERAL

K. Michael Conaway (R)	unopposed

PREVIOUS WINNING PERCENTAGES
2004 (77%)

Conaway is a small-government conservative who battles against industry regulations he sees as wrongheaded, calls for more fiscal discipline and abhors most programs he perceives as welfare or government handouts — unless it means subsidizing his farming constituents.

One anecdote sums up his political philosophy. A man in Harper once asked Conaway what the federal government could do for a couple in town who couldn't afford their medicine. "Why are you letting that happen to your neighbor?" Conaway responded. "You see the need. You see the family. You understand exactly what's going on, and you've got a better analysis of it than anyone else would have."

Conaway is among the most loyal Republicans in the House. He voted with his party on 98 percent of the votes that pitted a majority of Republicans against Democrats in the 110th Congress (2007-08). The former accountant continued his loyalty into 2009 as he opposed President Obama's early initiatives, including a $787 billion economic stimulus law, an expansion of a children's health insurance program, and a $3.56 trillion budget blueprint for fiscal 2010.

Republican leaders frequently turn to Conaway for his accounting skills. A member of the Armed Services Committee, he was named in 2009 as the top Republican on a panel charged with studying the Defense Department's problems in acquiring goods and services on time and on budget. During the 110th, he headed up an internal audit team for the National Republican Congressional Committee, the party's campaign finance arm. After the committee's treasurer, Christopher J. Ward, repeatedly canceled meetings with him, Conaway investigated and found Ward had been preparing false financial statements for years. The embezzlement was estimated to total $725,000.

Despite his calls for fiscal control, Conaway steers dollars to his district's farmers from his seat on the Agriculture Committee. In early 2007, he worked to protect commodity payments in the reauthorization of farm programs and battled the George W. Bush administration's efforts to impose stricter caps on such payments than those supported by the panel. He voted against the bill on the House floor in 2007 because it included a tax increase on foreign corporations, but he changed his vote on the final bill when that provision was dropped.

He opposes attempts to impose a federal ban on the use of antibiotics in livestock feed. The ranking Republican on the subcommittee on rural development, biotechnology and specialty crops, Conaway said in 2009 that no scientific evidence shows a clear link between such use of antibiotics and an increased resistance to antibiotics among humans.

Immigrant labor is important to his district's farmers, and Conaway in the past has backed a limited immigration policy overhaul that would have allowed illegal immigrants to register as temporary workers, but without the possibility of becoming citizens.

Although he opposed a fiscal 2009 omnibus spending bill, he touted the more than $14.5 million in earmarks — special funding set-asides for projects in members' districts — he helped obtain, including $1.7 million for the International Cotton Center to support research into "increasing the profitability and sustainability of cotton and other natural fiber production."

He also pushes for expanded oil and gas production. Conaway was once a "roughneck" — a worker on a drilling rig — and from 1981 to 1986 was chief financial officer of and an investor in Arbusto Energy Inc. (later Bush Exploration), a Midland-based energy company owned by George W. Bush.

He believes he understands the industry and its issues better than most of his colleagues, particularly Democrats who decry expanded drilling.

He derided a Democratic bill calling for the Organization of the Petroleum Exporting Countries to produce more oil as "a staggering twist of illogic," given the majority's opposition to U.S. oil production. And he voted against the Democrats' 2007 bill mandating new fuel economy standards for vehicles, calling it "one of the most onerous mandates placed on the American business community in recent years." He is a member of a GOP group tasked with devising an alternative energy plan. He opposes Democratic global warming legislation that includes a "cap and trade" system for greenhouse gas emissions.

Conaway is also a member of the Select Intelligence Committee, which in 2009 prepared to launch a probe into the interrogation practices used by Bush administration officials on terrorism suspects at the detention facility at Guantánamo Bay, Cuba. And in 2009 he picked up a seat on the ethics committee.

At least once each Congress, Conaway introduces legislation to require all members and senior staff to certify they had read and understood the Constitution. He carries a pocket version of it himself, noting inside the cover the dates he reads it, and requires his aides to read the document annually.

As a youth, Conaway played on Odessa Permian High School's first state championship football team as defensive end and offensive tackle. (The school's football program was the basis for the book "Friday Night Lights," which later became a film and television series.) He won a football scholarship after graduating, but of his limited college football career, he said, "I didn't play a lot on Saturdays."

He was a pre-law major in college, but a professor persuaded him to switch to accounting. He received his degree from East Texas State University (now Texas A&M University-Commerce) in 1970. He was a military police officer at the Army's Fort Hood in Texas, then worked for Price Waterhouse & Co., settling in Midland. After working in the energy industry, he opened his own accounting firm in 1993.

When Bush was in his first year as governor of Texas, he appointed Conaway to the state Board of Public Accountancy, where Conaway served for seven years. He also is an ordained deacon in the Baptist Church.

His first elective office was on the Midland school board. In 2003, he lost a House special-election race in the 19th District by just 587 votes to fellow Republican Randy Neugebauer. A GOP-inspired congressional redistricting allowed Conaway to breeze to victory in 2004 in the new 11th. He faced no major party opposition in 2006 or 2008.

KEY VOTES

2008
No   Delay consideration of Colombia free-trade agreement
Yes Override Bush veto of federal farm and nutrition programs reauthorization bill
Yes Overhaul surveillance laws and permit dismissal of suits against companies that conducted warrantless wiretapping
No   Grant mortgage relief to homeowners and funding for Fannie Mae and Freddie Mac
No   Approve initial $700 billion program to stabilize financial markets
Yes Approve final $700 billion program to stabilize financial markets
No   Provide $14 billion in loans to automakers

2007
No   Increase minimum wage by $2.10 an hour
No   Approve $124.2 billion in emergency war spending and set goal for redeployment of troops from Iraq
Yes Reject federal contraceptive assistance to international family planning groups
Yes Override Bush veto of $23.2 billion water projects authorization bill
Yes Implement Peru free-trade agreement
No   Approve energy policy overhaul with new fuel economy standards
Yes Clear $473.5 billion omnibus spending bill, including $70 billion for military operations

CQ VOTE STUDIES

	PARTY UNITY		PRESIDENTIAL SUPPORT	
	SUPPORT	OPPOSE	SUPPORT	OPPOSE
2008	97%	3%	76%	24%
2007	98%	2%	89%	11%
2006	98%	2%	93%	7%
2005	96%	4%	87%	13%

INTEREST GROUPS

	AFL-CIO	ADA	CCUS	ACU
2008	0%	5%	89%	92%
2007	4%	5%	70%	96%
2006	7%	0%	100%	88%
2005	13%	0%	93%	96%

TEXAS 11

West central — Midland, Odessa, San Angelo

Starting in Burnet County in the center of the state, the overwhelmingly white and Republican 11th District is characterized by stark plains, mesas and oil rigs. It slices from west of Austin to the New Mexico border, taking in San Angelo, Midland, Odessa and vast stretches of rural land.

In the west lies oil country and the Permian Basin, home to Midland and Odessa. Odessa's economy still relies heavily on petroleum, but the city has become a regional telecommunications and distribution hub. The area also has seen growing interest in "green" development and alternative energy production. Nationwide economic downturns have hurt oil-field workers as well as manufacturing centers to the east.

While the western portion of the 11th is mostly high desert plains, the southeastern section moves into the highland lakes region, taking in part of the state's hill country. Here, agriculture dominates, with cotton, row crops, cattle, sheep, goats and small grains key to the economy. This region also is popular with hunters, and tourism has grown at the area's resorts and lakes.

A growing Hispanic population makes up nearly one-third of the district, and immigration continues to be an issue throughout the region as illegal workers still play a heavy role in the oil and agricultural industries. The 11th also has the state's highest percentage of residents over age 65 (15 percent) due to a relatively inexpensive cost of living and good area health care. Improving transportation routes is also a priority for the district, as it is for much of West Texas.

The immense 11th gave Republican John McCain 75 percent of its 2008 presidential vote, the second-highest percentage he received in any Texas congressional district, and rural Glasscock County gave him 90 percent of its vote, his fourth-highest percentage in the state.

MAJOR INDUSTRY
Oil and gas, agriculture, cattle, tourism

MILITARY BASES
Goodfellow Air Force Base, 1,389 military, 769 civilian (2007)

CITIES
Midland, 94,996; Odessa, 90,943; San Angelo, 88,439; Brownwood, 18,813

NOTABLE
The Globe of the Great Southwest in Odessa is a replica of the famous Elizabethan-era theater used by William Shakespeare.

Rep. Kay Granger (R)

Elected 1996; 7th term

Granger is a former teacher, businesswoman and mayor whose ambitions keep her looking for a more prominent role in the GOP. She has stepped back from a brief stint in the Republican leadership, but has her sights set on reshaping her party's appeal to moderate voters and working with Democrats on high-profile economic and health care issues.

In 2009 she was given a key platform to help shape international policy when she was appointed top Republican on the State-Foreign Operations Appropriations Subcommittee. It was a new role for Granger, who has served on Appropriations since 1999, and she brings an understanding of the issues involved in sending U.S. dollars overseas, having traveled heavily while serving on the Defense and Military Construction-VA panels. But having touted herself as a "pro-choice Republican," she makes some conservatives uneasy.

Granger is more worried about helping her party rethink its image, particularly as it faces a larger Democratic majority in Congress and a Democratic administration. "I wouldn't call it compromise — I would call it working together," she said. "Issues like health care, transportation and defense were not partisan issues when I was first elected in 1996. They became partisan issues. We need to reach across the aisle."

Granger in 2008 tried to help Republicans reach out to moderate voters by attempting to craft policies that put less emphasis on hot-button issues such as abortion and same-sex marriage. She pushed to address family finances, advocating such ideas as full tax-deductibility for most medical expenses. Throughout President George W. Bush's tenure, however, she supported her party on 96 percent of the votes that pitted a majority of the two parties against each other. That included opposing a 2007 bill to expand the State Children's Health Insurance Program. On that vote, she was one of 45 Republicans targeted by union and political action groups to change her position. But she maintained her stance when Democrats moved similar legislation in 2009 that President Obama signed into law. In 2008, she supported a $700 billion law to shore up the ailing financial services industry, calling it the most difficult vote of her congressional career.

She expressed optimism in early 2009 regarding Obama's pledge toward bipartisanship in addressing the economic crisis and tightening spending. But she raised a warning against potential tax hikes and cuts to the armed forces. And she voted against Obama's $787 billion stimulus plan, saying she believed the bill should have focused on tax relief and provided more for transportation and water infrastructure projects. She also blamed Democrats for a lack of transparency in moving the bill.

Granger has spent the majority of her House career on Appropriations, tending to the needs of her middle-class district by sending home millions of dollars for local projects. She has kept federal dollars flowing to Lockheed Martin Corp. and Bell Helicopter Textron. She supports continued funding of the F-35 Joint Strike Fighter, the F-22 and the V-22 Osprey aircraft.

She has done extensive traveling as part of her job. She was part of the first congressional delegation to visit Iraq after the war began in 2003, and as co-chair of the bipartisan Iraqi Women's Caucus worked with female candidates there seeking a role in the new government.

Among the top issues she faces during the 111th Congress (2009-10) is the escalating drug war in Mexico. "If we do not support Mexico in its war against the drug cartels, the consequences may be grave … The problems in Mexico will inevitably spill into the United States," Granger said in April.

CAPITOL OFFICE
225-5071
kaygranger.house.gov
320 Cannon Bldg. 20515-4312; fax 225-5683

COMMITTEES
Appropriations

RESIDENCE
Fort Worth

BORN
Jan. 18, 1943; Greenville, Texas

RELIGION
Methodist

FAMILY
Divorced; three children

EDUCATION
Texas Wesleyan U., B.S. 1965

CAREER
Insurance agency owner; teacher

POLITICAL HIGHLIGHTS
Fort Worth Zoning Commission, 1981-89;
Fort Worth City Council, 1989-91; mayor of
Fort Worth, 1991-95

ELECTION RESULTS

2008 GENERAL
Kay Granger (R)	181,662	67.6%
Tracey Smith (D)	82,250	30.6%
Shiloh Sidney Shambaugh (LIBERT)	4,842	1.8%

2008 PRIMARY
Kay Granger (R)	unopposed

2006 GENERAL
Kay Granger (R)	98,371	66.9%
John R. Morris (D)	45,676	31.1%
Gardner C. Osborne (LIBERT)	2,888	2.0%

PREVIOUS WINNING PERCENTAGES
2004 (72%); 2002 (92%); 2000 (63%); 1998 (62%);
1996 (58%)

She has pledged to play conservatively when it comes to determining how many dollars to send overseas, yet some groups — such as the Family Research Council — are still nervous due to her past stance on abortion. Though a social conservative, Granger described herself in a September 2007 MSNBC interview as a "pro-choice Republican."

Obama in January 2009 overturned the "Mexico City" policy that prohibited funding of groups that perform or promote abortion overseas, and some conservatives are worried about how the issue will play out. But Granger has criticized Obama's move and said it flouts a consensus that the United States should support family planning, but nothing related to abortion, abroad.

She set her sights on the leadership in her freshman term, when she was named an assistant GOP whip. She made it to the elected leadership in late 2006, becoming vice chairwoman of the Republican Conference for the 110th Congress (2007-08). But in late 2008, she declined to serve a second term.

Her legislative priorities are shaped by her background. She worked her way through school and watched a favorite niece struggle to save to pay for her daughter's education. She champions tax-free education savings accounts and in 2008 supported a rewrite of the Higher Education Act that authorizes increases in federal financial aid programs and penalizes states that cut funding for institutions of higher education. Having raised three children alone, she has supported GOP efforts to allow compensatory time off in place of premium pay for overtime worked.

Granger was born in Greenville to two public school teachers who divorced when she was 13. After completing college, she became a teacher in the same Birdville school district that named an elementary school after her mother. She taught literature and journalism for 10 years. In 1978, she went into the insurance business, eventually founding her own agency. In 1981, she was appointed to the Fort Worth Zoning Commission, where she served until she won a seat on the city council in 1989. Two years later, she won a nonpartisan election to become mayor. As mayor, she helped cut city crime in half, lured new businesses to the city and reduced property taxes.

Both parties courted her when Democratic Rep. Pete Geren decided not to seek re-election in 1996. Granger chose to run as a Republican and resigned as mayor. She won the nomination handily, then defeated another former Fort Worth mayor, Hugh Parmer, by 17 percentage points. She was the first Republican woman elected to the House from Texas. Granger has not faced a real contest since. In early 2009, she considered a run for the Senate seat that Kay Bailey Hutchison is expected to vacate, but she reconsidered after getting her new Appropriations subcommittee assignment.

KEY VOTES

2008
- – Delay consideration of Colombia free-trade agreement
- No Override Bush veto of federal farm and nutrition programs reauthorization bill
- Yes Overhaul surveillance laws and permit dismissal of suits against companies that conducted warrantless wiretapping
- No Grant mortgage relief to homeowners and funding for Fannie Mae and Freddie Mac
- Yes Approve initial $700 billion program to stabilize financial markets
- Yes Approve final $700 billion program to stabilize financial markets
- No Provide $14 billion in loans to automakers

2007
- No Increase minimum wage by $2.10 an hour
- No Approve $124.2 billion in emergency war spending and set goal for redeployment of troops from Iraq
- Yes Reject federal contraceptive assistance to international family planning groups
- Yes Override Bush veto of $23.2 billion water projects authorization bill
- Yes Implement Peru free-trade agreement
- No Approve energy policy overhaul with new fuel economy standards
- Yes Clear $473.5 billion omnibus spending bill, including $70 billion for military operations

CQ VOTE STUDIES

	PARTY UNITY		PRESIDENTIAL SUPPORT	
	SUPPORT	OPPOSE	SUPPORT	OPPOSE
2008	96%	4%	80%	20%
2007	94%	6%	81%	19%
2006	97%	3%	95%	5%
2005	97%	3%	91%	9%
2004	96%	4%	94%	6%

INTEREST GROUPS

	AFL-CIO	ADA	CCUS	ACU
2008	7%	5%	100%	92%
2007	4%	10%	79%	92%
2006	8%	5%	100%	76%
2005	13%	0%	89%	80%
2004	15%	0%	100%	91%

TEXAS 12

Part of Fort Worth and suburbs; Parker and Wise counties

The Republican-leaning 12th takes in most of western Tarrant County, including two-thirds of Fort Worth, and all of rural Parker and Wise counties. The mostly white, middle-class district contains downtown Fort Worth, but also takes in a mix of suburban and rural areas.

The 12th's economy is built around transportation. A major airport, a naval air base, several main railroad lines and interstate highways are in or adjacent to the district, supporting aerospace, distribution services and retail sectors. The Burlington Northern Santa Fe Railroad has its headquarters in the 12th, and Union Pacific is active here.

The University of North Texas Health Science Center headlines the local medical services industry near Fort Worth, and defense contractor Lockheed Martin Corp. creates jobs and fuels economic growth. A diversifying economy in Fort Worth mostly has insulated the city from nationwide economic downturns, but there have been massive layoffs at Radio

Shack headquarters in recent years, and the national housing crisis hurt Fort Worth-based homebuilder D.R. Horton. The Stockyards district, once a stop on the cattle trails north into Oklahoma, is now a national historic district celebrating Fort Worth's role in the American West. The city's Sundance Square, named after the infamous outlaw, has become a downtown retail and entertainment destination.

There are still some Democratic areas in downtown Fort Worth, but areas in Tarrant County outside the city overwhelmingly favor the GOP, as do Parker and Wise counties. Parker includes Weatherford, which has become more Republican as the Forth Worth suburbs have encroached. John McCain took 63 percent of the district's 2008 presidential vote.

MAJOR INDUSTRY
Defense technology, transportation, health care

MILITARY BASES
Naval Air Station Fort Worth, 1,958 military, 1,800 civilian (2007)

CITIES
Fort Worth (pt.), 349,997; Haltom City, 39,018; Watauga, 21,908

NOTABLE
The National Cowgirl Museum and Billy Bob's Texas, a 127,000-square-foot honky tonk and rodeo, are in Fort Worth.

Rep. William M. "Mac" Thornberry (R)

Elected 1994; 8th term

CAPITOL OFFICE
225-3706
www.house.gov/thornberry
2209 Rayburn Bldg. 20515-4313; fax 225-3486

COMMITTEES
Armed Services
Select Intelligence

RESIDENCE
Clarendon

BORN
July 15, 1958; Clarendon, Texas

RELIGION
Presbyterian

FAMILY
Wife, Sally Thornberry; two children

EDUCATION
Texas Tech U., B.A. 1980 (history);
U. of Texas, J.D. 1983

CAREER
Lawyer; cattleman; U.S. State Department
official; congressional aide

POLITICAL HIGHLIGHTS
No previous office

ELECTION RESULTS

2008 GENERAL

William M. "Mac" Thornberry (R)	180,078	77.6%
Roger James Waun (D)	51,841	22.4%

2008 PRIMARY

William M. "Mac" Thornberry (R)	unopposed

2006 GENERAL

William M."Mac" Thornberry (R)	108,107	74.4%
Roger James Waun (D)	33,460	23.0%
Jim Thompson (LIBERT)	3,829	2.6%

PREVIOUS WINNING PERCENTAGES
2004 (92%); 2002 (79%); 2000 (68%); 1998 (68%);
1996 (67%); 1994 (55%)

Thornberry, elected in the watershed GOP year of 1994, is a Republican through and through. But even those opposed to his views describe him as a serious man — thoughtful, earnest and unassuming about finding ways the government can work better, especially on national security issues.

Thornberry backed Republicans on 96 percent of the votes in the 110th Congress (2007-08) in which they diverged from Democrats. He wants lower taxes, more controls on immigration, more domestic energy production and more defense spending. He traces his conservatism to his upbringing on the cattle ranch that has been in his family for more than 70 years. "Someone in the federal government was telling us what to do on a farm seven miles down a dirt road outside a town of 2,000 people," he said.

From his seat on the Armed Services Committee, Thornberry consistently has advocated for a strong defense while also seeking to protect his district's military bases and plants. He made a bid to serve as the panel's ranking Republican in the 111th Congress (2009-10), but lost to John M. McHugh of New York, who had more seniority. He also serves on the Select Intelligence Committee, where he is the top Republican on the Technical and Tactical Intelligence panel.

Thornberry has played a major role in reviewing how well spy agencies are responding to terrorism. Months before Sept. 11, 2001, he drafted a bill to create a new department to oversee homeland security. The idea became fashionable after the attacks, and in 2002 his measure became the foundation for legislation that created the new Department of Homeland Security. GOP leaders in 2003 rewarded him with a seat on the new Homeland Security Committee, giving him oversight of the new department as it was built from the ground up. After the department was launched, Thornberry saw another one of his ideas become reality in 2005 with the creation of an assistant secretary for "cybersecurity."

By then, Thornberry had moved from the Homeland Security Committee to Intelligence and was chairman of that panel's new oversight subcommittee during the 109th Congress (2005-06). The subcommittee was established to monitor effectiveness of the law uniting U.S. intelligence functions under one director, and in 2006 it issued a report concluding the law's implementation had been a "mixed bag," in Thornberry's words. He found fault with the Office of the Director of National Intelligence's approach to implementing the overhaul, and concluded the DNI should be focusing on high priorities such as information-sharing.

He has focused on developing what he calls "metrics" that can be used to measure progress on improving intelligence capabilities. He points, for example, to the ability to quantify the increase of Arabic language experts in the intelligence community. "We get these verbal assurances that you could replay year after year without the kind of hard measures we need," he said.

Thornberry has dug just as deep into the details of the Pentagon and its effectiveness. He is among those who say U.S. military power, for all its importance, is of limited utility in winning wars like the one against terrorism.

He served on a bipartisan Smart Power Commission in 2007 that drew up recommendations for winning the war with both lethal and non-lethal approaches. In 2008, Thornberry advocated adding a provision to the fiscal 2009 defense authorization bill that would improve coordination of the Defense Department's strategic communications. "We cannot beat terrorists with bullets alone," he said in a statement.

Thornberry was a strong supporter of President George W. Bush's conduct of the Iraq War, backing Bush even as much of the public turned against the administration's approach to the war. His support didn't end when Bush left office; when President Obama released memos in April 2009 detailing the harsh interrogation of terrorist detainees under the previous administration, Thornberry shied away from saying the detainees had been tortured. "I think people are too free with the use" of the word, he said on MSNBC. "I recommend folks go on the Internet and read these memos because you will get a real feel for the carefully controlled, doctor-supervised circumstances under which these things were used."

Thornberry also backed Bush on the $700 billion financial sector rescue law in fall 2008, switching his vote to "yes" after opposing an earlier version. "A former minister in my home church used to say that 'Sometimes you have to put aside your principles and do what's right,' " he said after the second version passed.

Thornberry has an interest in agricultural issues, as his district is among the nation's leading producers of cotton, wheat and peanuts. He has a keen interest in federal subsidies for those crops and supported the successful override of Bush's veto of the 2008 reauthorization of agriculture and nutrition programs, which the president said contained too much spending.

Thornberry is still in the ranching business with his brothers and owns a one-third stake in the Thornberry Brothers Cattle Partnership. He is a proponent of property owners' rights and says federal laws and regulations impinge unduly on farmers' land-use decisions.

But most of Thornberry's formative professional experiences were in Washington, D.C. He worked for five years as an aide on Capitol Hill after graduating from the University of Texas law school in 1983. He was a legislative aide to Texas GOP Rep. Tom Loeffler, then was chief of staff for Rep. Larry Combest, another Texas Republican. In 1988, he was deputy assistant secretary of State for legislative affairs in the Reagan administration, where he got to know the inner workings of the House.

Thornberry took a break from politics in 1989 to work in an Amarillo law firm while helping run his family's cattle ranch, but he was soon back in it, this time running for office. In 1994, he challenged Democratic incumbent Bill Sarpalius, who had become vulnerable in the conservative district because of his support for raising taxes as part of President Clinton's 1993 budget plan. Thornberry played up his family's close ties to the land and beat Sarpalius with 55 percent of the vote. He has won re-election easily since, taking 78 percent of the vote in 2008.

KEY VOTES

2008

No Delay consideration of Colombia free-trade agreement

Yes Override Bush veto of federal farm and nutrition programs reauthorization bill

Yes Overhaul surveillance laws and permit dismissal of suits against companies that conducted warrantless wiretapping

No Grant mortgage relief to homeowners and funding for Fannie Mae and Freddie Mac

No Approve initial $700 billion program to stabilize financial markets

Yes Approve final $700 billion program to stabilize financial markets

No Provide $14 billion in loans to automakers

2007

No Increase minimum wage by $2.10 an hour

No Approve $124.2 billion in emergency war spending and set goal for redeployment of troops from Iraq

Yes Reject federal contraceptive assistance to international family planning groups

Yes Override Bush veto of $23.2 billion water projects authorization bill

Yes Implement Peru free-trade agreement

No Approve energy policy overhaul with new fuel economy standards

Yes Clear $473.5 billion omnibus spending bill, including $70 billion for military operations

CQ VOTE STUDIES

	PARTY UNITY		PRESIDENTIAL SUPPORT	
	SUPPORT	OPPOSE	SUPPORT	OPPOSE
2008	98%	2%	82%	18%
2007	95%	5%	85%	15%
2006	97%	3%	95%	5%
2005	98%	2%	93%	7%
2004	98%	2%	97%	3%

INTEREST GROUPS

	AFL-CIO	ADA	CCUS	ACU
2008	0%	5%	89%	92%
2007	4%	5%	85%	100%
2006	7%	5%	100%	88%
2005	7%	0%	85%	100%
2004	7%	0%	100%	100%

TEXAS 13
Panhandle – Amarillo; Wichita Falls

The conservative and mostly white 13th covers much of the Texas Panhandle, including the city of Amarillo, then extends east along the Oklahoma border to take in the South Plains and much of the Red River Valley. It juts south twice to add more farmland as well as pick up Jones County's small portion of Abilene. The district takes in Wichita Falls and reaches east to haul in the western half of Cooke County, about 50 miles north of Fort Worth. Massive and mainly rural, the 13th includes all or part of 44 counties, 40 of which have a population of under 25,000.

Amarillo is still the Panhandle's economic hub despite declines in the once-dominant oil industry. Towers and pipes outside of the city produce a large supply of crude helium. Northeast of Amarillo, Pantex employs thousands at the nation's only nuclear weapons assembly and disassembly plant. The city also relies on military aircraft parts manufacturing for the V-22 Osprey and other Marine helicopters. A significant food processing sector includes key employer Tyson Foods.

Wichita Falls also was heavily dependent on the oil and gas industries,

but today factories are numerous. Sheppard Air Force Base is a major employer, but the base will lose thousands of jobs in light of the 2005 BRAC round. The city is a medical hub and a local prison provides stable jobs. The Ogallala Aquifer supports district farmers, who are among the nation's top producers of cotton, sorghum, peanuts and wheat.

The 13th is one of the state's most Republican districts, and the GOP excels in the rural towns that dot the area. In the 2008 presidential race, John McCain took 76 percent of the 13th's vote while winning eight of his 10 highest percentages statewide in the sparsely populated counties here, including his three highest in King, Roberts and Ochiltree. Blue-collar Wichita Falls also votes solidly GOP in state and national races.

MAJOR INDUSTRY
Agriculture, oil, defense

MILITARY BASES
Sheppard Air Force Base, 3,125 military, 4,023 civilian (2006)

CITIES
Amarillo, 173,627; Wichita Falls, 104,197; Pampa, 17,887

NOTABLE
Mineral Wells was a popular destination for people seeking to drink the water and soak themselves in specially constructed bathhouses.

Rep. Ron Paul (R)

Elected 1996; 10th full term
Also served 1976-77, 1979-85

After an improbable splash as a 70-something political rock star, "Dr. No" has returned to his old nay-saying ways in the House, where his absolutist stand against all things governmental has long limited his impact.

Paul was delighted to discover that his libertarian-leaning views struck a chord with GOP primary voters during his long-shot bid for the party's 2008 presidential nomination. But his enhanced national profile has done little to increase his clout on Capitol Hill. The Texas physician's vote is nearly always the one in the negative column when there is a House roll call with a single "no" vote.

Paul has called for reductions in government that go well beyond those advocated by other conservatives. He wants to abolish most federal agencies, including the IRS and Federal Reserve, and return to a gold standard. In fact, he's proposed a constitutional amendment that would abolish personal income, estate and gift taxes and prohibit the government from engaging in business in competition with its citizens.

Earnest and even-tempered, he nonetheless can be passionate about his views. When asked during one presidential primary debate whether as president he would work to phase out the IRS, Paul responded with a smile, "immediately," which brought laughter from the audience. He then added, "And you can only do that if you change our ideas about what the role of government ought to be."

He was among just six Republicans who voted in 2002 against giving President George W. Bush authority to use military force in Iraq. He says the resolution was unconstitutional because it transferred the right to declare war from Congress to the executive branch. He also was one of 17 Republicans who supported a February 2007 Democratic resolution that disapproved of Bush's plan to send more troops to Iraq.

A member of the Foreign Affairs Committee, Paul was the lone Republican dissenter — and one of only two "no" votes, the other being liberal Ohio Democrat Dennis J. Kucinich — on a 2007 resolution condemning the terrorist group Hezbollah and other pro-Syrian groups and backing the government of Lebanon. He takes a dim view of U.S. foreign aid, and he opposes U.S. support for the International Monetary Fund and the World Trade Organization. He also opposes free-trade deals and has sponsored legislation requiring the United States to withdraw from the United Nations.

Paul's views found support on the campaign trail. Before the presidential primaries had even started, he shocked political observers by raising a record $4.2 million on Nov. 5, 2007, a haul driven by Internet donations and supporters who tied the effort to the commemoration of a holiday celebrating Guy Fawkes, a British revolutionary who tried, unsuccessfully, to kill King James I in 1605. Paul raised $20 million during the last quarter of 2007, virtually all of it from individuals. It was twice as much as eventual nominee John McCain collected from individuals in the same period.

Paul's support in the primaries and caucuses never matched his fundraising — rarely breaching 10 percent — but he stayed in the race until June. Resisting calls to run as an independent, Paul used leftover contributions to create an organization called Campaign for Liberty, designed to channel the energies of his supporters into electing libertarian-leaning candidates to office. He also campaigned for GOP House candidates.

Paul's maverick streak goes back decades. He ran for the presidency in 1988 as a Libertarian, and received about 432,000 votes (0.5 percent of the

CAPITOL OFFICE
225-2831
www.house.gov/paul
203 Cannon Bldg. 20515-4314; fax

COMMITTEES
Financial Services
Foreign Affairs
Joint Economic

RESIDENCE
Lake Jackson

BORN
Aug. 20, 1935; Pittsburgh, Pa.

RELIGION
Protestant

FAMILY
Wife, Carol Wells Paul; five children

EDUCATION
Gettysburg College, B.S. 1957 (pre-med);
Duke U., M.D. 1961

MILITARY SERVICE
Air Force, 1963-65; Pa. Air National Guard, 1965-68

CAREER
Physician

POLITICAL HIGHLIGHTS
Republican nominee for U.S. House, 1974;
U.S. House, 1976-77; defeated for re-election to U.S. House, 1976; U.S. House, 1979-85; sought Republican nomination for U.S. Senate, 1984; Libertarian nominee for president, 1988; sought Republican nomination for president, 2008

ELECTION RESULTS

2008 GENERAL

Ron Paul (R)		unopposed

2008 PRIMARY

Ron Paul (R)	37,777	70.4%
W. Chris Peden (R)	15,859	29.6%

2006 GENERAL

Ron Paul (R)	94,380	60.2%
Shane Sklar (D)	62,429	39.8%

PREVIOUS WINNING PERCENTAGES
2004 (100%); 2002 (68%); 2000 (60%); 1998 (55%); 1996 (51%); 1982 (99%); 1980 (51%); 1978 (51%); 1976 Special Runoff Election (56%)

total) while he renounced the GOP, spoke out against "corporate welfare" and advocated drug legalization.

A member of the Financial Services and Joint Economic committees, Paul not surprisingly was a sharp critic of the $700 billion plan enacted in October 2008 to shore up the financial services sector. In 2009, he introduced legislation to require the Government Accountability Office to audit the Federal Reserve Board as it poured billions into the financial system — a proposal that Financial Services Chairman Barney Frank, a Massachusetts Democrat, endorsed.

Paul's libertarian beliefs make him an erratic ally of other GOP causes. He has said he believes marriage is the union of one man and one woman, yet voted in 2004 and 2006 against a proposed constitutional amendment to ban same-sex marriage, saying "everyone is an individual and ought to be treated equally." He also opposes a constitutional amendment to ban flag burning. But Paul, an obstetrician, parts company with many libertarians to oppose abortion.

The son of dairy farmers, Paul grew up in a small town west of Pittsburgh, Pa. Like his four brothers, he began working at the family's dairy at age 5. Later, he delivered newspapers, worked in a pharmacy and drove a milk delivery truck. In high school, he was a track and field star, played football and baseball and was on the wrestling team. He also was student body president.

In the early 1960s, he was a flight surgeon in the U.S. Air Force. He and his wife, Carol, moved to Texas in 1968, where he opened an obstetrical practice in Brazoria County.

Paul first won a seat in the House in an April 1976 special election to replace Democrat Bob Casey, defeating former Democratic state Rep. Bob Gammage. But in November's general election, Gammage felled Paul by 268 votes. In 1978, Paul won back the seat by 1,200 votes.

In 1984, Paul left his House seat for an unsuccessful Senate bid. He won election 12 years later in the 14th District, which included areas he had represented in his earlier House career. In the primary, he ousted Greg Laughlin, who had held the seat since 1989 but had switched from the Democratic Party in 1995. He won the general election by just 3 percentage points, despite criticism that he supported the legalization of drugs. He was unopposed in 2008 in a district that McCain carried by a 2-to-1 margin.

In the spring of 2009 Paul's son Rand, an ophthalmologist, expressed interest in seeking the Kentucky Senate seat held by Jim Bunning if the embattled GOP incumbent retired. "I've always encouraged my children to participate in the public debate," the elder Paul said.

KEY VOTES

2008

Yes	Delay consideration of Colombia free-trade agreement
No	Override Bush veto of federal farm and nutrition programs reauthorization bill
?	Overhaul surveillance laws and permit dismissal of suits against companies that conducted warrantless wiretapping
No	Grant mortgage relief to homeowners and funding for Fannie Mae and Freddie Mac
No	Approve initial $700 billion program to stabilize financial markets
No	Approve final $700 billion program to stabilize financial markets
No	Provide $14 billion in loans to automakers

2007

No	Increase minimum wage by $2.10 an hour
No	Approve $124.2 billion in emergency war spending and set goal for redeployment of troops from Iraq
?	Reject federal contraceptive assistance to international family planning groups
No	Override Bush veto of $23.2 billion water projects authorization bill
No	Implement Peru free-trade agreement
?	Approve energy policy overhaul with new fuel economy standards
?	Clear $473.5 billion omnibus spending bill, including $70 billion for military operations

CQ VOTE STUDIES

	PARTY UNITY		PRESIDENTIAL SUPPORT	
	SUPPORT	OPPOSE	SUPPORT	OPPOSE
2008	89%	11%	70%	30%
2007	84%	16%	71%	29%
2006	68%	32%	36%	64%
2005	72%	28%	38%	62%
2004	82%	18%	44%	56%

INTEREST GROUPS

	AFL-CIO	ADA	CCUS	ACU
2008	8%	10%	47%	90%
2007	21%	15%	47%	77%
2006	31%	45%	60%	76%
2005	50%	40%	33%	76%
2004	20%	50%	56%	78%

TEXAS 14

Northern Gulf Coast — Victoria, Galveston

Taking in a 200-mile stretch of the Gulf Coast, the 14th extends from north of Galveston to Rockport, which is just north of Corpus Christi. Dominated by farms and petrochemical plants, the district leans Republican and is overwhelmingly dependent on its coastal and agricultural industries.

The district's population center is located in its northeast. More than half of its residents live in Galveston and Brazoria counties (both shared with the 22nd). Chemical companies, such as Dow and Sterling, have facilities in Texas City, Freeport and North Seadrift, but a stalling national economy has forced layoffs. The Port of Galveston is a high-volume Gulf Coast cruise-ship port, and the University of Texas Medical Branch at Galveston is the city's largest employer. Plans call for a $1 billion improvement to the facility. Galveston was hit hard by Hurricane Ike in 2008, resulting in billions of dollars in property damage, and officials hope tourism and the medical center will help stabilize the economy.

Victoria, an oil and chemical center where Exelon Corp. plans to build two nuclear power plants, is the district's only city outside of Galveston

County that has more than 30,000 residents. Farther south, the 14th lures nature lovers to Goose Island State Park and the Aransas National Wildlife Refuge. Inland farming — rice, sorghum, corn and cattle — and commercial shrimping along the coast provide employment for many district residents, although imports threaten the local industry.

Now mostly Republican and socially conservative, the 14th has Democratic roots and a sizable minority population (38 percent) that is mostly Hispanic (25 percent overall). But, every county here backed John McCain in the 2008 presidential race, with Chambers County giving him 75 percent — McCain won the district as a whole with 66 percent. Locally, Republicans tend to do very well in rural counties, but factory jobs in the Galveston area allow unions to wield some political power.

MAJOR INDUSTRY
Petrochemicals, agriculture, shrimping

CITIES
Victoria, 60,603; Galveston, 57,247; League City (pt.), 45,279; Texas City (pt.), 31,979; Lake Jackson, 26,386

NOTABLE
Galveston claims to be the site of many Texas firsts, including the first telephone (1878), first medical college (1886) and first golf course (1898).

Rep. Rubén Hinojosa (D)

Elected 1996; 7th term

CAPITOL OFFICE
225-2531
hinojosa.house.gov
2463 Rayburn Bldg. 20515-4315; fax 225-5688

COMMITTEES
Education & Labor
 (Higher Education, Lifelong Learning
 & Competitiveness - chairman)
Financial Services

RESIDENCE
Mercedes

BORN
Aug. 20, 1940; Edcouch, Texas

RELIGION
Roman Catholic

FAMILY
Wife, Martha Hinojosa; five children

EDUCATION
U. of Texas, B.B.A. 1962; U. of Texas,
Pan American, M.B.A. 1980

CAREER
Food processing executive

POLITICAL HIGHLIGHTS
Mercedes school board, 1972-74; Texas State
Board of Education, 1974-84 (chairman of
special populations)

ELECTION RESULTS

2008 GENERAL

Rubén Hinojosa (D)	107,578	65.7%
Eddie Zamora (R)	52,303	31.9%
Gricha Raether (LIBERT)	3,827	2.3%

2008 PRIMARY

Rubén Hinojosa (D)	unopposed

2006 GENERAL

Rubén Hinojosa (D)	43,236	61.8%
Paul B. Haring (R)	16,601	23.7%
Eddie Zamora (R)	10,150	14.5%

PREVIOUS WINNING PERCENTAGES
2004 (58%); 2002 (100%); 2000 (88%); 1998 (58%);
1996 (62%)

Hinojosa is a soft-spoken, unassuming figure — until he's angered on any number of issues he holds close to his heart. Those issues include bilingual education, immigration and improving the treatment of migrant workers.

As chairman of an Education and Labor subcommittee, Hinojosa (full name: ru-BEN ee-na-HO-suh) is a formidable opponent of those who don't share his views, particularly when it comes to improving the lot of minority students. He has used his chairmanship, and his role as a member of the Congressional Hispanic Caucus, to strengthen education for minority students and English learners. He also has championed bills to address what education experts have dubbed the "dropout crisis."

Hinojosa is a staunch advocate of the Education Department's Trio programs of outreach and support for disadvantaged students. And he supported education bills in 2007 and 2008 that authorized $200 million in grants over five years to help increase the number of Latino graduates in science, technology, engineering and mathematics. "We need to increase the college know-how in the communities that have not had access to college opportunities," he said at a 2007 subcommittee hearing.

Hinojosa sees education, trade and transportation as the most powerful ways to improve life in his Texas border district. He attended a school where he and other Mexican-American children were segregated from white students. His parents, who had fled Mexico during the 1910 revolution, spoke only Spanish, as did Hinojosa and his 10 siblings. But his parents "understood intuitively that education was the path to a better life," he said.

Hinojosa took over the Subcommittee on Higher Education, Lifelong Learning and Competitiveness in 2007, after several years of successful efforts on education measures. During a 1997 debate to reauthorize the Higher Education Act, he was the driving force behind an effort to redirect existing programs to target resources to the neediest students, including Hispanics and American Indians.

Since then, he has helped win increases in aid to colleges that serve large numbers of Hispanic students, with funding ballooning from $12 million in 1998 to $95 million in 2006. In 2008, through a higher education bill he helped write, authorized levels jumped to $175 million in fiscal 2009. He also strengthened Head Start early-childhood development programs under a renewal of that law cleared in 2007.

Combating the tough economic situation in his district has also guided his agenda. When he took office in 1997, unemployment was 25 percent in some areas. Poverty is still pervasive; he said in 2007 that more than 7,500 households lack complete plumbing. As chairman of the Hispanic Caucus' task force on commerce and international relations, he praised President Obama's $787 billion economic stimulus law for its provisions aimed at helping small businesses.

A member of the Financial Services Committee, Hinojosa was a strong supporter in fall 2008 of the $700 billion plan to aid the nation's financial services sector. Though he said he disliked some aspects of the law, "it was a bipartisan compromise that could pass quickly and stop the downward spiral in our stock market, free up our credit system and get our economy back on track."

He supports a comprehensive immigration overhaul to secure U.S. borders, but also wants to address the plight of illegal immigrants already in the country and ensure their children have access to college and financial aid. He opposed legislation in 2006 that authorized the construction of 700 miles of fencing along the U.S.-Mexico border. "While a physical fence may work for certain parts of the border, at others it would choke off economic prosperity," Hinojosa said.

After initial efforts at a comprehensive immigration overhaul collapsed in 2007, a piecemeal approach was considered, including an enforcement-heavy bill by North Carolina Democrat Heath Shuler that drew the support of some conservative Democrats. Hinojosa and fellow Hispanic Caucus members fought against that bill and others, which Hinojosa told the Houston Chronicle were based on "pointless political stunts and fear-mongering."

He and other Hispanic leaders went public with their anger toward the Democratic leadership on immigration issues in 2008, threatening to entangle other measures and potentially draw down Hispanic support from presidential candidate Barack Obama. He and the caucus also battled back on the border fence, to no avail. He joined other South Texas lawmakers in urging Obama in early 2009 to temporarily suspend its construction to evaluate border security.

Hinojosa was one of four Texas Democrats who broke ranks with their party in 2002 to authorize the George W. Bush administration to negotiate trade agreements that Congress can approve or reject but cannot amend. He was one of just 15 Democrats who supported the Central America Free Trade Agreement in 2005. Hinojosa sees increased trade as offering the hope of improved highways, commerce and jobs for his constituents.

He also broke with fellow Democrats in backing a 2003 law banning a procedure opponents call "partial birth" abortion, supporting a 2005 GOP effort to limit the scope of the Endangered Species Act and voting for a 2006 bill to lift a moratorium on most offshore oil leasing nationwide.

After his education, Hinojosa joined the family business, H&H Foods, serving 20 years as its president and chief financial officer. He was elected to the local school board in the early 1970s. He served a decade on the Texas State Board of Education before making a successful bid for the U.S. House in 1996. He won a hotly contested five-way battle in the primary, then beat Republican minister Tom Haughey by 26 percentage points in November. He won a rematch with Haughey in 1998 by 17 percentage points and has won comfortably ever since.

Capitol Annex, a Texas political newsletter, quoted unnamed sources in February 2009 as saying that Obama was considering appointing Hinojosa as ambassador to Mexico. Hispanic Caucus members earlier had touted him as a potential secretary of Education.

KEY VOTES

2008
Yes Delay consideration of Colombia free-trade agreement
Yes Override Bush veto of federal farm and nutrition programs reauthorization bill
Yes Overhaul surveillance laws and permit dismissal of suits against companies that conducted warrantless wiretapping
Yes Grant mortgage relief to homeowners and funding for Fannie Mae and Freddie Mac
Yes Approve initial $700 billion program to stabilize financial markets
Yes Approve final $700 billion program to stabilize financial markets
Yes Provide $14 billion in loans to automakers

2007
Yes Increase minimum wage by $2.10 an hour
Yes Approve $124.2 billion in emergency war spending and set goal for redeployment of troops from Iraq
No   Reject federal contraceptive assistance to international family planning groups
Yes Override Bush veto of $23.2 billion water projects authorization bill
Yes Implement Peru free-trade agreement
Yes Approve energy policy overhaul with new fuel economy standards
Yes Clear $473.5 billion omnibus spending bill, including $70 billion for military operations

CQ VOTE STUDIES

	PARTY UNITY		PRESIDENTIAL SUPPORT	
	SUPPORT	OPPOSE	SUPPORT	OPPOSE
2008	97%	3%	22%	78%
2007	97%	3%	8%	92%
2006	78%	22%	49%	51%
2005	84%	16%	37%	63%
2004	90%	10%	36%	64%

INTEREST GROUPS

	AFL-CIO	ADA	CCUS	ACU
2008	100%	80%	59%	9%
2007	100%	90%	63%	4%
2006	93%	60%	87%	36%
2005	93%	80%	74%	44%
2004	93%	90%	63%	13%

TEXAS 15
South central — Harlingen, Edinburg, part of McAllen

Based in southern Texas, the 15th takes in agricultural and cattle areas southeast of San Antonio and then dips down to the state's border with Mexico. Consecutive years of intense drought have threatened the production from ranchers and farmers in the district.

A federal court redrew the 15th's lines in 2006 and restored its Hispanic population to 77.6 percent, the second-highest of any congressional district. The large minority presence adds to the district's Democratic lean. The less-populous northern counties back Republicans, and the southern counties vote strongly Democratic. Overall, the 15th gave Barack Obama 60 percent of its 2008 presidential vote.

While the 15th District reaches more than 225 miles north to south, its population is skewed to the south. Nearly 60 percent of the 15th's residents live in Hidalgo County (which is shared with the 28th), and nearly nine in 10 of Hidalgo's residents are Hispanic. This is one of the country's poorest areas, and community leaders struggle to establish jobs and provide job training.

Along the Mexican border, *maquiladoras* — plants that use low-cost labor and import many parts from the United States and export products back to the U.S. — are still the mainstay despite manufacturing slowdowns in both nations. Retail and trade with Mexican border cities add jobs. In 2009, UnitedHealth Group announced it would locate a new service center in Harlingen, at the southernmost tip of the district, that is expected to employ hundreds of workers. Federal funding for energy projects is expected to generate jobs in Hidalgo.

International trade has prompted local leaders in South Texas to push for improvements in transportation infrastructure — the region claims to be the largest populated area without easy access to an interstate highway, and many traffic problem spots are in the 15th's counties.

MAJOR INDUSTRY
Trade, manufacturing, agriculture, health care

CITIES
McAllen (pt.), 61,658; Harlingen, 57,564; Edinburg, 48,465; Weslaco, 26,935

NOTABLE
Caro Brown, the first woman to win a Pulitzer Prize for journalism, worked at the Alice Daily News during the 1940s and 1950s.

Rep. Silvestre Reyes (D)

Elected 1996; 7th term

A former Border Patrol agent and Army helicopter gunner, Reyes knows how to take orders. And as Speaker Nancy Pelosi's choice to head the Select Intelligence panel, he has worked hard to implement the wishes of Democratic leaders even while facing sometimes bruising fights with Republicans.

Reyes (full name: sil-VES-treh RAY-ess, with rolled R) is known for his friendly, easygoing manner, but he has had to survive some minor personal controversies which nearly cost him the job. Still, he's not someone party leaders typically have to worry about. He tends to follow their wishes on a range of votes that split the majority of Republicans and Democrats, including President Obama's initiatives in early 2009 to revive an ailing economy. He has parted ways on only a few crucial votes, particularly to support gun owners' rights. And he uses his seat on the Armed Services Committee to protect funding for El Paso's regional military facilities.

He hopes to bolster intelligence-gathering in Iraq and Afghanistan. He also wants to enact an intelligence authorization bill for the first time since 2004 and increase cybersecurity oversight, spy satellite programs, the security clearance process and the growth of the Office of the Director of National Intelligence, which critics say has become overly bureaucratic since its 2005 founding.

Reyes took some blame for himself and other Democrats in a 2009 letter to the CIA about controversial interrogation techniques of terrorism suspects held at Guantánamo Bay, Cuba. "One important lesson to me from the CIA's interrogation operations involves congressional oversight," he wrote. "I'm going to examine closely ways in which we can change the law to make our own oversight of CIA more meaningful; I want to move from mere notification to real discussion."

He was at the center of one of the Democrats' most devastating losses of the 110th Congress (2007-08), when President George W. Bush outmaneuvered them in securing a 2008 rewrite of the Foreign Intelligence Surveillance Act allowing warrantless surveillance of suspected foreign terrorists. Many of his Democratic colleagues castigated it as a violation of privacy and due process.

The first blow came in August 2007, when conservative House Democrats, in defiance of Reyes, sided with Republicans to push through a temporary measure that granted Bush expanded wiretapping authority. In the wake of that defeat, Reyes teamed with Judiciary Chairman John Conyers Jr. of Michigan on legislation to ensure more court oversight of intelligence-gathering while also refusing Bush's request that telecommunications companies be granted retroactive legal immunity for any cooperation they'd given government intelligence operatives after the Sept. 11 terrorist attacks. But the Senate was more in tune with Bush on the issue and, ultimately, the House and Reyes were forced to compromise. "I was under the illusion that, by doing the common-sense things, I could work and I could influence that committee to work in a bipartisan way to do what's best," he told the Dallas Morning News. "The reality is that politics unfortunately trumps everything else."

Internal House politics played a factor in Pelosi's selection of Reyes as chairman. In 2007, she passed over Jane Harman of California, the panel's senior Democrat and a political rival of hers, and rejected Florida's Alcee L. Hastings, whose federal judgeship in Florida had ended in scandal when Congress impeached and removed him in 1989. Reyes was third in line for the job.

But controversy dogged his selection. He told Newsweek that "20,000 to 30,000" more troops were needed in Iraq to "dismantle the militias," a view opposite Pelosi's. Then, in an interview with Congressional Quarterly that

CAPITOL OFFICE
225-4831
www.house.gov/reyes
2433 Rayburn Bldg. 20515-4316; fax 225-2016

COMMITTEES
Armed Services
Appropriations Select Intelligence Oversight Panel
Select Intelligence - chairman

RESIDENCE
El Paso

BORN
Nov. 10, 1944; Canutillo, Texas

RELIGION
Roman Catholic

FAMILY
Wife, Carolina Reyes; three children

EDUCATION
U. of Texas, attended 1964-65; Texas Western College, attended 1965-66 (criminal justice); El Paso Community College, A.A. 1977 (criminal justice)

MILITARY SERVICE
Army, 1966-68

CAREER
U.S. Border Patrol assistant regional official and agent

POLITICAL HIGHLIGHTS
Canutillo School Board, 1968-70

ELECTION RESULTS

2008 GENERAL
Silvestre Reyes (D)	130,375	82.1%
Benjamin Eloy "Ben" Mendoza (I)	16,348	10.3%
Mette A. Baker (LIBERT)	12,000	7.6%

2008 PRIMARY
Silvestre Reyes (D)	75,058	80.4%

2006 GENERAL
Silvestre Reyes (D)	61,116	78.7%
Gordon R. Strickland (LIBERT)	16,572	21.3%

PREVIOUS WINNING PERCENTAGES
2004 (68%); 2002 (100%); 2000 (68%); 1998 (88%); 1996 (71%)

received worldwide attention, Reyes failed a pop quiz. Asked whether al Qaeda was Sunni or Shiite, Reyes replied, "Al Qaeda, they have both." He added, "Predominately — probably Shiite." (The terrorist organization's Sunni roots are key to its founding.)

Reyes spent 26 years in the Border Patrol and has trod a careful line on immigration issues in Congress. He twice joined California Republican David Dreier on a bill to stiffen penalties for employers who hire illegal immigrants and to create a new worker identification system. But he opposed a 2006 law authorizing a 700-mile fence along the Mexican border, calling it neither smart nor effective. He continues to press for legislation to secure the border, legalize undocumented immigrants and offer a guest worker program.

When drug-related violence continued in Mexico in 2009, Reyes testified before the Senate Foreign Relations panel in support of continued funding to beef up border security and for hospital care. He assured lawmakers violence hadn't spilled across the border. But it had touched him personally. In June 2008, a relative of his by marriage was seized by gunmen in Ciudad Juarez, just across the border from El Paso. Notified by Reyes' staff, U.S. Immigration and Customs Enforcement agents helped arrange the relative's return after her family paid a $32,000 ransom.

On Capitol Hill, as in El Paso, Reyes is known as "Silver," a nickname given to him by a high school football coach who called him the "silver lining," based on his first name, Silvestre, and his linebacker position.

The oldest of 10 children, Reyes was born and raised on a farm in Canutillo, Texas, five miles outside El Paso. His father, grandfather and uncle grew cotton and alfalfa on two farms totaling 2,000 acres.

He briefly attended the University of Texas at Austin on a debate scholarship. Working while attending classes proved difficult, and after a year, he returned home and enrolled in what was then Texas Western College (now the University of Texas at El Paso). When he took a break from the spring semester in 1966, he was drafted into the Army, serving two and a half years, including 13 months in Vietnam as a helicopter crew chief and gunner. In 1969, he joined the Border Patrol, eventually becoming sector chief in McAllen and El Paso. He won national recognition for beginning "Operation Hold the Line" in El Paso, stationing more officers at the border.

El Paso community leaders persuaded Reyes to run for Congress when Democrat Ronald D. Coleman announced his retirement. Reyes became the district's first Hispanic representative after defeating a former Coleman aide in the primary and runoff and then winning the general election in 1996. Since then, he has easily won re-election.

KEY VOTES

2008

Yes Delay consideration of Colombia free-trade agreement

Yes Override Bush veto of federal farm and nutrition programs reauthorization bill

Yes Overhaul surveillance laws and permit dismissal of suits against companies that conducted warrantless wiretapping

Yes Grant mortgage relief to homeowners and funding for Fannie Mae and Freddie Mac

Yes Approve initial $700 billion program to stabilize financial markets

Yes Approve final $700 billion program to stabilize financial markets

Yes Provide $14 billion in loans to automakers

2007

Yes Increase minimum wage by $2.10 an hour

Yes Approve $124.2 billion in emergency war spending and set goal for redeployment of troops from Iraq

No Reject federal contraceptive assistance to international family planning groups

Yes Override Bush veto of $23.2 billion water projects authorization bill

Yes Implement Peru free-trade agreement

Yes Approve energy policy overhaul with new fuel economy standards

Yes Clear $473.5 billion omnibus spending bill, including $70 billion for military operations

CQ VOTE STUDIES

	PARTY UNITY		PRESIDENTIAL SUPPORT	
	SUPPORT	OPPOSE	SUPPORT	OPPOSE
2008	97%	3%	24%	76%
2007	96%	4%	9%	91%
2006	85%	15%	47%	53%
2005	81%	19%	39%	61%
2004	86%	14%	38%	62%

INTEREST GROUPS

	AFL-CIO	ADA	CCUS	ACU
2008	100%	70%	67%	8%
2007	96%	95%	63%	4%
2006	100%	80%	57%	36%
2005	100%	80%	60%	41%
2004	92%	70%	62%	26%

TEXAS 16
West — El Paso and suburbs

Situated along the Rio Grande in the desert landscape that characterizes the western reaches of Texas, the 16th takes in El Paso and some of its suburbs. The diverse district, joined to Mexico and El Paso's sister city, Ciudad Juarez, by the Bridge of the Americas, has a 77.7 percent Hispanic population, more than any other district in the nation.

Mexico has had a deep effect on the area's economy, culture and demographics, and growth in El Paso was fueled by trade with Mexico long before free-trade zones and global markets flourished. Companies on the U.S. side of the border provide supplies and services to plants in Mexico, and residents from Ciudad Juarez cross the border to shop in El Paso. NAFTA aided an explosion of *maquiladoras*, plants that use low-cost labor and import many parts from the United States and export products back to the U.S., but local leaders worry about increased competition from abroad and weak international manufacturing sectors. Residents and officials also worry about increasing drug cartel violence in Mexican border towns such as Ciudad Juarez, although El Paso has not experi-

enced large-scale problems yet. Decreases in recreational travel across the border and federal efforts to increase law and legal enforcement have affected the community.

Fort Bliss already is key to the 16th's economy, and the base is slated to grow dramatically as a result of the 2005 BRAC round. The area's growing population threatened to overwhelm its water supply, but conservation efforts largely have succeeded, and a desalination plant is set to meet the needs of the larger Fort Bliss community.

Democrats held the 16th's U.S. House seat for all but two years in the 20th century. In 2008, Barack Obama took 66 percent of the presidential vote here, his fourth-highest percentage in the state.

MAJOR INDUSTRY
Trade, defense, manufacturing

MILITARY BASES
Fort Bliss (Army), 17,000 military, 7,500 civilian (2006)

CITIES
El Paso, 563,662; Socorro, 27,152

NOTABLE
The National Border Patrol Museum boasts aircraft, vehicles and boats.

Rep. Chet Edwards (D)

Elected 1990; 10th term

CAPITOL OFFICE
225-6105
edwards.house.gov
2369 Rayburn Bldg. 20515-4317; fax 225-0350

COMMITTEES
Appropriations
(Military Construction-VA - chairman)
Budget

RESIDENCE
Waco

BORN
Nov. 24, 1951; Corpus Christi, Texas

RELIGION
Methodist

FAMILY
Wife, Lea Ann Edwards; two children

EDUCATION
Texas A&M U., B.A. 1974 (economics);
Harvard U., M.B.A. 1981

CAREER
Radio station executive; congressional aide

POLITICAL HIGHLIGHTS
Sought Democratic nomination for U.S. House,
1978; Texas Senate, 1983-91

ELECTION RESULTS

2008 GENERAL

Chet Edwards (D)	134,592	53.0%
Rob Curnock (R)	115,581	45.5%
Gardner C. Osborne (LIBERT)	3,849	1.5%

2008 PRIMARY

Chet Edwards (D)	unopposed

2006 GENERAL

Chet Edwards (D)	92,478	58.1%
Van Taylor (R)	64,142	40.3%
Guillermo Acosta (LIBERT)	2,504	1.6%

PREVIOUS WINNING PERCENTAGES
2004 (51%); 2002 (52%); 2000 (55%); 1998 (82%);
1996 (57%); 1994 (59%); 1992 (67%); 1990 (53%)

Edwards' prowess as a dealmaking Southern Democrat has raised his national profile — and his center-right politics and campaign skills have kept him popular in a GOP-dominated district that was drawn with the specific intention of undermining his chances to win.

His doggedness in increasing funding for veterans and military health care has won him awards from national advocacy groups. Speaker Nancy Pelosi of California suggested him as a potential running mate for Democrat Barack Obama in 2008; he subsequently was mentioned as a possible Veterans Affairs secretary before he took himself out of the running.

Edwards is a senior member of the Appropriations Committee and chairman of its Military Construction-VA Subcommittee. In the 110th Congress (2007-08), his first two years wielding the gavel, he helped secure a $16.3 billion increase in funding for veterans' health care and benefits. He said it was the largest increase in veterans' funding ever and a bigger boost in two years than the GOP-controlled Congress had provided in the preceding 12 years. The American Legion, the nation's largest veterans' organization, and the Veterans of Foreign Wars in 2008 each presented him their highest award, given to one member of Congress annually.

Edwards and other Democrats also beefed up funding for military health care and provided extra money for domestic base realignments, which his subcommittee shepherds. He also has been vigilant in seeking funds for nearby Fort Hood, and for research at Baylor and Texas A&M universities, both in his district.

As an appropriator and a member of the Budget Committee, Edwards defends earmarks — funding set-asides for members' favored projects. "Some have even made fun of our subcommittee's earmarks for daycare centers for the Department of Defense," he said at a March 2009 budget hearing. "Let me say for the record it's no laughing matter to troops from Fort Hood near my district in Texas who are on their third or fourth tour of duty in Iraq and have small children back home and a spouse working."

He also is the second-ranking Democrat on the Energy-Water Appropriations Subcommittee, where he has sought to boost funding for programs designed to protect nuclear material from falling into the wrong hands.

Energy has long been an important issue for Edwards, whose district includes part of the Barnett Shale, the largest natural gas field in the United States. The House in 2007 passed a bill he cosponsored with Colorado Democrat Mark Udall to set up pilot plants to test ways to treat water extracted during natural gas production in order to make it usable for irrigation and other purposes. He also worked behind the scenes on the energy bill that Democrats passed as part of their top-priority agenda at the start of the 110th to ensure it didn't harm independent gas and oil producers.

Edwards is a favorite of Pelosi. "I think Mr. Edwards is an extraordinarily talented person," she told reporters in June 2008 when touting him as a vice presidential candidate. Texas Republicans hope to hold that embrace against him in 2010, when they will try again — as they have unsuccessfully in the past — to tie him to liberal Democratic leaders.

From 1995 to 2003, Edwards served as a chief deputy whip for the House Democrats. He remains an important link between conservative Democrats and the more-liberal majority of his party.

Edwards generally votes with Democrats, backing the $700 billion financial sector rescue plan in 2008 and the $787 billion economic stimulus measure in 2009. But he departs on some key issues. He voted in 2006 to authorize warrantless electronic surveillance of terrorism suspects, and in 2008 he supported a bill to expand that authority and grant retroactive immunity for telecommunications companies that participated in surveillance; it became law. He also supports oil drilling in Alaska's Arctic National Wildlife Refuge. Edwards backed a proposed constitutional amendment to outlaw same-sex marriage, and in 2007 he was one of just 25 Democrats to vote against a bill banning employment discrimination based on sexual orientation.

In 1994, Edwards voted for a ban on 19 types of assault-style weapons in the wake of two mass killings in his district. In 1991, a man with an automatic pistol killed 22 people and wounded 20 in a Killeen cafeteria. Two years later, guns were involved in some of the deaths in a violent confrontation between federal agents and members of the Branch Davidian religious sect in Waco. In 2004, however, Edwards reversed his position on the assault weapons ban, saying it had not reduced crime.

As a student at Texas A&M, he was a leader in the Student Conference on National Affairs, where he got to know the local congressman, Democrat Olin E. "Tiger" Teague. As he was finishing college, Edwards accepted a job on Teague's congressional staff, intending to stay a year and then attend Harvard Business School. One year stretched into three. Teague told Edwards he planned to retire and that Edwards should run for his seat. The crowded Democratic primary in 1978 included a young Texas A&M economics professor, Phil Gramm, who edged past Edwards by fewer than 200 votes and went on to win election to the House and later the Senate.

Edwards earned a master's degree at Harvard, then returned to Texas, where he worked in real estate and owned a rural radio station. He was elected to the state Senate in 1982, and when Democratic Rep. Marvin Leath announced he would step down in 1990, Edwards moved to the 11th District to run for the House. He won with 53 percent of the vote.

In 2004 he was the sole survivor of eight Texas Democrats targeted by a 2003 redistricting plan engineered by House Majority Leader Tom DeLay and other Republicans; six lost and one retired. Edwards campaigned so diligently that he carried Crawford, the town nearest to President George W. Bush's ranch. "He was very good one-on-one," David Kent, a GOP county chairman, told the Waco Tribune-Herald. "His personality helped him win the race."

Having survived the 2004 remap, he had an easier time in 2006, winning with 58 percent. In 2008, he prevailed again despite GOP interest in the presidential race that enabled Arizona Republican Sen. John McCain to get two-thirds of the district's presidential vote.

KEY VOTES

2008
Yes Delay consideration of Colombia free-trade agreement
Yes Override Bush veto of federal farm and nutrition programs reauthorization bill
Yes Overhaul surveillance laws and permit dismissal of suits against companies that conducted warrantless wiretapping
Yes Grant mortgage relief to homeowners and funding for Fannie Mae and Freddie Mac
Yes Approve initial $700 billion program to stabilize financial markets
Yes Approve final $700 billion program to stabilize financial markets
Yes Provide $14 billion in loans to automakers

2007
Yes Increase minimum wage by $2.10 an hour
Yes Approve $124.2 billion in emergency war spending and set goal for redeployment of troops from Iraq
No   Reject federal contraceptive assistance to international family planning groups
Yes Override Bush veto of $23.2 billion water projects authorization bill
Yes Implement Peru free-trade agreement
Yes Approve energy policy overhaul with new fuel economy standards
Yes Clear $473.5 billion omnibus spending bill, including $70 billion for military operations

CQ VOTE STUDIES

	PARTY UNITY		PRESIDENTIAL SUPPORT	
	SUPPORT	OPPOSE	SUPPORT	OPPOSE
2008	97%	3%	22%	78%
2007	92%	8%	11%	89%
2006	66%	34%	60%	40%
2005	75%	25%	52%	48%
2004	73%	27%	50%	50%

INTEREST GROUPS

	AFL-CIO	ADA	CCUS	ACU
2008	100%	80%	67%	8%
2007	95%	85%	75%	12%
2006	71%	55%	87%	68%
2005	80%	85%	74%	36%
2004	73%	65%	81%	48%

TEXAS 17
East central — Waco, College Station, Bryan

The 17th begins south of Fort Worth and moves southeast mainly through fertile farmland to reach Bryan and College Station in Brazos County. On the way, it picks up Waco and Crawford, both in centrally located McLennan County.

One-third of district residents live in Waco or surrounding McLennan County, where foreclosure rates are rising. Waco, the 17th's largest city and the largest population center between Austin and Dallas, hosts Baylor University and a strong education sector. Defense-related firms, such as Waco's L-3 Communications, offer additional jobs in the county.

The district jogs east and then southeast from Waco, meandering through sparsely populated counties and into Brazos, where the district's southern portion is centered. College Station is home to Texas A&M University, which includes the George Bush Presidential Library and Museum, and is a major employer here. Unlike the more-liberal University of Texas at Austin, Texas A&M has a conservative agricultural and military tradition that favors GOP candidates.

Johnson County, in the 17th's northeastern corner, has become a bedroom community for Fort Worth and is home to some of the city's southern suburbs. The county's most populous city, Cleburne, and its neighboring communities rely on light manufacturing. Along the Squaw Creek Reservoir west of Johnson, a nuclear plant in Somervell County employs many district residents and is looking to expand. Other energy concerns also are important to the district, especially in the northern counties that cover parts of the Barnett Shale natural gas reservoir. Improving both roads and airports remains an issue.

The 17th has a distinct GOP lean, and John McCain took 67 percent of the 2008 presidential vote here. But Rep. Chet Edwards' comfortable 2008 re-election shows that conservative "Yellow Dog" Democrats and ticket splitters can still provide a winning margin for Democrats.

MAJOR INDUSTRY
Agriculture, higher education, light manufacturing, defense

CITIES
Waco, 113,726; College Station, 67,890; Bryan, 65,660; Cleburne, 26,005

NOTABLE
The soft drink Dr Pepper was invented in Waco in 1885, and the city hosts a museum celebrating the beverage.

Rep. Sheila Jackson Lee (D)

Elected 1994; 8th term

CAPITOL OFFICE
225-3816
www.jacksonlee.house.gov
2160 Rayburn Bldg. 20515-4318; fax 225-3317

COMMITTEES
Foreign Affairs
Homeland Security
   (Transportation Security & Infrastructure
   Protection - chairwoman)
Judiciary

RESIDENCE
Houston

BORN
Jan. 12, 1950; Queens, N.Y.

RELIGION
Seventh-day Adventist

FAMILY
Husband, Elwyn Lee; two children

EDUCATION
Yale U., B.A. 1972 (political science);
U. of Virginia, J.D. 1975

CAREER
Lawyer; congressional aide

POLITICAL HIGHLIGHTS
Democratic nominee for Texas District Court
judge, 1984; Democratic nominee for Harris
County Probate Court judge, 1986; Houston
municipal judge, 1987-89; Democratic nominee
for Texas District Court judge, 1988; Houston
City Council, 1990-95

ELECTION RESULTS

2008 GENERAL

Sheila Jackson Lee (D)	148,617	77.3%
John Faulk (R)	39,095	20.3%
Mike Taylor (LIBERT)	4,486	2.3%

2008 PRIMARY

Sheila Jackson Lee (D)	unopposed

2006 GENERAL

Sheila Jackson Lee (D)	65,936	76.6%
Ahmad R. Hassan (R)	16,448	19.1%
Patrick Warren (LIBERT)	3,667	4.3%

PREVIOUS WINNING PERCENTAGES
2004 (89%); 2002 (77%); 2000 (76%); 1998 (90%);
1996 (77%); 1994 (73%)

Jackson Lee, who has rarely encountered a topic she didn't want to address, is set to play a key role in upcoming debates over security measures for airplanes, trains and chemical plants. And as one of the most frequent speakers on the House floor, she is expected to make herself heard on many other issues as well.

She always has talked at length before C-SPAN cameras on any topic. She grabs a spot on the center aisle of the House for the president's State of the Union address every year so she can shake his hand in front of the TV cameras. A Houston Chronicle reporter called her "ubiquitous."

But her ability to get things done could be impeded by her abrasive personality. A 2008 Washingtonian magazine survey of Capitol Hill aides called her the "meanest" member of the House (along with high rankings in the "most talkative" and "show horse" categories). Ex-aides have told various publications that she berates staffers for minor failures and would call them at all hours and force them to drive her the short distance between her residence and the Capitol.

She is a loyal Democrat who sided with her party 98 percent of the time in the 110th Congress (2007-08) on votes that pitted the parties against each other. She broke with the House leadership, however, on the $700 billion financial rescue package that came to the floor in the fall of 2008. Joining 33 other Democrats who voted against the initial version of the bill, she said she wanted to ensure it included rigorous oversight and would benefit ordinary Americans. She backed a second version that was signed into law, telling the Chronicle she reluctantly voted for it because it was "the first step to putting our country on the right track economically."

Jackson Lee is chairwoman of Homeland Security's Subcommittee on Transportation Security and Infrastructure Protection. She said Congress needs to move away from an exclusive focus on aviation security and shore up vulnerable trains and bus systems. She introduced legislation in 2009 to overhaul and reauthorize the Transportation Security Administration.

She also champions legislation to grant TSA employees, including airport baggage screeners, the same personnel and collective bargaining rights as other government employees. And she will work in the 111th Congress (2009-10) to beef up chemical plant security.

In 2007, Jackson Lee helped shepherd through legislation aimed at improving security for rail and mass transit. It was signed into law as part of a broader measure to implement the recommendations of the Sept. 11 commission. Jackson Lee ensured that the bill would benefit her district by including a provision to establish a transportation security center at Texas Southern University.

As a member of the Judiciary Committee, Jackson Lee seeks to change laws that impose far stiffer sentences for crack cocaine offenses than for those involving powder cocaine. Critics say this disparity is unfair and has a disproportionate impact on minorities. "There are thousands upon thousands of incarcerated persons who have been adjudged unfairly," she told the Houston newspaper. With the Obama administration taking up the cause, her efforts could bear fruit in the 111th.

Jackson Lee also serves on the Foreign Affairs Committee. Her district contains a substantial number of immigrants from Pakistan, and she is co-chairwoman of the Congressional Pakistan Caucus. She was on good terms with the country's former prime minister, the late Benazir Bhutto. She flew to Pakistan to observe parliamentary elections in February 2008, and was back in the country again in spring 2009.

She also has been active in campaigns to call attention to genocide in Sudan. She traveled to the country in 2007 and voiced worries about the conditions for children there. In April 2006, she was among five members of Congress arrested for disorderly conduct at a protest at the Sudanese Embassy in Washington. They were released after paying a $50 fine.

After Hurricane Ike raged through the Houston region in the fall of 2008, causing widespread damage and leaving millions without power, Jackson Lee helped coordinate disaster relief and emergency aid, and worked with the governor to extend unemployment benefits. She also introduced legislation to help ensure electric utilities are prepared for disasters.

As a Houston representative, she is a strong advocate for the space program and believes NASA should consider using the space shuttle past its planned retirement date. When President George W. Bush walked down the aisle for his 2008 State of the Union address, she whispered to him, "Remember NASA."

Jackson Lee's role model was Democratic Rep. Barbara Jordan, the noted black liberal from Houston who served from 1973 to 1979. "I had the privilege of being part of the generation of people who were moved by movements and moved by the voices and messages of Medgar Evers, Martin Luther King and Fannie Lou Hamer," Jackson Lee once said. "I always viewed my charge from their history and stories to be a change-maker."

She was born in Queens, N.Y., and educated at Yale and the University of Virginia law school, where she was one of three African-Americans in her class. She moved to Texas when her husband took a job with the University of Houston. After two unsuccessful bids for local judgeships she was appointed a municipal judge in 1987. After another failed election campaign for a judgeship, in 1990 she won an at-large seat on the city council, where her initiatives included a law imposing penalties on gun owners who fail to keep guns away from children. She also pushed for expanded summer hours at city parks and recreation centers as a way to reduce gang activity.

She came to Congress after beating incumbent Democrat Craig Washington in the 1994 primary election. Washington had lost the support of the Houston business establishment and several other important constituencies, and Jackson Lee garnered 63 percent of the vote in the primary. In the heavily Democratic district, that win was tantamount to election.

Jackson Lee hasn't faced a primary challenger since 2002, and in the 2008 general election, she won by more than 50 percentage points.

KEY VOTES

2008
Yes Delay consideration of Colombia free-trade agreement
Yes Override Bush veto of federal farm and nutrition programs reauthorization bill
No   Overhaul surveillance laws and permit dismissal of suits against companies that conducted warrantless wiretapping
Yes Grant mortgage relief to homeowners and funding for Fannie Mae and Freddie Mac
No   Approve initial $700 billion program to stabilize financial markets
Yes Approve final $700 billion program to stabilize financial markets
Yes Provide $14 billion in loans to automakers

2007
Yes Increase minimum wage by $2.10 an hour
Yes Approve $124.2 billion in emergency war spending and set goal for redeployment of troops from Iraq
No   Reject federal contraceptive assistance to international family planning groups
Yes Override Bush veto of $23.2 billion water projects authorization bill
No   Implement Peru free-trade agreement
Yes Approve energy policy overhaul with new fuel economy standards
No   Clear $473.5 billion omnibus spending bill, including $70 billion for military operations

CQ VOTE STUDIES

	PARTY UNITY		PRESIDENTIAL SUPPORT	
	SUPPORT	OPPOSE	SUPPORT	OPPOSE
2008	98%	2%	14%	86%
2007	98%	2%	4%	96%
2006	93%	7%	34%	66%
2005	93%	7%	28%	72%
2004	96%	4%	21%	79%

INTEREST GROUPS

	AFL-CIO	ADA	CCUS	ACU
2008	100%	100%	59%	4%
2007	100%	100%	55%	0%
2006	100%	100%	53%	16%
2005	93%	100%	56%	14%
2004	93%	95%	53%	4%

TEXAS 18
Downtown Houston

The 18th takes in the central part of downtown Houston, with appendages spreading to the south and northeast, as well as a C-shaped swath out to the northwest and north. Downtown's older black neighborhoods and more-progressive residents make up the 18th, which includes some of the city's poorest areas. Downtown Houston has seen revitalization, with ongoing efforts in residential, retail and corporate construction.

The district is diverse: 40 percent of residents are black and 36 percent are Hispanic. Some of the district's most heavily black areas are just south of downtown, and rapidly growing Hispanic neighborhoods can be found just north of downtown, between Interstate 45 and the Eastex Freeway. While the 18th is mainly inner-city urban, it also includes the Heights, a trendier area populated with some young professionals. The northern arm of the 18th picks up George Bush Intercontinental Airport.

Downtown office buildings are filled with oil and gas employees and other white-collar businesses and service workers, but most commute here from outside the district. Downtown also hosts some corporate

giants, such as CenterPoint Energy, whose headquarters are housed in its iconic — and well-lit — skyscraper. Halliburton, currently operating out of downtown, announced in 2009 that it would be moving its headquarters to its campus near the airport and other operations to a facility in the 7th District by 2012. Downtown workers can avoid high daytime temperatures by using the miles of underground tunnels that connect many of Houston's buildings. The 18th also takes in the Theater District, with the Hobby Center for the Performing Arts, and is home to baseball's Astros, basketball's Rockets and Comets, and soccer's Dynamo.

The state's first minority-majority district, the 18th's large black and Hispanic populations make it one of the most strongly Democratic districts in Texas, and Texas Southern University and the University of Houston add to the area's liberal bent. Barack Obama won 77 percent of the 18th's 2008 presidential vote, his second-highest percentage statewide.

MAJOR INDUSTRY
Energy, government, business services, entertainment

CITIES
Houston (pt.), 507,631

NOTABLE
Houston's KUHT became the nation's first public TV station in May 1953.

Rep. Randy Neugebauer (R)

Elected June 2003; 3rd full term

CAPITOL OFFICE
225-4005
www.randy.house.gov
1424 Longworth Bldg. 20515-4319; fax 225-9615

COMMITTEES
Agriculture
Financial Services
Science & Technology

RESIDENCE
Lubbock

BORN
Dec. 24, 1949; St. Louis, Mo.

RELIGION
Baptist

FAMILY
Wife, Dana Neugebauer; two children

EDUCATION
Texas Tech U., B.B.A. 1972 (accounting)

CAREER
Land developer; homebuilding company
executive; bank executive

POLITICAL HIGHLIGHTS
Lubbock City Council, 1992-98

ELECTION RESULTS

2008 GENERAL

Randy Neugebauer (R)	168,501	72.4%
Dwight Fullingim (D)	58,030	24.9%
Richard "Chip" Peterson (LIBERT)	6,080	2.6%

2008 PRIMARY

Randy Neugebauer (R)	unopposed

2006 GENERAL

Randy Neugebauer (R)	94,785	67.7%
Robert Ricketts (D)	41,676	29.8%
Fred Jones (LIBERT)	3,349	2.4%

PREVIOUS WINNING PERCENTAGES
2004 (58%); 2003 Special Runoff Election (51%)

Neugebauer has experience bouncing up and down; he was a trampolinist in his youth who became so skilled at back flips, twists and other moves that in college he joined a touring trampoline group called The Flying Matadors. But as a lawmaker representing a GOP stronghold, his position on issues shows no similar flexibility — he always follows a rigid conservative line.

Neugebauer (NAW-geh-bow-er) is a member of the Republican Study Committee, the influential core of the House's most conservative members, and an unwavering advocate of lower taxes, less federal spending and smaller government. He most often makes his views known as a member of the Financial Services Committee, where he tries — usually without success — to thwart Democratic legislation he considers misguided and unnecessary.

Neugebauer gets along with liberal Financial Services Chairman Barney Frank of Massachusetts, but he strongly opposed the $700 billion financial sector rescue bill that Frank helped steer into law in fall 2008. "I do not believe that the people of the 19th District, who made conservative lending and investment decisions, should have to pay for the mistakes made on Wall Street, nor do I believe that ultimately our children and grandchildren should have to pay for these mistakes either," he said in explaining his vote.

Neugebauer also opposed an expansive housing package earlier in the year, even though he had managed to win a few changes during committee consideration. He said he opposed the final version because it created an affordable-housing trust fund to be financed through future revenues of Fannie Mae and Freddie Mac, government-sponsored mortage giants. The House defeated his efforts to amend that "Robin Hood" provision.

He was an active participant in the committee's subsequent hearings on what went wrong as Financial Services continued to explore ways to assist the ailing industry. "Certainly we need to consider some regulatory improvements," he said. But he cautioned, "This debate isn't simply about having more regulation or less regulation. It's about having effective regulation."

And as the committee approved a series of bills in the early months of President Obama's administration, Neugebauer regularly sided with financial industry groups that expressed concerns about Frank acting hastily. "I would hope that as we move down this road to regulatory reform, we would be extremely careful," he said in March 2009. "It's not going to be the speed in which we do our work, but the quality of that work."

One of his pet peeves is the frequent use of "emergency" spending to get around the limits on discretionary spending set by each year's budget resolution. (Emergency spending does not count against the annual caps, even though the money does add to the deficit.) "We need to stop spending money we don't have, and the emergency spending process needs to cease," he said in 2008. When the House passed a 2006 Iraq War emergency spending bill that also provided $19.2 billion in hurricane relief on top of the $51.8 billion in emergency spending appropriated soon after Hurricane Katrina in 2005, Neugebauer tried but failed to split off the hurricane money and require that it be offset.

On the Agriculture Committee, Neugebauer spent much of the 110th Congress (2007-08) working to protect his district's many cotton, wheat and peanut producers, along with its cattle ranchers, as the panel put together a five-year reauthorization of agriculture and nutrition programs. In one of his rare splits with the administration, he supported a successful override of President George W. Bush's veto of the final legislation.

He supports greater domestic oil and gas production, including drilling offshore. In the 110th, he cosponsored legislation to expedite judicial reviews of legal challenges to drilling on public lands. A member of the Science and Technology Committee, he also backs the development of alternative energy sources, including wind power. His district is home to the Horse Hollow Wind Energy Center, the nation's largest wind farm. But he is adamantly opposed to any attempts to curb greenhouse gas emissions that he believes would unduly burden businesses.

Neugebauer was born in St. Louis, where his parents met in college, but he was raised in his mother's hometown of Lubbock. His father sold insurance, and his mother worked as a real estate agent and interior designer. They divorced when Neugebauer was 9, and his father died soon thereafter.

He graduated from Texas Tech University with a degree in accounting and became a commercial real estate developer and homebuilder. He was elected to the Lubbock City Council in 1992 and served until 1998. A deacon in his Baptist church, he is married to his high school sweetheart.

Neugebauer arrived in the House in June 2003 after winning a special election to replace Republican Larry Combest, who resigned that year. He faced 13 Republicans and two Democrats in the special election. In an initial round of balloting, he and accountant K. Michael Conaway, who had close ties to Bush, finished first and second, respectively.

Conaway hailed from Midland, the district's second-largest city and Bush's former home. Neugebauer's home and political base was in Lubbock, the district's largest city, which helped him considerably in the runoff. He won by just 587 votes. (Conaway got a second chance in 2004, winning a seat of his own in the 11th District, after a Texas redistricting engineered by former House Majority Leader Tom DeLay and other state Republicans took effect.)

When Neugebauer ran for re-election in 2004, the redistricting had matched him against 26-year Democratic Rep. Charles W. Stenholm, the most conservative of congressional Democrats. Neugebauer campaigned vigorously, pumping hands at Friday night high school football games. He defeated Stenholm by 18 percentage points after spending $3 million. In 2006, he romped to re-election with more than two-thirds of the vote; two years later, he won with 72 percent — the same percentage that Arizona Republican Sen. John McCain received in carrying the district over Obama.

Neugebauer drew some publicity in 2009 when he asked the Federal Election Commission for permission to raise campaign funds in a family-owned recreational boat, possibly bringing a captain and staff for events aboard it.

KEY VOTES

2008

No Delay consideration of Colombia free-trade agreement

Yes Override Bush veto of federal farm and nutrition programs reauthorization bill

Yes Overhaul surveillance laws and permit dismissal of suits against companies that conducted warrantless wiretapping

No Grant mortgage relief to homeowners and funding for Fannie Mae and Freddie Mac

No Approve initial $700 billion program to stabilize financial markets

No Approve final $700 billion program to stabilize financial markets

No Provide $14 billion in loans to automakers

2007

No Increase minimum wage by $2.10 an hour

No Approve $124.2 billion in emergency war spending and set goal for redeployment of troops from Iraq

Yes Reject federal contraceptive assistance to international family planning groups

No Override Bush veto of $23.2 billion water projects authorization bill

Yes Implement Peru free-trade agreement

No Approve energy policy overhaul with new fuel economy standards

Yes Clear $473.5 billion omnibus spending bill, including $70 billion for military operations

CQ VOTE STUDIES

	PARTY UNITY		PRESIDENTIAL SUPPORT	
	SUPPORT	OPPOSE	SUPPORT	OPPOSE
2008	98%	2%	80%	20%
2007	99%	1%	88%	12%
2006	97%	3%	87%	13%
2005	99%	1%	87%	13%
2004	98%	2%	85%	15%

INTEREST GROUPS

	AFL-CIO	ADA	CCUS	ACU
2008	0%	5%	82%	96%
2007	4%	0%	70%	100%
2006	7%	5%	100%	100%
2005	13%	0%	93%	100%
2004	20%	5%	100%	96%

TEXAS 19

West central — Lubbock, Abilene, Big Spring

The conservative 19th begins in the Panhandle, then extends south and east through cattle and cotton country around Lubbock to Abilene. It swings north, almost reaching Wichita Falls. With ranches, cattle and remnants of the cowboy lifestyle, the 19th offers a taste of the Wild West.

The western part of the district, which includes Lubbock, is heavily agricultural, although that industry extends east through most of the district. Lubbock, the district's largest city, thrives on the surrounding acres of cotton, calling itself the world's largest cottonseed-processing center. Home to Texas Tech University, the city has become an educational and medical hub for the southwest Panhandle. Lubbock's Depot District has brought development and revenue to its downtown, and a growing wine industry outside the city provides a little boost to the economy. Lubbock County accounts for more than one-third of the district's population, which is majority white with growing numbers of Hispanic residents.

Abilene also has made an effort to revitalize its downtown, and local officials are seeing results as a telecommunications sector develops. A

nearby Air Force base is a stable part of the economy, and the prison industry has done well, with several state and contract facilities around the district. Peanut farms are found throughout the 19th, and Gaines County is one of the largest industry producers in the state. Famine and drought have hurt cattle and cotton over the past decade, and more-recent layoffs in the oil industry have impacted the district. In areas such as Shackelford County, wind power is a developing industry.

As in much of the South, conservative Democrats used to dominate the area: In 1978, George W. Bush lost a race for the Lubbock-area House seat to a Democrat. But the 19th has become a GOP stronghold at all levels. John McCain took 72 percent of the 19th's 2008 presidential vote.

MAJOR INDUSTRY
Cattle, agriculture, oil and gas, defense

MILITARY BASES
Dyess Air Force Base, 5,009 military, 407 civilian (2006)

CITIES
Lubbock, 199,564; Abilene (pt.), 110,442; Big Spring, 25,233

NOTABLE
Lubbock's Buddy Holly Center honors the native musician, who died in a February 1959 plane crash in Iowa.

Rep. Charlie Gonzalez (D)

Elected 1998; 6th term

CAPITOL OFFICE
225-3236
www.house.gov/gonzalez
303 Cannon Bldg. 20515-4320; fax 225-1915

COMMITTEES
Energy & Commerce
House Administration
Judiciary

RESIDENCE
San Antonio

BORN
May 5, 1945; San Antonio, Texas

RELIGION
Roman Catholic

FAMILY
Divorced; one child

EDUCATION
U. of Texas, B.A. 1969 (government);
St. Mary's U. (Texas), J.D. 1972

MILITARY SERVICE
Texas Air National Guard, 1969-75

CAREER
Lawyer; teacher

POLITICAL HIGHLIGHTS
Bexar County judge, 1982-87; Texas District
Court judge, 1988-97

ELECTION RESULTS

2008 GENERAL

Charlie Gonzalez (D)	127,298	71.9%
Robert Litoff (R)	44,585	25.2%
Michael Idrogo (LIBERT)	5,172	2.9%

2008 PRIMARY

Charlie Gonzalez (D)	unopposed

2006 GENERAL

Charlie Gonzalez (D)	68,348	87.4%
Michael Idrogo (LIBERT)	9,897	12.6%

PREVIOUS WINNING PERCENTAGES
2004 (65%); 2002 (100%); 2000 (88%); 1998 (63%)

Gonzalez prides himself on being an independent-minded moderate who seeks bipartisan solutions on immigration and other divisive issues. Though he is more pragmatic than his famously iconoclastic father, Henry B. Gonzalez, who served in the House for 37 years, he said he shares some of his father's individualistic spirit. "My style is entirely different, but I like to think that I have the same independent streak that just manifests itself a little differently," Gonzalez said. "I do believe in structure and process probably much more than Dad on the value of the Democratic Caucus."

Gonzalez belongs to the moderate New Democrat Coalition and is the second-ranking leader of the Congressional Hispanic Caucus behind New York Democrat Nydia M. Velázquez. He took a seat in 2009 on the Judiciary Committee, where his background as a state district court judge in San Antonio will serve him well on the panels overseeing the courts, border security and international law. And he can play a role in continuing discussions on comprehensive immigration reform, which he believes can be accomplished if heated rhetoric is subdued and economic and national interests are reconciled.

Gonzalez in 2006 supported President George W. Bush's immigration plan calling for stiffer penalties for employers coupled with a legal path to citizenship for illegal immigrants currently in the United States. He states on his Web site, "Our immigration system must secure our borders, work for employers and employees, and observe the laws of our land."

He generally votes with his party on most social issues. In 2009, he supported an expansion of federal hate crime law to cover offenses based on a victim's sexual orientation or gender identity. He also voted for 2007 legislation to ban job discrimination based on sexual orientation, and in 2006 voted to override a Bush veto of an expansion of federal funding for embryonic stem cell research. He led the Hispanic Caucus' successful campaigns in 2002 and 2003 against confirming Miguel A. Estrada as the first Latino on the U.S. Court of Appeals for the District of Columbia Circuit.

Even with an expanded House majority in the 111th Congress (2009-10), Gonzalez stresses the need for moderation. "The Democratic leadership is very aware that we didn't necessarily get hired by the American people, the old Republican majority got fired," he told the San Antonio Express-News in November 2008. "It's abundantly clear that moderates and conservative Democrats have been the margin in achieving the [House] majority."

He has served since 2004 on the Energy and Commerce Committee, which takes up broad energy legislation during the 111th. A member of the Subcommittee on Energy and the Environment, Gonzalez supports exploring a wide range of energy resources, including clean coal, nuclear, solar and wind, that can both provide energy independence and reduce global warming. But as lawmakers in 2009 weighed a way to reduce greenhouse gas emissions, Gonzalez questioned just how quickly the country could transition to battery-powered cars and trucks. "It does trouble me that we're not dealing with realistic expectations," he told The Dallas Morning News. "Let's be realistic about the need for domestic production and refining capacity in the United States."

Gonzalez also sits on the Health Subcommittee. He backed a 2009 law to expand the State Children's Health Insurance Program, which provides coverage to children whose families don't qualify for Medicaid.

He believes the use of information technology would improve the quality of medical care, help prevent mistakes and save the health care system billions of dollars. He joined with Republican Phil Gingrey of Georgia on legislation to boost the use of such technology in doctors' offices; aspects of it were included in a separate measure Energy and Commerce approved in July 2008, but which then languished in the Ways and Means Committee.

Gonzalez also sits on Commerce's panel on Commerce and Trade, an issue on which he has a mixed record. He enthusiastically touted the benefits of the 1993 North American Free Trade Agreement, which his father had virulently opposed. But in siding with labor unions, which had promoted his first congressional bid, he reversed course to vote against the 2002 fast-track law giving the president authority to negotiate trade deals that cannot be amended by Congress.

He again joined with the majority of his party in 2005 to vote against implementing a free-trade agreement with most Central American countries. Two years later, however, he supported a free-trade agreement with Peru, saying the strengthened economic ties "will truly improve the standard of living for Americans and Peruvians alike." And in 2008, he voted with nearly all House Democrats for a resolution to postpone fast-track action on a free-trade accord with Colombia.

Gonzalez's other committee assignment is House Administration, where he chaired a task force established to investigate allegations that voting machine errors contributed to the razor-thin 2006 victory by Republican Vern Buchanan in Florida's 13th District. The task force voted in 2008 to dismiss Democrat Christine Jennings' challenge based on a Government Accountability Office report.

Gonzalez is the third of eight children and the only one who followed his father into public life. He was a teenager when his father was first elected to Congress. After graduating from a public high school, Gonzalez earned a bachelor's degree in government from the University of Texas at Austin and a law degree from St. Mary's School of Law in San Antonio. After private law practice, he was elected to the county bench in 1982 and spent 15 years as a local and state trial judge.

When his father announced his retirement, Gonzalez jumped into a seven-way Democratic primary to succeed him in 1998. To let his son stand on his own, the elder Gonzalez declined to endorse his son until just before the primary. Gonzalez won the nomination with 62 percent of the vote in a runoff race. In the general election, he won with 63 percent. In 2000 and 2002 Gonzalez faced no major-party opposition, and he has cruised to victory ever since.

KEY VOTES

2008
Yes Delay consideration of Colombia free-trade agreement
Yes Override Bush veto of federal farm and nutrition programs reauthorization bill
No Overhaul surveillance laws and permit dismissal of suits against companies that conducted warrantless wiretapping
Yes Grant mortgage relief to homeowners and funding for Fannie Mae and Freddie Mac
Yes Approve initial $700 billion program to stabilize financial markets
Yes Approve final $700 billion program to stabilize financial markets
Yes Provide $14 billion in loans to automakers

2007
Yes Increase minimum wage by $2.10 an hour
Yes Approve $124.2 billion in emergency war spending and set goal for redeployment of troops from Iraq
No Reject federal contraceptive assistance to international family planning groups
Yes Override Bush veto of $23.2 billion water projects authorization bill
Yes Implement Peru free-trade agreement
Yes Approve energy policy overhaul with new fuel economy standards
Yes Clear $473.5 billion omnibus spending bill, including $70 billion for military operations

CQ VOTE STUDIES

	PARTY UNITY		PRESIDENTIAL SUPPORT	
	SUPPORT	OPPOSE	SUPPORT	OPPOSE
2008	98%	2%	23%	77%
2007	97%	3%	7%	93%
2006	89%	11%	33%	67%
2005	86%	14%	26%	74%
2004	88%	12%	35%	65%

INTEREST GROUPS

	AFL-CIO	ADA	CCUS	ACU
2008	100%	90%	61%	8%
2007	96%	95%	60%	4%
2006	100%	95%	57%	16%
2005	80%	90%	63%	16%
2004	87%	95%	62%	20%

TEXAS 20
Downtown San Antonio

While maintaining ties to its history, San Antonio — the heart of the 20th District — has grown into one of the nation's largest cities. The strongly Democratic 20th, which is located entirely in Bexar (pronounced BEAR) County, takes in majority of the city, including the heavily Hispanic West Side, downtown San Antonio and some close-in communities.

A huge military presence in San Antonio once fueled the economy here, but mid-1990s downsizing diminished its importance. The redeveloped Kelly Air Force Base is currently supervised by Port San Antonio. The KellyUSA business park's tenants include high-tech, aeronautics and manufacturing firms. The Baptist Medical Center and several Christus Santa Rosa facilities help make the district a regional health care hub. Key telecommunications employers AT&T and Clear Channel (located in the neighboring 21st) have been forced to cut jobs, but federal funding is expected to boost development of the city's solar energy infrastructure.

Tourism and convention business have bolstered the city's economy and contributed to a revitalization of the urban center. The Alamo, site of the

1836 battle with Mexico, is in the heart of downtown. The city's scenic Paseo del Rio, or Riverwalk, also draws visitors with its shops, hotels and restaurants that wind along the San Antonio River. Events at the Alamodome — less than one mile from the river — also draw crowds.

A mid-decade remap added several predominately black neighborhoods along the 20th's southeastern edge near downtown, adding Democratic strength in this Hispanic-majority district. The only significant GOP presence in the district is in the largely white, higher-income areas northwest and northeast of downtown San Antonio. The 20th gave Barack Obama 64 percent of its vote in the 2008 presidential election.

MAJOR INDUSTRY
Health care, tourism, military, telecommunications, trade

MILITARY BASES
Lackland Air Force Base, 27,123 military, 6,726 civilian (2005)

CITIES
San Antonio (pt.), 590,575

NOTABLE
Theodore Roosevelt recruited for the "Rough Riders," the 1st U.S. Volunteer Cavalry in the Spanish-American War, at the bar in the Menger Hotel (built 1859), which is adjacent to the Alamo and still open.

Rep. Lamar Smith (R)

Elected 1986; 12th term

CAPITOL OFFICE
225-4236
lamarsmith.house.gov
2409 Rayburn Bldg. 20515-4321; fax 225-8628

COMMITTEES
Homeland Security
Judiciary - ranking member
Science & Technology

RESIDENCE
San Antonio

BORN
Nov. 19, 1947; San Antonio, Texas

RELIGION
Christian Scientist

FAMILY
Wife, Beth Smith; two children

EDUCATION
Yale U., B.A. 1969 (American studies);
Southern Methodist U., J.D. 1975

CAREER
Lawyer; rancher; reporter

POLITICAL HIGHLIGHTS
Texas House, 1981-82; Bexar County
Commissioners Court, 1983-85

ELECTION RESULTS

2008 GENERAL

Lamar Smith (R)	243,471	80.0%
James Arthur Stohm (LIBERT)	60,879	20.0%

2008 PRIMARY

Lamar Smith (R)	unopposed

2006 GENERAL

Lamar Smith (R)	122,486	60.1%
John Courage (D)	49,957	24.5%
Gene Kelly (D)	18,355	9.0%
Tommy Calvert (I)	5,280	2.6%
James Arthur Strohm (LIBERT)	4,076	2.0%
James Lyle Peterson (I)	2,189	1.1%

PREVIOUS WINNING PERCENTAGES
2004 (62%); 2002 (73%); 2000 (76%); 1998 (91%);
1996 (76%); 1994 (90%); 1992 (72%); 1990 (75%);
1988 (93%); 1986 (61%)

The ranking Republican on the Judiciary Committee, Smith is the torchbearer of conservative GOP principles on immigration, "frivolous" lawsuits and gun owners' rights. He has limited opportunity to make headway on many of his priorities with Democrats in power, yet his frustrations rarely turn to outright anger or personal attacks; he prefers to use sly humor or sarcasm to push back against the majority.

"There's a way to be partisan and advocate for your side without attacking people personally," said Smith, who also sits on the Homeland Security and Science and Technology panels.

During Democratic investigations of the George W. Bush administration in 2007 and 2008, he consistently defended the White House and enforced his points with glib remarks. At a May 2007 hearing into allegations that Attorney General Alberto R. Gonzalez fired nine U.S. attorneys for political reasons, he said, "If there are no fish in this lake, we should reel in our lines of questions, dock our empty boat and turn to more pressing issues." When Judiciary turned discussions to deciding whether to commence impeachment proceedings against Bush, Smith said such a move "will only serve to impeach our own credibility."

In July 2008, Democrats tried to push a resolution citing senior White House aide Karl Rove for contempt of Congress for refusing to comply with a committee subpoena. Smith said the committee was opening "the curtain on its version of a Salem witch trial of Karl Rove." And when Judiciary Chairman John Conyers Jr. of Michigan indicated in early 2009 he would plow ahead with investigations of Bush officials for detainee interrogation, warrantless surveillance and allegations of politically motived prosecutions, Smith said: "No good purpose is served by persecuting those who are no longer in office."

When President Obama announced he would close the detention facilities at Guantánamo Bay, Cuba, Smith introduced a bill to bar the release of any of the detainees within the territorial United States. From his seats on Judiciary and Homeland Security, he spearheads a GOP effort to renew certain provisions of the Patriot Act anti-terrorism law. He led the fight during the 110th Congress (2007-08) to retain in a foreign surveillance bill provisions that effectively would grant immunity protections for telecommunications companies.

Smith is a reliable party supporter. He is a member of the conservative Republican Study Committee and the House Republican Steering Committee, which makes committee assignments. His opposition to a series of Democratic initiatives in early 2009 included his vote against a measure to expand federal hate crime law to cover offenses based on a victim's sexual orientation or gender identity. He also opposed a media shield law because of its potential to impede law enforcement and intelligence-gathering.

He said he supported Obama's intent to address drug-related violence in Mexico in 2009, but warned the effort shouldn't come at the expense of other federal programs such as immigration enforcement.

Smith constantly pushes for stronger border security. He believes lax enforcement of immigration laws contributed to the 2001 terrorist attacks, and he opposed Bush's 2007 proposal to create a path to citizenship for illegal immigrants. He joined with New York Republican Peter T. King to author the House Republicans' alternative, which would have barred illegal immigrants from obtaining legal status, made English the United States' official language and required tamper-proof birth certificates for all Americans. Smith authored a 1996 law that increased penalties for document fraud and the smuggling of illegal immigrants and made it easier for illegal immigrants to be detained at the border or deported.

He set aside partisanship during the 110th when he worked side-by-side with Democrat Howard L. Berman of California to push for his top legislative priority — an overhaul of the nation's patent laws, which he has been pushing since 2005 when he chaired Judiciary's panel on courts and intellectual property. The measure passed the House, yet stalled in the Senate after disagreements among the technology, pharmaceutical and biotechnology industries. Lawmakers set out to try again in 2009.

In 2007, he delayed passage of a bill to give the District of Columbia full voting rights in the House. Near the end of the debate, Smith offered a motion that called for adding language to repeal the District's ban on handguns and other local gun control laws. His motion caused the sponsors to pull the bill from the floor, but it later passed the House, without the gun control language. Efforts to repeal the gun ban stalled a similar D.C. voting bill in early 2009.

On the Science and Technology Committee, Smith in 2007 pushed for a permanent ban on state and local taxes on the Internet to ensure continued business investment and affordable access.

In the 110th, Smith was the Republican point man during consideration of a Democratic proposal to put a layer of outside review atop the internal House ethics process. Smith instead proposed expanding the current ethics committee to include four former House members, two from each party, and to rotate the chairmanship between the two parties.

Smith's family arrived in Texas around 1850, just five years after statehood, and the family's political involvement stretches back almost that long. His grandfather was district attorney in San Antonio and an unsuccessful House candidate. His great-grandfather was a San Antonio judge, and his great-great-grandfather was mayor of Galveston.

After graduating from Yale, he worked as a business reporter for the Christian Science Monitor in Boston. He then got a law degree and returned to San Antonio. He was first elected to a seat in the state legislature in Austin and then served on the Bexar County commission. He won election to Congress in 1986 when Republican Tom Loeffler left to run, unsuccessfully, for governor.

After Bush — then a Midland oilman with one losing congressional race under his belt — decided not to seek the seat, Smith won a six-way primary. He then defeated, with the help of Rove, former Democratic state Sen. Pete Snelson. Smith garnered at least 70 percent of the vote in subsequent elections until 2004 and 2006, when he won with just more than 60 percent. He had no Democratic opposition in 2008.

KEY VOTES

2008

No Delay consideration of Colombia free-trade agreement

No Override Bush veto of federal farm and nutrition programs reauthorization bill

Yes Overhaul surveillance laws and permit dismissal of suits against companies that conducted warrantless wiretapping

No Grant mortgage relief to homeowners and funding for Fannie Mae and Freddie Mac

Yes Approve initial $700 billion program to stabilize financial markets

Yes Approve final $700 billion program to stabilize financial markets

No Provide $14 billion in loans to automakers

2007

Yes Increase minimum wage by $2.10 an hour

No Approve $124.2 billion in emergency war spending and set goal for redeployment of troops from Iraq

Yes Reject federal contraceptive assistance to international family planning groups

Yes Override Bush veto of $23.2 billion water projects authorization bill

Yes Implement Peru free-trade agreement

Yes Approve energy policy overhaul with new fuel economy standards

Yes Clear $473.5 billion omnibus spending bill, including $70 billion for military operations

CQ VOTE STUDIES

	PARTY UNITY		PRESIDENTIAL SUPPORT	
	SUPPORT	OPPOSE	SUPPORT	OPPOSE
2008	95%	5%	70%	30%
2007	96%	4%	84%	16%
2006	97%	3%	97%	3%
2005	98%	2%	89%	11%
2004	97%	3%	88%	12%

INTEREST GROUPS

	AFL-CIO	ADA	CCUS	ACU
2008	20%	15%	100%	88%
2007	13%	15%	84%	88%
2006	7%	0%	100%	84%
2005	13%	0%	93%	96%
2004	7%	0%	100%	92%

TEXAS 21

Central — northeast San Antonio and suburbs, part of Austin and suburbs

The growing 21st is a Republican, mainly urban and suburban district that takes in most of San Antonio and part of Austin and also extends westward to scoop up some of Texas' rugged Hill Country.

A court-ordered 2006 remap of the 21st skewed the district's population toward Bexar (pronounced BEAR) County, where a slight majority of district residents now live. The 21st's share of Bexar takes in the mostly comfortable north and northeast parts of San Antonio and its suburbs, which have a strong Republican lean. The district also includes employment anchors San Antonio International Airport and Fort Sam Houston, as well as Canyon Lake, a popular recreation spot in the eastern portion of the 21st District.

Roughly one-fifth of district residents live in Austin's burgeoning Travis County. The 21st's share of the county encompasses the main University of Texas campus and parts of downtown Austin, including the Capitol

and governor's mansion as well as the Bob Bullock Texas State History Museum. The 21st also takes in some wealthy suburbs and rural areas in the western part of Travis County, including Lake Travis and surrounding attractions. Overall, the 21st is almost 70 percent white and has a growing Hispanic population.

Comal County, located northeast of San Antonio, makes up only one-eighth of the district's population, but it adds to the district's GOP tilt. The 21st's share of the Texas Hill County includes Bandera, Kerr and Real counties. The district favored Republican presidential candidate John McCain in 2008, giving him 58 percent of its vote.

MAJOR INDUSTRY
Technology, government, higher education, defense

MILITARY BASES
Fort Sam Houston (Army), 13,935 military, 8,594 civilian (2007)

CITIES
San Antonio (pt.), 259,488; Austin (pt.), 77,118; New Braunfels (pt.), 35,328

NOTABLE
Lyndon B. Johnson was born in Blanco County; Bandera bills itself as the cowboy capital of the world; Austin is home to North America's largest urban colony of Mexican free-tailed bats.

Rep. Pete Olson (R)

CAPITOL OFFICE
225-5951
olson.house.gov
514 Cannon Bldg. 20515-4322; fax 225-5241

COMMITTEES
Homeland Security
Science & Technology
Transportation & Infrastructure

RESIDENCE
Sugar Land

BORN
Dec. 9, 1962; Fort Lewis, Wash.

RELIGION
United Methodist

FAMILY
Wife, Nancy Olson; two children

EDUCATION
Rice U., B.A. 1985 (computer science);
U. of Texas, J.D. 1988

MILITARY SERVICE
Navy, 1988-98

CAREER
Congressional aide; Navy Senate liaison

POLITICAL HIGHLIGHTS
No previous office

ELECTION RESULTS

2008 GENERAL

Pete Olson (R)	161,996	52.4%
Nick Lampson (D)	140,160	45.4%
John Wieder (LIBERT)	6,839	2.2%

2008 PRIMARY RUNOFF

Pete Olson (R)	15,511	68.5%
Shelley Sekula Gibbs (R)	7,125	31.5%

Elected 2008; 1st term

Olson is a decorated naval aviator, a former aide to the Joint Chiefs of Staff and a seasoned U.S. Senate staffer. As a freshman House Republican, however, his claim to fame may have less to do with his credentials than with the high-profile seat he holds.

In 2008 Olson recaptured the 22nd District seat long held by House Majority Leader Tom DeLay, who resigned in early 2006 after being indicted the year before in a Texas campaign finance case. Nick Lampson, a Democrat who had held Texas' 9th District from 1997 to 2005, won the seat in 2006. But Olson grabbed it back. "The reason I was able to win has to do with the conservative values of the district," said Olson, who is staunchly to the right on fiscal and social policy issues alike.

The first bill he introduced sought to force state health departments to disclose whether any federal Medicaid funds they receive go to groups that perform, promote or refer for abortions. Taxpayers, Olson said, have a "right to know whether their money is being spent on activities or organizations to which they are morally opposed."

He is the sole Texas Republican on the Transportation and Infrastructure Committee, where he will join panel Democrats from Texas in looking out for the interests of his district and state. "Most certainly we have our differences, but if something's important to Texas, no one circles the wagon and works together like the Texas delegation," he said.

His seat on the Science and Technology Committee gives him a voice over space policy, crucial to his constituents. He also serves on the Homeland Security Committee, which helps write immigration laws. He hopes at some point to snag a seat on the Armed Services Committee.

During his nine-year Navy career, Olson flew missions over Iraq to enforce international sanctions following the first Gulf War, and in 1994 his aircrew was named Pacific Fleet's best in anti-submarine warfare. After a stint with the Joint Chiefs of Staff, he was assigned to the Senate as naval liaison. He then spent five years as chief of staff to Republican Sen. John Cornyn before making his own bid for elective office.

TEXAS 22

Southeast Houston and southern suburbs — Sugar Land, Pearland, part of Pasadena

Generally wealthy, white-collar and Republican, the 22nd includes most of Fort Bend County, a chunk of northern Brazoria County, a piece of Galveston County south of Houston and a slice of the city itself. Democrats took the House seat here in 2006, but the 22nd's 2008 congressional and presidential votes swung Republican. John McCain won with 58 percent of the vote.

The 22nd takes in the communities of Sugar Land and Pearland, as well as affluent areas surrounding the Lyndon B. Johnson Space Center. Wealthy NASA scientists and astronauts live nearby in Clear Lake. More than two-thirds of the population lives in Fort Bend County, which includes Sugar Land. The area has changed from a sugar-growing

hub into booming suburbia since the 1960s, and the 2003 closure of a key refinery did not stall economic growth.

On its northeastern edge, the 22nd takes in part of upscale southeastern Harris County, where 45 percent of district residents live. Some of the county's wealthiest areas are in southeastern Houston, near Ellington Airport, a former Air Force base that now hosts space center aircraft operations and a few commercial sites. The district sneaks north to grab Houston's Hobby Airport. Coastal areas in the 22nd sustained extensive damage in 2008 from Hurricane Ike, and inland areas received displaced residents.

MAJOR INDUSTRY
Aerospace, transportation, agriculture

CITIES
Houston (pt.), 109,880; Sugar Land, 63,328; Pasadena (pt.), 57,020; Pearland (pt.), 37,628; Missouri City (pt.), 32,855

NOTABLE
Fort Bend County's "Texian Market Days" include re-enactments of 1830s pioneer life.

Rep. Ciro D. Rodriguez (D)

Elected April 1997; 5th full term
Did not serve 2005-07

A Hispanic Democrat representing a conservative-to-moderate district along the border with Mexico, Rodriguez must keep an eye on the balance between following his liberal aspirations and meeting the concerns of his constituents.

It's a lesson he learned after being ousted from his seat in the neighboring 28th District in the 2004 election and fighting his way to a stunning comeback in a runoff election two years later. He has since worked to solidify his hold on his seat by making a nuanced shift to the center.

In the 110th Congress (2007-08), Rodriguez was one of the four least loyal members of the Congressional Hispanic Caucus, as measured by his "party unity" score in votes that pitted a majority of one party against the other. That was a reverse of his ranking during his previous tenure, when he was more loyal than the average Democrat.

His voting record is still solidly Democratic — he supported much of President Obama's early legislative agenda, including a $787 billion economic stimulus law and a $3.56 trillion budget blueprint for fiscal 2010. He also backed two bills to combat wage discrimination and a bill to expand a children's health insurance program. But his positions in the 110th on such high-profile matters as immigration and government bailouts of private industry were aimed at appealing more to his moderate constituency. "I'm responding to needs," Rodriguez told the San Antonio Express-News. "Part of it is looking at your district and who you represent." His district includes more than 700 miles of the Rio Grande border with Mexico and stretches from near El Paso to San Antonio.

Rodriguez was the only Hispanic member in 2007 to back an immigration-enforcement bill to hire another 8,000 border agents over five years and require employers to use an electronic verification system to catch undocumented workers. Hispanic groups criticized Rodriguez for supporting the measure, which was backed primarily by conservatives. Late in 2008, he bucked his party leaders to cast three votes against measures providing funding for the federal government to rescue the financial services and automobile industries. He was one of only 20 Democrats to break ranks on the funding for automakers.

Rodriguez said the differences are "day and night" between his current district and the last one he represented, where the dominant population center focused around San Antonio. He meets with small groups across his district, paying close attention to the needs of his conservative constituents in rural counties and Republican-leaning enclaves of San Antonio.

His seat on the Appropriations Committee also has helped him secure the trust of voters. As the committee's only member from the Texas-Mexico border, Rodriguez is well-positioned to secure funding for border communities and local law enforcement. This is especially important to his district, which is flooded with drug, weapon and human smuggling. In early 2009, he pushed for more federal dollars to boost border security and crack down on gun smuggling to stem drug-cartel related violence in Mexico and keep it from spilling across the border.

He was pleased when Obama announced an interim plan to commit $700 million for law enforcement on the border. But he warned that "these increased funds, in addition to what we have already passed, are unfortunately only the beginning of what we will need to combat this pervasive violence."

Rodriguez has directed millions of federal dollars back home to alleviate unemployment and improve infrastructure, including along the border.

CAPITOL OFFICE
225-4511
rodriguez.house.gov
2351 Rayburn Bldg. 20515-4323; fax 225-2237

COMMITTEES
Appropriations
Veterans' Affairs

RESIDENCE
San Antonio

BORN
Dec. 9, 1946; Piedras Negras, Mexico

RELIGION
Roman Catholic

FAMILY
Wife, Carolina Pena Rodriguez; one child

EDUCATION
St. Mary's U. (Texas), B.A. 1973 (political science); Our Lady of the Lake U., M.S.W. 1978

CAREER
Lobbyist; social worker; college instructor

POLITICAL HIGHLIGHTS
Harlandale Independent School District Board of Trustees, 1975-87; Texas House, 1987-97; U.S. House, 1997-2005; defeated in primary for re-election to U.S. House, 2004; sought Democratic nomination for U.S. House, 2006

ELECTION RESULTS

2008 GENERAL

Ciro D. Rodriguez (D)	134,090	55.8%
Lyle Larson (R)	100,799	41.9%
Lani Connolly (LIBERT)	5,581	2.3%

2008 PRIMARY

Ciro D. Rodriguez (D)	unopposed

2006 GENERAL RUNOFF

Ciro D. Rodriguez (D)	38,256	54.3%
Henry Bonilla (R)	32,217	45.7%

PREVIOUS WINNING PERCENTAGES
2002 (71%); 2000 (89%); 1998 (91%); 1997 Special Runoff Election (67%)

He also serves on the Veterans' Affairs Committee (as he did during his earlier service in the House), where he can look out for his district's two military bases and 55,000 veterans. He has helped pass proposals to extend benefits for substance-abuse treatment, expand access to mental health care services for Iraq and Afghanistan war veterans, and provide a cost-of-living increase in disability benefits. He pushed legislation in early 2009 to ensure such benefits are also provided to veterans not in the direct line of combat, but who still suffer post-traumatic symptoms.

Rodriguez was born on the Mexican side of the Rio Grande. His family moved back and forth across the border as his father took a series of jobs working on large industrial refrigeration units. They settled in the San Antonio area when Rodriguez was 3, and he became a U.S. citizen at 18.

He dropped out of school in the ninth grade and worked in a gas station. He returned to high school the next year, attended summer school and eventually graduated with his class. Of the six children in the family, he is the only one who attended college. He began his college studies intending to be a pharmacist but soon turned to social work. He has held jobs helping heroin addicts and patients in mental health clinics.

Rodriguez served a dozen years on a local school board and 10 years in the Texas House. In 1997, when Democratic Rep. Frank Tejeda of the 28th District died after a battle with brain cancer, Rodriguez ran for the seat. He finished first among 15 candidates in the special election, then defeated former Democratic San Antonio City Council member Juan Solis in the runoff.

He faced scant electoral opposition until 2004, when Henry Cuellar upset him in the primary. The contest was certified only after recounts, lawsuits and accusations of voting fraud lodged by Rodriguez and his supporters.

In March 2006, Rodriguez, who was doing community relations work and living off of his savings, lost a primary rematch with Cuellar by nearly 13 percentage points. But a court-ordered redistricting gave him a second chance by appending his political base in southern San Antonio to the 23rd.

In the race against GOP Rep. Henry Bonilla, he struggled to raise money. Bonilla took 49 percent of the vote, just short of the majority needed for an outright victory. That forced him into a December runoff with Rodriguez. The cash-rich Democratic Congressional Campaign Committee spent heavily on a television advertising campaign to attack Bonilla and promote Rodriguez, who took 54 percent of the vote in the low-turnout contest.

Rodriguez fought off a tough challenge in 2008 by Republican Lyle Larson, a former San Antonio City Council member and Bexar County commissioner, and won with 56 percent.

KEY VOTES

2008
Yes Delay consideration of Colombia free-trade agreement
Yes Override Bush veto of federal farm and nutrition programs reauthorization bill
Yes Overhaul surveillance laws and permit dismissal of suits against companies that conducted warrantless wiretapping
Yes Grant mortgage relief to homeowners and funding for Fannie Mae and Freddie Mac
No   Approve initial $700 billion program to stabilize financial markets
No   Approve final $700 billion program to stabilize financial markets
No   Provide $14 billion in loans to automakers

2007
Yes Increase minimum wage by $2.10 an hour
Yes Approve $124.2 billion in emergency war spending and set goal for redeployment of troops from Iraq
No   Reject federal contraceptive assistance to international family planning groups
Yes Override Bush veto of $23.2 billion water projects authorization bill
No   Implement Peru free-trade agreement
Yes Approve energy policy overhaul with new fuel economy standards
Yes Clear $473.5 billion omnibus spending bill, including $70 billion for military operations

CQ VOTE STUDIES

	PARTY UNITY		PRESIDENTIAL SUPPORT	
	SUPPORT	OPPOSE	SUPPORT	OPPOSE
2008	95%	5%	23%	77%
2007	95%	5%	11%	89%
2004	92%	8%	35%	65%
2003	92%	8%	20%	80%
2002	96%	4%	25%	75%

INTEREST GROUPS

	AFL-CIO	ADA	CCUS	ACU
2008	93%	80%	61%	24%
2007	96%	95%	60%	8%
2004	93%	90%	53%	13%
2003	100%	85%	40%	21%
2002	100%	95%	40%	0%

TEXAS 23

Southwest – south and northwest San Antonio and suburbs, Del Rio

Larger than most states east of the Mississippi River, the 23rd takes in more than 700 miles of border with Mexico along the Rio Grande River, skimming El Paso in the west and reaching as far east as San Antonio, the district's population center. Nearly 60 percent of residents live in San Antonio or in surrounding Bexar (pronounced BEAR) County.

Maverick and Val Verde counties on the 23rd's southern border — which includes some of the nation's poorest areas — are overwhelmingly Hispanic. Seasonal employment, an influx of immigrants and access to Mexican labor contribute to high unemployment, although trade and manufacturing bolster the economy.

In San Antonio, recent economic downturns forced a Toyota Tundra plant that opened in 2006 to delay plans for expansion and to cut jobs. The area economy also took a hit from the 2005 BRAC round, which ordered the Air Force's Brooks City-Base closed by 2011. Historically

lower home prices shielded much of San Antonio from the national housing market crisis, but economic growth has stalled due to layoffs.

The 23rd was the focal point of a legal challenge to a 2004 Republican-drawn congressional map. In August 2006, a federal court restored the 23rd's Hispanic population to 65 percent by moving the heavily Hispanic south side of San Antonio into the 23rd from the adjacent 28th. South San Antonio's Democratic lean contrasts with the Republican, mostly white areas in the city's north and in its suburbs. These changes lessened the 23rd's GOP tilt. In the 2008 presidential election, Barack Obama narrowly won the district's presidential vote in 2008 with 51 percent, earning four of his 10 highest percentages statewide in counties here.

MAJOR INDUSTRY
Agriculture, trade, tourism, defense

MILITARY BASES
Laughlin Air Force Base, 1,420 military, 1,800 civilian (2007); Brooks City-Base (Air Force), 1,297 military, 1,268 civilian (2005)

CITIES
San Antonio (pt.), 294,335; Del Rio, 33,867; Eagle Pass, 22,413

NOTABLE
Texas' largest county, Brewster, is roughly 6,200 square miles.

Rep. Kenny Marchant (R)

Elected 2004; 3rd term

CAPITOL OFFICE
225-6605
www.marchant.house.gov
227 Cannon Bldg. 20515-4324; fax 225-0074

COMMITTEES
Financial Services

RESIDENCE
Coppell

BORN
Feb. 23, 1951; Bonham, Texas

RELIGION
Nazarene

FAMILY
Wife, Donna Marchant; four children

EDUCATION
Southern Nazarene U., B.A. 1974 (religion);
Nazarene Theological Seminary, attended 1975-76

CAREER
Real estate developer; homebuilding
company owner

POLITICAL HIGHLIGHTS
Carrollton City Council, 1980-84 (mayor
pro tempore, 1983-84); mayor of Carrollton,
1984-86; Texas House, 1987-2005

ELECTION RESULTS

2008 GENERAL

Kenny Marchant (R)	151,434	56.0%
Tom Love (D)	111,089	41.1%
David A. Casey (LIBERT)	7,972	2.9%

2008 PRIMARY

Kenny Marchant (R)	unopposed

2006 GENERAL

Kenny Marchant (R)	83,835	59.8%
Gary R. Page (D)	52,075	37.2%
Mark Frohman (LIBERT)	4,228	3.0%

PREVIOUS WINNING PERCENTAGES
2004 (64%)

Marchant is a multimillionaire homebuilder who quietly supports business interests as well as his party. Despite a lengthy résumé in local and state government, he hews to the belief that the less taxpayer money politicians spend, the better.

Marchant (MARCH-unt) has voted against most major economic legislation since Democrats took control of Congress. That includes a 2008 measure to reauthorize farm programs, which President George W. Bush vetoed but many Republicans supported, as well as both versions of a $700 billion bill to aid the nation's ailing financial sector, the second of which became law. "He's about as fiscally conservative as a congressman can get," the Fort Worth Star-Telegram said in endorsing him for re-election in 2008.

An exception was his 2007 vote in favor of raising the minimum wage. He said it had broad support from constituents and was long overdue, though he complained Democrats rebuffed Republican attempts to link the increase to helping small businesses.

Not surprisingly, Marchant was a strong critic of President Obama's $787 billion economic stimulus law in early 2009. He denounced it as "payback to [Democrats'] special interests at the expense of the American people, who continue to suffer while Congress writes checks for programs we do not need with money we do not have." He compared the interest groups eagerly seeking provisions inserted in the measure to "people impatiently clamoring for beads at Mardi Gras."

He likewise opposed Obama's fiscal 2010 budget blueprint, which totalled $3.56 trillion when Congress passed it in April 2009.

Marchant is a member of the Republican Study Committee, the coalition of conservative House Republicans. In 2009 he also joined a new Property Rights Action Caucus, an informal group he said he hoped could "develop a groundswell of public sentiment for sensible legislation protecting private property from unnecessary and unconstitutional intrusion."

A member of the Financial Services Committee, Marchant rarely gives opening statements or poses questions to witnesses during hearings. But his seat in the hearing room is rarely empty, and he brings a state-level perspective to the panel's work. During his 18-year career in the Texas House, Marchant chaired the Financial Institutions Committee, among others.

He opposed the 2008 law to rescue troubled mortgage giants Fannie Mae and Freddie Mac and assist struggling homeowners. Though he favored a provision overhauling the Federal Housing Administration as well as other aspects, he said the law abdicated Congress' oversight ability and turned the government into a landlord. "Much of the good legislation that should pass into law is stuffed like a burrito with wasteful and unnecessary add-ons," he wrote in a letter to constituents. "I like burritos, but this was one burrito I could not bite into."

During his state government career, he also was the state House Republican Chairman in 2002 when his party won control of the chamber for the first time since Reconstruction. He effectively was the caucus chairman, the whip and policy chairman all in one, preferring to work behind the scenes and in committees. "I've never been much of an orator," Marchant said. "Probably, in 18 years in the Texas House, I gave eight speeches."

During his first two terms in Washington, Marchant was a reliable Republican vote, siding with Republicans 97 percent of the time on votes that divided the two parties in the 110th Congress (2007-08). He supports making the 2001 and 2003 Bush tax cuts permanent and is a strong voice on changes to immigration policy. "In my view, the proper approach to modern immigration policy rests on three pillars: security, responsibility and opportunity," he said.

Marchant's bona fides within the party were apparent even before his 2005 arrival on Capitol Hill with a party-building record. He helped draw the redistricting map that was planned by former House Majority Leader Tom DeLay of Texas to create more Republican seats, including the one Marchant now holds.

Though he largely remains in the background — he introduced just four bills in the 110th — Marchant took a major stand in 2008 on offshore drilling and clean energy. Joining a GOP revolt against holding the August congressional recess as gas prices soared, Marchant was among a group of Republicans who stayed in Washington to give speeches on the House floor. He sponsored an unsuccessful measure providing loan guarantees for companies seeking to build new nuclear power plants.

Marchant's assets were worth at least $9.9 million in 2007, according to the Center for Responsive Politics. He assists area churches through the Marchant Family Foundation, which also contributes funds for educational scholarships and assists local charities.

He grew up in Farmers Branch, where his father and two uncles owned a four-chair barbershop. "We went to church three or four times a week and I went to church camps," Marchant recalled. "All of my activities basically revolved around the church." He received a degree in religion from Southern Nazarene University in Bethany, Okla., and attended the Nazarene Theological Seminary in Kansas City, Mo. But after a year of study, as he and his wife, Donna, were expecting their first child, Marchant said he found that "I was not very happy, and began to doubt that was really, really what I should plan to do." The couple returned to Texas.

Marchant became a roofing contractor, work he had done to pay his way through college. From there, he began importing and installing wooden shingles, then building new homes and developing lots to sell to builders. He chaired the local homebuilders association, which suspected city inspectors of soliciting bribes. That spurred him to run for and win a seat on the Carrollton City Council in 1980. Four years later, he was elected mayor.

In 1987, he moved to the state House, where he served until he won his first congressional race in 2004 with 64 percent of the vote. He has had a relatively easy time with re-election, but his victory margin has dipped, hinting at the Democratic gains in parts of the district.

KEY VOTES

2008

No   Delay consideration of Colombia free-trade agreement

No   Override Bush veto of federal farm and nutrition programs reauthorization bill

Yes   Overhaul surveillance laws and permit dismissal of suits against companies that conducted warrantless wiretapping

No   Grant mortgage relief to homeowners and funding for Fannie Mae and Freddie Mac

No   Approve initial $700 billion program to stabilize financial markets

No   Approve final $700 billion program to stabilize financial markets

No   Provide $14 billion in loans to automakers

2007

Yes   Increase minimum wage by $2.10 an hour

No   Approve $124.2 billion in emergency war spending and set goal for redeployment of troops from Iraq

Yes   Reject federal contraceptive assistance to international family planning groups

No   Override Bush veto of $23.2 billion water projects authorization bill

Yes   Implement Peru free-trade agreement

No   Approve energy policy overhaul with new fuel economy standards

Yes   Clear $473.5 billion omnibus spending bill, including $70 billion for military operations

CQ VOTE STUDIES

	PARTY UNITY		PRESIDENTIAL SUPPORT	
	SUPPORT	OPPOSE	SUPPORT	OPPOSE
2008	98%	2%	82%	18%
2007	97%	3%	89%	11%
2006	98%	2%	97%	3%
2005	98%	2%	89%	11%

INTEREST GROUPS

	AFL-CIO	ADA	CCUS	ACU
2008	0%	0%	83%	100%
2007	9%	10%	78%	96%
2006	7%	0%	100%	92%
2005	13%	0%	93%	92%

TEXAS 24

Part of Dallas and western suburbs — Grand Prairie, Carrollton, part of Irving

Taking in most of the more affluent suburbs sandwiched between Dallas and Fort Worth, the 24th was designed to be a Republican stronghold, but the district gave John McCain only 55 percent of its 2008 presidential vote, 10 percentage points less than George W. Bush won here in 2004. The district as a whole is majority white (64 percent), although parts of it have a steadily growing Hispanic influence.

The district's economy revolves around Dallas-Fort Worth International Airport and the businesses the airport has attracted to the area. The airport, located in the middle of the 24th and a small part of which is in the neighboring 26th, is the largest employer in the district.

East of the airport, a corporate hub in Irving's Las Colinas financial district, which is shared with the 32nd, also fuels the district's economy. The area combines financial stability with low tax rates, high quality of life and good transportation — all of which contribute to its reputation as a

prime destination for domestic and international corporate relocation. The 12,000-acre business and residential planned community boasts thousands of companies. The local retail sector is expanding, and Everest Heights Mall, a South Asian-themed shopping center, is expected to open by 2010. Many residents from the wealthy suburbs commute into either Fort Worth or Dallas, making transportation policy, particularly plans for highway expansions, a major issue here.

Although most of the area's attractions and entertainment venues are in neighboring districts, the 24th hosts the Lone Star Park and the Nokia Theatre, both of which are in Grand Prairie, and the Gaylord Texan resort and convention center in Grapevine. The southern part of the district takes in almost all of Joe Pool Lake and its surrounding parks, an area with camping, marinas and expanding home development.

MAJOR INDUSTRY
Transportation, manufacturing, corporate headquarters

CITIES
Grand Prairie (pt.), 122,502; Carrollton, 109,576; Irving (pt.), 59,755; Bedford, 47,152; Euless, 46,005; Grapevine (pt.), 42,057; Dallas (pt.), 37,512

NOTABLE
Grand Prairie is home to the National Championship Indian Pow Wow.

Rep. Lloyd Doggett (D)

Elected 1994; 8th term

CAPITOL OFFICE
225-4865
www.house.gov/doggett
201 Cannon Bldg. 20515-4325; fax 225-3073

COMMITTEES
Budget
Ways & Means

RESIDENCE
Austin

BORN
Oct. 6, 1946; Austin, Texas

RELIGION
Methodist

FAMILY
Wife, Libby Belk Doggett; two children

EDUCATION
U. of Texas, B.B.A. 1967, J.D. 1970

CAREER
Lawyer

POLITICAL HIGHLIGHTS
Texas Senate, 1973-85; Democratic nominee
for U.S. Senate, 1984; Texas Supreme Court,
1989-94

ELECTION RESULTS

2008 GENERAL

Lloyd Doggett (D)	191,755	65.8%
George L. Morovich (R)	88,693	30.4%
Jim Stutsman (LIBERT)	10,848	3.7%

2008 PRIMARY

Lloyd Doggett (D)	unopposed

2006 GENERAL

Lloyd Doggett (D)	109,911	67.3%
Grant Rostig (R)	42,975	26.3%
Barbara Cunningham (LIBERT)	6,942	4.2%
Brian Parrett (I)	3,596	2.2%

PREVIOUS WINNING PERCENTAGES
2004 (68%); 2002 (84%); 2000 (85%); 1998 (85%);
1996 (56%); 1994 (56%)

Doggett has survived years of Republican attempts to unseat him and has emerged as one of Congress' most environment-friendly lawmakers. A strong supporter of Speaker Nancy Pelosi of California, he is also influential with other Democrats who respect his knowledge of tax policy and other issues.

He is generally loyal to his party but is not a rubber stamp. He authored climate change legislation that went further to reduce greenhouse gases than bills supported by his party's leaders, and he was a strong critic of the $700 billion financial rescue law that the Democratic leadership joined President George W. Bush in supporting in fall 2008. "Like the Iraq War and the [anti-terrorism] Patriot Act, this bill is fueled by fear and hinges on haste," he said.

From his senior position on the powerful Ways and Means Committee, Doggett has sought to force lobbyists seeking tax benefits to reveal their employers and to require "international tax dodgers" to pay more U.S. taxes. When President Obama unveiled his plan in May 2009 to significantly change how U.S.-based multinational corporations are taxed, it incorporated aspects of Doggett's proposal.

He also serves on the Budget Committee and has championed pay-as-you-go rules, which require offsets for new tax cuts or increased mandatory spending. He backed Obama's $787 billion economic stimulus law, calling it an "imperfect but responsible response" to the nation's economic woes.

Doggett said the House should lead by example on environmental issues by being more energy efficient. (He is diligent about recycling in his own Capitol Hill office.) He wants to direct more funding to renewable-energy initiatives and clean-energy research, and also advocates tax incentives aimed at conservation.

His climate change bill, introduced in the 110th Congress (2007-08), would create a "cap and trade" system to control emissions of carbon dioxide, aimed to reduce the nation's carbon emissions by 80 percent over the next 42 years, compared to 1990 levels. As lawmakers took up the issue in 2009, Doggett continued to propose a cap-and-trade plan that added "training wheels" for the early years of the program. It called for an oversight board to forecast and select emission allowance prices through 2019, with the market setting prices after that. He also said he wanted to ensure the legislation would cover costs that businesses pass on to consumers.

Another priority for Doggett has been the elderly. He is a strong defender of both the Medicare and Social Security programs, and advocates for a nationwide "Silver Alert" system, similar to a Texas program, to help authorities find missing seniors suffering from dementia or other impairments. The House passed the bill in 2008 and — when the bill didn't survive the Senate — again in 2009. He also got through the House in 2009 a bill to bar the government from printing seniors' Social Security numbers on their Medicare cards, a practice many lawmakers consider a security risk.

The technology industry has expanded Austin's economy, and Doggett pays attention to its needs. He founded and co-chairs the bipartisan House Information Technology Roundtable, a group that promotes dialogue among businesses, policy makers and the public on high-tech issues.

A liberal former Texas Supreme Court justice, Doggett spent his first 12 years in Congress in the minority, where he seldom missed an opportunity to upbraid, outmaneuver or otherwise confound Republican conservatives, particularly fellow Texan Tom DeLay, the former House majority leader.

He also devoted much of his time to opposing the Iraq War. During House consideration in late 2002 of a resolution authorizing the president to take military action against Iraq, he led an ad hoc whip organization to round up votes in opposition. In 2007, he argued for a "phased redeployment" that would pull U.S. troops out of Iraq and refocus U.S. military power on Afghanistan — an approach consistent with Obama's February 2009 policy.

Doggett's antipathy toward Republicans made him a top target when DeLay led a drive to redraw Texas' congressional districts in 2003 in a successful bid to enlarge the GOP majority in the House. The Republican redistricting plan dismantled Doggett's 10th District. Doggett quickly decided to run in the new 25th District, which stretched 350 miles from Austin to the Texas-Mexico border and was drawn to elect a Hispanic candidate. He gave up his hillside West Austin home and moved to the heavily Hispanic east side.

In June 2006, the U.S. Supreme Court ruled that the GOP-drawn map was unconstitutional because it diluted the political influence of Hispanic voters in the 23rd District. Subsequently, a three-judge panel redrew the 23rd and four nearby districts, including Doggett's 25th. The judges' map made Doggett's new district more compact and less Hispanic and added rural farming counties to his constituency. Because of his new agricultural interests, Doggett told the Austin American-Statesman that he supported the 2008 five-year rewrite of farm policy.

Born and raised in Austin, Doggett attended the University of Texas, where he was elected student body president. Within two years of earning his law degree in 1970, he won election to the state Senate and stayed until 1985. Colleagues knew he was ready to filibuster when he donned white leather tennis shoes, which kept him comfortable during long stints on his feet.

In 1984, he ran for the U.S. Senate, beating two veteran House members, Bob Krueger and Kent Hance, in the Democratic primary. But that November, he was crushed by GOP Rep. Phil Gramm. Four years later, Doggett won a seat on the Texas Supreme Court, which handles only civil cases. He was on the bench when 81-year-old Democratic Rep. J.J. Pickle announced his retirement in 1994.

Doggett was the first Democrat to announce his candidacy, and his quick start spared him a tough primary. Raising $1.2 million, he surmounted that year's GOP takeover tide and won by 16 percentage points over real estate consultant A. Jo Baylor. He has consistently won re-election by significant margins, even with his shifting districts. But he takes nothing for granted; in early 2009 he was among the House incumbents with the most campaign cash on hand — more than $2.7 million.

KEY VOTES

2008

Yes	Delay consideration of Colombia free-trade agreement
Yes	Override Bush veto of federal farm and nutrition programs reauthorization bill
No	Overhaul surveillance laws and permit dismissal of suits against companies that conducted warrantless wiretapping
Yes	Grant mortgage relief to homeowners and funding for Fannie Mae and Freddie Mac
No	Approve initial $700 billion program to stabilize financial markets
No	Approve final $700 billion program to stabilize financial markets
Yes	Provide $14 billion in loans to automakers

2007

Yes	Increase minimum wage by $2.10 an hour
Yes	Approve $124.2 billion in emergency war spending and set goal for redeployment of troops from Iraq
No	Reject federal contraceptive assistance to international family planning groups
Yes	Override Bush veto of $23.2 billion water projects authorization bill
Yes	Implement Peru free-trade agreement
Yes	Approve energy policy overhaul with new fuel economy standards
No	Clear $473.5 billion omnibus spending bill, including $70 billion for military operations

CQ VOTE STUDIES

	PARTY UNITY		PRESIDENTIAL SUPPORT	
	SUPPORT	OPPOSE	SUPPORT	OPPOSE
2008	97%	3%	11%	89%
2007	98%	2%	3%	97%
2006	97%	3%	21%	79%
2005	97%	3%	13%	87%
2004	95%	5%	27%	73%

INTEREST GROUPS

	AFL-CIO	ADA	CCUS	ACU
2008	100%	90%	50%	8%
2007	96%	95%	53%	4%
2006	92%	90%	23%	8%
2005	93%	90%	38%	4%
2004	93%	95%	39%	4%

TEXAS 25

South central — most of Austin

One of five Texas districts redrawn in 2006 by a federal court, the 25th is an Austin-dominated district that is much more compact than its 2004 antecedent, which stretched south in a narrow band from Austin to the Rio Grande River on the Mexican border.

More than 60 percent of district residents live in Travis County (Austin), nearly all of whom live within the city limits. The district takes in the southern portion of Travis, including Austin-Bergstrom International Airport. The economy here revolves around the University of Texas (located in the 21st), state government and the technology industry.

Austin's ties to the academic community and the public sector, coupled with its racial and ethnic diversity, give Travis, and thus the 25th District, a decidedly liberal tilt. Travis was the only one of Texas' 254 counties that voted against a state constitutional amendment banning same-sex marriage in November 2005.

Southwest of Travis lies Hays County, which was appended to the 25th in the 2006 remapping. Hays is growing rapidly: Its population increased by more than one-half between 2000 and 2008. Many of these new residents came from Travis County.

From Travis and Hays, the 25th fans southeast to scoop up less-populous areas. Bastrop County, located east of Austin, was added to the 25th in the 2006 remapping and has experienced robust population growth. Fayette, Gonzales, Lavaca and Colorado counties, which form the eastern half of the 25th, usually vote Republican — each gave John McCain at least a 30-percentage-point margin of victory over Barack Obama in the 2008 presidential election. But these conservative-leaning areas do not have the population to dislodge the 25th from its Democratic moorings — the district overall gave Obama 59 percent of its vote in 2008.

MAJOR INDUSTRY
Higher education, state government, technology, ranching, agriculture

CITIES
Austin (pt.), 358,434; San Marcos, 34,733; Lockhart, 11,615

NOTABLE
The Texas House deemed Lockhart the barbecue capital of Texas in 1999.

Rep. Michael C. Burgess (R)

Elected 2002; 4th term

CAPITOL OFFICE
225-7772
burgess.house.gov
229 Cannon Bldg. 20515-4326; fax 225-2919

COMMITTEES
Energy & Commerce
Joint Economic

RESIDENCE
Lewisville

BORN
Dec. 23, 1950; Rochester, Minn.

RELIGION
Episcopalian

FAMILY
Wife, Laura Burgess; three children

EDUCATION
North Texas State U., B.S. 1972 (biology), M.S.
1976 (physiology); U. of Texas Health Science
Center, Houston, M.D. 1977; U. of Texas
Southwestern Medical Center, Dallas,
M.S. 2000 (medical management)

CAREER
Physician

POLITICAL HIGHLIGHTS
No previous office

ELECTION RESULTS

2008 GENERAL

Michael C. Burgess (R)	195,181	60.2%
Ken Leach (D)	118,167	36.4%
Stephanie B. Weiss (LIBERT)	11,028	3.4%

2008 PRIMARY

Michael C. Burgess (R)	unopposed

2006 GENERAL

Michael C. Burgess (R)	94,219	60.2%
Tim Barnwell (D)	58,271	37.2%
Rich Haas (LIBERT)	3,993	2.6%

PREVIOUS WINNING PERCENTAGES
2004 (66%); 2002 (75%)

Burgess is a physician, like his forebears, and his background informs his views on health care. An obstetrician-gynecologist from the Republican Party's conservative wing, he is a relentless advocate of free-market solutions to the nation's health system woes.

Burgess' vote is just as reliably conservative on other issues. He pushes for a flat tax, generally supports free-trade agreements, and opposes abortion and embryonic stem cell research. His adherence to conservative principles led him to mount an unsuccessful challenge to Michigan's Thaddeus McCotter for the Republican Policy Committee chairmanship in November 2008 following his party's weak showing at the polls. "The GOP has always been a party of ideas; it's time we recapture that designation," he said in a statement.

Burgess sits on the Energy and Commerce Health Subcommittee, which began preparing in 2009 to tackle health care reform legislation. He was appointed to a GOP group charged with devising an alternative health care overhaul. He promotes longstanding GOP mainstays such as curbing medical-malpractice lawsuits, expanding the private sector's role in Medicare and tightening income eligibility for children to be covered by the State Children's Health Insurance Program.

Burgess fought Democratic efforts to expand the program, though they ultimately prevailed in early 2009 on a bill similar to two measures President George W. Bush vetoed. Burgess was particularly upset Democrats didn't restrict the program's access to illegal immigrants and loosened identity check and enrollment requirements in order to get more kids into the program. "You have to show your ID before you cash a check at the grocery store," Burgess said. "Why should we not require someone to show identification before they sign up for this benefit?"

On another health care issue — Medicare payments for physicians — Burgess aligned with Democrats in 2008. He joined in the successful override of Bush's veto of legislation that blocked a scheduled cut in Medicare payments to doctors. He warned that patient care would suffer if doctors get squeezed out of practice by shrinking Medicare payments and the costs of malpractice insurance. In 2008, the House passed his bill to create a loan program for hospitals to establish residency programs to train physicians in several specialties — primary care, emergency care, obstetrics and gynecology.

In the 110th Congress (2007-08), he worked with Texas Democrat Gene Green to push through the House a bill that became law to authorize $46 million over five years in matching grants to help develop state trauma networks.

But he didn't go for a 2009 Democratic bill to give the Food and Drug Administration broader powers to regulate nicotine, saying the agency was already spread too thin and didn't have the resources. He lamented that the House rejected his alternative to give the FDA power to ban nicotine entirely. "Giving the FDA the power to reduce nicotine levels to zero would be the single-most important tool we could provide the agency to control this dangerous product," he said.

He did get the House's support in March 2009 for a bill to require that people signing up for a health plan receive in writing an explanation of treatment limits or non-covered conditions, along with other plan restrictions, "in a form that is easily understandable."

Another of his priorities is reining in medical-malpractice suits, which to him is "an issue of fundamental fairness." Burgess, who estimates he has delivered more than 3,000 babies, was sued in the late 1980s by a family whose baby died during a difficult C-section. He was not in charge of the delivery, he said, but was called in to assist another obstetrician. He said the incident helped convince him the medical liability system needed to be overhauled.

Burgess holds both a commercial driver's license and a pilot's license. He's also a biker, something his aides didn't know until Burgess told them he wanted to do an event promoting motorcycle safety. "As a doctor, I've been in plenty of emergency rooms and trauma centers. Take it from me: You don't want to be involved in a crash of any kind, especially one involving a motorcycle," Burgess said at the May 2008 event. He introduced a bipartisan bill to fix a loophole in the law that allows insurers to deny payment for injuries resulting from recreational activities such as motorcycling.

Burgess also holds a seat on the Energy and Commerce panel on Energy and the Environment, which is charged with addressing climate change legislation. He supports conservation and the promotion of alternative-energy sources, but also backs drilling for oil in Alaska's Arctic National Wildlife Refuge "or any other federal lands where geologic data supports exploration."

Burgess has gone against his party on issues other than health care. In 2004, he voted against an intelligence overhaul that had been recommended by the independent, bipartisan commission that investigated the Sept. 11 terrorist attacks. He sided with F. James Sensenbrenner Jr. of Wisconsin, then-chairman of the Judiciary Committee, who said the bill didn't do enough to improve border security. Burgess was frustrated by the lack of action on immigration policy in the 110th, calling it "an abdication of responsibility."

Burgess stuck with his party in opposing President Obama's early economic agenda, however, including a $787 billion economic stimulus law that he said wouldn't offer any reprieve from the recession.

Burgess' grandfather was an obstetrician who worked at the Royal Victoria Hospital in Montreal. His father, Harry "Tim" Burgess, a general surgeon, moved to the United States to get away from Canada's government-run health care system. His sister is a nurse; his brother is a pathologist. "It's in my DNA," he said of medicine.

He had no prior political experience when he ran for former House Majority Leader Dick Armey's seat. To take his place, Burgess had to defeat the nine-term lawmaker's son, Scott Armey, in the 2002 primary. The district had just been redrawn to favor the younger Armey, who finished first in the six-way primary but faced a runoff. Burgess campaigned against him by handing out literature declaring, "My dad is not Dick Armey," and prevailed in the runoff with 55 percent of the vote. He won easily that November in the solidly GOP district. He has won re-election easily since.

KEY VOTES

2008
?	Delay consideration of Colombia free-trade agreement
No	Override Bush veto of federal farm and nutrition programs reauthorization bill
Yes	Overhaul surveillance laws and permit dismissal of suits against companies that conducted warrantless wiretapping
No	Grant mortgage relief to homeowners and funding for Fannie Mae and Freddie Mac
No	Approve initial $700 billion program to stabilize financial markets
No	Approve final $700 billion program to stabilize financial markets
No	Provide $14 billion in loans to automakers

2007
No	Increase minimum wage by $2.10 an hour
No	Approve $124.2 billion in emergency war spending and set goal for redeployment of troops from Iraq
Yes	Reject federal contraceptive assistance to international family planning groups
Yes	Override Bush veto of $23.2 billion water projects authorization bill
No	Implement Peru free-trade agreement
No	Approve energy policy overhaul with new fuel economy standards
Yes	Clear $473.5 billion omnibus spending bill, including $70 billion for military operations

CQ VOTE STUDIES

	PARTY UNITY		PRESIDENTIAL SUPPORT	
	SUPPORT	OPPOSE	SUPPORT	OPPOSE
2008	94%	6%	73%	27%
2007	94%	6%	82%	18%
2006	93%	7%	87%	13%
2005	97%	3%	89%	11%
2004	96%	4%	88%	12%

INTEREST GROUPS

	AFL-CIO	ADA	CCUS	ACU
2008	14%	10%	76%	96%
2007	8%	10%	74%	100%
2006	21%	5%	92%	83%
2005	13%	0%	88%	96%
2004	20%	5%	100%	96%

TEXAS 26

Eastern Fort Worth and suburbs; most of Denton County

The 26th stretches north from southeastern Fort Worth and its surrounding suburbs to take in almost all of Denton County and the eastern part of rural Cooke County. The district's economy depends mainly on transportation, with many white-collar industries providing jobs.

The heart of the district is fast-growing Denton County, the southern part of which is filled with burgeoning upper-middle-class Dallas-Fort Worth suburbs. Time Warner Cable has large facilities here, and education and technology are important. The University of North Texas engineering program emphasizes nanotech research and applications. Parts of the expansive Barnett Shale natural gas reservoir are located in Denton, and drilling provides thousands of jobs to the region.

Roughly 45 percent of residents live in Fort Worth and its Tarrant County suburbs, mainly in middle-class areas such as North Richland Hills. The 26th also grabs Forest Hill and Everman, areas south of downtown with large black populations. Much of Cooke is agricultural, relying mostly on cattle and dairy farms, with oat and wheat farms as well.

The area's interstates and highways carry the district's commuters to jobs elsewhere in the region. The 26th includes a small part of Dallas-Fort Worth International Airport, and Fort Worth Alliance Airport (shared with the 12th) was the nation's first airport to be built specifically to serve business needs. Bell Helicopter Textron's headquarters is in Hurst, although the company was hit by recent financial downturns.

Voters here support Republicans, and presidential candidate John McCain won 58 percent of the district's vote in 2008.

MAJOR INDUSTRY
Transportation, telecommunications

CITIES
Fort Worth (pt.), 153,549; Denton, 80,537; Lewisville (pt.), 58,106; North Richland Hills (pt.), 55,445; Flower Mound, 50,702; Hurst (pt.), 30,832

NOTABLE
The Texas Motor Speedway is in Denton County; The town council in Clark changed the town's name to DISH in 2005 to win 10 years of free basic satellite television from DISH Network for all 125 residents.

Rep. Solomon P. Ortiz (D)

Elected 1982; 14th term

Ortiz, one of the most senior members of the House, is a soft-spoken moderate. He leans conservative on social issues, opposing same-sex marriage. Yet he calls himself progressive on economic issues, hailing from a district that is home to many people in need of better educational and employment opportunities and health care services.

His allegiance is to the thousands of voters who work in his district's military installations and reside along the U.S.-Mexico border. The senior Democrat in the Texas House delegation, he is well-placed to help the civilians and military personnel in his district from his post on the Armed Services Committee, where he is the third-most-senior Democrat and the chairman of the Readiness Subcommittee. And he holds a seat on the powerful Transportation and Infrastructure Committee, where he can target funding for projects to aid the local economy.

The 27th District, which stretches wide along the Gulf of Mexico from Corpus Christi to Brownsville, is home to one Army and three Navy facilities. Much to Ortiz's disappointment, Naval Station Ingleside is slated for closure by 2011 — although plans are under way for redevelopment — and the number of employees at the Corpus Christi Naval Air Station is also scheduled to decline. Nonetheless, the defense facilities still largely define the district's identity and, to a large extent, Ortiz's.

He has drawn attention to the wear and tear on equipment and people caused by the wars in Iraq and Afghanistan. He talks about "a broken military" whose troops are staggering from multiple deployments, training difficulties and equipment bottlenecks. The depots in his district and elsewhere are critical to readiness because they keep equipment up to standards. But Ortiz has lamented that the facilities and their workers are struggling to keep pace with the volume of military hardware returning from Iraq for servicing.

In 2007, he helped write the defense authorization bill, which shifted funds from futuristic military modernization programs toward what Congress considered the more-pressing needs of U.S. troops and their families, including maintenance accounts and pay raises. In 2008, Ortiz lauded another defense authorization that called for $10.4 billion to repair and rebuild Army and Marine Corps equipment. "However," he said, "there is much work to be done."

Ortiz fights for the public employees who work at the military facilities in his district and beyond by resisting the Pentagon's attempts to outsource an increasing amount of the work done by civilian Defense employees.

As a young man, Ortiz served in the Army's military police, which set him on his path to a career in law enforcement and government. He has since looked out for military personnel and their families. He visits the families of killed and wounded soldiers from his district. He said many of those families are too poor to travel to the veterans' hospital in San Antonio, a two-and-a-half-hour drive from Corpus Christi and six or more hours from the Rio Grande Valley. He has long worked to get a VA hospital in South Texas.

In 2009 he picked up his seat on the Transportation panel, which was expected to take up a renewal of the surface transportation law. Early that year he accompanied Chairman James L. Oberstar of Minnesota on a visit to the 27th District, bringing some high-profile attention to the need for a new harbor bridge at Corpus Christi, estimated to cost $870 million. Ortiz applauded Obama's economic stimulus law of 2009 for including funding for transportation and infrastructure projects, as well as for health care, educa-

CAPITOL OFFICE
225-7742
www.house.gov/ortiz
2110 Rayburn Bldg. 20515-4327; fax 226-1134

COMMITTEES
Armed Services
 (Readiness - chairman)
Transportation & Infrastructure

RESIDENCE
Corpus Christi

BORN
June 3, 1937; Robstown, Texas

RELIGION
Methodist

FAMILY
Divorced; two children

EDUCATION
Institute of Applied Science, attended 1962;
Del Mar College, attended 1965-67

MILITARY SERVICE
Army, 1960-62

CAREER
Law enforcement official

POLITICAL HIGHLIGHTS
Nueces County constable, 1965-69; Nueces County Commission, 1969-77; Nueces County sheriff, 1977-83

ELECTION RESULTS

2008 GENERAL

Solomon P. Ortiz (D)	104,864	58.0%
William "Willie" Vaden (R)	69,458	38.4%
Robert E. Powell (LIBERT)	6,629	3.7%

2008 PRIMARY

Solomon P. Ortiz (D)	unopposed

2006 GENERAL

Solomon P. Ortiz (D)	62,058	56.8%
William "Willie" Vaden (R)	42,538	38.9%
Robert E. Powell (LIBERT)	4,718	4.3%

PREVIOUS WINNING PERCENTAGES
2004 (63%); 2002 (61%); 2000 (63%); 1998 (63%); 1996 (65%); 1994 (59%); 1992 (55%); 1990 (100%); 1988 (100%); 1986 (100%); 1984 (64%); 1982 (64%)

tion, housing assistance and energy-efficiency upgrades.

He sought Obama's help on another issue: halting construction of a 700-mile fence along the border with Mexico. Ortiz, who is the founder of the Congressional Border Caucus, joined several colleagues in the state delegation, along with Democrat Susan A. Davis of California, in a letter to the president early in 2009, stating: "In an era of advanced technologies, the border fence is an antiquated structure that has torn our communities apart and damaged our cross-border relationships."

With a drug war just across the border in Mexico, Ortiz was gratified by Obama's visits and his pledges to boost border security. But Ortiz told the Brownsville Herald that Americans need to be educated on how their drug use helps fund the drug cartels responsible for the violence.

Ortiz supported many of his party's initiatives in early 2009, including a bill to expand hate crime law to cover victims of violence due to their sexual preference or gender. But at times his votes are a bit unpredictable. In 2007, he was one of 59 House Democrats to oppose a bill to require a withdrawal of U.S. troops from Iraq by a certain date. But then he voted for a war funding bill that set a goal, not a requirement, for extricating U.S. forces.

In May 2008, he was the only Democrat on the Natural Resources panel to support drilling for oil in Alaska's Arctic National Wildlife Refuge. In 2005, he was one of only 15 Democrats to side with Republicans in approving the Central America Free Trade Agreement. And in fall 2008, he initially voted against a $700 billion law to help the ailing financial services industry. He supported a slightly revised version, although he said he didn't think it would be the "ultimate solution to our economic woes."

The child of a migrant family, Ortiz grew up poor near Corpus Christi, working a variety of odd jobs to help his family. His father died when he was 16. He then dropped out of high school and later joined the Army. "It was the one place that would give me free room and board and let me send my check back home to my mother," he recalled.

Ortiz left the Army in 1962 and two years later waged his first political campaign, defeating the incumbent Nueces County constable. In 1968, he became the first Hispanic elected to the county commission; in 1976, he was the first Hispanic to win election as county sheriff. A three-judge federal panel in charge of redistricting created the 27th District with a 60 percent Hispanic majority in 1982. He won the seat with 64 percent of the vote.

His district's boundaries haven't changed much since, and he typically cruises to victory with nearly 60 percent. His closest race was in 1992 when he took just 55 percent.

KEY VOTES

2008

Yes Delay consideration of Colombia free-trade agreement

Yes Override Bush veto of federal farm and nutrition programs reauthorization bill

Yes Overhaul surveillance laws and permit dismissal of suits against companies that conducted warrantless wiretapping

? Grant mortgage relief to homeowners and funding for Fannie Mae and Freddie Mac

No Approve initial $700 billion program to stabilize financial markets

Yes Approve final $700 billion program to stabilize financial markets

Yes Provide $14 billion in loans to automakers

2007

Yes Increase minimum wage by $2.10 an hour

Yes Approve $124.2 billion in emergency war spending and set goal for redeployment of troops from Iraq

? Reject federal contraceptive assistance to international family planning groups

Yes Override Bush veto of $23.2 billion water projects authorization bill

Yes Implement Peru free-trade agreement

+ Approve energy policy overhaul with new fuel economy standards

+ Clear $473.5 billion omnibus spending bill, including $70 billion for military operations

CQ VOTE STUDIES

	PARTY UNITY		PRESIDENTIAL SUPPORT	
	SUPPORT	OPPOSE	SUPPORT	OPPOSE
2008	95%	5%	27%	73%
2007	96%	4%	7%	93%
2006	76%	24%	57%	43%
2005	78%	22%	45%	55%
2004	83%	17%	47%	53%

INTEREST GROUPS

	AFL-CIO	ADA	CCUS	ACU
2008	100%	75%	65%	17%
2007	96%	80%	71%	10%
2006	100%	65%	80%	40%
2005	87%	70%	70%	40%
2004	93%	55%	47%	28%

TEXAS 27

Southern Gulf Coast — Corpus Christi, Brownsville

Anchored by Corpus Christi in the north, the 27th runs south to the Rio Grande River, with the Gulf of Mexico on its eastern coast. Ranches, as well as industries tied to the coast, are the mainstays between the two largest cities, Corpus Christi and Brownsville, which together take in nearly two-thirds of the 27th's population. Just north of Corpus Christi, the 27th also takes in more than half of San Patricio County's population.

Farther south, in the Rio Grande Valley, the port city of Brownsville struggles with an influx of illegal immigrants, drug smuggling and high poverty, but new manufacturing plants and *maquiladoras* — plants in Mexico that use low-cost labor and import many parts from the U.S. — have helped. Visitors from Mexico boost Brownsville's retail sectors, and ecotourism adds to the economy, luring bird- and turtle-watchers to local wetlands.

Corpus Christi relies on tourism, with oil and gas as other important industries. Petrochemical refining, also found up and down the coast, is

more common here, as is the storing and shipping of wind turbines out of the port. The area's military facilities are key to the region's economic health, and the 2005 BRAC round dealt the area a blow by ordering Naval Station Ingleside closed by 2011 and by reducing forces at the Corpus Christi naval air station. Rising energy prices have hurt companies tied to transportation and manufacturing.

The Hispanic-majority district (68 percent) supports Democrats, but the 27th's Democratic lean is not overwhelming — Barack Obama won 53 percent of the district's 2008 presidential vote.

MAJOR INDUSTRY
Manufacturing, trade, tourism, military, petrochemicals

MILITARY BASES
Naval Air Station Corpus Christi, 1,800 military, 2,700 civilian; Corpus Christi Army Depot, 12 military, 3,315 civilian (2004); Naval Station Ingleside, 2,559 military, 224 civilian (2006); Naval Air Station Kingsville, 754 military, 1,210 civilian (2004)

CITIES
Corpus Christi, 277,454; Brownsville, 139,722; Kingsville, 25,575

NOTABLE
Padre Island National Seashore runs most of the district's length.

Rep. Henry Cuellar (D)

Elected 2004; 3rd term

Pragmatism and accountability are the keys to Cuellar's work in Congress. He is one of the most conservative members of the Democratic Caucus, but he would rather work quietly behind the scenes than call attention to his differences with the more-liberal views of most House Democrats. And Cuellar wants to ensure government agencies and programs are held accountable for producing results.

His voting record in his first two terms on Capitol Hill shows Cuellar (KWAY-are) was among the two dozen least loyal Democrats on issues that split the two parties. Likewise, his support of President George W. Bush was among the highest posted by a House Democrat — no real stretch for a man who endorsed Bush, then governor of Texas, for the presidency in 2000 and took a plum job the next year as Texas secretary of state under Bush's successor, Republican Gov. Rick Perry.

His socially conservative bent can be explained in part by the influence of his Roman Catholic religion. Representing a largely Hispanic and poor constituency, he opposes abortion and gay marriage but is pro-immigration. A member of the fiscally conservative Blue Dog Coalition, Cuellar casts a generally pro-business vote.

Pragmatism is evident in his legislative work as well, as he focuses on issues important to his constituents, sometimes pushing for incremental changes. On the Agriculture Committee, he worked with Chairman Collin C. Peterson of Minnesota to win inclusion in the 2008 farm law of a funding authorization for a program to eradicate cattle tick fever, a major problem for South Texas ranchers. And he applauded the increase in funding for nutrition programs that help impoverished residents along the Texas border.

Cuellar looks out for his border district from the Homeland Security panel, where he chairs the Subcommittee on Emergency Communications. He has opposed construction of a border fence aimed at reducing illegal immigration, a measure he calls a "12th-century solution to a 21st-century problem." Instead, Cuellar argues the federal government should think of lower-cost solutions, such as removing invasive Carrizo cane that makes it difficult for sensors and cameras to operate.

As comprehensive immigration reform continued to stall, Cuellar, a member of the Hispanic Caucus, urged for the 111th Congress (2009-10) to complete an overhaul. "Right now, practically speaking, we have to focus on the economy. But immigration is a part of that — and addressing it can have an impact there," he said in March 2009.

He has sought additional funding for attorneys and support staff aimed at reducing the backlog of immigration and drug cases along the border. He praised the Obama administration's announcement that it would hire a "border czar," but also pushed for a federal agency to coordinate efforts on the border.

Cuellar also sits on the Oversight and Government Reform Committee. He has earned a number of advanced degrees, including a doctorate in government; his dissertation was on performance-based budgeting. "We should always measure for results, and not activity," he said.

In his accountability efforts, Cuellar, who grew up speaking Spanish at home, won approval of an amendment to a Head Start bill requiring program administrators to provide more understandable assessments of their progress in teaching English as a second language. He also won passage of a bill to require the government to develop performance measures and standards

CAPITOL OFFICE
225-1640
www.house.gov/cuellar
336 Cannon Bldg. 20515-4328; fax 225-1641

COMMITTEES
Agriculture
Homeland Security
(Emergency Communications - chairman)
Oversight & Government Reform

RESIDENCE
Laredo

BORN
Sept. 19, 1955; Laredo, Texas

RELIGION
Roman Catholic

FAMILY
Wife, Imelda Cuellar; two children

EDUCATION
Laredo Community College, A.A. 1976
(political science); Georgetown U., B.S.F.S. 1978;
U. of Texas, J.D. 1981; Laredo State U., M.B.A.
1982 (international trade); U. of Texas, Ph.D. 1998
(government)

CAREER
Lawyer; international trade firm owner

POLITICAL HIGHLIGHTS
Texas House, 1987-2001; Texas secretary of state,
2001; Democratic nominee for U.S. House, 2002

ELECTION RESULTS

2008 GENERAL

Henry Cuellar (D)	123,494	68.7%
Jim Fish (R)	52,524	29.2%
Ross Lynn Leone (LIBERT)	3,722	2.1%

2008 PRIMARY

Henry Cuellar (D)	unopposed

2006 GENERAL

Henry Cuellar (D)	52,574	67.6%
Frank Enriquez (D)	15,798	20.3%
Ron Avery (C)	9,383	12.1%

PREVIOUS WINNING PERCENTAGES
2004 (59%)

determine whether agencies are providing high-quality customer service, nd he was able to amend another measure to require a report to Congress n the effectiveness of a hotline that receives reports of child abuse.

Lack of accountability was one reason he cited for voting against the itial financial industry rescue bill in fall 2008. But a few days later, he voted r the second iteration of the package which became law, noting that "we ow have a new and improved bill that does not give the administration a lank check for $700 billion." And he backed President Obama's $787 billion conomic stimulus law, saying, "We're facing a once-in-a-lifetime crisis that emands a once-in-a-lifetime response."

Cuellar was the eldest of eight children born to migrant workers with nly an elementary school education. But they insisted their children obtain n education, and he went on to earn law and business degrees in addition o his doctorate in government.

He was elected to the Texas House in 1986, at 31, and served there 4 years. He was appointed Texas secretary of state in early 2001, but he esigned later that year to prepare for a 2002 campaign against Republican ep. Henry Bonilla in Texas' 23rd District. He lost by just a little more than percentage points.

In 2004, a new GOP-drawn congressional map moved part of Webb ounty (Laredo), Cuellar's base, to the 28th District, a heavily Hispanic and rimarily San Antonio-based district that had been represented since 1997 y Democrat Ciro D. Rodriguez. Cuellar challenged Rodriguez in the pri-ary, even though Rodriguez had backed Cuellar's 2002 campaign against onilla. Cuellar eked out a narrow win that was certified only after a series f recounts, lawsuits and accusations of voting fraud.

Rodriguez was back to challenge Cuellar in 2006. Liberal activists and bor unions sided with Rodriguez and circulated a photograph of Bush ffectionately taking Cuellar's face in his hands after the 2006 State of the Jnion address. But Cuellar, touting his accessibility and ability to bring fed-ral funds to the district, won the primary by almost 13 percentage points.

No Republican opposed Cuellar in the 2006 general election, but he had o wage another campaign after a federal court in August redrew his district nd four others to comply with a Supreme Court decision partially invalidat-g the Texas map.

The new map strengthened Cuellar by including all of Webb County in ne 28th District. He won 68 percent in a special November election. (Rodri-uez, meanwhile, took advantage of the second chance and unseated Bonil-in the adjacent 23rd District.) Cuellar slightly bettered that total in 2008.

KEY VOTES

2008
No Delay consideration of Colombia free-trade agreement
Yes Override Bush veto of federal farm and nutrition programs reauthorization bill
Yes Overhaul surveillance laws and permit dismissal of suits against companies that conducted warrantless wiretapping
Yes Grant mortgage relief to homeowners and funding for Fannie Mae and Freddie Mac
No Approve initial $700 billion program to stabilize financial markets
Yes Approve final $700 billion program to stabilize financial markets
Yes Provide $14 billion in loans to automakers

2007
Yes Increase minimum wage by $2.10 an hour
Yes Approve $124.2 billion in emergency war spending and set goal for redeployment of troops from Iraq
No Reject federal contraceptive assistance to international family planning groups
Yes Override Bush veto of $23.2 billion water projects authorization bill
Yes Implement Peru free-trade agreement
Yes Approve energy policy overhaul with new fuel economy standards
Yes Clear $473.5 billion omnibus spending bill, including $70 billion for military operations

CQ VOTE STUDIES

	PARTY UNITY		PRESIDENTIAL SUPPORT	
	SUPPORT	OPPOSE	SUPPORT	OPPOSE
2008	94%	6%	30%	70%
2007	88%	12%	16%	84%
2006	63%	37%	85%	15%
2005	70%	30%	57%	43%

INTEREST GROUPS

	AFL-CIO	ADA	CCUS	ACU
2008	87%	80%	72%	12%
2007	92%	90%	70%	20%
2006	64%	35%	100%	68%
2005	60%	70%	89%	52%

TEXAS 28
outh central — Laredo; part of McAllen

ebb and Hidalgo counties on the Mexican border are the two major opulation hubs in the 28th, a heavily Hispanic and Democratic-leaning strict that also skims north along Interstate 35 to take in a sliver of Bexar ounty northeast of San Antonio, including Randolph Air Force Base.

bout 30 percent of district residents live in Webb, where international ade is crucial for Laredo, the nation's largest inland port of entry and here the population has grown by more than 20 percent since 2000. rucking is key to Laredo's economy, and peanuts, cotton, sorghum, car-ots and beef dominate the region's agricultural market. Federal efforts to tem drug-related border violence have put a spotlight on Laredo, and ew border crossing rules may cause delays at Laredo bridges.

nother 30 percent of the 28th's population lives in Hidalgo County, nother fast-growing area where the district takes in nearly half of lcAllen and almost all of Mission. Like Webb, the 28th's share of Hidalgo he county is shared with the 15th) is overwhelmingly Hispanic. West of idalgo, Starr County is the nation's most heavily Hispanic county

(97.5 percent). At 77.5 percent, the 28th is the third-most heavily Hispanic district in the nation, just behind Texas' 16th and 15th districts. Hidalgo and Starr also are among the most economically depressed counties in the nation, and the 28th overall has a greater share of families below the poverty line than any other Texas district. But the economy is starting to show improvement as the number of small businesses rises.

Republican votes in Guadalupe, McMullen and Wilson counties to the north cannot counter the strongly Democratic southern counties. In the 2008 presidential race, Starr gave Barack Obama 85 percent, his highest percentage statewide, and Jim Hogg and Webb counties gave Obama his seventh- and eighth-highest margins of victory. The district gave Obama 56 percent of its vote overall in 2008.

MAJOR INDUSTRY
Agriculture, international trade, defense

MILITARY BASES
Randolph Air Force Base, 4,178 military, 4,000 civilian (2006)

CITIES
Laredo, 176,576; McAllen (pt.), 44,756; Mission (pt.), 42,721; Seguin, 22,011

NOTABLE
The "streets of Laredo" inspired titles for a cowboy ballad and a novel.

Rep. Gene Green (D)

Elected 1992; 9th term

The folksy Green juggles a mix of interests in his working-class, largely Hispanic district, which can sometimes lead him astray of his party. He is a classic liberal on some issues, a business advocate on others, but always a Texan to the bone. Democratic leaders understand the sometimes contradictory needs of his constituents and appreciate that he doesn't run around touting his disagreements with the party.

He sees areas to work with Republicans in energy and health care policy, two prime issues for him from his seat on the Energy and Commerce Committee. Unlike most Democrats, he seeks to protect the oil and gas industry, long prominent in Texas. He is generally a social conservative, but unites with his party on most spending, tax and trade policies.

Green for several years pushed Congress to open all U.S. offshore areas to drilling, and he and Republicans won a sweeping victory when an offshore drilling moratorium was dropped from the stopgap spending bill passed in September 2008. Although many Democrats vowed to try to reinstate the ban in 2009, policy experts said it was unlikely ever to be reinstated wholesale.

He faces a harder task during the 111th Congress (2009-10) in helping negotiate with Democratic leaders on climate change legislation likely to include some form of a "cap and trade" plan for greenhouse gas emissions. Green hopes to at least gain for the oil industry a free allocation of 5 percent of the available emissions permits under such a plan. He also supports research into environmental improvements for producing oil and gas, developing clean coal power, and newer renewable-energy technologies like wind power.

Green said in 2009 that his is a lonely voice in negotiations. "It's tough," he said. "We don't have near as many Democrats as we need from oil states."

In mid-2008, Democratic leaders tapped him to chair Energy and Commerce's panel on Environment and Hazardous Materials, replacing Maryland Democrat Albert R. Wynn, who resigned from Congress. Within six weeks of taking the helm, Green persuaded the Chemical Safety and Hazard Investigation Board to determine the cause of a fatal explosion at the Houston Goodyear plant. The board initially said it lacked the resources to do so, but it relented after pressure from Green. He did not return as chairman in 2009 after his panel was merged with another subcommittee.

Green also has worked with Republicans on health care. Early in 2007, he teamed with Republican and fellow Texan Michael C. Burgess, a physician, to pass a bill to upgrade states' trauma care systems. It was a victory Green had sought for years, since he heard about a man who was seriously injured in a car accident and could not get treatment at an overcrowded Houston trauma center. The man had to be taken to Austin, where he died the next day.

In 2008, Green won enactment of legislation to expand community clinics and to attack the spread of tuberculosis, a border health problem. He also sponsored legislation to eliminate a two-year waiting period for people designated as too ill or disabled to work to qualify for Medicare coverage.

Green also tends to constituent needs through his annual Immunization Day, which provides free vaccinations to children, and Citizenship Day, which helps legal immigrants obtain citizenship. Both efforts help cement the support of voters in his Hispanic-majority district.

When Hurricane Ike slammed the Texas coast and the Houston area in 2008, Green criticized the response of the Federal Emergency Management Agency and said Congress should revisit the idea of making FEMA an independent agency that answers directly to the president.

CAPITOL OFFICE
225-1688
www.house.gov/green
2372 Rayburn Bldg. 20515-4329; fax 225-9903

COMMITTEES
Standards of Official Conduct Rangel Inquiry
 - chairman)
Energy & Commerce
Foreign Affairs

RESIDENCE
Houston

BORN
Oct. 17, 1947; Houston, Texas

RELIGION
Methodist

FAMILY
Wife, Helen Albers Green; two children

EDUCATION
U. of Houston, B.B.A. 1971; Bates College of Law, attended 1971-77

CAREER
Lawyer

POLITICAL HIGHLIGHTS
Texas House, 1973-85; Texas Senate, 1985-92

ELECTION RESULTS

2008 GENERAL
Gene Green (D)	79,718	74.6%
Eric Story (R)	25,512	23.9%
Joel Grace (LIBERT)	1,564	1.5%

2008 PRIMARY
Gene Green (D)	unopposed

2006 GENERAL
Gene Green (D)	37,174	73.5%
Eric Story (R)	12,347	24.4%
Clifford Lee Messina (LIBERT)	1,029	2.0%

PREVIOUS WINNING PERCENTAGES
2004 (94%); 2002 (95%); 2000 (73%); 1998 (93%); 1996 (68%); 1994 (73%); 1992 (65%)

Green served his three-term limit on the ethics panel, but during the retained his role as chairman of an investigative panel looking into the financial dealings of Ways and Means Chairman Charles B. Rangel, a veteran New York Democrat. Green had also served at the end of 2008 as acting chairman of the full committee after Ohio Democrat Stephanie Tubbs Jones died of a brain aneurysm in August 2008.

He also sits on the Foreign Affairs Committee. In July 2008, he and other members of the Texas delegation met with Pakistani President Pervez Musharraf — before Musharraf's August resignation — and Prime Minister Yusaf Raza Gillani to urge further action against Islamic militants after violent attacks against U.S. forces in Afghanistan dramatically increased.

Green votes with his party more often than most white Southern Democrats, but party leaders can't take him for granted. He has voted for Republican-sponsored legislation to toughen criminal penalties for violent juvenile offenders and to overhaul public housing policies. He joins with Republicans in opposing new clean air standards and he generally opposes gun control proposals. He has sided with social conservatives to support the display of the Ten Commandments in public schools and government buildings.

But he supported President Obama's $787 billion economic stimulus law, as well as his $3.56 trillion budget blueprint for fiscal 2010 — only after cautioning the Budget Committee not to hinder oil and natural gas production through any tax changes.

He voted against President George W. Bush's tax cuts of 2001 and 2003. He also voted against the North American Free Trade Agreement in 1993, despite support for it from Houston's business community, and he opposed the Central America Free Trade Agreement in 2005. He voted against a Peru free-trade pact in 2007 "because of the jobs issue," he explained.

Born, raised and educated in Houston, Green grew up in an area called "Redneck Alley," home to mostly working-class whites. He attended the University of Houston where he obtained a degree in business administration. While attending law school, he won a seat in the Texas Legislature, where he served for nearly two decades before he made a bid for Congress in 1992.

He won a hard-fought five-way primary in a district that was drawn after the 1990 census to enhance the political power of Houston's growing Hispanic population. He bested Houston City Council member Ben Reyes in two runoffs; the first was voided after election officials found some Republicans had illegally crossed over and cast ballots. Green won the general election with 65 percent of the vote, defeated Reyes in a 1994 primary rematch and has won easily since then.

KEY VOTES

2008

Yes Delay consideration of Colombia free-trade agreement

Yes Override Bush veto of federal farm and nutrition programs reauthorization bill

Yes Overhaul surveillance laws and permit dismissal of suits against companies that conducted warrantless wiretapping

+ Grant mortgage relief to homeowners and funding for Fannie Mae and Freddie Mac

No Approve initial $700 billion program to stabilize financial markets

No Approve final $700 billion program to stabilize financial markets

Yes Provide $14 billion in loans to automakers

2007

Yes Increase minimum wage by $2.10 an hour

Yes Approve $124.2 billion in emergency war spending and set goal for redeployment of troops from Iraq

No Reject federal contraceptive assistance to international family planning groups

Yes Override Bush veto of $23.2 billion water projects authorization bill

No Implement Peru free-trade agreement

Yes Approve energy policy overhaul with new fuel economy standards

Yes Clear $473.5 billion omnibus spending bill, including $70 billion for military operations

CQ VOTE STUDIES

	PARTY UNITY		PRESIDENTIAL SUPPORT	
	SUPPORT	OPPOSE	SUPPORT	OPPOSE
2008	94%	6%	26%	74%
2007	94%	6%	7%	93%
2006	84%	16%	43%	57%
2005	82%	18%	35%	65%
2004	87%	13%	27%	73%

INTEREST GROUPS

	AFL-CIO	ADA	CCUS	ACU
2008	100%	80%	59%	26%
2007	100%	95%	63%	12%
2006	100%	85%	50%	33%
2005	100%	100%	48%	28%
2004	93%	85%	45%	20%

TEXAS 29

Part of Houston and eastern suburbs – most of Pasadena and Baytown

The blue-collar, Hispanic-majority 29th arcs from northern to southeastern Houston, with an eastern tail that extends to Baytown. The district is full of refineries and factories that employ union workers who help provide a solid Democratic lean, despite traditionally poor voter turnout in the Hispanic community. The district gave Barack Obama 62 percent of its 2008 presidential vote.

The 29th includes one-fifth of Harris County's population, and slightly more than half of the district's residents live in Houston. It takes in most of the Houston Ship Channel, which still handles high levels of foreign and domestic traffic despite a drop-off during the recession, and picks up most of middle-class Channelview. The heart of Houston's petrochemical complex is along the channel, which has caused concern among residents about possible health effects of living so close to an industrial corridor. Global oversupply of petrochemicals has hurt the local industry, and Hurricane Ike temporarily shut down the channel in 2008.

The 29th also includes working-class areas outside of the Interstate 610 loop such as Jacinto City, Galena Park, South Houston and much of Pasadena (shared with the 22nd) and Baytown (shared with the 2nd). Residents in these areas have seen widespread factory layoffs.

Hispanics make up more than two-thirds of the district's population. The heaviest concentrations of Hispanics are in South Houston, Jacinto City, Houston and Pasadena. According to 2000 census data, nearly one-fourth of district residents are not U.S. citizens, the highest percentage in Texas, and 60 percent speak a language other than English at home.

The 29th has the largest blue-collar workforce and the lowest high school graduation rate in Texas. One-third of district residents are age 17 or under, the highest percentage in the state.

MAJOR INDUSTRY
Petrochemicals, energy, shipping, construction

CITIES
Houston (pt.), 334,766; Pasadena (pt.), 84,654; Baytown (pt.), 35,003

NOTABLE
The Battleship Texas, docked at the San Jacinto Battleground state park, became the nation's first battleship memorial museum in 1948.

Rep. Eddie Bernice Johnson (D)

Elected 1992; 9th term

CAPITOL OFFICE
225-8885
www.house.gov/ebjohnson
1511 Longworth Bldg. 20515-4330; fax 226-1477

COMMITTEES
Science & Technology
Transportation & Infrastructure
   (Water Resources & Environment - chairwoman)

RESIDENCE
Dallas

BORN
Dec. 3, 1935; Waco, Texas

RELIGION
Baptist

FAMILY
Divorced; one child

EDUCATION
Texas Christian U., B.S. 1967 (nursing);
Southern Methodist U., M.P.A. 1976

CAREER
Business relocation company owner;
nurse; U.S. Health, Education & Welfare
Department official

POLITICAL HIGHLIGHTS
Texas House, 1973-77; Texas Senate, 1987-93

ELECTION RESULTS

2008 GENERAL

Eddie Bernice Johnson (D)	168,249	82.5%
Fred Wood (R)	32,361	15.9%
Jarrett Woods (LIBERT)	3,366	1.6%

2008 PRIMARY

Eddie Bernice Johnson (D)	unopposed

2006 GENERAL

Eddie Bernice Johnson (D)	81,348	80.2%
Wilson Aurbach (R)	17,850	17.6%
Ken Ashby (LIBERT)	2,250	2.2%

PREVIOUS WINNING PERCENTAGES
2004 (93%); 2002 (74%); 2000 (92%); 1998 (72%);
1996 (55%); 1994 (73%); 1992 (72%)

The first African-American elected to represent Dallas in Congress, Johnson has a strong commitment to liberal social causes. Yet she has shown a willingness to compromise with Republicans to get bills passed and to reach out to business interests that can help her district.

With eight terms behind her, she has promised to continue her trailblazing political career for at least one more term, although the septuagenarian lawmaker said she's taking elections one at a time.

Her attendance record for votes during the 110th Congress (2007-08) indicates the fast pace in Washington is becoming more difficult for Johnson. She missed more votes than all but two other Democrats serving full terms. Johnson told The Dallas Morning News in 2007 that she agreed to run for re-election in 2008 only after being "pushed and prodded" and her primary purpose in staying on was to secure funding for a major flood-control project around Dallas. She blew through the election with her typical wide margin of victory, taking 82 percent of the vote.

Johnson retains her role as chairwoman of the Transportation and Infrastructure Subcommittee on Water Resources and Environment. She had made some progress toward her goal for the flood-control project when she shepherded through in 2007 a major water projects bill — overcoming a presidential veto — that included authorization of $298 million for the Trinity River project in her district.

Johnson pushed through the House in 2009 a massive wastewater bill that included the first reauthorization of the Clean Water State Revolving Fund in 15 years. The reauthorization had stalled previously due to GOP attempts to remove a provision requiring contractors to pay union-scale wages to comply with a wage law known as the Davis-Bacon Act. The House passed the bill in March after Republicans were unsuccessful in another attempt to remove the language.

She also aims to provide more opportunities for minorities and the disadvantaged. During the 110th, she joined a Congressional Black Caucus committee established to help secure more earmarked funding for projects in black members' districts. And during the 2007 debate on reauthorizing the Head Start program for disadvantaged preschoolers, she sponsored an amendment that encourages collaboration between program administrators and historically black colleges.

She held sessions in her district in early 2009 on digital TV changes and "surviving a financial crisis." And she pushed a bill to provide housing and financial counseling for homeless and mentally ill people upon their release from an institution or residential program. She also offered a bill to apply the Community Reinvestment Act — which encourages banks and thrifts to offer loans in low-income communities — to all non-bank financial institutions.

Johnson hopes her legacy in Congress will include steering the Black Caucus toward effective coalitions with business groups rather than relying exclusively on its traditional allies in labor, the clergy and civil rights. As its chairwoman in 2001 and 2002, she hosted the caucus' first technology and energy summits to bridge the digital divide in poor communities and to encourage minority students to study science. In the 110th, she co-chaired a Black Caucus outreach task force to the South, where Democrats have struggled in recent years to hold onto their seats.

Civil rights have long been at the core of her agenda. In 2006, for example, she was arrested for disorderly conduct with six other caucus members at he Sudanese embassy in Washington while protesting the genocide in Darr by Janjaweed militias under the control of the Sudanese government. But uring the 108th Congress (2003-04), a former aide accused her of discrimnation. She invoked Congress' constitutional protection from being quesoned about "speech or debate" and asserted the former aide's duties were directly related to the due functioning of the legislative process." An appeals ourt ruled that lawmakers can mount a defense by claiming employment ecisions were based on legislative concerns, and a federal district court udge threw out the case for lack of evidence in October 2007.

On the Science and Technology Committee, she pushes legislation aimed t improving the number of women in math, science and engineering in niversities and colleges at both the student and staff level. She also has bbied for the expansion of minority participation in science research. In 007, she successfully amended a bill reauthorizing the National Science oundation and required the NSF and the National Academy of Sciences to eport on their support for minority institutions.

She is a member of the Congressional Caucus for Women's Issues and olds an annual conference in Dallas as part of her initiative, "A World of Vomen for World Peace."

As a young girl attending segregated schools in Waco, Johnson's goal was o go to medical school and become a doctor. But her high school counselor ncouraged her to become a nurse because "nurses were more feminine."

She earned an undergraduate degree in nursing, and a master's in public dministration from Southern Methodist University. She rose to be chief sychiatric nurse at the veterans' hospital in Dallas.

She won election to the state House in 1972 — the first black woman from Dallas to achieve the distinction. In the late 1970s, she turned to private usiness, setting up Eddie Bernice Johnson and Associates, which helped usinesses expand or relocate in the Dallas-Fort Worth area. She continued o run the business after her 1986 election to the state Senate, and expanded the company's reach in 1988 to include airport concessions management.

Wielding her power in the state legislature, she drew a House district reordained to elect her in 1992. Johnson generally has won re-election with ase. Initially, her electoral fate was caught up in the judicial and legislative vrangling over minority-majority House districts, including the 30th. After he U.S. Supreme Court in 1996 threw out some House districts in Texas s "racial gerrymanders," Johnson landed in a redrawn district that was 2 percent new to her. But she captured a 55 percent majority in an eightberson contest, and has won by wide margins since.

KEY VOTES

2008

Yes	Delay consideration of Colombia free-trade agreement
Yes	Override Bush veto of federal farm and nutrition programs reauthorization bill
No	Overhaul surveillance laws and permit dismissal of suits against companies that conducted warrantless wiretapping
Yes	Grant mortgage relief to homeowners and funding for Fannie Mae and Freddie Mac
Yes	Approve initial $700 billion program to stabilize financial markets
Yes	Approve final $700 billion program to stabilize financial markets
?	Provide $14 billion in loans to automakers

2007

Yes	Increase minimum wage by $2.10 an hour
Yes	Approve $124.2 billion in emergency war spending and set goal for redeployment of troops from Iraq
No	Reject federal contraceptive assistance to international family planning groups
Yes	Override Bush veto of $23.2 billion water projects authorization bill
Yes	Implement Peru free-trade agreement
+	Approve energy policy overhaul with new fuel economy standards
+	Clear $473.5 billion omnibus spending bill, including $70 billion for military operations

CQ VOTE STUDIES

	PARTY UNITY		PRESIDENTIAL SUPPORT	
	SUPPORT	OPPOSE	SUPPORT	OPPOSE
2008	99%	1%	14%	86%
2007	97%	3%	4%	96%
2006	94%	6%	35%	65%
2005	96%	4%	14%	86%
2004	93%	7%	34%	66%

INTEREST GROUPS

	AFL-CIO	ADA	CCUS	ACU
2008	100%	100%	56%	0%
2007	100%	80%	60%	0%
2006	100%	95%	60%	16%
2005	100%	100%	37%	0%
2004	87%	100%	63%	17%

TEXAS 30

Downtown Dallas and southern suburbs

onfined to Dallas County, the 30th stretches from Dallas Love Field outheast into downtown Dallas. It then dips south to take in some subrbs, such as Lancaster, where many black families have relocated after aving the city. Black residents account for 41 percent of the population — the highest percentage in any Texas district — and 34 percent of residents are Hispanic.

ove Field, an alternative to the large Dallas-Fort Worth International Airort (in the 24th and 26th), is a hub for Southwest Airlines, a low-cost airne whose headquarters are in the 30th. Federal restrictions on flight atterns and regional-only service are expected to completely phase out y 2014, and carrier American Airlines anticipates returning to Love Field 2013. The airport is also undergoing a more-than-$500 million capital nprovement project that is expected to double passenger traffic. Expanion at the airport, combined with a growing population, has made road ongestion and air pollution concerns for the area.

lthough only a slight majority of district residents hold white-collar jobs,

the Dallas-Fort Worth Metroplex is a banking, high-tech and transportation center. The district is home to several Fortune 500 firms, although national economic downturns have hurt several local companies. Downtown Dallas attracts visitors to the American Airlines Center, home to basketball's Mavericks and hockey's Stars, although the historic Cotton Bowl hosted its last namesake college football game in 2009. Dallas plans to develop a five-acre urban park and pedestrian paths connecting Uptown and Downtown Dallas.

Democrats run particularly well in the heavily black precincts just south of Illinois Avenue, and in largely Hispanic precincts near Love Field. In 2008, the 30th — the only Democratic district in the Dallas-Fort Worth area — gave Barack Obama 82 percent of its presidential vote, his highest percentage statewide.

MAJOR INDUSTRY
Transportation, banking, technology

CITIES
Dallas (pt.), 533,878; DeSoto, 37,646; Lancaster, 25,894

NOTABLE
Dealey Plaza and the Texas School Book Depository, where John F. Kennedy was assassinated in 1963, are in downtown Dallas.

Rep. John Carter (R)

Elected 2002; 4th term

CAPITOL OFFICE
225-3864
www.house.gov/carter
409 Cannon Bldg. 20515-4331; fax 225-5886

COMMITTEES
Appropriations

RESIDENCE
Round Rock

BORN
Nov. 6, 1941; Houston, Texas

RELIGION
Lutheran

FAMILY
Wife, Erika Carter; four children

EDUCATION
Texas Technological College, B.A. 1964
(history); U. of Texas, J.D. 1969

CAREER
Lawyer; state legislative aide

POLITICAL HIGHLIGHTS
Candidate for Texas House, 1980;
Texas District Court judge, 1981-2001

ELECTION RESULTS

2008 GENERAL

John Carter (R)	175,563	60.3%
Brian P. Ruiz (D)	106,559	36.6%
Barry N. Cooper (LIBERT)	9,182	3.2%

2008 PRIMARY

John Carter (R)	unopposed

2006 GENERAL

John Carter (R)	90,869	58.5%
Mary Beth Harrell (D)	60,293	38.8%
Matt McAdoo (LIBERT)	4,221	2.7%

PREVIOUS WINNING PERCENTAGES
2004 (65%); 2002 (69%)

As GOP conference secretary, Carter balances his responsibilities as a member of the House leadership team with his obligations to the conservative Republican Study Committee (RSC) and his role as an appropriator. It's a task perhaps uniquely suited for Carter, an ex-district court judge many simply call "Judge" — a nickname given to him by former Speaker J. Dennis Hastert.

A member of the Appropriations Committee, he espouses fiscal conservatism, seeking limited spending and continued tax cuts, though he's willing to send money back home. He also follows the party line on most social issues; he voted against a 2007 measure to ban job discrimination based on sexual orientation, supported a ban on a procedure opponents call "partial birth" abortion, and pushes for strong border security against illegal immigration.

Carter, who ran unopposed for conference secretary in each of the last two sessions of Congress, views his job as a liaison between the leadership and rank-and-file members, encouraging them to fall in line. He developed the first mentor program, joining members of his class of 2002 with freshman Republicans to show the newly elected "where the pitfalls are."

He also tries to serve as a liaison for the Study Committee, whose members often are at odds with the leadership and appropriators — particularly on earmarks, the funding set-asides put in bills to benefit members' districts. The RSC has pushed for reform of the process. Carter initially joined other appropriators resisting the idea; he said earmarks help set priorities for funding. But in late 2007, he and several other appropriators joined RSC leaders to propose a bicameral, bipartisan committee to study earmark reform. The plan, which was never adopted, would have put a moratorium on earmarks for six months while the panel studied the issue.

He's still willing to grab earmarks for his district — particularly for defense projects. In the fiscal 2009 spending bills, he helped acquire more than $18 million for projects in his district. More than $8 million of that was for military, defense and homeland security projects.

But Carter refused to back the $700 billion financial sector rescue law in fall 2008, telling Fox News that "overwhelmingly, the taxpayers back home think this is insane." And in 2009, he joined House GOP leaders in opposing President Obama's early priorities: a $787 billion economic stimulus package, which garnered no House GOP votes; an overhaul of the financial sector rescue program; wage discrimination legislation; and an expansion of the State Children's Health Insurance Program, which provides coverage to children whose families don't qualify for Medicaid.

Carter took on a high-profile task in 2009 as chief public antagonist of Ways and Means Chairman Charles B. Rangel of New York, who was the subject of an ethics committee investigation into his fundraising and personal finances. Carter sponsored an unsuccessful GOP resolution to force Rangel from his chairmanship until the committee reached a conclusion.

After the House adjourned for the August recess in 2008, Carter helped Minority Leader John A. Boehner of Ohio lead a small group of Republicans in protest against the Democrats' refusal to vote on a GOP energy plan to end a moratorium on oil and gas drilling along the outer continental shelf. He accused the Democratic party of being "an ostrich with its head in the sand."

Carter has been in the midst of some ethical debates since he came to the House in 2003 as an ally of former House Majority Leader Tom DeLay, who, like him, is from the Houston area. When DeLay ran into trouble with a campaign fundraising investigation, Carter was one of only 20 Republicans to vote in 2005 to retain Republican-written rules allowing leaders to keep their jobs if indicted. The rules were later withdrawn.

Carter also drew some negative press when it was revealed he was among eight lawmakers, including DeLay, who accepted trips to South Korea from a registered foreign agent, despite House rules prohibiting the practice. The lawmakers said they were unaware the organization that paid for the trip was an agent of the South Korean government.

He has concentrated particularly on military quality-of-life issues. In 2008, he sponsored legislation to make it easier for military spouses to claim residency in the state in which their spouses are stationed. His proposal was included as part of a larger veterans' benefits measure the House approved in July of that year, but which failed to get through the Senate.

Carter left the bench after 20 years to run for Congress, he said, because of the Sept. 11 terrorist attacks. Once in, he successfully lobbied for an amendment to apply the death penalty for an act of terrorism that results in deaths. It was passed as part of the 2005 reauthorization of the anti-terrorism law known as the Patriot Act. Another priority for Carter has been border security. He opposed President George W. Bush's proposal to allow some illegal immigrants to remain in the United States under a new guest worker program. In 2006, he opposed renewing parts of the 1965 Voting Rights Act requiring foreign language assistance at the polls. "I simply believe you should be able to read, write and speak English to be a voter in the United States," he said.

Carter grew up comfortably as the son of the general manager of Humble Oil and Refining Co., the precursor to Exxon. In high school the younger Carter worked summers on oil and gas pipelines. As a law student at the University of Texas at Austin, Carter said, he was one of a handful of conservatives. "I think I had the only Goldwater button in law school. I got criticized by several professors," he said.

During a summer in Holland, he worked on a pipeline project for Bechtel Corp. His interest in politics was sparked when he worked as a counsel for the Texas Legislature. He moved his family to the small town of Round Rock, set up a law practice, and in 1980 ran unsuccessfully for a seat in the Texas House. Carter then briefly resumed his practice until he was appointed district court judge of Williamson County in 1981. The following year he won election to the position. In his first House race in 2002, Carter won a GOP primary runoff with 57 percent of the vote. He then easily defeated Democrat David Bagley with 69 percent. He has had little trouble getting re-elected. In 2008, he won by 24 percentage points.

KEY VOTES

2008

No	Delay consideration of Colombia free-trade agreement
+	Override Bush veto of federal farm and nutrition programs reauthorization bill
Yes	Overhaul surveillance laws and permit dismissal of suits against companies that conducted warrantless wiretapping
No	Grant mortgage relief to homeowners and funding for Fannie Mae and Freddie Mac
No	Approve initial $700 billion program to stabilize financial markets
No	Approve final $700 billion program to stabilize financial markets
No	Provide $14 billion in loans to automakers

2007

No	Increase minimum wage by $2.10 an hour
No	Approve $124.2 billion in emergency war spending and set goal for redeployment of troops from Iraq
Yes	Reject federal contraceptive assistance to international family planning groups
Yes	Override Bush veto of $23.2 billion water projects authorization bill
Yes	Implement Peru free-trade agreement
No	Approve energy policy overhaul with new fuel economy standards
Yes	Clear $473.5 billion omnibus spending bill, including $70 billion for military operations

CQ VOTE STUDIES

	PARTY UNITY		PRESIDENTIAL SUPPORT	
	SUPPORT	OPPOSE	SUPPORT	OPPOSE
2008	99%	1%	80%	20%
2007	95%	5%	86%	14%
2006	97%	3%	95%	5%
2005	98%	2%	93%	7%
2004	98%	2%	94%	6%

INTEREST GROUPS

	AFL-CIO	ADA	CCUS	ACU
2008	0%	5%	94%	96%
2007	4%	0%	80%	100%
2006	15%	0%	100%	88%
2005	13%	0%	89%	92%
2004	7%	0%	100%	96%

TEXAS 31

East central – north Austin suburbs, Killeen

The Republican 31st District is made up of suburbs and rural areas extending from the northern Austin suburbs through fertile agricultural land in central Texas to Erath County, located about 60 miles southwest of Fort Worth.

In the south, the 31st takes in Williamson County, its largest population base and an area that has been one of Texas' fastest-growing. A suburban enclave north of Austin, the county enjoyed economic growth that attracted new residents, but massive layoffs at Round Rock-based computer giant Dell and other high-tech employers have hit the area hard. TECO-Westinghouse Motor Company also is based in Round Rock.

The 31st's other main population center is Bell County, located just north of Williamson. Fort Hood, a huge Army base near Killeen that is split with Coryell County, is a crucial part of the area's economy, contributing about $7 billion annually. The base is slated to lose a few thousand jobs as part of the 2005 BRAC round, but it will gain several new units as well. Six state correctional facilities in Coryell County also provide jobs.

Agriculture, especially dairy and grains, is a staple in rural Erath and Hamilton counties in the northern 31st. Cattle and poultry ranches and farms growing corn and sorghum dot the landscape of eastern counties. Plummeting aluminum prices and declining demand for aluminum products forced the closure of the Aluminum Company of America smelting plant near Rockdale. The plant had been Rockdale's primary employer since the discovery of lignite deposits in the 1950s.

The 31st favors the GOP in both its rural and suburban areas. Erath County, the district's northernmost county, gave John McCain 77 percent of its 2008 presidential vote. Williamson County, in the southern portion, gave McCain 56 percent. He won the 31st with 57 percent.

MAJOR INDUSTRY
Military, technology, agriculture, manufacturing

MILITARY BASES
Fort Hood (Army), 54,067 military, 5,580 civilian (2008)

CITIES
Killeen, 86,911; Round Rock (pt.), 60,060; Temple, 54,514

NOTABLE
Former baseball pitcher Nolan Ryan owns the Round Rock Express, a minor-league affiliate of the Houston Astros.

Rep. Pete Sessions (R)

Elected 1996; 7th term

Sessions is among the House's most devout conservatives, a confident Texan whose courtly manner belies his deep ambitions. A loyal ally of Minority Leader John A. Boehner of Ohio, he can be fierce in challenging Democratic initiatives he considers too liberal.

When he first arrived, he led an informal group called the House Results Caucus. The group doesn't exist anymore, but he still subscribes to its pithy motto: "Give the government the money it needs, but not a penny more." And he holds a prominent platform from which to promote his beliefs as chairman of the National Republican Congressional Committee (NRCC), the campaign arm of the House GOP that raises money and recruits candidates.

Upon winning the job in November 2008, he vowed to build an aggressive and modernized operation. In addition to erasing the Democrats' fundraising edge in recent elections, Sessions wants to improve candidate recruitment and update the group's communications. "Expect us to come back with [candidates] that will not only look and act like Republicans, but have ideas of how to sell," he vowed. But with his party ensconced in its deepest minority since 1994, he faces long odds.

Sessions sought the NRCC post in 2006 but lost to Tom Cole of Oklahoma, a former executive director of the organization. Cole originally expressed interest in returning as chairman, but he dropped out when it became clear Sessions had the votes to defeat him.

In what amounted to a tryout, Boehner tapped Sessions in June 2008 to provide fundraising help for Cole by raising cash for targeted races. During the 2007-08 election cycle, Sessions also donated more than $600,000 to other campaigns and committees from his own campaign funds and political action committee, known as PETE PAC. His methods sometimes raise questions; he held a 2007 fundraiser at a Las Vegas venue that aides said featured a mild burlesque show, but some conservative activists were dismayed the event was held at an adult club.

A member of the conservative Republican Study Committee (RSC), Sessions is outspoken against Democratic proposals, particularly when it comes to taxes and spending. He criticized a one-year "patch" to the alternative minimum tax adopted in 2008: "I have never, ever heard of a Democrat tax-and-spend bill that then touts how many jobs will be created, because they don't," he said. "They kill jobs in America every time we do what we're doing today."

And he decried a series of President Obama's early economic initiatives, including a $787 billion stimulus law, which became a theme of attack for the Republican Party. "We are united," Sessions told CNN. "The debt of this country is a national crisis and a national security issue."

But Sessions broke ranks with other RSC members to back both versions of the $700 billion proposal — the second of which became law — to shore up the nation's financial services sector in fall 2008. He also favors earmarks, which are funding requests for special projects in members' districts.

Sessions pushed hard in early 2009 against a Democratic proposal for a "cap and trade" program to limit greenhouse gas emissions, saying it effectively would create "a national energy tax that would increase energy prices, kill jobs and transfer wealth overseas." He instead encourages "opening American resources to energy production," promoting conservation and developing renewable sources.

On the Rules panel, which sets the parameters for floor debate on bills, he can be combative and relishes the spirited give-and-take with witnesses appear-

CAPITOL OFFICE
225-2231
sessions.house.gov
2233 Rayburn Bldg. 20515-4332; fax 225-5878

COMMITTEES
Rules

RESIDENCE
Dallas

BORN
March 22, 1955; Waco, Texas

RELIGION
United Methodist

FAMILY
Wife, Nete Sessions; two children

EDUCATION
Southwest Texas State U., attended 1973-74;
Southwestern U., B.S. 1978 (political science)

CAREER
Public policy analyst; telephone company executive

POLITICAL HIGHLIGHTS
Sought Republican nomination for U.S. House (special election), 1991; Republican nominee for U.S. House, 1994

ELECTION RESULTS

2008 GENERAL

Pete Sessions (R)	116,283	57.2%
Eric Roberson (D)	82,406	40.6%
Alex Bischoff (LIBERT)	4,421	2.2%

2008 PRIMARY

Pete Sessions (R)	unopposed

2006 GENERAL

Pete Sessions (R)	71,461	56.4%
Will Pryor (D)	52,269	41.3%
John B. Hawley (LIBERT)	2,922	2.3%

PREVIOUS WINNING PERCENTAGES
2004 (54%); 2002 (68%); 2000 (54%); 1998 (56%);
1996 (53%)

g before the committee, if not the restrictive rules Republicans complain shut ut the minority's hopes of shaping bills.

Sessions said in early 2009 that he and his GOP colleagues would like bama to adopt President Bill Clinton's triangulation strategy — splitting differences between the parties — and his penchant for pushing bipartisan deals, xe the 1996 welfare overhaul. "When Bill Clinton was president and Republicans were in charge, there used to be a lot of dialog even before the Rules ommittee about what the bill would look like," he said. (Ironically, Sessions ted in favor of four articles of impeachment against Clinton in 1998.)

There is one issue on which Sessions regularly reaches across the aisle. s the father of a son who has Down syndrome, Sessions has joined since 00 with Democrat Henry A. Waxman of California in an effort to help milies with incomes above the poverty line buy into Medicaid coverage r children with special needs. The bill passed in 2006 and was signed into w. He co-chairs the bipartisan Congressional Down Syndrome Caucus.

He pulls out a photo of his wife, Nete, who is Mexican, when asked about s political appeal to the Hispanic constituents in his district who are main-Democratic. "I am very aware of Hispanic needs and am in tune with their eds as parents on the issues of jobs, health care and education," he said. ke most Texas Republicans, he wants a crackdown on illegal immigration.

Sessions is the son of William S. Sessions, a former federal judge who rved as FBI director from 1987 to 1993. He was born in Waco and educated Southwestern University in Georgetown, Texas. After college, he went to ork at Southwestern Bell Telephone Co. and Bell Communications Research.

He ran for Congress in 1991, finishing sixth in a special election to suc-ed 3rd District GOP Rep. Steve Bartlett, who left to run for mayor of allas. In 1994, Sessions quit his job to make an unsuccessful bid against cumbent Democrat John Bryant of the 5th District. After that, he worked s vice president for public policy at the National Center for Policy Analysis, conservative think tank in Dallas.

When Bryant left in 1996 to run for the Senate, Sessions won his seat with 3 percent of the vote. After redistricting, Sessions ran in the newly created 2nd District in 2002, which had more GOP voters. His house was still in e 5th, but a mere two blocks from the boundary. Sessions cruised to vic-ry with 68 percent of the vote. In 2003, state Republicans, led by former ouse Majority Leader Tom DeLay of Texas, redrew the map. The new 2nd, which includes his home, pitted Sessions against 13-term Democrat artin Frost. Sessions prevailed with 54 percent in the costliest election of 04. He won in 2006 and 2008 by more than 15 percentage points.

KEY VOTES

2008

No	Delay consideration of Colombia free-trade agreement
No	Override Bush veto of federal farm and nutrition programs reauthorization bill
Yes	Overhaul surveillance laws and permit dismissal of suits against companies that conducted warrantless wiretapping
No	Grant mortgage relief to homeowners and funding for Fannie Mae and Freddie Mac
Yes	Approve initial $700 billion program to stabilize financial markets
Yes	Approve final $700 billion program to stabilize financial markets
No	Provide $14 billion in loans to automakers

2007

No	Increase minimum wage by $2.10 an hour
No	Approve $124.2 billion in emergency war spending and set goal for redeployment of troops from Iraq
Yes	Reject federal contraceptive assistance to international family planning groups
Yes	Override Bush veto of $23.2 billion water projects authorization bill
Yes	Implement Peru free-trade agreement
Yes	Approve energy policy overhaul with new fuel economy standards
Yes	Clear $473.5 billion omnibus spending bill, including $70 billion for military operations

CQ VOTE STUDIES

	PARTY UNITY		PRESIDENTIAL SUPPORT	
	SUPPORT	OPPOSE	SUPPORT	OPPOSE
2008	99%	1%	85%	15%
2007	98%	2%	91%	9%
2006	98%	2%	100%	0%
2005	99%	1%	90%	10%
2004	99%	1%	94%	6%

INTEREST GROUPS

	AFL-CIO	ADA	CCUS	ACU
2008	0%	5%	100%	92%
2007	4%	10%	94%	96%
2006	10%	0%	100%	96%
2005	13%	0%	93%	100%
2004	13%	0%	100%	100%

EXAS 32

orthern Dallas; most of Irving and Richardson

e hook-shaped 32nd is located in northern and western Dallas County d essentially encircles downtown Dallas. It includes a chunk of the ty and part of Dallas' northern and western suburbs. Although it does t include downtown, the 32nd is home to much of the Dallas business mmunity. Many district residents work downtown, and several Fortune 0 companies are located off the Lyndon B. Johnson Freeway, which ns as the northwestern border of the district.

eginning southwest of downtown, in the Hispanic area of Oak Cliff, the strict moves west through heavily Hispanic areas in Cockrell Hill and a ction of Grand Prairie into the southern part of Irving (shared with the th). South Irving has a vibrant Hispanic population, while central Irving becoming increasingly white with a blue-collar middle class. North ving is home to high-income, technology-oriented professionals in Las olinas, where many large companies are based. Texas Stadium, the for-er home of the Dallas Cowboys, is being leased to the state as a con-ruction staging site for a $500 million highway renovation project.

The district then curves east to re-enter Dallas and also take in the exclusive "Park Cities," made up of Highland Park and University Park. This area, almost entirely white, has its own school system and local government and is home to Southern Methodist University (SMU).

The 32nd continues north to the county line, through less-exclusive neigh-borhoods. The "telecom corridor" also is in northern Dallas, but standard-bearer Texas Instruments (based just in the nearby 3rd) has been forced into massive layoffs, as have other tech and finance firms in Richardson (shared with the 3rd). Many residents work at Dallas-Forth Worth Interna-tional Airport or Dallas Love Field airport, both of which border the 32nd.

The 32nd is Republican — the GOP is particularly strong in the wealthy communities near SMU — and John McCain took 53 percent of the vote here in the 2008 presidential race.

MAJOR INDUSTRY
Telecommunications, oil, retail, higher education

CITIES
Dallas (pt.), 393,211; Irving (pt.), 131,860; Richardson (pt.), 70,890

NOTABLE
George W. Bush is planning to build his presidential library at SMU.

Gov. Jon Huntsman Jr. (R)

Note: Gov. Huntsman has been nominated by President Obama to be ambassador to China.

First elected: 2004
Length of term: 4 years
Term expires: 1/13
Salary: $109,900
Phone: (801) 538-1000

Residence:
Salt Lake City
Born: March 26, 1960; Palo Alto, Calif.
Religion: Mormon
Family: Wife, Mary Kaye Huntsman; seven children
Education: U. of Utah, attended 1981-84; U. of Pennsylvania, B.A. 1987 (international politics)
Career: Chemical company CEO; U.S. Commerce Department official
Political highlights: U.S. ambassador to Singapore, 1992-93; deputy U.S. trade representative, 2001-03

Election results:
2008 GENERAL
Jon Huntsman Jr. (R)	734,049	77.6%
Bob Spingmeyer (D)	186,503	19.7%
Superdell Dell Schanze (LIBERT)	24,820	2.6%

Lt. Gov. Gary R. Herbert (R)

First elected: 2004
Length of term: 4 years
Term expires: 1/13
Salary: $104,405
Phone: (801) 538-1000

LEGISLATURE

Legislature: 45 days yearly January-March

Senate: 29 members, 4-year terms
2009 ratios: 21 R, 8 D; 24 men, 5 women
Salary: $117/day in session
Phone: (801) 538-1035

House: 75 members, 2-year terms
2009 ratios: 54 R, 21 D; 58 men, 17 women
Salary: $117/day in session
Phone: (801) 538-1029

TERM LIMITS

Governor: Yes, three terms
Senate: No
House: No

URBAN STATISTICS

CITY	POPULATION
Salt Lake City	181,743
West Valley City	108,896
Provo	105,166
Sandy	88,418
Orem	84,324

REGISTERED VOTERS

Registration by party began in May 1999, however, not all voters have declared an affiliation and the numbers are kept on a county basis.

POPULATION

2008 population (est.)	2,736,424
2000 population	2,233,169
1990 population	1,722,850
Percent change (1990-2000)	+29.6%
Rank among states (2008)	34

Median age	27.1
Born in state	62.9%
Foreign born	7.1%
Violent crime rate	256/100,000
Poverty level	9.4%
Federal workers	32,961
Military	16,621

ELECTIONS

STATE ELECTION OFFICIAL
(801) 538-1041
DEMOCRATIC PARTY
(801) 328-1212
REPUBLICAN PARTY
(801) 533-9777

MISCELLANEOUS

Web: www.utah.gov
Capital: Salt Lake City

U.S. CONGRESS

Senate: 2 Republicans
House: 2 Republicans, 1 Democrat

2000 Census Statistics by District

DIST.	2008 VOTE FOR PRESIDENT OBAMA	MCCAIN	WHITE	BLACK	ASIAN	HISP	MEDIAN INCOME	WHITE COLLAR	BLUE COLLAR	SERVICE INDUSTRY	OVER 64	UNDER 18	COLLEGE EDUCATION	RURAL	SQ. MILES
1	33%	64%	83%	1%	2%	11%	$45,058	59%	27%	14%	9%	32%	25%	11%	20,768
2	40	58	88	1	2	6	$45,583	66	21	14	11	30	31	15	45,624
3	29	67	85	0	2	10	$46,568	60	27	14	6	35	22	9	15,751
STATE	34	63	85	1	2	9	$45,726	61	25	14	9	32	26	12	82,144
U.S.	53	46	69	12	4	13	$41,994	60	25	15	12	26	24	21	3,537,438

Sen. Orrin G. Hatch (R)

Elected 1976; 6th term

CAPITOL OFFICE
224-5251
hatch.senate.gov
104 Hart Bldg. 20510-4402; fax 224-6331

COMMITTEES
Finance
Health, Education, Labor & Pensions
Judiciary
Select Intelligence
Special Aging
Joint Taxation

RESIDENCE
Salt Lake City

BORN
March 22, 1934; Pittsburgh, Pa.

RELIGION
Mormon

FAMILY
Wife, Elaine Hatch; six children

EDUCATION
Brigham Young U., B.S. 1959 (history);
U. of Pittsburgh, J.D. 1962

CAREER
Lawyer; songwriter

POLITICAL HIGHLIGHTS
Sought Republican nomination for
president, 2000

ELECTION RESULTS

2006 GENERAL

Orrin G. Hatch (R)	356,238	62.4%
Pete Ashdown (D)	177,459	31.1%
Scott N. Bradley (CNSTP)	21,526	3.8%
Roger I. Price (PC)	9,089	1.6%

2006 PRIMARY

PREVIOUS WINNING PERCENTAGES
2000 (66%); 1994 (69%); 1988 (67%); 1982 (58%);
1976 (54%)

Hatch combines an uncommon mix of tenacious conservatism and persistent graciousness that takes the rough edge off the partisan attacks he often launches against Democrats. He is an important player in fiscal and health care debates as well as battles over judicial nominees, and despite his harsh rhetoric, is often willing to extend a hand across the aisle. "I will work with anybody, if they do it the right way — if they are sincere, dedicated and act in good faith," Hatch said.

He and Indiana's Richard G. Lugar are the longest-serving Republicans currently in the Senate. Hatch looms as the likely successor in 2011 to Iowa's Charles E. Grassley, who holds the top GOP seat on the Finance Committee, which writes tax, trade and health measures. Hatch is active on the Health, Education, Labor and Pensions panel and is a former chairman of the Judiciary Committee, where he still serves. He also maintains close ties to another former Judiciary chairman, Vice President Joseph R. Biden Jr.

Hatch has led a lengthy life of political non-conformity and has been called everything from a right-wing partisan to a Republican turncoat — a situation he referenced in titling his 2002 autobiography "Square Peg." A frugal workaholic, he is also an urbane clotheshorse, art lover and successful songwriter whose work has been performed by the Osmonds and Gladys Knight. He is friendly with U2 singer Bono.

On Judiciary, Hatch has been in the middle of some of the Senate's most explosive fights, such as tort reform, the expansion of law enforcement's powers to fight terrorism and the confirmation of judges. Just as he supported conservatives Clarence Thomas and Robert Bork for Supreme Court appointments in an earlier era, Hatch backed President George W. Bush's high court nominees to the hilt.

In the early months of President Obama's administration, Hatch professed a desire to help the president fill key posts, including on the Supreme Court. But he criticized several of Obama's choices for various agencies and warned in March 2009, "I'm really getting alarmed at some of the — I don't want to call them all radicals — but some of the radical people who are being put into these sensitive, big-time positions."

As chairman of the Judiciary Subcommittee on Intellectual Property in 2005, Hatch won enactment of bipartisan legislation that outlawed the use of camcorders in movie theaters and punished the distribution of pirated movies or songs prior to their release. The successful bill also legalized movie-filtering technology that lets viewers skip objectionable material.

Much of Hatch's interest in copyright stems from his avocation as a songwriter. Hooked on music since he started taking piano lessons at age 6, he started writing poetry in college. In 1996, singer-songwriter Janice Kapp Perry asked him to write some hymns with her. He wrote 10 songs in a weekend, the core of the "My God Is Love" album. Since then, he's produced several discs of religious, romantic and patriotic songs. Bono once jokingly suggested that the straight-laced senator could boost his chances of getting airplay by changing his name to the catchier "Johnny Trapdoor."

Hatch is a GOP loyalist on many issues, siding with his party on 85 percent of the votes in the 110th Congress (2007-08) in which majorities of the two parties diverged. He splits with conservatives on embryonic stem cell research, which he considers the "most important biomedical research in the history of the planet." He also broke with most Republicans on legislation aimed at reauthorizing and expanding a federal children's health insurice program that Bush argued was too costly. Hatch and Grassley worked osely with Democrats in 2007 on an attempt to find consensus on the State hildren's Health Insurance Program legislation, which covers children om low-income families that do not qualify for Medicaid.

Nevertheless, when the measure resurfaced in 2009 as Obama took ffice, both senators opposed it; Hatch bitterly cited being excluded from the ocess and attacked several changes that had been made. He was equally smissive of Obama's early economic initiatives, including a $787 billion onomic stimulus law and a $3.56 trillion budget for fiscal 2010 that he called tragedy for Americans everywhere" because of its spending total.

Although he is often critical of Democratic plans, he will cooperate with lleagues on high-profile measures. He and Judiciary Chairman Patrick J. ahy of Vermont have for years pushed a bill to overhaul patent laws. He also orked with Judiciary member Dianne Feinstein of California in the 109th ngress (2005-06) on a bill to crack down on gangs, and with several Finance ommittee Democrats to combat elder abuse. He and liberal California Rep. enry A. Waxman were responsible for the landmark 1984 law that created a athway for the FDA to approve generic versions of traditional drugs.

He has had a long and fruitful relationship with liberal icon Edward M. ennedy of Massachusetts, with whom he has advanced a number of bills. heir ties have led some on the right to deem Hatch as someone not to be lly trusted. At Hatch's urging, senators named after Kennedy a March 009 Senate-passed bill they sponsored to significantly expand national and ommunity service programs. And at a White House summit on health care at month, Hatch asked participants to pray for Kennedy — suffering from ain cancer — because he "is the one guy who can bring all of the Demo- at major special interest groups together" to pass a major overhaul.

Hatch also serves on the Select Intelligence, Special Aging and Joint axation committees. As the National Republican Senatorial Committee's ce chairman, he seeks to help his party regain Senate seats in 2010.

Born in Pittsburgh, Hatch grew up in poverty. The family lost their home uring the Depression, so Hatch's father, a lather, borrowed $100 to buy an cre of land in the hills above Pittsburgh, where he built a home of black- ned lumber salvaged from a fire. The family grew their own food; Hatch nded the chickens and sold their eggs.

During World War II, when Hatch was 11, his beloved older brother, sse, a B-24 nose gunner, died in a bombing raid over Italy. Just weeks terward, a lock of hair over Hatch's forehead turned white. When it came ne for Hatch to serve his mission as a young Mormon, he chose to serve o, one for himself and one for Jesse.

He worked his way through college and law school as a janitor, an all- ght desk clerk in a girls' dormitory and a metal lather. To house a growing mily that included three of his six children by the time he finished law chool, he plastered the inside of his family's old chicken coop.

He returned to Utah in 1969. He was an attorney with a thriving private actice when he decided in 1976 to run for the Senate seat then being held y Democrat Frank Moss. In "Square Peg," Hatch said he ran because the untry was grappling with inflation, deficit spending, high unemployment, d a weakening military. He won the GOP nomination over Jack W. Carlson, former assistant secretary of Interior, then defeated incumbent Moss with 4 percent of the vote. He was re-elected in 1982 with 58 percent. In 1988, he efeated Brian H. Moss, son of the senator he had ousted, by a 2-1 ratio, and as won his past three re-elections by similarly impressive margins.

In 1999, Hatch launched a quixotic bid for the GOP presidential nomina- on. Lacking money and broad political support, he finished last in Iowa's OP caucuses and dropped out the next week, endorsing Bush.

KEY VOTES

2008

Yes Prohibit discrimination based on genetic information

Yes Reauthorize farm and nutrition programs for five years

No Limit debate on "cap and trade" system for greenhouse gas emissions

No Allow lawsuits against companies that participated in warrantless wiretapping

No Limit debate on a bill to block a scheduled cut in Medicare payments to doctors

No Grant mortgage relief to homeowners and funding for Fannie Mae and Freddie Mac

Yes Approve a nuclear cooperation agreement with India

Yes Approve final $700 billion program to stabilize financial markets

No Allow consideration of a $14 billion auto industry loan package

2007

Yes Increase minimum wage by $2.10 an hour

No Limit debate on a comprehensive immigration bill

Yes Overhaul congressional lobbying and ethics rules for members and their staffs

Yes Limit debate on considering a bill to add House seats for the District of Columbia and Utah

No Limit debate on restoring habeas corpus rights to detainees

No Mandate minimum breaks for troops between deployments to Iraq or Afghanistan

Yes Override Bush veto of $23.2 billion water projects authorization bill

Yes Confirm Michael B. Mukasey as attorney general

Yes Limit debate on an energy policy overhaul containing $21.8 billion in tax incentives and reduced oil and gas subsidies

CQ VOTE STUDIES

	PARTY UNITY		PRESIDENTIAL SUPPORT	
	SUPPORT	OPPOSE	SUPPORT	OPPOSE
2008	93%	7%	80%	20%
2007	82%	18%	76%	24%
2006	93%	7%	88%	12%
2005	96%	4%	93%	7%
2004	98%	2%	94%	6%
2003	98%	2%	99%	1%
2002	93%	7%	98%	2%
2001	95%	5%	97%	3%
2000	94%	6%	55%	45%
1999	92%	8%	30%	70%

INTEREST GROUPS

	AFL-CIO	ADA	CCUS	ACU
2008	20%	10%	100%	80%
2007	29%	30%	91%	76%
2006	20%	5%	92%	84%
2005	14%	5%	100%	92%
2004	8%	10%	100%	96%
2003	0%	10%	100%	80%
2002	23%	5%	100%	95%
2001	6%	5%	86%	96%
2000	0%	0%	100%	95%
1999	11%	0%	88%	84%

Sen. Robert F. Bennett (R)

Elected 1992; 3rd term

CAPITOL OFFICE
224-5444
bennett.senate.gov
431 Dirksen Bldg. 20510-4403; fax 228-1168

COMMITTEES
Appropriations
Banking, Housing & Urban Affairs
Energy & Natural Resources
Rules & Administration - ranking member
Joint Economic
Joint Library - ranking member
Joint Printing

RESIDENCE
Salt Lake City

BORN
Sept. 18, 1933; Salt Lake City, Utah

RELIGION
Mormon

FAMILY
Wife, Joyce Bennett; six children

EDUCATION
U. of Utah, B.S. 1957 (political science)

MILITARY SERVICE
Utah National Guard, 1957-60

CAREER
Time management company CEO;
management consultant; public relations
and marketing executive; U.S. Transportation
Department official; congressional aide

POLITICAL HIGHLIGHTS
No previous office

ELECTION RESULTS

2004 GENERAL

Robert F. Bennett (R)	626,640	68.7%
R. Paul Van Dam (D)	258,955	28.4%
Gary R. Van Horn (C)	17,289	1.9%

2004 PRIMARY

Robert F. Bennett (R)	unopposed

PREVIOUS WINNING PERCENTAGES
1998 (64%); 1992 (55%)

One of the Senate's most influential conservatives, Bennett adeptly juggles his divergent roles as a behind-the-scenes GOP strategist and bipartisan consensus builder. As counsel and adviser to his close friend, Minority Leader Mitch McConnell of Kentucky, Bennett has a seat at the table in leadership meetings and quietly reaches out to Republicans as well as Democrats at the minority leader's behest. "Mitch will call on me for various things that I do without anybody knowing about them," he said.

Such backroom assignments are a good fit for Bennett. He is more substance than flash; he measures his words carefully, doesn't get publicly ruffled and often leaves the television podium to others. Reporters approach him not for pithy sound bites but for reasoned explanations of business-friendly conservative positions and insights about the Senate's inner workings.

Bennett has a history of seeking common ground with Democrats on complex issues. Most recently, he teamed with Ron Wyden of Oregon on broad legislation to provide universal health care coverage. The bill would upend the nation's existing system of employer-based health insurance, providing subsidies for Americans to buy coverage directly from private insurers. The senators have sought cosponsors two at a time, one Democrat and one Republican.

Bennett also is heavily involved in financial issues as No. 2 Republican on the Banking, Housing and Urban Affairs Committee and a member of the Joint Economic Committee. He backed the $700 billion effort to shore up the ailing financial services sector in fall 2008, saying it was necessary to avoid a severe crisis. However, he opposed a subsequent $14 billion bailout for U.S. automakers and President Obama's $787 billion economic stimulus law; he said of the latter, "The only thing this bill will stimulate is the national debt."

Bennett is the top Republican on the Rules and Administration Committee, where he generally works well with Democrats. He introduced a bill in 2008 with then-Chairwoman Dianne Feinstein of California to permit states to verify results from electronic voting machines using electronic records rather than paper. They held hearings on the measure but didn't move it further in the 110th Congress (2007-08).

Bennett recently has taken a more active interest in energy issues. In 2009, he joined the Energy and Natural Resources Committee and became the top Republican on Appropriations' Energy and Water panel. He sought to include $50 billion in the economic stimulus for low-carbon energy producers, but the provision was dropped after environmental groups criticized it as an attempt to build more nuclear power plants.

He did please some environmentalists when a wilderness bill for one rapidly growing area of Utah was included in a massive public-lands bill Obama signed into law in March 2009. The provision made 256,000 acres off-limits to development or energy exploration, while letting the government sell 5,000 to 9,000 acres of non-sensitive land to developers.

Bennett also tangled with Interior Secretary Ken Salazar, his former Senate colleague, in May 2009 after placing legislative "holds" on two nominees to senior Interior posts. Bennett cited the Interior secretary's promise to review a controversial decision on oil and gas leasing in areas of the state.

He has a penchant for gadgets: In 2000, he was the first senator to drive a high-mileage, low-emissions gasoline-electric hybrid car. He and Wyden proposed a plan in September 2006 to reward drivers for buying fuel-efficient cars. Bennett said he liked the concept because it did not seek to raise Corporate Average Fuel Economy standards, something the auto industry has fought. He subsequently voted against a 2007 energy bill that increased the standards to 35 miles per gallon by 2020.

Bennett hopes to educate colleagues about finding solutions to complex problems, such as those surrounding Social Security. After President George W. Bush released a much-criticized proposal in 2005 to move some Social Security funds to personal savings accounts, Bennett unveiled an alternative to raise the eligibility age and index payments based on need. He reintroduced similar legislation in February 2009.

Bennett often takes the side of business interests that regard some Democratic proposals as overreaching. In 2007, as Democrats proposed legislation to require credit card companies to provide more details to consumers and to correct marketing practices they portrayed as predatory, Bennett urged lawmakers to avoid imposing requirements or sanctions that would amount to price controls over the industry. In the 110th Congress, he also opposed legislation that would block Wal-Mart Stores Inc. and other retailers from owning their own banks, as such charters are prevalent in Bennett's home state.

Although a solid conservative on regulatory and fiscal issues, Bennett breaks party ranks on occasion. He backs efforts to curb tobacco sales to youths and opposes a constitutional amendment to ban desecration of the U.S. flag. He also supports funding for the National Endowment for the Arts, citing his passion for preserving American culture.

Bennett's rangy 6-foot-6-inch physique is hard to miss around the Capitol. He inherited that trait from his father, Wallace F. Bennett, who preceded him as a senator from Utah. The senior Bennett served from 1951 to 1974, and people who knew both men say that though the son is taller, he is otherwise the image of his father in looks and mannerisms. His mother, Frances Grant Bennett, was the daughter of a Mormon church president and served on the church's board.

Bennett grew up in Salt Lake City and attended the University of Utah, where he was student body president. He managed his father's 1962 run and worked for him as an aide. In the 1970s, he was an adviser to President Richard M. Nixon and owned a public relations firm that employed E. Howard Hunt, who was indicted in the Watergate burglary that ultimately led to Nixon's resignation. He left Washington in 1974 to work for Howard Hughes at Summa Corp. and then at Hughes Airwest.

Bennett decided to run for office for the first time in 1992 after taking his company — makers of the Franklin Day Planner schedule organizer — from a four-person shop in 1984 to an $82 million company in 1991 with more than 700 on staff, according to Inc. magazine. He's been helped on the campaign trail by an endearing, homespun sense of humor. In 2004, his campaign billboards carried the slogan "Big Heart. Big Ideas. Big Ears."

In his first Senate bid, Bennett edged past steel company executive Joe Cannon in the primary and went on to beat Democratic Rep. Wayne Owens in the general election. Bennett raised $4.5 million and outspent Owens by more than 2-to-1. In 1996, Bennett paid a $55,000 fine to the Federal Election Commission for what he called "unintentional violations" during the 1992 campaign. That had little effect on his re-election in 1998, when he handily defeated Democratic surgeon Scott Leckman. In 2004, he easily beat former Utah Attorney General R. Paul Van Dam with 69 percent of the vote.

Bennett's support of the financial rescue law angered his state's conservatives and led some to mull a primary challenge to him in 2010, but he took steps to ward them off. He raised $474,000 during the first three months of 2009 and brought in fellow Mormon and 2008 GOP presidential candidate Mitt Romney to stump for him in the state.

KEY VOTES

2008
Yes Prohibit discrimination based on genetic information
No Reauthorize farm and nutrition programs for five years
No Limit debate on "cap and trade" system for greenhouse gas emissions
No Allow lawsuits against companies that participated in warrantless wiretapping
No Limit debate on a bill to block a scheduled cut in Medicare payments to doctors
Yes Grant mortgage relief to homeowners and funding for Fannie Mae and Freddie Mac
Yes Approve a nuclear cooperation agreement with India
Yes Approve final $700 billion program to stabilize financial markets
No Allow consideration of a $14 billion auto industry loan package

2007
Yes Increase minimum wage by $2.10 an hour
Yes Limit debate on a comprehensive immigration bill
No Overhaul congressional lobbying and ethics rules for members and their staffs
Yes Limit debate on considering a bill to add House seats for the District of Columbia and Utah
No Limit debate on restoring habeas corpus rights to detainees
No Mandate minimum breaks for troops between deployments to Iraq or Afghanistan
Yes Override Bush veto of $23.2 billion water projects authorization bill
Yes Confirm Michael B. Mukasey as attorney general
No Limit debate on an energy policy overhaul containing $21.8 billion in tax incentives and reduced oil and gas subsidies

CQ VOTE STUDIES

	PARTY UNITY		PRESIDENTIAL SUPPORT	
	SUPPORT	OPPOSE	SUPPORT	OPPOSE
2008	85%	15%	85%	15%
2007	87%	13%	84%	16%
2006	87%	13%	90%	10%
2005	96%	4%	93%	7%
2004	97%	3%	94%	6%
2003	97%	3%	97%	3%
2002	94%	6%	98%	2%
2001	96%	4%	96%	4%
2000	92%	8%	52%	48%
1999	93%	7%	31%	69%

INTEREST GROUPS

	AFL-CIO	ADA	CCUS	ACU
2008	10%	15%	100%	64%
2007	16%	15%	100%	75%
2006	20%	15%	100%	72%
2005	14%	5%	100%	92%
2004	8%	20%	100%	88%
2003	0%	10%	100%	80%
2002	23%	5%	100%	100%
2001	13%	5%	100%	100%
2000	0%	5%	100%	95%
1999	11%	0%	94%	84%

Rep. Rob Bishop (R)

Elected 2002; 4th term

CAPITOL OFFICE
225-0453
www.house.gov/robbishop
123 Cannon Bldg. 20515-4401; fax 225-5857

COMMITTEES
Armed Services
Education & Labor
Natural Resources

RESIDENCE
Brigham City

BORN
July 13, 1951; Salt Lake City, Utah

RELIGION
Mormon

FAMILY
Wife, Jeralynn Bishop; five children

EDUCATION
U. of Utah, B.A. 1974 (political science)

CAREER
Teacher; lobbyist

POLITICAL HIGHLIGHTS
Utah House, 1979-95 (Speaker, 1993-95);
Utah Republican Party chairman, 1997-2001

ELECTION RESULTS

2008 GENERAL

Rob Bishop (R)	196,799	64.8%
Morgan Bowen (D)	92,469	30.5%
Kirk D. Pearson (CNSTP)	7,397	2.4%
Joseph G. Buchman (LIBERT)	6,780	2.2%

2008 PRIMARY

Rob Bishop (R)	unopposed

2006 GENERAL

Rob Bishop (R)	112,546	63.1%
Steven Olsen (D)	57,922	32.5%
Mark Hudson (CNSTP)	5,539	3.1%
Lynn Badler (LIBERT)	2,467	1.4%

PREVIOUS WINNING PERCENTAGES
2004 (68%); 2002 (61%)

Bishop holds traditional conservative views on the role of government and spends much of his time challenging Democrats on property rights, gun rights and education when he's not seeking more defense dollars for his district. His favored weapon in partisan disputes is dry and irreverent humor; he can make other members laugh even when they disagree with him.

A consistent theme of Bishop's career is his aversion to big government. "I want to leave this office with less power to do things than when I came here," he once said. He contends the federal government is only good for "unification" and all issues except the military can be resolved at the state level: "Not everything has to be done in Washington."

He railed against the early spending initiatives of the Obama administration, saying of the $787 billion economic stimulus law: "The problem isn't just the amount of money spent, but that the money spent simply won't solve the problems." As top-ranking Republican on the Natural Resources panel on parks and public lands, Bishop noted the stimulus package's funding for national parks, but questioned how much it would stimulate the economy.

He criticized Interior Secretary Ken Salazar in 2009 for visiting Utah only to promote the recent legislative achievements rather than to explain why he rescinded oil and gas leases on 77 acres of land in Utah. "How about recognizing the merits in letting Utahns decide how, if and when we want to develop the natural resources in this state ... Deal?" he asked Salazar in an angry letter.

As chairman of the Congressional Western Caucus, he led the charge in 2009 against Democrats' climate change legislation aimed at creating new "green jobs" to boost the economy. "Some of those jobs are as real as the Jolly Green Giant: it is a great ad concept, but it doesn't exist," Bishop told the Salt Lake City Tribune.

Bishop said he thinks Democrats are turning away from oil and gas too quickly. He offered a bill aimed at boosting investment in renewable energy by increasing royalties on fossil fuels taken from federal lands.

He chastises those who want to turn large swaths of public land into conservation areas. In 2007, he questioned Democrat Barney Frank's bill to designate parts of a Massachusetts river as scenic or recreational, giving it special protections. "In fact, the only part of this river that's scenic is the graffiti that's found on the bridges and the human embankments that are part of this river system," he said. "The only thing that's wild about this river are the gangs that wrote this graffiti in the first place."

In 2006, he won enactment of a bill establishing a wilderness area near the Air Force's Utah Test and Training Range, blocking a proposed nuclear waste dump on the Skull Valley Goshute Indian Reservation. And in a catchall public-lands bill enacted into law in early 2009, he successfully included two bills allowing for a swap of about 1,600 acres between the U.S. Forest Service and Bountiful City, giving the city control over land where the Bountiful Lions Club gun range and the Davis Aqueduct are situated.

A former part-time lobbyist for the Utah Sports Council, Bishop is a strong believer that the 2nd Amendment allows average citizens to keep firearms. He has sought to ensure gun and hunting laws are not infringed on by the federal government when doing land transactions.

From his seat on Education and Labor, he intends to battle renewal of the No Child Left Behind Act, the 2001 rewrite of the elementary and secondary education law. Bishop said the measure is "incredibly stupid" and interferes with state and local decision-making on schools.

He also sits on the Armed Services Committee, where he looks out for the defense jobs in his district. It is home to Hill Air Force Base, which he helped save from the 2005 round of base closures. He promotes the F-35A Lightning II stealth fighter plane that is intended to replace the F-16 and A-10. Some of the planes would be stationed at Hill. In the 110th Congress (2007-08), he helped secure millions of dollars for other projects at the base and other military facilities in his district, including the Dugway Proving Ground.

Bishop has worked to add a fourth House seat to Utah's delegation. He collaborated during the 109th Congress (2005-06) on a bill to increase the size of the House to 437 members, giving one seat to Republican Utah and the other to the Democratic District of Columbia. GOP leaders refused to put the bill on the floor, and when the Democratic House passed a similar measure in 2007, Bishop chose to vote "present." He said he'd just as soon wait until after the 2010 census, when Utah is likely to get a new member anyway. A similar bill was pushed forward in 2009.

Bishop, a member of the conservative Republican Study Committee, is typically loyal to his leadership. But he was one of 13 Republicans to vote in 2006 against a reauthorization of the 2001 Patriot Act anti-terrorism law, arguing it didn't provide sufficient protection for civil liberties. In 2005, he voted to bar the use of federal funds to go after a person's library or bookstore records.

When Bishop was a boy, his father, an accountant, served as mayor of his hometown of Kaysville, as a GOP delegate and as a campaign volunteer. "I remember him vividly, sitting at the telephone at the kitchen table, calling delegates. I thought that everybody did that," he said.

After college, Bishop taught high school English, debate and history. He later added German and Advanced Placement government courses. He spent two years in Germany as part of his Mormon mission experience. Bishop also worked as a part-time lobbyist for several groups prior to his election to the House, even while he was a school teacher.

He continued teaching after he won election to the Utah House, where he served 16 years, the last two as Speaker. After a stint as state Republican Party chairman, Bishop jumped into the 2002 race to succeed retiring Republican James V. Hansen. He defeated state House Majority Leader Kevin Garn for the GOP nomination, then won the general election with 61 percent of the vote. He easily won his subsequent re-elections.

In Washington, he loves to play tour guide for Capitol visitors, telling one group that the Rayburn House Office Building has "the warmth of a mental institution" and later explaining the House's electronic voting system: "Green is yes, red is no and yellow is 'I don't know what I'm doing.'"

KEY VOTES

2008
? Delay consideration of Colombia free-trade agreement
? Override Bush veto of federal farm and nutrition programs reauthorization bill
Yes Overhaul surveillance laws and permit dismissal of suits against companies that conducted warrantless wiretapping
? Grant mortgage relief to homeowners and funding for Fannie Mae and Freddie Mac
No Approve initial $700 billion program to stabilize financial markets
No Approve final $700 billion program to stabilize financial markets
No Provide $14 billion in loans to automakers

2007
No Increase minimum wage by $2.10 an hour
No Approve $124.2 billion in emergency war spending and set goal for redeployment of troops from Iraq
Yes Reject federal contraceptive assistance to international family planning groups
Yes Override Bush veto of $23.2 billion water projects authorization bill
No Implement Peru free-trade agreement
No Approve energy policy overhaul with new fuel economy standards
Yes Clear $473.5 billion omnibus spending bill, including $70 billion for military operations

CQ VOTE STUDIES

	PARTY UNITY		PRESIDENTIAL SUPPORT	
	SUPPORT	OPPOSE	SUPPORT	OPPOSE
2008	96%	4%	78%	22%
2007	97%	3%	80%	20%
2006	97%	3%	89%	11%
2005	97%	3%	78%	22%
2004	97%	3%	85%	15%

INTEREST GROUPS

	AFL-CIO	ADA	CCUS	ACU
2008	8%	0%	81%	100%
2007	10%	10%	88%	100%
2006	15%	10%	93%	87%
2005	20%	10%	81%	100%
2004	14%	5%	95%	100%

UTAH 1
North — part of Salt Lake City, Ogden

In the late 1840s, Mormon pioneers led by Brigham Young journeyed into the mountainous terrain of northern Utah. Today, the 1st — covering the northernmost part of the state — remains the center of the Mormon world. The district contains more than half of Salt Lake City, bringing in most of downtown and Temple Square, which includes the Tabernacle and the headquarters of the Church of Jesus Christ of Latter-day Saints. Salt Lake City International Airport also is in the 1st District.

Ogden, the district's second-largest city, was once a lively railroad town but today includes facilities for such major employers as Autoliv, a car safety systems manufacturer, and the IRS, which operates a call center downtown. Defense is important to the 1st. The 2005 BRAC round saved Hill Air Force Base, one of the state's largest employers, but scheduled the closure of the Deseret Chemical Depot.

The 1st contains much of Utah's ski country in the north-central part of the state, including Park City, a wealthy resort town and winter sports destination. In rural areas, especially in Box Elder and Cache counties

along the Idaho border, agriculture is king. Utah State University is in Logan in Cache County.

Many areas of Salt Lake City lean Democratic at the state and federal levels, but wealthy suburbs in heavily populated Salt Lake and Davis counties give the district its solid Republican lean. Most of the rural areas favor Republicans, although Democrats pick up some votes in Park City and in Weber County. Overall, John McCain took 64 percent of the district's 2008 presidential vote.

MAJOR INDUSTRY
Manufacturing, defense, technology, tourism, agriculture

MILITARY BASES
Hill Air Force Base, 4,500 military, 11,854 civilian (2007); Dugway Proving Ground, 28 military, 754 civilian (2007); Tooele Army Depot, 2 military, 425 civilian (2007); Deseret Chemical Depot, 2 military, 150 civilian (2007)

CITIES
Salt Lake City (pt.), 94,049; Ogden, 77,226; Layton, 58,474; Logan, 42,670; Bountiful, 41,301; Roy, 32,885; Clearfield, 25,974; Tooele, 22,502

NOTABLE
Great Salt Lake is the largest saltwater lake in the Western Hemisphere; Park City is the home of the U.S. Ski and Snowboard Team.

Rep. Jim Matheson (D)

Elected 2000; 5th term

CAPITOL OFFICE
225-3011
www.house.gov/matheson
2434 Rayburn Bldg. 20515-4402; fax 225-5638

COMMITTEES
Energy & Commerce
Science & Technology

RESIDENCE
Salt Lake City

BORN
March 21, 1960; Salt Lake City, Utah

RELIGION
Mormon

FAMILY
Wife, Amy Matheson; two children

EDUCATION
Harvard U., A.B. 1982 (government);
U. of California, Los Angeles, M.B.A. 1987

CAREER
Energy consulting firm owner; energy
company project manager; environmental
policy think tank advocate

POLITICAL HIGHLIGHTS
No previous office

ELECTION RESULTS

2008 GENERAL

Jim Matheson (D)	220,666	63.4%
Bill Dew (R)	120,083	34.5%
Matthew Arndt (LIBERT)	4,576	1.3%

2008 PRIMARY

Jim Matheson (D)	unopposed

2006 GENERAL

Jim Matheson (D)	133,231	59.0%
LaVar Christensen (R)	84,234	37.3%
W. David Perry (CNSTP)	3,395	1.5%
Bob Brister (GREEN)	3,338	1.5%

PREVIOUS WINNING PERCENTAGES
2004 (55%); 2002 (49%); 2000 (56%)

Matheson, the only Democrat in a five-man congressional delegation, regularly plays down his party affiliation. Instead, he calls attention to his independent voting record and focus on issues that matter to his constituents, including the economy and environment.

A member of the fiscally conservative Blue Dog Coalition, his vote can at times elude Democratic leaders — as well as President Obama in early 2009. He generally votes with his party on education, health care and labor, but when it comes to addressing the high-profile issue of climate change, for example, Matheson can be a crucial swing vote for Democrats on the Energy and Commerce Committee and its Energy and the Environment panel.

During the 110th Congress (2007-08), he was among the House Democrats who split with a majority of their party most often on votes that pitted the two parties against each other. He also was among those who most frequently supported President George W. Bush. In 2009, he backed Obama's $787 billion economic stimulus law, saying he believed it would boost job creation. But, sticking with the Utah delegation, he was one of 17 House Democrats to oppose the new president's $3.56 trillion budget blueprint for fiscal 2010.

In late 2008, the Blue Dogs were deeply divided over a $700 billion measure to shore up the ailing financial services industry, and Matheson voted no both times the House took a vote. "What really needs to happen is for Wall Street, Main Street and ordinary citizens to come together and deal with the fact that we cannot continue to live high off the hog on credit," he said.

Matheson supported Bush's tax cuts of 2001 and 2003, as well as a 2004 corporate tax cut. He also joined Republicans to back a 2005 bill to repeal the federal estate tax. But in 2007, he refused to support a bill to keep the alternative minimum tax from hitting 21 million more Americans. He complained the bill's costs weren't offset with revenue increases.

Matheson also has consistently backed funding for the wars in Iraq and Afghanistan, even when a majority of Democrats balked. And he has backed measures to crack down on illegal immigration and to limit abortion rights.

A mid-level member of Energy and Commerce, Matheson tried unsuccessfully to save Michigan Democrat John D. Dingell's chairmanship of the committee from a vigorous challenge by the more liberal California Democrat Henry A. Waxman in late 2008. Matheson worked the phones for Dingell and suggested efforts to reach consensus on upcoming climate change legislation would be lost if there was a change from Dingell.

As efforts on that legislation got under way in 2009, Matheson — who leads the Blue Dogs' energy task force — gave Waxman credit for seeking consensus, including Matheson in some early talks. But he also warned Democrats might be moving too fast and not taking into consideration concerns of industry and regional differences. "I just want to make sure we are deliberate in how we go about this," he said in April 2009.

Matheson sticks with the Utah delegation on environmental issues. When legislation to advance construction of a nuclear waste dump at Nevada's Yucca Mountain came before the 107th Congress (2001-02), Matheson voted no, saying Westerners had been exposed to enough nuclear dangers. In 2009, he supported the idea of creating a blue-ribbon panel to discuss alternatives for nuclear waste disposal and pushed legislation to bar the import of foreign radioactive waste into the United States.

He and Utah Republican Sen. Robert F. Bennett saw passage of their bill to set 256,000 acres off-limits to energy exploration. The measure was includas part of an omnibus lands bill Obama signed into law in March 2009.

Matheson also sits on the Energy and Commerce Health Subcommittee, here he will take part in efforts to reform the health care system. He vocates tax credits for individuals and employers to purchase insurance d supports expanding existing federal programs.

Matheson joined with Utah Republicans in an effort to win resumption of deral compensation to people who became ill as a result of exposure to diation from atomic bomb testing in Nevada. Compensation for those "down-inders" was authorized in 1990, but funding had halted in 2000. The issue sonates with Matheson, whose father died in 1990 of bone marrow cancer, disease linked to radiation exposure. Scott Matheson, a two-term governor Utah, had lived in an area of southern Utah affected by the nuclear tests.

Matheson also sits on the trade subcommittee and departs from his party support free trade.

Party leaders give him leeway to vote how he needs. In 2007, when the ouse passed a bill to grant voting rights to the Democratic delegate from the istrict of Columbia and add a House seat for Republican-dominated Utah, emocratic leaders held up the bill until they were sure it couldn't jeopardize atheson's seat. The legislation ultimately was blocked in the Senate.

He also holds a seat on the Science and Technology panel. He co-thored a 2007 law designed to bolster math and science education.

Although his father was the governor, Matheson said his mother, Norma, as more responsible for his own interest in public service because she was volved in many civic projects. And he said his Mormon upbringing infused m with a sense of moral purpose.

While majoring in government at Harvard, he served a summer internship the office of House Speaker Thomas P. "Tip" O'Neill Jr., a Massachusetts emocrat. After college, he worked at an environmental policy think tank in ashington for three years. He returned to Utah after graduate school, orked in private sector energy jobs and started an energy consulting firm.

Matheson ran for Congress in 2000 for the seat held by GOP incumbent errill Cook, who subsequently lost the primary to Internet executive erek W. Smith. Smith received a dose of bad press over his past business actices, and Matheson sailed to victory by 15 percentage points. In post-00 census redistricting, Republicans redrew the 2nd District to guarantee GOP victory. But Matheson squeaked to victory in 2002 by 1,641 votes. e has solidified his grip since; he was elected in 2008 to a fifth term with percent, even as GOP presidential candidate Sen. John McCain of Ari-na carried the district with 58 percent.

KEY VOTES

2008
No   Delay consideration of Colombia free-trade agreement
No   Override Bush veto of federal farm and nutrition programs reauthorization bill
Yes Overhaul surveillance laws and permit dismissal of suits against companies that conducted warrantless wiretapping
Yes Grant mortgage relief to homeowners and funding for Fannie Mae and Freddie Mac
No   Approve initial $700 billion program to stabilize financial markets
No   Approve final $700 billion program to stabilize financial markets
No   Provide $14 billion in loans to automakers

2007
Yes Increase minimum wage by $2.10 an hour
No   Approve $124.2 billion in emergency war spending and set goal for redeployment of troops from Iraq
No   Reject federal contraceptive assistance to international family planning groups
Yes Override Bush veto of $23.2 billion water projects authorization bill
Yes Implement Peru free-trade agreement
Yes Approve energy policy overhaul with new fuel economy standards
Yes Clear $473.5 billion omnibus spending bill, including $70 billion for military operations

CQ VOTE STUDIES

	PARTY UNITY		PRESIDENTIAL SUPPORT	
	SUPPORT	OPPOSE	SUPPORT	OPPOSE
2008	86%	14%	32%	68%
2007	79%	21%	20%	80%
2006	66%	34%	67%	33%
2005	69%	31%	43%	57%
2004	64%	36%	50%	50%

INTEREST GROUPS

	AFL-CIO	ADA	CCUS	ACU
2008	67%	55%	78%	36%
2007	83%	75%	80%	36%
2006	57%	45%	87%	64%
2005	60%	75%	78%	40%
2004	60%	70%	86%	48%

TAH 2

outh and east – part of Salt Lake City, rural Utah

king in plateaus, towering cliffs, forests and mountain trails, the 2nd ts a reverse L-shaped swath across eastern and southern Utah from stern Salt Lake City in the north to Four Corners in the southeastern rner of the state and then west across Utah's southern tier.

uch of eastern Salt Lake County consists of bedroom communities ch as Murray. The area also is home to health care firms, a stadium for ccer's Real Salt Lake in Sandy and the University of Utah — the state's gest public university. In the southwestern portion of the district, St. orge in Washington County has attracted retirees for decades. But ge portions of the 2nd struggle. In the district's eastern and southern unties, population decline has slowed, but so has job growth. More an 30 percent of residents in San Juan County, home to part of the vajo Nation, live in poverty, by far the highest percentage in the state. rfield and Grand counties have the state's highest unemployment es. In Grand, artists and residents who rely on seasonal tourism-sed jobs populate Moab, a haven for outdoor enthusiasts.

Land-use issues are important in the 2nd, which includes all five of the state's national parks — Arches, Bryce Canyon, Canyonlands, Capitol Reef and Zion. Much of the district is federal land. San Juan County contains Utah's quadrant of Four Corners, the only point in the United States where four states meet. Carbon County in the middle of the state hosts a dwindling mining sector.

The district's part of Salt Lake County, where almost 60 percent of the 2nd's residents live, provides some Democratic votes. In the 2008 presidential election, Grand County gave Democrat Barack Obama a slim majority of 51 percent, his second-highest percentage in the state and one of only three counties that he won in Utah. John McCain, who took 58 percent of the 2nd's presidential vote overall, won his highest percentage statewide (83 percent) in Uintah County in the east.

MAJOR INDUSTRY
Manufacturing, tourism, ranching

CITIES
Sandy, 88,418; Salt Lake City (pt.), 87,694; St. George, 49,663; Murray, 34,024; Millcreek (unincorporated), 30,377

NOTABLE
San Juan County includes Utah's portion of Monument Valley.

Rep. Jason Chaffetz (R)

Elected 2008; 1st term

Assertive and energetic, Chaffetz is a strict fiscal conservative who wants to upend Congress' regular ways of doing business. Like his friend Arizona Republican Jeff Flake, he abhors earmarks, the member-driven spending requests for pet projects. Chaffetz (CHAY-fits) believes the federal government's role is "to get out of the way" of people's lives: "We are overregulated and overtaxed," he says.

Chaffetz serves on the same committees as his predecessor, Republican Chris Cannon: Oversight and Government Reform, Judiciary and Natural Resources. He sought the Oversight post so he could stress accountability on how the government spends money. "Washington is not known for shrinking," he said. "I often joke that a billion dollars is merely a rounding error here."

He made headlines in May 2009 as Oversight's top Republican on the Federal Workforce, Postal Service and the District of Columbia panel by seeking to counter a D.C. City Council vote to recognize the validity of same-sex marriages performed elsewhere. He also got involved in the debate over whether the District deserves full voting rights in Congress; he opposes the measure on constitutional grounds and said the city should be ceded back to Maryland.

Chaffetz is one of Judiciary's few non-lawyers. But one of the issues that propelled him to victory in his 2008 primary win over Cannon was his more conservative stance on illegal immigration. He also is a forceful advocate of personal privacy; when the Transportation Security Administration began testing whole-body imaging technology at some airports in spring 2009, he blasted the system as "TSA porn" and introduced a bill seeking to limit its use.

Chaffetz considered a run for Congress in 2006 against 2nd District Democrat Jim Matheson, but decided against it. He easily defeated Cannon in the 2008 GOP primary, then trounced Democratic journalist and professor Bennion L. Spencer in November.

Chaffetz's father's first wife was Katherine "Kitty" Dickson, who later married Massachusetts Democratic Gov. Michael S. Dukakis. In college, Chaffetz — then a Democrat — was a Utah co-chairman of Dukakis' 1988 presidential campaign.

CAPITOL OFFICE
225-7751
chaffetz.house.gov
1032 Longworth Bldg. 20515-4403; fax 225-5629

COMMITTEES
Judiciary
Natural Resources
Oversight & Government Reform

RESIDENCE
Alpine

BORN
March 26, 1967; Los Gatos, Calif.

RELIGION
Mormon

FAMILY
Wife, Julie Chaffetz; three children

EDUCATION
Brigham Young U., B.A. 1989 (communications)

CAREER
Public relations firm owner; gubernatorial and campaign aide; pharmaceutical company marketing executive; alternative fuel company marketing executive; personal care products company executive

POLITICAL HIGHLIGHTS
Utah Valley University Board of Trustees, 2007-08

ELECTION RESULTS

2008 GENERAL

Jason Chaffetz (R)	187,035	65.6%
Bennion L. Spencer (D)	80,626	28.3%
Jim Noorlander (CNSTP)	17,408	6.1%

2008 PRIMARY

Jason Chaffetz (R)	28,618	59.8%
Chris Cannon (R)	19,255	40.2%

UTAH 3
Central – part of Salt Lake County, Provo

Utah's centrally located 3rd takes in some Salt Lake City suburbs and then follows Interstate 15 south to Provo and Orem, the district's economic hubs. It stretches west to pick up rural Millard and Beaver counties on the state's western border. A heavily Mormon-influenced district, the 3rd has the nation's lowest median age (24.5).

Provo's predominately Mormon Brigham Young University, founded by its namesake in 1875, is one of the state's largest employers. Students and graduates from BYU and other district colleges have helped lure businesses to the Provo-Orem area. Some big-name software firms maintain key facilities here, and companies in the dietary supplement industry have headquarters in the 3rd. Salt Lake County's residents, in the northernmost

tip of the district, make up slightly less than half of the 3rd's population.

Outside Utah and Salt Lake counties, cattle ranching, farming, mining and tourism sustain small-town life. Ranchers in Millard County and hog farmers in Beaver County tend to vote Republican, but some mining communities like Magna will support Democratic candidates.

The district has a heavy GOP tilt, and John McCain received his best showing in the state here in the 2008 presidential election.

MAJOR INDUSTRY
Technology, mining, higher education, ranching

CITIES
West Valley City, 108,896; Provo, 105,166; Orem, 84,324; West Jordan, 68,336; Taylorsville, 57,439; Kearns (unincorporated), 33,659

NOTABLE
Philo T. Farnsworth, credited with inventing television, lived in Provo; Millard County, and its county seat Fillmore, are named after the 13th president.

Gov. Jim Douglas (R)

First elected: 2002
Length of term: 2 years
Term expires: 1/11
Salary: $150,051
Phone: (802) 828-3333

Residence: Middlebury
Born: June 21, 1951; East Longmeadow, Mass.
Religion: United Church of Christ
Family: Wife, Dorothy Douglas; two children
Education: Middlebury College, A.B. 1972 (Russian)
Career: Gubernatorial aide
Political highlights: Vt. House, 1973-79 (majority leader, 1977-79); Vt. secretary of state, 1981-93; Republican nominee for U.S. Senate, 1992; Vt. treasurer, 1995-2003

Election results:

2008 GENERAL

Jim Douglas (R)	170,492	53.4%
Anthony Pollina (I)	69,791	21.9%
Gaye Symington (D)	69,534	21.8%
Tony O'Connor (CRE)	3,106	1.0%

Lt. Gov. Brian Dubie (R)

First elected: 2002
Length of term: 2 years
Term expires: 1/11
Salary: $63,690
Phone: (802) 828-2226

LEGISLATURE

General Assembly: January-April

Senate: 30 members, 2-year terms
2009 ratios: 22 D, 7 R, 1 PRO; 20 men, 10 women
Salary: $625/week
Phone: (802) 828-2241

House: 150 members, 2-year terms
2009 ratios: 95 D, 48 R, 5 PRO, 2 I; 93 men, 57 women
Salary: $625/week
Phone: (802) 828-2247

TERM LIMITS

Governor: No
Senate: No
House: No

URBAN STATISTICS

CITY	POPULATION
Burlington	38,889
Essex	18,626
Rutland	17,292
Colchester	16,986
South Burlington	15,814

REGISTERED VOTERS

Voters do not register by party.

POPULATION

2008 population (est.)	621,270
2000 population	608,827
1990 population	562,758
Percent change (1990-2000)	+8.2%
Rank among states (2008)	49
Median age	37.7
Born in state	54.3%
Foreign born	3.8%
Violent crime rate	114/100,000
Poverty level	9.4%
Federal workers	5,630
Military	4,605

ELECTIONS

STATE ELECTION OFFICIAL
(802) 828-2304
DEMOCRATIC PARTY
(802) 229-1783
REPUBLICAN PARTY
(802) 223-3411

MISCELLANEOUS

Web: www.vermont.gov
Capital: Montpelier

U.S. CONGRESS

Senate: 1 Democrat, 1 independent
House: 1 Democrat

2000 Census Statistics by District

DIST.	2008 VOTE FOR PRESIDENT OBAMA	MCCAIN	WHITE	BLACK	ASIAN	HISP	MEDIAN INCOME	WHITE COLLAR	BLUE COLLAR	SERVICE INDUSTRY	OVER 64	UNDER 18	COLLEGE EDUCATION	RURAL	SQ. MILES
AL	67%	30%	96%	0%	1%	1%	$40,856	61%	25%	15%	13%	24%	29%	62%	9,250
STATE	67	30	96	0	1	1	$40,856	61	25	15	13	24	29	62	9,250
U.S.	53	46	69	12	4	13	$41,994	60	25	15	12	26	24	21	3,537,438

Grand Isle

Franklin

Orleans

Essex

Lamoille

● **Burlington**

Caledonia

Chittenden

Montpelier
★

Washington

● **Barre**

Addison

Orange

At Large

Rutland
●

Windsor

Rutland

Bennington

Windham

● **Bennington**

●**Brattleboro**

Sen. Patrick J. Leahy (D)

Elected 1974; 6th term

CAPITOL OFFICE
224-4242
leahy.senate.gov
433 Russell Bldg. 20510-4502; fax 224-3479

COMMITTEES
Agriculture, Nutrition & Forestry
Appropriations
   (State-Foreign Operations - chairman)
Judiciary - chairman

RESIDENCE
Middlesex

BORN
March 31, 1940; Montpelier, Vt.

RELIGION
Roman Catholic

FAMILY
Wife, Marcelle Leahy; three children

EDUCATION
St. Michael's College, B.A. 1961
(political science); Georgetown U., J.D. 1964

CAREER
Lawyer

POLITICAL HIGHLIGHTS
Chittenden County state's attorney, 1966-75

ELECTION RESULTS

2004 GENERAL

Patrick J. Leahy (D)	216,972	70.6%
John "Jack" McMullen (R)	75,398	24.5%
Cris Ericson (M)	6,486	2.1%
Craig Barclay Hill (GREEN)	3,999	1.3%
Keith Stern (I)	3,300	1.1%

2004 PRIMARY

Patrick J. Leahy (D)	27,459	94.3%
Craig Barclay Hill (D)	1,573	5.4%

PREVIOUS WINNING PERCENTAGES
1998 (72%); 1992 (54%); 1986 (63%); 1980 (50%);
1974 (50%)

Leahy employs a mixture of wry humor and partisan stubbornness as chairman of the Judiciary Committee, the site of some of the most brutal battles in Congress. He had lost more fights than he won as top-ranking Democrat on the panel when Republicans were in control. But he wasted no time taking on the George W. Bush administration after Democrats took the majority in the 2006 elections, and he is among the Obama administration's staunchest supporters against GOP attacks.

Leahy is fourth in seniority among current Senate Democrats. His political longevity allows him to pursue multiple policy interests — including ending the use of land mines, overhauling federal patent law and promoting civil liberties. But more recently he has expended tremendous sums of energy on vigorous oversight of the Bush administration, generating both headlines and push-back from Republicans. And he is intent on pursuing what he regards as the administration's many abuses of power.

But he must contend during the 111th Congress (2009-10) with a new top-ranking Republican on the panel — Jeff Sessions of Alabama, who is more conservative and combative than Pennsylvania's Arlen Specter, who announced in April 2009 that he was joining the Democratic caucus.

During the 110th Congress (2007-08), Leahy's committee led probes into issues ranging from warrantless surveillance of communications involving suspected terrorists to the firings of nine federal prosecutors for reasons that appeared suspiciously political. The Judiciary Committee's investigation of the prosecutor firings — on which Leahy allowed New York Democrat Charles E. Schumer to take the public lead — helped usher Attorney General Alberto R. Gonzales out of the Justice Department. Leahy didn't relent after Bush's departure; in February 2009, he proposed a "truth commission" to investigate everything from Bush's detainee and interrogation policies to the war in Iraq and the U.S. attorney firings. "We need to come to a shared understanding of the failures of the recent past," he said.

In early 2009, he offered a bill to narrow the "state secrets" privilege, a common-law doctrine allowing the federal government to withhold from the public materials that might harm national security.

He can draw criticism from Democratic allies who say he is too accommodating, particularly on judicial nominations. He caught a lot of flak from liberal groups in 2005 for his support of John G. Roberts Jr., Bush's nominee for chief justice of the Supreme Court. But Leahy later opposed conservative Supreme Court nominee Samuel A. Alito Jr., joining a quixotic filibuster attempt by Massachusetts Democrats John Kerry and Edward M. Kennedy.

He joined Democrats in pitched battles over the 1991 confirmation of Supreme Court Justice Clarence Thomas. Leahy elicited Thomas' assertions he had never discussed the landmark *Roe v. Wade* decision on abortion — statements Thomas' opponents exhibited as proof he was being evasive.

Leahy considers his long campaign against the use of land mines his most important issue, one on which he frequently clashed with the Bush administration as well as the Clinton administration. Leahy wrote legislation restricting the sale or transfer of cluster bombs. The Leahy War Victims Fund, established in 1989, provides millions of dollars in aid each year to civilian victims of armed conflict.

Leahy was drawn to that cause after a trip to Nicaragua. While there, he met a boy in a Red Cross field hospital who had lost a leg after stepping on a land mine. In a 2008 speech in Ireland, Leahy said, "I believe we should be guided by the conviction that this is, above all, a moral issue. Weapons that are inherently indiscriminate, whether by design or effect, should have no place in today's world."

Working with Utah Republican Orrin G. Hatch, he has pushed for a broad overhaul of federal patent law. It has foundered in part over a lack of compromise on provisions on calculating damages awards in patent infringement lawsuits. In 2008, Republicans openly threatened to block the bill in retaliation for the slow pace of appellate court confirmations.

Leahy opposed the U.S. invasion of Iraq and was a frequent critic of Bush's conduct of the war. As chairman of the Appropriations subcommittee in charge of the State Department's budget, he has sought to increase spending for humanitarian efforts overseas. "We can lead in the world, we can build new alliances and work to solve conflicts, promote stability and develop new markets, or we can turn inward," he said in April 2009 in successfully arguing for an additional $4 billion in international assistance in the fiscal 2010 budget.

Leahy was Judiciary chairman on Sept. 11, 2001, when terrorists attacked the World Trade Center in New York City and the Pentagon, and since then he has been a staunch advocate for civil liberties. "We fought two world wars to protect, we fought a civil war, we fought a revolutionary war to keep these values," he said.

The first major legislation enacted in response to the terrorist attacks was the Bush administration's Patriot Act, which greatly expanded law enforcement powers to investigate suspected terrorists. But Leahy worked to modify the measure, warning it infringed on civil liberties. "As draconian as it was, the terrorism bill was far more constitutional than it would have been had I not been chairman," he said. When the law came up for renewal in the 109th Congress (2005-06), he opposed extending several expiring provisions of the law, but the White House and congressional Republicans prevailed.

In November 2001, federal authorities intercepted an anonymous letter addressed to Leahy that was laced with deadly anthrax spores. But unlike an earlier letter to then-Senate Democratic leader Tom Daschle of South Dakota that created a bioterrorism scare in Congress, this one caused no harm.

He also protects the interests of his rural state. On the Agriculture Committee, he is a defender of Northeastern dairy farmers during conflicts with other dairy-producing areas. In 2008, he engineered the renewal of the Milk Income Loss Contract Program, a price-support subsidy for dairy farmers.

Almost 70 years old, Leahy still is plugged into pop culture and technology. A fan of the Batman comic character, he and his son had cameos in the 1997 film "Batman and Robin," and Leahy had another Batman movie cameo in "The Dark Knight" in 2008. An avid photographer, he has taken his camera all over the world and had his work published in newspapers and magazines.

Leahy's father was an Irish-American who ran a printing business in Montpelier, the state capital, out of the same building that housed the family. When he walked to school, he went by — and sometimes through — the Capitol building, and his mother rented rooms to state lawmakers when the legislature was in session. His mother's family, Italian immigrants, worked in Vermont's granite quarries.

His first exposure to the Senate was during the early 1960s when he was a student at Georgetown Law School and he observed the Senate in operation.

Leahy wanted to be a prosecutor or a U.S. senator. He ended up doing both, serving as a local prosecutor for eight years before being elected to the Senate in 1974 when a Watergate-fueled voter backlash helped him beat a favored Republican. At 34, he was the youngest elected senator in state history, and remains the only Democrat Vermont has ever elected to the Senate.

Leahy withstood the GOP landslide of 1980 to win his first re-election by just 2,500 votes. Since then he has been comfortably entrenched.

KEY VOTES

2008

Yes Prohibit discrimination based on genetic information
Yes Reauthorize farm and nutrition programs for five years
Yes Limit debate on "cap and trade" system for greenhouse gas emissions
Yes Allow lawsuits against companies that participated in warrantless wiretapping
Yes Limit debate on a bill to block a scheduled cut in Medicare payments to doctors
Yes Grant mortgage relief to homeowners and funding for Fannie Mae and Freddie Mac
No   Approve a nuclear cooperation agreement with India
Yes Approve final $700 billion program to stabilize financial markets
Yes Allow consideration of a $14 billion auto industry loan package

2007

Yes Increase minimum wage by $2.10 an hour
Yes Limit debate on a comprehensive immigration bill
Yes Overhaul congressional lobbying and ethics rules for members and their staffs
Yes Limit debate on considering a bill to add House seats for the District of Columbia and Utah
Yes Limit debate on restoring habeas corpus rights to detainees
Yes Mandate minimum breaks for troops between deployments to Iraq or Afghanistan
Yes Override Bush veto of $23.2 billion water projects authorization bill
No   Confirm Michael B. Mukasey as attorney general
Yes Limit debate on an energy policy overhaul containing $21.8 billion in tax incentives and reduced oil and gas subsidies

CQ VOTE STUDIES

	PARTY UNITY		PRESIDENTIAL SUPPORT	
	SUPPORT	OPPOSE	SUPPORT	OPPOSE
2008	98%	2%	30%	70%
2007	95%	5%	35%	65%
2006	97%	3%	46%	54%
2005	97%	3%	36%	64%
2004	94%	6%	58%	42%
2003	97%	3%	51%	49%
2002	98%	2%	67%	33%
2001	98%	2%	62%	38%
2000	94%	6%	89%	11%
1999	94%	6%	82%	18%

INTEREST GROUPS

	AFL-CIO	ADA	CCUS	ACU
2008	100%	100%	50%	4%
2007	100%	95%	36%	0%
2006	93%	95%	33%	0%
2005	86%	100%	28%	0%
2004	100%	100%	50%	8%
2003	85%	85%	35%	16%
2002	100%	95%	55%	0%
2001	100%	100%	38%	8%
2000	75%	85%	58%	8%
1999	100%	95%	41%	4%

Sen. Bernard Sanders (I)

Elected 2006; 1st term

CAPITOL OFFICE
224-5141
sanders.senate.gov
332 Dirksen Bldg. 20510-4503; fax 228-0776

COMMITTEES
Budget
Energy & Natural Resources
Environment & Public Works
   (Green Jobs & the New Economy - chairman)
Health, Education, Labor & Pensions
Veterans' Affairs

RESIDENCE
Burlington

BORN
Sept. 8, 1941; Brooklyn, N.Y.

RELIGION
Jewish

FAMILY
Wife, Jane O'Meara Sanders; four children

EDUCATION
Brooklyn College, attended 1959-60;
U. of Chicago, B.A. 1964 (political science)

CAREER
College instructor; freelance writer; documentary
filmmaker; carpenter

POLITICAL HIGHLIGHTS
Liberty Union candidate for U.S. Senate, 1972;
Liberty Union candidate for governor, 1972;
Liberty Union candidate for U.S. Senate, 1974;
Liberty Union candidate for governor, 1976; mayor
of Burlington, 1981-89; independent candidate for
governor, 1986; independent candidate for
U.S. House, 1988; U.S. House, 1991-2007

ELECTION RESULTS

2006 GENERAL

Bernard Sanders (I)	171,638	65.4%
Rich Tarrant (R)	84,924	32.4%

2006 PRIMARY

Bernard Sanders (D)	35,954	94.2%
others (D)	2,232	5.8%

PREVIOUS WINNING PERCENTAGES
2004 House Election (67%); 2002 House Election
(64%); 2000 House Election (69%); 1998 House
Election (63%); 1996 House Election (55%); 1994
House Election (50%); 1992 House Election (58%);
1990 House Election (56%)

As a first-term senator, Sanders has tailored his behavior as well as his dark suits in shifting from his bluster in the House to the more collegial atmosphere of the Senate. The Vermont independent — a self-described socialist who caucuses with Democrats — less often looks like a rumpled professor who spent half the night in the library and the other half tumbling in a dryer.

Sanders is often annoyed at the country's state of affairs in economic policy or civil liberties, but with Democrats in control of the White House and Congress, his voice is calmer and lower in decibel level. While he had been a lonely voice during his eight House terms, the ability of a single senator to block legislation has boosted his clout in committee and on the floor. But he has limited his battles, drawing attention to his concerns without stalling legislation entirely.

Sanders offered the only amendment allowed in either chamber to the $700 billion financial plan to shore up the ailing financial services industry in October 2008. But he settled for a voice vote, rather than a roll call vote, and his attempt to place a surtax on the wealthy was voted down. He did successfully attach to a $3.56 trillion budget resolution for fiscal 2010 an amendment requiring the Federal Reserve to disclose details about its emergency aid to various financial institutions.

With a seat on the Budget Committee, Sanders had heard about the economic crisis in anguished letters from constituents about high gas and heating-oil prices. But not all was bleak. The stopgap spending law passed at the end of 2008 doubled funding for the Low Income Home Energy Assistance Program to $5.1 billion, meaning Vermont could get $35 million.

He supported President Obama's $787 billion economic stimulus law in February 2009, though he said he thought the bill wasn't big enough. "Is it everything that I want? No. Is it a major step forward and a new direction for America? It is," Sanders said. "I wish there was a lot more. I'm disappointed. But nonetheless, you're talking about $800 billion invested in this country, creating millions of new jobs."

On the Environment and Public Works Committee, Sanders is a vocal advocate for limiting greenhouse gas emissions. In 2009 he was named chairman of the committee's panel on Green Jobs and the New Economy and said he would continue working to boost renewable energy sources and new job opportunities "through unprecedented green technologies, including Vermont-based weatherization and solar projects."

A member of the Energy and Natural Resources Committee, Sanders and then-Democratic Sen. Hillary Rodham Clinton of New York successfully included in the 2007 energy bill authorization of $100 million to train workers in energy-efficient "green-collar jobs."

He has had satisfaction in his ability to make such changes to legislation. "There is a reason why members in the House run for the Senate, but senators don't run for the House," said Sanders. "Here, there is a much greater opportunity to get provisions and language into a manager's amendment or a bill that we've been working very hard on."

He has focused on higher education from his seats on the Veterans' Affairs and Health, Education, Labor and Pensions (HELP) panels. During the 110th Congress (2007-08), he cosponsored with Virginia Democrat Jim Webb a new GI Bill to provide up to $90,000 to cover tuition at colleges in a veteran's home state.

And he helped obtain funding for a Vermont program that attempts to send a specialist to the home of every veteran returning from Iraq or Afghanistan, offering treatment for post-traumatic stress disorder, traumatic brain injuries and other mental health issues.

Sanders is an advocate of a national health care program. He was among 16 senators — the others all Democrats — who wrote a letter to chairmen of committees overseeing health care reform legislation, calling for the creation of a "public plan option" for insurance in legislation. And he has worked with HELP Chairman Edward M. Kennedy of Massachusetts to expand a federal program that provides funding for community health centers.

Sanders has long described himself as a socialist, and defends against its negative connotation. When Alabama GOP Rep. Spencer Bachus claimed in April 2009 at a local gathering in his district that he could count 17 socialists in Congress, Sanders responded with an opinion column in the Boston Globe: "Spencer Bachus is one of the few people I know from Alabama. I bet I'm the only socialist he knows, although he darkly claims there are 17 socialists lurking in the House of Representatives. I doubt there are any other socialists, let alone 17 more, in all of Congress. I also doubt that Bachus understands much about democratic socialism." He continued, "Washington is often a place where name-calling partisan politics too often trumps policy."

Sanders was the first identifiable socialist in the House since Wisconsin's Victor L. Berger, who served four terms in the early part of the 20th century. Sanders keeps a plaque on his office wall honoring Eugene V. Debs, founder of the American Socialist Party.

Sanders was born and raised in Brooklyn. His mother died at 46 when he was 19. His father, a Jewish immigrant from Poland whose family was killed in the Holocaust, was a paint salesman.

After college, he lived on a kibbutz in Israel. He returned briefly to New York before joining a wave of liberals abandoning urban life in 1968 for Vermont. Sanders held a variety of jobs in the Green Mountain state, from freelance writer to carpenter, and built a foundation in progressive politics.

While other transplants flocked to the Democratic Party, Sanders helped found the Liberty Union Party. He ran unsuccessfully for statewide office four times in the early 1970s. He then focused on local office and in 1981 unseated the Democratic mayor of Burlington by 10 votes. He became the city's first socialist mayor and won three more two-year terms by pursuing populist goals while presiding over the revitalization of the city's downtown.

Sanders was seen as a spoiler when he ran in 1988 for Vermont's lone House seat, vacated when Republican James M. Jeffords ran for the Senate. But Sanders lost to Republican Peter Smith by only 4 percentage points. During a rematch in 1990, Smith's efforts to portray Sanders as an admirer of Communist Cuban dictator Fidel Castro backfired, and Sanders won with 56 percent of the vote.

In 1992, Democrats avoided fielding a strong candidate, and Sanders won re-election against Tim Philbin, a favorite of state GOP conservatives.

Sanders barely held on during the national Republican wave of 1994 and had another anemic showing in 1996. In 2000, he captured his highest percentage yet with 69 percent of the vote.

When Jeffords announced his plans to retire from the Senate, Sanders jumped into the race to replace him. Campaigning as a Democrat, he had no trouble beating four political unknowns in the primary, then ran as an independent in the general election. His Republican rival, software magnate Rich Tarrant, spent $7 million of his own money to paint Sanders as a radical, but Sanders won with 65 percent of the vote. He enjoyed the financial backing of the Democratic Senatorial Campaign Committee headed by New York Sen. Charles E. Schumer, who had attended the same schools as Sanders in Brooklyn.

KEY VOTES

2008

Yes   Prohibit discrimination based on genetic information

Yes   Reauthorize farm and nutrition programs for five years

Yes   Limit debate on "cap and trade" system for greenhouse gas emissions

Yes   Allow lawsuits against companies that participated in warrantless wiretapping

Yes   Limit debate on a bill to block a scheduled cut in Medicare payments to doctors

Yes   Grant mortgage relief to homeowners and funding for Fannie Mae and Freddie Mac

No   Approve a nuclear cooperation agreement with India

No   Approve final $700 billion program to stabilize financial markets

Yes   Allow consideration of a $14 billion auto industry loan package

2007

Yes   Increase minimum wage by $2.10 an hour

No   Limit debate on a comprehensive immigration bill

Yes   Overhaul congressional lobbying and ethics rules for members and their staffs

Yes   Limit debate on considering a bill to add House seats for the District of Columbia and Utah

Yes   Limit debate on restoring habeas corpus rights to detainees

Yes   Mandate minimum breaks for troops between deployments to Iraq or Afghanistan

Yes   Override Bush veto of $23.2 billion water projects authorization bill

No   Confirm Michael B. Mukasey as attorney general

Yes   Limit debate on an energy policy overhaul containing $21.8 billion in tax incentives and reduced oil and gas subsidies

CQ VOTE STUDIES

	PARTY UNITY		PRESIDENTIAL SUPPORT	
	SUPPORT	OPPOSE	SUPPORT	OPPOSE
2008	98%	2%	30%	70%
2007	97%	3%	33%	67%
House Service:				
2006	98%	2%	15%	85%
2005	97%	3%	15%	85%
2004	98%	2%	29%	71%
2003	95%	5%	15%	85%
2002	98%	2%	18%	82%
2001	97%	3%	16%	84%
2000	96%	4%	78%	22%

INTEREST GROUPS

	AFL-CIO	ADA	CCUS	ACU
2008	100%	100%	38%	8%
2007	100%	95%	27%	4%
House Service:				
2006	100%	100%	27%	8%
2005	93%	100%	33%	8%
2004	100%	95%	30%	4%
2003	100%	100%	14%	20%
2002	100%	100%	16%	0%
2001	100%	100%	22%	8%
2000	100%	95%	23%	4%

Rep. Peter Welch (D)

Elected 2006; 2nd term

CAPITOL OFFICE
225-4115
welch.house.gov
1404 Longworth Bldg. 20515-4501; fax 225-6790

COMMITTEES
Energy & Commerce
Oversight & Government Reform
Standards of Official Conduct

RESIDENCE
Hartland

BORN
May 2, 1947; Springfield, Mass.

RELIGION
Roman Catholic

FAMILY
Wife, Margaret Cheney; eight children

EDUCATION
College of the Holy Cross, A.B. 1969 (history);
U. of California, Berkeley, J.D. 1973

CAREER
Lawyer; county public defender

POLITICAL HIGHLIGHTS
Vt. Senate, 1981-89 (minority leader, 1983-85;
president pro tempore, 1985-89); sought
Democratic nomination for U.S. House, 1988;
Democratic nominee for governor, 1990;
Vt. Senate, 2002-06 (president pro tempore,
2003-07)

ELECTION RESULTS

2008 GENERAL

Peter Welch (D)	248,203	83.2%
Mike Bethel (I)	14,349	4.8%
Jerry Trudell (EINDC)	10,818	3.6%
Thomas James Hermann (PRO)	9,081	3.0%
Cris Ericson (I)	7,841	2.6%
Jane Newton (LU)	5,307	1.8%

2008 PRIMARY

Peter Welch (D)	19,566	87.7%
Craig Barclay Hill (D)	2,635	11.8%

2006 GENERAL

Peter Welch (D)	139,815	53.2%
Martha Rainville (R)	117,023	44.5%

Welch is a loyal liberal whose views are influenced by his 1960s activist college days as well as his lengthy service in Vermont politics. He seeks to implement many of his progressive state's ideas on a national level.

In his first term, Welch sided with Democrats on 98 percent of the votes in which the two parties diverged. He was rewarded in 2009 with a seat on the prestigious Energy and Commerce Committee, where he seeks to align with its like-minded chairman, California's Henry A. Waxman. He also serves on the Oversight and Government Reform Committee and the House's ethics panel.

On Energy and Commerce, Welch pushed a bill to encourage the retrofitting of homes and government buildings to boost energy efficiency by 20 percent or more. The initiative was partly inspired by Efficiency Vermont, the nation's first statewide provider of energy efficiency services. "It's high time we bring this successful Vermont model to the national stage," Welch said in March 2009. "Investing in energy efficiency is a practical, common-sense strategy to create jobs, save on energy costs and do our part to fight climate change."

Soon after taking office, he began spending personal money to make his two offices carbon neutral after he discovered that every year they produce 56 tons of carbon dioxide — which most scientists contend contributes to global warming. Congressional rules prohibit members from spending office funds for such purposes. Welch offsets the greenhouse gas emissions related to his office activities by paying a carbon offset provider in Vermont.

With rising gas prices at the top of constituent concerns in mid-2008, Welch sponsored a bill to suspend depositing oil into the Strategic Petroleum Reserve for the rest of the year. He opposed the move at a time of high prices, arguing it takes supplies off the market and pushes prices even higher. A reluctant President George W. Bush signed Welch's bill into law.

Welch also sought to help constituents by cosponsoring a credit card holders' bill of rights that passed the House in April 2009. In debate on the measure, he unsuccessfully sought to cap credit card interest rates at 18 percent and increase transparency and oversight of the fees that companies charge merchants.

A member of Energy and Commerce's panel on Communications, Technology and the Internet, Welch wants to expand broadband access to more rural areas — something he likened in significance to rural electrification during Franklin D. Roosevelt's administration.

As Vermont's lone voice in the House, Welch brings up many issues that specifically concern his state. Vermont's economy is heavily dependent on agriculture, and during debate on the 2008 reauthorization of farm programs, Welch pushed proposals to help small family farms compete against larger corporate operations.

On the ethics panel, Welch became involved in a high-profile investigation of Ways and Means Chairman Charles B. Rangel's financial dealings. In early 2009, he returned political contributions he received from the New York Democrat and his political action committee.

Welch grew up in Springfield, Mass., the third of six children in an Irish Catholic family. His father was a dentist and his mother a homemaker. He attended Cathedral Catholic High School, where he received the school's scholar athlete award after helping his team win the 1964 and 1965 basketball city championships. He recalls public service being a prominent theme in his high school. "There was a sense that one of your opportunities in life was to do things that were good for the larger community," he said.

In 1965 Welch enrolled at the College of the Holy Cross in nearby Worcester, the oldest Catholic college in New England, which his father and three other siblings attended. But he became caught up in the country's political and social transformations at the time and left for Chicago, where he helped fight racial discrimination in housing.

Welch returned home briefly before returning to the city to continue his community work while taking a few classes at Loyola University — at the height of the Vietnam War and racial protests throughout the country. He also traveled to Georgia to hear the Rev. Dr. Martin Luther King Jr. preach.

Welch eventually returned to Holy Cross, graduating magna cum laude in 1969 with a degree in history. He quickly returned to Chicago, this time as an inaugural Robert Kennedy Fellow and spent the next year working for the Contract Buyers' League fighting discriminatory housing policies.

After earning a law degree at the University of California, Berkeley, Welch spent six months backpacking the length of the Pan-American Highway from Berkeley to Santiago, Chile. Back in the United States, Welch chose to work in general private practice in White River Junction. He later met his future wife, Joan Smith, a Dartmouth University sociology professor.

He entered politics in 1981, becoming the second Democrat ever elected to represent Windsor County in the state Senate. In 1982, he was elected minority leader and in 1984 led his party as it took over the majority for the first time in history. He was elected president pro tempore for two terms before making a failed bid for his district's seat in Congress in 1988.

After running unsuccessfully for governor in 1990, Welch dropped behind the scenes in politics while working in a law firm and caring for his wife, who was diagnosed with cancer in the mid-1990s and eventually succumbed to the disease in 2004. (Welch remarried in January 2009, to Margaret Cheney, a Vermont state representative.)

Welch supported Democrat Howard Dean's re-election gubernatorial bid in 2000 and was awarded with an appointment to the state Senate, where he again became president pro tempore in 2003. Welch then served as an adviser to Dean's unsuccessful presidential campaign in 2004.

When independent Rep. Bernard Sanders left open his seat in 2006 for a successful Senate bid, Welch was the choice to face GOP nominee Martha Rainville, the state's adjutant general. A tough political environment for Republicans helped Welch take 53 percent of the vote; two years later, he easily overcame a primary challenge and sailed to re-election in November.

KEY VOTES

2008

Yes Delay consideration of Colombia free-trade agreement

Yes Override Bush veto of federal farm and nutrition programs reauthorization bill

No Overhaul surveillance laws and permit dismissal of suits against companies that conducted warrantless wiretapping

Yes Grant mortgage relief to homeowners and funding for Fannie Mae and Freddie Mac

No Approve initial $700 billion program to stabilize financial markets

Yes Approve final $700 billion program to stabilize financial markets

Yes Provide $14 billion in loans to automakers

2007

Yes Increase minimum wage by $2.10 an hour

Yes Approve $124.2 billion in emergency war spending and set goal for redeployment of troops from Iraq

No Reject federal contraceptive assistance to international family planning groups

Yes Override Bush veto of $23.2 billion water projects authorization bill

No Implement Peru free-trade agreement

Yes Approve energy policy overhaul with new fuel economy standards

No Clear $473.5 billion omnibus spending bill, including $70 billion for military operations

CQ VOTE STUDIES

	PARTY UNITY		PRESIDENTIAL SUPPORT	
	SUPPORT	OPPOSE	SUPPORT	OPPOSE
2008	98%	2%	15%	85%
2007	98%	2%	5%	95%

INTEREST GROUPS

	AFL-CIO	ADA	CCUS	ACU
2008	100%	90%	56%	8%
2007	96%	95%	55%	0%

VERMONT

At Large

Resting on the shores of Lake Champlain and rolling through the rustic Green Mountains, the nation's second-least-populous state feels like a good, small-town neighbor.

Small businesses and family farms make up the majority of Vermont's workforce. The once prosperous dairy industry, which still comprises nearly 80 percent of the state's agricultural output, has been hit hard by increased production in the West combined with flagging demand, and loans and some federal funding have been promised to dairy farmers. The manufacturing sector is volatile, with both layoffs and new production at key employer IBM as well as the arrival of new manufacturers drawn by state incentives. Municipal and statewide budget shortfalls have cast doubt on the stability of government jobs.

Officials also hope to lure tourists, so prevalent on the ski slopes in the winter, to the state year-round. In addition, they continue to attempt to convince urban dwellers from other states — flatlanders, as they are called here — to buy summer homes, especially in the scenic northeast.

Once a remote rural bastion of Yankee Republicanism, Vermont moved solidly to the left 20 years ago as an influx of young liberal urbanites joined the remnants of the late-1960s counterculture settlers. In state and federal races, the strongly progressive voters in Burlington and surrounding Chittenden County — the state's most populous county — out vote libertarian conservatives. In some years, the state's liberal Progressive Party and other left-leaning independents have split Democratic voters, occasionally aiding GOP victories.

The state's rural areas, including the Northeast Kingdom, still hold small pockets of GOP votes, but Democrats dominate central Vermont and the southeastern corner. Many small urban centers, such as Montpelier and Rutland, now support Democrats. Still, Republicans can win here, as Gov. Jim Douglas has done since 2002. Barack Obama won 67 percent of the state's vote in the 2008 presidential election.

MAJOR INDUSTRY
Manufacturing, dairy farming, tourism

CITIES
Burlington, 38,889; Rutland, 17,292

NOTABLE
Ben & Jerry's ice cream began in Burlington in a renovated gas station.

VIRGINIA

Gov. Tim Kaine (D)

First elected: 2005
Length of term: 4 years
Term expires: 1/10
Salary: $175,000
Phone: (804) 786-2211

Residence: Richmond
Born: Feb. 26, 1958;
St. Paul, Minn.
Religion: Roman Catholic
Family: Wife, Anne Holton; three children
Education: U. of Missouri, A.B. 1979
(economics); Harvard U., J.D. 1983
Career: Lawyer
Political highlights: Richmond City Council,
1994-2001 (mayor, 1998-2001); lieutenant
governor, 2002-06

Election results:

2005 GENERAL

Tim Kaine (D)	1,025,942	51.7%
Jerry W. Kilgore (R)	912,327	46.0%
H. Russ Potts Jr. (I)	43,953	2.2%

Lt. Gov. Bill Bolling (R)

First elected: 2005
Length of term: 4 years
Term expires: 1/10
Salary: $36,321
Phone: (804) 786-2078

LEGISLATURE

General Assembly: 60 days
January-March in even-numbered
years; 40 days January-February in
odd-numbered years

Senate: 40 members, 4-year terms
2009 ratios: 21 D, 19 R; 32 men,
8 women
Salary: $18,000
Phone: (804) 698-7410

House: 100 members, 2-year terms
2009 ratios: 57 R, 40 D, 3 I; 84 men,
16 women
Salary: $17,640
Phone: (804) 698-1500

TERM LIMITS

Governor: No consecutive terms
Senate: No
House: No

URBAN STATISTICS

CITY	POPULATION
Virginia Beach	425,257
Norfolk	234,403
Chesapeake	199,184
Richmond	197,790
Newport News	180,150

REGISTERED VOTERS

Voters do not register by party.

POPULATION

2008 population (est.)	7,769,089
2000 population	7,078,515
1990 population	6,187,358
Percent change (1990-2000)	+14.4%
Rank among states (2008)	12

Median age	35.7
Born in state	51.9%
Foreign born	8.1%
Violent crime rate	282/100,000
Poverty level	9.6%
Federal workers	156,871
Military	170,046

ELECTIONS

STATE ELECTION OFFICIAL
(804) 864-8901
DEMOCRATIC PARTY
(804) 644-1966
REPUBLICAN PARTY
(804) 780-0111

MISCELLANEOUS

Web: www.virginia.gov
Capital: Richmond

U.S. CONGRESS

Senate: 2 Democrats
House: 6 Republicans, 5 Democrats

2000 Census Statistics by District

DIST.	2008 VOTE FOR PRESIDENT OBAMA	MCCAIN	WHITE	BLACK	ASIAN	HISP	MEDIAN INCOME	WHITE COLLAR	BLUE COLLAR	SERVICE INDUSTRY	OVER 64	UNDER 18	COLLEGE EDUCATION	RURAL	SQ. MILES
1	48%	51%	75%	18%	2%	3%	$50,257	63%	23%	14%	11%	26%	27%	36%	3,773
2	50	48	67	21	4	4	$44,193	63	22	15	9	26	26	8	961
3	76	24	38	56	1	3	$32,238	55	26	19	12	26	17	8	1,118
4	50	49	62	33	1	2	$45,249	58	28	14	11	27	20	29	4,489
5	48	51	72	24	1	2	$35,739	53	33	14	15	23	19	64	8,922
6	42	57	85	11	1	2	$37,773	56	29	15	15	22	21	35	5,647
7	46	53	78	16	2	2	$50,990	68	20	12	12	25	33	30	3,514
8	69	30	57	13	9	16	$63,430	77	11	12	9	20	54	0	123
9	40	59	93	4	1	1	$29,783	49	36	15	15	21	14	66	8,803
10	53	46	77	7	7	7	$71,560	72	16	11	7	28	43	17	1,856
11	57	42	67	10	11	9	$80,397	77	12	12	8	27	49	4	388
STATE	53	46	70	19	4	5	$46,677	64	23	14	11	25	30	27	39,594
U.S.	53	46	69	12	4	13	$41,994	60	25	15	12	26	24	21	3,537,438

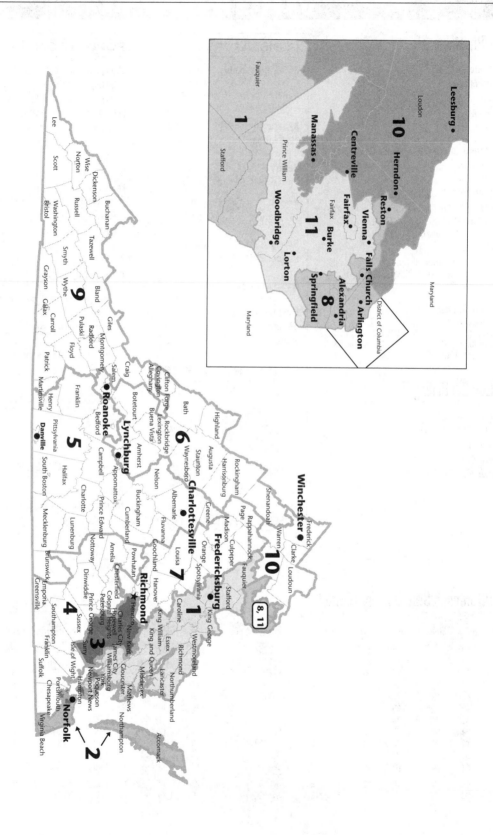

Sen. Jim Webb (D)

CAPITOL OFFICE
224-4024
webb.senate.gov
248 Russell Bldg. 20510-4604; fax 228-6363

COMMITTEES
Armed Services
Foreign Relations
  (East Asian & Pacific Affairs - chairman)
Veterans' Affairs
Joint Economic

RESIDENCE
Falls Church

BORN
Feb. 9, 1946; St. Joseph, Mo.

RELIGION
Protestant

FAMILY
Wife, Hong Le Webb; five children

EDUCATION
U. of Southern California, attended 1963-64;
U.S. Naval Academy, B.S. 1968; Georgetown U.,
J.D. 1975

MILITARY SERVICE
Marine Corps, 1968-72

CAREER
Author; screenwriter; journalist; U.S. Defense
Department official; congressional aide; lawyer

POLITICAL HIGHLIGHTS
Secretary of the Navy, 1987-88

ELECTION RESULTS

2006 GENERAL

Jim Webb (D)	1,175,606	49.6%
George Allen (R)	1,166,277	49.2%
Glenda Gail Parker (IGREEN)	26,102	1.1%

2006 PRIMARY

Jim Webb (D)	83,298	53.5%
Harris Miller (D)	72,486	46.5%

Elected 2006; 1st term

Webb stands out in the Senate, and not just for his shock of red hair. Novelist, lawyer and former Republican, he is first and last a Marine. His demeanor is ramrod-straight, and his style is candid and no-nonsense. Uncomfortable with the small talk and glad-handing of politics, he nonetheless was the unrivaled star of the Senate Democratic freshman class of 2006. In a 2008 political manifesto, "A Time to Fight: Reclaiming a Just and Fair America," Webb assessed his colorful career: "Financially and personally, my life has been one roll of the dice after another. I've had good years and bad years, but I've never lost my willingness to take a risk, and I've never been bored."

The decorated Vietnam veteran, a Navy secretary under President Ronald Reagan, has made his name as an expert on national security. He solidified that reputation during his first two years in the Senate; a member of the Veterans' Affairs Committee, he won enactment of enhanced education benefits for veterans and challenged President George W. Bush on the Iraq War.

Webb introduced the biggest expansion of the GI Bill in 25 years on his first day in the Senate, and he fought tenaciously to get it through the 110th Congress (2007-08). He triumphed over veteran Republican John McCain of Arizona, who pressed a more limited alternative. In September 2008, Esquire magazine labeled Webb one of the 75 most influential people of the 21st century for doing "more to repair his party's relationship with the military" than anyone since the Vietnam War.

Webb also champions improved benefits for military personnel, veterans and their families from his seat on the Armed Services Committee. But his work on defense issues goes beyond that. Webb, who also sits on the Foreign Relations panel, worked with fellow Democrat Claire McCaskill of Missouri to shepherd into law a Wartime Contracting Commission with a broad mandate to investigate waste, fraud and abuse in Iraq and Afghanistan.

He fought in vain to curb Bush's sweeping claims of executive war powers. He advocated a measure to require the president to seek prior congressional approval before attacking Iran. He also sought to require a vote on an agreement between the United States and Iraq governing the presence of U.S. forces in that country after 2008.

Webb served notice early in the 111th Congress (2009-10) that he wouldn't defer to President Obama on military matters. When the administration proposed cuts to Navy ships, many of which berth in Newport News, home to the Atlantic fleet, Webb pushed back hard. "I have a very strong view — one developed over many years — that we must grow the Navy's force structure in order for us to meet our strategic and security interests around the world now and those we are likely to face in the future," he said.

As Iraq has faded from the headlines, Webb has devoted more of his attention to domestic matters. In 2009, he introduced legislation to set up a National Criminal Justice Commission to come up with reform recommendations within 18 months. He knows changing the punishment regime will not be easy.

"Politically, this is like an electric wire with the insulation stripped off — few politicians want to touch it," he said. But, he told the Senate, "We have 5 percent of the world's population. We have 25 percent of the world's known prison population. We have an incarceration rate in the United States, the world's greatest democracy, that is five times as high as the incarceration rate in the rest of the world. There are only two possibilities. Either we have the most evil people on Earth living in the United States, or we are doing something dramatically wrong in terms of how we approach the issue of criminal justice."

He espouses a populist economic platform that highlights what he views as the perils of globalization and corporate excess. He wants to "re-regulate" U.S. financial systems in the wake of the Wall Street meltdown of 2008. He is especially concerned about sovereign wealth funds — foreign government involvement in speculative markets.

And he presses for a more comprehensive approach to energy independence than many Democrats are comfortable with, including nuclear power and development of domestic sources of oil. "I think the Democratic Party made a big mistake in opposing offshore drilling," he said.

If Webb is not destined to be a one-issue senator, neither is he a one-career senator. He has been a decorated Marine, a law school graduate, a congressional committee counsel, Navy secretary and award-winning writer. He is the author of eight books, perhaps the best-known of which was his 1978 Vietnam novel "Fields of Fire." He did some screenwriting and was an executive producer of the 2000 movie "Rules of Engagement," which was based on a story by Webb and starred Tommy Lee Jones.

He also wrote the highly praised "Born Fighting: How the Scots-Irish Shaped America," into which he weaved the history of his own family, which has its roots in Virginia's mountainous southwestern region.

But Webb comes off as more warrior than scholar. His frankness — some call it rudeness — earned him attention even before he was sworn in. At a post-election reception at the White House, Bush asked Webb about the senator-elect's son Jimmy, a Marine who was serving in Iraq. Webb tersely responded, "That's between me and my boy, Mr. President."

In March 2007, Webb was again in the news after an aide was arrested for carrying a loaded handgun into a Senate office building. The gun belonged to Webb, who described the incident as a mix-up. But he also used it to highlight his support for gun owners' rights and Virginia's concealed-carry law.

Webb's father was an Air Force pilot who fought in World War II, and the family hopped around the country during his youth. The Webbs were by and large Democratic, but he became a Republican because he agreed with that party's national security positions. After attending the University of Southern California, Webb transferred to the Naval Academy. In 1967, he lost an Academy boxing championship to Oliver L. North, who would later become a household name for his role in the Iran-Contra affair. "Both were popular and disliked each other," a Navy boxing coach told The Associated Press in 1991.

Webb graduated from Annapolis and from the Marine officers' school in Quantico, where he finished first in his class of 243. As an infantryman during the Vietnam War, he was awarded the Navy Cross, the Silver Star, two Bronze Stars and two Purple Hearts. Webb's third wife, whom he met long after his service, is Vietnamese, and he speaks the language fluently.

Webb emerged on the national political scene because of his concerns about the war in Iraq, writing in a newspaper column shortly before the Senate voted to authorize the war in 2002: "Those who are pushing for a unilateral war in Iraq know full well that there is no exit strategy if we invade and stay."

Less than a year before the 2006 election, it seemed unlikely Democrats could unseat George Allen, viewed as a potential GOP presidential candidate. Webb had even endorsed him for the Senate in 2000. He didn't join the race until February 2006, and began the campaign against Allen as a distinct underdog. The race shifted sharply in August when Allen used the word "macaca" to mock an Indian-American volunteer for Webb who had been videotaping him at a campaign stop. Critics skewered Allen for using an epithet that refers to a monkey, though Allen denied knowing it was a racial slur. The video streaked across the Internet and effectively doomed Allen's presidential ambitions and his Senate re-election. On Election Day, Webb pulled out a 9,329-vote victory that clinched the Democrats' Senate majority.

KEY VOTES

2008

Yes Prohibit discrimination based on genetic information
Yes Reauthorize farm and nutrition programs for five years
Yes Limit debate on "cap and trade" system for greenhouse gas emissions
No   Allow lawsuits against companies that participated in warrantless wiretapping
Yes Limit debate on a bill to block a scheduled cut in Medicare payments to doctors
Yes Grant mortgage relief to homeowners and funding for Fannie Mae and Freddie Mac
Yes Approve a nuclear cooperation agreement with India
Yes Approve final $700 billion program to stabilize financial markets
Yes Allow consideration of a $14 billion auto industry loan package

2007

Yes Increase minimum wage by $2.10 an hour
No   Limit debate on a comprehensive immigration bill
Yes Overhaul congressional lobbying and ethics rules for members and their staffs
Yes Limit debate on considering a bill to add House seats for the District of Columbia and Utah
Yes Limit debate on restoring habeas corpus rights to detainees
Yes Mandate minimum breaks for troops between deployments to Iraq or Afghanistan
Yes Override Bush veto of $23.2 billion water projects authorization bill
No   Confirm Michael B. Mukasey as attorney general
Yes Limit debate on an energy policy overhaul containing $21.8 billion in tax incentives and reduced oil and gas subsidies

CQ VOTE STUDIES

	PARTY UNITY		PRESIDENTIAL SUPPORT	
	SUPPORT	OPPOSE	SUPPORT	OPPOSE
2008	89%	11%	42%	58%
2007	87%	13%	41%	59%

INTEREST GROUPS

	AFL-CIO	ADA	CCUS	ACU
2008	100%	95%	63%	8%
2007	100%	85%	45%	16%

Sen. Mark Warner (D)

Elected 2008; 1st term

CAPITOL OFFICE
224-2023
warner.senate.gov
459A Russell Bldg. 20510; fax 224-6295

COMMITTEES
Banking, Housing & Urban Affairs
Budget
Commerce, Science & Transportation
Rules & Administration

RESIDENCE
Alexandria

BORN
Dec. 15, 1954; Indianapolis, Ind.

RELIGION
Presbyterian

FAMILY
Wife, Lisa Collis; three children

EDUCATION
George Washington U., B.A. 1977
(political science); Harvard U., J.D. 1980

CAREER
Technology venture capitalist; campaign aide
and party fundraiser

POLITICAL HIGHLIGHTS
Commonwealth Transportation Board, 1990-94;
Va. Democratic Party chairman, 1993-95;
Democratic nominee for U.S. Senate, 1996;
governor, 2002-06

ELECTION RESULTS

2008 GENERAL

Mark Warner (D)	2,369,327	65.0%
James S. Gilmore III (R)	1,228,830	33.7%

2008 PRIMARY

Mark Warner (D)	unopposed

As Virginia's popular governor, the self-described "radical centrist" Warner showed Democrats how to win in the South with moderate pro-business policies focused on cutting spending without harming government services. He hopes to repeat his success in the Senate by building bipartisan coalitions to tackle such issues as the economic and energy crises. "I was a governor that had a 2-1 Republican legislature. We had to find common ground. I think we still need to," Warner told CNBC in 2009.

Warner is an entrepreneur who made millions in business before entering politics, and he shares some of President Obama's youthful dynamism and avowed interest in bipartisanship. Those qualities helped make Warner a widely mentioned presidential candidate before he took himself out of the running. The Newport News Daily Press observed that his energy and intensity "make the Energizer Bunny look run-down."

Warner often talks about improving the nation's competitiveness to keep up with the rising economies of India and China. He calls for increased spending on infrastructure, including on transportation and broadband Internet access. "If we don't stand up and make sure that American business can compete in the global economy, we're going to be in real trouble," he said. He told The Associated Press in January 2009 that his business background would help him contribute to reshaping the economy "in a way that restores some trust and confidence in the system."

Part of that effort, he says, is greater transparency and accountability in the way government spends taxpayer dollars. A member of the Banking, Housing and Urban Affairs panel, Warner pressed Treasury Secretary Timothy F. Geithner in early 2009 to make public more details about what has happened to the $700 billion in financial sector rescue funds Congress approved in 2008. "A lot of folks in my state think that we've taken that money and are pouring it down a deep hole," he told Geithner at a hearing. To drive home his demands, Warner introduced legislation to require Treasury to use a single database, in a standardized format, to detail the actions of fund recipients and contractors.

Warner also serves on the Budget Committee, where he supports efforts by Chairman Kent Conrad of North Dakota to create a commission to recommend an overhaul of Social Security and Medicare that Congress would have to vote on, up or down. He also backs pay-as-you-go budget rules, which require any new tax cuts or mandatory spending to be offset. Along with other Senate moderates, he helped pare Obama's huge stimulus package in 2009 — ultimately enacted as a $787 billion law — and he later pressed Cabinet officers to ensure the money was spent efficiently and monitored carefully.

On energy issues, Warner supports an all-of-the-above approach that embraces clean-coal technology, nuclear power and expanded domestic oil drilling — including off Virginia's coastline — as well as alternative energy sources. Warner, who also serves on the Commerce, Science and Transportation Committee, said he wants the domestic auto industry to produce fuel-efficient vehicles and has called for government agencies to issue three years' worth of purchase orders for those vehicles. He has called for more private capital for energy, much like the infusion to the wireless and information technology industries two decades ago.

Warner works closely with Jim Webb, his Democratic Virginia colleague and a member of the Armed Services Committee, to protect the state's military installations. The two joined in November 2008 in calling for the Navy to modernize the Norfolk Naval Shipyard instead of adding to a Florida facility to house nuclear-powered aircraft carriers. Warner hailed the Obama administration's move to delay a decision on that shift until after a 2010 quadrennial review of the military's needs and challenges.

Warner grew up in Indiana and Connecticut, then attended college in Washington to be close to the city's political scene. After law school at Harvard, he took a job as a fundraiser for the Democratic National Committee. But he wanted to make money for himself. "After I graduated law school, it didn't take me long to realize that America wouldn't really miss me as a lawyer, so I started a business," he recalled. "My first company failed in six weeks. My next one was much more successful — it failed in six months."

Eventually, Warner convinced investors to purchase cellular telephone licenses the government was selling in the 1980s. He was an early investor in the cellular company Nextel. As he made money, he stayed active in the Democratic political scene, managing L. Douglas Wilder's successful campaign in 1989 to become the nation's first elected black governor. He also served as state party chairman from 1993 to 1995.

Warner first ran for the Senate in 1996, spending $10 million of his fortune in an unsuccessful campaign against Republican incumbent John W. Warner (no relation), whose seat he now holds. His close loss enhanced rather than diminished his standing in Virginia Democratic circles, and it helped lay the groundwork for his successful run for governor five years later.

As governor, Warner inherited a budget deficit that forced him to raise taxes — something that usually makes political enemies quickly. But he worked closely with GOP leaders in Richmond to produce a rescue package that included spending cuts, developing a reputation as a results-oriented pragmatist willing to listen to all sides. He implemented business-like reforms of state government, especially at Virginia's transportation department. As chairman of the National Governors Association in 2004 and 2005, he led a national high school reform initiative.

At the same time, Warner made political inroads in socially conservative rural Virginia. He praised the National Rifle Association, sponsored a NAS-CAR pickup and focused on job creation on the state's south side.

His efforts led Virginia to receive several honors for its financial management and prompted Time magazine to name him one of nation's five best governors in 2005. They also propelled his approval ratings to the mid-70s, unheard-of heights for a Democrat in a state that until 2008 had not supported a Democratic presidential nominee since 1964. When Warner left office in January 2006, speculation immediately arose that he would run for president. But after initial steps such as visiting key primary states, he abruptly backed out. "While politically this appears to be the right time for me to take the plunge, at this point, I want to have a real life," he said in October 2006.

Almost a year later, John W. Warner's retirement announcement led Warner to try for the Senate again. He faced Republican James S. Gilmore III, his predecessor as Virginia governor, who had a brief moment on the national stage when he waged a short-lived bid for the GOP presidential nomination in 2007. Gilmore sought to play up his conservative credentials, focusing on smaller government and lower taxes. But Warner led all the way, coasting to 65 percent of the vote. He received over 2.3 million votes — a record for a statewide candidate — while sweeping all 11 congressional districts and carrying 128 of the state's 134 cities and counties. His impressive showing was credited with helping Obama carry the state.

With so little trouble winning his own race, Warner had the luxury of being able to donate generously to the Democratic Senatorial Campaign Committee and through them to a host of other candidates; his campaign committee alone doled out more than $2.1 million during the 2007-08 election cycle. That largesse is likely to earn him additional goodwill down the road.

Rep. Rob Wittman (R)

Elected December 2007; 1st full term

CAPITOL OFFICE
225-4261
wittman.house.gov
1318 Longworth Bldg. 20515-4601; fax 225-4382

COMMITTEES
Armed Services
Natural Resources

RESIDENCE
Montross

BORN
Feb. 3, 1959; Washington, D.C.,

RELIGION
Episcopalian

FAMILY
Wife, Kathryn Wittman; two children

EDUCATION
Virginia Polytechnic Institute and State U.,
B.S. 1981 (biology); U. of North Carolina,
M.P.H. 1990 (health policy and administration);
Virginia Commonwealth U., Ph.D. 2002 (public
policy and administration)

CAREER
State health agency official; environmental
health inspector

POLITICAL HIGHLIGHTS
Montross Town Council, 1986-96 (mayor 1992-96);
Westmoreland County Board of Supervisors, 1996-
2005 (chairman 2004-05); Va. House, 2006-07

ELECTION RESULTS

2008 GENERAL

Rob Wittman (R)	203,839	56.6%
Bill S. Day Jr. (D)	150,432	41.8%
Nathan D. Larson (LIBERT)	5,265	1.5%

2008 PRIMARY

Rob Wittman (R)	unopposed

2007 SPECIAL

Rob Wittman (R)	42,772	60.8%
Philip Forgit (D)	26,282	37.3%
Lucky Narain (I)	1,253	1.8%

Wittman's soft-spoken nature and down-to-earth demeanor sit well with the residents in his district, where he has been a mainstay in local and state politics since 1986. In the small farming communities, he has a reputation as being both economically and socially conservative.

He pushes hard to limit government spending while looking out for his military-influenced district, where many constituents are heavily reliant on jobs related to the Marine Corps base at Quantico, a massive shipbuilding facility in Newport News and other military installations. And as a biologist and former environmental health official, he takes a special interest in the restoration of the Chesapeake Bay and the protection of its resources, which also are vital to the livelihood of area watermen.

As the top-ranking Republican on the Armed Services' Oversight and Investigations panel, he raised alarm when reports in early 2009 indicated Navy inspectors had found six ships unfit for their missions the previous year. He joined several of his Virginia colleagues in a letter drafted by Republican J. Randy Forbes to Defense Secretary Robert M. Gates, raising concern that such information was kept undercover. They said publicity about ship maintenance and operational problems is key to lawmakers' ability to solve problems. Wittman and freshman Democrat Glenn Nye also pushed the Pentagon to reconsider its proposal to move the base for an aircraft carrier from Norfolk to Mayport, Fla., fearing such a move would hurt the local economy and cost the department millions of dollars to prepare the site in Mayport.

Like other members, he was wary when President Obama announced his decision to close the detention center at Cuba's Guantánamo Bay. He supported a Forbes bill to ban federal dollars from being spent on moving the detainees to Virginia or housing them there. And he cosponsored another bill by Florida Republican Jeff Miller to forbid enemy combatants detained there from being treated at any armed forces or veterans' medical facility.

Wittman backed President George W. Bush's handling of the Iraq War and opposed efforts of others in Congress to call for a timeline for withdrawal, saying military leaders are the best to make such a call. After a late 2008 visit to the war zone, he expressed optimism over the progress that had been made.

Wittman also sits on the Natural Resources Committee and its Insular Affairs, Wildlife and Oceans Subcommittee, where he can apply his expertise in biology and environmental science. He holds a master's degree in health policy from the University of North Carolina and a doctorate in public policy and administration from Virginia Commonwealth University.

He applauded the Bush administration's designation in late 2008 of blue crab in the Chesapeake Bay as a "resources disaster," and a subsequent $20 million in funding to help address the disaster. Six months later, he announced reports indicating signs of a recovery. Also in 2008, he pushed legislation to better oversee the Chesapeake Bay oyster restoration project, and offered a bill to alter the management of all Chesapeake Bay restoration activities, seeking to improve coordination among various agencies and states.

While Wittman applauds such spending initiatives to help local projects, he is much more tightfisted when it comes to overall federal spending, lamenting the rise of the federal deficit. A member of the Republican Study Committee, a group of the House's most conservative members, he said he struggled on whether to support a $700 billion law in 2008 to shore up the nation's financial services sector. Minority Leader John A. Boehner of Ohio worked on him during the vote. "He said whatever I decide, I should be able to give a rational explanation back home," Wittman said. He ultimately opposed it, saying it "fell far short of my goals" Wittman also opposed Obama's $787 billion economic stimulus law, saying it was "not a fair shake for the hardworking taxpayer." A $410 billion catchall spending bill for fiscal 2009 and a $3.56 trillion budget blueprint for fiscal 2010 also failed to draw his support.

Wittman is the only current member of Congress who is an alumnus of Virginia Tech, which led the national news in April 2007 when student Seung-Hui Cho killed 32 students and faculty members and wounded several others before taking his own life. Reports subsequently indicated there had been growing concern about Cho's mental health. Wittman supported a measure to improve the availability of electronic data to states to check criminal and mental-health records of gun purchasers.

Wittman was born in Washington in 1959, and eight months later was adopted and moved to Richmond, Va. His mother was a homemaker before earning a teaching degree. His father, an auditor, often worked in the Northern Neck, a picturesque peninsula nestled between the Potomac and the Rappahannock rivers. Wittman now represents that area, where he spent summers working on fishing boats and tomato farms.

He attended Benedictine Military Institute, an all-boys military school in Richmond. He was active in the student government and newspaper. He then earned a bachelor's degree in biology in 1981 from Virginia Tech. After college, he worked as a fisherman in the Northern Neck before becoming an environmental specialist for Virginia's health department. He worked his way up from district supervisor to field director of the shellfish sanitation division.

He also served on the Montross Town Council for a decade, the last four years as the town's mayor. In 1995 he was elected to the Westmoreland County Board of Supervisors and won an election to the state legislature in 2005.

Wittman won a special election in December 2007 to replace Republican Rep. Jo Ann Davis, who had died of breast cancer just two months before. At the nominating convention he was one of 11 Republicans — and the only sitting elected official — who vied for the seat. More than 1,000 delegates traveled to Caroline High School in the tiny community of Milford. The hastily scheduled contest allowed little time to travel throughout the district, and candidates attracted voters by offering elaborate spreads, such as fried chicken and key lime bars. Wittman won in the fifth round of balloting, after two close contenders withdrew and threw their support behind him.

In the special election, he easily ousted Democrat Philip Forgit, an Iraq War veteran and former teacher, with 61 percent of the vote. In 2008, he took 57 percent in a district that Arizona GOP Sen. John McCain narrowly carried.

KEY VOTES

2008
No Delay consideration of Colombia free-trade agreement
Yes Override Bush veto of federal farm and nutrition programs reauthorization bill
Yes Overhaul surveillance laws and permit dismissal of suits against companies that conducted warrantless wiretapping
No Grant mortgage relief to homeowners and funding for Fannie Mae and Freddie Mac
No Approve initial $700 billion program to stabilize financial markets
No Approve final $700 billion program to stabilize financial markets
No Provide $14 billion in loans to automakers

2007
No Approve energy policy overhaul with new fuel economy standards
Yes Clear $473.5 billion omnibus spending bill, including $70 billion for military operations

CQ VOTE STUDIES

	PARTY UNITY		PRESIDENTIAL SUPPORT	
	SUPPORT	OPPOSE	SUPPORT	OPPOSE
2008	93%	7%	63%	37%
2007	100%	0%	75%	25%

INTEREST GROUPS

	AFL-CIO	ADA	CCUS	ACU
2008	20%	35%	83%	92%
2007	—	—	—	100%

VIRGINIA 1

East — parts of Newport News and Hampton, Fredericksburg

The GOP-friendly 1st lies along the Potomac River and Chesapeake Bay, stretching from the Northern Virginia suburbs and exurbs of Washington all the way south to the shipbuilding cities of Hampton and Newport News. Along the way, popular tourist destinations, such as Williamsburg, Jamestown and Yorktown, recall Virginia's colonial past.

Industry here revolves around military facilities and NASA sites, which have attracted private sector technology firms. Nearly one-fourth of workers in the 1st are employed by the government, which has helped insulate the area from widespread layoffs. Colleges and universities also stabilize the district's economic base, as do shipbuilding and tourism. Inland counties, such as Stafford, Spotsylvania and Caroline, are driven by education, health care and agriculture sectors.

The 1st's northern counties have absorbed Washington commuters who continue to move farther from the city. Spotsylvania County (one-fifth of which is in the 7th) has grown as a result of its proximity to both Richmond and Washington and its location on the Interstate 95 corridor. Fauquier County (shared with the 10th) and Stafford County, both north of Fredericksburg, had also grown quickly until a national housing market decline and economic downtown recently slowed expansion.

The 1st is solidly Republican, and the party controls local offices here, but John McCain won only 51 percent of the 1st's 2008 presidential vote.

MAJOR INDUSTRY
Defense, technology, agriculture, tourism, higher education

MILITARY BASES
Marine Corps Base Quantico, 8,137 military, 7,904 civilian (2009); Naval Surface Warfare Center, Dahlgren Division, 812 military, 3,873 civilian (2008); Naval Weapons Station Yorktown, 1,411 military, 839 civilian (2008); Fort A.P. Hill (Army), 2 military, 250 civilian (2009)

CITIES
Newport News (pt.), 71,800; Hampton (pt.), 31,755; Fredericksburg, 19,279

NOTABLE
George Washington and Robert E. Lee both were born in Westmoreland County, and their birth sites attract visitors; Jamestown, settled in 1607, was the first permanent English settlement in North America.

www.cqpress.com

Rep. Glenn Nye (D)

Elected 2008; 1st term

Nye is a centrist who may be young in years and short on formal political experience, but he might be the most internationally seasoned freshman in the 111th Congress (2009-10). A former Foreign Service officer who later worked with the U.S. Agency for International Development, he has served in Kosovo, the West Bank, Afghanistan and most recently Iraq, where he worked for nine months in 2006 on a USAID program to help employ Iraqis.

Nye said he ran for Congress because "there is only so much one can do on the executing end of foreign policy in terms of advancing American interests, and there's only so much you can do to influence the policy from the outside."

He secured a seat on the Armed Services Committee. His district includes numerous military installations and is home to tens of thousands of military personnel and retirees and their families. He wants to focus on long-term strategic budgeting for the military.

After an April 2009 trip to Kuwait and Afghanistan, Nye told The Virginian-Pilot that Congress and the Obama administration "need to get the Pakistani government to step up and do more" about Taliban forces in northern Pakistan that were launching attacks into Afghanistan.

He also serves on the Veterans' Affairs and Small Business committees. And he hopes to use his House seat to advocate for local infrastructure improvements, including a new third crossing of Hampton Roads in south-eastern Virginia.

A member of the Blue Dog Coalition, a group of about 50 fiscally conservative Democrats, Nye voted in February 2009 against a $410 billion catch-all spending bill, and he opposed the Obama administration's $3.56 trillion budget blueprint for fiscal 2010. He did support the president's $787 billion economic stimulus law and an expansion of a children's health insurance program.

Nye toppled two-term GOP incumbent Rep. Thelma Drake in 2008, taking advantage of the national Democratic tide that helped Barack Obama carry the conservative-leaning district.

CAPITOL OFFICE
225-4215
nye.house.gov
116 Cannon Bldg. 20515-4602; fax 225-4218

COMMITTEES
Armed Services
Small Business
 (Contracting & Technology - chairman)
Veterans' Affairs

RESIDENCE
Norfolk

BORN
Sept. 9, 1974; Philadelphia, Pa.

RELIGION
Presbyterian

FAMILY
Single

EDUCATION
Georgetown U., B.S. 1996 (foreign service)

CAREER
International development government liaison;
Foreign Service officer

POLITICAL HIGHLIGHTS
No previous office

ELECTION RESULTS

2008 GENERAL
Glenn Nye (D)	141,857	52.4%
Thelma Drake (R)	128,486	47.5%

2008 PRIMARY
Glenn Nye (D)	unopposed

VIRGINIA 2

Southeast – Virginia Beach, parts of Norfolk and Hampton, Eastern Shore

Taking in the state's Atlantic coastline, the 2nd is dominated by Virginia Beach, a center for white-collar military families and retirees. The district takes in parts of Norfolk and Hampton and crosses the Chesapeake Bay inlet to Virginia's Eastern Shore.

Growth in Virginia Beach slowed in the wake of military base closings and a national recession. The 2005 BRAC round ordered Fort Monroe, in Hampton, closed by 2011, but increases at the 2nd's other bases and commercial development at Fort Monroe may mean the 2nd will avoid job losses. The 2nd also includes half of largely blue-collar and Democratic-leaning Norfolk (shared with the 3rd). Its naval base, shipbuilding and shipping drive the economy.

Any conservatism here stems more from military and economic issues than from social questions, and the 2nd has followed the growing Democratic trend in Virginia. Barack Obama won the 2008 presidential race here with 50 percent of the vote.

MAJOR INDUSTRY
Military, tourism, shipbuilding

MILITARY BASES
Naval Station Norfolk, 51,413 military, 1,975 civilian (2008); Naval Air Station Oceana, 12,000 military, 2,500 civilian; Langley Air Force Base, 7,948 military, 2,100 civilian (2008); Naval Amphibious Base Little Creek, 7,700 military, 1,815 civilian; Naval Air Station Oceana Dam Neck Annex, 3,600 military, 1,300 civilian (2005); Fort Monroe (Army), 1,250 military, 1,680 civilian (2009); Fort Story (Army), 842 military, 71 civilian (2008)

CITIES
Virginia Beach, 425,257; Norfolk (pt.), 112,102; Hampton (pt.), 54,753

NOTABLE
The Norfolk Botanical Garden.

Rep. Robert C. Scott (D)

Elected 1992; 9th term

Scott is one of the stalwart liberals on the Judiciary Committee who long has espoused strong civil libertarian views. An active member of the Congressional Black Caucus, he pushes for equality across the board on education, jobs and health care and is active on budget issues as well.

While many Democrats may fear appearing soft on crime, he has for years loudly criticized tough mandatory minimum prison sentences that disproportionately affect African-American defendants. Though usually a stalwart Democrat — he backed his party on 99 percent of the votes in the 110th Congress (2007-08) in which majorities of the two parties diverged — he drops his liberal mantle when it comes to looking out for southeast Virginia's military interests.

As chairman of Judiciary's panel on Crime, Terrorism and Homeland Security, Scott has long argued that a tough-on-crime approach doesn't work and has backed programs to educate and provide jobs and family support for people in the criminal justice system. "It makes no sense, waiting for the children to mess up and then lock them up, when it is cheaper to invest in crime prevention programs and prevent them from getting into trouble in the first place," he once said.

Scott also has passionately decried the vast discrepancy in the amount of powdered vs. crack cocaine that would trigger a long mandatory prison sentence for convicted drug dealers. Since crack is more prevalent in cities, and a much smaller proportion of it draws a minimum five years of jail time, he and other critics say the law disproportionately affects poor blacks. President Obama and some key Republicans expressed support in 2009 for eliminating the disparity.

Scott won House passage in February of that year for his bill to require states receiving federal law enforcement grants to report prisoner deaths to attorneys general while mandating the federal government to provide details on inmate deaths in federal facilities. He also helped work on legislation to bolster the government's ability to combat financial fraud and to extend federal hate crime law to cover offenses based on sexual orientation.

During the George W. Bush administration, he was a persistent foe of proposals to expand law enforcement authority, fearing violations of individual rights. He often points out that federal wiretapping rules were created as "a tool of last resort" for investigations of organized crime, but said Bush's administration inappropriately relied on wiretapping to probe a broad array of crimes and possible terrorism links.

Scott was a vocal opponent of the 2001 anti-terrorism law known as the Patriot Act, which was enacted with overwhelming support by Congress six weeks after the Sept. 11 attacks. He said the new intelligence-gathering provisions in the statute trampled on individual liberties. He is also a persistent critic of Republican attempts to aid faith-based organizations. In 2007, Scott helped remove a provision from the Head Start reauthorization bill that would have allowed faith-based hiring. "If you allow discrimination in federally funded programs, you essentially lose your moral authority to enforce civil rights laws," Scott said.

A member of the Budget Committee and the Black Caucus' budget chairman, he supported Obama's early economic agenda. He praised the $3.56 trillion budget blueprint for fiscal 2010 because of its commitment to increased research on aeronautics that would benefit NASA's Langley Research Center in Hampton. But like many other liberals, he opposed a

CAPITOL OFFICE
225-8351
www.house.gov/scott
1201 Longworth Bldg. 20515-4603; fax 225-8354

COMMITTEES
Budget
Education & Labor
Judiciary
(Crime, Terrorism & Homeland Security
- chairman)

RESIDENCE
Newport News

BORN
April 30, 1947; Washington, D.C.

RELIGION
Episcopalian

FAMILY
Divorced

EDUCATION
Harvard U., A.B. 1969; Boston College, J.D. 1973

MILITARY SERVICE
Army Reserve, 1970-74; Mass. National Guard, 1974-76

CAREER
Lawyer

POLITICAL HIGHLIGHTS
Va. House, 1979-83; Va. Senate, 1983-93; Democratic nominee for U.S. House, 1986

ELECTION RESULTS

2008 GENERAL

Robert C. Scott (D)	239,911	97.0%
write-ins	7,377	3.0%

2008 PRIMARY

Robert C. Scott (D)	unopposed

2006 GENERAL

Robert C. Scott (D)	133,546	96.1%
write-ins	5,448	3.9%

PREVIOUS WINNING PERCENTAGES
2004 (69%); 2002 (96%); 2000 (98%); 1998 (76%); 1996 (82%); 1994 (79%); 1992 (79%)

$700 billion financial services sector rescue in fall 2008. He argued it did nothing to mitigate foreclosures on homeowners.

From his seat on the Education and Labor Committee, Scott argues that standardized test scores place low-income school districts and their students at a disadvantage. He voted against House passage of the 2001 No Child Left Behind Act requiring annual math and reading testing of students, although he did support the final version of the law. Scott argues the law gives schools a "perverse incentive" to obscure their dropouts when reporting graduation rates and wants that adjusted in any reauthorization of the law.

A former member of the Army Reserve and the National Guard, Scott is one of the stronger pro-Pentagon voices in the Black Caucus. He promotes the interests of his district's shipbuilders and military bases; Northrop Grumman Newport News and the Army's Fort Eustis are major employers. He joined other Virginia delegation members in late 2008 in urging president-elect Obama to block the proposed move of a Norfolk-based aircraft carrier to Florida. Scott feared the move would cost his state numerous jobs.

His district is also home to one of the nation's largest cigarette plants, a south Richmond facility operated by Philip Morris USA. But he backed an April 2009 House-passed bill allowing the Food and Drug Administration to regulate the manufacturing, sale and promotion of tobacco products.

Scott is the son of a surgeon and a teacher. When local white officials resisted court-ordered integration of the public schools, the Scotts, like other well-to-do black families, sent their son to Groton, the prestigious Massachusetts prep school, on a scholarship. He graduated from Harvard University and earned his law degree from Boston College. He returned to Newport News after law school and became active in local civic groups, which eventually led him into politics.

Scott won a seat in the state House in 1978 and in five years moved up to the state Senate. He was unsuccessful in his first run for Congress in 1986, but he tried again six years later after redistricting resulted in a 3rd District that was 64 percent black. With no incumbent running, he took two-thirds of the vote in a three-way Democratic primary and breezed to victory in November. He became the second black Virginian to serve in the House after John Mercer Langston, a Republican who served a few months in 1890 and 1891.

He won by lopsided margins again in 1994 and 1996, but when a federal panel struck down the 3rd District's boundaries in 1997, his political future seemed in jeopardy. The new lines drawn by the General Assembly kept the black population at 54 percent, but Scott won handily in 1998, with 76 percent of the vote, and has ever since. He ran unopposed in 2006 and 2008.

KEY VOTES

2008

Yes	Delay consideration of Colombia free-trade agreement
Yes	Override Bush veto of federal farm and nutrition programs reauthorization bill
No	Overhaul surveillance laws and permit dismissal of suits against companies that conducted warrantless wiretapping
Yes	Grant mortgage relief to homeowners and funding for Fannie Mae and Freddie Mac
No	Approve initial $700 billion program to stabilize financial markets
No	Approve final $700 billion program to stabilize financial markets
Yes	Provide $14 billion in loans to automakers

2007

Yes	Increase minimum wage by $2.10 an hour
Yes	Approve $124.2 billion in emergency war spending and set goal for redeployment of troops from Iraq
No	Reject federal contraceptive assistance to international family planning groups
Yes	Override Bush veto of $23.2 billion water projects authorization bill
No	Implement Peru free-trade agreement
Yes	Approve energy policy overhaul with new fuel economy standards
No	Clear $473.5 billion omnibus spending bill, including $70 billion for military operations

CQ VOTE STUDIES

	PARTY UNITY		PRESIDENTIAL SUPPORT	
	SUPPORT	OPPOSE	SUPPORT	OPPOSE
2008	99%	1%	11%	89%
2007	98%	2%	3%	97%
2006	95%	5%	27%	73%
2005	95%	5%	13%	87%
2004	98%	2%	12%	88%

INTEREST GROUPS

	AFL-CIO	ADA	CCUS	ACU
2008	100%	100%	53%	8%
2007	100%	100%	50%	4%
2006	100%	100%	27%	4%
2005	100%	100%	41%	4%
2004	100%	100%	29%	4%

VIRGINIA 3
Southeast — parts of Richmond, Norfolk and Newport News, Portsmouth

The black-majority 3rd begins in the state capital of Richmond and heads southeast into military and shipbuilding territory, taking in parts of Newport News, Hampton and Norfolk, and the entire city of Portsmouth.

The 3rd has long benefited from hosting one of the nation's largest ports, at Hampton Roads, and from Richmond's financial sector. While the district has not been immune to layoffs, state government jobs around Richmond and port-related jobs to the south have mitigated the impact of economic downturns. Richmond is home to one of the largest cigarette plants in the nation, a Philip Morris USA facility, but the company is struggling. Wachovia, now owned by Wells Fargo, has cut nearly 1,000 jobs from its major office in Richmond in the past several years.

The Hampton Roads area has a heavy concentration of naval installations as well as associated shipbuilding and ship repair firms. Among these is the nation's largest privately owned shipyard — Northrop Grum-

man Newport News — which builds aircraft carriers and submarines. All three of the 3rd's military bases were affected by personnel changes from the 2005 BRAC round, but none was slated for closure.

Richmond, Portsmouth and Norfolk, which have substantial black populations, all gave Barack Obama at least 70 percent of their 2008 presidential vote. Overall, Obama took 76 percent of the 3rd's vote, his best showing statewide. Despite Democrats' dominance of the 3rd, Republicans are strong in some areas, particularly in New Kent County and Prince George County, which is shared with the 4th District.

MAJOR INDUSTRY
Defense, shipbuilding and repair, shipping, government, tobacco

MILITARY BASES
Norfolk Naval Shipyard at Portsmouth, 50 military, 7,800 civilian (2007); Fort Eustis (Army), 4,777 military, 2,715 civilian (2008); Naval Medical Center Portsmouth, 3,026 military, 1,547 civilian (2005)

CITIES
Richmond (pt.), 144,520; Norfolk (pt.), 122,301; Newport News (pt.), 108,350; Portsmouth, 100,565; Hampton (pt.), 59,929

NOTABLE
The Edgar Allan Poe Museum is in Richmond, where Poe lived.

Rep. J. Randy Forbes (R)

Elected June 2001; 4th full term

CAPITOL OFFICE
225-6365
www.house.gov/forbes
2438 Rayburn Bldg. 20515-4604; fax 226-1170

COMMITTEES
Armed Services
Judiciary

RESIDENCE
Chesapeake

BORN
Feb. 17, 1952; Chesapeake, Va.

RELIGION
Baptist

FAMILY
Wife, Shirley Forbes; four children

EDUCATION
Randolph-Macon College, B.A. 1974
(political science); U. of Virginia, J.D. 1977

CAREER
Lawyer; state legislative aide

POLITICAL HIGHLIGHTS
Va. House, 1990-97 (Republican floor leader,
1994-97); Va. Republican Party chairman, 1996-
2000; Va. Senate, 1997-2001 (Republican
floor leader, 1998-2000)

ELECTION RESULTS

2008 GENERAL

J. Randy Forbes (R)	199,075	59.5%
Andrea Miller (D)	135,041	40.4%

2008 PRIMARY

J. Randy Forbes (R)	unopposed

2006 GENERAL

J. Randy Forbes (R)	150,967	76.1%
Albert P. Burckard Jr. (IGREEN)	46,487	23.4%

PREVIOUS WINNING PERCENTAGES
2004 (64%); 2002 (98%); 2001 Special Election (52%)

Forbes keeps a hold on his swing district by keeping a close eye on local issues and a strong dedication to fiscal conservatism, except when it threatens money for defense. And he occasionally supports a Democratic bill that might meet the expectations of constituents in his district who favored Barack Obama for president over Republican Sen. John McCain by a mere percentage point in 2008.

A Sunday school teacher for more than 20 years, Forbes also is co-founder of the Congressional Prayer Caucus and leads weekly prayer meetings just off the House floor. "We're working on changing the whole civility and demeanor of Congress," he said. "We've got to get out of this world where both leadership teams want to destroy the other."

A member of the conservative Republican Study Committee, Forbes takes a strong stance against heavy federal spending. He voted against a $700 billion law to aid the nation's financial services sector in fall 2008. He also opposed President Obama's $787 billion economic stimulus law in February 2009. "Americans understand that it is because of our economic situation that we cannot wastefully spend money," he said. He likewise opposed a $3.56 trillion budget resolution for fiscal 2010, saying, "At some point, the federal government must become effective at something other than spending money."

Yet when Defense Secretary Robert M. Gates indicated in April 2009 his proposed budget would reduce funding for various weapons systems, Forbes — top Republican on the Armed Services Subcommittee on Readiness — was outraged. "Our national security needs should be determined by strategic planning, not budgetary pressure," he said. He added that the proposed cuts were "a reaction to the fiscal strain caused by trillions in bailout and stimulus spending."

Forbes also took the lead in a letter from top Republicans on the full Armed Services Committee criticizing Gates for secrecy in the budget process by requiring Pentagon officials to sign a non-disclosure agreement. "Congress is mandated by the Constitution to raise and support armies and navies, including funding the budget for our defense," the letter stated. He criticized Gates for instituting a "gag order."

Forbes' district has one of the largest concentrations of military bases in the nation — it includes Army's Fort Lee and the a naval shipyard in Norfolk — and he is strongly protective of the jobs of constituents who work there. In 2005, his lobbying helped ensure Fort Lee was not only spared in the last round of base closings but was chosen for expansion instead.

Forbes was a strong supporter of President George W. Bush's Iraq War policy, and was appointed by House GOP leaders in 2007 to the top GOP slot on Armed Services' Readiness Subcommittee over the more senior Walter B. Jones of North Carolina, who was more critical of the war.

Forbes for years has expressed deep concern about Chinese militarism. "This is going to be a major, major superpower on the world scene in very short order. The frightening thing is they know much about us and we know very little about them," he once said. In March 2009, he raised alarm about a Defense report indicating further progress in China in building out its navy.

He has pressed for legislation to discourage foreign companies from selling sensitive military technology to China. He also has demanded the Navy take more seriously the threat of new Chinese missile technology and has encouraged the Pentagon to use modeling and simulation technology to prepare for potential threats. Forbes is a fan of computer modeling and simulation. He helped win inclusion of a provision in the 2008 overhaul of the Higher Education Act to provide grants to enhance university modeling and simulation study programs. In 2009, he and Democrat Patrick J. Kennedy of Rhode Island pushed legislation to spur the increased use of such technology to allow doctors to practice difficult medical procedures in lifelike situations.

A member of the Judiciary Committee, he takes a tough-on-crime approach, backing mandatory prison sentences. But he also supports prisoner rehabilitation and re-entry programs. He won House passage in 2006 of a bill targeting illegal immigrants who belong to criminal gangs.

Republican leaders can typically rely on Forbes for his vote, but there have been exceptions. He voted in 2009 for a Democratic bill setting mortgage standards and aiming to curb predatory lending practices. And he was one of three Judiciary Republicans who voted for a community policing bill when it went through the committee. He also voted for the Democrats' 2007 energy bill setting new fuel efficiency standards for vehicles.

Forbes pushes a "Manhattan Project" to end U.S. dependence on foreign energy sources. His bill went nowhere during the 110th Congress (2007-08), but its free-market incentives — big prize money for renewable energy innovations — earned him plaudits in his district and in national publications like The Wall Street Journal.

He grew up in what was then rural Chesapeake, where his grandparents farmed and returned to the area after law school and worked in private practice for several years. He won a seat in the Virginia House of Delegates in 1989, rising to become Republican floor leader, and later served in the state Senate.

When a former law school classmate, George Allen, became governor, he made Forbes chairman of the state Republican Party. Under Forbes' watch from 1996 to 2000, the party became the dominant power in Virginia politics. In 2001, he geared up to run for lieutenant governor. But when conservative Democrat Norman Sisisky died that March, Forbes ran for the House instead. He won the nomination at a contentious convention, then faced state Sen. Louise Lucas, a black Democrat and former shipyard worker. Both parties poured money into it, but Forbes won in balloting that broke along racial lines.

A controversial redistricting then moved several African-American neighborhoods into the neighboring 3rd District. Democrats sued, but a federal appeals court upheld the plan in September 2004. Forbes faced no competition in 2002, then garnered 64 percent of the vote in 2004. That percentage spiked to 76 percent in 2006 when he faced a minor party candidate. He had slightly tougher competition in Democrat Andrea Miller in 2008, but took nearly 60 percent of the vote.

KEY VOTES

2008
No Delay consideration of Colombia free-trade agreement
Yes Override Bush veto of federal farm and nutrition programs reauthorization bill
Yes Overhaul surveillance laws and permit dismissal of suits against companies that conducted warrantless wiretapping
No Grant mortgage relief to homeowners and funding for Fannie Mae and Freddie Mac
No Approve initial $700 billion program to stabilize financial markets
No Approve final $700 billion program to stabilize financial markets
No Provide $14 billion in loans to automakers

2007
Yes Increase minimum wage by $2.10 an hour
No Approve $124.2 billion in emergency war spending and set goal for redeployment of troops from Iraq
Yes Reject federal contraceptive assistance to international family planning groups
Yes Override Bush veto of $23.2 billion water projects authorization bill
Yes Implement Peru free-trade agreement
Yes Approve energy policy overhaul with new fuel economy standards
Yes Clear $473.5 billion omnibus spending bill, including $70 billion for military operations

CQ VOTE STUDIES

	PARTY UNITY		PRESIDENTIAL SUPPORT	
	SUPPORT	OPPOSE	SUPPORT	OPPOSE
2008	95%	5%	60%	40%
2007	94%	6%	77%	23%
2006	93%	7%	93%	7%
2005	95%	5%	89%	11%
2004	96%	4%	82%	18%

INTEREST GROUPS

	AFL-CIO	ADA	CCUS	ACU
2008	25%	25%	78%	91%
2007	13%	20%	79%	92%
2006	29%	10%	100%	92%
2005	20%	5%	89%	92%
2004	14%	5%	100%	100%

VIRGINIA 4
Southeast — Chesapeake, Petersburg

Located among the rivers and swamps of southeastern and south-central Virginia, the 4th begins in Hampton Roads in the growing city of Chesapeake before heading west into rural tobacco- and peanut-producing areas. The district then bends north to reach the Tri-Cities area — Petersburg, Hopewell and Colonial Heights — south of Richmond.

Chesapeake, by far the 4th's most-populous city, grew by nearly 45 percent after 1990 as manufacturing and other industries moved in alongside residents who commute to nearby Norfolk or Virginia Beach. But growth appears to be slowing and layoffs have caused rising unemployment rates throughout the metropolitan area.

Farther north, the Tri-Cities area received a boost from the 2005 BRAC round, which ordered a near doubling of personnel at Fort Lee by the end of 2011. Outside the 4th District's population centers, tobacco and peanut farming play a central role in the economy. There also are pork producing facilities here in sparsely populated counties such as Isle of Wight and Sussex.

The 4th traditionally votes Republican at the national and statewide levels, but Democrats fare better in areas with sizable black voting blocs — the district has the state's second-largest black population (33 percent) — and can win local elections across the 4th. Petersburg, which is nearly four-fifths black, gave Democrat Barack Obama 88 percent of its presidential vote in 2008, his best showing in the state. Overall, Obama won the district by just more than 1 percentage point.

MAJOR INDUSTRY
Military, agriculture, tobacco, health care, manufacturing

MILITARY BASES
Fort Lee (Army), 4,281 military, 2,539 civilian (2009); U.S. Joint Forces Command Joint Warfighting Center, 547 military, 120 civilian (2009); Defense Supply Center, Richmond, 38 military, 2,379 civilian (2009); Naval Support Activity Norfolk, Northwest Annex, 937 military, 775 civilian (2007)

CITIES
Chesapeake, 199,184; Suffolk, 63,677; Petersburg, 33,740; Hopewell, 22,354

NOTABLE
Suffolk, which calls itself the peanut capital of the world, is the birthplace of Planters' Mr. Peanut and hosts an annual Suffolk Peanut Festival.

Rep. Tom Perriello (D)

Elected 2008; 1st term

CAPITOL OFFICE
225-4711
perriello.house.gov
1520 Longworth Bldg. 20515-4605; fax 225-5681

COMMITTEES
Transportation & Infrastructure
Veterans' Affairs

RESIDENCE
Ivy

BORN
Oct. 9, 1974; Charlottesville, Va.

RELIGION
Roman Catholic

FAMILY
Single

EDUCATION
Yale U., B.A. 1996 (humanities), J.D. 2001

CAREER
Human rights nonprofit founder; international justice consultant;

POLITICAL HIGHLIGHTS
No previous office

ELECTION RESULTS

2008 GENERAL

Tom Perriello (D)	158,810	50.1%
Virgil H. Goode Jr. (R)	158,083	49.9%

2008 PRIMARY

Tom Perriello (D)	unopposed

Perriello, who says he was "called by my faith" to work for nonprofit organizations in conflict zones in Africa and Afghanistan, doesn't shy from talking about how his religious beliefs underpin his policy views. He spoke frequently during his 2008 campaign about replacing a "culture of corruption" in Congress with a "culture of service."

"For the last 20 years, so much of the great work has been done by our nonprofits and our houses of worship," Perriello said. "And I think we need to capture that spirit of service that still exists and bring it back into the public sector and bring it back into Washington."

As a Democrat in a historically conservative-leaning rural district — one that produced, in terms of percentage-point margin, the closest House race of the 2008 cycle in his razor-thin defeat of incumbent Republican Virgil H. Goode Jr. — Perriello will be bucking the Democratic leadership from time to time.

In early 2009, he backed Arizona Republican Jeff Flake's efforts to ask for an ethics committee inquiry into the relationship between campaign contributions and the narrowly tailored spending set-asides known as earmarks. Perriello (pear-ee-ELL-oh) also backed a bill to ban members of Congress from taking campaign contributions from companies on whose behalf they have requested earmarks.

He departs from many liberal colleagues in supporting gun owners' rights. In March 2009, he was one of eight signatories to a letter urging President Obama not to reinstate a ban on certain semiautomatic assault-style weapons.

But Perriello is a reliable Democratic vote on economic policy. He backed Obama's economic stimulus law as helpful to his district, which had jurisdictions suffering from unemployment rates of 20 percent or more early in 2009. He plans to seek money to upgrade roads and make other improvements through his seat on the Transportation and Infrastructure Committee.

Veterans are an abiding concern for Perriello, who in early 2009 used his seat on the Veterans' Affairs panel to push for a new veterans' hospital in his district. He also introduced legislation to increase vocational training benefits for veterans.

VIRGINIA 5

South central — Danville, Charlottesville

Rich in Civil War landmarks, the 5th extends from the central part of Virginia just north of Charlottesville to Southside on the south-central border with North Carolina.

The mostly rural 5th is relatively poor and relies on agriculture and textiles. Once the heart of tobacco country, the industry has suffered a decline, which has led to high unemployment in the district's southwestern corner. Manufacturing has taken a more prominent role, although jobs have dwindled in some areas. Officials hope the 5th can become a hub for new energy development. Danville is a tobacco and textile center on the North Carolina border and to the west Martinsville struggles with unemployment. Charlottesville, in the northern part of the 5th, has seen steadier employment, due in part to a growing public sector. The 5th's

northern tip also has several wineries.

While the 5th is reliably conservative, party labels hold little meaning here, as evidenced by former Rep. Virgil H. Goode Jr.'s ability to switch parties in 2002 and keep his U.S. House seat for six terms. In 2008, Goode lost to Democrat Tom Perriello, while 13 of the 18 counties wholly or partially in the district backed GOP presidential candidate John McCain. One notable exception to the 5th's conservative posture is Charlottesville, home to the University of Virginia, which gave Barack Obama 78 percent of its vote in the 2008 presidential election — his third-best showing statewide. Overall, McCain took 51 percent of the district's vote.

MAJOR INDUSTRY
Agriculture, manufacturing, textiles, service

CITIES
Danville, 48,411; Charlottesville, 45,049

NOTABLE
Appomattox Court House was where Confederate Gen. Robert E. Lee surrendered to end the Civil War.

Rep. Robert W. Goodlatte (R)

Elected 1992; 9th term

CAPITOL OFFICE
225-5431
www.house.gov/goodlatte
2240 Rayburn Bldg. 20515-4606; fax 225-9681

COMMITTEES
Agriculture
Judiciary

RESIDENCE
Roanoke

BORN
Sept. 22, 1952; Holyoke, Mass.

RELIGION
Christian Scientist

FAMILY
Wife, Maryellen Goodlatte; two children

EDUCATION
Bates College, B.A. 1974 (government);
Washington and Lee U., J.D. 1977

CAREER
Lawyer; congressional aide

POLITICAL HIGHLIGHTS
Roanoke City Republican Committee chairman,
1980-83; 6th Congressional District Republican
Party chairman, 1983-88

ELECTION RESULTS

2008 GENERAL

Robert W. Goodlatte (R)	192,350	61.6%
S. "Sam" Rasoul (D)	114,367	36.6%
Janice Lee Allen (I)	5,413	1.7%

2008 PRIMARY

Robert W. Goodlatte (R)	unopposed

2006 GENERAL

Robert W. Goodlatte (R)	153,187	75.1%
Barbara Jean Pryor (I)	25,129	12.3%
Andre D. Peery (I)	24,731	12.1%

PREVIOUS WINNING PERCENTAGES
2004 (97%); 2002 (97%); 2000 (99%); 1998 (69%);
1996 (67%); 1994 (100%); 1992 (60%)

Hardworking and unassuming, Goodlatte prefers to labor over the details of legislation rather than engage in partisan jousting. Though his voting record is solidly conservative, his willingness to reach across the aisle has made him a player on almost every major computer-related bill before Congress. He also teams with Democrats on agricultural issues.

Goodlatte (GOOD-lat) sees keeping budget deficits under control as his top priority. He has long advocated a balanced-budget constitutional amendment and adamantly opposed President Obama's early economic initiatives because he said they spent too much. "In these challenging economic times, it is even more important for government to be fiscally responsible," he wrote in a January 2009 opinion piece for The News Leader in Staunton.

A member of the Judiciary Committee and co-chairman of the Congressional Internet Caucus, Goodlatte has a special interest in technology policy as it affects rural areas. As a lawyer in Roanoke, he took advantage of the latest communications and information technology to build a competitive practice that included a specialty in immigration law. He sees communications technology today as comparable to the railroad in the 19th century. "If the railroad came through your town and connected you with the rest of the country, you'd boom. If it didn't, you'd go bust," he said.

He has worked on legislation aimed at protecting users' privacy, preserving intellectual copyright protections for artists and creators of software, shielding children from indecent material and safeguarding consumers from fraud. In 2004, the House overwhelmingly passed his measure setting criminal penalties for using privacy-invading "spyware" to tap into personal computers to steal information or damage hardware.

Two years later, he steered into law a bill to curb Internet gambling by prohibiting gambling businesses from accepting credit cards and electronic transfers for online betting. The measure also modified the 1961 Wire Act to clarify that its prohibitions also apply to Internet gambling, not just sports bets placed over telephone wires. When Financial Services Chairman Barney Frank, a Massachusetts Democrat, sought in 2009 to regulate online gambling through licensing outfits, Goodlatte was sharply critical. "Apparently Rep. Frank believes that [Treasury Secretary] Timothy Geithner can do a better job at enforcing our nation's criminal laws than the Department of Justice, which is scary considering [Geithner's] track record on complying with the tax code," he said.

Goodlatte's positions on technology are driven by the philosophy that government generally should stay out of the way of innovators and entrepreneurs. That is a conservative's perspective, but Goodlatte notes that many Internet-related issues lend themselves to bipartisanship. In 2007, he backed a bill sponsored by Democrat Anna G. Eshoo of California to permanently ban Internet access taxes, but the two wound up reluctantly endorsing a compromise seven-year extension of the existing moratorium on such taxes.

A frequent Goodlatte partner on technology matters is his Internet Caucus co-chairman, Democrat Rick Boucher of the neighboring 9th District, who also sits on the Judiciary Committee. Boucher and Goodlatte paired up to promote a bill making it easier for parties involved in some class action lawsuits to transfer cases from state to federal court. Proponents of the legislation said it would prevent "venue shopping" by trial lawyers who deliberately bring cases in jurisdictions friendly to plaintiffs. President George W. Bush signed the measure into law in 2005. The two also worked on legislation that passed the House in 2009 to protect journalists from being forced to reveal sources to government officials.

When he served as top Republican on the Agriculture Committee, Goodlatte helped write the five-year reauthorization of agriculture and nutrition programs enacted in 2008 over Bush's veto. He is proud of its focus on conservation, specialty crops and increased funding for food banks, and he urged the House to override the president. He defended the bill as containing "a long list of reforms that lower cost to the taxpayer and increase the efficiency and effectiveness of the programs." Goodlatte chaired the Agriculture Committee for four years before the Democrats regained the majority in the House in the 2006 elections. During that period, he helped pass Bush's so-called Healthy Forests Initiative, expediting the cutting of timber in areas prone to wildfires, and a long-sought buyout program for tobacco farmers.

Goodlatte takes a hard line against illegal immigration. He voted in 2006 to authorize construction of a 700-mile fence along the border with Mexico, and in 2007 he joined North Carolina Democrat Heath Shuler in sponsoring legislation to require employers to verify the legal status of all their workers.

In the summer of 2008, as record gasoline prices pushed energy policy to the political forefront, Goodlatte joined other House Republicans in assailing Democrats for their reluctance to allow a vote on legislation to permit oil and gas drilling on more public lands and offshore territory. He introduced legislation to authorize Virginia's governor to seek a waiver from the federal ban on offshore drilling, saying such a decision should rest with the state.

Goodlatte grew up in western Massachusetts. His father managed a Friendly's ice cream store, and his mother worked part time in a department store. His parents liked to visit places with historical significance, feeding his own lifelong interest in presidential history. Vacations for the lawmaker often include a stop at the home of a U.S. president. His favorite stop was President Ronald Reagan's California ranch. In 2006, the House passed Goodlatte's bill providing funds for a Woodrow Wilson presidential library in his district. (The 28th president was born in Staunton.)

Goodlatte was president of the College Republicans at Bates College in Maine. After getting a law degree at Washington and Lee University in Lexington, he entered private practice and also worked for the area's Republican congressman, M. Caldwell Butler. He considered running for Congress in 1986, but the birth of his second child at the start of the campaign season kept him out of the race. In 1992, however, when Democratic Rep. Jim Olin retired after five terms, Goodlatte decided the time was right. He won easily and has done so ever since.

KEY VOTES

2008

No	Delay consideration of Colombia free-trade agreement
Yes	Override Bush veto of federal farm and nutrition programs reauthorization bill
Yes	Overhaul surveillance laws and permit dismissal of suits against companies that conducted warrantless wiretapping
No	Grant mortgage relief to homeowners and funding for Fannie Mae and Freddie Mac
No	Approve initial $700 billion program to stabilize financial markets
No	Approve final $700 billion program to stabilize financial markets
No	Provide $14 billion in loans to automakers

2007

Yes	Increase minimum wage by $2.10 an hour
No	Approve $124.2 billion in emergency war spending and set goal for redeployment of troops from Iraq
Yes	Reject federal contraceptive assistance to international family planning groups
No	Override Bush veto of $23.2 billion water projects authorization bill
Yes	Implement Peru free-trade agreement
No	Approve energy policy overhaul with new fuel economy standards
Yes	Clear $473.5 billion omnibus spending bill, including $70 billion for military operations

CQ VOTE STUDIES

	PARTY UNITY		PRESIDENTIAL SUPPORT	
	SUPPORT	OPPOSE	SUPPORT	OPPOSE
2008	94%	6%	64%	36%
2007	95%	5%	78%	22%
2006	99%	1%	95%	5%
2005	96%	4%	85%	15%
2004	98%	2%	88%	12%

INTEREST GROUPS

	AFL-CIO	ADA	CCUS	ACU
2008	14%	15%	83%	96%
2007	17%	15%	75%	92%
2006	14%	0%	100%	92%
2005	20%	5%	93%	96%
2004	13%	0%	100%	100%

VIRGINIA 6
Northwest — Roanoke, Lynchburg

Running along the Shenandoah Valley, the conservative 6th slides down much of Virginia's western border with West Virginia, combining mountainous terrain, small towns, midsize cities and natural beauty.

Roanoke, the 6th District's most populous city, hosts several industries, including furniture and electrical products manufacturing. Roanoke had begun attracting biomedical and biotech companies to business parks in redeveloped areas of the city, but national economic downturns have stalled the construction sector, an industry that paralleled growth of expanding manufacturing and technology companies in the region. Rising bankruptcy and foreclosure rates have hit Lynchburg hard recently. Outside metropolitan Roanoke and Lynchburg, the 6th District depends mainly on dairy farming, livestock and poultry. Rockingham County in the north leads the state in livestock and hay production, although growing manufacturing interests have encroached on farmland and credit issues are of concern to local farmers.

The district has a sizable Mennonite population and attracts tourists to

see the scenic Blue Ridge Mountains and their natural caverns. The 6th also hosts colleges and universities, including James Madison University in Harrisonburg. The Harrisonburg area has seen service sector job growth fueled by businesses providing support to the area colleges.

The 6th has a large population of senior citizens, a mostly white-collar workforce and a generous dose of Republicans, although the rural valley's brand of Republicanism has traditionally been a moderate one, and Democrats and independents can win some local elections. Roanoke has a strong Democratic base with union ties, but Republicans have done well in Roanoke's suburbs, in Lynchburg and in most rural areas. Overall, John McCain took 57 percent of the 6th's vote in the 2008 presidential election, his second-best in the state.

MAJOR INDUSTRY
Agriculture, livestock, manufacturing, tourism, higher education

CITIES
Roanoke, 94,911; Lynchburg, 65,269; Harrisonburg, 40,468; Cave Spring (unincorporated), 24,941; Salem, 24,747; Staunton, 23,853

NOTABLE
Thomas Jefferson's Poplar Forest in Bedford County features tours of Jefferson's octagonal "other" home.

Rep. Eric Cantor (R)

CAPITOL OFFICE
225-2815
cantor.house.gov
329 Cannon Bldg. 20515-4607; fax 225-0011

COMMITTEES
Ways & Means

RESIDENCE
Glen Allen

BORN
June 6, 1963; Richmond, Va.

RELIGION
Jewish

FAMILY
Wife, Diana Fine Cantor; three children

EDUCATION
George Washington U., B.A. 1985 (political science); College of William & Mary, J.D. 1988; Columbia U., M.S. 1989 (real estate development)

CAREER
Lawyer; real estate developer; campaign aide

POLITICAL HIGHLIGHTS
Va. House, 1992-2001

ELECTION RESULTS

2008 GENERAL

Eric Cantor (R)	233,531	62.7%
Anita Hartke (D)	138,123	37.1%

2008 PRIMARY

Eric Cantor (R)	unopposed

2006 GENERAL

Eric Cantor (R)	163,706	63.8%
James M. Nachman (D)	88,206	34.4%
W. Brad Blanton (I)	4,213	1.6%

PREVIOUS WINNING PERCENTAGES
2004 (76%); 2002 (69%); 2000 (67%)

Elected 2000; 5th term

Cantor's vote-counting prowess, fundraising talents and aggressive debating skills have enabled him to rise rapidly through the ranks of House Republicans and command attention as one of his party's leading national figures. He is immersed in the challenge of rebuilding the GOP's tarnished image among independent voters and reconnecting the party to business groups without alienating its hard-core social conservatives.

Cantor is the minority whip, the House's No. 2 GOP leader, having earlier spent years helping other leaders count votes and playing the role of mediator between the leadership and sometimes-restive right-wing lawmakers. Youthful, articulate and relentlessly on message, he is seen by his admirers as an appealing fresh face for his party. His detractors accuse him of slickly marketing a tired philosophy that voters have shown a disinclination to embrace.

Cantor says Republicans must return to their free-market, limited-government roots to find solutions to problems facing middle-class voters. His inspiration has been the story of his paternal grandmother, who owned a grocery store in downtown Richmond. "It was that spirit of entrepreneurialism, that can-do spirit, that really, there were no bounds," he said.

In spring 2009 he helped launch a new organization, the National Council for a New America, that brought together party leaders to pursue new ideas from framing the GOP's policy agenda. It held a series of events in which participants gave talks and listened to voters while seeking to shy away from criticizing President Obama, whose popularity in the polls remained high. Conservative radio talk show host Rush Limbaugh ridiculed the concept, but Cantor defended it as a way to connect with the public. "The American people are very frustrated that they really see a government in Washington that doesn't hear them, that doesn't respond to their needs, and frankly are upset at a government that doesn't work," he told MSNBC.

As whip, Cantor kept House Republicans together in opposing Obama's early economic initiatives; not a single Republican voted for the president's $787 billion economic stimulus law or his subsequent $3.56 trillion budget blueprint for fiscal 2010. He brushed back charges from Democrats that the GOP had become a "party of no" and said his colleagues would offer alternative proposals on health care, energy and financial regulation. He headed the House Republicans' working group on the stimulus and assembled a substitute that pointedly omitted items from the old conservative playbook, such as an across-the-board tax-rate cut.

Using his connections to the financial and real estate sectors, Cantor is one of the GOP's most prolific fundraisers. In the first quarter of 2009 he took in more than $963,000 — more than double his take from the comparable first quarter of the last non-election year in 2007.

In 2002, GOP whip Roy Blunt of Missouri chose Cantor over several more-senior members of former Majority Leader Tom DeLay's operation to be his chief lieutenant — a position that is often a launching pad for elected leadership posts. Cantor had been favored to get the whip's job if Blunt defeated John A. Boehner of Ohio for the leader's job in 2006. But he cultivated Boehner's attention, too, becoming one of Boehner's closest allies and a link to conservatives who might otherwise try to topple the leader.

Cantor's own legislative focus tends to be on tax issues handled by the Ways and Means Committee, on which he serves. He favors lower corporate tax rates and led the successful 2007 fight against Democratic attempts to tax private equity managers' profit-sharing earnings as ordinary income instead of capital gains. Cantor assembled a coalition of real estate and business interests from across the country to lobby wavering members.

As the sole Jewish Republican in the House, Cantor is a natural nexus between the party's Christian conservatives and traditionally Democratic Jewish campaign donors they court with their stance on Israel. He ranks among the top beneficiaries of pro-Israel campaign dollars and is a spokesman for the party on Israel. He made trips to Jewish communities to talk up the presidential candidacy of Arizona Republican Sen. John McCain and was briefly mentioned as a possible McCain running mate. He chairs the Congressional Task Force on Terrorism and Unconventional Warfare, a policy forum for conservatives.

The low point for Cantor over the past few years was getting wrapped up in the Jack Abramoff influence-peddling scandal. Cantor was among the leaders who in 2003 signed a letter that helped an American Indian tribe represented by lobbyist Abramoff. That year, Cantor also held a fundraiser at an Abramoff-owned restaurant, and Abramoff named a sandwich after him. Cantor received $12,000 in campaign donations through him, though Cantor claimed to know the lobbyist on only a "casual" basis. He later gave $10,000 of the money to a Richmond-area charity.

Cantor grew up in a well-to-do, politically active Richmond family. His father, Eddie, was on the board of the Virginia Housing Development Authority, and his mother, Mary Lee, was a board member of the Family and Children's Trust Fund and the Science Museum of Virginia.

While in college, Cantor interned for Rep. Thomas J. Bliley Jr. of Virginia, driving the lawmaker's 1982 campaign car around the district he would one day represent. He also worked as an aide to Walter A. Stosch, a member of the Virginia House of Delegates.

Cantor is a lawyer with a master's degree in real estate development from Columbia University. Before he was elected to Congress, he worked in the family real estate business. His wife, Diana, is powerful in her own right. She was the founding executive director of the Virginia College Savings Plan and serves on the board of directors of Media General Inc. and Domino's Pizza.

When Stosch ran for the state Senate in 1991, Cantor made a bid for the open seat. The 28-year-old out-organized and outspent two rivals with more experience and won, becoming the youngest member of the House of Delegates. Bliley's campaign machinery stood behind Cantor when needed, and Cantor frequently served as Bliley's campaign chairman. When Bliley announced his retirement in 2000, Cantor joined the race to replace him. He won the primary by a scant 263 votes. But in November, he sailed to victory and his re-elections have been easy ever since.

KEY VOTES

2008
No Delay consideration of Colombia free-trade agreement
No Override Bush veto of federal farm and nutrition programs reauthorization bill
Yes Overhaul surveillance laws and permit dismissal of suits against companies that conducted warrantless wiretapping
No Grant mortgage relief to homeowners and funding for Fannie Mae and Freddie Mac
Yes Approve initial $700 billion program to stabilize financial markets
Yes Approve final $700 billion program to stabilize financial markets
No Provide $14 billion in loans to automakers

2007
No Increase minimum wage by $2.10 an hour
No Approve $124.2 billion in emergency war spending and set goal for redeployment of troops from Iraq
Yes Reject federal contraceptive assistance to international family planning groups
No Override Bush veto of $23.2 billion water projects authorization bill
Yes Implement Peru free-trade agreement
No Approve energy policy overhaul with new fuel economy standards
Yes Clear $473.5 billion omnibus spending bill, including $70 billion for military operations

CQ VOTE STUDIES

| | PARTY UNITY | | PRESIDENTIAL SUPPORT | |
	SUPPORT	OPPOSE	SUPPORT	OPPOSE
2008	98%	2%	79%	21%
2007	98%	2%	89%	11%
2006	98%	2%	95%	5%
2005	98%	2%	89%	11%
2004	98%	2%	97%	3%

INTEREST GROUPS

	AFL-CIO	ADA	CCUS	ACU
2008	7%	5%	94%	92%
2007	4%	0%	80%	100%
2006	7%	5%	100%	92%
2005	13%	0%	93%	96%
2004	7%	0%	100%	100%

VIRGINIA 7
Central — part of Richmond and suburbs

The solidly Republican 7th begins in part of Richmond and its affluent old-money suburbs, then reaches northwest to the Shenandoah Valley through farmland and new Washington exurbs.

Many of the 7th's residents work in Richmond, a longtime center of state government and commerce. Richmond also was one of the South's early manufacturing centers, concentrating on tobacco processing. Richmond-based Philip Morris USA continues to employ thousands of district residents despite some recent layoffs.

The northeastern stretch of the 7th is changing, as declining traditional farming communities transform into exurban areas filled with new residents with long commutes to Washington or its close-in suburbs. The northern 7th has a local wine industry, but manufacturing-dependent Page County has been hit by skyrocketing unemployment rates.

A plurality of district residents lives in Henrico County (shared with the 3rd), which cups Richmond in a backward C-shape. Henrico traditionally has voted Republican, although it backed Mark Warner in the U.S. Senate race and Barack Obama in the presidential election in 2008. Chesterfield County, which is shared with the 4th, borders Richmond to the south and west and has a stronger GOP lean. The 7th's portion of heavily Democratic-leaning Richmond includes some Republican voters who live in the city's western end.

As a whole, the 7th is reliably Republican, and it is difficult for any Democratic candidate to stitch together a victory here. All the counties that are located entirely in the district voted for Republican John McCain in the 2008 presidential election — only Caroline and Henrico counties, which are split with the 1st and 3rd districts, respectively, favored Obama. John McCain won 53 percent of the 7th's presidential vote.

MAJOR INDUSTRY
Agriculture, government, manufacturing

CITIES
Richmond (pt.), 53,270; Tuckahoe (unincorporated), 43,242; Mechanicsville (unincorporated), 30,464

NOTABLE
Luray Caverns, in Page County, features a pipe organ made of stalactites; James Madison's Montpelier estate is in Orange County.

Rep. James P. Moran (D)

Elected 1990; 10th term

CAPITOL OFFICE
225-4376
moran.house.gov
2239 Rayburn Bldg. 20515-4608; fax 225-0017

COMMITTEES
Appropriations

RESIDENCE
Arlington

BORN
May 16, 1945; Buffalo, N.Y.

RELIGION
Roman Catholic

FAMILY
Wife, LuAnn Bennett; four children

EDUCATION
College of the Holy Cross, B.A. 1967
(economics); City U. of New York, Bernard M.
Baruch School of Finance, attended 1967-68;
U. of Pittsburgh, M.P.A. 1970

CAREER
Investment broker; congressional aide;
U.S. Health, Education and Welfare
Department analyst

POLITICAL HIGHLIGHTS
Alexandria City Council, 1979-84 (vice mayor,
1982-84); mayor of Alexandria, 1985-90
(served as an independent 1985-88)

ELECTION RESULTS

2008 GENERAL

James P. Moran (D)	222,986	67.9%
Mark W. Ellmore (R)	97,425	29.7%
J. Ron Fisher (IGREEN)	6,829	2.1%

2008 PRIMARY

James P. Moran (D)	11,792	87.0%
Matthew T. Famiglietti (D)	1,764	13.0%

2006 GENERAL

James P. Moran (D)	144,700	66.4%
Tom M. O'Donoghue (R)	66,639	30.6%
James T. Hurysz (I)	6,094	2.8%

PREVIOUS WINNING PERCENTAGES
2004 (60%); 2002 (60%); 2000 (63%); 1998 (67%);
1996 (66%); 1994 (59%); 1992 (56%); 1990 (52%)

Moran has a reputation as a troubled politician, something attributed to his combative temperament, sometimes spotty personal finances and the occasional off-color or inflammatory remark. In recent years, though, he has sought to channel his passions into legislative work and is optimistic about what he can accomplish working with a Democratic White House.

The odds are in favor of Moran achieving some of his goals, because despite his sometimes confrontational manner, he also has a reputation as an able negotiator. From his seat on the Appropriations Committee, he has cut deals across party lines to bring in millions of dollars for local roads, education programs, law enforcement and low-income housing.

Moran's district is home to the Pentagon, but he has been a strong critic of the Iraq War and frequently supported calls for withdrawal. He supported President Obama's plan in early 2009 to withdraw U.S. combat troops from Iraq by August 2010, saying it meets the test of a gradual withdrawal.

Based on his feelings about the war, he found himself on the wrong side of the contest for majority leader in 2006. He sided with Pennsylvania Democrat John P. Murtha, a decorated Marine veteran who has led Democratic opposition to the war, in his challenge to Steny H. Hoyer of Maryland. If Murtha had won, Moran would have had a shot at the chairmanship of the Interior-Environment Appropriations Subcommittee. Instead, Moran holds his party's No. 2 slot on that panel behind Chairman Norm Dicks of Washington.

Moran also sits on the Labor-HHS-Education Appropriations Subcommittee. Moran hopes to address some of his longtime interests, such as early-childhood development, that many people don't associate with him. After graduate school, he worked for what was then the Department of Health, Education and Welfare. In his subsequent work as a staffer on the Senate Appropriations Committee, he handled health care and education.

On the Interior-Environment panel, Moran can take care of constituent needs such as the recreational areas along the George Washington Parkway, which shadows the Potomac River in his district.

He also tends to constituent needs on the Defense Appropriations panel. He is an energetic advocate for more pay and better health and retirement benefits for federal workers, including those in the Defense Department.

But Moran focuses on larger national security issues as well. He would prefer to see the Pentagon workforce be larger, more capable and conducting tougher oversight, with less outsourcing. He wants the Pentagon to buy weapons that are less expensive and better suited to current threats rather than Cold War ones.

And he is working to see agencies such as the State Department receive more resources — even if they must come from the Defense budget he oversees — to conduct development, diplomacy and nation-building. "Many conflicts are not going to lend themselves to military solutions," he said.

Moran joined with two House colleagues in 1997 to found the moderate New Democrat Coalition. He normally votes with the majority of his party, but he sometimes goes against the grain. He has voted for trade liberalization measures and supported a 2005 bill backed by President George W. Bush to rein in class action lawsuits.

For all of his legislative activity, Moran usually makes headlines in less flattering ways. In 2002, The Washington Post ran a Page One story about Moran borrowing $50,000 from an America Online executive and using the money to trade in stocks before repaying it months later.

Before the March 2003 invasion of Iraq, he told an audience at an event sponsored by a peace coalition, "If it were not for the strong support of the Jewish community for this war with Iraq, we would not be doing this." Moran apologized, but Democratic Leader Nancy Pelosi of California stripped him of his post in the whip organization. Four years later, he told the Jewish magazine Tikkun that the powerful American Israel Public Affairs Committee lobbying group "has pushed this war from the beginning." In April 2006, he and other Democrats were arrested by the U.S. Secret Service in front of the Embassy of Sudan for protesting the violence in Darfur.

That year, he poked fun at his reputation as a hothead by cooperating with a stunt on a popular late-night comedy show in which he pretended to throw a punch at host Stephen Colbert. Yet despite his willingness to make light of his image, news reports in 2009 indicated his impolitic behavior posed a challenge for his younger brother Brian — a veteran Virginia state legislator — as he sought the Democratic nomination for governor.

The son of a professional boxer who also was a Washington Redskins football player, he takes pride in his prowess as an amateur heavyweight, including college bouts at Holy Cross and an exhibition match with former heavyweight champion Joe Frazier. He comes by his pugilism honestly. Once, when he was a boy, someone came to the family's door with a petition to prevent an African-American family from moving into the neighborhood. "My father not only refused to sign it, he actually punched him in the nose," Moran said.

Moran grew up in a Boston suburb, one of seven siblings, all of whom have been involved in politics. First elected to the Alexandria City Council in 1979, Moran saw his career derailed briefly in 1984 when, after pleading no contest to a misdemeanor conflict-of-interest charge, he resigned as vice mayor. He ran as an independent the next year and unseated the incumbent mayor. He was serving as mayor in 1990 when he ran for Congress, upsetting six-term Republican Stan Parris with 52 percent of the vote.

Republicans tested Moran in 1992 and 1994 with a quality challenger in Kyle E. McSlarrow, but Moran prevailed by solid margins. In 2002 and 2004, he slipped to about 60 percent, a sign voters were tiring of his family problems and financial dealings. Moran's wife of 11 years, Mary, filed for divorce in 1999, a day after calling police during a domestic argument. In court filings, she blamed the couple's poor finances on $120,000 in bad stock trades Moran had made. He married for a third time in 2004 to LuAnn Bennett, a successful commercial real estate developer.

In the last two elections, Moran has bounced back, winning with 66 percent of the vote in 2006 and 68 percent in 2008.

KEY VOTES

2008

Yes Delay consideration of Colombia free-trade agreement

Yes Override Bush veto of federal farm and nutrition programs reauthorization bill

No Overhaul surveillance laws and permit dismissal of suits against companies that conducted warrantless wiretapping

Yes Grant mortgage relief to homeowners and funding for Fannie Mae and Freddie Mac

Yes Approve initial $700 billion program to stabilize financial markets

Yes Approve final $700 billion program to stabilize financial markets

Yes Provide $14 billion in loans to automakers

2007

Yes Increase minimum wage by $2.10 an hour

Yes Approve $124.2 billion in emergency war spending and set goal for redeployment of troops from Iraq

No Reject federal contraceptive assistance to international family planning groups

Yes Override Bush veto of $23.2 billion water projects authorization bill

Yes Implement Peru free-trade agreement

Yes Approve energy policy overhaul with new fuel economy standards

No Clear $473.5 billion omnibus spending bill, including $70 billion for military operations

CQ VOTE STUDIES

	PARTY UNITY		PRESIDENTIAL SUPPORT	
	SUPPORT	OPPOSE	SUPPORT	OPPOSE
2008	98%	2%	15%	85%
2007	98%	2%	5%	95%
2006	90%	10%	33%	67%
2005	92%	8%	24%	76%
2004	89%	11%	41%	59%

INTEREST GROUPS

	AFL-CIO	ADA	CCUS	ACU
2008	100%	95%	61%	0%
2007	96%	95%	55%	0%
2006	93%	95%	53%	16%
2005	80%	90%	65%	4%
2004	87%	95%	67%	24%

VIRGINIA 8

Washington suburbs — Arlington, Alexandria, part of Fairfax County

Taking in the close-in Northern Virginia suburbs of Washington, the 8th is mostly upper-income and strongly Democratic — in no small part because of a racially and ethnically diverse population of blacks, Asians and Hispanics, who together total about 40 percent of residents. The 8th also has the nation's fourth-largest number of residents of Arab ancestry.

The 8th bustles with high-tech firms and defense contractors, drawn to the district's substantial military presence, including the Pentagon and Fort Belvoir, which will receive nearly 20,000 new jobs as a result of the 2005 BRAC round. The government, defense and technology fields rely on well-educated employees, and 54 percent of the 8th's residents have a college degree, the second-highest mark in the nation.

Roughly half of the district's residents live in an elongated swath of growing Fairfax County that reaches from the Potomac River, near Mount Vernon (shared with the 11th), past Falls Church and Tysons Corner to Res-

ton. Gridlock plagues the commute into Washington, and local officials are looking to develop areas in the northern arm of the district into more self-contained urban areas.

Alexandria and Arlington tend to give Democratic statewide candidates some of their highest vote percentages in the state. A Republican presidential candidate has not won a majority in either jurisdiction since 1972, and the 8th gave Barack Obama 69 percent of its presidential vote in the 2008 election.

MAJOR INDUSTRY
Government, technology, defense, service

MILITARY BASES
Pentagon, 11,000 military, 13,000 civilian (2005); Fort Belvoir (Army), 6,800 military, 1,500 civilian (2008); Fort Myer (Army), 8,100 military, 422 civilian (2009); Henderson Hall, 2,156 military, 54 civilian (2007)

CITIES
Arlington (unincorporated), 189,453; Alexandria, 128,283; Reston (unincorporated) (pt.), 56,275; Franconia (unincorporated), 31,907

NOTABLE
The Torpedo Factory Art Center, in Alexandria, was a World War II munitions factory that has been converted into an art school and gallery.

Rep. Rick Boucher (D)

Elected 1982; 14th term

CAPITOL OFFICE
225-3861
www.house.gov/boucher
2187 Rayburn Bldg. 20515-4609; fax 225-0442

COMMITTEES
Energy & Commerce
 (Communications, Technology & the Internet
 - chairman)
Judiciary

RESIDENCE
Abingdon

BORN
Aug. 1, 1946; Abingdon, Va.

RELIGION
Methodist

FAMILY
Wife, Amy Boucher

EDUCATION
Roanoke College, B.A. 1968 (political science);
U. of Virginia, J.D. 1971

CAREER
Lawyer

POLITICAL HIGHLIGHTS
Va. Senate, 1976-82

ELECTION RESULTS

2008 GENERAL
Rick Boucher (D)	207,306	97.1%
write-ins	6,264	2.9%

2008 PRIMARY
Rick Boucher (D)	unopposed

2006 GENERAL
Rick Boucher (D)	129,705	67.8%
C.W. "Bill" Carrico (R)	61,574	32.2%

PREVIOUS WINNING PERCENTAGES
2004 (59%); 2002 (66%); 2000 (70%); 1998 (61%);
1996 (65%); 1994 (59%); 1992 (63%); 1990 (97%);
1988 (63%); 1986 (99%); 1984 (52%); 1982 (50%)

The wonkish Boucher has firmly entrenched himself in a strongly Republican district. He avoids partisanship, parts ways with his party on hot-button social issues and has persuaded constituents that his passion for technology can enable him to help diversify their economy.

A self-proclaimed "techno-geek" who once wired his backyard gazebo for Internet service, Boucher (BOW — rhymes with "now" — chur) has become an influential player on a range of technology-related issues in the House, particularly the high-profile push for Internet privacy and climate change legislation. He sits on the two powerful panels with broad and sometimes overlapping jurisdiction: the Energy and Commerce Committee and the Judiciary Committee.

He chairs the Energy and Commerce Subcommittee on Communications, Technology, and the Internet. Boucher, who co-founded the Congressional Internet Caucus, convinced voters in his rural district that high-speed Internet and other digital innovations will foster local jobs beyond the old pillars of coal mining, raising livestock and tobacco farming. By the early 2000s, communities throughout the area were wired with fiber-optic cable, and Abingdon was dubbed "the most wired small town in America" by Yahoo Life magazine.

But as Internet use expanded, so did Boucher's concern for user privacy. He launched in early 2009 an effort by multiple Energy and Commerce subcommittees to produce what he called "baseline" consumer privacy legislation to protect people's anonymity on the Internet, seeking to bar search engines and other Web-based companies from tracking users' online behavior. He said implementing such restrictions would encourage people to surf more, contrary to industry fears. "Right now, there's a huge reluctance on the part of the public to trust their Internet experience," he said.

He also seeks to protect fair-use rights for consumers of digital media. He said the 1998 Digital Millennium Copyright Act "has the seeds for the complete elimination of fair use with respect to digital media" because it empowers owners of intellectual property, such as the music and motion picture industries, to require a fee for access. He has advocated exceptions to the 1998 law when it comes to research or personal use.

Boucher is viewed as leaning toward satellite television providers over cable companies and favoring small rural phone companies that provide local service. But like the panel's former chairman, Democrat Edward J. Markey of Massachusetts, Boucher has been an advocate of "network neutrality," the idea that broadband providers should be barred from blocking certain traffic or establishing tiered pathways for Internet content. Major broadband carriers oppose such mandates.

Boucher also wants to overhaul the troubled Universal Service Fund, a government program that subsidizes construction and operation of rural telephone networks.

Boucher took over the communications panel from Markey in 2009 while Markey headed up the Energy and the Environment panel. But Boucher still sits on that subcommittee and became a key player in 2009 in negotiations on climate change legislation.

He seeks to protect the interests of Midwestern and Southern states still heavily reliant on coal-fired power plants. While Democratic leaders and President Obama insisted on a program to cap greenhouse gas emissions and set up a market-based emissions-trading system, Boucher led negotiations to ease the impact on industries. He and several Democratic colleagues want to be sure power plants can continue burning coal until carbon-capture technology is ready.

During the 110th Congress (2007-08), Boucher tried unsuccessfully to push legislation to provide a loan program for power plants to turn coal into liquid fuel for transportation, an idea unpopular with environmentalists. Later that year, he was one of 38 Democrats to oppose a House-passed measure requiring retail electricity suppliers to obtain a portion of their energy from alternative sources. When Obama said he wanted to push through similar legislation, Boucher said he would help move it along if he could be sure it wouldn't "harm ratepayers in regions with limited renewable sources."

On the Judiciary panel, Boucher parts ways with most Democrats on gun control and gay rights, siding with the overwhelming sentiment in his district. In September 2008, he voted to repeal District of Columbia laws prohibiting firearm possession.

One of his committee partners on intellectual property legislation is Republican Robert W. Goodlatte, his neighbor in Virginia's 6th District. The two also joined forces on legislation enacted in 2005 making it easier to transfer class action lawsuits from state to federal court.

With Goodlatte's support, he pushed through the House in early 2009 a media shield bill under which reporters would be forced to divulge sources or other information to government officials only if a judge decides it is necessary in certain circumstances. "The purpose of our legislation is not to protect reporters," Boucher said. "It is to protect the public's right to know."

Boucher has said that by age 12, he had decided to become a lawyer and pursue a career in public service. He recalls a couple of years later attending a John F. Kennedy rally in Abingdon where former President Truman spoke. After graduating from law school, he joined a Wall Street firm, worked as an advance man for Democrat George McGovern's 1972 presidential campaign, and joined the family law firm in 1978.

He won a seat in the state Senate before he turned 30, then took on Republican U.S. Rep. William C. Wampler in 1982. With high unemployment plaguing the district's coal fields, Boucher won by just 1,123 votes. Two years later, he edged to a 4-percentage-point victory over state Rep. Jefferson Stafford. Solid re-election victories then became Boucher's norm for awhile.

He faced only nominal opposition in 2006 and was unopposed in 2008 — a year in which Republican John McCain took 59 percent of the district's vote over Barack Obama in the presidential race.

Boucher and his wife bike as many as 50 miles a week during warm weather. He also jogs.

KEY VOTES

2008

Yes Delay consideration of Colombia free-trade agreement

Yes Override Bush veto of federal farm and nutrition programs reauthorization bill

Yes Overhaul surveillance laws and permit dismissal of suits against companies that conducted warrantless wiretapping

Yes Grant mortgage relief to homeowners and funding for Fannie Mae and Freddie Mac

Yes Approve initial $700 billion program to stabilize financial markets

Yes Approve final $700 billion program to stabilize financial markets

Yes Provide $14 billion in loans to automakers

2007

Yes Increase minimum wage by $2.10 an hour

Yes Approve $124.2 billion in emergency war spending and set goal for redeployment of troops from Iraq

No Reject federal contraceptive assistance to international family planning groups

Yes Override Bush veto of $23.2 billion water projects authorization bill

No Implement Peru free-trade agreement

Yes Approve energy policy overhaul with new fuel economy standards

Yes Clear $473.5 billion omnibus spending bill, including $70 billion for military operations

CQ VOTE STUDIES

	PARTY UNITY		PRESIDENTIAL SUPPORT	
	SUPPORT	OPPOSE	SUPPORT	OPPOSE
2008	96%	4%	23%	77%
2007	95%	5%	6%	94%
2006	79%	21%	33%	67%
2005	83%	17%	33%	67%
2004	81%	19%	38%	62%

INTEREST GROUPS

	AFL-CIO	ADA	CCUS	ACU
2008	100%	80%	61%	8%
2007	96%	95%	65%	8%
2006	93%	75%	60%	36%
2005	93%	90%	59%	25%
2004	73%	75%	67%	32%

VIRGINIA 9

Southwest — Blacksburg, Bristol

Encompassing the mountains and forests of Virginia's southwestern corner, the rural 9th District accommodates the college towns of Blacksburg and Radford, as well as the smaller coal and factory towns nestled close to neighboring West Virginia, North Carolina, Tennessee and Kentucky.

The district has struggled with high poverty rates and a weak economic base, and the 9th is Virginia's poorest congressional district, with a median income of less than $30,000. It also has the state's highest percentage of blue-collar workers, as coal mining and manufacturing provide many area jobs. Despite the presence of one of the state's largest universities — Virginia Tech in Blacksburg — the 9th has Virginia's lowest percentage of college-educated residents (14 percent).

Even with resources available from the district's colleges and universities, some counties perpetually struggle to provide residents with clean drinking water, and the district's local population has remained stagnant since the 1990s. State and local leaders have worked to improve district residents' quality of life by promoting the scenic Blue Ridge Parkway to attract tourism revenue, and by using federal wireless Internet-access grants in several counties to increase learning opportunities for residents.

Once known for its competitive congressional elections, the 9th is still characterized by its ornery isolation from the political establishment in Richmond. The district supports Republicans in presidential elections. Scott County gave Republican John McCain his second-highest margin of victory in the 2008 presidential election among all the state's counties and cities, providing a win of more than 43 percentage points. McCain won the district overall with 59 percent, his best showing statewide. But the 9th has elected a Democrat to Congress for more than two decades, and the party fares well in local races.

MAJOR INDUSTRY
Manufacturing, coal mining, agriculture

CITIES
Blacksburg, 39,573; Bristol, 17,367; Christiansburg, 16,947; Radford, 15,859

NOTABLE
Abingdon's still-thriving Barter Theatre allowed local residents to trade excess produce and livestock for admission during the Depression.

Rep. Frank R. Wolf (R)

Elected 1980; 15th term

CAPITOL OFFICE
225-5136
house.gov/wolf
241 Cannon Bldg. 20515-4610; fax 225-0437

COMMITTEES
Appropriations

RESIDENCE
Vienna

BORN
Jan. 30, 1939; Philadelphia, Pa.

RELIGION
Presbyterian

FAMILY
Wife, Carolyn Wolf; five children

EDUCATION
Pennsylvania State U., B.A. 1961
(political science); Georgetown U., LL.B. 1965

MILITARY SERVICE
Army Reserve, 1962-63

CAREER
Lawyer; U.S. Interior Department official;
congressional aide; lobbyist

POLITICAL HIGHLIGHTS
Sought Republican nomination for U.S. House,
1976; Republican nominee for U.S. House, 1978

ELECTION RESULTS

2008 GENERAL

Frank R. Wolf (R)	223,140	58.8%
Judy M. Feder (D)	147,357	38.8%
Neeraj C. Nigam (I)	8,457	2.2%

2008 PRIMARY

Frank R. Wolf (R)	16,762	91.8%
Vern P. McKinley (R)	1,506	8.2%

2006 GENERAL

Frank R. Wolf (R)	138,213	57.3%
Judy M. Feder (D)	98,769	41.0%

PREVIOUS WINNING PERCENTAGES
2004 (64%); 2002 (72%); 2000 (84%); 1998 (72%);
1996 (72%); 1994 (87%); 1992 (64%); 1990 (61%);
1988 (68%); 1986 (60%); 1984 (63%); 1982 (53%);
1980 (51%)

A fervent defender of human rights with deep Christian beliefs, Wolf isn't afraid to cross his own party when he deems it necessary. He advocates for religious freedom abroad and for the interests of his constituents at home.

One of his proudest accomplishments in his long career — he's now the 10th-most-senior Republican currently in the House — is a 1998 law that established a new government body to monitor religious freedom abroad. He said the International Religious Freedom Commission has given victims of persecution "a forum to speak truth" and to put pressure on U.S. policy makers to take action.

Wolf lobbied President George W. Bush, in vain, not to attend the 2008 Olympics in China. He compared the Beijing games to those held in 1936 in Nazi Germany, citing Chinese support for the regime in Sudan — widely believed to be culpable for genocide in its Darfur region — and China's domestic human rights record. "If any American is in the stands waving, they will go down in history as people cooperating in the genocide Olympics in 2008," Wolf said during a March 2008 hearing of the State-Foreign Operations Appropriations Subcommittee, where he was the top-ranking Republican during the 110th Congress (2007-08).

He is the top Republican on the Commerce-Justice-Science Appropriations Subcommittee, which he chaired earlier in the decade when Republicans controlled Congress. The panel oversees funding for the Commerce and Justice departments and science agencies, as well as the Commission on Civil Rights.

Wolf was a force behind the creation of the Iraq Study Group, an independent panel composed of policy experts that recommended a new course in Iraq in late 2006. Wolf was miffed that Bush chose to ignore many of its recommendations for diplomatic solutions, instead embracing a "surge" policy that involved increasing the number of U.S. troops. In protest, Wolf introduced a resolution in January 2007 calling for the recommendations of the study group to become U.S. strategy.

Wolf generally favors aggressive diplomacy. He traveled to Syria in 2007, in defiance of the Bush administration, to put pressure on the Syrian government to stay out of Lebanon. Before the Obama administration took office in January 2009, Wolf sent a letter to the president-elect calling on him to immediately appoint a high-level special envoy to the Middle East based in Jerusalem instead of relying on periodic "shuttle diplomacy."

Wolf also has long been known for his ardent opposition to gambling. He authored a law creating a national commission in the late 1990s to study gambling's impact on society, despite opposition from Republicans who received campaign contributions from the industry.

While generally conservative, he has shown an increased willingness to cross party lines. In the 110th Congress, he split with Republicans on almost one-fifth of the votes that pitted the two parties against each other. He joined Democrats in 2007 in an unsuccessful bid to override Bush's veto of a bill expanding the State Children's Health Insurance Program, which covers children whose families don't qualify for Medicaid; he was one of 40 House Republicans supporting the successful 2009 version of the bill. Also in 2007, Wolf sided with Democrats in a failed effort to override Bush's veto of a $150.7 billion bill funding labor, health and education programs. "What would you tell someone who doesn't have health care for their kids? What do you tell a 5-year-old kid with leukemia?" he said. "I have always tried to follow my conscience."

Wolf's Northern Virginia district is home to thousands of federal employees, and he has long fought for their interests. He was one of three original GOP cosponsors in 2009 of a bill to grant federal employees up to four weeks of paid parental leave. A leading proponent of telecommuting and its potential to relieve the area's clogged roads, Wolf has used his seat on the Appropriations Committee to send home millions of dollars for transportation projects. Earlier in his career, he fought for federal funds to complete the Washington area's subway system, and he was a staunch advocate of extending Metro service to Dulles International Airport, a project finally approved in January 2009.

A history buff, Wolf is often involved in efforts to preserve the many historic sites and battlefields in his district. Despite opposition from some conservatives who said it could impede local development decisions, he won enactment in 2008 of a law designating a 175-mile corridor from Gettysburg, Pa., to Charlottesville, Va., as a National Heritage Area. It is modeled after the Shenandoah Valley Battlefields National Historic District, which Wolf helped create in the late 1990s.

Wolf was born and raised in Philadelphia, the son of a police officer and a cafeteria worker. His interest in politics grew out of a boyhood fascination with history and a desire to overcome a stutter. He read biographies of George Washington, Thomas Jefferson and Abraham Lincoln and dreamed of winning respect by becoming a political leader.

In college Wolf majored in political science, then earned his law degree from Georgetown University in Washington. He became an aide to Pennsylvania GOP Rep. Edward G. Biester. He later served as a deputy assistant in the Interior Department during the Nixon and Ford administrations, and he was a lobbyist for baby food and farm implement manufacturers.

Though most members of his family were Democrats, Wolf said he became a Republican because of his beliefs in lower taxes, a strong national defense and a tough approach to fighting communism during the Cold War.

He credits President Ronald Reagan with getting him into office. Wolf was unsuccessful in his first two attempts to win a House seat, but edged closer each time. In a 1980 rematch with Rep. Joseph L. Fisher, the Democrat who had defeated him in 1978, Wolf rode the Reagan surge to a narrow victory. He had a tough re-election race in 1982, but then enjoyed smooth rides until his 2006 battle with former Georgetown University Public Policy Institute Dean Judy M. Feder. With the 10th District becoming incrementally more Democratic, Wolf had more of a struggle than he was accustomed to, as Feder attacked Wolf's initial support for the war in Iraq. He won 57 percent to 41 percent, a departure from his previous 30-point margins. However, he widened his margin against Feder in 2008, taking 59 percent.

KEY VOTES

2008

No Delay consideration of Colombia free-trade agreement

No Override Bush veto of federal farm and nutrition programs reauthorization bill

Yes Overhaul surveillance laws and permit dismissal of suits against companies that conducted warrantless wiretapping

No Grant mortgage relief to homeowners and funding for Fannie Mae and Freddie Mac

Yes Approve initial $700 billion program to stabilize financial markets

Yes Approve final $700 billion program to stabilize financial markets

No Provide $14 billion in loans to automakers

2007

Yes Increase minimum wage by $2.10 an hour

No Approve $124.2 billion in emergency war spending and set goal for redeployment of troops from Iraq

Yes Reject federal contraceptive assistance to international family planning groups

No Override Bush veto of $23.2 billion water projects authorization bill

Yes Implement Peru free-trade agreement

Yes Approve energy policy overhaul with new fuel economy standards

Yes Clear $473.5 billion omnibus spending bill, including $70 billion for military operations

CQ VOTE STUDIES

	PARTY UNITY		PRESIDENTIAL SUPPORT	
	SUPPORT	OPPOSE	SUPPORT	OPPOSE
2008	87%	13%	66%	34%
2007	79%	21%	58%	42%
2006	85%	15%	80%	20%
2005	90%	10%	84%	16%
2004	85%	15%	85%	15%

INTEREST GROUPS

	AFL-CIO	ADA	CCUS	ACU
2008	21%	30%	94%	79%
2007	38%	40%	80%	68%
2006	50%	10%	67%	64%
2005	20%	5%	89%	60%
2004	40%	25%	90%	76%

VIRGINIA 10
North – part of Fairfax County, Loudoun County

Located in the northern part of Virginia, the 10th District bridges a dizzying range of economies and lifestyles, with mountains and farmland at one end and congested Washington suburbs at the other. A hotbed of economic activity, the 10th is a mostly white-collar area that includes some of the nation's wealthiest counties — Loudoun and parts of Fairfax and Fauquier.

Most of the district's population resides in suburban Northern Virginia, and many residents commute to jobs in Washington or the inner suburbs just outside the nation's capital. Technology-magnet Loudoun County, which includes Leesburg and Washington Dulles International Airport, has tripled in population since 1990. About one-third of district residents live in Fairfax County (shared with the 8th and 11th).

Agriculture and manufacturing fuel the economy in the rest of the 10th, which is solidly Republican and less densely populated. Clarke and Frederick counties produce about half of Virginia's apples and peaches.

Winchester, in Frederick County, is the center of the state's apple-growing industry. Recently, outer areas such as Winchester and Manassas have seen an increase in methamphetamine use and distribution. The 10th also has seen a rise in violent gang activity in Northern Virginia, and slow-growth advocates have fared well in some recent elections here as the region grapples with its rapid expansion.

The 10th swung left in the 2008 presidential race, giving Democrat Barack Obama 53 percent of its vote, with parts of Fairfax and Frederick counties carrying the most Democratic weight. In presidential and state legislative races, Loudoun tends to vote Republican, but the county gave Obama 54 percent in 2008.

MAJOR INDUSTRY
Technology, government, manufacturing, agriculture

CITIES
Chantilly (unincorporated), 41,041; McLean (unincorporated) (pt.), 37,427; Manassas, 35,135; Centreville (unincorporated) (pt.), 33,053; Leesburg, 28,311; Winchester, 23,585

NOTABLE
The "Enola Gay," which dropped an atomic bomb in World War II, is at the National Air and Space Museum's Udvar-Hazy Center near Dulles.

Rep. Gerald E. Connolly (D)

Elected 2008; 1st term

Connolly calls himself a "radical pragmatist" who learned to compromise during more than a decade in local government and during a stint as a Senate Foreign Relations Committee staffer. A former seminary student, he said entering politics was a "logical extension" of his earlier study of religion.

"There is a pastoral element to what you do in politics," Connolly said. "I was infused with strong progressive Catholic values with respect to social justice and service to the community, and those are very strong values for me as a member of Congress."

Connolly entered the public eye in 1995 when he was elected to the Fairfax County Board of Supervisors, becoming its chairman in 2004. The position serves much like a mayor for the suburban Washington, D.C., county. He said he enjoyed the challenge of making things work at the local level and hopes Congress can be held to the same expectations — something he works toward as a member of the Oversight and Government Reform Committee.

He worked for the Foreign Relations Committee for 10 years before moving to the private sector. He hopes to pick up where he left off, working for peace in the Middle East on the Foreign Affairs Committee as a member of the Middle East and South Asia and terrorism panels.

Though he campaigned with President Obama and supported his early economic agenda, he said he doesn't blindly support the administration. As a Budget Committee member, he wrote a letter to President Obama with nine other freshman House Democrats opposing the release of the second half of the funds from the $700 billion financial sector rescue law of 2008. And he echoes GOP complaints that Obama's plan to extend the George W. Bush administration income tax cuts only for couples earning less than $250,000 will unfairly hit small-business owners and hurt a lot of his constituents, where the cost of living is particularly high. He also opposes Obama's proposal to limit the mortgage-interest deduction for wealthy families.

In the race to succeed retiring Republican Thomas M. Davis III, Connolly bested former Rep. Leslie L. Byrne in a heated Democratic primary, then had little trouble defeating Republican Keith Fimian in the general election.

CAPITOL OFFICE
225-1492
connolly.house.gov
327 Longworth Bldg. 20515; fax 225-3071

COMMITTEES
Budget
Foreign Affairs
Oversight & Government Reform

RESIDENCE
Fairfax

BORN
March 30, 1950; Boston, Mass.

RELIGION
Roman Catholic

FAMILY
Wife, Catherine Connolly; one child

EDUCATION
Maryknoll College, B.A. 1971 (literature);
Harvard U., M.P.A. 1979

CAREER
Government relations executive;
congressional aide; nonprofit international
aid organization director

POLITICAL HIGHLIGHTS
Fairfax County Board of Supervisors,
1995-2003; Fairfax County Board of
Supervisors chairman, 2004-09

ELECTION RESULTS

2008 GENERAL

Gerald E. Connolly (D)	196,598	54.7%
Keith Fimian (R)	154,758	43.0%
Joseph P. Oddo (IGREEN)	7,271	2.0%

2008 PRIMARY

Gerald E. Connolly (D)	14,233	57.9%
Leslie L. Byrne (D)	8,196	33.4%
Douglas J. Denneny (D)	1,508	6.1%
Lori P. Alexander (D)	638	2.6%

VIRGINIA 11

Washington suburbs — parts of Fairfax and Prince William counties

Anchored in the suburbs of Washington, the 11th is home to a well-educated, professional and upper-income workforce that boasts the nation's highest median income (more than $80,000). Like other nearby suburban areas, the 11th has become more racially and ethnically diverse — it has the state's largest Asian population.

Two-thirds of the population lives in Fairfax County (shared with the 8th and 10th districts). The balance lives in Prince William County, a burgeoning area south and west of Fairfax, or in Fairfax city, a separate jurisdiction within Fairfax County. Many residents work in Washington, either for the federal government or for private companies linked to the government. Technology

contributes to local economic growth, and Fairfax County's office parks are home to dozens of firms. Technology sector growth and related traffic woes have made telecommuting an increasingly attractive option for area workers.

The 11th's growth made it competitive and the district is now represented by a Democrat in the House. The 11th tends to lean left on social issues and right on fiscal issues. But traffic congestion is so rampant that some residents are willing to accept tax increases to pay for transportation improvements. In 2008, Barack Obama won 57 percent of the 11th's presidential vote.

MAJOR INDUSTRY
Government, technology, service

CITIES
Burke (unincorporated), 57,737; Dale City (unincorporated), 55,971; Annandale (unincorporated) (pt.), 51,350

NOTABLE
George Washington's estate, Mount Vernon, is on the Potomac River in Fairfax County.

Gov. Christine Gregoire (D)

Pronounced: GREG-wahr
First elected: 2004
Length of term: 4 years
Term expires: 1/09
Salary: $166,891
Phone: (360) 902-4111

Residence: Olympia
Born: March 24, 1947; Adrian, Mich.
Religion: Roman Catholic
Family: Husband, Mike Gregoire; two children
Education: U. of Washington, B.A. 1969 (speech & sociology); Gonzaga U., J.D. 1977
Career: Lawyer; state social services department caseworker; clerk typist
Political highlights: Wash. Department of Ecology director, 1988-92; Wash. attorney general, 1993-2004

Election results:
2008 GENERAL

Christine Gregoire (D)	1,598,738	53.2%
Dino Rossi (R)	1,404,124	46.8%

Lt. Gov. Brad Owen (D)

First elected: 1996
Length of term: 4 years
Term expires: 1/09
Salary: $93,948
Phone: (360) 786-7700

LEGISLATURE

Legislature: 105 days January-May in odd-numbered years; 60 days January-March in even-numbered years
Senate: 49 members, 4-year terms
2009 ratios: 31 D, 18 R; 30 men, 19 women
Salary: $42,106
Phone: (360) 786-7550

House: 98 members, 2-year terms
2009 ratios: 62 D, 36 R; 70 men, 28 women
Salary: $42,106
Phone: (360) 786-7750

TERM LIMITS

Governor: No
Senate: No
House: No

URBAN STATISTICS

CITY	POPULATION
Seattle	563,374
Spokane	195,629
Tacoma	193,556
Vancouver	143,560
Bellevue	109,569

REGISTERED VOTERS

Voters do not register by party.

POPULATION

2008 population (est.)	6,549,224
2000 population	5,894,121
1990 population	4,866,692
Percent change (1990-2000)	+21.1%
Rank among states (2008)	13

Median age	35.3
Born in state	47.2%
Foreign born	10.4%
Violent crime rate	370/100,000
Poverty level	10.6%
Federal workers	66,061
Military	74,250

ELECTIONS

STATE ELECTION OFFICIAL
(360) 902-4180
DEMOCRATIC PARTY
(206) 583-0664
REPUBLICAN PARTY
(206) 575-2900

MISCELLANEOUS

Web: www.access.wa.gov
Capital: Olympia

U.S. CONGRESS

Senate: 2 Democrats
House: 6 Democrats, 3 Republicans

2000 Census Statistics by District

DIST.	2008 VOTE FOR PRESIDENT OBAMA	MCCAIN	WHITE	BLACK	ASIAN	HISP	MEDIAN INCOME	WHITE COLLAR	BLUE COLLAR	SERVICE INDUSTRY	OVER 64	UNDER 18	COLLEGE EDUCATION	RURAL	SQ. MILES
1	62%	36%	82%	2%	8%	4%	$58,565	69%	18%	12%	10%	26%	36%	5%	439
2	56	42	86	1	3	6	$45,441	55	29	16	12	26	22	31	6,564
3	53	45	88	1	3	5	$44,426	57	28	15	11	27	21	29	7,515
4	40	58	68	1	1	26	$37,764	53	31	16	11	30	19	29	19,051
5	46	52	88	1	2	5	$35,720	60	23	17	13	25	24	28	22,864
6	57	40	78	6	4	5	$39,205	55	27	18	14	25	20	21	6,781
7	83	15	67	8	13	6	$45,864	71	15	14	12	17	44	2	141
8	56	42	82	2	8	4	$63,854	69	20	11	9	28	37	12	2,579
9	58	40	73	6	7	7	$46,495	59	25	15	10	26	22	5	608
STATE	58	41	79	3	5	7	$45,776	61	24	15	11	26	28	18	66,544
U.S.	53	46	69	12	4	13	$41,994	60	25	15	12	26	24	21	3,537,438

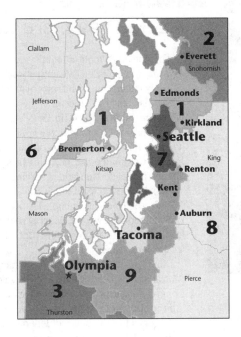

Sen. Patty Murray (D)

Elected 1992; 3rd term

The one-time "mom in tennis shoes" long ago replaced her trademark footwear with polished flats for her workdays on Capitol Hill, but the change has only underscored Murray's march to power in the Senate.

She has made a career of being underestimated. Dismissed as a fluke when she was first elected in 1992, Murray is now a seasoned insider on the Appropriations Committee, where she chairs the Transportation, Housing and Urban Development Subcommittee. She is the No. 2 Democrat on the Budget Committee and occupies the bottom rung of the elected Senate Democratic leadership ladder, serving as secretary of the party conference.

On a leadership team that includes media-savvy Majority Whip Richard J. Durbin of Illinois and voluble Democratic Caucus Vice Chairman Charles E. Schumer of New York, Murray seldom is at the microphones when the leaders interact with reporters. But when she is, Murray remains relentlessly on message.

Murray is methodical and has a hand in national issues ranging from Amtrak policy to education. But she said her political lodestar is ensuring Congress stays focused on things affecting everyday Americans.

From her post on the Appropriations Committee, she makes sure her state gets a healthy share of federal funding. Her prowess has prompted some to call her "Patty Magnuson," a reference to Washington's legendary Democratic Sen. Warren Magnuson, who was famed for securing billions of federal dollars for the state.

Murray once drew direct fire from Arizona Republican Sen. John McCain, a frequent critic of the funding set-asides known as earmarks, for attaching $3 million for a maritime museum to the transportation spending bill in 2001. Murray sat stone-faced in the Senate chamber as McCain blasted her project as an example of "pork barrel spending."

During the 110th Congress (2007-08), she emerged as a trusted lieutenant to ailing then-Appropriations Chairman Robert C. Byrd of West Virginia, who turned to her — rather than to several more-senior panel members — to serve as floor manager for key spending bills. In 2007, she steered both an Iraq War supplemental and the annual Homeland Security spending measure through the Senate. She was ready to step in again in 2008, but Byrd managed the war funding bill himself.

Her transportation spending bill for fiscal 2009 was rolled into a big stopgap package — but not before Murray successfully fought for approval of $8 billion in general revenues to shore up the faltering Highway Trust Fund. During debate on President Obama's economic stimulus package in early 2009, she proposed adding an additional $25 billion for infrastructure projects; the measure fell short of the 60 votes needed for passage after most Republicans balked.

One of the most active members of the Veterans' Affairs Committee, Murray has pushed for more funding for veterans' health care, particularly for those returning from war with traumatic brain injuries. When Obama proposed to collect money from private insurance companies for treating veterans with service-connected disabilities at VA hospitals, she said any budget request with the provision would be "dead on arrival"; the president eventually backed off.

Murray may not be as vocal as some of her colleagues, but she will go after what she wants in other ways. She was one of a few Democrats who threatened to block funding for some of President George W. Bush's pet

CAPITOL OFFICE
224-2621
murray.senate.gov
173 Russell Bldg. 20510-4704; fax 224-0238

COMMITTEES
Appropriations
 (Transportation-HUD - chairwoman)
Budget
Health, Education, Labor & Pensions
 (Employment & Workplace Safety - chairwoman)
Rules & Administration
Veterans' Affairs
Joint Printing

RESIDENCE
Seattle

BORN
Oct. 11, 1950; Bothell, Wash.

RELIGION
Roman Catholic

FAMILY
Husband, Rob Murray; two children

EDUCATION
Washington State U., B.A. 1972

CAREER
Parenting class instructor

POLITICAL HIGHLIGHTS
Candidate for Shoreline School Board, 1983;
Shoreline School Board, 1983-89; Wash. Senate, 1989-93

ELECTION RESULTS

2004 GENERAL

Patty Murray (D)	1,549,708	55.0%
George Nethercutt (R)	1,204,584	42.7%
J. Mills (LIBERT)	34,055	1.2%
Mark B. Wilson (GREEN)	30,304	1.1%

2004 PRIMARY

Patty Murray (D)	709,497	92.2%
Warren E. Hanson (D)	46,490	6.0%
Mohammad Hasan Said (D)	13,527	1.8%

PREVIOUS WINNING PERCENTAGES
1998 (58%); 1992 (54%)

projects until he agreed to include a full year's Iraq War funding estimate in his fiscal 2009 budget.

And though she eschews labels such as "feminist," Murray is nonetheless concerned with women's issues. She once vowed to hold up the nomination of the head of the Food and Drug Administration until the agency made a decision on approving over-the-counter sales of morning-after birth control pills.

She is a fierce promoter of Washington's two mega employers, Microsoft Corp. and Boeing Co. She repeatedly denounced the long-running federal antitrust case against Microsoft even though it was triggered by Democratic President Bill Clinton. And she flew into action when the Air Force in 2008 decided to award a $35 billion contract for a fleet of new aerial tankers to a consortium made up of Northrop Grumman Corp. and the North American arm of the European Aeronautic Defence and Space Co., or EADS, which owns the airplane manufacturer Airbus. Murray said U.S. tax dollars should not go to boost a foreign company. She threatened to withhold funds for the tankers or impose other penalties on the Air Force. After the Government Accountability Office concluded the Air Force had violated its own contracting rules, the deal was scrapped.

As the Senate moved forward in 2009 on legislation to overhaul the Pentagon's acquisitions process and tighten controls over how it buys weapons and other equipment, Murray successfully amended the legislation to require defense officials to consider the economic impact on defense industries when making program decisions.

Murray's backing of government social programs and her work ethic stem from her childhood. Her father managed a dime store, where she and her six siblings often put in long hours. They had to fend off ailments without health care because it was too expensive, and often they made their own clothes. When she was a teenager, Murray's father was diagnosed with multiple sclerosis and had to stop working. The family briefly went on welfare until her mother completed a government-funded program that enabled her to work as a bookkeeper. She credits the program with saving the family from financial ruin.

When Murray went to college, she went to work to try to help pay for it, taking any job she could find: in a glass shop, as a secretary and, one summer, cleaning bathrooms in a state park.

In the early 1980s, angered when the state legislature planned to eliminate a preschool program in which her children were enrolled, Murray packed the kids into the car and drove to the state capital to complain. She was dismissed by a legislator there who told her, "You can't make a difference. You're just a mom in tennis shoes." Murray said of the incident, "I drove home as angry as I could be, saying he has no right to tell me I can't make a difference." She organized a statewide parents' campaign to revive the program, an effort that succeeded in just three months. That led Murray to six years on her local school board and four years in the state Senate.

In her 1992 U.S. Senate quest, she bested two better-known moderates with years of congressional experience in the primary and general elections. She was re-elected in 1998 with 58 percent of the vote. In 2004, a prominent Washington state Republican said Murray would be no match for "giant killer" George Nethercutt, a Republican House member who had beaten Democratic Speaker Thomas S. Foley in 1994. Murray won by 12 percentage points. She sought to ward off any potential 2010 challengers by amassing more than $5.5 million in donations in the first three months of 2009.

Through it all, Murray has used her trademark tennis shoes to remind voters of her humble roots. She passes out "Golden Tennis Shoe" awards to constituents who, like her, have been community activists.

KEY VOTES

2008
Yes Prohibit discrimination based on genetic information
Yes Reauthorize farm and nutrition programs for five years
Yes Limit debate on "cap and trade" system for greenhouse gas emissions
Yes Allow lawsuits against companies that participated in warrantless wiretapping
Yes Limit debate on a bill to block a scheduled cut in Medicare payments to doctors
? Grant mortgage relief to homeowners and funding for Fannie Mae and Freddie Mac
Yes Approve a nuclear cooperation agreement with India
Yes Approve final $700 billion program to stabilize financial markets
Yes Allow consideration of a $14 billion auto industry loan package

2007
Yes Increase minimum wage by $2.10 an hour
Yes Limit debate on a comprehensive immigration bill
Yes Overhaul congressional lobbying and ethics rules for members and their staffs
Yes Limit debate on considering a bill to add House seats for the District of Columbia and Utah
Yes Limit debate on restoring habeas corpus rights to detainees
Yes Mandate minimum breaks for troops between deployments to Iraq or Afghanistan
Yes Override Bush veto of $23.2 billion water projects authorization bill
No Confirm Michael B. Mukasey as attorney general
Yes Limit debate on an energy policy overhaul containing $21.8 billion in tax incentives and reduced oil and gas subsidies

CQ VOTE STUDIES

	PARTY UNITY		PRESIDENTIAL SUPPORT	
	SUPPORT	OPPOSE	SUPPORT	OPPOSE
2008	99%	1%	28%	72%
2007	97%	3%	38%	62%
2006	92%	8%	59%	41%
2005	95%	5%	33%	67%
2004	91%	9%	63%	37%
2003	97%	3%	49%	51%
2002	86%	14%	75%	25%
2001	96%	4%	65%	35%
2000	94%	6%	87%	13%
1999	93%	7%	88%	12%

INTEREST GROUPS

	AFL-CIO	ADA	CCUS	ACU
2008	100%	95%	63%	0%
2007	100%	90%	64%	0%
2006	93%	95%	50%	4%
2005	79%	95%	44%	0%
2004	92%	90%	75%	8%
2003	85%	90%	43%	10%
2002	92%	90%	55%	10%
2001	100%	85%	64%	4%
2000	63%	90%	64%	8%
1999	88%	100%	59%	4%

Sen. Maria Cantwell (D)

Elected 2000; 2nd term

Cantwell has relied on her intellect and tenacity to fashion a reputation for herself as an emerging player on energy, tax and other issues and as a hard-working guardian of her state's interests. She often has strong opinions to share and likes to be involved in making deals.

Her voting record has been solidly Democratic, if just a shade less loyal to her party than that of her home-state colleague Patty Murray, a member of the Senate Democratic leadership. Cantwell's seats on panels dealing with energy, transportation, American Indian tribes and small businesses, as well as the powerful Finance Committee, give her ample opportunity to fulfill her goal of bringing more Pacific Northwest progressivism to Capitol Hill. "I'm here trying to get the rest of the country to think a little more like we [in Washington state] do," she told The Seattle Post-Intelligencer in 2006.

Her smarts and television-ready looks would seem to combine to make her a star in Democratic circles. Still, she has been criticized for exuding a sense of aloofness that makes her seem more like the dot-com executive she once was rather than the public figure she now is. In committee hearings, she sometimes passes up her chance to make an opening statement. In private, however, she is anything but aloof when discussing her love for the Seattle Mariners baseball team; she can rattle off her recollections of key plays in Mariners history.

Cantwell is chairwoman of the Energy and Natural Resources Committee's Subcommittee on Energy, where she has actively sought to expand the use of renewable energy sources. She worked to get $11 billion for "smart grid" technologies that control electricity flow to consumers while reducing costs included in President Obama's 2009 economic stimulus law.

Earlier, she also worked to include tax provisions on renewables in the $700 billion financial services rescue that became law in fall 2008 — but was one of nine Democrats to vote against the bill. "I do not support turning the keys of the U.S. Treasury over to the private sector," she said in explaining her decision.

She expressed concerns about a "cap and trade" proposal that the Senate began working on in spring 2009, saying its creation of a market for trading greenhouse gas emissions allowances among industries could trigger the same type of unregulated schemes that gave rise to the recession. She said she was more inclined to back a system that would cap carbon dioxide emissions and require companies to pay for their emissions credits or allowances.

In 2008, Cantwell decided the Commodity Futures Trading Commission wasn't doing enough to control speculation in energy futures markets, which many lawmakers believe was contributing to high gas prices. In retaliation, she blocked nominations to the agency. And she introduced a host of bills aimed at curbing speculation, including one to expand the commission's regulatory powers.

Similarly, she cheered when the Federal Trade Commission (FTC) in 2008 took steps to go after players in the petroleum futures market if their deceptive practices might be affecting prices in the market. Cantwell played a role in 2007 in the legislation that gave the FTC that authority.

She demanded in 2002 refunds from energy companies under investigation for allegedly driving up prices, and she confronted Federal Energy Regulatory Commission Chairman Patrick Wood III about the panel's regulation of electricity markets.

In 2005, she was the main Democratic opponent of a plan to open the Arctic

CAPITOL OFFICE
224-3441
cantwell.senate.gov
511 Dirksen Bldg. 20510-4705; fax 228-0514

COMMITTEES
Commerce, Science & Transportation
(Oceans, Atmosphere, Fisheries & Coast Guard
- chairwoman)
Energy & Natural Resources
(Energy - chairwoman)
Finance
Indian Affairs
Small Business & Entrepreneurship

RESIDENCE
Edmonds

BORN
Oct. 13, 1958; Indianapolis, Ind.

RELIGION
Roman Catholic

FAMILY
Single

EDUCATION
Miami U. (Ohio), B.A. 1980 (public policy)

CAREER
Internet audio company executive; public
relations consultant

POLITICAL HIGHLIGHTS
Wash. House, 1987-92; U.S. House, 1993-95;
defeated for re-election to U.S. House, 1994

ELECTION RESULTS

2006 GENERAL

Maria Cantwell (D)	1,184,659	56.9%
Mike McGavick (R)	832,106	39.9%
Bruce Guthrie (LIBERT)	29,331	1.4%
Aaron Dixon (GREEN)	21,254	1.0%

2006 PRIMARY

Maria Cantwell (D)	570,677	90.8%
Hong Tran (D)	33,124	5.3%
Mike the Mover (D)	11,274	1.8%
Goodspaceguy Nelson (D)	9,454	1.5%

PREVIOUS WINNING PERCENTAGES
2000 (49%); 1992 House Election (55%)

National Wildlife Refuge in Alaska to energy exploration, a move that won her the enmity of a powerful fellow senator at the time, Republican Ted Stevens of Alaska. He vowed to retaliate.

Cantwell also sits on the Commerce, Science and Transportation Committee, a position important for her state's international trade- and technology-dependent economy. She chairs its subcommittee on fisheries and the Coast Guard, where she looked into a troubled $24 billion, 25-year plan to upgrade the Coast Guard's fleet. Called Deepwater, the effort was plagued by errors, delays and cost overruns. The Senate passed her bill to overhaul the program and mandate stricter oversight in 2007.

On Finance, Cantwell has backed bipartisan health care legislation sponsored by Oregon Democrat Ron Wyden that some experts say could produce new revenue for the government. She favors restructuring the Medicare payment system to reward providers who offer well-managed primary care. She also sponsored a bill in 2009 granting trade preferences for Afghanistan and Pakistan to help combat militancy between the two countries.

Cantwell holds traditional Democratic views on social issues such as abortion rights. In all but one year in Congress, she has voted with fellow Democrats more than 90 percent of the time on votes that break along party lines. She also serves on the Indian Affairs and Small Business and Entrepreneurship panels.

On local matters, Cantwell has worked to gain federal benefits for former workers at the Hanford Nuclear Reservation in her state, some of whom became ill when they worked with plutonium used in the production of nuclear weapons. She has traveled to Cuba, Mexico and China to try to drum up interest for Washington's apples, potatoes and lentils.

Cantwell, a native of Indiana, was exposed early to politics by her father, Paul Cantwell, who brought the family to the nation's capital in 1965 when he took a job working for home-state Democratic Rep. Andrew Jacobs. After a year, he moved the family back to Indiana and took a seat as a county commissioner.

After earning a degree in public policy from Miami U. in Ohio, Cantwell worked on the unsuccessful gubernatorial campaign of Jerry Springer, who went on to talk-show fame. In 1983, she moved to the Seattle area to be a political organizer for Democratic presidential candidate Alan Cranston. She worked in public relations, then was elected to the state legislature, serving from 1987 to 1992. She was elected to the U.S. House in 1992, the same year her father was elected to the Indiana House. She served only one term before getting knocked out in the Republican tide of 1994.

Cantwell put politics aside for a few years, joining a Seattle Internet start-up, RealNetworks, the software company that invented RealPlayer and other online audio and video products. She rose to be senior vice president of consumer products, becoming a multimillionaire.

She tapped into her personal wealth in 2000 to run for the Senate, spending $10 million to unseat Republican Slade Gorton. She blew past the favored Democratic opponent, state Insurance Commissioner Deborah Senn, in Washington's open primary. But Cantwell carried only five of the state's 39 counties, all around Puget Sound, in her narrow general-election victory over Gorton. With just more than 2,000 votes separating the candidates, the results were so close that her victory was not declared official until nearly a month after the election.

In 2006, Stevens made good on his threat to campaign against her. But the Alaskan's support for Republican Mike McGavick backfired when the candidate had to return $14,000 Stevens helped him raise from an Alaska oil company that figured into an FBI criminal investigation. Cantwell won the race by 17 percentage points.

KEY VOTES

2008
Yes Prohibit discrimination based on genetic information
Yes Reauthorize farm and nutrition programs for five years
Yes Limit debate on "cap and trade" system for greenhouse gas emissions
Yes Allow lawsuits against companies that participated in warrantless wiretapping
Yes Limit debate on a bill to block a scheduled cut in Medicare payments to doctors
Yes Grant mortgage relief to homeowners and funding for Fannie Mae and Freddie Mac
Yes Approve a nuclear cooperation agreement with India
No Approve final $700 billion program to stabilize financial markets
Yes Allow consideration of a $14 billion auto industry loan package

2007
Yes Increase minimum wage by $2.10 an hour
Yes Limit debate on a comprehensive immigration bill
Yes Overhaul congressional lobbying and ethics rules for members and their staffs
Yes Limit debate on considering a bill to add House seats for the District of Columbia and Utah
Yes Limit debate on restoring habeas corpus rights to detainees
Yes Mandate minimum breaks for troops between deployments to Iraq or Afghanistan
Yes Override Bush veto of $23.2 billion water projects authorization bill
No Confirm Michael B. Mukasey as attorney general
Yes Limit debate on an energy policy overhaul containing $21.8 billion in tax incentives and reduced oil and gas subsidies

CQ VOTE STUDIES

	PARTY UNITY		PRESIDENTIAL SUPPORT	
	SUPPORT	OPPOSE	SUPPORT	OPPOSE
2008	97%	3%	28%	72%
2007	94%	6%	39%	61%
2006	92%	8%	54%	46%
2005	92%	8%	36%	64%
2004	90%	10%	66%	34%
2003	96%	4%	52%	48%
2002	82%	18%	81%	19%
2001	98%	2%	64%	36%
House Service:				
1994	92%	8%	86%	14%

INTEREST GROUPS

	AFL-CIO	ADA	CCUS	ACU
2008	100%	100%	50%	12%
2007	95%	95%	64%	4%
2006	87%	95%	58%	12%
2005	86%	95%	56%	8%
2004	83%	95%	65%	8%
2003	85%	90%	39%	15%
2002	85%	80%	55%	25%
2001	100%	100%	50%	12%
House Service:				
1994	67%	70%	83%	14%

Rep. Jay Inslee (D)

CAPITOL OFFICE
225-6311
www.house.gov/inslee
403 Cannon Bldg. 20515-4701; fax 226-1606

COMMITTEES
Energy & Commerce
Natural Resources
Select Energy Independence & Global Warming

RESIDENCE
Bainbridge Island

BORN
Feb. 9, 1951; Seattle, Wash.

RELIGION
Protestant

FAMILY
Wife, Trudi Inslee; three children

EDUCATION
Stanford U., attended 1969-70;
U. of Washington, B.A. 1973 (economics);
Willamette U., J.D. 1976

CAREER
Lawyer

POLITICAL HIGHLIGHTS
Wash. House, 1989-93; U.S. House, 1993-95;
defeated for re-election to U.S. House, 1994;
sought Democratic nomination for governor, 1996

ELECTION RESULTS

2008 GENERAL

Jay Inslee (D)	233,780	67.8%
Larry Ishmael (R)	111,240	32.2%

2008 PRIMARY (OPEN)

Jay Inslee (D)	104,342	66.4%
Larry Ishmael (R)	52,700	33.6%

2006 GENERAL

Jay Inslee (D)	163,832	67.7%
Larry Ishmael (R)	78,105	32.3%

PREVIOUS WINNING PERCENTAGES
2004 (62%); 2002 (56%); 2000 (55%); 1998 (50%);
1992 (51%)

Elected 1998; 7th term
Also served 1993-95

Inslee brings an air of calm into the partisan rancor that regularly heats up congressional debates over energy and climate change. His views on energy policy hew to the far left of his caucus. But while fellow West Coast liberals Henry A. Waxman and Speaker Nancy Pelosi are known to incite fury in oil-state Republicans, Inslee's friendly style can return rationality to the debate.

Inslee displays a detailed understanding of energy technology, something that was rumored to have put him on the short list of candidates for Interior secretary in an Obama administration in late 2008. It is an important quality given that his district gets its electricity from the Energy Department's giant Bonneville Power Administration and is home to workers in some of the nation's giant technology firms. He is optimistic about new forms of cutting-edge clean-energy technology, such as electricity generated from ocean waves.

With seats on the powerful Energy and Commerce Committee and the Natural Resources Committee, along with the Select Committee on Energy Independence and Global Warming, Inslee is in prime position to pursue his vision. He believes new technologies can keep global temperatures in check but that government must provide them with a boost. "When it comes to technology, what seems impossible looking forward often looks inevitable looking backward," he said. To bolster the point, he co-authored a 2008 book, "Apollo's Fire: Igniting America's Clean Energy Economy," that calls for a revolution in the way Americans produce and use energy, similar to President Kennedy's efforts in space exploration.

As the House began addressing global warming in 2009, Inslee cited as a need for action a 2007 Supreme Court ruling that carbon dioxide, a common greenhouse gas, qualifies as a pollutant. "People will have to recognize that there is a sword of Damocles out there mandated by the Supreme Court," he told The Washington Post in April 2009. He worked to soften the impact of any laws on steel, aluminum, cement and other heavy industries while proposing to give the Federal Energy Regulatory Commission authority to site electricity lines reserved exclusively for low-carbon generation. Inslee hopes to build on the success he had in 2007, when a new energy law included his provisions authorizing funding for the development of hybrid electric vehicles and for research aimed at harnessing energy from ocean waves. The next step, he said, is to ensure clean-energy producers can make a go of it by ensuring them a set rate for the power they create.

And as the nation's economic crisis continued in 2009, he planned to advocate initiatives to spur job growth by funneling money toward infrastructure projects and research that could lead to the creation of new energy-related jobs.

Inslee also was active with several other lawmakers on a "cash for clunkers" proposal that President Obama endorsed to offer incentives for consumers to trade in their old cars for newer, more fuel efficient models.

From his seat on Natural Resources, he has fought to protect the salmon-rich area of Bristol Bay off Alaska from oil and gas drilling. Energy exploration was temporarily banned following the *Exxon Valdez* spill in 1989, but the George W. Bush administration repeatedly tried to lift that ban. The moratorium was allowed to lapse in 2008.

Inslee also looks out for the thousands of Boeing Co. employees in his district, advocating for improved health care and workforce policies.

A member of the Energy and Commerce Subcommittee on Communications, Technology and the Internet, Inslee sponsored legislation during the

110th Congress (2007-08) to help Internet radio companies stay afloat and was a strong opponent of a Federal Communications Commission ruling allowing radio and TV broadcasters to own newspapers in large media markets.

Inslee is typically a strong supporter of his party but breaks with it on occasion. He is an occasional supporter of free trade; he defied the majority of his caucus in 2007 to support a trade deal with Peru. He was one of 14 Democrats to vote in May 2008 to sustain President Bush's veto of the reauthorization of farm programs, agreeing with Bush that the bill's generous subsidies for growers were in need of reform.

But more typically, Inslee's opinions were the opposite of Bush's. In late 2008, he refused to approve Bush's plan to use $700 billion in federal funds to rescue ailing banks, even as most Democrats signed on. Inslee said the law didn't provide enough taxpayer protections and failed to address the root causes of the economic collapse, such as declines in the housing market.

Inslee grew up in Seattle, where his father was a high school biology teacher and a coach. Inslee was a star football and basketball player and is still athletically active. He was accepted to Stanford University but left after only a year for the University of Washington because his savings from summer jobs during high school ran out. He then earned a law degree, married his high school sweetheart and settled in tiny Selah in south-central Washington, where he practiced law for 18 years. He ultimately ran successfully for a seat in the state legislature in 1988, serving four years there.

When 4th District Republican Rep. Sid Morrison announced he was giving up his House seat to run for governor in 1992, Inslee got into the race. His folksy style and tireless campaigning lifted him to a narrow primary victory and to an equally narrow win that November over Republican Doc Hastings. Once in the House, Inslee bucked his party on some high-visibility votes. He opposed a five-day waiting period for handgun purchases. But he also voted to ban some types of assault-style weapons, which provoked the National Rifle Association to pour resources into defeating him. Inslee lost a rematch with Hastings by almost 7 percentage points.

Inslee returned to the Seattle area, settled on Bainbridge Island and resumed legal work. He waged an unsuccessful primary bid for governor in 1996. Then in 1998, he unseated two-term Republican Rep. Rick White in the suburban Seattle 1st District. His victory was partly thanks to the third-party candidacy of Bruce Craswell, whose 6 percent tally was seen as coming largely from White's GOP base. Inslee has steadily increased his re-election victory margins, from nearly 6 percentage points in 1998 to a high of nearly 36 percentage points in 2008.

KEY VOTES

2008

Yes	Delay consideration of Colombia free-trade agreement
No	Override Bush veto of federal farm and nutrition programs reauthorization bill
No	Overhaul surveillance laws and permit dismissal of suits against companies that conducted warrantless wiretapping
Yes	Grant mortgage relief to homeowners and funding for Fannie Mae and Freddie Mac
No	Approve initial $700 billion program to stabilize financial markets
No	Approve final $700 billion program to stabilize financial markets
Yes	Provide $14 billion in loans to automakers

2007

Yes	Increase minimum wage by $2.10 an hour
Yes	Approve $124.2 billion in emergency war spending and set goal for redeployment of troops from Iraq
No	Reject federal contraceptive assistance to international family planning groups
Yes	Override Bush veto of $23.2 billion water projects authorization bill
Yes	Implement Peru free-trade agreement
Yes	Approve energy policy overhaul with new fuel economy standards
No	Clear $473.5 billion omnibus spending bill, including $70 billion for military operations

CQ VOTE STUDIES

	PARTY UNITY		PRESIDENTIAL SUPPORT	
	SUPPORT	OPPOSE	SUPPORT	OPPOSE
2008	99%	1%	15%	85%
2007	98%	2%	5%	95%
2006	93%	7%	28%	72%
2005	97%	3%	17%	83%
2004	94%	6%	26%	74%

INTEREST GROUPS

	AFL-CIO	ADA	CCUS	ACU
2008	100%	90%	61%	12%
2007	100%	80%	63%	4%
2006	93%	90%	47%	12%
2005	93%	95%	37%	0%
2004	93%	100%	43%	4%

WASHINGTON 1
Puget Sound (west and east) – North Seattle suburbs

Nestled on Washington's Puget Sound between mountain ranges to the east and west, the 1st District has become a suburban haven for employees of technology giants and biotech companies located throughout the greater Seattle area.

The eastern portion of the 1st, which includes the northern borders of Lake Washington and runs along the eastern coast of the sound, accounts for more than 80 percent of the district's population. The aviation industry, though waning in the region, is still a major employer in the district. Widespread layoffs at aviation, computer software and manufacturing companies have hurt the local economy. And the volatile biotech and biomedical equipment sector in the region is based near Bothell in southern Snohomish. Naval bases spur the economy on the west side of the sound, which also is home to a handful of high-tech firms.

Tourism is important to the 1st. Travelers can take a 35-minute ferry ride

from downtown Seattle to Bainbridge Island or drive north on Interstate 5 to one of the casinos in the 2nd District. The Sammamish River Valley is home to leading Washington state wineries and outdoor recreation sites, while the Future of Flight Aviation Center and Boeing Tour attracts visitors to Mukilteo.

Democrats have the edge in the district, with its well-educated, socially liberal professionals. The Snohomish portion is the most politically competitive of the three counties; the King and Kitsap county portions are slightly more Democratic.

MAJOR INDUSTRY
Software, military, tourism

MILITARY BASES
Naval Base Kitsap, 10,558 military, 13,661 civilian (shared with the 6th); Naval Undersea Warfare Center Keyport, 30 military, 1,400 civilian (2009)

CITIES
Kirkland (pt.), 44,406; Edmonds, 39,515; Shoreline (pt.), 35,694; Seattle Hill-Silver Firs (unincorporated), 35,311; Redmond (pt.), 34,759

NOTABLE
Poulsbo is home to the annual Scandinavian celebration Viking Fest; The Junior Softball World Series is played each summer in Kirkland.

Rep. Rick Larsen (D)

Elected 2000; 5th term

Larsen is a moderate — and modest — Democrat. In a chamber filled with supersized egos, he stands out mostly for not standing out. "This isn't my job," he said. "It belongs to my constituents. It's theirs to take."

He has occasionally voted with Republicans, but Larsen doesn't share their worldview. He said his political philosophy is firmly rooted in the Social Democratic ethos his Scandinavian forebears brought to the American Northwest. "I grew up believing that one's obligation to the community is equal to one's obligation to oneself," he said.

His unswerving attention to local needs paid off in 2008, when Larsen, working with local veterans' groups and Democratic Sen. Patty Murray, prevailed in a six-year campaign to secure a permanent Veterans Affairs outpatient clinic in northwest Washington, so the region's veterans won't have to spend hours in traffic to obtain medical care at the VA hospital in Seattle.

In the 110th Congress (2007-08), he also won enactment of his signature bill to designate more than 106,000 acres of land about 60 miles northeast of Seattle as a protected wilderness area. The new Wild Sky Wilderness, located in the Mt. Baker-Snoqualmie National Forest, is the first new wilderness area in Washington state in more than 20 years.

Larsen had sponsored the bill in four straight Congresses, and though it had bipartisan support in the state's congressional delegation and passed the Senate with Murray's help, then-Resources Chairman Richard W. Pombo — a conservative California Republican often at war with the environmental lobby — had refused to accept it. Once Pombo lost and Democrats took the majority in the 2006 elections, Larsen's bill won swift approval.

Larsen counts among his other legislative successes a law he helped pass in his freshman term to improve pipeline safety after a 1999 explosion in Bellingham killed three people. In 2005, he won enactment of provisions designed to provide safeguards to mail-order brides from abroad.

Larsen is a supporter of international trade, which benefits his export-oriented state and district. In 2002, he was one of only 25 Democrats who voted to give the president fast-track authority to negotiate trade agreements that Congress cannot amend. But he joined most of his party in opposing the 2005 Central America Free Trade Agreement, and has voted for only a couple of bilateral trade deals since then (with Oman and Peru) that were opposed by a majority of House Democrats.

He is the co-founder, with Illinois Republican Mark Steven Kirk, of the U.S.-China Working Group, and a co-founder of the Congressional Asia-Pacific Economic Cooperation Caucus. "Washington state has always maintained a good relationship with China," he said. "The first engineer hired by Boeing was a Chinese national."

A member of the Armed Services Committee, Larsen can watch out for Boeing Co., which houses a large aerospace facility in Everett. Yet he also supported a 2009 bill to transform the Defense Department's weapons acquisitions programs. The bill aims to add additional oversight to the procurement process and prevent conflicts of interest for the military's major acquisitions programs. Efforts to change the procurement practices were sparked after the Government Accountability Office reported that 96 of the largest acquisition programs had run $296 billion over budget since they began.

Larsen supported President Obama's plan to draw down U.S. troops in Iraq by August 2010, leaving in place up to 50,000 soldiers. Larsen said it would "reduce the strain on our military, allow us to refocus on Afghanistan,

CAPITOL OFFICE
225-2605
www.house.gov/larsen
108 Cannon Bldg. 20515-4702; fax 225-4420

COMMITTEES
Armed Services
Budget
Transportation & Infrastructure

RESIDENCE
Everett

BORN
June 15, 1965; Arlington, Wash.

RELIGION
Methodist

FAMILY
Wife, Tiia Karlen; two children

EDUCATION
Pacific Lutheran U., B.A. 1987 (political science);
U. of Minnesota, M.P.A. 1990

CAREER
Dental association lobbyist; port economic development official

POLITICAL HIGHLIGHTS
Snohomish County Council, 1998-2000
(chairman, 1999)

ELECTION RESULTS

2008 GENERAL

Rick Larsen (D)	217,416	62.4%
Rick Bart (R)	131,051	37.6%

2008 PRIMARY (OPEN)

Rick Larsen (D)	98,304	54.3%
Rick Bart (R)	68189	37.7%
Doug Schaffer (D)	8,857	4.9%
Glen S. Johnson (D)	5,590	3.1%

2006 GENERAL

Rick Larsen (D)	157,064	64.2%
Doug Roulstone (R)	87,730	35.8%

PREVIOUS WINNING PERCENTAGES
2004 (64%); 2002 (50%); 2000 (50%)

where the Sept. 11 attacks originated, and strengthen our ability to confront future threats to our security."

A member of the Budget Committee for the 111th Congress (2009-10), he supported Obama's $787 economic stimulus law in February 2009. And he backed the president's $3.56 trillion budget blueprint for fiscal 2010. On the House floor in April, he praised the budget for outlining investments in alternative energy sources, education and health care, as well as including a funding increase for the Defense Department and "transparent accounting" for costs of the continuing wars in Iraq and Afghanistan.

Larsen's vote does stray at times. He was among the minority of House Democrats who supported a 2005 bankruptcy overhaul making it harder for consumers to erase their debts. He has backed a permanent repeal of the estate tax. And he voted for President George W. Bush's 2001 tax cut package, although not for the 2003 follow-on or the 2004 extension of the earlier cuts.

Larsen, whose family is originally from Norway, was born and raised in Snohomish County, just north of Seattle. He was one of eight children of a utility company power line worker. Both of his parents were involved in community activities, and his father was a city councilman.

After earning a bachelor's degree in political science and a master's in public affairs, Larsen worked for the Port of Everett helping businesses comply with clean-water requirements. He then became the director of public affairs for the Washington Dental Association.

His first foray into electoral politics came in 1997, when he waged a successful door-to-door campaign for the Snohomish County Council. He chaired the council in 1999.

When three-term Republican Rep. Jack Metcalf retired in 2000, local Democratic Party strategists got behind Larsen, who also received campaign help from organized labor and other traditionally Democratic organizations, such as abortion rights and environmental groups. He prevailed by 12,000 votes against GOP state Rep. John Koster.

Redistricting did little to change the competitive nature of the 2nd District, and the 2002 race between Larsen and Norma Smith, a former aide to Metcalf, was hard-fought. Larsen squeaked through by fewer than 9,000 votes. He has won at least 62 percent of the vote in his past three elections.

In the early months of Obama's presidency, Larsen lobbied to play basketball with the president. Named by Washingtonian magazine in January 2009 as one of 12 potential "Dream Team" players, he said when he first endorsed Obama, "There's a short list of members of Congress who can go up and down the basketball court, and he should call me."

KEY VOTES

2008
Yes Delay consideration of Colombia free-trade agreement
Yes Override Bush veto of federal farm and nutrition programs reauthorization bill
No   Overhaul surveillance laws and permit dismissal of suits against companies that conducted warrantless wiretapping
Yes Grant mortgage relief to homeowners and funding for Fannie Mae and Freddie Mac
Yes Approve initial $700 billion program to stabilize financial markets
Yes Approve final $700 billion program to stabilize financial markets
Yes Provide $14 billion in loans to automakers

2007
Yes Increase minimum wage by $2.10 an hour
Yes Approve $124.2 billion in emergency war spending and set goal for redeployment of troops from Iraq
No   Reject federal contraceptive assistance to international family planning groups
Yes Override Bush veto of $23.2 billion water projects authorization bill
Yes Implement Peru free-trade agreement
Yes Approve energy policy overhaul with new fuel economy standards
Yes Clear $473.5 billion omnibus spending bill, including $70 billion for military operations

CQ VOTE STUDIES

	PARTY UNITY		PRESIDENTIAL SUPPORT	
	SUPPORT	OPPOSE	SUPPORT	OPPOSE
2008	98%	2%	16%	84%
2007	96%	4%	6%	94%
2006	89%	11%	35%	65%
2005	93%	7%	28%	72%
2004	92%	8%	29%	71%

INTEREST GROUPS

	AFL-CIO	ADA	CCUS	ACU
2008	100%	90%	56%	0%
2007	96%	95%	65%	0%
2006	86%	85%	67%	20%
2005	93%	90%	59%	16%
2004	93%	90%	48%	8%

WASHINGTON 2
Puget Sound – Bellingham, most of Everett

Extending from the Cascade Mountains to San Juan Island in the northwestern corner of the state, the 2nd covers an area that is mostly rural in its topography and moderate in its politics. Most residents live along Interstate 5, a technology corridor that runs alongside the Puget Sound, while rural areas just west of the mountains provide open expanses of land, much of it national forest. In between lies a fertile agricultural plain.

Everett, the district's most populous city, is home to Boeing's largest aerospace facility, which still employs thousands of district residents despite continuing layoffs in the face of domestic airline downturns. Firms linked to Seattle's technology industries are located in the district, and these white-collar jobs are integral to the local economy. The 2nd is home to several ports, including those in Everett and Bellingham.

Although no longer dominant, the 2nd's natural resources industries continue to provide some jobs in the rural east, and agriculture workers produce everything from raspberries to dairy products. Tourism also is a significant part of the economy, with visitors drawn to the state and national

forests that line the western slope of the Cascade Range in eastern Whatcom, Skagit and Snohomish counties. San Juan County, a collection of islands southwest of Bellingham, also lures tourists and has attracted retirees. But high foreclosure rates have hurt the slow-paced county. West of the mountains and north of Mount Vernon, residents are closer to Vancouver, British Columbia, than to Seattle.

The 2nd tends to be politically competitive and represented by centrists. The urban centers of Everett in the south and Bellingham in the north are liberal, while rural areas lean conservative. San Juan County, which has the highest median age in the state (47 years) votes Democratic. Barack Obama won 70 percent of the 2008 presidential vote here.

MAJOR INDUSTRY
Aviation, technology, shipping, agriculture, tourism

MILITARY BASES
Naval Air Station Whidbey Island, 7,600 military, 2,400 civilian (2009); Naval Station Everett, 4,305 military, 282 civilian (2007)

CITIES
Everett (pt.), 87,329; Bellingham, 67,171; Mount Vernon, 26,232

NOTABLE
There are no stop lights on the San Juan Islands.

Rep. Brian Baird (D)

CAPITOL OFFICE
225-3536
www.house.gov/baird
2350 Rayburn Bldg. 20515-4703; fax 225-3478

COMMITTEES
Science & Technology
(Energy & Environment - chairman)
Transportation & Infrastructure

RESIDENCE
Vancouver

BORN
March 7, 1956; Chama, N.M.

RELIGION
Protestant

FAMILY
Wife, Rachel Nugent; two children

EDUCATION
U. of Utah, B.S. 1977 (psychology);
U. of Wyoming, M.S. 1980 (clinical psychology),
Ph.D. 1984 (clinical psychology)

CAREER
Professor; psychologist

POLITICAL HIGHLIGHTS
Democratic nominee for U.S. House, 1996

ELECTION RESULTS

2008 GENERAL

Brian Baird (D)	216,701	64.0%
Michael Delavar (R)	121,828	36.0%

2008 PRIMARY (OPEN)

Brian Baird (D)	83,409	50.6%
Michael Delavar (R)	32,372	19.6%
Christine Webb (R)	27,738	16.8%
Cheryl Crist (D)	21,356	13.0%

2006 GENERAL

Brian Baird (D)	147,065	63.1%
Michael Messmore (R)	85,915	36.9%

PREVIOUS WINNING PERCENTAGES
2004 (62%); 2002 (62%); 2000 (56%); 1998 (55%)

Elected 1998; 6th term

Baird is a moderate-to-liberal Democrat with a reputation as one of the funnier members of Congress, known for dead-on imitations of some of his fellow politicians. Though he maintains a relatively low profile in the House as he assiduously seeks to help his district, his bluntness and independent stands don't always leave everyone laughing.

Baird greatly dismayed and angered friends and constituents when in 2007 — at the peak of opposition to the Iraq War — he broke from his party and said he could no longer advocate a speedy U.S. withdrawal from Iraq. Two years later, he became one of the first U.S. officials in nearly four years to visit the Palestinian Gaza Strip. He blasted the devastation there and blamed it on Israel's military, incensing that country's supporters. And he was candid in his subsequent criticism of Democratic efforts to pass legislation aimed at slowing global warming.

Though he serves on the House Democrats' whip team, he has at times gone his own way on other issues. In 2008, he voted to reauthorize and expand the law governing foreign surveillance wiretapping. He also voted with Republicans in 2006 to authorize construction of a 700-mile fence along the U.S.-Mexico border and urged the Supreme Court to uphold a ruling that the District of Columbia's gun ban violates the Second Amendment.

Baird chairs the Science and Technology's Subcommittee on Energy and Environment, putting him in position to shape global warming legislation. Like other Democrats from the Pacific Northwest, he struggles to balance protection of the environment with the need to help the timber industry, which is vital to his state's economy. He told an energy trade publication in April 2009 that a draft bill barring the use of biomass from forests and other federal lands for electricity generation was "foolish on environmental grounds and political grounds." He also expressed skepticism a bill could pass unless major modifications were made.

Baird sponsored legislation in 2009 to establish a panel to coordinate international science and technology cooperation across federal agencies. And he called on the Obama administration to take advanced vehicle research seriously, saying in March of that year that the Energy Department's program "has been a victim of drastic swings in priority between administrations."

Baird serves on the Transportation and Infrastructure Committee, which is expected to tackle an overhaul of the surface transportation law in the 111th Congress (2009-10). He previously served on the Budget Committee, and during fall 2008 negotiations on a rescue of the financial services industry, he joined with Tennessee Democrat John Tanner in an unsuccessful push for a trigger for a potential tax on investors in case the government lost money on the financial rescue.

He is a co-founder of a congressional caucus to fight methamphetamine abuse. "I have seen it destroy lives. Clearly we needed to get some more horsepower behind this effort, and the caucus is the way to do it," he said.

And though he doesn't serve on any committees dealing with national security, he considers it important to get a firsthand view of the world. After the uproar over his comments on the Gaza Strip, he told The Seattle Times that he felt compelled to report what he saw — just as he had with Iraq earlier. "I am learning through brutal experience not to let it get to me," he said of the subsequent backlash. Baird's broader interests tend to fall in the "good government" category. He supports direct popular election of presidents, calling the Electoral College system "a cockamamie, undemocratic process." He also espouses a constitutional amendment to allow each House member and senator to choose three potential successors to serve in the event of a catastrophe until a special election can be held; that proposal drew only 63 votes in 2004. He has pushed legislation to prohibit lawmakers and their staffs from using nonpublic information obtained through their official positions to benefit themselves financially.

He is known on the Hill for his humorous impersonations of politicians from both parties. Reprising an old joke, Baird-as-President George W. Bush once announced a new Operation Solar Landing initiative: "It's gonna put a man on the sun. Now, I know, I know, you pointy-headed academics and you liberal judges, you don't think we can do that. [Pause.] Heh. We're going at night!"

Baird grew up in a small town in western Colorado, where his father was a civics teacher and school principal and served on the city council. His mother owned a small business and was a community volunteer. An avid skier who holds an annual "Ski With Your Congressman Day," Baird said he went to the University of Utah for one reason: "Powder skiing. Period."

During his career as a clinical psychologist, he worked with troubled war veterans, juvenile offenders and drug addicts. He also taught at a community college and was a professor at Pacific Lutheran University in Tacoma.

When no Democrat chose to run against conservative GOP Rep. Linda Smith in 1996, Baird put together an underfunded grass-roots campaign. "People quite literally laughed," he recalls. But he lost by just 887 votes — and caught the political bug. He set about preparing for a second try.

In 1998, Smith gave up her House seat for an unsuccessful Senate bid. Baird was well-organized and better-financed this time around; he won by nearly 10 percentage points over GOP state Sen. Don Benton. He has won re-election with increasing ease since then.

After Baird announced his position against an Iraq withdrawal in 2007, the liberal political action group MoveOn.org attacked Baird in a TV ad, and anti-war activists said they would promote a serious primary challenger to Baird in 2008. But that threat fizzled. Baird finished first with 51 percent of the vote in Washington's open primary, in which all candidates regardless of party run on the same ballot. The other Democrat on the ballot got 13 percent.

He had to fight off another controversy in the months leading up to the November election — a taxpayer-financed trip to the Galapagos Islands with other lawmakers that was featured on the TV show "Inside Edition." But he still won with 64 percent of the vote, 11 percentage points above what Barack Obama took in carrying the district.

KEY VOTES

2008

Yes Delay consideration of Colombia free-trade agreement

Yes Override Bush veto of federal farm and nutrition programs reauthorization bill

Yes Overhaul surveillance laws and permit dismissal of suits against companies that conducted warrantless wiretapping

Yes Grant mortgage relief to homeowners and funding for Fannie Mae and Freddie Mac

Yes Approve initial $700 billion program to stabilize financial markets

Yes Approve final $700 billion program to stabilize financial markets

Yes Provide $14 billion in loans to automakers

2007

Yes Increase minimum wage by $2.10 an hour

Yes Approve $124.2 billion in emergency war spending and set goal for redeployment of troops from Iraq

No Reject federal contraceptive assistance to international family planning groups

Yes Override Bush veto of $23.2 billion water projects authorization bill

Yes Implement Peru free-trade agreement

Yes Approve energy policy overhaul with new fuel economy standards

Yes Clear $473.5 billion omnibus spending bill, including $70 billion for military operations

CQ VOTE STUDIES

	PARTY UNITY		PRESIDENTIAL SUPPORT	
	SUPPORT	OPPOSE	SUPPORT	OPPOSE
2008	94%	6%	16%	84%
2007	94%	6%	8%	92%
2006	89%	11%	37%	63%
2005	92%	8%	18%	82%
2004	89%	11%	37%	63%

INTEREST GROUPS

	AFL-CIO	ADA	CCUS	ACU
2008	100%	80%	50%	4%
2007	95%	95%	58%	0%
2006	86%	80%	53%	20%
2005	87%	95%	56%	9%
2004	92%	90%	53%	17%

WASHINGTON 3
Southwest – Vancouver, most of Olympia

Located in Washington's southwestern corner, the 3rd District is home to two enclaves of liberal Democratic voters — the state capital of Olympia and the city of Vancouver — and to Republican-leaning communities in the suburbs and countryside. The two cities are connected by Interstate 5, west and east of which lies considerable open rural territory.

The district's population center is Clark County (Vancouver), where slightly more than half of the 3rd's residents live. Tens of thousands of county residents cross the Columbia River each day to jobs in Oregon, many of them in Portland. But layoffs in construction and manufacturing sectors have hurt the area. Clark's considerable population growth over the last two decades made the home construction industry a cornerstone of the local economy, but recent economic downturns and a housing market crisis put the brakes on development.

The distressed economy and high foreclosure rates in the district affected the 3rd's extensive timber industry — the vast stretches of woodlands east in the Cascade Mountains and west in Wahkiakum and Pacific

counties supply the lumber for homes and commercial construction. Fishing and oyster harvesting are prominent on Pacific County's coast.

The district's other population pocket and cultural hub is Olympia in Thurston County at the 3rd's northern tip. Olympia's workforce relies on government and service industry jobs, but state budget shortfalls and rising unemployment rates concern local officials and residents.

Although recent presidential elections in the 3rd have been close, the district is trending left. Barack Obama took 53 percent of the vote in the 2008 presidential race, while Republican George W. Bush won the district in 2004 with 50 percent of the vote and in 2000 with 48 percent of the vote.

MAJOR INDUSTRY
Timber, computer hardware, manufacturing, mining

CITIES
Vancouver, 143,560; Olympia (pt.), 35,230; Longview 34,660

NOTABLE
Mount St. Helens erupted May 18, 1980, killing 57 people and destroying enough lumber for 300,000 two-bedroom homes; The World Kite Museum and Hall of Fame is located in Long Beach.

Rep. Doc Hastings (R)

CAPITOL OFFICE
225-5816
www.house.gov/hastings
1203 Longworth Bldg. 20515-4704; fax 225-3251

COMMITTEES
Standards of Official Conduct Rangel Inquiry
Natural Resources - ranking member

RESIDENCE
Pasco

BORN
Feb. 7, 1941; Spokane, Wash.

RELIGION
Protestant

FAMILY
Wife, Claire Hastings; three children

EDUCATION
Columbia Basin College, attended 1959-61;
Central Washington U., attended 1964

MILITARY SERVICE
Army Reserve, 1964-69

CAREER
Paper supply business owner

POLITICAL HIGHLIGHTS
Wash. House, 1979-87; Republican nominee
for U.S. House, 1992

ELECTION RESULTS

2008 GENERAL

Doc Hastings (R)	169,940	63.1%
George Fearing (D)	99,430	36.9%

2008 PRIMARY (OPEN)

Doc Hastings (R)	93,241	62.2%
George Fearing (D)	49,841	33.2%
Gordon Allen Pross (X)	6,842	4.6%

2006 GENERAL

Doc Hastings (R)	115,246	59.9%
Richard Wright (D)	77,054	40.1%

PREVIOUS WINNING PERCENTAGES
2004 (63%); 2002 (67%); 2000 (61%); 1998 (69%);
1996 (53%); 1994 (53%)

Elected 1994; 8th term

Hastings is subdued by nature but an expert tactician when it comes to navigating the legislative process. He skillfully tackles an assortment of challenging and often thankless assignments for the GOP, all while tending to his constituents' economic concerns.

Named the ranking Republican on the Natural Resources Committee in 2009, he can finally fulfill his desire to play a major role on legislation after completing an eight-year tenure on the ethics committee. Hastings supports drilling for oil in coastal waters and Alaska's Arctic National Wildlife Refuge as a way to promote energy independence. He also advocates an expansion of nuclear power and renewable energy sources, particularly hydroelectric.

Hastings hadn't served on Natural Resources since the 104th Congress (1995-96), but he beat out Utah Republican Rob Bishop for the post, which came open after embattled Alaska Republican Don Young pulled his name from consideration. Early in 2009, the committee began hearings into off-shore drilling along the Pacific and Atlantic coasts. Although it is unlikely Congress will reinstate a ban that was allowed to expire in 2008, the panel intended to look into oversight of leases for oil and gas companies.

As founder and chairman of the House Nuclear Cleanup Caucus, he seeks to expedite environmental restoration of radioactive waste sites. His district is home to the Hanford Nuclear Reservation, once a major employer. It now stands idle as the nation's most toxic relic of the Cold War, and Hastings has secured hundreds of millions of dollars to clean it up.

In 2004, he backed a law calling for a federal study of the potential for adding historic Manhattan Project sites, including the Hanford reactor, to the National Park system. He played an important role in the August 2008 designation of Hanford's B Reactor as a National Historic Landmark. The world's first full-scale plutonium production reactor, it was built as part of the top-secret project to produce the atomic bomb.

He is not among the GOP's rhetorical stars, but he puts up a fight against Democrats when he sees fit. He and other Republicans objected to the process of bringing a series of public-lands bills to the floor together in a single piece of legislation in early 2009. He complained that 100 of the measures in the package had never passed the House. The bill failed on an initial vote to reach a full two-thirds majority it needed to pass under a procedure that bars amendments, but passed on a second vote and was subsequently signed into law.

He also had an exchange with Rules Chairwoman Louise M. Slaughter of New York during debate on the bill. She had barred from debate his amendments to ensure wheelchair access to recreational areas. Her move spurred a shouting match with David Dreier of California in Hastings' absence, with Slaughter contending Hastings was making a ruse to stall the bill. Hastings subsequently wrote Slaughter a letter stating "deep personal regret" that she had made comments "about my truthfulness."

In mid-2008, as top-ranking Republican on the ethics panel, he led the call for an investigation of Ways and Means Chairman Charles B. Rangel of New York for alleged financial and fundraising improprieties. Although no longer on the committee, he continues to serve on the investigative panel reviewing Rangel's conduct. He had served on the ethics panel since 2001 and held its gavel from 2005 to 2006, at the behest of Speaker J. Dennis Hastert (who also reportedly included Hastings on a list of potential successors as Speaker in the event of a disaster). Hastert had ousted former Chairman Joel Hefley of Colorado and two other Republicans after the panel in 2004 admonished Republican

Majority Leader Tom DeLay of Texas for repeated breaches of the rules.

In a rare break from his party, Hastings in the fall of 2008 opposed a $700 billion law to rescue the nation's financial system, even though it included sweeteners, such as funding for rural schools, which he had supported. But he said "it still potentially leaves taxpayers holding the $700 billion bag for the reckless actions of Wall Street." He stuck with his party in voting against President Obama's economic stimulus bill in early 2009.

He funnels federal dollars to support farmers and protests what he sees as unfair foreign competition to Washington's lucrative apple industry. He wrote to Agriculture Secretary Tom Vilsack in May 2009 requesting the department purchase 1 million boxes of apples to support growers across the country. He also favors a proposed free-trade agreement with Colombia as a means to ease trade barriers and promote his state's agriculture products abroad. But in 2007, he was one of just 16 Republicans to vote against the U.S.-Peru free trade agreement, which he called unfair to the state's asparagus growers.

Central Washington's agriculture-based economy relies on the labor of seasonal workers, making immigration a major issue for his district. He opposes "blanket amnesty and automatic citizenship" and favors creating a path to citizenship for undocumented workers already in the country.

The potential taint of scandal touched Hastings' office early in 2007. John McKay, one of nine U.S. attorneys whose firings prompted congressional investigations, said Hastings' chief of staff called him in 2004 to ask whether he was investigating potential fraud in the disputed Washington state gubernatorial election. McKay told the aide it would be improper to answer, and that was the end of the matter. Hastings told the Lewiston (Idaho) Morning Tribune the call was "entirely appropriate," but several groups pressed for an investigation. In September 2008, a Justice Department report said the firings were improper, but couldn't determine why McKay was dismissed.

Born Richard Norman Hastings, he has been known as "Doc" since childhood. Before coming to Congress, Hastings ran his family's paper supply business in Pasco and was active in local GOP politics. He was elected to the Washington House in 1978 and served eight years, winning leadership posts as assistant majority leader and chairman of the GOP caucus.

In 1992, he was backed by GOP religious activists and considered the most conservative of the four Republicans running to succeed GOP Rep. Sid Morrison. Hastings won the primary handily, but narrowly lost to Democrat Jay Inslee. In a 1994 rematch, Hastings cast the campaign as a referendum on Inslee's support for President Clinton. Hastings ousted Inslee and has won handily ever since. (Inslee now represents the 1st District.)

KEY VOTES

2008
No Delay consideration of Colombia free-trade agreement
Yes Override Bush veto of federal farm and nutrition programs reauthorization bill
Yes Overhaul surveillance laws and permit dismissal of suits against companies that conducted warrantless wiretapping
No Grant mortgage relief to homeowners and funding for Fannie Mae and Freddie Mac
No Approve initial $700 billion program to stabilize financial markets
No Approve final $700 billion program to stabilize financial markets
No Provide $14 billion in loans to automakers

2007
No Increase minimum wage by $2.10 an hour
No Approve $124.2 billion in emergency war spending and set goal for redeployment of troops from Iraq
Yes Reject federal contraceptive assistance to international family planning groups
Yes Override Bush veto of $23.2 billion water projects authorization bill
No Implement Peru free-trade agreement
No Approve energy policy overhaul with new fuel economy standards
Yes Clear $473.5 billion omnibus spending bill, including $70 billion for military operations

CQ VOTE STUDIES

	PARTY UNITY		PRESIDENTIAL SUPPORT	
	SUPPORT	OPPOSE	SUPPORT	OPPOSE
2008	98%	2%	70%	30%
2007	95%	5%	81%	19%
2006	97%	3%	95%	5%
2005	96%	4%	87%	13%
2004	96%	4%	97%	3%

INTEREST GROUPS

	AFL-CIO	ADA	CCUS	ACU
2008	13%	15%	88%	96%
2007	9%	10%	74%	100%
2006	7%	0%	100%	88%
2005	29%	5%	96%	92%
2004	13%	0%	100%	100%

WASHINGTON 4
Central — Yakima and Tri-Cities

Lying just east of the Cascade Mountains, the 4th includes some of the state's most fertile land as well as large stretches of the Columbia River (shared with the 3rd and 5th), which works its way down the middle of the district before turning west to form the state's border with Oregon.

Yakima County is the 4th's largest, both in land area and population, and is home to the Yakima Valley, known as the fruit bowl of the Northwest. It includes Yakama Indian Reservation and part of the U.S. Army's Yakima Training Center, which spreads into Kittitas County. Heavily irrigated agriculture drives the valley, which is full of apple orchards and fields of hops. In fact, the valley produces more than 75 percent of the total U.S. hops crop and hosts the Hop Growers of America.

Benton County to the east takes in the 4th's other population center. The Tri-Cities of Kennewick, Richland and Pasco on the Columbia River are a hotbed for scientific research. It also is home to the Energy Department's Hanford nuclear site and Pacific Northwest National Laboratory, which is the district's largest employer. Hanford is the nation's most contaminated

nuclear site and has been targeted for accelerated cleanup. Projects to demolish parts of the site, transfer waste out of the district and protect groundwater are expected to create thousands of jobs in the area.

The Wenatchee National Forest still provides some timber jobs despite cutbacks over the past decade. The Columbia Basin Project delivers water to the area's wineries and potato, corn and fruit farms. Many of these agrarian areas have attracted populations that are more than 75 percent Hispanic.

The 4th is the state's most conservative district and gave Republican John McCain his highest percentage statewide (58 percent) in the 2008 presidential race. He won every county wholly in the district except for Kickitat, which he lost by about 20 votes.

MAJOR INDUSTRY
Scientific research, fruit orchards and other agriculture, timber

CITIES
Yakima, 71,845; Kennewick, 54,693; Richland, 38,708; Pasco, 32,066

NOTABLE
The oldest skeleton ever found in North America was discovered on the banks of the Columbia River near Kennewick in 1996.

Rep. Cathy McMorris Rodgers (R)

Elected 2004; 3rd term

CAPITOL OFFICE
225-2006
www.mcmorris.house.gov
1323 Longworth Bldg. 20515-4705; fax 225-3392

COMMITTEES
Armed Services
Education & Labor
Natural Resources

RESIDENCE
Spokane

BORN
May 22, 1969; Salem, Ore.

RELIGION
Christian non-denominational

FAMILY
Husband, Brian Rodgers; one child

EDUCATION
Pensacola Christian College, B.A. 1990
(pre-law); U. of Washington, M.B.A. 2002

CAREER
Fruit orchard worker; state legislative aide

POLITICAL HIGHLIGHTS
Wash. House, 1994-2004 (minority leader, 2002-03)

ELECTION RESULTS

2008 GENERAL

Cathy McMorris Rodgers (R)	211,305	65.3%
Mark Mays (D)	112,382	34.7%

2008 PRIMARY (OPEN)

Cathy McMorris Rodgers (R)	96,584	56.3%
Mark Mays (D)	34,251	20.0%
Barbara Lampert (D)	19,645	11.4%
Kurt Erickson (R)	12,155	7.1%
John H. Beck (LIBERT)	3,673	2.1%
Randall Yearout (CNSTP)	5,268	3.1%

2006 GENERAL

Cathy McMorris Rodgers (R)	134,967	56.4%
Peter J. Goldmark (D)	104,357	43.6%

PREVIOUS WINNING PERCENTAGES
2004 (60%)

McMorris Rodgers is the Republican Conference vice chairwoman and a trusted ally of Minority Leader John A. Boehner of Ohio, who values her allegiance to the GOP agenda and willingness to take on difficult backroom tasks. She seeks to put a family-friendly face on her party through her legislative work on education and health issues while looking out for her district's military and agricultural assets.

McMorris Rodgers has seen her life turned upside down in recent years. She has gotten married, had a son — and learned the boy has Down syndrome. She also has had to adjust to life in the minority, a situation she hopes to reverse by trying to improve how Republicans talk to voters. "We need to modernize our message," she told the Lewiston (Idaho) Morning Tribune in November 2008. "We've used terms like 'limited government' for a long time, but what do we mean by it?"

McMorris Rodgers embraces her party's preference for limited government. But she parts ways with conservatives on some issues, and split with President George W. Bush on several high-profile bills.

In 2007, she voted to override the president's veto of legislation to expand the State Children's Health Insurance Program, which covers children from low-income families that do not qualify for Medicaid, although the attempt failed. (She reversed course and opposed a similar measure in 2009 that President Obama signed into law.) She also supported three successful override attempts in 2007 and 2008, helping to enact over Bush's veto a water resources bill, a five-year farm program overhaul and a measure to block cuts in Medicare payments to physicians.

She has made it a point to stay on good terms with Democrats as well as Republicans, and notes that with the GOP in the minority, "relationships that I build with members of both sides become more important." In the 110th Congress (2007-08), she co-chaired the bipartisan Congressional Caucus for Women's Issues, where she and other members of that group strongly supported legislation enacted in 2008 to ban discrimination by insurers or employers based on genetic testing results.

As conference vice chairwoman, a job she won after running unopposed at Boehner's behest, McMorris Rodgers regularly uses social-networking tools such as Twitter and Facebook along with YouTube to communicate with voters. Boehner also tapped her in 2009 to head a Republican task force to come up with a policy on earmarks, funding set-asides for projects in member districts.

She uses her seat on the Armed Services Committee to look out for Fairchild Air Force Base, home to much of the Air Force's tanker fleet on the West Coast. On the Natural Resources Committee, where she serves as top Republican on the Water and Power Subcommittee, she promotes hydropower — plentiful in the Pacific Northwest — as clean, renewable energy. She launched a Congressional Hydropower Caucus in 2008 to advocate its expansion to boost domestic energy supplies and combat climate change.

On her third committee, Education and Labor, she won inclusion in the 2008 overhaul of the Higher Education Act provisions promoting scholarships for students pursuing studies in math, science, engineering and computer science and allowing school districts to enlist midcareer professionals as adjunct teachers. She has introduced legislation to amend federal labor laws to provide compensatory time for private-sector employees.

Though McMorris Rodgers acknowledges it has been difficult juggling her duties as a legislator and the mother of a developmentally disabled child, she considers herself lucky not to have to "punch a clock every day." The congressional schedule gives her some flexibility, and her husband, Brian, a retired career Navy officer, has pitched in to take care of their son, Cole.

Instead of drawing a veil of privacy around the family, McMorris Rodgers reached out, launching the Congressional Down Syndrome Caucus in 2008 to promote research, raise educational expectations and outcomes for children with Down syndrome, and help provide family and community support. "I think Cole gave me a whole new purpose to being in Congress," she said.

McMorris Rodgers is descended from pioneers who traveled the Oregon Trail to the Pacific Northwest in the 1850s. Her family lived in British Columbia for years, moving to Kettle Falls on the Columbia River 30 miles south of the Canadian border, as she and her brother, Jeff, were preparing to enter high school.

Her father, Wayne McMorris, bought an orchard and opened a fruit stand. She and her brother did every job on the farm, including pruning, thinning, picking and selling at the stand. Her father also chaired the Stevens County Republican Party and was president of the local Chamber of Commerce, setting "a good example," she said, by "making it a priority in his life to give back to the community." She was the first in her family to attend college, fulfilling her parents' dream for her. She worked her way through in jobs that ranged from stints at McDonald's to housekeeping.

When she graduated, a family friend, Bob Morton, asked her to manage his campaign for the state House. He won, and she became a legislative assistant in his office. When Morton was appointed to the state Senate in 1993, his young protégé — age 24 at the time — was appointed to replace him in the state House. She won the seat in her own right the next year and was elected minority leader in 2002.

Two years later, when Republican Rep. George Nethercutt unsuccessfully attempted to unseat Democratic Sen. Patty Murray, McMorris Rodgers won a three-way Republican primary for Nethercutt's House seat. She trounced the Democratic candidate, Spokane businessman Don Barbieri, by 19 percentage points.

In 2005, while she was home over the August recess, a campaign volunteer brought her brother, Brian Rodgers, to the congresswoman's "pink flamingo" summer fundraiser. The two talked only briefly, but Rodgers followed up with a letter. They married a year later, in the midst of her first re-election campaign. She won that race with 56 percent of the vote in a climate that had turned hostile to the GOP. In 2008, she won with 65 percent.

KEY VOTES

2008
No — Delay consideration of Colombia free-trade agreement
Yes — Override Bush veto of federal farm and nutrition programs reauthorization bill
Yes — Overhaul surveillance laws and permit dismissal of suits against companies that conducted warrantless wiretapping
No — Grant mortgage relief to homeowners and funding for Fannie Mae and Freddie Mac
No — Approve initial $700 billion program to stabilize financial markets
No — Approve final $700 billion program to stabilize financial markets
No — Provide $14 billion in loans to automakers

2007
No — Increase minimum wage by $2.10 an hour
No — Approve $124.2 billion in emergency war spending and set goal for redeployment of troops from Iraq
Yes — Reject federal contraceptive assistance to international family planning groups
Yes — Override Bush veto of $23.2 billion water projects authorization bill
No — Implement Peru free-trade agreement
Yes — Approve energy policy overhaul with new fuel economy standards
Yes — Clear $473.5 billion omnibus spending bill, including $70 billion for military operations

CQ VOTE STUDIES

	PARTY UNITY		PRESIDENTIAL SUPPORT	
	SUPPORT	OPPOSE	SUPPORT	OPPOSE
2008	95%	5%	64%	36%
2007	92%	8%	71%	29%
2006	98%	2%	92%	8%
2005	98%	2%	89%	11%

INTEREST GROUPS

	AFL-CIO	ADA	CCUS	ACU
2008	20%	20%	89%	92%
2007	9%	15%	75%	85%
2006	15%	5%	100%	96%
2005	20%	5%	93%	100%

WASHINGTON 5

East – Spokane

With beautiful forests and lush fields, the 5th is anchored by the greater Spokane region, which takes in nearly two-thirds of the district's population and is an economic hub for the Inland Northwest.

Spokane once revolved around manufacturing, but health care, finance and service jobs now dominate. Spokane, the largest city between Seattle and Minneapolis, also serves as a nexus for retail, trade and telecommunications businesses. Fairchild Air Force Base, 10 miles west of downtown, is one of the metropolitan area's key employers.

North of Spokane, among mountains and national and state forests, no city surpasses the 6,000-resident mark. Although logging and mining used to drive the economy, both industries have declined in recent decades. Okanogan County is known for ranches and orchards.

The Colville Indian Reservation, one of three reservations in the district, takes up large portions of Okanogan and Ferry counties. At the corner of Okanogan and Lincoln counties, the Grand Coulee Dam — the nation's

largest hydropower producer — crosses the Columbia River into the 4th.

The southern 5th's fertile soil produces some of the world's most sought-after wheat and the Walla Walla Sweet Onion. At the foot of the Blue Mountains near Oregon, Walla Walla hosts a thriving arts community and two colleges. Area wineries lure tourists, but economic slowdowns in the Northwest may hurt the city.

Spokane and Whitman counties can be politically competitive, but the 5th's rural areas tend to strongly favor the GOP. In the 2008 presidential race, John McCain won 11 of the district's 12 counties, including his four best Washington counties, and lost only Whitman.

MAJOR INDUSTRY
Agriculture, health care, service, finance

MILITARY BASES
Fairchild Air Force Base, 4,700 military, 700 civilian (2008)

CITIES
Spokane, 195,629; Walla Walla, 29,686

NOTABLE
The Fort Walla Walla Museum's "Living History" performances celebrate the city's heritage and the lives of 19th-century residents.

Rep. Norm Dicks (D)

Elected 1976; 17th term

CAPITOL OFFICE
225-5916
www.house.gov/dicks
2467 Rayburn Bldg. 20515-4706; fax 226-1176

COMMITTEES
Appropriations
(Interior-Environment - chairman)

RESIDENCE
Belfair

BORN
Dec. 16, 1940; Bremerton, Wash.

RELIGION
Lutheran

FAMILY
Wife, Suzanne Dicks; two children

EDUCATION
U. of Washington, B.A. 1963 (political science), J.D. 1968

CAREER
Congressional aide

POLITICAL HIGHLIGHTS
No previous office

ELECTION RESULTS

2008 GENERAL
Norm Dicks (D)	205,991	66.9%
Doug Cloud (R)	102,081	33.1%

2008 PRIMARY (OPEN)
Norm Dicks (D)	96,862	57.3%
Doug Cloud (R)	51,300	30.3%
Paul Richmond (D)	14,983	8.9%
Gary Murrell (GREEN)	6,014	3.6%

2006 GENERAL
Norm Dicks (D)	158,202	70.6%
Doug Cloud (R)	65,883	29.4%

PREVIOUS WINNING PERCENTAGES
2004 (69%); 2002 (64%); 2000 (65%); 1998 (68%);
1996 (66%); 1994 (58%); 1992 (64%); 1990 (61%);
1988 (68%); 1986 (71%); 1984 (66%); 1982 (63%);
1980 (54%); 1978 (61%); 1976 (74%)

Dicks has more than three decades' experience as an appropriator and has become a veteran inside player who delivers money to his state as an avid pro-defense Democrat. Beyond his historical hawkishness, though, his voting record is solidly within his party's mainstream.

Even before he came to Congress, the beefy former college linebacker with a booming voice was involved in spending. After graduating law school in 1968, he worked for former Washington Democrat Warren G. Magnuson, a Senate appropriator. He followed the path of his mentor, winning a bid for the U.S. House in 1976 and securing a seat on the Appropriations Committee in his first term, an unusual feat. He has stayed there since, funneling money back home for defense-related projects as well as for efforts to protect the region's vast natural resources.

As the third-most-senior Democrat on the Appropriations Committee, he steers spending to special projects whether or not the administration in power wants the funds. This practice, called earmarking, has many critics, but Dicks is not one of them. He has called earmarks "an important legislative tool that separates us from the executive branch."

Dicks has long been a player on national security and natural resource issues. He secured a gavel in 2007, becoming chairman of the Interior-Environment Appropriations Subcommittee. Dicks' district encompasses such scenic areas as Olympic National Park, Olympic National Forest, Puget Sound and mountain-rimmed coastlines along the Pacific. It also has a large American Indian constituency.

As subcommittee chairman, he has focused on boosting maintenance and staffing at national parks and increasing spending on health care for American Indians. He also has secured money to address the effects of global warming on public lands. He worked with Natural Resources Chairman Nick J. Rahall II of West Virginia to push a bill through the House in 2009 to create a separate wildfire account with the intent of freeing up funds for other priorities such as preventing forest fires. Termed the "Flame Fund," it would be used to set aside money for emergency wildfire suppression.

In early 2009, he proposed shifting the entire U.S. Forest Service to the Interior Department with the aim of improving public-lands management and potentially saving money by, in part, forcing collaboration. But the idea gained little traction. He also has been trying to restore funding to several programs — the Indian Health Service and Bureau of Indian Affairs — which were subject to years of cuts under George W. Bush's administration.

In 2000, Dicks sponsored a law adding vast tracts of wilderness to the federal conservation trust. He has secured billions of dollars for the Pacific Northwest, including millions for salmon protection and for the rehabilitation of the city of Tacoma.

Dicks also is the second-ranking Democrat on the Defense Appropriations Subcommittee — just behind his longtime friend, Chairman John P. Murtha of Pennsylvania. From that position, Dicks is attentive to Washington state's substantial military economy. Chicago-based aerospace giant Boeing Co. has major operations in the state.

In fact, Dicks is sometimes called "Mr. Boeing." He has long supported the company's bid to build midair refueling tankers for the U.S. military. Starting in late 2001, Dicks was among the members who pushed a program to obtain 100 tanker planes from Boeing, originally as a no-bid lease. The program was derailed in 2004 after a scandal that involved an Air Force official who was seeking a job with Boeing while she was overseeing the program and took steps to favor the company.

After the scandal, the Pentagon launched a competition to develop and build the tankers. In a surprise announcement in February 2008, the Air Force selected Northrop Grumman Corp., not Boeing, for the job. Boeing filed a formal protest of the decision with the Government Accountability Office (GAO). And in June 2008, the GAO determined the process had been unfair to Boeing — a point Dicks had long made — and urged the Pentagon to start over. "I've never felt more vindicated in anything I've ever done since I've been around here," he said at the time. The Pentagon decided in September 2008 to defer a decision on a follow-up competition.

Dicks usually supports his party; he took its side more than 90 percent of the time during the Bush administration. But as a strong supporter of Pentagon spending in his state and generally, it was not a stretch in 2002 for Dicks to back the invasion of Iraq. In fact, he was among a bipartisan group of nine House members hand-picked by the administration to help secure votes on the resolution authorizing the president to use force against Iraq.

But by 2006, his views on the war had changed. He joined his party's ranks by voting no on a resolution that rejected setting an "arbitrary" date for troop withdrawals. In early 2007, Dicks voted for a resolution opposing the White House plan to send more than 21,000 additional U.S. combat troops into Iraq. And he supported several attempts to set a target for withdrawal of U.S. troops.

In the 1990s, as the Intelligence Committee's top-ranking Democrat, Dicks was at the fore of early efforts to bring efficiencies to the nation's many-layered spy operations. In 1998 he and California Republican Rep. Christopher Cox led a bipartisan investigation of China's efforts to obtain U.S. technology. At Dicks' insistence, the panel examined security lapses at nuclear weapons laboratories that allegedly enabled China to obtain highly classified data.

Dicks grew up in Bremerton, population 37,000, the son of an electrician at Puget Sound Naval Shipyard. He excelled at sports and played football at the University of Washington, where his game name was "Dizzy Dicks." He wasn't good enough to go professional, so after graduating with a degree in political science, he went to law school with an eye on a career in politics.

He got his first taste of campaigning by pouring drinks aboard the campaign plane for the Democratic candidate for governor in 1968. In need of a job when his candidate lost, Dicks was quickly hired by Magnuson. When 6th District incumbent Rep. Floyd Hicks was named to the state Supreme Court in 1976, Dicks went home to run for the seat. He easily won that November and has carried his district with at least 60 percent of the vote in all but two elections.

KEY VOTES

2008
Yes Delay consideration of Colombia free-trade agreement

Yes Override Bush veto of federal farm and nutrition programs reauthorization bill

Yes Overhaul surveillance laws and permit dismissal of suits against companies that conducted warrantless wiretapping

Yes Grant mortgage relief to homeowners and funding for Fannie Mae and Freddie Mac

Yes Approve initial $700 billion program to stabilize financial markets

Yes Approve final $700 billion program to stabilize financial markets

Yes Provide $14 billion in loans to automakers

2007
Yes Increase minimum wage by $2.10 an hour

Yes Approve $124.2 billion in emergency war spending and set goal for redeployment of troops from Iraq

No   Reject federal contraceptive assistance to international family planning groups

Yes Override Bush veto of $23.2 billion water projects authorization bill

Yes Implement Peru free-trade agreement

Yes Approve energy policy overhaul with new fuel economy standards

Yes Clear $473.5 billion omnibus spending bill, including $70 billion for military operations

CQ VOTE STUDIES

	PARTY UNITY		PRESIDENTIAL SUPPORT	
	SUPPORT	OPPOSE	SUPPORT	OPPOSE
2008	98%	2%	19%	81%
2007	97%	3%	7%	93%
2006	86%	14%	33%	67%
2005	92%	8%	24%	76%
2004	90%	10%	31%	69%

INTEREST GROUPS

	AFL-CIO	ADA	CCUS	ACU
2008	100%	90%	67%	0%
2007	96%	95%	50%	0%
2006	93%	85%	50%	8%
2005	93%	85%	52%	0%
2004	93%	85%	48%	13%

WASHINGTON 6
West — Bremerton, Tacoma, Olympic Peninsula

The 6th includes the Olympic Mountains, which drop to the coast of the Pacific Ocean in the district's west. The lush Olympic National Park and Olympic National Forest constitute more than one-third of the 6th's land and make the area a very popular tourist destination. Surrounding the mountainous region, communities are striving to move beyond the lumber and fishing industries.

In the district's southwest, the Port of Grays Harbor is a shipping center, and Hoquiam is home to a biodiesel plant that opened to high expectations but has experienced recent layoffs. Port Angeles and Port Townsend along the Olympic Peninsula's northern and eastern shores rely on the ferries, airports and bridges that bring tourists to the region and connect residents to the central Puget Sound area.

More than half of the 6th's residents live near Tacoma and its suburbs in the south Puget Sound region. Revitalization efforts near the waterfront and the University of Washington-Tacoma have lured some people back to downtown. Once a key railroad terminus, the city's economy still relies on manufacturing and shipping jobs. Cargo shipping revenue losses have hurt the 6th, but a military presence in the eastern portion of the district stabilizes the economy. Bremerton, located north of Tacoma, is home to naval facilities, and the 6th has a large Coast Guard presence.

Tacoma's blue-collar, heavily unionized electorate generally gives Democrats the edge in the district's populated portion of Pierce County. But independent voters, who can be socially moderate, have prevented the 6th from moving out of the reach of the GOP. Barack Obama took 57 percent of the 2008 presidential vote and won every county in the 6th.

MAJOR INDUSTRY
Shipping, lumber, fishing, health care, tourism

MILITARY BASES
Puget Sound Naval Shipyard and Intermediate Maintenance Facility, 560 military, 9,900 civilian; Naval Base Kitsap, 10,558 military, 13,661 civilian (shared with the 1st) (2009)

CITIES
Tacoma (pt.), 176,853; Bremerton, 37,259; University Place, 29,933; Lakewood (pt.), 26,878; Port Angeles, 18,397

NOTABLE
Port Townsend celebrates the rhododendron bloom with "Rhody Fest."

Rep. Jim McDermott (D)

Elected 1988; 11th term

CAPITOL OFFICE
225-3106
www.house.gov/mcdermott
1035 Longworth Bldg. 20515-4707; fax 225-6197

COMMITTEES
Ways & Means
    (Income Security & Family Support - chairman)

RESIDENCE
Seattle

BORN
Dec. 28, 1936; Chicago, Ill.

RELIGION
Episcopalian

FAMILY
Wife, Therese Hansen; two children

EDUCATION
Wheaton College (Ill.), B.S. 1958;
U. of Illinois, M.D. 1963

MILITARY SERVICE
Navy Medical Service Corps, 1968-70

CAREER
Psychiatrist; Foreign Service officer

POLITICAL HIGHLIGHTS
Wash. House, 1971-73; sought Democratic
nomination for governor, 1972; Wash. Senate,
1975-87; Democratic nominee for governor, 1980;
sought Democratic nomination for governor, 1984

ELECTION RESULTS

2008 GENERAL

Jim McDermott (D)	291,963	83.6%
Steve Beren (R)	57,054	16.3%

2008 PRIMARY (OPEN)

Jim McDermott (D)	95,344	73.8%
Steve Beren (R)	19,307	14.9%
Donovan Rivers (D)	6,685	5.2%
Mark A. Goldman (X)	3,410	2.6%
Goodspaceguy Nelson (D)	3,199	2.5%

2006 GENERAL

Jim McDermott (D)	195,462	79.4%
Steve Beren (R)	38,715	15.7%
Linnea S. Noreen (I)	11,956	4.9%

PREVIOUS WINNING PERCENTAGES
2004 (81%); 2002 (74%); 2000 (73%); 1998 (88%);
1996 (81%); 1994 (75%); 1992 (78%); 1990 (72%);
1988 (76%)

One of the most liberal members of the House, McDermott is guided by a desire to help the poor. He struggled to make a mark during 12 years of Republican rule, but has shown he can be effective in the majority. Although several of his far-reaching bills have stalled, he has seen progress on others, from helping the economy in Africa to the unemployed in the United States.

Whatever maturity McDermott has achieved as a legislator, he still shows some of the bombastic tendencies that have marked much of his House career. And often his outlandish remarks make bigger headlines than his legislative accomplishments. Yet they don't dampen his enthusiasm for his agenda.

As chairman of the Ways and Means Income Security and Family Support Subcommittee, he has shepherded several bills and amendments aimed at helping people down on their luck. In July 2008, the House passed his bill to help African countries increase their exports to the United States by allowing them to obtain more of their raw materials from non-African suppliers.

The previous month, President George W. Bush signed legislation that included his provision extending unemployment benefits for people who had lost their jobs during the economic downturn. The House also moved his bill aimed at providing additional incentives for people to take in foster children.

He was less successful with other anti-poverty bills, including one to provide gasoline stamps to help low-income workers pay for their commuting costs. He also was unable to move a bill to legalize online gambling or one to require the Census Bureau to produce more-up-to-date poverty statistics.

But he is more often in the news — and in trouble — for his blunt remarks and inappropriate actions. He was formally admonished after he mocked Bush in a floor speech for saying the U.S. was "kicking ass" in Iraq. In December 2007, he voted against a House resolution honoring Christmas — an action he said he took to stick a finger in the eye of its sponsor, Iowa Republican Steve King, for voting against expanding a health care program for children.

McDermott was forced to pay House Republican Leader John A. Boehner of Ohio nearly $1.1 million in 2008 after McDermott received a copy of a recording of an intercepted cell phone call between Boehner and then-House Speaker Newt Gingrich and revealed it to the media. In May 2007, a federal appeals court ruled McDermott had violated House rules by leaking the call. McDermott insisted it was worth the fight — and the huge settlement — to protect what he contends was his First Amendment right to release the taped conversation.

He supported President Obama's early economic initiatives, backing a $787 billion economic stimulus law and a $3.56 trillion budget resolution for fiscal 2010. He initially voted in fall 2008 for a $700 billion measure to rescue the financial services sector, but changed his vote to "no" on a slightly altered version that became law. He said the Senate had ruined the bill by turning its back on Main Street even as unemployment figures continued to rise. "The Senate dug an enormous ditch alongside Main Street, and they want the House to drive into it."

During his years in the minority, McDermott relished throwing verbal bombshells at the GOP for policies he viewed as insensitive to the poor. During a floor speech in December 2005, he waved two red Christmas stockings to illustrate the impact of Republican fiscal policies. From the "poor" stocking, he transferred small presents representing benefits for the elderly and disabled, loans for college students, food stamp funds, and so on. "What's left for poor people?" McDermott asked with a flourish. "Look at that! A lump of coal!"

The only psychiatrist in Congress, he favors a universal government-run health system. But his bill to create a single-payer system foundered in 2008.

In 2009, he opposed plans to cap greenhouse gas emissions coupled with a market-based emissions credit trading system. He offered legislation to allow businesses to purchase emissions permits from the government that they couldn't trade. He said a trading system for emissions permits would be vulnerable to manipulation. He was one of just four Democrats to oppose a 2007 energy bill to raise fuel efficiency standards, arguing it didn't go far enough.

A veteran of the 1960s anti-war movement, McDermott voted against the 2002 resolution authorizing Bush to use force in Iraq and was featured as a critic of the war in filmmaker Michael Moore's 2004 documentary "Fahrenheit 9/11." Later, McDermott led efforts in the House to educate fellow members about the plight of ordinary Iraqis.

He spent years warning of the potential health risks that depleted uranium — used in bullets and armor-penetrating artillery shells — posed to U.S. soldiers and their families. Calling for a study of the health threat, he teamed with the punk rock group Anti-Flag, which in early 2006 released a song titled "Depleted Uranium Is a War Crime," and asked its fans to sign a petition supporting McDermott's measure. In 2006, the defense authorization bill contained his language calling for such a study.

Born and raised in Illinois, McDermott's family was poor, conservative and deeply religious. His father, a bond underwriter, and his mother, a telephone operator and homemaker, started a church in the garage of their two-bedroom home. His three siblings slept in one bedroom; his parents in the other. McDermott, the oldest child, had the couch.

He attended the conservative evangelical Wheaton College in Illinois. His liberal awakening began afterward, during medical school at the University of Illinois, when he voted for John F. Kennedy in the 1960 presidential election.

McDermott's residency training ultimately took him to Seattle. After a two-year stint in the Navy Medical Service Corps, he launched a career in medicine in Seattle. He won a seat in the state House in 1970 running on an abortion-rights platform. After two years in the state House and a two-year break, he won four state Senate elections. He also lost three bids for governor.

McDermott left the state Senate in 1987 to go to Africa as a Foreign Service medical officer. Less than a year later, when Democratic Rep. Mike Lowry announced his plans to run for the Senate, McDermott arranged to be released from his Foreign Service commitment to return to Washington to run for Lowry's seat in 1988. Since then, his re-election races have been runaways. In 2008 he garnered 84 percent of the vote.

KEY VOTES

2008

Yes Delay consideration of Colombia free-trade agreement

No Override Bush veto of federal farm and nutrition programs reauthorization bill

No Overhaul surveillance laws and permit dismissal of suits against companies that conducted warrantless wiretapping

Yes Grant mortgage relief to homeowners and funding for Fannie Mae and Freddie Mac

Yes Approve initial $700 billion program to stabilize financial markets

No Approve final $700 billion program to stabilize financial markets

Yes Provide $14 billion in loans to automakers

2007

Yes Increase minimum wage by $2.10 an hour

Yes Approve $124.2 billion in emergency war spending and set goal for redeployment of troops from Iraq

No Reject federal contraceptive assistance to international family planning groups

Yes Override Bush veto of $23.2 billion water projects authorization bill

Yes Implement Peru free-trade agreement

No Approve energy policy overhaul with new fuel economy standards

No Clear $473.5 billion omnibus spending bill, including $70 billion for military operations

CQ VOTE STUDIES

	PARTY UNITY		PRESIDENTIAL SUPPORT	
	SUPPORT	OPPOSE	SUPPORT	OPPOSE
2008	98%	2%	17%	83%
2007	98%	2%	7%	93%
2006	97%	3%	15%	85%
2005	99%	1%	14%	86%
2004	99%	1%	21%	79%

INTEREST GROUPS

	AFL-CIO	ADA	CCUS	ACU
2008	100%	95%	50%	8%
2007	96%	85%	50%	4%
2006	93%	95%	20%	4%
2005	93%	100%	37%	0%
2004	100%	95%	15%	0%

WASHINGTON 7
Seattle and suburbs

The most populous city in the Pacific Northwest, Seattle is nicknamed the "Emerald City," and it remains the gem of the Evergreen State. The city anchors the 7th, which is diverse, liberal and well-educated. From the top of the iconic Space Needle, tourists can see the Seattle skyline and both the Cascade and Olympic mountain ranges.

The 7th is home to technology-industry leaders such as Amazon.com and other large corporations such as coffee giant Starbucks. Seattle also has emphasized the development of biotech businesses. The maritime industry — centered around the bustling Port of Seattle — remains a major employer. Despite economic diversity here, widespread layoffs across all job sectors, including the once-prominent aviation sector, concern residents and local officials. The University of Washington and The Bill and Melinda Gates Foundation, which donates billions of dollars annually to global health and development projects and to national education and technology projects, are both in the 7th.

Seattle has some of the nation's worst traffic congestion, but local offi-

cials hope a multibillion-dollar expansion of the region's light-rail network will alleviate some of the pressure. The first link — from downtown to Seattle-Tacoma International Airport — is expected to open in 2009, and the overall expansion is planned to continue for at least a decade.

The percentage of Seattle residents who describe themselves as members of two races is nearly double the national average. At 13 percent, Asians make up Seattle's largest minority population and have influenced the International District. The Capitol Hill and University District neighborhoods are destinations for both residents and tourists.

The 7th's urban setting and large population of minorities and singles make it a liberal bastion. Democratic candidates regularly dominate the district in all races. In the 2008 presidential election, Barack Obama won 83 percent of the district's vote.

MAJOR INDUSTRY
Internet technology, computer software, trade, health care, aviation

CITIES
Seattle (pt.), 552,834; White Center (unincorporated), 20,975

NOTABLE
The Fraternal Order of Eagles was founded in 1898 at a Seattle shipyard.

Rep. Dave Reichert (R)

CAPITOL OFFICE
225-7761
www.house.gov/reichert
1730 Longworth Bldg. 20515-4708; fax 225-4282

COMMITTEES
Ways & Means

RESIDENCE
Auburn

BORN
Aug. 29, 1950; Detroit Lakes, Minn.

RELIGION
Lutheran - Missouri Synod

FAMILY
Wife, Julie Reichert; three children

EDUCATION
Concordia College (Ore.), A.A. 1970

MILITARY SERVICE
Air Force Reserve, 1971-76; Air Force, 1976

CAREER
Police officer; grocery warehouse worker

POLITICAL HIGHLIGHTS
King County sheriff, 1997-2005

ELECTION RESULTS

2008 GENERAL

Dave Reichert (R)	191,568	52.8%
Darcy Burner (D)	171,358	47.2%

2008 PRIMARY (OPEN)

Dave Reichert (R)	74,140	48.5%
Darcy Burner (D)	68,010	44.5%
James E. Vaughn (D)	5,051	3.3%
Richard Todd (X)	2,116	1.4%
Keith Arnold (D)	1,886	1.2%
Boleslaw "John" Orlinski (X)	1,523	1%

2006 GENERAL

Dave Reichert (R)	129,362	51.5%
Darcy Burner (D)	122,021	48.5%

PREVIOUS WINNING PERCENTAGES
2004 (52%)

Elected 2004; 3rd term

Reichert is a former sheriff who takes a cop's common-sense approach when it comes to legislating — not just out of habit, but for his political survival. His blend of fiscal conservatism and moderate views on the environment and social policy has kept him in office in a Democratic-leaning district that Barack Obama carried by 14 percentage points in the 2008 presidential election.

Reichert (RIKE-ert)was among the Republicans whom Obama wooed aggressively as he tried to win bipartisan backing for his economic recovery package in early 2009. But not a single House Republican supported the final $787 billion bill, claiming Democrats had shut them out of the drafting process. "It should be a trusting relationship, kind of like a marriage," Reichert said of the majority's responsibility to communicate. "If I look at my wife and listen, and then go and do whatever I want to do, it's not a partnership." In 2008 he voted against the $700 billion plan to shore up the financial services sector, asserting, "This proposed remedy could be more harmful than the illness."

Reichert was in tune with his party on those votes, but he aligns with Democrats on other matters. In 2008, he split with a majority of his fellow House Republicans on one-quarter of all floor votes pitting the two parties against each other — more often than all but nine other House GOP members.

That year, as lawmakers battled over ending a longstanding moratorium on oil and gas drilling off the Atlantic and Pacific coasts, Reichert was one of just 15 House Republicans to back a more limited Democratic alternative. And in May 2009 he supported a Democratic bill to set new mortgage standards and curb predatory lending practices.

He also has split with conservatives on some of their litmus-test social issues. In 2007, he was one of 35 Republicans to support legislation to outlaw job discrimination based on sexual orientation. He opposes abortion, but in 2006 he reversed his 2005 position and voted to override President George W. Bush's veto of a bill authorizing federal funding for stem cell research using surplus embryos from in vitro fertilization.

His decision was "the most difficult I have encountered as a member of Congress," he said, and came about after he visited a cancer research center and consulted with women in his life, including a daughter who underwent in vitro fertilization as well as six female aides in his office. He said he concluded that research using stem cells from embryos destined to be discarded was different from taking a life in an abortion.

But Republican leaders haven't scorned him because of his stands. In January 2009, they awarded him a prized slot on the Ways and Means Committee, which handles tax, trade and health care legislation. Since the trade-dependent 8th District's inception in 1980, its representatives have always eventually earned a seat on the panel. Reichert is a strong supporter of free-trade deals to help further jobs in his district.

He joins a universal call for reducing health care costs; he advocates expanding access, improving quality of care, and using advances in science to improve health care and prevention. He has particularly focused on childrens' health care. In 2009, he was one of 40 Republicans voting for a bill, which Obama signed into law, expanding the State Children's Health Insurance Program, which covers children from low-income families that don't qualify for Medicaid.

In his first term, when the GOP controlled the House, Reichert got his top-choice committee assignment — Homeland Security — and parlayed his law enforcement background into the chairmanship of the Emergency Communications, Preparedness and Response Subcommittee. He drafted high-profile bills to improve communication between first-responders and to restructure the Federal Emergency Management Agency within the Department of Homeland Security. In 2008, when he served as ranking member on that panel, he won enactment of a bill ensuring continued funding to pay security analysts at state and local "fusion centers" that share intelligence and other homeland security information with federal authorities.

The oldest of seven children of an abusive father, Reichert grew up in conditions that were far from ideal. The family lived in a two-bedroom duplex in a rough neighborhood; the boys slept in the garage. Reichert took on the role of protector. It stuck, and he began thinking about a career in police work.

A tuition waiver at a two-year college in Oregon got him on track, and spots as a pitcher on the baseball team and quarterback on the football team brought out his leadership skills.

Reichert tried six times before he passed the test required to get hired by the King County sheriff's office, but once there he thrived. He started as a patrol officer in 1972, later became an undercover agent and made sergeant in 1990. Seven years later, he was elected sheriff.

In a twist of fate, Reichert became sheriff just before the office in 2001 caught Green River serial killer Gary Ridgway, a case Reichert had supervised earlier in his career. Ridgway confessed to killing at least 48 women in the early 1980s in the Seattle area. Reichert published a book in 2004, "Chasing the Devil: My Twenty Year Quest to Capture the Green River Killer," and donated his $150,000 in royalties to a clinic that cares for drug-addicted babies. The clinic has a room named after Reichert, and according to the Seattle Times, the congressman is a frequent visitor.

The story made Reichert a media star, but he decided to see the case to its conclusion rather than run for governor, as he was being urged to do. Yet when six-term Republican Rep. Jennifer Dunn decided not to run for re-election in 2004, Reichert went for the 8th District seat. His name recognition gave him a huge advantage in the GOP primary. In the general election, he faced another local celebrity, radio commentator Dave Ross. The national parties' campaign committees spent more on the contest than on any other House race in 2004, and it turned out to be one of the closest of the year, with Reichert nabbing a 5-percentage-point win.

Two years later, he faced Microsoft executive Darcy Burner in a race that was even closer; after an arduous, weeks-long vote count, Reichert eked out a 3-percentage-point victory. Burner was back for a rematch in 2008, but despite the Democratic tide, Reichert widened his margin.

KEY VOTES

2008

No Delay consideration of Colombia free-trade agreement

No Override Bush veto of federal farm and nutrition programs reauthorization bill

Yes Overhaul surveillance laws and permit dismissal of suits against companies that conducted warrantless wiretapping

No Grant mortgage relief to homeowners and funding for Fannie Mae and Freddie Mac

No Approve initial $700 billion program to stabilize financial markets

No Approve final $700 billion program to stabilize financial markets

No Provide $14 billion in loans to automakers

2007

Yes Increase minimum wage by $2.10 an hour

No Approve $124.2 billion in emergency war spending and set goal for redeployment of troops from Iraq

Yes Reject federal contraceptive assistance to international family planning groups

Yes Override Bush veto of $23.2 billion water projects authorization bill

Yes Implement Peru free-trade agreement

Yes Approve energy policy overhaul with new fuel economy standards

Yes Clear $473.5 billion omnibus spending bill, including $70 billion for military operations

CQ VOTE STUDIES

	PARTY UNITY		PRESIDENTIAL SUPPORT	
	SUPPORT	OPPOSE	SUPPORT	OPPOSE
2008	75%	25%	53%	47%
2007	73%	27%	46%	54%
2006	80%	20%	82%	18%
2005	88%	12%	86%	14%

INTEREST GROUPS

	AFL-CIO	ADA	CCUS	ACU
2008	60%	60%	78%	56%
2007	54%	40%	85%	48%
2006	23%	25%	73%	56%
2005	20%	10%	88%	64%

WASHINGTON 8

Eastside Seattle suburbs; Bellevue; eastern Pierce County

Washington's wealthiest district, the 8th takes in the prosperous King County suburbs outside Seattle in its west as well as large rural areas in its east and south. Seattle's Eastside suburbs were fertile ground for technology businesses, and the area's development caused traffic congestion and fueled debates over infrastructure upgrades and "smart" growth.

The 8th's population center is Bellevue, which is one of the state's most diverse areas, nearly 20 percent of its population is Asian and one-fourth is foreign-born. Microsoft has a key presence in Bellevue, and its headquarters are in the 8th's portion of Redmond. Boeing Co. is still a major employer despite recent layoffs, and Bellevue's corporate residents also include the travel Web site Expedia and mobile phone company T-Mobile USA. The city also is a retail and financial services hub, but declining demand has stalled production at truck manufacturer PACCAR.

The 8th takes in most of the rest of King County to the east and a large

portion of Pierce County, including the fringes of Tacoma's suburbs. The less-populous portions of King and Pierce are home to wide-ranging agricultural production — including berries, vegetables, livestock and nursery plants — but the land faces pressures from development. The eastern halves of King and Pierce rise into the Cascade Range. Most of Mount Rainier National Park — including the peak itself, which is the highest point in Washington and in the Cascades — is within the 8th.

Once a GOP stronghold, the 8th's population boom has added to its urban and Democratic-minded constituency. Beyond the suburbs, voters tend to be fiscally conservative and socially moderate. Barack Obama took 56 percent of the vote in the 2008 presidential election, and the 8th's House seat has become more competitive over the last two decades. The area's growing number of minority voters will continue to influence elections.

MAJOR INDUSTRY
Aviation, manufacturing, computer software

CITIES
Bellevue, 109,569; Kent (pt.), 35,620; Sammamish, 34,104

NOTABLE
Mount Rainier, an active volcano, is the most heavily glaciated peak in the lower 48 states.

Rep. Adam Smith (D)

Elected 1996; 7th term

CAPITOL OFFICE
225-8901
www.house.gov/adamsmith
2402 Rayburn Bldg. 20515-4709; fax 225-5893

COMMITTEES
Armed Services
(Terrorism, Unconventional Threats &
Capabilities - chairman)
Select Intelligence

RESIDENCE
Tacoma

BORN
June 15, 1965; Washington, D.C.

RELIGION
Episcopalian

FAMILY
Wife, Sara Smith; two children

EDUCATION
Fordham U., B.A. 1987 (political science);
U. of Washington, J.D. 1990

CAREER
City prosecutor; lawyer

POLITICAL HIGHLIGHTS
Wash. Senate, 1991-97

ELECTION RESULTS

2008 GENERAL
Adam Smith (D)	176,295	65.4%
James Postma (R)	93,080	34.6%

2008 PRIMARY (OPEN)
Adam Smith (D)	81,503	64.7%
James Postma (R)	44,472	35.3%

2006 GENERAL
Adam Smith (D)	119,038	65.7%
Steven C. Cofchin (R)	62,082	34.3%

PREVIOUS WINNING PERCENTAGES
2004 (63%); 2002 (59%); 2000 (62%); 1998 (65%);
1996 (50%)

Smith considers himself a man in the middle, but he has moved noticeably closer to his party's liberal mainstream since Democrats took control of Congress in 2007. He still deviates occasionally on trade and certain national security issues, but he has increasingly supported party leaders on fiscal policy in hopes of addressing the nation's economic crisis.

He shares with President Barack Obama an interest in ending global poverty. And from his seats on the Armed Services and Select Intelligence committees, he can further the leadership's and the administration's plans for ending the threat of terrorism.

Once a strong supporter of President George W. Bush's policy in Iraq, Smith later became one of Bush's greatest critics and joined the Democratic chorus demanding a deadline for U.S. troop withdrawal, even offering his own resolution to terminate the congressional authorization for the war.

He praised Obama's early 2009 plan to withdraw U.S. troops from Iraq by August 2010 and boosting forces in Afghanistan and Packistan to try to defeat al Qaeda. "President Obama's strategy puts America's focus back where it should be: on the threat from al Qaeda," Smith said in March 2009. "For far too long, we had no strategy and failed to devote the resources and personnel needed to defeat al Qaeda and deny it safe haven in Afghanistan and Pakistan."

As chairman of the Armed Services panel on terrorism and unconventional threats, he also launched hearings in the 111th Congress (2009-10) into the issue of terrorism, including how to bust up terrorism financing. "We've had a lot of successes since 9/11. Certainly we have disrupted a lot of financing, but we have not been as successful as we could be," he said in March 2009.

His concerns about national security sometimes lead him astray of his party, however. In the 110th Congress (2007-08), he was among the minority of Democrats to vote for a measure to reauthorize the Foreign Intelligence Surveillance Act, enhancing the administration's spying authority and essentially guaranteeing immunity for telecommunications companies that assisted in a warrantless surveillance program.

Though he no longer serves on the Foreign Affairs Committee, he still takes a strong interest in the United States' relationship with other countries. He led a delegation on a trip to Africa and the Middle East in early 2009, where he said he believes several countries present "growing national security concerns and troubling humanitarian crises." He said upon his return: "From Kenya to Yemen, poverty and governance problems fuel instability, violence and extremism. This is a region that the United States cannot afford to neglect, both for national security and humanitarian reasons."

He pushed through the House a 2007 bill to establish a comprehensive foreign aid policy and making it U.S. policy to work to reduce global poverty. Obama, then an Illinois senator, sponsored the Senate companion bill.

Smith's membership on Armed Services also allows him to look out for the interests of defense contractor Boeing Co. and his district's two military installations: Fort Lewis, the Army's largest training base on the West Coast, and McChord Air Force Base. Like other Washington state lawmakers, he vigorously protested the Air Force's early 2008 decision to award a new multibillion-dollar air tanker contract to a consortium of Northrop Grumman Corp. and the North American division of the European Aeronautic Defence & Space Co., the parent company of Airbus. Boeing was the loser in that competition, which was later reopened.

Smith sides with his fellow Democrats on social issues and, while he continues to fret about the nation's increasing deficit, he endorsed Obama's early economic agenda, including a $787 billion economic stimulus measure in February 2009. "I am deeply concerned about our growing deficit and have been for a long time, but the threats to our economy are real, and doing nothing is simply not an option," he said. He also voted in late 2008 for a $700 billion law to rescue the financial services industry, saying he was concerned about the continuing credit crisis.

A leader of the business-friendly New Democrats, he is an advocate of intellectual property protections. In 2008, Smith and Democrat Ron Kind of Wisconsin led a group of lawmakers urging the U.S. trade representative to take a tougher line against Thailand, which had been granting exceptions to patent rights of U.S. pharmaceutical companies for cancer and cardiovascular drugs. Other Democrats disagreed, urging U.S. officials to support steps that make low-cost medicines available to citizens of poor developing nations.

Smith is a free-trade advocate. In 2002 he split with his party leaders and backed legislation giving the president fast-track authority to negotiate trade agreements that Congress cannot amend. In the 108th Congress (2003-04), he voted for trade accords with Australia, Chile, Morocco and Singapore. In 2005, however, he voted against the Central America Free Trade Agreement, pleasing unions that had criticized his earlier pro-trade votes. By 2007 he returned to the pro-trade side, backing a Peru trade deal that a majority of House Democrats opposed.

Smith's father, who worked as a baggage handler at the Seattle-Tacoma International Airport, died of a heart attack when Smith was 19. The family went on welfare, and Smith worked his way through college loading trucks for the United Parcel Service. He was a Teamsters union member and still supports organized labor on most issues other than trade.

After he earned his law degree in 1990, he won a state Senate seat in an upset and, at 25, became the youngest state senator in the country. The victory was bittersweet, however. Just days before his election, his mother suffered a stroke and died. A few weeks later, he received a letter from his father's sister revealing she was actually his birth mother and that he was adopted.

By 1996, at age 31, Smith was well-known as a tireless campaigner who had made repeat visits to many of the 40,000 homes in his legislative district. He challenged GOP Rep. Randy Tate, a favorite of social conservatives, who had ridden into office on the big GOP wave of 1994. Smith triumphed by 3 percentage points and has won fairly comfortably since then.

But he never gets too comfortable in Washington, D.C.: He sleeps in his office in the Rayburn Building, bedding down in a storeroom.

KEY VOTES

2008

Yes   Delay consideration of Colombia free-trade agreement

No   Override Bush veto of federal farm and nutrition programs reauthorization bill

Yes   Overhaul surveillance laws and permit dismissal of suits against companies that conducted warrantless wiretapping

Yes   Grant mortgage relief to homeowners and funding for Fannie Mae and Freddie Mac

Yes   Approve initial $700 billion program to stabilize financial markets

Yes   Approve final $700 billion program to stabilize financial markets

Yes   Provide $14 billion in loans to automakers

2007

Yes   Increase minimum wage by $2.10 an hour

Yes   Approve $124.2 billion in emergency war spending and set goal for redeployment of troops from Iraq

No   Reject federal contraceptive assistance to international family planning groups

Yes   Override Bush veto of $23.2 billion water projects authorization bill

Yes   Implement Peru free-trade agreement

Yes   Approve energy policy overhaul with new fuel economy standards

No   Clear $473.5 billion omnibus spending bill, including $70 billion for military operations

CQ VOTE STUDIES

	PARTY UNITY		PRESIDENTIAL SUPPORT	
	SUPPORT	OPPOSE	SUPPORT	OPPOSE
2008	97%	3%	20%	80%
2007	95%	5%	7%	93%
2006	88%	12%	45%	55%
2005	90%	10%	24%	76%
2004	84%	16%	38%	62%

INTEREST GROUPS

	AFL-CIO	ADA	CCUS	ACU
2008	100%	85%	67%	4%
2007	100%	95%	65%	0%
2006	85%	75%	57%	21%
2005	87%	85%	50%	12%
2004	86%	90%	55%	17%

WASHINGTON 9

South Seattle suburbs; small part of Tacoma

Taking in numerous cities in the south Puget Sound region, the 9th runs south of Seattle along Interstate 5 before picking up small parts of Tacoma and Olympia, the state capital, en route to rural areas that offer spectacular views of Mount Rainier's 14,410-foot peak (in the 8th).

Just south of the Seattle city line, the 9th's northern end takes in predominately middle-class King County suburbs, where half of the district's population lives. This area includes most of Burien, SeaTac and Tukwila (shared with the 7th), and Renton (shared with the 8th).

SeaTac, named after the area's major cities, includes the region's major airport and is home to the corporate headquarters for Alaska Air Group. Key district employers include Boeing's commercial airplane production facility in Renton, where the 737 is built, and timber giant Weyerhaeuser, which has headquarters in Federal Way. But mass layoffs have cost thousands of district residents their jobs.

South of King, Pierce County's suburbs account for about 40 percent of the 9th's population. Pierce also includes the deep-water Port of Tacoma, which helped diversify the area's economy and attract companies looking for fast distribution opportunities. The portion of Thurston County in the 9th includes part of Olympia (shared with the 3rd) as well as the most rural portion of the district.

Overall, Democrats have gained an edge in the 9th — Barack Obama won 58 percent of the 9th's 2008 presidential vote, 5 percentage points more than John Kerry took in 2004. Blue-collar aviation and port workers give the party a base throughout the district, but Democrats fare better in the 9th's portions of King and Thurston than in Pierce.

MAJOR INDUSTRY
Aviation manufacturing, trade, technology

MILITARY BASES
Fort Lewis (Army), 27,186 military, 2,454 civilian; McChord Air Force Base, 3,647 military, 1,176 civilian (2007)

CITIES
Federal Way, 83,259; Kent (pt.), 43,904; Puyallup, 33,011

NOTABLE
The 17-day Western Washington Fair in Puyallup is the largest annual event in the state.

Gov. Joe Manchin III (D)

First elected: 2004
Length of term: 4 years
Term expires: 1/13
Salary: $95,000
Phone: (304) 558-2000

Residence: Fairmont
Born: August 24, 1947; Fairmont, W.Va.
Religion: Roman Catholic
Family: Wife, Gayle Manchin; three children
Education: West Virginia U., B.A. 1970 (business administration)
Career: Coal brokerage company owner; carpet store owner
Political highlights: W.Va. House, 1983-85; W.Va. Senate, 1987-97; sought Democratic nomination for governor, 1996; W.Va. secretary of state, 2001-05

Election results:

2008 GENERAL

Joe Manchin III (D)	492,697	69.8%
Russ Weeks (R)	181,612	25.7%
Jesse Johnson (MOUNT)	31,486	4.5%

Senate President Earl Ray Tomblin (D)

(no lieutenant governor)
Phone: (304) 855-7270

LEGISLATURE

General Assembly: January-March, limit of 60 days

Senate: 34 members, 4-year terms
2009 ratios: 26 D, 8 R; 32 men, 2 women
Salary: $20,000
Phone: (304) 357-7800

House: 100 members, 2-year terms
2009 ratios: 71 D, 29 R; 80 men, 20 women
Salary: $20,000
Phone: (304) 340-3200

TERM LIMITS

Governor: 2 consecutive terms
Senate: No
House: No

URBAN STATISTICS

CITY	POPULATION
Charleston	53,421
Huntington	51,475
Parkersburg	33,099
Wheeling	31,419

REGISTERED VOTERS

Democrat	56%
Republican	29%
Unaffiliated	14%
Others	1%

POPULATION

2008 population (est.)	1,814,468
2000 population	1,808,344
1990 population	1,793,477
Percent change (1990-2000)	+0.8%
Rank among states (2008)	37
Median age	38.9
Born in state	74.2%
Foreign born	1.1%
Violent crime rate	317/100,000
Poverty level	17.9%
Federal workers	21,235
Military	10,203

ELECTIONS

STATE ELECTION OFFICIAL
(304) 558-6000
DEMOCRATIC PARTY
(304) 342-8121
REPUBLICAN PARTY
(304) 768-0493

MISCELLANEOUS

Web: www.wv.gov
Capital: Charleston

U.S. CONGRESS

Senate: 2 Democrats
House: 2 Democrats, 1 Republican

2000 Census Statistics by District

DIST.	2008 VOTE FOR PRESIDENT OBAMA	MCCAIN	WHITE	BLACK	ASIAN	HISP	MEDIAN INCOME	WHITE COLLAR	BLUE COLLAR	SERVICE INDUSTRY	OVER 64	UNDER 18	COLLEGE EDUCATION	RURAL	SQ. MILES
1	42%	57%	96%	2%	1%	1%	$30,303	54%	29%	17%	16%	22%	16%	46%	6,286
2	44	55	94	4	1	1	$33,198	55	30	15	15	23	16	54	8,459
3	42	56	94	4	0	1	$25,630	53	30	18	16	22	12	62	9,332
STATE	43	56	95	3	1	1	$29,696	54	29	17	15	22	15	54	24,078
U.S.	53	46	69	12	4	13	$41,994	60	25	15	12	26	24	21	3,537,438

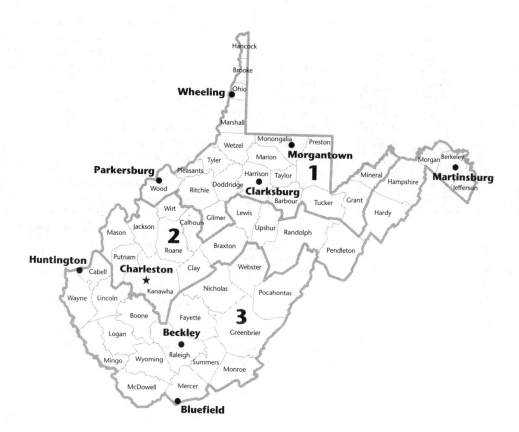

Sen. Robert C. Byrd (D)

Elected 1958; 9th term

The longest-serving senator in U.S. history, Byrd is spending his last years in Congress trying to prove he is more than an artifact. Because of his longevity, leadership roles, oratorical flourishes and reputation as the defender of Congress' constitutional prerogatives, he long ago took on the status of living legend. But being more than 90 years old has taken a toll — a wheelchair, trembling hands, reading from prepared scripts — and he was briefly hospitalized three times in 2008.

His situation led him to announce in November 2008 that he would step down as chairman of the Appropriations Committee, yielding the gavel to his 84-year-old friend Daniel K. Inouye of Hawaii. He had come under growing pressure to step down, though he remained as Senate president pro tempore, which places him third in line of succession to the presidency. "To everything there is a season and a time for every purpose under heaven," Byrd declared, turning to the Bible, a frequent oratorical source. Following Byrd's decision, then-Illinois Democratic Sen. Barack Obama, who had just won the presidential election, called Byrd "one of the greatest senators of all time."

But Byrd was anything but deferential to Obama in the subsequent early months of his administration. He voted against the president's $3.56 trillion budget for fiscal 2010 because it contained a shortcut known as "reconciliation" that could be used to fast-track policy proposals; as an author of the 1974 law that created the reconciliation process, he has been vocal in his opposition to using the process for matters unrelated to deficit reduction, arguing it was never intended to enact major policies.

When he announced his decision to step down on Appropriations, Byrd said he was confident Inouye and other Democrats would protect funding for his beloved West Virginia. Over his half-century of service, Byrd has funneled billions of dollars to his home state. After the Obama administration determined in May 2009 that funding for a $10 million road project in his state known as Corridor H was unnecessary, Byrd — who had once famously compared taking highway money from him to slapping his wife — was indignant. "While President Obama can submit his budget request to Congress, it is the Congress that has the power of the purse. And it is this senator's intention to ensure that funding for Corridor H stays in the purse," he said.

Byrd also joined some Democrats in calling for an investigation into President George W. Bush's conduct of the Iraq War and related matters, such as a procedure called "waterboarding" used on suspected terrorist detainees. No one was a sharper critic of the war; he voted against authorizing the conflict and tried in vain to persuade his colleagues it was folly. The day before the war began in 2003, Byrd told the Senate that Bush had chosen to channel the country's rage over the Sept. 11 terrorist attacks toward Iraqi dictator Saddam Hussein. "And villain he is," he said. "But he is the wrong villain. And this is the wrong war." Most Democrats came around to Byrd's view, and the party used its opposition to continuing the war to help take control of both chambers in the 2006 elections.

Byrd understands what goes into being a Senate leader; no one has ever been elected to more leadership posts. He has served as majority leader and minority leader, as majority whip and Democratic conference secretary. In 1971, he stunned outsiders when he ousted Edward M. Kennedy of Massachusetts as majority whip, the No. 2 post.

And those are not the only contests Byrd has won. In a political career that dates back to 1946, he has never lost an election. "There are four things

CAPITOL OFFICE
224-3954
byrd.senate.gov
311 Hart Bldg. 20510-4801; fax 228-0002

COMMITTEES
Appropriations
(Homeland Security - chairman)
Armed Services
Budget
Rules & Administration

RESIDENCE
Shepherdstown

BORN
Nov. 20, 1917; North Wilkesboro, N.C.

RELIGION
Baptist

FAMILY
Widowed; two children

EDUCATION
American U., J.D. 1963; Marshall U.,
B.A. 1994 (political science)

CAREER
Butcher

POLITICAL HIGHLIGHTS
W.Va. House, 1947-51; W.Va. Senate, 1951-53;
U.S. House, 1953-59

ELECTION RESULTS

2006 GENERAL

Robert C. Byrd (D)	296,276	64.4%
John R. Raese (R)	155,043	33.7%
Jesse Johnson (MOUNT)	8,565	1.9%

2006 PRIMARY

Robert C. Byrd (D)	159,154	85.7%
Billy Hendricks Jr. (D)	26,609	14.3%

PREVIOUS WINNING PERCENTAGES
2000 (78%); 1994 (69%); 1988 (65%); 1982 (69%);
1976 (100%); 1970 (78%); 1964 (68%); 1958 (59%);
1956 House Election (57%); 1954 House Election
(63%); 1952 House Election (56%)

people believe in in West Virginia," he has often said. "God Almighty; Sears, Roebuck; Carter's Little Liver Pills; and Robert C. Byrd."

First elected to the Senate in 1958 after serving six years in the House, Byrd on June 12, 2006, surpassed Republican Strom Thurmond of South Carolina as the longest-serving senator.

Byrd's political career has featured its share of mistakes, some quite spectacular. As a young man, he joined the Ku Klux Klan because, he said, of his alarm over communism. It was a decision he came to publicly regret. In 1964, he filibustered the landmark Civil Rights Act, at one point holding the floor with a 14-hour speech that is among the longest on record. He has also lamented that chapter of his career.

More important than his longevity is Byrd's pursuit of his self-appointed roles as guardian of the Senate's prerogatives and the grand master of its rules and procedures. He can be prickly and imperious, and is notoriously long-winded. But he literally wrote the book on the Senate — an authoritative four-volume history that began as a series of characteristically flowery speeches. "Sometimes I think Senate oratory is a lost art," he once said.

Byrd reveres the Constitution; he keeps a copy close at hand and can recite much of it from memory. Among his favorite passages is Article 1, Section 9, clause 7 — "No money shall be drawn from the Treasury, but in consequence of appropriations made by law."

In 1989, Byrd stepped down after 12 years as the Senate's top Democratic leader in order to claim the Appropriations Committee gavel. He vowed to steer $1 billion back home to West Virginia within five years, and he met that goal in less than three. Byrd served a second stint as chairman for 18 months starting in June 2001, when Democrats briefly regained control of the Senate, and took the gavel a third time in 2007.

Whether as chairman or as top minority member, he has ensured the stream of federal dollars to West Virginia continues unabated. The Charleston Gazette has called him a "one-man economic development program," and the Mountain State is dotted with highways, dams and other federal projects named for him. In 1997, his grateful state installed a 10-foot bronze statue of the senator in the state Capitol rotunda. Conservatives have assailed the special-project earmarks Byrd loves to insert for his state. The Senate voted in early 2007 to require disclosure of earmark sponsors, but that has not bothered Byrd, who happily takes credit for every dime he directs to his state.

Byrd was born Cornelius Calvin Sale Jr. When he was 1, his mother died and his father gave him to an aunt and uncle, Vlurma and Titus Byrd. The couple reared him in the hardscrabble coal country of southern West Virginia. Byrd graduated first in his high school class and married his high school sweetheart, Erma Ora. The very next day, he wrote in his 2005 autobiography, he handed her his wallet and said, "Here is the pocketbook. You keep it." Her death in March 2006 ended a partnership of almost 69 years. "She was God's greatest gift to me," Byrd told his Senate colleagues.

He worked as a gas station attendant, grocery store clerk, shipyard welder and butcher. It took him 12 years to save enough money to go to college. He learned to play the fiddle as a boy, and his talents helped him win a seat in the state legislature in 1946. Friends drove Byrd around the hills and hollows, where he brought the voters out by playing "Cripple Creek" and "Rye Whiskey." A picture of him as a boy, fiddle and bow in hand, is on the cover of his autobiography, "Child of the Appalachian Coalfields."

"I learned back in Wolf Creek Hollow that it was a sin to believe one was infallible," Byrd wrote in his most recent book. "Not even Jesus Christ himself claimed to be infallible. We humans are mortal beings, wracked with the knowledge that we are forever doomed to fall short in our aspirations, but also forever soaring with fresh hope that we can create ourselves anew."

KEY VOTES

2008

Yes Prohibit discrimination based on genetic information

Yes Reauthorize farm and nutrition programs for five years

? Limit debate on "cap and trade" system for greenhouse gas emissions

Yes Allow lawsuits against companies that participated in warrantless wiretapping

Yes Limit debate on a bill to block a scheduled cut in Medicare payments to doctors

Yes Grant mortgage relief to homeowners and funding for Fannie Mae and Freddie Mac

No Approve a nuclear cooperation agreement with India

Yes Approve final $700 billion program to stabilize financial markets

Yes Allow consideration of a $14 billion auto industry loan package

2007

Yes Increase minimum wage by $2.10 an hour

No Limit debate on a comprehensive immigration bill

Yes Overhaul congressional lobbying and ethics rules for members and their staffs

? Limit debate on considering a bill to add House seats for the District of Columbia and Utah

Yes Limit debate on restoring habeas corpus rights to detainees

Yes Mandate minimum breaks for troops between deployments to Iraq or Afghanistan

Yes Override Bush veto of $23.2 billion water projects authorization bill

No Confirm Michael B. Mukasey as attorney general

Yes Limit debate on an energy policy overhaul containing $21.8 billion in tax incentives and reduced oil and gas subsidies

CQ VOTE STUDIES

	PARTY UNITY		PRESIDENTIAL SUPPORT	
	SUPPORT	OPPOSE	SUPPORT	OPPOSE
2008	95%	5%	31%	69%
2007	86%	14%	35%	65%
2006	74%	26%	49%	51%
2005	84%	16%	44%	56%
2004	90%	10%	63%	37%
2003	93%	7%	54%	46%
2002	82%	18%	70%	30%
2001	86%	14%	71%	29%
2000	72%	28%	75%	25%
1999	80%	20%	70%	30%

INTEREST GROUPS

	AFL-CIO	ADA	CCUS	ACU
2008	100%	55%	57%	0%
2007	89%	80%	40%	8%
2006	80%	80%	25%	21%
2005	86%	95%	44%	20%
2004	100%	90%	38%	8%
2003	100%	95%	29%	30%
2002	85%	75%	40%	15%
2001	75%	85%	21%	40%
2000	63%	75%	40%	28%
1999	100%	80%	47%	20%

Sen. John D. Rockefeller IV (D)

Elected 1984; 5th term

CAPITOL OFFICE
224-6472
rockefeller.senate.gov
531 Hart Bldg. 20510-4802; fax 224-7665

COMMITTEES
Commerce, Science & Transportation - chairman
Finance
   (Health Care - chairman)
Veterans' Affairs
Select Intelligence
Joint Taxation

RESIDENCE
Charleston

BORN
June 18, 1937; Manhattan, N.Y.

RELIGION
Presbyterian

FAMILY
Wife, Sharon Percy; four children

EDUCATION
International Christian U. (Tokyo), attended
1957-60; Harvard U., A.B. 1961 (Asian languages
& history)

CAREER
College president; VISTA volunteer

POLITICAL HIGHLIGHTS
W.Va. House, 1967-69; W.Va. secretary
of state, 1969-73; Democratic nominee for
governor, 1972; governor, 1977-85

ELECTION RESULTS

2008 GENERAL

John D. Rockefeller IV (D)	447,560	63.7%
Jay Wolfe (R)	254,629	36.3%

2008 PRIMARY

John D. Rockefeller IV (D)	271,425	77.1%
Sheirl L. Fletcher (D)	51,073	14.5%
Billy Hendricks Jr. (D)	29,707	8.4%

PREVIOUS WINNING PERCENTAGES
2002 (63%); 1996 (77%); 1990 (68%); 1984 (52%)

Rockefeller is a faithful Democrat who can dispense partisan rhetoric when he considers it necessary, but he is more apt to rely on a sharp intellect, unpretentiousness and self-deprecating humor. He urges constituents to regard him as just plain "Jay," and his decisive re-election margins in the face of West Virginia's increasingly conservative tilt prove he has earned their trust.

Although Rockefeller's surname may be a symbol of American wealth, he represents one of the nation's poorest states and has devoted his career to helping those less fortunate than he is. Recalling his early experience as a young volunteer encountering extreme poverty in Appalachia, he said, "It just made me mad. I use that sustained outrage all the time ... There is so much injustice in the world. I felt it profoundly."

In the 111th Congress (2009-10), Rockefeller holds a position of greater influence than his senior West Virginia colleague, Democrat Robert C. Byrd. While Byrd relinquished his longtime perch atop the Appropriations Committee, Rockefeller became chairman of the Commerce, Science and Transportation Committee, making him a leading overseer of the corporate chiefs who have followed in the wake of his great-grandfather and namesake, the founder of Standard Oil Co.

Rockefeller can be protective of industry, particularly the coal and steel companies that are vital to his state. In West Virginia, he is called the "Senator of Steel." But he has a broader agenda. He wants to assist the Obama administration in bolstering the economy through rebuilding highways, bridges and other infrastructure while increasing oversight of railroads. His panel will have a role in rewriting the 2005 comprehensive surface transportation authorization bill as well as a measure to reauthorize NASA. Rockefeller also wants to revive a multi-year authorization of the Federal Aviation Administration that fell apart in the 110th Congress (2007-08).

Rockefeller promised that the Commerce panel will be a "very, very aggressive committee." He has given aides free rein to investigate anything that falls under its jurisdiction. Targets include the health insurance industry, transportation firms and companies that may have taken advantage of homeowners who lost their homes through foreclosure.

Rockefeller's most cherished cause remains health care. He is chairman of the Finance Subcommittee on Health Care, and favors chipping away at the problem of covering uninsured Americans to gradually build momentum for a larger overhaul. In the 110th, he worked with moderate GOP Sen. Olympia J. Snowe of Maine on legislation to expand the State Children's Health Insurance Program. President George W. Bush twice vetoed that legislation, but President Obama signed a version into law.

Rockefeller also joined some Democrats in endorsing a government-run insurance plan to compete with private insurers, despite warnings by Republicans, business groups and insurers that doing so would mean the end of employer-sponsored health insurance.

The increased emphasis on domestic issues is a switch for Rockefeller, who as the top Democrat on the Select Intelligence Committee spent the past several Congresses tangling with Republicans on vexing national security matters and the war in Iraq.

After the 2003 invasion of Iraq failed to produce any sign of the weapons of mass destruction that Bush had cited as a reason for war, the committee undertook an exhaustive review of prewar intelligence. In 2004, Rockefeller partnered with then-Chairman Pat Roberts, a Kansas Republican, to issue a scathing report on the CIA's information-gathering prior to the invasion. The détente did not last long. The two soon fought over a second phase of the probe examining the way top administration policy makers had used the prewar intelligence.

The investigation stalled, but after Democrats gained control of the Senate in the 2006 elections, Rockefeller vowed the committee would finish it. In June 2008, its second report concluded that the administration exaggerated available intelligence and ignored disagreements among spy agencies over Iraq's weapons programs and Saddam Hussein's links to al Qaeda. "It is my belief that the Bush administration was fixated on Iraq, and used the 9/11 attacks by al Qaeda as justification for overthrowing Saddam Hussein," he said. Some Republicans on the committee dissented.

Rockefeller also went head to head with GOP lawmakers on the National Security Agency's warrantless electronic surveillance of communications between Americans and terrorism suspects abroad. He eventually joined the Intelligence panel's top Republican, Christopher S. Bond of Missouri, in negotiating a deal with House leaders that Republicans said ended up being essentially what Bush wanted, drawing criticism from some Democrats.

Rockefeller also has served many years on Veterans' Affairs, where he was either chairman or ranking Democrat between 1993 and 2002. He has compiled a long list of legislative successes, including measures improving health care and expanding mortgage assistance for veterans.

Tall and bookish, Rockefeller has worked hard to gain the confidence of West Virginians from the day he arrived in 1964 as a 27-year-old volunteer in the Action for Appalachia Youth program of the Volunteers in Service to America. He was an unlikely transplant. He had been reared on Manhattan's Upper East Side, had been schooled at Exeter prep and Harvard University, and had just come from three years abroad studying Japanese. But Rockefeller loved the state. "What happened was, in a secular sense, I was reborn," he said. "Because everybody has to find what it is they do in life that has meaning to them."

He got involved in West Virginia politics, winning a seat in the state legislature, and he has lived in the state since. In a way, his wealth insulates him from suspicion back home. With no need to curry favor or solicit campaign cash in heavy doses, Rockefeller can devote all of his energy to the Senate.

In particular he considers the future of the domestic steel industry a "life or death" issue, and has waged knock-down fights with administrations of both parties when it has been threatened by low-cost imports. He also engages on policy affecting mining, another important local industry. After 12 miners died at West Virginia's Sago Mine in 2006, he and Byrd pushed a bill through that set stiff minimum penalties for negligent mine owners.

Rockefeller's ascent in West Virginia politics had some bumps. After serving in the state House and as secretary of state, he lost a race for governor in 1972. "I got clobbered; it was the best thing that ever happened to me," he recalled. He strengthened his ties to the state by taking a job as president of West Virginia Wesleyan College, then went on to win the governorship on his second try, in 1976, and serve two terms.

In the early 1980s, his popularity slid as the state's economy resisted his attempts to fulfill a campaign promise to fix it. He ran for the Senate in 1984, going after the seat of retiring Democrat Jennings Randolph. He won with just 52 percent of the vote despite spending $12 million against political neophyte John Raese. He has won more-easily since.

Given his wealth and experience, Rockefeller was sometimes mentioned as a potential presidential candidate; he mulled and declined a race in 1992. Asked about his interest in the 2004 campaign, Rockefeller told the Charleston Daily Mail in 2001, "I am sufficiently private to not want to do this."

KEY VOTES

2008
Yes Prohibit discrimination based on genetic information

Yes Reauthorize farm and nutrition programs for five years

Yes Limit debate on "cap and trade" system for greenhouse gas emissions

No Allow lawsuits against companies that participated in warrantless wiretapping

Yes Limit debate on a bill to block a scheduled cut in Medicare payments to doctors

Yes Grant mortgage relief to homeowners and funding for Fannie Mae and Freddie Mac

Yes Approve a nuclear cooperation agreement with India

Yes Approve final $700 billion program to stabilize financial markets

Yes Allow consideration of a $14 billion auto industry loan package

2007
Yes Increase minimum wage by $2.10 an hour

No Limit debate on a comprehensive immigration bill

Yes Overhaul congressional lobbying and ethics rules for members and their staffs

Yes Limit debate on considering a bill to add House seats for the District of Columbia and Utah

Yes Limit debate on restoring habeas corpus rights to detainees

Yes Mandate minimum breaks for troops between deployments to Iraq or Afghanistan

Yes Override Bush veto of $23.2 billion water projects authorization bill

No Confirm Michael B. Mukasey as attorney general

Yes Limit debate on an energy policy overhaul containing $21.8 billion in tax incentives and reduced oil and gas subsidies

CQ VOTE STUDIES

	PARTY UNITY		PRESIDENTIAL SUPPORT	
	SUPPORT	OPPOSE	SUPPORT	OPPOSE
2008	84%	16%	45%	55%
2007	91%	9%	35%	65%
2006	84%	16%	55%	45%
2005	93%	7%	40%	60%
2004	88%	12%	64%	36%
2003	96%	4%	50%	50%
2002	90%	10%	71%	29%
2001	97%	3%	66%	34%
2000	96%	4%	97%	3%
1999	94%	6%	89%	11%

INTEREST GROUPS

	AFL-CIO	ADA	CCUS	ACU
2008	100%	85%	63%	0%
2007	100%	85%	45%	8%
2006	100%	60%	83%	10%
2005	86%	100%	50%	4%
2004	100%	90%	41%	12%
2003	92%	100%	30%	15%
2002	100%	90%	45%	15%
2001	100%	100%	43%	12%
2000	75%	85%	60%	4%
1999	89%	100%	41%	4%

Rep. Alan B. Mollohan (D)

Elected 1982; 14th term

CAPITOL OFFICE
225-4172
www.house.gov/mollohan
2302 Rayburn Bldg. 20515-4801; fax 225-7564

COMMITTEES
Appropriations
(Commerce-Justice-Science - chairman)

RESIDENCE
Fairmont

BORN
May 14, 1943; Fairmont, W.Va.

RELIGION
Baptist

FAMILY
Wife, Barbara Mollohan; five children

EDUCATION
College of William & Mary, A.B. 1966
(political science); West Virginia U., J.D. 1970

MILITARY SERVICE
Army Reserve, 1970-83

CAREER
Lawyer

POLITICAL HIGHLIGHTS
No previous office

ELECTION RESULTS

2008 GENERAL

Alan B. Mollohan (D)	187,734	99.9%

2008 PRIMARY

Alan B. Mollohan (D)	unopposed

2006 GENERAL

Alan B. Mollohan (D)	100,939	64.3%
Chris Wakim (R)	55,963	35.6%

PREVIOUS WINNING PERCENTAGES
2004 (68%); 2002 (100%); 2000 (88%); 1998 (85%);
1996 (100%); 1994 (70%); 1992 (100%); 1990 (67%);
1988 (75%); 1986 (100%); 1984 (54%); 1982 (53%)

For more than a quarter-century, Mollohan has focused on diversifying West Virginia's economy, which was sputtering in the face of globalization's economic realities even when he first took office. Following the lead of the state's most revered politician, Sen. Robert C. Byrd, he adroitly secures federal dollars for projects ranging from prisons to industrial parks.

Mollohan tries to maintain a lower national profile than his Senate colleague, despite — and perhaps because of — publicity over allegations of ethical misconduct tied to his success at sending federal dollars home. But as chairman of the Commerce-Justice-Science Appropriations Subcommittee, he remains in a position to boost funding for climate change research, economic development programs and local law enforcement, and negotiate in the interest of his state.

Mollohan largely reflects the values of his state's residents. He tends to side with conservatives on some issues of environmental regulation, a stance that grows out of West Virginia's dependence on coal mining, steelmaking and other heavy industries. A member of the Interior-Environment Appropriations Subcommittee, he said he supports efforts to produce more renewable sources of energy but wants to be sure new regulations aren't biased against the carbon-based fuels important to his state. He also serves on the Homeland Security Appropriations Subcommittee.

He opposes free-trade agreements that he believes threaten his constituents' jobs; he voted against the 2005 Central America Free Trade Agreement. He also voted against President George W. Bush's tax cuts and authorizing the war in Iraq.

But the West Virginian maintains a more conservative stance on social issues than most Democrats. He strongly opposes abortion and chaired the House Pro-Life Caucus for many years. During the 110th Congress (2007-08), he supported language that would restrict the use of federal gun trace data, which put him at odds with gun control advocates.

Yet he has temporarily recused himself from all manners concerning the Justice Department's Office of the Attorney General, Criminal Division, Offices of the U.S. Attorneys or FBI in light of ongoing investigations connected to him, stemming back to a 2006 ethics complaint. A conservative watchdog group in Virginia, the National Legal and Policy Center, charged that Mollohan had directed numerous earmarks — funding set-asides for projects in member districts — to nonprofit organizations he set up in his district. The group also said he had failed to properly disclose various loans and assets, including interests in companies, on his financial reports over an eight-year period. In July 2006, he responded that he had unintentionally misstated more than a dozen transactions on his financial disclosure forms — discrepancies he called minor — and that the documents he released "also show that NLPC is dead wrong in implying that I have improperly benefited from my office."

Nevertheless, he resigned his seat from the ethics committee, and the Justice Department subpoenaed documents from the three West Virginia nonprofit organizations. Mollohan said he welcomed any review of his actions. The controversy led the watchdog group Citizens Against Government Waste to name Mollohan its "Porker of the Year" in 2006. But little more has surfaced since the issue first became public, and Mollohan maintains the allegations were unfounded from the start and that Justice has never contacted him about the matter. The allegations did not resonate with voters, who returned him to office in 2006 with 64 percent of the vote; Republicans didn't even bother to field an opponent in 2008.

Mollohan was also among several lawmakers who had received campaign donations from defense contractor MZM Inc. or its former owner, Mitchell Wade. Wade had pleaded guilty in 2006 to bribing former California Republican Rep. Randy "Duke" Cunningham, who resigned his seat in the wake of the scandal. Mollohan donated to charity the contributions he had received from MZM Inc. and Wade.

Mollohan also had been the focus of attention in 2004 when he became embroiled in a partisan dispute on the ethics panel. The dispute began when the House ethics committee admonished then-GOP Majority Leader Tom DeLay of Texas for three instances of inappropriate conduct. Mollohan was the committee's top-ranking Democrat at the time. Republican leaders retaliated, removing the committee's Republican chairman and two other GOP members and replacing them with party loyalists. The GOP also pushed new ethics rules through the House that Democrats said gutted the committee's powers. In response, Mollohan refused to allow the committee to organize or to function. GOP leaders eventually relented and rescinded the rules changes.

Mollohan worked as a lawyer in Washington before taking over the House seat of his father, Robert H. Mollohan, in 1983. Mollohan's father had first been elected to Congress when Alan was 9 years old. Mollohan remembers being on the House floor for his father's swearing-in ceremony. "I remember it like yesterday. I think it was kind of a biological imprinting on my brain. I said, 'This is what I want to do.' That's when I knew," he once told the Charleston Daily Mail. Mollohan struggled to claim his father's seat, as some voters questioned his career as a D.C.-based corporate attorney. But the elder Mollohan had close connections with party officials and with business and labor leaders; their support proved crucial to his son's narrow primary win in 1982. Mollohan won with just 53 percent of the vote that fall. In 1984, he was held to 54 percent. His general elections since have been easy.

Redistricting after the 1990 census threw him into a primary against colleague Harley O. Staggers Jr. While Staggers also had followed his father into Congress, he portrayed himself as the "outsider." Mollohan highlighted the importance of his seat on Appropriations. He won the 1992 primary by 24 percentage points and was unopposed in the general election.

Though mentioned as a possible successor to Byrd, Mollohan told the Virginia Informer — a newspaper at his alma mater, William & Mary — in March 2009 that he isn't interested. "I have seniority, and running for the Senate is something that I've never aspired to," he said.

KEY VOTES

2008
Yes Delay consideration of Colombia free-trade agreement
Yes Override Bush veto of federal farm and nutrition programs reauthorization bill
No   Overhaul surveillance laws and permit dismissal of suits against companies that conducted warrantless wiretapping
Yes Grant mortgage relief to homeowners and funding for Fannie Mae and Freddie Mac
Yes Approve initial $700 billion program to stabilize financial markets
Yes Approve final $700 billion program to stabilize financial markets
Yes Provide $14 billion in loans to automakers

2007
Yes Increase minimum wage by $2.10 an hour
Yes Approve $124.2 billion in emergency war spending and set goal for redeployment of troops from Iraq
Yes Reject federal contraceptive assistance to international family planning groups
Yes Override Bush veto of $23.2 billion water projects authorization bill
No   Implement Peru free-trade agreement
Yes Approve energy policy overhaul with new fuel economy standards
Yes Clear $473.5 billion omnibus spending bill, including $70 billion for military operations

CQ VOTE STUDIES

	PARTY UNITY		PRESIDENTIAL SUPPORT	
	SUPPORT	OPPOSE	SUPPORT	OPPOSE
2008	98%	2%	20%	80%
2007	94%	6%	11%	89%
2006	77%	23%	54%	46%
2005	78%	22%	36%	64%
2004	81%	19%	29%	71%

INTEREST GROUPS

	AFL-CIO	ADA	CCUS	ACU
2008	100%	85%	59%	4%
2007	96%	95%	55%	17%
2006	93%	60%	50%	46%
2005	93%	75%	56%	52%
2004	92%	65%	37%	24%

WEST VIRGINIA 1
North — Parkersburg, Wheeling, Morgantown

Located in the northernmost part of the state, the 1st has a large rural component but is the most urban of West Virginia's three districts. It contains six of the state's 10 largest cities and West Virginia University, the state's largest school. Wheeling, an industrial town and commercial center in the northern panhandle, and Parkersburg, a regional trade center in the west, are two of the main urban areas.

As factories shut down and coal mines began mechanizing operations in the 1980s, unemployment swept through the district and most counties experienced population loss. The 1st contains communities that again struggle with layoffs, as well as communities that are weathering economic downturns. Job losses in health care, chemicals and plastics manufacturing, and industries linked to the home construction sector have hurt Wheeling, Parkersburg and other areas along the Ohio border. To the east, West Virginia University drives Morgantown in Monongalia County, which has the state's lowest unemployment rate and a diversified economy hosting high-tech jobs and major interstate routes.

Waning coal and steel companies are still among the 1st's biggest employers, but a technology sector has developed. The FBI, Energy Department and NASA have facilities in the district, and Fairmont hosts the Institute for Scientific Research, a research and development facility.

The 1st has elected Democrats to Congress since 1969, but Republicans fare better in statewide and local elections, particularly in Doddridge County and areas to the southwest. Wheeling, in the Northern Panhandle, is often a target of national political campaigns because its media market reaches into neighboring Ohio and Pennsylvania. The 1st gave Republican John McCain 57 percent of the vote in the 2008 presidential election.

MAJOR INDUSTRY
Technology, coal, steel, chemicals

CITIES
Parkersburg, 33,099; Wheeling, 31,419; Morgantown, 26,809; Weirton, 20,411; Fairmont, 19,097; Clarksburg, 16,743

NOTABLE
The Wheeling Suspension Bridge, opened in 1849, is the oldest operating suspension bridge in the world; Confederate Gen. Thomas "Stonewall" Jackson was born in Clarksburg.

Rep. Shelley Moore Capito (R)

Elected 2000; 5th term

CAPITOL OFFICE
225-2711
capito.house.gov
2443 Rayburn Bldg. 20515-4802; fax 225-7856

COMMITTEES
Financial Services
Transportation & Infrastructure
Select Energy Independence & Global Warming

RESIDENCE
Charleston

BORN
Nov. 26, 1953; Glen Dale, W.Va.

RELIGION
Presbyterian

FAMILY
Husband, Charles L. Capito Jr.; three children

EDUCATION
Duke U., B.S. 1975 (zoology); U. of Virginia,
M.Ed. 1976 (counselor education)

CAREER
University system information center
director; college career counselor

POLITICAL HIGHLIGHTS
W.Va. House, 1997-2001

ELECTION RESULTS

2008 GENERAL

Shelley Moore Capito (R)	147,334	57.1%
Anne Barth (D)	110,819	42.9%

2008 PRIMARY

Shelley Moore Capito (R)	unopposed

2006 GENERAL

Shelley Moore Capito (R)	94,110	57.2%
Mike Callaghan (D)	70,470	42.8%

PREVIOUS WINNING PERCENTAGES
2004 (57%); 2002 (60%); 2000 (48%)

Capito is the lone woman and sole Republican in the state's congressional delegation. She has not only survived but thrived, thanks to a moderate voting record and devotion to her district's coal interests.

As a "blue" tide swept away GOP House members elsewhere in 2006 and 2008, she won re-election both times with 57 percent of the vote. After the first of those victories, she said her ability to "weather the storm ... certainly gives me a good feeling in terms of spreading my wings and going statewide." Yet as of early 2009, Capito (CAP-ih-toe) had refused all entreaties to take on either of West Virginia's veteran Democratic senators, preferring to wait them out.

Meanwhile, Capito has a full plate for the 111th Congress (2009-10). A member of the Financial Services Committee and the top Republican on its Housing and Community Opportunity Subcommittee, she will join in a sweeping overhaul of the nation's financial regulatory structure. While she supported a housing overhaul that became law in 2008, she opposed the subsequent $700 billion rescue package for the financial services industry, saying it lacked adequate protection for taxpayers.

Capito is married to an executive at Citigroup, one of the firms receiving money from the rescue. She told USA Today in February 2009 that she has "listened as much as a wife is going to listen to her husband" during their discussions about the crisis. "Policy-wise, the buck stops with me," she said.

Of more direct interest to West Virginia, Capito also serves on the Transportation and Infrastructure Committee, which will draft a multi-year surface transportation bill in the 111th. She is seeking additional funding for U.S. 35, an important route in the western part of her district that she says is plagued by floods and congestion. In the 109th Congress (2005-06), she won $87 million for the highway.

Capito sides with a majority of House Republicans on most tax, defense, regulatory and energy issues. But she split with President George W. Bush more often than the typical House Republican, backing him less than half the time on votes in the 110th Congress (2007-08) on which he staked out a position. She is a member of the moderate Republican Main Street Partnership, and she joins Democrats on a number of labor, trade and health care issues.

For example, Capito was one of just 17 Republicans to vote for five of the six bills in the Democrats' "first 100 hours" agenda at the beginning of the 110th Congress, including a measure to raise the minimum wage. Later in the 110th, she twice voted to override Bush's veto of legislation expanding the State Children's Health Insurance Program, which covers children from low-income families that do not qualify for Medicaid. The override efforts failed, but she supported a reworked version of the measure that President Obama signed into law in 2009.

Earlier in her House career, when Bush sought to overhaul Medicare by creating a prescription drug benefit for seniors, Capito was a close ally. Appointed vice chairwoman of a GOP prescription drug task force, Capito campaigned for the plan before its enactment in 2003.

But when Bush sought to overhaul Social Security in 2005, Capito balked. She called the administration's proposal to create individual investment accounts — which would partially privatize Social Security — a "tough sell."

She vigorously supports increased domestic energy production, especially from coal. "If it's good for coal mining, it's good for West Virginia," she said. Industry profits are not her only concern. In January 2006, a fire at the Sago Mine in Capito's district killed 12 miners. In response, she joined with

Democrats to push into law more-stringent mine safety rules. She was one of just seven House Republicans to vote for a follow-up bill in 2008.

She added a seat on a select committee on energy and global warming in 2009, enabling her to further represent the coal industry's interests.

As a member of the House Page Board, she was drawn into a controversy in 2006 after news reports that Florida GOP Rep. Mark Foley had sent sexually suggestive e-mails to male House pages. Capito said the House Republican leadership, including the GOP chairman of the Page Board, knew about Foley's behavior but had kept her in the dark. She worked on a measure that overhauled the Page Board, requiring equal party representation and more-frequent meetings. But in December 2007, she and Ginny Brown-Waite, a Florida Republican, resigned from the board, complaining that the page program still lacked supervision and that the board was not being adequately informed about instances of misconduct.

The daughter of former Gov. Arch A. Moore Jr., Capito was 2 when her father won his first House election. He was governor when she went to college. He served 12 years before his career ended when he pleaded guilty to federal charges that included taking illegal campaign contributions for his gubernatorial campaign. He served three years in prison and paid $750,000 to settle a lawsuit.

In 1972 Capito was a Cherry Blossom Princess for the annual festival in Washington, D.C. She missed being chosen queen by one notch on a spinning wheel. She said the experience "gave me nice exposure to Washington at that time." She was the first princess ever elected to Congress; Republican Sen. Lisa Murkowski of Alaska was the second.

Capito went to college planning to become a doctor, but she decided it would be tougher to balance motherhood with a career in medicine than with one in politics. She waited until her youngest child was 11 to enter politics, winning a seat in the state House of Delegates in 1996. There, she was recognized for her work on children's health issues.

Four years later, she ran for the 2nd District seat, which opened up when Democrat Bob Wise ran successfully for governor. She narrowly beat wealthy class action attorney Jim Humphreys, who plowed almost $7 million into the race. In their 2002 rematch, the most expensive House campaign that year, Capito prevailed by 20 percentage points. She has kept on winning since then, defeating Anne Barth, a veteran aide to Democratic Sen. Robert C. Byrd, in 2008. When she's not legislating or politicking, she remains an avid tennis player, a sport she pursued in college. She also runs, and she plays in the annual congressional softball game.

KEY VOTES

2008
No Delay consideration of Colombia free-trade agreement
Yes Override Bush veto of federal farm and nutrition programs reauthorization bill
Yes Overhaul surveillance laws and permit dismissal of suits against companies that conducted warrantless wiretapping
Yes Grant mortgage relief to homeowners and funding for Fannie Mae and Freddie Mac
No Approve initial $700 billion program to stabilize financial markets
No Approve final $700 billion program to stabilize financial markets
Yes Provide $14 billion in loans to automakers

2007
Yes Increase minimum wage by $2.10 an hour
No Approve $124.2 billion in emergency war spending and set goal for redeployment of troops from Iraq
Yes Reject federal contraceptive assistance to international family planning groups
Yes Override Bush veto of $23.2 billion water projects authorization bill
Yes Implement Peru free-trade agreement
Yes Approve energy policy overhaul with new fuel economy standards
Yes Clear $473.5 billion omnibus spending bill, including $70 billion for military operations

CQ VOTE STUDIES

| | PARTY UNITY | | PRESIDENTIAL SUPPORT | |
	SUPPORT	OPPOSE	SUPPORT	OPPOSE
2008	82%	18%	46%	54%
2007	79%	21%	49%	51%
2006	88%	12%	87%	13%
2005	90%	10%	75%	25%
2004	89%	11%	79%	21%

INTEREST GROUPS

	AFL-CIO	ADA	CCUS	ACU
2008	73%	60%	78%	48%
2007	67%	35%	90%	56%
2006	43%	15%	100%	80%
2005	38%	25%	85%	76%
2004	47%	30%	90%	72%

WEST VIRGINIA 2
Central – Charleston, Eastern Panhandle

The economically diverse 2nd stretches across the mountainous state from the Ohio border to the Eastern Panhandle at Harpers Ferry. It is home to poor, coal mining areas and isolated towns, as well as the more-prosperous capital city of Charleston and its commuters in the east.

Charleston, the district's pre-eminent city, is a center for chemical plants, state employees and retail shopping. Although chemical plants remain key employers, recent economic downturns have exacerbated decades of job loss in the sector. Telemarketing firms flocked to the state in the last decade, and call centers around the district still provide jobs despite competition from overseas locations and widespread layoffs. State government jobs offer stability in Kanawha County.

The mountainous regions north and east of Kanawha County remain dependent on coal, although production has dropped, particularly in Clay County. Federal rules and enforcement may continue to affect coal production. Putnam County takes in Buffalo, which is the site of a Toyota plant where precipitous declines in the domestic auto industry have

forced production slowdowns. Local sawmills shut down as the home construction sector waned and raw lumber exports dropped, and timber industry employers hope to diversify by marketing lumber byproducts and luring biomass production companies to the region.

Beginning in the 1990s, the district's eastern counties began filling with commuters from Washington, D.C., launching a sustained population growth. The district has the highest median income in the state, at just more than $33,000.

The 2nd was loyal to Democrats in U.S. House elections for 18 years before electing a Republican in 2000. Expanding GOP territories dot the district, and the 2nd now supports Republican presidential candidates. John McCain won 55 percent of the district's 2008 presidential vote.

MAJOR INDUSTRY
Chemicals, manufacturing, coal, lumber, telemarketing centers

CITIES
Charleston, 53,421; Martinsburg, 14,972; South Charleston, 13,390

NOTABLE
The Buffalo plant was Toyota's first automatic transmission production facility outside of Japan.

Rep. Nick J. Rahall II (D)

Elected 1976; 17th term

CAPITOL OFFICE
225-3452
www.rahall.house.gov
2307 Rayburn Bldg. 20515-4803; fax 225-9061

COMMITTEES
Natural Resources - chairman
Transportation & Infrastructure

RESIDENCE
Beckley

BORN
May 20, 1949; Beckley, W.Va.

RELIGION
Presbyterian

FAMILY
Wife, Melinda Rahall; three children

EDUCATION
Duke U., B.A. 1971 (political science);
George Washington U., attended 1972
(graduate studies)

CAREER
Broadcasting executive; travel agent;
congressional aide

POLITICAL HIGHLIGHTS
No previous office

ELECTION RESULTS

2008 GENERAL

Nick J. Rahall II (D)	133,522	66.9%
Marty Gearheart (R)	66,005	33.1%

2008 PRIMARY

Nick J. Rahall II (D)	unopposed

2006 GENERAL

Nick J. Rahall II (D)	92,413	69.4%
Kim Wolfe (R)	40,820	30.6%

PREVIOUS WINNING PERCENTAGES
2004 (65%); 2002 (70%); 2000 (91%); 1998 (87%);
1996 (100%); 1994 (64%); 1992 (66%); 1990 (52%);
1988 (61%); 1986 (71%); 1984 (67%); 1982 (81%);
1980 (77%); 1978 (100%); 1976 (46%)

Known as "Nicky Joe" back home in Beckley, Rahall built his reputation the West Virginia way: like his former boss and mentor, Sen. Robert C. Byrd, he brings home federal dollars and fiercely protects the interests of his rural coal-country district.

He has leveraged his more than 30 years in the House into the influential chairmanship of the Natural Resources Committee, a position increasingly in the spotlight as energy and fossil fuel dependence have become top political priorities. He is also a leader in transportation policy, as the No. 2 Democrat on the Transportation and Infrastructure Committee.

Rahall's sanguine, good-old-boy style serves him well, especially in his relationship with Speaker Nancy Pelosi of California. When record oil and gas prices drove energy to the top of the political agenda in the summer of 2008, Rahall (RAY-haul) helped Pelosi move legislation by acting as a go-between for the liberal Speaker and more-conservative Democrats, especially those in coal, oil and industrial states. His collegial style and reputation for protecting both the coal industry and the environment helped build support, and Democrats passed Rahall's bill to open new areas to drilling.

The Senate never moved on the measure, but a ban on drilling off the Pacific and Atlantic coasts was eventually allowed to lapse by way of a stopgap spending bill. While the change wasn't welcomed by environmentalists, Rahall has largely maintained their support by advocating for conservation and going after subsidies for oil drilling. He opposed a 2007 energy bill that increased fuel economy standards for new automobiles — one of just four House Democrats to do so — partly because the bill didn't include provisions to curtail the subsidies (or provisions promoting experimental clean-coal technology).

As a Democrat from a region of West Virginia particularly dependent on mining, he is in a more difficult position as the Obama administration and Democratic leaders move to push through sweeping climate change policy focused on a program to cap greenhouse gas emissions and set up a market-based trading program for emissions credits. He is reluctant to impose tough new burdens on the coal industry, but he's pledged his willingness to seek a middle ground to combat global warming. "It is incumbent on the industry to be at the table rather than to be on the menu," he said.

Rahall found more promise in Obama's fiscal 2010 budget proposal for the Interior Department that outlined proposals for billions of dollars in additional taxes on the oil and gas industry. He said the plan fit in nicely with his own priorities.

Rahall in early 2009 shepherded through the House and into law a large omnibus lands bill that had failed to move in previous years. The measure combined more than 150 separate bills to designate more than 2 million acres of new wilderness areas, expand national parks and designate new wild and scenic rivers. He also gained House passage of a bill he pushed with Interior-Environment Appropriations Chairman Norm Dicks of Washington, to create a separate wildfire account with the intent of freeing up funds for other priorities such as preventing forest fires. Termed the "Flame Fund," it would be used to set aside funds for emergency wildfire suppression.

It is on Transportation and Infrastructure that he most emulates Byrd, West Virginia's longtime senator and senior appropriator. Wielding his seniority on the panel, Rahall directs project funding to his home state. Rahall worked as an aide to Byrd in the 1970s. His office is filled with coal industry paraphernalia and pictures of the two men together. "Besides my own father, there's no man I'm closer to," said Rahall, who is often mentioned as a future contender for Byrd's Senate seat.

Rahall's ties to Byrd and close adherence to the mores of his district have helped him survive politically as a Democrat in an increasingly conservative part of the country. Though he has become more loyal to his party in recent years, he continues to deviate sharply from his fellow Democrats on social issues. In 2007, he voted to maintain a ban on federal funding for international organizations that perform abortions, and he opposed a ban on job discrimination based on sexual preference. A member of the National Rifle Association, he voted in 2008 to eliminate a restrictive District of Columbia handgun law.

Rahall also opposes most free-trade legislation, inspired by his interest in protecting jobs in his economically hard-pressed district. And in 2006, concerned about labor conditions in the West Virginia mines after accidents in the Sago and Aracoma mines killed 14 workers, Rahall supported passage of a mine safety law that raised fines for safety violations, required wireless communications equipment and tracking devices in all underground mines and established grants for new mine safety technology.

The grandson of Lebanese immigrants, Rahall is one of only a few outspoken critics of U.S. policy toward Israel in the House. He encourages closer ties with Arab countries and was one of only eight lawmakers who opposed a resolution expressing unconditional support for Israel in its 2006 conflict with the Lebanese Hezbollah group. He was one of five House members to vote against a January 2009 resolution supporting Israel in its attacks on Gaza.

Though Rahall grew up affluent, his family worked hard to get there. His paternal grandfather peddled goods in coal camps. Rahall's father ran a five-and-dime store and later a women's clothing shop, which eventually enabled him to invest in a chain of radio and television stations.

Rahall graduated from Duke University and, after working for Byrd, returned to his family's broadcasting business. In 1976 at age 27, he ran for the U.S. House, taking advantage of Democratic Rep. Ken Hechler's decision to run for governor. Rahall spent family money on a media campaign none of his foes could match and won the nomination with 37 percent of the vote. Hechler, who lost the governor's race, then mounted a write-in drive to keep his seat, but Rahall prevailed.

Rahall had some fits and starts — gambling debts in the mid-1980s, a guilty plea to an alcohol-related reckless driving charge in 1988, and bad publicity surrounding trips taken at lobbyists' expense in the 1990s. But he is the 13th-most-senior Democrat in the chamber and hasn't had a tough re-election race in many years.

KEY VOTES

2008

Yes Delay consideration of Colombia free-trade agreement

Yes Override Bush veto of federal farm and nutrition programs reauthorization bill

Yes Overhaul surveillance laws and permit dismissal of suits against companies that conducted warrantless wiretapping

Yes Grant mortgage relief to homeowners and funding for Fannie Mae and Freddie Mac

Yes Approve initial $700 billion program to stabilize financial markets

Yes Approve final $700 billion program to stabilize financial markets

No Provide $14 billion in loans to automakers

2007

Yes Increase minimum wage by $2.10 an hour

Yes Approve $124.2 billion in emergency war spending and set goal for redeployment of troops from Iraq

Yes Reject federal contraceptive assistance to international family planning groups

Yes Override Bush veto of $23.2 billion water projects authorization bill

No Implement Peru free-trade agreement

No Approve energy policy overhaul with new fuel economy standards

No Clear $473.5 billion omnibus spending bill, including $70 billion for military operations

CQ VOTE STUDIES

	PARTY UNITY		PRESIDENTIAL SUPPORT	
	SUPPORT	OPPOSE	SUPPORT	OPPOSE
2008	97%	3%	18%	82%
2007	94%	6%	9%	91%
2006	82%	18%	47%	53%
2005	87%	13%	33%	67%
2004	87%	13%	45%	55%

INTEREST GROUPS

	AFL-CIO	ADA	CCUS	ACU
2008	93%	85%	67%	8%
2007	96%	85%	60%	16%
2006	93%	65%	47%	48%
2005	93%	90%	56%	44%
2004	86%	75%	52%	28%

WEST VIRGINIA 3
South — Huntington, Beckley

The 3rd is a largely rural region that takes in the state's southern counties, sharing borders with Virginia, Kentucky and Ohio. Continuing layoffs and production slowdowns have hurt the region known as the "coal district," still home to the state's leading coal-producing counties.

The last 30 years have been hard on the 3rd District. As the coal industry mechanized production, the need for manpower was sharply reduced. Unemployment rates in counties along much of the border with Virginia are higher than the national average. These struggles have combined with persistent pockets of Appalachian poverty to give the district the third-lowest median income in the nation as of the last census, at slightly more than $25,600.

The 3rd attracts visitors with its ski resorts, whitewater rafting and The Greenbrier, a luxury resort in White Sulphur Springs that hosts golf tournaments, conferences and congressional party retreats. Raleigh County is home to Tamarack, a state and private cultural center featuring in-house artisans, live music, regional cuisine and retail shopping.

Huntington, by far the district's largest city and home to Marshall University, is cushioned by its location on the Ohio River, although local tobacco production and oil and steel company jobs are vulnerable.

Despite a continued Democratic lead in party registration in every county and an overall district-wide preference for Democrats elsewhere on the ballot, the 3rd has trended Republican at the presidential level. George W. Bush lost the 3rd by just 4 percentage points in 2000, but won the district in 2004 with 53 percent of the vote. In the 2008 presidential election, although Democrat Barack Obama's two highest percentages statewide were in Boone (54 percent) and McDowell (53 percent) counties, John McCain took 56 percent of the district's vote.

MAJOR INDUSTRY
Coal, wood products, tourism

CITIES
Huntington, 51,475; Beckley, 17,254; Bluefield, 11,451

NOTABLE
The New River Gorge Bridge, north of Fayetteville in Fayette County, is the second-longest steel-arch bridge in the world and the second-highest bridge in the United States; The Port of Huntington-Tristate is the largest inland shipping port in the United States.

WISCONSIN

Gov. James E. Doyle (D)

First elected: 2002
Length of term: 4 years
Term expires: 1/11
Salary: $137,094
Phone: (608) 266-1212

Residence: Madison
Born: Nov. 23, 1945;
Washington, D.C.
Religion: Roman Catholic
Family: Wife, Jessica Laird Doyle;
two children
Education: Stanford U., attended 1963-66;
U. of Wisconsin, B.A. 1967 (history); Harvard
U., J.D. 1972
Career: Lawyer; Peace Corps volunteer
Political highlights: Dane County district
attorney, 1977-82; Wis. attorney general,
1991-2003

Election results:
2006 GENERAL
James E. Doyle (D)	1,139,115	52.7%
Mark Green (R)	979,427	45.3%
Nelson Eisman (WG)	40,709	1.9%

Lt. Gov. Barbara Lawton (D)

First elected: 2002
Length of term: 4 years
Term expires: 1/11
Salary: $72,394
Phone: (608) 266-3516

LEGISLATURE

General Assembly: 10 floor periods
of varying lengths over a 2-year
session

Senate: 33 members, 4-year terms
2009 ratios: 18 D, 15 R; 26 men,
7 women
Salary: $49,943
Phone: (608) 266-2517

Assembly: 99 members, 2-year terms
2009 ratios: 52 D, 46 R, 1 I; 77 men,
22 women
Salary: $49,943
Phone: (608) 266-1501

TERM LIMITS

Governor: No
Senate: No
Assembly: No

URBAN STATISTICS

CITY	POPULATION
Milwaukee	596,974
Madison	208,054
Green Bay	102,313
Kenosha	90,352
Racine	81,855

REGISTERED VOTERS

Voters do not register by party.

POPULATION

2008 population (est.)	5,627,967
2000 population	5,363,675
1990 population	4,891,769
Percent change (1990-2000)	+9.6%
Rank among states (2008)	20

Median age	36
Born in state	73.4%
Foreign born	3.6%
Violent crime rate	237/100,000
Poverty level	8.7%
Federal workers	29,286
Military	18,937

ELECTIONS

STATE ELECTION OFFICIAL
(608) 266-8005
DEMOCRATIC PARTY
(608) 255-5172
REPUBLICAN PARTY
(608) 257-4765

MISCELLANEOUS

Web: www.wisconsin.gov
Capital: Madison

U.S. CONGRESS

Senate: 2 Democrats
House: 5 Democrats, 3 Republicans

2000 Census Statistics by District

DIST.	2008 VOTE FOR PRESIDENT OBAMA	MCCAIN	WHITE	BLACK	ASIAN	HISP	MEDIAN INCOME	WHITE COLLAR	BLUE COLLAR	SERVICE INDUSTRY	OVER 64	UNDER 18	COLLEGE EDUCATION	RURAL	SQ. MILES
1	51%	47%	87%	5%	1%	6%	$50,372	57%	30%	13%	12%	26%	22%	16%	1,680
2	69	30	89	4	2	3	$46,979	64	23	14	11	23	32	24	3,511
3	58	41	96	0	1	1	$40,006	53	31	16	13	25	20	57	13,565
4	75	24	50	33	3	11	$33,121	54	28	18	11	28	18	0	112
5	41	58	94	1	2	2	$58,594	68	22	10	14	25	35	15	1,273
6	50	49	94	1	1	2	$44,242	49	37	14	14	25	17	39	5,641
7	56	42	95	0	1	1	$39,026	52	34	15	15	25	17	58	18,787
8	53	45	92	1	1	2	$43,274	54	33	14	13	26	19	44	9,740
STATE	56	42	87	6	2	4	$43,791	57	29	14	13	26	22	32	54,310
U.S.	53	46	69	12	4	13	$41,994	60	25	15	12	26	24	21	3,537,438

Sen. Herb Kohl (D)

CAPITOL OFFICE
224-5653
kohl.senate.gov
330 Hart Bldg. 20510-4903; fax 224-9787

COMMITTEES
Appropriations
  (Agriculture - chairman)
Banking, Housing & Urban Affairs
Judiciary
  (Antitrust, Competition Policy & Consumer
  Rights - chairman)
Special Aging - chairman

RESIDENCE
Milwaukee

BORN
Feb. 7, 1935; Milwaukee, Wis.

RELIGION
Jewish

FAMILY
Single

EDUCATION
U. of Wisconsin, B.A. 1956; Harvard U.,
M.B.A. 1958

MILITARY SERVICE
Army Reserve, 1958-64

CAREER
Professional basketball team owner;
department and grocery store owner

POLITICAL HIGHLIGHTS
Wis. Democratic Party chairman, 1975-77

ELECTION RESULTS

2006 GENERAL
Herb Kohl (D)	1,439,214	67.3%
Robert Gerald Lorge (R)	630,299	29.5%
Rae Vogeler (WG)	42,434	2.0%
Ben J. Glatzel (I)	25,096	1.2%

2006 PRIMARY
Herb Kohl (D)	308,178	85.7%
Ben Masel (D)	51,245	14.2%

PREVIOUS WINNING PERCENTAGES
2000 (62%); 1994 (58%); 1988 (52%)

Elected 1988; 4th term

Kohl's background and personality offer a paradox in Washington politics. He has been a U.S. senator for more than two decades and is a multimillionaire who owns his hometown basketball team and once owned hundreds of department stores across the nation that still bear his name. Yet he is quiet, unassuming and professes no interest in the limelight.

"Everyone's different and being in front of cameras is not something that I seek, let alone enjoy," Kohl said. "I do it as a necessity." He finances his own campaigns — refusing to take money from special interests — and easily wins re-election. That, he said, allows him to vote the ways he sees best.

As chairman of the Agriculture Appropriations Subcommittee, Kohl presses for accountability and looks out for Wisconsin's economic mainstay — farming. In the 110th Congress (2007-08), he successfully included in the law to reauthorize farm programs a provision to permit interstate sales of state-inspected meat products, which he says will help smaller entrepreneurs expand their markets.

The law also includes an extension to the Milk Income Loss Contract program, which he helped create in 2002 to help dairy farmers pay for losses when the price of milk dips below a government target. At the Wisconsin State Fair, Kohl sells flavored milk at "Herb's Superb Milk House" for a quarter a glass.

Kohl in 2007 also pushed to boost funding for the Food and Drug Administration's food and drug safety enforcement efforts, eventually gaining $143 million more for the program than the previous fiscal year. And following a record-breaking recall of 143 million pounds of meat, his Appropriations panel held a February 2008 hearing with hopes of restoring consumer confidence. He also has pressed concerns about the treatment of cattle in slaughterhouses.

Kohl displayed his independence from corporate influence early in the 110th, taking on the pharmaceutical industry from two of his posts. As chairman of the Special Aging Committee, he held hearings to explore financial ties between the industry and doctors, and he is expected to keep calling for additional transparency in the way doctors interact with drug companies. Kohl and Republican Charles E. Grassley of Iowa in early 2009 introduced a bill to require pharmaceutical and medical device companies to disclose gifts and payments to physicians.

As chairman of Judiciary's Antitrust Competition Policy and Consumer Rights Subcommittee, he has pushed legislation to stop makers of brand-name drugs from making deals with would-be competitors to delay the market entry of cheaper generic versions of their products.

He also introduced a bill in 2009 to give Justice Department lawyers the ability to regulate railroad mergers and rate changes. The legislation sought to eliminate a longstanding exemption to antitrust laws allowing railroads to gain approval from the Surface Transportation Board for rail mergers, acquisitions and collective rate-making agreements. Kohl and other bill supporters said railroads have used the exemption to unfairly raise rates.

At the start of the 111th Congress (2009-10), Kohl picked up a seat on the Banking, Housing and Urban Affairs Committee. Though he supported the $700 billion financial sector rescue law of fall 2008, he immediately began to question the use of those funds to finance bank mergers. "We cannot countenance a situation in which the banking bailout leads to a highly concentrated industry with millions of consumers ... paying higher banking and credit card fees, higher loan rates, or lower interest rates on savings due to excessive consolidation," he said.

Kohl is typically a loyal party vote. Yet he considers himself a moderate who sees partisanship as the biggest obstacle to legislating, so at times he steps across the aisle to further his goals. Concerned about curbing the growing abuse of the elderly in long-term care facilities, he joined in 2007 with New Mexico Republican Pete V. Domenici (who retired in 2008) on a bill calling for a nationwide system of background checks to identify employee applicants with criminal histories.

In 2001, he was one of only a dozen Democrats to vote for President George W. Bush's $1.35 trillion tax cut in 2001 and one of 15 Democrats to back the initial version of the GOP's spending blueprint for the year. However, he opposed Bush's 2003 plan for $350 billion in tax cuts over 11 years.

He was one of 14 Democrats who backed a successful 2005 measure to shield gun manufacturers and dealers from liability for gun violence. Three years later, he was one of 17 Democrats to oppose a move to strike provisions from a spying bill providing retroactive immunity from civil liability to telecommunications firms that took part in Bush's warrantless surveillance program.

Kohl also has an interest in providing for education. He gave the University of Wisconsin, his alma mater, $25 million in 1995 to build a sports arena. And each year, his Herb Kohl Educational Foundation awards $1,000 grants to 100 teachers and their schools, and to high school seniors across Wisconsin. The fund had awarded more than $6.4 million as of August 2007.

Kohl doesn't worry about a personal legacy. "I hope when I'm finished people say, 'He was always there for us, he was always accessible,' " he said. He has routinely rejected pay raises since he entered the Senate.

Kohl's parents immigrated to the United States in the 1920s — his mother from Russia, his father from Poland. They opened a small food store in Milwaukee's south side, where Kohl worked after school and on weekends. One of his childhood friends (and later his college roommate) was Bud Selig, who went on to become a wealthy car dealer, owner of the Milwaukee Brewers baseball team and commissioner of Major League Baseball.

After earning a master's degree in business from Harvard, Kohl returned home and, with his two brothers, set about expanding the family grocery business into a department store chain in 1962 — the same year Sam Walton opened the first Wal-Mart Discount City store in Arkansas. Kohl and his brothers sold the chain in 1979.

Kohl decided in 1985 to buy the Milwaukee Bucks NBA franchise, primarily to keep the team in Milwaukee. He was a fan, and he saw the deal as "a combination of my own personal interest and public need." Kohl, the sole owner, purchased the team for $19 million; by 2008, Forbes magazine valued the team at $264 million. During Eric H. Holder Jr.'s confirmation hearing for attorney general in January 2009, Kohl drew laughter when he asked Holder if he could "promise us and the American people to defeat [Obama] as badly as you can" on the basketball court.

Kohl's first public involvement in politics came in 1975 when Democratic Gov. Patrick Lucey asked him to chair the state Democratic Party. He did the job for two years, despite his discomfort with some of its public aspects. In 1988, when Democrat William Proxmire stepped down after 31 years in the Senate, Democrats pressed an initially ambivalent Kohl to run. He had plenty of name recognition, and spent nearly $7.5 million (most of it his own money) on the campaign. Kohl's total outlay was double the previous state record.

He won a three-way Democratic primary with 47 percent of the vote and defeated GOP state Sen. Susan Engeleiter by 4 percentage points in the fall. Kohl has won with comfortable margins ever since. His slogan in every campaign has been the same — "Nobody's senator but yours."

KEY VOTES

2008

Yes Prohibit discrimination based on genetic information

Yes Reauthorize farm and nutrition programs for five years

Yes Limit debate on "cap and trade" system for greenhouse gas emissions

No Allow lawsuits against companies that participated in warrantless wiretapping

Yes Limit debate on a bill to block a scheduled cut in Medicare payments to doctors

Yes Grant mortgage relief to homeowners and funding for Fannie Mae and Freddie Mac

Yes Approve a nuclear cooperation agreement with India

Yes Approve final $700 billion program to stabilize financial markets

Yes Allow consideration of a $14 billion auto industry loan package

2007

Yes Increase minimum wage by $2.10 an hour

Yes Limit debate on a comprehensive immigration bill

Yes Overhaul congressional lobbying and ethics rules for members and their staffs

Yes Limit debate on considering a bill to add House seats for the District of Columbia and Utah

Yes Limit debate on restoring habeas corpus rights to detainees

Yes Mandate minimum breaks for troops between deployments to Iraq or Afghanistan

Yes Override Bush veto of $23.2 billion water projects authorization bill

No Confirm Michael B. Mukasey as attorney general

Yes Limit debate on an energy policy overhaul containing $21.8 billion in tax incentives and reduced oil and gas subsidies

CQ VOTE STUDIES

	PARTY UNITY		PRESIDENTIAL SUPPORT	
	SUPPORT	OPPOSE	SUPPORT	OPPOSE
2008	94%	6%	37%	63%
2007	96%	4%	38%	62%
2006	91%	9%	57%	43%
2005	89%	11%	45%	55%
2004	95%	5%	66%	34%
2003	94%	6%	50%	50%
2002	84%	16%	79%	21%
2001	89%	11%	69%	31%
2000	87%	13%	79%	21%
1999	90%	10%	91%	9%

INTEREST GROUPS

	AFL-CIO	ADA	CCUS	ACU
2008	100%	95%	63%	4%
2007	95%	95%	45%	0%
2006	87%	90%	50%	16%
2005	86%	100%	67%	13%
2004	92%	100%	44%	4%
2003	100%	95%	35%	25%
2002	92%	85%	60%	15%
2001	88%	90%	54%	16%
2000	63%	85%	60%	20%
1999	78%	100%	41%	4%

Sen. Russ Feingold (D)

CAPITOL OFFICE
224-5323
feingold.senate.gov
506 Hart Bldg. 20510-4904; fax 224-2725

COMMITTEES
Budget
Foreign Relations
  (African Affairs - chairman)
Judiciary
  (Constitution - chairman)
Select Intelligence

RESIDENCE
Middleton

BORN
March 2, 1953; Janesville, Wis.

RELIGION
Jewish

FAMILY
Divorced; two children

EDUCATION
U. of Wisconsin, B.A. 1975 (history & political science); Oxford U., B.A. 1977 (Rhodes scholar); Harvard U., J.D. 1979

CAREER
Lawyer

POLITICAL HIGHLIGHTS
Wis. Senate, 1983-93

ELECTION RESULTS

2004 GENERAL
Russ Feingold (D)	1,632,697	55.4%
Tim Michels (R)	1,301,183	44.1%

2004 PRIMARY
Russ Feingold (D)	unopposed

PREVIOUS WINNING PERCENTAGES
1998 (51%); 1992 (53%)

Elected 1992; 3rd term

Feingold has become a prolific legislator and maintained his reputation as a progressive gadfly, unafraid to shake up the customs of a governing body steeped in tradition — even if it causes discomfort among his colleagues. And with growing support for his reformist causes, he has seen his clout increase.

Feingold (FINE-gold) has pushed legislation on issues ranging from campaign finance reform to the redeployment of troops in Iraq to privacy protection for citizens. Holding the gavels of the Judiciary Committee's Constitution Subcommittee and the Foreign Relations panel on African Affairs, as well as seats on Budget and Select Intelligence, his legislative reach is wide.

As chairman of the Constitution Subcommittee, he urged President Obama in early 2009 to "restore the rule of law" that Feingold said had been lost during President George W. Bush's administration. Feingold had waged a fierce battle over the extension of the Bush White House's overhaul of the Foreign Intelligence Surveillance Act in 2008, seeking to curb the FISA courts' powers through a series of amendments, most of which were voted down. He joined Judiciary Chairman Patrick J. Leahy of Vermont in March 2009 in calling for a commission to review the Bush administration's alleged national security misdeeds.

Feingold is perhaps still best-known for a 2002 campaign finance overhaul that informally bears his name, along with that of Republican John McCain of Arizona. The two won enactment of the law after years of effort, overcoming strenuous objections of leaders of both parties. The Supreme Court subsequently upheld the law's major provisions, which set a number of new rules and banned "soft money," unregulated big-dollar donations to parties that were swamping political contests.

In 2007, Feingold was instrumental in pushing through an ethics and lobbying reform bill, helped along by the fallout from the scandal surrounding convicted lobbyist Jack Abramoff. The bill created more-stringent disclosure requirements for lobbying activities and outlawed certain ways lobbyists have sought to curry favor with lawmakers. He and McCain teamed with Missouri Democrat Claire McCaskill and Oklahoma Republican Tom Coburn in early 2009 on a bill to prevent unauthorized earmarks — member-added provisions for pet projects — in spending bills.

In 2002, Feingold was one of 21 Democrats to vote against authorizing Bush to use force in Iraq. Even fewer colleagues supported his subsequent calls for a deadline for withdrawing U.S. troops. But by April 2007, the political climate had changed, and Feingold's demand for a withdrawal timetable was included in a war funding bill that passed Congress. Bush vetoed the bill because of the deadline provision.

Feingold spoke favorably of Obama's decision in February 2009 to redeploy most troops out of Iraq by August 2010. But he was critical when the president announced he would increase the number of troops in Afghanistan; Feingold warned that a military escalation there without paying adequate attention to Pakistan could make the overall Middle East situation worse.

Feingold says his emphasis on government accountability is "all about being a Wisconsin progressive" based on the model of former Wisconsin Sen. Robert La Follette (1905-1925), a forefather of U.S. progressivism whose picture hangs in his office. "That was the political tradition that I was brought up in," Feingold said. "So making sure that the rules are fair, that government is transparent, and that those who are given the public trust in voting aren't benefiting in some private way in something that will twist their votes — that to me is the basis."

Feingold will take a public stand on issues even when the political winds are against him, such as when he cast the lone dissenting vote in the Senate on the anti-terrorism law known as the Patriot Act in 2001. He also was one of nine Democrats to vote in fall 2008 against a $700 billion law to rescue the financial services industry. But he backed Obama's $787 billion economic stimulus law and his $3.56 trillion budget blueprint for fiscal 2010. He said the economic crisis could encourage lawmakers to take more risks. "Most people around here don't like to rock the boat, but the boat's already been rocked," he said in March 2009.

His crusades have led some colleagues to view him as sanctimonious. When he was chairman of the Judiciary Committee in 2006, Pennsylvania Sen. Arlen Specter exploded when Feingold walked out of a 2006 meeting at which senators were voting on a proposed constitutional amendment to ban same-sex marriage. Feingold objected to holding the meeting in a room off the Senate chamber that was open to the press but not to the general public. "I do not need to be lectured by you," Specter snapped. "We have a quorum here and if you want to leave, good riddance." Feingold retorted, "I enjoyed your lecture, too. See ya, Mr. Chairman."

His stubbornness can tie up the Senate, a source of aggravation for his colleagues. In the final hours before Congress adjourned in 1999, Feingold and a handful of other Midwesterners fought provisions in a session-ending catchall spending measure that they claimed were unfair to home-state dairy interests. Feingold stalked the Senate floor with books of cheese recipes — among other potential filibuster reading materials — threatening a days-long delay in adjournment. He gave up only after overwhelmingly losing a test vote.

Feingold's paternal grandfather came from Russia, landing at Ellis Island and moving to Janesville in 1917, when the senator's father was 5 years old. Feingold says there were only 12 Jewish students in his high school, "and most of those were my relatives." His father, Leon, was an attorney; his mother, Sylvia, worked at a title company. Their family, he once told C-SPAN, regularly violated the old dinner-table dictum about avoiding discussions about religion and politics. "I'm a senator, and my little sister is the first woman rabbi in Wisconsin history," he said. "That's what happens when you talk about religion and politics at the table."

Elected to the state Senate in 1982, he entered the U.S. Senate primary a decade later. He scored a long-shot victory over better-known rivals and then knocked off incumbent GOP Sen. Bob Kasten. In the course of the campaign, he ran a series of humorous, offbeat television ads. One showed him using the back of his left hand as a map of his travels across Wisconsin, boasting he knew the state like the back of his hand.

Six years later, Feingold's tendency to buck the system nearly cost him his seat. He began his 1998 re-election campaign favored to beat GOP Rep. Mark W. Neumann. The McCain-Feingold restrictions were not yet law, but Feingold decided to play by the bill's rules anyway. He declined most forms of outside money and asked national Democrats not to run ads on his behalf paid for with the kind of money his bill would limit. Feingold barely held on, beating the well-financed Neumann by just 2 percentage points. In 2004, however, Feingold faced a weaker opponent in construction executive Tim Michels and won by 11 points.

Encouraged by liberal party activists, Feingold considered running for president in 2008, but announced in late 2006 that he would not join the crowded Democratic field, instead opting to begin building a movement of like-minded activists.

KEY VOTES

2008

Yes	Prohibit discrimination based on genetic information
Yes	Reauthorize farm and nutrition programs for five years
Yes	Limit debate on "cap and trade" system for greenhouse gas emissions
Yes	Allow lawsuits against companies that participated in warrantless wiretapping
Yes	Limit debate on a bill to block a scheduled cut in Medicare payments to doctors
Yes	Grant mortgage relief to homeowners and funding for Fannie Mae and Freddie Mac
No	Approve a nuclear cooperation agreement with India
No	Approve final $700 billion program to stabilize financial markets
Yes	Allow consideration of a $14 billion auto industry loan package

2007

Yes	Increase minimum wage by $2.10 an hour
Yes	Limit debate on a comprehensive immigration bill
Yes	Overhaul congressional lobbying and ethics rules for members and their staffs
Yes	Limit debate on considering a bill to add House seats for the District of Columbia and Utah
Yes	Limit debate on restoring habeas corpus rights to detainees
Yes	Mandate minimum breaks for troops between deployments to Iraq or Afghanistan
No	Override Bush veto of $23.2 billion water projects authorization bill
No	Confirm Michael B. Mukasey as attorney general
Yes	Limit debate on an energy policy overhaul containing $21.8 billion in tax incentives and reduced oil and gas subsidies

CQ VOTE STUDIES

	PARTY UNITY		PRESIDENTIAL SUPPORT	
	SUPPORT	OPPOSE	SUPPORT	OPPOSE
2008	93%	7%	30%	70%
2007	93%	7%	37%	63%
2006	92%	8%	47%	53%
2005	95%	5%	37%	63%
2004	95%	5%	66%	34%
2003	93%	7%	53%	47%
2002	84%	16%	67%	33%
2001	89%	11%	61%	39%
2000	92%	8%	90%	10%
1999	88%	12%	82%	18%

INTEREST GROUPS

	AFL-CIO	ADA	CCUS	ACU
2008	100%	100%	38%	24%
2007	100%	95%	18%	4%
2006	93%	100%	25%	8%
2005	86%	100%	17%	13%
2004	92%	100%	35%	8%
2003	100%	95%	26%	25%
2002	92%	90%	20%	5%
2001	94%	95%	29%	20%
2000	88%	100%	20%	8%
1999	100%	100%	24%	8%

Rep. Paul D. Ryan (R)

Elected 1998; 6th term

Articulate, telegenic and forward-thinking, Ryan has emerged as an important voice for Republicans on economic issues and as one of their most touted young stars. He is part of a group of "growth hawks" who consider it their job to drive home the conservative supply-side theory that lower taxes and less regulation help spur economic activity.

Ryan is undaunted by the inability of his ideas to gain traction in a government controlled by Democrats at both ends of Pennsylvania Avenue; he says he's thinking long term. "I would rather lose my election trying to do the right thing than win my election doing the small things," he said.

Ryan wasted no time in the 111th Congress (2009-10) launching an offensive against the ambitions of President Obama and the Democratic Congress. He was the keynote speaker at the Conservative Political Action Conference, the annual showcase for the political right. As the top Republican on the Budget Committee, he wrote the GOP alternative to Obama's fiscal 2010 plan, one that would have spent $4.8 trillion less than the Democrats' budget over 10 years and permanently extended the big 2001 and 2003 tax cuts. He penned opinion pieces for The Wall Street Journal and The New York Times and was all over the cable news shows.

"It's an obligation that if we don't think this administration is going in the right direction, if we're going to be offering criticism, we owe it to our employer, the American people, to show them a different pathway," he said.

Ryan says his philosophy of individualism and laissez faire capitalism was influenced most deeply by novelist Ayn Rand. He lists the late New York Rep. Jack F. Kemp, his former boss and the 1996 GOP vice presidential nominee, as his political role model. "Jack had a huge influence on me, his brand of inclusive conservatism, his pro-growth, happy-warrior style. That was infectious to me," Ryan told the Milwaukee Journal Sentinel in 2009.

Ryan was granted a seat on the Budget Committee at the start of his first term in 1999. He was 28, the youngest member of that year's freshman class. In the 110th Congress (2007-08), he became the committee's top Republican, vaulting over more-senior members to claim the spot. He also is a member of the powerful tax-writing Ways and Means Committee.

In May 2008 he introduced a proposal, "A Roadmap for America's Future," to rewrite portions of the tax code instead of, as Ryan says, "patching the holes." Among other things, it would establish universal health care through a refundable tax credit. The proposal drew attention from the Heritage Foundation and other conservative organizations, and Republican Sen. John McCain of Arizona used part of it in his presidential campaign plan.

Like other members of the conservative Republican Study Committee, Ryan is a sharp critic of earmarks, the spending provisions added by members to help their home districts. Ryan sponsored his party's fiscal 2009 budget proposal that advocated a one-year moratorium on earmarks. He steered a measure through the House in 2006 that would permit the president to target individual spending items in spending bills. The proposed cuts would have to go to Congress for an up-or-down vote, without amendment. Although that measure stalled in the Senate, Ryan reintroduced it in 2009 in concert with Wisconsin Democratic Sen. Russ Feingold.

In the 110th Congress, Ryan established the "Budget Boondoggle Award," a prize for lawmakers who wasted tax dollars. That was a takeoff from the "Golden Fleece Awards" given by late Wisconsin Democratic Sen. William Proxmire.

CAPITOL OFFICE
225-3031
www.house.gov/ryan
1113 Longworth Bldg. 20515-4901; fax 225-3393

COMMITTEES
Budget - ranking member
Ways & Means

RESIDENCE
Janesville

BORN
Jan. 29, 1970; Janesville, Wis.

RELIGION
Roman Catholic

FAMILY
Wife, Janna Ryan; three children

EDUCATION
Miami U. (Ohio), B.A. 1992 (political science & economics)

CAREER
Congressional aide; economic policy analyst

POLITICAL HIGHLIGHTS
No previous office

ELECTION RESULTS

2008 GENERAL
Paul D. Ryan (R)	231,009	64.0%
Marge Krupp (D)	125,268	34.7%
Joseph Kexel (LIBERT)	4,606	1.3%

2008 PRIMARY
Paul D. Ryan (R)	11,718	99.8%

2006 GENERAL
Paul D. Ryan (R)	161,320	62.6%
Jeffrey C. Thomas (D)	95,761	37.2%

PREVIOUS WINNING PERCENTAGES
2004 (65%); 2002 (67%); 2000 (67%); 1998 (57%)

While he is usually a dependable GOP vote, Ryan says on some issues he has a regional and "generational difference" with many in his party. He was one of 35 GOP lawmakers to support a 2007 bill to prohibit job discrimination based on sexual orientation. "Based on my personal friendships, I don't think every homosexual made a conscious decision to be a homosexual. I think many are just born with it," he said.

Ryan is an avid bow hunter who co-chairs the bipartisan Congressional Sportsmen's Caucus with Idaho Republican Sen. Michael D. Crapo, Nebraska Democratic Sen. Ben Nelson and Oklahoma Democratic Rep. Dan Boren.

The youngest of four children, Ryan was just 16 when his father died. His mother used Social Security survivor's benefits to help pay for his college education. He said that helped shape his personal and political beliefs. "I kind of grew up early," Ryan said. "It made me more of a self-starter and scrapper." He was a vocal proponent of President George W. Bush's plan to overhaul the Social Security system by allowing creation of private investment accounts. Ryan previously served on the Ways and Means subcommittee on Social Security, but is unlikely to find much support for his cause in the 111th.

Ryan said he "wasn't one of these guys who thought from second grade on that he wanted to run for Congress." But after college, he took a job as an aide to Wisconsin GOP Sen. Bob Kasten. His direct speaking style mirrors that of his two mentors, Kemp and William J. Bennett, former Republican Cabinet secretaries and co-founders of Empower America, a conservative think tank. Ryan also worked for Kansas Republican Sam Brownback in the House and Senate.

After five years in Washington, he returned to Wisconsin to join his family's earth-moving and construction business. When GOP Rep. Mark W. Neumann decided in late 1997 to run for the Senate, Ryan was persuaded to run for the open seat. His opponent in November was Democrat Lydia Spottswood, a former Kenosha City Council president who nearly beat Neumann in 1996. Ryan proved a superior campaigner — he earned the nickname "Robocandidate" — and won by more than 27,000 votes, a surprisingly large margin given that the previous three races in the district had been won by margins of 4,000 votes or fewer.

Ryan has since won each re-election with more than 62 percent of the vote. Bush offered to make him his budget director during his second term, an offer Ryan turned down. But he doesn't rule out a future Senate bid. He says he won't run against his friend Feingold. But if either Feingold or Democrat Herb Kohl should retire, "I'll take a hard look at it," Ryan told the Journal Sentinel.

KEY VOTES

2008

No Delay consideration of Colombia free-trade agreement

No Override Bush veto of federal farm and nutrition programs reauthorization bill

Yes Overhaul surveillance laws and permit dismissal of suits against companies that conducted warrantless wiretapping

No Grant mortgage relief to homeowners and funding for Fannie Mae and Freddie Mac

Yes Approve initial $700 billion program to stabilize financial markets

Yes Approve final $700 billion program to stabilize financial markets

Yes Provide $14 billion in loans to automakers

2007

No Increase minimum wage by $2.10 an hour

No Approve $124.2 billion in emergency war spending and set goal for redeployment of troops from Iraq

Yes Reject federal contraceptive assistance to international family planning groups

Yes Override Bush veto of $23.2 billion water projects authorization bill

Yes Implement Peru free-trade agreement

No Approve energy policy overhaul with new fuel economy standards

Yes Clear $473.5 billion omnibus spending bill, including $70 billion for military operations

CQ VOTE STUDIES

	PARTY UNITY		PRESIDENTIAL SUPPORT	
	SUPPORT	OPPOSE	SUPPORT	OPPOSE
2008	97%	3%	86%	14%
2007	96%	4%	80%	20%
2006	94%	6%	93%	7%
2005	94%	6%	80%	20%
2004	94%	6%	79%	21%

INTEREST GROUPS

	AFL-CIO	ADA	CCUS	ACU
2008	20%	15%	83%	84%
2007	26%	15%	75%	96%
2006	14%	0%	100%	92%
2005	13%	0%	89%	96%
2004	20%	20%	90%	92%

WISCONSIN 1

Southeast — Kenosha, Racine

From the wealthy Milwaukee suburbs on the coast of Lake Michigan to the center of Rock County in central Wisconsin, the 1st blends rural communities with some of the state's largest industrial areas. The district's two largest cities, Racine and Kenosha, are sandwiched between Milwaukee and Chicago along the lake and Interstate 94.

Kenosha and Walworth counties, two major manufacturing areas, have experienced faster population growth than the state's average. Much of this expansion is due to new residents attracted by lower housing prices and cheaper living and who commute to Milwaukee or Chicago, both less than an hour's drive away.

The 1st has been hit hard by manufacturing losses and recent economic downturns. Kenosha, Racine and Rock counties all have struggled with rising unemployment rates, and key regional employer Abbott Laboratories, an Illinois-based pharmaceutical company, has faced extensive layoffs. On the other side of the district, the General Motors plant in Janesville, a major employer in the area, will close in 2009. But SC Johnson and

Son, the consumer products manufacturer, continues to have a major presence in the area.

Resorts catering to wealthy visitors from Chicago ring Lake Geneva and Lake Delavan in Walworth County and have given the area a bit of an economic boost. But the future of Kenosha's Dairyland Greyhound Park remains uncertain as local Indian tribes negotiate gaming agreements.

The district is politically moderate and about evenly split between the two parties. Of the six counties wholly or partly in the 1st, two are strongly Democratic (Kenosha and Rock), two are strongly Republican (Walworth and Waukesha) and two tend to be competitive (Racine and Milwaukee). The district's even split was evident in the 2008 presidential election: Democrat Barack Obama carried 51 percent of the 1st's vote.

MAJOR INDUSTRY
Agriculture, manufacturing

CITIES
Kenosha, 90,352; Racine, 81,855; Janesville (pt.), 59,474; Greenfield, 35,476

NOTABLE
Racine hosts the Salmon-A-Rama annual fishing contest; C. Latham Sholes invented the typewriter in Kenosha.

Rep. Tammy Baldwin (D)

Elected 1998; 6th term

Baldwin is a self-styled "pragmatic progressive" who is one of the most liberal members of Congress, but who still reaches across the aisle. After eight years of criticizing President George W. Bush, she now has a president in Barack Obama whose politics are more to her liking, but whom she remains likely to challenge from the left.

Baldwin came to Congress with the overriding objective of providing universal health coverage for all Americans, followed closely by equal rights, justice and protections for all. She is well-positioned to advance her causes as a member of the Energy and Commerce Committee, which has jurisdiction over health legislation, and as a member of the Judiciary Committee.

Baldwin is the first woman elected to Congress from Wisconsin and the first openly gay woman to win a seat in either chamber. She exchanged marriage vows in 1998 with Lauren Azar, a lawyer, though same-sex unions are not legal in Wisconsin. With Democrat Barney Frank of Massachusetts, she founded the Lesbian, Gay, Bisexual, and Transgender Equality Caucus in 2008.

She concedes her preferred approach to health reform, a government-run single-payer system like Canada's, is unlikely to get through Congress. Still, she says, "I think we'll have a new opportunity in the 111th Congress to either make it the whole distance or at least enact bold and decisive reforms that will get us a long way towards universal health care."

As a Judiciary panel member, Baldwin in the 110th Congress (2007-08) was a cosponsor and vocal advocate of legislation expanding hate crime laws to cover crimes motivated by prejudice based on sexual orientation. The House passed the bill in 2007, but it failed to win enactment. Baldwin and other supporters were back again in the 111th Congress (2009-10), winning swift House passage of their new legislation. "Americans across the country, young and old alike, must hear Congress clearly affirm that hate-based violence targeting gays, lesbians, transgender individuals, women, and people with disabilities will not be tolerated," she told the House. To Republican critics who argued the bill could limit free speech or free religion, Baldwin said, "This is not a hate thought bill. This is not a hate speech bill. This is a hate crimes bill."

Baldwin also renewed in the 111th her push for another major gay rights measure. In 2007, she joined Frank and Republicans Deborah Pryce of Ohio and Christopher Shays of Connecticut in sponsoring legislation to outlaw employment discrimination based on sexual orientation or gender identity. The House passed the bill, but only after removing workplace protections for transgender individuals. The Senate did not call up the measure. Baldwin said she was pleased the bill had passed the House for the first time ever, but unhappy transgender individuals were "carved out."

Baldwin fared better with other legislative initiatives in the 110th Congress. In 2007, Bush signed into law two health bills she had sponsored. The first, which she considers one of her most significant achievements in Congress, reauthorized and expanded a screening program for breast and cervical cancer. The second expanded benefits for veterans with impaired vision. Another Baldwin-sponsored bill, to boost paralysis research, passed the House in 2007 and was rolled into a broader bill in the Senate in 2008.

Baldwin also takes pride in several provisions she helped craft during committee action on the 2007 energy law that raised vehicle fuel efficiency standards and promoted energy-efficient appliances. One required consumer appliances to have a standby mode using no more than 1 watt of electricity, while another promoted new technology to use excess steam from industrial

CAPITOL OFFICE
225-2906
tammybaldwin.house.gov
2446 Rayburn Bldg. 20515-4902; fax 225-6942

COMMITTEES
Energy & Commerce
Judiciary

RESIDENCE
Madison

BORN
Feb. 11, 1962; Madison, Wis.

RELIGION
Unspecified

FAMILY
Partner, Lauren Azar

EDUCATION
Smith College, A.B. 1984 (math & government);
U. of Wisconsin, J.D. 1989

CAREER
Lawyer

POLITICAL HIGHLIGHTS
Madison City Council, 1986; Dane County
Board of Supervisors, 1986-94; Wis. Assembly,
1993-99

ELECTION RESULTS

2008 GENERAL

Tammy Baldwin (D)	277,914	69.3%
Peter Theron (R)	122,513	30.6%

2008 PRIMARY

Tammy Baldwin (D)	18,414	99.3%

2006 GENERAL

Tammy Baldwin (D)	191,414	62.8%
Dave Magnum (R)	113,015	37.1%

PREVIOUS WINNING PERCENTAGES
2004 (63%); 2002 (66%); 2000 (51%); 1998 (52%)

processes for energy purposes. In 2000, she and her partner bought a historic home in Madison and set about updating it with energy-efficient appliances.

A member of the Progressive Caucus, Baldwin was one of six House members who cosponsored a 2008 resolution by Democrat Dennis J. Kucinich of Ohio calling for an impeachment inquiry of Bush. She said Bush should be held accountable for abuses of power by members of his administration.

But she also seeks common ground with Republicans. She has worked with Georgia Republican Tom Price — currently chairman of the Republican Study Committee, the House's most conservative faction — on legislation to allow states to use federal grants in a variety of ways to help provide health insurance. She and Iowa Republican Tom Latham also teamed on a measure aimed at reducing a nationwide nursing shortage.

Baldwin was a bipartisan hit in 1999, her first year in office, with a speech at the annual Congressional Dinner of the Washington Press Club. "I'm one of the first elected officials who represents a group historically discriminated against," Baldwin said. "A group that has been kept out of jobs, harassed at the workplace. A group that's been unfairly stereotyped and made the object of rude and base humor. Of course, I'm talking about blondes … especially blondes named Tammy."

Born and reared in Madison, home to the University of Wisconsin and a hotbed of liberalism, Baldwin reflects the progressive views of her constituency and the passion for politics of her upbringing. Her maternal grandparents raised her while her mother attended the University of Wisconsin and participated in the civil rights and anti-war demonstrations of the 1960s. Her grandfather, a biochemist, and grandmother, who worked at the costume lab at the university theater, lived through two world wars, the Depression and the attainment of women's suffrage. "Those experiences also informed their style of parenting — how important it was to be self-sufficient, to get a good education and to give back to one's community," Baldwin recalled.

Baldwin got into politics while she was still in law school. In 1986, at age 24, she won election as a Dane County supervisor. She says she had been inspired in part by the Democrats' nomination two years earlier of Geraldine Ferraro for vice president. After four terms as a county supervisor, in 1992 she was elected to the Wisconsin Assembly, where she served six years.

With her own impressive fundraising and help from EMILY's List, Baldwin edged out two well-known opponents in the 1998 primary for the House. She then beat former state Insurance Commissioner Josephine Musser by 6 percentage points. In 2000, she eked out a 3-point victory over Republican John Sharpless, a history professor. She has won handily in all subsequent elections.

KEY VOTES

2008

Yes   Delay consideration of Colombia free-trade agreement

Yes   Override Bush veto of federal farm and nutrition programs reauthorization bill

No   Overhaul surveillance laws and permit dismissal of suits against companies that conducted warrantless wiretapping

Yes   Grant mortgage relief to homeowners and funding for Fannie Mae and Freddie Mac

Yes   Approve initial $700 billion program to stabilize financial markets

Yes   Approve final $700 billion program to stabilize financial markets

Yes   Provide $14 billion in loans to automakers

2007

Yes   Increase minimum wage by $2.10 an hour

Yes   Approve $124.2 billion in emergency war spending and set goal for redeployment of troops from Iraq

No   Reject federal contraceptive assistance to international family planning groups

Yes   Override Bush veto of $23.2 billion water projects authorization bill

No   Implement Peru free-trade agreement

Yes   Approve energy policy overhaul with new fuel economy standards

No   Clear $473.5 billion omnibus spending bill, including $70 billion for military operations

CQ VOTE STUDIES

	PARTY UNITY		PRESIDENTIAL SUPPORT	
	SUPPORT	OPPOSE	SUPPORT	OPPOSE
2008	99%	1%	14%	86%
2007	99%	1%	3%	97%
2006	99%	1%	13%	87%
2005	99%	1%	13%	87%
2004	98%	2%	32%	68%

INTEREST GROUPS

	AFL-CIO	ADA	CCUS	ACU
2008	100%	100%	56%	0%
2007	96%	100%	45%	0%
2006	100%	95%	20%	0%
2005	93%	100%	30%	0%
2004	100%	100%	29%	4%

WISCONSIN 2

South – Madison

Once described by former GOP Gov. Lee Dreyfus as "78 square miles surrounded by reality," Madison has long been Wisconsin's liberal centerpiece. Madison, Wisconsin's capital city, is the 2nd's political heart, although growing numbers of socially liberal, fiscally conservative young professionals in the suburbs may have a future impact.

Located on an isthmus between two lakes — Mendota and Menona — Madison is known as one of the nation's most livable cities, diminished only by its biting winters. The state university system's flagship campus has a major influence on the city, and an educated, white-collar population fuels the local economy. University graduates, resources and expertise have boosted associated industries, such as biotech. The Madison area's relatively stable economy based around the university and government jobs mainly have insulated the district from drastic home foreclosure and unemployment rate spikes. Other large employment bases include light manufacturing firms.

Outside of Madison, the 2nd resembles most of the rest of Wisconsin.

Strong milk and grain production make the 2nd the state's top agricultural region. Tourists are lured to the district by New Glarus, touted as America's "Little Switzerland," in Green County in the district's southwest. The Wisconsin Dells — ancient natural limestone formations along the Wisconsin River — attract visitors to the district's north, which also features many commercial waterparks.

The 2nd generally is divided politically into Madison vs. everywhere else, with residents of the university- and government-dominated capital standing in contrast to social conservatives and residents of area farming communities. Overall, only the Milwaukee-based 4th District is more of a Democratic bastion than the 2nd. In the 2008 presidential election, Dane County gave Barack Obama 73 percent, his second-highest percentage statewide, as he took 69 percent of the 2nd as a whole.

MAJOR INDUSTRY
Higher education, agriculture, government

CITIES
Madison, 208,054; Beloit, 35,775; Fitchburg, 20,501; Sun Prairie, 20,369

NOTABLE
The Ringling Brothers started their circus — which later merged with Barnum and Bailey's "Greatest Show on Earth" — in Baraboo in 1884.

Rep. Ron Kind (D)

CAPITOL OFFICE
225-5506
www.house.gov/kind
1406 Longworth Bldg. 20515-4903; fax 225-5739

COMMITTEES
Natural Resources
Ways & Means

RESIDENCE
La Crosse

BORN
March 16, 1963; La Crosse, Wis.

RELIGION
Lutheran

FAMILY
Wife, Tawni Kind; two children

EDUCATION
Harvard U., A.B. 1985; London School of
Economics, M.A. 1986; U. of Minnesota, J.D. 1990

CAREER
Lawyer; county prosecutor

POLITICAL HIGHLIGHTS
No previous office

ELECTION RESULTS

2008 GENERAL

Ron Kind (D)	225,208	63.2%
Paul Stark (R)	122,760	34.4%
Kevin Barrett (LIBERT)	8,236	2.3%

2008 PRIMARY

Ron Kind (D)	unopposed

2006 GENERAL

Ron Kind (D)	163,322	64.8%
Paul R. Nelson (R)	88,523	35.1%

PREVIOUS WINNING PERCENTAGES
2004 (56%); 2002 (63%); 2000 (64%); 1998 (71%);
1996 (52%)

Elected 1996; 7th term

Kind, who represents Wisconsin's dairy country and boasts about how much he enjoys hunting, was the sort of rural Democrat who had become something of an endangered species when he first was elected in 1996. But as the Democrats have broadened their majority, he's become less of an outlier in his caucus.

Kind continues to emphasize frugality — both in his office and the federal budget — in the good-government tradition of former Democratic Wisconsin Sen. William Proxmire, for whom he once interned. He donates his congressional pay raises to charity, and returns about 10 percent of his office allotment to the federal Treasury each year. "Fiscal responsibility starts at home, the things you control. And for me, that's this office," he said.

In 2008, he swore off earmarks for the first time, deploring the funding set-asides for special projects as the equivalent of handing out billions in no-bid contracts each year. He introduced a bill to establish an independent commission to study the earmarking process in both Congress and the executive branch. He won notice in 2009 for his anti-earmark stand from the conservative Club for Growth.

And like Proxmire, Kind isn't afraid to embrace unpopular causes. During consideration of the massive reauthorization of agriculture and nutrition programs in the 110th Congress (2007-08), Kind joined forces with Wisconsin Republican Paul D. Ryan to try to cut sacrosanct farm subsidies and redirect the savings towards conservation, nutrition, rural development and deficit reduction. The effort failed, but Kind was unapologetic. In 2009, he praised President Obama for proposing to go after the same subsidies he had tried unsuccessfully to curtail.

As the Ways and Means Committee debated Obama's tax proposals in 2009, Kind sounded a cautionary note about tilting too far toward wage earners with too little income to pay federal income taxes. "I'm not a big subscriber to social engineering through the tax code," he said.

One area where Kind would like to see more federal spending, not less, is on public education. Kind, who worked his way through Harvard as a janitor on campus, calls education "the great equalizer." But he lost some of his ability to influence education policy when he gave up his seats on the Education and Labor and Budget committees in the 110th for a coveted spot on the Ways and Means panel. Earlier in his Capitol Hill career, his amendments to boost professional development for teachers and to help recruit teachers and principals were included in the 2001 No Child Left Behind Act. But he continues to advocate for schools to provide more physical fitness instruction.

Kind was allowed to retain his seat on the Natural Resources Committee, important for his rural western Wisconsin district as well as for Kind personally. Raised in La Crosse on the banks of the Mississippi river, Kind grew up hunting, fishing, camping and biking. "I am a river rat," he says. The outdoor life fostered "a greater appreciation of the importance of preserving and protecting our resources." Kind has taught his two young sons to hunt and fish and proudly shows off to visitors of his Capitol Hill office a picture of a buck they killed while bow hunting.

Only the third Democrat to represent his western, dairy-producing district in the past century, Kind is generally cooperative in his dealings with Republicans. He is one of four vice chairmen of the moderate New Democrat Coalition. But Kind sided with the Democratic majority more often in the 110th than in the past — 95 percent of the time on votes pitting the parties against each other. He typically had scored below 90 percent.

Perhaps his most lasting legislative legacy so far is the Veterans History Project at the Library of Congress. The volunteer-driven operation has collected more than 60,000 video and audio tapes, letters and cards, photographs, drawings, and other mementos from soldiers in the wars of the 20th and 21st centuries. Kind introduced the bill creating the project in September 2000, and it sped through Congress in less than a month. The collection of oral histories is now the nation's largest.

The idea for the project came to him on a Father's Day weekend as Kind was sitting in the yard with his father and uncle — veterans of the Korean conflict and of World War II, respectively — listening to them talk. He had never heard the stories before, and he grabbed a video camera to capture them for his boys.

The son of a union leader who lost his phone company job after a strike, Kind's views on trade issues have varied over the years. In 2002, he sided with labor and voted against a bill to grant the president expedited trade-negotiating authority, known as fast-track. He said it did not adequately address environmental concerns or the needs of displaced U.S. workers. In subsequent votes on individual trade agreements, Kind has voted for some and against others. He voted in favor of a free-trade agreement with Peru in the 110th after praising its environmental standards and labor protections.

Kind is an up-by-the-bootstraps success story. Reared in a blue-collar neighborhood, he was a high school football and basketball star and won an academic scholarship to Harvard University, where he was a quarterback on the football team before suffering a career-ending shoulder injury. As a summer intern for Proxmire in 1984, he did research for the senator's annual "Golden Fleece" awards, which showcased wasteful federal spending.

In addition to Proxmire's strong influence, Kind also was inspired to try politics by an experience he had backpacking through Eastern Europe just as communism was crumbling. In Berlin in 1990, Kind took a sledgehammer to the recently opened Berlin Wall and shook hands with new Czechoslovakian President Vaclav Havel. He still has a chunk of the wall, shaped like Wisconsin, on his desk.

He earned a master's degree at the London School of Economics, a law degree in Minnesota, worked two years at a Milwaukee law firm, then returned home to La Crosse to become a county prosecutor. When GOP Rep. Steve Gunderson announced his retirement, Kind entered the 1996 race. With little money, he waged a grass-roots campaign and beat Jim Harsdorf with 52 percent of the vote. He has won easily since.

KEY VOTES

2008

Yes   Delay consideration of Colombia free-trade agreement

No   Override Bush veto of federal farm and nutrition programs reauthorization bill

Yes   Overhaul surveillance laws and permit dismissal of suits against companies that conducted warrantless wiretapping

Yes   Grant mortgage relief to homeowners and funding for Fannie Mae and Freddie Mac

Yes   Approve initial $700 billion program to stabilize financial markets

Yes   Approve final $700 billion program to stabilize financial markets

Yes   Provide $14 billion in loans to automakers

2007

Yes   Increase minimum wage by $2.10 an hour

Yes   Approve $124.2 billion in emergency war spending and set goal for redeployment of troops from Iraq

No   Reject federal contraceptive assistance to international family planning groups

Yes   Override Bush veto of $23.2 billion water projects authorization bill

Yes   Implement Peru free-trade agreement

Yes   Approve energy policy overhaul with new fuel economy standards

Yes   Clear $473.5 billion omnibus spending bill, including $70 billion for military operations

CQ VOTE STUDIES

	PARTY UNITY		PRESIDENTIAL SUPPORT	
	SUPPORT	OPPOSE	SUPPORT	OPPOSE
2008	95%	5%	28%	72%
2007	96%	4%	7%	93%
2006	88%	12%	34%	66%
2005	89%	11%	23%	77%
2004	87%	13%	41%	59%

INTEREST GROUPS

	AFL-CIO	ADA	CCUS	ACU
2008	100%	80%	72%	8%
2007	96%	90%	60%	12%
2006	100%	85%	53%	25%
2005	87%	75%	59%	20%
2004	93%	90%	47%	24%

WISCONSIN 3
West – Eau Claire, La Crosse

Comprising most of western Wisconsin, the 3rd District is an agricultural and dairy powerhouse, home to hundreds of thousands of cows. The district still leads the state in dairy production even as corporate farming takes over and fewer family farms thrive.

Following declines in manufacturing, Eau Claire and La Crosse both now rely on their large hospital systems, which are the biggest employers in the district. The five branches of Wisconsin's state university system that are located in the district have placed an emphasis on computer and technology education.

Meanwhile, St. Croix County — filled with bedroom communities inhabited by commuters to Minneapolis-St. Paul, just across the Mississippi River from the Minnesota state line — is experiencing the fastest population growth in the state.

Recreational tourism also contributes to the 3rd's economy. The Mississippi River provides a 250-mile natural western border to the district,

snaking from near Minnesota's Twin Cities to the Illinois border along rolling prairies and nutrient-rich soil. Birdwatchers flock to the river to spot bald eagles perched on the steep bluffs, and lakes in the north attract sportsmen and retirees.

Made up of traditionally competitive counties, the 3rd has a slight Democratic lean overall and voted solidly for Barack Obama in the 2008 presidential election. Obama took 58 percent of the vote here, and he won every county wholly or partly in the 3rd except for St. Croix in the northwest, which supported John McCain with 51 percent of its vote.

MAJOR INDUSTRY
Dairy farming, tourism, technology, health care, manufacturing

MILITARY BASES
Fort McCoy (Army), 1,604 military, 1,122 civilian (2009)

CITIES
Eau Claire (pt.), 59,794; La Crosse, 51,818; Menomonie, 14,937

NOTABLE
Taliesin, Frank Lloyd Wright's estate, is in Spring Green; Pepin hosts the annual "Laura Ingalls Wilder Days," honoring the native-born author of the "Little House" books and holding demonstrations of the crafts, music and daily life of 1870s Wisconsin.

Rep. Gwen Moore (D)

Elected 2004; 3rd term

Moore is a steadfast liberal who works to combat poverty, hunger and homelessness, advocating for more government assistance for families and children for everything from vision care to pre-kindergarten to school breakfasts.

A former teenage single mother on welfare, Moore knows firsthand what it's like to face the fear of such conditions. "I am really in sync with people who struggle on a day-to-day basis," said Moore, who represents Milwaukee and a few of its working-class suburbs. "You don't have to have a 'D' after your name to understand that people have to eat."

She often recounts her stories of struggle as part of her campaign speeches. They surfaced again in 2008 when she stumped for Barack Obama for the Democratic presidential nomination, traveling through Wisconsin and 10 other states. And when his bid was secured on Election Night, she perhaps celebrated more for him than for her own landslide win.

A member of the Budget and Financial Services committees, she had attacked the George W. Bush administration for spending billions of dollars on the Iraq War and tax cuts for well-off Americans while cutting programs that provide food to the poor. After Obama took office, she supported his economic agenda wholeheartedly — including a $787 billion economic stimulus law that included provisions she advocated to expand the child tax credit and increase funding for Pell grants. She also backed a $3.56 trillion budget blueprint for fiscal 2010, calling it "a strong starting point to reversing the financial crisis left behind by the Bush legacy."

In fall 2008, she did support a $700 billion law to rescue the financial services sector, saying a credit crisis would hurt the poor.

Moore is proudest of her work with Democrat Paul W. Hodes of New Hampshire on a 2008 law that aims to ensure dependent students who take a medically necessary leave of absence don't lose their health insurance.

She has claimed some other modest victories. During the 109th Congress (2005-06), she won approval of her legislation to protect the identity of domestic violence victims who receive homeless assistance. And she successfully pressed for an amendment to help public housing assistance recipients become homeowners by allowing them to improve their creditworthiness with prompt rent payments.

She pushes legislation aimed at providing assistance to the homeless. A version of her bill drew criticism from advocacy groups during the 110th Congress (2007-08) when an amendment that she and California Democrat Maxine Waters offered didn't broaden the definition of "homeless" as much as they would have liked. Said Moore: "This amendment is not perfect, but few pieces of legislation are. At this time, this represents the most amount of resources that we can get for the people most in need." A version of that bill passed the House but didn't become law.

Moore has long supported an expansion of the State Children's Health Insurance Program, which covers children whose families don't qualify for Medicaid, and in February 2009 voted for the expansion that Obama signed into law. She also boasts of having steered millions of dollars in transportation improvements and funds for a new medical center to Milwaukee, along with more than $1 million for Milwaukee Public Schools programs.

Vice chairwoman of the bipartisan Congressional Caucus for Women's Issues, she applauded House passage in January 2009 of two bills aimed at strengthening the ability of workers to combat wage discrimination.

CAPITOL OFFICE
225-4572
www.house.gov/gwenmoore
1239 Longworth Bldg. 20515-4904; fax 225-8135

COMMITTEES
Budget
Financial Services

RESIDENCE
Milwaukee

BORN
April 18, 1951; Racine, Wis.

RELIGION
Baptist

FAMILY
Single; three children

EDUCATION
Marquette U., B.A. 1978 (political science)

CAREER
State agency legislative analyst;
city development specialist; VISTA volunteer

POLITICAL HIGHLIGHTS
Wis. Assembly, 1989-92; Wis. Senate, 1993-2004
(president pro tempore, 1997-98)

ELECTION RESULTS

2008 GENERAL

Gwen Moore (D)	222,728	87.6%
Michael D. LaForest (I)	29,282	11.5%

2008 PRIMARY

Gwen Moore (D)	18,342	96.4%
write-ins (D)	694	3.6%

2006 GENERAL

Gwen Moore (D)	136,735	71.3%
Perfecto Rivera (R)	54,486	28.4%

PREVIOUS WINNING PERCENTAGES
2004 (70%)

Moore was born in Racine, the eighth of nine children of a factory worker father and a teacher. She said her father taught her self-reliance, a trait that propelled her through school and her career. She has never married.

She got into politics as a student in Milwaukee's public schools in the late 1960s, inspired by the Rev. Martin Luther King Jr. and the civil rights movement. She served as student council president of North Division High School, where she pushed city officials to replace an aging building that lacked science labs and showers for athletes. Moore also organized a school walkout over a lack of textbooks describing black American history after slavery. A picture of a young Moore leading the protest is on display today inside America's Black Holocaust Museum in Milwaukee.

At age 18, Moore got pregnant during her freshman year at Marquette University. She went on government assistance, but continued her studies in political science, taking eight years to finally earn her bachelor's degree, struggling all the while to even pay for food. She then went to work as a VISTA volunteer and organized a community credit union in her North Milwaukee neighborhood, where traditional banks wouldn't lend money. She later worked in a variety of government jobs, including as a neighborhood development specialist for Milwaukee's city government. In 1988, she was elected to the state Assembly and later won a seat in the state Senate. She earned bipartisan praise for her work on Wisconsin's welfare reform program in the mid-1990s.

In 2004, when pro-labor Democrat Gerald D. Kleczka decided to retire after 20 years, Moore entered a highly competitive primary for his 4th District seat. She benefited from the recent mayoral race in which Tom Barrett, who is white, narrowly defeated acting Mayor Marvin Pratt, who is black, in a contest that divided the city's neighborhoods by race. That November, she prevailed over Republican Gerald H. Boyle, an Iraq War veteran, and became the first African-American member of Congress from Wisconsin. She took a symbolic oath of office from Wisconsin state Supreme Court Justice Louis Butler, who also is an African-American.

Her victory was marred by the arrest in January 2005 of her then 25-year-old son, Sowande Omokunde, one of five workers for the Kerry-Edwards presidential campaign charged with slashing the tires of GOP get-out-the-vote vehicles on Election Day. The judge sentenced Omokunde and three co-defendants to several months in jail. Moore got more unwanted press in 2005 when a local newspaper reported her election campaign had paid her sister $44,000 for work on the campaign, though she lives in Georgia. Moore's campaign treasurer said her sister had helped Moore cultivate relationships in Washington. Voters seemed unperturbed; she won easily in 2006 and 2008.

KEY VOTES

2008

Yes	Delay consideration of Colombia free-trade agreement
No	Override Bush veto of federal farm and nutrition programs reauthorization bill
No	Overhaul surveillance laws and permit dismissal of suits against companies that conducted warrantless wiretapping
Yes	Grant mortgage relief to homeowners and funding for Fannie Mae and Freddie Mac
Yes	Approve initial $700 billion program to stabilize financial markets
Yes	Approve final $700 billion program to stabilize financial markets
Yes	Provide $14 billion in loans to automakers

2007

Yes	Increase minimum wage by $2.10 an hour
Yes	Approve $124.2 billion in emergency war spending and set goal for redeployment of troops from Iraq
No	Reject federal contraceptive assistance to international family planning groups
Yes	Override Bush veto of $23.2 billion water projects authorization bill
?	Implement Peru free-trade agreement
Yes	Approve energy policy overhaul with new fuel economy standards
No	Clear $473.5 billion omnibus spending bill, including $70 billion for military operations

CQ VOTE STUDIES

	PARTY UNITY		PRESIDENTIAL SUPPORT	
	SUPPORT	OPPOSE	SUPPORT	OPPOSE
2008	99%	1%	19%	81%
2007	99%	1%	4%	96%
2006	98%	2%	13%	87%
2005	97%	3%	11%	89%

INTEREST GROUPS

	AFL-CIO	ADA	CCUS	ACU
2008	100%	95%	50%	4%
2007	96%	95%	53%	0%
2006	93%	100%	20%	4%
2005	93%	100%	38%	0%

WISCONSIN 4

Milwaukee

On the shores of Lake Michigan, the 4th takes in all of Milwaukee, Wisconsin's largest city. Once rooted in manufacturing, the city has become more cosmopolitan. It has a major art museum, the world's largest summer music festival and professional sports teams: basketball's Bucks, baseball's Brewers and minor league hockey's Admirals. The city is home to the original tap of Miller Brewing, now part of the MillerCoors conglomerate, and is the home of Harley-Davidson.

Milwaukee has lost residents since the 1960s, mainly due to a shrinking manufacturing base. But downtown revitalization efforts lured in new businesses and young professionals before double-digit unemployment rates jarred the local economy. The Milwaukee area hosts the headquarters for Fortune 500 firms — auto parts manufacturer Johnson Controls and global staffing firm Manpower both boast "green" headquarters in the area. Manpower's new corporate complex near northern Milwaukee created a multimillion-dollar development project and construction jobs. A large student population is spread among the city's colleges, including the local University of Wisconsin campus and Marquette University.

Milwaukee, once known for the stark racial, cultural and economic differences in formerly segregated parts of the city, is minority-majority: blacks (37 percent) and Hispanics (12 percent) together outnumber whites. It is not uncommon to find almost completely black areas in the north-central part of the city and exclusively white and Hispanic areas in the south, where Polish and German immigrants once settled.

Milwaukee once was the socialist hub of the country, even going so far as to elect the nation's first Socialist mayor. This history, combined with the city's remaining blue-collar enclaves, large minority population and strong union presence, make the 4th the state's most Democratic district. Milwaukee overwhelmingly supported Barack Obama in the 2008 presidential election, giving him 75 percent of its vote.

MAJOR INDUSTRY
Machinery manufacturing, service

CITIES
Milwaukee, 596,974; South Milwaukee, 21,256; West Allis (pt.), 20,936

NOTABLE
The world's largest four-sided clock is on the Allen-Bradley building.

Rep. F. James Sensenbrenner Jr. (R)

Elected 1978; 16th term

CAPITOL OFFICE
225-5101
sensenbrenner.house.gov
2449 Rayburn Bldg. 20515-4905; fax 225-3190

COMMITTEES
Judiciary
Science & Technology
Select Energy Independence & Global Warming
- ranking member

RESIDENCE
Menomonee Falls

BORN
June 14, 1943; Chicago, Ill.

RELIGION
Anglican Catholic

FAMILY
Wife, Cheryl Sensenbrenner; two children

EDUCATION
Stanford U., A.B. 1965 (political science);
U. of Wisconsin, J.D. 1968

CAREER
Lawyer

POLITICAL HIGHLIGHTS
Wis. Assembly, 1969-75; Wis. Senate, 1975-79

ELECTION RESULTS

2008 GENERAL

F. James Sensenbrenner Jr. (R)	275,271	79.6%
Robert R. Raymond (I)	69,715	20.2%

2008 PRIMARY

F. James Sensenbrenner Jr. (R)	47,144	78.3%
Jim Burkee (R)	13,078	21.7%

2006 GENERAL

F. James Sensenbrenner Jr. (R)	194,669	61.8%
Bryan Kennedy (D)	112,451	35.7%
Bob Levis (WG)	4,432	1.4%
Robert R. Raymond (I)	3,525	1.1%

PREVIOUS WINNING PERCENTAGES
2004 (67%); 2002 (86%); 2000 (74%); 1998 (91%);
1996 (74%); 1994 (100%); 1992 (70%); 1990 (100%);
1988 (75%); 1986 (78%); 1984 (73%); 1982 (100%);
1980 (78%); 1978 (61%)

Sensenbrenner is a former chairman of the Judiciary Committee whose forceful, articulate advocacy of conservative positions has won him admirers on the right; Human Events magazine named him "Man of the Year" in 2006. Though he has lost influence and now serves in the minority, he relishes playing the scold on issues ranging from the courts to climate change. "We remain relevant by being very vigorous, pointing out the shortcomings of the Democrats' agenda," he told the Milwaukee Journal Sentinel in 2008.

Sensenbrenner is known for his prickliness as much as his smarts. He doesn't suffer fools gladly; whether he holds the gavel or not, he can be downright ornery to colleagues, journalists, unprepared witnesses and even constituents. He abruptly adjourned a Judiciary hearing in 2005 when the questions irked him. A GOP colleague told The New York Times in 2006 that Sensenbrenner treats everyone equally — "like dogs." The following day, he circulated a basket of dog biscuits at a committee meeting.

Sensenbrenner has spent his entire career in politics and government since graduating from law school in 1968. He rose from the Wisconsin statehouse to the U.S. House and ultimately to his dream job of chairing the Judiciary Committee, where he had considerable power during a six-year reign and left his mark on several major pieces of legislation. He wrote the 2001 anti-terrorism law known as the Patriot Act after the attacks on New York and Washington. He also was a force behind changes in bankruptcy law in 2005 making it harder for people to escape their debts and was one of the House managers of the impeachment case against President Clinton in 1998.

But in 2007, when Democrats took control of the House, Sensenbrenner had to give up the Judiciary gavel, and he now ranks second on the minority side. In the 111th Congress (2009-10), he is the top Republican on the civil rights subcommittee, where he is likely to clash with panel chairman Jerrold Nadler of New York, a liberal who can match him in ferocity.

Sensenbrenner also serves as the top Republican on the Select Committee on Energy Independence and Global Warming. He pushes for a gradual approach to tackling climate change — an approach he advocated when he was chairman of the Science and Technology Committee. He says he feels putting too many restrictions on U.S.-based companies would hinder their ability to compete with foreign companies. "Despite having more than 50 hearings in the last Congress, the select committee never fully examined how legislated proposals to address global warming will truly affect the American economy," Sensenbrenner said at a January 2009 hearing.

And when the committee in April 2008 held a hearing to ask the five major U.S. oil companies to invest 10 percent of their profits in renewable energy and biofuels as a response to record-high prices for gasoline, Sensenbrenner defended the oil executives. Oil and gas companies, he said, "create a lot of good jobs, and their expanded investment in market-driven research and technology only serves to create more jobs."

But he isn't opposed to new energy technology. He sponsored a measure, which passed the House in 2008, designed to spur the development of plug-in hybrid utility and delivery trucks. Though it did not become law, Sensenbrenner re-introduced it in 2009 with bipartisan support.

He also will work across the aisle when it suits him. He worked with Majority Leader Steny H. Hoyer of Maryland to push through Congress in 2008 a bill to expand the category of people classified as disabled and ensure that protections under the 1990 Americans with Disabilities Act aren't withheld from anyone meeting those standards. Lawmakers said Supreme Court rulings had imposed unwarranted limits on the law's reach. Sensenbrenner's wife, Cheryl, is disabled and serves as the board chairwoman for the American Association of People with Disabilities.

In May 2009, Sensenbrenner crossed party lines again and teamed with Judiciary Democrat Howard L. Berman of California to steer through the House a bill expanding federal anti-fraud laws.

In his final months as Judiciary chairman in 2006, Sensenbrenner defied President George W. Bush on immigration policy, leading a hard-line group that favored a bill emphasizing border security and punishing illegal immigrants and the employers who hire them.

Some of Sensenbrenner's ideas made it into law, including a plan to build a 700-mile fence on the U.S.-Mexico border. The year before, in 2005, Congress cleared his bill compelling states to demand proof of legal U.S. residency when issuing driver's licenses.

On most social issues, he is an ardent conservative, opposing abortion, gun control and same-sex marriage. He was the only member of the Wisconsin delegation to support Bush's 2007 plan to send more than 21,000 additional U.S. troops into Iraq. But he has a soft spot for voting rights for minorities. In his final year as Judiciary chairman, Sensenbrenner won an extension of the 1965 Voting Rights Act and was riled that Republicans threw up roadblocks by trying to eliminate requirements for bilingual assistance at polling places.

Among the wealthiest lawmakers, Sensenbrenner is heir to the Kimberly-Clark paper and cellulose manufacturing fortune that began with his great-grandfather's invention of the Kotex sanitary napkin after World War I. As a teenager he helped his math teacher win a race for county surveyor.He studied political science at Stanford University, earned a law degree from the University of Wisconsin at Madison, then was elected to the state Assembly. He spent a decade in the legislature, part of it as assistant Senate minority leader.

When Republican Bob Kasten ran unsuccessfully for governor in 1978, Sensenbrenner, with a solid political base in the affluent suburbs bordering Lake Michigan, was the obvious successor. He dipped into family wealth to overcome a strong primary challenge from Susan Engeleiter, a state legislator, then won the general election with 61 percent of the vote.

In 2006, the Journal Sentinel reported he had accepted more than $200,000 in free world travel from private and nonprofit organizations since 2000; he still won with 62 percent. In 2008, he took 80 percent.

KEY VOTES

2008

No Delay consideration of Colombia free-trade agreement

No Override Bush veto of federal farm and nutrition programs reauthorization bill

Yes Overhaul surveillance laws and permit dismissal of suits against companies that conducted warrantless wiretapping

No Grant mortgage relief to homeowners and funding for Fannie Mae and Freddie Mac

No Approve initial $700 billion program to stabilize financial markets

No Approve final $700 billion program to stabilize financial markets

? Provide $14 billion in loans to automakers

2007

No Increase minimum wage by $2.10 an hour

No Approve $124.2 billion in emergency war spending and set goal for redeployment of troops from Iraq

Yes Reject federal contraceptive assistance to international family planning groups

No Override Bush veto of $23.2 billion water projects authorization bill

Yes Implement Peru free-trade agreement

No Approve energy policy overhaul with new fuel economy standards

Yes Clear $473.5 billion omnibus spending bill, including $70 billion for military operations

CQ VOTE STUDIES

	PARTY UNITY		PRESIDENTIAL SUPPORT	
	SUPPORT	OPPOSE	SUPPORT	OPPOSE
2008	98%	2%	82%	18%
2007	96%	4%	91%	9%
2006	92%	8%	84%	16%
2005	93%	7%	81%	19%
2004	94%	6%	79%	21%

INTEREST GROUPS

	AFL-CIO	ADA	CCUS	ACU
2008	0%	10%	67%	96%
2007	4%	0%	75%	96%
2006	21%	10%	87%	83%
2005	20%	0%	77%	96%
2004	27%	20%	86%	92%

WISCONSIN 5
Southeast — Milwaukee suburbs

A mix of suburbs, glacier-carved landscape and Lake Michigan shoreline, Wisconsin's 5th District experienced a decade of rapid job and population growth. Washington and Waukesha counties became destinations for Milwaukee-area white-collar workers leaving downtown and settling their families in the city's affluent suburbs.

These communities offer employment in all sectors and do not rely on Milwaukee's economy for jobs, although some residents still make the daily trip into the city along Interstate 94. Waukesha County's population has grown by 25 percent since 1990, while Washington County has grown by one-third over the same period. Most residents in Ozaukee County, north of Milwaukee, commute out of the county to service or office jobs.

Despite the nationwide decline in the manufacturing sector and some production cuts at district plants, the industry is still represented in Waukesha County, where most of the 5th's factory jobs are. Briggs and Stratton, located in Wauwatosa, manufactures engines for outdoor equipment. Other key employers in the county are Kohl's Department

Store, which has its headquarters in Menomonee Falls, and Quad/Graphics, a printing company based in Sussex that has been forced into several rounds of layoffs. The northern and western outskirts of the 5th are still mostly rural and populated with dairy farms and cattle ranches.

Many residents of the 5th still proudly celebrate their diverse European heritages — German, Belgian, Dutch and Eastern European folk festivals attract tourists almost every weekend of the summer. Vacationers travel to the Port Washington area in Ozaukee County for the recreational fishing and boating opportunities along Lake Michigan.

The 5th is the most heavily Republican district in Wisconsin and the only one in the state that supported GOP candidate John McCain in the 2008 presidential election, in which he won 58 percent of the district's vote.

MAJOR INDUSTRY
Service, manufacturing, retail

CITIES
Waukesha, 64,825; Wauwatosa, 47,271; West Allis (pt.), 40,318

NOTABLE
The Schurz Family in Watertown started the first kindergarten in America in 1856.

Rep. Tom Petri (R)

Elected April 1979; 15th full term

CAPITOL OFFICE
225-2476
www.house.gov/petri
2462 Rayburn Bldg. 20515-4906; fax 225-2356

COMMITTEES
Education & Labor
Transportation & Infrastructure

RESIDENCE
Fond du Lac

BORN
May 28, 1940; Marinette, Wis.

RELIGION
Lutheran

FAMILY
Wife, Anne Neal Petri; one child

EDUCATION
Harvard U., A.B. 1962 (government), J.D. 1965

CAREER
Lawyer; White House aide; Peace Corps volunteer

POLITICAL HIGHLIGHTS
Wis. Senate, 1973-79; Republican nominee
for U.S. Senate, 1974

ELECTION RESULTS

2008 GENERAL

Tom Petri (R)	221,875	63.7%
Roger A. Kittelson (D)	126,090	36.2%

2008 PRIMARY

Tom Petri (R)	21,839	99.6%

2006 GENERAL

Tom Petri (R)	201,367	98.9%
write-ins	2,190	1.1%

PREVIOUS WINNING PERCENTAGES
2004 (67%); 2002 (99%); 2000 (65%); 1998 (93%);
1996 (73%); 1994 (99%); 1992 (53%); 1990 (100%);
1988 (74%); 1986 (97%); 1984 (76%); 1982 (65%);
1980 (59%); 1979 Special Election (50%)

As a moderate Republican, Petri is in a minority of the minority party. He legislates as if he's from a different era, and he is — first elected in 1979, Petri remembers a time when the House was more collegial and less partisan.

Petri (PEA-try) is willing to back a Democratic bill if he likes it — particularly on education or infrastructure spending. "It seems kind of dumb to be against something just because someone from the other party comes up with it," he once said. But he also says the GOP can offer viable alternatives if Democrats move too far to the left. "I hope that means we are starting with the problems and coming up with sensible solutions to the problems, rather than starting with some ideology and some preconceived dogma and attempting to work the solutions into that dogma," he told the Milwaukee Journal Sentinel in December 2008.

During President George W. Bush's time in office, Petri's departures from the party line included votes to increase the minimum wage, to allow the federal government to negotiate prescription drug prices on behalf of Medicare recipients, and to require that all legislation be accompanied by a list of earmarks (funding set-asides for projects in member districts) and their sponsors.

And despite pressure from Bush, in fall 2008 he opposed both versions of a $700 billion bill — the second of which was signed into law — to aid the troubled financial services industry. "The plan, as it was presented to Congress, was a breathtaking grasp for power which should have alarmed everyone," he said. "The plan which was ultimately passed was a bit better, but still a cause for great concern."

Shortly after President Obama took office, Petri very nearly provided the Republican vote Obama was looking for on his economic stimulus plan to prove his yearning for bipartisanship. Yet Petri's complaint wasn't that the bill spent too much — as his GOP colleagues argued — but that it didn't spend enough, particularly on infrastructure. He is a member of the Transportation and Infrastructure Committee and said, "It seems to me that we ought to spend more on crumbling infrastructure and actually get something lasting for the spending." He joined with his party to vote against the bill, which became law.

Petri did in 2009 back a bill to set mortgage standards and curb predatory lending practices. And he was one of 40 Republicans to back an expansion of the State Children's Health Insurance Program, which covers children from families that do not qualify for Medicaid; Obama signed it into law.

He opposed Obama's $3.56 trillion budget blueprint for fiscal 2010, saying, "This is a bill that is going to come due." But Petri, who has had a lifelong interest in education policy and serves on the Education and Labor Committee, supported a proposal in the budget to end a program under which the government guarantees private student loans, while keeping in place direct loans from the government. Petri had previously teamed with Democrats George Miller of California and Sen. Edward M. Kennedy of Massachusetts, the chairmen of the House and Senate education committees, to push legislation to use market-based methods — such as auctions — to reduce taxpayer costs for federal guaranteed student loans. Lenders would have to bid for the business, and those willing to take the lowest government subsidy would have the right to offer loans.

Petri also pushes legislation to modify regulations that restrict the number of schools eligible for the Troops to Teachers program. The program helps veterans earn teaching certificates if they agree to work at public or charter schools that are academically needy or serve many low-income students.

Petri serves as the top Republican on the Transportation panel's Aviation Subcommittee, a seat that's good for his district. The 6th is home to Basler Turbo Conversions, Oshkosh Truck, a manufacturer of aircraft rescue and fire-fighting vehicles, and the Experimental Aircraft Association, which attracts 750,000 aviation enthusiasts to Oshkosh for its annual summer festival.

Petri, now No. 5 in seniority among House Republicans, has sometimes suffered for his moderate ways. He was passed over for the Education chairmanship in 2001, despite being next in line in seniority. He had hoped to become the top-ranking GOP member on Transportation and Infrastructure in 2007, when term limits forced Don Young of Alaska to step down. Petri had the support of Minority Leader John A. Boehner of Ohio, but the GOP Steering Committee passed him over once again, reaching several rungs down the seniority ladder to elevate Florida's John L. Mica.

Born Thomas Rudolph Everett Jr. in northern Wisconsin, Petri spent his early childhood in San Juan, Puerto Rico, where his father, a Navy pilot, was stationed. World War II changed his life forever — his father, who enlisted in the military shortly after graduating from Marquette University Law School, was killed in the conflict in 1944. His mother remarried after the war, and although Petri eventually took the name of his stepfather, he continued to be known to family and friends as "Tim," a nickname his paternal grandmother gave him at age 2 to distinguish him from his biological father.

As a teenager, Petri got his first job by marching down to the local radio station and asking to become a disc jockey. He soon became the host of "Teen Time," a weekly show that made him the Badger State's youngest on-air personality. He worked his way through Harvard as a teller at a local bank, then earned a law degree there. He clerked for Judge James E. Doyle Sr., the father of Wisconsin's current Democratic governor, before joining the Peace Corps for a stint in Somalia. Once home, Petri started a law practice in Fond du Lac. He won a state Senate seat in 1972 at age 32.

Petri was chosen to be the GOP Senate nominee against Democrat Gaylord Nelson in 1974, but he lost in the aftermath of the Watergate scandal. That exposure, however, helped him win a 1979 special election to replace GOP Rep. William A. Steiger, a fellow moderate who died after winning re-election in 1978. Petri easily won election to a full term in 1980 and coasted until 1992, when he was hit by negative publicity about 77 overdrafts at the private bank for House members. He pulled through with 53 percent of the vote, his worst re-election total ever. He has won easily ever since. He took 64 percent of the vote in 2008, and by the first quarter of 2009 had close to $900,000 in his campaign coffers, while no challengers had stepped forward for 2010.

KEY VOTES

2008

No   Delay consideration of Colombia free-trade agreement

No   Override Bush veto of federal farm and nutrition programs reauthorization bill

Yes Overhaul surveillance laws and permit dismissal of suits against companies that conducted warrantless wiretapping

No   Grant mortgage relief to homeowners and funding for Fannie Mae and Freddie Mac

No   Approve initial $700 billion program to stabilize financial markets

No   Approve final $700 billion program to stabilize financial markets

No   Provide $14 billion in loans to automakers

2007

Yes Increase minimum wage by $2.10 an hour

No   Approve $124.2 billion in emergency war spending and set goal for redeployment of troops from Iraq

Yes Reject federal contraceptive assistance to international family planning groups

Yes Override Bush veto of $23.2 billion water projects authorization bill

Yes Implement Peru free-trade agreement

Yes Approve energy policy overhaul with new fuel economy standards

Yes Clear $473.5 billion omnibus spending bill, including $70 billion for military operations

CQ VOTE STUDIES

	PARTY UNITY		PRESIDENTIAL SUPPORT	
	SUPPORT	OPPOSE	SUPPORT	OPPOSE
2008	91%	9%	62%	38%
2007	88%	12%	68%	32%
2006	90%	10%	85%	15%
2005	88%	12%	80%	20%
2004	89%	11%	85%	15%

INTEREST GROUPS

	AFL-CIO	ADA	CCUS	ACU
2008	33%	40%	72%	80%
2007	38%	30%	85%	72%
2006	14%	5%	87%	76%
2005	13%	5%	85%	72%
2004	33%	20%	95%	80%

WISCONSIN 6
East central — Oshkosh, Sheboygan, Fond du Lac

In 1854, a group of dissatisfied Whigs, Free Soilers and Democrats met in a Ripon schoolhouse in Fond du Lac County to dream up the Republican Party. Today, the 6th District's farms and small towns still hold primarily socially conservative Lutherans and Catholics, but the district also hosts the state's largest population of blue-collar workers. In the 2008 presidential election, Democrat Barack Obama edged out John McCain, but with only 49.7 percent of the vote.

Manitowoc County, on Lake Michigan, has a longstanding reputation as a shipbuilding center. South along the lake, Sheboygan County is famed for its meat processing, calling itself the "bratwurst capital of the world." The county once relied on manufacturing jobs, and it is home to plumbing company Kohler, which has cut hundreds of jobs recently as the national homebuilding market has slowed. Near the inland Lake Winnebago, Oshkosh — where the OshKosh B'Gosh overalls originated more than a century ago — still is one of the largest producers of military and specialty trucks in the world, but its construction-based industrial jobs have been threatened. The district's struggling paper industry is based mainly in Neenah and Menasha.

The 6th's west is farming territory. Milk products and grains are big contributors to the district's agriculture sector — one of the strongest in the nation. Large corporate farms have acquired some small farms, making them more profitable, and others have turned from dairy to new crops such as beans, peas and corn. Fruits and vegetables thrive in Adams County, and Marquette and Waushara counties grow Christmas trees.

Many of the 6th's residents are descendants of German immigrants who settled the area in the 1850s, and the district still claims more people of German ancestry (60 percent) than any other in the nation. In more-recent waves of immigration, the Hmong population continues to grow in Sheboygan, Manitowoc and Winnebago counties.

MAJOR INDUSTRY
Agriculture, tourism, manufacturing, paper

CITIES
Oshkosh, 62,916; Sheboygan, 50,792; Fond du Lac, 42,203

NOTABLE
The Wisconsin Maritime Museum is in Manitowoc.

Rep. David R. Obey (D)

Elected April 1969; 20th full term

CAPITOL OFFICE
225-3365
obey.house.gov
2314 Rayburn Bldg. 20515-4907; fax 225-3240

COMMITTEES
Appropriations - chairman
 (Labor-HHS-Education - chairman)

RESIDENCE
Wausau

BORN
Oct. 3, 1938; Okmulgee, Okla.

RELIGION
Roman Catholic

FAMILY
Wife, Joan Obey; two children

EDUCATION
U. of Wisconsin, B.S. 1960 (political science),
M.A. 1962 (political science)

CAREER
Real estate broker

POLITICAL HIGHLIGHTS
Wis. Assembly, 1963-69

ELECTION RESULTS

2008 GENERAL

David R. Obey (D)	212,666	60.8%
Dan Mielke (R)	136,938	39.1%

2008 PRIMARY

David R. Obey (D)	unopposed

2006 GENERAL

David R. Obey (D)	161,903	62.2%
Nick Reid (R)	91,069	35.0%
Mike Miles (WG)	7,391	2.8%

PREVIOUS WINNING PERCENTAGES
2004 (86%); 2002 (64%); 2000 (63%); 1998 (61%);
1996 (57%); 1994 (54%); 1992 (64%); 1990 (62%);
1988 (62%); 1986 (62%); 1984 (61%); 1982 (68%);
1980 (65%); 1978 (62%); 1976 (73%); 1974 (71%);
1972 (63%); 1970 (68%); 1969 Special Election (52%)

The hard-charging Obey combines his intelligence and institutional knowledge with a sharp tongue and reputation for suffering no fools as he drives spending decisions from his post atop the Appropriations Committee.

Obey, who says "indifference" is the biggest challenge facing the country, wears his old-style liberal views on his sleeve. He attributes his values to "the Catholic social gospel" and progressive tradition of legendary Wisconsin politician Robert La Follette, who emphasized social justice and workers' rights — neither of which always align with the liberalism of the nation's coasts.

Obey (OH-bee) prides himself on being a dealmaker who can get legislative business done, but also makes clear that he will always make his own decisions.

After years of clashing with President George W. Bush — particularly over the Iraq War — many observers expected a smoother relationship with the new Democratic White House, and Obey did shepherd through the House in early 2009 an economic stimulus package much in keeping with President Obama's requests, including spending on infrastructure, health care and education and some tax cuts. At the same time, he helped move along quickly a catchall measure containing nine fiscal 2009 spending bills that had not been acted on in the 110th Congress (2007-08).

But when the administration released details of a fiscal 2010 spending plan, Obey said Congress wouldn't be a rubber stamp. "We may belong to the same party, but we are an independent branch of government," he said in May 2009. He stepped a little too far for Speaker Nancy Pelosi of California when he released a supplemental war spending bill that month with instructions that the administration report within one year on whether the Afghan and Pakistani governments are progressing on building political consensus, combating corruption and fighting insurgents. When lawmakers of both parties and in both chambers — including Pelosi — raised alarm at setting a "timeline," he backed off, stating "there are no ultimatums in this bill, and there is not a fight against the administration."

Obey already had expressed concerns over whether those governments were committed to helping the fight against extremism. The administration planned an increase in forces in conjunction with a drawdown in Iraq to end the U.S. involvement in a war that had long been a source of contention between Obey and the Bush administration. Obey had led efforts in 2007 to condition the war's funding on troop withdrawal (Bush ultimately vetoed the measure.) Obey never sided, however, with war opponents who felt Congress should simply cut off funding for operations in Iraq; he argued such a move would harm the troops.

While Obey was unable to help Democrats change the Bush administration's war policy, he noted his party did significantly boost spending for veterans' programs. And as chairman of the Appropriations panel overseeing spending for the Health and Human Services Department, he has sought to increase funding for education, community health care clinics and medical research.

In the fall of 2008, he supported a $700 billion measure to shore up the nation's financial services sector. The law provided for the funding to be allocated in two installments, and when Obey in January 2009 introduced a plan for releasing the second portion, he said, "You have to look at this bill as not a salvation for the economy by any means. It is simply the largest effort by any legislative body on the planet to try to take government action to prevent economic catastrophe, and even that may be insufficient."

After more than 40 years in Washington, Obey still has no use for the sometimes awkwardly polite ways of Congress and makes no apologies for his hard-hitting style. "Washington is so full of BS," he told the Milwaukee Journal Sentinel in 2007. "I don't have the patience for it. And the day that I do, I'll quit."

He considers himself an institutionalist with respect for the ideals of orderly debate. Yet GOP tempers flared in December 2008 when Republican appropriators felt they weren't given the opportunity to bring forth their own witness to a hearing on an economic stimulus plan. California's Jerry Lewis, Appropriations' top Republican, requested another hearing to allow their concerns to be heard. Obey obliged, but wrote Lewis a letter stating he had given Republicans plenty of opportunity before the first hearing. "These are serious times for serious people," Obey wrote. "Political stunts do little to address the needs of the American people during this economic crisis."

Obey is not all growls and can easily play the role of jovial storyteller when the mood strikes him. He also is a fan of bluegrass music and plays harmonica in his band, the Capitol Offenses, with his two sons and some friends.

Obey considers himself a reformer. He directed a rewrite of the House ethics code after a series of scandals in the 1970s, when Democrats controlled the chamber, which in part limited the outside income members could collect. In 2007 he led efforts to overhaul earmarking — the setting aside of funding for projects in members' districts — which had been tainted by charges of waste and corruption. Obey sought to make information about the projects public and to cut the amount spent on earmarks. In January 2009, Obey and Senate Appropriations Chairman Daniel K. Inouye of Hawaii announced a plan to cut earmarks to about $8.5 billion in 2010 — down from $17 billion in 2006.

Obey is mindful of sentiment in his largely rural and small-town district and supports gun owners' rights and votes for some restrictions on abortion. He is the first Democrat to represent the 7th District and has won at least three-fifths of the vote in all but two re-election races.

Obey grew up in a Republican family in Wausau where money was tight, as he relates in his 2007 autobiography, "Raising Hell for Justice." His upbringing shaped his belief that government should help working families. When he was a boy, his father, who ran a local floor-covering business, had surgery that threatened his ability to work. Providing universal access to health care has been a goal throughout his career. He's been a politician almost all his adult life. At the University of Wisconsin, he majored in political science and was campus coordinator for 1960 presidential candidate Hubert H. Humphrey. At 24, he was elected to the state Assembly. At 30, he won his House seat in a 1969 special election to succeed Melvin R. Laird, President Richard M. Nixon's first Defense secretary.

KEY VOTES

2008

Yes Delay consideration of Colombia free-trade agreement

Yes Override Bush veto of federal farm and nutrition programs reauthorization bill

No Overhaul surveillance laws and permit dismissal of suits against companies that conducted warrantless wiretapping

Yes Grant mortgage relief to homeowners and funding for Fannie Mae and Freddie Mac

Yes Approve initial $700 billion program to stabilize financial markets

Yes Approve final $700 billion program to stabilize financial markets

Yes Provide $14 billion in loans to automakers

2007

Yes Increase minimum wage by $2.10 an hour

Yes Approve $124.2 billion in emergency war spending and set goal for redeployment of troops from Iraq

No Reject federal contraceptive assistance to international family planning groups

Yes Override Bush veto of $23.2 billion water projects authorization bill

No Implement Peru free-trade agreement

Yes Approve energy policy overhaul with new fuel economy standards

No Clear $473.5 billion omnibus spending bill, including $70 billion for military operations

CQ VOTE STUDIES

	PARTY UNITY		PRESIDENTIAL SUPPORT	
	SUPPORT	OPPOSE	SUPPORT	OPPOSE
2008	99%	1%	13%	87%
2007	98%	2%	3%	97%
2006	94%	6%	22%	78%
2005	95%	5%	18%	82%
2004	93%	7%	26%	74%

INTEREST GROUPS

	AFL-CIO	ADA	CCUS	ACU
2008	100%	95%	56%	0%
2007	95%	100%	50%	0%
2006	100%	90%	20%	20%
2005	93%	100%	35%	16%
2004	100%	90%	25%	4%

WISCONSIN 7
Northwest — Wausau, Superior, Stevens Point

Wisconsin's 7th District, the state's largest and most rural, stretches north and west from the state's central counties to the Apostle Islands in the waters of southern Lake Superior. Small towns and family farms checker the district, carrying a populist flavor and retaining threads of mid-20th-century LaFollette progressivism.

Farming sustains the district's economy, although cold weather in the north shaves a full month off the growing season. Dairy farms are the agricultural heart of the 7th District. Centrally located Marathon County leads Wisconsin in dairy production. The nutrient-rich soil in the Central Sands country in the state's midsection produces seed potatoes, cranberries, vegetables and ginseng. Some small metalworking and paper factories — the industries that attracted immigrants to the 7th in the 19th century — still produce their goods, although the district has lost blue-collar and paper mill jobs recently. Stevens Point and Wausau continue to be local insurance hubs.

The tranquil lifestyle in the small towns appeals to senior citizens, and the 7th's hundreds of lakes in the north are a natural draw for tourists. The University of Wisconsin campuses at Stevens Point and Superior attract young people to the area. A large number of Hmong immigrants has settled in Marathon County. One fast-growing area of the district is Polk County, which capitalizes on its proximity to the Minneapolis-St. Paul metropolitan area.

Blue-collar regions around Stevens Point and Wausau, and along Lake Superior in the north, consistently vote Democratic, while some descendants of Scandinavian immigrants and a Christian Right contingent favor the GOP. Democrat Barack Obama carried the 7th with 56 percent of its vote in the 2008 presidential election. He won every county wholly or partly in the district except for Polk and Taylor, and four of his 10 highest percentages in the state were in counties in the 7th.

MAJOR INDUSTRY
Agriculture, paper, manufacturing

CITIES
Wausau, 38,426; Superior, 27,368; Stevens Point, 24,551

NOTABLE
The American Birkebeiner, from Cable to Hayward, is North America's largest cross-country ski marathon.

Rep. Steve Kagen (D)

Elected 2006; 2nd term

CAPITOL OFFICE
225-5665
kagen.house.gov
1232 Longworth Bldg. 20515-4908; fax 225-5729

COMMITTEES
Agriculture
Transportation & Infrastructure

RESIDENCE
Appleton

BORN
Dec. 12, 1949; Neenah, Wis.

RELIGION
Jewish

FAMILY
Wife, Gayle Kagen; four children

EDUCATION
U. of Wisconsin, B.S. 1972 (molecular biology),
M.D. 1976

CAREER
Allergy clinic owner; physician

POLITICAL HIGHLIGHTS
No previous office

ELECTION RESULTS

2008 GENERAL		
Steve Kagen (D)	193,662	54.0%
John Gard (R)	164,621	45.9%
2008 PRIMARY		
Steve Kagen (D)		unopposed
2006 GENERAL		
Steve Kagen (D)	141,570	50.9%
John Gard (R)	135,622	48.8%

Kagen is a physician whose string of allergy clinics around Wisconsin made him a multimillionaire, but he emphasizes a range of issues of interest to blue-collar Wisconsin voters. He criticizes free-trade agreements, which he blames as the "source of the bleeding" of manufacturing jobs in his district, and works to protect the state's dairy farmers.

He is motivated by political survival; even though Barack Obama carried the district in 2008, it went for George W. Bush in 2000 and 2004, and Kagen is an occasional target of advertising campaigns fueled by GOP-sympathetic causes and interests. Though generally a reliable Democratic vote, he supports gun owners' rights and parts company with his party on some high-profile economic issues.

With a seat on the Agriculture Committee, Kagen was well-positioned to help his state's dairy industry as that panel worked on a major rewrite of farm policy in the 110th Congress (2007-08). Kagen, whose first job was bagging whey and sugar at a Wisconsin dairy, backed an increase in payments to dairy producers when domestic milk prices fall. The final bill, cleared over President Bush's veto in June 2008, extends the Milk Income Loss Contract program through 2012 and increases the payment rate.

He also successfully pushed for a provision in the bill that calls for the education of food stamp recipients and authorizes $10 million annually through fiscal 2012 to provide grants to study the problem of obesity.

Kagen voted against the Peru free-trade agreement in 2007 and joined Wisconsin Republican Tom Petri in writing Commerce Secretary Carlos Gutierrez to complain about cheap foreign imports they blamed for the closure of a local paper plant.

In May 2008, the House passed his bill that would amend antitrust law to allow legal action against the Organization of the Petroleum Exporting Countries for manipulating supplies and fixing prices. The vote was largely symbolic since the White House threatened to veto the measure.

When the House passed a bill later that year aimed at bailing out struggling U.S. automakers, Kagen was one of just 20 Democrats to vote against the measure (which ultimately died in the Senate), in part because it would benefit Cerberus Capital Management, Chrysler's parent company. Cerberus is the parent company of NewPage Corp., which earlier had closed two local paper mills.

He also opposed a $700 billion law to aid the ailing financial services industry. "Not just because I didn't think it would work, but also because there was something missing, and that was the oversight necessary to make sure taxpayer dollars are accounted for," he told the Green Bay Press-Gazette.

Kagen did support President Obama's early economic initiatives, including a $3.56 trillion budget blueprint for fiscal 2010 and a $787 billion economic stimulus law. He said both would create jobs in his district. He plans to further help the area through his seat on the Transportation and Infrastructure Committee when it takes up a reauthorization of the 2005 surface transportation law.

Given his background, Kagen would like to be a player on health issues, though he does not currently serve on any of the relevant committees. He has introduced legislation to ban insurers from denying coverage based on pre-existing conditions. To press his point that everybody deserves health coverage, Kagen has refused to accept the health insurance provided to members of Congress. "If every member of Congress had the same sense of uneasiness, we'd begin to address this problem this year and solve it in several weeks," he said.

During his first months in office he drew unwelcome publicity for his version of a White House confrontation with Bush's political adviser Karl Rove. He told a small group of hometown peace activists that during a reception for freshman lawmakers, he had bragged to Rove, "I kicked your ass." The White House dismissed Kagen's account as "ridiculous," and Kagen was peppered with editorial criticism back home. The Appleton Post-Crescent reported that he apologized in a letter to constituents, calling his remarks a "mishandled attempt at humor."

Kagen, who sold his interests in his clinic business in January 2007, got in hot water the same month with the Food and Drug Administration, which told him to stop making and selling allergy vaccines across state lines without the required "biologics" license.

Kagen comes from a medical family, boasting that he is the seventh generation in his family to enter the health care field. His father was a dermatologist who would continue practicing medicine until age 90, and his mother worked as an infection control nurse. Politics is another family tradition; his father preceded him in an unsuccessful run for Congress in 1966. Kagen recalls prominent Wisconsin Democrats such as Sens. Gaylord Nelson and William Proxmire were regular guests in his living room.

As a college student, Kagen took part in protests against the Vietnam War and in favor of establishing an African-American studies program at the University of Wisconsin at Madison. But he largely swore off politics after embarking on a medical career. The closest Kagen came to campaign work was helping Bill Clinton find an allergist when he lost his voice during his 1992 presidential campaign.

Kagen later ran four Wisconsin allergy clinics and served as an assistant clinical professor of allergy and immunology at the Medical College of Wisconsin and as an allergy consultant for CNN.

The 8th District seat came open when Republican Mark Green left to make an unsuccessful bid for governor. Kagen ran as an outsider, while John Gard, his GOP foe, was the Speaker of the state Assembly and had been a lawmaker since 1987. Kagen raised nearly $3.2 million, $2.5 million of it from his own pocket, in what became the costliest House race in state history. He won by 2 percentage points.

Gard came back two years later for a rematch, but Kagen again was able to out-raise his opponent and benefitted from the national Democratic tide, broadening his margin of victory to 8 percentage points.

KEY VOTES

2008
Yes Delay consideration of Colombia free-trade agreement
Yes Override Bush veto of federal farm and nutrition programs reauthorization bill
No Overhaul surveillance laws and permit dismissal of suits against companies that conducted warrantless wiretapping
Yes Grant mortgage relief to homeowners and funding for Fannie Mae and Freddie Mac
No Approve initial $700 billion program to stabilize financial markets
No Approve final $700 billion program to stabilize financial markets
No Provide $14 billion in loans to automakers

2007
Yes Increase minimum wage by $2.10 an hour
Yes Approve $124.2 billion in emergency war spending and set goal for redeployment of troops from Iraq
No Reject federal contraceptive assistance to international family planning groups
Yes Override Bush veto of $23.2 billion water projects authorization bill
No Implement Peru free-trade agreement
Yes Approve energy policy overhaul with new fuel economy standards
No Clear $473.5 billion omnibus spending bill, including $70 billion for military operations

CQ VOTE STUDIES

	PARTY UNITY		PRESIDENTIAL SUPPORT	
	SUPPORT	OPPOSE	SUPPORT	OPPOSE
2008	96%	4%	11%	89%
2007	95%	5%	3%	97%

INTEREST GROUPS

	AFL-CIO	ADA	CCUS	ACU
2008	93%	90%	50%	16%
2007	96%	95%	50%	4%

WISCONSIN 8

Northeast – Green Bay, Appleton

On autumn Sundays, all eyes in Wisconsin turn to the 8th to watch football's Green Bay Packers. Regardless of the team's fortunes, the Packers represent the emotional heart of the state, and they pull in millions of dollars. The waiting list for Packers season tickets exceeds 75,000, and home games at Lambeau Field draw tourists from across the country as well as fans from the region. But the district's blue-collar tradition stems from more than a century of production at paper mills in the Fox River Valley, which stretches southwest from Green Bay.

The 8th's economy depends on natural resources. The sparsely populated north contains the state's largest tracts of forests, historically supplying the local paper industry. Local paper manufacturers, who had invested millions of dollars into modernizing their equipment over the past decade, are now shutting down plants, reducing production and cutting jobs. Fertile soil in the district's south supports grain, and the open land hosts ranches. Appleton still hosts some high-skill manufacturing plants, as do Green Bay and other towns in Brown County.

Forests and lakes in Vilas County, near the Michigan border, attract outdoorsmen and nature lovers in the more temperate seasons. Despite economic downturns affecting the region — especially the market for upscale second homes for wealthier vacationers from Milwaukee and Chicago — the Door County peninsula jutting into Lake Michigan has 250 miles of shore that lure tourists to vineyards, apple and cherry orchards, and artists' colonies. The 8th also is home to six American Indian tribes, each of which boasts a reservation-based casino.

The largely Catholic 8th has a long history of social conservatism. Although the district has historically leaned GOP, residents here are shifting their support to Democratic candidates at the federal level. Brown County has competitive areas, and Democrats dominate Menominee County, which gave Barack Obama his highest percentage statewide in the 2008 presidential race. Obama won the 8th overall with 53 percent.

MAJOR INDUSTRY
Agriculture, casinos, paper products, tourism

CITIES
Green Bay, 102,313; Appleton (pt.) 69,270

NOTABLE
The snowmobile was invented in Sayner.

WYOMING

Gov. Dave Freudenthal (D)

Pronounced: FREED-en-thal
First elected: 2002
Length of term: 4 years
Term expires: 1/11
Salary: $105,000
Phone: (307) 777-7434

Residence: Cheyenne
Born: Oct. 12, 1950; Thermopolis, Wyo.
Religion: Episcopalian
Family: Wife, Nancy Freudenthal; four children
Education: Amherst College, B.A. 1973 (economics); U. of Wyoming, J.D. 1980
Career: Lawyer; gubernatorial aide; state economic development official
Political highlights: Wyo. State Planning Coordinator, 1975-77; U.S. attorney, 1994-2001

Election results:
2006 GENERAL

Dave Freudenthal (D)	135,516	70.0%
Ray Hunkins (R)	58,100	30.0%

Secretary of State
Max Maxfield (R)

(no lieutenant governor)
First elected: 2006
Length of term: 4 years
Term expires: 1/11
Salary: $92,000
Phone: (307) 777-5333

LEGISLATURE

General Assembly: 40 days January-March in odd-numbered years; 20 days February-March in even-numbered years

Senate: 30 members, 4-year terms
2009 ratios: 23 R, 7 D; 29 men, 1 women
Salary: $150/day in session
Phone: (307) 777-7711

House: 60 members, 2-year terms
2009 ratios: 41 R, 19 D; 45 men, 15 women
Salary: $150/day in session
Phone: (307) 777-7852

TERM LIMITS

Governor: 2 terms
Senate: No
House: No

URBAN STATISTICS

CITY	POPULATION
Cheyenne	53,011
Casper	49,644
Laramie	27,204
Gillette	19,646

REGISTERED VOTERS

Republican	60%
Democrat	25%
Others/unaffiliated	14%

POPULATION

2008 population (est.)	532,668
2000 population	493,782
1990 population	453,588
Percent change (1990-2000)	+8.9%
Rank among states (2008)	50

Median age	36.2
Born in state	42.5%
Foreign born	2.3%
Violent crime rate	267/100,000
Poverty level	11.4%
Federal workers	7,186
Military	6,224

ELECTIONS

STATE ELECTION OFFICIAL
(307) 777-7186
DEMOCRATIC PARTY
(307) 473-1457
REPUBLICAN PARTY
(307) 234-9166

MISCELLANEOUS

Web: www.wyoming.gov
Capital: Cheyenne

U.S. CONGRESS

Senate: 2 Republicans
House: 1 Republican

2000 Census Statistics by District

DIST.	2008 VOTE FOR PRESIDENT OBAMA	MCCAIN	WHITE	BLACK	ASIAN	HISP	MEDIAN INCOME	WHITE COLLAR	BLUE COLLAR	SERVICE INDUSTRY	OVER 64	UNDER 18	COLLEGE EDUCATION	RURAL	SQ. MILES
AL	33%	65%	89%	1%	1%	6%	$37,892	54%	29%	17%	12%	26%	22%	35%	97,100
STATE	33	65	89	1	1	6	$37,892	54	29	17	12	26	22	35	97,100
U.S.	53	46	69	12	4	13	$41,994	60	25	15	12	26	24	21	3,537,438

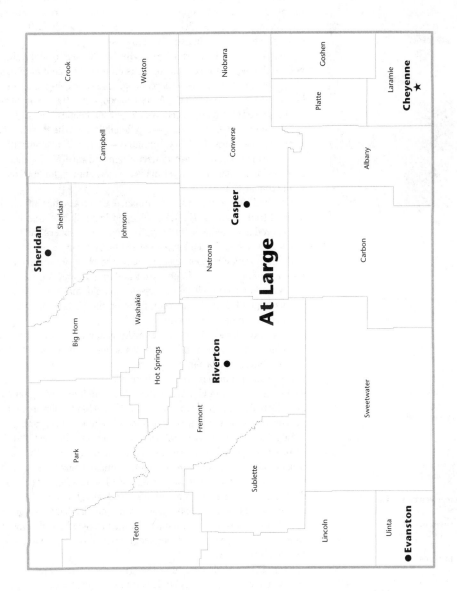

Sen. Michael B. Enzi (R)

Elected 1996; 3rd term

CAPITOL OFFICE
224-3424
enzi.senate.gov
379A Russell Bldg. 20510-5004; fax 228-0359

COMMITTEES
Budget
Finance
Health, Education, Labor & Pensions - ranking
  member
Small Business & Entrepreneurship

RESIDENCE
Gillette

BORN
Feb. 1, 1944; Bremerton, Wash.

RELIGION
Presbyterian

FAMILY
Wife, Diana Enzi; three children

EDUCATION
George Washington U., B.A. 1966 (accounting);
U. of Denver, M.S. 1968 (retail marketing)

MILITARY SERVICE
Wyoming Air National Guard, 1967-73

CAREER
Accountant; computer programmer;
shoe store owner

POLITICAL HIGHLIGHTS
Mayor of Gillette, 1975-83; Wyo. House,
1987-91; Wyo. Senate, 1991-96

ELECTION RESULTS

2008 GENERAL

Michael B. Enzi (R)	189,046	75.6%
Chris Rothfuss (D)	60,631	24.3%

2008 PRIMARY

Michael B. Enzi (R)	unopposed

PREVIOUS WINNING PERCENTAGES
2002 (73%); 1996 (54%)

Enzi's voting record marks him one of the Senate's most conservative members, but he is the opposite of a firebrand. The former shoe salesman and accountant shuns divisive rhetoric and frequently strikes bipartisan deals on health, pension and education issues.

Enzi (EN-zee) follows what he calls the "80/20 rule" of legislating. "I truly believe that if senators choose to focus on the 80 percent of things we can all agree on instead of the 20 percent we are never going to agree on, we'll be able to achieve more for the American people and the people of Wyoming ... It also works in many aspects of life beyond politics," he said.

That approach enables Enzi — top Republican on the Health, Education, Labor and Pensions (HELP) Committee — to regularly team with the panel's chairman, liberal Massachusetts Sen. Edward M. Kennedy. It also makes him an influential player in his new assignment for 2009 on the powerful Finance Committee.

Enzi had long sought a seat on Finance, which also has jurisdiction over tax and trade matters. He acknowledged in April 2008 that he seriously considered not seeking a third term because GOP leaders had twice denied him a spot. When the leadership passed him over in January 2008 in favor of the less senior but politically endangered New Hampshire Republican John E. Sununu, Enzi told The Associated Press it was "a down time" in his life. Sununu ended up losing his re-election bid, making room for Enzi. "I always hoped I could be a liaison between the HELP Committee and the Finance Committee," Enzi said.

He shares Democrats' desire to make health care more affordable. But he wants a fair hearing for his party's suggestions. In spring 2009, Enzi warned that using a fast-track process on health care — enabling legislation to pass with a simple majority without allowing opponents an opportunity for filibusters — would amount to a "declaration of war" against Republicans. Enzi also criticized Obama's fiscal 2010 budget blueprint for curtailing the role of private lenders in the federal student loan program.

Enzi backed his party on 97 percent of the votes in the 110th Congress (2007-08) in which the two parties diverged and displays the typical Western conservative's aversion to government regulation and taxation. A member of the Budget Committee, he was one of 15 Senate Republicans to oppose the George W. Bush administration's $700 billion law to assist the financial services industry in October 2008, saying the plan lacked "a guarantee of proper oversight and accountability for the taxpayer." He also voted against an earlier bill to create an independent regulator for mortgage giants Fannie Mae and Freddie Mac.

Even so, he and Kennedy do a remarkable job of cooperating, given their different backgrounds. Despite Kennedy's frequent absences due to brain cancer in the 110th, they got several major pieces of legislation into law, including measures to expand mental health insurance coverage and the first overhaul in a decade of the law governing federal aid to higher education.

When Enzi chaired the HELP Committee in the 109th Congress (2005-06), his knack for numbers came in handy as he led congressional negotiations with Kennedy on a complex overhaul of the law governing the pension system. They also have worked for years on legislation to increase the use of information technology in health care.

That's not to say the two senators always agree. Enzi has clashed with Kennedy over plans to give the Food and Drug Administration the power to regulate tobacco products. Enzi opposes any tobacco regulation bill that does not give the FDA the power to ban cigarettes, which Democratic bills wouldn't do. Supporters of giving the agency jurisdiction say Enzi's approach is a legislative overreach designed to kill efforts to boost government regulation of tobacco.

Before taking the HELP gavel in 2005, Enzi had served four years as chairman of the Banking Committee's Securities and Investment Subcommittee. From that perch, he worked in 2002 with Maryland Democrat Paul S. Sarbanes, then chairman of the full Banking panel, to pass new federal standards for accounting and corporate governance of companies whose stock is sold to the public.

Enzi generally favors liberalized foreign trade, including agricultural trade with Cuba and expanded ties with China, which could help his state's farmers and ranchers. In 2007 he supported the trade agreement between the United States and Peru and cast the only dissenting vote on extending a ban on U.S. imports from Myanmar; he said unilateral sanctions often hurt U.S. businesses. But he voted against the 2005 Central America Free Trade Agreement.

A member of the Small Business and Entrepreneurship Committee, Enzi regularly goes to bat for small businesses and says many lawmakers have no notion of the problems faced by such firms. While some lawmakers refer to companies with 100 to 500 workers as small businesses, he says, "To me, a small business is when the person who writes the checks also sweeps the front walk, cleans the toilets and waits on the customers."

A former computer programmer, Enzi created a stir in his first year in office by announcing his intention to bring his laptop computer onto the Senate floor, where there is a ban on mechanical devices that might be distracting. The Rules and Administration Committee refused to grant his request. Enzi continues to press for a rules change, but he's also found a way around it — the BlackBerry, which allows him to send and receive e-mail messages while he's on the floor. Although the little communications devices are also theoretically banned, Enzi said he finds them useful. "I actually think [senators] would stay on the floor, debate more, if we could communicate with our staff," he once said.

Enzi was born in Bremerton, Wash., where his father had worked in the naval shipyards during World War II. The family moved to Wyoming soon after his birth. After graduating from high school in Sheridan, Enzi headed east to George Washington University in Washington, D.C., where he earned an accounting degree. He returned west to the University of Denver, where he collected a master's in retail marketing in 1968. The following year, he married and moved back to Wyoming with his wife, Diana, settling in Gillette, where they started their own small business, NZ Shoes. They later added stores in Sheridan and Miles City, Mont.

Enzi began his political career by winning election as mayor of Gillette in 1974, when he was 30. In 1986, he won a seat in the state House, and by 1991 was serving in the state Senate.

When Alan K. Simpson retired after 18 years, Enzi went after his Senate seat. He narrowly won the 1996 primary by building a network of supporters drawn in part from the Wyoming Christian Coalition and stressing his opposition to abortion. He took the general election by 12 percentage points over Kathy Karpan, a former two-term Wyoming secretary of state.

In 2002, he won re-election with 73 percent of the vote over Democrat Joyce Jansa Corcoran, the former mayor of Lander. Six years later, he took 77 percent against University of Wyoming professor Chris Rothfuss. Enzi's re-election was never in doubt, but he refused to have his campaign take any polls. "I don't do polls because, on a weekend, I talk to more people than a pollster does," he told The Associated Press.

KEY VOTES

2008

Yes	Prohibit discrimination based on genetic information
Yes	Reauthorize farm and nutrition programs for five years
No	Limit debate on "cap and trade" system for greenhouse gas emissions
No	Allow lawsuits against companies that participated in warrantless wiretapping
No	Limit debate on a bill to block a scheduled cut in Medicare payments to doctors
No	Grant mortgage relief to homeowners and funding for Fannie Mae and Freddie Mac
Yes	Approve a nuclear cooperation agreement with India
No	Approve final $700 billion program to stabilize financial markets
No	Allow consideration of a $14 billion auto industry loan package

2007

Yes	Increase minimum wage by $2.10 an hour
No	Limit debate on a comprehensive immigration bill
Yes	Overhaul congressional lobbying and ethics rules for members and their staffs
No	Limit debate on considering a bill to add House seats for the District of Columbia and Utah
No	Limit debate on restoring habeas corpus rights to detainees
No	Mandate minimum breaks for troops between deployments to Iraq or Afghanistan
No	Override Bush veto of $23.2 billion water projects authorization bill
Yes	Confirm Michael B. Mukasey as attorney general
No	Limit debate on an energy policy overhaul containing $21.8 billion in tax incentives and reduced oil and gas subsidies

CQ VOTE STUDIES

	PARTY UNITY		PRESIDENTIAL SUPPORT	
	SUPPORT	OPPOSE	SUPPORT	OPPOSE
2008	99%	1%	78%	22%
2007	96%	4%	89%	11%
2006	98%	2%	91%	9%
2005	94%	6%	84%	16%
2004	97%	3%	98%	2%
2003	99%	1%	97%	3%
2002	95%	5%	93%	7%
2001	95%	5%	99%	1%
2000	97%	3%	35%	65%
1999	95%	5%	24%	76%

INTEREST GROUPS

	AFL-CIO	ADA	CCUS	ACU
2008	10%	5%	75%	96%
2007	5%	10%	55%	96%
2006	8%	5%	91%	96%
2005	21%	10%	78%	96%
2004	9%	5%	100%	96%
2003	0%	5%	100%	80%
2002	17%	10%	89%	100%
2001	20%	10%	100%	92%
2000	0%	0%	100%	92%
1999	0%	0%	94%	92%

Sen. John Barrasso (R)

CAPITOL OFFICE
224-6441
barrasso.senate.gov
307 Dirksen Bldg. 20510-5003; fax 224-1724

COMMITTEES
Energy & Natural Resources
Environment & Public Works
Foreign Relations
Indian Affairs - vice chairman

RESIDENCE
Casper

BORN
July 21, 1952; Reading, Pa.

RELIGION
Presbyterian

FAMILY
Wife, Bobbi Barrasso; three children

EDUCATION
Georgetown U., B.S. 1974 (biology), M.D. 1978

CAREER
Surgeon

POLITICAL HIGHLIGHTS
Sought Republican nomination for U.S. Senate,
1996; Wyo. Senate, 2003-07

ELECTION RESULTS

2008 GENERAL

John Barrasso (R)	183,063	73.4%
Nick Carter (D)	66,202	26.5%

2008 PRIMARY

John Barrasso (R)	unopposed

Elected 2008; 1st term
Appointed June 2007

Though he was reared in the East, Barrasso has embraced his wide-open adoptive state right down to a self-effacing country manner. On the Senate floor, he has the air of a pastor reading the Sunday psalm. His views are strictly conservative, whether the issue is environmental, fiscal, social or foreign policy — a philosophy that tracks that of his predecessor, the late Republican Craig Thomas.

Barrasso (buh-RASS-o), an orthopedic surgeon, was appointed to replace Thomas, a former farm bureau executive who died of leukemia in June 2007, just into his third term. Barrasso's background is vastly different from his predecessor's, but his priorities are so in keeping that he easily won a November 2008 special election to serve the remainder of Thomas' term, which runs through 2012. He also serves as a GOP deputy whip.

When Barrasso took office, he vowed to continue Thomas' work. He took a seat on the Energy and Natural Resources Committee, where Thomas had served; Wyoming has had a senator on the committee overseeing natural resources since 1899. The first bill he introduced was a measure — which Thomas had been preparing to introduce before he died — to protect 1.2 million acres in the Wyoming Range of west-central Wyoming's Bridger-Teton National Forest from oil and gas development. The measure was signed into law as part of an omnibus lands measure in March 2009. That same catchall measure also included Barrasso's bill to create a five-year grant program to provide compensation for ranchers who have lost livestock to wolves.

Barrasso also favors allowing snowmobile users access to Yellowstone and Grand Teton parks, something Thomas had long advocated.

He sits on the Environment and Public Works Committee, where he looks out for his state's coal industry in the face of the Obama administration's interest in passing aggressive climate change legislation. He opposes a proposal to cap greenhouse gas emissions and set up a market-based trading system for emissions credits.

In spring 2009, Barrasso blocked the nomination of Regina McCarthy to be assistant administrator for air and radiation at the EPA. He said McCarthy, commissioner of the Connecticut Department of Environmental Protection, hadn't fully answered his questions about the impact of the administration's proposal to label carbon dioxide and five other gases as threats to public health because of their role in contributing to global climate change. That proposal would open the door to regulating such gases under the Clean Air Act, which he said would place sweeping restrictions on hospitals, schools, farms, commercial buildings and nursing homes. "The people and businesses of Wyoming need to know how they will be protected from the long arm of Washington," he said.

Barrasso also champions federal help for health care in rural areas. He was a cosponsor of the Craig Thomas Rural Hospital and Provider Equity Act and played a role in the inclusion of rural health care provisions in legislation late in 2007 to prevent a cut to doctors' Medicare payment rates. But he voted against a 2009 bill to expand the State Children's Health Insurance Program, which provides coverage to children whose low-income families don't qualify for Medicaid.

Barrasso also serves on the Foreign Relations and Indian Affairs committees. When drug-related violence in Mexico threatened to spill over the border in early 2009, he said gun owners' rights should not be weakened in the name of increased security.

On fiscal matters, he supports abolishing the estate tax and creating a "fairer and simpler" tax system. He has opposed every major spending bill to address the nation's economic crisis, including a $700 billion law — enacted in fall 2008 — to aid the financial services sector, and President Obama's $787 billion economic stimulus law in 2009. He said of Obama's $3.56 trillion budget blueprint for fiscal 2010: "This bill is the exact opposite of fiscal responsibility."

Barrasso also is far from Democrats' views on social policy. In 2007, he opposed expanding federal funding for stem cell research, which uses surplus embryos from in vitro fertilization procedures. His stance was a blow for some proponents of the research, who had hoped their colleague would support the measure. Senate Majority Leader Harry Reid of Nevada had even postponed a vote on the issue until after Thomas' vacancy was filled, hoping Thomas' successor would help Democrats override a Bush veto of expanded embryonic stem cell research funding.

In a 1996 GOP primary race for the Senate — which Michael B. Enzi won — Barrasso took a more moderate position on abortion than he does today. He opposed federal funding for abortions through Medicaid but said a decision on the procedure should be between a woman and her doctor. Subsequently, during four years in the state Senate, he took increasingly conservative positions and sponsored a bill to increase the penalty for killing a pregnant woman. He said most forms of abortion should be banned.

In the state Senate he also sponsored the "I'm Sorry" law, which protects physicians from lawsuits based on communications with their patients when unforeseen complications arise.

Barrasso grew up in Reading, Pa., part of a blue-collar family of committed Republicans. His grandfather worked as a cement finisher after emigrating from Italy in the early 1900s. His father joined the industry after quitting school in the ninth grade to supplement the family's income during the Great Depression. During World War II, Barrasso's father, also named John, joined the Army and fought in the Battle of the Bulge, the largest land battle of World War II in which the United States participated. (The younger Barrasso carried his late father's dog tags with him when he was sworn into Congress.)

After the war, his father returned to cement finishing, and his mother stayed home with their three children. At age 8, Barrasso made his first trip to Washington, for the January 1961 inauguration of Massachusetts Democrat John F. Kennedy as president, though, as Barrasso recalls, his father voted for Kennedy's Republican opponent, Vice President Richard Nixon. Barrasso later returned to study at Georgetown University, where he majored in biology and went on to earn a medical degree.

He spent summers in Reading, laying cement during the week and working at an auto racetrack on weekends. As a college student, he visited Wyoming and fell in love with the western landscape. After finishing his postgraduate medical residency in New Haven, Conn., he and his now-ex-wife moved to Casper, where they raised two children.

Barrasso wrote a newspaper column called "Keeping Wyoming Healthy" and gave health and fitness commentaries on television, where he would sign off with the tag line, "I'm Dr. John Barrasso, helping you care for yourself." For two decades, he hosted state broadcasts of the annual Jerry Lewis Telethon, which raises money for the Muscular Dystrophy Association.

Barrasso's 1996 bid to replace Republican Sen. Alan K. Simpson was his first campaign for public office; he signed on as Enzi's finance chairman after losing to him in the primary. Barrasso's appointment to the U.S. Senate came under unusual political circumstances. Unlike most states, Wyoming effectively requires the governor to select someone from the previous senator's party.

On a personal level, on New Year's Day 2008, Barrasso married longtime friend Bobbi Brown, who had been Thomas' state director for nearly 17 years.

KEY VOTES

2008

Yes Prohibit discrimination based on genetic information

Yes Reauthorize farm and nutrition programs for five years

No Limit debate on "cap and trade" system for greenhouse gas emissions

No Allow lawsuits against companies that participated in warrantless wiretapping

No Limit debate on a bill to block a scheduled cut in Medicare payments to doctors

No Grant mortgage relief to homeowners and funding for Fannie Mae and Freddie Mac

Yes Approve a nuclear cooperation agreement with India

No Approve final $700 billion program to stabilize financial markets

No Allow consideration of a $14 billion auto industry loan package

2007

No Limit debate on a comprehensive immigration bill

Yes Overhaul congressional lobbying and ethics rules for members and their staffs

No Limit debate on considering a bill to add House seats for the District of Columbia and Utah

No Limit debate on restoring habeas corpus rights to detainees

No Mandate minimum breaks for troops between deployments to Iraq or Afghanistan

Yes Override Bush veto of $23.2 billion water projects authorization bill

Yes Confirm Michael B. Mukasey as attorney general

No Limit debate on an energy policy overhaul containing $21.8 billion in tax incentives and reduced oil and gas subsidies

CQ VOTE STUDIES

	PARTY UNITY		PRESIDENTIAL SUPPORT	
	SUPPORT	OPPOSE	SUPPORT	OPPOSE
2008	99%	1%	76%	24%
2007	96%	4%	84%	16%

INTEREST GROUPS

	AFL-CIO	ADA	CCUS	ACU
2008	10%	5%	75%	96%
2007	0%	10%	75%	100%

Rep. Cynthia M. Lummis (R)

Elected 2008; 1st term

Lummis may be new to Congress, but over the last three decades she has spent time in a variety of posts in Wyoming politics. That experience, she said, helped make her a strong advocate of states' rights — one of many positions she holds that are prevalent among Western conservatives. "I see states as the great innovators and the great incubators of ideas," she said.

Lummis served eight years as state treasurer, a job she said gave her "hands-on experience" in dealing with the economic crisis confronting Congress when she took office. A member of the Budget Committee, she opposed President Obama's early economic initiatives and said his emphasis on more spending "takes it out of the hides of the American people, placing a tax on their dreams." She also serves on a House GOP task force that looks at ways to help rural areas.

She plans to advocate for her state's natural resource-rich economy as a member of the Natural Resources Committee dealing with energy matters.

"Wyoming has what America needs," Lummis said. "We have oil, gas, coal, uranium, solar, biomass, and the technology is being developed in Wyoming to recover these resources, renewable and non-renewable."

As a member of the Agriculture Committee, she hopes to focus on the "slow food" movement, which serves as an alternative to fast food and centers around healthy eating choices and homegrown ingredients to help small-business owners. Lummis believes a focus on the movement will help family farms and ranches without the need for government spending.

Her experience as a college intern for Wyoming's Senate agriculture committee prompted her entry into politics. She became the youngest woman ever elected to the state legislature at 24. An early assignment to the state Senate Judiciary Committee convinced her to attend law school, but she later returned to the legislature.

She won the race to succeed retiring seven-term GOP Rep. Barbara Cubin with 53 percent of the vote, boosted by turnout in the heavily Republican state that enabled Arizona GOP Sen. John McCain to carry Wyoming with nearly two-thirds of the vote.

CAPITOL OFFICE
225-2311
lummis.house.gov
1004 Longworth Bldg. 20515-5001; fax 225-3057

COMMITTEES
Agriculture
Budget
Natural Resources

RESIDENCE
Cheyenne

BORN
Sept. 10, 1954; Cheyenne, Wyo.

RELIGION
Lutheran - Missouri Synod

FAMILY
Husband, Al Wiederspahn; one child

EDUCATION
U. of Wyoming, B.S. 1976 (animal science),
B.S. 1978 (biology), J.D. 1985

CAREER
Rancher; lawyer; gubernatorial aide

POLITICAL HIGHLIGHTS
Wyo. House, 1979-83, 1985-93; Wyo. Senate,
1993-95; Wyo. State Lands and Investment
acting director, 1997-98; Wyo. treasurer, 1999-2007

ELECTION RESULTS

2008 GENERAL

Cynthia M. Lummis (R)	131,244	52.6%
Gary Trauner (D)	106,758	42.8%
W. David Herbert (LIBERT)	11,030	4.4%

2008 PRIMARY

Cynthia M. Lummis (R)	33,149	46.2%
Mark Gordon (R)	26,827	37.4%
Bill Winney (R)	8,537	11.9%
Michael S. Holland (R)	3,171	4.4%

WYOMING

At Large

Wyoming, the least populated state, basks in its wide-open spaces, which define its libertarian politics and natural-resources-based economy. The Grand Tetons' jagged peaks rise from the floor of the Jackson Hole Valley to their 13,000-foot apex.

Tourist attractions such as Yellowstone National Park, the first national park, are economic staples. The state relies on ranching and mining, but wind turbines have been popping up along the landscape. Although the state lacks a highly diversified economy, stability in retail and government jobs has attracted some out-of-state workers from areas hit hard by the nationwide recession.

Residents savor their land and resources and reject government intrusion, especially regarding land use. Most residents are happy with relative seclusion, a tranquil lifestyle and little population growth. State lawmakers are loath to raise taxes. Wyoming, with a statewide 4 percent sales tax, has no corporate or personal income taxes.

Voters favor the GOP but will sometimes allow personality to triumph over party if a Democrat is moderate and unaffiliated with the national party. Wyoming has not elected a Democrat to Congress since 1976, but has elected a Democratic governor in 7 of the last 9 elections. John McCain took 65 percent of Wyoming's 2008 presidential vote, his second-best state showing.

MAJOR INDUSTRY
Mining, tourism, agriculture

MILITARY BASES
Francis E. Warren Air Force Base,
3,361 military, 964 civilian (2009)

CITIES
Cheyenne, 53,011; Casper, 49,644;
Laramie, 27,204; Gillette, 19,646

NOTABLE
Jackson was the first U.S. town ever (1920) to elect an all-female slate — mayor, council and marshal.

Del. Eni F.H. Faleomavaega (D)

CAPITOL OFFICE
225-8577
www.house.gov/faleomavaega
2422 Rayburn Bldg. 20515-5201; fax 225-8757

COMMITTEES
Foreign Affairs
(Asia, the Pacific & the Global Environment
- chairman)
Natural Resources

RESIDENCE
Pago Pago

BORN
Aug. 15, 1943; Vailoatai, Am. Samoa

RELIGION
Mormon

FAMILY
Wife, Hinanui Bambridge Hunkin; five children

EDUCATION
Brigham Young U., A.A. 1964, B.A. 1966
(political science); Texas Southern U.,
attended 1969 (law); U. of Houston, J.D. 1972;
U. of California, Berkeley, LL.M. 1973

MILITARY SERVICE
Army, 1966-69; Army Reserve, 1983-2001

CAREER
Lawyer; territorial prosecutor; congressional aide

POLITICAL HIGHLIGHTS
Democratic candidate for U.S. House, 1984;
lieutenant governor, 1985-89

ELECTION RESULTS

2008 GENERAL

Eni F.H. Faleomavaega (D)	7,498	60.4%
Aumua Amata (R)	4,349	35.0%
Rosie F. Tago Lancaster (I)	570	4.6%

2006 GENERAL

Eni F.H. Faleomavaega (D)	5,195	47.1%
Aumua Amata (R)	4,493	40.7%
Ae Ae Muavaefaatasi Jr. (I)	1,345	12.2%

PREVIOUS WINNING PERCENTAGES
2004 (65%); 2002 General Election Runoff (55%);
2000 General Election Runoff (61%); 1998 (86%);
1996 General Election Runoff (56%); 1994 (64%);
1992 (65%); 1990 (55%); 1988 (51%)

Elected 1988; 11th term

Faleomavaega has spent more than two decades in the House seeking to protect and improve his island territory's economy, which is dominated by tuna fishing and processing. With a calm manner, he openly discusses the challenges workers in American Samoa face in foreign competition.

Faleomavaega (full name: EN-ee FOL-ee-oh-mav-ah-ENG-uh) is the third-ranking Democrat on the Foreign Affairs Committee and chairs the panel on Asia, the Pacific and the Global Environment. He also sits on the Natural Resources Committee. He struggles to satisfy both constituents and companies. "No fish means no canneries and no canneries means no jobs for our workers," he said.

In early 2009, Faleomavaega appealed for a delay in a 2007 minimum wage hike — which he had reluctantly supported — contending worsening economic conditions would hamper companies' ability to comply. And he included in President Obama's economic stimulus law a provision requiring a report on the effects of the wage hike on the territories.

In 2008, he came under fire from local officials for attaching a provision in the annual Coast Guard funding bill to allow foreign-built tuna boats to operate under the U.S. flag and fish off the islands near American Samoa. Fishermen argued that would foreclose the possibility of restoring a U.S. tuna-boat-building industry. The bill ultimately stalled in the Senate. He also hopes to gain a tsunami monitoring and early warning system for the islands, and he pushes to remove the limit on Medicaid funding territories can receive.

Faleomavaega attended high school in Hawaii, where his father was stationed in the Navy. After college, he joined the Army and served in Vietnam before returning to the mainland for law school. He worked for eight years in Washington, first as an executive assistant to American Samoa's first elected representative to the Capitol, A.U. Fuimaono, then for California Democratic Rep. Phillip Burton, the Interior Committee chairman at the time.

He returned to Pago Pago in 1981, serving as a deputy attorney general, then lieutenant governor. He is a "matai," a Samoan chief, a title he's held since 1988. Faleomavaega is also his title; his family name is Hunkin. He has typically had tough re-election battles, but in 2008 he took 60 percent of the vote.

TERRITORIES

American Samoa

In the heart of Polynesia, American Samoa is the nation's southernmost territory and the least populated entity represented in the U.S. House. Located about 2,500 miles southwest of Hawaii, it is composed of five volcanic islands and two outlying coral atolls. Its total land area is 76 square miles, slightly more than the District of Columbia. Tourists venture here for snorkeling, fishing, hiking and the islands' secluded beaches.

An 1899 treaty gave the United States control over the islands in the eastern portion of the Samoan archipelago. During World War II, the U.S. Marine Corps, attracted by the deep-water harbor at Pago Pago, made the island an advanced training and staging center. Today it is an unincorporated territory of the United States, administered by the Interior Department. Residents are U.S. nationals, not citizens, and the territory has had a non-voting delegate since 1981.

Most land here is communally owned. Per capita income is very low, and federal aid, including welfare and food stamps, is vital. Economic growth, even in the promising tourism sector, is hindered by American Samoa's isolation, limited transportation and susceptibility to hurricanes. In recent years, there has been a concerted government effort to cope with the islands' limited resources of fresh water.

Tuna fishing is key to the private sector economy, but one of the islands' two canneries is closing. The loss of thousands of jobs and uncertainty about the overall health of the market concern officials and residents.

MAJOR INDUSTRY
Government, handicrafts, tourism, fishing

VILLAGES
Tafuna, 8,409; Nu'uuli, 5,154; Pago Pago, 4,278

NOTABLE
Anthropologist Margaret Mead studied on Ta'u and wrote "Coming of Age in Samoa."

Del. Eleanor Holmes Norton (D)

Elected 1990; 10th term

Norton is a savvy politician with a keen understanding of the legislative process. Her emphasis on results over ideology has won her respect from Republicans, while her determination to be a vocal advocate for her constituents has repeatedly won her re-election.

Her longtime goal has been full representation in the House, which would change her own title from delegate to representative. In April 2007, the House passed a measure to give the D.C. delegate floor voting privileges while adding one more House seat for Utah, which barely missed getting another seat after the last census reapportionment. But the measure collapsed in the Senate after supporters were unable to get the 60 votes needed to limit debate. Congress took up the measure again in 2009, but negotiations got bogged down when the Senate passed a version including language to repeal the District's restrictions on semiautomatic weapons.

From her seat on the Oversight and Government Reform Committee, she has worked on giving the city government midyear budget autonomy, allowing it to spend locally raised funds without returning to secure congressional approval. She also wants to reform the Government Services Administration, which she said has failed to restructure itself into a modern agency that is cost-effective and environmentally friendly.

From her Homeland Security panel seat, Norton has worked to rejuvenate southeast D.C.'s economy by relocating the department's headquarters to the area. And on the Transportation and Infrastructure panel, she chairs the Subcommittee on Economic Development, Public Buildings and Emergency Management. She hopes repairing infrastructure can stimulate the economy.

A native Washingtonian, Norton graduated in the last segregated class at Dunbar High School. Her father was a city employee, and her mother a teacher. After earning a law degree at Yale and working in Mississippi with civil rights groups, she took a job with the American Civil Liberties Union. She was teaching law at Georgetown University in 1990 when D.C. Delegate Walter E. Fauntroy stepped down to run for mayor. She routinely wins with more than 90 percent of the vote.

CAPITOL OFFICE
225-8050
www.norton.house.gov
2136 Rayburn Bldg. 20515-5101; fax 225-3002

COMMITTEES
Homeland Security
Oversight & Government Reform
Transportation & Infrastructure
(Economic Development, Public Buildings
& Emergency Management - chairwoman)

RESIDENCE
Washington

BORN
June 13, 1937; Washington, D.C.

RELIGION
Episcopalian

FAMILY
Divorced; two children

EDUCATION
Antioch College, B.A. 1960 (history); Yale U.,
M.A. 1963 (American studies); LL.B. 1964;

CAREER
Professor; lawyer

POLITICAL HIGHLIGHTS
New York City Human Rights Commission,
1971-77; Equal Employment Opportunity
Commission chairwoman, 1977-81

ELECTION RESULTS

2008 GENERAL

Eleanor Holmes Norton (D)	228,376	92.3%
Maude Louise Hills (GREEN)	16,693	6.7%

2008 PRIMARY

Eleanor Holmes Norton (D)	38,999	98.3%
write-ins (D)	682	1.7%

2006 GENERAL

Eleanor Holmes Norton (D)	111,726	97.3%
write-ins	3,051	2.7%

PREVIOUS WINNING PERCENTAGES
2004 (91%); 2002 (93%); 2000 (90%); 1998 (90%);
1996 (90%); 1994 (89%); 1992 (85%); 1990 (62%)

District of Columbia

"Taxation Without Representation." That slogan on the District's license plates sums up succinctly residents' displeasure at not being able to participate fully in a democracy that they host. The city's budget and laws are subject to review and veto by Congress, a body in which the residents have no vote.

Although residents have a vote for president, a non-voting delegate in the House and an elected mayor, efforts to gain full participation in the U.S. government — including bids for statehood — have not yet succeeded.

It is no surprise that the main business of the nation's capital is the government. Hundreds of thousands work for the federal or local governments or in related private sector fields, such as lobbying, law and journalism. It also is no surprise that the District draws hordes of tourists who come to see the White House, Smithsonian museums and national monuments.

Although the city has one of the wealthier and most-educated populations in the nation, that wealth is not spread evenly throughout the District, with the wealthiest areas in the northwest quadrant. Some revitalized enclaves, such as those just east of the U.S. Capitol, attract national chains and young professionals. Local officials hope planned development along the Anacostia River, on Georgia Avenue and in the northeast quadrant will spur further economic growth.

MAJOR INDUSTRY
Government, professional services

MILITARY BASES
Walter Reed Army Medical Center, 1,679 military, 2,206 civilian; Bolling Air Force Base, 1,961 military, 1,007 civilian; Fort McNair (Army), 1,017 military, 1,033 civilian (2004)

2008 POPULATION (EST.)
Washington, 591,833

NOTABLE
Since residents first began casting votes for president in 1964, the Republican candidate's share has ranged from a high of 22 percent in 1972 to a low of 7 percent in 2008.

Del. Madeleine Z. Bordallo (D)

Elected 2002; 4th term

A Minnesota native who has lived most of her life in Guam, Bordallo protects the Pacific island's interests as chairwoman of a Natural Resources panel and serves as point person for a multibillion-dollar military buildup that will continue to feed the island's economy. She has garnered wide support back home and has run unopposed since her initial election in 2002.

As chairwoman of the Insular Affairs, Oceans & Wildlife Subcommittee, Bordallo (bore-DAA-yo) pushes legislation to curb overfishing, clamp down on illegal fishing and protect coral reefs.

Her top legislative focus is protecting Guam's military bases. On the Armed Services panel, she watches over a $15 billion military buildup that will include the transfer of thousands of troops from Okinawa, Japan. She has steered defense funds home. The fiscal 2009 defense authorization included $180 million in military construction spending for Guam and created an account within the U.S. Treasury to manage Japan's $6 billion contribution for the buildup. Bordallo also prods the U.S. government to provide restitution for islanders who spent 32 months under Japanese occupation during World War II.

Dubbed "Miss Guam" by her House colleagues, she educates fellow members about the 212-square-mile island. Her family had moved to Guam from Minnesota when she was 15 so her father could take a job as the principal of the island's only high school. She returned after attending college in the Midwest to study music.

She married Ricardo J. Bordallo, the son of a wealthy and politically connected island family. Ricardo served as the island's governor, and Bordallo won a seat in the island's legislature. But in 1990, caught up in a corruption case, Ricardo wrapped himself in the Guam flag, chained himself to a statue of Chief Kepuha on the island's main thoroughfare and shot himself in the head.

That same year she lost the gubernatorial race to Republican Joseph F. Ada. She remained in the island's legislature and later served as lieutenant governor. In 2002, when five-term Democratic Del. Robert A. Underwood ran unsuccessfully for governor of Guam, Bordallo became the first woman to seek the delegate post. She won with 65 percent of the vote.

CAPITOL OFFICE
225-1188
www.house.gov/bordallo
427 Cannon Bldg. 20515-5301; fax 226-0341

COMMITTEES
Armed Services
Natural Resources
(Insular Affairs, Oceans & Wildlife - chairwoman)

RESIDENCE
Tumuning

BORN
May 31, 1933; Graceville, Minn.

RELIGION
Roman Catholic

FAMILY
Widowed; one child

EDUCATION
Saint Mary's College (Ind.), attended 1952-53;
The College of St. Catherine, A.A. 1953
(music & voice)

CAREER
Guam first lady; shoe company founder;
radio show host

POLITICAL HIGHLIGHTS
Guam Senate, 1981-83, 1987-95; Democratic
nominee for governor, 1990; lieutenant
governor, 1995-2003

ELECTION RESULTS

2008 GENERAL

Madeleine Z. Bordallo (D)	28,247	94.6%
write-ins	1,617	5.4%

2008 PRIMARY

Madeleine Z. Bordallo (D)	8,716	69.0%
Jonathan B. Diaz (D)	2,904	23.0%

2006 GENERAL

Madeleine Z. Bordallo (D)	32,677	96.5%
write-ins	1,201	3.5%

PREVIOUS WINNING PERCENTAGES
2004 (97%); 2002 (65%)

TERRITORIES

Guam

"Where America's day begins," Guam is the largest and most southerly island in the Marianas archipelago. At 212 square miles, it is about three times the size of the District of Columbia. More than 3,800 miles west of Hawaii and across the International Date Line from the U.S. mainland, Guam is closer to Tokyo than Honolulu.

The indigenous people, the Chamorros, first had contact with Europeans in 1521 with the visit of Ferdinand Magellan. Spain ceded Guam to the United States in 1898, and the U.S. Navy administered Guam until 1950, when residents were granted U.S. citizenship and elected a local government. Guam has had a non-voting delegate in the House since 1973. Although residents are citizens, they may not vote in presidential elections.

Guam's economy is heavily dependent on a U.S. military presence, which is expected to increase here by 2014, when tens of thousands of Marines will be relocated to Guam from bases in Japan. A tropical climate, pristine beaches and a picturesque countryside make the island an ideal vacation spot, and tourism is vital to the local economy. Per capita income in 2005 was $12,768.

Most food and other consumer goods are imported. In recent years, Guam has had to cope with large influxes of illegal immigrants, who pay smugglers to sneak them onto the island to seek asylum in the United States.

MAJOR INDUSTRY
Military, tourism, construction, shipping

MILITARY BASES
Naval Station Guam, 4,050 military, 1,806 civilian; Andersen Air Force Base, 2,170 military, 400 civilian (2004)

DISTRICTS
Dededo, 42,980; Yigo, 19,474; Tamuning, 18,012

NOTABLE
If measured from its undersea base in the Marianas Trench, Mount Humuyong Manglo would be the highest mountain in the world.

Del. Gregorio Kilili Camacho Sablan (D)

CAPITOL OFFICE
225-2646
sablan.house.gov
423 Cannon Bldg. 20515; fax

COMMITTEES
Education & Labor
Natural Resources

RESIDENCE
Saipan

BORN
Jan. 19, 1955; Saipan, N. Marianas

RELIGION
Roman Catholic

FAMILY
Wife, Andrea C. Sablan; six children

EDUCATION
U. of Hawaii, Manoa, attended 1989-90

MILITARY SERVICE
Army, 1981-86

CAREER
Election commission director; gubernatorial aide

POLITICAL HIGHLIGHTS
N. Marianas House, 1982-86

ELECTION RESULTS

2008 GENERAL

Gregorio Kilili Camacho Sablan (I)	2,474	24.3%
Pete A. Tenorio (R)	2,117	20.8%
John Oliver Delos Reyes Gonzalez (I)	1,855	18.3%
Juan Tudela Lizama (I)	1,819	17.9%
Luis Palacios Crisostimo (I)	946	9.3%
David Mendiola Cing (D)	307	3.0%
Felipe Quitugua Atalig (I)	249	2.4%
Chong Man Won (I)	230	2.3%
John Henry Davis Jr. (I)	164	1.6%

Elected 2008; 1st term

A lifelong public servant, Sablan has pledged to take a diplomatic approach to represent his constituents' concerns for improved infrastructure, health care and education. As a former special assistant to Democratic Sen. Daniel K. Inouye of Hawaii, he's no stranger to the ways of Washington.

Sablan holds the first seat added to the small group of non-voting House delegates since American Samoa elected its first delegate in 1981. President George W. Bush signed legislation creating the Northern Marianas delegate position in May 2008. Sablan (full name: greg-OREO key-LEE-lee ka-MAH-cho sab-LAHN) said during his campaign, which he ran as an independent, that party affiliation shouldn't matter, as he would work with anyone. But soon after he took office, he joined the Democratic Caucus.

He sits on the Education and Labor Committee, where he can look out for concerns back home. In his first months, Sablan — a member of the Congressional Hispanic Caucus task force on immigration — helped persuade the federal government to delay by six months the application of federal immigration law to the commonwealth. The law had been scheduled to take effect in the islands in June. It includes an exemption for local employers from a cap on the number of H-1B and H-2B visas, and would effectively restrict travel to the commonwealth from Russia and China — both valuable tourist markets — and would institute a visa waiver program to allow Hong Kong tourists and other eligible visitors longer visits here. Sablan and other local officials said the commonwealth needed more time to make preparations.

A member of the Natural Resources panel, he also introduced a bill in 2009 to convey to the commonwealth the submerged lands surrounding each of the Northern Mariana Islands out to three miles from the coastline.

Sablan was born on the island of Saipan, and at age 11 his family moved to Micronesia. He later finished high school in Saipan, and attended college in Guam and in Berkeley, Calif. He served in several gubernatorial administrations in the Marianas. He was a two-term member of the commonwealth House before being named the executive director of the Commonwealth Election Commission. He won a nine-way race for the U.S. House seat in 2008.

TERRITORIES

Northern Mariana Islands

A string of more than a dozen mostly volcanic islands forming the eastern boundary of the Philippine Sea in the tropical Pacific Ocean, the Northern Mariana Islands rely on the federal government and tourism. Saipan, the commonwealth's largest island and capital, supports more than 90 percent of the population and most of the local economy. Tinian and Rota are the commonwealth's other inhabited islands.

After three centuries of colonization by Spain, decades of control by Germany and then Japan, and participation in a territorial structure with other Micronesian islands, the Northern Marianas in 1976 became a commonwealth of the United States. Residents are U.S. citizens but cannot vote in presidential elections. Formerly represented in Washington by a resident representative, the Northern Marianas gained a two-year term delegate to the U.S. House in 2009.

Tourists and prospective members of the workforce arrive in large numbers from Asia, and Asians make up more than half of the population. Filipinos and Chamorros, a native island population, make up the largest individual ethnic groups and 8 percent of residents here are of multiple ethnicities.

The federal government is a stable source of jobs, as well as a source of economic subsidies. Hotels are among the largest employers on the islands, but employment rates, family incomes and population have decreased over the past decade. The median household income in the Northern Marianas was roughly $17,000 in 2004.

MAJOR INDUSTRY
Government, tourism

ISLANDS
Saipan, 60,608; Tinian, 2,829; Rota, 2,490

NOTABLE
More than three-fourths of the population speaks a language other than English at home.

Res. Cmsr. Pedro R. Pierluisi (D)

Elected 2008; 1st term

CAPITOL OFFICE
225-2615
pierluisi.house.gov
1218 Longworth Bldg. 20515-5401; fax 225-2154

COMMITTEES
Education & Labor
Judiciary
Natural Resources

RESIDENCE
San Juan

BORN
April 26, 1959; San Juan, P.R.

RELIGION
Roman Catholic

FAMILY
Wife, Maria Elena Carrión; four children

EDUCATION
Tulane U., B.A. 1981 (American history);
George Washington U., J.D. 1984

CAREER
Lawyer

POLITICAL HIGHLIGHTS
P.R. secretary of Justice, 1993-96

ELECTION RESULTS

2008 GENERAL

Pedro R. Pierluisi (NP)	1,010,285	53.1%
Alfredo Salazar (POPDEM)	810,093	42.5%
Carlos A. Velázquez López (PR)	46,123	2.4%
Jessica Martínez Birriel (PRI)	37,865	2.0%

2008 PRIMARY

Pedro R. Pierluisi (NP)	440,672	59.6%
Charlie Rodríguez (NP)	248,127	33.6%
Miriam Ramírez (X)	50,590	6.8%

Pierluisi hails from Puerto Rico, but he's familiar with Washington; the resident commissioner graduated from George Washington University's law school and served as a part-time aide to former resident commissioner Baltasar Corrada del Rio during the 1980s.

The only House member with a four-year term, Pierluisi will have plenty of opportunities to forge relationships and work on his priorities, which include looking after the island's banking and housing sectors hit by the economic crisis. He also said he wants to lift a cap on the level of federal Medicaid funding Puerto Rico can receive. And in March 2009, Pierluisi introduced a bill to require that military veterans in Guam and Puerto Rico have access to the same health services available in the states.

From his seat on the Education and Labor Committee, Pierluisi (pea-air-loo-EE-see) supported a bill in May 2009 to authorize billions of dollars for "green" school renovation and modernization projects.

He also sits on the Judiciary Committee. He served as Puerto Rico's attorney general for roughly four years during the 1990s and was recruited by White House officials to lobby key members of Congress voting on President Clinton's 1994 crime bill. He also helped obtain Puerto Rico's designation as a High Intensity Drug Trafficking area.

Pierluisi, a member of the Congressional Hispanic Caucus, cosponsored a 2009 bill by Tennessee Democrat Steve Cohen to create a pilot program to study the causes of racial and ethnic disparities in the judicial system.

A member of the Natural Resources Committee, he also backed legislation by Democratic Del. Madeleine Z. Bordallo of Guam to authorize increased funding for programs and research aimed at protecting coral reefs.

He was born in San Juan, and said his interest in public service stems from his father, Jorge, a former secretary of housing for Puerto Rico. Pierluisi is a member of the New Progressive Party in Puerto Rico, which advocates statehood for the island territory. In November 2008, he defeated Democrat Alfredo Salazar to succeed Republican Luis Fortuño, who ran a successful campaign for governor — also on the New Progressive Party ticket.

TERRITORIES

Puerto Rico

Puerto Rico, the largest and most populated (3.8 million) of the territories, has been a self-governing commonwealth of the United States since 1952. Median household income here in 2007 was about $18,000 — high by Caribbean standards, but still only about half that of the poorest state.

Christopher Columbus arrived in Puerto Rico in 1493, and the Spanish arrived 15 years later. The Spanish brought slaves to work in the sugar cane fields, and slavery was not abolished on the island until 1873. Spain ceded the territory to the United States in 1898 following the Spanish-American War. Its residents became U.S. citizens in 1917, but they cannot vote for president. Since 1901, Puerto Ricans have been represented in the House by a resident commissioner.

The island's political status has been a long-standing issue, with various factions favoring continued commonwealth status, statehood or independence. In 2008, Puerto Ricans elected a pro-statehood ticket as former Res. Cmsr. Luis Fortuño, who caucused with the GOP, was elected governor and Pedro R. Pierluisi won the U.S. House seat.

Puerto Rico's economy, one of the most stable in the Caribbean, thrives off its tourism industry and industrial sector. Nearly 5 million tourists visit Puerto Rico each year; El Yunque tropical forest and local beaches are popular destinations. Mainland U.S. firms also invest heavily here, encouraged by tax incentives and by duty-free access to the United States.

MAJOR INDUSTRY
Manufacturing, service, tourism

MILITARY BASES
Fort Buchanan, 190 military, 699 civilian (2004)

CITIES
San Juan (unincorporated), 434,374;
Bayamón (unincorporated), 224,044

NOTABLE
Coliseo Roberto Clemente was named after the baseball star and Puerto Rico native.

Del. Donna M.C. Christensen (D)

Elected 1996; 7th term

Christensen has seen her role broaden since Democrats assumed control of the House in 2007. Along with her fellow delegates from the territories and the District of Columbia, she now has limited voting rights on the House floor. And in 2009 she was granted a seat on the Energy and Commerce Committee, which she had long sought so she could help develop health care legislation.

A physician by training, Christensen sits on the Energy and Commerce Committee's Health panel and seeks to lift a cap on federal Medicaid funding for the U.S. territories. She is a vice chairwoman of the Congressional Black Caucus and former chairwoman of its Health Braintrust, where she has fought to eliminate health care disparities suffered by minority groups.

She also sits on the Natural Resources Committee, where during the 110th Congress (2007-08) she was chairwoman of the panel on Insular Affairs. In 2009, she applauded passage of President Obama's $787 billion economic stimulus law that included nearly $1.7 million for national parks in the Virgin Islands.

Among her other priorities is a constitutional amendment to grant the territories the right to vote in presidential elections.

During the 110th Congress, President George W. Bush signed into law her measure creating a new House delegate for the Northern Mariana Islands — a seat filled by Gregorio Kilili Camacho Sablan, who ran as an independent but later joined the Democratic Caucus.

The daughter of a St. Croix judge, Christensen was inspired by a booklet encouraging African-American students to consider careers in medicine. She attended medical school at George Washington University and did post-graduate training in San Francisco and Washington, D.C., before returning to the Virgin Islands. Over her 20-year medical career she worked in clinics and hospitals on St. Croix and later became acting commissioner of health.

She lost her first race for delegate in 1994. But in 1996 she edged out Del. Victor O. Frazer, who ran as an independent, and Republican Kenneth Mapp in a three-way battle. She has won easily since.

CAPITOL OFFICE
225-1790
donnachristensen.house.gov
1510 Longworth Bldg. 20515-5501; fax 225-5517

COMMITTEES
Energy & Commerce
Natural Resources

RESIDENCE
St. Croix

BORN
Sept. 19, 1945; Teaneck, N.J.

RELIGION
Moravian

FAMILY
Husband, Chris Christensen; two children, four stepchildren

EDUCATION
Saint Mary's College (Ind.), B.S. 1966 (biology); George Washington U., M.D. 1970

CAREER
Physician; health official

POLITICAL HIGHLIGHTS
Virgin Is. Democratic Territorial Committee, 1980-97 (chairwoman, 1980-82); Virgin Is. Board of Education, 1984-86; Virgin Is. acting commissioner of health, 1993-94; sought Democratic nomination for U.S. House, 1994

ELECTION RESULTS

2008 GENERAL

Donna M.C. Christensen (D)		unopposed

2006 GENERAL

Donna M.C. Christensen (D)	18,322	62.9%
Warren B. Mosler (I)	10,800	37.1%

PREVIOUS WINNING PERCENTAGES
2004 (66%); 2002 (68%); 2000 (78%); 1998 (80%); 1996 General Runoff Election (52%)

TERRITORIES

Virgin Islands

The Virgin Islands, just east of Puerto Rico, are known for their subtropical climate, beautiful beaches, duty-free shopping and — far too often — being in the path of tropical storms. The first three attributes have helped build a tourism industry, while the storms and, more recently, budget shortfalls, have made economic development an uneven and difficult process.

Spain asserted its authority over the islands after Christopher Columbus arrived in 1493, and over the next century Spanish settlers killed or drove out the native Indians. But, Spain showed no real interest in setting up a colony on the Virgin Islands.

Denmark established a colony on St. Thomas in the mid-17th century, and sugar plantations drove the islands' economy until slavery was abolished in 1848. The U.S. government bought the islands from Denmark for $25 million in 1917.

The Virgin Islands is an unincorporated territory and is under the jurisdiction of the Interior Department. The territory is composed of 68 islands and cays, but only four are inhabited. Its population in 2000 was 108,612. Residents are U.S. citizens but may not vote for president. The Virgin Islands has had a non-voting House delegate since 1973.

Cruise ships make regular stops at the islands, principally at the capital of Charlotte Amalie on St. Thomas but also in neighboring St. Croix. Passengers stream ashore to take advantage of duty-free shopping, and most of the Virgin Islands' tourists leave without spending a night. A large petroleum refinery and a rum distillery on St. Croix, as well as light industry on other islands, provide other bases of economic stability.

MAJOR INDUSTRY
Tourism, petroleum refining, rum distilling

CITIES
Charlotte Amalie, 11,004; Christiansted, 2,637

NOTABLE
The Virgin Islands is the only U.S. territory where traffic travels on the left.

Member Statistics

The 2008 election was the first in 16 years in which voters elected a Democratic president, House and Senate. The 111th Congress includes the oldest Senate in history and the oldest House in more than a century, and the average tenure of a member of Congress — 13 years among current senators and 11 years for House members — is the longest ever.

Over time, Congress has gained more women (a record 90 female senators and representatives serve in the 111th) as well as a little more diversity. But a demographic analysis shows that the 111th, like those before it, is still dominated by white, middle-aged men.

The following pages offer some facts and figures about the men and women of the 111th Congress.

111th Congress by the Numbers

1981   The year the youngest member of Congress, Illinois Republican Rep. Aaron Schock, was born. He is the only current House member born after the launch of C-SPAN, which went live on March 19, 1979.

541   The total membership of Congress, including the new delegate from the Northern Mariana Islands.

160   The number of Roman Catholics in Congress. Protestants make up the largest religious group, but Catholics are the largest single denomination.

21   The number of years Delaware Democrat Ted Kaufman worked as an aide for his immediate predecessor in the Senate, Joseph R. Biden Jr., who is now vice president.

17   The number of members who were born abroad. Freshman Lousiana Republican Rep. Anh "Joseph" Cao is the first member of Congress to be born in Vietnam.

13   The number of former governors in the 111th Congress. Four of them — Sens. Mike Johanns, R-Neb.; Jim Risch, R-Idaho; Jeanne Shaheen, D-N.H.; and Mark Warner, D-Va. — were elected to Congress in 2008.

6   The number of states whose congressional delegations are represented entirely by one party. Hawaii, Massachusetts, New Mexico, North Dakota and Rhode Isand are all-Democratic, while Wyoming is represented solely by the GOP. Connecticut and Vermont would be all Democratic delegations, but for Sens. Joseph I. Lieberman and Bernard Sanders, who are independents that caucus with the Democrats.

5   The number of Rhodes scholars currently in Congress — Reps. Jim Cooper, D-Tenn., and Jim Himes, D-Conn., and Sens. Russ Feingold, D-Wis., Richard G. Lugar, R-Ind., and David Vitter, R-La.

1   The number of African-Americans in the Senate. Illinois Democrat Roland W. Burris was appointed to the seat previously held by President Obama.

Get to know the 111th Congress with these fact files, charts, statistics and other handy reference guides. Immerse yourself in campaign finance numbers.

Check out who's a member of which caucus, scope out who's a doctor, a pilot or born overseas. Plus, you can test your congressional IQ with "Did You Know?"

SENIORITY ... 1134	MOST/LEAST BILLS ... 1146	COMMITTEE FACTS ... 1161
FORMER GOVERNORS ... 1139	FAMILIES IN CONGRESS ... 1147	DISTRICT DEMOGRAPHICS ... 1162
WOMEN IN CONGRESS ... 1140	PRONUNCIATION GUIDE ... 1148	CLOSEST ELECTIONS ... 1164
OLDEST/YOUNGEST ... 1140	HALF-LIFE IN CONGRESS ... 1149	SPLIT TICKETS ... 1165
MINORITIES IN CONGRESS ... 1141	SENATORS UP IN 2010 ... 1150	TOP SPENDERS ... 1166
BORN ABROAD ... 1141	DEANS OF DELEGATIONS ... 1151	CAMPAIGN FINANCE ... 1168
FORMER HILL AIDES ... 1142	OCCUPATIONS ... 1152	HOUSE COMMITTEES ... 1184
BORN IN D.C. ... 1143	RELIGIONS ... 1153	SENATE COMMITTEES ... 1197
MILITARY SERVICE ... 1144	VOTE STUDIES CHARTS ... 1154	JOINT COMMITTEES ... 1205
FASTEST MEMBERS ... 1146	INFORMAL CAUCUSES ... 1158	DID YOU KNOW? ... 1206

House Seniority

DEMOCRATS

House Democrats determine seniority by length of service. Members who previously served in the House are given some credit for that service — when they return they are ranked above other members of that entering class.

For members who join at the start of a Congress, service is credited from the session's first day. Seniority for members who won special elections is credited from the election's date. No credit is given for prior service, such as serving as a senator or governor.

1. John D. Dingell, Mich.	Dec. 13, 1955
2. John Conyers Jr., Mich.	Jan. 4, 1965
3. David R. Obey, Wis.	April 1, 1969
4. Charles B. Rangel, N.Y.	Jan. 21, 1971
5. Pete Stark, Calif.	Jan. 3, 1973
6. John P. Murtha, Pa.	Feb. 5, 1974
7. George Miller, Calif.	Jan. 14, 1975
8. James L. Oberstar, Minn.	Jan. 14, 1975
9. Henry A. Waxman, Calif.	Jan. 14, 1975
10. Edward J. Markey, Mass.	Nov. 2, 1976
11. Norm Dicks, Wash.	Jan. 4, 1977
12. Dale E. Kildee, Mich.	Jan. 4, 1977
13. Nick J. Rahall II, W.Va.	Jan. 4, 1977
14. Ike Skelton, Mo.	Jan. 4, 1977
15. Barney Frank, Mass.	Jan. 5, 1981
16. Steny H. Hoyer, Md.	May 19, 1981
17. Howard L. Berman, Calif.	Jan. 3, 1983
18. Rick Boucher, Va.	Jan. 3, 1983
19. Marcy Kaptur, Ohio	Jan. 3, 1983
20. Sander M. Levin, Mich.	Jan. 3, 1983
21. Alan B. Mollohan, W.Va.	Jan. 3, 1983
22. Solomon P. Ortiz, Texas	Jan. 3, 1983
23. John M. Spratt Jr., S.C.	Jan. 3, 1983
24. Edolphus Towns, N.Y.	Jan. 3, 1983
25. Gary L. Ackerman, N.Y.	March 1, 1983
26. Bart Gordon, Tenn.	Jan. 3, 1985
27. Paul E. Kanjorski, Pa.	Jan. 3, 1985
28. Peter J. Visclosky, Ind.	Jan. 3, 1985
29. Peter A. DeFazio, Ore.	Jan. 6, 1987
30. John Lewis, Ga.	Jan. 6, 1987
31. Louise M. Slaughter, N.Y.	Jan. 6, 1987
32. Nancy Pelosi, Calif.	June 2, 1987
33. Jerry F. Costello, Ill.	Aug. 9, 1988
34. Frank Pallone Jr., N.J.	Nov. 8, 1988
35. Eliot L. Engel, N.Y.	Jan. 3, 1989
36. Nita M. Lowey, N.Y.	Jan. 3, 1989
37. Jim McDermott, Wash.	Jan. 3, 1989
38. Richard E. Neal, Mass.	Jan. 3, 1989
39. Donald M. Payne, N.J.	Jan. 3, 1989
40. John Tanner, Tenn.	Jan. 3, 1989
41. Gene Taylor, Miss.	Oct. 17, 1989
42. José E. Serrano, N.Y.	March 20, 1990
43. Robert E. Andrews, N.J.	Nov. 6, 1990
44. Neil Abercrombie, Hawaii	Jan. 3, 1991
Also served Sept. 1986-Jan. 1987	
45. Rosa DeLauro, Conn.	Jan. 3, 1991
46. Chet Edwards, Texas	Jan. 3, 1991
47. James P. Moran, Va.	Jan. 3, 1991
48. Collin C. Peterson, Minn.	Jan. 3, 1991
49. Maxine Waters, Calif.	Jan. 3, 1991
50. John W. Olver, Mass.	June 4, 1991
51. Ed Pastor, Ariz.	Sept. 24, 1991
52. Jerrold Nadler, N.Y.	Nov. 3, 1992
53. Xavier Becerra, Calif.	Jan. 5, 1993
54. Sanford D. Bishop Jr., Ga.	Jan. 5, 1993
55. Corrine Brown, Fla.	Jan. 5, 1993

56. James E. Clyburn, S.C.	Jan. 5, 1993
57. Anna G. Eshoo, Calif.	Jan. 5, 1993
58. Bob Filner, Calif.	Jan. 5, 1993
59. Gene Green, Texas	Jan. 5, 1993
60. Luis V. Gutierrez, Ill.	Jan. 5, 1993
61. Alcee L. Hastings, Fla.	Jan. 5, 1993
62. Maurice D. Hinchey, N.Y.	Jan. 5, 1993
63. Tim Holden, Pa.	Jan. 5, 1993
64. Eddie Bernice Johnson, Texas	Jan. 5, 1993
65. Carolyn B. Maloney, N.Y.	Jan. 5, 1993
66. Earl Pomeroy, N.D.	Jan. 5, 1993
67. Lucille Roybal-Allard, Calif.	Jan. 5, 1993
68. Bobby L. Rush, Ill.	Jan. 5, 1993
69. Robert C. Scott, Va.	Jan. 5, 1993
70. Bart Stupak, Mich.	Jan. 5, 1993
71. Nydia M. Velázquez, N.Y.	Jan. 5, 1993
72. Melvin Watt, N.C.	Jan. 5, 1993
73. Lynn Woolsey, Calif.	Jan. 5, 1993
74. Bennie Thompson, Miss.	April 13, 1993
75. Sam Farr, Calif.	June 8, 1993
76. Lloyd Doggett, Texas	Jan. 4, 1995
77. Mike Doyle, Pa.	Jan. 4, 1995
78. Chaka Fattah, Pa.	Jan. 4, 1995
79. Sheila Jackson Lee, Texas	Jan. 4, 1995
80. Patrick J. Kennedy, R.I.	Jan. 4, 1995
81. Zoe Lofgren, Calif.	Jan. 4, 1995
82. Jesse L. Jackson Jr., Ill.	Dec. 12, 1995
83. Elijah E. Cummings, Md.	April 16, 1996
84. Earl Blumenauer, Ore.	May 21, 1996
85. David E. Price, N.C.	Jan. 6, 1997
Also served 1987-95	
86. Marion Berry, Ark.	Jan. 6, 1997
87. Leonard L. Boswell, Iowa	Jan. 6, 1997
88. Allen Boyd, Fla.	Jan. 6, 1997
89. Danny K. Davis, Ill.	Jan. 6, 1997
90. Diana DeGette, Colo.	Jan. 6, 1997
91. Bill Delahunt, Mass.	Jan. 6, 1997
92. Bob Etheridge, N.C.	Jan. 6, 1997
93. Rubén Hinojosa, Texas	Jan. 6, 1997
94. Carolyn Cheeks Kilpatrick, Mich.	Jan. 6, 1997
95. Ron Kind, Wis.	Jan. 6, 1997
96. Dennis J. Kucinich, Ohio	Jan. 6, 1997
97. Carolyn McCarthy, N.Y.	Jan. 6, 1997
98. Jim McGovern, Mass.	Jan. 6, 1997
99. Mike McIntyre, N.C.	Jan. 6, 1997
100. Bill Pascrell Jr., N.J.	Jan. 6, 1997
101. Silvestre Reyes, Texas	Jan. 6, 1997
102. Steven R. Rothman, N.J.	Jan. 6, 1997
103. Loretta Sanchez, Calif.	Jan. 6, 1997
104. Brad Sherman, Calif.	Jan. 6, 1997
105. Adam Smith, Wash.	Jan. 6, 1997
106. Vic Snyder, Ark.	Jan. 6, 1997
107. Ellen O. Tauscher, Calif.	Jan. 6, 1997
108. John F. Tierney, Mass.	Jan. 6, 1997
109. Robert Wexler, Fla.	Jan. 6, 1997
110. Gregory W. Meeks, N.Y.	Feb. 3, 1998

111. Lois Capps, Calif.	March 10, 1998
112. Barbara Lee, Calif.	April 7, 1998
113. Robert A. Brady, Pa.	May 19, 1998
114. Jay Inslee, Wash.	Jan. 6, 1999
	Also served 1993-95
115. Brian Baird, Wash.	Jan. 6, 1999
116. Tammy Baldwin, Wis.	Jan. 6, 1999
117. Shelley Berkley, Nev.	Jan. 6, 1999
118. Michael E. Capuano, Mass.	Jan. 6, 1999
119. Joseph Crowley, N.Y.	Jan. 6, 1999
120. Charlie Gonzalez, Texas	Jan. 6, 1999
121. Rush D. Holt, N.J.	Jan. 6, 1999
122. John B. Larson, Conn.	Jan. 6, 1999
123. Dennis Moore, Kan.	Jan. 6, 1999
124. Grace F. Napolitano, Calif.	Jan. 6, 1999
125. Jan Schakowsky, Ill.	Jan. 6, 1999
126. Mike Thompson, Calif.	Jan. 6, 1999
127. Anthony Weiner, N.Y.	Jan. 6, 1999
128. David Wu, Ore.	Jan. 6, 1999
129. Joe Baca, Calif.	Nov. 16, 1999
130. Jane Harman, Calif.	Jan. 3, 2001
	Also served 1993-99
131. William Lacy Clay, Mo.	Jan. 3, 2001
132. Susan A. Davis, Calif.	Jan. 3, 2001
133. Michael M. Honda, Calif.	Jan. 3, 2001
134. Steve Israel, N.Y.	Jan. 3, 2001
135. Jim Langevin, R.I.	Jan. 3, 2001
136. Rick Larsen, Wash.	Jan. 3, 2001
137. Jim Matheson, Utah	Jan. 3, 2001
138. Betty McCollum, Minn.	Jan. 3, 2001
139. Mike Ross, Ark.	Jan. 3, 2001
140. Adam B. Schiff, Calif.	Jan. 3, 2001
141. Diane Watson, Calif.	June 5, 2001
142. Stephen F. Lynch, Mass.	Oct. 16, 2001
143. Jim Cooper, Tenn.	Jan. 7, 2003
	Also served 1983-95
144. Timothy H. Bishop, N.Y.	Jan. 7, 2003
145. Dennis Cardoza, Calif.	Jan. 7, 2003
146. Artur Davis, Ala.	Jan. 7, 2003
147. Lincoln Davis, Tenn.	Jan. 7, 2003
148. Raúl M. Grijalva, Ariz.	Jan. 7, 2003
149. Jim Marshall, Ga.	Jan. 7, 2003
150. Kendrick B. Meek, Fla.	Jan. 7, 2003
151. Michael H. Michaud, Maine	Jan. 7, 2003
152. Brad Miller, N.C.	Jan. 7, 2003
153. C.A. Dutch Ruppersberger, Md.	Jan. 7, 2003
154. Tim Ryan, Ohio	Jan. 7, 2003
155. Linda T. Sánchez, Calif.	Jan. 7, 2003
156. David Scott, Ga.	Jan. 7, 2003
157. Chris Van Hollen, Md.	Jan. 7, 2003
158. Ben Chandler, Ky.	Feb. 17, 2004
159. Stephanie Herseth Sandlin, S.D.	June 1, 2004
160. G.K. Butterfield, N.C.	July 20, 2004
161. John Barrow, Ga.	Jan. 4, 2005
162. Melissa Bean, Ill.	Jan. 4, 2005
163. Dan Boren, Okla.	Jan. 4, 2005
164. Russ Carnahan, Mo.	Jan. 4, 2005
165. Emanuel Cleaver II, Mo.	Jan. 4, 2005
166. Jim Costa, Calif.	Jan. 4, 2005
167. Henry Cuellar, Texas	Jan. 4, 2005
168. Al Green, Texas	Jan. 4, 2005
169. Brian Higgins, N.Y.	Jan. 4, 2005
170. Daniel Lipinski, Ill.	Jan. 4, 2005
171. Charlie Melancon, La.	Jan. 4, 2005
172. Gwen Moore, Wis.	Jan. 4, 2005

173. John Salazar, Colo.	Jan. 4, 2005
174. Allyson Y. Schwartz, Pa.	Jan. 4, 2005
175. Debbie Wasserman Schultz, Fla.	Jan. 4, 2005
176. Doris Matsui, Calif.	March 10, 2005
177. Albio Sires, N.J.	Nov. 13, 2006
178. Ciro D. Rodriguez, Texas	Jan. 4, 2007
	Also served 1997-2005
179. Baron P. Hill, Ind.	Jan. 4, 2007
	Also served 1999-2005
180. Jason Altmire, Pa.	Jan. 4, 2007
181. Michael Arcuri, N.Y.	Jan. 4, 2007
182. Bruce Braley, Iowa	Jan. 4, 2007
183. Chris Carney, Pa.	Jan. 4, 2007
184. Kathy Castor, Fla.	Jan. 4, 2007
185. Yvette D. Clarke, N.Y.	Jan. 4, 2007
186. Steve Cohen, Tenn.	Jan. 4, 2007
187. Joe Courtney, Conn.	Jan. 4, 2007
188. Joe Donnelly, Ind.	Jan. 4, 2007
189. Keith Ellison, Minn.	Jan. 4, 2007
190. Brad Ellsworth, Ind.	Jan. 4, 2007
191. Gabrielle Giffords, Ariz.	Jan. 4, 2007
192. John Hall, N.Y.	Jan. 4, 2007
193. Phil Hare, Ill.	Jan. 4, 2007
194. Mazie K. Hirono, Hawaii	Jan. 4, 2007
195. Paul W. Hodes, N.H.	Jan. 4, 2007
196. Hank Johnson, Fla.	Jan. 4, 2007
197. Steve Kagen, Wis.	Jan. 4, 2007
198. Ron Klein, Fla.	Jan. 4, 2007
199. Dave Loebsack, Iowa	Jan. 4, 2007
200. Jerry McNerney, Calif.	Jan. 4, 2007
201. Harry E. Mitchell, Ariz.	Jan. 4, 2007
202. Christopher S. Murphy, Conn.	Jan. 4, 2007
203. Patrick J. Murphy, Pa.	Jan. 4, 2007
204. Ed Perlmutter, Colo.	Jan. 4, 2007
205. John Sarbanes, Md.	Jan. 4, 2007
206. Joe Sestak, Pa.	Jan. 4, 2007
207. Heath Shuler, N.C.	Jan. 4, 2007
208. Carol Shea-Porter, N.H.	Jan. 4, 2007
209. Zack Space, Ohio	Jan. 4, 2007
210. Betty Sutton, Ohio	Jan. 4, 2007
211. Tim Walz, Minn.	Jan. 4, 2007
212. Peter Welch, Vt.	Jan. 4, 2007
213. Charlie Wilson, Ohio	Jan. 4, 2007
214. John Yarmuth, Ky.	Jan. 4, 2007
215. Laura Richardson, Calif.	Sept. 4, 2007
216. Niki Tsongas, Mass.	Oct. 18, 2007
217. Bill Foster, Ill.	March 11, 2008
218. André Carson, Ind.	March 13, 2008
219. Jackie Speier, Calif.	April 10, 2008
220. Travis W. Childers, Miss.	May 20, 2008
221. Donna Edwards, Md.	June 19, 2008
222. Marcia L. Fudge, Ohio	Nov. 19, 2008
223. John Adler, N.J.	Jan. 6, 2009
224. John Boccieri, Ohio	Jan. 6, 2009
225. Bobby N. Bright, Ala.	Jan. 6, 2009
226. Gerald E. Connolly, Va.	Jan. 6, 2009
227. Kathy Dahlkemper, Pa.	Jan. 6, 2009
228. Steve Driehaus, Ohio	Jan. 6, 2009
229. Debbie Halvorson, Ill.	Jan. 6, 2009
230. Martin Heinrich, N.M.	Jan. 6, 2009
231. Jim Himes, Conn.	Jan. 6, 2009
232. Alan Grayson, Fla.	Jan. 6, 2009
233. Parker Griffith, Ala.	Jan. 6, 2009
234. Mary Jo Kilroy, Ohio	Jan. 6, 2009
235. Ann Kirkpatrick, Ariz.	Jan. 6, 2009

236. Larry Kissel, N.C.	Jan. 6, 2009
237. Suzanne M. Kosmas, Fla.	Jan. 6, 2009
238. Frank Kratovil Jr., Md.	Jan. 6, 2009
239. Ben Ray Luján, N.M.	Jan. 6, 2009
240. Dan Maffei, N.Y.	Jan. 6, 2009
241. Betsy Markey, Colo.	Jan. 6, 2009
242. Eric Massa, N.Y.	Jan. 6, 2009
243. Michael E. McMahon, N.Y.	Jan. 6, 2009
244. Walt Minnick, Idaho	Jan. 6, 2009
245. Glenn Nye, Va.	Jan. 6, 2009
246. Tom Perriello, Va.	Jan. 6, 2009
247. Gary Peters, Mich.	Jan. 6, 2009
248. Chellie Pingree, Maine	Jan. 6, 2009
249. Jared Polis, Colo.	Jan. 6, 2009
250. Mark Schauer, Mich.	Jan. 6, 2009
251. Kurt Schrader, Ore.	Jan. 6, 2009
252. Harry Teague, N.M.	Jan. 6, 2009
253. Dina Titus, Nev.	Jan. 6, 2009
254. Paul Tonko, N.Y.	Jan. 6, 2009
255. Mike Quigley, Ill.	April 21, 2009
256. Scott Murphy, N.Y.	April 29, 2009

REPUBLICANS

House Republicans determine seniority by length of service. Members who previously served in the House are usually given credit for most of that service.

For members who joined at the beginning of a Congress, service is credited from the first day of the session. Seniority for members who won special elections is credited from the date of the election.

Reps. Rodney Alexander, Nathan Deal, and Ralph M. Hall began their tenure as Democrats. The GOP Conference credited their service as Democrats toward their seniority. No credit is given for other prior service, such as serving as a governor.

1. C.W. Bill Young, Fla.	Jan. 21, 1971
2. Don Young, Alaska	March 6, 1973
3. Jerry Lewis, Calif.	Jan. 15, 1979
4. F. James Sensenbrenner Jr., Wis.	Jan. 15, 1979
5. Tom Petri, Wis.	April 3, 1979
6. David Dreier, Calif.	Jan. 5, 1981
7. Ralph M. Hall, Texas	Jan. 5, 1981
8. Harold Rogers, Ky.	Jan. 5, 1981
9. Christopher H. Smith, N.J.	Jan. 5, 1981
10. Frank R. Wolf, Va.	Jan. 5, 1981
11. Dan Burton, Ind.	Jan. 3, 1983
12. Joe L. Barton, Texas	Jan. 3, 1985
13. Howard Coble, N.C.	Jan. 3, 1985
14. Elton Gallegly, Calif.	Jan. 6, 1987
15. Wally Herger, Calif.	Jan. 6, 1987
16. Lamar Smith, Texas	Jan. 6, 1987
17. Fred Upton, Mich.	Jan. 6, 1987
18. John J. "Jimmy" Duncan Jr., Tenn.	Nov. 8, 1988
19. Dana Rohrabacher, Calif.	Jan. 3, 1989
20. Cliff Stearns, Fla.	Jan. 3, 1989
21. Ileana Ros-Lehtinen, Fla.	Aug. 29, 1989
22. Ron Paul, Texas	Jan. 6, 1997
Also served 1976-77, 1979-85	
23. John A. Boehner, Ohio	Jan. 3, 1991
24. Dave Camp, Mich.	Jan. 3, 1991
25. Sam Johnson, Texas	May 18, 1991
26. Spencer Bachus, Ala.	Jan. 5, 1993
27. Roscoe G. Bartlett, Md.	Jan. 5, 1993
28. Steve Buyer, Ind.	Jan. 5, 1993
29. Ken Calvert, Calif.	Jan. 5, 1993
30. Michael N. Castle, Del.	Jan. 5, 1993
31. Nathan Deal, Ga.	Jan. 5, 1993
32. Lincoln Diaz-Balart, Fla.	Jan. 5, 1993
33. Robert W. Goodlatte, Va.	Jan. 5, 1993
34. Peter Hoekstra, Mich.	Jan. 5, 1993
35. Peter T. King, N.Y.	Jan. 5, 1993
36. Jack Kingston, Ga.	Jan. 5, 1993
37. John Linder, Ga.	Jan. 5, 1993
38. Donald Manzullo, Ill.	Jan. 5, 1993
39. John M. McHugh, N.Y.	Jan. 5, 1993
40. Howard P. "Buck" McKeon, Calif.	Jan. 5, 1993
41. John L. Mica, Fla.	Jan. 5, 1993
42. Ed Royce, Calif.	Jan. 5, 1993
43. Vernon J. Ehlers, Mich.	Dec. 7, 1993
44. Frank D. Lucas, Okla.	May 10, 1994
45. Rodney Frelinghuysen, N.J.	Jan. 4, 1995
46. Doc Hastings, Wash.	Jan. 4, 1995
47. Walter B. Jones, N.C.	Jan. 4, 1995
48. Tom Latham, Iowa	Jan. 4, 1995
49. Steven C. LaTourette, Ohio	Jan. 4, 1995
50. Frank A. LoBiondo, N.J.	Jan. 4, 1995
51. Dan Lungren, Calif.	Jan. 4, 2005
Also served 1979-89	
52. Sue Myrick, N.C.	Jan. 4, 1995
53. George P. Radanovich, Calif.	Jan. 4, 1995
54. John Shadegg, Ariz.	Jan. 4, 1995
55. Mark Souder, Ind.	Jan. 4, 1995
56. William M. "Mac" Thornberry, Texas	Jan. 4, 1995
57. Todd Tiahrt, Kan.	Jan. 4, 1995
58. Zach Wamp, Tenn.	Jan. 4, 1995
59. Edward Whitfield, Ky.	Jan. 4, 1995
60. Jo Ann Emerson, Mo.	Nov. 5, 1996
61. Robert B. Aderholt, Ala.	Jan. 6, 1997
62. Roy Blunt, Mo.	Jan. 6, 1997
63. Kevin Brady, Texas	Jan. 6, 1997
64. Kay Granger, Texas	Jan. 6, 1997
65. Jerry Moran, Kan.	Jan. 6, 1997
66. Joe Pitts, Pa.	Jan. 6, 1997
67. Pete Sessions, Texas	Jan. 6, 1997
68. John Shimkus, Ill.	Jan. 6, 1997
69. Mary Bono Mack, Calif.	April 7, 1998
70. Judy Biggert, Ill.	Jan. 6, 1999
71. Bob Inglis, S.C.	Jan. 4, 2005
Also served 1993-99	
72. Gary G. Miller, Calif.	Jan. 6, 1999
73. Paul D. Ryan, Wis.	Jan. 6, 1999
74. Mike Simpson, Idaho	Jan. 6, 1999
75. Lee Terry, Neb.	Jan. 6, 1999
76. Greg Walden, Ore.	Jan. 6, 1999
77. Brian P. Bilbray, Calif.	June 13, 2006
Also served 1995-2001	
78. Todd Akin, Mo.	Jan. 3, 2001
79. Henry E. Brown Jr., S.C.	Jan. 3, 2001
80. Eric Cantor, Va.	Jan. 3, 2001
81. Shelley Moore Capito, W.Va.	Jan. 3, 2001
82. Ander Crenshaw, Fla.	Jan. 3, 2001

83. John Culberson, Texas	Jan. 3, 2001		147. Dean Heller, Nev.	Jan. 4, 2007
84. Jeff Flake, Ariz.	Jan. 3, 2001		148. Jim Jordan, Ohio	Jan. 4, 2007
85. Sam Graves, Mo.	Jan. 3, 2001		149. Doug Lamborn, Colo.	Jan. 4, 2007
86. Darrell Issa, Calif.	Jan. 3, 2001		150. Kevin McCarthy, Calif.	Jan. 4, 2007
87. Timothy V. Johnson, Ill.	Jan. 3, 2001		151. Peter Roskam, Ill.	Jan. 4, 2007
88. Mark Steven Kirk, Ill.	Jan. 3, 2001		152. Adrian Smith, Neb.	Jan. 4, 2007
89. Mike Pence, Ind.	Jan. 3, 2001		153. Paul Broun, Ga.	July 25, 2007
90. Todd R. Platts, Pa.	Jan. 3, 2001		154. Bob Latta, Ohio	Dec. 13, 2007
91. Adam H. Putnam, Fla.	Jan. 3, 2001		155. Rob Wittman, Va.	Dec. 13, 2007
92. Denny Rehberg, Mont.	Jan. 3, 2001		156. Steve Scalise, La.	May 7, 2008
93. Mike Rogers, Mich.	Jan. 3, 2001		157. Steve Austria, Ohio	Jan. 6, 2009
94. Pat Tiberi, Ohio	Jan. 3, 2001		158. Anh "Joseph" Cao, La.	Jan. 6, 2009
95. Bill Shuster, Pa.	May 15, 2001		159. Bill Cassidy, La.	Jan. 6, 2009
96. J. Randy Forbes, Va.	June 19, 2001		160. Jason Chaffetz, Utah	Jan. 6, 2009
97. Jeff Miller, Fla.	Oct. 16, 2001		161. Mike Coffman, Colo.	Jan. 6, 2009
98. John Boozman, Ark.	Nov. 20, 2001		162. John Fleming, La.	Jan. 6, 2009
99. Joe Wilson, S.C.	Dec. 18, 2001		163. Brett Guthrie, Ky.	Jan. 6, 2009
100. John Sullivan, Okla.	Feb. 15, 2002		164. Gregg Harper, Miss.	Jan. 6, 2009
101. Rodney Alexander, La.	Jan. 7, 2003		165. Duncan Hunter, Calif.	Jan. 6, 2009
102. J. Gresham Barrett, S.C.	Jan. 7, 2003		166. Lynn Jenkins, Kan.	Jan. 6, 2009
103. Rob Bishop, Utah	Jan. 7, 2003		167. Leonard Lance, N.J.	Jan. 6, 2009
104. Marsha Blackburn, Tenn.	Jan. 7, 2003		168. Christopher Lee, N.Y.	Jan. 6, 2009
105. Jo Bonner, Ala.	Jan. 7, 2003		169. Blaine Luetkemeyer, Mo.	Jan. 6, 2009
106. Ginny Brown-Waite, Fla.	Jan. 7, 2003		170. Cynthia M. Lummis, Wyo.	Jan. 6, 2009
107. Michael C. Burgess, Texas	Jan. 7, 2003		171. Tom McClintock, Calif.	Jan. 6, 2009
108. John Carter, Texas	Jan. 7, 2003		172. Pete Olson, Texas	Jan. 6, 2009
109. Tom Cole, Okla.	Jan. 7, 2003		173. Erik Paulsen, Minn.	Jan. 6, 2009
110. Mario Diaz-Balart, Fla.	Jan. 7, 2003		174. Bill Posey, Fla.	Jan. 6, 2009
111. Trent Franks, Ariz.	Jan. 7, 2003		175. Phil Roe, Tenn.	Jan. 6, 2009
112. Scott Garrett, N.J.	Jan. 7, 2003		176. Tom Rooney, Fla.	Jan. 6, 2009
113. Jim Gerlach, Pa.	Jan. 7, 2003		177. Aaron Schock, Ill.	Jan. 6, 2009
114. Phil Gingrey, Ga.	Jan. 7, 2003		178. Glenn Thompson, Pa.	Jan. 6, 2009
115. Jeb Hensarling, Texas	Jan. 7, 2003			
116. Steve King, Iowa	Jan. 7, 2003			
117. John Kline, Minn.	Jan. 7, 2003			
118. Thaddeus McCotter, Mich.	Jan. 7, 2003			
119. Candice S. Miller, Mich.	Jan. 7, 2003			
120. Tim Murphy, Pa.	Jan. 7, 2003			
121. Devin Nunes, Calif.	Jan. 7, 2003			
122. Mike D. Rogers, Ala.	Jan. 7, 2003			
123. Michael R. Turner, Ohio	Jan. 7, 2003			
124. Randy Neugebauer, Texas	June 3, 2003			
125. Charles Boustany Jr., La.	Jan. 4, 2005			
126. K. Michael Conaway, Texas	Jan. 4, 2005			
127. Geoff Davis, Ky.	Jan. 4, 2005			
128. Charlie Dent, Pa.	Jan. 4, 2005			
129. Jeff Fortenberry, Neb.	Jan. 4, 2005			
130. Virginia Foxx, N.C.	Jan. 4, 2005			
131. Louie Gohmert, Texas	Jan. 4, 2005			
132. Connie Mack, Fla.	Jan. 4, 2005			
133. Kenny Marchant, Texas	Jan. 4, 2005			
134. Michael McCaul, Texas	Jan. 4, 2005			
135. Patrick T. McHenry, N.C.	Jan. 4, 2005			
136. Cathy McMorris Rodgers, Wash.	Jan. 4, 2005			
137. Ted Poe, Texas	Jan. 4, 2005			
138. Tom Price, Ga.	Jan. 4, 2005			
139. Dave Reichert, Wash.	Jan. 4, 2005			
140. Lynn Westmoreland, Ga.	Jan. 4, 2005			
141. Jean Schmidt, Ohio	Aug. 3, 2005			
142. John Campbell, Calif.	Dec. 7, 2005			
143. Michele Bachmann, Minn.	Jan. 4, 2007			
144. Gus Bilirakis, Fla.	Jan. 4, 2007			
145. Vern Buchanan, Fla.	Jan. 4, 2007			
146. Mary Fallin, Okla.	Jan. 4, 2007			

Party Switchers

Six current members changed their party affiliation after their election to Congress. Several other members switched before coming to Congress; they are not listed below.

House

Rep. Rodney Alexander, La.
Democrat to Republican as of Sept. 7, 2004

Rep. Ralph M. Hall, Texas
Democrat to Republican as of Jan. 5, 2004

Rep. Nathan Deal, Ga.
Democrat to Republican as of April 10, 1995

Senate

Sen. Arlen Specter, Pa.
Republican to Democrat as of April 30, 2009

Sen. Joseph I. Lieberman, Conn.
Democrat to independent as of Jan. 4, 2007

Sen. Richard C. Shelby, Ala.
Democrat to Republican as of Nov. 9, 1994

Senate Seniority

Seniority is determined by the length of consecutive Senate service. Tie-breakers for those who join the Senate on the same day, in order of precedence, are: previous Senate service, service as the vice president, previous House service, service in the Cabinet, service as a state governor. If a tie still exists, they are ranked according to their state's population at the time of swearing in.

Independents Joseph I. Lieberman and Bernard Sanders caucus with the Democrats. Richard C. Shelby was a Democrat and the GOP Conference credited that service toward his seniority ranking. Arlen Specter was Republican and Democrats credited his prior Republican service.

DEMOCRATS

1. Robert C. Byrd, W.Va.	Jan. 7, 1959
2. Edward M. Kennedy, Mass.	Nov. 7, 1962
3. Daniel K. Inouye, Hawaii	Jan. 9, 1963
4. Patrick J. Leahy, Vt.	Jan. 14, 1975
5. Max Baucus, Mont.	Dec. 15, 1978
6. Carl Levin, Mich.	Jan. 15, 1979
7. Christopher J. Dodd, Conn.	Jan. 5, 1981
8. Arlen Specter, Pa.	Jan. 5, 1981
9. Jeff Bingaman, N.M.	Jan. 3, 1983
10. John Kerry, Mass.	Jan. 2, 1985
11. Tom Harkin, Iowa	Jan. 3, 1985
12. John D. Rockefeller IV, W.Va.	Jan. 15, 1985
13. Barbara A. Mikulski, Md.	Jan. 6, 1987
14. Harry Reid, Nev.	Jan. 6, 1987
15. Kent Conrad, N.D.	Jan. 6, 1987
16. Herb Kohl, Wis.	Jan. 3, 1989
17. Daniel K. Akaka, Hawaii	April 28, 1990
18. Dianne Feinstein, Calif.	Nov. 4, 1992
19. Byron L. Dorgan, N.D.	Dec. 15, 1992
20. Barbara Boxer, Calif.	Jan. 5, 1993
21. Russ Feingold, Wis.	Jan. 5, 1993
22. Patty Murray, Wash.	Jan. 5, 1993
23. Ron Wyden, Ore.	Feb. 6, 1996
24. Richard J. Durbin, Ill.	Jan. 7, 1997
25. Tim Johnson, S.D.	Jan. 7, 1997
26. Jack Reed, R.I.	Jan. 7, 1997
27. Mary L. Landrieu, La.	Jan. 7, 1997
28. Charles E. Schumer, N.Y.	Jan. 6, 1999
29. Blanche Lincoln, Ark.	Jan. 6, 1999
30. Evan Bayh, Ind.	Jan. 6, 1999
31. Bill Nelson, Fla.	Jan. 3, 2001
32. Thomas R. Carper, Del.	Jan. 3, 2001
33. Debbie Stabenow, Mich.	Jan. 3, 2001
34. Maria Cantwell, Wash.	Jan. 3, 2001
35. Ben Nelson, Neb.	Jan. 3, 2001
36. Frank R. Lautenberg, N.J.	Jan. 7, 2003
	Also served 1983-2001
37. Mark Pryor, Ark.	Jan. 7, 2003
38. Robert Menendez, N.J.	Jan. 18, 2006
39. Benjamin L. Cardin, Md.	Jan. 4, 2007
40. Sherrod Brown, Ohio	Jan. 4, 2007
41. Bob Casey, Pa.	Jan. 4, 2007
42. Jim Webb, Va.	Jan. 4, 2007
43. Claire McCaskill, Mo.	Jan. 4, 2007
44. Amy Klobuchar, Minn.	Jan. 4, 2007
45. Sheldon Whitehouse, R.I.	Jan. 4, 2007
46. Jon Tester, Mont.	Jan. 4, 2007
47. Mark Udall, Colo.	Jan. 6, 2009
48. Tom Udall, N.M.	Jan. 6, 2009
49. Jeanne Shaheen, N.H.	Jan. 6, 2009
50. Mark Warner, Va.	Jan. 6, 2009
51. Kay Hagan, N.C.	Jan. 6, 2009
52. Jeff Merkley, Ore.	Jan. 6, 2009
53. Mark Begich, Alaska	Jan. 6, 2009
54. Roland W. Burris, Ill.	Jan. 15, 2009
55. Ted Kaufman, Del.	Jan. 16, 2009
56. Michael Bennet, Colo.	Jan. 22, 2009
57. Kirsten Gillibrand, N.Y.	Jan. 27, 2009

REPUBLICANS

1. Richard G. Lugar, Ind.	Jan. 4, 1977
2. Orrin G. Hatch, Utah	Jan. 4, 1977
3. Thad Cochran, Miss.	Dec. 27, 1978
4. Charles E. Grassley, Iowa	Jan. 5, 1981
5. Mitch McConnell, Ky.	Jan. 3, 1985
6. Richard C. Shelby, Ala.	Jan. 6, 1987
7. John McCain, Ariz.	Jan. 6, 1987
8. Christopher S. Bond, Mo.	Jan. 6, 1987
9. Judd Gregg, N.H.	Jan. 5, 1993
10. Robert F. Bennett, Utah	Jan. 5, 1993
11. Kay Bailey Hutchison, Texas	June 14, 1993
12. James M. Inhofe, Okla.	Nov. 30, 1994
13. Olympia J. Snowe, Maine	Jan. 4, 1995
14. Jon Kyl, Ariz.	Jan. 4, 1995
15. Sam Brownback, Kan.	Nov. 27, 1996
16. Pat Roberts, Kan.	Jan. 7, 1997
17. Jeff Sessions, Ala.	Jan. 7, 1997
18. Susan Collins, Maine	Jan. 7, 1997
19. Michael B. Enzi, Wyo.	Jan. 7, 1997
20. Jim Bunning, Ky.	Jan. 6, 1999
21. Michael D. Crapo, Idaho	Jan. 6, 1999
22. George V. Voinovich, Ohio	Jan. 6, 1999
23. John Ensign, Nev.	Jan. 3, 2001
24. Lisa Murkowski, Alaska	Dec. 20, 2002
25. Saxby Chambliss, Ga.	Jan. 7, 2003
26. Lindsey Graham, S.C.	Jan. 7, 2003
27. Lamar Alexander, Tenn.	Jan. 7, 2003
28. John Cornyn, Texas	Jan. 7, 2003
29. Richard M. Burr, N.C.	Jan. 3, 2005
30. Jim DeMint, S.C.	Jan. 3, 2005
31. Tom Coburn, Okla.	Jan. 3, 2005
32. John Thune, S.D.	Jan. 3, 2005
33. Johnny Isakson, Ga.	Jan. 3, 2005
34. David Vitter, La.	Jan. 3, 2005
35. Mel Martinez, Fla.	Jan. 3, 2005
36. Bob Corker, Tenn.	Jan. 4, 2007
37. John Barrasso, Wyo.	June 25, 2007
38. Roger Wicker, Miss.	Dec. 31, 2007
39. Mike Johanns, Neb.	Jan. 6, 2009
40. Jim Risch, Idaho	Jan. 6, 2009

INDEPENDENTS

1. Joseph I. Lieberman, Conn.	Jan. 3, 1989	2. Bernard Sanders, Vt.	Jan. 4, 2007

Former Governors

Thirteen members have served as a governor.

Member	Years	Member	Years
Sen. Lamar Alexander, R-Tenn.	1979-87	Sen. Ben Nelson, D-Neb.	1991-99
Sen. Evan Bayh, D-Ind.	1989-97	Sen. Jim Risch, R-Idaho	2006
Sen. Christopher S. Bond, R-Mo.	1973-77, 1981-85	Sen. John D. Rockefeller IV, D-W.Va.	1977-85
Sen. Thomas R. Carper, D-Del.	1993-2001	Sen. Jeanne Shaheen, D-N.H.	1997-2003
Rep. Michael N. Castle, R-Del.	1985-93	Sen. George V. Voinovich, R-Ohio	1991-99
Sen. Judd Gregg, R-N.H.	1989-93	Sen. Mark Warner, D-Va.	2002-06
Sen. Mike Johanns, R-Neb.	1999-2005		

Former Lieutenant Governors

Five members and two delegates have served as a lieutenant governor.

Member	Years	Member	Years
Del. Madeleine Z. Bordallo, D-Guam	1995-2003	Rep. Mazie K. Hirono, D-Hawaii	1994-2002
Rep. Michael N. Castle, R-Del.	1981-85	Sen. Jim Risch, R-Idaho	2003-06, 2007-09
Del. Eni F.H. Faleomavaega, D-Am. Samoa	1985-89	Sen. George V. Voinovich, R-Ohio	1979
Rep. Mary Fallin, R-Okla.	1995-2007		

Former Representatives in the Senate

26 Democrats, 22 Republicans, 1 Independent

Member	House Service	Member	House Service
Daniel K. Akaka, D-Hawaii	1977-90	James M. Inhofe, R-Okla.	1987-94
Max Baucus, D-Mont.	1975-78	Daniel K. Inouye, D-Hawaii	1959-63
Barbara Boxer, D-Calif.	1983-93	Johnny Isakson, R-Ga.	1999-2005
Sherrod Brown, D-Ohio	1993-2007	Tim Johnson, D-S.D.	1987-97
Sam Brownback, R-Kan.	1995-96	Jon Kyl, R-Ariz.	1987-95
Jim Bunning, R-Ky.	1987-99	Blanche Lincoln, D-Ark.	1993-97
Richard M. Burr, R-N.C.	1995-2005	John McCain, R-Ariz.	1983-87
Robert C. Byrd, D-W.Va.	1953-59	Robert Menendez, D-N.J.	1993-2006
Maria Cantwell, D-Wash.	1993-95	Barbara A. Mikulski, D-Md.	1977-87
Benjamin L. Cardin, D-Md.	1987-2007	Bill Nelson, D-Fla.	1979-91
Thomas R. Carper, D-Del.	1983-93	Jack Reed, D-R.I.	1991-97
Saxby Chambliss, R-Ga.	1995-2003	Harry Reid, D-Nev.	1983-87
Tom Coburn, R-Okla.	1995-2001	Pat Roberts, R-Kan.	1981-97
Thad Cochran, R-Miss.	1973-78	Bernard Sanders, I-Vt.	1991-2007
Michael D. Crapo, R-Idaho	1993-99	Charles E. Schumer, D-N.Y.	1981-99
Jim DeMint, R-S.C.	1999-2005	Richard C. Shelby, R-Ala.	1979-87
Christopher J. Dodd, D-Conn.	1975-81	Olympia J. Snowe, R-Maine	1979-95
Byron L. Dorgan, D-N.D.	1981-92	Debbie Stabenow, D-Mich.	1997-2001
Richard J. Durbin, D-Ill.	1983-97	John Thune, R-S.D.	1997-2003
John Ensign, R-Nev.	1995-99	Mark Udall, D-Colo.	1999-2009
Kirsten Gillibrand, D-N.Y.	2007-09	Tom Udall, D-N.M.	1999-2009
Lindsey Graham, R-S.C.	1995-2003	David Vitter, R-La.	1999-2005
Charles E. Grassley, R-Iowa	1975-81	Roger Wicker, R-Miss.	1995-2007
Judd Gregg, R-N.H.	1981-89	Ron Wyden, D-Ore.	1981-96
Tom Harkin, D-Iowa	1975-85		

Women in Congress

Senate (13 D, 4 R)
Barbara Boxer, D-Calif.
Maria Cantwell, D-Wash.
Susan Collins, R-Maine
Dianne Feinstein, D-Calif.
Kirsten Gillibrand, D-N.Y.*
Kay Hagan, D-N.C.*
Kay Bailey Hutchison, R-Texas
Amy Klobuchar, D-Minn.
Mary L. Landrieu, D-La.
Blanche Lincoln, D-Ark.
Claire McCaskill, D-Mo.
Barbara A. Mikulski, D-Md.
Lisa Murkowski, R-Alaska
Patty Murray, D-Wash.
Jeanne Shaheen, D-N.H.*
Olympia J. Snowe, R-Maine
Debbie Stabenow, D-Mich.

House (59 D, 17 R)
Michele Bachmann, R-Minn.
Tammy Baldwin, D-Wis.
Melissa Bean, D-Ill.
Shelley Berkley, D-Nev.
Judy Biggert, R-Ill.
Marsha Blackburn, R-Tenn.
Mary Bono Mack, R-Calif.
Del. Madeleine Z. Bordallo, D-Guam
Corrine Brown, D-Fla.
Ginny Brown-Waite, R-Fla.
Shelley Moore Capito, R-W.Va.
Lois Capps, D-Calif.

Kathy Castor, D-Fla.
Del. Donna M.C. Christensen, D-V.I.
Yvette D. Clarke, D-N.Y.
Kathy Dahlkemper, D-Pa.*
Susan A. Davis, D-Calif.
Diana DeGette, D-Colo.
Rosa DeLauro, D-Conn.
Donna Edwards, D-Md.
Jo Ann Emerson, R-Mo.
Anna G. Eshoo, D-Calif.
Mary Fallin, R-Okla.
Virginia Foxx, R-N.C.
Marcia L. Fudge, D-Ohio
Gabrielle Giffords, D-Ariz.
Kay Granger, R-Texas
Debbie Halvorson, D-Ill.*
Jane Harman, D-Calif.
Stephanie Herseth Sandlin, D-S.D.
Mazie K. Hirono, D-Hawaii
Sheila Jackson Lee, D-Texas
Lynn Jenkins, R-Kan.*
Eddie Bernice Johnson, D-Texas
Marcy Kaptur, D-Ohio
Carolyn Cheeks Kilpatrick, D-Mich.
Mary Jo Kilroy, D-Ohio*
Ann Kirkpatrick, D-Ariz.*
Suzanne M. Kosmas, D-Fla.*
Barbara Lee, D-Calif.
Zoe Lofgren, D-Calif.
Nita M. Lowey, D-N.Y.
Cynthia M. Lummis, R-Wyo.*
Carolyn B. Maloney, D-N.Y.

Betsy Markey, D-Colo.*
Doris Matsui, D-Calif.
Carolyn McCarthy, D-N.Y.
Betty McCollum, D-Minn.
Cathy McMorris Rodgers, R-Wash.
Candice S. Miller, R-Mich.
Gwen Moore, D-Wis.
Sue Myrick, R-N.C.
Grace F. Napolitano, D-Calif.
Del. Eleanor Holmes Norton, D-D.C.
Nancy Pelosi, D-Calif.
Chellie Pingree, D-Maine*
Laura Richardson, D-Calif.
Ileana Ros-Lehtinen, R-Fla.
Lucille Roybal-Allard, D-Calif.
Linda T. Sánchez, D-Calif.
Loretta Sanchez, D-Calif.
Jan Schakowsky, D-Ill.
Jean Schmidt, R-Ohio
Allyson Y. Schwartz, D-Pa.
Carol Shea-Porter, D-N.H.
Louise M. Slaughter, D-N.Y.
Jackie Speier, D-Calif.
Betty Sutton, D-Ohio
Ellen O. Tauscher, D-Calif.
Dina Titus, D-Nev. *
Niki Tsongas, D-Mass.
Nydia M. Velázquez, D-N.Y.
Debbie Wasserman Schultz, D-Fla.
Maxine Waters, D-Calif.
Diane Watson, D-Calif.
Lynn Woolsey, D-Calif.

15 Oldest Members of Congress

Member	Birthdate
Sen. Robert C. Byrd, D-W.Va.	11/20/1917
Rep. Ralph M. Hall, R-Texas	5/3/1923
Sen. Frank R. Lautenberg, D-N.J.	1/23/1924
Sen. Daniel K. Inouye, D-Hawaii	9/7/1924
Sen. Daniel K. Akaka, D-Hawaii	9/11/1924
Rep. Roscoe G. Bartlett, R-Md.	6/3/1926
Rep. John D. Dingell, D-Mich.	7/8/1926
Rep. John Conyers Jr., D-Mich.	5/16/1929
Rep. Louise M. Slaughter, D-N.Y.	8/14/1929
Rep. Dale E. Kildee, D-Mich.	9/16/1929
Sen. Arlen Specter, D-Pa.	2/12/1930
Rep. Charles B. Rangel, D-N.Y.	6/11/1930
Rep. Sam Johnson, R-Texas	10/11/1930
Rep. C.W. Bill Young, R-Fla.	12/16/1930
Rep. Howard Coble, R-N.C.	3/18/1931

15 Youngest Members of Congress

Member	Birthdate
Rep. Aaron Schock, R-Ill.*	5/28/1981
Rep. Duncan Hunter, R-Calif.*	12/7/1976
Rep. Patrick T. McHenry, R-N.C.	10/22/1975
Rep. Jared Polis, D-Colo.*	5/12/1975
Rep. André Carson, D-Ind.	10/16/1974
Rep. Tom Perriello, D-Va.*	10/9/1974
Rep. Glenn Nye, D-Va.*	9/9/1974
Rep. Adam H. Putnam, R-Fla.	7/31/1974
Rep. Patrick J. Murphy, D-Pa.	10/19/1973
Rep. Devin Nunes, R-Calif.	10/1/1973
Rep. Christopher S. Murphy, D-Conn.	8/3/1973
Rep. Dan Boren, D-Okla.	8/2/1973
Rep. Tim Ryan, D-Ohio	7/16/1973
Rep. Ben Ray Luján, D-N.M.*	6/7/1972
Rep. Heath Shuler, D-N.C.	12/31/1971

* New to Congress

Minorities in Congress

American Indian
House (1 R)
Tom Cole, R-Okla.

Asian
Senate (2 D)
Daniel K. Akaka, D-Hawaii
Daniel K. Inouye, D-Hawaii

House (6 D, 2 R)
Steve Austria, R-Ohio*
Anh "Joseph" Cao, R-La.*
Del. Eni F.H. Faleomavaega,
 D-Am. Samoa
Mazie K. Hirono, D-Hawaii
Michael M. Honda, D-Calif.
Doris Matsui, D-Calif.
Del. Gregorio Kilili Camacho Sablan,
 D-N. Marianas*
David Wu, D-Ore.

Hispanic
Senate (1 D, 1 R)
Mel Martinez, R-Fla.
Robert Menendez, D-N.J.

House (21 D, 3 R)
Joe Baca, D-Calif.
Xavier Becerra, D-Calif.
Henry Cuellar, D-Texas
Lincoln Diaz-Balart, R-Fla.
Mario Diaz-Balart, R-Fla.
Charlie Gonzalez, D-Texas
Raúl M. Grijalva, D-Ariz.
Luis V. Gutierrez, D-Ill.
Rubén Hinojosa, D-Texas
Ben Ray Luján, D-N.M.*
Grace F. Napolitano, D-Calif.
Solomon P. Ortiz, D-Texas
Ed Pastor, D-Ariz.
Res. Cmsr. Pedro R. Pierluisi, D-P.R.*
Silvestre Reyes, D-Texas
Ciro D. Rodriguez, D-Texas
Ileana Ros-Lehtinen, R-Fla.
Lucille Roybal-Allard, D-Calif.
John Salazar, D-Colo.
Linda T. Sánchez, D-Calif.
Loretta Sanchez, D-Calif.
José E. Serrano, D-N.Y.
Albio Sires, D-N.J.
Nydia M. Velázquez, D-N.Y.

Black
Senate (1 D)
Roland W. Burris, D-Ill.*

House (41 D)
Sanford D. Bishop Jr., D-Ga.
Corrine Brown, D-Fla.
G.K. Butterfield, D-N.C.
André Carson, D-Ind.
Del. Donna M.C. Christensen, D-V.I.
Yvette D. Clarke, D-N.Y.
William Lacy Clay, D-Mo.
Emanuel Cleaver II, D-Mo.
James E. Clyburn, D-S.C.
John Conyers Jr., D-Mich.
Elijah E. Cummings, D-Md.
Artur Davis, D-Ala.
Danny K. Davis, D-Ill.
Donna Edwards, D-Md.
Keith Ellison, D-Minn.
Chaka Fattah, D-Pa.
Marcia L. Fudge, D-Ohio
Al Green, D-Texas
Alcee L. Hastings, D-Fla.
Jesse L. Jackson Jr., D-Ill.
Sheila Jackson Lee, D-Texas
Eddie Bernice Johnson, D-Texas
Hank Johnson, D-Ga.
Carolyn Cheeks Kilpatrick, D-Mich.
Barbara Lee, D-Calif.
John Lewis, D-Ga.
Kendrick B. Meek, D-Fla.
Gregory W. Meeks, D-N.Y.
Gwen Moore, D-Wis.
Del. Eleanor Holmes Norton, D-D.C.
Donald M. Payne, D-N.J.
Charles B. Rangel, D-N.Y.
Laura Richardson, D-Calif.
Bobby L. Rush, D-Ill.
David Scott, D-Ga.
Robert C. Scott, D-Va.
Bennie Thompson, D-Miss.
Edolphus Towns, D-N.Y.
Maxine Waters, D-Calif.
Diane Watson, D-Calif.
Melvin Watt, D-N.C.

Born Abroad

There are 17 lawmakers and 3 delegates who were born outside the 50 states and Washington, D.C.

Member	Country	Member	Country
Del. Eni F.H. Faleomavaega, D-Am. Samoa	Am. Samoa	Rep. Ciro D. Rodriguez, D-Texas	Mexico
Rep. Geoff Davis, R-Ky.	Canada	Rep. Peter Hoekstra, R-Mich.	Netherlands
Rep. Lincoln Diaz-Balart, R-Fla.	Cuba	Rep. Chris Van Hollen, D-Md.	Pakistan
Sen. Mel Martinez, R-Fla.	Cuba	Sen. John McCain, R-Ariz.	Panama Canal Zone
Rep. Ileana Ros-Lehtinen, R-Fla.	Cuba	Rep. Jim Himes, D-Conn.*	Peru
Rep. Albio Sires, D-N.J.	Cuba	Res. Cmsr. Pedro R. Pierluisi, D-P.R.*	Puerto Rico
Sen. Michael Bennet, D-Colo.*	India	Rep. José E. Serrano, D-N.Y.	Puerto Rico
Rep. Diana DeGette, D-Colo.	Japan	Rep. Nydia M. Velázquez, D-N.Y.	Puerto Rico
Rep. Mazie K. Hirono, D-Hawaii	Japan	Rep. David Wu, D-Ore.	Taiwan
Del. Gregorio Kilili Camacho Sablan, D-N. Marianas*	N. Marianas	Rep. Anh "Joseph" Cao, R-La.*	Vietnam

* New to Congress

Former Congressional Staffers

Below are the 75 members who previously worked as paid, full-time congressional aides. Internships, fellowships and campaign work are not included.

Member	Congressional Office	Years
Sen. Lamar Alexander, R-Tenn.	Sen. Howard H. Baker Jr., R-Tenn.	1967-68
Rep. Jason Altmire, D-Pa.	Rep. Pete Peterson, D-Fla.	1991-96
Sen. Robert F. Bennett, R-Utah	Rep. Sherman P. Lloyd, R-Utah	1963
	Sen. Wallace F. Bennett, R-Utah	1963-64
Rep. Jo Bonner, R-Ala.	Rep. Sonny Callahan, R-Ala.	1985-2002
Rep. Dan Boren, D-Okla.	Rep. Wes Watkins, R-Okla.	2000-01
Sen. Barbara Boxer, D-Calif.	Rep. John L. Burton, D-Calif.	1974-76
Rep. Dave Camp, R-Mich.	Rep. Bill Schuette, R-Mich.	1984-87
Rep. Dennis Cardoza, D-Calif.	Rep. Gary A. Condit, D-Calif.	1989
Rep. William Lacy Clay, D-Mo.	House Clerk	1977-83
Rep. Tom Cole, R-Okla.	Rep. Mickey Edwards, R-Okla.	1982-84
Sen. Susan Collins, R-Maine	Rep./Sen. William S. Cohen, R-Maine	1975-87
Rep. Gerald E. Connolly, D-Va.	Senate Foreign Relations Committee	1979-89
Rep. John Conyers Jr., D-Mich.	Rep. John D. Dingell, D-Mich.	1958-61
Rep. Jim Costa, D-Calif.	Rep. John Krebs, D-Calif.	1975-76
Rep. Peter A. DeFazio, D-Ore.	Rep. James Weaver, D-Ore.	1977-82
Rep. Rosa DeLauro, D-Conn.	Sen. Christopher J. Dodd, D-Conn.	1981-87
Rep. Charlie Dent, R-Pa.	Rep. Don Ritter, R-Pa.	1982
Rep. Norm Dicks, D-Wash.	Sen. Warren G. Magnuson, D-Wash.	1968-76
Rep. Steve Driehaus, D-Ohio	Rep. Charles Luken, D-Ohio	1991-92
Rep. Chet Edwards, D-Texas	Rep. Olin E. Teague, D-Texas	1974-77
Del. Eni F.H. Faleomavaega, D-Am. Samoa	Del. A.U. Fuimaono, D-Am. Samoa	1973-75
	House Interior and Insular Affairs Committee	1975-81
Rep. Bob Filner, D-Calif.	Sen. Hubert H. Humphrey, D-Minn.	1975
	Rep. Donald M. Fraser, D-Minn.	1976
	Rep. Jim Bates, D-Calif.	1984
Rep. Jeff Fortenberry, R-Neb.	Senate Governmental Affairs subcommittee	1985-86
Rep. Barney Frank, D-Mass.	Rep. Michael Harrington, D-Mass.	1971-72
Rep. Marcia L. Fudge, D-Ohio	Rep. Stephanie Tubbs Jones, D-Ohio	1999
Rep. Robert W. Goodlatte, R-Va.	Rep. M. Caldwell Butler, R-Va.	1977-79
Rep. Phil Hare, D-Ill.	Rep. Lane Evans, D-Ill.	1983-2006
Sen. Tom Harkin, D-Iowa	Rep. Neal Smith, D-Iowa	1969-70
Rep. Jane Harman, D-Calif.	Sen. John V. Tunney, D-Calif.	1972-73
	Senate Judiciary Committee	1975-77
Rep. Jeb Hensarling, R-Texas	Sen. Phil Gramm, R-Texas	1985-89
Rep. Steve Israel, D-N.Y.	Rep. Richard L. Ottinger, D-N.Y.	1980-83
Rep. Sheila Jackson Lee, D-Texas	House Select Committee on Assassinations	1977-78
Sen. Ted Kaufman, D-Del.	Sen. Joseph R. Biden Jr., D-Del.	1973-94
Rep. Mark Steven Kirk, R-Ill.	Rep. John Edward Porter, R-Ill.	1984-89
	House International Relations Committee	1995-2000
Rep. Barbara Lee, D-Calif.	Rep. Ronald V. Dellums, D-Calif.	1975-86
Rep. Jerry Lewis, R-Calif.	Rep. Jerry L. Pettis, R-Calif.	1967
Sen. Blanche Lincoln, D-Ark.	Rep. Bill Alexander, D-Ark.	1982-84
Rep. Daniel Lipinski, D-Ill.	Rep. Rod R. Blagojevich, D-Ill.	1999-2000
Rep. Zoe Lofgren, D-Calif.	Rep. Don Edwards, D-Calif.	1970-79
Rep. Dan Maffei, D-N.Y.	Sen. Bill Bradley, D-N.J.	1995-96
	Sen. Daniel Patrick Moynihan, D-N.Y.	1997-98
	House Ways and Means Committee	1999-2005
Rep. Betsy Markey, D-Colo.	Sen. John A. Durkin, D-N.H.	1979
	Rep. Herb Harris, D-Va.	1979-81
	Sen. Ken Salazar, D-Colo.	2005-07
Rep. Eric Massa, D-N.Y.	House Armed Service Committee	2003
Rep. Kevin McCarthy, R-Calif.	Rep. Bill Thomas, R-Calif.	1987-2002
Sen. Mitch McConnell, R-Ky.	Sen. Marlow W. Cook, R-Ky.	1969-70
Rep. Jim McGovern, D-Mass.	Rep. Joe Moakley, D-Mass.	1981-93
Sen. Jeff Merkley, D-Ore.	Congressional Budget Office	1985-89
Rep. John L. Mica, R-Fla.	Sen. Paula Hawkins, R-Fla.	1981-85

Rep. James P. Moran, D-Va.	Senate Appropriations Committee	1976-79
Rep. James L. Oberstar, D-Minn.	Rep. John A. Blatnik, D-Minn.	1964-74
Rep. Pete Olson, R-Texas	Sen. Phil Gramm, R-Texas	1998-2002
	Sen. John Cornyn, R-Texas	2002-07
Rep. Erik Paulsen, R-Minn.	Rep. Jim Ramstad, R-Minn.	1990-94
Rep. Nick J. Rahall II, D-W.Va.	Sen. Robert C. Byrd, D-W.Va.	1971-74
Rep. Denny Rehberg, R-Mont.	Rep. Ron Marlenee, R-Mont.	1979-82
	Sen. Conrad Burns, R-Mont.	1989-91
Sen. Pat Roberts, R-Kan.	Sen. Frank Carlson, R-Kan.	1967-68
	Rep. Keith G. Sebelius, R-Kan.	1968-80
Rep. Tom Rooney, R-Fla.	Sen. Connie Mack, R-Fla.	1993
Rep. Peter Roskam, R-Ill.	Rep. Tom DeLay, R-Texas	1985-86
	Rep. Henry J. Hyde, R-Ill.	1986-87
Rep. Paul D. Ryan, R-Wis.	Sen. Bob Kasten, R-Wis.	1992
	Rep./Sen. Sam Brownback, R-Kan.	1995-97
Rep. Tim Ryan, D-Ohio	Rep. James A. Traficant Jr., D-Ohio	1995-97
Sen. Olympia J. Snowe, R-Maine	Rep. William S. Cohen, R-Maine	1973
Rep. Mark Souder, R-Ind.	Rep./Sen. Daniel R. Coats, R-Ind.	1983-85, 89-93
	House Select Committee on Children, Youth & Families	1985-89
Rep. Jackie Speier	Rep. Leo Ryan, D-Calif.	1976-78
Rep. William M. "Mac" Thornberry, R-Texas	Rep. Tom Loeffler, R-Texas	1983-85
	Rep. Larry Combest, R-Texas	1985-88
Sen. John Thune, R-S.D.	Sen. James Abdnor, R-S.D.	1985-86
	Senate Small Business Committee	1989
Rep. Pat Tiberi, R-Ohio	Rep. John R. Kasich, R-Ohio	1983-91
Sen. Tom Udall, D-N.M.	Sen. Joseph R. Biden Jr., D-Del.	1973
Rep. Fred Upton, R-Mich.	Rep. David A. Stockman, R-Mich.	1977-81
Rep. Chris Van Hollen, D-Md.	Sen. Charles McC. Mathias Jr., R-Md.	1985-87
	Senate Foreign Relations Committee	1987-89
Rep. Nydia M. Velázquez, D-N.Y.	Rep. Edolphus Towns, D-N.Y.	1983
Rep. Peter J. Visclosky, D-Ind.	Rep. Adam Benjamin Jr., D-Ind.	1977-82
Rep. Greg Walden, R-Ore.	Rep. Denny Smith, R-Ore.	1981-86
Sen. Jim Webb, D-Va.	House Veterans' Affairs Committee	1977-81
Rep. Anthony Weiner, D-N.Y.	Rep. Charles E. Schumer, D-N.Y.	1985-91
Sen. Roger Wicker, R-Miss.	Rep. Trent Lott, R-Miss.	1980-82
Rep. Frank R. Wolf, R-Va.	Rep. Edward G. Biester, R-Pa.	1968-71
Rep. John Yarmuth, D-Ky.	Sen. Marlow W. Cook, R-Ky.	1971-74

Born in D.C.

Member
Rep. Jo Ann Emerson, R-Mo.
Rep. Hank Johnson, D-Ga.
Rep. Suzanne M. Kosmas, D-Fla.
Del. Eleanor Holmes Norton, D-D.C.
Rep. Bill Posey, R-Fla.
Rep. Robert C. Scott, D-Va.
Rep. Adam Smith, D-Wash.
Rep. Cliff Stearns, R-Fla.
Rep. Rob Wittman, R-Va.

Former Pages

There are 10 members of Congress who once served as congressional pages:

Member	Years
Sen. Michael Bennet, D-Colo.	—
Rep. Dan Boren, D-Okla.	1989
Rep. Jim Cooper, D-Tenn.	1970
Rep. Ander Crenshaw, R-Fla.	1961
Rep. John D. Dingell, D-Mich.	1938-42
Sen. Christopher J. Dodd, D-Conn.	c. 1960
Rep. Rush D. Holt, D-N.J.	1963-64
Rep. Paul E. Kanjorski, D-Pa.	1953-54
Sen. Mark Pryor, D-Ark.	1982
Sen. Roger Wicker, R-Miss.	1967

Members Who Served in the Military

There are 121 members with military service. Included is service in the National Guard and reserve. The years of service includes both active and inactive duty, and an asterisk denotes a combat veteran.

Senate (11 R, 14 D)	Years
Daniel K. Akaka, D-Hawaii *	1945-47
Robert F. Bennett, R-Utah	1957-60
Jeff Bingaman, D-N.M.	1968-74
Thomas R. Carper, D-Del. *	1968-91
Thad Cochran, R-Miss.	1959-61
Christopher J. Dodd, D-Conn.	1969-75
Michael B. Enzi, R-Wyo.	1967-73
Lindsey Graham, R-S.C.	1982-present
Tom Harkin, D-Iowa	1962-74
James M. Inhofe, R-Okla.	1957-58
Daniel K. Inouye, D-Hawaii *	1943-47
Johnny Isakson, R-Ga.	1966-72
Edward M. Kennedy, D-Mass.	1951-53
John Kerry, D-Mass. *	1966-70
Herb Kohl, D-Wis.	1958-64
Frank R. Lautenberg, D-N.J.	1942-46
Richard G. Lugar, R-Ind.	1957-60
John McCain, R-Ariz. *	1958-81
Bill Nelson, D-Fla.	1965-71
Jack Reed, D-R.I.	1971-91
Pat Roberts, R-Kan.	1958-62
Jeff Sessions, R-Ala.	1973-86
Arlen Specter, D-Pa.	1951-53
Jim Webb, D-Va. *	1968-72
Roger Wicker, R-Miss.	1976-2004

House (48 R, 48 D)	Years
Todd Akin, R-Mo.	1972-80
Rodney Alexander, R-La.	1965-71
Joe Baca, D-Calif.	1966-68
Spencer Bachus, R-Ala.	1969-71
J. Gresham Barrett, R-S.C.	1983-87
Sanford D. Bishop Jr., D-Ga.	1971
John Boccieri, D-Ohio	1994-present
John A. Boehner, R-Ohio	1968
Leonard L. Boswell, D-Iowa *	1956-76
Allen Boyd, D-Fla. *	1969-71
Paul Broun, R-Ga.	1964-73
Henry E. Brown Jr., R-S.C.	1953-62
Vern Buchanan, R-Fla.	1970-76
Dan Burton, R-Ind.	1956-62
G.K. Butterfield, D-N.C.	1968-70
Steve Buyer, R-Ind. *	1980-present
Christopher Carney, D-Pa.	1995-present
Howard Coble, R-N.C. *	1952-56, 1960-82
Mike Coffman, R-Colo. *	1972-2006
K. Michael Conaway, R-Texas	1970-72
John Conyers Jr., D-Mich. *	1948-57
Geoff Davis, R-Ky.	1976-87
Nathan Deal, R-Ga.	1966-68

	Years
Peter A. DeFazio, D-Ore.	1967-71
Bill Delahunt, D-Mass.	1963-71
John D. Dingell, D-Mich. *	1944-46
John J. "Jimmy" Duncan Jr., R-Tenn.	1970-87
Bob Etheridge, D-N.C.	1965-67
Eni F.H. Faleomavaega, D-Am. Samoa	1966-69, 1983-2001
John Fleming, R-La.	1976-82
Rodney Frelinghuysen, R-N.J. *	1969-71
Louie Gohmert, R-Texas	1978-82
Charlie Gonzalez, D-Texas	1969-75
Bart Gordon, D-Tenn.	1971-72
Parker Griffith, D-Ala.	1970-73
Brett Guthrie, R-Ky.	1987-2002
Ralph M. Hall, R-Texas *	1942-45
Phil Hare, D-Ill.	1969-75
Doc Hastings, R-Wash.	1964-69
Maurice D. Hinchey, D-N.Y.	1956-59
Duncan Hunter, R-Calif. *	2002-08
Darrell Issa, R-Calif.	1970-72, 1976-88
Sam Johnson, R-Texas *	1951-79
Walter B. Jones, R-N.C.	1967-71
Paul E. Kanjorski, D-Pa.	1960-61
Peter T. King, R-N.Y.	1968-73
Mark Steven Kirk, R-Ill. *	1989-present
John Kline, R-Minn. *	1969-94
John Linder, R-Ga.	1967-69
Edward J. Markey, D-Mass.	1968-73
Jim Marshall, D-Ga. *	1968-70
Eric Massa, D-N.Y.*	1981-2001
Jim McDermott, D-Wash.	1968-70
Gary G. Miller, R-Calif.	1967-68
Walt Minnick, D-Idaho	1970-72
Alan B. Mollohan, D-W.Va.	1970-83
Dennis Moore, D-Kan.	1970-73
Patrick J. Murphy, D-Pa. *	1996-2007
John P. Murtha, D-Pa. *	1952-55, 1966-90
Pete Olson, R-Texas	1988-98
Solomon P. Ortiz, D-Texas	1960-62
Bill Pascrell Jr., D-N.J.	1961-67
Ron Paul, R-Texas	1963-68
Gary Peters, D-Mich.	1993-2000
Collin C. Peterson, D-Minn.	1963-69
Joe Pitts, R-Pa. *	1963-69
Ted Poe, R-Texas	1970-76
Charles B. Rangel, D-N.Y. *	1948-52
Dave Reichert, R-Wash.	1971-76
Silvestre Reyes, D-Texas *	1966-68
Phil Roe, R-Tenn.	1973-74
Harold Rogers, R-Ky.	1956-63
Mike Rogers, R-Mich.	1985-88
Tom Rooney, R-Fla.	2000-04

Bobby L. Rush, D-Ill.	1963-68	Cliff Stearns, R-Fla.	1963-67
Gregorio Kilili Camacho Sablan, D-M.P.	1981-86	John Tanner, D-Tenn.	1968-72, 1974-2000
John Salazar, D-Colo.	1973-76	Gene Taylor, D-Miss.	1971-84
Robert C. Scott, D-Va.	1970-76	Mike Thompson, D-Calif. *	1969-73
José E. Serrano, D-N.Y.	1964-66	Edolphus Towns, D-N.Y.	1956-58
Joe Sestak, D-Pa. *	1974-2005	Tim Walz, D-Minn.	1981-2005
John Shadegg, R-Ariz.	1969-75	Edward Whitfield, R-Ky.	1967-73
John Shimkus, R-Ill.	1980-2008	Joe Wilson, R-S.C.	1972-2003
Vic Snyder, D-Ark.	1967-69	Frank R. Wolf, R-Va.	1962-63
John M. Spratt Jr., D-S.C.	1969-71	C.W. Bill Young, R-Fla.	1948-57
Pete Stark, D-Calif.	1955-57	Don Young, R-Alaska	1955-57

Members Whose Kids Served in Iraq or Afghanistan

Member	Child's Name	Relationship	Branch
Rep. Todd Akin, R-Mo.	Perry Akin	son	Marines
Sen. Christopher S. Bond, R-Mo.	Sam Bond	son	Marines
Rep. Jo Ann Emerson, R-Mo.	Jessica Gladney	stepchild	Army
Rep. Debbie Halvorson, D-Ill.	Jay Bush	stepson	Army
Sen. Tim Johnson, D-S.D.	Brooks Johnson	son	Army
Rep. John Kline, R-Minn.	John Daniel Kline	son	Army
Rep. Ileana Ros-Lehtinen, R-Fla.	Douglas Lehtinen	stepchild	Marines
	Lindsey Nelson Lehtinen	daughter-in-law	Marines
Rep. Lucille Roybal-Allard, D-Calif.	Guy Mark Allard	stepchild	Army
Sen. Jim Webb, D-Va.	Jimmy Webb	son	Marines
Rep. Joe Wilson, R-S.C.	Alan Wilson	son	S.C. National Guard

Peace Corps Volunteers

Members of Congress who have served in the Peace Corps:

Member	Country	Years
Sen. Christopher J. Dodd, D-Conn.	Dominican Republic	1966-68
Rep. Sam Farr, D-Calif.	Colombia	1964-66
Rep. Michael M. Honda, D-Calif.	El Salvador	1965-67
Rep. Tom Petri, R-Wis.	Somalia	1966-67
Rep. Steve Driehaus, D-Ohio	Senegal	1988-90

Fastest Members of Congress

Some members participate in an annual 3.2 mile footrace in Washington, D.C. Here are the times posted by the 32 members who ran in the April 2009 race, when Rep. Gordon outpaced his congressional colleagues for a 20th year.

Member	Time	Member	Time
Rep. Bart Gordon, D-Tenn.	18:49	Rep. Peter A. DeFazio, D-Ore.	26:35
Sen. John Thune, R-S.D.	19:47	Rep. Bill Cassidy, R-La.	27:00
Rep. Aaron Schock, R-Ill.	20:02	Rep. José E. Serrano, D-N.Y.	27:34
Sen. John Ensign, R-Nev.	20:10	Sen. Mark Udall, D-Colo.	28:51
Rep. Bob Inglis, R-S.C.	20:21	Sen. Jack Reed, D-R.I.	29:30
Rep. Jim Marshall, D-Ga.	22:13	Rep. Doug Lamborn, R-Colo.	29:33
Rep. Jean Schmidt, R-Ohio	23:11	Rep. Mike Pence, R-Ind.	30:16
Rep. Baron P. Hill, D-Ind.	23:34	Sen. Jeff Bingaman, D-N.M.	30:27
Sen. Jim DeMint, R-S.C.	23:50	Rep. Jane Harman, D-Calif.	30:41
Rep. Charlie Dent, R-Pa.	24:34	Rep. Dave Reichert, R-Wash.	30:42
Rep. Brad Ellsworth, D-Ind.	24:41	Rep. Larry Kissell, D-N.C.	35:09
Rep. Dave Loebsack, D-Iowa	24:57	Rep. Todd Tiahrt, R-Kan.	35:30
Rep. Anh "Joseph" Cao, R-La.	25:04	Sen. Kay Bailey Hutchison, R-Texas	39:32
Rep. Earl Blumenauer, D-Ore.	25:17	Sen. Richard G. Lugar, R-Ind.	42:10
Rep. Shelley Moore Capito, R-W.Va.	25:34	Rep. Cynthia M. Lummis, R-Wyo.	42:16
Rep. Russ Carnahan, D-Mo.	25:56	Rep. Mazie K. Hirono, D-Hawaii	50:00

Most and Least Legislation

These current members served in the entire 110th Congress (2007-08) and introduced the most and least legislation.

Most — Senate

Dianne Feinstein, D-Calif.*	138
Harry Reid, D-Nev.	130
John Kerry, D-Mass.	115
Charles E. Schumer, D-N.Y.*	113
Richard J. Durbin, D-Ill.*	110
Christopher J. Dodd, D-Conn.	99
Edward M. Kennedy, D-Mass.	97
Olympia J. Snowe, R-Maine*	92
Russ Feingold, D-Wis.	91
Barbara Boxer, D-Calif.	83
Jeff Bingaman, D-N.M.	83

Most — House

Carolyn B. Maloney, D-N.Y.*	88
Charles B. Rangel, D-N.Y.*	84
Ron Paul, R-Texas *	70
Barbara Lee, D-Calif.	69
Sheila Jackson Lee, D-Texas	67
Alcee L. Hastings, D-Fla.	63
Bob Filner, D-Calif.	63
Dan Burton, R-Ind.	62
Ellen O. Tauscher, D-Calif.	61
Louise M. Slaughter, D-N.Y.	60

Least — Senate

Bob Corker, R-Tenn.	2
Richard C. Shelby, R-Ala. †	3
Robert F. Bennett, R-Utah †	4
Thad Cochran, R-Miss. †	10
Robert C. Byrd, D-W.Va. †	12
Jim Webb, D-Va.	12
Tom Coburn, R-Okla. †	16
Sheldon Whitehouse, D-R.I.	16
Jon Tester, D-Mont.	17
Jim Bunning, R-Ky.	18
Lindsey Graham, R-S.C.	18

Least — House

Ander Crenshaw, R-Fla.	2
John Linder, R-Ga.	2
C.W. Bill Young, R-Fla. †	2
Spencer Bachus, R-Ala.	3
Lincoln Diaz-Balart, R-Fla.	3
Harold Rogers, R-Ky. †	3
Gene Taylor, D-Miss. †	3
Jerry Lewis, R-Calif.	4
Frank D. Lucas, R-Okla.	4
Kenny Marchant, R-Texas	4
Lynn Westmoreland, R-Ga. †	4

* Also in the top 10 in the 109th Congress.

† Also in the bottom 10 in the 109th Congress.

Members With a Parent Who Served in Congress

There are 31 members with a parent who served in Congress. Walter B. Jones is the only one on the list who belongs to a different political party than his parent. * Directly succeeded their parent in the same seat.

Member	Parent	Years Parent Served
Sen. Evan Bayh, D-Ind.	Sen. Birch Bayh, D-Ind.	1963-81
Sen. Mark Begich, D-Alaska	Rep. Nick Begich, D-Alaska	1971-72
Sen. Robert F. Bennett, R-Utah	Sen. Wallace F. Bennett, R-Utah	1951-74
Rep. Gus Bilirakis, R-Fla.*	Rep. Michael Bilirakis, R-Fla	1983-2007
Rep. Dan Boren, D-Okla.	Sen. David L. Boren, D-Okla.	1979-94
Rep. Shelley Moore Capito, R-W.Va.	Rep. Arch A. Moore Jr., R-W.Va.	1957-69
Rep. Russ Carnahan, D-Mo.	Sen. Jean Carnahan, D-Mo.	2001-02
Rep. William Lacy Clay, D-Mo.*	Rep. William L. Clay, D-Mo.	1969-2001
Rep. John D. Dingell, D-Mich.*	Rep. John D. Dingell Sr., D-Mich.	1933-55
Sen. Christopher J. Dodd, D-Conn.	Rep./Sen. Thomas J. Dodd, D-Conn.	1953-57, 1959-71
Rep. John J. "Jimmy" Duncan Jr., R-Tenn.*	Rep. John J. Duncan, R-Tenn.	1965-88
Rep. Rodney Frelinghuysen, R-N.J.	Rep. Peter H. Frelinguysen, R-N.J.	1953-75
Rep. Charlie Gonzalez, D-Texas*	Rep. Henry B. Gonzalez, D-Texas	1961-99
Rep. Rush D. Holt, D-N.J.	Sen. Rush Dew Holt, D-W.Va.	1935-41
Rep. Duncan Hunter, R-Calif.*	Rep. Duncan Hunter, R-Calif.	1981-2009
Rep. Walter B. Jones, R-N.C.	Rep. Walter B. Jones Sr., D-N.C.	1966-92
Rep. Patrick J. Kennedy, D-R.I.	Sen. Edward M. Kennedy, D-Mass.	1962-present
Sen. Jon Kyl, R-Ariz.	Rep. John H. Kyl, R-Iowa	1959-65, 1967-73
Rep. Bob Latta, R-Ohio	Rep. Delbert L. Latta, R-Ohio	1959-89
Rep. Daniel Lipinski, D-Ill.*	Rep. William O. Lipinski, D-Ill.	1983-2005
Rep. Connie Mack, R-Fla.	Rep./Sen. Connie Mack, R-Fla.	1983-2001
Rep. Kendrick B. Meek, D-Fla.*	Rep. Carrie P. Meek, D-Fla.	1993-2003
Rep. Alan B. Mollohan, D-W.Va.*	Rep. Robert H. Mollohan, D-W.Va.	1953-57, 1969-83
Sen. Lisa Murkowski, R-Alaska*	Sen. Frank H. Murkowski, R-Alaska	1981-2002
Rep. Nancy Pelosi, D-Calif.	Rep. Thomas D'Alesandro Jr., D-Md.	1939-47
Sen. Mark Pryor, D-Ark.	Rep./Sen. David Pryor, D-Ark.	1966-73, 1979-97
Rep. Lucille Roybal-Allard, D-Calif.	Rep. Edward R. Roybal, D-Calif.	1963-93
Rep. John Sarbanes, D-Md.	Rep./Sen. Paul S. Sarbanes, D-Md.	1971-2007
Rep. Bill Shuster, R-Pa.*	Rep. Bud Shuster, R-Pa.	1973-2001
Sen. Mark Udall, D-Colo.	Rep. Morris K. Udall, D-Ariz.	1961-91
Sen. Tom Udall, D-N.M.	Rep. Stewart L. Udall, D-Ariz.	1955-61

Members Whose Spouse Served in Congress

Member	Spouse	Spouse's Service
Rep. Mary Bono Mack, R-Calif.*	Rep. Sonny Bono, R-Calif.	1995-98
Rep. Lois Capps, D-Calif.	Rep. Walter Capps, D-Calif.	1997
Rep. Jo Ann Emerson, R-Mo.	Rep. Bill Emerson, R-Mo.	1981-96
Rep. Stephanie Herseth Sandlin, D-S.D.	Rep. Max Sandlin, D-Texas	1997-2005
Rep. Doris Matsui, D-Calif.	Rep. Robert T. Matsui, D-Calif.	1979-2005
Sen. Olympia J. Snowe, R-Maine	Rep. John R. McKernan Jr., R-Maine	1983-87
Rep. Niki Tsongas, D-Mass.	Rep./Sen. Paul E. Tsongas, D-Mass.	1975-85

* Current Republican Reps. Mary Bono Mack, Calif., and Connie Mack, Fla., are married to each other.

Siblings in Congress

Rep. Lincoln Diaz-Balart, R-Fla.   Rep. Mario Diaz-Balart, R-Fla.
Rep. Sander M. Levin, D-Mich.   Sen. Carl Levin, D-Mich.
Rep. Loretta Sanchez, D-Calif.   Rep. Linda T. Sánchez, D-Calif.

Cousins in Congress

Sen. Mark Udall, D-Colo.
Sen. Tom Udall, D-N.M.

Pronunciation Guide for Congress

Some members of Congress whose names are frequently mispronounced:

Rep. Robert B. Aderholt, R-Ala. – ADD-er-holt
Sen. Daniel K. Akaka, D-Hawaii – uh-KAH-kuh
Rep. Michael Arcuri, D-N.Y. – are-CURE-ee
Rep. Michele Bachmann, R-Minn. – BOCK-man
Rep. Spencer Bachus, R-Ala. – BACK-us
Sen. John Barrasso, R-Wyo. – buh-RASS-o
Rep. John Barrow, D-Ga. – BEAR-oh (rhymes with "arrow")
Sen. Evan Bayh, D-Ind. – BY
Rep. Xavier Becerra, D-Calif. – HAH-vee-air beh-SEH-ra
Rep. Gus Bilirakis, R-Fla. – bil-uh-RACK-iss
Rep. Earl Blumenauer, D-Ore. – BLUE-men-hour
Rep. John Boccieri, D-Ohio – bo-CHAIR-ee
Rep. John A. Boehner, R-Ohio – BAY-ner
Rep. John Boozman, R-Ark. – BOZE-man
Del. Madeleine Z. Bordallo, D-Guam – bore-DAA-yo
Rep. Rick Boucher, D-Va. – BOW (rhymes with "now")-chur
Rep. Charles Boustany Jr., R-La. – boo-STAN-knee
Rep. Paul Broun, R-Ga. – BROWN
Rep. Steve Buyer, R-Ind. – BOO-yer
Rep. Anh "Joseph" Cao, R-La. – GOW
Rep. Shelley Moore Capito, R-W.Va. – CAP-ih-toe
Rep. Michael E. Capuano, D-Mass. – KAP-you-AH-no
Rep. Jason Chaffetz, R-Utah – CHAY-fits
Sen. Saxby Chambliss, R-Ga. – SAX-bee CHAM-bliss
Rep. Travis W. Childers, D-Miss. – CHILL-ders
Sen. John Cornyn, R-Texas – CORE-nin
Sen. Michael D. Crapo, R-Idaho – CRAY-poe
Rep. Joseph Crowley, D-N.Y. – KRAU-lee
Rep. Henry Cuellar, D-Texas – KWAY-are
Rep. Artur Davis, D-Ala. – ar-TOUR
Rep. Peter A. DeFazio, D-Ore. – da-FAH-zee-o
Rep. Diana DeGette, D-Colo. – de-GETT
Rep. Bill Delahunt, D-Mass. – DELL-a-hunt
Rep. Rosa DeLauro, D-Conn. – da-LAUR-o
Rep. Lincoln Diaz-Balart, R-Fla. – DEE-az ba-LART
Rep. Mario Diaz-Balart, R-Fla. – DEE-az ba-LART
Rep. Steve Driehaus, D-Ohio – DREE-house
Rep. Vernon J. Ehlers, R-Mich. – AY-lurz
Sen. Michael B. Enzi, R-Wyo. – EN-zee
Rep. Anna G. Eshoo, D-Calif. – EH-shoo
Del. Eni F.H. Faleomavaega, D-Am.Samoa –
    EN-ee FOL-ee-oh-mav-ah-ENG-uh
Rep. Mary Fallin, R-Okla. – FAL-in (rhymes with "Allen")
Rep. Chaka Fattah, D-Pa. – SHOCK-ah fa-TAH
Sen. Russ Feingold, D-Wis. – FINE-gold
Sen. Dianne Feinstein, D-Calif. – FINE-stine
Rep. Rodney Frelinghuysen, R-N.J. – FREE-ling-high-zen
Rep. Elton Gallegly, R-Calif. – GAL-uh-glee
Rep. Jim Gerlach, R-Pa. – GUR-lock
Sen. Kirsten Gillibrand, D-N.Y. – KEER-sten JILL-uh-brand
Rep. Robert W. Goodlatte, R-Va. – GOOD-lat
Rep. Raúl M. Grijalva, D-Ariz. – gree-HAHL-va
Rep. Luis V. Gutierrez, D-Ill. – loo-EES goo-tee-AIR-ez
Rep. Martin Heinrich, D-N.M. – HINE-rick
Rep. Jeb Hensarling, R-Texas – HENN-sur-ling
Rep. Ruben Hinojosa, D-Texas – ru-BEN ee-na-HO-suh
Rep. Mazie K. Hirono, D-Hawaii – may-ZEE hee-RO-no
Rep. Paul W. Hodes, D-N.H. – rhymes with "roads"
Rep. Peter Hoekstra, R-Mich. – HOOK-struh
Rep. Bob Inglis, R-S.C. – ING-lis
Sen. James M. Inhofe, R-Okla. – IN-hoff

Sen. Daniel K. Inouye, D-Hawaii – in-NO-ay
Rep. Darrell Issa, R-Calif. – EYE-sah
Sen. Mike Johanns, R-Neb. – JOE-hannes
    (rhymes with "cans")
Rep. Larry Kissell, D-N.C. – KISS-ell
Sen. Amy Klobuchar, D-Minn. – KLO-buh-shar
Rep. Suzanne M. Kosmas, D-Fla. – KOSS-muss
Rep. Frank Kratovil Jr., D-Md. – KRAT-oh-vil
Rep. Dennis J. Kucinich, D-Ohio – ku-SIN-itch
Sen. Jon Kyl, R-Ariz. – KILE
Rep. Doug Lamborn, R-Colo. – LAMB-born
Sen. Mary L. Landrieu, D-La. – LAN-drew
Rep. Jim Langevin, D-R.I. – LAN-juh-vin
Rep. Steven C. LaTourette, R-Ohio – la-tuh-RETT
Rep. Frank A. LoBiondo, R-N.J. – lo-bee-ON-dough
Rep. Dave Loebsack, D-Iowa – LOBE-sack
Rep. Zoe Lofgren, D-Calif. – ZO LOFF-gren
Rep. Nita M. Lowey, D-N.Y. – LO-ee
Rep. Blaine Luetkemeyer, R-Mo. – LUTE-ka-myer
Rep. Ben Ray Luján, D-N.M. – loo-HAHN
Rep. Dan Maffei, D-N.Y. – muh-FAY
Rep. Donald Manzullo, R-Ill. – man-ZOO-low
Rep. Kenny Marchant, R-Texas – MARCH-unt
Rep. Eric Massa, D-N.Y. – MASS-uh
Rep. Charlie Melancon, D-La. – meh-LAW-sawn
Rep. John L. Mica, R-Fla. – MY-cah
Rep. Michael H. Michaud, D-Maine – ME-shoo
Rep. Jerrold Nadler, D-N.Y. – NAD-ler
Rep. Randy Neugebauer, R-Texas – NAW-geh-bow-er
Rep. Devin Nunes, R-Calif. – NEW-ness
Rep. David R. Obey, D-Wis. – OH-bee
Rep. Frank Pallone Jr., D-N.J. – puh-LOAN
Rep. Bill Pascrell Jr., D-N.J. – pass-KRELL
Rep. Ed Pastor, D-Ariz. – pas-TORE
Rep. Nancy Pelosi, D-Calif. – pa-LO-see
Rep. Tom Perriello, D-Va. – pear-ee-ELL-oh
Rep. Tom Petri, R-Wis. – PEA-try
Res. Cmsr. Pedro R. Pierluisi, D-P.R. – pea-air-loo-EE-see
Rep. Chellie Pingree, D-Maine – Like "Shelley"
Rep. Jared Polis, D-Colo. – POE-liss
Rep. George Radanovich, R-Calif. – ruh-DON-o-vitch
Rep. Nick J. Rahall II, D-W.Va. – RAY-haul
Rep. Denny Rehberg, R-Mont. – REE-berg
Rep. Dave Reichert, R-Wash. – RIKE-ert
Rep. Silvestre Reyes, D-Texas – sil-VES-treh RAY-ess
    (rolled 'R')
Sen. Jim Risch, R-Idaho – Rhymes with "wish"
Rep. Dana Rohrabacher, R-Calif. – ROAR-ah-BAH-ker
Rep. Ileana Ros-Lehtinen, R-Fla. – il-ee-AH-na ross-LAY-tin-nen
Del. Gregorio Kilili Camacho Sablan, D-N. Marianas –
    greg-OREO key-LEE-lee ka-MAH-cho sab-LAHN
Rep. Steve Scalise, R-La. – skuh-LEASE
Rep. Jan Schakowsky, D-Ill. – shuh-KOW-ski
Rep. Mark Schauer, D-Mich. – SCHAU (rhymes with "now")-ur
Rep. José E. Serrano, D-N.Y. – ho-ZAY sa-RAH-no (rolled 'R')
Rep. Joe Sestak, D-Pa. – SESS-tack
Rep. John Shadegg, R-Ariz. – SHAD-egg
Rep. John Shimkus, R-Ill. – SHIM-kus
Rep. Heath Shuler, D-N.C. – SHOO-lur
Rep. Albio Sires, D-N.J. – SEAR-eez (like "series")
Rep. Mark Souder, R-Ind. – SOW (rhymes with "now")-dur

Rep. Jackie Speier, D-Calif. – SPEAR
Sen. Debbie Stabenow, D-Mich. – STAB-uh-now
Rep. Bart Stupak, D-Mich. – STU-pack
Sen. John Thune, R-S.D. – THOON
Rep. Todd Tiahrt, R-Kan. – TEE-hart
Rep. Pat Tiberi, R-Ohio – TEA-berry
Rep. Niki Tsongas, D-Mass. – SONG-gus

Rep. Nydia M. Velázquez, D-N.Y. – NID-ee-uh veh-LASS-kez
Rep. Peter J. Visclosky, D-Ind. – vis-KLOSS-key
Sen. George V. Voinovich, R-Ohio – VOY-no-vitch
Rep. Tim Walz, D-Minn. – WALLS
Rep. Anthony Weiner, D-N.Y. – WEE-ner
Rep. Lynn Woolsey, D-Calif. – WOOL-zee

Congressional Half-Life

Members who have served more than half of their life in Congress. Length of service and percentage figures are as of the start of the 111th Congress.

Member	Age at Swearing-in	Length of Service	Percent of Life in Congress
Rep. John D. Dingell, D-Mich.	29 years, 158 days	53 years, 22 days	64
Sen. Robert C. Byrd, D-W.Va.	35 years, 44 days	56 years	61
Sen. Edward M. Kennedy, D-Mass.	30 years, 258 days	46 years, 58 days	60
Sen. Daniel K. Inouye, D-Hawaii	34 years, 348 days	49 years, 136 days	59
Rep. David R. Obey, D-Wis.	30 years, 180 days	39 years, 278 days	57
Rep. John Conyers Jr., D-Mich.	35 years, 233 days	44 years	55
Rep. Nick J. Rahall II, D-W.Va.	27 years, 229 days	32 years	54
Rep. George Miller, D-Calif.	29 years, 242 days	34 years	53
Sen. Christopher J. Dodd, D-Conn.	30 years, 233 days	34 years	53
Rep. Edward J. Markey, D-Mass.	30 years, 114 days	32 years, 63 days	52
Sen. Max Baucus, D-Mont.	33 years, 34 days	34 years	51
Sen. Thad Cochran, R-Miss.	35 years, 28 days	36 years	51
Rep. Christopher H. Smith, R-N.J.	27 years, 308 days	28 years	50

Note: Rep. David Dreier, R-Calif., will reach the half-life mark on July 9, 2009. Other lawmakers who will join the list during the 111th Congress include Sen. Patrick J. Leahy, D-Vt. (Oct. 31, 2009), Sen. Tom Harkin, D-Iowa (March 12, 2010), Rep. Henry A. Waxman, D-Calif. (May 19, 2010), and Sen. Olympia J. Snowe, R-Maine (Dec. 10, 2010).

High Fliers

Members who have a current pilot's license:

Rep. Leonard L. Boswell, D-Iowa
Rep. Allen Boyd, D-Fla.
Rep. Sam Graves, R-Mo.
Sen. Tom Harkin, D-Iowa
Sen. James M. Inhofe, R-Okla.
Rep. Collin C. Peterson, D-Minn.
Rep. John Salazar, D-Colo.

Members Who Have A Twin

Member	Sibling
Rep. John Barrow, D-Ga.	brother
Rep. Leonard Lance, R-N.J.	brother
Rep. Jerry McNerney, D-Calif.	brother
Sen. Patty Murray, D-Wash.	sister
Rep. Steven R. Rothman, D-N.J.	brother
Rep. Jean Schmidt, R-Ohio	sister
Rep. Nydia M. Velázquez, D-N.Y.	sister

New to Congress

Senate (8 D, 2 R)
Mark Begich, D-Alaska
Michael Bennet, D-Colo.
Roland W. Burris, D-Ill.
Kay Hagan, D-N.C.
Mike Johanns, R-Neb.
Ted Kaufman, D-Del.
Jeff Merkley, D-Ore.
Jim Risch, R-Idaho
Jeanne Shaheen, D-N.H.
Mark Warner, D-Va.

House (36 D, 22 R)
John Adler, D-N.J.
Steve Austria, R-Ohio
John Boccieri, D-Ohio
Bobby Bright, D-Ala.
Anh "Joseph" Cao, R-La.
Bill Cassidy, R-La.
Jason Chaffetz, R-Utah
Mike Coffman, R-Colo.
Gerald E. Connolly, D-Va.
Kathy Dahlkemper, D-Pa.
Steve Driehaus, D-Ohio

John Fleming, R-La.
Alan Grayson, D-Fla.
Parker Griffith, D-Ala.
Brett Guthrie, R-Ky.
Debbie Halvorson, D-Ill.
Gregg Harper, R-Miss.
Martin Heinrich, D-N.M.
Jim Himes, D-Conn.
Duncan Hunter, R-Calif.
Lynn Jenkins, R-Kan.
Mary Jo Kilroy, D-Ohio
Ann Kirkpatrick, D-Ariz.
Larry Kissell, D-N.C.
Suzanne M. Kosmas, D-Fla.
Frank Kratovil Jr., D-Md.
Leonard Lance, R-N.J.
Christopher Lee, R-N.Y.
Blaine Luetkemeyer, R-Mo.
Ben Ray Luján, D-N.M.
Cynthia M. Lummis, R-Wyo.
Dan Maffei, D-N.Y.
Betsy Markey, D-Colo.
Eric Massa, D-N.Y.
Tom McClintock, R-Calif.

Michael E. McMahon, D-N.Y.
Walt Minnick, D-Idaho
Scott Murphy, D-N.Y.
Glenn Nye, D-Va.
Pete Olson, R-Texas
Erik Paulsen, R-Minn.
Tom Perriello, D-Va.
Gary Peters, D-Mich.
Res. Cmsr. Pedro R. Pierluisi, D-P.R.
Chellie Pingree, D-Maine
Jared Polis, D-Colo.
Bill Posey, R-Fla.
Mike Quigley, D-Ill.
Phil Roe, R-Tenn.
Tom Rooney, R-Fla.
Del. Gregorio Kilili Camacho Sablan, D-N. Marianas
Mark Schauer, D-Mich.
Aaron Schock, R-Ill.
Kurt Schrader, D-Ore.
Harry Teague, D-N.M.
Glenn Thompson, R-Pa.
Dina Titus, D-Nev.
Paul Tonko, D-N.Y.

Senators Up for Election in 2010

18 Republicans, 18 Democrats

Evan Bayh, D-Ind.
Michael Bennet, D-Colo.***
Robert F. Bennett, R-Utah
Christopher S. Bond, R-Mo.*
Barbara Boxer, D-Calif.
Sam Brownback, R-Kan.*
Jim Bunning, R-Ky.
Richard M. Burr, R-N.C.
Roland W. Burris, D-Ill.***
Tom Coburn, R-Okla.
Michael D. Crapo, R-Idaho
Jim DeMint, R-S.C.
Christopher J. Dodd, D-Conn.
Byron L. Dorgan, D-N.D.

Russ Feingold, D-Wis.
Kirsten Gillibrand, D-N.Y.***
Charles E. Grassley, R-Iowa
Judd Gregg, R-N.H.*
Daniel K. Inouye, D-Hawaii
Johnny Isakson, R-Ga.
Ted Kaufman, D-Del.**
Patrick J. Leahy, D-Vt.
Blanche Lincoln, D-Ark.
Mel Martinez, R-Fla.*
John McCain, R-Ariz.
Barbara A. Mikulski, D-Md.
Lisa Murkowski, R-Alaska
Patty Murray, D-Wash.

Harry Reid, D-Nev.
Charles E. Schumer, D-N.Y.
Richard C. Shelby, R-Ala.
Arlen Specter, D-Pa.
John Thune, R-S.D.
David Vitter, R-La.
George V. Voinovich, R-Ohio*
Ron Wyden, D-Ore.

* Not running for re-election
** Not running for election
*** Appointed and expected to stand for election in 2010

Dean of The Delegation

State	Member	First Elected	State	Member	First Elected
Alabama	Sen. Richard C. Shelby, R	*1978	Montana	Sen. Max Baucus, D	*1974
Alaska	Rep. Don Young, R	1973	Nebraska	Rep. Lee Terry, R	1998
Arizona	Sen. John McCain, R	1982	Nevada	Sen. Harry Reid, D	*1982
Arkansas	Sen. Blanche Lincoln, D	*1992	New Hampshire	Sen. Judd Gregg, R	*1980
California	Rep. Pete Stark, D	1972	New Jersey	Rep. Christopher H. Smith, R	1980
Colorado	Rep. Diana DeGette, D	1996	New Mexico	Sen. Jeff Bingaman, D	1982
Connecticut	Sen. Christopher J. Dodd, D	*1974	New York	Rep. Charles B. Rangel, D	1970
Delaware	Sen. Thomas R. Carper, D	*1982	North Carolina	Rep. Howard Coble, R	1984
Florida	Rep. C.W. Bill Young, R	1970	North Dakota	Sen. Byron L. Dorgan, D	*1980
Georgia	Rep. John Lewis, D	1986	Ohio	Rep. Marcy Kaptur, D	1982
Hawaii	Sen. Daniel K. Inouye, D	*1959	Oklahoma	Sen. James M. Inhofe, R	*1986
Idaho	Sen. Michael D. Crapo, D	*1992	Oregon	Sen. Ron Wyden, D	*1980
Illinois	Sen. Richard J. Durbin, D	*1982	Pennsylvania	Rep. John P. Murtha, D	1974
Indiana	Sen. Richard G. Lugar, R	1976	Rhode Island	Sen. Jack Reed, D	*1990
Iowa	Sen. Charles E. Grassley, R	†*1974	South Carolina	Rep. John M. Spratt Jr., D	1982
Kansas	Sen. Pat Roberts, R	*1980	South Dakota	Sen. Tim Johnson, D	*1986
Kentucky	Rep. Harold Rogers, R	1980	Tennessee	Rep. Bart Gordon, D	1984
Louisiana	Sen. Mary L. Landrieu, D	1996	Texas	Rep. Ralph M. Hall, R	1980
Maine	Sen. Olympia J. Snowe, R	*1978	Utah	Sen. Orrin G. Hatch, R	1976
Maryland	Sen. Barbara A. Mikulski, D	*1976	Vermont	Sen. Patrick J. Leahy, D	1974
Massachusetts	Sen. Edward M. Kennedy, D	1962	Virginia	Rep. Frank R. Wolf, R	1980
Michigan	Rep. John D. Dingell, D	1955	Washington	Rep. Norm Dicks, D	1976
Minnesota	Rep. James L. Oberstar, D	1974	West Virginia	Sen. Robert C. Byrd, D	*1952
Mississippi	Sen. Thad Cochran, R	*1972	Wisconsin	Rep. David R. Obey, D	1969
Missouri	Rep. Ike Skelton, D	1976	Wyoming	Sen. Michael B. Enzi, R	1996

*First elected to the House.

† Sen. Tom Harkin, D, also was elected to the House in 1974, but Grassley reached the Senate four years before Harkin.

M.D.s

Member	Field
Sen. John Barrasso, R-Wyo.	Orthopedic surgeon
Sen. Tom Coburn, R-Okla.	Obstetrician
Rep. Charles Boustany Jr., R-La.	Heart surgeon
Rep. Paul Broun, R-Ga.	Physician
Rep. Michael C. Burgess, R-Texas	Obstetrician
Rep. Bill Cassidy, R-La.	Gastroenterologist
Del. Donna M.C. Christensen, D-Virgin Is.	Physician
Rep. John Fleming, R-La.	Family practice
Rep. Phil Gingrey, R-Ga.	Obstetrician
Rep. Parker Griffith, D-Ala.	Radiation oncologist
Rep. Steve Kagen, D-Wis.	Allergy/Immunology
Rep. Jim McDermott, D- Wash.	Psychiatrist
Rep. Ron Paul, R-Texas	Obstetrician
Rep. Tom Price, R-Ga.	Orthopedic surgeon
Rep. Phil Roe, R-Tenn.	Physician
Rep. Vic Snyder, D-Ark.	Family practice

Physicists

Rep. Vernon J. Ehlers, R-Mich.
Rep. Bill Foster, D-Ill.
Rep. Rush D. Holt., D-N.J.

Engineers

These House members have held engineering jobs:

Member	Job
Roscoe G. Bartlett, R-Md.	biomedical engineer
Joe L. Barton, R-Texas	engineering consultant
Martin Heinrich, D-N.M.	mechanical draftsman
Eric Massa, D-N.Y.	photonics engineer
Jerry McNerney, D-Calif.	wind engineer
Bill Posey, R-Fla.	space program inspector
Steve Scalise, R-La.	software engineer
Paul Tonko, D-N.Y.	state public works engineer

Member Occupations

	HOUSE			SENATE			111th
	Democrat	Republican	Total	Democrat	Republican	Total	CONGRESS
Public Service/Politics	169	80	249	32	16	48	297
Business	114	113	227	16	20	36	263
Law	115	64	179	37*	27	64	243
Education	59	25	84	13*	7	20	104
Real Estate	10	27	37	2	5	7	44
Agriculture	12	15	27	1	3	4	31
Medicine/Doctor	5	12	17		3	3	20
Labor/Blue Collar	9	5	14	2*	1	3	17
Journalism	5	4	9	3*	2	5	14
Homemaker/Domestic	8	4	12	1		1	13
Law Enforcement	8	3	11				11
Secretarial/Clerical	7	4	11				11
Health Care	7	3	10				10
Military	3	4	7		1	1	8
Engineering	5	2	7				7
Science	3	3	6				6
Entertainment/Actor	3		3	1	1	2	5
Technical	2	2	4				4
Artistic/Creative				2*		2	2
Professional Sports	1		1		1	1	2
Miscellaneous	1		1	1		1	2
Clergy	1		1				1

Notes: Some members have had more than one occupation, and some members
have had more than one separate occupation within a catergory. Delegates are not included.

* Total includes independents Joseph I. Lieberman, Conn., and Bernard Sanders, Vt.

Member Religious Affiliations

	HOUSE			SENATE			111th
	Democrat	Republican	Total	Democrat	Republican	Total	CONGRESS
Roman Catholic	97	37	134	17	9	26	160
Baptist	28	26	54	2	6	8	62
Methodist	23	22	45	4	5	9	54
Protestant - Unspecified	13	30	43	7	3	10	53
Jewish	30	1	31	12*		13 **	44
Presbyterian	15	16	31	4	8	12	43
Episcopalian	13	18	31	3	3	6	37
Lutheran	11	9	20	4		4	24
Mormon	1	7	8	2	3	5	13
Eastern Orthodox	4	2	6		1	1	7
United Church of Christ/ Congregationalist		3	3	2	2	4	7
Unspecified	6		6	1		1	7
African Methodist Episcopal	4		4				4
Christian Scientist		3	3				3
Unitarian	2		2	1		1	3
Buddhist	2		2				2
Christian Reformed Church		2	2				2
Muslim	2		2				2
Seventh-day Adventist	1	1	2				2
Christian Church	1		1				1
Community of Christ	1		1				1
Disciples of Christ	1		1				1
Pentecostal		1	1				1
Quaker	1		1				1

Delegates are not included.

* Includes independents Joseph I. Lieberman, Conn., and Bernard Sanders, Vt.

** Both Norm Coleman and Al Franken are Jewish. This tally reflects a Jewish Senator from Minnesota regardless of the race's outcome.

Senate Presidential Support and Opposition

Support scores represent how often a senator sided with President George W. Bush on roll call votes on which the president took a clear position beforehand. Opposition scores represent how often a senator voted against the president's position. During the 110th Congress (2007-08), there were 151 such votes in the Senate. Only members of the 111th Congress who voted more than half the time in 2007 and 2008 are listed.

110th Congress: Top Scorers

Support — Democrats

Joseph I. Lieberman, Conn.*	58.5
Mary L. Landrieu, La.	49.3
Ben Nelson, Neb.	49.0
Mark Pryor, Ark.	46.4
Thomas R. Carper, Del.	45.9
Evan Bayh, Ind.	44.7
Blanche Lincoln, Ark.	43.8
Kent Conrad, N.D.	42.7
Claire McCaskill, Mo.	42.3
Barbara A. Mikulski, Md.	42.0
Bill Nelson, Fla.	41.6
Bob Casey, Pa.	41.1
Jim Webb, Va.	40.9
Harry Reid, Nev.	40.4
Daniel K. Inouye, Hawaii	39.7
Max Baucus, Mont.	39.1
John D. Rockefeller IV, W.Va.	38.9
Jack Reed, R.I.	38.7
Dianne Feinstein, Calif.	38.6
Tim Johnson, S.D.	37.9
Herb Kohl, Wis.	37.7

Support — Republicans

Tom Coburn, Okla.	87.9
Jim DeMint, S.C.	87.8
Judd Gregg, N.H.	87.5
Jon Kyl, Ariz.	87.2
John Ensign, Nev.	86.5
Richard M. Burr, N.C.	86.3
Michael B. Enzi, Wyo.	84.8
Robert F. Bennett, Utah	84.5
John Cornyn, Texas	84.4
Sam Brownback, Kan.	84.0
Jim Bunning, Ky.	82.8
James M. Inhofe, Okla.	82.7
Lindsey Graham, S.C.	82.6
Mitch McConnell, Ky.	82.1
David Vitter, La.	81.8
Jeff Sessions, Ala.	81.2
Richard G. Lugar, Ind.	81.1
Johnny Isakson, Ga.	80.7
John Barrasso, Wyo.	80.2
John Thune, S.D.	79.9

Opposition — Democrats

Tom Harkin, Iowa	68.8
Debbie Stabenow, Mich.	68.5
Bernard Sanders, Vt.*	68.2
Barbara Boxer, Calif.	67.6
Patrick J. Leahy, Vt.	67.1
Sherrod Brown, Ohio	66.9
Charles E. Schumer, N.Y.	66.7
Robert C. Byrd, W.Va.	66.0
Russ Feingold, Wis.	65.6
Richard J. Durbin, Ill.	65.5
Byron L. Dorgan, N.D.	65.5
Jon Tester, Mont.	65.3
Frank R. Lautenberg, N.J.	65.3
Robert Menendez, N.J.	65.3
Patty Murray, Wash.	65.3
Maria Cantwell, Wash.	65.1
Ron Wyden, Ore.	64.9
Benjamin L. Cardin, Md.	64.7
Jeff Bingaman, N.M.	64.7
Edward M. Kennedy, Mass.	64.6

Opposition — Republicans

Olympia J. Snowe, Maine	46.4
Susan Collins, Maine	39.7
Arlen Specter, Pa. †	38.5
Norm Coleman, Minn.**	35.6
Roger Wicker, Miss.	29.6
Chuck Hagel, Neb.	25.4
Lisa Murkowski, Alaska	25.0
Pat Roberts, Kan.	25.0
Kay Bailey Hutchison, Texas	24.7
Charles E. Grassley, Iowa	23.2
Orrin G. Hatch, Utah	23.0
George V. Voinovich, Ohio	22.1
Richard C. Shelby, Ala.	21.9
Mel Martinez, Fla.	21.9
Lamar Alexander, Tenn.	21.9
Saxby Chambliss, Ga.	21.1
Michael D. Crapo, Idaho	20.8
Thad Cochran, Miss.	20.8
Bob Corker, Tenn.	20.7
Christopher S. Bond, Mo.	20.4

* Independents in the 111th Congress, Lieberman and Sanders, caucus with the Democrats.
** Trailing in his re-election bid, not currently a member of the 111th Congress
† Served as a Republican in the 110th Congress.

www.cqpress.com

Senate Party Unity and Opposition

Support scores represent how often a senator voted with his or her party's majority against a majority of the other party. Opposition scores represent how often a senator voted against his or her party's majority. In the 110th Congress (2007-08), there were 377 such "party unity" votes in the Senate. Only members of the 111th Congress who voted more than half the time in 2007 and 2008 are listed.

110th Congress: Top Scorers

Support — Democrats
Frank R. Lautenberg, N.J.	98.4
Richard J. Durbin, Ill.	98.1
Robert Menendez, N.J.	97.6
Barbara Boxer, Calif.	97.5
Benjamin L. Cardin, Md.	97.3
Charles E. Schumer, N.Y.	97.3
Sherrod Brown, Ohio	97.3
Jack Reed, R.I.	97.3
Sheldon Whitehouse, R.I.	97.3
Bernard Sanders, Vt.*	97.3
Patty Murray, Wash.	97.3
Christopher J. Dodd, Conn.	96.5
Tom Harkin, Iowa	96.5
Patrick J. Leahy, Vt.	96.3
Jeff Bingaman, N.M.	96.2
Daniel K. Akaka, Hawaii	96.0
Ron Wyden, Ore.	95.7
John Kerry, Mass.	95.6
Carl Levin, Mich.	95.4
Debbie Stabenow, Mich.	95.2
Herb Kohl, Wis.	95.2

Support — Republicans
Jim DeMint, S.C.	98.9
James M. Inhofe, Okla.	98.1
Richard M. Burr, N.C.	97.8
John Ensign, Nev.	97.5
John Cornyn, Texas	97.5
John Barrasso, Wyo.	97.5
Tom Coburn, Okla.	96.8
Michael B. Enzi, Wyo.	96.8
Johnny Isakson, Ga.	95.9
Mitch McConnell, Ky.	95.5
Jon Kyl, Ariz.	95.4
Saxby Chambliss, Ga.	95.4
Jim Bunning, Ky.	95.1
David Vitter, La.	94.6
Jeff Sessions, Ala.	93.8
Roger Wicker, Miss.	93.6
Lindsey Graham, S.C.	93.2
Michael D. Crapo, Idaho	92.5
Sam Brownback, Kan.	90.8
John Thune, S.D.	90.5

Opposition — Democrats
Ben Nelson, Neb.	29.7
Evan Bayh, Ind.	24.7
Mary L. Landrieu, La.	24.7
Mark Pryor, Ark.	19.4
Joseph I. Lieberman, Conn.*	18.9
Claire McCaskill, Mo.	18.8
Tim Johnson, S.D.	16.8
Max Baucus, Mont.	15.2
Blanche Lincoln, Ark.	15.0
Thomas R. Carper, Del.	14.2
Jon Tester, Mont.	13.8
Byron L. Dorgan, N.D.	12.6
Jim Webb, Va.	12.4
Kent Conrad, N.D.	12.1
Robert C. Byrd, W.Va.	12.0
John D. Rockefeller IV, W.Va.	10.8
Bill Nelson, Fla.	10.0
Daniel K. Inouye, Hawaii	9.1
Harry Reid, Nev.	8.2
Barbara A. Mikulski, Md.	7.8

Opposition — Republicans
Olympia J. Snowe, Maine	57.8
Susan Collins, Maine	50.9
Arlen Specter, Pa. †	47.0
Norm Coleman, Minn.**	34.7
George V. Voinovich, Ohio	31.8
Richard G. Lugar, Ind.	28.7
Lisa Murkowski, Alaska	28.4
Chuck Hagel, Neb.	25.6
Charles E. Grassley, Iowa	17.2
Mel Martinez, Fla.	15.3
Pat Roberts, Kan.	15.2
Christopher S. Bond, Mo.	15.2
Thad Cochran, Miss.	15.1
Orrin G. Hatch, Utah	14.6
Robert F. Bennett, Utah	14.0
Lamar Alexander, Tenn.	13.5
Bob Corker, Tenn.	12.5
Judd Gregg, N.H.	11.4
Kay Bailey Hutchison, Texas	10.2
Richard C. Shelby, Ala.	9.9

* Independents in the 111th Congress, Lieberman and Sanders, caucus with the Democrats.
** Trailing in his re-election bid, not currently a member of the 111th Congress.
† Served as a Republican in the 110th Congress.

House Presidential Support and Opposition

Support scores represent how often a House member sided with President George W. Bush on roll call votes on which the president took a clear position beforehand. Opposition scores represent how often a member voted against the president's position. During the 110th Congress (2007-08), there were 197 such votes in the House. Only members of the 111th Congress who voted more than half the time in 2007 and 2008 are listed.

110th Congress: Top Scorers

Support — Democrats

Dan Boren, Okla.	35.8
Jim Marshall, Ga.	35.1
Nick Lampson, Texas	31.7
Travis W. Childers, Miss.	26.4
John Barrow, Ga.	25.3
Jim Matheson, Utah	24.9
Charlie Melancon, La.	24.5
Melissa Bean, Ill.	24.0
Gene Taylor, Miss.	23.5
Lincoln Davis, Tenn.	23.1
Henry Cuellar, Texas	21.9
Joe Donnelly, Ind.	21.3
Brad Ellsworth, Ind.	21.3
Bill Foster, Ill.	20.6
Jim Cooper, Tenn.	20.5
John Tanner, Tenn.	20.5
Mike McIntyre, N.C.	20.3
Christopher Carney, Pa.	20.1
Jason Altmire, Pa.	18.8
Heath Shuler, N.C.	18.7

Support — Republicans

John Campbell, Calif.	90.9
Mike Pence, Ind.	90.5
Doug Lamborn, Colo.	90.2
Jeb Hensarling, Texas	90.1
John A. Boehner, Ohio	89.8
John Shadegg, Ariz.	89.6
Jim Jordan, Ohio	88.7
Pete Sessions, Texas	88.5
J. Gresham Barrett, S.C.	88.4
Virginia Foxx, N.C.	88.2
Jeff Flake, Ariz.	87.5
Sam Johnson, Texas	87.2
Paul Broun, Ga.	87.1
Joe Pitts, Pa.	87.0
F. James Sensenbrenner Jr., Wis.	87.0
Dan Lungren, Calif.	86.8
Jeff Miller, Fla.	86.6
Joe Wilson, S.C.	86.6
Ed Royce, Calif.	86.5
Patrick T. McHenry, N.C.	86.5

Opposition — Democrats

Linda T. Sánchez, Calif.	94.4
Bill Delahunt, Mass.	94.4
Peter A. DeFazio, Ore.	94.4
Lloyd Doggett, Texas	94.2
Joe Courtney, Conn.	93.9
Robert C. Scott, Va.	93.9
Xavier Becerra, Calif.	93.8
Grace F. Napolitano, Calif.	93.8
Ed Pastor, Ariz.	93.7
Lucille Roybal-Allard, Calif.	93.4
Steve Kagen, Wis.	93.4
Raúl M. Grijalva, Ariz.	93.3
Elijah E. Cummings, Md.	93.3
Hank Johnson, Ga.	93.2
Loretta Sanchez, Calif.	93.1
Alcee L. Hastings, Fla.	93.0
John Conyers Jr., Mich.	93.0
Edward J. Markey, Mass.	92.9
Phil Hare, Ill.	92.8
John Yarmuth, Ky.	92.8
Stephen F. Lynch, Mass.	92.8
John F. Tierney, Mass.	92.8
David Wu, Ore.	92.8
David R. Obey, Wis.	92.8

Opposition — Republicans

Christopher H. Smith, N.J.	64.9
Frank A. LoBiondo, N.J.	61.5
Walter B. Jones, N.C.	59.4
Michael N. Castle, Del.	59.2
Timothy V. Johnson, Ill.	56.7
Jim Gerlach, Pa.	55.6
Steven C. LaTourette, Ohio	55.2
Mark Steven Kirk, Ill.	54.2
Tim Murphy, Pa.	53.1
John M. McHugh, N.Y.	52.6
Shelley Moore Capito, W.Va.	52.1
Candice S. Miller, Mich.	51.5
Jo Ann Emerson, Mo.	51.3
Charlie Dent, Pa.	51.0
Dave Reichert, Wash.	51.0
Ileana Ros-Lehtinen, Fla.	49.2
Fred Upton, Mich.	49.0
Todd R. Platts, Pa.	47.9
Lincoln Diaz-Balart, Fla.	42.9
Vern Buchanan, Fla.	42.6

House Party Unity and Opposition

Support scores represent how often a House member voted with his or her party's majority against a majority of the other party. Opposition scores represent how often a member voted against his or her party's majority on such party unity tests. In the 110th Congress (2007-08) there were 1,097 such "party unity" votes in the House. Only members of the 111th Congress who voted more than half the time in 2007 and 2008 are listed.

110th Congress: Top Scorers

Support — Democrats

Niki Tsongas, Mass.	99.8
Tammy Baldwin, Wis.	99.7
Richard E. Neal, Mass.	99.6
George Miller, Calif.	99.5
Jesse L. Jackson Jr., Ill.	99.5
John W. Olver, Mass.	99.5
Doris Matsui, Calif.	99.4
Lois Capps, Calif.	99.4
Linda T. Sánchez, Calif.	99.4
Jim McGovern, Mass.	99.4
Edward J. Markey, Mass.	99.4
Louise M. Slaughter, N.Y.	99.4
Raúl M. Grijalva, Ariz.	99.3
Jan Schakowsky, Ill.	99.3
Yvette D. Clarke, N.Y.	99.3
Nita M. Lowey, N.Y.	99.3
David E. Price, N.C.	99.3
Eight members tied:	99.2

Michael M. Honda, Calif.; Xavier Becerra, Calif.; Rosa DeLauro, Conn.; Danny K. Davis, Ill.; John Sarbanes, Md.; Barney Frank, Mass.; Betty McCollum, Minn.; and Robert A. Brady, Pa.

Support — Republicans

Paul Broun, Ga.	99.5
Doug Lamborn, Colo.	99.4
Trent Franks, Ariz.	99.2
John A. Boehner, Ohio	99.1
Marsha Blackburn, Tenn.	99.1
Sam Johnson, Texas	98.9
Patrick T. McHenry, N.C.	98.8
Lynn Westmoreland, Ga.	98.7
Nathan Deal, Ga.	98.7
Steve Scalise, La.	98.7
Bob Latta, Ohio	98.7
Mike Pence, Ind.	98.6
Todd Akin, Mo.	98.6
J. Gresham Barrett, S.C.	98.5
Tom Price, Ga.	98.4
Joe Pitts, Pa.	98.4
Jeb Hensarling, Texas	98.4
Randy Neugebauer, Texas	98.4
Pete Sessions, Texas	98.4
Dan Burton, Ind.	98.3
Steve King, Iowa	98.3
Adrian Smith, Neb.	98.3
Eric Cantor, Va.	98.3

Opposition — Democrats

Nick Lampson, Texas	29.7
John Barrow, Ga.	25.3
Joe Donnelly, Ind.	22.2
Jim Marshall, Ga.	22.0
Heath Shuler, N.C.	22.0
Baron P. Hill, Ind.	21.4
Gene Taylor, Miss.	21.4
Jason Altmire, Pa.	20.4
Brad Ellsworth, Ind.	19.7
Christopher Carney, Pa.	18.7
Jim Matheson, Utah	18.4
Harry E. Mitchell, Ariz.	18.1
Dan Boren, Okla.	17.0
Melissa Bean, Ill.	14.9
Gabrielle Giffords, Ariz.	13.3
Mike McIntyre, N.C.	12.8
Charlie Melancon, La.	11.8
Collin C. Peterson, Minn.	11.7
John Tanner, Tenn.	11.5
Tied: Zack Space, Ohio, Lincoln Davis, Tenn.	11.1

Opposition — Republicans

Christopher H. Smith, N.J.	36.2
Frank A. LoBiondo, N.J.	32.8
Timothy V. Johnson, Ill.	30.1
Michael N. Castle, Del.	29.3
Mark Steven Kirk, Ill.	29.2
Walter B. Jones, N.C.	27.2
Dave Reichert, Wash.	26.4
John M. McHugh, N.Y.	26.2
Jim Gerlach, Pa.	25.8
Tim Murphy, Pa.	25.3
Ileana Ros-Lehtinen, Fla.	25.1
Steven C. LaTourette, Ohio	25.1
Charlie Dent, Pa.	23.9
Todd R. Platts, Pa.	21.9
Vernon J. Ehlers, Mich.	20.9
Jo Ann Emerson, Mo.	20.8
Shelley Moore Capito, W.Va.	20.2
Jeff Fortenberry, Neb.	18.8
Frank R. Wolf, Va.	18.6
Rodney Frelinghuysen, N.J.	18.5

New Democrat Coalition

The New Democrats are a group of pro-business Democratic House moderates.

Chairwoman: Ellen O. Tauscher, Calif.

John Adler, N.J.	Gabrielle Giffords, Ariz.	Gregory W. Meeks, N.Y.
Jason Altmire, Pa.	Charlie Gonzalez, Texas	Charlie Melancon, La.
Michael Arcuri, N.Y.	Parker Griffith, Ala.	Harry E. Mitchell, Ariz.
Brian Baird, Wash.	Debbie Halvorson, Ill.	Dennis Moore, Kan.
John Barrow, Ga.	Jane Harman, Calif.	James P. Moran, Va.
Melissa Bean, Ill.	Martin Heinrich, N.M.	Christopher S. Murphy, Conn.
Shelley Berkley, Nev.	Brian Higgins, N.Y.	Patrick J. Murphy, Pa.
John Boccieri, Ohio	Baron P. Hill, Ind.	Scott Murphy, N.Y.
Bruce Braley, Iowa	Jim Himes, Conn.	Ed Perlmutter, Colo.
Bobby Bright, Ala.	Rush D. Holt, N.J.	Gary Peters, Mich.
Lois Capps, Calif.	Jay Inslee, Wash.	Laura Richardson, Calif.
Russ Carnahan, Mo.	Steve Israel, N.Y.	Loretta Sanchez, Calif.
Christopher Carney, Pa.	Ron Kind, Wis.	Mark Schauer, Mich.
André Carson, Ind.	Ron Klein, Fla.	Adam B. Schiff, Calif.
Travis W. Childers, Miss.	Suzanne M. Kosmas, Fla.	Kurt Schrader, Ore.
Gerald E. Connolly, Va.	Frank Kratovil Jr., Md.	David Scott, Ga.
Joe Courtney, Conn.	Rick Larsen, Wash.	Allyson Y. Schwartz, Pa.
Joseph Crowley, N.Y.	John B. Larson, Conn.	Joe Sestak, Pa.
Susan A. Davis, Calif.	Dan Maffei, N.Y.	Adam Smith, Wash.
Artur Davis, Ala.	Carolyn McCarthy, N.Y.	Debbie Wasserman Schultz, Fla.
Eliot L. Engel, N.Y.	Mike McIntyre, N.C.	Charlie Wilson, Ohio
Bob Etheridge, N.C.	Michael E. McMahon, N.Y.	David Wu, Ore.
Bill Foster, Ill.	Kendrick B. Meek, Fla.	

Blue Dog Coalition

The Blue Dogs are a group of the House's most fiscally conservative Democrats.

Co-Chairs: Stephanie Herseth Sandlin, S.D., Baron P. Hill, Ind., Charlie Melancon, La.

Jason Altmire, Pa.	Henry Cuellar, Texas	Dennis Moore, Kan.
Michael Arcuri, N.Y.	Lincoln Davis, Tenn.	Patrick J. Murphy, Pa.
Joe Baca, Calif.	Joe Donnelly, Ind.	Glenn Nye, Va.
John Barrow, Ga.	Brad Ellsworth, Ind.	Collin C. Peterson, Minn.
Marion Berry, Ark.	Gabrielle Giffords, Ariz.	Earl Pomeroy, N.D.
Sanford D. Bishop Jr., Ga.	Bart Gordon, Tenn.	Mike Ross, Ark.
Dan Boren, Okla.	Parker Griffith, Ala.	John Salazar, Colo.
Leonard L. Boswell, Iowa	Jane Harman, Calif.	Loretta Sanchez, Calif.
Allen Boyd, Fla.	Tim Holden, Pa.	Adam B. Schiff, Calif.
Bobby Bright, Ala.	Frank Kratovil Jr., Md.	David Scott, Ga.
Dennis Cardoza, Calif.	Jim Marshall, Ga.	Heath Shuler, N.C.
Christopher Carney, Pa.	Jim Matheson, Utah	Zack Space, Ohio
Ben Chandler, Ky.	Mike McIntyre, N.C.	John Tanner, Tenn.
Travis W. Childers, Miss.	Michael H. Michaud, Maine	Gene Taylor, Miss.
Jim Cooper, Tenn.	Walt Minnick, Idaho	Mike Thompson, Calif.
Jim Costa, Calif.	Harry E. Mitchell, Ariz.	Charlie Wilson, Ohio

Progressive Caucus

The Progressive Caucus is a group of the most liberal-minded Democrats. All members are House Democrats, except independent Sen. Bernard Sanders and Democratic Sen. Tom Udall.

Co-Chairs: Raúl M. Grijalva, Ariz., and Lynn Woolsey, Calif.

Neil Abercrombie, Hawaii
Tammy Baldwin, Wis.
Xavier Becerra, Calif.
Earl Blumenauer, Ore.
Robert A. Brady, Pa.
Corrine Brown, Fla.
Michael E. Capuano, Mass.
André Carson, Ind.
Del. Donna M.C. Christensen, V.I.
Yvette D. Clarke, N.Y.
William Lacy Clay, Mo.
Emanuel Cleaver II, Mo.
Steve Cohen, Tenn.
John Conyers Jr., Mich.
Elijah E. Cummings, Md.
Danny K. Davis, Ill.
Peter A. DeFazio, Ore.
Rosa DeLauro, Conn.
Donna Edwards, Md.
Keith Ellison, Minn.
Sam Farr, Calif.
Chaka Fattah, Pa.
Bob Filner, Calif.
Barney Frank, Mass.
Marcia L. Fudge, Ohio
Alan Grayson, Fla.
Luis V. Gutierrez, Ill.
John Hall, N.Y.
Phil Hare, Ill.
Maurice D. Hinchey, N.Y.
Mazie K. Hirono, Hawaii
Michael M. Honda, Calif.
Jesse L. Jackson Jr., Ill.
Sheila Jackson Lee, Texas
Eddie Bernice Johnson, Texas
Hank Johnson, Ga.
Marcy Kaptur, Ohio
Carolyn Cheeks Kilpatrick, Mich.
Dennis J. Kucinich, Ohio

Barbara Lee, Calif.
John Lewis, Ga.
Dave Loebsack, Iowa
Ben Ray Luján, N.M.
Carolyn B. Maloney, N.Y.
Edward J. Markey, Mass.
Jim McDermott, Wash.
Jim McGovern, Mass.
George Miller, Calif.
Gwen Moore, Wis.
James P. Moran, Va.
Jerrold Nadler, N.Y.
Eleanor Holmes Norton, D.C.
John W. Olver, Mass.
Frank Pallone Jr., N.J.
Ed Pastor, Ariz.
Donald M. Payne, N.J.
Chellie Pingree, Maine
Jared Polis, Colo.
Charles B. Rangel, N.Y.
Laura Richardson, Calif.
Lucille Roybal-Allard, Calif.
Bobby L. Rush, Ill.
Linda T. Sánchez, Calif.
Bernard Sanders, Vt.
Jan Schakowsky, Ill.
José E. Serrano, N.Y.
Louise M. Slaughter, N.Y.
Pete Stark, Calif.
Bennie Thompson, Miss.
John F. Tierney, Mass.
Tom Udall, N.M.
Nydia M. Velázquez, N.Y.
Maxine Waters, Calif.
Diane Watson, Calif.
Melvin Watt, N.C.
Henry A. Waxman, Calif.
Peter Welch, Vt.
Robert Wexler, Fla.

Republican Study Committee

The RSC is the most conservative bloc and dominant force within the House Republican caucus. The list below is not comprehensive, as the caucus permits individual members to decide whether to publicize their membership.

Chairman: Tom Price, Ga.

Robert B. Aderholt, Ala.
Todd Akin, Mo.
Rodney Alexander, La.
Steve Austria, Ohio
Michele Bachmann, Minn.
Spencer Bachus, Ala.
J. Gresham Barrett, S.C.
Roscoe G. Bartlett, Md.
Joe L. Barton, Texas
Brian P. Bilbray, Calif.
Rob Bishop, Utah
Marsha Blackburn, Tenn.
Jo Bonner, Ala.
John Boozman, Ark.
Kevin Brady, Texas
Paul Broun, Ga.
Henry E. Brown Jr., S.C.
Vern Buchanan, Fla.
Michael C. Burgess, Texas
Dan Burton, Ind.
Dave Camp, Mich.
John Campbell, Calif.
Eric Cantor, Va.
John Carter, Texas
Bill Cassidy, La.
Jason Chaffetz, Utah
Mike Coffman, Colo.
Tom Cole, Okla.
K. Michael Conaway, Texas
John Culberson, Texas
Geoff Davis, Ky.
Mary Fallin, Okla.
Jeff Flake, Ariz.
John Fleming, La.
J. Randy Forbes, Va.
Jeff Fortenberry, Neb.

Virginia Foxx, N.C.
Trent Franks, Ariz.
Scott Garrett, N.J.
Phil Gingrey, Ga.
Louie Gohmert, Texas
Robert W. Goodlatte, Va.
Sam Graves, Mo.
Brett Guthrie, Ky.
Gregg Harper, Miss.
Jeb Hensarling, Texas
Wally Herger, Calif.
Peter Hoekstra, Mich.
Duncan Hunter, Calif.
Bob Inglis, S.C.
Darrell Issa, Calif.
Sam Johnson, Texas
Jim Jordan, Ohio
Steve King, Iowa
Jack Kingston, Ga.
John Kline, Minn.
Doug Lamborn, Colo.
Bob Latta, Ohio
Christopher Lee, N.Y.
John Linder, Ga.
Frank D. Lucas, Okla.
Blaine Luetkemeyer, Mo.
Cynthia M. Lummis, Wyo.
Dan Lungren, Calif.
Connie Mack, Fla.
Donald Manzullo, Ill.
Kenny Marchant, Texas
Michael McCaul, Texas
Tom McClintock, Calif.
Thaddeus McCotter, Mich.
Patrick T. McHenry, N.C.
Howard P. "Buck" McKeon, Calif.

Cathy McMorris Rodgers, Wash.
Gary G. Miller, Calif.
Jeff Miller, Fla.
Jerry Moran, Kan.
Sue Myrick, N.C.
Randy Neugebauer, Texas
Pete Olson, Texas
Mike Pence, Ind.
Joe Pitts, Pa.
Ted Poe, Texas
Bill Posey, Fla.
George Radanovich, Calif.
Denny Rehberg, Mont.
Phil Roe, Tenn.
Tom Rooney, Fla.
Peter Roskam, Ill.
Ed Royce, Calif.
Paul D. Ryan, Wis.
Steve Scalise, La.
Jean Schmidt, Ohio
Aaron Schock, Ill.
Pete Sessions, Texas
John Shadegg, Ariz.
John Shimkus, Ill.
Lamar Smith, Texas
Mark Souder, Ind.
Cliff Stearns, Fla.
John Sullivan, Okla.
Glenn Thompson, Pa.
William M. "Mac" Thornberry, Texas
Todd Tiahrt, Kan.
Michael R. Turner, Ohio
Zach Wamp, Tenn.
Lynn Westmoreland, Ga.
Joe Wilson, S.C.
Rob Wittman, Va.

Other Caucus Leadership

Moderate Dems Working Group
Sen. Evan Bayh, D-Ind., co-founder
Sen. Thomas R. Carper, D-Del., co-founder
Sen. Blanche Lincoln, D-Ark., co-founder

Congressional Black Caucus
Rep. Barbara Lee, D-Calif., chairwoman

Congressional Caucus for Women's Issues
Rep. Jan Schakowsky, D-Ill., co-chairwoman
Rep. Mary Fallin, R-Okla., co-chairwoman

Congressional Hispanic Caucus
Rep. Nydia M. Velázquez, D-N.Y., chairwoman

Committees by the Numbers

75   Members on the House Transportation and Infrastructure panel, the largest committee in this Congress.

23   House gavels held by Californians, more members than from any other state. New Yorkers have 13, Massachusetts lawmakers 10, Texans eight, Pennsylvanians seven.

17   Freshmen on the House Agriculture Committee, more than one-third of the panel membership. No other committee in Congress has more freshmen.

17   Subcommittees in either chamber with the word "oversight" in their name. There are 13 with the word "health" or "healthy" in the name, eight with "energy," eight with "environment" or "environmental," eight with "international" and six with "water."

6   Members on the Senate Select Ethics Committee, the smallest panel in Congress. The smallest in the House is House Administration, with nine members.

2   Senators from a state serving together on a committee: Agriculture (Iowa and Nebraska); Armed Services (Florida and North Carolina); Budget (Oregon); Commerce, Science and Transportation (Florida); HELP (North Carolina and Rhode Island); Indian Affairs (Hawaii and North Dakota); Judiciary (Wisconsin); Small Business and Entrepreneurship (Louisiana); and Special Aging (Colorado, Florida and Pennsylvania).

Better Know a Chairman

Who is the most senior Democratic senator who does not chair a full committee?

> That would be West Virginia's **Robert C. Byrd**, who was elected in 1958.

Who is the most junior senator who is a full committee chairman?

> It's **Charles E. Schumer** of New York, who chairs both the Joint Printing Committee and the Rules and Administration Committee. Schumer was elected in 1998.

Which senator has the most committee gavels?

> It's a four-way tie. California's **Barbara Boxer** and New York's **Charles E. Schumer** each chair two committees and one subcommittee. North Dakota's **Byron L. Dorgan** and Wisconsin's **Herb Kohl** each chair one committee and two subcommittees.

Name the most senior House Democrat who is not a full committee chairman.

> That's **John D. Dingell** of Michigan, who is in his 27th term but does not have chairmanship in the 111th Congress and is not in the leadership. Dingell doesn't have a formal gavel, but he is chairman emeritus of the Energy and Commerce Committee.

Who is the most junior House Democrat who chairs a committee?

> **Robert A. Brady** of Pennsylvania, who was elected in 1998, chairs the House Administration Committee.

Hispanic Districts

Congressional districts with the largest percentage of Hispanics (Hispanics may be of any race):

District	Hispanic	Member
Texas 16	77.7%	Reyes, D
Texas 15	77.6%	Hinojosa, D
Texas 28	77.5%	Cuellar, D
California 34	77.2%	Roybal-Allard, D
Illinois 4	74.5%	Gutierrez, D
California 38	70.6%	Napolitano, D
California 31	70.2%	Becerra, D
Florida 21	69.7%	Diaz-Balart, R
Texas 27	68.1%	Ortiz, D
Texas 20	67.1%	Gonzalez, D

Black Districts

Congressional districts with the largest percentage of African-Americans:

District	Black	Member
Illinois 1	65.2%	Rush, D
Louisiana 2	63.7%	Cao, R
Mississippi 2	63.2%	Thompson, D
Illinois 2	62.0%	Jackson, D
Alabama 7	61.7%	Davis, D
Illinois 7	61.6%	Davis, D
Michigan 14	61.1%	Conyers, D
Pennsylvania 2	60.7%	Fattah, D
Michigan 13	60.5%	Kilpatrick, D
New York 10	60.2%	Towns, D

Asian Districts

Congressional districts with the largest percentage of Asians:

District	Asian	Member
Hawaii 1	53.6%	Abercrombie, D
California 15	29.2%	Honda, D
California 8	28.7%	Pelosi, D
California 12	28.5%	Speier, D
California 13	28.2%	Stark, D
Hawaii 2	28.0%	Hirono, D
New York 5	24.5%	Ackerman, D
California 29	23.7%	Schiff, D
California 16	23.4%	Lofgren, D
California 32	18.4%	Vacant

American Indian Districts

Congressional districts with the largest percentage of American Indians:

District	Indian	Member
Arizona 1	22.1%	Kirkpatrick, D
New Mexico 3	18.9%	Luján, D
Oklahoma 2	16.8%	Boren, D
Alaska AL	15.4%	Young, R
North Carolina 7	8.5%	McIntyre, D
South Dakota AL	8.1%	Herseth Sandlin, D
Montana AL	6.0%	Rehberg, R
Oklahoma 3	6.0%	Lucas, R
Oklahoma 1	5.8%	Sullivan, R
Oklahoma 4	5.5%	Cole, R

Oldest Districts

Congressional districts with the highest median age:

District	Median Age	Member
Florida 13	47.4	Buchanan, R
Florida 14	47.4	Mack, R
Florida 5	45.5	Brown-Waite, R
Florida 19	45.1	Wexler, D
Florida 16	44.5	Rooney, R
Florida 10	43.9	Young, R
Florida 22	43.0	Klein, D
Florida 9	41.1	Bilirakis, R
Florida 15	41.0	Posey, R
Pennsylvania 18	41.0	Murphy, R

Youngest Districts

Congressional districts with the lowest median age:

District	Median Age	Member
Utah 3	24.5	Chaffetz, R
California 43	26.7	Baca, D
California 20	26.9	Costa, D
Arizona 4	27.1	Pastor, D
Illinois 4	27.2	Gutierrez, D
Texas 29	27.4	Green, D
New York 16	27.5	Serrano, D
California 47	27.6	Sanchez, D
Utah 1	27.6	Bishop, R
California 34	27.9	Roybal-Allard, D

Statistics in the boxes appearing on pp. 1162-1163 are from the U.S. Census Bureau.

Richest Districts

Congressional districts with the highest median household income in 1999:

District	Income	Member
Virginia 11	$80,397	Connolly, D
New Jersey 11	$79,009	Frelinghuysen, R
California 14	$77,985	Eshoo, D
Georgia 6	$75,611	Price, R
California 15	$74,947	Honda, D
New Jersey 7	$74,823	Lance, R
Colorado 6	$73,393	Coffman, R
New Jersey 5	$72,781	Garrett, R
Illinois 13	$71,686	Biggert, R
Illinois 10	$71,663	Kirk, R

Poorest Districts

Congressional districts with the lowest median household income in 1999:

District	Income	Member
New York 16	$19,311	Serrano, D
Kentucky 5	$21,915	Rogers, R
West Virginia 3	$25,630	Rahall, D
California 31	$26,093	Becerra, D
Alabama 7	$26,672	Davis, D
California 20	$26,800	Costa, D
Texas 15	$26,840	Hinojosa, D
Mississippi 2	$26,894	Thompson, D
Louisiana 5	$27,453	Alexander, R
Louisiana 2	$27,514	Cao, R

Districts With Most Government Workers

Congressional districts with the largest percentage of workers employed by local, state, federal or international government organizations:

District	Workers	Member
Maryland 4	29.0%	Edwards, D
Maryland 5	28.8%	Hoyer, D
Florida 2	28.5%	Boyd, D
Alaska AL	26.8%	Young, R
New Mexico 3	25.8%	Luján, D
California 5	24.8%	Matsui, D
New York 10	24.6%	Towns, D
Arizona 1	24.4%	Kirkpatrick, D
Maryland 7	24.3%	Cummings, D
Virginia 11	24.2%	Connolly, D

Most Educated Districts

Congressional districts with the largest percentage of people 25 and older with at least a bachelor's degree:

District	Degree	Member
New York 14	56.9%	Maloney, D
Virginia 8	53.8%	Moran, D
Maryland 8	53.7%	Van Hollen, D
California 30	53.5%	Waxman, D
California 14	52.2%	Eshoo, D
Georgia 6	50.7%	Price, R
Texas 7	50.0%	Culberson, R
Virginia 11	48.9%	Connolly, D
North Carolina 4	48.0%	Price, D
New York 8	47.8%	Nadler, D

Least Educated Districts

Congressional districts with the largest percentage of people 25 and older without a high school diploma:

District	No Diploma	Member
California 34	53.7%	Roybal-Allard, D
California 31	52.5%	Becerra, D
California 20	49.8%	Costa, D
Texas 29	49.8%	Green, D
California 47	49.6%	Sanchez, D
New York 16	49.5%	Serrano, D
Illinois 4	48.3%	Gutierrez, D
Texas 28	44.0%	Cuellar, D
New York 12	43.6%	Velázquez, D
California 38	41.6%	Napolitano, D

Districts With Most Foreign Born

Congressional districts with the largest percentage of residents born outside the United States (Americans born abroad are not included):

District	Foreign Born	Member
Florida 21	56.6%	Diaz-Balart, R
California 31	56.2%	Becerra, D
Florida 18	54.0%	Ros-Lehtinen, R
California 47	50.7%	Sanchez, D
California 34	47.2%	Roybal-Allard, D
Florida 25	46.6%	Diaz-Balart, R
New York 5	45.6%	Ackerman, D
California 28	44.0%	Berman, D
California 29	43.8%	Schiff, D
California 32	41.7%	Vacant

Closest Elections of 2008

Race	Winner	Votes	Loser	Votes	Margin
Minnesota Senate	Al Franken, D (leading)	1,212,629	Norm Coleman, R	1,212,317	312
Louisiana 4†	John Fleming, R	44,501	Paul J. Carmouche, D	44,151	350
Virginia 5	Tom Perriello, D	158,810	Rep. Virgil H. Goode Jr., R	158,083	727
Alabama 2	Bobby Bright, D	144,368	Jay Love, R	142,578	1,790
California 4	Tom McClintock, R	185,790	Charlie Brown, D	183,990	1,800
Louisiana 2†	Anh "Joseph" Cao, R	33,132	Rep. William J. Jefferson, D	31,318	1,814
Ohio 15*	Mary Jo Kilroy, D	139,584	Steve Stivers, R	137,272	2,312
Maryland 1	Frank Kratovil Jr., D	177,065	Andy Harris, R	174,213	2,852
Alaska Senate	Mark Begich, D	151,767	Sen. Ted Stevens, R	147,814	3,953
Idaho 1	Walt Minnick, D	175,898	Rep. Bill Sali, R	171,687	4,211

† Dec. race

* Also finished in the top 10 in the 2006 election.

Fewest Votes Received

Winning House candidates in contested elections who received the fewest votes in 2008:

Member	Votes Received
Anh "Joseph" Cao, R-La. (2)†	33,132
John Fleming, R-La (4)†	44,501
Gene Green, D-Texas (29)*	79,718
Loretta Sanchez, D-Calif. (47)*	85,878
Ed Pastor, D-Ariz. (4)*	89,721
Jim Costa, D-Calif. (20)	93,023
Lucille Roybal-Allard, D-Calif. (34)*	98,503
Solomon P. Ortiz, D-Texas (27)	104,864
Rubén Hinojosa, D-Texas (15)*	107,578
Joe Baca, D-Calif. (43) *	108,259

* Also finished in the top 10 in the 2006 election. † Dec. race

Most Votes Received

Winning House candidates who received the most votes in 2008:

Member	Votes Received
Denny Rehberg, R-Mont. (AL)*	308,470
Jim McDermott, D-Wash. (7)	291,963
Spencer Bachus, R-Ala. (6)	280,902
Tammy Baldwin, D-Wis. (2)*	277,914
Chaka Fattah, D-Pa. (2)	276,870
F. James Sensenbrenner Jr., R-Wis. (5)*	275,271
Peter A. DeFazio, D-Ore. (4)	275,143
Bill Delahunt, D-Mass. (10)	272,899
David E. Price, D-N.C. (4)	265,751
Ginny Brown-Waite, R-Fla. (5)	265,186

* Also finished in the top 10 in the 2006 election. † Dec. race

Most Votes Cast

The 10 congressional districts in which the most votes were cast in 2008:

District	Votes Cast
Montana AL	480,900
Florida 5	433,632
North Carolina 4	419,698
Colorado 6	413,516
Minnesota 6	404,725
Wisconsin 2	400,841
North Carolina 9	386,483
Minnesota 2	385,656
Florida 7	385,013
Virginia 10	379,480

Fewest Votes Cast

The 10 districts in which the fewest votes were cast in 2008 in contested elections:

District	Votes Cast
Louisiana 2†	66,882
Louisiana 4†	92,572
Texas 29	106,794
California 47	123,584
Arizona 4	124,427
California 20	125,141
California 34	127,769
New York 16	131,667
New York 12	136,793
Illinois 4	139,606

† Dec. election

Under 49 Percent

Winners of 2008 elections who got less than 49 percent of the votes cast:

Member	Percent
Al Franken, D-Minn (leading)	41.5
Jean Schmidt, R-Ohio	44.8
Mary Jo Kilroy, D-Ohio	45.9
Michele Bachmann, R-Minn.	46.4
Dina Titus, D-Nev.	47.4
Mark Begich, D-Alaska	47.8
John Fleming, R-La.†	48.1
Bill Cassidy, R-La.	48.1
Erik Paulsen, R-Minn.	48.5
Mark Schauer, D-Mich.	48.8
Jeff Merkley, D-Ore.	48.9

† Dec. election

Republican Wins in Obama Districts

In 2008, 34 Republicans won in districts whose voters preferred Democrat Barack Obama for president. The second column of numbers shows the percentage with which Obama won in the district, and the last column shows how far the House Republican ran ahead or behind Obama in the district.

	Member's Win	Obama	+/-		Member's Win	Obama	+/-
Tom Petri (Wis. 6)	64%	50%	+14%	Charlie Dent (Pa. 15)	59%	56%	+3%
John M. McHugh (N.Y. 23)	65	52	+13	David Dreier (Calif. 26)	53	51	+2
Paul D. Ryan (Wis. 1)	64	51	+13	Peter Roskam (Ill. 6)	58	56	+2
Dave Camp (Mich. 4)	62	50	+12	Lee Terry (Neb. 2)	52	50	+2
J. Randy Forbes (Va. 4)	60	50	+10	Ken Calvert (Calif. 44)	51	50	+1
Howard P. "Buck" McKeon (Calif. 25)	58	49	+9	Pat Tiberi (Ohio 12)	55	54	+1
C.W. Bill Young (Fla. 10)	61	52	+9	Dan Lungren (Calif. 3)	49	49	–
Donald Manzullo (Ill. 16)	61	53	+8	Judy Biggert (Ill. 13)	54	54	–
Tom Latham (Iowa 4)	61	53	+8	Leonard Lance (N.J. 7)	50	50	–
Elton Gallegly (Calif. 24)	58	51	+7	Brian P. Bilbray (Calif. 50)	50	51	-1
John Campbell (Calif. 48)	56	49	+7	Michael N. Castle (Del. AL)	61	62	-1
Ileana Ros-Lehtinen (Fla. 18)	58	51	+7	Thaddeus McCotter (Mich.11)	51	54	-3
Mary Bono Mack (Calif. 45)	58	52	+6	Dave Reichert (Wash. 8)	53	56	-3
Frank R. Wolf (Va. 10)	59	53	+6	Erik Paulsen (Minn. 3)	48	52	-4
Fred Upton (Mich. 6)	59	54	+5	Jim Gerlach (Pa. 6)	52	58	-6
Frank A. LoBiondo (N.J. 2)	59	54	+5	Mark Steven Kirk (Ill. 10)	53	61	-8
Mike Rogers (Mich. 8)	57	53	+4	Anh "Joseph" Cao (La. 2)*	50	75	-25

* Elected in December; not on the same ballot as Obama

Democratic Wins in McCain Districts

In 2008, 49 Democrats won in districts whose voters preferred Republican John McCain for president. The second column of numbers shows the percentage with which McCain won in the district, and the last column shows how far the House Democrat ran ahead or behind McCain in the district.

	Member's Win	McCain	+/-		Member's Win	McCain	+/-
John Tanner (Tenn. 8)	100%	56%	+44%	Zack Space (Ohio 18)	60%	53%	+7%
Alan B. Mollohan (W.Va. 1)	100	57	+43	Betsy Markey (Colo. 4)	56	50	+6
Marion Berry (Ark. 1)	100	59	+41	Suzanne M. Kosmas (Fla. 24)	57	51	+6
Charlie Melancon (La. 3)	100	61	+39	Harry Teague (N.M. 2)	56	50	+6
Rick Boucher (Va. 9)	97	59	+38	Ike Skelton (Mo. 4)	66	61	+5
Mike Ross (Ark. 4)	86	58	+28	John Boccieri (Ohio 16)	55	50	+5
Vic Snyder (Ark. 2)	77	54	+23	Jim Matheson (Utah 2)	63	58	+5
Collin C. Peterson (Minn. 7)	72	50	+22	Dan Boren (Okla. 2)	70	66	+4
Mike McIntyre (N.C. 7)	69	52	+17	Gabrielle Giffords (Ariz. 8)	55	52	+3
Stephanie Herseth Sandlin (S.D. AL)	68	53	+15	Kathy Dahlkemper (Pa. 3)	51	49	+2
Brad Ellsworth (Ind. 8)	65	51	+14	Christopher Carney (Pa. 10)	56	54	+2
Tim Holden (Pa. 17)	64	51	+13	Ann Kirkpatrick (Ariz. 1)	56	54	+2
John Salazar (Colo. 3)	62	50	+12	Harry E. Mitchell (Ariz. 5)	53	52	+1
Charlie Wilson (Ohio 6)	62	50	+12	Jim Marshall (Ga. 8)	57	56	+1
Bart Gordon (Tenn. 6)	74	62	+12	Eric Massa (N.Y. 29)	51	50	+1
Nick J. Rahall II (W.Va. 3)	67	56	+11	Jason Altmire (Pa. 4)	56	55	+1
Ben Chandler (Ky. 6)	65	55	+10	Tom Perriello (Va. 5)	50	51	-1
Michael E. McMahon (N.Y. 13)	61	51	+10	Lincoln Davis (Tenn. 4)	59	64	-5
Heath Shuler (N.C. 11)	62	52	+10	Travis W. Childers (Miss. 1)	54	62	-8
Earl Pomeroy (N.D. AL)	62	53	+9	Frank Kratovil Jr. (Md. 1)	49	58	-9
John P. Murtha (Pa. 12)	58	49	+9	Parker Griffith (Ala. 5)	51	61	-10
John M. Spratt Jr. (S.C. 5)	62	53	+9	Walt Minnick (Idaho 1)	51	62	-11
Allen Boyd (Fla. 2)	62	54	+8	Bobby Bright (Ala. 2)	50	63	-13
Baron P. Hill (Ind. 9)	58	50	+8	Chet Edwards (Texas 17)	53	67	-14
Gene Taylor (Miss. 4)	75	67	+8				

CAMPAIGN FINANCE

Top 10 Senate Spenders in 2008

Based on FEC reports of expenditures from Jan. 1, 2007, through Dec. 31, 2008, the first column lists the top spenders who were elected or re-elected in the 2008 election. Losing incumbents are in italics.

Member	Expenditures	Opponent	Expenditures
Mitch McConnell, R-Ky.	$21,306,296	Bruce Lunsford, D	$10,801,203
Al Franken, D-Minn. (leading)	$21,066,834	Norm Coleman, R	$19,011,108
John Cornyn, R-Texas	$16,454,518	Rick Noriega, D	$4,157,553
Saxby Chambliss, R-Ga.	$15,692,294	James Martin, D	$7,508,505
Mark Udall, D-Colo.	$12,987,562	Bob Schaffer, R	$7,205,644
Mark Warner, D-Va.	$12,515,479	James S. Gilmore III, R	$2,420,635
John Kerry, D-Mass.	$12,279,425	Jeff Beatty, R	$2,070,528
Mary L. Landrieu, D-La.	$10,146,669	John Kennedy, R	$4,795,281
Kay Hagan, D-N.C.	$8,953,274	*Elizabeth Dole, R*	$17,468,134
Jeanne Shaheen, D-N.H	$8,225,580	*John E. Sununu, R*	$8,010,010

CAMPAIGN FINANCE

Top 10 House Spenders in 2008

Based on FEC reports of expenditures from Jan. 1, 2007, through Dec. 31, 2008, the first column lists the top spenders who were elected or re-elected in the 2008 election. Losing incumbents are in italics.

Member	Expenditures	Opponent	Expenditures
Jared Polis, D-Colo. (2)	$7,323,502	Scott Starin, R	$90,252
Mark Steven Kirk, R-Ill. (10)	$5,450,659	Dan Seals, D	$3,566,123
John A. Boehner, R-Ohio (8)	$5,342,022	Nicholas von Stein, D	$15,425
Bill Foster, D-Ill. (14)*	$5,047,815	Jim Oberweis, R	$5,084,489
Kirsten Gillibrand, D-N.Y. (20)	$4,488,475	Sandy Treadwell, R	$7,038,552
Vern Buchanan, R-Fla. (13)	$4,345,554	Christine Jennings, D	$2,434,002
Charles B. Rangel, D-N.Y. (15)	$4,209,400	Edward Daniels, R	$0
Jim Himes, D-Conn.(4)	$3,909,937	*Christopher Shays, R*	$3,828,300
Patrick J. Murphy, D-Pa. (8)	$3,834,971	Tom Manion, R	$1,138,048
Eric Cantor, R-Va. (7)	$3,823,907	Anita Hartke, D	$63,152

* Includes special-election expenditures

CAMPAIGN FINANCE

10 Least-Expensive Winning 2008 House Campaigns

The chart is based on expenditures from Jan. 1, 2007, through Dec. 31, 2008, for contested elections.

Member	Expenditures	Member	Expenditures
Marcia L. Fudge, D-Ohio (11)*	$94,049	Anh "Joseph" Cao, R-La. (2)†	$234,559
Luis V. Gutierrez, D-Ill. (4)	$188,438	Timothy V. Johnson, R-Ill. (15)	$295,919
Todd R. Platts, R-Pa. (19)	$192,495	Vic Snyder, D-Ark. (2)	$307,060
Roscoe G. Bartlett, R-Md. (6)	$204,443	Vernon J. Ehlers, R-Mich. (3)	$319,953
Diane Watson, D-Calif. (33)	$229,692	Gary G. Miller, R-Calif., (42)	$325,244

* Includes special-election expenditures   † Runoff

CAMPAIGN FINANCE

Winners Outspent by Opponents

General-election winners in 2008 who spent less than their opponents. Totals cover the period Jan. 1, 2007, through Dec. 31, 2008. Losing incumbents are in italics.

(in order of spending margin)

Senate

Name, Party, State	Expenditures	Opponent	Expenditures
Kay Hagan, D-N.C.	$8,953,274	*Elizabeth Dole, R*	$17,468,134
Jeff Merkley, D-Ore.	$6,501,315	*Gordon H. Smith, R*	$11,405,378

House

Member	Expenditures	Opponent	Expenditures
David Scott, D-Ga. (13)	$1,433,435	Deborah Honeycutt, R	$5,204,670
Kirsten Gillibrand, D-N.Y. (20)	$4,488,475	Sandy Treadwell, R	$7,038,552
Larry Kissell, D-N.C. (8)	$1,509,753	*Robin Hayes, R*	$3,808,201
Dave Reichert, R-Wash. (8)	$2,852,514	Darcy Burner, D	$4,462,884
Dale E. Kildee, D-Mich. (5)	$2,528,897	Matt Sawicki, R	$4,135,864
Bill Cassidy, R-La. (6)	$1,252,457	*Don Cazayoux, D**	$2,766,865
Dina Titus, D-Nev. (3)	$1,777,641	*Jon Porter, R*	$3,182,799
Kathy Dahlkemper, D-Pa. (3)	$1,301,838	*Phil English, R*	$2,633,349
John Culberson, R-Texas (7)	$1,757,226	Michael Skelly, D	$3,080,655
Tom Rooney, R-Fla. (16)	$1,819,259	*Tim Mahoney, D*	$3,101,491
Bobby Bright, D-Ala. (2)	$1,193,166	Jay Love, R	$2,444,627
Kurt Schrader, D-Ore. (5)	$1,389,044	Mike Erickson, R	$2,594,663
Leonard Lance, R-N.J. (7)	$1,419,698	Linda Stender, D	$2,621,407
Frank Kratovil Jr., D-Md. (1)	$1,994,553	Andy Harris, R	$3,024,144
Steve Driehaus, D-Ohio (1)	$1,447,544	*Steve Chabot, R*	$2,410,292
Henry E. Brown Jr., R-S.C. (1)	$1,287,308	Linda Ketner, D	$2,248,361
Glenn Nye, D-Va. (2)	$1,333,931	*Thelma Drake, R*	$2,033,543
Jean Schmidt, R-Ohio (2)	$1,276,573	Victoria Wulsin, D	$1,972,691
Steve Scalise, R-La. (1)*	$1,628,134	Jim Harlan, D	$2,296,392
Howard Coble, R-N.C. (6)	$778,037	Teresa Bratton, D	$1,266,429
Christopher Carney, D-Pa. (10)	$2,333,358	Chris Hackett, R	$2,553,644
Cynthia M. Lummis, R-Wyo. (AL)	$1,517,018	Gary Trauner, D	$1,716,008
Sam Graves, R-Mo. (6)	$2,633,443	Kay Barnes, D	$2,801,656
Frank R. Wolf, R-Va. (10)	$2,053,375	Judy Feder, D	$2,206,307
Earl Pomeroy, D-N.D. (AL)	$1,795,714	Duane Sand, R	$1,944,095
Tom Perriello, D-Va. (5)	$1,822,148	*Virgil H. Goode Jr., R*	$1,939,824
Anh "Joseph" Cao, R-La., (2) †	$234,559	*William J. Jefferson, D*	$342,240
Lynn Jenkins, R-Kan. (2)	$1,666,239	*Nancy Boyda, D*	$1,760,726
Gerald E. Connolly, D-Va. (11)	$1,974,640	Keith Fimian, R	$2,010,087
Bart Stupak, D-Mich. (1)	$2,158,006	Tom Casperson, R	$2,180,725
Gary G. Miller, R-Calif. (42)	$325,244	Edwin Chau, D	$347,351
Pete Olson, R-Texas (22)	$2,366,149	*Nick Lampson, D*	$2,385,202
John Fleming, R-La. (4)	$1,828,695	Paul J. Carmouche, D	$1,844,290

* Includes special-election expenditures

† Runoff

Campaign Finance

Figures are given for all members of Congress and their general election opponents as reported by the FEC. Only candidates who raised at least $5,000 are shown. For senators, figures are for their most recent election.

The data covers receipts and expenditures from Jan. 1, 2007, to Dec. 31, 2008. Candidates who ran in special elections in the two-year election cycle are marked with a † and in these cases figures may include money spent on those races. Activity for runoff races also may be included.

Senate data for 2006 covers the period Jan. 1, 2005, to Dec. 31, 2006 and for 2004 covers the period Jan. 1, 2003, to Dec. 31, 2004. Figures may include amended filings.

The figures for political action committee receipts are based on the FEC summary report for each candidate. Expenditures can exceed receipts if a candidate raised funds before the start of the two-year campaign cycle. Amounts listed include contributions from both PACs and candidate committees, but not party committees.

The FEC is constantly receiving amended reports. The figures listed were the latest available as of April 2009.

Alabama

	RECEIPTS	FROM PACS		EXPENDITURES
SENIOR SENATOR - 2004				
Shelby (R)	$6,610,117	$1,480,707	(22%)	$1,922,646
JUNIOR SENATOR - 2008				
Sessions (R)	$4,956,130	$1,166,621	(24%)	$3,240,151
Figures (D)	$332,670	$36,983	(11%)	$333,721
DISTRICT 1				
Bonner (R)	$842,270	$397,323	(47%)	$736,705
Lodmell (D)	$72,110	$0	(0%)	$49,822
DISTRICT 2				
Bright (D)	$1,218,680	$537,766	(44%)	$1,193,166
Love (R)	$2,446,492	$560,323	(23%)	$2,444,627
DISTRICT 3				
Rogers (R)	$1,480,933	$517,440	(35%)	$2,056,912
Segall (D)	$1,090,145	$115,294	(11%)	$1,089,890
DISTRICT 4				
Aderholt (R)	$666,973	$269,299	(40%)	$688,864
Sparks (D)	$24,879	$500	(2%)	$22,701
DISTRICT 5				
Griffith (D)	$1,843,945	$691,450	(37%)	$1,786,989
Parker (R)	$1,279,164	$357,907	(28%)	$1,276,538
DISTRICT 6				
Bachus (R)	$1,460,646	$895,867	(61%)	$1,414,799
DISTRICT 7				
Davis (D)	$1,692,708	$1,109,289	(66%)	$820,467

Alaska

	RECEIPTS	FROM PACS		EXPENDITURES
SENIOR SENATOR - 2004				
Murkowski (R)	$5,702,709	$1,991,677	(35%)	$5,429,904
Knowles (D)	$5,834,694	$784,870	(13%)	$5,767,707
Millican (NON)	$187,850	$0	(0%)	$190,379
Sykes (GREEN)	$15,247	$0	(0%)	$8,771
JUNIOR SENATOR - 2008				
Begich (D)	$4,576,970	$659,920	(14%)	$4,453,292
Stevens (R)	$3,858,991	$1,199,654	(31%)	$4,050,791
Bird (AKI)	$33,788	$0	(0%)	$33,019
AT LARGE				
Berkowitz (D)	$1,646,057	$249,550	(15%)	$1,634,981
Young (R)	$1,412,026	$389,646	(28%)	$3,213,532

Arizona

	RECEIPTS	FROM PACS		EXPENDITURES
SENIOR SENATOR - 2004				
McCain (R)	$3,419,717	$658,093	(19%)	$2,140,807
Starky (D)	$12,956	$7,000	(54%)	$12,716
JUNIOR SENATOR - 2006				
Kyl (R)	$14,123,880	$2,802,011	(20%)	$15,571,727
Pederson (D)	$14,707,261	$422,057	(3%)	$14,703,074
DISTRICT 1				
Kirkpatrick (D)	$2,016,929	$593,061	(29%)	$1,997,089
Hay (R)	$676,823	$126,601	(19%)	$675,723
Maupin (I)	$30,491	$0	(0%)	$30,467
DISTRICT 2				
Franks (R)	$485,040	$201,784	(42%)	$442,232
Thrasher (D)	$36,803	$1,990	(5%)	$37,187
DISTRICT 3				
Shadegg (R)	$2,892,553	$1,001,213	(35%)	$2,911,880
Lord (D)	$1,831,410	$393,385	(21%)	$1,813,648
DISTRICT 4				
Pastor (D)	$1,174,759	$581,843	(50%)	$815,864
DISTRICT 5				
Mitchell (D)	$2,437,569	$871,859	(36%)	$2,324,598
Schweikert (R)	$1,421,599	$83,369	(6%)	$1,416,883
DISTRICT 6				
Flake (R)	$1,289,321	$157,150	(12%)	$845,005
Gramazio (D)	$7,099	$2,500	(35%)	$7,088
DISTRICT 7				
Grijalva (D)	$708,514	$323,534	(46%)	$720,896
Chewning (R)	$8,455	$0	(0%)	$8,504
DISTRICT 8				
Giffords (D)	$3,303,130	$1,086,217	(33%)	$2,775,313
Bee (R)	$1,949,493	$241,700	(12%)	$1,932,103

Arkansas

	RECEIPTS	FROM PACS		EXPENDITURES
SENIOR SENATOR - 2004				
Lincoln (D)	$5,489,103	$2,427,554	(44%)	$5,816,913
Holt (R)	$153,628	$7,000	(5%)	$148,682
JUNIOR SENATOR - 2008				
Pryor (D)	$4,998,992	$1,931,800	(39%)	$3,284,632
Kennedy (GREEN)	$13,745	$0	(0%)	$13,392
DISTRICT 1				
Berry (D)	$1,166,377	$788,086	(68%)	$848,986
DISTRICT 2				
Snyder (D)	$301,981	$152,000	(50%)	$307,060

DISTRICT 3

	RECEIPTS	FROM PACS		EXPENDITURES
Boozman (R)	$396,807	$258,406	(65%)	$325,926
Tomlinson (GREEN)	$5,948	$0	(0%)	$7,131

DISTRICT 4

Ross (D)	$1,791,656	$1,160,385	(65%)	$1,722,151

California

	RECEIPTS	FROM PACS		EXPENDITURES
SENIOR SENATOR - 2006				
Feinstein (D)	$8,238,616	$1,327,479	(16%)	$8,030,489
Mountjoy (R)	$198,630	$3,360	(2%)	$195,265
Chretien (GREEN)	$61,549	$0	(0%)	$59,435
JUNIOR SENATOR - 2004				
Boxer (D)	$14,301,289	$1,290,551	(9%)	$14,886,426
Jones (R)	$7,766,693	$559,414	(7%)	$7,774,352
Gray (LIBERT)	$251,832	$9,500	(4%)	$250,244
DISTRICT 1				
Thompson (D)	$1,916,753	$851,714	(44%)	$1,391,605
Wolman (GREEN)	$6,428	$0	(0%)	$6,428
DISTRICT 2				
Herger (R)	$970,055	$660,228	(68%)	$1,256,602
Morris (D)	$59,065	$2,617	(4%)	$33,371
DISTRICT 3				
Lungren (R)	$904,196	$478,419	(53%)	$1,325,036
Durston (D)	$729,272	$61,278	(8%)	$731,513
DISTRICT 4				
McClintock (R)	$3,671,853	$292,650	(8%)	$3,532,595
Brown (D)	$2,570,015	$515,463	(20%)	$2,598,080
DISTRICT 5				
Matsui (D)	$964,536	$551,823	(57%)	$889,113
DISTRICT 6				
Woolsey (D)	$732,486	$308,464	(42%)	$686,383
Halliwell (R)	$56,448	$0	(0%)	$49,657
DISTRICT 7				
Miller (D)	$1,155,882	$649,857	(56%)	$948,684
Petersen (R)	$13,161	$0	(0%)	$13,167
DISTRICT 8				
Pelosi (D)	$2,856,945	$1,511,730	(53%)	$2,727,177
Walsh (R)	$720,921	$650	(0%)	$637,731
Sheehan (I)	$601,821	$5,158	(1%)	$578,718
DISTRICT 9				
Lee (D)	$1,051,437	$284,247	(27%)	$1,048,228
Dulk (R)	$5,409	$0	(0%)	$5,667
DISTRICT 10				
Tauscher (D)	$1,289,082	$890,638	(69%)	$1,049,777
Gerber (R)	$102,197	$500	(0%)	$104,128
DISTRICT 11				
McNerney (D)	$3,047,771	$1,006,460	(33%)	$2,957,100
Andal (R)	$1,422,822	$346,083	(24%)	$1,406,404
DISTRICT 12 †				
Speier (D)	$1,569,225	$351,476	(22%)	$893,615
Conlon (R)	$107,093	$4,400	(4%)	$103,889
Hermanson (GREEN)	$26,411	$0	(0%)	$26,378
McMurry (D)	$14,470	$0	(0%)	$4,250
DISTRICT 13				
Stark (D)	$913,166	$605,495	(66%)	$659,570
DISTRICT 14				
Eshoo (D)	$1,579,249	$799,750	(51%)	$1,476,279

	RECEIPTS	FROM PACS		EXPENDITURES
DISTRICT 15				
Honda (D)	$1,001,001	$400,855	(40%)	$833,894
DISTRICT 16				
Lofgren (D)	$797,809	$472,333	(59%)	$592,974
DISTRICT 17				
Farr (D)	$743,122	$472,588	(64%)	$775,793
Taylor (R)	$41,698	$0	(0%)	$41,568
DISTRICT 18				
Cardoza (D)	$1,042,839	$616,846	(59%)	$962,057
DISTRICT 19				
Radanovich (R)	$728,770	$361,129	(50%)	$712,277
DISTRICT 20				
Costa (D)	$1,026,588	$546,059	(53%)	$922,364
Lopez (R)	$17,015	$0	(0%)	$14,112
DISTRICT 21				
Nunes (R)	$1,195,789	$632,796	(53%)	$734,226
Johnson (D)	$34,469	$824	(2%)	$33,825
DISTRICT 22				
McCarthy (R)	$1,040,018	$502,888	(48%)	$709,687
DISTRICT 23				
Capps (D)	$1,054,974	$489,139	(46%)	$957,695
Kokkonen (R)	$61,178	$4,000	(7%)	$61,178
DISTRICT 24				
Gallegly (R)	$743,200	$177,519	(24%)	$737,060
Jorgensen (D)	$12,655	$800	(6%)	$11,927
DISTRICT 25				
McKeon (R)	$1,053,740	$540,623	(51%)	$903,400
Conaway (D)	$10,989	$0	(0%)	$10,486
DISTRICT 26				
Dreier (R)	$1,594,341	$562,605	(35%)	$2,919,351
Warner (D)	$1,309,327	$46,750	(4%)	$1,331,293
DISTRICT 27				
Sherman (D)	$1,267,706	$509,701	(40%)	$565,838
Singh (R)	$37,677	$0	(0%)	$32,645
DISTRICT 28				
Berman (D)	$1,191,003	$471,320	(40%)	$1,287,898
DISTRICT 29				
Schiff (D)	$1,192,230	$471,697	(40%)	$909,396
Hahn (R)	$76,101	$2,300	(3%)	$76,097
DISTRICT 30				
Waxman (D)	$990,870	$705,735	(71%)	$745,084
DISTRICT 31				
Becerra (D)	$1,557,660	$1,055,954	(68%)	$1,396,520
DISTRICT 32				
Solis (D)	$800,763	$559,040	(70%)	$659,981
DISTRICT 33				
Watson (D)	$233,831	$153,535	(66%)	$229,692
Crowley (R)	$6,307	$0	(0%)	$5,773
DISTRICT 34				
Roybal-Allard (D)	$579,484	$333,667	(58%)	$594,045
DISTRICT 35				
Waters (D)	$777,231	$170,245	(22%)	$829,614
Hayes (R)	$13,227	$0	(0%)	$13,282
DISTRICT 36				
Harman (D)	$600,682	$344,628	(57%)	$687,693
Gibson (R)	$8,962	$500	(6%)	$8,988

DISTRICT 37†

Richardson (D)	$1,104,662	$768,134 (70%)	$1,075,767
Oropeza (D)	$392,165	$117,600 (30%)	$390,966
Mathews (D)	$97,687	$0 (0%)	$98,036
Dibs (I)	$65,943	$0 (0%)	$64,894
Grisolia (D)	$54,697	$0 (0%)	$54,671
McDonald (D)	$52,547	$21,350 (41%)	$52,517
Wilson (D)	$26,370	$0 (0%)	$26,398
Guillory (R)	$11,144	$0 (0%)	$11,767

DISTRICT 38

Napolitano (D)	$425,757	$269,575 (63%)	$385,568

DISTRICT 39

Sánchez (D)	$616,883	$376,850 (61%)	$439,587
Lenning (R)	$14,949	$0 (0%)	$18,479

DISTRICT 40

Royce (R)	$1,644,376	$567,010 (34%)	$1,172,942
Hoffman (D)	$20,584	$0 (0%)	$23,882

DISTRICT 41

Lewis (R)	$1,185,600	$429,612 (36%)	$1,192,618
Prince (D)	$132,416	$2,789 (2%)	$123,655

DISTRICT 42

Miller (R)	$620,752	$295,044 (48%)	$325,244
Chau (D)	$359,175	$53,032 (15%)	$347,351

DISTRICT 43

Baca (D)	$941,695	$580,927 (62%)	$885,963
Roberts (R)	$78,519	$2,000 (3%)	$64,941

DISTRICT 44

Calvert (R)	$1,048,730	$360,139 (34%)	$1,150,432
Hedrick (D)	$212,394	$53,470 (25%)	$191,461

DISTRICT 45

Bono Mack (R)	$1,795,640	$548,203 (31%)	$1,622,511
Bornstein (D)	$488,830	$83,924 (17%)	$487,826

DISTRICT 46

Rohrabacher (R)	$746,799	$148,470 (20%)	$741,821
Cook (D)	$482,069	$58,820 (12%)	$481,660

DISTRICT 47

Sanchez (D)	$1,244,415	$623,993 (50%)	$1,258,594
Avila (R)	$52,767	$500 (1%)	$52,639

DISTRICT 48

Campbell (R)	$1,008,970	$359,999 (36%)	$776,452
Young (D)	$268,159	$25,945 (10%)	$268,129

DISTRICT 49

Issa (R)	$1,035,312	$438,015 (42%)	$950,631
Hamilton (D)	$63,219	$3,794 (6%)	$63,217

DISTRICT 50

Bilbray (R)	$1,366,324	$388,600 (28%)	$1,456,454
Leibham (D)	$1,315,936	$259,835 (20%)	$1,282,943

DISTRICT 51

Filner (D)	$990,586	$478,239 (48%)	$927,615

DISTRICT 52

Hunter (R)	$1,305,020	$393,817 (30%)	$1,280,755
Lumpkin (D)	$482,065	$86,901 (18%)	$482,063

DISTRICT 53

Davis (D)	$591,715	$237,157 (40%)	$455,081
Crimmins (R)	$24,241	$0 (0%)	$23,617

Colorado

	RECEIPTS	FROM PACS	EXPENDITURES
SENIOR SENATOR - 2008			
Udall (D)	$11,787,048	$2,186,292 (19%)	$12,987,562
Schaffer (R)	$7,387,843	$1,006,379 (14%)	$7,205,644
DISTRICT 1			
DeGette (D)	$808,491	$537,744 (67%)	$925,776
Lilly (R)	$13,746	$0 (0%)	$14,060
DISTRICT 2			
Polis (D)	$7,353,034	$24,250 (0%)	$7,323,502
Starin (R)	$93,293	$5,500 (6%)	$90,252
DISTRICT 3			
Salazar (D)	$1,335,166	$741,386 (56%)	$901,272
Wolf (R)	$21,704	$0 (0%)	$21,669
DISTRICT 4			
Markey (D)	$2,918,744	$629,306 (22%)	$2,897,153
Musgrave (R)	$2,869,957	$832,131 (29%)	$2,876,753
DISTRICT 5			
Lamborn (R)	$611,755	$318,540 (52%)	$606,051
Bidlack (D)	$241,785	$21,042 (9%)	$240,798
DISTRICT 6			
Coffman (R)	$1,488,310	$217,566 (15%)	$1,325,282
Eng (D)	$273,696	$16,000 (6%)	$270,609
DISTRICT 7			
Perlmutter (D)	$1,770,087	$805,145 (45%)	$1,276,238
Lerew (R)	$37,121	$0 (0%)	$37,121

Connecticut

	RECEIPTS	FROM PACS	EXPENDITURES
SENIOR SENATOR - 2004			
Dodd (D)	$4,676,379	$1,368,210 (29%)	$3,938,132
Orchulli (R)	$1,476,876	$800 (0%)	$1,462,401
JUNIOR SENATOR - 2006			
Lieberman (CFL)	$18,996,689	$2,324,109 (12%)	$17,210,710
Lamont (D)	$20,524,133	$53,599 (0%)	$20,614,353
Schlesinger (R)	$221,019	$5,650 (3%)	$204,113
DISTRICT 1			
Larson (D)	$1,605,192	$776,298 (48%)	$1,381,640
Visconti (R)	$15,840	$0 (0%)	$15,816
DISTRICT 2			
Courtney (D)	$2,370,575	$893,057 (38%)	$1,792,920
Sullivan (R)	$399,208	$16,955 (4%)	$395,207
DISTRICT 3			
DeLauro (D)	$1,151,850	$744,295 (65%)	$1,098,930
DISTRICT 4			
Himes (D)	$3,940,028	$411,844 (10%)	$3,909,937
Shays (R)	$3,774,740	$953,689 (25%)	$3,828,300
DISTRICT 5			
Murphy (D)	$3,080,818	$1,024,612 (33%)	$3,056,641
Cappiello (R)	$1,357,444	$212,167 (16%)	$1,330,995

Delaware

	RECEIPTS	FROM PACS		EXPENDITURES
SENIOR SENATOR - 2008				
Biden (D)	$1,453,307	$5,010	(0%)	$4,907,245
O'Donnell (R)	$116,471	$1,750	(2%)	$116,050
JUNIOR SENATOR - 2006				
Carper (D)	$3,177,275	$1,564,498	(49%)	$2,632,478
Ting (R)	$212,766	$5,700	(3%)	$212,765
O'Donnell (X)	$62,575	$0	(0%)	$63,629
AT LARGE				
Castle (R)	$1,480,591	$661,089	(45%)	$1,808,076
Hartley-Nagle (D)	$27,845	$15,100	(54%)	$27,785

Florida

	RECEIPTS	FROM PACS		EXPENDITURES
SENIOR SENATOR - 2006				
Nelson (D)	$15,355,490	$1,804,712	(12%)	$16,116,224
Harris (R)	$9,341,803	$277,500	(3%)	$9,334,232
Moore (I)	$16,234	$0	(0%)	$12,177
Tanner (X)	$13,000	$0	(0%)	$12,968
JUNIOR SENATOR - 2004				
Martinez (R)	$12,856,384	$2,245,433	(17%)	$12,837,220
Castor (D)	$11,645,379	$880,326	(8%)	$11,472,071
Bradley (VET)	$15,793	$1,552	(10%)	$15,794
DISTRICT 1				
Miller (R)	$360,055	$170,738	(47%)	$458,359
Bryan (D)	$18,784	$0	(0%)	$18,358
DISTRICT 2				
Boyd (D)	$1,450,645	$959,987	(66%)	$962,421
Mulligan (R)	$33,411	$0	(0%)	$33,430
DISTRICT 3				
Brown (D)	$559,627	$318,335	(57%)	$562,421
DISTRICT 4				
Crenshaw (R)	$681,603	$202,300	(30%)	$613,594
McGovern (D)	$143,086	$29,500	(21%)	$152,624
DISTRICT 5				
Brown-Waite (R)	$722,174	$372,296	(52%)	$563,685
Russell (D)	$36,218	$625	(2%)	$37,220
Castagnero (D)	$12,203	$0	(0%)	$12,479
DISTRICT 6				
Stearns (R)	$806,444	$372,987	(46%)	$789,774
Cunha (D)	$249,755	$21,350	(9%)	$249,754
DISTRICT 7				
Mica (R)	$1,125,803	$601,275	(53%)	$1,031,911
Armitage (D)	$32,929	$0	(0%)	$34,241
DISTRICT 8				
Grayson (D)	$3,376,076	$272,900	(8%)	$3,062,686
Keller (R)	$1,619,406	$910,153	(56%)	$1,774,992
DISTRICT 9				
Bilirakis (R)	$1,494,533	$347,167	(23%)	$1,542,342
Mitchell (D)	$280,623	$12,524	(4%)	$394,756
Emmons (PTY)	$38,015	$0	(0%)	$36,082
DISTRICT 10				
Young (R)	$944,430	$376,533	(40%)	$969,224
Hackworth (D)	$155,698	$500	(0%)	$155,590
DISTRICT 11				
Castor (D)	$631,095	$300,992	(48%)	$662,366
Adams (R)	$57,640	$0	(0%)	$57,650
DISTRICT 12				
Putnam (R)	$1,843,688	$967,884	(52%)	$2,054,571
Tudor (D)	$125,219	$20,042	(16%)	$121,851
DISTRICT 13				
Buchanan (R)	$4,434,205	$630,572	(14%)	$4,345,554
Jennings (D)	$2,229,184	$625,313	(28%)	$2,434,002
Schneider (X)	$30,658	$0	(0%)	$50,212
Baldauf (X)	$9,020	$0	(0%)	$9,009
DISTRICT 14				
Mack (R)	$1,307,189	$310,072	(24%)	$1,008,108
Saunders (X)	$165,409	$7,750	(5%)	$165,327
George (X)	$20,326	$0	(0%)	$20,325
Neeld (D)	$15,781	$0	(0%)	$15,252
DISTRICT 15				
Posey (R)	$944,893	$348,800	(37%)	$909,257
Blythe (D)	$113,371	$5,500	(5%)	$113,372
Zilaitis (X)	$38,693	$233	(1%)	$38,694
Lowing (X)	$7,100	$0	(0%)	$7,100
DISTRICT 16				
Rooney (R)	$1,837,390	$264,728	(14%)	$1,819,259
Mahoney (D)	$3,056,964	$1,182,734	(39%)	$3,101,491
DISTRICT 17				
Meek (D)	$1,552,012	$991,650	(64%)	$1,311,327
DISTRICT 18				
Ros-Lehtinen (R)	$1,834,650	$475,769	(26%)	$2,838,976
Taddeo (D)	$1,177,017	$193,927	(16%)	$1,177,003
DISTRICT 19				
Wexler (D)	$2,908,098	$547,756	(19%)	$2,372,548
Graber (X)	$425,788	$1,000	(0%)	$425,784
Lynch (R)	$136,707	$0	(0%)	$61,352
DISTRICT 20				
Wasserman Schultz (D)	$1,721,750	$922,795	(54%)	$1,475,436
Hostetter (X)	$8,784	$0	(0%)	$8,621
DISTRICT 21				
Diaz-Balart (R)	$2,284,221	$727,278	(32%)	$3,390,478
Martinez (D)	$1,893,437	$268,600	(14%)	$1,881,108
DISTRICT 22				
Klein (D)	$3,955,503	$1,200,835	(30%)	$2,372,293
West (R)	$584,980	$21,850	(4%)	$555,543
DISTRICT 23				
Hastings (D)	$820,458	$466,416	(57%)	$671,962
Thorpe (R)	$51,635	$1,250	(2%)	$50,970
DISTRICT 24				
Kosmas (D)	$2,108,182	$593,325	(28%)	$2,083,810
Feeney (R)	$2,157,264	$1,184,133	(55%)	$2,002,969
Bhola (X)	$6,725	$0	(0%)	$390
DISTRICT 25				
Diaz-Balart (R)	$1,982,909	$780,008	(39%)	$2,583,098
Garcia (D)	$1,788,034	$324,474	(18%)	$1,787,834

Georgia

	RECEIPTS	FROM PACS		EXPENDITURES
SENIOR SENATOR - 2008				
Chambliss (R)	$13,969,329	$4,120,748	(29%)	$15,692,294
Martin (D)	$7,490,201	$724,659	(10%)	$7,508,505
Buckley (LIBERT)	$26,628	$2,000	(8%)	$28,666

JUNIOR SENATOR - 2004

	RECEIPTS	FROM PACS		EXPENDITURES
Isakson (R)	$8,577,130	$1,713,570	(20%)	$8,038,200
Majette (D)	$2,084,294	$602,604	(29%)	$2,470,272
Buckley (LIBERT)	$42,377	$0	(0%)	$42,376

DISTRICT 1

Kingston (R)	$968,547	$404,522	(42%)	$873,385
Gillespie (D)	$136,940	$20,550	(15%)	$136,150

DISTRICT 2

Bishop (D)	$1,062,311	$641,543	(60%)	$1,034,540
Ferrell (R)	$8,979	$0	(0%)	$10

DISTRICT 3

Westmoreland (R)	$762,003	$359,110	(47%)	$920,966
Camp (D)	$56,248	$2,000	(4%)	$54,855

DISTRICT 4

Johnson (D)	$380,346	$245,492	(65%)	$381,100

DISTRICT 5

Lewis (D)	$1,267,597	$824,609	(65%)	$1,195,110

DISTRICT 6

Price (R)	$1,622,318	$795,263	(49%)	$1,607,716
Jones (D)	$642,645	$50,600	(8%)	$640,883

DISTRICT 7

Linder (R)	$581,976	$220,150	(38%)	$375,540
Heckman (D)	$174,673	$16,650	(10%)	$120,979

DISTRICT 8

Marshall (D)	$1,816,862	$962,725	(53%)	$1,736,540
Goddard (R)	$1,201,389	$298,965	(25%)	$1,192,303

DISTRICT 9

Deal (R)	$912,801	$600,550	(66%)	$898,875
Scott (D)	$23,708	$0	(0%)	$23,708

DISTRICT 10[†]

Broun (R)	$1,832,814	$322,622	(18%)	$1,800,502
Saxon (D)	$135,638	$7,750	(6%)	$128,894

DISTRICT 11

Gingrey (R)	$1,630,863	$412,188	(25%)	$1,242,887

DISTRICT 12

Barrow (D)	$2,299,743	$1,294,657	(56%)	$2,502,783
Stone (R)	$319,659	$37,925	(12%)	$265,171

DISTRICT 13

Scott (D)	$1,435,970	$1,165,429	(81%)	$1,433,435
Honeycutt (R)	$5,280,370	$5,500	(0%)	$5,204,670

Hawaii

	RECEIPTS	FROM PACS		EXPENDITURES
SENIOR SENATOR - 2004				
Inouye (D)	$2,788,703	$957,571	(34%)	$1,768,886
Cavasso (R)	$57,514	$8,500	(15%)	$57,122
JUNIOR SENATOR - 2006				
Akaka (D)	$2,648,898	$921,664	(35%)	$2,651,026
Thielen (R)	$356,419	$15,253	(4%)	$356,413
DISTRICT 1				
Abercrombie (D)	$1,444,071	$688,355	(48%)	$1,005,218
DISTRICT 2				
Hirono (D)	$1,240,402	$476,500	(38%)	$970,819

Idaho

	RECEIPTS	FROM PACS		EXPENDITURES
SENIOR SENATOR - 2004				
Crapo (R)	$1,948,398	$1,241,988	(64%)	$1,031,912
JUNIOR SENATOR - 2008				
Risch (R)	$3,594,815	$850,873	(24%)	$3,573,256
LaRocco (D)	$1,424,818	$281,591	(20%)	$1,421,746
Rammell (I)	$439,360	$0	(0%)	$439,397
Pro-Life (I)	$20,464	$0	(0%)	$20,465
DISTRICT 1				
Minnick (D)	$2,656,356	$422,803	(16%)	$2,649,953
Sali (R)	$1,178,118	$679,866	(58%)	$1,168,536
DISTRICT 2				
Simpson (R)	$707,482	$420,300	(59%)	$649,431
Holmes (D)	$16,765	$550	(3%)	$16,765

Illinois

	RECEIPTS	FROM PACS		EXPENDITURES
SENIOR SENATOR - 2008				
Durbin (D)	$8,116,764	$1,971,284	(24%)	$8,016,455
Sauerberg (R)	$2,060,788	$22,923	(1%)	$1,974,832
Koppie (CNSTP)	$20,340	$0	(0%)	$18,115
DISTRICT 1				
Rush (D)	$431,209	$266,543	(62%)	$435,961
Members (R)	$469,469	$4,000	(1%)	$422,267
DISTRICT 2				
Jackson (D)	$1,189,930	$480,651	(40%)	$1,673,968
DISTRICT 3				
Lipinski (D)	$707,824	$393,983	(56%)	$553,030
Pohlen (GREEN)	$7,054	$0	(0%)	$6,960
DISTRICT 4				
Gutierrez (D)	$323,493	$89,752	(28%)	$188,438
DISTRICT 5				
Emanuel (D)	$2,878,252	$1,173,066	(41%)	$2,105,109
DISTRICT 6				
Roskam (R)	$2,659,880	$1,063,515	(40%)	$2,708,859
Morgenthaler (D)	$833,593	$155,975	(19%)	$827,457
DISTRICT 7				
Davis (D)	$531,842	$298,123	(56%)	$413,001
DISTRICT 8				
Bean (D)	$3,107,765	$1,714,778	(55%)	$2,985,976
Greenberg (R)	$991,547	$114,653	(12%)	$990,574
DISTRICT 9				
Schakowsky (D)	$1,408,942	$375,435	(27%)	$1,227,724
Younan (R)	$13,721	$0	(0%)	$6,686
DISTRICT 10				
Kirk (R)	$5,456,604	$1,158,601	(21%)	$5,450,659
Seals (D)	$3,532,528	$486,132	(14%)	$3,566,123
DISTRICT 11				
Halvorson (D)	$2,317,190	$960,188	(41%)	$2,266,615
Ozinga (R)	$1,969,363	$166,025	(8%)	$1,969,363
Wallace (GREEN)	$7,130	$0	(0%)	$6,742
DISTRICT 12				
Costello (D)	$1,475,768	$710,423	(48%)	$830,944
Jennings (GREEN)	$6,783	$0	(0%)	$8,229

DISTRICT 13

Biggert (R)	$1,424,178	$715,491	(50%)	$1,585,536
Harper (D)	$1,086,105	$108,170	(10%)	$1,070,201

DISTRICT 14[†]

Foster (D)	$5,061,265	$881,335	(17%)	$5,047,815
Oberweis (R)	$5,091,510	$228,543	(4%)	$5,084,489
Stein (D)	$228,409	$0	(0%)	$228,172
Laesch (D)	$173,245	$13,400	(8%)	$176,477

DISTRICT 15

Johnson (R)	$321,390	$211,675	(66%)	$295,919

DISTRICT 16

Manzullo (R)	$1,352,576	$440,256	(33%)	$1,346,244
Abboud (D)	$516,010	$17,000	(3%)	$501,317
Summers (GREEN)	$5,547	$0	(0%)	$5,027

DISTRICT 17

Hare (D)	$896,347	$556,085	(62%)	$556,136

DISTRICT 18

Schock (R)	$2,618,129	$574,782	(22%)	$2,619,861
Callahan (D)	$624,526	$216,348	(35%)	$607,734
Schafer (GREEN)	$9,184	$0	(0%)	$9,074

DISTRICT 19

Shimkus (R)	$1,333,108	$847,841	(64%)	$1,209,093
Davis (D)	$69,270	$1,865	(3%)	$68,004

Indiana

	RECEIPTS	FROM PACS		EXPENDITURES
SENIOR SENATOR - 2006				
Lugar (R)	$2,925,923	$771,820	(26%)	$3,133,830
JUNIOR SENATOR - 2004				
Bayh (D)	$4,820,160	$1,583,913	(33%)	$2,250,428
Scott (R)	2,265,166	$6,450	0%	$2,242,526
DISTRICT 1				
Visclosky (D)	$1,758,060	$602,942	(34%)	$1,664,250
Leyva (R)	$11,732	$0	(0%)	$12,024
DISTRICT 2				
Donnelly (D)	$1,846,892	$1,121,658	(61%)	$1,599,268
Puckett (R)	$301,368	$1,159	(0%)	$286,350
DISTRICT 3				
Souder (R)	$1,077,170	$508,865	(47%)	$1,064,302
Montagano (D)	$854,428	$332,611	(39%)	$854,573
DISTRICT 4				
Buyer (R)	$870,667	$558,564	(64%)	$969,469
Ackerson (D)	$871,450	$40,700	(5%)	$870,680
DISTRICT 5				
Burton (R)	$1,417,754	$329,208	(23%)	$1,810,296
Ruley (D)	$16,195	$2,500	(15%)	$18,624
DISTRICT 6				
Pence (R)	$1,612,797	$514,771	(32%)	$1,575,412
Welsh (D)	$23,625	$3,000	(13%)	$24,935
DISTRICT 7[†]				
Carson (D)	$1,652,313	$1,038,816	(63%)	$1,600,840
Elrod (R)	$199,624	$30,760	(15%)	$198,260
Campo (R)	$38,923	$1,100	(3%)	$38,684
DISTRICT 8				
Ellsworth (D)	$1,571,814	$999,968	(64%)	$1,366,664
Goode (R)	$223,728	$6,045	(3%)	$223,729

DISTRICT 9

Hill (D)	$2,151,725	$1,348,072	(63%)	$2,185,740
Sodrel (R)	$1,007,289	$173,157	(17%)	$1,045,379
Schansberg (LIBERT)	$31,022	$0	(0%)	$35,565

Iowa

	RECEIPTS	FROM PACS		EXPENDITURES
SENIOR SENATOR - 2004				
Grassley (R)	$5,655,068	$2,146,135	(38%)	$6,403,445
Small (D)	$140,204	$1,200	(1%)	$135,503
JUNIOR SENATOR - 2008				
Harkin (D)	$6,358,882	$1,835,130	(29%)	$5,022,490
Reed (R)	$59,087	$0	(0%)	$58,793
DISTRICT 1				
Braley (D)	$1,150,967	$543,275	(47%)	$979,333
Hartsuch (R)	$55,222	$5,036	(9%)	$54,604
DISTRICT 2				
Loebsack (D)	$887,184	$544,574	(61%)	$805,024
Miller-Meeks (R)	$371,695	$49,194	(13%)	$367,694
White (X)	$6,883	$0	(0%)	$6,882
DISTRICT 3				
Boswell (D)	$1,537,390	$1,022,669	(67%)	$1,547,567
Schmett (R)	$157,300	$38,450	(24%)	$155,895
DISTRICT 4				
Latham (R)	$1,573,136	$824,589	(52%)	$1,627,654
Greenwald (D)	$635,581	$126,100	(20%)	$654,736
DISTRICT 5				
King (R)	$1,025,574	$350,240	(34%)	$873,230
Hubler (D)	$298,626	$59,610	(20%)	$290,089

Kansas

	RECEIPTS	FROM PACS		EXPENDITURES
SENIOR SENATOR - 2004				
Brownback (R)	$2,730,682	$893,588	(33%)	$2,476,585
Jones (D)	$71,102	$32,000	(45%)	$31,147
JUNIOR SENATOR - 2008				
Roberts (R)	$5,752,220	$2,489,463	(43%)	$6,297,288
Slattery (D)	$1,677,907	$260,810	(16%)	$1,677,905
DISTRICT 1				
Moran (R)	$1,586,150	$608,041	(38%)	$2,769,946
Bordonaro (D)	$7,791	$0	(0%)	$6,057
DISTRICT 2				
Jenkins (R)	$1,803,971	$377,971	(21%)	$1,666,239
Boyda (D)	$1,726,192	$599,493	(35%)	$1,760,726
DISTRICT 3				
Moore (D)	$1,864,356	$1,017,551	(55%)	$1,868,504
Jordan (R)	$1,114,912	$166,562	(15%)	$1,114,721
DISTRICT 4				
Tiahrt (R)	$1,334,556	$620,300	(46%)	$964,059
Betts (D)	$215,497	$6,500	(3%)	$210,358

Kentucky

	RECEIPTS	FROM PACS		EXPENDITURES
SENIOR SENATOR - 2008				
McConnell (R)	$18,681,961	$3,754,331	(20%)	$21,306,296
Lunsford (D)	$10,883,172	$421,285	(4%)	$10,801,203

JUNIOR SENATOR - 2004

Bunning (R)	$5,120,291	$1,903,137	(37%)	$6,075,399
Mongiardo (D)	$3,127,490	$484,365	(15%)	$3,104,981

DISTRICT 1

Whitfield (R)	$1,020,193	$597,680	(59%)	$1,052,635
Ryan (D)	$27,939	$5,000	(18%)	$21,203

DISTRICT 2

Guthrie (R)	$1,282,672	$497,291	(39%)	$1,257,624
Boswell (D)	$916,853	$360,100	(39%)	$900,518

DISTRICT 3

Yarmuth (D)	$2,136,760	$644,212	(30%)	$2,138,457
Northup (R)	$1,705,223	$371,060	(22%)	$1,708,081

DISTRICT 4

Davis (R)	$2,100,351	$805,418	(38%)	$1,811,169
Kelley (D)	$20,492	$1,000	(5%)	$19,531

DISTRICT 5

Rogers (R)	$611,926	$373,879	(61%)	$796,760

DISTRICT 6

Chandler (D)	$1,034,153	$520,751	(50%)	$481,994

Louisiana

	RECEIPTS	FROM PACS		EXPENDITURES
SENIOR SENATOR - 2008				
Landrieu (D)	$9,210,825	$2,634,351	(29%)	$10,146,669
Kennedy (R)	$4,828,936	$474,175	(10%)	$4,795,281
JUNIOR SENATOR - 2004				
Vitter (R)	$7,743,804	$1,182,643	(15%)	$7,206,714
John (D)	$4,893,113	$1,065,880	(22%)	$4,868,165
Kennedy (D)	$1,919,879	$122,570	(6%)	$1,919,774
Morrell (D)	$68,653	$12,050	(18%)	$67,214
DISTRICT 1[†]				
Scalise (R)	$1,608,688	$317,107	(20%)	$1,628,134
Harlan (D)	$2,158,629	$56,500	(3%)	$2,158,185
Reed (D)	$141,244	$23,850	(17%)	$138,207
DISTRICT 2				
Cao (R)	$242,529	$19,100	(8%)	$234,559
Jefferson (D)	$350,862	$14,500	(4%)	$342,240
Rahim (GREEN)	$10,985	$0	(0%)	$945
DISTRICT 3				
Melancon (D)	$1,544,912	$942,656	(61%)	$904,878
DISTRICT 4				
Fleming (R)	$1,833,027	$243,646	(13%)	$1,828,695
Carmouche (D)	$1,849,102	$892,250	(48%)	$1,844,290
Kelley (X)	$31,473	$0	(0%)	$39,510
DISTRICT 5				
Alexander (R)	$911,236	$286,945	(31%)	$1,021,984
DISTRICT 6[†]				
Cassidy (R)	$1,295,442	$242,094	(19%)	$1,252,457
Cazayoux (D)	$2,740,163	$1,459,876	(53%)	$2,766,865
Jackson (X)	$217,325	$4,800	(2%)	$212,215
DISTRICT 7				
Boustany (R)	$1,569,139	$677,610	(43%)	$1,606,461
Cravins (D)	$624,762	$255,893	(41%)	$623,426

Maine

	RECEIPTS	FROM PACS		EXPENDITURES
SENIOR SENATOR - 2006				
Snowe (R)	$3,434,635	$1,247,685	(36%)	$2,773,431
Bright (D)	$127,767	$12,382	(10%)	$126,823
Slavick (I)	$1,931	$0	(0%)	$5,580
JUNIOR SENATOR - 2008				
Collins (R)	$7,593,350	$2,696,845	(36%)	$7,765,295
Allen (D)	$5,998,773	$573,340	(10%)	$6,462,451
Hoffman (I)	$43,301	$0	(0%)	$42,657
Dobson (I)	$14,262	$0	(0%)	$13,787
DISTRICT 1				
Pingree (D)	$2,239,046	$250,190	(11%)	$2,213,642
Summers (R)	$655,635	$65,456	(10%)	$644,690
DISTRICT 2				
Michaud (D)	$792,499	$567,075	(72%)	$569,114
Frary (R)	$256,059	$0	(0%)	$311,470

Maryland

	RECEIPTS	FROM PACS		EXPENDITURES
SENIOR SENATOR - 2004				
Mikulski (D)	$5,911,959	$1,133,700	(19%)	$5,997,093
Pipkin (R)	$2,313,360	$16,310	(1%)	$2,298,709
JUNIOR SENATOR - 2006				
Cardin (D)	$8,770,424	$1,480,090	(17%)	$8,676,056
Steele (R)	$8,432,622	$1,212,942	(14%)	$8,219,686
Zeese (GREEN)	$68,909	$0	(0%)	$68,908
DISTRICT 1				
Kratovil (D)	$2,011,387	$600,307	(30%)	$1,994,553
Harris (R)	$3,088,490	$548,117	(18%)	$3,024,144
DISTRICT 2				
Ruppersberger (D)	$1,030,869	$526,846	(51%)	$636,162
Matthews (R)	$11,028	$1,800	(16%)	$9,836
DISTRICT 3				
Sarbanes (D)	$1,012,936	$171,349	(17%)	$799,506
DISTRICT 4[†]				
Edwards (D)	$1,457,357	$313,137	(21%)	$1,443,942
James (R)	$23,564	$0	(0%)	$23,514
DISTRICT 5				
Hoyer (D)	$3,677,188	$2,394,264	(65%)	$3,435,232
Bailey (R)	$26,870	$2,200	(8%)	$27,681
DISTRICT 6				
Bartlett (R)	$323,051	$121,451	(38%)	$204,443
Dougherty (D)	$172,862	$11,844	(7%)	$172,381
DISTRICT 7				
Cummings (D)	$951,855	$517,650	(54%)	$684,420
Hargadon (R)	$23,703	$1,720	(7%)	$23,702
DISTRICT 8				
Van Hollen (D)	$2,375,319	$965,167	(41%)	$1,279,456
Hudson (R)	$60,608	$2,000	(3%)	$59,213
Clark (GREEN)	$36,541	$0	(0%)	$36,305

Massachusetts

	RECEIPTS	FROM PACS		EXPENDITURES
SENIOR SENATOR - 2006				
Kennedy (D)	$8,931,742	$1,012,376	(11%)	$7,043,877
Chase (R)	$873,982	$0	(0%)	$853,730
JUNIOR SENATOR - 2008				
Kerry (D)	$16,116,152	$1,079,262	(7%)	$12,279,425
Beatty (R)	$2,078,533	$3,910	(0%)	$2,070,528
DISTRICT 1				
Olver (D)	$817,743	$419,055	(51%)	$857,631
Bech (R)	$161,389	$7,300	(5%)	$157,611
DISTRICT 2				
Neal (D)	$1,621,922	$1,007,436	(62%)	$766,166
DISTRICT 3				
McGovern (D)	$1,085,779	$317,551	(29%)	$848,694
DISTRICT 4				
Frank (D)	$2,297,677	$1,019,013	(44%)	$2,953,741
Sholley (R)	$40,248	$0	(0%)	$39,038
DISTRICT 5†				
Tsongas (D)	$3,302,898	$655,404	(20%)	$3,287,403
Ogonowski (R)	$696,898	$72,150	(10%)	$696,535
Hayes (R)	$24,530	$100	(0%)	$24,378
DISTRICT 6				
Tierney (D)	$735,813	$242,070	(33%)	$498,041
Baker (R)	$29,174	$70	(0%)	$28,082
DISTRICT 7				
Markey (D)	$1,454,661	$587,620	(40%)	$1,021,890
Cunningham (R)	$23,219	$400	(2%)	$23,134
DISTRICT 8				
Capuano (D)	$1,084,081	$522,203	(48%)	$554,013
DISTRICT 9				
Lynch (D)	$1,066,677	$349,223	(33%)	$739,421
DISTRICT 10				
Delahunt (D)	$117,097	$133,048	(114%)	$1,217,875

Michigan

	RECEIPTS	FROM PACS		EXPENDITURES
SENIOR SENATOR - 2008				
Levin (D)	$8,276,479	$1,282,058	(15%)	$5,784,520
Hoogendyk (R)	$302,747	$3,740	(1%)	$301,993
JUNIOR SENATOR - 2006				
Stabenow (D)	$9,211,206	$1,566,316	(17%)	$11,220,506
Bouchard (R)	$6,065,160	$709,826	(12%)	$6,050,148
Sole (GREEN)	$5,527	$0	(0%)	$5,508
DISTRICT 1				
Stupak (D)	$1,326,898	$818,005	(62%)	$1,281,683
Casperson (R)	$237,063	$23,709	(10%)	$236,254
DISTRICT 2				
Hoekstra (R)	$742,440	$321,763	(43%)	$828,852
Johnson (D)	$115,011	$19,300	(17%)	$111,801
DISTRICT 3				
Ehlers (R)	$413,365	$188,130	(46%)	$319,953
DISTRICT 4				
Camp (R)	$2,237,726	$1,642,029	(73%)	$2,568,143
Concannon (D)	$122,041	$23,000	(19%)	$121,971

DISTRICT 5

Kildee (D)	$606,568	$338,545	(56%)	$559,948
DISTRICT 6				
Upton (R)	$1,413,946	$827,199	(59%)	$1,527,587
Cooney (D)	$82,761	$3,000	(4%)	$84,883
DISTRICT 7				
Schauer (D)	$2,344,492	$787,046	(34%)	$2,331,667
Walberg (R)	$2,112,214	$833,684	(39%)	$2,128,559
DISTRICT 8				
Rogers (R)	$1,384,974	$815,981	(59%)	$1,565,888
Alexander (D)	$218,544	$30,775	(14%)	$214,282
DISTRICT 9				
Peters (D)	$2,540,363	$756,098	(30%)	$2,528,897
Knollenberg (R)	$3,790,742	$1,243,928	(33%)	$4,135,864
DISTRICT 10				
Miller (R)	$835,527	$417,227	(50%)	$756,978
DISTRICT 11				
McCotter (R)	$1,133,779	$664,474	(59%)	$1,058,502
Larkin (D)	$29,066	$4,728	(16%)	$28,957
DISTRICT 12				
Levin (D)	$725,438	$555,295	(77%)	$660,710
DISTRICT 13				
Kilpatrick (D)	$1,027,101	$587,339	(57%)	$1,066,838
DISTRICT 14				
Conyers (D)	$1,111,753	$657,696	(59%)	$1,196,772
DISTRICT 15				
Dingell (D)	$2,736,892	$2,038,633	(74%)	$2,522,180
Lynch (R)	$20,096	$800	(4%)	$19,870

Minnesota

	RECEIPTS	FROM PACS		EXPENDITURES
SENATOR - 2006				
Klobuchar (D)	$9,202,052	$905,058	(10%)	$9,155,313
Kennedy (R)	$10,211,119	$2,245,415	(22%)	$10,308,273
Fitzgerald (INDC)	$13,652	$0	(0%)	$13,350
Cavlan (GREEN)	$9,378	$0	(0%)	$8,544
SENATOR - 2008				
Franken (D)	$22,502,124	$589,866	(3%)	$21,066,834
Coleman (R)	$19,298,843	$3,254,080	(17%)	$19,011,108
Barkley (INDC)	$163,358	$4,946	(3%)	$162,387
DISTRICT 1				
Walz (D)	$2,732,738	$937,548	(34%)	$2,707,385
Davis (R)	$1,097,200	$69,800	(6%)	$1,094,278
DISTRICT 2				
Kline (R)	$1,464,906	$590,965	(40%)	$1,484,962
Sarvi (D)	$559,473	$168,161	(30%)	$559,474
DISTRICT 3				
Paulsen (R)	$2,781,437	$771,383	(28%)	$2,744,927
Madia (D)	$2,734,890	$673,315	(25%)	$2,711,899
Dillon (INDC)	$161,185	$1,000	(1%)	$161,181
DISTRICT 4				
McCollum (D)	$722,054	$385,826	(53%)	$719,710
Matthews (R)	$86,561	$5,000	(6%)	$79,648
DISTRICT 5				
Ellison (D)	$1,530,396	$335,384	(22%)	$1,476,449
White (R)	$62,099	$0	(0%)	$55,796

DISTRICT 6

Bachmann (R)	$3,494,045	$975,875	(28%)	$3,565,248
Tinklenberg (D)	$2,968,319	$416,613	(14%)	$2,515,420

DISTRICT 7

Peterson (D)	$1,218,264	$889,565	(73%)	$1,036,463
Menze (R)	$12,875	$2,472	(19%)	$13,401

DISTRICT 8

Oberstar (D)	$1,995,753	$1,126,244	(56%)	$1,409,685
Grams (R)	$14,499	$0	(0%)	$14,933

Mississippi

	RECEIPTS	FROM PACS		EXPENDITURES
SENIOR SENATOR - 2008				
Cochran (R)	$2,212,827	$960,950	(43%)	$2,063,627
JUNIOR SENATOR - 2008				
Wicker (R)	$6,227,613	$1,779,536	(29%)	$6,160,116
Musgrove (D)	$2,686,206	$468,116	(17%)	$2,685,515
DISTRICT 1[†]				
Childers (D)	$1,851,648	$1,023,349	(55%)	$1,822,307
Davis (R)	$1,534,915	$364,350	(24%)	$1,435,971
McCullough (R)	$745,298	$96,000	(13%)	$744,754
Holland (D)	$340,457	$9,500	(3%)	$335,699
DISTRICT 2				
Thompson (D)	$2,147,392	$1,227,245	(57%)	$1,081,785
DISTRICT 3				
Harper (R)	$1,160,476	$97,450	(8%)	$1,143,197
Gill (D)	$93,262	$0	(0%)	$93,191
DISTRICT 4				
Taylor (D)	$521,148	$366,129	(70%)	$513,266
McCay (R)	$17,686	$1,000	(6%)	$11,141

Missouri

	RECEIPTS	FROM PACS		EXPENDITURES
SENIOR SENATOR - 2004				
Bond (R)	$8,093,952	$2,098,125	(26%)	$7,848,506
Farmer (D)	$3,600,882	$512,409	(14%)	$3,548,116
JUNIOR SENATOR - 2006				
McCaskill (D)	$11,935,806	$1,058,519	(9%)	$11,705,967
Talent (R)	$14,098,563	$3,472,930	(25%)	$14,340,762
Lewis (PRO)	$5,937	$0	(0%)	$5,938
DISTRICT 1				
Clay (D)	$674,852	$459,699	(68%)	$622,529
DISTRICT 2				
Akin (R)	$966,369	$267,943	(28%)	$838,986
Haas (D)	$54,868	$13,350	(24%)	$52,218
DISTRICT 3				
Carnahan (D)	$952,442	$623,430	(65%)	$883,674
Sander (R)	$36,148	$1,250	(3%)	$32,444
DISTRICT 4				
Skelton (D)	$1,127,899	$765,801	(68%)	$1,203,525
DISTRICT 5				
Cleaver (D)	$554,095	$335,848	(61%)	$554,037
Turk (R)	$57,055	$430	(1%)	$56,599
DISTRICT 6				
Graves (R)	$2,667,310	$1,210,750	(45%)	$2,633,443
Barnes (D)	$2,814,780	$590,824	(21%)	$2,801,656

DISTRICT 7

Blunt (R)	$2,580,060	$1,553,538	(60%)	$2,597,311
Monroe (D)	$62,563	$0	(0%)	$55,453

DISTRICT 8

Emerson (R)	$1,246,268	$627,050	(50%)	$1,285,597
Allen (D)	$63,369	$18,030	(28%)	$62,069

DISTRICT 9

Luetkemeyer (R)	$2,784,442	$429,503	(15%)	$2,778,724
Baker (D)	$1,702,214	$531,187	(31%)	$1,669,071

Montana

	RECEIPTS	FROM PACS		EXPENDITURES
SENIOR SENATOR - 2008				
Baucus (D)	$8,433,751	$3,257,396	(39%)	$8,164,703
JUNIOR SENATOR - 2006				
Tester (D)	$5,588,548	$565,531	(10%)	$5,588,292
Burns (R)	$8,057,326	$2,586,600	(32%)	$8,516,022
AT LARGE				
Rehberg (R)	$1,164,171	$387,094	(33%)	$897,187

Nebraska

	RECEIPTS	FROM PACS		EXPENDITURES
SENIOR SENATOR - 2006				
Nelson (D)	$6,451,279	$2,683,758	(42%)	$7,492,134
Ricketts (R)	$13,424,896	$197,700	(1%)	$13,417,690
JUNIOR SENATOR - 2008				
Johanns (R)	$3,907,749	$1,534,896	(39%)	$3,781,316
Kleeb (D)	$1,852,094	$141,140	(8%)	$1,911,771
DISTRICT 1				
Fortenberry (R)	$725,529	$174,000	(24%)	$341,030
Yashirin (D)	$24,725	$3,175	(13%)	$24,232
DISTRICT 2				
Terry (R)	$1,746,226	$805,074	(46%)	$1,838,836
Esch (D)	$849,545	$195,269	(23%)	$842,986
DISTRICT 3				
Smith (R)	$806,088	$397,892	(49%)	$623,810

Nevada

	RECEIPTS	FROM PACS		EXPENDITURES
SENIOR SENATOR - 2004				
Reid (D)	$7,015,254	$2,103,980	(30%)	$7,040,588
Ziser (R)	$648,792	$9,343	(1%)	$647,500
JUNIOR SENATOR - 2006				
Ensign (R)	$5,305,606	$1,851,877	(35%)	$4,456,881
Carter (D)	$2,266,273	$186,856	(8%)	$2,264,708
DISTRICT 1				
Berkley (D)	$2,164,787	$842,443	(39%)	$1,985,063
Wegner (R)	$15,747	$0	(0%)	$15,794
DISTRICT 2				
Heller (R)	$1,713,909	$746,809	(44%)	$1,605,810
Derby (D)	$1,119,169	$364,986	(33%)	$1,131,582
DISTRICT 3				
Titus (D)	$1,856,736	$676,299	(36%)	$1,777,641
Porter (R)	$3,100,864	$1,516,500	(49%)	$3,182,799

New Hampshire

	RECEIPTS	FROM PACS		EXPENDITURES
SENIOR SENATOR - 2004				
Gregg (R)	$2,982,530	$1,654,297	(55%)	$1,897,466
Haddock (D)	$177,594	$0	(0%)	$177,199
JUNIOR SENATOR - 2008				
Shaheen (D)	$8,264,353	$1,140,192	(14%)	$8,225,580
Sununu (R)	$7,376,457	$2,443,144	(33%)	$8,010,010
DISTRICT 1				
Shea-Porter (D)	$1,543,513	$584,019	(38%)	$1,576,897
Bradley (R)	$1,377,090	$506,043	(37%)	$1,447,187
DISTRICT 2				
Hodes (D)	$2,031,760	$854,680	(42%)	$2,022,042
Horn (R)	$555,500	$70,607	(13%)	$552,317

New Jersey

	RECEIPTS	FROM PACS		EXPENDITURES
SENIOR SENATOR - 2008				
Lautenberg (D)	$7,219,668	$1,374,321	(19%)	$8,135,752
Zimmer (R)	$1,542,809	$166,324	(11%)	$1,498,731
JUNIOR SENATOR - 2006				
Menendez (D)	$11,950,586	$2,151,084	(18%)	$13,328,665
Kean (R)	$7,879,050	$1,250,612	(16%)	$7,762,370
Flynn (LIBERT)	$5,172	$0	(0%)	$5,632
DISTRICT 1				
Andrews (D)	$1,618,559	$741,526	(46%)	$3,502,678
Glading (R)	$26,709	$65	(0%)	$26,034
DISTRICT 2				
LoBiondo (R)	$1,365,485	$598,764	(44%)	$1,520,178
Kurkowski (D)	$192,123	$5,525	(3%)	$192,143
DISTRICT 3				
Adler (D)	$2,883,253	$1,026,472	(36%)	$2,863,993
Myers (R)	$1,264,872	$181,698	(14%)	$1,259,800
DISTRICT 4				
Smith (R)	$928,729	$229,308	(25%)	$1,076,919
Zeitz (D)	$483,229	$35,900	(7%)	$481,166
DISTRICT 5				
Garrett (R)	$1,550,308	$579,490	(37%)	$1,726,631
Shulman (D)	$1,221,943	$197,660	(16%)	$1,194,535
DISTRICT 6				
Pallone (D)	$2,601,120	$1,255,295	(48%)	$1,542,502
McLeod (R)	$12,364	$0	(0%)	$12,364
DISTRICT 7				
Lance (R)	$1,450,189	$352,512	(24%)	$1,419,698
Stender (D)	$2,632,497	$893,189	(34%)	$2,621,407
Hsing (HFC)	$219,039	$0	(0%)	$213,817
DISTRICT 8				
Pascrell (D)	$1,450,970	$654,252	(45%)	$1,137,316
Straten (R)	$84,075	$750	(1%)	$82,227
DISTRICT 9				
Rothman (D)	$1,426,865	$495,419	(35%)	$1,288,656
Micco (R)	$33,890	$1,435	(4%)	$34,363
DISTRICT 10				
Payne (D)	$804,186	$440,471	(55%)	$502,611

DISTRICT 11				
Frelinghuysen (R)	$1,084,231	$378,225	(35%)	$1,206,615
Wyka (D)	$88,199	$3,834	(4%)	$93,651
DISTRICT 12				
Holt (D)	$1,181,465	$340,630	(29%)	$1,268,760
Bateman (R)	$36,731	$9,100	(25%)	$32,959
DISTRICT 13				
Sires (D)	$993,228	$313,160	(32%)	$802,335

New Mexico

	RECEIPTS	FROM PACS		EXPENDITURES
SENIOR SENATOR - 2006				
Bingaman (D)	$3,310,009	$1,609,084	(49%)	$2,628,276
McCulloch (R)	$559,138	$10,230	(2%)	$555,511
JUNIOR SENATOR - 2008				
Udall (D)	$7,447,684	$1,270,798	(17%)	$7,841,887
Pearce (R)	$4,632,311	$676,725	(15%)	$4,626,706
DISTRICT 1				
Heinrich (D)	$2,513,759	$633,286	(25%)	$2,481,040
White (R)	$1,798,891	$404,117	(22%)	$1,778,319
DISTRICT 2				
Teague (D)	$3,480,455	$365,087	(10%)	$3,458,821
Tinsley (R)	$2,402,283	$353,750	(15%)	$2,389,508
DISTRICT 3				
Luján (D)	$1,570,993	$388,345	(25%)	$1,520,908
East (R)	$193,911	$23,500	(12%)	$190,884
Miller (I)	$42,156	$0	(0%)	$42,154

New York

	RECEIPTS	FROM PACS		EXPENDITURES
SENIOR SENATOR - 2004				
Schumer (D)	$11,921,568	$928,698	(8%)	$15,467,530
Mills (R)	$632,319	$51,350	(8%)	$629,170
Hirschfeld (BLD)	$702,000	$0	(0%)	$87,293
O'Grady (C)	$47,143	$0	(0%)	$15,628
McReynolds (GREEN)	$14,275	$0	(0%)	$7,209
Silberger (LIBERT)	$9,999	$0	(0%)	$9,594
DISTRICT 1				
Bishop (D)	$1,391,804	$512,295	(37%)	$1,478,623
Zeldin (R)	$871,275	$24,200	(3%)	$864,720
DISTRICT 2				
Israel (D)	$2,144,797	$546,622	(25%)	$1,436,880
Stalzer (R)	$10,000	$0	(0%)	$15,500
DISTRICT 3				
King (R)	$1,791,786	$613,778	(34%)	$875,084
Long (D)	$45,593	$2,500	(5%)	$42,361
DISTRICT 4				
McCarthy (D)	$1,336,619	$524,571	(39%)	$1,520,492
Martins (R)	$503,789	$0	(0%)	$496,029
DISTRICT 5				
Ackerman (D)	$1,313,440	$372,295	(28%)	$988,775
Berney (R)	$25,098	$500	(2%)	$24,367
Policarpio (C)	$18,546	$0	(0%)	$17,737
DISTRICT 6				
Meeks (D)	$1,308,844	$742,110	(57%)	$1,343,648
DISTRICT 7				
Crowley (D)	$2,058,150	$1,274,260	(62%)	$1,729,732

DISTRICT 8
Nadler (D) | $1,381,995 | $448,734 (32%) | $1,044,454

DISTRICT 9
Weiner (D) | $379,311 | $189,660 (50%) | $524,607

DISTRICT 10
Towns (D) | $1,545,288 | $890,962 (58%) | $1,568,247

DISTRICT 11
Clarke (D) | $537,750 | $239,360 (45%) | $545,983

DISTRICT 12
Velázquez (D) | $1,136,163 | $858,394 (76%) | $816,108

DISTRICT 13
McMahon (D) | $1,481,524 | $617,447 (42%) | $1,272,811
Straniere (R) | $166,214 | $14,350 (9%) | $162,474
Morano (INDC) | $51,075 | $0 (0%) | $51,424

DISTRICT 14
Maloney (D) | $1,692,319 | $702,962 (42%) | $1,257,989

DISTRICT 15
Rangel (D) | $5,093,239 | $2,346,847 (46%) | $4,209,400

DISTRICT 16
Serrano (D) | $410,512 | $280,345 (68%) | $386,734

DISTRICT 17
Engel (D) | $1,000,776 | $463,506 (46%) | $776,808

DISTRICT 18
Lowey (D) | $1,394,481 | $290,570 (21%) | $1,489,302
Russell (R) | $18,405 | $500 (3%) | $19,906

DISTRICT 19
Hall (D) | $2,239,376 | $678,461 (30%) | $2,136,773
Lalor (R) | $637,983 | $12,499 (2%) | $612,220

DISTRICT 20
Gillibrand (D) | $4,649,651 | $1,173,389 (25%) | $4,488,475
Treadwell (R) | $7,043,425 | $192,538 (3%) | $7,038,552

DISTRICT 21
Tonko (D) | $748,250 | $312,207 (42%) | $753,520
Steck (INDC) | $552,608 | $4,850 (1%) | $552,513
Buhrmaster (R) | $504,380 | $24,545 (5%) | $504,378

DISTRICT 22
Hinchey (D) | $698,167 | $265,605 (38%) | $735,253
Phillips (R) | $148,326 | $7,620 (5%) | $150,490

DISTRICT 23
McHugh (R) | $708,604 | $511,612 (72%) | $645,795
Oot (D) | $107,809 | $0 (0%) | $107,714

DISTRICT 24
Arcuri (D) | $1,612,038 | $942,604 (58%) | $1,616,138
Hanna (R) | $1,092,861 | $49,204 (5%) | $1,090,713

DISTRICT 25
Maffei (D) | $2,366,299 | $974,221 (41%) | $2,410,865
Sweetland (R) | $406,316 | $59,518 (15%) | $403,189
Hawkins (GRP) | $8,485 | $0 (0%) | $6,132

DISTRICT 26
Lee (R) | $2,247,742 | $352,099 (16%) | $2,220,960
Kryzan (D) | $1,235,756 | $327,627 (27%) | $1,206,640
Powers (WFM) | $1,207,091 | $270,357 (22%) | $1,174,679

DISTRICT 27
Higgins (D) | $1,088,825 | $409,776 (38%) | $844,699
Humiston (R) | $192,960 | $10,400 (5%) | $190,451

DISTRICT 28
Slaughter (D) | $822,542 | $574,183 (70%) | $756,579

DISTRICT 29
Massa (D) | $2,161,657 | $557,142 (26%) | $2,159,314
Kuhl (R) | $1,500,971 | $857,377 (57%) | $1,500,324

North Carolina

	RECEIPTS	FROM PACS	EXPENDITURES
SENIOR SENATOR - 2004			
Burr (R)	$12,951,226	$2,796,484 (22%)	$12,853,110
Bowles (D)	$13,405,743	$822,974 (6%)	$13,357,851
JUNIOR SENATOR - 2008			
Hagan (D)	$8,975,412	$920,069 (10%)	$8,953,274
Dole (R)	$17,268,326	$2,103,266 (12%)	$17,468,134
DISTRICT 1			
Butterfield (D)	$792,329	$564,773 (71%)	$703,692
DISTRICT 2			
Etheridge (D)	$1,270,858	$679,212 (53%)	$984,575
Mansell (R)	$22,008	$0 (0%)	$21,861
DISTRICT 3			
Jones (R)	$670,132	$395,591 (59%)	$915,298
Weber (D)	$18,616	$0 (0%)	$21,761
DISTRICT 4			
Price (D)	$1,152,754	$505,425 (44%)	$940,570
Lawson (R)	$576,023	$3,250 (1%)	$573,569
DISTRICT 5			
Foxx (R)	$1,096,759	$320,214 (29%)	$852,649
Carter (D)	$238,163	$10,695 (4%)	$238,153
DISTRICT 6			
Coble (R)	$569,684	$347,075 (61%)	$688,818
Bratton (D)	$117,114	$1,000 (1%)	$105,750
DISTRICT 7			
McIntyre (D)	$895,676	$385,650 (43%)	$1,160,679
Breazeale (R)	$86,402	$4,500 (5%)	$89,219
DISTRICT 8			
Kissell (D)	$1,513,740	$585,273 (39%)	$1,509,753
Hayes (R)	$3,768,678	$1,306,279 (35%)	$3,808,201
DISTRICT 9			
Myrick (R)	$1,198,840	$563,622 (47%)	$1,164,506
Taylor (D)	$252,143	$1,800 (1%)	$252,020
DISTRICT 10			
McHenry (R)	$1,525,720	$661,460 (43%)	$1,587,880
Johnson (D)	$693,910	$121,200 (17%)	$684,167
DISTRICT 11			
Shuler (D)	$1,670,728	$815,298 (49%)	$769,941
Mumpower (R)	$134,307	$0 (0%)	$134,199
DISTRICT 12			
Watt (D)	$680,471	$458,142 (67%)	$646,075
Cobb (R)	$25,306	$3,300 (13%)	$25,584
DISTRICT 13			
Miller (D)	$938,767	$447,895 (48%)	$907,519
Webster (R)	$44,847	$3,750 (8%)	$34,655

North Dakota

	RECEIPTS	FROM PACS	EXPENDITURES
SENIOR SENATOR - 2006			
Conrad (D)	$4,664,878	$2,033,240 (44%)	$3,532,732
Grotberg (R)	$259,080	$125 (0%)	$259,081

JUNIOR SENATOR - 2004

	RECEIPTS	FROM PACS		EXPENDITURES
Dorgan (D)	$2,941,662	$1,410,617	(48%)	$2,676,756
Liffrig (R)	$380,351	$12,299	(3%)	$381,125

AT LARGE

Pomeroy (D)	$2,090,327	$1,530,640	(73%)	$1,795,714
Sand (R)	$1,963,453	$15,703	(1%)	$1,944,095

Ohio

	RECEIPTS	FROM PACS		EXPENDITURES
SENIOR SENATOR - 2004				
Voinovich (R)	$7,326,196	$1,670,976	(23%)	$8,956,380
Fingerhut (D)	$1,171,554	$97,837	(8%)	$1,166,538
JUNIOR SENATOR - 2006				
Brown (D)	$8,937,004	$1,471,968	(16%)	$10,751,765
DeWine (R)	$12,094,898	$2,906,920	(24%)	$14,161,402
DISTRICT 1				
Driehaus (D)	$1,489,648	$637,095	(43%)	$1,447,544
Chabot (R)	$2,349,745	$1,122,411	(48%)	$2,410,292
DISTRICT 2				
Schmidt (R)	$1,289,300	$472,179	(37%)	$1,276,573
Wulsin (D)	$1,929,589	$370,352	(19%)	$1,972,691
Krikorian (I)	$203,437	$1,000	(0%)	$191,083
DISTRICT 3				
Turner (R)	$1,211,637	$334,175	(28%)	$1,058,000
Mitakides (D)	$462,026	$86,546	(19%)	$462,075
DISTRICT 4				
Jordan (R)	$950,218	$357,435	(38%)	$436,919
Carroll (D)	$30,658	$6,150	(20%)	$27,697
DISTRICT 5[†]				
Latta (R)	$1,991,571	$1,040,891	(52%)	$2,051,669
Weirauch (D)	$545,833	$312,214	(57%)	$548,796
Mays (D)	$7,200	$0	(0%)	$8,217
DISTRICT 7				
Austria (R)	$1,209,739	$603,324	(50%)	$1,196,189
Neuhardt (D)	$861,992	$163,308	(19%)	$855,329
DISTRICT 8				
Boehner (R)	$5,144,481	$2,280,558	(44%)	$5,342,022
von Stein (D)	$16,708	$24	(0%)	$15,425
DISTRICT 9				
Kaptur (D)	$640,879	$327,875	(51%)	$501,404
DISTRICT 10				
Kucinich (D)	$2,408,616	$173,760	(7%)	$2,430,560
Trakas (R)	$383,987	$41,119	(11%)	$381,135
DISTRICT 11[†]				
Fudge (D)	$330,361	$168,150	(51%)	$94,049
DISTRICT 12				
Tiberi (R)	$2,068,833	$1,150,060	(56%)	$1,714,042
Robinson (D)	$187,800	$30,262	(16%)	$180,974
DISTRICT 13				
Sutton (D)	$739,118	$463,992	(63%)	$719,608
Potter (R)	$31,549	$1,000	(3%)	$28,165
DISTRICT 14				
LaTourette (R)	$1,476,187	$862,918	(58%)	$1,425,133
O'Neill (D)	$556,177	$84,070	(15%)	$556,388
DISTRICT 15				
Kilroy (D)	$2,592,756	$704,248	(27%)	$2,611,122
Stivers (R)	$2,407,038	$1,261,136	(52%)	$2,244,221

Eckhart (I)	$34,172	$0	(0%)	$33,596
DISTRICT 16				
Boccieri (D)	$1,794,110	$830,879	(46%)	$1,722,377
Schuring (R)	$1,225,858	$232,768	(19%)	$1,208,527
DISTRICT 17				
Ryan (D)	$1,360,624	$658,350	(48%)	$1,151,775
DISTRICT 18				
Space (D)	$2,265,350	$1,162,985	(51%)	$2,041,891
Dailey (R)	$392,126	$34,359	(9%)	$391,524

Oklahoma

	RECEIPTS	FROM PACS		EXPENDITURES
SENIOR SENATOR - 2008				
Inhofe (R)	$5,408,751	$1,642,852	(30%)	$5,477,730
Rice (D)	$2,869,433	$231,426	(8%)	$2,868,819
JUNIOR SENATOR - 2004				
Coburn (R)	$5,106,058	$895,428	(18%)	$5,078,647
Carson (D)	$6,345,497	$1,016,490	(16%)	$6,256,444
DISTRICT 1				
Sullivan (R)	$1,093,526	$528,501	(48%)	$1,171,990
Oliver (D)	$566,308	$22,000	(4%)	$566,307
DISTRICT 2				
Boren (D)	$1,748,479	$983,550	(56%)	$960,350
DISTRICT 3				
Lucas (R)	$543,187	$339,512	(63%)	$644,446
Michael (I)	$74,676	$0	(0%)	$73,167
Robbins (D)	$27,103	$0	(0%)	$28,612
DISTRICT 4				
Cole (R)	$1,124,657	$431,492	(38%)	$1,116,842
Cummings (D)	$10,033	$253	(3%)	$12,369
DISTRICT 5				
Fallin (R)	$1,140,478	$249,751	(22%)	$1,081,684

Oregon

	RECEIPTS	FROM PACS		EXPENDITURES
SENIOR SENATOR - 2004				
Wyden (D)	$3,802,681	$1,111,758	(29%)	$2,817,706
King (R)	$33,012	$5,250	(16%)	$32,930
Keane (I)	$9,940	$0	(0%)	$8,511
JUNIOR SENATOR - 2008				
Merkley (D)	$6,512,231	$708,040	(11%)	$6,501,315
Smith (R)	$9,252,337	$2,956,267	(32%)	$11,405,378
DISTRICT 1				
Wu (D)	$1,029,675	$383,947	(37%)	$1,214,535
Haugen (R)	$8,370	$0	(0%)	$7,563
DISTRICT 2				
Walden (R)	$1,582,984	$706,085	(45%)	$1,646,853
DISTRICT 3				
Blumenauer (D)	$1,181,680	$639,240	(54%)	$1,132,494
Walsh (D)	$12,672	$0	(0%)	$11,942
DISTRICT 4				
DeFazio (D)	$729,421	$467,636	(64%)	$471,179
DISTRICT 5				
Schrader (D)	$1,438,450	$664,118	(46%)	$1,389,044
Erickson (R)	$2,595,628	$14,067	(1%)	$2,594,663

Pennsylvania

	RECEIPTS	FROM PACS		EXPENDITURES
SENIOR SENATOR - 2004				
Specter (R)	$14,952,496	$2,605,116	(17%)	$20,307,099
Hoeffel (D)	$4,556,417	$405,686	(9%)	$4,540,209
Clymer (CNSTP)	$218,996	$4,500	(2%)	$212,896
JUNIOR SENATOR - 2006				
Casey (D)	$17,941,270	$1,328,861	(7%)	$17,592,212
Santorum (R)	$24,796,718	$4,007,539	(16%)	$25,832,567
DISTRICT 1				
Brady (D)	$764,048	$363,950	(48%)	$1,013,835
DISTRICT 2				
Fattah (D)	$274,080	$204,157	(74%)	$699,411
Livingston (R)	$12,825	$1,000	(8%)	$12,824
DISTRICT 3				
Dahlkemper (D)	$1,313,237	$470,187	(36%)	$1,301,838
English (R)	$2,659,966	$1,805,387	(68%)	$2,633,349
DISTRICT 4				
Altmire (D)	$2,945,099	$1,482,631	(50%)	$2,986,360
Hart (R)	$1,362,707	$358,043	(26%)	$1,362,528
DISTRICT 5				
Thompson (R)	$445,736	$200,233	(45%)	$442,425
McCracken (D)	$98,895	$31,600	(32%)	$98,895
DISTRICT 6				
Gerlach (R)	$2,370,625	$1,171,984	(49%)	$2,310,342
Roggio (D)	$667,507	$68,800	(10%)	$663,236
DISTRICT 7				
Sestak (D)	$3,889,073	$1,008,143	(26%)	$1,162,719
Williams (R)	$610,740	$53,100	(9%)	$598,846
DISTRICT 8				
Murphy (D)	$3,967,303	$1,157,266	(29%)	$3,834,971
Manion (R)	$1,143,292	$223,290	(20%)	$1,138,048
DISTRICT 9				
Shuster (R)	$988,776	$466,175	(47%)	$979,174
Barr (D)	$43,864	$14,000	(32%)	$47,417
DISTRICT 10				
Carney (D)	$2,348,306	$1,145,890	(49%)	$2,333,358
Hackett (R)	$2,565,110	$269,356	(11%)	$2,553,644
DISTRICT 11				
Kanjorski (D)	$2,517,285	$1,531,728	(61%)	$3,153,006
Barletta (R)	$1,324,951	$257,925	(19%)	$1,315,969
DISTRICT 12				
Murtha (D)	$3,523,106	$1,245,675	(35%)	$3,656,397
Russell (R)	$3,513,269	$12,500	(0%)	$3,492,873
DISTRICT 13				
Schwartz (D)	$3,161,116	$1,095,960	(35%)	$1,745,577
Kats (R)	$500,140	$16,668	(3%)	$500,141
DISTRICT 14				
Doyle (D)	$915,671	$562,668	(61%)	$838,611
DISTRICT 15				
Dent (R)	$1,881,014	$703,353	(37%)	$1,775,398
Bennett (D)	$956,164	$252,855	(26%)	$950,043
DISTRICT 16				
Pitts (R)	$625,290	$420,754	(67%)	$621,729
Slater (D)	$98,458	$14,757	(15%)	$92,274
DISTRICT 17				
Holden (D)	$1,038,657	$684,648	(66%)	$1,096,079
Gilhooley (R)	$106,906	$7,000	(7%)	$104,485

DISTRICT 18				
Murphy (R)	$1,825,275	$954,725	(52%)	$2,073,251
O'Donnell (D)	$552,521	$32,657	(6%)	$556,306
DISTRICT 19				
Platts (R)	$214,284	$0	(0%)	$192,495
Avillo (D)	$59,654	$0	(0%)	$66,601

Rhode Island

	RECEIPTS	FROM PACS		EXPENDITURES
SENIOR SENATOR - 2008				
Reed (D)	$3,962,443	$1,575,299	(40%)	$2,258,706
JUNIOR SENATOR - 2006				
Whitehouse (D)	$6,580,257	$746,035	(11%)	$6,426,874
Chafee (R)	$4,782,343	$1,349,397	(28%)	$5,381,488
DISTRICT 1				
Kennedy (D)	$1,496,417	$459,517	(31%)	$1,791,870
DISTRICT 2				
Langevin (D)	$804,924	$369,325	(46%)	$679,026
Zaccaria (R)	$53,498	$2,325	(4%)	$52,545

South Carolina

	RECEIPTS	FROM PACS		EXPENDITURES
SENIOR SENATOR - 2008				
Graham (R)	$4,634,992	$1,330,505	(29%)	$4,463,619
Conley (D)	$17,105	$0	(0%)	$15,202
JUNIOR SENATOR - 2004				
DeMint (R)	$9,040,100	$2,347,943	(26%)	$9,036,086
Tenenbaum (D)	$6,275,269	$644,938	(10%)	$6,156,183
Tyndall (CNSTP)	$13,319	$0	(0%)	$13,318
DISTRICT 1				
Brown (R)	$976,846	$288,900	(30%)	$1,287,308
Ketner (D)	$2,249,241	$132,175	(6%)	$2,248,361
DISTRICT 2				
Wilson (R)	$1,161,187	$369,515	(32%)	$1,266,821
Miller (D)	$629,487	$40,368	(6%)	$624,365
DISTRICT 3				
Barrett (R)	$1,182,187	$607,931	(51%)	$765,832
Dyer (D)	$84,399	$39,400	(47%)	$82,865
DISTRICT 4				
Inglis (R)	$454,141	$121,124	(27%)	$495,289
Corden (D)	$77,795	$0	(0%)	$75,167
DISTRICT 5				
Spratt (D)	$1,225,278	$819,427	(67%)	$829,176
DISTRICT 6				
Clyburn (D)	$3,076,315	$2,165,470	(70%)	$2,391,430

South Dakota

	RECEIPTS	FROM PACS		EXPENDITURES
SENIOR SENATOR - 2008				
Johnson (D)	$4,473,960	$2,003,588	(45%)	$4,550,590
Dykstra (R)	$906,630	$62,600	(7%)	$905,366
JUNIOR SENATOR - 2004				
Thune (R)	$16,103,023	$1,183,602	(7%)	$14,666,225
Daschle (D)	$19,333,685	$2,807,562	(15%)	$19,975,170
AT LARGE				
Herseth Sandlin (D)	$1,456,448	$829,787	(57%)	$1,568,455
Lien (R)	$606,801	$25,600	(4%)	$606,776

Tennessee

	RECEIPTS	FROM PACS		EXPENDITURES
SENIOR SENATOR - 2008				
Alexander (R)	$5,791,640	$1,688,532	(29%)	$4,571,728
Tuke (D)	$730,299	$33,085	(5%)	$751,915
Lugo (I)	$5,238	$0	(0%)	$5,236
JUNIOR SENATOR - 2006				
Corker (R)	$16,831,072	$1,599,958	(10%)	$18,565,935
Ford (D)	$14,306,467	$1,503,653	(11%)	$15,302,455
DISTRICT 1				
Roe (R)	$803,433	$1,000	(0%)	$717,171
Russell (D)	$10,361	$0	(0%)	$10,354
DISTRICT 2				
Duncan (R)	$658,169	$413,424	(63%)	$511,959
DISTRICT 3				
Wamp (R)	$1,239,746	$361,790	(29%)	$1,440,107
DISTRICT 4				
Davis (D)	$1,062,420	$680,860	(64%)	$1,074,524
Lankford (R)	$532,172	$10,700	(2%)	$528,945
DISTRICT 5				
Cooper (D)	$637,404	$297,445	(47%)	$429,556
Donovan (R)	$12,455	$600	(5%)	$14,240
DISTRICT 6				
Gordon (D)	$1,704,626	$1,225,500	(72%)	$1,123,083
DISTRICT 7				
Blackburn (R)	$1,246,326	$567,148	(46%)	$1,558,273
DISTRICT 8				
Tanner (D)	$1,462,297	$1,229,499	(84%)	$923,816
DISTRICT 9				
Cohen (D)	$1,238,073	$491,574	(40%)	$886,339
Wright (I)	$295,302	$5,410	(2%)	$47,715

Texas

	RECEIPTS	FROM PACS		EXPENDITURES
SENIOR SENATOR - 2006				
Hutchison (R)	$6,378,589	$1,023,385	(16%)	$5,734,146
Radnofsky (D)	$1,482,207	$49,890	(3%)	$1,432,107
JUNIOR SENATOR - 2008				
Cornyn (R)	$13,727,473	$2,613,361	(19%)	$16,454,518
Noriega (D)	$4,166,286	$320,892	(8%)	$4,157,553
Schick (LIBERT)	$8,130	$0	(0%)	$7,370
DISTRICT 1				
Gohmert (R)	$888,649	$181,862	(20%)	$834,732
DISTRICT 2				
Poe (R)	$800,692	$257,250	(32%)	$391,238
DISTRICT 3				
Johnson (R)	$1,213,670	$633,146	(52%)	$1,569,813
Daley (D)	$74,514	$2,250	(3%)	$73,653
DISTRICT 4				
Hall (R)	$1,097,928	$515,847	(47%)	$939,674
Melancon (D)	$83,756	$6,566	(8%)	$83,243
DISTRICT 5				
Hensarling (R)	$1,598,453	$574,876	(36%)	$1,005,714
DISTRICT 6				
Barton (R)	$1,517,025	$1,340,597	(88%)	$1,934,766
Otto (D)	$29,568	$0	(0%)	$29,634

	RECEIPTS	FROM PACS		EXPENDITURES
DISTRICT 7				
Culberson (R)	$1,747,989	$565,235	(32%)	$1,757,226
Skelly (D)	$3,083,681	$89,572	(3%)	$3,080,655
DISTRICT 8				
Brady (R)	$621,911	$537,718	(86%)	$610,288
DISTRICT 9				
Green (D)	$369,156	$269,600	(73%)	$384,442
DISTRICT 10				
Mccaul (R)	$1,723,165	$554,884	(32%)	$1,728,339
Doherty (D)	$1,201,084	$73,685	(6%)	$1,189,406
Finkel (LIBERT)	$13,442	$0	(0%)	$14,673
DISTRICT 11				
Conaway (R)	$1,137,066	$482,587	(42%)	$951,802
DISTRICT 12				
Granger (R)	$1,380,779	$567,812	(41%)	$1,452,977
Smith (D)	$17,172	$2,500	(15%)	$16,300
DISTRICT 13				
Thornberry (R)	$778,206	$170,650	(22%)	$789,264
Waun (D)	$13,149	$2,400	(18%)	$13,211
DISTRICT 14				
Paul (R)	$5,014,283	$36,017	(1%)	$2,735,129
DISTRICT 15				
Hinojosa (D)	$616,104	$335,250	(54%)	$388,362
Zamora (R)	$22,446	$0	(0%)	$23,843
DISTRICT 16				
Reyes (D)	$1,033,251	$440,761	(43%)	$1,034,725
DISTRICT 17				
Edwards (D)	$2,267,333	$1,127,079	(50%)	$2,114,653
Curnock (R)	$110,597	$5,250	(5%)	$109,335
DISTRICT 18				
Jackson Lee (D)	$930,270	$264,517	(28%)	$562,704
Faulk (R)	$59,018	$1,200	(2%)	$59,213
DISTRICT 19				
Neugebauer (R)	$1,283,209	$524,930	(41%)	$1,052,072
Fullingim (D)	$42,225	$0	(0%)	$41,374
DISTRICT 20				
Gonzalez (D)	$870,831	$600,025	(69%)	$821,805
DISTRICT 21				
Smith (R)	$1,242,140	$505,416	(41%)	$1,069,346
DISTRICT 22				
Olson (R)	$2,431,979	$564,767	(23%)	$2,366,149
Lampson (D)	$2,300,044	$1,072,661	(47%)	$2,385,202
Wieder (LIBERT)	$31,088	$0	(0%)	$21,704
DISTRICT 23				
Rodriguez (D)	$2,347,718	$1,308,632	(56%)	$2,356,020
Larson (R)	$814,616	$112,681	(14%)	$813,774
DISTRICT 24				
Marchant (R)	$651,065	$437,050	(67%)	$644,822
Love (D)	$23,226	$2,500	(11%)	$21,990
DISTRICT 25				
Doggett (D)	$1,150,661	$476,343	(41%)	$401,449
Morovich (R)	$68,919	$500	(1%)	$64,134
DISTRICT 26				
Burgess (R)	$1,049,108	$696,873	(66%)	$1,021,104
Leach (D)	$7,421	$0	(0%)	$974
DISTRICT 27				
Ortiz (D)	$794,981	$373,800	(47%)	$719,709
Benavidez (R)	$87,082	$250	(0%)	$81,500

DISTRICT 28			
Cuellar (D)	$1,371,508	$548,182 (40%)	$1,171,941
Fish (R)	$7,453	$0 (0%)	$7,028
DISTRICT 29			
Green (D)	$1,077,277	$842,656 (78%)	$860,643
Story (R)	$14,010	$600 (4%)	$13,200
DISTRICT 30			
Johnson (D)	$527,856	$333,196 (63%)	$459,462
DISTRICT 31			
Carter (R)	$947,701	$365,825 (39%)	$1,053,850
Ruiz (D)	$23,156	$0 (0%)	$23,020
DISTRICT 32			
Sessions (R)	$1,808,588	$742,250 (41%)	$1,629,824
Roberson (D)	$109,996	$1,500 (1%)	$110,003

Utah

	RECEIPTS	FROM PACS	EXPENDITURES
SENIOR SENATOR - 2006			
Hatch (R)	$4,880,281	$1,765,142 (36%)	$3,340,902
Ashdown (D)	$256,050	$9,500 (4%)	$255,729
Bradley (CNSTP)	$24,733	$0 (0%)	$8,225
Price (PC)	$6,172	$200 (3%)	$1,375
JUNIOR SENATOR - 2004			
Bennett (R)	$2,755,838	$1,093,642 (40%)	$2,649,234
Van Dam (D)	$118,226	$18,750 (16%)	$116,959
DISTRICT 1			
Bishop (R)	$309,556	$167,850 (54%)	$325,769
Bowen (D)	$24,278	$2,350 (10%)	$24,587
DISTRICT 2			
Matheson (D)	$1,789,766	$1,378,754 (77%)	$1,389,004
Dew (R)	$665,429	$15,250 (2%)	$632,101
DISTRICT 3			
Chaffetz (R)	$443,395	$166,269 (37%)	$409,628
Spencer (D)	$42,886	$20,495 (48%)	$41,601
Noorlander (CNSTP)	$6,249	$0 (0%)	$6,160

Vermont

	RECEIPTS	FROM PACS	EXPENDITURES
SENIOR SENATOR - 2004			
Leahy (D)	$2,292,393	$1,500 (0%)	$1,531,833
McMullen (R)	$731,028	$2,100 (0%)	$736,126
JUNIOR SENATOR - 2006			
Sanders (I)	$6,179,359	$551,038 (9%)	$6,004,222
Tarrant (R)	$7,315,854	$0 (0%)	$7,300,392
AT LARGE			
Welch (D)	$956,124	$282,470 (30%)	$654,436

Virginia

	RECEIPTS	FROM PACS	EXPENDITURES
SENIOR SENATOR - 2006			
Webb (D)	$8,590,412	$468,957 (5%)	$8,558,861
Allen (R)	$14,994,264	$2,843,031 (19%)	$16,071,564
Parker (IGREEN)	$22,784	$0 (0%)	$19,992

JUNIOR SENATOR - 2008			
Warner (D)	$13,663,049	$2,224,939 (16%)	$12,515,479
Gilmore (R)	$2,437,715	$192,244 (8%)	$2,420,635
Parker (IGREEN)	$48,313	$0 (0%)	$16,946
Redpath (LIBERT)	$44,718	$2,300 (5%)	$49,598
DISTRICT 1†			
Wittman (R)	$998,693	$509,915 (51%)	$952,691
Day (D)	$218,890	$31,703 (14%)	$218,889
Forgit (D)	$120,325	$34,000 (28%)	$126,986
DISTRICT 2			
Nye (D)	$1,360,676	$369,592 (27%)	$1,333,931
Drake (R)	$2,046,092	$943,564 (46%)	$2,033,543
DISTRICT 3			
Scott (D)	$525,140	$240,100 (46%)	$506,728
DISTRICT 4			
Forbes (R)	$729,040	$251,028 (34%)	$942,026
Miller (D)	$48,073	$4,442 (9%)	$37,670
DISTRICT 5			
Perriello (D)	$1,866,778	$203,281 (11%)	$1,822,148
Goode (R)	$1,797,226	$509,602 (28%)	$1,939,824
DISTRICT 6			
Goodlatte (R)	$1,407,767	$632,534 (45%)	$1,996,993
Rasoul (D)	$389,666	$3,107 (1%)	$382,473
Allen (I)	$10,005	$0 (0%)	$10,005
DISTRICT 7			
Cantor (R)	$3,990,894	$1,848,199 (46%)	$3,823,907
Hartke (D)	$75,116	$13,215 (18%)	$63,152
DISTRICT 8			
Moran (D)	$1,286,993	$501,979 (39%)	$1,207,945
Ellmore (R)	$59,385	$0 (0%)	$65,940
DISTRICT 9			
Boucher (D)	$1,750,965	$1,226,947 (70%)	$1,153,918
DISTRICT 10			
Wolf (R)	$2,051,358	$439,525 (21%)	$2,053,375
Feder (D)	$2,201,291	$237,850 (11%)	$2,206,307
Nigam (I)	$7,845	$0 (0%)	$8,815
DISTRICT 11			
Connolly (D)	$1,997,494	$646,596 (32%)	$1,974,640
Fimian (R)	$2,020,214	$130,714 (6%)	$2,010,087

Washington

	RECEIPTS	FROM PACS	EXPENDITURES
SENIOR SENATOR - 2004			
Murray (D)	$11,081,050	$1,691,587 (15%)	$11,556,148
Nethercutt (R)	$8,011,311	$1,326,952 (17%)	$7,726,296
JUNIOR SENATOR - 2006			
Cantwell (D)	$13,725,773	$55,514 (0%)	$14,013,932
McGavick (R)	$10,853,230	$978,417 (9%)	$10,842,132
Guthrie (LIBERT)	$1,255,235	$0 (0%)	$1,243,606
Dixon (GREEN)	$87,749	$0 (0%)	$87,118
Adair (I)	$16,199	$0 (0%)	$16,079
DISTRICT 1			
Inslee (D)	$1,033,928	$508,011 (49%)	$777,233
Ishmael (R)	$51,730	$0 (0%)	$49,230
DISTRICT 2			
Larsen (D)	$1,336,438	$763,024 (57%)	$1,147,005
Bart (R)	$47,105	$1,000 (2%)	$44,576

DISTRICT 3
Baird (D)	$741,621	$379,277 (51%)	$926,288
Delavar (R)	$78,437	$2,106 (3%)	$78,385

DISTRICT 4
Hastings (R)	$615,270	$281,600 (46%)	$682,931
Fearing (D)	$334,382	$32,250 (10%)	$291,784

DISTRICT 5
McMorris Rodgers (R)	$1,442,687	$629,128 (44%)	$1,139,376
Mays (D)	$105,623	$0 (0%)	$101,027

DISTRICT 6
Dicks (D)	$1,390,406	$625,445 (45%)	$1,159,160
Cloud (R)	$17,949	$0 (0%)	$18,408

DISTRICT 7
McDermott (D)	$614,932	$305,991 (50%)	$1,033,233
Beren (R)	$30,879	$1,037 (3%)	$32,329

DISTRICT 8
Reichert (R)	$2,855,897	$952,770 (33%)	$2,852,514
Burner (D)	$4,450,646	$563,557 (13%)	$4,462,884

DISTRICT 9
Smith (D)	$648,477	$384,587 (59%)	$612,066
Postma (R)	$12,679	$0 (0%)	$12,421

West Virginia

	RECEIPTS	FROM PACS	EXPENDITURES
SENIOR SENATOR - 2006			
Byrd (D)	$5,114,217	$1,158,555 (23%)	$4,944,546
Raese (R)	$3,163,848	$128,184 (4%)	$3,147,967
JUNIOR SENATOR - 2008			
Rockefeller (D)	$5,189,461	$1,727,456 (33%)	$4,820,379
Wolfe (R)	$123,862	$1,000 (1%)	$123,720
DISTRICT 1			
Mollohan (D)	$794,864	$369,878 (47%)	$793,612
DISTRICT 2			
Capito (R)	$2,217,838	$912,850 (41%)	$2,283,316
Barth (D)	$1,207,712	$377,763 (31%)	$1,182,701
DISTRICT 3			
Rahall (D)	$794,933	$404,681 (51%)	$592,264

Wisconsin

	RECEIPTS	FROM PACS	EXPENDITURES
SENIOR SENATOR - 2006			
Kohl (D)	$6,438,431	$450 (0%)	$6,347,126
Lorge (R)	$175,772	$0 (0%)	$176,987
Vogeler (WG)	$49,733	$227 (0%)	$48,669
JUNIOR SENATOR - 2004			
Feingold (D)	$8,377,885	$684,717 (8%)	$9,239,908
Michels (R)	$5,547,838	$397,532 (7%)	$5,542,087
DISTRICT 1			
Ryan (R)	$1,653,204	$722,184 (44%)	$2,251,389
Krupp (D)	$161,564	$32,615 (20%)	$143,292
DISTRICT 2			
Baldwin (D)	$1,471,218	$418,559 (28%)	$1,159,239
Theron (R)	$27,430	$0 (0%)	$27,213
DISTRICT 3			
Kind (D)	$1,301,638	$891,940 (69%)	$916,105
Stark (R)	$46,071	$0 (0%)	$34,657

DISTRICT 4
Moore (D)	$546,188	$397,295 (73%)	$559,761

DISTRICT 5
Sensenbrenner (R)	$479,866	$231,298 (48%)	$567,709
Burkee (R)	$80,476	$0 (0%)	$80,601

DISTRICT 6
Petri (R)	$769,225	$549,733 (71%)	$635,888
Kittelson (D)	$18,202	$500 (3%)	$17,207

DISTRICT 7
Obey (D)	$1,749,164	$1,065,634 (61%)	$1,560,229
Mielke (R)	$93,682	$1,300 (1%)	$92,501

DISTRICT 8
Kagen (D)	$2,170,739	$1,094,227 (50%)	$2,218,166
Gard (R)	$1,604,691	$461,589 (29%)	$1,597,322

Wyoming

	RECEIPTS	FROM PACS	EXPENDITURES
SENIOR SENATOR - 2008			
Enzi (R)	$1,648,563	$1,190,521 (72%)	$1,247,841
Rothfuss (D)	$32,326	$0 (0%)	$27,258
JUNIOR SENATOR - 2008			
Barrasso (R)	$2,585,977	$1,340,567 (52%)	$1,981,441
Carter (D)	$210,914	$81,000 (38%)	$273,688
AT LARGE			
Lummis (R)	$1,530,454	$386,500 (25%)	$1,517,018
Trauner (D)	$1,672,702	$377,838 (23%)	$1,716,008

Delegates

	RECEIPTS	FROM PACS	EXPENDITURES
AMERICAN SAMOA			
Faleomavaega (D)	$119,020	$17,500 (15%)	$115,861
Lancaster (I)	$7,400	$0 (0%)	$9,181
DISTRICT OF COLUMBIA			
Norton (D)	$446,781	$170,425 (38%)	$380,917
GUAM			
Bordallo (D)	$262,275	$45,850 (17%)	$152,538
NORTHERN MARIANA ISLANDS			
Sablan (I)	$22,931	$0 (0%)	$22,803
Lizama (I)	$75,302	$0 (0%)	$75,201
Tenorio (R)	$54,565	$0 (0%)	$60,730
Gonzales (I)	$21,165	$0 (0%)	$18,982
Cing (D)	$10,756	$0 (0%)	$6,025
PUERTO RICO			
Pierluisi (D)	$1,597,246	$18,050 (1%)	$1,528,434
Salazar (D)	$470,827	$10,800 (2%)	$527,119
Martinez-Birriel (I)	$13,475	$0 (0%)	$13,390
VIRGIN ISLANDS			
Christensen (D)	$233,098	$121,300 (52%)	$220,090

House Committees

House standing and select committees are listed alphabetically. Membership is in order of seniority on the panel. Subcommittee membership is listed in order of seniority. Partisan committees are on page 1195.

In the full committee rosters Democrats are in roman type and Republicans are in *italics*. A vacancy indicates that a committee or subcommittee seat had not been filled at press time, May 2009. Subcommittee vacancies do not necessarily indicate vacancies on full committees or vice versa.

The telephone area code for Washington, D.C., is 202. The ZIP code for all House office buildings is 20515.

AGRICULTURE

Phone: 225-2171   Office: 1301 Longworth

DEMOCRATS (28)	REPUBLICANS (18)
Collin C. Peterson, Minn., chairman	*Frank D. Lucas, Okla.*
Tim Holden, Pa.	*Robert W. Goodlatte, Va.*
Mike McIntyre, N.C.	*Jerry Moran, Kan.*
Leonard L. Boswell, Iowa	*Timothy V. Johnson, Ill.*
Joe Baca, Calif.	*Sam Graves, Mo.*
Dennis Cardoza, Calif.	*Mike D. Rogers, Ala.*
David Scott, Ga.	*Steve King, Iowa*
Jim Marshall, Ga.	*Randy Neugebauer, Texas*
Stephanie Herseth Sandlin, S.D.	*K. Michael Conaway, Texas*
Henry Cuellar, Texas	*Jeff Fortenberry, Neb.*
Jim Costa, Calif.	*Jean Schmidt, Ohio*
Brad Ellsworth, Ind.	*Adrian Smith, Neb.*
Tim Walz, Minn.	*Bob Latta, Ohio*
Steve Kagen, Wis.	*Phil Roe, Tenn.*
Kurt Schrader, Ore.	*Blaine Luetkemeyer, Mo.*
Debbie Halvorson, Ill.	*Glenn Thompson, Pa.*
Kathy Dahlkemper, Pa.	*Bill Cassidy, La.*
Eric Massa, N.Y.	*Cynthia M. Lummis, Wyo.*
Bobby Bright, Ala.	
Betsy Markey, Colo.	
Frank Kratovil Jr., Md.	
Mark Schauer, Mich.	
Larry Kissell, N.C.	
John Boccieri, Ohio	
Scott Murphy, N.Y.	
Earl Pomeroy, N.D.	
Travis W. Childers, Miss.	
Walt Minnick, Idaho	

CONSERVATION, CREDIT, ENERGY & RESEARCH

Holden (chairman), Herseth Sandlin, Halvorson, Dahlkemper, Markey, Schauer, Kissell, Boccieri, McIntyre, Costa, Ellsworth, Walz, Massa, Bright, Kratovil, Minnick, Pomeroy, Vacancy
Goodlatte, Moran, Graves, Rogers, King, Neugebauer, Schmidt, Smith, Latta, Luetkemeyer, Thompson, Cassidy

GENERAL FARM COMMODITIES & RISK MANAGEMENT

Boswell (chairman), Marshall, Ellsworth, Walz, Schrader, Herseth Sandlin, Markey, Kissell, Halvorson, Pomeroy, Childers
Moran, Johnson, Graves, King, Conaway, Latta, Luetkemeyer

HORTICULTURE & ORGANIC AGRICULTURE

Cardoza (chairman), Massa, Costa, Schrader, Kratovil, Vacancy
Schmidt, Moran, Johnson, Lummis

LIVESTOCK, DAIRY & POULTRY

Scott (chairman), Costa, Kagen, Kratovil, Holden, Boswell, Baca, Cardoza, Markey, Minnick, Vacancy
Neugebauer, Goodlatte, Rogers, King, Conaway, Smith, Roe

OPERATIONS, OVERSIGHT, NUTRITION & FORESTRY

Baca (chairman), Cuellar, Kagen, Schrader, Dahlkemper, Childers
Fortenberry, King Schmidt, Lummis

RURAL DEVELOPMENT, BIOTECHNOLOGY, SPECIALTY CROPS & FOREIGN AGRICULTURE

McIntyre (chairman), Bright, Marshall, Cuellar, Kissell, Minnick
Conaway, Roe, Thompson, Cassidy

APPROPRIATIONS

Phone: 225-2771 Office: H-218 Capitol

DEMOCRATS (37)

David R. Obey, Wis., chairman
John P. Murtha, Pa.
Norm Dicks, Wash.
Alan B. Mollohan, W.Va.
Marcy Kaptur, Ohio
Peter J. Visclosky, Ind.
Nita M. Lowey, N.Y.
José E. Serrano, N.Y.
Rosa DeLauro, Conn.
James P. Moran, Va.
John W. Olver, Mass.
Ed Pastor, Ariz.
David E. Price, N.C.
Chet Edwards, Texas
Patrick J. Kennedy, R.I.
Maurice D. Hinchey, N.Y.
Lucille Roybal-Allard, Calif.
Sam Farr, Calif.
Jesse L. Jackson Jr., Ill.
Carolyn
   Cheeks Kilpatrick, Mich.
Allen Boyd, Fla.
Chaka Fattah, Pa.
Steven R. Rothman, N.J.
Sanford D. Bishop Jr., Ga.
Marion Berry, Ark.
Barbara Lee, Calif.
Adam B. Schiff, Calif.
Michael M. Honda, Calif.
Betty McCollum, Minn.
Steve Israel, N.Y.
Tim Ryan, Ohio
C.A. Dutch
   Ruppersberger, Md.
Ben Chandler, Ky.
Debbie
   Wasserman Schultz, Fla.
Ciro D. Rodriguez, Texas
Lincoln Davis, Tenn.
John Salazar, Colo.

REPUBLICANS (23)

Jerry Lewis, Calif.
C.W. Bill Young, Fla.
Harold Rogers, Ky.
Frank R. Wolf, Va.
Jack Kingston, Ga.
Rodney Frelinghuysen, N.J.
Todd Tiahrt, Kan.
Zach Wamp, Tenn.
Tom Latham, Iowa
Robert B. Aderholt, Ala.
Jo Ann Emerson, Mo.
Kay Granger, Texas
Mike Simpson, Idaho
John Culberson, Texas
Mark Steven Kirk, Ill.
Ander Crenshaw, Fla.
Denny Rehberg, Mont.
John Carter, Texas
Rodney Alexander, La.
Ken Calvert, Calif.
Jo Bonner, Ala.
Steven C. LaTourette, Ohio
Tom Cole, Okla.

AGRICULTURE

DeLauro (chairwoman), Farr, Boyd, Bishop, Davis, Kaptur, Hinchey, Jackson
Kingston, Latham, Emerson, Alexander

COMMERCE-JUSTICE-SCIENCE

Mollohan (chairman), Kennedy, Fattah, Schiff, Honda, Ruppersberger, Visclosky, Serrano
Wolf, Culberson, Aderholt, Bonner

DEFENSE

Murtha (chairman), Dicks, Visclosky, Moran, Kaptur, Boyd, Rothman, Bishop, Hinchey, Kilpatrick
Young, Frelinghuysen, Tiahrt, Kingston, Granger, Rogers

ENERGY-WATER

Visclosky (chairman), Edwards, Pastor, Berry, Fattah, Israel, Ryan, Olver, Davis, Salazar
Frelinghuysen, Wamp, Simpson, Rehberg, Calvert, Alexander

FINANCIAL SERVICES

Serrano (chairman), Wasserman Schultz, DeLauro, Edwards, Boyd, Fattah, Lee, Schiff
Emerson, Culberson, Kirk, Crenshaw

HOMELAND SECURITY

Price (chairman), Serrano, Rodriguez, Ruppersberger, Mollohan, Lowey, Roybal-Allard, Farr, Rothman
Rogers, Carter, Culberson, Kirk, Calvert

INTERIOR-ENVIRONMENT

Dicks (chairman), Moran, Mollohan, Chandler, Hinchey, Olver, Pastor, Price
Simpson, Calvert, LaTourette, Cole

LABOR-HHS-EDUCATION

Obey (chairman), Lowey, DeLauro, Jackson, Kennedy, Roybal-Allard, Lee, Honda, McCollum, Ryan, Moran
Tiahrt, Rehberg, Alexander, Bonner, Cole

LEGISLATIVE BRANCH

Wasserman Schultz (chairwoman), Honda, McCollum, Ryan, Ruppersberger, Rodriguez
Aderholt, LaTourette, Cole

MILITARY CONSTRUCTION-VA

Edwards (chairman), Farr, Salazar, Dicks, Kennedy, Bishop, Berry, Israel
Wamp, Crenshaw, Young, Carter

STATE-FOREIGN OPERATIONS

Lowey (chairwoman), Jackson, Schiff, Israel, Chandler, Rothman, Lee, McCollum
Granger, Kirk, Crenshaw, Rehberg

TRANSPORTATION-HUD

Olver (chairman), Pastor, Rodriguez, Kaptur, Price, Roybal-Allard, Berry, Kilpatrick
Latham, Wolf, Carter, LaTourette

SELECT INTELLIGENCE OVERSIGHT*

Holt (chairman), Obey, Murtha, Reyes, Dicks, Lowey, Schiff, Israel
Calvert, Lewis, Young, Hoekstra, Frelinghuysen

* The panel's required designees from the Select Intelligence Committee are Peter Hoekstra, R-Mich., Rush D. Holt, D-N.J., and Silvestre Reyes, D-Texas.

ARMED SERVICES

Phone: 225-4151   Office: 2120 Rayburn

DEMOCRATS (37)	REPUBLICANS (25)
Ike Skelton, Mo., chairman	John M. McHugh, N.Y.
John M. Spratt Jr., S.C.	Roscoe G. Bartlett, Md.
Solomon P. Ortiz, Texas	Howard P. "Buck"
Gene Taylor, Miss.	McKeon, Calif.
Neil Abercrombie, Hawaii	William M. "Mac"
Silvestre Reyes, Texas	Thornberry, Texas
Vic Snyder, Ark.	Walter B. Jones, N.C.
Adam Smith, Wash.	Todd Akin, Mo.
Loretta Sanchez, Calif.	J. Randy Forbes, Va.
Mike McIntyre, N.C.	Jeff Miller, Fla.
Ellen O. Tauscher, Calif.	Joe Wilson, S.C.
Robert A. Brady, Pa.	Frank A. LoBiondo, N.J.
Robert E. Andrews, N.J.	Rob Bishop, Utah
Susan A. Davis, Calif.	Michael R. Turner, Ohio
Jim Langevin, R.I.	John Kline, Minn.
Rick Larsen, Wash.	Mike D. Rogers, Ala.
Jim Cooper, Tenn.	Trent Franks, Ariz.
Jim Marshall, Ga.	Bill Shuster, Pa.
Madeleine Z. Bordallo, Guam	Cathy
Brad Ellsworth, Ind.	McMorris Rodgers, Wash.
Patrick J. Murphy, Pa.	K. Michael Conaway, Texas
Hank Johnson, Ga.	Doug Lamborn, Colo.
Carol Shea-Porter, N.H.	Rob Wittman, Va.
Joe Courtney, Conn.	Mary Fallin, Okla.
Dave Loebsack, Iowa	Duncan Hunter, Calif.
Joe Sestak, Pa.	John Fleming, La.
Gabrielle Giffords, Ariz.	Mike Coffman, Colo.
Niki Tsongas, Mass.	Tom Rooney, Fla.
Glenn Nye, Va.	
Chellie Pingree, Maine	
Larry Kissell, N.C.	
Martin Heinrich, N.M.	
Frank Kratovil Jr., Md.	
Eric Massa, N.Y.	
Bobby Bright, Ala.	
Scott Murphy, N.Y.	
Dan Boren, Okla.	

AIR & LAND FORCES

Abercrombie (chairman), Spratt, Reyes, Smith, McIntyre, Tauscher, Brady, Cooper, Marshall, Sestak, Giffords, Tsongas, Kissell, Kratovil, Massa, Bright, Vacancy
Bartlett, McMorris Rodgers, Fallin, Hunter, Fleming, Coffman, McKeon, Akin, Miller, Wilson, LoBiondo, Bishop, Turner

MILITARY PERSONNEL

Davis (chairwoman), Snyder, Sanchez, Bordallo, Murphy, Johnson, Shea-Porter, Loebsack, Tsongas
Wilson, Jones, Kline, Rooney, Fallin, Fleming

OVERSIGHT & INVESTIGATIONS

Snyder (chairman), Spratt, Sanchez, Tauscher, Davis, Cooper, Sestak, Nye, Pingree
Wittman, Jones, Rogers, Franks, McMorris Rodgers, Lamborn, Hunter

READINESS

Ortiz (chairman), Taylor, Abercrombie, Reyes, Marshall, Bordallo, Johnson, Shea-Porter, Courtney, Loebsack, Giffords, Nye, Kissell, Heinrich, Kratovil, Bright, Vacancy
Forbes, Bishop, Rogers, Franks, Shuster, McMorris Rodgers, Conaway, Lamborn, Wittman, Fallin, Fleming, LoBiondo

SEAPOWER & EXPEDITIONARY FORCES

Taylor (chairman), Ortiz, Langevin, Larsen, Ellsworth, Courtney, Sestak, Nye, Pingree, Massa
Akin, Wittman, Bartlett, Forbes, Hunter, Coffman, Rooney

STRATEGIC FORCES

Tauscher (chairwoman), Spratt, Sanchez, Andrews, Langevin, Larsen, Heinrich, Vacancy
Turner, McKeon, Thornberry, Franks, Lamborn

TERRORISM, UNCONVENTIONAL THREATS & CAPABILITIES

Smith (chairman), McIntyre, Andrews, Langevin, Cooper, Marshall, Ellsworth, Murphy, Bright, Vacancy
Miller, LoBiondo, Kline, Shuster, Conaway, Rooney, Thornberry

DEFENSE ACQUISITION REFORM

Andrews (chairman), Cooper, Ellsworth, Sestak
Conaway, Hunter, Coffman

BUDGET

Phone: 226-7200   Office: 207 Cannon

DEMOCRATS (24)	REPUBLICANS (15)
John M. Spratt Jr., S.C., chairman	Paul D. Ryan, Wis.
Allyson Y. Schwartz, Pa.	Jeb Hensarling, Texas
Marcy Kaptur, Ohio	Scott Garrett, N.J.
Xavier Becerra, Calif.	Mario Diaz-Balart, Fla.
Lloyd Doggett, Texas	Mike Simpson, Idaho
Earl Blumenauer, Ore.	Patrick T. McHenry, N.C.
Marion Berry, Ark.	Connie Mack, Fla.
Allen Boyd, Fla.	John Campbell, Calif.
Jim McGovern, Mass.	Jim Jordan, Ohio
Niki Tsongas, Mass.	Cynthia M. Lummis, Wyo.
Bob Etheridge, N.C.	Steve Austria, Ohio
Betty McCollum, Minn.	Robert B. Aderholt, Ala.
Charlie Melancon, La.	Devin Nunes, Calif.
John Yarmuth, Ky.	Gregg Harper, Miss.
Robert E. Andrews, N.J.	Bob Latta, Ohio
Rosa DeLauro, Conn.	
Chet Edwards, Texas	
Robert C. Scott, Va.	
Jim Langevin, R.I.	
Rick Larsen, Wash.	
Timothy H. Bishop, N.Y.	
Gwen Moore, Wis.	
Gerald E. Connolly, Va.	
Kurt Schrader, Ore.	

EDUCATION & LABOR
Phone: 225-3725 Office: 2181 Rayburn

DEMOCRATS (30)
George Miller, Calif., chairman
Dale E. Kildee, Mich.
Donald M. Payne, N.J.
Robert E. Andrews, N.J.
Robert C. Scott, Va.
Lynn Woolsey, Calif.
Rubén Hinojosa, Texas
Carolyn McCarthy, N.Y.
John F. Tierney, Mass.
Dennis J. Kucinich, Ohio
David Wu, Ore.
Rush D. Holt, N.J.
Susan A. Davis, Calif.
Raúl M. Grijalva, Ariz.
Timothy H. Bishop, N.Y.
Joe Sestak, Pa.
Dave Loebsack, Iowa
Mazie K. Hirono, Hawaii
Jason Altmire, Pa.
Phil Hare, Ill.
Yvette D. Clarke, N.Y.
Joe Courtney, Conn.
Carol Shea-Porter, N.H.
Marcia L. Fudge, Ohio
Jared Polis, Colo.
Paul Tonko, N.Y.
Pedro R. Pierluisi, P.R.
Gregorio Kilili Camacho
Sablan, N. Marianas
Dina Titus, Nev.
Vacancy

REPUBLICANS (19)
Howard P. "Buck"
McKeon, Calif.
Tom Petri, Wis.
Peter Hoekstra, Mich.
Michael N. Castle, Del.
Mark Souder, Ind.
Vernon J. Ehlers, Mich.
Judy Biggert, Ill.
Todd R. Platts, Pa.
Joe Wilson, S.C.
John Kline, Minn.
Cathy
McMorris Rodgers, Wash.
Tom Price, Ga.
Rob Bishop, Utah
Brett Guthrie, Ky.
Bill Cassidy, La.
Tom McClintock, Calif.
Duncan Hunter, Calif.
Phil Roe, Tenn.
Glenn Thompson, Pa.

EARLY CHILDHOOD, ELEMENTARY & SECONDARY EDUCATION
Kildee (chairman), Payne, Scott, Holt, Davis, Grijalva, Sestak, Loebsack, Hirono, Polis, Pierluisi, Sablan, Woolsey, Hinojosa, Kucinich, Altmire, Titus, Vacancy
Castle, Petri, Hoekstra, Souder, Ehlers, Biggert, Platts, McMorris Rodgers, Bishop, Cassidy, McClintock, Hunter

HEALTH, EMPLOYMENT, LABOR & PENSIONS
Andrews (chairman), Wu, Hare, Tierney, Kucinich, Fudge, Kildee, McCarthy, Holt, Sestak, Loebsack, Clarke, Courtney
Kline, Wilson, McMorris Rodgers, Price, Guthrie, McClintock, Hunter, Roe

HEALTHY FAMILIES & COMMUNITIES
McCarthy (chairwoman), Clarke, Scott, Shea-Porter, Tonko, Polis, Miller, Vacancy
Platts, McKeon, Guthrie, Roe, Thompson

HIGHER EDUCATION, LIFELONG LEARNING & COMPETITIVENESS
Hinojosa (chairman), Bishop , Altmire, Courtney, Tonko, Titus, Andrews, Tierney, Wu, Davis, Hirono, Fudge, Polis, Pierluisi
Guthrie, McKeon, Castle, Souder, Ehlers, Biggert, Cassidy, Roe, Thompson

WORKFORCE PROTECTIONS
Woolsey (chairwoman), Shea-Porter, Payne, Grijalva, Bishop, Hare, Sablan
Price, Hoekstra, Wilson, Kline

ENERGY & COMMERCE
Phone: 225-2927 Office: 2125 Rayburn

DEMOCRATS (36)
Henry A. Waxman, Calif., chairman
John D. Dingell, Mich.
Edward J. Markey, Mass.
Rick Boucher, Va.
Frank Pallone Jr., N.J.
Bart Gordon, Tenn.
Bobby L. Rush, Ill.
Anna G. Eshoo, Calif.
Bart Stupak, Mich.
Eliot L. Engel, N.Y.
Gene Green, Texas
Diana DeGette, Colo.
Lois Capps, Calif.
Mike Doyle, Pa.
Jane Harman, Calif.
Jan Schakowsky, Ill.
Charlie Gonzalez, Texas
Jay Inslee, Wash.
Tammy Baldwin, Wis.
Mike Ross, Ark.
Anthony Weiner, N.Y.
Jim Matheson, Utah
G.K. Butterfield, N.C.
Charlie Melancon, La.
John Barrow, Ga.
Baron P. Hill, Ind.
Doris Matsui, Calif.
Donna M.C. Christensen, V.I.
Kathy Castor, Fla.
John Sarbanes, Md.
Christopher S. Murphy, Conn.
Zack Space, Ohio
Jerry McNerney, Calif.
Betty Sutton, Ohio
Bruce Braley, Iowa
Peter Welch, Vt.

REPUBLICANS (23)
Joe L. Barton, Texas
Ralph M. Hall, Texas
Fred Upton, Mich.
Cliff Stearns, Fla.
Nathan Deal, Ga.
Ed Whitfield, Ky.
John Shimkus, Ill.
John Shadegg, Ariz.
Roy Blunt, Mo.
Steve Buyer, Ind.
George Radanovich, Calif.
Joe Pitts, Pa.
Mary Bono Mack, Calif.
Greg Walden, Ore.
Lee Terry, Neb.
Mike Rogers, Mich.
Sue Myrick, N.C.
John Sullivan, Okla.
Tim Murphy, Pa.
Michael C. Burgess, Texas
Marsha Blackburn, Tenn.
Phil Gingrey, Ga.
Steve Scalise, La.

COMMERCE, TRADE & CONSUMER PROTECTION
Rush (chairman), Schakowsky, Sarbanes, Sutton, Pallone, Gordon, Stupak, Green, Gonzalez, Weiner, Matheson, Butterfield, Barrow, Matsui, Castor, Space, Braley, DeGette
Radanovich, Stearns, Whitfield, Pitts, Bono Mack, Terry, Myrick, Sullivan, Murphy, Gingrey, Scalise

COMMUNICATIONS, TECHNOLOGY & THE INTERNET
Boucher (chairman), Markey, Gordon, Rush, Eshoo, Stupak, DeGette, Doyle, Inslee, Weiner, Butterfield, Melancon, Hill, Matsui, Christensen, Castor, Murphy, Space, McNerney, Welch, Dingell
Stearns, Upton, Deal, Shimkus, Shadegg, Blunt, Buyer, Radanovich, Bono Mack, Walden, Terry, Rogers, Blackburn

ENERGY & THE ENVIRONMENT
Markey (chairman), Doyle, Inslee, Butterfield, Melancon, Hill, Matsui, McNerney, Welch, Dingell, Boucher, Pallone, Engel, Green, Capps, Harman, Gonzalez, Baldwin, Ross, Matheson, Barrow
Upton, Hall, Stearns, Whitfield, Shimkus, Shadegg, Blunt, Pitts, Bono Mack, Walden, Sullivan, Burgess, Scalise

HEALTH

Pallone (chairman), Dingell, Gordon, Eshoo, Engel, Green, DeGette, Capps, Schakowsky, Baldwin, Ross, Weiner, Matheson, Harman, Gonzalez, Barrow, Christensen, Castor, Sarbanes, Murphy, Space, Sutton, Braley
Deal, Hall, Whitfield, Shimkus, Shadegg, Blunt, Buyer, Pitts, Rogers, Myrick, Murphy, Burgess, Blackburn, Gingrey

OVERSIGHT & INVESTIGATIONS

Stupak (chairman), Braley, Markey, DeGette, Doyle, Schakowsky, Ross, Christensen, Welch, Green, Sutton
Walden, Deal, Radanovich, Sullivan, Burgess, Blackburn, Gingrey

FINANCIAL SERVICES

Phone: 225-4247   Office: 2129 Rayburn

DEMOCRATS (42)	REPUBLICANS (29)
Barney Frank, Mass., chairman	*Spencer Bachus, Ala.*
Paul E. Kanjorski, Pa.	*Michael N. Castle, Del.*
Maxine Waters, Calif.	*Peter T. King, N.Y.*
Carolyn B. Maloney, N.Y.	*Ed Royce, Calif.*
Luis V. Gutierrez, Ill.	*Frank D. Lucas, Okla.*
Nydia M. Velázquez, N.Y.	*Ron Paul, Texas*
Melvin Watt, N.C.	*Donald Manzullo, Ill.*
Gary L. Ackerman, N.Y.	*Walter B. Jones, N.C.*
Brad Sherman, Calif.	*Judy Biggert, Ill.*
Gregory W. Meeks, N.Y.	*Gary G. Miller, Calif.*
Dennis Moore, Kan.	*Shelley Moore Capito, W.Va.*
Michael E. Capuano, Mass.	*Jeb Hensarling, Texas*
Rubén Hinojosa, Texas	*Scott Garrett, N.J.*
William Lacy Clay, Mo.	*J. Gresham Barrett, S.C.*
Carolyn McCarthy, N.Y.	*Jim Gerlach, Pa.*
Joe Baca, Calif.	*Randy Neugebauer, Texas*
Stephen F. Lynch, Mass.	*Tom Price, Ga.*
Brad Miller, N.C.	*Patrick T. McHenry, N.C.*
David Scott, Ga.	*John Campbell, Calif.*
Al Green, Texas	*Adam H. Putnam, Fla.*
Emanuel Cleaver II, Mo.	*Michele Bachmann, Minn.*
Melissa Bean, Ill.	*Kenny Marchant, Texas*
Gwen Moore, Wis.	*Thaddeus McCotter, Mich.*
Paul W. Hodes, N.H.	*Kevin McCarthy, Calif.*
Keith Ellison, Minn.	*Bill Posey, Fla.*
Ron Klein, Fla.	*Lynn Jenkins, Kan.*
Charlie Wilson, Ohio	*Christopher Lee, N.Y.*
Ed Perlmutter, Colo.	*Erik Paulsen, Minn.*
Joe Donnelly, Ind.	*Leonard Lance, N.J.*
Bill Foster, Ill.	
André Carson, Ind.	
Jackie Speier, Calif.	
Travis W. Childers, Miss.	
Walt Minnick, Idaho	
John Adler, N.J.	
Mary Jo Kilroy, Ohio	
Steve Driehaus, Ohio	
Suzanne M. Kosmas, Fla.	
Alan Grayson, Fla.	
Jim Himes, Conn.	
Gary Peters, Mich.	
Dan Maffei, N.Y.	

CAPITAL MARKETS, INSURANCE & GSES

Kanjorski (chairman), Ackerman, Sherman, Capuano, Hinojosa, McCarthy , Baca, Lynch, Miller, Scott, Velázquez, Maloney, Bean, Moore (Wis.), Hodes, Klein, Perlmutter, Donnelly, Carson, Speier, Childers, Wilson, Foster, Minnick, Adler, Kilroy, Kosmas, Grayson, Himes, Peters
Garrett, Price, Castle, King, Lucas, Manzullo, Royce, Biggert, Capito, Hensarling, Putnam, Barrett, Gerlach, Campbell, Bachmann, McCotter, Neugebauer, McCarthy, Posey, Jenkins

DOMESTIC MONETARY POLICY & TECHNOLOGY

Watt (chairman), Maloney, Meeks, Clay, Sherman, Green, Cleaver, Ellison, Adler, Kosmas
Paul, Castle, Lucas, Gerlach, Price, Posey, Lance

FINANCIAL INSTITUTIONS & CONSUMER CREDIT

Gutierrez (chairman), Maloney, Watt, Ackerman, Sherman, Moore (Kan.), Kanjorski, Waters, Hinojosa, McCarthy, Baca, Green, Clay, Miller, Scott, Cleaver, Bean, Hodes, Ellison, Klein, Wilson, Meeks, Foster, Perlmutter, Speier, Childers, Minnick
Hensarling, Barrett, Castle, King, Royce, Jones, Capito, Garrett, Gerlach, Neugebauer, Price, McHenry, Campbell, McCarthy, Marchant, Lee, Paulsen, Lance

HOUSING & COMMUNITY OPPORTUNITY

Waters (chairwoman), Velázquez, Lynch, Cleaver, Green, Clay, Ellison, Donnelly, Capuano, Kanjorski, Gutierrez, Driehaus, Kilroy, Himes, Maffei
Capito, McCotter, Biggert, Miller, Neugebauer, Jones, Putnam, Marchant, Jenkins, Lee

OVERSIGHT & INVESTIGATIONS

Moore (Kan.) (chairman), Lynch, Klein, Speier, Moore (Wis.), Adler, Kilroy, Driehaus, Grayson
Biggert, McHenry, Paul, Bachmann, Lee, Paulsen

INTERNATIONAL MONETARY POLICY & TRADE

Meeks (chairman), Gutierrez, Waters, Watt, Moore (Wis.), Carson, Driehaus, Peters, Maffei
Miller, Royce, Paul, Manzullo, Bachmann, Paulsen

FOREIGN AFFAIRS

Phone: 225-5021   Office: 2170 Rayburn

DEMOCRATS (28)	REPUBLICANS (19)
Howard L. Berman, Calif., chairman	*Ileana Ros-Lehtinen, Fla.*
Gary L. Ackerman, N.Y.	*Christopher H. Smith, N.J.*
Eni F.H. Faleomavaega, A.S.	*Dan Burton, Ind.*
Donald M. Payne, N.J.	*Elton Gallegly, Calif.*
Brad Sherman, Calif.	*Dana Rohrabacher, Calif.*
Robert Wexler, Fla.	*Donald Manzullo, Ill.*
Eliot L. Engel, N.Y.	*Ed Royce, Calif.*
Bill Delahunt, Mass.	*Ron Paul, Texas*
Gregory W. Meeks, N.Y.	*Jeff Flake, Ariz.*
Diane Watson, Calif.	*Mike Pence, Ind.*
Russ Carnahan, Mo.	*Joe Wilson, S.C.*
Albio Sires, N.J.	*John Boozman, Ark.*
Gerald E. Connolly, Va.	*J. Gresham Barrett, S.C.*
Michael E. McMahon, N.Y.	*Connie Mack, Fla.*
John Tanner, Tenn.	*Jeff Fortenberry, Neb.*
Gene Green, Texas	*Michael McCaul, Texas*
Lynn Woolsey, Calif.	*Ted Poe, Texas*
Sheila Jackson Lee, Texas	*Bob Inglis, S.C.*
Barbara Lee, Calif.	*Gus Bilirakis, Fla.*
Shelley Berkley, Nev.	
Joseph Crowley, N.Y.	
Mike Ross, Ark.	
Brad Miller, N.C.	
David Scott, Ga.	
Jim Costa, Calif.	
Keith Ellison, Minn.	
Gabrielle Giffords, Ariz.	
Ron Klein, Fla.	

AFRICA & GLOBAL HEALTH

Payne (chairman), Watson, Woolsey, Lee, Miller, Meeks, Jackson Lee
Smith, Flake, Boozman, Fortenberry

ASIA, THE PACIFIC & THE GLOBAL ENVIRONMENT

Faleomavaega (chairman), Ackerman, Watson, Ross, Sherman, Engel, Meeks
Manzullo, Inglis, Rohrabacher, Royce, Flake

EUROPE

Wexler (chairman), Tanner, Delahunt, Sires, McMahon, Berkley, Miller, Scott, Costa
Gallegly, Bilirakis, Wilson, Poe, Boozman, Inglis, Barrett

INTERNATIONAL ORGANIZATIONS, HUMAN RIGHTS & OVERSIGHT

Delahunt (chairman), Carnahan, Ellison, Payne, Wexler
Rohrabacher, Paul, Poe

MIDDLE EAST & SOUTH ASIA

Ackerman (chairman), Carnahan, McMahon, Jackson Lee, Berkley, Crowley, Ross, Costa, Ellison, Klein, Sherman, Wexler, Engel, Connolly, Green
Burton, Wilson, Barrett, Fortenberry, McCaul, Inglis, Bilirakis, Rohrabacher, Royce

TERRORISM, NONPROLIFERATION & TRADE

Sherman (chairman), Connolly, Scott, Watson, McMahon, Jackson Lee, Klein
Royce, Poe, Manzullo, Boozman, Barrett

WESTERN HEMISPHERE

Engel (chairman), Meeks, Sires, Green, Giffords, Faleomavaega, Payne, Tanner, Lee, Crowley, Klein
Mack, McCaul, Smith, Burton, Gallegly, Paul, Fortenberry, Bilirakis

HOMELAND SECURITY

Phone: 226-2616   Office: H2-176 Ford

DEMOCRATS (21)	REPUBLICANS (13)
Bennie Thompson, Miss., chairman	*Peter T. King, N.Y.*
Loretta Sanchez, Calif.	*Lamar Smith, Texas*
Jane Harman, Calif.	*Mark Souder, Ind.*
Peter A. DeFazio, Ore.	*Dan Lungren, Calif.*
Eleanor Holmes Norton, D.C.	*Mike D. Rogers, Ala.*
Zoe Lofgren, Calif.	*Michael McCaul, Texas*
Sheila Jackson Lee, Texas	*Charlie Dent, Pa.*
Henry Cuellar, Texas	*Gus Bilirakis, Fla.*
Christopher Carney, Pa.	*Paul Broun, Ga.*
Yvette D. Clarke, N.Y.	*Candice S. Miller, Mich.*
Laura Richardson, Calif.	*Pete Olson, Texas*
Ann Kirkpatrick, Ariz.	*Anh "Joseph" Cao, La.*
Ben Ray Luján, N.M.	*Steve Austria, Ohio*
Bill Pascrell Jr., N.J.	
Emanuel Cleaver II, Mo.	
Al Green, Texas	
Jim Himes, Conn.	
Mary Jo Kilroy, Ohio	
Eric Massa, N.Y.	
Dina Titus, Nev.	
Vacancy	

BORDER, MARITIME & GLOBAL COUNTERTERRORISM

Sanchez (chairwoman), Harman, Lofgren, Jackson Lee, Cuellar, Kirkpatrick, Pascrell, Green, Massa
Souder, McCaul, Bilirakis, Rogers, Miller

EMERGENCY COMMUNICATIONS

Cuellar (chairman), Norton, Richardson, Pascrell, Cleaver, Titus, Vacancy
Rogers, Olson, Cao, McCaul

EMERGING THREATS

Clarke (chairwoman), Sanchez, Richardson, Luján, Kilroy
Lungren, Broun, Austria

INTELLIGENCE, INFORMATION SHARING & TERRORISM RISK ASSESSMENT

Harman (chairwoman), Carney, Clarke, Kirkpatrick, Green, Himes, Vacancy
McCaul, Dent, Broun, Souder

MANAGEMENT & OVERSIGHT

Carney (chairman), DeFazio, Pascrell, Green, Kilroy
Bilirakis, Cao, Lungren

TRANSPORTATION SECURITY & INFRASTRUCTURE PROTECTION
Jackson Lee (chairwoman), DeFazio, Norton, Kirkpatrick, Luján, Cleaver, Himes, Massa, Titus
Dent, Lungren, Olson, Miller, Austria

HOUSE ADMINISTRATION
Phone: 225-2061   Office: 1309 Longworth

DEMOCRATS (6)	REPUBLICANS (3)
Robert A. Brady, Pa., chairman	*Dan Lungren, Calif.*
Zoe Lofgren, Calif.	*Kevin McCarthy, Calif.*
Michael E. Capuano, Mass.	*Gregg Harper, Miss.*
Charlie Gonzalez, Texas	
Susan A. Davis, Calif.	
Artur Davis, Ala.	

CAPITOL SECURITY
Capuano (chairman), Brady
Lungren

ELECTIONS
Lofgren (chairwoman), Gonzalez, Davis (Calif.), Davis (Ala.)
McCarthy, Harper

JUDICIARY
Phone: 225-3951   Office: 2138 Rayburn

DEMOCRATS (24)	REPUBLICANS (16)
John Conyers Jr., Mich., chairman	*Lamar Smith, Texas*
Howard L. Berman, Calif.	*F. James Sensenbrenner Jr., Wis.*
Rick Boucher, Va.	*Howard Coble, N.C.*
Jerrold Nadler, N.Y.	*Elton Gallegly, Calif.*
Robert C. Scott, Va.	*Robert W. Goodlatte, Va.*
Melvin Watt, N.C.	*Dan Lungren, Calif.*
Zoe Lofgren, Calif.	*Darrell Issa, Calif.*
Sheila Jackson Lee, Texas	*J. Randy Forbes, Va.*
Maxine Waters, Calif.	*Steve King, Iowa*
Bill Delahunt, Mass.	*Trent Franks, Ariz.*
Robert Wexler, Fla.	*Louie Gohmert, Texas*
Steve Cohen, Tenn.	*Jim Jordan, Ohio*
Hank Johnson, Ga.	*Ted Poe, Texas*
Pedro R. Pierluisi, P.R.	*Jason Chaffetz, Utah*
Mike Quigley, Ill.	*Tom Rooney, Fla.*
Luis V. Gutierrez, Ill.	*Gregg Harper, Miss.*
Brad Sherman, Calif.	
Tammy Baldwin, Wis.	
Charlie Gonzalez, Texas	
Anthony Weiner, N.Y.	
Adam B. Schiff, Calif.	
Linda T. Sánchez, Calif.	
Debbie Wasserman Schultz, Fla.	
Dan Maffei, N.Y.	

COMMERCIAL & ADMINISTRATIVE LAW
Cohen (chairman), Delahunt, Watt, Sherman, Maffei, Lofgren, Johnson, Scott, Conyers
Franks, Jordan, Coble, Issa, Forbes, King

CONSTITUTION, CIVIL RIGHTS & CIVIL LIBERTIES
Nadler (chairman), Watt, Scott, Delahunt, Johnson, Baldwin, Conyers, Cohen, Sherman, Jackson Lee
Sensenbrenner, Rooney, King, Franks, Gohmert, Jordan

COURTS & COMPETITION POLICY
Johnson (chairman), Conyers, Boucher, Wexler, Gonzalez, Jackson Lee, Watt, Sherman, Quigley
Coble, Chaffetz, Sensenbrenner, Goodlatte, Issa, Harper

CRIME, TERRORISM & HOMELAND SECURITY
Scott (chairman), Pierluisi, Nadler, Lofgren, Jackson Lee, Waters, Cohen, Weiner, Wasserman Schultz, Quigley
Gohmert, Poe, Goodlatte, Lungren, Forbes, Rooney

IMMIGRATION, CITIZENSHIP, REFUGEES, BORDER SECURITY & INTERNATIONAL LAW
Lofgren (chairwoman), Berman, Jackson Lee, Waters, Pierluisi, Gutierrez, Sánchez, Weiner, Gonzalez, Delahunt
King, Harper, Gallegly, Lungren, Poe, Chaffetz

PORTEOUS IMPEACHMENT INQUIRY
Schiff (chairman), Jackson Lee, Delahunt, Cohen, Johnson, Gonzalez, Pierluisi
Goodlatte, Lungren, Forbes, Gohmert, Sensenbrenner

NATURAL RESOURCES
Phone: 225-6065   Office: 1324 Longworth

DEMOCRATS (29)	REPUBLICANS (20)
Nick J. Rahall II, W.Va., chairman	*Doc Hastings, Wash.*
Dale E. Kildee, Mich.	*Don Young, Alaska*
Eni F.H. Faleomavaega, A.S.	*Elton Gallegly, Calif.*
Neil Abercrombie, Hawaii	*John J. "Jimmy" Duncan Jr., Tenn.*
Frank Pallone Jr., N.J.	*Jeff Flake, Ariz.*
Grace F. Napolitano, Calif.	*Henry E. Brown Jr., S.C.*
Rush D. Holt, N.J.	*Cathy McMorris Rodgers, Wash.*
Raúl M. Grijalva, Ariz.	*Louie Gohmert, Texas*
Madeleine Z. Bordallo, Guam	*Rob Bishop, Utah*
Jim Costa, Calif.	*Bill Shuster, Pa.*
Dan Boren, Okla.	*Doug Lamborn, Colo.*
Gregorio Kilili Camacho Sablan, N. Marianas	*Adrian Smith, Neb.*
Martin Heinrich, N.M.	*Rob Wittman, Va.*
George Miller, Calif.	*Paul Broun, Ga.*
Edward J. Markey, Mass.	*John Fleming, La.*
Peter A. DeFazio, Ore.	*Mike Coffman, Colo.*
Maurice D. Hinchey, N.Y.	*Jason Chaffetz, Utah*
Donna M.C. Christensen, V.I.	*Cynthia M. Lummis, Wyo.*
Diana DeGette, Colo.	*Tom McClintock, Calif.*
Ron Kind, Wis.	*Bill Cassidy, La.*
Lois Capps, Calif.	
Jay Inslee, Wash.	
Joe Baca, Calif.	
Stephanie Herseth Sandlin, S.D.	
John Sarbanes, Md.	
Carol Shea-Porter, N.H.	
Niki Tsongas, Mass.	
Frank Kratovil Jr., Md.	
Pedro R. Pierluisi, P.R.	

ENERGY & MINERAL RESOURCES
Costa (chairman), Faleomavaega, Holt, Boren, Sablan, Heinrich, Markey, Hinchey, Sarbanes, Tsongas
Lamborn, Young, Gohmert, Gallegly, Flake, Fleming, Chaffetz, Lummis

INSULAR AFFAIRS, OCEANS & WILDLIFE
Bordallo (chairwoman), Kildee, Faleomavaega, Abercrombie, Pallone, Sablan, Christensen, DeGette, Kind, Capps, Shea-Porter, Kratovil, Pierluisi
Brown, Young, Flake, Lamborn, Wittman, Fleming, Chaffetz, Cassidy

NATIONAL PARKS, FORESTS & PUBLIC LANDS
Grijalva (chairman), Kildee, Abercrombie, Napolitano, Holt, Bordallo, Boren, Heinrich, DeFazio, Hinchey, Christensen, DeGette, Kind, Capps, Inslee, Herseth Sandlin, Sarbanes, Shea-Porter, Tsongas, Pierluisi
Bishop, Young, Gallegly, Duncan, Flake, Brown, Gohmert, Shuster, Wittman, Broun, Coffman, Lummis, McClintock

WATER & POWER
Napolitano (chairwoman), Miller, Grijalva, Costa, DeFazio, Inslee, Baca
McMorris Rodgers, Smith, Coffman, McClintock

OVERSIGHT & GOVERNMENT REFORM
Phone: 225-5051   Office: 2157 Rayburn

DEMOCRATS (25)
Edolphus Towns, N.Y., chairman
Paul E. Kanjorski, Pa.
Carolyn B. Maloney, N.Y.
Elijah E. Cummings, Md.
Dennis J. Kucinich, Ohio
John F. Tierney, Mass.
William Lacy Clay, Mo.
Diane Watson, Calif.
Stephen F. Lynch, Mass.
Jim Cooper, Tenn.
Gerald E. Connolly, Va.
Mike Quigley, Ill.
Marcy Kaptur, Ohio
Eleanor Holmes Norton, D.C.
Patrick J. Kennedy, R.I.
Danny K. Davis, Ill.
Chris Van Hollen, Md.
Henry Cuellar, Texas
Paul W. Hodes, N.H.
Christopher S. Murphy, Conn.
Peter Welch, Vt.
Bill Foster, Ill.
Jackie Speier, Calif.
Steve Driehaus, Ohio
Vacancy

REPUBLICANS (16)
Darrell Issa, Calif.
Dan Burton, Ind.
John M. McHugh, N.Y.
John L. Mica, Fla.
Mark Souder, Ind.
Todd R. Platts, Pa.
John J. "Jimmy" Duncan Jr., Tenn.
Michael R. Turner, Ohio
Lynn Westmoreland, Ga.
Patrick T. McHenry, N.C.
Brian P. Bilbray, Calif.
Jim Jordan, Ohio
Jeff Flake, Ariz.
Jeff Fortenberry, Neb.
Jason Chaffetz, Utah
Aaron Schock, Ill.

DOMESTIC POLICY
Kucinich (chairman), Cummings, Tierney, Watson, Cooper, Kennedy, Welch, Foster
Jordan, Souder, Burton, Turner, Fortenberry, Schock

FEDERAL WORKFORCE, POSTAL SERVICE & THE DISTRICT OF COLUMBIA
Lynch (chairman), Norton, Davis, Cummings, Kucinich, Clay, Connolly
Chaffetz, McHugh, Souder, Bilbray

GOVERNMENT MANAGEMENT, ORGANIZATION & PROCUREMENT
Watson (chairwoman), Kanjorski, Cooper, Connolly, Cuellar, Speier, Hodes, Murphy
Bilbray, Schock, Platts, Duncan, Flake

INFORMATION POLICY, CENSUS & NATIONAL ARCHIVES
Clay (chairman), Kanjorski, Maloney, Norton, Davis, Driehaus, Watson
McHenry, Westmoreland, Mica, Chaffetz

NATIONAL SECURITY & FOREIGN AFFAIRS
Tierney (chairman), Maloney, Kennedy, Van Hollen, Hodes, Murphy, Welch, Foster, Driehaus, Lynch, Cuellar, Kucinich
Flake, Platts, Burton, Mica, Duncan, Turner, Westmoreland, McHenry, Jordan, Fortenberry

RULES
Phone: 225-9091   Office: H-312 Capitol

DEMOCRATS (9)
Louise M. Slaughter, N.Y., chairwoman
Jim McGovern, Mass.
Alcee L. Hastings, Fla.
Doris Matsui, Calif.
Dennis Cardoza, Calif.
Michael Arcuri, N.Y.
Ed Perlmutter, Colo.
Chellie Pingree, Maine
Jared Polis, Colo.

REPUBLICANS (4)
David Dreier, Calif.
Lincoln Diaz-Balart, Fla.
Pete Sessions, Texas
Virginia Foxx, N.C.

LEGISLATIVE & BUDGET PROCESS
Hastings (chairman), Cardoza, Pingree, Polis, Slaughter
Diaz-Balart, Dreier

RULES & THE ORGANIZATION OF THE HOUSE
McGovern (chairman), Matsui, Arcuri, Perlmutter, Slaughter
Sessions, Foxx

SCIENCE & TECHNOLOGY

Phone: 225-6375   Office: 2321 Rayburn

DEMOCRATS (27)	REPUBLICANS (17)
Bart Gordon, Tenn., chairman	*Ralph M. Hall, Texas*
Jerry F. Costello, Ill.	*F. James*
Eddie Bernice Johnson, Texas	*Sensenbrenner Jr., Wis.*
Lynn Woolsey, Calif.	*Lamar Smith, Texas*
David Wu, Ore.	*Dana Rohrabacher, Calif.*
Brian Baird, Wash.	*Roscoe G. Bartlett, Md.*
Brad Miller, N.C.	*Vernon J. Ehlers, Mich.*
Daniel Lipinski, Ill.	*Frank D. Lucas, Okla.*
Gabrielle Giffords, Ariz.	*Judy Biggert, Ill.*
Donna Edwards, Md.	*Todd Akin, Mo.*
Marcia L. Fudge, Ohio	*Randy Neugebauer, Texas*
Ben Ray Luján, N.M.	*Bob Inglis, S.C.*
Paul Tonko, N.Y.	*Michael McCaul, Texas*
Parker Griffith, Ala.	*Mario Diaz-Balart, Fla.*
Steven R. Rothman, N.J.	*Brian P. Bilbray, Calif.*
Jim Matheson, Utah	*Adrian Smith, Neb.*
Lincoln Davis, Tenn.	*Paul Broun, Ga.*
Ben Chandler, Ky.	*Pete Olson, Texas*
Russ Carnahan, Mo.	
Baron P. Hill, Ind.	
Harry E. Mitchell, Ariz.	
Charlie Wilson, Ohio	
Kathy Dahlkemper, Pa.	
Alan Grayson, Fla.	
Suzanne M. Kosmas, Fla.	
Gary Peters, Mich.	
Vacancy	

ENERGY & ENVIRONMENT

Baird (chairman), Costello, Woolsey, Edwards, Luján, Tonko, Johnson, Lipinski, Giffords, Matheson, Davis, Chandler
Inglis, Bartlett, Ehlers, Biggert, Akin, Neugebauer, Diaz-Balart

INVESTIGATIONS & OVERSIGHT

Miller (chairman), Dahlkemper, Rothman, Davis, Wilson, Grayson
Broun, Bilbray, Vacancy

RESEARCH & SCIENCE EDUCATION

Lipinski (chairman), Johnson, Baird, Fudge, Griffith, Tonko, Carnahan
Ehlers, Neugebauer, Bilbray, Inglis

SPACE & AERONAUTICS

Giffords (chairwoman), Fudge, Griffith, Wu, Edwards, Rothman, Hill, Wilson, Grayson, Kosmas
Olson, Rohrabacher, Sensenbrenner, Lucas, McCaul

TECHNOLOGY & INNOVATION

Wu (chairman), Edwards, Luján, Tonko, Lipinski, Mitchell, Peters
Smith (Neb.), Biggert, Akin, Broun

SELECT ENERGY INDEPENDENCE & GLOBAL WARMING

Phone: 225-4012   Office: B-243 Longworth

DEMOCRATS (9)	REPUBLICANS (6)
Edward J. Markey, Mass., chairman	*F. James*
Earl Blumenauer, Ore.	*Sensenbrenner Jr., Wis.*
Jay Inslee, Wash.	*John Shadegg, Ariz.*
John B. Larson, Conn.	*Candice S. Miller, Mich.*
Stephanie	*John Sullivan, Okla.*
Herseth Sandlin, S.D.	*Marsha Blackburn, Tenn.*
Emanuel Cleaver II, Mo.	*Shelley Moore Capito, W.Va.*
John Hall, N.Y.	
John Salazar, Colo.	
Jackie Speier, Calif.	

SELECT INTELLIGENCE

Phone: 225-7690   Office: HVC-304 Capitol

DEMOCRATS (13)	REPUBLICANS (9)
Silvestre Reyes, Texas, chairman	*Peter Hoekstra, Mich.*
Alcee L. Hastings, Fla.	*Elton Gallegly, Calif.*
Anna G. Eshoo, Calif.	*William M. "Mac"*
Rush D. Holt, N.J.	*Thornberry, Texas*
C.A. Dutch	*Mike Rogers, Mich.*
Ruppersberger, Md.	*Sue Myrick, N.C.*
John F. Tierney, Mass.	*Roy Blunt, Mo.*
Mike Thompson, Calif.	*Jeff Miller, Fla.*
Jan Schakowsky, Ill.	*John Kline, Minn.*
Jim Langevin, R.I.	*K. Michael Conaway, Texas*
Patrick J. Murphy, Pa.	
Adam B. Schiff, Calif.	
Adam Smith, Wash.	
Dan Boren, Okla.	

INTELLIGENCE COMMUNITY MANAGEMENT

Eshoo (chairwoman), Holt, Hastings, Schakowsky, Murphy
Myrick, Blunt, Conaway

OVERSIGHT & INVESTIGATIONS

Schakowsky (chairwoman), Tierney, Murphy, Ruppersberger, Thompson, Schiff, Boren
Miller, Thornberry, Rogers, Blunt, Kline

TECHNICAL & TACTICAL INTELLIGENCE

Ruppersberger (chairman), Holt, Langevin, Murphy, Schiff, Smith
Thornberry, Rogers, Miller, Kline

TERRORISM, HUMAN INTELLIGENCE, ANALYSIS & COUNTERINTELLIGENCE

Thompson (chairman), Hastings, Ruppersberger, Langevin, Schiff, Smith, Boren
Rogers, Gallegly, Myrick, Miller, Conaway

SMALL BUSINESS

Phone: 225-4038   Office: 2361 Rayburn

DEMOCRATS (17)	REPUBLICANS (12)
Nydia M. Velázquez, N.Y., chairwoman	Sam Graves, Mo.
Dennis Moore, Kan.	Roscoe G. Bartlett, Md.
Heath Shuler, N.C.	Todd Akin, Mo.
Kathy Dahlkemper, Pa.	Steve King, Iowa
Kurt Schrader, Ore.	Lynn Westmoreland, Ga.
Ann Kirkpatrick, Ariz.	Louie Gohmert, Texas
Glenn Nye, Va.	Mary Fallin, Okla.
Michael H. Michaud, Maine	Vern Buchanan, Fla.
Melissa Bean, Ill.	Blaine Luetkemeyer, Mo.
Daniel Lipinski, Ill.	Aaron Schock, Ill.
Jason Altmire, Pa.	Glenn Thompson, Pa.
Yvette D. Clarke, N.Y.	Mike Coffman, Colo.
Brad Ellsworth, Ind.	
Joe Sestak, Pa.	
Bobby Bright, Ala.	
Parker Griffith, Ala.	
Debbie Halvorson, Ill.	

FINANCE & TAX
Schrader (chairman), Moore, Kirkpatrick, Bean, Sestak, Halvorson, Nye, Michaud
Buchanan, King, Akin, Luetkemeyer, Coffman

INVESTIGATIONS & OVERSIGHT
Altmire (chairman), Shuler, Ellsworth, Griffith
Fallin, Gohmert, Vacancy

REGULATIONS & HEALTHCARE
Dahlkemper (chairwoman), Lipinski, Griffith, Bean, Altmire, Sestak, Bright
Westmoreland, King, Buchanan, Thompson, Coffman

RURAL DEVELOPMENT, ENTREPRENEURSHIP & TRADE
Shuler (chairman), Michaud, Bright, Dahlkemper, Kirkpatrick, Clarke
Luetkemeyer, King, Schock, Thompson

CONTRACTING & TECHNOLOGY
Nye (chairman), Clarke, Ellsworth, Schrader, Halvorson, Bean, Sestak, Griffith
Schock, Bartlett, Akin, Fallin, Thompson

STANDARDS OF OFFICIAL CONDUCT

Phone: 225-7103   Office: HT-2 Capitol

DEMOCRATS (5)	REPUBLICANS (5)
Zoe Lofgren, Calif., chairwoman	Jo Bonner, Ala.
Ben Chandler, Ky.	J. Gresham Barrett, S.C.
G.K. Butterfield, N.C.	John Kline, Minn.
Kathy Castor, Fla.	K. Michael Conaway, Texas
Peter Welch, Vt.	Charlie Dent, Pa.

RANGEL INQUIRY
Gene Green (Texas) (chairman), Robert C. Scott (Va.)
Bonner, Doc Hastings (Wash.)

TRANSPORTATION & INFRASTRUCTURE

Phone: 225-4472   Office: 2165 Rayburn

DEMOCRATS (45)	REPUBLICANS (30)
James L. Oberstar, Minn., chairman	John L. Mica, Fla.
Nick J. Rahall II, W.Va.	Don Young, Alaska
Peter A. DeFazio, Ore.	Tom Petri, Wis.
Jerry F. Costello, Ill.	Howard Coble, N.C.
Eleanor Holmes Norton, D.C.	John J. "Jimmy" Duncan Jr., Tenn.
Jerrold Nadler, N.Y.	Vernon J. Ehlers, Mich.
Corrine Brown, Fla.	Frank A. LoBiondo, N.J.
Bob Filner, Calif.	Jerry Moran, Kan.
Eddie Bernice Johnson, Texas	Gary G. Miller, Calif.
Gene Taylor, Miss.	Henry E. Brown Jr., S.C.
Elijah E. Cummings, Md.	Timothy V. Johnson, Ill.
Ellen O. Tauscher, Calif.	Todd R. Platts, Pa.
Leonard L. Boswell, Iowa	Sam Graves, Mo.
Tim Holden, Pa.	Bill Shuster, Pa.
Brian Baird, Wash.	John Boozman, Ark.
Rick Larsen, Wash.	Shelley Moore Capito, W.Va.
Michael E. Capuano, Mass.	Jim Gerlach, Pa.
Timothy H. Bishop, N.Y.	Mario Diaz-Balart, Fla.
Michael H. Michaud, Maine	Charlie Dent, Pa.
Russ Carnahan, Mo.	Connie Mack, Fla.
Grace F. Napolitano, Calif.	Lynn Westmoreland, Ga.
Daniel Lipinski, Ill.	Jean Schmidt, Ohio
Mazie K. Hirono, Hawaii	Candice S. Miller, Mich.
Jason Altmire, Pa.	Mary Fallin, Okla.
Tim Walz, Minn.	Vern Buchanan, Fla.
Heath Shuler, N.C.	Bob Latta, Ohio
Michael Arcuri, N.Y.	Brett Guthrie, Ky.
Harry E. Mitchell, Ariz.	Anh "Joseph" Cao, La.
Christopher Carney, Pa.	Aaron Schock, Ill.
John Hall, N.Y.	Pete Olson, Texas
Steve Kagen, Wis.	
Steve Cohen, Tenn.	
Laura Richardson, Calif.	
Albio Sires, N.J.	
Donna Edwards, Md.	
Solomon P. Ortiz, Texas	
Phil Hare, Ill.	
John Boccieri, Ohio	
Mark Schauer, Mich.	
Betsy Markey, Colo.	
Parker Griffith, Ala.	
Michael E. McMahon, N.Y.	
Tom Perriello, Va.	
Dina Titus, Nev.	
Harry Teague, N.M.	

AVIATION
Costello (chairman), Carnahan, Griffith, McMahon, DeFazio, Norton, Filner, Johnson, Boswell, Holden, Capuano, Lipinski, Hirono, Mitchell, Hall, Cohen, Richardson, Boccieri, Rahall, Brown, Cummings, Tauscher, Altmire, Ortiz, Schauer
Petri, Coble, Duncan, Ehlers, LoBiondo, Moran, Graves, Boozman, Capito, Gerlach, Dent, Mack, Westmoreland, Schmidt, Fallin, Buchanan, Guthrie

COAST GUARD & MARITIME TRANSPORTATION

Cummings (chairman), Brown, Larsen, Taylor, Baird, Bishop, Kagen, McMahon, Richardson

LoBiondo, Young, Coble, Ehlers, Platts, Olson

ECONOMIC DEVELOPMENT, PUBLIC BUILDINGS & EMERGENCY MANAGEMENT

Norton (chairwoman), Markey, Michaud, Shuler, Griffith, Carnahan, Walz, Arcuri, Carney, Edwards, Perriello

Diaz-Balart, Johnson, Graves, Capito, Fallin, Guthrie, Cao, Vacancy

HIGHWAYS & TRANSIT

DeFazio (chairman), Rahall, Nadler, Filner, Tauscher, Holden, Baird, Capuano, Bishop , Michaud, Napolitano, Lipinski, Hirono, Altmire, Walz, Shuler, Arcuri, Mitchell, Carney, Cohen, Richardson, Sires, Edwards, Taylor, Boswell, Larsen, Hall, Kagen, Ortiz, Hare, Boccieri, Schauer

Duncan, Young, Petri, Coble, Moran, Miller (Calif.), Brown, Johnson,, Platts, Shuster, Boozman, Capito, Gerlach, Diaz-Balart, Dent, Mack, Schmidt, Miller (Mich.), Fallin, Buchanan, Latta, Schock

RAILROADS, PIPELINES & HAZARDOUS MATERIALS

Brown (chairwoman), Titus, Teague, Rahall, Nadler, Cummings, Napolitano, Altmire, Walz, Arcuri, Carney, Sires, Schauer, Markey, McMahon, Perriello, DeFazio, Costello, Filner, Johnson, Boswell, Larsen, Michaud, Lipinski, Cohen, Richardson

Shuster, Petri, Moran, Miller (Calif.), Brown, Johnson, Graves, Gerlach, Dent, Westmoreland, Schmidt, Miller (Mich.), Buchanan, Latta, Guthrie, Schock, Cao, Olson

WATER RESOURCES & ENVIRONMENT

Johnson (chairwoman), Perriello, Costello, Taylor, Tauscher, Baird, Bishop, Carnahan, Kagen, Edwards, Ortiz, Hare, Titus, Teague, Norton, Capuano, Napolitano, Hirono, Mitchell, Hall, Griffith, Filner, Brown

Boozman, Young, Duncan, Ehlers, LoBiondo, Miller (Calif.), Brown, Platts, Shuster, Diaz-Balart, Mack, Westmoreland, Miller (Mich.), Latta, Cao, Olson

VETERANS' AFFAIRS

Phone: 225-9756   Office: 335 Cannon

DEMOCRATS (18)

Bob Filner, Calif., chairman
Corrine Brown, Fla.
Vic Snyder, Ark.
Michael H. Michaud, Maine
Stephanie
 Herseth Sandlin, S.D.
Harry E. Mitchell, Ariz.
John Hall, N.Y.
Debbie Halvorson, Ill.
Tom Perriello, Va.
Harry Teague, N.M.
Ciro D. Rodriguez, Texas
Joe Donnelly, Ind.
Jerry McNerney, Calif.
Zack Space, Ohio
Tim Walz, Minn.
John Adler, N.J.
Ann Kirkpatrick, Ariz.
Glenn Nye, Va.

REPUBLICANS (11)

Steve Buyer, Ind.
Cliff Stearns, Fla.
Jerry Moran, Kan.
Henry E. Brown Jr., S.C.
Jeff Miller, Fla.
John Boozman, Ark.
Brian P. Bilbray, Calif.
Doug Lamborn, Colo.
Gus Bilirakis, Fla.
Vern Buchanan, Fla.
Phil Roe, Tenn.

DISABILITY ASSISTANCE & MEMORIAL AFFAIRS

Hall (chairman), Halvorson, Donnelly, Rodriguez, Kirkpatrick

Lamborn, Miller, Bilbray

ECONOMIC OPPORTUNITY

Herseth Sandlin (chairwoman), Perriello, Adler, Kirkpatrick, Teague

Boozman, Moran, Bilirakis

HEALTH

Michaud (chairman), Brown, Snyder, Teague, Rodriguez, Donnelly, McNerney, Nye, Halvorson, Perriello

Brown, Stearns, Moran, Boozman, Bilirakis, Buchanan

OVERSIGHT & INVESTIGATIONS

Mitchell (chairman), Space, Walz, Adler, Hall

Roe, Stearns, Bilbray

WAYS & MEANS
Phone: 225-3625   Office: 1102 Longworth

DEMOCRATS (26)
Charles B. Rangel, N.Y., chairman
Pete Stark, Calif.
Sander M. Levin, Mich.
Jim McDermott, Wash.
John Lewis, Ga.
Richard E. Neal, Mass.
John Tanner, Tenn.
Xavier Becerra, Calif.
Lloyd Doggett, Texas
Earl Pomeroy, N.D.
Mike Thompson, Calif.
John B. Larson, Conn.
Earl Blumenauer, Ore.
Ron Kind, Wis.
Bill Pascrell Jr., N.J.
Shelley Berkley, Nev.
Joseph Crowley, N.Y.
Chris Van Hollen, Md.
Kendrick B. Meek, Fla.
Allyson Y. Schwartz, Pa.
Artur Davis, Ala.
Danny K. Davis, Ill.
Bob Etheridge, N.C.
Linda T. Sánchez, Calif.
Brian Higgins, N.Y.
John Yarmuth, Ky.

REPUBLICANS (15)
Dave Camp, Mich.
Wally Herger, Calif.
Sam Johnson, Texas
Kevin Brady, Texas
Paul D. Ryan, Wis.
Eric Cantor, Va.
John Linder, Ga.
Devin Nunes, Calif.
Pat Tiberi, Ohio
Ginny Brown-Waite, Fla.
Geoff Davis, Ky.
Dave Reichert, Wash.
Charles Boustany Jr., La.
Dean Heller, Nev.
Peter Roskam, Ill.

HEALTH
Stark (chairman), Doggett, Thompson, Becerra, Pomeroy, Kind, Blumenauer, Pascrell, Berkley
Herger, Johnson, Ryan, Nunes, Brown-Waite

INCOME SECURITY & FAMILY SUPPORT
McDermott (chairman), Stark, Davis (Ala.), Lewis, Berkley, Van Hollen, Meek, Levin, Davis (Ill.)
Linder, Boustany, Heller, Roskam, Tiberi

OVERSIGHT
Lewis (chairman), Becerra, Kind, Pascrell, Larson, Davis (Ala.), Davis (Ill.), Etheridge, Higgins
Boustany, Reichert, Roskam, Ryan, Linder

SELECT REVENUE MEASURES
Neal (chairman), Thompson, Larson, Schwartz, Blumenauer, Crowley, Meek, Higgins, Yarmuth
Tiberi, Linder, Heller, Roskam, Davis

SOCIAL SECURITY
Tanner (chairman), Pomeroy, Schwartz, Becerra, Doggett, Kind, Crowley, Sánchez, Yarmuth
Johnson, Brady, Tiberi, Brown-Waite, Reichert

TRADE
Levin (chairman), Tanner, Van Hollen, McDermott, Neal, Doggett, Pomeroy, Etheridge, Sánchez
Brady, Davis, Reichert, Herger, Nunes

Partisan House Committees

DEMOCRATIC LEADERS

Speaker .... Nancy Pelosi
Majority Leader .... Steny H. Hoyer
Majority Whip .... James E. Clyburn
Caucus Chairman .... John B. Larson
Caucus Vice Chairman................. Xavier Beccera
Assistant to the Speaker.............. Chris Van Hollen
Chief Deputy Whips: John Lewis (senior), G.K. Butterfield, Joseph Crowley, Diana DeGette, Ed Pastor, Jan Schakowsky, John Tanner, Debbie Wasserman Schultz, Maxine Waters

DEMOCRATIC CONGRESSIONAL CAMPAIGN COMMITTEE
863-1500 430 S. Capitol St. S.E. 20003

Chairman .... Chris Van Hollen
Vice Chairpersons:............. Bruce Braley, Albio Sires,
.... Debbie Wasserman Schultz
Business Council Co-Chairmen: . Dennis Cardoza, Ron Klein
Frontline Democrats Co-Chairs ..... Christopher S. Murphy
.... Debbie Wasserman Schultz
Recruitment Chairman..................... Steve Israel

HOUSE DEMOCRATIC STEERING & POLICY COMMITTEE
225-0100 235 Cannon

Chairwoman .... Nancy Pelosi
Co-Chairwoman....................... Rosa DeLauro
Co-Chairman .... George Miller
Vice Chairman .... Marion Berry
Freshman Class Representative .... Jared Polis
Members: Chris Van Hollen, Robert A. Brady, Jerrold Nadler, John F. Tierney, Jan Schakowsky, Tammy Baldwin, Jerry McNerney, Ron Klein, Rick Larsen, James P. Moran, Linda T. Sanchez, Bob Etheridge, Eddie Bernice Johnson, Xavier Becerra, G.K. Butterfield, Michael E. Capuano, Dennis Cardoza, Kathy Castor, James E. Clyburn, Jerry F. Costello, Joseph Crowley, Artur Davis, Diana DeGette, Lloyd Doggett, Barney Frank, Debbie Halvorson, Rush D. Holt, Steny H. Hoyer, Marcy Kaptur, John B. Larson, John Lewis, Zoe Lofgren, Doris Matsui, Kendrick B. Meek, David R. Obey, Ed Pastor, Collin C. Peterson, Charles B. Rangel, Tim Ryan, Louise M. Slaughter, John M. Spratt Jr., John Tanner, Mike Thompson, Nydia M. Velázquez, Debbie Wasserman Schultz, Maxine Waters, Henry A. Waxmann

REPUBLICAN LEADERS

Minority Leader .... John A. Boehner
Minority Whip .... Eric Cantor
Conference Chairman .... Mike Pence
Conference Vice Chairwoman.... Cathy McMorris Rodgers
Conference Secretary .... John Carter
Chief Deputy Whip .... Kevin McCarthy

NATIONAL REPUBLICAN CONGRESSIONAL COMMITTEE
479-7070 320 First St. S.E. 20003

Chairman........................... Pete Sessions
Vice Chairman .... Greg Walden
Finance Chairman .... Jeb Hensarling
Communications Chairwoman .... Mary Fallin
Candidate Recruitment Chairman .... Kevin McCarthy
Incumbent Retention Chairman .... Mike Rogers
Redistricting Chairman .... Lynn Westmoreland
Coalitions Chairman...................... Devin Nunes
Regional Chairs: Charles Boustany Jr., Michael N. Castle, Geoff Davis, Jack Kingston, Denny Rehberg, Ed Royce, John Shadegg, Bill Shuster, Lee Terry, Fred Upton
Ex Officio Members: John A. Boehner, Eric Canto, John Carter, David Dreier, Thaddeus McCotter, Cathy McMorris Rodgers Mike Pence

POLICY COMMITTEE
225-6168 2471 Rayburn

Chairman....................... Thaddeus McCotter

HOUSE REPUBLICAN STEERING COMMITTEE
225-4000 H-204 Capitol

Chairman........................... John A. Boehner
Members: Spencer Bachus, Joe L. Barton, Ken Calvert, Dave Camp, Eric Cantor, John Carter, Tom Cole, David Dreier, Gregg Harper, Doc Hastings, Steven C. LaTourette, Jerry Lewis, John Linder, Kevin McCarthy, Thaddeus McCotter, John M. McHugh, Cathy McMorris Rodgers, Jeff Miller, Mike Pence, Harold Rogers, Mike Rogers, Pete Sessions, John Shimkus, Mike Simpson, Lamar Smith, Adrian Smith, Lee Terry

www.cqpress.com

Senate Committees

The standing and select committees of the U.S. Senate are listed below in alphabetical order. The listings include a telephone number, room number and party ratio for each full committee. Membership is given in order of seniority on the committee. Subcommittee membership is listed in order of seniority.

On full committee rosters, Democrats are shown in roman type; members of the minority party, Republicans, are shown in *italic* type; independents are labeled.

The word "vacancy" indicates that a committee or subcommittee seat had not been filled at press time, May 2009. Subcommittee vacancies do not necessarily indicate vacancies on full committees or vice versa.

The telephone area code for Washington, D.C., is 202. The ZIP code for all Senate offices is 20510.

Partisan committees are listed on page 1203.

ARMED SERVICES

Phone: 224-3871   Office: 228 Russell

DEMOCRATS (15)	REPUBLICANS (11)
Carl Levin, Mich., chairman	*John McCain, Ariz.*
Edward M. Kennedy, Mass.	*James M. Inhofe, Okla.*
Robert C. Byrd, W.Va.	*Jeff Sessions, Ala.*
Joseph I. Lieberman, Conn. (I)	*Saxby Chambliss, Ga.*
Jack Reed, R.I.	*Lindsey Graham, S.C.*
Daniel K. Akaka, Hawaii	*John Thune, S.D.*
Bill Nelson, Fla.	*Mel Martinez, Fla.*
Ben Nelson, Neb.	*Roger Wicker, Miss.*
Evan Bayh, Ind.	*Richard M. Burr, N.C.*
Jim Webb, Va.	*David Vitter, La.*
Claire McCaskill, Mo.	*Susan Collins, Maine*
Mark Udall, Colo.	
Kay Hagan, N.C.	
Mark Begich, Alaska	
Roland W. Burris, Ill.	

AGRICULTURE, NUTRITION & FORESTRY

Phone: 224-2035   Office: 328A Russell

DEMOCRATS (12)	REPUBLICANS (9)
Tom Harkin, Iowa, chairman	*Saxby Chambliss, Ga.*
Patrick J. Leahy, Vt.	*Richard G. Lugar, Ind.*
Kent Conrad, N.D.	*Thad Cochran, Miss.*
Max Baucus, Mont.	*Mitch McConnell, Ky.*
Blanche Lincoln, Ark.	*Pat Roberts, Kan.*
Debbie Stabenow, Mich.	*Mike Johanns, Neb.*
Ben Nelson, Neb.	*Charles E. Grassley, Iowa*
Sherrod Brown, Ohio	*John Thune, S.D.*
Bob Casey, Pa.	*Vacancy*
Amy Klobuchar, Minn.	
Kirsten Gillibrand, N.Y.	
Michael Bennet, Colo.	

AIRLAND

Lieberman (I) (chairman), Bayh, Webb, McCaskill, Hagan, Begich, Burris
Thune, Inhofe, Sessions, Chambliss, Burr

EMERGING THREATS & CAPABILITIES

Reed (chairman), Kennedy, Byrd, Nelson (Fla.), Nelson (Neb.), Bayh, Udall
Wicker, Graham, Martinez, Burr, Collins

PERSONNEL

Nelson (Neb.) (chairman), Kennedy, Lieberman (I), Akaka, Webb, McCaskill, Hagan, Begich, Burris
Graham, Chambliss, Thune, Martinez, Wicker, Vitter, Collins

READINESS & MANAGEMENT SUPPORT

Bayh (chairman), Byrd, Akaka, McCaskill, Udall, Burris
Burr, Inhofe, Chambliss, Thune

SEAPOWER

Kennedy (chairman), Lieberman (I), Reed, Akaka, Nelson (Fla.), Webb, Hagan
Martinez, Sessions, Wicker, Vitter, Collins

STRATEGIC FORCES

Nelson (Fla.) (chairman), Byrd, Reed, Nelson (Neb.), Udall, Begich
Vitter, Sessions, Inhofe, Graham

APPROPRIATIONS
Phone: 224-7363   Office: S-128 Capitol

DEMOCRATS (18)
Daniel K. Inouye, Hawaii, chairman
Robert C. Byrd, W.Va.
Patrick J. Leahy, Vt.
Tom Harkin, Iowa
Barbara A. Mikulski, Md.
Herb Kohl, Wis.
Patty Murray, Wash.
Byron L. Dorgan, N.D.
Dianne Feinstein, Calif.
Richard J. Durbin, Ill.
Tim Johnson, S.D.
Mary L. Landrieu, La.
Jack Reed, R.I.
Frank R. Lautenberg, N.J.
Ben Nelson, Neb.
Mark Pryor, Ark.
Jon Tester, Mont.
Arlen Specter, Pa.

REPUBLICANS (12)
Thad Cochran, Miss.
Christopher S. Bond, Mo.
Mitch McConnell, Ky.
Richard C. Shelby, Ala.
Judd Gregg, N.H.
Robert F. Bennett, Utah
Kay Bailey Hutchison, Texas
Sam Brownback, Kan.
Lamar Alexander, Tenn.
Susan Collins, Maine
George V. Voinovich, Ohio
Lisa Murkowski, Alaska

AGRICULTURE
Kohl (chairman), Harkin, Dorgan, Feinstein, Durbin, Johnson, Nelson, Reed, Pryor, Specter
Brownback, Bennett, Cochran, Bond, McConnell, Collins

COMMERCE-JUSTICE-SCIENCE
Mikulski (chairwoman), Inouye, Leahy, Kohl, Dorgan, Feinstein, Reed, Lautenberg, Nelson, Pryor
Shelby, Gregg, McConnell, Hutchison, Brownback, Alexander, Voinovich, Murkowski

DEFENSE
Inouye (chairman), Byrd, Leahy, Harkin, Dorgan, Durbin, Feinstein, Mikulski, Kohl, Murray, Specter
Cochran, Bond, McConnell, Shelby, Gregg, Hutchison, Bennett

ENERGY-WATER
Dorgan (chairman), Byrd, Murray, Feinstein, Johnson, Landrieu, Reed, Lautenberg, Harkin, Tester
Bennett, Cochran, McConnell, Bond, Hutchison, Shelby, Alexander, Voinovich

FINANCIAL SERVICES
Durbin (chairman), Landrieu, Lautenberg, Nelson, Tester
Collins, Bond, Murkowski

HOMELAND SECURITY
Byrd (chairman), Inouye, Leahy, Mikulski, Murray, Landrieu, Lautenberg, Tester, Specter
Voinovich, Cochran, Gregg, Shelby, Brownback

INTERIOR-ENVIRONMENT
Feinstein (chairwoman), Byrd, Leahy, Dorgan, Mikulski, Kohl, Johnson, Reed, Nelson, Tester
Alexander, Cochran, Bennett, Gregg, Murkowski, Collins, Voinovich

LABOR-HHS-EDUCATION
Harkin (chairman), Inouye, Kohl, Murray, Landrieu, Durbin, Reed, Pryor, Specter
Cochran, Gregg, Hutchison, Shelby, Alexander

LEGISLATIVE BRANCH
Nelson (chairman), Pryor, Tester
Murkowski

MILITARY CONSTRUCTION-VA
Johnson (chairman), Inouye, Landrieu, Byrd, Murray, Reed, Nelson, Pryor
Hutchison, Brownback, McConnell, Collins, Alexander, Murkowski

STATE-FOREIGN OPERATIONS
Leahy (chairman), Inouye, Harkin, Mikulski, Durbin, Johnson, Landrieu, Lautenberg, Specter
Gregg, McConnell, Bennett, Bond, Brownback

TRANSPORTATION-HUD
Murray (chairwoman), Byrd, Mikulski, Kohl, Durbin, Dorgan, Leahy, Harkin, Feinstein, Johnson, Lautenberg, Specter
Bond, Shelby, Bennett, Hutchison, Brownback, Alexander, Collins, Voinovich

BANKING, HOUSING & URBAN AFFAIRS

Phone: 224-7391   Office: 534 Dirksen

DEMOCRATS (13)	REPUBLICANS (10)
Christopher J. Dodd, Conn., chairman	*Richard C. Shelby, Ala.*
Tim Johnson, S.D.	*Robert F. Bennett, Utah*
Jack Reed, R.I.	*Jim Bunning, Ky.*
Charles E. Schumer, N.Y.	*Michael D. Crapo, Idaho*
Evan Bayh, Ind.	*Mel Martinez, Fla.*
Robert Menendez, N.J.	*Bob Corker, Tenn.*
Daniel K. Akaka, Hawaii	*Jim DeMint, S.C.*
Sherrod Brown, Ohio	*David Vitter, La.*
Jon Tester, Mont.	*Mike Johanns, Neb.*
Herb Kohl, Wis.	*Kay Bailey Hutchison, Texas*
Mark Warner, Va.	
Jeff Merkley, Ore.	
Michael Bennet, Colo.	

ECONOMIC POLICY
Brown (chairman), Tester, Merkley, Dodd
DeMint

FINANCIAL INSTITUTIONS
Johnson (chairman), Reed, Schumer, Bayh, Menendez, Akaka, Tester, Kohl, Merkley, Bennet
Crapo, Bennett, Hutchison, Bunning, Martinez, Corker, DeMint

HOUSING, TRANSPORTATION & COMMUNITY DEVELOPMENT
Menendez (chairman), Johnson, Reed, Schumer, Akaka, Brown, Tester, Kohl, Warner, Merkley
Vitter, Hutchison, Bennett, Johanns, Crapo, Martinez, DeMint

SECURITIES, INSURANCE & INVESTMENT
Reed (chairman), Johnson, Schumer, Bayh, Menendez, Akaka, Brown, Warner, Bennet, Dodd
Bunning, Martinez, Bennett, Crapo, Vitter, Johanns, Corker

SECURITY & INTERNATIONAL TRADE
Bayh (chairman), Kohl, Warner, Bennet, Dodd
Corker, Johanns

BUDGET

Phone: 224-0642   Office: 624 Dirksen

DEMOCRATS (13)	REPUBLICANS (10)
Kent Conrad, N.D., chairman	*Judd Gregg, N.H.*
Patty Murray, Wash.	*Charles E. Grassley, Iowa*
Ron Wyden, Ore.	*Michael B. Enzi, Wyo.*
Russ Feingold, Wis.	*Jeff Sessions, Ala.*
Robert C. Byrd, W.Va.	*Jim Bunning, Ky.*
Bill Nelson, Fla.	*Michael D. Crapo, Idaho*
Debbie Stabenow, Mich.	*John Ensign, Nev.*
Robert Menendez, N.J.	*John Cornyn, Texas*
Benjamin L. Cardin, Md.	*Lindsey Graham, S.C.*
Bernard Sanders, Vt. (I)	*Lamar Alexander, Tenn.*
Sheldon Whitehouse, R.I.	
Mark Warner, Va.	
Jeff Merkley, Ore.	

COMMERCE, SCIENCE & TRANSPORTATION

Phone: 224-0411   Office: 254 Russell

DEMOCRATS (14)	REPUBLICANS (11)
John D. Rockefeller IV, W.Va., chairman	*Kay Bailey Hutchison, Texas*
Daniel K. Inouye, Hawaii	*Olympia J. Snowe, Maine*
John Kerry, Mass.	*John Ensign, Nev.*
Byron L. Dorgan, N.D.	*Jim DeMint, S.C.*
Barbara Boxer, Calif.	*John Thune, S.D.*
Bill Nelson, Fla.	*Roger Wicker, Miss.*
Maria Cantwell, Wash.	*Johnny Isakson, Ga.*
Frank R. Lautenberg, N.J.	*David Vitter, La.*
Mark Pryor, Ark.	*Sam Brownback, Kan.*
Claire McCaskill, Mo.	*Mel Martinez, Fla.*
Amy Klobuchar, Minn.	*Mike Johanns, Neb.*
Tom Udall, N.M.	
Mark Warner, Va.	
Mark Begich, Alaska	

AVIATION OPERATIONS, SAFETY & SECURITY
Dorgan (chairman), Inouye, Kerry, Boxer, Nelson, Cantwell, Lautenberg, Pryor, McCaskill, Klobuchar, Warner, Begich
DeMint, Snowe, Ensign, Thune, Wicker, Isakson, Vitter, Brownback, Martinez, Johanns

COMMUNICATIONS, TECHNOLOGY & THE INTERNET
Kerry (chairman), Inouye, Dorgan, Nelson, Cantwell, Lautenberg, Pryor, McCaskill, Klobuchar, Udall, Warner, Begich
Ensign, Snowe, DeMint, Thune, Wicker, Isakson, Vitter, Brownback, Martinez, Johanns

COMPETITIVENESS, INNOVATION & EXPORT PROMOTION
Klobuchar (chairwoman), Kerry, Dorgan, McCaskill, Udall, Warner, Begich
Martinez, Ensign, DeMint, Thune, Brownback, Johanns

CONSUMER PROTECTION, PRODUCT SAFETY & INSURANCE
Pryor (chairman), Dorgan, Boxer, Nelson, McCaskill, Klobuchar, Udall
Wicker, Snowe, DeMint, Thune, Isakson, Vitter

OCEANS, ATMOSPHERE, FISHERIES & COAST GUARD
Cantwell (chairwoman), Inouye, Kerry, Boxer, Lautenberg, Begich
Snowe, Wicker, Isakson, Vitter, Martinez

SCIENCE & SPACE
Nelson (chairman), Inouye, Kerry, Boxer, Pryor, Udall, Warner
Vitter, Snowe, Ensign, Thune, Isakson, Johanns

SURFACE TRANSPORTATION & MERCHANT MARINE
Lautenberg (chairman), Inouye, Kerry, Dorgan, Boxer, Cantwell, Pryor, UdalL, Warner, Begich
Thune, Snowe, Ensign, DeMint, Wicker, Isakson, Vitter, Brownback, Johanns

ENERGY & NATURAL RESOURCES
Phone: 224-4971   Office: 304 Dirksen

DEMOCRATS (13)
Jeff Bingaman, N.M., chairman
Byron L. Dorgan, N.D.
Ron Wyden, Ore.
Tim Johnson, S.D.
Mary L. Landrieu, La.
Maria Cantwell, Wash.
Robert Menendez, N.J.
Blanche Lincoln, Ark.
Bernard Sanders, Vt. (I)
Evan Bayh, Ind.
Debbie Stabenow, Mich.
Mark Udall, Colo.
Jeanne Shaheen, N.H.

REPUBLICANS (10)
Lisa Murkowski, Alaska
Richard M. Burr, N.C.
John Barrasso, Wyo.
Sam Brownback, Kan.
Jim Risch, Idaho
John McCain, Ariz.
Robert F. Bennett, Utah
Jim Bunning, Ky.
Jeff Sessions, Ala.
Bob Corker, Tenn.

ENERGY
Cantwell (chairwoman), Dorgan, Wyden, Landrieu,
   Menendez, Sanders (I), Bayh, Stabenow, Udall, Shaheen
Risch, Burr, Barrasso, Brownback, Bennett, Bunning,
   Sessions, Corker

NATIONAL PARKS
Udall (chairman), Dorgan, Landrieu, Menendez, Lincoln,
   Sanders (I), Bayh, Stabenow
Burr, Barrasso, Brownback, McCain, Bunning, Corker

PUBLIC LANDS & FORESTS
Wyden (chairman), Johnson, Landrieu, Cantwell, Menendez,
   Lincoln, Udall, Shaheen
Barrasso, Risch, McCain, Bennett, Sessions, Corker

WATER & POWER
Stabenow (chairwoman), Dorgan, Johnson, Cantwell,
   Lincoln, Sanders (I), Bayh, Shaheen
Brownback, Risch, McCain, Bennett, Bunning, Sessions

ENVIRONMENT & PUBLIC WORKS
Phone: 224-8832   Office: 410 Dirksen

DEMOCRATS (12)
Barbara Boxer, Calif.,
   chairwoman
Max Baucus, Mont.
Thomas R. Carper, Del.
Frank R. Lautenberg, N.J.
Benjamin L. Cardin, Md.
Bernard Sanders, Vt. (I)
Amy Klobuchar, Minn.
Sheldon Whitehouse, R.I.
Tom Udall, N.M.
Jeff Merkley, Ore.
Kirsten Gillibrand, N.Y.
Arlen Specter, Pa.

REPUBLICANS (7)
James M. Inhofe, Okla.
George V. Voinovich, Ohio
David Vitter, La.
John Barrasso, Wyo.
Michael D. Crapo, Idaho
Christopher S. Bond, Mo.
Lamar Alexander, Tenn.

CHILDREN'S HEALTH
Klobuchar (chairwoman), Udall, Merkley, Specter
Alexander

CLEAN AIR & NUCLEAR SAFETY
Carper (chairman), Baucus, Cardin, Sanders (I), Merkley
Vitter, Voinovich, Bond

GREEN JOBS & THE NEW ECONOMY
Sanders (I) (chairman), Carper, Gillibrand
Bond, Voinovich

OVERSIGHT
Whitehouse (chairman), Udall, Gillibrand
Barrasso, Vitter

SUPERFUND, TOXICS & ENVIRONMENTAL HEALTH
Lautenberg (chairman), Baucus, Klobuchar, Whitehouse,
   Gillibrand, Specter
Crapo, Bond

TRANSPORTATION & INFRASTRUCTURE
Baucus (chairman), Carper, Lautenberg, Cardin, Sanders (I),
   Klobuchar, Specter
Voinovich, Vitter, Barrasso

WATER & WILDLIFE
Cardin (chairman), Lautenberg, Whitehouse, Udall, Merkley
Crapo, Barrasso, Alexander

FINANCE

Phone: 224-4515   Office: 219 Dirksen

DEMOCRATS (13)
Max Baucus, Mont., chairman
John D. Rockefeller IV, W.Va.
Kent Conrad, N.D.
Jeff Bingaman, N.M.
John Kerry, Mass.
Blanche Lincoln, Ark.
Ron Wyden, Ore.
Charles E. Schumer, N.Y.
Debbie Stabenow, Mich.
Maria Cantwell, Wash.
Bill Nelson, Fla.
Robert Menendez, N.J.
Thomas R. Carper, Del.

REPUBLICANS (10)
Charles E. Grassley, Iowa
Orrin G. Hatch, Utah
Olympia J. Snowe, Maine
Jon Kyl, Ariz.
Jim Bunning, Ky.
Michael D. Crapo, Idaho
Pat Roberts, Kan.
John Ensign, Nev.
Michael B. Enzi, Wyo.
John Cornyn, Texas

ENERGY, NATURAL RESOURCES & INFRASTRUCTURE
Bingaman (chairman), Conrad, Kerry, Lincoln, Stabenow, Cantwell, Nelson, Carper
Bunning, Crapo, Cornyn, Hatch, Enzi

HEALTH CARE
Rockefeller (chairman), Bingaman, Kerry, Lincoln, Wyden, Schumer, Stabenow, Cantwell, Nelson, Menendez, Carper
Hatch, Snowe, Ensign, Enzi, Cornyn, Kyl, Bunning, Crapo

INTERNATIONAL TRADE, CUSTOMS & GLOBAL COMPETITIVENESS
Wyden (chairman), Rockefeller, Bingaman, Kerry, Stabenow, Cantwell, Menendez
Crapo, Snowe, Bunning, Roberts

SOCIAL SECURITY, PENSIONS & FAMILY POLICY
Lincoln (chairwoman), Rockefeller, Conrad, Schumer, Nelson
Roberts, Kyl, Ensign

TAXATION, IRS OVERSIGHT & LONG-TERM GROWTH
Conrad (chairman), Baucus, Rockefeller, Wyden, Schumer, Stabenow, Cantwell, Menendez, Carper
Kyl, Hatch, Snowe, Roberts, Ensign, Enzi, Cornyn

FOREIGN RELATIONS

Phone: 224-4651   Office: 446 Dirksen

DEMOCRATS (11)
John Kerry, Mass., chairman
Christopher J. Dodd, Conn.
Russ Feingold, Wis.
Barbara Boxer, Calif.
Robert Menendez, N.J.
Benjamin L. Cardin, Md.
Bob Casey, Pa.
Jim Webb, Va.
Jeanne Shaheen, N.H.
Ted Kaufman, Del.
Kirsten Gillibrand, N.Y.

REPUBLICANS (8)
Richard G. Lugar, Ind.
Vacancy
Bob Corker, Tenn.
Johnny Isakson, Ga.
Jim Risch, Idaho
Jim DeMint, S.C.
John Barrasso, Wyo.
Roger Wicker, Miss.

AFRICAN AFFAIRS
Feingold (chairman), Cardin, Webb, Kaufman, Shaheen
Isakson, DeMint, Corker, Risch

EAST ASIAN & PACIFIC AFFAIRS
Webb (chairman), Dodd, Feingold, Boxer, Casey, Gillibrand
Vacancy, Isakson, Barrasso, Wicker

EUROPEAN AFFAIRS
Shaheen (chairwoman), Dodd, Menendez, Casey, Webb, Kaufman
DeMint, Risch, Corker, Wicker

INTERNATIONAL DEVELOPMENT
Menendez (chairman), Boxer, Cardin, Casey, Shaheen, Gillibrand
Corker, Wicker, DeMint, Vacancy

INTERNATIONAL OPERATIONS & ORGANIZATIONS
Boxer (chairwoman), Feingold, Menendez, Kaufman, Shaheen, Gillibrand
Wicker, DeMint, Barrasso, Vacancy

NEAR EASTERN & SOUTH & CENTRAL ASIAN AFFAIRS
Casey (chairman), Dodd, Feingold, Boxer, Cardin, Kaufman
Risch, Corker, Barrasso, Isakson

WESTERN HEMISPHERE, PEACE CORPS & GLOBAL NARCOTICS AFFAIRS
Dodd (chairman), Menendez, Webb, Cardin, Gillibrand
Barrasso, Isakson, Risch, Vacancy

HOMELAND SECURITY & GOVERNMENTAL AFFAIRS

Phone: 224-2627   Office: 340 Dirksen

DEMOCRATS (10)
Joseph I. Lieberman, Conn. (I), chairman
Carl Levin, Mich.
Daniel K. Akaka, Hawaii
Thomas R. Carper, Del.
Mark Pryor, Ark.
Mary L. Landrieu, La.
Claire McCaskill, Mo.
Jon Tester, Mont.
Roland W. Burris, Ill.
Michael Bennet, Colo.

REPUBLICANS (7)
Susan Collins, Maine
Tom Coburn, Okla.
John McCain, Ariz.
George V. Voinovich, Ohio
John Ensign, Nev.
Lindsey Graham, S.C.
Vacancy

CONTRACTING OVERSIGHT
McCaskill (chairwoman), Levin, Carper, Pryor, Tester
Vacancy, Coburn, McCain

DISASTER RECOVERY
Landrieu (chairwoman), McCaskill, Burris
Graham

FEDERAL FINANCIAL MANAGEMENT
Carper (chairman), Levin, Akaka, Pryor, McCaskill, Burris
McCain, Coburn, Voinovich, Ensign, Vacancy

OVERSIGHT OF GOVERNMENT MANAGEMENT
Akaka (chairman), Levin, Landrieu, Burris, Bennet
Voinovich, Graham, Vacancy

PERMANENT INVESTIGATIONS
Levin (chairman), Carper, Pryor, McCaskill, Tester, Bennet
Coburn, Collins, McCain, Ensign, Vacancy

STATE, LOCAL & PRIVATE SECTOR PREPAREDNESS
Pryor (chairman), Akaka, Landrieu, Tester, Bennet
Ensign, Voinovich, Graham

HEALTH, EDUCATION, LABOR & PENSIONS

Phone: 224-5375   Office: 428 Dirksen

DEMOCRATS (13)
Edward M. Kennedy, Mass., chairman
Christopher J. Dodd, Conn.
Tom Harkin, Iowa
Barbara A. Mikulski, Md.
Jeff Bingaman, N.M.
Patty Murray, Wash.
Jack Reed, R.I.
Bernard Sanders, Vt. (I)
Sherrod Brown, Ohio
Bob Casey, Pa.
Kay Hagan, N.C.
Jeff Merkley, Ore.
Sheldon Whitehouse, R.I.

REPUBLICANS (10)
Michael B. Enzi, Wyo.
Judd Gregg, N.H.
Lamar Alexander, Tenn.
Richard M. Burr, N.C.
Johnny Isakson, Ga.
John McCain, Ariz.
Orrin G. Hatch, Utah
Lisa Murkowski, Alaska
Tom Coburn, Okla.
Pat Roberts, Kan.

INDIAN AFFAIRS

Phone: 224-2251   Office: 838 Hart

DEMOCRATS (9)
Byron L. Dorgan, N.D., chairman
Daniel K. Inouye, Hawaii
Kent Conrad, N.D.
Daniel K. Akaka, Hawaii
Tim Johnson, S.D.
Maria Cantwell, Wash.
Jon Tester, Mont.
Tom Udall, N.M.
Vacancy

REPUBLICANS (6)
John Barrasso, Wyo.,
John McCain, Ariz.
Lisa Murkowski, Alaska
Tom Coburn, Okla.
Michael D. Crapo, Idaho
Mike Johanns, Neb.

JUDICIARY

Phone: 224-7703   Office: 224 Dirksen

DEMOCRATS (12)
Patrick J. Leahy, Vt., chairman
Herb Kohl, Wis.
Dianne Feinstein, Calif.
Russ Feingold, Wis.
Charles E. Schumer, N.Y.
Richard J. Durbin, Ill.
Benjamin L. Cardin, Md.
Sheldon Whitehouse, R.I.
Ron Wyden, Ore.
Amy Klobuchar, Minn.
Ted Kaufman, Del.
Arlen Specter, Pa.

REPUBLICANS (7)
Jeff Sessions, Ala.
Orrin G. Hatch, Utah
Charles E. Grassley, Iowa
Jon Kyl, Ariz.
Lindsey Graham, S.C.
John Cornyn, Texas
Tom Coburn, Okla.

ADMINISTRATIVE OVERSIGHT & THE COURTS
Whitehouse (chairman), Feinstein, Feingold, Schumer, Cardin, Kaufman
Sessions, Grassley, Kyl, Graham

ANTITRUST, COMPETITION POLICY & CONSUMER RIGHTS
Kohl (chairman), Schumer, Whitehouse, Wyden, Klobuchar, Kaufman, Specter
Hatch, Grassley, Cornyn

CONSTITUTION
Feingold (chairman), Feinstein, Durbin, Cardin, Whitehouse, Specter
Coburn, Kyl, Graham, Cornyn

CRIME & DRUGS
Specter (chairman), Kohl, Feinstein, Feingold, Schumer, Durbin, Cardin, Klobuchar, Kaufman
Graham, Hatch, Grassley, Sessions, Coburn

HUMAN RIGHTS & THE LAW
Durbin (chairman), Feingold, Cardin, Kaufman, Specter
Coburn, Graham, Cornyn

IMMIGRATION, REFUGEES & BORDER SECURITY
Schumer (chairman), Leahy, Feinstein, Durbin, Whitehouse, Wyden
Cornyn, Grassley, Kyl, Sessions

TERRORISM & HOMELAND SECURITY
Cardin (chairman), Kohl, Feinstein, Schumer, Durbin, Wyden, Kaufman
Kyl, Hatch, Sessions, Cornyn, Coburn

RULES & ADMINISTRATION
Phone: 224-6352   Office: 305 Russell

DEMOCRATS (11)	REPUBLICANS (8)
Charles E. Schumer, N.Y., chairman	*Robert F. Bennett, Utah*
Robert C. Byrd, W.Va.	*Mitch McConnell, Ky.*
Daniel K. Inouye, Hawaii	*Thad Cochran, Miss.*
Christopher J. Dodd, Conn.	*Kay Bailey Hutchison, Texas*
Dianne Feinstein, Calif.	*Saxby Chambliss, Ga.*
Richard J. Durbin, Ill.	*Lamar Alexander, Tenn.*
Ben Nelson, Neb.	*John Ensign, Nev.*
Patty Murray, Wash.	*Pat Roberts, Kan.*
Mark Pryor, Ark.	
Tom Udall, N.M.	
Mark Warner, Va.	

SELECT ETHICS
Phone: 224-2981   Office: 220 Hart

DEMOCRATS (3)	REPUBLICANS (3)
Barbara Boxer, Calif., chairwoman	*Johnny Isakson, Ga., vice chairman*
Mark Pryor, Ark.	*Pat Roberts, Kan.*
Sherrod Brown, Ohio	*Jim Risch, Idaho*

SELECT INTELLIGENCE
Phone: 224-1700   Office: 211 Hart

DEMOCRATS (8)	REPUBLICANS (7)
Dianne Feinstein, Calif., chairwoman	*Christopher S. Bond, Mo., vice chairman*
John D. Rockefeller IV, W.Va.	*Orrin G. Hatch, Utah*
Ron Wyden, Ore.	*Olympia J. Snowe, Maine*
Evan Bayh, Ind.	*Saxby Chambliss, Ga.*
Barbara A. Mikulski, Md.	*Richard M. Burr, N.C.*
Russ Feingold, Wis.	*Tom Coburn, Okla.*
Bill Nelson, Fla.	*Jim Risch, Idaho*
Sheldon Whitehouse, R.I.	

SMALL BUSINESS & ENTREPRENEURSHIP
Phone: 224-5175   Office: 428A Russell

DEMOCRATS (11)	REPUBLICANS (8)
Mary L. Landrieu, La., chairwoman	*Olympia J. Snowe, Maine*
John Kerry, Mass.	*Christopher S. Bond, Mo.*
Carl Levin, Mich.	*Vacancy*
Tom Harkin, Iowa	*David Vitter, La.*
Joseph I. Lieberman, Conn. (I)	*John Thune, S.D.*
Maria Cantwell, Wash.	*Michael B. Enzi, Wyo.*
Evan Bayh, Ind.	*Johnny Isakson, Ga.*
Mark Pryor, Ark.	*Roger Wicker, Miss.*
Benjamin L. Cardin, Md.	
Jeanne Shaheen, N.H.	
Kay Hagan, N.C.	

SPECIAL AGING
Phone: 224-5364   Office: G31 Dirksen

DEMOCRATS (13)
Herb Kohl, Wis., chairman
Ron Wyden, Ore.
Blanche Lincoln, Ark.
Evan Bayh, Ind.
Bill Nelson, Fla.
Bob Casey, Pa.
Claire McCaskill, Mo.
Sheldon Whitehouse, R.I.
Mark Udall, Colo.
Michael Bennet, Colo.
Kirsten Gillibrand, N.Y.
Arlen Specter, Pa.
Vacancy

REPUBLICANS (8)
Mel Martinez, Fla.
Richard C. Shelby, Ala.
Susan Collins, Maine
Vacancy
Bob Corker, Tenn.
Orrin G. Hatch, Utah
Sam Brownback, Kan.
Lindsey Graham, S.C.

VETERANS' AFFAIRS
Phone: 224-9126   Office: 412 Russell

DEMOCRATS (10)
Daniel K. Akaka, Hawaii, chairman
John D. Rockefeller IV, W.Va.
Patty Murray, Wash.
Bernard Sanders, Vt. (I)
Sherrod Brown, Ohio
Jim Webb, Va.
Jon Tester, Mont.
Mark Begich, Alaska
Roland W. Burris, Ill.
Arlen Specter, Pa.

REPUBLICANS (5)
Richard M. Burr, N.C.
Johnny Isakson, Ga.
Roger Wicker, Miss.
Mike Johanns, Neb.
Lindsey Graham, S.C.

Partisan Senate Committees

DEMOCRATIC LEADERS

President . . . . Vice President Joseph R. Biden Jr.
President Pro Tempore . . . . Robert C. Byrd
Majority Leader . . . . .Harry Reid
Majority Whip . . . . Richard J. Durbin
Caucus Vice Chairman. . . . . Charles E. Schumer
Conference Secretary . . . . Patty Murray
Committee Steering & Outreach Chairwoman . . . .
. . . . .Debbie Stabenow
Chief Deputy Whip . . . . .Barbara Boxer
Deputy Whips: Thomas R. Carper, Russ Feingold, Bill Nelson

DEMOCRATIC SENATORIAL CAMPAIGN COMMITTEE
224-2447   120 Maryland Ave. N.E. 20002

Chairman. . . . . .Robert Menendez

POLICY COMMITTEE
224-3232   419 Hart

Chairman. . . . . Byron L. Dorgan
Regional Chairs: Evan Bayh, Mary L. Landrieu, Patty Murray, Jack Reed
Members: Daniel K. Akaka, Sherrod Brown, Thomas R. Carper, Russ Feingold, Dianne Feinstein, Tim Johnson, Frank R. Lautenberg, Joseph I. Lieberman, Blanche Lincoln, Barbara A. Mikulski, Bill Nelson, Harry Reid, Charles E. Schumer, Ron Wyden
Ex-Officio Member. . . . . Richard J. Durbin

STEERING AND OUTREACH COMMITTEE
224-9048   712 Hart

Chairwoman . . . . .Debbie Stabenow
Members: Max Baucus, Jeff Bingaman Barbara Boxer Robert C. Byrd, Kent Conrad, Christopher J. Dodd, Richard J. Durbin, Tom Harkin, Daniel K. Inouye Edward M. Kennedy, John Kerry, Herb Kohl, Patrick J. Leahy, Carl Levin, Mark Pryor, Harry Reid, John D. Rockefeller IV

REPUBLICAN LEADERS
Minority Leader . . . . Mitch McConnell
Minority Whip . . . . Jon Kyl
Conference Chairman . . . . .Lamar Alexander
Conference Vice Chairman . . . . .John Thune
Counsel & Adviser to the Leader . . . . Robert F. Bennett
Chief Deputy Whip . . . . Richard M. Burr
Deputy Whips: John Barrasso, Michael D. Crapo, Saxby Chambliss, Jeff Sessions, Olympia J. Snowe, David Vitter

NATIONAL REPUBLICAN SENATORIAL COMMITTEE
675-6000   425 Second St. N.E. 20002

Chairman. . . . . John Cornyn
Vice Chairman . . . . .Orrin G. Hatch
Program Chairmen: John Barrasso, Christopher S. Bond, Saxby Chambliss, Jon Kyl, Jim Risch, Pat Roberts, Jeff Sessions, John Thune

POLICY COMMITTEE
224-2946   347 Russell

Chairman. . . . . John Ensign

COMMITTEE ON COMMITTEES
224-6142   239 Dirksen

Chairman. . . . . Michael D. Crapo

www.cqpress.com

Joint Committees

JOINT ECONOMIC
Phone: 224-5171   Office: G-01 Dirksen

SENATE MEMBERS
DEMOCRATS (6)
Charles E. Schumer, N.Y. vice chairman
Edward M. Kennedy, Mass.
Jeff Bingaman, N.M.
Amy Klobuchar, Minn.
Bob Casey, Pa.
Jim Webb, Va

REPUBLICANS (4)
Sam Brownback, Kan.
Jim DeMint, S.C.
Jim Risch, Idaho
Robert F. Bennett, Utah

HOUSE MEMBERS
DEMOCRATS (6)
Carolyn B. Maloney, N.Y., chairwoman
Maurice D. Hinchey, N.Y.
Baron P. Hill, Ind.
Loretta Sanchez, Calif.
Elijah E. Cummings, Md.
Vic Snyder, Ark

REPUBLICANS (2)
Kevin Brady, Texas
Ron Paul, Texas
Michael C. Burgess, Texas
John Campbell, Calif.

JOINT LIBRARY
Phone: 225-2061   Office: 1309 Longworth

SENATE MEMBERS
DEMOCRATS (3)
Charles E. Schumer, N.Y.,
   vice chairman
Christopher J. Dodd, Conn.
Richard J. Durbin, Ill.

REPUBLICANS (2)
Robert F. Bennett, Utah
Thad Cochran, Miss.

HOUSE MEMBERS
DEMOCRATS (2)
Robert A. Brady, Pa., chairman
Zoe Lofgren, Calif.

REPUBLICANS (2)
Dan Lungren, Calif.
Gregg Harper, Miss.

JOINT PRINTING
Phone: 224-6352   Office: 305 Russell

SENATE MEMBERS
DEMOCRATS (3)
Charles E. Schumer, N.Y.,
   chairman
Patty Murray, Wash.
Tom Udall, N.M.

REPUBLICANS (2)
Robert F. Bennett, Utah
Saxby Chambliss, Ga.

HOUSE MEMBE RS
DEMOCRATS (3)
Robert A. Brady, Pa.,
   vice chairman
Michael E. Capuano, Mass.
Susan A. Davis, Calif.

REPUBLICANS (2)
Dan Lungren, Calif.
Kevin McCarthy, Calif.

JOINT TAXATION
Phone: 225-3621   Office: 1015 Longworth

SENATE MEMBERS
DEMOCRATS (3)
Max Baucus, Mont.,
   vice-chairman
John D. Rockefeller IV, W.Va.
Kent Conrad, N.D.

REPUBLICANS (2)
Charles E. Grassley, Iowa
Orrin G. Hatch, Utah

HOUSE MEMBERS
DEMOCRATS (3)
Charles B. Rangel, N.Y.,
   chairman
Pete Stark, Calif.
Sander M. Levin, Mich.

REPUBLICANS (2)
Dave Camp, Mich.
Wally Herger, Calif.

Did You Know?

It's common knowledge that Arizona Sen. John McCain was a prisoner of war in Vietnam and Massachusetts Sen. Edward M. Kennedy's brother was president, but many other members of Congress also have noteworthy and occasionally quirky backgrounds that can provide insight into their behavior as lawmakers.

Iowa Sen. Tom Harkin, for instance, has long been interested in legislation affecting people with disabilities.

Rep. **Gary L. Ackerman**, D-N.Y., used to live on a houseboat named "Unsinkable." It sank.

Tennessee Republican Sen. **Lamar Alexander** is an accomplished musician. He played trombone, tuba and washboard at a Bourbon Street nightclub while clerking for a federal judge in New Orleans.

Rep. **Robert E. Andrews**, D-N.J., used Rahm Emanuel — later his House colleague and now White House chief of staff — as an opposition researcher in his first campaign for the House in 1990.

A collection of campaign buttons, started by his father, adorns a wall in New York Democratic Rep. **Michael Arcuri**'s Capitol Hill office. It includes buttons from almost every presidential candidate since the 1900 election. Arcuri is missing only 1904 Democratic candidate Alton B. Parker, who suffered a landslide defeat at the hands of incumbent President Theodore Roosevelt. He may want to talk to Oklahoma Republican Rep. **John Sullivan**, who used to run a political memorabilia business.

Rep. **Roscoe G. Bartlett**, R-Md., holds 20 patents, including ones for components in breathing equipment used by pilots, astronauts and rescue workers.

Sen. **Max Baucus**, D-Mont., has served on the Finance Committee since shortly after he arrived in the Senate in 1978. If he completes his current term, he will have been on the panel longer than any senator in history, eclipsing legendary Louisiana Democrat Russell Long, a former chairman and Finance member for 34 years.

One of Indiana Democratic Sen. **Evan Bayh**'s babysitters was Lynda Bird Johnson, the president's daughter.

Ohio Democratic Rep. **John Boccieri**'s promising baseball career ended after he threw a snowball at a Franciscan friar at St. Bonaventure University and the friar turned around and tackled him, breaking his leg. The Ohio Democrat never played baseball as well afterward.

An athlete in his younger days, Pennsylvania Democratic Rep. **Robert A. Brady** once teamed up with Wilt Chamberlain in a neighborhood pickup basketball game and sparred with Muhammad Ali.

Freshman House Democrat **Bobby Bright** of Alabama is the 13th of 14 children of a sharecropper.

The son of a longtime Georgia state senator, Republican Rep. **Paul Broun** used to give up his bedroom when his father's colleague, Jimmy Carter from Plains, would visit his home in Athens.

Kentucky Republican Sen. **Jim Bunning** is a member of the Baseball Hall of Fame. He was the first pitcher to record 100 wins and 1,000 strikeouts in each league.

Sen. **Richard M. Burr**, R-N.C., is descended from Aaron Burr, the New York senator and vice president who survived a famous 1804 duel with Alexander Hamilton.

California Republican Rep. **John Campbell** is a member of the Sons of Union Veterans and has occasionally participated in Civil War re-enactments. His great-grandfather on his father's side, Alexander, was elected to the California Assembly in 1860 on the same GOP ticket as Abraham Lincoln.

Sen. **Thomas R. Carper**, D-Del., is known for keeping a list of several hundred birthdays of current and former colleagues, staffers and others and for dialing them on that day to wish them well.

Rep. **André Carson**, D-Ind., was an aspiring rapper during high school, performing at local variety shows under the stage name "Juggernaut."

Utah Republican Rep. **Jason Chaffetz**'s father's first wife was Katherine "Kitty" Dickson, who later married Massachusetts Gov. Michael S. Dukakis. In college, Chaffetz — then a Democrat — was a Utah co-chairman of Dukakis' 1988 presidential campaign.

To pay for his education at the University of Maryland, Rep. **William Lacy Clay**, D-Mo., was a U.S. House of Representatives doorman for seven years.

Rep. **James E. Clyburn**, D-S.C., is the first African-American elected to Congress from South Carolina since 1896, when his great-uncle, George Washington Murray, was in the House.

Rep. **Steve Cohen**, D-Tenn., was diagnosed with polio as a child, but was too young to take the same vaccine that his father, a doctor, was helping Jonas Salk test.

At least once each Congress, GOP Rep. **K. Michael Conaway** of Texas introduces legislation to require all members and senior staff to certify they had read and understood the Constitution. He carries a pocket version of it himself, noting inside the cover the dates he reads it, and requires his aides to read the document annually.

One of Democratic North Dakota Sen. **Kent Conrad**'s committee assignments is Indian Affairs, and on the wall of his office back in Bismark hangs a gift from North Dakota's Standing Rock American Indian Tribe: a framed resolution bearing his honorary Sioux name, Namni Sni, or Never Turns Back.

In Texas Republican Rep. **John Culberson**'s office is a refurbished mahogany roll-top desk that he bought at an antiques store when he discovered it had once belonged

---

His inspiration was his late brother Frank, who was deaf.

A lawmaker's past can provide clues as to why they got into politics in the first place. For example, two members — Washington Sen. Patty Murray and Minnesota Rep. Betty McCollum — can point to their dissatisfaction with the way their local officials dealt with playground equipment. Sometimes these personal tidbits offer a fascinating humanizing touch. Did you know that:

to his great-great-uncle, Charles Culberson, who was governor of Texas from 1895 to 1899 and a U.S. senator from 1899 to 1923.

An aunt of Florida GOP Reps. **Lincoln Diaz-Balart** and **Mario Diaz-Balart**, who are brothers, was once married to Fidel Castro.

When Rep. **Anna G. Eshoo**, D-Calif., was in high school in Connecticut, President Harry S Truman gave her a ride home from school one day.

California Democratic House members **Anna G. Eshoo** and **Jackie Speier** are the only two Armenian-American members of Congress.

Rep. **Chaka Fattah**, D-Pa., was born Arthur Davenport. Fattah's mother changed his name when she married community activist David Fattah. She called him "Chaka"in honor of a Zulu warrior.

Democratic Illinois Rep. **Bill Foster** was a physicist on the small team that discovered the top quark, the heaviest known form of matter.

Rep. **Marcia L. Fudge**, D-Ohio, was the national president of Delta Sigma Theta, a sorority of predominately black college-educated women.

Rep. **Rodney Frelinghuysen**, R-N.J., is the sixth member of his family to serve in Congress.

New York Democratic Sen. **Kirsten Gillibrand** studied abroad in China and Taiwan in college. She also spent a month on a fellowship in India where she interviewed the Dalai Lama and Tibetan refugees for a senior project.

Septuagenarian Sen. **Charles Grassley**, R-Iowa, runs two to three miles nearly every day at a 9 ½ minute pace.

Sen. **Judd Gregg**, R-N.H., Rep. **F. James Sensenbrenner Jr.**, R-Wis., and Rep. **Kevin McCarthy**, R-Calif., are all lottery winners. Gregg donated some of his $853,492 to charity, Sensenbrenner put his $250,000 toward charities and investments, and McCarthy invested the $5,000 from his scratch-off ticket to open "Kevin O's Deli."

New York Democratic Rep. **John Hall** was the lead singer of the 1970s rock-and-roll band Orleans when he penned the pop standard "Still the One," which hit the Top 10 on the Billboard charts.

Democratic Rep. **Debbie Halvorson** of Illinois worked as a Mary Kay cosmetics saleswoman for 14 years.

Sen. **Orrin G. Hatch**, R-Utah, has written songs and movie soundtracks performed by the Osmonds and Gladys Knight; he often scribbles song lyrics between Senate votes and has produced several discs of religious, romantic and patriotic songs

Rep. **Rush D. Holt**, D-N.J., is a former champion on the TV quiz show "Jeopardy." New York Sen. **Charles E. Schumer** appeared on the high school quiz program "It's Academic" in 1967 and was captain of his team.

As a young Hill aide on a 1969 trip to Vietnam, Sen. **Tom Harkin**, D-Iowa, discovered the "tiger cages," squalid underground cells where the South Vietnamese government secretly kept prisoners of war. Harkin's

revelations got worldwide attention.

In 1993, Oklahoma Republican Sen. **James M. Inhofe** became the only member of Congress to fly an airplane around the world. He retraced Wiley Post's journey, the first solo flight around the world.

Democratic Sen. **Daniel K. Inouye** of Hawaii was awarded a Medal of Honor in 2000 for heroism in World War II. A member of the famed all-Nisei "Go for Broke" 442nd Regimental Combat Team, he lost his right arm when he advanced alone to take out a machine gun that had pinned down his men.

Rep. **Jesse L. Jackson Jr.**, D-Ill., vacuums his office carpet for relaxation.

Rep. **Sam Johnson**, R-Texas, spent almost seven years in a North Vietnamese prison camp. For a brief stretch, he shared a cell with fellow prisoner of war Sen. **John McCain**, R-Ariz.

Rep. **Paul E. Kanjorski**, D-Pa., a licensed attorney since 1966, never graduated from law school. He didn't graduate from college, either.

Michigan Democratic Rep. **Dale E. Kildee** founded the Native American Caucus. In honor of his efforts, the Grand Traverse Band of Ottawa and Chippewa Indians in 1998 designated April 15 "Dale Kildee Day."

Rep. **Ron Kind**, D-Wis., was inspired to try politics while backpacking in Berlin in 1990, when he took a sledgehammer to the recently opened Berlin Wall and shook hands with new Czechoslovakian President Vaclav Havel. He still has a chunk of the wall, shaped like Wisconsin, on his desk.

During his service in the Marine Corps, Minnesota Republican Rep. **John Kline** carried the "football" — the briefcase with nuclear war codes — for Presidents Jimmy Carter and Ronald Reagan and flew the presidential helicopter, Marine One.

Ohio Democratic Rep. **Dennis J. Kucinich** was so unpopular as Cleveland's mayor that he wore a bulletproof vest to throw out the first pitch at an Indians game.

Louisiana Democrat **Mary L. Landrieu** and Maine Republican **Olympia J. Snowe** are the first female duo to lead a committee in either chamber. They head up the Senate Small Business and Entrepreneurship Committee.

An avid photographer, Sen. **Patrick J. Leahy**, D-Vt., has taken his camera all over the world and regularly takes it to presidential inaugurations and other historic events. His work has appeared in U.S. News & World Report as well as other publications.

Connecticut Independent Sen. **Joseph I. Lieberman** taught Democratic Sens. **Sherrod Brown** of Ohio and **Amy Klobuchar** of Minnesota in separate seminar classes at Yale University. Klobuchar's program was about the Democratic Party.

Rep. **Stephen F. Lynch**, D-Mass., donated more than half his liver to his brother-in-law.

House Republicans **Connie Mack** of Florida and **Peter**

Hoekstra of Michigan and Democratic West Virginia Sen. **Robert C. Byrd** were all born with the first name Cornelius.

Reps. **George Miller**, D-Calif., and **Bill Delahunt**, D-Mass., and Sens. **Charles E. Schumer**, D-N.Y., and **Richard J. Durbin**, D-Ill., share a Capitol Hill rowhouse of such notorious disarray that it merited a New York Times write-up and a visit from an ABC News television crew in early 2007.

Rep. **Dennis Moore**, D-Kan., has played guitar since high school and once shared the stage at a Farm Aid concert with Willie Nelson and David Crosby. Pennsylvania GOP Rep. **Tim Murphy**, R-Pa., taught himself to play guitar and once opened for banjo legend Earl Scruggs.

Rep. **Patrick J. Murphy**, D-Pa., was the first Iraq War veteran elected to Congress.

Rep. **Tim Murphy**, R-Pa., a psychologist, gave out medical advice as "Dr. Tim" on Pittsburgh radio and television stations.

Democratic Rep. **John P. Murtha** of Pennsylvania acted in high school plays. His most memorable moment was as a professor in "Little Women" when he split his pants and never turned his back to the audience.

Michigan House Republican **Thaddeus McCotter** once played in a band called Sir Funk-a-Lot and the Knights of the Terrestrial Jam.

Rep. **Candice S. Miller**, R-Mich., earned the honorary title "Old Goat" in 2001 when she competed in her 25th Port Huron to Mackinac Island sailboat race.

Democratic Rep. **Harry E. Mitchell** of Arizona was such a popular mayor in his hometown of Tempe that city officials established the Harry E. Mitchell Government Complex and erected a 35-foot abstract steel statue of him near city hall.

Sen. **Lisa Murkowski**, R-Alaska, is the first woman to represent Alaska in Congress. She is also the first person ever appointed to the Senate by her father.

Rep. **Randy Neugebauer**, R-Texas, was so skilled at back flips, twists and other moves that while at Texas Tech he joined the Flying Matadors trampoline troupe.

As a girl, Speaker **Nancy Pelosi**, D-Calif., slept above stacks of the Congressional Record. Her father, Thomas D'Alesandro Jr., was a Maryland congressman and stored them under her bed in their Baltimore rowhouse.

Republican Rep. **Tom Petri**'s first job was hosting a radio show called "Teen Time," a weekly program that made him the Badger State's youngest on-air personality.

Freshman Republican Rep. **Bill Posey** of Florida is an accomplished stock-car racer and won an award for short-track driver achievement. Nevada Republican Rep. **Dean Heller** also enjoys racing and competes in several stock car races each year in Nevada and California.

Political science professor and now Rep. **David E. Price**, D-N.C., helped judge Illinois Democratic Rep. **Daniel Lipinski**'s doctoral thesis at Duke University.

Rep. **Dave Reichert**, R-Wash., was the original lead detective in the Green River serial killer task force. Almost 20 years later, as the King County sheriff, he announced the arrest of Gary Ridgway in 2001.

Senate Democratic Majority Leader **Harry Reid** of Nevada took on organized crime as chairman of the Nevada Gaming Commission. A bomb was once found under the hood of his car.

Rep. **Dana Rohrabacher**, R-Calif., says John Wayne taught him how to drink tequila.

Illinois Democratic Rep. **Bobby L. Rush** is a former Black Panther who served six months in prison on a weapons charge.

Wisconsin Republican Rep. **Paul D. Ryan** once took a summer job in college as an Oscar Mayer salesman and drove the Wienermobile as he promoted a new line called "Lunchables."

Rep. **José E. Serrano**, D-N.Y., learned English by listening to Frank Sinatra records.

Democratic Pennsylvania Rep. **Joe Sestak**, a retired Navy vice admiral, is the highest-ranking military officer ever elected to Congress. Minnesota Democratic Rep. **Tim Walz** spent two decades in the Army National Guard and rose to command sergeant major, making him the highest-ranking enlisted soldier ever to serve in Congress.

As of April 2009, Ohio Republican Rep. **Jean Schmidt** had run in 76 marathons.

New York Democratic Rep. **Louise M. Slaughter** was born in Harlan County, Ky., and is a descendant of Daniel Boone.

In the 1960s, Sen. **Arlen Specter**, D-Pa., as a top aide to the Warren Commission, helped devise the "single bullet" theory that a lone gunman was responsible for the 1963 assassination of President John F. Kennedy.

While a member of the California Senate, Democratic Rep. **Jackie Speier** spent a night at Valley State Prison for Women in Chowchilla to find out what the living conditions for female inmates were like.

Rep. **Pete Stark**, a California Democrat, is recognized by the American Humanist Association as the highest-ranking U.S. official and the first member of Congress to proclaim he is an atheist. Stark says he's a Unitarian who does not believe in a supreme being.

Rep. **Harry Teague**, D-N.M., is the only current member of Congress who did not graduate from high school; he dropped out at age 17 to work in the oil fields.

In 1982, while working as a White House aide, Republican Michigan Rep. **Fred Upton** proposed to his wife during a Baltimore Orioles baseball game, hiring an airplane to fly overhead with a banner reading, "Amey this is the inning to say yes."

In 1967, Virginia Democratic Sen. **Jim Webb**, as a student at the U.S. Naval Academy, lost a boxing championship to Oliver L. North, who would later become a household name for his role in the Iran-Contra affair.

Index

A

Abercrombie, Neil, D-Hawaii (1), 279, **307**, 657
Ackerman, Gary L., D-N.Y. (5), **693**
Aderholt, Robert B., R-Ala. (4), **12**
Adler, John, D-N.J. (3), **649**
Akaka, Daniel K., D-Hawaii, 24, **305**, 310
Akin, Todd, R-Mo. (2), **582**
Alexander, Lamar, R-Tenn., 53, 566, **927**, 929, 940
Alexander, Rodney, R-La. (5), **445**
Altmire, Jason, D-Pa. (4), 813, **858**
Andrews, Robert E., D-N.J. (1), 641, **645**
Arcuri, Michael, D-N.Y. (24), 684, **728**
Austria, Steve, R-Ohio (7), **793**

B

Baca, Joe, D-Calif. (43), 146, **154**, 162, 708
Bachmann, Michele, R-Minn. (6), **555**
Bachus, Spencer, R-Ala. (6), 11, **15**, 795, 1034
Baird, Brian, D-Wash. (3), **1072**
Baldwin, Tammy, D-Wis. (2), **1106**
Barrasso, John, R-Wyo., **1124**
Barrett, J. Gresham, R-S.C. (3), **909**
Barrow, John, D-Ga. (12), 290, **297**
Bartlett, Roscoe G., R-Md. (6), **474**
Barton, Joe L., R-Texas (6), 232, 374, 538, 952, **965**
Baucus, Max, D-Mont., 95, 313, 388, 483, **599**, 601, 603
Bayh, Evan, D-Ind., 51, **366**, 382, 455, 607
Bean, Melissa, D-Ill. (8), 148, 204, **340**
Becerra, Xavier, D-Calif. (31), 85, **131**, 137, 698, 797
Begich, Mark, D-Alaska, **23**, 26
Bennet, Michael, D-Colo., **179**
Bennett, Robert F., R-Utah, 833, **1022**, 1026
Berkley, Shelley, D-Nev. (1), **624**, 626
Berman, Howard L., D-Calif. (28), **125**, 130, 253, 693, 996, 1113
Berry, Marion, D-Ark. (1), **55**
Biggert, Judy, R-Ill. (13), 337, **349**, 667
Bilbray, Brian P., R-Calif. (50), **168**, 174
Bilirakis, Gus, R-Fla. (9), **237**
Bingaman, Jeff, D-N.M., 21, **671**, 673, 675
Bishop, Rob, R-Utah (1), **1024**, 1074
Bishop, Sanford D. Jr., D-Ga. (2), 275, **277**
Bishop, Timothy H., D-N.Y. (1), 647, **685**
Blackburn, Marsha, R-Tenn. (7), **942**
Blumenauer, Earl, D-Ore. (3), 836, 839, **841**
Blunt, Roy, R-Mo. (7), 37, 228, 344, 414, 448, 577, 579, **592**, 795, 803, 1053
Boccieri, John, D-Ohio (16), **810**
Boehner, John A., R-Ohio (8), 15, 38, 43, 74, 76, 111, 119, 228, 230, 253, 378, 398, 413, 571, 592, 789, **794**, 803, 807, 827, 963, 965, 1014, 1016, 1043, 1053, 1076, 1080, 1115
Bond, Christopher S., R-Mo., **576**, 584, 591-592, 892, 1091
Bonner, Jo, R-Ala. (1), **7**
Bono Mack, Mary, R-Calif. (45), 115, **158**, 247, 877
Boozman, John, R-Ark. (3), **59**
Bordallo, Madeleine Z., D-Guam (AL), **1129**, 1131
Boren, Dan, D-Okla. (2), 289, **823**, 1105
Boswell, Leonard L., D-Iowa (3), **396**
Boucher, Rick, D-Va. (9), 613, 1051, **1057**
Boustany, Charles Jr., R-La. (7), **448**
Boxer, Barbara, D-Calif., **70**, 72, 82, 158, 209, 542, 671

Boyd, Allen, D-Fla. (2), **224**
Brady, Kevin, R-Texas (8), **969**
Brady, Robert A., D-Pa. (1), **853**, 856
Braley, Bruce, D-Iowa (1), **392**, 805
Bright, Bobby, D-Ala. (2), **9**
Broun, Paul, R-Ga. (10), 275, **293**
Brown, Sherrod, D-Ohio, 457, **780**, 806
Brown, Corrine, D-Fla. (3), **226**
Brown, Henry E. Jr., R-S.C. (1), **905**
Brown-Waite, Ginny, R-Fla. (5), **230**, 1095
Brownback, Sam, R-Kan., **404**, 408, 413, 1105
Buchanan, Vern, R-Fla. (13), **245**, 994
Bunning, Jim, R-Ky., 417, **420**, 432, 982,
Burgess, Michael C., R-Texas (26), **1004**, 1010
Burr, Richard M., R-N.C., 398, 543, 672, **739**, 851, 927
Burris, Roland W., D-Ill., 68, **325**, 327, 336, 339, 343, 358
Burton, Dan, R-Ind. (5), **376**
Butterfield, G.K., D-N.C. (1), **743**
Buyer, Steve, R-Ind. (4), 170, **374**
Byrd, Robert C., D-W.Va., 197, 303, 461, 482, 819, 1064, **1088**-1090, 1092, 1095-1096

C

Calvert, Ken, R-Calif. (44), **156**
Camp, Dave, R-Mich. (4), 74, **518**, 713
Campbell, John, R-Calif. (48), **164**
Cantor, Eric, R-Va. (7), 113, 160, 413, 518, 794, 921, **1053**
Cantwell, Maria, D-Wash. (1), **1066**
Cao, Anh "Joseph", R-La. (2), **441**
Capito, Shelley Moore, R-W.Va. (2), **1094**
Capps, Lois, D-Calif. (23), **115**
Capuano, Michael E., D-Mass. (8), **500**
Cardin, Benjamin L., D-Md., 263, **463**, 469, 478
Cardoza, Dennis, D-Calif. (18), **105**
Carnahan, Russ, D-Mo. (3), **584**
Carney, Christopher, D-Pa. (10), **869**
Carper, Thomas R., D-Del., 51, 53, **209**, 213, 928
Carson, André, D-Ind. (7), **380**
Carter, John, R-Texas (31), **1014**
Casey, Bob, D-Pa. (1), 221, **851**, 982
Cassidy, Bill, R-La. (6), **447**
Castle, Michael N., R-Del. (AL), 210, **213**, 945
Castor, Kathy, D-Fla. (11), **241**, 245
Chaffetz, Jason, R-Utah (3), **1028**
Chambliss, Saxby, R-Ga., **271**, 276, 290, 398, 407, 771
Chandler, Ben, D-Ky. (6), **431**
Childers, Travis W., D-Miss. (1), **567**
Christensen, Donna M.C., D-V.I. (AL), **1132**
Clarke, Yvette D., D-N.Y. (11), **705**
Clay, William Lacy, D-Mo. (1), **580**
Cleaver, Emanuel II, D-Mo. (5), **588**
Clyburn, James E., D-S.C. (6), **915**
Coble, Howard, R-N.C. (6), **753**
Coburn, Tom, R-Okla., 390, 619, 817, **819**, 904, 968, 1102
Cochran, Thad, R-Miss., 435, **563**, 565, 568
Coffman, Mike, R-Colo. (6), **189**
Cohen, Steve, D-Tenn. (9), **946**, 1131
Cole, Tom, R-Okla. (4), **827**, 1016
Coleman, Norm, R-Minn., 543, **545**, 953
Collins, Susan, R-Maine, 96, 452, **454**, 456, 578, 607, 633
Conaway, K. Michael, R-Texas (11), **975**, 992
Connolly, Gerald E., D-Va. (11), **1061**

Conrad, Kent, D-N.D., 195, 272-273, 483, 600, 609, 631, **770**, 773, 775, 913, 922, 1041
Conyers, John Jr., D-Mich. (14), 17, 504, 535, **536**, 946, 985, 995
Cooper, Jim, D-Tenn. (5), 431, **938**
Corker, Bob, R-Tenn., **929**
Cornyn, John, R-Texas, 5, 30, 421, 921, 951, **953**, 966, 974, 997
Costa, Jim, D-Calif. (20), **109**, 243
Costello, Jerry F., D-Ill. (12), **347**, 361
Courtney, Joe, D-Conn. (2), **200**, 243
Crapo, Michael D., R-Idaho, **313**, 315, 319, 1105
Crenshaw, Ander, R-Fla. (4), **228**
Crowley, Joseph, D-N.Y. (7), 198, 355, **697**, 701
Cuellar, Henry, D-Texas (28), 999, **1008**
Culberson, John, R-Texas (7), 43, 160, **967**
Cummings, Elijah E., D-Md. (7), 394, **476**
Dahlkemper, Kathy, D-Pa. (3), **857**

D

Davis, Artur, D-Ala. (7), **17**, 478
Davis, Danny K., D-Ill. (7), 326, **338**
Davis, Geoff, R-Ky. (4), **427**
Davis, Lincoln, D-Tenn. (4), **936**
Davis, Susan A., D-Calif. (53), 171, **173**, 1007
Deal, Nathan, R-Ga. (9), **291**
DeFazio, Peter A., D-Ore. (4), 834, 836, 839, **843**
DeGette, Diana, D-Colo. (1), **181**
Delahunt, Bill, D-Mass. (10), 323, **504**
DeLauro, Rosa, D-Conn. (3), **202**, 205, 398, 812
DeMint, Jim, R-S.C., 437, **903**, 912
Dent, Charlie, R-Pa. (15), **879**
Diaz-Balart, Lincoln, R-Fla. (21), **259**, 266, 667
Diaz-Balart, Mario, R-Fla. (25), 257, **266**, 667
Dicks, Norm, D-Wash. (6), 413, 1055, **1078**, 1096
Dingell, John D., D-Mich. (15), 129, 181, 476, 512, 535, 537, **538**, 573, 654, 885, 1026
Dodd, Christopher J., D-Conn., 3, **194**, 200, 202, 313, 435, 564, 771, 835, 929
Doggett, Lloyd, D-Texas (25), **1002**
Donnelly, Joe, D-Ind. (2), **370**
Dorgan, Byron L., D-N.D., 22, 771, **772**, 775, 922
Doyle, Mike, D-Pa. (14), **877**
Dreier, David, R-Calif. (26), **121**, 144, 287, 734, 986, 1074
Driehaus, Steve, D-Ohio (1), **782**
Duncan, John J. "Jimmy" Jr., R-Tenn. (2), **932**
Durbin, Richard J., D-Ill., **323**, 325, 327, 361, 388, 505, 566, 681, 724, 773, 849, 1064

E

Edwards, Chet, D-Texas (17), **987**
Edwards, Donna, D-Md. (4), **470**
Ehlers, Vernon J., R-Mich. (3), 351, **516**
Ellison, Keith, D-Minn. (5), 99, 381, **553**, 935
Ellsworth, Brad, D-Ind. (8), **382**-383
Emerson, Jo Ann, R-Mo. (8), **594**
Engel, Eliot L., D-N.Y. (17), **716**
Ensign, John, R-Nev., 179, 619, **622**, 625
Enzi, Michael B., R-Wyo., 273, **1122**, 1125
Eshoo, Anna G., D-Calif. (14), 93, **97**, 1051
Etheridge, Bob, D-N.C. (2), **745**

F

Faleomavaega, Eni F.H., D-A.S. (AL), **1127**
Fallin, Mary, R-Okla. (5), 342, **829**
Farr, Sam, D-Calif. (17), **103**
Fattah, Chaka, D-Pa. (2), 785, **855**
Feingold, Russ, D-Wis., 30, 180, **1102**, 1104
Feinstein, Dianne, D-Calif., 33, **68**, 157, 221, 542, 893, 1021-1022
Filner, Bob, D-Calif. (51), **170**, 174, 374, 457
Flake, Jeff, R-Ariz. (6), 36, 39, **43**, 93, 127, 164, 333, 911, 963, 1028, 1050
Fleming, John, R-La. (4), **444**
Forbes, J. Randy, R-Va. (4), 1043, **1048**
Fortenberry, Jeff, R-Neb. (1), **611**
Foster, Bill, D-Ill. (14), **351**
Foxx, Virginia, R-N.C. (5), **751**
Frank, Barney, D-Mass. (4), 15, 152, 190, 194, 406, 490, **492**, 496, 502, 505, 635, 652, 727, 871, 982, 991, 1024, 1051, 1106
Franken, Al, D-Minn., 543, **544**, 545, 953
Franks, Trent, R-Ariz. (2), **35**, 38
Frelinghuysen, Rodney, R-N.J. (11), 652, **663**
Fudge, Marcia L., D-Ohio (11), **801**

G

Gallegly, Elton, R-Calif. (24), **117**
Garrett, Scott, R-N.J. (5), 25, 492, **652**
Gerlach, Jim, R-Pa. (6), **861**, 882
Giffords, Gabrielle, D-Ariz. (8), **47**
Gillibrand, Kirsten, D-N.Y., **683**, 688, 690-691, 722, 733
Gingrey, Phil, R-Ga. (11), **295**, 938, 994
Gohmert, Louie, R-Texas (1), **955**
Gonzalez, Charlie, D-Texas (20), **993**
Goodlatte, Robert W., R-Va. (6), **1051**, 1058
Gordon, Bart, D-Tenn. (6), **940**, 943
Graham, Lindsey, R-S.C., 68, 399, 773, **901**, 910
Granger, Kay, R-Texas (12), 718, **977**
Grassley, Charles E., R-Iowa, 313, **388**, 394, 564, 599, 833, 1020, 1100
Graves, Sam, R-Mo. (6), **590**
Grayson, Alan, D-Fla. (8), **236**
Green, Al, D-Texas (9), **971**
Green, Gene, D-Texas (29), 1004, **1010**
Gregg, Judd, R-N.H., 3, 88, 314, **631**, 636-637, 770, 833
Griffith, Parker, D-Ala. (5), **14**
Grijalva, Raúl M., D-Ariz. (7), **45**
Guthrie, Brett, R-Ky. (2), **424**
Gutierrez, Luis V., D-Ill. (4), 43, **333**

H

Hagan, Kay, D-N.C., **741**
Hall, John, D-N.Y. (19), **720**
Hall, Ralph M., R-Texas (4), **961**
Halvorson, Debbie, D-Ill. (11), **337**, 346
Hare, Phil, D-Ill. (17), **357**, 590
Harkin, Tom, D-Iowa, 83, **390**, 399, 609, 770
Harman, Jane, D-Calif. (36), 77, **140** 785, 911, 985
Harper, Gregg, R-Miss. (3), **571**
Hastings, Alcee L., D-Fla. (23), **263**, 985
Hastings, Doc, R-Wash. (4), 25, 932, 1069, **1074**
Hatch, Orrin G., R-Utah, **1020**, 1032

Heinrich, Martin, D-N.M. (1), **675**
Heller, Dean, R-Nev. (2), **624**, 626
Hensarling, Jeb, R-Texas (5), 55, 413, 652, 797, **963**
Herger, Wally, R-Calif. (2), **74**, 518
Herseth Sandlin, Stephanie, D-S.D. (AL), 60, **923**
Higgins, Brian, D-N.Y. (27), **732**
Hill, Baron P., D-Ind. (9), 379, **384**, 923
Himes, Jim, D-Conn. (4), **204**
Hinchey, Maurice D., D-N.Y. (22), 720, **724**
Hinojosa, Ruben, D-Texas (15), 803, **983**
Hirono, Mazie K., D-Hawaii (2), 281, **309**
Hodes, Paul W., D-N.H. (2), 636-**637**, 1110
Hoekstra, Peter, R-Mich. (2), 466, **514**
Holden, Tim, D-Pa. (17), **883**
Holt, Rush D., D-N.J. (12), 351, **665**
Honda, Michael M., D-Calif. (15), **99**
Hoyer, Steny H., D-Md. (5), 85, 142, 283, 466, **472**, 592, 657, 874, 1055, 1112
Hunter, Duncan, R-Calif. (52), **172**
Hutchison, Kay Bailey, R-Texas, 781, **951**, 978

I

Inglis, Bob, R-S.C. (4), 331, 904, **911**
Inhofe, James M., R-Okla., 70, **817**, 830, 927
Inouye, Daniel K., D-Hawaii, 69, 219, **303**, 305, 1088, 1117, 1130
Inslee, Jay, D-Wash. (1), **1068**, 1075
Isakson, Johnny, R-Ga., 272-**273**, 286
Israel, Steve, D-N.Y. (2), 354, **687**, 873
Issa, Darrell, R-Calif. (49), **166**, 703

J

Jackson, Jesse L. Jr., D-Ill. (2), 326, **329**, 613, 935
Jackson Lee, Sheila, D-Texas (18), **989**
Jenkins, Lynn, R-Kan. (2), **410**
Johanns, Mike, R-Neb., **609**
Johnson, Tim, D-S.D., **919**, 922
Johnson, Timothy V., R-Ill. (15), **353**, 688
Johnson, Sam, R-Texas (3), **959**, 969
Johnson, Hank, D-Ga. (4), **281**, 310
Johnson, Eddie Bernice, D-Texas (30), **1012**
Jones, Walter B., R-N.C. (3), **747**, 1048
Jordan, Jim, R-Ohio (4), **787**

K

Kagen, Steve, D-Wis. (8), **1118**
Kanjorski, Paul E., D-Pa. (11), **871**
Kaptur, Marcy, D-Ohio (9), 131, **797**
Kaufman, Ted, D-Del., **211**
Kennedy, Edward M., D-Mass., 45, 194, 220, 273, 304, 390, 461, **482**, 490, 495, 564, 632, 643, 672, 781, 895, 1021, 1031, 1034, 1088, 1114, 1122
Kennedy, Patrick J., D-R.I. (1), 483, **895**, 1049
Kerry, John, D-Mass., 191, 206, 262, 366, 436, 482, **484**, 490-491, 527, 547, 634, 642, 702, 790, 844, 866, 879, 1031, 1085
Kildee, Dale E., D-Mich. (5), **520**, 522, 692
Kilpatrick, Carolyn Cheeks, D-Mich. (13), **534**
Kilroy, Mary Jo, D-Ohio (15), **809**
Kind, Ron, D-Wis. (3), 1085, **1108**
King, Steve, R-Iowa (5), **400**, 1080
King, Peter T., R-N.Y. (3), 652, **689**, 710

Kingston, Jack, R-Ga. (1), 244, **275**, 717
Kirk, Mark Steven, R-Ill. (10), 336, **344**, 395, 585, 879, 1070
Kirkpatrick, Ann, D-Ariz. (1), **34**
Kissell, Larry, D-N.C. (8), **757**
Klein, Ron, D-Fla. (22), **261**
Kline, John, R-Minn. (2), **548**, 556
Klobuchar, Amy, D-Minn., **542**
Kohl, Herb, D-Wis., **1100**, 1105
Kosmas, Suzanne M., D-Fla. (24), **265**
Kratovil, Frank Jr., D-Md. (1), **465**
Kucinich, Dennis J., D-Ohio (10), 537, **779**, 787, 799, 806, 981, 1107
Kyl, Jon, R-Ariz., **32**, 38, 44, 420, 452, 553, 927, 954

L

Lamborn, Doug, R-Colo. (5), **187**
Lance, Leonard, R-N.J. (7), **656**
Landrieu, Mary L., D-La., 418, **435**, 438, 445, 453, 563, 607
Langevin, Jim, D-R.I. (2), **897**
Larsen, Rick, D-Wash. (2), **1070**
Larson, John B., D-Conn. (1), 131, 146, **198**, 200, 205, 657, 698
Latham, Tom, R-Iowa (4), **398**, 401, 1107
LaTourette, Steven C., R-Ohio (14), **807**
Latta, Bob, R-Ohio (5), **789**
Lautenberg, Frank R., D-N.J., **641**, 645, 658-659
Leahy, Patrick J., D-Vt., 5, 32, 211, 577, 644, 1021, **1031**, 1102
Lee, Barbara, D-Calif. (9), 81, **88**, 715
Lee, Christopher, R-N.Y. (26), **731**
Levin, Carl, D-Mich., 69, **508**, 510, 519, 533, 891
Levin, Sander M., D-Mich. (12), 509, **532**
Lewis, Jerry, R-Calif. (41), 137, **150**, 280, 430, 1117, 1125
Lewis, John, D-Ga. (5), 18, 171, 275, **283**, 488, 853
Lieberman, Joseph I., I-Conn., 30, **196**, 454, 578, 619, 641
Lincoln, Blanche, D-Ark., **51**, 53, 56, 60, 313
Linder, John, R-Ga. (7), **287**, 296
Lipinski, Daniel, D-Ill. (3), **331**, 911
LoBiondo, Frank A., R-N.J. (2), **647**, 685
Loebsack, Dave, D-Iowa (2), **394**
Lofgren, Zoe, D-Calif. (16), **101**
Lowey, Nita M., D-N.Y. (18), **718**
Lucas, Frank D., R-Okla. (3), **825**
Luetkemeyer, Blaine, R-Mo. (9), **596**
Lugar, Richard G., R-Ind., **364**, 380, 851, 1020
Luján, Ben Ray, D-N.M. (3), **677**
Lummis, Cynthia M., R-Wyo. (AL), **1126**
Lungren, Dan, R-Calif. (3), **76**, 161
Lynch, Stephen F., D-Mass. (9), 492, **502**

M

Mack, Connie, R-Fla. (14), 158, **247**
Maffei, Dan, D-N.Y. (25), **730**
Maloney, Carolyn B., D-N.Y. (14), **710**
Manzullo, Donald, R-Ill. (16), **355**, 812
Marchant, Kenny, R-Texas (24), **1000**
Markey, Betsy, D-Colo. (4), **186**
Markey, Edward J., D-Mass. (7), 232, 243, 496, **498**, 505, 523, 887, 1057
Marshall, Jim, D-Ga. (8), **289**
Martinez, Mel, R-Fla., 218, **220**, 242, 245, 248, 251, 262
Massa, Eric, D-N.Y. (29), **736**
Matheson, Jim, D-Utah (2), **1026**, 1028
Matsui, Doris, D-Calif. (5), **79**

McCain, John, R-Ariz., 5, 8, 11, 21, 24, **30**, 32, 34, 36, 38-39, 42, 44-45, 56, 58, 60, 62, 73, 75, 78, 108, 112, 114, 118, 133, 147-149, 151, 153, 157, 161, 167, 169, 172, 185, 186, 188-189, 196, 221, 223, 225, 229, 231, 233, 235, 238, 244, 246, 248-249, 252, 260, 265, 267, 276, 280, 283, 286, 288, 290-292, 294, 296, 317, 319, 323, 327, 352, 354, 359, 361, 364, 371, 373, 375, 377, 379, 385, 401, 405, 409, 410, 413-414, 417, 423, 424, 427-428, 430-432, 435, 440, 443, 444, 446-447, 449, 452, 465, 475, 485, 515, 517, 549, 555-556, 558, 560, 563, 568, 571-573, 587, 591, 593, 595, 596, 604, 614, 616, 619, 627, 651, 653, 664, 666, 690, 700, 709, 720, 722, 727, 730, 731, 736, 772, 775, 778, 784, 786, 788, 790, 792-793, 796, 804, 808-809, 810, 814, 817, 822-823, 825-826, 828, 830, 840, 857, 859, 860, 867-868, 870, 872, 874, 882, 884, 886, 888, 901, 906, 908, 910, 912, 924, 931, 933, 935, 937, 941, 943, 945, 956, 958-960, 962-964, 966, 968, 970, 974, 976, 978, 980-982, 988, 992, 996-997, 1001, 1003, 1005, 1015, 1017, 1025, 1027, 1028, 1039, 1044, 1048, 1050, 1052, 1054, 1058, 1064, 1075, 1077, 1093, 1095, 1097, 1102, 1104, 1109, 1113, 1115, 1126
McCarthy, Carolyn, D-N.Y. (4), **691**
McCarthy, Kevin, R-Calif. (22), **113**
McCaskill, Claire, D-Mo., 577-**578**, 1039, 1102
McCaul, Michael, R-Texas (10), 898, **973**
McClintock, Tom, R-Calif. (4), **78**
McCollum, Betty, D-Minn. (4), **551**
McConnell, Mitch, R-Ky., 3, 21, 313, 366, **417**, 421-422, 426, 431, 619, 631, 927, 1022
McCotter, Thaddeus, R-Mich. (11), **530**, 558, 1004
McDermott, Jim, D-Wash. (7), 149, 796, **1080**
McGovern, Jim, D-Mass. (3), 77, **490**, 715
McHenry, Patrick T., R-N.C. (10), 43, **760**
McHugh, John M., R-N.Y. (23), **726**, 785, 979
McIntyre, Mike, D-N.C. (7), **755**
McKeon, Howard P. "Buck", R-Calif. (25), **119**
McMahon, Michael E., D-N.Y. (13), **709**
McMorris Rodgers, Cathy, R-Wash. (5), **1076**
McNerney, Jerry, D-Calif. (11), **91**
Meek, Kendrick B., D-Fla. (17), 74, **251**
Meeks, Gregory W., D-N.Y. (6), **695**
Melancon, Charlie, D-La. (3), **442**
Menendez, Robert, D-N.J., 218, 220, **643**, 646, 667, 681
Merkley, Jeff, D-Ore., **835**
Mica, John L., R-Fla. (7), **234**, 559, 932, 1115
Michaud, Michael H., D-Maine (2), **457**
Mikulski, Barbara A., D-Md., **461**, 463, 469, 577
Miller, Brad, D-N.C. (13), **766**, 785
Miller, Candice S., R-Mich. (10), **528**
Miller, Gary G., R-Calif. (42), **152**
Miller, George, D-Calif. (7), 26, **83**, 96, 119, 298, 323, 505, 645, 888, 1114
Miller, Jeff, R-Fla. (1), **222**, 907, 1043
Minnick, Walt, D-Idaho (1), **317**
Mitchell, Harry E., D-Ariz. (5), **41**
Mollohan, Alan B., D-W.Va. (1), **1092**
Moore, Dennis, D-Kan. (3), **411**
Moore, Gwen, D-Wis. (4), **1110**
Moran, James P., D-Va. (8), 368, **1055**
Moran, Jerry, R-Kan. (1), **408**, 413
Murkowski, Lisa, R-Alaska, **21**, 23, 671, 1095
Murphy, Christopher S., D-Conn. (5), **205**, 882
Murphy, Patrick J., D-Pa. (8), 352, **865**
Murphy, Scott , D-N.Y. (20), **722**
Murphy, Tim, R-Pa. (18), 289, **885**

Murray, Patty, D-Wash., 271, **1064**, 1066, 1070, 1077
Murtha, John P., D-Pa. (12), 85, 145, 164, 198, 200, 239, 472, 657, 783, 853, 865, **873**, 877, 884, 886, 1055, 1078
Myrick, Sue, R-N.C. (9), **758**

N

Nadler, Jerrold, D-N.Y. (8), **699**, 1112
Napolitano, Grace F., D-Calif. (38), **144**
Neal, Richard E., D-Mass. (2), **488**
Nelson, Bill, D-Fla., **218**, 220, 264
Nelson, Ben, D-Neb., 421, 455, **607**, 610 1105
Neugebauer, Randy, R-Texas (19), 976, **991**
Norton, Eleanor Holmes, D-D.C. (AL), 372, 568, **1128**
Nunes, Devin, R-Calif. (21), **111**, 113
Nye, Glenn, D-Va. (2), 1043, **1045**

O

Oberstar, James L., D-Minn. (8), 234, 341, 546, **559**, 569, 732, 807, 1006
Obey, David R., D-Wis. (7), 151, 257, 303, **1116**
Olson, Pete, R-Texas (22), **997**
Olver, John W., D-Mass. (1), **486**, 715
Ortiz, Solomon P., D-Texas (27), **1006**

P

Pallone, Frank Jr., D-N.J. (6), **654**
Pascrell, Bill Jr., D-N.J. (8), **657**, 664, 681
Pastor, Ed, D-Ariz. (4), **39**
Paul, Ron, R-Texas (14), 41, 293, 932, **981**
Paulsen, Erik, R-Minn. (3), **550**
Payne, Donald M., D-N.J. (10), **661**
Pelosi, Nancy, D-Calif. (8), 26, 71-72, 79, 83, **85**, 91, 95, 97, 104-105, 119, 125, 127, 129, 131, 136, 140, 144, 154, 156, 162, 174, 198, 203, 230, 241, 243, 261, 263, 285, 289, 342, 383, 385, 397, 456, 472, 478, 492, 495-496, 498, 500, 519, 522, 534, 551, 588, 635, 657, 674, 684, 689, 697, 703, 734, 786, 795, 798, 823, 860, 874, 909, 915, 923, 936, 945, 961, 985, 987, 1002, 1056, 1068, 1096, 1116
Pence, Mike, R-Ind. (6), 111, 261, **378**, 794, 803, 910, 963
Perlmutter, Ed, D-Colo. (7), **190**
Perriello, Tom, D-Va. (5), **1050**
Peters, Gary, D-Mich. (9), **527**
Peterson, Collin C., D-Minn. (7), 448, 530, 546, **557**, 774, 1008
Petri, Tom, R-Wis. (6), **1114**, 1118
Pierluisi, Pedro R., D-P.R. (AL), **1131**
Pingree, Chellie, D-Maine (1), 454-455, **456**
Pitts, Joe, R-Pa. (16), **881**, 883
Platts, Todd R., R-Pa. (19), **887**
Poe, Ted, R-Texas (2), **957**, 972
Polis, Jared, D-Colo. (2), **183**
Pomeroy, Earl, D-N.D. (AL), 590, **774**
Posey, Bill, R-Fla. (15), **249**
Price, David E., D-N.C. (4), 122, 332, **749**
Price, Tom, R-Ga. (6), **285**, 1107
Pryor, Mark, D-Ark., 51, **53**, 62, 929
Putnam, Adam H., R-Fla. (12), 55, **243**, 276, 943

Q

Quigley, Mike, D-Ill. (5), **335**

R

Radanovich, George, R-Calif. (19), **107**, 111
Rahall, Nick J. II, D-W.Va. (3), 559, 1078, **1096**
Rangel, Charles B., D-N.Y. (15), 7, 18, 56, 101, 338, 389, 432, 488, 532, 600, **712**, 1011, 1014, 1035, 1074
Reed, Jack, D-R.I., 211, 508, **891**, 894,
Rehberg, Denny, R-Mont. (AL), 600, **603**
Reichert, Dave, R-Wash. (8), **1082**
Reid, Harry, D-Nev., 68, 195, 323, 418, 435, 437, 452, 601, **619**, 623, 625, 672, 681, 819, 849, 1125
Reyes, Silvestre, D-Texas (16), **985**
Richardson, Laura , D-Calif. (37), **142**
Risch, Jim, R-Idaho, **315**
Roberts, Pat, R-Kan., 404, **406**, 409, 1090
Rockefeller, John D. IV, D-W.Va., 273, 406, 576, 817, **1090**
Rodriguez, Ciro D., D-Texas (23), **998**, 1009
Roe, Phil, R-Tenn. (1), **931**
Rogers, Harold, R-Ky. (5), **429**
Rogers, Mike, R-Mich. (8), 10, **525**
Rogers, Mike D., R-Ala. (3), **10**, 86
Rohrabacher, Dana, R-Calif. (46), **160**
Rooney, Tom, R-Fla. (16), **250**
Roskam, Peter, R-Ill. (6), **336**
Ros-Lehtinen, Ileana, R-Fla. (18), **253**, 257, 266, 717
Ross, Mike, D-Ark. (4), **61**
Rothman, Steven R., D-N.J. (9), **659**
Roybal-Allard, Lucille, D-Calif. (34), **136**
Royce, Ed, R-Calif. (40), **148**
Ruppersberger, C.A. Dutch, D-Md. (2), **466**, 469
Rush, Bobby L., D-Ill. (1), **327**
Ryan, Paul D., R-Wis. (1), 228, 518, 652, **1104**, 1108
Ryan, Tim, D-Ohio (17), **811**

S

Sablan, Gregorio Kilili Camacho, D-N. Marianas (AL), **1130**, 1132
Salazar, John, D-Colo. (3), **184**
Sánchez, Linda T., D-Calif. (39), 46, **146**, 154, 162
Sanchez, Loretta, D-Calif. (47), 133, 146, 154, **162**
Sanders, Bernard, I-Vt., 196, **1033**, 1036
Sarbanes, John, D-Md. (3), **468**
Scalise, Steve, R-La. (1), **439**
Schakowsky, Jan, D-Ill. (9), 198, **342**
Schauer, Mark, D-Mich. (7), **524**
Schiff, Adam B., D-Calif. (29), **127**, 878
Schmidt, Jean, R-Ohio (2), **783**
Schock, Aaron, R-Ill. (18), **359**
Schrader, Kurt, D-Ore. (5), **845**
Schumer, Charles E., D-N.Y., 323, 505, 545, 643, **681**, 702, 727, 852, 954, 1031, 1034, 1064
Schwartz, Allyson Y., D-Pa. (13), **875**
Scott, David, D-Ga. (13), 277, **299**
Scott, Robert C., D-Va. (3), **1046**
Sensenbrenner, F. James Jr., R-Wis. (5), 536, 1005, **1112**
Serrano, José E., D-N.Y. (16), **714**
Sessions, Jeff, R-Ala., **5**, 1031
Sessions, Pete, R-Texas (32), 964, **1016**
Sestak, Joe, D-Pa. (7), 862, **863**, 864
Shadegg, John, R-Ariz. (3), 36, **37**-39, 593
Shaheen, Jeanne, D-N.H., **633**, 638
Shea-Porter, Carol, D-N.H. (1), **635**
Shelby, Richard C., R-Ala., **3**, 8, 11, 631
Sherman, Brad, D-Calif. (27), **123**, 355

Shimkus, John, R-Ill. (19), 347, **360**
Shuler, Heath, D-N.C. (11), 168, 225, **762**, 923, 941, 984, 1052
Shuster, Bill, R-Pa. (9), **867**
Simpson, Mike, R-Idaho (2), 317-**318**
Sires, Albio, D-N.J. (13), **667**
Skelton, Ike, D-Mo. (4), 289, **586**
Slaughter, Louise M., D-N.Y. (28), 349, 452, 490, **734**, 1074
Smith, Adam, D-Wash. (9), **1084**
Smith, Adrian, R-Neb. (3), 610, **615**
Smith, Christopher H., R-N.J. (4), 513, **650**
Smith, Lamar, R-Texas (21), 536, 973, **995**
Snowe, Olympia J., R-Maine, 69, 417, 435, **452**, 454, 458, 464, 484, 542, 590, 633, 1090
Snyder, Vic, D-Ark. (2), **57**
Souder, Mark, R-Ind. (3), 370, **372**, 665, 692, 855,
Space, Zack, D-Ohio (18), **813**
Specter, Arlen, D-Pa., 5, 32, 324, 390, 417, 452, 454, 544, 619, 671, **849**, 852, 863, 876, 880, 903, 921, 951, 1031, 1103
Speier, Jackie, D-Calif. (12), 73, **93**
Spratt, John M. Jr., D-S.C. (5), 494, **913**
Stabenow, Debbie, D-Mich., 461, **510**, 526
Stark, Pete, D-Calif. (13), **95**, 713
Stearns, Cliff, R-Fla. (6), **232**
Stupak, Bart, D-Mich. (1), **512**
Sullivan, John, R-Okla. (1), **821**
Sutton, Betty, D-Ohio (13), 528, 687, **805**

T

Tanner, John, D-Tenn. (8), 568, 935, **944**, 1072
Tauscher, Ellen O., D-Calif. (10), **90**
Taylor, Gene, D-Miss. (4), **572**
Teague, Harry, D-N.M. (2), **676**
Terry, Lee, R-Neb. (2), **613**
Tester, Jon, D-Mont., **601**, 603
Thompson, Bennie, D-Miss. (2), **569**, 689, 724
Thompson, Glenn, R-Pa. (5), **860**
Thompson, Mike, D-Calif. (1), **72**, 865
Thornberry, William M. "Mac", R-Texas (13), **979**
Thune, John, R-S.D., 919, **921**, 924
Tiahrt, Todd, R-Kan. (4), 408, **413**, 963
Tiberi, Pat, R-Ohio (12), **803**
Tierney, John F., D-Mass. (6), **496**
Titus, Dina, D-Nev. (3), 624, **628**
Tonko, Paul, D-N.Y. (21), **723**
Towns, Edolphus, D-N.Y. (10), 166, 196, 476, **703**, 706, 708
Tsongas, Niki, D-Mass. (5), **494**
Turner, Michael R., R-Ohio (3), 732, **785**

U

Udall, Mark, D-Colo., **177**, 180, 188, 190, 673, 935, 961, 987
Udall, Tom, D-N.M., **673**, 675, 677
Upton, Fred, R-Mich. (6), **522**, 911

V

Van Hollen, Chris, D-Md. (8), 85, 392, **478**
Velázquez, Nydia M., D-N.Y. (12), 146, 154, 162, **707**, 993
Visclosky, Peter J., D-Ind. (1), **368**
Vitter, David, R-La., 436-**437**, 440, 442
Voinovich, George V., R-Ohio, 53, **778**, 800, 812, 814

W

Walden, Greg, R-Ore. (2), **839**, 843
Walz, Tim, D-Minn. (1), **546**, 813, 923
Wamp, Zach, R-Tenn. (3), 329, 878, **934**, 943
Warner, Mark, D-Va., **1041**, 1054
Wasserman Schultz, Debbie, D-Fla. (20), 230, **257**, 261, 714
Waters, Maxine, D-Calif. (35), 16, 81, **138**, 160, 1110
Watson, Diane, D-Calif. (33), **134**
Watt, Melvin, D-N.C. (12), **764**
Waxman, Henry A., D-Calif. (30), 91, 108, 126, **129**, 166, 181,
    196, 205, 213, 342, 392, 476, 498, 512, 538, 654, 703, 1017,
    1021, 1026, 1035, 1068
Webb, Jim, D-Va., 41, 578, 1033, **1039**, 1041
Weiner, Anthony, D-N.Y. (9), 613, 697, **701**
Welch, Peter, D-Vt. (AL), 205, **1035**
Westmoreland, Lynn, R-Ga. (3), **279**
Wexler, Robert, D-Fla. (19), **255**
Whitehouse, Sheldon, D-R.I., **893**
Whitfield, Ed, R-Ky. (1), **422**
Wicker, Roger, R-Miss., 7, 239, **565**, 567, 827
Wilson, Charlie, D-Ohio (6), **791**
Wilson, Joe, R-S.C. (2), **907**, 937
Wittman, Rob, R-Va. (1), **1043**
Wolf, Frank R., R-Va. (10), 12, 938, **1059**
Woolsey, Lynn, D-Calif. (6), **81**
Wu, David, D-Ore. (1), **837**
Wyden, Ron, D-Ore., 209, 271, 306, 452, **833**, 835, 839, 842-843,
    939, 1022, 1067

Y

Yarmuth, John, D-Ky. (3), **425**
Young, Don, R-Alaska (AL), 21, 23, **25**, 558, 652, 932, 1074, 1115
Young, C.W. Bill, R-Fla. (10), 25, 150, **239**, 710